THE

# BOOK of DAYS

A MISCELLANY

OF

POPULAR ANTIQUITIES

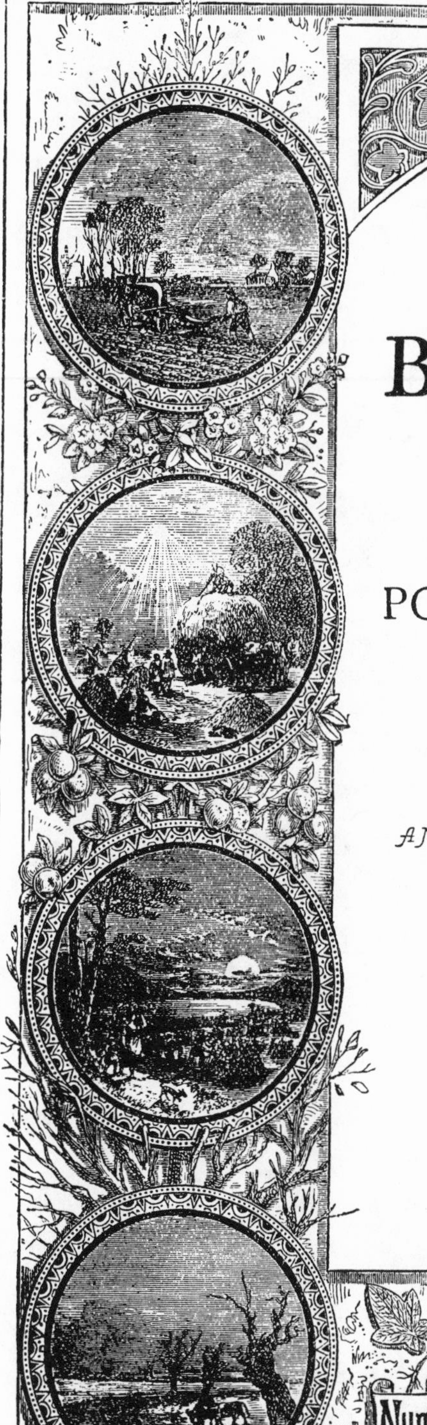


# THE BOOK of DAYS

A MISCELLANY

OF

POPULAR ANTIQUITIES

IN CONNECTION WITH

THE CALENDAR

INCLUDING

*ANECDOTE, BIOGRAPHY, & HISTORY*

*CURIOSITIES of LITERATURE*

*and ODDITIES of HUMAN LIFE and CHARACTER.*

EDITED BY R. CHAMBERS

IN TWO VOLS.—VOL. II.

W. & R. CHAMBERS, L[TD] LONDON, & EDINBURGH

J. B. LIPPINCOTT COMPANY, PHILADELPHIA

REPUBLISHED BY GALE RESEARCH COMPANY, BOOK TOWER, DETROIT, 1967

ISBN 0-8103-3002-4

Library of Congress Catalog Card Number 67-13009

# List of Illustrations.

# LIST OF ILLUSTRATIONS.

Then came hot JULY, boiling like to fire,
  That all his garments he had cast away;
Upon a lion raging yet with ire
  He boldly rode, and made him to obey:
(It was the beast that whilom did foray
  The Nemæan forest, till the Amphitrionide
Him slew, and with his hide did him array:)
  Behind his back a scythe, and by his side
Under his belt he bore a sickle circling wide.

SPENSER.

(DESCRIPTIVE.)

JULY is now what our old poets loved to call 'sweet summer-time, when the leaves are green and long,' for in such brief word-painting did they picture this pleasant season of the year; and, during this hot month, we sigh while perusing the ancient ballad-lore, and wish we could recall the past, were it only to enjoy a week with Robin Hood and his merry men in the free old forests

'All under the greenwood tree.'

We feel the harness chafe in which we have hitherto so willingly worked, amid the 'fever and the fret' of the busy city, and pine to get away to some place where we can hear the murmur of the sea, or what is nearest the sound—the rustle of the summer leaves. We long to lie down beneath the low-bending, and high overhanging branches beside the stream, that runs dark and bright through shade and sunshine, and watch the blue dragon-flies sport above the bluer forget-me-nots, that nod their tufted heads to every breeze which ripples the water. There fancy floats away, and where the drooping willow gives a white shiver as the under part of the leaves is turned to the light, and the brook rolls along 'singing a quiet tune,' we conjure up the image of sweet Ophelia, 'her clothes spread wide' upon the glassy stream, and seem again to hear her warbling 'snatches of old tunes' till, mermaid-like, she sinks beneath the 'weeping brook.' Then we hear the bleating of sheep that come down from some hidden bending of the water-course, and journeying along we see an old-world picture, such as the gray patriarchs had often looked on, and which is familiar to us, through the Bible pages, unaltered through thousands of years; for there we find them washing sheep, just as they did when David and Solomon paused to look at the sheep-washers, beside the brooks that flow through the valleys around Jerusalem. The mind wanders away into the twilight of those remote ages, and we wonder who she was whose teeth Solomon in his Song compared to a flock of sheep 'which come up from the washing.' In our wanderings through the nooks and corners of England, we have seen sheep-washing in such pleasant places, that had they been selected purposely to harmonise with this picturesque occupation, it would scarcely have been possible to have added a new beauty to the scene, though trees are always beautiful when reflected in water, especially when they also overhang a ground of green. The wattled hurdles, running in lines beneath the wide-spreading branches, which enclose the white sheep, making gray patches of light under the boughs, and upon the greensward; the sheep-washer standing in the pool, and the idlers in every variety of coloured costume assembled on the banks, and all mirrored in the water, make as pretty a rural picture as the eye can delight to dwell upon, and which seems ever changing its hue under the shifting lights of heaven. Then those brown sinewy labourers clutch at the fleecy sheep as they are driven down the bank—keeping their heads clear of the water, while they roll them to and fro, making incessant circles of ripples, for as one releases a sheep, another seizes upon it, until the immersion is completed, when it swims to the opposite bank, and there stands bleating, while the water drops from its heavy-hanging wool. Now and then you hear a loud laugh from the spectators, for the chubby farmer's-boy, who has to drive the sheep into the water for the men to wash, finds one that is obstinate, at which he pushes with all his might, when the animal gives a sudden spring, and the boy falls headlong into the pool.

About a week or so after the washing, sheep-shearing commences; the reason why 'clipping' is delayed for this length of time is, that the fleece may regain its oily nature, which it can only do through the wool becoming thoroughly dry, when the shears cut through it easily. This also is a busy time, and we have seen half a score sheep-shearers at work at once, the large barn-door having been lifted off its hinges and raised about a foot above the ground, to place the sheep upon, while they were shorn. By night the barn looks like a large wool warehouse, so high rise the piles of rolled up fleeces, and some of our English sheep yield as much as fifteen pounds of wool each. It is amusing to watch the lambs after the dams are clipped, the way they go smelling about them, and the pitiful bleating they make, until the mother answers, when they at once recognise her voice, and all doubt in a moment ceases.

Sheep-shearing feasts, like harvest-homes, are of ancient date; for we read in the Bible of Nabal, who had three thousand sheep in Carmel, holding a sheep-shearing feast in his house 'like the feast of a king,' and the custom still remains amongst many of our English sheep-breeders in the present day. It is pleasant to know that such old-world customs are still kept up; that when the owner has gathered the wool that clothes him, and the corn that feeds him, he should make glad the hearts of those who 'have borne the burden and heat of the day.' While this busy work is going on, the bean-fields are in bloom, and fill the air around with such a perfume as makes the wayfarer feel languid, longing to lie down in the midst of it, and with half-shut eyes dream dreams.

At every passing gust which ripples the fields, the corn now makes a husky whisper, and there are white spots on the long ears, which tell that it is fast ripening, and that bending reapers will soon be busy with their crooked sickles in the harvest-field. We now see amid the grass that is powdered with summer-dust, the most beautiful of all our wayside-flowers, the pretty pimpernel, which, though but little larger than the bloom of the common chickweed, fairly dazzles the eye like a gem with its rich crimson petals. By the very rim of the cart-rut, and close by the dent of the horse's hoof on the brown highway, it blows, a thing of beauty, that has no peer in garden or green-house, whether blood-red, crimson, or scarlet, for nothing but the flashing blaze of the red poppy of the cornfield, can be compared with it a moment for richness of colour. Country-people call this wayside beauty the poor man's weather-glass, and the shepherd's clock; and it never errs in announcing the approach of rain, for long before we can discover any sign of the coming shower, we find its deep-dyed petals folded up in its green cup. As a time-keeper, it may be relied upon, always closing at noon, no matter how fine the day may be, and never opening again before seven on the following morning. Its leaves are also very beautiful, of a fine clean oval shape, and on the underpart spotted. Often near to it, on the sunny-side of the hedge, may now be found the dull golden-coloured agrimony, with its long spiked head up-coned with little flowers, the favourite 'tea' of the poor cottagers, and a thousand times more delicious than some of the rubbish sold as tea in low neighbourhoods, for it makes a most refreshing beverage. Scarcely a leaf can be found on tree, shrub, or plant, to equal in beauty of form that of the agrimony, so deeply and elegantly are the edges cut, and so richly veined, that they carry the eye from the up-piled head of five-petaled golden flowers, which so gracefully overtop the foliage. The fragrance, too, is quite refreshing; only bruise this elegant leaf between the fingers, and it throws out an aroma that can no more be forgotten than the smell of roses. The next favourite as a tea-making herb among our old country-women, is the wood betony, now in bloom, and which forms a winding terrace of flowers, as the whorls rise step above step, a pile of rose-coloured flowers, beautiful to look upon in the sunshine. Nor does the charm of each little bloom diminish, when examined closely, as it is found to belong to the lipped family of flowers, the most exquisite of all the many orders; and quaint old Culpepper, writing about it at his house in Spitalfields above two centuries ago, says, 'the leaves and flowers, by their sweet spicy taste, are comfortable both in meat and medicine;' he also calls it 'a very precious herb;' and in his curious book, he tells us where he found choice wild-flowers growing in the summer sun about London, in the very places where long miles of streets now spread, and not even a blade of grass can be seen.

Through long leagues of untrodden flowers the golden-belted bees now go with a pleasant murmuring, over sunny openings in the bowery underwood, which shrub and bramble guard, and beneath overhanging branches by the water-courses, where the foot of man cannot tread. Up lanes that lead nowhere, saving to green fields, and over which a wheel seldom passes, saving at hay-time, or during the garnering of harvest, they grow and run. Up the hillsides they climb, over the fences, and into the old woods, where they play at hide-and-seek behind every bank and shaded hollow. Great trees throw their green arms over them, and make a shelter for their beauty under their shadows. From the faces of steep crags, inaccessible to man, they droop and wave in all their beauty; and in their bells the insects find a home, and at the golden entrances they play in the sunshine. They lean over and listen to the singing of the river all day long, and when they are folded, still hear its soothing lullaby go rippling over the reflected stars. The gentle dews alight upon them with silver feet in the moon-light, and hang golden drops about their petals to sparkle in the sun, in hidden nooks which the eye of man never penetrates; for nature leaves no crypt in her great temple undecorated. Place any flower under a microscope, and it becomes a world of wonder: the petals are vast plains, the stamens stately trees, many of them formed of gold; and deep down, on a pavement richer than any that was ever inlaid by the hand of man, move the inhabitants of this beautiful world, winged, and dazzling to look upon—fitting forms to sip nectar, and find a dwelling-place in the fragrant flowers. And what know we of their delights? The mari-gold may be to them a land of the sun, and its golden petals the beams that ever shine upon them without setting.

What tranquillity reigns around a green secluded village on the Sabbath! There seems a Sunday breath in the very air, so calm and quiet sleeps everything we look upon, compared with the unceasing hum of far-away cities, whose streets are never silent. The very fields are still, and we have often fancied that the flocks and herds take more rest on this old Holy day than at any other time. Not a sound of labour is heard. The creaking wagon, with its shafts turned up, stands under the thatched shed; and the busy wheel of the old water-mill rests, gray, and dry, and motion-less, in the summer sun. No far-sounding ring comes from the blacksmith's forge, at the door of which a few peasants linger in their clean smock-frocks, waiting until the village-bells sound from the hoary tower to summon them to church. Even the bells, as they come and go in the shifting breeze, seem like sounding messengers sent out everyway—up the valley, and over the hill—now heard, then lost—as if they left no nook unvisited, but carried their Sabbath tidings every-where. The childish voices that come floating on the air from the low, white-washed, village Sunday-school, where they are singing some simple hymn, bring before us His image, who said: 'Suffer little children to come unto me,' and who walked out in the fields with His disciples, to enjoy the calm of the holy Sabbath. The very murmur that Nature makes, in the low rustling of the leaves, and the subdued ripple of the stream, seems—because they are audible—to leave the stillness more profound, as her voice would not be heard if the grit of the wain, the tramp of the hoof on the dry rutted road, and the ring of the anvil, broke the repose which rests here—almost noiseless as the dew falling on the fleece of a sleeping lamb—throughout the Sabbath-day. The very gardens appear asleep, the spade is stuck motionless in the ground, hoe and rake are laid aside, and, saving the murmuring of a bee among the flowers, or the twittering of a bird from the orchard-trees, all around lie images of rest—a land of peace from which brown Labour seems to have retired in silence, and left no sound of his whereabout, but sunk in slumber somewhere, folds his sinewy arms.

How tempting those great ripe round-bellied gooseberries look on a hot July day; we wonder there is one left on the bushes, when we see so many children about! The red currants, too, hang down like drops of rich carnelian; while the black currants look like great ebony beads, half-hidden by their fragrant leaves—for all the early garden-fruits are now ripe to perfection. Down the long rows the pretty strawberries peep out, shewing like red-breasted robins at hide-and-seek under the foliage; while overhead the melting cherries hang down, leading even the very birds to commit trespass, for they cannot resist such a tempting banquet. Sweet Summer has now attained her perfect loveliness; the roses on her cheeks will never look more beautiful than they do now, nor will her sky-blue eyes ever beam with sweeter lustre. She has wreathed her sunny hair with the sweetest and fairest of flowers; and when they have faded, there will be no more found to make a frame of blossoms round her matchless countenance until the leaves of Autumn have fallen, white Winter awakened from his cold sleep, and young Spring gone dancing away, hold-ing up her green kirtle as she trips over the daisies. As yet, there is no sign of decay around her, only a few birds are silent, but they have not yet departed; there are myriads of flowers in bloom, and great armies of insects hurrying along every way, as they go sounding through the warm and fragrant air. Few writers had a deeper apprecia-tion of the beauties of nature than honest Izaak Walton; we can almost hear the rain-drops fall while reading that beautiful passage where he describes himself sitting under the hedge of honey-suckles, sheltering from the shower, 'which fell so gently on the teeming earth, and gave yet a sweeter smell to the lovely flowers that adorned those verdant meadows;' and listening 'to the birds in the adjoining grove that seemed to have a friendly contention with an echo, whose dead voice seemed to live in a hollow tree, near the brow of that primrose-hill.'

What dreams have we dreamed, and what visions have we seen, lying idly with half-shut eyes in some 'greenwood shaw,' sheltering from July's noonday sun, while we seemed to hear 'airy tongues that syllable men's names,' in the husky whispering of the leaves! Golden forms have seemed to spring up in the sun-lighted stems of the trees, whose high heads were buried among the lofty foliage, through which were seen openings to the sky. The deep-dyed pheasant, shooting over the underwood with streaming plumage, became a fair maiden in our eyes; and the skulking fox, noiselessly threading the brake, the grim enchanter from whom she was escaping. The twining ivy, with discoloured leaves, coiled round the stem in the far distance, became the fanged serpent, which we feared would untwine and crush her in its scaly folds. Scouts were sent out after her in the form of bees and butterflies, and seemed not to leave a flowery nook unvisited in which there was room enough for her to hide. Bird called to bird in sweet confusion, from leafy hollows, open glades, and wooded knolls, as if to tell that she had passed this way and that, until their songs became so mingled, we could not tell from which quarter the voices came. Then, as the sun burst out in all its brightness, the grim enchanter seemed to throw a golden net over the whole wood, the meshes of which were formed of the checkered lights that fell through leaf and branch, and, as we closed our eyes, we felt that she could not escape, so lay silent until the shadows around us deepened, and gray twilight stole noiselessly over the scene:

'A pleasing land of drowsyhead it was,
Of dreams that wave before the half-shut eye;
And of gay castles in the clouds that pass,
For ever flushing round a summer sky.'
THOMSON.

What imaginative mind has not enjoyed these summer dreams, these poetical flashes of purple, gold, and azure, that play on the 'inward eye' like colours on a cathedral pavement, streaming through some triple-arched window, richly stained with 'twilight saints, and dim emblazonings!'

Towards the close of July, most of our birds are silent—even the robin and the wren are but rarely heard again till the end of August. Large flocks of young birds may now be seen flying together, and many think that they have been driven away by the old ones, so congregate for company; their assembling has nothing to do with migration, as it is the case with those that never leave us, as well as with others that will soon migrate. It is just possible that they may have become so numerous in the places where they were hatched as to find food scarce, so set out together in flocks, to seek their living where fare is more plentiful. The chiff-chaff is one of the few birds that neither the heat of summer nor the advance of the season can silence, for it sings better in July than in any of the earlier months; leaving off the two shrill monotonous notes, which in sound resemble its name, and giving a peculiar whistle, unlike that of any other bird. One of the earliest singers in the morning is the chaffinch, which may often be heard before three o'clock during the long days of summer. The clean white on his wings gives him a splendid appearance. These birds build their nests with such an eye to the harmony of colour, that they are difficult to distinguish from the branches and leaves amid which they are placed, as they will match the green moss on the bough, and the yellow lichen on the bark, so closely, that only the little bright eyes of the bird betray its whereabout by their glittering. In the midland counties they are called 'pinks,' from their constant repetition of the note conveying that sound. Though most birds display great courage in defending their young, yet hundreds of little nestlings perish during the absence of their parents in search of food. Then their stealthy enemies, who are ever on the watch, pounce upon the little half-naked things, tear them out of their nests, and devour them. It is pitiable to hear the cry of the female on her return, when she finds her nest empty, and parts of the remains of her little ones hanging to the thorns they have been dragged through. We have sometimes fancied those wailing notes convey the feeling of Shakspeare's Macduff, when he exclaimed:

'All my pretty ones. All at one fell swoop!'

(HISTORICAL.)

July was originally the fifth month of the Roman year, and thence denominated *Quintilis.* In the Alban Calendar, it had a complement of thirty-six days. Romulus reduced it to thirty-one, and Numa to thirty days, and it stood thus for many centuries. At length, it was restored to thirty-one days by *Julius Cæsar*, who felt a personal interest in it as his natal month. After the death of this great reformer of the calendar, Mark Antony changed the name to July, in honour of the family-name of Cæsar. 'This month he selected for such honorary distinction, when the sun was generally most potent, the more effectually to denote that Julius was the emperor of the world, and therefore the appropriate leader of one-half of the year.'—*Brady.*

Our Saxon ancestors called July *Hey Monath*, 'because therein they usually mowed and made their hay-harvest; and also *Maed Monath*, from the meads being then in their bloom.'—*Verstegan.*

CHARACTERISTICS OF JULY.

July is allowed all over the northern hemisphere to be the warmest month of the year, notwithstanding that the sun has then commenced his course of recession from the tropic of Cancer. This is owing to the accumulating effect of the heat, while the sun is still so long above the horizon. In a table formed from the careful observations of the Rev. Dr Robert Gordon, at Kinfauns, Perthshire, the mean temperature of the air during the month, in that part of Great Britain, appears to be 61°. The same average has been stated for England; but in London 62° would probably be more correct.

At London, the sun rises on 1st July at 3.46 morning, and sets at 8.14 evening; on the 31st, the respective times are 4.18 morning and 7.42 evening. At Edinburgh, it rises on the 1st at 3.20 and sets at 8.46; on the 31st, the respective times are 4 4, and 8.8. The sun is in Cancer for the greater part of the month, and enters Leo about the 22d.

The great heat of the month led to a superstition among the Romans: they conceived that this pre-eminent warmth, and the diseases and other calamities flowing from it, were somehow connected with the rising and setting of the star Canicula—the Little Dog—in coincidence with the sun. They accordingly conferred the name of DOG-DAYS upon the period between the 3d of July and the 11th of August. Horace, it will be remembered, makes allusion to this in his address to the Blandusian Fountain—

'Te flagrantis atrox hora Caniculæ
Nescit tangere.'

The fact truly being that a spring necessarily preserves a mean heat all the year round—in Britain, about 47°. The utter baselessness of the Roman superstition has been well shewn by the ordinary processes of nature, for Canicula does not now rise in coincidence with the sun till the latter end of August, while, of course, the days between 3d July and 11th August are what they have ever been. Dr Hutton, remarking how the heliacal rising of Canicula is getting later and later every year in all latitudes, says that, on the Roman principle, the star may in time come to be charged with bringing frost and snow. Yet the *Dog-days* continues to be a popular phrase, and probably will long continue so. It is undoubtedly under some lingering regard for the old notion, as much as from a consideration of the effect of extreme heat upon canine flesh and blood, that magistrates of towns so often order dogs to be muzzled about the beginning of July. The verity of the Roman superstition is brought home to us by an antique

ANTIQUE GEM—THE DOG STAR.

garnet gem in the Bessborough Collection, representing the face of a tongue-lolling dog, surrounded by solar rays, as in the accompanying illustration.

# First of July.

Saints Julius and Aaron, martyrs, about 303. St Thierri, abbot of Mont-d'Hor, 533. St Calais or Carilephus, abbot of Anille, 542. St Gal the First, bishop of Clermont, about 553. St Cybar, recluse at Angouleme, 581. St Simeon, surnamed Salus, 6th century. St Leonorus or Lunaire, bishop. St Rumold, patron of Mechlin, bishop and martyr, 775. St Theobald or Thibault, confessor, 1066.

*Born.*—Bishop (Joseph) Hall, 1574, *Bristow Park, Leicestershire;* Louis Joseph, Duc de Vendome, 1654; Jean Baptiste, Comte de Rochambeau, 1725, *Vendome;* Adam Viscount Duncan, admiral, 1731, *Dundee.*

*Died.*—Edgar, king of England, 975; Admirable Crichton, assassinated at Mantua, 1582; Isaac Casaubon, learned scholar, editor of ancient classics, 1614, *bur. Westminster Abbey;* Frederick, Duke Schomberg, killed at the Battle of the Boyne, 1690; Edward Lluyd, antiquary, 1709, *Oxford;* Henry Fox, Lord Holland, 1774; William Huntingdon, 1813, *Tunbridge Wells;* G. F. von Schubert, German philosophical writer, 1860, *Laufzorn*, near *Munich.*

## ISAAC CASAUBON—WALTON'S INITIALS.

Isaac Casaubon was a foreign scholar of the highest eminence, who came to England in 1610, along with Sir Henry Wotton, the English ambassador at Paris, who had lodged in his house at Geneva, and 'there contracted,' as Izaak Walton tells us, 'a most worthy friendship with that man of rare learning and ingenuity.' Casaubon did not survive his arrival in England above four years. He was buried in the south transept of Westminster Abbey, where a marble mural tablet was erected to him by Bishop Morton.

While we have ample record of the friendship—and it was an *angling* friendship—which subsisted between Izaak Walton and Sir Henry Wotton, we have none regarding any between Walton and

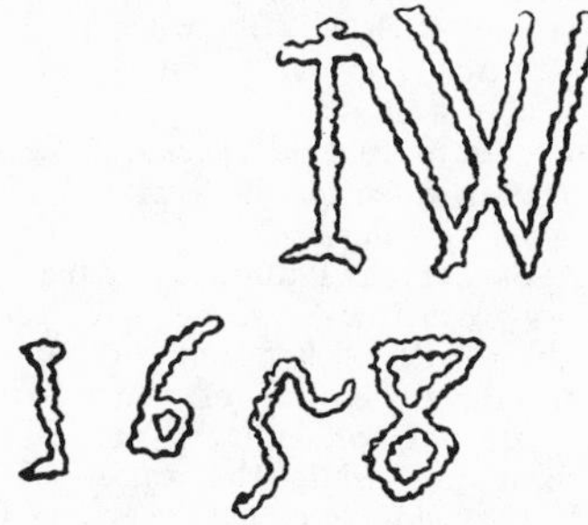


Casaubon, beyond the respectful reference to him above quoted, and the presumption arising from Walton having been the friend of Casaubon's friend Wotton. There is, however, some reason in the

traditions of Westminster Abbey for believing that Walton, from affection for Casaubon's memory, scratched his initials upon the mural tablet just adverted to. We do find upon the tablet a rude cutting of initials, with a date, as represented on the preceding page. For the mere probability of this being a veritable work of the hand of one so dear to English literature as good Izaak Walton, we have thought the matter worthy of the present notice.*

## HOLY WELLS.

July 1, 1652, the eccentric John Taylor, commonly called the Water Poet, from his having been a waterman on the Thames, paid a visit to St Winifred's Well, at Holywell, in Flintshire. This was a place held in no small veneration even in Taylor's days; but in Catholic times, it filled a great space indeed.

There is something at once so beautiful and so bountiful in a spring of pure water, that no wonder it should become an object of some regard among a simple people. We all feel the force of Horace's abrupt and enthusiastic address, 'O Fons Blandusiæ, splendidior vitro,' and do not wonder that he should resolve upon sacrificing a kid to it. In the middle ages, when a Christian tinge was given to everything, the discovery of a spring in a romantic situation, or remarkable for the brightness, purity, or taste of its water, was forthwith followed by its dedication to some saint; and once placed among the category of holy wells, its waters were endued, by popular faith, with powers more or less miraculous. Shrewd Thomas Powell, writing in 1631, says: 'Let them find out some strange water, some unheard-of spring; it is an easy matter to discolour or alter the taste of it in some measure, it makes no matter how little. Report strange cures that it hath done; beget a superstitious opinion of it. Good-fellowship shall uphold it, and the neighbouring towns shall all swear for it.' So early as 963, the Saxon king Edgar thought it necessary to forbid the 'worshipping of fountains,' and the canons of Anselm (1102) lay it down as a rule, that no one is to attribute reverence or sanctity to a fountain *without the bishop's authority*. Canons, however powerful to foster superstition, were powerless to control it; ignorance invested springs with sanctity without the aid of the church, and every county could boast of its holy well.

Some of these were held specially efficacious for certain diseases. St Tegla's Well was patronised by sufferers from 'the falling sickness;' St John's, Balmanno, Kincardineshire, by mothers whose children were troubled with rickets or sore eyes. The Tobirnimbuadh, or spring of many virtues, in St Kilda's Isle, was pre-eminent in deafness and nervous disorders; while the waters of Trinity Gask Well, Perthshire, enabled every one baptized therein to face the plague without fear. Others, again, possessed peculiar properties. Thus, St Loy's Well, Tottenham, was said to be always full but never overflowing; the waters of St Non's ebbed and flowed with the sea; and those of the Toberi-clerich, St Kilda, although covered twice in the day by the sea, never became brackish.

The most famous holy well in the three kingdoms is undoubtedly that dedicated to St Winifred (Holywell, Flintshire), at whose shrine Giraldus Cambrensis offered his devotions in the twelfth century, when he says she seemed 'still to retain her miraculous powers.' Winifred was a noble British maiden of the seventh century; a certain Prince Cradocus fell in love with her, and finding his rough advances repulsed, cut off the lady's head. Immediately he had done this, the prince was struck dead, and the earth opening, swallowed up his body. Meanwhile, Winifred's head rolled down the hill; where it stopped, a spring gushed forth, the blood from the head colouring the pebbles over which it flowed, and rendering fragrant the moss growing around. St Bueno picked up the head, and skilfully reunited it to the body to which it belonged, after which Winifred lived a life of sanctity for fifteen years, while the spring to which she gave her name became famous in the land for its curative powers.

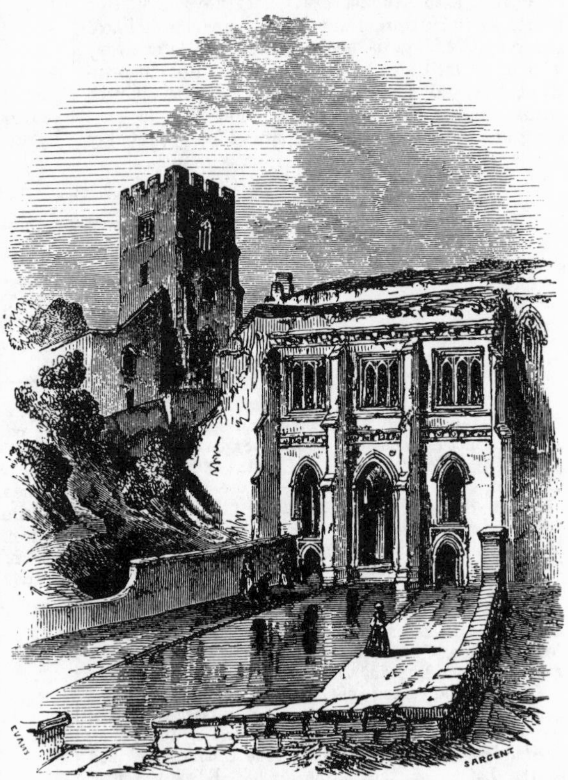

ST WINIFRED'S WELL, FLINTSHIRE.

The spring rises from a bed of shingle at the foot of a steep hill, the water rushing out with great impetuosity, and flowing into and over the main basin into a smaller one in front. The well is enclosed by a building in the perpendicular Gothic style (dating from the beginning of the reign of Henry VII.), which 'forms a crypt under a small

* The initials and date were first introduced to public notice, by Frank T. Buckland, Esq., 2d Life Guards, in the *Field* newspaper.

chapel contiguous to the parish church, and on a level with it, the entrance to the well being by a descent of about twenty steps from the street. The well itself is a star-shaped basin, ten feet in diameter, canopied by a most graceful stellar vault, and originally enclosed by stone traceried screens filling up the spaces between the supports. Round the basin is an ambulatory similarly vaulted.'* The sculptural ornaments consisted of grotesque animals, and the armorial-bearings of various benefactors of the shrine; among them being Catharine of Aragon, Margaret, mother of Henry VII., and different members of the Stanley family, the founders both of the crypt and the chapel above it. Formerly, the former contained statues of the Virgin Mary and St Winifred. The first was removed in 1635; the fate of Winifred's effigy, to which a Countess of Warwick (1439) bequeathed her russet velvet gown, is unknown. On the stones at the bottom of the well grow the *Bissus iolethus*, and a species of red *Jungermania* moss, known in the vulgar tongue as Winifred's hair and blood. In the seventeenth century, St Winifred could boast thousands of votaries. James II. paid a visit to the shrine in 1688, and received the shift worn by his great-grandmother at her execution, for his pains. Pennant found the roof of the vault hung with the crutches of grateful cripples. He says, 'the resort of pilgrims of late years to these Fontanalia has considerably decreased; the greatest number are from Lancashire. In the summer, still a few are to be seen in the water, in deep devotion up to their chins for hours, sending up their prayers, or performing a number of evolutions round the polygonal well; or threading the arches between and the well a prescribed number of times.' An attempt to revive the public faith in the Flintshire saint was made in 1805, when a pamphlet was published, detailing how one Winefred White, of Wolverhampton, experienced the benefit of the virtue of the spring. The cure is certified by a resident of Holywell, named Elizabeth Jones, in the following terms: 'I hereby declare that, about three months ago, I saw a young woman calling herself Winefred White, walking with great difficulty on a crutch; and that on the following morning, the said Winefred White came to me running, and without any appearance of lameness, having, as she told me, been immediately cured after once bathing in St Winifred's Well.' It was of no avail; a dead belief was not to be brought again to life even by Elizabeth Jones of Holywell.

St Madern's Well, Cornwall, was another popular resort for those who sought to be relieved from aches and pains. Bishop Hall, in his *Mystery of Godliness*, bears testimony to the reality of a cure wrought upon a cripple by its waters. He says he 'took strict and impartial examination' of the evidence, and 'found neither art nor collusion—the cure done, the author an invisible God.' In the seventeenth century, however, the well seems to have lost its reputation. St Madern was always propitiated by offerings of pins or pebbles. This custom prevailed in many other places beside; Mr Haslam assures us, that pins may be collected by the handful near most Cornish wells. At St Kilda, none dared approach with empty hands, or without making some offering to the genius of the place, either in the shape of shells, pins, needles, pebbles, coins, or rags. A well near Newcastle obtained the name of Ragwell, from the quantity of rags left upon the adjacent bushes as thank-offerings. St Tegla, of Denbighshire, required greater sacrifices from her votaries. To obtain her good offices, it was necessary to bathe in the well, walk round it three times, repeating the Lord's Prayer at each circuit, and leave fourpence at the shrine. A cock or hen (according to the patient's sex) was then placed in a basket, and carried round the well, into the churchyard, and round the church. The patient then entered the church, and ensconced him or herself under the communion-table, with a Bible for a pillow, and so remained till daybreak. If the fowl, kept all this while imprisoned, died, the disease was supposed to have been transferred to it, and, as a matter of course, the believer in St Tegla was made whole.

Wells were also used as divining-pools. By taking a shirt or a shift off a sick person, and throwing it into the well of St Oswald (near Newton), the end of the illness could easily be known—if the garment floated, all would be well; if it sank, it was useless to hope. The same result was arrived at by placing a wooden bowl softly on the surface of St Andrew's Well (Isle of Lewis), and watching if it turned from or towards the sun; the latter being the favourable omen. A foreknowledge of the future, too, was to be gained by shaking the ground round St Madern's Spring, and reading fate in the rising bubbles. At St Michael's (Banffshire), an immortal fly was ever at his post as guardian of the well. 'If the sober matron wished to know the issue of her husband's ailment, or the love-sick nymph that of her languishing swain, they visited the well of St Michael. Every movement of the sympathetic fly was regarded with silent awe, and as he appeared cheerful or dejected, the anxious votaries drew their presages.'*

Of St Keyne's Well, Cornwall, Carew in his *Survey* quotes the following descriptive rhymes:

'In name, in shape, in quality,
  This well is very quaint;
The name to lot of Keyne befell,
  No over-holy saint.
The shape—four trees of divers kind,
  Withy, oak, elm, and ash,
Make with their roots an arched roof,
  Whose floor the spring doth wash.
The quality—that man and wife,
  Whose chance or choice attains,
First of this sacred stream to drink,
  Thereby the mastery gains.'

Southey sang of St Keyne—how the traveller drank a double draught when the Cornishman enlightened him respecting the properties of the spring, and how

'You drank of the well I warrant betimes?
  He to the Cornishman said;
But the Cornishman smiled as the stranger spake,
  And sheepishly shook his head.

'I hastened as soon as the wedding was done,
  And left my wife in the porch;
But i' faith she had been wiser than me,
  For she took a bottle to church!'

* *Archæological Journal*, iii. 148.

* *Statistical Account of Scotland.*

When Erasmus visited the wells of Walsingham (Norfolk), they were the favourite resort of people afflicted with diseases of the head and stomach. The belief in their medicinal powers afterwards declined, but they were invested with the more wonderful power of bringing about the fulfilment of wishes. Between the two wells lay a stone on which the votary of our Lady of Walsingham knelt with his right knee bare; he then plunged one hand in each well, so that the water reached the wrist, and silently wished his wish, after which he drank as much of the water as he could hold in the hollows of his hands. This done, his wishes would infallibly be fulfilled within the year, provided he never mentioned it to any one or uttered it aloud to himself.

While the Routing Well of Inveresk rumbled before a storm of nature's making, the well of Oundle, Northamptonshire, gave warning of perturbations in the world of politics. Baxter writes (*World of Spirits*, p. 157)—'When I was a schoolmaster at Oundle, about the Scots coming into England, I heard a well in one Dob's yard, drum like any drum beating a march. I heard it at a distance; then I went and put my head into the mouth of the well, and heard it distinctly, and nobody in the well. It lasted several days and nights, so as all the country-people came to hear it. And so it drummed on several changes of tunes. When King Charles II. died, I went to the Oundle carrier at the Ram Inn, Smithfield, who told me the well had drummed, and many people came to hear it.'

Not many years ago, the young folks of Bromfield, Cumberland, and the neighbouring villages, used to meet on a Sunday afternoon in May, at the holywell, near St Cuthbert's Stane, and indulge in various rural sports, during which not one was permitted to drink anything but water from the well. This seems to have been a custom common to the whole county at one time, according to *The June Days Jingle.*—

'The wells of rocky Cumberland
 Have each a saint or patron,
Who holds an annual festival,
 The joy of maid and matron.

And to this day, as erst they wont,
 The youths and maids repair,
To certain wells on certain days,
 And hold a revel there.

Of sugar-stick and liquorice,
 With water from the spring,
They mix a pleasant beverage,
 And May-day carols sing.'

London was not without its holy wells; there was one dedicated to St John, in Shoreditch, which Stow says was spoiled by rubbish and filth laid down to heighten the plots of garden-ground near it. A pump now represents St Clement's Well (Strand), which in Henry II.'s reign was a favourite idling-place of scholars and city youths in the summer evenings when they walked forth to take the air.

## THE BATTLE OF THE BOYNE.

This conflict, by which it might be said the Revolution was completed and confirmed, took place on the 1st of July 1690. The Irish Catholic army, with its French supporters, to the number in all of about 30,000, was posted along with King James on the right bank of the Boyne river, about 25 miles north of Dublin. The army of King William, of rather greater numbers, partly English regiments, partly Protestants of various continental countries, approached the river from the north. Although the river was fordable, it was considered that James's army occupied a favourable position for resistance.

MEDAL STRUCK TO COMMEMORATE THE BATTLE OF THE BOYNE.

In the course of the day before the battle, the Irish army got an opportunity of firing a cannon at King William, as he was on horseback inspecting their position; and he was slightly wounded in the shoulder. The news that he was slain spread to Paris, Rome, and other strongholds of the Catholic religion, diffusing great joy; but it was quickly followed by intelligence which changed that joy into sorrow.

At an early hour on Tuesday, the 1st of July—a bright and beautiful summer morning—the right wing of the Protestant army made a detour by the bridge of Slane, to fall upon the left of the Irish host, while William conducted his left across the river by a ford, several miles in the other direction. The main body crossed directly, and found some difficulty in doing so, so that if well met by the enemy, they might have easily been defeated. But the great mass of the Irish foot did not stop to fight; they ran away. For this their want of discipline, aided by lawless habits, is sufficient to account, without supposing that they were deficient in courage. Such panics, as we now know better than ever, are apt to happen with the raw troops of all countries. The Irish horse made a stout resistance; but when King William, having crossed the river, came upon them in flank, they were forced to retire. Thus, in a few hours, a goodly army was completely dissipated. King James pusillanimously fled to Dublin, as soon as he saw that the day was going against him. Nor did he stop till he had reached France, bringing everywhere the news of his own defeat. So it was that King William completed the triumph of the Protestant religion in these islands.

The anniversary of the day has ever since been held in great regard by the Protestants in Ireland. As it gave them relief from the rule of the Catholic majority, the holding of the day in affectionate remembrance was but natural and allowable. Almost down to our time, however, the celebration has been managed with such strong external demonstrations—armed musterings, bannered processions, glaring insignia, and insulting party-cries—as could not but be felt as grievous by the Catholics; and the consequence has been that the fight begun on Boyne Water in 1690, has been in some degree renewed every year since. In private life, to remind a neighbour periodically of some humiliation he once incurred, would be accounted the perfection of bad-manners—how strange that a set of gallant gentlemen, numbering hundreds of thousands, should be unable to see how unpolite it is to keep up this 1st of July celebration, in the midst of a people whose feelings it cannot fail to wound!

## MISADVENTURES OF A STATUE.

The services of King William in securing the predominance of the Protestant religion in Ireland, were acknowledged by the erection of an equestrian statue of him in College Green, Dublin. This work of art, composed of iron with a coating of lead, and solemnly inaugurated in 1701, has lived a very controversial life ever since—never, it may be said, out of hot water. Rather oddly, while looked on with intensest hatred by Catholics, even the Protestant lads of the college did not like it—for why, it turned its tail upon the university!

So, ever since that solemn affair in 1701, this unfortunate semblance of the hook-nosed Nassau has been subjected to incessant maltreatment and indignity, all magisterial denunciations notwithstanding. Some of the outrages committed upon it were of a nature rather to be imagined than described. On the 27th of June 1710, it was found to have been feloniously robbed of its regal sword and martial baton. The act was too gross to be overlooked. The corporation offered a reward of a hundred pounds for the discovery of the culprit or culprits; and three students of Trinity College were consequently accused, tried, and condemned to suffer six months' imprisonment, to pay a fine of one hundred pounds each, and to be carried to College Green, and there to stand before the statue, for half an hour, with this inscription on each of their breasts:—'I stand here for defacing the statue of our glorious deliverer, the late King William.' On account of their loss of prospects by expulsion from the college, and loss of health by incarceration in a noisome dungeon, the latter part of the sentence was remitted, and the fine reduced to five shillings. But neither severity nor lenity in the authorities seemed to afford the statue any protection; just four years after the students' affair, the baton was again taken away, and though

EQUESTRIAN STATUE OF WILLIAM III.

another reward of one hundred pounds was offered, the evil-doers were not discovered.

Twice a year, on the anniversaries of the battle of the Boyne, and birthday of King William, the statue was cleaned, white-washed, and decorated with a scarlet cloak, orange sash, and other appurtenances; while a bunch of green ribbons and shamrocks was symbolically placed beneath the horse's uplifted foot. Garlands of orange lilies, and streamers of orange ribbons, bedecked the honoured horse, while drums, trumpets, and volleys of musketry made the welkin ring in honour of the royal hero. Moreover, every person who chanced to pass that way, and did not humbly take off his hat, was knocked down, and then mercilessly kicked for presuming to fall in the presence of so noble a prince. As a natural consequence of these proceedings, during the other 363 days of the year, the then undressed and unprotected statue was so liberally besmeared with filth by the anti-Orange party, as to be a disgrace to a civilised city.

To chronicle all the mishaps of this statue, would require a volume. Many must be passed over; but one that occurred in the eventful year 1798, is worthy of notice. A well-known eccentric character, named Watty Cox, for many years the editor of *The Irish Magazine*, having been originally a gunsmith, was expert in the use of tools, and being much annoyed by the helpless statue, he tried, one dark night, to file off the monarch's head. But the inner frame of iron *foiled*, as the Dublin wits said, the literary filer's foul attempt.

In 1805, the 4th of November falling upon a Sunday, the usual riotous demonstration around the statue was postponed till the following day. On the Saturday night, however, the watchman on College Green was accosted by a man, seemingly a painter, who stated that he had been sent by the city authorities to decorate the statue for the approaching festivities of the Monday; adding that the apprehended violence of the disaffected portion of the populace rendered it advisable to have the work done by night. The unsuspecting watchman assisted the painter in mounting the statue, and the latter plied his brush most industriously for some time. Then descending, he coolly requested the watchman to keep an eye to his painting utensils, while he went to his master's house for some more colours, necessary to complete the work. The night, however, passed away without the return of the painter, and at daybreak, on Sunday morning, the statue was found to be completely covered with an unctuous black pigment, composed of grease and tar, most difficult to remove; while the bucket that had contained the mixture was suspended by a halter fixed round the insulted monarch's neck. This act caused the greatest excitement among the Orange societies; but most fortunately for himself and friends, the adventurous artist was never discovered.

The annual custom of decorating the statue, so provocative of religious and political rancour, and the fertile source of innumerable riots, not unattended with loss of life, was put down by the enlightened judgment of the authorities, combined with the strong arm of the law, in 1822; and the miserable monument suffered less rough usage, until its crowning catastrophe happened in 1836. One midnight, in the April of that year, the statue blew up, with a terrific explosion, smashing and extinguishing the lamps for a considerable distance. The body was blown in one direction, the broken legs and arms in another, and the wretched horse, that had suffered so many previous injuries, was shattered to pieces. An offered reward of £200 failed to discover the perpetrators of this deed.

The statue was repaired and replaced in its old position. Like an old warrior, who had seen long service and suffered many wounds, it gradually acquired a certain degree of respect, even from its enemies. The late Daniel O'Connell, during his year of mayoralty, caused it to be bronzed, thereby greatly improving its appearance: and ever since it has remained an ornament, instead of a disgrace, to the capital of Ireland.

## THE CHEVALIER DE LA BARRE.

The case of Thomas Aikenhead, a youth hanged in Scotland in 1695, at the instigation of the clergy, for the imaginary crime of blasphemy, finds an exact parallel in a later age in France. A youth of nineteen, named the Chevalier de la Barre, was decapitated and then burned at Abbeville, on the 1st of July 1765, for mutilating a figure of Christ, which stood on the bridge of that town, this offence being regarded as sacrilege, for which a decree of Louis XIV. had assigned a capital punishment. Even when the local judgment on this unfortunate young man was brought for review before the parliament of Paris, there was a majority of fifteen to ten for confirming the sentence; so strongly did superstition still hold the minds of the upper classes in France. Does it not in some measure explain the spirit under which Voltaire, Diderot, and others were then writing?

It is to be admitted of the first of these writers, amidst all that is to be reprobated in his conduct, that he stood forth as the friend of humanity on several remarkable occasions. His energy in obtaining the vindication of the Calas family will always redound to his praise. He published an account of the case of the Chevalier de la Barre, from which it appears that his persecutors gave him at the last for a confessor and assistant a Dominican monk, the friend of his aunt, an abbess in whose convent he had often supped. When the good man wept, the chevalier consoled him. At their last dinner, the Dominican being unable to eat, the chevalier said to him: 'Pray, take a little nourishment; you have as much need of it as I to bear the spectacle which I am to give.' The scaffold, on which five Parisian executioners were gathered, was mounted by the victim with a calm courage; he did not change colour, and he uttered no complaint, beyond the remark: 'I did not believe they could have taken the life of a young man for so small a matter.'

## THE FIRST STEAMER ON THE THAMES.

The London newspapers in 1801 contained the following very simple announcement, in reference to an event which took place on the 1st of July, and which was destined to be the precursor of achievements highly important to the wellbeing of society: 'An experiment took place on the river Thames, for the purpose of working a barge or any other heavy craft against tide by means of a steam-engine on a very simple construction. The moment the engine was set to work, the barge was brought about, answering her helm quickly; and she made way against a strong current, at the rate of two miles and a half an hour.'

The historians of steam-navigation seem to have lost sight of this incident. But in truth it was only a small episode in a series, the more important items of which had already appeared in Scotland. Mr Patrick Miller, banker, Edinburgh, made literally the first experiments in steam-navigation in this hemisphere. [There were some similarly obscure experiments at an earlier date in America.] Mr Miller's own plan at the first was to have a double boat, with a wheel in the centre, to be driven by man's labour. Annexed is a copy of a contemporary drawing of his vessel, which was ninety feet long, and cost £3000. It proved a failure by reason of the insupportable labour required to drive the wheel. His sons' tutor, Mr James Taylor, then suggested the application of the steam-engine as all that was necessary for a triumph over wind and tide, and he was induced, with the practical help of a mechanician named Symington, recommended by Taylor, to get a smaller vessel so fitted up, which was actually tried with success upon the lake near his mansion of Dalswinton, in Dumfriesshire, in October 1788, the boat going at the rate of five miles an hour.

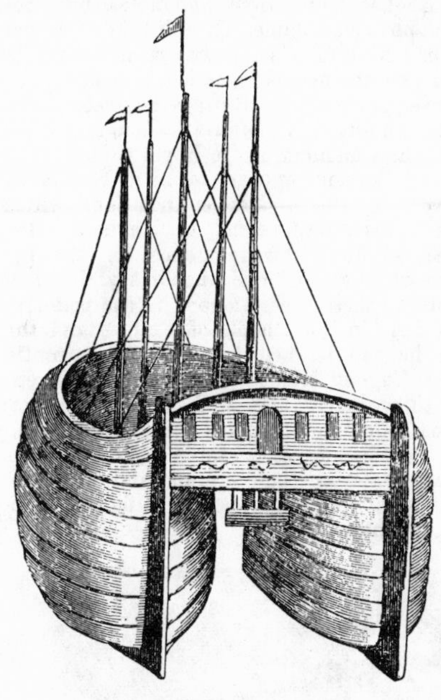

DOUBLE BOAT.

The little steam-engine used in this interesting vessel is preserved in the Andersonian Museum at Glasgow.

Encouraged by this happy trial and the applause of his friends, Mr Miller bought one of the boats used upon the Forth and Clyde Canal, and employed the Carron Iron Company to make a steam-engine on a plan devised and superintended by Symington. On the 26th of December 1789, the steamer thus prepared, tugged a heavy load on the above-named canal, at the speed of seven miles an hour. For some reason or other, nothing further was done for many years; the boat was dismantled and laid up. From this time we hear no more of Mr Miller; he turned his attention to other pursuits, chiefly of an agricultural nature. Mr Taylor, without his patron, could do nothing. In 1801, Lord Dundas, who was largely interested in the success of the canal, employed Symington to make experiments for working the canal trade by steam-power instead of horse-power. A steamer was built, called the *Charlotte Dundas*—the first ever constructed expressly for steam-navigation, its predecessors having been mere make-shifts. A steam-engine was made suitable for it; and early in 1802, the boat drew a load of no less than seventy tons at a rate of three miles and a quarter per hour, against a strong gale. An unexpected obstacle dashed the hopes of the experimenters; some one asserted that the surf or wave occasioned by the motion of the steamer would damage the banks of the canal; the assertion was believed, and the company declined any further experiments. What took place after another interval of discouragement and inaction will be related in another place.

# JULY 2.

The Visitation of the Blessed Virgin. Saints Processus and Martinian, martyrs, 1st century. St Monegondes, recluse at Tours, 570. St Oudoceus, bishop of Llandaff, 6th century. St Otho, bishop of Bamberg, confessor, 1139.

## Visitation of the Virgin Mary.

In the Romish church, the visit paid by the Virgin Mary to her cousin Elizabeth (St Luke i. 39, 40) is celebrated by a festival on this day, instituted by Pope Urban VI. in 1383; which festival continues to be set down in the calendar of the reformed Anglican Church.

*Born.*—Christian II., king of Denmark, 1480; Archbishop Cranmer, 1489, *Aslacton, Notts;* Frederick Theophilus Klopstock, German poet, 1724, *Quedlinburg, Saxony;* Henry, third Marquis of Lansdowne, statesman, 1780.

*Died.*—Henry I., emperor of Germany (*the Fowler*), 936; Michel Nostradamus (predictions), 1566, *Salon;* Jean Jacques Rousseau, 1778, *Ermenonville;* Dionysius Diderot, philosophical writer, 1784, *Paris;* Dr Hahnemann, originator of homœopathy, 1843, *Paris;* Sir Robert Peel, statesman, 1850, *London;* William Berry (works on heraldry), 1851, *Brixton.*

### KLOPSTOCK.

The German poet Klopstock enjoyed a great celebrity in his own day, not less on account of his *Odes*, many of which are excellent, than for that more ambitious sacred poem, called *The Messiah*, upon which the fabric of his fame was first built. This celebrated epic was written in hexameters, a species of verse little employed by his predecessors, but not uncongenial to German rhythm. Klopstock formed himself on Milton and Young, and is styled in his own country the *Milton* of Germany: but he soars rather with the wing of the owl than the wing of the eagle. His ode *To Young*, as the composition of a stranger, will be interesting to English readers, and serves very well as a clue to his genius.

TO YOUNG—1752.

Die, aged prophet: lo, thy crown of palms
Has long been springing, and the tear of joy
    Quivers on angel-lids
    Astart to welcome thee.
Why linger? Hast thou not already built
Above the clouds thy lasting monument?
    Over thy night-thoughts, too,
    The pale free-thinkers watch,
And feel there's prophecy amid the song,
When of the dead-awakening trump it speaks,
    Of coming final doom,
    And the wise will of heaven.
Die: thou hast taught me that the name of death
Is to the just a glorious sound of joy:
    But be my teacher still,
    Become my genius there.

The language of this ode approaches to a style which in English is termed *bathos.* As a proof of the wide-spread fame which Klopstock acquired in his own country, we briefly subjoin the account of his funeral, in the words of Mr Taylor's *Historical Survey of German Poetry:* 'Klopstock died in 1803, and was buried with great solemnity on the 22d of March, eight days after his decease. The cities of Hamburg and Altona concurred to vote him a public mourning; and the residents of Denmark, France, Austria, Prussia, and Russia joined in the funeral-procession. Thirty-six carriages brought the senate and magistracy, all the bells tolling; a military procession contributed to the order and dignity of the scene; vast bands of music, aided by the voices of the theatre, performed appropriate symphonies, or accompanied passages of the poet's works. The coffin having been placed over the grave, the preacher, Meyer, lifted the lid, and deposited in it a copy of *The Messiah;* laurels were then heaped on it; and the death of Martha, from the fourteenth book, was recited with chaunt. The ceremony concluded with the dead mass of Mozart.'

## THE PROPHECIES OF NOSTRADAMUS.

Princes, and other great people, besides many learned men, three centuries ago, paid studious attention to a set of mystic prophecies in French quatrains, which had proceeded from a Provençal physician, named Nostradamus, and were believed to foreshadow great historical events. These predictions had been published in a series of little books, containing each a hundred, and they were afterwards collected into one volume. Our copy of Nostradamus is one published in London in 1672, with English translations and notes, by a refugee French physician, named Theophilus de Garencieres, who had himself a somewhat remarkable history. Wood informs us that he died of a broken heart, in consequence of the ill-usage he received from a certain knight. He himself, though a doctor of Oxford, and member of the Royal College of Physicians of London, appears to have been a devout believer in the mystic enunciations which he endeavoured to represent in English. He had, indeed, imbibed this reverence for the prophet in his earliest years, for, strange to say, the brochures containing these predictions were the primers used about 1618 in the schools of France, and through them he had learned to read. The frontispiece of the English translation represents Garencieres as a thin elderly man with a sensitive, nervous-bilious countenance, seated, in a black gown with wig and bands, at a table, with a book and writing materials before him, and also a carafe bottle containing what appears as figures of the sun and crescent moon.

DR GARENCIERES, THE TRANSLATOR OF NOSTRADAMUS.

Michael Nostradamus (the name was a real one) saw the light at St Remy, on the 14th of December 1503, and died, as our prefatory list informs us, on the 2d of July 1566. He studied mathematics, philosophy, and physic, and appears to have gained reputation as a medical man before becoming noted as a mystogogue. He was twice married, and had several children; he latterly was settled at Salon, a town between Marseille and Avignon. It was with the view of improving his medical gifts that he studied astrology, and thus was led to foretell events. His first efforts in this line took the humble form of almanac-making. His almanacs became popular; so much so, that imitations of them appeared, which, being thought his, and containing nothing but folly, brought him discredit, and caused the poet Jodelle to salute him with a satirical couplet:

> '*Nostra damus* cum falsa damus, nam fallere nostra est,
> Et cum falsa damus, nil nisi *Nostra damus*.'

That is: 'We give our own things when we give false things, for it is our peculiarity to deceive, and when we give false things, we are only giving our own things.' His reputation was confirmed by the publication, in 1555, of some of his prophecies, which attracted so much regard, that Henry II.

sent for him to Paris, and consulted him about his children. One of these, when king under the name of Charles IX., making a progress in Provence in 1564, did not fail to go to Salon to visit the prophet, who was commissioned by his fellow-townsmen to give the young monarch a formal reception. Charles, and his mother, Catharine de' Medici, also sent for him on one occasion to Lyon, where each gave him a considerable present in gold, and the king appointed him his physician. Many of his contemporaries thought him only a doting fool; but that the great bulk of French society was impressed by his effusions, there is no room to doubt.

The quatrains of the Salon mystic, are set forth by himself as arising from judicial astrology, with the aid of a divine inspiration. 'I am,' he said, 'but a mortal man, and the greatest sinner in the world; but, being surprised occasionally by a prophetical humour, and by a long calculation, pleasing myself in my study, I have made books of prophecies, each one containing a hundred astronomical stanzas.' We are to understand that Nostradamus lived much in solitude—spent whole nights in his study, withdrawn into intense meditation—and considered himself as thus attaining to a participation in a supernatural knowledge flowing directly from God. He was probably quite sincere in believing that coming events cast their shadows on his mind.

Nor are we left without instances of his acting much as the seer of the Scottish Highlands in the midst of the ordinary affairs of life. One day, being at the castle of Faim, in Lorraine, attending on the sick mother of its proprietor the Lord of Florinville, he chanced to walk through the yard, where there were two little pigs, one white, the other black. 'The lord inquired in jest, what should come of these two pigs. He answered presently: "We shall eat the black, and the wolf shall eat the white." The Lord Florinville, intending to make him a liar, did secretly command the cook to dress the white for supper. The cook then killed the white, dressed it, and spitted it ready to be roasted, when it should be time. In the meantime, having some business out of the kitchen, a young tame wolf came in and ate up the buttocks of the white pig. The cook coming in, and fearing lest his master should be angry, took the black one, killed, and dressed it, and offered it at supper. The lord, thinking he had got the victory, not knowing what was befallen, said to Nostradamus: "Well, sir, we are now eating the white pig, and the wolf shall not touch it." "I do not believe it," said Nostradamus; "it is the black one that is upon the table." Presently the cook was sent for, who confessed the accident, the relation of which was as pleasing to them as any meat.' *

The prophecies of the Salon seer appear to us, in these modern days, as vague and incoherent rhapsodies, extremely ill adapted for being identified with any actual event. And even when it is possible to say that some particular event seems faintly intimated in one of these quatrains, it is generally accompanied by something else so irrelevant, that we are induced almost irresistibly to trace it to accident. One of the predictions which most conduced to raise his reputation, was the following:

> Le Lion jeune le vieux surmontera,
> En champ bellique par singulier duelle,
> Dans cage d'or l'œil il lui crevera,
> Deux playes une puis mourir mort cruelle.

> [The young lion shall overcome the old one,
> In martial field by a single duel,
> In a golden cage he shall put out his eye,
> Two wounds from one; then shall he die a cruel death.]

It was thought that this prophecy, uttered in 1555, was fulfilled when Henry II., in 1559, tilting with a young captain of his guard, at a tournament, received a wound from the splinter of a lance in the right eye, and died of it in great pain, ten days after. But here we must consider these two combatants as properly called lions; we must take the king's gilt helmet for the golden cage; and consider the imposthume which the wound created, as a second wound; all of them concessions somewhat beyond what we can regard as fair.

Another of the predictions thought to be clearly fulfilled, was the following:

> Le sang de juste à Londres sera faute,
> Brulez par feu, de vingt et trois, les Six,
> La Dame antique cherra de place haute
> De meme secte plusieurs seront occis.

> [The blood of the just shall be wanting in London,
> Burnt by fire of three and twenty, the Six,
> The ancient dame shall fall from her high place,
> Of the same sect many shall be killed.]

It was supposed that the death of Charles I., and the fire of London, were here adumbrated; but the correspondence between the language and the facts is of the most shadowy kind. Another line, 'Le Senat de Londres metteront à mort le Roy,' appears a nearer hit at the bloody scene in front of Whitehall. There is also some felicity in 'Le Oliver se plantera en terra firme,' if we can render it as, 'Oliver will get a footing on the continent,' and imagine it as referring to Cromwell's success in Flanders. Still, even these may be regarded as only chance hits amongst a thousand misses. One learns with some surprise that, well on in the eighteenth century, there was a lingering respect for the dark sayings of Nostradamus. Poor Charles Edward Stuart, in his latter days, scanned the mystic volume, anxious to find in it some hint at a restoration of the right royal line of Britain.

Connected with Nostradamus and the town of Salon, there is a ghost-story of a striking character, which we believe is not much known, and may probably amuse the faculty of wonder in a considerable portion of the readers of the *Book of Days*.

It was in the month of April 1697, that a spirit, which some believed to be no other than that of the great prophet, appeared to a man of the humbler class at Salon, commanding him on pain of death to observe inviolable secrecy in regard of what he was about to deliver. 'This done, it ordered him to go to the intendant of the province, and require, in its name, letters of recommendation, that should enable him, on his arrival at Versailles, to obtain a private audience of the king. "What thou art to say to the king," continued the apparition, "thou wilt not be informed of till the day of thy being at court, when I shall

* Garencieres's Life of Nostradamus, prefixed to English edition of the Prophecies, 1672.

appear to thee again, and give thee full instructions. But forget not that thy life depends upon the secrecy which I enjoin thee on what has passed between us, towards every one, only not towards the intendant." At these words the spirit vanished, leaving the poor man half dead with terror. Scarcely was he come a little to himself, when his wife entered the apartment where he was, perceived his uneasiness, and inquired after the cause. But the threat of the spectre was yet too much present to his mind, to let her draw a satisfactory answer from him. The repeated refusals of the husband did but serve to sharpen the curiosity of the wife; the poor man, for the sake of quietness, had at length the indiscretion to tell her all, even to the minutest particulars: and the moment he had finished his confession, he paid for his weakness by the loss of his life. The wife, violently terrified at this unexpected catastrophe, persuaded herself, however, that what had happened to her husband might be merely the effect of an overheated imagination, or some other accident; and thought it best, as well on her own account, as in regard to the memory of her deceased husband, to confide the secret of this event only to a few relations and intimate friends.

'But another inhabitant of the town, having, shortly after, the same apparition, imparted the strange occurrence to his brother; and his imprudence was in like manner punished by a sudden death. And now, not only at Salon, but for more than twenty miles around, these two surprising deaths became the subject of general conversation.

'The same ghost again appeared, after some days, to a farrier, who lived only at the distance of a couple of houses * from the two that had so quickly died; and who, having learned wisdom from the misfortune of his neighbours, did not delay one moment to repair to the intendant. It cost him great trouble to get the private audience, as ordered by the spectre, being treated by the magistrate as a person not right in the head. "I easily conceive, so please your excellency," replied the farrier, who was a sensible man, and much respected as such at Salon, "that I must seem in your eyes to be playing an extremely ridiculous part; but if you would be pleased to order your sub-delegates to enter upon an examination into the hasty death of the two inhabitants of Salon, who received the same commission from the ghost as I, I flatter myself that your excellency, before the week be out, will have me called."

'In fact, François Michel, for that was the farrier's name, after information had been taken concerning the death of the two persons mentioned by him, was sent for again to the intendant, who now listened to him with far greater attention than he had done before; then giving him dispatches to Mons. de Baobefieux, minister and secretary of state for Provence, and at the same time presenting him with money to defray his travelling expenses, wished him a happy journey.

'The intendant, fearing lest so young a minister as M. de Baobefieux might accuse him of too great credulity, and give occasion to the court to make themselves merry at his expense, had enclosed with the dispatches, not only the records of the examinations taken by his sub-delegates at Salon, but also added the certificate of the lieutenant-general de justice, which was attested and subscribed by all the officers of the department.

Michel arrived at Versailles, and was not a little perplexed about what he should say to the minister, as the spirit had not yet appeared to him again according to its promise. But in that very night the spectre threw open the curtains of his bed, bid him take courage, and dictated to him, word for word, what he was to deliver to the minister, and what to the king, and to them alone. "Many difficulties will be laid in thy way," added the ghost, "in obtaining this private audience; but beware of desisting from thy purpose, and of letting the secret be drawn from thee by the minister or by any one else, as thou wouldst not fall dead upon the spot."

'The minister, as may easily be imagined, did his utmost to worm out the mystery: but the farrier was firm, and kept silence, swore that his life was at stake, and at last concluded with these words: that he might not think that what he had to tell the king was all a mere farce, he need only mention to his majesty, in his name, "that his majesty, at the last hunting-party at Fontainebleau, had himself seen the spectre; that his horse took fright at it, and started aside; that his majesty, as the apparition lasted only a moment, took it for a deception of sight, and therefore spoke of it to no one."

'This last circumstance struck the minister; and he now thought it his duty to acquaint the king of the farrier's arrival at Versailles, and to give him an account of the wonderful tale he related. But how great was his surprise, when the monarch, after a momentary silence, required to speak with the farrier in private, and that immediately!

'What passed during this extraordinary interview never transpired. All that is known is, that the spirit-seer, after having stayed three or four days at court, publicly took leave of the king, by his own permission, as he was setting out for the chase.

'It was even asserted that the Duc de Duras, captain of the guard in waiting, was heard to say aloud on the occasion: "Sire, if your majesty had not expressly ordered me to bring this man to your presence, I should never have done it, for most assuredly he is a fool!" The king answered smiling: "Dear Duras, thus it is that men frequently judge falsely of their neighbour; he is a more sensible man than you and many others imagine."

'This speech of the king's made great impression. People exerted all their ingenuity, but in vain, to decipher the purport of the conference between the farrier and the king and the minister Baobefieux. The vulgar, always credulous, and consequently fond of the marvellous, took it into their heads that the imposts, which had been laid on by reason of the long and burdensome war, were the real motives of it, and drew from it happy omens of a speedy relief; but they, nevertheless, were continued till the peace.

'The spirit-seer having thus taken leave of the king, returned to his province. He received money of the minister, and a strict command never to mention anything of the matter to any person, be he who he would. Roullet, one of the best artists of the time, drew and engraved the portrait of this

* Might not perhaps this circumstance, properly seized, have conduced to trace out the affair?

farrier. Copies are still existing in several collections of prints in Paris. That which the writer of this piece has seen, represented the visage of a man from about thirty-five to forty years of age; an open countenance, rather pensive, and had what the French term *physionomie de caractere.*'

## THE TIR FEDERAL, OR RIFLE-SHOOTING MATCH IN SOLEURE.

THE Swiss have been famed for the use of the rifle long before English volunteers disputed the prize of all nations with them. Their national gathering is the greatest festival in the year, and is got up in so picturesque a style, that the tourist may well tarry a few days in order to have an opportunity of witnessing it, when he may also observe the national manners and costume more closely than he will be able to do in a hasty tour through the country. It is held at each of the capitals of the cantons in turn the first week in July, commencing invariably on a Sunday. On Saturday evening, all the hotels are crowded for the opening procession next Sunday morning. From six A.M. on that day until nine, on the occasion when the writer was present, the broad flight of steps leading up to the cathedral at Soleure was crowded by worshippers. Mass was repeated again and again to each relay, and then, the religious duties of the day being over, all gave themselves up to pleasure. The streets were one mass of people waiting for the procession. The burning sun of a beautiful summer-day lightened up the scene, the cannon roared, bands of music added their sweet tones, and the variety of a hundred gay and fantastic costumes dazzled the eye of the amused spectator in the windows. Then came the cry: 'Here is the procession.' At its head walked the juniors, with two pieces of cannon and fifty guns; behind them a man in the costume of William Tell, the patron of riflemen, preceded the body of markers, who were dressed in bright-red blouses with white cordings, carrying at the end of a stick the white disks which serve to mark the shots. Then came the military band, followed by the committee carrying the federal banner, bearing the motto: 'LIBERTY, EQUALITY, FRATERNITY.' The deputations of marksmen from each canton, in the greatest variety of picturesque costume, followed: those of Soleure wearing gray felt-hats, adorned with green ribbons; the Hanseatic towns, Bremen and Lubeck, sent their quota, dressed in rich green and gold coats, with a high-crowned hat

SWISS PEASANTS AT THE TIR FEDERAL.

adorned with a plume of feathers. Most of those present had a bouquet of flowers in the front of their hats, no doubt given by some fair friend.

The shooting-ground was about half a mile from the city, a beautiful plain, surrounded by the Vosges Mountains. A splendid avenue of trees led up to the gay pavilion of glass (see illustration on the following page), where the prizes for the successful competitors were hung. They consisted of watches, rifles, cups, gold and silver dishes, coffers, and purses filled with gold Napoleons, amounting in all to a hundred and fifty thousand francs. To the left was the stand for the shooters, a long covered shed opposite twenty-seven targets, furnished with long tables for the convenience of loading. At each successful shot a paper ticket was given to the marksman, which he stuck in the ribbon of his hat; at the end of the day they were presented and counted up, and he who could return into the city in the evening with a hatful received much applause. Not the least amusing part was to turn to the right, and walk through the magnificent dining-room, and then into the temporary kitchens, where hundreds of cooks were preparing substantial roast and boiled joints of meat, with puddings and pies innumerable. The writer could not help thinking how much better they manage the commissariat department abroad than in England, where the cold pork-pie and glass of ale is the usual refreshment at rifle reviews. The women take a very active part in the success of their brothers or lovers. Most of them were without bonnets: the Unterwalden, in their singular fan-like lace head-dress; the Bernese, in their wide-brimmed hats; the Loèche, with the circle of plaited ribbon, giving a most singular aspect to the scene; whilst the velvet corsage, white habit-shirt and sleeves, silver chains, and short petticoat bordered with red, is the picturesque costume of most of the women (see illustration

HALL OF PRIZES AT THE TIR FEDERAL.

on the preceding page). The shooting usually lasts from Sunday to Sunday, though sometimes, from the number of competitors, it is prolonged for a few days. The holders of prizes receive an enthusiastic ovation, each returning to his family and business with the reassuring sentiment that he belongs to one vast family, bearing this device: 'One for all, and all for one.'

## OLD SCARLETT.

Died, July 2, 1591, Robert Scarlett, sexton of Peterborough Cathedral, at the age of 98, having buried two generations of his fellow-creatures. A portrait of him, hung up at the west end of that noble church, has perpetuated his fame, and caused him to be introduced in effigy in various works besides the present. And what a lively effigy—short, stout, hardy, and self-complacent, perfectly satisfied, and perhaps even proud of his profession, and content to be exhibited with all its insignia about him! Two queens had passed through his hands into that bed which gives a lasting rest to queens and to peasants alike. An officer of Death, who had so long defied his principal, could not but have made some impression on the minds of bishop, dean, prebends, and other magnates of the cathedral, and hence we may suppose the erection of this lively portraiture of the old man, which is believed to have been only once renewed since it was first put up. Dr Dibdin, who last copied it, tells us that 'old Scarlett's jacket and trunk-hose are of a brownish red, his stockings blue, his shoes black, tied with blue ribbands, and the soles of his shoes red. The cap upon his head is red, and so also is the ground of the coat armour.'

The following verses below the portrait are characteristic of his age:

'You see old Scarlett's picture stand on hie;
But at your feet here doth his body lye.
His gravestone doth his age and death-time shew,
His office by heis token [s] you may know.
Second to none for strength and sturdy lymm,
A scare-babe mighty voice, with visage grim;
He had interd two queenes within this place
And this townes householders in his life's space
Twice over, but at length his own time came,
What he for others did, for him the same
Was done:' no doubt his soule doth live for aye,
In heaven, though here his body clad in clay.'

The first of the queens interred by Scarlett was Catharine, the divorced wife of Henry VIII., who died in 1535 at Kimbolton Castle, in Huntingdonshire. The second was Mary Queen of Scots, who was beheaded at Fotheringay in 1587, and first interred here, though subsequently transported to Westminster Abbey.

A droll circumstance, not very prominent in Scarlett's portrait, is his wearing a short whip under his girdle. Why should a sexton be invested with such an article? The writer has not the least doubt that old Robert required a whip to keep off the boys, while engaged in his professional operations. The curiosity of boys regarding graves and funerals is one of their most irrepressible passions. Every grave-digger who works in a churchyard open to the public, knows this well by troublesome experience. An old man, who about fifty years

OLD SCARLETT, THE PETERBOROUGH SEXTON.

ago pursued this melancholy trade at Falkirk, in Scotland, always made a paction with the boys before beginning—'Noo, laddies, ye maun bide awa for a while, and no tramp back the mools into the grave, and I'll be sure to bring ye a' forrit, and let ye see the grave, when it's dune.'

## CHILDREN DETAINED FOR A FATHER'S DEBT.

On the 2d of July 1839, a singular trial came on before the Tribunal de Première Instance, at Paris, to determine whether the children of a debtor may be detained by the creditor as a pledge for the debt. Mr and Mrs ——, with five children, and some domestic servants, lived for a time at a large hotel at Paris; and as they could not or would not pay their account, they removed to a smaller establishment, the Hôtel Britannique, the owner of which consented to make himself responsible for the debt to the other house. After the family had remained with him for a considerable time, Mr —— disappeared, and never returned to the hotel, sending merely a letter of excuses. Then Mrs —— went away, leaving the children and servants behind. The servants were discharged; but the hotel-keeper kindly supported the five children thus strangely left on his hands, until his bill had run up to the large sum of 20,000 francs (about £800). A demand was then made upon him (without revealing to him the present dwelling-place of the parents) to deliver up the children; he refused, unless the bill was paid; whereupon a suit was instituted against him. M. Charles Ledru, the advocate for the parents, passed the highest encomiums on the generous hotel-keeper, and said that he himself would use all his influence to induce the father to pay the debt so indisputably due; but added, that his own present duty was to contend against the detention of the children as a pledge for the debt. The president of the tribunal, M. Debelleyme, equally praised the hotel-keeper, but decided that the law of France would not permit the detention of the children. They were given up, irrespective of the payment of the debt, which was left to be enforced by other tribunals.

## JULY 3.

St Phocas, martyr, 303. St Gunthiern, abbot in Brittany, 6th century. St Bertran, bishop of Mans, 623. St Guthagon, recluse at Oostkerk, 8th century.

*Born.*—Louis XI. of France, 1423, *Bourges;* Henry Grattan, Irish parliamentary orator, 1746, *Dublin.*

*Died.*—Mary de Medicis, mother of Louis XIII. of France, 1642, *Cologne;* Ferdinand, Duke of Brunswick, 1792, *Brunswick.*

### HENRY GRATTAN.

Ireland has great honour in producing Henry Grattan, and she will never be politically beyond hope while she continues to venerate his memory. With every temptation to become the tool of the British ministry, he came forward as the unflinching advocate of the just rights and independence of his country; a Protestant, he never ceased to claim equal rights for an opposite class of believers. In the blotted page of Irish history, it is truly a bright spot where Grattan (1780) obtains in the native parliament the celebrated resolution as to its sole competency to make laws for Ireland. An irreproachable private life admirably supports the grandeur of his public career.

An anecdote of Grattan's boyhood shews the possession of that powerful will without which there can be no true greatness: 'When very young, Mr Grattan had been frightened by stories of ghosts and hobgoblins, which nurses are in the habit of relating to children, so much so, as to affect his nerves in the highest degree. He could not bear being left alone, or remaining long without any person, in the dark. This feeling he determined to overcome, and he adopted a bold plan. In the dead of night he used to resort to a churchyard near his father's house, and there he used to sit upon the gravestones, whilst the perspiration poured down his face; but by these efforts he at length succeeded and overcame his nervous sensation. This certainly was a strong proof of courage in a child.'—*Memoirs of Henry Grattan by his Son* (1848), v. 212.

### EXPIRATION OF THE CORNISH LANGUAGE.

The 3d of July is connected (in a very slight manner, it must be acknowledged) with an event of some importance—the utter death and extinction of one of the ancient provincial languages of England.

Many have been the conjectures as to the person and to the locality, where lived the last individual who could speak Cornish. Dr Borlase, who published his History in 1758, says that 'the language had altogether ceased, so as not to be spoken anywhere in conversation;' while Dr Bryce of Redruth affirms that the language had its last struggles for life, at or about the wild prominences of the Land's End. This fact Lhwyd, in a letter, March 10, 1701, corroborates. Our doubts are, however, settled by the detailed account of Dorothy Pentreath, *alias* Jeffries, who, born in 1681, lived at Mouse-hole, near Penzance, and conversed most fluently in the Cornish tongue. Her father, a fisherman, sent this young Sibyl at the age of twelve with fish to Penzance. In Cornish she sold them, no improbability, as not until over twenty could she speak a word of English. The name Pentreath signifies *the end of the sand.* The following lines, giving Cornish and English alternately, will serve to confirm the occupation of the Pentreaths:

TO NEIGHBOUR NICHOLAS PENTREATH.

Contreoak Nicholas Pentreath,
*Neighbour Nicholas Pentreath,*
Pa resso why doaz war an treath
*When you come upon the sand,*
Gen puseas, komero why wryth
*With fish, take you care,*
Tha geil compez, hedna yw fŷr
*To do right, that is wise,*
Ha cowz meaz Dega, dega,
*And speak aloud Tythe, Tythe,*
Enna ew ol guz dega gûr.
*There is all your true tythe.*

The Hon. Daines Barrington, who travelled in Cornwall in 1768, had an interview with her, which is described in the *Archæologia*, vol. iii.: 'When we reached Mouse-hole, I desired to be introduced as a person who had laid a wager, that there was no one who could converse in Cornish. Upon which Dolly Pentreath spoke in an angry tone of voice for two or three minutes, in a language which sounded very much like Welsh. The hut in which she lived was in a very narrow lane, opposite to two rather better cottages, at the doors of which two other women stood, advanced in years, and who, I observed, were laughing at what Dolly Pentreath said to me. Upon this, I asked them whether she had not been abusing me; to which they answered: "Yes, very heartily, and because I supposed she could not speak Cornish." I then said they must be able to talk it; to which they answered, they could not speak it readily, but that they understood it, being only ten or twelve years younger than Dolly Pentreath.'

Six years after this visit, though bending with old age, and in her 87th year, Dolly Pentreath could walk six miles in bad weather, her intellect was unimpaired, and her memory so good that she recollected the gentleman who had such a curiosity to hear the Cornish language. The parish maintained her in her poverty, while her fortune-telling and gabbling Cornish also contributed to her maintenance. She was short of stature, and towards the end of her life somewhat deaf, but positive that she was the only person who could speak or know anything about the ancient tongue of her country. She died January 1778, and was buried in Paul Churchyard, where her epitaph, supposed to have been written by Mr Thomson of Truro, ran thus:

'Coth Doll Pentreath eans ha dean,
Marow ha kledyz ed Paul pleu,
Na ed an Egloz, gan pobel brâs,
Bes ed Egloz—hay coth Dolly es.'

Old Doll Pentreath, one hundred aged and two,
Deceased, and buried in Paul parish too,
Not in the church with folks great,
But in the churchyard, doth old Dolly lie.

Thus much for Dolly. We also learn that the language was not entirely lost by her death; for a fisherman of Mouse-hole, in 1797, informed Mr Barrington, that one William Bodenoer was the last person of that place who could speak in Cornish. This man, some years younger than Dolly, frequently conversed with her, but their conversation was scarcely understood by any one of that place. Impossible as it is precisely to fix upon the very last conversationalist, all accounts agree in making Dorothy the latest fluent speaker. Though her successors may have understood the language, they were unable to maintain a dialogue in the manner in which she did. A letter from Bodenoer, dated July 3, 1776 (two years before Dorothy's death), will shew the condition of the language:

'Bluth vee Eue try Gevree a pemp,
Theatra vee pean boadjack an poscas
Me rig deskey Cornoack termen me vee mave,
Cornoack ewe all ne,
Cea ves yen pobble younk.

My age is threescore-and-five,
I am a poor fisherman,
I learned Cornish when I was a boy.
Cornish is all forgot
With young people.'

*Archæologia*, vol. v.

Bodenoer died in 1794, leaving two sons, who knew not enough of the Cornish to converse in it. If the visitor to Penzance will direct his steps three miles west of that place, he will hear somewhat of Dorothy Pentreath, and of that language, which, now forgotten, found in her its last efficient representative.

## EXTRAORDINARY CALCULATORS.

On the 3d of July 1839, some of the eminent members of the Academy of Sciences at Paris, including MM. Arago, Lacroix, Libri, and Sturm, met to examine a remarkable boy, whose powers of mental calculation were deemed quite inexplicable. The boy, named Vito Mangiamele, a Sicilian, was the son of a shepherd, and was about eleven years old. The examiners asked him several questions which they knew, under ordinary circumstances, to be tedious of solution—such as, the cube root of 3,796,416, and the 10th root of 282,475,249; the first of these he answered in half a minute, the second in three minutes. One question was of the following complicated character: 'What number has the following proportions, that if its cube is added to 5 times its square, and then 42 times the number, and the number 40 be subtracted from the result, the remainder is equal to 0 or zero?' M. Arago repeated this question a second time, but while he was finishing the last word, the boy replied: 'The number is 5!'

Such cases greatly puzzle ordinary mathematicians. Buxton, Colburn, and Bidder, have at different times exhibited this unaccountable power of accounting. Jedediah Buxton, although his grandfather was a clergyman and his father a schoolmaster, was so neglected in his education that he could not even write; his mental faculties were slow, with the one wonderful exception of his power of mental arithmetic. After hearing a sermon, he remembered and cared for nothing concerning it except the number of words, which he had counted during their delivery. If a period of time, or the size of an object, were mentioned in his hearing, he almost unconsciously began to count how many seconds, or how many hair's-breadths there were in it. He walked from Chesterfield to London on purpose to have the gratification of seeing George II.; and while in the metropolis, he was taken much notice of by members of the Royal Society. On one occasion he went to see Garrick in *Richard III.;* but instead of attending to the performance in the usual way, he found occupation in counting the number of words uttered by each performer. After striding over a field in two or three directions, he would tell the number of square inches it contained. He could number all the pints of beer he had drunk at all the houses he had ever visited during half a century. He once set himself to reckon how much a farthing would amount to if doubled 140 times; the result came out in such a stupendous number of pounds sterling as required 39 places of figures to represent it. In 1750 this problem was put to him: to find how many cubical eighths of an inch there are in a quadrangular mass measuring 23,145,789 yards long, 5,642,732 yards wide, and 54,965 yards thick; he answered this, as all the others, mentally. On one occasion he made himself what he called 'drunk with reckoning' the following: 'In 200,000 million cubic miles, how many grains of eight different kinds of corn and pulse, and how many hairs one inch long?' He ascertained by actual counting how many of each kind of grain, and how many hairs an inch long, would go to an inch cube, and then set himself about his enormous self-imposed task. He could suspend any of his problems for any length of time, and resume it at the point where he left off; and could converse on other subjects while thus employed. He could never give any account of the way in which he worked out his problems; nor did his singular but exceptional faculty bring him any other advantage than that of being invited to the houses of the gentry as a kind of show.

Zerah Colburn, who excited much interest in London in 1812, was a native of Vermont, in the United States. At six years old, he suddenly shewed extraordinary powers of mental calculation. By processes which seemed to be almost unconscious to himself, and were wholly so to others, he answered arithmetical questions of considerable difficulty. When eight years old, he was brought to London, where he astonished many learned auditors and spectators by giving correct solutions to such problems as the following: raise 8 up to the 16th power; give the square root of 106,929: give the cube root of 268,336,125; how many seconds are there in 48 years? The answers were always given in a very few minutes—sometimes in a few seconds. He was ignorant of the ordinary rules of arithmetic, and did not know how or why particular modes of process came into his mind. On one occasion, the Duke of Gloucester asked him to multiply 21,734 by 543; something in the boy's manner induced the duke to ask how he did it, from which it appeared that the boy arrived at the result by multiplying 65,202 by 181, an equivalent process; but why he made this change in the factors, neither he nor any one else could tell. Zerah Colburn was unlike other boys also in this, that he had more than the usual number of toes and fingers; a peculiarity observable also in his father and in some of his brothers.

An exceptional instance is presented in the case of Mr Bidder, of this faculty being cultivated to a highly useful purpose. George Parker Bidder, when six years old, used to amuse himself by counting up to 100, then to 1000, then to 1,000,000; by degrees he accustomed himself to contemplate the relations of high numbers, and used to build up peas, marbles, and shot, into squares, cubes, and other regular figures. He invented processes of his own, distinct from those given in books on arithmetic, and could solve all the usual questions mentally more rapidly than other boys with the aid of pen and paper. When he became eminent as a civil engineer, he was wont to embarrass and baffle the parliamentary counsel on contested railway bills, by confuting their statements of figures almost before the words were out of their mouths. In 1856, he gave to the Institution of Civil Engineers an interesting account of this singular arithmetical faculty—so far, at least, as to shew that *memory* has less to do with it than is generally supposed; the processes are actually worked out *seriatim*, but with a rapidity almost inconceivable.

## JULY 4.

St Finbar, abbot. St Bolcan, abbot. St Sisoes or Sisoy, anchoret in Egypt, about 429. St Bertha, widow, abbess of Blangy, in Artois, about 725. St Ulric, bishop of Augsburg, confessor, 973. St Odo, archbishop of Canterbury, confessor, 10th century.

### Translation of St Martin.

That the Church of Rome should not only celebrate the day of St Martin's death (November 11), but also that of the transference of his remains from their original humble resting-place to the cathedral of Tours, shews conclusively the veneration in which this soldier-saint was held. (See under November 11.) The day continues to have a place in the Church of England calendar.

In Scotland, this used to be called St Martin of Bullion's Day, and the weather which prevailed upon it was supposed to have a prophetic character. It was a proverb, that if the deer rise dry and lie down dry on Bullion's Day, it was a sign there would be a good gose-harvest—gose being a term for the latter end of summer; hence gose-harvest was an early harvest. It was believed generally over Europe that rain on this day betokened wet weather for the twenty ensuing days.

*Born.*—Christian Gellert, German poet and fabulist, 1715, *Chemnitz, Saxony*.

*Died.*—Lord Saye and Seal, beheaded, 1450, *London*; William Birde, English composer of sacred music, 1623; Meric Casaubon, learned and controversial writer, 1671, *bur. Canterbury Cathedral*; Henry Bentinck, first Duke of Portland, 1726, *Jamaica*; Samuel Richardson, novelist, 1761; Fisher Ames, American statesman, President of Harvard College, 1808, *Boston, U. S.*; Richard Watson, bishop of Llandaff, 1816; John Adams, second president of the United States, 1826; Thomas Jefferson, third president of the United States, 1826; Rev. William Kirby, naturalist, 1850, *Barham, Suffolk*; Richard Grainger, the re-edifier of Newcastle-on-Tyne, 1861, *Newcastle*.

### THOMAS JEFFERSON.

The celebrated author of the American Declaration of Independence, entered life as a Virginian barrister, and, while still a young man, was elected a member of the House of Burgesses for his state. When the disputes between the colonies and mother-country began, he took an active part in the measures for the resistance of taxation, and for diffusing the same spirit through the other provinces. Elected in 1775 to the Continental Congress, he zealously promoted the movement for a complete separation from England, and in the Declaration of Independence, which was adopted on the 4th of July 1776, he laid down the propositions, since so often quoted, that 'all men are created equal,' with 'an inalienable right' to 'life, liberty, and the pursuit of happiness,' and that 'governments derive their just powers from the consent of the governed.' When the cause of independence became triumphant, Mr Jefferson naturally took a high place in the administration of the new government. He successively filled the posts of governor of Virginia, secretary of state under the presidency of Washington, and vice-president under that of John Adams; finally, in 1801, attaining to the presidency, which he held for two terms or eight years. While Washington and Adams aimed at a strong, an aristocratic, and a centralising government, Jefferson stood up as the advocate of popular rights and measures. He headed the Liberal Republican, or, as it was afterwards called, the Democratic party. He laboured for civil and religious liberty and education. He secured the prohibition of the slave trade, and of slavery over a vast territory, and was in favour of universal emancipation. In Virginia, he secured the abolition of a religious establishment, and of entails, and the equal rights of both sexes to inheritance. The most important measure of his administration was the acquisition of Louisiana, including the whole territory west of the Mississippi, which was purchased of France for 15,000,000 dollars. His administration was singularly free from political favouritism. It is remembered as one of his sayings, that 'he could always find better men for every place than his own connections.'

After retiring from the presidency, he founded the university of Virginia, carried on an extensive correspondence, entertained visitors from all parts of the world, and enjoyed his literary and philosophical pursuits. He was married early in life, and had one daughter, whose numerous children were the solace of his old age. At the age of eighty, he wrote to John Adams, with whom, in spite of political differences, he maintained a warm personal friendship: 'I have ever dreaded a doting age; and my health has been generally so good, and is now so good, that I dread it still. The rapid decline of my strength, during the last winter, has made me hope sometimes that I see land. During summer I enjoy its temperature; but I shudder at the approach of winter, and wish I could sleep through it with the dormouse, and only wake with him in the spring, if ever. They say that Stark could walk about his room.* I am told you walk well and firmly. I can only reach my garden, and that with sensible fatigue. I ride, however, daily, but reading is my delight.—God bless you, and give you health, strength, good spirits, and as much life as you think worth having.'

The death of Jefferson, at the age of eighty-three, was remarkable. Both he and his friend John Adams, the one the author and the other the chief advocate of the Declaration of Independence—each having filled the highest offices in the Republic they founded—died on the 4th of July 1826, giving a singular solemnity to its fiftieth anniversary.

On the tomb of Jefferson, at Monticello, he is described as the author of the Declaration of Independence, the founder of religious freedom in Virginia, and of the university of Virginia; but there is a significant omission of the fact, that he was twice president of the United States.

## 'THE FOURTH OF JULY.'

Where a country or a government has been baffled in its efforts to attain or preserve a hated rule over another people, it must be content to see its failure made the subject of never-ending triumph and exultation. The joy attached to the sense of escape or emancipation tends to perpetuate itself by periodical celebrations, in which it is not likely that the motives of the other party, or the general justice of the case, will be very carefully considered or allowed for. We may doubt if it be morally expedient thus to keep alive the memory of facts which as certainly infer mortification to one party as they do glorification to another: but we must all admit that it is only natural, and in a measure to be expected.

The anniversary of the Declaration of Independence, July 4, 1776, has ever since been celebrated as a great national festival throughout the United States, and wherever Americans are assembled over the world. From Maine to Oregon, from the Great Lakes to the Gulf of Mexico, in every town and village, this birthday of the Republic has always hitherto been ushered in with the ringing of bells, the firing of cannon, the display of the national flag, and other evidences of public rejoicing. A national salute is fired at sunrise, noon, and at sunset, from every fort and man of war. The army, militia, and volunteer troops parade, with bands of music, and join with the citizens in patriotic processions. The famous Declaration is solemnly read, and orators, appointed for the occasion, deliver what are termed *Fourth of July Orations*, in which the history of the country is reviewed, and its past and coming glories proclaimed. The virtues of the Pilgrim Fathers, the heroic exertions and sufferings of the soldiers of the Revolution, the growth and power of the Republic, and the great future which expands before her, are the staple ideas of these orations. Dinners, toasts, and speeches follow, and at night the whole country blazes with bonfires, rockets, Roman candles, and fireworks of every description. In a great city like New York, Boston, or Philadelphia, the day, and even the night previous, is insufferably noisy with the constant rattle of Chinese-crackers and firearms. In the evening, the displays of fireworks in the public squares, provided by the authorities, are often magnificent.

John Adams, second president of the United States, and one of the most distinguished signers of the Declaration of Independence, in a letter written at the time, predicted the manner in which it would be celebrated, and his prediction has doubtless done something to insure its own fulfilment. Adams and Jefferson, two of the signers, both in turn presidents, by a most remarkable coincidence died on the fiftieth anniversary of Independence, in the midst of the national celebration, which, being semi-centennial, was one of extraordinary splendour.

* General Stark, 'the victor of Bennington,' had just died at the age of ninety-three.

## THE FAIRLOP OAK FESTIVAL.

The first Friday in July used to be marked by a local festival in Essex, arising through a simple yet curious chain of circumstances.

In Hainault Forest, in Essex, there formerly was an oak of prodigious size, known far and wide as the Fairlop Oak. It came to be a ruin about the beginning of the present century, and in June 1805 was in great part destroyed by an accidental fire. When entire—though the statement seems hardly credible—it is said to have had a girth of thirty-six feet, and to have had seventeen branches, each as large as an ordinary tree of its species. A vegetable prodigy of such a character could not fail to become a most notable and venerated object in the district where it grew.

Far back in the last century, there lived an estimable block and pump maker in Wapping, Daniel Day by name, but generally known by the quaint appellative of *Good Day*. Haunting a small rural retreat which he had acquired in Essex, not far from Fairlop, Mr Day became deeply interested in the grand old tree above described, and began a practice of resorting to it on the first Friday of July, in order to eat a rustic dinner with a few friends under its branches. His dinner was composed of the good old English fare, beans and bacon, which he never changed, and which no guest ever complained of. Indeed, beans and bacon became identified with the festival, and it would have been an interference with many hallowed associations to make any change or even addition. By and by, the neighbours caught Mr Day's spirit, and came in multitudes to join in his festivities. As a necessary consequence, trafficking-people came to sell refreshments on the spot; afterwards commerce in hard and soft wares found its way thither; shows and tumbling followed; in short, a regular fair was at last concentrated around the Fairlop Oak, such as Gay describes:

'Pedlars' stalls with glitt'ring toys are laid,
The various fairings of the country-maid.
Long silken laces hang upon the twine,
And rows of pins and amber bracelets shine.

Here the tight lass, knives, combs, and scissors spies,
And *looks* on thimbles with desiring eyes.
The mountebank now treads the stage, and sells
His pills, his balsams, and his ague-spells:
Now o'er and o'er the nimble tumbler springs,
And on the rope the vent'rous maiden swings;
Jack Pudding, in his party-coloured jacket,
Tosses the glove, and jokes at ev'ry packet:
*Here* raree-shows are seen, and Punch's feats,
And pockets picked in crowds and various cheats.'

Mr Day had thus the satisfaction of introducing the appearances of civilisation in a district which had heretofore been chiefly noted as a haunt of banditti.

Fun of this kind, like fame, naturally gathers force as it goes along. We learn that for some years before the death of Mr Day, which took place in 1767, the pump-and-block-makers of Wapping, to the amount of thirty or forty, used to come each first Friday of July to the Fairlop beans-and-bacon feast, seated in a boat formed of a single piece of wood, and mounted upon wheels, covered with an awning, and drawn by six horses. As they went accompanied by a band of musicians,

FAIRLOP OAK.

it may be readily supposed how the country-people would flock round, attend, and stare at their anomalous vehicle, as it hurled madly along the way to the forest. A local poet, who had been one of the company, gives us just a faint hint of the feelings connected with this journey:

'O'er land our vessel bent its course,
Guarded by troops of foot and horse;
Our anchors they were all a-peak,
Our crew were baling from each leak,
On Stratford bridge it made me quiver,
Lest they should spill us in the river.'

The founder of the Fairlop Festival was remarkable for benevolence and a few innocent eccentricities. He was never married, but bestowed as much kindness upon the children of a sister as he could have spent upon his own. He had a female servant, a widow, who had been eight-and-twenty years with him. As she had in life loved two things in especial, her wedding-ring and her tea, he caused her to be buried with the former on her finger, and a pound of tea in each hand—the latter circumstance being the more remarkable, as he himself disliked tea, and made no use of it. He had a number of little aversions, but no resentments. It changed the usual composed and amiable expression of his countenance to hear of any one going to law. He literally every day relieved the poor at his gate. He often lent sums of money to deserving persons, charging no interest for it. When he had attained a considerable age, the Fairlop Oak lost one of its branches. Accepting the fact as an omen of his own approaching end, he caused the detached limb of the tree to be fashioned into a coffin for himself, and this convenience he took care to *try*, lest it should prove too short. By his request, his body was borne in its coffin to Barking churchyard by water, in a boat, the worthy old gentleman having contracted a prejudice against all land vehicles, the living horse included, in consequence of being so often thrown from them in his various journeys.*

* *Fairlop and its Founder*, printed at Totham, 1847.

## WILLIAM HUTTON'S 'STRONG WOMAN.'

William Hutton, the quaint but sensible Birmingham manufacturer, was accustomed to take a month's tour every summer, and to note down his observations on places and people. Some of the results appeared in distinct books, some in his autobiography, and some in the *Gentleman's Magazine*, towards the close of the last century and the beginning of the present. One year he would be accompanied by his father, a tough old man, who was not frightened at a twenty-mile walk; another year he would go alone; while on one occasion his daughter went with him, she riding on horseback, and he trudging on foot by her side. Various parts of England and Wales were thus visited, at a time when tourists' facilities were slender indeed. It appears from his lists of distances that he could 'do' fifteen or twenty miles a day for weeks together; although his mode of examining places led to a much slower rate of progress. One of the odd characters which he met with at Matlock, in Derbyshire, in July 1801, is worth describing in his own words. After noticing the rocks and caves at that town, he said: 'The greatest wonder I saw was Miss Phœbe Bown, in person five feet six, about thirty, well-proportioned, round-faced and ruddy; a dark penetrating eye, which, the moment it fixes upon your face, stamps your character, and that with precision. Her step (pardon the Irishism) is more manly than a man's, and can easily cover forty miles a day. Her common dress is a man's hat, coat, with a spencer above it, and men's shoes; I believe she is a stranger to breeches. She can lift one hundred-weight with each hand, and carry fourteen score. Can sew, knit, cook, and spin, but hates them all, and every accompaniment to the female character, except that of modesty. A gentleman at the New Bath recently treated her so rudely, that "she had a good mind to have knocked him down." She positively assured me she did not know what fear is. She never gives an affront, but will offer to fight any one who gives her one. If she has not fought, perhaps it is owing to the insulter being a coward, for none else would *give* an affront [to a woman]. She has strong sense, an excellent judgment, says smart things, and supports an easy freedom in all companies. Her voice is more than masculine, it is deep toned; the wind in her face, she can send it a mile; has no beard; accepts any kind of manual labour, as holding the plough, driving the team, thatching the ricks, &c. But her chief avocation is breaking-in horses, at a guinea a week; always rides without a saddle; and is supposed the best judge of a horse, cow, &c., in the country; and is frequently requested to purchase for others at the neighbouring fairs. She is fond of Milton, Pope, Shakspeare, also of music; is self-taught; performs on several instruments, as the flute, violin, harpsichord, and supports the bass-viol in Matlock church. She is an excellent markswoman, and, like her brother-sportsmen, carries her gun upon her shoulder. She eats no beef or pork, and but little mutton; her chief food is milk, and also her drink—discarding wine, ale, and spirits.

## BISHOP WATSON.

Richard Watson was eminent as a prelate, politician, natural philosopher, and controversial theologian; but his popular fame may be said to depend solely on one little book, his *Apology for the Bible*, written as a reply to Paine's *Age of Reason.* A curious error has been, more than once, lately promulgated respecting this prelate. At a telegraphic soiree, held in the Free-trade Hall, Manchester, during the meeting of the British Association for the Advancement of Science, at that city, in 1861, it was confidently asserted that Bishop Watson had given the first idea of the electric telegraph. The only probable method of accounting for so egregious an error, is that Bishop Watson had been confounded with Sir William Watson, who, when an apothecary in London, conducted some electrical experiments in 1747, and succeeded in sending the electric current from a Leyden-jar through a considerable range of earth, or water, and along wires suspended in the open air on sticks. But, even he never had the slightest idea of applying his experiments to telegraphic purposes. In his own account of these experiments, he says: 'If it should be asked to what useful purposes the effects of electricity can be applied, it may be answered that we are not yet so far advanced in these discoveries as to render them conducive to the service of mankind.'

Bishop Watson was elected professor of chemistry at the university of Cambridge in 1769; and he gives us the following statement on the subject: 'At the time this honour was conferred upon me, I knew nothing at all of chemistry, had never read a syllable on the subject, nor seen a single experiment in it!' A very fair specimen of the consideration in which physical science was held at the English universities, during the dark ages of the last century. After studying chemistry for fourteen months, Watson commenced his lectures; but in all his printed works on chemistry, and other subjects, the word electricity is never once mentioned!

# JULY 5.

St Modwena, virgin, of Ireland, 9th century. St Edana or Edæne, virgin, of same country. St Peter of Luxemburg, confessor, cardinal, and bishop of Metz, 1387.

*Born.*—John Broughton, noted pugilist, 1704, *London;* Mrs Sarah Siddons (*née* Kemble), tragic actress, 1755; C. A. Stothard, antiquarian draughtsman, 1786, *London.*

*Died.*—Queen Magdalen of Scotland, 1537; Cardinal Passionei, librarian of the Vatican, 1761; Sir Robert Strange, the 'prince of British line-engravers,' 1792, *London;* Mrs Dorothea Jordan (*née* Bland), comic actress, 1816, *St Cloud.*

## JOHN BROUGHTON.

That regulated system of combat with the closed fists, which bears the name of Boxing, and which may be said to be peculiar to England, dates only from the earlier half of the eighteenth century. The rules, including those notable ones regarding rounds, and the interval of half a minute between each, which give such a marked character to the practice—a sort of humanity relieving its barbarism—were the production of John Broughton, who kept a booth for the exhibition of boxing in the Tottenham Court Road; they are dated the 10th of August 1743. It seems to have been on the decline of sword-combat exhibitions in the reign of George I., that the *comparatively* harmless amusement of boxing arose. There appears to be no such thing known at an earlier date.

Broughton was the first who stood in the position of Champion—a distinction which he held for eighteen years. It gives a curious idea of the tastes of the English of his day, that his most notable patron was the king's second son, the Duke of Cumberland, so noted for his butcheries after the battle of Culloden. The duke probably attended Broughton's boxing-booth within a week of his going forth upon that famous expedition, in which the fate of a dynasty was decided; probably, it was one of the first places of amusement he went to after his triumphant return. He once took Broughton with him on a journey to the continent, and on shewing him the grenadier guards at Berlin, asked the pugilist what he thought of any of those fellows for a 'set-to;' to which Broughton is said to have answered, that he would have no objection to take up the whole regiment, if he were only allowed a breakfast between each two battles.

Broughton was admitted to have a constant originality, as well as great power, in his style of boxing, and he seems to have been a man of sense and ability, apart from his profession. He was at the very acme of his reputation, when he was so unfortunate as to fall into a quarrel with a butcher named Slack, who consequently challenged him. The champion himself, and the whole circle of his friends and admirers, regarded the challenger with contempt, and when the combat commenced, the betting was ten to one in Broughton's favour. But Slack contrived, at an early period of the contest, to hit Broughton between the eyes, and blinded him. The poor man had undiminished strength, but he was not able to see his antagonist. His royal patron, with characteristic brutality, called out to him: 'Why, Broughton, you can't fight—you are beat!'

['Proud Cumberland prances, insulting the slain.']

It was too true. The fight closed in fourteen minutes, with the defeat of the hitherto unmatched hero. 'The faces in the amphitheatre,' says the historian of the day, 'were of all manner of colours and lengths.' The duke was understood to have lost thousands on the occasion. Slack, by his adroit blow, gained six hundred pounds.

Broughton survived in obscurity, but in comparative affluence, for thirty-nine years, dying on the 8th of January 1789, at a very advanced age. The father, as he may well be called, of this 'truly English art,' lies buried in Lambeth churchyard.

## QUEEN MAGDALEN.

The death of the French princess, Magdalen, consort of James V. of Scotland, is a very affecting incident. The young Scottish monarch had voyaged to France in the summer of 1536, to see the daughter of the Duc de Vendome, with a view to marriage; but, not affecting her on intimate acquaintance, he turned his thoughts to the royal family as likely to furnish him a better bride. The king, Francis I., received him with great kindness at a place to the south of Lyon, and thence conducted him to a castle where his family was residing. He found the Princess Magdalen unable to ride on horseback, as her mother and other ladies did, but obliged by weakness of health to be carried in a chariot. 'Yet, notwithstanding her sickness'—so the contemporary Scottish historian Lindsay informs us—'fra the time she saw the king of Scotland, and spak with him, she became so enamoured of him, and loved him so weel, that she wold have no man alive to her husband, but he allenarly [only].' Sage counsellors of both countries discommended the union; but the young princess easily induced her father to consent, and the consent of the king of Scotland followed. On the 1st of January, the pair were united in the church of Notre Dame, in the presence of seven cardinals and a great assemblage of the French nobility, amidst circumstances of great pomp and popular joy. 'Through all France that day, there was jousting and running of horse proclaimed, with all other manly exercise; as also skirmishing of ships through all the coasts; so that in towns, lands, seas, firths, castles, and towers, there was no man that might have heard for the *raird* [uproar] and noise of cannons, nor scarcely have seen for the vapours thereof. There was also within the town of Paris, cunning carvers and profound necromancers, who by their art caused things appear whilk wes not, as follows: fowls flying in the air spouting fire on others, rivers of water running through the town and ships fechtand therupon.'

With his young bride, and a hundred thousand crowns by way of dowry, gifted moreover with twenty war-horses, as many suits of elegant mail, two great war-ships, and a vast quantity of jewels and other minor articles, the young Scottish monarch set sail for his own country. Landing at Leith on Whit Sunday, the young queen, full of love for her husband and his country, knelt on the shore, took up a handful of sand, and kissed it, invoking God's blessing upon Scotland. She was received in Edinburgh with triumphs and shows of unexampled grandeur, with, what was far better, the affectionate reverence of the entire people. But the doom had already been passed upon her. She withered like an uprooted flower, and only forty days from her arrival, lay a corpse in her husband's palace. The death of this beautiful young creature in such interesting circumstances, made a deep impression on the national heart, and it is understood to have been the first occasion of a general mourning being assumed in Scotland.

# JULY 6.

St Julian, anchoret, about 370. St Palladius, apostle of the Scots, bishop and confessor, about 450. St Moninna, of Ireland, virgin, 518. St Goar, priest and confessor, 575. St Sexburgh, abbess of Ely, 7th century.

---

*Born.*—John Flaxman, sculptor, 1755, *York;* Sir Thomas Stamford Raffles, governor of Java (1811—1816), author of a *History of Java*, founder of the Zoological Society, 1781.

*Died.*—Henry II. of England, 1189, *Chinon Castle;* Pope Benedict XI., 1304; Sir Thomas More, Chancellor of England, beheaded 1535, *London;* Edward VI. of England, 1553, *Greenwich;* Archbishop Grindal, 1583, *Croydon;* Humphry Wanley, learned scholar, 1726; Michael Bruce, poet, 1767, *Kinnesswood, Kinross-shire;* George Augustus Elliot, Lord Heathfield, military commander, 1790; Granville Sharpe, philanthropist, 1813, *Fulham;* Samuel Whitbread, statesman, 1815; Sir Henry Raeburn, painter, 1823, *Edinburgh;* Sir Thomas Munro, 1827, *Madras;* D. M. Moir, poet and miscellaneous writer, 1851, *Musselburgh, Scotland;* Andrew Crosse, electrician, 1855; Sir Francis Palgrave, historian, 1861.

## SIR THOMAS MORE.

When Sir Thomas More was installed as lord chancellor, in the room of Cardinal Wolsey, the Duke of Norfolk, by the king's express command, commended him 'unto the people, there with great applause and joy gathered together,' for his *admirable wisdome, integritie, and innocencie, joined with most pleasant facilitie of witt;* praise which perfectly suited its subject.

Sir Thomas More united prudence with pleasantry, great and singular learning with simplicity of life, and unaffected humility with the proudest temporal greatness; he preferred the love of his family, and the quiet pleasures of his own household, to the favours of kings or delights of courts. It was only after the repeated urging of Henry, that at last he consented to relinquish his studious and secluded life at Chelsea; and it may truly be said that he was never happy after; for, besides his natural shrinking from public responsibility, and his disregard of worldly notoriety, he had a remarkably clear insight into Henry's character, and never put much faith in his abundant favours.

More was retained in the king's household like a personal friend, except that there must have been a degree of tyranny in his being kept thus continually from his own family. But his pleasantries amused the king and his queen, and his learning was useful to a monarch, who was writing a book which was to be the wonder of Christendom, and which had to be looked over, corrected, and arranged by Sir Thomas, as Sir Thomas himself admits, before Europe could be honoured with a glance at it. He was employed on several embassies alone, and in company with Wolsey; and finally, much against his will, he succeeded in 1529, to the highest honours, upon Wolsey's fall.

He filled the office of chancellor with a wisdom and unspotted integrity which were unexampled in his own time; and yet united with these virtues such graceful ease and agreeable manners, that it seemed to him no effort to be honest, and no difficulty to be just. When one woman sought to bribe him, by presenting him with a valuable cup, he ordered his butler to fill it with wine, and having drunk her health, returned it; and when another presented him with a pair of gloves, containing forty pounds, he accepted the gloves and returned the gold, declaring that 'he preferred his gloves without lining?'

More, though liberal-minded, was a stanch believer in the pope's supremacy, and had a great dread of heresy; and when Henry opposed the pope's will and decree by marrying Anne Boleyn, More resigned his chancellorship. He did not do so ostensibly on that account, but the king was shrewd enough to surmise his true reason. Henry really loved his servant, and did his utmost to obtain his approval of the new marriage, but the ex-chancellor preserved a discreet silence. The king, piqued by the neutrality of one whose opinion he valued, and on whom he fancied he had bestowed so many inestimable benefits, determined to make the late favourite acquiesce in his sovereign's will. More was invited to the coronation, and urged to appear, but he refused. He was threatened, but he only smiled. His name was put in the bill of attainder against the supposed accomplices of Joan of Kent, and then erased as a favour. But when the oath was put to him, which declared the lawfulness of the king's marriage, he would not take it, and so was committed to the Tower; and after many attempts, first to change him, and then to make him betray himself, so as to afford just ground for condemnation, he was tried and condemned unjustly, and beheaded, to the regret and shame of the whole nation, and all the world's astonishment and disgust.

The body of Sir Thomas More was first interred in St Peter's Church, in the Tower, and afterwards in Chelsea Church; but his head was stuck on a pole, and placed on London Bridge, where it remained fourteen days. His eldest and favourite daughter, Margaret Roper, much grieved and shocked at this exposure of her father's head, determined, if possible, to gain possession of it. She succeeded; and, according to Aubrey, in a very remarkable manner. 'One day,' says he, 'as she was passing under the bridge, looking on her father's head, she exclaimed: "That head has lain many a time in my lap, would to God it would fall into my lap as I pass under!" She had her wish, and it did fall into her lap!' Improbable as this incident may appear, it is not unlikely that it really occurred. For having tried in vain to gain possession of the head by open and direct means, she bribed or persuaded one of the bridge-keepers to throw it over the bridge, as if to make room for another, just when he should see her passing in a boat beneath. And she doubtless made the above exclamation to her boatmen, to prevent the suspicion of a concerted scheme between her and the bridge-keeper. However some of these particulars may be questioned, it appears certain that Margaret Roper gained possession of her father's head by some such means, for when summoned before the council for having it in her custody, she boldly declared that 'her father's head should not be food for fishes!' For this she was imprisoned, but was soon liberated, and allowed to retain her father's head, which she had enclosed in a leaden box, and preserved it with the tenderest devotion. She died in 1544, aged 36, and was buried in the Roper vault, in St Dunstan's Church,

Canterbury; and, according to her own desire, her father's head was placed in her coffin. But subsequently, for some cause not now known, it was removed from its leaden case, and deposited in a small niche in the wall of the vault, with an iron grating before it, where it now remains in the condition of a fleshless skull.

Margaret Roper was well skilled in Greek, Latin, and other languages; a proficient in the arts and sciences as then known; and a woman of remarkable determination and strength of character. A tradition, preserved in the Roper family, records that Queen Elizabeth offered her a ducal coronet, which she refused, lest it should be considered as a compromise for what she regarded as the judicial murder of her father.

## HUMPHRY WANLEY, THE ANTIQUARY.

This laborious worker in the field of antiquarianism was the son of the author of that strange collection of curious, but ill-authenticated matters, the *Wonders of the Little World*, and was born March 21, 1671-2. He was placed to some mechanical business; but all the time he could command, he employed in searching for and reading ancient manuscripts, by copying and imitating which he acquired a particular facility in judging of their authenticity and dates. Dr Lloyd, bishop of Worcester, pleased with this extraordinary taste in so young a person, sent him to Oxford. He was next appointed by Harley, Earl of Oxford, to arrange his valuable collections of manuscripts and books; and his lordship's eldest son allowed Wanley a pension, and continued him in his situation of librarian till his death. His industry as a bibliographer was untiring, and various public libraries and collections of manuscripts benefited from his labours.

Humphry was a very unselfish being, and extremely faithful to his patrons. He was in the habit of collecting scarce articles for Lord Oxford's library. One day, having procured a rarity, he went to his lordship's town-house, where several cabinet ministers were assembled, and Wanley was desired to wait a few minutes. The weather was cold, and he became irritated by the delay; so he determined to retaliate by increasing the price for his treasure. When the ministers departed, Wanley was admitted to Lord Oxford.

'I have, my lord,' said Wanley, 'a most rare article, but it is very dear. It is the property of a widow, who has two daughters; they have seen better days. She would scarcely permit me to bring it, though I left a promissory-note for the hundred pounds she demanded, in case I did not return it.'

'A hundred pounds, Wanley; that is a great sum for so small a thing!'

'It is, my lord; but you have so often asked me to get it, that I thought I could not do less than shew it your lordship, particularly as it is quite perfect, and is the only copy known.'

'It is a large sum; however, I must have it. Give me pen, ink, and paper.' A draught was drawn for a hundred pounds, in presenting which his lordship said: 'Now, Wanley, perhaps you purchased this at some bookstall!'

Humphry expressed a seeming surprise, shrugged up his shoulders, and left the book with the peer, for what he really did give for it at a bookstall—*sixpence!*

Wanley died July 6, 1726, and was buried in the old church of St Marylebone, under a flat stone.

## ANDREW CROSSE.

Andrew Crosse was a country gentleman, who spent his whole life at Fyne Court, on his patrimonial acres, six miles from Taunton, on the Quantock Hills. His leisure he employed in electrical experiments made on a gigantic scale. Shewing a large party, that had come from a distance to see his apparatus, two enormous Leyden-jars, which he charged by means of wires stretched for miles among the forest-trees, an old gentleman contemplated the arrangement with a look of grave disapprobation, and at length, with much solemnity, observed: 'Mr Crosse, don't you think it is rather impious to bottle the lightning?'

'Let me answer your question by asking another,' replied Mr Crosse, laughing. 'Don't you think, sir, it might be considered rather impious to bottle the rain-water?'

Whilst engaged in the construction of a variety of minerals, by subjecting various matters held in solution to electrical action, he, in 1837, hit on a discovery, which, blazoned abroad in the newspapers, raised round his name a storm of obloquy which happily his hearty good-nature enabled him to endure without discomfort.

Having mixed two ounces of powdered flint with six ounces of carbonate of potassa, fused them together in a strong heat, then reduced the compound to powder, and dissolved it in boiling-water, he obtained silicate of potassa, a portion of which he diluted in boiling water, slowly adding hydrochloric acid to super-saturation. This fluid he subjected to a long-continued electric action, through the intervention of a porous stone, in order to form, if possible, crystals of silica, but this failed. On the fourteenth day from the commencement of the experiment, he observed, through a lens, a few small whitish excrescences projecting from the middle of the electrified stone. On the eighteenth day, these projections had become enlarged, and struck out seven or eight filaments. On the twenty-sixth day, they assumed the forms of perfect insects, standing erect on a few bristles, which were their tails. On the twenty-eighth day they moved their legs, and soon after detached themselves from the stone, and began to move about. In the course of a few weeks, about a hundred insects had made their appearance. The smaller ones had six legs and the larger eight, and were pronounced as belonging to the genus *Acarus*.

At first Mr Crosse imagined that these insects must have originated from some *ova* in the water. He repeated the experiment, taking every conceivable care to subject his materials to processes destructive of life, but the *acari* duly reappeared under the same conditions. Others tried the experiment, with even more rigid pains to exclude and destroy imperceptible ova, but still *acari* came to life, walked about, fed, multiplied, and only died after frost, which always proved fatal to them. The discussion which followed these remarkable experiments still continues. Some hold that they are clear proofs of spontaneous generation, and of the possibility of animal creation wherever the requisite conditions are supplied. Others firmly maintain the impossibility of such new creation, and assert that ova must needs be present, having eluded the contrivances to destroy or to strain them out. About the *Acarus Crossii*, as it was called, Crosse himself put forth no theory, drew no inferences, and attacked no established belief. He was very little of a theorist; he simply said, I did so and so, and so and so was the result. The abuse lavished on him for the inferences that might be drawn from his discovery was singularly out of place.

Mr Crosse was not wealthy, and his secluded life at home among the Somersetshire hills was first a necessity and then a habit. He was far from unsocial, and he excited in all who knew him the heartiest friendship. He was twice married; and died on the 6th July 1855, in the room in which, seventy-one years before, he had been born.

## A MODERN HERMIT.

In the village of Newton Burgoland, which is a hamlet of the parish of Swepstone, near Ashby-de-la-Zouch, Leicestershire, is now (1863) living* an eccentric character, who styles himself 'The Old Hermit of Newton Burgoland.' Though he has resided here nearly fifteen years, his real name, William Lole, is scarcely known; and a stranger might search for him in vain, even in his own hamlet, unless he inquired for 'The Old Hermit.' Yet he is no recluse, no ascetic. It cannot be said of him:

'The moss his bed, the cave his humble cell;
His food the fruits, his drink the crystal well.'

He lives among the haunts of men, in a comfortable cottage; he can enjoy a good dinner, can drink his glass of beer, and smoke his pipe with as much relish as any man. Yet, according to his own definition, he is entitled to the appellation of a hermit. 'True hermits,' says he, 'throughout every age, have been the firm abettors of freedom.' And, as regards his appearance, his fancies, and his habits, he is a hermit—a *solitaire*, in the midst of his fellow-beings. He wears a long beard, and has a very venerable appearance. In his dress he is the veriest dandy, if we regard its profuseness and singularity. He has a multitude of suits, all of an original and very fantastical description. They must have cost more than half his income, and have exhausted his utmost ingenuity to devise. He has no less than twenty different kinds of hats, each of which has its own name and form, with some emblem or motto on it—sometimes both. Here are a few examples:

| No. | Name. | Motto or Emblem. |
|---|---|---|
| 1. | Odd Fellows. | Without money, without friends, without credit. |
| 5. | Bellows. | Blow the flames of freedom with God's word of truth. |
| 7. | Helmet. | Will fight for the birthright of conscience, love, life, property, and national independence. |
| 13. | Patent Tea-pot. | To draw out the flavour of the tea best—Union and Goodwill. |
| 17. | Wash-basin of Reform. | White-washed face, and collyed heart. |
| 20. | Bee-hive. | The toils of industry are sweet; a wise people live at peace. |

* The Modern Hermit died in 1875.

The shapes of the hats, and the devices on them, are intended to symbolise some fact or sentiment.

The rest of his dress is as fantastical as his hats. He has twelve suits of clothes, each with a peculiar name, differing from the others, and, like his hats, intended to be emblematical. One dress, which he calls 'Odd Fellows,' is of white cotton or linen. It hangs loosely over the body, except

being bound round the waist with a white girdle, buckled in the front. Over his left breast is a heart-shaped badge, bearing the words, 'Liberty of conscience,' which he calls his 'Order of the Star.' The hat which he wears with this dress is nearly white, and of common shape, but has on it four fanciful devices, bound with black ribbon, and inscribed, severally, with these words: 'Bless, feed—good allowance—well clothed—all working-men.'

Another dress, which he calls 'Foresters,' is a kind of frock-coat, made of soft brown leather, slightly embroidered with braid. This coat is closed down the front with white buttons, and bound round the waist with a white girdle, fastened with a white buckle. The hat, slightly resembling a turban, is divided into black and white stripes, running round it.

Another dress, which he has named 'Military,' has some resemblance to the military costume at the beginning of the present century. The coat is sloped off at the waist, and faced with fur; dark knee-breeches, and buckled shoes. The hat belonging to this dress is no longer in existence. It was a large conspicuous article, a composition between the old-fashioned cocked-hat, and that worn by military commanders; but instead of the military plume, it had two upright peaks on the crown, not unlike the tips of a horse's ears. This hat, which he asserts cost five pounds, was the pride of his heart. He considered it a perfect specimen of exquisite taste and ingenuity. He preserved it with religious care, and never wore it but on important occasions.

On one of these occasions he arrayed himself in his 'Military,' and adjusted his pet-hat with consequential precision. Exulting in his fancied dignity, he sallied forth from his hermitage: but, forgetful of the hermit's humility, he strode along the road with a somewhat martial air. When, lo! he met a group of giddy, mischievous youths who were just looking out for a frolic. The old hermit's queer appearance, of course, attracted their notice. His fantastical hat, his antiquated military costume,

the whimsical mixture of his reverent and defiant air, might have conquered the gravity of a Stoic. No wonder the merry youths were convulsed with laughter. But nothing less than a practical joke would satisfy them. So they rushed round the old hermit, knocked off his hat, tossed it into the air, kicked it about for a football, and finally tore it into tatters. Thus perished our sage's pet-hat. Alas! for pets, whether old hermits' hats or young ladies' pug-dogs, they are sure to come to an untimely end. The old hermit still mourns over his lost hat, and descants of its glories with melancholy pleasure. 'Ah!' says he, 'it was a perfect beauty—a wonderful production! It cost me many a sleepless night to invent it. Many a meal I lost to save money to pay for it. I shall never have its like again. I cannot afford it. I grow old, and times grow harder with me, Ah! those audacious lads. Would they had had something better to do! It was downright cruelty to rob the poor old hermit of such a noble hat!' His mania for symbolisation pervades all his thoughts and doings. His garden is a complete collection of emblems. The trees, the walks, the squares, the beds, the flowers, the seats and arbours—are all symbolically arranged. In the passage leading into the garden are 'the three seats of Self-inquiry,' each inscribed with one of these questions: 'Am I vile? Am I a hypocrite? Am I a Christian?' Among the emblems and mottoes, which are marked by different-coloured pebbles or flowers, are these: 'The vessels of the tabernacle;' 'The Christian's armour—olive-branch, baptismal-font, breastplate of righteousness, shield of faith,' &c. 'Mount Pisgah;' a circle enclosing the motto—'Eternal love has wed my soul;' 'A bee-hive;' 'A church;' 'Sacred urn;' 'Universal grave;' 'Bed of diamonds;' 'A heart, enclosing the rose of Sharon;' All the implements used in gardening. 'The two hearts' bowers;' 'The lovers' prayer;' 'Conjugal bliss;' 'The Hermit's coat of arms;' 'Gossips' Court,' with motto: 'Don't tell anybody!' 'The kitchen-walk' contains representations of culinary utensils, with mottoes. 'Feast square' contains—'Venison pasty, Round of beef,' &c.; 'The Odd Fellow's Square,' with 'The hen-pecked husband put on water-gruel.' 'The oratory,' with various mottoes; 'The orchestry,' mottoes, 'God save our noble queen; Britons never shall be slaves,' &c. 'The sand-glass of Time;' 'The assembly-room;' 'The wedding-walk;' 'The Holy Mount;' 'Noah's ark, Rainbow, Jacob's ladder,' &c. 'The Bank of Faith;' 'The Saloon;' 'The Enchanted Ground;' 'The Exit'—all with their respective emblems and mottoes. Besides these fantastical devices, there are, or were, in his garden, representations of the inquisition and purgatory; effigies of the apostles; and mounds covered with flowers, to represent the graves of the Reformers. In the midst of the religious emblems stood a large tub, with a queer desk before it, to represent a pulpit. When his garden was full of visitors, as it often used to be, he would clamber into this tub, and harangue them in a long rambling tirade against popery, and all kinds of real or fancied religious and political oppression. He declaims vociferously against the pope as Antichrist and the enemy of humanity; and when he fled from Rome in the guise of a servant, our old hermit decked his hat with laurels, and, thus equipped, went to the Independent chapel, declaring that 'the reign of the man of sin was over.' He also raised a mock-gallows in his garden, and suspended on it an effigy of the pope, whimsically dressed, with many books sticking out of his pockets, which, he said, contained the doctrines of popery. Though he professes Christianity, and owns the Bible to be a divine revelation, yet he belongs to no religious community, and very rarely enters a place of worship. He is extremely poor, and how he ekes out a livelihood is a marvel; for though his house and garden are his own property, they yield him no income. His garden, which might have been made profitable, is so fully occupied with his whimsical devices, that it produces scarcely any fruit or vegetables. And often, when laying out some new fancy in his garden, he would be so engrossed with it, that he would have passed day after day without food, had not one kind neighbour and another carried him a ready-dressed meal. He gains a little, however, by opening his garden to tea-parties, on which occasions he supplies the visitors with tea-services, and charges them one shilling or sixpence a head, according to their condition in life. But this income, which is very scanty and precarious, lasts only during the summer season. Occasionally he prints little pamphlets or tracts, consisting of mottoes and trite sayings; but these, though sold at a high price, can scarcely pay the expense of printing. He is now in such poverty that he is thankful for any assistance, which does not require him to relinquish his present mode of living. He has a brother in competent circumstances, who has offered to share his home with him; but, 'No,' says the old hermit, 'for what would then become of my garden? My heart is in my garden. I cannot leave it!'

## JULY 7.

St Pantaenus, father of the church, 3d century. St Felix, bishop of Nantes, confessor, 584. St Edelburga, virgin, of Kent. St Hedda, bishop of the West Saxons, confessor, 705. St Willibald, bishop of Aichstadt, confessor, 790. St Benedict XI., pope and confessor, 1304.

*Born.*—Thomas, Earl of Arundel, collector of ancient sculptures, 1592; Emperor Nicolas of Russia, 1796.

*Died.*—Edward I. of England, 1307, *Burgh-on-Sands;* John Huss, burned at Constance, 1415; Dr John Eachard, 1697, *Cambridge;* Bishop Compton, 1713; Dr Thomas Blacklock, 'the blind poet,' 1791, *Edinburgh;* Richard Brinsley Sheridan, 1816, *London.*

### THOMAS, EARL OF ARUNDEL—THE ARUNDELIAN MARBLES.

There is such a singularity in the idea of an English nobleman of the early part of the seventeenth century interesting himself in art and its treasures, that this peer stands out in a prominence much beyond what either his rank or personal qualities would have otherwise entitled him to. It does not seem to have been from any high conception of the value of beautiful things, that he busied himself so much in collecting relics of ancient sculpture in Italy. He was travelling there—the objects struck his fancy, and he thought of getting them brought home to England. Clarendon speaks of him as a rather illiterate man. More certainly, he was a man of great formality and stateliness—unbending—even a little austere —all of them qualities that one does not naturally associate with a lover of the fine arts for their own sake. From whatever motive, however, he acted, it was undoubtedly a remarkable service he performed to his country, to collect so many sculptures, medals, &c., at the time when such things were yet abundant, and when as yet his countrymen were so indifferent to them.

The Arundelian Marbles, as they came to be called, were all stored in and about a mansion which the earl possessed in the Strand, on the river side, between Essex House and Somerset House. His lordship's descendants acceding to the dukedom of Norfolk, the curiosities and their mansion became in time the property of that family. There is something melancholy, and a good deal that is surprising, in the ultimate history of the marbles.

An act of parliament having been obtained, empowering the then Duke of Norfolk, to let part of the site of the house and gardens to builders, at a reserved ground-rent, which was to accumulate in order to raise a fund for building a mansion-house for the family, on that part of the gardens which lay next the river—preparations were made for taking down the old buildings. The Royal Society, who had hitherto, by permission of the duke, held their meetings in Arundel House, had removed to Gresham College, taking with them the noble library which the duke had liberally presented to them.

'Arundel House,' says Mr Theobald,* 'being now about to be pulled down, great part of the furniture was removed to Stafford House, with the museum, &c. And as there were many fine statues, bas-reliefs, and marbles, they were received into the lower part of the gardens, and many of them placed under a colonnade there; and the upper part of the ground next the Strand let to builders, who continued the street, next the Strand, from Temple Bar towards Westminster; and also to build thereon the several streets called Arundel, Norfolk, and Surrey Streets, leading from the Strand towards the river, as far as the cross-street, called Howard Street, which ran parallel with the Strand.

'When the workmen began to build next the Strand, in order to prevent encroachments, a cross-wall was built to separate the ground let to builders from that reserved for the family mansion; and many of the workmen, to save the expense of carrying away the rubbish, threw it over this cross-wall, where it fell upon the colonnade; and at last, by its weight, broke it down, and falling on the statues placed there, broke several of them. A great part of these in that sad condition, was purchased by Sir William Fermor, from whom the present Earl of Pomfret is descended. He removed these down to his seat at Easton Neston, in Northamptonshire, where he employed some statuary to repair such as were not too much demolished.

'Here these continued till the year 1755, when the countess made a present of them to the university of Oxford, for which she received their thanks in due state; and in the year following, the university celebrated a public act, where, in a set oration, and a full theatre, the countess was again complimented. Among this collection was the famous sleeping Cupid, lying on a lion's skin, strewed with roses, as emblems of silence and secrecy; Cupid having presented that flower to Harpocrates, the god of Silence, as a bribe to him to conceal the amours of his mother. Below the foot of Cupid, on the bed, is a lizard—by some supposed to be placed here as a known ingredient in love-charms; by others, as a watchful attendant to wake the sleeper on the approach of danger; and by others imagined to be an emblem of sleep itself, from its being torpid during great part of the year, and placed near a statue of Somnus on a monument at Rome. But the real design of the sculptor was rather to perpetuate his name by this symbol, which was Saurus, signifying a lizard.'

Some other of the broken statues, not thought worth replacing, were begged by Boyder Cuper, who had been gardener to the Arundel family, and were removed by him to decorate a piece of garden-ground, which he had taken opposite Somerset House water-gate, in the parish of Lambeth; this being then a place of resort for the citizens in holiday-time: in Mr Theobald's time, 1757, it was still called Cuper's, corruptly Cupid's gardens, and which Mr Theobald describes as 'much of the same nature as Sadler's Wells and Marylebone Gardens, called also a music-house, as they had always

* Letter to the president of the Society of Antiquaries 1757.

music attending, and a large room for dancing, when the company were so disposed.' However, these 'broken statues' must have been of great merit; for Mr Freeman, of Fawley Court, near Henley, and Mr Edmund Waller, of Beaconsfield, happening to see the marbles, were struck with their beauty, and commissioned Mr Theobald to treat with Cuper for their purchase, leaving in his hands a bank-note of £100; eventually they were bought by Mr Theobald for £75, and were sent, part to Fawley Court, and part to Beaconsfield.

The remaining statues and fragments in Arundel gardens were removed, by permission of the crown, to a piece of waste-ground in the manor of Kennington, belonging to the Principality of Wales; of which piece of ground a grant was obtained, at a small rent, for a term of years, which was renewed. Such fragments as were thought not worth removing, were buried in the foundations of the buildings in the lower parts of Norfolk Street, and in the gardens. Mr Aislabie, who inhabited one of these houses, as Mr Theobald was told by the duke's steward, found a broken statue in his cellar, which he carried down to his seat in Yorkshire; and upon the same authority, Mr Theobald states, there was a sarcophagus placed in the cellar of the corner house, on the left hand, in the lower part of Norfolk Street.

The ground at Kennington, whither some of the marbles had been removed, was subsequently let for a timber-yard, and a wharf built thereon; and when the ground was cleared for rebuilding St Paul's Cathedral, great quantities of the rubbish were taken there, to raise the ground, which used to be overflowed every spring-tide; so that, by degrees, the statues and fragments were buried under the rubbish, and there lay almost forgotten for many years. About the year 1712, this piece of ground was rented by Mr Theobald's father, who, in digging foundations for buildings, frequently met with some of the fragments; of which the Earl of Burlington hearing, his lordship went to Kennington, to inspect the remains, and prevailed upon Mr Theobald to permit him to take his choice of a few specimens; these were conveyed to Chiswick House, where one piece of bas-relief was placed in the pedestal of an obelisk which he erected in his grounds. Mr Theobald next allowed Lord Petre to dig for fragments at Kennington, when six statues, some colossal, without heads or arms, were found lying close to each other, and were soon after sent to Worksop, the seat of the Duke of Norfolk, in Nottinghamshire.

Mr Theobald also found several blocks of grayish-veined marble, out of which he cut chimney-pieces and slabs for his house, the Belvedere, in Lambeth. He also found the fragment of a column, which he had conveyed to his seat, Waltham Place, in Berkshire, and there converted this fragment of precious art into a roller for his bowling-green!

These, however, were but a portion of the Arundel collection. The Duchess of Norfolk, who was divorced from the seventh duke in 1700, carried with her a fine collection of cameos, belonging to the Norfolk family, and valued at £10,000.

In 1720, a sale was made of another part of the collection at Stafford House. Mr Charles Howard, of Greystock, had a priced catalogue of this sale, with the names of the purchasers. The amounts were: Pictures sold for £812, 17*s.*; prints, £168, 17*s.* 4*d.*; drawings, £299, 4*s.* 7*d.*; japan, £698, 11*s.*; gilt and other plate, £462, 1*s.* 11¾*d.*; crystal vases, £364, 3*s.*; agate cups, £163, 16*s.*; jewels and other curiosities, £2467, 7*s.* 10*d.*; medals, £50, 10*s.* 6*d.*; odd lots of plate, £170, 6*s.* 7*d.*; cabinets and china, £1256, 19*s.*; household furniture, £1199, 3*s.*; several other odd lots, £738, 13*s.* 2*d.*—total, £8852, 0*s.* 11¾*d.* Besides which, there still remained, in several branches of the Norfolk family, many curious pieces of plate, jewels, &c. Mr Charles Howard possessed what was termed Archbishop Thomas à Becket's grace-cup, but which is really of Elizabethan work. Mr Howard also possessed the high-constable's staff, which he presented to the then Earl of Strafford.

At the revolution, in 1688, Henry, then Duke of Norfolk, who was a Protestant, came over with King William, and soon after obtained an act of parliament, by which the remainder of the Arundel garden-ground was leased for a term of forty-one years; which he accordingly let to Mr Stone, of New Inn, an attorney. The design of building a mansion was then laid aside, and the money which had accumulated for the purpose was paid over to the then duke; and thus disappeared Arundel House, never to be rebuilt; while its treasures were dispersed with little regard for their artistic value or interest.

## RICHARD BRINSLEY SHERIDAN.

The remark of Buffon, that Genius is Patience, was well illustrated in the case of Sheridan. It fully appears from Moore's biography, that all the brilliant passages in Sheridan's plays were very carefully elaborated, written over and over again, and not left till they were incapable of further polish. So, also, the written draughts of his speeches remain to prove that all the showy passages were written two or three times over upon small detached pieces of paper or cards, often without any material change in their form. 'It is certain, says Moore, 'that even his *bon mots* in society were not always to be set down to the credit of the occasion; but that frequently, like skilful priests, he prepared the miracle of the moment beforehand. Nothing, indeed, could be more remarkable than the patience and tact with which he would wait through a whole evening for the exact moment when the shaft which he had ready feathered, might be let fly with effect.

'A curious instance,' adds the biographer, 'of the care with which he treasured up the felicities of his wit, appears in the use he made of one of those epigrammatic passages, which the reader may remember among the memorandums for his comedy of Affectation, and which in its first form ran thus:—"He certainly has a great deal of fancy and a very good memory; but, with a perverse ingenuity, he employs these qualities as no other person does—for he employs his fancy in his narratives, and keeps his recollection for his wit:—when he makes his jokes, you applaud the accuracy of his memory, and 'tis only when he states his facts that you admire the flights of his imagination.' After many efforts to express this thought more concisely, and to reduce the language of it to that condensed and elastic state, in which alone it gives force to the projectiles of wit, he kept the passage by him patiently for some years—till he at length found an opportunity of turning it to account, in a reply, I believe, to Mr Dundas, in the House of Commons, when, with the most extemporaneous air, he brought it forth, in the following compact and pointed form:—"The right honourable gentleman is indebted to his memory for his jests, and to his imagination for his facts."'*

### SHERIDAN'S FUNERAL.

The brilliant assemblage at Westminster Abbey on the day of Sheridan's funeral bore testimony to the estimation in which genius was held, apart from the special merit or usefulness of the purposes to which the genius had been applied. Those who looked to the dramatic career of Richard Brinsley Sheridan recognised in him the most brilliant writer of comedy that had appeared since the days of Congreve and Farquhar. Sheridan takes rank among those who belie their school-day reputation by their after-career. Both at Dublin and at Harrow, where he received his education, he was pronounced to be an 'impenetrable dunce,' with whom neither severity nor indulgence would avail; yet this was the 'dunce' who produced *The Rivals* in 1775, *The Duenna* and *St Patrick's Day* in 1776, *The School for Scandal* and *The Trip to Scarborough* in 1777, and *The Critic* in 1778; and then passed through a political career which spread over the period from 1780 to 1816. His celebrated Begum Speech, in connection with the trial of Warren Hastings, is ranked among the most brilliant orations ever known; and there can be little doubt that he might have risen to a high position among statesmen had he been true to himself. But his moral character was weak, even depraved. Though he sometimes aided the Whig party by his eloquence, he gradually degenerated into a mere amusing speaker, much enjoyed and much admired, but winning for himself very little esteem. His life, by degrees, became an ineffectual struggle against poverty. He borrowed from all who would lend to him, and had neither the will nor the power to redeem the debts. The Prince of Wales welcomed him to Carlton House as long as his flashes of brilliant wit were ready to enliven the assembled guests; but when Sheridan began to fail in health and spirits, the doors were closed against him. The like occurred at other mansions where he had been admired but never really esteemed. He was steeped in poverty for some time before his death. Leigh Hunt mentions that Sheridan on one occasion burst into tears at the degradation of being touched by a bailiff when arrested; while all the time he was callous to the moral degradation involved in that conduct which led to the arrest. When he was dead, some of those in high places regretted that they had deserted the brilliant wit during his declining years of poverty; while others, knowing that he had not really deserved their esteem, wished, nevertheless, to honour the memory of a man of undoubted though ill-regulated genius. A public funeral was resolved upon. The body was removed from Sheridan's house, in Saville Row, to Mr Peter Moore's residence in Great George Street, Westminster; and on the 13th of July, a funeral procession walked from thence to the abbey. Arrived at the chief entrance at the west end of the nave, the procession was received by the dignitaries of the abbey, who preceded it to the place of sepulture in that celebrated nook of the abbey known as Poet's Corner. The pall was supported by the Duke of Argyle, the Duke of Bedford, the Earl of Lauderdale, Lord Mulgrave, Lord Holland, and the bishop of London. The chief mourner, as representing the family, was Mr Charles Sheridan; while among the other mourners were their Royal Highnesses the Dukes of York and Sussex, the Marquis of Anglesea, the Earl of Rosslyn, the Earl of Harrington, the Earl of Bessborough, Earl Gower, the Earl of Yarmouth, Lord Sidmouth, Lord Grenville, Lord Lynedoch, Lord Erskine, Lord George Cavendish—together with Canning, Romilly, and others, who belonged rather to the aristocracy of intellect than to that of birth. A small space was found between the monuments of Shakspeare and Addison, and close to the grave of Garrick. There lies Sheridan, under the roof of the venerable building which contains the bones of Chatham, Pitt, Fox, Canning, Chaucer, Spenser, Ben Jonson, Congreve, Addison, Rowe, Gay, Betterton, Garrick, Purcell, Handel, Newton, Johnson, Barrow, South, Camden, Usher, and many others known to fame.

* Moore's *Life of Sheridan*, ii. 471.

---

### THE MACARONIS.

In all periods and countries there have been persons, and even groups or classes of people, who sought to attract attention by eccentricities in dress. In England, during the last two centuries, we have had gallants, bloods, bucks, beaux, fribbles, macaronis, fops, monstrosities, corinthians, dandies, exquisites, and swells. Reeves, in his *God's Plea for Nineveh*, gives a curious vocabulary of dandyism in his account of a 'gallant' of the seventeenth century. 'He is, indeed,' says our Puritan author,

'the buffoon and baboon of the times. His mind is wholly set upon cuts and slashes, knots and roses, patchings and pinkings, jaggings and taggings, borderings and brimmings; half-shirts, half-arms, yawning breasts, gaping knees, arithmetical middles, geometrical sides, mathematical waists, musical heels, and logical toes.'

Amongst the dress-eccentricities of the eighteenth

century, none was more signal than the macaronis, though their reign was short, commencing about 1770, and coming to a close about 1775. The year of their ascendant was 1772, and the engraving on the preceding page represents a macaroni of that period; distinguished by an immense knot of artificial hair behind, a very small cocked-hat, an enormous walking-stick with long tassels, and a jacket, waistcoat, and small-clothes cut to fit the person as closely as possible. Their most remarkable peculiarity was the large knot of hair, thus celebrated in a satirical song:

'Five pounds of hair they wear behind,
  The ladies to delight, O,
Their senses give unto the wind,
  To make themselves a fright, O.
This fashion, who does e'er pursue,
  I think a simple-tony;
For he's a fool, say what you will,
  Who is a macaroni.'

It would appear that the macaronis originated among a number of young men, who had made the grand tour, and on their return, formed themselves into a club, which, from a dish of macaroni, then little known in England, being always placed upon the dinner-table, was called the Macaroni Club. A magazine writer of the time, evidently alluding to this origin, says: 'The macaronis are the offspring of a body, a many-headed monster in Pall Mall, produced by a demoniac committee of depraved taste and exaggerated fancy, conceived in the courts of France and Italy, and brought forth in England.' Horace Walpole, however, writing about the same time, gives the macaronis a different pedigree, ascribing their origin to the enormous wealth, lately gained by certain persons, through Clive's conquests in India, and asserts that their boundless extravagance soon dissipated it, and brought them to poverty. 'Lord Chatham,' he says, 'begot the East India Company, the East India Company begot Lord Clive, Lord Clive begot the macaronis, the macaronis begot Poverty, and all the race are still living.' In the following year, 1773, he writes: 'A winter without politics—even our macaronis entertain the town with nothing but new dresses, and the size of their nosegays. They have lost all their money, and exhausted their credit, and can no longer game for £20,000 a night.'

The macaronis took the town by storm. Nothing was fashionable that was not *à la macaroni*. Even the clergy had their wigs combed, their clothes cut, and their delivery refined *à la macaroni*. The shop-windows were filled with prints of the new tribe; there were engraved portraits of turf macaronis, military macaronis, college macaronis, and other varieties of the great macaroni race. At balls, no other than macaroni music could be danced to; at places of public amusements, macaroni songs, of which the following is a specimen, alone were sung to divert the company:

THE MACARONI.

AIR—*Nancy Dawson.*

Come listen all, and you shall hear,
Of all the beauties that appear,
And move in fashion's motley sphere,
  The fat, the lean, the bony;
The boast, the glory of the age,
How young and old can now engage;
Each master, miss, and parent sage,
  Is now a macaroni.

Each tries the other to outvie,
With foretops mounting to the sky,
And some you oft with tails may spy,
  As thick as any pony;
Insipid gait, affected sneer,
With side-curls high above the ear,
That each may more the ass appear
  Or shew the macaroni.

Each doctor's now become a prig,
That used to look so wise and big,
With stiffenéd and swingeing wig,
  That got him all his money;
They've all thrown off the grave disguise,
Which made each quaking owl look wise,
For wig, of Whip the coachman's size,
  To shew the macaroni.

The lawyer too's become a crop,
Instead of tail, a Tyburn top,
Alack-a-day! each barber's shop
  Now looks but half so funny,
As when the windows once were graced,
Where stately wigs in rows were placed—
But these are days of wit and taste,
  Huzza, for macaroni!

The priest that once with rose and band,
With formal wig, and hat in hand,
Sagacious phiz that might demand,
  A bow from any tony;
Behold him now all debonair,
With tiny hat and tortured hair,
And while he prattles to the fair,
  He shews the macaroni.

The cits that used, like Jerry Sneak,
To dress and walk out once a week,
And durst not to their betters speak,
  Are all grown jolly crony;
Each sneak is now a buckish blade,
When in the Park, but talk of trade,
He thinks you mean him to degrade—
  Each cit's a macaroni.

Who would not live in days like these,
In days of jollity and ease,
There's no exception to degrees,
  My lord and John are cronies.
Each order and profession claim,
An equal right, an equal fame,
For nothing's equal to the name
  Of modern macaronis.

The periodical literature, such as it was, of the time is very severe on the macaronis. 'No handsome fellow,' we read, 'will belong to them, because their dress is calculated to make the handsome ugly, and the ugly ridiculous. His hat, like his understanding, is very little, and he wears it in direct opposition to the manly beaver of our ancient heroes. He has generally an abundant quantity of hair, and well he may, for his head produces nothing else; if he has not a sufficient quantity of his own, he borrows it from his neighbours. His coat slouches down behind, and his shoes are reduced to the shape of slippers, on the surface of which appears a small circle of silver, which he tells us is a buckle. His manners are still more strange than his dress. He is the sworn foe of learning, and even sets simple orthography at defiance; for all learned fellows that can spell or write are either queer dogs or poor rogues. If you see him at a theatre, he will scarcely wink without his opera-glass, which he will thrust into a lady's face, and then simper, and be "pruddigisly enteerteen'd with her confusion."'

After all, it is by no means improbable that the macaronis, eccentric fops as they certainly were, added somewhat to the progress of national refinement. Living in the days of six-bottle men, one grave charge brought against them was that they hated 'all drinking, except tea, capillaire, and posset.' In a very successful five-act drama of the day, entitled *The Macaroni*, the hero of the piece —the macaroni *par excellence*—is held up to ridicule, principally because he respects female virtue, and swears by such mild and milk-and-water oaths as, 'May I be deaf at the opera!' We now know how to appreciate these distinctions.

## JULY 8.

St Procopius, martyr, about 303. Saints Kilian, Colman, and Totnan, martyrs, 688. St Withburge, virgin, of Norfolk, 743. St Grimbald, abbot of New Minstre, 903. Blessed Theobald, abbot of Vaux de Cernay, 1247. St Elizabeth, queen of Portugal, 1336.

*Born.*—John de la Fontaine, French writer of tales and fables, 1621, *Château-Thierry*.

*Died.*—Peter the Hermit, preacher of the first Crusade, 1115; Pope Gregory XV., 1623; Dr Robert South, eminent English preacher, 1716; Second Marshal Villeroi, 1730; Jean Pierre Niceron, useful writer, 1738, *Paris;* Jean Baseillac (Frere Côme), eminent French lithotomist, 1781; Torbern Bergmann, Swedish chemist and naturalist, 1784, *Medevi, near Upsala;* Edmund Burke, statesman, orator, and miscellaneous writer, 1797, *Beaconsfield, Bucks;* Sir Edward Parry, arctic voyager, 1855, *Ems.*

### PETER THE HERMIT.

There is no more extraordinary episode in the annals of the world, than the History of the Crusades. To understand it, we must previously have some sense of the leading form which had been given to religion in the eleventh and twelfth centuries—an intense contemplation of the sufferings and merits of Christ, with a boundless feeling of gratitude and affection towards his name. Already had this feeling caused multitudes to pilgrimise through barbarous countries to pay their devotions on the scene of his passion. It needed but an accident to make the universal European sentiment take the form of some wild and wonderful series of acts.

In the north of France, there lived a man of low origin, named Peter, naturally active and restless, but who by various causes was drawn at last into a religious and anchoritic life, in which he became liable to visions and spiritual impulses, all thought by him to be divine. It was impressed upon him that the Deity had constituted him one of His special instruments on earth, and, as usual, others soon came to view him in that character, to thrill under his preachings, and to believe in his miraculous gifts.

The rage for pilgrimages to the East drew the hermit Peter from his retreat, and, like the rest, he went to Jerusalem, where his indignation was moved by the manner in which the Christians were treated by the infidels. He heard the relation of their sufferings from the lips of the patriarch Simeon, and with him in private lamented over them, and talked of the possibility of rescuing the sufferers. It was in these conversations that the project was formed of exciting the warriors of the West to unite together for the recovery of the Holy Land from the power of the infidels. Peter's enthusiasm now led him to believe that he was himself the man destined for this great work, and on one occasion, when he was kneeling before the holy sepulchre, he believed that he had a vision, in which Jesus Christ appeared to him, announced to him his mission, and ordered him to lose no time in setting about it. Impressed with this idea, he left Palestine, and proceeded to Rome, where Urban II. was then pope. Urban embraced the project with ardour, treated Peter the Hermit as a prophet, and enjoined him to go abroad and announce the approaching deliverance of Jerusalem. Peter thereupon set out on his new pilgrimage. He rode on a mule, bare-headed and bare-foot, clothed in a long frock and a hermit's mantle of coarse woollen cloth, girded with a rope. In this manner he proceeded through Italy, crossed the Alps, and wandered through France and the greater part of Europe, everywhere received as a saint, and spreading among all classes an amazing amount of zeal for the Crusade, which he was now openly preaching. The enthusiasm which followed his steps was wonderful; people crowded to obtain the favour of touching his garments, and even the hairs of his mule were preserved as holy relics. His miracles were a subject of general conversation, and nobody doubted for a moment the truth of his mission.

It was at this moment that the ambassadors of the Emperor Alexis Comnenus arrived in Rome, to represent to the pope the danger to which Constantinople was exposed from the invasions of the Turks, and to implore the assistance of the Western Christians. Pope Urban called a council, which met at Placenza, in Lombardy, at the beginning of March 1095. So great had been the effect of Peter's preaching, that no less than 200 archbishops and bishops, 4000 other ecclesiastics, and 30,000 laymen attended this council, which was held in the open air, in a plain near the city; but various subjects divided its attention, and it came to no decision relative to the war against the infidels. The pope found that the Italians, who were, even at this early period, less bigoted Catholics than the other peoples of Western Europe, were not very enthusiastic in the cause, and he resolved on calling another council, for the especial object of deliberating on the holy war, and in a country where he was likely to find more zeal. Accordingly, this council assembled in the November of the same year, at Clermont, in Auvergne; it was equally numerous with that of Placenza, and, which was of most importance, Peter the Hermit attended in person, seated on his mule, and in the costume in which he had preached the Crusade through so many countries. After some preliminary business had been transacted, Peter was brought forward, and he described the sufferings of the Christians in the East in such moving language, and was so well seconded by the eloquence of the pope, that the whole assembly was seized with a fit of wild enthusiasm, and burst into shouts of, 'God wills it! God wills it!' 'It is true,' exclaimed the pope, 'God wills it, indeed, and you here see fulfilled the words of our Saviour, who promised to be present in the midst of the faithful when assembled in his name; it is he who puts into your mouths the words I have just heard; let them be your war-cry, and may they announce everywhere the presence of the God of armies!' The pope then held forth a cross, and told them all to take that as their sign, and wear it upon their breasts, and the proposal was adopted amid a scene of the most violent agitation. Ademar de Monteil, bishop of Puy, advanced, and was the first to assume the cross, and multitudes hastened to follow his example. They called upon Urban to take the command of the expedition, but he excused himself personally, and appointed to the command, as his delegate, the zealous bishop of Puy, who is said to have been distinguished as a warrior before he became an ecclesiastic.

Thus began the first Crusade. Armies—or rather crowds of men in arms—began now to assemble in various parts, in order to direct their march towards Constantinople. Among the first of these was the multitude who followed the preaching of Peter the Hermit, and who, impatient of delay, chose him for their leader, and were clamorous to commence their march. Peter, blinded by his zeal, accepted a position for which he was totally without capacity, and placed himself at their head, mounted on the same mule and in the same costume in which he had preached. His troop, starting from the banks of the Maas and the Moselle, and consisting originally of people of Champagne and Burgundy, was soon increased by recruits from the adjacent districts, until he numbered under his command from 80,000 to 100,000 men. They came chiefly from the simpler and more ignorant classes of society, and they had been told so much of God's direct interference, that they were led to believe that he would feed and protect them on the road, and they did not even take the precaution to carry provisions or money with them. They expected to be supported by alms, and they begged on the way. Peter's army was divided into two bodies, of which the first, commanded by a man whose mean social position may be conjectured by his name of Walter the Penniless (Gaultier sans Avoir), marched in advance. They were received with enthusiasm by the Germans, who crowded to the same standard, and all went well until they came to the banks of the Morava and the Danube, and encountered the Hungarians and Bulgarians, both which peoples were nominally Christians; but the former took no interest in the Crusades, and the latter were not much better than savages. Walter's band of Crusaders passed through Hungary without any serious accident, and reached the country of the Bulgarians, where, finding themselves entirely destitute of provisions, they spread over the country, plundering, murdering, and destroying, until the population, flying to arms, fell upon them, and made a great slaughter. Those who escaped, fled with their leader towards Greece, and reached Nissa, the governor of which place administered to their pressing necessities; and, having learned by misfortune the advantage of observing something like discipline, they proceeded with more order till at length they reached Constantinople, where they were treated well, and allowed to encamp and await the other division, which was approaching under the command of Peter the Hermit.

The zeal and incapacity of the latter led him into still greater disasters. In their passage through Hungary, the spots where some of the followers of Walter the Moneyless had been slaughtered, were pointed out to the Crusaders, and they were told that the Hungarians had entered into a plot for their destruction. Instead of enforcing the necessity of caution and discipline, Peter talked of vengeance, and sought only to inflame the passions of his followers. On their arrival at Semlin, they beheld the arms of some of the first band of Crusaders, who had been slain, suspended as a trophy over the gates, and Peter himself encouraged them to revenge their comrades. The inhabitants abandoned the town, fled, were overtaken, and 4000 of them slain, and their bodies thrown into the Danube, the waters of which carried them down to Belgrade. The Crusaders returned to Semlin, which was given up to plunder, and they lived there in the most licentious manner, until news came that the Hungarians had assembled a great army to attack them, and then they abandoned the town, and hastened their march across Bulgaria. Everywhere the violence and licentiousness of the Crusaders had spread terror, and they now found the country abandoned, and suffered fearfully from the want of provisions. The people of Nissa had armed and fortified themselves, so that the Crusaders did not venture to attack them, but, having obtained a supply of provisions, had continued their march, when the ill-behaviour of their rear-guard provoked a collision, in which a considerable number of the Crusaders were slaughtered. Peter, informed of this affair, instead of hastening his march, returned to obtain satisfaction, and the irritating behaviour of his troops provoked a still greater conflict, in which 10,000 of the Crusaders were slaughtered, and the rest fled and took refuge in the woods and marshes of the surrounding country. That night, Peter the Hermit, who had taken refuge on a hill, had only 500 men about him, but next day his band numbered 7000, and a few days afterwards the number had been increased to 30,000. With these he continued his march, and, as their disasters had rendered them more prudent, they reached Constantinople without further misfortunes, and rejoined their companions.

As the Emperor Alexis rather despised this undisciplined horde than otherwise, he received them with favour, and treated Peter the Hermit with the greatest distinction; but he lost no time in ridding himself of such troublesome visitors by transporting them to the other side of the Bosphorus. Those who had marched under the banner of Peter the Hermit, had now been joined by the remains of other similar hordes who had followed them, and who had experienced still greater disasters in passing through Hungary and Bulgaria; and, in addition to the other causes of disorder, they now experienced that of jealousy among themselves. They not only laid waste the country, and committed every sort of atrocity, but they quarrelled about the plunder; and, Peter himself having lost his authority, various individuals sought to be their leaders. The Italians and Germans, under the conduct of a chieftain named Renaud, separated from the rest of the army, left the camp which was established in the fertile country bordering on the Gulf of Nicomedia, and penetrated into the mountains in the neighbourhood of Nicæa, where they were destroyed by the Turks. The main army of the Crusaders, who now acknowledged the nominal authority of Walter, but who paid little attention to the orders of their chieftains, hastened imprudently to revenge the Italians and Germans, and had reached the plain of Nicæa, when they found themselves unexpectedly surrounded by the numerous and better disciplined army of the Turks, and, after a useless resistance, the whole army was put to the sword, or carried into captivity, and a vast mound of their bones was raised in the midst of the plain.

Thus disastrously ended the expedition of Peter the Hermit. Of 300,000 men who had marched from Europe in the belief that they were going to conquer the Holy Land, all had perished, either in the disasters of the route, or in the battle of Nicæa. Peter had left them before this great battle, disgusted with their vices and disorders, and had returned to Constantinople, to declaim against them as a horde of brigands, whose enormous sins had caused God to desert them. From this time the Hermit became a second-rate actor in the events of the Crusade. When the more noble army of the Crusaders, under the princes and great warriors of the West, arrived at Constantinople, he joined them, and accompanied them in their march, performing merely the part of an eloquent and zealous preacher; but at the siege of Antioch, he attempted to escape the sufferings of the Christian camp by flight, and was pursued and overtaken by Tancred, brought back, and compelled to take an oath to remain faithful to the army. This disgrace appears to have been wiped out by his subsequent conduct; and he was among the first ranks of the Crusaders who came in sight of Jerusalem. The wearied warriors were cheered by the enthusiastic eloquence with which he addressed them on the summit of the Mount of Olives; and in the midst of the slaughter, when the holy city was taken, the Christian soldiers crowded round him, as people had crowded round him when he first proclaimed the Crusade, and congratulated him on the fulfilment of his prophecies.

Peter remained in the Holy Land until 1102, when he returned to Europe, with the Count of Montaign, a baron of the territory of Liege. On their way they were overtaken by a dreadful tempest, in which the Hermit made a vow to found a monastery if they escaped shipwreck. It was in fulfilment of this vow, that he founded the abbey of Neufmoutier, at Huy, on the Maas, in honour of the holy sepulchre. Here he passed the latter years of his life, and died in 1115. In the last century, his tomb was still preserved there, with a monumental inscription.

## BURKE'S ESTATE—HIS DAGGER-SCENE IN THE HOUSE OF COMMONS.

It is very clear from the authentic biographies of Burke, that he entered upon literary and political life in London with little or no endowment beyond that which nature and a good education had given him. He wrote for his bread for several years, as many able but penniless Irishmen have since done and continue to do. At length, when several years past thirty, merging into a political career as private secretary, first to Single-speech Hamilton, and afterwards to the Marquis of Rockingham, he enters parliament for a small English burgh, and soon after—all at once—in 1767—he purchases an estate worth £23,000! In a large elegant house, furnished with all the adjuncts of a luxurious establishment, surrounded by 600 acres of his own land, driving a carriage and *four*, Burke henceforth appeared as a man of liberal and independent fortune. When surly but pure-hearted Samuel Johnson was shewn by him over all the splendours of Beaconsfield, he said: 'Non equidem invideo—miror magis'—I do not envy, I am only astonished; and then added, still more significantly: 'I wish you all the success which can be wished—by an honest man.' There was an unpleasant mystery here, which it was reserved for modern times to penetrate.

One theory on the subject, set forth so lately as 1853, by an ingenious though anonymous writer,* was that Burke was mainly indebted for the ability to purchase his estate to successful speculations in Indian stock. In Macknight's able work, *The Life and Times of Edward Burke*, published in 1858, an account of the transaction is given in tolerably explicit terms, but without leaving the character of Burke in the position which his admirers might wish. 'In 1767,' says this writer, 'when Lord Rockingham refused to return again to office, and Burke, though in very straitened circumstances, adhered faithfully to his noble leader, it then occurred to the marquis that it was incumbent on him to do something for the fortune of his devoted friend. He advanced £10,000 to Burke, on a bond that it was understood would never be reclaimed. With those £10,000, £5000 raised on mortgage from a Dr Saunders in Spring Gardens, and other £8000, doubtless obtained from the successful speculations of William and Richard Burke [his brothers] in Indian stock, Burke purchased the estate of Gregories. After the reverses of his relatives in the year 1769, all the money they had advanced to him was required. Lord Rockingham again came forward. From that time through many years of opposition, as Burke's fortune, so far from increasing, actually diminished under his unvarying generosity and the requirements of his position, this noble friend was his constant and unfailing resource. The loss of the agency for New York [by which Burke had £1000 a year for a short time] the marquis endeavoured to compensate by frequent loans. At the time of Lord Rockingham's death [1782], he may, on different occasions extending over fourteen years, have perhaps advanced on bonds, which though never formally required, Burke insisted on giving, the sum of about thirty thousand pounds.' It appears, in short, that this brilliant statesman and orator maintained his high historical place for thirty years, wholly through pecuniary means drawn by him from a generous friend. The splendid mansion, the vineries and statuary, the four-horsed carriage, even the kind-hearted patronage to such men of genius as Barry and Crabbe, were all supported in a way that implies the entire sacrifice of Burke's independence. It is very sad to think of in one whom there was so much reason

* See *Athenæum*, Nos. 1363 and 1364.

to admire; but it only adds another and heretofore undetected example to those we have, illustrating a fact in our political system, that it is no sphere for clever adventurers, independence in personal circumstances being the indispensable pre-requisite of political independence.

Burke's dagger-scene in the House of Commons is an obscure point in his life—no one at the time gave any good account of it. On this matter also we have latterly obtained some new light. The great Whig, as is well known, was carried by the French Revolution out of all power of sober judgment, and made a traitor, it might be said, to all his old affections. When at the height of the rabies, having to speak on the second reading of the Alien Bill, December 28, 1792, he called, in passing, at the office of Sir Charles M. Lamb, under-secretary of state. It was only three months from the massacres of Paris. England was in high excitement about the supposed existence of a party amongst ourselves, who were disposed to fraternise with the ensanguined reformers of France, and imitate their acts. Some agent for that party had sent a dagger to a Birmingham manufacturer,

BURKE'S DAGGER-SCENE IN THE HOUSE OF COMMONS.

with an order for a large quantity after the same pattern. It was a coarsely-made weapon, a foot long in the blade, and fitted to serve equally as a stiletto and as a pike-head. The Birmingham manufacturer, disliking the commission, had come up to the under-secretary's office, to exhibit the pattern dagger, and ask advice. He had left the weapon, which Burke was thus enabled to see. The illustrious orator, with the under-secretary's permission, took it along with him to the House, and, in the course of a flaming tirade about French atrocities, and probable imitations of them in England, he drew the dagger from his bosom, and threw it down on the floor, as an illustration of what every man might shortly expect to see levelled at his own throat. There were of course sentiments of alarm raised by this scene; but probably the more general feeling was one of derision. In this way the matter was taken up by Gillray, whose caricature on the subject we here reproduce in miniature, as a curious memorial of a crisis in our history, and also as giving a characteristic portrait of one of our greatest men.

## WILLIAM HUNTINGTON'S EPITAPH.

When a man's epitaph is written by himself in anticipation of his death, there may generally be found in it some indication of his character, such as probably would not otherwise have transpired. Such was certainly the case in reference to William or the Rev. William Huntington, who loved to couple the designations 'coal-heaver' and 'sinner saved' with his name. On the 8th of July 1813, the remains of this eccentric man were transferred from a temporary grave at Tunbridge Wells to a permanent one at Lewes. The stone at the head of the grave was inscribed with an epitaph which he himself had written a few days before his death—leaving a space, of course, for the exact date. 'Here lies the Coal-heaver, who departed this life (July 1, 1813), in the (69th) year of his age; beloved of his God, but abhorred by men. The Omniscient Judge, at the Great Assize, shall ratify and confirm this, to the confusion of many thousands; for England and its metropolis shall know that there hath been a prophet among them. W. H. S. S.'—This S. S. meant 'sinner saved.'

The career of the man affords a clue to the state of mind which could lead to the production of such an epitaph. William Hunt was born in the Weald of Kent, of very poor parents. He complained, in later life, that 'unsanctified critics' laughed at him for his ignorance; and certain it is that he never could get over the defects of his education. He struggled for a living as an errand-boy, then as a labourer, then as a cobbler. While engaged in the last-named trade, he took up the business of a preacher. He would place his work on his lap, and a Bible on a chair beside him; and, while working for his family, he collected materials for his next sermon. At what time, or for what reason, he changed his name from Hunt to Huntington, is not clear; but we find him coming up from Thames-Ditton to London, 'bringing two large carts with furniture and other necessaries, besides a post-chaise well filled with children and cats.' He became a preacher at Margaret Street Chapel, and attached a considerable number of persons to him by his peculiar denunciatory style. In 1788, his admirers built him a chapel in Gray's Inn Road, which he named 'Providence Chapel.' When a person attributes to Providence the good that comes to him, his sentiment is at all events worthy of respect; but the peculiarity in Huntington's case was the whimsical way in which everyday matters were thus treated. When £9000 had been spent on the chapel, various gifts of chairs, a tea-caddy full of tea, a looking-glass, a bed and bedstead for the vestry, 'that I might not be under the necessity of walking home in the cold winter nights'—are spoken of by him as things that Providence had sent him. He had a keen appreciation of worldly goods, however; for he refused to officiate in the chapel until the freehold had been made over absolutely to himself. Wishing afterwards to enlarge his chapel a little, he applied for a bit of ground near it from the Duke of Portland, but demurred at the ground-rent asked. Therefore, says he, 'finding nothing could be done with the earth-holders, I turned my eyes another way, and determined to build my stories in the heavens, where I should find more room and less cost'—in plain English, he raised the building another story. His manner towards his hearers was dogmatic and arrogant. Having once taken the designation of 'Sinner Saved,' he observed no bounds in addressing others. His pulpit-oratory, always vigorous, was not unfrequently interlarded with such expressions as—'Take care of your pockets!'—'Wake that snoring sinner!'—'Silence that noisy numbskull!'—'Turn out that drunken dog!' With a certain class of minds, however, Huntington had great influence. Some time after the death of his first wife, he married the widow of Sir James Sanderson, at one time lord mayor of London: by which alliance he became possessed of much property. On one occasion, a sale of some of his effects took place at his residence at Pentonville, when sixty guineas were given for an old arm-chair by one of his many admirers. Two or three books which he published were quite in character with the epitaph he afterwards wrote—an intense personal vanity pervading all else that might be good in him.

---

## A KING AND HIS DUMB FAVOURITES.

King James I., although a remorseless destroyer of animals in the chase, had, like many modern sportsmen,* an intense fondness for seeing them around him, happy and well cared for, in a state of domesticity. In 1623, John Bannal obtained a grant of the king's interest in the leases of two gardens and a tenement in the Minories, on the condition of building and maintaining a house, wherein to keep and rear his majesty's newly imported silkworms.† Sir Thomas Dale, one of the settlers of the then newly formed colony of Virginia, returning to Europe on leave, brought with him many living specimens of American zoology; amongst them, some flying squirrels. This coming to his majesty's ears, he was seized with a boyish impatience to add them to the private menagerie in St James's Park. At the council-table, and in the circle of his courtiers, he recurs again and again to the subject, wondering that Sir Thomas had not given him the 'first pick' of his cargo of curiosities. He reminded them how the recently arrived Muscovite ambassador had brought him live sables, and, what he loved even better, splendid white gyrfalcons of Iceland; and when Buckingham suggested that, in the whole of her reign, Queen Elizabeth had never received live sables from the czar, James made special inquiries if such were really the case.

Henry Wriothesley, fourth Earl of Southampton, one of the council, and governor and treasurer of the Virginia Company, better known to us as the friend and patron of Shakspeare, wrote as follows to the state secretary, the Earl of Salisbury: 'Talking with the king by chance, I told him of the Virginian squirrels, which they say will fly, whereof there are now divers brought into England, and he presently and very earnestly asked me if none of them was provided for him, and whether your lordship had none for him—saying he was sure Salisbury would get him one of them. I would not have troubled you with this, but that you know full well how he is affected to these toys; and with a little inquiry of any of your folks, you may furnish yourself to present him at his coming to London, which will not be before Wednesday next—the Monday before to Theobald's, and the Saturday before to Royston.'

Some one of his loving subjects, desirous of ministering to his favourite hobby, had presented him with a cream-coloured fawn. A nurse was immediately hired for it, and the Earl of Shrewsbury commissioned to write as follows to Miles Whytakers, signifying the royal pleasure as to future procedure: 'The king's majesty hath commissioned me to send this rare beast, a white hind calf, unto you, together with a woman, his nurse, that hath kept it, and bred it up. His majesty would have you see it be kept in every respect as this good woman doth desire, and that the woman may be lodged and boarded by you, until his majesty come to Theobald's on Monday next, and then you shall know further of his pleasure. What account his majesty maketh of this fine beast you may guess, and no man can suppose it to be more rare than it is, therefore I know that your care of it will be accordingly. So in haste I bid you very heartily farewell. At Whitehall, this 6th Nov. 1611.

'*P.S.* The wagon and the men are to be sent home; only the woman is to stay with you, until his majesty's coming hither, and as long after as it shall please his majesty.'

About the year 1629, the king of Spain effected an important diversion in his own favour, by sending the king—priceless gift!—an elephant and five camels. 'Going through London, after midnight,' says a state-paper letter, 'they could not pass unseen,' and the clamour and outcry raised by some street-loiterers at sight of their ponderous bulk and ungainly step, roused the sleepers from their beds in every district through which they passed. News of this unlooked-for addition to the Royal Zoological Garden in St James' Park, is conveyed to Theobald's as speedily as horse-flesh, whip, and spur could do the work. Then arose an interchange of missives to and fro, betwixt the king, my lord treasurer, and Mr Secretary Conway, grave, earnest, and deliberate, as though involving the settlement or refusal of some treaty of peace. In muttered sentences, not loud but deep, the thrifty lord treasurer shews 'how little he is in love with royal presents, which cost his master as much to maintain as would a garrison.' No matter. Warrants are issued to the officers of the Mews, and to Buckingham, master of the horse, 'that the elephant is to be daily well dressed and fed. but that he should not be led forth to water,

* The Honourable Grantley Berkeley, Gage Earle Freeman, known as 'Premier Falconer of England,' &c.

† This article is the result of original research in the state papers.

nor any admitted to see him, without directions from his keeper, which they were to observe and follow in all things concerning that beast, as they will answer for the contrary at their uttermost peril.' The camels are to be daily grazed in the park, but brought back at night, with all possible precautions to screen them from the vulgar gaze. 'In the blessed graciousness of his majesty's disposition,' £150 was to be presented to Francisco Romano, who brought them over—though the meagre treasury was hardly able to yield up that sum, and her majesty's visit to 'the Bath' must be put off to a more convenient season, for want of money to bear her charges. Then Sir Richard Weston was commissioned by Mr Secretary Conway to estimate the annual cost of maintaining the royal quadruped, his master having decided to take the business into his own hands. He suggested economy, but does not seem to have succeeded, for the state papers for August 1623 furnish the following 'breefe noate what the chardges of the elephant and his keepers are in the yeare:

| | |
|---|---|
| ffeeding for the elephant at 10s. per diem, is per an., . . . . . . | £180 |
| To the 2 Spaniards that keep him, xx$^s$. per week, . . . . . . | 52 |
| To the 2 Englishmen, his keepers, xvi$^s$. per week, . . . . . . | 41 |
| Sum per ann. in toto . | £275, 12s. |

Such is the gross amount, according to the manuscript, but not according to Cocker. Should the above be a specimen of Mr Secretary Conway's arithmetic, we can only hope his foreign policy was somewhat better than his figures. This calculation, however, by no means embraced every item of the costly bill of fare—'Besides,' adds the manuscript, 'his keepers afirme that from the month of September until April, he must drink (not water) but wyne—and from April unto September, he must have a gallon of wyne the daye.'

A pleasant time of it must this same elephant have had, with his modest winter-allowance of six bottles per diem, in exchange for the Spaniard's lenten quarters.

## JULY 9.

St Ephrem of Edessa, doctor and confessor, 378. St Everildis, virgin, of England, 7th century. The martyrs of Gorcum, 1572.

*Born.*—Thomas Butler, Earl of Ossory, 1634, *Kilkenny Castle*; Alexis Piron, 1689, *Dijon*; Anne Radcliffe, novelist, 1764, *London*; Henry Hallam, historian, 1777, *Windsor*.

*Died.*—Emperor Anastasius I., 518; Archbishop (Stephen) Langton, 1228; Emperor Leopold III. of Austria, killed at Sempach, 1386; John Oldmixon (English history), 1742, *Bridgewater*; Philip V. of Spain, 1746, *San Ildefonso*; General Braddock, killed at Du Quesne, North America, 1755; William Strachan, publisher, 1785; Zachary Taylor, President of the United States, 1850, *Washington, U.S.*

### HENRY HALLAM.

Hallam holds a sort of coldly monumental place in the modern literary annals of England. His historical works on the Middle Ages, the English Constitution, and the progress of literature in Europe, are models of research, justness of generalisation, and elegance of expression. The writer, however, always seems to sit aloof. Like many other men of letters, whose work accorded with their taste, and who were safe by fortune or frugality from the more trying cares of life, he reached a great age, being at his death, in January 1859, eighty-two years old. In one respect, he resembled Burke—he had to submit, near the close of his own life, to the loss of a son whom he held to be a youth of the highest promise, and whom he regarded with doting affection. There is scarcely a more affecting chapter in English biography, than the account of the death of the younger Hallam, when travelling for the recovery of health under his father's care, and the account of the bringing home of the corpse by the sorrow-stricken old man, himself conscious that he must soon follow him into the dark and narrow house appointed for all living.

Perhaps the most valuable service Mr Hallam has rendered to his country, was the careful view he gave it of the progress of its political system. The grand virtue of that system—its distribution of power amongst a variety of forces, which check and counterpoise each other, so that liberty and order result in strict co-ordination—has been fully asserted and held up by him. Somewhat to the surprise of the Whig party, to which he had always been attached, he deprecated the great change which they proposed in the parliamentary representation in 1831. Conversing on this subject with one of the most influential members of the cabinet, he said: 'I am a Whig, as you are: a reform appears to me to be needed, but the reform you attempt is unreasonable. The object should be to perfect, not to change. To suppress certain abuses in the electoral system, and to extend the right of voting, is doubtless in conformity with the spirit of our institutions, and may be advantageous to the development of our public life; but it would be dangerous to give too large an extension to this measure. To grant universal suffrage, would be to hazard a change in the English constitution, and to disturb the harmonious working of a system which we owe to the sagacity and good-fortune of our forefathers. It is in the House of Commons that the union of the Crown, Lords, and Commons is at present effected, that their concerted action is initiated, and, in a word, the equilibrium of power is maintained. This equilibrium constitutes the very essence of the government of England. If the composition of the House of Commons is too essentially altered, by rendering elections too democratic, a risk is incurred of destroying this balance, and giving an irregular impulse to the state by introducing new elements. If once the principle of this bill be admitted, its consequences will extend; change will succeed to change, and the reform of one day will necessitate a fresh one the next. The government will gradually be transferred to the hustings. The representatives, elected by the democracy, will look to the quarter from which the wind of popular favour blows, in order to follow its direction; and English politics, abandoned to popular caprice, will deviate from their proper course, whilst the English constitution will be shaken to its foundation.'*

---

### LUNACY AND ASTRONOMY.

On the 9th of July 1787, a Dr Elliott, described in the journals of the day as 'one of the literati,' fired two pistols, apparently, at a lady and gentleman, while walking in Prince's Street, London. Neither, however, was injured, though both were very much frightened, and the lady's dress was singed by the closeness of the explosion. Elliott was arrested, committed to Newgate, and, a few days after, tried for an attempted murder, but acquitted on the technical point, that there was no proof of the pistols having been loaded with ball.

Unforeseeing this decision, Elliott's friends had set up a plea of insanity, and among other witnesses in support thereof, Dr Simmons, of St Luke's hospital for lunatics, was examined. This gentleman, whose long and extensive experience in cases of insanity, gave great weight to his evidence, testified that he had been intimately acquainted with Dr Elliott for more than ten years, and fully believed him to be insane. On being further pressed by the recorder to adduce any particular instance of Elliott's insanity, the witness stated that he had lately received a letter from the prisoner on the light of the celestial bodies, which indisputably proved his aberration of mind. The letter, which had been intended by the prisoner to have been laid before the Royal Society, was then produced and read in court. The part more particularly depended upon by the witness as a proof of the insanity of the writer, was an assertion that the sun is not a body of fire, as alleged by astronomers, 'but its light proceeds from a dense and universal aurora, which may afford ample light to the inhabitants of the surface (of the sun) beneath, and yet be at such a distance aloft as not to annoy them.' The recorder objected to this being proof of insanity, saying that if an extravagant hypothesis were to be considered a proof of lunacy, many learned and perfectly sane astronomers might be stigmatised as madmen.

Though the defence of insanity was not received, Elliott, as already observed, was acquitted on a legal point, but the unfortunate man died in prison, of self-inflicted starvation, on the 22d of July, having resolutely refused to take any food during the thirteen days which intervened between his arrest and death.

The story in itself is little more than a common newspaper report of an Old Bailey trial; but as Elliott's idea respecting the sun is that held by the first astronomers of the present day, we are afforded a curious instance of a not very generally recognised fact—namely, that the madness of one century may be the wisdom of its successor; while it is not improbable that the converse of the proposition may be equally as certain, so that a great deal of what we consider wisdom now, may be condemned as rank folly 'a hundred years hence.'

* Mignet's *Sketch of the Life of Mr Hallam*, read before the Institut of France, Jan. 4, 1862.

### SUPERSTITIONS ABOUT NEW-BORN CHILDREN.

It is unlucky to weigh them. If you do, they will probably die, and, at anyrate, will not thrive. I have caused great concern in the mind of a worthy old monthly nurse by insisting on weighing mine. They have, however, all done very well, with the exception of one, the weighing of whom was accidentally forgotten to be performed.

The nurses always protested against the weighing, though in a timorous sort of way; saying that, no doubt it was all nonsense, but still it had better not be done.

It is not good for children to sleep upon bones—that is, upon the lap. There seems to be some sense in this notion; it is doubtless better for a child to be supported throughout its whole length, instead of hanging down its head or legs, as it might probably do if sleeping on the lap.

Hesiod, in his *Works and Days*, forbids children of twelve months, or twelve years old, to be placed ἐπ' ἀκινήτοισι—upon things not to be moved—which some have understood to mean *sepulchres*: if this is right, perhaps there is some connection between his injunction, and that which condemns the sleeping upon bones, though the modern bones are those of the living, and not of the dead.

Cats suck the breath of infants, and so kill them. This extremely unphilosophical notion of cats preferring exhausted to pure air, is frequently a cause of great annoyance to poor pussy, when, after having established herself close to baby, in a snug warm cradle, she finds herself ignominiously hustled out under suspicion of compassing the death of her quiet new acquaintance, who is not yet big enough to pull her tail.

When children first leave their mother's room, they must go *upstairs* before they go *down-stairs*, otherwise they will never rise in the world.

Of course it frequently happens that there is no 'upstairs,' that the mother's room is the highest in the house. In this case the difficulty is met by the nurse setting a *chair*, and stepping upon that with the child in her arms as she leaves the room. I have seen this done.

A mother must not go outside her own house-door till she goes to be 'churched.' Of course the *principle* of this is a good one. It is right, under such circumstances, the first use a woman should make of her restored strength, should be to go to church, and thank God for her recovery; but in practice this principle sometimes degenerates into mere superstition.

If you rock an *empty* cradle, you will rock a new baby into it. This is a superstition *in viridi observantiâ*, and it is quite curious to see the face of alarm with which a poor woman, with her tenth baby in her arms, will dash across a room to prevent the 'baby-but-one' from engaging in such a dangerous amusement as rocking the empty cradle.

In connection with this subject, it may be mentioned that there is a widely-spread notion among the poorer classes, that rice, as an article of food, prevents the increase of the population. How the populousness of India and China are accounted for on this theory, I cannot say; probably those who entertain it never fully realise the existence of 'foreign parts,' but it is certain that there was not long ago a great outcry against the giving of rice to poor people under the poor law, as it was said to be done with a purpose.

*Suffolk.* C. W. J.

## JULY 10.

**The Seven Brothers, martyrs, 2d century. Saints Rufina and Secunda, virgins and martyrs, 3d century.**

### The Korban Beiram.

The Korban Beïram, or feast of sacrifices, is one of the greatest solemnities of the Mohammedan religion. On this day every family of the true believers offers a sheep to God, and the streets of their cities are filled with men carrying the destined victim on their backs. Among the Arabs the festival begins at the early hour of four A.M., when immense crowds collect at the residence of the nearest pacha or bey, awaiting his appearance in the court of the palace. The fanciful style of eastern costume renders the scene both original and picturesque. All the sheiks are arranged on one side: in the front stand the officers and ministers of the pacha. At five o'clock his highness, accompanied by the members of his family and his staff, makes his entrée: cannon are fired, the peculiar bands of the East play airs suitable for this religious ceremony. The chief-captain of the hussars of the palace announces to the crowd, in a solemn voice, that the hour of sacrifice has arrived, and that his highness, after prayer, will be present at this important act. All then adjourn to the mosque, the body of imams or priests entering with the suite of the pacha. As soon as the sacrifice is over, the pacha re-enters the court, and seated on an elevated throne, all those of high rank have the privilege of kissing his hand; the inferiors slightly touch it with their lips. This occupies an hour, when all retire to take coffee; the captain thanking the crowd for their presence as a mark of attachment to their ruler.

---

*Born.*—John Calvin, theologian, 1509, *Noyon, Picardy;* John Ernest Grabe, religious controversialist, 1666, *Konigsberg;* Sir William Blackstone, writer on English law, 1723, *Cheapside, London;* Frederick Marryatt, novelist, 1792, *London.*

*Died.*—Emperor Adrian, 138; Pope Benedict VII., 983; Pope Benedict VIII., 1024; Henry II. of France, 1559; William, first Prince of Orange, assassinated at Delft, 1584; Louis Moreri (Historical and Critical Dictionary), 1680, *Lyon;* Francois Eudes de Mezerai, historian, 1683; Bishop Fell, 1686, *Oxford;* Dr Alexander Monro, professor of anatomy, 1767, *Edinburgh;* David Rittenhouse, astronomer, 1796, *Philadelphia, U. S.*

### DON PANTALEON SA.

On the 10th of July 1653, Don Pantaleon Sa, a Portuguese nobleman, brother of the ambassador from that country to England, and a Knight of Malta, was beheaded on Tower Hill. The peculiar circumstances of Don Pantaleon's untimely fate, and a remarkable coincidence connected with the affair, render it not unworthy of our notice.

At that time there was, on the south side of the Strand, a kind of bazaar called the New Exchange; the buildings of the Adelphi now cover its site. It was opened in 1608 by James I., who named it 'Britain's Burse,' but in popular parlance it never received any other designation than the New Exchange. It consisted of four rows or walks—two on the ground-floor, and two upstairs, each being lined with small shops, where all kinds of fancy articles were sold. As a place to lounge in, to walk, and talk, and hear the news, as our American cousins say, the New Exchange succeeded to Paul's Walk; but, with this difference, Paul's Walk was only used by gentlemen; while the shops in the New Exchange being especially devoted to the sale of gloves, perfumes, fans, and other feminine necessities or luxuries, its walks were frequented by the gay and fashionable of both sexes. Many scenes in our old comedies are laid in this place; and most old libraries contain whity-brown pamphlets, entitled *News from the New Exchange,* or *New News from the New Exchange;* but as in most of these scurrility and indecency take the place of wit and humour, the less we say about them the better.

It happened that, in the November of 1652, Don Pantaleon was walking in the New Exchange, with some of his countrymen, when a quarrel arose between them and a young English gentleman of good family, named Gerrard. The cause of the quarrel, as is usual in such occurrences, was of a

DON PANTALEON SA.

most trivial kind. Mr Gerrard accused the Portuguese of speaking, in French, disparagingly of England; they, on the other hand, alleged that he rudely pushed between them, without any provocation. Whatever may have been the original cause, swords were drawn, and passes exchanged; but the good sense of a few unarmed Englishmen, who were present, stopped the fray, by separating the combatants, and hustling the Portuguese out of the Exchange, one of them with a cut cheek, leaving Gerrard slightly wounded in the shoulder. The next day, Don Pantaleon, with fifty well-armed followers, came to the Exchange, to take his revenge. Fortunately, few Englishmen were there at the time, but of these, four were severely wounded by the Portuguese, and a Mr Greenway, while walking with his sister and a lady to whom he was betrothed, being mistaken for Gerrard, was killed by a pistol-shot through the head. A great and enraged crowd soon collected, before which the Portuguese retreated, taking shelter in their house of embassy.

Colonel Whaley, who commanded the horse-guard on duty, proceeded to disperse the crowd, and demand the criminals from the Portuguese ambassador. The latter insisted that, by the law of nations, his house was an inviolable sanctuary for all his countrymen; and begged that the circumstances should be at once made known to the Lord Protector. Cromwell sent a messenger, in reply, to state that if the criminals were not given up to the civil authorities, the soldiers would be withdrawn, and the mob left to do as they pleased in the matter. Under this threat, Don Pantaleon, three Portuguese, and 'an English boy,' were given up; they were confined in the guard-house for the night, and next day committed to Newgate. By the intercession of the Portuguese merchants, their trial was delayed till the 6th of July in the following year, when they were arraigned for the crime of murder.

At first, Don Pantaleon refused to plead, claiming the immunity of an ambassador; he holding a commission to act in that high capacity, in the event of his brother's death, or absence from England. On being told that, if he did not plead he would be submitted to the *press*, he pleaded not guilty. A mixed jury, of Englishmen and foreigners, brought in a verdict of guilty, and the five prisoners were sentenced to be hanged on the 8th. Every effort was made, by the Portuguese and other ambassadors, to save Don Pantaleon's life, but without avail. Either to supplications or threats, Cromwell made no other reply than, 'Blood has been shed, and justice must be satisfied.' The only mercy granted to Don Pantaleon was a respite of two days, from the 8th to the 10th, and a reprieve from the disgraceful death of hanging, Don Guimarez, the ambassador, having requested that he might be permitted to kill his brother with his own sword, rather than he should be hanged.

In the meantime, while Don Pantaleon was a prisoner in Newgate, awaiting his trial, Gerrard, with whom the unhappy quarrel had arisen, becoming concerned in a plot to assassinate Cromwell, was tried and condemned to be hanged also. And in his case, too, his gentle blood and profession of arms being taken into consideration, the punishment of hanging was changed to beheading. So, as Don Pantaleon, attended by a number of his brother's followers, was being conveyed in a mourning-coach with six horses, from Newgate to the place of execution, Gerrard was expiating his crime on the same scaffold to which the other was hastening. It has been said that they met on the scaffold, but without truth, though Don Pantaleon suffered immediately after Gerrard. The three other Portuguese were pardoned, but the person described as the 'English boy,' was hanged at Tyburn on the same day. The inflexible conduct of Cromwell on this occasion, gave him great credit, even among his enemies in England, for his justice; while it impressed foreign nations with a salutary sense of his power; and the case has ever since been considered as a precedent in all questions respecting the privileges of ambassadors.

### THE TWO COUNTESSES OF KELLIE.

On this day, in the year 1781, Mr Methven Erskine, a cadet of the Kellie family, married at Edinburgh Joanna, daughter of the deceased Adam Gordon, of Ardoch, in Aberdeenshire. A brother of the gentleman, named Thomas, had, ten years before, married Anne, another daughter of Mr Gordon. These gentlemen were in the position of merchants, and there were at one time seventeen persons between them and the family titles; yet they lived to become, in succession, Earls of Kellie, being the last who enjoyed that peerage, separately from any other.*

It was by a series of very singular circumstances, hitherto unnarrated, that these two marriages came about. The facts were thus related to the writer in 1845, by a lady then upwards of ninety years of age, who had had opportunities of becoming well acquainted with all the particulars.

At Ardoch Castle—which is situated upon a tall rock overlooking the sea—the proprietor, Mr Gordon, was one evening, a little after the middle of the last century, alarmed by the firing of a gun, evidently from a vessel in distress near shore. A storm was raging, and he had every reason to fear that the vessel was about to be dashed against that iron-bound coast. Hastening down to the beach with lights and ropes, he and his servants looked in vain for the distressed vessel. Its fate was already accomplished, as the floating spars but too plainly shewed; but they looked in vain for any, dead or alive, who might have come from the wreck. At length they found a sort of crib which had been rudely cast ashore, containing, strange to say, a still live infant. The little creature, whose singular fate it had been to survive where so many stronger people perished, was carefully taken to the house and nursed. It proved to be a female child, evidently from its wrappings the offspring of persons of no mean condition, but with nothing about it to afford a trace as to whom these were.

Mr Gordon made some attempts to find the relatives of this foundling, but without effect. Hoping that she in time might be claimed, he caused her to be brought up along with his own daughters, and treated in all respects as one of them. The personal graces and amiable character of the child in time made him feel towards her as if she had actually stood in that relation to him. When she had attained to womanhood, a storm similar to that already spoken of occurred. An alarm-gun was fired, and Mr Gordon, as was his wont, hurried down to the beach, but this time to receive a ship-wrecked party, whom he immediately conducted to his house, and treated with his characteristic kindness. Amongst them was one gentleman-passenger, whom he took into his own parlour, and entertained at supper. After a comfortable night spent in the castle, this stranger was surprised at breakfast by the entrance of a troop of blooming young ladies, the daughters of his host, as he understood, but one of whom attracted his attention in a special manner. 'Is this young lady your daughter too?' he inquired of Mr Gordon. 'No,' replied his

* The title, in 1829, fell to the head of the Erskine family, John Francis, Earl of Mar.

host; 'but she is as dear to me as if she were.' And he then related her story. The stranger listened with increasing emotion, and at the close of the narration, said he had reason to believe that the young lady was his own niece. He then related the circumstances of a sister's return from India, corresponding to the time of the shipwreck, and explained how it might happen that Mr Gordon's inquiries for her relations had failed. 'She is now,' said he, 'an orphan; but, if I am not mistaken in my supposition, she is entitled to a handsome provision which her father bequeathed to her in the hope of her yet being found.'

Ere long, sufficient evidence was afforded to make it certain that the gentleman had really, by the strange accident of the shipwreck, found his long missing niece. It became necessary, of course, that she should pass under his care, and leave Ardoch—a bitter necessity to her, as it inferred a parting with so many friends dear to her. To mitigate the anguish of this separation, it was arranged that one of her so-called sisters, the Misses Gordon, should accompany her. Their destination was Gottenburg, where the uncle had long been settled as a merchant. Here closes all that was romantic in the history of the foundling, but there was to be a sequel of that nature in favour of Mr Gordon's children. Amongst the Scotch merchants settled in the Swedish port, was Mr Thomas Erskine, a younger son of a younger brother of Sir William Erskine of Cambo, in Fife, an offshoot of the family of the Earl of Kellie. To him was Miss Anne Gordon of Ardoch married in 1771. A younger brother, named Methven, who had pursued merchandise in Bengal, ten years later, married a sister of Miss Gordon, as has been stated. No one then dreamed that these gentlemen would ever come near to the peerage of their family; but in 1797 the baronet of Cambo became Earl of Kellie, and two years later, the title lighted on the shoulders of the husband of Anne Gordon. In short, these two daughters of Mr Gordon of Ardoch, became, in succession, Countesses of Kellie in consequence of the incident of the shipwrecked foundling, whom their father's humanity had rescued from the waves, and for whom an owner had so unexpectedly been found.

## DRESS OF A LADY OF FASHION IN THE SEVENTEENTH CENTURY.

In a dramatic pastoral, entitled *Rhodon and Iris*, first acted at Norwich in 1631, we find the following list of the dress, ornaments, and toilet requisites of a fashionable lady of the period.

Chains, coronets, pendants, bracelets, and earrings;
Pins, girdles, spangles, embroideries, and rings;
Shadows, rebatoes, ribbands, ruffs, cuffs, falls,
Scarfs, feathers, fans, masks, muffs, laces, cauls,
Thin tiffanies, cobweb lawn, and farthingales,
Sweet falls, veils, wimples, glasses, crisping-pins,
Pots of ointment, combs, with poking sticks, and
bodkins,
Coifs, gorgets, fringes, rolls, fillets, and hair-laces.
Silks, damasks, velvets, tinsels, cloth of gold,
Of tissues, with colours of a hundredfold.
But in her tires so new-fangled is she,
That which doth with her humour now agree,
To-morrow she dislikes. Now doth she swear
That a loose body is the neatest wear;
But, ere an hour be gone, she will protest,
A strait gown graces her proportion best;
Now calls she for a boisterous farthingale,
Then to her haunch she 'll have her garments fall;
Now doth she praise a sleeve that 's long and wide,
Yet by and by that fashion doth deride;
Sometimes, she applauds a pavement-sweeping train,
And presently dispraiseth it again;
Now she commends a shallow band so small,
That it may seem scarce any band at all;
But soon to a new fancy she doth reel,
And calls for one as big as a coach-wheel.
She 'll wear a flowing coronet to-day,
The symbol of her beauty's sad decay;
To-morrow, she a waving plume will try,
The emblem of all female levity,
Now in her hat, now in her hair is drest;
Now, of all fashions, she thinks change the best,
Nor in her weeds alone, is she so nice,
But rich perfumes she buys at any price;
Storax and spikenard, she burns in her chamber,
And daubs herself with civet, musk, and amber.

* * * *

Waters she hath to make her face to shine,
Confections, eke, to clarify her skin;
Lip-salve and cloths of a rich scarlet dye
She hath, which to her cheeks she doth apply;
Ointment, wherewith she sprinkles o'er her face,
And lustrifies her beauty's dying grace.

FASHIONABLE LADY OF THE SEVENTEENTH CENTURY.

## CHILD SUCKLED BY A GOAT.

Whether the old story of Romulus and Remus is a myth or a record of genuine fact, we shall never know: most probably the former; but incidents of the same nature are sufficiently vouched. The *Swallow* frigate was, in July 1812, engaged in a severe action with a French frigate near Majorca. One of the sailors, named Phelan, had his wife on board. In such circumstances, the woman is always expected to assist the surgeons in attending on the sick and wounded. The two ships being engaged yard-arm and yard-arm, the slaughter was great, and the cockpit became crowded with poor fellows in need of attention. While engaged in her service of kindness, the woman heard that her husband was wounded on deck. She rushed up, and reached the spot in time to catch poor Phelan in her arms. They kissed and embraced; but next instant a cannon-ball took off the unfortunate woman's head. The husband gave one agonised look at his dead wife, and then expired. When the rage of the battle was over, the two bodies were sewed up in a hammock and consigned to the deep. The hapless wife had, only three weeks before, given birth to an infant. The child was thus left an orphan, with no woman near it, and none but rough-handed, though kind-hearted, tars to tend it. They all declared their willingness to be fathers to the little one; but a mother was still wanting. It happened, however, that one of the officers had a female Maltese goat on board. The child was put to the goat, and followed his natural instinct by sucking. The animal became so accustomed to this proceeding, that she would lie down voluntarily to suckle the infant. Goat's milk is known to be very nourishing; and little Tommy (as the sailors called him) prospered with this substitute for a natural parent.

---

# JULY 11.

St Pius I., pope and martyr, 157. St James, bishop of Nisibis, confessor, 350. St Hidulphus, bishop and abbot, 707. St Drostan, abbot of Dalcongaile, about 809.

---

*Born.*—Robert I. of Scotland, 1274, *Lochmaben;* Lalande, French mathematician, 1732, *Bourg en Bresse.*

*Died.*—Emperor Anthemius, murdered at Rome, 472; Jack Cade, leader of a peasant rebellion in England, killed near Lewes, 1450; Charles Macklin, comedian, 1797, *London;* General Alexander Hamilton, Vice-president of United States, killed in a duel, 1804.

## CHARLES MACKLIN.

A rare and remarkable instance of length of days, combined with an arduous and successful theatrical career, is exhibited in the great age of Macklin, who died in his one hundred and seventh year. Born two months before his father was killed, fighting for King James at the battle of the Boyne, in 1690, Macklin died in 1797, thus witnessing the extremities of two centuries, and nearly having lived in three. As an actor, he was distinguished for his performance of Shylock, Sir Archy in his own comedy of *Love-à-la-Mode,* and other parts in which sarcasm forms the leading trait of character. His writings display the same sarcastic tone, and his best performances seem to have been reflections of his own personal disposition. Even his repartees were generally of the severe kind. For instance, on a dignitary of the church, who had a doubtful reputation for veracity, telling Macklin that a tradesman in the parish had called him a liar, the actor asked: 'What reply did you make?' 'I told him,' said the clergyman, 'that a lie was one of the things I dared not commit.' 'And why, doctor,' retorted Macklin, 'why did you give the fellow so mean an opinion of your courage?'

Macklin's shrewdness, knowledge of the world, long experience of life, and liberal ideas rendered his conversation peculiarly pleasant and instructive, when he was not in the sarcastic mood. Nor was he unaware of his failing in the latter respect. Alluding to it on one occasion, he said: 'It takes a long time for a man to learn the art of *neutralising* in conversation. I have, for a great part of my life, been endeavouring at it, but was never able to act up to it as I wished. I could never sit still hearing people assert what I thought wrong, without labouring to set them right, not considering how difficult it is to correct the errors of others, when we are so wedded to our own. But this folly generally attaches to men of inexperience and lively imagination: your dull fellows know better; they have little but neutrality to trust to, and soon find out the policy of it.'

Macklin's recollections of the very different manners and customs that prevailed in the earlier part of the last century, were very interesting. Then, the east and west of London were as totally distinct as two cities one hundred miles apart. The merchant then scarcely ever lived out of the city, his residence being invariably attached to his counting-house; his credit, in a great degree, depending upon the observance of this long-established practice. The first emigration of the city merchants westwards was about 1747, and then only as far as Hatton Garden; and even this removal was ventured upon by such only as had already realised large fortunes, and possessed reputations for wealth beyond any shadow of doubt. 'The lawyers, too,' said Macklin, 'lived mostly in the Inns of Court, or about Westminster Hall, and the players all resided in the vicinity of the theatres, so that they could attend rehearsal without inconvenience, or expense of coach-hire. But I do not know how the change has been effected; we, the actors, are all now looking out for high ground, squares, and genteel neighbourhoods, no matter how far distant from the theatres, as if local selection could give rhythm to the profession, or genteel neighbourhoods instantaneously produce good-manners.'

Macklin's last appearance on the stage, was in his hundredth year, in the character of Shylock. Even at that very great age, he was physically capable of performing the part with considerable vigour; but his mental powers were almost gone. In the second act, his memory totally failing him, he with great grace and solemnity came forward, and apologised to the audience. For a few years afterwards, he scarcely felt the infirmities of advanced age. He lived then, as he always had been accustomed to do, much from home; taking long walks, and frequenting a tavern in Duke's Court, every evening, where, though still by no means unready at putting down an impudent questioner by a biting sarcasm, he used to relate, with tolerable distinctness, many interesting anecdotes to gratified listeners. As his infirmities increased, he wandered feebly about the vicinity of Covent Garden, and often visited the theatre, more, apparently, from the force of habit, than from any amusement he derived from the performance. On these occasions, however full the house might be, the pit audience always made room for him in his accustomed seat—the centre of the last row, next to the orchestra.

Mr Kirkman relates a conversation he had with Macklin, less than a year before he died, which forms an interesting and not unpleasing picture of faculties still shrewd and vivacious, though fast fading into decay. As a specimen of the conversation of a man upwards of one hundred and six years old, it is probably unique.

*Kirkman.* Are you not pleased when your friends come and converse with you?

*Macklin.* I am always very happy to see my friends, and I should be very happy to hold a—a—a—see there now——

*Kirkman.* A conversation you mean, sir?

*Macklin.* Ay, a conversation. Alas, sir! you see the wretched state of my memory; see there now, I could not recollect that common word—but I cannot converse. I used to go to a house very near this, where my friends assemble.... It was a—a—a [a company]; no that's not the word, a—a—club, I mean. I was the father of it, but I could not hear all; and what I did hear, I did not a—a—under—under—understand; they were all very attentive to me, but I could not be one of them. Indeed, I found, sir, that I was not fit to keep company, so I stay away.

*Kirkman.* But I perceive with satisfaction, sir, that your sight is good.

*Macklin.* O, sir! my sight like everything else begins to fail too; about two days ago, I felt a—a—a—there now—— I have lost it; a pain just above my left eye.

*Kirkman.* I think you appear at present free from pain.

*Macklin.* Yes, sir, I am pretty comfortable now; but I find my, my—a—a—my strength is all gone. I feel myself going gradually.

*Kirkman.* But you are not afraid to die?

*Macklin.* Not in the least, sir. I never did any person any serious mischief in my life; even when I gambled, I never cheated: I know that a—a—a—see there now—— death, I mean, must come, and I am ready to give it up.

*Kirkman.* I understand you were at Drury Lane Theatre last night.

*Macklin.* Yes, sir, I was there.

*Kirkman.* Yes, sir, the newspapers of this morning take notice of it.

*Macklin.* Do they?

*Kirkman.* Yes, sir;—the paragraph runs thus: 'Among the numerous visitors at Drury Lane Theatre last night, we observed the Duke of Queensberry and the veteran Macklin, whose ages together amount to one hundred and ninety-six.'

*Macklin.* The Duke of who?

*Kirkman.* The Duke of Queensberry, sir.

*Macklin.* I don't know that man. The Duke of Queensberry! The Duke of Queensberry! Oh! ay, I remember him now very well. The Duke of Queensberry old! Why, sir, I might be his father!* Ha, ha, ha!

*Kirkman.* Well, sir, I understand that you went to the Haymarket Theatre to see the *Merchant of Venice.*

*Macklin.* I did, sir.

*Kirkman.* What is your opinion of Mr Palmer's Shylock?

*Macklin.* Why, sir, my opinion is, that Mr Palmer played the character of Shylock in *one style.* In this scene there was a sameness, in that scene a sameness, and in every scene a sameness: it was all same, same, same!—no variation. He did not look the character, nor laugh the character, nor speak the character of Shakspeare's Jew. In the trial-scene, where he comes to cut the pound of flesh, he was no Jew. Indeed, sir, *he did not hit the part, nor did the part hit him.*'

Macklin seems to have been mainly indebted for his long life to a vigorous constitution. He never was an abstemious man. His favourite beverage was ale, porter, or white wine thickened to the consistence of a syrup with sugar. For many years before he died, his loss of teeth compelled him to eat only fish, hash, and other spoon-meats. For the last ten years of his existence, he had no fixed hour for meals. He ate when he was hungry, at any hour of the day or night, drank when he was thirsty, and went to bed or arose just as he felt inclined, without any reference to time. There can be no doubt that the constant care and attention of his devoted wife, combined with her thorough knowledge of his disposition, constitution, and temper, was partly the cause of the prolongation of his life.

* Macklin was right, and the newspaper wrong. The duke was then only in his seventy-first year.

## ALEXANDER HAMILTON.

Although the name of Alexander Hamilton is not so popularly familiar as several others concerned in the construction of the American Union, yet there is scarcely another which so closely interests the profounder students of that momentous passage in the world's history. Of Hamilton's share in that work, Guizot testifies, 'that there is not one element of order, strength, and durability in the constitution which he did not powerfully contribute to introduce into the scheme and cause to be adopted.'

Hamilton's father was a Scotsman, and his mother a member of a Huguenot family, banished from France. He was born in 1757, on the island of Nevis; and whilst a youth serving as clerk in a merchant's office, a hurricane of more than ordinary violence occurred, and Hamilton drew up an account of its ravages, which was inserted in a West Indian newspaper. The narrative was so well written, and excited so much attention, that the writer was deemed born for something better than mercantile drudgery, and was sent to New York to prosecute his education. The dispute between Great Britain and the colonies had begun to grow very warm, and Hamilton soon distinguished himself by eloquent speeches in advocacy of resistance. With the ardour of youth he commenced the study of military tactics, and turned his learning to good account in the first action between the British and Americans at Lexington in 1775. In the course of the unhappy war which followed, Hamilton was Washington's most trusted and confidential aid. At the conclusion of hostilities he commenced practice at the bar, became secretary of the treasury under President Washington, and a leading actor in all those intricate, delicate, and perplexing discussions, which attended the consolidation of the thirteen independent colonies into one nation. Hamilton was the most conservative of republicans. He opposed the ultra-democratic doctrines of Jefferson, he was an ardent admirer of the English constitution, and he beheld the course of the French Revolution with abhorrence and dismay. But all the blessings which lay in store for America in the treasury of Hamilton's fine intellect, were lost by a cruel mischance ere he had attained his forty-seventh year. With the feelings of an upright man, he had expressed his sense of the profligacy of Aaron Burr, who thereon challenged him to a duel. Hamilton had all reasonable contempt for such a mode of settling differences, but fearing, as he wrote, that 'his ability to be in future useful either in preventing mischief or effecting good was inseparable from a conformity to prejudice in this particular,' he weakly yielded. With every precaution of secrecy, he met his adversary at Weehardken, near New York. Colonel Burr fired, and his ball entered Hamilton's side, who fell mortally wounded, his pistol going involuntarily off as he staggered to the ground. After a day of agony, he expired on the 11th of July 1804. Never, except at Washington's death, was there such mourning in America.

Hamilton was a man under middle height, spare, erect, and of a most dignified presence. His writings in *The Federalist* are read by political philosophers with admiration to this day. He wrote rapidly, but with precision and method. His habit was to think well over his subject, and then, at whatever time of night, to go to bed and sleep for six or seven hours. On awaking, he drank a cup of strong coffee, sat down at his desk, and for five, six, seven, or even eight hours continued writing, until he had cleared the whole matter off his mind.

---

## HURLING THE WHETSTONE:
## THE COUTEAU RODOMONT.

Our ancestors, with a strong love for practical jokes, and an equally strong aversion to falsehood and boasting, checked an indulgence in such

vices, when they became offensive, by very plain satire. A confirmed liar was presented with *a whetstone*, to jocularly infer that his invention, if he continued to use it so freely, would require sharpening. Hence, to 'win the whetstone,' was equivalent to being proclaimed the greatest liar in the company.

Annexed is a cut representing a man offering the whetstone to 'a pack of knaves,' being one of a series of twenty copper-plates of foreign execution (probably Dutch or Flemish) without date or name, but evidently of the time of Charles I., preserved in the Bridgewater Library. It is thus described in Mr Payne Collier's catalogue thereof: 'Hurling the whetstone,' was a phrase apparently equivalent to 'throwing the hatchet,' and the latter is derived from the tale of a man who was so incredibly skilful, that he was able to throw a hatchet at a distant object, and sever it; perhaps 'hurling the whetstone' was an exaggeration of a similar kind, easily connected with the hatchet. Underneath the preceding engraving are the following lines:—

'The whettstone is a knave that all men know,  
Yet many on him doe much cost bestowe:  
Hee's us'd almost in every shoppe, but whye?  
An edge must needs be set on every lye.'

Shakspeare has an illustrative allusion to this satirical custom. In *As You Like It* (Act I. sc. 2), the entrance of the fool, Touchstone, is greeted by

OLD WHETSTONE IN BRITISH MUSEUM.

Celia as a lucky event, 'fortune's work, who, perceiving our natural wits too dull to reason, hath sent this natural* for our whetstone: for always the dulness of the fool is the whetstone of his

* The old term for a born-fool.

wits.' In *Troilus and Cressida* (Act V. sc. 2), the same idea occurs when Thersites satirically alludes to the duplicity of Cressida in the words:

'Now she sharpens;—well said, *whetstone*.'

Ben Jonson has a more direct allusion to it, when he makes one of his characters declare of another, 'he will lie cheaper than any beggar, and louder than most clocks; for which he is right properly accommodated to the *whetstone*, his page!' thus branding both master and man as liars by collusion. A confirmed slanderer, whose allegations were his own invention, was sometimes publicly exposed with the whetstone hanging round his neck in the pillory, or on the stool of repentance.

The form of the old whetstone differed in some points from the modern one, as may be seen in our engraving on the preceding page, from one preserved in the British Museum. It is supplied with a loop for suspension at one end, and thus could be readily hung to the girdle of a butcher or artisan whose tools required sharpening, and might be as easily attached to the neck of any convicted liar.

Boasters, who occupied the time, or exhausted the patience of the company at a social gathering, were silenced in France and Germany by having delivered to them a wooden knife, called *couteau rodomont*, and *rodomont messer*, from the word *rodomontado*, applied to a rambling boastful narrative. They were kept at taverns, and placed beside the president of the table, and he stopped the troublesome speaker by ringing the bell in the blade, or blowing a whistle concealed in the handle of the knife, and then delivering it into the hands of the offender to guard until a greater boaster was found; this ceremony being greeted by peals of laughter, and words of mockery. Our engraving depicts one of these curious carving-knives, made at Nuremberg in the early part of the sixteenth century, bearing upon the bell the arms of the emperor, and on the blade descriptive verses from the pen of the renowned cobbler-poet, Hans Sachs. The rhymes are of the homeliest description, and allude as well to the folly as the immorality of falsehood. The utility of the implement is enforced in a couplet which runs along the back of the blade, and may be thus translated:

'Though made from wood, this knife is good,
To cut short tales from the lying brood.'

This knife was probably made about 1550. Sachs was born in 1494, and lived till 1576; he wrote abundantly, and on all subjects, in the early part of his century, and reckons his works in 1561 at 'a sum-total of six thousand and forty-eight pieces, great and small.' During the whole of his life he continued to work at his trade, although he found leisure enough to spin out a greater mass of rhyme than was ever produced by one man, if Lope de Vega, the Spaniard, be excepted. Very many of Sachs's poems were called forth by temporary circumstances; several are satirical; and those which he levelled at the Church of Rome, from the popularity of their style, did much in aid of the Reformation.

## JULY 12.

Saints Nabor and Felix, martyrs, about 304. St John Gualbert, abbot, 1073.

*Born.*—Caius Julius Cæsar, 100 B.C.

*Died.*—Desiderius Erasmus, scholar, 1536, *Basel;* General St Ruth, killed at Aghrim, Ireland, 1691; Titus Oates, 1704; Christian G. Heyne (illustrator of ancient writings), 1814, *Gottingen;* Dr John Jamieson (Scottish Dictionary), 1838, *Edinburgh;* Mrs Tonna ('Charlotte Elizabeth'), controversial writer, 1846; Horace Smith, novelist, comic poet, 1849; Robert Stevenson, engineer of Bell Rock light-house, &c., 1850.

### MRS TONNA.

It is quite possible to be an author and have one's books sold by thousands, and yet only attain a limited and sectional fame. Such was Mrs Tonna's case. We remember overhearing a conversation between a young lady and a gentleman of almost encyclopædic information, in which a book by Charlotte Elizabeth was mentioned. 'Charlotte Elizabeth!' exclaimed he; 'who is Charlotte Elizabeth?' 'Don't you know Charlotte Elizabeth?' rejoined she; 'the writer of so many very nice books.' She was amazed at his ignorance, and probably estimated his acquirements at a much lower rate afterwards.

'Charlotte Elizabeth,' Miss Browne, Mrs Phelan, finally Mrs Tonna, was the daughter of the rector of St Giles, Norwich, and was born in that city on the 1st of October 1790. As soon as she could read she became an indiscriminate devourer of books, and when yet a child, once read herself blind for a season. Her favourite volume was *Fox's Martyrs*, and its spirit may be said to have become her spirit. Shortly after her father's death, she entered into an unhappy marriage with one Captain Pelhan, whose regiment she accompanied to Canada for three years. On her return, she settled on her husband's estate in Kilkenny, and mingling with the peasantry, she came to the conclusion that all their miseries sprang out of their religion. She thereon commenced to write tracts and tales illustrative of that conviction, which attracted the notice and favour of the Orange party, with whom she cordially identified herself. As her writings became remunerative, her husband laid claim to the proceeds, and to preserve them from sequestration, she assumed the name of 'Charlotte Elizabeth.' Her life henceforward is merely a tale of unceasing literary activity. Having become totally deaf, her days were spent between her desk and her garden. In the editorship of magazines, and in a host of publications, she advocated her religious and Protestant principles with a fervour which it would not be unjust to designate as, occasionally at least, fanatical. In 1837, Captain Pelhan died, and in 1841 she formed a happier union with Mr Tonna, which terminated with her death at Ramsgate on the 12th of July 1846. Mrs Tonna had a handsome countenance and in its radiance of intelligence and kindliness, a stranger would never imagine that he was in the presence of one whose religion and politics, theoretically, were those of the days of Elizabeth rather than of Victoria, and who was capable of saying in all earnestness, as she once did say to a young Protestant Irish lady of our acquaintance, on their being introduced to each other, "Well, my dear, I hope you hate the Paapists!'

## THE FEMALE HEAD-DRESSES OF 1776.

On the 12th of July 1776, Samuel Foote appeared at the Haymarket theatre in the character of Lady Pentweazle, wearing one of the enormous female head-dresses which were then fashionable—not meaning, probably, anything so serious as the reform of an absurdity, but only to raise a laugh, and bring an audience to his play-house. The dress is stated to have been stuck full of feathers of an extravagant size; it extended a yard wide; and the whole fabric of feathers, hair, and wool dropped off his head as he left the stage. King George and Queen Charlotte, who were present,

A FEMALE HEAD-DRESS OF 1776.

laughed heartily at the exhibition; and her majesty, wearing an elegant and becoming head-dress, supplied a very fitting rebuke to the absurdity which the actor had thus satirised. There are numerous representations to be met with in books of fashions, and descriptions in books of various kinds, of the head-dress of that period. Sometimes it was remarkable simply for its enormous height; a lofty pad or cushion being placed on the top of the head, and the hair combed up over it, and slightly confined in some way at the top. Frequently, however, this tower was bedizened in a most extravagant manner, necessarily causing it to be broad as well as high, and rendering the whole fabric a mass of absurdity. It was a mountain of wool, hair, powder, lawn, muslin, net, lace, gauze, ribbon, flowers, feathers, and wire. Sometimes these varied materials were built up, tier after tier, like the successive stages of a pagoda. The *London Magazine*, in satirizing the fashions of 1777, said:

'Give Chloe a bushel of horse-hair and wool,
 Of paste and pomatum a pound,
Ten yards of gay ribbon to deck her sweet skull,
 And gauze to encompass it round.
Of all the bright colours the rainbow displays,
 Be those ribbons which hang on the head;
Be her flounces adapted to make the folks gaze,
 And about the whole work be they spread;
Let her flaps fly behind for a yard at the least,
 Let her curls meet just under her chin;
Let these curls be supported, to keep up the jest,
 With an hundred instead of one pin.'

The *New Bath Guide*, which hits off the follies of that period with a good deal of sarcastic humour, attacked the ladies' head-dresses in a somewhat similar strain:

'A cap like a hat
 (Which was once a cravat)
Part gracefully plaited and pin'd is,
 Part stuck upon gauze,
 Resembles macaws
And all the fine birds of the Indies.

 But above all the rest,
 A bold Amazon's crest
Waves nodding from shoulder to shoulder;
 At once to surprise
 And to ravish all eyes
To frighten and charm the beholder.

 In short, head and feather,
 And wig altogether,
With wonder and joy would delight ye;
 Like the picture I've seen
 Of th' adorable queen
Of the beautiful bless'd Otaheite.

 Yet Miss at the Rooms *
 Must beware of her plumes,
For if Vulcan her feather embraces,
 Like poor Lady Laycock,
 She'd burn like a haycock,
And roast all the Loves and the Graces.'

The last stanza refers to an incident in which a lady's monstrous head-dress caught fire, leading to calamitous results.

## BELL LEGENDS.

Church-bells are beginning to awake a regard that has long slumbered. They have been deemed, too, recently, fit memorial of the mighty dead. Turrets, whose echoes have repeated but few footfalls for a century, have been intrepidly ascended, and their clanging tenants diligently scanned for word or sign to tell their story. Country clergymen, shewing the lions of their parishes to archæological excursionists, have thought themselves happy in the choice of church-bells as the subject of the address expected of them. And it will be felt that some of the magic of the International

* The Pump-rooms at Bath, a place of great resort for fashionables.

Exhibition was due to the tumultuous reverberations of the deep, filling, quivering tones of the many bells.

In monkish medieval times, church-bells enjoyed peculiar esteem. They were treated in great measure as voices, and were inscribed with Latin ejaculations and prayers, such as—Hail, Mary, full of grace, pray for us; St Peter, pray for us; St Paul, pray for us; St Katharine, pray for us; Jesus of Nazareth, have mercy upon us; their tones, swung out into the air, would, ecstatically, appear to give utterence to the supplication with which they were inscribed. A bell in St Michael's church, Alnwick, says, in quaint letters on a belt that is diapered with studs, 'Archangel Michael, come to the help of the people of God.' A bell at Compton Basset, which has two shields upon it, each bearing a chevron between three trefoils, says, 'Blessed be the name of the Lord.' Many bells are found to have identical inscriptions; there is, however, great variety, and further search would bring much more to light.

In those old times, pious queens and gentlewomen threw into the mass of metal that was to be cast into a bell their gold and silver ornaments; and a feeling of reverence for the interceding voices was common to gentle and simple. At Sudeley Castle, in the chapel, there is a bell, dated 1573, that tells us of the concern which the gentle dames of the olden time would take in this manufacture. It says, 'St George, pray for us. The Ladie Doratie Chandos, Widdowe, made this.' They were sometimes cast in monasteries under the superintendence of ecclesiastics of rank. It is written that Sir William Corvehill, 'priest of the service of our Lady,' was a 'good bell-founder and maker of frames;' and on a bell at Sealton, in Yorkshire, we may read that it was made by John, archbishop of Graf. One of the ancient windows on the north side of the nave of York minster is filled with stained-glass, which is divided into subjects representing the various processes of bell-casting, bell-cleaning, and bell-tuning, and has for a border a series of bells, one below another; proving that the associations with which bells were regarded rendered them both ecclesiastical and pictorial in the eyes of the artists of old.

The inscriptions on ancient bells were generally placed immediately below the haunch or shoulder, although they are sometimes found nearer the sound bow. The legends are, with few exceptions, preceded by crosses. Coats of arms are also of frequent occurrence, probably indicating the donors. The tones of ancient bells are incomparably richer and softer, more dulcet, mellow, and sufficing to the ear than those of the present iron age.

King Henry VIII., however, looked upon church-bells only as so much metal that could be melted down and sold. Hence, in the general destruction and distribution of church-property in his reign, countless bells disappeared, to be sold as mere metal. Many curious coincidences attended this wholesale appropriation. Ships attempting to carry bells across the seas, foundered in several havens, as at Lynn, and at Yarmouth; and, fourteen of the Jersey bells being wrecked at the entrance of the harbour of St Malo, a saying arose to the effect, that when the wind blows the drowned bells are ringing. A certain bishop of Bangor, too, who sold the bells of his cathedral, was stricken with blindness when he went to see them shipped; and Sir Miles Partridge, who won the Jesus bells of St Paul's, London, from King Henry, at dice, was, not long afterwards hanged on Tower Hill. Notwithstanding the regal and archiepiscopal disregard of bells, they did not, altogether, pass from popular esteem. Within the last half century, at Brenckburne, in Northumberland, old people pointed out a tree beneath which, they had been told when they were young, a treasure was buried. And when this treasure was sought and found, it turned out to be nothing more than fragments of the bell of the ruined priory church close by. Tradition recounts that a foraging-party of moss-trooping Scots once sought far and near for this secluded priory, counting upon the contents of the larders of the canons. But not a sign or a track revealed its position, for it stands in a cleft between the wooded banks of the Coquet, and is invisible from the high lands around. The enraged and hungry marauders—says the legend—had given up the search in despair, and were leaving the locality, when the monks, believing their danger past, bethought themselves to offer up thanksgivings for their escape. Unfortunately, the sound of the bell, rung to call them to this ceremony, reached the ears of the receding Scots in the forest above, and made known to them the situation of the priory. They retraced their steps, pillaged it, and then set it on fire.

After the Reformation, the inscriptions on bells were addressed to man, not to Heaven; and were rendered in English. There is an exception to this rule, however, at Sherborne, where there is a fire-bell, 1652, addressed conjointly to Heaven and man: 'Lord, quench this furious flame; Arise, run, help, put out the same.' Many of the legends on seventeenth-century bells reflect the quaint times of George Herbert:

'When I ring, God's prayses sing;
When I toule, pray heart and soule;'

and, 'O man be meeke, and lyve in rest;' 'Geve thanks to God;'

'I, sweetly tolling, men do call
To taste on meate that feeds the soule,

are specimens of this period. More vulgar sentiments subsequently found place. 'I am the first, although but small, I will be heard above you all,' say many bells coarsely. A bell at Alvechurch says still more uncouthly, 'If you would know when we was run, it was March the twenty-second 1701.' 'God save the queen,' occurs on an Elizabethan bell at Bury, Sussex, bearing date 1599; and on several others of the reign of Queen Anne, in Devonshire, and on one in Magdalen College, Oxford. 'God save our king,' is found first written on a bell at Stanford-upon-Soar, at the date of the accession of James I., 1603; it is of frequent occurrence on later bells; and the same sentiment is found produced in other forms, one of which is 'Feare God and honner the king, for obedience is a vertuous thing.'

We have one bell that is dedicated to a particular service. It is the great bell of St Paul's, London, which is only tolled on the death of sovereigns. The ordinary passing bell, now commonly called the dead-bell, used to be rung when the dying person was receiving the sacrament, so that those who wished to do so could pray for him at this moment; but it is now only rung after death, simply to inform the neighbourhood of the fact. In the same way the sanctus-bell used to be rung in the performance of mass, when the priest came to the words 'Sancte, Sancte, Sancte, Deus Sabaoth,' so that those persons unable to attend, might yet be able to bow down and worship at this particular moment. For this reason, the bell was always placed in a position where it might be heard as far as possible. In the gables of the chancel arches of ancient churches, are seen small square apertures, whose use few people can divine. It was through these that the ringers watched the services below, so as to be able to ring at the right time.

The great bell of Bow owes its reputation to the nursery legend of 'Oranges and lemons, said the bells of St Clement's;' not to any superior characteristics, for it is exceeded in size and weight by many others. English bells, generally, are smaller than those of foreign countries; perhaps for the reason that scientific ringing is not practised abroad; and all effect must be produced by the bells themselves, not by the mode in which they are handled. The more polite the nation, it is argued, the smaller their bells. The Italians have few bells, and those that they have are small. The Flemish and Germans, on the other hand, have great numbers of large bells. The Chinese once boasted of possessing the largest bells in the world; but Russia has borne off the palm, or in other words carried away the bell, by hanging one in Moscow Cathedral, measuring 19 feet in height, and 63 feet 11 inches round the rim. By the side of these proportions our Big Lens and Big Toms are diminutive. The great bell of St Paul's is but 9 feet in diameter, and weighs but 12,000 lbs. The largest bell in Exeter Cathedral weighs 17,470 lbs.; the famous Bow Bell but 5800 lbs. York, Gloucester, Canterbury, Lincoln, and Oxford, can also eclipse our familiar friend.

France possesses a few ancient bells; some of them are ornamented with small bas-relievos of the Crucifixion, of the descent from the Cross, fleurs-de-lis, seals of abbeys and donors; and others have inscriptions of the same character as our own, each letter being raised on a small tablet more or less decorated. There was a bell in the abbey-church of Moissac (unfortunately recast in 1845), which was of a very rare and early date. An inscription on it, preceded by a cross, read, *Salve Regina misericordiæ.* Between the two last words was a bas-relief of the Virgin, and after them three seals; then followed a line in much smaller characters, 'Anno Domini millesimo cc° LXX. tercio Gofridus me fecit et socios meos. Paulus vocor.' French bells were sometimes the gifts of kings and abbots; and were in every way held in as great esteem as those of our own country. In the accounts of the building of Troyes Cathedral, there is mention of two men coming to cast the bells, and of the canons visiting them at their work and stimulating them to perform it well, by harangues and by chanting the Te Deum. The canons finally assisted at the consecration of the bells.

Bells have their literature as well as legends. Their histories are written in many russet-coloured volumes, in Latin, in French, and in Italian. These have been published in different parts of Europe, in Paris, in Leipsic, in Geneva, in Rome, in Frankfort, in Pisa, in Dresden, in Naples, in the fifteenth, sixteenth, seventeenth, and eighteenth centuries. They take the forms of dissertations, treatises, descriptions, and notes. Early English writers confined themselves more especially to elucidating the art of ringing in essays bewilderingly technical. The names of the different permutations read like the reverie of a lunatic—single bob, plain bob, grandsire bob, single bob minor, grandsire treble, bob major, caters, bob royal, and bob maximus; and the names of the parts of a bell are quite as puzzling to the uninitiated. There are the canons, called also *ansa*, the haunch, otherwise *cerebrum vel caput*, the waist, *latus*, the sound-bow, the mouth, or labium, the brim, and the clapper. There is a manuscript in the British Museum of the 'Orders of the Company of ringers in Cheapside, 1603,' the year of Queen Elizabeth's death. And a work published in 1684, the last year of the reign of Charles II., called *The School of Recreation, or Gentleman's Tutor*, gives ringing as one of the exercises in vogue. There are, besides these, *True Guides for Ringers, and Plain Hints for Ringers*, a poem in praise of ringing, written in 1761, by the author of *Shrubs of Parnassus*, and other curious tracts of no value beyond their quaintness. Schiller has sung the song of the bell in vigorous verse; and in our own day the subject has received much literary care at the hands of more than one country clergyman.

There is another bell legend to be told. On the eve of the feast of Corpus Christi, to this day, the choristers of Durham Cathedral ascend the tower, and in their fluttering white robes sing the Te Deum. This ceremony is in commemoration of the miraculous extinguishing of a conflagration on that night, A.D. 1429. The monks were at midnight prayer when the belfry was struck by lightning and set on fire; but though the flames raged all that night and till the middle of the next day, the tower escaped serious damage and the bells were uninjured—an escape that was imputed to the special interference of the incorruptible St Cuthbert, enshrined in the cathedral. These bells, thus spared, are not those that now reverberate among the house-tops on the steep banks of the Wear. The registry of the church of St Mary le Bow, Durham, tells of the burial of Thomas Bartlet, February 3, 1632, and adds, 'this man did cast the abbey bells the summer before he dyed.'

The great bell in Glasgow Cathedral, tells its own history, mournfully, in the following inscription: 'In the year of grace, 1583, Marcus Knox, a merchant in Glasgow, zealous for the interest of the Reformed Religion, caused me to be fabricated in Holland, for the use of his fellow-citizens of Glasgow, and placed me with solemnity in the Tower of their Cathedral. My function was announced by the impress on my bosom: ME AUDITO, VENIAS, DOCTRINAM SANCTAM UT DISCAS, and I was taught to proclaim the hours of unheeded time. One hundred and ninety-five years had I sounded these awful warnings, when I was broken by the hands of inconsiderate and unskilful men. In the year 1790, I was cast into the furnace, refounded at London, and returned to my sacred vocation. Reader! thou also shalt know a resurrection; may it be to eternal life! Thomas Mears fecit, London, 1790.'

### SIGNALS FOR SERVANTS.

The history of the invention and improvement of the manifold appliances for comfort and convenience in a modern house of the better class, would not only be very curious and instructive, but would also teach us to be grateful for much that has become cheap to our use, though it would have been troublesome and costly to our ancestors, and looked on by them as luxurious. We turn a tap, and pure water flows from a distant river into our dressing-room; we turn another, and gas for lighting or firing is at our immediate command. We pull a handle in one apartment, and the bell rings in a far-distant one. We can even, by directing our mouth to a small opening beside the parlour fireplace, send a whisper along a tube to the servants' hall or kitchen, and thus obtain what we want still more readily. We can now scarcely appreciate the time and trouble thus saved. Hand-bells or whistles were the only signals used in a house a century and a half ago. In an old comedy of the reign of Charles II., the company supposed to be assembled at a country-house of the better class, are summoned to dinner by the cook knocking on the dresser with a rolling-pin! It was usual to call servants by ringing hand-bells; which, thus becoming table-ornaments, were frequently enriched by chasing. Walpole possessed a very fine one, which he believed to be the work of Cellini, and made for Pope Clement VII.* He also had a pair of very curious silver owls, seated on perches formed into whistles, which were blown when servants were wanted. They were curious and quaint specimens of the workmanship of the early part of the seventeenth century; and one of them is here engraved for the first time, from a

sketch made during the celebrated sale at Strawberry Hill in 1842. It may be worth noting, as a curious instance of the value attached by connoisseurs to rare curiosities, that these owls were bought at prices considerably above their weight in gold; and the taste for collecting has so much increased, that there is little doubt they would now realise even higher prices.

* See cut of this article at p. 324, vol. i.



---

## JULY 13.

St Anacletus, martyr, 2d century. St Eugenius, bishop of Carthage, and his companions, martyrs, 505. St Turiaf, Turiave or Thivisiau, bishop of Dol, in Brittany, about 749.

### Festival of the Miracles.

This day (July 13), if Sunday, or the first Sunday after the 13th, begins the festival of the Miracles at Brussels, which lasts for fifteen days. The first day, Sunday, however, is the grand day of celebration; for on this takes place the public procession of the Holy Sacrament of the Miracles. We had an opportunity of witnessing this locally celebrated affair on Sunday, July 15, 1860, and next day procured from one of the ecclesiastical officials a historical account of the festival, of which we offer an abridgment.

In the year 1369, there lived at Enghien, in Hainault, a rich Jew, named Jonathan, who, for purposes of profanation, desired to procure some consecrated wafers. In this object he was assisted by another Jew, named Jean de Louvain, who resided in Brussels, and had hypocritically renounced Judaism. Jean was poor, and in the hope of reward gladly undertook to steal some of the wafers from one of the churches. After examination, he found that the church of St Catherine, at Brussels, offered the best opportunity for the theft. Gaining access by a window on a dark night in October, he secured and carried off the pix containing the consecrated wafers; and the whole were handed to Jonathan, who gave his appointed reward. Jonathan did not long survive this act of sacrilege. He was assassinated in his garden, and his murderers remained unknown. After his death, his widow gave the pix, with the wafers, to a body of Jews in Brussels, who, in hatred of Christianity, were anxious to do the utmost indignity to the wafers. The day they selected for the purpose was Good Friday, 1370. On that day, meeting in their synagogue, they spread the holy wafers, sixteen in number, on a table, and with horrid imprecations proceeded to stab them with poniards. To their amazement, the wounded wafers spouted out blood, and in consternation they fled from the spot! Anxious to rid themselves of objects on which so very extraordinary a miracle had been wrought, these wicked Jews engaged a woman, named Catherine, to carry the wafers to Cologne, though what she was to do with them there is not mentioned. Catherine fulfilled her engagement, but with an oppressed conscience she, on her return, went and revealed all to the rector of the parish church. The Jews concerned in the sacrilege were forthwith brought to justice. They were condemned to be burned, and their execution took place May 22, 1370. Three of the wafers were restored to the clergy of St Guduli, where they have ever since remained as objects of extreme veneration. On several occasions they have done good service to the inhabitants of Brussels, in the way of stopping epidemics. On being appealed to by a solemn procession in 1529, a grievous epidemic at once ceased. From 1579 to 1585, during certain political troubles in the Netherlands, there were no processions in their honour; and they were similarly neglected for some years after the great revolution of 1789—92. But since Sunday, July 14, 1804, the annual procession has been resumed, and the three wafers shewing the miraculous marks of blood, have been exposed to the adoration of the faithful in the church of St Guduli. It is added in the authoritative account, that certain indulgences are granted by order of Pius VI. to all who take part in the procession, and repeat daily throughout the year, praises and thanks for the most holy sacrament of the Miracles. In the openings of the pillars along both sides of the choir of St Guduli, is suspended a series of Gobelin tapestries, vividly representing the chief incidents in the history of the Miracles, including the scene of stabbing the wafers.

---

*Born.*—Regnier de Graaf, 1641, *Schoenhaven, in Holland;* Richard Cumberland, bishop of Peterborough, 1632.

*Died.*—Pope John III., 573; Emperor Henry II., 1024; Du Guesclin, constable of France, illustrious warrior, 1380, *Châteauneuf-Randon;* Sir William Berkley, 1677, *Twickenham;* Richard Cromwell, ex-Protector of the three kingdoms, 1712, *Cheshunt;* Elijah Fenton, poet, 1730, *Easthampstead;* Bishop John Conybeare, 1755, *Bristol;* Dr James Bradley, astronomer, 1762; Jean Paul Marat, French Revolutionary leader and writer, 1793, *Paris;* Rev. John Lingard, author of a History of England, 1851, *Hornby, near Lancaster.*

## BERTRAND DU GUESCLIN.

This flower of French chivalry was of a noble but poor family in Brittany. 'Never was there so bad a boy in the world,' said his mother, 'he is always wounded, his face disfigured, fighting or being fought; his father and I wish he were peaceably underground.' All the masters engaged to teach him, gave up the task in despair, and to the end of his life he could neither read nor write. A tournay was held one day at Rennes, to which his father went; his son, then about fourteen, secretly followed him, riding on a miserable pony: the first knight who retired from the lists found the young hero in his hostelry, who, throwing himself at his knees, besought him to lend him his horse and arms. The request was granted, and Du Guesclin, preparing in all haste, flew to the combat, and overthrew fifteen adversaries with such address and good grace as to surprise all the spectators. His father presented himself to run a course with him, but Bertrand threw down his lance. When persuaded to raise his visor, the paternal joy knew no bounds; he kissed him tenderly, and henceforward took every means to insure his advancement.

His first campaign with the French army was made in 1359, where he gave full proof of his rare valour, and from that time he was the much-feared enemy of the English army, until taken prisoner by the Black Prince at the battle of Navarete, in Spain, in 1367. In spite of the repeated entreaties of both French and English nobles, the prince kept him more than a year at Bordeaux, until it was whispered that he feared his rival too much to set him free. Hearing this, Edward sent for Du Guesclin and said. 'Messire Bertrand, they pretend that I dare not give you your liberty, because I am afraid of you.' 'There are those who say so,' replied the knight, 'and I feel myself much honoured by it.' The prince coloured, and desired him to name his own ransom. 'A hundred thousand florins,' was the reply. 'But where can you get so much money?' 'The king of France and Castile, the pope, and the Duke of Anjou will lend it to me, and were I in my own country, the women would earn it with their distaffs.' All were charmed with his frankness, and the Princess of Wales invited him to dinner, and offered to pay twenty thousand francs towards the ransom. Du Guesclin, kneeling before her, said: 'Madame, I believed myself to be the ugliest knight in the world, but now I need not be so displeased with myself.' Many of the English forced their purses on him, and he set off to raise the sum; but on the way he gave with such profusion to the soldiers he met that all disappeared. On reaching home, he asked his wife for a hundred thousand francs he had left with her, but she also had disposed of them to needy soldiers; this her husband approved of, and returning to the Duke of Anjou and the pope, he received from them forty thousand francs, but on his way to Bordeaux these were all disposed of, and the Prince of Wales asking if he had brought the ransom, he carelessly replied: 'That he had not a doubloon.' 'You do the magnificent!' said the prince. 'You give to everybody, and have not what will support yourself; you must go back to prison.' Du Guesclin withdrew, but at the same time a gentleman arrived from the French king prepared to pay the sum required. He was raised to the highest post in the kingdom, that of Connétable de France, in 1370, amidst the acclamations and joy of the whole nation; yet, strange to say, after all his services, he lost the confidence of the king a few years after, who listened to his traducers, and wrote a letter most offensive to the hero's fidelity. Du Guesclin immediately sent back the sword belonging to his office of Connétable; but the cry of the whole nation was in his favour. The superiority of his military talents, his generosity and modesty had extinguished the feelings of jealousy which his promotion might have created. Charles acknowledged that he had been deceived, and sent the Dukes of Anjou and Bourbon to restore the sword, and appoint him to the command of the army in Auvergne, where his old enemies the English were pillaging. He besieged the castle of Randan, and was there attacked with mortal disease, which he met with the intrepid firmness which characterised him, and with the sincere piety of a Christian. At the news of his death, the camp resounded with groans, his enemies even paying homage to his memory; for they had promised to surrender on a certain day if not relieved, and the commander marched out, followed by his garrison, and kneeling beside the bier, laid the keys upon it.

The king ordered him to be buried at St Denis, at the foot of the mausoleum prepared for himself. The funeral cortège passed through France amidst the lamentations of the people, followed by the princes of the blood, and crowds of the nobility. This modest epitaph was placed on his grave: 'Ici gist noble homme, Messire Bertrand du Guesclin, Comte de Longueville et Connétable de France, qui trépassa au Chastel neuf de Randan le 13me Jour de Juillet 1380. Priez Dieu pour lui.'

A very rare phenomenon was seen after his death—the chief place in the state was vacant, and no one would take it. The king offered it to the Sire de Couci; he excused himself, recommending Du Guesclin's brother-in-arms, De Clisson; but he and Sancerre both declared that after the grand deeds that had been wrought, they could not satisfy the king, and it was only filled up at the beginning of the following reign by Clisson accepting the dignity.

## RICHARD CROMWELL.

This day, 1712, died Richard Cromwell, eldest son of Oliver, and who, for a short time after his father (between September 3, 1658, and May 25, 1659), was acknowledged Protector of these realms. He had lived in peaceful obscurity for fifty-three years after giving up the government, and was ninety when he died. The ex-Protector, Richard, has usually been spoken of lightly for resigning without any decisive effort to maintain himself in his place; but, perhaps, it is rather to the credit of his good sense, that he retired as he did, for the spirit in which the restoration of Charles II. was soon after effected, may be regarded as tolerable proof that any obstinate attempt to keep up the Cromwellian rule, would have been attended with great hazard. While it never has been, and cannot be, pretended that Richard was aught of a great man, one cannot but admit that his perfect negativeness after the Restoration, had in it something of dignity. That he could scarcely ever be induced to speak of politics, was fitting in one who had been at the summit of state, and found all vanity and instability. There was, moreover, a profound humour under his external negativeness. His conduct in respect of the addresses which had come to him during his short rule, was not that of a common-place character. When obliged to leave Whitehall, he carried these documents with him in a large hair-covered trunk, of which he requested his servants to take particular care.

'Why so much care of an old trunk?' inquired some one; 'what on earth is in it?'

'Nothing less,' quoth Richard, 'than the lives and fortunes of all the good people of England.'

Long after, he kept up the same joke, and even made it a standing subject of mirth among his friends. Two new neighbours, being introduced to his house, were very hospitably entertained in the usual manner, along with some others, till the company having become merry, Richard started up with a candle in his hand, desiring all the rest to follow him. The party proceeded with bottles and glasses in hand, to the garret, where, somewhat to the surprise of the new guests, who alone were uninitiated, the ex-Protector pulled out an old hairy trunk to the middle of the floor, and seating himself on it, proposed as a toast, 'Prosperity to Old England.' Each man in succession seated himself on the trunk, and drank the toast; one of the new guests coming last, to whom Mr Cromwell called out: 'Now, sit light, for you have the lives and fortunes of all the good people of England under you.' Finally, he explained the freak by taking out the addresses, and reading some of them, amidst the laughter of the company.

RICHARD CROMWELL.

## SUPERSTITIONS, SAYINGS, &C., CONCERNING DEATH.

If a grave is open on Sunday, there will be another dug in the week.

This I believe to be a very narrowly limited superstition, as Sunday is generally a favourite day for funerals among the poor. I have, however, met with it in one parish, where Sunday funerals are the exception, and I recollect one instance in particular. A woman coming down from church, and observing an open grave, remarked: 'Ah, there will be somebody else wanting a grave before the week is out!' Strangely enough (the population of the place was then under a thousand), her words came true, and the grave was dug for *her*.

If a corpse does not stiffen after death, or if the *rigor mortis* disappears before burial, it is a sign that there will be a death in the family before the end of the year.

In the case of a child of my own, every joint of the corpse was as flexible as in life. I was perplexed at this, thinking that perhaps the little fellow might, after all, be in a trance. While I was considering the matter, I perceived a bystander looking very grave, and evidently having something on her mind. On asking her what she wished to say, I received for answer that, though she did not put any faith in it herself, yet people *did* say that such a thing was the sign of another death in the family within the twelvemonth.

If every remnant of Christmas decoration is not cleared out of church before Candlemas-day (the Purification, February 2), there will be a death that year in the family occupying the pew where a leaf or berry is left.

An old lady (now dead) whom I knew, was so persuaded of the truth of this superstition, that she would not be contented to leave the clearing of her pew to the constituted authorities, but used to send her servant on Candlemas-eve to see that her own seat at anyrate was thoroughly freed from danger.

Fires and candles also afford presages of death. Coffins flying out of the former, and winding-sheets guttering down from the latter. A winding-sheet is produced from a candle, if, after it has guttered, the strip, which has run down, instead of being absorbed into the general tallow, remains unmelted: if, under these circumstances, it curls over away from the flame, it is a presage of death to the person in whose direction it points.

Coffins out of the fire are hollow *oblong* cinders spirted from it, and are a sign of a coming death in the family. I have seen cinders, which have flown out of the fire, picked up and examined to see what they presaged; for coffins are not the only things that are thus produced. If the cinder, instead of being *oblong*, is *oval*, it is a cradle, and predicts the advent of a baby; while, if it is *round*, it is a purse, and means prosperity.

The howling of a dog at night under the window of a sick-room, is looked upon as a warning of death's being near.

Perhaps there may be some truth in this notion. Everybody knows the peculiar odour which frequently precedes death, and it is possible that the acute nose of the dog may perceive this, and that it may render him uneasy: but the same can hardly be alleged in favour of the notion, that the screech of an owl flying past signifies the same, for, if the owl did scent death, and was in hopes of prey, it is not likely that it would screech, and so *give notice of its presence*.

*Suffolk.* C. W. J.

## THE HOT WEDNESDAY OF 1808.

Farmers, and others engaged in outdoor pursuits, men of science, and others engaged in observations on meteorological phenomena, have much reason to doubt whether the reported temperatures of past years are worthy of reliance. In looking through the old journals and magazines, degrees of winter cold and summer heat are found recorded, which, to say the best of it, need to be received with much caution; seeing that the sources of fallacy were numerous. There was one particular Wednesday in 1808, for instance, which was marked by so high a temperature, as to obtain for itself the name of the 'Hot Wednesday;' there is no doubt the heat was great, even if its degree were overstated. At Hayes, in Middlesex, two thermometers, the one made by Ramsden, and the other by Cary, were observed at noon, and were found to record 90° F. in the shade. Men of middle age at that time, called to mind the 'Hot Tuesday' of 1790, which, however, was several degrees below the temperature of this particular Wednesday. Remembering that the average heat, winter and summer, of the West Indies, is about 82°, it is not surprising that men fainted, and horses and other animals died under the pressure of a temperature so unusual in England as 8° above this amount. In the shade, at an open window looking into St James's Park, a temperature of 94° was observed. In a shop-window, on the shady side of the Strand, a thermometer marked 101°; but this was under the influence of conducted and radiant warmth from surrounding objects. At Gainsborough, in Lincolnshire, two thermometers, made by Nairne and Blunt respectively, hanging in the shade with a northern aspect, marked 94° at one o'clock on the day in question. In the corresponding month of 1825, observers were surprised to find a temperature of 85° marked in the quadrangle of the Royal Exchange at four o'clock in the 19th, 86¼° at one o'clock on the same day, 87° at Paris, and 91° at Hull; but all these were below the indications noticed, or alleged to be noticed, in 1808. It is now known, however, better than it was in those days, that numerous precautions are necessary to the obtainment of reliable observations on temperature. The height from the ground, the nature and state of the ground, the direction in reference to the points of the compass, the vicinity of other objects, the nature of those objects as heat-reflectors, the covered or uncovered state of the space overhead—all affect the degree to which the mercury in the tube of a thermometer will be expanded by heat: even if the graduation of the tube be reliable, which is seldom the case, except in high-priced instruments. On this account all the old newspaper statements on such matters must be received with caution, though there is no reason to doubt that the Hot Wednesday of 1808 was really a very formidable day.

---

# JULY 14.

St Idus, bishop of Ath-Fadha, in Leinster. St Bonaventura, cardinal and bishop, 1274. St Camillus de Lellis, confessor, 1614.

*Born.*—Cardinal Mazarin, 1602, *Pescina, in Abruzzo;* Sir Robert Strange, engraver, 1721, *Orkney;* John Hunter, eminent surgeon, 1728, *Long Calderwood;* Aaron Arrowsmith, publisher of maps, 1750, *Winston, Durham;* John S. Bowerbank, naturalist, 1797, *London;* John Frederick Lewis, R.A., painter, 1805.

*Died.*—Philip Augustus of France, 1223, *Mantes;* Dr William Bates, eminent physician, 1699, *Hackney;* Dr Richard Bentley, editor, controversialist, 1742, *Cambridge;* General Laudohn, 1790; Gœrtner, German botanist, 1791; Baroness De Staël Holstein (*née* Anne Necker), 1817, *Paris;* Lady Duff Gordon, authoress of *Letters from Egypt*, 1863–65, 1869.

## PHILIP AUGUSTUS OF FRANCE.

The name of Philip Augustus is better known in English history than those of most of the earlier French monarchs, on account of his relations with the chivalrous Richard Cœur-de-Lion and the unpopular King John. Philip's reign was a benefit to France, as he laboured successfully to overcome feudalism, and strengthen and consolidate the power of the crown. He came to the throne when he was only fifteen years of age, and already displayed a vigour of mind which was beyond his years. One of the earlier acts of his reign, was the persecution of the Jews, who, on the charge of having crucified a Christian child at Easter, were stripped of their possessions, and banished from France; but this was less an act of religious bigotry, than probably an expedient for enriching his treasury. While King Henry II. of England lived, Philip encouraged the two young English princes, Geoffrey and Richard, in rebelling against their father, because he aimed at getting possession of the English territories in France; and after Henry's death, he professed the closest friendship for Richard, who succeeded him on the throne, and joined with him in the third Crusade. This, however, was the result neither of religious zeal nor of sincere friendship; for, as is well known to all readers, he quarrelled with King Richard on the way to the East, and became his bitter enemy, and soon abandoned the crusade and returned home. He was restrained by his oath, and still more by the threats of the pope, and by the fear of incurring the odium of all Western Europe, from attacking King Richard's possessions during his absence; but he intrigued against him, incited his subjects to rebellion, assisted his brother John in his attempt to usurp his throne, and when Richard had been seized and imprisoned by the emperor of Austria, he offered money to that monarch to induce him to keep him in confinement.

By the death of Richard Cœur-de-Lion, Philip was released from a powerful and dangerous enemy, and he soon commenced hostilities against his successor, King John, with whom he had previously been in secret and not very honourable alliance. The result of this war was, that in 1204, King John was stripped of his Norman duchy, which was reunited to the crown of France, and the English king gained from his Norman subjects the derisive title of Jehan sans Terre, which was Anglicised by the later English annalists into John Lack-land. Philip's plans of aggrandisement in the north and west were no doubt assisted by the absence of the great barons of the south, who might have embarrassed him in another crusade, in which they conquered not Jerusalem, but Constantinople and Greece. Philip invaded and occupied Brittany, and other provinces which were under English influence and rule, while King John made a feeble and very short attempt at resistance. These events were followed by the terrible crusade against the heretical Albigeois, which Philip encouraged, no doubt from motives of crafty policy, and not from either religious bigotry or attachment to the pope. Nevertheless, the pope, as is well known, was so well satisfied with Philip's conduct in this cause, that he struck the English nation with the interdict, and nominally deposed King John from his throne, transferred the crown of England by his authority to the head of Philip Augustus, and authorised him to go and take possession of it by force, promising the privilege of crusaders in this world and the next to all who should assist him in this undertaking. This expedition was retarded by a war with the Count of Flanders, which led to a coalition between the count, the emperor of Germany, and the king of England, against the French king; but the war was ended advantageously for Philip, by his victory in the battle of Bouvines. Philip now found sufficient occupation for a while in regulating the internal affairs of his own country, and in resisting the rather undisguised aspirations of his subjects for popular liberty; while his enemy, King John, was engaged in a fiercer struggle with his own barons; but there had been a change which Philip did not expect, for the pope, who hated everything like popular liberty, no sooner saw that it was for this object, in some degree, that the English barons were fighting, than he altered his policy, took King John under his protection, and forbade the king of France to interfere further. Philip had no love for the pope, and was seldom inclined to submit to any control upon his own will; and when the English barons, in their discouragement, sought his assistance, and offered the crown of England to his son, the prince Louis (afterwards King Louis VIII. of France), he accepted and sent Louis with an army to England, in defiance of the pope's direct prohibition. The death of King John, and the change of feelings in England which followed that event, finally put an end to his ambitious hopes in that direction. The remainder of Philip's reign presented no events of any great importance except the renewal of the war in the south, in which the first Simon de Montford was slain in the year 1218. Philip Augustus died at Mantes, on the 14th of July 1223, at the age of fifty-eight, leaving the crown of France far more powerful than he had found it.

Philip's accession to the throne of France, when he was only a child, was accompanied by a rather romantic incident. His father, who, as was then usual, was preparing to secure the throne to his son by crowning him during his lifetime, and who was residing, in a declining state of health, at Compiègne, gave the young prince permission to go to the chase with his huntsmen. They had hardly entered the forest, before they found a boar, and the hunters uncoupled the hounds, and pursued it till they were dispersed in different directions among the wildest parts of the woods. Philip, on a swift horse, followed eagerly the boar, until his steed slackened its pace through fatigue, and then the young prince found that he was entirely separated from his companions, and ignorant of the direction in which he might hope to find them. After he had ridden backwards and forwards for some time, night set in, and the prince, left thus alone in the midst of a vast and dreary forest, became seriously alarmed. In this condition he wandered about for several hours, until at last, attracted by the appearance of a light, he perceived at a distance a peasant who was blowing the fire of a charcoal kiln. Philip rode up to him, and told him who he was, and the accident which had happened to him, though his fear was not much abated by the collier's personal appearance, for he was a large, strong, and rough-looking man, with a forbidding face, rendered more ferocious by being blackened with the dust of his charcoal, and he was armed with a formidable axe. His behaviour, however, did not accord with his appearance, for he immediately left his charcoal, and conducted the prince safely back to Compiègne; but fear and fatigue threw the child into so violent an illness, that it was found necessary to postpone the coronation more than two months.

## MARAT.

The sanguinary fanaticism of the French Revolution has no representative of such odious and repulsive figure as Marat, the original self-styled 'Friend of the People.' By birth a Swiss, of Calvinistic parents, he had led a strange skulking life for five-and-forty years—latterly, a sort of quack mediciner—when the great national crisis brought him to the surface as a journalist and member of the Convention. Less than five feet high, with a frightful countenance, and maniacal eye, he was shrunk from by most people as men shrink from a toad; but he had frantic earnestness, and hesitated at no violence against the enemies of liberty, and so he came to possess the entire confidence and affection of the mob of Paris. His constant cry was for blood; he literally desired to see every well-dressed person put to death. Every day his paper, *L'Ami du Peuple*, was filled with clamorous demands for slaughter, and the wish of his heart was but too well fulfilled. By the time that the summer of 1793 arrived, he was wading in the blood of his enemies. It was then that the young enthusiastic girl, Charlotte Corday, left her native province, for Paris, to avenge the fate of her friend, Barbaroux. She sought Marat at his house—was admitted to see him in his hot bath—and stuck a knife into his heart. His death was treated as a prodigious public calamity, and his body was deposited, with extravagant honours, in the Pantheon; but public feeling took a turn for the better ere long, and the carcass of the wretch was then ignominiously extruded.

MARAT.

To contemporaries, the revolutionary figure of Marat had risen like a frightful nightmare: nobody seemed to know whence he had come, or how he had spent his previous life. There was, however, one notice of his past history published in a Glasgow newspaper,* four months before his death, rather startling in its tenor; which, nevertheless, would now appear to have been true. It was as follows: 'From an investigation lately taken at Edinburgh, it is said that Marat, the celebrated orator of the French National Convention, the humane, the mild, the gentle Marat, is the same person who, a few years ago, taught tambouring in this city under the name of John White. His conduct while he was here was equally unprincipled, if not as atrocious, as it has been since his elevation to the legislatorship. After contracting debts to a very considerable amount, he absconded, but was apprehended at Newcastle, and brought back to this city, where he was imprisoned. He soon afterwards executed a summons of *cessio bonorum* against his creditors, in the prosecution of which, it was found that he had once taught in the academy at Warrington, in which Dr Priestley was tutor; that he left Warrington for Oxford, where, after some time, he found means to rob a museum of a number of gold coins, and medallions; that he was traced to Ireland, apprehended at an assembly there in the character of a German count; brought back to this country, tried, convicted, and sentenced to some years' hard labour on the Thames. He was refused a *cessio*, and his creditors, tired of detaining him in jail, after a confinement of several months, set him at liberty. He then took up his residence in this neighbourhood, where he continued about nine months, and took his final leave of this country about the beginning of the year 1787.

'He was very ill-looked, of a diminutive size, a man of uncommon vivacity, a very turbulent disposition, and possessed of a very uncommon share of legal knowledge. It is said that, while here, he used to call his children Marat, which he said was his family name.'

These revelations regarding Marat were certainly calculated to excite attention. Probably, however, resting only on an anonymous newspaper paragraph, they were little regarded at the time of their publication. It is only of late years that we have got any tolerably certain light regarding Marat's life in England. It now appears that he was in this country in 1774, when thirty years of age, being just the time when the differences between the American colonists and the mother-country were coming to a crisis. In that year he published, in English, a huge pamphlet (royal 8vo, price 12*s.*), under the title of '*The Chains of Slavery*: a work wherein the clandestine and villainous attempts of princes to ruin liberty are pointed out, and the dreadful scenes of despotism disclosed; to which is prefixed An Address to the Electors of Great Britain, in order to draw their timely attention to the choice of proper representatives in the next Parliament.—Becket, London.' Most likely, this work would meet with but little encouragement in England, for the current of public feeling ran in the opposite direction. In 1776, we find him dating from 'Church Street, Soho,' a second and much less bulky pamphlet on a wholly different subject—*An Inquiry into the Nature, Cause,*

* *Star* of March 4, 1793: see *Notes and Queries*, September 24, 1859.

*and Cure of a Singular Disease of the Eyes, hitherto unknown, and yet common, produced by the use of certain Mercurial Preparations.* By J. P. Marat, M.D. He here vented some quackish ideas he had regarding eye-disease, and out of which he is said at one time to have made a kind of living in Paris. In the prefatory address to the Royal Society, he lets out that he had been in Edinburgh in the previous August (1775). It is stated, but we do not know on what authority, that, in the Scottish capital, he tried to support himself by giving lessons in French.* He probably was not there long, but quickly migrated to the academy at Warrington. Nor was he there long either. The next incident in his life was the Oxford felony, adverted to in the Glasgow *Star*. At least there can be little doubt that the following extract from a letter of Mr Edward Creswell, of Oxford, dated February 12, 1776, refers to Marat under an assumed name:

'. . . I shall now tell you a piece of news respecting a robbery which was committed here lately. . . . About a week ago, a native of France, who calls himself M. le Maitre, and was formerly a teacher in Warrington Academy, being invited here by a gentleman of this college to teach the French language, came over, and met with great encouragement in the university, but, happening to get acquainted with Mr Milnes, a gentleman of Corpus Christi College, who is the keeper of the museum and several other natural curiosities, he prevailed on him, by repeated importunities, to let him have a view of them. Accordingly, they both went together, and after M. le Maitre had viewed them a great while, Mr Milnes, from the suspicions he entertained of his behaviour, under pretence of getting rid of him, told him that several gentlemen were waiting at the door for admittance, and that he must now go out immediately; but the Frenchman excused himself by saying he would retire into the other apartments, and whilst the strangers that were admitted were surveying the curiosities with more than ordinary attention, this artful villain retired from them, and concealed himself under a dark staircase that led into the street, where he stayed till the company had gone out, after which he stole away medals and other coins to the amount of two hundred pounds and upwards, and got clear off with his booty. It was somewhat observable that he was often seen lurking near the museum some time before this affair happened, and very frequently desired to be admitted as soon as he had got a view of the medals. I am sorry I have not time to tell you a few more particulars concerning this transaction, but shall defer it till I know further about it.'

In a subsequent letter, Mr Creswell informed his correspondent that the Frenchman who robbed the museum was tried, and being found guilty, was 'sentenced to work on the river Thames for five years.'

These extracts appear, with due authentication, in the *Notes and Queries* (September 16, 1860), and they are supported in their tenor by the publications of the day. The robbery of the Ashmolean Museum at Oxford by a person styled at first 'a Swiss hair-dresser,' and afterwards 'Le Mair, now a prisoner in Dublin,' is noticed in the *Gentleman's Magazine* for February and March 1776. Subsequently, it is stated in the same work under September 1, that 'Petre le Maitre, the French hair-dresser, who robbed the museum at Oxford of medals, &c., to a considerable amount, was brought by *habeas corpus* from Dublin, and lodged in Oxford Castle.' Unfortunately, this record fails to take notice of the trial.

What a strange career for a Swiss adventurer from first to last! A pamphleteer for the illumination of British electors, a pamphleteer for a quack cure for the eyes, a teacher of languages at Edinburgh, an usher at the Warrington Academy under the sincere and profound Priestley, a felon at Oxford, a *forçat* for five years on the Thames, afterwards a teacher of tambouring at Glasgow, running into debt, and going through a struggle for white-washing by the peculiar Scotch process of *cessio bonorum*, which involves the preliminary necessity of imprisonment; finally, for a brief space, the most powerful man in France, and, in that pride of place, struck down by a romantic assassination—seldom has there been such a life. One can imagine, however, what bitterness would be implanted in such a nature by the felon's brand and the long penal servitude, and even by the humiliation of the *cessio bonorum*, and how, with these experiences rankling beyond sympathy in the wretch's lonely bosom, he might at length come to revel in the destruction of all who had deserved better than himself.

* *Biographie Universelle*, art. 'Marat.'

## 'DE HERETICO COMBURENDO.'

Amongst the last victims of the religious persecution under Mary, were six persons who formed part of a congregation caught praying and reading the Bible, in a by-place at Islington, in May 1558. Seven of the party had been burned at Smithfield on the 27th of June; the six who remained were kept in a miserable confinement at the palace of Bonner, bishop of London, at Fulham, whence they were taken on the 14th of July, and despatched in a similar manner at Brentford.

While these six unfortunates lay in their vile captivity at Fulham, Bonner felt annoyed at their presence, and wished to get them out of the way; but he was sensible, at the same time, of there being a need for getting these sacrifices to the true church effected in as quiet a way as possible. He therefore penned an epistle to (apparently) Cardinal Pole, which has lately come to light, and certainly gives a curious idea of the coolness with which a fanatic will treat of the destruction of a few of his fellow-creatures when satisfied that it is all right.

'Further,' he says, 'may it please your Grace concerning these obstinate heretics that do remain in my house, pestering the same, and doing much hurt many ways, some order may be taken with them, and in mine opinion, as I shewed your Grace and my Lord Chancellor, it should do well to have them brent in Hammersmith, a mile from my house here, for then I can give sentence against them here in the parish church very quietly, and without tumult, and having the sheriff present, as I can have him, he, without business or stir, [can] put them to execution in the said place, when otherwise the thing [will need a] day in [St] Paul's, and with more comberance than now it needeth. Scribbled in haste, &c.'

Bonner was a man of jolly appearance, and

usually of mild and placid speech, though liable to fits of anger. In the ordinary course of life, he would probably have rather done one a kindness than an injury. See, however, what fanaticism made him. He scribbles *in haste* a letter dealing with the lives of six persons guilty of no real crime, and has no choice to make in the case but that their condemnation and execution may be conducted in a manner as little calculated to excite the populace as possible.

---

## BEAR-BAITING.

In the account which Robert Laneham gives of the festivities at Kenilworth Castle, in 1575, on the reception of Queen Elizabeth by her favourite minister, the Earl of Leicester, there is a lively though conceited description of the bear and dog combats which formed part of the entertainments prepared for her majesty, and which took place on the sixth day of her stay (Friday, 14th July). There were assembled on this occasion thirteen bears, all tied up in the inner court, and a number of ban-dogs (a small kind of mastiff). 'The bears were brought forth into the court, the dogs set to them, to argue the points even face to face. They had learned counsel also o' both parts; what, may they be counted partial that are retain[ed] but a to [to one] side? I ween no. Very fierce both tone and tother, and eager in argument; if the dog, in pleading, would pluck the bear by the throat, the bear, with traverse, would claw him again by the scalp; confess an a [he] list, but avoid a [he] could not, that was bound to the bar; and his counsel told him that it could be to him no policy in pleading. Therefore thus with fending and fearing, with plucking and tugging, scratching and biting, by plain tooth and nail to [the one] side and tother, such expense of blood and leather was there between them, as a month's licking, I ween, will not recover; and yet [they] remain as far out as ever they were. It was a sport very pleasant of these beasts, to see the bear with his pink eyes leering after his enemy's approach, the nimbleness and weight of the dog to take his advantage, and the force and experience of the bear again to avoid the assaults; if he were bitten in one place, how he would pinch in another to get free; if he were taken once, then what shift, with biting, with clawing, with roaring, tossing, and tumbling, he would work to wind himself from them, and when he was loose, to shake his ears twice or thrice, with the blood and the slaver about his phisnomy, was a matter of goodly relief.'

In the twelfth century, the baiting of bulls and bears was the favourite holiday pastime of Londoners; and although it was included in a proclamation of Edward III., among 'dishonest, trivial, and useless games,' the sport increased in popularity

BEAR-GARDEN, BANKSIDE, SOUTHWARK.

with all classes. Erasmus, who visited England in the reign of Henry VIII., speaks of 'many herds' of bears regularly trained for the arena; the rich nobles had their bearwards, and the royal establishment its 'master of the king's bears.' For the better accommodation of the lovers of the rude amusement, the Paris Garden Theatre was erected at Bankside, the public being admitted at the charge of a penny at the gate, a penny at the entry of the scaffold, and a penny for quiet standing. When Queen Mary visited her sister during her confinement at Hatfield House, the royal ladies were entertained with a grand baiting of bulls and bears, with which they declared themselves 'right well contented.' Elizabeth took especial delight in seeing the courage of her English mastiffs pitted against the cunning of Ursa and the strength of Taurus. On the 25th of May 1559, the French ambassadors 'were brought to court with music to dinner, and after a splendid dinner, were entertained with the baiting of bears and bulls with English dogs. The queen's grace herself, and the ambassadors, stood in the gallery looking on the pastime till six at night.' The diplomatists were so gratified, that her majesty never failed to provide a similar show for any foreign visitors she wished to honour.

Much as the royal patron of Shakspeare and Burbage was inclined to favour the players, she waxed indignant when the attractions of the bear-garden paled before those of the theatre; and in 1591 an order issued from the privy-council forbidding plays to be acted on Thursdays, because bear-baiting and such pastimes had usually been practised on that day. This order was followed by an injunction from the lord mayor to the same effect, in which his lordship complained, 'that in divers places, the players do use to recite their plays to the great hurt and destruction of the game of bear-baiting, and such-like pastimes, which are maintained for her majesty's pleasure.'

An accident at the Paris Garden in 1583, afforded the Puritans an opportunity for declaring the popular sport to be under the ban of Heaven—a mode of argument anticipated years before by Sir Thomas More in his Dialogue. 'At Beverley late, much of the people being at a bear-baiting, the church fell suddenly down at evening-time, and overwhelmed some that were in it. A good fellow that after heard the tale told, "So," quoth he, "now you may see what it is to be at evening-prayers when you should be at the bear-baiting!"' Some of the ursine heroes of those palmy-days of bear-baiting have been enshrined in verse. Sir John Davy reproaches the law-students with

'Leaving old Plowden, Dyer, and Brooke alone,
To see old Harry Hunks and Sackerson.'

The last named has been immortalised by Shakspeare in his *Merry Wives of Windsor*—Slender boasts to sweet Anne Page, 'I have seen Sackerson loose twenty times; and have taken him by the chain: but, I warrant you, the women have so cried and shrieked at it, that it passed.'

James I. prohibited baiting on Sundays, although he did not otherwise discourage the sport. In Charles I.'s reign, the Garden at Bankside was still a favourite resort, but the Commonwealth ordered the bear to be killed, and forbade the amusement. However, with the Restoration it revived, and Burton speaks of bull and bear baiting as a pastime 'in which our countrymen and citizens greatly delight and frequently use.' On the 14th of August 1666, Mr Pepys went to the Paris Garden, and saw 'some good sports of the bulls tossing the dogs, one into the very boxes;' and that it had not lost the countenance of royalty, is proved by the existence of a warrant of Lord Arlington's for the payment of ten pounds to James Davies, Esq., master of his majesty's bears, bulls, and dogs, 'for making ready the rooms at the bear-garden, and baiting the bears before the Spanish ambassadors, the 7th of January last' (1675).

After a coming bear-baiting had been duly advertised, the bearward used to parade the streets with his champions. 'I'll set up my bills,' says the sham bearward in *The Humorous Lovers*, 'that the gamesters of London, Horsleydown, Southwark, and Newmarket may come in, and bait him before the ladies. But first, boy, go fetch me a bagpipe; we will walk the streets in triumph, and give the people notice of our sport.' Sometimes the bull or bear was decorated with flowers, or coloured ribbons fastened with pitch on their foreheads, the dog who pulled off the favour being especially cheered by the spectators. The French advocate, Misson, who lived in England during William III.'s reign, gives a vivid description of 'the manner of these bull-baitings, which are so much talked of. They tie a rope to the root of the horns of the bull, and fasten the other end of the cord to an iron ring fixed to a stake driven into the ground; so that this cord, being about fifteen feet long, the bull is confined to a space of about thirty feet diameter. Several butchers, *or other gentlemen*, that are desirous to exercise their dogs, stand round about, each holding his own by the ears; and when the sport begins, they let loose one of the dogs. The dog runs at the bull; the bull, immovable, looks down upon the dog with an eye of scorn, and only turns a horn to him, to hinder him from coming near. The dog is not daunted at this, he runs round him, and tries to get beneath his belly. The bull then puts himself into a posture of defence; he beats the ground with his feet, which he joins together as closely as possible, and his chief aim is not to gore the dog with the point of his horn (which, when too sharp, is put into a kind of wooden sheath), but to slide one of them under the dog's belly, who creeps close to the ground, to hinder it, and to throw him so high in the air that he may break his neck in the fall. To avoid this danger, the dog's friends are ready beneath him, some with their backs, to give him a soft reception; and others with long poles, which they offer him slantways, to the intent that, sliding down them, it may break the force of his fall. Notwithstanding all this care, a toss generally makes him sing to a very scurvy tune, and draw his phiz into a pitiful grimace. But unless he is totally stunned with the fall, he is sure to crawl again towards the bull, come on't what will. Sometimes a second frisk into the air disables him for ever; but sometimes, too, he fastens upon his enemy, and when once he has seized him with his eye-teeth, he sticks to him like a leech, and would sooner die than leave his hold. Then the bull bellows and bounds and kicks, all to shake off the dog. In the end, either the dog tears out the piece he has laid hold on, and falls, or else remains fixed to him with an obstinacy that would never end, did they not pull him off. To call him away, would be in vain; to give him a hundred blows, would be as much so; you might cut him to pieces, joint by joint, before he would let him loose. What is to be done then? While some hold the bull, others thrust staves into the dog's mouth, and open it by main force.'

In the time of Addison, the scene of these animal combats was at Hockley in the Hole, near Clerkenwell. The *Spectator* of August 11, 1711, desires those who frequent the theatres merely for a laugh, would 'seek their diversion at the bear-garden, where reason and good-manners have no right to disturb them.' Gay, in his *Trivia*, says:

'Experienced men, inured to city ways,
Need not the calendar to count their days.
When through the town, with slow and solemn air,
Led by the nostril walks the muzzled bear;
Behind him moves, majestically dull,
The pride of Hockley Hole, the surly bull.
Learn hence the periods of the week to name—
Mondays and Thursdays are the days of game.'

The over-fashionable amusement had fallen from its high estate, and was no longer upheld by the patronage of the higher classes of society. In 1802, a bill was introduced into the Commons for the suppression of the practice altogether. Mr Windham opposed the measure, as the first result of a conspiracy of the Jacobins and Methodists to render the people grave and serious, preparatory to obtaining their assistance in the furtherance of other anti-national schemes, and argued as if the British Constitution must stand or fall with the bear-garden; and Colonel Grosvenor asked, if 'the higher orders had their Billington, why not the lower orders their Bull?' This extraordinary reasoning prevailed against the sarcasm of Courtenay, the earnestness of Wilberforce, and the eloquence of Sheridan, and the House refused, by a majority of thirteen, to abolish what the last-named orator called 'the most mischievous of all amusements.' This decision of the legislature doubtless received the silent approval of Dr Parr, for that learned talker was a great admirer of the sport. A bull-baiting being advertised in Cambridge, during one of his last visits there, the doctor hired a garret near the scene of action, and taking off his academic attire, and changing his notorious wig for a night-cap, enjoyed the exhibition *incog.* from the windows. This predilection was unconquerable. 'You see,' said he, on one occasion, exposing his muscular hirsute arm to the company, 'that I am a kind of taurine man, and must therefore be naturally addicted to the sport.'

It was not till the year 1835 that baiting was finally put down by an act of parliament, forbidding the keeping of any house, pit, or other place for baiting or fighting any bull, bear, dog, or other animal; and after an existence of at least seven centuries, this ceased to rank among the amusements of the English people.

## AN EXPLOSION IN THE COURT OF KING'S BENCH.

On the 14th of July 1737, when the courts were sitting in Westminster Hall, between one and two o'clock in the afternoon, a large brown-paper parcel, containing fireworks, which had been placed, unobserved, near the side-bar of the Court of King's Bench, exploded with a loud noise, creating great confusion and terror among the persons attending the several courts. As the crackers rattled and burst, they threw out balls of printed bills, purporting that, on the last day of term, five libels would be publicly burned in Westminster Hall. The libels specified in the bills were five very salutary but most unpopular acts of parliament, lately passed by the legislature. One of these printed bills, being taken to the Court of King's Bench, the grand-jury presented it as a wicked, false, and scandalous libel; and a proclamation was issued for discovering the persons concerned in this 'wicked and audacious outrage.' A reward of £200 was offered for the detection of the author, printer, or publisher of the bills; but the contrivers of this curious mode of testifying popular aversion to the measures of parliament were never discovered.

## DESTRUCTION OF THE BASTILE—THE MAN IN THE IRON MASK.

The 14th of July will ever be a memorable day in French history, as having witnessed, in 1789, the demolition, by the Paris populace, of the grim old fortress identified with the despotism and cruelty of the falling monarchy. It was a typical incident, representing, as it were, the end of a wicked system, but unfortunately not inaugurating the beginning of one milder and better. Much heroism was shewn by the multitude in their attack upon the Bastile, for the defenders did not readily submit, and had a great advantage behind their lofty walls. But their triumph was sadly stained by the massacre of the governor, Delaunay, and many of his corps.

'It was now,' says Lamartine, 'that the mysteries of this state-prison were unveiled—its bolts broken—its iron doors burst open—its dungeons and subterranean cells penetrated—from the gates of the towers to their very deepest foundations and their summits. The iron rings and the chains, rusting in their strong masonry, were pointed out, from which the victims were never released, except to be tortured, to be executed, or to die. On those walls they read the names of prisoners, the dates of their confinement, their griefs and their prayers—miserable men, who had left behind only those poor memorials in their dungeons to attest their prolonged existence and their innocence! It was surprising to find almost all these dungeons empty. The people ran from one to the other: they penetrated into the most secret recesses and caverns, to carry thither the word of release, and to bring a ray of the free light of heaven to eyes long lost to it; they tore the locks from the heavy doors, and those heavy doors from the hinges; they carried off the heavy keys; all these things were displayed in triumph in the open court. They then broke into the archives, and read the entries of committals. These papers, then ignominiously scattered, were afterwards collected. They were the annals of arbitrary times, the records of the fears or vengeance of ministers, or of the meaner intrigues of their favourites, here faithfully kept to justify a late exposure and reproach. The people expected to see a spectre come forth from these ruins, to testify against these iniquities of kings. The Bastile, however, long cleared of all guilt by the gentle spirit of Louis XVI., and by the humane disposition of his ministers, disappointed these gloomy expectations. The dungeons, the cells, the iron collars, the chains, were only worn-out symbols of antique secret incarcerations, torture, and burials alive. They now represented only recollections of old horrors. These vaults restored to light but seven prisoners—three of whom, gray-headed men, were shut up legitimately, and whom family motives had withdrawn from the judgments of the ordinary courts of law. Tavernier and Withe, two of them, had become insane. They saw the light of the sun with surprise; and their incurable insanity caused them to be sent to the madhouse of Charenton, a few days after they had enjoyed fresh air and freedom. The third was the Count de Solages, thirty-two years before sent to this prison at his father's request. When restored free to Toulouse, his home, he was recognised by none, and died in poverty. Whether he had been guilty of some crime, or was the victim of oppression, was an inexplicable enigma. The other four prisoners had been confined only four years, and on purely civil grounds. They had forged bills of exchange, and were arrested in Holland on the requisition of the bankers they had defrauded. A

DESTRUCTION OF THE BASTILE.

royal commission had reported on their cases; but nothing was now listened to against them. Whatever had been branded by absolute authority, must be innocent in the eyes of the prejudiced people. These seven prisoners of the Bastile became victims—released, caressed, even crowned with laurels, carried in triumph by their liberators like living spoil snatched from the hands of tyranny, they were paraded about the streets, and their sufferings avenged by the people's shouts and tears. The intoxication of the victors broke out against the very stones of the place, and the embrasures, torn from the towers, were soon hurled with indignation into the ditches.'

It was asserted at the time, and long afterwards believed—though there was no foundation for the averment—that the wasted body of the famous state-prisoner, called the Man in the Iron Mask, had been found chained in a lower dungeon, with the awful mask still upon the skull!

Speculations had long been rife among French historians, all tending to elucidate the mystery connected with that celebrated prisoner. By some, it was hinted that he was the twin-brother of Louis XIV., thus frightfully sacrificed to make his senior safe on his throne; others affirmed him to be the English Duke of Monmouth; others, a son of Oliver Cromwell; many, with more reason, inclining to think him a state-prisoner of France, such as the Duke de Beaufort, or the Count de Vermandois. It was reserved for M. Delort, at a comparatively recent period, to penetrate the mystery, and enable the late Lord Dover to compile and publish, in 1825, his *True History* of this unfortunate man; the facts being gathered from the state archives of France, and documentary evidence of conclusive authority.

It appears that this mysterious prisoner was Count Anthony Matthioli, secretary of state to Charles III., Duke of Mantua, and afterwards to his son Ferdinand, whose debauched habits, and consequent need, laid him open to a bribe from Louis XIV. for permission to place an army of occupation in his territory, with a view to establish French influence in Italy. Matthioli had expressed his readiness to aid the plot; had visited Paris, and had a secret interview with the king, who presented him with a valuable ring and a considerable sum of money; but when the time came for vigorous action, Matthioli, who appears to have been intriguing with the Spanish court for a better bribe, placed all obstacles and delays in the way of France. The French envoy, the Baron Asfeld, was arrested by the Spanish governor of the Milanese; and the French court found that their diplomacy was betrayed. Louis determined to satisfy his wounded pride and frustrated ambition, by taking the most signal vengeance on Matthioli. The unfortunate secretary was entrapped at a secret interview on the frontier, and carried to the French garrison at Pignerol, afterwards to the fortress of Exiles; when his jailer, St Mars, was appointed governor of the island of St Marguérite (opposite Cannes), he was immured in the fortress there, and so remained for eleven years. In the autumn of 1698, St Mars was made governor of the Bastile, and thither Matthioli was conveyed, dying within its gloomy walls on the 19th of November 1703. He had then been twenty-four years in this rigorous confinement, and had reached the age of sixty-three.

Throughout this long captivity, Louis never shewed him any clemency. The extraordinary precautions against his discovery, and the one which appears to have been afterwards resorted to, of obliging him to wear a mask during his journeys, or when he saw any one, are not wonderful, when we reflect upon the violent breach of the law of nations which had been committed by his imprisonment. Matthioli, at the time of his arrest, was actually the plenipotentiary of the Duke of Mantua for concluding a treaty with the king of France; and for that very sovereign to kidnap him, and confine him in a dungeon, was one of the most flagrant acts of violence that could be committed; one which, if known, would have had the most injurious effects upon the negotiations of Louis with other sovereigns; nay, would probably have indisposed other sovereigns from treating at all with him. The confinement of Matthioli is decidedly one of the deadliest stains that blot the character of Louis XIV.

The prison of Matthioli, in the fortress of St Marguérite, is now, for the first time, engraved from an original sketch. It is one of a series of five, built in a row on the scarp of the rocky cliff. The

PRISON OF MAN IN IRON MASK.

walls are fourteen feet thick; there are three rows of strong iron gratings placed equidistant within the arched window of Matthioli's room, a large apartment with vaulted roof, and no feature to break its monotony, except a small fireplace beside the window, and a few shelves above it. The Bay of Cannes, and the beautiful range of the Esterel mountains, may be seen from the window; a lovely view, that must have given but a maddening sense of confinement to the solitary prisoner. It is on record, that his mind was seriously deranged during the early part of his imprisonment; what he became ultimately, when all hope failed, and a long succession of years deadened his senses, none can know—the secret died with his jailers.

There is a tradition, that he attempted to make his captivity known, by scratching his melancholy tale on a metal dish, and casting it from the window; that it was found by a fisherman of Cannes, who brought it to the governor, St Mars, thereby jeopardising his own life or liberty, for he was at once imprisoned, and only liberated on incontestable proof being given of his inability to read. After this, all fishermen were prohibited from casting their nets within a mile of the island. Matthioli was debarred, on pain of death, from speaking to any but his jailer; he was conveyed from one dungeon to the other in a sedan-chair, closely covered with oil-cloth, into which he entered in his cell, where it was fastened so that no one should see him; his jailers nearly smothered him on his journey to St Marguérite; and afterwards the black mask seems to have been adopted on all occasions of the kind. Lord Dover assures us, that it has been a popular mistake to affirm this famed mask was of iron; that, in reality, it was formed of velvet, strengthened by bands of whalebone, and secured by a padlock behind the head.

The same extraordinary precautions for concealment followed his death that had awaited him in life. The walls of his dungeon were scraped to the stone, and the doors and windows burned, lest any scratch or inscription should betray the secret. His bedding, and all the furniture of the room, were also burned to cinders, then reduced to powder, and thrown into the drains; and all articles of metal melted into an indistinguishable mass. By this means it was hoped that oblivion might surely follow one of the grossest acts of political cruelty in the dark record of history.

---

## JULY 15.

St Plechelm, bishop and confessor, apostle of Guelderland, 732. St Swithin or Swithun, confessor, bishop and patron of Winchester, 862. St Henry II., emperor of Germany, 1024.

### St Swithin's Day.

The pranks played by tradition with the memory of various noted individuals, saintly and otherwise, display not unfrequently the most whimsical anomalies both as regards praise and blame. Whilst the sordid and heretical George of Cappadocia has been transformed into the gallant and chivalrous St George, the patron saint of England, and the mirror of all knightly virtues, it has been the misfortune of the patriotic and virtuous St Swithin to be associated in the popular mind with drunkenness and excess, and at best to enjoy only a mythical reputation as the hero of a well-known saying in connection with the state of the weather on the anniversary of his so-called translation.

The common adage regarding St Swithin, as every one knows, is to the effect that, as it rains or is fair on St Swithin's Day, the 15th of July, there will be a continuous track of wet or dry weather for the forty days ensuing.

'St Swithin's Day, if thou dost rain,
For forty days it will remain:
St Swithin's Day, if thou be fair,
For forty days 'twill rain nae mair.'

The explanation given by Brand in his *Popular Antiquities* of this saying—an explanation which has been pretty currently received as correct—is as follows. St Swithin, bishop of Winchester, was a man equally noted for his uprightness and humility. So far did he carry the latter quality, that, on his death-bed, he requested to be buried, not within the church, but outside in the churchyard, on the north of the sacred building, where his corpse might receive the eaves-droppings from the roof, and his grave be trodden by the feet of the passers-by. His lowly request was complied with, and in this neglected spot his remains reposed till about a hundred years afterwards, when a fit of indignation seized the clergy at the body of so pious a member of their order being allowed to occupy such a position; and on an appointed day they all assembled to convey it with great pomp into the adjoining cathedral of Winchester. When they were about to commence the ceremony, a heavy rain burst forth, and continued without intermission for the forty succeeding days. The monks interpreted this tempest as a warning from Heaven of the blasphemous nature of their attempt to contravene the directions of St Swithin, and, instead of disturbing his remains, they erected a chapel over his grave, at which many astounding miracles were performed. From this circumstance, it is stated, arose the popular belief of the anniversary of the attempted translation of St Swithin being invested with a prophetic character in reference to the condition of the weather for the ensuing six weeks.

This statement is specious, but unfortunately rests on no authority whatever, and indeed has been traced by an annotator on Brand to no more trustworthy source than a cutting from an old newspaper. So far from the account of the repugnance of the saint to his transference from the churchyard to the church being borne out by the real facts of the case, these are diametrically the other way; and from what has been actually ascertained, the translation of St Swithin was, instead of being a disastrous failure, accomplished with the utmost *éclat* and success. For the most recent history of this celebrated personage we are indebted to the Rev. John Earle, professor of Anglo-Saxon in the university of Oxford, who has published a fac-simile and translation of a Saxon manuscript of the tenth century—the earliest fragment which we possess regarding St Swithin—along with an ingenious essay, in which he has collected all the reliable data connected with the saint that can be obtained. These are far indeed from being either numerous or ample, but, such as they are, may be considered as exhaustive on this subject.

Swithin, or Swithun, was born in the neighbourhood of Winchester, probably about the year 800. He became a monk of the Old Abbey of Winchester, and gradually rose to be prior of that community. He seems to have gained the favour of Egbert, king of Wessex, who intrusted him with the education of his son and successor, Ethelwulf. An authentic record of Swithin at this period is furnished by a charter granted by King Egbert in 838, and bearing the signatures of Elmstan, *episcopus*, and Swithunus, *diaconus*. Elmstan dying in 852, Swithin was appointed his successor in the see of Winchester, a situation which he filled with great credit and usefulness. Through his endeavours great improvements were effected on the city, including the erection of several churches, and the spanning of the Itchen by a fine stone bridge, the first of the kind which had been seen in these parts. After the accession of Ethelwulf, he acted as that monarch's counsellor in all matters relating to religion and the peaceful arts, whilst the charge of military and foreign affairs was assumed by Alstan, bishop of Sherbourne. It has been imagined that he was chosen by Ethelwulf to accompany his son, the great Alfred, then a boy, on his visit to Rome, and also that he acted as mediator betwixt Ethelwulf and his eldest son, the rebellious Ethelbald. Swithin seems to have died about 862, leaving directions that he should be buried in a vile place, under the eaves-droppings on the north side of Winchester church. Mr Earle conjectures that he may have chosen this locality for sepulture, to put a stop to the common superstitious prejudices against burial in that part of the churchyard. Whatever may have been his reasons, his request was acceded to, and there he would probably have been permitted to rest undisturbed, had it not suited the policy of Dunstan, more than a hundred years afterwards, to revive the popular veneration for Swithin, in furtherance of his own schemes for the establishment of monastic discipline, for Swithin appears to have been a maintainer of the stricter conventual rule, which Dunstan zealously sought to enforce; and he had, moreover, earned a most enduring mark of distinction, by being the first to get introduced the system of tithes as a provision for the clergy. This was during the reign of Ethelwulf, who was induced by Swithin to set apart a tenth of his lands for religious uses, though the payment of tithes as a legal obligation was not introduced till the time of Athelstan, nor finally established till under King Edgar. In addition to the reasons just detailed, the cathedral of Winchester was then rebuilding under Bishop Ethelwold, a confederate of Archbishop Dunstan; and the enrichment of the new temple by the possession of some distinguished relics was a most desirable object. The organised plan was now accordingly put into execution, and ingenious reports were circulated regarding certain miraculous appearances made by Swithin. The account of these forms the subject of the Saxon fragment above referred to, edited by Mr Earle. According to this, Bishop Swithin appeared one night in a dream to a poor decrepit smith, and requested him to go to a certain priest, named Eadsige, who, with others, had been ejected for misconduct from the abbey of Old-Minster, and desire him, from Swithin, to repair to Bishop Ethelwold, and command him to open his (Swithin's) grave, and bring his bones within the church. The smith, in reply to the orders of his ghostly visitant, stated that Eadsige would not believe him, whereupon Swithin rejoined that he would find the reality of the vision confirmed by going to his stone coffin, and pulling therefrom an iron ring, which would yield without the least difficulty. The smith was still unconvinced, and Swithin had to repeat his visit twice; after which the smith went to the bishop's tomb, and withdrew the ring from the coffin with the greatest ease, as had been foretold. He then delivered Swithin's message to Eadsige, who hesitated for a while, but at last communicated it to Bishop Ethelwold. Contemporaneously, various wonderful miracles took place at Bishop Swithin's tomb, including the cure of a deformed man, who was relieved of his hump, in the most astonishing manner, by praying at the grave; and of another individual, who recovered by the same means from a grievous ailment in his eyes. These preternatural occurrences were all duly reported to King Edgar, who thereupon gave directions for the formal translation of the relics of St Swithin from the grave in the churchyard to the interior of the cathedral, where they were enclosed in a magnificent shrine, and placed in a conspicuous position. A few years afterwards, the church, which had previously been dedicated to the apostles Peter and Paul, changed these guardians for St Swithin, who continued its patron saint till the time of Henry VIII., who ordered the name of the Holy Trinity to be substituted. A splendid ceremonial and feast accompanied the translation, which was effected on 15th July 971, 108 years after the death of Swithin. It ought to be remarked, that, though distinguished by the prefix of *Saint*, Swithin was never regularly canonised by the pope, a practice not introduced till nearly 200 years after his translation, which is the only ceremony on which he rests his claim to the title. He is thus emphatically what Mr Earle calls 'a home-made saint.' It will be noticed that the above narrative completely contradicts Mr Brand's account of a supposed supernatural interposition on the part of Swithin to prevent his translation. No event or natural phenomenon, which could be construed into such, is alluded to by any of the various authors—Monk Wolstan and others—who subsequently wrote histories of St Swithin. On the contrary, the weather seems to have been most propitious, whilst the community at large, so far from regarding these proceedings of their rulers as an unhallowed contravention of the wishes of the holy man, seemed rather to have rejoiced in the honours bestowed on his relics, and to have feasted and revelled to the utmost. How, then, did the popular notion about St Swithin's Day arise? Most probably, as Mr Earle remarks, it was derived from some primeval pagan belief regarding the meteorologically prophetic character of some day about the same period of the year as St Swithin's. Such adaptations, it is well known, were very frequent on the supplanting throughout Europe of heathenism by Christianity. Many of our popular customs and beliefs can indeed be only satisfactorily explained by tracing them to such a source.

In further confirmation of this view, it is to be observed, that in various countries of the European continent the same belief prevails, though differences exist as to the period of the particular day in question. Thus, in France, St Médard's Day (June 8), and the day of Saints Gervais and Protais (June 19), have a similar character ascribed to them:

'S'il pleut le jour de Saint Médard,
Il pleut quarante jours plus tard;
S'il pleut le jour de Saint Gervais et de
  Saint Protais,
Il pleut quarante jours après.'

It is a little curious that St Médard should have the post of a rainy saint assigned him, as the celebrated fête at Salency, where the young maiden who has enjoyed the highest reputation during the preceding year for good-conduct receives a prize, and is crowned with a chaplet of roses, takes place on his day, and is said to have been instituted by him. A somewhat ludicrous account is given of the origin of the peculiar characteristic of St Médard's Day. It is said that, Médard being out with a large party one hot day in summer, a heavy fall of rain suddenly took place, by which all were thoroughly drenched, with the exception of the saint himself, round whose head an eagle kept continually fluttering; and by sheltering him with his wings till his return home, accomplished effectually the purposes of an umbrella. In Belgium they have a rainy saint, named St Godelieve; whilst in Germany, among others, a character of this description is ascribed to the day of the Seven Sleepers.

The belief in the peculiar characteristics of St Swithin's Day is thus alluded to in *Poor Robin's Almanac* for 1697:

'In this month is St Swithin's Day,
On which, if that it rain, they say,
Full forty days after it will,
Or more or less, some rain distil.
This Swithin was a saint, I trow,
And Winchester's bishop also,
Who in his time did many a feat,
As popish legends do repeat:
A woman having broke her eggs,
By stumbling at another's legs,
For which she made a woful cry.
St Swithin chanced for to come by,
Who made them all as sound or more,
Than ever that they were before.
But whether this were so or no,
'Tis more than you or I do know.
Better it is to rise betime,
And to make hay while sun doth shine,
Than to believe in tales and lies,
Which idle monks and friars devise.'

In the next century, Gay remarks in his *Trivia*—

'Now if on Swithin's feast the welkin lours,
And every penthouse streams with hasty showers,
Twice twenty days shall clouds their fleeces drain,
And wash the pavement with incessant rain.
Let not such vulgar tales debase thy mind;
Nor Paul nor Swithin rule the clouds and wind!'

The question now remains to be answered, whether the popular belief we have been considering has any foundation in fact, and here the observations at Greenwich for the 20 years preceding 1861, must be adduced to demonstrate its fallacy. From these we learn that St Swithin's Day was wet in 1841, and there were 23 rainy days up to the 24th of August; 1845, 26 rainy days; 1851, 13 rainy days; 1853, 18 rainy days; 1854, 16 rainy days; and, in 1856, 14 rainy days. In 1842, and following years, St Swithin's Day was dry, and the result was in 1842, 12 rainy days; 1843, 22 rainy days; 1844, 20 rainy days; 1846, 21 rainy days; 1847, 17 rainy days; 1848, 31 rainy days; 1849, 20 rainy days; 1850, 17 rainy days; 1852, 19 rainy days; 1855, 18 rainy days; 1857, 14 rainy days; 1858, 14 rainy days; 1859, 13 rainy days; and, in 1860, 29 rainy days. It will thus be seen, by the average of the foregoing 20 years, that the greatest number of rainy days, after St Swithin's Day, had taken place when the 15th of July was dry. It is, indeed, likely enough that a track of wet weather, or the opposite, may occur at this period of the year, as a change generally takes place soon after midsummer, the character of which will depend much on the state of the previous spring. If this has been for the greater part dry, it is very probable that the weather may change to wet about the middle of July, and *vice versâ*. But that any critical meteorological influence resides in the 15th, seems wholly erroneous.

Hone, in his *Everyday Book*, quotes an amusing instance of a lady, a stanch believer in St Swithin, who, on his day one year being fine, expressed her belief in an approaching term of fine weather, but, a few drops of rain having fallen in the evening, changed her tune, and maintained that the next six weeks would be wet. Her prediction was not accomplished, the weather having been remarkably fine. 'No matter,' she would say, when pressed on the point, 'if there has been no rain during the day, there certainly has been during the night.' Her opinion of St Swithin's infallibility was in nowise to be shaken. The same author mentions a pretty saying current in some parts of the country when rain falls on St Swithin's Day: 'St Swithin is christening the apples.'

It is only to be remarked, in conclusion, that the epithet of the 'drunken saint,' sometimes applied to St Swithin, is a base slander on the worthy bishop's memory. True, the Saxons were rather noted for their convivial habits, and St Swithin, doubtless, had no objection to a cheerful glass in moderation. But no aberrations whatever, on the score of temperance, are recorded of him. The charge belongs clearly to the same category as that veracious statement in the popular ditty, by which St Patrick, the apostle of Ireland, is represented as a lover of potheen, and initiating his converts in the art of manufacturing that liquor.

---

*Born.*—Gerard Langbaine, the Younger (bibliography of the English drama), 1656, *Oxford;* Henry Edward Manning, Cardinal, 1808, *Totteridge, Hertfordshire.*

*Died.*—Anne of Cleves, consort of Henry VIII., 1567, *Chelsea;* James, Duke of Monmouth, executed on Tower Hill, 1685; John Wilson, botanist, 1751; Bryan Edwards, author of *History of the West Indies*, 1800, *Southampton;* Thomas Dermody, peasant-poet, 1802; Winthrop Mackworth Praed (comic poetry), and contributor to the *Etonian* and *Quarterly Magazine*, 1839; Prince Adam Czartoryski, Polish patriot, 1861, *Paris;* Gustav Rose, German chemist, 1873.

## JAMES, DUKE OF MONMOUTH.

Monmouth's tragic history has redeemed from contempt a person who was naturally a mediocrity, and something of a fool. Born in 1650, the eldest natural son of the young exiled Charles II., brought into prominence as a beautiful boy at the Restoration, he was thought to have his fortune made by being married to the girl Countess of Buccleuch, then considered the greatest heiress in the three kingdoms, seeing that her family estates were reckoned at five thousand a year! But there was something horrible and revolting in uniting two mere children in marriage for interested reasons, and nature avenged herself by introducing alienation between them, though not till they had become the direct ancestors of the line of the Dukes of Buccleuch.

There was always a hankering notion that a secret marriage had existed between Charles II. and Lucy Waters, the mother of Monmouth. Charles took formal steps for declaring the contrary to be the truth; but, nevertheless, the love the king had for his handsome son, and perhaps a few suspicious facts, kept alive the idea in the young man's heart. The oppressed dissenters took him up as one in whom they might have hopes, if legitimacy could be established. So it was not wonderful, when his essentially weak character is considered, that he should have set up pretensions to the throne against his uncle James II., though nothing could be for himself more ruinously unfortunate.

His ill-starred expedition in June 1685, the rebellion he headed, his defeat at Sedgemore, and the subsequent circumstances, have all been rendered familiar to the present generation by the animated narration of Macaulay. The exact particulars of his capture are less known, and are very interesting. It appears that the duke rode from the field along with Lord Gray, and proceeded to Woodyates, where they quitted their horses, and the duke assumed the clothes of a peasant. He then walked on with the design of reaching Bournemouth, in order, if possible, to get shipping for the continent. An alarm from the appearance of his enemies interrupted this plan, and he fled across the country to a wild tract of ground called Shag's Heath. There was here a patch of cultivated ground, divided by hedges, enclosed by a ditch, and bearing crops of rye and pease in full summer growth. It bore the name of the Island, by reason that it was entirely surrounded by ground in an opposite condition. On the report of a woman, that she had seen a man enter that enclosure, the dragoons surrounded it—'beat' it in all directions—and at length, on the ensuing day, when about to depart in despair, lighted upon the would-be king, skulking in a ditch under fern. The spot is still indicated with precision by a tree, which is popularly called Monmouth's Ash. It was with some difficulty he was identified, so great was the change which the mean attire and three days of personal neglect, starvation, and terror had wrought upon his once graceful form. The woman, Ann Farrant, who had given the information regarding his entering the Island, was considered by the peasantry to have never thriven after her ungracious act.

Amongst the articles found upon Monmouth's person, was a little pocket-book containing notes of various journeys, and a number of charms or spells. This volume, recovered from a book-stall at Paris, was shewn in 1849, at a meeting of the Royal Irish Academy in Dublin, and is now in the British Museum. The charms are found to be for such purposes as learning how a sickness is to end, and whether a friend will continue faithful; to heal certain maladies, and make gray hair turn black. There are also cabalistic and astrological figures, which have not been explained. The character of this part of the contents of the book is in conformity with a statement which has come from Colonel William Legge, the officer who conducted Monmouth to London after his capture. This gentleman reported that, on their journey, the duke shewed him several charms he had about his person, which he said he had got when in Scotland, but which he now saw to be only 'foolish conceits.'* It must be admitted that Monmouth was not singular in trusting to such conceits. We may here well remember that his

* Note in Dartmouth's edition of Burnet.

truly 'cruel uncle,' James II., a very few years afterwards, was induced to pause in his advance against the Prince of Orange, and to return from Salisbury to London, by a bleeding at his nose!

## WINTHROP MACKWORTH PRAED.

The name of Praed is one far less familiar to the public than it deserves to be. Some writers with great natural gifts have obstinately stood in their own light—have written so obscurely that the world would not be at the trouble of deciphering their meaning; but the subject of our present notice wrote as clearly as Cowper, and yet remains comparatively unknown on this side of the Atlantic. The Americans, with their usual quickness, long ago perceived his merits, and published his poetical works, but have included in the edition many poems which Praed never wrote, and many which, for his literary fame, he had better not have written. A small volume might, however, be made up of his selected writings, which would, in its line, be without a rival. As an author of Verses of Society—and those not of transitory interest, or on altogether frivolous themes—he is far superior to Thomas Moore, to the Hon. William Spencer (a writer far more widely known than Praed), and indeed to any poet of the class, whom we can call to mind, whether celebrated for those efforts alone, or exercising powerful pinions, as in Moore's case, in such short 'swallow flights of song.' He combined no small portion of the wit of Hood, with an elegance to which Hood could not lay claim; while in his soberer pieces he reminds one of Crabbe dancing—that is to say, they have all the naturalness of the *Tales of the Hall*, mingled with a certain graceful humour. *The Vicar* is a charming poem of the latter class.

His talk was like a stream which runs
  With rapid change from rocks to roses;
It slipped from politics to puns;
  It passed from Mahomet to Moses;
Beginning with the laws which keep
  The planets in their radiant courses,
And ending with some precept deep
  For dressing eels or shoeing horses.

He was a shrewd and sound divine,
  Of loud dissent the mortal terror;
And when by dint of page and line,
  He 'stablished truth or startled error,
The Baptist found him far too deep;
  The Deist sighed with saving sorrow,
And the lean Levite went to sleep
  And dreamt of eating pork to-morrow.

He wrote, too, in a quiet way,
  Small treatises and smaller verses,
And sage remarks on chalk and clay,
  And hints to noble lords and nurses;
True histories of last year's ghost;
  Lines to a ringlet or a turban,
And trifles for the *Morning Post*,
  And nothings for Sylvanus Urban.

He did not think all mischief fair,
  Although he had a knack of joking;
He did not make himself a bear,
  Although he had a taste for smoking.
And when religious sects ran mad,
  He held, in spite of all his learning,
That if a man's belief is bad,
  It will not be improved by burning.



And he was kind, and loved to sit
  In the low hut or garnished cottage,
And praise the farmer's homely wit,
  And share the widow's homelier pottage.
At his approach complaint grew mild,
  And when his hand unbarred the shutter,
The clammy lips of fever smiled
  The welcome that they could not utter.

He always had a tale for me
  Of Julius Cæsar or of Venus;
From him I learned the rule of three,
  Cat's-cradle, leap-frog, and Quæ genus;
I used to singe his powdered wig,
  To steal the staff he put such trust in,
And make the puppy dance a jig
  When he began to quote Augustine.

That Praed should have gathered so little fame is the more remarkable as, when alive, he had a reputation even superior to his merits. The friend and contemporary of Macaulay at Cambridge, he awakened an equal expectation of future greatness in all who knew them both. He carried off as many university prizes as the embryo historian; he divided with him the applause of the undergraduate audience in *the Union;* and in the poems which the friendly rivals contributed at that period to *Knight's Magazine*, Praed (with one glorious exception, *The Battle of Naseby*) surpassed Macaulay altogether. It is only in the pages of that extinct serial, and here and there in other dead periodicals, that the treasures of Praed's muse can be found. In politics, Praed was a Conservative, and in the Songs of the Civil Wars which Macaulay and he contributed to the pages of Mr Knight, took the Cavalier side, as will be seen in the following passage from his ballad of *Marston Moor*.

'To horse! to horse! Sir Nicholas, the clarion's note is high!
To horse! to horse! Sir Nicholas, the big drum makes reply!
Ere this hath Lucas marched, with his gallant cavaliers,
And the bray of Rupert's trumpets grows fainter in our ears.
To horse! to horse! Sir Nicholas! White Guy is at the door,
And the Raven whets his beak o'er the field of Marston Moor.

Up rose the Lady Alice from her brief and broken prayer,
And she brought a silken banner down the narrow turret-stair;
Oh! many were the tears that those radiant eyes had shed,
As she traced the bright word "Glory" in the gay and glancing thread;
And mournful was the smile which o'er those lovely features ran.
As she said, "It is your lady's gift, unfurl it in the van!"

"It shall flutter, noble wench, where the best and boldest ride,
Midst the steel-clad files of Skippon, the black dragoons of Pride;
The recreant heart of Fairfax shall feel a sicklier qualm,
And the rebel lips of Oliver give out a louder psalm;

When they see my lady's gewgaw flaunt proudly on their wing,
And hear the loyal soldier's shout, "For God and for the King!"

'Tis noon. The ranks are broken, along the royal line
They fly, the braggarts of the court! the bullies of the Rhine!
Stout Langdale's cheer is heard no more, and Astley's helm is down,
And Rupert sheaths his rapier, with a curse and with a frown,
And cold Newcastle mutters, as he follows in their flight,
"The German boar had better far have supped in York to-night!"

The knight is left alone, his steel-cap cleft in twain,
His good buff jerkin crimson'd o'er with many a gory stain:
Yet still he waves his banner, and cries amid the rout,
"For Church and King, fair gentlemen! spur on, and fight it out!"
And now he wards a Roundhead's pike, and now he hums a stave,
And now he quotes a stage-play, and now he fells a knave.

God aid thee now, Sir Nicholas! thou hast no thought of fear;
God aid thee now, Sir Nicholas! for fearful odds are here!
The rebels hem thee in, and at every cut and thrust,
"Down, down," they cry, "with Belial! down with him to the dust!"
"I would," quoth grim old Oliver, "that Belial's trusty sword,
This day were doing battle for the Saints and for the Lord!"

The tendencies of Praed induced the Conservative party to entertain great hopes of him in parliament; but in that arena, although he sat for some years, he made no figure. In 1830, he was elected for Truro; in 1835, for Yarmouth, and finally for Aylesbury; he was Secretary of the Board of Control under the Conservative government in 1835. When he died, still young, a lament arose from a large circle of friends that he had done so little, and that little only as a fashionable poet. But a first-rate fashionable poet is surely equal to a second-rate politician, and more than this, there was really no reason to suppose that Praed would ever become. He exercised his talents in the direction for which they were best fitted, and acquitted himself excellently well. He wrote at least half-a-dozen poems which deserve to live as long as the language, and to be popular while humour, elegance, and pathos still command a welcome.

The biography of Winthrop Mackworth Praed is comprised in his poems. They are all he *did* with which mankind at large has any concern. The darling of a fashionable and intellectual circle, he lived the usual butterfly life of his class, except for the parliamentary experiments above alluded to. His influence upon his contemporaries—clearly traceable, by the by, in Macaulay's early poetic efforts—was doubtless very considerable, but we have no means of estimating it.

There are certain men to whom the public is not introduced except by proxy—such as Sidney Walker, and Arthur H. Hallam—and whose merits we are required to take upon trust. Men of judgment to whom they were justly dear, and who estimated them highly, evidence warmly in their favour; at last, half irritated that we refuse to welcome a shadow, they publish their Literary Remains. In nine cases out of ten, the disappointment of the public thereupon is made rudely manifest, and the reputation that has been sought to be established is blown to the winds. At the head of all authors of this class stands Mackworth Praed, but with this important difference, that his Remains—although no pious British hand has yet collected them—more than bear out all that we hear of his merits from private sources. It is impossible to question the social charms of the man who could write the following poem, which fitly concludes this sketch—'a poem,' says Miss Mitford, 'as truthful as if it had been written in prose by Jane Austen.'

### THE BELLE OF THE BALL.

'Years, years ago, ere yet my dreams,
Had been of being wise or witty;
Ere I had done with writing themes,
Or yawned o'er this infernal "Chitty,"
Years, years ago, while all my joys
Were in my fowling-piece and filly,
In short, while I was yet a boy,
I fell in love with Laura Lily.

I saw her at a country ball
There where the sound of flute and fiddle,
Gave signal, sweet in that old hall,
Of hands across and down the middle;
Hers was the subtlest spell by far,
Of all that sets young hearts romancing,
She was our queen, our rose, our star,
And when she danced—Oh, heaven! her dancing!

She talked of politics or prayers,
Of Southey's prose, or Wordsworth's sonnets,
Of daggers, or of dancing bears,
Of battles, or the last new bonnets;
By candle-light, at twelve o'clock,
To me it mattered not a tittle,
If those bright lips had quoted Locke,
I might have thought they murmured Little.

Through sunny May, through sultry June,
I loved her with a love eternal;
I spoke her praises to the moon,
I wrote them for the Sunday journal.
My mother laughed; I soon found out
That ancient ladies have no feeling.
My father frowned; but how should gout
Find any happiness in kneeling?

She was the daughter of a dean,
Rich, fat, and rather apoplectic;
She had one brother just thirteen,
Whose colour was extremely hectic;
Her grandmother, for many a year,
Had fed the parish with her bounty;
Her second-cousin was a peer,
And lord-lieutenant of the county.

But titles and the three-per-cents,
And mortgages and great relations,
And India Bonds, and tithes and rents,
Oh! what are they to love's sensations?
Black eyes, fair foreheads, clustering locks,
Such wealth, such honours Cupid chooses;
He cares as little for the stocks,
As Baron Rothschild for the Muses.

She sketched: the vale, the wood, the beach
Grew lovelier from her pencil's shading;
She botanised: I envied each
Young blossom on her boudoir fading;
She warbled Handel: it was grand,
She made the Catalani jealous;
She touched the organ: I could stand
For hours and hours and blow the bellows.

She kept an album, too, at home,
Well filled with all an album's glories;
Paintings of butterflies and Rome;
Pattern for trimming; Persian stories;
Soft songs to Julia's cockatoo;
Fierce odes to famine and to slaughter,
And autographs of Prince Le Boo,
And recipes for elder-water.

And she was flattered, worshipped, bored,
Her steps were watched, her dress was noted,
Her poodle-dog was quite adored,
Her sayings were extremely quoted.
She laughed, and every heart was glad,
As if the taxes were abolished:
She frowned, and every look was sad,
As if the opera were demolished.

She smiled on many just for fun—
I knew that there was nothing in it:
I was the first, the only one,
Her heart had thought of for a minute.
I knew it, for she told me so,
In phrase that was divinely moulded;
She wrote a charming hand, and oh!
How neatly all her notes were folded.

Our love was like most other loves—
A little glow, a little shiver;
A rosebud and a pair of gloves,
And "Fly not yet," upon the river;
Some jealousy of some one's heir;
Some hopes of dying broken-hearted;
A miniature; a lock of hair;
The usual vows; and then we parted.

We parted: months and years rolled by,
We met again some summers after;
Our parting was all sob and sigh!
Our meeting was all mirth and laughter!
For in my heart's most secret cell
There had been many other lodgers;
And she was not the ball-room belle,
But only Mistress—something—Rogers!

W. M. Praed was born in 1802 and died in 1839.

---

## THE FIRST HULKS ON THE THAMES.

English statesmen, in past days, felt a difficulty which the lapse of time has rendered very little more soluble than before: viz., the best kind of secondary punishment to adopt for offenders against the law—the most effective mode of dealing with criminals, who deserve some punishment less awful than that of death. Whipping, transportation, silent imprisonment, and imprisonment with hard labour, have all had their advocates, as being most effective for the purpose in view; and if the first of these four has given way before the advanced humanity of English society, the other three still form a debatable ground among thinking persons. Early in the reign of George III., there were so many kinds of crime for which capital punishments were inflicted, that executions used to take place in London nearly every week, giving rise to a very unhealthy tone of feeling among the lower class. It was as a means of devising a severe mode of punishment short of death, that the *Hulks* on the Thames were introduced, in 1776. 'Hulk' is a nautical name for any old ship, applied to temporary purposes after its sea-going qualities have become impaired; it has often been applied to prison-ships, fashioned out of old men-of-war; but these prison-ships have sometimes been constructed for this special purpose, and yet the term 'hulk' remains in use as a short and easy designation. The avowed object in 1776, was 'to employ prisoners in some kind of hard labour for the public benefit;' the severity and the continuance of the labour being made dependent on the good-conduct of each prisoner. Special care was to be taken that the imprisonment, while on the one hand not cruel, should on the other not be *comfortable*. 'They [the prisoners] are to be employed in as much labour as they can sustain; to be fed with legs and shins of beef, ox-cheek, and such other coarse food; to have nothing to drink but water or small-beer; to be clad in some squalid uniform; never to be visited without the consent of the overseers; and never to be supplied with any gifts from other persons, either in money or otherwise.' The Thames between Woolwich and Barking being much choked with mud, it was deemed a useful work to employ convicts in dredging. A vessel was built, neither a ship, tender, nor lighter, but combining something of all three: on a plan approved by the king in council. Part of the stern was decked in as a sleeping-place for the convicts, part of the forecastle was enclosed for the overseer, and the rest of the vessel was open. There were overhanging platforms, on which the men could stand to work; and on one of these was 'a machine called a David, with a windlass, for raising the ballast'—which was probably the same thing as sailors now call a *davit*. The vessel had space for about thirty tons of sand, mud, or ballast, dredged up from the Thames.

Such was the hulk or prison-ship, which was placed under the management of Mr Duncan Campbell, a sort of superintendent of convicts. On the 15th of July, in the above-named year, the first party of convicts, chained two and two by the leg, entered the ship, and commenced their labours off Barking Creek. Many violent encounters took place before the convicts could be brought to understand the reality of the system. On one occasion, several of them attempted to get off their chains; they were flogged, and made to work harder as a consequence. On another occasion, five of them slipped down into a boat, and rowed off; they were pursued, and fired at; two were killed, one wounded, and two recaptured. One day, during a violent north wind, the hulk was driven across from Barking Creek to Woolwich; fourteen of the convicts rose on the keepers, compelled them to keep below, and escaped; a naval officer meeting them on the Greenwich road, persuaded eight of them to return to the vessel; of the six who refused, some were afterwards captured and hanged. In a further instance, eight convicts effectually escaped; they seized the arm-chest, took pistols, intimidated the keepers, and made off in an open boat. This system of working in hulks had a long trial on the Thames, but gradually gave way to other arrangements.

# JULY 16.

St Eustathius, confessor, patriarch of Antioch, 338. St Elier, or Helier, hermit and martyr.

*Born.*—Carneades, founder of the 'New Academy' school of philosophy, 217 B. C., *Cyrene;* Joseph Wilton, sculptor, 1722, *London;* Sir Joshua Reynolds, celebrated painter, 1723, *Plympton, Devonshire.*

*Died.*—Anne Askew, martyred at Smithfield, 1546; Tommaso Aniello (by contraction *Masaniello*), celebrated revolutionary leader, murdered by the populace at Naples, 1647; John Pearson, bishop of Chester, author of *Exposition of the Creed,* 1686, *Chester;* François Le Tellier, Marquis de Louvois, chancellor of France, 1691, *Paris;* Dr Thomas Yalden, poet, 1736; Peter III., czar of Russia, husband to the Empress Catharine, strangled, 1762; Jean Louis Delolme, writer on the British constitution, 1806; John Adolphus, historical writer, 1845, *London;* Margaret Fuller Ossoli, American authoress, perished at sea, 1850; Pierre Jean de Beranger, distinguished French lyrical poet, 1857, *Paris.*

## MARGARET FULLER OSSOLI.

Not in England nor in France is the influence of women on society so active and so manifest as in New England. The agitation there for Women's Rights is merely an evidence of actual power, seeking its recognition in civic insignia. Every student of American society has noted the wide diffusion of intellectual ability, along with an absence of genius, or the concentration of eminent mental gifts in individuals. There is an abundance of cleverness displayed in politics, letters, and arts—there is no want of daring and ambition—but there is a strange lack of originality and greatness. The same is true of the feminine side of the people. A larger number of educated women, able to write well and talk well, it would be difficult to find in any European country, but among them all it would be vain to look for a Madame de Staël, or a Miss Martineau. Perhaps those are right who cite Margaret Fuller as the fairest representative of the excellences, defects, and aspirations of the women of New England.

She was the daughter of a lawyer, and was born at Cambridge Port, Massachusetts, on the 23d of May 1810. Her father undertook to educate her himself, and finding her a willing and an able scholar, he crammed her with learning, early and late, in season and out of season. Her intellect became preternaturally developed, to the life-long cost of her health. By day, she was shewn about as a youthful prodigy; and by night, she was a somnambulist, and a prey to spectral illusions and nightmare. As she advanced into womanhood, she pursued her studies with incessant energy. 'Very early I knew,' she once wrote, 'that the only object in life is to grow.' She learned German, and made an intimate acquaintance with the writings of Goethe, which she passionately admired. Her father died in 1835, leaving her no fortune, and to maintain herself, she turned schoolmistress. Her reputation for learning, and for extraordinary eloquence in conversation, had become widely diffused in and around Boston, and her acquaintance was sought by most people with any literary pretensions. About this time, she was introduced to Mr Emerson, who describes her as rather under the middle height, with fair complexion and fair strong hair, of extreme plainness, with a trick of perpetually opening and shutting her eyelids, and a nasal tone of voice. She made a disagreeable impression on most persons, including those who subsequently became her best friends; and to such an extreme, that they did not wish to be in the same room with her. This was partly the effect of her manners, which expressed an overweening sense of power, and slight esteem of others, and partly the prejudice of her fame, for she had many jealous rivals. She was a wonderful mimic, and could send children into ecstasies with her impersonations; but to this faculty she joined a dangerous repute for satire, which made her a terror to grown people. 'The men thought she carried too many guns, and the women did not like one who despised them.' Mr Emerson, at their first meeting, was repelled. 'We shall never get far,' said he to himself, but he was mistaken. Her appearance, unlike that of many people, was the worst of Miss Fuller. Her faults and weaknesses were all superficial, and obvious to the most casual observer. They dwindled, or were lost sight of, in fuller knowledge. When the first repulse was over, she revealed new excellences every day to those who happily made her their friend. 'The day was never long enough,' says Mr Emerson, 'to exhaust her opulent memory; and I, who knew her intimately for ten years—from July 1836 to August 1846—never saw her without surprise at her new powers. She was an active, inspiring companion and correspondent. All the art, the thought, and the nobleness in New England, seemed related to her and she to them.'

The expression of her self-complacency was startling in its thoroughness and frankness. She spoke in the quietest manner of the girls she had formed, the young men who owed everything to her, and the fine companions she had long ago exhausted. In the coolest way she said to her friends: 'I now know all the people worth knowing in America, and I find no intellect comparable to my own!' Some, who felt most offence at these arrogant displays, were yet, on further reflection, compelled to admit, that if boastful, they were at anyrate not far from true. Her sympathies were manifold, and wonderfully subtle and delicate; and young and old resorted to her for confession, comfort, and counsel. Her influence was indeed powerful and far-reaching. She was no flatterer. With an absolute truthfulness, she spoke out her heart to all her confidants, and from her lips they heard their faults recited with submission, and received advice as though from an oracle.

It was in conversation that Miss Fuller shone. She would enter a party, and commence talking to a neighbour. Gradually, listeners would collect around her until the whole room became her audience. On such occasions she is said to have discoursed as one inspired; and her face, lighted up with feeling and intellect, dissolved its plainness, if not deformity, in beauty of expression. Some of her friends turned this faculty to account, by opening a conversation-class in Boston in 1839, over which Miss Fuller presided. She opened the proceedings with an extempore address, after which discussion followed. The class was attended by some of the most intellectual women of the American Athens, and very favourable memories are preserved of the grace and ability with which the president did her share of duty.

Much of Miss Fuller's freedom and force of utterance deserted her when she essayed to write, and her friends protest against her papers being regarded as any fair index of her powers. She edited for two years *The Dial*, a quarterly given to the discussion of transcendental and recondite themes, and then resigned her office to Mr Emerson. In 1844, she removed to New York, and accepted service as literary reviewer to the *New York Tribune;* a post for which she was singularly unfitted. The hack-writer of the daily press is always ready to spin a column or two on any new book on instant notice, but Miss Fuller could only write in ample leisure, and when in a proper mood, which mood had often to be waited for through several days. Happily, Mr Horace Greeley, the editor of the *Tribune*, appreciated the genius of the reviewer, and allowed her to work in her own way.

In 1846, an opportunity occurred for a visit to Europe, long an object of desire; and after a tour through England, Scotland, and France, she made a prolonged stay in Italy, and in December 1847, she was married to Count Ossoli, a poor Roman noble, attached to the papal household. Concerning him she wrote to her mother: 'He is not in any respect such a person as people in general expect to find with me. He had no instructor except an old priest, who entirely neglected his education; and of all that is contained in books he is absolutely ignorant, and he has no enthusiasm. On the other hand, he has excellent practical sense; has been a judicious observer of all that has passed before his eyes; has a nice sense of duty, a very sweet temper, and great native refinement. His love for me has been unswerving and most tender.' The conjunction of the intellectual Yankee woman with the slow Roman noble, utterly destitute of that culture which she had set above all price, seemed to many as odd as inexplicable. It was only another illustration of the saying, that extremes meet; and those who know how impossible it is for books and the proudest fame to fill a woman's heart (and Margaret Fuller had a great and very tender heart), will not wonder that she felt a strange and happy peace in Ossoli's simple love.

She was a friend of Mazzini's, and when, in 1848, revolution convulsed almost every kingdom on the continent, she rejoiced that Italy's day of redemption had at last dawned. During the siege of Rome by the French, she acted as a hospital nurse, and her courage and activity inspired extraordinary admiration among the Italians. When Rome fell, her hopes for her chosen country vanished, and she resolved to return to America. 'Beware of the sea!' had been the warning of a fortune-teller to Ossoli when a boy. In spite of gloomy forebodings, they set sail from Leghorn in a merchant-ship. At the outset of the voyage, the captain sickened and died of confluent small-pox in its most malignant form. Ossoli was next seized, and then their infant boy, but both recovered, though their lives were despaired of. At last the coast of America was reached, when, on the very morning of the day they would have landed, 16th July 1850, the ship struck on Fire Island beach. For twelve hours, during which the vessel went to pieces, they faced death. At last crew and passengers were engulfed in the waves, only one or two reaching the land alive. The bodies of Ossoli and his wife were never found, but their child was washed ashore, and carried to Margaret's sorrowing mother.

## DE BERANGER.

Notwithstanding the 'De' prefixed to his name, the illustrious French songster was of the humblest origin. In youth, the natural energies of his intellect led him to authorship; but he was at first like to starve by it, and had at one moment serious thoughts of enlisting as a soldier in the expedition to Egypt, when he was succoured by the generosity of Lucien Bonaparte, who conferred on him the income he was entitled to as a member of the Institute. It was not without cause, and a cause honourable to his feelings, that Béranger was ever after a zealous Bonapartist. Béranger is, without doubt, the most popular poet of France: men of literature, citizens, workmen, peasants, everybody, in fact, sings his songs. Yet his modesty was never spoiled by flattery; when a professor of high standing spoke in his presence of his 'immortal works;' he replied: 'My dear friend, I believe really that I am overpraised; permit me to doubt the immortality of my poems. At the opening of my career, the French song had no other pretension than to enliven a dessert. I asked if it would not be possible to raise its tone, and use it as the interpreter of the ideas and feelings of a generous nation. At a dinner given by M. Laffitte, where Benjamin Constant was present, I sang one of my first songs, when the latter declared that a new horizon was opened to poetry. This encouraged me to persevere.'

The circumstances of the times favoured the poet; he never ceased to sing the glories of France, and particularly of the Empire. Yet he is most truly himself in those little dramas, where, placing a single person on the scene, he expresses the national feeling, such as *Le Vieux Sergent*, *Le Roi d'Ivetôt;* whilst he was said to be the only man who knew how to make riches popular, he had another secret, how to render his own poverty almost as inexhaustible in kindnesses as the rich. He never would receive anything, and lived to the last on the profits of his works, leaving his small fortune to be divided among a few poor and old friends.

---

## ROYAL VISIT TO MERCHANT TAILORS' HALL.

On the 16th of July 1607, James I., accompanied by Henry, Prince of Wales, visited the Merchant Tailors' Company of London, at their hall, in Threadneedle Street. The records of the company contain several interesting notices of this royal visit. A short time previous to its taking place, a meeting was held to consult how the king could be best entertained; and Alderman Sir John Swynnerton was entreated 'to confer with Mr Benjamin Jonson, the poet, about a speech to be made to welcome his majesty, and for music, and other inventions.' From the same source we also glean the following account of the entertainment:

'At the upper end of the hall, there was a chair of estate, where his majesty sat; and a very proper child, well-spoken, being clothed like an Angel of Gladness, with a taper of frankincense burning in his hand, delivered a short speech, containing eighteen verses, devised by Mr Ben. Jonson, which pleased his majesty marvellously well. And upon either side of the hall, in the windows near the upper end, were galleries made for music, in either of which were seven singular choice musicians, playing on their lutes, and in the ship, which did hang aloft in the hall, were three rare men and very skilful, who sung to his majesty; wherein it is to be remembered, that the multitude and noise was so great, that the lutes and songs could scarcely be heard or understood. And then his majesty went up into the king's chamber, where he dined alone at a table which was provided only for his majesty, in which chamber were placed a very rich pair of organs, whereupon Mr John Bull, doctor of music, and brother of this company, did play all the dinner-time.'

After dinner, James was presented with a purse of gold; but on being shewn a list of the eight kings, and other great men, who had been members of the company, he declined to add his name to it; stating that he already belonged to another guild, but that his son, the Prince of Wales, should at once become a Merchant Tailor. Then all descended to the great hall, where the prince, having dined, was presented with a purse of gold, and the garland being put on his head, he was made free of the company amidst loud acclamations of joy. During this ceremony, the king stood in a new window made for the purpose, 'beholding all with a gracious kingly aspect.'

'After all which, his majesty came down to the great hall, and sitting in his chair of estate, did hear a melodious song of farewell by the three rare men in the ship, being apparelled in watchet* silk, like seamen, which song so pleased his majesty, that he caused it to be sung three times over.'

## MOCK-ELECTION IN THE KING'S BENCH.

In the old bad system of imprisonment for debt, there were many evils, but none worse than the enforced idleness undergone by the prisoners. It is easy to understand how a man who had been long kept in prison came out a worse member of society than he went in. The sufferers, in general, made wonderful struggles to get their time filled up, though it was too often with things little calculated for their benefit. Sometimes special amusements were got up amongst them. In 1827, the inmates of the King's Bench Prison, in London, devised one of such a nature, that public attention was attracted by it. It was proposed that they should elect a member to represent '*Tenterden*' (a slang name for the prison) in parliament. Three candidates were put up, one of whom was Lieutenant Meredith, an eccentric naval officer. All the characteristics of a regular election were burlesqued. Addresses from the candidates to the 'worthy and independent electors' were printed and placarded about the walls of the prison; squibs were written, and songs sung, disparaging the contending parties; processions were organised with flags, trappings, and music, to take the several candidates to visit the several 'Collegians' (i.e., prisoners) in their rooms; speeches were made in the courtyards, full of grotesque humour; a high-sheriff and other officers were chosen to conduct the proceedings in a dignified way; and the electors were invited to 'rush to the poll' early on Monday morning, the 16th of July. The turnkeys of the prison entered into the fun. While these preliminary plans were engaging attention, a creditor happened to enter the prison; and seeing the prisoners so exceedingly joyous, declared that such a kind of imprisonment for debt could be no punishment; and he therefore liberated his debtor. Whether owing to this singular result of prison-discipline (or indiscipline), or an apprehension of evils that might follow, Mr Jones, marshal of the prison, stopped the whole proceedings on the morning of the 16th. This, however, he did in so violent and injudicious a way as to exasperate the whole of the prisoners—some of whom, although debtors, were still men of education and self-respect. They resented the language used towards them, and the treatment to which they were subjected; until at length a squad of Foot-guards, with fixed bayonets, forcibly drove some of the leaders into a filthy 'black-hole' or place of confinement. The matter caused a few days' further excitement, both within and without the prison; and it was generally thought that a more good-humoured course of proceeding on the part of the marshal would have brought the whole affair to a better ending.

* Blue.

## AN APPLE-STALL DISCUSSED IN PARLIAMENT.

A case which attracted some notice and created some amusement in 1851, serves, although trifling in itself, to illustrate the tenacity with which *rights* of any kind are maintained in England. During a period of several years, strollers in Hyde Park, particularly children, were familiar with the 'White Cottage,' a small structure near the east end of the Serpentine, at the junction of several footpaths. In this cottage Ann Hicks dispensed apples, nuts, gingerbread, cakes, ginger-beer, &c. It had grown up from a mere open stall to something like a small tenement, simply through the pertinacious applications of the stall-keeper to persons in office. Until 1843, there was an old conduit at that spot, once connected with a miniature water-fall, but occupied then by Ann Hicks for the purposes of her small dealings. This was pulled down, and her establishment was reduced to a mere open stall. Ann Hicks, who appears to have been an apt letter-writer, wrote to Lord Lincoln, at that time Chief Commissioner of Woods and Forests, stating that her stall consisted merely of a table with a canvas awning, and begging for permission to have some kind of lock-up into which she could place her wares at night. She was therefore allowed to make some such wooden erection as those which have long existed near the Spring Garden corner of St James' Park. She wrote again, after a time, begging for a very small brick enclosure, as being more secure at night than one of wood; this was unwillingly granted, because quite contrary to the general arrangements for the management of the park; but as she was importunate, and persuaded other persons to support her appeal, permission was given. Ann Hicks put a wide interpretation on this kindness, for she not only built a little brick room, but she built a little window as well as a little door to it. She wrote again, saying that her locker was not large enough; might she make it a little higher, to afford space for her ginger-beer bottles? Yes, provided the total height did not exceed five feet. She wrote again, might she repair the roof, which was becoming leaky? Obtaining permission, she not only repaired the roof, but protruded a little brick chimney through it; and advancing still further, she made a little brick fireplace, whereon she could conduct small cooking operations. She wrote again, stating that the boys annoyed her by looking in at the little window: might she put up a few hurdles, to keep them at a distance? This being allowed, she gradually moved the hurdles further and further outwards, till she had enclosed a little garden. Thus the open stall developed into a miniature tenement. Lord Seymour came into office as chief-commissioner in 1850, and found that Ann Hicks had given the officials as much trouble as if she had been a person of the first consequence. Preparations were at that time being made for the great Exhibition of 1851, and it was deemed proper to remove obstructions as much as possible from the Park. Ann Hicks was requested to remove the white cottage. She flatly refused, asserting that the ground was her own by vested right. She told a story to the effect that, about a hundred years earlier, her grandfather had saved George II. from peril in the Serpentine; that, as a reward, he had obtained permission to hold a permanent stall in the park; that he had held this during a long life, and then his son, and then Ann Hicks; and that she had incurred an expenditure of £130 in building the white cottage. After due inquiry, no evidence could be found other than that Ann Hicks had long had a stall in that spot. Lord Seymour, wishing to be on the right side, applied to the Duke of Wellington, as ranger of Hyde Park; and the veteran, punctual and precise in small matters as in great, caused the whole matter to be investigated by a solicitor. The result was that Ann Hicks's story was utterly discredited, and she was ordered to remove—receiving, at the same time, a small allowance for twelve months as a recompense. She resisted to the last, and became a source of perpetual annoyance to every one connected with the park. When the cottage was removed, and the money paid, she placarded the trees in the park with accusations against the commissioners for robbing her of her rights. She pestered noblemen and members of parliament to intercede in her favour, and even wrote to the Queen. She gradually gave up the pretended vested right, and put in a claim for mere charity. Nevertheless, in July of the following year, when the Exhibition was open, the case was brought before parliament by Mr Bernal Osborne. Full explanations were given by the government, and the agitation died out. Many foreigners were in England at the time, and the matter afforded them rather a striking proof of the jealousy with which the nation regards any supposed infractions by the government of the rights of private persons—even to so small a matter as an apple-stall.

---

## OLD SUBURBAN TEA-GARDENS.

London has so steadily enlarged on all sides, and notably so within the present century, that the old suburbs are embraced in new streets; and a comparatively young person may look in vain for the fields of his youthful days. 'The march of brick and mortar' has invaded them, and the quiet country tea-garden to which the Londoner wended across grass, may now be transformed to a glaring gin-palace in the midst of a busy trading thoroughfare.

Readers of our old dramatic literature may be amused with the rustic character which invests the residents of that portion of the outskirts of old London comprehended between King's Cross and St John's Wood, as they are depicted by Ben Jonson in his *Tale of a Tub*. The action of the drama takes place in St Pancras Fields, the country near Kentish Town, Tottenham Court, and Marylebone. The *dramatis personæ* seem as innocent of London and its manners as if they were inhabiting Berkshire, and talk a broad-country dialect. This northern side of London preserved its pastoral character until a comparatively recent time, it being not more than twenty years since some of the marks used by the Finsbury archers of the days of Charles II., remained in the Shepherd and Shepherdess Fields, between the Regent's Canal and Islington. From White Conduit House, the view was unobstructed over fields to Highgate. The pretorium of a Roman camp was visible where Barnsbury Terrace now stands; the remains of another, as described by Stukely, were situated opposite old St Pancras Church; and hordes of cows grazed where the Euston Square terminus of our great midland railway is now placed, and which was then Rhodes' Farm. At the commencement of the present century, the country was open from the back of the British Museum to Kentish Town; the New Road, from Tottenham to Battlebridge, was considered unsafe after dark; and parties used to collect at stated points to take the chance of the escort of the watchman in his half-hour round. Hampstead and Highgate could only be reached by 'short stages,' going twice a day; and a journey there, once or twice in the summer, was the furthest and most ambitious expedition of a Cockney's year. Both villages abounded in inns, with large gardens in their rear, overlooking the pleasant country fields towards Harrow, or the extensive and more open land towards St Alban's and the valley of the Thames. 'Jack Straw's Castle' and 'The Spaniards' still remain as samples of these old 'rural delights.' The features of the latter place, as they existed more than a century since, have been preserved by Chatelaine, in a

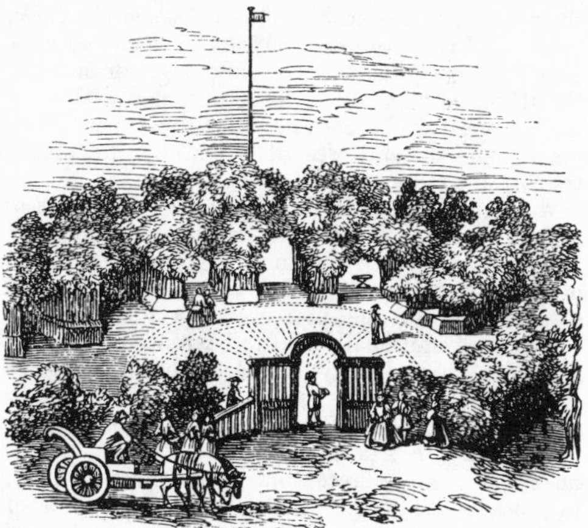

THE SPANIARDS, 1745.

small engraving he executed about 1745, and which we here copy. The formal arrangement of trees and turf, in humble imitation of the Dutch taste introduced by William III., and exhibited at Hampton Court and Kensington palaces, may be noted in this humbler garden.

For those who cared not for such distant pleasures, and who could not spare time and money to climb the hills that bounded the Londoner's northern horizon, there were 'Arcadian bowers' almost beneath the city walls. Following the unfragrant Fleet ditch until it became a comparatively clear stream in the fields beyond Clerkenwell, the citizen found many other wells, each within its own shady garden. The Fleet was anciently known as 'the river of wells,' from the abundance of these rills, which were situated on its sloping banks, and swelled its tiny stream. 'The London Spa' gave the name to the district now known as Spa-fields, Rosomon's Row being built on its site. The only representation of the gardens occurs in the frontispiece to an exceedingly rare pamphlet, published in 1720, entitled *May-day, or the Origin of Garlands*, which appears to be an elaborate puff for the establishment, as we are told in grandiloquent rhymes:

'Now ninepin alleys and now skittles grace
The late forlorn, sad, desolated place;
Arbours of jasmine, fragrant shades compose,
And numerous blended companies enclose.
The spring is gratefully adorn'd with rails,
Whose fame shall last till the New River fails!'

Situated in the low land near by (sometimes termed Bagnigge Marsh), was a well and its pleasure-grounds, known as 'Black Mary's Hole.' Spring Place, adjoining Exmouth Street, marks its locality now; it obtained its name from a black woman named Mary Woolaston, who rented it in the days of Charles II. Another 'hole,' of worse repute, was in the immediate vicinity, and is better known to the reader of London literature as 'Hockley-in-the-Hole.' There assembled on Sundays and holidays the Smithfield butchers, the knackers of Turnmill Street, and the less respectable denizens of Field Lane, for dog-fights and pugilistic encounters. 'That men may be instructed by brutes, Æsop, Lemuel Gulliver, and Hockley-in-the-Hole, shew us,' says the author of *The Taste of the Town*, 1731; adding, with satiric slyness: 'Who can view dogs tearing bulls, bulls goring dogs, or mastiffs throttling bears, without being animated with their daring spirits.' It became the very type of low blackguardism, and was abolished by the magistracy at the close of the last century.

A short distance further north, in the midst of ground encircled by the Fleet River, stood the more famous Bagnigge Wells, long the favoured resort of Londoners, as it added the attraction of a concert-room to the pleasure of a garden. The house was traditionally said to have been a country residence of Nell Gwynn, the celebrated mistress of Charles II.; and her bust was consequently placed in the post of honour, in the Long Room, where the concerts were given. The house was opened for public reception about the year 1757, in consequence of the discovery, by Mr Hughes, of two mineral springs (one chalybeate, the other cathartic), which had been covered over, but by their percolation, injured his favourite flower-beds. Mineral waters being then much sought after, he took advantage of his springs, and opened his gardens to the public with much success. In *The Shrubs of Parnassus*, 1760, is a curious poetical description of the company usually seen:

'Here ambulates th' Attorney, looking grave,
And Rake, from Bacchanalian rout uprose,
And mad festivity. Here, too, the Cit,
With belly turtle-stuffed, and Man of Gout
With leg of size enormous. Hobbling on,
The pump-room he salutes, and in the chair
He squats himself unwieldy. Much he drinks,
And much he laughs, to see the females quaff
The friendly beverage.'

There is a pleasing mezzotint engraving (now very scarce), which was published by the great printseller of the day, Carington Bowles, in St Paul's Churchyard, 1780, depicting two fair visitors

A BAGNIGGE WELLS SCENE, 1780.

to the gardens, breaking through the laws against plucking flowers. It is entitled, 'A Bagnigge Wells Scene, or no resisting Temptation.' It is copied above. The gardens at that time were extensive, and laid out in the old-fashioned manner, with clipped trees, walks in formal lines, and a profusion of leaden statues. A fountain was placed in the centre, as shewn in our cut. A Dutch Cupid half-choking a swan was the brilliant idea it shadowed forth. The roof of the temple is seen above the trees to the left; it was a circular domed colonnade, formed by a double row of pillars and pilasters; in its centre was a double pump, one piston supplying the chalybeate, the other the cathartic water; it was encircled by a low balustrade. A grotto was the other great feature of the garden; it was a little castellated building of irregular hexagonal form, covered with shells, stones, glass, &c., forming two apartments open to the gardens. The waters were drunk for the charge of threepence each person, or delivered from the pump-room at eightpence per gallon. As a noted place for tea-drinking, it is frequently alluded to by authors of the last century. In the prologue to Colman's comedy, *Bon Ton*, 1776, a vulgar city-madam from Spitalfields thus defines that phrase:

'*Bone Tone's* the space 'twixt Saturday and Monday,
And riding in a one-horse chair on Sunday.
'Tis drinking tea on summer afternoons
At Bagnigge Wells with china and gilt spoons.'

There is a print of the company in the great room, styled, 'The Bread and Butter Manufactory, or the

Humours of Bagnigge Wells.' Miss Edgeworth alludes to it in one of her tales as a place of vulgar resort; and a writer of 1780 says:

'The Cits to Bagnigge Wells repair,
To swallow dust, and call it air.'

The gardens were much curtailed in 1813, when the bankruptcy of the proprietors compelled a general sale on the premises. They gradually sank in repute; the Long-room was devoted to threepenny concerts; and the whole was ultimately destroyed in 1841, when a public-house was erected on the site of the old tavern. A relic of the oldest house remained over a side-door at the end of the garden, consisting of a head in high-relief, and an inscription: 'S. T. This is Bagnigge House neare the Pinder a Wakefeilde. 1680.' The latter was the sign of another house of entertainment in Gray's Inn Lane; and nearly opposite to it, within a short distance of King's Cross, was another garden, where St Chad's Well offered its cure to invalids. The New Underground Railway cuts through the whole of this marshy district, once so redolent of healing springs, and to which we may bid adieu in the grandiloquent words of the author quoted above:

'Farewell, sweet vale! how much dost thou excel
Arno or Andalusia!'

Passing along the great main-road to Islington from Smithfield (St John Street Road), we find on the banks of the New River, at that point where it crosses the road, a theatre still bearing the name of Sadler's Wells, and occupying the site of that

SADLER'S WELLS, 1745.

old sanatorium. The aspect of the house in 1745 is shewn in our engraving, from a view published at that period. The reader who is familiar with the works of Hogarth, will recognise the entrance-gate and portion of the house in the background to his print of 'Evening,' one of the 'Four Times of the Day.' The well was a medicinal spring, once the property of the monks of Clerkenwell, reputed for its cures before the dissolution of the priory in Henry VIII.'s reign, when this well was ordered to be stopped up as a relic of superstition. In the reign of Charles II., the house and grounds were in the hands of a surveyor of the highway named Sadler, who employed men to dig gravel in his garden, leading to the rediscovery of the well under an arch of stone. This happened in 1683. With great business tact, Mr Sadler engaged a certain 'T.G., Doctor of Physick,' to write 'A True and Exact Account of Sadler's Well; or, the New Mineral Waters lately found at Islington,' in which it was recommended as equal in virtue to that of Tunbridge. He built a music-house, and succeeded in making it 'so frequented, that there are five or six hundred people there constantly every morning.' After a few years, that attraction ceased; but as a place of amusement, it never failed in popularity. In 1690, it was known as Miles's Music-house; to him succeeded Francis Forcer, the son of a musician, who introduced rope-dancers, tumblers, &c., for the public amusement; no charge was made for this, but only paid for in the drink visitors ordered. While under these managements, the premises appear to have been a tea-garden with a music-room, on the plan of Bagnigge Wells; but in 1765, one Rosoman, an eminent builder, took the lease, pulled down the old building, and erected a theatre on the site. Opposite to the Wells, on the south side of the New River, was another favourite tea-garden, 'The Sir Hugh Middleton,' which still exists as an ordinary public-house, minus the garden. In Hogarth's print, already alluded to, it appears as a country hostel, with a luxuriant vine trained over its wooden front; the scenery beyond is a Cockney arcadia, with milk-maids and cows, open fields and farm-tenements, to the Middlesex alps at Highgate.

Turning round the New River head, 'Merlin's Cave,' another tea-garden, wooed the traveller; but if he resolutely crossed the New Road, he came to White Conduit House, on the extreme verge of London, situated on the high land just above the tunnel connecting the Regent's and Paddington canals. It took its name from the contiguous conduit originally constructed for the use of the Charter-house, and once bore the initials of Thomas

WHITE CONDUIT HOUSE, 1827.

Sutton, its founder, and the date 1641. Our cut represents the aspect of both buildings, as they stood in 1827. The Conduit was then in a pitiable state of neglect—denuded of the outer case of stone, a mere core of rubble; the house was a low-roofed building, with a row of clipped trees in front, and a large garden in the rear, well supplied with arbours all round for tea-drinking; and such was its popularity at the commencement of this century, that fifty pounds was often taken on a Sunday afternoon for sixpenny tea-tickets. Its bread was as popular as the buns of Chelsea; and 'White Conduit loaves' was a London cry, listened for by such old ladies as wished to furnish a tea-table luxury to their friends. On week-days, it was a kind of minor Vauxhall, with singing and fire-works; on great occasions, the ascent of a balloon crowded the gardens, and collected thousands of persons in the fields around. It was usual for London 'roughs' to assemble in large numbers in these fields for foot-ball play on Easter Monday; occasionally 'the fun' was diversified by Irish faction-fights; the whole neighbourhood is now covered with houses. The old tea-garden was built upon and the house destroyed in 1849; a large public-house marking the site of the older building we engrave.

Field-paths, with uninterrupted views over the country, led toward St Pancras, where another well and public garden invited strollers with its sanitary promises. The way between this place and London was particularly unsafe to pedestrians after dark, and robberies between here and Gray's Inn Lane were common in the early part of the last century. About half a mile to the west, the Jew's Harp Tavern invited wayfarers to Primrose Hill, being situated close to the south of the present Regent's Park Barracks.

Marylebone Gardens was the most important of these north-western places of amusement. It was situated opposite the old parish church, on ground now covered by Devonshire Street and Beaumont Street. It is mentioned by Pepys, two years after the great fire of London, as 'a pretty place' to walk in. Its bowling-alleys were famous, and here Sheffield, Duke of Buckingham, 'bowled time away' in the days of Pope and Gay. The latter author alludes to this place more than once in the *Beggar's Opera*, as a rendezvous for the dissipated, putting it on a level with one of bad repute already mentioned. He alludes to the dog-fights allowed here in one of his Fables:

> 'Both Hockley-hole and Marybone
> The combats of my dog have known.'

After 1740, it became more respectable—a shilling was charged for admission, an orchestra was erected; the gardens were occasionally illuminated, fêtes given, and a rivalry to Vauxhall attempted, which achieved a certain amount of success. Balls and concerts were given; Handel's music was played under Dr Arne's direction; Chatterton wrote a burlesque burletta after the fashion of *Midas*, entitled *The Revenge*, which was performed in 1770; but after many vicissitudes, the gardens were closed within the next eight years, and the site turned to more useful purposes.

Pursuing the road toward Paddington, 'The Yorkshire Stingo,' opposite Lisson Grove, invited the wayfarer to its tea-garden and bowling-green; it was much crowded on Sundays, when an admission fee of sixpence was demanded at the doors. For that a ticket was given, to be exchanged with the waiters for its value in refreshments; a plan very constantly adopted in these gardens, to prevent the intrusion of the lowest classes, or of such as might only stroll about them without spending anything. The Edgeware Road would point the way to Kilburn Wells, which an advertisement of 1773 assures us were then 'in the utmost perfection, the gardens enlarged and greatly improved, the great room being particularly adapted to the use and amusement of the politest companies, fit for either music, dancing, or entertainment.'

The south-western suburb had also its places of resort. 'Cromwell Gardens,' and 'The Hoop and Toy,' at Brompton; 'The Fun,' at Pimlico, celebrated for its ale; 'The Monster,' and 'Jenny's Whim,' in the fields near Chelsea. Walpole, in one of his letters, says that at Vauxhall he 'picked up Lord Granby, arrived very drunk from Jenny's Whim.' Angelo, in his *Pic-nic* or *Table-talk*, describes it as 'a tea-garden, situated, after passing a wooden bridge on the left, previous to entering the long avenue, the coach-way to where Ranelagh once stood.' This place was much frequented from its novelty, being an inducement to allure the curious by its amusing deceptions, particularly on their first appearance there. Here was a large garden, in different parts of which were recesses; and treading on a spring, taking you by surprise, up started different figures, some ugly enough to frighten you; like a Harlequin, Mother Shipton, or some terrific animal. In a large piece of water, facing the tea-alcoves, large fish or mermaids were shewing themselves above the surface. This queer spectacle was kept by a famous mechanist, who had been employed at one of the winter theatres.' The water served less reputable purposes in 1755. when, according to a notice in *The Connoisseur*, it was devoted to 'the royal diversion of duck-hunting.'

This disgraceful 'diversion' gave celebrity to a house in St George's Fields, which took for its sign 'The Dog and Duck,' though originally known as

THE DOG AND DUCK, 1780.

'St George's Spa.' It was established, like so many of these places, after the discovery of a mineral spring, about the middle of the last century. 'As a public tea-garden,' says a writer in 1813, 'it was within a few years past a favourite resort of the vilest dregs of society, until properly suppressed by the magistrates.' The site forms part of the ground upon which the great lunatic asylum, known as New Bethlehem Hospital, now stands; and in the boundary-wall is still to be seen the sculptured figure of a seated dog holding a duck in his mouth, which once formed the sign of the tea-garden. The 'sport' consisted in hunting unfortunate ducks in a pond by dogs; the diving of the one, and the pursuit of the others, gratifying the brutal spectators, who were allowed to bring their dogs to 'the hunt,' on the payment of sixpence each; the owner of the dog who caught and killed the duck might claim that prize.

Closer to London, but on the same side of the Thames, was Lambeth Wells, where concerts were occasionally given; 'The Apollo Gardens' (on the site of Maudsley's factory, in the Westminster Road), with an orchestra in its centre, and alcoves for tea-drinking, the walls of which were covered with pictures—a very common decoration to the wooden boxes in all these gardens, giving amusement to visitors in examining them. 'Cuper's Gardens' were opposite Somerset House, the present Waterloo Bridge Road running over what was once its centre. They were called after the original proprietor, a gardener, named Boydell Cuper, who had been in the service of the famous collector, Thomas, Earl of Arundel, whose antique marbles are still at Oxford. Cuper begged from him such as were mutilated, and stuck them about his walks. In 1736, an orchestra was added to its attractions; it subsequently became famed for its fireworks; but ultimately most so for the loose society it harboured, and for which it was deprived of its licence in 1753.

In addition to these the inhabitants of Southwark might disport in 'Finch's Grotto,' situated in Gravel Lane, Southwark; 'The Jamaica Tavern,' or 'St Helena Gardens,' Rotherhithe; so that London was literally surrounded with these popular places of resort; as alluded to by the Prussian D'Archenholz, who, in his account of England (published toward the close of the last century), observes: 'The English take a great delight in the public gardens, near the metropolis, where they assemble and drink tea together in the open air. The number of these in the neighbourhood of the capital is amazing, and the order, regularity, neatness, and even elegance of them are truly admirable. They are, however, very rarely frequented by people of fashion; but the middle and lower ranks go there often, and seem much delighted with the music of an organ, which is usually played in an adjoining building.' Now, owing to the altered tastes of the age, scarcely one of them exists, and they will be remembered only in the pages of the topographer.

---

# JULY 17.

Saints Speratus and his companions, martyrs, 3d century. St Marcellina, eldest sister of St Ambrose, about 400. St Alexius, confessor, 5th century. St Ennodius, bishop of Pavia, confessor, 521. St Turninus, confessor, 8th century. St Leo IV., pope and confessor, 855.

---

*Born.*—Dr Isaac Watts, well-known divine and writer of hymns, 1674, *Southampton;* Adrian Reland, oriental scholar and author, 1676, *Ryp, North Holland.*

*Died.*—Robert Guiscard the Norman, Duke of Apulia, 1085, *Corfu;* Jacques Arteveldt, brewer in Ghent, and popular leader, slain, 1344; Janet, Lady Glammis, burnt as a witch on Castle Hill of Edinburgh, 1537; Marchioness of Brinvilliers, noted poisoner, executed at Paris, 1676; Sir William Wyndham, noted Tory orator, 1740, *Wells, Somersetshire;* Charlotte Corday, assassin of Marat, guillotined, 1793; Dr John Roebuck, distinguished manufacturing chemist, and founder of the Carron Ironworks, 1794; Charles, second Earl Grey, prime minister to William IV., 1845; Sir Francis Nathaniel Conyngham, Marquis Conyngham, 1876, *London.*

## THE MARCHIONESS OF BRINVILLIERS.

It is a melancholy fact that the progress of civilisation, along with the innumerable benefits which it confers on the human race, tends to develop and bring forth a class of offences and crimes which are almost, if not wholly, unknown in the earlier and less sophisticated stages of society. Whilst violence and rapine are characteristics of primitive barbarism and savage independence, commercial fraud and murder by treachery but too often spring up as their substitutes in peaceful and enlightened times. As long as human nature continues the same, and its leading principles have ever hitherto been unchanging, so long must the spirit of evil find some mode of expression, veiled though it may be under an infinite variety of disguises, and yet not without undergoing a gradual softening down which optimists would fondly regard as a promise of its ultimate suppression.

The crime of poisoning, it has often been remarked, is like assassination—the offspring of a polished and voluptuous age. In proof of this, we need only look to its horrible and astounding frequency in Italy and France during the sixteenth and seventeenth centuries. One of the most notable instances of its occurrence is the case of the Marchioness of Brinvilliers, whose nefarious practices, coupled with her distinguished rank, have exalted her to the very pinnacle of infamy. She was the daughter of M. Dreux d'Aubray, who held the office of lieutenant-civil in the capital of France during the reign of Louis XIV. In 1651, she was married to the Marquis of Brinvilliers, a son of the president of the Chamber of Accounts, and the heir of an immense fortune, to which his wife brought a very considerable accession. The marchioness is described as a woman of most prepossessing appearance, both as regards agreeableness of person and as impressing the beholder with a sense of virtue and amiability. Never was the science of physiognomy more completely stultified. Beneath that fair and attractive exterior was concealed one of the blackest and most depraved hearts that ever beat within a female bosom. A career of degrading sensuality had, as afterwards appeared by her own confession, exerted on her its natural and corrupting influence almost from her childhood. No special evidence of its fruits, however, became prominently manifest till her acquaintance with a certain Sieur Godin, commonly called St Croix, who had made her husband's acquaintance in the course of military service, and for whom the latter conceived such an overweening affection that he introduced him into, and made him an inmate of, his house. An intimacy, which was soon converted into a criminal one, sprang up between him and the marchioness, who also not long afterwards procured a separation from her husband on the ground of his pecuniary recklessness and mismanagement. Freed now from all the restraints by which she had hitherto been held, she indulged so shamelessly her unlawful passion for St Croix, that public decency was scandalised, and her father, after several ineffectual attempts to rouse M. de Brinvilliers to a sense of his conjugal degradation, procured a *lettre de cachet*, by which her paramour was committed to the Bastile. Here St Croix became acquainted with an Italian named Exili, an adept in poisons, who taught him his arts, and on their release, after about a twelvemonth's confinement, became an inmate of his house. The intimacy of St Croix with the marchioness was at the same time renewed, but more cautiously, so as to save appearances, and even to enable the latter to regain the affection of her father; a necessary step towards the accomplishment of the schemes in view. Avarice and revenge now conspired with illicit love, and the horrid design was conceived of poisoning her father and the other members of her family, so as to render herself sole heir to his property. Tutored by St Croix, she mixed up poison with some biscuits which she distributed to the poor, and, more especially, to the patients of the Hôtel Dieu, as an experiment to test the quantity necessary for a fatal effect.

Having thus prepared herself for action, the marchioness commenced with the murder of her father, which she effected by mixing some poison with his broth when he was residing at his country seat. The symptoms ordinarily exhibited in such cases ensued, but the patient did not die till after his return to Paris. No suspicions on this occasion seem to have rested on the marchioness, who forthwith proceeded to effect the deaths of her two brothers, one of whom succeeded their father in his office of lieutenant-civil, and the other was a counsellor of the parliament of Paris. This she accomplished by means of a man named La Chaussée, who had formerly lived as a footman with St Croix, and then transferred his services to the brothers D'Aubray, who occupied together the same house. Under the guidance of his former master, this miscreant administered poison to them on various occasions, which destroyed first the lieutenant and then the counsellor; but so well had the semblance of fidelity been maintained, that the latter bequeathed to La Chaussée a legacy of a hundred crowns in consideration of his services. One member of the marchioness's family still remained, her sister Mademoiselle D'Aubray, whose suspicions, however, were now aroused against her sister, and by her vigilance and circumspection she escaped the snares laid for her life.

The singular deaths of M. D'Aubray and his sons excited considerable attention, and the belief came to be strongly entertained that they had been poisoned. Yet no suspicion alighted on the marchioness or St Croix, and they might have succeeded in escaping the punishment due to their crimes, had it not been for a singular accident. Whilst the latter was busied one day with the preparation of his poisons, the mask which he wore to protect himself from their effects dropped off, and he was immediately suffocated by the pernicious vapours. Having no relations to look after his property, it was taken possession of by the public authorities, who, in the course of their rummaging, discovered a casket, disclosing first a paper in the handwriting of the deceased, requesting all the articles contained in it to be delivered unexamined to the Marchioness de Brinvilliers. These consisted of packets of various kinds of poison, a promissory-note by the marchioness in St Croix's favour for 1500 livres, and a number of her letters to him, written in the most extravagantly amatory strain. Even now, had it not been for the imprudence of La Chaussée in presenting sundry claims on St Croix's succession, it might have been difficult to substantiate his guilt and that of his employers. He was indicted at the instance of the widow of the lieutenant-civil, the younger D'Aubray; and having been brought before the parliament of Paris, was condemned to be broken alive on the wheel, after having been first subjected to the torture for the discovery of his accomplices. On the rack, he made a full confession; in consequence of which a demand was made on the authorities of Liege for the tradition to the French government of the Marchioness of Brinvilliers, who had fled thither on hearing of the proceedings instituted after the death of St Croix. This abandoned woman had, previous to quitting Paris, made various attempts, by bribery and otherwise, to obtain possession of the fatal casket; but finding all these ineffectual, made her escape by night across the frontier into the Netherlands. Given up here by the Council of Sixty of Liege to a company of French archers, she was conducted by them to Paris, not without many offers, on her part, of large sums of money to the officers to let her go, and also an endeavour to commit suicide by swallowing a pin. Previous to, and during her trial, she made the most strenuous declarations of her innocence; but the accumulated proof against her was overwhelming; and, notwithstanding the very ingenious defence of her counsel, M. Nivelle, she was found guilty by the parliament, and condemned to be first beheaded and then burned. This sentence was pronounced on the 16th of July 1676, and executed the following day. On hearing the verdict against her, she retracted her former protestations, and made a full and ample confession of her crimes. One of the doctors of the Sorbonne, M. Pirot, who attended her as spiritual adviser during the twenty-four hours' interval between her sentence and death, has left a most fervid description of her last moments. According to his account, she manifested so sincere and pious a contrition for her enormities, and gave such satisfactory evidences of her conversion, that he, the confessor, would have been willing to exchange places with the penitent! The great painter, Le Brun, secured a good place for himself at her execution, with the view of studying the features of a condemned criminal in her position, and transferring them to his canvas. We are informed also, that among the crowds who thronged to see her die were several ladies of distinction. This last circumstance can hardly surprise us, when we recollect that, three quarters of a century later, the fashion and beauty of Paris sat for a whole day to witness, as a curious spectacle, the barbarities of the execution of Damiens.

## CHARLES VII. OF FRANCE AND JEANNE DARC.

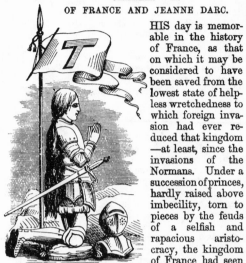

LA PUCELLE, FROM HER MONUMENT AT ORLEANS.

THIS day is memorable in the history of France, as that on which it may be considered to have been saved from the lowest state of helpless wretchedness to which foreign invasion had ever reduced that kingdom—at least, since the invasions of the Normans. Under a succession of princes, hardly raised above imbecility, torn to pieces by the feuds of a selfish and rapacious aristocracy, the kingdom of France had seen its crown surrendered to a foreigner, the king of England; its legitimate monarch, a weak-minded and slothful prince, had been driven into almost the last corner of his kingdom which was able to give him a shelter, and almost his last stronghold of any importance was in imminent danger of falling into the hands of his enemies, when, by a sudden turn of fortune, on the 17th of July 1429, Charles VII., relieved from his dangers, was crowned at Rheims, and all this wonderful revolution was the work of a simple peasant-girl.

The very origin, and much of the private history of this personage are involved in mystery, and have furnished abundant subjects of discussion for historians. There is even some doubt as to her real name; but the French antiquaries seem now to be agreed that it was Darc, and not D'Arc, and that it had no relation whatever to the village of Arc, from which it was formerly supposed to be derived. Hence the name of Joan of Arc, by which she is popularly known in England, is a mere mistake. There was the more room for doubt about her name, because in France, during her lifetime, she was usually spoken of as La Pucelle, or The Maid; or at most she was called Jeanne la Pucelle—Jeanne the Maid. Jeanne was born at Domremi, a small village on the river Meuse, at the extremity of the province of Champagne, it is supposed in the latter part of the year 1410, and was the youngest child of a respectable family of labouring peasants, named Jacques and Isabelle Darc. The girl appears to have laboured from childhood under a certain derangement of constitution, physically and mentally, which rendered her mind peculiarly open to superstitious feelings, and made her subject to trances and visions. The prince within whose territory her native village stood, the Duke of Bar, was a stanch partisan of Charles VII., who, as he had never been crowned, was still only spoken of as the dauphin, while on the other side of the river lay the territory of the Duke of Lorraine, an equally violent adherent of the Duke of Burgundy and the English party. It is not surprising, therefore, if the mind of the young Jeanne became preoccupied with the troubles of her unhappy country; the more so as she appears to have possessed much that was masculine in form and character. Under such feelings she believed at length that she saw in her visions St Michael the Archangel, who came to announce to her that she was destined to be the saviour of France, and subsequently introduced to her two female saints, Catherine and Margaret, who were to be her guides and protectors. She believed that her future communications came from these, either by their appearance to her in her trances, or more frequently by simple communications by a voice, which was audible only to herself.

She stated that she had been accustomed to these communications four or five years, when, in June 1428, she first communicated the circumstance to her parents, and declared that the voice informed her that she was to go into France to the Dauphin Charles, and that she was to conduct him to Rheims, and cause him to be crowned there. An uncle, who believed at once in her mission, took her to Vaucouleurs, the only town of any consequence in the neighbourhood, to ask its governor, Robert de Baudricourt, to send her with an escort to the court of the dauphin; but he treated her statement with derision, and Jeanne returned with her uncle to his home. However, the story of the Maid's visions had now been spread abroad, and created a considerable sensation; and Robert de Baudricourt, thinking that her story and her enthusiasm might be turned to some account, sent a report of the whole affair to court. News arrived about this time of the extreme danger of Orleans, closely besieged by the English, and, in the midst of the excitement caused by this intelligence, Jeanne spoke with so much vehemence of the necessity of being immediately sent to the dauphin, that two young gentlemen of the country, named Jean de Novelonpont and Bertrand de Poulengi, moved by her words, offered to conduct her to Chinon, where Charles was then holding his court. This, however, was rendered unnecessary by the arrival of orders from the court, addressed to Robert de Baudricourt. It appears that Charles's advisers thought also that some use might be made of the maiden's visions, and Baudricourt was directed to send her immediately to Chinon. The inhabitants of Vaucouleurs subscribed the money to pay the expenses of her journey, her uncle and another friend bought her a horse, and Robert de Baudricourt gave her a sword; and she cut her hair short, and adopted the dress of a man. Thus equipped, with six attendants, among whom were the two young gentlemen just mentioned, Jeanne left Vaucouleurs on the 18th of February 1429, and, after escaping some dangers on the way, arrived at Chinon on the 24th of the same month.

Such is the account of the commencement of Jeanne's mission, as it came out at a subsequent period on her trial. On her arrival at Chinon, Charles VII. appears to have become ashamed of the whole affair, and it was not till the 27th, after various consultations with his courtiers and ecclesiastics, that he at length consented to see her. No doubt, every care had been taken to give effect to the interview, and when first introduced, although Charles had disguised himself so as not to be distinguished from his courtiers, among whom he had placed himself, she is said to have gone direct to him, and fallen on her knees before him, and, among other things to have said: 'I tell thee from the Lord, that thou art the true heir of France, and the son of the king. This declaration had a particular importance, because it had been reported abroad, and seems to have been very extensively believed, that Charles was illegitimate. Charles now acknowledged that he was perfectly satisfied of the truth of the Maid's mission, and the belief in it became general, and was confirmed by the pretended discovery of a prophecy of Merlin, which foretold that France was to be saved by a virgin, who was to come from the Bosc-Chesnu. This, which meant the Wood of Oaks, was the name of the wood on the edge of which her native village of Domremi stood. Other precautions were taken, for it was necessary to dispel a prejudice which was rising against her—namely, that she was a witch—and she was carried to Poitiers, to be examined before a meeting of the ecclesiastics of Charles's party, who were assembled there, and who gave their opinion in her favour. She then returned to Chinon, while the young Duke of Alençon went to Blois, to collect the soldiers and the convoy of provisions and munitions of war, which the maiden was to conduct into Orleans. Jeanne now assumed the equipment and arms of a soldier, and was furnished with the usual attendance of the commander of an army. She went to Tours, to prepare for her undertaking; and while there, caused an emblematical standard to be made, and announced, on the authority of information received from her voices, that near the altar of St Catherine, in the church of Fierbois, a sword lay buried, which had five crosses engraved on the blade, and which was destined for her use. An armourer of Tours was sent to the spot, and he brought back a rusty sword, which he said had been found under the circumstances she described, and which answered to her description.

Reports of these proceedings had been carried into Orleans, and had raised the courage and resolution of the inhabitants and garrison, while the besiegers were greatly alarmed, for they also seem to have believed in Jeanne's mission in one sense, and expected that they would have to contend with Satanic agency. They believed from the first that she was a witch. At length, on the 27th of April, Jeanne left Blois with the convoy, accompanied by some of the military chiefs of the dauphin's party, and leading a force of 6000 or 7000 men. The enthusiasm she created produced an effect beyond anything that could be expected, and after serious disasters, the English were obliged, on the 8th of May, to raise the siege. The Maid herself carried the news of this great triumph to Charles VII., who was at Loche, and insisted on his repairing immediately to Rheims to be crowned. But, though he received her with honour, he exhibited none of her enthusiasm, and refused to follow her advice. In fact, his council had decided on following a totally different course of military operations to that which she wished; but they were at length persuaded to agree to the proposal for hastening the coronation, as soon as the course of the Loire between them and Rheims could be cleared of its English garrisons. The army was accordingly placed under the command of the Duke of Alençon, with orders to act by Jeanne's counsels. Gergeau, where the Duke of Suffolk commanded, was soon taken, and the garrison massacred. Having received considerable reinforcements, commanded by the Count of Vendôme, the Maid marched against the English forces, under the command of the celebrated Talbot, carried the bridge of Meung by force on the 15th of June, and reduced Beaugenci to capitulate in the night of the 17th. In their retreat, the English were overtaken and defeated with great slaughter, and Talbot himself was made prisoner. Charles shewed no gratitude for all these services, but listened to the councils of favourites, who were jealous of the maiden's fame, and who now began to throw obstacles in her way. He refused to yield to her proposal to attack Auxerre, and Troyes was only taken in contradiction to the dauphin's intentions. Châlons surrendered without resistance, and on the 16th, the French army came in view of Rheims, which was immediately abandoned by the English and Burgundian troops which formed its garrison. Next day, Charles VII. was crowned in the cathedral of Rheims with the usual ceremonies, and from this moment he received more openly the title of king.

From this moment the history of Jeanne Darc is one only of ingratitude and treachery on the part of those whom she had served, and who, intending only to use her as an instrument, seem to have believed that her utility was now at an end. Further successes, however, attended the march of the army to Paris, where the mass of the English forces were collected, under the command of the regent, Bedford. To the great grief of the Maid, the attack upon Paris was abandoned; and during the operations against the French capital, an accident happened, which was felt as an unfortunate omen, and disturbed the mind of the Maid herself. In anger at some soldiers who had disobeyed her orders, she struck them with the flat of the sword of Fierbois, which was supposed to have been sent to her from Heaven, and the blade broke. It seemed to many as though her principal charm was broken with it. The events which occurred during the winter were comparatively of small importance, but on the approach of spring, Jeanne, who was detained unwillingly at court, made her escape from it, and hastened to Lagni, on the Marne, which was besieged by the English and Burgundians, where she displayed her usual enthusiasm, though she was haunted by sinister thoughts, and believed that her voices told her of approaching disaster. After the Easter of 1430, the Duke of Bedford prepared to attack the important town of Compiègne, and on his way had laid siege to Choisi; whereupon Jeanne left Lagni, repaired to Compiègne, and immediately hastened with a body of troops to relieve Choisi. But she was ill seconded, was frustrated in her design, and deserted by her troops, and was obliged to retire sorrowfully into Compiègne, which was soon afterwards regularly besieged. Jeanne displayed her usual courage, but she was an object of dislike to the French governor, and was no longer regarded with the same enthusiasm by the soldiery as before. On the 23d of May, Jeanne went out of Compiègne at the head of a detachment of troops, to attack an English post, but after a desperate combat, she was obliged to retreat before superior numbers. As they approached Compiègne, one division of their pursuers made a rush to get before them, and cut off their retreat; on which the French fled in disorder, and, to their consternation, when they reached the head of the bridge of Compiègne, they found the barrier closed, and were left for some time in this terrible position. At length the barrier was opened, and the French struggled through, and then it was as suddenly closed again, before Jeanne—who, as usual, had taken her post in the rear—could get through. Whether this were done intentionally or not, is uncertain, but only a few soldiers were left with her, who were all killed or taken, while she managed to get clear of her assailants, and rode back to the bridge, but no notice was taken of her cries for assistance. In despair, she attempted to ride across the plain, but she was surrounded by her enemies, and one of the archers dragged her from her horse. She was thus secured and carried a prisoner to Marigni, where the Duke of Burgundy came to her. She was finally sold to the English, and delivered up as their prisoner in the month of October. During the intermediate period, the court of France had made no effort to obtain her liberation, or even shewn any sympathy for her fate.

The latter may be soon told. The question as to what should be done with the prisoner was soon taken out of the hands of her captors. No sooner was it known that the Maid was taken, than the vicar-general of the inquisition in France claimed her as a person suspected of heresy, under which name the crime of sorcery was included. When no attention had been paid to this demand—for it seems to have been thought doubtful on which of the two political sides of the great dispute the inquisition stood—another ecclesiastic, the bishop of Beauvais, a man of unscrupulous character, who was at this time devoted to the English interests, claimed her as having been taken within his diocese, and therefore under his ecclesiastical jurisdiction. After apparently some hesitation, it was determined to yield to this demand, and she was removed to Rouen, where Bedford had decided that the trial should take place, and where she appears to have been treated in her prison with great rigour and cruelty. Justice was as little observed in the proceedings on her trial, which began on the 21st of February 1431, and which ended, as might be expected, in her condemnation. The conduct of Bishop Cauchon and his creatures throughout was infamous in the extreme, but, on the whole, the proceedings resembled very much those of trials for witchcraft and heresy in general, and probably a very large portion of the inhabitants of England and France conscientiously believed her to be a witch. We judge, in such cases, by the sentiments of the age in which they occurred, and not by our own. On the morning of the 30th of May, Jeanne the Maiden was burned as a witch and heretic in the old market of Rouen, where a memorial to her has since been erected.*

## A COMFORTABLE BISHOP OF OLD TIMES.

July 17, 1506, James Stanley was made bishop of Ely. He was third son of the noted Thomas Stanley, who was created Earl of Derby in 1485, for his conduct on Bosworth Field. It is thought to have been by the influence of his step-mother, the Countess of Richmond, the king's mother, that he attained the dignity; and her historian calls it 'the worst thing she ever did.' Stanley was, indeed, a worldly enough churchman—*armis quam libris peritior*, more skilled in arms than in books, he has been described—'ane great viander as any in his days,' so another contemporary calls him—yet not wanting in the hospitality and the bountifulness to churches and colleges, which ranked high among the clerical virtues of his age. Having been warden of Manchester, he lies buried in the old collegiate (now cathedral) church there, in a side-chapel built by himself. Some lines about him, which occur in a manuscript History of the Derby Family, are worth quoting for the quaintness of their style, and the pleasant tenderness with which they touch upon his character:

'. . . . little priest's metal was in him . . . .
A goodly tall man, as was in all England,
And sped well in matters that he took in hand.
Of Ely many a day was he bishop there,
Builded Somersame, the bishop's chief manere:
Ane great viander as was in his days:
To bishops that then was this was no dispraise.
Because he was a priest, I dare do no less,
But leave, as I know not of his hardiness:
What priest hath a blow on the one ear, [will] suddenly
Turn the other likewise, for humility?
He would not do so, by the cross in my purse;
Yet I trust his soul fareth never the worse.
For he did acts boldly, divers, in his days,
If he had been no priest, had been worthy praise.
God send his soul to the heavenly company,
Farewell, godly James, Bishop of Ely!'

## A DANISH KING'S VISIT TO ENGLAND IN 1606.

On the 17th of July 1606, King Christian IV. of Denmark arrived in England, on a visit to his brother-in-law and sister, the king and queen of Great Britain. Christian was a hearty man, in the prime of life, fond of magnificence, and disposed to enjoy the world while it lasted. His relative, King James, was of similar disposition, though of somewhat different tastes. To him nothing was more delightful than a buck-hunt. Christian had more relish for gay suppers, and the society of gay ladies. During the three weeks he spent in England, he was incessantly active in seeing sights and giving and receiving entertainments. 'The month of his stay,' says Wilson, 'carried with it a pleasing countenance on every side, and recreations and pastimes flew as high a flight as love mounted on the wings of art and fancy, the suitable nature of the season on time's swift foot, could possibly arrive at. The court, city, and some parts of the country, with banquetings, barriers, and other gallantry, besides the manly sports of wrestling and brutish sports of baiting wild beasts, swelled to such a greatness, as if there were an intention in every particular man, this way, to have blown up himself.'

Another writer, named Roberts, describes the dresses of the king of Denmark's followers with all the gusto of a man-milliner. 'His pages and guard of his person were dressed in blue velvet embroidered with silver lace; they wore white

* See *Book of Days*, vol. i. p. 702, for a brief article stating grounds of doubt which have lately risen among French antiquaries as to the heretofore unquestioned fact of the death of La Pucelle at Rouen.

hats with silver bands, and white and blue stockings. His trumpeters had white satin doublets, and blue velvet hose, trimmed with silk and silver lace; their cloaks were of sundry colours, their hats white with blue and gold bands. His common soldiers wore white doublets, and blue hose trimmed with white lace. His trumpeters were led by a sergeant in a coat of carnation velvet, and his drummer rode upon a horse, with two drums, one of each side the horse's neck, whereon he struck two little mallets of wood, a thing very admirable to the common sort, and much admired. His trunks, boxes, and other provision for carriage were covered with red velvet trimmed with blue silk.'

Sir John Harrington, in a letter which has been printed in Park's *Nugæ Antiquæ*, gives us a lively picture of the carousals which marked the presence of this northern potentate at the British court.

'I came here,' says Sir John, 'a day or two before the Danish king came; and from the day he did come, until this hour, I have been well-nigh overwhelmed with carousals and sports of all kinds. The sports began each day in such manner and such sort as well-nigh persuaded me of Mohammed's paradise. We had women, and indeed wine too, in such plenty as would have astonished each sober beholder. Our feasts were magnificent, and the two royal guests did most lovingly embrace each other at table. I think the Dane hath strangely wrought on our good English nobles; for those, whom I never could get to taste good liquor, now follow the fashion, and wallow in beastly delights. The ladies abandon their sobriety, and seem to roll about in intoxication. One day a great feast was held, and after dinner the representation of Solomon's temple, and the coming of the queen of Sheba, was made, or (as I may better say) was meant to have been made before their majesties, by device of the Earl of Salisbury and others. But, alas! as all earthly things do fail to poor mortals in enjoyment, so did prove our presentment thereof. The lady who did play the queen's part, did carry most precious gifts to both their majesties; but, forgetting the steps arising to the canopy, overset her caskets into his Danish majesty's lap, and fell at his feet, though I rather think it was in his face. Much was the hurry and confusion; cloths and napkins were at hand, to make all clean. His majesty then got up, and would dance with the queen of Sheba; but he fell down and humbled himself before her, and was carried to an inner chamber, and laid on a bed of state; which was not a little defiled with the presents of the queen, which had been bestowed upon his garments; such as wine, cream, beverage, jellies, cakes, spices, and other good matters. The entertainment and show went forward, and most of the presenters went backward, or fell down; wine did so occupy their upper chambers. Now did appear, in rich dress, Hope, Faith, and Charity. Hope did essay to speak, but wine rendered her endeavours so feeble that she withdrew, and hoped the king would excuse her brevity; Faith was then all alone, for I am certain she was not joined with good works, and left the court in a staggering condition; Charity came to the king's feet, and seemed to cover the multitude of sins her sisters had committed: in some sort she made obeisance, and brought gifts; but said she would return home, as there was no gift which Heaven had not already given his majesty. She then returned to Hope and Faith, who were both in the lower hall. Next came Victory, in bright armour, and presented a rich sword to the king, who did not accept it, but put it by with his hand; and by a strange medley of versification, did endeavour to make suit to the king. But Victory did not triumph long; for, after much lamentable utterance, she was led away, like a silly captive, and laid to sleep on the outer steps of the ante-chamber. Now, did Peace make entrance, and strive to get forward to the king; but I grieve to tell how great wrath she did discover unto those of her attendants; and, much contrary to her semblance, most rudely made war with her olive-branch, and laid on the pates of those who did oppose her coming.'

It is supposed to have been from the fact of the extreme bacchanalianism practised by Christian at home, that Shakspeare attributed such habits to the king in *Hamlet*. The northern monarch was, however, duly anxious that his servants should practise sobriety. While he was in England, a marshal took care that any of them getting drunk should be sharply punished.

Christian appears to have been quite an enthusiastic sight-seer. Although he was observed to express no approbation, he wandered incessantly about the metropolis, 'so that neither Powles, Westminster, nor the Exchange escaped him.' He was also fond of the amusements of the tilting-yard. 'On a solemn tilting-day,' writes Sir Dudley Carleton, 'the king of Denmark would needs make one; and in an old black armour, without plume or basses, or any rest for his lance, he played his prizes so well, that Ogerio himself never did better. At a match between our king and him, running at the ring, it was his hap never almost to miss it; while ours had the ill-luck scarce ever to come near it, which put him in no small impatience.'

The custom of making extravagant gifts at leave-takings was a characteristic feature of that sumptuous style of living amongst the high-born and wealthy, prevalent during the seventeenth century. James, so long as his exchequer continued pretty well replenished, distinguished himself by the magnificence of his princely largess. Indeed, taking into account the vast sums lavished on favourites, in addition to the debts of impoverished nobles, paid by him once and again, we are no ways astonished at the unkingly pecuniary straits to which he was continually reduced. A letter preserved amongst the state-papers, dated August 20, 1606, descriptive of the leave-taking between James and Christian of Denmark, narrates the following specimen of reckless profusion in the former, at a time when his necessities were so notoriously great, that his own subjects caricatured him as a beggar with his pockets turned inside out. 'The two kings,' says Sir Dudley Carleton, 'parted on Monday sevennight, as well pleased with each other as kings usually are upon interview. The gifts were great on our king's side, and only tolerable on the other. Imprimis, a girdle and hangers, with rapiers and daggers set with stones, which I heard valued by a goldsmith at £15,000. Then the old cup of state, which was the chief ornament of Queen Elizabeth's rich cupboard, of £1000 price; Item, a George, as rich as could be made in proportion; Item, a saddle embroidered with rich pearls; four war-steeds with their appropriate furniture and caparisons; two ambling geldings and two nags. To the king of Denmark's six counsellors were given £2000 worth of plate, and each of them a chain of £100; and to twenty-two gentlemen, chains of £50 apiece; and £1000 in money to the servants, the guard, and the sailors in the ship the king went in. The king of Denmark gave nothing to the king, as I heard, but made an offer of his second ship, in hope to have it requited with the *White Bear;* but that match was broken off by my Lord of Salisbury, and he had his own given back with thanks. To the king's children he gave £6000, and as much to the king's household.' Then follows a word-picture of a royal naval banquet in the year 1606, sketched with infinite humour, and strikingly illustrative of the social habits of that age. James takes leave of his brother on shipboard. 'The feasting was plenteous, but not riotous at court; but at the ships they played the seamen for good-fellowship. First at Chatham, where twenty-two of the king's were set out in their best equipage, and two especially, the *Elizabeth Jonas* and the *Bear*, trimmed up to feast in, betwixt which there was a large railed bridge built upon masts, and in the midst betwixt them both, butteries and kitchens built upon lighters and flat-boats. All things were there performed with such order and sumptuousness, that the king of Denmark confessed that he would not have believed such a thing could have been done, unless he had seen it. At the Danish ships, where was the last farewell, what was wanting in meat and other ceremony was helped out with drink and gunshot; for at every health—of which there were twenty—the ship the kings were in made nine shot; and every other, there being eight in all, three; and the two blockhouses at Gravesend, where the fleet lay, each of them, six; at which I must tell you, by the way, our king was little pleased, and took such order in his own ships as not to be annoyed by the smell of powder; but good store of healths made him so hearty, that he bid them at the last "shoot and spare not," and very resolutely commanded the trumpets to sound him a point of war.'

'Give me the cups;
And let the kettle to the trumpet speak,
The trumpet to the cannoneer without,
The cannons to the heaven, the heaven to earth,
Now the king drinks to Hamlet.'

## RICH BEGGARS.

There are multitudes of instances of beggars who, amid squalor, rags, and dirt utterly miserable, contrive to amass considerable sums of money. For obvious reasons, they generally conceal their wealth during life, and it is only when the breath is out of their body that the golden hypocrisy is discovered. Usually, the hoarded coins are found sewn up in rags or straw-beds, or otherwise hidden in holes and corners; it is only in a few instances that the beggar ventures to invest his money in a bank. Among the many recorded examples of rich beggars, have been Daniel Eagle, who begged for thirty years in London, and lived in a room which was never entered by any one but himself, and never cleaned during the whole period; after his death, coins to the value of £25 were found there.—Margaret Coles, who died in wretched filth in St Giles's, at the age of 101, and in whose hovel was found £30 in gold and silver, and £10 in copper.—Margaret Everett, an equally squalid beggar, who left £150 behind her.—Esther Davies, who died in London at the advanced age of 103, and who for thirty years had the double chances of a street-beggar and a parish pauper; she left £160.—Mary Wilkinson, beggar and bone-grubber, whose rags of clothing concealed £300 in money.—Alice Bond, who had risen to the dignity of £300 in the funds, besides £50 in guineas, half-guineas, and seven-shilling pieces, and £23 in silver.—Frances Beet, whose bed and rickety furniture yielded a booty of no less than £800.—And 'Poor Joe all alone,' a famous character about a century ago, who wore a long beard, and had not lain in a bed for fifty years; he left £3000, and with it a will, by which he bequeathed all the money to certain widows and orphans. Foreign countries are not without instances of like kind. Witness the case of Dandon, of Berlin, who died in 1812; he was competent to teach as a professor of languages during the day, and went out begging at night. After his death, 20,000 crowns were found secreted under the floor of his room. He had refused to see a brother for thirty-seven years, because he once sent him a letter without prepaying the postage. This Dandon, however, was an example rather of the miser than of the beggar, popularly so considered.

Some beggars have been remarkable quite as much for their eccentricity, as for the amount of money they left behind them. Such was the case with William Stevenson, who died at Kilmarnock on the 17th of July 1817. Although bred a mason, the greater part of his life was spent as a beggar. About the year 1787, he and his wife separated, making this strange agreement—that whichever of them was the first to propose a reunion, should forfeit £100 to the other. According to the statements in the Scotch newspapers, there is no evidence that they ever saw each other again. In 1815, when about 85 years old, Stevenson was seized with an incurable disease, and was confined to his bed. A few days before his death, feeling his end to be near, he sent for a baker, and ordered twelve dozen burial-cakes, a large quantity of sugared biscuit, and a good supply of wine and spirits. He next sent for a joiner, and instructed him to make a good, sound, dry, roomy, 'comfortable' coffin. Next he summoned a grave-digger, whom he requested to select a favourable spot in the churchyard of Riccarton, and there dig a roomy and comfortable grave. This done, he ordered an old woman who attended him, to go to a certain nook, and bring out £9, to pay all these preliminary expenses: assuring her that she was remembered in his will. Shortly after this he died. A neighbour came in to search for his wealth, which had been shrouded in much mystery. In one bag was found large silver pieces, such as dollars and half-dollars, crowns and half-crowns; in a heap of musty rags, was found a collection of guineas and seven-shilling pieces; and in a box were found bonds of various amounts, including one for £300—giving altogether a sum of about £900. A will was also found, bequeathing £20 to the old woman, and most of the remainder to distant relations, setting aside sufficient to give a feast to all the beggars who chose to come and see his body 'lie in state.' The influx was immense; and after the funeral, all retired to a barn which had been fitted up for the occasion; and there they indulged in revelries but little in accordance with the solemn season of death.

One curious circumstance regarding a beggar connected with the town of Dumfries, we can mention on excellent authority: a son of his passed through the class of Humanity (Latin), in the university of Edinburgh, under the superintendence of Professor Pillans.

# JULY 18.

St Symphorosa, and her seven sons, martyrs, 120. St Philastrius, bishop of Brescia, confessor, 4th century. St Arnoul, martyr, about 534. St Arnoul, bishop of Metz, confessor, 640. St Frederic, bishop of Utrecht, martyr, 838. St Odulph, canon of Utrecht, confessor, 9th century. St Bruno, bishop of Segni, confessor, 1125.

---

*Born.*—Dr John Dee, astrologer and mathematician, 1527, *London;* Zachary Ursinus, celebrated German divine, 1534, *Breslau;* Dr Robert Hooke, natural philosopher, 1635, *Freshwater, Isle of Wight;* Saverio Bettinelli, Italian author, 1718, *Mantua;* Gilbert White, naturalist, 1720, *Selborne.*

*Died.*—Pope John XVIII., 1009; Godfrey of Bouillon, king of Jerusalem, 1100; Francesco Petrarca (*Petrarch*), great Italian poet and sonneteer, 1374, *Arqua, near Padua;* Abraham Sharp, mechanist and calculator, 1742, *Little Horton, Yorkshire;* Thomas Sherlock, bishop of London, 1761, *Fulham.*

## REV. GILBERT WHITE.

Gilbert White is one of those happy souls who without painful effort, in the quiet pursuit of their own pleasures, have registered their names among the *dii minores* of literature. Biography scarcely records a finer instance of prolonged peaceful and healthful activity. His life seems to have been a perfect idyll.

Selborne, with which White's name is indissolubly associated, is a village of one straggling street, about fifty miles from London, situated in a corner of Hampshire, bordering on Sussex. In the house in which he spent his life and in which he died, White was born on the 18th July 1720. His father was a gentleman of comfortable income, who educated him for a clergyman. He gained a fellowship at Oxford, and served as a proctor, to the surprise of his family, who thought it a strange office for one of his habits, and that he would be more observant of the swallows in the Christchurch meadows than the undergraduates in the High Street. He had frequent opportunities of accepting college livings, but his fondness for 'the shades of old Selborne, so lovely and sweet,' outweighed every desire for preferment. In his native village he settled, and the ample leisure secured from clerical duty he devoted to the minute and assiduous study of nature. He was an outdoor naturalist, and kept diaries in which the progression of the seasons, and every fact which fell under his eye, were entered with the exactness which a merchant gives to his ledger. The state of the weather, hot or cold, sunny or cloudy, the variations of the wind, of the thermometer and barometer, the quantity of rain-fall, the dates on which the trees burst into leaf and plants into blossom, the appearance and disappearance of birds and insects, were all accurately recorded. On the 21st of June, he tells us that house-martins, which had laid their eggs in an old nest, had hatched them, and got the start of those which had built new nests by ten days or a fortnight. He relates that dogs come into his garden at night, and eat his gooseberries; that rooks and crows destroy an immense number of chaffers; and that, but for them, the chaffers would destroy everything. His neighbours' crops, fields, and gardens, cattle, pigs, poultry, and bees were all looked after. He chronicled his ale and beer, as they were brewed by his man Thomas. The births of his nephews and nieces were duly entered, to the number of sixty-three.

Selborne was a choice home for a naturalist. It is a place of great rural beauty, and of thorough seclusion. The country around is threaded with deep sandy lanes overgrown with stunted oaks, hazels, hawthorns, and dog-roses, and the banks are covered with primroses, strawberries, ferns, and almost every English wild-flower. In White's time, the roads were usually impassable for carriages in winter, and Selborne held little intercourse with the world. Once a year, White used to visit Oxford, leaving the registration of the weather to Thomas, who was well versed in his master's business. Happily, White's brothers had an interest in natural history only second to his own, and with them and other congenial friends he kept up a lively correspondence. It was by the persuasion of his brother Thomas, a fellow of the Royal Society, that he was induced to overcome a horror of publicity and reviewers, and to issue in quarto, in 1789, the *Natural History of Selborne*, compiled from a series of letters addressed to Thomas Pennant and Daines Barrington. Four years afterwards, he died, 26th June 1793, aged seventy-three. His habits were regular and temperate, his disposition social and cheerful; he was a good story-teller, and a favourite with young and old, at home and abroad. His autobiography is in his book, and ardent admirers who have haunted Selborne for further particulars concerning the philosophical old bachelor, have learned little more than was spoken by an old dame, who had nursed several of the White family: 'He was a still, quiet body: there wasn't a bit of harm in him, I'll assure ye, sir; there wasn't indeed!'

The paternal acres of White at Selborne are, of course, to the great body of British naturalists, a classic ground. By a happy chance, they were long in the possession of Professor Bell, an eminent naturalist, fully competent to appreciate the sentimental charm which invests them, and of a social character to banish envy among his brethren even for such an extraordinary piece of good-fortune. In 1877, Bell published an edition of White's classical work, in two volumes. Since the death of Professor Bell in 1879, the home of the naturalist has passed into other hands.

---

## WAYLAND SMITH'S CAVE.

This now well-known monument of a remote antiquity stands in the parish of Ashbury, on the western boundaries of Berkshire, among the chalk-hills which form a continuation of the Wiltshire downs, in a district covered with ancient remains. It is simply a primitive sepulchre, which, though now much dilapidated, has originally consisted of a rather long rectangular apartment, with two lateral chambers, formed by upright stones, and roofed with large slabs. It was, no doubt, originally covered with a mound of earth, which in course of time has been in great part removed. It belongs to a class of monuments which is usually called Celtic, but, if this be a correct denomination, we must take it, no doubt, as meaning Celtic during the Roman period, for it stands near a Roman road, the Ridgway, which was the position the Romans chose above all others, while the Britons in the earlier period, if they had any high-roads at all, which is very doubtful, chose in preference the tops of hills for their burial-place. A number of early sepulchral monuments might be pointed out in different parts of our island, of the same class, and more important than Wayland Smith's Cave, but it has obtained an especial celebrity through two or three circumstances.

In the first place, this is the only monument of the kind which we find directly named in an Anglo-Saxon document. It happened to be on the

WAYLAND SMITH'S CAVE.

line of boundary between two Anglo-Saxon estates, and, therefore, became a marked object. In the deed of conveyance of the estate in which this monument is mentioned, of a date some time previous to the Norman Conquest, it is called Welandes Smiththan, which means Weland's Smithy, or forge, so that its modern name, which is a mere slight corruption from the Anglo-Saxon one, dates itself from a very remote period. In the time of Lysons, to judge from his account of it, it was still known merely by the name of Wayland Smith, so that the further corruption into Wayland Smith's Cave appears to be of very recent date. It is also worthy of remark, that the Anglo-Saxon name appears to prove that in those early times the monument had been already uncovered of its earth, and was no longer recognised as a sepulchral monument, for the Anglo-Saxons would hardly have given the name of a forge, or smithy, to what they knew to be a tomb; so that we have reason for believing that many of our cromlechs and monuments of this description had already been uncovered of their mounds in Anglo-Saxon times. They were probably opened in search of treasure.

But, perhaps, the most curious circumstance of all connected with this monument is its legend. It has been the popular belief among the peasantry in modern times, that should it happen to a traveller passing this way that his horse cast a shoe, he had only to take the animal to the 'cave,' which they supposed to be inhabited by an invisible, to place a groat on the copestone, and to withdraw to a distance from which he could not see the operation, and on his return, after a short absence, he would find his horse properly shod, and the money taken away. To explain this, it is necessary only to state that, in the primitive Anglo-Saxon and Teutonic mythology, Weland was the mythic smith, the representative of the ancient Vulcan, the Greek Hephaistos. We have a singular proof, too, of the extreme antiquity of the Berkshire story, in a Grecian popular legend which has been preserved by the Greek scholiast on Apollonius Rhodius. We are told that one of the localities which Hephaistos, or Vulcan, especially haunted was the Vulcanian islands, near Sicily; and the scholiast tells us, that 'it was formerly said that, whoever chose to carry there a piece of unwrought iron, and at the same time deposit the value of the labour, would, on presenting himself there on the following morning, find it made into a sword, or whatever other object he had desired.' We have here, at this very remote period, precisely the same legend, and connected with the representative of the same mythic character, as that of the Berkshire cromlech; and we have a right, therefore, to assume that the same legend had existed in connection with the same character, at that far-distant period before the first separation of the different branches of the Teutonic family, and when Weland, and Hephaistos, and Vulcan were one.

All our readers know how skilfully our great northern bard, Sir Walter Scott, introduced the Berkshire legend of Wayland Smith into the romance of *Kenilworth*, and he has thus given a celebrity to the monument which it would never otherwise have enjoyed. Yet, although in his story the mythic character of Wayland Smith is lost, and he stands before us a rather commonplace piece of humanity, yet every reader must feel interested in knowing something of the real character of the personage, whose name is famous through all medieval poetry in the west, and who held a prominent place in the heathen mythology of our early Saxon forefathers. His story is given in the *Eddas*.

Weland, as we have said, was the Vulcan of the Teutonic mythology. He was the youngest of the three sons of Wade, the alf, or demi-god; and when a child, his father intrusted him to the dwarfs in the interior of the mountains, who lived among the metals, that they might instruct him in their wonderful skill in forging, and in making weapons and jewellery, so that, under their teaching, the youth became a wonderful smith. The scene of this legend is placed by the Edda in Iceland, where the three brothers, like all Scandinavian heroes, passed much of their time in hunting, in which they pursued the game on skates. In the course of these expeditions, they settled for a while in Ulfdal, where, one morning, finding on the banks of a lake three Valkyrier, or nymphs, with their elf-garments beside them, they seized and took them for their wives, and lived with them eight years, at the end of which period the Valkyrier became tired of their domestic life, and flew away during the absence of their husbands. When the three brothers returned, two of them set off in search of their fugitive spouses; but Weland remained patiently at home, working in his forge to make gold rings, which he strung upon a willow-wand, to keep them till the expected return of his wife. There lived at this time a king of Sweden, named Niduth, who had two sons, and a daughter named Baudvild, or, in the Anglo-Saxon form of the name, Beadohild. The possession of a skilful smith, and the consequent command of his labour, was looked upon as a great prize; and when Niduth heard that Weland was in Ulfdal, he set off, with a strong body of his armed followers, to seek him. They arrived at his hut while he was away hunting, and, entering it, examined his rings, and the king took one of them as a gift for his daughter, Baudvild. Weland returned at night, and made a fire in his hut to roast a piece of bear's flesh for his supper; and when the flames arose, they gave light to the chamber, and Weland's eyes fell on his rings, which he took down and counted, and thus found that one was missing. This circumstance was to him a cause of joy, for he supposed that his wife had returned and taken the ring, and he laid him down to slumber; but while he was asleep, King Niduth and his men returned, and bound him, and carried him away to the king's palace in Sweden. At the suggestion of the queen, they hamstringed him, that he might not be able to escape, and placed him in a forge in a small island, where he was compelled to work for the king, and where anybody but the latter was forbidden to go under severe penalties. Weland brooded over his revenge, and accident offered him the first opportunity of indulging it. The greediness of the king's two sons had been excited by the reported wealth of Weland's forge, and they paid a secret visit to it, and were astonished at the treasures which the wily smith presented to their view. He promised that they should have them all, if they would come to him in the utmost secrecy early next morning; but when they arrived, he suddenly closed the door, cut off their heads, and buried their bodies in the marshy ground on which the forge was built. He made of the skulls, plated with silver, drinking-cups for the king's table; of their eyes, gems for the queen; and of their teeth, a collar of pearls, which he sent as a present to the princess. The latter was encouraged to seek Weland's assistance to mend her ring, which had been accidentally broken; and, to conceal the accident from her father, she went secretly to the forge, where the smith completed his vengeance by offering violence to her person, and sent her away dishonoured. While he had been meditating vengeance, Weland had also been preparing the means of escape, and now, having fitted on a pair of wings of his own construction, he took flight from his forge. He halted for a moment on the wall of the enclosure of the palace, where he called for the king and queen, told them all the circumstances of the murder of their sons and the dishonour of their daughter, and then continued his flight, and was heard of no more. The Princess Baudvild, in due time, gave birth to a daughter, who also was a celebrated hero of the early German mythology. It will be remarked, that the lameness of Weland is accounted for in a different manner from that of Vulcan in the more refined mythology of the classical ages.

As the various branches of the Teutonic race spread towards the west, they carried with them their common legends, but soon located them in the countries in which they settled, and after a few generations they became established as local legends. Thus, among the Scandinavians, the scene of Weland's adventures was laid in Iceland and Sweden; while among the earlier Teutons, it appears to have been fixed in some part of Germany; and the Anglo-Saxons, no doubt, placed it in England. We have found the name, and one of the legends connected with it, fixed in a remote corner of Berkshire, where they have been preserved long after their original import was forgotten. It is one of the most curious examples of the great durability of popular legends of all kinds. We know that the whole legend of Weland the smith was perfectly well known to the Anglo-Saxons to a late period of their monarchy.

## THE AUTHOR OF 'BARON MUNCHAUSEN.'

Who is there that has not, in his youth, enjoyed *The Surprising Travels and Adventures of Baron Munchausen, in Russia, the Caspian Sea, Iceland, Turkey, &c.*, a slim volume—all too short, indeed—illustrated by a formidable portrait of the baron in front, with his broad-sword laid over his shoulder, and several deep gashes on his manly countenance? I presume they must be few.

This book appears to have been first published, in a restricted form, by one Kearsley, a bookseller in Fleet Street, in 1786; a few years afterwards, it was reprinted, with a considerable addition of palpably inferior matter, by H. D. Symonds of Paternoster Row. The author's name was not given, and it has, till a very recent date, remained little or not at all known. There can hardly be a more curious piece of neglected biography.

The author of the baron's wonderful adventures is now ascertained to have been Rodolph Eric Raspe, a learned and scientific German, who died in the latter part of 1794 at Mucross, in the south of Ireland, while conducting some mining operations there. Much there was of both good and ill about poor Raspe. Let us not press matters too hard against one who has been able to contribute so much to the enjoyment of his fellow-creatures. But, yet, let the truth be told. Be it known, then, that this ingenious man, who was born at Hanover in 1737, commenced life in the service of the landgrave of Hesse Cassel as professor of archæology, inspector of the public cabinet of medals, keeper of the national library, and a councillor, but disgraced himself by putting some of the valuables intrusted to him in pawn, to raise money for some temporary necessities. He disappeared, and was advertised for by the police as the Councillor Raspe, a man with red hair, who usually appeared in a scarlet dress embroidered with gold, but sometimes in black, blue, or gray clothes.* He was arrested at Clausthal, but escaped during the night, and made his way to England, where he chiefly resided for the remainder of his days.

It will be heard with pain, that before this lamentable downbreak in life, Raspe had manifested decided talents in the investigation of questions in geology and mineralogy. He published at Leipsic, in 1763, a curious volume in Latin, on the formation of volcanic islands, and the nature of petrified bodies. In 1769, there was read at the Royal Society in London, a Latin paper of his, on the teeth of elephantine and other animals found in North America, and it is surprising at what rational and just conclusions he had arrived. Raspe had detected the specific peculiarities, distinguishing these teeth from those of the living elephant, and saw no reason for disbelieving that some large kinds of elephants might formerly live in cold climates; being exactly the views long after generally adopted on this subject.

The exact time of the flight to England is not known; but in 1776, he is found publishing in London a volume on *Some German Volcanoes and their Productions*—necessarily extinct volcanoes—thus again shewing his early apprehension of facts then little if at all understood, though now familiar.

* *Biographie Universelle.*

And in the ensuing year, he gave forth a translation of the Baron Born's Travels in Tameswar, Transylvania, and Hungary—a mineralogical work of high reputation. In 1780, Horace Walpole speaks of him as 'a Dutch savant,' who has come over here, and who was preparing to publish two old manuscripts 'in infernal Latin,' on oil-painting, which proved Walpole's own idea that the use of oil-colours was known before the days of Van Eyck. 'He is poor,' says the virtuoso of Strawberry Hill; the natural sequel to which statement is another three months later: 'Poor Raspe is arrested by his tailor.' 'I have sent him a little money,' adds Walpole, 'and he hopes to recover his liberty; but I question whether he will be able to struggle on here.'* By Walpole's patronage, the book was actually published in April 1781.

In this year, Raspe announced a design of travelling in Egypt, to collect its antiquities; but while the scheme was pending, he obtained employment in certain mines in Cornwall. He was residing as 'storemaster' at Dalcoath Mines, in that district, when he wrote and published his *Travels of Baron Munchausen.*† Previously to this time, his delinquency at Cassel having become known, the Royal Society erased his name from their honorary list; and he threatened, in revenge, to print in the form of their Philosophical Transactions the *Unphilosophical Transactions* of the English savans, with their characters. This matter seems to have blown over.

And now we have to introduce our hero in a new connection with English literature. The facts are fully known to us, and there can be no harm in stating them. Be it understood, then, that Raspe paid a visit to Scotland in the summer and autumn of 1789, for the professed purpose of searching in various districts for minerals. It was announced in the *Scots Magazine* for October, that he had discovered copper, lead, iron, cobalt, manganese, &c.; that the marble of Tiree, the iron of Glengarry, and the lead on the Breadalbane property were all likely to turn out extremely well. From Sutherland he had brought specimens of the finest clay; there was 'every symptom of coal,' and a fine vein of heavy spar had been discovered. He had now begun his survey of Caithness. From another source we learn that a white saline marble in Icolmkill had received his attention.‡ As to Caithness, here lay probably the loadstone that had brought him into Scotland, in the person of Sir John Sinclair of Ulbster, a most benevolent gentleman, who, during a long life, was continually engaged in useful projects, chiefly designed for the public benefit, and of novel kinds. With him Raspe took up his abode for a considerable time, at his spray-beaten castle on the Pentland Firth; and members of the family still speak of their father's unfailing appreciation of the infinite intelligence and facetiousness of his visitor's conversation. Sir John had, some years before, discovered a small vein of yellow mundick on the moor of Skinnet, four miles from Thurso. The Cornish miners he consulted told him that the mundick was itself of no value, but a good sign of other valuable minerals not far off. In

* See *Index to Walpole's Correspondence.*

† *Gentleman's Magazine*, Nov. 1856.

‡ Walker's *Econ. Hist. of Hebrides*, ii. 379.

their peculiar jargon, 'white mundick was a good *horseman*, and always rode on *a good load*.'* Sir John now employed Raspe to examine the ground, not designing to mine it himself, but to let it to others if it should turn out favourably. For a time, this investigation gave the proprietor very good hopes. Masses of a bright heavy mineral were brought to Thurso Castle, as foretastes of what was coming. But, in time the bubble burst, and it was fully concluded by Sir John Sinclair, that the ores which appeared were all brought from Cornwall, and planted in the places where they were found. Miss Catherine Sinclair has often heard her father relate the story, but never with the slightest trace of bitterness. On the contrary, both he and Lady Sinclair always said, that the little loss they made on the occasion was amply compensated by the amusement which the mineralogist had given them, while a guest in their house.

Such was the author of *Baron Munchausen*, a man of great natural penetration and attainments, possessed of lively general faculties, and well fitted for a prominent position in life. Wanting, however, the crowning grace of probity, he never quite got his head above water, and died in poverty and obscurity. It will be observed that, in his mining operations in Caithness, he answers to the character of Dousterswivel in the *Antiquary;* and there is every reason to believe that he gave Scott the idea of that character, albeit the baronet of Ulbster did not prove to be so extremely imposed upon as Sir Arthur Wardour, or in any other respect a prototype of that ideal personage. Of all Raspe's acknowledged works, learned, ingenious, and far-seeing, not one is now remembered, and his literary fame must rest with what he probably regarded as a mere *jeu d'esprit*. It may be remarked that a translation of the Baron into German was published by the ingenious Bürger in 1787. This was very proper, for most of the marvels were of German origin. Some of those connected with hunting are to be found, 'in a dull prosy form, in Henry Bebel's *Facetiæ*, printed in Strasburg in 1508; others of the tales are borrowed from Castiglioni's *Cortegians*, and other known sources.'†

# JULY 19.

St Macrina, virgin, 379. St Arsenius, anchoret, 449. St Symmachus, pope and confessor, 514. St Vincent de Paul, founder of the Lazarites, confessor, 1660.

*Born.*—Conrad Vorstius, or Vorst, celebrated German divine, 1569, *Cologne;* Gilbert Sheldon, archbishop of Canterbury, erecter of the Sheldon theatre at Oxford, 1598, *Staunton, Staffordshire;* John Martin, celebrated painter, 1789, *Haydon Bridge, Northumberland.*

*Died.*—Dr John Caius, physician and author, founder of Caius College, Cambridge, 1573, *Cambridge;* William Somerville, author of *The Chase*, 1742, *Edstone, Warwickshire;* Nathaniel Hooke, author of the *Roman History*, 1764, *Hedsor;* Captain Matthew Flinders, Australian explorer, 1814; Professor John Playfair, writings in natural philosophy, geology, &c., 1819, *Edinburgh;* Iturbide, Mexican leader, shot at Padillo, 1824.

* *Stat. Account of Scotland*, xx. 538.
† F. N., in *Gentleman's Magazine*, Nov. 1856.

## BATTLE OF HALIDON HILL.

July 19, 1333, is the date of a remarkable battle between the Scots and English at Halidon Hill. Stowe's account of the conflict is picturesque and interesting, though not in every particular to be depended on. The youthful Edward III. had laid siege to Berwick; and a large Scottish army, animated, doubtless, by recollections of Bannockburn, came to relieve the town. 'At length,' says Stowe, 'the two armies appointed to fight, and setting out upon Halidon Hill [near Berwick], there cometh forth of the Scots camp a certain stout champion of great stature, who, for a fact by him done, was called *Turnbull*. He, standing in the midst between the two armies, challenged all the Englishmen, any one, to fight with him a combat. At length Robert Venale, knight, a Norfolk-man, requesting licence of the king, being armed, with his sword drawn, marcheth toward the champion, meeting by the way a certain black mastiff dog, which waited on the champion, whom with his sword he suddenly strake, and cut him off at his loins; at the sight whereof the master of the dog slain was much abashed, and in his battle more wary and fearful; whose left hand and head also afterward this worthy knight cut off. After this combat both the armies met, but they fighting scarce half an hour, certain of the Scots being slain, they closed their army (which was in three) all in one battle; but at length flying, the king followed them, taking and chasing them into lakes and pits for the space of five miles.' The honest chronicler sets down the loss of the Scots infantry on this occasion at 35,000, besides 1300* horsemen, being more than ten times the loss of the British at Waterloo. Such exaggerations are common among the old chroniclers, and historians generally, before the days of statistics. More probably, the slain on the side of the vanquished did not exceed two thousand. It will be heard with some surprise, that there is preserved a song, in the English language, written at the time upon this victory of King Edward. It appears as one of a series, composed upon the king's wars, by one Lawrence Minot, of whom nothing else is known.* It opens with a strain of exultation over the fallen pride of the Scots, and then proceeds to a kind of recital of facts—

'A little fro that foresaid town [Berwick],
Halidon Hill, that is the name,
There was crackèd many a crown
Of wild Scots,† and als of tame.‡
There was their banner borne all down,
To mak sic boast they war' to blame;
But, nevertheless, ay are they boune
To wait England with sorrow and shame.

Shame they have, as I hear say;
At Dundee now is done their dance;
And went they must another way,
Even through Flanders into France.
On Philip Valois fast cry they,
There for to dwell, and him avance;
And nothing list them than of play,
Sin' them is tide this sary chance.

* See *Political Poems and Songs relating to English History*. Published under direction of the Master of the Rolls. 1859. Vol. i.
† Highlanders. ‡ Lowlanders.

This sary chance is them betide,
For they were false and wonder fell;
For cursed caitiffs are they kid,
And full of treason, sooth to tell.
Sir John the Cumin had they hid,
In haly kirk they did him quell; *
And therefore many a Scottis bride
With dole are dight that they must dwell.'

The bard then changes to another strain, in which he joyfully proclaims how King Edward had revenged Bannockburn:

'Scots out of Berwick and of Aberdeen,
At the Bannockburn war ye too keen;
There slew ye many saikless, as it was seen,
And now has King Edward wroken it, I ween:
It is wroken, I ween, weel worth the while,
War it with the Scots, for they are full of guile.

Where are the Scots of St John's town?
The boast of your banner is beaten all down;
When ye boasting will bide, Sir Edward is boune
For to kindle you care, and crack your crown;
He has cracked your crown, well worth the while;
Shame betide the Scots, for they are full of guile.'

* * * *

## THE CAMPAGNA OF ROME DURING THE MONTH OF JULY.

In Italy, July is the month of bread; August, the month of wine: in the first, the Roman peasants reap; in the second, they gather the grapes. The harvest-people come, for the most part, from

MASS IN THE CAMPAGNA.

the Neapolitan provinces, especially the Abruzzi mountains; they leave their homes, carrying their families with them, pitch their tents every night for sleeping, and might be taken for Bedouin hordes or gipsy tribes. They hire their labour for the small sum of twenty baiocchi a day, out of which they manage to save in order to carry home a little treasure. The Roman Campagna is by no means an uncultivated desert; the greater part is ploughed, and produces wheat, but, on account of miasma, it is uninhabited and uninhabitable, and the cultivators of the ground are obliged to come from great distances. On Sunday, the priests attend and perform mass for the reapers in a kind of movable church drawn by oxen, and provided with all the necessary apparatus for the celebration of the service. Mass in the Campagna is a very picturesque scene: strong brawny men in their shirt-sleeves and short trousers; women in the satin dress which was the one worn at their marriage, and is used for the Sunday costume ever after; children of every age, from the nursling playing on its mother's breast or peacefully sleeping in the cradle; hunters, who sometimes join the assembly with their dogs; the priest officiating in the wooden chapel suspended between the two-wheeled wagon; still further, the tents supported by two poles; the horses tranquilly grazing; the harnessed oxen, which will soon carry away the nomade edifice to another spot; the beautiful blue hills which surround the verdant, golden landscape; the burning sun shedding torrents of light and fire over all nature; the deep silence, scarcely interrupted by the words of the priest, the prayers of the crowd, the neighing of the horses, or the humming of insects—all unite to form a scene interesting both in a physical and moral sense.

When the reaping is over, then comes the operation of thrashing, which they call *la trita.* For this purpose, they prepare a level thrashing-floor on which to spread the sheaves; fasten together six horses, and make them tread over the straw until the grain has all fallen out. When finished, they rake up the straw, stack it, and pile up the grain into heaps, on the top of which they place a cross.

## LETTER FRANKING.

Long before the legal settlements of the post-office in the seventeenth century, the establishment of the *post* was kept up at the instance of the reigning sovereign for his special service and behoof. Under the Stuarts, the postal resources of the kingdom were greatly developed, and all classes were made to share alike in the benefits of the post. Cromwell made many improvements in the post-office, though the reasons which he assigned for so doing, 'that they will be the best means to discover and prevent many dangerous and wicked designs against the commonwealth,' are open to exception and censure, viewed as we view post-office espionage at this date. In the reign of the second Charles, the post-office for the first time became the subject of parliamentary enactments, and it was at this time that the franking privilege, hitherto enjoyed by the sovereign and the executive alone, was extended to parliament. A committee of the House of Commons, in the year 1735, reported 'that the privilege of franking letters by the knights, &c., chosen to represent the Commons in parliament, began with the creating of a post-office in the kingdom by act of parliament.' The bill here referred to was introduced into the House of Commons in 1660, and it contained a proviso

* Alluding to the murder of Cumin by Robert Bruce in the Greyfriars' Church at Dumfries.

securing the privilege. The account of the discussion on the clause in question is somewhat amusing. Sir Walter Earle proposed that 'members' letters should come and go free during the time of their sittings.' Sir Heneage Finch (afterwards Lord Chancellor Finch) said, indignantly, 'It is a real *poor mendicant* proviso, and below the honour of the House.' Many members spoke in favour of the measure, Serjeant Charlton urging that 'letters for counsel on circuit went free.' The debate was nearly one-sided, but the speaker, Sir Harbottle Grimstone, on the question being called, refused for a considerable time to put it, saying, 'He felt ashamed of it.' The clause, however, was eventually put, and carried by a great majority. When the bill, with its franking proviso, was sent up to the Lords, they threw out the clause, as there was no provision made in it, 'that the Lords' own letters should pass free!' Some years later, this omission was supplied, and both Houses had the privilege guaranteed to them, neither Lords nor Commons feeling the arrangement below their dignity. It is important to notice, that at the time of which we are speaking, the post-office authorities had much more control over the means of conveyance than they have at the present day. With both inland and packet conveyance the postmasters-general had entire control. At the present day, contracts are made with the different railway companies, &c., for inland conveyance, and the packet-service is under the management of the Board of Admiralty. Without this knowledge, it would be difficult to account for the vast and heterogeneous mass of articles which were passed free through the post-office by a wide stretch of the privilege under notice. In old records of the English post-office still preserved, we find lists of these franked consignments; the following, culled from a number of such, is sufficient to indicate their character:

'Fifteen couple of hounds, going to the king of the Romans with a free pass.' 'Two maid-servants, going as laundresses to my Lord Ambassador Methuen.' 'Docter Crichton, carrying with him a *cow* and divers necessaries.' 'Three suits of *cloaths*, for some nobleman's lady at the court of Portugal.' 'Two bales of stockings for the use (?) of the ambassador to the crown of Portugal.' 'A deal-case, with four flitches of bacon, for Mr Pennington of Rotterdam.'

When the control of the packet-service passed out of the hands of the post-office authorities, and when the right of franking letters became properly sanctioned and systematised, we hear no more of this kind of abuses of privilege. The franking system was henceforth confined to passing free through the post any letter which should be endorsed on the cover with the signature of a member of either house of parliament. It was not necessary, however, that parliament should be in session, or that the correspondence should be on the affairs of the nation (though this was the original design of the privilege) to insure this immunity from postage; and this arrangement, as might have been expected, led to various forms of abuse. Members signed large packets of covers at once, and supplied them to friends in large quantities; sometimes they were sold; they have been known to have been given to servants in lieu of wages, the servants selling them again in the ordinary way of business. Nor was this all. So little precaution seems to have been used, that thousands of letters passed through the post-office with forged signatures of members. To such an extent did these and kindred abuses accumulate, that whereas in 1715, £24,000 worth of franked correspondence passed through the post-office, in 1763 the amount had increased to £170,000. During the next year, viz., in 1764, parliament enacted that no letter should pass free through the post-office unless the whole address was in the member's own handwriting, and his signature attached likewise. It is obvious that this arrangement would materially lessen the frauds practised upon the public revenue of the country. But even these precautions were not sufficient, for fresh regulations were rendered necessary in the year 1784. This time it was ordered that all franks should be dated—the month to be given in full—and further, that all such letters should be put into the post on the same day.

From 1784 to the date of the penny-postage era, the estimated value of franked letters was £80,000 annually. No further reforms were, however, attempted, till Sir Rowland Hill advocated the very radical and indispensable reform of entirely abrogating the privilege. In the bill, which through his unceasing energy was introduced into parliament in 1839, no provision was made such as had existed for a couple of centuries.

Writing on this subject, and having mentioned the name of the founder of the penny-post system, we may advert to an anecdote which has been mistakingly reported regarding him.

Coleridge the poet, when a young man, visiting the Lake District, halted at the door of a wayside inn at the moment when the rural post-messenger was delivering a letter to the barmaid of the place. Upon receiving it, she turned it over and over in her hand, and then asked the postage of it. The postman demanded a shilling. Sighing deeply, however, the girl handed the letter back, saying she was too poor to pay the required sum. The young poet at once offered to pay the postage, and in spite of the girl's resistance, which the humane tourist deemed quite natural, did so. The postman had scarce left the place, when the young barmaid confessed that she had learned all that she was likely to know from the letter; that she had only been practising a preconceived trick; she and her brother having agreed that a few hieroglyphics on the back of a post-letter should tell her all she wanted to know, whilst the letter would contain no writing. 'We are so poor,' she added, 'that we have invented this manner of corresponding and franking our letters.' Mr Hill, having heard of this incident, introduced it into his first pamphlet on postal reform, as a lively illustration of the absurdity of the old system. It was by an inadvertency on the part of a modern historical writer that Mr Hill was ever described as the person to whom the incident happened.

## DRINKING-FOUNTAIN IN 1685.

The desirableness of providing public drinking-fountains, similar to those which originated a few years ago in Liverpool, and are now becoming general in London and other large towns, seems to have occurred to some benevolent persons almost two centuries ago.

Sir Samuel Morland, who was a most ingenious as well as benevolent character, purchased a house at Hammersmith in 1684, where, for many years, he chiefly resided. Observing the scarcity of good drinking-water in his neighbourhood, and knowing how seriously the poor would suffer from the want of such a necessary of life, he had a well sunk near his own house, and constructed over it an ingenious pump, a rare convenience in those days, and consigned it gratuitously for the use of the public. A tablet, fixed in the wall of his own house, bore the following record of his benefaction: 'Sir Samuel Morland's Well, the use of which he freely gives to all persons, hoping that none who shall come after him will adventure to incur God's displeasure, by denying a cup of cold water (provided at another's cost, and not their own) to either neighbour, stranger, passenger, or poor thirsty beggar. July 8, 1685.' The pump has been removed, but the stone bearing the inscription was preserved in the garden of the house, afterwards known by the name of Walbrough House. Sir Samuel Morland was an interesting character. He was the son of a country clergyman in Berkshire, and was born about 1625. He was educated at Winchester School, and at Magdalen College, Cambridge. In 1653, he went to Sweden in the famous embassy of Bulstrode Whitelock, and subsequently became assistant to Secretary Thurloe. Afterwards he was sent by Cromwell to the Duke of Savoy, to remonstrate against the persecution of the Waldenses; and, on his return, he published a *History of the Evangelical Churches of the Valley of Piedmont.* But he distinguished himself chiefly by his mechanical inventions; among which are enumerated the speaking-trumpet, the fire-engine, a capstan for heaving anchors, and the steam-engine. If not the original inventor of these, as is questioned, he certainly effected great improvements in them. He constructed for himself a coach, with a movable kitchen in it, so fitted with clockwork machinery, that he could broil steaks, roast a joint of meat, and make soup, as he travelled along the road. The side-table in his dining-room was furnished with a large fountain of water; and every part of his house bore evidence of his ingenuity. He was created a baronet by Charles II. in 1660, and died in 1696, having been four times married.

## LARGE-WHEEL VEHICLES IN 1771.

Many ingenious inventions go completely out of sight, when the accounts relating to them are confined to newspapers and journals of temporary interest; unless some historian of industrial matters fixes them in a book, or in a cyclopædic article, down they go, and subsequent inventors may re-invent the self-same things, quite unconscious of what had been done. We believe that this is, to a considerable extent, the case with Mr Moore's large-wheel vehicles brought out in London in 1771. Of course, few readers now a days need to be told that a vehicle with large wheels will move more easily than one with wheels of smaller diameter; like as the latter will move more easily than one that rests upon mere rollers. Reduced friction and greater leverage result; and it depends upon other considerations how far this enlargement of wheel may be carried: in other words, a great number of circumstances combine to settle the best size for a carriage-wheel to work in the streets of London. Mr Moore has no halo of glory around him; but he certainly succeeded in shewing, to the wonderment of many Londoners, that large wheels do enable vehicles to roll with comparative ease over the ground. The journals and magazines of that year contain many such announcements as the following: 'On Saturday evening, Mr Moore's new constructed coach, which is very large and roomy, and is drawn by one horse, carried six persons and the driver, with amazing ease, from Cheapside to the top of Highgate Hill. It came back at the rate of ten miles an hour, passing coaches-and-four, and all other carriages it came near on the road.' Another account gives a description of the vehicle itself, which was evidently a remarkable one on other accounts besides the size of wheel: 'Mr Moore has hung the body, which is like that of a common coach reversed, between two large wheels, nine feet and a half in diameter, and draws it with a horse in shafts. The passengers sit sideways within; and the driver is placed upon the top of the coach.' On one occasion, Mr Moore went in his curious coach, with five friends, to Richmond, where he had the honour of being presented to George III., who passed great commendations on the vehicle. Mr Moore appears not to have forgotten the exigencies of good traffic, and the heavy pull to which horses are often subjected in the streets of the metropolis. We read (19th July) that Mr Moore experimented on a cart with two wheels, and drawn by two horses, which conveyed twenty-six sacks of coals from Mr De Paiba's wharf, in Thames Street, to Mr Moore's house in Cheapside, and repeated this in four successive journeys—an amount of work which, it was said, would require twice as many horses with a cart of ordinary construction. On another day, we are told something about the construction of the vehicle: 'Mr Moore's new invented coal-carriage, the wheels of which are fifteen feet high, passed through the streets, attended by a great concourse of people. Two horses abreast drew two chaldrons and two sacks of coals with more ease and expedition than the common carts do one chaldron with three horses at length.' And on another occasion, 'the coal-carriage was tried on Friday evening, with thirty-one sacks, making two chaldrons and a half, drawn by two horses only to the foot of Holborn Hill, when a third was put to it, to help them up the hill. This they performed with as much ease as one chaldron is commonly done by three horses.' Notices of this kind ceased to appear about the autumn of the year; and Mr Moore, for reasons to us unknown, passed into the limbo of forgotten inventors.

# JULY 20.

**St Joseph Barsabas, confessor, 1st century. Saints Justa and Rufina, martyrs, 304. St Margaret, virgin and martyr, beginning of 4th century. St Aurelius, archbishop of Carthage, confessor, 423. St Ulmar, or Wulmar, abbot of Samer, 710. St Ceslas, confessor, of the order of St Dominic, 1242. St Jerom Aemiliani, confessor, 1537.**

*Born.*—Petrarch, Italian poet, 1304 (O. S.), *Arezzo, in Tuscany;* Eusebius Renaudot, oriental scholar, 1646, *Paris;* James Harris, author of *Hermes*, 1709, *Salisbury;* Auguste de Marmont, Duke of Ragusa, Bonapartist general, 1774, *Chatillon-sur-Seine;* Sultan Mahmoud II., 1785; Sir James Phillips Kay-Shuttleworth, noted for his exertions in promoting education, 1804; John Sterling, poet and essayist, 1806, *Kames Castle, Bute.*

*Died.*—Robert the Wise, king of France, 1031, *Melun;* Peter Lombard, bishop of Paris, 1164; Thomas Randolph, Earl of Moray, 1332, *Musselburgh;* Talbot, Earl of Shrewsbury, distinguished warrior, 1452; John Prideaux, bishop of Worcester, scholar and author, 1650, *Bredon, Worcestershire;* William Scrope, author of *Days and Nights of Salmon Fishing*, 1852, *London;* Caroline Anne Southey (*née* Bowles), poetess and novelist, 1854, *Buckland, near Lymington.*

## THE NORFOLK COMMOTION.

The intolerable tyranny of the feudal system, aggravated by the enclosure of common lands by those who obtained grants of ecclesiastical estates, at the suppression of monastries, drove the people of several of the English counties into open, though unconnected insurrection. The most formidable of these risings taking place in the county of Norfolk, local historians and ancient chroniclers have given it the distinctive appellation of 'the Norfolk Commotion!' The first outbreak, early in the summer of 1549, was merely a village riot, in which some fences were destroyed; but one Robert Kett, a tanner, an energetic man of rude and ready eloquence, taking the leadership, the number of insurgents increased so rapidly, that, in a few days, he encamped on Mousehold Heath, about a mile from the city of Norwich, with a following of some twenty thousand men. Kett's first duty in this position being to feed his forces, he, styling himself the king's friend and deputy, issued warrants licensing 'all men to provide and bring into the camp at Mousehold, all manner of cattle and provision of victuals in what place soever they may find the same, so that no violence or injury be done to any honest or poor man.' Such was the effects of these warrants, that a fat sheep was sold in the camp for fourpence; and bullocks, deer, and other provisions at proportionate prices. Having thus provided for his commissariat, Kett drew up, in form of a petition to the king, a list of the grievances under which the populace laboured, praying for their immediate redress. This petition is remarkably suggestive of its period, when a great part of the agricultural population were in a state of serfdom, one item praying 'that all bondmen may be made free, for God made all free, with his precious blood-shedding.' Strange to say, two of the grievances have been cause of complaint in our own day; namely, the great number of rabbits kept by large landed proprietors, and the differences in the size of the bushel measure in various localities.

KETT, THE REBEL, UNDER THE OAK OF REFORMATION.

While waiting the result of the petition, Kett maintained good order among his followers, daily holding a court and administering justice under the wide-spreading branches of a tree, named in consequence the Oak of Reformation. The reformed liturgy was read at the same place night and morning, by one of the vicars of Norwich, whom the insurgents had pressed into their service as chaplain; and other clergymen were not only invited to address them, but permitted to rebuke their rebellious conduct in the boldest manner.

The 20th of July 1549 was, for good or evil, the turning-point of the rebellion. On that day, the king's reply to the petition was delivered to Kett, with all due formality, by the York herald. It was to the effect that a parliament would be called in the following October, to consider and redress the petitioners' grievances; and that a general pardon would be granted to all, who should at once lay down their arms, and return to their respective homes. When York herald read the proclamation of pardon at the Oak of Reformation, some of the insurgents cried out, 'God save the king!' But Kett said, 'Kings are won't to pardon wicked persons, not just and innocent men!' The herald then called Kett a traitor, and ordered his sword-bearer to arrest 'that captain of mischief;' but, the crowd beginning a great stir on every side, he was glad to depart in safety. The departure of the herald being considered tantamount to a declaration of war, the people of Norwich attempted to fortify and defend their city. But Kett attacking it with cannon, soon gained possession of it, leading the mayor and some of the principal inhabitants prisoners to the camp at Mousehold. And, with a grim kind of humour, the insurgents issued a mock-proclamation, stating such was their store of provisions, especially of fish, that a cod's head could be sold, at the Oak of Reformation, for one half-penny—the name of the unfortunate mayor being Codd. But his imprisonment was of the lightest kind, and, indeed, it does not appear that the rebels put any one to death in cold blood. There was one person, however, a lawyer, who had the reputation of being able to raise spirits, with fearful signs and wonders. It is not clear what they would have done to him; on his hiding-place among thorns and briers being made known to them by a woman; but as they were hauling him with all reproach and contumely, he caused a tempest to arise, 'mighty showers fell mixed with hail,' and thus he made his escape.

It is uncertain how long this lawless state of affairs had lasted, before government made a serious attempt to restore order. The dates given of the events connected with Kett's rebellion, are exceedingly contradictory and confused. Early in August, the Marquis of Northampton, with Lord Sheffield, many knights, and 1500 men, arrived at Norwich, sent by the council to put down the rebellion. Kett did not dispute the entrance of the royal troops into the city, but attacked them the same night, when the wearied soldiers were reposing after their long march. He again attacked them in the following morning, when Lord Sheffield and a great number being killed, the remainder fled back to London, 'hiding themselves in caves, groves, and woods by the way.'

The unexpected defeat of Northampton rendered the strongest measures necessary. An army, that had been prepared to march against Scotland, was sent, under the Earl of Warwick, to subdue the rebels in Norfolk. Warwick, entering Norwich, encamped his troops in the market-place; but Kett succeeded in capturing the royal ammunition and artillery. This loss compelled the earl to shut himself up in the city, and act on the defensive, while the rebels played upon him with his own artillery. At this juncture, Warwick's officers, considering the city to be untenable, urged upon him the immediate necessity of his leaving it. To this the stout earl 'valiantly answered, by God's grace not to depart the city, but would deliver it or leave his life. With these words he drew his sword, as did also the rest of the nobles, who were all there gathered together, and commanded after a warlike manner—and, as is usually done in greatest danger—that they should kiss one another's swords, making the sign of the holy cross, and by an oath, and solemn promise by word of mouth, every man to bind himself to other, not to depart from the city, before they had utterly banished the enemy, or else fighting manfully, had bestowed their lives cheerfully for the king's majesty.'

A welcome reinforcement of 1400 German mercenaries, determined Warwick to attack the rebels in their strong position on Mousehold Heath. But the infatuated men did not wait for the attack. Relying on an ancient prophecy, which foretold that

'The country gnoffes, Hob, Dick, and Hick,
With clubs and clouted shoon,
Shall fill the vale,
Of Dussinsdale,
With slaughtered bodies soon;
The heedless men, within the dale,
Shall there be slain both great and small'—

Kett left his vantage-ground upon the hill, and with twenty ensigns of war displayed, marched down into the vale. Warwick at once saw and embraced the opportunity offered by his enemy's folly. In the battle which ensued, the insurgents were defeated with great slaughter. Two thousand of the insurgents were killed in Dussinsdale, and 1500 more were destroyed by Warwick's cavalry, in the wild flight that followed. A few, barricading themselves among their carts and wagons, fought desperately; and Warwick, wishing to spare their lives, sent a herald to summon them to surrender. But they, drinking to one another, in sign of good-luck, vowed to spend their lives fighting manfully, rather than trust to false promises of pardon. The earl, grieved, however, at the thought of so many brave men perishing, went to them himself, and pledged his honour that their lives would be spared. 'Then every man laid down his weapons, and, as with one mouth cried: "God save King Edward!"'

A great number were hanged on the Oak of Reformation. Kett was made prisoner, and conveyed to London, but was subsequently sent back to Norwich, and hanged alive in chains on the top of the castle. His brother William, a butcher, who had also taken a leading part in the insurrection, was hanged in the same barbarous manner on the steeple of Wymondham church. Yet the rebellion, thus fiercely trampled out, led to important results, which it is not our province but that of the historian to enumerate and explain.

## CURIOUS ADVERTISEMENTS OF TWO CENTURIES AGO.

It was in the reign of Charles II. that the public journals first began to be, to any considerable extent, the vehicles of advertisements. In that era many *annonces* of an extremely curious kind were made, as will fully appear from the following examples, freshly selected by a correspondent:

'Whereas John Pippin, whose grandfather, father, and himself have been for above 190 years past famous throughout all England for curing the rupture, making the most easie trusses of all sorts, both for men, women, and children, being lately deceased; This is to certifie to all persons that Eleanor Pippin, the widow, who in his lifetime made all the trusses which he sold, lives still at "The Three Naked Boys," near the Strand Bridge, where she makes all manner of trusses. She also hath a gentleman to assist in the fitting of them upon men, he being intrusted by the said John Pippin in his lifetime.'—1679-80.

'At the sign of the "Golden Pall and Coffin," a coffin-maker's shop, at the upper end of the Old Change, near Cheapside, there are ready made to be sold, very fashionable laced and plain dressings for the dead of all sizes, with very fashionable coffins, that will secure any corps above ground without any ill scent or other annoyance as long as shall be required.'—1679-80.

'The much approved necklaces of Joynts, of the great traveller J. C., which absolutely eases children in breeding teeth, by cutting them, and thereby preventing feavers, convulsions, &c., are sold by T. Burrel, at the "Golden Ball," under St Dunstan's Church, in Fleet Street.'—1679.

'One Robert Taylor, a dancing-master, being in company of several neighbours in Covent Garden on Monday night last, about 10 of the clock, upon occasion of some words, killed one Mr Price, of the same place, at the "Three Tuns'" Tavern, in Shandois Street. The said R. Taylor is a person of middle stature, hath a cut across his chin, a scar in his left cheek, having two fingers and a thumb of one hand burnt at the ends shorter than the other, round visaged, thick lipt, his own hair being of a light brown under a periwig; he lived in James Street, in Covent Garden. Whoever apprehends him, and gives notice thereof to Mr Reynolds, bookseller, in Henrietta Street, Covent Garden, shall have 10 pounds reward. And whereas it was printed in last week's *Intelligence* that he was taken, you are to take notice that it is most notoriously false.'—1679.

'The certain cure of agues of all sorts is performed by a physitian of known integrity; they who desire his assistance may repair to his house, which is the first door on the right hand in Gun-Yard, in Houndsditch. His hours are from 8 in the morning till 2 in the afternoon.'—1680.

'William Deval, at the sign of the "Angel and Stilliards," in St Ann's Lane, near Aldersgate, London, maketh Castile, marble, and white sope, as good as any man sells; tryed and proved, and sold at very reasonable rates.'—1680.

'Whereas one John Stuart, of a tall stature, black brows, a wart upon his cheek, in a black periwig, and a tawny or black suit, and campaign coat, has been lately intrusted to sell several pieces of black worsted, crapes, hair chamblets, black philemot, and sky-coloured mohairs, watered and unwatered; with which goods he is run away, and cannot yet be heard of. Whoever gives notice of the man and goods (who, it is thought, is gone towards Ireland) to Mr Howard, in Milk Street Market, shall have 40*s.* reward.'—1680.

'A book in quarto, bound in parchment, about a quire of paper, near all writ out, being several accompts for work done, being missing out of a shop near Cheapside Conduit: supposed to fall off the stall, or other wayes, by some accident, lost about the middle of September last. If any will bring the said book to Mr Hifftell's Coffee-house, in Cheapside, near the Nagg's Head Tavern, shall have 10*s.* reward.'—1680.

'October the 29th.—There was dropt out of a balcony, in Cheapside, a very large watch-case, studded with gold; if any person hath taken it up, and will bring it to Mr Fells, a goldsmith, at the sign of the "Bunch of Grapes," in the Strand; or to Mr Benj. Harris, at the sign of the "Stationers' Armes," in the Piaza, under Royal Exchange, in Cornhill, shall have a guinney reward.'—1680.

'This is to give notice to all the *Marshals*, both in the city and countrey, that may be desirous to come to their namesake's feast, which will be the 13th of November 1679, at Mr Edward *Marshal's* house, at the sign of the "Cock," in Fleet Street, where the tickets are delivered, and at Mr *Marshal's*, bookseller, at the "Bible," in Newgate Street.'—1680.

'There is a side of a shop, ready furnished with all sorts of millinary goods, to be sold, and the said side of a shop to be let, all at reasonable rates; at the "Naked Boy," near Strand Bridge. Inquire at the said shop, or at the house of Mr Van Auker, merchant, in Lime Street.'—1680.

'At Tobias' Coffee-house, in Pye Corner, is sold the right drink, called Dr Butler's Ale, it being the same that was sold by Mr Lansdale in Newgate Market. It is an excellent stomack drink, it helps digestion, expels wind, and dissolves congealed phlegm upon the lungs, and is therefore good against colds, coughs, ptisical and consumptive distempers; and being drunk in the evening, it moderately fortifies nature, causeth good rest, and hugely corroborates the brain and memory.'—1680.

'At the "Miter," near the west end of St Paul's, is to be seen a rare collection of curiosityes, much resorted to, and admired by persons of great learning and quality; amongst which a choyce *Egyptian Mummy*, with hieroglyphics; the *Ant-Beare* of Brazil; a *Remora*; a *Torpedo*; the huge *Thigh-bone of a Gyant*; a *Moon-Fish*; a *Tropick-bird*, &c.'—1664.

'Without Bishopsgate, near Hog Lane, over against the Watch-house, liveth one Jacob Summers, a weaver; who maketh and selleth town-velvets at reasonable rates.'—1664.

'Lost upon the 13th inst., a little blackamoor boy in a blew livery, about 10 years old, his hair not much curled, with a silver collar about his neck, inscribed "Mrs Manby's blackamoor, in Warwick Lane." Whoever shall give notice of him to Mrs Manby, living in the said lane, or to the "Three Cranes," in Pater-Noster Row, shall be well rewarded for his peynes.'—1664.

'Whereas his sacred majesty (Charles II.) has been pleased, after the example of his roya' ancestors, to incorporate the musitians in England, for the encouragement of that excellent quality, and the said corporation to impower all that profess the said science, and to allow and make free such as they shall think fit. This is to give notice to persons concern'd, that the said corporation sits once a week in "Durham Yard," in pursuance of the trust and authority to them committed by his most gracious majesty.'—1664.

'At the "Angel and Sun," in the Strand, near Strand Bridge, is to be sold every day, fresh *Epsum-water*, *Barnet-water*, and *Tunbridge-water; Epsum-ale*, and *Spruce-beer*.'—1664.

'These are to give notice to the heirs and trustees of *William Hinton*, some time one of the servants of the late king; and to the heirs or trustees of the estate of one *Christopher King*, and *Mr Francis Braddock*, sometimes of *London*, gent.; that there is a discovery of a concealment of some estate belonging to them or some of them, or to some persons claiming from them; whereof they may be informed if they repair to Mr *John Bellinger* at his house in Clifford's Inn Lane, in Fleet Street.'—1663.

'Stolne on Fryday night, the 10th instant, from *Peter Bennier*, his majesty's sculptor, between Whitehall and Charing Cross, one blackmore cast from the life, and three or four other heads. If any person can bring notice of the blackmore to the said *Peter Bennier*, at his house over against the signe of the "Golden Balle," they shall be very well payd for their payns.'—1663.

'*Fortescutus Illustratus*: or, a commentary on that nervous treatise—*De Laudibus Legum Angliæ*. Written by Sir John Fortescue, knight; first, Lord Chief-justice; after, Lord Chancellor to King Henry Sixth. Which treatise was dedicated to Prince Edward, that king's son and heir; whom he attended in his retirement into France, and to whom he legally and affectionately imparted himself in the vertue and variety of his excellent discourse. He purposely wrote to consolidate his princely minde in the love and approbation of the good laws of England, and of the laudible customes of this his native country. The heroicke designe of whose excellent judgment and loyal addiction to his prince, is humbly endeavoured to be revived, admired, and advanced. By *Edward Waterhouse*, Esq. Sold by *Thomas Dicas*, at the *Hen and Chickens*, in St Paul's Church-yard.'—1663.

'A young brindled mastiff, cropt with three notches on the rump, four white feet, and a white streak down the face, was lost on Fryday was seven-night, July 31. 'Tis one of the king's dogs, and whoever gives notice of him at the porter's lodge in Whitehall, shall have a very good reward.' —1663.

## A TORNADO IN CHESHIRE.

The 20th of July 1662, was marked in Lancashire and Cheshire by a storm of prodigious violence, accompanied by a fall of heavy hailstones. What, however, chiefly distinguished the day, was a travelling vortex or whirlwind, which produced some remarkable effects, and is thus vividly described in a volume, entitled *Admirable Curiosities*, &c., published in London in 1682.

'In the same day,' says this narration, 'in the afternoon, in the forest of Maxfield [Macclesfield], there arose a great pillar of smoke, in height like a steeple, and judged twenty yards broad, which, making a most hideous noise, went along the ground six or seven miles, levelling all the way; it threw down fences and stone walls, and carried the stones a great distance from their places, but happening upon moorish ground [moor-land] not inhabited, it did the less hurt. The terrible noise it made so frightened the cattle, that they ran away, and were thereby preserved; it passed over a cornfield, and laid it as low with the ground as if it had been trodden down by feet; it went through a wood, and turned up above an hundred trees by the roots; coming into a field full of cocks of hay ready to be carried in, it swept all away, so that scarce a handful of it could afterwards be found, only it left a great tree in the middle of the field, which it had brought from some other place. From the forest of Maxfield, it went up by a town called Taxal, and thence to Wailey Bridge [Whaley Bridge], where, and nowhere else, it overthrew an house or two, yet the people that were in them received not much hurt, but the timber was carried away nobody knew whither. From thence it went up the hills into Derbyshire, and so vanished. This account was given by Mr Hurst, minister of Taxal, who had it from an eye-witness.'

## FORMIDABLE ATTACK BY BEES.

Huber, Bevan, and other naturalists who have studied the extraordinary habits and instincts of bees, have not yet succeeded in discovering the various circumstances which lead those insects to attack man in a hostile spirit. How far revenge, or retaliation for injuries received, influences them, is but imperfectly known. There is proof that, when the queen-bee dies, the hive is thrown into confusion and agitation; and it has been supposed by many persons that the insects, at such a time, would seek to attack any one who may have been concerned in the death of the great mother. This, whether right or wrong, was the suggested explanation of an extraordinary attack by bees in Prussia, in 1820. As narrated in the *Berliner Zeitung*, the incident was as follows: On the 20th of July, M. Eulert, a merchant of Berlin, was travelling with his wife from Wittenberg to that city; they were in a private carriage, and a coachman was driving. While passing along the high-road, between Kroppstadt and Schmogelsdorf, the coachman observed the horses to rub uneasily against each other, as if stung by a horse-fly. Suddenly a swarm of bees appeared, or a collection of swarms, numerous beyond all reckoning. They covered the carriage, horses, travellers, and coachman, but especially the living beings. They attacked the mouth, nose, eyes, and ears of each horse, until the poor animals, quite overcome, lay down unresisting. The coachman lost his hat while endeavouring to aid the horses, and the bees then fastened upon his head with such avidity, that his poor skull became covered with a matted mass of bees, hair, and blood; he threw himself on the ground in desperation, and became for a time insensible. Madame Eulert, as soon as the attack began, covered her face with her hood, got out of the carriage, hastened to a neighbouring field, and threw herself, face downwards, on the grass. M. Eulert then alighted, and shouted for help; but while his mouth was open, some of the bees entered it, and increased his troubles. He then covered his face and neck with a handkerchief, and ran to a place where he saw three peasants looking on; but they were too much alarmed to help him, and so he ran on further. He then met a woodman, a carrier with a cart, and three horses, and some labourers. After much entreaty, the carrier agreed to put his horses into a neighbouring stable, and to accompany M. Eulert, as did the others, all carrying dry hay and straw to burn. Arrived at the spot, they found Madame Eulert still lying, face downward, on the grass, very little injured. The poor coachman was lying nearly insensible, and for forty-eight hours his case was precarious. After burning much hay and straw to drive away the bees, M. Eulert and his helpers were able to examine the suffering horses; one was so maddened by the stinging it had received, that it died the same day; the other was taken to Schmogelsdorf, and placed under the care of a veterinary surgeon, but the poor animal died on the following day. M. Eulert, in attempting afterwards to assign a probable reason for this fierce attack, supposed that when the horses had been seen to rub against each other, a queen-bee was annoying one of them; that the rubbing crushed her; and that the attack by the swarm was an expression of the bees' resentment for the murder of their queen. Others sought no further than this for an explanation—that there were, at that time, no less than 2000 hives of bees in the commune of Schmogelsdorf; and that this number (greatly beyond the usual limit) increased the probability of attacks on men and animals.

## JULY 21.

St Praxedes, virgin, 2d century. St Zoticus, bishop and martyr, about 204. St Victor of Marseilles, martyr, beginning of 4th century. St Barhadbeschiabas, deacon and martyr, 354. St Arbogastus, bishop of Strasburg, confessor, about 678.

*Born.*—Matthew Prior, English poet, 1664, *Winborne, Dorsetshire.*

*Died.*—Darius III., king of Persia, murdered by Bessus, 330 B. C.; Pope Nicholas II., 1061; William Lord Russell, beheaded in Lincoln's-Inn-Fields, 1683; James Butler, Duke of Ormond, 1688; Daniel Sennertus, learned physician, 1637, *Wittemberg;* Robert Burns, national poet of Scotland, 1796, *Dumfries;* Peter Thelusson, celebrated *millionaire*, 1797, *Plastow, Essex.*

### THE DEATH AND FUNERAL OF BURNS, FROM THE NEWSPAPERS OF THE TIME.

'On the 21st [July, 1796] died, at Dumfries, after a lingering illness, the celebrated Robert Burns. His poetical compositions, distinguished equally by the force of native humour, by the warmth and tenderness of passion, and by the glowing touches of a descriptive pencil, will remain a lasting monument of the vigour and the versatility of a mind guided only by the lights of nature and the inspiration of genius. The public, to whose amusement he has so largely contributed, will learn with regret that his extraordinary endowments were accompanied with frailties which rendered him useless to himself and family. The last months of his short life were spent in sickness and indigence, and his widow, with five infant children, and the hourly expectation of a sixth, is now left without any resource but what she may hope from the regard due to the memory of her husband.

BURNS'S MONUMENT AT DUMFRIES.

'A subscription for the widow and children of poor Burns is immediately to be set on foot, and there is little doubt of its being an ample one.

'Actuated by the regard which is due to the shade of such a genius, his remains were interred on Monday last, the 25th July, with military honours and every suitable respect. The corpse having been previously conveyed to the town-hall of Dumfries, remained there till the following ceremony took place: The military there, consisting of the Cinque Port Cavalry, and the Angusshire Fencibles, having handsomely tendered their services, lined the streets on both sides to the burial-ground. The Royal Dumfries Volunteers, of which he was a member—in uniform, with crape on their left arms, supported the bier; a party of that corps, appointed to perform the military obsequies, moving in slow, solemn time to the "Dead March in Saul," which was played by the military band—preceded in mournful array with arms reversed. The principal part of the inhabitants and neighbourhood, with a number of particular friends of the bard, from remote parts, followed in procession; the great bells of the churches tolling at intervals. Arrived at the churchyard gate, the funeral-party, according to the rules of that exercise, formed two lines, and leaned their heads on their firelocks, pointed to the ground. Through this space the corpse was carried. The party drew up alongside the grave, and, after the interment, fired three volleys over it. The whole ceremony presented a solemn, grand, and affecting spectacle, and accorded with the general regret for the loss of a man whose like we shall scarce see again.'

EPITAPH.

'Consigned to earth, here rests the lifeless clay,
Which once a vital spark from Heaven inspired;
The lamp of genius shone full bright as day,
Then left the world to mourn its light retired.
While beams that splendid orb which lights the spheres—
While mountain streams descend to swell the main—
While changeful seasons mark the rolling years—
Thy fame, O Burns, let Scotia still retain!'

To these interesting notices may here be fitly appended, what, apart from intrinsic merit, may be considered the most remarkable production ever penned regarding Burns. It was at the centenary of his birth, January 25, 1859, that a great festival was held at the Crystal Palace, Sydenham, in honour of the memory of the Scottish national poet. Many personal relics of the illustrious dead were shewn; there was a concert of his best songs. Then it was announced to the vast and highly-strung auditory, that the offered prize of fifty guineas had brought together 621 poems by different authors, in honour of Burns's memory; out of which the three gentlemen judges had selected one as the best; and this was forthwith read by Mr Phelps, the eminent tragedian, with thrilling effect. It proved to be the composition of a young countrywoman of Burns, up to that time scarcely known, but who was in some respects not less wonderful, as an example of genius springing up in the lowly paths of life—her name, ISA CRAIG. There was an enthusiastic call for the youthful prize-holder, and had she been present, she would have received honours exceeding in fervour those at the laureation of Petrarch; but Miss Craig was then pursuing her modest duties in a distant part of London, unthinking of the proceedings at Sydenham. The poem was as follows:

We hail this morn,
A century's noblest birth;
A Poet peasant-born,
Who more of Fame's immortal dower
Unto his country brings,
Than all her Kings!

As lamps high set
Upon some earthly eminence—
And to the gazer brighter thence
Than the sphere-lights they flout—
Dwindle in distance and die out,
While no star waneth yet;
So through the past's far-reaching night
Only the star-souls keep their light.

A gentle boy—
With moods of sadness and of mirth,
Quick tears and sudden joy—
Grew up beside the peasant's hearth.
His father's toil he shares;
But half his mother's cares
From his dark searching eyes,
Too swift to sympathise,
Hid in her heart she bears.

At early morn,
His father calls him to the field;
Through the stiff soil that clogs his feet,
Chill rain and harvest heat,
He plods all day; returns at eve outworn,
To the rude fare a peasant's lot doth yield;
To what else was he born?

The God-made King
Of every living thing
(For his great heart in love could hold them all);
The dumb eyes meeting his by hearth and stall—
Gifted to understand!—
Knew it and sought his hand;
And the most timorous creature had not fled,
Could she his heart have read,
Which fain all feeble things had bless'd and sheltered.

To Nature's feast—
Who knew her noblest guest
And entertain'd him best—
Kingly he came. Her chambers of the east
She drap'd with crimson and with gold,
And pour'd her pure joy-wines
For him the poet-soul'd.
For him her anthem roll'd
From the storm-wind among the winter pines,
Down to the slenderest note
Of a love-warble, from the linnet's throat.

But when begins
The array for battle, and the trumpet blows,
A King must leave the feast, and lead the fight.
And with its mortal foes—
Grim gathering hosts of sorrows and of sins—
Each human soul must close.
And Fame her trumpet blew
Before him; wrapp'd him in her purple state;
And made him mark for all the shafts of fate,
That henceforth round him flew.

Though he may yield
Hard-press'd, and wounded fall
Forsaken on the field;
His regal vestments soil'd;
His crown of half its jewels spoil'd;
He is a king for all.

Had he but stood aloof!
Had he array'd himself in armour-proof
Against temptation's darts!
So yearn the good; so those the world calls wise,
With vain presumptuous hearts,
Triumphant moralise.

Of martyr-woe
A sacred shadow on his memory rests;
Tears have not ceas'd to flow;
Indignant grief yet stirs impetuous breasts,
To think—above that noble soul brought low,
That wise and soaring spirit, fool'd, enslav'd—
Thus, thus he had been saved!

It might not be
That heart of harmony
Had been too rudely rent;
Its silver chords, which any hand could wound,
By no hand could be tun'd,
Save by the Maker of the instrument,
Its every string who knew,
And from profaning touch his heavenly gift withdrew.

Regretful love
His country fain would prove,
By grateful honours lavish'd on his grave;
Would fain redeem her blame
That he so little at her hands can claim,
Who unrewarded gave
To her his life-bought gift of song and fame.

The land he trod
Hath now become a place of pilgrimage;
Where dearer are the daisies of the sod
That could his song engage.
The hoary hawthorn, wreath'd
Above the bank on which his limbs he flung
While some sweet plaint he breath'd;
The streams he wander'd near;
The maidens whom he lov'd; the songs he sung;
All, all are dear!

The arch blue eyes—
Arch but for love's disguise—
Of Scotland's daughters, soften at his strain;
Her hardy sons, sent forth across the main
To drive the ploughshare through earth's virgin soils,
Lighten with it their toils;
And sister-lands have learn'd to love the tongue
In which such songs are sung.

For doth not Song
To the whole world belong!
Is it not given wherever tears can fall,
Wherever hearts can melt, or blushes glow,
Or mirth and sadness mingle as they flow,
A heritage to all?

The widow of Burns survived him a time equal to his own entire life—thirty-eight years—and died in the same room in which he had died, in their humble home at Dumfries, in March 1834. The celebrity he gave her as his 'bonnie Jean,' rendered her an object of much local interest; and it is pleasant to record, that her conduct throughout her long widowhood was marked by so much good sense, good principle, and general amiableness and worth, as to secure for her the entire esteem of society. One is naturally curious about the personality of a poet's goddess; and much silent criticism had Mrs Burns accordingly to endure. A sense of being the subject of so much curiosity made her shrink from having any portraiture of herself taken; but one day she was induced, out of curiosity regarding silhouettes, to go to the studio of a wandering artist in that style, and sit to him. The result is here represented. The reader will

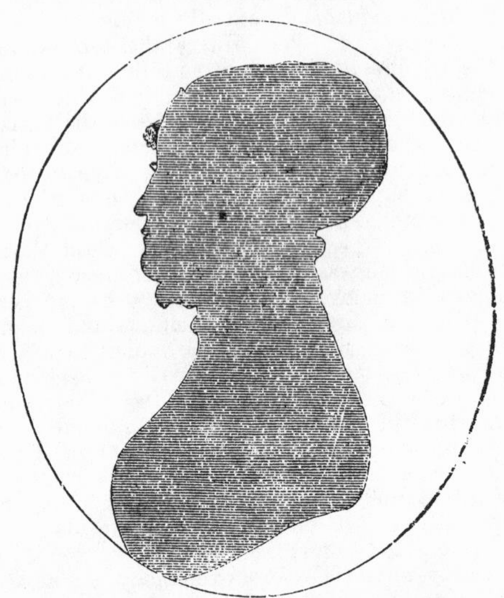

SILHOUETTE OF MRS BURNS, WIDOW OF THE POET.

probably have to regret the absence of regularity in the mould of the features; yet the writer can assure him that, even at the age of fifty-eight, Jean was a sightly and agreeable woman. It is understood that, in her youth, while decidedly comely, her greatest attractions were those of a handsome figure—a charm which came out strongly when engaged in her favourite amusement of dancing.

## PETER THELUSSON.

Peter Thelusson was born in France, of a Genevese family, and as a London merchant trading in Philpot Lane, he acquired an enormous fortune. He died on the 21st of July 1797, and when his will was opened, its provisions excited in the public mind mingled wonder, indignation, and alarm. To his dear wife, Ann, and children he left £100,000; and the residue of his property, amounting to upwards of £600,000, he committed to trustees, to accumulate during the lives of his three sons, and the lives of their sons, and when sons and grandsons were all dead, then the entire property was to be transferred to his eldest great-grandson. Should no heir exist, the accumulated property was to be conveyed to the sinking fund for the reduction of the national debt. Various calculations were made as to the probable result of the accumulation. According to the lowest computation, it was reckoned that, at the end of seventy years, it would amount to £19,000,000. Some estimated the result at far higher figures, and saw, in the fulfilment of the bequest, nothing short of a national disaster. The will was generally stigmatised as unwise or absurd, and, moreover, illegal. The Thelusson family resolved to test its legality, and raised the question in Chancery. Lord Chancellor Loughborough, in 1799, pronounced the will valid, and on appeal to the House of Lords, his decision was unanimously affirmed. The will, though within the letter of the law, was certainly adverse to its spirit, which 'abhors perpetuities,' and an act was passed by parliament in 1800, rendering null all bequests for the purposes of accumulation for longer than twenty years after the testator's death.

Thelusson's last grandson died in 1856. A dispute then arose whether Thelusson's eldest great-grandson, or the grandson of Thelusson's eldest son, should inherit. The House of Lords decided, on appeal in 1859, that Charles S. Thelusson, the grandson of Thelusson's eldest son, was the heir. It is said that, instead of about a score of millions, by reason of legal expenses and accidents of management, little more than the original sum of £600,000 fell to his lot.

### HAMPDEN'S BURIAL AND DISINTERMENT.

The parish church of Great Hampden, the burial-place of the Hampden family, is situated in the south-eastern part of Buckinghamshire, three miles from Great Missenden, through which passes the turnpike-road from Aylesbury to London. It is a pretty village church, with a flamboyant window at the west end, and other interesting features; and, standing embosomed in trees, in a secluded but elevated position, has a strikingly picturesque and pleasing appearance. The chancel contains many memorials of the Hampden family, whose bodies lie interred beneath. Here also was buried John Hampden, commonly called 'the Patriot.'

HAMPDEN CHURCH.

On Sunday morning, June 18, 1643, while encamped at Watlington, in Oxfordshire, he received intelligence that Prince Rupert, with a large body of troopers, had been ravaging, during the night, the neighbourhood of Chinnor and Wycombe, and was returning to Oxford, laden with spoil, and carrying off two hundred prisoners. Hampden, without waiting for his own regiment of infantry, placed himself at the head of a body of troopers, and galloped off with all speed in pursuit of the plunderers. On arriving at Chalgrove, instead of finding, as he expected, a retreating enemy, he beheld them drawn up in order of battle in the open field, waiting his approach. An encounter ensued, and, in the first onset, Hampden was severely wounded. Finding himself powerless, and seeing his troops in disorder and consternation, he left the battle-field. While the bells of his peaceful little church were chiming for morning-worship, Hampden was riding, in agonies of pain, to Thame, where he placed himself under surgical care. On the following Sunday, a large company of soldiers, chiefly Hampden's 'green coats,' entered the park-gates which opened into that noble avenue of beeches, nearly a mile in extent, which still forms the magnificent approach to Hampden House, and its adjoining church. With their drums and banners muffled, with their arms reversed and their heads uncovered, those soldiers moved slowly up the avenue, chanting the 90th Psalm, and carrying with them the dead body of their lamented colonel. The bell tolled solemnly as they approached, and crowds of mourners were assembled to receive the melancholy cortege. Hampden was much beloved, especially in his own county, and by his own tenantry and dependants. The weather-beaten faces of many sturdy yeomen were that day bedewed with tears. 'Never,' says Clough, 'were heard such piteous cries at the death of one man as at Master Hampden's.' 'His death,' says Clarendon, 'was as great a consternation to his party as if their whole army had been defeated, or cut off.' A grave was dug for him near his first wife's, in the chancel of the little church, where from childhood he had been wont to worship. And there, in the forty-ninth year of his age, was buried 'John Hampden, the patriot,' June 25, 1643.*

Nearly two centuries later, on July 21, 1828, Hampden's death was the occasion of a more extraordinary scene in this church, owing to the actual cause of it having been differently stated. Clarendon, and other contemporary writers, attributed it to the effects of two musket-balls received in his shoulder from the fire of his adversaries; whereas Sir Robert Pye, who married Hampden's daughter, asserted that his death was caused by the bursting of his own pistol, which so shattered his hand, that he died from the effects of the wound. To decide which of these statements was correct, Lord Nugent, who was about to write the biography of Hampden, obtained permission to examine his body, and for this purpose a large party, on the day above named, assembled in Hampden church, among whom were Lord Nugent; Counsellor, afterwards Lord Denman; the rector of the parish; Mr Heron, the Earl of Buckinghamshire's agent; Mr George Coventry, and 'six other young gentlemen;

* Hampden's burial occurred on Sunday, June 25, and is thus recorded in the parish register: '1643: *N.B.*—John Hampden, Esquire, Lord of Hampden, buried June 25th.' The writer is indebted for this extract to the Rev. F. Aspitel, the present rector, who thus remarks on the entry: 'It is in the handwriting of Lenthall, the successor of Spurtow, in this rectory, who appears to have found, on his coming into the living in November 30, 1643, that the register had not been kept since May of the year before, and who therefore proceeded to post it up, forgetting, at first, the burial of Hampden, and then inserting it at the head of the entries in its proper place, with "*N.B.*" at the beginning of the line.'

twelve grave-diggers and assistants, a plumber, and the parish clerk.'

The work began at an early hour in the morning, by turning up the floor of the church. The dates and initials on several leaden coffins were examined; but on coming to the coffin supposed to be Hampden's, the plate was found 'so corroded that it crumbled and fell into small pieces on being touched,' which rendered the inscription illegible. But from this coffin lying near the feet of Hampden's first wife, to whom he had himself erected a memorial, it was concluded to be his; and 'it was unanimously agreed that the lid should be cut open, to ascertain the fact.' The plumber descended 'and commenced cutting across the coffin, then longitudinally, until the whole was sufficiently loosened to roll back the lead, in order to lift off the wooden lid beneath, which came off nearly entire. Beneath this was another wooden lid, which was also raised without being much broken. The coffin was filled up with saw-dust, 'which was removed, and the process of examination commenced. Silence reigned. Not a whisper or a breath was heard. Each stood on the tiptoe of expectation, awaiting the result. Lord Nugent descended into the grave, and first removed the outer cloth, which was firmly wrapped round the body, then the second, and a third. Here a very singular scene presented itself. No regular features were apparent, although the face retained a deathlike whiteness, and shewed the various windings of the blood-vessels beneath the skin. The upper row of teeth was perfect, and those that remained in the under-jaw, on being taken out and examined, were found

JOHN HAMPDEN.

quite sound. A little beard remained on the lower part of the chin; and the whiskers were strong, and somewhat lighter than his hair, which was a full auburn brown.' The coffin was now raised from the grave, and placed on a trestle in the centre of the church. The arms, which 'nearly retained their original size, and presented a very muscular appearance,' were examined. The right arm was without its hand, which had apparently been amputated. On searching under the clothes, the hand, or rather a number of small bones enclosed in a separate cloth, was found, but no finger-nails were discovered, although on the left hand they remained almost perfect. The resurrectionists 'were now perfectly satisfied' that Hampden's hand had been shattered by the bursting of his pistol. Still it was possible that he might have been wounded at the same time in the shoulder by a musket-ball from the enemy; and to corroborate or disprove this statement, a closer examination was made. 'It was adjudged necessary to remove the arms, which were amputated with a penknife.' The result was, that the right arm was found properly connected with the shoulder, but the left, being 'loose and disunited from the scapula, proved that dislocation had taken place' 'In order to examine the head and hair, the body was raised up and supported with a shovel.' 'We found the hair in a complete state of preservation. It was a dark auburn colour, and, according to the custom of the times, was very long, from five to six inches. It was drawn up, and tied round at the top of the head with black thread or silk. On taking hold of the top-knot, it soon gave way, and came off like a wig.' 'He was five feet nine inches in height, apparently of great muscular strength, of a vigorous and robust frame, forehead broad and high, the skull altogether well formed—such an one as the imagination would conceive capable of great exploits.'

The body was duly re-interred, and shortly afterwards a full description of the examination, from which the foregoing has been abridged, appeared in the *Gentleman's Magazine*, when, to the discomposure of the party concerned, it was confidently asserted that the disinterred body was not John Hampden's, but that of a lady who died *durante partu*, and that the bones, mistaken for a hand, were those of her infant. Inconsistent as this assertion may appear with the whiskered body examined, it is evident Lord Nugent did not consider it wholly irrelevant; for in a letter on the subject to Mr Murray, he says: 'I certainly did see, in 1828, while the pavement of the chancel of Hampden church was undergoing repair, a skeleton, which I have many reasons for believing was not John Hampden's, but that of some gentleman or *lady* who probably died a quiet death in bed, certainly with no wound in the wrist.' Thus, after the rude violation of the Hampden sepulchre, and the mutilation of a human body, it still remained a mystery whether that body was a gentleman's or a lady's; and the problem, if any, respecting the cause of Hampden's death, was as far from solution as ever.* Lord Nugent, in his *Life of Hampden*, makes no allusion to this opening of the grave, but adopts

* Since the foregoing account was written, the subject of Hampden's death, and the exhumation of his body, has been elaborately discussed in the *Times*, and other newspapers, and letters have appeared from the Rev. G. W. Brooks, and others who were present at the exhumation, but nothing has been elicited to affect materially the account here given. The general opinion, however, appears to be, that the body examined on July 21, 1828, was that of 'the patriot.' An interesting paper on the subject by Mr Robert Gibbs of Aylesbury, who, from private sources of information, is strongly inclined to this opinion, appeared in the *Aylesbury News* of January 24, 1863.

the statement given by Clarendon. 'In the first charge,' says he, 'Hampden received his death. He was struck in the shoulder with two carbine balls, which, breaking the bone, entered his body, and his arm hung powerless and shattered by his side.'

It is remarkable that 'the patriot's grave should have been left without any monument or inscription, when such pains were taken to give him honourable burial in the sepulchre of his fathers. He is, however, commemorated by a monument against the north wall of the chancel. This memorial consists of a large sarcophagus between two weeping boys—one holding a staff, with the cap of Liberty, the other with a scroll inscribed "MAGNA CHARTA." Above this, in an oval medallion, is a representation in basso-relievo, of the Chalgrove fight, with a village and church in the background, and Hampden, as the prominent figure, bending over his horse, as having just received his fatal wound. Above the medallion is a genealogical tree, bearing on its several branches the heraldic shields of the successive generations of the Hampdens and their alliances.

John Hampden, the last male heir of the family, died unmarried in 1754, and is described in his epitaph as the twenty-fourth hereditary lord of Hampden manor. The property, after passing through female descendants, was possessed by Lady Vere Cameron, who generally resided in Hampden House, which is a large handsome mansion, retaining, as Lord Nugent thought, 'traces of the different styles of architecture, from the early Norman to the Tudor, though deformed by the innovations of the eighteenth century.' It stands finely grouped among ancestral trees, on a branch of the Chiltern Hills, and commands a beautiful and extensive view over a richly wooded country, diversified by hill and dale, and lacking only water to make the scenery complete.

## LARGE MEN.

'Some,' reads Malvolio, 'are born great, some achieve greatness, and some have greatness thrust upon them.' Among the latter class, we may place Mr Daniel Lambert, who died at Stamford on the 21st of July 1809, at the advanced weight of 739 pounds. In 1806, Lambert exhibited himself in London, and the following is a copy of one of his bills.

'*Exhibition*.—Mr Daniel Lambert, of Leicester, the heaviest man that ever lived; who, at the age of thirty-six years, weighs upwards of fifty stone (fourteen pounds to the stone), or eighty-seven stones four pounds, London weight, which is ninety-one pounds more than the great Mr Bright weighed. Mr Lambert will see company at his house, No. 53 Piccadilly, next Albany, nearly opposite St James's Church, from eleven to five o'clock. Tickets of Admission, One Shilling each.'

Lambert died suddenly. He went to bed well at night, but expired before nine o'clock of the following morning. A country newspaper of the day, aiming at fine writing, observes: 'Nature had endured all the trespass she could admit; the poor man's corpulency had constantly increased, until, at the time we have mentioned, the clogged machinery of life stood still, and this prodigy of mammon (*sic*) was numbered with the dead.' His coffin contained 112 superficial feet of elm, and was 6 feet 4 inches long, 4 feet 4 inches wide, and 2 feet 4 inches deep; and the immense substance of his legs necessitated it to be made in the form of a square case. It was built upon two axle-trees, and four clog-wheels, and upon these the remains of the great man were rolled into his grave in St Martin's Churchyard. A regular descent was made to the grave by cutting away the earth for some distance. The apartments which he occupied were on the ground-floor, as he had been long incapable of ascending a staircase. The window, and part of the wall of the room in which he died, had to be taken down, to make a passage for the coffin. A vast multitude followed the remains to the grave, the most perfect decorum was preserved, and not the slightest accident occurred.

The 'great Mr Bright,' mentioned in Lambert's exhibition-bill, was a grocer at Maldon, in Essex. He may partly be said to 'have been born great,' for he was of a family noted for the great size and great appetites of its members. Bright enjoyed good health, married at the age of twenty-two, and had five children. An amiable mind inhabited his overgrown body. He was a cheerful companion, a kind husband, a tender father, a good master, a friendly neighbour, and an honest man. 'So,' says his biographer, 'it cannot be surprising if he was universally loved and respected.'

PORTRAIT OF MR BRIGHT.

Bright died in his thirtieth year, at the net weight of 616 pounds, or 44 stone, jockey weight, His neighbours considered that death was a happy release to him, 'and so much the more as he thought so himself, and wished to be released.

His coffin was 3 feet 6 inches broad at the shoulders, and more than 3 feet in depth. A way was cut through the wall and staircase of his house to let it down into the shop. It was drawn to the church on a low-wheeled carriage, by twelve men; and was let down into the grave by an engine, fixed up on the church for that purpose, amidst a vast concourse of spectators from distant parts of the country. After his death, a wager was laid that five men, each twenty-one years of age, could be buttoned in his waistcoat. It was decided at the Black Bull Inn, at Maldon, when not only five, as proposed, but seven men were enclosed in it, without breaking a stitch or straining a button.

A Mr Palmer, landlord of the Golden Lion Inn at Brompton, in Kent, was another great man in his way, though not fit to be compared with either Bright or Lambert; weighing but 25 stone, a matter of some 380 pounds less than the great Daniel. Palmer came to London to see Lambert; yet, though five men could be buttoned in his waistcoat, he looked like a pigmy beside the great Leicestershire man. It is said that the superior grossness of his more corpulent rival in greatness, so affected Palmer as to cause his death. However that may be, he certainly died three weeks after his journey to London. A part of the Golden Lion had to be taken down to allow egress for his coffin, which was drawn to the grave in a timber wagon, as no hearse could be procured either large enough to admit it, or sufficiently strong to bear its weight.

A sad episode in the history of crime is exhibited in the forgeries and subsequent execution of Ryland, a celebrated engraver, who exercised his profession in London during the latter part of the last century. Ryland had an apprentice named John Love, who, terrified by his master's shameful death, gave up the business he was learning, and returned to his native place in Dorsetshire. At that time being exceedingly meagre and emaciated, his friends, fearing he was falling into a consumption, applied to a physician, who recommended an abundance of nutritious food, as the best medicine under the circumstances of the case. Love thus acquired a relish for the pleasures of the table, which he was soon enabled to gratify to its fullest extent, by success in business as a bookseller at Weymouth: where he soon grew as remarkably heavy and corpulent as he had previously been light and lean. So, he may have been said to have achieved his own greatness, but he did not live long to enjoy it; suffocated by fat, he died in his fortieth year, at the weight of 364 pounds.

---

## CURIOUS OLD DIVISIONS OF THE LIFE OF MAN.

Since the mythical days of Œdipus and the Sphinx, many curious attempts have been made to partition out the life of a man into distinct periods, and to assign to each its own peculiar duties or characteristics.

From a series of valuable and pleasing reflections upon youth and age, with the virtues and offices appropriate to each, to be found in Dante's prose work, called the *Convito* or *Banquet*, a philosophic commentary on certain of his own songs, Mr Lyell, the translator of Dante's *Lyrical Poems*, has drawn the following table:

TABLE OF DANTE'S FIVE AGES OF MAN, AND OF THE DUTY PARTICULARLY CALLED FOR IN EACH.

| Years. | | Period of life. | Peculiar Duty of each Period. |
|---|---|---|---|
| From. | To. | | |
| 1 | 10 | Childhood. | To acquire life. |
| 10 | 25 | Adolescence. | To confirm it. |
| 25 | | Youth: summit of the arch of life. | To employ it well. |
| 35 | | | To attain its summit. |
| | 45 | | To perfect it. |
| 45 | 70 | Old age. | To direct it to its ultimate end; i. e., to God. |
| 70 | 80 | Extreme old age. | To end it in peace. |

We find another such scheme, less instructive, but more amusing, in the pages of an old English poet. Many readers, to whom the name of Dante will be quite familiar, will be strangers to Thomas Tusser. He was born in Essex, about 1520, and wrote a curious book of jingling rhymes, called *Five Hundred Points of Good Husbandry;* intended chiefly to be useful to the poorer sort—farmers, housewives, plough-boys, and the like. Southey, in whose collection of *Early English Poets*, Tusser's work was reprinted, relates of Lord Molesworth, that having proposed (in 1723) that a school of husbandry should be set up in every county, he advised that 'Tusser's old book of husbandry should be taught to the boys, to read, to copy, and to get by heart.' Tusser's book, the most curious book, says Southey, in the English language, was once very popular. It catalogues all weather-signs, all farm and field work, all farmer's duties, peculiarities, and wise saws, under the several heads of the appropriate months; and winds up with a strange medley of curious household rhymes—of evil neighbours; of religious maxims and creeds; or concerning household physic—evidently meant to become popular among country labourers. Our table forms a part of this medley.

*Man's age divided here ye have,*
*By 'prenticeships, from birth to grave.*

7. The first seven years bring up as a child:
14. The next, to learning, for waxing too wild.
21. The next, keep under Sir Hobbard de Hoy:
28. The next, a man, no longer a boy.
35. The next, let Lusty lay wisely to wive:
42. The next, lay now, or else never, to thrive.
49. The next, make sure, for term of thy life:
56. The next, save somewhat for children and wife.
63. The next, be stayed; give over thy lust:
70. The next, think hourly whither thou must.
77. The next, get chair and crutches to stay;
84. The next, to heaven God send us the way.

Who loseth their youth, shall rue it in age:
Who hateth the truth, in sorrow shall rage.

Not satisfied with this, Tusser is pleased to add, for the sake of variety, another edition, from a somewhat different point of view:

*Another division of the nature of man's age.*

The Ape, the Lion, the Fox, the Ass,
Thus sets forth man as in a glass.

*Ape.* Like apes we be toying, till twenty-and-one;
*Lion.* Then hasty as lions, till forty be gone:
*Fox.* Then wily as foxes, till threescore-and-three;
*Ass.* Then after for asses accounted we be.

Certainly, this last takes a most humiliating view of man: and in that division of his book, which the writer calls *The Points of Huswifery*, we are favoured with one, not much more favourable, of woman.

THE DESCRIPTION OF A WOMAN'S AGE.

*By six times fourteen years 'prenticeship, with a lesson to the same.*

14. Two first seven years for a rod they do whine:
28. Two next as a pearl in the world they do shine.
42. Two next trim beauty beginneth to swerve:
56. Two next for matrons or drudges they serve.
70. Two next doth crave a staff for a stay:
84. Two next a bier to fetch them away.

*A lesson.*

Then purchase some pelt
By fifty and three;
Or buckle thyself
A drudge for to be.

THE CITIZEN AND THE THIEVES.

The general apparel of a citizen of London—the friendly custom of borrowing and lending—and the danger and difficulty of travelling that prevailed at the period—are all humorously sketched in the following lines from a popular pamphlet, published in 1609:

'A citizen, for recreation's sake,
To see the country would a journey take
Some dozen miles, or very little more;
Taking his leave with friends two months before,
With drinking healths and shaking by the hand,
As he had travelled to some new-found land.
Well, taking horse, with very much ado,
London he leaveth for a day or two:
And as he rideth, meets upon the way
Such as (what haste soever) bid men stay.
"Sirrah," says one, "stand and your purse deliver,
I am a *taker*, thou must be a *giver*."

Unto a wood, hard by, they hale him in,
And rifle him unto his very skin.
"Maisters," quoth he, "pray hear me ere you go;
For you have robbed me more than you do know,
My horse, in truth, I borrowed of my brother;
The bridle and the saddle of another;
The jerkin and the bases, be a tailor's;
The scarf, I do assure you, is a sailor's;
The falling band is likewise none of mine,
Nor cuffs, as true as this good light doth shine.
The satin doublet, and raised velvet hose
Are our churchwarden's, all the parish knows.
The boots are John the grocer's at the Swan;
The spurs were lent me by a serving-man.
One of my rings—that with the great red stone—
In sooth, I borrowed of my gossip Joan:
Her husband knows not of it, gentle men!
Thus stands my case—I pray shew favour then."

"Why," quoth the thieves, "thou needst not greatly care,
Since in thy loss so many bear a share;
The world goes hard, and many good folks lack,
Look not, at this time, for a penny back.
Go, tell at London thou didst meet with four,
That, rifling thee, have robbed at least a score."'

# JULY 22.

St Mary Magdalen. St Joseph of Palestine (Count Joseph), about 356. St Vandrille or Wandregisilus, abbot of Fontenelles, 666. St Meneve, abbot of Menat, 720. St Dabius or Davius, of Ireland, confessor.

## MARY MAGDALEN.

THE beautiful story of Mary Magdalen—for such it is, though so obscurely related in Scripture—has always made her a popular saint among the Roman Catholics, and Italian painters and sculptors have found an inspiration in her display of the profound moral beauty of repentance. A medieval legend connected with her name represents her as ending her days in France. It is said that, after the crucifixion of Jesus, she, in company with the Virgin and Mary Salome, being much persecuted by the Jews, set sail on the Mediterranean in a leaky boat, and after a miraculous deliverance, landed in the south of Gaul. There, the party separated, the Magdalen retired to St Baume, to spend the remainder of her days in penitence and prayer; and in that retreat, in the odour of sanctity, she closed her earthly pilgrimage.

The rise of saintly histories forms a curious chapter in that of human belief. There has always been much less of positive deliberate deception in them than most persons would now be disposed to admit. Some appearances were presented—a supposition was hazarded about them—this, instantly translated by well-meaning credulity into a fact, set the story agoing. In an age when no one thought of sifting evidence, the tale took wing unchecked, and erelong it became invested with such sanctity, that challenge or doubt was out of the question. In some such way it probably was, that the remains of a dead body found by the monks of Vezelai under their high-altar, were accepted as those of Mary Magdalen. The news soon spread through France; the monks were delighted at the opportunity it afforded them of enriching their monastery, as the celebrity of the saint would certainly draw a great multitude of people; and they determined to encase these relics with a pomp which should dazzle the simple. The king of France, St Louis, who was always interested in anything relating to religion, determined to be present at the festival, and went to Vezelai accompanied by his whole court. The body was drawn from its coffin, and placed in a silver shrine; the legate took a part; and the king several bones, which he had enshrined, some with two of the thorns of Christ's crown, and a morsel of the cross in an arm of gold enriched with pearls and ninety precious stones; others in a reliquary, silver gilt, supported by an angel, and richly ornamented.

But Vezelai was not long in possession of this sacred deposit without Provence disputing it; their tradition was, that St Maximin, bishop of Aix, had buried it at La Baume in an alabaster tomb; and Charles, Prince of Salerno, the eldest son of the king of Sicily, commenced a search for the body, and had the happiness to find it. The legend relates that a delicious odour spread through the chapel, and that from the tongue there sprang a branch of fennel, which, divided into several bits, became as many relics. Near the body were two writings; one on a board covered with wax containing these words: 'Here rests Mary Magdalen:' the other on incorruptible wood, with these words: 'The seven hundredth year of the nativity of our Lord, on the sixteenth day of December, Odoin being the reigning king of France, at the time of the invasion of the Saracens, the body of Saint Mary Magdalen was transferred secretly in the night from her alabaster sepulchre into this of marble for fear of the infidels.' The young prince immediately assembled the nobility and clergy of Provence, raised the body in their presence, enshrined it, and placed the head in a reliquary of pure gold. Then Vezelai lost much of its credit, in spite of the pope, who declared himself on its side. La Baume carried the day, and the preaching friars who held the deposit, triumphed loudly over the monks who kept possession of the other. It gave birth to a long and acrimonious discussion: the latter party objected that dates were never used in France before the middle of the eighth century, under Pepin and Charlemagne. No trace could be found in history of this incursion of the Saracens; and who was Odoin? No king of that name ever reigned in France. So many absurdities discredited the Provençal tradition, yet La Sainte Baume was still frequented by a great concourse of people: now, nothing remains but a grotto celebrated for the fables to which it has given rise.

---

*Born.*—Anthony Ashley Cooper, first Earl of Shaftesbury, celebrated politician in the reign of Charles II., 1621, *Winborne, Dorsetshire.*

*Died.*—Sir John Graham, Scottish patriot, killed at the battle of Falkirk, 1298; Sir Henry Percy (Hotspur), killed at the battle of Shrewsbury, 1403; Charles VII., king of France, 1461, *Meun, in Berri;* Henry III., king of France, assassinated at Paris, 1589; Henry Carey, Lord Hunsdon, 1596, *London;* Gerbrant Vander Eeckhout, Dutch painter, 1674; Pope Clement X., 1676; Francis Lord Gardenstone, Scottish judge, miscellaneous writer, 1793; Marie François Xavier Bichat, eminent French anatomist, 1802, *Paris;* Dr George Shaw, naturalist, 1813, *London;* Joseph Piazzi, eminent astronomer, 1826, *Palermo.*

## THE PERCY INSURRECTION—BATTLE OF SHREWSBURY—DEATH OF HOTSPUR.

Happy are the heroes who are immortalised by the poets of their country. The brave, headstrong, irascible Hotspur; the rousing of Prince Henry to noble deeds from the wild roystering companionship of Falstaff and his friends; the imaginative, superstitious Glendower—all stand as lifelike characters before the eye of hundreds of Englishmen, who would never have heard their names had it not been for the bard of Avon. The powerful Percies, who had been Henry IV.'s greatest friends in the day of distress, became discontented subjects after he ascended the throne. The Hotspur, of whom Henry had said:

> 'O that it could be proved
> That some night-tripping fairy had exchanged
> In cradle-clothes our children where they lay,
> And called mine Percy, his Plantagenet!
> Then would I have his Harry and he mine,'

took dire offence at the refusal of the king to permit him to pay the ransom of his brother-in-law, Sir Edmund Mortimer, who had been taken captive by Owen Glendower. Joining himself to his uncle, the Earl of Worcester, Scroop, archbishop of York, the Scottish Earl of Douglas, and the Welsh chieftain, he entered on the fatal insurrection which cost his life, and that of many thousands of brave men. The earl, his father, being dangerously ill, could not join the rendezvous; but Douglas crossed the border with a goodly array, and the Earl of Worcester collected a picked body of Cheshire archers, all making their way to the borders of Wales, where Glendower's army was to meet them. Henry IV.'s skilful generalship probably saved his crown; for hastening his army with all speed from Burton-upon-Trent, he contrived to get between the two rebel forces, and prevent their junction. Having reached Shrewsbury, and finding Hotspur's army close at hand, he determined to give battle on the following day. During the night, the insurgents sent in a long list of their grievances, in the shape of a defiance: 'For which causes,' said they, 'we do mortally defy thee, thy fautors, and accomplices, as common traitors and destroyers of the realm, and invaders, oppressors, and confounders of the very true and right heir to the crown of England and France; and we intend to prove it this day by force of arms, Almighty God blessing us.'

Early in the morning (July 22, 1403), the eager combatants drew up in battle-array; about 14,000 on each side, brothers in language and country, thus sadly opposed. The martial strains of the trumpets were sounded, the war-cry of 'St George for us!' which had led to many a victory, was answered by, 'Esperance, Percy!' and the bravest knights in Christendom, Hotspur and Douglas, led the charge. Had they been well supported, nothing could have resisted the shock. As it was, many noble knights were slain; the two leaders seeking the king everywhere in vain, he having put on plain clothes, and forcing Hotspur to say: 'The king hath many marching in his coats;' and Douglas to reply:

> 'Another king! they grow like Hydra's heads;
> I am the Douglas, fatal to all those
> That wear those colours on them.'

The Prince of Wales, though wounded in the face, fought with desperate courage, and for three hours the battle raged fearfully; but Hotspur, being shot through the head, fell mortally wounded, and the king's cry of 'Victory and St George!' put the assailants to flight. Douglas, falling from a hill, was so bruised that his pursuers took him; but he was soon after set at liberty. The Earl of Worcester, Sir Richard Vernon, and some others, were executed on the field, and the great but dearly-bought victory of Shrewsbury settled the usurper Henry firmly on the throne. The body of Hotspur, found among the dead, was by Henry's command taken from the grave, where Lord Furnival had laid it, and placed between two millstones in the market-place of Shrewsbury, quartered, and hung upon the gates, after the barbarous fashion of the times. Otterbourne tells us that the courage of the brave Percy was much damped before the battle by an incident which marks the superstitious feeling of the times. When preparing for the field, he called for his favourite sword, and was informed that he had left it at the village of Berwick, where he had rested the previous night. Startled at the name of the place, he heaved a deep sigh, and exclaimed: 'Alas! then my death is near at hand, for a wizard once told me that I should not live long after I had seen Berwick, which I thought was the town in the north.—Yet will I not be cheaply won.'

When the king had put an end to the pursuit and slaughter, he returned thanks for his victory on the field of battle, and commanded the erection of the collegiate church of Battlefield, of which more than half is now in ruins.

## RAT LEGENDS.

On the 22d day of July, in the year of our Lord 1376, according to old Verstegan, a terrible calamity befell the town of Hamel, in Brunswick:

'There came into the town of Hamel an old kind of companion, who, for the fantastical coat which he wore being wrought with sundry colours, was called the Pied Piper. This fellow, forsooth, offered the townsmen, for a certain sum of money, to rid the town of all the rats that were in it (for at that time the burghers were with that vermin greatly annoyed). The accord, in fine, being made, the Pied Piper, with a shrill pipe, went thorow all the streets, and forthwith the rats came all running out of the houses in great numbers after him; all which he led into the river of Weaser, and therein drowned them. This done, and no one rat more perceived to be left in the town, he afterward came to demand his reward according to his bargain; but being told that the bargain was not made with him in good earnest, to wit, with an opinion that he could be able to do such a feat, they cared not what they accorded unto, when they imagined it could never be deserved, and so never be demanded; but, nevertheless, seeing he had done such an unlikely thing indeed, they were content to give him a good reward; and so offered him far less than he looked for. He, therewith discontented, said he would have his full recompense according to his bargain; but they utterly denied to give it him. He threatened them with revenge; they bade him do his worst, whereupon he betakes him again to his pipe, and going thorow the streets as before, was followed by a number of boys out of one of the gates of the city, and coming to a little hill, there opened in the side thereof a wide hole, into the which himself and all the children did enter; and being entered, the hill did close up again, and became as before. A boy, that, being lame, came somewhat lagging behind the rest, seeing this that happened, returned presently back, and told what he had seen; forthwith began great lamentation among the parents for their children, and the men were sent out with all diligence, both by land and by water, to inquire if aught could be heard of them; but with all the inquiry they could possibly use, nothing more than is aforesaid could of them be understood. And this great wonder happened on the 22d day of July, in the year of our Lord 1376.'*

The rat seems altogether a mystical sort of creature; at least, very mystical things are current everywhere regarding it. It is one of the simplest of these, that there are districts where rats do not dwell and cannot be introduced. Not only are we told by the credulous Hector Boece, that there are no rats in Buchan (Aberdeenshire), but a later and more intelligent author, Sir Robert Gordon, makes the same statement regarding Sutherlandshire: 'If,' says he, 'they come thither in ships from other parts, they die presently, how soon they do smell the air of that country.' Sir Robert at the same time asserts, that the species abounds in the neighbouring province of Caithness. But this is not all. The reverend gentlemen who contributed to Sir John Sinclair's *Statistical Account of Scotland*, about 1794, the articles on Morven and Roseneath, the one in the north, the other in the south of Argyleshire, avouch that rats have been introduced into those parishes in vain. The author of the article on Roseneath seems to have been something of a wag, though quite in earnest on the point of fact. 'From a prevailing opinion,' says he, 'that the soil of this parish is hostile to that animal, some years ago, a West India planter actually carried out to Jamaica several casks of Roseneath earth, with a view to kill the rats that were destroying his sugar-canes. It is said this had not the desired effect; so we lost a valuable export. Had the experiment succeeded, this would have been a new and profitable trade for the proprietors; but perhaps by this time, the parish of Roseneath might have been no more!'

It was a prevalent notion in past ages, that you might extirpate rats by a persevering course of anathematising in rhyme. Reginald Scot says that the Irish thought they could rhyme any beast to death; but the notion was, in general, restricted to the rat. It is with reference to this belief, or practice, that Rosalind, in *As You Like It*, says: 'I never was so berhymed since Pythagoras's time, that I was an Irish rat, which I can hardly remember.'

Another prevalent notion regarding rats was, that they had a presentiment of coming evil, and always deserted in time a ship about to be wrecked, or a house about to be flooded or burned. So lately as 1854, it was seriously reported in a Scotch provincial newspaper that, the night before a town mill was burned, the rats belonging to the establishment were met migrating in a body to a neighbouring pease-field. The notion acquires importance as the basis of a new verb in the English language—to rat—much used in political party janglings.

Mr Bewick, the ingenious wood-engraver, has put on record a fact regarding rats nearly as mystical as any of the above. He alleges that 'the skins of such of them as have been devoured in their holes [for they are cannibals to a sad extent] have frequently been found curiously turned inside out, every part of them being completely inverted, even to the ends of the toes.'

It may be added as a more pleasing trait of these too much despised animals, that they are, nevertheless, of a social turn, and have their sports and

* *Restitution of Decayed Intelligence*, chap. iii. edit. 1673, p. 92.

pastimes by themselves. 'They play at hide-and-seek with each other, and have been known to hide themselves in the folds of linen, where they have remained quite still until their playmates have discovered them, in the same manner as kittens. Most readers will recollect the fable, where a young mouse suggests that the cat should have a bell fastened to his neck, so that his companions might be aware of her approach. This idea was scouted by one of their wise-heads, who asked, who was to tie the bell round the cat's neck? This experiment has actually been tried upon a rat. A bell was fastened round his neck, and he was replaced in his hole, with full expectation of his frightening the rest away; but it turned out that, instead of their continuing to be alarmed at his approach, he was heard for the space of a year to frolic and scamper with them.'*

The profession of the rat-catcher is an old and a universal one. In Italy, in the seventeenth

VISCHER'S RAT-CATCHER: SEVENTEENTH CENTURY.

century, as we learn from Annibal Caracci's illustrations of the Cries of Bologna, this kind of professional went about with a pole bearing a square flag, on which were representations of rats and mice. The Chinese rat-catcher carries, as the outward ensign of his craft, a cat in a bag. One of the many exquisite engravings of Cornelius Vischer (born at Haarlem, 1610), gives us the Dutch rat-catcher of that day with all his paraphernalia—a sketch so lifelike and so characteristic that its fidelity cannot be doubted. Our artist here gives what we are happy to consider a tolerable transcript of this humorous print. In the original, the following inscription is given in prose form:

Fele fugas mures: magnis si furibus arces
Exiguos fures, furor est; me respice, vilis
Si modo nummus adest, mures felesque fugabo.

[i. e. 'By the cat you put rats to flight. If you drive away little thieves by great ones, it is utter folly. Look at me; provided only a little coin is forthcoming, I will put both rats and cats to flight.']

## HOUSEHOLD SUPERSTITIONS.

If a fire does not burn well, and you want to 'draw it up,' you should set the poker across the hearth, with the fore part leaning across the top bar of the grate, and you will have a good fire—if you wait long enough; but you must not be unreasonable, and refuse to give time for the charm to work. For a charm it is, the poker and top bar combined, forming *a cross*, and so defeating the malice of the gnomes, who are jealous of our possession of their subterranean treasures; or else of the witches and demons, who preside over smoky chimneys. I had seen the thing done scores of times; and understanding that it was supposed to create a draught, like a poor weak rationalist as I was, I once thought to improve the matter by setting up the *shovel* instead of the poker; but I

* Smith's *Cries of London*, 4to, 1839, p. 33.

might as well have left it alone—the fire wasn't to be taken in, or the witches balked, by such a shallow contrivance, and I was left in the cold.

This poker-superstition is at least harmless, and we may admit that among those belonging to the household there are some which are positively beneficial—for example, those referring to the breakage of glass and crockery.

You have a valuable mirror, we will say. Do you know what is its greatest safeguard from the handles of housemaids' brooms, &c.? It is the belief, that if a looking-glass is broken, there will be a death in the family within the year. This fear is, of course, most operative in small households, where there are but few persons to divide the risk with the delinquent.

I once had a servant who was very much given to breaking glass and crockery. Plates and wine-glasses used to slip out of her hands, as if they had been soaped; even spoons (which it was hardly worth while to drop, for they would not break) came jingling to the ground in rapid succession.

'Let her buy something,' said the cook, 'and that will change the luck.' 'Decidedly,' said the mistress, 'it will be as well that she feel the inconvenience herself.' 'Oh, I didn't mean that, ma'am,' was the reply; 'I meant that it would change the luck.'

'Well, have you broken anything more?' I asked, a few days after this conversation. 'No, sir,' the girl answered, 'I hav'nt broken nothing since I bout the 'tater dish.' Unluckily, however, this was too good to last; the breaking recommenced, and we were obliged to part.

If you break two things, you will break a third.

A neighbour saw one of her servants take up a coarse earthenware basin, and deliberately throw it down upon the brick floor.

'What *did* you do that for?' asked the mistress. 'Because, ma'am, I'd broke tew things,' answered the servant, 'so I thout the third 'd better be this here,' pointing to the remains of the least valuable piece of pottery in the establishment, which had been sacrificed to glut the vengeance of the offended Ceramic deities.

*Suffolk.* C. W. J.

## JULY 23.

St Apollinaris, bishop of Ravenna, martyr, 1st century.
St Liborius, bishop of Mans, confessor, about 397.

*Born.*—Godfrey Olearius, the younger, German divine, 1672, *Leipsic.*

*Died.*—St Bridget of Sweden, 1372; Sir Robert Sherley, English military adventurer in Persia, 1627; Richard Gibson, artist, 1690; Gilles Menage, grammarian and versifier, 1692, *Paris;* Vicomte Alexandre de Beauharnais, first husband of the Empress Josephine, guillotined, 1794; Jean Francois Vauvilliers, eminent French scholar, 1800, *St Petersburg;* Arthur Wolfe, Lord Kilwarden, murdered by the populace in Dublin, 1803; Mrs Elizabeth Hamilton, authoress of the *Cottagers of Glenburnie*, 1816, *Harrowgate.*

### ST BRIDGET OF SWEDEN.

Birgir, widow of Ulpho, Prince of Nericia, died on the 23d of July 1372, and, a few years afterwards, was canonised by Pope Boniface IX., under the appellation of St Bridget of Sweden. Unlike most other saints, there seems to have been little more miraculous in her character and career, than the simple fact, that she was a pious woman, a scholar, and writer on religious subjects, at a period of general barbarism. She founded the monastic order of Bridgetines, peculiar of its kind, as it included both nuns and monks under the same roof. The regular establishment of a house of Bridgetines numbered sixty nuns, thirteen monks, four deacons, and eight lay-brothers; the lady-abbess controlling and superintending the whole. The mortified and religious life to which they had bound themselves, by the most solemn engagements, was supposed to render the mixed inmates of these convents superior to temptation, and free from the slightest suspicion of evil. Strange stories, nevertheless, have been told of these communities, and the greater part, if not all, of the convents of the order that now exist, are of one sex alone.

There is an ancient wood-cut, formerly in the possession of Earl Spencer, representing St Bridget of Sweden writing her works. A pilgrim's staff, hat, and scrip, raised behind her, alluded to her many pilgrimages. The letters S.P.Q.R., in the upper corner, denoted that she died at Rome. The lion of Sweden, and crown at her feet, shewed that she was a princess of that country, as well as her contempt for worldly dignities. A legend above her head consisted of a brief invocation in German: '*O, Brigita, bit Got fur uns!*'—O, Bridget, pray to God for us!

A striking illustration of the inherent vitality of extreme weakness, not unfrequently met with, both in the moral and physical world, is exhibited in the history of the first and only house of Bridgetines established in England. About 1420, Henry V., as a memorial of the battle of Agincourt, founded the Bridgetine House of Sion, on that pleasant bank of the Thames, now so well known by the palatial residence of the Duke of Northumberland. And there, with broad lands, fisheries, mill-sites, water-courses, and other valuable endowments, the establishment—the female part consisting principally of ladies of rank—flourished in peace and plenty till the dissolution of monasteries in 1539. Even then the inmates were not thrown helpless on the world; all were allowed pensions, more or less according to their stations, from Dame Agnes Jordan, the abbess, who received £200 per annum, for life, down to the humble lay-brother, whose yearly dole was £2, 13*s.* 4*d.* The community thus broken up, did not all separate. A few holding together, joined a convent of their order at Dermond, in Flanders; from whence they were brought back, and triumphantly reinstated in their original residence of Sion, by Queen Mary, in 1557. Of those who had remained in England at the dissolution, few were found, after a lapse of eighteen years, to join their old community. Some were dead; some, renouncing their ancient faith, or yielding to the dictates of nature, had married. As old Fuller quaintly phrases it, 'the elder nuns were in their graves, the younger in the arms of their husbands;' but with the addition of new members, the proper number was again made up. But scarcely had they been settled in their ancient abode, ere the accession of Elizabeth once more dissolved the establishment; and at this second dissolution, all the nuns, with the exception of the abbess, left England, to seek a place of rest and refuge at Dermond. The convent at Dermond being too poor to support so many, the Duchess of Parma gave the English nuns a monastery in

Zealand, to which they transferred the House of Sion; but the place being unendowed and unhealthy, poverty and sickness compelled them to abandon it, and they were fortunate enough to obtain a house and church near Antwerp. Here the fugitives thought they had at last found a shelter and a home, but they soon were undeceived. In a popular tumult, their house and furniture were destroyed, and only by a timely flight did they themselves escape insult and injury from the rudest of the populace. Their next establishment was at Mechlin, where they lived for seven years, till that city was taken by the Prince of Orange. In the misery and confusion consequent thereon, the nuns were accidentally discovered by some English officers in the service of the prince, who preserved and protected them; and learning that they might find a shelter at Rouen, the officers, though of the reformed faith, protected their countrywomen in all honour and safety to Antwerp, and provided them with a passage to France. Arriving at Rouen in 1589, the sisters of Sion, though sunk in poverty, had another brief rest, till that city was besieged by Henry IV. At its capture, their house was confiscated, but they were assisted to hire a ship to convey them to Lisbon. They arrived at Lisbon in 1594, and were well received; soon finding themselves comfortably situated, with a pension from the king of Spain, a church, monastery, and other endowments. With the exception of being burned out in 1651, and the demolition of their convent by the great earthquake in 1755, the nuns of Sion, continually recruited by accessions from the British Islands, lived at Lisbon, in peaceful and easy circumstances, till the revolutionary wars of 1809. In that year, ten of them fled for refuge to England; and receiving a small pension from government, managed to subsist, through various vicissitudes and changes of residence, till finally dispersed by death and other causes. But those who remained at Lisbon, after suffering great privations—their convent being made an hospital for the Duke of Wellington's army—recovered all their former privileges at the end of the war; and being joined by several English ladies, became a flourishing community. The last scene of this eventful history is not the least strange, nor can it be better or more concisely told, than in the following paragraph from a London newspaper, published in September 1861:

'NUNS PER LISBON STEAMER.—The *Sultan*, on Saturday, brought over twelve nuns of the ancient convent of Sion House, who return to England, having purchased an establishment at Spetisbury, in Dorsetshire. The sisters bring with them the antique stone cross which formerly stood over the gateway of Sion House at Isleworth, also several ancient statues which adorned the original church, and a portrait of Henry V. of England, their founder, which is said to be a likeness, and to have been painted during the monarch's lifetime. This order of Bridgetines has been settled at Lisbon since the year 1595; but there being now more religious liberty in England than in Portugal, and more prospects here for the prosperity of the order, the sisterhood have determined to return to their native land. The Duke of Northumberland, to whose ancestors the ancient Sion House, with its lands, was granted by Henry VIII., has given the poor nuns a handsome donation to assist them in defraying the expenses of their journey and change of establishment.'

## SIR ROBERT SHERLEY.

Among the remarkable travellers of the fifteenth and sixteenth centuries, not the least so was the youngest son of Sir Thomas Sherley, of Wistenston, in Sussex. A love of adventure seems to have inspired both himself and his elder brother, Sir Anthony, from an early age; for who in those days could fail to be roused when the discoveries of Columbus, Sir Walter Raleigh, and other adventurous seamen were the daily topic? As soon as Robert Sherley was of sufficient age he set off on his travels, and wishing to understand the politics of various European courts, he attached himself to their sovereigns, and, for five years, was employed by them in various missions. The Emperor Rodolf, of Germany, was so much satisfied by the talents he evinced on one of his embassies, that he created him a count of the empire. His brother Anthony had, during this time, been in Persia, and thither Robert followed him, and was introduced at the court. The king, acknowledging the abilities of the stranger who had arrived, made him a general of artillery, and for ten years he fought against the Turks with distinguished bravery; bringing the newest improvements in cannon and arms generally under the notice of the government; but, at the same time, getting into considerable trouble through the envy of the Persian nobles, who could not bear to see honours showered upon a stranger.

A life in the east cannot be passed without romance, and so it fell out that the valour and noble conduct of Sir Robert inflamed the hearts of many a fair Persian, but above all of Teresia, the daughter of Ismay Hawn, prince of the city of Hercassia Major, whose sister was one of the queens of Persia. Much difficulty and opposition did the true lovers meet with, but at length they were married. After this, Sir Robert seems to have left the army, and returned to his former life as ambassador to various countries; among the rest, to Rome, where he went in 1609, and was received with every mark of distinction, magnificent entertainments being given to him. He then came to England, bringing his wife with him, who must have been much astonished with the manners of a country which probably none of her countrywomen had ever seen before. They were, however, received with great favour by James I., and especially by Henry, Prince of Wales, a young man always ready to welcome enterprising countrymen. Here his wife presented him with a son on the 4th of November 1611, on which occasion the happy father wrote the following letter to the prince, requesting him to stand godfather:

'MOST RENOWNEDE PRINCE—The great hounors and favors it hath pleased your Highnes to use towards me, hathe embouldede me to wrighte thes fewe lyns, which shal be to beseeche your Highnes to Christen a sonn which God hath geven me. Your Highnes in this shal make your servant happy, whose whole loudginge is to doe your Highnes some segniolated servis worthy to be esteemed in your Prinsly breast. I have not the pen of Sissero [Cicero], yet want I not menes to sownde your Highnesse's worthy prayses into the ears of forran nattions and mighty princes;

and I assure myselfe your high-borne sperrit thirstes after Fame, the period of great princes' ambissiones. And further I will ever be your Highnes' most humbele and observaunt servant, ROBERT SHERLEY.'

This letter certainly does not give us a very high opinion of the ambassador's learning. He was said to be 'a famous general, but a wretched scholar; his patience was more philosophical than his intellect, having small acquaintance with the muses. Many cities he saw, many hills climbed over, and tasted many waters; yet Athens, Parnassus, Hippocrene, were strangers to him: his notion prompted him to other employments.' Yet in spite of this, the prince gave his godchild his own name, the queen taking the office of godmother; and when the father returned to Persia, he left his little boy under her care. Sherley was again in England in 1624, but with very sad results. A quarrel arose between him and the Persian ambassador, which caused the king to send them both back to Persia, to reconcile their differences. Whether the ambassador felt himself in the wrong, and durst not face his master, certain it is that he poisoned himself on the way; and Sir Robert being unable to gain a hearing and proper satisfaction from the court, died of a broken heart at the age of sixty-three. There is a portrait of him at Petworth, in his Persian dress; for it seems that he liked to appear in England in these foreign garments, as more graceful and picturesque than his national garb.

## GILLES MENAGE.

Menage, in the earlier part of his life, was a lawyer, but though eminently successful as a pleader, he entered the church to acquire more leisure for his favourite pursuit of literature. A curious trial, on which he was engaged, affords a remarkable instance of justice overtaking a criminal, in what may be termed an unjust manner.

A country priest, of a notoriously violent and vicious character, had a dispute about money-matters with the tax-collector of the district; who soon afterwards disappearing, a strong suspicion arose that he had been murdered by the priest. About the same time, a man was executed for highway robbery, and his body gibbeted in chains by the roadside, as a warning to others. The relations of the highwayman came one night and took the body down, with the intention of burying it; but, being frightened by a passing patrol, they could do no more than sink it in a pond, not far from the priest's residence. Some fishermen, when drawing their nets, found the body, and the neighbours applying their previous suspicions to the then much disfigured body of the highwayman, alleged that it was that of the tax-collector. The priest was arrested, tried, and condemned, solemnly protesting against the injustice of his sentence, but, when the day of execution arrived, he admitted that he had perpetrated the crime for which he was about to suffer. Nevertheless, he said, I am unjustly condemned, for the tax-collector's body, with that of his dog, still lies buried in my garden, where I killed them both. On search being made, the bodies of the man and dog were found in the place described by the priest; and subsequent inquiries brought to light the secret of the body found in the pond.

## RICHARD GIBSON.

On the 23d of July 1690, died Richard Gibson, aged seventy-five; and nineteen years afterwards, his widow died at the advanced age of eighty-nine. Nature thus, by length of years, compensated this compendious couple, as Evelyn terms them, for shortness of stature—the united heights of the two amounting to no more than seven feet. Gibson

RICHARD GIBSON.

was miniature-painter, in every sense of the phrase, as well as court-dwarf, to Charles I.; his wife, Ann Shepherd, was court-dwarf to Queen Henrietta Maria. Her majesty encouraged a marriage between these two clever but diminutive persons; the king giving away the bride, the queen presenting her with a diamond ring; while Waller, the court-poet, celebrated the nuptials in one of his prettiest poems.

'Design or chance make others wive,
But nature did this match contrive;
Eve might as well have Adam fled,
As she denied her little bed
To him, for whom Heaven seemed to frame
And measure out this little dame.'

The conclusion of the poem is very elegant.

'Ah Chloris! that kind nature, thus,
From all the world had severed us;
Creating for ourselves, us two,
As Love has me, for only you.'

The marriage was an eminently happy one. The little couple had nine children, five of whom lived to years of maturity, and full ordinary stature. Gibson had the honour of being drawing-master to Queen Mary and her sister Queen Anne. His works were much valued, and one of them was the innocent cause of a tragical event. This painting, representing the parable of the lost sheep, was highly prized by Charles I., who gave it into the charge of Vandervort, the keeper of the royal pictures, with strict orders to take the greatest care of it. In obedience to these orders, the unfortunate man put the picture away so carefully, that he could not find it himself when the king asked for it a short time afterwards. Afraid or ashamed to say that he had mislaid it, Vandervort committed suicide by hanging. A few days after his death, the picture was found in the spot where he had placed it.

The courts of the Sultan and Czar are, we believe, the only European ones where dwarfs are still retained as fitting adjuncts to imperial state. The last court-dwarf in England was a German, named Coppernin, retained by the Princess of Wales, mother to George III.

## CHRISTOBELLA, VISCOUNTESS SAY AND SELE.

This lady, who died on 23d of July 1789, in the ninety-fifth year of her age, was remarkable for her vivacity and sprightliness, even to extreme old age. She was the eldest daughter and coheir of Sir Thomas Tyrrell, Bart. of Castlethorpe, Bucks. She was thrice married: first, to John Knapp, Esq., of Cumner, Berkshire; secondly, to John Pigott, Esq., of Doddershall House, in the parish of Quainton, Bucks; and lastly, to Richard Fiennes, Viscount Say and Sele. Mr Pigott, her second husband, left her, in dowry for life, his family estates, and Doddershall House became her ordinary place of residence. It is a fine old mansion, built in 1639, in the Elizabethan style, and contains some spacious rooms, with much curious and interesting carvings, and antique furniture. Here it was that, after the death of her third husband, when she was at least eighty-six years old, she used frequently to entertain large social parties, and her balls were the gayest and pleasantest in the county. She was the life of all her parties; she still loved the company of the young, and often seemed the sprightliest among them; she was still passionately devoted to dancing, and practised it with grace and elegance, even when many far her juniors, were sinking into the decrepitude of age. Gray, wishing to have a fling at Sir Christopher Hatton's late love of gaiety, sings:

'Full oft within these spacious walls,
When he had fifty winters o'er him,
My grave lord-keeper led the brawls,
The seals and maces danced before him.'

But men of fifty were mere boys to Lady Say and Sele, when she gaily tripped it 'on the light fantastic toe,' in her own ball-room at Doddershall. It was truly delicious to see her ladyship at eighty-eight, and her youthful partner of sixty-five, merrily leading the country-dance, or bounding away in the cotillon, or gracefully figuring a fashionable minuet.

'And around, and around, and around they go,
Heel to heel, and toe to toe,
Prance and caper, curvet and wheel,
Toe to toe, and heel to heel.
'Tis merry, 'tis merry, Sir Giles, I trow,
To dance thus at sixty, as we do now.'

When her ladyship was about ninety, she used to say, that she 'had chosen her first husband for love, her second for riches, and her third for rank, and that she had now some thoughts of beginning again in the same order.' 'I have always hitherto,' she continued, 'been able to secure the best dancer in the neighbourhood for my partner, by sending him an annual present of a haunch or two of venison; but latterly, I begin to think he has shewn a preference for younger ladies; so, I suppose, I must increase my bribe, and send him a whole buck at a time, instead of a haunch.' Her exact age was not known, for she most carefully concealed it, and it is said, even caused the record of her baptism to be erased from the parish-register. She was buried in the church at Grendon-Underwood, the burial-place of the Pigott family, and the inscription on her monument describes her as ninety-four, but it was generally believed that she was above a hundred when she died.

There is a portrait of her at Doddershall, and Pope, who visited her in the time of her second husband, is said to have written some verses in her praise with a diamond on the pane of a window, which unfortunately has been destroyed. Addison, who also visited at Doddershall, is supposed to have taken it as his model for an old manor-house. It is only an act of justice to Lady Say and Sele to mention, that while she loved gay recreations, she was not unmindful of the wants of the poor. She was benevolent while living, and in her will, dated two years before her death, she bequeathed large sums of money for the endowment of some excellent charities for the poor of the several parishes with which she was connected.

## 'THE CASTING OF THE STOOLS.'

The 23d of July 1637 is the date of an event of a semi-ludicrous character, which may be considered as the opening of the civil war. By a series of adroit measures, James I. contrived to introduce bishops into the Scotch church. His son, Charles I., who was altogether a less dexterous, as well as a more arbitrary ruler, wished to complete the change by bringing in a book of canons and a liturgy. He was backed up by his great councillor Archbishop Laud, whose tendencies were to something like Romanising even the English church. Between them, a service-book, on the basis of the English one, but said to include a few Romish peculiarities besides, was prepared in 1636 for the Scotch church, which was thought to be too much under awe of the royal power to make any resistance. In reality, while a certain deference had been paid to the king's will in religious matters, there was a large amount of discontent in the minds of both clergy and people. The Scotch had all along, from the Reformation, had a strong predilection for evangelical doctrines and a simple and informal style of worship. Bishops ruling in the church-courts they had, with more or less unwillingness, submitted to; but an interference with their ordinary Sunday-worship in the churches was too much for their patience. The king was ill-informed on the subject, or he would never have committed himself to such a dangerous innovation.

On the day mentioned, being Sunday, the service-book was, by an imperious command from the king, to be read in every parish-church in Scotland. Before the day arrived, the symptoms of popular opposition appeared almost everywhere so ominous, that few of the clergy were prepared to obey the order. In the principal church of Edinburgh, the chancel of the old cathedral of St Giles, which contained the seats of the judges, magistrates, and other authorities, the liturgy was formally introduced under the auspices of the bishop, dean, and other clergy. Here, if anywhere, it might have been expected that the royal will would have been implicitly carried out. And so it would, perhaps, if there had been only a congregation of official dignitaries. But the body of the church was, in reality, filled by a body of the common sort of people, including a large proportion of citizens' wives and their maid-servants—Christians of vast zeal, and comparatively safe by their sex and their obscurity. There were no pews in those days; each godly dame sat on her own chair or clasp-stool, brought to church on purpose. When the dean, Mr James Hannay, opened the service-book and began to read the prayers, this multitude was struck with a horror which defied all control. They raised their voices in discordant clamours and abusive language, denouncing the dean as of the progeny of the devil, and the bishop as a belly-god, calling out that it was rank popery they were bringing in. A strenuous female (Jenny Geddes) threw her stool at the dean's head, and whole

'JENNY GEDDES'S STOOL.'
From the Antiquarian Museum, Edinburgh.*

sackfuls of small clasp-Bibles followed. The bishop from the pulpit endeavoured to calm the people, but in vain. A similar 'ticket of remembrance' to that aimed at the dean was levelled at him, but fell short of its object. The magistrates from their gallery made efforts to quell the disturbance—all in vain; and they were obliged to clear out the multitude by main force, before the reading of the liturgy could be proceeded with.

After the formal dismissal of the congregation, the bishop was mobbed on the street, and narrowly escaped with his life. It became apparent to the authorities that they could not safely carry out the royal instructions, and they wrote to court in great anxiety, shewing in what difficulties they were placed. Had the king tacitly withdrawn the service-book, the episcopal arrangements might have held their ground. He pressed on; a formal opposition from the people of Scotland arose, and never rested till the whole policy of the last forty years had been undone. In short, the civil war, which ended in the destruction of the royal government twelve years after, might be said to have begun with the Casting of the Stools in St Giles's Kirk.

* Strange as it may appear, there is tolerably good evidence that the stool here depicted is identical with the one which was thrown at the dean.

## LONDON MUG-HOUSES AND THE MUG-HOUSE RIOTS.

On the 23d of July 1716, a tavern in Salisbury Court, Fleet Street, was assailed by a great mob, evidently animated by a deadly purpose. The house was defended, and bloodshed took place before quiet was restored. This affair was a result of the recent change of dynasty. The tavern was one of a set in which the friends of the newly acceded Hanover family assembled, to express their sentiments and organise their measures. The mob was a Jacobite mob, to which such houses were a ground of offence. But we must trace the affair more in detail.

Amongst the various clubs which existed in London at the commencement of the eighteenth century, there was not one in greater favour than the Mug-house Club, which met in a great hall in Long Acre, every Wednesday and Saturday, during the winter. The house had got its name from the simple circumstance, that each member drank his ale (the only liquor used) out of a separate mug. There was a president, who is described in 1722 as 'a grave old gentleman in his own gray hairs, now full ninety years of age.' A harper sat occasionally playing at the bottom of the room. From time to time, a member would give a song. Healths were drunk, and jokes transmitted along the table. Miscellaneous as the company was—and it included barristers as well as trades-people—great harmony prevailed. In the early days of this fraternity there was no room for politics, or anything that could sour conversation.*

By and by, the death of Anne brought on the Hanover succession. The Tories had then so much the better of the other party, that they gained the mob on all public occasions to their side. It became necessary for King George's friends to do something in counteraction of this tendency. No better expedient occurred to them, than the establishing of mug-houses, like that of Long Acre, throughout the metropolis, wherein the friends of the Protestant succession might rally against the partizans of a popish pretender. First, they had one in St John's Lane, chiefly under the patronage of a Mr Blenman, a member of the Middle Temple, who took for his motto, 'Pro rege et lege;' then arose the Roebuck mug-house in Cheapside, the haunt of a fraternity of young men who had been organised for political action before the end of the late reign. According to a pamphlet on the subject, dated in 1717, 'The next mug-houses opened in the city were at Mrs Read's coffee-house in Salisbury Court, in Fleet Street, and at the Harp in Tower Street, and another at the Roebuck in Whitechapel. About the same time, several other mug-houses were erected in the suburbs, for the reception and entertainment of the like loyal societies; viz., one at the Ship, in Tavistock Street, Covent Garden, which is

* [Macky's] *Journey through England*, i. 271.

mostly frequented by loyal officers of the army; another at the Black Horse, in Queen Street, near Lincoln's-Inn-Fields, set up and carried on by gentlemen, servants to that noble patron of loyalty, to whom this vindication of it is inscribed [the Duke of Newcastle]; a third was set up at the Nag's Head, in James's Street, Covent Garden; a fourth at the Fleece, in Burleigh Street, near Exeter Exchange; a fifth at the Hand and Tench, near the Seven Dials; several in Spittlefields, by the French refugees; one in Southwark Park; and another in the Artillery Ground.' Another of the rather celebrated mug-houses was the Magpie, without Newgate, which still exists in the Magpie and Stump, in the Old Bailey. At all of these houses

A LONDON MUG-HOUSE.

it was customary in the forenoon to exhibit the whole of the mugs belonging to the establishment in a range over the door—the best sign and attraction for the loyal that could have been adopted, for the White Horse of Hanover itself was not more emblematic of the new dynasty than was—the Mug.

It was the especial age of clubs, and the frequenters of these mug-houses formed themselves into societies, or clubs, known generally as the Mug-house Clubs, and severally by some distinctive name or other, and each club had its president to rule its meetings and keep order. The president was treated with great ceremony and respect: he was conducted to his chair every evening at about seven o'clock, or between that and eight, by members carrying candles before and behind him, and accompanied with music. Having taken a seat, he appointed a vice-president, and drank the health of the company assembled, a compliment which the company returned. The evening was then passed in drinking successively loyal and other healths, and in singing songs. Soon after ten, they broke up, the president naming his successor for the next evening, and, before he left the chair, a collection was made for the musicians.

These clubs played a very active part in the violent political struggles of the time. The Jacobites had laboured with much zeal to secure the alliance of the street-mob, and they had used it with great effect, in connection with Dr Sacheverell, in overthrowing Queen Anne's Whig government, and paving the way for the return of the exiled family. Disappointment at the accession of George I. rendered the party of the Pretender more unscrupulous, the mob was excited to go to greater lengths, and the streets of London were occupied by an infuriated rabble, and presented nightly a scene of riot such as can hardly be imagined in our quiet times. It was under these circumstances that the mug-house clubs volunteered, in a very disorderly manner, to be the champions of order, and with this purpose it became a part of their evening's entertainment to march into the street and fight the Jacobite mob. This practice commenced in the autumn of 1715, when the club called the Loyal Society, which met at the Roebuck, in Cheapside, distinguished itself by its hostility to Jacobitism. On one occasion, at the period of which we are now speaking, the members of this society, or the Mug-house Club of the Roebuck, had burned the Pretender in effigy. Their first conflict with the mob recorded in the newspapers occurred on the 31st of October 1715. It was the birthday of the Prince of Wales, and was celebrated by illuminations and bonfires. There were a few Jacobite alehouses, chiefly situated on Holborn Hill [Sacheverell's parish], and in Ludgate Street; and it was probably the frequenters of the Jacobite public-house in the latter locality who stirred up the mob on this occasion to raise a riot on Ludgate Hill, put out the bonfire there, and break the windows which were illuminated. The Loyal Society men, receiving intelligence of what was going on, hurried to the spot, and, in the words of the newspaper report, 'soundly thrashed and dispersed' the rioters. The 4th of November was the anniversary of the birth of King William III., and the Jacobite mob made a large bonfire in the Old Jury, to burn an effigy of that monarch; but the mug-house men came upon them again, gave them 'due chastisement with oaken plants,' demolished their bonfire, and carried King William in triumph to the Roebuck. Next day was the commemoration of gunpowder treason, and the loyal mob had its pageant. A long procession was formed, having in front a figure of the infant Pretender, accompanied by two men bearing each a warming-pan, in allusion to the story about his birth, and followed by effigies, in gross caricature, of the pope, the Pretender, the Duke of Ormond, Lord Bolingbroke, and the Earl of Mar, with halters round their necks, and all of which were to be burned in a large bonfire made in Cheapside. The procession, starting from the Roebuck, went through Newgate Street, and up Holborn Hill, where they compelled the bells of St Andrew's Church, of which Sacheverell was incumbent, to ring; thence through Lincoln's-Inn-Fields and Covent Garden to the gate of St James's palace; returning by way of Pall-Mall and the Strand, and through St Paul's Churchyard. They had met with no interruption on their way, but on their return to Cheapside, they found that, during their absence, that quarter had been invaded by the Jacobite mob, who had carried away all the materials which had been collected for the bonfire. Thus the various anniversaries became, by such demonstrations, the occasions for the greatest turbulence; and these riots became more alarming, in consequence of the efforts which were made to increase the force of the Jacobite mob.

On the 17th of November, of the year just mentioned, the Loyal Society met at the Roebuck, to celebrate the anniversary of the accession of Queen Elizabeth; and, while busy with their mugs, they received information that the Jacobites, or, as they commonly called them, the Jacks, were assembled in great force in St Martin's-le-Grand, and preparing to burn the effigies of King William and King George, along with the Duke of Marlborough. They were so near, in fact, that their party-shouts of High Church, Ormond, and King James, must have been audible at the Roebuck, which stood opposite Bow Church. The 'Jacks' were starting on their procession, when they were overtaken in Newgate Street by the mug-house men from the Roebuck, and a desperate encounter took place, in which the Jacobites were defeated, and many of them were seriously injured. Meanwhile the Roebuck itself had been the scene of a much more serious tumult. During the absence of

MUG-HOUSE RIOT.

the great mass of the members of the club, another body of Jacobites, much more numerous than those engaged in Newgate Street, suddenly assembled and attacked the Roebuck mug-house, broke its windows and those of the adjoining houses, and with terrible threats, attempted to force the door. One of the few members of the Loyal Society who remained at home, discharged a gun upon those of the assailants who were attacking the door, and killed one of their leaders. This, and the approach of the lord mayor and city officers, caused the mob to disperse; but the Roebuck was exposed to continued attacks during several following nights, after which the mobs remained tolerably quiet through the winter.

With the month of February 1716, these riots began to be renewed with greater violence than ever, and large preparations were made for an active mob-campaign in the spring. The mug-houses were refitted, and re-opened with ceremonious entertainments, and new songs were composed to encourage and animate the clubs. Collections of these mug-house songs were printed in little volumes, of which copies are still preserved, though they now come under the class of rare books. The Jacobite mob was again heard gathering in the streets by its well-known signal of the beating of marrow-bones and cleavers, and both sides were well furnished with staves of oak, their usual arms, for the combat, although other weapons, and missiles of various descriptions, were in common use One of the mug-house songs gives the following account of the way in which these riots were carried on:

'Since the Tories could not fight,
And their master took his flight,
They labour to keep up their faction;
With a bough and a stick,
And a stone and a brick,
They equip their roaring crew for action.

Thus in battle-array,
At the close of the day,
After wisely debating their plot,
Upon windows and stall
They courageously fall,
And boast a great victory they 've got.

But, alas! silly boys!
For all the mighty noise
Of their "High Church and Ormond for ever!"
A brave Whig, with one hand,
At George's command,
Can make their mightiest hero to quiver.'

One of the great anniversaries of the Whigs was the 8th of March, the day of the death of King William; and with this the more serious mug-house riots of the year 1716 appear to have commenced. A large Jacobite mob assembled to their old watchword, and marched along Cheapside to attack the Roebuck; but they were soon driven away by a small party of the Loyal Society, who met there. The latter then marched in procession through Newgate Street, paid their respects to the Magpie as they passed, and went through the Old Bailey to Ludgate Hill. On their return, they found that the Jacobite mob had collected in great force in their rear, and a much more serious engagement took place in Newgate Street, in which the 'Jacks' were again beaten, and many persons sustained serious personal injury. Another great tumult, or rather series of tumults, occurred on the evening of the 23d of April, the anniversary of the birth of Queen Anne, during which there were great battles both in Cheapside and at the end of Giltspur Street, in the immediate neighbourhood of the two celebrated mug-houses, the Roebuck and the Magpie, which shews that the Jacobites had now become enterprising. Other great tumults took place on the 29th of May, the anniversary of the Restoration, and on the 10th of June, the Pretender's birthday. From this time the Roebuck is rarely mentioned, and the attacks of the mob appear to have been directed against other houses. On the 12th of July, the mug-house in Southwark, and, on the 20th, that in Salisbury Court (Read's Coffee-house), were fiercely assailed, but successfully defended. The latter was attacked by a much more numerous mob on the evening of the 23d of July, and after a resistance which lasted all night, the assailants forced their way in, and kept the Loyal Society imprisoned in the upper rooms of the house while they gutted the lower part, drank as much ale out of the cellar as they could, and let the rest run out. Read, in desperation, had shot their ringleader with a blunderbuss, in revenge for which they left the coffeehouse-keeper for dead; and they were at last with difficulty dispersed by the arrival of the military. The inquest on the dead man found a verdict of wilful murder against Read; but, when put upon his trial, he was acquitted, while several of the rioters, who had been taken, were hanged. This result appears to have damped the courage of the rioters, and to have alarmed all parties, and we hear no more of the mug-house riots. Their incompatibility with the preservation of public order was very generally felt, and they became the subject of great complaints. A few months later, a pamphlet appeared, under the title of *Down with the Mug, or Reasons for Suppressing the Mug-houses*, by an author who only gave his name as Sir H. M.; but who seems to have shewn so much of what was thought to be Jacobite spirit, that it provoked a reply, entitled *The Mug Vindicated.*

But the mug-houses, left to themselves, soon became very harmless.

## BLOOMER COSTUME.

The originator of this style of dress was Mrs Amelia Bloomer, the editor of a temperance journal named *The Lily*, which was published at Seneca Falls, New York. A portrait of her, exemplifying her favourite costume, is given on the following page, from a photograph taken by Mr T. W. Brown, Auburn, New York. The dress was first brought practically before the notice of the world, at a ball held on the 23d of July 1851, at the cotton-manufacturing town of Lowell, Massachusetts. It was an attempt to substitute for the cumbrous, inconvenient, inelegant, and in many other respects objectionable dress which then and has since prevailed, one of a light, graceful, and convenient character. In no part of the world, perhaps, would such a reform have been attempted but in one where women had for some time been endeavouring to assert an individuality and independence heretofore unknown to the meeker sex. But, like many other reformers, Mrs Bloomer lived before her proper day. In the pleading which she made for the proposed change in her magazine, she defended it from the charge of being either immodest or inelegant. She there adverts to the picturesque dress of the Polish ladies, with high fur-trimmed boots, and short tunic skirt: and she asks: 'If delicacy requires that the skirt should be long, why do our ladies, a dozen times a day, commit the indelicacy of raising their dresses, which have already been sweeping the side-walks, to prevent their draggling in the mud of the streets? Surely a few spots of mud added to the refuse of the side-walks, on the hem of their garment, are not to be compared to the charge of indelicacy, to which the display they make might subject them!' It may here be mentioned, in illustration of this matter, that the streets of American cities are kept much less carefully cleaned than those of our British cities.

The authorities in the new fashion left the upper portion of the dress to be determined according to the individual taste of the wearer; but Mrs Bloomer described the essential portion as follows: 'We would have a skirt reaching down to nearly half-way between the knee and the ankle, and not made quite so full as is the present fashion. Underneath this skirt, trousers moderately full, in fair, mild weather, coming down to the ankle (not instep), and there gathered in with an elastic band. The shoes or slippers to suit the occasion. For winter, or wet weather, the trousers also full, but coming down into a boot, which should rise some three or four inches at least above the ankle. This boot should be gracefully sloped at the upper edge, and trimmed with fur, or fancifully embroidered, according to the taste of the wearer. The material might be cloth, morocco, moose-skin, &c., and water-proof, if desirable.' The costume-reformer adduced many advantages which would follow the use of this kind of dress. There would be less soiling from the muddy state of the streets; it would be cheaper than an ordinary dress, as having a less quantity of material in it; it would be more durable, because the lower edge of the skirt would not be exposed to attrition upon the ground; it would be more convenient, owing to less frequent changes to suit the weather; it would require a less bulky wardrobe; it could more easily be made cooler in summer, and warmer in winter, than ladies' ordinary dresses; and it would be conducive to health, by the avoidance of damp skirts hanging about the feet and ankles in wet weather. Some of these arguments, it may be mentioned, were adduced by the editress herself, some by a Boston physician, who wrote in the *Lily*.

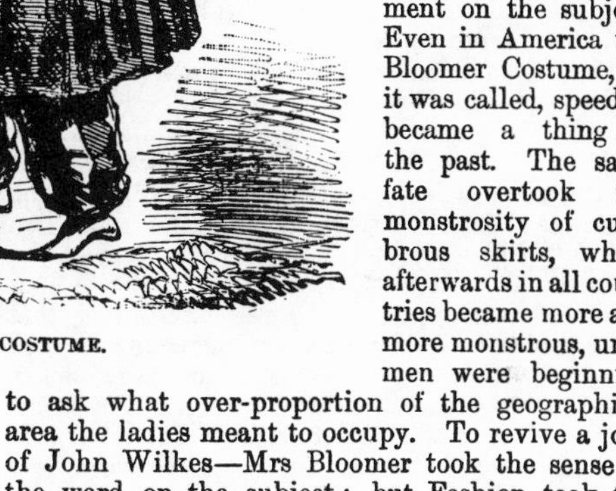

BLOOMER COSTUME.

The fashion did not fail to make itself apparent in various parts of the United States. The *Washington Telegraph*, the *Lycoming Gazette*, the *Hartford Times*, the *Rochester Daily Times*, the *Syracuse Journal*, and other newspapers, noticed the adoption of the costume at those places; and generally with much commendation, as having both elegance and convenience to recommend it, and not being open to any charge of indelicacy, except by a misuse of that word. In the autumn of the same year, an American lady lectured on the subject in London, dressed in black satin jacket, skirt, and trousers, and urged upon English ladies the adoption of the new costume; but this, and all similar attempts in England, failed to do more than raise a foolish merriment on the subject. Even in America the Bloomer Costume, as it was called, speedily became a thing of the past. The same fate overtook the monstrosity of cumbrous skirts, which afterwards in all countries became more and more monstrous, until men were beginning to ask what over-proportion of the geographical area the ladies meant to occupy. To revive a joke of John Wilkes—Mrs Bloomer took the sense of the ward on the subject; but Fashion took the *non*-sense, and carried it ten to one.

---

# JULY 24.

St Christina, virgin and martyr, beginning of 4th century. St Lewine of Britain, virgin and martyr. St Declan, first bishop of Ardmore, Ireland, 5th century. St Lupus, bishop of Troyes, confessor, 478. Saints Wulfhad and Ruffin, martyrs, about 670. Saints Romanus and David, patrons of Muscovy, martyrs, 1010. St Kinga or Cunegundes of Poland, 1292. St Francis Solano, confessor, 16th century.

*Born.*—Roger Dodsworth, eminent antiquary, 1585, *Newton Grange, Yorkshire;* Rev. John Newton, evangelical divine, 1725, *London;* John Philpot Curran, distinguished Irish barrister, 1750.

*Died.*—Caliph Abubeker, first successor of Mohammed, 634, *Medina;* Don Carlos, son of Philip II. of Spain, died in prison, 1568; Alphonse des Vignoles, chronologist, 1744, *Berlin;* George Vertue, eminent engraver and antiquary, 1756, *London;* John Dyer, poet, author of *Grongar Hill*, 1758, *Coningsby, Lincolnshire;* Dr Nathaniel Lardner, author of *Credibility of the Gospel History*, 1768, *Hawkhurst, Kent;* Jane Austen, novelist, 1817, *Winchester;* Armand Carrel, French political writer, died in consequence of wounds in a duel, 1836.

## DON CARLOS.

The uncertainty which hangs over the fate of many historical personages, is strikingly exemplified in the case of Don Carlos. That he died in prison at Madrid, on the 24th or 25th of July, is undoubted; but much discrepancy of opinion has prevailed as to whether this event arose from natural causes, or the death-stroke of the executioner, inflicted by the order of his own father, Philip II.

The popular account—and, it must also be added, that given by the majority of historians—is that the heir to the Spanish throne met his death by violent means. A wayward and impulsive youth, but, at the same time, brave, generous, and true hearted, his character presents a most marked contrast to that of the cold-blooded and bigoted Philip, between whom and his son it was impossible that any sympathy could exist. The whole course of the youth's upbringing seems to have been in a great measure a warfare with his father; but the first deadly cause of variance, was the marriage of the latter with the Princess Elizabeth of France, who had already been destined as the bride of Don Carlos himself. This was the third time that Philip II. had entered the bonds of matrimony. His first wife, Mary of Portugal, died in childbed of Don Carlos; his second was Mary of England, of persecuting memory; and his third, the French princess. By thus selfishly appropriating the affianced bride of another, whose love for her appears to have been of no ordinary description, the overpowering passion of jealousy was added to the many feelings of aversion with which he regarded his son. Many interviews are reported to have taken place between the queen and Don Carlos, but their intercourse appears always to have been of the purest and most Platonic kind. Other causes were contributing, however, to hurry the young prince to his fate. Naturally free and outspoken, his sympathies were readily engaged both on behalf of his father's revolted subjects in the Low Countries, and the Protestant reformers in his own and other nations. Part of his latter predilections has been traced to his residence in the monastery of St Just with his grandfather, the abdicated Charles V., with whom he was a great favourite, and who, as is alleged, betrayed a leaning to the Lutheran doctrines in his latter days. In regard to his connection with the burghers of the Netherlands, it is not easy to form a definite conclusion; but it appears to be well ascertained, that he regarded the blood-thirsty character of the Duke of Alva with abhorrence, and was determined to free the Flemings from his tyrannical sway. A sympathising letter from Don Carlos to the celebrated Count Egmont is said to have been found among the latter's papers when he and Count Horn were arrested. There seems, also, little reason to doubt that the prince had revolved a plan for proceeding to the Netherlands, and assuming the principal command there in person. This design was communicated by him to his uncle, Don Juan, a natural son of Charles V., who thereupon imparted it to King Philip. The jealous monarch lost no time in causing Don Carlos to be arrested and committed to prison, himself, it is said, accompanying the officers on the occasion. Subsequently to this, there is a considerable diversity in the accounts given by historians. By one class of writers, it is stated that the prince chafed so under the confinement to which he was subjected, that he threw himself into a burning fever, which shortly brought about his death, but not until he had made his peace with his father and the church. The more generally received account is that Philip, anxious to get rid of a son who thwarted so sensibly his favourite schemes of domination, consulted on the subject the authorities of the Inquisition, who gladly gave their sanction to Carlos's death, having long regarded him with aversion for his heretical leanings. Such a deed on the part of a parent, was represented to Philip as a most meritorious act of self sacrifice, and a reference was made to the paternal abnegation recorded in Scripture of Abraham. The fanaticism and interest of the Spanish monarch thus combined to overcome any scruples of conscience and filial love still abiding in his breast, and he signed the warrant for the execution of his son, which forthwith took place. The mode in which this was effected is also differently represented: one statement being that he was strangled, and another, that his veins were opened in a bath, after the manner of the Roman philosopher Seneca. The real truth of the sad story must ever remain a mystery; but enough has transpired to invest with a deep and romantic interest the history of the gallant Don Carlos, who perished in the flower of youthful vigour, at the early age of twenty-three, and to cast a dark shade on the memory of the vindictive and unscrupulous Philip II.

The story of Don Carlos has formed the subject of at least two tragedies—by Campustron, who transferred the scene to Constantinople, and, in room of Philip II., substituted one of the Greek emperors; and by Schiller, whose noble drama is one of the most imperishable monuments of his genius.

## JOHN PHILPOT CURRAN.

Oratory is the peculiar gift of the Emerald Isle, and, among the crowd of celebrated men whom she can proudly point to, the name of Curran stands pre-eminent, whether we look at him as a most able lawyer, a first-rate debater, and, in a society boasting of Erskine, Macintosh, and Sheridan, the gayest wit and most brilliant conversationalist of the day. From the village of Newmarket, in Cork, of a poor and low origin, he, at nine years of age, attracted the attention of the rector, the Rev. Mr Boyse, who sent him to Middleton School, and then to Dublin, where he was 'the wildest, wittiest, dreamiest student of old Trinity;' and, in the event of his being called before the fellows for wearing a dirty shirt, could only plead as an excuse, that he had but one. Poverty followed his steps for some years after this; instead of briefs to argue before the judge, he was amusing the idle crowd in the hall with his wit and eloquence. 'I had a family for whom I had no dinner,' he says, 'and a landlady for whom I had no rent. I had gone abroad in despondence, I came home almost in desperation. When I opened the door of my study, where Lavater could alone have found a library, the first object that presented itself was an immense folio of a brief, and twenty gold guineas wrapped up beside it.'

As with many other great lawyers, this was the turning-point; his skill in cross-examination was wonderful, judge and jury were alike amused, while the perjured witness trembled before his power, and the audience were entranced by his eloquence. His first great effort was in 1794, in defence of Archibald Rowan, who had signed an address in favour of Catholic emancipation. In spite of the splendid speech of his advocate, he was convicted; but the mob outside were determined to chair their favourite speaker. Curran implored them to desist, but a great brawny fellow roared out: 'Arrah, blood and turf! Pat, don't mind the little cratur; here, pitch him up this minute upon my showlder!' and thus was he carried to his carriage, and then drawn home. After the miserable rebellion of 1798, it fell to Curran's part to defend almost all the prisoners; and, being reminded by Lord Carleton that he would lose his gown, he replied with scorn: 'Well, my lord, his majesty may take the silk, but he must leave the *stuff* behind!' Most distressing was the task to a man of his sense of justice; the government arrayed against him, and every court filled with the military, yet with swords pointed at him, he cried: 'Assassinate me, you may; intimidate me, you cannot!' Added to this, came domestic sorrow. His beautiful daughter fell in love with the unfortunate Emmet, who was executed in 1803, and she could not survive the shock, but drooped gradually and died; an event which Moore immortalised in his songs, 'O breathe not his name, let it sleep in the shade;' and, 'She is far from the land where her young hero sleeps.' The gloom which had always affected Curran's mind became more settled; he resigned the Mastership of the Rolls in 1813, and sought alleviation in travelling, but in vain, his death took place at Brompton, on the 14th of October 1817. The witticisms which are attributed to him are numberless. 'Curran,' said a judge to him, whose wig being a little awry, caused some laughter in court, 'do you see anything ridiculous in this wig?' 'Nothing but the head, my lord;' was the reply. One day, at dinner, he sat opposite to Toler, who was called the 'hanging judge.' 'Curran,' said Toler, 'is that hung-beef before you?' 'Do you *try* it, my lord, and then it's sure to be!' Lundy Foot, the celebrated tobacconist, asked Curran for a Latin motto for his coach. 'I have just hit on it,' said Curran, 'it is only two words, and it will explain your profession, your elevation, and contempt for the people's ridicule; and it has the advantage of being in two languages, Latin and English, just as the reader chooses. Put up, "Quid rides," upon your carriage.' The hatred he always felt for those who betrayed their country by voting for the Union, is shewn in the answer he gave to a lord who got his title for his support of the government measure. Meeting Curran near the Parliament House, in College Green, he said: 'Curran, what do they mean to do with this useless building? For my part, I hate the very sight of it.' 'I do not wonder at it, my lord,' said Curran contemptuously, 'I never yet heard of a *murderer* who was not afraid of a *ghost*.'

---

## CAPTURE AND DEFENCE OF GIBRALTAR BY THE BRITISH.

In July 1704, a capture was made, the importance of which has never ceased to be felt: viz., that of Gibraltar by the British. No other rock or headland in Europe, perhaps, equals Gibraltar for commanding position and importance. Situated at the mouth of the Mediterranean, where that celebrated sea is little more than twenty miles wide, the rock has a dominating influence over the maritime traffic of those waters. Not that a cannon-ball could reach a ship at even half that distance; but still the owners of a fortified headland so placed, must necessarily possess great advantages in the event of any hostilities in that sea. The rock is almost an island, for it is connected with the mainland of Spain only by a low isthmus of sand; it is, in fact, a promontory about seven miles in circumference, and 1300 feet high. At present, a bit of neutral-ground on the sandy isthmus separates Spain from it, politically though not geographically; but in former times, it always belonged to the government, whatever it may have been, of the neighbouring region. The Moors crossed over from Africa, in the eighth century, dethroned the Christian king of Spain, and built a castle on the rock, the ruins of which may still be seen. The Moslems held their rule for 600 years. Gibraltar then changed hands three times during the fourteenth century. After 1492, the Moors never held it. The Christian kings of Spain made various additions to the fortifications during the sixteenth and seventeenth centuries; but still the defences bore no comparison with those which have become familiar to later generations. Early in the eighteenth century, there was a political contest among the European courts, which led England to support the pretensions of an Austrian prince, instead of those of a Bourbon, to the crown of Spain; and, as a part of the arrangement then made, a combined force proceeded to attack Gibraltar. The Prince of Hesse Darmstadt commanded the troops, and Sir George Rooke the fleet. It is evident either that the Spaniards did not regard the place as of sufficient importance to justify a strenuous defence, or that the defence was very ill-managed; for the attack, commenced on the 21st of July, terminated on the 24th by the surrender of the stronghold. From that day to this, Gibraltar has never for one moment been out of English hands. When it was lost, the Spaniards were mortified and alarmed at their discomfiture; and for the next nine years they made repeated attempts to recapture it, by force and stratagem. On one occasion they very nearly succeeded. A French and Spanish force having been collected on the isthmus, a goat-herd offered to shew them a path up the sloping sides of the rock, which he had reason to believe was unknown to the English. This offer being accepted, 500 troops ascended quietly one dark night, and took shelter in an indenture or hollow called by the Spaniards the *silleta*, or 'little chair.' At day-break, next morning, they ascended higher, took the signal-station, killed the guard, and anxiously looked round for the reinforcements which were to follow. These reinforcements, however, never came, and to this remissness was due the failure of the attack; for the English garrison, aroused by the surprise, sallied forth, and drove the invaders down the rock again. The *silleta* was quickly filled up, and the whole place made stronger than ever. When the Peace of Utrecht was signed in 1713, Gibraltar was confirmed to the English in the most thorough and complete way; for the tenth article of that celebrated treaty says:—'The Catholic king (i. e., of Spain) doth hereby, for himself, his heirs, and successors, yield to the crown of Great Britain the full and entire property of the town and castle of Gibraltar, together with the port, fortifications, and forts thereunto belonging; and he gives up the said property to be held and enjoyed absolutely, with all manner of right, for ever, without any exception or impediment whatsoever.' Towards the close of the reign of George I., about 1726, there were great apprehensions that the government would yield to the haughty demands of the king of Spain, that Gibraltar should be given up; addresses to the king, deprecating such a step, were presented by lord mayors and mayors, in the names of the inhabitants of London, York, Exeter, Yarmouth, Winchester, Honiton, Dover, Southampton, Tiverton, Hertford, Malmesbury, Taunton, Marlborough, and other cities and towns. Owing to this or other causes, the king remained firm, and Gibraltar was not surrendered. In 1749, a singular attempt was

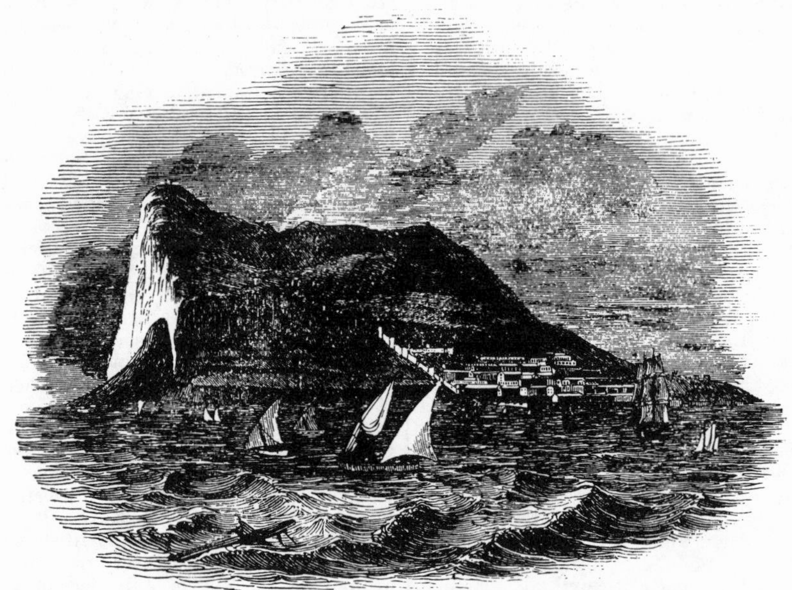

ROCK OF GIBRALTAR.

made in England to advocate such a surrender. A pamphlet appeared under the title, *Reasons for Giving up Gibraltar*, in which the writer said: 'I can demonstrate that the use of Gibraltar is only to support and enrich this or that particular man; that it is a great expense to the nation; that the nation is thereby singularly dishonoured, and our trade rather injured, than protected.' It appears that there was gross corruption at that time on the part of the governor and other officials; and that merchants, incensed at the profligate and vexatious management of the port, asserted that trade would be better if the place were in Spanish hands than English—differing so far from a few modern theorists, who have advocated the surrender of Gibraltar on grounds of moral right and fairness towards Spain. There must have been some other agitations, of a similar kind, at that period; for both Houses of parliament addressed George II., praying him not to cede Gibraltar. The 'Key to the Mediterranean,' as it has been well called, was besieged unavailingly by Spain in 1727, and by Spain and France in 1779—since which date no similar attempt has been made. The siege, which was commenced in 1779, and not terminated till 1783, was one of the greatest on record. The grand attack was on the 13th of September 1782. On the land-side were stupendous batteries, mounting 200 pieces of heavy ordnance, supported by a well-appointed army of 40,000 men, under the Duc de Crillon; on the sea-side were the combined fleets of France and Spain, numbering 47 sail of the line, besides numerous frigates and smaller vessels, and 10 battering-ships of formidable strength. General Elliott's garrison threw 5000 *red-hot* shot on that memorable day; and the attack was utterly defeated at all points.

## THE FIRST ROAD-TRAMWAY.

On the 24th of July 1801, a joint-stock undertaking was completed, which marks an important era in the history of railways. It was the Surrey Iron Railway, from Wandsworth to Croydon, and thence southward in the direction of Merstham. We should regard it as a trifling affair if witnessed now: a train of donkeys or mules drawing small wagons of stone along a very narrow-gauge railway; but its significance is to be estimated in reference to the things of that day. At the coal-mines in the north of England, the fact had long been recognised, that wheels will roll over smooth iron more easily than over rough gravel or earth; and to take advantage of this circumstance, rails were laid down on the galleries, adits, and staiths. Certain improvements made in these arrangements in 1800 by Mr Benjamin Outram, led to the roads being termed *Outram roads;* and this, by an easy abbreviation, was changed to *tramroads*, a name that has lived ever since. Persons in various parts of England advocated the laying of tram-rails on common roads, or on roads purposely made from town to town; in order that upper-ground traffic might share the benefits already reaped by mining operations. In 1800, Mr Thomas, of Denton, read a paper before the Literary and Philosophical Society of Newcastle-upon-Tyne, in which this view of the matter was ably advocated. In 1801, Dr James Anderson, of Edinburgh, in his *Recreations of Agriculture*, set forth, in very glowing terms, the anticipated value of horse-tramways.* 'Diminish carriage expenses by one farthing,' he said, 'and you widen the circle of intercourse; you form, as it were, a new creation, not only of stones and earth, trees and plants, but of men also, and, what is more, of industry, happiness, and joy.' In a less enthusiastic, and more practical strain, he proceeded to argue that the use of such tramways would lessen distances as measured by time, economise horse-power, lead to the improvement of agriculture, and lower the prices of commodities. The Surrey Iron Railway was not a very successful affair, commercially considered; but this was not due to any failure in the principle of construction adopted. In 1802, Mr Lovell Edgeworth, father of the eminent writer, Maria Edgeworth, proposed that passengers as well as minerals should be conveyed on such tramways: a suggestion, however, that was many years in advance of public opinion. When, however, it was found that one horse could draw a very heavy load of stone on the Surrey tramway, and that a smooth road was the only magic employed, engineers began to speculate on the vast advantages that must accrue from the use, on similar or better roads, of trains drawn by steam-power instead of horse-power. Hence the wonderful railway-system of our day. The Surrey iron-path has long been obliterated; it was bought up, and removed by the Brighton and Croydon Railway Companies.

## FLEET MARRIAGES.

The *Weekly Journal* of June 29, 1723, says: 'From an inspection into the several registers for marriages kept at the several alehouses, brandy-shops, &c., within the Rules of the Fleet Prison, we find no less than thirty-two couples joined together from Monday to Thursday last without licenses, contrary to an express act of parliament against clandestine marriages, that lays a severe fine of £200 on the minister so offending, and £100 each on the persons so married in contradiction to the said statute. Several of the above-named brandy-men and victuallers keep clergymen in their houses at 20*s*. per week, hit or miss; but it is reported that one there will stoop to no such low conditions, but makes, at least, £500 per annum, of divinity-jobs after that manner.'

These marriages, rather unlicensed than clandestine, seem to have originated with the incumbents of Trinity Minories and St James's, Duke's Place, who claimed to be exempt from the jurisdiction of the bishop of London, and performed marriages without banns or license, till Elliot, rector of St James, was suspended in 1616, when the trade was taken up by clerical prisoners living within the Rules of the Fleet, and who, having neither cash, character, nor liberty to lose, became the ready instruments of vice, greed, extravagance, and libertinism. Mr Burn, who has exhausted the subject in his *History of Fleet Marriages*, enumerates eighty-nine Fleet parsons by name, of whom the most famous were John Gayman or Gainham, known as the 'Bishop of Hell'—a lusty, jolly man, vain of his learning; Edward Ashwell, a thorough rogue and vagabond; Walter Wyatt, whose certificate was rendered in the great case of Saye and Sele; Peter Symson; William Dan; D. Wigmore, convicted for selling spirituous liquors unlawfully; Starkey, who ran away to Scotland to escape examination in a trial for bigamy; and James Lando, one of the last of the tribe. The following are specimens of the style in which these matrimonial hucksters appealed for public patronage:

'G. R.—At the true chapel, at the old Red Hand and Mitre, three doors up Fleet Lane, and next door to the White Swan, marriages are performed by authority by the Rev. Mr Symson, educated at the university of Cambridge, and late chaplain to the Earl of Rothes.—*N.B.* Without imposition.'

'J. Lilley, at ye Hand and Pen, next door to the China-shop, Fleet Bridge, London, will be performed the solemnisation of marriages by a gentleman regularly bred at one of our universities, and lawfully ordained according to the institutions of the Church of England, and is ready to wait on any person in town or country.'

'Marriages with a license, certificate, and crown-stamp, at a guinea, at the New Chapel, next door to the China-shop, near Fleet Bridge, London, by a regular bred clergyman, and not by a Fleet parson, as is insinuated in the public papers; and that the town may be freed mistakes, no clergyman being a prisoner within the Rules of the Fleet, dare marry; and to obviate all doubts, the chapel is not on the verge of the Fleet, but kept by a gentleman who was lately chaplain on board one of his majesty's men-of-war,* and likewise has gloriously distinguished himself in defence of his king and country, and is above committing those little mean actions that some men impose on people, being determined to have everything conducted with the utmost decorum and regularity, such as shall always be supported on law and equity.'

Some carried on the business at their own lodgings, where the clocks were kept always at the canonical hour; but the majority were employed by the keepers of marriage-houses, who were generally tavern-keepers. The Swan, the Lamb, the Horse-shoe and Magpie, the Bishop-Blaise, the Two Sawyers, the Fighting-cocks, the Hand and Pen, were places of this description, as were the Bull and Garter and King's Head, kept by warders of the prison. The parson and landlord (who usually acted as clerk) divided the fee between them—unless the former received a weekly wage—after paying a shilling to the plyer or tout who brought in the customers. The marriages were entered in a pocket-book by the parson, and afterwards, on payment of a small fee, copied into the regular register of the house, unless the interested parties desired the affair to be kept secret.

The manners and customs prevalent in this

* Dr James Anderson, originally a Scotch farmer, by his periodical work, *The Bee*, published all through the years 1791, 2, and 3, might be considered as the first to exemplify a respectable cheap literature. His daughter was the wife of Mr Benjamin Outram, and these were the parents of the Bayard of India, Sir James Outram. Mrs Outram died recently at an advanced age.

* Lando, ex-chaplain to H.M.S. *Falkland*.

matrimonial mart are thus described by a correspondent of *The Grub Street Journal*, in 1735: 'These ministers of wickedness ply about Ludgate Hill, pulling and forcing people to some pedling alehouse or a brandy-shop to be married, even on a Sunday stopping them as they go to church, and almost tearing their clothes off their backs. To confirm the truth of these facts, I will give you a case or two which lately happened. Since midsummer last, a young lady of birth and fortune was deluded and forced from her friends, and by the assistance of a wry-necked, swearing parson, married to an atheistical wretch, whose life is a continued practice of all manner of vice and debauchery. And since the ruin of my relative, another lady of my acquaintance had like to have been trepanned in the following manner: This lady had appointed to meet a gentlewoman at the Old Play-house, in Drury Lane; but extraordinary business prevented her coming. Being alone when the play was done, she bade a boy call a coach for the city. One dressed like a gentleman helps her into it, and jumps in after her. "Madam," says he, "this coach was called for me, and since the

FLEET MARRIAGES.

weather is so bad, and there is no other, I beg leave to bear you company; I am going into the city, and will set you down wherever you please." The lady begged to be excused, but he bade the coachman drive on. Being come to Ludgate Hill, he told her his sister, who waited his coming but five doors up the court, would go with her in two minutes. He went, and returned with his pretended sister, who asked her to step in one minute, and she would wait upon her in the coach. The poor lady foolishly followed her into the house, when instantly the sister vanished, and a tawny fellow, in a black coat and a black wig, appeared. "Madam, you are come in good time, the doctor was just agoing!" "The doctor," says she, horribly frighted, fearing it was a madhouse, "what has the doctor to do with me?" "To marry you to that gentleman. The doctor has waited for you these three hours, and will be paid by you or that gentleman before you go!" "That gentleman," says she, recovering herself, "is worthy a better fortune than mine;" and begged hard to be gone. But Doctor Wryneck swore she should be married; or if she would not, he would still have his fee, and register the marriage for that night. The lady, finding she could not escape without money or a pledge, told them she liked the gentleman so well, she would certainly meet him to-morrow night, and gave them a ring as a pledge, "Which," says she, "was my mother's gift on her death-bed, enjoining that, if ever I married, it should be my wedding-ring;" by which cunning contrivance she was delivered from the black doctor and his tawny crew. Some time after this, I went with this lady and her brother in a coach to Ludgate Hill in the daytime, to see the manner of their picking up people to be married. As soon as our coach stopped near Fleet Bridge, up comes one of the myrmidons. "Madam," says he, "you want a parson?" "Who are you?" says I. "I am the clerk and register of the Fleet." "Shew me the chapel." At which comes a second, desiring me to go along with him. Says he: "That fellow will carry you to a pedling alehouse." Says a third: "Go with me, he will carry you to a brandy-shop." In the interim comes the doctor. "Madam," says he, "I'll do your job for you presently!" "Well, gentlemen," says I, "since you can't agree, and I can't be married quietly, I'll put it off till another time;" and so drove away.' The truthfulness of this description is attested by Pennant: 'In walking along the street, in my youth, on the side next the prison, I have often been tempted by the question: "*Sir, will you be pleased to walk in and be married?*" Along this most lawless space was hung up the frequent sign of a male and female hand enjoined, with *Marriages performed within*, written beneath. A dirty fellow invited you in. The parson was seen walking before his shop; a squalid profligate figure, clad in a tattered plaid nightgown, with a fiery face, and ready to couple you for a dram of gin or a roll of tobacco.'—*Some Account of London*, 1793.

In 1719, Mrs Anne Leigh, an heiress, was decoyed from her friends in Buckinghamshire, married at the Fleet chapel against her consent, and barbarously ill-used by her abductors. In 1737, one Richard Leaver, being tried for bigamy, declared he knew nothing of the woman claiming to be his wife, except that one night he got drunk, and 'next morning found myself abed with a strange woman. "Who are you? how came you here?" says I. "Oh, my dear," says she, "we were married last night at the Fleet!"' These are but two of many instances in which waifs of the church and self-ordained clergymen, picking up a livelihood in the purlieus of the Fleet, aided and abetted nefarious schemers. For a consideration, they not only provided bride or bridegroom, but antedated marriages, and even gave certificates where no marriage took place. In 1821, the government purchased the registers of several of the marriage-houses, and deposited them with the Registrar of the Consistory Court of London; and in these registers we have proofs, under the hands of themselves and their clerks, of the malpractices of the Fleet parsons, as the following extracts will shew:

'5 Nov. 1742, was married Benjamin Richards, of the parish of St Martin's-in-the-Fields, Br. and Judith Lance, Do. sp. at the Bull and Garter, and gave [a guinea] for an antedate to March ye 11th in the same year, which Lilley comply'd with, and put 'em in his book accordingly, there being a vacancy in the book suitable to the time.'

'June 10, 1729.—John Nelson, of ye parish of St George, Hanover, batchelor and gardener, and Mary Barnes of ye same, sp. married. Cer. dated 5 November 1727, to please their parents.'

'Mr Comyngs gave me half-a-guinea to find a bridegroom, and defray all expenses. Parson, 2*s*. 6*d*. Husband do., and 5. 6 myself.' [We find one man married four times under different names, receiving five shillings on each occasion 'for his trouble.']

'1742, May 24.—A soldier brought a barber to the Cock, who, I think, said his name was James, barber by trade, was in part married to Elizabeth: they said they were married enough.'

'A coachman came, and was half-married, and would give but 3*s*. 6*d*., and went off.'

'Edward —— and Elizabeth —— were married, and would not let me know their names.'

'The woman ran across Ludgate Hill in her shift.' [Under the popular delusion that, by so doing, her husband would not be answerable for her debts.]

'April 20, 1742, came a man and woman to the Bull and Garter, the man pretended he would marry ye woman, by w'ch pretence he got money to pay for marrying and to buy a ring, but left the woman by herself, and never returned; upon which J. Lilley takes the woman from the Bull and Garter to his own house, and gave her a certifycate, as if she had been married to the man.'

'1 Oct. 1747.—John Ferren, gent. ser. of St Andrew's, Holborn, Br and Deborah Nolan, do. sp. The supposed J. F. was discovered, after the ceremonies were over, to be in person a woman.'

'To be kept a secret, the lady having a jointure during the time she continued a widow.'

Sometimes the parsons met with rough treatment, and were glad to get off by sacrificing their fees. One happy couple stole the clergyman's clothes-brush, and another ran away with the certificate, leaving a pint of wine unpaid for. The following memorandums speak for themselves:

'Had a noise for four hours about the money.'

'Married at a barber's shop one Kerrils, for half-a-guinea, after which it was extorted out of my pocket, and for fear of my life, delivered.'

'The said Harronson swore most bitterly, and was pleased to say that he was fully determined to kill the minister, etc., that married him. *N.B.*—He came from Gravesend, and was sober!'

Upon one occasion the parson, thinking his clients were not what they professed to be, ventured to press some inquiries. He tells the result in a *Nota Bene*: 'I took upon me to ask what ye gentleman's name was, his age, and likewise the lady's name and age. Answer was made me, G— d— me, if I did not immediately marry them, he would use me ill; in short, apprehending it to be a conspiracy, I found myself obliged to marry them *in terrorem*.' However, the frightened rascal took his revenge, for he adds in a second *N.B.*, 'some material part was omitted!' Dare's *Register* contains the following: 'Oct. 2, 1743.—John Figg, of St John the Evangelist, gent., a widower, and Rebecca Wordwand, of ditto, spinster. *At ye same time gave her ye sacrament*.' This, however, is the only instance recorded of such blasphemous audacity.

The hymeneal market was not supported only by needy fortune-hunters and conscienceless profligates, ladies troubled with duns, and spinsters wanting husbands for reputation's sake. All classes flocked to the Fleet to marry in haste. Its registers contain the names of men of all professions, from the barber to the officer in the Guards, from the pauper to the peer of the realm. Among the aristocratic patrons of its unlicensed chapels we find Edward, Lord Abergavenny; the Hon. John Bourke, afterwards Viscount Mayo; Sir Marmaduke Gresham; Anthony Henley, Esq., brother of Lord Chancellor Northington; Lord Banff; Lord Montagu, afterwards Duke of Manchester; Viscount Sligo; the Marquis of Annandale; William Shipp, Esq., father of the first Lord Mulgrave; and Henry Fox, afterwards Lord Holland, of whose marriage Walpole thus writes to Sir Horace Mann: 'The town has been in a great bustle about a private match; but which, by the ingenuity of the ministry, has been made politics. Mr Fox fell in love with Lady Caroline Lenox (eldest daughter of the Duke of Richmond), asked her, was refused, and stole her. His father was a footman, her great-grandfather, a king—*hinc illæ lachrymæ!* All the blood-royal have been up in arms.' A few foreigners figure in the Fleet records, the most notable entry in which an alien is concerned being this: '10 Aug. 1742. —Don Dominian Bonaventura, Baron of Spiterii, Abbott of St Mary, in Præto Nobary, chaplain of hon. to the king of the Two Sicilies, and knt. of the order of St Salvator, St James, and Martha Alexander, ditto, Br. and sp.' Magistrates and parochial authorities helped to swell the gains of the Fleet parsons; the former settling certain cases by sending the accused to the altar instead of the gallows, and the latter getting rid of a female pauper, by giving a gratuity to some poor wretch belonging to another parish to take her for better for worse.

From time to time, the legislature attempted to check these marriages; but the infliction of pains and penalties were of no avail so long as the law recognised such unions. At length Chancellor Hardwicke took the matter in hand, and in 1753 a bill was introduced, making the solemnisation of matrimony in any other but a church or chapel, and without banns or license, felony punishable by transportation, and declaring all such marriages null and void. Great was the excitement created; handbills for and against the measure were thrown broadcast into the streets. The bill was strenuously opposed by the opposition, led by Henry Fox and the Duke of Bedford, but eventually passed by a large majority, and became the law of the land from Lady-Day 1754, and so the scandalous matrimonial-market of the Fleet came to an end.*

### MINT, SAVOY, AND MAY-FAIR MARRIAGES.

The Fleet chapels had competitors in the Mint, May-Fair, and the Savoy. In 1715, an Irishman, named Briand, was fined £2000 for marrying an orphan about thirteen years of age, whom he decoyed into the Mint. The following curious certificate was produced at his trial: 'Feb. 16, 1715, These are therefore, whom it may concern, that Isaac Briand and Watson Anne Astone were joined together in the holy state of matrimony (*Nemine contradicente*) the day and year above written, according to the rites and ceremonies of the church of Great Britain. Witness my hand, Jos. Smith, Cler.' In 1730, a chapel was built in May Fair, into which the Rev. Alexander Keith was inducted. He advertised in the public papers, and carried on a flourishing trade till 1742, when he was prosecuted by Dr Trebeck, and excommunicated. In return, he excommunicated the doctor, the bishop of London, and the judge of the Ecclesiastical Court. The following year, he was committed to the Fleet Prison; but he had a house opposite his old chapel fitted up, and carried on the business through the agency of curates. At this chapel, Lady Mary Wortley Montagu's worthless son was married; and here the impatient Duke of Hamilton was wedded with a ring from a bed-curtain, to the youngest of the beautiful Gunnings, at half-past twelve at night. When the marriage act was mooted, Keith swore that he would revenge himself upon the bishops, by taking some acres of land for a burying-ground, and underburying them all. He published a pamphlet against the measure, in which he states it was a common thing to marry from 200 to 300 sailors when the fleet came in, and consoles himself with the reflection, that if the alteration in the law should prove beneficial to the country, he will have the satisfaction of having been the cause of it, the compilers of the act having done it 'with the pure design' of suppressing his chapel. No less than sixty-one couples were united at Keith's chapel the day before the act came into operation. He himself died in prison in 1758. The Savoy Chapel did not come into vogue till after the passing of the marriage bill. On the 2d January 1754, the *Public Advertiser* contained this advertisement: 'By Authority.—Marriages performed with the utmost privacy, decency, and regularity at the Ancient Royal Chapel of St John the Baptist, in the Savoy, where regular and authentic registers have been kept from the time of the Reformation (being two hundred years and upwards) to this day. The expense not more than one guinea, the five-shilling stamp included. There are five private ways by land to this chapel, and two by water.' The proprietor of this chapel was the Rev. John Wilkinson (father of Tate Wilkinson, of theatrical fame), who fancying (as the Savoy was extra-parochial) that he was privileged to issue licenses upon his own authority, took no notice of the new law. In 1755, he married no less than 1190 couples. The authorities began at last to bestir themselves, and Wilkinson thought it prudent to conceal himself. He engaged a curate, named Grierson, to perform the ceremony, the licenses being still issued by himself, by which arrangement he thought to hold his assistant harmless. Among those united by the latter, were two members of the Drury Lane company. Garrick, obtaining the certificate, made such use of it that Grierson was arrested, tried, convicted, and sentenced to fourteen years' transportation, by which sentence 1400 marriages were declared void. In 1756, Wilkinson, making sure of acquittal, surrendered himself, and received the same sentence as Grierson, but died on board the convict-ship as she lay in Plymouth harbour, whither she had been driven by stress of weather.

* 'It is well you are married! How would my Lady Ailesbury have liked to be asked in a parish church for three Sundays running? I really believe she would have worn her weeds for ever rather than have passed through so impudent a ceremony! What do *you* think? But you will want to know the interpretation of this preamble. Why, there is a new bill, which, under the notion of preventing clandestine marriages, has made such a general rummage and reform in the office of matrimony, that every Strephon and Chloe will have as many impediments and formalities to undergo as a treaty of peace. Lord Bath invented the bill, but had drawn it so ill, that the chancellor was forced to draw a new one, and then grew so fond of his own creature, that he has crammed it down the throats of both Houses, though they gave many a gulp before they could swallow it.'—*Horace Walpole to Mr Conway, 22d May* 1753.

## JULY 25.

**St James the Great, the Apostle. St Christopher, martyr, 3d century. St Cucufas, martyr in Spain, 304. Saints Thea and Valentina, virgins, and St Paul, martyrs, 308. St Nissen, abbot of Mountgarret, Ireland.**

### ST JAMES THE GREAT.

The 25th of July is dedicated to St James the Great, the patron saint of Spain. According to legendary lore, James preached the gospel in Spain, and afterwards returning to Palestine, was made the first bishop of Jerusalem. He suffered martyrdom by order of Herod Agrippa, in the year 44 A.D., shortly before the day of the Passover. Some Spanish converts, however, who had followed him to Jerusalem, rescued his holy relics, and conveyed them to Spain, where they were miraculously discovered in the eighth century. The Spaniards hold St James in the highest veneration, and if their history was to be believed, with good reason. At the battle of Clavijo, fought in the year 841 between Ramiro, king of Leon, and the Moors, when the day was going hard against the Christians, St James appeared in the field, in his own proper person, armed with a sword of dazzling splendour, and mounted on a white horse, having housings charged with scallop shells, the saint's peculiar heraldic cognizance; he slew sixty thousand of the Moorish infidels, gaining the day for Spain and Christianity. The great Spanish order of knighthood, Santiago de Espada—St James of the Sword—was founded in commemoration of the miraculous event; giving our historian Gibbon occasion to observe that, 'a stupendous metamorphosis was performed in the ninth century, when from a peaceful fisherman of the Lake of Gennesareth, the apostle James was transformed into a valorous knight, who charged at the head of Spanish chivalry in battles against the Moors. The gravest historians have celebrated his exploits; the miraculous shrine of Compostella displayed his power; and the sword of a military order, assisted by the terrors of the inquisition, was sufficient to remove every objection of profane criticism.'

The city of Compostella, in Galicia, became the chief seat of the order of St James, from the legend of his body having been discovered there. The peculiar badge of the order is a blood-stained sword in the form of a cross, charged, as heralds term it, with a white scallop shell; the motto is *Rubet ensis sanguine Arabum*—Red is the sword with the blood of the Moors. The banner of the order, preserved in the royal armory at Madrid, is said to be the very standard which was used by Ferdinand and Isabella at the conquest of Granada. But, as it bears the imperial, double-headed eagle of the Emperor Charles V., we may accept the story, like many other Spanish ones, with some reservation. On this banner, St James is represented as he appeared at the battle of Clavijo; and the accompanying engraving is a correct copy of the marvellous apparition. But it was not at Clavijo alone that St James has appeared and fought for Spain; he has been seen fighting, at subsequent times, in Flanders, Italy, India, and America. And, indeed, his powerful aid and

ST JAMES THE GREAT.

influence has been felt even when his actual presence was not visible. St James's Day has ever been considered auspicious to the arms of Spain. Grotius happily terms it, a day the Spaniards believed fortunate, and through their belief made it so. Charles V. conquered Tunis on that day; but on the following anniversary, when he invaded Provence, he was not by any means so successful.

The shrine of St James, at Compostella, was a great resort of pilgrims, from all parts of Christendom, during the medieval period; and the distinguishing badge of pilgrims to this shrine, was a scallop shell worn on the cloak or hat. In the old ballad of the *Friar of Orders Gray*, the lady describes her lover as clad, like herself, in 'a pilgrim's weedes:'

'And how should I know your true love
From many another one?
Oh, by his scallop shell and hat,
And by his sandal shoon.'

The adoption of the shell by the pilgrims to the shrine of St James, is accounted for in a legend, which relates, that when the relics of the saint were being miraculously conveyed from Jerusalem to Spain, in a ship built of marble, the horse of a Portuguese knight, alarmed, we may presume, at so extraordinary a barge, plunged into the sea with its rider. The knight was rescued, and taken on board of the ship, when his clothes were found to be covered with scallop shells. Erasmus, however, in his *Pilgrimages*, has given us a more feasible account. One of his interlocutors meets a pilgrim, and says: 'What country has sent you safely back to us, covered with shells, laden with tin and leaden images, and adorned with straw necklaces, while your arms display a row of serpents' eggs?'

'I have been to St James of Compostella,' replies the pilgrim.

'What answer did St James give to your professions?'

'None; but he was seen to smile, and nod his head, when I offered my presents; and he held out to me this imbricated shell.'

'Why that shell rather than any other kind?'

'Because the adjacent sea abounds in them.'

Curiously enough, a scallop shell is borne at the present day by pilgrims in Japan; and in all probability its origin, as a pilgrim's badge, both in Europe and the East, was derived from its use as a primitive cup, dish, or spoon. And this idea is corroborated by the crest of Dishington, an old English family, being a scallop shell—a punning allusion to the name and the ancient use of the shell as a dish. And we may add, as a proof of the once ancient popularity of pilgrimages to Compostella, that seventeen English peers and eight baronets carry scallop shells in their arms as heraldic charges.

There is some folk lore connected with St James's Day. They say in Herefordshire:

'Till St James's Day is past and gone,
There may be hops or they may be none;'

implying the noted uncertainty of that local crop. Another proverb more general is—'Whoever eats oysters on St James's Day, will never want money.' In point of fact, it is customary in London to begin eating oysters on St James's Day, when they are necessarily somewhat dearer than afterwards; so we may presume that the saying is only meant as a jocular encouragement to a little piece of extravagance and self-indulgence. In this connection of oysters with St James's Day, we trace the ancient association of the apostle with pilgrims' shells. There is a custom in London which makes this relation more evident. In the course of the few days following upon the introduction of oysters for the season, the children of the humbler class employ themselves diligently in collecting the shells which have been cast out from taverns and fish-shops, and of these they make piles in various rude forms. By the time that old St James's Day (the 5th of August) has come about, they have these little fabrics in nice order, with a candle stuck in the top, to be lighted at night. As you thread your way through some of the denser parts of the metropolis, you are apt to find a cone of shells, with its votive light, in the nook of some retired court, with a group of youngsters around it, some of whom will be sure to assail the stranger with a whining claim—*Mind the grotto!* by which is meant a demand for a penny wherewith professedly to keep up the candle. It cannot be doubted that we have here, at the distance of upwards of three hundred years from the Reformation, a relic of the habits of our Catholic ancestors.

OYSTER-SHELL DAY.

## The Legend of St Christopher.

This is a very early and obscure saint. He is generally represented as a native of Lycia, who suffered martyrdom under Decius, in the third century. Butler conceives that he took the name of Christopher (q. d. *Christum fero*), to express his ardent love for the Redeemer, as implying that he carried that sacred image constantly in his breast. When a taking religious idea was once fairly set agoing in the middle ages, it grew under favour of the popular imagination, always tending more and more to a tangible form. In time, a legend obtained currency, being obviously a mere fiction suggested by the saint's name. It was said that his original occupation was to carry people across a stream, on the banks of which he lived. As such, it was obviously necessary he should be a strong man; *ergo*, he was represented as a man of gigantic stature and strength. One evening, a child presented himself to be conveyed over the stream. At first his weight was what might be expected from his infant years; but presently it began to increase, and so went on till the ferryman was like to sink under his burden. The child then said: 'Wonder not, my friend, I am Jesus, and you have the weight of the sins of the whole world on your back!'

When this legend had become thoroughly established, the stalwart figure of Christopher wading the stream, with the infant Jesus on his shoulder.

became a favourite object for painting and carving in churches. St Christopher was in time regarded as a kind of symbol of the Christian church. A tutelage over fishing came to be one of his minor attributes, and it was believed that where his image was, the plague could not enter. The saint has come to have an interesting place in the history of typography, in consequence of a wood-engraving of his figure, supposed to be of date about 1423, being the earliest known example of that art. Besides the figure of the saint, there is a mill-scene on one side of the river, and a hermit holding out a lantern for the saint's guidance on the other, all remarkably well drawn for the age. Underneath is an inscription, assuring the reader that on the day he sees this picture, he could die no evil death:

> 'Christofori faciem die quacunque tueris,
> Illa nempe die morte malâ non morieris.'

None of the many carved figures of St Christopher approached in magnitude one which was placed in the church of Notre Dame at Paris. It was erected by a knight of the name of Antoine des Essars, who was arrested with his brother for some malversation; the latter was beheaded, but the former dreamed that the saint broke his prison-bars and carried him off in his arms. The dream was verified, for in a few days he was declared innocent. He in consequence erected this wooden giant, which, after being an object of popular wonder for many generations, was removed in 1785.

Erasmus, in his *Colloquy of the Shipwreck*, describing a company threatened with that calamity, says: 'Did no one think of Christopher? I heard one, and could not help smiling, who, with a shout, lest he should not be heard, promised to Christopher who dwells in the great Church at Paris, and is a mountain rather than a statue, a wax image as great as himself. He had repeated this more than once, bellowing as loud as he could, when the man who happened to be next to him, touched him with his finger, and hinted: "You could not pay that, even if you set all your goods to auction." Then the other, in a voice now low enough, that Christopher might not hear him, whispered: "Be still, you fool! Do you fancy I am speaking in earnest? If I once touch the shore, I shall not give him a tallow candle!"

LEGEND OF ST CHRISTOPHER.

*Born.*—Rev. William Burkitt, author of *Expository Notes on the New Testament*, 1650, *Hitcham, Northamptonshire;* Mrs Elizabeth Hamilton, authoress of the *Cottagers of Glenburnie*, 1758, *Belfast.*

*Died.*—Constantius Chlorus, Roman emperor, 306, *York* (*Eboracum*); Nicephorus I., Greek emperor, killed in Bulgaria, 811; Thomas à Kempis, reputed author of the *Imitation of Christ*, 1471, *Mount St Agnes, near Zwoll;* Philip Beroaldus (the elder), eminent classic commentator, 1505, *Bologna;* Ferdinand I., emperor of Germany, 1564, *Vienna;* Robert Fleming, author of *The Fulfilling of the Scripture*, 1694, *Rotterdam;* Baron Friederich von der Trenck, author of the *Memoirs*, guillotined at Paris, 1794; William Romaine, eminent divine, 1795, *London;* Charles Dibdin, celebrated author of sea-songs, 1814, *Camden Town, London;* William Sharp, engraver, 1824, *Chiswick;* William Savage (*Dictionary of the Art of Printing*), 1844, *Kennington;* James Kenney, dramatic writer, 1849, *London.*

## CHARLES DIBDIN.

Southampton has had the peculiar honour of giving to England two most prolific and popular versifiers—Isaac Watts and Charles Dibdin were born there. Unlike in character and calling, they were curiously akin in activity and versatility, and specially in the readiness and ease with which they wrote rhymes, which now and then broke into genuine poetry.

Dibdin was the eighteenth child of a Southampton silversmith; and his mother was nearly fifty years of age at his birth, in 1745. His parents designed him for the church, and sent him to Winchester, but his love for music was an overpowering passion; and, to be near the theatres, he ran off to London, and, while a boy of sixteen, managed to bring out at Covent Garden *The Shepherd's Artifice*, an opera in two acts, written and composed by himself. A few years afterwards he made his appearance as an actor with fair success. In 1778, he was appointed musical director of Covent Garden theatre at a salary of £10 a week. As a playwright, a composer of operas, a theatrical manager, and a builder of theatres, he spent his years with chequered fortune. In 1796, he opened the Sans Souci in Leicester Street, Leicester Square; and in an entertainment, entitled *The Whim of the Moment*, he occupied the stage for nearly ten years as sole performer, author, and composer. For the Sans Souci, he wrote about a thousand songs. The naval war with France was meanwhile at its height, Nelson was in his full career of glory, and the nation was wild with delight and pride in the exploits of its seamen. Dibdin became the bard of the British navy. He sang his multitudinous songs in Leicester Fields with a patriotic fervour truly contagious; his notes were caught up and repeated over sea and land; and, it is said, did more to recruit the navy than all the press-gangs. To Dibdin the beau-ideal of the English sailor—a being of reckless courage, generosity, and simple-heartedness—is largely attributable.

In 1805, he sold Sans Souci, and opened a music-shop in the Strand, which landed him in bankruptcy. The government gave him a pension of £200, which was withdrawn in a fit of parsimony, and then restored. He was attacked with paralysis at the end of 1813, and died in 1814 at his house in Camden Town, in those days a rural suburb of London.

The great mass of Dibdin's songs are now forgotten, but a choice few the world will not willingly let die. Some of his operas still keep the stage, and are always heard with pleasure; for no musician has ever excelled him in sweetness of melody and just adaptation of sound to sense. He wrote about a dozen novels, a *History of the Stage*, and an account of his professional life. One of his sons, Thomas Dibdin, pursued a similar life to his father, producing a host of theatrical pieces, but with less success. He died in indigence in 1841. Dr Dibdin, the celebrated bibliographer, was a nephew of Charles Dibdin; and it was on the death of Thomas, the doctor's father, that Charles wrote the fine ballad of *Poor Tom Bowling*.

## WILLIAM SHARP, THE ENGRAVER.

'This celebrated engraver-in-line was born on the 29th of January 1749, at Haydon Yard, in the Minories, where his father carried on the business of a gunmaker. Apprenticed to *a bright engraver*, his first essay was made upon a pewter-pot, and one of his earliest essays was a small plate of an old lion which had been in the Tower menagerie for thirty years. He next began to engrave pictures from the old masters, and some plates from designs by Stothard; but he greatly excelled in copying the original feeling of Sir Joshua Reynolds; his portrait of John Hunter, the surgeon, is one of the finest prints in the world.

Sharp, though he attained the highest excellence in his profession, was in politics and religious belief a visionary and an enthusiast. He was several times arrested and examined before the privy-council, on suspicion of treasonable practices; and on one occasion, after he had been plagued with many irrelevant questions, he pulled out of his pocket a prospectus for subscribing to his portrait of General Kosciusko, after West, which he was then engraving; and handing it to Mr Pitt and Mr Dundas, he requested them to put their names down as subscribers, which set the council laughing, and he was soon liberated.

He shewed less shrewdness in other matters. No imposture was too great for his belief, and no evidence sufficiently strong to disabuse his mind. The doctrines of Mesmer, the rhapsodies of the notorious Richard Brothers, and the gross delusion of Joanna Southcott, in turn found in him a warm disciple; and in the last case an easy dupe. For Jacob Bryan, an irregular Quaker, but a fervid fanatic, Sharp professed a fraternal regard; so he set him up in business as a copper-plate printer; and one morning, Sharp found Jacob on the floor, between his two printing-presses, groaning for the sins of the people. Sharp believed the millennium to be at hand, and that he and Brothers were to march with their squadrons for the New Jerusalem, in which, by anticipation, Sharp effected purchases of estates! Upon a friend remonstrating with him, that none of his preparations for the journey provided for the marine passage, Sharp replied, 'Oh, you'll see, there will be an earthquake; and a miraculous transportation will take place.' Nor can Sharp's faith or sincerity on this point be distrusted; for he actually engraved *two* plates of the portrait of the prophet Brothers, fully believing that one plate would not print the great number of impressions that would be wanted when the advent should arrive; and he added to each this inscription: 'Fully believing this to be the man appointed by God, I engrave his likeness.—W. SHARP.' The wags of the day generally chose to put the comma-pause after the word 'appointed.' Sharp's belief in Joanna Southcott's delusion was equally absurd; when the surgeons were proceeding to an anatomical investigation of the causes of her dissolution, Sharp maintained that she was not dead, but in a trance! And, subsequently, when he was sitting to Mr Haydon for his portrait, he predicted that Joanna would reappear in the month of July 1822. 'But, suppose she should not?' said Haydon. 'I tell you she will,' retorted Sharp; 'but if she should not, nothing should shake my faith in her divine mission.' And those who were near Sharp's person during his last illness, state that in this belief he died. He lies interred near Dr Loutherbourg and Hogarth, in Chiswick church-yard.

---

# JULY 26.

St Anne, mother of the Blessed Virgin. St Germanus, bishop of Auxerre, confessor, 448.

---

*Born.*—Henry VII., king of England, 1456, *Pembroke, South Wales.*

*Died.*—King Roderick of Spain, killed in battle with the Moors, 711; Ladislaus I., king of Poland, 1102; Pope Paul II., 1471; Jacopo Bonfadio, historian and poet, executed at Genoa, 1560; Armand de Gontaut-Biron, Marshal of France, killed at siege of Epernai, 1592; Charles Emmanuel the Great, Duke of Savoy, 1630; John Wilmot, Earl of Rochester, noted debauchee and poet, 1680, *Woodstock, Oxfordshire;* Thomas Osborne, Duke of Leeds, statesman, 1712; Dr John Freind, eminent scholar, 1728; John Emery, comic actor, 1822; Baron Gourgaud, distinguished general under Napoleon, 1852, *Paris.*

## LEGEND OF DON RODERICK.

One of the most romantic episodes of medieval history, is the conquest of Spain by the Moors or Saracens, in the beginning of the eighth century. There is perhaps no nation whose early chronicles are more shrouded in the robe of chivalrous legend and fiction, or invested with a brighter halo of poetic luxuriance. The story of the fate of Don Roderick, the last of its Gothic kings, forms one of the most curious of these semi-mythical narrations, and has in recent times been made by Sir

Walter Scott the groundwork of one of his poems. It has also been told with singular attractiveness by Washington Irving, in his *Legends of the Conquest of Spain.*

Witiza, the predecessor of Don Roderick on the Spanish throne, had alienated the hearts of his subjects by his shameful debaucheries and misgovernment; and an insurrection having taken place, the latter, who had previously signalised himself greatly by his military achievements, was put in possession of the crown. His conduct in this exalted position was at first all that could be desired; but the deteriorating influences of prosperity and a life of ease gradually corrupted his disposition, and he became almost as noted as Witiza for his voluptuous and irregular life. One of the most noted victims of his lawless passions was Florinda, who had been placed at Don Roderick's court as one of the attendants on his queen. Her father, Count Julian, held the post of military governor of Ceuta, in the Spanish dominions in Barbary; but having been high in favour under the administration of Witiza, he had never cherished much affection for the government of his successor. The intelligence of this outrage on his daughter roused in him the most strenuous determination of vengeance, for obtaining which the conjuncture of affairs presented ready facilities. The religion of Mohammed, which had been promulgated less than a century previous, had now established itself over the greater part of Western Asia and North Africa. In its career of conquest, it had already penetrated to the western shores of the Mediterranean, and made encroachments on the African territories of Spain. Here, however, it had sustained some severe checks from the valour of Count Julian, and its further progress in this direction might have been stayed. But the irreparable insults offered to his family overcame all feelings of loyalty or patriotism in the breast of Julian, and he opened a correspondence with Muza, the Moorish general, for the betrayal of his country to the Saracens. Muza readily listened to his proposals, and a preliminary expedition was organised, under the celebrated Taric, who, by the direction of Julian, made a predatory descent on the Spanish coast, and returned to his master, Muza, with such glowing accounts of the wealth and fertility of the country, that its conquest was forthwith resolved on.

Don Roderick was, in the meantime, consuming his days in inglorious ease in the ancient city of Toledo. Not long after the disaster of the hapless Florinda, he had received a singular warning of the calamities which were about to overtake himself and kingdom. While seated on his throne one day, in the audience-chamber, two venerable old men, with long white beards, presented themselves before him. Their mission, they said, was to request from the king the performance of a behest which had been complied with by all his predecessors. As the guardians of the enchanted tower, which had been founded by the great hero Hercules, in the course of his western peregrinations, they besought Don Roderick to repair thither and affix an additional lock on the portal, as had been done by all former Spanish kings. A terrible mystery, on which the fate of the monarchy depended, was concealed in the building, which the founder had, after constructing it with immense strength and magic art, secured by a massive iron door and a lock of steel. He had further left injunctions that each succeeding king should add another lock to the portal, and refrain religiously from violating its mysteries. Various Spanish sovereigns had, from time to time, ventured to force an entrance into the building, but they had either perished on the threshold, or been so appalled by the fearful sights and sounds which were encountered, that they had rapidly retreated and reclosed the ponderous barrier. No one had yet succeeded in penetrating to the inmost recesses of the sanctuary, the secrets of which had thus remained inviolate since the days of Hercules. Having delivered their message, the venerable guardians of the tower made an obeisance and withdrew.

The curiosity of Don Roderick was greatly excited by what he had just heard, and he declared his determination to see the interior of this marvellous tower. The archbishop of Toledo vainly endeavoured to make him desist from his purpose, assuring him that the violation of a mystery which had been so carefully respected by his predecessors, would only draw down destruction on his head. But the evil star of Don Roderick was in the ascendant, and he marched on blindly to his fate.

The following morning, a gay cavalcade of courtiers, with the king at its head, rode out at one of the gates of Toledo, and took the road to the mountains. They soon reached the mysterious tower, which was situated on a lofty rock, and supported by four magnificent bronze lions. The walls were constructed of marbles of various colours, so disposed as to represent the famous battles and heroic deeds of antiquity. The door was strongly secured by locks and bars, and before it stood the two aged men who had visited the court on the previous day. The king alighted with his train, and requested the old men to open the gate. They remained for a moment astonished, and then falling down on their knees, besought him that he would refrain from so rash an attempt. He was, however, inexorable, and a pair of huge keys having been produced from their girdles, the locks, one after another, were opened, but with such difficulty that a great part of the day was spent before the task was completed. When every barrier was removed, an endeavour was made to open the gate; but it remained immovable, notwithstanding all the efforts of the king's attendants. Don Roderick himself then went forward and placed his hand on it, when it at once moved, as obedient to his touch, and swung open with a dismal groan. A damp cold wind rushed forth, and some of the eager young courtiers pressed into the tower, but quickly returned as if overcome by some magic influence. The king then led the way and entered a hall, on one side of which was an open door. Beside that door stood on a pedestal a gigantic figure whirling furiously a mace, which he, however, dropped to his side on the approach of Don Roderick, allowing him and his train to pass. They then entered a vast and magnificent chamber, the walls of which were composed of the rarest and most brilliant gems, and surmounted by a splendid dome. There were no windows in the hall; but a light, dazzling beyond description, proceeded from the walls, rendering the place as bright as day. Beneath the centre of the dome stood a table bearing the inscription, that Hercules, the Theban hero, had founded this tower in the year of the world three thousand and six. On a golden casket on the table, richly adorned with precious stones, was another inscription, to the effect that herein was contained the mystery of the tower, but warning the intruder from proceeding further. The king had now, however, gone too far to recede, and he opened the casket, which only contained a piece of linen interposed between two plates of copper. It had painted on it figures of men and horses, which, as Don Roderick gazed on it, seemed to enlarge and become animated. A misty panoramic vision of an engagement gradually displayed itself, in which Christians and Moslems seemed to be struggling in deadly conflict, while to complete the scene, the cries of the combatants, the clash of arms, and the roar of battle, were all distinctly audible. The Christians were seen to retreat, broken and discomfited, before the Saracens; and among the numerous figures, Don Roderick could descry his own war-steed, Orelia, galloping frantically about without a rider. Astounded and terrified, the king and his attendants rushed out of the tower, at the entrance of which they found the two aged guardians stricken dead, as if by a thunderbolt. A fearful blackness now spread over the landscape, turning rapidly to a terrible tempest, in the midst of which the royal party reached Toledo. The next day the king returned to the tower, resolved to replace the barriers which confined its dreadful secrets. On coming within sight of it, an eagle was descried soaring aloft, bearing a lighted brand, with which he swooped down upon the tower. The structure at once burst into a flame, and was speedily reduced to ashes, around which congregated a vast array of birds, who caught them up and scattered them over the country. Wherever these ashes fell, they were converted into drops of blood, and the places so stained became the scenes of slaughter and desolation in the ensuing conflicts with the Moors.

The remainder of the legend of Don Roderick is soon told. The warning received from the vision in the tower seems to have been gradually effaced from his mind, when one day he received the unexpected intelligence of the Moorish general, Taric, having effected a landing in Andalusia with a numerous and well-appointed army. To repel the invaders he despatched, in the first place, his kinsman Ataulpho, a gallant young nobleman, who at the head of an armed force encountered the enemy, near the rock of Calpe, the modern Gibraltar, but was discomfited and slain. The victorious Saracens now advanced into Andalusia, and encamped by the river Guadalete, in the plain of Xeres. Thither the king himself marched with the flower of the Spanish chivalry. A great battle ensued, in which the Christians fought with the most determined bravery, but were at length routed and dispersed by the superior generalship of Taric, aided by a Spanish force under the command of the recreant Julian. In the heat of battle Don Roderick was suddenly lost sight of; he was never heard of more, but it was conjectured that, having been slain near the Guadalete, his body had been washed away by the stream. The belief was long current in Spain that he had escaped from the battle, and would return one day to vindicate his own and his country's rights against the invading foe. This fond dream, however, was never to be realised; and it has happened to Don Roderick, as to some other men, that the courage shewn by him in the last struggle has redeemed his name from much of the reproach previously resting on it, whilst the remarkable change of dynasty which the battle of the Guadalete inaugurated, has invested the fate of the last Gothic king of Spain with a romantic and abiding interest.

## EARL OF ROCHESTER.

Among all the gay courtiers who crowded round Charles II., none was more celebrated for his conviviality and wit than the Earl of Rochester. He early displayed remarkable talent, and was much distinguished at Oxford: had he lived in better times, he would probably have graced his high birth; but, after making the grand tour, as it was called, he came to court at the early age of eighteen, there quickly to become the leader of every excess. As his companions found that his wit was greater at the close of a long debauch than at the beginning, it was their amusement to make him drink deeply, and he himself confessed that for five years he was never sober. During this time he was writing satires and squibs upon all around him, and, as may be supposed, making himself many enemies. In one instance he handed the king a paper which Charles opened in the expectation of finding a droll description of some ladies, but it proved to be a witticism on the monarch himself. On another occasion, he scribbled on Charles's bedroom door the well-known mock epitaph:

> 'Here lies our sovereign lord the king,
> Whose word no man relies on;
> Who never says a foolish thing,
> Nor ever does a wise one.'

He joined Charles in many of his wild pranks in the streets of London. At one time he disappeared from the court. Just then stories were circulated about a wonderful physician, necromancer, or Italian mountebank, who was practising on Tower Hill; those who consulted him were startled when they found him disclosing secrets which they hoped were known to none but their most intimate friends; the life of the court seemed laid bare by his wonderful powers; and nothing was talked of for some time, until the shrewder minds felt sure that only Rochester's talent could carry on such a game, and so it proved. At other times, he was inimitable as a porter or a beggar; indeed, he could personate any character to perfection.

That he had a spirit for better things, had he been wisely directed, is evident from his volunteering to join the Earl of Sandwich when he went to sea in 1665; during the engagement that followed, it was necessary that a dispatch should be carried from one ship to another in the very heat of the fight, and in an open boat. Rochester went on this mission, at the imminent risk of his life; yet the rufflers of the court used to taunt him with cowardice in avoiding the duels which his satires brought upon him. Sir C. Scrope thus wrote of him:

> 'Thou canst hurt no man's fame with thy ill word,
> Thy pen is full as harmless as thy sword.'

His constitution was not strong enough to bear his excesses, and early broke up; then, convinced of his past folly, he sent for Dr Burnet, made confession of his reckless life and negation of all religion, and entreated to have his doubts about Christianity dispelled. Burnet has left a touching account of the unfortunate nobleman's last days; he desired that all his wicked writings should be destroyed, and longed to undo the evil he had done by making his deep repentance known to all the world. He died at the early age of thirty-three.

---

# JULY 27.

Saints Maximian, Malchus, Martinian, Dionysius, John Serapion, and Constantine, martyrs, commonly called 'The Seven Sleepers,' 250. St Pantaleon, martyr, 303. St Congall, abbot of Iabhnallivin, Ireland. St Luican, confessor, of Ireland.

## Legend of the Seven Sleepers.

The festival of the Seven Sleepers, commemorated on the 27th of July, was introduced into the Christian church at a very early period. The legend on which it is founded, relates that the Emperor Decius, having set up a statue in the city of Ephesus, commanded all the inhabitants to worship it. Seven young men, disobeying this mandate, and being unambitious of the honour of martyrdom, fled to Mount Cœlius, where they concealed themselves in a cavern (anno 250). Decius, enraged, caused all the various caverns on the mount to be closed up, and nothing was heard of the fugitives till the year 479, when a person, digging foundations for a stable, broke into the cavern, and discovered them. Disturbed by the unwonted noise, the young men, who had been asleep all the time, awakened; feeling very hungry, and thinking they had slept but one night, they despatched one of their number into Ephesus to learn the news, and purchase some provisions. The antiquity of the coin proffered by the messenger at a baker's shop attracted suspicion, and the notice of the authorities. After an investigation, the whole affair was declared to be a miracle, and in its commemoration the festival was instituted.

This legend, which is merely an adaptation of a more ancient one, has found a place in the Koran. According to the Mohammedan account, the sleepers were accompanied by a dog, named Kratim. This animal, after its long sleep, becoming a great prophet and philosopher, has been admitted into the Mussulman's paradise, where it sits beside the ass of Balaam. The other eight animals that enjoy this high privilege, are the ant of Solomon, the whale of Jonah, the ram of Isaac, the calf of Abraham, the camel of Saleh, the cuckoo of Belkis, the ox of Moses, and the mare of Mohammed.

Alban Butler gives a rational cast to the legend of the Seven Sleepers. He conceives that the young men were put to death, by being walled up in a cave, and that only their relics were discovered in 479. These relics he states to be preserved in a large stone coffin, in the church of St Victor, at Marseilles. He further cites from Spon's *Travels*, that the cave of the Seven Sleepers continued in modern times to be the object of devout pilgrimages.

---

*Born.*—Isaac Maddox, bishop of Worcester (*Vindication of Government, &c., of Church of England*), 1697, *London;* Thomas Campbell, poet (*Pleasures of Hope*), 1777, *Glasgow;* George Biddell Airy, astronomer-royal of England, 1801, *Alnwick.*

*Died.*—James I., king of Aragon, 1276, *Xativa;* Henri, Maréchal de Turenne, killed near Saltzbach in Alsace, 1675; Pierre Louis de Maupertuis, natural philosopher, 1759, *Basel;* Samuel Gottlieb Gmelin, naturalist, 1774, *Achmetkent, in the Caucasus;* George Burnet, Scottish painter, 1816; Dr John Dalton, eminent chemist, 1844, *Manchester.*

## DR DALTON.

At one of the early meetings of the British Association for the Advancement of Science, it drew out into prominence, and directed great reverence to, an old man from Manchester, who had been, up to that time, but little known to his fellow-citizens. For a long course of years, he had been an obscure teacher of mathematics—he was a Quaker—he was an unobtrusive and, to all outward appearance, an insignificant person. It was now learned, for the first time, by many of the Manchester people, that this quiet little old man enjoyed high esteem in the scientific world, as the originator of a theory of the utmost importance in chemistry, and was indeed one of the great men of his age, living there, as it were, in a disguise framed of his own superabundant modesty.

John Dalton, the son of a Cumberland yeoman, was born at Eaglesfield, near Cockermouth, on the 5th of September 1766. At the age of thirteen, he began to earn his living by teaching, and at twenty-seven he went to Manchester as a lecturer on mathematics. Until pensioned by government in 1833, he gave lessons at eighteenpence an hour in mathematics. He declined several offers to provide him with a competency, so that he might give his undivided attention to chemistry; asserting 'that teaching was a kind of recreation, and that if richer, he would not probably spend more time in investigation than he was accustomed to do.' He was of course frugal and provident. The apparatus of his laboratory was of the simplest, and indeed rudest kind; scarcely superior to that of Wollaston, who, on a foreign chemist expressing an anxious desire to see his laboratory, produced a small tray containing some glass tubes, a blow-pipe, two or three watch-glasses, a slip of platina, and a few test-tubes. Dalton was a bachelor, altogether of most quiet and regular habits. Twice each Sunday he took his seat in the Friends' meeting-house, and for forty years he ate his Sunday-dinner at one friend's table. The afternoon of every Thursday he spent in a bowling-green, assigning as a reason that he liked to take his Saturday in the middle of the week. He was fond of exercise in the open air, and made an annual excursion among the mountains of Cumberland and Westmoreland. He did not read many books, and was singularly indifferent to all that was written concerning himself. His words were few and truthful. A student who had missed one lecture of a course, applied to him for a certificate of full attendance. He declined to give it, and then relenting, said: 'If thou wilt come to-morrow, I will go over the lecture thou hast missed.' Dalton enjoyed robust health; he was middle-sized, and of a figure more sturdy than elegant. His head and face bore a striking resemblance to the portraits of Sir Isaac Newton. Like Newton, he referred his success, not to genius, but to patience and industry. 'These, in my opinion, make one man succeed better than another.'

It is in connection with the *Atomic Theory* that the name of Dalton promises to go down to posterity. The constitution of matter with respect to divisibility, has been debated from very ancient times. Some hold that its divisibility is infinite, and others, that its reduction is only possible to the extent of atoms (from the Greek Ατομος, that which cannot be cut or divided). Newton expressed the latter opinion in these words: 'All things considered, it seems probable that God, in the beginning, formed matter in solid, massy, hard, impenetrable, movable particles, of such sizes, figures, and with such other properties, and in such proportion to space, as most conduced to the end for which he formed them; and that these primitive particles, being solids, are incomparably harder than any porous bodies compounded of them; even so very hard as never to wear or break to pieces, no ordinary power being able to divide what God made one in the first creation.'

At this point Dalton took up the question. He began by assuming that matter, although it may in essence be infinitely divisible, is in fact only finitely divided, so that each element consists of particles or molecules of a definite and unchangeable weight, size, and shape. He had observed that in certain chemical compounds the elements united in a constant proportion; for example, water, when decomposed, yields one part by weight of hydrogen, and eight parts by weight of oxygen; and it would be useless to try to combine eleven parts of oxygen with one part of hydrogen; water would be formed, but three parts of oxygen would be left free as overplus. What is the reason for the maintenance of this combining proportion? asked Dalton. In his answer, we have the atomic theory, or rather hypothesis.

Taking for granted the existence of atoms, he went on to conceive that in the several elements they vary in weight; atoms of gold from atoms of silver, atoms of iodine from atoms of chlorine; but, on the other hand, that all atoms of the same element are of uniform weight; thus, that any atom of iron is equal to any other atom of iron the world over. We have observed that water is compounded of eight parts by weight of oxygen to one part by weight of hydrogen, and an explanation of the combination is offered in the supposition, that each atom of oxygen is eight times as heavy as one of hydrogen. Further, it is presumed, that in the union of oxygen with hydrogen, the atoms of each are not interfused, but lie side by side, complete in their individuality. If, therefore, the weight of an atom of hydrogen be 1, and an atom of oxygen be 8, it is impossible that their smallest combining proportion, by weight, can be other than 1 and 8. The smallest quantity of water, in this view, must then consist of one atom of hydrogen and one atom of oxygen, bound together in that mystic tie which we term chemical affinity.

The example we have chosen from the constitution of water is a simple illustration of the constant proportion which exists throughout chemical compounds with infinite, complex, and multiple variations. It was in 1803 that the great cosmic idea entered Dalton's mind. In 1804, he explained it in conversation to Dr Thomas Thomson of Glasgow, who, in 1807, gave a short sketch of the hypothesis in the third edition of his *System of Chemistry*. The asserted law of combination in constant proportions was quickly tested in a multitude of experiments, and the facts clustered to its confirmation. It was discovered that there was as little chance or haphazard in the concourse of atoms as in the motions of planets. The hypothesis gave a prodigious impulse to the science of chemistry; it shot light through all its realms, and reduced a chaos of observations to purpose and system. Before Dalton's happy conception there was not a single analysis which could be trusted as correct, or a single gas whose specific gravity was known with accuracy. In the arts, his service was beyond value. He gave the manufacturing chemist a rule whereby he could preclude waste, teaching him how to effect combinations without the loss of an ounce of material. Even supposing that in the future Dalton's notion of the coacervation of infinitesimal atoms should prove erroneous, his merit will remain untouched; for that properly consists in the discovery and promulgation of the law of constant proportion in chemical unions, where before law was unknown, or at anyrate only dimly surmised. The theory of atoms was merely an attempt to reveal the mystery of the law, which will abide, whatever may be the fate of the theory.

Dalton was almost insensible to differences in colours. Whereas most persons see seven colours in the rainbow, he saw only two—yellow and blue; or at most, three—yellow, blue, and purple He saw no difference between red and green, so that he thought 'the face of a laurel-leaf a good match to a stick of red sealing-wax; and the back of the leaf to the lighter red of wafers.' When, at Oxford, Dr Whewell asked him what he would compare his scarlet doctor's gown to, he pointed to the leaves of the trees around them. When a young man, 31st October 1794, he read a paper before the Manchester Literary and Philosophical Society, entitled *Extraordinary Facts Relating to the Vision of Colours*, drawing attention to his own deficiency, which thenceforth became known under the name of Daltonism. Colour-blindness is by no means an uncommon affection. Dalton was acquainted with nearly twenty people in his own case. Dugald Stewart, the metaphysician, was one of them: he could not distinguish the crimson fruit of the Siberian crab from the leaves of the tree on which it grew otherwise than by the difference in form. Dalton tried to account for his peculiarity by supposing that it arose from the vitreous humour of his eyes having a blue tint instead of being colourless like water, as in the majority of mankind. After his death, in obedience to his instructions, his eyes were dissected; but no peculiarity could be detected. The true explanation of colour-blindness is, we apprehend, a phrenological one—namely, that in persons insensible to colours there is a deficiency or mal-organisation in that portion of the brain which receives impressions of colour; just as there are some similarly deficient in the sense of tune, and who cannot distinguish between one piece of music and another. In one thus insensible to melody, we do not assume any defect in his ears, but a deficiency in that part of his brain assigned to the organ of tune.

## THOMAS CAMPBELL.

The author of *The Pleasures of Hope* died at Boulogne, June 15, 1844, at the age of sixty-seven, and was interred in Poets' Corner, Westminster Abbey. He had held for forty-five years a place in the first rank of living poets. He was born at Glasgow, of West Highland parentage; but the most remarkable circumstance connected with his entrance into the world was the fact that his father,

THOMAS CAMPBELL.

at the time of his birth, numbered as many years as he himself was destined to attain. The poet was a man of small stature, of handsome face and figure, animated in conversation, liberal in his political and religious ideas, fond of old friends, could sing a droll song and tell a pleasant story at table, had a very good power of formal public address, and was altogether an amiable and respectable man through life.

Of his pleasant table-anecdotes we remember one regarding himself. He tarried at a London book-stall one day, and after some conversation with the bookseller, purchased a book, which he requested to be sent home. The bookseller, who had previously appeared interested in his conversation, no sooner saw his name on the card he handed, than he seemed to become additionally excited, and finally he blundered out: 'May I inquire, sir?—but—are you, sir—are you the *great* Mr Campbell?' The poet had the caution to ask who it was he considered as the *great* Mr Campbell, but not without a tolerably safe conclusion in his own mind that the author of the *Pleasures of Hope* was the man in question. The answer was: 'Oh! Mr Campbell, the missionary and author of *Travels in South Africa*, to be sure!'

For a few years previous to 1824, a Danish litterateur, named Feldborg, resided in Britain—chiefly in Scotland, where he brought out a book of considerable merit, entitled *Denmark Delineated.* He was good-natured, clever, and entertaining, and much a favourite with Wilson, Lockhart, and other illuminati of the north. It appears that he had also made the acquaintance of Campbell, who, on giving him a copy of his poems containing the ode on the *Battle of the Baltic*, thought proper to address him in the following lines (heretofore, as we believe, inedited):

'Think me not, Danish stranger, a hard-hearted pagan,
If you find, mid'st my war-songs, one called "Copenhagen,"
For I thought when your state join'd the Emperor Paul,
We'd a right to play with you the devil and all;
But the next time our fleet went your city to batter,
That attack, I allow, was a scandalous matter,
And I gave it my curse—and I wrote on't a satire.
To bepraise such an action of sin, shame, and sorrow,
I'll be —— if I would be the laureate to-morrow.
There is not (take my word) a true Englishman glories
In that deed—'twas a deed of our merciless Tories,
Whom we hate though they rule us, and I can assure ye,
They had swung for 't if England had sat as their jury.
But a truce to remembrances blackened with pain,
Here's a health to yourself, and your country, dear Dane.
As our nations are kindred in language and kind,
May the ties of our blood be the ties of our mind,
And perdition on him who our peace would unbind!

May we struggle not who shall in fight be the foremost,
But the boldest in sense—in humanity warmest;
May you leave us with something like love for our nation;
Though we're still curs'd by Castlereagh's administration,
But whatever you think, or wherever you ramble,
Think there's one who has loved you in England'
—Tom Campbell.

London, 30 Foley Place,
Great Portland Street,
*July* 11, 1822.

At a public dinner, in those days when England and France were at mortal enmity, Campbell proposed the health of Napoleon Bonaparte, Emperor of the French. The company was astounded, and on the poet being asked why he could give such a toast, he replied: 'Because he once shot a bookseller!' Campbell sadly forgot, on this occasion, the handsome and even generous treatment he had experienced from the first booksellers with whom he had any important transaction.

His poem, *The Pleasures of Hope*, was written before he had attained his twenty-second year, and while earning his living as a tutor in Edinburgh. In long walks about Arthur's Seat, he conned over its lines until they satisfied his fastidious ear. When the poem was finished, the question arose, how to get it printed without expense or risk of loss? The title had nothing to commend it in the way of originality. Akenside's *Pleasures of Imagination* had long been published, and Rogers's *Pleasures of Memory* had been familiar to the world for six years. He had some acquaintance with the firm of Mundell & Son, for whom he had abridged Bryan Edwards's *West Indies* for £20, and to them he offered his manuscript. Pleased with the poem, yet with slight expectation of pecuniary advantage, they agreed to publish it on condition that Campbell should assign to them the copyright, in return for which they would give him two hundred copies of his book in quires—that is, unbound. Judged by the event, this may seem to have been a niggard bargain; but a better it would be very difficult to make with a manuscript poem, of whatever merit, by an unknown author, though the salesman should trot from east to west of London, and try Edinburgh and Dublin to boot. *The Pleasures of Hope* made its appearance in May 1799. A few copies spread from hand to hand, and were read in Edinburgh with delight and astonishment. Quickly the news flashed through the world of letters, that a poet had appeared whose prime, should it realise the promise of his youth, would register his name among the immortals. Edition after edition of the poem was bought up, and Mundell & Son shared the profits of their speculation with the author, giving him £25 on every thousand printed, or a royalty of sixpence a copy. Further, in 1802, they allowed him to print, in quarto, for his own benefit, a seventh edition, containing *The Battle of Hohenlinden*, *Ye Mariners of England*, *The Exile of Erin*, and *Lochiel's Warning*. By this venture, it is said, he cleared £600. Mundell & Son only ceased to pay their voluntary tribute after a quarrel with the poet. It is estimated that from *The Pleasures of Hope* he derived at least £900, which, as the poem contains 1100 lines, is at the rate of 15*s*. a line—not poor pay, certainly. Campbell wrote little and at long intervals, and nothing in marked excess of his early efforts. His powers appear to have been paralysed with a dread that he should produce anything beneath the standard of his youth. But the fame of *The Pleasures of Hope* was a source of easy income to him through life. For his name as editor of books and magazines, publishers paid him large sums; and in 1806, before he was thirty, the Fox ministry endowed him with a pension of £200 a year. Poetry, if it was a hard mistress to Burns, was a most bountiful one to Campbell.

Reverting to Campbell's feeling about booksellers, it is to be admitted that he shared it with many authors. For what cause we know not, it is an opinion commonly entertained that a publisher is unjust if he on any occasion profits more than the author. If he buys a doubtful manuscript on speculation, and its publication proves remunerative, the author goes about proclaiming that he has been outwitted or defrauded. If, on the other hand, the publication had proved a dead loss, it would never enter the author's head to refund the cash he had received, or to divide the deficit with the publisher. It must be obvious, that such conduct is childish in the extreme. In no trade, except literature, would such an outcry be heard with the least tolerance. No commercial men, except publishers, are ever found sharing the gains of a speculation with those from whom they made their purchase. If Mundell & Son had bought a piece of land from Campbell, and in their hands its rental had multiplied however prodigiously, they would never have dreamed of sharing the increase with Campbell, nor would Campbell have ventured to expect a dividend. It is eminently unreasonable that publishers should incur odium for conducting their business on ordinary commercial principles. Happy is that author by whom a publisher is able to make a successful speculation! If *The Pleasures of Hope* had not been remunerative, Campbell would never have received great sums for editing magazines, nor a pension of £200 a year from government whilst quite a young man.

## STORY OF JANE M'REA.

On the 27th of July 1777, an incident occurred on the Hudson River, which temporarily threw a sad discredit on the British arms, then engaged in the hopeless attempt to preserve America to the British crown. An American army under Schuyler, was posted on the Hudson, with a rear-guard occupying Fort Edward on that river. The British army of General Burgoyne was in possession of the chain of lakes extending towards Canada. At this crisis, there resided with a widow close to Fort Edwards, a young lady of New York, named Jane M'Rea, who had a lover named Jones, a native loyalist, serving under Burgoyne. Her brother wished her to come to him in a safer part of the country; but it is supposed that she lingered at her friend Mrs M'Neil's house at Fort Edward, in a dreamy hope of meeting her loyalist lover. She was a lovely girl of twenty, extremely intelligent, and of charming manners.

The British army had a number of red Indians in its employment, to assist in harassing the unfortunate colonists. They were strictly enjoined only to make captures, and not to commit murder; but it was impossible, by an injunction, to control such wild natures. The fact is, that they shed blood in many instances, and so left an indelible disgrace on the British name in that country. On the day above stated, a party of them assailed Mrs M'Neil's house, and bore off herself and her guest Miss M'Rea, as prisoners, designing apparently to carry them both to the British camp. They were, however, pursued by some American soldiery, who fired upon them. Mrs M'Neil was brought into camp, but of Jane M'Rea only the scalp, with her long flowing hair, was forthcoming. The poor girl had been shot by her own countrymen, and the Indians, seeing her dead, had brought away the bloody trophy, which they are accustomed to tear from the bodies of their enemies.

This tale of woe made a deep impression on the minds of the American people. It was universally believed, that the Indians had murdered Miss M'Rea, notwithstanding the palpably contradictory fact, that they had preserved the elder lady. The love affair added romance to the tragic story. It was held as a terrible example of the wickedness of employing the Indians in a civilised warfare. Poor Jones withdrew in extreme grief to Canada, where he lived to grow old, but was always sad, and never married. Jane lies buried in the small village cemetery, near Fort Edward, beside the grave of her friend Mrs M'Neil.*

* This account of the tragedy of Jane M'Rea, is chiefly taken from a book of remarkable merit and interest, Lossing's *Field-book of the Revolution*, i. 98.

## LEGENDARY ACCOUNT OF GERBERT, MAGICIAN AND POPE.

It was a peculiar feature of the middle ages, that, amid the general mass of ignorance, individuals arose possessed of such enormous mental powers, and so far in advance of their age, that, while the real effects of their great understanding were lost, their names became enveloped in a mist of superstitious wonder which gave them the repute of supernatural giants. A very remarkable example was furnished by the latter part of the tenth century, a period in the history of Western Europe which was not remarkable for its intellectual development. It was France which then produced a youth named Gerbert, of whom the old chroniclers tell us that the highest science then known seemed to be beneath his notice, while his mechanical inventions were the world's wonder. From the account which William of Malmesbury gives of his organ worked by hot water, we might be led to believe that he was not unacquainted with the power of steam. We cannot be surprised if such a man became the subject of innumerable legends, even in his own time, and the historian just quoted, who lived in the middle of the twelfth century, has collected some of them, which are not only curious in themselves, but place in an interesting light the manner in which science was then generally regarded.

According to these legends, Gerbert made his *debût* in the world as a monk of Fleury; but, dissatisfied with the unintellectual life which he led there, he fled from his monastery by night, and went to Spain, to study, among other things, the occult sciences at Toledo. This place was the great seat of learning among the Arabs of Spain; and, among the Christians of the middle ages, Arabian science was equivalent with magic and sorcery. Gerbert, according to the legend, lodged at Toledo with a Saracenic 'philosopher,' whose friendship he gained by his liberality (for he seems to have been possessed of wealth) and by the prospect of advancement in the world, and whose fair daughter became attached to the young student by more tender feelings. The philosopher instructed Gerbert in all hidden knowledge, and communicated to him freely all his books, with the exception of one volume, containing 'the knowledge of his whole art,' which nothing could induce him to impart to his pupil, while the latter became more eager to obtain what was so strictly forbidden. At length, with the assistance of the young lady, Gerbert treacherously plied the Saracen with wine, and, while he was asleep in his bed, took the book from under his pillow, where it was concealed, and fled. The Saracen awoke, perceived his loss, and having discovered, by his knowledge of the stars, the robber and the road he had taken, pursued him without delay. Gerbert also had become acquainted with the stars, and through them he was made aware of the nearness of his pursuer, and of the danger which threatened him, and he adopted an ingenious stratagem. Coming to a wooden bridge, he took shelter under it, and suspended himself to the woodwork, so as to touch neither earth nor water. Then the Saracen, whose knowledge of Gerbert's movements reached only to those two elements, found himself suddenly at fault, and returned home to make further experiments in his art. He soon obtained the further knowledge he required, and again went in pursuit of Gerbert, who meanwhile had arrived on the sea-coast, and there, by means apparently of his stolen book, called up the Evil One, to whom he sold himself, on the condition that the latter should protect him from the Saracen, and convey him safely over the sea to France.

William of Malmesbury here interrupts his narrative to state his reasons for believing that Gerbert had really entered into a league with the devil; and then goes on to state that, on his arrival in France, he opened a school at Orleans, where he was respected by all the great scholars of the age, and had among his pupils the sons of Hugh Capet and the Emperor Otho, and other remarkable persons. When Robert, the son of the former, became king of France (A.D. 997), he made his old instructor, Gerbert, archbishop of Rheims. His other pupil, Otho, who had succeeded his father, Otho, as Emperor of Germany, afterwards raised Gerbert to the archbishopric of Ravenna, and, through that emperor's influence, he was subsequently (in 999) elected pope. 'Thus,' says William of Malmesbury, 'he followed up his fortune so successfully, with the aid of the devil, that he left nothing unexecuted which he had once conceived.'

The same old historian gives another story of Gerbert's shrewdness. There stood in the Campus Martius at Rome, a statue, having the forefinger of the right hand extended, and inscribed on the head the words, 'Strike here!' Many had believed that by obeying this injunction, they would discover a treasure, and the statue had thus been much mutilated by ignorant people; but Gerbert saw at once its meaning. Marking where the shadow of the finger fell at noonday, when the sun was on the meridian, he placed a mark on the spot, and returning thither at night, accompanied only by a trusty servant carrying a lantern, he caused the earth to open by his accustomed arts, and a spacious entrance was displayed. Advancing, they saw before them a vast palace, with walls of gold, golden roofs—in fact, everything of gold; golden soldiers playing with golden dice; a king of the same metal at table with his queen; delicacies set before them, and servants waiting; vessels of great weight and value, the sculpture of which surpassed nature herself. In the innermost part of the mansion, a carbuncle of the first quality, though small in appearance, dispelled the darkness of night. In the opposite corner stood a boy, with a bow bent, and the arrow drawn to the head. When, however, the visitors attempted to touch any of these objects, all the figures appeared to rush forward to repel their presumption. Gerbert took warning, and controlled his desires; but his man, possessing less self-control, attempted to purloin a knife from the table, and instantly the figures all started up with loud clamour, the boy let fly his arrow at the carbuncle, and in a moment all was darkness. Gerbert compelled his servant to restore the knife, and then, with the aid of the lantern, succeeded in making their escape. It is hardly necessary to add that the entrance, then closed up, has never since been found.

This, as well as the next story, has been repeated in different forms, and in relation to different persons. Before Gerbert's great advancement in the world, he cast the head of a statue, which, by means of astrology, he endowed with the property that, if questioned, it would return an answer, and, moreover, would speak nothing but the truth. The first question put by Gerbert was: 'Shall I be pope?' to which the head replied, 'Yes!' He then asked when he should die, and was told that he would not die until he had sung mass in Jerusalem. Gerbert believed he had thus, in his own hands, the power of prolonging his life indefinitely, simply by not going to Jerusalem. He became pope in due time; but he was ignorant of the fact that there was a church in Rome which was popularly called Jerusalem. One day, while in the height of his prosperity, he performed mass in that church, and was at the same time suddenly seized with sickness. On inquiry, he learned the name of the church, and then, remembering the prophecy, he perceived it was fulfilled, and prepared for his death, which soon followed.

The same story is told in a more romantic form by another early writer, Walter Mapes. Mapes's version introduces a fairy-like being, named Meridiana, as greatly affecting the destiny of Gerbert. It also states that Gerbert, when pope, 'out of fear or reverence,' always avoided partaking of the Eucharist, using sleight-of-hand to keep up appearances before the people. It concludes as follows: Gerbert, when assured he was soon to die, called together, in a great meeting, the cardinals, the clergy, and the populace, and there publicly made a full confession of his life. He afterwards made an order that, in future, when the pope in person consecrated the bread and wine, instead of taking it himself with his back turned to the congregation, he should turn round and do it in the view of everybody. The few days which remained to him he passed in sincere penitence, and he made at last a very religious death. He was buried in the church of St John Lateran, and it was said that his marble tomb in that church sweated, or exuded water before the death of people of note; the water becoming a perfect stream when it prognosticated the death of the pope, and at other times varying in quantity according to the rank of the individual whose death was thus announced.

Most of our readers will remember how this story of the equivocation of dying in Jerusalem was, at a much later period, transferred to our King Henry IV.

---

# JULY 28.

Saints Nazarius and Celsus, martyrs, about 68. St Victor, pope and martyr, 201. St Innocent I., pope and confessor, 417. St Sampson, bishop and confessor, about 564.

---

*Born.*—Jacopo Sannazaro, Italian poet, 1458, *Naples;* Joseph I., Emperor of Germany, 1678, *Vienna.*

*Died.*—Theodosius the Younger, Roman emperor, 450, *Constantinople;* Pope Innocent VIII., 1492; Thomas Cromwell, Earl of Essex, beheaded on Tower Hill, 1540; John Speed, historical writer, 1629, *Cripplegate, London;* Richard Corbet, bishop of Norwich, humorous poet, 1635; Abraham Cowley, metaphysical poet, 1667, *Chertsey, Surrey;* Conyers Middleton, philosophical and historical author, 1750, *Hildersham;* George Bubb Dodington, intriguing politician, 1762; Maximilien Isidore Robespierre, terrorist autocrat, guillotined at Paris, 1794; Giuseppe Sarti, musical composer, 1802, *Berlin;* Sultan Selim III., assassinated at Constantinople, 1808; Andoche Junot, Duc d'Abrantes, Bonapartist general, 1813, *Montpelier;* Marshal Mortier, Bonapartist general, killed at Paris by Fieschi's 'infernal machine,' 1835; John George Lambton, Earl of Durham, Liberal statesman, 1840, *Cowes, Isle of Wight;* Joseph Bonaparte, ex-king of Spain, 1844, *Florence;* John Walter, proprietor and conductor of *The Times* newspaper, 1847, *London;* Charles Albert, ex-king of Sardinia, 1849, *Oporto;* Mortimer Collins, poet and novelist, contributor to *Punch*, and author of *Sweet Anne Page*, &c., 1876.

## JACOPO SANNAZARO.

Among the highest sums ever paid for poetical composition, must be included the 6000 golden crowns, given by the citizens of Venice to Sannazaro, for his six eulogistic lines on their city, thus translated by John Evelyn, the amiable author of *Sylva.*

'Neptune saw Venice on the Adria stand
Firm as a rock, and all the sea command,
"Think'st thou, O Jove!" said he, "Rome's walls excel?
Or that proud cliff, whence false Tarpeia fell?
Grant Tyber best, view both; and you will say,
That men did those, gods these foundations lay."'

Howel's lines on the 'stupendous site and structure' of London Bridge, are evidently imitations of Sannazaro's on Venice:

'When Neptune from his billows London spied,
Brought proudly thither by a high spring-tide,
As through a floating wood, he steered along,
And dancing castles clustered in a throng;
When he beheld a mighty bridge give law
Unto his surges, and their fury awe,
When such a shelf of cataracts did roar,
As if the Thames with Nile had changed her shore;
When he such massy walls, such towers did eye,
Such posts, such irons upon his back to lie;
When such vast arches he observed, that might
Nineteen Rialtos make, for depth and height;
When the cerulean god these things surveyed,
He shook his trident, and astonished said:
"Let the whole earth now all her wonders count,
This bridge of wonders is the paramount!"'

## THOMAS CROMWELL, EARL OF ESSEX.

English history boasts of two great men who bore the name of Cromwell, each of whom was the instrument of a great revolution, not only political, but which affected the whole frame of society. The first of these men, Thomas Cromwell, is said to have been the son of a blacksmith at Putney, who, having saved money, became, according to some, a brewer; or, according to others, a fuller. His son Thomas received a tolerable school education, after which he spent some years on the continent, and made himself master of several foreign languages. His original occupation appears to have been of a mercantile character, but he turned soldier, served in Italy under the Constable Bourbon, and was present in 1527 at his death and the sack of Rome. He afterwards resumed his original calling of a merchant, and, returning to England, embraced the profession of the law. He soon attracted the attention of Cardinal Wolsey, who made him his solicitor, and employed him as his chief agent in the dissolution of the monasteries, which the pope had abandoned to the powerful minister for the foundation of colleges. On Wolsey's fall, Cromwell accompanied him in his retirement to Esher; but he was soon tired of inactivity, and he went back to court, determined to push his own fortunes. As far as is known, he never deserted his old master, but spoke eloquently in his defence in the House of Commons, of which he was a member, and where his talents for business were highly commended. Cromwell now made his way into the royal favour, which he secured by his bold and able counsels in the king's final breach with Rome, and he soon became the principal and confidential minister of the crown. To Cromwell, indeed, more than to anybody else, we owe the dissolution of the monasteries, and the establishment of the Reformation in England; and these great measures were carried through entirely by his great abilities, courage, and perseverance. Of course the whole hatred of the Catholic party was directed against him; but he was strong in the king's favour, and was raised rapidly to wealth and honours. The estates of the dissolved monasteries contributed towards the former; and, besides holding some of the highest and most lucrative offices of state, he was raised to the peerage in 1536 under the title of Baron Cromwell of Okeham, and three years afterwards he was created Earl of Essex, having been invested with the order of the Garter, and advanced to the office of lord-high chamberlain of England. This great man eventually experienced the fate of most of Henry's confidential ministers, who were overloaded with favours so long as they pleased him, but the first loss of confidence was but a step to the scaffold. He was actively instrumental in promoting the marriage with Anne of Cleves, and the king, disappointed in his wife, wreaked his vengeance upon his minister. Archbishop Cranmer pled for him in vain, and Cromwell was committed to the Tower on the 10th of June 1540, attainted, after the mere shadow of a trial, of high treason, and beheaded on the 28th of July.

A nephew of Cromwell, Sir Robert Williams, obtained court-favour through his means, and assumed his name. He received a grant from the crown of the lands of the dissolved monasteries in Huntingdonshire, and established his family at Hinchinbroke, in that county. He was the great-grandfather of Oliver Cromwell, the Protector.

## RICHARD CORBET.

Richard Corbet, successively bishop of Oxford and Norwich, was one of the most eminent English poets of his day. Born in the reign of Elizabeth, his wit and eloquence recommended him to the favour of James, and his advancement in the church was commensurate with his abilities. Benevolent, generous, and spirited in his public character—amiable and affectionate in private life—he deservedly enjoyed the patronage of the great, the applause and estimation of the good. The following lines, found written on the fly-leaf of a volume of Corbet's poems, convey an excellent idea of his general character

'If flowing wit, if verses writ with ease,
If learning void of pedantry can please;
If much good-humour joined to solid sense,
And mirth accompanied with innocence,
Can give a poet a just right to fame,
Then Corbet may immortal honour claim;
For he these virtues had, and in his lines
Poetic and heroic spirit shines;
Though bright, yet solid, pleasant but not rude,
With wit and wisdom equally imbued.
Be silent, Muse, thy praises are too faint,
Thou want'st a power, the prodigy to paint,
At once a poet, prelate, and a saint.'

## ROBESPIERRE.

The 10th Thermidor was the revolutionary name for the day (the 28th July 1794) which brought the termination of the celebrated Reign of Terror. While pressing dangers from foreign invaders and internal enemies surrounded the Revolution, the extreme party, headed by Robespierre, Barrere, St Just, &c., had full sway, and were able to dictate numberless atrocities, under pretence of consulting the public safety. But when the Revolution became comparatively safe, a reaction set in, and a majority in the Convention arrayed themselves against the Terrorists. A struggle of two days between the two parties produced the arrest of Robespierre, Couthon, St Just, Lebas, and a younger brother of Robespierre; and finally, in the afternoon of the 28th, these men, with some others, their accomplices, mounted the scaffold to which they had, during eighteen months, consigned so many better men. Robespierre died at the age of thirty-five.

It is undoubted that many of the most frightful outrages on humanity have been perpetrated, not in wanton malignity, or from pleasure in inflicting pain, but in the blind fervour of religious and patriotic feeling. We do not charge St Paul with cruelty when, as Saul, he went about 'breathing threatenings and slaughter,' and 'making havoc of the church.' St Dominic, who led on the massacre of the Albigenses, is said to have been a kindly man, but for a heretic he had no more heart than a stone. Indeed, the catalogue of persecutors contains some of the noblest names in history.

Had Robespierre himself not been sent as deputy from Arras to Paris, he probably would have lived a useful citizen, respected for his probity, benevolence, and intelligence. When an enterprising spirit in Arras set up a Franklin lightning-conductor, there arose a popular outcry against his impiety. 'What! shall we rend the very lightnings from the hand of God?' exclaimed the terrified people. Robespierre defended Science against Superstition, and won a verdict for the innovator. He was appointed a judge in the Criminal Court of Arras, but he actually resigned his office rather than sentence a murderer to death. In Paris, he dwelt with Madame Duplay, who idolised her lodger. His evenings he occasionally spent in conversation with her and her daughter; sometimes he read them a play from Racine, and sometimes took them to the theatre, to see some favourite tragedy. Once he proposed to leave the house, saying: 'I compromise your family, and my enemies will construe your children's attachment to me into a crime.' 'No, no,' replied Duplay, 'we will die together, or the people will triumph.' Similar testimonies of esteem come from others who knew Robespierre privately; yet we cannot suppose he ever commanded any deeper feeling in any human breast than respect. He had no geniality; his virtues were all severe; he was a Puritan and Precisian, and perhaps the most perfect type of the fanatic to be found in biography. As Mr G. H. Lewes, in his *Life and Correspondence of Robespierre*, observes: 'All that is great and estimable in fanaticism—its sincerity, its singleness of purpose, its exalted aims, its vigorous consistency, its disdain of worldly temptations—all may be found in Robespierre; and those who only contemplate that aspect of the man will venerate him. But there is another aspect of fanaticism, presenting narrow-mindedness, want of feeling, of consideration, and of sympathy; unscrupulousness of means, pedantic wilfulness, and relentless ferocity; and whoso contemplates this aspect also, will look on Robespierre with strangely mingled feelings of admiration and abhorrence.'

It was the intense unity and energy of his character that carried Robespierre so quickly to power. His mind was small but single; not any of its force was wasted. When he first spoke in the Assembly, he was laughed at; but, said Mirabeau, with the prescience of genius: 'That man will do somewhat; he believes every word he says.' It is to be remembered that he ran the career by which he is infamous in the short space of five years; he arrived in Paris as deputy from Arras in 1789, and was guillotined in 1794.

Robespierre's person was in striking correspondence with his mind. He was little, lean, and

ROBESPIERRE.

feeble. His face was sharp; his forehead good, but narrow, and largely developed in the perceptive organs; his mouth was large, and the lips thin and compressed; his nose was straight and small, and very wide at the nostrils. His voice was hoarse in the lower, and discordant in the higher, tones, and when in a rage, it seemed to change into a howl. He was bilious, and his complexion livid, and thus Carlyle, in his *French Revolution*, always marks him out as 'the sea-green.'

His wants were few and his habits simple. For money he had as little desire as necessity; and at his death his worth in cash was no more than £8. Thus as easily as justly did he win his title of 'The Incorruptible.' He drank nothing but water; his only excess was in oranges; these he ate summer and winter with strange voracity, and never did his features relax into such pleasantness as when his mouth was engrossed in one. His lodgings with Duplay were very humble; his bed-room and study were one apartment. There might be seen a bedstead, covered with blue damask and white flowers, a table, and four straw-bottomed chairs. The walls were studded with busts and portraits of himself; and two or three deal-shelves contained the few books he cared to read, and his manuscripts carefully written, and with many erasures. On the table there usually lay a volume of Racine or Rousseau, open at the place he was reading. He went to bed early, rising in the night to write. His recreation was a solitary walk in the Champs Elysées, or about the environs of Paris, with his great dog Brount, who nightly kept guard on the mat at his master's door. A striking picture might be made of the lean, anxious, bilious, precise tribune, playing with his colossal mastiff.

Considering the extent of his infamy, there are singularly few anecdotes preserved of Robespierre. Mr Lewes describes, in the words of a certain M. Legrand, who was living in Paris in 1849, an interview with Robespierre, at which you are puzzled whether to laugh or shudder. 'M. Legrand,' writes Mr Lewes, 'boasts of his acquaintance with Robespierre, whom he regards as the best abused man of his acquaintance. To him Robespierre was a very agreeable man in society. He only thinks of him in that light. The Reign of Terror is a sort of nightmare—he no longer thinks of it. There is one story he always tells, and I regret that I must spoil it in the telling, wherein so much of the effect depends upon the gesture and the quiet senile tone of voice; but such as it is, it will, I think, amuse the reader.' M. Legrand speaks—'I recollect one time being at Lebas . . . . where he went very often . . . . I heard a noise upon the stairs. "Stop," cried I. I thought it was that *farceur* (jester) Robespierre . . . . for he was very merry . . . . in society [This epithet of *farceur* is very piquant]. In fact, it was he. He came into the parlour . . . . I go up to him, and say: "Citizen, you know . . . . or you ought to know . . . . that M. Legrand, my kinsman—alas! he is condemned, and to-morrow morning . . . . [Here a very significant gesture imitative of the guillotine completes the sentence] . . . . A man, citizen, whose innocence is certain! for whom I can answer as for myself! . . . . And the life of an innocent man, citizen, it is of some account!" Then he answers me: "Let us see, let us see, what is your business?" . . . . (for he was very agreeable in society—M. de Robespierre). I tell him the tale; then he asks me, "At what hour does your friend die?" . . . . (for he was very agreeable in society—M. de Robespierre). "Citizen," I reply, "at nine o'clock precisely!"—"At nine o'clock! that is unfortunate! for you know I work late; and as I go to bed late, I rise late. I am much afraid I shall not be up in time to save your friend . . . . but we shall see, we shall see!" . . . . (for he was very agreeable in society—M. de Robespierre). [After a short pause the old gentleman continues.] It appeared . . . . that M. de Robespierre had worked *very hard* that night; for my poor friend! [Here again he makes the guillotine gesture]. It is all the same! I am sure that if he had not worked so late, he would have saved my poor friend; for he was very agreeable in society—M. de Robespierre.'

## MARSHAL MORTIER:
## FIESCHI'S INFERNAL MACHINE.

It was on the 28th July 1835, that this infernal machine was discharged, with intent to destroy the French king, Louis Philippe, as he rode along the lines of the National Guard, on the Boulevard du Temple, accompanied by his three sons and suite. The machine consisted of twenty-five barrels, charged with various species of missiles, which were fired simultaneously by a train of gunpowder. The king and his sons escaped; but Marshal Mortier, Duc de Treviso, was shot dead, and many other persons were dangerously wounded. Such were the circumstances under which one of Napoleon's marshals, after escaping the perils of the battle-field, perished in a time of peace, in the streets of the capital, while in the service, suite, and favour of a king of the Orleans branch of the Bourbons! It is as an introduction to some little known facts of his earlier life, that we have thus briefly stated the circumstances of his death.

Biography, like history, is at times written after a strange fashion. Like the fabled shield, gold on one side and silver on the other, not only the colouring but the facts of a life seem to depend on the stand-point of the writer. Before us lies a little publication of the year 1813, professing to give *An interesting Account of Buonaparte and his Family; with the Original Name, Pedigree, and present Title of the Marshals and Generals who fought his Battles in Spain, Portugal, Russia, Germany, &c.; chiefly extracted from the Literary Panorama, with Additions to the present Time, by the Editor.* Some idea may be formed of the character of this *brochure*, from the fact that it charges most of the family of Napoleon, and many of his marshals and generals, with the foulest crimes; as murder, incest, adultery, forgery, wholesale robberies, &c. In an introductory note, its editor says: 'Nor perhaps will it be believed that Brissot, who dethroned Louis XVI., had been employed in a printing-office in London, at the rate of 30*s*. per week, as corrector of the press!' We have not elsewhere seen this statement, and of course cannot pronounce it either true or false. But if true, it is noteworthy that Brissot was not the only one of those bespattered with abuse by 'the editor' aforesaid, who passed some time in England. This is what he writes on the subject of our sketch:

'Marshal Mortier, Duke of Treviso, was clerk to a merchant at Dunkirk, Mr James Bell, now of Angel Court, Throgmorton Street, London, who took him to Alicante, at £25 per annum. There he learned the Spanish language, and behaved remarkably well. He then left his situation at the beginning of the French revolution, and went back to France, where he was made a sergeant in the National Guard. He committed great depredations in Hanover. The Duchess of Treviso is an inn-keeper's daughter.'

Looking at most of the other portraits in this wretched picture-gallery, it seems clear that the limner had not been able to find any of his darker hues with which to smear the character of Mortier. But, leaving this statement with the expression of a doubt as to its veracity in two or three important features, we turn to a much more pleasing sketch from another English pen.

In that amusing book, entitled *Music and Friends*, by the late Mr Gardiner, of Leicester, the author gives the following account of a visit he made to Paris in July 1802: 'One of my first objects in Paris was to be present at the *fête* on the 14th of July, the anniversary of the revolution, and for this purpose my friend, Mr Cape, procured me a letter of introduction to General Mortier from Mr Sylvester, of Manchester, with whom Mortier had served his clerkship as a merchant. On my arrival I found the general was commander of the city, residing at the Etat Major, what we should call the Horse Guards of Paris. . . . I had received a note from General Mortier, afterwards Duke of Treviso, to dine with him, and bring my friend. This was very agreeable to me, as Mr Fichet spoke the language like a native. My friend was overjoyed at the thoughts of this visit, and was in a hundred perplexities how he should dress for the occasion. The first article laid out was an embroidered shirt that cost twelve guineas, with loads of rings, chains, and trinkets. When attired, I confess we did not look as if we belonged to the same species. Having driven to the Etat Major, we were received by a file of soldiers at the gate, who presented arms. We were ushered into the drawing-room, and introduced to the general, to Madame Mortier, another lady, and the general officers, Menou, Soult, and Lefevre. The coats of these warriors were covered with gold upon the arms from the shoulder to the wrist; you could scarcely see the scarlet cloth for oak-leaves and acorns wrought in gold. When we had sat down to dinner, I noticed two vacant places at table, which were soon filled up by the sergeant and corporal upon guard, who had just received us at the door. This was one of the outward signs of liberty and equality; they behaved well, and retired just before the dessert was brought in. We had an elegant dinner; some things surprised me—the eating of ripe melon to boiled beef, and drinking sixteen sorts of wine at dinner. A fine embroidered *garçon* was incessantly bawling in my ear some new sort he had upon his tray. I satisfied him by tasting all, and it was well I did so, for you get no wine afterwards. My friend was the admiration of the ladies, and had the whole of their conversation—a sort of small-talk in which he greatly excelled. For my part, I was compelled to be silent, not having that enviable fluency; and my taciturnity excited the attention of Menou, who asked me "What the English thought of the French?" Mortier, who spoke our language perfectly, was kind enough to be my interpreter, and I replied: "We thought them a fine gallant nation, great in science and in arms." This produced a smile of satisfaction, and was probably the first sentiment of the kind they had heard from an Englishman. "We have the same opinion of you," replied the Egyptian general; "you are as great upon sea as we are upon land. What folly is this fighting! Could we but agree, the world might be at peace; England and France could govern Europe. What do you think of the Consul?" continued he. "Why, we think him rather an ambitious gentleman; we have a notion that he will not long be satisfied with being Prime Consul, but will declare himself sole Consul;

and, if you wish for my private opinion, I think shortly he will make himself king!" The general turned round with a supercilious smile, and addressing himself to the company, said the credulity of the English was a proverb all over Europe.'

From this narrative, it appears that Mr Gardiner had not been introduced to Mortier before July 1802, and that it is only on hearsay that he states that the marshal had been a clerk in the establishment of a Manchester merchant, named Sylvester. This is an error, which the present writer is enabled to correct. In the year 1786, an academy was established in Manchester, entitled the Manchester Academy, chiefly in connection with the Presbyterian or Unitarian denomination of dissenters. Its principal was the Rev. Thomas Barnes, D.D., then the senior minister of the Manchester Presbyterian Chapel, Cross Street. Its tutor for the Belles-Lettres, &c., was Mr Lewis Loyd, then a dissenting minister, who preached at Dob Lane Chapel, Failsworth, about three miles from Manchester. He subsequently married Miss Jones, the daughter of a Manchester banker, and became a partner in the since well-known firm of Jones, Loyd, & Co., of London and Manchester. His son, Samuel Jones Loyd, was, a few years ago, elevated to the peerage by the title of Lord Overstone. When it is added that the mathematical tutor at the Manchester Academy, at the same period, was Dr Dalton, afterwards so celebrated for his chemical discoveries, and especially for what has been termed the law of definite proportions, or the atomic theory—enough has been said to shew that this provincial academical institution of the last century was worthy of its high reputation.

Some years ago, the writer had several conversations on the subject of this academy, its principal, its tutors, and *alumni*, with a venerable survivor of the latter body, the late John Moore, Esq., F.L.S., in whose words is the following too brief account of the subject of this notice: 'Another student of the Manchester Academy, whose military talents advanced him to high rank in the service of his country, was the celebrated Marshal Mortier. He was the son of a merchant at Lyons, who, being desirous that his son should acquire an insight into the English methods of manufacturing and of doing business, sent him over to Manchester, and he was placed in the academy, but some time before I entered it. It has been erroneously stated that Mortier was a clerk in the house of Messrs Sylvester & Co., and Colonel Sylvester (of the volunteers) has been mentioned in connection with him. But it was the colonel's brother with whom Mortier was intimate, and there was no commercial connection whatever—nothing but personal friendship between them. It is supposed, however, that Mortier was, for a short time, in more than one Manchester house; not, however, as a clerk, but as a young gentleman seeking to obtain information as to their modes of doing business. Mortier did not remain long in Manchester, but returned to France when the war broke out. He joined the army, where his military talents led to his rapid rise, now a matter of history. It is to his honour that, learning, after he had risen to a high military rank and position, that his old friend James Sylvester was in embarrassed circumstances, he wrote to him; intimating that he could never forget his friendship while in Manchester, and (it is believed) sent him some very substantial present, to enable him to improve his fortunes.'

From another friend in Manchester, the writer derived the following interesting anecdote of Mortier: 'I knew a young man named Wild, in the volunteers—a very modest, shy lad; but he afterwards joined the army, rose by merit, and became lieutenant. He was with the British army in Spain, where he was appointed adjutant of the 29th Regiment, and was in that slaughtering affair—I think Salamanca—where Colonel White was shot; Wild being wounded at the same time. Colonel White became delirious from the effects of the wound, and as he was being carried to the rear, he began singing. The Duke of Wellington, passing at the time, stopped, and when he saw poor White's condition, tears came into the eyes of the man who has been called "The Iron Duke." Subsequently, Wild being at an outpost, was taken prisoner with some of his men, by the French troops, and they were marched up the country. The officers were very civil to Wild, and, as it was their custom to march at the head of their men, in order to avoid the dust, they invited him to join them. After some days' march they reached head-quarters, and on reporting themselves, received the honour of an invitation to dine with Marshal Mortier, then commanding a garrison town. The invitation contained the words: "Bring your English prisoner with you." Poor Wild was in no plight to dine with a marshal of France; but his captors were most considerately kind. One lent him a shirt; another some other article of attire; and by their courteous aid he found himself at length presentable. The dinner was *recherché*, everything *en grand regle;* and at length, after coffee, the guests rose to retire. The marshal requested them to leave their prisoner with him; and when the French officers had withdrawn, Wild was astonished to hear himself addressed in plain English: "Well, and where do you come from?" His reply was, "From beyond Rochdale, in Lancashire." "Well; and how's Dick Crompton?" In this familiar style Mortier chatted with his astonished guest, naming Smithy-door and other well-remembered localities, and appearing much amused to learn that his old acquaintance, Dick Crompton, was then town-major of Lisbon. After a pleasant conversation on Lancashire men and places, Wild was reconducted to his quarters, and remained some time in prison. He succeeded, with the aid of a kindly girl, in effecting his escape, and long rambled about the country, under great risks, till at length, by the aid of friendly contrabandistas, he made his way back to the head-quarters of the British army. After attaining a captaincy he was placed on half-pay; returned to Manchester; took the White Lion Inn, Long Millgate; and subsequently went to keep what were then called Tinker's Gardens (afterwards Vauxhall Gardens), Collyhurst. He married a very beautiful girl, who did not assist him in the inn; all went wrong; and poor Wild was taken as a debtor to Lancaster Castle. Hearing a bell ring in the evening, he asked what it was, and was told it was the time for the prisoners to be locked up. He fell down, and expired on the spot. Dick

Crompton became Captain Crompton, and on my telling him about Mortier asking after him, he said, "Oh, I knew Mortier very well in Manchester."'

## JOHN WALTER, OF 'THE TIMES.'

The perfection of literary success involves the conjunction of the man of letters with the man of business. Next to the author is the publisher, who carries the author's wares to market, and suggests to him what ought to be produced, and indicates what can be sold. A publisher is often a mere seller of books irrespective of their contents, but it must be obvious that for the due fulfilment of his functions, a taste for and delight in literature are essential. It was through a happy union of business tact with literary taste that the House of Murray was crowned with honour and fortune; and the same truth we find illustrated with equal brilliancy in the story of the House of Walter.

As there have been three John Murrays, there have been three John Walters—father, son, and grandson. John Walter, the father, was born in 1739, and was known as the 'logographic printer.' He held a patent for Logography, or the art of printing with entire words, and their roots and terminations, in addition to the use of types for single letters; and persevered with his scheme through much opposition and many difficulties. In joke it used to be said that his orders to the typefounder ran in this fashion: 'Send me a hundredweight of type made up in separate pounds, of *heat, cold, wet, dry, murder, fire, dreadful, robbery, atrocious outrage, fearful calamity, alarming explosion, honourable gentleman, loud cheers, gracious majesty, interesting female*,' and so on. He brought out, in 1785, *The Daily Universal Register*, the title of which he changed on the 1st of January 1788, to (world-famous name!) *The Times*. The heading of the early numbers was as follows: *The Times, or Daily Universal Register, printed Logographically*. Its price was 3*d*. For many years the *Times* existed in quiet equality with its daily brethren; now and then falling into trouble from actions at law through incautious writing. In 1790, Mr Walter was fined £200 for a couple of libels on the Prince of Wales, and the Dukes of York and Clarence, but was released from Newgate at the end of sixteen months by the intercession of the Prince of Wales. John Walter I. died in 1812.

It was under John Walter II., born in 1784, that the *Times* rose to the place of the first newspaper in the world. Whilst yet a youth, in 1803, he became joint-proprietor and sole manager of the *Times*, and very soon his hand became manifest in the vigour and independence of its politics, and the freshness of its news. Free speech, however, had its penalties. The *Times* denounced the malpractices of Lord Melville, and the government revenged itself by withdrawing from the Walters the office of printers to the Customs, which had been held by the family for eighteen years. During the war between Napoleon and Austria in 1805, the desire for news was intense. To thwart the *Times*, the packets for Walter were stopped at the outports, whilst those for the ministerial journals were hurried to London. Complaint was made, and the reply was given that the editor might receive his foreign papers as a *favour*; meaning thereby that if the government was gracious to the *Times*, the *Times* should be gracious to the government; but Walter would accept no favours on such terms. Thrown on his own resources, he contrived, by means of superior activity and stratagem, to surpass the ministry in early intelligence of events. The capitulation of Flushing, in August 1809, was announced by the *Times* two days before the news had arrived through any other channel. In the editorship of the paper he spared neither pains nor expense. The best writers were employed; and wherever a correspondent or a reporter displayed marked ability, he was carefully looked after, and his faculty utilised. Correspondents were posted in every great city in the world, and well-qualified reporters were despatched to every scene of public interest. The debates in parliament, law proceedings, public meetings, and commercial affairs were all reported with a fulness and accuracy which filled readers with wonder. What a visionary could scarcely dare to ask, the *Times* gave. To other journals, imitation alone was left. They might be more consistent politicians, but in the staple of a newspaper, to be nearly as good as the *Times* was their highest praise.

The public were not slow to appreciate such service, and to reward the *Times* with a yearly increase of circulation. Next to Mr Walter's desire to occupy its columns worthily, was his anxiety to print it off so rapidly as to be able to meet any demand. The hand-press was of course inadequate. As early as 1804, he assisted Thomas Martyn, an ingenious compositor, in devising a new machine, and only gave up when he had exhausted his available funds. Shortly after, Frederick Koenig, a German, came to England with some novel ideas about printing, which met the approval of two or three enterprising London tradesmen; and after several years of patient and expensive experiment, Koenig and his patrons were gratified by success. Mr Walter gave an order for two of Koenig's machines, to be worked by a steam-engine. The *Times'* pressmen were enraged at the innovation, and Mr Walter had actually to set up the new apparatus in adjoining premises, to be safe from their violence. On the 29th November 1814, a memorable day, the *Times* was printed for the first time by steam-power. The number impressed per hour was 1100. Improvement on improvement followed on Koenig's invention, until at this day 15,000 sheets of the *Times* are printed off in a single hour!

Mr Walter acquired a noble fortune through his enterprise, and purchased a fine estate in Berkshire, for which county he was returned as member of parliament in 1832; he resigned his seat in 1837, in consequence of a difference with his constituents on the question of the new Poor Law. He died on the 28th July 1847, at his house in Printing House Square, Blackfriars, the scene of his labours and triumphs.

Mr Walter was succeeded by his son, John Walter III., born 1818. He sat in the House of Commons, as member for Nottingham, from 1847 till 1859; when he was elected for Berks. Under his care the *Times* has continued to flourish.

# JULY 29.

St Martha, virgin, sister of Mary and Lazarus. Saints Simplicius and Faustinus, brothers, and their sister Beatrice, martyrs, 303. St Olaus, king of Sweden, martyr. St Olaus or Olave, king of Norway, martyr, 1030. St William, bishop of St Brieuc, in Brittany, confessor, about 1234.

---

*Born.*—Albert I., emperor of Germany, 1248.

*Died.*—Philip I., king of France, 1108, *Melun;* Sebastian, king of Portugal, killed near Tangiers, 1578; Thomas Stukely, adventurer, 1578; Pope Urban VIII., 1644; Andrew Marvell, poet and politician, 1678, *London;* Benjamin Robins, celebrated mathematician and experimenter on projectiles, 1751, *Madras; Augustus* William Ernesti, editor of Livy, 1801, *Leipsic;* Anna Selina Storace, favourite singer, 1814, *London;* William Wilberforce, philanthropist, 1833, *London;* Dr Thomas Dick, author of various scientific works, 1857, *Broughty Ferry, Forfarshire.*

## DISAPPEARANCE OF DON SEBASTIAN OF PORTUGAL.

The students of modern European history, and the readers of Anna Maria Porter's novels, are well aware of the romantic circumstances under which Don Sebastian, king of Portugal, disappeared from the face of the earth in 1578. This enthusiastic young king—he was only two-and-twenty—chose to conduct the best military strength of his country into Marocco, in order to put down a usurping sovereign of that country; an expedition utterly extravagant and foolish, against which all his best friends counselled him in vain. He fought a desperate battle with the Moors at Alcazar, performed prodigies of valour, and was nevertheless so thoroughly defeated, that it is said scarcely fifty of his army escaped alive. A body, said to be his, was rendered up by the Moors, and interred at Belem; but the fact of his death, nevertheless, remained doubtful. His countrymen, who admired and loved him, considered him as having mysteriously disappeared, and an idea took possession of them that he would by and by reappear and resume his throne. Strange to say, this notion continued in vigour after the expiration of the time within which the natural life of Sebastian must have been circumscribed; indeed, it became a kind of religious belief, which passed on from one generation of Portuguese to another, and has even survived to very recent times. In the *Times*, December 1825, it is stated as 'a singular species of infatuation, that many persons residing in Brazil, as well as Portugal, still believe in the coming of Sebastian. Some of these old visionaries will go out, wrapped in their large cloaks, on a windy night, to watch the movements of the heavens; and frequently if an exhalation is seen flitting in the air, resembling a fallen star, they will cry out, "There he comes!" Sales of horses and other things are sometimes effected, payable at the coming of King Sebastian. It was this fact that induced Junot, when asked what he would be able to do with the Portuguese, to answer: "What can I do with a people who were still waiting for the coming of the Messiah and King Sebastian?"'



## THOMAS STUKELY.

The romantic career of this extraordinary adventurer has furnished materials for the novelist, dramatist, and poet. He was of a good family in the west of England; and a relative, probably brother, of the Sir Lewis Stukely, sheriff of Devonshire, who arrested Sir Walter Raleigh. His father is said to have been a wealthy clothier or manufacturer of woollen cloths. This being the most lucrative trade of the period, requiring large capital to carry it on, the clothiers were considered as gentlemen, and allowed the privilege of wearing coat-armour. Stukely's place of birth is doubtful. The long popular ballad on him commences thus:

> 'In the west of England,
> Born there was, I understand,
> A famous gallant in his days,
> By birth a worthy clothier's son;
> Deeds of wonder hath he done,
> To purchase him a long and lasting praise.'

But in the drama ascribed to George Peele, entitled *The Battle of Alcazar*, he is represented saying:

> 'Thus Stukely, slain with many a deadly stab,
> Dies in these desert fields of Africa.
> Hark, friends! and, with the story of my life,
> Let me beguile the torment of my death.
> In England's London, lordings, was I born,
> On that brave bridge, the bar that thwarts the Thames.'

Other accounts say that Stukely was a natural son of Henry VIII.; and again, it is stated that he was the son of an English knight, by an Irish mother of the regal race of Mac Murrough, and he certainly had family connections with the principal nobility of Ireland. It is certain, also, that he was bred a merchant, and acquired an immense fortune by marrying the daughter of an Alderman Curtis. This lady, whose fortune supplied Stukely's inordinate extravagance, represented to him one day that he 'ought to make more of her.' 'I will,' he replied, 'make as much of thee, believe me, as it is possible for any man to do;' and he kept his word, in one sense at least, for having dissipated all her fortune, he stripped her of even her wearing apparel before he finally left her.

Sir Walter Scott says, that this 'distinguished gallant' ruffled it at the court of Queen Elizabeth with Raleigh, and the best of the time. And it would seem that his inordinate pride, vanity, and ambition were considered an amusement, rather than an insult to the court. His first, but abortive enterprise, was to found a kingdom for himself in Florida; and he presumed to tell Elizabeth, that he would rather be the independent sovereign of a molehill, than the highest subject of the greatest monarch in Christendom. At another time, he said, in hearing of the queen, that he was determined to be a prince before he died. 'I hope,' ironically observed Elizabeth, 'that you will let us hear from you, when you are settled in your principality.' 'I will write unto your majesty,' Stukely replied. 'And how will you address me?' she asked. 'Oh! in the style of a prince,' the adventurer with great coolness replied. To our dear sister!'

Stukely, having squandered the greater part of his wealth, went to Ireland in 1563, with the apparent intention of settling in that kingdom.

He soon obtained considerable influence over Shane O'Neill, the most powerful of the native chieftains, and was employed by the government to negotiate with him. When Shane defeated the Hebridean Scots at Ballycastle, Stukely was with the Irish chief, and there is every probability that it was by his generalship the victory was gained. Stukely applied for high office in Ireland, but only obtained the seneschalship of Wexford. During his Irish career, he never completely gave up his character of merchant; he still retained ships, which, under the guise of peaceful traders, committed infamous piracies. These depredations being at last traced to Stukely, he sailed to Spain, and assuming to be a person of great consequence, was well received at the Spanish court.

'There did Tom Stukely glitter all in gold,
Mounted upon his jennet, white as snow,
Shining as Phœbus in King Philip's court;
There, like a lord, famous Don Stukely lived.'

From Spain, Stukely went to Rome, where he was also well received; and at the great naval battle of Lepanto, gained by Don John of Austria over the Turks, he commanded one of the papal ships. And as Taylor, the Water-poet, in his *Church's Deliverance*, tells us:

'Rome's malice and Spain's practice still concur
To vex and trouble blest Elizabeth;
With Stukely they combine to raise new stirs;
And Ireland-bragging Stukely promiseth
To give unto the pope's brave bastard son,
James Boncompagno, an ambitious boy;
And Stukely from the pope a prize hath won,
A holy peacock's tail (a proper toy):
But Stukely was in Mauritania slain,
In that great battle at Alcazar fought.'

Gregory XIII., having created Stukely Baron Ross, Viscount Murrough, Earl of Wexford, Marquis of Leinster, and Duke of Ireland, supplied him with a small army of 800 men, with which our adventurer sailed from Ostia, with the intention of conquering Ireland, and annexing it to the pope's dominions. Calling at Lisbon on his way, he found Sebastian, king of Portugal, on the point of sailing with a large force for the invasion of Marocco. Being invited to join this expedition, the chivalrous spirit of Stukely at once assented—the rest is a matter of history. Though Stukely was a traitor and a pirate, his dashing, gallant, fearless career has caused him to be remembered, when many a better man has sunk into oblivion. The ballad, entitled *The Life and Death of the Famous Lord Stukely*, was commonly sold by pedlers in the writer's boyhood; it thus describes Stukely's last and fatal battle-field:

'Upon this day of honour,
Each man did shew his banner,
Morocco and the king of Barbary,
Portugal and all his train,
Bravely glittering on the plain,
And gave the onset there most valiantly.

Bloody was the slaughter,
Or rather wilful murder,
Where sixscore thousand fighting-men were slain.
Three kings within this battle died,
With forty dukes and earls beside,
The like will never more be fought again.'

Besides Peele's drama, already mentioned, there was another play published in 1605, entitled *The Famous History of the Life and Death of Captain Thomas Stukely:* and our hero is thus noticed in Heywood's drama of *If you know not Me, you know Nobody:*

'That renowned battle,
Swift Fame desires to carry round the world,
The battle of Alcazar; wherein two kings,
Besides this king of Barbary, was slain,
King of Morocco, and of Portugal,
With Stukely, that renowned Englishman,
That had a spirit equal to a king,
Made fellow with these kings in warlike strife,
Honoured his country, and concluded life.'

## THE GOOD WILBERFORCE.

An appellation which was never more worthily bestowed. The century can boast of greater politicians and abler men; but none ingrafted himself so peculiarly in the affections of the masses—who were ever ready to trust his measures, because of the certainty they felt that he acted from the highest principles. His flow of words, so classic and pure in their arrangement, added to a remarkably sweet voice—so beautiful, that he was called 'the Nightingale of the House of Commons'—made him a very persuasive orator. Not less than forty members were influenced by his speech on Lord Melville's prosecution.

He was born in the High Street, Hull, where his ancestors had long carried on a successful trade, and educated at Rochlington, and then at St John's College, Cambridge, where his life-long friendship with William Pitt and Dr Milner commenced. In their company, he travelled on the continent, at which time the religious convictions he afterwards professed were fully formed, as expressed in the work he published—*A Practical View of Christianity*. Only a few weeks after attaining his majority, he was elected member for his native town, and for forty-five years he was never without a seat in the House, exercising there the greatest influence of any one not in office: supporting Catholic emancipation and parliamentary reform; the abolishing of lotteries and of climbing-boys; and last, not least, the great object of his life—the abolition of the slave trade. It was through the persuasion of the venerable Clarkson that he first turned his attention to this subject; and at a dinner given by Bennet Langton, he consented to join the society which had been established for the purpose of carrying out the scheme. He brought the matter before parliament in a most eloquent speech in May 1789, declaring that 38,000 negroes were annually imported to our West Indian colonies. Year after year was the unpopular bill brought forward by its unwearied advocate, and with ever-lessening majorities. Out of the House, Granville, Sharp, Clarkson, Macaulay, Stephen, and many others were working with all their strength. The Irish members joined the cause; but seventeen years passed, and it was not until the death of Pitt that, on the motion of Mr Fox, the immediate abolition of the slave trade was carried by a majority of 114 to 15. How enviable must have been the feelings at that moment of him who had devoted his whole energies to so sacred and humane a cause!

Four times he had been elected member for the

county of York; but in the year 1807, he encountered a most powerful competition from the two great families of Fitzwilliam and Lascelles. Such a period of excitement has seldom been seen in electioneering annals. Party-spirit was at its highest; Mr Pitt had, some little time before his death, offended the cloth-manufacturers of the West Riding; they were, in those days, hand-loom weavers, each possessing his own little freehold, and to a man they declared for the Whig interest. For fifteen days the poll was carried on at York, whither the voters had to be conveyed in wagons and coaches as best they might from the more distant places; and thousands walked many miles to vote, making the election expenses most serious for the members. A large collection was made for Mr Wilberforce, and from the first his seat was sure. Eleven thousand votes placed him at the head of the poll, whilst the other two each numbered 10,000, the largest number of votes ever given at an election; but Lord Milton secured the triumph to the Whigs. Many were squeezed to death in the polling-booths. Riots were daily expected in Leeds, the streets were filled with the mob, and the appearance of a man with the Tory colours made the mayor order out the military. This was the last time Mr Wilberforce stood for Yorkshire; at the next two elections, he chose the borough of Bramber, and he accepted the Chiltern Hundreds in 1825.

WILBERFORCE.

In 1797, he married the eldest daughter of Isaac Spooner, Esq., of Elmdon House, and found in his domestic life a happy relaxation from political fatigues. His fondness for children made him their playful and joyous companion; whilst his conversation was so pleasing and varied, that he was as much at home with deep-thinking senators as with the gravest divines, and never forgot to give the truest consolation to the poor, the sufferer, or the mourner. Though he married a lady of large fortune, his latter days were impoverished by the immense expenses of his Yorkshire elections and unfortunate speculations; whilst the loss of his younger daughter, to whom he was fondly attached, inflicted upon him a wound which he never recovered during the few months he survived her.

He had directed his funeral to be conducted in the quietest manner; but the most eminent statesmen entreated his family to allow a public ceremony in Westminster Abbey, where he rests close to his old friends, Pitt, Canning, and Fox. The large meeting which was held in York the same year, for paying a suitable tribute to the memory of one who had represented the county for thirty years, resulted in the establishment of a School for the Blind.

---

## AQUA TUFANIA.

On the 29th of July 1717, Addison, as secretary of state, addressed a letter to the Commissioners of Customs in England, requiring them to take measures for checking the introduction of a poisoned liqueur of which the British envoys at Naples and Genoa had sent home accounts. It appears from the communications of these gentlemen, that this liqueur, called *Aqua Tufania*, from the Greek woman who invented it, was introduced in large quantities into Italy, and also in part distilled there, and was extensively used as a poison. It was stated that six hundred persons had been destroyed by it at Naples, and there had been many punished capitally for selling and administering it. The culprits engaged in the making and sale of the liquor pretended a religious and conscientious object—they desired to keep the world in ease and quiet, by furnishing husbands with the means of getting quit of troublesome wives, fathers of unruly sons, a man of his enemy, and so forth. The Inquisitors of State, not entering at all into these views, used the strictest measures to put down the Aqua Tufania, but apparently with only partial success.

Such cases as that of the Marchioness Brinvilliers—which are far from being rare—we may remember that of Catherine Wilson in 1862—shew that when an apparently secret and safe means of murder by poison can be obtained, there is that in human nature that will put it to use. It would almost appear that, after one or two successes, a sort of fascination or mania takes possession of the experimenter; and victims are at length struck down, from hardly any motive beyond that of gratifying a morbid feeling. Indulgence in a wickedness so great, and at the same time so cowardly, certainly presents human nature in one of its least amiable aspects.

## RISE IN THE PRICE OF RUE AND WORMWOOD.

On the 29th of July 1760, a rumour arose in London—no one could afterwards tell how—to the effect that the plague had broken out in St Thomas's Hospital! Commerce, notoriously, has no bowels; and Adam Smith justifies it for its visceral deficiency. Next morning, the price of rue and wormwood, in Covent Garden Market, had risen forty per cent.! The authorities saw the necessity of an instant contradiction to the rumour. They put an advertisement in the public journals: 'Whereas the town has been alarmed with a false and wicked report that the *plague* is broke out in St Thomas's Hospital: we, the underwritten (in pursuance of an order of the grand committee of the governors, held this day), do hereby certify that the said report is absolutely without foundation; and that there are no other diseases amongst the patients than what are usual in this and all other hospitals.

'(Signed.) THOMAS MILNER, M. AKENSIDE, ALEXANDER RUSSELL, JOHN HADLEY, *physicians* to St Thomas's Hospital; T. BAKER, BENJAMIN COWELL, THOMAS SMITH, *surgeons* to the said hospital; GEORGE WHITFIELD, *apothecary* to the said hospital.'

It may be remarked, that the M. Akenside here named is much better remembered by the world as a poet (*Pleasures of Imagination*) than as a physician.

St Thomas's Hospital—a magnificent establishment, with lecture-theatres, a dissecting-room, and other accommodations for medical teaching—is now, alas! no more, having been taken down in 1862, in consequence of its purchase by the Croydon, Brighton, and South-Eastern Railway Companies. By these corporations a mere angle of the hospital property was required for the railway line proposed to be extended to Charing Cross; and the governors obtained the insertion of a clause in the act, empowering them to insist on the purchase of the entire hospital by the companies, if they so pleased. It was a reasonable exaction, for the noise of the passing trains could not have failed to be hurtful to the patients. The companies bowed to the claim, but were startled when the sum of £750,000 was demanded for the hospital. On the matter being submitted, the sum of £296,000 was awarded, being considerably less, as is understood, than what might have been obtained on a reasonable private negotiation with the company. The hospital thus lost a site in which it was eminently useful, and for a compensation which may prove hardly sufficient to replace it in some one probably less advantageous. The association of the institution with rue and wormwood a century before seems to have been ominous.

## LEGEND OF THE GREEN LADY OF THORPE HALL.

Hard by the neat old town of Louth, in Lincolnshire, which lies nestling at the foot of the famous 'Wolds,' and is noted for possessing one of the most beautiful parish churches in the kingdom, stands Thorpe Hall, an old mansion, charmingly situated amidst most delightful scenery, and connected with which is an old legend but comparatively little known.

It appears that the elder branch of the ancient family of Bolles, or Bolle, settled at this Thorpe Hall, and at Haugh, a small village near the town of Alford, also in Lincolnshire, many members of it lying buried in both Louth and Haugh churches. The earliest mention of any monumental inscription respecting this family, in either of these churches, is of Richard Bolle, of Haugh, who married, 1stly, a daughter of Sir William Skypwith, of Ormesby, Knight, Lincolnshire; 2dly, a daughter of —— Risbye, Esq., of Yorkshire; and 3dly, a daughter of —— Hutton, Esq., of Cambridgeshire. He served the office of sheriff of the county of Lincoln, in 4th Edward VI. and 11th Elizabeth. He had by his first wife a son, Charles, and four daughters; and by his second wife, two sons. Charles Bolle, Esq., his eldest son, had four wives; he died in the lifetime of his father, in 1590, and was buried in Haugh church, where, on the outside of the chancel, is a mural monument of marble, surrounded with the arms of Bolle, and those of his four wives, with a somewhat lengthy inscription in Latin.

His only son and heir, Sir John Bolle, of Thorpe Hall, Knight, lived in the reigns of Elizabeth and James, and was celebrated as well for the gallantry with which he signalised himself as an officer in the army, in the memorable expedition against Cadiz, in 1596, as for his activity, bravery, and good conduct in Ireland. He commanded at the taking of the castles of Donolong and Lifford, during the administration of the Earl of Essex, by whom he was appointed governor of Kinsale. Queen Elizabeth conferred upon him the honour of knighthood after his return from Cadiz; and it is in connection with this gallant knight, and his exploits at this place, that the legend of *The Green Lady* has its origin.

Tradition assures us that, amongst the prisoners taken at Cadiz, it fell to the lot of Sir John Bolle to take charge of a lady of extraordinary beauty, and of distinguished family and great wealth. This lady the noble knight treated with the care and tenderness which was the right of her sex, by endeavouring to soften and alleviate the heavy weary hours of her captivity. This generous care naturally evoked feelings of gratitude, and these ultimately warmed into love. This resulted in her throwing at the feet of the warrior her riches and her person, and such was her ardent passion, that, when released, she entreated him to permit her to accompany him to England as his page. But the gallant knight had a wife at home, and neither the charms of the beautiful Spaniard, nor the powerful influence of her gold, could prevail. Like a true knight, therefore, he returned whither duty and honour alike called him, and the beautiful and inconsolable lady retired to a nunnery, there to spend the remainder of her days in sorrow and seclusion.

On Sir John Bolle's departure from Cadiz, the devoted Spaniard sent, as presents to his wife, a profusion of jewels and other valuables, amongst which was her portrait, taken as she was, *dressed in green*; a beautiful tapestry-bed, wrought in gold by her own hands; and several casks full of plate, money, and other treasure. Some of these articles, it is said, were, at the commencement of the present century, still in possession of the family; but the portrait was unfortunately lost, or disposed of in some way, half a century before. The picture being thus in *green*, led to her being called, in the neighbourhood of Thorpe Hall, *The Green Lady*. Tradition further records the superstitious belief, that the old hall was haunted by her, and that she used nightly to take her seat in a particular tree near the mansion. It was also said that, during the life of his son, Sir Charles Bolle, a knife and fork were always laid for her at table, if she chose to make her appearance!

The compiler of this account, who was then resident in Louth, well remembers the belief in many superstitious minds, some thirty-five years ago, that *The Green Lady* was occasionally to be seen walking about the grounds at midnight!

But to continue with our story. It seems that the attachment of the beautiful Spaniard to Sir John was such, that it became the subject of a ballad, which was subsequently published in *Percy's Reliques of Ancient English Poetry*, and which was called—

THE SPANISH LADYE'S LOVE FOR AN ENGLISHMAN.

'Will you hear a Spanish lady,
How she wooed an English man?
Garments gay as rich as may be,
Decked with jewels, she had on.
Of a comely countenance and grace was she,
And by birth and parentage of high degree.

As his prisoner there he kept her,
In his hands her life did lye;
Cupid's bands did tye them faster
By the liking of an eye.
In his courteous company was all her joy,
To favour him in anything she was not coy.

But at last there came commandment
For to set the ladies free,
With their jewels still adornèd,
None to do them injury.
Then said this lady mild: "Full woe is me,
O! let me still sustain this kind captivity!

Gallant captain, shew some pity
To a lady in distresse;
Leave me not within this city,
For to dye in heavinesse:
Thou hast set this present day my body free,
But my heart in prison still remains with thee."

"How shouldst thou, fair lady, love me,
Whom thou know'st thy country's foe?
Thy fair wordes make me suspect thee:
Serpents lie where flowers grow."
"All the harme I wishe to thee, most courteous knight,
God grant the same upon my head may fully light.

Blessed be the time and season
That you came on Spanish ground;
If you may our foes be termed,
Gentle foes we have you found:
With our city, you have won our hearts each one,
Then to your country bear away, that is your own."

"Rest you still, most gallant lady;
Rest you still, and weep no more;
Of fair lovers there are plenty,
Spain doth yield you wonderous store."
"Spaniards fraught with jealousy we oft do find,
But Englishmen throughout the world are counted kind.

Leave me not unto a Spaniard,
Thou alone enjoy'st my heart;
I am lovely, young, and tender,
Love is likewise my desert.
Still to serve thee day and night my mind is prest;
The wife of every Englishman is counted blest."

"It would be a shame, fair lady,
For to bear a woman hence;
English soldiers never carry
Any such without offence."
"I'll quickly change myself, if it be so,
And like a page will follow thee, where'er thou go."

"I have neither gold nor silver
To maintain thee in this case,
And to travel is great charges
As you know in every place."
"My chains and jewels every one shall be thy own,
And eke ten thousand pounds in gold that lies unknown."

"On the seas are many dangers,
Many storms do there arise,
Which will be to ladies dreadful,
And force tears from watery eyes."
"Well in troth I shall endure extremity,
For I could find in heart to lose my life for thee."

"Courteous ladye, leave this fancy,
Here comes all that breeds the strife;
I in England have already
A sweet woman to my wife!
I will not falsify my vow for gold nor gain,
Nor yet for all the fairest dames that live in Spain."

"O how happy is that woman
That enjoys so true a friend!
Many happy days God send her;
Of my suit I make an end:
On my knees I pardon crave for my offence,
Which did from love and true affection first commence.

Commend me to thy lovely lady,
Bear to her this chain of gold;
And these bracelets for a token;
Grieving that I was so bold:
All my jewels in like sort bear them with thee;
For they are fitting for thy wife, but not for me.

I will spend my days in prayer,
Love and all his laws defye;
In a nunnery will I shroud me
Far from any companye:
But ere my prayers have an end, be sure of this,
To pray for thee and for thy love I will not miss.

Thus farewell, most gallant captain!
Farewell, too, my heart's content!
Count not Spanish ladies wanton,
Though to thee my love was bent:
Joy and true prosperity goe still with thee!"
"The like fall ever to thy share, most fair ladye!"'

Shenstone had also an elegant poem on the same

subject, entitled *Love and Honour*, concluding with the lines :—

> 'And to the cloister's pensive scene
> Elvira shaped her solitary way.'

Sir John died in 1606, in the forty-sixth year of his age, and was interred in the chancel of Haugh church, where a monument was erected to him, with a Latin inscription, bespeaking his accomplishments as a scholar and a soldier. His portrait,

SIR JOHN BOLLE.

taken in 1596, when thirty-six years of age, having on the 'chain of gold' spoken of in the poem, and a curious thumb-ring, set in massive gold, with the arms of the family, bearing sixteen quarterings, elegantly engraven and emblazoned, came into the possession of the Birch family, descendants of the Bolles. Captain T. Birch, of the 1st Life Guards, lived at Thorpe Hall about 1808.

---

# JULY 30.

Saints Abdon and Sennen, martyrs, 250. St Julitta, martyr, about 303.

---

*Born.*—Angelo Poliziano, poet and classic commentator, 1454, *Montepulciano, Tuscany;* Samuel Rogers, poet (*Pleasures of Memory*), 1763, *Stoke Newington, London.*

*Died.*—Pope Benedict I., 577; Ladislaus I., king of Hungary, 1095; Robert, Earl of Kingston, 1643; Maria Theresa, queen of Louis XIV., 1683; William Penn, coloniser of Pennsylvania, 1718, *Ruscombe, Berkshire;* John Sebastian Bach, eminent composer, 1750, *Leipsic;* Thomas Gray, poet, 1771; Prince Charles Lucien Bonaparte, naturalist, 1857, *Paris;* Sir C. Hastings, founder of British Medical Association, 1866.

## THE GOOD EARL OF KINGSTON.

Robert Pierrepoint, Earl of Kingston, surnamed the Good, being not less celebrated for his great wealth than the benevolent use he made of it, was killed on the 30th of July 1643, under circumstances which either confirmed a rash asseveration, or gave rise to a curious story. As the wealth, abilities, influence, and popular reputation of the earl would render him a most powerful and valuable auxiliary, to whichever party he might join at the breaking out of the great civil war, each side was equally anxious to secure his adherence. He remained neutral so long that it was considered his mind was undecided as to which cause he would eventually support. At last, seeing that war was inevitable, he joined the king, bringing with him the valuable aid of 2000 men, and £24,000 in money. Vigorously opposing the Parliamentarians in the field, he was surprised and taken prisoner by Lord Willoughby of Parham, at Gainsborough. A prize of so great value was not to be lightly guarded, at such an uncertain time. To make him perfectly secure, Willoughby placed the earl in a pinnace, to be conveyed to the stronghold of Hull. On the vessel's passage thither, the royalist Sir Charles Cavendish ordered it to be fired upon by a cannon, and the unlucky ball killed the Earl of Kingston and his servant. The vessel being brought-to, and Cavendish learning that his rash procedure had destroyed his friend and the most valuable man of his party, he, in a paroxysm of rage and blind revenge, ordered all the crew of the pinnace to be put to death. Such is the account of this untoward affair given in history; but Mrs Lucy Hutchinson, in her memoir of her husband, gives us the popular account, perfectly in keeping with the beliefs and opinions of the period. It would from this appear that the last parliamentary agent sent to the Earl of Kingston, to induce him to join their party, was a Captain Lomax, to whom the earl expressed his solemn determination not to join either side. And to quote the words of Mrs Hutchinson: 'he made a serious imprecation on himself: "When," said he, "I take arms with the king against the parliament, or with the parliament against the king, let a cannon bullet divide me between them;" which God was pleased to bring to pass a few months after; for he going into Gainsborough, and there taking up arms for the king, was surprised by my Lord Willoughby, and, after a handsome defence of himself, yielded, and was put prisoner into a pinnace, and sent down the river to Hull, when my Lord Newcastle's army, marching along the shore, shot at the pinnace, and, being in danger, the Earl of Kingston went up upon the deck to shew himself, and to prevail of them to forbare shooting; but as soon as he appeared, a cannon bullet flew from the king's army, and divided him in the middle, being then in the parliament's pinnace, who thus perished according to his own unhappy imprecation.'

## WILLIAM PENN.

William Penn was born on Tower Hill, London, 14th October 1644. His father was Sir William Penn, an admiral who had fought with distinction the fleets of Holland and Spain. His mother was a Dutchwoman, the daughter of a rich Rotterdam merchant. Penn received an excellent education, and whilst at Oxford he was tempted to go and hear one Thomas Loe, a Quaker, preach. Quakerism, in our time the meekest of faiths, was in those days regarded by churchmen and dissenters alike, as an active spirit of evil deserving no mercy or forbearance: there was contamination and disgrace in everything connected with it. Loe's ministry so affected Penn, that he began to think of becoming a Quaker himself. His father heard of the impending metamorphosis with horror, and sent him off to France, to avert the change. The policy was successful. Penn soon forgot the Quaker in the gaiety of Paris, and returned, to his father's delight, a fine gentleman, with all the airs and accomplishments of a courtier. The terrors of the plague of London in 1665, however, revived the youth's pious tendencies, and again his father tried change of scene, and sent him to Ireland. There he distinguished himself in subduing an insurrection; and it is a curious fact, that the only authentic portrait of the great apostle of peace existing, represents him at this period a young man armed and accoutred as a soldier. It so happened, that the Quakers were growing numerous in the larger Irish cities, and one day Penn strolled into their meeting in Cork. To his surprise, Thomas Loe, from Oxford, arose and spoke from the text, 'There is a faith that overcomes the world, and there is a faith that is overcome by the world.' From that meeting is dated Penn's thorough conversion to Quakerism. His father heard of his relapse with dismay, and ordered him back to London. They had a long and painful discussion, but the young man was immovable; neither the hope of honour nor the prospect of degradation had any effect on his resolution; and the admiral, after exhausting his whole armory of persuasion, ended by turning his son out of doors.

This conduct threw Penn completely over to the Quakers. He began to preach at their meetings, to write numerous pamphlets in defence of their doctrines, to hold public debates with their adversaries, and to make propagandist tours over England and the continent, sometimes alone, and sometimes in company with George Fox, Robert Barclay, and others. Of persecution and imprisonment he had his share. A tract, *The Sandy Foundation Shaken*, in which he set forth Unitarian opinions, so excited the bishop of London, that he had him committed to the Tower, where he lay for nearly nine months. King Charles sent Stillingfleet to talk him out of his errors; but, said Penn, 'The Tower is to me the worst argument in the world.' During this confinement he wrote, *No Cross, no Crown*, the most popular of his works. 'Tell my father, who I know will ask thee,' said he one day to his servant, 'that my prison shall be my grave before I will budge a jot: for I owe my conscience to no mortal man.' Actuated by a spirit as patient as it was resolute, Penn and his brethren fairly wore out the malice of their persecutors, so that in sheer despair intolerance abandoned Quakerism to its own devices.

Happily, the admiral had the good sense to reconcile himself to his son. It is said that, in spite of his irritation, he came to admire the steady front William shewed to an adverse and mocking world. The admiral's disappointment was indeed severe. He stood high in favour with Charles II. and the Duke of York, and had his son co-operated with him, there was no telling what eminence they might not have attained. 'Son William,' said the veteran, only a day or two before his death, 'I am weary of the world: I would not live my days over again, if I could command them with a wish; for the snares of life are greater than the fears of death.' Almost the last words he uttered were, 'Son William, if you and your friends keep to your plain way of preaching, and also keep to your plain way of living, you will make an end of priests to the end of the world.'

Penn, by his learning and logic, did more than any man, excepting Barclay, author of the *Apology*, to shape Quaker sentiment into formal theology; but the service by which the world will remember him, was his settlement of Pennsylvania. His father had bequeathed him a claim on the government of £16,000 for arrears of pay and cash advanced to the navy. Penn very well knew that such a sum was irrecoverable from Charles II.; he had long dreamed of founding a colony where peace and righteousness might dwell together; and he decided to compound his debt for a tract of country in North America. The block of land he selected lay to the north of the Catholic province of Maryland, owned by Lord Baltimore; its length was nearly 300 miles, its width about 160, and its area little less than the whole of England. Objections were raised; but Charles was only too glad to get rid of a debt on such easy terms. At the council, where the charter was granted, Penn stood in the royal presence, it is said, with his hat on. The king thereupon took off his; at which Penn observed, 'Friend Charles, why dost thou not keep on thy hat?' to which his majesty replied, laughing: 'It is the custom of this place for only one person to remain covered at a time.' The name which Penn had fixed on for his province was New Wales; but Secretary Blathwayte, a Welshman, objected to have the Quaker-country called after his land. He then proposed Sylvania, and to this the king added Penn, in honour of the admiral.

The fine country thus secured became the resort of large numbers of Quakers, who, to their desire for the free profession of their faith, united a spirit of enterprise; and very quickly Pennsylvania rose to high importance among the American plantations. Its political constitution was drawn up by Penn, aided by Algernon Sidney, on extreme democratic principles. Perfect toleration to all sects was accorded. 'Whoever is right,' Penn used to say, 'the persecutor must be wrong.' The world thought him a visionary; but his resolution to treat the Indians as friends, and not as vermin to be extirpated, seemed that of a madman. So far as he could prevent, no instrument of war was allowed to appear in Pennsylvania. He met the Indians, spoke kindly to them, promised to pay a fair price for whatever land he and his friends might occupy, and assured them of his good-will. If offences should unhappily arise, a jury of six Indians and six Englishmen should decide upon them. The Indians met Penn in his own spirit. No oaths, no seals, no official mummeries were used; the treaty was ratified on both sides with a yea, yea—the only one, says Voltaire, 'that the world has known, never sworn to, and never broken.' A strong evidence of Penn's sagacity is the fact, that not one drop of Quaker blood was ever shed by an Indian; and forty years elapsed from the date of the treaty, ere a red man was slain by a white in Pennsylvania. The murder was an atrocious one, but the Indians themselves prayed that the murderer's life might be spared. It was spared; but he died in a very short time, and they then said, the Great Spirit had avenged their brother.

It will be thought that Penn made a capital bargain, in the purchase of Pennsylvania for £16,000; but in his lifetime, he drew little but trouble from his investment. The settlers withheld his dues, disobeyed his orders, and invaded his rights; and he was kept in constant disquiet by intrigues for the nullification of his charter. Distracted by these cares, he left his English property to the care of a steward, who plundered him mercilessly; and his later years were saddened with severe pecuniary distress. He was twice married, and in both cases to admirable women. His eldest son, a promising youth, he lost just as he verged on manhood; and a second son, by riotous living, brought himself to an early grave, trying Penn's fatherly heart with many sorrows. Multiplied afflictions did not, however, sour his noble nature, nor weaken his settled faith in truth and goodness.

Penn's intimacy with James II. exposed him, in his own day, to much suspicion, which yet survives. It ought to be remembered, that Admiral Penn and James were friends; that the admiral, at death, consigned his son William to his guardianship; and that between James and his ward there sprung up feelings apparently amounting to affection. While James was king, Penn sometimes visited him daily, and persuaded him to acts of clemency, otherwise unattainable. Penn scorned as a Quaker, James hated as a Catholic, could sympathise as brothers in adversity. Penn, by nature, was kindly, and abounding in that charity which thinketh no evil; and taking the worst view of James's character, it is in nowise surprising that Penn should have been the victim of his duplicity. It is well known that rogues could do little mischief, if it were not so easy to make good men their tools.

There was very little of that asceticism about Penn which is thought to belong to—at least early—Quakerism. The furniture of his houses was equal in ornament and comfort to that of any gentleman of his time. His table abounded in every real luxury. He was fond of fine horses, and had a passion for boating. The ladies of his household dressed like gentlewomen—wore caps and buckles, silk gowns and golden ornaments. Penn had no less than four wigs in America, all purchased the same year, at a cost of nearly £20. To innocent dances and country fairs he not only made no objection, but patronised them with his own and his family's presence.

William Penn, after a lingering illness of three or four years, in which his mind suffered, but not painfully, died at Ruscombe on the 30th July 1718, and was buried at the secluded village of Jordans, in Buckinghamshire. No stone marks the spot, although many a pilgrim visits the grave.



## GRAY AND HIS ELEGY.

Sprung of a harsh and unamiable father, but favoured with a mother of opposite character—rising from a youth spent in comparatively humble circumstances—Thomas Gray became, in his mature years, a devoted college-student, a poet, a man of refined taste, and an exemplifier of all the virtues. There is not a more irreproachable character in English literature. The portraits of the bard give us the idea of a very good-looking man. He was unfitted, however, for success in society, by an insuperable taciturnity. The only reproach ever intimated against him by his college-associates, was that of fastidiousness. We may fairly suspect the truth on this point to be, that he shrunk from the coarse and boisterous enjoyments in which the greater number of them indulged.

He had a weakness, in the form of a nervous dread of fire. His chamber in St Peter's College, Cambridge, being in a second-floor, he thought it very likely that, in case of a conflagration, his exit by the stairs might be cut off. He therefore caused an iron bar to be fixed by arms projecting from the outside of his window, designing by a rope tied

GRAY'S WINDOW, ST PETER'S COLLEGE, CAMBRIDGE.

thereto to descend to the ground, in the event of a fire occurring. This excessive caution, as it appeared to his brother-collegiates, raised a spirit of practical joking in them; and one evening, not long after the fire-escape had been fixed up, a party of them came from a merry-making, and thundered at the door of Gray, with loud cries of 'Fire! fire! fire!' The nervous poet started from bed, flew to his window, and descended by his rope into the vacant ground below, where of course he was saluted with bursts of laughter by his friends. Gray's delicate nature was so much shocked by this rough affair, that he deserted Peter's College, and took up his residence in Pembroke. The window with the iron apparatus is still shewn, and is faithfully represented on the preceding page.

Among popular English poems, there is none more deservedly distinguished than Gray's *Elegy.* It appeals to a feeling which is all but universal—a tendency to moralise when alone in a churchyard; and thus it is enabled to take hold of the most common-place minds.

There are several curious circumstances connected with its publication worth recording. For some time after it was written, Gray shewed it round among his friends, but said nothing about publishing it. After a time, he became bolder, and even allowed copies of it to circulate in manuscript, until, at last, through the carelessness of Horace Walpole—or it may have been from a friendly wish of his to see it universally admired, as he felt it would be—a copy fell into the hands of the editor of *The Magazine of Magazines*, who immediately sent the poet word that he meant to print it. Gray had now no alternative but to print it himself; and accordingly wrote at once to Horace Walpole, with special directions to that end. 'I have but one *bad* way left,' he writes, 'to *escape* the honour they would *inflict* upon me: and therefore am *obliged* to desire you would *make* Dodsley print it immediately (which may be done in less than a week's time) from your copy, but without my name.' It seems, he would have us think it a great infliction to be admired by the public. However, Walpole did as he was bid, and had it printed in all haste; adding an *advertisement*, at Gray's request, in which he informs the reader that the publication is entirely due to an unavoidable accident. But Dodsley, after all, was too late. It first saw the light in *The Magazine of Magazines*, February 1751. Some imaginary literary wag is made to rise in a convivial assembly, and thus announce it: 'Gentlemen, give me leave to soothe my own melancholy, and amuse you in a most noble manner, with a full copy of verses by the very ingenious Mr Gray, of Peterhouse, Cambridge. They are stanzas written in a country churchyard.' Then follow the verses. A few days afterwards, Dodsley's edition appeared, in quarto, anonymously, price sixpence, entitled *An Elegy wrote in a Country Churchyard*, and the title-page duly adorned with cross-bones, skulls, and hour-glasses.

There are several copies of the original manuscript of the *Elegy* in existence; one of them is at Pembroke College, Cambridge; another in the British Museum; another, which has been frequently resold, is written on four sides of a doubled half-sheet of yellow foolscap, in a neat legible hand, with a crow-quill. Gray bequeathed it to Mr Mason, who wrote his life; Mr Mason left it to his curate, Mr Bright; and Mr Bright's son sold the lot in 1845, when the *Elegy* fell to Mr Penn, of Stoke Pogeis, for £100. In 1854, it was purchased for £131 by Mr Wrightson; it was again sold in 1875.

A photographed *Facsimile of the Original Autograph Manuscript of Gray's Elegy*, was published in 1862, by Messrs Sampson Low and Son. Curious and interesting differences exist between the first draft and the printed copy: numerous alterations were afterwards made, and as many as six verses, which appear in the manuscript, were omitted.

Perhaps the most interesting of all the emendations was that made in verse 15 of the printed poem; in which *Hampden*, *Milton*, and *Cromwell* were severally substituted for *Cato*, *Tully*, and *Cæsar:* it is said that this judicious change was suggested by Mason.

Verse 19, as the poem now stands, is—

'Far from the madding crowd's ignoble strife
  Their sober wishes never learned to stray;
Along the cool sequestered vale of life
  They kept the noiseless tenor of their way.'

Verse 24 is—

'For thee, who, mindful of th' unhonour'd dead,
  Dost in these lines their artless tale relate;
If chance, by lonely contemplation led,
  Some kindred spirit shall inquire thy fate.'

Verse 24 originally stood thus—

'If chance, that e'er some pensive spirit more,
  By sympathetic musings here delay'd,
With vain, tho' kind inquiry shall explore
  Thy once-loved haunt, this long deserted shade.'

And before verse 19 came these four verses—

'The thoughtless World to majesty may bow,
  Exalt the brave, and idolise success;
But more to Innocence their safety owe
  Than Power and Genius e'er conspired to bless.

And thou who, mindful of the unhonoured Dead,
  Dost in these notes their artless tale relate,
By night and lonely contemplation led
  To linger in the lonely walks of Fate,

Hark how the sacred calm that reigns around
  Bids every fierce tumultuous passion cease;
In still small accents whisp'ring from the ground
  A grateful earnest of eternal peace.

No more with Reason and thyself at strife,
  Give anxious cares and endless wishes room;
But through the cool, sequester'd vale of life
  Pursue the silent tenor of thy doom.'

The change which Gray made is tolerably clear. The four verses were struck out and replaced by verse 19, and the second of the four substituted for the old 24th, with some necessary changes.

After verse 25 followed, originally—

'Him have we seen the greenwood side along,
  While o'er the heath we hied, our labours done,
Oft as the woodlark piped her farewell song,
  With wistful eyes pursue the setting sun.'

And after verse 29, now the last, once followed—

'There scatter'd oft the earliest of ye year,
  By hands unseen are frequent vi'lets found;
The robin loves to build and warble there,
  And little footsteps lightly print the ground.'

In the summer of 1759, Gray lodged at Mr Jauncey's, in Southampton Row, Bloomsbury, to be near the British Museum, of which he was a diligent explorer. He told his friend Mason that in this 'peaceful settlement' he had an uninterrupted view of Hampstead, Highgate, and the Bedford Gardens! a space now covered with miles of uninterrupted brick and mortar. The contrast which the Reading Room, with its hundreds of constant readers, now presents with the corresponding establishment in Gray's time, is not less remarkable.

The company that then assembled to study and pursue research, was composed of 'a man that writes for Lord Royston, a man that writes for Dr Burton of York, a third that writes for the emperor of Germany or Dr Pocock; Dr Stukely, who writes for himself, the very worst person he could write for; and I, who only read to know if there is anything worth writing.' Gray further mentions a comfortable fact. 'The keepers have broken off all intercourse with one another, and only lower a silent defiance as they pass by.'

The admirable mother of Gray—who had set up a millinery shop to support her children, when deserted by her unworthy husband—was buried in the churchyard of Stoke Pogeis, near Eton, with an epitaph by the poet containing this most touching passage: 'The careful tender mother of many children, one of whom alone had the misfortune to survive her.' It seems to be generally concluded that he conceived himself as musing in this burial-ground when he composed the *Elegy*. He himself was interred there beside the worshipped grave of his mother.

In one of the final verses of the *Elegy* there is a clause not unworthy of comment, as a historical expression of the intellectual condition of the English peasantry in the eighteenth century. 'Approach and read—*for thou canst read*,' says the hoary-headed swain to the stranger. It is here assumed that, as a rule, an English peasant was unable to read. A Scottish poet would not have had occasion to make the same assumption regarding his humble countrymen—thanks to the Scottish parish schools, instituted at the Revolution.

## SALE OF THE OLD GATES OF LONDON.

A sale of three of the City gates, on the 30th of July 1760, marked, in a singular way, a dividing-point between the old and the modern history of London. The English metropolis, like most large and important cities in the middle ages, was bounded by a wall and a ditch; and in this wall were openings or gates for the passage of foot and vehicle traffic. Beginning from the east, this fortified boundary commenced with the famous Tower of London, itself a vast assemblage of gates and fortified posts. Advancing thence nearly northward, the wall extended to *Æld-gate* or *Aldgate*, which defended the approach by the great highway from Essex. This was probably the oldest of all the City gates. In 1215, during the civil war between King John and the barons, the citizens aided the latter in entering London by Aldgate; and soon afterwards, the gate, being very ruinous and dilapidated, was replaced by one strongly built of stone. This new one (a double gate with portcullis) remained till the time of Queen Elizabeth, when it was replaced by another more ornamental than warlike. This was one of the three gates finally removed in 1760. The wall extended nearly north-west from Aldgate to *Bishopsgate*, which guarded the great road from Cambridge. This gate was not among the oldest of the series, but is supposed to have been built about the reign of Henry II. At first there were no means of exit from the City between Aldgate and Aldersgate; and this extra gate was opened rather to furnish additional accommodation, than for any defensive purpose. The gate was in a ruinous state from the time of Edward VI. to that of James I., when it was replaced by a new one; and this latter was finally removed early in the last century. The wall stretched westward from Bishopsgate to *Moorgate;* of which Stow says: 'I find that Thomas Falconer, mayor about the year 1415, the third of Henry V., caused the wall of the city to be broken near unto Coleman Street, and there builded a postern, now called Moorgate, upon the moor-side, where was never gate before. This gate he made for ease of the citizens that way to pass upon causeys [causeways] into the fields for their recreation; for the same field was at that time a marsh.' Indeed, all the country immediately outside the city, from Bishopsgate to Aldersgate, was very fenny and marshy, giving rise to the names Moorfields and Finsbury (Fensbury). Moorgate was rebuilt in 1472, and pulled down about the middle of the last century, the stones being used to repair the piers of London Bridge. The next gate was *Cripplegate*, a postern or minor gate like Moorgate, but much more ancient; it was many times rebuilt, and was, like the other gates, used as a prison. The name, Stow says, 'so called of cripples begging there.' This was one of the three gates finally pulled down in 1760. The City wall extended thence to *Ælders-gate* or *Aldersgate*, one of the oldest of the series, and also one of the largest. The ancient structure, crumbling with age, was replaced by a new and very ornamental one in the time of James I.; and this latter gave way to the street improvers early in the last century. The next gate was *Newgate*. In the Anglo-Norman times, there were only three City gates—Aldgate, Aldersgate, and Ludgate; and no person could leave the city westward at any point between the two last-named gates. To remedy this inconvenience, Newgate was built about the time of Henry I., the designation 'new' being, of course, only comparative. After being rebuilt and repaired several times, Newgate and its prison were burned down by Lord George Gordon's mob in 1780; the prison was replaced by a much larger and stronger one, but the gate was not rebuilt. The City wall extended from Newgate to *Ludgate*, which was the oldest of the series except Aldgate and Aldersgate, and the one with which the greatest number of historical events was connected. After many rebuildings and repairings, Ludgate was one of the three which were pulled down in 1760.

It must not be supposed that *Dowgate*, *Billingsgate*, and *St John's Gate* were necessarily City gates; the first and second were landing-places on the river-side, the third was the gate belonging to the Hospital of St John of Jerusalem. As to the *Bars*—such as *Temple Bar*, *Holborn Bar*, and *Smithfield Bar*—they were subsidiary or exterior barriers, bearing some such relation to 'the City without the walls,' as the gates bore to 'the City within the walls,' but smaller, and of inferior strength.

The announcement in the public journals, concerning the destruction of three of the gates on the 30th of July 1760, was simply to the effect that Mr Blagden, a carpenter of Coleman Street, gave £91 for the old materials of *Cripplegate*, £148 for *Ludgate*, and £177, 10*s*. for *Aldgate;* undertaking to have all the rubbish removed by the end of September. Thus ended our old City gates, except *Newgate*, which the rioters put an end to twenty years later.

## JULY 31.

**St Helen of Skofde, in Sweden, martyr, about 1160. St John Columbini, confessor, founder of the order of the Jesuati, 1367. St Ignatius of Loyola, founder of the Society of Jesus, 1556.**

*Born.*—Princess Augusta of Brunswick, 1737.

*Died.*—Ignatius Loyola, founder of the Jesuits, 1556, *Rome;* Charles de Gontaut, Duc de Biron, favourite commander of Henri IV., beheaded in the Bastile, 1602; Martin Harpertzoon Van Tromp, Dutch admiral, killed in an engagement near Texel, 1653; John V., king of Portugal, 1750; Denis Diderot, French encyclopædist, 1784, *Paris;* William T. Lowndes, bibliographer, 1843.

### IGNATIUS LOYOLA.

Ignatius Loyola, 'a Spanish soldier and hidalgo with hot Biscayan blood,' was, in 1521, assisting in the defence of Pampeluna against the French, when a cannon-ball fractured his right leg and a splinter injured his left. He was carried to the neighbouring castle of Loyola, and in the weary months during which he lay stretched upon his couch, he tried to while away the time in reading the *Lives of the Saints.* He was only thirty; he had a strong and vehement will; he had led a wild and vicious life; and had burned for military glory. As it was evident that for him henceforward the part of the soldier was barred, the question arose, Why might he not be a saint, and rival St Francis and St Dominic? He decided to try. He tore himself from his kindred and friends, and made a pilgrimage to the Holy Land. In the church of the Virgin at Mount Serrat, he hung up his arms, and vowed constant obedience to God and the church. Dressed as a beggar, and in the practice of the severest austerities, he reached Jerusalem on the 4th of September 1523. On his return to Spain, at the age of thirty-three, he resumed his education, which had been neglected from childhood, and laboriously from the rudiments of grammar worked his way through a full university course, making no secret of his ignorance. The rigour of his life, and the rebukes he administered to lax ecclesiastics, not unfrequently brought him into trouble as a Pharisaic meddler.

He went to Paris in 1528, and at the university he made the acquaintance of Xavier, Faber, Lainez, Bobadilla, and Rodriguez, five students whom he inspired with his own devout fervour. In an underground chapel of the church of Montmartre, on the 15th of August 1534, the six enthusiasts took the solemn vows of celibacy, poverty, and the devotion of their lives to the care of Christians, and the conversion of infidels. Such was the beginning of the famous Society of Jesus.

The plan of the new order was laid before Pope Paul III., who raised several objections to it; but, on the engagement that Jesuits should in all matters yield implicit obedience to the holy see, he granted them a constitution in a bull, dated the 27th of September 1540. Loyola was elected president, and was established at Rome as director of the movements of the society. Very opportunely did the Jesuits come to the service of the popedom. Unhampered by the routine of other ecclesiastical orders, they undertook services for which they alone were fit; and, as sharp-shooters and skirmishers, became the most annoying and dangerous antagonists of Protestantism. To a certain freedom of action the Jesuit united the advantages of perfect discipline; obedience was his primary duty. He used his faculties, but their action was controlled by a central authority; every command had to be wrought out with all his skill and energy, without questioning, and at all hazards. It was the aim of the society to discover and develop the peculiar genius of all its members, and then to apply them to the aggrandisement of the church. Soon the presence of the new order, and the fame of its missionaries, spread throughout the world, and successive popes gladly increased the numbers and enlarged the privileges of the society. Loyola brought more ardour than intellect to the institution of Jesuitism. The perfection of its mechanism, which Cardinal Richelieu pronounced a masterpiece of policy, was due to James Lainez, who succeeded Loyola as president.

Worn out with labours and privations, Loyola died on the 31st of July 1556, aged sixty-five. He was canonised as a saint in 1622, and his festival is celebrated on the 31st of July.

Ignatius

An original autograph of the founder of the order of Jesus is subjoined—taken from his signature to a document, dated 1554, preserved in the public library of the city of Treves, on the Moselle.

### TWO LOVERS KILLED BY LIGHTNING.

It was on the 31st of July 1718, that the affecting incident occurred to which Pope, Gay, and Thomson severally adverted—the instantaneous killing of two rustic lovers by a lightning-stroke. At Stanton-Harcourt, about nine miles west of Oxford, are the remains of a very old mansion, belonging to the family of the Harcourts, consisting chiefly of a domestic chapel in a tower, and two or three rooms over it. Pope spent two summers in this old building, with the hearty assent of the Harcourts, who had been lords of the manor for more than seven hundred years. One room, in which he finished the Fifth Book of his *Iliad*, obtained, on that account, the name of 'Pope's Study.' Gay often visited him there; and it is in one of Gay's letters that the catastrophe, which occurred in a neighbouring field, is thus narrated: 'John Hewit was a well-set man of about twenty-five. Sarah Drew might be called comely rather than beautiful, and was about the same age. They had passed through the various labours of the year together with the greatest satisfaction. Their love was the talk of the whole neighbourhood, for scandal never affirmed that they had other views than the lawful possession of each other in marriage. It was that very morning that they had obtained the consent of her parents; and it was but till the next week that they had to wait to be happy. Perhaps in the interval of their work they were talking of their wedding-clothes, and John was suiting several sorts of poppies and wild-flowers to her complexion, to choose her a hat for the wedding-day. While they were thus busied (it was between two and three o'clock in the afternoon), the clouds grew black, and such a storm of lightning and thunder ensued, that all the labourers made the best of their way to what shelter the trees and hedges afforded. Sarah was frighted, and fell down in a swoon on a heap of barley; John, who never separated from her, having raked together two or three heaps, the better to secure her from the storm. Immediately after was heard so loud a crash as if the heavens had split asunder. Every one was now solicitous for the safety of his neighbour, and they called to one another throughout the field. No answer being returned to those who called to our lovers, they stepped to the place where they lay. They perceived the barley all in a smoke, and then spied the faithful pair; John, with one arm about Sarah's neck, and the other held over her, as if to screen her from the lightning. They were struck dead, and stiffened in this tender posture. Sarah's left eye was injured, and there appeared a black spot on her breast. Her lover was all over black; but not the least sign of life was found in either. Attended by their melancholy companions, they were conveyed to the town, and next day were interred in Stanton-Harcourt churchyard.'

Pope, whether or not he was at Stanton-Harcourt at the time, soon afterwards wrote an epitaph on the hapless young couple:

ON TWO LOVERS STRUCK DEAD BY LIGHTNING.

'When eastern lovers feed the funeral fire,
On the same pile the faithful pair expire:
Here pitying heav'n, that virtue mutual found,
And blasted both, that it might neither wound.
Hearts so sincere th' Almighty saw well pleased,
Sent his own lightning, and the victims seized.'

'Lord Harcourt,' says Mr Robert Carruthers, in his edition of Pope, 'on whose estate the unfortunate pair lived, was apprehensive that the country-people would not understand the above, and Pope wrote the subjoined:

'NEAR THIS PLACE LIE THE BODIES
OF JOHN HEWIT AND SARAH DREW,
AN INDUSTRIOUS YOUNG MAN
AND VIRTUOUS YOUNG MAIDEN OF THIS PARISH;
WHO, BEING AT HARVEST-WORK
(WITH SEVERAL OTHERS),
WERE IN ONE INSTANT KILLED BY LIGHTNING,
THE LAST DAY OF JULY 1718.

Think not, by rigorous judgment seized,
A pair so faithful could expire;
Victims so pure Heav'n saw well pleas'd,
And snatch'd them in eternal fire.

Live well, and fear no sudden fate;
When God calls victims to the grave,
Alike 'tis justice soon or late,
Mercy alike to kill or save,

Virtue unmov'd can hear the call,
And face the flash that melts the ball.'

This second epitaph was engraved on a stone in the parish church of Stanton-Harcourt.

Thomson appears to have had this incident in his view when he wrote the *Seasons*, about nine years afterwards. The fifty lines (in 'Summer') beginning

'Young Celadon
And his Amelia were a matchless pair,'

relate an episode of the same character as the sad story of John Hewit and Sarah Drew, with the exception that the poet kills the maiden but not the lover.

## TESTIMONIALS TWO HUNDRED AND SIXTY YEARS AGO.

The following present made to the new recorder of Nottingham, 1603 A. D., by order of the Hall, affords a curious instance of the taste and habit of the times, in respect to what are now dignified by the name of *Testimonials*. 'It is agreed that the *town* shall, on Wednesday next, present the recorder, Sir Henry Pierrepont, with a sugar-loaf, 9*s.*; lemons, 1*s.* 8*d.*; white wine, one gallon, 2*s.* 8*d.*; claret, one gallon, 2*s.* 8*d.*; muskadyne, one pottle, 2*s.* 8*d.*; sack, one pottle, 2*s.*; total 20*s.* 8*d.*'

Another testimonial was presented by the same town, in the year following, the object of public admiration and bounty in this instance being no less a personage than the Earl of Shrewsbury. Of course the present, intended to convey to his lordship the sense entertained by the burgesses of his high worth and character, must be of a more weighty description than that bestowed on the recorder. Accordingly, it was ordered that 'a veal, a mutton, a lamb, a dozen of chickens, two dozen of rabbits, two dozen of pigeons, and four capons, should be presented to his lordship.'

Ours is a day beyond all others for the presentation of Testimonials, but we have never yet heard of a celebrity of the nineteenth century being invited to a public meeting to receive from his friends a testimonial of their esteem, and then having laid at his feet sundry bottles of wine, with sugar and lemons to flavour it; or a good fat calf, a wedder-sheep, and a lamb of a year old, with dozens of chickens and rabbits to garnish the same, as appears to have been the favourite course with our 'good-living' ancestors.

## PARTRIDGE, THE ALMANAC-MAKER.

Partridge, the almanac-maker, of whom mention is made in the article on 'Written and Printed Almanacs' (page 9, vol. i.), has been so fortunate as to be embalmed in one of the most pleasing poems in the English language—Pope's *Rape of the Lock*. With a consummation of surprising power and appropriate character, the poet, after the robbery of Belinda's 'wavy curl' has been effected, proceeds to place the stolen object among the constellations. The poem says:

'This the beau-monde shall from the Mall survey,
And hail with music its propitious ray;
This the blest lover shall for Venus take,
And send up prayers from Rosamunda's lake;
This PARTRIDGE soon shall view in cloudless skies,
When next he looks through Galileo's eyes;
And hence the egregious wizard shall foredoom,
The fate of Louis and the fall of Rome.'

It is strange how sometimes the most worthless of men, as regards posterity, are handed down to fame for the very qualities which it might be hoped would be left in oblivion. What sacrifices would many a sage or poet have made, to be connected with all time through Pope and the charming Belinda! Yet here, in this case, we find the almanac-making shoemaker enjoying a companionship and a celebrity for qualities which, morally, have no virtue or endurance in them, but quite the reverse.

The eighth was August, being rich arrayed
  In garment all of gold, down to the ground:
Yet rode he not, but led a lovely maid
  Forth by the lily hand, the which was crowned
  With ears of corn, and full her hand was found.
That was the righteous Virgin, which of old
  Lived here on earth, and plenty made abound;
But after wrong was loved, and justice sold,
  She left th' unrighteous world, and was to heaven extolled.

SPENSER.

(DESCRIPTIVE.)

AUGUST comes, and though the harvest-fields are nearly ripe and ready for the sickle, cheering the heart of man with the prospect of plenty that surrounds him, yet there are signs on every hand that summer is on the wane, and that the time is fast approaching when she will take her departure. We catch faint glances of autumn peeping stealthily through openings where the leaves have already fallen, and among berries where summer hung out her blossoms; and sometimes hear his rustling footstep among the dry seed-vessels, which have usurped the place of her flowers. Though the convolvulus still throws its straggling bells about the hedges, the sweet May-buds are dead and gone, and in their place the green haws hang crudely upon the branches. The winds come not a-Maying amongst them now. Nearly all the field-flowers are gone; the beautiful feathered grasses that waved like gorgeous plumes in the breeze and sunshine are cut down and carried away, and in their place there is only a green flowerless after-math. Many of the birds that sung in the green chambers which she hung for them with her richest arras, have left her and gone over the sea. What few singers remain are silent, and preparing for their departure; and when she hears the robin, his song comforts her not, for she knows that he will chant a sweeter lay to autumn, when she lies buried beneath the fallen leaves. Musing at times over her approaching end, upon the hillsides, they are touched by her beauty, and crimson up with the flowers of the heather, and long leagues of wild moorland catch the reflected blush, which goes reddening up like sunshine along the mountain slopes. The blue harebell peeps out in wonder to see such a land of beauty, and seems to shake its fragile bells with delight. In waste-places, the tall golden-rod, the scarlet poppy, and the large ox-eyed daisy muster, as if for a procession, and there wave their mingled banners of gold, crimson, and silver, as summer passes by, while the little eyebright, nestling among the grass, looks up and shews its white petals, streaked with green and gold.

But, far as summer has advanced, several of her beautiful flowers and curious plants may still be found in perfection in the water-courses, and beside the streams—pleasanter places to ramble along than the dusty and all but flowerless waysides in August. There we find the wild-mint, with its lilac-coloured blossoms, standing like a nymph knee-deep in water, and making all the air around fragrant. And all along the margin by where it grows, there is a flush of green, fresh as April; and perhaps we find a few of the grand water-flags still in flower, for they often bloom late, and seem like gold and purple banners hanging out over some ancient keep, whose colours are mirrored in the moat below. There also the beautiful arrow-head, with its snow-white flowers and arrow-pointed leaves, may be found, looking like ivy growing about the water. Many a rare plant, too little known, flourishes beside and in our sedge-fringed meres and bright meadow streams, where the overhanging trees throw cooling shadows over their grassy margins, and the burning noon of summer never penetrates. Such pleasant places are always cool, for there the grass never withers, nor are the paths ever wholly dry; and when we come upon them unaware, after having quitted the heat and glare of the brown dusty highway, it seems like travelling into another country, whose season is spring. And there the water-plantain spreads its branches, and throws out its pretty broad leaves and rose-tinted flowers, which spread up to the very border of the brook, and run in among the pink-flowers of the knot-grass, which every ripple sets in motion. Further on, the purple loosestrife shews its gorgeous spikes of flowers, seeming like a border woven by the moist fingers of the Naiads, to curtain their crystal baths; while the water-violets appear as if growing to the roofs of their caves, the foliage clinging to the vaulted-silver, and only the dark-blue flowers shewing their heads above the water. There, too, is the bog-pimpernel, almost as pretty as its scarlet sister, which may still be found in bloom by the wayside, though its flowers are not so large. Beautiful it looks, a very flower in arms, nursed by the yielding moss, on which it leans, as if its slender stem and prettily-formed leaves were too delicate to rest on common earth, so had a soft pillow provided for its exquisite flowers to repose upon. Nor does it change, when properly dried, if transferred to the herbarium, but there looks as fresh and beautiful as it did while growing—the very fairy of flowers. Nor will the splendid silver-weed be overlooked, with its prettily-notched leaves, which underneath have a rich silvery appearance; while the golden-coloured flowers, which spread out every way, are soft as velvet to the feel. Then the water has its grass like the field, and is sometimes covered with great meadows of green, among which are seen flowers as beautiful as grow on the inland pastures. The common duck-weed covers miles of water with its little oval-shaped leaves, and will from one tiny root soon send out buds enough to cover a large pool, for every shoot it sends forth becomes flower and seed while forming part of the original stem, and these are reproduced by myriads, and would soon cover even the broad Atlantic, were the water favourable to its growth, for only the land could prevent it from multiplying further. Row a boat through this green land-looking-like meadow, and almost by the time you have reached the opposite shore—though you have sundered millions of leaves, and made a glassy course wide enough for a carriage to pass through the water, not a trace will be left, where all was bright and clear as a broad silver mirror, but all again be covered with green, as with a smooth carpet. Beside its velvet-meadows, the water has its tall forests and spreading underwood, and stateliest amongst its trees are the flower-bearing rushes, one of which is the very Lady of the Lake, crowned with a red tiara of blossoms. The sword-leaved bur-weed, and many another aquatic plant, are like bramble, fern, and shrub, the underwood of the tall sedge, which the nodding bulrushes overtop. Nor is forest or field frequented with more beautiful birds or insects than those found among our water-plants.

Then we have the beautiful white water-lily, which seems to bring an old world before us, for it belongs to the same species which the Egyptians held sacred, and the Indians worshipped. To them it must have seemed strange, in the dim twilight of early years, when nature was so little understood, to see a flower disappear at night, leaving on the surface no trace of where it bloomed—to re-appear again in all its beauty, as it still does, on the following morning. And lovely it looks, floating double lily and shadow, with its rounded leaves, looking like green resting-places for this Queen of the Waters to sit upon, while dipping at pleasure her ivory sandals in the yielding silver; or, when rocked by a gentle breeze we have fancied they looked like a moving fairy-fleet on the water, with low green hulls, and white sails, slowly making for the shore. The curious little bladder-wort is another plant that immerses itself until the time for flowering arrives, when it empties all its water-cells, fills them with air, and rises to the surface. It may now be seen almost everywhere among water-plants. In a few more weeks it will disappear, eject the air, fill its little bladders once more with water, and, sinking down, ripen its seed in its watery bed, where it will lie until another summer warns and wakens it to life, when it will once more empty its water-barrels, fill them with air, and rising to the light and sunshine, again beautify the surface with its flowers. Sometimes water-insects open the valves of these tiny bladders, and get inside; but they cannot get out again until the cells are once more unlocked to receive air. Many another rare and curious plant may be found by the water-side in August, where sometimes the meadow-sweet still throws out a few late heads of creamy-coloured bloom, that scent the air with a fragrance delicious as May throws out, when all her hawthorns are in blossom, for though June is a season

'Half-pranked with spring, with summer half-embrowned,'

August is a month richly flushed with the last touches of summer, toned down here and there with the faint grays of autumn, before the latter has taken up his palette of kindled colours.

Still, we cannot look around, and miss so many favourite flowers, which met our eye on every side a few weeks ago, without noticing many other changes. The sun sinks earlier in the evening; mists rise here and there and dim the clear blue of twilight; we see wider rents through the foliage of the trees and hedges, and, above all, we miss the voices of those sweet singers, whose pretty throats seemed never at rest, but from morning to night shook their speckled feathers with swellings of music. Yet how almost imperceptibly the days draw in, like the hands of a large clock, that appear motionless, yet move on with true measured footsteps to the march beaten by Time. So do the days come out and go in, and move through the land of light and darkness, to the shelving steep, down which undated centuries have shot and been forgotten. Soon those pleasant meadows that are still so green, and where the bleating of white flocks, and the lowing of brindled herds, are yet heard, will be silent, the hedges naked, and not even the hum of an insect sound in the air. Where the nearly ripe harvest, when the breeze blows, now murmurs like the sea in its sleep, and where the merry voices of sun-tanned reapers will soon be heard, the trampled stubble only will be seen, and brown bare patches of miry earth, where the straw has blackened and rotted, shew like the coverings of newly-made graves. Even now unseen hands are tearing down the tapestry of flowers which summer had hung up to shelter her orchestra of birds in the hedges. What few flowers the woodbine again throws out—children of its old age—have none of the bloom and beauty about them like those born in the lusty sunshine of early summer. For even she is getting gray, and the white down of thistles, dandelion, groundsel, and many other hoary seeds streak her sun-browned hair. There are blotches of russet upon the ferns that before only unfolded great fans of green, and in the sunset the fields of lavender seem all on fire, as if the purple heads of the flowers had been kindled by the golden blaze which fires the western sky. Fainter, and further between each note, the shrill chithering of the grasshopper may still be heard; and as we endeavour to obtain a sight of him, the voice fades away beyond the beautiful cluster of red-coloured pheasant's-eye, which country maidens still call rose-a-ruby, believing that if they have not a sweetheart before it goes out of flower, they will have to wait for another year until it blooms again. The dwarf convolvulus twines around the corn, and the bear-bine coils about the hedges, the former winding round in the direction of the sun, and the latter twining in a contrary direction. Sometimes, where the little pink convolvulus has bound several stems of corn together, and formed such a tasteful wreath as a young lady would be proud to wear on her bonnet, the nest of the pretty harvest-mouse may be found. This is the smallest quadruped known to exist—the very humming-bird of mammalia—for when full-grown it will scarcely weigh down a worn farthing, while the tiny nest, often containing as many as eight or nine young ones, may be shut up easily within the palm of the hand, though so compactly made, that if rolled along the floor like a ball, not a single fibre of which it is formed will be displaced. How the little mother manages to suckle so large a family within a much less compass than a common cricket-ball, is still a puzzle to our greatest naturalists. It is well worth hiding yourself for half an hour among the standing-corn, just for the pleasure of seeing it run up stalks of wheat to its nest, which it does much easier than we could climb a wide and easy staircase, for its weight does not even shake a grain out of the ripened ears that surmount its pretty chamber. It may be kept in a little cage, like a white mouse, and fed upon corn; water it laps like a dog; and it will turn a wheel as well as any squirrel. Often it amuses itself by coiling its tail around anything it can get at, and hanging with its mite of a body downward, will swing to and fro for many minutes together. One, while thus swinging, would time its motions to the ticking of the clock that stood in the apartment, and fall asleep while suspended.

There are now thousands of lady-birds about, affording endless amusement to children; only a few years ago, they invaded our southern coast in such clouds, that the piers had to be swept, and millions of them perished in the sea; many vessels crossing over from France had their decks covered with them. That pretty blue butterfly, which looks like a winged harebell, is now seen everywhere; and as it balances itself beside some late cluster of purple sweet-peas, it is difficult to tell which is the insect and which the flower, until it springs up and darts off with a jerk along its zigzag way. On some of the trees we now see a new crop of leaves quite as fresh and beautiful as ever made green the boughs in vernal May, and a pleasant appearance they have beside the early-changing foliage that soonest falls, looking in some places as if spring, summer, and autumn had combined their varied foliage together. And never does the country look more beautiful than now, if the eye can at once take in a wide range of scenery from some steep hillside. Patches of green, where the cattle are feeding on the second crop of grass, are all one emerald—looking in the distance as if April had come again, and tinted them with the softest flush of spring; and if you are near enough, you may still hear the milkmaid's carol morning and night, for that green eddish causes the cows to yield as much milk as they did when feeding knee-deep amid the flowers of May. Then great fields of ripe corn rush in like floods of sunshine between these green spaces, widening and yellowing out on every hand, shewing here and there a thin dark band, which would hardly arrest the eye, were it not beaded with trees that shoot up from amid these low hedgerows.

And in the remote distance, where the same dark lines run between the cornfields, they look like streaks of grass on a yellow clay land in spring—a fallow, sun-lighted land, where beside these thin lines no green thing grows. The roofs of the little cottages are all that is seen to float amid this golden ocean of corn, which appears to have washed over wall, window, and door, and left but the sloping thatch on the face of that great yellow sea of waving and rolling ears. That old roadside alehouse, which we thought so picturesque while eating our bread and cheese in the sunny porch an hour ago, is, excepting the roof and the tall sign-post, lost in the long perspective of sweeping acres of cornfields; and the winding road we passed, which leads to it, seems to have been filled up by the long eary ranks that, from here, appear to have closed since we came by. We no longer hear the creaking of the old sign, though the gust that just now swept by and sent a white wave over the corn, must have made the old Green Dragon sigh again as it swung before the door. Soon that great bay-window, which looks so pleasantly over the long range of corn-lands, will be filled with thirsty reapers in the evening, and well-to-do farmers in the daytime, as they ride down to see how the work of harvest progresses, while great bottles and wooden flagons will be passing all day long, out full, and in empty, at that old porch, until all the corn is garnered. Children, who come with their parents, because they have no other home, until harvest is over, will be hanging about that great long trough before the door, filling bottles with water for the reapers, and throwing it over one another, and wetting the hay that stands ever ready in those movable racks for any mounted horseman who chooses to give his nag a bite as well as a sup, when he pulls up at that well-known halting-place. Right proud is mine host of his great kitchen, with its clean sanded floor, and white long settles, that will seat a score or more of customers. You may see your face in the brass copper and block-tin cooking utensils that hang around, for often during the hay and corn harvest, the great farmers call and dine or lunch there, whose homes lie a long way from those open miles of cornfields. It would make a hungry man's mouth water to see what juicy hams and fine streaky flitches ever hang up on the oaken beams which span the ceiling of that vast kitchen. As to poultry—finer chickens were never eaten than those we saw picking about the horse-trough, nor do plumper ducks swim than those we sent quacking into the green pond—covered with duck-weed—when our ragged terrier barked at them as we left the porch.

In some places, if it has been what the country-people call a forward summer, harvest has already commenced, though it is more general about the beginning of next month, which heralds in autumn. And now the fruit is ripe on the great orchard-trees, the plums are ready to drop through very mellowness, and there is a rich redness on the sunny-side of the pears, and on many of the apples. What strangely-shaped trees are still standing in many of our old English orchards, some of them so aged, that all record of when they were first planted was lost a century or two ago! Apple-trees so old that their arms have to be supported on crutches, as the decayed trunk would not bear the branches when they are weighed down with fruit, for some of these codlins are as big as a baby's head. Many of these hoary trees are covered with misletoe, or wrapped about with great flakes of silver moss, causing them in the distance to look like bearded Druids, while some of the trunks are bent and humped with knots, and stoop until they are almost double under the weight of fruit and years. And when does pear ever taste so sweet or plum so rich and mellow, as those which have fallen through very ripeness, and are picked up from the clean green after-math under the orchard-trees, as soon as they have fallen?—few that are gathered can ever be compared with these. A hot day in August, a parching thirst, and a dozen golden-drop plums, picked up fresh from the cool grass, is a thing to be remembered, and talked about after, like Justice Shallow's pippins, in Shakspeare. They must not be shaken down by the wind, but slip off the boughs through sheer ripeness, and leave the stalks behind, so rich are they then that they would even melt in the crevice of an iceberg. But we have now reached the borders of a fruitful land, where the corn is ready for the sickle, and the wild fruits hang free for all; for though the time of summer's departure has arrived, she has left plenty behind for all, forgetting neither beast nor bird in her bounty. And now the voices of the labourers who are coming up to the great gathering, may be heard through the length and breadth of the land, for the harvest-cry has sounded.

## (HISTORICAL.)

In the old Roman calendar, August bore the name of *Sextilis*, as the sixth month of the series, and consisted but of twenty-nine days. Julius Cæsar, in reforming the calendar of his nation, extended it to thirty days. When, not long after, Augustus conferred on it his own name, he took a day from February, and added it to August, which has consequently ever since consisted of thirty-one days. This great ruler was born in September, and it might have been expected that he would take that month under his patronage; but a number of lucky things had happened to him in August, which, moreover, stood next to the month of his illustrious predecessor, Julius; so he preferred Sextilis as the month which should be honoured by bearing his name, and August it has ever since been among all nations deriving their civilisation from the Romans.

## CHARACTERISTICS OF AUGUST.

In height of mean temperature, August comes only second, and scarcely second, to July; it has been stated, for London, as 61° 6′. The sun, which enters the constellation Virgo on the 23d, is, on the 1st of the month, above the horizon at London for 15 hours 22 minutes; on the last, for 13 hours 34 minutes: at Edinburgh, for 16 hours 40 minutes, and 14 hours 20 minutes, on these days respectively.

# First of August.

St Peter ad Vincula, or St Peter's Chains. The Seven Machabees, brothers, and their mother, martyrs. Saints Faith, Hope, and Charity, virgins and martyrs, 2d century. St Pellegrini or Peregrinus, hermit, 643. St Ethelwold, bishop of Winchester, confessor, 984.

## Lammas.

This was one of the four great pagan festivals of Britain, the others being on 1st November, 1st February, and 1st May. The festival of the *Gule of August*,* as it was called, probably celebrated the realisation of the first-fruits of the earth, and more particularly that of the grain-harvest. When Christianity was introduced, the day continued to be observed as a festival on these grounds, and, from a loaf being the usual offering at church, the service, and consequently the day, came to be called *Hlaf-mass*, subsequently shortened into Lammas, just as *hlaf-dig* (bread-dispenser), applicable to the mistress of a house, came to be softened into the familiar and extensively used term, lady. This we would call the rational definition of the word Lammas. There is another, but in our opinion utterly inadmissible derivation, pointing to the custom of bringing a lamb on this day, as an offering to the cathedral church of York. Without doubt, this custom, which was purely local, would take its rise with reference to the term Lammas, after the true original signification of that word had been forgotten.

'It was once customary in England, in contravention of the proverb, that a cat in mittens catches no mice, to give money to servants on Lammas-day, to buy gloves; hence the term *Glove-Silver*. It is mentioned among the ancient customs of the abbey of St Edmund's, in which the clerk of the cellarer had 2*d.*; the cellarer's squire, 11*d.*; the granger, 11*d.*; and the cowherd a penny. Anciently, too, it was customary for every family to give annually to the pope on this day one penny, which was thence called *Denarius Sancti Petri*, or Peter's Penny.'—*Hampson's Medii Ævi Kalendarium.*

What appears as a relic of the ancient pagan festival of the Gule of August, was practised in Lothian till about the middle of the eighteenth century. From the unenclosed state of the country, the tending of cattle then employed a great number of hands, and the cow-boys, being more than half idle, were much disposed to unite in seeking and creating amusement. In each little district, a group of them built, against Lammas-day, a tower of stones and sods in some conspicuous place. On Lammas-morning, they assembled here, bearing flags, and blowing cow-horns—breakfasted together on bread and cheese, or other provisions—then set out on a march or procession, which usually ended in a foot-race for some trifling prize. The most remarkable feature of these rustic fêtes was a practice of each party trying, before or on the day, to demolish the sod fortalice of some other party near by. This, of course, led to great fights and brawls, in which blood was occasionally spilt. But, on the whole, the Lammas Festival of Lothian was a pleasant affair, characteristic of an age which, with less to gain, had perhaps rather more to enjoy than the present.*

* *Gwyl*, Brit. a festival.

* A minute account of the Lammas Festival was written by Dr James Anderson, and published in the *Transactions of the Antiquarian Society of Scotland*, vol. i. p. 194.

---

*Born.*—Tiberius Claudius Drusus, Roman emperor, uncle and successor of Caligula, B.C. 11, *Lyons;* Edward Kelley, alchemist and necromancer, 1555.

*Died.*—Marcus Ulpius Trajanus Crinitus (Trajan), Roman emperor, 117, *Selinus, in Cilicia;* Louis VI., surnamed Le Gros, king of France, 1137; Stephen Marcel, insurrectionary leader, slain at Paris, 1358; Cosmo de' Medici, the elder, grandfather of Lorenzo the Magnificent, 1464, *Florence;* Lorenzo Valla, distinguished Latin scholar, 1457 or 1465, *Rome;* Jacques Clement, monk, 1589; Anne, queen of England, 1714; Jacques Boileau, theologian, brother of the satirist, 1716, *Paris;* Admiral Sir John Leake, great naval commander, 1720, *Greenwich;* Richard Savage, poet and friend of Johnson, 1743, *Bristol;* Dr Shebbeare, notorious political writer, 1788; Mrs Elizabeth Inchbald, actress and dramatist, 1821; Rev. Robert Morrison, D.D., first Protestant missionary to China, 1834, *Canton;* Harriet Lee, novelist, 1851, *Clifton;* Bayle St John, miscellaneous writer, 1859, *London.*

### COSMO DE' MEDICI.

The Florentine family of the Medici, which made itself in various ways so notable in the fifteenth, sixteenth, and seventeenth centuries, may be said to have been founded by Cosmo, who died in 1464. This gentleman, for he was of no higher rank, by commerce acquired wealth comparable to that of kings, which enabled him to be the friend of the poor, to enrich his friends, to ornament his native city with superb edifices, and to call to Florence the Greek savans chased out of Constantinople. His counsels were, during thirty years, the laws of the republic, and his benefactions its sole intrigues. Florence, by common consent, inscribed his tomb with the noble legend: 'THE FATHER OF HIS COUNTRY.'

### MRS INCHBALD.

Biography does not perhaps afford a finer example of industry, prudence, self-denial, and beneficence, than the story of Mrs Inchbald. Starting in life with the merest rudiments of education, she managed to make a living in literature; her personal expenditure she governed with a severity which Franklin's 'Poor Richard' might have applauded; her charity she dispensed with a lavish generosity; her path lay through scenes proverbial for their dangers, yet she preserved a spotless name; and the world's copious flattery of her beauty and abilities—an intoxication which but few of the strongest heads can wholly withstand—left the even tenor of her conduct unaffected. It was not that she was a block of indifference; she was a woman of warm affections and delicate sensibilities; but a lively common-sense, cultivated by much experience in the hard school of adversity, ruled supreme in her mind, and when success and honour fell to her lot, she stood proof to all their wiles.

Elizabeth Inchbald was the daughter of Simpson, a Suffolk farmer, and was born at Standingfield, near Bury St Edmunds, on the 15th of October 1753. She very early took a fancy for the stage, and when about eighteen, she eloped from her mother's care, and made her way to London in search of an engagement as an actress. After sundry perilous adventures among the theatres, she married, in 1772, Mr Inchbald, a second-rate actor, twice her own age. With him she strolled for seven years from city to city of the three kingdoms, sometimes in the enjoyment of plenty, and sometimes in such poverty that they were glad to make a dinner by the roadside out of a turnip-field. In 1779, Mr Inchbald died suddenly at Leeds, leaving his young widow with funds in hand to the amount of £350. She started for London, and was engaged at Covent Garden for 26*s.* 8*d.* a week, and subsequently by Colman at the Haymarket for 30*s.* Whilst acting for Colman in 1784, she took it into her head to write a farce, *The Mogul Tale*, which not only pleased the town, but drew from Colman the grateful assurance that, as a dramatist, she might earn as much money as she wanted. Thus encouraged, she went on writing play after play to the number of about a score, and for some of which she received large sums. *Every One has His Fault* brought her £700, and *To Marry or Not to Marry*, £600. She was a favourite performer, but she owed her popularity more to her piquant beauty than to her histrionic powers. She had, moreover, an impediment in her speech, which only with great difficulty she could conceal. Having therefore discovered an easier means of livelihood, she retired from the stage in 1789. She next tried her hand as a novelist, and in 1791, published *A Simple Story*, and in 1796, *Nature and Art*, which carried her fame into regions where her dramas were unknown. Respected by all, and loved by those who intimately knew her, she died in Kensington on the 1st of August 1821, leaving a little fortune in the funds which had been yielding her £260 a year.

Mrs Inchbald's relations were poor, and some unfortunate, and she ministered to their necessities with a liberality which, measured by her income, was really extraordinary. To a widowed sister, Mrs Hunt, she allowed a pension of £100 a year. To meet such sacrifices, she pinched herself to a degree that would have done credit to a saint of the Catholic church, to which church, by birth and conviction, she belonged. On the death of Mrs Hunt, she wrote to a friend: 'Many a time this winter, when I cried with cold, I said to myself—but, thank God, my sister has not to stir from her room: she has her fire lighted every morning; all her provisions bought, and brought to her ready cooked: she would be less able to bear what I bear; and how much more should I have to suffer but for this reflection! It almost made me warm when I thought that *she* suffered no cold.' To save money for the use of others, she lived in cheap lodgings, migrating from one neighbourhood to another, in the hope of discomforts as amusing as pitiful. With a milliner in the Strand she stayed some years, and she thus depicts the accommodation she enjoyed: 'My present apartment is so small, that I am all over black and blue with thumping my body and limbs against my furniture on every side; but, then, I have not far to *walk* to reach anything I want, for I can kindle my fire as I lie in bed, and put on my cap as I dine, for the looking-glass is obliged to stand on the same table with my dinner. To be sure, if there was a fire in the night, I must inevitably be burned, for I am at the top of the house, and so removed from the front part of it, that I cannot hear the least sound of anything from the street; *but, then*, I have a great deal of fresh air, more daylight than most people in London, and the enchanting view of the Thames and the Surrey Hills.' She was accustomed to wait on herself and clean out her room, as the following passage from one of her letters will prove: 'I have been very ill indeed, and looked worse than I was; but since the weather has permitted me to leave off making my fire, scouring the grate, sifting the cinders, and all the *et cetera* of going up and down three pair of long stairs with water and dirt, I feel quite another creature.' And again: 'Last Thursday morning, I finished scouring my bed-chamber, while a coach with a coronet and two footmen waited at the door to take me an airing.'

Money, so precious to her, she was able to decline when its purchase was at the cost of good taste. She had written her *Memoirs*, and twice was offered £1000 for the manuscript; but it seemed to her that its publication would cause suffering and irritation, and she took counsel with her spiritual adviser. Her diary thus records her heroic decision:

'*Query*. What I should wish *done* at the instant of death?

*Dr Pointer*. Do it *now*.

*Four volumes destroyed*.'

Mrs Inchbald was rather tall, and of a striking figure. She was fair, slightly freckled, and her hair of a sandy-auburn hue. Her face was lovely, and full of spirit and sweetness. 'Her dress,' records one of her admirers, 'was always becoming, and very seldom worth so much as *eightpence*.' She had many suitors, young, rich, and noble, but none among them did she care to accept. She fell in love with her physician, Dr Warren, but he was a married man; and whilst, like a true woman, she suppressed her feelings, she sometimes yielded so far as to pace Sackville Street at night, for the pleasure of seeing the light in his window.

With all her prudence she was frank in speech, and loved gaiety and frolic. Here is what Leigh Hunt calls 'a delicious memorandum' from her diary: 'On Sunday, dined, drank tea, and supped with Mrs Whitfield. At dark, she, and I, and her son William walked out; and *I rapped at doors in New Street and King Street, and ran away*.' This was in 1788, when she was five-and-thirty. 'But,' says Leigh Hunt, 'such people never grow old. Imagine what the tenants would have thought, could anybody have told them that the runaway-knocks were given by one of the most respectable of women—a lady midway between thirty and forty, and authoress of the *Simple Story*!'

## GREAT FIRES A CAUSE OF RAIN: ESPY'S THEORY.

There is extant a letter, dated the 1st of August 1636, from the Earl of Pembroke and Montgomery to the high-sheriff of Staffordshire, stating that the king was about to pass through that county, and having heard there was an opinion in it that the burning of fern brought down rain, he desired that such practice should be forborne for the time, 'that the country and himself may enjoy fair weather as long as he remains in those parts.'

In Scotland, it is customary in spring to burn large tracts of heather, in order that herbage may grow in its place; and there also it is a common remark that the *moor-burn*, as it is called, generally brings rain.

The idea looks very like a piece of mere folk-lore, devoid of a foundation in truth; but it is very remarkable that, in our own age, a scientific American announced a theory involving this amongst other conclusions, that extensive fires on the surface of the earth were apt to produce rainy weather. He was a simple-hearted man, named James P. Espy, who for many years before his death in 1860 had occupied a post under the American government at Washington. It is undoubted that he made an immense collection of facts in support of his views, and though most of his scientific friends thought he was too ready to adopt conclusions, and too little disposed to review and test them, yet it must be admitted that his 'law of storms,' as he called it, was entitled to some measure of consideration. It may be thus briefly stated:

When a body passes from a solid to a fluid state, it absorbs a large amount of caloric. In passing from a liquid to a solid state, this *caloric of fluidity* is given out. In the same manner liquids passing into vapour absorb, and vapours condensed to liquids give out the *caloric of elasticity*. The former is 140°, the latter no less than 1030°. The evaporation of water cools the earth, by its absorption of this caloric of elasticity. The condensation of vapour into clouds sets free this latent caloric, which rarefies the surrounding atmosphere, and produces an upward current of air.

When the atmosphere is well charged with vapour, an ascending current, however produced, causes condensation, by exposing the vapour to cold. This condensation, setting free latent caloric, produces a further upward movement and condensation. The air rushes in on every side to fill the partial vacuum. This air takes the upward movement, with the accompanying phenomena of condensation and the attendant rarefaction, until the clouds so formed are precipitated in rain; or where the movement is more powerful, in hail, sometimes accompanied by water-spouts and tornadoes.

All storms, Mr Espy held, have these characteristics. There is a central upward movement, with condensation of vapour, forming clouds. The wind blows from every side toward the centre. When the movement is very powerful, in level countries and hot climates, it has the character of a tornado, in the track of which he always found trees fallen in every direction, but always toward the centre. The water-spout forms the centre of the tornado at sea.

The formation of hail has long puzzled men of science. Why should drops of water, falling from a cloud, be frozen while passing through a still warmer atmosphere, and even in hot climates? Mr Espy's upward current solves the difficulty. The rain-drops are first carried up into the region of congelation, and being thrown outward, fall to the earth. So great masses of water, carried up in water-spouts, fall in a frozen state, in lumps which have sometimes measured fifteen inches in circumference. In the same manner Mr Espy accounts for the occasional raining of frogs, fishes, sand, seeds, and stranger substances; but he does not account for such matters being kept in the clouds for several days, and carried over hundreds of miles' distance from the place where they were carried up in tornado or water-spout. They may have been carried up by the force of aërial currents, but it does not appear that they could be kept up for any length of time by such currents. Thousands of tons of water are swept into the clouds by water-spouts, but what power prevents it from pouring down again in torrents?

Still the theory of Mr Espy is very ingenious, and has the merit of affording a reasonable explanation to many, if not all, phenomena. The committee of the French Academy called his attention to the connection of electricity with meteoric phenomena, but he does not appear to have pursued that branch of investigation. It is our opinion that a certain electrical condition of bodies in the atmosphere gives them a repulsion to the earth, and that gravitation has no effect upon such bodies, until there is a change in their electrical condition. The earth is a magnet which may either attract or repel bodies, as they are positive or negative to it. Only in this, or in some such way, can we account for solid bodies, often of considerable density, being sustained for days in the atmosphere. It may be admitted, in conformity with Mr Espy's theory, that such bodies may have been carried upward in a tornado, and it may be that the atmospheric movements may develop their electrical condition. It was to these matters, doubtless, that the French Academy wished to direct his attention.

Mr Espy was very anxious that the American government should make appropriations to test the utility of a practical application of his theory. He always asserted that, in a certain condition of the atmosphere, as of a high dew-point in a season of drouth, it was practicable to make it rain by artificial means. *Nothing was necessary but to make an immense fire.* This would produce an upward current, vapour would condense, the upward movement would thereby be increased, currents of air would flow in, with more condensation, until clouds and rain would spread over a great surface of country, so that for a few thousands of dollars a rain would fall worth millions. Mr Espy had observed that the burning of forests and prairies in America is often followed by rain. He believed that the frequent showers in London and other large cities have a similar origin. Rains have even been supposed to be caused by great battles. There is little doubt that they are caused by volcanic eruptions. An eruption in Iceland has been followed by rains over all Europe. In 1815, during an eruption of a volcano in one of the East India Islands, of a population of 12,000, all but 26 were killed by a series of terrific tornadoes.

In this case there were phenomena strongly corroborative of Mr Espy's theory. Large trees, torn up by the tornadoes, appear to have been carried upward by an ascending current formed first by the heat of the volcano, and then by the rush of winds from every quarter, for these trees, after being carried up to a vast height, were thrown outward and descended, scorched by the volcanic fires.

## INSTITUTION OF THE ORDER OF ST MICHAEL.

AUGUST 1, 1469.

There had been an order of the Star in France, but it had fallen into oblivion. When Louis XI. resolved that it was necessary there should be an order of knighthood in his kingdom, he reflected that it was easier to create a new, than to revive the lustre of an old one. As to a name for his proposed fraternity, there was no being of reality held in greater esteem in that age than the archangel Michael. It was believed that this celestial personage had fought visibly for the French at Orleans. The superstitious king worshipped him probably more vehemently than he did his God. Accordingly, he chose for his new order the name of St Michael. The knights, thirty-six in number, all men of name and of birth, could only be degraded for three crimes—heresy, treason, and cowardice.

## THOMAS DOGGET AND THE WATERMEN'S ROWING-MATCH.

Annually, on the 1st of August, there takes place one of the great rowing-matches, or races, on the Thames. The competitors are six young watermen, whose apprenticeship ends in the same year—the prize, a waterman's coat and silver badge. The distance rowed extends from the Old Swan at London Bridge, to the White Swan at Chelsea, against an adverse tide; so none but men of great strength, skill, and endurance need attempt the arduous struggle. The prize, though not of much intrinsic value, may be termed the Red Ribbon of the river, being an important step towards the grand *Cordon Bleu*—the championship of the Thames.

The founder of this annual contest was one Thomas Dogget, a native of Dublin, and a very popular actor in the early part of the eighteenth century. He is described as 'a little, lively, spract man, who danced the *Cheshire Rounds* full as well as the famous Captain George, but with more nature and nimbleness.' Tony Aston, in the rarest of theatrical pamphlets, tells us that he travelled with Dogget when the latter was manager of a strolling-company, and he gives a very different idea of a stroller's life, as it was then, from that generally entertained. Each member of the company wore a brocaded waistcoat, kept his own horse, on which he rode from town to town, and was everywhere respected as a gentleman—seemingly better off than even those in the old ballad quoted by Hamlet, when he says: 'Then came each actor on his ass.'

Colley Cibber describes Dogget as the most original and the strictest observer of nature of all his contemporaries. He borrowed from none, though he was imitated by many. In dressing a character to the greatest exactness, he was remarkably skilful; the least article of whatever habit he wore, seemed in some degree to speak and mark the different humour he represented. He could be extremely ridiculous without stepping into the least impropriety, and knew exactly when and where to stop the current of his jokes. He could, with great exactness, paint his face to resemble any age from manhood to extreme senility, which caused Sir Godfrey Kneller to say that Dogget excelled him in his own art; for he could only copy nature from the originals before him, while the actor could vary them at pleasure, and yet always preserve a true resemblance.

Dogget was an ardent politician, and an enthusiastic advocate of the Hanoverian succession. It was in honour of this event that he gave a waterman's coat and badge to be rowed for on the first anniversary of the accession of the First George to the British throne. And at his death he bequeathed a sum of money, the interest of which was to be appropriated annually, for ever, to the purchase of a like coat and badge, to be rowed for on the 1st of August, in honour of the day. And with the minute attention to matters of dress which distinguished him as an actor, and in accordance with his political principles, he directed that the coat should be of an orange colour, and the badge should represent the white horse of Hanover.

Almost as we write, on the 12th of February 1863, the Prince of Wales visits the worshipful company of Fishmongers, in their own magnificent hall at London Bridge. And a newspaper paragraph, describing the festival, says, 'With singular appropriateness and good taste, eighteen watermen, who had at various periods, since the year 1824, been winners of Dogget's coat and badge, arrayed in the garb which testifies to their prowess, and of which the Fishmongers' Company are trustees, were substituted for the usual military guard of honour in the vestibule.'

A more stalwart set of fellows, in more quaintly antique costume, could scarcely be found in any country, to serve as an honorary guard on 'the expectancy and rose of the fair state.'

## LONDON BRIDGE—NEW AND OLD.

On the day when William IV. and Queen Adelaide opened New London Bridge (August 1, 1831), the vitality of the old bridge may be said to have ceased; a bridge which had had more commerce under and over it perhaps than any other in the world. Eight centuries at least had elapsed since the commencement of that bridge-traffic. There were three or four bridges of wood successively built at this spot before 1176 A. D., in which year the stone structure was commenced; and this was the veritable 'Old London Bridge,' which served the citizens for more than six hundred and fifty years. A curious fabric it was, containing an immense quantity of stone arches of various shapes and sizes, piers so bulky as to render the navigation between them very dangerous, and (until 1754) a row of buildings a-top. The bridge suffered by fire in 1212, again in 1666, and again in 1683. So many were the evils which accumulated upon, around, and under it, that a new bridge was resolved upon in 1823—against strong opposition on the part of the corporation. John Rennie furnished the plans, and his son, Sir John, carried them out. The foundation-stone was laid in 1825 by the Duke of York and the lord mayor; and the bridge took six years in building. The cost, with the approaches at both ends, was not less than two millions sterling, and was defrayed by a particular application of the coal-tax. The ceremonial attending the opening, on the 1st of August 1831, comprised the usual routine of flags, music, procession, addresses, speeches, &c. The old bridge finally disappeared towards the end of 1832; and then began in earnest the career of that noble structure, the new bridge, which is now crossed every day by a number of persons equal to the whole population of some of our largest manufacturing towns.

Strictly, the Old London Bridge, for a water-way of 900 feet, had eighteen solid stone piers, varying from 25 to 34 feet in thickness; thus confining the flow of the river within less than half its natural channel. That this arose simply from bad engineering, is very probable; but it admitted of huge blocks of building being placed on the bridge, with only a few inter-spaces, from one end to the other. These formed houses of four stories in height, spanning across the passage-way for traffic, most of which was, of course, as dark as a railway-tunnel. Nestling about the basement-floors of these buildings were shops, some of which, as we learn from old title-pages, were devoted to the business of bookselling and publishing. It is obvious that the inhabitants of these dwellings must have been sadly pent up and confined; it would be, above all, a miserable field for infant life; yet nothing can be more certain than that they were packed with people as full as they could hold. About the centre, on a pier larger than the rest, was reared a chapel, of Gothic architecture of the twelfth century, 60 feet by 20, and of two floors, dedicated to St Thomas of Canterbury, and styled St Peter's of the Bridge; a strange site, one would think, for an edifice of that sacred character, and yet we are assured that to rear religious houses upon bridges was by no means an uncommon practice in medieval times.

TRAITORS' GATE, OLD LONDON BRIDGE.

In the earlier days of London Bridge, the gate at the end towards the city was that on which the heads of executed traitors were exhibited; but in the reign of Elizabeth, this grisly show was transferred to the gate at the Southwark end, which consequently became recognised as the TRAITORS' GATE. A representation of this gate, with the row of heads above it, is here given, mainly as it appears in Vischer's View of London (seventeenth century).

There was one clear space upon the bridge, of such extent that it was deemed a proper place for joustings or tournaments; and here, on St George's Day 1390, was performed a tilting of extraordinary character. John de Wells, the English ambassador in Scotland, having boasted of the prowess of his countrymen at the Scottish court, a famous knight of that country, David Lindsay, Earl of Crawford, offered to put all questions on that point to trial by a combat on London Bridge. He was enabled by a royal safe-conduct to travel to London with a retinue of twenty-nine persons. The ground was duly prepared, and a great concourse of spectators took possession of the adjacent houses. To follow the narrative of Hector Bœce: 'The signal being given, tearing their barbed horses with their spurs, they rushed hastily together, with a mighty force, and with square-ground spears, to the conflict. Neither party was moved by the vehement impulse and breaking of the spears; so that the common people affected to cry out that David was bound to the saddle of his horse, contrary to the law of arms, because he sat unmoved amidst the splintering of the lances on his helmet and visage. When Earl David heard this, he presently leaped off his charger, and then as quickly vaulted again upon his back without any assistance; and, taking a second hasty course, the spears were a second time shivered by the shock, through their burning desire to conquer. And now a third time were these valorous enemies stretched out and running together; but then the English knight was cast down breathless to the earth, with great sounds of mourning from his countrymen that he was killed. Earl David, when victory appeared, hastened to leap suddenly to the ground; for he had fought without anger, and but for glory, that he might shew himself to be the strongest of the champions, and casting himself upon Lord Wells, tenderly embraced him until he revived, and the surgeon came to attend him. Nor, after this, did he omit one day to visit him in the gentlest manner during his sickness, even like the most courteous companion. He remained in England three months, by the king's desire, and there was not one person of nobility who was not well affected towards him.'

### EMANCIPATION OF BRITISH SLAVES.

The 1st of August 1834 was the day on which the slaves in the British colonies were assigned, not to their actual freedom, but to a so-called 'apprenticeship' which was to precede and prepare for freedom. Lord (then Mr) Brougham brought forward a measure to this great end in 1830; and Mr Fowell Buxton another in 1832; but no act was passed till 1833. It provided that on the 1st of August in the following year, all slaves should become 'apprenticed labourers' to their masters, in two classes; that in 1838 and 1840, respectively, these two classes should receive their actual freedom; that twenty millions sterling should ultimately be paid to the masters, who would then lose the services of their slaves; and that this sum would be distributed rateably, according to the market-price of slaves in each colony, during the eight years 1823—1830. Many subsequent statutes modified the minor details, but left the main principle untouched. It was found, on a careful analysis, that on the 1st of August 1834 (all negroes born after that date, were born free), there were 770,280 slaves in the colonies affected by the Emancipation Act.

A remarkable address was issued on this occasion by the Marquis of Sligo, governor of Jamaica: remarkable in relation to the paternal tone in which the negroes were addressed, as children to whom freedom was an unknown privilege, and who might possibly like a lazy life better than an industrious one, when enforced labour should cease:

'My Friends!—Our good king, who was himself in Jamaica long time ago, still thinks and talks a great deal of this island. He has sent me out here to take care of you, and to protect your rights; but he has also ordered me to see justice done to your owners, and to punish those who do wrong. Take my advice, for I am your friend, be sober, honest, and work well when you become apprentices; for should you behave ill, and refuse to work because you are no longer slaves, you will assuredly render yourselves liable to punishment. The people of England are your friends and fellow-subjects; they have shewn themselves such by passing a bill to make you all free. Your masters are also your friends; they have proved their kind feeling towards you all, by passing in the House of Assembly the same bill. The way to prove that you are deserving of all this goodness, is by labouring diligently during your apprenticeship. You will, on the 1st of August next, no longer be slaves; from that day you will be apprenticed to your former owners, for a few years, in order to fit you all for freedom. It will therefore depend entirely upon your own conduct, whether your apprenticeship shall be short or long; for should you run away, you will be brought back by the Maroons and the police, and have to remain in apprenticeship longer than those who behave well. You will only be required to work four days and a half in each week; the remaining day and a half in each week will be your own time, and you may employ it for your own benefit. Bear in mind, that every one is obliged to work: some work with their hands, some with their heads; but no one can live and be considered respectable without some employment. Your lot is to work with your hands. I pray you, therefore, do your part faithfully; for if you neglect your duty, you will be brought before the magistrates whom the king has sent out to watch you; and they must act fairly, and do justice to all, by punishing those who are badly disposed. Do not listen to the advice of bad people; for should any of you refuse to do what the law requires of you, you will bitterly repent it; for when at the end of the appointed time, all your fellow-labourers are released from apprenticeship, you will find yourselves condemned to hard labour in the workhouse for a lengthened period, as a punishment for your disobedience. If you follow my advice, and conduct yourselves well, nothing can prevent your being your own masters, and to labour only for yourselves, your wives and children, at the end of four or six years, according to your respective classes. I have not time to go about to all the properties in this island, and tell you this myself. I have ordered this letter of advice to be printed, and to be read to you all, that you may not be deceived, and bring yourselves into trouble by bad advice or mistaken motives. I trust you will be obedient and diligent subjects to our good king, so that he may never have reason to be sorry for all the good he has done for you.'

---

## AUGUST 2.

St Stephen, pope and martyr, 257; St Etheldritha or Alfrida, virgin, about 834.

*Born.*—Pope Leo XII., 1760; Cardinal Nicholas Wiseman, 1802; J. J. Gurney, philanthropist, 1788.

*Died.*—Archidamus III., king of Sparta, son of Agesilaus, B.C. 338, *Lucania, in Italy;* Quintilius Varus, Roman governor in Germany, A.D. 10; William II. (Rufus) of England, killed in the New Forest, Hampshire, 1100; Henry III., king of France, stabbed the previous day by Jacques Clément, 1589, *St Cloud;* Etienne Bonnot de Condillac, abbé, author of *Traité des Sensations, Cours d'Etudes,* &c., 1780, *Flux, near Beaugenci;* Thomas Gainsborough, great landscape painter, 1788; Mehemet Ali, pacha of Egypt, 1849; Lord Herbert of Lea, British statesman, 1861, *Wilton House, Salisbury.*

### DEATH OF WILLIAM RUFUS.

Few Englishmen of the nineteenth century can realise a correct idea of the miseries endured by their forefathers, from the game-laws, under despotic princes. Constant encroachments upon private property, cruel punishments—such as tearing out the offender's eyes, or mutilating his limbs—inflicted for the infraction of forest law; extravagant payments in the shape of heavy tolls levied by the rangers on all merchandise passing within the purlieus of a royal chase; frequent and arbitrary changes of boundary, in order to bring offences within the forest jurisdiction, were only a portion of the evils submitted to by the victims of feudal tyranny. No dogs, however valuable or dear to their owners—except mastiffs for household defence—were allowed to exist within miles of the outskirts, and even the poor watch-dog, by a 'Court of Regard' held for that special purpose every three years, was crippled by the amputation of three claws of the forefeet close to the skin—an operation, in woodland parlance, termed expeditation, intended to render impossible the chasing or otherwise incommoding the deer in their coverts.

Of all our monarchs of Norman race, none more rigorously enforced these tyrannous game-laws than William Rufus; none so remorselessly punished his English subjects for their infraction. Even the Conqueror himself, who introduced them, was more indulgent. No man of Saxon descent dared to approach the royal preserves, except at the peril of his life. The old forest rhyme:

'Dog draw—stable stand,
Back berand—bloody hand,' *

provided for every possible contingency; and the trespasser was hung up to the nearest convenient tree with his own bowstring.

The poor Saxons, thus worried, adopted the impotent revenge of nicknaming Rufus 'Woodkeeper,' and 'Herdsmen of wild beasts.' Their minds, too, were possessed with a rude and not unnatural superstition, that the devil in various shapes, and under the most appalling circumstances, appeared to their persecutors when chasing the deer in these newly-formed hunting-grounds. Chance had made the English forests—the New Forest especially—fatal to no less than three descendants of their Norman invader, and the popular belief in these demon visitations received additional confirmation from each recurring catastrophe; Richard, the Conqueror's eldest son, hunting there, was gored to death by a stag; the son of Duke Robert, and nephew of Rufus, lost his life by being dashed against a tree by his unruly horse; and we shall now shew how Rufus himself died by a hunting casualty in the same place.

Near Chormingham, and close to the turnpike-road leading from Lymington to Salisbury, there is a lovely secluded dell, into which the western sun alone shines brightly, for heavy masses of foliage encircle it on every other side. It is, indeed, a popular saying of the neighbourhood: that in ancient days a squirrel might be hunted for the distance of six miles, without coming to the ground; and a traveller journey through a long July day without seeing the sun. Long avenues open away on all sides into the deep recesses of those dark woods; and, altogether, it forms just the spot where the hunter following his chase after the ancient Norman fashion of woodcraft, would secrete himself to await the passing game—a fashion which Shakspeare has thus graphically described:

'*Enter* SKINKLO *and* HUMPHREY, *with cross-bows in their hands.*

*Skinklo.* Under this thick grown brake we'll hide ourselves,
For through this laund anon the deer will come;
And in this covert we will take our stand,
Culling the principal of all the deer.

*Humphrey.* I'll stay above the hill, so both may shoot.

*Skinklo.* That cannot be—the noise of thy cross-bow
Will scare the herd, and so my shot is lost.
Here stand we both and shoot we at the best.'

His friends had dispersed to various coverts, and there remained alone with Rufus, Sir Walter Tyrrel, a French knight, whose unrivalled adroitness in archery raised him high in the Norman Nimrod's favour. That morning, a workman had brought to the palace six cross-bow quarrels* of superior manufacture, and keenly pointed, as an offering to his prince. They pleased him well, and after presenting to the fellow a suitable guerdon, he handed three of the arrows to Tyrrel—saying, jocosely, 'Bon archer, bonnes flèches.'

The Red King and his accomplished attendant now separated, each stationing himself, still on horseback, in some leafy covert, but nearly opposite; their cross-bows bent, and with an arrow upon the nut. The deep mellow cry of a staghound, mingled with the shouts of attendant foresters, comes freshening on the breeze. There is a crash amongst the underwood, and out bounds 'a stag of ten,' that after listening and gazing about him, as deer are wont to do, commenced feeding behind the stem of a tall oak. Rufus drew the trigger of his weapon, but, owing to the string breaking, his arrow fell short. Enraged at this, and fearful the animal would escape, he exclaimed, 'Tirez donc, Walter! tirez donc! si même c'etoit le diable'—Shoot, Walter! shoot! even were it the devil. His behest was too well obeyed; for the arrow glancing off from the tree at an angle, flew towards the spot where Rufus was concealed. A good arrow, and moreover a royal gift, is always worth the trouble of searching for, and the archer went to look for his. The king's horse, grazing at large, first attracted attention; then the hounds cowering over their prostrate master; the fallen cross-bow; and, last of all, the king himself prone upon his face, still struggling with the arrow, which he had broken off short in the wound. Terrified at the accident, the unintentional homicide spurred his horse to the shore, embarked for France, and joined the Crusade then just setting for the East.

About sun-down, one Purkiss, a charcoal-burner, driving homewards with his cart, discovered a gentleman lying weltering in blood, with an arrow driven deep into his breast. The peasant knew him not, but conjecturing him to be one of the royal train, he lifted the body into his vehicle, and proceeded towards Winchester Palace, the blood all the way oozing out between the boards, and leaving its traces upon the road. There is a tradition, that for this service he had some rods of land, to the amount of an acre or two, given to

* That is:—1. Holding a dog in leash. 2. Standing concealed with bow ready drawn. 3. Detected carrying off a dead deer. 4. The hands stained with blood. Any one of these circumstances was deemed conclusive evidence of guilt.

* Cross-bow arrows, so called.

him; and it is very remarkable that a lineal descendant of this charcoal-burner, bearing the same name, does now live in the hut, and in possession of the land, and is himself a charcoal-man; that all the family, from the first, have been of the same calling, and never richer or poorer, the one than the other; always possessed of a horse and cart, but never of a team; the little patrimony of land given to their celebrated ancestor having descended undiminished from father to son. This

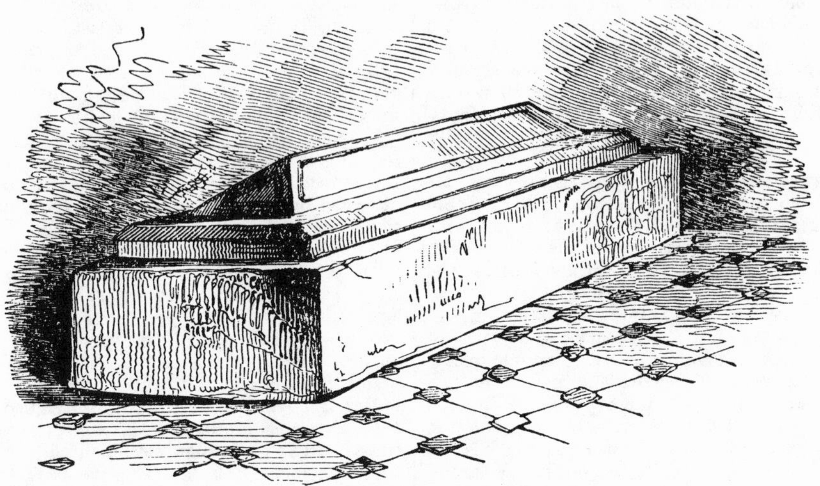

TOMB OF WILLIAM RUFUS, WINCHESTER CATHEDRAL.

family, therefore, is rightly esteemed the most ancient in the county of Hants. A Purkiss of the last century, kept suspended in his hovel the identical axletree made of yew, which had belonged to the aforesaid cart; but which, in a fit of anger, on its accidentally falling on his foot, he reduced to a bag of charcoal, much to the chagrin of the late Duke of Gloucester, who, when appointed ranger of New Forest, was desirous of purchasing it. As to the famous Rufus Oak, after being reduced to a stump by the mutilations of relic-seekers, it was privately burned by one William House from mere wantonness. The circumstance was unknown until after his death, otherwise his safety would have been endangered, so highly did the foresters prize the tree, on account of the profits accruing from a host of sight-seekers. Some fragments of the root were preserved, one of which is still extant, inscribed—'Dec[r] 16th, 1751; part of the oak under which King Rufus died, Aug. 2d, 1100; given me by Lord de la War, C. Lyttleton, Nov. 30th, 1768; given by C. Lyttleton, bishop of Carlisle, to Hen. Baker.' In the year 1745, Lord de la War being head-ranger of New Forest, erected a triangular pillar, bearing suitable inscriptions, on the site of this historical tree, in one of which he states that he had seen the oak growing there. But his lordship's erection has proved a far more evanescent memorial than the oak, it having also been chipped and defaced by relic-hunters; so that it is now as silent on all points of history as the quondom tree.

## MEHEMET ALI.

Oriental history presents us with numerous instances of men, who have ascended to the highest stations from the humblest grades of society. The throne itself has been attained by individuals, whose antecedents did not differ greatly from those of the *Arabian Nights* hero, Aladdin. And just as strange and sudden as was their elevation, has often been their downfall.

The life of Mehemet Ali, viceroy of Egypt, affords a striking illustration of the first of these remarks, though his success in establishing himself and descendants as hereditary rulers of the country, furnishes an exception to the general slipperiness of the tenure of power in the East. He was of Turkish origin, being a native of the town of Cavalla, in Roumelia, the ancient Macedonia, where he was born about the year 1769. He adopted the trade of a tobacconist, but after carrying it on for a time, abandoned it to enter the army. By his bravery and military skill, he soon received promotion, and on the death of his commander, was appointed his successor, and afterwards married his widow. During the French invasion of Egypt, he was sent thither as the second in command of a contingent of 300 furnished by the town of Cavalla, and greatly distinguished himself in the various engagements with the troops of Bonaparte. For several years after the evacuation of the country by the French, Egypt was distracted by contending factions, Mehemet Ali uniting himself to that of the Mamelukes. At last, in an outbreak at Cairo in 1806, the viceroy, Khoorshid Pasha, was deposed by the populace, who insisted on Mehemet Ali taking the vacant post. This tumultuary election was ratified by a firman from the sultan, who probably saw that the only means of preserving the tranquillity of the country, was by placing Mehemet at the head of affairs. It was wholly disregarded, however, by the old allies of the latter, the Mameluke Beys, and with them, for several years, Mehemet was engaged in a perpetual struggle for supremacy. What he might perhaps have found some difficulty in accomplishing by open hostilities, he determined to effect by treachery. During an interval of tranquillity between the contending parties, the Mamelukes were invited to attend the ceremony of the investiture of Toussoon, Mehemet Ali's son, with the command of the army. About 470 of them, with their chief Ibrahim Bey, responded to the summons, and entered the citadel of Cairo. At the conclusion of the ceremony, they mounted their horses and were proceeding to depart, when a murderous fire of musketry was opened upon them by the viceroy's soldiers, stationed on various commanding positions. The unfortunate Mameluke guests were shot down to a man, for literally only one effected his escape, and that was by the extraordinary feat of leaping his horse over the ramparts. The gallant steed was killed by the fall, but his rider managed, though, it is said, with a broken ankle, to escape to a place of safety. The whole affair leaves an indelible blot on the memory of Mehemet Ali. After this act of treachery, he proceeded to consolidate his power, and gradually became undisputed master of Egypt and its dependencies, though still with nominal recognition of the supremacy of the Sublime Porte.

So powerful a vassal might well excite the apprehensions of his superior. In 1831, on the pretext of vindicating a claim against Abdallah Pasha, governor of Acre, he despatched a strong army into Syria, under the command of his son, Ibrahim Pasha, who, in the course of a few months, effected a complete subjugation of the country. The sultan thereupon declared Mehemet Ali a rebel, and sent troops against him into Syria, but the result was only further discomfiture. The powers of Europe then interfered, and through their mediation a treaty of peace was signed, by which Syria was made over to Mehemet Ali, to be held as a fief of the Sublime Porte. After a few years, hostilities were resumed with the sultan, who sought to expel the viceroy from Syria, a project in which he had the countenance of the four European powers—Great Britain, Austria, Russia, and Prussia. Against so formidable a combination Mehemet Ali had no chance, and accordingly, after sustaining a signal defeat near Beyrout, and the blockade of Alexandria by an English squadron, he found himself compelled to come to terms and evacuate Syria in favour of Turkey, the latter power recognising formally the hereditary right to the pashalic of Egypt as vested in him and his family. This agreement was concluded in 1841, eight years before the death of Mehemet Ali, and was the last public event of importance in his life. That Syria was a gainer by the change of masters, is very doubtful. The vigorous administration of the Egyptian potentate was succeeded by the effete imbecility of the Turkish sway, which in recent years found itself unable to avert the atrocious massacres of Damascus and the Lebanon.

As an Oriental and a Mohammedan, Mehemet Ali displays himself wonderfully in advance of the views and tendencies generally characteristic of his race and sect. Instead of superciliously ignoring the superior progress and attainments of European nations, he made it his sedulous study to cope with and derive instruction from them, in all matters of commercial and social improvement. Through the liberal-minded policy carried into practice by him, Egypt, after the slumber and decay of ages, has again taken her place as a flourishing and well-ordered state, and regained in some measure the *prestige* which she enjoyed in ancient times. Trade with foreign countries has been encouraged and extended, financial and military affairs placed on an organised and improved footing, the cultivation of cotton and mulberries introduced and fostered, and various important public works, such as canals and railways, successfully executed. With the view of initiating his subjects in the arts of European civilisation, young men of intelligence were sent by him to Britain and other countries, and maintained there at his expense, for the purpose of studying the arts and sciences. A perfect toleration in religious matters was observed by him, and under his government Christians were frequently raised to the highest offices of state, and admitted to his intimate friendship.

In personal appearance Mehemet Ali was of short stature, with features so intelligent and agreeable as greatly to prepossess strangers in his favour. He enjoyed till the year before his death an iron constitution, but was so enfeebled by a severe illness which attacked him then, that the duties of government had to be resigned by him to his son Ibrahim Pasha, who survived the transfer little more than two months. In disposition Mehemet Ali is said to have been frank and open, though the treacherous massacre of the Mamelukes militates strongly against his character in this respect. His magnanimity, as well as commercial discernment, was conspicuous in his permission of the transit of the Indian mails through Egypt, whilst he himself was at war with Britain. The undoubted abilities and sagacity which he displayed, were almost entirely the results of the exertions of an unaided vigorous mind, as even the elementary acquirement of reading was only attained by him at the age of forty-five. In the earlier years of his government, Mehemet employed an old lady of his seraglio to read any writing of importance that came to him, and it was only when left without that confidential secretary by her death, that he had himself instructed in a knowledge of writing.

## DEATH OF JOHN PALMER, THE ACTOR.

Once now and then the stage has witnessed the death of some of its best ornaments in a very affecting way. This was especially so in the case of Mr John Palmer, who, during the latter half of the last century, rose to high distinction as an actor, identifying himself with a greater variety of characters than any who had preceded him, except David Garrick. Palmer had a wife and eight children, and indulged in a style of living that kept him always on the verge of poverty. The death of his wife affected him deeply; and when, shortly afterwards, the death of a favourite son occurred, his system received a shock from which he never fully recovered. He was about that time, in 1798, performing at Liverpool. On the 2d of August, it fell to his duty to perform the character of the Stranger, in Kotzebue's morbid play of the same name. He went through the first and second acts with his usual success; but during the third he became very much depressed in spirits. Among the incidents in the fourth act, Baron Steinfort obtains an interview with the Stranger, discovers that he is an old and valued friend, and entreats him to relate the history of his career—especially in relation to his (the Stranger's) moody exclusion from the world. Just as the children began to be spoken of, the man overcame the actor; poor Palmer trembled with agitation, his voice faltered; he fell down on the stage, breathed a convulsive sigh, and died. He had just before had to utter the words:

'Oh, God! oh, God!
There is another and a better world!'

The audience, supposing that the intensity of his feeling had led him to *acting* a swoon, applauded the scene, though it was a painful one; but when the real truth was announced, a mournful dismay seized upon all. The above two lines were afterwards engraved on Palmer's tombstone, in Walton churchyard, near Liverpool.

---

## ANCIENT WRITING-MATERIALS.

Sculptured records on stone are the earliest memorials of history we possess. When portable manuscripts became desirable, the skins of animals, the leaves or membraneous tissues of plants, even fragments of stone and tile, were all pressed into the service of the scribe. Notwithstanding the abundant and universal use of paper, some of these ancient utilities still serve modern necessities. Vellum is universally used for important legal documents, and many bibliomaniacs put themselves and the printer to trouble and expense over vellum-printed copies of a favourite book. There is a peculiarly sacred tree grown in China, the leaves of which are used to portray sacred subjects and pious inscriptions upon; other eastern nations still make use of fibrous plants upon which to write, and sometimes to engrave, with a sharp finely-pointed implement, the words they desire to record. The ancient Egyptians wrote upon linen, or wood, with a brush or reed pen, but chiefly and commonly used the delicate membrane obtained by unrolling the fibrous stem of the papyrus; a water-plant once abundant, but now almost extinct in the Nile. Fragile as this material may at first thought appear, it is very enduring; European museums furnish abundant specimens of manuscripts executed in these delicate films three thousand years ago, that appear less changed than many do that were written with ordinary modern ink in the last century. It was usual with these early scribes to make use of fragments of stone and tile, upon which to write memorandums of small importance, or to cast up accounts; to use them, indeed, as we use 'scribbling-paper.' The abundance of potsherds usually thrown in the streets of eastern towns, afforded a ready material for this purpose; and the mounds of antique fragments of tiles, &c., in the island of Elephantine, on the Nile, opposite Assouan (the extreme limit of ancient Egypt), has furnished more than a hundred specimens to our British museums, consisting chiefly of accountants' memoranda.

The use of papyrus as a writing-material, descended to the Greeks and Romans. The thin concentric coats of this useful rush were carefully dried and pasted cross-ways over each other, to give firmness to the whole; the surface was then burnished smooth with a polishing-stone, and written upon with a reed cut to a point similar to the modern pen. The ink was made from lamp-black or the cuttle-fish, like the Indian ink of our own era. Indeed, it is curious to reflect on the little change that occurs in articles of simple utility in the course of ages, and how slightly the terms have altered by which we distinguish them; thus the *papyrus*-reed gives the name to *paper*, and the roll or *volumen* of manuscript is the origin of the term *volume* applied to a book. These rolls were packed away on the library shelves, and to one end was attached a label, telling of its contents. When the excavations at Pompeii were first conducted, many of these charred rolls were thought to be half-burned sticks, and disregarded; now, by very careful processes they are gradually unrolled, and have furnished us with very valuable additions to classic literature. Boxes of these rolls were carried from place to place as wanted, and representations of them, packed for the use of the student, are seen in the wall-paintings of Pompeii; they were cylindrical, with a cover (like a modern hat-box), and were slung by a strap across the shoulders.

The Romans greatly advanced the convenience of the scribe, by the more general adoption of tablets of wood, metal, and ivory. These square tablets exactly resembled the slates now used in schools; having a raised frame, and a sunk centre for writing upon; which centre was coated with wax, and upon this an iron pen or stylus inscribed the writing; which was preserved from obliteration by the raised edge or frame when the tables were shut together. Hinges, or a string, could readily unite any quantity of these tablets, and form a very near approach to a modern volume. In excavating for the foundation of the Royal Exchange, in London, some of these tablets of the Roman era were found, and are now to be seen in the library at Guildhall.

The semi-barbaric nations that flourished after the fall of Rome, could do no better than follow the fashions set by the older masters of the world. A curious drawing in a fine manuscript, once the property of Charlemagne, and now preserved in the public library of the ancient city of Treves, on the Moselle, furnishes the annexed representation of a *tabula* held by a handle in the left hand of a scribe, exactly resembling the old horn-book of our village schools; the surface is covered with wax, partly inscribed by the metal style held in the right hand. These *styli* sometimes were surmounted by a knob, but frequently were beaten out into a broad, flat eraser, to press down the waxen surface for a new inscription. The style in our cut combines both.

Useful as these tablets might be, their clumsiness was sufficiently apparent; books composed of vellum leaves superseded them soon after the Carlovingian era. The finest medieval manuscripts we possess, we owe to the unwearied assiduity of the clergy, whose 'learned leisure' was insured by monastic seclusion. Books that demanded a life-long labour to complete, were patiently worked upon, and often decorated with initial letters and ornament of the most gorgeous and elaborate kind. Enriched often by drawings, which give us living pictures of past manners, they are the most valuable relics of our ancestry, justly prized as the gems of our national libraries.

Attached to all large monasteries was a *scriptorium*, or apartment expressly devoted to the use of such persons as worked upon these coveted volumes. The scribes of the middle ages frequently carried their writing-materials appended to their girdles, consisting of an ink-pot, and a case for pens; the latter, usually formed of *cuirboulli* (leather softened by hot water, then impressed with ornament, and hardened by baking), which was strong as horn, of which latter material the ink-pot was generally formed. Hence the old term, 'ink-horn phrases,' for learned affectations in discourse. The incised brass to the memory of a notary of the time of Edward IV., in the church of St Mary Key, at Ipswich, furnishes us with the excellent representation here given of a penner and ink-horn, slung across the man's girdle; they are held together by cords, which slip freely through loops at the side of each implement, the knob and tassel at each end preventing them from falling.

When book-learning was rare, and the greatest and wisest sovereigns, such as Charlemagne and our William I., could do no more than make a mark as an autograph that now would shame a common peasant, the possession of knowledge gave an important position to a man, and granted him many immunities; hence was derived 'the benefit of clergy' as a plea against the punishment of crime; and the scraps of Latin a criminal was sometimes taught to repeat, was termed his 'neck-verse,' as it saved him from hanging. The printing-press put all these notions aside, and a very general spread of knowledge broke down the exclusiveness of monastic life altogether. Books multiplied abundantly, and produced active thinking. The laborious process of producing them by hand-writing had gone for ever, and we take leave of this subject with a representation of the working-table of a scribe, contemporary with the invention of printing. The pages upon which he is at work lie upon the sloping desk; on the flat table above he has stuck his penknife; the pens lie on the standish in front of him. Bottles for ink of both colours are seen, and an hour-glass to give him due note of time. A pair of scissors, and a case for a glass to assist his eyes, are on the right side. This interesting group is copied from a picture in the gallery of the Museo Borbonico, at Naples.

WRITING-MATERIALS.

## AUGUST 3.

St Nicodemus. St Gamaliel. The Invention of St Stephen, or the Discovery of his Relics, 415. St Walthen or Waltheof, confessor, and abbot of Melrose, 1160.

*Born.*—John Henley (Orator Henley), preacher satirised by Pope, 1692, *Melton Mowbray;* Charles, Earl Stanhope, reforming statesman, and ingenious in mechanics, 1753; Frederick William III. of Prussia, 1770.

*Died.*—James II. of Scotland, killed before Roxburgh, 1460; Stephen Dolet, eminent scholar and typographer, burned at Lyon, 1546; Jeremy Taylor, bishop of Down and Connor, celebrated author of *Holy Living* and other works, 1667, *Lisburn, Ireland;* John Matthias Gesner, distinguished classical scholar and editor, 1761, *Göttingen;* Archbishop Thomas Secker, learned prelate, *Lambeth Palace;* Sir Richard Arkwright, celebrated inventor or applier of the roller machine for spinning cotton, 1792, *Crumford, Derbyshire;* Christopher Anstey, author of *The New Bath Guide*, 1805, *Chippenham;* Michael Adanson, French naturalist, 1806, *Paris;* Eugene Sue, eminent French novelist, 1857, *Annecy, Savoy;* Father Ventura, Catholic controversial writer, 1861, *Versailles.*

### CHARLES, EARL STANHOPE.

This nobleman merits a passing notice here as the inventor of the printing-press which bears his name. It is rather a remarkable circumstance in connection with the typographical art, that from the period of its first introduction up to the latter half of the eighteenth century, no alteration took place in the form or mode of working the press. The same clumsy wooden machine which it was in the hands of Faust and Gutenberg it continued to be in those of Baskerville and Bensley. The improvements devised by Lord Stanhope have been followed by the wonderful achievements of the printing-machine, but the value of his ingenious invention is still recognised.

Besides the printing-press, the earl's engineering turn led him to the construction of various other mechanical implements, all displaying a considerable amount of practical genius. They include, among others, a machine for performing arithmetical operations, and a contrivance for the management of locks on canals. He also entered the literary arena, and published a reply to Burke's *Reflections on the French Revolution*, with other political treatises. As a statesman, Lord Stanhope is noted for the violence and extremeness of his democratic views, leading him, on one occasion, in a fit of republican enthusiasm, to lay aside his carriage, and cause the armorial-bearings to be erased from his plate and furniture. His eccentric character seems to have been inherited in another form by his eldest daughter, the celebrated Lady Hester Stanhope, whose mother, the earl's first wife, was the eldest daughter of Pitt, the great Earl of Chatham.

## STEPHEN DOLET.

The lives of the early printers are full of sorrows and vicissitudes; always men of high literary attainments, they had to wage the battle of learning against ignorance, of liberty against tradition, of the rights of law against the brutality of actual life, of the renaissance against routine. The stories of Fust, Shröeder, Etienne, and Aldus give confirmation to this statement, and that of Dolet is still more striking, as his was one of those ardent impetuous natures that are incapable of calculation and circumspection, and his life was full of trouble and sorrow, ending in the dreadful punishment of the stake.

Etienne Dolet, or according to the fashion of those days, Stephanus Doletus Aurelius, was born in the city of Orleans, on that day of the year on which he afterwards suffered death. He was said to be an illegitimate child of Francis I. He early shewed the germs of the great talent which was afterwards developed. At twelve years of age, he arrived in Paris for the sake of study, and there followed assiduously the lectures on Latin eloquence given by his compatriot Nicolas Bérauld, and especially devoted himself to the works of Cicero. From Paris he proceeded to Padua, where for three years he laboured night and day under the direction of Simon de Villeneuve, to gain a pure Latin style and the art of rhetoric. He was then inclined to return to France; but Du Bellay-Langey, one of the most learned, eloquent, and wise diplomatists of the day, offered him the post of secretary in his political mission to Venice; the opportunity was too good to refuse, his classical studies would not suffer, and as for society, the famous Rabelais was one of his companions, as surgeon to the ambassador. In 1530, he returned to France, and though devotedly attached to literary pursuits, he did not find that they would give him a position, so he determined to study law at Toulouse. This celebrated city had besides its university many societies which had been in existence for centuries, in which various nations—French, Spaniards, and Aquitanians—discussed any subject brought before them, and on which the government cast no favourable eye. The parliament of Toulouse seized upon the pretext of some disorders committed by the students to dissolve the associations, and Dolet, who had been elected orator of the French section, was cast into prison; the first of a long series of incarcerations which made one of his enemies remark, 'that the prison was his country.' Nor need it excite our wonder when he spoke thus of the city. 'This place,' said he, 'which arrogates to itself the monopoly of the true faith, and bears aloft the torch of Catholicism, is still in the lowest rudiments of the Christian faith, and altogether given up to the ridiculous superstitions of the Turks. How otherwise can we speak of the yearly ceremony of the feast of St George, which consists in galloping nine times round the church tower? or of the cross which on certain days is plunged into the Garonne, with vows and prayers addressed to it to be preserved from inundations? What are we to say in summer of the statues of the saints, bits of dried wood which children carry through the street to bring down rain after a long drought? Yet this city, so shamefully ignorant of true religion, dares to impose on all its own way of thinking, and treats as heretics those free spirits who will not submit.' After a few days, he was released, to the great discontent of some narrow minds, who published atrocious libels against him, and even hired assassins to kill him, at the same time parading a pig, mounted on a car, through the streets, bearing a label, on which was written in large letters the name—Dolet. Amidst such animosity the place was no longer tenable, and he took refuge in Lyon, where he published his two harangues against Toulouse; but they issued from a private press, and were prefaced 'without the permission of the author.' This was all he wanted, a little vengeance, and then he returned to Paris, and his early love, Cicero, which he regretted having abandoned for such wretched rivals as the Pandects. At the age of twenty-five, he solicited permission to print the first volume of his *Commentaries on the Latin Language*, a work of immense erudition, but it was with the greatest difficulty that he obtained leave: many were of opinion that printing was an invention of the devil, and they feared the rapid extension of knowledge. His friend, Sebastian Gryphius, brought it out, with all the splendour that suited a book of those times, and with the strict correction that marked so conscientious a printer; but from this time Dolet would have his own presses, and the second volume, which appeared soon after, was of his own printing.

He had at this time taken a wife, and in 1539 his little son Claude was born, yet nothing could make him prudent; he was heaping up fagots for his funeral-pyre. He dared to attack the voluptuous character of the monks, and then published *The Holy Scripture in the Vulgar Tongue*. Such a man became too dangerous; he was accused of eating meat in Lent, and given up to the Inquisition. On the 2d of October 1542, the vicar-general pronounced the sentence of 'heretic, schismatic, scandalous defender of errors and heresies' upon him, and for fifteen months he lay in the dungeons of the holy church, from which the bishop of Tulle released him, taking care to revenge himself on thirteen of his books, which were burned. Once more free, but not for long; in nine months, two packets addressed to him were seized at the gates of Paris, containing prohibited books from the press of Geneva; he was arrested, but after three days contrived to escape into Piedmont; yet the longing to see his wife, his dear books and manuscripts, and to print some articles he had written in his exile, brought him back to Lyon, where he was immediately arrested and condemned, for a false translation of a line from Plato, to be tortured, put to the question, hung and burned, with his books, in the Place Maubert. In his prison he composed a noble canticle, in which he declares his firm adherence to the doctrines he had believed for years; but his enemies say that he recanted on the scaffold, and begged those present to read his books with much circumspection. Of the likelihood of this final concession, the reader may judge for himself.

## RICHARD ARKWRIGHT.

It is not uncommon to hear Arkwright's merits as an inventor questioned. It is said that at the est he merely completed other men's conceptions and reduced them to practice. To trace such assertions to their roots in fact or fancy is no easy matter. Unquestionably Arkwright held converse with many mechanicians, and what he owed to them, and what to himself, it would be impossible for us to determine. Probably Arkwright himself would have been unable to disentangle precisely the hints of others from his own ideas. That he was a man of amazing ingenuity, energy, and originality there can be no doubt; these qualities were written out large in his prosperous career; and the claims he made as an inventor are certainly consistent with the known power and range of his faculties. Nor, even accepting the lowest estimate of Arkwright's genius, need we esteem it a slight

RICHARD ARKWRIGHT.

service to mankind, that he perfected the contrivances of amateurs, and shaped them to use, transforming mechanical dreams into operative realities. Those alone who have introduced some new engine or process to the world, can duly appreciate Arkwright's merit on that score.

Richard Arkwright was born in Preston on the 23d of December 1732, the youngest of thirteen children. His parents were poor, and little Dick was bred up a barber. When a young man, he opened shop in Bolton, where, as Carlyle observes, 'in stropping of razors, in shaving of dirty beards, and the contradictions and confusions attendant thereon, the man had notions in that rough head of his! Spindles, shuttles, wheels, and contrivances plying ideally within the same.' In 1760, he gave up the shop and commenced travelling about the country, buying fine heads of hair from women willing to sell, which, when clipped, he prepared for the wig-makers. By this traffic, and a recipe for hair-dye, he managed to accumulate a little money.

There was much talk in Lancashire, in those days, about improvements in spinning and weaving. Employment was abundant, and wages were high. Traders in linen and cotton cloths were anxious to have them produced more rapidly and cheaply, whilst, on the other hand, the makers were jealous of improvements, lest their craft should be endangered, and their gains diminished. The trader's desire for cheapness, and the worker's interest in dearness, were the stimulus and the terror of inventors. Hargreaves, the Blackburn carpenter, who contrived the spinning-jenny, by means of which twenty or thirty threads could be produced with the labour formerly requisite for one, was persecuted and ruined by the populace for his pains.

The yarn spun by the jenny of poor Hargreaves could only be used for *weft*, being destitute of the firmness required in the long threads, or *warp*. It was at this point Arkwright came in. One day, while watching some workmen elongating a red-hot bar of iron between rollers, the idea suddenly suggested itself, that cotton might be treated in a similar manner. As he was no mechanic, he applied to Kay, a Warrington clockmaker, to help him, and with the aid of Kay's fingers he constructed a machine, in which, by means of a double set of rollers, one moving three times as fast as the other, cotton was spun into a firm fine thread, as fit for *warp* as though it had been linen. Whilst prosecuting his experiments, he gave out that he was in pursuit of perpetual motion; a ruse, Dr Ure imagines, to avert popular animosity from his true design. His first machine was completed at Preston in 1768; and so close had he cut into his funds, that he was unable to vote as a burgess of Preston at a contested election, until the party who sought his support had given him a decent suit of clothes. To be safe from Lancashire rioters, Arkwright removed to Nottingham, where he had the happy fortune to find a partner in Jedediah Strutt, the patentee and improver of the ribbed-stocking frame. Strutt was able to indicate several useful alterations in Arkwright's spinning-frame, for which a patent was secured in 1769. In the same year, they opened a mill at Nottingham, which they worked by horses. Horse-power, however, was found too costly, and Arkwright thereon advised that they should move to Cromford, in Derbyshire, and use the river to turn their mill. The suggestion was acted on; a factory was there built and opened in 1771, and through many discouragements it grew into a great success. Cromford has been justly styled 'the nursing-place of the factory power and opulence of Great Britain.'

Manufacturers, at the outset, refused to buy the water-twist, as the Cromford yarn was called. To meet this difficulty, the partners wove it into cloth; but here a new attempt was made to checkmate them. There was a duty of 6*d.* a yard levied on calicoes imported from India, and the Excise was set on to claim 6*d.* on every yard of the Cromford cloth; for it was alleged to be the same kind of fabric as the Hindu, and therefore liable to pay the same duty. Parliament, however, had the grace to pass an act, in which it was obligingly conceded, that the making of calicoes was 'not only a lawful but a laudable manufacture,' and fixed the duty at '3*d.* per square yard on cotton printed, painted, or stained with colours;' thus placing the Cromford company on a level with other manufacturers. Arkwright's patent was repeatedly infringed, and great sums were expended for its defence in Chancery, with varying results. Yet, spite of all, large profits were realised, and Arkwright became the dictator of the cotton-market. Factories on the Cromford model were set up in other places. Mobs occasionally tore them down, sometimes with the connivance of the authorities; but where money is to be made, the enterprise of Englishmen is not to be defeated.

Arkwright died in his sixtieth year in 1792, leaving behind him a fortune of about half a million sterling. He was succeeded by his son Richard, who inherited a full share of his father's tact. He died in 1843, at the age of eighty-eight, with the reputation of the richest commoner in England. On the proving of his will, his property was sworn to exceed one million, that being merely a nominal sum, because the scale of stamp-duties goes no higher. The probate bore a stamp of £15,750.

Asthma plagued Arkwright nearly all his life, but nothing seemed to arrest his energy and devotion to work. He was a very early riser, a severe economist of time, and one who seemed to consider nothing impossible. His administrative skill was extraordinary, and would have done credit to a statesman; his plans of factory management were entirely his own; and the experience of a century has done little to improve them. He had passed his fiftieth birthday when, to retrieve the deficiency of his early education, he devoted an hour in the morning to grammar, and an hour in the evening to writing and spelling. King George knighted him in 1786, when, as high-sheriff of Derbyshire, he presented an address to his majesty, congratulating him on his escape from the knife of Margaret Nicolson.

---

## POWEL'S PUPPET-SHOW.

Jointed dolls have amused the world for ages. Originally intended to gratify children, they ended in being a diversion for adults; and puppet-shows attracted a due amount of attention in the middle ages, arriving at such a perfection in the sixteenth century, that their performances rivalled in attraction that of living actors. Readers of Cervantes's immortal work will remember the zest with which the puppet-show is described, and the reality with which Don Quixote invests the performance; and the student of our early dramatic literature will be equally familiar with the amusing close of Ben Jonson's play, *Bartholomew Fair*, which takes place at the performance of a drama on the adventures of Hero and Leander, acted by puppets in one of the booths there.

The great French novelist, Le Sage, produced dramas for the Theatre de la Foire; and on this being silenced in 1721, he and his fellow-labourer, Francisque, procured puppets instead of living actors, and devoted their talents to the production of puppet-plays. These became exceedingly popular in England in the early part of the last century, but none more so than those under the conduct of Robert Powel, whose performances were not restricted to London, but were given in 'the season' at Bath, &c., and at Oxford on great public occasions. He has a certain immortality from the fact of being mentioned in the pages of the *Tatler* and the *Spectator*.

The first notice of Powel's performances occurs in No. 16 of the *Tatler* (published May 15, 1709), describing the rivalry between his show and 'the play of *Alexander the Great* to be acted by the company of strollers.' To insure due attention to the wooden actors, we are told 'the puppet-drummer, Adam and Eve, and several others who lived before the flood, passed through the streets on horseback, to invite us all to the pastime, and the representation of such things as we all knew to be true; and Mr Mayor was so wise as to prefer these innocent people, the puppets, who, he said, were to represent Christians, before the wicked players, who were to shew Alexander, a heathen philosopher.' At ten in the morning, all the fashionables of Bath honoured the show, which seems to have been constructed on the principles of the old religious Mysteries and Moralities, with all their absurdities mixed with modern incongruities. Thus, 'when we came to Noah's Flood in the show, Punch and his wife were introduced dancing in the ark. An honest plain friend of Florimel's, but a critic withal, rose up in the midst of the representation, and made very many good exceptions to the drama itself, and told us it was against all morality, as well as the rules of the stage, that Punch should be in jest in the deluge, or indeed that he should appear at all. This was certainly a just remark, and I thought to second him, but he was hissed by Prudentia's party; upon which, really, we, who were his friends, hissed him too. Old Mrs Petulant desired both her daughters to mind the moral: then whispered Mrs Mayoress: "This is very proper for young people to see." Punch, at the end of the play, made Madam Prudentia a compliment, and was very civil to the whole company, making bows till his buttons touched the ground.'

The delight with which the appearance of Punch was greeted at all times, proper or improper, has been humorously noted in Swift's *Dialogue between Mad Mullinix and Timothy*:

'Observe, the audience is in pain,
While Punch is hid behind the scene;
But when they hear his rusty voice,
With what impatience they rejoice!
And then they value not two straws,
How Solomon decides the cause;
Which the true mother—which, pretender.'

This obtrusive minister of fun appears to have been brought forward whenever the interest of the scene flagged. He entered and seated himself in the queen of Sheba's lap, when 'Solomon in all his glory' was exhibited to gaping spectators. He fights the Duke of Lorraine, 'sells the king of Spain' a bargain—

'St George himself he plays the wag on,
And mounts astride upon the dragon.'

The engraving on next page, copied from the frontispiece to *A Second Tale of a Tub, or the History of Robert Powel the Puppet-Showman*, 1715, represents Punch and his wife on the stage. It will be noted that Punch partakes more fully of his Italian character than in more modern impersonations; and his wife (then called Joan) is but a simple elderly woman, without the grotesque characteristics of the Judy of the present day. The stage is furnished with a set-scene, wings, and sky-borders; the performance takes place by lamplight; and Powel, wand in hand, takes his place, like the Chorus of a Greek play, to illustrate the performance. He appears to have been humpbacked, and otherwise slightly deformed. It must be stated that this book is, in reality, a severe satire on the ministry of Robert Harley, Earl of Oxford, under the name of Powel; and was written by Thomas Burnet, son of the famous bishop. In his dedication, he alludes to the great popularity of Powel's show; and asks 'what man, woman, or child that lives within the verge of Covent Garden, or what beau or belle, visitant at Bath, knows not Mr Powel? Have England, Scotland, France, and Ireland; have not even the Orcades—the utmost limits of Cæsar's conquests—been filled with the fame of Mr Powel's mechanical achievements? The Dutch, the most expert nation in the world for puppet-shows, must now confess themselves to be shamefully outdone. It would be trifling after this to recount to you how Mr Powel has melted a whole audience into pity and tears, when he has made the poor starved children in the wood miserably depart in peace, and a robin bury them. It would be tedious to enumerate how often he has made Punch the diversion of all the spectators, by putting into his mouth many bulls and flat contradictions, to the dear joy of all true Teagues. Or to what end should I attempt to describe how heroically he makes King Bladud perform the part of a British prince?' So great a favourite was he in Bath, that 'he was mightily frequented by all sorts of quality, and Punch, with his gang, soon broke the strollers, and enjoyed the city of Bath to themselves. Money coming in apace, Mr Powel bought him several new scenes, for the diversion of his audience, and the better acting of several incomparable dramas of his own composing; such as, *Whittington and his Cat*, *The Children in the Wood*, *Dr Faustus*, *Friar Bacon and Friar Bungay*, *Robin Hood and Little John Mother Shipton*, *Mother Goose*, together with the pleasant and comical humours of Valentini, Nicolini, and the tuneful warbling-pig of Italian race.'

POWEL'S PUPPET-SHOW.

Powel set up his puppet-show in London, under the Piazza at Covent Garden. It was humorously announced by Steele, that Powel would gratify the town with the performance of his drama on the story of *Chaste Susannah*, which would be graced by 'the addition of two new elders.' In the *Spectator* (No. 14), a letter was introduced, purporting to come from the sexton of the parish of St Paul's, Covent Garden, complaining that when he tolls to prayers, 'I find my congregation take the warning of my bell, morning and evening, to go to a puppet-show, set forth by one Powel under the Piazzas. By this means I have not only lost my two best customers, whom I used to place, for sixpence apiece, over-against Mrs Rachel Eyebright, but Mrs Rachel herself has gone thither also. There now appear among us none but a few ordinary people, who come to church only to say their prayers, so that I have no work worth speaking of but on Sundays. I have placed my son at the Piazzas, to acquaint the ladies that the bell rings for church, and that it stands on the other side of the garden; but they only laugh at the child!'

The literary celebrity that has thus invested Powel's show, has not been shared by his rivals. The *Tatler*, however, announces, in the account of the downfall of May-fair, that 'Mrs Saraband, so famous for her ingenious puppet-show, has set up a shop in the Exchange, where she sells her little troop under the name of jointed babies.' Penkethman, the comedian, was also proprietor of a puppet-show, and regularly attended the great fairs; where 'Crawley's Booth' was also fixed, and exhibited 'the Creation of the World, yet newly revived, with the addition of Noah's Flood,' where, according to his own advertisement, might be seen 'six angels ringing of bells, with Dives rising out of hell, and Lazarus seen in Abraham's bosom, besides several figures dancing jigs, sarabands, and country-dances (with Punch among them), to the admiration of the spectators!'

When the Scottish lords and others were executed for their share in the Rebellion of 1745, 'the beheading of puppets' made one of the exhibitions at May-fair, and was continued for some years. The last 'great' proprietor of puppets was Flockton, whose puppet-show was in high repute about 1790, and enabled him in time to retire on a handsome competence.

---

# AUGUST 4.

St Luanus or Lugid, sometimes called Molua, abbot in Ireland, 622. St Dominic, confessor, and founder of the Friar Preachers, 1221.

## ST DOMINIC.

The Romish church has been for nothing more remarkable than the many revivals of energy within her pale under the impulse of particular enthusiasts. One of these took place at the beginning of the thirteenth century, through the zeal of a Spanish gentleman, named Dominic de Guzman, born at Calaruega, in Old Castile, in the year 1170. Had Dominic chosen an ordinary course of life, he would have been a man of station and dignity in the eye of the world. But, being from his infant years of a religious frame of mind, he was content to resign all worldly honour, that he might devote himself wholly to the service of God. Protestants hardly do justice to such men. Think of their objects as we will, we must own that, in confining themselves to a diet of pulse and a bed of boards, in giving away everything they had to the poor, in chastising themselves out of every earthly indulgence, and giving nearly their whole time to religious exercises, they established such a claim to popular admiration, that the influence they acquired was not to be wondered at. As an example of the self-devotion of Dominic, he offered to go as a slave into Marocco, that so he might purchase the liberation of another person. The purpose of all his devotions was to secure the eternal welfare of others. It was the Waldensian 'heresy' that first put him into great activity. His success in restoring many of the Vaudois to the church seems to have suggested to him that he, and others associated with him, might greatly advance the interests of religion by a practice of going about preaching and praying continually, while at the same time visibly abstaining in their own persons from every sort of indulgence. In the course of a few years, he had thus established a new order of religious called the *Black* or *Preaching Friars*, or shortly, from his own name, the *Dominicans* (the term black referred to the hue of the cloak and hood which they wore). This order was sanctioned by Pope Innocent III. in 1215, and very soon it had its establishments in most European countries. There were in England, at the Reformation, forty-three monasteries of Blackfriars, and in Scotland fifteen. Dominic was unremitting in his exertions to extend, sustain, and animate his institution. He performed many journeys, always on foot, and on bare feet. He braved every sort of danger. He never shewed the slightest symptom of pride in his success: all with him was for the glory of God and the saving of men. The contemporary memoirs which describe his life are full of miracles attributed to him. He on several occasions restored to life persons believed to be dead. Often, in holy raptures at the altar, he appeared to the bystanders elevated into the air. It was his ardent desire to shed his blood for the cause he had espoused; but in this he was not gratified. The founder of the Dominicans calmly expired of a fever at Bologna, at the age of fifty-one. He was canonized by Gregory IX. in 1234.

---

*Born.*—Joseph Justus Scaliger, eminent critic, 1540, *Agen, France;* John Augustus Ernesti, classical editor, 1707, *Tennstadt, in Thuringia;* Percy Bysshe Shelley, poet, 1792, *Field Place, near Horsham, Sussex.*

*Died.*—Pope Martin III., 946; Henry I. of France, 1060, *Vitry en Brie;* Simon de Montfort, Earl of Leicester, killed at battle of Evesham, 1265; Wenceslaus III., king of Bohemia, stabbed at Olmutz, 1306; Jacques d'Armagnac, Duc de Nemours, beheaded by Louis XI., 1477; William Cecil, Lord Burleigh, 1598; George Abbot, archbishop of Canterbury, 1633, *Croydon;* William Cave, eminent scholar and divine (Lives of the Apostles), 1713, *Windsor;* William Fleetwood, bishop of Ely, 1723, *Tottenham;* John Bacon, sculptor, 1799; Viscount Adam Duncan, admiral and hero of Camperdown, 1804; John Banim, Irish novelist, 1842, *near Kilkenny.*

## SIMON DE MONTFORT

Simon de Montfort, Earl of Leicester—the *Cromwell of the thirteenth century*—was a French noble possessed of English property and rank through his mother. We know little of the early years he spent in France; but, after establishing himself at the English court, he soon comes into notice. By the favour of the young king, Henry III., he was united to the monarch's widowed sister Eleanor, notwithstanding a difficulty arising from a vow of the lady's never to wed a second husband. This marriage involved De Montfort in many troubles, and lost him, for a time, the friendship of the king. After a temporary absence from England, he returned to raise the means of going on a pilgrimage to the Holy Land. Duly provided, he journeyed to Syria, where he greatly distinguished himself by his military talents and achievements, and became extremely popular with the Christians. He returned to England in 1241, and appeared to have recovered all the favour at court which he had formerly enjoyed. In 1242, he distinguished himself in the war against the French. But he had now become well known as a political reformer, and as a champion of popular liberties; and it is not improbable that his known principles had been partly the means of raising him enemies at court. His name stood second among the signatures to the bold remonstrance against papal extortion and oppression in 1246, and in 1248 the king was driven by his remonstrances into a temporary fit of economy. Earl Simon had formed a design to return to the Holy Land, but King Henry, embarrassed at this time by the turbulence of his subjects in Gascony, persuaded him to remain and undertake the government of that country, where he soon reduced the rebels to submission. In consequence of King Henry's imprudence, the rebellion broke out with more fury than ever, and it not only required all the earl's military talents to suppress it a second time, but he was obliged to raise money on his own estates to carry on the war, in consequence of the miserable condition of the royal treasury. The rebel leaders now sought to injure in another way the governor with whom they could no longer contend openly, and they sent a deputation to England, to accuse him to the king of tyranny and extortion in his administration—charges which seem, if true at all, to have been excessively exaggerated. Yet the king listened to them eagerly, and when Earl Simon arrived at court to plead his own cause, a violent scene took place, which shewed that the king could lose his dignity as easily as the earl his temper, and they were only reconciled by the interference of Prince Richard and the Earls of Gloucester and Hereford. From this moment the king no longer disguised his hatred to Simon de Montfort. Nevertheless, the latter consented to resume the command in Gascony, where he found affairs in greater confusion than ever. He was proceeding to execute his difficult task with his usual ability, when the king sent directions to his subjects in Gascony not to obey him, and appointed his young son, Edward, to govern in his stead. When the earl became aware of this treacherous conduct, he left Gascony and repaired to Paris, where he was held in such esteem that the regency of France, in the absence of its king, was offered him. But he remained steady in his duties to his adopted country, declined this great honour, and soon afterwards, when Gascony was nearly lost by the misconduct of King Henry's officers, he voluntarily offered his services in restoring it, which were gladly accepted. When the province was by his means reduced to obedience and order, the earl, now reconciled with the king, returned to England, where King Henry's misgovernment had brought the kingdom to the eve of a civil war.

Such were the antecedents of the great baron who was now to assume a still more exalted character. The events of the Barons' War are given in every history of England, and can only be told very briefly here. At the parliament of Oxford in 1258, the barons of the popular party overpowered the court, and compelled the king to consent to statutes which took the government out of his hands and placed it in those of twenty-four persons, twelve of whom were to be chosen by each of the two parties. The first name on the baronial list was that of Simon de Montfort, whom the barons now looked upon as their leader. The insolent and oppressive foreigners, who, under Henry's favour, had eaten up the land, were now driven out of England, and the government was carried on with a degree of justice and vigour which was quite new.

The king, meanwhile, was behaving basely and treacherously, and he had taken steps to induce the pope not only to absolve him from all oaths he had taken, or might take, but to interfere in his favour in a more direct manner. The pope's brief arrived in 1261, when the king, whose friends had gained over some of the less patriotic of the barons, ventured to throw off the mask, and proclaimed all to be null and void which had been done since the parliament of Oxford. The result of all this, after two or three years of turbulence and confusion, was the great battle of Lewes, Wednesday, May 14, 1264, in which the barons, under the command of Simon de Montfort, obtained so sanguinary and decisive a victory, that the king, his son Edward (afterwards Edward I.), and the king's brother, Richard, King of the Romans, remained among the prisoners, and the royal cause was for the time utterly ruined. The principles now proclaimed by Earl Simon and the barons, involved principles of political freedom of the most exalted character; which we can only understand by supposing that they were founded partly on older Anglo-Saxon sentiments, and that they were moulded under the influence of men of learning who had studied not in vain the writers of the classic ages. A rather long Latin poem, written by one on the baronial side soon after the battle of Lewes, and intended, no doubt, to be recited among the clergy of that party, who were very numerous, in order to keep constantly before their minds the principles which the barons fought for, gives a complete exposition of the political doctrines of what we may call the constitutional party of the middle of the thirteenth century, and they are doctrines of which we need not be ashamed at the present day. This curious poem, which is printed in Mr Wright's *Political Songs* (published by the Camden Society), lays it down very clearly, that the king derives his power from the people; that he holds it for the public good; and that he is under control, and responsible for his actions. Even feudalism is totally ignored in it, and it was the *plebs plurima*, the mass of the people, for whom Earl Simon and his barons fought, it was *salutem communitatis*, the weal of the community, he sought, and the king's defeat was a just judgment upon him, because he was 'a transgressor of the laws.' 'For,' we are here told, 'every king is ruled by the laws.' The nobles are spoken of as placed between the people and the king as guardians of their liberties, to watch over the exercise of the royal power and prevent its abuse. 'If the king should adopt measures destructive to the kingdom, or should nourish the desire of setting his own power above the laws—if thus or otherwise the kingdom should be in danger—then the magnates of the kingdom are bound to look to it, 'that the land be purged of all errors.' The constraint to which a king is rightly subjected, is only a just power held over him to prevent his doing wrong, or choosing bad ministers—it is not making him a slave. 'He who should be in truth a king,' the poem says, 'he is truly free if he rule rightly himself and the people; let him know that all things are permitted him which are in governing convenient to the kingdom, but not such as are injurious to it. It is one thing to rule according to a king's duty, and another to destroy by resisting the law.' 'If,' it goes on to say, 'a king is less wise than he ought to be, what advantage will the kingdom gain by his reign? If he alone has the right to choose, he will be easily deceived, since he is not capable of knowing who will be useful. Therefore, let the community of the kingdom advise; and let it be known what the generality thinks, to whom their own laws are best known. . . . . it concerns the community to see what sort of men ought justly to be chosen for the utility of the kingdom. . . . . It is a thing which concerns the whole community, to see that miserable wretches be not made the leaders of the royal dignity, but that they be good and chosen men, and the most approved that can be found.'

In accordance with these sentiments, a summons was issued, dated from Worcester, on the 14th of December 1264, calling a parliament to meet on the 20th of January following, addressed to the barons, both lay and ecclesiastic, and two representatives from each county. Ten days later, on the 24th of December, new writs were issued, calling upon each city and town in the kingdom 'to choose and send two discreet, loyal, and honest men,' to represent them in the same parliament. This second summons was dated from Woodstock, and is the first instance in which the commons, properly speaking, were ever called to sit in an English parliament. If there were nothing else for which we have reason to be grateful to Simon de Montfort, Earl of Leicester, we certainly have reason to be thankful to him for laying the foundation of the English House of Commons.

This great revolution was too advanced for an age in which feudalism, though in a weakened form, was established in our island, and physical force was distributed into too few hands to remain united. Success only made place for personal jealousies, and selfish motives led many of the barons to desert the popular cause, while others were quarrelling among themselves. A succession of intrigues followed, and new leagues were formed among the barons, until, on the 4th of August 1265, the decisive battle of Evesham was fought, in which Simon de Montfort was slain, and the barons sustained a ruinous defeat. The joy of the royalists was shewn in the indignities which they heaped upon the body of the great statesman, but his work remained, and none of the substantial advantages of the baronial war of the middle of the thirteenth century have ever been lost. The short period of the battles of Lewes and Evesham stands as a marked division between two periods of English constitutional history.

## CHRISTOPHER COLUMBUS.

At the hour of eight, on the morning of Friday, 3d of August 1492, Columbus, with his little squadron of three ships, sailed from the port of Palos, in Spain, with the object of reaching India by a westerly course. The result of this voyage was, as is well known, the discovery of the continent now termed America; and thus the remarkable prediction of the old pagan philosopher and poet, Seneca, was almost literally fulfilled:

'Venient annis secula seris,
Quibus Oceanus vincula rerum
Laxet, et ingens pateat tellus,
Tethysque novos detegat orbes;
Nec sit terris ultima Thule.'

The life and voyages of Columbus, being matters of history, are without the pale of our limited sphere. It is not generally known, however, that a very obscure point in the history of his first voyage, has lately been most satisfactorily cleared up, Captain Becher, of the Royal Navy, aided by the practical skill of a thorough seaman, and the scientific acquirements of an accomplished hydrographer, having clearly proved that Watling's Island, one of the Bahamas, was the first land, in the New World, seen by Columbus, and not the Island of Guanahani, as had previously been generally supposed.

The precise meaning of the curious form of signature, adopted by the great navigator, is still a subject for doubtful speculation; that he himself considered it to be of weighty importance, is evident from the following injunction in his will: 'Don Diego, my son, or any other, who may inherit this estate, on coming into possession of the inheritance, shall sign with the signature which I now make use of; which is an S, with an X under it, and an M, with a Roman A over it, and over that an S, and a great Y, with an S over it, with its lines and points as is my custom, as may be seen by my signature, of which there are many, and it will be seen by the present one. He shall only write The Admiral, whatever titles the king may have conferred upon him. This is to be understood, as respects his signature; but not the enumeration of his titles, which he can make at full length if agreeable; only the signature is to be The Admiral'—*El Almirante.* The signature thus specified, is the following:

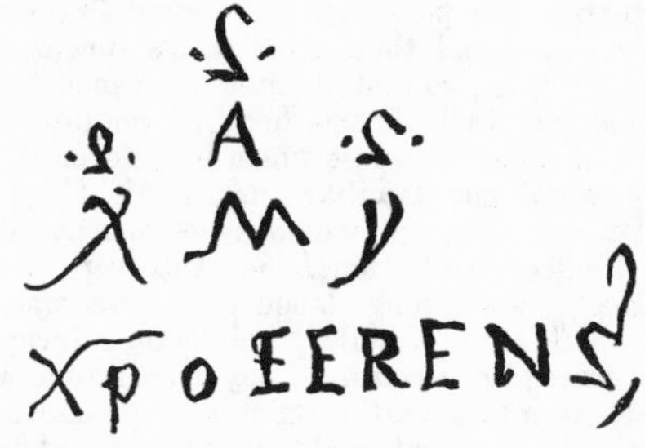


The Xpo, signifying Christo, is in Greek letters; and, indeed, it is not unusual at the present day, in Spain, to find a mixture of Greek and Roman letters and languages in signatures and inscriptions. This signature of Columbus exemplifies the peculiar character of the man, who, considering himself selected and set apart from all others, by the will of Providence, for the accomplishment of a great purpose—great in a temporal, greater still in a spiritual point of view—adopted a correspondent formality and solemnity in all his actions. Named after St Christopher, whose legendary history is comprised in his name *Christophorus*—the bearer of Christ—being said to have carried the infant Saviour on his shoulders over an arm of the sea—Columbus felt that he, too, was destined to carry over the sea the glad tidings of the gospel, to nations dwelling in the darkness of paganism.

Spotorno, commencing with the lower letters of the mysterious signature, and connecting them with those above, conjectures them to represent the words Xristus Sancta Maria Josephus. Captain Becher, however, has given a much simpler, and, in all probability, the correct solution of the enigma. It was from Queen Isabella that Columbus, after many disappointments, first received the welcome intelligence, that he should be sent on his voyage, and that his son would be received into the royal service during his absence. Moved to tears of joy and gratitude at the prospect of realising the grand object of his life, and the advancement and protection offered to his son, the great man, as soon as his feelings allowed utterance, exclaimed: 'I shall ever be the servant of your majesty!' We may readily believe that Columbus would retain this sentiment of devoted service, and bequeath it as a sacred heir-loom to his successors; and assuming that the concealed words are Spanish, and the letters are to be read in their regular order, they, in all probability, signify:

SERVIDOR
SUS ALTEZAS SACRAS
JESUS MARIA ISABEL.

Or in English and in full:

THE SERVANT
OF THEIR SACRED HIGHNESSES
JESUS MARY AND ISABELLA,
CHRIST BEARING.
THE ADMIRAL.

## SHELLEY.

It would be difficult to point out a career, as recent and familiar to us as that of Shelley, involved in so many obscurities. From some peculiar bias of temperament, or constitutional irregularity, his imagination stamped much more vivid impressions on his own mind than most men's imaginations are wont to do; so that it often happened to him that old fancies took the form of reminiscences, and he believed in a past which had never existed. His personal and familiar friends, Mr Hogg and Mr Peacock, both of whom have written down their kindly recollections, shew this very clearly. Mr Hogg uses strong language. 'He was,' he says, speaking of Shelley, 'altogether incapable of rendering an account of any transaction whatsoever, according to the strict and precise truth, and the bare naked realities of actual life; not through an addiction to falsehood, which he cordially detested, but because he was the creature —the unsuspecting and unresisting victim—of his irresistible imagination. Had he written to ten different individuals the history of some proceeding in which he was himself a party and an eye-witness, each of his ten reports would have varied from the rest in essential and important particulars.' Though this statement looks somewhat exaggerated, Mr Peacock, who quotes it, does not contradict it, and many of his anecdotes go to shew that it is, in the main, true; and the result is, that many stories, confidently reported—many tragic histories of nightly attempts to assassinate the poet, or mysterious visitants to his abode, or singular events in his ordinary life, resting only on his own testimony—will have to be quietly, though often, doubtless, reluctantly, passed over by a cautious biographer. Concerning Shelley, already much error has been corrected, and probably more remains to correct; even as many more particulars have still to be revealed. Strictly speaking, Shelley's life is still unwritten, and at present it will remain so, though the leading events are well known.

Percy Bysshe Shelley came of an aristocratic stock. At the time of his birth, the 4th of August 1792, his grandfather was a baronet, and before Shelley was many years old, his father succeeded to the title, as also did Shelley's son, Sir Percy, after the poet's death. At ten years old, he was sent to Zion House Academy, near Brentford, and in his fifteenth year he went to Eton. Being of a sensitive nature, he had to pass through many troubles, and his eccentricities brought him into more, before he had been at Oxford many terms. He and Mr Hogg, a college-friend, concocted a little pamphlet on religious subjects, and printed it for private circulation; and the master and fellows of University College saw good, in a fit of rigid orthodoxy, to expel both of them. Men who think little are often severely orthodox, but deep thinkers are mostly lenient towards the scruples of others.

Nevertheless, we must admit that Shelley went far enough to startle more than mediocrity. Even at Zion House Academy he was given to raising the devil, and throughout his life he remained, let us say, a philosopher. That earnestness and love of truth which made comedy repulsive to him, conspired, with independent and original thinking, to make him very fearless in expressing and maintaining his many eccentric opinions. Young thinkers are generally sanguine and self-important; they seem to fancy that the world never existed till they themselves set eyes on it, and deem themselves inspired apostles specially raised up to set truth on its feet again.

Shelley's circumstances, after his expulsion from Oxford, became straitened. His father, who was never kind to him, refused supplies, and he had to live on secret remittances from his kind-hearted sisters. They sent them to his lodging in London by the willing hand of a school-fellow, Harriet Westbrook, and the sympathy she shewed won the heart of the grateful youth. The two children, as we may call them, came to an understanding, and eloped to Scotland, and their marriage-ceremony was performed at Edinburgh in August 1811, Shelley being nineteen, and his wife not so old.

Matters went on pleasantly for a time, and Harriet Shelley made an affectionate wife; but she did not prove exactly the partner fully to correspond to her husband. Love cannot do all the household-work, but requires some handmaidens. There was still a void, as the future revealed, ungraciously enough. Shelley did not allow it to himself, and in 1814, the marriage-ceremony was performed again, according to the English form; but soon afterwards he met with Mary Wollstonecraft Godwin, and the strong current of his feelings changed. Mary Godwin was a woman of great intellectual energy and congenial tastes; and so, at once—let no man judge him!—he left his wife without her consent; he left her sister, whom he disliked intensely; and his children, whom he loved to carry in his arms, singing a strange lullaby of 'Ya'hmani, Ya'hmani, Ya'hmani, Ya'hmani;' and went abroad with the other lady. Harriet drowned herself in the Serpentine two years later, and Miss Godwin became Mrs Shelley.

Shelley's children by his first wife were taken from him, on the plea that their father held, and acted upon, opinions with respect to marriage 'injurious to the best interests of society.' It is not correct, as usually stated, that this deprivation was made because of his heterodox religious opinions. His first wife's tragical end, as well as the loss of his little ones, affected Shelley with the most lively grief; although the same considerations, which will make many readers smile at the statement, sealed his lips.

Much of the rest of Shelley's short life was spent in Italy. His father had finally arranged to allow him a thousand a year, so that anxiety on that score was taken away. Surrounded with the grand features and exquisite beauties of prodigal nature, he fed the unceasing stream of his spiritual fancy, and filled the world with the luxurious music of strains, wild as Arion's; all the time drawing visibly nearer—so say some who knew him, though not all—to the evident catastrophe, premature death. Inevitable as early death was to his failing constitution, it came before the expected time; for a squall sank his boat in the bay of Spezzia, and the waves received him, together with his friend, Captain Williams. After long search, the bodies were found and burned—that of Captain Williams on August 15, 1822, and that of Shelley on the following day—according to the requirements of quarantine regulations. Byron, Leigh Hunt, and Trelawny performed the last obsequies, and Trelawny and Hunt have left us an account of them. His ashes were interred in the Protestant cemetery at Rome.

Shelley had three children by his second wife; William and Clara, who died before him, and the one who was afterwards Sir Percy. Mrs Shelley survived him many years, and lived to publish his *Memorials*. The poet's lines on his little boy are worthy of a place in this brief sketch:

TO WILLIAM SHELLEY.

(With what truth I may say—
Roma! Roma! Roma!
Non è piu come era prima!)

My lost William, thou in whom
Some bright spirit lived, and did
That decaying robe consume
Which its lustre faintly hid,
Here its ashes find a tomb,
But beneath this pyramid
Thou art not—if a thing divine
Like thee can die, thy funeral shrine
Is thy mother's grief and mine.

Where art thou, my gentle child?
Let me think thy spirit feeds,
With its life intense and mild,
The love of living leaves and weeds,
Among these tombs and ruins wild;
Let me think that through low seeds
Of the sweet flowers and sunny grass,
Into their hues and scents may pass
A portion '——

Let the reader decide why the verse is left unfinished.

A familiar acquaintance existed between Shelley and Byron. They made an excursion together round the Lake of Geneva, and afterwards saw a great deal of each other in Italy. Shelley believed implicitly in Byron's genius, yet their natures were not, in many respects, congenial. Byron was a problem to Shelley, and sometimes a source of amusement. We meet with a playful instance of his quiet sarcasm in a letter to Peacock, written in August 1821, which will also afford a curious illustration of their manner of life: 'Lord Byron gets up at two. I get up, quite contrary to my usual custom, but one must sleep or die, like Southey's sea-snake in *Kehama*, at twelve. After breakfast, we sit talking till six. From six till eight we gallop through the pine-forests which divide Ravenna from the sea; then come home and dine, and sit up gossiping till six in the morning. I do not think this will kill me in a week or fortnight, but I shall not try it longer. Lord B.'s establishment consists, besides servants, of ten horses, eight enormous dogs, three monkeys, five cats, an eagle, a crow, and a falcon; and all these, except the horses, walk about the house, which every now and then resounds with their unarbitrated quarrels, as if they were the masters of it. . . . . P.S.—After I have sealed my letter, I find that my enumeration of the animals in this Circean palace was defective, and that in a material point. I have just met on the grand staircase five peacocks, two guinea-hens, and an Egyptian crane. I wonder who all these animals were before they were changed into these shapes.'

A most brotherly and affectionate friendship existed between Shelley and Leigh Hunt. Leigh Hunt went to Italy at Shelley's instigation, to share in the preparation of a quarterly magazine—*The Liberal*—which Shelley, Byron, and Hunt were mainly to support: he lost his friend soon after his arrival. Leigh Hunt well knew—knew perhaps better than any one—the generous, kind, and noble, and loving nature so tragically taken from the earth.

Shelley was a genius in the highest sense of the word. His spiritual, impressible soul was little fitted to be penned up in a common-place world. Though he lived but a brief period, his pen was prolific, wild, and musical, beyond anything written since, if not before. His poems will maintain a place in the literature of his country, although, from their subtlety, and their philosophic tendency, many of them are tiresome to read, and will remain unread except by a few. His earliest effort, *Queen Mab*, was inspired by Southey's *Thalaba*, and contains much speculative matter. *The Revolt of Islam* is his longest poem: it met with virulent censure in its first form, and under its earlier title of *Laon and Cythna*. The *Cenci* was one of the few productions of his pen which were popular in his own time. A drama, harrowing in its details, taking for its subject the horrible story of Beatrice Cenci, it is less mystical than most of Shelley's writings, and possesses more human interest, though it cannot be considered in any sense fit for the stage. The *Adonais*, or lament for Keats, is a favourite with every one; and many of his smaller poems, such as *The Skylark*, *The Invitation*, and others, figure in every selection of English poetry. Had he lived longer, it is more than probable he would have acquired a firmer tone, and a more popular and enduring manner.

We may append, in conclusion, Shelley's own lines:

'Music, when soft voices die,
Vibrates on the memory—
Odours, when sweet violets sicken.
Live within the sense they quicken.

Rose leaves, when the rose is dead,
Are heaped for the beloved's bed;
And so thy thoughts, when thou art gone,
Love itself shall slumber on.'

It would not be right to omit Robert Browning's beautiful tribute to the memory of the poet:

*Memorabilia.*

'Ah, did you once see Shelley plain,
And did he stop and speak to you?
And did you speak to him again?
How strange it seems, and new!

But you were living before that,
And you are living after,
And the memory I started at—
My starting moves your laughter!

I crossed a moor with a name of its own,
And a use in the world, no doubt,
Yet a hand's-breadth of it shines alone
'Mid the blank miles round about—

For there I picked up on the heather,
And there I put inside my breast
A moulted feather, an eagle feather—
Well, I forget the rest.'

## ARCHBISHOP ABBOT'S LAST HUNT.

On the 4th of August 1621, Mr John Chamberlain writing, as he was accustomed to do, to Sir Dudley Carleton, adverted to a strange accident which had just fallen out in the hands of the Archbishop of Canterbury (George Abbot). In those days, when hunting was the favourite and almost the only amusement of the English nobility, the gay train of huntsmen, falconers, verderers, and rangers seldom left the courtyard without ecclesiastics among them. The purity of 'the cloth' was not thought to be in the least stained by partaking in such sport. Even the Archbishop of Canterbury of the time above indicated—all Calvinist as he was—did not scruple to join in the pleasures of the chase. He was now on the borders of sixty, and his declining health made such recreation the more desirable. Paying a visit to Lord Zouch, at his seat of Bramshill, in Hampshire, the archbishop accompanied a hunting-party to the field, furnished with a cross-bow, the weapon then usually employed against deer.

A buck being started, his Grace discharged an arrow, which, instead of hitting the animal, struck the arm of Peter Hawkins, one of Lord Zouch's gamekeepers. An artery was divided, and the poor man bled to death in half an hour, to the inexpressible grief and distress of the archbishop, although the bystanders acquitted him of everything save awkwardness. His Grace made all the reparation in his power by settling an annuity on the widow and children of the deceased. He also thenceforth held a monthly fast on account of the sad event.

Casualty as the act obviously was, there were not wanting some who urged that the archbishop should be tried for it as a crime. King James knew too well the chances of the hunting-field to allow of any such course being taken. He remarked that he had once himself shot a keeper's horse under him; the queen, too, had on another occasion killed him one of the best braches (hounds) he ever possessed. It was a mere misfortune which might befall any man. In this light the accident was viewed by the inquest held on the body of Hawkins; nay, in their verdict, they found that the man's death came '*per infortunium suâ propriâ culpâ*.'

It was, nevertheless, an accident not easily to be passed over in an archbishop. Many doubted if, with blood on his hands, he could henceforth exercise the functions of a prelate. To settle this point, a mixed commission was appointed by the king, and this court sat five months deliberating on the many subtleties connected with the question, at length pronouncing that the archbishop required both a royal pardon, and a re-instatement in his metropolitan authority. After all this was done, Laud and three other clergymen, elected to bishoprics, refused to accept consecration from Abbot, and the rite was accordingly performed by a congregation of prelates in the Bishop of London's chapel. There can be little doubt that dislike for the archbishop's puritanic leanings actuated these scrupulous divines fully as much as a horror for the blood of Hawkins.

Archbishop Abbot was of humble extraction, his father being a cloth-worker at Guildford, in Surrey. It is told that his mother, a short while before his birth, dreamed that if she could have a pike or jack to eat, the baby she was expecting would rise to greatness. Some time after, fetching water from the river, a jack came into her pail, which she immediately cooked and ate. Some persons of rank hearing of this, offered themselves as sponsors to the child; and a gentleman one day passing over Guildford Bridge, noticed George and his brother Robert playing, and struck with their appearance, offered to put them to school, and then sent them to the university. In 1599, George was installed Dean of Winchester; ten years after, advanced to the see of Lichfield, thence to London, and the year after to the Primacy.

He took a leading part in completing the Reformation; assisted materially in the translation of the Bible; counselled his king wisely in many difficult matters; opposing him fearlessly in his declaration of sports and pastimes on Sunday, and in the divorce which was granted to the Countess of Essex. He died on the 4th of August 1633, at the age of seventy-one, and was buried in the old church at Guildford: an altar tomb, with a canopy supported by six black marble pillars, under which is his full-length figure in his robes, marks the spot: at the west end is a curious representation of a sepulchre filled with skulls and bones, and a grating before it carved in the stone.

## DISSOLUTION OF THE PRIORY, WALSINGHAM.

### AUGUST 4, 1538.

'Give me my scallop-shell of quiet,
My staff of faith to walk upon,
My scrip of joy, immortal diet,
My bottle of salvation,
My gown of glory (hope's true gage),
And then I'll take my pilgrimage.'

Let us hope that these beautiful lines of Sir Walter

Raleigh were the sincere feelings of many a pious soul, on pilgrimage to the far-famed shrine of our Ladye at Walsingham; a little spot in Norfolk, lying a few miles distant from the sea, which was the rival of our Ladye of Loretto, or St James of Compostella, in the number of pilgrims who were yearly attracted to it; indeed, the town was created and subsisted solely upon these travellers, being nothing but a collection of inns and hostelries for their accommodation. Walsingham Chapel was founded in 1061, by the widow of Ricoldie de Faverches, and owed its reputation to the fact of its being an exact fac-simile of the Santa Casa, or home of the Virgin Mary, at Nazareth; which house was, three hundred years after, said to have been carried by angels to Loretto. The Crusaders and pilgrims to Palestine transferred their affections to the Norfolk shrine, after the Mohammedans had conquered Nazareth; believing that the Virgin had deserted her real home, and established herself in England, when the infidels desecrated the Holy Land. The splendid priory which soon arose beside the chapel was founded by Godfrey de Faverches, and granted to the order of St Augustine; and in 1420, a large and handsome church was built at the side of the low-roofed shrine of which Erasmus speaks in his famous *Colloquy upon Pilgrimages*. He says, 'The church is splendid and beautiful, but the Virgin dwells not in it; that veneration and respect is only granted to her Son. She has her church so contrived as to be on the right hand of her Son, but neither in that doth she live, the building not being finished.' The original shrine he describes as being 'built of wood, pilgrims are admitted through a narrow door at each side. There is but little or no light in it, but what proceeds from wax-tapers yielding a most pleasant and odoriferous smell; but if you look in, you will say it is the seat of the gods, so bright and shining as it is all over with jewels, gold, and silver.' That the treasures of the place, arising from gifts and benefactions, were very great, we have abundant evidence. Lord Burghersh, K.G., left in his will, in 1369, that a statue of himself on horseback should be made in silver, and offered to the Virgin; Henry VII. had the same kind of image made, above three feet high, of his own effigy, kneeling on a table, with 'a brode border, and in the same graven and written with large letters, blake enameled, theis words: "Sancte Thoma, intercede pro me."' The Plantagenet kings were great benefactors to it. Henry III., Edwards I. and II., were among those who made the Walsingham pilgrimage. Charles V., when he came secretly to gain Wolsey's ear, made this pilgrimage his ostensible reason. At no time was it more popular than just before its destruction: Henry VIII. walked there barefoot,* to present a costly necklace to the Virgin, and made it his favourite place of devotion, with Catharine of Aragon, perhaps partly induced by his minister Wolsey's great affection for the neighbourhood of his birth: yet the caprice, which is perhaps a truer word than principle, of this monarch induced him not long after to order this famous chapel to be desecrated. The dying tyrant is said to have felt this sin lie more heavily on his conscience than many others, and, after all, unable to throw off his early superstitions, he left his soul in charge of the Lady of Walsingham: his poor divorced Catharine did the same with much more sincerity, and ordered two hundred nobles to be given by a pilgrim in charity on his way there.

* From Barsham.

Erasmus gives us a very amusing account of the wonders of the place, and the miracle performed there. 'On the north side there is a gate, which has a very small wicket, so that any one wanting to enter is obliged first to subject his limbs to attack, and then must stoop his head. Our reverend guide related that once a knight, seated on his horse, escaped by this door from the hands of his enemy, who was at the time closely pressing upon him. The wretched man, thinking himself lost, by a sudden aspiration commended his safety to the Virgin who was so near; and, lo!—the unheard of occurrence!—on a sudden the man and horse were together within the precincts of the church, and the pursuer fruitlessly storming without.

"And did he make you swallow such a wonderful story?"

"Unquestionably. He pointed out a brass-plate nailed to the gate, representing the scene; the knight had a beard as long as a goat's, and his dress fitted tightly without a wrinkle."

'It would be wrong to doubt any longer.

'To the east of this is a chapel full of wonders. A joint of a man's finger is exhibited to us: I kiss it, and then ask: "Whose relics were these?" He says: "St Peter's." Then observing the size of the joint, which might have been that of a giant, I remarked: "Peter must have been a man of very large size." At this one of my companions burst into a laugh, which I certainly took ill, and pacified the attendant by offering him a few pence. Before the chapel was a shed, under which are two wells full to the brink; the water is wonderfully cold and efficacious in curing pains in the head. They affirm that the spring suddenly burst from the earth at the command of the most holy Virgin.' (These still exist, and are called the Wishing-wells, as it was believed that the Virgin granted to the pilgrims what they desired when drinking.) 'I asked how many years it might be since that little house was brought thither. He answered: "Some centuries." "But the walls," I remarked, "do not bear any signs of age." He did not dispute the matter. "But the wooden posts, the roof, and the thatch are new, how, then, do you prove that this was the cottage which was brought from a great distance?" He immediately shewed us a very old bear's skin fixed to the rafters, and almost ridiculed our dulness in not having observed so manifest a proof.' In a more satirical spirit Erasmus goes on to speak of the heavenly milk of the blessed Virgin, which had been brought from the Holy Land through many dangers, making the canon to look aghast at him as if possessed by fury and horrified at his blasphemous inquiries. He next saw 'the wonderful jewel at the feet of the Virgin, which the French named toad-stone, because it so imitates the figure of a toad as no art could do the like; and what makes the miracle greater, the stone is very small, the figure does not project, but shines as it enclosed in the jewel itself.'

Among other superstitions belonging to the place, was one that the Milky-way pointed directly to the home of the Virgin, in order to guide pilgrims on their road, hence it was called the Walsingham-

Way, which had its counterpart on earth in the broad road which led through Norfolk: at every town that it passed through a cross was erected, pointing out the path to the holy spot; some of these elegant structures still remain.

Let us now take a glance at the pilgrims themselves; a class of persons who played no unimportant part in the social life of the middle ages. An example of the corps was clad in a long coat of

AN ENGLISH PILGRIM.

russet hue, a sort of broad flapped hat, which was as often thrown back as worn on the head, with a long staff in his hand, and silver scallop-shells embroidered on his coat; an armorial bearing, supposed, in the first instance, to have been assumed, because these shells were used as drinking-cups and dishes in Palestine. Tin and leaden images were stuck all over his hat and dress, to mark what holy shrines he had visited; this is alluded to in a poem ascribed to Chaucer:

'Then as manere and custom is, signes there they bought,
For men of contré should knowe whome they had sought,
Eche man set his silver in such thing as they liked.
And in the meen while the millar had y-picked
His bosom full of signys of Caunterbury brochis.
They set their signys upon their hedes and some oppon their capp,
And sith to the dyner ward they gan for to stapp.'

The reader will remember the hat of Louis XI. of France, described in *Quentin Durward* as full of these leaden images of the Virgin. In addition to these, the rosary was always hung over the arm, that name being given in consequence of the legend which relates that the Virgin presented her chaplet of beads to St Dominic, and that it was scented with the sweet perfume of roses. It ought to contain one hundred and fifty beads, in which one Pater-noster comes after every ten Ave-Marias. It was often made of jet or wood, but those of Cordova were exquisitely worked in gold-filigree. A bottle slung at the back, and a pouch in front, completed the orthodox costume.

The abuses of these pilgrimages occupy many a page in the old writers; they led to lying, idleness, and mendicancy. A sermon of the year 1407 thus remarks upon them: 'Also I knowe well that when divers men and women will goe thus after their own willes and finding out on pilgrimage, they will ordaine with them before to have with them both men and women that can well sing wanton songs, and some other pilgrimes will have with them bagge-pipes; so that everie town that they come through, what with the noise of their singing and with the sound of their piping, and with the jangling of their Canturburie-bells, and with the barking out of dogges after them, that they make more noice then if the king came there away with all his clarions and many other minstrels. And if these men and women be a moneth out in their pilgrimage, many of them shall be a halfe yeare after great janglers, tale-tellers, and liers.' All which is borne out by mine Host of the Tabarde:

'Ye gon to Caunterbury; God you spede,
The blisful martir quyte you youre mede!
And wel I wot, as ye gon by the way
Ye schapen you to talken and to play,
For trewely comfort ne mirthe is non,
To ryden by the way dumb as a ston:
And therefore wold I maken you disport.'

It will be readily imagined how great was the distress when Henry despoiled this valuable shrine. The people of Norfolk rose in insurrection, as they gained so great a profit from the travellers who passed through the county, and who would now be prevented coming. 'Indeed,' says one, 'it would have made a heart of flint to have melted and wept, to have seen the breaking up of the house, and the sorrowful departure of the monks, every person bent himself to filch and spoil what he could.' The abbey became the property of Thomas Sydney, whose son married the sister of Sir Francis Walsingham, and died very wealthy. In the Bodleian library there is a poem, entitled a *Lament for Walsingham*, from which we take a short specimen.

'Bitter, bitter oh to behoulde,
The grasse to growe,
Where the walles of Walsingham
So stately did shewe.

Oules doe scrike where the sweetest himmes
Lately wear songe,
Toades and serpents hold their dennes
Where the palmers did throng.

Weepe, weepe, O Walsingham,
Whose dayes are nightes,
Blessings turned to blasphemies,
Holy deedes to despites.

Sinne is where our Lady sate,
Heaven turned is to helle,
Sathan sitte where our Lord did swaye,
Walsingham, O farewell!'

But few ruins remain of this once 'holy lande of blessed Walsingham.' A part of the east front of the priory church, with a circular window of flowing tracery, and four windows of the refectory, are standing in the prettily laid-out grounds of the

GATEWAY OF WALSINGHAM PRIORY.

present owner of the estate, the Lee-Warners, by whom it was purchased in 1766.

## HARROW SHOOTINGS AND HARROW SPEECHES.

The 4th of August is associated with a very old custom at Harrow School—now obsolete, and superseded by a celebration of another kind. The practice of *archery* was coeval with the establishment of this celebrated institution. Indeed, by the rules laid down by John Lyon, the founder of the school, the necessary implements for the proper exercise of this amusement were required to be furnished by the parents of every boy on his entering the school. 'You shall allow your child,' said the ordinances drawn up in 1592, 'at all times bow-shafts, bow-strings, and a bracer.' The *Butts* at Harrow was, in former days, a beautiful spot a little to the west of the London road, backed by a lofty insulated knoll, crowned with trees, and having rows of grassy seats, cut on the slopes, for spectators. In the early ages of the school, it was customary for the boys to contend for the prize of a silver arrow; the number of competitors being at first six, but afterwards increased to twelve. The competitors were attired in fancy-dresses, white, green, or red satin, decked with spangles; with green silk sashes and caps. In the *Harrow Calendar* it is stated that one of these dresses is still preserved in the school-library, where it has been for nearly a hundred years. Whoever shot within the three circles which surrounded the bull's-eye, was saluted with a concert of French-horns; and he who first shot twelve times nearest the mark, was proclaimed victor, and marched back in triumph from the Butts to the town, at the head of a procession of boys, carrying and waving the silver arrow. The entertainments of the day were concluded with a ball, given by the winner, in the school-room, to which all the neighbouring families were invited. The late master, the Rev. Dr Drury, spoke of an old print or drawing of the Butts on the day of celebration, in these terms: 'The village barber is seen walking off, like one of Homer's heroes, with an arrow in his eye, stooping forward, and evidently in great pain, with his hand applied to the wound. It is perfectly true that this Tom of Coventry was so punished; and I have somewhere a ludicrous account of it in Dr Parr's all but illegible holograph.' Scattered through the early volumes of the *Gentleman's Magazine* are many notices of the Harrow shootings, with the names of the successful competitors. The gossip of the school comprises a story that, in the last century, three brothers successively carried off three silver arrows, which their father stuck up in three corners of his drawing-room; it became a matter of family pride to fill up the fourth corner; and this was effected by the success of a fourth brother in 1766. Another anecdote was communicated to the Dean of Peterborough by the Hon. Archibald Macdonald. On one particular 4th of August, two boys, Merry and Love, were equal or nearly so, and both of them decidedly superior to the rest. Love, having shot his last arrow into the bull's eye, was greeted by his school-fellows with a shout, '*Omnia vincit Amor.*' 'Not so,' said Merry in an under voice, '*Nos non cedamus Amori;*' and carefully adjusting his shaft, shot it into the bull's eye, a full inch nearer to the centre than his exulting competitor. So he gained the day.

The Harrow Shootings were abolished in 1771. Dr Heath, the head-master at that time, was dissatisfied with the frequent exemptions from the regular business of the school, which those who practised as competitors for the prize claimed as a privilege not to be infringed upon. He also observed, as other masters had done before him, that the contest usually brought down a band of profligate and disorderly persons from the metropolis, to the demoralisation of the village. The Harrovians deeply regretted the ending of their old amusement; and, as a record of it, they still preserve the silver arrow made for 1772, but not used. The annual shootings were succeeded by annual speeches, which, under many modifications, have continued ever since.

# AUGUST 5.

**St Memmius or Menge, first bishop and apostle of Chalons-sur-Marne, end of 3d century. St Afra and her companions, martyrs, 304. St Oswald, king and martyr, 642. The Dedication of St Mary ad Nives, about 435.**

## THE ARM OF ST OSWALD.

Incredible sums were sometimes given by the monastic bodies, in the dark ages, for relics of saints. Amongst such valuables, the arm of St Oswald, preserved in Peterborough Cathedral, was in especial esteem, insomuch that King Stephen once came to see it; on which occasion, besides presenting his ring, he remitted a debt of forty marks to the abbey. 'The story told of the arm is, that Oswald, who was king of Northumberland, and a very liberal benefactor to the poor, sitting at meat one day, a great number of beggars came to the gate for relief, upon which Oswald sent them meat from his own table, and there not being enough to serve them all, he caused one of his silver dishes to be cut in pieces, and distributed among the rest; "which Aidanus, a bishop who came out of Scotland to instruct and convert these northern parts of England, beholding, took the king by the right hand, saying: *Nunquam inveterascat haec manus!*" Poor Oswald, however, quarrelling with one of his neighbours, Pender, king of Murcia, and encountering his army at Oswestre, or as others say at Burne, was vanquished and slain, when some, remembering Bishop Aidanus's blessing, took care to preserve his arm, which was finally treasured up at Peterborough.'—Bliss's *Notes to Hearne's Diary.*

---

*Born.*—John, Lord Wrottesley, distinguished astronomer, and president of the Royal Society, 1798.

*Died.*—Xerxes I., king of Persia, murdered by Artabanus 465 B.C.; Louis III. of France, 882 A.D.; Sir Reginald Bray, architect, 1503; John, Earl of Gowrie, slain at Perth, 1600; Frederick, Lord North, statesman, 1792; Richard, Lord Howe, naval hero, 1799; Charles James Blomfield, bishop of London, 1857, *Fulham.*

## THE GOWRIE CONSPIRACY.

It is little known that the 5th of August was once observed in England as a holiday, exactly in the same manner as the 5th of November, and for a cause of the same nature. On that day, in the year 1600, King James, then ruling Scotland alone, narrowly escaped death at the hands of two conspirators of his own people—the Earl of Gowrie, and his brother Alexander Ruthven. It was a strange confused affair, which the death of the two conspirators prevented from being thoroughly cleared up; and there have not been wanting individuals, both at the time and since, to doubt the reality of the alleged design against the king. It is, however, not difficult for an unprejudiced person to accept the conspiracy as real, and to comprehend even its scope and drift.

The king, on that August morning, was mounting his horse at Falkland, to go out a-hunting—his almost daily practice—when Alexander Ruthven, who was a youth barely twenty, came up and entered into private conversation with him. The young man told a wild-looking story, about a vagrant Highlander who knew of a secret treasure, and who might be conversed with at Gowrie House, in Perth. The king's curiosity and love of money were excited, and he agreed to go to Perth after the hunt. He then rode from the field in company with Ruthven, followed by some of his courtiers, to one of whom (the Duke of Lennox) he imparted the object in view. It appears that Lennox did not like the expedition, and he told the king so; but the king, nevertheless, proceeded, only asking the duke to have an eye upon Alexander Ruthven, to keep close, and be ready to give assistance, if needful.

The king and his followers, about a dozen in number, came to Gowrie House in time for the early dinner of that age, and, after the meal was concluded, he allowed himself to be conducted by Alexander Ruthven through a series of chambers, the doors of which the young man locked behind him, till they came to a small turret closet, connected

GOWRIE HOUSE.

with an upper room at the end of the house, where James found, instead of the man with 'the pose' he had expected, one completely armed, a servant of the earl. Ruthven now clapped his hat upon his head, and snatching a dagger from the armed man, said to the king: 'Sir, ye maun be my prisoner! Remember on my father's deid [death]!' alluding to the execution of his father for a similar treason to this, sixteen years before. The king remonstrated, shewing that he, as a minor at the time, was not concerned in his father's death, and had of his own accord restored the family to its rank and estates; and he asked meekly of the young man what he aimed at by his present proceedings. Ruthven said he would bring his brother to tell what they wanted: meanwhile the king must promise to stay quietly there till he returned. During his brief absence, the king induced the armed man to open one of the windows, looking to the neighbouring street; and while the man was proceeding to open the other, which looked to the courtyard below, Ruthven rushed in, crying there was no remede, and attempted to bind the king's hands with a garter. A struggle ensued, in which the armed servant gave the king some useful help, and James was just able to get near the window, and call out 'Treason!' It appeared from the deposition of the servant, that he had been placed there by his master, without any attempt to prepare him for the part he was to play, or to ascertain if he could be depended upon. In point of fact, the sight of the king and of Alexander Ruthven's acts filled him with terror. He opened the door, and let in Sir John Ramsay, one of the royal attendants, who immediately relieved his struggling master by stabbing Ruthven, and thrusting him down the stair. As the conspirator descended, wounded and bleeding, he was met by two or three others of the king's attendants coming up upon the alarm, and by them was despatched, saying as he fell: 'Alas! I had not the wyte [blame] of it!'

Immediately after the king left the dining-room, an officer or friend of the Earl of Gowrie had raised a sudden report among the royal attendants, that their master was gone home—was by this time past the Mid Inch (an adjacent public green)—so that they all rushed forth to follow him. The porter, on being asked by some of them if the king had gone forth, denied it; but the earl called him liar, and insisted that his highness had departed. It was while they were hurrying to mount and follow, that the king was heard to cry 'Treason!' from the turret-window. The earl now drew his sword, and, summoning his retinue, about eighty in number, to follow him, he entered the house, and appeared in the room where his brother had just received his first wound. The four gentlemen of the royal train, having first thrust the king for his safety into the little closet, encountered the earl and the seven attendants who entered with him, and in brief space Gowrie was pierced through the heart by Ramsay, and his servants sent wounded and discomfited down stairs. Soon after, the Earl of Mar and other friends of the king, who had been trying for some time to force an entrance by the locked-up gallery, came in, and then James knelt down on the bloody floor, with his friends about him, and returned thanks to God for his deliverance.

It was a wild and hardly intelligible scene. Gowrie and his brother were accomplished young men, in good favour at court, and popular in Perth; they had the best prospects for their future life; it seemed unaccountable that, without giving any previous hint of such a design, they should have plunged suddenly into a murderous conspiracy against their sovereign, and yet been so ill provided with the means of carrying it out successfully. Yet the facts were clear and palpable, that the king had been enticed, first to their own town of Perth, and then into a remote part of their house, and there murderously assaulted. Evidence afterwards came out, to shew that they had been led to frame a plan for the seizure of the royal person, though whether for the sake of the influence they could thereby exercise in the government, or with some hazy design of taking vengeance for their father's death, cannot be ascertained. It also appeared that, at Padua University, whence they were only of late returned, they had studied necromancy, which they continued to practise in Scotland. It seems not unlikely that they were partly incited by some response, paltering with them in a double sense, which they conceived they had obtained to some ambitious question. Their attainder—nay, the attainder of the whole family—followed. The people generally rejoiced in the king's deliverance, and his popularity was manifestly increased by the dangers he had passed. Yet a few of the clergy professed to entertain doubts about the transaction; and one of eminence, named Robert Bruce, underwent a banishment of thirty years rather than give these up. His spirit has reappeared in a few modern writers, of the kind who habitually feel a preference for the side of a question which has least to say for itself. That a king, constitutionally devoid of physical courage, should have gone with only a hunting-horn hanging from his neck, and a handful of attendants in the guise of the chase, to attack the life of a powerful noble in his own house, and in the midst of armed retainers and an attached burgal populace; that he should have adventured solitarily into a retired part of his intended victim's house, to effect this object, while none of his courtiers knew where he was or what he was going to do; meets an easy faith with this party; while in the fact of Alexander Ruthven coming to conduct the king to Perth, in the glaring attempt of the earl, by false reports and lies, to send away the royal train from his house; in the fact that the two brothers and their retainers were armed, while the king was not; and in the clear evidence which the armed man of the turret-chamber gave in support of the king's statements; they can see no manner of force. Minds of this kind are governed by prejudices, and not by the love of truth, and it is vain to reason with them.

## LONDON SHOEBLACKS.

Ten years before the cry of 'Clean your boots, sir!' became familiar to the ears of the present generation of Londoners, Mr Charles Knight described 'the last of the shoeblacks,' as a short, large-headed son of Africa, rendered melancholy by impending bankruptcy, who might be seen, about the year 1820, plying his calling in one of the many courts on the north side of Fleet Street, till driven into the workhouse by the desertion of his last customer. This unfortunate was probably the individual alluded to by a correspondent of Mr Hone as sitting under the covered entrance of Red Lion Court. He attributes the ruin of the fraternity to Messrs Day and Martin, and says he remembered the time when they were to be seen, as now, at the corner of every street. Their favourite pitches then were the steps of St Andrew's Church, Holborn, and the site of Finsbury Square, at that period a large open space of ground. Instead of the square box used by our scarlet-coated brigade, their predecessors employed a tripod, or three-legged stool, and carried their implements in a large tin kettle. Their stock in trade consisted of an earthen pot filled with blacking (compounded of ivory black, brown sugar, vinegar, and water), a knife, two or three brushes, a stick with a piece of rag at the end, and an old wig; the latter being used to whisk the dust or wipe the wet dirt from the shoes. The operation, in those days of shoes and shoebuckles, was one requiring some dexterity to avoid soiling the stocking or buckle. Some liberal shoeblackers, as Johnson calls them, provided an old pair of shoes and yesterday's paper for the convenience and entertainment of their patrons while the foot grew 'black that was with dirt embrowned.'

The author of the *Art of Living in London* (1784) counsels his readers to

'Avoid the miser's narrow care,
Which robs the shoeblack of his early fare;
No—let some son of Fleet Street or the Strand,
Some sooty son, with implements at hand,
Who hourly watches with no other view,
Than to repolish the bespattered shoe;
Earn by his labour the offensive gains,
Nor grudge the trifle that rewards his pains.'

A writer in *The World* for the 31st January 1754, humorously exalts the shoeblack's calling above his own. He complains that 'once an author, always an author,' is the dictum of the world—'A man convicted of being a wit is disqualified for business during life; no city apprentice will trust him with his shoes, nor will the poor beau set a foot upon his stool, from an opinion that for want of skill in his calling his blacking must be bad, or for want of attention be applied to the stocking instead of the shoe. That almost every author would choose to set up in this business, if he had wherewithal to begin with, must appear very plainly to all candid observers, from the natural propensity which he discovers towards blackening.' Shoeblacks were also known as japanners. Pope says:

'The poor have the same itch;
They change their weekly barber, weekly news,
Prefer a new japanner to their shoes.'

Gay, not content with telling how

'The black youth at chosen stands rejoice,
And "clean your shoes" resounds from every voice,'

seeks to make the shoeblack of more importance, by giving him a goddess, though an unsavoury one, for a mother. According to the poet, this deity, shocked at finding her son grow up a beggar, entreated the gods to teach him some art:

'The gods her suit allowed,
And made him useful to the walking crowd.
To cleanse the miry feet, and o'er the shoe,
With nimble skill the glossy black renew.
Each power contributes to relieve the poor;
With the strong bristles of the mighty boar
Diana forms his brush; the god of day
A tripod gives, amid the crowded way
To raise the dirty foot and ease his toil;
Kind Neptune fills his vase with fetid oil,
Pressed from the enormous whale; the god of fire,
From whose dominions smoky clouds aspire,
Among these generous presents joins his part,
And aids with soot the new japanning art.'
—*Trivia.*

The art, however, was scarcely new in Gay's time, for Middleton, in his *Roaring Girl* (1611), speaks of shoes 'stinking of blacking;' and Kitely, in *Every Man in his Humour*, exclaims:

'Mock me all over,
From my flat cap unto my shining shoes.'

In 1851, some gentlemen connected with the Ragged Schools determined to revive the brotherhood of boot-cleaners for the convenience of foreign visitors to the Exhibition, and commenced the experiment by sending out five boys in the now well-known red uniform. The scheme succeeded beyond expectation; the boys were patronised by natives as well as aliens, and the Shoeblack Society and its brigade were regularly organised. During the Exhibition season, about twenty-five boys were kept constantly employed, and cleaned no less than 101,000 pair of boots. The receipts of the brigade during its first year amounted to £656. Since that time, thanks to a wise combination of discipline and liberality, the Shoeblack Society has gone on and prospered, and proved the parent of other societies. Every district in London now has its corps of shoeblacks in every variety of uniform, and while the number of boys has increased from tens to hundreds, their earnings have increased from hundreds to thousands. Numbers of London waifs and strays have been rescued from idleness and crime, and metropolitan pedestrians deprived of any excuse for being dirtily shod.

---

# AUGUST 6.

The Transfiguration of our Lord. St Xystus or Sixtus II., pope and martyr, about 258. Saints Justus and Pastor, martyrs, 304.

---

*Born.*—Matthew Parker, archbishop of Canterbury, eminent divine, 1504, *Norwich;* Bulstrode Whitelock, eminent parliamentarian, 1605, *London;* Nicholas Malebranche, distinguished French philosopher (*Recherche de la Verité*), 1638, *Paris;* François-de-Salignac-de-Lamothe Fenelon, archbishop of Cambray, and author of *Telemaque*, 1651, *Château de Fenelon, Perigord;* Jean Baptiste Bessières, French general, 1768, *Preissac, near Cahors;* Dr William Hyde Wollaston, chemist, 1766.

*Died.*—St Dominic de Guzman, founder of the Dominicans, 1221, *Bologna;* Anne Shakspeare, widow of the dramatist, 1623, *Stratford-upon-Avon;* Ben Jonson, dramatist, 1637, *London;* Diego Rodriguez de Silva y Velasquez, celebrated Spanish painter, 1660, *Madrid;* James Petit Andrews, author of *History of Great Britain*, 1797, *London.* General Robert Cunningham, Baron Rossmore, eminent public character in Ireland, 1801.

## SHAKSPEARE'S WIFE.

Obscure as are many of the points in Shakspeare's life, it is known that his wife's maiden name was Anne Hathaway, and that her father was a substantial yeoman at Shottery, near Stratford-on-Avon. Shakspeare was barely nineteen, and his bride about six-and-twenty, when they married. The marriage-bond has been brought to light, dated November 1582. Singularly little is known of their domestic life; and it is only by putting together a number of small indications that the various editors of Shakspeare's works have arrived at any definite conclusions concerning the family. One circumstance seems rather to tell against the supposition of strong affection on his side: Shakspeare drew out his whole will without once mentioning his wife, and then put in a few words interlined. The will points out what shall be bequeathed to his daughter Judith (Mrs Quiney), his daughter Susanna (Mrs Hall), his sister Joan Hart, her three sons, William, and Thomas, and Michael, and a considerable number of friends and acquaintances at Stratford; but the sole mention of Anne Shakspeare is in the item: 'I give unto my wife my second-best bed, with the furniture.' Malone accepted this interlined bequest as a proof that Shakspeare had, in making his will, forgot his wife, and then only remembered her with what was equivalent to an insult. Mr Knight has, on the other hand, pointed out that Mrs Shakspeare would, by law, have a third part of her husband's means; so that there was presumably the less reason to remember her with special gifts of affection. She died on the 6th of August 1623, and was buried on the 8th, in Stratford church. Her gravestone is next to the stone with the doggrel inscription,* but nearer to the north wall, upon which Shakspeare's monument is placed. The stone has a brass plate, with the following inscription:

'Heere lyeth interred the body of Anne, wife of William Shakespeare, who dep.ted this Life the 6th day of Avgv. 1623, being of the age of 67 Yeares.

Vbera tu mater, tu lac vitamque dedisti;
Væ mihi! pro tanto munere saxa dabo.
Quam mallem amoveat lapidem bonus Angelus ore',
Exeat [ut] Christi corpus, imago tua;
Sed nil vota valent, venias cito, Christe, resurget,
Clausa licet tumulo, mater, et astra petet.'

Mr Knight considers this as a strong evidence of the love in which Shakspeare's wife was regarded by her daughter, with whom, he thinks it probable, she lived during her latter years.

## BEN JONSON.

Ben Jonson occupies a prominent position on the British Parnassus; yet his works are little read, because there is something of roughness and boldness in his style, which repels that class of readers who read poetry for recreation, rather than critically. But hundreds, who find little pleasure in reading his verses, feel an interest in his personal history.

Jonson's poetical career was one of great activity. His was a prolific muse: his pen was seldom still. Much of his writing is lost, and yet his surviving works may be described as voluminous. All that labour which he expended in dramatic composition, in conjunction with brothers of the craft, many poems, some plays, and most of his prose, have passed into oblivion; yet there still remain to us upwards of twenty plays, about forty masques, a book of epigrams, many small poems, epistles, and translations, a book of *Discoveries*, as he calls a collection of prose scraps, and an unfinished Grammar of the English Language, written in English and Latin.

Much of Jonson's life is involved in obscurity; partly from the usual neglect of his age in recording contemporary history, but still more from the scandals and misrepresentations of those numerous maligners, which his fame or his bluntness raised up against him. For Ben spoke out his whole mind, whether others liked it or not; and probably, like his great namesake in later times, somewhat overpowered and oppressed the lesser wits.

Ben, or Benjamin Jonson, was born in Westminster, in 1574, a month after the death of his father, but his family was of Scotch extraction. They came of the *Johnstons* of Annandale, the name having been so far changed in its migration southwards. The dramatist's mother married again, and, whatever might have been his father's position in life, his step-father was a master-bricklayer. This second parent allowed him to obtain a good education; he went to Westminster school, and in due time proceeded to Cambridge. But before he had been long at the university, the necessary funds were found wanting, and Ben returned home with a heavy heart, to become a bricklayer. This employment, of which, in after-years, he was often derisively reminded, proved uncongenial. He 'could not endure,' he tells us, 'the occupation of a bricklayer:' so he tried the military profession, and joined the army in Flanders. Before long our valiant hero sickened of the sword, and returned home, 'bringing with him,' says Gifford, 'the reputation of a brave man, a smattering of Dutch, and an empty purse.'

At this critical juncture, being a good scholar, and passionately devoted to learning and literature, Jonson commenced writing for the stage. Before he had acquired any great literary notoriety, he attained to one less satisfactory, by getting into prison, for killing a man in a duel. While he remained in confinement, a priest drew him over to the Roman Catholic church, which he conscientiously persisted in for twelve years, in the meantime marrying a Roman Catholic wife. Gradually his fame became established, and for many years—after the death of Shakspeare—he retained undisputed possession of the highest poetic eminence. He grew into great favour with James I., and found constant employment in writing the court masques, and similar compositions for great occasions, which among the nobility and public bodies, in those days afforded occupation for the pens of poets. He also went to France for a short time in 1613, as tutor to the son of Sir Walter Raleigh, with whom, as with many other great ones, Ben lived on intimate and honourable terms.

About the time of Jonson's visit to France, the king, among other proofs of kindness, made him poet-laureate, with a life-pension of a hundred marks.

'Learned James,
Who favoured quiet and the arts of peace,
Which in his halcyon-days found large increase,
Friend to the humblest, if deserving, swain,
Who was himself a part of Phœbus' train,
Declared great Jonson worthiest to receive
The garland which the Muses' hands did weave;
And though his bounty did sustain his days,
Gave a most welcome pension to his praise.'

In 1618, the poet made a pedestrian tour into Scotland, mainly, it has been surmised, to visit his friend the poet Drummond. Taylor, the so-called Water-poet, had come to Scotland at the same time on a tour, designed to prove whether he could peregrinate beyond the Tweed without money; a question which he solved in the

* 'Good Frend for Jesus sake forbeare,
To digg the dust encloased heare:
Bleste be $\frac{e}{y}$ man $\frac{t}{y}$ spares thes stones,
And curst be he $\frac{t}{y}$ moves my bones.'

affirmative, as the well-known *Penniless Pilgrimage* avouches. He found his 'approved good friend,' Jonson, living with Mr John Stuart at Leith, and received from him a gold piece of the value of twenty-two shillings; a solid proof of the kind feelings of honest Ben towards his brethren of Parnassus. Jonson, on this occasion, spent some time with the Duke of Lennox in the west, and formed a design of writing a piscatorial play, with Loch Lomond as its scene. He passed the winter in Scotland, and in April was for three weeks the guest of Drummond at his romantic seat of Hawthornden, on the Esk. Here he drank freely—perhaps the bacchanalian habits of the north had somewhat corrupted him—indulged in the hearty egotism of a roysterer, and spoke disparagingly of many of his contemporaries, a little to the disgust of the modest Scottish poet, who took memoranda of his conversation, since published. On this subject there has been, in our day, a good deal of unnecessary discussion, to which it would be useless further to advert.

It is observable how little Jonson cared for worldly dignity. James had a wish to knight him, but he eluded the honour. He liked the love of men better. A jovial boon-companion, an affectionate

friend, he was ever as open-handed as he was open-hearted. When he had money, his friends shared it, or feasted on it. Towards the close of his life, when sickness overtook him, and his popularity somewhat declined, after the death of James, he fell into poverty. He was even reduced so far as to have to ask for assistance; but he did it in a manly way. There is nothing unworthy of a man in the following letter; how superior is it to the meanness of other scribblers in those days!

'MY NOBLEST LORD AND BEST PATRON—

I send no borrowing epistle to provoke your lordship, for I have neither fortune to repay, nor security to engage, that will be taken; but I make a most humble petition to your lordship's bounty, to succour my present necessities this good time of Easter, and it shall conclude all begging-requests hereafter on the behalf of your Truest Beadsman and most Humble Servant, B. J.

TO THE EARL OF NEWCASTLE.'

The Earl of Newcastle was now Jonson's chief patron. Hearing of the poet's distress, Charles I., who had gradually taken him into favour, sent him a hundred pounds. He also willingly renewed the pension bestowed by his father, increasing the one hundred marks to one hundred pounds, adding from his own stores a tierce of Canary (Ben's favourite wine).

Ben's sickness grew upon him, and he died on the 6th of August 1637, and was buried in Westminster Abbey on the 9th. The curious inscription, by which his grave was marked—

'O RARE BEN JONSON!'—

and which formed the concluding words of the verses written and displayed in the celebrated club-room of Ben's clique, is said to have been a temporary memorandum, until such time as a fitting monument could be erected. The story says that one of Ben's friends gave a mason, who was on the spot, eighteenpence to cut it. The troubles of the civil wars prevented the execution of a more ambitious memorial. Some have spoken of the brief legend as if it were a thing profane in that sacred place of tombs; we must confess that we think otherwise. By whatever accident or freak it came to be placed there, we fancy that it contains a true vein of pathos, and feel it to exercise a thrilling influence over us each time we look at it and read it.

If Ben, by his freeness, as well as his greatness, made enemies, he secured to himself innumerable friends by the same means. No man possessed more loving friends than he among the great or among the unregarded; no man wrote more loving verses to those whom he loved. The club at the Mermaid was the meeting-place of all those brothers of song; there they held their jovial literary orgies, which have made the Mermaid a place and a name never to be forgotten.

'Souls of poets dead and gone,
What Elysium have ye known,
Happy field, or mossy-cavern,
Choicer than the Mermaid Tavern?'

So Keats expresses the unanimous feeling of all who loved Ben. Shakspeare, Sir Walter Raleigh, the learned Selden, Dr Donne, Beaumont, Fletcher, Carew, Cotton, Herrick, and innumerable other worthies, waited religiously on the far-famed oracle; and the recollection of their meetings, and of Ben's oracular utterances, dwelt in their minds when all was over, like the remembrance of a lost Eden, as Herrick, in conclusion, shall bear witness:

AN ODE FOR BEN JONSON.

Ah, Ben!
Say how, or when
Shall we thy guests
Meet at those lyric feasts,
Made at the Sun,
The Dog, the Triple Tun?
Where we such clusters had,
As made us nobly wild, not mad;
And yet each verse of thine
Outdid the meat, outdid the frolic wine.

My Ben,
Or come agen,
Or send to us
Thy wit's great overplus:
But teach us yet
Wisely to husband it;
Lest we that talent spend:
And having once brought to an end
That precious stock; the store
Of such a wit: the world should have no more.

---

## A CABINET OF GEMS, FROM BEN JONSON'S DISCOVERIES.

Very few books contain as much wisdom in as little space as Ben Jonson's book of *Discoveries.* And yet, as we never hear it spoken of or quoted, it seems very clear that no one ever reads it. We grace our store-house of useful curiosities with one or two specimens of the bright golden ore hid in abundance in this unexplored mine. As the extracts are made as short as possible, the reader will observe that the words at the head of each are not always our author's, but often merely our own nomenclature for the gems in our little cabinet:

*Fortune.*—Ill-fortune never crushed that man whom good-fortune deceived not.

*Self-reliance.*—He knows not his own strength, that hath not met adversity.

*Counsel.*—No man is so foolish, but may give another good counsel sometimes; and no man is so wise, but may easily err, if he will take no other's counsel but his own.

*True Wisdom.*—Wisdom without honesty is mere craft and cozenage.

*Discernment.*—There are many that, with more ease, will find fault with what is spoken foolishly, than can give allowance to that wherein you are wise silently.

*Stupidity.*—A man cannot imagine that thing so foolish, or rude, but will find or enjoy an admirer.

*Short-sightedness of Discontent.*—If we would consider what our affairs are indeed, not what they are called, we should find more evils belonging to us, than happen to us.

*Man, a Mimetic Animal.*—I have considered our whole life is like a play: wherein every man, forgetful of himself, is in travail with expression of another.

*A Bricklayer's Cunning.*—I have discovered that a feigned familiarity in great ones, is a note of certain usurpation on the less.

*Vice and Virtue.*—If we will look with our understanding, and not our senses, we may behold virtue and beauty (though covered with rags) in their brightness; and vice and deformity so much the fouler, in having all the splendour of riches to gild them, or the false light of honour and power to help them.

*Self-approval.*—The worst opinion gotten for doing well should delight us.

*Being above seeming.*—I am glad when I see any man avoid the infamy of a vice; but to shun the vice itself were better.

*The best Writer.*—The order of God's creatures in themselves is not only admirable and glorious, but eloquent: then he who could apprehend the consequence of things in their truth, and utter his apprehensions as truly, were the best writer or speaker.

*Poesy.*—A dulcet and gentle philosophy, which leads on and guides us by the hand to action, with a ravishing delight, and incredible sweetness.

## DEATH OF LORD ROSSMORE.

Lord Rossmore, who, for many years in the latter part of the last century, was commander-in-chief of the forces in Ireland, died suddenly during the night, between the 5th and 6th of August 1801, at his house in Dublin, having attended a viceregal drawing-room at the Castle till so late as eleven o'clock on the preceding evening. Sir Jonah Barrington, who was Lord Rossmore's neighbour in the country, relates, in his *Personal Sketches of his Own Times,** an occurrence connected with his lordship's unlooked-for death, which he frankly calls 'the most extraordinary and inexplicable' of his whole existence. It may be premised that his lordship was a remarkably healthy old man, and Sir Jonah states that he 'never heard of him having a single day's indisposition.' Lady Barrington had met Lord Rossmore at the drawing-room, and received a cheerful message from him for her husband, regarding a party they were invited to at his country-house of Mount Kennedy, in the county of Wicklow.

Sir Jonah and Lady Barrington retired to their chamber about twelve, and 'towards two,' says Sir Jonah, 'I was awakened by a sound of a very extraordinary nature. I listened: it occurred first at short intervals; it resembled neither a voice nor an instrument; it was softer than any voice, and wilder than any music, and seemed to float in the air. I don't know wherefore, but my heart beat forcibly; the sound became still more plaintive, till it almost died away in the air; when a sudden change, as if excited by a pang, altered its tone: it seemed *descending.* I felt every nerve tremble: it was not a *natural* sound, nor could I make out the point whence it came.

'At length I awakened Lady Barrington, she heard it as well as myself, and suggested that it might be an Eolian harp: but to that instrument it bore no similitude: it was altogether a different *character of sound.* She at first appeared less affected than myself, but was subsequently more so.

'We now went to a large window in our bedroom, which looked directly upon a small garden underneath: the sound, which first appeared *descending,* now seemed obviously to *ascend* from a grassplot immediately below our window. It continued; Lady Barrington requested that I would call up her maid, which I did, and she was evidently much more affected than either of us. The sounds lasted for more than half an hour. At last a deep, heavy, throbbing sigh seemed to issue from the spot, and was as shortly succeeded by a sharp but low cry, and by the distinct exclamation, thrice repeated, of "Rossmore! Rossmore! Rossmore!" I will not attempt to describe my own sensations; indeed I cannot. The maid fled in terror from the window, and it was with difficulty I prevailed on Lady Barrington to return to bed: in about a minute after, the sound died gradually away, until all was silent.

'Lady Barrington, who is not *superstitious,* as I am, attributed this circumstance to a hundred different causes, and made me promise that I would not mention it next day at Mount Kennedy, since we should thereby be rendered *laughing-stocks.*

* 2 vols. London, 1827. Vol. ii. pp. 151-155.

At length, wearied with speculations, we fell into a sound slumber.

'About seven the ensuing morning, a strong rap at my chamber-door awakened me. The recollection of the past night's adventure rushed instantly upon my mind, and rendered me very unfit to be taken suddenly on any subject.

'It was light: I went to the door, when my faithful servant, Lawler, exclaimed on the other side: "Oh Lord, sir!"

"What is the matter?" said I hurriedly.

"Oh, sir!" ejaculated he, "Lord Rossmore's footman was running past the door in great haste, and told me in passing that my lord, after coming from the Castle, had gone to bed in perfect health, but that, about *half after two* this morning, his own man, hearing a noise in his master's bed (he slept in the same room), went to him, and found him in the agonies of death; and before he could alarm the other servants, all was over!"

'I conjecture nothing. I only relate the incident as unequivocally *matter of fact*. Lord Rossmore *was absolutely dying at the moment I heard his name pronounced!*'

Sir Jonah was very much quizzed for publishing this story; many letters were sent to him on the subject, some of them abusing him as an enemy to religion. He consequently, in a third volume of his Sketches, published five years afterwards, thus referred to his former narration: 'I absolutely persist unequivocally as to the matters therein recited, and shall do so to the day of my death, after which I shall be able to ascertain individually the matter of fact to a downright certainty, though I fear I shall be enjoined to absolute secrecy.' *

It may be interesting to Scottish readers to know, that Lord Rossmore was identical with a youth named Robert Cunningham, who makes some appearance in the history of 'the Forty-five.' Having attached himself, with some other young men, as volunteers to General Cope's army, on its landing at Dunbar, he and a Mr Francis Garden acted as scouts to ascertain the movements of the approaching Highlanders, but, in consequence of tarrying to solace themselves with oysters and sherry in a hostelry at Fisherrow, were captured by a Jacobite party. They were at first threatened with the death due to spies, but ultimately allowed to slip away,† and lived to be, the one an Irish peer, the other a Scotch judge.

---

## THE SEA-SERPENT.

On the 6th of August 1848, H. M. S. *Dædalus*, on her way from the Cape of Good Hope to St Helena, came near a singular-looking object in the water. Captain M'Quhae attempted to wear the ship close up to it, but the state of the wind prevented a nearer approach than two hundred yards. The officers, watching carefully through their glasses, could trace eye, mouth, nostril, and form, in the floating mass to which their attention was directed. The general impression produced was, that the animal belonged rather to the lizard than to the serpent tribe; its movement was steady, rapid, and uniform, as if propelled by fins rather than by undulating power. The size appeared to be very great; but as only a portion of the animal was above water, no exact estimate of dimensions could be made. Neither officers nor seamen ever saw anything similar to it before.

The report of this incident caused a stir among the British naturalists, who were eager to meet the popular fancy of the sea-serpent with facts shewing the extreme improbability of the existence of any such creature. Captain M'Quhae, nevertheless, insisted on the correctness of his report, and many professed to attach little consequence to the merely negative evidence brought against it.

On the 12th of December 1857, the ship *Castilian*, bound from Bombay to Liverpool, was, at six in the evening, about ten miles distant from St Helena. A monster that suddenly appeared in the water was described by the three chief officers of the ship—Captain G. H. Harrington, Mr W. Davies, and Mr E. Wheeler; the description was entered by Captain Harrington in his Official Meteorological Journal, and was forwarded to the Board of Trade. Nothing can be more plain than the honest good faith in which the narrative is written. The chief facts, in the captain's own words, are as follows: 'While myself and officers were standing on the lee-side of the poop, looking towards the island, we were startled by the sight of a huge marine animal, which reared its head out of the water, within twenty yards of the ship; when it suddenly disappeared for about half a minute, and then made its appearance in the same manner again—shewing us distinctly its neck and head, about ten or twelve feet out of the water. Its head was shaped like a long nun-buoy; and I suppose the diameter to have been seven or eight feet in the largest part, with a kind of scroll, or tuft of loose skin, encircling it about two feet from the top. The water was discoloured for several hundred feet from its head: so much so, that on its first appearance my impression was that the ship was in broken water, produced, as I supposed, by some volcanic agency since the last time I passed the island; but the second appearance completely dispelled those fears, and assured us that it was a monster of extraordinary length, which appeared to be moving slowly towards the land. The ship was going too fast, to enable us to reach the mast-head in time to form a correct estimate of its extreme length; but from what we saw from the deck, we conclude that it must have been over two hundred feet long. The boatswain and several of the crew who observed it from the top-gallant fore-castle, state that it was more than double the length of the ship, in which case it must have been five hundred feet. Be that as it may, I am convinced that it belonged to the serpent tribe; it was of a dark colour about the head, and was covered with several white spots.' Captain Harrington, some time afterwards, strengthened his testimony by that of other persons.

These are but examples of many confident reports made by persons professing to have seen the sea-serpent. Between 1844 and 1846, there were reported several appearances of this monster, in the seas fronting the United States and Canada. About the same time, a similar creature was stated to have presented itself near the shores of Norway, considered as identical with one depicted in Pontoppidan's *Natural History of Norway* (1752), of which

* *Sketches, &c.* Vol. iii., 1832, preface, p. xiii.

† See Scott's amusing account of this affair, *Quarterly Review*, xxxvi. 177. See also Home's Works, iii. 84.

a transcript is here given. Twenty years earlier, the sea-serpent was repeatedly seen on the coasts of the United States, also about 1818, and in 1806. It is remarkable with what distinctness, and with what confidence, the observers state their notions of what they saw—not meaning, we suppose, to deceive, but in all good faith taking hasty and

THE SEA-SERPENT—FROM PONTOPPIDAN.

excited impressions for serious and exact observation.

It chances that a creature, described by the beholders in as wonderful terms as were employed in any of the above instances, came ashore on the coast of Orkney in the year 1808. Even then exaggerated and most erroneous accounts of its decaying carcass were transmitted to scientific persons in Edinburgh, so that Dr Barclay, the ablest anatomist of his day, was completely misled in regard to the nature of the animal. Some of the bones of the vertebral column having fortunately been sent to Sir Everard Home, in London, he was able to determine that the creature was a shark, of the species *Squalus Maximus*, but one certainly of uncommon size, for it had been carefully measured by a carpenter with a foot-rule, and found to be fifty-five feet long.

It is not, however, the prevalent belief of naturalists, that the sea-serpent has been in all cases the *Squalus Maximus*. It seems to be now concluded, that the animal actually seen by M'Quhae and Harrington was more probably a certain species of seal known to inhabit the South Seas. The creature so often seen on the American coasts, was in all probability a shark, similar to that stranded in Orkney.

## AUGUST 7.

St Donatus, bishop of Arezzo, in Tuscany, martyr, 361. St Cajetan of Thienna, confessor, 1547.

*Born.*—Adam von Bartsch, engraver, 1757, *Vienna;* Princess Amelia, daughter of George III. of England, 1783; John Ayrton Paris, distinguished physician, 1785, *Cambridge.*

*Died.*—Leonidas, Spartan hero, slain at Thermopylæ, 480 B.C.; Herod Agrippa, persecutor of the Apostles, 44 A.D., *Cœsarea;* Henry IV. the Great, Emperor of Germany, 1106, *Liege;* Caroline of Brunswick, consort of George IV., 1821, *Hammersmith.*

### QUEEN CAROLINE.

On the 7th of August 1821, expired the ill-starred Caroline of Brunswick, stricken down, as was generally alleged, by vexation at being refused admission to Westminster Abbey in the previous month of July, when she desired to participate in the coronation ceremonies of her consort George IV. The immediate cause, however, was an illness by which she was suddenly attacked at Drury Lane Theatre, and which ran its course in the space of a few days.

The marriage of the Prince of Wales with his cousin Caroline Amelia Elizabeth, daughter of the Duke of Brunswick, was essentially one of those unions in which political motives form the leading element, to the almost entire exclusion of personal affection and regard. By his reckless prodigality and mismanagement, he had contracted debts to the amount nearly of £650,000, after having had only a few years before obtained a large parliamentary grant for the discharge of his obligations. His father, George III., who was determined that he should contract this alliance, had engaged that, on his complying with this requisition, another application would be made to the Commons, and a release effected for him out of his difficulties. The prince, thus beset, agreed to complete the match, though he used frequently to intimate his scorn of all *mariages de convênance.* A more serious impediment, such as in the case of an ordinary individual, would have acted as an effectual bar to the nuptials, existed in the union which, a few years before, he had contracted with Mrs Fitzherbert, a Roman Catholic lady, but which the Royal Marriage Act rendered in his case nugatory. This circumstance in his history was long a matter of doubt, but is now known to be a certainty. With such antecedents, it is easy to understand how his new matrimonial connection would be productive of anything but happiness.

Caroline herself is said to have unwillingly consented to the match, her affections being already engaged to another, but is reported to have expressed an enthusiastic admiration of the personal graces and generous qualities of her cousin. Her portrait had been forwarded to him, and he shewed it to one of his friends, asking him at the same time what he thought of it. The answer was that it gave the idea of a very handsome woman. Some joking then followed about 'buying a pig in a poke;' but, observed the prince, 'Lennox and Fitzroy have seen her, and they tell me she is even handsomer than her miniature.' The newspapers lauded her charms to the skies, descanting on the elegance of her figure, style of dress, her intelligent eyes and light auburn hair, and the blended gentleness and majesty by which her demeanour was characterised. They also extolled her performance on the harpsichord, and remarked that, as the prince was passionately fond of music, the harmony of the pair was insured. Great talk was made of the magnificent dressing-room fitted up for the young bride at a cost of twenty-five thousand pounds, and of a magnificent cap, presented by the bridegroom, adorned with a plume in imitation of his own crest, studded with brilliants. Her journey from her father's court to England was beset by many ill-omened delays and mischances, and not less than three months were consumed from various causes on the route. On the noon of Sunday, the 5th of April 1795, she landed at Greenwich, after a tempestuous voyage from Cuxhaven. An enthusiastic ovation attended her progress to London, where she was conducted in triumph to St James's Palace, and received by the Prince of Wales. On his first introduction to her, his nerves are reported to have received as great a shock as Henry VIII. experienced on meeting Anne of Cleves, and according to a well-known anecdote, he turned round to a friend, and whispered a request for a glass of brandy. Outwardly, however, he manifested the most complete satisfaction, and the rest of the royal family having arrived to pay their respects, a domestic party, such as George III. delighted in, was formed, and protracted till midnight. Three days afterwards, on the 8th of April, the marriage took place, evidently to the immense gratification of the king, who ever testified the utmost respect for his daughter-in-law, and acted through life her guardian and champion.

But this blink of sunshine was destined to be sadly evanescent. The honeymoon was scarcely over ere rumours began to be circulated of disagreements between the Prince and Princess of Wales, and at the end of a twelvemonth, a formal and lasting separation took place. One daughter had been born of the marriage, the Princess Charlotte, whose untimely end, twenty-two years afterwards, has invested her memory with so melancholy an interest. The circumstances attending the disunion of her parents have never been thoroughly explained, and by many the blame has been laid exclusively on the shoulders of her husband. That he was ill fitted for enjoying or preserving the felicities of domestic life, is indisputable; but there can now be no doubt, however much party zeal may have denied or extenuated the fact, that Caroline was a woman of such coarseness of mind, and such vulgarity of tastes, as would have disgusted many men of less refinement than the Prince of Wales. Her personal habits were even filthy, and of this well-authenticated stories are related, which dispose us to regard with a more lenient eye the aversion, and in many respects indefensible conduct, of her husband. His declaration on the subject was, after all, a gentle one: 'Nature has not made us suitable to each other.'

Through all her trials, her father-in-law proved a powerful and constant friend, but her own levity and want of circumspection involved her in meshes from which she did not extricate herself with much credit. On quitting her husband's abode at Carlton House, she retired to the village of Charlton, near Blackheath, where she continued for many years. Here her imprudence in adopting the child of one of the labourers in the Deptford dock-yard, gave rise to many injurious suspicions, and occasioned the issue of a royal commission, obtained at the instance of the prince, for the investigation of her conduct in regard to this and other matters. The results of this inquiry were to clear her from the imputation of any flagitious conduct; but the commissioners who conducted it, passed a censure in their report on the 'carelessness of appearances' and 'levity' of the Princess of Wales. On being thus absolved from the serious charges brought against her, the paternal kindness of George III. was redoubled, and he assigned her apartments in Kensington Palace, and directed that at court she should be received with marked attention. With old Queen Charlotte, however, who is said to have been thwarted from the first in the project of wedding her son to Princess Louisa of Mecklenburg, afterwards the amiable and unfortunate queen of Prussia, Caroline never lived on cordial terms.

In 1814, the Princess of Wales quitted England for the continent, where she continued for six years, residing chiefly in Italy. Her return from thence in 1820, on hearing of the accession of her husband to the throne, and the omission of her name from the liturgy of the English Church, with her celebrated trial on the charge of an adulterous intercourse with her courier or *valet de place*, Bartolomo Bergami, are matters of history. The question of her innocence or guilt is still a disputed point, and will probably ever remain so. She was certainly, in many respects, an ill-used woman, but that the misfortunes and obloquy which she underwent were in a great measure traceable to her own imprudent conduct and want of womanly delicacy, there can also exist no reasonable doubt.

In considering the history of Queen Caroline, an impressive lesson is gained regarding the evils attending ill-assorted marriages, and more especially those contracted from motives of state policy, where all questions of suitability on the ground of love and affection are ignored. As a necessary result of such a system, royal marriages have been rarely productive of domestic happiness. It is satisfactory, however, to reflect that in the case of our beloved sovereign, Queen Victoria and her family, a different procedure has been followed, and the distinct and immutable laws of God, indicated by the voice of nature, accepted as the true guides in the formation of the nuptial tie. The legitimate consequence has been, the exhibition of an amount of domestic purity and happiness on the part of the royal family of Great Britain which leaves nothing to be desired. Her happy and exemplary family life has been clouded by the death of her husband the Prince Consort, and her two children Princess Alice and Prince Leopold. She is the fourth English sovereign whose reign has extended to fifty years.

---

## THE FENMEN.

The Fenmen, or inhabitants of the Fens lying along the east coast of England, were notorious for their obstinate opposition to all schemes of drainage.* The earliest inhabitants would break down embankments, because the exclusion of the water damaged their fishing; and the more enlightened landowners of later days invariably dreaded trouble, and change, and risk of expense, more than annual destruction of property. The fact affords a curious illustration of that indolent spirit, apparently inherent in human nature, which clings, at any cost, to what is familiar.

In one of those schemes for improving matters, which were set on foot from time to time, so far back as the time of the Romans, and which usually assumed considerable importance whenever a more destructive flood than ordinary had produced more than ordinary complaints, we find James I. writing from Theobald's, and urging the undertakers of the work to do their utmost; describing the cause

* An interesting and excellent sketch of the history of the fen drainage is to be found in N. Walker and T. Craddock's *History of Wisbech and the Fens*, published at Wisbech in 1849.

as one in which he himself was much interested, and enjoining them, among other things, to inform him of '*any mutinous speeches which might be raised concerning this business*, so generally intended for the public good.' In any attempt of this kind, it seems, a fair amount of opposition was of course anticipated.

On this occasion the undertakers, four in number, began operations on the 7th of August 1605, with so important a person as Sir John Popham, Lord Chief-Justice, as one of the four; yet, although the scheme was carefully organised, and regularly arranged with the proper commissioners, the Fenmen, after all, brought it to nothing. The undertakers engaged to drain 307,242 acres, in seven years, and to accept in payment 130,000 acres, 'to be taken out of the worst sort of every particular fen proportionably.' The prospect of so handsome a reward was too much for the Fenmen; and so many grievances did they make out, so many objections had they to raise to the scheme, that a commission of inquiry had to be appointed. This commission decided against them; declaring, amongst other plain truths, that 'whereas an objection had been made of much prejudice that might redound to the poor by such draining, they had information by persons of good credit, that in several places of recovered grounds, within the Isle of Ely, &c., such as before that time had lived upon alms, having no help but by fishing and fowling, and such poor means, out of the common fens while they lay drowned, were since come to good and supportable estates.' Yet, although the king had taken up the scheme, and the good of it was self-evident, the plan duly laid, and the operations even commenced, the work had to be discontinued; chiefly because of 'the opposition which divers perverse-spirited people made thereto, by bringing turbulent suits in law, as well against the commissioners as those whom they employed therein, and *making of libellous songs to disparage the work*.'

This instance of the Fenmen's stupid opposition was not peculiar: the following song, which went under the title of *The Powte's Complaint*,* will afford a specimen of the 'libellous' effusions above alluded to:

'Come, brethren of the water, and let us all assemble,
To treat upon this matter, which makes us quake and tremble;
For we shall rue it, if 't be true, that the Fens be undertaken,
And where we feed in Fen and reed, they 'll feed both beef and bacon.

They 'll sow both beans and oats, where never man yet thought it,
Where men did row in boats, ere undertakers bought it:
But Ceres, thou behold us now, let wild-oats be their venture,
Oh let the frogs and miry bogs destroy where they do enter!

* * * * *

Away with boats and rudders; farewell both boots and skatches,
No need of one nor th' other, men now make better matches;
Stilt-makers all and tanners shall complain of this disaster;
For they will make each muddy lake for Essex calves a pasture.

Wherefore let us entreat our ancient winter nurses,
To shew their power so great as t' help to drain their purses;
And send us good old Captain Flood to lead us out to battle,
Then Twopenny Jack, with skales on 's back, will drive out all the cattle.

This noble captain yet was never known to fail us,
But did the conquest get of all that did assail us;
His furious rage who could assuage? but, to the world's great wonder,
He bears down banks, and breaks their cranks and whirlygigs asunder.

* * * * *

Great Neptune (god of seas!), this work must need provoke thee,
They mean thee to disease, and with fen-water choke thee:
But with thy mace do thou deface and quite confound this matter,
And send thy sands to make dry lands, when they shall want fresh water.

* *Poult*, a young trout.

---

## GENERAL PUTNAM'S TREATMENT OF A SPY.

In the course of the transactions of the second year of the American war of independence, General Putnam caught a man lurking about his post at Peekskill, on the Hudson. A flag of truce came from Sir Henry Clinton, claiming the prisoner as a lieutenant in the British service. The answer of the old general was equally brief, and to the point:

'HEAD-QUARTERS, *7th August* 1777.

'Edmund Palmer, an officer in the enemy's service, was taken as a spy lurking within our lines. He has been tried as a spy, condemned as a spy, and shall be executed as a spy; and the flag is ordered to depart immediately.

ISRAEL PUTNAM.

'*P. S.*—He has, accordingly, been executed.'

Diction somewhat similar to this regarding the treatment of an offender in Scotland fifty years earlier, is on record. It proceeded from the Earl of Islay, who ruled Scotland for Sir Robert Walpole, in the reign of George II., and was, amongst other things, an extraordinary lord of session:

'EDINBURGH, *February* 28, 1728

'I, Archibald, Earl of Islay, do hereby prorogate and continue the life of John Ruddell, writer in Edinburgh, to the term of Whitsunday next, and no longer, by ——. ISLAY, I.P.D.'

The letters following the signature mean, 'In presentia Dominorum,' in the presence of the Lords; *i. e.*, the judges of the criminal court over which Islay presided; so that we must presume this trenchant rescript to have been produced in sufficiently dignified circumstances.

## LADY CLERK'S DREAM-STORY.

Lady Clerk, of Penicuick, *née* Mary Dacre, who spent a long widowhood in Edinburgh,* where some little singularities of dress made her extremely well known, used to relate (and ultimately communicated to *Blackwood's Magazine*†) a dream-story, of the general truth of which she was well assured. It represented her father, a Cumberland gentleman,‡ as attending classes in Edinburgh about the year 1731, and residing under the care of an uncle, Major Griffiths, of the regiment then stationed in the castle. The young man, who was accustomed to take rambles with some companions, announced to his uncle and aunt one night, that he and his friends had agreed to join a fishing-party, which was to go out in a boat from Leith the next morning at six o'clock. No objection being made, they separated for the night; but during her sleep Mrs Griffiths screamed out: 'The boat is sinking; save, oh save them!' To pursue Lady Clerk's relation: 'The major awaked her, and said, "Were you uneasy about the fishing-party?" "Oh, no," she said, "I had not once thought of them." She then composed herself, and soon fell asleep again; in about another hour, she cried out, in a dreadful fright: "I see the boat is going down!" The major again awoke her, and she said: "It has been owing to the other dream I had; for I feel no uneasiness about it." After some conversation, they both fell sound asleep; but no rest could be obtained for her; in the most extreme agony, she again exclaimed: "They are gone—the boat is sunk!" When the major awaked her, she said: "Now I cannot rest: Mr Dacre must not go, for I feel, should he go, I would be miserable till his return; the thoughts of it would almost kill me."' In short, on the strength of this dream, Mrs Griffiths induced her nephew to send a note of apology to his companions, who, going out, were caught in a sudden storm, and perished.

Unlike many stories of the same kind, this one can be traced to an actual occurrence, which was duly chronicled in the brief records of the time. On the 7th of August 1734 (Lady Clerk's suggested date being three years too early), five men of respectable positions in life, including Patrick Cuming, a merchant, and Colin Campbell, a shipmaster, accompanied by two boys, one of whom was 'John Cleland, a nephew of Captain Campbell's,' went out in a boat with two sailors, to fish in the Firth of Forth. All was well till eleven o'clock, when a squall came on from the south-west, and they were forced to run for Prestonpans. On their way, Captain Campbell, observing a *flan* coming on, called to a sailor to loose the sail; but the man failed to acquit himself rightly, and the boat went over on its side. The party clung to it for a while, but one after another fell off, or sunk in trying to swim to land, all except Captain Campbell, who was taken up by a boat, and brought ashore nearly dead with fatigue, after being five hours in the water.§

* See some reference to Lady Clerk in our first volume, page 520.

† *Blackwood*, June 1826.

‡ Dacre, of Kirklinton.

§ *Caledonian Mercury*, August 12, 1734.



## The Welsh Man's Inventory.

In one of the miscellaneous collections of the British Museum Library, there is a quaint old broadside, adorned with a coarse wood-cut, designed to burlesque the goods and chattels of a Welsh gentleman or yeoman, at the same time raising mirth at his style of language and pronunciation. It is remarkable how strong a resemblance the whole bears to the *jeux d'esprit* indulged in by the Lowland Scots at the expense of the simple mountaineers of the north, who are a people kindred to the Welsh. The *Infentory* and its quaint vignette are here reproduced:

'Han Infentory of the Couds of William Morgan, *ap* Renald, *ap* Hugh, *ap* Richard, *ap* Thomas, *ap* Evan, *ap* Rice, in the county of Clamorgan, Shentleman.

*Imprimis*, in the *Pantry of Poultry* (for hur own eating).—One creat pig four week old, one coose, two black-puddings, three cow-foot.

*Item*, in the *Pantry of Plate*—One cridiron, one fripan, one tripan, three wooden ladle, three cann.

*Item*, in the *Napery*—Two towel, two table-cloath, four napkin, one for hurself, one for hur wife Shone, two for cusen *ap* Powell, and Thomas *ap* Hugh, when was come to hur house.

*Item*, in the *Wardrope*—One Irish rugg, one frize shirkin, one sheep-skin tublet, two Irish stocking, two shooe, six leather point.

*Item*, in the *Tary*—One toasting shees, three oaten-cake, three pint of cow-milk, one pound cow-putter.

*Item*, in the *Kitchen*—One pan with white curd, two white pot, two red herring, nine sprat.

*Item*, in the *Cellar*—One firkin of wiggan, two gallon sower sider, one pint of perry, one little pottle of *Carmarden* sack, *alias* Metheglin.

*Item*, in the *Armory of Weapon* to kill hur enemy—One pack-sword, two-edge, two Welsh-hook, three long club, one cun, one mouse-trap.

*Item*, in the *Carden*—One ped carlike, nine onion, twelve leek, twelve worm, six frog.

*Item*, in the *Leas-way*—Two tun cow, one mountain calf.

*Item*, in the *Common-Field*—Two Welsh nag, twelve long-leg'd sheep, fourteen and twenty coat.

*Item*, in the *Proom-close*—Three robin-run-hole, four hare: *hur own coods, if you can catch hur.*

*Item*, in the *Parn*—One half heblet of oate, seven pea, two pean.

*Item*, in the *Study* (*hur was almost forgot hur!*)—One Welsh Pible, two almanac, one *Erra Pater*, one Seven Champions, for St Taffy sake, twelve pallat, one pedigree.

*Item*, in the *Closet*—Two straw-hat, one pouse.

*Item*, more Cattle apout the house—Two tog, three cat, twelve mouse (*hur was eat hur toast cheese*), 1000 white flea with plack pack.

*Item*, more Lumber about the house—One wife, two shild, one call hur plack *Shack*, and t'other little *Morgan*.

*Item*, in the *Yard*, under the wall—One wheel, two pucket, one ladder, two rope.

*This Infentory taken Note in the Presence of hur own Cusen Rowland Merideth ap Howel, and Lewellin Morgan ap William, in* 1749, *upon the Ten and Thirtieth of Shun.*

*The above-named William Morgan dyed when hur had threescore-and-twenty years, thirteen months, one week, and seven days.*

*A Note of some Legacy of a creat deal of Coods bequeathed to hur Wife and hur two Shild, and all hur Cusens, and Friends, and Kindred, in manner as followeth:*

*Imprimis*—Was to give hur teer wife, *Shone Morgan*, all the coods in the ped-room.

*Item*—Was to give hur eldest sun, *Plack Shack*, 40 and 12 card to play at Whipper-shinny, 4 ty to sheat hur cusen; beside awl hur land to the full value of 20 and 10 shillings 3 groats per annum.

*Item*—Was to give to hur second sun, little *Morgan* ap *Morgan*, hur short ladder under the wall in the yard, and two rope.

*Item*—Was to give to hur Cusen Rowland *Merideth* ap *Howell* and *Lewellin Morgan*, whom was made hur executor, full power to pay awl hur tets, when hur can get money.

**Seal'd and delivered in the Presence of Evan ap Richard ap Shinkin ap Shone, hur own Cusen, the Day and Year above written.**

London: Licensed, entered, printed, &c.'

W. E.

# AUGUST 8.

Saints Cyriacus, Largus, Smaragdus, and their companions, martyrs, 303. St Hormisdas, martyr.

*Born.*—Dominic Baudius, jurist and philologist, 1561, *Lisle;* Jacques Basnage de Beauval, Protestant theologian and historian, 1653, *Rouen;* Francis Hutcheson, moral philosopher, 1694, *North of Ireland.*

*Died.*—Cardinal Peter d'Ailly, ecclesiastic and author, 1419, *Compiègne;* Pope Alexander VI. (Roderic Borgia), infamous pontiff, 1503; Dr Antoine Arnauld, celebrated opponent of the Jesuits, and friend of Pascal, 1694, *Brussels;* Louis François Armand du Plessis, Duke of Richelieu, captor of Minorca, 1788; Sir Richard Worsley (*History of the Isle of Wight*), 1805, *Appledurcombe in Wight;* George Canning, statesman, 1827, *Chiswick;* Thomas Crofton Croker, author of *Irish Fairy Tales*, 1854, *London;* John Austin, jurist, 1867.

## GEORGE CANNING.

There is a certain moral grandeur popularly ascribed to the *doctrinaire* which is denied to the statesman. There are few politicians who receive the unreserved admiration accorded to those who have done nothing but write books, or yielded their lives to the advocacy of a single cause. The *doctrinaire*—the propounder of a fixed set of opinions—advises mankind, but does not undertake to manage them. Through a long series of years he may publish his convictions with pertinacious uniformity, without hindrance and without responsibility. Such consistency is sometimes contrasted with the wavering tactics of the statesman, to the unfair disadvantage of the latter. A statesman sets himself to lead a people, and is less careful to entertain them with his private convictions than to discover what principles they are inclined to accept and to commit to practice. The *doctrinaire's* business is to proclaim what is true, whether men hear or reject; the statesman's is to ascertain and recommend what is practicable. The statesman is often compelled to defer his private judgment to popular prejudice, and to rest content with bending what cannot be broken. Sir Robert Peel was a free-trader long before free-trade was possible. These reserves are inseparable from statesmanship, nor need they involve dissimulation. A statesman, being a practical man, regards all speech as lost labour which is not likely to be reproduced in action. There is, as all know, a base statesmanship, which does not aspire to lead from good to better, but which panders to popular folly for selfish ends. Of this we do not speak. We merely note the fact, that the consistency of the *doctrinaire* is an easy virtue compared with the statesman's arduous art: the first *tells* what is right; the other *persuades* millions to do it. A statesman who has led with any credit a free people, has necessarily encountered difficulties and temptations of which the solitary student has had no experience, and possibly no conception.

George Canning, whilst one of the ablest European statesmen of the present century, was not doctrinally far in advance of his generation; yet for England he did much worthy service, and through his genius English principles acquired new influence the world over. He was born in Marylebone, London, on the 11th of April 1770. His father was a young gentleman, whose family had cast him off for making a poor marriage; and, while Canning was an infant, he died, it is said, of a broken heart. His mother commenced school-keeping for her support, but it did not pay, and then she tried the stage, but with little better success. An uncle meanwhile intervened, and sent Canning to Eton, where he quickly made his mark by his aptitude for learning, and by starting, at the age of sixteen, a small periodical work, entitled *The Microcosm.* It was written by himself and three school-fellows, and was published at Windsor, weekly, from November 1786 to August 1787. Canning's articles, in their elegance and wit, foreshadowed the future man. *The Microcosm* provoked the Westminster boys to commence *The Trifler.* To their first number they prefixed a caricature representing Justice in the act of weighing their merits against the Etonians, the latter being aloft, while their rivals rested on the ground. Young Canning took his pen, and thus interpreted the symbol:

'What mean ye by this print so rare,
Ye wits—of Eton jealous—
But that *we* soar aloft in air,
And *ye* are heavy fellows?'

From Eton he passed to Oxford, and thence to Lincoln's Inn, with the intention of studying for the bar; but such was his readiness in debate, that his friends persuaded him that politics were his true vocation. At this time he was on familiar terms with Sheridan and Fox, and other leading Whigs, but to their disappointment he sought alliance with Pitt, and under his auspices he entered parliament in 1793. As soon as by trial Pitt had tested the quality of his young recruit, he placed him on active service, and left him to bear the brunt of some formidable attacks. Canning enjoyed and grew under this discipline, and found wit and eloquence equal to all demands. With the *Anti-Jacobin* periodical—begun in 1797 and concluded in 1798, to resist and ridicule democratic opinions—he was largely concerned, and its best verses and *jeux d'esprit* were written by him. His *Needy Knife-Grinder,* a burlesque of a poem by Southey, is known to everybody, being a stock-piece in all collections of humorous poetry. In 1800, Canning was married to Joan Scott, a daughter of General Scott, who brought with her a dowry of £100,000.

Canning's life, from 1793 to 1827, is inwrought with the parliamentary history of England, sometimes in office, and sometimes in opposition. He was a steady enemy of the French Revolution and of Napoleon; he advocated the Irish union, the abolition of the slave trade, and Catholic emancipation; but resisted parliamentary reform, and the repeal of the Test and Corporation Acts. As secretary of state for foreign affairs, he was peculiarly distinguished. His sympathies were heartily liberal; and the assertion of Lord Holland, that Canning had 'the finest logical intellect in Europe,' seemed to find justification in his state-papers and correspondence, which were models of lucid and spirited composition. Against the craft of the Holy Alliance he set his face steadily, and was always ready to afford counsel and help to those who were struggling after constitutional freedom. With real joy he recognised the republics formed from the dissolution of Spanish dominion in America, and one of his last public acts was the treaty which led to the deliverance of Greece from the Turks.

Canning was only prime minister during a few months preceding his death. On the resignation of the Earl of Liverpool, through illness, Canning, in April 1827, succeeded him as premier; and as a consequence of his known favour for the Catholics, Lord Eldon, the Duke of Wellington, Sir Robert Peel, and other Tories threw up their places. Canning had, therefore, to look for support to the Whigs, and with much anxiety and in weak health he fought bravely through the session to its close in July, when he retired to the Duke of Devonshire's villa at Chiswick, and there died on the 8th of August 1827.

M. Guizot, in an account of *An Embassy to the Court of St James's in* 1840, relates a curious anecdote of Canning's death, in connection with a description of Lady Holland. He writes: 'Lady Holland was much more purely English than her husband. Sharing with him the philosophic ideas of the eighteenth French century, in politics she was a thoroughly aristocratic Whig, without the slightest Radical tendency, proudly liberal, and as strongly attached to social hierarchy, as faithful to her party and her friends. . . . . This person, so decidedly incredulous, was accessible, for her friends and for herself, to fears childishly superstitious. She had been slightly ill, was better, and admitted it. "Do not speak of this," she said to me, "it is unlucky." She told me that, in 1827, Mr Canning, then ill, mentioned to her that he was going for change and repose to Chiswick. She said to him: "Do not go there; if I were your wife, I would not allow you to do so." "Why not?" asked Mr Canning. "Mr Fox died there." Mr Canning smiled; and an hour after, on leaving Holland House, he returned to Lady Holland, and said to her in a low tone: "Do not speak of this to any one; it might disturb them." "And he died at Chiswick," concluded Lady Holland with emotion.'

## NEWSPAPER MANAGEMENT IN THE SEVENTEENTH CENTURY.

In the seventeenth century, there was no such term as editor, implying a literary man devoted to the general management of a journal, with a share in such original composition as it required. We only hear of the printer, or at most of the publisher. In those days, the printer found himself surrounded with difficulties, and often, from the imperfection and simplicity of his arrangements, he was thrown into positions by no means dignified.

The following curious notices, &c., are from some of the earliest English newspapers; *circ.* 1620—1626.

'*The Stationer to the Reader.*—We should also present you with the French News, but for that some, who neither know what hath past before, nor how businesses depend one vpon another, haue patcht vp a Pamphlet with broken relations, contradicted newes of Sea-fights, and most non-sence Translations of matters of State, wee cannot but informe you, how you haue been wronged, and wee preuented, by those who would thrust out any falsitie, if they were but persuaded that the nouelty will sell it.'

The above is from a paper published in 1622. It is not very clear, certainly, but at anyrate that which the 'stationer' (publisher) means to convey to his readers may be arrived at without much difficulty. We have copied it literally, as illustrative at once of the typography, orthography, and punctuation of that age.

The annexed quaint notice is from a correspondent of one of these periodicals in the same year. Having given intelligence of the wars at that time being waged abroad, with running comments thereon, the writer concludes by saying to the editor: 'And thus, sir, I end a long letter, wherein I haue dilated the discourse, by attempting to giue the reasons of each motion, and to describe the persons and places, to giue light to the storie, which you shall doe well to keepe by you, for it will make you the better to vnderstand whatsoeuer shall be written of these wars.'

Here is another (same year) from a military correspondent to a similar journal, and who seems to have suffered some loss in his calling: 'Now, courteous Reader, hauing heard the truth of the matter, moderate your griefe, and doe not discourage a young braue warrior, by lamenting for some small losse by him sustained, seeing also that commonly the issues of battailes and warlike actions are variable and inconstant, and that many times it happeneth, that those that the one day haue the worst, the next day haue the better hand.'

In publishing an account of what had occurred to the Spanish fleet in America, in 1623, the translator (and printer) thus apologetically introduces his intelligence:

'*The Printer to the Reader*.—This Spanish originall comming to my hands most opportunely, tooke the aduantage of my liking it, and sudden apprehension, that it would please the Reader, whosoeuer: not so much because thereby is proposed a kinde of variety of newes, as in that the glory of God is made apparant in His workes, and wonderfull Prouidence, that can preserue men out of raging seas, and afford His mercy when wee thinke that it is quite denied vs: and although I may incurre an imputation by leaning more to the true sense then to the words as they lye in order: yet I will be bold to say, that the sentences here extended, shall neither receiue exoticke interpretation, nor bee carryed with any wanton hand from the true meaning: be therefore thus fauorable, I pray, to reade it without a strict comparison of the originall: and accept of an honest intent, that aymeth as much at the satisfaction of worthy deseruers, as any profit can arise out of so meane a worke.'

Another writer of the same period, at the conclusion of his intelligence as to 'the State of Affairs of Europe,' oddly says: 'In this manner stand the affaires of Europe, which I cannot compare better then to a wounded man, newly drest, and in great danger of life, so that vntill his second opening, and taking the aire, the surgion himselfe cannot tell what will become of him: but if you, gentle Reader, affect to vnderstand (by way of indulgencie and desire of his well-doing) the state of his health & body, I wil myselfe attend the next dressing, & according to the effect of the surgery certifie you, what hope there is of recouery, that is to say, if euer these commanders take the field; these threatning armies meet one another; these prepared forces make any encounter; and these martial affairs come to deciding, I will come toward you with honest information, and not hide my talent in a napkin, but acquaint you with as much as falls to my poore portion to know.'

Here is an apology for some news-letters omitted for want of space: 'Reader, I cannot let thee haue the letters for want of roome vntill next weeke.'

Another journal, of a date somewhat later, contains the following apologetic notice on account of an error: 'Whereas there is notice given in the *Gazette* published yesterday, that one Mr Fox has been scandalized in this paper: This is to certify that there was never any such relation printed in any intelligence published by Benjamin Harris; but by some others that have counterfeited his title. But as for the mistakes in the elections at *Rye*, and other places, we do once for all acknowledge that, taking them up on common fame, we have sometimes been mistaken; but we are resolved for the future to be so very cautious and careful, as to endeavour not to give the least offence upon this or any other account to any person whatsoever.'

'Touching for the King's Evil.—In 1664 occurs the following announcement on this subject, of course with the direct cognizance of his majesty Charles II.:—'His sacred majesty having declared it to be his royal will and purpose to continue the healing of his people for the evil, during this month of May; and then to give over till Michaelmas next. I am commanded to give notice thereof, that the people may not come up to the town in the interim, and loose their labour.'

'Notice to Correspondents' in Olden Times.—At the foot of a newspaper of the early part of the seventeenth century, an invitation to amateurs is given in the following quaint terms:—'Ale persons who are pleased to favour us with any comical or sollid stories, may repair to the "Three Kings," Ludgate, and they shall have them very carefully put in.'

The circulation of newspapers may be considered as having reached perfection, when a penny could buy the sheet and another penny insure its quick and safe transmission to any part of the country. In such a state of things, it becomes difficult to imagine or recall the difficulties which beset the obtaining of a newspaper only a few years ago. When we cast back our thoughts twenty years, we find the sheet costing fourpence-halfpenny at the least; when we go back twenty or thirty years more, we find it was sevenpence, the greater part of which sum went into the public exchequer. The number of sheets printed by any journal up to 1814 was usually a few hundreds; only two or three came to thousands. It was, indeed, mechanically impossible that there should be a newspaper circulation above two or three thousand, for, before any larger number could be thrown off, the news would have been cold, and the next number in requisition.

When we go back a century, or a century and a half, we find that the journals of the empire were but a handful. There was not one north of Edinburgh till 1746; there was not one established on a permanent basis in Edinburgh till 1718. News were in those days sent about in private letters, and in the gossip of conversation. The wandering beggar, who came to the farmer's house craving a supper and bed, was the principal intelligencer of the rural population of Scotland so late as 1780. In Queen Anne's time, to receive a regular news-sheet from the metropolis was the privilege of lords, squires, and men of official importance. At an earlier time, this communication was not a printed sheet at all, but a written sheet, called a *News-letter*, prepared in London, copied by some process or by the hand, and so circulated from a recognised centre. When such a sheet arrived at the hall, with any intelligence unusually interesting, the proprietor would cause his immediate dependants to be summoned, and would from his porch read out the principal paragraphs (see illustration on the following page). So did the news of William's landing at Torbay, of King Charles's restoration, of his father's tragic death, reach the ears of a large part of the people of England. The reader of our national history will have a very imperfect comprehension of it, if he does not bear in mind how slowly and imperfectly intelligence of public matters was conveyed in all times which we now call past, and how much of false news was circulated. In the case of an insurrection, the whole surrounding circumstances might be changed before a fourth of the nation was apprised of what had taken place, or was prepared to move. Or, supposing that a landing was expected on the south coast, in connection with party-movements within the empire, the heads of the conspiracy might all be in the Tower before any one could be sure that the fleet was even in sight.

One peculiarity of the newspaper management of old days is sufficiently obvious to any one who examines the files. There was no adequate system of home-reporting. It seems to have been mainly by private and arbitrary means that a domestic paragraph came to the office. An amusing illustration of this primitive system of reporting occurs in the *Caledonian Mercury* for March 3, 1724: 'We hear,' says the paper, 'that my Lord Arniston, one of the ordinary lords of session, is dead.' In next number appears this apologetic, but certainly very awkward, paragraph:

ENGLISH COUNTY GENTLEMAN READING THE NEWS.

'It was by mistake in our last that Lord Arniston was dead, occasioned by the rendezvous of coaches hard by his lordship's lodging, that were to attend the funeral of a son of the Right Honourable the Earl of Galloway; wherefore his lordship's pardon and family is humbly craved.' W. E.

---

## AUGUST 9.

St Romanus, martyr. St Nathy, or David, priest in Ireland. St Fedlimid, or Felimy, bishop of Kilmore, confessor, 6th century.

*Born.*—Izaak Walton, author of *The Complete Angler*, 1593, *Stafford;* John Dryden, poet, 1631, *Aldwinkle, Northamptonshire;* John Oldham, satirical poet, 1653, *Shipton, Gloucestershire;* Thomas Telford, eminent engineer, 1757, *Westerkirk, Dumfriesshire.*

*Died.*—Simon Ockley, orientalist (*History of the Saracens*), 1720, *Swavesey;* Robert Potter, translator of *Æschylus*, &c., 1804, *Lowestoff, Norfolk;* Mrs Charles Mathews (Madame Vestris), celebrated vocalist and actress, 1856, *Fulham.*

### IZAAK WALTON.

Uncanonized, Izaak Walton is the patron saint of anglers. About scarce another author centre memories of such unmixed gentleness and peace. To speak of Walton is to fall to praising him. As Charles Lamb says: 'It might sweeten a man's temper at any time to read the *Complete Angler.*'

Of Walton's early life little is known beyond the fact that he was born at Stafford in 1593. It is presumed he was apprenticed in London to a sempster or linen-draper, for soon after coming of age he had a shop of his own in the Royal Exchange, Cornhill. In this situation he could hardly have had elbow-room, for the shops in the Exchange were but 7½ feet long by 5 wide. From this, in 1624, he moved to a house 'on the north side of Fleet Street, two doors west of the end of Chancery Lane,' thus under the very shadow of Temple Bar. In the crowd and din of the junction there of Fleet Street and the Strand, it is a piquant reflection at this day, that an author whose name is wedded with green fields and quiet waters once abode. Subsequently he removed round the corner to the seventh house on the west side of Chancery Lane.

In this neighbourhood Walton tasted much sorrow. He married at Canterbury, in 1626,

Rachel Floud, maternally descended from Archbishop Cranmer. Seven children were the fruit of this union, but they all died in childhood, and last of all the mother also, in 1640. The narrow accommodations which London tradesmen then assigned to their families are sufficient to account for such tragic results. Meanwhile Walton's business as linen-draper prospered; and for recreation he used 'to go a-fishing with honest Nat, and R. Roe.' His favourite stream was the Lea, a river which has its source above Ware, in Hertfordshire, and gliding about the country to the north-east of London, falls into the Thames a little above Blackwall.

Amidst the troubles of the civil war, while London was generally parliamentarian, worthy Izaak remained a steady royalist and churchman. Having accumulated a small independence, and anxious, it is supposed, to escape from the scene of so many domestic afflictions, and from possible annoyance on the score of his faith and politics, he gave up shopkeeping, about 1643, and retired into the country. In 1646, he contracted a second marriage with Anne Ken, sister of the saintly bishop of Bath and Wells. She died in 1662, leaving her husband a son Izaak and a daughter Anne to comfort him in his prolonged old age.

Walton was fifty when he gave up business, and forty years of leisure remained for his enjoyment. Authorship he had begun before he left his shop. In the parish church of St Dunstan he had been a hearer and, as he says, 'a convert' to the preaching of Dean Donne, the poet. An intimate friendship ensued between the divine and the linen-draper, and when Donne died in 1631, Walton was tempted into writing his elegy; and to a collection of the dean's *Sermons*, published in 1640, he prefixed *The Life of Dr John Donne.* His success in this piece of biography led on to other efforts of the same kind, as inclination and opportunity offered. In 1651, appeared his *Life of Sir Henry Wotton;* in 1662, *The Life of Mr Richard Hooker;* in 1670, *The Life of Mr George Herbert;* and in 1678, *The Life of Dr Sanderson.* These five biographies, brief yet full, written in sympathy yet with faithfulness, with reverence, modesty, and discretion, have been accepted as choice miniatures of the several worthies who are their subjects, and are reprinted and read to this day with unabated admiration.

Not the *Lives*, however, but *The Complete Angler or Contemplative Man's Recreation* is Walton's true title to fame. It was published in 1653, the year in which Oliver Cromwell was declared Protector, and Walton lived to see it pass through four other editions—namely, in 1655, 1664, 1668, and 1676. How often it has since been reprinted, annotated by admiring editors, and extolled by critics of every mind, time would fail to tell. The *Angler* has long ago taken an undisputed place among English classics, and to speak of its abounding poetry, wisdom, and piety would be to repeat criticism which has passed into commonplace.

The advices which Walton gives for the treatment of live-bait—as, for instance, the dressing of a frog with hook and wire, needle and thread, '*using him as though you loved him*, that is, harm him as little as you may possible, that he may live the longer,' and the recommendation of a perch for taking pike, as 'the longest-lived fish on a hook' —have subjected him to the charge of cruelty. Hence Byron writes in *Don Juan* of—

'Angling, too, that solitary vice,
Whatever Izaak Walton sings or says;
The quaint, old, cruel coxcomb, in his gullet
Should have a hook, and a small trout to pull it.'

But people in the seventeenth century concerned themselves little or nothing with animal suffering. Boyle, a good Christian and contemporary of Walton's, records experiments with animals in the air-pump with a coolness which makes us shudder. The Puritans objected to bull and bear baiting, not, as Lord Macaulay observes, in pity for bull or bear, but in aversion and envy at the pleasure of the spectators. Strange as it may seem, compassion for animals is a virtue, the coming in of which may be remembered by living men.

Blessed with fine health, Walton carried the vigour of manhood into old age; in his eighty-third year, we find him professing a resolution to begin a pilgrimage of more than a hundred miles, to visit his friend Cotton on the Dove in Derbyshire. In the great frost of 1683, which covered the Thames with ice eleven inches thick, split oaks and forest trees, and killed the hollies, and in which nearly all the birds perished, old Izaak died in his ninety-first year. He was at the time on a visit to his daughter Anne, at Winchester, and in Winchester Cathedral he lies buried. In a will made a few months before, he declared his 'belief to be, in all points of faith, as the Church of England now professeth;' a declaration of some consequence, he asserts, on account of 'a very long and very true friendship with some of the Roman Church.'

## DRYDEN—THE WEAPON SALVE.

What a blurred page is presented to us in the life of Dryden—in one short year bemoaning Cromwell and hailing Charles—afterwards changing his religion, not without a suspicion of its being done for the sake of court-favour—a noble, energetic poet, yet capable of writing licentious plays to please the debased society of his age—a gentleman by birth, yet fain to write poetical translations from the classics for Jacob Tonson at so much a line! Notwithstanding all short-comings, Dryden is not merely a venerated figure in the literary Pantheon of England, but one not a little loved. We all enter heartily into the praise of 'Glorious John.'

Dryden had many enemies; no man could write in those days without incurring hatred. Hence it arose that the following notice appeared in a London newspaper in December 1679. 'Upon the 17th instant, in the evening, *Mr Dryden*, the great poet, was set upon in Rose Street, in Covent-Garden, by three persons, who called him a rogue, and other bad names, knockt him down, and dangerously wounded him, but upon his crying out "Murther!" they made their escape. It is conceived that they had their pay beforehand, and designed not to rob him, but to execute on him some cruelty, if not popish vengeance.' Soon afterwards the following advertisement was issued: 'Whereas, &c., &c., if any person shall make discovery of the said offenders, to the said *Mr Dryden*, or to any justice of peace for the liberty of Westminster, he shall not only receive fifty pounds, which is deposited in the hands of Mr Blandard, goldsmith, next door to Temple Bar, for the said purpose; but if the discoverer himself be one of the actors, he shall have the fifty pounds, without letting his name be known, or receiving the least trouble by any prosecution.'

In Dryden's version of Shakspeare's *Tempest*, Ariel is made to save Hippolito's life by directing Ferdinand's sword to be anointed with weapon-salve and wrapped up close from the air. Believers were not wanting in this extraordinary nostrum, so well suited to an age when every gentleman carried a sword as a matter of course, which, equally as a matter of course, he was ready to draw on the slightest provocation. Sconce, the hero of Glapthorne's comedy of *The Hollander*, knew a captain reported to have obtained some of the precious ointment from the witches of Lapland, and is extremely anxious to get some himself, that he may safely 'confront the glistering steel, outface the sharpest weapon.' An apothecary's man gives him an unguent which he warrants genuine, thirty citizens blown up by an explosion of gunpowder having been saved by dressing the smoke of the powder with the salve! Sconce is so convinced by this evidence, that when he has occasion to test the efficacy of the ointment, and finds it of little avail, he attributes the failure to some impediment in his blood, and fully credits the doctor's assertion that—

'The same salve will cure
At any distance—as if a person hurt
Should be at York, the weapon dressed at London
On which the blood is.'

Davenant says (*The Unfortunate Lovers*, Act II., scene I.):

'Greatness hath still a little taint i' th' blood;
And often 'tis corrupted near the heart;
But these are not diseases held, till by
The monarch spied who our ambition feeds,
Till at surfeits with his love; nor do we strive
To cure or take it from ourselves, but from
His eyes, and then our medicine we apply
Like the weapon-salve, not to ourselves but him
Who was the sword that made the wound.'

The 'ever-memorable' John Hales, of Eton, thought it worth while to make a serious attack on the weapon-salve, in a 'letter to an honourable person' (1630). He declares it is but 'a child of yesterday's birth,' one amongst the many pleasant phantasies of the Rosicrucians; and as for the cures it has worked, 'the effect is wrought by one thing, and another carries the glory of it. A man is wounded; the weapon taken, and a wound-working salve applied to it; in the meanwhile, the wounded person is commanded to use abstinence as much as may be, and to keep the wound clean. Whilst he thus doth, he heals, and the weapon-salve bears the bell away.' No man in his right senses would ever have thought of curing a wound by anointing the weapon that inflicted it; therefore the discovery must have been the result of experience, in which case there must have been a fortuitous concurrence of circumstances scarcely credible. 'First the salve, made for some other end, must fall on the weapon, and that upon the place where the blood was, and there rest, and then some man must observe it, and find that it wrought the cure.' He then shews that if the doctrine be true, that it is through the blood that the cure is worked, the salve would be just as efficacious applied whereon the blood fell, and is therefore foolishly called weapon-salve; and having thus deprived it both of reputation and name, he winds up his letter triumphantly thus: 'I have read that a learned Jew undertook to persuade Albertus, one of the Dukes of Saxony, that by certain Hebrew letters and words, taken out of the Psalms, and written on parchment, strange cures might be done upon any wound; as he one day walked with the duke, and laboured him much to give credit to what he discoursed in that argument, the duke suddenly drew his sword, and wounding him in divers places, tells him he would now see the conclusion tried upon himself. But the poor Jew could find no help in his Semhamphoras, nor his Hebrew characters, but was constrained to betake himself to more real chirurgery. I wish no man any harm, and therefore I desire not the like fortune might befall them who stand for the use of weapon-salve; only this much I will say, that if they should meet with some Duke of Saxony, he would go near to cure them of their errors, howsoever they would shift to cure their wounds.'

The latest allusion to this wonderful medicine we can find, is in Mrs Behn's *Young King*, published in 1690, in which play one of the characters is cured of a wound by a balm—

'That like the weapon-salve
Heals at a distance.'

## QUEEN ELIZABETH AT TILBURY FORT.

During the first week of August, in the eventful year 1588, there was doubt in England whether the much-dreaded Spanish Armada would or would not enter the Thames, in its attack upon the freedom and religion of England. Both sides of the Thames were hastily fortified, especially at Gravesend and Tilbury, where a chain of boats was established across the river to bar the passage. There was a great camp at Tilbury Fort, in which more than twenty thousand troops were assembled. After having reviewed the troops assembled in London, the queen went down to encourage those encamped at Tilbury, where her energetic demeanour filled the soldiery with enthusiasm. Riding on a war-charger, wearing armour on her back, and holding a marshal's truncheon in her hand—with the Earls of Essex and Leicester holding her bridle-rein, she harangued them thus:—'My loving people, we have been persuaded by some that are careful of our safety, to take heed how we commit ourselves to armed multitudes, for fear of treachery. But I assure you I do not desire to live to distrust my faithful and loving people. Let tyrants fear! I have always so behaved myself that, under God, I have placed my chiefest strength and safeguard in the loyal hearts and good-will of my subjects; and, therefore, I have come amongst you at this time, not as for my recreation and sport, but being resolved in the midst and heat of the battle to live or die amongst you all—to lay down for my God, for my kingdom, and for my people, my honour and my blood, even in the dust. I know that I have but the body of a weak and feeble woman; but I have the heart of a king, and of a king of England too, and think foul scorn that Parma, or Spain, or any prince of Europe, should dare to invade the borders of my realm! To which, rather than any dishonour shall grow by me, I myself will take up arms, I myself will be your general, the judge and rewarder of every one of your virtues in the field. I know already by your forwardness, that you have deserved rewards and crowns; and we do assure you, on the word of a prince, they shall be duly paid you. In the meantime, my lieutenant-general shall be in my stead, than whom never prince commanded more noble or more worthy subject. Nor will I suffer myself to doubt, but that by your obedience to my general, by the concord in the camp, and your valour in the field, we shall shortly have a famous victory over those enemies of my God, my kingdom, and my people.' The harangue is given in slightly different form by different historians; but the substance is the same in all.

However much historians may have differed, and still do differ, concerning the character of Elizabeth, there can be no doubt of the fitness of such an harangue to rouse the people to an heroic resistance. She was no longer youthful; but her sex and her high spirit recommended her to the hearts of her people. 'By the spirited behaviour,' says Hume, 'she revived the tenderness and admiration of the soldiery; an attachment to her person became a kind of enthusiasm among them; and they asked one another, whether it were possible Englishmen could abandon this glorious cause, could display less fortitude than appeared in the female sex, or could ever by any dangers be induced to relinquish the defence of their heroic princess?' The so-called 'Invincible Armada,' as most English readers are aware, did not afford an opportunity for Elizabeth's land-forces to shew their valour; its destruction was due to other agencies.

## THE DUKE OF SUSSEX'S ANNULLED MARRIAGE.

The annulling of the late Duke of Sussex's first marriage, in August 1794, was one of the sad consequences of the Royal Marriage Act. That statute was passed about twenty years before, at the request, and almost at the command, of George III. The king, who held very high notions concerning royal prerogatives, had been annoyed by the marriages of two of his brothers with English ladies. He wished to see the regal dignity maintained in a twofold way—by forbidding the marriage of English princes and princesses with English subjects; and by rendering the consent of the reigning sovereign necessary, even when the alliance was with persons of royal blood. The Royal Marriage Act, by making provision for the last-named condition, virtually insured the first-named so long as the king should live: seeing that he had resolved never to give his consent to the marriage of any of his children with any of his own subjects. The nation sympathised deeply with the amiable prince whose happiness was so severely marred on this particular occasion. While travelling in Italy in 1792, the duke formed an attachment to Lady Augusta Murray, daughter of the Earl of Dunmore. The earl was not in Italy at that time; but Lady Dunmore consented to a private marriage of her daughter with the Duke of Sussex (who was then about twenty years of age). The duke could not have been ignorant of the Royal Marriage Act, nor is it likely that the existence of such a statute could have been unknown to Lady Dunmore; this afterwards afforded an argument in the hands of the king's party. The young couple, after a residence at Rome of several months, came to England. At the desire of the lady and her friends, the duke consented to a second marriage-ceremony, more public and regular than the first. The couple took lodgings in South Molton Street, at the house of a coal-merchant; merely that they might, by a residence of one month in the parish of St George's, Hanover Square, be entitled to have their banns asked in the church of that parish. They were regularly married on the 5th of December 1793, under the names of Augustus Frederick, and Augusta Murray. It was an anxious time for the lady, seeing that she was about to become a mother, and had every motive for wishing to be recognised as a true wife. She was, however, destined to disappointment. The king never forgave the duke for this marriage, which he inflexibly determined not to recognise. In his own name, as if personally aggrieved in the matter, the obstinate monarch instituted a suit against his own son in the Court of Arches, for a nullity of the marriage. Within one week of Lady Augusta's confinement, the king's proctor served a citation on the Duke of Sussex, to answer the charges of the suit. The investigations underwent many costly changes. At one time the privy-council made searching inquiries; at other times other tribunals; and the fact of the marriage at St George's Church had to be rendered manifest by the testimony of the mother and sister of Lady Augusta, the clergyman who had performed the marriage-ceremony, the coal-merchant and his wife, and another witness who was present. So far as the church was concerned, the marriage was in all respects a valid one; but the terms of the Royal Marriage Act were clear and decided; and after many months of anxious doubt, the duke and Lady Augusta were informed, by the irreversible judgment of the courts, that their marriage was no marriage at all in the eyes of the English law, and that their infant son was illegitimate. Later sovereigns sought to alleviate the misery thus occasioned to an amiable family (a daughter was born before the Duke of Sussex and Lady Augusta finally separated), by giving a certain degree of rank and position to those who were *taboo'd* from the royal circle; but nothing could fully compensate for the misery and disappointment that had been occasioned. Lady Augusta, in a letter to a friend written in 1811, said: 'Lord Thurlow told me my marriage was good in law; religion taught me it was good at home; and not one device of my powerful enemies could make me believe otherwise, nor ever will.' The Duke of Sussex settled an income on Lady Augusta, out of the allowance he received from parliament; and the king took care, during the whole remainder of his life, not to give the duke a single office or post that would augment his resources. In 1826, Lord (then Mr) Brougham, in a speech relating to the duke, characterised the Royal Marriage Act, which had produced so much misery, as 'the most unfortunate of all acts;' while Mr Wilberforce stigmatised it as 'the most unconstitutional act that ever disgraced the statute-book.'

# AUGUST 10.

St Lawrence, martyr, 258. St Deusdedit, confessor. St Blaan, bishop of Kinngaradha among the Picts, in Scotland, about 446.

## ST LAWRENCE.

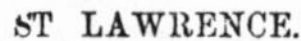

THIS being a very early saint, his history is obscure. The Spaniards, however, with whom he is a great favourite, claim him as a native of the kingdom of Aragon, and even go so far as remark, that his heroism under unheard-of sufferings was *partly* owing to the dignity and fortitude inherent in him as a Spanish gentleman. Being taken to Rome, and appointed one of the deacons under Bishop Xystus, he accompanied that pious prelate to his martyrdom, anno 257, and only expressed regret that he was not consigned to the same glorious death. The bishop enjoined him, after he should be no more, to take possession of the church-treasures, and distribute them among the poor. He did so, and thus drew upon himself the wrath of the Roman prefect. He was called upon to account for the money and valuables which had been in his possession; 'The emperor needs them,' said he, 'and you Christians always profess that the things which are Cæsar's should be rendered to Cæsar.' Lawrence promised, on a particular day, to shew him the treasures of the church; and when the day came, he exhibited the whole body of the poor of Rome, as being the true treasures of a Christian community. 'What mockery is this?' cried the officer. 'You desire, in your vanity and folly, to be put to death—you shall be so, but it will be by inches.' So Lawrence was laid upon a gridiron over a slow fire. He tranquilly bore his sufferings; he even jested with his tormentor, telling him he was now done enough on one side—it was time to turn him. While retaining his presence of mind, he breathed out his soul in prayers, which the Christians heard with admiration. They professed to have seen an extraordinary light emanating from his countenance, and alleged that the smell of his burning was grateful to the sense. It was thought that the martyrdom of Lawrence had a great effect in turning the Romans to Christianity.

The extreme veneration paid to Lawrence in his native country, led to one remarkable result, which is patent to observation at the present day. The bigoted Philip II., having gained the battle of St Quintin on the 10th of August 1557, vowed to build a magnificent temple and palace in honour of the holy Lawrence. The Escurial, which was constructed in fulfilment of this vow, arose in the course of twenty-four years, at a cost of eight millions, on a ground-plan which was designed, by its resemblance to a gridiron, to mark in a special manner the glory of that great martyrdom. The palace represents the handle. In its front stood a silver statue of St Lawrence, with a gold gridiron in his hand; but this mass of the valuable metals was carried off by the soldiers of Napoleon. The only very precious article now preserved in the place, is a bar of the original gridiron, which Pope Gregory is said to have found in the martyr's tomb at Tivoli. The cathedral at Exeter boasted, before the Reformation, of possessing some of the coals which had been employed in broiling St Lawrence.

---

*Born.*—Bernard Nieuwentyt, eminent Dutch mathematician, &c., 1654; Armand Gensonné, noted Girondist, 1758, *Bordeaux;* Sir Charles James Napier, conqueror of Scinde, 1782, *Whitehall.*

*Died.*—Magnentius, usurper of Roman empire, 353, *Lyon;* John de Witt and his brother Cornelius, eminent Dutch statesmen, murdered by the mob at the Hague, 1672; Cardinal Dubois, intriguing statesman, 1723, *Versailles;* Gabrielle Emilie de Breteuil, Marquise du Chastelet, translator of Newton's *Principia*, 1749, *palace of Luneville;* Dr Benjamin Hoadly, eldest son of the bishop, and author of the *Suspicious Husband*, 1757, *Chelsea;* Ferdinand VI. of Spain, 1759, *Madrid;* John Wilson Croker, Tory politician and reviewer, 1857; Sir George Thomas Staunton, wrote on Chinese affairs, 1859.

## BERNARD NIEUWENTYT, THE REAL AUTHOR OF PALEY'S 'NATURAL THEOLOGY.'

On the 10th of August 1654, the pastor of Westgraafdyke, an obscure village in the north of Holland, had a son born to him. This child, named Bernard Nieuwentyt, was educated for the ministry, but to the great disappointment of his reverend father, the youth resolutely declined to enter the church. Studying medicine, he acquired the degree of doctor; and then settled down contentedly in his native place in the humble capacity of village leech. Nieuwentyt, however, was very far from being an ordinary man. While the boorish villagers considered him an addle-pated dunce, unable to acquire sufficient learning to fit him for the duties of a country minister, he was sedulously pursuing abstruse mathematical and philosophical studies; when he became a contributor to the *Leipsic Transactions*, the principal scientific periodical of the day, the learned men of Europe admired the abilities of the man who, by his neighbours, was considered to be little better than a fool. The talents of Nieuwentyt were at last recognised by his countrymen, and he was offered lucrative and honourable employment in the service of the state; but the unambitious student, finding in science its own reward, could never be persuaded to leave the seclusion of his native village.

Though the name of Nieuwentyt is scarcely known in this country, yet the patient student of the obscure Dutch hamlet has left an important impress on English literature. Towards the close of the seventeenth century, he contributed a series of papers to the *Leipsic Transactions*, the object of which was to prove the existence and wisdom of God from the works of creation. These papers were collected, and published in Dutch, and subsequently translated into French and German. Mr Chamberlayne, a Fellow of the Royal Society, translated the work into English, and it was published by the evergreen house of Longman in 1718, under the title of *The Religious Philosopher.* The work achieved considerable popularity in its day, but, another line of argument becoming more fashionable, it fell into oblivion, and until a few years ago was utterly forgotten. In 1802, the well-known English churchman and author, William Paley, published his equally well-known *Natural Theology.* The well-merited popularity of this last work need not be noticed here; it has gone through many editions, and had many commentators, not one of whom seems ever to have suspected that it was not the genuine mental offspring of Archdeacon Paley. But, sad to say, for common honesty's sake, it must be proclaimed that Paley's *Natural Theology* is little more than a version or abstract, with a running commentary, of Nieuwentyt's *Religious Philosopher!*

Many must remember the exquisite gratification experienced, when reading, for the first time, Paley's admirably interesting illustration of the watch. Alas! that watch was stolen, shamefully stolen, from Bernard Nieuwentyt, and unblushingly vended as his own, by William Paley! As a fair specimen of this great and gross plagiarism, a few passages on the watch-argument may be here adduced. The Dutchman finds the watch 'in the middle of a sandy down, a desert, or solitary place;' the Englishman on 'a heath;' and thus they describe it:

*Nieuwentyt.* So many different wheels, nicely adapted by their teeth to each other.

*Paley.* A series of wheels, the teeth of which catch in and apply to each other.

*Nieuwentyt.* Those wheels are made of brass, in order to keep them from rust; the spring is steel, no other metal being so proper for that purpose.

*Paley.* The wheels are made of brass, in order to keep them from rust; the spring of steel, no other metal being so elastic.

*Nieuwentyt.* Over the hand there is placed a clear glass, in the place of which if there were any other than a transparent substance, he must be at the pains of opening it every time to look upon the hand.

*Paley.* Over the face of the watch there is placed a glass, a material employed in no other part of the work, but in the room of which if there had been any other than a transparent substance, the hour could not have been seen without opening the case.

The preceding quotations are quite sufficient to prove the identity of the two works. Paley, in putting forth the *Natural Theology* as his own, may have been guided by his favourite doctrine of expediency; but if he did not succumb to the temptation of wilful fraud, he must have had very confused ideas on the all-important subject of *meum* and *tuum.* And no one can have any hesitation in naming Bernard Nieuwentyt the author of Paley's *Natural Theology.*

In conclusion, it may be added that, though everybody knows the meaning of the words plagiarist and plagiarism, yet few persons are acquainted with their derivation. Among the more depraved classes in ancient Rome, there existed a nefarious custom of stealing children and selling them as slaves. According to law, the child-stealers, when detected, were liable to the penalty of being severely flogged; and as the Latin word *plaga* signifies a stripe or lash, the ancient kidnappers were, in Cicero's time, termed *plagiari*—that is to say, deserving of, or liable to, stripes; and thus both the crime and criminals received their names from the punishment inflicted.

## SIR CHARLES JAMES NAPIER.

When one recalls the character and expressions of this person and his brother William, author of *The History of the Peninsular War,* he cannot but feel a curiosity to learn whence was derived ability so vivid and blood so hot. They were two of the numerous sons of the Hon. George Napier, 'comptroller of accounts in Ireland,' a descendant of the celebrated inventor of the logarithms, but more immediately of Sir William Scott of Thirlstain, a scholar and poet of the reign of Queen Anne. Their mother was the Lady Sarah Lennox, who has been noticed in this work (under February 14) as a great-grand-daughter of Charles II., and the object of a boyish flame of George III. The attachment of Charles Napier to his mother was deep and lasting, as his many letters to her attest; she lived to see him advance to middle life, and one envies the pride which a woman must have had in such a son.

In childhood, the future conqueror of Scinde was sickly, and of a demure and thoughtful turn, but he early displayed an ardent enthusiasm for a military life. When only ten years of age, he rejoiced to find he was short-sighted, because a portrait of Frederick the Great, which hung up in his father's room, had strange eyes, and he had heard Plutarch's statement mentioned, that Philip, Sertorius, and Hannibal had each only one eye, and that Alexander's eyes were of different colours. The young aspirant for military fame even wished to lose one of his own eyes, as the token of a great general; a species of philosophy which recalls to mind the promising youth, depicted by Swift, who had all the *defects* characterising the great heroes of antiquity. Though naturally of a very sensitive temperament, he overcame all his tendencies to timidity by his wonderful force of will, and became almost case-hardened both to fear and pain. Throughout life, from boyhood to old age, he was constantly meeting with accidents, which, however, had no effect in diminishing his passion for perilous adventures. On one occasion, when a mere boy, he struck his leg in leaping against a bank of stones, so as to inflict a frightful wound, which, however, he bore with such stoical calmness as to excite the admiration of many rough and stern natures. Another time, at the age of seventeen, he broke his right leg leaping over a ditch when shooting, and by making a further scramble after being thus disabled, to get hold of his gun, produced such a laceration of the flesh, and extravasation of blood, that it was feared by the surgeons that amputation would be necessary. This was terrible news to the youth, as he rather piqued himself on a pair of good legs, and he resolved, according to his own account, to commit suicide rather than survive such a mutilation. The servant was sent out by him for a bottle of laudanum, which he hid under his pillow; but in the meantime a change for the better took place in the condition of his limb, and the future hero was saved to his country. But the pains of this misfortune were not yet over; the leg was set crooked,' and it became necessary to bend it straight by bandages, an operation which fortunately succeeded, and left the limb, to use his own words, 'as straight a one, I flatter myself, as ever bore up the body of a gentleman, or kicked a blackguard.' His narration of this adventure, written many years afterwards, affords a striking specimen of the wonderful vigour of his character, and we have only to regret that our space does not allow us to transcribe it at full length.

A curious incident connected with his boyish days, which the ancients would have regarded as a presage of his future greatness, ought not to be omitted. Having been out angling one day, he had caught a fish, and was examining his prize, when a huge eagle flopped down upon him, and carried off the prey out of his hands. Far, however, from being frightened, he continued his sport, and on catching another fish, held it up to the royal bird, who was seated on an adjoining tree, and invited him to try his luck again.

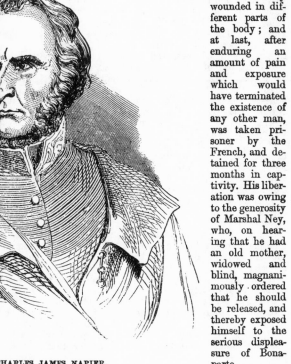

In the days of which we write, mere boys were often gazetted to commissions in the army; an abuse in connection with which many of our readers will remember the story of the nursery-maid announcing to the inquiring mamma, who had been disturbed one morning by an uproar overhead, 'that it was only the major greeting for his porridge.' In 1794, when only twelve years old, young Napier obtained a commission in the 33d, or Duke of Wellington's Regiment, but was afterwards successively transferred to the 89th and 4th Regiments. After this he attended a school at Celbridge, a few miles from Dublin, and made himself conspicuous there by raising, among the boys, a corps of volunteers. In 1799, he first entered really on the duties of his profession by becoming aide-de-camp to Sir James Duff, a staff situation, which he afterwards resigned to his brother George, to enter as a lieutenant the 95th or Rifle Corps. After the peace of Amiens he made further changes, and in 1806 entered the 50th Regiment as major, a capacity in which he was present at the battle of Corunna, of his share in which he subsequently penned a most graphic and interesting account. He was here severely wounded in different parts of the body; and at last, after enduring an amount of pain and exposure which would have terminated the existence of any other man, was taken prisoner by the French, and detained for three months in captivity. His liberation was owing to the generosity of Marshal Ney, who, on hearing that he had an old mother, widowed and blind, magnanimously ordered that he should be released, and thereby exposed himself to the serious displeasure of Bonaparte.

SIR CHARLES JAMES NAPIER.

Rejoining, after a while, his regiment in the Peninsula, Charles Napier received a dreadful wound at the battle of Busaco, by which his upper jaw-bone was shattered to pieces, causing unspeakable agony, both at the time of extraction of the bullet, and for many months afterwards. The gaiety, however, and elasticity of spirit which he manifested on no occasion more conspicuously than during pain and suffering, are most whimsically given utterance to in a letter to a friend at home, in which he says that he offered a piece of his jaw-bone, which came away with the bullet, to a monk for a relic; telling him, at the same time, that it was a piece of St Paul's wisdom-tooth, which he had received from the Virgin Mary in a dream! The holy man, he adds, would have carried it off to his convent, but on being demanded a price for it, said he never gave money for relics, upon which Napier returned it to his pocket In another letter he compares himself, with six wounds in two years, to General Kellarman, who had as many wounds as he was years old—thirty-two. On recovering to a certain extent from his Busaco wound, he again took the field, was present at the battle of Fuentes d'Onoro and the second siege of Badajos; and in 1811 was promoted to a lieutenant-colonelcy in a colonial corps, and sent out to Bermuda. Towards the end of 1814 he returned to England, was placed on half-pay, and with the view of studying the theory of his profession, entered, with his brother William, the Military College at Farnham, where he remained for two years. A period of comparative inaction followed, but in 1822 he received the appointment of military governor of Cephalonia—a situation in which he was more successful in gaining the affections of the inhabitants than pleasing the authorities at home, and his vocation consequently came to an end in 1830.

The most important epoch in Sir Charles Napier's life was yet to come, and in 1842, at the age of sixty, he was appointed as major-general to the command of the Indian army within the Bombay presidency. Here Lord Ellenborough's policy led Napier to Scinde, for the purpose of quelling the Ameers, who had made various hostile demonstrations against the British government after the termination of the Afghan war. His campaign against these chieftains resulted, as is well known, after the victories of Meanee and Hyderabad, in the complete subjugation of the province of Scinde, and its annexation to our eastern dominions. Appointed its governor by Lord Ellenborough, his administration was not such as pleased the directors of the East India Company, and he accordingly returned home in disgust, but was sent out again by the acclamatory voice of the nation, in the spring of 1849, to reduce the Sikhs to submission. On arriving once more in India, he found that the object of his mission had already been accomplished by Lord Gough. He remained for a time as commander-in-chief; quarrelled with Lord Dalhousie, the governor-general; then throwing up his post, he returned home for the last time. Broken down with infirmities, the result of his former wounds in the Peninsular campaign, he expired about two years afterwards at his seat of Oaklands, near Portsmouth, in August 1853, at the age of seventy-one.

The letters of Sir Charles Napier, as published by his brother and biographer, Sir William Napier, the distinguished military historian, exhibit very decidedly the stamp of an original and vigorous mind, blended with a certain degree of eccentricity, which evinces itself no less in him than in his eminent cousin and namesake, Admiral Sir Charles Napier, of naval and parliamentary celebrity. A curious specimen of this quality is given in the following letter, addressed by him to a private soldier:

'Private James N——y,—I have your letter. You tell me you give satisfaction to your officers, which is just what you ought to do; and I am very glad to hear it, because of my regard for every one reared at Castletown, for I was reared there myself. However, as I and all belonging to me have left that part of the country for more than twenty years, I neither know who Mr *Tom Kelly* is, nor who your father is; but I would go far any day in the year to serve a Celbridge man; or any man from the barony of Salt, in which Celbridge stands: that is to say, if such a man behaves himself like a good soldier, and not a drunken vagabond, like James J——e, whom you knew very well, if you are a Castletown man. Now, Mr James N——y, as I am sure you are, and must be a remarkably sober man, as I am myself, or I should not have got on so well in the world as I have done: I say, as you are a remarkably sober man, I desire you to take this letter to your captain, and ask him to shew it to your lieutenant-colonel, and ask the lieutenant-colonel, with my best compliments, to have you in his memory; and if you are a remarkably sober man, mind that, James N——y, a remarkably sober man, like I am, and in all ways fit to be a lance-corporal, I will be obliged to him for promoting you now and hereafter. But if you are like James J——e, then I sincerely hope he will give you a double allowance of punishment, as you will deserve for taking up my time, which I am always ready to spare for a good soldier but not for a bad one. Now, if you behave well, this letter will give you a fair start in life; and if you do behave well, I hope soon to hear of your being a corporal. Mind what you are about, and believe me your well-wisher, Charles Napier, major-general and governor of Scinde, because I have always been a remarkably sober man.'

The sobriety to which the writer of the above refers in such whimsical terms was eminently characteristic of Sir Charles Napier through life. He abstained habitually from the use of wine or other fermented liquor, and was even a sparing consumer of animal food, restricting himself entirely, at times, to a vegetable diet. Though of an ardent enthusiastic temperament, impetuous in all his actions, and a most devoted champion of the fair sex, his moral deportment throughout was of the most unblemished description, even in the fiery and unbridled season of youth. His attachment to his mother has already been alluded to, and no finer exhibition of filial love and respect can be presented than the letters written home to her from the midst of war and bloodshed, by her gallant son. As an officer and gentleman, he was the soul of honour, and devoted above all things to promoting the welfare of the army, and the elevation of the military profession. And the uprightness and generous nature of the man were not more conspicuous than the energy, zeal, and courage of the soldier.

## MURDER OF THE DE WITTS.

The murder of the De Witts, on the 10th of August 1672, was an atrocity which attracted much attention throughout Europe. John and Cornelius de Witt, born at Dort, in Holland, were the sons of a burgomaster of that town. John, in 1652, was made Grand Pensioner of Holland. At a time when the Seven United Provinces formed a republic, John de Witt was favourable to a lessening of the power which was possessed by the stadtholder or president, and which was gradually becoming too much assimilated to sovereign power to be palatable to true republicans. During the minority of William, Prince of Orange (afterwards king of England), the office of stadtholder was held in suspension, and the United Provinces were ruled by the states-general, in which John de Witt was all-powerful. It was virtually he who negotiated a peace with Cromwell in 1652; who afterwards carried on war with England; who sent the fleet which shamed the English by burning some of the royal ships in the Medway; who concluded the peace of Breda in 1667; and who formed a triple alliance with England and Sweden, to guarantee the possessions of Spain against the ambition of Louis XIV. De Witt's plans concerning foreign policy were cut short by a manœuvre on the part of France to rekindle animosity between

England and Holland. A French army suddenly entered the United Provinces in 1672, took Utrecht, and advanced to within a few miles of Amsterdam. It was just at this crisis that home-politics turned out unfavourably for De Witt. He had given offence previously by causing a treaty to be ratified directly by the states-general, instead of first referring it, according to the provision of the Federation, to the acceptance of the seven provinces separately—a question, translated into the language of another country and a later date, of 'States' rights' as against 'Federal rights.' He had also raised up a party against him by procuring the passing of an edict, abolishing for ever the office of stadtholder. When the French suddenly appeared at the gates of the republican capital, those who had before been discontented with De Witt accused him of neglecting the military defences of the country. William, the young Prince of Orange, was suddenly invested with the command of the land and sea forces. About this time, Cornelius de Witt, who had filled several important civil and military offices, was accused of plotting against the life of William of Orange; he was thrown into prison, tortured, and sentenced to banishment. The charge appears to have been wholly unfounded, and to have originated in party malice. John de Witt, whose life had already been attempted by assassins, resigned his office, and went to the Hague in his carriage to receive his brother as he came out of prison. A popular tumult ensued, during which a furious mob forced their way into the prison, and murdered both the brothers with circumstances of peculiar ferocity. John de Witt, by far the more important man of the two, appears to have possessed all the characteristics of a patriotic, pure, and noble nature. The times in which he lived were too precarious and exciting to allow him to avoid making enemies, or to enable him, under all difficulties, to see what was best for his country; but posterity has done him justice, as one of the great men of the seventeenth century.

---

## FOUNDING OF GREENWICH OBSERVATORY.

On the 10th of August 1675, a commencement was made of that structure which has done more for astronomy, perhaps, than any other building in the world—Greenwich Observatory. It was one of the few good deeds that marked the public career of Charles II. In about a year the building was completed; and then the king made Flamsteed his astronomer-royal, or 'astronomical observator,'

GREENWICH OBSERVATORY.

with a salary of £100 a year. The duties of Flamsteed were thus defined—'forthwith to apply himself, with the most exact care and diligence, to the rectifying the table of the motions of the heavens, and the places of the fixed stars, so as to find out the so much-desired longitude of places for the perfecting the art of navigation.' It will thus be seen that the object in view was a directly practical one, and did not contemplate any study of this noble science for its own sake. How the sphere of operations extended during the periods of service of the successive astronomers-royal—Flamsteed, Halley, Bradley, Bliss, Maskelyne, Pond, and Airy—it is the province of the historians of astronomy to tell. Flamsteed laboriously collected a catalogue of nearly three thousand stars; Halley directed his attention chiefly to observations of the moon; Bradley carried the methods of minute measurements of the heavenly bodies to a degree of perfection never before equalled; Bliss confined his attention chiefly to tabulating the relative positions of sun, moon, and planets; Maskelyne was the first to measure such minute portions of time as tenths of a second, in the passage of stars across the meridian; Pond was enabled to apply the wonderful powers of Troughton's instruments to the starry heavens; while Airy's name is associated with the very highest class of observations and registration in every department of astronomy.

Considered as a building, Greenwich Observatory has undergone frequent changes, to adapt it to the reception of instruments either new in form, large in size, or specially delicate in action. Electricity has introduced a whole series of instruments entirely unknown to the early astronomers; akin in principle to the electric telegraph, and enabling the observers to record their observations in a truly wonderful way. Again, photography is enabling astronomers to take maps of the moon and other heavenly bodies with a degree of accuracy which no pencil could equal. Meteorology, a comparatively new science, has been placed under the care of the astronomer-royal in recent years—so far as concerns the use of an exquisite series of instruments for recording (and most of them *self*-recording) the various phenomena of the weather. The large ball which surmounts one part of Greenwich Observatory falls at precisely one o'clock (mean solar time) every day, and thus serves as a signal or monitor whereby the captains of ships about to depart from the Thames can regulate the chronometers, on which the calculation of their longitudes, during their distant voyages, so much depends. The fall of this ball, too, by a series of truly wonderful electrical arrangements, causes the instantaneous fall of similar balls in London, at Deal, and elsewhere, so that Greenwich time can be known with extreme accuracy over a large portion of the kingdom. During every clear night, experienced observers are watching the stars, planets, moon, &c. with telescopes of wonderful power and accuracy; and during the day, a staff of computers are calculating and tabulating the results thus obtained, to be published annually at the expense of the nation. The internal organisation of the observatory is of the most perfect kind; but it can be seen by very few persons, except those officially employed, owing to the necessity of keeping the observers and computers as free as possible from interruption.

---

John Flamsteed, who presided over the founding of the Greenwich Observatory, and from whom it was popularly called Flamsteed House, was of humble origin, and weakly and unhealthy in childhood (born 19th August 1646; died December 31, 1719). His father, a maltster at Derby, set him to carry out malt with the brewing-pan, which he found a very tiresome way of effecting the object; so he set to, and framed a wheel-barrow to carry the malt. The father then gave him a larger quantity to carry, and young Flamsteed felt the disappointment so great, that he never after could bear the thoughts of a wheel-barrow. Many years after, when he reigned as the astronomer-royal in the Greenwich Observatory, he chanced once more to come into unpleasant relations with a wheel-barrow. Having one day spent some time in the Ship Tavern with two gentlemen-artists, of his acquaintance, he was taking a rather ceremonious leave of them at the door, when, stepping backwards, he plumped into a wheel-barrow. The vehicle immediately moved off down-hill with the philosopher in it; nor did it stop till it had reached the bottom, much to the amusement of the by-standers, but not less to the discomposure of the astronomer-royal.*

## 'THE TENTH OF AUGUST.'

The 10th of August 1792 is memorable in modern European history, as the day which saw the abolition of the ancient monarchy of France in the person of the unfortunate Louis XVI. The measures entered upon by prince and people for constitutionalising this monarchy had been confounded by a mutual distrust which was almost inevitable. When the leading reformers, and the populace which gave them their strength, found at length that Austria and Prussia were to break in upon them with a reaction, they grew desperate; and the position of the king became seriously dangerous. In our day, such attempts at intervention are discouraged, for we know how apt they are to produce fatal effects. In 1792, there was no such wisdom in the world.

It was at the end of July that the celebrated manifesto announcing the plans of Austria and Prussia reached Paris. The people broke out in fury at the idea of such insulting menaces. Louis himself was in dismay at this manifesto, for it went far beyond anything that he had himself wished or expected. But his people would not believe him. An indescribable madness seized the nation; and 'Death to the aristocrats!' was everywhere the cry. 'Whatever,' says Carlyle, 'is cruel in the panic-fury of twenty-five million men, whatsoever is great in the simultaneous death-defiance of twenty-five million men, stand here in abrupt contrast, near by one another.' During the night between the 9th and 10th of August, the tocsin sounded all over Paris, and the rabble were invited to scenes of violence by the more unscrupulous leaders—against the wish of many who would even have gone so far as to dethrone the king. Danton gave out the fearful words: 'We must strike, or be stricken!' Nothing more was needed. The danger to the royal family being now imminent, numbers of loyal men hastened to the Tuileries with an offer of their swords and lives. There were also at the palace several hundred Swiss Guards, national guards, and gens d'armes. The commandant, Mandat, placed detachments to guard the approaches to the palace as best he could. When, at six o'clock in the morning, the insurgent mob, armed with cannon as well as other weapons, came near the Tuileries, the unfortunate Louis found that none of his troops were trustworthy save the Swiss Guards: the rest betrayed their trust at the critical moment. A day of horror then commenced. Mandat, the commander of the national guard, going to consult the authorities at the Hôtel de Ville, was knocked down with clubs, and butchered by the mob. They then put to death four persons in the Champs Elysées, whose only fault was that they wore rapiers, and looked like royalists; the heads of these hapless persons, stuck on pikes, were paraded about. The lives of the unhappy royal family were placed in such peril, that they were compelled to take refuge within the walls of the Legislative Assembly, hostile as that assembly was to the king. Louis, his queen, and their children walked

* *Reliquiæ Hearnianæ*, i. 354.

the short distance from the palace-doors to the assembly-doors; but even in this short distance the king had to bear the jeers and hisses of the populace; while the queen, who was an object of intense national hatred, was met with a torrent of loathsome epithets. All through the remainder of that distressing day, the royal family remained ignobly cooped up in a reporter's box at the Legislative Assembly, where, without being seen, they had to listen to speeches and resolutions levelled against kingly power in all its forms; for the assembly, though at this moment protecting the king, was on the eve of dethroning him. Meanwhile blood was flowing at the Tuileries. None of the troops remained faithful to the royal cause except the Swiss Guards, who defended the palace with undaunted resolution, and laid more than a thousand of the insurgents in the dust. A young man, destined to world-wide notoriety, Napoleon Bonaparte, who was in the crowd, declared that the Swiss Guards would have gained the day had they been well commanded. But a fatal indecision ruined all. The poor king was persuaded to send an order to them, commanding them to desist from firing upon 'his faithful people,' as the insurgents were called. The end soon arrived. The rabble forced an entrance into the palace, and even dragged a cannon upstairs to the state-rooms. The Swiss Guards were butchered almost to a man; many of the courtiers and servants were killed while attempting to escape by the windows; some were killed and mutilated after they had leaped from the windows to the ground; while others were slaughtered in the apartments. The Parisians had not yet tasted so much blood as to be rabid against the lives of tender women. Madame Campan, the Princess de Tarente, and a few other ladies were saved from slaughter by a band of men whose hands were still gory, and who said: 'Respite to the women! do not dishonour the nation!' They were escorted safely to a private house; but they had to walk over several dead bodies, to see murder going on around them, to find their dresses trailing in pools of blood, and to see a band of hideous women carrying the head of Mandat on a pike!

This terrible day inaugurated the French Revolution. The king and queen were never again free.

## THE MODERN SAMSON.

Thomas Topham, born in London about 1710, and brought up to the trade of a carpenter, though by no means remarkable in size or outward appearance, was endowed by nature with extraordinary muscular powers, and for several years exhibited wonderful feats of strength in London and the provinces. The most authentic account of his performances was written by the celebrated William Hutton, who witnessed them at Derby. We learned, says Mr Hutton, that Thomas Topham, a man who kept a public-house at Islington, performed surprising feats of strength, such as breaking a broomstick of the largest size by striking it against his bare arm, lifting three hogsheads of water, heaving his horse over a turnpike-gate, carrying the beam of a house, as a soldier does his firelock, and others of a similar description. However belief might at first be staggered, all doubt was removed when this second Samson came to Derby, as a performer in public.

The regular performances of this wonderful person, in whom was united the strength of twelve ordinary men, were such as the following: Rolling up a pewter dish, seven pounds in weight, as a man would roll up a sheet of paper; holding a pewter-quart at arm's length, and squeezing the sides together like an egg-shell; lifting two hundred weights on his little-finger, and moving them gently over his head. The bodies he touched seemed to have lost their quality of gravitation. He broke a rope that could sustain twenty hundredweight. He lifted an oaken-table, six feet in length, with his teeth, though half a hundred-weight was hung to its opposite extremity. Weakness and feeling seemed to have left him altogether. He smashed a cocoa-nut by striking it against his own ear; and he struck a round bar of iron, one inch in diameter, against his naked arm, and at one blow bent it into a semicircle.

Though of a pacific temper, says Mr Hutton, and with the appearance of a gentleman, yet he was liable to the insults of the rude. The ostler at the Virgin's Inn, where he resided, having given him some cause of displeasure, he took one of the kitchen-spits from the mantel-piece, and bent it round the ostler's neck like a handkerchief; where it excited the laughter of the company, till he condescended to untie it.

This remarkable man's fortitude of mind was by no means equal to his strength of body. Like his ancient prototype, he was not exempt from the wiles of a Delilah, which brought him to a miserable and untimely end (August 10, 1749).

## SUPERSTITIONS AND SAYINGS REGARDING THE MOON AND THE WEATHER.

In connection with Greenwich Observatory, it may not be improper to advert to one of the false notions which that institution has helped to dispel—namely, the supposed effect of the moon in determining the weather. It is a very prevalent belief, that the general condition of the atmosphere throughout the world during any lunation depends on whether the moon changed before or after midnight. Almanacs sometimes contain a scientific-looking table constructed on this principle, the absurdity of which appears, if on no other grounds, from the consideration that what is calculated for the meridian of Greenwich may not be correct elsewhere, for the moon may even change before twelve o'clock at Westminster, and after it at St Paul's. If I recollect rightly, this was actually the case with regard to the Paschal full-moon a few years ago, the consequence of which (unless Greenwich-time had been silently assumed to be correct) would have been that Easter-day must have fallen at different times in London and Westminster. There are other notions about the moon which are of a still more superstitious nature.

In this part of the world (Suffolk), it is considered unlucky to kill a pig in the wane of the moon; if it is done, the pork will waste in boiling. I have known the shrinking of bacon in the pot attributed to the fact of the pig having been killed in the moon's decrease; and I have also known the death of poor piggy delayed, or hastened, so as to happen during its increase.

The worship of the moon (a part of, perhaps, the oldest of false religions) has not entirely died out in this nineteenth century of the Christian era. Many persons will courtesy to the new moon on its first appearance, and turn the money in their pockets 'for luck.' Last winter, I had a set of rough country lads in a night-school; they happened to catch sight of the new moon through the window, and all (I think) that had any money in their pockets turned it 'for luck.' As may be supposed, it was done in a joking sort of way, but still it *was* done. The boys could not agree what was the right form of words to use on the occasion, but it seemed to be understood that there was a proper formula for it.

Another superstition was acknowledged by them at the same time—namely, that it was unlucky to see the new moon for the first time *through glass*. This must, of course, be comparatively modern. I do not know what is the origin of it, nor can I tell that of the saying:

'A Saturday moon,
If it comes once in seven years,
Comes once too soon.'

The application of this is, that if the new moon happens on a Saturday, the weather will be bad for the ensuing month. The average of the last seven years gives exactly two Saturday moons per annum, which is rather above the general average due from the facts of there being seven days to the week, and twenty-nine and a half to the lunation. This year, however (1863), there is but one Saturday moon, which brings the average nearer to the truth. I mention this to illustrate the utter want of observation which can reckon a septennial recurrence of a Saturday moon as something abnormal. Yet many sayings about the weather are, no doubt, founded upon observation; such appears to be the following:

'Rain before seven,
Fine before eleven.'

At anyrate, I have hardly ever known it fail in this district; but it must be borne in mind it is only about ten miles from Thetford, where the annual rainfall is no more than nineteen inches, the lowest registered at any place in the kingdom. Another saying is, that 'There never is a Saturday without sunshine.' This is almost always true, but, as might be supposed from the low annual rainfall, the same might be said of any day in the week with an equal amount of truth.

The character of St Swithin's Day is much regarded here as a prognostication of fine or wet weather; but I am happy to think that the saint failed to keep his promise this year, and though he rained on his own day, did not feel himself obliged to go on with it for the regulation forty days.

Another weather-guide connected with the moon is, that to see 'the old moon in the arms of the new one' is reckoned a sign of fine weather; and so is the turning up of the horns of the new moon. In this position it is supposed to retain the water, which is imagined to be in it, and which would run out if the horns were turned down.

The streaks of light often seen when the sun shines through broken clouds are believed to be pipes reaching into the sea, and the water is supposed to be drawn up through them into the clouds, ready to be discharged in the shape of rain. With this may be compared Virgil's notion, 'Et bibit ingens Arcus' (*Georg.* I. 380); but it is more interesting, perhaps, as an instance of the truth sometimes contained in popular superstitions; for, though the streaks of sunlight are no actual pipes, yet they are visible signs of the sun's action, which, by evaporating the waters, provides a store of vapour to be converted into rain.

*Suffolk.* C. W. J.

---

# AUGUST 11.

St Tiburtius, martyr, and St Chromatius, confessor, 286. St Susanna, virgin and martyr, about 295. St Gery or Gaugericus, confessor, 619. St Equitius, abbot, about 540.

*Born.*—Thomas Betterton, celebrated actor, 1635, *Westminster;* Dr Richard Mead, distinguished physician, 1673, *Stepney, London;* Joseph Nollekens, sculptor, 1737, *London;* Jean Victor Moreau, French republican general, 1763, *Morlaix, in Brittany;* Viscount Rowland Hill, Peninsular general, 1772, *Prees, Shropshire.*

*Died.*—General Sir Samuel Auchmuty, captor of Monte Video, 1822; James Wilson, eminent financial statesman, founder of the *Economist* newspaper, 1860, *Calcutta.*

## DR MEAD—ROUGH DOCTORS.

Although a brief general memoir of Dr Mead has been presented under the day of his death, February 16, it may be allowable to open so interesting a subject with a few more particulars.

Mead was a stanch Whig of the old school, and was fortunate enough to render his party a most important service, in a very extraordinary manner. When called in to see Queen Anne on her death-bed, he boldly asserted that she could not live an hour. Though this proved not to be literally true—for the queen lived to the next day—it was substantially so. Intentionally on Mead's part or not, it roused the energies of the Whigs, who made immediate preparations for securing the Hanoverian succession; for which important event, according to Miss Strickland, we are mainly indebted to the physician's prognosis.

The immense difference between the habits and feelings of the present and past century, seems like a wide ocean, dividing two continents, inhabited by distinct races. We can, with a little force to our feelings, imagine a courtly physician, like Mead, visiting his patients with a sword by his side; but we are shocked to hear of two medical men, of high standing, drawing their swords upon each other, and fighting like a couple of bravos, in the open street. Yet such a duello actually took place between Mead and Woodward. The latter, making a false step, fell, and Mead called

DUEL SCENE AT GRESHAM COLLEGE.

upon him to submit, and beg his life. 'Not till I am your patient,' satirically replied the other. He did next moment yield by laying his sword at Mead's feet. Vertue's engraving of Gresham College, in Ward's *Lives of the Professors*, commemorates this duel, Woodward being represented on his knees, with his sword dropped, and Mead standing over him, with his sword raised. The admission of these figures into the engraving is a significant sign of the period. Ward, the author of the work, was a protégé of Mead, and probably aimed at flattering him in this manner. It may be noted that, many years after the encounter of Mead and Woodward, two London physicians in high practice had a duel—bloodless—in Hyde Park, in consequence of merely some slighting remark by the one regarding the other.

The gulf between the present and the past century is no greater than that between the latter and its predecessor. A celebrated Dorsetshire physician and master of arts, named Grey, who was buried at Swyre in 1612, is described as 'a little desperate doctor, commonly wearing a pistol about his neck.' Mr Roberts in his *Social History of the People*, informs us that, one day, a sheriff's officer, disguised as a pedler, served Grey with a writ. The doctor caught the fellow by both ends of his collar, and, drawing out a great run-dagger, broke his head in three places; so the man slipped his head through his cloak, and ran away, leaving the garment in the doctor's hands. The officer then complained to a magistrate, that Grey had stolen his cloak, which the doctor, being sent for, denied, and tearing the cloak in many pieces, told the fellow to look for his lousy rags in the kennel. Most of the gentlemen in the county who were young, strong, and convivially inclined, were adopted by Grey as his sons. When the sheriff was attending the assizes with sixty men, this desperate doctor came with twenty of his 'sons,' and drank before the sheriff and his men, daring any one to touch them. And then Grey, in bravado, blew his horn (a curious appendage for a physician), and rode away with his friends.

A very rough-living doctor of the seventeenth century was John Lambe, confidential physician to Villiers, Duke of Buckingham. This man had been indicted and found guilty, at Worcester assizes, for being 'a sorcerer and juggling person, absolutely given over to lewd, wicked, and diabolical courses, an invocator and adorer of impious and wicked spirits.' At this assize the jail-fever broke out with fatal effect upon many persons, and the sagacious authorities, suspecting that Lambe, by his magical arts, had caused the pestilence, were afraid to carry his sentence into execution, lest he might, in a spirit of revenge, make matters worse. They accordingly sent him to London, where he was confined for some time in the King's Bench Prison. He there practised as a doctor, with great success, till, having committed an outrage on a young woman, he was tried at the Old Bailey, but saved from punishment by the powerful influence of his patron and protector, Buckingham. The popular voice accused Lambe of several grave offences, particularly against women; and on the very same day that the duke was denounced in the House of Commons as the cause of England's calamities, his dependent and doctor was murdered by an infuriated mob in the city of London. The story of his death, from a rare contemporary pamphlet, is worth transcribing, as a sample of the lawless conduct of the people and insecure state of the streets of London at the period.

'On Friday, he (Dr Lambe) went to see a play at the Fortune,* where the boys of the town, and other unruly people, having observed him present, after the play was ended flocked about him, and (after the manner of the common people, who follow a hubbub when it is once set on foot) began in a confused manner to assault and offer him violence. He, in affright, made towards the city as fast as he could, and hired a company of sailors that were there to be his guard. But so great was the fury of the people, who pelted him with stones and other things that came next to hand, that the sailors had much to do to bring him in safety as far as Moorgate. The rage of the people about that place increased so much, that the sailors, for their own sake, were forced to leave the protection of him; and then the multitude pursued him through Coleman Street to the Old Jewry, no house being able or daring to give him protection, though he attempted many. Four constables were there raised to appease the tumult; who, all too late for his safety, brought him to the Counter in the Poultry, where he was bestowed upon command of the lord mayor. For, before he was brought thither, the people had had him down, and with stones and cudgels, and other weapons, had so beaten him that his skull was broken, and all parts of his body bruised and wounded, whereupon, though surgeons in vain were sent for, he never spoke a word, but lay languishing till the next morning, and then died.'

On the day of Lambe's death, placards containing the following words were displayed on the walls of London: 'Who rules the kingdom?—The king. Who rules the king?—The duke. Who rules the duke?—The devil. Let the duke look to it, or he will be served as his doctor was served.' A few weeks afterwards, the duke was assassinated by Felton.

## JAMES WILSON.

As a rule, the aristocratic-democratic government of Britain does not favour the rise to high official position of men unendowed with fortune. Clever but poor men, who make their way into prominent political situations, are too much under necessities perilous to their honesty, or at least to their independence, to allow of their usually leading that straight course which alone gives success in public life in England. The men of the upper and wealthy circles, who possess the requisite ability and industry, have an advantage over them against which it seems almost impossible for them to make head. The instances, therefore, of high office attained by such men, and administered worthily, are very few. Among the exceptions of our own times, there has been none more remarkable than that presented by the career of the Right Hon. James Wilson, who was from 1853 to 1858 Financial Secretary of the Treasury, and died in 1860 in the position of Financial Member of the Council in India. Mr Wilson—one of the sons of a Quaker manufacturer at Hawick, Roxburghshire, and born there in 1805—commenced life as a hat-manufacturer, first at his native town, and subsequently in London; was prosperous through close application and business talents; gave his mind at leisure time to political economy; in time set up a weekly

* The Fortune Theatre was near the present Whitecross Street.

business paper, *The Economist*; prospered in that too; and so went on, step by step, till in 1847 he obtained a seat in the House of Commons. Wilson was a serious, considerate, earnest man. Whatever he set his hand to, he did with all his might; every point he gained, he always turned to the best advantage for his further progress. It would be a great mistake, however, to suppose that he succeeded purely by industry and application. He was a man of penetrating and original mind. Coming forward in public life at the great crisis when protection and hostile tariffs were to yield to free trade, he was able to give his writings on these subjects a character which did not belong to those of any other person. He always held to the practical points: 'What did business-men do in such and such circumstances?' 'Why did they do it?' and 'Why it was right that they should do it?' His mind, at the same time, could grasp great principles; when Mr Cobden and others, for example, were representing the struggle with protection as a conflict of class with class, and thus making landlords hold their ground with the most desperate tenacity, Mr Wilson saw and avowed that it was a system disadvantageous for all classes, since all classes, in reality, have but one interest. He thus added immense force to the cause of free trade; and it is unnecessary to say, that the soundness of his views has been fully proved by the event.

Mr Wilson might be considered, in 1859, as in the fair way for erelong taking an honoured place in the cabinet. It was a most extraordinary fact in our administrative system; but Mr Wilson's success in his own affairs had overcome all those obstacles to which we have adverted. He would have been hailed among the immediate advisers of his sovereign, as one who had never sacrificed one point of probity or one jot of consistency on the shrine of ambition. At this juncture, a necessity arose for a finance minister for India, and as the difficulties were great, a man of Mr Wilson's talents was thought necessary for the position. He was induced to undertake this duty, and for some time he pursued at Calcutta the same career of assiduous application which had given him distinction at home. His health, however gave way, and this remarkable man sank at the comparatively early age of fifty-six, when just about to complete his plans for the regeneration of the Indian revenue.

There are men who will be heard with one breath complaining of the aristocratic character of our institutions, and with another sneering at the rise of a statesman like James Wilson. It is not for us to reconcile their inconsistencies. It may be remarked, however, that an insinuation often made by such persons, to the effect that he had creditors who remained unsatisfied at the time of his taking office, was untrue. On an embarrassment arising in his firm through losses in indigo speculations, he from his own personal means discharged one-half of the obligations, and the plant of the firm was accepted in full satisfaction for the remainder. On this turning out less favourably than was expected, Mr Wilson devoted a part of the means subsequently acquired to make up for the deficiency; so that, at the time in question, he was entirely free of the slightest imputation of indebtedness. His conduct on this occasion was, indeed, such as to do honour to the place he gained, rather than to detract from it.

### KITTY CANNON.

On the 11th of August 1755, died John Lord Dalmeny, eldest son of James, second Earl of Rosebery, in the thirty-first year of his age. In the life of this young nobleman there was a romantic circumstance which has been handed down to us by an English provincial newspaper, and appears to be authentic. In London, some years before his death, he casually encountered a lady who made a deep impression on him, and whom he induced to marry him, and accompany him on a tour of the continent. This union was without the knowledge of relations on either side, but it apparently fulfilled all the essential conditions of matrimony, and the pair lived in great harmony and happiness till the lady was overtaken by a mortal illness. When assured that she was dying, she asked for pen and paper, and wrote the words: 'I am the wife of the Rev. Mr Gough, rector of Thorpe, in Essex; my maiden name was C. Cannon, and my last request is, to be buried at Thorpe.' How she had happened to desert her husband does not appear; but Lord Dalmeny, while full of grief for her loss, protested that he was utterly ignorant of this previous marriage. In compliance with her last wishes, he embalmed her body, and brought it in a chest to England. Under the feigned name of Williams, he landed at Colchester, where the chest was opened by the custom-house officers under suspicion of its containing smuggled goods. The young nobleman manifested the greatest grief on the occasion, and seemed distracted under the further and darker suspicions which now arose. The body being placed uncovered in the church, he took his place beside it, absorbed in profound sorrow; the scene reminded a bystander of Romeo and Juliet. At length he gave full explanation of the circumstances, and Mr Gough was sent for to come and identify his wife. The first meeting of the indignant husband with the sorrow-struck young man who had unwittingly injured him, was very moving to all who beheld it. Of the two, the latter appeared the most solicitous to do honour to the deceased. He had a splendid coffin made for her, and attended her corpse to Thorpe, where Mr Gough met him, and the burial was performed with all due solemnity. Lord Dalmeny immediately after departed for London, apparently inconsolable for his loss. 'Kitty Cannon,' says the local narrator, 'is, I believe, the first woman in England that had two husbands to attend her to the grave together.' In the Peerages, Lord Dalmeny is said to have died unmarried.

---

## AUGUST 12.

St Euplius, martyr, 304. St Muredach, first bishop of Killala, in Ireland, 5th century. St Clare, virgin and abbess, 1253.

---

*Born.*—John George Gmelin, naturalist and Siberian traveller, 1709, *Tubingen*; Rev. Rowland Hill, divine, 1745 (O. S.); Thomas Bewick, celebrated wood engraver, 1753, *Cherry Burn, Northumberland*; George IV., king of England, 1762; Robert Southey, poet, 1774, *Bristol*; Francis Horner, politician, 1778, *Edinburgh*.

*Died.*—Pope Gregory IX., 1241; Sir Thomas Smith, distinguished scholar, and author of *The English Commonwealth*, 1577; Pope Innocent XI., 1689; Nahum

Tate, versifier of the Psalms, 1715, *Southwark;* William Sherard, founder of the botanical chair at Oxford, 1728, *Eltham;* Robert Stewart, Marquis of Londonderry (Lord Castlereagh), Tory statesman, died by his own hand at North Cray, Kent, 1822; George Stephenson, engineer, 1848; Dean Conybeare, geologist, 1857, *Itchinstoke, Hants.*

## REV. ROWLAND HILL.

Society, at the present day, rarely witnesses the exhibition of striking and eccentric traits of character on the part of individuals. The figures in the great picture of the human family seldom stand prominently forth from the canvas; angularities and roughnesses are gradually being smoothed, and the tendency to a fixed and unvarying uniformity is continually becoming more and more manifest.

This observation applies with very decided emphasis to the ministrations of the pulpit and the deportment of clergymen. True, we have the vagaries of Mr Spurgeon, and one or two others of a similar class, though even these fall far short of the piquancy to which our ancestors were formerly accustomed under similar circumstances. The innumerable quaintnesses and witty sayings recorded of pulpit oratory in ancient times, the odd *contretemps* and whimsical incidents narrated by the jest-books in connection with clerical functions and services, are now almost entirely reminiscences of the past. And doubtless it is well that it should be so. The penny-postage, cheap newspapers, and railways, have been as efficacious in banishing them from the present generation, as they have been influential in the extinction of popular superstitions and observances in the remote parts of the kingdom.

One of the last of the old school of divines to which we have just referred was the Rev. Rowland Hill. The son of a Shropshire baronet, whose ancestors had held estates in the county from at least the days of Edward I., he presented to the close of his life, with all his peculiarities, the perfect model of the English gentleman—tall, vigorous, and energetic. Having received a good education at Eton and Cambridge, his eccentricities were prevented from degenerating into offensive displays of ignorance and bad taste; whilst his natural abilities and real kindliness of heart enabled him both to exercise the most extended and beneficial influence in his preaching, and gain the affections and esteem of those with whom he was brought in contact.

In his youthful days, the religious views of Wesley were just making their way amid opprobrium and ridicule to the extensive adoption which they afterwards attained. Their Arminianism, however, was too mild a nutriment for Hill, and he fastened with enthusiastic preference on the tenets of Whitefield, Berridge, and similar preachers of the more fiery sort. The religious convictions which had been impressed on him when still a boy at Eton, were renewed and strengthened during his sojourn at Cambridge, where his incessant activity in endeavouring to gain converts to Calvinism among the students, holding meetings for religious conversation and prayer, and occasionally preaching in the town and neighbourhood, drew down upon him severe rebukes from the college-authorities. He persisted, nevertheless, in his procedure; and having now satisfied himself, from the audiences which he attracted, that preaching was his vocation, he resolved to adopt it as his profession in life. Though retaining a strong attachment to the Church of England, he differed so much from her in many points of discipline and religious worship, that he was unable to bind himself by any pledge to refrain from deviating from her rules. Consequently, though he succeeded in being admitted to deacon's orders, he was refused episcopal ordination by one prelate after another, till at last he abandoned the attempt as hopeless. During the subsequent part of his life, he must therefore be regarded as a Dissenter; but, like Whitefield, he never promulgated any special form of orthodox doctrine, or attached himself to any particular sect. At first, he was entirely itinerary, preaching as opportunity offered; but, latterly, on the Surrey chapel being built for him in London, he assumed the functions of a settled charge, and he is chiefly known in connection with his ministrations in that place of worship.

The anecdotes recorded of Rowland Hill and his pulpit discourse are numerous and piquant. On one occasion, he was preaching for a public charity, when a note was handed up to him, inquiring if it would be right for a bankrupt to contribute. He noticed the matter in the course of his sermon, and pronounced decidedly that such a person could not do so in Christian honesty. 'But, my friends,' he added, 'I would advise you who are not insolvent, not to pass the plate this evening, as the people will be sure to say: "There goes the bankrupt!"' Another time, at the church of St John's, Wapping, he declared: 'I am come to preach to great sinners, notorious sinners, profane sinners—yea, to *Wapping* sinners.' And one day, on announcing from the pulpit the amount of a liberal collection which had been contributed by his hearers, he remarked: 'You have behaved so well on this occasion, that we mean to have another collection next Sunday. I have heard it said of a good cow, that the more you milk her the more she will give.' One wet day he observed a number of persons enter his chapel to take shelter from a heavy shower of rain, and remarked pithily, that many people were blamed for making religion a *cloak;* but he did not think those were much better who made it an *umbrella!* Petitions were frequently handed to him in the pulpit, requesting the prayers of the congregation for certain persons. A wag one day handed up, 'The prayers of the congregation are requested for the Reverend Rowland Hill, that he will not ride in his carriage on Sunday.' Not being aware of the peculiar nature of the request till he had read it too far to recede, he went on to the end, and then added: 'If the writer of this piece of folly and impertinence is at present in the congregation, and will come into the vestry after service, and allow me to put a saddle on his back, I shall be willing to ride home upon him instead of in my carriage.'

He was very kind and charitable to the poor, but had a great intolerance of dirt and slovenliness. On noticing anything of the kind, he would say: 'Here, mistress, is a trifle for you to buy some soap and a scrubbing-brush: there is plenty of water to be had for nothing. Good Mr Whitefield used to say: "Cleanliness is next to godliness."' In impressing upon his hearers the duty of owing no man anything, he would remark: 'I never pay my debts, and for the best of all reasons, because I never have any debts to pay.' Speaking to tradesmen, he would say: 'You are sometimes more in the path of duty in looking into your ledgers, than into your Bibles. All things should be done decently and in order.' Ludicrous stories are told of people who, from hearing so much about him, imagined his influence must be paramount in every quarter. A sentimental-looking lady one morning made her *entrée* into his study in the most solemn manner. Advancing by measured steps towards the preacher, she began: 'Divine shepherd'——

''Pon my word, ma'am!'

'I hear you have great influence with the royal family.'

'Well, ma'am, and did you hear anything else?'

'Now, seriously, sir—my son has most wonderful poetic powers. Sir, his poetry is of a sublime order—noble, original, fine!'

Hill muttered to himself: 'Well, I wonder what will come next?' and his visitor continued:

'Yes, sir, pardon the liberty, and I therefore called to ask you to get him made *poet laureate!*'

'Ma'am, you might as well ask me to get him made archbishop of Canterbury!' Whereupon the colloquy terminated.

Another day, a foreigner was announced, who entered with: 'Meester Hill, I have heard you are a wonderful great, goot man—can do anyting.'

'Mercy on us! then I must be a wonderful man indeed.'

'Yes, sare, so you are a very wonderful man; so I call to ask you to *make my ambassador do his duty by me.*'

'Sir, I can assure you I have not the honour of knowing him.'

'Oh, sare, but he regard a letter from you.'

'Sir, I can have no possible influence with him, and cannot take the liberty of writing to him on a subject about which I know nothing.'

'But, sare, I will tell you.'

Then seeing no other way of getting rid of his visitor, he concluded by saying: 'Well, sir, you may give my compliments to the ambassador, and say that *I advise him to do his duty;* and that will do as well as writing.'

'Very goot, sare—goot-day.'

He was very severe in rebuking hypocrisy, and those persons who had disgraced their religious profession by some discreditable action. An individual in this predicament met him one morning as he was going out, and saluted him with: 'How do you do, Mr Hill, I am delighted to see you once more?'

'What! ar'n't you hanged yet?' was the reply.

An adherent of Antinomianism, who was rather given to the bottle, asked him one day: 'Now, do you think, Mr Hill, a glass of spirits will drive grace out of my heart?'

'No,' he replied, 'for there is none in it!'

A lady, who led rather a gay and worldly life, once remarked to him: 'Oh! I am afraid lest, after all, I should not be saved!'

'I am glad to hear you say so,' answered Hill, 'for I have been long afraid for you, I assure you.'

On one occasion he was addressing a number of candidates for the ministry, and said: 'I will tell you a story. A barber, having amassed a comfortable independence, retired to his native place, where he became a preacher in a small chapel. Another person from the same village being similarly fortunate, settled there also, and attended the ministry of the barber. Wanting a new wig, he said to his pastor: "*You* might as well make it for me," to which he assented. The wig was sent home, badly made, but charged at nearly double the usual price. The good man said nothing; but when anything particularly profitable escaped the lips of the preacher, he observed to himself: "Excellent—but, *oh! the wig.*" When the barber prayed with apparent unction, he also thought this should touch my heart, but, *oh! the wig.* Now, my dear young brethren, whenever you are placed, *remember the wig!*'

The anecdotes recorded above of this celebrated divine may be depended on for their authenticity; but it is otherwise with a host of other sayings ascribed to him. It is related that he used, in the pulpit, to make personal allusions to his wife, as an example of the transitoriness of beauty and the necessity of humility and self-depreciation. In lecturing on the vanities of dress, he is reported to have said: 'Ladies love fine caps; so does Mrs Hill. Yesterday, came home a five-guinea one; but she will never wear it, for I poked it into the fire, bandbox and all.' On one Sunday morning, the same veracious chroniclers represent him as apostrophising his wife, when entering chapel, with: 'Here comes my wife with a chest of drawers on her head! She went out to buy them, and spent all her money in that hoity-toity bonnet!'

These pleasant little stories, like, unfortunately, many other good things related of different people, are purely fictitious. The subject of them was amused with the generality of them, but expressed great indignation on learning the speeches ascribed to him in reference to Mrs Hill. 'It is an abominable untruth,' he would exclaim, 'derogatory to my character as a Christian and a gentleman—they would make me out a bear!'

In the course of his ministry, Rowland Hill paid three visits to Scotland, the last in 1824. On the first two occasions he delivered sermons to immense crowds in the Edinburgh Circus, and also on the Calton Hill, besides visiting Glasgow and Paisley. His style of preaching was rather a novelty in the north, where the smooth rounded periods of Blair and Robertson had, for many years, formed the models of pulpit eloquence. It was, moreover, made the subject of animadversion by the General Assembly of the Church, who issued a 'pastoral admonition' against countenancing such irregular and itinerant preachers as Rowland Hill and his coadjutors, the Haldanes. In connection with this subject, it is related of him that, on his being asked the reason why his carriage-horses bore such strange names (one of the quadrupeds being denominated *Order*, and the other *Decorum*), he answered: 'Oh, they said in the north, "Mr Hill rides upon the backs of *order* and *decorum;*" so I called one of my horses *Order*, and the other *Decorum*, that they might tell the truth in one way, if they did not in another.'

Rowland Hill married, in 1773, Miss Mary Tudway, of Somersetshire, with whom he lived happily for a space of nearly sixty years. She died in August 1830, and was followed shortly afterwards by her husband, who departed on 11th

April 1833, in his eighty-eighth year. Almost to the last he maintained his mental vigour unimpaired, and delivered his last sermon in Surrey chapel little more than a week previous to his decease. Though so popular and renowned as a preacher, his literary productions are few; but the principal one, his *Village Dialogues*, will, from the vigour and raciness of humour which it displays, interest all classes of readers, apart from any religious predilections.

## THE LAST OF THE GEORGES.

The faults of character belonging to George IV. have of late years been largely insisted on, and perhaps it is not possible to extenuate them in any great degree. It is, however, a mistake to suppose that, because a man is a voluptuary, and more remarkable for good manners than good morals, he *therefore* is a person wholly bad. There really is no such being as one wholly bad, or wholly good either. A human being is a mixture of various and often apparently incongruous elements, one relieving and redeeming another, sometimes one assuming a predominance and sometimes another, very much as the accidental provocations of external circumstances may determine. It was so with this monarch, as it was with the humblest of his subjects. *In his lifetime*, one often heard both of pleasant things said, and of amiable things done, by the king. His restoration of the forfeited Scotch peerages in 1824 was a piece of pure generosity towards men who were suffering through no faults of their own. When that measure was determined on, the representative of a forfeited baronet of 1715 applied for a like extension of the royal grace. Though equally suitable from the fact of the family having purchased back their ancestral lands, it was refused by the ministers; but the king, on hearing of it, insisted on the gentleman being gratified. This we can tell on the authority of a person very nearly concerned in the matter.

In Mrs Mathews's Memoirs of her husband is an anecdote shewing conclusively a very great deal of good-nature in the king. The old Polish dwarf, Count Boruwlaski, was, through Mathews's exertions, brought to Carlton House to see the king, who had known him many years before. The two visitors, a dwarf and a player, were treated by the king with great kindness, and, moro than this, with much considerate delicacy. It was in July 1821, when the approaching coronation and some less pleasant matters were greatly occupying the royal mind. When Boruwlaski came away, Mathews found him in tears, and learned that it was entirely owing to the kindness the king had manifested towards him. While the two were for a little while apart, the king had taken the opportunity to inquire if the little count required any pecuniary help to make his latter days comfortable, avowing his desire to supply whatever was necessary. The king had also offered to shew his coronation-robes to the dwarf, and further asked if he retained any recollection of a favourite valet of his, whom he named. 'The count professing a perfect remembrance of the man, the king said: "He is now, poor fellow, on his death-bed. I saw him this morning, and mentioned your expected visit. He expressed a great desire to see you, which I ventured to promise he should do; for I have such a regard for him, that I would gratify his last hours as much as possible. Will you, count, do me the favour of paying my poor faithful servant a short visit? He is even now expecting you. I hope you will not refuse to indulge a poor, suffering, dying creature." The count of course expressed his perfect readiness to obey the king's wishes.

'Boruwlaski was first shewn the robes, and then conducted to the chamber of the sick man, which was fitted up with every comfort and care; a nurse and another attendant in waiting upon the sufferer. When the count was announced, the poor invalid desired to be propped up in his bed. He was so changed by time and sickness, that the count no longer recognised the face with which his memory was familiar. The nurse and attendant having retired into an adjoining room, the dying man (for such he was, and felt himself to be) expressed the great obligation he felt at such a visit, and spoke most gratefully of him whom he designated the *best of masters;* told the count of all the king's goodness to him, and, indeed, of his uniform benevolence to all that depended upon him; mentioned that his majesty, during the long course of his poor servant's illness, notwithstanding the circumstances that had agitated himself so long, his numerous duties and cares, his present anxieties and forthcoming ceremonies, had never omitted to visit his bedside *twice every day*, not for a moment merely, but long enough to soothe and comfort him, and to see that he had everything necessary and desirable, telling him all particulars of himself that were interesting to an old and attached servant and humble friend. This account was so genuine in its style, and so affecting in its relation, that it deeply touched the heart of the listener. The dying man, feeling exhaustion, put an end to the interview by telling the count that he only prayed to live long enough to greet his dear master after his *coronation*—to hear that the ceremony had been performed with due honour, and without any interruption to his dignity—and that then he was ready to die in peace.'

Mrs Mathews adds: 'Poor Boruwlaski returned to the royal presence, as I have related, utterly subdued by the foregoing scene; upon which every feeling heart will, I am persuaded, make its own comment, unmixed with party-spirit or prejudice.'*

## FRANCIS HORNER.

To the rising generation, the name of Francis Horner is comparatively little known, though as the friend of Jeffrey, Brougham, and Sydney Smith, a contributor to the *Edinburgh Review*, and a brilliant and influential speaker on the side of the Whigs, in the House of Commons, his name is intimately connected with the political and literary history of the early part of the present century. Cut off by an insidious and consuming disease at the premature age of thirty-eight, in the very flower of his parliamentary reputation, he had not yet so far matured his powers as to leave behind a durable impress of his character and abilities. Yet the universal regret by which the tidings of his death were received at the time, testify how exalted were the hopes which the intelligence of his countrymen had entertained respecting him—

* *Memoirs of Charles Mathews*, 1839, iii. 227.

hopes which a perusal of his literary remains, limited in amount as these are, induce us to pronounce to have been thoroughly justifiable.

The history of this brilliant young man is not much diversified by incident. His father was a wealthy merchant in the city of Edinburgh, and Francis received his education in the High School there, then under the rectorship of the distinguished classical scholar, Dr Adam. Always of a studious, retiring disposition, he rarely mingled in the sports of the other boys, among whom, however, he held the proud pre-eminence of being the *dux* or head-scholar. The bent of his mind, from the first, seems to have been towards a profession to which the art of oratory formed a leading adjunct, and he accordingly chose that of an advocate at the Scottish bar. With the view of getting rid of his northern accent, his father sent him, when about seventeen, to an academy at Shacklewell, near London, conducted by a Mr Hewlett, who succeeded so well in smoothing down the young Scotchman's Doric, that in after-life it is said to have been perfectly indistinguishable. Returning to Edinburgh, he commenced his legal studies, and in due time was admitted a member of the Faculty of Advocates. Here his avocations and sympathies naturally brought him into close fellowship with Francis Jeffrey, and the rest of that brilliant coterie which embraced so enthusiastically the cause of progress, and established the *Edinburgh Review* as the promulgator of their sentiments. He was also one of the most distinguished members of the Speculative Society, a debating association in Edinburgh, which then included some of the most splendid oratorical and literary talent in Great Britain.

After practising for some time as an advocate, he resolved on qualifying himself for the English bar, as affording a better field for his talents, and also as opening up to him more readily the path of distinction in public life. He accordingly proceeded to London, where he entered himself as a student at Lincoln's Inn, and was called to the bar in 1807, having the previous year been returned to parliament for the borough of St Ives, in Cornwall, through the influence of Lord Henry Petty, afterwards the Marquis of Lansdowne. He subsequently sat successively in three other parliaments, the last place for which he was returned being St Mawes, in Cornwall. During a period of about ten years, he distinguished himself as one of the most effective members of the Opposition, on all questions of commercial polity, and more especially those relating to the currency. Towards the end of 1816, his constitution, never robust, began visibly to give way, and in the hope of re-establishing his health, he was recommended to try the curative influences of a southern climate. He accordingly proceeded to Italy, and took up his abode at Pisa, where for a time he was cheered by the appearances of convalescence. These, however, proved fallacious, and the difficulty of breathing, and other symptoms of his malady, having returned with renewed severity, he expired on the evening of Saturday, 8th February 1817.

The regret occasioned in England by his death was great and profound. Eloquent tributes to his memory were rendered in the House of Commons by Lord Morpeth, Mr Canning, and others; but it was in private life, among the personal friends to whom he had endeared himself by the uprightness and amiability of his disposition, that his loss was most sensibly felt. Sydney Smith used to declare of him, that he had the ten commandments written in his face, which bore so thoroughly the impress of virtue and honesty, that as the clerical wag remarked, no jury could possibly convict him on any charge, and he might consequently commit all sorts of crimes with impunity. His talents as an orator, statesman, and scholar were only exceeded by the modesty which characterised his whole deportment. Had he survived, there is little doubt that he would have attained to the highest offices in the state, and handed down his name to posterity as one of the ablest and most industrious of our political economists. But, like Henry Kirke White and John Keats, whom, however, he only resembled in the gentleness and goodness of his disposition, the brightness of the morning of his life was prematurely extinguished, and his sun went down whilst it was yet day.

---

## THE OLD AND NEW VERSIONS OF THE PSALMS.

Nahum Tate has a place in literary history solely on account of his connection with one of the two authorised versions of the Psalms, printed in the Book of Common Prayer. His merits would never have given him a niche in the Temple of Fame, but for that authorisation.

The Psalms of David have, individually and partially, been translated into an English lyrical form by many persons; but the collections best known are the 'old version' and the 'new version'—the one under the names of Sternhold and Hopkins, the other under those of Brady and Tate. Thomas Sternhold, in the reign of Henry VIII., being, as Warton says, 'of a serious disposition, and an enthusiast to the reformation, was much offended at the lascivious ballads which prevailed among the courtiers; and with a laudable desire to check these indecencies, undertook a metrical version of the Psalter—"thinking thereby," says Anthony Wood, "that the courtiers would sing them instead of their sonnets; *but they did not*, only some few excepting."' Sternhold translated thirty-seven of the Psalms; and they were published collectively in 1549—'drawen into English metre,' as the title-page expressed it. Some few years after this, John Hopkins (of whom very little is known) translated fifty-eight Psalms from the Hebrew, different from those which had been taken in hand by Sternhold; and in 1562 appeared *The Whole Book of Psalms, collected into English metre, by Thomas Sternhold, John Hopkins, and others. Set forth and allowed to be sung in all Churches before and after Morning and Evening Prayer, and also before and after Sermons.* To this day, it is a matter of controversy how the word 'allowed' is to be understood here; but whether the collection received Episcopal authorisation or not, it came into general use, and was in after-years regularly printed with the Book of Common Prayer. The Psalms, however, underwent such repeated changes in words and general style, that Sternhold and Hopkins would hardly have recognised their own work. As originally written, some of the words and phrases were of such a character that, though perhaps not noticeable at the time, they grated on the taste of a later age. The following examples are from four of the Psalms:

For why their hartes were nothyng bent,
To him *nor to his trade;*
Nor yet to keep nor to performe
The Covenant that was made!

What! is his goodness clean decaid
*For ever and a day?*
Or is his promise now delaid,
And doth his truth decay?

Confound them that do apply
And seeke to make my shame;
And at my harme do laugh, and cry
*So, so, there goes the game!*

Why dost withdraw thy hand aback,
And hide it in thy lappe?
O pluck it out, and be not slack,
To *give thy foe a rappe!*

The last of these four verses is addressed to the Deity! The old version, even after all the dressing-up it received, was a very poor affair; but Bishop Secker said a good word for it. He contended that the Psalms, thus set, suited the common people, for whom they were intended. 'The plainer they are, the sooner they understand them; the lower their style is, the better is it levelled to their capacities; and the heavier they go, the more easily can they keep pace with them.'

Nicholas Brady, born in Ireland in 1659, made a new metrical translation of some of the Psalms; and Nahum Tate, also born in Ireland about the same year, translated others. It is, however, not now known who prepared that 'new version' which comprises the labours of Brady, Tate, and others left unmentioned. Tate was, for a time, poet-laureate. A severe critic has characterised him as 'the author of the worst alterations of Shakspeare, the worst version of the Psalms of David, and the worst continuation of a great poem (*Absalom and Achitophel*) extant;' but this is going a little too far in reference to the Psalms. These translations are, nevertheless, rather spiritless. Dr Watts received a letter from his brother, in which the latter said:—'Tate and Brady still keep near the same pace. I know not what beast they ride (one that will be content to carry double); but I am sure it is no Pegasus. There is in them a mighty deficiency of that life and soul which are necessary to rouse our fancies and kindle and fire our passions.' More modern versions of the Psalms are now very largely used in English churches; but as the ecclesiastical authorities have not made any combined move in the matter, the version of Brady and Tate is still bound up with the Book of Common Prayer.

---

## AUGUST 13.

St Hippolytus, martyr, 252. St Cassian, martyr. St Radegundes, queen of France, 587. St Wigbert, abbot and confessor, about 747.

---

*Born.*—Dr William Wotton, author of *Reflections on Ancient and Modern Learning*, 1666, *Wrentham, Suffolk;* Matthew Terrasson, jurist, 1669, *Lyons;* Antoine-Laurent Lavoisier, eminent chemist, 1743, *Paris;* Adelaide, consort of William IV. of England, 1792, *Upper Saxony.*



*Died.*—Tiberius II., Roman emperor, 582, *Constantinople;* Emperor Louis II., 875, *Milan;* Pope Sixtus IV., 1484; Francis Peck, antiquary, 1743, *Godeby, Leicestershire;* Henri Louis du Hamel, natural philosopher, 1782, *Paris;* Dr Gilbert Stuart, historian, 1786, *Musselburgh;* Robert Plumer Ward, novelist, 1846.

### AN EARTHQUAKE IN SCOTLAND.

Earthquakes are of very rare occurrence in the British Isles, or, at least, such as are of sufficient violence to attract attention. Scientific observers have not yet arrived at any very definite result as to the causes of these phenomena; but it is known that, when begun, they take the form of an earth-*wave*, propagated over a large area in a very small space of time. Observers in distant towns, frightened by what they see and hear, seldom can tell to a second, or even a minute, when these shocks occur; but if the times were accurately noted, it would probably be found that the shocks occur at consecutive instants along a line of country. Among the small number of recorded earthquakes in Great Britain, that of 1816 takes rather a notable place. At about eleven o'clock on the evening of the 13th of August, shocks were felt over nearly the whole of the north of Scotland. The Scottish newspapers gave accounts which, varying in detail, agreed in general results. From Aberdeen, a letter said: 'Where we sat, the house was shaken to the foundation; the heaviest articles of furniture were moved; and a rumbling noise was heard, such as if some heavy bodies were rolling along the roof. In many houses the bells were set ringing, and the agitation of the wires continued visible for some time after the cessation of the shock. It has been described to us, by one who was in Lisbon at that time, as exactly resembling the commencement of the earthquake in that city on the 6th of June 1807.' This Aberdeen letter states that the shock lasted only six seconds, and seemed to travel from south-south-east to north-north-west. A letter from Perth said: 'Persons in bed felt a sensible agitation, or rather concussion, in an upward direction; and if the bed happened to be in contact with the wall, a lateral shock was also felt. In some houses, the chairs and tables moved backwards and forwards, and even the bells were set ringing. Birds in cages were thrown down from the sticks on which they were perched, and exhibited evident signs of fear.' A writer at Montrose said: 'The leaves of folding-tables were heard to rattle; the fire-irons rang against the fenders, bells in rooms and passages were set ringing, in many kitchens the cooking utensils and dishes made a noise, and next morning many of the doors were found difficult to open. One gentleman observed his bookcase move from the wall, and fall back again to it. . . . Many leaped from bed, imagining their houses were falling; while others ran down stairs in great anxiety, supposing that some accident had happened in the lower part of their houses. In this neighbourhood, two excisemen, who were on the watch for smugglers, whom they expected in a certain direction, had lain down on the ground; and when the shock took place, one of them leaped up, calling to his companion: "There they are, for I feel the ground shaking under their horses' feet."' Forres, Strathearn, Dingwall, the Carse of Gowrie, and other towns and districts, had a similar tale to tell. At Dunkeld, the liquor was shaken out of the glasses as a family sat at supper. At Dornoch, there was a mound crossing a narrow part of the Firth, with three arches at one end for small vessels to go under; those arches were thrown down. At Inverness, women fainted, and many were seen in the streets almost naked, calling out that their children had been killed in their arms. Many houses were damaged, and almost the whole were forsaken by the inhabitants, who fled under an impression that a second shock might occur. . . . The walls of many houses were rent from top to bottom, and several of the largest stones thrown down on the roof.' One of the scared inhabitants declared, that 'he was tossed in his bed, as he had never been tossed out at sea, for full five minutes;' and other ludicrous misstatements of a similar kind were made. There is no evidence that any lives were lost.

## HAWKING IN THE OLDEN TIME.

Of all the country sports appertaining to the upper classes during the middle ages, hawking may be fairly considered as the most distinctively aristocratic. It was attended with great expense; its practice was overlaid with a jargon of terms, all necessary to be learned by the gentleman who would fit himself for the company of others in the field; and thus hawking, in the course of centuries, became a semi-science, to be acquired by a considerable amount of patience and study.

Hawking in Europe appears to have originated with the northern nations, and to have grown into importance along with themselves. The training of a hawk for the field was an essential part of the education of a young Saxon nobleman; and a present of a well-trained hawk was a gift to be welcomed by a king. Our Edward the Confessor spent the larger part of the time he did not consume in study in the sports of hunting or hawking; and Alfred the Great is reported to have written a treatise on the last-named sport. It was, however, those enthusiastic sportsmen, the early Norman kings and nobles, who carried the art to perfection, and established its rules and customs; inventing a language for falconry, and surrounding it with all the formalism of the stately rule of feudality.

To be seen bearing a hawk on the hand, was to be seen in the true character of a gentleman; and the grade of the hawk-bearer was known also by the bird he bore. Thus, the gerfalcon was appropriated to a king; the falcon-gentle, to a prince; the falcon of the rock, to a duke; the peregrine-falcon, to an earl; the merlin, to a lady; and so on through the various ranks. The goshawk was permitted to the yeoman; the nobby, to a young man; while the ordinary serving-men were allowed to practise with the kestrel. Priests were permitted the sparrow-hawk, but the higher clergy were, of course, allowed to use the birds pertaining to their rank; and their love of the sport, and pride of display, are satirised by many writers of their own era. In a poem on the evil times of Edward II., preserved in the Auchenleck MS. (Advocates' Library, Edinburgh), the author complains that—

'These abbots and priors do again* their rights,
They ride with hawk and hound, and counterfeit knights.'

* That is, act against.

Piers Plowman is equally loud against their appearing with 'an heap of houndes at their heels;' and Chaucer says:

'They ride coursers like knights,
With hawks and with hounds.'

In the reign of Edward III., the bishop of Ely attended the service of the church in the great abbey at Bermondsey, Southwark, leaving his hawk on its perch in the cloister; the hawk was stolen while there, and the bishop solemnly excommunicated the thieves. Had they been caught, they would have been rigorously treated by the laws, for their crime had been made felony. If a hawk was on any occasion lost, the finder was compelled to make it known to the sheriff of his county, that its noble owner might recover it, or the finder was liable to two years' imprisonment, and payment of the full value of the bird; if he could not do that, his punishment was increased. Fines also awaited such as carried hawks awarded by the laws of the chase to the use only of men higher in rank, and all kinds of protective restrictions surrounded the bird and the pastime.

'A knowledge of hunting and hawking was an essential requisite in accomplishing the character of a knight,' says Warton; and a gentleman rarely appeared in public without his hawk on his fist. The custom was carried to the extreme; and a satirist of the fifteenth century very properly censures such as bring their birds to church with them:

'Into the church there comes another sot,
Without devotion strutting up and down,
For to be seen, and shew his braided coat;
Upon his fist sits sparrow-hawk or falcon.'

This constant connection of man and bird was in some degree necessitated, that it might know its master's voice, and be sufficiently familiar with, and obedient to him. It was laid down as a rule in all old manuals of falconry, that the sportsman constantly attend to the bird, feed him, and train him daily; and very minute are the rules laid down by authors who have, like Dame Juliana Berners, written on field-sports. To part with the hawk, even in circumstances of the utmost extremity, was deemed highly ignominious; and by the ancient laws of France, a knight was forbidden to give up his sword and his hawk, even as the price of his ransom.

The engraving on the following page, copied from the book on field-sports, published in 1614, and entitled *A Jewell for Gentrie*, gives us the full costume of a hawker, as well as a curious specimen of the fashion of the day. It represents King James I., as his majesty appeared in the field. He wears a high copatain hat and feather; a close-fitting jerkin, slashed and decorated with bands of lace; his breeches are in the very height of fashion, stuffed and padded to an enormous extent about the hip, tapering toward the knee, and covered with lace and embroidery. To his girdle is hung the large purse in which the hawker carried the implements necessary to the sport, or the hood and jesses removed from the hawk, which was perched on the left hand. This hand was protected from the talons of the bird by being covered with a thick glove, often highly enriched with needle-work and spangles. In his right hand the king carries a staff, which was used to assist the bearer when following the flight of the hawk on foot, in leaping a rivulet or ditch. Our Henry VIII. had once a very narrow escape of his life when following his bird at Hitchin, in Hertfordshire. In jumping a ditch, the pole broke, and he fell head first into a mass of mud, which must have smothered him, had not one of his followers leaped in after him, and with some difficulty rescued him from his perilous situation.

JAMES I. IN HAWKING COSTUME.

The dress of the hawk may now be described. It consisted of a close-fitting hood of leather or velvet, enriched with needle-work, and surmounted with a tuft of coloured feathers, for use as well as ornament, inasmuch as they assisted the hand in removing the hood when 'the quarry' (or birds for the hawk's attack) came in sight. A series of leathern and silken straps were affixed to the legs, to train the hawk in short flights, and bring him back to hand; or to hold him there, and free him entirely for a course at the game, by means of the jesses and tyrrits or rings. Othello uses a forcible simile from the practice of hawking, when speaking of his wife, he says:

'If I do prove her haggard,
Though that her jesses were my dear heart-strings,
I'd whistle her off, and let her down the wind,
To prey at fortune.'

A small strap, fastened with rings of leather, passed round each leg of the hawk, just above the talons; they were termed bewets, and each of them had a bell attached. In a flight of hawks, it was so arranged that the different bells varied in tone, so that 'a consort of sweet sounds' might be produced. We engrave two specimens of hawk's bells of mixed metal, which were found in the mud of the Thames, and are still sonorous, one being an octave under the other.

The imagination kindles at the idea of a hawking-party going abroad on a cheerful April morning, over the pleasant fields around an English baronial castle, ladies and gentlemen riding gaily together, while their attendants followed, bearing the perches of the birds, and a motley throng would come after

HAWK'S BELLS.

at a respectful distance, to get a peep at the sports of their betters. The aërial stage on which the play was played gave a peculiar elevation and liveliness to the scene. A sad affair it was for the poor herons and cranes of the neighbouring meres, but a right blithsome time for the gentlefolks who aimed at making them a prey. For the pacific King James, the sport had a fascination that seems to have thrown every other pleasure of life into the shade.

In Heywood's curious play, entitled *A Woman Killed with Kindness*, 1617, is a hawking scene, containing a striking allusion to these bells. It is a vivid picture of country nobles at this favourite sport, and the dialogue is curious for the jargon of hunting-terms used in it. The following is as much of the scene as will assist the reader in reproducing, to 'his mind's eye,' the glories of the hawking-ground in the days of James I.:

'*Sir Charles Mountford.* So; well cast off: aloft, aloft! well flown!
Oh now she takes her at the *sowse*, and strikes her down
To th' earth, like a swift thunder-clap.
*Wendall.* She hath struck ten angels * out of my way!
*Sir Francis Acton.* A hundred pound from me!
*Sir Charles.* What, falconer?
*Falconer.* At hand, sir!
*Sir Charles.* Now hath she seiz'd the fowl, and 'gins to *plume* her;
*Rebeck* her not: rather stand still and *check* her.
So, seize her *gets*, her *jesses*, and her *bells*:
Away!
*Sir Francis.* My hawk kill'd too!
*Sir Charles.* Aye; but 'twas at the *querre*,
Not at the *mount*, like mine.
*Sir Francis.* Judgment, my masters.
*Cranwell.* Yours missed her at the *ferre*.
*Wendall.* Aye, but our Merlin first had *plum'd* the fowl.
And twice *renew'd* her from the river, too:
Her bells, Sir Francis, had not both one weight,
Nor was one semi-tune above the other:
Methinks these Milan bells do sound too full,†
And spoil the mounting of your hawk.

* It should be noted, that these gentlemen are betting on the prowess of their hawks. The angel was a gold coin of the value of 6*s.* 8*d.*, and had its name from the figure of the archangel Michael piercing the dragon, which was impressed on the obverse.

† The bells manufactured at Milan were considered to be of the best quality and sweetest sound. A portion of silver was mixed with the metal used in their fabrication.

*Sir Charles.* 'Tis lost!
*Sir Francis.* I grant it not. Mine likewise seiz'd a fowl
Within her talons; and you saw her paws
Full of the feathers: both her *petty singles*,
And her *long singles*, grip'd her more than other;
The *terrials* of her legs were stain'd with blood
Not of the fowl only; she did *discomfit*
Some of her feathers; but she brake away.'

The care necessary to the proper training of a hawk has already been alluded to. A continuous attention was given to a favourite bird, so that its natural wildness should be subdued, and it become familiar to its master. 'It can be no more disgrace to a great lord,' says Peacham, 'to draw a fair picture, than to cut his hawk's meat.' The hawk was trained to fly at the game, by means of a lure made in the shape of birds' wings, and partially formed of wing-feathers, inserted in a pad of leather or velvet, quilted with needle-work, and having a swivel-hook on the upper part, to which a long cord was attached; the lure being thrown upward in the air, and guided like a boy's kite; the hawk was trained to fly at, and strike it, as if it was a real bird; he was also trained at the same time to desist, and return to his master's fist, at his whistle. The bird could not get entirely away during this practice, as the long creance or string was appended to one leg by which he might be drawn back. The form of the lure is very clearly given in the wood-cut here copied from Geffry Whitney's *Choice of Emblems and other Devises*, printed at Leyden in 1586. This emblem typifies *spes vana;* and is thus quaintly elucidated by the author:

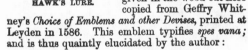

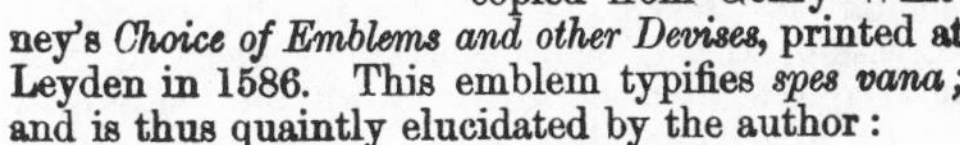

HAWK'S LURE.

'The eager hawk, with sudden sight of lure,
Doth stoop, in hope to have her wished prey:
So many men do stoope to sights unsure:
And courteous speech doth keep them at the bay.
Let such beware, lest friendly looks be like
The lure, to which the soaring hawk did strike!'

The practice of hawking appears to have suddenly declined in the early part of the seventeenth century. The expense and trouble of training the birds were great, and the improvement effected in firearms made shooting a more convenient and certain sport. Fowling-pieces of a light and elegant kind were manufactured, and to suit the tastes of the wealthy, were inlaid with gold and silver, or enriched by carving the stock with elaborate ornament in relief. 'The art of shooting flying' was cultivated with assiduity, giving a novel interest to field-sports, and hawking lost its charm for ever.

The office of Grand Falconer of England is still a hereditary service of the crown, and held by the Duke of St Alban's. The King's Mews at Charing Cross—the site of the building in which the king's hawks were kept while they *mewed* or moulted—has given a term to the English language, a stable-lane in any of our large cities being commonly called a mews-lane.

giving great clearness to the tone. Others, of a cheaper kind, were made at Dort, in Holland; they emitted a shrill but pleasant sound. Of the ordinary bells, the book of St Albans informs us, 'there is great choice, and they are cheap enough.'

---

# AUGUST 14.

St Eusebius, priest and martyr, about end of 3d century. St Eusebius, priest and confessor at Rome, 4th century.

*Born.*—Dr Meric Casaubon, eminent Protestant divine, 1599, *Geneva;* C. J. Vernet, French painter, 1714, *Avignon;* Dr Charles Hutton, distinguished mathematician, 1737, *Newcastle-on-Tyne.*

*Died.*—John I. of Portugal, 1433; Pope Pius II. (Aeneas Silvius Piccolomini), 1464, *Ancona;* Edmund Law, bishop of Carlisle, editor of Locke, 1787, *Rose Castle, Cumberland;* Thomas Sheridan, author of the *Pronouncing Dictionary*, and father of the dramatist, 1788, *Thanet;* George Colman (the elder), dramatist, 1794, *Paddington;* Marquis Luigi Cagnola, distinguished Italian architect, 1833; Rev. Henry Francis Cary, translator of Dante, 1844, *London;* Dr William Buckland, eminent geologist, 1856; George Combe, phrenologist, author of *Essay on the Constitution of Man in Relation to External Objects*, 1858, *Moor Park, Surrey;* A. M. C. Domeril, eminent French naturalist, 1860, *Paris.*

## GEORGE COMBE

Was one of those men who, from various causes, do not fill a very conspicuous place in society, and yet exercise a great influence on their own and on future ages. He was a native of Edinburgh, and spent there nearly the whole of his life of seventy years. Having, in his profession of a writer to the Signet, equivalent to solicitor in England, attained, at about forty-five, to a moderate competency, he retired to devote the remainder of his days to literary and philosophical pursuits. An alliance he formed about that time with an elegant woman, the daughter of the celebrated Mrs Siddons, enabled him to do this in a style of dignity and comfort which made his house thenceforth one of the centres of refined society in the northern capital. In his youth, Mr Combe had entered heartily into the then young science of phrenology, and, in company with his accomplished brother, Dr Andrew Combe, and a few other men of talent, he diffused a large amount of knowledge on this subject, and made it for some years a popular study. The bases of the science, however, have never been established to the satisfaction of the philosophic world, and even its popularity has, in the course of years, somewhat faded. Had Mr Combe been a mere vaticinator upon heads, he would not now be of much account in the rolls of fame. He was, in reality, a man of profound philosophical conceptions; one whose views reached far beyond those of the ordinary men of science and letters of his day. Phrenology, and its great patron, Dr Spurzheim, whatever other effect they might have upon his mind, had at least impressed him with the idea that man is, in one important respect, simply a part of nature, depending on the conditions of his original constitution, and his subsequent nurture and education, for the character he is to bear through life, and on his harmonious action with the other parts of nature surrounding him for success in securing his secular happiness. He put these ideas into a form in which they could be readily apprehended, in his *Essay on the Constitution of Man in relation to External Objects*, and the sale of upwards of a hundred thousand copies in Britain, and its almost equal diffusion in America and Germany, have amply attested that he had here laid hold of a most important, however partial, truth. Inspired by the same views, he wrote several treatises on education, in which the value of a knowledge of the world which surrounds us is eloquently expounded. He everywhere maintained that the brain is the organ of the mind, and as he made no further profession on the subject, it was felt by many that he too much countenanced materialistic doctrines. Against this, however, it ought to be observed, that Mr Combe invariably traced natural affairs to a divine origin and upholding, and never failed to inculcate that God has so constituted the world that the moral faculties of man are certain of an ultimate supremacy. Matter is a thing which may be undervalued as well as overvalued. To say that there is nothing in this world but matter and certain laws impressed upon it, is to take but a poor and narrow view of the *cosmos*. But, on the other hand, matter is a far more respectable thing than many, from their language, seem to consider it. Only think of the endless worlds it constitutes, of the wonderful relations of its chemical elements, of the admirable psychical operations and sentiments of which it is the observable vehicle in organised beings, and we must be lost in admiration of the magnificent purposes with which the Creator has charged it. A memoir of George Combe, by Charles Gibbon, appeared in 1878.

The subject of this notice was tall and thin, with a handsome cast of countenance, and a head of fine proportions. He was generally in weak health, but by great care avoided serious ailments, and succeeded in protracting the thread of life to the Psalmist's period. He was cheerful. social, and benevolent, with a large infusion of the simplicity which seems to form a necessary element in true greatness. From the effect of professional habits, he was methodical to a degree which often provoked a smile; but the fault was essentially connected with the conscientiousness which formed a conspicuous part of his character.

## THE FUNERAL OF QUEEN CAROLINE.

Tuesday, the 14th August 1821, presented a singular scene of commotion in London. That day had been fixed by the authorities for the removal of the remains of Queen Caroline from Brandenburgh House, where she had expired a week previously, to Harwich, for the purpose of embarking them there for the continent, in terms of the instructions contained in her own will, which directed that her body should be deposited among those of her ancestors at Brunswick. A military guard had been provided by government for the funeral cortège; but, with the view of avoiding as much as possible, in the circumstances, any popular demonstrations, it was resolved that the procession should not pass through the city, a determination which gave the greatest offence both to the queen's executors and a large portion of the community at large. According to the prescribed route, the procession was to go from Hammersmith, through Kensington, into the Uxbridge Road, then down the Edgeware Road, into the New Road; along the City Road, Old Street, and Mile-end to Romford; and thence through Chelmsford and Colchester to Harwich. On the appointed day, an immense crowd congregated about Hammersmith, though the rain was falling in torrents. On the funeral reaching the gravel-pits at Kensington, and proceeding to turn off to the left, the way was blocked up with carts and wagons, to prevent further advance towards the Uxbridge Road, and the procession, after halting for an hour and a half, was compelled to move on towards London. Arriving at Kensington Gore, an attempt was made by the head of the police force, Sir R. Baker, with a detachment of Life Guards, to force open the park-gates, but in vain, the crowd, which had already given way to many hostile demonstrations, shouting loudly all the while: 'To the City—to the City!' Hyde Park Corner being reached, the gate there was found barricaded, and the procession moved up Park Lane, but was shortly met by similar obstructions. It then returned to the Corner, where the soldiers had, in the meantime, succeeded in clearing an entrance, and made its way through Hyde Park. On reaching Cumberland Gate, this was found closed, and a furious conflict ensued with the mob, who hurled at the troops the stones of the park-wall, which had been thrown down by the pressure of the crowd. Many of the soldiers were severely hurt, and their comrades were provoked to use their firearms, by which two persons were killed and several wounded. After some further clearing away of obstructions, the procession moved down the Edgeware and along the New Roads till it reached the Tottenham Court Road, where the mob made so determined a stand against it proceeding further in the prescribed direction, that Sir R. Baker deemed it most advisable to turn the cortège down the Tottenham Court Road, and thence by Drury Lane through the Strand and the City. So resolute was the popular determination to compel the procession to traverse the city, that every street, including Holborn, through which a detour could have been made to reach the New Road or the City Road, was carefully blocked up and rendered impassable. Having emerged from the City, the funeral train proceeded quietly on its way to Chelmsford, where it arrived at two o'clock on the following morning. From Chelmsford it proceeded to Colchester, and thence to Harwich, where it embarked for the continent on the evening of the 16th. The remains reached Brunswick on the 24th, and were deposited the following day in the cathedral, in the vault of the ducal family. An inscription had been directed by the deceased to be placed on her coffin in the following terms: 'Here lies Caroline of Brunswick, the injured Queen of England,' but the British authorities refused to allow this to be done. While the coffin, however, was lying at Chelmsford, on its way to the coast, the queen's executors affixed to it an engraved plate with the obnoxious title, but it was discovered, and removed by the authorities in charge, notwithstanding a vehement protest from the other party. Thus closed the tomb on this unfortunate queen, whom, even after death, the storms which had visited her so fiercely while in life, did not cease to pursue.

## AUGUST 15.

The Assumption of the Blessed Virgin Mary. St Alipius, bishop and confessor, 5th century. St Mac-cartin, Aid or Aed, bishop and confessor in Ireland, 506. St Arnoul or Arnulphus, confessor and bishop of Soissons, 1087.

*Born.*—Robert Blake, celebrated admiral, 1599, *Bridgewater;* Gilles Menage, miscellaneous writer (*Dictionnaire Etymologique*), 1613, *Angers;* Frederick William I. of Prussia, 1688; Napoleon Bonaparte, French emperor, 1769, *Ajaccio, France;* Sir Walter Scott, poet and novelist, 1771, *Edinburgh;* Thomas de Quincey, author of *Confessions of an Opium Eater*, 1785, *Manchester.*

*Died.*—Honorius, Roman emperor, 423; St Stephen, first king of Hungary, 1038, *Buda;* Alexius Comnenus, Greek emperor, 1118; Philippa, queen of Edward III. of England, 1369; James, Earl of Douglas, 1388, *Otterburn;* Gerard Noodt, distinguished jurist, 1725, *Leyden;* Joseph Miller, comedian, 1738; Nicolas Hubert de Mongault, translator of Cicero's Letters, 1746, *Paris;* Dr Thomas Shaw, traveller, 1751, *Oxford;* Thomas Tyrwhitt, editor of Chaucer, 1786; Dr Herbert Mayo, eminent physiologist, 1852, *Bad-Weilbach, near Mayence.*

### NAPOLEON BONAPARTE.

After all that has been said and written on the subject of Napoleon Bonaparte, the conclusion is forced upon us, that he had few of the elements in his composition which go to make up the character of a true hero. Of unbounded ambition, perfectly unscrupulous as to the means by which he might accomplish his ends, and tinged throughout by an utter selfishness and regardlessness of others, we can deem him no more entitled to a real and intelligent admiration, than a previous occupant of the French throne, Louis XIV., brilliant in many respects though the reigns of both these men undoubtedly were.

That the first Napoleon was in many ways a benefactor to France, cannot reasonably be denied. By his military and administrative abilities he raised himself to supreme power at a time when the country was emerging from the lawlessness and terrorism to which she had been subjected after the death of Louis XVI. The divided and profligate government of the Directorate had succeeded the anarchy and violence of the leaders of the Convention. Some powerful hand was required as a dictator to hold the reins of state, and arrange in a harmonious and well-adjusted train the various jarring and unstable systems of government. Had he conducted himself with the same prudence as his nephew, the late emperor, he might have died absolute sovereign of France, and the history of that country been written without the narrative of the Restoration of the Bourbons, the Three Days of July 1830, and the Revolution of February 1848. But vaulting ambition with him overleaped itself, and his impetuous self-willed nature, or what he himself used to consider his destiny, drove him headlong to his ruin. Regardless of the warnings addressed to him by the most sagacious of his counsellors, contemptuously defiant of the coalitions formed to impede his progress, and careless, lastly, of the odium which his tyrannical sway in the end excited among his own subjects, he found himself at length left utterly destitute of resources, and obliged to submit to such terms as his enemies chose to impose. His career presents one of the most melancholy and impressive lessons that history affords. And yet how eagerly would a large portion of the French nation revert to a policy which, in his hands, overwhelmed it only with vexation and disaster!

Napoleon's character may be contemplated in three phases—as a statesman, as a commander, and as a private individual. In the first of these capacities, he displayed, as regards France, much that was worthy of commendation in point of political and social reform. A vigorous administration of the laws, a simplification of legal ordinances and forms, a wise and tolerating system in religious matters, many important and judicious sanitary measures, the embellishment of the capital, and patronage afforded to art and science, must all be allowed to have been distinguishing attributes of his sway. But how little did he understand the art of conciliating and securing the allegiance of the countries which he had conquered! A total ignoring of all national predilections and tendencies seems to have been here habitually practised by him, and nowhere was this more conspicuous than in his treatment of Germany. That system of centralisation, by which he sought to render Paris the capital of a vast empire, at the expense of the dignity and treasures of other cities and kingdoms, might flatter very sensibly the national vanity of France, but was certain, at the same time, to exasperate the degraded and plundered countries beyond all hopes of forgiveness. And the outrages which he tacitly permitted his troops to exercise on the unfortunate inhabitants, argue ill for the solidity or wisdom of his views as a governor or statesman.

The military genius of Bonaparte has been, and still is, a fruitful theme for discussion. In the early part of his career, he achieved such successes as rendered his name a terror to Europe, and gained for him a *prestige* which a series of continuous and overwhelming defeats in the latter period of his history was unable to destroy. But in the game of war, results alone can form the criterion, and the victories of Marengo, of Austerlitz, and of Wagram can scarcely be admitted in compensation for the blunders of the Russian campaign and the overthrow at Waterloo. One qualification, however, of a great general, the capacity of recognising and rewarding merit, in whatever position it might be found, was eminently conspicuous in Napoleon. Favouritism, and the influence of rank or fortune, were almost entirely unknown in his army. Few of his generals could boast much of family descent, and the circumstance that bravery and military talent were certain to receive their due reward in promotion or otherwise, gave every man a personal interest in the triumph of the emperor's arms.

An inquiry into the personal character of Bonaparte exhibits him perhaps in a still less favourable light than that in which we have hitherto been considering him. Of a cold-blooded and impassible temperament, and engrossed exclusively by the master-passion, ambition, he betrayed no tendencies towards any of those aberrations by which the characters of so many other great men have been stained. But the very cause which kept his moral purity inviolate, rendered him totally insensible to the promptings of love and affection when his interest seemed to require that they should be disregarded. His ruthless abandonment of Josephine is a proof of this. And the insensibility with which he appears to have regarded the sacrifice of myriads of Frenchmen to his lust for power, leads us to form a very low estimate of the kindness or goodness of his heart. Two facts of his life stand prominently forward as evidence—the one of the dark and arbitrary injustice of his nature, the other of a contemptible jealousy and littleness. These are the judicial murder of the Duke d'Enghien, and the vindictive and unchivalrous persecution of the talented Madame de Staël, and the amiable Louisa, queen of Prussia.

## JOE MILLER.

It would be curious to note in how many cases the principle of *lucus a non lucendo* has been used, sometimes unintentionally, and sometimes perhaps as a joke, in the application of names. The man whose name is now the representative of the very idea of joking, Joe Miller, is said never to have uttered a joke. This reputed hero of all jokes, in reality an eminent comic actor of the earlier part of the last century, was born in the year 1684; he was no doubt of obscure origin, but even the place of his birth appears to be unknown. In the year 1715, his name occurs for the first time on the bills of Drury Lane theatre as performing, on the last day of April, the part of Young Clincher in Farquhar's comedy of *The Constant Couple; or a Trip to the Jubilee.* Whatever may have been his previous career, it appears certain that his début was a successful one, for from this time he became regularly engaged on the boards of Drury. It was the custom at that time, during the season when the regular theatres were closed, for the actors of perform in temporary theatres, or in booths erected at the several fairs in and near the metropolis, as in Bartholomew's Fair, Smithfield May Fair, Greenwich Fair, and, in this particular year, at the Frost Fair on the frozen Thames, for it was an extraordinary severe season. We find Joe Miller performing with one of the most celebrated of these movable companies—that of the well-known Pinkethman. At Drury Lane, Miller rose constantly in public esteem. At his benefit on the 25th of April 1717, when he played the part of Sir Joseph Whittol, in Congreve's *Old Bachelor*, the tickets were adorned with a design from the pencil of Hogarth, which represented the scene in which Whittol's bully, Noll, is kicked by Sharper. The original engraving is now extremely rare, and therefore, of course, very valuable.

JOE MILLER.

For a rather long period we find Joe Miller acting as a member of the Drury Lane company, and, in the vacation intervals, first associated with Pinkethman, and subsequently established as an independent booth-theatre manager himself. Joe appears also to have been a favourite among the members of his profession, and it has been handed down to us, through tradition and anecdote, that he was a regular attendant at the tavern, still known as the 'Black Jack,' in Portsmouth Street, Clare Market, then the favourite resort of the performers at Drury Lane and Lincoln's Inn Fields' theatres, and of the wits who came to enjoy their society. It is said that at these meetings Miller was remarkable for the gravity of his demeanour, and that he was so completely innocent of anything like joking, that his companions, as a jest, ascribed every new jest that was made to him. Joe

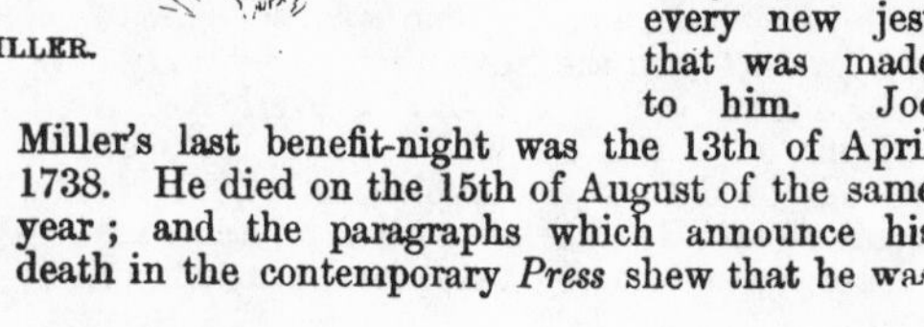

Miller's last benefit-night was the 13th of April 1738. He died on the 15th of August of the same year; and the paragraphs which announce his death in the contemporary *Press* shew that he was

not only greatly admired as an actor, but that he was much esteemed for his personal character.

Miller was interred in the burial-ground of the parish of St Clement Danes, in Portugal Street, where a tombstone was erected to his memory.

JOE MILLER'S TOMBSTONE, ST CLEMENT DANES CHURCHYARD.

About thirty years ago, that burial-ground, by the removal of the mortuary remains, and the demolition of the monuments, was converted into a site for King's College Hospital. Whilst this not unnecessary, yet undesirable, desecration was in progress, the writer saw Joe's tombstone lying on the ground; and, being told that it would be broken up and used as materials for the new building, he took an exact copy of the inscription, which was as follows:

'Here lye the Remains of
Honest Jo: Miller,
who was
a tender Husband,
a sincere Friend,
a facetious Companion,
and an excellent Comedian.
He departed this Life the 15th day of
August 1738, aged 54 years.

*If humour, wit, and honesty could save*
*The humorous, witty, honest, from the grave,*
*The grave had not so soon this tenant found,*
*Whom honesty, and wit, and humour, crowned;*
*Could but esteem, and love preserve our breath,*
*And guard us longer from the stroke of Death,*
*The stroke of Death on him had later fell,*
*Whom all mankind esteemed and loved so well.*

S. Duck.

From respect to social worth,
mirthful qualities, and histrionic excellence,
commemorated by poetic talent in humble life,
the above inscription, which Time
had nearly obliterated, has been preserved
and transferred to this Stone, by order of
Mr Jarvis Buck, *Churchwarden*.
A.D. 1816.'

The 'merry memory' of the comedian, the phrase used in one of the newspaper-paragraphs announcing Joe Miller's death, and the wit and humour ascribed to him in the epitaph, perhaps relate especially to his acting, or they would seem to contradict the tradition of his incapacity for making a joke. It was after his death, however, that he gained his fame as a jester. Among the society in which he usually mixed was a dramatic writer of no great merit, named John Mottley, the son of a Jacobite officer. This man was reduced to the position of living on the town by his wits, and in doing this he depended in a great measure on his pen. Among the popular publications of that time, was a kind easy of compilation, consisting substantially of the same jests, ever newly vamped up, with a few additions and variations. It was a common trick to place on the title of one of these brochures the name of some person of recent celebrity, in order to give it an appearance of novelty. Thus, there had appeared in the sixteenth century, *Scogan's Jests* and *Skelton's Jests;* in the seventeenth, *Tarlton's Jests*, *Hobson's Jests*, *Peele's Jests*, *Hugh Peter's Jests*, and a multitude of others; and in the century following, previous to the death of Joe Miller in 1738, *Pinkethman's Jests*, *Polly Peachum's Jests*, and *Ben Jonson's Jests*. It speaks strongly for the celebrity of Joe Miller, that he had hardly lain a year in his grave, when his name was thought sufficiently popular to grace the title of a jest-book; and it was Mottley who, no doubt pressed by necessity, undertook to compile a new collection which was to appear under it. The title of this volume, which was published in 1739, and sold for one shilling, was *Joe Miller's Jests: or, the Wit's Vade-mecum.* It was stated in the title to have been 'first carefully collected in the company, and many of them transcribed from the mouth, of the facetious gentleman whose name they bear; and now set forth and published by his lamentable friend and former companion, Elijah Jenkins, Esq.' This was of course a fictitious name, under which Mottley chose to conceal his own. It must not be concealed that there is considerable originality in Mottley's collection—that it is not a mere republication, under a different name, of what had been published a score of times before; in fact, it is evidently a selection from the jokes which were then current about the town, and some of them apparently new ones. This was perhaps the reason of its sudden and great popularity. A second and third edition appeared in the same year, and it was not only frequently reprinted during the same century, but a number of spurious books appeared under the same title, as well as similar collections, under such titles as *The New Joe Miller*, and the like.

It appears to have been the custom, during at least two centuries, for people who were going to social parties, to prepare themselves by committing to memory a selection of jokes from some popular jest-book; the result of which would of course be, that the ears of the guests were subjected to the old jokes over and over again. People whose ears were thus wearied, would often express their annoyance, by reminding the repeater of the joke of the book he had taken it from; and, when the popularity of Joe Miller's jests had eclipsed that of all its rivals, the repetition of every old joke would draw forth from some one the exclamation: 'That's a Joe Miller!' until the title was given indiscriminately to every jest which was recognised as not being a new one. Hence arose the modern fame of the old comedian, and the adoption of his name in our language as synonymous with 'an old joke.'

The S. Duck, whose name figures as author of the verses on Miller's tombstone, and who is alluded to on the same tablet, by Mr Churchwarden Buck, as an instance of 'poetic talent in humble life,' deserves a short notice. He was a thresher in the service of a farmer near Kew, in Surrey. Imbued with an eager desire for learning, he, under most adverse circumstances, managed to obtain a few books, and educate himself to a limited degree. Becoming known as a rustic rhymer, he attracted the attention of Caroline, queen of George II., who, with her accustomed liberality, settled on him a pension of £30 per annum; she made him a yeoman of the Guard, and installed him as keeper of a kind of museum she had in Richmond Park, called Merlin's Cave. Not content with these promotions, the generous, but perhaps inconsiderate queen, caused Duck to be admitted to holy orders, and preferred to the living of Byfleet, in Surrey, where he became a popular preacher among the lower classes, chiefly through the novelty of being the 'Thresher Parson.' This gave Swift occasion to write the following quibbling epigram:

'The thresher Duck could o'er the queen prevail;
The proverb says—"No fence against a flail."
From threshing corn, he turns to thresh his brains,
For which her majesty allows him grains;
Though 'tis confest, that those who ever saw
His poems, think 'em all not worth a straw.
Thrice happy Duck! employed in threshing stubble!
Thy toil is lessened, and thy profits double.'

One would suppose the poor thresher to have been beneath Swift's notice, but the provocation was great, and the chastisement, such as it was, merited. For, though few men had ever less pretensions to poetical genius than Duck, yet the court-party actually set him up as a rival, nay, as superior, to Pope. And the saddest part of the affair was, that Duck, in his utter simplicity and ignorance of what really constituted poetry, was led to fancy himself the greatest poet of the age. Consequently, considering that his genius was neglected, that he was not rewarded according to his poetical deserts, by being made the clergyman of an obscure village, he fell into a state of melancholy, which ended in suicide; affording another to the numerous instances of the very great difficulty of doing good. If the well-meaning queen had elevated Duck to the position of farm-bailiff, he might have led a long and happy life, amongst the scenes and the classes of society in which his youth had passed, and thus been spared the pangs of disappointed vanity and misdirected ambition.

---

## THE BATTLE OF OTTERBOURNE AND CHEVY CHASE.

The famous old ballad of *Chevy Chase* is subject to twofold confusion. There are two, if not three, wholly different versions of the ballad; and two wholly independent incidents mixed up by an anachronism. The battle of Otterbourne was a real event. In 1388, the border chieftains carried on a ruthless warfare. The Scots ravaged the country about Carlisle, and carried off many hundred prisoners. They then crossed into Northumberland, and committed further ravages. On their return home, they attacked a castle at Otterbourne, close to the Scottish border; but they were here overtaken, on the 15th of August, by an English force under Henry Percy, surnamed Hotspur, son of the Earl of Northumberland. James, Earl of Douglas, rallied the Scots; and there ensued a desperately fierce battle. The earl was killed on the spot; Lord Murray was mortally wounded; while Hotspur and his brother, Ralph Percy, were taken prisoners. It appears, moreover, that nearly fifty years after this battle, a private conflict took place between Hotspur's *son* and *William*, Earl of Douglas. There was a tacit understanding among the border families, that none should hunt in the domains of the others without permission; but the martial families of Percy and Douglas being perpetually at feud, were only too ready to break through this rule. Percy crossed the Cheviots on one occasion to hunt without the leave of Douglas, who was either lord of the soil or warden of the marches; Douglas resisted him, and a fierce conflict ensued, the particulars of which were not historically recorded. Now, it appears that some ballad-writers of later date mixed up these two events in such a way as to produce a rugged, exciting story out of them. The earliest title of the ballad was, *The Hunting a' the Cheviat;* this underwent changes until it came simply to *Chevy Chase.* In the Rev. George Gilfillan's edition of Percy's *Reliques of Ancient English Poetry,* the oldest known version of the ballad is copied from Hearne, who printed it in 1719 from an old manuscript, to which the name of Rychard Sheale was attached. Hearne believed this to be one Richard Sheale, who was living in 1588; but Percy, judging from the language and idiom, and from an allusion to the ballad in an old Scottish prose work, printed about 1548, inferred that the poet was of earlier date. Various circumstances led Percy to believe that the ballad was written in the time of Henry VI. As given by Hearne and Percy, the *Hunting a' the Cheviat* occupies forty-five stanzas, mostly of four lines each, but some of six, and is divided into two 'Fits' or Sections. The ruggedness of the style is sufficiently shewn in the first stanza:

'The Persè owt of Northombarlande,
And a vowe to God mayde he,
That he wolde hunte in the mountayns
Off Chyviat within dayes thre,
In the mauger * of doughtè Dogles,
And all that ever with him be.'

The ballad relates almost wholly to the conflict arising out of this hunting, and only includes a few incidents which are known to have occurred at the battle of Otterbourne—such as the death of Douglas and the captivity of Hotspur. One of the stanzas runs thus:

'Worde ys commyn to Eaden-burrowe,
To Jamy the Skottishe kyng,
That dougheti Duglas, leyff-tennante of the Merchis,
He lay slayne Cheviat within.'

Percy printed another version from an old manuscript in the Cotton Library. There is also another

* In spite of.

manuscript of this same version, but with fewer stanzas, among the Harleian Collection. This ballad is not confined to the incidents arising out of the hunting by Percy, but relates to the raids and counter-raids of the border-chieftains. Indeed, it accords much better with the historical battle of Otterbourne than with the private feud between the Douglas and the Percy. It consists of seventy stanzas, of four lines each; one stanza will suffice to shew the metre and general style:

'Thus Syr Hary Percye toke the fylde,
For soth, as I you saye:
Jesu Cryste in hevyn on hyght
Dyd helpe hym well that daye.'

But the *Chevy Chase* which has gained so much renown among old ballads, is neither of the above. Addison's critique in the *Spectator* (Nos. 70 and 74) related to a *third* ballad, which Percy supposes cannot be older than the reign of Elizabeth, and which was probably written after—perhaps in consequence of—the eulogium passed by Sir Philip Sidney on the older ballad. Sidney's words were: 'I never heard the old song of Percy and Douglas, that I found not my heart more moved than with a trumpet; and yet it is sung by some blind crowder with no rougher voice than rude style, which being so evil-apparel'd in the dust and cobweb of that uncivil age, what would it work trimmed in the gorgeous eloquence of Pindar!' Addison, approving of the praise here given, dissents from the censure. 'I must, however,' he says, 'beg leave to dissent from so great an authority as that of Sir Philip Sidney, in the judgment which he has passed as to the rude style and evil apparel of this antiquated song; for there are several parts in it where not only the thought but the language is majestic, and the numbers sonorous; at least the apparel is much more gorgeous than many of the poets made use of in Queen Elizabeth's time.' This is taken as a proof that Addison was not speaking of the older versions. Nothing certain is known of the name of the third balladist, nor of the time when he lived; but there is internal evidence that he took one or both of the older versions, and threw them into a more modern garb. His *Chevy Chase* consists of seventy-two stanzas, of four lines each, beginning with the well-known words:

'God prosper long our noble king,
Our lives and safetyes all;
A woful hunting once there did
In Chevy Chase befall.'

The ballad relates mainly to the hunting-exploit, and what followed it: not to the battle of Otterbourne, or to the border-raids generally. Addison does not seem to refer in his criticism to the original ballad; he praises the third ballad for its excellences, without comparing it with any other. Those who have made that comparison, generally admit that the later balladist improved the versification, the sentiment, and the diction in most cases; but Bishop Percy contents that in some few passages the older version has more dignity of expression than the later. He adduces the exploit of the gallant Witherington:

'For Wetharryngton my harte was wo,
That ever he slayne shulde be;
For when both hys leggis were hewyne in to,
Yet he knyled and fought on hys kne.'

The bishop contends that, if this spelling be a little modernised, the stanza becomes much more dignified than the corresponding stanza in the later version:

'For Witherington needs must I wayle,
As one in doleful dumpes;
For when his leggs were smitten off,
He fought upon his stumpes.'

In any sense, however, both the versions—or rather all three versions—take rank among our finest specimens of heroic ballad-poetry.

It will be learned, not without interest, that certain relics or memorials of the fight of Otterbourne are still preserved in Scotland. The story of the battle represents Douglas as having, in a personal encounter with Percy in front of Newcastle, taken from him his spear and its pennon or hanging flag, saying he would carry it home with

THE DOUGLAS BANNER.

him, and plant it on his castle of Dalkeith. The battle itself was an effort of Percy to recover this valued piece of spoil, which, however, found its way to Scotland, notwithstanding the death of its captor. One of the two natural sons of Douglas founded the family of Douglas of Cavers, in Roxburghshire, which still exists in credit and renown; and in their hands are the relics of Otterbourne, now nearly five hundred years old. It is found, however, that history has somewhat misrepresented the matter. The Otterbourne flag proves to be, not a spear-pennon, but a standard thirteen feet long, bearing the Douglas arms: it evidently has been Douglas's own banner, which of course his son would be most anxious to preserve and carry home. The other relic consists of a pair of, apparently, lady's gauntlets, bearing the white lion of the Percies in pearls, and fringed with filigree-work in silver. It now seems most probable that this had been a love-pledge carried by Percy, hanging from his helmet or his spear, as was the fashion of those chivalrous times, and that it was the loss of this cherished memorial which caused the Northumbrian knight to pursue and fight the Earl of Douglas. We owe the clearing up of this matter to a paper presented by Mr J. A. H. Murray, of Hawick, to the Hawick Archæological Society, when the Douglas banner and the Percy gauntlets were exhibited. It may be said to indicate a peculiar and surely very interesting element in British society, that a family should exist which has preserved such relics as these for half a thousand years. Let American readers remark, in particular, the banner was laid up in store at Cavers more than a hundred years before America was discovered. The writer recalls with curious feelings having been, a few years ago, at a party in Edinburgh where were present the Duke of Northumberland, representative of the Percy of Otterbourne celebrity, and the younger Laird of Cavers, representative of the Douglas whose name, even when dead, won that hard-fought field.

## FIRST BRITISH STEAM PASSAGE-BOAT.

On the 15th of August 1812, there appeared in the *Greenock Advertiser*, an *annonce* signed Henry Bell, and dated from the Helensburgh Baths, making the public aware that thereafter a steam passage-boat, the COMET, would ply on the Clyde, between Glasgow and Greenock, leaving the former city on Tuesdays, Thursdays, and Saturdays, and the latter on the other lawful days of the week; the terms 4*s*. for the best cabin, and 3*s*. for the second. This vessel, one of only twenty-five tons burden, had been prepared in the building-yard of John and Charles Wood, Port-Glasgow, during the previous winter, at the instance of the above-mentioned Henry Bell, who was a simple uneducated man, of an inventive and speculative turn of mind, who amused himself with projects, while his more practical wife kept a hotel and suite of baths at a Clyde watering-place. The application of steam to navigation had been experimentally proved twenty-four years before, by Mr Patrick Miller, a Dumfriesshire gentleman, under the suggestions of Mr James Taylor, and with the engineering assistance of Mr Alexander Symington: more recently, a steamer had been put into regular use by Mr Robert Fulton, on the Hudson river in America. But this little *Comet* of Henry Bell, of the Helensburgh Baths, was the first example of a steam-boat brought into serviceable use within European waters. In its proposed trips of five-and-twenty miles, it is understood to have been successful as a commercial speculation; insomuch that, presently after, other and larger vessels of the same kind were built and set agoing on the Clyde. It is an interesting circumstance, that steam-navigation thus sprung up in a practical form, almost on the spot where James Watt, the illustrious improver of the steam-engine, was born. This eminent man appears never to have taken any active concern in the origination of steam-navigation; but, so early as 1816, when he, in old age, paid a visit to his native town of Greenock, he went in one of the new vessels to Rothesay and back, an excursion which then occupied the greater portion of a whole day. Mr Williamson, in his *Memorials of James Watt*, relates an anecdote of this trip. 'Mr Watt entered into conversation with the engineer of the boat, pointing out to him the method of *backing* the engine. With a foot-rule he demonstrated to him what was meant. Not succeeding, however, he at last, under the impulse of the ruling passion, threw off his overcoat, and putting his hand to the engine himself, shewed the practical application of his lecture. Previously to this, the *back-stroke* of the steam-boat engine was either unknown, or not generally acted on. The practice was to stop the engine entirely, a considerable time before the vessel reached the point of mooring, in order to allow for the gradual and natural diminution of her speed.'

THE COMET—FIRST BRITISH STEAM PASSAGE-BOAT.

It is a great pity that Henry Bell's *Comet* was not preserved, which it would have been entitled to be, as a curiosity. It was wrecked one day, by running ashore on the Highland coast, when Bell himself was on board—no lives, however, being lost. The annexed representation of the proto-steamer of Europe, was obtained by Mr Williamson, from an original drawing which had been in the possession of Henry Bell, and was marked with his signature.

## BALLAD-SINGERS AND GRUB-STREET POETS.

It was in reality Montaigne, who made the shrewd but now somewhat musty remark: 'Let me have the making of a nation's ballads, and I care little who makes its laws.' The old Frenchman had observed the powerful effect of caustic satire wedded to popular tunes. It has been told, with truth, how *Lilliburlero* gave the finishing-stroke to the Great Revolution of 1688, and 'sung King James II. out of his three kingdoms;' and it is equally historic, that Béranger was a power in the state, seriously damaging to the stability of the restored Bourbon dynasty.

Shakspeare has happily delineated the popular love of ballads, in the sheep-shearer's feast-scene of *The Winter's Tale.* The rustics love 'a ballad in print,' for then they 'are sure they are true;' and listen with easy credulity to those which tell of 'strange fish,' and stranger monstrosities. It must not be imagined that Autolycus's pack contains caricatured resemblances of popular ballads; for the Roxburghe, Pepysian, and other collections, preserve specimens of lyrics, seriously published and sold, which are quite as absurd as anything mentioned by Shakspeare. In the British Museum is one entitled *Pride's Fall: or a Warning for all English Women, by the example of a Strange Monster, lately born in Germany, by a Merchant's proud Wife at Geneva;* which is adorned with a grim wood-cut of the monster, and is intended to frighten women from extravagant fashions in dress.

'From the head to the foot
Monster-like was it born,
Every part had the shape
Of Fashions daily worn.'

The moral of the story is, that all women should 'take heed of wanton pride,' and remember that this sin is rapidly bringing forth a day of judgment, and the end of the world. Such moralities were like the ballad of Autolycus, 'written to a very doleful tune,' and chanted by a blind fiddler to an equally doleful fiddle. Shakspeare has expressed his contempt for the literary merits of these effusions, when he makes Benedick speak of picking out his eyes 'with a ballad-maker's pen;' but the pages of Percy, Ritson, and Evans are sufficient to establish the claim of many balladists to attention and respect, for the simple imagery and natural beauty of their effusions.

Gifford says, 'in Jonson's time, scarcely any ballad was printed without a wood-cut illustrative of its subject. If it was a ballad of "pure love," or of "good life," which afforded no scope for the graphic talents of the Grub-Street Apelles, the portrait of "good Queen Elizabeth," magnificently adorned with the globe and sceptre, formed no unwelcome substitute for her loyal subjects.' Ballad-buyers were fond of seeing these familiar wood-cuts, they were 'old favourites,' and so well-worn by printers, that it is not unusual to find cuts, evidently executed in the days of James I., worked by ballad-printers during the reign of Anne; so indestructible were the coarse old wood-engravings which were then used 'to adorn' the 'doleful tragedies,' or 'merry new ballads' of the Grub-Street school of sentiment.

The constables kept a wary eye on the political or immoral ballad-singer of London; but Chettle, in *Kind Heart's Dream,* 1592, notes 'that idle, upstart generation of ballad-singers,' who ramble in the outskirts, and are 'able to spread more pamphlets, by the state forbidden, than all the booksellers in London; for only in this city is straight search; abroad, small suspicion; especially of such petty pedlars.' A dozen groats' worth of ballads is said to be their stock in trade; but they all dealt in the pamphlets of a few leaves, that were industriously concocted on all popular subjects by the hack-writers of the day.

In the curious view of the interior of the Royal Exchange, executed by Hollar in 1644, and depicting its aspect when crowded by merchants and visitors, we see one of these itinerant ballad and pamphlet mongers plying her trade among the

BALLAD-SELLER.

busy group. This figure we copy above, on a larger scale than the original, which gives, with minute truthfulness, the popular form of the ballads of that day, printed on a broad sheet, in double columns, with a wood-cut at the head of the story.

The great Civil War was a prolific source of ballad-writing and pamphleteering. It would not be easy to carry libel to greater length than it was then carried, and especially by ballad-singers. These 'waifs and strays,' many of them being the productions of men of some literary eminence, have been gathered into volumes, affording most vivid reminiscences of the strong party-hatred of the time. The earliest of these collections was published in 1660, and is entitled *Ratts Rhimed to Death: or, the Rump-parliament hang'd up in the Shambles*—the title sufficiently indicating the violent character of the songs, gathered under this strange heading. 'They were formerly printed on loose sheets,' says the collector to the reader; adding, 'I hope you will pardon the ill tunes to which they are to be sung, there being none bad enough for them.' Most of them are too coarse for modern quotation; the spirit of all may be gathered from the opening stanza of one:

'Since sixteen hundred forty and odd,
We have soundly been lash'd with our own rod,
And have bow'd ourselves down at a tyrant's nod—
Which nobody can deny.'

The violent personality of others may be understood in reading a few stanzas of *A Hymn to the Gentle Craft, or Hewson's Lamentation.* Colonel Hewson was one of Cromwell's most active officers, and said to have originally been a shoemaker; he had by accident lost an eye.

'Listen awhile to what I shall say,
Of a blind cobbler that's gone astray,
Out of the parliament's highway.
*Good people, pity the blind!*

His name you wot well is Sir John Hewson,
Whom I intend to set my muse on,
As great a warrior as Sir Miles Lewson.
*Good people, pity the blind!*

He'd now give all the shoes in his shop,
The parliament's fury for to stop,
Whip cobbler, like any town-top.
*Good people, pity the blind!*

Oliver made him a famous lord,
That he forgot his cutting-board;
But now his thread's twisted to a cord.
*Good people, pity the blind!*

Sing hi, ho, Hewson!—the state ne'er went upright,
Since cobblers could pray, preach, govern, and fight;
We shall see what they'll do now you're out of sight.
*Good people, pity the blind!*'

For some time after the Restoration, the popular songs were all on the court-side, and it was not until Charles II.'s most flagrant violations of political liberty and public decency, that they took an opposite turn. The court then guarded itself by imposing a licence upon all ballad-singers and pamphleteers. One John Clarke, a bookseller, held this right to license of Charles Killigrew, the Master of the Revels, and advertised in the *London Gazette* of 1682 as follows: 'These are to give notice to all ballad-singers, that they take out licences for singing and selling of ballads and small books, according to an ancient custom. And all persons concerned are hereby desired to take notice of, and to suppress, all mountebanks, rope-dancers, prize-players, and such as make shew of motions and strange sights, that have not a licence in red and black letter, under the hand and seal of the said Charles Killigrew, Master of Revels to his Majesty.' In 1684, a similar advertisement orders all such persons 'to come to the office to change their licences as they are now altered.' The court had reason for all this, for the ballad-singers had become as wide-mouthed as in the days of Cromwell; while the court-life gave scope to obscene allusion that exceeded anything before attempted. The short reign of James II., the birth of the Prince of Wales, and advent of the Prince of Orange, gave new scope for personal satire. Of all the popular songs ever written, none had greater effect than *Lilliburlero* (attributed to Lord Wharton), which Burnet tells us 'made an impression on the king's army that cannot be imagined by those that saw it not. The whole army, and at last the people, both in city and country, were singing it perpetually. And perhaps never had so slight a thing so great an effect.' Some of these songs were written to popular old tunes; that of *Old Simon the King* accompanied the *Sale of Old State Household Stuff*, when James II. was reported to have had an intention to remove the hangings in the Houses of Parliament, and wainscot the rooms; one stanza of this ditty we give as a sample of the whole:

'Come, buy the old tapestry-hangings
Which hung in the House of Lords,
That kept the Spanish invasion
And powder plot on records:
A musty old Magna Charta
That wants new scouring and cleaning,
Writ so long since and so dark too,
That 'tis hard to pick out the meaning.
Quoth Jemmy, the bigoted king,
Quoth Jemmy, the politick thing;
With a threadbare-oath,
And a Catholic troth,
That never was worth a farthing!'

The birth of the Prince of Wales was a fertile theme for popular rhymes, written to equally popular tunes. The first verse of one, entitled *Father Petre's Policy Discovered; or the Prince of Wales proved to be a Popish Perkin*, runs thus:

'In Rome there is a most fearful rout;
And what do you think it is about?
Because the birth of the babe's come out.
Sing lullaby baby, by, by, by.'

The zest with which such songs would be sung in times of great popular excitement can still be imagined, though scarcely to its full extent. Another, on *The Orange*, contains this strong stanza:

'When the Army retreats,
And the Parliament sits,
To vote our King the true use of his wits;
'Twill be a sad means,
When all he obtains
Is to have his Calves-head dress'd with other men's brains;
And *an Orange.*'

No enactments could reach these lampoons, nor the fine or imprisonment of a few wretched ballad-singers stop their circulation. Lauron, a Dutch

BALLAD-SELLER.—TEMP. WILLIAM III.

artist, then resident in London, has preserved a representation of one of these women offering 'a merry new ballad,' to her customers; and she has a bundle of others in her apron pocket. To furnish these 'wandering stationers,' as they were termed, with their literary wants, a band of Grub-street authors existed, in a state of poverty and degradation of which we now can have little idea, except by referring to contemporary writers. The half-starved hacks are declared to fix their highest ideas of luxurious plenty in

'Gallons of beer and pounds of bullock's liver.'

Pope in the *Dunciad*, has given a very low picture of the class:

'Not with less glory mighty Dulness crown'd,
Shall take through Grub Street her triumphant round:
And, her Parnassus glancing o'er at once,
Behold a hundred sons, and each a dunce.'

In Fielding's *Author's Farce*, 1730, we are introduced to a bookseller's workroom, where his hacks are busy concocting books for his shop. One of them complains that he 'has not dined these two days,' and the rest find fault with the disagreeable character of their employment; when the bookseller enters, and the following conversation ensues:

'*Book.* Fie upon it, gentlemen!—what, not at your pens? Do you consider, Mr Quibble, that it is above a fortnight since your *Letter from a Friend in the Country* was published? Is it not high time for an answer to come out? At this rate, before your answer is printed, your letter will be forgot: I love to keep a controversy up warm. I have had authors who have writ a pamphlet in the morning, answered it in the afternoon, and compromised the matter at night.

*Quibble.* Sir, I will be as expeditious as possible.

*Book.* Well, Mr Dash, have you done that murder yet?

*Dash.* Yes, sir; the murder is done. I am only about a few moral reflections to place before it.

*Book.* Very well; then let me have a ghost finished by this day seven-night.

*Dash.* What sort of a ghost would you have, sir? The last was a pale one.

*Book.* Then let this be a bloody one.'

GRUB STREET.

This last hit seems levelled at Defoe, who in reality concocted a very seriously-told ghost-story, *The Apparition of Mrs Veal*, to enable a bookseller to get rid of an unsaleable book, *Drelincourt on Death*, which was directly puffed by the ghost assuring her friend, Mrs Bargrave, that it was the best work on the subject.

Pope and his friends amused and revenged themselves on Curll the bookseller, who was the chief publisher of trashy literature in their day, by an imaginary account of his poisoning and preparation for death, as related by 'a faithful, though unpolite historian of Grub Street.' In the course of the narrative, instructions are given how to find Mr Curll's authors, which indicates the poverty-stricken character of the tribe: 'At a tallow-chandler's in Petty France, half-way under the blind arch, ask for the historian; at the Bedstead and Bolster, a music-house in Moorfields, two translators in a bed together; at a blacksmith's shop in the Friars, a Pindaric writer in red stockings; at Mr Summers's, a thief-catcher's in Lewkner's Lane, the man that wrote against the impiety of Mr Rowe's plays; at the farthing pie-house, in Tooting Fields, the young man who is writing my new pastorals; at the laundress's, at the Hole-in-the-wall, in Cursitor's Alley, up three pair of stairs, the author of my church history; you may also speak to the gentleman who lies by him in the flock-bed, my index-maker.'

Grub Street no longer appears by name in any London Directory; yet it still exists and preserves some of its antique features, though it has for the last forty years been called Milton Street. It is situated in the parish of St Giles's, Cripplegate, leading from Fore Street northerly to Chiswell Street.*

* Our view is of the Fore Street entry, which has remained almost unchanged from the days of Steele. The street still preserves its original squalor. Many of the houses are as old as the time of Charles I. A labyrinth of filthy courts, packed with dirty and half-ruined

Its contiguity to the artillery-ground in Bunhill Fields, where the city trainband exercised, is amusingly alluded to in *The Tatler*, No. 41, where their redoubtable doings are narrated: 'Happy was it that the greatest part of the achievements of this day was to be performed near Grub Street, that there might not be wanting a sufficient number of faithful historians, who being eye-witnesses of these wonders, should impartially transmit them to posterity.'

The concocters of News-letters were among the most prolific and unblushing authors of 'Grub-street literature.' Steele, in the periodical just quoted, alludes to some of them by name: 'Where Prince Eugene has slain his thousands, Boyer has slain his ten thousands; this gentleman can, indeed, be never enough commended for his courage and intrepidity during this whole war.' 'Mr Buckley has shed as much blood as the former.' 'Mr Dyer was particularly famous for dealing in whales, insomuch that in five months' time he brought three into the mouth of the Thames, besides two porpuses and a sturgeon. The judicious and wary Mr I. Dawks hath all along been the rival of this great writer, and got himself a reputation from plagues and famines, by which he destroyed as great multitudes, as he has lately done by the sword. In every dearth of news, Grand Cairo was sure to be unpeopled.'

This mob of unscrupulous scribblers, and the ballad-singers who gave voice to their political pasquinades, occasioned the government much annoyance at times. The pillory and the jail were tried in vain.

'Earless on high stood unabashed Defoe.'

It was the ambition of speculative booksellers to get a government prosecution, for it insured the sale of large editions. Vamp, the bookseller in Foote's play, called the *Author*, 1757, makes that worthy shew the side of his head and his ears, cropped in the pillory for his publications; yet he has a certain business pride, and declares, 'in the year forty-five, when I was in the treasonable way, I never squeaked; I never gave up but one author in my life, and he was dying of a consumption, so it never came to a trial.' The poor ballad-singers, less fortunate, could be seized at once, and summarily punished by any magistrate.

The newspapers of the day often allude to these persecutors. The Middlesex grand jury, in 1716, denounced 'the singing of scandalous ballads about the streets as a common nuisance; tending to alienate the minds of the people.' The *Weekly Packet*, which gives this information, adds, 'we hear an order will be published to apprehend those who cry about, or sing, such scandalous papers.' Read's *Weekly Journal* tells us, in July 1731, that 'three hawkers were committed to Tothill Fields Bridewell, for crying about the streets a printed paper called *Robin's Game, or Seven's the Main*;' a satire on the ministry of Sir Robert Walpole. In July 1763, we are told 'yesterday evening two women were sent to Bridewell, by Lord Bute's order, for singing political ballads before his lordship's door in South Audley Street.' State prosecutions have never succeeded in repressing political satire; it has died a natural death for want of strong food!

old houses, are on both sides the way; and the whole neighbourhood is depressing to the spirits, through its hopeless air of poverty.

## The Minstrels' Festival at Tutbury.

The castle of Tutbury was a place of great strength, built shortly after the Conquest by Henry de Ferrars, one of William's Norman noblemen, who had received the gift of large possessions in Derbyshire, Staffordshire, and the neighbouring counties. It stands upon a hill so steep on one side that it there needs no defence, whilst the other three were strongly walled by the first owner, who lost his property by joining in the rebellion of Simon de Montfort against Henry III. It was afterwards in the possession of the Dukes of Lancaster, one of whom, the celebrated John of Gaunt, added to its fortifications. During the civil war, it was taken and destroyed by the parliamentary forces; and the ruins only now remain.

During the time of the Dukes of Lancaster, the little town of Tutbury was so enlivened by the noble hospitality they kept up, and the great concourse of people who gathered there, that some regulations became necessary for keeping them in order; more especially those disorderly favourites of both the high and low, the wandering jongleurs or minstrels, who displayed their talents at all festive-boards, weddings, and tournaments. A court was therefore appointed by John of Gaunt, to be held every year on the day after the festival of the Assumption of the Virgin, being the 16th of August, to elect a king of the minstrels, try those who had been guilty of misdemeanours during the year, and grant licences for the future year, all which were accompanied by many curious observances.

The wood-master and rangers of Needwood Forest began the festivities by meeting at Berkley Lodge, in the forest, to arrange for the dinner which was given them at this time at Tutbury Castle, and where the buck they were allowed for it should be killed, as also another which was their yearly present to the prior of Tutbury for his dinner. These animals having received their death-blow, the master, keepers, and deputies met on the Day of Assumption, and rode in gay procession, two and two, into the town, to the High Cross, each carrying a green bough in his hand, and one bearing the buck's head, cut off behind the ears, garnished with a rye of pease and a piece of fat fastened to each of the antlers. The minstrels went on foot, two and two, before them, and when they reached the cross, the keeper blew on his horn the various hunting signals, which were answered by the others; all passed on to the churchyard, where, alighting from their horses, they went into the church, the minstrels playing on their instruments during the time of the offering of the buck's head, and whilst each keeper paid one penny as an offering to the church. Mass was then celebrated, and all adjourned to the good dinner which was prepared for them in the castle; towards the expenses of which the prior gave them thirty shillings.

On the following day, the minstrels met at the bailiff's house, in Tutbury, where the steward of the court, and the bailiff of the manor, who were noblemen of high rank, such as the Dukes of Lancaster, Ormond, or Devonshire, with the wood-master, met them. A procession was formed to go to church, two trumpeters walking first, and then the musicians on stringed instruments, all playing; their king, whose office ended on that day, had the privilege of walking between the steward and bailiff, thus, for once at least, taking rank with nobility; after them came the four stewards of music, each carrying a white wand, followed by the rest of the company. The psalms and lessons were chosen in accordance with the occasion, and each minstrel paid a penny, as a due to the vicar of Tutbury.

FESTIVAL AT TUTBURY.

On their return to the castle-hall, the business of the day began by one of the minstrels performing the part of a herald, and crying: 'Oyez, oyez, oyez! all minstrels within this honour, residing in the counties of Stafford, Derby, Nottingham, Leicester, and Warwick, come in and do your suit and service, or you will be amerced.' All were then sworn to keep the King of Music's counsel, their fellows', and their own. A lengthy charge from the steward followed, in which he expatiated on the antiquity and excellence of their noble science, passing from Orpheus to Apollo, Jubal, David, and Timotheus, instancing the effect it had upon beasts by the story of a gentleman once travelling near Royston, who met a herd of stags upon the road following a bagpipe and violin: when the music played, they went forward; when it ceased, they all stood still; and in this way they were conducted out of Yorkshire to the king's palace at Hampton Court. The jurors then proceeded to choose a new king, who was taken alternately from the minstrels of Staffordshire and Derbyshire, as well as four stewards, and retired to consider the offences which were alleged against any minstrel, and fine him, if necessary. During this time, the old stewards brought into the court a treat of wine, ale, and cakes, and the minstrels diverted themselves and the company by playing their merriest airs. The new king entered, and was presented by the jurors, the old one rising from his place, and giving the white wand to his successor, pledging him in a cup of wine, and bidding him joy of the honour he had received; the old stewards followed his example, and at noon all entered into a fair room within the castle, where the old king had prepared for them a plentiful dinner.

The conclusion of the day was much in accordance with the barbarous taste of the times: a bull being given them by the prior of Tutbury, they all adjourned to the abbey gate, where the poor beast had the tips of his horns sawed off, his ears and tail cut off, the body smeared over with soap, and his nose filled with pepper. The minstrels rushed after the maddened creature, and if any of them could succeed in cutting off a piece of his skin before he crossed the river Dove into Derbyshire, he became the property of the King of Music, but if not, he was returned sound and uncut to the prior again. After becoming the king's own, he was brought to the High Street, and there baited with dogs three times; the bailiff then gave the king five nobles, equal to about £1, 13*s.* 4*d.*, for his right, and sent the bull to the Earl of Devon's manor of Hardwick, to be fed and given to the poor at Christmas. It has been supposed that John of Gaunt, who assumed the title of King of Castile and Leon in right of his wife, introduced this sport in imitation of the Spanish bull-fights; but in the end the young men of the neighbourhood, who flocked in great numbers to the festival, could not help interfering with the minstrels, and, taking cudgels of about a yard in length, the one party endeavoured to drive the bull into Derbyshire, the other to keep him in Staffordshire, and this led to such outrage, that many returned home with broken heads. Gradually, as 'old times were changed, old manners gone,' the minstrels fell into disrepute; the castles were destroyed in the civil wars, the nobility spent their time and sought their amusements in London, and harpers were no longer needed to charm away the ennui of their ladies and retainers; the court of minstrels found no employment, and the bull-baiting was strongly objected to by the inhabitants. The Duke of Devonshire consequently abolished the whole proceeding in 1778, after it had lasted through the long period of four hundred years.

The manor of Tutbury was one of those held by cornage tenure: in 1569, Walter Achard claimed to be hereditary steward of Leek and Tutbury, in proof of which he shewed a white hunter's horn, decorated with silver gilt ornaments. It was hung to a girdle of fine black silk, adorned with buckles of silver, on which were the arms and the fleurs-de-lis of the Duke of Lancaster, from whom it descended. The Stanhopes of Elvaston were recently in possession of the badge.

---

## AUGUST 16.

St Hyacinth, confessor, 1257. St Roch, confessor, 14th century.

### ST ROCH OR ROQUE

Was a French gentleman, possessing estates near Montpelier, which, however, he abandoned in order to devote himself to a religious life. The date of his death is stated with some uncertainty as 1327. In consequence of working miraculous cures of the plague, while himself stricken with the disease at Placentia, in Italy, Roque was held as a saint specially to be invoked by persons so afflicted. There were many churches dedicated to him in Germany and other countries, and it seems to have been a custom that persons dying of plague should be buried there.

St Roch's Day was celebrated in England as a general harvest-home.

---

*Born.*—Ralph Thoresby, antiquary, author of *Ducatus Leodiensis*, 1658, *Leeds;* Catharine Cockburn, dramatist and moral writer, 1679, *London;* Pierre Mechain, mathematician and astronomer, 1744, *Laon;* Frederick, Duke of York, second son of George III., 1763.

*Died.*—Dr Thomas Fuller, celebrated divine and author, 1661, *Cranford, Middlesex;* Jacques Bernouilli, mathematician and natural philosopher, 1705, *Basel;* Dr Matthew Tindal, freethinking writer, 1733, *London;* Bartholomew Joubert, French general, killed at Novi, 1799; John Palmer, post-reformer, 1818.

### TINDAL AND BUDGEL.

Dr Matthew Tindal, a clergyman's son, and a fellow of All Souls' College, Oxford, made himself notable, in the early part of the eighteenth century, by a series of books and pamphlets assailing the pretensions of High Church, and latterly endeavouring to take away the supernatural element from Christianity itself. His writings gave rise to prodigious controversies, which whizzed and sputtered and fumed about the ears of mankind for a good many years, and by and by subsided into the silence of oblivion, in which for fully a hundred years past they have remained.

Tindal cannot be mentioned without some notice of Eustace Budgel, his friend and follower as far as regards religious ideas. Budgel was a relation of Addison, a man of fair talents, and a contributor to the *Spectator* and *Guardian.* Through Addison's influence, when secretary of state, Budgel obtained confidential and lucrative political offices, and his abilities as a writer and speaker promised his speedy rise to distinction. But, cursed with an unhappy temper, an irregular ambition, and an inability to control splenetic, revengeful passions, he lost his official position; and the bursting of the South-sea Bubble left him, in the prime of life, ruined alike in fortune and political influence. His reputation was to follow. At Tindal's death, it was found that he had made Budgel his heir, to the exclusion of his nephew. Budgel was accused of forging the will, which was written by an alleged female accomplice, a Mrs Price; and whether innocent or otherwise, there can be no doubt that he was guilty of dishonesty regarding a considerable sum he had borrowed from Tindal, just previous to his death, and the receipt of which he strenuously denied, till the notes were traced to his possession. The subject was a fruitful one for the wits of the day. Pope writes—

'Let Budgel charge all Grub Street on my quill,
And write whate'er he please, except my will.'

The best epigram on Tindal's will, however, is the following:

'Hundreds of years, th' Old Testament and New
By general consent have passed for true;
In this learn'd age, a doctor, 'god-like great!'*
By dint of reason proved them both a cheat:
A *third* he made,† which, sinking nature's share,
Gave more than he died worth to Reason's heir.
Mal-practice to prevent, of his last thought,
A female scribe engrossed the genuine draught.
But, oh! 'gainst Testaments such reasons shown,
Have taught the world to question e'en his own.
Those seventeen centuries old he scarce could raze,
His own remained unshook not seventeen days.
Yet all perhaps are true; if none, the third,
Of three forged Testaments, seems most absurd.'

Budgel boldly attempted to outface the obloquy of this affair, and for a while seemed to have succeeded; but at length, succumbing to popular indignation, he committed suicide. The evils of undisciplined temper and passions are nowhere more clearly evinced than in the unhappy career of Eustace Budgel.

### PALMER, THE POST-REFORMER.

Three hundred years ago, travellers had no choice but to ride on horseback or walk. Kings, queens, and gentlefolk all mounted to the saddle. The practice had existed for generations and centuries. Chaucer's ride to Canterbury is made famous by his own lucid account of that celebrated journey. Ladies were accustomed to ride on pillions fixed on the horse, and generally behind

* So Budgel termed Tindal.

† His own testament, the alleged forged will.

some relative or serving-man. In this way Queen Elizabeth, when she rode into the city from her residence at Greenwich, placed herself behind her lord-chancellor. Judges rode the circuit in jack-boots for centuries, and continued to do so long after other means of conveyance were in general use.*

The first improvement consisted in a kind of rude wagon, which was, in reality, nothing but a cart without springs, the body of it resting solidly upon the axle. In such a vehicle did Elizabeth drive to the opening of her fifth parliament. Mr Smiles, in his interesting *Lives of the Engineers*, relates that, 'that valyant knyght, Sir Harry Sydney, on a certain day in 1583, entered Shrewsbury in his *wagon*, with his trompeter blowynge, verey joyfull to behold and see.' Bad as these conveyances must have been, they had scarcely fair-play on the execrable roads of the period. Even up to the end of the seventeenth century, the roads in most parts of the country were not unlike broad ditches, much water-worn and carelessly strewn with loose stones. It is on record, that on one occasion eight hundred horses were taken prisoners by Cromwell's forces *while sticking in the mud!* During the seventeenth century, it was common, when a long journey was contemplated, for servants to be sent on beforehand, to investigate the country, and report upon the most promising tract. In 1640, the road from Dover to London was the best in England, owing, of course, to the amount of continental traffic continually kept up, and yet the journey of Queen Henrietta and household occupied four long weary days over that short distance.

It was not till towards the close of the sixteenth century that the wagon became used as a public conveyance, and only very rarely then. Fifty years after, we find that a string of stage-wagons travelled regularly between London and Liverpool, each one starting from the Axe Inn, Aldermanbury, every Monday and Thursday, and occupying ten days on the road during summer, and generally about twelve days during winter. About the same time, three men started every Friday morning for Liverpool, from Lad's Lane, London, with a gang of horses for the conveyance of light goods and passengers, usually reaching Liverpool on the Monday evening following.

Stage-coaches were great improvements on all the then existing conveyances, and were destined to work great changes in travelling. A kind of stage-coach was first used in London early in the seventeenth century. Towards the middle of the same century, they were generally adopted in the metropolis, and on the better highways around London, travelling at the rate of two or three miles an hour. Before 1698, stage-coaches were placed on three of the principal roads in the kingdom. The original announcement for that between London and York still exists, and runs as follows:—'Whoever is desirous of going between London and York or York and London, Let them Repair to the Black Swan in Holboorn, or the Black Swan in Coney Street, York, where they will be conveyed in a Stage Coach (if God permits), which starts every Thursday at Five in the morning.' This was only, however, for the summer season; during winter, they did not run at all, but were laid up for the season like ships during arctic frosts. Even in summer, the passengers very frequently got out and walked long distances, the state of the roads in some places compelling them to do so. With the York coach especially, the difficulties were really formidable. Passing through the low Midland counties was sometimes entirely impracticable, and during the time of floods, it was nothing unusual for passengers to remain at some town *en route* for days together, until the roads were dry again. Notwithstanding these drawbacks, stage-coaches increased in number and in popularity, and so decidedly was travelling on the increase, that they now became the subjects of grave discussion; news-letters encouraged or reviled them, and pamphlets were written concerning them. For instance, in one entitled *The Grand Concern of England Explained in Several Proposals to Parliament*, these same stage-coaches are denounced as the greatest evil that had happened of late years to the kingdom, mischievous to trade, and destructive to the public health. Curious to know in what way these sad consequences are brought about, we read on, and find it stated that 'those who travel in these coaches contracted an idle habit of body; became weary and listless when they rode a few miles, and were then unable or unwilling to travel on horseback, and not able to endure frost, snow, or rain, or to lodge in the field!' Opinions on even such a subject as this differed most materially. In the very same year that produced the book to which we have just referred, another writer, descanting on the improvements which had been brought about in the *postal* arrangements of the country, goes on to say, that, 'besides the excellent arrangement of conveying men and letters on horseback, there is of late such an admirable commodiousness, both for men and women, to travel from London to the principal towns in the country, *that the like hath not been known in the world*, and that is by *stage-coaches*, wherein any one may be transported to any place, sheltered from foul weather and foul ways; free from endamaging of one's health and one's body by the hard jogging or over-violent motion; and this not only at a low price (about a shilling for every five miles), but with such velocity and speed in one hour, as that the posts in some forraign countreys make in a day.'

From the information which we have been able to gather on the subject, it would appear that at first stage-coaches were not regarded as very great improvements upon the old stage-wagons. M. Soubrière, a Frenchman of letters, who landed at Dover in the reign of Charles II., alludes to the existence of stage-coaches, but he would seem to have been well acquainted with their demerits, as we may learn from an account which he has left: 'That I might not take post, or again be obliged to use the stage-coach, I went from Dover to London in a wagon. I was drawn by six horses placed in a line, one after another, and driven by a wagoner, who walked by the side of it. He was clothed in black, and appointed in all things like another St George. He had a brave monteror on his head, and was a merry fellow, fancied he

* Lord Cockburn, in his *Memorials*, describes very graphically the difficulties encountered by the Bar travelling in Scotland so late as the last century, and states that he always rode circuits when he was an advocate-depute between 1807 and 1810.

made a figure, and seemed mightily pleased with himself.'

The speed at which the coaches travelled was a great marvel at that time. In 1700, York was a week distant from the metropolis. Between London and Edinburgh, even so late as 1763, a fortnight was consumed, the coach only starting once a month. The intermediate Sunday was quietly spent at Boroughbridge, in Yorkshire, as much for the sake of relief to exhausted nature as from motives of piety. The first vehicle which plied between Edinburgh and Glasgow was started in 1749. It was called 'The Edinburgh and Glasgow Caravan,' and performed the journey of forty-four miles in two days. Ten years after, another vehicle was started, and called the 'Fly,' because it contrived to perform this same journey in a day and a half. Latterly, it took the daylight of one day. It is a perfectly authentic anecdote that, about 1780, a gentleman, anxious to make favour with a young lady, learning that she was to travel from Glasgow to Edinburgh, on a particular day, took the whole remaining inside-seats, had her all to himself of course, and succeeded in winning her as his wife. Mr Smiles tells us that, during the last century, the Fly coach from London to Exeter stopped at the latter place the fifth night from town; the coach proceeded next morning to Axminster, and there a woman-barber '*shaved the coach*.' The fact was that, on any of the roads, the difference of half a day, or even a day, was a small matter. Time was of less consequence than safety. The coaches were advertised to start 'God willing,' or about such and such an hour as shall seem good to the majority of the passengers. Thoresby tells us, that he was even accustomed to leave the coach (on the journey from London to York) and go in search of fossil shells in the fields, on either side of the road, while making the journey between these two places. Whether or not the coach was to stop at some favourite inn, was determined, in most cases, by a vote of the passengers, who would generally appoint a chairman at the beginning of the journey. Under such circumstances, we cannot wonder that disputes, especially about stopping at wayside-inns, should be of frequent occurrence. Perhaps the driver had a pecuniary interest in some particular posting-house, and would exert an influence, sometimes tyrannical, to obtain the consent of the passengers to a place of his choosing. In 1760, an action was tried before the Court of King's Bench to recover damages, on the plea that, during a stage-coach journey, the driver wished to compel the passengers to dine at some low inn on the road. They preferred to walk on to a respectable inn at some little distance, and desired the driver to call for them, as he must pass the place. Instead of doing so, he drove past the inn at full speed, leaving them to get up to London as best they could. The jury found for the passengers in £20 damages. On another occasion, a dispute arose, which resulted in a quarrel between the guard and a passenger, the coach stopping to see the two fight it out on the road!

While yet the ordinary stage-coach was found equal to all the requirements on most of the old coach-roads, the speed at which it travelled did not at all satisfy the enterprising merchants of Lancashire and Yorkshire. In 1754, a company of merchants in Manchester started a new vehicle, called the 'Flying Coach,' which seems to have earned its designation by the fact, that it proposed to travel at the rate of four or five miles an hour! The proprietors, at the commencement, issued the following remarkable prospectus: 'However incredible it may appear, this coach will actually (barring accidents) arrive in London in four days and a half after leaving Manchester.' Three years afterwards, the Liverpool merchants established another of these 'flying machines on steel springs,' as the newspapers of the period called them, which was intended to eclipse the Manchester one in the matter of speed. It started from Warrington (Liverpool passengers reaching the former place the night previous to starting), and only *three* days had to be taken up in the journey to London. 'Each passenger to pay two guineas—one guinea as earnest, and the other on taking coach; 14lbs. of luggage allowed, and 3*d.* per pound for all luggage in excess.' About as much more money as was required for the fare was expended in living and lodgings on the road, not to speak of fees to guard and driver. Sheffield and Leeds followed with their respective 'flying coaches,' and before the last century closed, the whole of them had acquired the respectable velocity of eight miles an hour.

These flying-coaches were the precursors of a great reform effected by a man of energetic nature in 1784. John Palmer, a person of substance at Bath, having been pleased to establish and conduct a theatre there, became strongly impressed with a sense of the antiquated system for both sending human beings and letters along the road between his town and the metropolis. He often desired to have occasional assistance from a London star, but was balked by the dilatoriness of the coach-travelling. Even to communicate with the London houses was insufferably tedious, for then the post starting in London on Monday did not reach Bath till Wednesday. Palmer travelled all over the country, and found everywhere the same insufficiency; he memorialised the government; he took means to inform the public; he clearly shewed how easy it would be to effect vast improvements tending to economise the time and money of the public. As usual, he was set down as a half-crazed enthusiast and *bore;* the post-office authorities were against him to a man; even those who saw and admitted his data, could not be brought to say more than that, while sure on the whole to fail, his system might give a slight impulse in the right direction. It was only through the enlightened judgment of Pitt, that he was able to commence, in the year mentioned, that system of rapid mail-coaches which lasted up to the days of railways. The first mail-coach in accordance with Mr Palmer's plan, was one from London to Bristol, which started at eight in the morning of the 8th of August 1784, and reached its destination at eleven at night. The benefits to the public quickly became too manifest to be denied even by the most inveterate of his opponents, and—mark the national gratitude! The government had entered into a regular contract with him, engaging to give him two-and-a-half per cent. upon the saving effected in the transmission of the letters. It was clearly shewn soon after that this saving amounted to £20,000 a year. Parliament, however, would not vote the fulfilment of the bargain, and Mr Palmer was *cheated* with grant of only £50,000.

The history of Palmer's reform was precisely that of Rowland Hill fifty years later—the same enlightened energy in one man, the same official conservatism of antiquated absurdities, the same sluggishness on the part of the public whose benefit was sought—not exactly the same reward. Hill's reward, too, was slight compared with his work; he received a public testimonial of £13,360 in 1842; and in 1864, now a K.C.B., he retired on his full salary of £2000 a year for life, while parliament in the same year voted him £20,000.

## EUGENE ARAM.

Seldom has there been a robber and murderer, in the middle station of society, unconnected with great political movements, whose life has become the theme both of a novel and a poem. Eugene Aram is among these few. His case has attracted the attention of writers of fiction, both from the extraordinary circumstances connected with it, and the cultivated mind of the man himself.

Eugene Aram was born in Yorkshire. He received a fair school education; then became clerk in a London counting-house; then returned to his native place, set up a school, and married unfortunately. He next lived at Knaresborough, where, by great application, he obtained an extensive knowledge of the Greek, Hebrew, and Latin languages and literature. All this took place before 1744. In that year he came again to London, and was engaged as usher at a school in Piccadilly. Here he worked laboriously, and added a considerable knowledge of Chaldee and Arabic to his previous store of information, intending to apply it to the production of a lexicon. During his subsequent engagement at various other schools, he studied Celtic, and also acquired a very extensive knowledge of botany.

Such a man appeared to be among the last who would commit a robbery and a murder; and hence the intense surprise and pain that followed certain disclosures. In 1758, some workmen, digging about St Robert's Cave, near Knaresborough, found the remains of a man who appeared to have been murdered. Fourteen years before, a shoemaker, named Daniel Clark, had mysteriously disappeared from Knaresborough, and had not since been seen or heard of. It was recollected that one Richard Housman was the last person seen in his company; and the finding of the dead body (which was believed to be that of Clark) led to the apprehension of Housman. On his examination, Housman stated that the body was not Clark's, but that Clark's body, nevertheless, lay buried at a spot which he named. This admission led to further inquiries, which implicated Eugene Aram; and about the middle of August, Housman and Aram were committed for trial. The trial, which did not take place till the following year, disclosed a strange history. Clark married in 1744. Aram was living at Knaresborough at the time, poor, and united to a wife with whom he appears to have lived very unhappily. Three needy men—Clark, Aram, and Housman—entered into a conspiracy for borrowing as much valuable property as possible, as if for Clark's wedding, and then dividing the spoil amongst them. Clark was soon afterwards missing, and suspicion fell upon the other two, but nothing definite was found out. Aram deserted his wife, who had some suspicion of what he had done. Housman, at the inquest, stated that Aram murdered Clark, to conceal the evidence about the robbery; but Aram (who owned to the fraud) denied all knowledge of the murder. At the trial, Housman was acquitted of murder, and was admitted as king's evidence against Aram. Everything told heavily against the unhappy usher. He made a most elaborate defence, which could only have proceeded from an educated man. This remarkable defence was read before the court from manuscript; and in it he endeavoured to shew that all the facts against him had the usual defect of mere circumstantial evidence. He was found guilty, and condemned to death; he made a partial confession, then attempted to end his existence with a razor, and was finally brought out to the place of execution at York, and hanged on 6th August 1759.

This almost inexplicable history has attracted many pens, as we have said. In 1828, the late Thomas Hood wrote *The Dream of Eugene Aram*, a poem of thirty-six stanzas. In a preface to the poem, Hood described how the subject was suggested to his mind by a horrible dream. 'A lifeless body, in love and relationship the nearest and dearest, was imposed upon my back, with an overwhelming sense of obligation, not of filial piety merely, but some awful responsibility, equally vague and intense, and involving, as it seemed, inexpiable sin, horrors unutterable, torments intolerable—to bury my dead, like Abraham, out of my sight. In vain I attempted, again and again, to obey the mysterious mandate; by some dreadful process the burden was replaced with a more stupendous weight of imagination, and an appalling conviction of the impossibility of its fulfilment. My mental anguish was indescribable; the mighty agonies of souls tortured on the supernatural racks of sleep, are not to be penned.' Eugene Aram, it was known, when an usher in a school at Lynn, was accustomed to talk to the boys frequently on the subject of murder—for a reason which they could not understand, but which was probably the result of remorse in his own heart. Hood's horrible dream, and this fact, together suggested the idea of the poem. School-boys are represented at sport in the evening. Near them was the usher, 'a melancholy man,' alternately reading and brooding. He sees a gentle lad reading a book, and asks what it is. *The Death of Abel.* The usher started, and then said that he himself had dreamed, on the preceding night, that he had committed a murder. He narrated the dream, and a terrible one it is. Once in the course of his narration, he felt that his manner was too intensely earnest, and said—

'My gentle boy, remember this
Is nothing but a dream!'

And again he said—

'Oh, God! that horrid, horrid dream
Besets me now awake!
Again, again with busy brain,
The human life I take;
And my red right hand grows raging hot,
Like Cranmer's at the stake.'

Sir E. B. Lytton (when Mr Bulwer) published his romance of *Eugene Aram* in 1831, and dedicated it to Sir Walter Scott. In his preface he said: 'During Aram's residence at Lynn, his reputation for learning had attracted the notice of my grandfather—a country gentleman living in the same county, and of more intelligence and accomplishments than, at that day, usually characterised his class. Aram frequently visited at Heydon, my grandfather's house, and gave lessons, probably in no very elevated branches of erudition, to the younger members of the family.' Sir Edward expresses a belief, that though there cannot be much *moral* doubt of the guilt of Eugene Aram, the *legal* evidence was not such as would suffice to convict him at the present day. He at first intended his *Eugene Aram* for the stage, but made it into a romance instead of a drama. Mr Godwin, author of *Caleb Williams*, once told Sir Edward that 'he had always thought the story of Eugene Aram peculiarly adapted for fiction, and that he had more than once entertained the notion of making it the foundation of a novel.'

## AUGUST 17.

St Mamas, martyr, about 275. Saints Liberatus, Abbot, and six monks, martyrs, 483.

*Born*—Thomas Stothard, artist, 1755, *Longacre, London;* Dr William Carey, missionary and oriental scholar, 1761, *Paulerspury, Northamptonshire;* Richard Lalor Shiel, politician and dramatist, 1791, *Dublin.*

*Died.*—Carloman of Austrasia, eldest son of Charles Martel, 755, *Vienne, Dauphiné;* John Gower, early English poet, 1408; Edward V. and his brother Richard, Duke of York, smothered in the Tower, 1483; Admiral Robert Blake, 1657, *Plymouth;* Madame Anne le Fevre Dacier, translator of Homer and other classic authors, 1720; Frederick II. (the Great) of Prussia, 1786, *Potsdam;* Matthew Boulton, engineer and partner of Watt, 1809, *Soho, Birmingham;* Dr Edward Pearson, Arminian champion, 1811, *Rempstone, Nottinghamshire.*

### FREDERICK THE GREAT.

On the 17th of August 1786, died the most remarkable sovereign which Prussia has yet produced, and one of the most remarkable sovereigns of Europe in the eighteenth century. Mr Carlyle, whose most elaborate and extensive work is his *History of Frederick II., called Frederick the Great*, gives a graphic picture of his hero, as he is supposed to have been about the year 1776. Writing in 1856, Mr Carlyle says: 'About fourscore years ago, there used to be seen sauntering on the terraces of Sans Souci, for a short time in the afternoon—or you might have met him elsewhere at an earlier hour, riding or driving in a rapid business manner on the open roads, or through the scraggy woods and avenues of that intricate amphibious Potsdam region—a highly interesting lean little old man, of alert though slightly stooping figure; whose name among strangers was King Frederick II., or Frederick the Great of Prussia, and at home, among the common people, who much loved and esteemed him, was *Vater Fritz*—Father Fred—a name of familiarity which had not bred contempt in that instance. He is a king every inch of him, though without the trappings of a king. Presents himself in a Spartan simplicity of vesture: no crown but an old military cocked-hat—generally old, or trampled and kneaded into absolute softness, if new; no sceptre but one like Agamemnon's, a walking-stick cut from the woods, which serves also as a riding-stick (with which he hits the horse 'between the ears,' say authors); and for royal robes, a mere soldier's blue coat with red facings, coat likely to be old, and sure to have a good deal of Spanish snuff on the breast of it; rest of the apparel dim, unobtrusive in colour or cut, ending in high over-knee military boots, which may be brushed (and, I hope, kept soft with an underhand suspicion of oil), but are not permitted to be blackened or varnished; Day and Martin with their soot-pots forbidden to approach.

'The man is not of godlike physiognomy, any more than of imposing stature or costume: close-shut mouth with thin lips, prominent jaws and nose, receding brow, by no means of Olympian height; head, however, is of long form, and has superlative gray eyes in it. Not what is called a beautiful man; nor yet, by all appearance, what is called a happy. On the contrary, the face bears evidence of many sorrows, as they are termed, of much hard labour done in this world; and seems to anticipate nothing but more still coming. Quiet stoicism, capable enough of what joy there were, but not expecting any worth mention; great unconscious and some conscious pride, tempered with a cheery mockery of humour—are written on that old face; which carries its chin well forward, in spite of the slight stoop about the neck; snuffy nose rather flung into the air, under its old cocked-hat—like an old snuffy lion on the watch; and such a pair of eyes as no man or lion or lynx of that century bore elsewhere, according to all the testimony we have.' After quoting a few words from Mirabeau, Carlyle proceeds: 'Most excellent potent brilliant eyes, swift-darting as the stars, steadfast as the sun; gray, we said, of the azure-gray colour; large enough, not of glaring size; the habitual expression of them vigilance and penetrating sense, rapidity resting on depth. Which is an excellent combination; and gives us the notion

AUTOGRAPH OF FREDERICK THE GREAT.

of a lambent outer radiance springing from some great inner sea of light and fire in the man. The voice, if he speaks to you, is of similar physiognomy: clear, melodious, and sonorous; all tones are in it, from that of ingenuous inquiry, graceful sociality, light-flowing banter (rather prickly for most part), up to definite word of command, up to desolating word of rebuke and reprobation.'

---

## THE WASHING TALLY.

A washing tally, here engraved of a reduced size, was found not many months ago behind some oak-panelling in the old Chaplain's Room at Haddon Hall, in Derbyshire, in the same room in which many other curious relics are preserved—jack-boots, pewter-plates, fire-dogs, cradles, and other things, which each tell their tale of bygone-times, and of the home-life of the Vernons—the once noble owners of the place. It is, judging from the style of the engraving, the lettering, and ornamentation, of the time of King Charles I., and the names of the articles of dress enumerated upon it well accord with that period. This 'tally' was first made public in the *Reliquary*, where it is fully described, and where also the engraving here given appears. From that account the following description and particulars as to costume, &c., are selected under the care of the author: 'The Washing Tally, here engraved of a reduced size, is five inches and a half in length, and four and a half inches in depth. It is formed of a piece of beech-wood of the size described, and of a quarter of an inch in thickness, covered with linen at the back and sides. In construction, it is

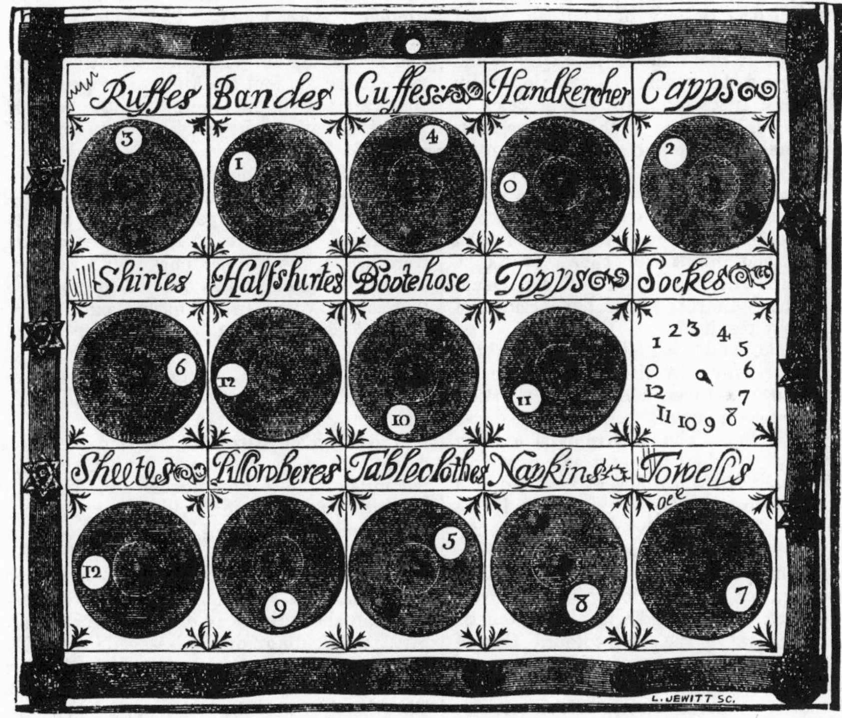


THE WASHING TALLY.

precisely similar to a "Hornbook"—in front, the different articles are printed from copper-plate, and protected by a sheet of horn. Around the edge a narrow strip of thin brass, fastened down with highly-ornamental nails, attaches the horn, the paper, and the linen to the wood. The tally is divided into fifteen squares, in each of which is a dial numbered from 0 to 12, and above each square is the name of the article intended to be taken into account. The articles are "ruffes," "bandes," "cuffes," "handkercher," "capps," "shirtes," "halfshirtes," "bootehose," "topps," "sockes," "sheetes," "pillowberes," "tableclothes," "napkins," and "towells." On each of the dials is a circular brass indicator, fastened by a little pin in its centre, so as to turn round at pleasure. Each of these indicators is pierced on one side, close to its outer edge, with a round hole through which one number on the dial is visible. Opposite to this opening is a raised point by which the indicator may be turned.

'In keeping an account of the articles "sent to the wash," it was, as will be seen, simply necessary to turn each indicator to the figure representing the number of each article looked out, and when none were sent, the 0 was brought in requisition. I have, for the purpose of this illustration, turned the indicator so as to shew each number, and as one of the indicators is fortunately missing, I am also enabled to shew one of the dials in full. As the tally now stands, the account of washing would be as follows:—

| | | | |
|---|---|---|---|
| Ruffes, | 3 | Topps, | 11 |
| Bandes, | 1 | Sockes (indicator removed) | |
| Cuffes, | 4 | Sheetes, | 12 |
| Handkercher, | none | Pillowberes, | 9 |
| Capps, | 2 | Tableclothes, | 5 |
| Shirtes, | 6 | Napkins, | 8 |
| Halfshirtes, | 12 | Towells, | 7 |
| Bootehose, | 10 | | |

'Towels, however, do not appear at all times to have belonged to the domestic arrangements of the owner of this interesting relic, for in place of that name the words *laced bands* has been written on the horn, in the olden times. The writing is now nearly obliterated, but may be seen by a careful observer.'

A similar tally, in the possession of a gentleman of Liverpool, has been figured in the *Transactions* of the Historic Society of Lancashire and Cheshire:

'Washing-days, at the time of the Tudors and Stuarts (the period to which the washing tally belongs), though a little more important than in the preceding ages, had none of those unpleasantnesses and terrors which are said now to accompany them. Articles which required washing were "few and far between," whilst those of a texture which would not "stand a wash" were usually worn. The dyer was far more commonly employed than the laundress, and his trade thus covered a "multitude of sins" of omission of personal cleanliness, which the laundress would have remedied with more healthy results.

'Velvets, taffeta, and rich silks were, in the middle ages, often worn by the wealthy without any underclothing whatever, while the domestics, and people of lower order, wore coarse woollen, also without underclothing. The possession of a linen shirt, even with the highest nobles, was a matter of note, and it was but few wardrobes which contained them. Night-gowns were not known, and the custom was to sleep entirely without clothing. Under the Tudors, night-gowns were worn, but they were formed mostly of silk or velvet, so that no washing was required. Anne Boleyn's night-dress was made of black satin, bound with black taffeta, and edged with velvet of the same colour. One of Queen Elizabeth's night-gowns was of black velvet, trimmed with silk lace, and lined with fur; and in 1568, her majesty ordered George Bradyman to deliver "threescore-and-sixe of the best sable skynnes, to furnish us a night-gowne." In another warrant from her majesty in 1572, she orders the delivery of "twelve yards of purple velvet, frized on the backe syde with white and russet silke," for a night-gown for herself, and also orders the delivery of fourteen yards of murry damask for the "makyng of a nyght-gown for the Erle of Leycester." Night-dresses for ladies were, at a later period, called "night-rails," and, in the reign of Queen Anne, it became the fashion for them to be worn in the daytime in the streets, over the usual dress. This gave rise to many curious satires. Night-caps, too, were mostly of velvet and silk, and these, with the velvet night-dresses, the silken shirts, and other matters of a like kind, eased the laundress, though they must have added to the discomfort of the wearer.

'Clothes were, in former times, usually washed in the river, but not unfrequently in the common wells of towns, from which the water was fetched for culinary purposes and for drinking. In 1467, the corporation of Leicester, to prevent the constant fouling of the water, ordered that no woman do wash clothes or other corruption in the common wells. At Lyme, an order by court was given in 1608, that none do wash their bucks in the street (*i. e.* in the stream of running water which supplied the town), under a penalty of 6*s.* 8*d.* The "buck" here alluded to, was the quantity of family linen put to wash. "Buck," was "to wash," and was also used for the quantity of linen washed at once —a tub full of linen "in buck." Thus "to wash a buck," was to wash a tub of clothes; "buck ashes," were the ashes of which the lye for washing was made; "buck-basket," the basket in which the linen was carried; "buck-pan," the washing tub; and to be "bucked," was to be soaked or drenched with water. The "buck-basket" will be familiar to every reader, as described by Sir John Falstaff, as "rammed with foul shirts and smocks, socks, foul stockings, and greasy napkins, that, Master Brook, there was the rankest compound of villainous smells that ever offended nostril."

'The clothes being placed in the tub, the women, sometimes several in number, with their dresses tucked up, danced upon them to beat out the impurities. When washed at the river-side, they were beaten on wood or stones. Under Henry VIII., the royal laundress was ordered to procure enough "sweet powder, sweet herbs, and other sweet things," as might be requisite for the "sweet keeping" of the linen.'

A word or two on the different articles enumerated on the tablet, may not be out of place. The 'ruffe' was the frill, or plaited collar so generally worn in the reign of Elizabeth, and in the succeeding reign, and which are made familiar by the many portraits of the 'virgin queen' and the 'illustrious notables' of her reign which are extant. They were sometimes worn of gigantic size, and propped up, and made to keep in form by a framework of wire, which, with the strong starch—which Stubbes called '*the devil's own liquor, I mean starch*'—held them up about the neck of the wearer. Under the Stuarts, the ruffs gradually lessened in size. The ruffs worn by men were of similar shape to those worn by women, and almost of an equally extravagant size. The 'band,' from which the small bands still worn by the clergy took their origin, were collars of linen, cambric, or other material, worn around the neck. When starched to stand up, they were simply 'bands;' when allowed to lie flat on the shoulders, they were called 'falling-bands.' The 'laced bands' were the richly worked lace neckcloths so frequently seen in portraits of the Stuart period. It may interest our fair readers to know, that the origin of the name of 'band-box' is traced to these articles of attire—the boxes originally being made to keep ruffs and bands in.

The 'cuffe' was the lower part of the sleeve, which was sometimes quite plain, and at others richly embroidered, or formed of lace, and was worn turned back over the wrist. '"Handkerchers," or handkerchiefs, were, in the days when this tally was first used, costly articles. Laced handkerchiefs "first came in vogue" under Queen

Elizabeth, and in that and the succeeding reigns were "laced round with gold." Also

> "Handkerchiefs were wrought
> With names and true-love knots,"

and many of the pretty devices are given and worn as love-tokens—the gallants sometimes wearing them as favours in their hats. The term "cap" would, of course, include night-caps, and these were, under both Tudors and Stuarts, frequently most elegantly embroidered, worked in filigree on velvet or silk, and trimmed with costly lace.

"Shirt" was a term applied equally to that part of both male and female attire worn next the skin. They were made usually of fine Holland, but not unfrequently of silk, and were occasionally embroidered. The Holland-shirts of both male and female had, in some instances, the ruffs and hand-ruffs, the bands and wrist-bands, of cambric or lace attached to them. "Half-shirts" were stomachers, more richly decorated with embroidery and lace, over which the boddice was laced from side to side. "Boot-hose." Hose formerly were not stockings as we now wear them, but were drawn up the full length of the leg, and sometimes even to the waist, and had pockets in their sides. In the time of the Tudors and Stuarts, they were worn of great variety of materials and of colour, and were in some instances very costly. They were often termed "nether stocks."

"Tops" were the Holland, linen, and lace-linings and frills, worn around the full-hanging boots of the Cavaliers. The tops were exceedingly full and rich among the higher class, and their "getting-up" must have been a somewhat tiresome operation for the laundress. The "sock" was frequently beautifully worked, and was drawn on over the hose or stocking, and reached up to the calf of the leg.

"Pillowberes" is the old term for what we call "pillow-cases;" that is, the covering of the pillow, sometimes also called "pillow-slips," or "pillow-ties."

"Table-cloths" have been in use in England certainly since the Saxon period, and in that and every succeeding age.

'The word "napkin" was formerly applied to handkerchiefs and table-linen, as well as to cloths for head-dresses, &c. "Napery" was the general term for linen, especially that for the table. "Towel" requires no explanation.'

As the 'Horn-book' gradually gave way to the 'Battledore' and the 'Primer,' so the 'Washing Tally' has given place to the 'Lady's and Gentleman's Washing-books,' to be found in the shop of every stationer. But, like the Horn-book, the original was far more lasting, more useful, and, in the end, much less expensive, than the modern books are which have been substituted for them.

L. L. J.

---

# AUGUST 18.

St Agapetus, martyr, about 275. St Helen, empress, 328. St Clare of Monte Falco, virgin, 1308.

*Born.*—Dr Henry Hammond, eminent English divine, 1605, *Chertsey;* Brook Taylor, mathematician, 1685, *Edmonton;* John, Earl Russell, from 1846 to 1852 Prime Minister of Great Britain, 1792, *London.*

*Died.*—Empress Helena, mother of Constantine, 328, *Rome;* Sir Richard Empson and Edmund Dudley, ministers to the rapacity of Henry VII., executed on Tower Hill, 1510; Pope Paul IV., 1559; Guido Reni, celebrated painter, 1642, *Bologna;* William Boyd, Earl of Kilmarnock, and Arthur, Lord Balmerino, beheaded for high treason, 1746, *London;* Francis I., Emperor of Germany, 1765, *Innspruck;* Dr James Beattie, poet (*The Minstrel*), 1803, *Aberdeen;* Sir William Fairbairn, Engineer, 1874, Farnham, Surrey.

## THE REBEL LORDS OF 1746.

Four of the Scotch nobility, who had joined in the insurrection of 1745, were condemned to death. One, the Earl of Cromarty, was pardoned, very much out of pity for his wife and large family. A second, Lord Lovat, was executed in 1747. The remaining two suffered decapitation on Tower Hill, on the 18th of August 1746, while the country was still tingling with the fear it had sustained from the rising. Of these, the Earl of Kilmarnock, a gentle-natured man of two-and-forty, professed penitence. The other, Lord Balmerino, a bluff old dragoon, met death with cheerful resignation, avowing his zeal for the House of Stuart to the last. The scaffold erected for this execution was immediately in front of a house which still exists, marked as No. 14 Tower Hill. The two lords were in succession led out of this house on to the scaffold, Kilmarnock suffering before Balmerino, in melancholy reference to his higher rank in the peerage. Their mutilated bodies, after being deposited in their respective coffins, are said to have been brought back into the house, and in proof of this, a trail of blood is still visible along the hall and up the first flight of stairs. There is a contemporary print of the execution, representing the scaffold as surrounded by a wide square of dragoons, beyond which are great multitudes of people, many of them seated in wooden galleries. The decapitated lords were all respectfully buried in St Peter's Chapel within the Tower.

There were in all between eighty and ninety men put to death for their concern in the Forty-five. Many of them suffered on Kennington Common, including two English gentlemen, named Francis Townley and George Fletcher, who had joined the prince at Manchester. The heads of these two were fixed at the top of poles, and stuck over Temple Bar, where they remained till 1772, when one of them fell down, and in a storm, the other soon followed. There were people living in London not long ago, who remembered having in their childhood seen these grisly memorials of civil strife. Many readers will remember the jocular remark made by Goldsmith to Johnson, with reference to the rebel heads of Temple Bar. Johnson, who was well known to be of Jacobite inclinations, had just quoted to Goldsmith from *Ovid,* when among the poets' tombs at Westminister Abbey—

> 'Forsitan et nostrum nomen miscebitur istis.'

Passing on their way home under Temple Bar, Goldsmith slily whispered in Johnson's ear, pointing to the heads—

> 'Forsitan et nostrum nomen miscebitur *istis.*'

Previous to the rebellion of 1745, Temple Bar, for about thirty years, exhibited the head of a barrister named Layer, who had been executed for a Jacobite conspiracy, soon after Atterbury's Plot. At length, one stormy night, the head of Layer was tumbled down from its station, and being found in the morning by a gentleman named Pearce, was taken into a neighbouring public-house. It is said to have there been buried in the cellar; nevertheless, a skull was purchased as Layer's by Dr Rawlinson, an antiquary, and, on his death in 1755, was buried in his right hand.*

## DECLINE AND END OF THE JACOBITE PARTY.

It is scarcely necessary to remark that Jacobitism proceeded upon a principle, which is not now in any degree owned by anybody in the United Kingdom—that a certain family had a simply hereditary right to the crown and all the associated benefits, and could not be deprived of it without the same degree of injustice which attends the taking of a man's land, or his goods, or anything else that is his. 'The king shall enjoy *his own* again!' was the burden of a song of the Commonwealth, which continued in vogue among the Stuart party as long as it existed. Those who made and sang it, had no idea of any right in the many controlling this supposed right of one; and there, of course, lay their great mistake. Granting, however, that the Jacobites viewed the case of the Stuarts as that of a family deprived of a right by unjust means, we must admit that their conduct in trying to effect its restoration was not merely logical, but generous. In the heat of contention, the Revolution party could not so regard it; but *we* may. We may—while deploring the short-sightedness of their principles—admire their sacrifices and efforts, and pity their sufferings.

After the House of Brunswick had been well settled in England, the chance of a restoration of the Stuarts became extremely small. The attempt of 1745, brilliant as it was in some respects, was a thing out of time, a mere temporary and, as it were, impertinent interruption of a state of things quite in a contrary strain. The Jacobites were chiefly country gentlemen—men of the same type who are now known as ultra-conservatives. They were important in their own local circles, but could exercise little influence on the masses. The essential weakness of their cause is shewn in the necessity they were under of putting a mask upon it.

A constant correspondence was kept up between them and the Stuarts, but under profound secrecy. Portraits and medals of the royal exiles were continually coming to them, to keep alive their bootless loyalty. An old lady would have the face of James III. so arranged in her bedroom, that it was the first thing she saw on opening her eyes in the morning. The writer has seen a copy of the Bible, with a print of that personage pasted on the inside of the first board. The contemplation of it had been a part of the owner's devotions. There was also a way of shewing the Stuart face by a curious optical device, calculated to screen the possessor from any unpleasant consequences. The face was painted on a piece of canvas, in such a way that no lineament of humanity was visible upon it; but when a polished steel cylinder was erected in the midst, a beautiful portrait of 'the king' or 'the prince' was visible by reflection on the metal surface. There were also occasional presents of peculiar choice articles from the Stuarts to their adherents. A gentleman in Perthshire still possesses the silver collar of an Italian greyhound, which was sent to his grandmother, considerably more than a hundred years ago, the collar being thus inscribed: 'C. STEWARTUS PRINCEPS JUVENTUTIS.' On the other hand, when some ingenious manufacturer produced a ribbon or a garter coloured tartan-wise, and containing allusive inscriptions, initials, or other objects, samples of it would be duly transmitted to the expatriated court.

The Jacobites dealt largely in songs metaphorically conveying their sentiments, and some of these, from this very additional necessity of metaphor, are tolerably effective as samples of poetry. Dr William King, president of St Mary's Hall, Oxford, and Dr John Byrom of Manchester, were the chief bards of the party about the middle of the century. The Jacobites also dealt largely in mystically significant toasts. If the old squire, in giving 'The king,' brought his glass across a water-jug, it was held to be a very clever way of shewing that he meant 'The king over the water.' If some Will-Wimble-like dependent, on being asked for his toast, proposed, 'The king *again*,' it was accepted as a dexterous hint at a Restoration. One of Dr Byrom's toasts was really a clever equivoque:

'God bless the king—I mean the Faith's Defender.
God bless—no harm in blessing—the Pretender.
Who that Pretender is, and who that king,
God bless us all, is quite another thing.'

This was set forth in Byrom's works, as 'intended to allay the violence of party-spirit.' One of the hopeful sons of the squire was sure of an additional apple, if he could clearly enunciate to the company at table the following alphabet:

| | |
|---|---|
| A. B. C. | A Blessed Change. |
| D. E. F. | D— Every Foreigner. |
| G. H. J. | Get Home James. |
| K. L. M. | Keep Loyal Ministers. |
| N. O. P. | No Oppressive Parliaments. |
| Q. R. S. | Quickly Return, Stuart. |
| T. U. W. | Tuck Up Whelps (Guelphs). |
| X. Y. Z. | 'Xert Your Zeal. |

As another specimen of their system of equivocation, take the following verses, as given on the fly-leaf of a book which had belonged to a Jacobite partisan:

| | |
|---|---|
| I love with all my heart | The Tory party here |
| The Hanoverian part | Most hateful doth appear |
| And for their settlement | I ever have denied |
| My conscience gives consent | To be on James's side |
| Most glorious is the cause | To be with such a king |
| To fight for George's laws | Will Britain's ruin bring |
| This is my mind and heart | In this opinion I |
| Though none should take my part | Resolve to live and die |

To appearance, this was a long poem of short lines, conveying nothing but loyalty to the Hanover family, while, in reality, it was a short poem in long lines, pronouncing zealously for the Stuarts.

* *Temple Bar, the City Golgotha.* By a Member of the Inner Temple. 1853.

Mr Richard Almack, F. S. A., Melford, exhibited at a meeting of the Archæological Institute, a very affecting memorial of the Jacobite party, in the form of an impression from a secretly engraved plate, supposed to have been executed by Sir Robert Strange, and of which a copy is here reproduced on wood. It professedly is a sort of cenotaph of the so-called 'Martyrs for King and Country in 1746.' The form, as will be observed, is that of a full-blown five-petalled rose, on which are thirty-five small circles, containing each the

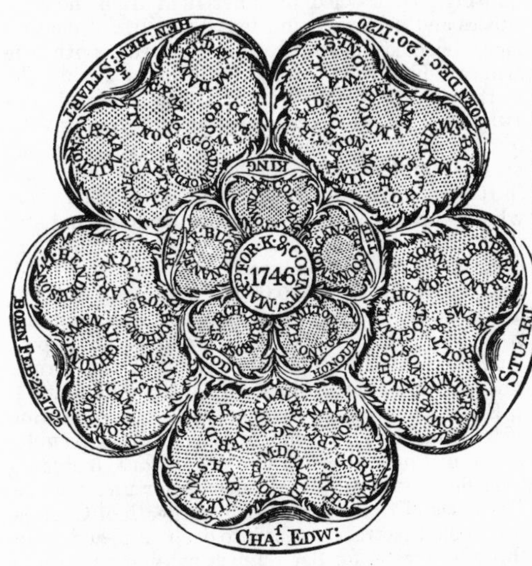


MEMORIAL OF JACOBITE MARTYRS.

name of some one who suffered for the cause at the close of the insurrection of 1745-6; as also, on the extremities, those of Prince Charles and Prince Henry Benedict, with the dates of their births. Amongst the names of the sufferers are those of Captain John Hamilton, who had been governor of Carlisle for the Prince, and surrendered it to the Duke of Cumberland, Sir Archibald Primrose, Francis Buchanan of Arnprior, Colonel Townley, who had raised a rebel regiment at Manchester, and Captain David Morgan, originally a barrister. The others were persons of less account; most of them were put to death in barbarous circumstances on Kennington Common. [A second plate, similar in form to the one engraved above, was in 1884 in the possession of Miss Foster, Larkholm, near Liverpool. This plate contains a different set of names, amongst which appear those of Lords Balmerino and Kilmarnock.] Jacobitism may be said to have ceased to have a profession of faith at the death of Charles Edward in 1788. Little of it survived in favour of Cardinal York, who, at the death of his brother, was content to issue a medal bearing his name as 'Henricus Nonus Dei Gratia Rex,' with the meek addition, 'Haud desideriis Hominum, sed voluntate Dei.' The feeling may be said to have merged in an attachment to George III., on his taking so strong a part against the French Revolution and Friends of the People—a position which made him something like a Stuart himself.

# AUGUST 19.

Saints Timothy, Agapius, and Thecla, martyrs, 304. St Mochteus, bishop and confessor, 535. St Cumin, bishop in Ireland, 7th century. St Lewis, bishop of Toulouse, confessor, 1297.

*Born.*—Elizabeth Stuart, Electress-Palatine of the Rhine, queen of Bohemia, daughter of James VI. of Scotland, 1596; Gerbrant Vander Eeckhout, painter, 1621, *Amsterdam;* John Flamsteed, astronomer, 1646, *Denby, Derbyshire;* Francis I., king of the Two Sicilies, 1777; James Nasmyth, engineer, 1808, *Edinburgh.*

*Died.*—Octavius Cæsar Augustus, first Roman emperor, 14 A. D., *Nola;* Geoffrey Plantagenet, brother of Richard Cœur-de-Lion, killed at Paris, 1186; Blaise Pascal, author of the *Provincial Letters*, 1662, *Paris;* John Eudes, priest, founder of the Congregation of Jesus and Mary, 1680, *Caen;* Sir Benjamin Thompson, Count Rumford, practical philosopher, 1814, *Auteuil;* Robert Bloomfield, poet (*The Farmer's Boy*), 1823, *Shefford, Bedfordshire;* Sir Martin A. Shee, president of Royal Academy, 1850, *Brighton;* Honoré de Balzac, French novelist, 1850, *Paris.*

## ELIZABETH, ELECTRESS PALATINE.

Happiness such as rarely falls to the lot of crowned heads, might have been the portion of this lovely and interesting woman, had not a foolish ambition of being called a queen blighted in a moment the whole tenor of her life. The eldest child of James VI. of Scotland, she was born at the palace of Falkland, and when baptized, had for a sponsor the city of Edinburgh, in the proxies of its provost and bailies, who stoutly held to their right of seeing the princess brought up in the Protestant faith. When her father departed, in 1603, to take possession of the English throne, he left his consort and young family to follow him; and their progress through the counties was marked by festivals and pageants nearly as grand as those which had signalised the king's own progress. After a short stay at Windsor, it was deemed necessary that the little princess should be withdrawn from her father's palace and placed under the superintendence of Lord and Lady Harrington, at Combe Abbey. Very pleasant is the picture of the life led at this lovely spot, where beautiful gardens, aviaries, park, and river, charmed the eyes of those who had been accustomed to the wild, desolate Scottish scenery. Many noble young ladies were sent to share in the education of Elizabeth, which seems to have been admirably conducted by Lord Harrington: a sincere Christian and learned man, he strove to instruct his pupil more thoroughly in life and its duties, than in mere outside show, and but for the lavish expenditure, arising from her generosity, which he could not subdue, we may say that he succeeded well.

At the age of fifteen, the young princess was removed to London, and proposals of marriage came from all the countries in Europe. France and Spain drew back, on the ground of religious differences, and at length Frederick V., Elector palatine, was the accepted suitor, who, though snubbed by the queen for his want of a kingly title, was yet the first in rank of the German princes, ruling those wide and fertile Rhenish Provinces which now form so valuable a part of the Prussian dominions. His reception in October 1612 was of a most joyous kind; water-processions, tiltings, masques, and feasts filled up the days, until the sad death of Prince Henry threw the royal family into mourning. He and his sister had always been strongly attached, and his last words were for her. The opportunity was, however, given for her lover to offer his best consolations, and the deep attachment formed at this period was never abated during the many trials of their married life. St Valentine's Day was appropriately chosen for the marriage-ceremony; the first royal one that had ever been performed according to the liturgy of the Church of England. James's vanity induced him to load himself on this joyous occasion with six hundred thousand pounds worth of jewels, and the bride's white satin dress was embroidered with pearls and gems, and her coronet set in pinnacles of diamonds and pearls. Having taken a sad farewell of her parents, whom she was never to see again, she sailed to Flushing, and proceeded on a sort of triumphal march through Holland and Germany, arriving at her beautiful palace of Heidelberg amidst arches of flowers and hearty welcomes from her subjects. Frederick lifted her over the threshold in his arms, according to old German custom, and introduced her to his mother and relatives in rooms furnished with solid silver. The great tun of wine stood on the terrace, and was twice drunk dry by the scholars, soldiers, and citizens, who dined in the meadows beneath, by the banks of the Neckar. For six years this happy couple reigned in equal prosperity and popularity; three lovely children rejoiced their parents' hearts; when the Bohemians, roused to insurrection by the oppression of the emperor of Germany, offered their crown to Frederick.

Very thankful would the Elector have been to decline such a desperate venture as that of matching his strength with the Imperial forces: but Elizabeth urged him on with the question, 'Why he had married a king's daughter, if he dreaded being a king?' The stadtholder, Maurice, was on her side of the question; while the Electress-Dowager supported her son. Maurice one day abruptly asked the Electress-Dowager: 'If there were any green baize to be got in Heidelberg?' 'Yes, surely,' answered she; 'but what for, Maurice?' 'To make a fool's cap for him who might be a king and will not!' was the reply of Maurice. Thus overcome, Frederick signed the acceptance of the ancient crown of Bohemia, and in October he and his family made a ceremonial entry into the old city of Prague, where Taborites, Hussites, Lutherans, and Catholics were soon at daggers-drawing with each other and their chosen sovereign. The Spanish army immediately seized on Heidelberg and the Palatinate, whilst the Duke of Bavaria's cannon boomed over the Weissenberg, and his soldiers descended on Prague. The unfortunate king assisted his wife into the carriage in which she had to fly for her life, saying: 'Now I know what I am. We princes seldom hear the truth until we are taught it by adversity.' The Catholics broke out into songs of exultation. Mr Floyd, a member of parliament in England, was expelled from the House, branded, and flogged, for repeating a squib, 'that the king's daughter fled from Prague like an Irish beggar-woman with her babe at her back.' Placards were fixed on the walls of Brussels, offering a reward for 'a king run-away a few days since, of adolescent age, sanguine colour, middle height, a cast in one of his eyes, no moustache, only down on his lip, not badly disposed when a stolen kingdom did not lie in his way—his name, Frederick.' Henceforth this royal pair, with their large family of little princes and princesses, were only indebted to charity for a home.

By the kindness of the States-General, Elizabeth found refuge at the Hague. She maintained a brave heart, indulged in her favourite sport of hunting, and seemed to suffer little from the difficulties and privations incidental to a life of penury. Her dejected husband was generally with the armies which were desolating Germany during the fearful Thirty Years' War, until death carried him away in 1632, at a distance from his loving wife, in the castle of Mentz: sorrow at witnessing the miseries of his people broke his heart when but thirty-six years of age. The sad tidings were wholly unexpected by his poor widow, and for three days she was unable to speak; her brother, Charles I., shewed her great sympathy and kindness, allowing her £20,000 a year, and begging her to come to him. This she declined; but her two elder sons, Prince Charles and Rupert, spent much time at the English court, until the former was once more settled in a part of the Palatinate.

Elizabeth occupied herself with the education of her daughters and younger sons, until the troubles began in England, when two of her sons, including 'the fiery Rupert,' joined their unfortunate uncle. The close of the struggle with the death of Charles, threw the Electress at once into deep grief, and something like want, for her English pension necessarily ceased. Her court, nevertheless, became a refuge for the persecuted loyalists, whilst her kind, affectionate temper, made her friends among all sects and parties. Louisa, one of her daughters, shewed such talent for painting, that her pictures were often disposed of to assist the needy household; this clever woman afterwards became a nun at Chaillot, much to her mother's sorrow.

The restoration in 1660, brought a last ray of hope to the sorrowful life of Elizabeth. She longed to see her native country once more; and when her nephew, the king, declared his inability to bear the expense of a state-visit, she determined to come incognito, to her generous friend, Lord Craven, who offered her his house in Drury Lane. We soon hear of her entering into the gaieties of London, and being the first lady of the court; £12,000 a year was settled upon her, and happiness seemed in store; but in less than a year after her arrival, inflammation of the lungs attacked her, and she died on the eve of St Valentine's Day, just forty-nine years after she had been made a happy bride, and was buried at Westminster Abbey, with a torchlight procession on the Thames. Of her seven sons, not one left a grandson; and it was through her youngest daughter, Sophia, that the present royal family came to the British throne.

---

### COUNT RUMFORD.

Sir Benjamin Thompson, better known as Count Rumford, was one of those few but fortunate men who have both the means and the inclination to be useful to society generally. He was continually doing something or other, that had for its object, or one of its objects, public or individual improvement. He was an American, born at Rumford, in New England, in 1752. After receiving a good education, and marrying advantageously, he espoused the cause of the mother-country against the colonies during the American war, and was knighted by George III. for his services. Sir Benjamin, in 1784, made a continental tour, and eventually entered the service of the king of Bavaria, in the singular capacity of a general reformer. He remodelled the whole military system of the country; he suppressed a most pernicious system of mendicancy that prevailed in Munich; he taught the people to like and to cultivate potatoes, against which they had before had a prejudice; he organised a plan for employing the poor in useful pursuits; and he introduced a multitude of new and curious contrivances of various kinds. He was made a count for his services. He returned to England in 1799, but lived mostly in France, till his death on the 19th of August 1814. Count Rumford's papers in the *Philosophical Transactions*, and his detached scientific essays, range over the subjects of food, cooking, fuel, fireplaces, ventilation, smoky chimneys, sources of heat, conduction of heat, warm baths, uses of steam, artificial illumination, portable lamps, sources of light, broad-wheeled carriages, &c. He was well-versed in English, French, German, Spanish, and Italian. He founded the 'Rumford Medal' of the Royal Society: leaving £1000 stock in the three per cents, the interest of which is applied biennially, in payment for a gold medal, to reward the best discoverers in light and heat; and he benefited many other scientific institutions.

Count Rumford adopted a singular winter-dress while at Paris—white from head to foot. This he did in obedience to the ascertained fact, that the natural heat of the body radiates and wastes less quickly through light than dark-coloured substances. But the most remarkable achievement of Rumford's life, perhaps, was the suppression of the beggars at Munich. Mendicancy had risen to a deplorable evil, sapping the industrial progress of the people, and leading to idleness, robbery, and the most shameless debauchery. The civil power could not battle against the evil; but Rumford took it in hand. He caused a large building to be constructed, and filled it with useful implements of trade—but without letting the beggars into the secret. Having instructed the garrison and the magistrates in the parts they were to fill, he fixed on the 1st of January 1790, as the day for a *coup d'état*, when the beggars would be more than usually on the look-out for New-year's gifts. 'Count Rumford began by arresting the first beggar he met with his own hand. No sooner had their commander set the example, than the officers and soldiers cleared the streets with equal promptitude and success, but at the same time with all imaginable good-nature; so that before night, not a single beggar was to be seen in the whole metropolis. As fast as they were arrested, they were conducted to the town-hall, where their names were inscribed, and they were then dismissed with directions to repair the next day to the new workhouse provided for them, where they would find employment, and a sufficiency of wholesome food. By persevering in this plan, and by the establishment of the most excellent practical regulations, the count so far overcame prejudice, habit, and attachment, that these heretofore miserable objects began to cherish the idea of independence—to feel a pride in obtaining an honest livelihood—to prefer industry to idleness, and decency to filth, rags, and the squalid wretchedness attendant on beggary. In order to attain these important objects, he introduced new manufactures into the electoral dominions.'*

## ROBERT BLOOMFIELD.

Robert Bloomfield, when he wrote his *Farmer's Boy*, drew upon his own experience. His father was a tailor, his mother a village-schoolmistress, his uncle a farmer, and under this uncle the fatherless lad was placed. But the labour of his employment, it is said, proved too much for a delicate constitution; so he went to live in London with an elder brother, and learned the trade of a shoemaker. The Muses whispered their secrets in his ear, as he sat working in his garret, and he wrote down what they said: in due time, with the help of a patron, the shoemaker's verses were published, and the polite world was astonished.

In these days, when the advantages and opportunities of education have been extended to the humblest in the land, and the simplest village letter-carrier is expected to be informed as to higher matters than mere numbers of houses and names of streets, poems from the pens of men of humble origin are not such a wonderful thing as they were in Bloomfield's time. The art of writing verses is as simple to acquire as the art of mending shoes. Further than this, all men, from whatever classes they may have sprung, and how differently soever they may have been reared to manhood, have inherently the same passions, hopes, feelings, and tendencies. The sweet influences of nature sway the farmer's boy and the lord's heir alike, if in different degrees, or after different fashions. The difficulty which stands in the way of a rustic, when he takes a pen in his hand, is not how to find thoughts, or feel emotions, but how to give expression to them. This difficulty education has tended much to remove, and hence we now encounter poetic post-boys and rhyming shoemakers much more often than we used to do.

Poor Robert Bloomfield! Ambition led him astray! He was lifted off his feet. When the great smiled on him, he thought himself famous; when they forgot him in due course, he sickened and despaired, and only preserved his reason by surrendering his life. It is a sad thing not to distinguish clearly what one is, and what one is not, and a most dangerous thing for one who is deserving to hanker after notoriety.

## THE SCRATCH-BACK.

The curious little instruments here figured are of extreme rarity, and probably not many of our readers have ever heard of, much less seen, any examples of them. The name, 'Scratch-back,' is not very euphonious, but it is remarkably expressive, and conveys a correct notion of the use of the curious little instrument to which it belongs. The

* *Gentleman's Magazine*, vol. lxiv. part 2. p. 395.

'scratch-back' was literally, as its name implies, formed for the purpose of scratching the backs of our fair and stately great and great-great-grand-mothers, and their ancestresses from the time of Queen Elizabeth; and very choicely set and carved some of them assuredly were. Sometimes the handles were of silver elegantly chased, and we have seen one example where a ring on the finger of the hand was set with brilliants. But few of these relics have passed down to our times, and even in instances where they are preserved, their original use has been forgotten. At one time, scratch-backs were almost as indispensable an accompaniment to a lady of quality as her fan and her patch-box. They were kept in her toilet, and carried with her even to her box at the play.

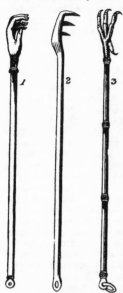

SCRATCH-BACKS.

The first one, engraved on the accompanying illustration, is twelve inches in length. At the upper end is an ivory knob, with a hole, through which a cord could be passed for suspension to the waist, or for hanging in the dressing-room. The handle or shaft is mottled, and the *practical* end, or scratcher, is a beautifully carved hand of ivory. The fingers are placed in the proper position for the operation, and would lead one to believe that the carver must have studied pretty closely from nature. The finger-nails are particularly sharp and well formed, and designed to scratch in the most approved fashion. This seems to have been the most favourite form for this strange instrument, of which form I have seen three examples.

The second example in our engraving is of about the same length as the one just described. This instrument is made entirely of horn, one end being pierced for suspension, and the other formed into three teeth or claws, sharp at the ends and bent forward. It is particularly simple in construction, but evidently would be as effective as the more artistic and elaborate example just described.

The third specimen which I give is, like the first, partly of ivory, and beautifully carved. The stick or shaft is of tortoise-shell, and it has a little silver ring at the top, and a rim of silver to cover the junction of the tortoise-shell and ivory. The scratcher is formed like the foot of a bird, with the claws set, and, of course, made very sharp at the points. The foot is beautifully carved, and remarkably well formed; and the instrument must have been one of the best of its class. On the under-side of the foot of this example are the initials of its fair owner, A. W., cut into the ivory.

It would add to the interest of this little notice could we tell our readers to whom these precious little relics had belonged, and whose fair backs they had scratched; but this we cannot do. All we can do is, to give them representations of these curious instruments, explain their uses, describe their construction, and heartily congratulate our fair friends on their not being required in our day. In former times, when personal cleanliness was not considered essential, when the style of dress worn was anything but conducive to comfort and ease—for it must be remembered that, in the last century, ladies' immensely-high head-dresses, when once fixed, were frequently not disturbed or altered for a month, and not until they had become almost intolerable to the wearer and to her friends—and when the domestic manners of the aristocracy, as well as others, were not of the most refined and delicate kind, the use of these little instruments, with many other matters which we may yet take the opportunity of describing, became almost essential. In our day they are not so, and we have no fear of seeing their use revived.

L. L. J.

# AUGUST 20.

St Oswin, king of Deira and martyr, 651. St Bernard, abbot of Clairvaux, 1153.

## ST BERNARD.

St Bernard, often styled by Catholics 'the last of the Fathers,' was unquestionably one of the greatest men of the middle ages. He was the son of a knight, and was born at the castle of Fontaines, in Burgundy, in 1091. His mother was a pious woman, who encouraged his inclination for religious thought and study, and he had scarcely passed out of boyhood, when he formed the resolution to be a monk. His capacity for leadership displayed itself very early. He drew thirty companions, including his brothers, after him into the Cistercian monastery of Citeaux; and such was his persuasive eloquence, that mothers hid their sons, and wives their husbands, lest he should steal them from them. The discipline of the Cistercians was very severe, but it did not reach the mark of Bernard's ardour. He determined not only to extirpate the desires of the flesh, but the sense of enjoyment itself. He seldom ate except to save himself from fainting, and passed whole days in ecstatic contemplation, 'so that seeing he saw not, and hearing he heard not.' To escape the worldly talk of friends who visited him, he stopped his ears with flax, and burying his head in his cowl, allowed them to go on as they chose, every now and then addressing them in some sentence of admonition. When he worked, he selected the most menial occupations, such as digging, hewing wood, and carrying burdens. In spite of these austerities, his mind found comfort and relaxation in nature. He was accustomed to say, that whatever knowledge he had of the Scriptures, he had chiefly acquired in the woods and fields, and that beeches and oaks had ever been his best teachers in the Word of God. By centuries anticipating Wordsworth, he wrote to a pupil: 'Trust to one who has had experience. You will find something far greater in the woods than you will find in books. Stones and trees will teach you that which you will never learn from masters. Think you not you can suck honey from the rock, and oil from the flinty rock? Do not the mountains drop sweetness, the hills run with milk and honey, and the valleys stand thick with corn?'

A capable man like Bernard was not to be lost in privacy. As Citeaux became crowded with devotees, the abbot, a shrewd judge of character, selected Bernard, and sent him into the wilderness at the head of twelve companions to found a new settlement. After wandering northwards for ninety miles, they fixed their abode in a woody valley, called Wormwood, in Champagne, and erected a log-hut, which, under Bernard's genius, grew into the renowned Abbey of Clairvaux. This was in 1115, when Bernard was a young man of twenty-four.

The saintly rigour of his life, his eloquence as a preacher, and his courage in attacking civil and ecclesiastical wrong-doers, gradually raised Bernard into European fame, and letters and visitors from far and near drifted to Clairvaux. The force of his influence became especially manifest in 1130, when, on the death of Pope Honorius II., two popes—Innocent II. and Anacletus II.—each claimed to be the true and only vicar of Christ. The rulers of Europe were at a loss to decide between the rivals. Louis VI. of France convened a council to consider the question, to which Bernard was invited. The assembly waited with awe for his opinion, believing that the Holy Spirit would speak through his mouth. He declared for Innocent, and the council at once broke up perfectly satisfied. Henry I. of England he convinced as easily. 'Are you afraid,' said Bernard, 'of incurring sin if you acknowledge Innocent? Bethink you how to answer for your *other* sins to God, *that one* I will take and account for.' Henry accepted the offer, and yielded supremacy to Innocent.

Bernard troubled himself less with errors of opinion than errors of conduct, and though he had many contests with heretics, they appear to have been prompted by others rather than undertaken from choice. One of his most notable controversies was with Abelard, the Rationalist of the twelfth century, who was accused of unsound doctrine, and dangerous speculation on the mystery of the Trinity. Abelard challenged Bernard to a public logical disputation. Bernard hesitated, and refused. 'When all fly before his face,' said Bernard, 'he selects me, the least, for single combat. I refuse, because I am but a child, and he a man of war from his youth.' These fears were overcome by his friends, and a council was called at Sens, to which the king of France and a crowd of nobles and ecclesiastics repaired. Abelard came with a troop of disciples; Bernard, with two or three monks, as it behoved a Cistercian abbot to travel. Abelard seems to have discovered that he had made a mistake. He was used to address the reason of scholars, and the gathering at Sens was made up of men on whose minds his logic would have slight effect, whilst his adversary's impassioned oratory would be irresistible. Bernard had scarcely opened his discourse, when, to the speechless astonishment of all, Abelard rose up, said he refused to hear more, or answer any questions. He appealed to Rome, and at once left the assembly. The council, nevertheless, proceeded to condemn Abelard, and the pope affirmed the decree. Two years afterwards, in 1142, Abelard died.

Perhaps the greatest business of Bernard's life was the preaching-up of the second Crusade. He was fifty-five, and worn and old for his years, and thought his time for rest had come, when an order arrived from Rome, that he should bestir himself and raise the spirit of Europe against the Turks. Pale and attenuated to a degree which seemed almost supernatural, he made a tour among the towns of France and Germany, preaching with a success so prodigious that in some districts scarcely one man was left to seven women.

The times of crusade fever were usually sad times for the Jews. Simultaneously with the growth of the passion for fighting and slaughtering the infidels abroad, hatred was developed against the Jews at home. Following in the wake of Bernard's preaching, a monk named Rodolph travelled through the towns on the Rhine inciting the people to the massacre of the Jews. Bernard, hearing of the atrocities committed in the name of Christ, with a humanity far in advance of his age, at once intervened. 'Does not the church,' he inquired, 'triumph more fully over the Jews by convincing or converting them from day to day, than if she, once and for ever, were to slay them all with the edge of the sword?' Rodolph he denounced as a child of the devil, and meeting him at Mayence, managed to send him home to his monastery. A Jewish contemporary attests Bernard's service, saying: 'Had not the tender mercy of the Lord sent priest Bernard, none of us would have survived.'

Miracles without end are related of Bernard, with an amount of minute and authentic testimony which it is puzzling to deal with. 'His faithful disciples,' writes Gibbon, 'enumerate twenty or thirty miracles wrought by him in a day, and appeal to the public assemblies of France and Germany, in which they were performed. At the present hour, such prodigies will not obtain credit beyond the precincts of Clairvaux; but in the preternatural cures of the blind, the lame, and the sick, who were presented to the man of God, it is impossible for us to ascertain the separate shares of accident, of fancy, of imposture, and of fiction.'

He died in 1153, and was canonised in 1174. The Roman Church celebrates his festival on the 20th of August. St Bernard's writings have been repeatedly published, and contain passages of great vigour, eloquence and pathos, and abound in interesting references to the modes of life in the fierce and gloomy century in which his lot was cast.

---

*Born.*—Robert Herrick, English poet, 1591; George Villiers, Duke of Buckingham, favourite of James I. and Charles I., 1592, *Brookesley, Leicestershire;* Louis Bourdaloue, celebrated preacher, 1632, *Bourges;* Thomas Simpson, distinguished mathematician, 1710, *Market-Bosworth, Leicestershire;* George Eden, Earl of Auckland, governor general of India, 1784.

*Died.*—Count Ricimer, celebrated Roman general, 472; Pope John XIV., 984; St Bernard, abbot of Clairvaux, 1153; Jerome Osorio, Portuguese prelate and author, 1580, *Tavila;* Martin Opitz, poet and philologist, 1639, *Dantzic;* Edward, Lord Herbert, of Cherbury, philosophical writer, 1648, *London;* Sir Charles Sedley, poet and dramatist, 1701, *Haverstock Hill, London;* Joseph Spence, critic, drowned at Weybridge, 1768; Pope Pius VII., 1823; William Maginn, LL.D., miscellaneous writer, 1842, *Walton on Thames;* John Thomas Quekett, eminent microscopist, 1861, *Pangbourne, Berkshire.*

## ROBERT HERRICK.

No one makes himself familiar with the merry, melancholy Robin Herrick without loving him. It is better not to analyse the feeling: perhaps we should find in it more elements of love than either respect or admiration.

Robert Herrick, Errick, Heyrick, or, as he himself wrote his name, Hearick, was the son of a goldsmith, and born in Cheapside. Very little is known of him, though his poems gained him, in his own time, considerable reputation. He seems to have been educated at Westminster, and undoubtedly entered as a Fellow-Commoner of St John's College, Cambridge—the college of Wordsworth. Ultimately taking holy orders, he received from Charles I. the living of Dean Priors, in Devonshire, from which he was ejected in 1648, but to which he was afterwards restored by Charles II.

We ought to accept the general dissoluteness of morals in Herrick's day as some sort of excuse for certain tendencies of his which he naïvely denominates 'jocund.' Facts have handed down nothing to his discredit, and it is but charitable to receive his own testimony :—

'To his book's end this last line he 'd have placed :
Jocund his muse was, but his life was chaste.'

So sings Ovid, so Martial, so Catullus. Muretus justly comments : 'Whoever is like Catullus in his poems, is seldom like Cato in his morals.'

Herrick lived to be over eighty, in celibacy, and his maid 'Prue' seems to have gained his affection by taking excellent care of him. In his hearty, indolent, little verses he does not forget to praise her.

While residing occasionally in London, he became one of Ben Jonson's famous clique, and seems almost to have worshipped the burly demigod. Indeed he has canonised him in twelve honest lines, with his usual poet's love of rites and forms.

### HIS PRAYER TO BEN JONSON.

When I a verse shall make,
Know I have prayed thee,
For old religion's sake,
Saint Ben, to aid me.

Make the way smooth for me,
When I, thy Herrick,
Honouring thee, on my knee
Offer my lyric.

Candles I 'll give to thee,
And a new altar:
And thou, Saint Ben, shall be
Writ in my psalter.

Herrick's poetry was for more than a century in complete oblivion, and much of it was worthy of no better fate ; but a selection of it ought not to be wanting in any library of English literature. His *Nuptial Song* is inferior to none ; and his *Fairy Land* is full of the daintiest thoughts, fresh coined by an exquisite fancy. Saint Ben was far behind him in pathos and simple tenderness : his *Charms and Ceremonials* are a storehouse of quaint old English customs ; and Wordsworth could not have written a sweeter epitaph than this :



### UPON A VIRGIN.

Here a solemn fast we keep,
While all beauty lies asleep.
Hush'd be all things ; no noise here,
But the toning of a tear :
Or a sigh of such as bring
Cowslips for her covering.

## TALENT WITHOUT CONDUCT :
## THE LIFE OF WILLIAM MAGINN, LL.D.

Amid the many melancholy instances of genius and talent impeded and finally extinguished by the want of a little ordinary prudence and circumspectness of conduct, Dr Maginn is prominently conspicuous. Possessed of one of the most versatile of minds, which enabled him to pass with the utmost ease from grave to gay, from the rollicking fun of 'The Story without a Tail,' and 'Bob Burke's Duel,' to the staidness and delicate discrimination of the 'Shakspeare Papers,' and the classic elegance of the

WILLIAM MAGINN, LL.D.

'Homeric Ballads,' he yet found himself incompetent to the proper husbanding and turning to account of these gifts, and, after enduring the last miseries of a debtor's prison, fell a victim soon afterwards to consumption. The leading events of his biography are few and soon told.

He was a native of Cork, and born there in 1794. His father was proprietor of a school of considerable reputation in that city, to the management of which the son succeeded when little more than twenty, having previously passed with distinguished reputation through a course of study at Trinity College, Dublin. He continued to discharge the duties of this office with much credit for some years till he abandoned it to devote himself entirely to a literary life. Some of his first essays were trifles and *jeux d'esprit*, written in connection with a literary society in Cork, of which he was a member. They excited a good deal of local attention. In 1816, he obtained the degree of LL.D., and soon after became a contributor to the *Literary Gazette*, then under the management of Mr William Jerdan, who says that Maginn was in the habit of sending him 'a perfect shower of varieties; classic paraphrases, anecdotes, illustrations of famous ancient authors, displaying a vast acquaintance with, and fine appreciation of them.' It is principally, however, with *Blackwood's* and *Fraser's Magazines* that his name is associated, being a contributor to the former almost from its commencement, whilst the latter owed mainly its existence to him, being projected by him in company with Mr Hugh Fraser. A characteristic anecdote is related of his first meeting with Mr Blackwood. He had already contributed to the *Magazine* several biting papers, which had excited a considerable ferment both in Edinburgh and Cork; but the intercourse between him and his publisher had as yet been wholly epistolary, the latter not even knowing the name of his correspondent. Determined now to have an interview with Mr Blackwood, Maginn set out for Edinburgh, where he arrived on a Sunday evening, and on the ensuing forenoon he presented himself in the shop in Princes Street, where the following conversation took place. It must be observed, in passing, that Mr Blackwood had received numerous furious communications, more especially from Ireland, demanding the name of the writer of the obnoxious articles, and he now believed that this was a visit from one of them to obtain redress *in propriâ personâ*.

'You are Mr Blackwood, I presume?'

'I am.'

'I have rather an unpleasant business, then, with you regarding some things which appeared in your magazine. They are so and so' (mentioning them); 'would you be so kind as to give me the name of the author?'

'That requires consideration, and I must first be satisfied that'——

'Your correspondent resides in Cork, doesn't he? You need not make any mystery about that.'

'I decline at present giving any information on that head, before I know more of this business—of your purpose—and who you are.'

'You are very shy, sir. I thought you corresponded with Mr Scott of Cork' (the assumed name which he had used).

'I beg to decline giving any information on that subject.'

'If you don't know him, then, perhaps you *could* know your own handwriting' (drawing forth a bundle of letters from his pocket). 'You need not deny your correspondence with that gentleman—I am that gentleman.'

Such, as related by Dr Moir, was Dr Maginn's introduction to the proprietor of this noted periodical, the pages of which, for several years afterwards, continued to be enriched with some of his most original and piquant articles. A disagreement, however, in process of time, took place between him and Mr Blackwood, and led him to the projection of *Fraser's Magazine*, to which, amid innumerable other articles, he supplied nearly all the letter-press of the celebrated 'Gallery of Literary Portraits.' One of his articles, a review of the novel entitled *Berkeley Castle*, led to a duel with the Hon. Grantley Berkeley, which, after three rounds of shots had been exchanged without doing further damage than grazing the heel of Dr Maginn's boot and the collar of Mr Berkeley's coat, ended in the parties quitting the ground, on the interference of the seconds, without speaking a word, or making any explanation.

Notwithstanding the many sources of livelihood which our author's prolific and versatile genius opened up to him, his improvident habits kept him constantly in difficulties, which at last so thickened upon him, that he repeatedly became the inmate of a jail; and in the spring of 1842, the misery and depression of spirits which he had undergone, terminated in a rapid decline. In the vain hope of re-establishing his health, he retired from London to Walton-on-Thames, where, however, his disease gradually gained strength; his frame wasted to a shadow; and in the month of August 1842, he expired. To the last he retained almost undiminished his wonderful flow of humour and animal spirits, and talked and jested with his friends as far as his reduced strength and emaciated frame would permit. He complained bitterly of the neglect with which he had been treated by his party (the Tories); and there can be no doubt that, to a certain extent, the reproach was well founded, though the generosity of Sir Robert Peel was liberally displayed a few days before Maginn's death, on his unfortunate situation being brought under the notice of the premier.

Maginn's character presents much of the conventional characteristics of the Irishman—warm-hearted, generous, and impulsive, freely imparting of his substance to his friends in their need, and as readily borrowing from them to supply his wants in his own. The reckless conviviality of his nature disposed him not unfrequently to excesses which ultimately shattered and destroyed his constitution. Such a vein, however, of *bonhommie* and real kindliness of heart was perfectly irresistible. His conversation is described as a jumble of incongruous subjects, theology, politics, and general literature, all cemented together in an overpowering style of drollery, which, however, not unfrequently left the listeners at a loss whether to surrender themselves unconditionally to the influence of the ludicrous or admire the great common-sense and profound vein of philosophy conspicuous in all his remarks. The ease and rapidity with which he wrote were astonishing. Jumping out of bed, he would seat himself in his shirt at his desk, and run off in an hour one of his brilliant papers for *Blackwood* or *Fraser*. Not unfrequently, it must be added, he composed with the pen in one hand and a glass of brandy-and-water in the other. Much of what he wrote was necessarily of an ephemeral character, and his works will therefore, probably, in a succeeding generation, be comparatively little read; whilst his memory, like that of Foote, is preserved as that of a brilliant wit and conversationalist. Yet he was far from being a mere droll or after-dinner talker. His 'Shakspeare Papers' contain some of the most delicately appreciative touches which have ever been presented on the subject of our great national dramatist; and his 'Homeric Ballads' will fairly rival in vigour and classic genius the *Lays of Ancient Rome* of Macaulay.

The following epitaph was written for Maginn by his friend, John G. Lockhart:

WALTON-ON-THAMES, AUGUST 1842.

Here, early to bed, lies kind WILLIAM MAGINN,
Who, with genius, wit, learning, life's trophies to win,
Had neither great lord nor rich cit of his kin,
Nor discretion to set himself up as to tin;
So, his portion soon spent—like the poor heir of Lynn—
He turned author ere yet there was beard on his chin,
And, whoever was out, or whoever was in,
For your Tories his fine Irish brains he would spin;
Who received prose and rhyme with a promising grin—
'Go ahead, you queer fish, and more power to your fin,'
But to save from starvation stirred never a pin.
Light for long was his heart, though his breeches were thin,
Else his acting, for certain, was equal to Quin;
But at last he was beat, and sought help of the bin
(All the same to the doctor, from claret to gin),
Which led swiftly to jail, and consumption therein.
It was much, when the bones rattled loose in the skin,
He got leave to die here, out of Babylon's din.
Barring drink and the girls, I ne'er heard a sin:
Many worse, better few, than bright, broken Maginn.

---

## AUGUST 21.

Saints Bonosus and Maximilian, martyrs, 363. St Richard, bishop of Andria, confessor, 12th century. St Bernard Ptolemy, founder of the Olivetans, 1348. St Jane Frances de Chantal, widow and abbess, 1641.

*Born.*—James Crichton (*The Admirable*), celebrated scholar, 1561; St Francis de Sales, celebrated Catholic divine, 1567, *Sales, Savoy;* Dionysius Petau, chronologer (*De Doctrinâ Temporum*), 1583, *Orleans;* King William IV. of England, 1765, *St James's Palace;* Augustin Louis Cauchy, mathematician, 1789, *Paris.*

*Died.*—John Dudley, Duke of Northumberland, statesman, beheaded in the Tower, 1553; Lady Mary Wortley Montagu, celebrated letter-writer, 1762.

### LADY MARY WORTLEY MONTAGU.

Lady Mary Pierrepont (afterwards Lady Mary Wortley Montagu) was the eldest daughter of the Earl of Kingston (created Marquis of Dorchester in 1706, and Duke of Kingston in 1715) and Lady Mary Fielding. She was born in 1690, at Thoresby, in Nottinghamshire. She had one brother and two sisters. Her mother died in 1694. As she grew up, she became remarkable for the beauty of her person, an obvious superiority of intellect, and a fondness for reading and study. With some assistance from Burnet, bishop of Salisbury, she acquired a knowledge of the Latin language, and in 1710, had completed a translation of *Epictetus* from the Latin version. Mr Edward Wortley Montagu, eldest son of the Hon. Sydney Montagu, and grandson of the Earl of Sandwich, happened one day to meet Lady Mary Pierrepont in the apartment of his sister Miss Anne Wortley. He was charmed with her beauty, her cultivated mind, her wit; and when he learned that she could read Latin, and wanted to peruse *Quintus Curtius*, but did not possess a copy, he sent her in a few days a superb edition of that author, together with some complimentary verses. This introduction led to a correspondence, a courtship, and proposals of marriage,

LADY MARY WORTLEY MONTAGU.

which were at first accepted by Lord Dorchester, but finally rejected when Mr Wortley refused to settle his landed estates on his eldest son, if he should have one, irrevocably, whatever might be the character and conduct of that son. Lord Dorchester chose a person for husband to Lady Mary, to whom she had a decided aversion. The consequence was, that she eloped with Mr Wortley Montagu, and they were married in 1712. Their only son was born in 1713, their only daughter in 1716.

Edward Wortley Montagu was a good scholar, and having travelled much, was skilled in modern languages. He was a man of clear understanding, much attached to polite literature, and was acquainted with Garth, Congreve, Steele, and Addison. He was a member of parliament for the borough of Huntingdon, and soon after the accession of George I., obtained a seat at the Treasury-board. For some years after her marriage, Lady Mary resided in various places, at Hinchinbroke (the seat of Lord Sandwich), at Huntingdon, at hired houses in Yorkshire, and in London. She was then 'beautiful exceedingly,' and was distinguished for her wit and gaiety. Lady Mary and her husband kept up an intercourse with the wits above mentioned and others, including Pope, with whom, however, during this period, they seem to have had only a very general acquaintance. In August 1716, Mr Wortley Montagu being appointed ambassador to Turkey, he and his wife proceeded to Constantinople, a part of the world then very unfamiliar, compared with what it has since become. Lady Mary's quick and penetrating mind could not fail to be struck by a social scene so different from anything else in Europe, and she wrote of all she saw to her sister, the Countess of Mar. When the pair returned from the East in 1718, they took a furnished house at Twickenham, at the suggestion of Pope, who had entered into a correspondence with Lady Mary during her absence; but even then the intercourse between Lady Mary and Pope does not appear to have been frequent. In a letter to her sister, the Countess of Mar, dated Twickenham, 1720, she says: 'I see sometimes Mr Congreve, but very seldom Mr Pope, who continues to embellish his house at Twickenham He has made a subterranean grotto, which he has furnished with looking-glasses, and they tell me it has a very good effect.' Pope, however, visited Lady Mary occasionally till 1721, when the estrangement between them seems to have originated with Pope, who, in a well-known letter to Lord Hervey, says, 'neither had I the least misunderstanding with that lady, till after I was the author of my own misfortune by discontinuing her acquaintance.' The causes of the subsequent quarrel between them are only conjecturally and imperfectly known. Mr W. Moy Thomas, in the first volume of his new edition (the third) of Lord Wharncliffe's *Letters and Works of Lady Mary Wortley Montagu*, 1861, has entered into a full and minute investigation of her character and conduct; and has been enabled, with the aid of letters and other manuscripts which remain, to wipe away or neutralise the stains of filthy slander with which Pope, Horace Walpole, and others, had befouled her. It is to be fully admitted that this clever woman was wanting in delicacy, and sometimes allowed her love of satire and pleasantry to outrun her discretion; but of gross errors of conduct there is no reason to believe her guilty.

One grievous blight to her happiness arose from the conduct of her son, which was eccentric almost to madness. Shocked by his depravity, the father ultimately made use of the power which he had reserved to himself, and disinherited his son, leaving his vast property, amounting to £1,300,000, to the family of the Earl of Bute (the prime-minister of George III.), who in 1736 had married his only daughter.

Lady Mary had, for some time, suffered from ill health, and about 1738, her face became disfigured by an eruption, which shut her out from general society, and from which she continued to suffer during the rest of her life. Her husband was almost constantly absent, looking after the great coal-fields in Yorkshire and Durham, which had fallen to him by inheritance; the conduct of her son had become a source of scandal and extreme grief; her sister, Lady Mar, had become insane; and the coarse slanders of Pope and his party were a constant annoyance. Under these circumstances, and probably with the hope of recovering her health, she took the resolution of residing in the warm south. She left England in July 1739, and after visiting the principal cities of Italy, fixed her residence at Louvere, on the shore of Lake Iseo, north-west of Brescia. There she occupied a palace, and amused herself with her garden, her silk-worms, and her vineyard. About 1758, she settled at Venice, where she resided till the death of Mr Wortley Montagu in 1761. She was now upwards of seventy-one years of age, but in compliance with the solicitations of her daughter, Lady Bute, to whom she wrote on the subject of their common loss in terms of deep grief, she set out for England in the winter of 1761. She reached the shores of her native land in January 1762, and on the 21st of August following, died of a cancer in her breast.

Lady Mary kept a journal or diary, which was begun at the time of her marriage, and was continued almost to the day of her death. It was very voluminous, and passed, after her decease, into the hands of Lady Bute, who always kept it under lock and key, and shortly before her death committed it to the flames. In this diary, during her first absence from England, she had copied her own letters to her correspondents, and from it, after her return home, she compiled the celebrated *Turkish Letters*, which were circulated in manuscript among her friends during her lifetime, but were not published till 1763. On her last return home she had given a copy to Mr Sowden, a clergyman of Rotterdam, 'to do what he pleased with,' and he sold it for £500 to Lord Bute, who intended to suppress it. In the interval between the gift and the sale, the manuscript had been copied (without Mr Sowden's knowledge, as he affirmed), and was published in three volumes, under the editorship of Captain Cleland, a literary man of notoriety at that time, who in 1767, published a fourth volume, which is suspected to have been a forgery of his own.

The first publication of Lady Mary Wortley Montagu's works, was under the editorship of Mr Dallaway in 1803, in five volumes. He professed to have printed them from the original manuscripts in the possession of the Marquis of Bute, and the works were preceded by an indifferently written life. In 1837, appeared *The Letters and Works of Lady Mary Wortley Montagu, Edited by her Great-Grandson, Lord Wharncliffe*, 3 vols. 8vo. The chief value of this edition, which is little more than a reprint of Dallaway's, with a few notes of correction and explanation, is an introduction under the title of *Biographical Anecdotes*, by Lady Louisa Stuart, daughter of Lord and Lady Bute, and granddaughter of Lady Mary. Lady Louisa was born in 1757, and was consequently in her eightieth year when these lively and interesting 'Anecdotes' were published in 1837.

## CURIOUS PRAYER.

A gentleman in America has projected a work to be published under the title of *The Book of Uncommon Prayer*. Any one conversant with books of anecdote, will readily bethink him of much suitable material for such a volume. Perhaps no more appropriate example than the following, from an old copy of *Fog's Journal*, has ever appeared: 'O Lord, thou knowest that I have nine houses in the city of London, and likewise that I have lately purchased an estate in fee-simple in the county of Essex. Lord, I beseech Thee to preserve the two counties of Essex and Middlesex from fires and earthquakes; and as I have a mortgage in Hertfordshire, I beg Thee likewise to have an eye of compassion on that county. And, Lord, for the rest of the counties, Thou mayest deal with them as Thou art pleased. O Lord, enable the Bank to answer all their bills, and make all my debtors good men. Give a prosperous voyage and return to the *Mermaid* sloop, which I have insured; and Lord, Thou hast said, "That the days of the wicked are short," and I trust Thou wilt not forget Thy promises, having purchased an estate in reversion of Sir J. P., a profligate young man. Lord, keep our funds from sinking; and if it be Thy will, let there be no *sinking* fund. Keep my son Caleb out of evil company, and from gaming-houses. And sanctify, O Lord, this night to me, by preserving me from thieves and fire, and make my servant honest and careful, whilst I, Thy servant, lie down in Thee, O Lord. Amen.'

PUPPETS A HUNDRED AND FIFTY YEARS AGO.

The annexed singular hand-bill, which we find, with its curious vignette heading, in an odd volume of literary curiosities, was published probably towards the end of the seventeenth century. It presents an interesting illustration of the amusements of that period.

'At PUNCH'S Theatre.

For the Entertainment of the

Four Indian Kings, viz.

(A) The Emperor *Tee Yee Neen Ho Ga Row.*
(B) King *Sa Ga Yean Qua Rah Tow.*
(C) King *E Tow oh Koam.*
(D) King *Oh Nee Yeath Tow no Riow.*

This present *Munday, May* 1, at Seven a-Clock

T the Upper End of *St. Martin's Lane,* joyning to *Litchfield-Street,* will be Presented a NEW OPERA, Performed by a Company of *Artificial Actors,* who will *present you* with an *incomparable Entertainment,* call'd

The Last Year's CAMPAIGNE.

With the Famous Battle fought between the Confederate Army (Commanded by the Duke of *Marlborough*) and the *French* in the *Woods* near *Blaguiers.* With *several Comic Entertainments of*

Punch *in the* Camp. Also, *variety of* Scenes; with a *most Glorious Prospect of both Armies, the French in their Entrenchments and the Confederates out; where will be seen several Regiments of Horse and Foot Engaged in Forcing* the French *Lines. With the Admirable Entertainments of a Girl of Five Years old Dancing with Swords.*

Note.—*This* Play *will continue all the Week.*

Box 2*s.* Pit 1*s.* Gallery 6*d.*'

W. E.

## AUGUST 22.

St Symphorian, martyr, about 178. St Hippolytus, bishop and martyr, 3d century. St Timothy, martyr, 311. St Philibert, abbot of Jumièges, 684. St Andrew, deacon and confessor, about 880.

*Born.*—Philip Augustus II. of France, 1165; Aimé Bonpland, distinguished naturalist and friend of Humboldt, 1773, *La Rochelle;* Thomas Tredgold, engineer, 1788, *Brandon, near Durham;* John B. Gough, temperance orator, 1817, *Sandgate, Kent.*

*Died.*—Pope Nicholas III., 1280; Philippe de Valois, king of France, 1350, *Nogent-le-Roi, near Chartres;* Richard III. of England, killed at Bosworth Field, 1485; Guillaume Budé (Budæus), scholar and author, 1540; Thomas Percy, Earl of Northumberland, beheaded at York, 1572; Dominic Baudius, jurist and philologist, 1613, *Leyden;* Pierre le Moine, Jesuit and poet, 1672, *Paris;* Louis Francois de Boufflers, duke and marshal of France, distinguished commander, 1711, *Fontainbleau;* William Whiston, celebrated divine and translator of Josephus, 1752, *London;* George, Lord Lyttelton, author of *Dialogues of the Dead,* 1773, *Hagley, near Stourbridge;* John Henry Tischbein, eminent painter, 1789, *Cassel;* Warren Hastings, governor general of India, 1818, *Daylesford, Worcestershire;* Dr Franz Joseph Gall, founder of phrenology, 1828, *Paris;* Richard Oastler, 'The Factory King,' leader of the 'Ten-hours' Movement,' 1861, *Harrogate.*

### WILLIAM WHISTON.

We are afraid that, except as an affix to a translation of *Josephus*—a stock-book in every ordinary library—the name of William Whiston suggests very little to modern memories. Yet at the beginning of the eighteenth century he—a restless, indiscreet, and loquacious man of learning—was in everybody's mouth, and by his heresies contrived to keep the Church of England for years in a fidget.

He was the son of a clergyman, and was born at Norton, near Twycross, in Leicestershire, in 1667. At Cambridge, he greatly distinguished himself by his mathematical attainments, and won the friendship of Newton, whose *Principia* he studied and appreciated. In 1696, he published his first work, the forerunner of a multitude, entitled *A New Theory of the Earth from its Original to the Consummation of all Things, wherein the Creation of the World in Six Days, the Universal Deluge, and the General Conflagration as laid down in the Holy Scriptures are shewn to be perfectly agreeable to Reason and Philosophy*; it ran through six editions. The flood he accounted for by a comet, but the wits objected, that while he had covered the earth with water, he had provided no means for drawing it off. Newton, in 1701, made him his deputy in the duties of the Lucasian chair, and in 1703, resigned the chair itself, and procured the election of Whiston as his successor. Gradually he began to broach and promulgate Arian doctrine on the subject of the Trinity, and the result was, that in 1710, he was banished from the university, and the year after his professorship was declared vacant. These penalties only added fuel to his zeal; so that he provoked Convocation to censure his writings, and for five years to keep his case dangling before the public. Meanwhile Whiston sought his living by teaching mathematics in London, and Steele and Addison found him an audience at Button's coffee-house for a series of astronomical lectures. He tried to establish a sect, and held a meeting for worship in his house in Cross Street, Hatton Garden, but he could never get beyond a dozen or score of disciples. Apparently without any power of considerate reticence, he published his fancies as quickly as they were formed. He turned Baptist; he asserted the Jews would be restored to Palestine and the millennium begin in 1766, and that an earthquake in London would swallow up 7000 men, and the remainder would be converted. He had a method for finding the longitude, by means of signal-vessels moored at various points in the ocean, which he held was everywhere fathomable. In fact, his brain teemed with odd notions, theological, literary, and scientific.

There was no lack of friends who respected his honesty and learning, but his habit of blunt, free speech and immovable self-will, rendered it very difficult to assist him effectually. His Arianism was shared by many ecclesiastics, who regretted his retreat from the church as wholly unnecessary. Whiston, one day talking with Chief-Justice King, entered into a discussion about signing articles which were not believed, for the sake of preferment. King freely sanctioned the latitudinarian practice, saying: 'We must not lose our usefulness for scruples.' Whiston expressed his sorrow to hear his lordship say so, and proceeded to inquire, whether he permitted similar prevarication in the law-courts. The chief-justice said, 'No,' whereon Whiston rejoined: 'Suppose God Almighty should be as just in the next world as my lord chief-justice is in this, where are we then?' King was silent. When Queen Caroline heard the story, she said: 'No answer was to be made to it.'

With Caroline, wife of George II., Whiston was somewhat of a favourite. She allowed him £50 a year, and usually sent for him every summer when she was out of town, to spend a day or two with her. At Richmond, on one occasion, she asked him what people thought of her. He told her that she was esteemed as a lady of great abilities, a patron of learned men, and a kind friend of the poor. 'But,' said she, 'no one is without faults, what are mine?' Whiston begged to be excused, but she insisting, he informed her majesty that she did not behave with proper reverence in church. She pleaded in excuse that the king would talk to her. He asked her to remember, that during worship, she was in the presence of One greater than kings. Confessing her fault, she went on: 'Pray tell me what is my next?' With fine tact Whiston evaded the dangerous topic with the promise: 'When your majesty has amended the fault of which we have spoken, we shall then proceed to the next.'

Another good story is told of his frank speech. A party, in which Addison, Pope, Walpole, and Secretary Craggs were included, was debating whether a secretary of state could be an honest man, and Whiston was appealed to for his opinion, which may be imagined. Craggs said: 'It might do for a fortnight, but not longer.' With much simplicity Whiston inquired: 'Mr Secretary, did you ever try it for a fortnight?'

Whiston lived till he was eighty-five, dying in London in 1752. His long life was one of great literary activity, but his multitudinous publications, amongst which was an autobiography abounding in injudicious revelations, have long been neglected. Vain yet sincere, sceptical yet credulous, insensible alike to fear and favour, where he thought the interests of truth concerned; many laughed at Whiston's eccentricities, but those who knew him most intimately, were those who held him in highest honour for substantial virtue and uprightness.

## WARREN HASTINGS:

### THE GREY GEESE OF ADDLESTROP HILL.

The brilliant but mud-streaked history of Warren Hastings has been made familiar to the present generation by a masterly pen. It is not necessary here to repeat the tale of him who was the subject of a ruthless, though futile party prosecution of ten years by the House of Commons, and lived to enjoy the unexampled honour of having that House to *rise* to him on his entering it, an act of unpremeditated veneration. He enjoyed a long retirement from the cares of office at his seat of Daylesford, in Worcestershire, those paternal acres, to recover which for his family had been the great impulse and inspiration of his early life. There he died at the advanced age of eighty-five.

We find a simple circumstance in the private latter life of Mr Hastings, which has come into a curious connection with modern literature. It will be remembered that the first of the *Tales of My Landlord* opens with the description of a moor on the Scottish border, which was encumbered with a number of huge blocks, called the *Grey Geese of Mucklestane Moor*, and connected with which was a legend, to the effect that a noted witch was driving her geese to market, when, losing patience with their waywardness, she suddenly exclaimed: 'Deevil! that neither they nor I ever stir from this spot more!' and instantly she and her flock were transformed into blocks of stone, as they had ever since remained, until the Black Dwarf appropriated them for the building of his lonely cottage. In the annotated edition of his novels, Sir Walter fails to tell that he took up this idea from a communication to the *Gentleman's Magazine* of April 1808. In this paper it is stated that, on the top of an eminence in the parish of Addlestrop, in Gloucestershire, there was a number of blocks of stone, which had stood there from time immemorial, under the name of the *Grey Geese of Addlestrop Hill*, until they had lately been taken by Mr Warren Hastings, and formed into a rock-work for the decoration of his grounds at Daylesford. There was added a ballad which had been composed evidently for the amusement of the circle at Daylesford—as follows:

'Beneath the gray shroud of a wintry cloud
  The day-star dimly shone;
And the wind it blew chill upon Addlestrop Hill,
  And over the Four-shire Stone.

But the wind and the rain they threaten'd in vain;
  Dame Alice was up and away:
For she knew to be healthy, and wealthy, and wise,
Was early to bed, and early to rise,
  Though never so foul the day.

O foul was the day, and dreary the way;
  St Swithin the good woman shield!
For she quitted her bower in an evil hour
  To drive her geese a-field.

To rival this flock, howe'er they might mock,
  Was never a wight could aspire;
The geese of Dame Alice bred envy and malice
  Through many a bordering shire.

No wonder she eyed with delight and with pride
  Their plumes of glossy gray:
And she counted them o'er, and she counted a score,
  And thus to herself 'gan say:

"A score of gray geese at a groat a piece,*
  Makes six-and-eightpence clear;
Add a groat, 'tis enow to furnish a cow,
  And I warrant, we'll make good cheer.'

But ah! well-a-day, no mortal may say
  What fate and fortune ordain;
Or Alice, I ween, had her loss foreseen,
  Where most she look'd for gain.

And didst thou not mark the warnings dark?
  'Twas all on a Friday morn—
She tripp'd unawares as she hurried down stairs,
  And thrice was her kirtle torn.

And thrice by the way went the gander astray
  Ere she reach'd the foot of the hill;
And the raven's croak from a neighbouring oak
  Proclaim'd approaching ill.

* 'We are told that at an early period of our history, a goose was sold for 3*d.*, and a cow for 7*s.* The superiority of Dame Alice's geese in their original state, to judge of them by their present size, must plead her excuse for estimating them at a penny above the market-price.'

And now and O now had she climb'd the steep brow
  To fatten her flock on the common,
When full in her path, to work her scath.
  She met with a weird woman.

This hag she was foul both in body and soul,
  All wild and tatter'd in trim,
And pale was the sheen of her age-wither'd een—
  Was never a witch so grim.

And "Give me," quoth she, "of thy fair poultry—
  Or dear shalt thou rue this day."
So hoarse was the note of the beldam's throat,
  That the geese they hiss'd with dismay.

But the dame she was stout, and could fleer and could flout:
  "Gramercy! good gossip," she cried,
"Would ye taste of my fry, ye must barter and buy,
  Though weal or woe betide.

"'Twere pity in sooth, 'gin ye had but a tooth,
  Ye should lack for a giblet to chew:
Belike of the claw, and the rump, and the maw,
  A hell-broth ye mean to brew."

O sour look'd the hag; and thrice did she wag
  Her hoar head scatter'd with snow:
And her eye through the gloom of wrath and of rheum
  Like a comet predicted woe.

And anon she began to curse and to ban
  With loud and frantic din.
But the spell which she mutter'd must never be utter'd,
  For that were a deadly sin.

Then sudden she soars in the whirlwind, and roars
  To the deep-voic'd thunder amain;
And the lightning's glare envelops the air,
  And shivers the rocks in twain.

But Alice she lay 'mid the wrack and the fray
  Entranc'd in a deathlike swoon,
Till the sheep were in fold, and the curfew toll'd;
  She arose by the light of the moon.

And much did she muse at the cold evening's dews
  That reflected the pale moonbeam;
But more at the sight that appeared by its light—
  And she counted it all a dream.

O what is yon heap that peers o'er the steep,
  'Mid the furze and the hawthorn glen!
With trembling and fear the dame she drew near,
  And she knew her own geese again!

But, alas! the whole flock stood as stiff as a stock;
  And she number'd them one by one.
All grisly they lay, and they lie to this day
  A flock, as it were, of gray stone!

"Thy birds are not flown," cried a voice to her moan;
  "O never again shall they fly,
Till Evenlode flow to the steeple at Stow
  And Oddington mount as high.

"But here shall they stand, forlorn on dry land,
  And parch in the drought and the blast,
Nor e'er bathe a feather, save in fog and foul weather,
  Till many an age be past.

"More fetter'd and bound than geese in a pound,
Could aught their bondage atone;
They shall ne'er dread the feast of St Michael at least,
Like geese of flesh and bone.

"But pitying fate at length shall abate
The rigour of this decree,
By the aid of a sage in a far-distant age;
And he comes from the East country.

"A pundit his art to this seer shall impart;
Where'er he shall wave his wand,
The hills shall retire, and the valleys aspire,
And the waters usurp the land.

"Then, Alice, thy flock their charm shall unlock,
And pace with majestic stride,
From Addlestrop heath, to Daylesford beneath,
To lave in their native tide.

"And one shall go peep like an isle o'er the deep,
Another delighted wade,
At the call of this wizard, to moisten her gizzard
By the side of a fair cascade.

"This sage to a dame shall be wedded, whose name
Praise, honour, and love shall command;
By poets renown'd, and by courtesy crown'd
The queen of that fairy-land!"

Here ceased the high strain—but seek not in vain
To unravel the dark record:
Enough that ye wot, 'twas traced to the spot
By a clerk of Oxenford.'

## THE BATTLE OF BOSWORTH :
## WELSH TALES CONNECTED THEREWITH.

The 22d of August 1485 was an important day for England, not merely in putting an end to the reign and the life of a usurper and murderer, whose rule was a disgrace to it, but in finally freeing it from the civil contentions comprehended under the title of the Wars of the Roses. It must, after all, be admitted that the atrocious Crookback somewhat redeemed his life by the way he ended it. It was worthy of his brave race, and of the pretensions he had set up, that he should perish in the thick of a fight which was to conclude his dynasty.

On the other hand, the gallant adventure of Henry of Richmond in landing with only two thousand Frenchmen to fight his way to the English crown, his stout struggle at Bosworth, and the picturesque incident of Stanley picking up Richard's crown, and placing it on the brows of Henry on the battle-field, raise expectations with which the subsequent events are somewhat out of harmony.

It should be more borne in mind than it is, that the first of the Tudor sovereigns was a Welsh noble, and owed much to the friendship of his warm-blooded countrymen. He was particularly indebted to the men of Pembrokeshire, his native county. At the time of the battle of Tewkesbury, Henry was a boy at Pembroke Castle, but this place not being thought one of safety, he was removed by his uncle, Jasper, Earl of Pembroke, to Tenby. Here he was received with much hospitality by the mayor, John White, who secretly conveyed him to Britanny in one of his own vessels. Afterwards, when he returned, it was at Milford he landed, marching thence to meet 'the bloody and usurping boar' at Bosworth-field. Henry, upon coming to the throne, was not unmindful of the assistance he had received. He rewarded the mayor of Tenby with a lease, at a nominal rent, of all the crown-lands about that town; 'a good recompense,' says the historian of Pembrokeshire, 'to one man for a good deede done to the whole realme.' It is a rather curious circumstance, that Mr George White, the present mayor of Tenby (1863), is a descendant of him who aided Henry in his escape; is, like his ancestor, a wine-merchant; and resides on the spot occupied by his family more than four centuries ago.

The treacherous Stanley may have placed the crown upon Richmond's head on Bosworth field, but the hand that virtually crowned him was that which dealt the gallant Richard his death-wound. According to Welsh tradition, the deed was done by Rhys ap Thomas, commonly called 'the valiant Welshman.' This hero of the principality came of a warlike stock. His grandfather fell fighting for the white rose, at Mortimer's Cross; his father was murdered as he lay spent and wounded by the side of the corpse of David Gough, whom he had killed in single-combat. Rhys himself was brought up at the court of Philip of Burgundy, and did credit to his knightly training. The death of his two elder brothers, killed in some petty border skirmishes, left him the representative of his race, and lord of the greater part of Carmarthenshire. During the latter part of Edward IV.'s reign, and through the minority of his successor, the Welsh chieftain occupied himself in training his tenantry in the art of war, that he might be ready for the troublous times he foresaw must come.

When Richard III. became aware of the intention of the Earl of Richmond to dispute his right to the English throne, he wished to assure himself of the support of Rhys ap Thomas. To that end he sent commissioners to Carmarthen, to administer the oath of allegiance to Rhys, and demand the surrender of his son and heir, a boy of four years old, as hostage for his fidelity. Not caring to defy Richard's anger, the Welshman took the oath, though much against his will, but declined to give up his child. To mollify the king for this disobedience, he (or rather the abbot of Talye for him) wrote a letter to Richard, asserting his loyalty, and promising to obey his majesty's commands by preventing the landing of Richmond at Milford Haven. He says he 'deems it not unseasonable to annex this voluntary protestation: that, whoever, ill affected to the state, shall dare to land in those parts of Wales, where I have employments under your majesty, must resolve with himself *to make his entrance and irruption over my belly!*' As for the delivery of his heir, he pleads his infancy, 'more fit to be embosomed in a mother's care, than exposed to the world; nature as yet not having the leisure to initiate him in that first lecture of feeding himself;' concluding significantly by declaring that if the king persisted in depriving him of the sole prop of his house, the better part of himself, 'I were then divided in my strength, which, united, might perhaps, serve as most useful were I called to some weighty employments for the good of your service.'

Not long after the despatch of this politic letter, the abbot of Talye and the bishop of St David's employed all their influence with Rhys to persuade him to join the party of the Earl of Richmond. The latter promised him full absolution for breaking his oath, a matter which did not trouble the soldier's conscience so much as violating the promises he had given under his hand and seal. The wily ecclesiastic set him at ease on that point, by shewing that Richmond could not be looked upon as ill affected to the state, seeing he came to relieve it from an unrighteous ruler, while it would not be difficult to keep to the letter of the remaining clause of his voluntary protestation. While Rhys was debating with himself, a letter arrived from Richmond soliciting his assistance, and promising great rewards in the event of success. This decided the Welsh captain's course of action. He at once took the field with two thousand men, kinsmen and friends flocked to his standard, and setting out for Milford Haven, he welcomed Richmond ashore, and tendered his services to him, at the same time satisfying his own scruples by lying down on the ground and allowing the earl to pass over his body.

Of the part he played in the battle of Bosworth, his biographer gives the following account: 'While the avant-guards were in hot chase, the one of the other, King Richard held not his hands in his pockets; but, grinding and gnashing his teeth, up and down he goes in quest of Richmond, whom, no sooner espying, than he makes at him, and, by the way, in his fury, manfully overthrew Sir William Brandon, the earl's standard-bearer, as also Sir John Cheney, both men of mighty force and known valiancy. In Wales we say, that Rice ap Thomas, who from the beginning closely followed the earl, and ever had an eye to his person, seeing his party begin to quail, and the king's to gain ground, took the occasion to send unto Sir William Stanley, giving him to understand the danger they were in, and entreating him to join his forces for the disengaging of the earl, who was not only in despair of victory, but almost of his life. Whereupon (for it seems he understood not the danger before) Sir William Stanley made up to Rice ap Thomas, and joining both together, rushed in upon their adversaries and routed them, by which means the glory of the day fell on the earl's side; King Richard, as a just guerdon for all his facinorous acts and horrible murders, being slain on the field. One Welsh tradition says that Rice ap Thomas slew Richard, manfully fighting with him hand to hand, and we have one strong argument in defence of our tradition, to prove that he was the man who in all likelihood had done the deed; for from that time forward, the Earl of Richmond, as long as he lived, did ever honour him with the title of Father Rhys.'

Be this as it may, Rhys ap Thomas was knighted on the field, and was afterwards employed in the war with France and the rebellions at home. He was made a knight of the Garter and privy-councillor, and appointed constable and lieutenant of Brecknock, chamberlain of Carmarthen and Cardigan, seneschal and chancellor of Haverfordwest, Ross, and Builth, justiciar of South Wales, and governor of the principality. At the end of Henry VII.'s reign, the recipient of so many honours retired to Wales, where he practised the national virtue of hospitality in a style of great magnificence till his death, at the good old age of seventy-six. His tomb, although sadly ruinated, may still be seen in St Peter's Church, Carmarthen; while his memory is preserved in the poetic literature of his countrymen, whose bards have delighted to sing of Rhys-ap-Thomas as the sword and buckler of his country, the champion of Cambria, the shield of Britain, the scourge of the obstinate, the protector of the innocent, and the flower of Cambro-Britons.

## RICHARD WATTS'S BEQUEST.

The tendency of Englishmen to follow out the instincts of the individual character has been strikingly shewn in what may be called odd and whimsical bequests. It is no unusual thing amongst us, to see some singularity of opinion or fancy thus carried out, in the case of some obscure citizen, for hundreds of years after he has ceased to breathe.

Richard Watts, recorder of Rochester in the reign of Queen Elizabeth, was a man of large property, who had represented his city in parliament, and entertained his sovereign in his house. It is said that, on Elizabeth taking leave of him as a guest, he expressed regret that his house had not been larger and more commodious; when she replied '*Satis*' (enough); in consequence of which royal laconism, the house was afterwards called Satis House. Part of the old building, standing on Bully Hill, still retains the name.

By his will, dated August 22, 1579, this house, with its furniture, was left to be sold for the maintenance of some almshouses in the High Street, and especially to provide 'six good matrices or flock-beds and other sufficient furniture, to harbour or lodge poor travellers or wayfaring men, being no common rogues, *nor procters*, and they, the said wayfaring men, to harbour and lodge therein no longer than one night, unless sickness be the further cause thereof; and these poor folk there dwelling to keep the same sweet, and courteously intreat the said poor travellers; and every one of them, at their first coming in, to have fourpence; and to warm them at the fire of the resident within the said house, if need be.' It is said that the objection made in the above will to proctors, thus fixing a lasting stigma on the legal profession, arose from the fact that when Mr Watts was travelling on the continent, he was seized with a serious illness, and calling in a proctor to make his will, he found, on his recovery, that the traitorous man of law had conveyed all the estates to himself, instead of writing the wishes of his client. Another author has, however, suggested that the word proctor or procurator was applied to those itinerant priests, who in the reign of Queen Elizabeth travelled secretly about England, with dispensations from the pope to absolve her subjects from their allegiance.

A few years after the death of Mr Watts, his widow, who married a second time, disputed the will, and was allowed to retain Satis House, on condition of paying over land to the value of twenty pounds a year; an immense increase has since arisen in the value of the property, so that the annual income is above £1000: one large estate which was then a marsh in Chatham, is now drained and covered with houses. The almshouses are of brick, three stories high, with large square windows and projecting centre. They were fully repaired in 1771, by Nathaniel Hood, then mayor of Rochester, and an inscription, describing the nature of the bequest, engraved on a tablet in front; but now, alas! a poor traveller will knock in vain for admittance, the wishes of the hospitable founder having been altogether set aside though the four pennies may be obtained on application to the mayor. Among the file of orders retained by the provider, or man who distributes this money, is one dated 1677, as follows: 'Brother Wade: Pray relieve these two gentlemen, who have the king's letters recommendatory, and give them twelve pence a man, and foure a piece to the other five.'

The remainder of the income is appropriated to the payment of the poor's rates. Over the monument in the cathedral to the memory of Watts is a bust taken during his lifetime, and representing a man with a bald head, short hair, and a long flowing beard. It will be remembered by many of our readers that our distinguished countryman, Charles Dickens, has chosen this house at Rochester as the groundwork of one of his Christmas stories.

## THE HYDES—CURIOSITIES OF THEIR GENEALOGY.

Alexander Hyde, who died bishop of Salisbury, August 22, 1667, was son of Sir Lawrence Hyde, of the Close of Sarum. He had been, at the Restoration, made dean of Winchester, 'through the recommendation of his kinsman, Lord Chancellor Clarendon.' *

This is nearly all that can now be learned regarding Bishop Hyde, of whom we may fairly presume that he would never have risen to great prominence but for the power and influence of his eminent nephew, the chancellor.

The fact of two queens-regnant of England being granddaughters of the Chancellor Earl of Clarendon, has made the genealogy of the Hydes of some interest to poking antiquaries. It appears beyond question that the paternal ancestry was respectable, Lawrence Hyde, the grandfather of the chancellor, and father of the bishop of Salisbury, being a younger son of Robert Hyde of Norbury and Hyde, in Cheshire, a family which had been settled there from the time of Henry III. There is, however, a sort of legendary account of a humble *ancestress*, which has several times been adverted to in print. In a manuscript note of apparently a century old, now in our possession, it is stated that the common ancestor of the chancellor and bishop 'married a tub-woman, and retired to Dinton, in the county of Wilts [the birthplace of the chancellor].' If this were true, it would be a curious consideration that the grandfather's grandmother of the queens Mary and Anne was of such plebeian origin. Some years ago, there was a discussion of this subject in the *Notes and Queries* The fact alleged was, that Lord Clarendon, when a young lawyer, had married a wealthy brewer's widow, who had originally come into her future husband's employment as a tub-woman, 'to carry out beer from the brewhouse.' And it was conclusively shewn that this could not be true, as both of the chancellor's wives were women of family. There was, however, nothing brought forward on that occasion at issue with the old genealogical note in our possession, which makes the alleged tub-woman the mother of the bishop, and consequently grandmother of the chancellor. Nor in that version of the tale is there anything difficult to be believed. A younger son of Sir Robert Hyde of Norbury might very fairly have married a rich brewer's widow, and that widow might very fairly have risen from the humble condition ascribed to her by the tradition. Generally, where a story of this kind has taken root, there is some foundation for it.

Another genealogical particular connected with the two queens is equally remarkable, and can be better authenticated—namely, that a cousin of their mother, the Duchess of York, died in Emanuel Hospital, Tothill Fields, Westminster, so recently as December 1771. She was named Mrs Windymore, or Windlemore, and stated to be 108 years of age at the time of her death. The *Gentleman's Magazine* and *Annual Register* both notice her demise, and her connection with royalty, and our old genealogical note enters her as next in descent from the son of the bishop of Salisbury.

* Hoare's *Wiltshire*, § *Salisbury*, p. 628.

## THE FATE OF RUTH OSBORNE.

It is a curious proof of the ignorance in which the English populace was allowed to rest down to very recent times that, so lately as the 22d of August 1751, a man was executed at Tring for being concerned in the murder of a poor woman suspected of witchcraft. It was in the year 1745 that this poor woman, Ruth Osborne by name, having vainly besought one Butterfield for a little milk, went away muttering, that she wished the Pretender would soon come and carry off his cattle. He soon after fell into ill health and adversity, and it became impressed on his mind that the ill-will of Mrs Osborne was the cause of all his misfortunes. To counteract her evil influence, a renowned wise-woman or white-witch was fetched all the way from Northamptonshire. This sagacious female, on her arrival at Tring, confirmed the general opinion, and at once took measures to remove the spell; and as a preliminary step, she appointed six able men, armed with pitchforks, to guard Butterfield's house night and day; taking care, as a necessary precaution, to hang certain charms round the watchers' necks, to prevent them from being bewitched also. The wise-woman's mode of treatment proving expensive, and not producing the desired effect of improving Butterfield's health and circumstances, it was determined to try another plan; one that, by a severe punishment, would deter the assumed witch from her evil courses, as well as, at the same time, produce a profit to Butterfield and the neighbouring publicans, by collecting a mob of thirsty beer-drinkers. Accordingly, the public-criers of the adjoining towns of Hemel-Hempstead, Leighton-Buzzard, and Winslow, were employed to make the following announcement on their respective market-days: '*This is to give notice, that on Monday next a man and woman are to be publicly ducked at Tring, in this county, for their wicked crimes.*'

The parish overseer of Tring, learning that John Osborne and his wife Ruth, both upwards of seventy years of age, were the persons alluded to in the above notice, determined to protect them as far as he could, and for their better safety, lodged them in the workhouse. The master of the workhouse, to make the poor creatures more secure, secretly removed them, late on Sunday night, to the vestry of the parish church, vainly hoping that the sacred character of the edifice might have some effect in restraining their lawless persecutors. On the Monday, however, a mob, consisting of more than five thousand persons—not all of the lowest class, for about one half were well mounted on horseback—assembled, and, proceeding to the workhouse, demanded that the Osbornes should be delivered up to them. The master assured the crowd that the persons sought for were not in the house, but the rabble disbelieving him, broke open the doors, and searched all parts of the building, looking into drawers, trunks, and even the salt-box, supposing, in their dense ignorance, that the alleged witch and wizard could conceal themselves in the same space as would contain two cats. Disappointed of their victims, the mob, becoming infuriated, proceeded to demolish the workhouse; and having collected a quantity of straw, they lighted firebrands, threatening to murder the master, and burn down the whole town of Tring, if their demand were not instantly complied with. Thus threatened, the master told where the Osbornes were concealed, and then the mob, with yells of fiendish delight, broke open the church-doors, seized their helpless victims, and carried them off to a neighbouring pond. Decency and humanity imperatively forbid any description of the horrible scene of brutal cruelty that ensued. Suffice it to say, that the woman was murdered in the pond, and the man, still breathing, was tied to the dead body of his wife, and expired soon afterwards.

Neither the clergyman of Tring, nor those of the adjoining parishes, interfered to save these wretched victims of superstition. But the legal authorities determined to punish some, at least, of the perpetrators of the brutal crime. A coroner's inquest was held on the body of Ruth Osborne, twelve of the principal gentlemen of Hertfordshire being summoned as the jury. For at an inquest held a short time previously on a similar case of murder at Frome, in Somersetshire, the jurors, selected, as is usual, from the lower middle class, would not convict the prisoner. The Hertfordshire gentlemen, however, brought in a verdict of wilful murder against one Thomas Colley and twenty-one other known and unknown persons. At the ensuing county assizes, Colley being tried and found guilty, was sentenced to be executed, and hung in chains at the place where the murder was committed. To prevent a rescue, and impress on the ignorant minds of the country-people the power of the law, and an idea of the crime that had been perpetrated, the arrangements for the execution were conducted with military display and unusual solemnity. In the *Universal Magazine* of that year, we read as follows:

'Thursday, August 22d.—About ten in the morning, Mr Thomas Colley, condemned for the murder of Ruth Osborne, as a supposed witch, received the sacrament at Hertford, administered to him by the Rev. Mr Edward Bouchier, when he signed a solemn declaration of his faith relating to witchcraft; which he desired might be carried to the place of execution, and was there publicly read at his earnest request, just before he was turned off, by the Rev. Mr Randall, minister of Tring, who attended him in his last moments. He was escorted by one hundred and eight men belonging to the regiment of Horse Guards Blue, with their officers and two trumpets; and the procession was slow, solemn, and moving. Friday night he was lodged in St Alban's jail, and at five the next morning, he was put in a one-horse chaise with the executioner, and came to the place of execution about eleven; and after half an hour spent in prayer, he was executed, and immediately after hung up in chains on the same gibbet he was hanged on. The infatuation of the greater part of the people in that country was so great, that they would not be seen near the place of execution, insisting that it was a hard case to hang a man for destroying an old wicked woman, that had done so much damage by her witchcraft. A very odd accident happened in Tring town; which was, that just as the prisoner's wife and daughter were permitted to speak to him, one of the trooper's pistols in his holsters went off, occasioned by his handkerchief accidentally getting into the holster, which he pulling out, drew the trigger, and the ball went into the ground; but no other damage ensued than putting the corps in some disorder, it being at first imagined to have been fired out of a window.'

## THE FIRST ROYAL TELEGRAM ACROSS THE ATLANTIC.

In the month of August 1858, the first royal telegraphic message crossed the Atlantic from Europe to America. In 1854, the colonial government of Newfoundland offered certain terms, in the form of guarantee, to a company undertaking to lay a submerged telegraph beneath the Atlantic from that colony to Ireland. This offer was followed, during that and the next two years, by elaborate experiments on the best form and size of cable, and by soundings to determine the depth of the Atlantic at various places. The greatest depth plumbed reached the vast amount of 25,000 feet (about five miles). A company was then definitely formed, and a cable manufactured. The cable weighed about one ton per mile, and was 2500 miles long—1700 miles for the direct distance from Valentia in Ireland to Cape Race in Newfoundland, and 800 miles for bendings, deviations, and unforeseen contingencies; there were 350,000 miles of wire altogether in the cable, taxing the wire-drawers of the United Kingdom to the utmost to produce it in time. The British government lent the war-ship *Agamemnon* to take out half the cable, while the American government lent the *Niagara* to take out the other half. All being ready, operations commenced on the 5th of August 1857. The two magnificent ships, attended by the *Susquehanna*, *Leopold*, *Willing Mind*, and *Advice* set forth from Valentia. The portion of the cable on board the *Agamemnon* was uncoiled; and by means of central blocks, grooved-sheaves, friction-rollers, cramps, breaks, grips, and other mechanical appliances, it was lowered into the ocean as fast as the ship progressed. But disaster was impending. By the morning of the 11th, the engineer found that the cable had too much 'slack'—that is, too much of it had run out in proportion to the straight line traversed; it lay at the bottom of the ocean in too serpentine or zigzag a way. He therefore caused the grip-machinery to be tightened; this was unskilfully done, and the cable snapped. Thus, at a distance, in a straight line, of 350 miles from Ireland, the broken end of the cable sank to the bottom in 12,000 feet depth of water—more than forty times the height of St Paul's Cathedral!

One whole year was lost, in addition to a large sum of money. During the winter and spring months, many attempts were made to raise the broken end of the cable, splice it to the unused portion, and pursue the voyage to America; but the cable broke again and again, chiefly owing to the uneasy movement of the ship in stormy weather. At length the *Agamemnon* and the *Niagara* made another attempt under better auspices. They steamed out to mid-ocean, spliced together their two portions of the cable, and then parted company—the one returning to Valentia, the other proceeding onward to Cape Race. It was on the 29th of July 1858 that this parting of the two ships commenced; and as the distance between them increased, the officials on board the two ships interchanged telegraphic messages with each other, through the submerged portion of cable. Notwithstanding the perils and obstacles afforded by a tremendous sea, both vessels reached their destinations on the 5th of August—the *Agamemnon* having payed-out 1020 nautical miles of cable, and the *Niagara* 1030—equal altogether to about 2400 English statute miles. Each ship sent a telegraphic message to the other through this wonderful length of submerged cable; but the actual connection from shore to shore could not be made, because the land ends of the cable were not yet adjusted. At length the necessary attachments were made; and the submarine cable was placed in unbroken connection with the whole telegraphic system of England at one end, and with that of America at the other. The directors of the company in London exchanged compliments with their agents and coadjutors in New York; the lord mayor of London did the same with the mayor of New York. On the 20th, the cable communicated the first *commercial* news from the New World to the Old, in the form of a telegram announcing a collision between the *Arabia* and *Europa* mail-steamers near Cape Race. On the 22d, Queen Victoria and President Buchanan exchanged compliments. The Queen sent the following message: 'The Queen desires to congratulate the President upon the successful completion of this great international work, in which the Queen has taken the greatest interest. The Queen is convinced that the President will join with her in fervently hoping that the electric cable, which now connects Great Britain with the United States, will prove an additional link between the two nations, whose friendship is founded upon their common interests and reciprocal esteem. The Queen has much pleasure in thus directly communicating with the President, and in renewing to him her best wishes for the prosperity of the United States.' This message occupied about two hours in transmission from London to Washington. The President replied to it in a suitable strain.

The bright hopes thus raised were destined to be cruelly damped, as the cable ceased to act on the 3d of September. The experience gained by this failure was no doubt a help towards the success of 1866, and since that time telegraphic communication with America has been uninterrupted.

# AUGUST 23.

**Saints Claudius, Asterius, Neon, Domnina, and Theonilla, martyrs, 285. St Theonas, archbishop of Alexandria, 300. St Justinian, hermit and martyr, about 529. St Apollinaris Sidonius, confessor, bishop of Clermont, 482. St Eugenius, bishop in Ireland, 618. St Philip Beniti, confessor, 1285.**

*Born.*—**Louis XVI., king of France, 1754,** *Versailles*; **Sir Astley Cooper, eminent surgeon, 1768,** *Brooke, Norfolk*; William Frederick I., king of the Netherlands, 1772; Friedrich Tiedemann, physiologist, 1781, *Cassel*; **Frank Stone, artist, 1800,** *Manchester*.

*Died.*—**Flavius Stilicho, great Roman general,** beheaded at *Ravenna*, 408; Sir William Wallace, Scottish hero, 1305, executed at *Smithfield, London*; William Warham, archbishop of Canterbury, 1532; George Villiers, Duke of Buckingham, assassinated at *Portsmouth*, 1628; Jacques Vergier, poet and tale-writer, assassinated at *Paris*, 1720.

## WILLIAM WALLACE.

Edward I. of England having by craft and violence taken military possession of Scotland; the chief nobles of the land having submitted to him; it was left to a young gentleman of Renfrewshire, the celebrated William Wallace, to stand forth in defence of the expiring liberties of his country. He was, in some respects, well fitted to be a guerilla chief, being of lofty stature and hardy frame, patient of fatigue and hardship, frank in his manners, and liberal to his associates, while at the same time of sound judgment and a lover of truth and justice. The natural ascendancy of such qualities quickly put him at the head of large, though irregular forces, and he won an important victory at Stirling over some of Edward's principal officers (Sept. 11, 1297). A month later, he and Andrew of Moray are found, under the title of *Duces exercitus regni Scotiæ*, administering in national affairs—sending two eminent merchants to negotiate with the two Hanse towns of Lubeck and Hamburg. Next year, in a public document, Wallace appears by himself under the title of *Custos regni Scotiæ*. During this interval of authority, acting upon a cruel though perhaps unavoidable policy, he executed a complete devastation of the three northern counties of England, leaving them a mere wilderness. Edward led an army against him in person, and gaining a victory over him at Falkirk (July 22, 1298), dispersed his forces, and put an end to his power.

While most of the considerable men submitted to the English monarch, Wallace proceeded to France, to make interest with its king, Philip the Fair, in behalf of Scotland. Philip gave him some encouragement, and furnished him (this fact has only of late become known) with a letter of recommendation to the pope. Afterwards, being glad to make peace with Edward for the sake of the recovery of his authority over Flanders, Philip entered into an agreement to deliver up the ex-governor of Scotland to his enemy. The fact, however, was not accomplished, and Wallace was able to return to his own country. Being there betrayed by Sir John Monteith into the hands of the English, he was led to London; subjected to a mock-trial at Westminster, as if he had been a traitor to his sovereign Edward I.; and, on the

23d of August 1305, put to a cruel death on Smithfield.

The Scottish people have ever since cherished the memory of Wallace as the assertor of the liberties of their country—their great and ill-requited chief. What Tell is to the Swiss, and Washington to the Americans, Wallace is to them. It is true that he had little or no mercy for the English who fell into his hands, and that he ravaged the north of England. If, however, the English put themselves into the position of robbers and oppressors in a country which did not belong to them, they were scarcely entitled to much mercy; and, certainly, at a time so rude as the close of the thirteenth century, they were not very likely to receive it.

## GEORGE VILLIERS, FIRST DUKE OF BUCKINGHAM.

'Princes and lords are but the breath of kings.' Seldom has this sentiment been more strikingly exemplified than in the case of this nobleman. His rapid and unmerited advancement, effected solely by a sovereign's capricious will, stands almost, if not entirely, unparalleled in history. His father was Sir George Villiers of Brokesby, in Leicestershire, who possessed but a moderate property, was twice married, and had nine children. The duke—his father's fourth son—was by his second wife, Mary, daughter of Anthony Beaumont of Glenfield, Leicestershire, and was born on the 20th of August 1592. He was educated at home in fencing, riding, dancing, and other gentlemanly accomplishments of the period, and, at the age of eighteen, went to France for his further improvement. After travelling there for about three years, he returned to England in 1613, and obtained an appointment at court as cup-bearer to King James I., 'who of all wise men living,' says Clarendon, 'was the most delighted and taken with handsome persons in fine clothes.' Young Villiers was remarkable for the beauty of his person, the gracefulness of his air, the elegance of his dress, the suavity and sprightliness of his conversation. The king was delighted with him, and, in token of his admiration, gave him the familiar name of Steenie, in allusion to a beautiful portrait in Whitehall representing St Stephen, the proto-martyr. Honours now fell rapidly upon him. Here is a glance at his progress:

1615.—Knighted, and made one of the Gentlemen of the Bedchamber.

1616.—Master of the Horse; Knight of the Garter; Baron of Whaddon; Viscount Villiers.

1617.—Earl of Buckingham; Marquis of Buckingham; Lord High Admiral; Chief-justice in Eyre, south of Trent; Master of the King's Bench; High Steward of Westminster; Constable of Windsor Castle.

1623.—Earl of Coventry; Duke of Buckingham; Warden of the Cinque Ports; Steward of the Manor of Hampton Court.

Thus, in the course of ten years, King James raised his favourite from a poor cup-bearer to the highest title a sovereign has to bestow. Nor did he lavish on him merely titles and lucrative appointments; he enriched him with magnificent grants from the royal domains; thus placing him not only among the highest, but among the wealthiest, noblemen in the land. The royal lordship of Whaddon alone, from which the duke derived his first title, contained four thousand acres and a chase sufficient for a thousand deer. To gratify his favourite still more, the king extended his patronage to his whole family. His mother was, in 1618, created Countess of Buckingham; his elder brother, John, was made Baron Villiers and Viscount Purbeck; his younger brother, Christopher, was, in 1623, created Earl of Anglesey and Baron of Daventry; his half-brother, William, was, in 1619, created a baronet; and his other half-brother, Edward, was knighted in 1616, and in 1622 was appointed president of Munster, in Ireland—a lucrative post of great honour, which had previously always been held by a nobleman. The duke's influence at court was not diminished by the death of King James, for he had become no less a favourite with the succeeding monarch, Charles I.; so much so, indeed, that Clarendon, who, on the whole, speaks favourably of Villiers, asserts that 'all preferments in church and state were given by him; all his kindred and friends promoted to the degree in honour, or riches, or offices that he thought fit; and all his enemies and enviers discountenanced as he appointed.'

'To him the church, the realm, their powers consign;
Through him the rays of regal bounty shine;
Turned by his nod the stream of honour flows;
His smile alone security bestows:
Still to new heights his restless wishes tower,
Claim leads to claim, and power advances power,
Till conquest, unresisted, ceased to please,
And rights submitted left him none to seize.'

—DR JOHNSON *on Wolsey.*

Raised to this pinnacle of power, the duke displayed a presumption perfectly intolerable. One or two instances will amply illustrate this. When sent to France, by Charles I., to bring over Henrietta, his betrothed wife, the queen of France, being indisposed, was confined to her bed, and the duke was permitted to have an interview with her in her chamber. But, instead of approaching her as an ambassador, he had 'the insolence to converse with her as a lover!' The Marchioness of Sencey, the queen's lady of honour, who was present, gave the duke a severe reproof, saying: 'Sir, you must learn to be silent; it is not thus we address the queen of France!' Afterwards, when the duke would have gone on another embassy to the French court, it was signified to him, that for reasons *well known to himself*, his presence would not be agreeable to the king of France. The duke exclaimed: 'He would go and see the queen in spite of the French court!' 'And to this pretty affair,' remarks our authority, 'is to be ascribed the war between the two nations!' His insolence to Henrietta herself, when queen of England, was even more audacious. 'One day,' says Clarendon, 'when he unjustly apprehended that the queen had shewn some disrespect to his mother, in not going to her lodging at an hour she had intended to go, and was hindered by mere accident, he came into her chamber in much passion, and after some expostulations rude enough, he told her, she should repent it. Her majesty answering with some quickness, he thereupon replied insolently to her—that there had been queens in England who had lost their heads!'

The duke had a strong passion for magnificence. In 1617, only three or four years after his first entrance at court, he gave a most sumptuous entertainment on his being created a marquis. The banquet, which was held in Whitehall, was served up in the French fashion, under the auspices of Sir Thomas Edmondes, who had recently returned from France. 'You may judge,' writes an eyewitness of the feast, 'by this scantling, that there were said to be seventeen dozens of pheasants, and twelve partridges in a dish; throughout which, methinks, were more spoil than largesse. In spite of many presents,' the feast cost six hundred pounds.* Buckingham was equally excessive in the splendour of his equipage. Coaches, which were first introduced into England in 1580, were at first only used with a pair of horses, but Buckingham, about 1619, had his coach drawn by six horses, which was, says Wilson, 'wondered at as a novelty, and imputed to him as a mastering pride.' He was also remarkable for his extravagance in dress. 'He had twenty-seven suits of clothes made, the richest that embroidery, lace, silk, velvet, silver, gold, and gems could contribute; one of which was a white uncut velvet, set all over, both suit and cloak, with diamonds valued at fourscore thousand pounds, besides a great feather stuck all over with diamonds, as were also his sword, girdle, hat, and spurs.' He could also afford to have his diamonds so loosely tacked on, that when he chose to shake a few off on the ground, he obtained all the fame he desired from the pickers-up; for he never condescended to take back those which he had dropped. In the masques and banquets with which he entertained the court, he is said to have usually expended for the evening from one to five thousand pounds.†

The consequences of the duke's rise were most disastrous to the kingdom. He had little or no genuine patriotism, and either did not understand, or would not heed, the rights and requirements of his fellow-subjects. Indebted for his own position to mere favouritism, he, who was now sovereign all but in name, dispensed posts of importance and responsibility on the same baneful principles. Discontent became general. The ancient peers were indignant at having a man thrust over their heads with little to recommend him but his personal appearance and demeanour. The House of Commons were still more indignant at having measures, which they knew to be ruinous to the country, forced on them by a minister who, to gain his own ends, would not hesitate to hazard the honour and prosperity of the whole nation. This was especially manifested in two of his proceedings. From a private pique of his own, he involved his country first in a war with Spain, and afterwards with France, both of which wars brought discredit and perplexity on England. The House of Commons prepared a bill of impeachment against him, containing no less than sixteen charges; and the king only warded off the blow by suddenly dissolving parliament. This, as Clarendon admits, was not only irregular but impolitic. The country became exasperated, and Buckingham's life was known to be in danger. 'Some of his friends,' says Sir Symonds d'Ewes, 'had advised him how generally he was hated in England, and how needful it would be for his greater safety to wear some coat-of-mail, or some secret defensive armour, but the duke, sighing, said: "It needs not—there are no Roman spirits left!"' Warnings and threatenings were alike unheeded, and the duke proceeded to head a new expedition, which he had planned to relieve the Protestants of Rochelle. Having engaged a house at Portsmouth, to superintend the embarkation of his forces, he passed the night there with the duchess, and others of his family, and on Saturday, August 23, 1628, "he did rise up," says Howell, "in a well-disposed humour out of his bed, and cut a caper or two, and being ready, and having been under the barber's hands, he went to breakfast, attended by a great company,' among whom were some Frenchmen, whose eager tones and gesticulations were mistaken by some of the bystanders for anger. The duke, being in private conversation with Sir Thomas Fryar, was stooping down to take leave of him, when he was suddenly struck over his shoulder with a knife, which penetrated his heart. He exclaimed: 'The villain has killed me!' and at the same moment pulling out the knife, which had been left in his breast, he fell down dead.

Many of the attendants at first thought he had fallen from apoplexy, but, on seeing the effusion of blood from his breast and mouth, they perceived that he had been assassinated, and at once attributed the act to one of the Frenchmen who had just before been so eagerly conversing with him. Some hasty spirits, drawing their swords, rushed towards the Frenchmen, to take summary vengeance on them all, and were restrained with so much difficulty, that, according to Clarendon, 'it was a kind of a miracle that the Frenchmen were not all killed in that instant.' The Duchess of Buckingham and the Countess of Anglesey, having entered a gallery looking into the hall, beheld the lifeless body of the duke. 'Ah, poor ladies!' writes Lord Carlton, who was present at the murder, 'such were their screechings, tears, and distractions, that I never in my life heard the like before, and hope never to hear the like again.' Amid this distracting scene, a man's hat was found near the door where the murder was committed, and in the crown of it was sewn a written paper containing these words: 'That man is cowardly base, and deserveth not the name of a gentleman or souldier, that is not willinge to sacrifice his life for the honor of his God, his Kinge, and his Countrie. Lett no man Commend me for doeinge of it, but rather discommend themselves as the cause of it, for if God had not taken away o[r] hartes for o[r] sinnes, he would not have gone so longe vnpunished. Jo: felton.'

Felton, the owner of the hat, was found, says Lord Carlton, 'standing in the kitchen of the same house, and after inquiry made by a multitude of captains and gentlemen, then pressing into the house and court, and crying out amain, "Where is the villain? Where is the butcher?" he most audaciously and resolutely drawing forth his sword, came out, and went amongst them, saying boldly: "I am the man; here I am!" Upon which divers drew upon him, with an intent to have then despatched him; but Sir Thomas Morton, myself, and some others used such means (though with much trouble and difficulty) that we drew him out of their hands,' and he was conveyed by a guard

* Mrs Thomson's *Life of the Duke of Buckingham.*

† See Disraeli's *Curiosities of Literature*, vol. vi. 237.

of musketeers to the governor's house. John Felton, who was a younger son of a Suffolk gentleman, 'was by nature,' says Sir Henry Wotton, 'of a deep melancholy, silent, and gloomy constitution, but bred in the active way of a soldier, and thereby raised to the place of lieutenant to a foot company, in the regiment of Sir James Ramsay.' On being questioned as to his motives for committing the murder, he replied, that he was dissatisfied, partly because his pay was in arrear, and partly because the duke had promoted a junior officer over him, but that his chief motive was to 'do his country a great good service;' and that he 'verily thought, in his soul and conscience, the remonstrance of the parliament was a sufficient warrant for what he did upon the duke's person.' He underwent several examinations, always asserting that he had no accomplices; and when the Earl of Dorset threatened, in the king's name, to examine him on the rack; he said: 'I do again affirm, upon my salvation, that my purpose was known to no man living; and more than I have said before, I cannot. But if it be his majesty's pleasure, I am ready to suffer whatever his majesty will have inflicted upon me. Yet this I must tell you by the way, that if I be put upon the rack, I will accuse you, my Lord Dorset, and none but yourself.' This bold resolve astounded the examiners. They hesitated, and consulted the judges, who unanimously replied, that 'torture was not justifiable according to the law of England.' So that by this firmness Felton did, indeed, 'great good service to his country.' He forced from the judges an avowal of a law which condemned all their former practice. He was imbued with fanaticism, had a revengeful spirit, and gloried in manifesting it. Having once been offended by a gentleman, he cut off a piece of his own finger, and enclosing it with a challenge, sent it to him, to shew how little he heeded pain provided he could have vengeance. He continued in prison till November, passing the time in deep penitence and devotion, and was executed at Tyburn towards the end of the month, and was afterwards hung in chains at Portsmouth.

The Duke of Buckingham, who had married Catherine, daughter and sole heir of Francis, Earl of Rutland, was thirty-six years old at his death. His body was buried, by command of the king, in Westminster Abbey, and a sumptuous monument was erected within the communion rails of the church at Portsmouth; but it has recently been removed into the north aisle of the chancel. The house in which Buckingham was assassinated still exists, with but slight modern alterations, being marked No. 10 in the High Street of Portsmouth. The kitchen to which Felton retired is a distinct building at the further end, according to our view.

HOUSE AT PORTSMOUTH IN WHICH THE DUKE OF BUCKINGHAM WAS ASSASSINATED.

The duke's murder is said to have been preceded by many supernatural warnings, the most curious of which was the reputed appearance of his father's ghost. The story, which is gravely and circumstantially related by Clarendon, is long and tedious, but the substance of it is as follows:

About six months before the duke's murder, as one Mr Towse, an officer of the king's wardrobe, was lying awake in his bed at Windsor, about midnight there appeared at his bedside, 'a man of a very venerable aspect, who drew the curtains of his bed, and fixing his eyes upon him, asked him, if he knew him. The poor man, half-dead with fear,' on being asked the second time, said, he thought he was Sir George Villiers, the father of the Duke of Buckingham.

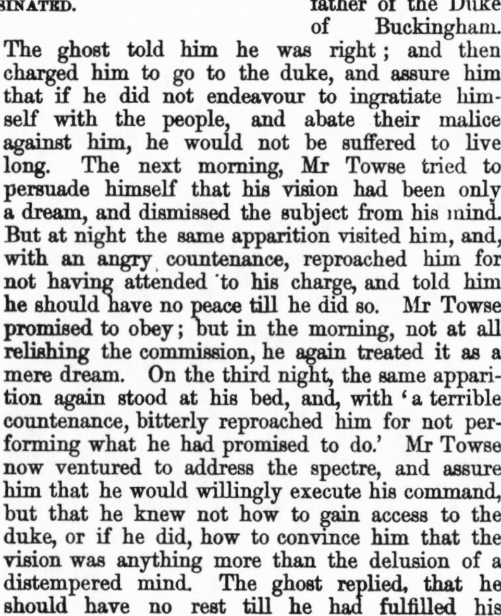

The ghost told him he was right; and then charged him to go to the duke, and assure him that if he did not endeavour to ingratiate himself with the people, and abate their malice against him, he would not be suffered to live long. The next morning, Mr Towse tried to persuade himself that his vision had been only a dream, and dismissed the subject from his mind. But at night the same apparition visited him, and, with an angry countenance, reproached him for not having attended to his charge, and told him he should have no peace till he did so. Mr Towse promised to obey; but in the morning, not at all relishing the commission, he again treated it as a mere dream. On the third night, the same apparition again stood at his bed, and, with 'a terrible countenance, bitterly reproached him for not performing what he had promised to do.' Mr Towse now ventured to address the spectre, and assure him that he would willingly execute his command, but that he knew not how to gain access to the duke, or if he did, how to convince him that the vision was anything more than the delusion of a distempered mind. The ghost replied, that he should have no rest till he had fulfilled his commission; that access to the duke was easy; and that he would tell him two or three particulars, in strict secrecy, to repeat to him, which would at once insure confidence in all he should say, 'and so repeating his threats, he left him. Mr Towse obtained an interview with the duke, who, on being told "the secret particulars," changed colour, and swore no one could have come to that knowledge except by the devil; for that those particulars were known only to himself, and to one person more, who he was sure would never speak of it.' After this interview, the duke appeared unusually thoughtful, and in the course of the day he had a long conference with his mother. But he made no change in his conduct; nor is it known whether or not he gave any credit to the story of the apparition, though it is supposed that his repetition of it to his mother, made a strong impression on her, for when the news of his murder was brought her, 'she seemed not in the least degree surprised, but received it as if she had foreseen it.'

## THE PIG-FACED LADY.

There can be few that have not heard of the celebrated pig-faced lady, whose mythical story is common to several European languages, and is most generally related in the following manner: A newly-married lady of rank and fashion, being annoyed by the importunities of a wretched beggar-woman, accompanied by a dirty, squalling child, exclaimed: 'Take away your nasty pig, I shall not give you anything!' Whereupon, the enraged beggar, with a bitter imprecation, retorted: 'May your own child, when it is born, be more like a pig than mine!' And so, shortly afterwards, the lady gave birth to a girl, perfectly, indeed beautifully, formed in every respect, save that its face, some say the whole head, exactly resembled that of a pig. This strange child thrived apace, and grew to be a woman, giving the unhappy parents great trouble and affliction—not by its disgusting features alone, but by its hoggish manners in general, much easier to be imagined than minutely described. The fond and wealthy parents, however, paid every attention to this hideous creature, their only child. Its voracious and indelicate appetite was appeased by food, placed in a silver trough. To the waiting-maid, who attended on the creature, risking the savage snaps of its beastly jaws, and enduring the horrid grunts and squeaks of its discordant voice, a small fortune had to be paid as annual wages, yet seldom could a person be obtained to fill the disagreeable situation longer than a month. A still greater perplexity ever troubled the wealthy parents, namely, what would become of the unfortunate creature after their decease? Counsel learned in the law were consulted, and it was determined that she should be married, the father, besides giving a magnificent dowry in hand, settling a handsome annuity on the happy husband for as long as she should live. But experience proving, that after the first introduction, the boldest fortune-hunters declined any further acquaintance, another course was suggested. This was to found a hospital, the trustees of which were bound to protect and cherish the pig-faced damsel, until her death relieved them from the unpleasing guardianship. And thus it is that, after long and careful research on the printed and legendary histories of pig-faced ladies, the writer has always found them wanting either a husband or a waiting-maid, or connected with the foundation of a hospital. But as there are exceptions to all general rules, so there is an exceptional story of a pig-faced lady; according to which, it appears that a gentleman, whose religious ideas were greatly confused by the many jarring sects during the Commonwealth, ended his perplexity by adopting the Jewish faith. And the first child born to him, after his change of religion, was a pig-faced girl! Years passed, the child grew to womanhood before the wretched father perceived that her hideous countenance was a divine punishment, inflicted on him for his grievous apostasy. Then a holy priest reconverted the father, and on the daughter being baptized, a glorious miracle occurred; a copious ablution of holy-water changing the beastly features to the human face divine. This remarkable story is said to be recorded by a choice piece of monumental sculpture, erected in some one of the grand old cathedrals in Belgium. It might, however, be better to take it *cum grano salis*—with a whole bushel thereof—rather than go so far, on so uncertain a direction, to look for evidence.

There are several old works, considered sound scientific treatises in their day, filled with the wildest and most extravagant stories of monsters, but none of them, as far as the writer's researches extend, mentions a pig-faced man or woman. St Hilaire, the celebrated French physiologist, in his remarkable work on the anomalies of organisation, though he ransacks all nature, ancient and modern, for his illustrations, never notices such a being. What, then, it may be asked, has caused this very prevalent myth? Probably some unhappy malformation, exaggerated, as all such things are, by vulgar report, gave origin to the absurd story; which was subsequently enlarged and disseminated by the agency of lying catch-penny publications of the chap-book kind. There was exhibited in London, a few years ago, a person who, at an earlier period, might readily have passed for a pig-faced lady, though the lower part of her countenance resembled that of a dog more than a pig. This unfortunate creature, named Julia Pastorana, was said to be of Spanish-American birth. After being exhibited in London, she was taken to the continent, where she died; and such is the indecent cupidity of showmen, so great is the morbid curiosity of sight-seers, that her embalmed remains were re-exhibited in the metropolis during the last year!

The earliest printed account of a pig-faced lady that the writer has met with, was published at London in 1641, and entitled *A Certain Relation of the Hog-faced Gentlewoman.* From this veracious production, we learn that her name was Tanakin Skinker, and she was born at Wirkham, on the Rhine, in 1618. As might be expected, in a contemporary Dutch work, which is either a translation or the original of the English one, she is said to have been born at Windsor on the Thames. Miss Skinker is described as having 'all the limbs and lineaments of her body well featured and proportioned, only her face, which is the ornament and beauty of all the rest, has the nose of a hog or swine, which is not only a stain and blemish, but a deformed ugliness, making all the rest loathsome, contemptible, and odious to all that look upon her.' Her language, we are further informed, is only 'the hoggish Dutch *ough, ough!* or the French *owee, owee!*' Forty thousand pounds, we are told, was the sum offered to the man who would consent to marry her, and the author says: 'This was a bait sufficient to make every fish bite at, for no sooner was this publicly divulged, but there came suitors of all sorts, every one in hope to carry away the great prize, for it was not the person but the prize they aimed at.' Gallants, we are told, came from Italy, France, Scotland, and England—were there no Irish fortune-hunters in those days?—but all ultimately refused to marry her. The accompanying illustration is a *fac-simile* of a wood-cut on the title-page of the work, representing a gallant politely addressing her with a 'God save you, sweet mistress,' while she replies only with the characteristic 'Ough!' Unlike some other pig-faced ladies, Miss Skinker always dressed well, and was 'courteous and kind in her way to all.' And the pamphlet ends by stating, that she has come to look for a husband in London, but whether she resides at Blackfriars or Covent Garden, the writer will 'say little,' lest the multitude of people who would flock to see her might, in their eagerness, pull the house down in which she resides.

In the earlier part of this century, there was a kind of publication in vogue, somewhat resembling the more ancient broadside, but better printed, and

THE LADY WITH A PIG'S HEAD.

adorned with a rather pretentious coloured engraving. One of those, published by Fairburn in 1815, and sold for a shilling, gives a portrait of the pig-faced lady, her silver trough placed on a table beside her. In the accompanying letter-press, we are informed that she was then twenty years of age, lived in Manchester Square, had been born in Ireland, of a high and wealthy family, and on her life and issue by marriage a very large property depended. 'This prodigy of nature,' says the author, 'is the general topic of conversation in the metropolis. In almost every company you join, the pig-faced lady is introduced, and her existence is firmly believed in by thousands, particularly those in the west end of the town. Her person is most delicately formed, and of the greatest symmetry; her hands and arms are delicately modelled in the happiest mould of nature; and the carriage of her body indicative of superior birth. Her manners are, in general, simple and unoffending; but when she is in want of food, she articulates, certainly, something like the sound of pigs when eating, and which, to those who are not acquainted with her, may perhaps be a little disagreeable.'

She seems, however, to have been disagreeable enough to the servant who attended upon her and slept with her; for this attendant, though receiving one thousand pounds per annum, as wages, left the situation, and gave the foregoing particulars to the publisher. And there can be little doubt that this absurd publication caused a poor simpleton to pay for the following advertisement, which appeared in the *Times* of Thursday, the 9th of February 1815:

'For the Attention of Gentlemen and Ladies.—A young gentlewoman having heard of an advertisement for a person to undertake the care of a lady, who is heavily afflicted in the face, whose friends have offered a handsome income yearly, and a premium for residing with her for seven years, would do all in her power to render her life most comfortable; an undeniable character can be obtained from a respectable circle of friends; an answer to this advertisement is requested, as the advertiser will keep herself disengaged. Address, post paid, to X. Y., at Mr Ford's, Baker, 12 Judd Street, Brunswick Square.'

Another simpleton, probably misled in the same manner, but aspiring to a nearer connection with the pig-faced lady, thus advertised in the *Morning Herald* of February 16, 1815:

'Secrecy.—A single gentleman, aged thirty-one, of a respectable family, and in whom the utmost confidence may be reposed, is desirous of explaining his mind to the friends of a person who has a misfortune in her face, but is prevented for want of an introduction. Being perfectly aware of the principal particulars, and understanding that a final settlement would be preferred to a temporary one, presumes he would be found to answer the full extent of their wishes. His intentions are sincere, honourable, and firmly resolved. References of great respectability can be given. Address to M. D., at Mr Spencer's, 22 Great Ormond Street, Queen's Square.'

For oral relations of the pig-faced lady, we must go to Dublin. If we make inquiries there respecting her, we shall be shewn the hospital that was founded on her account. We will be told that her picture and silver trough are to be seen in the building, and that she was christened Grisly, on account of her hideous appearance. Any further doubts, after receiving this information, will be considered as insults to common sense. Now, the history of Steevens's Hospital, the institution referred to, is simply this: In 1710, Dr Steevens, a benevolent physician, bequeathed his real estate, producing £650 per annum, to his only sister, Griselda, during her life; and, after her death, vested it in trustees for the erection and endowment of a hospital. Miss Steevens, being a lady of active benevolence—a very unusual character in those days, though happily not an uncommon one now—determined to build the hospital in her lifetime. Devoting £450 of her income to this purpose, she collected subscriptions and donations, and by dint of unceasing exertion, succeeded in a few years in opening a part of the building, equal to the accommodation of forty patients. Whether it was the uncommon name of Grizelda, or the uncommon benevolence of this lady, that gave rise to the vulgar notion respecting her face, will probably be never satisfactorily explained. But her portrait hangs in the library of the hospital, proving her to have been a very pleasant-looking-lady, with a peculiarly benevolent cast of countenance.

A lady, to whom the writer applied for information, thus writes from Dublin: 'The idea that Miss Steevens was a pig-faced lady still prevails among the vulgar; when I was young, everybody believed it. When this century was in its teens, it was customary, in genteel society, for parties to be made up to go to the hospital, to see the silver trough and pig-faced picture. The matron, or housekeeper, that shewed the establishment, never denied the existence of those curiosities, but always alleged she *could* not shew them, implying, by her mode of saying it, that she dared not, that to do so would be contrary to the stringent orders she had received. The housekeeper, no doubt, obtained many shillings and tenpennies by this equivocating mode of keeping up the delusion. Besides, many persons who had gone to the hospital to see the trough and picture, did not like to acknowledge that they had not seen them. I can form no opinion of the origin of the myth, but can give you another instance of its dissemination. Old Mr B., whom you may just recollect, had an enormous silver punch-bowl, much bruised and battered by long service in the cause of Bacchus. The crest of a former proprietor, representing a boar's head, was engraved upon it: and my poor aunt, not inappropriately, considering the purposes for which the bowl was used and the scenes it led to, used to call it the pig-trough. Every child and servant in the house believed that it was one of the pig-faced lady's troughs; and the crest, her correct likeness. The servants always shewed it as a great curiosity to their kitchen-visitors, who firmly believed the stupid story. And I have always found, in the course of a long life, that ignorant minds accept fiction as readily as they reject truth.'

The pig-faced lady is not unfrequently exhibited, in travelling-caravans, by showmen at fairs, country-wakes, races, and places of general resort. The lady is represented by a bear, having its head carefully shaved, and adorned with cap, bonnet, ringlets, flowers, &c. The animal is securely tied in an upright position, into a large arm-chair, the cords being concealed by the shawl, gown, and other parts of the *lady's* dress.

---

# AUGUST 24.

St Bartholomew, apostle. The Martyrs of Utica, or The White Mass, 258. St Ouen or Audoen, archbishop of Rouen, confessor, 683. St Irchard or Erthad, bishop and confessor in Scotland, 10th century.

## ST BARTHOLOMEW,

One of the twelve apostles, is believed to have travelled on a mission into Armenia, and to have there suffered martyrdom by being flayed alive. A knife, consequently, became the emblem of St Bartholomew, as may be seen on many of the old clog almanacks, described in a former part of this work. At the abbey of Croyland, there used to be a distribution of knives each St Bartholomew's Day, in honour of the saint.

The insetting of chilly evenings is noted at this season of the year, and has been expressed in a popular distich:

St Bartholomew
Brings the cold dew.

---

*Born.*—Letizia Bonaparte (*née* Ramolini), mother of Napoleon, 1750, *Ajaccio, Corsica;* William Wilberforce, philanthropist and religious writer, 1759, *Hull.*

*Died.*—Cneius Julius Agricola, Roman general, 93, *Rome;* Alphonso V., of Portugal, 1481, *Cintra;* Admiral Gaspard de Coligni, murdered at Paris, 1572; Colonel Thomas Blood, noted for his attempt to steal the regalia from the Tower, 1680; John, Duke of Lauderdale, minister of Charles II., 1682; Dr John Owen, eminent divine, 1683, *Ealing;* Theodore Hook, novelist, 1841.

## THEODORE HOOK.

If fine personal qualities, as a handsome figure and agreeable countenance, quick intelligence and brilliant wit, with an unfailing flow of animal spirits, were alone able to secure happiness, Theodore Hook ought to have been amongst the happiest and most fortunate of mankind, for he possessed them all. We know, however, that something more is needed—above all, conscientiousness, sense of duty, or at least common prudence—to make life a true success. No man could more thoroughly illustrate the vanity of all gifts where this is wanting, than Theodore Hook.

His early days were spent in an atmosphere which naturally tended to foster and develop his peculiar genius. His father was a favourite musical composer, whose house was the resort of all the popular characters of the day—musical, theatrical, and otherwise. Theodore was found to have an exquisite ear for music, and soon became noted among his father's coteries as a first-rate singer and player on the pianoforte. One night he astonished the old gentleman by singing and accompanying on the instrument two songs, one serious and the other comic, which the latter had never heard before. On inquiry, they turned out to be original compositions, both as regarded words and music. Here an assistant was unexpectedly discovered, by the elder Hook, to aid him in his labours, as hitherto he had always been obliged to employ the services of some poetaster to furnish the libretto of his musical pieces. Thus encouraged, Theodore set to work, and produced *The Soldier's Return; or, What can Beauty do?* a comic opera, in two acts, first represented at Drury Lane in 1805. Its success was such as to stimulate him to further efforts, and at the age of sixteen he became a successful dramatist and song-writer, the pet of the *coulisses* and green-room, to which he had a free entrée, and the recipient of a handsome income, rarely procurable by a man's personal exertions at so early an age. The pieces written by him at this period comprise—*Catch Him who Can; The Invisible Girl; Tekeli, or the Siege of Mongratz; Killing no Murder*, and others; but few, if any, of these now keep possession of the stage.

As may have been expected, the more solid branches of education seem to have been little attended to in the case of Hook. The first school to which he was sent, was a 'seminary for young gentlemen' in Soho Square, where, by his own account, he used regularly to play the truant, amusing himself by wandering about the streets, and devising all sorts of excuses to account to his teacher for his absence. On one occasion, unfortunately for him, he had remained at home, asserting to his parents that a general holiday had been granted to the scholars. His brother on the same day, which happened to be the rejoicing for the peace of Amiens, was passing Theodore's school, and seeing it open, was induced to go in and make inquiries, from which he learned that the young vagabond had not shewn face there for the last three weeks. The result was his being locked up for the remainder of the day in the garret, and debarred from seeing the illuminations and fireworks in the evening. From this academy he was sent to a school in Cambridgeshire, and afterwards to Harrow, where he had Lord Byron and Sir Robert Peel for his companions, but made little progress in classic learning, study and application being to him a most irksome drudgery. On the death of his stepmother in 1802, he was prematurely withdrawn from school, and from this period remained at home, in the enjoyment of the congenial atmosphere of his father's house, and the reputation and more solid advantages which the brilliancy of his talents enabled him to secure.

Hook's turn for quizzing and practical jokes was very early displayed, and innumerable anecdotes are recorded of this propensity. They are connected chiefly with the theatre, to which his occupations constantly led him, and where he was the soul and mirth-inspirer of the motley community behind the scenes. On one occasion he nearly frightened Dowton, the comedian, out of his wits, by walking up to him instead of the proper personator of the part, and delivering a letter. On another, when Sheridan was contesting the seat for Westminster, the cry of 'Sheridan for ever!' was heard by the astonished audience proceeding apparently from the evil spirit in the 'Wood-Demon,' and producing one of those incongruous effects which are so much relied on for raising a laugh in pantomime or burlesque. A mischievous trick of another kind, in which he was aided by Liston, may also be mentioned. A young gentleman of Hook's acquaintance had a great desire to witness a play, and also escort a fair cousin thither, but was terrified lest his going to a theatre should come to the knowledge of his father, a rigid Presbyterian, who held such places in abhorrence. He communicated his difficulties to his gay friend. 'Never mind the governor, my dear fellow,' was the reply; 'trust to me; I'll arrange everything—get you a couple of orders, secure places—front-row; and nobody need know anything about it.' The tickets were procured, and received with great thankfulness by Mr B——, who started with his relative for the playhouse, and the pair soon found themselves absorbed in an ecstasy of delight in witnessing the drolleries of Liston. But what was their confusion when the comedian, advancing to the foot-lights during a burst of laughter at one of his performances, looked round the dress-circle with a mock-offended air, and exclaimed: 'I don't understand this conduct, ladies and gentlemen! I am not accustomed to be laughed at; I can't imagine what you can see ridiculous in *me*; why, I declare' (pointing at the centre box with his finger), 'there's Harry B——, too, and his cousin Martha J——; what business have they to come here and laugh at me, I should like to know? I'll go and tell his father, and hear what *he* thinks of it!' The consternation caused to the truant couple by this unexpected address, and the eyes of the whole audience being turned on them, may be more readily imagined than described, and they fled from the house in dismay.

In the days of which we write, the abstraction of pump-handles and street-knockers was a favourite amusement of the young blades about town, some of whom prided themselves not a little in forming a museum of these trophies. Hook was behind no one in such freaks. One of them was the carrying off the figure of a Highlander, as large as life, from the door of a tobacconist, wrapping it up in a cloak, and tumbling it into a hackney-coach as 'a friend, a very respectable man, but a little tipsy,' with a request to the coachman to drive on. The following anecdote is related in the *Ingoldsby Legends*, but will well bear repetition. On the occasion of the trial of Lord Melville, Hook had gone with a friend to Westminster Hall to witness the proceedings. As the peers began to enter, a simple-looking lady from the country touched his arm, and said: 'I beg your pardon, sir, but pray who are those gentlemen in red now coming in?'

'Those, ma'am,' he replied, 'are the barons of

England; in these cases, the junior peers always come first.'

'Thank you, sir, much obliged to you. Louisa, my dear (turning to her daughter, who accompanied her), tell Jane these are the barons of England; and the juniors (that's the youngest, you know) always goes first. Tell her to be sure and remember that when we get home.'

'Dear me, ma,' said Louisa, 'can that gentleman be one of the *youngest?* I am sure he looks very old.'

This *naiveté* held out an irresistible temptation to Theodore, who, on the old lady pointing to the bishops, who came next in order, with scarlet and lawn sleeves over their doctors' robes, and asking, 'What gentlemen are those?' replied: 'Gentlemen, ma'am! these are not gentlemen; these are *ladies*, elderly ladies—the dowager-peeresses in their own right.'

His interrogator looked at him rather suspiciously, as if to find out whether or not he was quizzing her; but reassured by the imperturbable air of gravity with which her glance was met, turned round again to her daughter, and whispered: 'Louisa, dear, the gentleman says that these are elderly ladies and dowager-peeresses in their own right; tell Jane not to forget *that*.'

Shortly afterwards, her attention was drawn to the speaker of the House of Commons, with his richly-embroidered robes. 'Pray, sir,' she exclaimed, 'who is that fine-looking person opposite?'

'That, ma'am, is Cardinal Wolsey.'

'No, sir!' was the angry rejoinder, 'we knows a good deal better than that; Cardinal Wolsey has been dead and buried these many years.'

'No such thing, my dear madam,' replied Hook, with the most extraordinary *sang froid;* 'it has indeed been so reported in the country, but without the least foundation in truth; in fact, these rascally newspapers will say anything!'

The good lady looked thunderstruck, opened her eyes and mouth to their widest compass, and then, unable to say another word, or remain longer on the spot, hurried off with a daughter in each hand, leaving the mischievous wag and his friend to enjoy the joke.

A well-known story is told of Hook and Terry the actor making their way into a gentleman's house with whom they had no acquaintance whatever, but the appetising steams issuing from whose area gave indications of a glorious feast being in the course of preparation. The anecdote is perfectly true, though the real scene of the adventure was not, as commonly represented, a suburban villa on the banks of the Thames, but a town-mansion somewhere in the neighbourhood of Soho Square. Hook caught at the idea suggested by Terry, that he should like to make one of so jovial a party; and arranging with his friend that he should call for him there that evening at ten o'clock, hurried up the steps, gave a brisk rap with the knocker, and was at once admitted to the drawing-room. The room being full, no notice was taken of him at first, and before the host discovered him, he had already made his way to the hearts of a knot of guests by his sallies of drollery. The master of the house at last perceiving a stranger, went up, and politely begged his name, as he felt rather at a loss. Hook replied with a perfect torrent of volubility, but expressed in the suavest and most fascinating terms, and effectually preventing any interruption to his discourse. An explanation at last came out, that he had mistaken both the house and the hour at which he ought to have dined with a friend. The old gentleman's civility then could not allow him to depart, as his friend's dinner-hour must now be long past, and a guest with such a flow of spirits must prove a most agreeable acquisition to his own table. Hook professed great reluctance to trespass thus on the hospitality of a perfect stranger, but was induced, seemingly with much difficulty, to remain, and partake of dinner. So delightful a companion and so droll a fellow had never been met before, and so much mirth and jollity had never till now enlivened the mansion. At ten o'clock, Mr Terry was announced, and Hook, who had seated himself at the pianoforte, in the performance of one of his famous extemporaneous effusions, brought his song to a close as follows:

'I am very much pleased with your fare;
Your cellar's as prime as your cook;
My friend's Mr Terry the player,
And I'm Mr Theodore Hook!'

Nor was this by any means the only entertainment of the kind which his assurance and farcical powers enabled him to obtain. Passing one day in a gig with a friend by the villa of a retired chronometer-maker, he suddenly reined up, remarked to his friend what a comfortable little box that was, and that they might do worse than dine there. He then alighted, rang the bell, and on being admitted to the presence of the worthy old citizen, said that he had often heard his name, which was celebrated throughout the civilised world, and that being in the neighbourhood, he could not resist the temptation of calling and making the acquaintance of so distinguished a public character. The good man was quite tickled with the compliment; pressed his admirer and friend to stay dinner, which was just ready; and a most jovial afternoon was spent, though on the way home the gig containing Hook and his companion was smashed to pieces by the refractory horse, and the two occupants had a narrow escape of their lives. Another of his adventures, in which he seems to have taken his cue from Tony Lumpkin, was driving up to an old gentleman's house, ordering the servant who appeared to take his mare to the stable and rub her down well, and then proceeding to the parlour, stretched himself at full-length on the sofa, and called for a glass of brandy and water. On the master of the house making his appearance and inquiring the business of his visitor, Hook became more vociferous than ever, declared that he had never before met with such treatment in any inn, or from any landlord, and ended by saying that his host must be drunk, and he should certainly feel it his duty to report the circumstance to the bench. The old gentleman was confounded, but in a short time Hook pretended to discover his blunder of having taken the house for an inn, and made ten thousand apologies, adding that he had been induced to commit the mistake by seeing over the entrance-gate a large vase of flowers, which, he imagined, indicated the sign of the Flower-pot. This said vase happened to be cherished by its owner with special complacency as a most unique and chaste ornament.

and here was it degraded to the level of a pot-house sign!

Another story is told of Hook, in which he improved on a well-known device related of Sheridan. Getting into a hackney-coach one day, and being unable to pay the fare, he bethought himself of the plan adopted by the celebrated wit just mentioned on a similar occasion, and hailed a friend whom he observed passing along the street. He made him get into the carriage beside him, but on comparing notes he found his companion equally devoid of cash as himself, and it was necessary to think of some other expedient. Presently they approached the house of a celebrated surgeon. Hook alighted, rushed to the door, and exclaimed hurriedly to the servant who opened it: 'Is Mr —— at home? I must see him immediately. For God's sake do not lose an instant.' Ushered into the consulting-room, he exclaimed wildly to the surgeon: 'Thank heaven! Pardon my incoherence, sir; make allowance for the feelings of a husband, *perhaps a father*—your attendance, sir, is instantly required—instantly—by Mrs ——. For mercy's sake, sir, be off.' 'I'll be on my way immediately,' replied the medical man. 'I have only to get my instruments, and step into my carriage.' 'Don't wait for your carriage,' cried the pseudo-distressed parent; 'get into mine, which is waiting at the door.' Esculapius readily complied, was hurried into the coach, and conveyed in a trice to the residence of an aged spinster, whose indignation and horror at the purport of his visit was beyond all bounds. The poor man was glad to beat a speedy retreat, but the fury of the old maiden-lady was not all he was destined to undergo, as the hackney-coachman kept hold of him, and mulcted him in the full amount of the fare which Hook ought to have paid.

All these and similar escapades, however, were fairly eclipsed by the famous Berners-street hoax, which created such a sensation in London in 1809. By despatching several thousands of letters to innumerable quarters, he completely blocked up the entrances to the street, by an assemblage of the most heterogeneous kind. The parties written to had been requested to call on a certain day at the house of a lady, residing at No. 54 Berners Street, against whom Hook and one or two of his friends had conceived a grudge. So successful was the trick, that nearly all obeyed the summons. Coal-wagons, heavily laden, carts of upholstery, vans with pianos and other articles, wedding and funeral coaches, all rumbled through, and filled up the adjoining streets and lanes; sweeps assembled with the implements of their trade; tailors with clothes that had been ordered; pastry-cooks with wedding-cakes; undertakers with coffins; fishmongers with cod-fishes, and butchers with legs of mutton. There were surgeons with their instruments; lawyers with their papers and parchments; and clergymen with their books of devotion. Such a babel was never heard before in London, and to complete the business, who should drive up but the lord mayor in his state-carriage; the governor of the Bank of England; the chairman of the East India Company; and even a scion of royalty itself, in the person of the Duke of Gloucester. Hook and his confederates were meantime enjoying the fun from a window in the neighbourhood, but the consternation occasioned to the poor lady who had been made the victim of the jest, was nearly becoming too serious a matter. He never avowed himself as the originator of this trick, though there is no doubt of his being the prime actor in it. It was made the subject of a solemn investigation by many of the parties who had been duped, but so carefully had the precautions been taken to avoid detection, that the inquiry proved entirely fruitless.

In 1813, Hook received the appointment, with a salary of £2000 a year, of accountant-general and treasurer of the Mauritius, an office which one would have supposed to be the very antipodes to all his capacities and predilections. How it came to be conferred on him, does not clearly appear; but it exhibits a memorable instance, among others, of the reckless selection, too often displayed in those days, in the choice of public officials. What might have been expected followed. The treasurer was about as fitted by nature for discharging the duties of such an office as a clown in a pantomime, and the five years spent by him in the island were little more than a round of merriment and festivities. An investigation of his accounts at last took place, and a large deficit, ultimately fixed at about £12,000, was discovered. There seems no reason for believing that Hook had been guilty of the least embezzlement or mal-appropriation of the government funds; but there can be no doubt that his negligence in regard to his duties was most reprehensible, trusting their performance entirely to a deputy, who committed suicide about the time of the inquiry being instituted. A criminal charge was made out against the unfortunate accountant-general, and in 1818, he was sent home under arrest. His buoyancy of spirits, however, never failed him, and meeting at St Helena one of his old friends, who asked him if he was going home for his health, he replied: 'Yes, I believe there's something wrong with the chest!'

On landing in England, it was found that there was no ground for a criminal action against him, but that as responsible for the acts of his deputy, his person and estate were amenable to civil proceedings. The whole of his property in the Mauritius and elsewhere was accordingly confiscated, and he underwent a long confinement, first in a sponging-house in Shire-Lane, and afterwards in the King's Bench Prison. Thrown again on his own resources, he produced several dramatic pieces, which achieved a respectable amount of success. The great event, however, at this period of his life, was his becoming editor of the *John Bull* newspaper, which, under his management, made itself conspicuous by its stinging and too often scurrilous attacks on the Whig party. An inexhaustible fund of metrical lampoon and satire was ever at the command of its conductor, and he certainly dealt out his sarcasm with no sparing hand. Some of the most famous of his effusions were directed against Queen Caroline and her party at the time of the celebrated trial. *Whyttington and his Catte*, the *Hunting of the Hare*, and *Mrs Muggins's Visit to the Queen*, were reckoned in their day by the Tories as uncommonly smart things.

Have you been to Brandenburgh? heigh! ma'am,
ho! ma'am;
Have you been to Brandenburgh! ho!
O yes! I have been, ma'am, to visit the queen, ma'am,
With the rest of the gallantee show.

What did you see, ma'am? heigh! ma'am, ho! ma'am,
What did you see, ma'am? ho!
We saw a great dame, with a face as red as flame,
And a character spotless as snow.

* * * *

*Mrs Muggins's Visit* was a satire on Queen Caroline's drawing-room, at Brandenburgh House, and is said to be a very good specimen of Hook's style in improvisation, an art which he possessed in a wonderful degree.

Some years before Hook's obtaining his disastrous appointment at the Mauritius, he had published, under an assumed name, a novel entitled *The Man of Sorrow*, but its success was very doubtful. It was not till after he had passed through the furnace of adversity, and undergone the pains of incarceration, that he gave to the world that series of works of fiction which, prior to the days of Dickens and Thackeray, had so unbounded a popularity as the exponents of middle-class life. With great smartness and liveliness of description, they partake eminently of the character of the author whose gifts were much more brilliant than solid. Deficient in the latter element, and possessing, in a great measure, an ephemeral interest, it becomes, therefore, doubtful whether they will be much heard of in a succeeding generation.

The *bons mots* recorded of Theodore Hook are multifarious, but they have all more or less a dash of the flippancy and impudence by which, especially in early life, he was characterised. Walking along the Strand one day, he accosted, with much gravity, a very pompous-looking gentleman. 'I beg your pardon, sir, but may I ask, are you anybody particular?' and passed on before the astonished individual could collect himself sufficiently to reply. In the midst of his London career of gaiety, when a stripling, he was induced by his brother James, who was seventeen years his senior, to enter himself at St Mary's Hall, Oxford, where his sojourn, however, was but brief. On being presented for matriculation to the vice-chancellor, that dignitary inquired if he was prepared to sign the Thirty-nine Articles.

'O yes,' replied Theodore, 'forty, if you like!' It required all his brother's interest with Dr Parsons to induce him to pardon this petulant sally. The first evening, it is said, of his arrival at Oxford, he had joined a party of old schoolfellows at a tavern, and the fun had become fast and furious. Just then the proctor, that terror of university evil-doers, made his appearance, and advancing to the table where Hook was sitting, addressed him with the customary question: 'Pray, sir, are you a member of this university?' 'No, sir,' was the reply (rising and bowing respectfully); 'pray, sir, are you?'

Somewhat discomposed by this unexpected query, the proctor held out his sleeve, 'You see this, sir?'

'Ah,' replied the young freshman, after examining with much apparent interest for a few moments the quality of the stuff. 'Yes, I perceive, Manchester velvet; and may I take the liberty, sir, of inquiring how much you may have paid per yard for the article?' Discomfited by so much imperturbable coolness, the academical dignitary was forced to retire amid a storm of laughter.

The Mauritius affair proved a calamity, from the effects of which Hook never recovered. With a crushing debt constantly suspended *in terrorem* over him, and an enfeebled frame, the result of his confinement in prison, and partly also of the unwholesome style of living, as regards food, in which he had indulged when abroad, his last years were sadly embittered by ill health, mental depression, and pecuniary embarrassment. Outwardly, he seemed still to enjoy the same flow of spirits; but a worm was gnawing at the heart, and his diary at this period discloses a degree of mental anguish and anxiety which few of those about him suspected. He died at Fulham, on 24th August 1841, in his fifty-third year.

## THE ST BARTHOLOMEW MASSACRE.

The prodigious event bearing this well-known name, was mainly an expression of the feelings with which Protestantism was regarded in France in the first age after the Reformation; but the private views of the queen-mother, the atrocious Catharine de' Medici, were also largely concerned. After the death of her husband, Henry II., she had an incessant struggle, during the reigns of the boy-kings, her sons, who succeeded, for the supreme power. It seemed within her grasp, but for the influence which the Protestant leader, the Admiral Coligni, had acquired over the mind of Charles IX. This young monarch was a semi-maniac. He was never happy but when taking the most violent exercise, riding for twelve or fourteen hours consecutively, hunting the same stag for two or three days, only stopping to eat, and reposing but a few hours in the night. He had, during the absence of Catharine, listened to Coligni, and agreed to an expedition against the Spaniards in alliance with the Prince of Orange. When the proud mother returned, she found herself supplanted by the chief of the Huguenot party, whose triumph in her eyes would be absolute ruin to her family. The king had accepted the idea of war with delight; he demanded the constant presence of the admiral, and kept him half the night in his bedroom, calculating the number of his armies, and laying down plans for marching. From this moment the death of the Protestant leader was determined on.

The opportunity of the marriage between Henry of Navarre and the Princess Margaret, which took place on the 18th of August 1572, was seized upon; the Huguenots of rank had followed their leader to Paris; a gallery was erected for them outside Notre Dame, that their prejudices might not be wounded, and nothing was seen but festivity and concord between the disagreeing parties. But on the 22d, Coligni was shot at from a window by a follower of the Duke de Guise, and wounded in two places; his party were highly indignant at the outrage, crowded round the house, and threats of vengeance were heard; these were used by the king's relatives to convince him that he and all about him were in danger of immediate destruction, if he did not permit a general massacre. The Dukes de Guise, Anjou, Aumale, and others agreed to carry out the dreadful decree; the bell of St Germain de l'Auxerrois was to toll out the signal in the dead of the night. From a balcony in the Louvre, which opened out of the ball-room, and looked into the Seine, the guilty mother and trembling son watched the proceedings. The house where Coligni lay wounded was first attacked; he met his fate with the heroism of a Christian hero; his body was thrown from the window, and his followers shared the same fate. All the streets in Paris rang with the dreadful cry: 'Death to the Huguenot! kill every man! kill! kill!' Neither men, women, nor children were spared; some asleep, some kneeling in supplication to their savage assailants; about thirty thousand innocent persons were thus butchered by a furious mob, allowed to give vent to their fanatical passion. All that day it continued; towards evening the king sent out his trumpeter to command a cessation; but the people were not so easily controlled, and murders were committed during the two following days. Five hundred men of rank, with many ladies of equally high birth, and ministers of religion, were among the victims; every man, indeed, might kill his personal enemy without inquiry being made as to his religion, and Catholics suffered as well as Huguenots. The large cities of the provinces, Rouen, Lyon, &c., caught the infection, which the queen-mother took no steps to prevent, and France was steeped in blood and mourning.

The king at first laid the blame on the Houses of Guise and Coligni, but he afterwards went to the parliament, and acknowledged himself as the author, claiming the merit of having given peace to France by the destruction of the Protestants. But his life was ever after one of bitter remorse and horror. Not many days after, he said to his surgeon: 'I feel like one in a fever, my body and mind are both disturbed; every moment, whether asleep or awake, visions of murdered corpses, covered with blood, and hideous to the sight, haunt me. Oh, I wish they had spared the innocent and imbecile!' In less than two years, the unfortunate young king had joined his victims; a prey to every mental and physical suffering that could be imagined.

The black turpitude and wickedness of the Bartholomew Massacre is very obvious; but it is not less true that it was a great blunder. The facts were heard of all over Europe with a shudder of horror. They have been a theme of reproach against Catholics ever since. It may be considered as a serious misfortune for any code of opinions whatever to have such a terrible affair associated with it.

### THE BARTHOLOMEW ACT, 1662.

When High Church had the upper hand in the reign of Charles I., it did not scruple to pillory the Puritans, excise their ears, and banish them. When the Puritans got the ascendancy afterwards, they treated high-churchmen with an equally conscientious severity. At the Restoration, all the reforming plans of the last twenty years were found utterly worn out of public favour, and the public submitted very quietly to a reconstitution of the church under what was called the Act of Uniformity, which made things very unpleasant once more for the Puritans. By its provisions, every clergyman was to be expelled from his charge on the 24th of August 1662, if, by that time, he did not declare his assent to everything contained in the revised Book of Common Prayer; every clergyman who, during the period of the Commonwealth, had been unable to obtain episcopal ordination, was commanded now to obtain that kind of sanction; all were to take an oath of canonical obedience; all were to give up the theory on which the old 'Solemn League and Covenant' had been based; and all were to accept the doctrine of the king's supremacy over the church. The result was, that two thousand of the clergy signalised this Bartholomew Day by coming out of the church. Baxter, Alleyne, Calamy, Owen, and Bates, were among them; while Milton, Bunyan, and Andrew Marvell, were among the laymen who adhered to their cause. The act became the more harsh from its coming into operation just before one whole year's tithes were due. Two thousand families, hitherto dependent on stipends for support, were driven hither and thither in the search for a livelihood; and this was rendered more and more difficult by a number of subordinate statutes passed in rapid succession. The ejected ministers were not allowed to exercise, even in private houses, the religious functions to which they had been accustomed. Their books could not be published without episcopal sanction, previously applied for and obtained. A statute, called the 'Conventicle Act,' punished with fine, imprisonment, or transportation, every one present in any private house where religious worship was carried on—if the total number exceeded by more than five the regular members of the household. Another, called the 'Oxford Act,' imposed on these unfortunate ministers an oath of passive obedience and non-resistance; and if they refused to take it, they were prohibited from living within five miles of any place where they had ever resided, or of any corporate town, and from eking out their scanty incomes by keeping schools, or taking in boarders. A second and stricter version of the Conventicle Act deprived the ministers of the right of trial by jury, and empowered any justice of the peace to convict them on the oath of a single informer, who was to be rewarded with one-third of the fines levied; no flaw in the legal document, called the *mittimus*, was allowed to vitiate it; and the 'benefit of the doubt,' in any uncertain cases, was to be given to the accusers, not to the accused.

Writers who take opposite sides on this subject naturally differ as to the causes and justification to be assigned for the ejection; but there is very little difference of opinion as to the misery suffered during the years intervening between 1662 and 1688. Those who, in one way or other, suffered homelessness, hunger, and penury on account of the Act of Uniformity and the ejection that followed it, have been estimated at 60,000 persons, and the amount of pecuniary loss at twelve or fourteen millions sterling. Defoe, Penn, and other contemporary writers, set down upwards of 5000 Nonconformists as the number who perished within the walls of prisons; and many, like Baxter, were hunted from house to house, from chapel to chapel, by informers, whose only motive was to obtain a portion of the fines levied for infringement of numerous statutes.

Considered as a historical fact, *dissent* may be said to have begun in England on this 24th August 1662, when the Puritans, who had before formed a body *within* the church, now ranged themselves as a dissenting or Nonconformist sect *outside* it.

## BARTHOLOMEW FAIR.

The great London Saturnalia—the Smithfield fair on the anniversary of St Bartholomew's Day —died a lingering death in 1855, after flourishing for seven centuries and a half. Originally established for useful trading purposes, it had long survived its claim to tolerance, and as London increased, had become a great public nuisance, with its scenes of riot and obstruction in the very heart of the city.

When Rahere, minstrel and jester to Henry I., left the gaieties of the court for the proprieties of the cloister, he exhibited much worldly prudence in arranging his future career. He affirmed that he had seen Bartholomew the apostle in a vision, and that he had directed him to found a church and hospital in his honour in the suburbs of London, at Smithfield. The land was the more readily granted by the king, Henry II.; for it was waste and marshy, and would be improved by the proposed foundation. Osier Lane (now spelled in Cockney form with an H) marks the site of a small brook, lined with osiers, which emptied itself in the Fleet River. The marsh was drained, and the monastery founded on its site in 1123; Rahere was made prior, and great success attended the shrine of St Bartholomew, where many miracles were affirmed to have been effected in aid of the afflicted. But the new prior, having been an active man of the world, looked to temporal as well as spiritual aid; he therefore included the right to hold a great fair on the festival of his patron saint, and this brought traders from all parts to Smithfield, for they had the royal safeguard—'firm peace to all persons coming to and returning from the fair'—during the three days it was held. Cattle and merchandise were the staple of such fairs. The safeguard given to traders in days when travelling was difficult and dangerous, and the ease with which men might combine to go in companies to them, made them generally useful; hence shopkeepers laid in their stock from them, and housekeepers furnished their homes with articles not readily obtained elsewhere. The pious might join in a great church-festival, the pleasure-seekers find amusement in the wandering minstrels and jesters who were drawn to the busy scene, or stare with wonder at some performing-monkey or other 'outlandish beast,' who was sure to find favour with the sight-loving Londoners.

Several centuries elapsed, and the whole character of English life altered, before the trading-fair became exclusively a pleasure-fair. It was not until the cessation of our civil wars, and the quiet establishment of the House of Tudor upon the throne, that trade assumed its important position, and commercial enterprise elevated and enlarged its boundaries. In the reign of Queen Elizabeth, Bartholomew Fair ceased to be a cloth-fair of any importance; but its name and fame is still preserved in the lane running parallel to Bartholomew Close, termed 'Cloth-fair,' which was 'generally inhabited by drapers and mercers' in the days of Strype, and which still preserves many antique features, and includes, in a somewhat modernised form, some of the old houses founded by Lord Rich and his successors, who obtained the grant of the hospital property in the reign of Henry VIII. The fair was always proclaimed by the lord mayor, beneath the arch shewn in our cut, to the very end of its existence; and its original connection with the cloth trade was also shewn in a burlesque proclamation the evening before by a company of drapers and tailors, who met at 'the Hand and Shears,' a house-of-call for their fraternity

CLOTH-FAIR.

in Cloth-fair, from whence they marched, shears in hand, to this archway, and announced the opening of the fair, concluding the ceremony by a general shout and 'snapping of shears.'

Keutzner, the German traveller, who visited England in 1598, tells us, 'that every year, upon St Bartholomew's Day, when the fair is held, it is usual for the mayor, attended by the twelve principal aldermen, to walk in a neighbouring field, dressed in his scarlet gown, and about his neck a golden chain.' A tent was pitched for their accommodation, and wrestling provided for their amusement. 'After this is over, a parcel of live rabbits are turned loose among the crowd, which are pursued by a number of boys, who endeavoured to catch them with all the noise they can make.' The next vivid picture of the fair we obtain from an eye-witness, shews how great the change in its character during the progress of the reign of Elizabeth. This photograph of the fair in 1614, we obtain in Ben Jonson's comedy, which takes its title from, and is supposed to be chiefly enacted in, the precincts of the fair. There was hardly a trace now left of its old business character—it was all eating, drinking, and amusement. It had become an established custom to eat roast-pig here; shows were established for the exhibition of 'motions' or puppet-plays, sometimes constructed on religious history, such as 'the Fall of Nineveh,' 'the History of the Chaste Susanna,' &c.; others were constructed in classic story, as 'the Siege of Troy,' or 'the Loves of Hero and Leander;' which is enacted in the last act of Ben Jonson's play, and bears striking resemblances to the burlesques so constantly played in our modern theatres. Shows of other kinds abounded, and zoology was always in high favour. One of Ben's characters says: 'I have been at the Eagle and the Black Wolf, and the Bull with the five legs, and the Dogs that dance the Morrice, and the Hare with the Tabor.' Some of these performances are still popular 'sights:' the hare beating the tabor amused our Anglo-Saxon forefathers, as it may amuse generations yet unborn. Over-dressed dolls ('Bartholomew-Fair babies'), and 'gilt gingerbread,' with drums, trumpets, and other toys were abundantly provided for children's 'fairings.'

In 1641, the fair had increased greatly, and become solely devoted to pleasure —such as it was. In a descriptive tract of that date, we are told it was 'of so vast an extent that it is contained in no less than four several parishes—namely, Christchurch, Great and Little St Bartholomew's, and St Sepulchre's. Hither resort people of all sorts and conditions. Christchurch cloisters are now hung full of pictures. It is remarkable, and worth your observation to behold, and hear the strange sights, and confused noise in the fair. Here, a knave, in a fool's coat, with a trumpet sounding, or on a drum beating, invites you to see his puppets; there, a rogue like a wild woodman, or in an antic shape like an incubus, desires your company to view his motion; on the other side, Hocuspocus, with three yards of tape or ribbon in his hand, shews his art of legerdemain to the admiration and astonishment of a company of cockloaches. Amongst these, you shall see a gray goose-cap (as wise as the rest), with a "what do ye lacke" in his mouth, stand in his booth, shaking a rattle or scraping a fiddle, with which children are so taken, that they presently cry out for these fopperies; and all these together make such a distracted noise, that you would think Babel not comparable to it.'

In the reign of Charles II., the fair became a London carnival of the grossest kind. The licence was extended from three to fourteen days, the theatres were closed during this time, and the actors brought to Smithfield. All classes, high and low, visited the place. Evelyn records his visit there, so does John Locke, and garrulous Pepys went often. On August 28, 1667, he notes that he 'went twice round Bartholomew Fair, which I was glad to see again.' Two days afterwards, he writes: 'I went to Bartholomew Fair, to walk up and down; and there, among other things, find my Lady Castlemaine at a puppet-play (*Patient Grisel*), and a street full of people expecting her coming out.' This infamous woman divided her affections between the king, Charles II., and Jacob Hall, the rope-dancer, who was a great favourite at the fair, and salaried by her ladyship. In 1668, Pepys again notes two visits he paid to the fair, in company with Lord Brouncker and others, to see 'The mare that tells money, and many things to admiration—and then the dancing of the ropes, and also the little stage-play, which is very ridiculous.'

LEE AND HARPER'S BOOTH, BARTHOLOMEW FAIR.

In 1699, Ned Ward notes in his *London Spy*, a visit he paid to the fair, viewing it from a public-house near the Hospital Gate, under the influence of a pipe. 'The first objects, when we were seated at the window, that lay within our observation, were the quality of the fair, strutting round their balconies in their tinsel robes, and golden leather buskins, expressing such pride in their buffoonery stateliness, that I could but reasonably believe they were as much elevated with the thought of their fortnight's pageantry, as ever Alexander was with the thought of a new conquest; looking with great contempt on their split deal-thrones upon the admiring mobility gazing in the dirt at our ostentatious heroes, and their most supercilious doxies, who looked as awkward and ungainly in their gorgeous accoutrements, as an alderman's lady in her stiff-bodied gown upon a lord-mayor's festival.' One of the most famous of these great theatrical booths was that owned by Lee and Harper, and represented in the above engraving, copied from a curious general view of the fair, designed to form a fan-mount, and probably published about 1728.*

* It was re-engraved and printed by Mr Setchel, of King's Street, Covent Garden, 1824, but that print is now rare. It was accompanied by a few descriptive lines of letter-press, in which the date of 1721 was assigned to

Here one of the old favourite sacred dramas is being performed on the history of Judith and Holophernes, and both these characters parade the stage in front; the hero in the stage-dress of a Roman general; the heroine in that of a Versailles court-masque, with a feathered head-dress, a laced stomacher, and a hooped petticoat of crimson silk, with white rosettes in large triangles over its ample surface. A few of these Bartholomew-fair dramas found their way into print, the most remarkable of the series being the *Siege of Troy*, by Elkanah Settle, once the favourite court-poet of Charles II., and the rival of Dryden; ultimately a poor writer for Mrs Mynn's booth, compelled in old age to roar in a dragon of his own invention, in a play founded on the tale of St George. These dramas are curiously indicative of popular tastes, filled with bombast interspersed with buffoonery, and gorgeous in dress and decoration. There is an anecdote on record of the proprietress of this show refusing to pay Oram, the scene-painter, for a splendid set of scenes he was engaged to paint, because he had used Dutch metal instead of leaf-gold in their decoration. Settle's *Siege of Troy* is a good specimen of these productions, and we are told in the preface, 'is no ways inferior to any one opera yet seen in either of the royal theatres.' One of the gorgeous displays offered to the sightseers is thus described: 'The scene opens and discovers Paris and Helen, fronting the audience, riding in a triumphant chariot, drawn by two white elephants, mounted by two pages in embroidered livery. The side-wings are ten elephants more, bearing on their backs open castles, umbrayed with canopies of gold; the ten castles filled with ten persons richly drest, the retinue of Paris; and on the elephants' necks ride ten more pages in the like rich dress. Beyond and over the chariot is seen a Vistoe* of the city of Troy, in the walls of which stand several trumpeters, seen behind and over the head of Paris, who sound at the opening of the scene.' Of course such magnificent people talk 'brave words,' like Ancient Pistol. Paris declares:

'Now when the tired world's long discords cease,  
We 'll tune our Trumps of War to Songs of Peace.  
Where Hector dragg'd in blood, I 'll drive around  
The walls of Troy; with love and laurels crown'd.'

All this magniloquence is relieved by comic scenes between a cobbler (with the appropriate name of Bristles) and his wife, one 'Captain Tom,' and 'a numerous train of Trojan mob.'

FAUX THE CONJUROR'S BOOTH.

The regular actors, as we have before observed, were transplanted to the fair during its continuance, and some of them were *pro-tem* proprietors and managers of the great theatrical booths. Penkethman, Mills, Booth, and Doggett were of the number. The great novelist, Henry Fielding, commenced his career as part-proprietor of one of these booths, continuing for nine years in company with Hippisley, the favourite comedian, and others. It was at his booth, in 1733, that the famous actress, Mrs Pritchard, made her great success, in an adaptation by Fielding, of Molière's *Cheats of Scapin*.

The fan-mount, already described, furnishes us with another representation of a booth in the fair; and it will be perceived that they were solid erections of timber, walled and roofed with planks, and perfectly weather-proof. In this booth 'Faux's dexterity of hand' is displayed, as well as a 'famous posture-master,' whose evolutions are exhibited in a picture outside the show. Faux was the Robert Houdin of his day, and is recorded to have died worth £10,000, which he had accumulated during his career. *The Gentleman's Magazine* for February 1731, tells us that the Algerine ambassadors visited him, and at their request he shewed them a view of Algiers, 'and raised up an apple-tree which bore ripe apples in less than a minute's time, which several of the company tasted of.' There was abundance of other shows to gratify the great British public; wild beasts, monsters, learned pigs, dwarfs, giants, *et hoc genus omne* abounded. 'A prodigious monster

the original; but inasmuch as 'The Siege of Gibraltar' is exhibited in one of the peep-shows, and that siege did not occur till 1727, the earlier date is assuredly wrong. This error was first pointed out by Mr Morley in his elaborate and beautiful volume, *Memoirs of Bartholomew Fair*, which contains 500 pages of curious reading for all who wish to go fully into its history and associations.

* A vista, or long perspective view.

is advertised, 'with one head and two distinct bodies;' and 'An admirable work of nature, a woman having three breasts.' Then there was to be seen, 'A child alive, about a year and a half old, that has three legs.' It appears that nobility and even royalty patronised these sights, thus 'The tall Essex woman,' in the reign of George I., 'had the honour to shew herself before their Royal Highnesses the Prince and Princess of Wales, and the rest of the royal family, last Bartholomew Fair.' A distinguished visitor is seen in our last engraving decorated with the ribbon and star of the Garter. The figure is by some supposed to represent the premier, Sir Robert Walpole, who was a frequent visitor to the fair; his attention is directed to Faux's booth by an attendant; but these figures may be intended to depict the Prince of Wales, who visited the fair in company with Rich, the manager and actor, who did duty as cicerone on the occasion.

The licence and riot which characterised the proceedings in Smithfield, at last aroused the civic authorities, and after much rioting and many ineffectual attempts, the fair was again limited to three days' duration, by a resolution of the court of common council in 1708. The theatrical booths were still important features in the fair, and in 1715, we hear of 'one great playhouse erected for the king's players—the booth is the largest that ever was built.' During the run of the *Beggar's Opera*, it was reproduced by Rayner and Pullen's company at the fair. In 1728, Lee and Harper produced a ballad-opera on the adventures of Jack Sheppard, and in 1730, another devoted to the popular hero—Robin Hood. Dramatic entertainments ultimately declined, but monstrosities never failed, and gratified the Londoners to the last day of the existence of the fair. Pig-faced ladies were advertised, if not seen; but learned pigs were never wanting, who could do sums in arithmetic, tell fortunes by cards, &c. Wild-beast shows ended in being the principal attraction, though they were the most expensive exhibitions in the fair; a shilling being charged for admission.

The mayor endeavoured to stem the irregularities of the fair in 1769, by appointing seventy-two officers to keep the peace and prevent gambling, as well as to hinder the performance of plays and puppet-shows. In 1776, the mayor refused permission to erect booths at all, which occasioned great rioting. Some years before this, the deputy-marshal lost his life in endeavouring to enforce order in the fair. The most dangerous rioters were a body of blackguards, who termed themselves 'Lady Holland's Mob,' and assembled to proclaim the fair after their own fashion, the night before the mayor did so. Hone says, 'the year 1822 was the last year wherein they appeared in any alarming force, and then the inmates of the houses they assailed, or before which they paraded, were aroused and kept in terror by their violence. In Skinner Street especially, they rioted undisturbed until between three and four in the morning: at one period that morning, their number was not less than five thousand, but it varied as parties went off or came in to and from the assault of other places. Their force was so overwhelming, that the patrol and watchmen feared to interfere, and the riot continued till they had exhausted their fury.'

The last royal visit to the fair took place in 1778, when the Duke and Duchess of Gloucester rode through it. Flockton's puppets were at this time a great attraction. Mr Lane, 'his majesty's conjuror,' and Mr Robinson, 'conjuror to the queen,' divided the attention of amateurs of their art. Polito's 'Grand collection of wild beasts' were brought from Exeter Change; 'The famous ram with six legs,' 'The unicorn ram,' 'The performing-serpents,' and other wonders in natural history, also invited visitors; as well as 'A surprising large fish,' affirmed to have 'had in her belly, when found, one thousand seven hundred mackerel.'

When Hone visited the fair in 1825, he saw, in a penny-show, the mermaid which had been exhibited about a year before in Piccadilly, at the charge of half-a-crown each person. This imposture was a hideous combination of a dried monkey's head and body, and the tail of a fish, believed to have been manufactured on the coast of China, and exhibited as the product of the seas there.* George Cruikshank has preserved its features, and we are tempted to reproduce his spirited etching.

THE MERMAID.

'A mare with seven feet' was a *lusus naturæ* also then exhibited, giants and dwarfs of course abounded, as they ever do at fairs!

Atkin's and Wombwell's menageries were the great shows of the fair in its expiring glory. They still charged the high price of one shilling admission. Richardson's theatre was the only successful rival in price and popularity—here was a charge of boxes 2*s*., pit 1*s*., gallery 6*d*.; but the deluded

* This was in the summer of 1822, and afterwards, when the price was reduced to a shilling, a contemporary journal described it as 'now the great source of attraction in the British metropolis; and three to four hundred people every day pay their shilling each, to see a disgusting sort of a compound animal, which contains in itself everything that is odious and disagreeable.' Though naturalists and journalists fully exposed the imposture, we are at the same time assured, that 'this circumstance does not appear to affect the exhibition, which continues as crowded as ever.'

exclusives who paid for box or pit seats, found on entering only a steep row of planks elevated above each other in front of the stage, without any distinction of parties, or anything to prevent those on the top row from falling between the supports to the bottom! Here, in the course of a quarter of an hour, a melodrama, with a ghost and several murders—a comic song by way of interlude, and a pantomime—were all got through to admiring and crowded audiences; by which the manager died rich.* Richardson was also proprietor of another 'show' in the fair; this was 'The beautiful spotted negro boy,' a child whose skin was naturally mottled with black, and whose form has been carefully delineated in a good engraving, here copied.

THE SPOTTED BOY.

He was a child of amiable manners, much attached to Richardson, who behaved with great kindness toward him; consequently both of them were in high favour with the public.† He was the last of the great natural curiosities exhibited there, for the fair gradually dwindled to death, opposed by the civic authorities and all decent people. It was at one time resolved to refuse all permission to remove stones from pavement or roadway, for the erection of booths; but the showmen evaded the restriction by sticking their poles in large and heavy tubs of earth. Then high ground-rents were fixed, which proved more effectual; and in 1850, when the mayor went as usual to Clothfair-gate to proclaim the opening of the fair, he found nothing awaiting to make it worth that trouble. No mayor went after, and until 1855, the year of its suppression, the proclamation was read by a deputy.

* Mr George Daniel, in his *Merrie England in the Olden Time*, says: 'The following account of Bartholomew Fair receipts, in 1828, may be relied on. Wombwell's Menagerie, £1700; Atkin's ditto, £1000; and Richardson's Theatre, £1200—the price to each being sixpence. Morgan's Menagerie, £150; admission, threepence. Balls, £80; Ballard, £89; Keyes, £20; Frazer, £26; Pike, £40; Pig-faced Lady, £150; Corder's Head, £100; Chinese Juggler's, £50; Fat Boy and Girl, £140; Salamander, £30; Diorama of Navarino, £60; Scotch Giant, £20. The admission to the last twelve shows varied from twopence to one halfpenny.'

† This remarkable child was born in the island of St Vincent, in 1808; his parents were natives of Africa, and both black; the child's skin and hair were spotted or mottled all over dark-brown and white; it was brought to Bristol when only fifteen months old, and an arrangement made with Richardson for its exhibition. The showman took an affectionate interest in the child, and had it christened Geo. Alex. Gratton. It lived to the age of four years and three-quarters, and was buried at Great Marlow, in Buckinghamshire, where a monument was placed to record its death and Richardson's attachment.

---

# AUGUST 25.

St Ebba or Tabbs, virgin and abbess, 683. St Gregory, abbot and confessor, 776. St Louis, king of France, 1270.

---

*Born.*—Charles Etienne Louis Camus, mathematician and author, 1699, *Crécy en Brie.*

*Died.*—Gratianus, Roman emperor, assassinated, 383, *Lyon;* Louis IX. of France (St Louis), 1270, *Tunis, Africa;* Henry VII., emperor of Germany, 1313, *Sienna;* Margaret of Anjou, queen of Henry VI. of England, 1482, *France;* Dr David Hartley, philosopher (*Observations on Man*), 1757, *Bath;* Thomas Chatterton, poet, 1770, *London;* David Hume, philosopher and historian, 1776, *Edinburgh;* James Watt, celebrated improver of the steam-engine, 1819, *Heathfield, near Birmingham;* Sir William Herschel, eminent astronomer, 1822, *Slough;* Daniel Stuart, noted improver of the newspaper-press, 1846.

## CHATTERTON.

The crowd through which we had to elbow our way, a few years ago, at the Manchester Art Exhibition, in order to get a sight of the picture of Chatterton, lying on his bed in his little London garret, set us thinking. It was not from any absolute merit in the picture, though that was great, that it attracted so many eyes. How was it then? No doubt the morbid feeling, which pushes through a crowd, to see the mangled remains of some traveller killed by an accident, drew some; doubtless that fondness for the horrible, which leads women to read all the tragic tales in newspapers, to the neglect of brilliant leading articles, drew many more; but in every connoisseur, more or less, there must have been mixed up a human sympathy with genius, and an interest in its fate, which the pitifulness of the sad history of the marvellous boy roused into activity.

Thomas Chatterton was born in Bristol, on the 20th of November 1752. His father was successively a writing-master, one of the cathedral choir, and master of a free school in the city, and died a short time before Chatterton was born; his mother, after her husband's death, supported herself by sewing, and keeping a small day-school. She seems to have been a very worthy and respectable person: beyond her fondness for her son, we hear little of her.

The boy, at first mistaken for a dunce, finally learned his letters from an old illuminated manuscript: then a change took place in him, and at eight years old, it is said, he would read without urging, and read anything and everything, from morning till night.

He was a moping boy. He would shut himself up in his bedroom, and cared for no companions. Sometimes, he would burst into tears; at others, stare in some one's face for many minutes together, without appearing to observe them. There were neighbours wise enough to see madness in these peculiarities, but none who discerned the self-absorption of genius. Indeed, until the lad was dead, no one seems to have regarded his eccentricities in that light.

In August 1760, being nearly eight years of age, Chatterton was admitted into a Bristol charity-school. While here, he would express disgust at being taught nothing but reading, writing, and arithmetic, and privately, though not neglecting school-tasks, turned his attention to other studies.

CHATTERTON.

He read incessantly, and amongst other acquirements, made himself an adept in heraldry. And when he could, he haunted the buildings and the meadows of St Mary Redcliffe, where he would lie and look fixedly at the church, as if he were 'in a kind of trance.' He betrayed an intense love of everything which was old. It is interesting to speculate as to what civilising influences the advantages of a classical education, if he had been so favoured, would have exercised over him.

Before he had been at this school three years, certain poems made their appearance. Some verses of his, on a sacred subject, figured in *Felix Farley's Bristol Journal* for January 8, 1763; in less than a year after this he indulged a satirical vein, to the exposure of hypocrisy. He was a precocious boy, and his genius developed itself with astounding rapidity.

Chatterton's next feat was to provide Mr Burgum, a pewterer, and 'fond of talking about his family,' with the following document: '*Account of the family of the De Berghams, from the Norman Conquest to this time, collected from Original Records, Tournament Rolls, and the Heralds of March and Garters' Records.* By Thomas Chatterton.' This account, though unfinished, gave great satisfaction, and procured Chatterton five shillings; upon which he produced a continuation of it to the time of Charles II., at which point he paused. In this last portion, appeared the name of a poet, John de Bergham, and, as a specimen of his style, a poem, *The Romaunte of the Cnyghte*, with a modern rendering. Where did this poem come from? it was asked. Chatterton answered—from the manuscripts and old parchments, which his father had taken from the chest called Canynge's chest, in St Mary Redcliffe's. That his father had taken such manuscripts was a known fact, and that Chatterton had the remains of them locked up in his garret, was admitted by his mother and sister: yet when foolish Mr Burgum went up to London with his pedigree to the Herald's office, after Chatterton's death, it appears that he was laughed at.

On the 1st of July 1767, Chatterton was made apprentice to Mr Lambert, an attorney. He slept with the footboy, and took his meals with the servants, and he never liked the place: he was very proud. But he had not much employment; so he pored over Spenser, and Chaucer, and old English chronicles, and scribbled satirical poems of a loose, irreligious tendency. Chatterton has been charged with dissolute habits, and Masson, in his *Story of the Year* 1770, produces a curious proof that there was some ground for the charge, so far as regarded some female companion; but little, if anything, has been clearly established. His habits were regular, his diet simple, his intimate friends few; let any precocious boy of sixteen, who never had a father, whose moral training has been deficient, and whose too prying intellect has ranged through so many books for and against religion, that it leans to infidelity—if he finds himself with strong passions, and without sin, first cast a stone.

In September 1768, Chatterton blazed out into notoriety. A new bridge superseded an old one, with appropriate ceremonies, and to *Felix Farley's Bristol Journal* a certain Dunhelmus Bristoliensis contributed a 'Description of the Mayor's first passing over the Old Bridge, taken from an old Manuscript.' Astonished antiquarians besieged the editor, and Dunhelmus Bristoliensis turned out to be Thomas Chatterton. The original was demanded, and Dunhelmus prevaricated. Upon this the boy was treated roughly; till, drawing himself up to the height of his proud self-assurance, he referred them to those same old relics in his garret, and obstinately retained the key.

The attention which he excited by these matters introduced Chatterton to the pewterer's partner, a Mr Catcott, and to Mr Barrett, a surgeon, both respectable men, and the latter at the time busy compiling a history of Bristol. From the stores in the garret the boy supplied both these worthy literati with matter at once curious and valuable. Mr Catcott was furnished with *The Bristowe Tragedy, Rowley's Epitaph*, and other pieces of ancient poetry, by Thomas Rowley, poet-laureate to 'Maistre Canynge,' the wealthy founder of St Mary Redcliffe, and quondam mayor of the city; and Mr Barrett with interesting information, hitherto unknown, to be used in his history.

Some specimens of the original parchments were also produced in the boy's more generous moments, and were never in the least suspected, although, as it appears, their antiquity will wash off with a sponge.

But ere long the ambitious boy grew much dissatisfied with Bristol. His friends remunerated him, indeed, but inadequately; and as he had a deep affection for his mother and sister, and a curious desire to provide them with articles of dress better than their wont, he tried other means of raising funds and becoming a notoriety. He first expresses his dissatisfaction with Mr Catcott by a little bill:

Mr G. Catcott,

To the exors. of T. Rowley,

| | | | |
|---|---|---|---|
| To pleasure rec[d] in read[g] his Historic works, . . | £5 | 5 | 0 |
| ——— his poetic works, . . . | 5 | 5 | 0 |
| | £10 | 10 | 0 |

Having given vent to his spleen by this humorous document, which was probably never sent, nor meant to be sent, he wrote to Dodsley, the London publisher. The old parchments, it seems, had proved by this time so productive, that he had by him quite a stock of poems by Thomas Rowley: these he offered to Dodsley for publication. But nothing could be made of Dodsley. Upon which it occurred to Chatterton that Horace Walpole, recently much deceived in certain poems, styled Ossian's, which the boy had read, might feel an interest in Rowley; upon which a correspondence was commenced. He began by sending Walpole a series of notices of ancient painters, for his *History of Painting*, and receives a letter of thanks. Upon this he sends other notices, and also accounts of hitherto unknown poets, with specimens of their style, and the mind of Walpole became uneasy. Nevertheless he waited, to see if any fresh material would turn up; upon which Chatterton, growing indignant at Mr Walpole's delay, and characteristically attributing the apparent neglect to his having confessed himself a poor woman's son, demanded his manuscripts. The author of *The Castle of Otranto* at once returned them, with a letter of advice about the extreme vileness of literary forging.

During this time the apprentice's views on religious subjects underwent further changes. He finally rejected Christianity, though not irreligiously. The man who draws and carries in his pocket articles of belief, entirely for his own private use, is in our opinion a religious man. Such a document, in Chatterton's handwriting, and much soiled, may be seen in the British Museum. Chatterton also, during this period, formed a connection with a London magazine, and wrote a considerable quantity of verse, chiefly satirical.

Early in 1770, Chatterton was dismissed from the service of Mr Lambert, and the occasion was this: In some strange humour of mind, made up of vexation and satirical spleen, with a temporary touch, it may be, of that infirmity, lunacy, under which his sister afterwards laboured, he penned a document professing to be his will, and 'wrote between 12 and 2 o'clock, Saturday, in the utmost distress of mind.' This will he enclosed in a letter to a Mr Clayfield, with information that the writer, by the time it should reach that gentleman, would 'be no more.' In some way or other this letter fell into Mr Lambert's hands, and a boy of seventeen, who could meditate suicide, was considered much too dangerous an individual to be retained in the house.

What object Chatterton had in composing this will, or whether, 'between 12 and 2 o'clock,' he was really in earnest about putting an end to his life, must remain an unsolved problem; but certainly a more singular document we never read. He satirises a few friends, in some fifty lines of verse; gives directions about his body and tombstone; furnishes inscriptions for the latter in French, Latin, and English; describes how his arms are to be quartered; leaves Mr Catcott his 'vigour and fire of youth;' the Rev. Mr Camplin his humility; his moderation 'to the politicians on both sides of the question;' and so on. Gleams of pathetic earnestness flash at intervals through the solemn banter:

'I give and bequeath to Mr Matthew Mease, a mourning-ring, with this motto—

*Alas, poor Chatterton!*

provided he pays for it himself.'

'I leave my mother and sister to the protection of my friends, if I have any.'

And one of his epitaphs, which, in fact, was afterwards adopted for his monument in Bristol, ran thus:

'To the Memory of

THOMAS CHATTERTON.

Reader, judge not; if thou art a Christian, believe that he shall be judged by a superior Power: to that Power alone is he now answerable.'

However, the end was not yet, for Chatterton went to London—with a friendly group, to see him start, let us mention, though it may seem somewhat of a reproach to his pride—and having found lodgings in Shoreditch—which he afterwards changed for No. 4 Brook Street, Holborn—proceeded with great assurance to look up his London correspondents—Dodsley and others. Chatterton's London career only extended over four months, and the records of his life during that period are obscure and untrustworthy. It is true that he sent glowing descriptions of his rising fame to friends in Bristol; it is true that he found money to purchase useless articles of finery for his mother and sister; and also that he did his utmost to form profitable connections; but that any large amount of success or remuneration encouraged his extraordinary efforts, is more than doubtful. He wrote political letters 'on both sides,' and numerous articles in prose and verse. At one time he seemed in a fair way to fame, for Beckford, lord mayor, received him with favour, and allowed him to dedicate an essay to him; but before the essay could appear, Beckford died. The accounts sent home to friends and relatives were probably chiefly intended to produce an impression that he could well afford to live without Bristol help. As an evidence of his scanty resources, we find a small memorandum extracted from his pocket-book:

| | | | |
|---|---|---|---|
| Received to May 23, of Mr Hamilton, for Middlesex, | £1 | 11 | 6 |
| of B. | 1 | 2 | 3 |
| of Fell, for the Consuliad [some 250 lines], | | 10 | 6 |
| of Mr Hamilton, for Candedus and Foreign Journal, | | 2 | 0 |
| of Mr Fell, | | 10 | 6 |
| Middlesex Journal, | | 8 | 6 |
| Mr Hamilton, *for* 16 *songs* (!!), | | 10 | 6 |
| | £4 | 15 | 9 |

There is tolerably clear proof that when he had sent home the finery for his mother and sister, and *the pipe for his grandmother*, Chatterton did not find himself many shillings in pocket. At length work failed him. Ere long he began to starve. He grew so sickly and famished in appearance, that his landlady, as also a neighbour, ventured, in spite of his pride, to offer him a meal. These ill-managed charities he indignantly refused. Once only, when the invitation must have been made with peculiar delicacy, did he sit down at another's table. Day after day he remained shut up in his room, and said he was not hungry; and, on the morning of the 25th of August 1770, he was found lying on his bed, stiff and cold, with remains of arsenic between his teeth. He was interred, after the inquest, in the paupers' burial-ground: at least so it was believed, but after-evidence went far to prove that his body was removed to Bristol, and secretly stowed away in the churchyard of St Mary Redcliffe. It will be remarked that the life of Chatterton, filled as it was with incident and a variety of works, extended to only seventeen years and three-quarters.

Pride will ruin angels, we are told, and pride destroyed Chatterton, who was not by any means an angel. He exhibited in his career extraordinary recklessness about the little niceties of literary morality. He could write, as we have seen, 'on either side' of a question; he could corrupt learned histories by forged documents; he could invent pedigrees; he could put his case in a letter, as he wished it to appear, without in the least being impeded by the stubborn facts; all which things, nevertheless, seem to us signs, not so much of a corrupt nature, as of a nature too rapidly developed in the midst of corruption, without adequate bias of moral training, joined to a pride of intellectual power, which led him to unloosen for himself all the ties of religion, and to despise his fellow-beings.

We say, to forge documents and invent pedigrees. We have traced the course of Chatterton's literary life without comment, and much controversy raged after his death as to the genuineness of the Rowley poems; but now the fact is universally admitted, that Chatterton himself was Thomas Rowley. It is indeed difficult to read the poems, with the least previous suspicion, without feeling the fact of their modernness take irresistible hold upon us. There is nothing ancient about them, except the spelling, and at times the phraseology. The great difficulty is, how did he write them? By moonlight, said his sister; in the Redcliffe meadows, says Masson; and both statements are true. Every man has two souls—an outer, which all men can read; an inner, which he hides. Every man lives two lives—a relative life, to suit his friends, his circumstances, his baser nature; and an essential life, which is his real life. The inner soul and essential life of Chatterton brooded purely and intensely over visions of noble truth and exquisite beauty, which he felt that he could share with none; and these, to keep them pure, he clothed in antique form; his outer and relative life led him to scatter round him, carelessly and recklessly, the lighter products of his pen, such as expressed the baser and evanescent passion or weakness of the moment, and which seemed to him good enough for those for whom they were intended.

## THE MONTYON PRIZE FOR VIRTUE.

On the 25th of August 1823, took place one of those distributions of the Montyon prizes which form so pleasant a feature in the social condition of France. The Baron de Montyon, or Monthyon, was a wealthy man, who, during the second half of the last century, occupied a distinguished place in the estimation of his countrymen; chiefly in various judicial capacities, in which his probity and honour were universally admitted. He established, at various periods of his life, no less than eight prizes, to be awarded to worthy recipients by the Académie des Sciences, the Académie Française, and the Faculté de Médecine. They were briefly as follows: In 1780, he invested 12,000 francs, the interest to be spent as an annual prize for inventions and discoveries useful in the arts. In 1782, he invested an equal sum, for an annual prize for any literary work likely to be most useful to society; and a similar one for lessening the unhealthiness of trades and manufactures. In 1783, another of equal amount for the benefit of the poor of Poitou and Berri; one for assisting poor men of letters; one for simplifying certain special mechanical arts; and one for rewarding acts of virtue among the poor. In 1787, and subsequent years, he established other prizes—all for good and worthy objects. The revolution drove him to Switzerland, and then to England, whence he did not return to France till 1815. His prize for virtue had been suppressed by the revolutionists; but he took care, by his will, to remodel it on a permanent and enlarged basis. This good man died in 1820, at the advanced age of eighty-seven.

The distribution in 1823 will serve as well as any other, to shew the mode in which the Montyon prize for virtue is awarded. Five prizes were given to five persons—four women and one man. One of the women, although her husband earned but sixteenpence a day, had taken into her house and supported a poor destitute female neighbour. Another, a milliner, had for twelve years supported the mistress under whom she had served as an apprentice, and who was afflicted with an incurable malady. A third had, in a similar way, supported for seventeen years a mistress under whom she had acted as a servant, and who had fallen into abject poverty. A fourth, who was a portress, had shewn her charity in a somewhat similar way. These four persons received one thousand francs each. But the chief prize was awarded to an old clothesman, Joseph Bécard. During the French Revolution, one M. Chavilliac, of Arras, had first been imprisoned, and then put to death. Many years afterwards, in 1812, his widow came to Paris, to obtain, if possible, some property which had belonged to her husband. In this she failed, and she was reduced to the lowest pitch of want. Bécard, when a servant to the Marquis de Steinfort, at Arras, had known the Chavilliacs as persons of some consideration in the place; and happening now to meet the poor lady in her adversity, he resolved to struggle for her as well as for himself, for grief had made her blind and helpless. He begged coarse food for himself, in order that he might buy better food for her out of his small incomings as an old clothesman. She became ill, and occupied the only bed he possessed; and he slept on a chair for three months—or rather kept resolutely awake during the greater part of the night, in order that he might attend upon the sick lady. Pain and suffering made her peevish and sour of temper; but he bore it all patiently, never once departing from his custom of treating her as a lady—higher in birth and natural condition than himself. This life continued for eleven years, she being the whole of the time entirely dependent on that noble-spirited but humble man. The lady died in May 1823. Bécard gave a small sum to a curé, to offer up prayers for her soul; he carved with his own hands a small wooden cross; and he placed it, together with an inscription, on her grave. Such was the man to whom the Académie Française, acting under the provisions of the Montyon bequest, awarded a prize of fifteen hundred francs, a gold medal, and honourable commendation in presence of the assembled academicians.

---

## AUGUST 26.

St Zephyrinus, pope and martyr, 219. St Gelasinus, martyr, 297. St Genesius (a comedian), martyr, end of 3d century. St Genesius of Arles, martyr.

*Born.*—Sir Robert Walpole (Earl of Orford), eminent statesman, 1676, *Houghton, Norfolk;* Prince Albert, consort of Queen Victoria, 1819.

*Died.*—Lopez Felix de la Vega, Spanish poet and dramatist, 1635, *Madrid;* Lord George Sackville, commander and statesman, 1785; Christopher Christian Sturm, author of the *Reflections*, 1786; Elizabeth Chudleigh, Duchess of Kingston, 1788, *France;* Karl Theodor Körner, martial lyrist, killed, 1813; Dr Adam Clarke, eminent divine and author, 1832, *Haydon Hall, Middlesex;* Louis Philippe, ex-king of France, 1850, *Claremont, Surrey.*

### LOPE DE VEGA'S EIGHTEEN HUNDRED PLAYS.

Lope de Vega, or more fully Lope Felix de Vega-Carpio, may be said to enjoy the distinction of having been the most fertile of all authors of imaginative literature. Born at Madrid in 1562, he was so precocious that, if we are to believe his disciple and biographer, Montalvan, he dictated poetry at five years old, before he could write. At seventeen, while in the university of Alcala, he wrote his dramatic romance of *Dorothea*, in which he depicted himself as one of the characters, leading a wild and dissolute life. Now a poet, now a soldier, now a courtier, now an adventurer, Lope appeared under various aspects—one of which was that of a subordinate officer in the far-famed Armada, which made a vain attempt to invade England. But wherever he was, and whatever other work he was engaged in, he always contrived to write poems and plays. After many more fluctuations in position, he became an ecclesiastic in 1609, and officiated in daily church-offices for the rest of his life. It will serve to illustrate the tone of moral and social life in Spain, at that time, that Lope de Vega not only continued to pour forth plays with amazing rapidity, but that some of them were very licentious in character. Poems, too, appeared in almost equal abundance: some sacred, some immoral; some based upon his own ideas, some in imitation of Dante, Petrarch, Tasso, or Boccaccio. The words seemed to flow almost spontaneously from his pen; for not only are his works almost incredibly numerous, but some of them are very long. One, called *Gatomachia, or the Battle of the Cats*—in which two cats quarrel and fight about a third—consists of no less than 2500 verses, 'rather long,' as one of his biographers admits, 'for a badinage.' If his chief productions had not been dramas, he would still have been one of the most prolific poets ever known; but his plays far outnumbered his poems, and were the means of giving something like nationality to the Spanish drama. In 1603, when forty-one years of age, he found that his dramatic compositions reached the number of 341; it swelled to 483 in 1609, about 800 in 1618, nearly 900 in 1619, 1070 in 1624, and 1800 at the time of his death (August 26, 1635). According to ordinary experience, this would be almost incredible; but we must believe that the dramas were mostly very short. Montalvan, one of the biographers of Lope de Vega, states that, while at Toledo, Lope wrote five dramas in a fortnight; and that half a morning was often enough for him to produce an entire act of a play. It is asserted that every one of these 1800 plays was acted in his lifetime. No less than 500 of them have been printed, and occupy a place among the literature of Spain. Some of them are interludes, or short farces in prose; but the greater number are comedies in verse, mostly in three portions or acts. Of no other writer can it be said that his printed plays fill twenty-six quarto volumes (published between 1609 and 1647); and yet that his *un*published plays were nearly thrice as many. Lope de Vega gave that tone to the Spanish drama, brilliant but immoral, which has been made so familiar to the public by the various forms of *Don Juan* and the *Barber of Seville*.

### THE DUCHESS OF KINGSTON.

As an example of the *adventuress*, amid several notabilities of a like kind, in the earlier half of the reign of George III., Elizabeth Chudleigh, Duchess of Kingston, is prominently distinguished. She was the daughter of Colonel Chudleigh, a gentleman of good family in Devonshire, who, through his friendship with Mr Pulteney, obtained for his daughter the post of maid of honour to the Princess of Wales, mother of George III. Her natural talents and attractions were here cultivated and developed, and the charms of her manners and conversation soon surrounded her with a host of distinguished and enthusiastic admirers. One of the most conspicuous of these was the Duke of Hamilton, who made her an offer of his hand, and was accepted. Circumstances, however, prevented their immediate union; the parties agreed to hold themselves as engaged, and the duke set out on a tour on the continent, from which he regularly corresponded with Miss Chudleigh. In the meantime, Captain Hervey, son of the Earl of Bristol, came forward as a suitor, under the auspices of Miss Chudleigh's aunt, Mrs Hanmer, who is said to have intercepted the Duke of Hamilton's letters, and otherwise exerted her influence to the utmost with her niece, to induce her to discard him for the captain. A volatile and impetuous disposition, guided apparently by no high or abiding principle, induced Miss Chudleigh, without much difficulty, to receive Hervey's addresses, and they were privately married at Lainston, near Winchester. This ill-advised step proved the foundation of all her subsequent perplexities. Fearing the effects of his father's anger, Captain Hervey dared not venture to acknowledge his marriage, and his wife had to endure all the inconveniences which a woman must submit to, who is placed in such a position. She seems almost immediately after the conclusion of the match, to have repented of her precipitancy. Indifference was followed by positive aversion, and though one son was born of the union, who soon quitted the world, as he had entered it, in secrecy and obscurity, a lasting estrangement took place between the parents. Captain Hervey, whose jealousy was violently excited by the attentions paid to his wife as Miss Chudleigh, gradually changed his line of conduct, and threatened to proclaim their marriage to the public, whilst she became only more determined to find some pretext for its legal dissolution. With this view, she is said to have gained access to the register in which her wedding was recorded, and destroyed the evidence of it, by tearing out the leaf. The officiating clergyman was now dead. But not long afterwards, her husband succeeded, by the death of his father, to the earldom of Bristol, upon which a revulsion took place in her crooked policy, and she contrived, by bribing the officiating clerk, to get her marriage reinserted in the same register from which she had previously torn the record. So far for the first acts of this singular drama.

From the aristocratic circles amid which Miss Chudleigh reigned as queen, the Duke of Kingston now stepped forth, and proffered her his hand. He appears to have possessed many good qualities, being mild and unassuming in his manners, the very reverse of his mistress, whose love of admiration had been the great occasion of her errors. There can be no doubt that an illicit intercourse had subsisted for some time betwixt them; but the duke's attachment to her seems to have been sincere. The Earl of Bristol had now himself become desirous of severing his nuptial ties, and he therefore was readily induced to concur in a process of jactitation of marriage in the ecclesiastical courts, which, by an adroit suppression of evidence, terminated in a decree of nullification. The path being thus, in their opinion, cleared, the union of the duke and Miss Chudleigh was publicly solemnised. For some years the duchess basked in all the sunshine of wealth and exalted position, when at last her husband died. By his will the duke was found to have devised his estates to one of his younger nephews, excluding the heir at law, and bequeathing to his wife the enjoyment of the rents of the property during her life. The duchess being aware of the contents of the will, and of certain restrictions which had been imposed on her marrying again, had endeavoured, though ineffectually, to procure before the duke's death the execution of a more favourable deed. The elder nephew, whose claims to the succession had been ignored, resolved to dispute the validity of his uncle's will. Through information received from a Mrs Cradock, who had been one of the witnesses to the marriage of Miss Chudleigh with Captain Hervey, and had afterwards, as she deemed, been rather shabbily treated by the duchess, he instituted against the latter an indictment for bigamy. She had previously to this quitted the kingdom for the continent, but on receiving intelligence of these proceedings, deemed it prudent to return to England, to avoid an outlawry. The trial commenced on 15th April 1776, before the House of Peers, in Westminster Hall, which was filled by a distinguished audience, including Queen Charlotte and several members of the royal family. The evidence of the marriage with Captain Hervey having been produced, and the whole matter carefully sifted, the peers unanimously found the duchess guilty of bigamy, with the exception of the Duke of Newcastle, who pronounced her guilty 'erroneously but not intentionally.' The consequences of this sentence would have been the issuing of a writ *Ne exeat regno* to prevent her quitting the country, but before it could be completed, she contrived to escape to Calais, from which she never returned. The heirs of the Duke of Kingston, having thus succeeded in nullifying his marriage, now endeavoured to get his will set aside; but in this they were thoroughly unsuccessful. The duchess was left to the undisturbed enjoyment of her large income, which she dissipated in the indulgence of all sorts of luxury. She had already purchased a house at Calais, but it was inadequate to her ideas of splendour, and she accordingly entered into terms for the purchase of another at Montmartre, in the suburbs of Paris. A dispute with the owner of this property gave rise to a litigation, during the dependence of which she made a journey to St Petersburg, and there entered into some speculations connected with the distilling of brandy. She subsequently returned to France, and became the purchaser of a fine domain in the neighbourhood of Paris, belonging to a brother of Louis XVI., the reigning sovereign The investment proved a good one, the immense number of rabbits on the property furnishing a most lucrative return. As much as 300 guineas is said to have been realised by her from this source alone in the first week of her possession. But the end was now approaching. In the midst of this temporal prosperity, intelligence was one day brought her, that judgment had been pronounced against her in the suit regarding the house at Montmartre. So great an agitation was produced on her by this news, that she ruptured a blood-vessel, and was obliged to confine herself to her bed. In the course of a few days she seemed to rally, and insisted on getting up and having herself dressed. Her attendant vainly endeavoured to dissuade her, and she then called for a glass of Madeira, which she drank, and insisted on a second being brought. This also she drank off, and then said she should like to lie down. Having stretched herself on a couch, she soon appeared to fall asleep, and remained in this state for some time, when her servants felt an unusual coldness in her hands, and on examining more closely, found that she had passed away. Such was her end, to die among strangers in a foreign land—a fitting termination, perhaps, to her chequered and singular career.

One circumstance in connection with the Duchess of Kingston ought not to be passed over in silence. We allude to her well-known *fracas* with Mr Foote. That celebrated wit and dramatist, who derived a considerable portion of his fame from the personalities which he introduced into his literary lucubrations, produced a farce, entitled *A Trip to Calais*, in which he brought forward the duchess under the title of 'Lady Kitty Crocodile.' His procedure in this transaction reflects little credit either on his character as a man or policy as a schemer. The duchess would have willingly paid him a handsome sum to withdraw the piece; but, in the hopes of obtaining a larger consideration, he out-manœuvred himself; whilst she, by her interest with parties in power, contrived to have the representation of the play interdicted by the lord-chamberlain, and also its publication, for the time at least, prevented.

## BATTLE OF CRECY—WERE CANNON FIRST EMPLOYED THERE?

This extraordinary conflict, to which the English for ages looked back as they have latterly looked back to Waterloo, was fought on the 26th of August 1346, in an angle of ground lying between the river Somme and the sea, in Picardy. Edward III. had invaded France, in pursuit of his imagined right to the throne, and for some weeks conducted his small army along the valley of the Seine, in considerable danger from the much larger one of Philip, the French king. At length he made a stand on a favourable piece of ground at the village of Crecy, and awaited in calmness and good order the precipitate and disorderly attack of the opposite host. By virtue of coolness and some hard fighting, he gained the battle, and was able to destroy an immense number of the enemy. The prowess shewn on the occasion by his son the Black Prince, and other particulars of the well-fought field, are generally familiar to the readers of English history.

It is said there is still to be seen upon the field a tower-like wind-mill, which existed at the time of the action, and marking the station of the English king.

There is a doubtful statement, to the effect that cannon were first used in military encounter at the Battle of Crecy. It must be considered as liable to great doubt. Our own chroniclers make no allusion to such a circumstance; neither is it mentioned in the ordinary copies of Froissart, although his account of the battle is remarkably ample and detailed. It has been surmised that only some comparatively recent French writers have introduced the assertion into their narratives, as a sort of excuse for the panic which the troops of King Philip exhibited on the occasion. On the other hand, there appears to be a manuscript copy of Froissart, preserved at Amiens, from which the present emperor of France has quoted the following passage in his work on artillery: 'Et li Angles descliquèrent aucuns canons qu'il avaient en la bataille pour esbahir les Genevois.' And it is alleged that Villani, a contemporary Italian writer, states that cannon were used by the English at Crecy.* If these statements are correct, we may consider it established that artillery—though probably of a very simple and portable kind—were first employed on this interesting occasion.

## 'THE MARRIAGE OF THE ARTS.'

On Sunday, the 26th of August 1621, a comedy, entitled *Technogamia, or the Marriage of the Arts*, written by Barton Holiday, M. A., of Christ's Church, Oxford, was performed by students of the same college, before James I. at Woodstock. As a typical specimen of the allegorical piece of the olden time, this drama is not unworthy of notice. The *dramatis personæ* consist of Polites, a magistrate; Physica, and her daughter Astronomia; Ethicus, with his wife Economa; Geographicus, a traveller, with his servant Phantastes; Logicus, and his servant Phlegmaticus; Grammaticus, a schoolmaster, and his usher Choler; Poeta, and his servant Melancholia; Medicus, and his servant Sanguis; Historia; Rhetorica; Geometres; Arithmetica; Musica; Causidicus; Magus, and his wife Astrologia; Physiognomus and Cheiromantes, two cheating gipsies. All these are attired in goodly and appropriate fashion. Astronomia, for instance, wearing 'white gloves and pumps, an azure gown, and a mantle seeded with stars; on her head a tiara, bearing on the front the seven stars, and behind stars promiscuously; on the right side, the sun; on the left, the moon.' Astronomia is the brilliant heroine of the play—the heaven to which Geographicus aspires to travel, of which Geometres endeavours to take the measure, in which Poeta desires to repose. On the other hand, Arithmetica has a more natural passion for Geometres, and Historia anxiously wishes to be united to Poeta. Grammaticus, in an amorous mood, solicits Rhetorica, whose flowers bloom only for Logicus. These conflicting attachments cause great confusion in the commonwealth of learning; each of the enamoured personages endeavouring to obtain the object of his or her affections. Polites assists Geographicus; Magus employs his occult art in favour of Geometres; while the Nine Muses, as in duty bound, assist Poeta. Polites can with difficulty keep the peace. The gipsies, Physiognomus and Cheiromantes, pick Poeta's pocket, but find nothing therein but a copy of Anacreon and a manuscript translation of Horace. Physiognomus is appropriately branded on the face, that all men may know him to be a rogue; and Cheiromantes receives the same punishment on the hand; and the two, with Magus and Astrologia, who had attempted to strangle Astronomia, are justly banished the commonwealth of the Sciences. Then Geographicus, discharging his servant Phantastes, marries Astronomia; Grammaticus espouses Rhetorica; Melancholia obtains the hand of Musica, and takes Phantastes into his service; Logicus, old and heartless, being left without a mate, becomes an assistant to Polites; and thus peace and harmony is restored among the Sciences. There is

* See *Notes and Queries*, x. 306, 412, 534.

considerable ingenuity displayed in the invention of this plot, the dialogue is witty, and the professors of the sciences represented are humorously satirised.

One would have supposed, that the pedantic spirit of James would have been delighted with this production, but such was not the case. Anthony à Wood tells us that the king 'offered several times to withdraw, but being persuaded by some of those that were near him to have patience till it were ended, lest the young men should be discouraged, [he] adventured it, though much against his will.' And the Cambridge students, pleased that the Oxford drama did not interest the king, produced the following epigram:

'At Christ-church marriage, played before the king,
Lest these learned mates should want an offering,
The king, himself, did offer—What, I pray?
He offered twice or thrice to go away.'

It is not difficult to perceive what it was that displeased the king. Phlegmaticus was dressed 'in a pale russet suit, on the back whereof was represented one filling a pipe of tobacco, his hat beset round about with tobacco-pipes, with a can of drink hanging at his girdle.' He entered, exclaiming: 'Fore Jove, most meteorological tobacco! Pure Indian! not a jot sophisticated; a tobacco-pipe is the chimney of perpetual hospitality. Fore Jove, most metropolitan tobacco.' And then, rather unphlegmatically, he broke out into the following song:

Tobacco's a Musician,
And in a pipe delighteth;
It descends in a close,
Through the organs of the nose,
With a relish that inviteth.
This makes me sing, So ho, so ho, boys,
Ho, boys, sound I loudly;
Earth ne'er did breed
Such a jovial weed,
Whereof to boast so proudly.

Tobacco is a Lawyer,
His pipes do love long cases;
When our brains it enters,
Our feet do make indentures;
While we seal with stamping paces,
This makes me sing, &c.

Tobacco's a Physician,
Good both for sound and sickly;
'Tis a hot perfume,
That expels cold rheum,
And makes it flow down quickly.
This makes me sing, &c.

Tobacco is a Traveller,
Come from the Indies hither;
It passed sea and land,
Ere it came to my hand,
And 'scaped the wind and weather,
This makes me sing, &c.

Tobacco is a Critic,
That still old paper turneth,
Whose labour and care,
Is as smoke in the air,
That ascends from a rag when it burneth.
This makes me sing, &c.

Tobacco's an Ignis-fatuus,
A fat and fiery vapour,
That leads men about,
Till the fire be out,
Consuming like a taper.
This makes me sing, &c.

Tobacco is a Whiffler,*
And cries huff snuff with fury,
His pipe's his club and link,
He's the wiser that does drink; †
Thus armed I fear not a fury.
This makes me sing, So ho, so ho, boys,
Ho, boys, sound I loudly;
Earth ne'er did breed
Such a jovial weed,
Whereof to boast so proudly.

The royal author of the *Counterblast to Tobacco* must have felt himself insulted by such a song. Ben Jonson was wiser, when, in his *Gipsies' Metamorphosis*, he abused 'the devil's own weed,' in language totally unpresentable at the present day; and the delighted monarch ordered the filthy, slangy, low play, to be performed three several times in his kingly presence.

## THE LAST OF THE ARCTIC VOYAGERS.

The nation has given £20,000 in prizes to the gallant men who have solved (so far as it is yet solved) the problem of the North-West Passage—that is, a navigable channel from the Atlantic to the Pacific round the northern margin of America. There were twenty-two attempts made to discover such a passage in the sixteenth century, twenty in the seventeenth, and twenty-one in the eighteenth—nearly the whole of these sixty-three attempts being made by natives of this country, and most of them without any material aid from the government. In the present century, the regular arctic expeditions, planned and supported by the government, began in 1817; and during the next forty years, Parry, John Ross, James Ross, Back, Franklin, Lyons, Beecher, Austin, Kellett, Osborne, Collinson, M'Clure, Rae, Simpson, M'Clintock, and other gallant men, made those discoveries which cost the nation more than a million sterling, besides many valuable lives. Sir John Franklin headed one of the expeditions; and his stay being strangely protracted, ships were sent out in search of him year after year. Captain M'Clure did not obtain any information concerning poor Franklin's fate; but he made such discoveries as justify us in asserting that *a North-West Passage is found.* So far back as 1745, parliament offered a reward of £20,000 to the discoverer of the much-coveted passage; this reward was never paid or claimed, and its offer was withdrawn in 1828; but Parry and John Ross each received £5000, in recognition of what they had done—leaving to the country to reward other discoverers as it might choose.

The reasons why Captain (afterwards Sir Robert) M'Clure may be considered as having practically solved the problem, may be stated in a few words. In 1850, Captains M'Clure and Collinson were sent out in the *Investigation* and the *Enterprize*, to assist in searching for Sir John Franklin and his hapless companions. They proceeded by the Pacific to Behring's Strait, and thence worked their way eastward to the frozen regions. Collinson's labours were confined chiefly to such open water as could be found close to the American shores; but M'Clure pushed forward in a more northern route. What he endured during four

* A person who cleared the way for processions by flourishing or *whiffling* a sword.

† The old phrase for smoking, was drinking tobacco.

years, mostly in regions where no civilised man had ever before been, his narrative must tell—so far as *any* narrative can do justice to such labour. He returned to England from Davis's Strait in the autumn of 1854. True, he had to leave his ship behind him, hopelessly locked in among mountains of ice; and he had to walk and sledge over hundreds of miles of ice to reach other ships which had entered the frozen regions in the opposite direction; but still he had *water under him* all the way; and he was thus the first commander of a vessel who really made the passage. A 'navigable' passage it certainly was not, in the proper meaning of the term, but still it solved the main problem. In 1855, a committee of the House of Commons investigated the matter, and decided that a grant of £10,000 should be made for this discovery—making, with the £5000 given to Parry, and a sum of equal amount to John Ross, a total of £20,000; equivalent to that which, more than a century earlier, had been offered for the discovery of this North-West Passage. Parliament and the government agreeing to this, the £10,000 was paid to the hardy explorers in August 1855—£5000 to Captain M'Clure himself, and £5000 to his officers and crew.

This was entirely distinct from the reward given —not for the discovery of the North-West Passage —but for any authentic tidings of the fate of Sir John Franklin. After an enormous sum had been spent in fitting out expeditions for the last-named purpose, the government offered £20,000 to any one who should 'discover and effectually relieve the crews of H. M. ships *Erebus* and *Terror*' (those which Franklin commanded); £10,000 to any one who 'should give such intelligence as might lead to the succour of the crews of those ships;' and £10,000 to any person who should, 'in the judgment of the Board of Admiralty, first succeed in ascertaining the fate of those crews.' The first and second of these prizes were never earned; but the third prize was given in 1856 to Dr Rae, who, by a daring overland journey from the Hudson Bay Company's Settlements, found circumstantial, though not unmistakable evidences of the deplorable deaths of Franklin and some of his companions. The investigation was continued by Captain M'Clintock in 1858 and 1859, and Dr Rae's discovery was certified. The researches of former expeditions were confirmed by Hall in 1869, and Lieutenant Schwatka in 1879. The latter found numerous relics of the Franklin expedition on the west coast of King William's Land. The bones of several of these heroes, who had died on the eve of the discovery of the North-West Passage, were carefully buried; the remains of Lieutenant Irving, third officer of the *Terror*, were transmitted to Edinburgh, and reinterred there, January 7, 1881.

# AUGUST 27.

St Pœman or Pastor, abbot, about 451. St Cæsarius, archbishop of Arles, confessor, 542. St Syagrius, bishop of Autun, 600. St Malrubius, hermit and martyr in Scotland, about 1040. St Hugh of Lincoln, martyr, 1255. St Joseph Calasanctius, confessor, 1648.

*Born.*—William Woollett, engraver, 1735, *Maidstone*.

*Died.*—Pope Sixtus V., 1590; James Thomson, poet, 1748, *Richmond;* Dr John Jortin, critic, 1770; Countess Craven (*née* Louisa Brunton), once a favourite actress, 1860; J. H. Foley, R.A., eminent sculptor, 1874.

## POPE SIXTUS V.

Many of the popes have been of the humblest extraction. Pope Sixtus V. was the son of a poor pig-dealer at Montalto—born there in 1521. It may fairly be said that no occupant of the Holy See has ever left a stronger mark upon his age. Elizabeth upon the throne of England, Henry IV. upon that of France, and Sixtus V. upon that of Rome, was a wonderful cluster of great sovereigns for one period. Having, as a cardinal, long appeared imbecile, he was elected by the concurrent voices of several who hoped to reign in his name, and knew they could not individually command a majority. It seemed, too, as if so feeble and sickly a man could not long postpone another election. When at length informed that he was pope, Sixtus threw by his staff, smoothed away his wrinkles, and joined the *Te Deum* with a voice so powerful as to make his electors tremble. He at the same time informed them that his age was seven years less than had been supposed. Immediately there commenced an administration of extraordinary vigour. The banditti perished and disappeared before the sternness of his justice. He entered upon wonderful measures for the decoration of Rome. He excommunicated several Protestant princes; yet afterwards, it is said, coming to know Henry of France, and Elizabeth of England, conceived a respect for them both, and actually won one over to the Romish Church. Of Elizabeth, he characteristically remarked: 'She is a *big-head* —that queen. Could I have espoused her, what a breed of great princes we might have had!'

His severity to the vicious had something eccentric in it. While making adultery a capital crime, he extended the same punishment to a husband who did not complain. It seemed, too, as if a cruel disposition made him take a positive pleasure in the infliction of death. 'I wish justice to be done before dinner,' he said to the governor of Rome; 'so make haste, for I am very hungry.' On one occasion, when some friends of a Spanish gentleman-criminal pleaded that, if he must die, it should be by decapitation: 'No,' said Sixtus, 'he shall be hanged, but I will ennoble his execution by attending it myself.' He looked on attentively, and declared the affair had given him a good appetite. It was to him a recommendation for a judgeship, if the candidate had a severe countenance. He was full of jokes about his own severity. Some people pleading for mercy to a criminal of sixteen—alleging that the execution of so young a person was not according to law—the holy father only replied: 'I will give him ten of my own years to make him subject to the law;' and, of course, the lad suffered.

On the whole, he was one of the greatest of the popes, and no one can visit Rome without becoming aware how much it owes to him.

## LANDING OF CÆSAR IN BRITAIN.

Sunday, the 27th of August, 55 B.C., may, upon good grounds, be set down as the day on which Cæsar invaded the island of Britain. His own account of the event being vague and general, there has been room for discussion both as to the place where, and the day on which, the landing was effected. In a late volume, however, by a very painstaking and ingenious inquirer,* both points are tolerably well determined, as it also is that the Roman commander embarked on his expedition at the port since called Boulogne, using the adjacent lesser harbour of Ambleteuse for shipping his cavalry.

The day is thus ascertained. Cæsar himself tells that he proceeded on his expedition when little of summer remained—when the people of the south of Britain were engaged in their harvest—and we learn that he returned three weeks after, *before the equinox.* Thus, the day must have been in August. He further tells us that the full moon occurred on the fourth day after his landing. The full moon of August in that year is ascertained from astronomical tables to have been at 3 A.M. of the 31st. Hence Cæsar landed on the 27th. He had set out from Boulogne at midnight, with 8000 men in 80 transports, besides a few swift-moving war-galleys or trirémes, and arrived at a point near the British coast about ten in the forenoon.

He found himself in front of a bold coast, covered by enemies who could throw their javelins from the higher ground to the shore. The description answers to the well-known high chalk-cliffs between Sandgate and the South Foreland. He necessarily made a lateral movement to find a more favourable place of landing, and wind and tide enabled him to do so. The question is, was it eastward to Deal, or westward towards Hythe. It has very generally been assumed that he took the former course, and landed at Deal. But Mr Lewin shews that the tide which enabled Cæsar to make this movement did not go in that direction. High water at Dover on the 27th of August, 55 B.C., was at 7.31 A.M. Four hours later, the tide would begin, as it now does, to move westward, and would so continue for seven hours. Cæsar, therefore, in his shift of place that afternoon, went westward—namely, towards Hythe. There we find in Romney Marsh precisely such a plain as that on which he describes himself as having landed. Mr Lewin conjectures that the name Romney may have been affixed to the place in commemoration of its having been the site of the first encampment made by the Romans on the British shore.

It is well known that Cæsar met with greater difficulty in landing and making good his first footing on the island than he expected. The truth is, although we, as well as he, are apt to forget or be ignorant of it, that the southern Britons were a people well advanced in a native civilisation at the time of Cæsar's invasion. 'In the first place,' says Mr Lewin, 'there was a crowded population, which is never found in a state of barbarism. Even in literary attainments the Britons were in advance of the Gauls, for the priests are universally the depositaries of learning, and the Gauls were in the habit of sending their youth to Britain, to perfect themselves in the knowledge of Druidism. Then there was great commercial intercourse carried on between Britain and Gaul, not to mention that a partial trade existed between Britain and more distant nations, as the Phœnicians. It was only about a century after this that London, by its present name, was a city crowded with merchants and of world-wide celebrity. The country also to the south had been cleared of its forests, and was under the plough. . . . . But I do not know a greater confirmation of British advancement than the circumstance mentioned by Cæsar, that when he made war upon the Veneti, to the west of Gaul, the Britains sent a fleet of ships to their assistance.'

* *The Invasion of Britain by Julius Cæsar.* By Thomas Lewin, Esq., M.A. London, 1859.

## BURNING OF MILTON'S BOOKS BY THE HANGMAN.

Milton was all his life a liberal, in the best sense of the word, resisting with his powerful pen the encroachments of unwarrantable power, whether political or ecclesiastical. When the restoration of Charles II. became imminent, Milton's position was perilous. Amongst other books, his *Iconoclastes* and his *Defensio pro Populo Anglicano*, contained sentiments which Charles and his court could not be expected to tolerate. In 1660, just before Charles's return, Milton added another to his many works against monarchy, in a letter addressed to General Monk, under the title of *The Ready and Easy Way to Establish a Free Commonwealth;* and he also combated the reasonings of one Dr Matthew Griffith, in *Brief Notes upon a Late Sermon, titled The Fear of God and the King.* All would not do, however; the people were wearied of the Commonwealth, and welcomed Charles home again. Milton felt that he could not safely appear in public at this crisis. He quitted his home in Petty France, and sought an asylum with a friend in Bartholomew Close. Many writers have said that his friends got up a mock-funeral for him, to keep him well out of sight; and that when this fact came to the ears of Charles, the 'Merry Monarch' laughed heartily, and 'applauded his policy in escaping the punishment of death by a seasonable show of dying.' Whether this were or were not the case, no very diligent search appears to have been made for him. 'There were among the royalists,' says Mr Keightley, 'men of humanity who could feel compassion for him, who was deprived of nature's prime blessing [Milton had then been quite blind about seven years], and men of taste who were capable of admiration for exalted genius.'* But, although Milton escaped, his books did not. On the 16th of June 1660, the House of Commons passed a resolution, that his majesty should be 'humbly moved to call in Milton's two books [the *Iconoclastes* and the *Defensio*], and that of John Goodwin [*The Obstructors of Justice*], written in justification of the murder of the late king, and order them to be burned by the common hangman; and that the attorney-general do proceed against them by indictment or otherwise.' On the 27th of August following, as many copies of the three offending books as could be met with, were publicly burned, in conformity with this resolution. During the intervening ten weeks a proclamation appeared, in which it was stated that 'the said John Milton and John Goodwin are so fled, or so obscure themselves, that no endeavours used for their apprehension can take effect, whereby they may be brought to legal tryal, and deservedly receive condign punishment for their treasons and offences.' As has just been said, however, there is reason to believe that the search

* *Life, Opinions, and Writings of Milton.*

was purposely allowed to slacken; and within three days after the burning of the books, an act of indemnity relieved the poet from any further necessity for concealment.

---

# AUGUST 28.

St Hermes, martyr, about 132. St Julian, martyr at Brioude. St Augustine or Austin, bishop of Hippo, confessor, and doctor of the church, 430.

## ST AUGUSTINE.

St Augustine, usually styled 'the greatest of the fathers,' is held in about equal reverence by Catholics and Protestants. Calvinists and Jansenists especially have resorted to his writings for sympathy and authority.

Augustine was an African, being born at Tagaste, a city of Numidia, in 354. His father was a pagan, and his mother, Monica, a Christian of earnest piety, who longed with exceeding desire for her son's conversion. In his boyhood, falling seriously ill, he desired to submit to the rite of baptism, but, the danger being averted, the rite was deferred. As he grew up, his morals became corrupted, and he lapsed into profligate habits. The perusal, in his nineteenth year, of Cicero's *Hortensius* (a work now lost), made a deep impression on his mind, and stirred within him aspirations after a nobler life. At this juncture he became a convert of the Manichæans, and for nine years an able advocate of their opinions. The Manichæans were a sect founded by one Manes about 261. He confounded the teaching of Christ with that of Zoroaster, and held that the government of the universe was shared by two powers, one good and the other bad: the first, which he called Light, did nothing but good; the second, which he called Darkness, did nothing but evil. Meanwhile, Augustine taught grammar at Tagaste, and then rhetoric at Carthage, but growing disgusted with the vicious character of his pupils, he determined to go to Rome, much against the will of his mother. In Rome he attracted many scholars, but finding them no better than on the other side of the Mediterranean, he removed to Milan, where he was elected professor of rhetoric. The intrepid Ambrose ruled at that time as archbishop in Milan, and by his ministry Augustine was delivered from the Manichæan heresy. The vacation of 386, he spent at the country-seat of his friend Verecundus, in the diligent study of the Scriptures; and, in the Easter of the following year, he, with his son Adeodatus, a youth of singular genius, was baptized by Ambrose. Shortly after, his faithful mother, rejoicing in the fulfilment of her prayers, visited Milan, and persuaded him to return to Africa, but on their way thither she fell sick, and died at Ostia. Augustine, associating himself with eleven pious men, retired to a villa outside the walls of Hippo, and passed three years in monastic seclusion, in fasting, prayer, study, and meditation. He entered the priesthood in 391; and at a church council he spoke with such vigour and learning that he was, with common consent, raised to the bishopric of Hippo in 396. In defence and illustration of the Christian faith, his tongue and pen during the remainder of his life were incessantly engaged. The composition of his great work, *De Civitate Dei*, is believed to have occupied him seventeen years. In 430, the Vandals, having overrun Africa, laid siege to Hippo, and Augustine, an old man of seventy-six, prayed for death ere the city was taken. In the third month of the siege, on the 28th of August, a fever cut him off. When the city, some months after his death, was captured and burned, the library was fortunately saved which contained his voluminous writings—two hundred and thirty-two separate books or treatises on theological subjects, besides a complete exposition of the psalter and the gospels, and a copious magazine of epistles and homilies. The best account of Augustine is found in his *Confessions*, in which, with unflinching and sorrowful courage, he records the excesses of his youth and the progress of his life in Christ.

---

## RESISTANCE TO FIRE.

The Augustinian or Austin Friars took their name from the holy bishop of Hippo. Camerarius, in his *Horæ Subsecivæ*, tells a curious story, relating to the decision of a controversy, between this brotherhood and the Jesuits. It appears that, one day, the father-general of the Augustinians, with some of his friars, was receiving the hospitality of a Jesuits' college; on the cloth being removed, he entered into a formal discourse on the super-excellence of his order, in comparison with that of the Jesuits; insisting particularly on the surpassing discipline of the friars, caused by their more stringent and solemn vows of obedience. The Augustinian, being very eloquent, learned, and a skilled debater, had the best of the argument; but the superior of the Jesuits, foreseeing the discussion, had prepared to meet his opponent in another fashion. Words, he replied, were mere wind, but he could at once give a decided and practical, if not miraculous proof, of the more implicit obedience and greater sanctity of the Jesuits. 'I shall be very glad to witness such a proof,' sneeringly replied the unwary Augustinian. 'Then,' said the Jesuit to one of his inferiors, 'Brother Mark, my hands are cold, fetch me some fire from the kitchen to warm them. Do not wait to put the burning coals in a chafing-dish, but just carry them hither in your hands.' Mark gave a cheerful response, left the room, and immediately returned, to the surprise and dismay of the Augustinians, carrying burning coals of fire in his naked hands; which he held to his superior to warm himself at, and, when commanded, took them back to the kitchen-hearth. The superior of the Jesuits, then, without speaking, bestowed a peculiarly triumphant and inquiring look on the general of the Augustinians, as much as to say, will any of your inferiors do that for you? The Augustinian, in turn, looked wistfully on one of the most docile of his friars, as if he wished to command him to do the like. But the friar, perfectly understanding the look, and seeing there was no time for hesitation, hurriedly exclaimed: 'Reverend Father, forbear; do not command me to tempt God! I am ready to fetch you fire in a chafing-dish, but not in my bare hands.'

The art or trick of handling fire with impunity has been so often practised by jugglers and mountebanks, during the last fifty years, that it has now lost its attraction as an exhibition; though at an earlier period it created great wonder, affording an ample remuneration to its professors. One Richardson, an Englishman, astonished the greater part of Europe by his tricks with fire; and, though a mere juggler, acquired a sort of semi-scientific position, by a notice of his feats in the *Journal des Scavans* for 1680. Evelyn saw this man, and gives the following account of his performances. Having called upon Lady Sutherland, he says: 'She made me stay dinner, and sent for Richardson, the famous fire-eater. He devoured brimstone on glowing coals before us, chewing and swallowing them; he melted a beer-glass, and eat it quite up; then taking a live coal on his tongue, he put on it a raw oyster, the coal was blown with bellows, till it flamed and sparkled in his mouth, and so remained till the oyster gaped and was quite boiled. Then he melted pitch and wax together with sulphur, which he drank down as it flamed. I saw it flaming in his mouth a good while; he also took up a thick piece of iron, such as laundresses use to put in their smoothing-boxes, when it was fiery hot, he held it between his teeth, then in his hand, and threw it about like a stone; but this, I observed, he cared not to hold very long.'

In ancient history, we find several examples of people, who possessed the art of touching fire without being burned. The priestesses of Diana, at Castabala, in Cappadocia, commanded public veneration, by walking over red-hot iron. The Hirpi, a people of Etruria, walked among glowing embers, at an annual festival held on Mount Soracte; and thus proving their sacred character, received certain privileges—among others, exemption from military service—from the Roman senate. One of the most astounding stories of antiquity is related in the *Zend-Avesta*, to the effect that Zoroaster, to confute his calumniators, allowed fluid lead to be poured over his body, without receiving any injury. Yet M. Boutigny, the discoverer of the science of bodies in a spheroidal state, has amply proved in his own person the extreme easiness of the feat.

The fiery ordeals of the middle ages, in which accused persons proved their innocence of the crimes imputed to them, by walking blindfold among red-hot ploughshares, or holding heated irons in their hands without receiving injury, were always conducted by the clergy; who, no doubt, had sufficient knowledge of the trick to turn the result as best accorded with their own views. Richardi, queen of Charles le Gros of France, Cunegonda, empress of Germany, and Emma, mother of Edward the Confessor, all proved their innocence by the ordeal of fire. Albertus Magnus, after trial by ordeal had been abolished, published the secret of the art; which merely consisted in rubbing the hands and feet with certain compositions.

A Signora Josephine Girardelli, attracted most fashionable metropolitan audiences, in the early part of the present century, by her feats with fire. She stood with her naked feet on a plate of red-hot iron, and subsequently drew the same plate over her hair and tongue. She washed her hands in boiling oil; and placing melting lead in her mouth, after a few moments, produced it again solidified, and bearing the impression of her teeth.

M. Boutigny, in his work on the spheroidal state of bodies, and Mr Pepper of the Polytechnic Institution, London, in an amusing lecture, have fully exemplified the principles on which these feats are performed. Some of them, however, being mere juggling tricks, are not for scientific explanation. For instance, the performer taking an iron spoon, holds it up to the spectators, to shew that it is empty; then, dipping it into a pot containing melted lead, he again shews it to the spectators full of the molten metal; then, after putting the spoon to his mouth, he once more shews it to be empty; and after compressing his lips, with a look expressive of pain, he, in a few moments, ejects from his mouth a piece of lead, impressed by the exact form of his teeth. Ask a spectator what he saw, and he will say that the performer took a spoonful of molten lead, placed it in his mouth, and soon afterwards shewed it in a solid state, bearing the exact form and impression of his teeth. If deception be insinuated, the spectator will say, 'No! having the evidence of my senses, I cannot be deceived; if it had been a matter of opinion I might, but seeing, you know, is believing.' Now, the piece of lead, cast from a plaster mould of the performer's teeth, has probably officiated in a thousand previous performances, and is placed in the mouth, between the gum and cheek, just before the trick commences. The spoon is made with a hollow handle containing quicksilver, which, by a simple motion, can be let run into the bowl, or back again into the handle at will. The spoon is first shewn with the quicksilver concealed in the handle, the bowl is then dipped just within the rim of the pot containing the molten lead, but not into the lead itself, and, at the same instant, the quicksilver is allowed to run into the bowl. The spoon is then shewn with the quicksilver (which the audience take to be melted lead) in the bowl, and when placed in the mouth, the quicksilver is again allowed to run into the handle. The performer, in fact, takes a spoonful of nothing, and soon after exhibits the lead.

---

*Died.*—Emperor Louis I. of Germany, 'the Pious,' 876, *Frankfort;* Sir Francis Vere, distinguished military commander and author, 1608, *Portsmouth;* Hugo Grotius, eminent jurist, 1645, *Rostock;* Count Axel Oxenstiern, Swedish chancellor under Gustavus Adolphus, 1654; Charles Boyle, Earl of Orrery, celebrated antagonist of Bentley, 1731; John Hutchinson, mystic theologian, 1737, *London;* Leigh Hunt, poet, critic, miscellaneous writer, 1859, *Putney;* William Lyon Mackenzie, leader in the Canadian Rebellion of 1837, 1861, *Toronto.*

## LEIGH HUNT.

Among the numerous distinguished literary characters of the first half of the nineteenth century, no man more fully answered to the appellation of 'a man of letters' than Leigh Hunt. He exercised no inconsiderable influence on the literature of his day. As a political writer, he stood at one time almost alone in a resolute advocacy of an independent and enlightened spirit of journalism, as distinguished from mere party-scribbling; as a critic of poetry and art, he contributed much to the overthrow of the pedantry and narrow maxims of the Johnsonian era; and, as an entertaining and popular writer, he figures in the van of that illustrious army, which has since, with such singular success, fought the battle of the people, and established the right of labouring-men to educational advantages.

Leigh Hunt was born on the 19th of October 1784. His father, Isaac Hunt, was descended from some of the earliest settlers in Barbadoes, and practised successfully as an advocate; but, espousing the cause of the king in the American struggle, he was seized and put in prison; and probably only saved himself from unpleasant handling by bribing the jailer. He made his escape to England, leaving his wife and family behind, and some time elapsed before they could join him. Mrs Isaac Hunt came of a Quaker stock, and would have done honour to any sect. Her husband became a clergyman and popular preacher, but behaving with too imprudent generosity on a certain occasion, in which royalty was implicated, he never secured the promotion which he confidently expected.

Leigh Hunt was sent to Christ Hospital, where he remained some years, but he did not proceed to the university from that foundation, because a habit of stammering which he had, as well as a laxness of orthodoxy, derived from changes in the views of both parents, led him honestly to refuse to promise to enter the ministry. For some time he did nothing, not knowing what profession to take up; then he entered the office of an attorney, his elder brother; in the next place, he became a clerk in the War-Office, through the patronage of Mr Addington; and, finally, he decided, and decided wisely, to become a man of letters.

In 1802, when Leigh Hunt was only eighteen, the Rev. Isaac Hunt was so pleased with his verses, that he published them, by subscription, under the title of *Juvenilia*. He ought to have known better, for the boy's vanity was by no means lessened by the notice that was taken of him.

Leigh Hunt made his first great advance towards celebrity as a dramatic critic. He diligently attended the theatres; resolutely refused to form any acquaintances with actors or managers, in order to preserve his independence; and bringing his extensive reading and liberal views to bear on the emptiness of dramatic productions, he made such a stir by his papers in the *Traveller*, that playgoers learned to accept his dictum without demur, and play-performers to hate him.

His next career was that of a journalist. He joined with his brother John in setting up a weekly paper, named the *Examiner*. The noble and independent, and, at the same time, liberal spirit in which the paper was conducted, drew all eyes upon it. It took no side; it stood alone. The Tories execrated it; and the Whigs, although, in the main, it advocated their views, were afraid to support it. Nevertheless, it succeeded in acquiring, by its honest plain-speaking, sufficient influence to make it troublesome, and at length the government of the day felt the necessity of punishing disinterestedness so glaring, and watched its opportunity. On three successive occasions the attempt was made, and on each the editors escaped. The *Examiner's* first offence was defending a certain Major Hogan, who accused the Duke of York, as commander-in-chief, of favouritism and corruption. The second was the following curious remark: 'Of all monarchs since the Revolution, the successor of George III. will have the finest opportunity of becoming nobly popular.' The third was an article against military flogging.

These three cases of prosecution were not carried out; but a fourth was to come. The government was exasperated by failure, and when it struck at last, the blow was severe. We cannot do better than record the affair in the words of Leigh Hunt's eldest son:

'The occurrence which prompted the article was a public dinner on St Patrick's Day, at which the chairman, Lord Moira, a generous man, made not the slightest allusion to the Prince Regent; and Mr Sheridan, who manfully stood up for his royal friend, declaring that he still sustained the principles of the Prince Regent, was saluted by angry shouts, and cries of "Change the subject!" The Whig *Morning Chronicle* moralised this theme; and the *Morning Post*, which then affected to be the organ of the court, replied to the *Chronicle*, partly in vapid prose railing, and partly in a wretched poem, graced with epithets, intending to be extravagantly flattering to the prince. To this reply the *Examiner* rejoined in a paper of considerable length, analysing the whole facts, and translating the language of adulation into that of truth. The close of the article shews its spirit and purpose, and is a fair specimen of Leigh Hunt's political writing at that time:

"What person, unacquainted with the true state of the case, would imagine, in reading these astounding eulogies, that this 'glory of the people' was the subject of millions of shrugs and reproaches?—that this 'protector of the arts' had named a wretched foreigner his historical painter, in disparagement or in ignorance of the merits of his own countrymen?—that this 'Mæcenas of the age' patronised not a single deserving writer?—that this 'breather of eloquence' could not say a few decent extempore words, if we are to judge, at least, from what he said to his regiment on its embarkation for Portugal?—that this 'conqueror of hearts' was the disappointer of hopes?—that this 'exciter of desire' [bravo! Messieurs of the *Post*!]—this 'Adonis in loveliness' was a corpulent man of fifty? in short, this *delightful*, *blissful*, *wise*, *pleasurable*, *honourable*, *virtuous*, *true*, and *immortal* prince, was a violator of his word, a libertine, over head and ears in disgrace, a despiser of domestic ties, the companion of gamblers and demireps, a man who has just closed half a century without one single claim on the gratitude of his country, or the respect of posterity?" . . . . .

'This article, no doubt,' says Leigh Hunt at a later period, 'was very bitter and contemptuous; therefore, in the legal sense of the term, very libellous; the more so, inasmuch as it was very true!' Admit that it was true, and that words of truth, however bitter and blasting, if the speaker can substantiate them, ought not to be held as a libel. One, nevertheless, cannot wonder that the authors of such language against a reigning prince received castigation. The punishment was cruel: the brothers were fined a thousand pounds, and imprisoned for two years in separate cells. It is a noble fact in their favour, that, being promised privately a remission of the punishment, if they would abstain for the future from unpleasant remarks, John and Leigh Hunt refused the offer. They also declined to allow a generous stranger to pay the fine in their stead.

Leigh Hunt's account of his prison-life is very interesting. He was ill when he entered on it, and this illness, and want of exercise, permanently injured his constitution; but he passed the time pleasantly enough. He papered his prison-walls with roses, and painted the ceiling like a sky; he furnished his room with a piano, with bookshelves, with his wife and all his children, and turned a little yard into an arbour of summer loveliness by the help of flowers and paint. We should have been pleased to possess a fuller history of what was said and done in this noteworthy prison-cell. Charles Lamb was a daily visitor. Thomas Moore introduced Byron, who afterwards came frequently to dine or chat, and was very courteous to the prisoner. And many other worthies, whom Leigh Hunt had not previously known, on this occasion introduced themselves, among whom were Charles Cowden Clarke, William Hazlitt, and Jeremy Bentham. He lost no old friends, and made many new ones. Shelley, though almost a stranger to him, made him what he calls 'a princely offer,' and Keats penned a sonnet, which was all he could do:

'WRITTEN ON THE DAY THAT MR LEIGH HUNT LEFT PRISON.

What though, for shewing truth to flattered state,
Kind Hunt was shut in prison, yet has he,
In his immortal spirit, been as free
As the sky-searching lark, and as elate.
Minion of grandeur! think you he did wait?
Think you he nought but prison-walls did see,
Till, so unwilling, thou unturn'dst the key?
Ah, no! far happier, nobler was his fate!
In Spenser's halls he strayed, and bowers fair,
Culling enchanted flowers; and he flew
With daring Milton through the fields of air;
To regions of his own his genius true
Took happy flights. Who shall his fame impair,
When thou art dead, and all thy wretched crew?'

Leigh Hunt entered prison on the 3d of February 1813, and left it on the same day two years later. The next most noticeable event of his personal history is his friendship with Shelley. It was by Shelley's inducement that he undertook a journey to Italy, to co-operate with Shelley and Byron in a liberal periodical which they proposed to bring out. The voyage proved a troublesome one. He engaged to embark in September 1821, he actually embarked on November 16 of that year, and, after narrowly escaping shipwreck with his family, the whole of which he had on board, he was landed at Dartmouth. He embarked again in May 1822, and reached Italy in June. Before he had been many days in Italy, his friend was drowned, and Byron shewed signs of relenting in the matter of the periodical. It was but a short connection, as might have been expected. Byron went to Greece, and Leigh Hunt stayed in Italy till 1825, after which he returned to England.

The rest of his life was passed in literary projects, in getting into debt, and getting out of it, in pleasant communing with his numerous literary friends, among whom were Barry Cornwall, Thomas Carlyle, the Brownings, and many others, in attempts to live cheerfully under affliction, and, chief of all, in accumulating book-lore. His closing years were rendered more happy by an opportune pension of £200 a year, which Lord John Russell obtained for him. He died on the 28th of August 1859, and was buried, according to his wish, in Kensal Green Cemetery.

Leigh Hunt had a kind heart and a cheerful spirit; he was a man of simple tastes and no inclination to expense. If he could have gone through life as a child under tutelage, he might have smiled on to its close, and died as the gay insects do at the close of the season. As a man with responsibilities to his fellow-men, and to a wife and children, he failed in duty, and consequently lost in happiness. It was quite impossible, however, for any one with the most ordinary share of generosity to know him and not love him. In literature he might be said to take a high place among the *dii minores*. His poetry, though burdened with mannerism, charms by its sparkling vivacity; and of his many essays it would be possible to select at least a hundred which reach a degree of classic excellence.

---

## THE EGLINTOUN TOURNAMENT.

It was an idea not unworthy of a young nobleman of ancient lineage and ample possessions, to set forth a living picture, as it were, of the medieval tournament before the eyes of a modern generation. When the public learned that such an idea had occurred to the Earl of Eglintoun, and that it was to be carried out in the beautiful park surrounding his castle in Ayrshire, it felt as if a new pleasure had been at length invented. And, undoubtedly, if only good weather could have been secured, the result could not have fallen short of the expectations which were formed.

Nearly two years were spent in making the necessary preparations, and on the 28th of August 1839, the proceedings commenced in the presence of an immense concourse of spectators, many of whom, in obedience to a hint previously given, had come in fancy-costumes. The spot chosen for the tourney was about a quarter of a mile eastward of the castle, surrounded by beautiful scenery; it comprised an arena of four acres, with a boarded fence all round. At convenient places, were galleries to hold 3000 persons, one for private friends of the earl and the knights who were to take part in the mimic contest, and the other for visitors of a less privileged kind. In the middle of the arena were barriers to regulate the jousts of the combatants. Each of the knights had a separate marquee or pavilion for himself and his attendants. The decorations everywhere were of the most costly character, being aided by many trappings which had recently been used at the Queen's coronation. Besides keeping 'open house' at the castle, the earl provided two temporary saloons, each 250 feet long, for banquets and balls. But the weather was unfavourable to the 'brave knights;' the rain fell heavily; spectators marred the medievalism of the scene by hoisting umbrellas; and the 'Queen of Beauty' and her ladies, who were to have ridden on elegantly-caparisoned palfreys, were forced to take refuge in carriages. A procession started from the castle in the midst of a drenching shower. It comprised men-at-arms clad in demi-suits of armour, musicians, trumpeters, banner-bearers, marshals, heralds, pursuivants, a 'judge of the peace,' retainers, halberdiers, a knight-marshal, a jester, archers, servitors, swordsmen, and chamberlains—all attired in the most splendid costumes that befitted their several characters. These were mostly subordinates. The chiefs were fifteen knights, and about double as many esquires and pages—nearly all in magnificent armour, whole or demi. The knights were the Marquis of Waterford, the Earls of Eglintoun, Craven, and Cassilis; Viscounts Alford and Glenlyon; Captains Gage, Fairlie, and Beresford; Sirs Frederick Johnstone and Francis Hopkins; and Messrs Jerningham, Lamb, Boothby, and Lechmere. These knights all bore chivalric appellations—such as the Knights of the Dragon, the Griffin, the Black Lion, the Dolphin, the Crane, the Ram, the Swan, the Golden Lion, the White Rose, the Stag's Head, the Burning Tower, the Lion's Paw, &c.; these emblems and symbols being emblazoned on the trappings of the several knights and their retainers. Some of the dresses were exceedingly gorgeous. The Marquis of Londonderry, as 'King of the Tournament,' wore a magnificent train of green velvet, embroidered with gold, covered by a crimson-velvet cloak trimmed with gold and ermine, and having a crown covered in with crimson velvet; the Earl of Eglintoun, as 'Lord of the Tournament,' had a rich damasked suit of gilt armour, with a skirt of chain-mail; and Sir Charles Lamb, as 'Knight Marshal,' had a suit of black armour, embossed and gilt, and covered by a richly-emblazoned surcoat. The esquires and pages were all gentlemen of fortune and position. Lady Seymour, as 'Queen of Beauty,' wore a robe of crimson velvet, with the Seymour crest embroidered in silver on blue velvet, and a cloak of cerise velvet trimmed with gold and ermine. The ladies in the chief gallery were mostly attired in the costumes of the fourteenth and fifteenth centuries.

Under most discouraging circumstances the cavalcade set forth—the gaily-trimmed horses splashing in the dirt, the armour washed with pitiless rain, and the velvets and laces saturated with wet. The knights with their esquires entered their several pavilions, while the rest of the personages took up the posts allotted to them. The knights issued forth from their pavilions two and two, paid their devoirs to the fair ladies in the galleries, and then fought to the sound of trumpet. This fighting consisted in galloping against each other, and each striking his lance against the armour of the other; the lances were so made of wood as to be easily broken, and thus there was no great danger incurred. After several couples had thus jousted, the Earl of Eglintoun and the Marquis of Waterford (the 'Lord of the Tournament' and the 'Knight of the Dragon') came forward, most gorgeously arrayed and armed, and attended by no fewer than eight esquires and pages. After running at each other until two lances were broken, the earl was declared the best knight of the day, and was rewarded by the 'Queen of Beauty' with a crown of victory. But the incessant rain sadly marred the whole affair; and the day's jousting ended with a very unpicturesque broadsword combat between an actor and a soldier, engaged for the purpose. In every sense was the day's joyousness damped; for when the guests were quite ready for a grand banquet and ball in the evening, it was found that the two temporary pavilions, fitted up in the most splendid manner, were flooded with water from the heavy rains, and were quite useless for the purposes intended. On the 29th, the weather was nearly as bad; no jousting in the lists was attempted, but some mimic tilts took place under cover, in which one personage took part who was destined to fill an important place in the history of Europe—Prince Louis Napoleon, afterwards the Emperor Napoleon III. of France. On the 30th, the skies were more favourable; the joustings were renewed, and were wound up by a tourney of eight knights armed with swords—used in some inoffensive way against each other's armour. Measures had been taken to render the banqueting-hall and ball-room available, and the day ended with a banquet for 300 persons and a ball for 1000. The 31st came, and with it weather so stormy and ungenial that any further proceedings with the tournament were abandoned. And thus ended this most costly affair. The spot had been so selected that, outside the fence, an enormous number of spectators might witness the proceedings; and it was estimated that little under 200,000 persons availed themselves of this opportunity on one or other of the four days—coming from almost every county in Scotland, and from various parts of England and Ireland. The Ardrossan Railway Company trebled their fares; and whoever had a gig or other vehicle to let at Glasgow, could command extravagant terms for it.

---

# AUGUST 29.

The Decollation of St John the Baptist. St Sabina, martyr, 2d century. St Sebbi or Sebba, king of Essex, 697. St Merri or Medericus, abbot of St Martin's, about 700.

*Born.*—John Locke, philosopher (*Essay on the Human Understanding*), 1632, *Wrington, Somersetshire;* John Henry Lambert, distinguished natural philosopher of Germany, 1728, *Mülhausen.*

*Died.*—St John the Baptist, beheaded, 30 A. D.; John Lilburne, zealous parliamentarian, 1657, *Eltham;* Edmund Hoyle, author of the book on Games, 1769, *London;* Joseph Wright, historical painter, 1797, *Derby;* Pope Pius VI., 1799; William Brockedon, painter, 1854.

## LILBURNE THE PAMPHLETEER.

In the pamphleteering age of Charles I. and the Commonwealth, no man pamphleteered like John Lilburne. The British Museum contains at least a hundred and fifty *brochures* by him, all written in an exaggerated tone—besides many *fasciculi* which others wrote in his favour. Lilburne was impartial towards Cavaliers and Roundheads; his great aim was to advance his own opinions and defend himself from the comments which they excited.

In 1637, ere the troubles began, Lilburne was accused before the Star-Chamber of publishing and dispersing seditious pamphlets. He refused to take the usual oath in that court, to the effect that he would answer *all* interrogatories, even though they inculpated himself; and for this refusal he was condemned to be whipped, pilloried, and imprisoned. During the very processes of whipping and pillorying, he harangued the populace against the tyranny of the court-party, and scattered pamphlets from his pocket. The Star-Chamber, which was sitting at that very moment, ordered him to be gagged; but he still stamped and gesticulated, to shew that he would again have harangued the people if he could. The Star-Chamber, more and more provoked, condemned him to be imprisoned in a dungeon and ironed. When the parliament gained ascendency over the king, Lilburne, as well as Prynne, Bastwick, and many other liberals, received their liberty, and were welcomed with joyful acclamations by the people. Then followed the downfall of the king, the Protectorate of Cromwell, and the gradual resuscitation of measures deemed almost as inimical to liberty as those of Charles had been. Lilburne was at his post as usual, fighting the cause of freedom by means of pamphlets, with unquestioned honesty of purpose, but with intemperate zeal. In 1649, he was again thrown into prison, but this time by order of the parliament instead of by that of the crown; even the women of London petitioned for his release, but the parliament was deaf to their arguments. When the case was brought on for regular trial, a London jury found him not guilty of the 'sedition' charged against him by the parliament. Again, after Cromwell had dissolved the Long Parliament, Lilburne was once more imprisoned for his outspoken pamphlets; again was he liberated when the voice of the people obtained expression through the verdict of a jury; and again was there great popular delight displayed at his liberation.

There is reason to doubt whether Lilburne was so steady and sagacious a liberal, as to be able to render real services to the cause which he so energetically advocated; but his public life well illustrated the pamphleteering tendencies of the age. One among the pamphlets published in 1653, when Lilburne was opposing the assumption of arbitrary power by Cromwell, was in the form of a pretended catalogue of books, to be sold in 'Little Britain.' First came about forty books, every one with some sarcastic political hit contained in the title. Then came a series of pretended 'Acts and Orders' of parliament, among which the following are samples:—'An act for the speedy suppressing all plays, the Fools being all termed commanders or parliament-men.'—'An act for a speedy drawing up of a petition to Lucifer on behalf of Cromwell: that, seeing he hath done such eminent services for him in this world, he may not want a place of preferment in his dominions!'—'An act forbidding any to stamp the Lord General's [Cromwell's] image on gingerbread, lest the valour of it should bite the children by the tongue.'—'An act ordering that Vavasour Powell shall preach the devil out of hell, that there may be room for the members.'—'An act for the regulating of names, that the well-affected may not be abased by nicknames, but that every syllable may have its full pronunciation—as General Monke must hereafter be rightly called General Monkey.' And then follow a series of 'Cases of Conscience,' such as the following: 'Whether Whitehall may not properly be called a den of thieves.'—'Whether the countenances of Miles Corbet and Mr Gurden do not speak their mothers to be blackamoors and their fathers Jews.'—'Whether Alderman Atkins his imbecility had ever been found out, if Sir Walter Earl had not smelt it.'—'Whether Balaam's beating his own ass were a sufficient warrant for the footman's cudgelling Sir Henry Mildmay.'—'Whether Cromwell had not gotten a patent for brimstone, which makes his nose so fiery.'—'Whether there was not an ironmonger spoil'd when Harry Walker was made a priest; and whether he, being a priest, can tell what stands for pillory in Hebrew.'—'Whether our Saviour's riding into Jerusalem upon an ass's foal, were any more than a type of our deliverer Cromwell's riding into his throne, upon the backs of a hundred and twenty asses, elected out of the several counties for that purpose.'

It is not stated that these audacious sarcasms were actually by Lilburne, for the pamphlet has neither author nor editor, neither printer nor publisher, named; but they will serve to illustrate the spirit of the times, when such pamphlets could be produced.

### EDMUND HOYLE.

Of this celebrated writer of treatises on games of chance, including among others whist, piquet, quadrille, and backgammon, and whose name has become so familiar, as to be immortalised in the well-known proverb, 'According to Hoyle,' little more is known, than that he appears to have been born in 1672, and died in Cavendish Square, London, on 29th August 1769, at the advanced age of ninety-seven. In the *Gentleman's Magazine* of December 1742, we find among the list of promotions 'Edmund Hoyle, Esq., made by the Primate of Ireland, register of the Prerogative Court, there, worth £600 per annum.' From another source, we learn that he was a barrister by profession. His treatise on *Whist*, for which he received from the publisher the sum of £1000, was first published in 1743, and attained such a popularity that it ran through five editions in a year, besides being extensively pirated. He has even been called the inventor of the game of whist, but this is certainly a mistake, though there can be no doubt that it was indebted to him for being first treated of, and introduced to the public in a scientific manner. It first began to be popular in England about 1730, when it was particularly studied by a party of gentlemen, who used to assemble in the Crown Coffee House, in Bedford Row. Hoyle is said to have given instructions in the game, for which his charge was a guinea a lesson.

---

### BEQUESTS FOR THE GUIDANCE OF TRAVELLERS.

Some of the old charitable bequests of England form striking memorials of times when travelling, especially at night, and even a night-walk in the streets of a large city, was attended with difficulties unknown to the present generation. For example—the corporation of Woodstock, Oxfordshire, pay ten shillings yearly, the bequest of one Carey, for the ringing of a bell at eight o'clock every evening, for the guide and direction of travellers. By the bequest of Richard Palmer, in 1664, the sexton of Wokingham, Berks, has a sum for ringing every evening at eight, and every morning at four, for this among other purposes, 'that strangers and others who should happen, in winter-nights, within hearing of the ringing of the said bell, to lose their way in the country, might be informed of the time of night, and receive some guidance into the right way.' There is also an endowment of land at Barton, Lincolnshire, and 'the common tradition of the parish is, that a worthy old lady, in ancient times, being accidentally benighted on the Wolds, was directed in her course by the sound of the evening-bell of St Peter's Church, where, after much alarm, she found herself in safety, and out of gratitude she gave this land to the parish-clerk, on condition that he should ring one of the church bells from seven to eight o'clock every evening, except Sundays, commencing on the day of the carrying of the first load of barley in every year till Shrove Tuesday next ensuing inclusive.'*

By his will, dated 29th August 1656, John Wardall gave £4 yearly to the churchwardens of St Botolph's, Billingsgate, 'to provide a good and sufficient iron and glass lanthorn, with a candle, for the direction of passengers to go with more security to and from the water-side, all night long, to be fixed at the north-east corner of the parish church, from the feast-day of St Bartholomew to Lady-Day; out of which sum £1 was to be paid to the sexton for taking care of the lanthorn.' A similar bequest of John Cooke, in 1662, has provided a lamp—now of gas—at the corner of St Michael's Lane, next Thames Street.

The schoolmaster of the parish of Corstorphine, Edinburghshire, enjoys the profits of an acre of ground on the banks of the Water of Leith, near Coltbridge. This piece of ground is called the Lamp Acre, because it was formerly destined for the support of a lamp in the east end of the church of Corstorphine, believed to have served as 'a beacon to direct travellers going from Edinburgh along a road, which in those times was both difficult and dangerous.'*

## EARL OF MARCH'S CARRIAGE RACE.

August 29, 1750, there was decided a bet of that original kind for which the noted Earl of March (subsequently fourth Duke of Queensberry) shewed such a genius. It came off at Newmarket at seven o'clock in the morning. The matter undertaken by the earl, in conjunction with the Earl of Eglintoun, on a wager for a thousand guineas against Mr Theobald Taafe, was to furnish a four-wheeled carriage, with four horses, to be driven by a man, nineteen miles within an hour. A contemporary authority thus describes the carriage: 'The pole was small, but lapped with fine wire; the perch had a plate underneath; two cords went on each side, from the back-carriage to the fore-carriage, fastened to springs. The harness was of fine leather covered with silk. The seat for the man to sit on was of leather straps, and covered with velvet. The boxes of the wheel were brass, and had tins of oil to drop slowly for an hour. The breechings for the horses were whalebone. The bars were small wood, strengthened with steel springs, as were most parts of the carriage, but all so light, that a man could carry the whole with the harness.' Before this carriage was decided on, several others had been tried. Several horses were killed in the course of the preliminary experiments, which cost in all about seven hundred pounds. The two earls, however, won their thousand guineas, for the carriage performed the distance in 53 minutes 27 seconds, leaving fully time enough to have achieved another mile.

THE EARL OF MARCH'S RACING CARRIAGE.

## LOSS OF THE 'ROYAL GEORGE.'

Cowper's lines on this disastrous event very well embody the painful feeling which occupied the public mind in reference to it. When Lord Howe's fleet returned to Portsmouth in 1782, after varied service in the Atlantic, it was found that the *Royal George*, 108 guns, commanded by Admiral Kempenfeldt, required cleaning on the exterior and some repairs near the keel. In order to get at this portion of the hull, the ship was 'heeled over'—that is, thrown so much on one side as to expose a good deal of the other side above the surface of the water. In recent times, the examination is made in a less perilous way; but in those days heeling was always adopted, if the defects were not so serious as to require the ship to go into dock. On the 29th of August, the workmen proceeded to deal with the *Royal George* in this fashion; but

* Edwards's *Remarkable Charities*, 99, 203, 223.

* Sinclair's *Statistical Acc. Scotland*, xiv. 449.

they heeled it over too much, water entered the port-holes, the ship filled, and down she went with all on board—the admiral, captain, officers, crew, about three hundred women and children who were temporarily on board, guns, ammunition, provisions, water, and stores. So sudden was the terrible calamity, that a smaller vessel lying alongside the *Royal George* was swallowed up in the gulf thus occasioned, and other vessels were placed in imminent danger. Of the total number of eleven hundred souls on board, very nearly nine hundred at once found a watery grave; the rest were saved. The ship had carried the loftiest masts, the heaviest metal, and the greatest number of admirals' flags, of any in the navy; it had been commanded by some of the best officers in the service; and Admiral Kempenfeldt, who was among those drowned, was a general favourite. A court-martial on Captain Waghorn (who had escaped with his life), for negligence in the careening operation, resulted in his acquittal: a liberal subscription for the widows and children of those who had perished; and a monument in Portsea Churchyard to Kempenfeldt and his hapless companions—quickly followed. Cowper mourned over the event in a short poem, monody, or elegy:

'ON THE LOSS OF THE ROYAL GEORGE.

(*To the March in Scipio.*)

WRITTEN WHEN THE NEWS ARRIVED.

Toll for the brave!
The brave that are no more!
All sunk beneath the wave,
Fast by their native shore!

Eight hundred of the brave,
Whose courage well was tried,
Had made the vessel heel,
And laid her on her side;

A land-breeze shook the shrouds,
And she was overset;
Down went the *Royal George*,
With all her crew complete.

Toll for the brave!
Brave Kempenfeldt is gone;
His last sea-fight is fought;
His work of glory done.

It was not in the battle;
No tempest gave the shock;
She sprang no fatal leak;
She ran upon no rock;

His sword was in his sheath;
His fingers held the pen,
When Kempenfeldt went down
With twice four hundred men.

Weigh the vessel up,
Once dreaded by our foes!
And mingle with our cup
The tear that England owes.

Her timbers yet are sound,
And she may float again,
Full charged with England's thunder,
And plough the distant main.

But Kempenfeldt is gone;
His victories are o'er;
And he and his eight hundred men
Shall plough the wave no more.'

Cowper also gave a Latin translation of these stanzas, beginning:

'Plangimus fortes. Periere fortes,
Patrium propter periere littus
Bis quater centum; subito sub alto
Æquore mersi.'

The hapless *Royal George* has been the subject of many interesting submarine operations. During the three months which immediately followed the disaster, several divers succeeded in fishing up sixteen guns out of the ship, by the aid of a diving-bell. In the next year, a projector brought forward a scheme for raising the ship itself, but it failed. In 1817, after the ship had been submerged thirty-five years, it underwent a thorough examination by men who descended in a diving-bell. It was found to be little other than a pile of ruinous timber-work—the guns, anchors, spars, and masts having fallen into a confused mass among the timbers. She was too dilapidated to be raised in a body, by any arrangement however ingenious. Twenty-two years afterwards, in 1839, General (then Colonel) Pasley devised a mode of discharging enormous masses of gunpowder, by means of electricity, against the submerged hull, so as to shatter it utterly, to let all the timbers float that would float, and to afford opportunity for divers to bring up the heavier valuables. This plan succeeded completely. Enormous submarine charges of powder, in metal cases containing 2000 lbs. each, were fired, and the anchorage was gradually cleared of an obstruction which had lain there nearly sixty years. The value of the brass guns fished up was equal to the whole cost of the operations.

# AUGUST 30.

Saints Felix and Adauctus, martyrs, about 303. St Pammachius, confessor, 410. St Agilus or Aile, abbot of Rebais, about 650. St Fiaker, Fiacre, or Fefre, anchoret and confessor, about 670. St Rose of Lima, virgin, 1617.

*Born.*—Giovanni Battista Nani, flower and foliage painter, 1616, *Venice;* Dr David Hartley, moral philosopher, author of *Observations on Man*, 1705, *Armley, Yorkshire;* Johann Christoph Adelung, grammarian and linguist, 1734, *Spantekow, in Pomerania;* Archdeacon William Paley, author of *Natural Theology*, *Evidences of Christianity*, &c., 1743, *Peterborough.*

*Died.*—Queen Cleopatra of Egypt, committed suicide, 30 B. C., *Alexandria;* Theodoric the Great, king of the Goths, 526, *Ravenna;* Pope Alexander III., 1181; Louis XI., king of France, 1483, *Plessis-les-Tours;* Sultan Soliman II., the Magnificent, 1566; Francis Baily, astronomer, 1844, *London;* Sir John Ross, Arctic navigator, 1856, *London;* Sir Richard Westmacott, sculptor, *London;* John Francis, sculptor, 1861, *London.*

## ARCHDEACON PALEY.

The character of Dr Paley is strikingly illustrative of the province to which he belonged: strong shrewd sense, great economy, and much persevering industry, without the graces of refinement, are still the prevailing features of the inhabitants of the north of Yorkshire. Though born at Peterborough, where his father was a minor canon, he was, at the age of one year, carried to Giggleswick, in Craven, on his mother's lap, she being seated on a pillion behind her husband. The primitive habits of the family were strictly kept up by this clever woman, who taught her son to knit his own stockings, a practice he continued after he was archdeacon of Carlisle. His father being the head-master of the grammar-school of Giggleswick, he received his education there; and to prevent his being made a baker, as Mrs Paley wished, he was carried by his father to Cambridge, and entered on the books at the early age of fifteen. His falling from his pony no less than seven times on the road there, and the parental carelessness in not even turning his head to see if his son were hurt, merely remarking: 'Take care of thy money, lad,' confirm the opening remarks. His uncouth awkwardness created the greatest mirth among the under-graduates, who dignified him with the sobriquet of 'Tommy Potts.' Idle and extravagant during the first two years, lying in bed until noon, and frequenting fairs, strolling-players, and puppet-shows, he was roused from these habits by the remonstrance of one of his gay companions, who at four o'clock one morning came to him in bed, and shewed how much better his talents might be employed. In consequence of that word spoken in season, he entirely reformed; began a practice of rising at five, and in a year came out senior-wrangler. In 1766, he was elected fellow of Christ's College, and became one of the tutors, giving lectures on moral philosophy, the substance of which he embodied afterwards in his book on that subject. His friendship with the son of the bishop of Carlisle procured him the living of Musgrave, worth but eighty pounds a year, upon which he married: happily, preferment of various kinds flowed in, and in 1782 he was made arch-deacon of Carlisle. Soon after he began his celebrated works; but the first, *Principles of Moral Philosophy*, had to wait some time until the author was rich enough to publish it, no one in the trade being willing to run the risk: the sale from the first was so great that Faulder, the publisher, to whom it had been offered for one hundred pounds, was willing to give two hundred and fifty. Whilst the negotiation was pending, another offer came of a thousand pounds, and Paley's distress lest his friend should have concluded the bargain for the lesser sum was sufficiently ludicrous. *Horæ Paulinæ* and some smaller works followed; but the highest commendations were reserved for his *View of the Evidences of Christianity*, which was greeted by all ranks, from George III. downwards, as an antidote to the infidelity which then prevailed. He was immediately made prebend of St Paul's, and subdean of Lincoln, with the valuable living of Bishop-Wearmouth, raising his income to more than two thousand a year. After eleven years spent in the enjoyment of these good things, and in the society of the distinguished men of the day, among whom were Ellenborough and Mackintosh, he died on the 25th of May 1805.

## AN OBSTINATE PRISONER.

When the system of imprisonment for debt was in full force, instances were frequent in which men were incarcerated for a long series of years—either because they were too poor to work out their deliverance, or because they disputed the justice of the claim under which they had been captured. A singular case of the latter kind occurred towards the close of the last century. Mr Benjamin Pope, a tanner in Southwark, made £70,000 by success in trade, and then became a money-lender, discounter, and mortgagee. When his fortune reached £100,000, he was familiarly known as 'Plum Pope.' His good-fortune gradually deserted him, however. His grasping disposition led him to offend against the usury laws, and he was frequently before the courts. In one serious case he was cast in £10,000 damages. He never ceased throughout the remainder of his life from complaining of this sentence; he went to France for a time, with his property and effects; and when he returned to England in 1782, he voluntarily went to prison rather than pay the above-named damages. In the King's Bench Prison he remained for the last twelve years of his life. At one time he might have got off by paying £1000 instead of £10,000; but this he refused to do, as 'this would be acknowledging the justice of the debt, which he would die sooner than do'—and he kept his word. While in prison he carried on his avocation of a money-lender, on a more limited and cautious scale than before. Always penurious and eccentric, he had become still more so. A pint of small-beer lasted him two days, and he always looked at the fulness of the measure before he paid for it. He would drink strong-beer with any one who would give it to him; but he never bought any. If he bought his three-farthing candle at eight to the pound, he would always select the *heaviest* of the eight, to obtain the most tallow he could for his money. He never had a joint of meat on his table during the whole twelve years of his voluntary imprisonment; a fourpenny-plate from a cook's shop served him for two meals. His friends, though living at a distance, knowing of his penurious habits, often sent him articles of food which he refused to buy for himself. When he died, at the end of August 1794, Mr Pope still owed the debt which had embittered so many years of his strange life.

## JOHN CAMDEN NEILD.

In the autumn of 1852, general curiosity was excited by an announcement in the newspapers that an eccentric gentleman, who had died on the 30th of August in that year, had bequeathed an immense legacy to the Queen. This gentleman was John Camden Neild, whose name had hitherto been all unknown to the public; but now reports respecting his eccentricities and the vast amount of his bequest were everywhere rife, and were eagerly devoured. Many of these reports, however, were contradictory, and instead of satisfying, only perplexed and mortified sober inquirers. Nor has any authentic memoir of Mr Neild since been published. It is therefore hoped that the following biographical sketch, compiled from credible sources, and containing many unpublished anecdotes, will be read with interest.

His father, James Neild, was a native of Knutsford, in Cheshire, and becoming a goldsmith in London, amassed considerable wealth, and purchased estates in the counties of Buckingham, Middlesex, Kent, and Surrey. In these several counties he held the office of magistrate for many years, and in 1804, he was appointed high-sheriff of Buckinghamshire. He was eminently benevolent, especially in his efforts for the improvement of prisons, and originated a society for the relief of persons imprisoned for small debts. He married Elizabeth, daughter of John Camden, Esq., of Battersea, in Surrey, a direct descendant of the renowned antiquary of the same name. He died in 1814, and was buried at Chelsea.

John Camden Neild, the only surviving son of the above, was born in 1780, and after receiving a good classical and general education, was entered at Trinity College, Cambridge, where he took the degree of B.A. in 1801, and M.A. in 1804. He afterwards became a student at Lincoln's Inn, and in 1808 was called to the bar. Succeeding in 1814 to the whole of his father's property, estimated at £250,000, it was at first hoped that he would walk in the paternal footsteps, and prove a benevolent and public-spirited country gentleman. Soon, however, it began to appear that avarice was his ruling passion. His parsimonious spirit increased till he became a confirmed miser, and for the last thirty years of his life, it may be said that he was entirely given over to the accumulation of wealth. His habits and appearance became very peculiar. He lived in a large house in Cheyne Walk, Chelsea; but it was meanly and scantily furnished. At one time, it is said, he slept on a bare board, but latterly on an old stump-bedstead, on which he died. His favourite companion was a large black cat, which was present in his chamber when he breathed his last. He kept two female servants, one as housekeeper, whom he placed on low board-wages when he left home, and it was on such occasions that he gave the fullest scope to his penurious inclinations.

He had considerable property at North Marston, in Buckinghamshire, and here he often stayed for days together, besides his half-yearly visits to receive rents. As lessee of the rectory, it was incumbent on him to repair the chancel of the church, and this he did in a very original manner. On one occasion, the leaded roof having become full of chinks and fissures, he had them covered with strips of painted calico, to the number of forty, saying, 'they would last his time.' While these repairs were in progress, he sat all day on the roof, to keep the workmen employed, and even ate his dinner there, which consisted of hard eggs, dry bread, and butter-milk. It may be remarked that he seldom paid his workmen or trades-people without disputing their account, and protesting that they would ruin him with their high charges.

His dress, which was extremely old-fashioned and shabby, consisted of a blue 'swallow-tailed' coat, with gilt buttons, brown trousers, short gaiters, and shoes which were patched and generally down at the heels. He never allowed his clothes to be brushed, because, he said, it destroyed the nap, and made them wear out faster. His stockings and linen were generally full of holes; but when he stayed a night at a tenant's, the mistress often mended them while he was in bed. On one occasion a night-shirt, which he accidentally left at a tenant's house, was found to be so tattered and rotten, that the mistress, finding repair impossible, burned it. His personal appearance was unprepossessing. He was short and punchy, scarcely above five feet in height, with a large round head, and short neck. He always carried with him an old green cotton umbrella, but never, even in the coldest or wettest weather, wore a greatcoat, considering such a luxury far too extravagant for his slender means. Often has he been seen, in a piercingly cold winter's evening, entering Aylesbury on the outside of a coach without the slightest addition to his ordinary clothing; while a poor labourer, sitting by his side, appeared warmly clad in a thick greatcoat. His appearance on such occasions often excited the compassion of his fellow-travellers, who mistook him for a decayed gentleman in extreme poverty. Just before the introduction of railway-travelling, he had been visiting some of his Kentish property, when, as he was returning to London, the coach stopped at Farningham. It was a bitterly cold day, and, with the exception of Mr Neild, all the outside passengers, though well wrapped in greatcoats and rugs, entered the inn 'to take something to warm them.' As they sat in the comfortable parlour drinking their brandy and water, they saw with pity their thinly-clad companion still sitting on the coach. Thinking he only remained there in the cold because he was ashamed to enter the inn when he had no money to spend, they subscribed for a good glass of brandy and water, and sent it to the 'poor gentleman,' who drank it off, and thanked his benefactors for their kindness. He often took rather long journeys on foot, especially in Buckinghamshire, where he had estates in different parts, which he could not visit by any public conveyance.

In these walking-journeys he never scrupled to avail himself of any proffered 'lift,' even in the dirtiest farm-cart, and he has been known to sit on a load of coal, to enable him to proceed a little further without expense; though, after all, he would probably give the driver a penny or two for the accommodation; for it is a fact that, miser as he was, he never liked to receive anything without paying for it, though his ideas of remuneration were certainly on a very restricted scale. When he called on the clergymen of the parishes where his estates lay, he always refused to partake of a meal or any refreshment; giving his declinature in a hasty, sharp tone, as if he had been annoyed or surprised at the invitation. With his tenants, especially those of a lower grade, the case was different. With one tenant, whose condition was scarcely above that of a labourer, he remained some days, sharing with the family their coarse meals and lodging. When business required his presence at North Marston, he used to reside with his tenant on the rectory-farm. While staying here about the year 1828, he attempted self-destruction by cutting his throat, and his life was saved chiefly by the prompt assistance of his tenant's wife, a Mrs Neal. This rash act was supposed to have been caused by a sudden declension in the stocks, in which he had just made a large investment.

During the year 1848, an enclosure was taking place in another parish in which he had a farm, and he often visited it to attend meetings on the subject. On these occasions he generally slept at Tring, or at the railway station, but ate his dinner at his tenant's. Before entering the house, he was often observed to walk up to the dairy-window, and stand on tip-toe to see what was within. He would then enter the house, and say to his tenant's wife: 'Could you let me have a basin of your nice milk?' As he sipped it up, he would keep repeating: 'O how good, how rich! Have you any eggs?' 'No, sir, but I can easily get some.' 'How do they sell now?' 'Eighteen for sixpence, sir.' 'Then that will be three for a penny. Will you get me three?' The eggs were procured, and he had two boiled very hard, and began to eat them, asking for another basin of milk. The third egg he put in his pocket for his breakfast next morning. Sometimes he used to take out of his pocket some sandwiches or bread and butter, and ask leave to place them in a cupboard. Having deposited them there, he would examine if they were safe every time he returned to the house after an absence of even half an hour. His Sundays he often spent in walking over the farm with his tenant, who, by Mr Neild's desire, used to carry a pickaxe for examining the quality of the soil at different places. He used to investigate very minutely the nature of his land, and the manner of its cultivation, and keep an account of the number of trees on his estates. He has been known to walk from twelve to fifteen miles to a small portion of his property, and, after counting over the few trees on it, to return the same distance, with no other apparent object for his journey. An idea of Mr Neild's extreme caution in purchasing land, may be gathered from the following extracts from his letters: 'Lot 3 is described as "exceedingly rich grazing-land." Does the tenant stock it with oxen or with cows—and if with oxen, are they large or small beasts? or does he dairy the land, and feed one half and mow the other half? .... I have never seen the close .... but I feel assured that if Mr —— had an idea that I was desirous of purchasing it, he would put such a price upon it as to render all treaty for it nugatory; and therefore, until I can see my way a little more in the matter than I do at present, and until the mortgagees shall feel themselves under an absolute necessity of selling the estate, which they have a power to do, what I have here written should not be suffered to transpire, but be kept within ourselves.... Six hundred pounds for little more than nine acres of land, and of land, perhaps, not of first-rate quality, and subject to a corn-rent of ——— in lieu of tithes, is a long price; and the offer, suppose you feel inclined to make it, can only at first be of a conditional nature, for I must see the close (although you need not tell Mr —— so) before anything can be concluded.'

Some misers have occasional feasts, though, like angels' visits, short and far between. Such was the case with Mr Neild. Having some business with a clergyman (perhaps to his own advantage), he invited him to dine with him at an inn where he was staying in Buckinghamshire. On this occasion, he was both courteous and hospitable, having provided for their dinner a leg of lamb, a tart, cheese, beer, and a bottle of sherry. He also *once* invited another clergyman, with two or three other persons connected with his property, to dine with him at an inn in another Buckinghamshire town, and provided for the occasion quite a generous entertainment. But when the same clergymen applied to him for some charitable assistance for their parishes, to one he gave a very uncourteous refusal, and to the other he sent the following characteristic letter:

'CHELSEA, *April* 24, 1852.

REV. AND DEAR SIR—When you last saw me, I was very infirm, and that infirmity has been increasing ever since, and still is upon the increase, until I am at last arrived at almost the last stage of decrepitude. I am confined to my bedroom, and cannot stir from my chair, except in exquisite pain. Without the summer shall work, I may say, on me a miraculous change, I do not expect ever to be at —— again.

'All that is wanting at ——, and, indeed, in all parishes purely agricultural, is a Sunday-school. Mr P—— tried to establish a daily school there, but did not succeed. I don't know that you are aware that where a daily school is established, it generally brings about with it a heavy pecuniary burden upon the clergyman; subscriptions, although ample at first, yearly fall off, are badly paid, and by degrees discontinued, until the whole charge, or nearly so, falls upon the minister; and then the school is necessarily discontinued. Such has been the fate of many of the parish schools in Bucks; and such, very recently, of one in Kent, the rector of the parish declining, on account of the charge upon him (as by letters he informs me), to superintend it any longer.

'You may suppose that, in the state in which I am, I do not see any one except upon business of a most urgent nature.—Your most obedient servant,

J. CAMDEN NEILD.'

Mr Neild's ordinary answer to all applications for charitable contributions was a refusal; but in some few instances it was otherwise. He once, but only once, gave a pound for the Sunday-school at North Marston; he contributed £5 or £10 towards building a school at Aton Clinton, Bucks; he sent £50 to the Culham Training College; he was an annual subscriber to the London Asylum for the Blind; and he promised £300 towards the building of an infirmary for Buckinghamshire, but withheld it from an objection to the site. Thus it appears that Mr Neild, as a miser, did not quite reach the perfection of the character which we see displayed in Dancer, Elwes, and other examples of this deplorable kind of eccentricity. Neither was it true of him, as said in various obituary notices, that his mind had no intellectuality—that nature had no beauty or endearments for him—that he was 'a frigid, spiritless specimen of humanity.' Mr Neild, in reality, possessed considerable knowledge of legal and general literature; and, despite his narrow-mindedness on the subject of money, he retained to the last a love for the ancient classics, and enjoyed poetical pathos and elegant phraseology, both in ancient and modern authors. So late as the year 1849, the writer of this notice received from him a letter containing a Latin inscription, with his own comments on it, fully evincing his knowledge of the language, and his taste for refined and elegant diction, and even pointing out the exquisite tenderness of one idea, and the well-chosen words used to express it. Although he might not duly appreciate works of art or the beauties of nature, yet he was not blind to their charms, nor altogether devoid of a certain regard for them. There is one anecdote which, if true, as there is reason to believe it is, presents a pleasing contrast to his general character. It is said that, finding the son of one of his tenants an exceedingly clever boy, he persuaded his father to bring him up for one of the learned professions, and paid himself, either wholly or in part, the expenses of his school and college education. That boy became a distinguished scholar, and a dignitary in the Church of England.

In February 1850, Mr Neild became subject to a very painful disorder, from which he suffered more or less to the end of his life. After that event, among those who were aware of his wealth, his will necessarily came to light, and great was the sensation which it occasioned. After bequeathing a few trifling legacies to different persons, he left the whole of his vast property, which was sworn to as under £250,000, to 'Her Most Gracious Majesty, Queen Victoria, begging Her Majesty's most gracious acceptance of the same, for her sole use and benefit, and her heirs, &c.' The executors were the Keeper of the Privy Purse, for the time being; Dr Henry Tattam, archdeacon of Bedford; and Mr Stevens, of Willesborough; to each of whom he bequeathed £100. He was buried, on 16th September, in the chancel of North Marston Church—in that very chancel which he had so elaborately repaired with strips of calico. His will had excited such curiosity that, though his life had passed almost unnoticed, a large concourse of persons assembled at Chelsea to witness the removal of his body, and the church and churchyard at North Marston were crowded with wondering—not lamenting—spectators. Among them were many of his tenants, of his workmen, and of the poor of the parish in which he possessed so much property; but not a tear was shed, not a regret uttered, as his body was committed to its last resting-place. He had done nothing to excite their gratitude, to win their sympathy, or to lay them under the slightest obligation. His property had passed into other hands, and they felt it was almost impossible they could suffer by the change. The only remark heard was: 'Poor creature! had he known so much would have been spent on his funeral, he would have come down here to die to save the expense!'

After the death of Mr Neild, his will was duly proved, and the Queen was left to take undisputed possession of his property. She immediately increased Mr Neild's bequest to his executors to £1000 each; she provided for his old housekeeper, for whom he had made no provision, though she had lived with him twenty-six years; and she secured an annuity on Mrs Neal, who had frustrated Mr Neild's attempt at suicide. Her Majesty has since, in 1855, thoroughly and judiciously restored the chancel of North Marston Church, and inserted an east window of beautifully stained glass, beneath which is a reredos sculptured in Caen stone, and bearing this inscription: 'This Reredos, and the stained-glass window above it, were erected by Her Majesty Victoria (D. G. B. R. F. D.) in the eighteenth year of her reign, in memory of John Camden Neild, Esq., of this parish, who died August 30, 1852, aged 72.' The chancel, which was built by the offerings made at the shrine of Sir John Schorne, a sainted rector of the parish in the thirteenth century, is a fine specimen of the perpendicular style, at its best period. It contains sedilia, piscina, niches, &c.—all richly ornamented with elaborate sculpture, so that now, with these all carefully restored, and the addition of its elegant memorial-window, there is perhaps not a more handsome chancel to be found in any village church. The rest of the church, however, is of an earlier and a plainer style of architecture.

# AUGUST 31.

St Aidan or Aedan, bishop of Lindisfarne, confessor, 651. St Cuthburge, queen of Northumbria, virgin and abbess, beginning of 8th century. St Raymund Nonnatus, confessor, 1240. St Isabel, virgin, 1270.

*Born.*—Caius Cæsar Caligula, Roman emperor, 12 A. D., *Antium.*

*Died.*—Henry V., king of England, 1422, *Vincennes, near Paris;* Etienne Pasquier, French jurist and historian, 1615, *Paris;* John Bunyan, author of the *Pilgrim's Progress*, 1688, *Snowhill, London;* Dr William Borlase, antiquary, 1772, *Ludgran, Cornwall;* F. A. Danican (Phillidor), noted for his skill in chess-playing, 1795; Dr James Currie, biographer of Burns, 1805, *Sidmouth;* Admiral Sir John Thomas Duckworth, 1817, *Devonport.*

## JOHN BUNYAN.

Everybody has heard of his birth at Elstow, about a mile from Bedford, in 1628; that he was bred a tinker; that his childhood was afflicted with remorse and dreams of fiends flying away with him; that, as he grew up, he 'danced, rang church-bells, played at tip-cat, and read *Sir Bevis of Southampton*,' for which he suffered many stings of conscience; that his indulgence in profanity was such, that a woman of loose character told him 'he was the ungodliest fellow for swearing she had ever heard in all her life,' and that 'he made her tremble to hear him;' that he entered the Parliamentary army, and served against the king in the decisive campaign of 1645; that, after terrible mental conflicts, he became converted, a Baptist, and a preacher; that at the Restoration in 1660 he was cast into Bedford jail, where, with intervals of precarious liberty, he remained for twelve years, refusing to be set at large on the condition of silence, with the brave answer: 'If you let me out to-day, I'll preach again to-morrow;' that, on his release, the fame of his writings, and his ability as a speaker, drew about him large audiences in London and elsewhere, and that, a few months before the Revolution of 1688, he caught a fever in consequence of a long ride from Reading in the rain, and died at the house of his friend, Mr Strudwick, a grocer at the sign of the Star, on Snowhill, London.

Bunyan was buried in Bunhill Fields, called by Southey, 'the Campo Santo of the Dissenters.' There sleep Dr John Owen and Dr Thomas Goodwin, Cromwell's preachers; George Fox, the Quaker; Daniel Defoe, Dr Isaac Watts, Susannah Wesley, the mother of the Wesleys; Ritson, the antiquary; William Blake, the visionary poet and painter; Thomas Stothard, and a host of others of greater or lesser fame in their separate sects. A monument, with a recumbent statue of Bunyan, was erected over his grave in 1862.

'It is a significant fact,' observes Macaulay, 'that, till a recent period, all the numerous editions of the *Pilgrim's Progress* were evidently meant for the cottage and the servants' hall. The paper, the printing, the plates were of the meanest description. In general, when the educated minority differs [with the uneducated majority] about the merit of a book, the opinion of the educated minority finally prevails. The *Pilgrim's Progress* is perhaps the only book about which, after the lapse of a hundred years, the educated minority has come over to the opinion of the common people.'

The literary history of the *Pilgrim's Progress* is indeed remarkable. It attained quick popularity. The first edition was 'Printed for Nath. Ponder, at the Peacock in the Poultry, 1678,' and before the year closed a second edition was called for. In the four following years it was reprinted six times. The eighth edition, which contains the last improvements made by the author, was published in 1682, the ninth in 1684, the tenth in 1685. In Scotland and the colonies, it was even more popular than in England. Bunyan tells that in New England his dream was the daily subject of conversation of thousands, and was thought worthy to appear in the most superb binding. It had numerous admirers, too, in Holland and among the Huguenots in France. Envy started the rumour that Bunyan did not, or could not have written the book, to which, 'with scorn to tell a lie,' he answered:

'It came from mine own heart, so to my head,
And thence into my fingers trickled;
Then to my pen, from whence immediately
On paper I did dribble it daintily.
Manner and matter too was all mine own,
Nor was it unto any mortal known,
Till I had done it. Nor did any then
By books, by wits, by tongues, or hand, or pen,
Add five words to it, or write half a line
Thereof: the whole and every whit is mine.'

Yet the favour and enormous circulation of the *Pilgrim's Progress* was limited to those who read for religious edification and made no pretence to critical tastes. When the *literati* spoke of the book, it was usually with contempt. Swift observes in his *Letter to a Young Divine:* 'I have been better entertained and more informed by a few pages in the *Pilgrim's Progress* than by a long discourse upon the will and intellect, and simple and complex ideas;' but we apprehend the remark was designed rather to depreciate metaphysics than to exalt Bunyan. Young, of the *Night Thoughts*, coupled Bunyan's prose with D'Urfey's doggerel, and in the *Spiritual Quixote* the adventures of Christian are classed with those of Jack the Giant Killer and John Hickathrift. But the most curious evidence of the rank assigned to Bunyan in the eighteenth century appears in Cowper's couplet, written so late as 1782:

'I name thee not, lest so despised a name
Should move a sneer at thy deserved fame.'

It was only with the growth of purer and more Catholic principles of criticism towards the close of the last century and the beginning of the present, that the popular verdict was affirmed and the *Pilgrim's Progress* registered among the choicest English classics. Almost every year there now appears one or more beautiful editions of the *Pilgrim*. Ancient editions are sought for with eager rivalry by collectors; but, until 1886, only one perfect copy of the first edition of 1678 was known to be extant. Originally published for a shilling, this rare edition was bought in its old sheep-skin cover, for twenty guineas. Two copies changed hands in 1886; one was added to the Library of the British Museum at the price of £65; the other was sold for £25. A fac-simile reprint of the first edition was published in 1875, and a statue to its author was unveiled at Bedford in 1874.

A curious anecdote of Bunyan appeared in the *Morning Advertiser* a few years ago. To pass away the gloomy hours in prison, Bunyan took a rail out of the stool belonging to his cell, and, with his knife, fashioned it into a flute. The keeper, hearing music, followed the sound to Bunyan's cell; but, while they were unlocking the door, the ingenious prisoner replaced the rail in the stool, so that the searchers were unable to solve the mystery; nor, during the remainder of Bunyan's residence in the jail, did they ever discover how the music had been produced.

In an old account of Bedford, there is an equally good anecdote, to the effect that a Quaker called upon Bunyan in jail one day, with what he professed to be a message from the Lord. 'After searching for thee,' said he, 'in half the jails of England, I am glad to have found thee at last.'

JOHN • BVNYAN • 1662.

AUTOGRAPH OF BUNYAN, FROM A BOOK.

'If the Lord sent thee,' said Bunyan sarcastically, 'you would not have needed to take so much trouble to find me out, for He knows that I have been in Bedford jail these seven years past.'

The portrait of Bunyan represents a robust man, with a large well-formed head, of massive but not unhandsome features, and a profusion of dark hair falling in curls upon his shoulders. The head is well carried, and the expression of the face open and manly—altogether a prepossessing, honest-looking man.

In an obscure part of the borough of Southwark—in Zoar Street, Gravel Lane—there is an old dissenting meeting-house, now used as a carpenter's shop, which tradition affirms to have been occupied by John Bunyan for worship. It is known to have been erected a short while before the Revolution, by a few earnest Protestant Christians, as a means of counteracting a Catholic school which had been established in the neighbourhood under the auspices of James II. But Bunyan may have once or twice

BUNYAN'S MEETING-HOUSE, ZOAR STREET, SOUTHWARK.

or occasionally preached in it during the year preceding his death. From respect for the name of the illustrious Nonconformist, we have had a view taken of the interior of the chapel in its present state.

## PHILLIDOR, THE CHESS-PLAYER.

Phillidor is known, in the present day, not under his real name, but under one voluntarily assumed; and not for the studies to which he devoted most time and thought, but for a special and exceptional talent. François André Danican, born at Dreux, in France, in 1726, was in his youth one of the pages to Louis XIV., and was educated as a court-musician. He composed a motet for the Royal Chapel at the early age of fifteen. Having by some means lost the sunshine of regal favour, he earned a living chiefly by teaching music, filling up vacant time as a music-copyist for the theatres and concerts, and occasionally as a composer. He composed music to Dryden's *Alexander's Feast;* in 1754, he composed a *Lauda Jerusalem* for the chapel at Versailles; in 1759, an operetta called *Blaise le Savetier;* and then followed, in subsequent years, *Le Maréchal-ferrant*, *Le Sorcier*, *Ernelinde*, *Persée*, *Thémistoclée*, *Alceste*, and many other operas—the whole of which are now forgotten.

Danican, or—to give the name by which he was generally known—Phillidor, lives in fame through his chess-playing, not his music. When quite a young man, an intense love of chess seized him; and at one time he entertained a hope of adding to his income by exhibiting his chess-playing powers, and giving instructions in the game. With this view he visited Holland, Germany, and England. While in England, in 1749, he published his *Analyse des Echecs*—a work which has taken its place among the classics of chess. During five or six years of residence in London, his remarkable play attracted much attention. Forty years passed over his head, marked by many vicissitudes as a chess-player as well as a composer, when the French Revolution drove him again to England, where he died on the 31st August 1795. The art of playing chess *blindfold* was one by which Phillidor greatly astonished his contemporaries, though he was not the first to do it. Buzecca, in 1266, played three games at once, looking at one board, but not at the other two; all three of his competitors were skilful players; and his winning of two games, and drawing a third, naturally excited much astonishment. Ruy Lopez, Mangiolini, Terone, Medrano, Leonardi da Cutis, Paoli Boi, Salvio, and others who lived between the thirteenth and the seventeenth centuries, were also able to play at chess without seeing the board. Father Sacchieri, who was professor of mathematics at Pavia early in the last century, could play three games at once against three players, without seeing any of the boards. Many of these exploits were not well known until recently; and, on that account, Phillidor was regarded as a prodigy. While yet a youth, he used to play imaginary games of chess as he lay awake in bed. His first real game of this kind he won of a French abbé. He afterwards became so skilful in this special knack, that he could play nearly as well without as with seeing the board, even when playing two games at once. Forty years of wear and tear did not deprive him of this faculty; for when in England, in 1783, he competed blindfold against three of the best players then living, Count Bruhl, Baron Maseres, and Mr Bowdler: winning two of the games and drawing the third. On another occasion he did the same thing, even giving the odds of 'the pawn and move' (as it is called) to one of his antagonists. What surprised the lookers-on most was, that Phillidor could keep up a lively conversation during these severe labours. Phillidor's achievement has been far outdone in recent years by Morphy, Paulsen, and Blackburne, in respect to the number of games played at once; but the lively Frenchman carried off the palm as a gossip and a player at the same time.

---

## DREAD OF SCOTCH COMPETITION:

### SCOTCH NON-TRADING LEAGUE AGAINST ENGLAND.

On this day, in 1527, is dated the 'ordinary' of the corporation of weavers in Newcastle, in which, amongst other regulations, there is a strict one that no member should take a Scotsman to apprentice, or set any of that nation to work, under a penalty of forty shillings. To call a brother, 'Scot' or 'mansworn,' inferred a forfeit of 6*s.* 8*d.*, 'without any forgiveness.'—Brand's *Hist. of Newcastle.*

The superior ability of the Scottish nation, in the competitions of life, seems to have made an unusual impression on their Newcastle neighbours. To be serious—we can fortunately shew our freedom from national partiality by following up the above with an example of the like illiberality on the part of Scotland towards England. It consists of a sort of covenant entered into in the year 1752 by the drapers, mercers, milliners, &c., of Edinburgh, to cease dealing with commercial travellers from England—what were then called English Riders. 'Considering'—so runs the language of this document—'that the giving orders or commissions to English Riders (or clerks to English merchants), when they come to this city, tends greatly to the destruction of the wonted wholesale trade thereof, from which most of the towns in Scotland used to be furnished with goods, and that some of these English Riders not only enhances the said wholesale trade, but also corresponds with, and sells goods to private families and persons, at the same prices and rates as if to us in a wholesale way, and that their frequent journeys to this place are attended with high charges, which consequently must be laid on the cost of those goods we buy from them, and that we can be as well served in goods by a written commission by post (as little or no regard is had by them to the patterns or colours of goods which we order them to send when they are here), therefore, and *for the promoting of trade*, we hereby voluntarily bind and oblige ourselves that, in no time coming, we shall give any personal order or commission for any goods we deal in to any English dealer, clerk, or rider whatever who shall come to Scotland.' They add an obligation to have no dealings 'with any people in England who shall make a practice of coming themselves or sending clerks or riders into Scotland.' The penalty was to be two pounds two shillings for every breach of the obligations.

This covenant was drawn out on a good sheet of vellum bearing a stamp, and which was to be duly registered, in order to give it validity at law against the obligants in case of infraction. It bears one hundred and fifty-four signatures, partly of men, generally in good and partly of women in bad holograph.* It is endorsed, 'Resolution and Agreement of the Merchants of Edinburgh for Discouraging English Riders from Coming into Scotland.'

This strange covenant, as it appears to us, seems to have made some noise, for, several months after its date, the following paragraph regarding it appeared in an English newspaper: 'We hear from Scotland, that the trading people throughout that kingdom have agreed, by a general association, not to give any orders for the future to any English riders that may be sent among them by the English tradesmen. This resolution is owing to the unfair behaviour of the itinerants, whose constant practice it is to undermine and undersell each other, without procuring any benefit to the trading interest of the nation in general, by such behaviour; which, on the contrary, only tends to unsettle the course of business and destroy that connection and good understanding between people, who had better not deal together at all, than not do it with spirit and mutual confidence. It is said also that several towns in England have already copied this example.'—*London Daily Advertiser*, January 27, 1753.

* Amongst the male signatures are those of James Lindsay, Cleghorn and Livingston, David Inglis, Edward Caithness, Patrick Inglis, Hugh Hamilton, Adam Anderson, Murray and Lindsay, George Dunsmure, George Pitcairne, James Beveridge, Bertram and Williamson, Alexander Hepburn, Arbuthnott and Scott, James Stirling, Thomas Trotter, Jun[r]., William Clapperton, Archibald Bowie, James Allan, William Burn, Nicol Swan, Archibald M'Coull, John Hope, Stuart and Wallace, Walter Hamilton, John Grieve, Oliver Tod. Several of these were wealthy citizens; some became magistrates. Amongst the female names are those of Katherine Ramsay and sisters, Peg Bowie, Betty Murray, Christy Balfour, and many others thus familiarly expressed. The Misses Ramsay were milliners of great business, who ultimately realised some wealth, and built a handsome suburban villa, in which to spend their latter days.

Next him September marched eke on foot,
  Yet was he hoary, laden with the spoil
Of harvest riches, which he made his boot,
  And him enriched with bounty of the soil;
  In his one hand, as fit for harvest's toil,
He held a knife-hook; and in th' other hand
  A pair of weights, with which he did assoil
Both more and less, where it in doubt did stand,
And equal gave to each as justice duly scanned.

SPENSER.

(DESCRIPTIVE.)

SEPTEMBER FAR inland, within sight of our wave-washed shores, along the margins of our pleasant rivers, in level meadows and sinking valleys, on gentle uplands and sloping hill-sides, there is now a busy movement, for men and maidens are out, with their bended sickles, to gather in the golden harvest. The village streets are comparatively silent. Scores of cottages are shut up—one old woman perhaps only left to look after the whole row—for even the children have gone to glean, and many of the village artizans find it pleasant to quit their usual employment for a few days, and go out to reap the corn. There will be no getting a coat mended or a shoe cobbled for days to come. If there is a stir of life in the village street, those who move along are either coming from or going to the reapers, bringing back empty bottles and baskets, or carrying them filled with ale and provisions. A delicate Cockney, who can only eat the lean of his overdone mutton-chop, with the aid of pickles, would stand aghast at the great cold dinner spread out for the farmer and his house-servants—men, each with the appetite of three, and maidens who can eat meat that is all fat. Pounds of fat beef, bacon, and ham, great wedges of cheese, cold apple-pies, with crusts two inches thick, huge brown loaves, lumps of butter, and a continually gurgling ale, are the viands which a well-to-do farmer places before his servants, and shares with them, for he argues, he cannot expect to get the proper quantity of work out of them unless they live well. To get his harvest in quick, while the weather is fine, is the study of the great corn-grower; and such a far-seeing man scarcely gives the cost a consideration, for he knows that those who delay will, if the weather changes, be ready to pay almost any price for reapers; so he gets in his corn 'while the sun shines.' If well got in, what a price it will fetch in the market, compared with that which was left out in the rain, until it became discoloured and sprouted! And as he points to his ricks with pride, he asks what's the value of the extra bullock, the pig or two, and the few barrels of ale the reapers consumed, compared to such a crop as that; and he is right. It is an anxious time for the farmer. He is continually looking at his weather-glass, and watching those out-of-door signs which denote a change in the weather, and which none are better acquainted with than those who pass so much of their life in the fields. Unlike the manufacturer, who carries on his business indoors whatever the changes of the season may be, the farmer is dependent on the weather for the safety of his crop, and can never say what that will be, no matter how beautiful it may look while standing, until it is safely garnered. Somehow he seems to live nearer to God than the busy indwellers of cities, for he puts his trust in Him who has promised that He will always send 'seed-time and harvest.'

How gracefully a good reaper handles his sickle, and clutches the corn—one sweep, and the whole armful is down, and laid so neat and level, that when the band is put round the sheaf, the bottom of almost every straw touches the ground when it is reared up, and the ears look as level as they did while growing! It is a nice art to make those corn-bands well, which bind the sheaves—to twist the ears of corn so that they shall all cluster together without shaking out the grain, and then to tie up the sheaves, so round and plump, that they may be rolled over, when stacking or loading, without hardly a head becoming loose. There are rich morsels of colour about the cornfield where the reapers are at work. The handkerchiefs which they bind around their foreheads, to keep off the sun—the white of their shirt-sleeves, making spots of light amid the yellow corn—the gleaners in costumes of every hue, blue, red, and gray, stooping or standing here and there, near the overhanging trees in the hedgerows—make such a diversity of colour as please the eye, while the great blue heaven spans over all, and a few loose silver clouds float gently over the scene. In such a light, the white horses seem cut out of silver, the chestnuts of ruddy gold, while the black horses stand out against the sky, as if cut in black marble. What great gaps half-a-dozen reapers soon make in the standing corn! Half-an-hour ago, where the eye dwelt on a broad furrow of upstanding ears, there is now a low road of stubble, where trails of the ground-convolvulus may be seen, and the cyanus of every hue, which the country children call corn-flowers. Pretty is it, too, to see the little children gleaning, each with a rough bag or pocket before it, and a pair of old scissors dangling by its side, to cut off the straw, for only the ears are to be placed in the gleaner's little bag. Then there is the large poke, under the hedge, into which their mother empties the tiny glean-bags, and that by night will be filled, and a heavy load it is for the poor woman to carry home on her head, for a mile or two, while the little ones trot along by her side, the largest perhaps carrying a small sheaf, which she has gleaned, and from which the straw has not been cut, while the ears hang down and mingle with her flowing hair. A good, kind-hearted farmer will, like Boaz of old, when he spoke kindly to pretty Ruth, let his poor neighbours glean 'even amongst the sheaves.' The dry hard stubble, amid which they glean, cuts the bare legs and naked arms of the poor children like wires, making them as rough at times as fresh-plucked geese. Rare gleaning there is where the 'stooks' have stood, when the wagons come to 'lead' the corn out of the field. The men stick the sheaves on their forks as fast as you can count them, throw them into the wagon, then move on to the next 'stook'—each of which consists of eight or ten sheaves—then there is a rush and scramble to the spot that is just cleared, for there the great ears of loose and fallen corn lie thick and close together, and that is the richest gleaning harvest yields.

Who has not paused to see the high-piled wagons come rocking over the furrowed fields, and sweeping through the green lanes, at the leading-home of harvest? All the village turns out to see the last load carried into the rick-yard; the toothless old grandmother, in spectacles, stands at her cottage-door; the poor old labourer, who has been long ailing, and who will never more help to reap the harvest, leans on his stick in the sunshine; while the feeble huzzas of the children mingle with the deep-chested cheers of the men, and the silvery ring of maiden-voices—all welcoming home the last load with cheery voices, especially where the farmer is respected, and has allowed his poor neighbours to glean. Some are mounted on the sheaves, and one sheaf is often decorated with flowers and ribbons, the last that was in the field; and sometime a pretty girl sits sideways on one of the great fat horses, her straw-hat ornamented with flowers and ears of corn. Right proud she is when hailed by the rustics as the Harvest Queen! Then there are the farmer, his wife, and daughters, all standing and smiling at the open gate of the stack-yard; and proud is the driver as he cocks his hat aside, and giving the horses a slight touch, sends the last load with a sweep into the yard, that almost makes you feel afraid it will topple over, so much does it rock coming in at this grand finish. Rare gleaning is there, too, for the birds, and many a little animal, in the long lanes through which the wagons have passed during the harvest, for almost every overhanging branch has taken toll from the loads, while the hawthorn-hedges have swept over them like rakes. The long-tailed field-mouse will carry off many an ear to add to his winter-store, and stow away in his snug nest under the embankment. What grand subjects, mellowed by the setting suns of departed centuries, do these harvest-fields bring before a picture-loving eye!

Abraham among his reapers—Isaac musing in the fields at even-tide—Jacob labouring to win Rachel—Joseph and the great granaries of Egypt—Ruth

'Standing in tears among the alien corn'—

and the harvests of Palestine, amid which our Saviour walked by the side of His disciples. All these scenes pass before a meditative mind while gazing over the harvest-field, filled with busy reapers and gleaners, and we think how, thousands of years ago, the same picture was seen by the patriarchs, and that Ruth herself may have led David by the hand, while yet a child, through the very fields in which she herself had gleaned. But the frames in which these old pictures were placed were not carved into such beautiful park-like scenery and green pastoral spots as we see in England, for there the harvest-fields were hemmed in by rocky hills, and engirded with deserts, where few trees waved, and the villages lay far and wide apart. And, instead of the sound of the thrasher's flail, oxen went treading their weary round to trample out the corn, which in spring shot up in green circles where they had trodden.

Winged seeds now ride upon the air, like insects, many of them balanced like balloons, the broad top uppermost, and armed with hooked grapnels, which take fast hold of whatever they alight upon. We see the net-work of the spider suspended from leaf to branch, which in the early morning is hung with rounded crystals, for such seem the glittering dew-drops as they catch the light of the rising sun. The hawthorn-berries begin to shew red in the hedges, and we see scarlet heps where, a few weeks ago, the clustering wild-roses bloomed. Here and there, in sunny places, the bramble-berries have began to blacken, though many yet wear a crude red, while some are green, nor is it unusual, in a mild September, to see a few of the satin-like bramble blossoms, putting out here and there, amid a profusion of berries. The bee seems to move wearily from flower to flower, for they lie wider asunder now than they did a month ago, and the little hillocks covered with wild-thyme, which he scarcely deigned to notice then, he now gladly alights upon, and revels amid the tiny sprigs of lavender-coloured bloom. The spotted wood-leopard moth may still be seen, and the goat-moth, whose larva is called the oak-piercer, and sometimes the splendid tiger-moth comes sailing by on Tyrian wings, that fairly dazzle the eye with their beauty. But at no season of the year are the sunsets so beautiful as now; and many who have travelled far say, that nowhere in the world do the clouds hang in such gaudy colours of ruby and gold, about the western sky, as they do in England during autumn, and that these rich effects are produced through our being surrounded by the sea. Nor is sunrise less beautiful een from the summit of some hill, while the valleys are still covered with a white mist. The tops of the trees seem at first to rise above a country that is flooded, while the church-spire appears like some sea-mark, heaving out of the mist. Then comes a great wedge-like beam of gold, cutting deep down into the hollows, shewing the stems of the trees, and the roofs of cottages, gilding barn and outhouse, making a golden road through a land of white mist, which seems to rise on either hand, like the sea which Moses divided for the people of Israel to pass through dryshod. The dew-drops on the sun-lighted summit the feet rest upon are coloured like precious stones of every dye, and every blade of grass is beaded with these gorgeous gems. Sometimes the autumnal mists do not rise more than four or five feet above the earth, revealing only the heads of horse and rider, who seem to move up as if breasting a river, while the shepherd and milkmaid shew like floating busts. The following word-painting was made in the early sunrise, while we were wanderers, many long years ago:

On the far sky leans the old ruined mill;
  Through its rent sails the broken sunbeams glow;
Gilding the trees that belt the lower hill,
  And the old oaks which on its summit grow;
Only the reedy marsh that sleeps below,
  With its dwarf bushes is concealed from view;
And now a straggling thorn its head doth shew,
  Another half shakes off the misty blue
  Just where the smoky gold streams through the heavy dew.

And there the hidden river lingering dreams,
  You scarce can see the banks that round it lie;
That withered trunk, a tree, or shepherd seems,
  Just as the light or fancy strikes the eye.
  Even the very sheep which graze hard by,
So blend their fleeces with the misty haze,
  They look like clouds shook from the cold gray sky
Ere morning o'er the unsunned hill did blaze—
The vision fades as they move further off to graze.

We have often fancied that deer never look so beautiful, as when in autumn they move about, or couch amid the rich russet-coloured fern—when there is a blue atmosphere in the distance, and the trees scattered around are of many changing hues. There is a majesty in the movements of these graceful animals, both in the manner of their walk, and the way they carry their heads, crowned with picturesque antlers. Then they are so particular in their choice of pasture, refusing to eat where the verdure is rank or trampled down, also feeding very slowly, and when satisfied, lying down to chew the cud at their ease. Their eyes are also very beautiful, having a sparkling softness about them like the eyes of a woman, while the senses of sight, smelling, and hearing are more perfect than that of the generality of quadrupeds. Watch their attitude while listening! that raised head, and those erect ears, catch sounds so distant that they would not be within our own hearing, were we half a mile nearer the sound from the spot where the herd is feeding.

Beautiful are the fern and heath covered wastes in September—with their bushes bearing wild-fruits, sloe, and bullace, and crab; and where one may lie hidden for hours, watching how beast, bird, and insect pass their time away, and what they do in these solitudes. In such spots, we have seen great gorse-bushes in bloom, high as the head of a mounted horseman; impenetrable places where the bramble and the sloe had become entangled with the furze and the branches of stunted hawthorns, that had never been able to grow clear of the wild waste of underwood—spots where the boldest hunter is compelled to draw in his rein, and leave the hounds to work their way through the tangled maze. Many of these hawthorns were old and gray, and looked as if some giant hand had twisted a dozen iron stems into one, and left them to grow and harden together in ridges, and knots, and coils, that looked like the relics of some older world—peopled with other creations than those the eye now dwells upon. Some few such spots we yet know in England, of which no record can be found that they were ever cultivated. And over these bowery hollows, and this dense underwood, giant oaks threw their arms so far out, that we marvelled how the hoary trunks, which were often hollow, could bear such weights without other support than the bole from which they sprang—shewing a strength which the builder man, with all his devices, is unable to imitate. Others there were—gnarled, hoary trunks—which, undated centuries ago, the bolt had blackened, and the lightning burned, so monstrous that they took several men, joined hand-to-hand, to girth them, yet still they sent out a few green leaves from their branchless tops, like aged ruins whose summits the ivy often covers. And in these haunts the red fox sheltered, and the gray badger had its home, and there the wild-cat might sometimes be seen glaring like a tiger, through the branches, on the invader of its solitude. It seemed like a spot in which vegetation had struggled for the mastery for ages, and where the tall trees having overtopped the assailing underwood, were hemmed in every way, and besieged until they perished from the rank growth below. But every here and there were sunny spots, and open glades, where the turf rose elastic from the tread, and great green walls of hazel shot up more like trees than shrubs. There were no such nuts to be found anywhere as on these aged hazels, which, when ripe, we could shake out of their husks, or cups—nothing to be found in our planted Nutteries so firm and sweet as those grown in this wildwood, and Nutting-Day is still kept up as a rural holiday in September in many parts of England, in the neighbourhood of merry greenwoods. Towards the end of the month, old and young, maidens and their sweethearts, generally accompanied by a troop of happy boys and girls, sally out with bags and crooks, bottles and baskets, containing drink and food, pipes and tobacco for the old people, and all that is required for a rough rustic repast 'all under the greenwood tree.' One great feature of this old rural merry-making, is their going out in their very homeliest attire, and many there were who had worn the same nutting-dress for years. Old Royster's leather-shorts had been the heirloom of two generations, and when last we heard of them, were still able to bid defiance to brake or brier. A fashionable picnic is shorn of all that heart-happiness which is enjoyed by homely country-people, for, in the former, people are afraid of appearing natural. Pretty country girls were not called 'young ladies' at these rural holidays, but by their sweet-sounding Christian names; and oh what music there is in Mary' compared with 'Miss!' What merry laughter have we heard ringing through those old woods, as some pretty maiden was uplifted by her sweetheart to reach the ripe cluster of nuts which hung on the topmost bough, where they had been browned by the sun, when, overbalancing himself, they came down among the soft wood-grass, to the great merriment of every beholder! Some were sure to get lost, and there was such shouting and hallooing as awakened every echo, and sent the white owls sailing half asleep in search of some quieter nook, where they could finish their nap in peace.

Then what a beautiful banquet-hall they find in some open sunny spot, surrounded with hazels, and overtopped by tall trees, where the golden rays, shining through the leaves, throw a warm mellow light on all around! Nothing throws out smoother or more beautifully coloured branches than the hazel, the bark of which shines as if it had been polished. And who has not admired its graceful catkins in spring, that droop and wave like elegant laburnums, and are seen long before its leaves appear? Nor does autumn, amid all its rich coloured foliage, shew a more beautiful object than a golden hued hazel-copse, which remains in leaf later than many of the trees. When this clear yellow tint of the leaves is seen, the nuts are ripe, and never before—one shake at a branch, and down they come rattling out of their cups by scores—real 'brown sheelers,' as they are called by country-people. Wood-nuts gathered at the end of September or the beginning of October, have the true 'nutty' flavour, which is never tasted if they are gathered before. These wild-nuts are seldom found 'hollow'—so they are called when the kernel is eaten by the white grub, the egg of which was laid while the nut was in a soft state early in summer. And unless this grub has eaten its way out, and left visible the hole by which it escaped, we have never yet been able to discover what part of the shell the fly pierced when depositing its egg. This grub is still a puzzle, nor do we remember to have ever seen its re-appearance as a perfect weevil in spring, though we have often looked on while letting itself down from the nut by the thread it had spun after escaping from the shell. How long it remains in the earth is not at present known; nor is there a certainty that the grub buries itself in the earth at all while in a state of pupa, though it must find something to feed on somewhere before reaching a state of imago, some imagine, unless it obtain nourishment enough in the kernel it had eaten, prior to undergoing this later change. This, we believe, is a nut which none of our many clever naturalists have yet cracked to their own satisfaction.

---

## (HISTORICAL.)

When the year began in March, this was the seventh of its months; consequently, was properly termed September. By the commencement of the year two months earlier, the name is now become inappropriate, as is likewise the case with its three followers—October, November, and December. When Julius Cæsar reformed the calendar, he gave this month a 31st day, which Augustus subsequently took from it; and so it has since remained. Our Saxon ancestors called it *Gerst monat*, or barley-month, because they then realised this crop; one of unusual importance to them, on account of the favourite beverage which they brewed from it.

On the 23d, the sun enters the constellation *Libra*, and passes to the southward of the equator, thus producing the autumnal equinox; a period usually followed by a course of stormy weather. September, however, is often with us a month of steady and pleasant weather, notwithstanding that in the mornings and evenings the first chills of winter begin to be felt. On the 1st of the month, at London, the sun is up 12h 28m, and on the 30th, 11h 38m.

# First of September.

**Saints Felix, Donatus, Arontius, Honoratus, Fortunatus, Sabinianus, Septimius, Januarius, Felix, Vitalis, Satyrus, and Repositus, twelve brothers, martyrs at Benevento, in Italy. St Firminus II. bishop and confessor, 4th century. St Lupus or Lew, archbishop of Sens, confessor, about 623. St Giles, abbot, about 700.**

## ST GILES.

Giles or Ægidius, a very eminent saint of the seventh century, is believed to have been a Greek who migrated to France under the influence of a desire of greater retirement than he could enjoy in his own country. Settling in a hermitage, first in one of the deserts near the mouth of the Rhone, finally in a forest in the diocese of Nismes, he gave himself to solitude and heavenly contemplation with such entire devotion of spirit as raised him to the highest reputation. There is a romantic story of his being partly indebted for his subsistence to a Heaven-directed hind, which came daily to give him its milk; and it is added that his retirement was discovered by the king of the country, who, starting this animal in the chase, followed it till it took refuge at the feet of the holy anchorite. In time, admitting disciples, St Giles became, almost against his own will, the head of a little monastic establishment, which in time grew to be a regular Benedictine monastery, and was surrounded by a town taking its name from the saint.

Veneration for St Giles caused many churches to be dedicated to him in various countries. In reference to a legend of his having once refused to be cured of lameness, the better to mortify in him all fleshly appetites, he became, as it were, the patron saint of cripples. It was customary that Giles's Church should be on the outskirts of a town, on one of the great thoroughfares leading into it, in order that cripples might the more conveniently come to and cluster around it. We have a memorial of this association of facts in the interesting old church of *St Giles, Cripplegate*, in the eastern part of the city of London. So early as 1101, Matilda, the queen of Henry I., founded a hospital for lepers at another inlet of the metropolis, where now exists the modern church of St Giles-in-the-Fields. From an early, but unascertained time, the parish church of Edinburgh was dedicated to this French saint. After it had been undergoing gradual extension and improvement for ages, one William Preston of Gorton, travelling in France, succeeded, with great pains and expense, in obtaining a most holy relic—an arm-bone of St Giles—and brought it home to Scotland, to be placed for perpetuity in St Giles's Church. The municipality, in gratitude, allowed him to raise an aisle in the church, and granted that he and his successors should have the privilege of carrying the bone in all processions. It is curious to trace such past matters amidst a state of things now so different. So lately as 1556, the Dean of Guild of Edinburgh expended 12*d.* in 'mending and polishing Saint Geles arme.' A great change was at that very time impending. When the time for the annual procession of St Giles came about in 1558 (1st September), the populace were found to have stolen the wooden image of the saint, usually carried on those occasions, and to have ignominiously burned it. An attempt was made to effect the procession in the usual style with a borrowed image; but the proceedings were interrupted by a riot, and after that time we hear no more of any religious rites connected with St Giles in Scotland. How difficult it is, however, altogether to eradicate anything religious that has ever once taken root in a country! There, to this day, on one side of the coat-armorial of the city of Edinburgh, you see figuring as a supporter, the hind which ancient legend represents as nurturing the holy anchorite in the forests of Languedoc twelve hundred years ago.

*Born.*—Edward Alleyn, founder of Dulwich College, 1566, *London;* Margaret, Countess of Blessington, novelist, 1789, *Knockbrit, near Clonmel.*

*Died.*—Pope Adrian IV., 1159; Dr Henry More, theologian and philosopher, 1687, *Cambridge;* Louis XIV. of France, 1715, *Versailles;* Eusebius Renaudot, oriental scholar, 1720, *Paris;* Sir Richard Steele, essayist and dramatist, 1729, *Llangunnor, near Caermarthen;* Dr Maurice Greene, ecclesiastical composer, 1755; John Ireland, dean of Westminster, theological writer, 1842; William Yarrell, distinguished naturalist, 1856, *Yarmouth.*

## LAST MOMENTS OF A GREAT KING.

Louis XIV. had reigned over France for seventy-two years. He had been allowed to assume power beyond his predecessors; he had been idolised to a degree unknown to any other European sovereign. His wars, though latterly unfortunate, had greatly contributed to raise him in the eyes of his subjects. He had enlarged his dominions, and planted a grandson on the throne of Spain. As specially *Le Grand Monarque* amongst all contemporary sovereigns, he was viewed even by neighbouring nations as a being somewhat superior to common humanity. It becomes curious to see how such a demi-god could die.

Up to the 23d of August 1715, Louis was able to attend council and transact business; for two days more, he could listen to music and converse with his courtiers. About seven in the evening of the 25th, the musicians came as usual to entertain him; but he felt himself too unwell to receive them, and his medical advisers were called instead. It was seen that his hour was approaching, and the last offices of religion were that night administered to him.

Next day, after mass, he called to his bedside the cardinals De Rohan and De Billi, in presence of Madame de Maintenon (his wife), the Father

Tellier, the chancellor, and other officers, and said to them: 'I die in the faith and submission of the church. I am not instructed in the matters which trouble her, but have followed your counsels, and uniformly done what you desired. If I have done amiss, you will be answerable before God, who is now my witness.' [What awfully wrong things *were* done!] The two cardinals made no other answer than by eulogiums on his conduct: he was destined to be flattered to the last moment of his life.

Immediately after, the king said: 'I again take God to witness that I have never borne hatred to the Cardinal de Noailles; I have always been distressed by what I have done against him; but it was what they told me I ought to do.' Thereupon, Blouin, Fagon, and Mareschal asked in elevated tones: 'Will they not allow the king to see his archbishop, to mark the reconciliation?' The king, who understood them, declared that, far from having any objection, he desired it, and ordered the chancellor to make the archbishop come to him—'If these gentlemen,' he said, looking to the two cardinals, 'do not find it inconvenient.' It was a critical moment for them. To leave the conqueror of heresy to die in the arms of a heretic was a great scandal in their eyes. They withdrew into the recess of a window to deliberate with the confessor, the chancellor, and Madame de Maintenon. Tellier and Billi judged the interview too dangerous, and induced Madame de Maintenon to think so likewise; Rohan and the chancellor, having the future in view, neither opposed nor approved; all, once more approaching the bed, renewed their praises of the delicacy of the royal conscience, and told him that such a step could not but subject the good cause to the triumph of its enemies—nevertheless, they were willing to see the archbishop come, if he would give the king his promise to accept the constitution. The timid prince submitted to their advice, and the chancellor wrote in consequence to the archbishop. Noailles felt keenly this last stroke of his enemies, answered with respect, but did not accept the conditions, and could not see the king. From that time he was nothing but an ingrate and a rebel, and they spoke of him no more, in order that the king might die in peace.

The same morning, the king had the infant dauphin (his great-grandchild, subsequently Louis XV.) brought to him by the Duchess de Ventadour, and addressed him in these words: 'My child, you will soon be the sovereign of a great kingdom: what I most strongly recommend to you, is that you never forget your obligations to God; remember you owe Him all that you are. Endeavour to preserve peace with your neighbours. I have loved war too much. Do not imitate me in that, nor in my too great expenditure. Take counsel in all things; seek to know the best, that you may follow it. Relieve your people as much as you can, and do for them that which I have had the misfortune not to be able to do for them myself. Do not forget the great obligations you are under to Madame de Ventadour. For me, madam,' turning to her, 'I am sorry not to be in a condition more emphatically to mark my gratitude to you.' He ended by saying to the dauphin: 'My dear child, I give you my blessing with all my heart;' and he then embraced him twice with the greatest marks of tenderness.

The Duchess de Ventadour, seeing the king so moved, took away the dauphin. The king then received, in succession, the princes and princesses of the blood, and spoke to them all, but separately to the Duc d'Orleans and the legitimate children, whom he had made come first. He rewarded all his domestics for the services they had rendered him, and recommended them to shew the same attachment to the dauphin.

After dinner, the king addressed those about him. 'Gentlemen, I ask your pardon for the bad example I have given you. I would wish to shew my sense of the manner in which you have always served me, my sense of your invariable attachment and fidelity. I am extremely vexed not to have been able to do for you all I wished to do. I ask you for my great-grandson the same attachment and fidelity you have shewn to me. I hope you will all stand unitedly round him, and that, if any one breaks away, you will aid in bringing him back. I feel that I am giving way too much, and making you give way too—pray, pardon me. Adieu, gentlemen; I reckon upon your occasionally remembering me.'

On Tuesday the 27th, when the king had no one beside him but Madame de Maintenon and the chancellor, he caused to be brought to him two caskets, from which he directed numerous papers to be taken out and burned, and gave orders to the chancellor regarding the remainder. Subsequently to this, he ordered his confessor to be called, and after speaking to him in a low voice, made the Count of Pouchartrain approach, and instructed him to carry out his commands relative to conveying his heart to the Jesuits' convent, and depositing it there opposite that of his father, Louis XIII.

With the same composure, Louis caused the plan of the castle of Vincennes to be taken from a casket, and sent to the grand marshal of the household, to enable him to make preparations for the residence of the court, and conducting thither *the young king*—such were the words used. He employed also occasionally the expression, *In the time that I was king;* and then, addressing himself to Madame de Maintenon, said: 'I have always heard that it is a difficult thing to die; I am now on the verge of this predicament, and I do not find the process of dissolution so painful a one.' Madame de Maintenon replied, that such a moment was terrible when we still cherished an attachment to the world and had restitutions to make. 'As an individual,' rejoined the king, 'I owe restitution to no one; and as regards what I owe the kingdom, I trust in the mercy of God. I have duly confessed myself; my confessor declares that I have a great reliance in God; I have it with all my heart.' How indubitable a security was Father Tellier for the conscience of a king! The following day (Wednesday) Louis, as he was conversing with his confessor, beheld in the glass two of his servants who were weeping at the foot of his bed. 'Why do you weep,' said he, 'did you think I was immortal? My age should have prepared you for my death.' Then looking to Madame de Maintenon, 'What consoles me in quitting you, is the hope that we shall soon be reunited in eternity.' She made no reply to this farewell, which did not appear at all agreeable to her. 'Bolduc, the first apothecary, assured me,' says Duclos, 'that Madame de Maintenon said, as she left the room: "See the appointment which he makes with me! this man has never loved any one but himself." Such an expression, the authenticity of which I would not guarantee, as the principal domestics bore her no good-will, is more suitable to the widow of Scarron than to 'a queen.' However this may be, Madame de Maintenon departed immediately for Saint-Cyr, with the intention of remaining there.

A Marseille empiric, named Lebrun, made his appearance with an elixir, which he announced as a remedy for the gangrene which was advancing so rapidly in the king's leg. The physicians, having abandoned all hope, allowed the king to take a few drops of this liquid, which seemed to revive him, but he speedily relapsed; a second dose was presented, his attendants telling him at the same time that it was to recall him to life. 'To life or to death,' said the king, taking the glass, 'whatever pleases God.' He then asked his confessor for a general absolution.

Since the king had taken to his bed, the court had gathered in a marked manner around the Duke of Orleans [the future regent]; but the king having apparently rallied on Thursday, this favourable symptom was so exaggerated, that the duke found himself alone.

The king having noticed the absence of Madame de Maintenon, exhibited some chagrin, and asked for her several times. She returned speedily, and said that she had gone to unite her prayers with those of her daughters, the virgins of Saint-Cyr. Throughout the following day, the 30th, she remained beside the king till the evening, and then seeing his faculties becoming confused, she went to her own room, divided her furniture among her servants, and returned to Saint-Cyr, from which she no more emerged.

From this time, Louis had but slight intervals of consciousness, and thus was spent Saturday the 31st. About eleven o'clock at night, the curé, the Cardinal de Rohan, and the ecclesiastics of the palace came to repeat the prayers appointed for those in the agonies of death. The ceremony recalled the dying monarch to himself; he uttered the responses to the prayers with a loud voice, and still recognising the Cardinal de Rohan, said to him: 'These are the last benefits of the church.' Several times he repeated: 'My God, come to my aid; haste to succour me!' and thereupon fell into an agony, which terminated in death on Sunday the 1st September, at eight o'clock in the morning.

'Although,' remarks Voltaire, 'the life and death of Louis XIV. were glorious, he was not so deeply regretted as he deserved. The love of novelty, the approach of a minority in which each one anticipated to make his fortune, the *constitution* dispute which soured men's minds, all made the intelligence of his death be received with a feeling which went further than indifference. We have seen the same people, which, in 1686, had besought from Heaven with tears the recovery of its sick king, follow his funeral procession with very different demonstrations . . . . Notwithstanding his being blamed for littleness, for severities in his zeal against Jansenism, an overweening degree of arrogance in success towards foreigners, a weakness in female relationships, too much rigour in personal matters, wars lightly entered upon, the Palatinate given over to the flames, and the persecution of the adherents of the reformed doctrines, still his great qualities and actions, when placed in the balance, outweigh his defects. Time, which ripens the opinions of men, has set its seal on his reputation; and in despite of all that has been written against him, his name will never be pronounced without respect, and without conjuring up the idea of an epoch memorable through all ages. If we regard this prince in his private life, we see him, it is true, too full of his exalted position, but withal affable, refusing to his mother any share in the government, but fulfilling towards her all the duties of a son, and observing towards his wife all the externals of good-breeding; a good father, a good master, always decorous in public, hard-working in council, exact in business, just in thought, eloquent in speech, and amiable with dignity.'*

## SPORTSMEN'S SHOOTING-SEASON.

The customary usages in England concerning the dates for commencing the shooting of game in each year, doubtless had their origin in the habits of the birds themselves: each kind of bird being, in reference to its qualities for the table, and still more for the degree of pleasure which it affords to the sportsman, best fitted for attention at certain seasons of the year. There are, nevertheless, other reasons why shooting is especially welcome as a sport in connection with the mode of apportioning time among the wealthy classes in this country. A writer in the *Encyclopædia Britannica* (art. 'Shooting'), while alluding to the commencement of grouse-shooting in August, says: 'Many circumstances contribute to the popularity of grouse-shooting; among which may be enumerated the following. It commences during the parliamentary recess and long vacation—the legislator's, lawyer's, and collegian's holiday; and it is no wonder that, after being cooped up all the summer, these or any other classes of society should seek relaxation in the sports of the field. August is the season when every one, from the peer to the shopkeeper, who can afford the indulgence, either rusticates or travels. In that month the casual tourist, the laker, and the angler, are often in the north, where the temptation to draw a trigger is irresistible.' It remains not the less true, however, that the precise days for beginning and ending each kind of game-shooting is determined by the legislature. The seasons fixed are—August 12 to December 10 for *grouse;* August 20 to December 10 for *black-cock;* September 1 to February 1 for *partridge;* September 1 to March 1 for *bustard;* October 1 to February 1 for *pheasant.* One further restriction is made in regard to black-cock shooting; that, in Somerset, Devon, and the New Forest, instead of commencing on August 20, the opening day must not be earlier than September 1. This last-named date is an important one, therefore, in connection with shooting; seeing that it concerns the fate of partridges, bustards, and (in some parts of the kingdom) black-cock. The game-laws, in determining these dates, were possibly made to bear some relation to the convenience of farmers, as well as to the habits of the game. A landowner

* This article is translated from a French work, *Ephémérides, Politiques, Littéraires, et Religieuses.* Paris, 1812.

has certain rights in *letting* out the 'shooting' on his estate. A game-certificate empowers a sportsman to *shoot* game; a game-licence enables a dealer to *buy* game from the sportsman; none may shoot or buy but those who hold these documents, for which duties or fees are paid; and as farmers are often much troubled by the proceedings of these sportsmen, it is necessary that the legislature (if such statutes as game-laws are needed at all) should define the season *before* which and *after* which the field-ramblings for game shall not be allowed. The reader, by noticing the civil suits and the criminal trials reported in the public journals, will see how frequently there are collisions between sportsmen, gamekeepers, farmers, and poachers, arising in various ways out of these matters. Definite days certainly must be fixed, as the subject now stands; but there is evidently no natural necessity that the days should actually be those which have been selected. Colonel Hawker, a great authority on these matters, recommends that, except in relation to black-game, moor-game, and ptarmigan, shooting should not be allowed until the month of October. His reasons are as follow: 'By such an arrangement, thousands of very young partridges, that are not fair game, would escape being shot by the gentlemen-poachers, or falling a prey, when in hedges and hassocks, to the dogs of the pot-hunter. There would be avoided many disputes between farmers and eager young sportsmen (perhaps the sons of their landlords), who sometimes cannot resist following their game into the corn. There would be an end of destroying a whole *nide* of young pheasants in standing barley, which is so frequently and so easily done in September. The hot month of September was never meant for hard fagging. September is a month that the agriculturist should devote to his harvest, and the man of pleasure to sailing, sea-bathing, fishing, and other summer pursuits. But when October arrives, the farmer has leisure to enjoy a little sport after all his hard labour, without neglecting his business; and the gentleman, by a day's shooting at that time, becomes refreshed and invigorated, instead of wearing out himself and his dogs by slaving after partridges under the broiling sun of the preceding month. The evenings begin to close; and he then enjoys his home and his fireside, after a day's shooting of sufficient duration to brace his nerves and make everything agreeable.'* It appears, therefore, that though the 'First of September' is an important day in the laws of game, those laws do not *necessarily* partake of the inflexibility of the oft-quoted laws of the Medes and Persians.

---

# SEPTEMBER 2.

**St Justus, archbishop of Lyon, confessor, about 390. St Stephen, king of Hungary, confessor, 1038. St William, bishop of Roschild, confessor, 1067. Blessed Margaret, virgin and martyr, 13th century.**

---

***Born.*—John Howard, philanthropist, 1726, *Hackney.***
***Died.*—Alice Lisle, executed for sheltering a rebel, 1685; Marie Therese, Princesse de Lamballe, murdered by a revolutionary mob, 1792, *Paris;*** General Jean Victor **Moreau, mortally wounded at battle of Dresden, 1813.**

* *Hints to Young Sportsmen.*

## LADY HERVEY—DREAD OF HAPPINESS.

September 2, 1768, died Mary Lepell, Lady Hervey, celebrated for her beauty, wit, and good sense at the court of the second George.

In one of her letters, dated April 5, 1750, after expressing her pity for the Countess of Dalkeith in losing her husband, she says: 'I dread to see people I care for quite easy and happy. I always wish them some little disappointment or rub, for fear of a greater; for I look upon felicity in this world not to be a natural state, and consequently what cannot subsist: the further, therefore, we are put out of our natural position, with the more violence we return to it.'*

It is worthy of note, that Sir Humphry Davy entertained a similar view of human happiness. He enters in his journal, in the midst of the most triumphant period of his life: 'Beware of too much prosperity and popularity. Life is made up of mixed passages—dark and bright, sunshine and gloom. The unnatural and excessive greatness of fortune of Alexander, Cæsar, and Napoleon—the first died after divine honours were paid him; the second gained empire, the consummation of his ambition, and lost his life immediately; the third, from a private individual, became master of continental Europe, and allied to the oldest dynasty, and after his elevation, his fortune immediately began to fall. Even in private life too much prosperity either injures the moral man and occasions conduct which ends in suffering, or is accompanied by the workings of envy, calumny, and malevolence of others.'†

## JOHN HOWARD.

To the service of a heart of the tenderest pity, John Howard united consummate skill in business, and a conscientiousness which no danger nor tedium could baffle. Burke's summary of his labours, happily spoken in parliament whilst Howard lived to hear them recognised, has never been superseded in grace and faithfulness: 'He has visited all Europe—not to survey the sumptuousness of palaces, or the stateliness of temples; not to make accurate measurements of the remains of ancient grandeur, nor to form a scale of the curiosities of modern art; not to collect medals or to collate manuscripts; but, to dive into the depths of dungeons, to plunge into the infection of hospitals, to survey the mansions of sorrow and pain; to take the gauge and dimensions of misery, depression, and contempt; to remember the forgotten, to attend to the neglected, to visit the forsaken, and to compare and collate the distresses of all men in all countries. His plan is original: it is as full of genius as of humanity. It was a voyage of discovery; a circumnavigation of charity.'

Howard came of a mercantile stock, and his commercial training was not the least element in his usefulness. His father was a retired London merchant, who, when his son's schooling was over, bound him apprentice to Newnham and Shipley, wholesale grocers of Watling Street, City, paying down

* *Letters of Lady Hervey*, p. 176.
† *Life of Sir Humphry Davy*, by his brother.

£700 as premium. In the warehouse and counting-room, Howard continued until his father's death, in 1742, placed fortune in his hands. From a child he had been delicate, he had lost his mother in infancy, and city air and hard work had reduced his strength almost to prostration. He, therefore, purchased the remnant of his apprenticeship, and, in order to recruit his vigour, set out on a French and Italian tour.

On his return to London, he retired to lodgings in the suburban village of Stoke Newington. He was an invalid, weak, low-spirited, and restless, and falling seriously ill, was confined to bed for several weeks. His landlady, Mrs Sarah Lardeau, a widow, eked out a narrow income by letting apartments. To Howard, in his sickness, she behaved with all the tenderness of a mother, and the young man, on his recovery, questioned with himself how he should reward her. Overcome with gratitude, he decided to offer her his hand and fortune in marriage. He was twenty-five, she was fifty-two. She was a good and prudent woman, and refused him with all natural and obvious reasons. He, however, was determined, asserted that he felt it his duty to make her his wife, and that yield she must. In the end she consented, and, strange to say, the odd union proved a happy one. For three years they dwelt together in perfect amity, until her death made him a widower so miserable, that Stoke Newington became unendurable, and for change of scene and relief, he set sail for Lisbon, with the design of relieving the sufferers by the terrible earthquake of that year, 1755; but Lisbon he never reached. England and France were at war, and on the voyage thither, his vessel was captured, and the crew and passengers carried into the port of Brest, where they were treated with the utmost barbarity, and Howard experienced the horrors of prison-life for the first time in his own person.

On his release and return to England, he settled on a small patrimonial estate at Cardington, near Bedford, and, in 1758, contracted his second marriage with Henrietta Leeds, the daughter of a lawyer, with whom he made the stipulation, that, in all matters in which there should be a difference of opinion between them, his voice should rule. She appears to have made him an admirable wife, and to have entered heartily into the charitable schemes whereby he blessed his neighbourhood and expended a large portion of his income. They built improved cottages, established schools, administered to the sick, and relieved the necessitous. Howard likewise dabbled in science, and was elected a member of the Royal Society. Medicine he was compelled to study in his care of the poor, but astronomy and meteorology were his favourite pursuits. As an illustration of the rigorous and methodical spirit he brought to every undertaking, it is related that, at the bottom of his garden, he had placed a thermometer, and, as soon as the frosty weather set in, he used to leave his warm bed at two o'clock every morning, walk in the bitter air to his thermometer, examine it by his lamp, and write down its register—which done to his satisfaction, he would coolly betake himself again to bed.

The quiet usefulness of his life at Cardington came to a melancholy termination by the death of his beloved wife in 1765, after giving birth to their only child, a son. Weak health and a heavy heart again induced him to seek relief in continental travel. On his renewed settlement at Cardington, he was, in 1773, elected sheriff of Bedford, and though ineligible, being a dissenter, he accepted, and was permitted to retain the office. Such a position to a man of Howard's temper could not possibly remain a sinecure, but at once drove him into active contact with the prisons of his county. Their inspection outraged alike his benevolence and justice. The cells were frequently damp, wet, dark, and ill ventilated, so that the phrase, 'to rot in prison,' was anything but a metaphor. In such noisome holes, innocence, misfortune, and vice were huddled together, and it was hard to say whether the physical or moral corruption was greater. Over these holds of wretchedness a jailer sat as extortioner of bribes and fees, and under him turnkeys, cruel and vicious, operated on their own account. From Bedford, Howard passed into the adjoining counties, and from thence into more distant parts, until he effected the tour of England, discovering everywhere abuses and horrors of which few had any conception. Howard's vocation was now fixed; the inspection and reformation of prisons became his business, and to the work he gave all his energies with a singleness of purpose and an assiduity which have placed his name in the first line of philanthropists. England alone was insufficient to exhaust his zeal; Europe he tracked from east to west, from north to south, and through the lazarettos of the Levant he passed as a ministering angel. The age was ripe for Howard. Kings and statesmen listened to his complaints and suggestions, and promised amendment. The revelations he was enabled to make stirred the feelings of the good and enlightened to the uttermost, and provided material for philosophers like Bentham, and stimulus and direction for the kind-hearted, like Mrs Fry.

Howard printed his work, on the *State of Prisons*, at Warrington. He was attracted thither by the skill of Mr Eyre, a printer, and the promise of literary assistance from Dr Aiken, the brother of Mrs Barbauld, then practising as surgeon in that town; and of Howard's habits, Dr Aiken has recorded some interesting particulars. Every morning—though it was then in the depth of a severe winter—he rose at two o'clock precisely, washed, said his prayers, and then worked at his papers until seven, when he breakfasted and dressed for the day. Punctually at eight he repaired to the printing-office, to inspect the progress of his sheets through the press. There he remained until one, when the compositors went to dinner. While they were absent, he would walk to his lodgings, and, putting some bread and dried fruit into his pocket, sally out for a stroll in the outskirts of the town, eating his hermit-fare as he trudged along, and drinking a glass of water begged at some cottage-door. This was his only dinner. By the time that the printers returned to the office, he had usually, but not always, wandered back. Sometimes he would call upon a friend on his way, and spend an hour or two in pleasant chat, for though severe with himself, the social instincts were largely developed in his nature. At the press, he remained until the men left off their day's toil, and then retired to his lodgings to tea or coffee, went through his religious exercises, and retired to rest at an early hour. Such was the usual course of a day at

Warrington. Sometimes a doubt would suggest itself as to the precise truth of some statement, and though it might cost a journey of some hundreds of miles, off Howard would set, and the result would appear in a note of some insignificant modification of the text. Truth, Howard thought cheap at any price.

Like Wesley, he ate no flesh and drank no wine or spirits. He bathed in cold water daily, ate little and at fixed intervals, went to bed early and rose early. Of this asceticism he made no show. After fair trial, he found that it suited his delicate constitution, and he persevered in it with unvarying resolution. Innkeepers would not welcome such a guest, but Howard was no niggard, and paid them as if he had fared on their meat and wine. He used to say, that in the expenses of a journey which must necessarily cost three or four hundred pounds, twenty or thirty pounds extra was not worth a thought.

Beyond the safeguard of his simple regimen, the precautions Howard took to repel contagious diseases were no more than smelling at a phial of vinegar while in the infected cell, and washing and changing his apparel afterwards; but even these, in process of time, he abandoned as unnecessary. He was often pressed for his secret means of escaping infection, and usually replied: 'Next to the free goodness and mercy of the Author of my being, temperance and cleanliness are my preservatives. Trusting in divine Providence, and believing myself in the way of my duty, I visit the most noxious cells, and while thus employed, I fear no evil.'

Howard died on the 20th of January 1790, at Kherson, in South Russia.

## THE GREAT FIRE OF LONDON.

London was only a few months freed from a desolating pestilence, it was suffering, with the country generally, under a most imprudent and ill-conducted war with Holland, when, on the evening of the 2d of September 1666, a fire commenced by which about two-thirds of it were burned down, including the cathedral, the Royal Exchange, about a hundred parish churches, and a vast number of other public buildings. The conflagration commenced in the house of a baker named Farryner, at Pudding Lane, near the Tower, and, being favoured by a high wind, it continued for three nights and days, spreading gradually eastward, till it ended at a spot called Pye Corner, in Giltspur Street. Mr John Evelyn has left us a very interesting description of the event, from his own observation, as follows:

'*Sept.* 2, 1666.—This fatal night, about ten, began that deplorable fire near Fish Streete in London.

'*Sept.* 3.—The fire continuing, after dinner I took coach with my wife and sonn, and went to the Bankside in Southwark, where we beheld that dismal spectacle, the whole City in dreadful flames neare ye water side; all the houses from the Bridge, all Thames Street, and upwards towards Cheapeside downe to the Three Cranes, were now consum'd.

'The fire having continu'd all this night (if I may call that night which was as light as day for ten miles round about, after a dreadful manner) when conspiring with a fierce eastern wind in a very drie season; I went on foote to the same place, and saw the whole South part of ye Citty burning from Cheapeside to ye Thames, and all along Cornehill (for it kindl'd back against ye wind as well as forward), Tower Streete, Fenchurch Streete, Gracious Streete, and so along to Bainard's Castle, and was now taking hold of St Paule's Church, to which the scaffolds contributed exceedingly. The conflagration was so universal, and the people so astonish'd, that from the beginning, I know not by what despondency or fate, they hardly stirr'd to quench it, so that there was nothing heard or seene but crying out and lamentation, running about like distracted creatures, without at all attempting to save even their goods, such a strange consternation there was upon them, so as it burned both in breadth and length, the Churches, Publiq Halls, Exchange, Hospitals, Monuments, and ornaments, leaping after a prodigious manner from house to house and streete to streete, at greate distances one from ye other; for ye heate with a long set of faire and warme weather, had even ignited the air, and prepar'd the materials to conceive the fire, which devour'd after an incredible manner, houses, furniture, and every thing. Here we saw the Thames cover'd with goods floating, all the barges and boates laden with what some had time and courage to save, as, on ye other, ye carts, &c., carrying out to the fields, which for many miles were strew'd with moveables of all sorts, and tents erecting to shelter both people and what goods they could get away. Oh the miserable and calamitous spectacle! such as haply the world had not seene the like since the foundation of it, nor to be outdone till the universal conflagration. All the skie was of a fiery aspect, like the top of a burning oven, the light seene above forty miles round about for many nights. God grant my eyes may never behold the like, now seeing above 10,000 houses all in one flame; the noise and cracking and thunder of the impetuous flames, ye shrieking of women and children, the hurry of people, the fall of Towers, Houses, and Churches, was like an hideous storme, and the aire all about so hot and inflam'd that at last one was not able to approach it, so that they were forc'd to stand still and let ye flames burn on, wch they did for neere two miles in length and one in bredth. The clouds of smoke were dismall, and reach'd upon computation neer fifty miles in length. Thus I left it this afternoone burning, a resemblance of Sodom, or the last day. London was, but is no more!

'*Sept.* 4.—The burning still rages, and it was now gotten as far as the Inner Temple, all Fleet Streete, the Old Bailey, Ludgate Hill, Warwick Lane, Newgate, Paul's Chain, Watling Streete, now flaming, and most of it reduc'd to ashes; the stones of Paules flew like granados, ye melting lead running downe the streetes in a streame, and the very pavements glowing with fiery rednesse, so as no horse nor man was able to tread on them, and the demolition had stopp'd all the passages, so that no help could be applied. The Eastern wind still more impetuously drove the flames forward. Nothing but ye Almighty power of God was able to stop them, for vaine was ye help of man.

'*Sept.* 5.—It crossed towards Whitehall; Oh the confusion there was then at that Court! It pleas'd his Maty* to command me among ye rest to looke after the quenching of Fetter Lane, and to preserve if possible that part of Holborn, while the rest of ye gentlemen tooke their several posts (for now they began to bestir themselves, and not till now, who hitherto had stood as men intoxicated, with their hands acrosse), and began to consider that nothing was likely to put a stop but the blowing up of so many houses as might make a wider gap than any had yet ben made by the ordinary method of pulling them down with engines; this some stout seamen propos'd early enough to have sav'd neare ye whole Citty, but this some tenacious and avaritious men, aldermen, &c., would not permit, because their houses must have ben of the first. It was therefore now commanded to be practic'd, and my concern being particularly for the hospital of St Bartholomew neere Smithfield, where I had many wounded and sick men, made me the more diligent to promote it, nor was my care for the Savoy lesse. It now pleas'd God by abating the wind, and by the industry of ye people, infusing a new spirit into them, that the fury of it began sensibly to abate about noone, so as it came no farther than ye Temple Westward, nor than ye entrance of Smithfield North; but continu'd all this day and night so impetuous towards Cripplegate and the Tower, as made us all despaire: it also broke out againe in the Temple, but the courage of the multitude persisting, and many houses being blown up, such gaps and desolations were soone made, as with the former three days' consumption, the back fire did not so vehemently urge upon the rest as formerly. There was yet no standing neere the burning and glowing ruines by neere a furlong's space.

LONDON, AS IT APPEARED FROM BANKSIDE, SOUTHWARK, DURING THE GREAT FIRE.—FROM A PRINT OF THE PERIOD BY VISSCHER.

'The poore inhabitants were dispers'd about St George's Fields, and Moorefields, as far as Highgate, and severall miles in circle, some under tents, some under miserable hutts and hovells, many without a rag or any necessary utensills, bed or board, who from delicatenesse, riches, and easy accommodations in stately and well-furnish'd houses, were now reduc'd to extreamest misery and poverty.

'In this calamitous condition I return'd with a sad heart to my house, blessing and adoring the mercy of God to me and mine, who in the midst of all this ruine was like Lot, in my little Zoar, safe and sound.

'*Sept.* 7.—I went this morning on foote from Whitehall as far as London Bridge, thro' the late Fleete Streete, Ludgate Hill, by St Paules, Cheapeside, Exchange, Bishopsgate, Aldersgate, and out to Moorefields, thence thro' Cornehille, &c., with extraordinary difficulty, clambering over heaps of yet smoking rubbish, and frequently mistaking where I was. The ground under my feete was so hot, that it even burnt the soles of my shoes. In the mean time his Maty got to the Tower by water, to demolish ye houses about the graff, which being built intirely about it, had they taken fire and attack'd the White Tower where the magazine of powder lay, would undoubtedly not only have beaten downe and destroy'd all ye bridge, but sunke and torne the vessells in ye river, and render'd ye demolition beyond all expression for several miles about the countrey.

'At my return I was infinitely concern'd to find that goodly Church St Paules now a sad ruine, and that beautifull portico (for structure comparable to any in Europe, as not long before repair'd by the King) now rent in pieces, flakes of vast stone split asunder, and nothing remaining intire but the inscription in the architrave, shewing by whom it was built, which had not one letter of it defac'd. It was astonishing to see what immense stones the heat had in a manner calcin'd, so that all ye ornaments, columns, freezes, and projectures of massie Portland stone flew off, even to ye very

* An abbreviation for his majesty.

roofe, where a sheet of lead covering a great space was totally mealted; the ruines of the vaulted roofe falling broke into St Faith's, which being fill'd with the magazines of bookes belonging to ye stationers, and carried thither for safety, they were all consum'd, burning for a weeke following. It is also observable that ye lead over ye altar at ye East end was untouch'd, and among the divers monuments, the body of one Bishop remain'd intire. Thus lay in ashes that most venerable Church, one of the most antient pieces of early piety in ye Christian world, besides neere 100 more. The lead, yron worke, bells, plate, &c. mealted; the exquisitely wrought Mercers Chapell, the sumptuous Exchange, ye august fabriq of Christ Church, all ye rest of the Companies Halls, sumptuous buildings, arches, all in dust; the fountaines dried up and ruin'd whilst the very waters remain'd boiling; the vorrago's of subterranean cellars, wells, and dungeons, formerly warehouses, still burning in stench and dark clouds of smoke, so that in five or six miles traversing about I did not see one load of timber unconsum'd, nor many stones but what were calcin'd white as snow. The people who now walk'd about ye ruines appear'd like men in a dismal desart, or rather in some greate citty laid waste by a cruel enemy; to which was added the stench that came from some poore creatures bodies, beds, &c. Sir Tho. Gresham's statue, tho' fallen from its nich in the Royal Exchange, remain'd intire, when all those of ye Kings since ye Conquest were broken to pieces, also the standard in Cornehill, and Q. Elizabeth's effigies, with some armes on Ludgate, continued with but little detriment, whilst the vast yron chaines of the Cittie streetes, hinges, bars and gates of prisons, were many of them mealted and reduced to cinders by ye vehement heate. I was not able to passe through any of the narrow streetes, but kept the widest, the ground and aire, smoake and fiery vapour, continu'd so intense that my haire was almost sing'd, and my feete unsufferably surheated. The bie lanes and narrower streetes were quite fill'd up with rubbish, nor could one have knowne where he was, but by ye ruines of some Church or Hall, that had some remarkable tower or pinnacle remaining. I then went towards Islington and Highgate, where one might have seene 200,000 people of all ranks and degrees dispers'd and lying along by their heapes of what they could save from the fire, deploring their losse, and tho' ready to perish for hunger and destitution, yet not asking one penny for relief, which to me appear'd a stranger sight than any I had yet beheld.'

## RELICS OF LONDON SURVIVING THE FIRE.

At the time of the Great Fire, the walls of the City enfolded the larger number of its inhabitants. Densely packed they were in fetid lanes, overhung by old wooden houses, where pestilence had committed the most fearful ravages, and may be said to have always remained in a subdued form ready to burst forth. Suburban houses straggled along the great highways to the north; but the greater quantity lined the bank of the Thames toward Westminster, where court and parliament continually drew strangers. George Wither, the Puritan poet, speaks of this in his *Britain's Remembrancer* 1628:

> 'The Strand, that goodly thorow-fare betweene
> The Court and City; and where I have seene
> Well-nigh a million passing in one day.'

That industrious and accurate artist, Wenceslaus Hollar, busied himself from his old point of view, the tower of St Mary Overies, or, as it is now called, St Saviour's, Southwark, in delineating the appearance of the city as it lay in ruins. He afterwards engraved this, contrasting it with its appearance before the fire. From its contemplation, the awful character of the visitation can be fully felt. Within the City walls, and stretching beyond them to Fetter Lane westwardly, little but ruins remain; a few walls of public buildings, and a few church towers, mark certain great points for the eye to detect where busy streets once were. The whole of the City was burned to the walls, except a small portion to the north-east. We have, consequently, lost in London all those ancient edifices of historic interest—churches crowded with memorials of its inhabitants, and buildings consecrated by their associations—that give so great a charm to many old cities. The few relics of these left by the fire have become fewer, as changes have been made in our streets, or general alterations demanded by modern taste. It will be, however, a curious and not unworthy labour to briefly examine what still remains of Old London edifices erected before the fire, by which we may gain some idea of the general character of the old city.

Of its grand centre—the Cathedral of St Paul—we can now form a mental photograph when contemplating the excellent views of interior and exterior, as executed by Hollar for Dugdale's noble history of the sacred edifice.* It was the pride of the citizens, although they permitted its 'long-drawn aisles' to be degraded into a public promenade, a general rendezvous for the idle and the dissolute. The authors, particularly the dramatic, of the Elizabethan and Jacobean eras, abound with allusions to 'the walks in Paul's;' and Dekker, in his *Gull's Hornbook*, devotes due space to the instruction of a young gallant, new upon town, how he is to behave in this test of London dandyism. The poor hangers-on of these new-fledged gulls, the Captains Bobadil, *et hoc genus omne*, hung about the aisles all day if they found no one to sponge upon. Hence came the phrase, to 'dine with Duke Humphrey,' as the tomb of that nobleman was the chief feature of the middle aisle; despite, however, of its general appropriation to him, it was in reality the tomb of Sir John Beauchamp, son to the Earl of Warwick, who died in 1538—having lived at Baynard's Castle, a palatial residence on the banks of the Thames, also destroyed in the fire. The next important monument in the Old Cathedral was that of Sir Christopher Hatton, the famous 'dancing chancellor' of Queen Elizabeth; and of this some few fragments remain, and are still preserved in the crypt of the present building. Along with them are placed other portions of monuments, to Sir Nicholas, the father of the great Lord Bacon; of Dean Colet, the founder of St Paul's School; and of the poet,

* See a picture of Old St Paul's in our first volume, p. 423.

Dr John Donne. The reflective eye will rest with much interest on these relics of the past, but especially on that of Donne, which has wonderfully withstood the action of the fire, and exactly agrees with Walton's description, in his memoir of the poet-dean, who lapped himself in his shroud, and so stood as a model to Nicholas Stone as he sculptured the work.

Near St Paul's, on the south side of Basing Lane, there existed, until a very few years since, the pillared vaults of an old Norman house, known as Gerrard's Hall; it is mentioned by Stow as the residence of John Gisors, mayor of London, 1245. It was an interesting and beautiful fragment; but after having withstood the changes of centuries, and the great fire in all its fury, it succumbed to the city improvements, and New Cannon Street now passes over its site.

The old Guildhall, a favourable specimen of the architecture of the fifteenth century, withstood the fire bravely; portions of the old walls were incorporated with the restorations, and from a window in the library may still be seen one of the ancient south windows of the hall; it is a fair example of the perpendicular style, measuring 21 feet in height by 7 in width. The crypt beneath the hall is worth inspection, and so is the eastern side of the building.*

Such are the few fragments left us of all that the devouring element passed over. We shall, however, still find much of interest in that small eastern side of the city which escaped its ravages. At the angle where Mark Lane meets Fenchurch

CHURCH OF ALL-HALLOWS STAINING.

Street, behind the houses, is the picturesque church of All-hallows Staining, in the midst of a quaint old square of houses, with a churchyard and a few trees, giving it a singularly old-world look. The tower and a portion of the west end alone are ancient; the church escaped the fire, but the body of the building fell in, 1671 A. D. In this church, the Princess (afterwards Queen) Elizabeth performed her devotions, May 19, 1554, on her release from the Tower.* The churchwarden's accounts contain some curious entries of rejoicings by bell-ringing on great public events.†

The church of All-hallows, Barking, at the end of Tower Street, presents many features of interest, and helps us best to understand what we have lost by the Great Fire. One of the finest Flemish brasses in England is still upon its floor; it is most elaborately engraved and enamelled, and is to the memory of one Andrew Evyngar and his wife (circa 1535). Another, to that of William Thynne, calls up a grateful remembrance, that to him we owe, in 1532, the first edition of the works of that 'well of English undefiled'—Geoffrey Chaucer. Other brasses and quaint old tombs cover floor and walls.

Here the poetic Earl of Surrey was hurriedly buried after his execution; so was Bishop Fisher, the friend of More; and Archbishop Laud ignominiously in the churchyard, but afterwards removed to honourable sepulture in St John's College, Oxford.

Keeping northward, across Tower Hill, we enter Crutched-friars, where stand the alms-houses erected by Sir John Milborn in 1535. He built them 'in honor of God, and of the Virgin;' and it is a somewhat remarkable thing, that a bas-relief representing the Assumption of the Virgin, in the conventional style of the middle ages, still remains over the entrance-gate. St Olave, Hart Street, is the next nearest old church. Seen from the churchyard, it is a quaint and curious bit of Old London, with its churchyard-path and trees. Here lies Samuel Pepys, the diarist, to whom we all are so much indebted for the striking picture of the days of Charles II. he has left to us. He lived in the parish, and often mentions 'our own church' in his diary. Upon the walls, we still see the tablet he placed to the memory of his wife. There are also tablets to William Turner, who published the first English Herbal in 1568; and to the witty and poetic comptroller of the navy, Sir John Mennys, who wrote some of the best poems in the *Musarum Deliciæ*, 1656.

St Catherine Cree, on the north side of Leadenhall Street, was rebuilt in 1629, and is chiefly remarkable for its consecration by Archbishop Laud, with an amount of ceremonial observance, particularly as regarded the communion, which led to an idea of his belief in transubstantiation, and was made one of the principal charges against him. The church contains a good recumbent effigy of Queen Elizabeth's chief butler, Sir Nicholas Throgmorton; and an inscription to R. Spencer, Turkey

* The crypt of Bow Church is of early work, so early as to have been called Roman—but it is very probably Saxon—and has been carefully drawn and published by the Society of Antiquaries in their *Vetusta Monumenta*. Wren chose it for the substructure of this church when he re-erected it after the fire; and when the security of his famous steeple was mooted, declared there was no safer place he wished to be in during any hurricane.

* It is an old London tradition, that she dined at the King's Head Tavern, in Fenchurch Street, after the service, 'off pork and peas;' an ancient metal dish and cover is still preserved in the tavern, and shewn as that used by her.

† Among them are payments for peals 'for joye of y[e] execution of y[e] Queene of Scots;' for the return to London from Feversham of King James II.; and only two days afterwards, with ready subservience, another peal as merrily announced the arrival of the Prince of Orange. This church was one of the four London churches in which James's unpopular 'Declaration of Indulgence' was read.

merchant, recording his death in 1667, after he had 'seen the prodigious changes in the state, the dreadful triumphs of death by pestilence, and the astonishing conflagration of the city by fire.'*

A little to the west, stands St Andrew Undershaft, abounding with quaint old associations. It takes its name from the high shaft of the May-pole, which the citizens used to set up before it, on every May-day, and which overtopped its tower. John Stow, who narrates this, lies buried within; and his monument, representing him at his literary labours, is one of the most interesting of its kind in London.† It is not the only quaint mortuary memorial here worth looking on; there is among them the curious tomb of Sir Hugh Hammersley, with armed figures on each side. Opposite this church is a very fine Elizabethan house, from the windows of which the old inhabitants may have seen the setting-up of the old May-pole, and laughed at the tricks of the hobby-horse and fool, as they capered among the dancers. Passing up St Mary Axe, we shall notice many good old mansions of the resident merchantmen of the last two centuries; and at the corner of Bevis Marks, a very old public-house, rejoicing in the sign of 'the Blue Pig.'‡ The parish of St Helen's, Bishopsgate, is the most interesting in London for its many old houses. The area and courts known as Great St Helen's are particularly rich in fine examples, ranging from the time of Elizabeth to James II. No. 2 has a good doorway and staircase of the time of Charles I.; Nos. 3 and 4 are of Elizabethan date, with characteristic corbels; while Nos. 8 and 9 are modern subdivisions of a very fine brick mansion, dated 1646, and most probably the work of Inigo Jones. No. 9 still possesses a very fine chimney-piece and staircase of carved oak. Crosby Hall is of course the great feature of this district, and is one of the finest architectural relics of the fifteenth century left in London; yet, after escaping the great fire, and the many vicissitudes every building in the heart of London is subjected to, it had a very narrow escape in 1831 of being ruthlessly destroyed; and had it not been for the public spirit of a lady, Miss Hackett, who lived beside it, and who by her munificence shamed others into aiding her, this historic mansion would have passed away from sight. It is now used as a lecture-hall or for public meetings; and an excellently designed modern house, in antique taste, leads into it from Bishopsgate Street. The timber roof, with its elegant open tracery, and enriched octagonal corbels hanging therefrom, cannot be exceeded by any architectural relic of its age; the Oriel window is also of great beauty. It was built by Sir John Crosby, a rich merchant, between 1466–1475, and his widow parted with it to Richard Plantagenet, Duke of Gloucester, afterwards Richard III. Its contiguity to the Tower, where the king, Henry VI., was confined, and the unfortunate princes after him, rendered this a peculiarly convenient residence for the unscrupulous duke. Shakspeare has immortalised the place by laying one of the scenes of his great historical drama there. Gloucester, after directing the assassins to murder Clarence, adds:

'When you have done, repair to Crosby Place.'

Here, indeed, were the guilty plots hatched and consummated that led Richard through blood to the crown; and Shakspeare must have pondered over this old place, then more perfect and beautiful than now, for we know from the parish assessments, that he was a resident in St Helen's in 1598, and must have lived in a house of importance from the sum levied. The tomb of Sir John Crosby is in the adjoining church of St Helen's, and is one of the finest remaining in any London church; it has upon it the recumbent figures of himself and wife. The knight is fully armed, but wears over all his mantle as alderman, and round his neck a collar of suns and roses, the badge of the House of York. In this church also lies Sir Thomas Gresham, another of our noblest old merchantmen; and 'the rich' Sir John Spencer, from whom the Marquises of Northampton have derived—by marriage—so large a portion of their revenues.

Passing up Bishopsgate Street, we may note many old houses, and a few inns, as well as the quaint church of St Ethelburgha. In the house known as Crosby Hall Chambers, is a very fine chimney-piece, dated 1635. Many houses in this district are old, but have been new fronted and modernised. There is an Elizabethan house at the north corner of Houndsditch, and another at the corner of Devonshire Street, which has over one of its fire-places the arms of Henry Wriothesley, Earl of Southampton, the friend of Shakspeare. But the glory of the neighbourhood is the house of Sir Paul Pinder, nearly opposite; the finest old private house remaining in London. The quaint beauty of the *façade* is enhanced by an abundance of rich ornamental details, and the ceiling of the first-floor is a wonder of elaboration and beauty. Sir Paul was a Turkey merchant of great wealth, resident ambassador at Constantinople for upwards of nine years, in the early part of the reign of James I. He died in 1650, 'a worthie benefactor to the poore.'

Returning a few hundred yards, we get again within the Old-London boundary; and crossing Broad Street, the small church of Allhallows-on-the-Wall marks the site of a still smaller one of very ancient date; the wall beside it is upon the foundation of the old wall that encircled London, and which may be still traced at various parts of its course round the city, and is always met with in deep excavations.* Passing the church, we see to

* There is a curious old gate to what was once the watch-house, at the east end of the church. It bears the inscription, 'This gate was built at the cost and charges of William Avenon, Citizen and Gouldsmith of London, who died December, anno dni 1631.' Above it is sculptured a representation of the donor, as a skeleton in a shroud lying on a mattress.

† Stow lived in Aldgate; the district still retains a few old houses near the famous pump, and the remains of the once celebrated Saracen's Head Inn. Some of the butchers' shops just past the Minories are very old, and one bears the badges of the French ambassador, temp. Eliz.

‡ This is evidently a vulgar corruption of 'the Blue Boar,' the badge of King Richard III., who resided in the immediate neighbourhood when Duke of Gloucester. This is a curious instance of the long endurance of an old party-memorial, transformed into a London vulgarism.

* In digging for the foundations of the railway arches across Haydon Square, in the Minories, a very perfect portion of the old Roman Wall was exhumed; and a still more interesting fragment remained on Tower Hill but a very few years since. It has now been converted into a party-wall for enormous factories. In digging for their

our left Great Winchester Street, which, in spite of some recent modernisation, is the most curious old street remaining within the city boundary, inasmuch as all its houses are old on both sides of

GREAT WINCHESTER STREET.

the way; about forty years ago, when the above sketch was made, it gave a perfect idea of a better-class street before the great fire. In the angle of this street, leading into Broad Street, are some fine old brick mansions of the Jacobean era; and to the west lies Carpenter's Hall, with curious paintings of the sixteenth century on its walls, ancient records and plate in its muniment-room, and a large garden; joining on to the still larger Drapers' Garden, interesting examples of 'town-gardens' existing untouched from the middle ages. Austin Friars is contiguous: the old church here is a portion of the monastic building erected in 1354; the window-tracery is extremely elegant. Unfortunately, it is now a roofless ruin, injured by a fire last year, and no steps yet taken for its reparation; and thus another of our few historic monuments may soon pass away from the City. Keeping again to the line of the Old-London wall westward, we pass Coleman Street, and note some few good Elizabethan houses. Then comes Sion College, which was seriously injured, and one-third of the library consumed by the great fire. Aldermanbury Postern, nearly opposite, marks the site of a small gate, or 'postern' in the City wall leading to Finsbury Fields; the favourite resort of the Londoners in the summer evenings.

'And Hogsdone, Islington, and Tothnam-court,
For cakes and creame, had then no small resort.'

So says George Wither, writing in 1628. To the eagerness of those in 'populous city pent,' to get out of its bounds, he testifies from his own observation:

'Some coached were, some horsed, and some walked,
Here citizens, there students, many a one;
Here two together; and, yon, one alone.
Of Nymphes and Ladies, I have often ey'd
A thousand walking at one evening-tide;
As many gentlemen; and young and old
Of meaner sort, as many ten times told.'

The alms-houses of the Clothworkers' Company occupy the angle of the City wall at Cripplegate; beneath the small chapel is a fine crypt in the Norman style, built of Caen stone, the groining decorated with zigzag moulding and spiral ornament. It is a fragment of the old 'Hermitage of St James on the Wall,' and is a graceful and interesting close to our survey, for the fire travelled thus far to the north-west, and left the City no other early relics.

Passing outside the City bounds, and into the churchyard of St Giles's, Cripplegate, a very fine piece of the old wall may be seen, with a circular bastion at the angle, the upper part now converted into a garden for the alms-houses just spoken of. Another bastion, to the south, was converted by Inigo Jones into an apsidal termination of Barber-Surgeon's Hall. The church tower is a stone erection, the body of the church of brick, inside are monuments, second in interest to none. Here lies Fox, the martyrologist; Frobisher, the traveller; Speed, the historian; and one of England's greatest poets and noblest men—John Milton. The church-register records the marriage here of Oliver Cromwell. The range of houses in the main street, and the quaint old church-gate, were built in the year 1660; so short a time before the fire, that we may study in them the 'latest fashions' of London-street architecture at that period.

As there are some quaint and interesting buildings in the suburbs of this side of London, we may bestow a brief notice upon them, more particularly as they help us to comprehend its past state. There are still some Elizabethan houses leading toward Barbican; a few years ago, there were very many in this district. In Golden Lane, opposite, is the front of the old theatre, by some London topographers considered to be 'The Fortune,' by which Edward Alleyn, the founder of Dulwich College, made his estate; others say it is Killigrew's playhouse, called 'The Nursery,' intended to be used as a school for young actors. Pepys records a visit there, in his quaint style, when 'he found the musique better than we looked for, and the acting not much worse, because I expected as bad as could be.' There is a very old stucco representation of the Royal Arms and supporters over the door.

Aldersgate Street preserves the remains of a noble town-house, erected by Inigo Jones for the Earls of Thanet; its name soon changed to Shaftesbury House, by which it is best known. On the opposite side, higher up the street, 'the City Auction-rooms' are in a fine old mansion, with some pleasing enrichments of Elizabethan character. A short street beyond Barbican leads into a quiet square, and the entrance to Sutton's noble foundation—the Charter House. It still preserves much of its monastic look. The entrance-gate is of the fifteenth century, and over it was once placed the mangled

foundation, the workmen came down to virgin soil, and exposed the Roman substructure, supporting the medieval work. It was founded on enormous blocks, projecting beyond its face; the rows of bounding tiles, and the original facing-stones of the wall, were perfect to the height of fifteen feet, and above that the additions rose as high again.

limbs of its last prior, who was executed at Tyburn by command of Henry VIII. The chapel, hall, and governor's room have fine old original enrichments. At the Smithfield end of Long Lane, are some old houses, but the best are in Cloth-fair and St Bartholomew's Close. The churchyard entrance, with the old edifice, and row of ancient houses looking down upon it, seems not to belong to the present day, but to carry the visitor entirely back to the seventeenth century. There is a back-alley encroaching on the chancel, with tumble-down old houses supported on wooden pillars, which gives so perfect an idea of the crowded and filthy passages, once common in Old London, that we here engrave it. The houses are part of those

BACK-ALLEY, ST BARTHOLOMEW'S.

erected by the Lord Rich, one of the most wicked and unscrupulous of the favourites of Henry VIII., and to whom the priory and precinct was given with great privileges. The church is one of the most ancient and interesting in London, with many fine fragments of its original Norman architecture; the houses of the neighbourhood are built over the conventual buildings, and include portions of them, such as the cloisters and refectory.

Ascending Holborn Hill, we see in Ely Place the remains of the old chapel of the mansion once there, with a very fine decorated window. This was the town residence of the bishops of Ely from 1388. It was a pleasantly situated spot in the olden time, with its large orchards and gardens sloping toward the river Fleet. Shakspeare, on the authority of Holinshed, makes the crafty Duke of Gloucester (afterwards Richard III.) pleasantly allude to its produce:

'My Lord of Ely, when I was last in Holborn,
I saw good strawberries in your garden there;
I do beseech you send for some of them.'

Saffron Hill, in the immediate neighbourhood, carries in its name the memory of its past floral glories; and Gerard, whose *Great Herbal* was published in the latter days of Elizabeth, dates his preface 'from my house in Holborn, in the suburbs of London.' We may walk as far as Staples Inn, opposite Gray's Inn Lane, to see the finest row of old houses of the early part of the seventeenth century remaining in London. The quaint old hall behind them, with its garden and fig-trees, preserves still a most antique air. In Chancery Lane, the fine old gate-house bears the date of 1518, and the brick-houses beside it have an extra interest in consequence of Fuller's assertion that Ben Jonson, when a young man, 'helped in the building, when having a trowel in one hand, he had a book in his pocket.' Passing toward Fleet Street, we meet with no old vestige, where, a few years since, they abounded. Beside the Temple Gate, is a good old Elizabethan house, with a fine plaster ceiling, with the initials and badges of Henry, Prince of Wales, son of James I. The Temple, with its round church and unique series of fine monumental effigies, brings us to the margin of the Thames, and is a noble conclusion to our survey, which the chances and changes of busy London may alter every forthcoming year.

## SEPTEMBER 3.

St Mansuet, first bishop of Toul, in Lorraine, about 375. St Macnisius, first bishop of Connor, in Ireland, 513. St Simeon Stylites, the Younger, 592. St Remaclus, bishop of Maestricht, confessor, about 664.

*Born.*—Matthew Boulton, partner of James Watt, 1728, *Birmingham;* Sir John Soane, architect, 1753, *Reading;* Prince Eugene de Beauharnois, step-son of Napoleon Bonaparte, 1781, *Paris.*

*Died.*—Richard Tarleton, celebrated comedian, 1588; Sir Edward Coke, eminent lawyer, 1634, *Stoke Pogeis;* Claudius Salmasius, author of a Defence of Charles I., 1653; Oliver Cromwell, Protector of England, 1658, *Whitehall, London;* David Ancillon, eminent Protestant divine, 1692, *Berlin;* George Lillo, dramatist, 1739; Joseph Ritson, antiquary, 1803, *Hoxton;* Clara Reeve, novelist, 1807, *Ipswich;* George Richardson Porter, statist, 1852, *Tunbridge Wells.*

### DICK TARLETON.

In the morning of the English stage, just before Shakspeare gave it form and finish, the most favourite comic actor was Richard Tarleton. Of peasant origin in Shropshire, this quaint person seems to have spent most of his early life in the business of tavern-keeping, first in the country, afterwards in London. He had, at one time, an hostelry in Gracechurch Street; at another time, an ordinary in Paternoster Row—it has been surmised that the latter establishment has come down to more recent times, under the well-known name of Dolly's Chop-house. Dick could write ballads for the streets; he could make witty answers in rhyme; his aspect—which included a flattened nose—was provocative of mirth wherever it shewed itself; he was full of the mimetic gift. After living some years in London by tavern-keeping, he was adopted into the service of Queen Elizabeth, that he might enliven her at supper-time by his jests and his gossip. We must imagine this grand old woman, at the very time when she was perhaps counter-conspiring against Mary and Babington, or giving orders for meeting the Armada, or devising plans for preserving her rule in Ireland, prone to listen to the 'quips, and cranks, and wanton wiles' of this poor fellow: a wise thing, too, for even the life of a sovereign will be the better of occasional condescensions to simple natural merriment and outbreaks of laughter. Latterly, Dick was a performer at the Curtain Theatre, in Shoreditch—a favourite one in low comedy, as we should now call it, though in plain truth there was then no other. His face was half his fortune in professional respects. It was so droll, that the moment he appeared—before he had said a word—it took the audience with laughter that scarcely subsided for an hour. He could regale them with dexterous fencing, an accomplishment in which he had attained some fame; but his most popular single performance was the playing of what was in those days called a *Jig*. This was not simply a merry dance, as it still is, but also a song or ballad. In came the irresistible Dick, quaintly attired, playing a little tabor with one hand, and ready to finger a pipe with the other: curveting, skipping,

DICK TARLETON.

shuffling round and round before the bewitched audience, he would then chant forth a long string of verses, referring in comic or satiric terms to some persons or things of the day, all with such droll expression as was in itself charm enough. We have fortunately preserved to us one of Tarleton's jigs, entitled *A Horseload of Fools*, in which he takes off a great variety of persons, as the Puritan, the Courtier, the Poet, the Lover, and at length comes to the corporation dignitary—a class which made itself odious to the players by constant efforts to repress theatricals in the city.

'This fool comes of the citizens,
Nay, prithee, do not frown;
I know him as well as you
By his livery gown:
Of a rare horn-mad family.

He is a fool by 'prenticeship
And servitude, he says;
And hates all kinds of wisdom,
But most of all in plays:
Of a very obstinate family.

You have him in his livery gown,
But presently he can
Qualify for a mule or mare,
Or for an alderman:
With a gold chain in his family.

Being born and bred for a fool,
Why should he be wise?
It should make him not fit to sit
With his brethren of Ass-ize:
Of a very long-eared family,' &c.

The contemporary portrait of Tarleton, here copied, represents him in the act of performing one of his jigs; and one can readily see in the face that homely comicality which made him the delight of the Shoreditch groundlings of his day, and enabled him to cure his queen of melancholy 'better,' as old Fuller tells us, 'than all her physicians.'

Poor Tarleton is supposed to have been cut off suddenly by the plague, for he made his will, died, and was buried all on one day. His remains were deposited in the churchyard of St Leonard's, Shoreditch. He could not have reached any considerable age, for from his will it appears that his mother was still alive, and the son to whom he left his property is spoken of as under tutelage. His wife Kate, who is often alluded to in his jests, and who appears to have been of loose life, is not adverted to in the will. She had probably by that time departed from this sublunary sphere.

Dick is alluded to by several contemporary writers, always in kindly terms. It is pleasant to think of one who made so many laugh, that he passed through life unoffendingly. The London populace are said to have kept his memory alive for a century; they named game-cocks after him; they had an ale-house in Southwark adorned with his portrait. Tarleton's jests were collected and published after his death, and have been reproduced with much illustrative matter by the Shakspeare Society. In vain, however, do we look in them for any very brilliant wit or profound humour. We must presume that the droll countenance, voice, and manner of the man were mainly what his contemporaries enjoyed.

## OLIVER CROMWELL—HIS DEATH—A QUEER PECULIARITY OF HIS CHARACTER.

The 3d of September had become a day very memorable to Cromwell. In his expedition to reduce the Scotch Presbyterians, who had taken up the son of the late king as their sovereign, he gained his first great success in the battle of Dunbar, fought on the 3d of September 1650. The affair was closed triumphantly for him at Worcester on the 3d of September 1651. In an age when individuals were believed to have days specially connected with their destiny, the 3d of September might well appear auspicious to the Protector. A strange turn, however, was given to these superstitious ideas in his case, when, on the 3d of September 1658, the Protector died. It is usually stated that his decease took place amidst a storm of singular violence, which was tearing and flooding the whole country, and which fittingly marked the occasion; but the storm, in reality, happened on Monday the 30th of August, and must have been pretty well spent before the Friday afternoon, when Oliver breathed his last.

M. Guizot, in his *Life of Cromwell*, describes the Protectoral court as confined within rather narrow limits, and having his own family as its 'centre and chief element.' His wife, Elizabeth Bouchier, was a simple and timid woman, anxious about her children, and a little jealous (not without cause) of himself. Two or three ladies of rank—one in particular, the Lady Dysart, subsequently Duchess of Lauderdale—were now and then seen at court. The other principal figures were the Protector's children. 'He summoned his son Richard to London, and obtained his election as a member of parliament, a privy-councillor, and chancellor of the university of Oxford. His son-in-law, John Claypole, was a man of elegant tastes, and, like Richard Cromwell, was on friendly terms with a great many Cavaliers. After the marriage of his two younger daughters with Lord Falconbridge and Mr Rich, Cromwell had about him four young and wealthy families, desirous to enjoy life, and to share their enjoyments with all who came near them in rank and fortune. The Protector himself was fond of social amusements and brilliant assemblies; he was also passionately fond of music, and took delight in surrounding himself with musicians, and in listening to their performances. His court became, under the direction of his daughters, numerous and gay. One of them, the widow of Ireton and wife of Fleetwood, was a zealous and austere republican, and took but little part in their festivities, and deplored the monarchical and worldly tendencies which prevailed in the household as well as in the policy of the Protector. In the midst of his public labours, Cromwell exulted in the enjoyment of this domestic prosperity.'

After making full allowance for the verity of what M. Guizot states, it is necessary to look at a certain fact considerably derogating from the dignity of the Protector's court. He was, in reality, a man of a coarse humour, fond of playing off jokes equally rough and childish. It will scarcely be believed, but it is well authenticated, that, at the marriage of his daughter Frances to Mr Rich, November 1657, not a twelvemonth before his death, he amused himself by throwing about sack-posset among the ladies, to soil their rich clothes; flung wet sweetmeats about, and with the same article daubed the stools on which the ladies were to sit. He also pulled off the bridegroom's peruke, and made as if he would have thrown it in the fire, but did not: he only sat upon it. These pranks appear to have been viewed by the company with the usual complaisance shewn to even the *mauvaises plaisanteries* of the great, for we are told that the ladies took their share of the sack-posset sent them in so irregular a manner as 'a favour.'

Dr Bates, in his book on the Troubles in England, records an anecdote of Cromwell's youth, which we might have set down as a royalist fiction but for the pranks above described. It is to the effect that, when Sir Oliver Cromwell was holding Christmas in the old English fashion at Hitchenbrook, his nephew and namesake, the future Protector, mingled amongst the dancers, with gloves and leggings befouled in the most horrible manner, that he might spread contamination amongst the company, thus spoiling innocent mirth, and rendering the house itself insufferable. A writer in the *Gentleman's Magazine*,* who brought forward this unpleasant story, adds the observation: 'I have noticed this itch in certain boys at school, who were invariably tyrants in their nature.'

## COCKER'S ARITHMETIC.

The 3d of September 1677 is the date of the licensing (by Sir Roger L'Estrange) of *Cocker's Arithmetick*. The fifty-first edition was published in 1745 by 'R. Ware, at the Bible and Sun, Amen Corner;' marking the extraordinary success which attended the book during the first seventy years of its existence. There had been manuals of arithmetic before; but Cocker's had a superior completeness, which threw all others into the shade. In his original 'proeme or preface,' the author, who described himself as a 'practitioner in the arts of writing, arithmetick, and engraving' (to which he had been directed by 'the secret influence of Divine Providence'), says: 'For you, the pretended Numerists of this vapouring age, who are more disingeniously witty to propound unnecessary questions, than ingeniously judicious to resolve such as are necessary; for you was this book composed and published, if you will deny yourselves so much as not to invert the streams of your ingenuity, but by studiously conferring with the Notes, Names, Orders, Progress, Species, Properties, Proprieties, Proportions, Powers, Affections and Applications of Numbers delivered herein, become such Artists indeed, as you now only seem to be.' He further assured the world that all the rules in his book are 'grounded on Verity and delivered with Sincerity; the Examples built up gradually from the smallest Consideration to the greatest—

'Zoilus and Momus, lie you down and die,
For these inventions your whole force defy.'

Cocker, however, was not destined to see anything of the success which has since made his name proverbial in England in connection with arithmetical subjects. The little book was edited from a manuscript he had left, by 'Mr John Hawkins, writing-master, near St George's Church, in Southwark;' bearing, nevertheless, a wood-cut portrait of the author, with the following inscription below:

'Ingenious Cocker, now to rest thou 'rt gone,
No art can shew thee fully, but thine own;
Thy rare *Arithmetick* alone can shew
Th' vast sum of thanks we for thy labours owe.'

It appears that Cocker died in the year of the publication of his book, and was buried in St George's Church, Southwark, 'in the passage at the west end, within the church.' He was rather a caligrapher, a writer and engraver of 'letters,

* *Gentleman's Magazine*, November 1840.

knots, and flourishes,' than an arithmetician, and valued himself chiefly on the former accomplishments. His life seems to have been one of struggle: there is extant a petition sent by him, some years before his death, to the Treasurer, Earl of Southampton, entreating payment of £150, granted to him by the king for his encouragement in the arts of writing and engraving, as he was hindered in his operations 'by reason of extreme want and necessity.'* He probably could have gone through a second life in handsome style on the profits of his *Arithmetick*.

Connected with the life of Cocker, it may be allowable to introduce a set of remarks, by the great novelist of our age, upon an ancient mode of keeping accounts which was kept up in the British Exchequer long after better modes were in use everywhere else.

'Ages ago, a savage mode of keeping accounts on notched sticks was introduced into the Court of Exchequer, and the accounts were kept much as Robinson Crusoe kept his calendar on the desert island. In the course of considerable revolutions of time, the celebrated Cocker was born, and died. Walkinghame of the *Tutor's Assistant*, well versed in figures, was also born, and died—a multitude of accountants, book-keepers, and actuaries were born, and died. Still official routine inclined to these notched sticks, as if they were the pillars of the constitution, and still the Exchequer accounts continued to be kept on certain splints of elm-wood called "tallies." In the reign of George III. an inquiry was made by some revolutionary spirit whether—pens, ink, and paper, and slates and pencils being in existence—this obstinate adherence to an obsolete custom ought to be continued, and whether a change ought not to be effected. All the red tape in the country grew redder at the bare mention of this bold and original conception, and it took till 1826 to get these sticks abolished. In 1834, it was found that there was a considerable accumulation of them, and the question then arose, what was to be done with such worn-out, wormeaten, rotten old bits of wood? I daresay there was a vast amount of minuting, memorandum-ing, and despatch-boxing on this mighty subject. The sticks were housed at Westminster, and it would naturally occur to any intelligent person that nothing could be easier than to allow them to be carried away for firewood by the miserable people who live in that neighbourhood. However, they never had been useful, and official routine required that they never should be, and so the order went forth that they were to be privately and confidentially burned. It came to pass that they were to be burned in a stove in the House of Lords. The stove, overgorged with these preposterous sticks, set fire to the panelling; the panelling set fire to the House of Lords; the House of Lords set fire to the House of Commons; the two houses were reduced to ashes; architects were called in to build others; we are now in the second million of the cost thereof; the national pig is not nearly over the stile yet, and the little old woman, Britannia, hasn't got home to-night. Now, I think we may reasonably remark, in conclusion, that all obstinate adherence to rubbish which the time has long outlived, is certain to have in the soul of it more or less that is pernicious and destructive, and that will some day set fire to something or other, which, if given boldly to the winds, would have been harmless, but which, obstinately retained, is ruinous.'

AN EXCHEQUER TALLY.

* *Gentleman's Magazine*, May 1840.

An example of the Exchequer notched sticks is here depicted for the amusement of the reader. It contains a half-intelligible legend in Latin, indicating that it is the record of an East Indian loan. Of course the reader will understand that there is, after all, a sort of rationality in the system, the one stick being for the creditor, the other for the lender, and the tallying of the notches a proof that both are genuine. In Scotland, till the early days of the editor, it was customary for the baker's lad to bring the *Nick-sticks* with his bread, a notch being made for each loaf he left. While the notches on his stick corresponded with those on the one left with the family, both parties were satisfied that the account was justly kept.

## 'STRANGE FISH.'

When Trinculo (in Shakspeare's *Tempest*) mistakes Caliban for 'a strange fish,' he at once exclaims: 'Were I in England now, and had but this fish painted, not a holiday fool there but would give a piece of silver: there would this monster make a man; any strange beast there makes a man: when they will not give a doit to relieve a lame beggar, they will lay out ten to see a dead Indian. This love of the English populace for strange sights is frequently alluded to by other writers of the Elizabethan era; a time fertile of travel, and abounding in discoveries which required very little exaggeration to carry them into the marvellous. This taste for the wonderful was well supplied—shows, ballads, and broadsides fostered and fed the public appetite. Occasionally, the 'monster' was a very mild form of monster indeed! A shark or a polypus was, by dint of rhetorical flourishes, converted into a very alarming monster, of which instances occur in Halliwell's folio edition of Shakspeare. The continental artists and authors went far beyond all this; the inland people particularly, from their inexperience of the sea, appear to have been thought capable of believing anything. Gesner, Rondeletius, and other authors of the sixteenth century, narrate the capture of marine monsters of a very 'strange' order, and among them one that was 'taken in Polonia in 1531,' which bore a general resemblance to a bishop! In the rare and curious little volume on *Costume*, by Johannes Sluper, published at Antwerp in 1572, is a picture of this fish, here reproduced in fac-simile. The *quatrain* appended to this cut assures us that bishops are not confined to land alone, but

THE SEA-BISHOP.

that the sea has the full advantage of their presence; and that though they may not speak, they wear a mitre. This 'monster,' we are told, was brought to the king, 'and after a while seemed very much to express to him, that his mind was to return to his own element again: which, the king perceiving, commanded that it should be

THE SEA-MONK.

so; and the bishop was carried back to the sea, and cast himself into it immediately.' The bishop once established in the popular mind, the clergy might follow of course, the more particularly as it would seem to countenance a sort of divine creation of monkery in the sea. So accordingly we find in the same work, this equally extraordinary representation of 'The Sea-Monk,' to which the following stanza is appended:

'La Mer poissons en abondance apporte,
Par dons devins que devous estimer.
Mais fert estrange est le Moyne de Mer,
Qui est ainsè que ce pourtrait le porte.'

In the office-book of the master of the revels, Sir Henry Herbert, is the entry of 'a licence to James Leale to shew a strange fish for half a yeare, the 3d of September 1632.' The records of London exhibitions, and the chronicles of Bartholomew, and other fairs, supply a constant succession of these favourite shows. A most amusing underplot in Jasper Mayne's comedy, *The City Match*, 1659, is founded on this popular weakness. A silly young Cockney is intoxicated by revellers, upon whom he forces his company for the sake of learning fashionable follies, and is dressed up and exhibited at a tavern, as 'a strange fish,' to wondering sight-seers at a shilling a head. One asks, if it is a whale, that the charge is so high; and another declares, 'We gave but a groat to see the last fish;' the showman replies with quiet dignity:

'Gentlewoman, that was but an Irish Sturgeon!
This came from the Indies; and eats five crowns a day,
In fry, ox-livers, and brown paste!'

But we must not laugh too freely at our ancestors. It is not more than three years since a 'talking fish' was profitably exhibited in London, and the principal provincial towns, at a shilling a head. The fish was a species of seal, and the 'talking' consisted of a free translation of its natural cry into the words *ma-ma* or *pa-pa*, according to the fancy of the showman or spectator.

---

# SEPTEMBER 4.

Saints Marcellus and Valerian, martyrs, 179. St Ultan, first bishop of Ardbraccan, in Meath, 656. St Ida, widow, 9th century. The Translation of St Cuthbert, about 995. St Rosalia, virgin, 1160. St Rosa of Viterbo, virgin, about 1252.

## TRANSLATION OF ST CUTHBERT.

Cuthbert—originally a shepherd-boy in Lauderdale, afterwards a monk at Old Melrose on the Tweed, finally bishop of the Northumbrian island of Lindisfarne, in which capacity he died in the year 688—is remarkable for the thousand-years' long history which he had, after experiencing that which brings most men their quietus. Fearing future incursions of the Danes, he charged his little religious community that, in case any such event should take place, they would quit the island, taking his bones along with them. Eleven years after his death, having raised his body to give it a more honourable place, they were amazed to find it had undergone not the slightest decay. In consequence of this miraculous circumstance, it became, in its new shrine, an object of great popular veneration, and the cause of many other miracles; and so it continued till the year 875, when at length, to escape the Danes, the monks had to carry it away, and commence a wandering life on the mainland. After seven years of constant movement, the body of St Cuthbert found rest at Chester-le-Street; but it was, in a sense, only temporary, for in 995, a new incursion of the Danes sent it off once more upon its travels. It was kept some time at Rippon, in Yorkshire, and when the danger was past, the monks set out on their return to Chester-le-Street. They were miraculously arrested, however, at a spot called Duirholm (the deer's meadow), on the river Wear, and there finally settled with the precious corpse of their holy patron, giving rise to what has since been one of the grandest religious establishments of the British empire, the cathedral of Durham. This is the event which was for some ages celebrated as the Translation of St Cuthbert.

For upwards of a hundred years, the tomb of St Cuthbert, with his uncorrupted body, continued to be visited by devout pilgrims, and in 1104, on the erection of the present cathedral of Durham, it was determined to remove his remains to a shrine within the new structure. Some doubts had been expressed as to the permanence of his incorruptibility, and to silence all such misgivings, the clergy of the church, having met in conclave beside the saint's coffin the night before its intended removal, resolved to satisfy themselves by an actual inspection. After preparing themselves for the task by prayer, they removed, with trembling hands, the external fastenings, and opened the first coffin, within which a second was found, covered with rough hides, and enclosing a third coffin, enveloped in several folds of linen. On removing the lid of this last receptacle, a second lid appeared, which on being raised with much fear and agitation, the swathed body of the saint lay before them 'in a perfect state.' According to the narrative, the monks were appalled as if by some fearful interposition of Heaven; but after a short interval, they all fell flat on the ground, repeated amid a deluge of tears the seven penitential psalms, and prayed the Lord not to correct them in his anger, nor chasten them in his displeasure. The next day the miraculous body was shewn to the multitude, though it is honestly stated by the chronicler that the whole of it, including the face, was covered with linen, the only flesh visible being through a chink left in the cerecloths at the neck. Thereafter it was placed in the shrine destined for it behind the great altar, where it remained undisturbed for the ensuing *four hundred and twenty-six years*, and proved the source of immense revenues to the cathedral. No shrine in England was more lavishly adorned or maintained than that of St Cuthbert; it literally blazed with ornaments of gold, silver, and precious stones, and to enrich the possessions of the holy man, and his representative the bishop of Durham, many a fair estate was impoverished or diverted from the natural heirs. The *corporax cloth*, which the saint had used to cover the chalice when he said mass, was enclosed in a silk banner, and employed in gaining victories for the Plantagenet kings of England. It turned the fate of the day at the battle of Neville's Cross, in 1346, when David of Scotland was defeated; and it soon after witnessed the taking of Berwick by Edward III. But all the glories of St Cuthbert were to be extinguished at the Reformation, when his tomb was irreverently disturbed. It had, however, a better fate than many other holy places at this eventful epoch, as the coffin, instead of being ignominiously broken up, and its contents dispersed, was carefully closed, a new exterior coffin added, and the whole buried underneath the defaced shrine.

For the greater part of *three centuries more*, the body of St Cuthbert lay here undisturbed. He was not forgotten during this time, but a legend prevailed that the site of his tomb was known only to the Catholic clergy, three of whom, it was alleged, and no more, were intrusted with the secret at a time, one being admitted to a knowledge of it as another died—all this being in the hope of a time arriving when the shrine might be re-erected, and the incorrupt body presented once more to the veneration of the people. It is hardly necessary to observe, that this story of a secret was pure fiction, as the exact site of the tomb could be easily ascertained.

The next appearance of St Cuthbert was in May 1827, when, in presence of a distinguished assemblage, including the dignitaries of Durham Cathedral, his remains were again exhumed from their triple encasement of coffins. After the larger fragments of the lid, sides, and ends of the last coffin had been removed, there appeared below a dark substance of the length of a human body, which proved to be a skeleton, lying with its feet to the east, swathed apparently in one or more shrouds of linen or silk, through which there projected the brow of the skull and the lower part of the leg bones. On the breast lay a small golden cross, of which a representation is here given. The

GOLDEN CROSS.—WORN BY ST CUTHBERT, AND FOUND ON HIS BODY AT THE OPENING OF HIS TOMB IN 1827.

whole body was perfectly dry, and no offensive smell was perceptible. From all the appearances, it was plain that the swathings had been wrapped round a dry skeleton, and not round a complete body, for not only was there no space left between the swathing and the bones, but not the least trace of the decomposition of flesh was to be found. It was thus clear that a fraud had been practised, and a skeleton dressed up in the habiliments of the grave, for the purpose of imposing on popular credulity, and benefiting thereby the influence and temporal interests of the church. In charity, however, to the monks of Durham, it may be surmised that the perpetration of the fraud was originally the work of a few, but having been successful in the first instance, the belief in the incorruptibility of St Cuthbert's body came soon to be universally acquiesced in, by clergy as well as laity. Perhaps the history of the saint is not yet finished, and after the lapse of another cycle of years, a similar curiosity may lead to a re-examination of his relics, and Macaulay's New Zealander, after sketching the ruins of St Paul's from a broken arch of London Bridge, may travel northwards to Durham, to witness the disinterment from the battered and grass-grown precincts of its cathedral, of the bones of the Lauderdale shepherd of the seventh century.

## ST CUTHBERT'S BEADS.

On a rock, by Lindisfarne,
Saint Cuthbert sits, and toils to frame
The sea-born beads that bear his name:
Such tales had Whitby's fishers told,
And said they might his shape behold,
And hear his anvil sound;
A deadened clang—a huge dim form,
Seen but, and heard, when gathering storm,
And night were closing round.

*Marmion.*

There is a Northumbrian legend, to the effect that, on dark nights, when the sea was running high, and the winds roaring fitfully, the spirit of St Cuthbert was heard on the recurring lulls forging beads for the faithful. He used to sit in the storm-mist, among the spray and sea-weeds, on a fragment of rock on the shore of the island of Lindisfarne, and solemnly hammer away, using another fragment of rock as his anvil. A remarkable circumstance connected with the legend is, that after a storm the shore was found strewed with the beads St Cuthbert was said to have so forged. And a still more remarkable circumstance connected with the legend consists in the fact that, although St Cuthbert is, now, neither seen nor heard at work, the shore is still found strewed with the beads after a storm. The objects which are called beads are, in fact, certain portions of the fossilised remains of animals, called crinoids, which once inhabited the deep in myriads. Whole specimens of a crinoid are rare, but several parts of it are common enough. It consisted of a long stem supporting a cup or head; and out of the head grew five arms or branches. The stem and the branches were flexible, and waved to and fro in the waters; but the base was firmly attached to the sea-bottom. The flexibility of the stems and branches was gained by peculiar formation; they were made of a series of flat plates or ossicula, like thick wafers piled one above another, and all strung together by a cord of animal matter, which passed through the entire animal. These plates, in their fossilised form detached from one another, are the beads in question. The absence of the animal matter leaves a hole in the centre of each piece, through which they can be strung together, rosary-fashion. They vary in size; some are about the diameter of a pea, others of a sixpence. They are most frequently found in fragments of the stems, an inch or two long, each inch containing about a dozen joints or beads. Crinoids

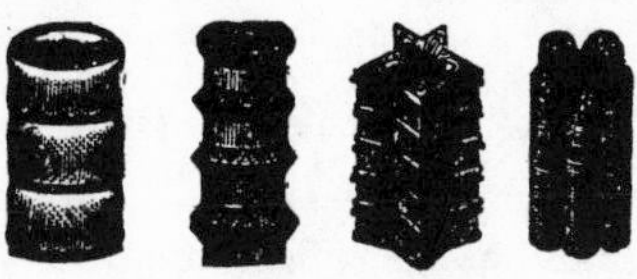

ST CUTHBERT'S BEADS.

are classed by modern naturalists with the order *echinodermata*—that is to say, among the sea-stars and sea-urchins. The entrochal marble of Derbyshire, used for chimney-pieces and ornamental purposes, includes a vast quantity of the fragments of crinoids. Those found at Lindisfarne have been embedded in shale, out of which they have been washed by the sea, and cast ashore.

---

*Born.*—Pindar, lyric poet, 518 B.C., *Thebes;* Alexander III. of Scotland, 1241, *Roxburgh;* Gian Galeazzo Visconti, celebrated Duke of Milan, founder of the cathedral, 1402; François Réné, Vicomte de Chateaubriand, moral and romantic writer, 1768, *St Malo.*

*Died.*—John Corvinus Huniades, Hungarian general, 1456, *Zemlin;* Robert Dudley, Earl of Leicester, favourite of Queen Elizabeth, 1588; John James Heidegger, Master of the Revels to George II., 1749; Charles Townshend, orator and statesman, 1767.

## A MASTER OF THE REVELS.

John James Heidegger, a native of Switzerland, after wandering, in various capacities, through the greater part of Europe, came to England early in the eighteenth century; and by his witty conversation and consummate address, soon gained the good graces of the gay and fashionable, who gave him the appellation of the Swiss Count. His first achievement was to bring out an opera (*Thomyres*), then a novel and not very popular kind of entertainment in England. By his excellent arrangements, and judicious improvements on all previous performances, Heidegger may be said to have established the opera in public favour. Becoming manager of the Opera House in the Haymarket, he acquired the favour of George II.; and introducing the then novel amusement of masquerades, he was appointed master of the revels, and superintendent of masquerades and operas to the royal household. Heidegger now became the fashion; the first nobility in the land vied in bestowing their caresses upon him. From a favourite, he became an autocrat; no public or private festival, ball, assembly, or concert was considered complete, if not submitted to the superintendence of the Swiss adventurer. Installed by common consent as *arbiter elegantiarum*, Heidegger, for a long period, realised an income of £5000 per annum, which he freely squandered in a most luxurious style of life, and in the exercise of a most liberal charity.

Though tall and well made, Heidegger was characterised by a surpassing ugliness of face. He had the good sense to joke on his own peculiar hardness of countenance, and one day laid a wager with the Earl of Chesterfield, that the latter could not produce, in all London, an uglier face than his own. The earl, after a strict search, found a woman in St Giles's, whose features were, at first sight, thought to be as ill-favoured as those of the master of the revels; but when Heidegger put on the woman's head-dress, it was unanimously admitted that he had won the wager.

Jolly, a fashionable tailor of the period, is said to have also been rather conspicuous by a Caravaggio style of countenance. One day, when pressingly and inconveniently dunning a noble duke, his Grace exclaimed: 'I will not pay you, till you shew me an uglier man than yourself.' Jolly bowed, retired, went home, and wrote a polite note to Heidegger, stating that the duke particularly wished to see him, at a certain hour, on the following morning. Heidegger duly attended; the duke denied having sent for him; but the mystery was unravelled by Jolly making his appearance. The duke then saw the joke, and with laughter acknowledging the condition he stipulated was fulfilled, paid the bill.

As might be supposed, Heidegger was the constant butt of the satirists and caricaturists of his time. Hogarth introduces him into several of his works, and a well-known sketch of 'Heidegger in a Rage,' attributed to Hogarth, illustrates a remarkable practical joke played upon the master of the revels. The Duke of Montague gave a dinner at the 'Devil Tavern' to several of the nobility and gentry, who were all in the plot, and to which Heidegger was invited. As previously arranged, the bottle was passed round with such celerity, that the Swiss became helplessly intoxicated, and was removed to another room, and placed upon a bed, where he soon fell into a profound sleep. A modeller, who was in readiness, then took a mould of his face, from which a wax mask was made. An expert mimic and actor, resembling Heidegger in height and figure, was instructed in the part he had to perform, and a suit of clothes, exactly similar to that worn by the master of the revels on public occasions, being procured, everything was in readiness for the next masquerade. The eventful evening having arrived, George II., who was in the secret, being present, Heidegger, as soon as his majesty was seated, ordered the orchestra to play *God Save the King;* but his back was no sooner turned, than his counterfeit commanded the musicians to play *Over the Water to Charlie.* The mask, the dress, the imitation of voice and attitude, were so perfect, that no one suspected a trick, and all the astonished courtiers, not in the plot, were thrown into a state of stupid consternation. Heidegger hearing the change of music, ran to the music-gallery, stamped and raved at the musicians, accusing them of drunkenness, or of a design to ruin him, while the king and royal party laughed immoderately. While Heidegger stood in the gallery, *God Save the King* was played, but when he went among the dancers, to see if proper decorum were kept by the company, the counterfeit stepped forward, swore at the musicians, and asked: had he not just told them to play *Over the Water to Charlie?* A pause ensued, the musicians believing Heidegger to be either drunk or mad, but as the mimic continued his vociferations, *Charlie* was played again. The company was by this time in complete confusion. Several officers of the guards, who were present, believing a studied insult was intended to the king, and that worse was to follow, drew their swords, and cries of shame and treason resounded from all sides. Heidegger, in a violent rage, rushed towards the orchestra, but he was stayed by the Duke of Montague, who artfully whispered that the king was enraged, and his best plan was first to apologise to the monarch, and then discharge the drunken musicians. Heidegger went, accordingly, to the circle immediately before the king, and made a humble apology for the unaccountable insolence of the musicians; but he had scarcely spoken ere the counterfeit approaching, said in a plaintive voice: 'Indeed, sire, it is not my fault, but,' pointing to the real Heidegger, 'that devil in my likeness.' The master of the revels, turning round and seeing his counterpart, stared, staggered, turned pale, and nearly swooned from fright. The joke having gone far enough, the king ordered the counterfeit to unmask; and then Heidegger's fear turning into rage, he retired to his private apartment, and seating himself in an arm-chair, ordered the lights to be extinguished, vowing he would never conduct another masquerade unless the surreptitiously-obtained mask were immediately broken in his presence. The mask was delivered up, and Hogarth's sketch represents Heidegger in his chair, attended by his porter, carpenter, and candle-snuffer, the obnoxious mask lying at his feet.

Heidegger gave grand entertainments to his friends; the king even condescended to visit him in his house at Barn-Elms. One day, a discussion took place at his table as to which nation in Europe had the best-founded claim to ingenuity. After various opinions had been given, Heidegger claimed that character for the Swiss, appealing to himself as a case in point. 'I was,' said he, 'born a Swiss, in a country where, had I continued to tread in the steps of my simple but honest forefathers, twenty pounds a year would have been the utmost that art or industry could have procured me. With an empty purse, a solitary coat on my back, and *almost* two shirts, I arrived in England, and by the munificence of a generous prince, and the liberality of a wealthy nation, am now at the head of a table, covered with the delicacies of the season, and wines from different quarters of the globe; I am honoured with the company, and enjoy the approbation, of the first characters of the age, in rank, learning, arms, and arts, with an income of five thousand pounds a year. Now, I defy any Englishman or native of any other country in Europe, how highly soever he may be gifted, to go to Switzerland, and raise such a sum there, or even to spend it.'

Although an epicure and a wine-bibber, Heidegger lived to the age of ninety years. He died on the 4th of September 1749, and was buried in the church of Richmond, in Surrey. With all his faults, it must not be forgotten that he gave away large sums in charity. And in spite of his proverbial ugliness—

> 'With a hundred deep wrinkles impressed on his front,
> Like a map with a great many rivers upon 't'—

an engraving of his face, taken from a mask after death, and inserted in Lavater's *Physiognomy,* exhibits strong marks of a benevolent character, and features by no means displeasing or disagreeable.

## SEPTEMBER 5.

St Alto, abbot. St Bertin, abbot, 709. St Laurence Justinian, confessor, first patriarch of Venice, 1455.

*Born.*—Tommaso Campanella, philosophical writer, 1568, *Stilo in Calabria;* Cardinal Richelieu, celebrated French statesman, 1585, *Paris;* Louis XIV. of France, 1638, *St Germains;* Jean Benjamin Laborde, musician and historical writer, 1734, *Paris;* Robert Fergusson, Scottish poet, 1750, *Edinburgh;* Dr John Dalton, eminent chemist, 1766, *Eaglesfield, Cumberland.*

*Died.*—Catharine Parr, queen of Henry VIII., 1548; Edmund Bonner, persecuting bishop, 1569, *Marshalsea Prison;* Matthew Stuart, Earl of Lennox, regent of Scotland, shot at Stirling, 1571; Cardinal du Perron, statesman and man of letters, 1618; Jean François Regnard, comic poet, 1710, *near Paris;* John Home, author of *Douglas*, 1808; James Wyatt, architect, 1813; Dr Patrick Neill, author of works on natural history, &c., 1851, *Edinburgh;* Dr William Macgillivray, distinguished naturalist, 1852, *Aberdeen.*

### JOHN HOME.

The public has been made pretty well acquainted with the history of the author of *Douglas*—how the bringing out of his play in Edinburgh, in the year 1756, exposed him to censure among his brethren in the Scotch Church—how he finally retired from clerical duty upon a pension granted him by Lord Bute—how he failed in every other literary undertaking, but spent, on the whole, a happy, as well as a long life, in the enjoyment of the friendship of all the eminent men of his day. Home's tragedy is not now looked upon as the marvel of genius which it once was; and yet, one would think, there must be some peculiar merit in a play of which so many portions remain so strongly impressed upon so many memories. The author was acknowledged, in his lifetime, to be vain up to the full average of poets; yet it was equally admitted regarding him, that he loved his friends as warmly as he loved himself, and was untiring in his exertions for their good. His vanity seems to have been of a very inoffensive kind.

Sir Adam Ferguson, the son of Home's friend, Dr Ferguson, used to relate an anecdote of the venerable dramatist with great comic effect. It cannot be set forth in print with nearly the same force, but it may, nevertheless, be worthy of a place in this miscellany. Mrs Siddons, on visiting the Edinburgh theatre, always spent an afternoon with her worthy friends, Mr and Mrs Home, at their neat house in North Hanover Street (latterly, Robertson's upholstery wareroom). On one occasion, they were seated at an early dinner, attended by Mr Home's old man-servant John, and a little 'lassie,' whose usual place was the kitchen, and who did not as yet know much about waiting at table.

'And what will you take to drink, Mrs Siddons?' inquired the host.

'A little porter,' answered the tragedy queen in her impressive voice.

John, unobservant of the lady's wishes, was ordered by his master to get a little porter for Mrs Siddons, and immediately left the room, apparently to obtain the desired beverage. Two or three minutes having elapsed, Mr Home was heard complaining to his wife of John's absence. 'My dear, John is getting very stupid—I think we shall have to part with him. There he has been out of the room for some minutes, and we are all at a stand.' A few more minutes passed, and Mr Home's patience was rapidly ebbing, notwithstanding that Mrs Siddons did all in her power to put him at his ease. The absence of John, however, had become the subject of concentrated thought to the company, when all at once the outer-door was heard to open, hasty steps crossed the lobby, and John presented himself in the dining-room, with a flushed face, crying: 'I've found ane, ma'am! he's the least I could get!' Then emerged into view a short, thick-set Highlander, whose band of ropes and leaden badge betokened his profession, but who seemed greatly bewildered on finding himself in a gentleman's dining-room, surveyed by the curious eyes of one of the grandest women that ever walked the earth. The truth flashed first upon Mrs Siddons, who, unwonted to laugh, was for once overcome by a sense of the ludicrous, and broke forth into something like shouts of mirth, while as yet Mr Home was but beginning to apprehend what his servant meant, and Mrs Home had evidently not the least chance of ever understanding it—for this lady was by no means a bright specimen of her sex, as the second of Sir Adam's anecdotes will help to make more clear to the reader.

Fallen, as *Douglas* is now, to the rank of a second-rate play, it is scarce possible for modern men to imagine that it was once the subject of enthusiastic admiration, even beyond the limits of the author's country. A middle-aged Englishman came to Edinburgh in the summer of 1802, mainly for the purpose of seeing the author of this, his favourite tragedy. He found his way to a modest tenement in a court off the principal street called Canongate, and tremulously knocked at the door. A 'lassie' came.

'Is Mr Home within?'

'Na, sir.'

'Will he be at home soon?'

'Oh, na, sir; he's in the Hielands.'

This was true—Mr Home, attended by his man John, generally spent some weeks in the Highlands every summer.

'And when will he be at home?'

'I canna tell, sir; and John's awa' too—I suppose you had better come in and see Mrs Home.'

'Oh, then, Mrs Home is not gone? I should be glad to see her for a few minutes.' He reflected that, next to seeing a poet, was seeing a poet's love. She must doubtless be a very interesting woman. So he sent in his card, with a message stating that he had come to Edinburgh almost on purpose to see Mr Home—and would the lady be so obliging as allow him a few minutes' conversation? He was presently ushered in, when he beheld a withered old lady, with her head wrapped up in flannel, and looking in the last stage of stupidity and decrepitude. She had a little hot wine and water in a tumbler beside her, and was engaged in grating into it a few grains of nutmeg, such being her ordinary solacement after an early dinner. The heart of the ardent Douglassomaniac sank within him, but he mustered strength to engage in conversation with the old lady, whom he found sadly deficient in knowledge regarding matters of the day, and, indeed, hardly able to converse at all, time having made havoc of the few faculties she once possessed. After trying her with various topics, he came upon one which had lately been in great vogue—the peace concluded with France.

'Oh, yes, I've heard o' the peace. Ay, it's come at last.'

'It must make a great change in many things,' said the Englishman; 'we may all be thankful for it. England will be able to breathe again, madam.' The old lady paused—she had not a single idea in her head, but she naturally felt the necessity of saying something. So she asked, in the slow deliberate manner of old paralytic people: '*Do you think, sir, it will mak' ony difference in the price o' nitmugs?*' Hereupon, the lion-hunting Englishman, it is said, uttered a hasty expression unsuitable for print, bade the lady a hasty adieu, and made the best of his way back to his hotel, whence he next day set out for England.

---

## BANBURY AND ITS REMARKABLES.

The *Tatler* for September 5, 1710, gives a jocular account of an *Ecclesiastical Thermometer*, which had been invented for testing the degrees of zeal of particular places in behalf of the church. The writer states that the town of Banbury, Oxfordshire, which had been singled out by Dr Fuller a century before for its *cakes* and *zeal*, proved itself by 'the glass,' i. e., the above-mentioned thermometer, to be still characterised in a marked manner by the latter peculiarity. It may be suspected that Banbury at that time equally maintained its ancient distinction in respect of cakes, for the town is still noted for this article, insomuch that they are exported to the most distant parts of the world, one baker alone in 1839 disposing of 139,500 twopenny ones. However this may be, we find that, in the days of Fuller, the material things which the town was remarkable for were—*veal, cheese*, and *cakes;* while it is not less certain, that in the abstract article *zeal*, Banbury was also notable. Thereby hangs a jest. When Philemon Holland was printing his English edition of Camden's *Britannia*, he added to the author's statement of Banbury being famous for cheese, the words 'cakes and ale;' and so it was passing through the press, when, Mr Camden coming in, and seeing the change, thinking 'ale' a somewhat disrespectful reference, substituted for it the word 'zeal,' very unluckily, as it proved, for the Puritans, who abounded in the town, were greatly offended by the allusion, and so more was lost than gained by the change.

Modern research has not failed to discover the early traces of the extreme Puritanism of Banbury.

The advent of Queen Elizabeth to power brought evil days to the Roman Catholics; and in 1571, Mr Anthony Cope, of Hanwell, a zealous Puritan, was chosen parliamentary representative for the borough by its eighteen electors, an office which he filled for upwards of thirty years. The Rev. Thomas Bracebridge, an eminent Puritan divine, was also at this time vicar of Banbury, and was suspended by the bishop in 1590, for denouncing that usurpation of power in ecclesiastical matters which most of the Tudors were so fond of taking on themselves. There can be no doubt that he laid the foundation of those principles of Puritanism which displayed themselves in Banbury, towards the close of the reign in question, and which Mr Johnson describes as follows:

'From the date of the execution of the Earl of Essex—the last and best-beloved favourite of the queen—an event which took place in 1601, the active mind of Elizabeth became seriously impaired, and the transaction of public business was disagreeable and irksome. The oppressed and consequently dissatisfied adherents of the church of Rome, taking advantage of this altered state of things, began to wax bolder in the expression of their opinions. Under the strict rule of the Puritans, the shows and pageants had been suppressed, and an attempt was now made by the Catholics to revive them. The dresses were procured, the characters rehearsed, and a day fixed for the performance in Banbury. The procession of the performers had reached the high cross, and the actors were engaged in the prologue of the play, when a counter-demonstration issued from High Street, and a collision ensued between the excited partisans of the conflicting creeds. A regular mêlée is described as having taken place; but the supporters of the reformed doctrines, having both numbers and the law upon their side, seem eventually to have had the best of the fray. Having succeeded in driving their antagonists out of the town, the rage of the populace took a new direction. Hammers and pickaxes were procured, and the "goodly cross," the symbol of the faith of the Roman-Catholic world, was strewed in ruins through the Horse Fair. . . . So thorough was the work of destruction, that a writer of the time compares the state in which the crosses were left—for there were at least four of them—to the stumps of trees when the trunks are cut down, or to the conveniences by a roadside inn, to aid a lazy horseman in mounting to the saddle. To the church the crowd repaired next, and worked their frantic will upon the stately temple. The magnificent windows of stained glass were shivered to atoms, as savouring too strongly of idolatry, and the statuary and sculpture mutilated and defaced by the hands of those insensible to forms of beauty. Corbet charges the rioters with not having left the leg or arm of an apostle, and says that the names of the churchwardens were the only inscriptions to be seen upon the walls.

'The reputed sanctity of manners drew upon the town the cutting sarcasms of the wits of the age. The "rare Ben Jonson," in his comedy of *Bartholomew Fair*, represents one of his characters, "Zeal-o'-the-Land Busy," as a Banbury baker, who had abandoned the dough-tub and oven for the more lucrative avocation of "seeing visions and dreaming dreams." Braithwaite, in his *Drunken Barnaby's Four Journeys*, refers to the town in the well-known strain:

"To Banbury came I, O profane one!
There I saw a Puritane one
Hanging of his cat on Monday,
For killing of a mouse on Sunday."

The same writer, in his *Strappado for the Devil*, calls Bradford in Yorkshire, the "Banbury of the

North," and says that it also is famous for its "twanging ale, zeal, cakes, and cheese." Richard Corbet, subsequently bishop of Oxford, in his *Iter Boreale*, thus refers to the walks in and around Banbury church:

"If not for God's, for Mr Whateley's sake,
Level the walks; suppose these pitfalls make
Him sprain a lecture, or displace a joint
In his long prayer, or in his fifteenth point."'

This William Whateley was an eminent Puritan divine, of the Richard-Baxter school, who succeeded to the vicarage in 1610, and held the office for about thirty years. The Rev. Samuel Wells, another clergyman holding similar views, was inducted to the vicarage in 1648, and held the office until 1662, when, on 'Black Bartholomew,' he threw the emoluments of his living to the winds, and preached his farewell sermon from the words, 'And now, behold, I go bound in the spirit to Jerusalem, not knowing the things which shall befall me there.'

Sir William Davenant, in his comedy *The Wits*, in speaking of a certain lady, says:

'She is more devout
Than a weaver of Banbury, that hopes
To entice heaven, by singing, to make him lord
Of twenty looms.'

The following lines of Thomas Jordan, in his *Royal Arbor of Loyal Poesie*, may have had some reference to the doings already mentioned:

'They pluckt communion-tables down,
And broke our painted glasses;
They threw our altars to the ground,
And tumbled down the crosses.

They set up Cromwell and his heir—
The Lord and Lady Claypole—
Because they hated common-prayer,
The organ, and the May-pole.'

Most persons who have a feeling for the literature of their early years, will lament the destruction of the cross of Banbury, the locality of the famous nursery rhyme:

'Ride a cock-horse to Banbury Cross,
To see a black lady ride on a white horse,
Rings on her fingers and bells on her toes,
That she may have music wherever she goes.'

---

## SEPTEMBER 6.

St Pambo of Nitria, abbot, 385. St Macculindus, bishop of Lusk, 497. St Eleutherius, abbot, about 585. St Bega or Bees, virgin, 7th century.

---

*Born.*—Dr Robert Whytt, eminent medical writer, 1714, *Edinburgh*.

*Died.*—Pope John XIII., 972; Jean Baptiste Colbert, celebrated minister of finance to Louis XIV., 1683; Bishop Edmund Gibson, 1748, *Bath;* Sir John Fielding, notable police magistrate, 1780, *Brompton, London;* George Alexander Stevens, song and burlesque writer, 1784; Louis Peter Anquetil, historical writer, 1808; Dr Vicesimus Knox, miscellaneous writer, 1821, *Tunbridge;* John Bird Sumner, archbishop of Canterbury, author of *Records of Creation*, and other works, 1862.

### THE STRATFORD JUBILEE, OR SHAKSPEARE COMMEMORATION FESTIVAL IN 1769.

On Wednesday, the 6th of September 1769, and two following days, Stratford-upon-Avon, in Warwickshire, witnessed a succession of festivities such as seldom befall in an English country town. The object of these remarkable doings was the commemoration of the great Shakspeare, whose remains, upwards of a hundred and fifty years before, had been deposited in the chancel of the parish church of this his native place. To the scarcely less famous exponent of the national dramatist, the celebrated actor, David Garrick, belongs the credit, such as it is, of having devised this festive ceremonial, which, from the novelty as well as popularity of the scheme, created an immense sensation throughout the kingdom. The idea had been suggested to him by a request conveyed from the corporation of Stratford, that he would honour them by becoming a burgess, and accepting of the freedom of the town. Having intimated his willingness to do so, the freedom of the borough was, in May of this year, presented to him in an elegant box, made out of the famous mulberry-tree which Shakspeare himself had planted, but which, a short time previously, had been cut down by its proprietor, a splenetic clergyman, who, in addition to this act of Vandalism, had also pulled down the house in which Shakspeare lived. Vanity and enthusiasm alike stimulating Garrick, he now set himself arduously to work in the carrying out of the idea which he had conceived, and in its accomplishment he was aided by the zealous co-operation both of the authorities of the town of Stratford, and the most influential personages in point of rank and distinction in the realm. The most extensive preparations were made for the proper celebration of the festival; crowds of persons from all parts of England pressed forward to be present on the occasion, and the eventful morning at length dawned. The newspapers and magazines of the day have detailed at considerable length the events which took place, and from these we have compiled the following narrative.

On the morning of Wednesday, at five o'clock, the proceedings were inaugurated by a serenade performed through the streets by a band of musicians and singers from Drury Lane Theatre. Several guns were then fired, and the magistrates assembled about eight o'clock in one of the principal streets. A public breakfast was prepared in the new town-hall at nine, presided over by Mr Garrick as steward, who, previous to the reception of the general company, was formally waited on by the mayor and corporation of Stratford, and presented with a medallion of Shakspeare, carved on a piece of the famous mulberry-tree, and richly set in gold. At breakfast, favours in honour of the great dramatist were universally worn by ladies as well as gentlemen, and the assemblage numbered the most distinguished of the aristocracy amid its guests. This entertainment having been concluded, the company proceeded to the church, where the oratorio of *Judith* was performed under the superintendence of Dr Arne. A procession, with music, led by Mr Garrick, was then formed from the church to the amphitheatre, a wooden building erected for the occasion on the bank of the Avon, constructed after the manner of the Rotunda at Ranelagh, in the form of an octagon, with a roof supported by eight pillars, and elegantly painted and gilded. Here dinner was served up at three o'clock, and a suitable interval having elapsed, a musical performance took place, at which several songs, chiefly written by Garrick, were received

THE AMPHITHEATRE: STRATFORD JUBILEE, 1769.

with the greatest applause by the audience. One of these, which was greatly commended for its liveliness and spirit, is here inserted:

THE WARWICKSHIRE LAD.

Ye Warwickshire lads, and ye lasses,
See what at our jubilee passes;
Come, revel away, rejoice, and be glad,
For the lad of all lads, was a Warwickshire lad,
Warwickshire lad,
All be glad,
For the lad of all lads, was a Warwickshire lad.

Be proud of the charms of your county,
Where nature has lavished her bounty,
Where much she has given, and some to be spar'd,
For the bard of all bards, was a Warwickshire bard,
Warwickshire bard,
Never pair'd,
For the bard of all bards, was a Warwickshire bard.

Each shire has its different pleasures,
Each shire has its different treasures,
But to rare Warwickshire, all must submit,
For the wit of all wits, was a Warwickshire wit,
Warwickshire wit,
How he writ!
For the wit of all wits, was a Warwickshire wit.

Old Ben, Thomas Otway, John Dryden,
And half a score more we take pride in,
Of famous Will Congreve we boast too the skill,
But the Will of all Wills, was a Warwickshire Will,
Warwickshire Will,
Matchless still,
For the Will of all Wills, was a Warwickshire Will.

Our Shakspeare compared is to no man,
Nor Frenchman, nor Grecian, nor Roman,
Their swans are all geese, to the Avon's sweet swan,
And the man of all men, was a Warwickshire man,
Warwickshire man,
Avon's swan,
And the man of all men, was a Warwickshire man.

As ven'son is very inviting,
To steal it our bard took delight in,
To make his friends merry, he never was lag,
For the wag of all wags, was a Warwickshire wag,
Warwickshire wag,
Ever brag,
For the wag of all wags, was a Warwickshire wag.

There never was seen such a creature,
Of all she was worth he robbed Nature;
He took all her smiles, and he took all her grief,
And the thief of all thieves, was a Warwickshire thief,
Warwickshire thief,
He 's the chief,
For the thief of all thieves, was a Warwickshire thief.

A grand ball commenced in the amphitheatre in the evening, and was kept up till three o'clock next morning. In front of the building, an ambitious transparency was exhibited, representing Time leading Shakspeare to immortality, with Tragedy on one side, and Comedy on the other. A general illumination took place in the town, along with a brilliant display of fireworks, under the management of Mr Angelo. The next morning was ushered in like the former by firing of cannon, serenading, and ringing of bells. A public breakfast was again served in the town-hall, and at eleven o'clock the company repaired to the amphitheatre, to hear performed Garrick's *Shakspeare Ode*, which he had composed for the dedication of the town-hall, and placing there a statue of the great bard presented by Garrick to the corporation. We quote the grandiloquent language of Boswell, the biographer of Johnson, regarding this production.

'The performance of the Dedication Ode was noble and affecting: it was like an exhibition in Athens or Rome. The whole audience were fixed in the most earnest attention; and I do believe, that if one had attempted to disturb the performance, he would have been in danger of his life. Garrick, in the front of the orchestra, filled with the first musicians of the nation, with Dr Arne at their head, and inspired with an awful elevation of soul, while he looked from time to time at the venerable statue of Shakspeare, appeared more than himself. While he repeated the ode, and saw the various passions and feelings which it contains fully transfused into all around him, he seemed in ecstasy, and gave us the idea of a mortal transformed into a demigod, as we read in the pagan mythology.'

The statue of Shakspeare, above referred to, was raised in a conspicuous position above the assembled company, and Garrick, we are told, was stationed in the centre of the orchestra, dressed in a brown suit, richly embroidered with gold lace, with his steward's wand of the mulberry-wood in his hand, and the medallion, presented him by the corporation, suspended from his breast. Our space does not permit us to transcribe here the Dedication Ode, which is a piece of considerable length. Declaimed by Garrick, with the airs and choruses set to music by Arne, and performed under the personal direction of that gifted composer, it must have formed the most attractive part of the jubilee festivities. On its completion, its author stood up and delivered a eulogium on Shakspeare, in which the enemies of the dramatist (if he had any) were called on to state anything which they knew to his prejudice. Upon this, King, the celebrated comedian, ascended to the orchestra, and in the character of a *macaroni*, the reigning type of fop of the day, commenced a denunciatory attack on Shakspeare, as an ill-bred uncultivated fellow, who made people laugh or cry as *he* thought proper—in short, quite unsuited for the refinement of the present age. It is said to have been a highly-amusing exhibition, though many of the audience, unable to understand a joke, and believing it a real onslaught upon Shakspeare, testified visibly their dissatisfaction. An epilogue addressed to the ladies, and delivered by Garrick, closed this part of the ceremonial, which did not terminate without a mishap—the composure of the meeting being unexpectedly disturbed by the giving way of a number of the benches on which the audience sat, with a terrible crash. A nobleman was at the same time hurt by the falling of a door, but fortunately no one received any serious detriment.

The remainder of Thursday was, like the previous day, spent in dining, listening to a concert, and witnessing illuminations and fireworks. At midnight commenced a grand masquerade, said to have been one of the finest entertainments of the kind ever witnessed in Britain. Three ladies, we are informed, who personated Macbeth's witches, and another, who appeared as Dame Quickly, excited universal admiration. An Oxford gentleman assumed, with great effect, the character of Lord Ogleby ; but a person dressed as the Devil gave inexpressible offence ! One individual, whose costume attracted special attention, was James Boswell, already referred to, whom the accompanying engraving represents as he appeared at the Stratford jubilee masquerade, in the character of an armed chief of Corsica, an island of which he had published an account, and regarding which he had, as his countrymen in the north would say, 'a bee in his bonnet.' The dress consisted of a short, dark-coloured coat of coarse cloth, scarlet waistcoat and breeches, and black spatterdashes, and a cap of black cloth, bearing on its front, embroidered in gold letters, VIVA LA LIBERTA, and on its side a blue feather and cockade. The device was in allusion to the struggles of the Corsicans for national independence under General Paoli, Boswell's friend. On the breast of the coat was sewed a Moor's head, the crest of Corsica, surrounded with branches of laurel. Mr Boswell wore also a cartridge-pouch, into which was stuck a stiletto, and on his left side a pistol. A musket was slung across his shoulder, and his hair, which was unpowdered, hung plaited down his neck, ending in a knot of blue ribbons. In his right hand he carried a long vine staff, with a bird curiously carved at the upper end, as 'emblematical of the sweet bard of Avon.' He wore no mask, saying that it was not proper for a gallant Corsican. In this character he also delivered a

JAMES BOSWELL, AT THE STRATFORD JUBILEE, 1769.
FROM THE LONDON MAGAZINE.

poetical address, sufficiently grandiose and Cambysean, on the united subjects of Corsica and the Stratford jubilee. There can be no doubt, as Mr Croker remarks, that poor Bozzy made a sad fool of himself, both on this and other occasions during the jubilee, and would have done well to have followed the advice of his blunt-spoken Mentor, 'to clear his head of Corsica.' During his stay at Stratford, he is said to have gone about with the words CORSICA BOSWELL printed in large letters outside his hat, that no one might remain in ignorance of the presence of so illustrious a personage.

On the masquerade revellers awaking from their slumbers on the following day (Friday), they found a deluge of rain, which had continued unintermittedly from the previous night, descending on the town of Stratford. All prospect, therefore, of carrying out the proposed Shakspeare pageant, in which the principal characters in his plays were to have been represented in a triumphal procession, *al fresco*, with chariots, banners, and all proper adjuncts, was rendered hopeless. There was, however, a jubilee horse-race, which was well attended, though the animals were up to their knees in water. In the evening another grand ball took place in the town-hall, in which the graceful minuet-dancing of Mrs Garrick, who in her youth had been a distinguished Terpsichorean performer on the London stage, won the highest encomiums. The assembly broke up at four o'clock on Saturday morning, and so ended the Stratford jubilee.

As might have been expected, this festive celebration did not escape satire and animadversion, both before and after the event; the jealousy felt against its author, Garrick, being sufficient to call forth many pungent attacks. In the *Devil on Two Sticks*, Foote introduced the following sarcastic description: 'A jubilee, as it hath lately appeared, is a public invitation, circulated and urged by puffing, to go post without horses, to an obscure borough without representatives, governed by a mayor and aldermen who are no magistrates, to celebrate a great poet, whose own works have made him immortal, by an ode without poetry, music without melody, dinners without victuals, and lodgings without beds; a masquerade where half the people appeared barefaced, a horse-race up to the knees in water, fireworks extinguished as soon as they were lighted, and a gingerbread amphitheatre, which, like a house of cards, tumbled to pieces as soon as it was finished.' Other squibs appeared in the form of parodies and epigrams; and also a farce, entitled *The Stratford Jubilee*, intended to have been performed at Foote's theatre, in the Haymarket, but which, though printed and published, seems to have never been placed on the boards. Strictures of a different description were passed on the whole festival by certain of the inhabitants of Stratford, who imputed the violent rains which fell during the jubilee to the judgment of Heaven on such impious demonstrations. This circumstance may recall to some of our readers the worthy minister of Leith, recorded by Hugh Miller in his *Schools and Schoolmasters*, who ascribed the great fire in Edinburgh in 1824, to the Musical Festival which had a short time previously been celebrated there!

In the month of October following the Stratford jubilee, the Shakspeare pageant devised by Garrick, but the representation of which had been prevented by the unfavourable weather, was brought out by him with great magnificence and success at Drury Lane Theatre, and had a run of nearly a hundred nights. On the 6th of September in the ensuing year, the anniversary of the ceremonial was celebrated at Stratford with great festivity; but the custom seems afterwards to have fallen into desuetude, and no further public commemoration of our great national poet was attempted in the place of his birth for upwards of fifty years. At last, in 1824, the Shakspeare Club was established, and an annual celebration in his honour appointed to be held on the 23d of April, the (erroneously) assumed day of his birth,* and which we know, upon good evidence, to have been that of his death. Under the auspices of this association, a splendid gala, after the manner of the jubilee of 1769, was conducted in Stratford, on 23d April 1827 and two following days. A similarly magnificent commemoration took place in 1830, when, among other festive ceremonies, an ode, written for the occasion by Mr Alaric A. Watts, was recited, and a series of dramatic performances exhibited, in which the principal characters were sustained by Mr Charles Kean. At the celebration in 1836, an oration was delivered in the theatre by Mr George Jones, the American tragedian, and in 1837 by Mr Sheridan Knowles. A memorial theatre, including a library and picture gallery, the foundation stone of which was laid in 1877, has been erected at Stratford for the occasional celebration of the poet's birthday, and for the representation of his plays.

The Shakspeare jubilee was the first of those commemorative festivals which have since become so familiar to all of us. In 1785, a grand musical celebration took place in Westminster Abbey in honour of Handel. Centenary festivities were performed in nearly every part of the world, in honour of Robert Burns, in January 1859. Although the 15th August was Sir Walter Scott's real birthday, for various reasons his centenary was celebrated on 9th August 1871, with great enthusiasm in Edinburgh, Glasgow, Dundee, and Dumfries.

* See *Book of Days*, i. 543.

---

# SEPTEMBER 7.

St Regina or Reine, virgin and martyr, 3d century. St Evurtius, bishop of Orleans, confessor, about 340. St Grimonia or Germana, virgin and martyr. St Eunan, first bishop of Raphoe, in Ireland. St Cloud, confessor, 560. St Madelberte, virgin, about 705. Saints Alchmund and Tilberht, confessors, 8th century.

*Born.*—Queen Elizabeth of England, 1533, *Greenwich;* Thomas Erpenius, celebrated orientalist, 1584, *Gorcum, Holland;* Louis de Bourbon, Prince de Condé, great commander, 1621, *Paris;* George Louis, Count de Buffon, distinguished naturalist, 1707, *Montbard, Burgundy;* Dr Samuel Johnson, lexicographer and author, 1709, *Lichfield;* Arthur Young, agricultural writer, 1741.

*Died.*—Emperor Frederick IV. of Germany, 1493, *Vienna;* Cardinal Guido Bentivoglio, historical writer, 1644, *Rome;* Captain Porteous, murdered by the Edinburgh mob, 1736; Dr John Armstrong, author of *The Art of Preserving Health*, 1779, *London;* Leonard Euler, eminent mathematician, 1783, *St Petersburg;* Mrs Hannah More, religious and moral writer, 1833, *Clifton.*

## ARTHUR YOUNG.

The most popular and prolific of writers on rural affairs was Arthur Young. No great discovery or improvement in agriculture bears his name: his merit consists in the fact, that he was an agitator. He had a passion for novelties, and such was the vigour of his mind, that he succeeded in affecting the most stolid and conservative of classes with something of his own enthusiasm. He set landlords thinking, enticed and drove them into experiments, and persuaded farmers everywhere to break from the dull routine of centuries. More than any man, England owes to Arthur Young that impulse which, within the last hundred years, has transformed her wastes into rich pastures and fruitful fields, and multiplied the produce of her harvests by many fold.

Young was the son of a Suffolk clergyman, and was born in 1741. He was apprenticed to a merchant in Lynn, but an inordinate taste for reading and scribbling interfered sadly with his mercantile progress. At the age of seventeen, he wrote a pamphlet on the war against the French in America, for which a publisher gave him ten pounds' worth of books. He next started a periodical, called the *Universal Museum*, which, by the advice of Dr Johnson, he discontinued at the sixth number. Four novels, about the same time, flowed from his facile pen. At his father's death, in 1769, he wished to enter the army, but at his mother's entreaty refrained, and turned farmer instead, without any practical knowledge of husbandry, and, as he afterwards confessed, with his head bursting with wild notions of improvements. Farming supplied matter and direction for his literary activity, and in 1770 he published, in two thick volumes quarto, *A Course of Experimental Agriculture, containing an exact Register of the Business transacted during five years on near* 300 *acres of various Soils.* A few years before, he had printed *A Tour through the Southern Counties of England*, which proved so popular that he was led to undertake similar surveys in the east, west, and north, and Ireland. These tours excited the liveliest interest in all connected with agriculture: soils, methods of culture, crops, farm-buildings, cattle, plantations, roads, were all discussed in a most vivacious style, and praised or blamed with bluff honesty. Between 1766 and 1775, he relates that he realised £3000 by his agricultural writings, a large sum for works of that order in those times. His own farming was far from profitable, and the terms in which he describes a hundred acres he rented in Hertfordshire, may be taken as a fair specimen of his outspoken manner: 'I know not what epithet to give this soil; sterility falls short of the idea; a hungry vitriolic gravel—I occupied for nine years the jaws of a wolf. A nabob's fortune would sink in the attempt to raise good arable crops in such a country: my experience and knowledge had increased from travelling and practice; but all was lost when exerted on such a spot. I hardly wonder at a losing account, after fate had fixed me on land calculated to swallow, without return, all that folly or imprudence could bestow upon it.' Finding that his income was barely sufficient to meet his expenditure, he engaged to report the parliamentary debates for the *Morning Post*. This he continued to perform for several years; and after the labours of the week, he walked every Saturday evening to his wretched farm, a distance of seventeen miles from London, from which he as regularly returned every Monday morning. This was the most anxious and laborious part of his life. 'I worked,' he writes, 'like a coal-heaver, though without his reward.'

In 1784, he commenced a periodical work under the title of the *Annals of Agriculture*, which he continued through forty-five volumes. He admitted no papers unless signed by the author, a regulation which added alike to the interest and authority of the publication. The rule was relaxed, however, in the case of the king, George III., who contributed to the seventh volume a description of the farm of Mr Ducket at Petersham, under the signature of 'Ralph Robinson of Windsor.'

Young's English *Tours* possess considerable historic interest, which will increase with the lapse of years; but their present, and probably future, value in that respect is thrown into the shade by his *Agricultural Survey of France*, made on horseback, in 1788. The French admit that Young was the first who opened their eyes to the very low condition of their husbandry, but his observations on the social and political state of the peasantry, their poverty and hardships, are of peculiar and unique importance, as made on the very verge of the revolution; and no student of the circumstances which led up to that tremendous catastrophe, will ever neglect Arthur Young's *Survey.* In his French travel he displays a liberal and reforming spirit, but the excesses and atrocities of the revolutionists drove Young, as it did Burke and a host of others, into Toryism, and a pamphlet he published in 1793, entitled *The Example of France a Warning to Britain*, had a great sale, and attests the depth of his horror and disgust.

The fame of Young as an agriculturist was greater even abroad than at home, and many were the tokens of admiration he received. The French Directory, in 1801, ordered the translation of all his agricultural writings, and in twenty volumes they were published in Paris, under the title of *Le Cultivateur Anglais.* The Empress Catherine sent three young Russians to be instructed by him, and made him the present of a gold snuff-box, with rich ermine cloaks for his wife and daughter. His son, too, was employed by the Czar Alexander, in 1805, to make an agricultural survey around Moscow, and was rewarded with a sum which enabled him to purchase an estate of 10,000 acres of very fertile land in the Crimea, where he settled. Pupils flocked to Arthur Young from all parts of the world. The Duke of Bedford one morning, at his breakfast-table, counted representatives from France, Poland, Austria, Russia, Italy, Portugal, and America.

Sir John Sinclair, in 1793, persuaded the government to establish a Board of Agriculture, of which Young was appointed secretary, with a free house and a salary of £400 a year. It was a post for which he was admirably suited, and was the means of preserving him from a very hazardous speculation—a tract of Yorkshire moorland he purposed cultivating. 'What a change in the destination of a man's life!' he exclaims. 'Instead of entering, as I proposed, the solitary lord of 4000 acres, in the keen atmosphere of lofty rocks and mountain torrents, with a little creation rising gradually around me, making the desert smile with cultivation, and grouse give way to industrious population, active and energetic, though remote and tranquil, and every instant of my existence *making two blades of grass to grow where not one was found before*—behold me at a desk in the fog, the smoke, the din of Whitehall!'

About 1808, his sight grew dim, terminating in blindness, but his busy career did not close until the 12th of April 1820, when he had nearly reached his eightieth year.

## OLD SAYINGS AS TO CLOTHES.

It is lucky to put on any article of dress, particularly stockings, inside out: but if you wish the omen to hold good, you must continue to wear the reversed portion of your attire in that condition, till the regular time comes for putting it off—that is, either bedtime or 'cleaning yourself.' If you set it right, you will 'change the luck.' It will be of no use to put on anything with the wrong side out *on purpose.*

It is worthy of remark, in connection with this superstition, that when William the Conqueror, in arming himself for the battle of Hastings, happened to put on his shirt of mail with the hind-side before, the bystanders seem to have been shocked by it, as by an ill omen, till William claimed it as a good one, betokening that he was to be changed from a duke to a king. The phenomenon of the 'hind-side before' is so closely related to that of 'inside out,' that one can hardly understand their being taken for contrary omens.

The clothes of the dead will never wear long.

When a person dies, and his or her clothes are given away to the poor, it is frequently remarked: 'Ah, they may look very well, but they won't wear; they belong to the dead.'

If a mother gives away *all* the baby's clothes she has (or the cradle), she will be sure to have another baby, though she may have thought herself above such vanities.

If a girl's petticoats are longer than her frock, that is a sign that her father loves her better than her mother does—perhaps because it is plain that her mother does not attend so much to her dress as she ought to do, whereas her father may love her as much as you please, and at the same time be very ignorant or unobservant of the rights and wrongs of female attire.

If you would have good-luck, you must wear something new on 'Whitsun-Sunday' (pronounced Wissun-Sunday). More generally, Easter Day is the one thus honoured, but a glance round a church or Sunday-school in Suffolk, on Whitsunday, shews very plainly that it is the one chosen for beginning to wear new 'things.'

While upon the subject of clothes, I may mention a ludicrous Suffolk phrase descriptive of a person not quite so sharp as he might be: he is spoken of as 'short of buttons,' being, I suppose, considered an unfinished article.

## MISCELLANEOUS SAYINGS.

It is unlucky to enter a house, which you are going to occupy, by the *back*-door.

I knew of a family who had hired a house, and went to look over it, accompanied by an old Scotch servant. The family, innocently enough, finding the front-door 'done up,' went in at the back-door, which was open; but great was their surprise to see the servant burst into tears, and sit down on a stone outside, refusing to go in with them. If I recollect rightly (the circumstance happened several years ago), she had the front-door opened, and went in at that herself, hoping, I suppose, that the spell would be dissolved, if *all* the family did not go in at the back-door.

The Cross was made of elder-wood.

Speaking to some little children one day about the danger of taking shelter under trees during a thunderstorm, one of them said that it was not so with all trees, 'For,' said he, 'you will be quite safe under an *eldern*-tree, because the cross was made of that, and so the lightning never strikes it.'

With this may be contrasted a superstition mentioned by Dean Trench in one of the notes to his *Sacred Latin Poetry*, and accounting for the trembling of the leaves of the aspen-tree, by saying that the cross was made of its wood, and that, since then, the tree has never ceased to shudder.

Hot cross-buns, if properly made, will never get mouldy.

To make them properly, you must do the whole of the business on the Good-Friday itself; the materials must be mixed, the dough made, and the buns baked on that day, and this, I think, before a certain hour; but whether this hour is sunrise or church-time, I cannot say. Perhaps the spice which enters into the composition of hot cross-buns, has as much to do with the result as anything, but, *experto crede*, you may keep them for years without their getting mouldy.

In the appendix to Forby's *Vocabulary of East Anglia*, are given several local superstitions. One of them, regarding the cutting of the nails, is such a very elaborate one, that I give entire the formula in which it is embodied. The version that I have heard is nearly word for word the same as that which he has printed, and is as follows:

'Cut 'em on Monday, you cut 'em for health;
Cut 'em on Tuesday, you cut 'em for wealth;
Cut 'em on Wednesday, you cut 'em for news;
Cut 'em on Thursday, a new pair of shoes;
Cut 'em on Friday, you cut 'em for sorrow;
Cut 'em on Saturday, you'll see your true love to-morrow;
Cut 'em on Sunday, and you'll have the devil with you all the week.'

I must confess that I cannot divine the origin of any of these notions, but of the last two. Sunday is, of course, the chief day for courting among the labouring-classes, and what can be more natural than that the cutting of the nails on a Saturday, should be followed by the meeting of true-lovers on the next day? the most likely one for such an event, whether the nails had been cut or not.

The last, again, seems to have arisen from considering the cutting of nails to be a kind of *work*, and so to be a sin, which would render the breaker of the Sabbath more liable to the attacks of the devil. This view is strengthened by the fact of the Sunday being placed not at the *beginning*, but at the *end* of the week, and thus identified with the Jewish Sabbath. Indeed, I have found that among poor people generally, it is reckoned as the seventh day, and that on the Sunday, they speak of the remainder of the week as the *next* week.

Superstitions with respect to the cutting of the nails are of very ancient date. We find one in Hesiod's *Works and Day* (742–3), where he tells you: 'Not to cut from the five-branched with glittering iron the dry from the quick in the rich feast of the gods,' a direction which may be compared with the warning against Sunday nail-cutting in the East-Anglian saw given above.

Mushrooms will not grow after they have been seen. Very naturally, the first person that sees them, gathers them.

The price of corn rises and falls with Barton Mere—an eccentric piece of water, which varies in size from twelve or fourteen acres to a small pond, and is sometimes entirely dried up. It lies about four miles from Bury St Edmunds, and a worthy old farmer, now deceased, used frequently to ride to Barton Mere to observe the state of the water there, before proceeding to Bury market. I do not know of any one who does this now, but it is an observed fact that the price of corn, and the height of the water, frequently *do* vary together: for instance, corn is now (October 1862) very low, and the mere is nearly dry. Probably the character of the weather may affect both in common, and in this manner the notion can be explained, as the saying that: 'If the rain-drops hang on the window, more will come to join them,' may be accounted for by the fact, that it is a sign of slow evaporation, of the presence of abundant moisture, which will be likely to precipitate itself in the form of more rain.

If, when you are fishing, you count what you have taken, you will not catch any more.

This may be paralleled with the prejudice against counting lambs, mentioned in a former paper. It is a western superstition, and was communicated to me by a gentleman, who, when out with professional fishermen, has been prevented by them from counting the fish caught till the day's sport was over.

The same gentleman also told me a method which he had seen practised in the same locality to discover the body of a person who had been drowned in a river. An apple was sent down the stream from above the spot where the body was supposed to be, and it was expected that the apple would stop above the place where the corpse lay. He could not, however, take upon himself to say that the expedient was a successful one.

*Suffolk.* C. W. J.

---

# SEPTEMBER 8.

The Nativity of the blessed Virgin. St Adrian, martyr. St Sidronius, martyr, 3d century. Saints Eusebius, Nestablus, Zeno, and Nestor, martyrs, 4th century. St Disen or Disibode, bishop and confessor, about 700. St Corbinian, bishop of Frisingen, confessor, 730. The Holy Name of the Blessed Virgin Mary.

---

*Born.*—Lodovico Ariosto, Italian poet, 1474, *Reggio, in Lombardy;* John Leyden, poet, 1775, *Denholm, Roxburghshire.*

*Died.*—Thomas, Duke of Gloucester, murdered at Calais, 1397; Amy Robsart, wife of the Earl of Leicester, 1560, *Cumnor;* Francis Quarles, poet, 1644; Princess Elizabeth, daughter of Charles I., 1650, *Carisbrooke Castle;* Bishop Joseph Hall, author of the *Contemplations* and *Satires*, 1656, *Higham, near Norwich.*

## LODOVICO ARIOSTO.

The author of *Orlando Furioso* was born at the castle of Reggio, in Lombardy, on the 8th of September 1474. Of all the Italian poets, he is considered to be the most eminent, and his name is held in the same veneration in his native country as that of Shakspeare is in England. Preferring comfort and independence to splendour and servility, he refused several invitations to live at the courts of crowned heads, and built a commodious, but small house, for his own residence, at Ferrara. Being asked how he, who had described so many magnificent palaces in his poems, could be satisfied with so small a house, he replied that it was much easier to put words and sentences together than stones and mortar. Then leading the inquirer to the front of his house, he pointed out the following inscription on the lintel below the windows, extending along the whole front of the house.

'Parva sed apta mihi, sed nulli obnoxia, sed non
Sordida, parta meo sed tamen ære domus.'

Which may be translated—

Small is my humble roof, but well designed
To suit the temper of the master's mind;
Hurtful to none, it boasts a decent pride,
That my poor purse the modest cost supplied.

Ferrara derives its principal celebrity from the house of Ariosto, which is maintained in good condition at the public expense. The first edition of the *Orlando* was published in that city in 1516, and there, too, the poet died and was buried in the Benedictine Church, in 1533. Some time in the last century, the tomb of Ariosto was struck by lightning, and the iron laurels that wreathed the brows of the poet's bust were melted by the electric fluid. And so Byron tells us:

'The lightning rent from Ariosto's bust
The iron crown of laurels' mimick'd leaves;
Nor was the ominous element unjust,
For the true laurel wreath, which glory weaves,
Is of the tree no bolt of thunder cleaves,
And the false semblance but disgraced his brow;
Yet still, if fondly superstition grieves,
Know that the lightning sanctifies below,
Whate'er it strikes—Yon head is doubly sacred now.'

In 1801, the French general, Miollis, removed Ariosto's tomb and remains to the gallery of the public library of Ferrara; and there, too, are preserved his chair, ink-stand, and an imperfect copy of the *Orlando* in his own handwriting.

## THE DEATH OF THOMAS, DUKE OF GLOUCESTER, 1397.

The arrest and murder of Thomas of Woodstock, Duke of Gloucester, is one of the most tragical episodes of English history. However guilty he might be, the proceedings against him were executed with such treachery and cruelty, as to render them revolting to humanity. He was the seventh and youngest son of Edward III., and consequently the uncle of Richard II. Being himself a resolute and warlike man, he was dissatisfied with what he considered the unprincipled and pusillanimous conduct of his nephew, and, either from a spirit of patriotism or ambition, or, more probably, a combination of both, he promoted two or three measures against the king, more by mere words than by acts. On confessing this to the king, and expressing his sorrow for it, he was promised forgiveness, and restored to the royal favour. Trusting to this reconciliation, he was residing peaceably in his castle at Pleshy, near London, where he received a visit from the king, not only without suspicion, but with the fullest confidence of his friendly intentions. The incident is thus touchingly related by Froissart, a contemporary chronicler:

'The king went after dinner, with part of his retinue, to Pleshy, about five o'clock. The Duke of Gloucester had already supped; for he was very sober, and sat but a short time at table, either at dinner or supper. He came to meet the king, and honoured him as we ought to honour our lord, so did the duchess and her children, who were there. The king entered the hall, and thence into the chamber. A table was spread for the king, and he supped a little. He said to the duke: "Fair uncle! have your horses saddled: but not all; only five or six; you must accompany me to London; we shall find there my uncles Lancaster and York, and I mean to be governed by your advice on a request they intend making to me. Bid your maître-d'hotel follow you with your people to London." The duke, who thought no ill from it, assented to it pleasantly enough. As soon as the king had supped, and all were ready, the king took leave of the duchess and her children, and mounted his horse. So did the duke, who left Pleshy with only three esquires and four varlets. They avoided the high-road to London, but rode with speed, conversing on various topics, till they came to Stratford. The king then pushed on before him, and the earl marshal came suddenly behind him, with a great body of horsemen, and springing on the duke, said: "I arrest you in the king's name!" The duke, astonished, saw that he was betrayed, and cried with a loud voice after the king. I do not know if the king heard him or not, but he did not return, but rode away.'

The duke was then hurried off to Calais, where he was placed in the hands of some of the king's minions, under the Duke of Norfolk. Two of these ruffians, Serle, a valet of the king's, and Franceys, a valet of the Duke of Albemarle, then told the Duke of Gloucester, that 'it was the king's will that he should die. He answered, that if it was his will, it must be so. They asked him to have a chaplain, he agreed, and confessed. They then made him lie down on a bed; the two valets threw a feather-bed upon him; three other persons held down the sides of it, while Serle and Franceys pressed on the mouth of the duke till he expired, three others of the assistants all the while on their knees weeping and praying for his soul, and Halle keeping guard at the door. When he was dead, the Duke of Norfolk came to them, and saw the dead body.'* The body of the Duke of Gloucester was conveyed with great pomp to England, and first buried in the abbey of Pleshy, his own foundation, in a tomb which he himself had provided for the purpose. Subsequently, his remains were removed to Westminster, and deposited in the king's chapel, under a marble slab inlaid with brass. Immediately after his murder, his widow, who was the daughter of Humphry de Bohun, Earl of Hereford, became a nun in the abbey of Barking; at her death she was buried beside her husband in Westminster Abbey. Gower, in his work entitled *Vox Clamantis*, has a Latin poem on the Duke of Gloucester, in which occur the following lines respecting the manner of his death:

'Heu quam tortorum quidam de sorte malorum,
Sic Ducis electi plumarum pondere lecti,
Corpus quassatum jugulantque necant jugulatum.'†

## QUARLES AND HIS EMBLEMS.

Francis Quarles, who, at one time, enjoyed the post of 'chronologer to the city of London,' and is supposed to have had a pension from Charles I., has a sort of side-place in English literature in consequence of his writing a book of *Emblems*, delighted in by the common people, but despised by the learned and the refined. The Protestantism of the first hundred and fifty years following upon the Reformation took a strong turn in favour of hour-glasses, cross-bones, and all other things which tended to make humanity sensible of its miserable defects, and its deplorable destinies. There was quite a tribe of churchyard poets, who only professed to be great in dismal things, and of whom we must presume that they never smiled or joked, or condescended to be in any degree happy, but spent their whole lives in conscientiously making other people miserable. The emblematists were of this order. It was their business to get up little allegorical pictures, founded on some of the distressing characteristics of mortality, carved on wood blocks in the most unlovely style, and accompanied by verses of such harshness as to set the moral teeth on edge, and leave a bitter ideal taste in the mouth for some hours after. An extract of a letter from Pope to Bishop Atterbury, in which he refers to Quarles's work, will give some idea of the system practised by this grim class of preachers: '"*Tinnit, inane est*" [It rings, and is empty], with the picture of one ringing on the globe with his finger, is the best thing that I have the luck to remember in that great poet Quarles (not that I forget the Devil at Bowls, which I know to be your lordship's favourite cut, as well as favourite diversion). But the greatest part of them are of a very different character from these: one of them, on, "O wretched man that I am, who shall deliver me from the body of this death?" represents a man sitting in a melancholy posture, in a large skeleton. Another, on, "O that my head were waters, and mine eyes a fountain of tears!" exhibits a human figure, with several spouts gushing from it, like the spouts of a fountain.' Mr Grainger, quoting this from Pope, adds: 'This reminds me of an emblem, which I have seen in a German author, on Matt. vii. 3, in which are two men, one of whom has a beam almost as big as himself with a peaked end sticking in his left eye; and the other has only a small hole sticking in his right. Hence it appears that metaphor and allegory, however beautiful in themselves, will not always admit of a sensible representation.'*

There is just this to be said of Quarles, that he had a vein of real poetry in him, and so far was not rightly qualified for the duty of depressing the spirits of his fellow-creatures. One is struck, too, by hearing of him a fact so like natural and happy life, as that he was the father of eighteen children by one wife. A vine would be *her* proper emblem, we may presume. His end, again, was duly sad. A false accusation, of a political nature, was brought against him, and he took it so much to heart, that he said it would be his death, which proved true. He died at the age of fifty-two.

Quarles's *Emblems* was frequently printed in the seventeenth century, for the use of the vulgar, who generally rather like things which remind them that, in some essential respects, the great and the cultured are upon their own level. After more than a century of utter neglect, it was reprinted about fifty years ago; and this reprint has also now become scarce.

## THE PRINCESS ELIZABETH STUART.

Elizabeth, the second of the ill-fated daughters of the ill-fated Charles I., was born in 1635, in the palace of St James. The states of Holland, as a congratulatory gift to her father, sent ambergris, rare porcelain, and choice pictures. Scarcely was the child six years old, when the horrors of civil war separated her from her parents, and the remaining nine years of her short life were passed in the custody of strangers. A few interviews with her father cheered those dreary years, and then the last sad meeting of all took place, the day preceding the ever-memorable 30th of January. With attempts at self-control far beyond her tender years, she listened to the last words she ever was to hear from parental lips. The king, we are told, took

* From the deposition of Halle, who was afterwards hanged and quartered for the murder.

† Weever's *Funeral Monuments*, page 639.

* *Biographical History of England*, iii. 135.

her in his arms, embraced her, and placing her on his knees, soothed her by his caresses, requesting her to listen to his last instructions, as he had that to confide to her ears which he could tell no one else, and it was important she should hear and remember his words. Among other things, he told her to tell her mother that his thoughts never strayed from her, and that his love should be the same to the last. This message of undying love remained undelivered, for the gentle girl never again saw her mother.

How the wretched child passed the day of her father's execution in the ancient house of Sion, at Brentford, God, who tempers the wind to the shorn lamb, alone knows. From Sion, she was removed to the classic shades of Penshurst, and from thence her jealous custodians sent her to Carisbrooke Castle. About eighteen months after her father's death, she accidentally got wet in the bowling-green of the castle; fever and cold ensued, and the frail form succumbed to death. Supposing her to have fallen asleep, her attendants left the apartment for a short time; on their return, she was dead, her hands clasped in the attitude of prayer, and her face resting on an open Bible, her father's last and cherished gift.

A statement has found its way into Hume's and other histories, to the effect that the parliament designed to apprentice this poor child to a button-maker at Newport. But it is believed that such an idea never went beyond a joke in the mouth of Cromwell; in point of fact, the conduct of the parliament towards the little princess was humane and liberal, excepting in the matter of personal restraint. At the time of her death, she had an allowance of £1000 per annum for her maintenance; and she was treated with almost all the ceremonious attendance due to her rank.

Her remains were embalmed, and buried with considerable pomp, in the church of St Thomas, at Newport. The letters E. S., on an adjacent wall, alone pointing out the spot. In time, the obscure resting-place of a king's daughter was forgotten; and it came upon people like a discovery, when, in 1793, while a grave was being prepared for a son of Lord de la Warr, a leaden coffin, in excellent preservation, was found, bearing the inscription:

Elizabeth, 2^d^ daughter
of the late King Charles.
Deceased September 8^th^ MDCL.

Clarendon says that the princess was a 'lady of excellent parts, great observation, and an early understanding.' Fuller, speaking of her in his quaint style, says: 'The hawks of Norway, where a winter's day is hardly an hour of clear light, are the swiftest of wing of any fowl under the firmament, nature teaching them to bestir themselves to lengthen the shortness of the time with their swiftness. Such was the active piety of this lady, improving the little life allotted to her, in running the way of God's commandments.'

The church at Newport becoming ruinous, it was found necessary to rebuild it a few years ago; and her Majesty the Queen, with the sympathy of a woman and a princess, took the opportunity of erecting a monument to the unhappy Elizabeth. Baron Marochetti was commissioned to execute the work, and well has he performed his task. It represents the princess, lying on a mattress, her cheek resting on an open page of the sacred volume, bearing the words, 'Come unto me, all ye that labour and are heavy laden, and I will give you rest.' From the Gothic arch, beneath which the figure reposes, hangs an iron grating with its bars broken asunder, emblematising the prisoner's release by death. Two side-windows, with stained glass to temper the light falling on the monument, have been added by her Majesty's desire. And the inscription thus gracefully records a graceful act: 'To the Memory of the Princess Elizabeth, Daughter of Charles I., who died at Carisbrooke Castle on Sunday, September 8, 1650, and is interred beneath the Chancel of this Church. This Monument is erected, a token of respect for her Virtues, and of sympathy for her Misfortunes, by Victoria R., 1856.'

---

## PATRICK COTTER:
### ANCIENT AND MODERN GIANTS.

Henrion, a learned French academician, published a work in 1718, with the object of shewing the very great decrease, in height, of the human race, between the periods of the creation and Christian era. Adam, he tells us, was one hundred and twenty-three feet nine inches, and Eve one hundred and eighteen feet nine inches and nine lines in height. The degeneration, however, was rapid. Noah reached only twenty-seven, while Abraham did not measure more than twenty, and Moses was but thirteen feet in height. Still, in comparison with those, Alexander was misnamed the Great, for he was no more than six feet; and Julius Cæsar reached only to five. According to this erudite French dreamer, the Christian dispensation stopped all further decrease; if it had not, mankind by this time would have been mere microscopic objects. So much for the giants of high antiquity: those of the medieval period may be passed over with almost as slight a notice. Funnam, a Scotsman, who lived in the time of Eugene II., is said to have been more than eleven feet high. The remains of that puissant lord, the Chevalier Rincon, were discovered at Rouen in 1509; the skull held a bushel of wheat, the shin-bone was four feet long, and the others in proportion. The skeleton of a hero, named Bucart, found at Valence in 1705, was twenty-two feet long, and we read of others reaching from thirty to thirty-six feet. But even these last, when in the flesh, were, to use a homely expression, not fit to hold a candle to the proprietor of a skeleton, said to be found in Sicily, which measured three hundred feet in length! Relaters of strange stories not unfrequently throw discredit on their own assertions. With this last skeleton was found his walking-stick, thirty feet in length, and thick as the main-mast of a first-rate. But a walking-stick only thirty feet in length for a man who measured three hundred, would be as ridiculously short, as one of seven inches for a person of ordinary stature.

Sir Hans Sloane was one of the first who expressed an opinion, that these skeletons of giants were not human remains. This was, at the time, considered rank heresy, and the philosopher was asked if he would dare to contradict the sacred Scriptures. But Cuvier, since then, has fully proved that these so-termed bones of giants were in reality fossil remains of mammoths, megatheriums, mastodons, and similar extinct brutes; and that the 'giant's teeth' found in many museums, had once graced the jaw-bones of spermaceti whales.

Of the ancient giants, it is said that they were mighty men of valour, their strength being commensurate with their proportions. But the modern giants are generally a sickly, knock-kneed, splay-footed, shambling race, feeble in both mental and bodily organisation. Such was Patrick Cotter, who died at Clifton on the 8th September 1804. He was exhibited as being eight feet seven inches in height, but this was simply a showman's exaggeration. A memorial-tablet in the Roman Catholic Chapel, Trenchard Street, Bristol, informs us that:

'Here lie the remains of Mr Patrick Cotter O'Brien, a native of Kinsale, in the kingdom of Ireland. He was a man of gigantic stature, exceeding eight feet three inches in height, and proportionably large.'

Cotter was born in 1761, of poor parents, whose stature was not above the common size. When eighteen years of age, a speculative showman bought him from his father, for three years, at £50 per annum. On arriving at Bristol with his proprietor, Cotter demurred to being exhibited, without some remuneration for himself, besides the mere food, clothing, and lodging stipulated in the contract with his father. The showman, taking advantage of the iniquitous law of the period, flung his recalcitrant giant into a debtor's prison, thinking that the latter would soon be terrified into submission. But the circumstances coming to the ears of a benevolent man, he at once proved the contract to be illegal; and Cotter, being liberated, began to exhibit himself for his own profit, with such success that he earned £30 in three days.

Showmen well know the value of fine names and specious assertions. So the plebeian name of Cotter was soon changed to the regal appellation of O'Brien. The alleged descendants of Irish monarchs have figured in many capacities; the following copy of a hand-bill records the appearance of one in the guise of a giant:

'Just arrived in Town, and to be seen in a commodious room, at No. 11 Haymarket, nearly opposite the Opera House, the celebrated Irish Giant, Mr O'Brien, of the kingdom of Ireland, indisputably the tallest man ever shewn; he is a lineal descendant of the old puissant King Brien Boreau, and has in person and appearance all the similitude of that great and grand potentate. It is remarkable of this family, that, however various the revolutions in point of fortune and alliance, the lineal descendants thereof have been favoured by Providence with the original size and stature which have been so peculiar to their family. The gentleman alluded to measures near nine feet high. Admittance, one shilling.'

Cotter, *alias* O'Brien, conducted himself with prudence, and having realised a small competence by exhibiting himself, retired to Clifton, where he died at the very advanced age, for a giant, of forty-seven years. He seems to have had less imbecility of mind than the generality of overgrown persons, but all the weakness of body by which they are characterised. He walked with difficulty, and felt considerable pain when rising up or sitting down. Previous to his death, he expressed great anxiety lest his body should fall into the hands of the anatomists, and gave particular directions for securing his remains with brickwork and strong iron bars in the grave. A few years ago, when some alterations were being made in the chapel where he was buried, it was found that his grave had not been disturbed.

PATRICK COTTER O'BRIEN.

Cotter probably adopted the name of O'Brien, from a giant of a somewhat similar appellation, who attracted a good deal of attention, and died about the time the former commenced to exhibit. This person's death is thus recorded in the *British Magazine* for 1783.

'In Cockspur Street, Charing Cross, aged only twenty-two, Mr Charles Byrne, the famous Irish Giant, whose death is said to have been precipitated by excessive drinking, to which he was always addicted, but more particularly since his late loss of almost all his property, which he had simply invested in a single bank-note of £700. In his last moments, he requested that his remains might be thrown into the sea, in order that his bones might be removed far out of the reach of the chirurgical fraternity; in consequence of which the body was put on board a vessel, conveyed to the Downs, and sunk in twenty fathoms water. Mr Byrne, about the month of August 1780, measured exactly eight feet; in 1782, his stature had gained two inches; and when dead, his full length was eight feet four inches.'

Another account states that Byrne, apprehensive of being robbed, concealed his bank-note in the fireplace on going to bed, and a servant lighting a fire in the morning, the valuable document was consumed. There is no truth in the statement that his remains were thrown into the sea, for his skeleton, measuring seven feet eight inches, is now in the museum of the College of Surgeons. And the tradition of the college is, that the indefatigable anatomist, William Hunter, gave no less a sum than five hundred pounds for Byrne's body. The skeleton shews that the man was very 'knock-kneed,' and the arms are relatively shorter than the legs. Byrne certainly created considerable sensation during the short period he was exhibited in London. In 1782, the summer pantomime, at the Haymarket Theatre—for there were summer pantomimes in those days—was entitled, in reference to Byrne, *Harlequin Teague, or The Giant's Causeway!*

In the museum of Trinity College, Dublin, there is preserved the skeleton of one Magrath, who is said to have attained the height of seven feet eight inches. A most absurd story is related of this person in a *Philosophical Survey of Ireland,* written by a Dr Campbell, who gravely states that Magrath's overgrowth was the result of a course of experimental feeding from infancy, carried out by the celebrated philosopher Berkeley, bishop of Cloyne. The truth of the matter is, Magrath, at the age of sixteen, being then more than six feet in height, had, probably by his abnormal growth, lost the use of his limbs, and the charitable prelate, concluding that a change from the wretched food of an Irish peasant would be beneficial to the overgrown lad, caused him to be well fed for the space of one month, a proceeding which had the desired effect of literally placing the helpless creature on his legs again. This is the sole foundation for the ridiculous and often-repeated story of Bishop Berkeley's experimental giant.

It is a remarkable, little-known, but well-established fact, that while giants are almost invariably characterised by mental and bodily weakness, the opposite anomaly of humanity, the dwarfs, are generally active, intelligent, healthy, and long-lived persons. Guy Patin, a celebrated French surgeon, relates that, in the seventeenth century, to gratify a whim of the empress of Austria, all the giants and dwarfs in the Germanic empire were assembled at Vienna. As circumstances required that all should be housed in one extensive building, it was feared lest the imposing proportions of the giants would terrify the dwarfs, and means were taken to assure the latter of their perfect freedom and safety. But the result was very different to that contemplated. The dwarfs teased, insulted, and even robbed the giants to such an extent, that the overgrown mortals, with tears in their eyes, complained of their stunted persecutors; and, as a consequence, sentinels had to be stationed in the building, to protect the giants from the dwarfs!

## SEPTEMBER 9.

Saints Gorgonius, Dorotheus, and Companions, martyrs, 304. St Kiaran, abbot in Ireland, 549. St Omer, bishop and confessor, 670. St Osmanna, virgin, about 7th century. St Bettelin, hermit and confessor.

*Born.*—Richard Chenevix Trench, dean of Westminster, etymologist, 1807.

*Died.*—James IV. of Scotland, killed at Flodden, 1513; Charles de St Evremond, wit and letter-writer, 1703, *London;* Bernard Siegfried Albinus, eminent anatomist, 1770, *Leyden;* Robert Wood ('Palmyra' Wood), traveller and archæologist, 1771, *Putney;* Rev. Gilbert Wakefield, theological and political writer, 1801; John Brand, author of *Observations on Popular Antiquities,* 1806.

### BATTLE OF FLODDEN.

On the 9th of September 1513, was fought the battle of Flodden, resulting in the defeat and death of the Scottish king, James IV., the slaughter of nearly thirty of his nobles and chiefs, and the loss of about 10,000 men. It was an overthrow which spread sorrow and dismay through Scotland, and was long remembered as one of the greatest calamities ever sustained by the nation. With all tenderness for romantic impulse and chivalric principle, a modern man, even of the Scottish nation, is forced to admit that the Flodden enterprise of James IV. was an example of gigantic folly, righteously punished. The king of Scots had no just occasion for going to war with England. The war he entered upon he conducted like an imbecile, only going three or four miles into the English territory, and there dallying till the opportunity of striking an effective blow was lost. When the English army, under the Earl of Surrey, came against him, he, from a foolish sentiment of chivalry, or mere vanity, would not allow his troops to take the fair advantages of the ground. So he fought at a disadvantage, and lost all, including his own life. It is pitiable, even at this distance of time, to think of a people having their interests committed to the care of one so ill qualified for the trust; the Many suffering so much through the infatuation of One.

### LYDFORD LAW.

An old English proverb says: 'First hang and draw, then hear the cause by Lydford Law.' A Devonshire poet, anxious for the reputation of his county, attempts to shew that this summary method of procedure originated from merciful motives:

'I oft have heard of Lydford Law,
How in the morn they hang and draw,
And sit in judgment after:
At first I wondered at it much;
But since, I find the reason such,
As it deserves no laughter.

They have a castle on a hill;
I took it for an old wind-mill,
The vanes blown off by weather.
To lie therein one night, 'tis guessed
'Twere better to be stoned and pressed,
Or hanged, now chose you whether.

Ten men less room within this cave,
Than five mice in a lantern have,
The keepers they are sly ones.
If any could devise by art
To get it up into a cart,
'Twere fit to carry lions.

When I beheld it, Lord! thought I,
What justice and what clemency
Hath Lydford when I saw all!
I know none gladly there would stay,
But rather hang out of the way,
Than tarry for a trial!

This curious vindication of Devonshire justice is ascribed to Browne, the author of *Britannia's*

*Pastorals*. Lydford itself is the chief town of the Stannaries, and the proverb probably was levelled at the summary decisions of the Stannary Courts which, under a charter of Edward I., had sole jurisdiction over all cases in which the natives were concerned, that did not affect land, life, or limb.

## SEPTEMBER 10.

Saints Nemesianus, Felix, Lucius, another Felix, Litteus, Polianus, Victor, Jader, and Dativus, bishops, and their companions, part martyrs, and part confessors, 3d century. St Pulcheria, virgin and empress, 453. St Finian or Winin, bishop and confessor, 6th century. St Salvius, bishop of Albi, 6th century. St Nicholas of Tolentino, confessor, 1306.

*Born.*—Mungo Park, African traveller, 1771, *Fowlshields, Selkirkshire.*

*Died.*—Louis d'Outremer, king of France, killed, 954; William the Conqueror, 1087, *Rouen;* John, Duke of Burgundy, murdered at Montereau, 1419; Dr Edward Pococke, traveller and oriental scholar, 1691, *Oxford;* Dr Thomas Sheridan, Irish scholar, translator of *Persius*, 1738; Mrs Godwin (Mary Wollstonecraft), authoress of *Rights of Woman*, 1797, *London;* Ugo Foscolo, Italian republican and writer, 1827, *London;* Grace Aguilar, Jewish authoress, 1847, *Frankfort.*

### THE END OF THE CONQUEROR.

During his reign of twenty years subsequent to the Conquest, William had succeeded in planting his Norman followers and adherents upon the property of England. They might be described as an armed militia occupying the country, and owning a devoted allegiance to their sovereign for the lands they severally possessed. It was a grand position for a man to have achieved in a short lifetime; but it had been attained by pure violence, and was only upheld by force against the will of a noble though subjugated people. The Conqueror was, accordingly, not a happy man. He never felt any confidence in the continuance of the system of things which he had organised. He probably felt that he had been only a successful robber, and perhaps often envied the serener feelings of those whom he oppressed.

While sojourning in Normandy, early in 1087, he addressed himself to the recovery from King Philip I. of France of a piece of territory which had been appropriated by that sovereign some years before. He was at the same time submitting to medical regimen for the reduction of the extreme corpulence to which he had become subject. Philip put off his demand for the territory, and made a jest of the Conqueror's obesity. 'It is a long lying-in,' said he; 'there will doubtless be a ceremonious churching.' William, hearing of this speech, swore he would hold his churching at Notre Dame, in Paris, with ten thousand lances for tapers. He got up, and led an expedition of fire and sword into the French territory, feasting his eyes with the havoc and destruction which his soldiers spread around. It was while so engaged that his horse, chancing to plant his feet on some burning timber concealed by ashes, plunged and fell, causing a rupture in the belly of the overgrown king. He languished under this hurt for some weeks at Rouen, and fearing death, made some efforts to repair the cruel wrongs he had inflicted in the course of his life. He also made some arrangements regarding the fortunes of his children. On the 10th of September 1087, the great king breathed his last, in the sixty-first year of his age.

William had only been feared, never loved. Now that he was no more, his servants and great officers thought only of their own interests. His body was left almost naked on the floor, and was buried by monks, without the presence of any relative, or any one who cared for the deceased. There being no coffin, and the body proving too large for the grave of masonry designed for it, it was necessary to force it down; in doing which it burst. Incense and perfumes failed to drown the stench thus diffused through the church, and the people dispersed in horror and disgust. Such was the end of one of the greatest potentates who ever lived—one who had driven human beings before him like cattle, but never induced any one to love him, not even one of his own children.

### LEGEND OF THE SONS OF THE CONQUEROR.

One day, it being observed that William was absorbed in deep thought, his courtiers ventured to inquire the cause of such profound abstraction. 'I am speculating,' said the monarch, 'on what may be the fate of my sons after my death.' 'Your majesty,' replied the wise men of the court, 'the fate of your sons will depend upon their conduct, and their conduct will depend upon their respective characters; permit us to make a few inquiries, and we shall soon be able to tell you that which you wish to know.' The king signifying his approbation, the wise men consulted together, and agreed to put questions separately to the three princes, who were then young. The first who entered the room was Robert, afterwards known by the surname of Courthose. 'Fair sir,' said one of the wise men, 'answer me a question—If God had made you a bird, what bird would you wish to have been?' Robert answered: 'A hawk, because it resembles most a courteous and gallant knight.' William Rufus next entered, and his answer to the same question was: 'I would be an eagle, because it is a strong and powerful bird, and feared by all other birds, and therefore it is king over them all.' Lastly, came the younger brother Henry, who had received a learned education, and was on that account known by the surname of Beauclerc. His choice was a starling, 'Because it is a debonnaire and simple bird, and gains its living without injury to any one, and never seeks to rob or grieve its neighbour.' The wise men returned immediately to the king. Robert, they said, would be bold and valiant, and would gain renown and honour, but he would finally be overcome by violence, and die in prison. William would be powerful and strong as the eagle, but feared and hated for his cruelty and violence, until he ended a wicked life by a bad death. But Henry would be wise, prudent, and peaceful, unless when actually compelled to engage in war, and would die in peace after gaining wide possessions. So when King William lay on his death-bed, he remembered the saying of his wise men, and bequeathed Normandy to Robert, England to William, and his own treasures, without land, to his younger son Henry, who eventually became king of both countries, and reigned long and prosperously.

This story, which most probably is of Eastern origin, is frequently told under various circumstances by medieval writers. A Latin manuscript, of the thirteenth century, relates it in the following form:

A wealthy English baron, whose broad lands extended over a large extent of England and Wales, had three sons; when lying on his deathbed, he called them to him, and said: 'If you were compelled to become birds, tell me what bird each of you would choose to resemble?' The eldest said: 'I would be a hawk, because it is a noble bird, and lives by rapine.' The second said: 'I would be a starling, because it is a social bird, and flies in coveys.' The youngest said: 'I would be a swan, because it has a long neck, so that if I had anything in my heart to say, I should have plenty of time for reflection before it came to my mouth.' When the father had heard them, he said to the first: 'Thou, my son, as I perceive, desirest to live by rapine; I will therefore bequeath thee my possessions in England, because it is a land of peace and justice, and thou canst not rob in it with impunity.' To the second, he said: 'Because thou lovest society, I will bequeath thee my lands in Wales, which is a land of discord and war, in order that thy courtesy may soften down the malice of the natives.' And then turning to the youngest, he said: 'To thee I bequeath no land at all, because thou art wise, and will gain enough by thy wisdom.' And as he foretold, the youngest son profited by his wisdom, and became Lord Chief-Justice of England, which in those times was the next dignity to that of king.

## DR THOMAS SHERIDAN.

On the 10th of September 1738, Dr Sheridan was sitting, after dinner, in the house of a friend. The conversation happening to turn on the force and direction of the wind, Sheridan said: 'Let the wind blow east, west, north, or south, the immortal soul will take its flight to the destined point;' and leaning back in his chair, instantly expired. Dr Sheridan was the intimate friend and choice companion of Jonathan Swift; the father of 'Manager Tom,' as his son was termed in Ireland; and the grandfather of the Right Honourable Richard Brinsley Sheridan. He was born in the county of Cavan, about 1684, and, having completed his education at Trinity College, set up a classical school in Dublin. Entering into orders, he received the degree of D.D., and was appointed to a church-living in the south of Ireland. But by a singular act of inadvertence, he lost all chance of further preferment, by preaching a sermon on the anniversary of George I.'s birthday, from the text: '*Sufficient for the day is the evil thereof.*' On this becoming known, he was struck off the list of the Lord-Lieutenant's chaplains; parents hastened to take their children from his school; and, in short, as Swift said: 'He had killed his own fortunes by a chance-shot from an unlucky text.'

No reverse of fortune, however, could damp or discourage the high spirits of Dr Sheridan. Such, it is said, was his perpetual flow of ready wit and humour, that it was impossible for the most splenetic man to be unhappy in his company. When Swift, in a morbid state of disappointment, was condemned to live, as he considered it, an exile in Ireland, the companionship of Sheridan formed the great solace of his life. For one whole year they carried on a daily correspondence, and, according to previous stipulation, each letter was the unpremeditated effusion of five minutes' writing. Some of the funny nonsense thus composed, is preserved in Swift's miscellaneous works, though the greater part has fallen into merited oblivion.

Dr Sheridan was an excellent classical scholar, and wrote a prose translation of *Persius*, which was published after his death. Though indolent, good-natured, careless, and not particularly strict in his own conduct, he took good care of the morals of his scholars, whom he sent to the university well grounded in classical lore, and not ill instructed in the social duties of life. He was slovenly, indigent, and cheerful, knowing books better than men, and totally ignorant of the value of money. Ill-starred, improvident, but not unhappy, he was a fiddler, punster, quibbler, and wit; and his pen and fiddle-stick were in continual motion. As might be supposed, Sheridan's house, at Quilca, was such as Swift has described it in the following lines; and the writer may add, that, in his youth, he often saw the *ménage* of an Irish gentleman and scholar, to which the same description would be as justly applicable.

QUILCA.

'Let me thy properties explain:
A rotten cabin dropping rain;
Chimneys with scorn rejecting smoke;
Stools, tables, chairs, and bedsteads broke.
Here elements have lost their uses,
Air ripens not, nor earth produces;
In vain, we make poor Shela toil,
Fire will not roast, nor water boil;
Through all the valleys, hills, and plains,
The goddess Want, in triumph reigns,
And her chief officers of state,
Sloth, Dirt, and Theft, around her wait.'

## UGO FOSCOLO.

Early in this century, the name of Ugo Foscolo enjoyed as extensive a reputation as that of the most enthusiastic champion of Italian independence, and one of the greatest and brightest ornaments of modern Italian literature. What he actually effected, however, in the first of these characters, was but trifling, and in the second, he has left little, not even excepting his celebrated *Letters of Jacopo Ortis*, which can commend itself to the tastes of this practical and unsentimental age. He was descended from a noble Venetian family, and was himself born on board a frigate, lying off the island of Zante, of which his father was governor for the republic of Venice. Entering life as a young man, just when the French Revolution was stirring the social life of Europe from its very depths, young Foscolo ardently embraced the new doctrines, and became so conspicuous a maintainer of them, that he was arrested and carried before the terrible inquisition of state, as a partisan in a conspiracy for overthrowing the government. No proof, however, appeared against him, and he was acquitted. It is related that his mother, a Greek lady, on seeing him led off as a prisoner, exclaimed to him, in a spirit worthy of a Spartan matron of old:

'Die; but do not dishonour thyself by betraying thy friends!' After gaining considerable renown by the representation of his tragedy of *Tieste*, when he was yet little more than twenty, he received the appointment of secretary to Battaglia, the Venetian ambassador to Bonaparte. The treacherous manner in which the latter transferred the republic to Austria, disgusted him for a time with political life, and he retired into Lombardy, then styled the 'Cisalpine Republic,' and penned there his celebrated romance, entitled *Ultime Lettere di Jacopo Ortis*. This created nearly as great a sensation as Goethe's *Sorrows of Werther*, to which, in point of subject-matter and style, it is very similar, though differing from it in the amount of political allusion by which Foscolo's work is throughout characterised. It has been translated into various languages, and contains much beautiful and pathetic writing, but imbued with an extremely morbid spirit.

Emerging from his retreat, Foscolo again sought the busy world, and served for some years in Bonaparte's army; but finding himself obnoxious to the authorities, on account of his republican principles, he resigned his commission, and returned once more to private life. Various literary works, including his edition of the writings of General Montecuccoli, and a translation of the first book of the *Iliad*, now occupied his leisure, and about 1809, he was appointed professor of literature in the university of Pavia, where the spirited style of his lectures to the young men so alarmed the sensitive absolutism of Bonaparte, that, in two months afterwards, the three Italian universities, Pavia, Padua, and Bologna, were closed. On the restoration of the Austrian government, Foscolo was suspected of being accessory to a conspiracy for its overthrow, and found it expedient to retire, first to Switzerland, and then to England, where he took up his abode for the remainder of his days.

Such are the leading events in the history of the Mazzini and Victor Hugo of his day. While in England, he enjoyed ready access to the first society in the metropolis, being both a man of great classical attainments, and most brilliant conversational powers. He built for himself a cottage in the neighbourhood of the Regent's Park, which, in allusion to the controversy on the use of the digamma in Greek, and his own large share in the dispute, he christened 'Digamma Cottage.' The furniture and decorations of his habitation were of the most magnificent order, including casts of the most celebrated works of sculpture, which were scattered through every apartment, and were contemplated by their owner with an enthusiasm little short of adoration. In excuse for this lavishness, he would observe, in reference to his costly articles of furniture: 'They encompass me with an air of respectability, and they give me the illusion of not having fallen into the lowest circumstances. I must also declare, that I will die like a gentleman, on a clean bed, surrounded by the Venuses, Apollos, and the Graces, and the busts of great men; nay, even among flowers, and if possible, while music is breathing around me.' It is easy to infer from this that Foscolo had much of the Epicurean in his composition. He is said, however, to have been remarkably abstemious in his habits, and laid claim himself to vying with Pythagoras for sobriety, and Scipio for purity of morals. Unfortunately, his means, eked out as they were by writing for the various reviews, and publishing essays on Petrarch, and a commentary on Dante, proved wholly inadequate to the maintenance of the luxurious style of living which he affected; and, after a brief period, the temple which he had reared to the Graces, with its gorgeous appliances, was brought to the hammer. His latter years were sorely disturbed by pecuniary embarrassment, a source of vexation which was greatly aggravated by a violent and fretful temper. He seems, indeed, to have been both true and generous hearted; but, as even an intimate friend admitted, his virtues were those of a savage nature. When in good-humour and spirits, nothing could be more entertaining than his conversation, though he displayed great peevishness if any irrelevant question were asked. He used to say: 'I have three miseries—smoke, flies, and to be asked a foolish question.'

## MARY WOLLSTONECRAFT.

It is impossible for human laws to do more than minister to the greatest good of the greatest number; no skill can avert their oppressive action in singular cases. The law decrees that the contract of marriage shall only terminate with the decease of either partner, and few will dispute, that the law decrees wisely. But there are cases—and we do not allude to those in which divorce is the permitted remedy—where life-long marriage is life-long misery; yet, for the relief of such sufferers no thoughtful legislator advocates the abrogation of a law which, in its broad sweep, affords assured protection and security to the weaker half of humanity—to wives and children. Again, the law consigns children to the absolute government of their parents, and though there are many who neglect and abuse their trust, yet we feel that it is better to tolerate partial wrong, than invade an order which, on the whole, coincides with the greatest good of the greatest number. So, again, we permit the spendthrift to waste and the miser to hoard rather than infringe on that sense of independence and ownership, which more than doubles the joy of possession and gives spur and purpose to enterprise. Similar illustrations of exceptional sufferings and mischiefs might be multiplied indefinitely, for wherever there is a just and kind law, there is, at the same time, a possible shelter for injustice and cruelty. Whoever, therefore, will defend the best law, must be content to prove its general, not its universal excellence. This truth is continually forgotten by enthusiastic and generous natures. They encounter some case of hardship under the law, and at once raise a cry for its modification or abolition, never considering, whether if the cord were relaxed on one side it might not cut deeper and more dangerously on the other; and sometimes not satisfied with their verbal protest, they enter into actual rebellion, and in their own persons endure social obloquy and outlawry, in the vain endeavour to compass a universal, a Utopian justice. Among the boldest and noblest of such mistaken innovators must be ranked Mary Wollstonecraft.

She was born on the 27th of April 1759, but whether in London or Epping Forest, she could never ascertain. Her father was the son of a Spitalfields manufacturer, from whom he inherited about £10,000: her mother was an Irishwoman, a Miss Dixon of Ballyshannon. Mr Wollstonecraft was a rolling stone which not only gathered no moss, but wore away its substance in rolling. He moved from London to Yorkshire, and from Yorkshire to London, and thence to Wales, sometimes farming and sometimes trading, and always losing. His temper was abominable; when in a rage, he would strike his wife, flog his children, and kick his dogs, finishing up with a fit of maudlin affection. Mary had frequently to throw herself between her father and mother to save her from his blows. Regular education was out of the question under these circumstances, and the young Wollstonecrafts were left to pick up what learning they could at a variety of day-schools. Mary was a handsome girl, lively and intelligent, with a proud spirit and ardent affections. For dolls and needle-work she had a thorough contempt, preferring to join in the sports of her brothers.

Among the wanderings of the family, they settled for a while at Queen's Row, Hoxton, in the neighbourhood of which William Godwin was a student at the Dissenters' College. Reflecting, in after-years, on his unconscious proximity to Mary, he observes: 'It is perhaps a question of curious speculation to inquire, what would have been the amount of difference in the pursuits and enjoyments of each party had they met, and considered each other with the same distinguishing regard in 1776, as they were afterwards impressed with in the year 1796.'

While at Queen's Row, Mary made the friendship of Frances Blood, a young lady of many accomplishments, who inspired her with a fervent desire for intellectual improvement. Tired of her wretched home, she became companion to Mrs Dawson, a lady of Bath, who was reputed to have such a temper that no one could abide with her. Mary forewarned was forearmed; she stayed with the virago two years, taught her better manners, and only left her side to nurse her mother in a mortal illness. Her next important step in life was to open a school in Islington, in company with her sisters and Frances Blood. Mary proved an excellent teacher; the school flourished, and was removed to Newington Green. Near by lived Dr Price, who became a visitor, and Mary's cordial friend. She was introduced to Dr Johnson, but his death prevented further acquaintance. Just as life was growing prosperous, Miss Blood fell into a decline, and was ordered to Portugal. Hearing that there was no hope of her recovery, Mary, in the strength of her affection, left the school to its fate, and sailed for Lisbon that she might be near her dear companion in her last hours. On her return, she went to Ireland as governess in the family of Lord Kingsborough, and there won golden opinions for her intelligence and amiability. One of her pupils, Countess Mount Cashel, remained Mary's friend through good and evil report till death divided them.

Conscious of powers which as yet had found no outlet, Miss Wollstonecraft came to London in August 1787, with the daring hope of acquiring a livelihood by authorship. The year before, she had made her advent in the world of letters by the publication of *Thoughts on the Education of Daughters*, for which her publisher, Mr Johnson, had given her ten guineas. She took humble lodgings in George Street, Blackfriars Bridge, and set to work. She contributed largely to the *Analytical Review;* abridged Lavater's *Physiognomy;* translated from the German Salzmann's *Elements of Morality;* from the French, Necker's *Importance of Religious Opinions;* and from the Dutch, *Young Grandison;* wrote tales for children, and executed a variety of other literary business: and not only did she earn her own living, but was able to assist her father, find situations for her brothers and sisters, and adopt an orphan girl of seven.

In such labours she might have spent many years in comparative obscurity, had not Burke's *Reflections on the Revolution in France*, published in November 1790, stirred in her such indignation, that she determined to answer the recreant Whig. She brought out a *Vindication of the Rights of Man*, in which she trounced her adversary with no little vehemence and much natural eloquence. It was among the first of the many replies to which Burke was treated, and it had a very large sale. Miss Wollstonecraft from that hour was a marked woman. By one set she was regarded with horror as a sort of monster, and by another was extolled as a divinity. Unhappily, her admirers stimulated her worst tendencies, and provoked her to issue a *Vindication of the Rights of Women*, wherein much that was true and excellent was nullified by extravagant sentiment and language. Her increased income allowed her, in 1791, to remove to better apartments in Store Street, Tottenham Court Road, where she was visited by the most distinguished republicans and freethinkers of that sanguine age. Godwin then met her for the first time at a dinner-party where Thomas Paine was present, and disliked her. Paine was not much of a talker, and the little he had to say Godwin was anxious to catch, but Mary interrupted his purpose by her almost incessant conversation.

Along with Godwin she had begun to entertain the opinion that marriage was an unjust monopoly; that marriage ought only to exist as long as there was heartfelt sympathy between a husband and wife; and that wherever that sympathy sprung up, the licence of marriage should be allowed. Poor Mary was doomed, in her own person, to illustrate the peril to women that lay in such a creed.

Her first attachment was to Fuseli, the painter. A lively affection developed between them, but Mrs Fuseli, like a dragon, lay in the way, and Mary, as a diversion to her feelings, made a trip to Paris, which extended into a residence of two years. By Paine she was introduced to the principal revolutionary leaders, and found a congenial spirit in Helen Maria Williams. From her window she saw Louis XVI. pass in a hackney-coach to execution, 'with more dignity,' she wrote, 'than I expected from his character.' Whilst in the spring of her enjoyment in Paris, she met Gilbert Imlay, an American merchant, and put in practice her theory by living with him as his wife without the legal forms of matrimony. All for a time went on smoothly. In a pleasant retreat at Neuilly she worked industriously on her most finished work, *A Historical and Moral View of the French Revolution.* Imlay left her nominally for a few weeks to look after some business at Havre. One day, on entering Paris, she passed the guillotine, whilst the blood streamed over the pavement. She burst at once into loud exclamations of horror and indignation. A kind bystander checked and implored her to hasten and hide herself from all who had heard her words. The agony she experienced on being informed of the death of Brissot, Vergniaud, and the twenty deputies, she vowed was greater than any pain she had ever felt. Meanwhile Imlay did not return. She followed him to Havre, and there gave birth to a daughter, named Frances, in memory of her old friend, Miss Blood. Imlay then went to London, persuading his wife to return to Paris, with the promise that he would rejoin her shortly. Half a year elapsed, but no Imlay made his appearance. Anxious and suspicious, Mary crossed to England, and arrived in London to find her worst fears realised, and the father of her child in the arms of another mistress. She prayed that he would return to her, and was only prevented committing suicide by his timely arrival. By renewed seductions he induced her to start for Norway, and there transact some business for him. He made an assignation at Hamburg, which he did not keep, and on her return to London, it became at last apparent that she was betrayed and befooled. Distracted with anguish, she took a boat to Putney, and walking about in the rain till her clothes were drenched through, she leaped over the bridge into the Thames. Happily, she was observed and rescued. Again she saw Imlay, and made the extraordinary proposal that she and his paramour should live together. 'I think it important,' she wrote to him, 'that you should learn habitually to feel for your child the affection of a father.' Imlay, who seems to have been an irresolute scoundrel, at first assented and afterwards refused, and Mary then summoned up resolution, and dismissed him from her thoughts for ever.

Well-nigh broken-hearted, she went to live in Pentonville, and renewed her acquaintance with Godwin. Acquaintance melted into friendship, and friendship into love, and again she ventured to become a wife without the ceremonies of marriage. Finding, however, the pains and penalties attached to such a relation unendurable, they yielded to what they thought popular prejudice, and were married. Godwin's account of the method of their conjugal life is worth reading. He writes: 'Ours was not an idle happiness, a paradise of selfish and transitory pleasures. It is perhaps scarcely necessary to mention, that, influenced by the ideas I had long entertained on the subject of cohabitation, I engaged an apartment about twenty doors from our house in the Polygon, Somers Town, which I designed for the purpose of my study and literary occupations. Trifles, however, will be interesting to some readers, when they relate to the last period of the life of such a person as Mary. I will add, therefore, that we were both of us of opinion, that it was possible for two persons to be too uniformly in each other's society. Influenced by that opinion, it was my practice to repair to the apartment I have mentioned as soon as I rose, and frequently not to make my appearance in the Polygon till the hour of dinner. We agreed in condemning the notion, prevalent in many situations in life, that a man and his wife cannot visit in mixed society but in company with each other, and we rather sought occasions of deviating from, than of complying with, this rule. By these means, though for the most part we spent the latter half of each day in one another's society, yet we were in no danger of satiety. We seemed to combine, in a considerable degree, the novelty and lively sensation of a visit, with the more delicious and heartfelt pleasures of domestic life.'

This philosophic union, to Godwin's inexpressible affliction, did not extend over more than eighteen months. Mrs Godwin died in childbed, on the 10th of September 1797, at the age of thirty-eight. Her infant grew to womanhood, and became the wife of the poet Shelley, and the author of *Frankenstein.*

The errors of Mary Wollstonecraft's life lie on the surface, and many will be quick to supply the ready commentary of condemnation. If, however, we are more careful to be just than vindictive, we shall not leave her without many allowances, some admiration, and much pity. Considering the unhappy circumstances of her childhood, and her imperfect education, we shall regard with wonder and respect the energy and self-control by which she transformed herself into the successful schoolmistress, the governess, the writer for the press, the antagonist of Burke, and the esteemed associate of politicians and philosophers. Nor shall we forget her generosity, almost wild in its excess; her free sacrifice of money and opportunity to her family and friends. Nor shall we fail to observe that the painful eccentricities of her career were confined within seven years, 1790-1797; a time of abnormal excitement, when the mind of Europe broke loose from the moorings of ages, and every maxim of law and morals was put to inquisition. Mary Wollstonecraft found herself in this mælström of revolution, and determined to realise that new moral world about which so many were content to theorise. Godwin himself bears witness that she did not reason, but darted to conclusions. In the matter of her cohabitation with Imlay and Godwin, she must receive the full benefit which charity accords to those who do wrong believing they do right. In her conduct there was nothing clandestine; indeed, she took superfluous pains to inform her acquaintance that she was not legally married, and thus drove from her presence many who were very willing to enjoy the charm of her society, if only she would condescend to subterfuge.

---

## INCIDENTAL TO A JOURNEY TO PARIS IN 1723.

On the 10th of September 1723, three English gentlemen, named Sebright, Davis, and Mompesson, set out from Calais for Boulogne, on their way to Paris. Sebright and Davis travelled in one coach, Mompesson and a servant in another: another servant rode on horseback. Before leaving the *Lion d'Argent* hotel in Calais, Mr Sebright changed twenty-five guineas into French silver money, for the use of the party on the road. Hence, it was supposed, the sad accident which overtook them in their journey.

About seven miles from Calais, they were beset by six mounted highwaymen, who demanded the money they were believed to have in their possession. The English gentlemen, having no arms but their swords, made no resistance. All the money they possessed, being about one hundred and twenty pounds, was surrendered, as also their swords, watches, and other trinkets. They were commanded to come out of the chaises, and lie down with their faces to the ground, and when their persons had in these circumstances been more effectually searched, the word to kill was given, and the whole five were then shot and hacked in the most cruel manner. Another English gentleman, named Locke, coming up at the moment on his way from Paris, was shot in his vehicle, and with difficulty his Swiss valet was enabled to beg his life. When the murderous work appeared to be complete, the six banditti rode off with their booty. It then appeared that Mr Mompesson, notwithstanding his throat had been cut, was still alive; and so was Mr Sebright's servant, Richard Spendelow. But the unfortunate gentleman survived only a few hours. Six persons in all lost their lives on this occasion. It was supposed that the incident of the changing of the twenty-five guineas was what attracted the attention of the predatory party to the travellers. We do not learn that more than one person was ever brought to justice for this horrid outrage, notwithstanding that the Regent d'Orleans offered large rewards for their apprehension.*

## The Curfew.

The lengthening evenings bring naturally to our minds their discomforts in the olden times, and the various customs and observations connected with them. Among these was the curfew-bell, which has been made well known to all ears by the frequent allusions to it in our poets, but which has been the subject of not a few 'vulgar errors.' In those old times, people, in general, possessed nothing like clocks or watches; they learned, by the practice of observation, to judge roughly of the time of the day, but in cases where it was necessary to know the exact hour, they were entirely at a loss. Any implement for measuring time was rare, and belonged only to a public body, or institution, or to some very remarkable individual, and the only means of imparting to the public the knowledge gained from it, was by ringing a bell, or blowing a horn, at certain hours of the day. This practice was first introduced in the monastic establishments, where the inmates required to know the hours for celebrating the various services. It was probably adopted also in the great houses of the aristocracy, and in towns. There were, in fact, many customs to be observed at stated hours, besides the religious services, and some of these were required by public safety.

In the middle ages there was a very much larger proportion of society which lived by cheating, plundering, and ill treating the rest, than in modern times. Owing to the want of any effective police, there was no safety out of doors at night; and even people who, by daylight, appeared to live honestly, sallied forth after dark to rob and assassinate. It was attempted, in towns especially, to meet this evil, by making it criminal to be found out of doors after a certain hour; and, as otherwise offenders might plead ignorance, it was ordered that the hour should be publicly sounded, generally by the town-bell, and when that was heard, all people were compelled to shut the doors of their houses, put out their fires, and retire to bed, those who were out of bed after the sounding of the bell being liable to severe punishment. It was an efficacious way of clearing the streets. The bell sounded for this purpose was, in France, called popularly the *couvre-feu*, or cover-fire, which, in the Latin documents in which it was alluded to, was translated by *ignitegium*. Something of the same kind, probably, existed in the Anglo-Saxon times, but the name just mentioned was, of course, introduced by the Normans, and we have no express allusion to the practice in this country before the Anglo-Norman period. Hence, no doubt, has arisen the erroneous notion that the *couvre-feu* bell, corrupted into the *curfew*-bell, was invented by William the Conqueror as an instrument of tyranny. It was, apparently, a municipal and not a state institution, and the utility of a general covering of fires at a reasonable hour is obvious. In those days, most houses were constructed wholly or mostly of wood, and were extremely liable to take fire when fire was used carelessly. To cover up the fire was an important regulation for safety, and a utensil was employed for the purpose—here represented.

CURFEW.

The curfew-bell was used in the monastic establishments as well as in the towns. In the great abbey of St Alban's, it was ordered that the monks should not remain assembled in conversation after the ringing of the curfew-bell. In Lichfield Cathedral, according to the statutes of that church, quoted in Ducange, the curfew-bell was sounded at seven o'clock in the evening, and this appears to have been the usual hour at the earlier period, for ordinary people went to bed very early, and rose before daybreak; but in course of time, seven o'clock seems to have been thought too early, and it was moved onwards an hour to eight o'clock, which seems, down to a very late period, to have been the most common hour of the curfew in England, though in many places it was still further advanced to nine o'clock. The curfew is still rung in many towns and parishes in England, in some at eight o'clock, and in others at nine. At the end of the last century, as we learn from the *Gentleman's Magazine* for 1790, the curfew was announced at the latter hour at Ripon, in Yorkshire, by a man with a horn, which he blew, first at the market-cross, and then at the mayor's door. In Scotland, the hour of curfew was similarly retarded, until it

* *Hearne's Diaries*, ii. 507. Newspapers of the time.

was fixed, not at nine, but at ten o'clock, and that seems to have been, in later times, the usual hour of the Scottish curfew.

It is quite a mistake to suppose that the curfew-bell was peculiar to this island—it was a natural expedient for serving a generally useful purpose, and was adopted in France, Italy, and Spain, and probably in all parts of continental Europe. Moreover, a corresponding bell was rung in the morning, to inform people of the hour at which it was customary to rise. In some instances, this is merely said to have taken place at daybreak, but a more usual hour appears to have been four o'clock in the morning. At Ludlow, in Shropshire, this bell still rings at six o'clock, and the evening-curfew at nine. It is kept up merely because it has been customary, and because there is provision for it in the old corporation or parish orders. At London, as we learn from records of the end of the fifteenth century, the curfew was sounded at the same time from the three churches of Bow in Cheapside, St Bride's, and St Giles's without Cripplegate, and the clerks of all the other parish churches in the metropolis were obliged to begin ringing the moment they heard one of these, or, for neglect, were to be presented to the quest of wardmote. At Oxford, the curfew was rung at Carfax at eight o'clock, and there was a foolish tradition that it was established, not by William the Conqueror, but by King Alfred. Here, a refinement of the ordinary curfew had been introduced, for, after the bell of Carfax had sounded the curfew, it rung deliberately the day of the month.

## SEPTEMBER 11.

Saints Protus and Hyacinthus, martyrs. St Paphnutius, bishop and confessor, 4th century. St Patiens, archbishop of Lyon, confessor, about 480.

*Born.*—Ulysses Aldrovandus, distinguished naturalist, 1522, *Bologna;* Henri, Vicomte de Turenne, great French commander, 1611, *Sedan Castle on the Meuse;* William Lowth, divine and commentator, 1661; James Thomson, poet, 1700, *Ednam, Roxburghshire.*

*Died.*—Treasurer Cressingham, slain at battle of Stirling, 1297; James Harrington, author of *Oceana,* 1677, *London;* John Augustus Ernesti, classical editor, 1781, *Leipsic;* David Ricardo, political economist, 1823, *Gatcombe Park, Gloucestershire;* Captain Basil Hall, author of books of voyages and travels, 1844, *Portsmouth.*

### THE TAKING OF DROGHEDA, SEPTEMBER 11, 1649.

In the summer following on the death of Charles I., Cromwell was sent into Ireland to bring it under obedience to the English parliament. The country was composed of factions—Catholics, Episcopalians, Presbyterians, &c.—agreeing in hardly anything but their opposition to the new Commonwealth. It was the policy of Cromwell to strike terror into these various parties by one thunderbolt of vigorous action; and his assault upon the town of Drogheda afforded him the opportunity. There were here about 3000 royalists assembled under Sir Arthur Ashton. The town had some tolerably strong defences. Cromwell, on the 10th of September, summoned the town, but was answered only with a defiance. He set his cannon a-playing on the walls, and, having made some breaches, sent in a large armed force next day, who, however, were for that time repulsed. Renewing the assault, they drove the garrison into confined places, where the whole were that evening put to the sword, with merely a trifling exception. Cromwell, in his dispatch to Lenthall, describes this affair as a 'righteous judgment' and a 'great mercy,' and with equal coolness relates how any that he spared from death were immediately shipped off for Barbadoes—that is, deported as slaves. The policy of the English Attila was successful. It cut through the heart of the national resistance, and laid Ireland at the feet of the English parliment.

### ROGER CRAB.

Among the many crazy sectaries produced from the yeasty froth of the fermenting caldron of the great civil war, there was not one more oddly crazy than Roger Crab. This man had served for seven years in the Parliamentary army, and though he had his 'skull cloven' by a royalist trooper, yet, for some breach of discipline, Cromwell sentenced him to death, a punishment subsequently commuted to two years' imprisonment. After his release from jail, Crab set up in business as 'a haberdasher of hats' at Chesham,

ROGER CRAB.

in Buckinghamshire. His wandering mind, probably not improved by the skull-cleaving operation, then imbibed the idea, that it was sinful to eat any kind of animal food, or to drink anything stronger than water. Determined to follow, literally, the injunctions given to the young man in the gospel, he sold off his stock in trade, distributing the proceeds among the poor, and took up his residence in a hut, situated on a rood of ground near Ickenham, where for some time he lived on the small sum of three-farthings a week. His food consisted of bran, dock-leaves, mallows, and grass; and how it agreed with him we learn from a rare pamphlet, principally written by himself, entitled *The English Hermit, or the Wonder of the Age.* 'Instead of strong drinks and wines,' says the eccentric Roger, 'I give the old man a cup of water; and instead of roast mutton and rabbit, and other dainty dishes, I give him broth thickened with bran, and pudding made with bran and turnip-leaves chopped together, at which the old man (meaning my body) being moved, would know what he had done, that I used him so hardly. Then I shewed him his transgressions, and so the wars began. The law of the old man in my fleshly members rebelled against the law of my mind, and had a shrewd skirmish; but the mind, being well enlightened, held it so that the old man grew sick and weak with the flux, like to fall to the dust. But the wonderful love of God, well pleased with the battle, raised him up again, and filled him full of love, peace, and content of mind, and he is now become more humble, for now he will eat dock-leaves, mallows, or grass.'

The persecutions the poor man inflicted on himself, caused him to be persecuted by others. Though he states that he was neither a Quaker, a Shaker, nor a Ranter, he was cudgelled and put in the stocks; the wretched sackcloth frock he wore was torn from his back, and he was mercilessly whipped. He was four times arrested on suspicion of being a wizard, and he was sent from prison to prison; yet still he would persist in his course of life, not hesitating to term all those whose opinion differed from his by the most opprobrious names. He published another pamphlet, entitled *Dagon's Downfall; or the great Idol digged up Root and Branch; The English Hermit's Spade at the Ground and Root of Idolatry.* This work shews that the man was simply insane. We last hear of him residing in Bethnal Green. He died on the 11th of September 1680, and was buried in Stepney Churchyard, where his tombstone exhibits the following quaint epitaph:

'Tread gently, reader, near the dust
Committed to this tomb-stone's trust:
For while 'twas flesh, it held a guest
With universal love possest:
A soul that stemmed opinion's tide,
Did over sects in triumph ride;
Yet separate from the giddy crowd,
And paths tradition had allowed.
Through good and ill reports he past,
Oft censured, yet approved at last.
Wouldst thou his religion know?
In brief 'twas this: to all to do
Just as he would be done unto.
So in kind Nature's law he stood,
A temple, undefiled with blood,
A friend to everything that 's good.
The rest angels alone can fitly tell;
Haste then to them and him; and so farewell!'

## SEPTEMBER 12.

**St Albeus, bishop and confessor, 525. St Eanswide, virgin and abbess, 7th century. St Guy, confessor, 11th century.**

*Born.*—**Francis I. of France, 1494; Sir William Dugdale, antiquary, 1605, *Shustoke, Warwickshire*; Jean-Philippe Rameau, writer of operas, 1683, *Dijon.***

*Died.*—**Pope Innocent VI., 1362; Cinq-Mars, favourite of Louis XIII., executed at Lyon, along with De Thou, on charge of conspiracy, 1642; Griffith Jones, miscellaneous writer, 1786, *London*; Edward, Lord Thurlow, chancellor of England, 1806, *Brighton*; Lebrecht von Blücher, field-marshal of Prussia, 1819, *Kriblowitz, Silesia*; Lord Metcalfe, statesman, 1846, *Basingstoke*; William Cooke Taylor, miscellaneous writer, 1849, *Dublin*; James Fillans, sculptor, 1852, *Glasgow*; Sir James Stephen, historical and miscellaneous writer, 1859, *Coblentz.***

### CINQ-MARS.

Youth and comeliness of person not unfrequently serve as palliations of serious delinquencies, and what in the case of an ordinary criminal would have been looked on as simply a fitting punishment for his misdeeds, is apt to be regarded as harsh and oppressive, when the penalties of the law come to be inflicted on a young and handsome transgressor. A feeling of this sort has thrown a romantic interest around the fate of the Marquis de Cinq-Mars, the favourite of Louis XIII., though it is but justice to his memory to admit that, in putting him to death, the principles both of law and equity were grossly violated.

It is well known that the weak and irresolute Louis XIII. was entirely subject to his prime minister, the crafty and ambitious Cardinal Richelieu. Yet in the opinion of the latter, it was necessary to watch the sovereign closely, lest some stranger should gain such a sway over his heart, as to render nugatory the influence wielded by himself. It was necessary to provide him with some favourite, who might act as a spy on his actions, and duly report all his proceedings. A fitting instrument for such an employment, the cardinal believed he had discovered in M. de Cinq-Mars, a young gentleman of Auvergne, who joined the most unique graces of personal appearance to the most brilliant wit and captivating manners. Having been introduced at court by Richelieu, he rapidly gained the favour of the king, who had him appointed, when only nineteen, to the offices of grand equerry and master of the robes. Never was a favourite's advancement more speedy, nor the sunshine of royal friendship more liberally dispensed. Yet the gay and volatile Cinq-Mars chafed under the restraints to which the constant attention claimed by an invalid monarch subjected him, and he not unfrequently involved himself in disgrace by transgressing the rules of court. A mistress of his, the beautiful Marion de Lorme, occupied a large share of his thoughts to the exclusion of the king; and Louis was often irritated in the mornings, on sending for his equerry, by the announcement, that he had not yet risen, the real fact being, that he had just lain down to sleep after a night spent in visiting Mademoiselle de Lorme. Cinq-Mars was at first gently reprimanded for his indolence, but the truth at last came out, and a most uncourtly altercation ensued between him and the king. High words passed on both sides, and at last Louis ordered him from his presence. After a short absence from court, he made a humble submission to Richelieu, and through his influence was reinstated in royal favour. But the relation between these two men soon assumed a different phase. Cinq-Mars was beginning to insinuate himself too intimately into the king's good graces, and by aiming at freeing himself from dependence on Richelieu, rendered himself an object of suspicion and hatred to the jealous priest.

Then the latter mortally offended the favourite, by interposing to prevent his marriage with the Princess Gonzaga, to whose hand Cinq-Mars had ventured to aspire. The result of all these counter-agencies was a rancorous and deadly feud, which nothing but blood could appease. The assassination of Richelieu was meditated by Cinq-Mars, and suggested by him to the king, who certainly did not manifest any decided aversion to a scheme which would have rid him of a minister who exercised over him so thorough a control. But the project was never carried out. In the meantime, some of the leading French nobles, including among others the Duke of Orleans, Louis's brother, and the Duke de Bouillon, had entered into a conspiracy for the overthrow of Cardinal Richelieu, and the securing to the first-named duke the regency of the kingdom, in the event of the king's death, an occurrence which the state of his health rendered probable at no distant date. Into this confederacy Cinq-Mars readily entered along with a friend of his, the councillor De Thou, a son of the celebrated historian. The real mover, however, in the plot was Louis, Duke of Orleans. With the view of strengthening their cause, the conspirators entered into a secret treaty with the Spanish court, and everything was looking favourable for the success of their design. The cardinal, however, had his spies and informers everywhere, and having received intelligence of what was going on, refrained from taking any active steps till he could strike the final blow. At last he contrived to get possession of a copy of the Spanish treaty, and laid it before the king, who thereupon granted a warrant for the arrest of the parties implicated. The real ringleader, Louis of Orleans, a man aged forty-six, had the baseness to throw the entire guilt of the transaction upon Cinq-Mars, a youth of twenty-two, and by burning, as is said, the original treaty, managed to destroy the legal proof of his treason. The Duke de Bouillon escaped by forfeiting his principality of Sedan. But Richelieu was bent on having the lives of Cinq-Mars and De Thou, the demerits of the latter consisting in the circumstance of his father, the historian, having made in his work some unpleasant revelations regarding one of the cardinal's ancestors. The two friends were arrested at Narbonne, conveyed to Perpignan, and from thence up the Rhone towards Lyon. It is said Richelieu preceded them in a triumphal progress as far as Valence, having his two victims placed in a barge, which was attached to the stern of his own as he sailed up the river. On reaching Lyon, the prisoners were brought to trial, and after a mockery of the forms of justice, the evidence against both, more especially De Thou, being very incomplete, they were condemned to lose their heads as traitors. To gratify Richelieu, who dreaded the effect of the intercession of their friends and relatives with the king, the proceedings were hurried through as rapidly as possible, and the execution took place on the same day that sentence was pronounced. Both Cinq-Mars and De Thou behaved with great courage, though the decapitation of the latter was accomplished in a most bungling and repulsive manner, the proper executioner having broken his leg a few days before, and his place being supplied by a novice to the business, who was rewarded with a hundred crowns for his work. Such was the history of Cinq-Mars, whose fate has supplied materials both to the romance-writer and dramatist. That he was illegally condemned, is certainly true; but it is no less so, that he had plotted Richelieu's overthrow, and at one period meditated his death, so that he could scarcely complain of being entangled in the same net which he had already spread for another. The cardinal did not long survive the gratification of his vengeance, and, broken down by disease and bodily suffering, followed his victims in a few months to that unseen world where the forgiveness, which he had so inexorably withheld from them, would have to be solicited, it is to be hoped successfully, by himself, from a higher and more merciful Power.

## GRIFFITH JONES.

The readers of the *Vicar of Wakefield*—and who has not read it?—must remember how poor Primrose, when sick and penniless at a little alehouse seventy miles from home, was rescued from his distressing situation by 'the philanthropic bookseller of St Paul's Churchyard, who has written so many little books for children'—who called himself the friend of children, 'but was the friend of all mankind'— then engaged in a journey of importance, namely, to gather 'materials for the history of one Mr Thomas Trip.' The person here meant was Mr John Newbery, who carried on business as a publisher in the last house of Ludgate Hill, adjoining to St Paul's Churchyard, and who was one of the chief bibliopolic patrons of Goldsmith himself. It was, indeed, he to whom Dr Johnson sold for sixty pounds the manuscript of the *Vicar of Wakefield*, thereby redeeming its author from a position of difficulty with which Boswell has made the public sufficiently familiar.

The little books for children published by Mr Newbery are now entirely unknown. We remember them still in great favour about fifty years ago. Rather plain in respect of paper they were; the embellishments were somewhat rude; and perhaps the variant-hued paper-covers, with a slight gold lackering, would be sneered at by the juveniles of the present age. Nevertheless, we cannot look back upon them without respect. The *History of Goody Two-shoes*, the *History of Giles Gingerbread*, and the *Travels of Tommy Trip*, were all charming narrations.

If it was worth while to advert to M. Perrault as the author of the *Contes des Fées*, it seems equally proper, in a book of this kind, to put into some prominence the writers of this English literature for the young. Let it be observed, then, that the chief of these was a Welshman of considerable learning and talent, Mr Griffith Jones, who had been reared as a printer under Mr Bowyer, but advanced to be a journalist of repute, and a notable contributor to periodical works supported by Johnson, Smollett, Goldsmith, and other eminent men. He was many years editor of the *Daily Advertiser*, the paper in which the letters of Junius appeared. He resided at one time in Bolt Court, Fleet Street, and thus was a near neighbour of Johnson. A small work of his, entitled *Great Events from Little Causes*, is said to have had an extensive sale. Being, however, a modest man, he was content to publish anonymously, and thus it has happened that his name is hardly known in our literary history. His brother, Giles Jones, was another worker in the humble field wherein Mr Newbery acquired his fame, and his son, Stephen Jones, was the editor of the *Biographia Dramatica*, 1812.

---

### RAISING OF THE SIEGE OF VIENNA.

SEPTEMBER 12, 1683.

Depressed as the Turks now are, it is difficult to imagine how formidable they were two hundred years ago. The Hungarians, threatened by their sovereign, the Emperor Leopold, with the loss of their privileges, revolted against him, and called in the Turks to their aid. An Ottoman army, about two hundred thousand strong, augmented by a body of Hungarian troops, consequently advanced into Austria, and, finding no adequate resistance, laid siege to Vienna.

The emperor, quitting his capital with precipitation, retired first to Lintz, afterwards to Passau, leaving the Duke of Lorraine at the head of a little army to sustain, as he best might, the fortunes of the empire. All Europe was at gaze at this singular conjuncture, none doubting that the Austrian capital would speedily be in the hands of the Turks, for it had hardly any defence beyond what was furnished by a weak garrison of citizens and students. The avarice of the grand vizier, Kara-Mustapha, the commander of the Turks, saved Vienna. He had calculated that the emperor's capital ought to contain immense treasures, and he hesitated to order a general assault, lest these should be appropriated by the soldiery. This allowed time for John Sobieski, king of Poland, to bring up his army, and for the princes of the empire to gather their troops. The Janissaries murmured. Discouragement followed upon indignation. They wrote, 'Come, infidels; the mere sight of your hats will put us to flight!'

In effect, when the king of Poland and the Duke of Lorraine descended the Colemberg mountain with their troops, the Turks retired without fighting. The vizier, who had expected to obtain so much treasure in Vienna, left his own in the hands of Sobieski, and went to surrender his head to the sultan. The retreat of his army was so precipitate, that they left behind them the grand standard of the Prophet, which Sobieski, with practical wit, sent to the pope.

---

## SEPTEMBER 13.

St Maurilius, bishop of Angers, confessor, 5th century. St Eulogius, confessor and patriarch of Alexandria, 608. St Amatus, abbot and confessor, about 627. Another St Amatus, bishop and confessor, about 690.

---

*Born.*—Sir William Cecil, Lord Burleigh, 1520, *Bourn, Leicestershire.*

*Died.*—Titus, Roman emperor, 81 A.D.; Sir John Cheke, eminent Greek scholar, 1557, *London;* William Farel, coadjutor of Calvin, 1565, *Neufchatel;* Michael de Montaigne, celebrated essayist, 1592, *Montaigne, near Bordeaux;* Philip II. of Spain, 1598; John Buxtorf the Elder, eminent Hebrew scholar, 1629, *Basel;* General James Wolfe, killed at capture of Quebec, 1759; Charles James Fox, eminent statesman, 1806, *Chiswick House;* Saverio Bettinelli, Italian writer (Risorgimento d'Italia), 1808, *Mantua.*

### MONTAIGNE.

Montaigne was born in 1533, and died in 1592, his life of sixty years coinciding with one of the gloomiest eras in French history—a time of widespread and implacable dissensions, of civil war, massacre and murder. Yet, as the name of Izaak Walton suggests little or nothing of the strife between Cavalier and Roundhead, so neither does that of Montaigne recall the merciless antagonism of Catholic and Huguenot. Walton and Montaigne alike sought refuge from public broils in rural quiet, and in their solitude produced writings which have been a joy to the contemplative of many generations; but here the likeness between the London linen-draper and the Gascon lawyer ends: they were men of very different characters.

The father of Montaigne was a baron of Perigord. Having found Latin a dreary and difficult study in his youth, he determined to make it an easy one for his son. He procured a tutor from Germany, ignorant of French, and gave orders that he should converse with the boy in nothing but Latin, and directed, moreover, that none of the household should address him otherwise than in that tongue. 'They all became Latinised,' says Montaigne; 'and even the villagers in the neighbourhood learned words in that language, some of which took root in the country, and became of common use among the people.' Greek he was taught by similar artifice, feeling it a pastime rather than a task. At the age of six, he was sent to the college of Guyenne, then reputed the best in France, and, strange as it seems, his biographers relate, that at thirteen he had run through the prescribed course of studies, and completed his education. He next turned his attention to law, and at twenty-one was made *conseiller*, or judge, in the parliament of Bordeaux. He visited Paris, of which he wrote: 'I love it for itself; I love it tenderly, even to its warts and blemishes. I am not a Frenchman, but by this great city—great in people, great in the felicity of her situation, but above all, great and incomparable in variety and diversity of commodities; the glory of France, and one of the most noble ornaments of the world.' He was received at court, enjoyed the favour of Henri II., saw Mary Stuart, Queen of Scots, and entered fully into the delights and dissipations of gay society. At thirty-three he was married—though had he been left free to his choice, he 'would not have wedded with Wisdom herself had she been willing. But 'tis not much to the purpose,' he writes, 'to resist custom, for the common usance of life will be so. Most of my actions are guided by example, not choice.' Of women, indeed, he seldom speaks save in terms of easy contempt, and for the hardships of married life he has frequent jeers.

In 1571, in his thirty-eighth year, the death of his father enabled Montaigne to retire from the practice of law, and to settle on the patrimonial estate. It was predicted he would soon exhaust his fortune, but, on the contrary, he proved a good economist, and turned his farms to excellent account. His good sense, his probity, and liberal soul, won for him the esteem of his province; and though the civil wars of the League converted every house into a fort, he kept his gates open, and the neighbouring gentry brought him their jewels and papers to hold in safe-keeping. He placed his library in a tower overlooking the entrance to his court-yard, and there spent his leisure in reading, meditation, and writing. On the central rafter he inscribed : *I do not understand; I pause; I examine.* He took to writing for want of something to do, and having nothing else to write about, he began to write about himself, jotting down what came into his head when not too lazy. He found paper a patient listener, and excused his egotism by the consideration, that if his grandchildren were of the same mind as himself, they would be glad to know what sort of man he was. 'What should I give to listen to some one who could tell me the ways, the look, the bearing, the commonest words of my ancestors!' If the world should complain that he talked too much about himself, he would answer the world that it talked and thought of everything but itself.

A volume of these egotistic gossips he published at Bordeaux in 1580, and the book quickly passed into circulation. About this time he was attacked with stone, a disease he had held in dread from childhood, and the pleasure of the remainder of his life was broken with paroxysms of severe pain. 'When they suppose me to be most cast down,' he writes, 'and spare me, I often try my strength, and start subjects of conversation quite foreign to my state. I can do everything by a sudden effort, but, oh! take away duration. I am tried severely, for I have suddenly passed from a very sweet and happy condition of life, to the most painful that can be imagined.' Abhorring doctors and drugs, he sought diversion and relief in a journey through Germany, Switzerland, and Italy. At Rome he was kindly received by the pope and cardinals, and invested with the freedom of the city, an honour of which he was very proud. He kept a journal of this tour, which, after lying concealed in an old chest in his chateau for nearly two hundred years, was brought to light and published in 1774; and, as may be supposed, it contains a stock of curious and original information. While he was travelling, he was elected mayor of Bordeaux, an office for which he had no inclination, but Henri III. insisted that he should accept it, and at the end of two years he was re-elected for the same period. During a visit to Paris, he became acquainted with Mademoiselle de Gournay, a young lady who had conceived an ardent friendship for him through reading his *Essays.* She visited him, accompanied by her mother, and he reciprocated her attachment by treating her as his daughter. Meanwhile, his health grew worse, and feeling his end was drawing near, and sick of the intolerance and bloodshed which devastated France, he kept at home, correcting and retouching his writings. A quinsy terminated his life. He gathered his friends round his bedside, and bade them farewell. A priest said mass, and at the elevation of the host he raised himself in bed, and with hands clasped in prayer, expired. Mademoiselle de Gournay and her mother crossed half France, risking the perils of the roads, that they might condole with his widow and daughter.

It is superfluous to praise Montaigne's *Essays;* they have long passed the ordeal of time into assured immortality. He was one of the earliest discoverers of the power and genius of the French language, and may be said to have been the inventor of that charming form of literature—the essay. At a time when authorship was stiff, solemn, and exhaustive, confined to Latin and the learned, he broke into the vernacular, and wrote for everybody with the ease and nonchalance of conversation. The *Essays* furnish a rambling autobiography of their author, and not even Rousseau turned himself inside out with more completeness. He gives, with inimitable candour, an account of his likes and dislikes, his habits, foibles, and virtues. He pretends to most of the vices; and if there be any goodness in him, he says he got it by stealth. In his opinion, there is no man who has not deserved hanging five or six times, and he claims no exception in his own behalf. 'Five or six as ridiculous stories,' he says, 'may be told of me as of any man living.' This very frankness has caused some to question his sincerity, but his dissection of his own inconsistent self is too consistent with flesh and blood to be anything but natural. Bit by bit the reader of the *Essays* grows familiar with Montaigne; and he must have a dull imagination indeed who fails to conceive a distinct picture of the thick-set, square-built, clumsy little man, so undersized that he did not like walking, because the mud of the streets bespattered him to the middle, and the rude crowd jostled and elbowed him. He disliked Protestantism, but his mind was wholly averse to bigotry and persecution. Gibbon, indeed, reckons Montaigne and Henri IV. as the only two men of liberality in the France of the sixteenth century. Nothing more distinguishes Montaigne than his deep sense of the uncertainty and provisional character of human knowledge; and Mr Emerson has well chosen him for a type of the sceptic. Montaigne's device—a pair of scales evenly balanced, with the motto, *Que scais-je?* (What do I know?)—perfectly symbolises the man.

The only book we have which we certainly know was handled by Shakspeare, is a copy of Florio's translation of Montaigne's *Essays.* It contains the poet's autograph, and was purchased by the British Museum for one hundred and twenty guineas. A second copy of the same translation in the Museum has Ben Jonson's name on the fly-leaf.

## ANCIENT BOOKS.

Before the invention of printing, the labour requisite for the production of a manuscript volume was so great, that such volume, when completed, became a treasured heir-loom. Half-a-dozen such books made a remarkable library for a nobleman to possess; and a score of them would furnish a monastery. Many years must have been occupied in writing the large folio volumes that are still the most valued books in the great public libraries of Europe; vast as is the labour of the literary portion, the artistic decoration of these elaborate pages of elegantly-formed letters, is equally wonderful. Richly-painted and gilt letters are at the head of chapters and paragraphs, from which vignette decoration flows down the sides, and about the margins, often enclosing grotesque figures of men and animals, exhibiting the fertile fancies of these old artists. Miniature drawings, frequently of the greatest beauty, illustrating the subject of each page, are sometimes spread with a lavish hand through these old volumes, and often furnish us with the only contemporary pictures we possess of the everyday-life of the men of the middle ages.

When the vellum leaves completing the book had been written and decorated, the binder then commenced his work; and he occasionally displayed a costly taste and manipulative ability of a kind no moderns attempt. A valued volume was literally encased in gold and gems. The monks of the ninth and tenth centuries were clever adepts in working the precious metals; and one of the number—St Dunstan—became sufficiently celebrated for his ability this way, to be chosen the patron-saint of the goldsmiths. Our engraving will convey some idea of one of the finest existing

ANTIQUE BOOKBINDING.

specimens of antique bookbinding in the national collection, Paris. It is a work of the eleventh century, and encases a book of prayers in a mass of gold, jewels, and enamels. The central subject is sunk like a framed picture, and represents the Crucifixion, the Virgin and St John on each side the cross, and above it the veiled busts of Apollo and Diana; thus exhibiting the influence of the older Byzantine school, which is, indeed, visible throughout the entire design. This subject is executed on a thin sheet of gold, beaten up from behind into high relief, and chased upon its surface. A rich frame of jewelled ornament surrounds this subject, portions of the decoration being further enriched with coloured enamels; the angles are filled with enamelled emblems of the evangelists; the ground of the whole design enriched by threads and foliations of delicate gold wire.

Such books were jealously guarded. They represented a considerable sum of money in a merely mercantile sense; but they often had additional value impressed by some individual skill. Loans of such volumes, even to royalty, were rare, and never accorded without the strictest regard to their safety and sure return. Gifts of such books were the noblest presents a monastery could offer to a prince; and such gifts were often made the subject of the first picture on the opening page of the volume. Thus the volume of romances, known as *The Shrewsbury Book*, in the British Museum, has upon its first page an elaborate drawing, representing the famed Talbot, Earl of Shrewsbury, presenting this book to King Henry VI., seated on his throne, and surrounded by his courtiers. Many instances might readily be cited of similar scenes in other manuscripts preserved in the same collection.

Smaller and less ambitious volumes, intended for the use of the student, or for church-services, were more simply bound; but they frequently were enriched by an ivory carving let into the cover—a practice that seems to have ceased in the sixteenth century, when leather of different kinds was used, generally enriched by ornament stamped in relief. A quaint fancy was sometimes indulged

ANCIENT BOOK.

in the form of books, such as is seen in the first figure of the cut just given. The original occurs in a portrait of a nobleman of that era, engaged in devotion, his book of prayers taking the conventional form of a heart, when the volume is opened. For the use of the religious, books of prayers were bound, in the fifteenth century, in a very peculiar way, which will be best understood by a glance at the second figure in our cut. The leathern covering of the volume was lengthened beyond the margin of the boards, and then gathered (a loose flap of skin) into a large knot at the end. When the book was closed and secured by the clasp, this leathern flap was passed under the owner's girdle, and the knot brought over it, to prevent its slipping. Thus a volume of prayers might be conveniently carried, and such books were very constantly seen at a monk's girdle.

There is another class of books for which great durability, during rough usage, was desired. These were volumes of accounts, registers, and law records. Strong boards sometimes formed their only covering, or the boards were covered with hog-skins, and strengthened by bosses of metal. The town of Southampton still possesses a volume containing a complete code of naval legislation, written in Norman-French, on vellum, in a hand apparently of the earlier half of the fourteenth century. It is preserved in its original binding, consisting of two oak boards, about half an inch thick, one of them being much longer than the other, the latter having a square hole in the lower part, to put the hand through, in order to hold it up while citing the laws in court. These boards are held together by the strong cords upon which the back of the book is stitched, and which pass through holes in the wooden covers. These are again secured by bands of leather and rows of nails. Paper-books, intended for ordinary use, were sometimes simply

ANCIENT BOOK.

covered with thick hog-skin, stitched at the back with strong thongs of leather. Binding, as a fine art, seems to have declined just before the invention of printing: after that, libraries became common, and collectors prided themselves on good book-binding; but into this more modern history of the art we do not propose to enter.

---

## SEPTEMBER 14.

**The Exaltation of the Holy Cross, 629. St Cormac, bishop of Cashel, 908. St Catherine of Genoa, widow, 1510.**

### EXALTATION OF THE HOLY CROSS.

The discovery of the cross on which Christ was supposed to have suffered, by the Empress Helena (see under May 3), led to the sacred relic being raised or exalted in view of the people, in a magnificent church built by her son the Emperor Constantine, at Jerusalem; and this ceremony of the exaltation of the holy cross, which took place on the 14th September 335, was commemorated in a festival held on every recurrence of that day, by both the Greek and Latin churches. The cross was afterwards (*anno* 614) carried away by Chosroes, king of Persia, but recovered by the Emperor Heraclius, and replaced amidst circumstances of great pomp and expressions of the highest devotion.

Many churches in Britain were dedicated to the Holy Rood or Cross. One at Edinburgh became the nucleus of the palace of the Scottish kings. Holyrood Day was one of much sacred observance all through the middle ages. The same feeling led to a custom of framing, between the nave and choir of churches, what was called a rood-screen or rood-loft, presenting centrally a large crucifix, with images of the Holy Virgin and St John on each side. A winding stair led up to it, and the epistle and gospel were often read from it. Some of these screens still remain, models of architectural beauty; but numbers were destroyed with reckless fanaticism at the Reformation, the people not distinguishing between the objects which had caused what they deemed idolatry and the beautifully carved work which was free from such a charge.

One of the most famous of these roods or crucifixes was that at the abbey of Boxley, in Kent, which was entitled the *Rood of Grace.* The legend is, that an English carpenter, having been taken prisoner in the French wars, and wishing to employ his leisure as well as obtain his ransom, made a very skilful piece of workmanship of wood, wire, paste, and paper, in the form of a cross of exquisite proportion, on which hung the figure of our Saviour, which, by means of springs, could bow down, lift itself up, shake its hands and feet, nod the head, roll its eyes, and smile or frown. The carpenter, getting permission to return and sell his work, put it on a horse, and drove it before him; but stopping near Rochester at an alehouse for refreshment, the animal passed on, and missing the straight road, galloped south to Boxley, and being driven by some 'divine furie,' never stopped until it reached the church-door, when it kicked so loudly with its heels, that the monks ran out to see the wonder. No sooner was the door opened, than the horse rushed in, and stood still by a pillar. The monks were proceeding to unload, when the owner appeared, and claimed his property; but in vain did he try to lead the horse from the sanctuary; it seemed nailed to the spot. He next attempted to remove the rood, but was equally unsuccessful; so that in the end, through sheer weariness and the entreaties of the monks to have the image left with them, he consented to sell it to them for a piece of money.

The accounts transmitted to us by the Reformers—although to be taken as one-sided—leave us little room to doubt that, in the corrupt age preceding the great change in the sixteenth century, many deceptious practices had come to be connected with the images on the rood-galleries. 'If you were to benefit by the Rood of Grace, the first visit to be paid was to one of the priests, who would hear your confession and give you shrift, in return for a piece of money. You must next do honour to another image of St Rumwald or Grumbald, a little picture of a boy-saint, which, by means of a pin of wood put through a pillar behind, made certain contortions, by which the monks could tell whether all sins had been atoned for in the previous confession. Those who stretched their purse-strings, and made liberal offerings, gained St Rumwald to their side, and were pronounced to be living a pure life. If the poor pilgrim had done all this with sufficient honour to himself and the saints, he was prepared to go to the holy rood and gain plenary absolution.'

At the dissolution of the abbeys, Cromwell and his associates laid their ruthless hands on Boxley; and Nicholas Partridge, suspecting some cheat in the Rood of Grace, made an examination, and soon discovered the spring which turned the mechanism. It was taken to Maidstone, and there exposed to the people; from thence to London, where the king and his court laughed at the object they had once deemed holy; and, finally, it was brought before an immense multitude at St Paul's Cross, by Hilsey, bishop of Rochester, on Sunday, the

24th of February 1538, when it was broken to pieces and buried, the bishop preaching a sermon on the subject.

---

*Born.*—Henry Cornelius Agrippa, alchemist and author, 1486, *Cologne;* Browne Willis, antiquary, 1682, *Blandford, Dorsetshire;* Alexander Baron von Humboldt, celebrated traveller and natural philosopher, 1769, *Berlin;* Lord William Henry Cavendish Bentinck, governor-general of India, 1774.

*Died.*—St Cyprian, archbishop of Carthage, Christian writer and martyr, 258, *Carthage;* St Chrysostom, renowned preacher and writer, 407, *near Comana;* Dante Alighieri, great Italian poet, 1321, *Ravenna;* John Plantagenet, Duke of Bedford, English commander in France, 1435, *Rouen;* Pope Adrian VI., 1523; Robert, Earl of Essex, parliamentary general, 1646; John Dominic Cassini, astronomer, 1712; Charles Rollin, historian, 1741, *Paris;* Louis Joseph de Montcalm, French commander, 1759, *Quebec;* James Fenimore Cooper, American novelist, 1851, *Cooperstown, New York;* Arthur, Duke of Wellington, illustrious British commander, 1852, *Walmer Castle, Kent;* Augustin W. N. Pugin, ecclesiastical architect, 1852, *Ramsgate.*

---

## AN ANTIQUARY OF THE OLDEN TYPE.

In the early part of the eighteenth century, when few were paying any attention to antiquities, and ancient remains were consequently exposed to reckless damage and neglect, there arose in England a quaint, uncouth sort of country gentleman, who, to the scorn of his neighbours, devoted himself, with an Old-Mortality-like zeal, to the study and care-taking of old churches. Browne Willis, so was he hight, inherited a competent fortune from his grandfather, Dr Thomas Willis, the celebrated physician. While a boy at Westminster School, by frequently walking in the adjacent abbey, he acquired a taste for ecclesiastical and architectural antiquities, which formed the sole pursuit and pleasure of his blameless life. For many years, he constantly employed himself in making pilgrimages to the various cathedrals and churches in England and Wales; always endeavouring, if possible, to visit each on the festival-day of the saint to which it was dedicated. As an amusing instance of his veneration for saints' days, it may be mentioned that he dedicated to St Martin a chapel, which he gratefully erected, at Fenny-Stratford, in honour of his grandfather, who was born in St Martin's Lane, upon St Martin's Day, placing the following inscription on a conspicuous part of the building:

'In honour to thy memory, blessed shade!
Were the foundations of this chapel laid.
Purchased by thee, thy son and present heir
Owes these three manors to thy sacred care.
For this may all thy race thanks ever pay,
And yearly celebrate St Martin's Day.'

Though succeeding to an income of £4000 per annum, our amiable antiquary almost impoverished himself, by the extreme ardour with which he gave himself to his favourite pursuits. He expended large sums in beautifying and restoring ancient edifices of an ecclesiastical character, sometimes, indeed, with greater enthusiasm than good taste. He erected an ornamental tower on Buckingham Church, without first correctly estimating the supporting capabilities of the substructure; and, not long after, the tower fell, utterly demolishing the sacred edifice which it was intended to decorate. A curious instance of the not uncommon insensibility to danger, which arises from habit, is told of the downfall of this tower. A person who worshipped in the church, and whose architectural knowledge enabled him to foresee the impending fall, being asked if he had ever taken any precautions, or notified to his neighbours the probability of such a catastrophe, replied that he always had desired his family and friends to shut their pew-doors as softly as possible!

The personal appearance of Mr Willis has been described as resembling that of a beggar more than a country gentleman of fortune. He wore three, sometimes four, coats, surmounted by an old blue cloak, the whole bound round his body by a common leathern girdle. His boots were covered with patches, as they well might be after a wear of forty years; and his carriage, being painted black, and studded with brass plates, on which were incised the various armorial bearings of the Willis family, was frequently mistaken for a hearse. Antiquarian pilgrimages in this guise could scarcely fail to give rise to many amusing mistakes. Mr Willis, one day, when passing an old building that had been converted into a farmhouse, stopped his carriage, and cried to a female he saw engaged in domestic occupations: 'Woman, have ye any arms in this house?'—meaning coats of arms painted or carved on the walls or windows. But, the period being the eventful year of 1745, when the English peasantry were terrified by the most absurd rumours, the woman, thinking that arms of a different description were required, barricaded her door, and replied to the question with a volley of vulgar abuse from an upper window. On another occasion, Mr Willis, observing a building that exhibited appearances of better days, asked the good woman: 'Has this ever been a religious house?' 'I don't know what you mean by a religious house,' was the reply of the enraged matron, 'but I know it is as decent and honest a house as any that a dirty old rascal like you could have.'

While incessantly engaged in repairing churches, Mr Willis as earnestly insisted upon clergymen fulfilling their particular duties. This spirit led to many disputes and references to courts of law, where antiquarian lore invariably gained the day; the defeated parties generally revenging themselves by satirical squibs on the enthusiastic antiquary. From the best of these, embodying the principal peculiarities of a worthy, though eccentric man, we extract the following verses:

'Whilome there dwelt near Buckingham,
That famous county town,
At a known place, hight Whaddon Chase,
A squire of odd renown.

A Druid's sacred form he bore,
His robes a girdle bound:
Deep versed he was in ancient lore,
In customs old, profound.

A stick, torn from that hallowed tree
Where Chaucer used to sit,
And tell his tales with leering glee,
Supports his tottering feet.

No prophet he, like Sydrophel,
Could future times explore;
But what had happened, he could tell,
Five hundred years and more.

A walking almanac, he appears,
Stepped from some mouldy wall,
Worn out of use through dust and years
Like scutcheons in his hall.

His boots were made of that cow's hide,
By Guy of Warwick slain;
Time's choicest gifts, aye to abide
Among the chosen train.

His car himself he did provide,
To stand in double stead;
That it should carry him alive,
And bury him when dead.

By rusty coins, old kings he 'd trace,
And know their air and mien;
King Alfred he knew well by face,
Though George he ne'er had seen.

This wight th' outside of churches loved,
Almost unto a sin;
Spires Gothic of more use he proved
Than pulpits are within.

Whene'er the fatal day shall come,
For come, alas! it must,
When this good squire must stay at home,
And turn to ancient dust,

The solemn dirge, ye owls, prepare,
Ye bats more hoarsely shriek,
Croak, all ye ravens, round the bier,
And all ye church-mice squeak!'

## ROLLIN AND HIS ANCIENT HISTORY.

Charles Rollin, born in Paris in 1661, the son of a cutler, rose to be, at thirty-three, rector of the university of Paris, a position of the highest dignity, which he adorned by the sweetness of his character, his learning, probity, and moderation. He is now chiefly memorable for a work, entitled *Ancient History*, in which he gave such information regarding the Egyptians, Assyrians, Carthaginians, and other ancient nations, as was obtainable in his day, in a style distinguished by its purity and elegance. The English translation of this work was a stock-book in the English market down to about thirty years ago, when at length it began to be neglected, in consequence of the many discoveries giving a new cast to our knowledge of ancient history. Voltaire praises the work highly, though he alleges that it would have been better if the author had been a philosopher, able to distinguish better the false from the true, the incredible from the probable, and to sacrifice the useless. It is the best compilation, he says, in any language, because compilers are seldom eloquent, and Rollin was.

## THE DUKE OF WELLINGTON.

On the 14th of September 1852, died Arthur, Duke of Wellington, the most illustrious Englishman of his time, at the age of eighty-three. He had performed the highest services to his country, and indeed to Europe, and the honours he had consequently received were such as would tire even a Spaniard. While so much honoured, the duke was a man of such simplicity of nature, that he never appeared in the slightest degree uplifted. His leading idea in life was the duty he owed to his country and its government, and with the performance of *that* he always appeared perfectly satisfied. He was the *truest* of men, and even in the dispatches and bulletins which he had occasion to compose amidst the excitements of victory, there is never to be traced a feeling in the slightest degree allied to vapouring or even self-complacency. It was not in respect of stricken fields alone, that he proved himself the superior of Napoleon. He was his superior in every moral attribute.

The duke was the younger son of an Irish peer remarkable only for his musical compositions. To a clever and thoughtful mother, early left a widow, it is owing, that two men so remarkable as Richard, Marquis Wellesley, and Arthur, Duke of Wellington, were included in one family. Arthur entered the army in 1787, as an ensign of foot. He passed through various regiments of foot and horse, and at four-and-twenty had attained the lieutenant-colonelcy of the 33d Regiment of infantry. His first conspicuous appearance in our military history is as the chief of a little British army, which (September 23, 1803) overthrew a large Mahrattas force at Assaye, in the Deccan, by which the British power was established in that part of India. It is not required here that we should recite the series of campaigns in Spain and Portugal, extending between April 1809 and November 1813, by which he expelled the superior armies of Napoleon from the Peninsula, and enabled his troops to bivouac in unopposed triumph on the soil of France. Neither is it necessary here to repeat the particulars of his Belgian campaign of 1815, ending in his triumph over Napoleon in person at Waterloo. All of these transactions are already written deeply in the hearts of his countrymen.

When Arthur Wellesley completed his military career in 1815, with the title of Duke, and a multitude of other marks of the public gratitude, he was only forty-six years of age. Throughout the remainder of his long life, he devoted himself to the service of his country, as a member of the House of Peers and occasionally as a minister. It cannot be said that he shone as a politician, and his sagacity, for once, made a dismal failure in the estimate he formed of the necessity for parliamentary reform in 1830. Yet no one ever for a moment hesitated to admit, that the duke was perfectly honest and unselfish in his political, as he had been in his military career.

The death of this eminently great man was the result of natural decay, taking finally the form of a fit of epilepsy. He was interred with the highest public honours in St Paul's Cathedral.

## THE DUKE OF WELLINGTON AT WALMER.

The death of the Duke of Wellington was associated with much of that soldierly simplicity which marked his character generally. From 1829 till 1852, he was accustomed to pass two months of each autumn at Walmer Castle, away from the turmoil of parliamentary and official life in the metropolis. As Lord Warden of the Cinque Ports, Walmer was one of his official residences. Those ports have long survived the state of affairs which once gave them celebrity as a naval fraternity; but still the title of Lord Warden is kept up, with a few unimportant duties—Dover being the head-quarters, but Walmer the official residence. The castle, built in the time of Henry VIII., is one of three which defend the low coast near Walmer and Deal; it has had alterations made in it from time to time, to adapt it as a domestic residence. Here the Great Duke, as we have said, passed a portion of each year. His apartments were furnished in the simplest possible way; especially his bedroom, which besides an iron military bedstead and a coverlet, contained very few articles. The one window of that room looked out upon the sea; while a door, in an adjoining apartment, gave access to the ramparts of the castle, where the duke was accustomed to walk at an early hour every morning—a few guns around him, but a very lovely prospect in front. His habits were as plain and simple as his rooms. On many of the doors in the passages and apartments was written, in intelligible letters, 'SHUT THIS DOOR,' a command likely to be the more scrupulously obeyed in being issued in this uncompromising way. The Queen, and some of the most illustrious persons in the kingdom, visited the great general here; but whoever it might be, and at whatever time, all felt a desire to fall in with (or, at least, not to interrupt) his daily mode of life. From morning until night, every hour was apportioned with the utmost regularity. That faculty for order and organisation, which had enabled him, in earlier years, to manage large armies, still remained with him till his death, when he was in his eighty-fourth year.

On Monday the 13th of September 1852, the duke rode and walked out as usual, dined as usual, and retired to rest at his usual hour. On Tuesday the 14th, his valet called him at the customary hour of six o'clock. Half an hour afterwards, hearing a kind of moaning, the valet entered the room, and found his master ill. The duke requested that his apothecary, Mr Hulke of Deal, should be sent for. Lord and Lady Charles Wellesley, the son and daughter-in-law of the duke, happened to be stopping at the castle at the time, and they were at once apprised that something was wrong. When the apothecary arrived between eight and nine o'clock, the duke was in an epileptic fit, something similar to one from which he had suffered a few years before. The apothecary went back to Deal to prepare some medicines; but while he was gone, the symptoms became worse, and Dr Macarthur of Walmer attended. As the day advanced, the urgency of the case led to the despatching of telegrams to London, summoning any one of three eminent physicians; two were in Scotland, and the third did not arrive at Walmer till all was over. The veteran suffered much during the day; he spoke frequently, but his words could not be understood. At four o'clock on that same afternoon, he breathed his last. So little did he or any one anticipate that his end was near, that he had appointed to meet the Countess of Westmoreland at Dover on that day, to see her off by a steam-packet to Ostend. Thus the Duke of Wellington died, with nobody near him, among all his crowd of illustrious and distinguished friends, except one son, one daughter-in-law, a physician, an apothecary, and the ordinary domestics of the castle.

When all the glitter of a lying-in-state and a public funeral were occupying men's thoughts, the simplicity of the duke's life at Walmer was well-nigh forgotten; but many facts came to light by degrees, illustrative of this matter. He made his little bedroom serve also for his library and his study. His iron-bedstead was only three feet wide, and had a mattress three inches thick; he had one coverlet, but no blankets, and was accustomed to carry his pillow with him when he travelled. He rose between six and seven, walked on the ramparts, and at nine breakfasted on plain tea and bread and butter. When the Queen and Prince Albert visited the veteran in 1842, the only changes he made in the apartments appropriated to them were—to put a plate-glass window where the Queen could have a better view of the sea, and to get a common carpenter to make a deal stand for a time-piece in the Prince's room. The Queen was so delighted with the simplicity of the whole affair, that she begged permission to stop for a week longer than the time originally intended—a compliment, of course, flattering to the duke, but possibly regarded by him as a departure from order and regularity.

The duke's death suggested to Mr Longfellow a subject for the following stanzas:

THE WARDEN OF THE CINQUE PORTS.

A mist was driving down the British Channel,
  The day was just begun,
And through the window-panes, on wall and panel,
  Stream'd the red autumn sun.

It glanc'd on flowing flag and rippling pennon,
  And the white sails of ships;
And from the frowning rampart the black cannon
  Hail'd it with fev'rish lips.

Sandwich and Romney, Hastings, Hythe, and Dover,
  Were all alert that day,
To see the French war-steamer speeding over,
  When the fog clear'd away.

Sullen and silent, and like couchant lions,
  Their cannon through the night,
Holding their breath, had watch'd in grim defiance
  The sea-coast opposite.

And now they roar'd at drum-beat from their stations,
  On every citadel;
Each answ'ring each with morning salutations
  That all was well.

And down the coast, all taking up the burden,
  Replied the distant forts;
As if to summon from his sleep the Warden
  And Lord of the Cinque Ports.

Him shall no sunshine from the fields of azure,
  No drum-beat from the wall,
No morning-gun from the black fort's embrasure,
  Awaken with their call.

No more surveying with an eye impartial
  The long line of the coast,
Shall the gaunt figure of the old field-marshal
  Be seen upon his post.

For in the night, unseen, a single warrior,
In sombre harness mailed,
Dreaded of man, and surnamed the Destroyer,
The rampart-wall had scaled.

He passed into the chamber of the sleeper,
The dark and silent room;
And as he enter'd, darker grew and deeper
The silence of the gloom.

He did not pause to parley or dissemble,
But smote the warder hoar:
Ah, what a blow! that made all England tremble,
And groan from shore to shore.

Meanwhile, without the surly cannon waited,
The sun rose bright o'erhead;
Nothing in nature's aspect intimated
That a great man was dead.

## THE DUKE'S COOLNESS.

'Lord Aylmer,' says Mr Larpent in his *Journal*, 'gave me two striking instances of Lord Wellington's coolness: one, when in a fog in the morning, as he was pursuing the French, he found a division of our men, under Sir William Erskine, much exposed in advance, and nearly separated from the rest of the army, and the French in a village within a mile of where he was standing. He could see nothing. But, on some prisoners being brought in, and being asked what French division, and how many men were in the village, they, to the dismay of every one except Wellington, said that the whole French army were there. All he said was, quite coolly: "Oh! they are all there, are they? Well, we must mind a little what we are about, then." Another time, soon after the battle of Fuentes d'Onoro, and when we were waiting in our position near them to risk an attack, to protect the siege of Almeida, one morning suddenly and early, Lord Aylmer came in to him, whilst he was shaving, to tell him "the French were all off, and the last cavalry mounting to be gone;" the consequence of which movement relieved him entirely, gave him Almeida, and preserved Portugal. He only took the razor off for one moment, and said: "Ay, I thought they meant to be off; very well," and then another shave, just as before, and not another word till he was dressed.'

'Of the duke's perfect coolness on the most trying occasions,' so said Mr Rogers, 'Colonel Gurwood gave me this instance. He was once in great danger of being drowned at sea. It was bedtime, when the captain of the vessel came to him, and said: "It will soon be all over with us." "Very well," answered the duke, "then I shall not take off my boots."—*Table-Talk of Samuel Rogers*.

'His coolness in danger,' says the *Edinburgh Review* in an article on Brialmont's *Life of the Duke of Wellington*, 'and his personal escapes, are as striking attributes of the individual man as his tactics are attributes of the general. During the battle of Talavera, Albuquerque sent him, by a staff-officer, a letter, informing him that Cuesta, the commander of the Spanish army in the action, was a traitor, and was actually playing into the enemy's hands. He was intently watching the progress of the action as the dispatch reached him; he took the letter, read it, and turning to the aid-de-camp, coolly said: "Very well, colonel, you may go back to your brigade." On another occasion, just before the siege of Rodrigo, when the proximity of the allies to Marmont's army placed them in considerable danger by reason of the non-arrival of their flank divisions, a Spanish general was astonished to find the English commander lying on the ground in front of his troops, serenely and imperturbably awaiting the issue of the peril. "Well, general," said the Spaniard, "you are here with two weak divisions, and you seem to be quite at your ease; it is enough to put one in a fever." "I have done the best," the duke replied, "that could be done according to my own judgment, and hence it is that I don't disturb myself, either about the enemy in my front, or about what they may say in England." On several instances he very narrowly escaped being taken prisoner. Once at Talavera, in the midst of the action; once, just before the battle of Maya, being surprised by a party of French while looking at his maps; once at Quatre Bras, again during the battle. In the latter action, as he was carried away on the tide of a retreating body of young troops, the French lancers suddenly charged on its flank, and his only chance was in his horse's speed. "He arrived," Mr Gleig writes, "hotly pursued, at the edge of a ditch, within which the 92d Highlanders were lying, and the points of their bayonets bristled over the edge. He called out to them as he approached, "Lie down, men!" and the order was obeyed, whereupon he leaped his horse across the ditch, and immediately pulled up with a smile on his countenance." . . . . The duke's success no doubt was largely owing to his special mastery of details. In camp and on the march, equally methodical, he relied for victory on the preparations he had made. From the smallest incident to the greatest, he made himself acquainted with all that could affect the organisation of his army, and the comfort of his men individually. Even the cooking of mess-dinners was his constant care; in the Crimea, he would almost have supplanted Soyer. Upon the first publication of his *Dispatches*, one of his friends said to him, on reading the records of his Indian campaigns: "It seems to me, duke, that your chief business in India was to procure rice and bullocks." "And so it was," replied Wellington; "for if I had rice and bullocks, I had men, and if I had men, I knew I could beat the enemy." Like Napoleon, though with a vast difference in scale, his army was the work of his own hands. "Its staff," Mr Gleig writes, "its commissariat, its siege apparatus, its bridge equipment, its means of transport, its intelligence department, its knowledge of outpost and other duties, were all of his creation." This mental activity, of course, widened the range of his achievements. Like Cæsar, who is said to have written an essay on Latin rhetoric as he was crossing the Alps, Wellington passed the night previous to one of his battles in devising a scheme for a Portuguese bank.'

# SEPTEMBER 15.

St Nicomedes, martyr, about 90. St Nicetas, martyr, 4th century. St John the Dwarf, anchoret of Scete. St Aper or Evre, bishop and confessor, 5th century. St Aicard or Achart, abbot and confessor, about 687.

*Born.*—Jean Sylvain Bailly, distinguished astronomer, 1736, *Paris;* James Fenimore Cooper, American novelist, 1789, *Burlington, New Jersey;* John, Lord Campbell, chancellor of England, 1779, *Cupar-in-Fife.*

*Died.*—Philip of Austria, father of Charles V., 1506; Sir Thomas Overbury, poisoned in the Tower, 1613; Lady Arabella Stuart, 1615; Richard Boyle, Earl of Cork, eminent statesman, 1643, *Youghal;* Sidney, Earl of Godolphin, premier to Queen Anne, 1712, *St Albans;* Abbé Terrasson, translator of Diodorus Siculus, 1750; General Lazarus Hoche, French commander, 1797, *Wetzlar;* William Huskisson, distinguished politician and economist, killed at the opening of the Liverpool and Manchester Railway, 1830; I. K. Brunel, eminent civil engineer, 1859, *Westminster.*

## ROMANCE OF THE LADY ARABELLA.

Although Lady Arabella Stuart plays no very prominent part amid the public characters of her time, her history presents a series of romantic incidents and disasters, scarcely surpassed even by those of her celebrated relative, Mary Queen of Scots. She was the daughter of Charles Stuart, Earl of Lennox, younger brother of Lord Darnley, and stood thus next in succession to the crown, after her cousin, James VI., through their common ancestor Margaret Tudor, sister of Henry VIII., and grandmother, by her second marriage with the Earl of Angus, to Lord Darnley. Brought up in England, Arabella excited the watchful care and jealousy of Elizabeth, who, on the king of Scotland proposing to marry her to Lord Esmé Stuart, interposed to prevent the match, and afterwards imprisoned her, on hearing of her intention to wed a son of the Earl of Northumberland. Meantime she formed the subject of eager aspirations on the continent, the pope entertaining the idea of uniting her to some Catholic prince, and setting her up as the legitimate heir to the English throne. Among her suitors appear the Duke of Parma, and the Prince of Farnese; but it would seem that the idea which prevailed abroad of her predilections for the old religion was quite unfounded. Shortly after the accession of James I., a clumsy conspiracy, in which Sir Walter Raleigh is said to have been concerned, was formed for raising her to the throne. It proved quite abortive, and does not seem to have been shared in by Arabella herself, who continued to live on amicable terms with the court, and had a yearly pension allowed her by James. At last, about 1609, when she could not have been less than thirty-three years of age, she formed an attachment to William Seymour, son of Lord Beauchamp, and a private marriage took place. On this being discovered, Seymour was committed to the Tower for his presumption in allying himself with a member of the royal family, and his wife was detained a prisoner in the house of Sir Thomas Parry, in Lambeth. The wedded pair, nevertheless, managed to correspond with each other; whereupon, it was resolved to remove Arabella to a distance, and place her under the custody of the bishop of Durham. Her northward journey commenced, but, either feeling or affecting indisposition, she advanced no further than Highgate, where she was allowed to remain under surveillance, in the house of Mr Conyers. A plot to effect her escape was now concocted on the part of herself and Seymour.

The subsequent mishaps of this ill-starred couple read like a tale of romance. One afternoon she contrived to obtain leave from her female guardian at Highgate to pay a visit to her husband, on the plea of seeing him for the last time. She then disguised herself in man's clothes, with a doublet, boots, and rapier, and proceeded with a gentleman named Markham to a little inn, where they obtained horses. On arriving there, she looked so pale and exhausted that the ostler who held her stirrup, declared the gentleman would never hold out to London. The ride, however, revived her, and she reached Blackwall in safety, where she found a boat waiting. Mr Seymour, who was to have joined her here, had not yet arrived, and, in opposition to her earnest entreaties, her attendants insisted on pushing off, saying that he would be sure to follow them. They then crossed over towards Woolwich, pulled down from thence to Gravesend, and afterwards, by the promise of double fare, induced the rowers to take them to Lee, which they reached just as day was breaking. A French vessel was descried lying at anchor for them about a mile beyond, and Arabella, who again wished to abide here her husband's arrival, was forced on board by the importunity of her followers. In the meantime, Seymour, disguised in a wig and black cloak, had walked out of his lodgings at the west door of the Tower, and followed a cart which was returning after having deposited a load of wood. He proceeded by the Tower wharf to the iron gate, and finding a boat there lying for him, dropped down the river to Lee, with an attendant. Here he found the French ship gone; but, imagining that a vessel which he saw under sail was the craft in question, he hired a fisherman for twenty shillings to convey him thither. The disappointment of the luckless husband may be imagined when he discovered that this was not the ship he was in quest of. He then made for another, which proved to be from Newcastle, and an offer of £40 induced the master to convey Seymour to Calais, from which he proceeded safely into Flanders. The vessel conveying Arabella was overtaken off Calais harbour by a pink despatched by the English authorities on hearing of her flight, and she was conveyed back to London, subjected to an examination, and committed to the Tower. She professed great indifference to her fate, and only expressed anxiety for the safety of her husband.

To the end of her days Arabella Stuart remained a prisoner. She died in confinement in 1615, and rumours were circulated of her having fallen a victim to poison; but these would seem to have been wholly unwarranted. Such unmerited misfortunes did her near relationship to the crown entail. Her husband afterwards procured his pardon, distinguished himself by his loyalty to Charles I. during the civil wars, and, surviving the Restoration, was invested by Charles II. with the dukedom of Somerset, the forfeited title of his ancestor, the Protector.

---

## FIRST BALLOON ASCENTS IN BRITAIN:

### LUNARDI—TYTLER.

The inventions and discoveries ultimately proving least beneficial to mankind, have generally been received with greater warmth and enthusiasm than those of a more useful character. The aëronautical experiments of the Montgolfiers and others, in France, created an immense excitement, which soon found its way across the Channel to the shores of England. Horace Walpole, writing at the close of 1783, says: 'Balloons occupy senators, philosophers, ladies, everybody.' While some entirely disbelieved the accounts of men, floating, as it were, in the regions of upper air, others indulged in the wildest speculations. The author of a poem, entitled *The Air Balloon, or Flying Mortal*, published early in 1784, exclaims:

'How few the worldly evils now I dread,
No more confined this narrow earth to tread!

Should fire or water spread destruction drear,
Or earthquake shake this sublunary sphere,
In air-balloon to distant realms I fly,
And leave the creeping world to sink and die.'

Besides doubt and wonder, an unpleasant feeling of insecurity prevailed over England at the time. The balloon was a French invention: might it not be used as a means of invasion by the natural enemies of the British race! A caricature, published in 1784, is entitled *Montgolfier in the Clouds, constructing Air Balloons for the Grand Monarque.* In this, the French inventor is represented blowing soap-bubbles, and saying: 'O by Gar, dis be de grand invention. Dis will immortalise my king, my country, and myself. We will declare the war against our enimie; we will made des English quake, by Gar. We will inspect their camp, we will intercept their fleet, and we will set fire to their dock-yards, and, by Gar, we will take Gibraltar, in de air-balloon; and when we have conquer de English, den we conquer de other countrie, and make them all colonie to de Grand Monarque.'

Several small balloons had been sent up from various parts of England; but no person, adventurous enough to explore the realms of air, had ascended, till Vincent Lunardi, a youthful attaché of the Neapolitan embassy, made the first ascent in England from the Artillery Ground, at Moorfields, September 15, 1784. It was Lunardi's original intention to ascend from the garden of Chelsea Hospital, having acquired permission to do so; but the permission was subsequently rescinded, on account of a riot caused by another balloon adventurer, a Frenchman named De Moret. This man proposed to ascend from a tea-garden, in the Five-fields, a place now known by the general term of Belgravia. His balloon seems, from an engraving of the period, to have resembled one of the large, old-fashioned, wooden summer-houses still to be seen in suburban gardens; and the car was provided with wheels, so that it could, if required, be used as a travelling-carriage! Whether he ever intended to attempt an ascension in such an unwieldy machine, has never been clearly ascertained. The balloon, such as it was, was constructed on the Montgolfier, or fire, principle—that is to say, the ascending agent was air rarefied by the application of artificial heat. De Moret, having collected a considerable sum of money, was preparing for an ascent on the 10th of August 1784, when his machine caught fire, and was burned, the unruly mob revenging their disappointment by destroying the adjoining property. The adventurer, however, made a timely escape, and a caricature of the day represents him flying off to Ostend with a bag of British guineas, leaving the Stockwell Ghost, the Bottle Conjuror, Elizabeth Canning, Mary Toft, and other cheats, enveloped in the smoke of his burning balloon.

The authorities, being apprehensive that, in case of failure, Chelsea Hospital might be destroyed in a similar riot, rescinded their permission; but Lunardi was, eventually, accommodated with the use of the Artillery Ground, the members of the City Artillery Company being under arms, to protect their property. When the eventful day arrived, Moorfields, then an open space of ground, was thronged by a dense mob of spectators; such a crowd had never previously been collected in London. As the morning hours wore away, silent expectation was followed by impatient clamour, soon succeeded by yells of angry threatenings, to be in a moment changed to loud acclamations of applause, as the balloon rose majestically into the air. Lunardi himself said: 'The effect was that of a miracle on the multitude which surrounded the place, and they passed from incredulity and menace into the most extravagant expressions of approbation and joy.'

Lunardi first touched earth in a field at North Mimms; after lightening the balloon, he again rose in the air, and finally descended in the parish of Standon, near Ware, in Hertfordshire. Some labourers, who were working close by, were so

LUNARDI'S BALLOON.

frightened at the balloon, that no promises of reward would induce them to approach it; not even when a young woman had courageously set the example by taking hold of a cord, which the aëronaut had thrown out.

The adventurer came down from the clouds to find himself the hero of the day. He was presented at court, and at once became the fashion; wigs, coats, hats, and bonnets were named after him; and a very popular bow of bright scarlet ribbons, that had previously been called Gibraltar, from the heroic defence of that fortress, was now termed the Lunardi. By exhibiting his balloon at the Pantheon, he soon gained a large sum of money; and the popular applause might readily have turned the head of a less vain person than the impulsive Italian.

Mr Lunardi's publications exhibit him as a vain excitable young man, utterly carried away by the singularity of his position. He tells us how a woman dropped down dead through fright, caused by beholding his wondrous apparition in the air;

but, on the other hand, he saved a man's life, for a jury brought in a verdict of Not guilty on a notorious highwayman, that they might rush out of court to witness the balloon. When Lunardi arose, a cabinet council was engaged on most important state deliberations; but the king said: 'My lords, we shall have an opportunity of discussing this question at another time, but we may never again see poor Lunardi; so let us adjourn the council, and observe the balloon!'

Ignorance, combined with vanity, led Lunardi into some strange assertions. He professed to be able to lower his balloon, at pleasure, by using a kind of oar. When he subsequently ascended at Edinburgh, he affirmed that, at the height of 1100 feet, he saw the city of Glasgow, and also the town of Paisley, which are, at least, forty miles distant, with a hilly country between. The following paragraph from the *General Advertiser* of September 24, 1784, has a sly reference to these and the like allegations. 'As several of our correspondents seem to disbelieve that part of Mr Lunardi's tale, wherein he states that he saw the neck of a quart bottle four miles' distance, all we can inform them on the subject is, that Mr Lunardi *was above lying*.'

Lunardi's success was, in all probability, due to the suggestions of another, rather than to his own scientific acquirements. His original intention was to have used a Montgolfier or fire balloon, the inherent perils of which would almost imperatively forbid a successful result. But the celebrated chemist, Dr George Fordyce, informed him of the buoyant nature of hydrogen gas, with the mode of its manufacture; and to this information Lunardi's successful ascents may be attributed. Three days before Lunardi ascended, Mr Sadler made an ineffectual attempt at Shotover Hill, near Oxford, but was defeated, by using a balloon on the Montgolfier principle.

It is generally supposed that Lunardi was the first person who ascended by means of a balloon in Great Britain, but he certainly was not. A very poor man, named James Tytler, who then lived in Edinburgh, supporting himself and family in the humblest style of garret or cottage life by the exercise of his pen, had this honour. He had effected an ascent at Edinburgh on the 27th of August 1784, just nineteen days previous to Lunardi. Tytler's ascent, however, was almost a failure, by his employing the dangerous and unmanageable Montgolfier principle. After several ineffectual attempts, Tytler, finding that he could not carry up his fire-stove with him, determined, in the maddening desperation of disappointment, to go without this his sole sustaining power. Jumping into his car, which was no other than a common crate used for packing earthenware, he and the balloon ascended from Comely Garden, and immediately afterwards fell in the Restalrig Road. For a wonder, Tytler was uninjured; and though he did not reach a greater altitude than three hundred feet, nor traverse a greater distance than half a mile, yet his name must ever be mentioned as that of the first Briton who ascended with a balloon, and the first man who ascended in Britain.

Tytler was the son of a clergyman of the Church of Scotland, and had been educated as a surgeon; but being of an eccentric and erratic genius, he adopted literature as a profession, and was the principal editor of the first edition of the *Encyclopædia Britannica*. Becoming embroiled in politics, he published a handbill of a seditious tendency, and consequently was compelled to seek a refuge in America, where he died in 1805, after conducting a newspaper at Salem, in New England, for several years.

A prophet acquires little honour in his own country. While poor Tytler was being overwhelmed by the coarse jeers of his compatriots, Lunardi came to Edinburgh in 1785, and was received with the utmost enthusiasm. His first ascent in Scotland was made from the garden of Heriot's Hospital, and he came down at Ceres, near Cupar, in Fife. The clergyman of the parish, who witnessed his descent, writing to an Edinburgh newspaper, says: 'As it' [the balloon] 'drew near the earth, and sailed along with a kind of awful grandeur and majesty, the sight gave much pleasure to such as knew what it was, but terribly alarmed such as were unacquainted with the nature of this celestial vehicle.' A writer in the *Glasgow Advertiser* thus describes the sensation caused by Lunardi's first ascent from that city: 'Many were amazingly affected. Some shed tears, and some fainted, while others insisted that he was in compact with the devil, and ought to be looked upon as a man reprobated by the Almighty.' The hospitality and attention Lunardi received in Scotland seems to have completely turned his weak head. When publicly entertained in Edinburgh, and asked to propose a toast, he gave, 'Lunardi, the favourite of the ladies!' to the infinite amusement of the assemblage. His last appearance in England, previous to his return to Italy, was as the inventor of what he termed a water-balloon, a sort of tin life-buoy, with which he made several excursions on the Thames.

## OPENING OF THE LIVERPOOL AND MANCHESTER RAILWAY.

One of the 'red-letter' days in the history of railways, a day that stamped the railway-system as a triumphant success, was marked by a catastrophe which threw gloom over an event in other ways most satisfactory. The Liverpool and Manchester Railway was the first on which the powers of the steam-locomotive for purposes of traction were fully established. On the Stockton and Darlington line, formed a few years earlier, traction by animal power, by fixed engines, and by locomotives, had all been tried; and the experience thereby obtained had determined George Stephenson to recommend the locomotive system for adoption on the Liverpool and Manchester line. When this railway was in progress, in 1829, the directors offered a premium of £500 for the best form of locomotive, to be determined by public competition, on conditions very clearly laid down. In October of that year the contest took place; and Mr Robert Stephenson's locomotive, *Rocket*, carried off the prize against Mr Hackworth's *Sanspareil*, and Messrs Braithwaite and Ericsson's *Novelty*. A period of eleven months then elapsed for the finishing of the railway and the manufacture of a store of locomotives and carriages.

On the 15th of September 1830, the Liverpool and Manchester Railway was opened with great ceremony. The Duke of Wellington, Sir Robert Peel, Mr Huskisson, and many other distinguished persons were invited. Eight locomotives, all built by Robert Stephenson, on the model of the *Rocket*, took part in the procession. The *Northumbrian* took the lead, drawing a splendid carriage, in which the duke, Sir Robert, and other distinguished visitors were seated. Each of the other locomotives drew four carriages; and the whole of the twenty-nine carriages conveyed six hundred persons. They formed eight distinct trains; the first one, with the more distinguished guests, having one line of rails to itself; and the other seven following each other on the second line. The procession, which started from Liverpool about eleven o'clock, was an exceedingly brilliant one, with the aid of flags, music, &c.; and the sides of the railway were lined with thousands of enthusiastic spectators. The trains went on past Wavertree Station, Olive Mount Cutting, Rainhill Bridge, the Sutton Incline, and the Sankey Viaduct, to Parkhurst. Here it was (seventeen miles from Liverpool) that the trains stopped to enable the locomotives to take in water; and here it was that the deplorable accident occurred, which threw a cloud over the brilliant scene. In order to afford the Duke of Wellington an opportunity of seeing the other parts of the procession, it was determined that the seven locomotives, with their trains, should pass him; his carriage, with the *Northumbrian*, being for a while stationary. Several gentlemen alighted from the carriages while the locomotives were taking in water. Mr Huskisson, who was one of them, went up to shake hands with the duke; and while they were together, the *Rocket* passed rapidly on the other line. The unfortunate gentleman, who happened to be in a weak state of health, became flurried, and ran to and fro in doubt as to the best means of escaping danger. The engine-driver endeavoured to stop the train in time, but without success; and Mr Huskisson, unable to escape, was knocked down by the *Rocket*, the wheels of which went over his leg and thigh. The same locomotive which had triumphed at the competition, now caused the death of the statesman. The directors deemed it necessary to complete the remainder of the journey to Manchester, as a means of shewing that the railway, in all its engineering elements, was thoroughly successful; but it was a sad procession for those who thought of the wounded statesman. He expired that same evening.

Mr Huskisson was born March 11, 1770. In 1790, he first entered government service, as private secretary to the British ambassador at Paris. In 1793, he was appointed to an office for managing the claims of French emigrants; in 1795, Under Secretary of State for War and the Colonies; in 1804, Secretary of the Treasury; and in 1807, he resumed the same office, after a short period in opposition. In 1814, he was made Chief Commissioner of Woods and Forests; in 1823, President of the Board of Trade and Treasurer of the Navy; and in 1829, Secretary of State for the Colonies. He had thus, during about forty years, rather a varied experience of official life. Mr Huskisson, in the House of Commons, was not a speaker of any great eloquence; but he is favourably remembered as having advocated a free-trade policy at a time when such policy had few advocates in parliament.

# SEPTEMBER 16.

**St Cornelius, pope and martyr, 252. St Cyprian, archbishop of Carthage, martyr, 258. Saints Lucia and Geminianus, martyrs, about 303. St Euphemia, virgin and martyr, about 307. St Ninian or Ninyas, bishop and confessor, and apostle of the southern Picts, 432. St Editha, virgin, 984.**

## ST CYPRIAN,

One of the most famous of the Latin fathers, and reputed to be second in point of eloquence only to Lactantius, was a native of Carthage, and became a convert to Christianity at an advanced period of life, having been led to renounce paganism through conversation with an aged presbyter, called Cecilius, whose name he adopted as an addition to his own. The enthusiasm which he displayed on behalf of his new faith caused him soon to be admitted as a priest, and, within less than a year afterwards, to be raised to the dignity of bishop of Carthage, as successor to Donatus. In the exercise of his office he manifested such zeal, that the pagans, in derision, styled him *Coprianus*, in allusion to a Greek term for filth; and on the commencement of the Christian persecution under the Emperor Decius, the heathen populace rushed into the market-place shouting: 'Cyprian to the lions! Cyprian to the wild-beasts!' The danger that threatened him seemed so imminent, that he deemed it expedient for a time to retire from Carthage, though in doing so he exposed himself to some severe animadversions from his brother-clergy of Rome for thus shrinking from the storm, and suffering his flock to perish. From his place of retreat, however, which seems to have been carefully concealed, he despatched numerous letters to guide and animate his people under their trials. At last, on an abatement of the persecution taking place, Cyprian returned to Carthage, and continued his episcopal ministrations with great zeal and success, till a fresh season of tribulation commenced for the church under the Emperor Valerian, in 257 A.D. On this occasion, the bishop of Carthage shewed no disposition to cower before the blast, but bravely remained at his post to encourage and strengthen his hearers. In the autumn of the last-mentioned year, he was himself apprehended, and brought before the African proconsul, who ordered him into banishment to the city of Curubis, about fifty miles from Carthage. After remaining there for about a twelvemonth, the expectation of still bloodier edicts arriving from Rome, caused him to be brought back to Carthage, and lodged for a time under surveillance in his own country-house near the city. On the reception of the fatal orders, the Proconsul Galerius Maximus caused Cyprian to be brought before him at his country-seat of Sextus, six miles from Carthage. The tide of popular opinion had now turned entirely in favour of the bishop, who, while a pestilence was raging in the city, had exerted himself with the most heroic ardour, both personally and by calling forth the co-operation of others, in relieving the sufferings and ministering to the necessities of the sick. A noble large-heartedness had also been shewn by him in proclaiming to his people the duty of assisting all sufferers in this terrible visitation, without regard to the circumstance of their being Christian or pagan. An immense and sympathising crowd accompanied him on the road to the proconsul's house. The proceedings before that functionary appear to have been of a very summary description, as Cyprian, on having replied to a few interrogations, and steadily refused to conform to the pagan ceremonies, was forthwith ordered to be beheaded. He was led a short distance into the country, to an extensive plain, planted with trees, which were ascended by numerous spectators, and was there put to death. His relics are said to have been exhumed in the beginning of the ninth century, by ambassadors of Charlemagne, on their return from a mission to Persia, and conveyed by them to France.

*Born.*—James Francis Stephens, entomologist, 1792, *Shoreham, Sussex.*

*Died.*—Pope Martin I., 655; Pope Victor III., 1087; Charles V. the Wise, king of France, 1380, *Vincennes;* Dean (John) Colet, 1519; Michael Baius, theologian, 1589, *Louvain;* James II., ex-king of England, 1701, *St Germains, France;* Gabriel Daniel Fahrenheit, constructor of thermometers, 1736; Allen, Earl Bathurst, statesman and man of letters, 1775; Louis XVIII., king of France, 1824.

## GABRIEL DANIEL FAHRENHEIT.

The name of Fahrenheit has been familiarised to a large part of mankind, in consequence of his invention of a thermometer, which has come into almost universal use.

Before the seventeenth century, men could only judge of the amount of heat prevailing at any place by their personal sensations. They could only speak of the weather as hot or very hot, as cold or very cold. In that century, there were several attempts made, by tubes containing oil, spirits of wine, and other substances, to establish a satisfactory means of measuring heat; but none of them could be considered as very successful, although both Halley and Newton applied their great minds to the subject. It was reserved for an obscure and poor man to give us the instrument which has since been found so specially serviceable for this purpose.

Fahrenheit was a native of Danzig, who, having failed in business as a merchant, and having a turn for mechanics and chemistry—possibly, that was what made him fail as a merchant—was fain to take to the making of thermometers for his bread. He at first made his thermometers with spirits of wine, but ere long became convinced that mercury was a more suitable article to be put in the tube; about the same time, finding Danzig a narrow field for his business, he removed to Amsterdam. There, about the year 1720, this patient, humble man completed the arrangement for a mercury-thermometer, very much as it has ever since been fashioned. His instruments were speedily spread throughout the world, everywhere carrying his name along with them. The basis of the plan of Fahrenheit's instrument, was to mark on the tube the two points at which, respectively, water is congealed and boiled, and to graduate the space between. Through a chain of circumstances, which it would here be tedious to explain, he put 180° between these two points, commencing, however, with 32°, because he found that the mercury descended 32° more, before coming to what he thought the *extreme* cold resulting from a mixture of ice, water, and sal-ammoniac. The Royal Society gladly received from Fahrenheit accounts of his experiments, the value of which it acknowledged by making him one of its members (a fact overlooked in all his biographies); and in 1724, he published a distinct treatise on the subject. Celsius, of Stockholm, soon after suggested the obviously more rational graduation of a hundred degrees between freezing and boiling points—the Centigrade Thermometer: the Frenchman, Reaumur, proposed another graduation, which has been accepted by his countrymen. But with by far the larger part of civilised mankind, Fahrenheit's scale is the only one in use, and probably will be so for a long time to come. To speak, accordingly, of 32° as freezing, of 55° as temperate, 96° as blood-heat, and 212° as the boiling-point, is part of the ordinary habits of Englishmen all over the world. Very true, that the zero of Fahrenheit's scale is a solecism, since it does *not* mark the extreme to which heat can be abstracted. This little blemish, however, seems never to have been found of any practical consequence. The arctic voyagers of the last forty years, have all persisted in describing certain low temperatures as below zero of Fahrenheit, the said degrees of temperature being such as the Amsterdam thermometer-maker never dreamed of, as being part of the existing system of things.

It is a pity that we know so little of the personal history of this remarkable man. There is even some doubt as to the year of his death; some authors placing it in 1740.

## ORDERS OF A SCHOOL IN THE SIXTEENTH CENTURY.

The statutes which Dean Colet concocted for St Paul's School, at its founding in the early part of the sixteenth century, afford a picture of his mind, and in fact of the times in which he lived. 'The children,' he says, 'shall come into the school at seven of the clock, both winter and summer, and tarry there until eleven; and return against one of the clock, and depart at five. In the school, no time in the year, they shall use tallow candle in nowise, at the cost of their friends. Also, I will they bring no meat nor drink, nor bottle, nor use in the school no breakfasts, nor drinkings, in the time of learning, in nowise. I will they use no cock-fightings, nor riding about of victory, nor disputing at St Bartholomew, which is but foolish babbling and loss of time.' There were to be no holidays granted at desire, unless for the king, or a bishop. The studies for the youth were Erasmus's *Copia;* Lactantius, Prudentius, and a few such authors; no classic is mentioned; yet the learned dean professes his zeal for 'the true Latin speech;' adding: 'all barbary, all corruption, all Latin adulterate, which ignorant blind fools brought into this world, and with the same hath distained and poisoned the old Latin speech, and the *veray* Roman tongue which in the time of Sallust and Virgil was used—I say that filthiness and all such *abusion,* which the later blind world brought in, which more rather may be called *Bloterature* than Literature, I utterly banish and exclude out of this school.' *

* Extracted into Dibdin's *Bibliomania,* i. 15, from Knight's *Life of Colet.*

# SEPTEMBER 17.

**Saints Socrates and Stephen, martyrs, beginning of 4th century. St Rouin, Rodingus, or Chrodingus, abbot of Beaulieu, about 680. St Lambert, bishop of Maestricht, and patron of Liege, martyr, 709. St Columba, virgin and martyr, 853. St Hildegardis, virgin and abbess, 1179.**

*Born.*—Jean Antoine, Marquis de Condorcet, distinguished mathematician, 1743, *Picardy;* Samuel Prout, painter in water-colours, 1783, *London.*

*Died.*—Henry Bullinger, Swiss Reformer, 1575, *Zurich;* Cardinal Robert Bellarmin, celebrated controversialist, 1621, *Rome;* Philip IV. of Spain, 1665; Dr John Kidd, mineralogical and medical writer, 1851, *Oxford.*

## CONDORCET.

Than the Marquis de Condorcet the French Revolution had no more sincere and enthusiastic promoter. Writing to Franklin, in 1788, concerning American affairs, he observes: 'The very name of king is hateful, and in France words are more than things. I see with pain that the aristocratic spirit seeks to introduce itself among you in spite of so many wise precautions. At this moment it is throwing everything into confusion here. Priests, magistrates, nobles, all unite against the poor citizens.' When 'the poor citizens' came into power, and proscribed those who served them, Condorcet's faith in democracy remained unaffected. In the words of Lamartine, 'the hope of the philosopher survived the despair of the citizen. He knew that the passions are fleeting, and that reason is eternal. He confessed it, even as the astronomer confesses the star in its eclipse.'

Condorcet was born in Picardy in 1743. Early in life he distinguished himself as a mathematician, and his labours in the development of the differential and integral calculus, will preserve his name in the history of science. Associating with Voltaire, Helvetius, and D'Alembert, he became a sharer in their opinions, and a social reformer with an almost fanatical abhorrence of the present and the past, and with an invincible assurance in a glorious destiny for humanity in the future. The outbreak of the revolution was to him as the dawn of this new era when old wrongs should pass away and justice and goodness should rule the world. He wrote for the revolutionary newspapers, and was an indefatigable member of the Jacobin club, but he was less effective with his tongue than his pen. A cold and impassive exterior, a stoical Roman countenance, imperfectly expressed the fiery energy of his heart, and caused D'Alembert to describe him as 'a volcano covered with snow.' When the rough and bloody business of the revolution came on, he was unable, either from timidity or gentle breeding, to hold his own against the desperadoes who rose uppermost. During the violent struggle between the Girondist and Mountain party, he took a decided part with neither, provoking Madame Roland to write of him, 'the genius of Condorcet is equal to the comprehension of the greatest truths, but he has no other characteristic besides fear. It may be said of his understanding combined with his person, that he is a fine spirit absorbed in cotton. Thus, after having deduced a principle or demonstrated a fact in the Assembly, he would give a vote decidedly opposite, overawed by the thunder of the tribunes, armed with insults and lavish of menaces. Such men should be employed to write, but never permitted to act.' This mingling of courage with gentleness and irresolution caused him, says Carlyle, 'to be styled, in irreverent language, *mouton enragé*—peaceablest of creatures bitten rabid.'

Robespierre, in July 1793, issued a decree of accusation against Condorcet. At the entreaty of his wife he hid himself in an attic in an obscure quarter of Paris, and there remained for eight months without once venturing abroad. He relieved the weariness of his confinement by writing a treatise on his favourite idea, *The Perfectibility of the Human Race;* and had he been able to endure restraint for a few months longer, he would have been saved; but he grew anxious for the safety of the good woman who risked her life in giving him shelter, and the first verdure of the trees of the Luxembourg, of which he had a glimpse from his window, brought on an overpowering desire for fresh air and exercise. He escaped into the streets, passed the barriers, and wandered among thickets and stone-quarries in the outskirts of Paris. Wounded with a fall, and half-dead with hunger and fatigue, he entered a cabaret in the village of Clamart, and asked for an omelet. 'How many eggs will you have in it?' inquired the waiter. 'A dozen,' replied the starving philosopher, ignorant of the proper dimensions of a working-man's breakfast. The extraordinary omelet excited suspicion. Some present requested to know his trade. He said, a carpenter, but his delicate hands belied him. He was searched, and a Latin *Horace* and an elegant pocket-book furnished unquestionable evidence that he was a skulking aristocrat. He was forthwith arrested, and marched off to prison at Bourg-la-Reine. On the way, he fainted with exhaustion, and was set on a peasant's horse. Flung into a damp cell, he was found dead on the floor next morning, 24th March 1794. He had saved his neck from the guillotine by a dose of poison he always carried about with him in case of such an emergency.

Condorcet's works have been collected and published in twenty-one volumes. The Marquise de Condorcet long survived her husband. She was one of the most beautiful and accomplished women of her day, and distinguished herself by an elegant and correct translation into French of Adam Smith's *Theory of the Moral Sentiments.*

## CURIOUS TESTAMENTARY DIRECTIONS ABOUT THE BODY.

Sir Lewis Clifford, a member of the senior branch of this ancient and distinguished family, who lived in the reign of Henry IV., became a Protestant, or, to use the language of an ancient writer, was 'seduced by those zealots of that time, called Lollards (amongst which he was one of the chief); but being at length sensible of those schismatical tenets, he confessed his error to Thomas Arundel, archbishop of Canterbury, and did cordially repent.' By way of atoning for his error, he left the following directions respecting his burial, in his last will, which begins thus:—'In nomine Patris et Filii et Spiritus Sancti, Amen. The sevententhe day of September, the yer of our Lord Jesu Christ, a thousand four hundred and four, I Lowys Clyftorth, fals and traytor to my Lord God, and to alle the blessed company of Hevene, and unworthi to be clepyd Cristen man, make and ordeyn my testament and my last wille in this manere.—At the begynnynge, I most unworthi and Goddys traytour, recommaund my wretchid and synfule sowle hooly to the grace and to the mercy of the blessful Trynytie; and my wretchid careyne to be beryed in the ferthest corner of the chirche-zerd, in which pariche my wretchid soule departeth fro my body. And I prey and charge my survivors and myne executors, as they wollen answere to fore God, and as all myne hoole trest in this matere is in them, that on my stinking careyne be neyther leyd clothe of gold ne of silke, but a black clothe, and a taper at myne hed, and another at my fete; ne stone ne other thinge, whereby eny man may witte where my stinking careyne liggeth. And to that chirche do myne executors all thingis, which owen duly in such caas to be don, without eny more cost saaf to pore men. And also, I prey my survivors and myne executors, that eny dette that eny man kan axe me by true title, that hit be payd. And yf eny man can trewly say, that I have don hym eny harme in body or in good, that ye make largely his gree whyles the goodys wole stretche. And I wole alsoe, that none of myne executors meddle or mynystre eny thinge of my goodys withoutyn avyse and consent of my survivors or of sum of hem.'

The rest of the will is in Latin, and contains Sir Lewis's directions for the disposal of his property.

---

## THE GERMAN PRINCESS.

Two hundred years ago, all London interested itself in the sayings and doings of a sharp-witted adventuress, known as 'the German Princess.' Mary Moders was the daughter of a Canterbury fiddler. After serving as waiting-woman to a lady travelling on the continent, and acquiring a smattering of foreign languages, she returned to England with a determination to turn her talents to account in the metropolis, where, on arriving, she took up her quarters at 'the Exchange Tavern, next the Stocks,' kept by a Mr King. Taking her hostess into confidence, she confessed that she was Henrietta Maria de Wolway, the only daughter and heiress of John de Wolway, Earl of Roscia, in Colonia, Germany, and had fled from home to avoid a marriage with an old count. If Mr King and his wife had any doubts as to the truth of her story, they were reassured by the receipt of a letter from the earl's steward, thanking them for the kindness they had shewn to his young mistress.

Mrs King had a brother, John Carleton, of the Middle Temple, whom she soon introduced to her interesting guest as a young nobleman. He played his part well, plied the mock-princess with presents, took her in his coach to Holloway and Islington, and vowed himself the victim of disinterested love. On Easter-Day, he proposed to take her to St Paul's, 'to hear the organs and very excellent anthems performed by rare voices;' but, instead of going there, he persuaded the lady to accompany him to Great St Bartholomew's Church, where he had a clergyman ready, and Miss Moders became Mrs Carleton, to the great rejoicing of his relatives. After the wedding, the happy couple went to Barnet for a couple of days, after which they returned, and to make assurance doubly sure, were re-married by licence, and went home to Durham Yard.

For a time all went smoothly enough, although the newly-made Benedict found his wife's notions of economy more befitting a princess than the spouse of a younger brother. As weeks, however, passed by without the Carletons deriving any of the expected benefits from the great match, they grew suspicious; good-natured friends, taken into the secret, expressed their doubts of the genuineness of Mrs John Carleton, and set inquiries on foot. Before long, old Carleton received a letter from Dover, in which his daughter-in-law was stigmatised as the greatest cheat in the world, having already two husbands living in that town, where she had been tried for bigamy, and only escaped conviction by preventing her real husband from putting in an appearance at the trial. Great was the indignation of the family at having their ambitious dream dispelled so rudely. Carleton père, at the head of a posse of male and female friends, marched to Durham Yard, and, as soon as they gained admittance, set upon the offender, knocked her down, despoiled her of all her counterfeit rings, false pearls, and gilded brass-wire worked bracelets, and left her almost as bare as Mother Eve ere the invention of the apron. She strenuously denied her identity with the Dover damsel, but was taken before the magistrates, and committed to the Gatehouse, at Westminster, to await her trial for bigamy. Here for six weeks she held her levees, and exercised her wit in wordy warfare with her visitors. When one complimented her upon her breeding and education, she replied: 'I have left that in the city amongst my kindred, because they want it;' and upon a gentleman observing that 'marrying and hanging went by destiny,' told him, she had received marriage from the destinies, and probably he might receive hanging. Among her visitors were Pepys and his friend Creed.

Upon the 4th of June 1663, our heroine was brought up at the Old Bailey, before the Lord Chief-Justice of Common Pleas, the lord mayor, and aldermen. If the account of the trial contained in *The Great Tryal and Arraignment of the late Distressed Lady, otherwise called the late German Princess*, be correct, the result was a foregone conclusion. She was indicted in the name of Mary Moders, for marrying John Carleton, having two husbands, Ford and Stedman, alive at the time. The prosecution failed to prove either of the marriages, and one incident occurred which must have told greatly in her favour. 'There came in a bricklayer with a pretended interest that she was his wife; but Providence or policy ordered it another way. There was a fair gentlewoman, standing at the bar by her, much like unto her, to whom he addressed himself, saying: "This is my wife;" to which the judge said: "Are you sure she is yours?" and the old man, taking his spectacles out of his pocket, looked her in the face again, and said: "Yes; she is my wife, for I saw her in the street the other day." Then said the lady: "Good, my lord, observe this doting fellow's words, and mark his mistake, for he doth not know me here with his four eyes; how then is it possible that he should now know me with his two!" At which expression all the bench smiled. Again said she: "My lord, and all you grave senators, if you rightly behold my face, that I should match with such a simple piece of mortality!" Then the old fellow drew back, and said no more.'

The accused bore herself bravely at the bar, bewitching all auditors as she played with her fan, and defended herself in broken English. She insisted on her German birth, saying she came to England to better her fortunes—and if there was any fraud in the business, it lay on the other side; 'for they thought by marrying of me, to dignify themselves, and advance all their relations, and upon that account, were there any cheat, they cheated themselves.' She divided the witnesses against her into two classes—

those who came against her for want of wit, and those who appeared for want of money. The jury acquitted her, and when she applied for an order for the restoration of her jewelry, the judge told her she had a husband to see after them. The verdict seems to have pleased the public, and we find lady-loving Pepys recording, 'after church to Sir W. Batten's; where my Lady Batten inveighed mightily against the German Princess, and I as high in defence of her wit and spirit, and glad that she is cleared at the sessions.' The author of *An Encomiastick Poem*, after comparing his subject to divers famous ladies, proceeds to tell us that—

'Her most illustrious worth
Through all impediments of hate brake forth;
Which her detracters sought within a prison,
T' eclipse, whereby her fame 's the higher risen.
As gems i' th' dark do cast a brighter ray
Than when obstructed by the rival day;
So did the lustre of her mind appear
Through this obscure condition, more clear.
And when they thought by bringing to the bar
To gain her public shame, they raised her far
More noble trophies—she being cleared quite
Both by her innocence and excellent wit.'

Mr Carleton, however, refused to acknowledge his wife, and published his *Ultima Vale*, in which, after abusing her to his heart's content, he grows sentimental, and indites a poetical farewell to his 'perjured Maria;' whose next appearance before the public was as an actress in a play founded upon her own adventures. Mr Pepys records: '15 April 1664.—To the Duke's House, and there saw *The German Princess* acted by the woman herself; but never was anything so well done in earnest, worse performed in jest upon the stage.' The theatre failing her, Mary Carleton took to thieving, was detected, tried, and sentenced to transportation to Jamaica. By discovering a plot against the life of the captain of the convict-ship, she obtained her liberty upon arriving at Port Royal, but becoming tired of West-Indian life, she contrived to find her way back to England, and resumed her old life. For some time she appears to have done so with impunity, in one case succeeding in getting clear off with £600 worth of property belonging to a watchmaker. The manner of her arrest was curious. A brewer, named Freeman, having been robbed, employed Lowman, a keeper of the Marshalsea, to trace out the thieves. With this object in view, Lowman called at a house in New Spring Gardens, and there spied a gentlewoman walking in one of the rooms, two pair of stairs high, in her night-gown, with her maid waiting upon her. He presently enters the room, and spies three letters lying upon the table, casts his eye upon the superscription of one of them, directed to a prisoner of his; upon which the lady began to abuse him in no measured terms, and so drew him to look at her more closely than he had done, and thereby recognise her as Mrs Carleton. He at once took her into custody for the watch-robbery; she was tried at the Old Bailey, found guilty, and sentenced to death.

She was executed at Tyburn on the 22d of January 1672–3, with five young men, 'who could not, among them all, complete the number of 120 years.' She made a short exhortation to the people, sent some words of good advice to her husband, whose portrait she placed in her bosom at the last moment. Her body was given up to her friends, by whom it was interred in the churchyard of St Martin's, and 'thus,' says her biographer, 'exit German Princess, in the thirty-eighth year of her age, and the same month she was born in.'

In Luttrell's *Collection of Eulogies and Elegies*, there is preserved an 'Elegie on the famous and renowned Lady,' Madame Mary Carleton, which concludes with

HER EPITAPH.

Here lieth one was hurried hence,
To make the world a recompense
For actions wrought by wit and lust,
Whose closet now is in the dust.
Then let her sleep, for she hath wit
Will give disturbers hit for hit.

---

# SEPTEMBER 18.

St Ferreol, martyr, about 304. St Methodius, bishop of Tyre, martyr, 4th century. St Thomas of Villanova, confessor, archbishop of Valentia, 1555. St Joseph of Cupertino, confessor, 1663.

*Born.*—Trajan, Roman Emperor, 56 A.D.; Gilbert, Bishop Burnet, historian, 1643, *Edinburgh;* William Collins, artist, 1787, *London.*

*Died.*—Domitian, Roman emperor, slain 96 A.D.; Louis VII. of France, 1180, *Paris;* Hugo Vander Goes, Flemish painter, 1684; Matthew Prior, poet, 1721, *Wimpole, Cambridgeshire;* André Dacier, classic commentator, 1722, *Paris;* Olaf Swartz, eminent botanist, 1817, *Stockholm;* William Hazlitt, miscellaneous writer, 1830; Joseph Locke, eminent engineer, 1860, *Moffat.*

## THE EMPEROR DOMITIAN.

The obituary for this day includes the name of one of those monsters, who disgrace so frequently the annals of the ancient Roman empire. On 18th September, 96 A. D., the Emperor Domitian was assassinated by a band of conspirators, after having rendered himself for many years the terror and detestation of his subjects. The son of Vespasian, and the brother and successor of Titus, he exhibited in the commencement of his reign a great show of righteous severity, and came forward as a reformer of public morals. Several persons who had transgressed the laws of conjugal fidelity, as well as some vestal virgins who had violated their vows, were punished with death. It was not long, however, before his real character shewed itself, and he became a disgrace to humanity by his acts of cruelty and avarice. Cowardice and falsehood entered largely into his disposition, which, if we are to credit all the accounts that have descended to us, seems to have scarcely had a redeeming point. Multitudes of persons were put to death, either because the emperor desired their wealth, or from his having become apprehensive of their popularity or influence. Secret informers were encouraged, but philosophers and literary men were slaughtered or banished, though Martial and Silius Italicus could so far degrade poetry, as make it the vehicle for flattery of the imperial monster. A favourite amusement of his, it is said, was killing flies, in which he would spend whole hours, and nothing seemed to give him greater pleasure than to witness the effects of terror on his fellow-creatures. On one occasion, he invited formally the members of the senate to a grand feast, and caused them on their arrival to be ushered into a large hall, hung with black and lighted with funeral torches, such as only served to exhibit to the awe-struck guests an array of coffins, on which each read his own name. Whilst they contemplated this ghastly spectacle, a troop of horrid forms, habited like furies, burst into the apartment, each with a lighted torch in one hand, and a poniard in the other. After having terrified for some time the members of Rome's legislative body, these demon-masqueraders opened the door of the hall, through which the senators were only too happy to make a speedy exit. Who can doubt that the character of Domitian had as much of the madman as the wretch in its composition?

At length human patience was exhausted, and a conspiracy was formed for his destruction, in which his wife and some of his nearest friends were concerned. For a long time, the emperor had entertained a presentiment of his approaching end, and even of the hour and manner of his death. Becoming every day more and more fearful, he caused the galleries in which he walked to be lined with polished stones, so that he might see, as in a mirror, all that passed behind him. He never conversed with prisoners but alone and in secret, and it was his practice whilst he talked with them, to hold their chains in his hands. To inculcate on his servants a dread of compassing the death of their master, even with his own consent, he caused Epaphroditus to be put to death, because he had assisted Nero to commit suicide.

The evening before his death, some truffles were brought, which he directed to be laid aside till the next day, adding, '*If I am there;*' and then turning to his courtiers said, that the next day the moon would be made bloody in the sign of Aquarius, and an event would take place of which all the world should speak. In the middle of the night, he awoke in an agony of fear, and started from his bed. The following morning, he had a consultation with a soothsayer from Germany, regarding a flash of lightning; the seer predicted a revolution in the empire, and was forthwith ordered off to execution. In scratching a pimple on his forehead, Domitian drew a little blood, and exclaimed: 'Too happy should I be were this to compensate for all the blood that I cause to be shed!' He asked what o'clock it was, and as he had a dread of the fifth hour, his attendants informed him that the sixth had arrived. On hearing this he appeared reassured, as if all danger were past, and he was preparing to go to the bath, when he was stopped by Parthenius, the principal chamberlain, who informed him that a person demanded to speak with him on momentous business of state. He caused every one to retire, and entered his private closet. Here he found the person in question waiting for him, and whilst he listened with terror to the pretended revelation of some secret plot against himself, he was stabbed by this individual, and fell wounded to the ground. A band of conspirators, including the distinguished veteran Clodianus, Maximus a freedman, and Saturius the decurion of the palace, rushed in and despatched him with seven blows of a dagger. He was in the forty-fifth year of his age, and fifteenth of his reign. On receiving intelligence of his death, the senate elected Nerva as his successor.

## LANDING OF GEORGE I. IN ENGLAND.

The death of Queen Anne on the 1st of August 1714 had ended the dynasty of the Stuarts. Although she left a Tory ministry, understood to be well affected to the restoration of her brother James, the 'Pretender,' yet the parliamentary enactments for the succession of the House of Hanover, in accordance with the Protestant predilections of the people, were quietly carried out; and, on the 16th of September, the Elector of Hanover, now styled George I. of Great Britain, embarked for England, and landing at Greenwich two days after, in the evening, was there duly received by the lords of the Regency, who had been conducting the government since the queen's death. Next day, there was a great court held in the palace of Greenwich, at which the Lord Treasurer Oxford was barely permitted to kiss the king's hand, the Lord Chancellor Harcourt was turned out of office, and the Duke of Ormond was not even admitted to the royal presence. It was evident there was to be a complete change of administration under the new sovereign. What made the treatment experienced by Ormond the more galling, was that he had come in a style of uncommon splendour and parade as captain-general, to pay his respects to the king.

Although George I., as a man of fifty-four years of age and a foreigner, was not calculated to awaken much popular enthusiasm, he was received next day in London with all external demonstrations of honour. Two hundred coaches of nobles and great officials preceded his own. The city authorities met him at St Margaret's Hill, Southwark, in all their paraphernalia, to congratulate him on his taking possession of his kingdoms. There can be no doubt, that of those present, with loyalty on their lips, there were many ill affected to the new house; and of this the zealous friends of the Protestant succession must have been well aware. At the court held that day in St James's, the Whig Colonel Chudleigh, branded with the name of Jacobite Mr Charles Aldworth, M.P. for New Windsor; and a duel ensued in Marylebone Fields, where Mr Aldworth was killed.

So began a series of two reigns which were on the whole happy for England. The two monarchs were certainly men of a mediocre stamp, who had little power of engaging the affections of their subjects; but they had the good sense to leave the ministers who enjoyed the confidence of parliament to rule, contenting themselves with a quiet life amongst the mere routine matters of a court.

Walpole relates that on one of George I.'s journeys to Hanover, his coach broke down. At a distance in view was the château of a considerable German nobleman. The king sent to borrow assistance. The possessor came, conveyed the king to his house, and begged the honour of his majesty accepting a dinner while his carriage was repairing; and, while the dinner was preparing, begged leave to amuse his majesty with a collection of pictures, which he had formed in several tours to Italy. But what did the king see in one of the rooms, but an unknown portrait of a person in the robe and with the regalia of the sovereigns of Great Britain? George asked whom it represented. The nobleman replied, with much diffident but decent respect, that in various journeys to Rome, he had been acquainted with the Chevalier de St George, who had done him the honour of sending him that picture. 'Upon my word,' said the king, instantly, 'it is very like to the family.' It was impossible to remove the embarrassment of the proprietor with more good-breeding.

## FIRST DISMEMBERMENT OF POLAND.

The iniquitous partition of this country between the three powers of Russia, Prussia, and Austria, was first accomplished on the 18th September 1772. For many years previous, the distracted condition of the kingdom had rendered it but too easy and tempting a prey to such ambitious and active neighbours as the Empress Catherine and Frederick the Great.

A war was on the point of breaking out between Russia and Austria, and Prussia would have been unable to avoid being drawn into the conflict. It was the interest of Frederick at the time to preserve peace, and he accordingly sent his brother, Prince Henry of Prussia, to St Petersburg, to endeavour to bring about an adjustment of matters. Some overtures made to Frederick by the Prince of Kaunitz at the conference of Neustadt, and some expressions which escaped from Catherine, had induced Prince Henry to form the idea that a dismemberment of Poland might satisfy the ambitious aspirations of all the potentates, and prevent the contingency of war.

Austria, on her part, demanded that Russia should restore to the Turks the conquests which she had made from them during the late war, and insisted more especially on the reddition of Moldavia and Wallachia. Russia, on the other hand, far from shewing a disposition to be dictated to, claimed the right herself of exercising this privilege; and hostilities were about to commence, when Prince Henry of Prussia suggested to Catherine the project of dismembering Poland. The empress was at first astonished, and probably chagrined, at being expected to share with others what she already regarded as her own property. She condescended, nevertheless, after some reflection, to entertain the subject which had been mooted to her by the prince. It was agreed between them that Austria should be invited to accede to the arrangement; and in case of her refusing to do so, the king of Prussia engaged to furnish Russia with assistance against Austria.

This last-mentioned power was at that moment in alliance with Turkey, and by acceding to the proposed partition, laid herself open to the resentment of France; but, finding herself obliged to choose between partition and war, deemed it most advisable to adopt the former alternative. The plenipotentiaries of the three courts signed at St Petersburg, on 5th August 1772, the formal stipulations of the Partition Treaty. In this document, the boundaries of the territories which should be assigned in the division to each of the three powers were settled and reciprocally guaranteed. The actual execution of the dismemberment was deferred to September, on the 18th of which month it was completed. The Empress of Russia, by the same convention, bound herself to restore Moldavia and Wallachia to Turkey.

Since the previous year, the governments of Vienna and Berlin had been advancing their troops to the frontiers of Poland. The king of Prussia had carried off from Great Poland more than twelve thousand families, and sent them to people the barren sands of his hereditary territories. Austria had laid hold of the salt-mines, which supplied one of the most valuable sources of revenue to the Polish crown. Soon a manifesto was handed to King Stanislaus and the senate by the Austrian and Prussian ministers, declaring that their respective sovereigns had come to the resolution to make available certain ancient rights which they possessed over a portion of the Polish territory. Some days afterwards the envoy of the Empress Catherine made a similar declaration on the part of his mistress. The three powers specified subsequently in individual notes the provinces which they desired to appropriate in virtue of their pretended rights, and in pursuance of this announcement proceeded forthwith to take possession.

The king of Poland and his ministers protested in vain against this act of spoliation, and sought, but ineffectually, the assistance of those powers by whom the integrity of their territories had been assured. The leading powers of Western Europe, Great Britain and France, remained shamefully passive, and permitted a flagrant breach of the law of nations to be perpetrated almost without remonstrance. Too feeble, then, to offer any effectual resistance, and finding no help in any quarter, the unfortunate Stanislaus was compelled to accede to any terms which the trio of crowned robbers chose to impose. A diet summoned at Warsaw appointed a commission to conclude with the plenipotentiaries of the three sovereigns the necessary treaty of dismemberment. The convention was signed at Warsaw, and afterwards ratified in the Polish diet. Of the territory thus seized and distributed, Austria received as her share about 1300 German square miles (15 to the degree), and a population of 700,000; Russia, 4157 square miles, and a population of 3,050,000; and Prussia, 1060 square miles, and a population of 1,150,000. It included about a third of the whole kingdom, and some of its richest provinces. The three plunderers—Catherine, Frederick, and Joseph—bound themselves in the most solemn manner to refrain from asserting any further claims on the provinces retained by Stanislaus. It is well known, however, how shamefully this compact was violated, and how, by a second partition in 1793, and a third in 1795, the remaining territories of Poland were divided between the three powers, her king deposed, and herself obliterated from the map of Europe.

# SEPTEMBER 19.

St Januarius, bishop of Benevento, and his companions, martyrs, 305. Saints Peleus, Pa-Termuthes, and companions, martyrs, beginning of 4th century. St Eustochius, bishop of Tours, 461. St Sequanus or Seine, abbot, about 580. St Theodore, archbishop of Canterbury, confessor, 690. St Lucy, virgin, 1090.

*Born.*—Henry III. of France, 1551, *Fontainebleau;* Robert Sanderson, bishop of Lincoln, and high-church divine, 1587, *Rotherham, Yorkshire;* Rev. William Kirby, entomologist, 1759, *Witnesham Hall, Suffolk;* Henry, Lord Brougham and Vaux, 1779, *Edinburgh.*

*Died.*—Charles Edward Poulett Thomson, Lord Sydenham, governor of Canada, 1841; Professor John P. Nichol, author of *The Architecture of the Heavens, &c.*, 1859, *Rothesay.*

## THE BATTLE OF POITIERS.

On 19th September 1356, the second great battle fought by the English on French soil, in assertion of their chimerical claim to the crown of that country, was won by the Black Prince, in the face, as at Crécy, of an overwhelming superiority of numbers. Whilst the army of the French king mustered sixty thousand horse alone, besides foot soldiers, the whole force of Edward, horse and foot together, did not exceed ten thousand men. The engagement was not of his own seeking, but forced upon him, in consequence of his having come unexpectedly on the rear of the French army in the neighbourhood of Poitiers, to which town he had advanced in the course of a devastating expedition from Guienne, without being aware of the proximity of the French monarch. Finding that the whole of the surrounding country swarmed with the enemy, and that his retreat was effectually cut off, his first feeling seems to have been one of consternation. 'God help us!' he exclaimed; and then added undauntedly: 'We must consider how we can best fight them.' A strong position amid hedges and vineyards was taken up by him, and as night was then approaching, the English troops prepared themselves for repose in expectation of to-morrow's battle. In the morning, King John marshalled his forces for the combat, but just as the engagement was about to commence, Cardinal Talleyrand, the pope's legate, arrived at the French camp, and obtained a reluctant permission to employ his offices, as mediator, to prevent bloodshed. The whole of that day (Sunday) was spent by him in trotting between the two armies, but to no effect. The English leader made the very liberal offer to John, to restore all the towns and castles which he had taken in the course of his campaign, to give up, unransomed, all his prisoners, and to bind himself by oath to refrain for seven years from bearing arms against the king of France. But the latter, confiding in his superiority of numbers, insisted on the Black Prince and a hundred of his best knights surrendering themselves prisoners, a proposition which Edward and his army indignantly rejected. Next morning at early dawn, the trumpets sounded for battle, and even then the indefatigable cardinal made another attempt to stay hostilities; but on riding over to the French camp for that purpose, he was cavalierly told to go back to where he came from, with the significant addition, that he had better bring no more treaties or pacifications, or it would be the worse for himself. Thus repulsed, the worthy prelate made his way to the English army, and told the Black Prince that he must do his best, as he had found it impossible to move the French king from his resolution. 'Then God defend the right!' replied Edward, and prepared at once for action. The attack was commenced by the French, a body of whose cavalry came charging down a narrow lane with the view of dislodging the English from their position; but they encountered such a galling fire from the archers posted behind the hedges, that they turned and fled in dismay. It was now Edward's turn to assail, and six hundred of his bowmen suddenly appeared on the flank and rear of John's second division, which was thrown into irretrievable confusion by the discharge of arrows. The English knights, with the prince at their head, next charged across the open plain upon the main body of the French army. A division of cavalry, under the Constable of France, for a time stood firm, but ere long was broken and dispersed, their leader and most of his knights being slain. A body of reserve, under the Duke of Orleans, fled shamefully without striking a blow. King John did his best to turn the fortune of the day, and, accompanied by his youngest son, Philip, a boy of sixteen, who fought by his side, he led upon foot a division of troops to the encounter. After having received two wounds in the face, and been thrown to the ground, he rose, and for a time defended himself manfully with his battle-axe against the crowd of assailants by whom he was surrounded. The brave monarch would certainly have been slain had not a French knight, named Sir Denis, who had been banished for killing a man in a fray, and in consequence joined the English service, burst through the press of combatants, and exclaimed to John in French: 'Sire, surrender.' The king, who now felt that his position was desperate, replied: 'To whom shall I surrender? Where is my cousin, the Prince of Wales?' 'He is not here,' answered Sir Denis; 'but surrender to me, and I will conduct you to him.' 'But who are you?' rejoined the king. 'Denis de Morbecque,' was the reply; 'a knight of Artois; but I serve the king of England because I cannot belong to France, having forfeited all I had there.' 'I surrender to you,' said John, extending his right-hand glove; but this submission was almost too late to save his life, for the English were disputing with Sir Denis and the Gascons the honour of his capture, and the French king was in the utmost danger from their violence. At last, Earl Warwick and Lord Cobham came up, and with every demonstration of respect conducted John and his son Philip to the Black Prince, who received them with the utmost courtesy. He invited them to supper, waited himself at table on John, as his superior in age and rank, praised his valour and endeavoured by every means in his power to diminish the humiliation of the royal captive.

The day after the victory of Poitiers, the Black Prince set out on his march to Bordeaux, which he reached without meeting any resistance. He remained during the ensuing winter in that city; concluded a truce with the Dauphin, Charles, John's eldest son; and, in the spring of 1357, crossed over to England with the king and Prince Philip as the trophies of his prowess. A magnificent entrance was made into London, John being mounted on a cream-coloured charger, whilst the Prince of Wales rode by his side on a little black palfrey as his page. Doubtless the French king would have willingly dispensed with this ostentatious mode of respect. He was lodged as a prisoner in the Savoy Palace, and continued there till 1360, when, in consequence of the treaty of Bretigny, he was enabled to return to France. The stipulations of this compact having been broken by John's sons and nobles, he conceived himself bound in honour to surrender himself again a prisoner to England, and actually returned thither, when Edward III. received him with great affection, and assigned him again his old quarters in the Savoy. His motives in displaying so nice a sense of honour, a proceeding so unusual in those times, when oaths and treaties seemed made only to be broken, have been variously construed. In charity, however, and as affording a pleasing exception to the general maxims of the age, we may, in default of any positive evidence to the contrary, assume that John was really actuated by what most persons deemed then a gratuitous and romantic scruple. He did not long survive his second transference to the Savoy, and died there in April 1364.

## THE GREAT PLAGUE OF LONDON.

The week ending the 19th of September 1665, was that in which this memorable calamity reached its greatest destructiveness. It was on the 26th of the previous April that the first official notice announcing that the plague had established itself in the parish of St Giles-in-the-Fields, appeared in the form of an order of council, directing the precautions to be taken to arrest its progress. The evil had at this time been gradually gaining head during several weeks. Vague suspicions of danger had existed during the latter part of the previous year, and serious alarm was felt, which however gradually abated. But the suspicions proved to be too true ; the infection, believed to have been brought over from Holland, had established itself in the parish of St Giles, remained concealed during the winter, and began to shew itself in that and the adjoining parishes at the approach of spring, by the increase in their usual bills of mortality. At the date of the order of council just alluded to, there could be no longer any doubt that the parishes of St Giles, St Andrews, Holborn, and one or two others adjoining, were infected by the plague.

During the months of May and June, the infection spread in spite of all the precautions to arrest its progress, but, towards the end of the latter month, the general alarm was increased by the certainty that it had not only spread into the other parishes outside the walls, but that several fatal cases had occurred in the city. People now began to hurry out of town in great numbers, while it was yet easy to escape, for as soon as the infection had become general, the strictest measures were enforced to prevent any of the inhabitants leaving London, lest they might communicate the dreadful pestilence to the towns and villages in the country. One of the most interesting episodes in the thrilling narrative of Defoe is the story of the adventures of three men of Wapping, and the difficulties they encountered in seeking a place of refuge in the country to the north-east of London, during the period while the plague was at its height in the metropolis. The alarm in London was increased when, in July, the king with the court also fled, and took refuge in Salisbury, leaving the care of the capital to the Duke of Albemarle. The circumstance of the summer being unusually hot and calm, nourished and increased the disease. An extract or two from Defoe's narrative will give the best notion of the internal state of London at this melancholy period. Speaking of the month in which the court departed for Salisbury, he tells us that already 'the face of London was strangely altered—I mean the whole mass of buildings, city, liberties, suburbs, Westminster, Southwark, and altogether ; for, as to the particular part called the City, or within the walls, that was not yet much infected ; but, in the whole, the face of things, I say, was much altered ; sorrow and sadness sat upon every face, and though some part were not yet overwhelmed, yet all looked deeply concerned, and as we saw it apparently coming on, so every one looked on himself and his family as in the utmost danger: were it possible to represent those times exactly, to those that did not see them, and give the reader due ideas of the horror that everywhere presented itself, it must make just impressions upon their minds, and fill them with surprise. London might well be said to be all in tears ; the mourners did not go about the streets indeed, for nobody put on black, or made a formal dress of mourning for their nearest friends ; but the voice of mourning was truly heard in the streets ; the shrieks of women and children at the windows and doors of their houses, where their nearest relations were perhaps dying, or just dead, were so frequent to be heard, as we passed the streets, that it was enough to pierce the stoutest heart in the world to hear them. Tears and lamentations were seen almost in every house, especially in the first part of the visitation ; for towards the latter end, men's hearts were hardened, and death was so always before their eyes, that they did not so much concern themselves for the loss of their friends, expecting that themselves should be summoned the next hour.'

As the infection spread, and families under the slightest suspicion were shut up in their houses, the streets became deserted and overgrown with grass, trade and commerce ceased almost wholly, and, although many had succeeded in laying up stores in time, the town soon began to suffer from scarcity of provisions. This was felt the more as the stoppage of trade had thrown workmen and shopmen out of employment, and families reduced their numbers by dismissing many of their servants, so that a great mass of the population was thrown into a state of absolute destitution. 'This necessity of going out of our houses to buy provisions, was, in a great measure, the ruin of the whole city, for the people catched the distemper, on these occasions, one of another, and even the provisions themselves were often tainted, at least I have great reason to believe so ; and, therefore, I cannot say with satisfaction, what I know is repeated with great assurance, that the market-people, and such as brought provisions to town, were never infected. I am certain the butchers of Whitechapel, where the greatest part of the flesh-meat was killed, were dreadfully visited, and that at last to such a degree, that few of their shops were kept open, and those that remained of them killed their meat at Mile-end and that way, and brought it to market upon horses. . . . . It is true people used all possible precautions ; when any one bought a joint of meat in the market, they would not take it out of the butcher's hand, but took it off the hooks themselves. On the other hand, the butcher would not touch the money, but have it put into a pot full of vinegar, which he kept for that purpose. The buyer carried always small money to make up any odd sum, that they might take no change. They carried bottles for scents and perfumes in their hands, and all the means that could be used were employed ; but then the poor could not do even these things, and they went at all hazards. Innumerable dismal stories we heard every day on this very account. Sometimes a man or woman dropped down dead in the very markets; for many people that had the plague upon them knew nothing of it till the inward gangrene had affected their vitals, and they died in a few moments; this caused that many died frequently in that manner in the street suddenly, without any warning; others, perhaps, had time to go to the next bulk or stall, or to any door or porch, and just sit down and die, as I have said before. These objects were so frequent in the streets, that when the plague came

PEST-HOUSE IN TOTHILL FIELDS, WESTMINSTER—FROM A PRINT BY HOLLAR.

to be very raging on one side, there was scarce any passing by the streets, but that several dead bodies would be lying here and there upon the ground; on the other hand, it is observable that though at first, the people would stop as they went along and call to the neighbours to come out on such an occasion, yet, afterwards, no notice was taken of them; but that if at any time we found a corpse lying, go across the way and not come near it; or if in a narrow lane or passage, go back again, and seek some other way to go on the business we were upon; and in those cases the corpse was always left, till the officers had notice to come and take them away; or till night, when the bearers attending the dead-cart would take them up, and carry them away. Nor did those undaunted creatures, who performed these offices, fail to search their pockets, and sometimes strip off their clothes if they were well dressed, as sometimes they were, and carry off what they could get.'

As the plague increased in intensity, the markets themselves were abandoned, and the country-people brought their provisions to places appointed in the fields outside the town, where the citizens went to purchase them with extraordinary precautions. There were stations of this kind in Spitalfields, at St George's Fields in Southwark, in Bunhill-fields, and especially at Islington. The appearance of the town became still more frightful as the summer advanced. 'It is scarcely credible,' continues the remarkable writer we are quoting, 'what dreadful cases happened in particular families every day; people, in the rage of the distemper, or in the torment of their rackings, which was indeed intolerable, running out of their own government, raving and distracted, and oftentimes laying violent hands upon themselves, throwing themselves out of their windows, shooting themselves, &c. Mothers murdering their own children, in their lunacy; some dying of mere grief, as a passion; some of mere fright and surprise, without any infection at all; others frightened into idiotism and foolish distractions; some into despair and lunacy; others into melancholy madness. The pain of the swelling was in particular very violent, and to some intolerable; the physicians and surgeons may be said to have tortured many poor creatures even to death. The swellings in some grew hard, and they applied violent drawing plasters or poultices to break them; and, if these did not do, they cut and scarified them in a terrible manner. In some, those swellings were made hard, partly by the force of the distemper, and partly by their being too violently drawn, and were so hard, that no instrument could cut them, and then they burned them with caustics, so that many died raving mad with the torment, and some in the very operation. In these distresses, some, for want of help to hold them down in their beds, or to look to them, laid hands upon themselves, as above; some broke out into the streets, perhaps naked, and would run directly down to the river, if they were not stopped by the watchmen, or other officers, and plunge themselves into the water, wherever they found it. It often pierced my very soul to hear the groans and cries of those who were thus tormented.' 'This running of distempered people about the streets,' Defoe adds, 'was very dismal, and the magistrates did their utmost to prevent it; but, as it was generally in the night, and always sudden, when such attempts were made, the officers could not be at hand to prevent it; and, even when any got out in the day, the officers appointed did not care to meddle with them, because, as they were all grievously infected, to be sure, when they were come to that height, so they were more than ordinarily infectious, and it was one of the most dangerous things that could be to touch them; on the other hand, they generally ran on, not knowing what they did, till they dropped down stark dead, or till they had exhausted their spirits so, as that they would fall and then die in perhaps half an hour or an hour; and, which was most piteous to hear, they were sure to come to themselves entirely in that half hour or hour, and then to make most grievous and piercing cries and lamentations, in the deep afflicting sense of the condition they were in.' 'After a while, the fury of the infection appeared to be so increased that, in short, they shut up no houses at all; it seemed enough that all the remedies of that kind had been used till they were found fruitless, and that the plague spread itself with an irresistible fury, so that it came at last to such violence, that the people sat still looking at one another, and seemed quite abandoned to despair. Whole streets seemed to be desolated, and not to be shut up only, but to be emptied of their inhabitants; doors were left open, windows stood shattering with the wind in empty houses, for want of people to shut them; in a word, people began to give up themselves to their fears, and to think that all regulations and methods were in vain, and that there was nothing to be hoped for but an universal desolation.'

In spite of this horrible state of things, the town was filled with men desperate in their wickedness; robbers and murderers prowled about in search of plunder, and riotous people, as if in despair, indulged more than ever in their vices. One house, in special, the Pye Tavern, at the end of Houndsditch, was the haunt of men who openly mocked at religion and death. In the middle of these scenes, two incidents occurred of an almost ludicrous character. Such is the story of the piper, which Defoe appears to have heard from one of the men who carted the dead to the burial-places, whose name was John Hayward, and in whose cart the accident happened. 'It was under this John Hayward's care,' he says, 'and within his bounds, that the story of the piper, with which people have made themselves so merry, happened, and he assured me that it was true. It is said that it was a blind piper; but, as John told me, the fellow was not blind, but an ignorant, weak, poor man, and usually went his rounds about ten o'clock at night, and went piping along from door to door, and the people usually took him in at public-houses where they knew him, and would give him drink and victuals, and sometimes farthings; and he in return would pipe and sing, and talk simply, which diverted the people, and thus he lived. It was but a very bad time for this diversion, while things were as I have told, yet the poor fellow went about as usual, but was almost starved; and when anybody asked how he did, he would answer, the dead cart had not taken him yet, but that they had promised to call for him next week. It happened one night that this poor fellow, whether somebody had given him too much drink or no (John Hayward said he had not drink in his house, but that they had given him a little more victuals than ordinary at a public-house in Colman Street), and the poor fellow having not usually had a bellyfull, or, perhaps, not a good while, was laid all along upon the top of a bulk or stall, and fast asleep, at a door in the street near London-wall, towards Cripplegate, and that, upon the same bulk or stall, the people of some house in the alley, of which the house was a corner, hearing a bell, which they always rung before the cart came, had laid a body really dead of the plague just by him, thinking, too, that this poor fellow had been a dead body as the other was, and laid there by some of the neighbours. Accordingly, when John Hayward with his bell and the cart came along, finding two dead bodies lie upon the stall, they took them up with the instrument they used, and threw them into the cart; and all this while the piper slept soundly. From hence they passed along, and took in other dead bodies, till, as honest John Hayward told me, they almost buried him alive in the cart, yet all this while he slept soundly; at length the cart came to the place where the bodies were to be thrown into the ground, which, as I do remember, was at Mountmill; and, as the cart usually stopped some time before they were ready to shoot out the melancholy load they had in it, as soon as the cart stopped, the fellow awaked, and struggled a little to get his head out from among the dead bodies, when, raising himself up in the cart, he called out, "Hey, where am I?" This frighted the fellow that attended about the work, but, after some pause, John Hayward recovering himself, said: "Lord bless us! there's somebody in the cart not quite dead!" So another called to him, and said: "Who are you?" The fellow answered: "I am the poor piper: where am I?" "Where are you!" says Hayward: "why, you are in the dead cart, and we are going to bury you." "But I an't dead, though, am I?" says the piper; which made them laugh a little, though, as John said, they were heartily frightened at first; so they helped the poor fellow down, and he went about his business.'

The number of deaths in the week ending the 19th September, was upwards of ten thousand. The weather then began to change, and the air became cooled and purified by the equinoctial winds. It took a good part of the winter, however, to allay the infection entirely, and it was only late in December that the people who had fled began to crowd back to the metropolis. The king and court only returned at the beginning of the following February. It has been calculated that considerably above a hundred thousand persons perished by this terrible visitation.

---

## SEPTEMBER 20.

St Eustachius and companions, martyrs, 2d century. St Agapetus, pope and confessor, 536.

---

*Born.*—Alexander the Great, Macedonian conqueror, 356 B.C., *Pella;* Emperor Antoninus Pius, 86 A.D.; Prince Arthur, elder brother of Henry VIII., 1486, *Winchester;* Maria Paulina Bonaparte, sister of Napoleon, 1780, *Ajaccio.*

*Died.*—Lucius Crassus, orator, 91 B.C., *Rome;* Owen Glendower, Welsh patriot, 1415, *Monnington;* John Gruter, eminent scholar and critic, 1527, *Heidelberg;* Jerome Cardan, physician, 1576; Lucius Carey, Lord Falkland, royalist statesman, killed at Newbury, 1643; John Gauden, bishop of Worcester, supposed author of the *Eikon Basilikê*, 1662; Charles VI., emperor of Germany, 1740, *Vienna;* William Hutton, self-taught man, and miscellaneous writer, 1815, *Birmingham;* Dr José Gaspar Rodriguez Francia, dictator of Paraguay, 1840; William Finden, engraver, 1852.

## OWEN GLENDOWER.

This celebrated chieftain, the Paladin of Welsh nationality, forms a prominent character during the reign of Henry IV., and has been immortalised by Shakspeare, in his play of that name. The injury inflicted on him by Lord Grey de Ruthyn, who treacherously maligned him to the king, and afterwards, under pretext of forfeiture, took possession of his lands, first prompted Glendower to seek, by force of arms, the redress denied him by the English government. Claiming to be the representative of the ancient Welsh kings, through his mother, who was lineally descended from Llewelyn, the last of these princes, he asserted his right to the crown of the principality, and, about 1400, raised the standard of insurrection. Among his own countrymen he enjoyed an unbounded influence, both from his enterprising and energetic character, and the reputation of possessing supernatural powers. This latter attribute our readers will remember is forcibly made use of by Shakspeare, in the discussion which he represents as taking place between Glendower and Hotspur.

*Glend.* I can call spirits from the vasty deep.
*Hots.* Why, so can I, or so can any man;
But will they come, when you do call for them?
*Glend.* Why, I can teach thee, cousin, to command the devil.
*Hots.* And I can teach thee, coz, to shame the devil,
By telling truth; tell truth, and shame the devil.

For some years, fortune favoured Glendower's arms, and having taken prisoner his enemy Lord Grey, he compelled him to ransom himself by the payment of a large sum of money, and give one of his daughters in marriage to his captor. A complaint was made by the English House of Commons, that the Welsh scholars had left the universities, and Welsh labourers, their masters, to join in the rebellion at home. With Sir Edmund Mortimer and the Northumbrian Percies, Glendower formed a close alliance, and so sanguine were the expectations of the confederacy, that they formally partitioned among themselves the whole dominions of Henry IV., the country to the west of the Severn being assigned as the share of the Welsh champion. After the battle of Shrewsbury, however, in which his allies, the Percies, were overthrown, his star of success appears to have waned, and having sustained two signal defeats in 1405, he was compelled for a time to wander up and down the country, with a few faithful followers, concealing himself in remote and untravelled districts. One of his places of refuge, a cave in Merionethshire, is known to this day, by the name of Ogof Owain or Owen's Cave. From this retreat he emerged to appear again at the head of an army, and being joined by a large body of French troops, whose king had formed an alliance with the Welsh insurgents, he made a devastating march through Glamorganshire, and advanced as far as the environs of Worcester. Here, he took up a strong position, and maintained for three days a succession of skirmishes with the royal troops, but was at last obliged, from want of supplies, to retire with his allies into Wales. No further enterprise of any importance was from this time attempted by him, but to the close of his life, he continued to harass the English by predatory incursions from the mountain-fastnesses. In the reign of Henry V., an offer of pardon was made by the king to Glendower and his followers, and negotiations were accordingly entered into, to be interrupted by the death of the aged chief; he expired peacefully on 20th September 1415, at the house of one of his daughters. A tombstone, but without any inscription, in the churchyard of Monnington-on-Wye, is said to mark his place of sepulture.

The very name of Glendower has a romantic interest attached to it, and we would gladly attribute to its owner all the shining qualities of a hero and patriot. Yet truth compels us to state, that, though brave, active, and vigilant, Glendower is charged with both cruelty and rapacity. The portrait of him, engraved in the *Archæologia* from his great seal, represents a man of majestic and intellectual mien, such as is generally attributed to those destined by nature to the leadership of their fellows.

## JEROME CARDAN.

One of the most voluminous authors that ever wrote, perhaps the ablest physician of his day, and certainly a man of the most decided and versatile genius, Jerome Cardan, or to designate him more properly by his Italian name, Girolamo Cardano, presents, in his singular history, a curious epitome of the sixteenth century, its eccentricities, energies, and modes of thought. The natural son of an eminent jurisconsult of Milan, he found himself thrown on the world as a waif and vagabond, and for many long and weary years had to battle with it in that character, though he ultimately succeeded in winning for himself a place amid the most favoured of its children. Few men who have risen to eminence and distinction, have had so protracted a period of probation as Cardan, or exhibited such perseverance and tenacity of purpose in prosecution of the fame to which they believed themselves destined. Though regularly educated at the universities of Pavia and Padua, his stain of illegitimacy prevented his admission as a member of the Milanese College of Physicians; and it was not till after he had gained, by his literary and medical abilities, some powerful friends, that he was enabled by their aid to force his entrance into that learned body. The appointment of professor of medicine at the university of Pavia, with a salary of two hundred and forty, afterwards raised to four hundred gold crowns, followed shortly after this victory, and from this time fortune may be said to have smiled on Cardan. His fame as a physician diffused itself not only over Italy, but throughout Europe. Pope Paul III. offered him a handsome pension if he would enter his service, and a proffer of an annual stipend of eight hundred crowns, with the maintenance of his household, was forwarded to him by the king of Denmark; but with neither of these invitations would he accord compliance, the uncertainty of the papal tenure of office, and the cold and moist climate of Scandinavia, being both insuperable objections. To another offer, however, which he received, he lent a more ready ear, and the journey which he undertook in consequence forms, to a Briton, more especially, one of the most curious episodes in the life of the Italian physician.

In the middle of the sixteenth century, the regency of the kingdom of Scotland was held by James Hamilton, Earl of Arran, whose weak and vacillating disposition was very markedly controlled by his more decided and energetic brother John, abbot of Paisley, and afterwards archbishop of St Andrews. The health of the latter, whose course of life was by no means consonant to his ecclesiastical character, had for some years been in a declining condition, and he laboured under a 'periodic asthma.' Benefiting apparently little by the ministration of his own physician, William Cassanate, a Frenchman, of Spanish extraction, settled in Edinburgh, Hamilton was recommended to consult the famous Cardan, who had now quitted Pavia for Milan. The suggestion was readily accepted by the archbishop, and a flattering letter was forthwith despatched by Cassanate to Italy, in which he besought Cardan to travel to Paris or at least to Lyon, where he would be met by Archbishop Hamilton, who had resolved to make this journey for the sake of his health. Such an invitation happened to fall in with Jerome's humour at the time, and he returned a favourable reply. The sum of two hundred crowns was paid him, in name of travelling expenses, by the archbishop's messenger, and on 23d February 1552, he started on his journey across the Alps, taking the Simplon Pass into Switzerland, and proceeding from thence through Geneva to Lyon. At the latter town, he expected to meet either the archbishop or his physician, but neither made appearance, and he remained upwards of a month in the place, where he reaped a golden harvest from the exercise of his profession of the healing art, nobles and distinguished persons eagerly pressing to him to avail themselves of his services. At last Cassanate arrived, bearing a letter from Archbishop Hamilton, in which that prelate, after apologising for his inability from cares of church and state to visit France at present, besought the learned Cardanus to give him the benefit of his professional skill, by extending his journey to Scotland. He further intimated that Cassanate would provide him with a safe-conduct, and also give him the security of any banker in Milan, for such suitable remuneration as might be agreed on.

It was not without considerable difficulty that Cardan was prevailed on to enter on this new undertaking, as he entertained the perfectly natural belief that the archbishop had inveigled him so far on the way, knowing well that he would have absolutely refused to visit Scotland had he been invited to do so at Milan. However, a reluctant consent was at last given, and after receiving an additional guerdon of three hundred crowns, Cardan and Cassanate set out together on their journey northward. Having arrived at Paris, the travellers made a stay of a few weeks, during which the most flattering attentions were paid to Cardan, including a request from Henry II. that he would take up his abode with him as court-physician, but the Milanese professor declined thus to expatriate himself. In like manner as he had practised at Lyon, however, he held numerous and crowded levees of patients, and realised large sums of money in shape of fees. Towards the end of May, he and Cassanate quitted Paris, a place of which Cardan seems to have carried away no exalted opinion in point of cleanliness and salubrity. He suggests sarcastically, indeed, that its ancient name, *Lutetia*, may have been derived from the dirt (*lutum*) which formed, in his opinion, one of the leading characteristics of the place. They then proceeded down the Seine to Rouen, of which our physician speaks in the most eulogistic terms, and from thence journeyed to Boulogne and Calais, where they took ship for London, and arrived there on 3d June. After a rest in the English metropolis of three days, they set out on their overland journey to Edinburgh, which they reached at the end of twenty-three days.

From the end of June to the middle of September, Cardan remained in Edinburgh in attendance on Archbishop Hamilton, who seems to have benefited greatly by the prescriptions of his Italian doctor. A full account has been left us by the latter of the remedies employed and the regimen prescribed for his distinguished patient, much of which seems sufficiently absurd at the present day, but is, nevertheless, accompanied by numerous sensible and judicious injunctions. Among these were recommendations to use frequently the cold bath (the water to be poured from a pail or pitcher over the archiepiscopal head and shoulders), featherbeds and pillows to be avoided, a sufficient amount of sleep to be taken, moderation and regularity to be observed as regards meals, and the mind to be kept free from harassing cares. So sensible was Hamilton of the benefits which he had received from this treatment, that he would gladly have detained Cardan for a much longer period; but the latter was inexorable, being both impatient to return to his country and family, and unwilling to face the inclement skies of a Scottish winter. He, accordingly, quitted Edinburgh for London, after receiving from the archbishop the princely remuneration of eighteen hundred gold crowns, of which four hundred went to Cardan's attendants. The subsequent history of the prelate, to whom a renewed lease of life had thus been granted, is well known to all readers of Scottish history. After endeavouring ineffectually to avert the change in religion and ecclesiastical establishments which shortly afterwards took place in the country, he became, on the arrival of Queen Mary in Scotland, one of her most favoured counsellors; and on her deposition and subsequent confinement in Loch Leven, an active member of that party which sought to reinstate her on the throne. Doomed to see all his hopes disappointed, he took refuge in Dumbarton Castle, and on the capture of that fortress by the government forces in 1571, was tried and condemned on the charge, among others, of participating in the murder of the Regent Murray. In pursuance of this sentence, Hamilton was ignominiously hanged in his pontifical robes on the common gibbet at Stirling, being both the last Roman Catholic primate of Scotland, and the first of its prelates to suffer capital punishment.

In passing through London on his return home, Cardan was summoned to attend the young king, Edward VI., then in a declining state of health, and who fell a victim to consumption in the ensuing summer. He had several interviews and conversations with the youthful sovereign, whose generally received reputation for distinguished abilities and goodness of heart he amply confirms. Probably he foresaw that Edward's life must ere long come to a termination, but to have expressed any opinion to that effect would have been both perilous to himself and cruel towards the amiable prince. After a short stay in London, he proceeded to Dover, crossed over from thence into Belgium, and passing through the Low Countries, reached Cologne, from which he sailed up the Rhine to Strasburg and Basel. He then continued his journey through Switzerland, crossed the Alps, and re-entered Milan, on 3d January 1553, after an absence of nearly a year.

The sunshine of prosperity continued for several years to beam on Cardan, but his latter days were embittered by a terrible calamity. Gianbatista, his eldest son, had married a worthless girl, and thereby occasioned his father the most poignant sorrow; but the indignation which he expressed at the event gradually relented, and he allowed the disreputable couple a maintenance. Soon fearful quarrels arose between husband and wife, the latter of whom did not scruple to glory in her infidelities, and thereby roused the implacable resentment of Gianbatista, who conceived the design of poisoning her, and effected it through the medium of a cake. His wife died, and thereupon he and his brother Aldo were arrested as her murderers. As regarded the latter, the charge was abandoned, but the proofs of Gianbatista's criminality were strong, and notwithstanding all the efforts of his father to save him, he was condemned, and put to death in prison at the early age of twenty-six. Desolation and misery were now the portion of Cardan. The disgrace which had fallen on his house told even on his worldly fortunes, and, afflicted and depressed, he accepted a professorship in the university of Bologna; after residing in which town for several years, he was thrown into prison in 1570 on the charge of impiety, but was liberated after a detention of eighty-six days, the condition of his release being that he should publish no more books. At this time, he resigned his chair by the advice of his friends, who obtained for him a pension from Pope Pius V. On this arrangement being made, he left Bologna for Rome, where the remaining six years of his life were spent. He died on 20th September 1576, at the age of seventy-five, his birth having been on 24th September 1501.

Throughout life, Cardan never enjoyed robust health, but his literary activity was excessive, and it is said that he left behind him no less than one hundred and thirty-one printed works and one hundred and eleven in manuscript, besides having written a large amount of matter which he had committed to the flames. Among his productions may be mentioned *De Malo Recentiorum Medicorum Medendi usu* (On the Bad Practice of the Healing Art among Modern Physicians), which, as might be expected, occasioned a tremendous outcry from the profession against its author; his philosophical books on *Wisdom* and *Consolation*; his *Practice of Arithmetic*; and his *Algebra*. Of all his works, the last has tended most to perpetuate his fame, being the first in which the whole doctrine of cubic equations was given to the world, and which also made known for the first time some most important rules and principles. The value of his contributions to mathematical science is still recognised, but most of his disquisitions on medicine and philosophy, which excited such attention in his own day, have long ago been completely forgotten. Of his personal character, it is not possible to speak very favourably, as he seems to have been loose in morals, and to have been imbued to an ample extent with all the objectionable tendencies of his time. But he appears to have been a kind and affectionate husband and parent, and a genial and agreeable companion, though his manners, like his person, are said to have been unprepossessing. Considering the misfortune of his birth, the defects of his education, and the period in which he lived, we may fairly give our tribute of admiration to his undoubted genius; and while making the most of the good points, cast the mantle of charity over the defects in the character of Jerome Cardan.

## A BLUE-COAT MARRIAGE.

Pepys, in a letter to Mrs Steward, dated September 20, 1695, notes that the extreme depression of the London public at that time, under a grievous war and heavy losses at sea, was enlivened by an extraordinary occurrence in connection with Christ's Hospital (the Blue-Coat School). Two wealthy citizens, lately deceased, had left their estates, the one to a Blue-coat boy, the other to a Blue-coat girl, and this had led some of the magistrates to bring about a match between these two young persons. The boy, in a habit of blue satin, led by two of the girls; the girl, in blue, with a green apron, and yellow petticoat, all of sarsenet, led by two of the boys; proceeded in procession along Cheapside to Guildhall, where (in the chapel) they were united in wedlock by the dean of St Paul's, the lord mayor giving away the bride. Then there was an entertainment in the hall of the hospital, Bow bells ringing out a merry peal all the time. The high patronage thus bestowed upon the union of two persons in nonage, gives a strange idea of the taste and morals of the age. It would be easy to shew that the incident was far from being unique.

## SHOWERS OF ANIMALS.

On the 20th of September 1839, an English officer, residing in the neighbourhood of Calcutta, saw a quantity of live fish descend in a smart shower of rain. They were about three inches in length, and all of one kind. Some, falling on hard ground, were killed; some, which fell on soft grass, continued in life. 'The most strange thing that struck me in connection with this event,' said the officer, 'was that the fish did not fall helter-skelter, everywhere, or here and there: they fell in a straight line, not more than a cubit in breadth.' Shortly after this event, at a village near Allahabad, 3000 or 4000 fish were found on the ground, of a well-known species, and about a span in length, but all dead and dry.

The instances are more numerous than most observers would suppose, of animals falling to the ground in the manner of rain, sometimes accompanied by real rain. On the 14th of April 1828, Major Forbes Mackenzie, of Fodderty, in Ross-shire, while walking in a field on his farm, saw a great portion of the ground covered with herring-fry, three to four inches in length, fresh and entire. The spot was three miles from the Firth of Dingwall. About two years afterwards, in the island of Islay, in Argyleshire, after a day of very heavy rain, the inhabitants were surprised to find a large number of small herrings strewed over the fields, perfectly fresh, and some of them alive. On another occasion, during a strong gale, herrings and other fish were carried from the Firth of Forth so far as Loch Leven, eight or ten miles distant. More recently, a Wick newspaper stated that, on a particular morning, a large quantity of herrings were found lying scattered in a garden about half a mile from the shore at that town. The peasants cooked and ate them—not without misgiving on the part of others as to the possibility of some Satanic agency having been concerned in the transfer of herrings to such a spot.

Hasted, in his *History of Kent*, narrates that about Easter, 1666, in the parish of Stanstead, which is at a considerable distance from the sea, and has no fish-ponds near it, a pasture-field was found strewed over with small fish.

Frogs and insects have similarly rained down upon the fields, but more rarely. Professor Pontus, of Cahors, communicated to the French Academy in 1804 the particulars of a shower of frogs near Toulouse. Pontus saw the young frogs on the cloaks of two gentlemen, who were caught in the storm on the road. When the diligence in which he was travelling arrived at the place where the storm burst, the road and fields were observed to be full of frogs, in some places three or four deep; the horses' hoofs killed thousands during the passage of the vehicle along this spot. Concerning showers of insects, we will simply notice one instance recorded in the *Journal de St Petersbourg*, 1827. A heavy snow-storm occurred on the 17th of October, at Pakroff, in the government of Tver. The snow was accompanied by a prodigious number of black insects about an inch and a quarter in length; they had flat shining heads, antennæ, a velvety kind of skin marked with rings or bands, and feet which enabled them to crawl rapidly over the snow. Such of them as were carried into a warm place, died presently; but the rest remained alive for a considerable time in a very severe temperature.

How are these phenomena to be accounted for? There seems little doubt that winds, whirlwinds, and waterspouts are the chief source of their production. Waterspouts are not unknown in that portion of Ross-shire where the shower of herrings took place in 1828. The herring fall at Islay occurred after a day of very heavy rain; and that at Loch Leven during a strong gale from the Firth of Forth. The occurrence at Wick was attributed by the more intelligent inhabitants to a waterspout. At Stanstead, a thunder-storm preceded the fall of fish. At Calcutta, the fish-shower was both preceded and accompanied by a smart shower of rain. At Allahabad, a blast of wind came on suddenly, so violently as to blow down several large trees; and it was after this wind that the fish were found on the ground. At Toulouse, the shower of frogs was preceded by the sudden appearance of a very thick cloud from the horizon, and the bursting out of a thunder-storm. In all these instances, the results were probably due, wholly or in part, to this fact (ascertained by modern science), that wind has a strong tendency to become circular or rotatory, sucking up from beneath any small light objects that may be in the way, carrying them to a distance, and depositing them when the force is allayed. If this occurs on land, we have a *whirlwind;* if on sea, a *waterspout*. There is one case on record, in Norway, of a colony of rats, while migrating in vast numbers from the high to the low countries, having been overtaken by a whirlwind; they were caught up, carried to a neighbouring valley, and there fell as a rat-shower.

---

## SEPTEMBER 21.

St Matthew, apostle and evangelist. St Maura, virgin, 850. St Lo or Laudus, bishop of Coutances, 568.

*Born.*—John Loudon M'Adam, improver of roads, 1756; Louis Bonaparte, king of Holland, 1778, *Ajaccio, Corsica.*

*Died.*—Edward II. of England, murdered at Berkeley Castle, 1327; Sultan Selim I. 1520; Emperor Charles V., 1558, *Monastery of St Just, Spain;* Colonel James Gardiner, killed at Prestonpans, 1745; John Balguy, eminent divine and controversial writer, 1748, *Harrowgate.*

### QUEEN ISABELLA: ENGLISH DOMESTIC LIFE OF FIVE HUNDRED YEARS SINCE.

One of the most interesting records of the domestic life of our ancestors that we remember to have read of late, consists of certain notices of the last days of Isabella, queen of Edward II., drawn from an account of the expenses of her household, in one of the Cottonian manuscripts in the British Museum, and lately communicated to the Society of Antiquaries by Mr E. A. Bond. No Court Circular ever recorded the movements of royalty more minutely than does this memorial of the domestic manners of the middle of the fourteenth century—*the private life of five hundred years since!*

It will be recollected that after the deposition and murder of King Edward II., we hear little of the history of the chief mover of these fearful events. The ambitious Mortimer expiates his crimes on the scaffold. Isabella, the instigator of sedition against her king, the betrayer of her husband, survives her accomplice; but from the moment that her career of guilt is arrested, she is no more spoken of. After mentioning the execution of Mortimer, Froissart tells us that 'the king, by the advice of his council, ordered his mother to be confined in a goodly castle, and gave her plenty of ladies to wait and attend on her, as well as knights and esquires of honour. He made her a handsome allowance to keep and maintain the state she had been used to, but forbade that she should ever go out, or drive herself abroad, except at certain times, when any shows were exhibited in the court of the castle; the queen thus passed her time there meekly, and the king, her son, visited her twice or thrice a year.' Castle Rising was the place of her confinement. After the first two years, the strictness of her seclusion was relaxed, and thence she was removed to Hertford Castle.

The account of the expenses of her household embraces, in distinct divisions, the queen's general daily expenses; sums given in alms; miscellaneous necessary expenses; disbursements for dress, purchases of plate and jewellery, gifts, payments to messengers, and imprests for various services. In the margin of the general daily expenses are entered the names of the visitors during the day, together with the movements of the household from place to place. From these entries we gain some insight into the degree of personal freedom enjoyed by the queen and her connections; the consideration she obtained at the court of the great King Edward III., her son; and even into her personal disposition and occupations.

It appears, then, that at the beginning of October 1357, the queen was residing at her castle at Hertford, having not very long before been at Rising. The first visitor mentioned, and who supped with her, was Joan, her niece, who visited the queen constantly, and nursed her in her last illness.

About the middle of October, the queen set out from Hertford on a pilgrimage to Canterbury. She rested at Tottenham, London, Eltham, Dartford, and Rochester, in going or returning, visited Leeds Castle, and was again at Hertford at the beginning of November. She gave alms to the nuns-minoresses without Aldgate; to the rector of St Edmund's, London, in whose parish her hostel was situated—it was in Lombard Street; and to the prisoners in Newgate. On the 26th of October, she entertained the king and Prince of Wales at her house in Lombard Street; and we find recorded a gift of 13*s.* 4*d.* to four minstrels, who played in their presence.

After her return to Hertford Castle, the queen was visited by the renowned Gascon writer, the Captal de Buche, cousin of the Comte de Foix. He had recently come over to England with the Prince of Wales, having taken part, on the English side, in the great battle of Poitiers; and there are also entries of the visits of several noble captives, who were taken in the above engagement. On the 10th of February, messengers arrive from the king of Navarre, to announce, as it appears elsewhere, his escape from captivity; an indication that Isabella was still busy in the stirring events of her native country. On the 20th of March, the king comes to supper. On each day of the first half of the month of May, during the queen's stay in London, the entries shew her guests at dinner, her visitors after dinner, and at supper, as formally as in a Court Circular of our time.

On May 14, Isabella left London, and rested at Tottenham, on her way to Hertford; and there is entered a gift of 6*s.* 8*d.* to the nuns of Cheshunt, who met the queen at the cross, in the high-road, in front of their house.

On the 4th of June, the queen made another pilgrimage to Canterbury, where she entertained the abbot of St Augustine's; under 'Alms' are recorded the queen's oblations at the tomb of St Thomas; here, too, are entered a payment to minstrels, her oblations in the church of St Augustine, and her donations to various hospitals and religious houses in Canterbury.

The entries of 'alms' amount to the considerable sum of £298, equivalent to about £3000 of present money. They consist of chapel-offerings, donations to religious houses, to clergymen preaching in the queen's presence, to special applicants for charity, and to paupers. The most interesting entry, perhaps, is that of a donation of 40*s.* to the abbess and minoresses Without Aldgate, in London, to purchase for themselves two pittances on the anniversaries of Edward, late king of England, and Sir John, of Eltham (the queen's son), given on the 20th of November. And this is the sole instance of any mention of the unhappy Edward II.

Among these items is a payment to the nuns of Cheshunt, whenever the queen passed the priory, in going to or from Hertford. There is more than one entry of alms given to poor scholars of Oxford, who had come to ask aid of the queen. A distribution is made amongst a hundred or fifty poor persons on the principal festivals of the year, amongst which that of Queen Katherine is included; and doles are made among paupers daily and weekly throughout the year, amounting in one year and a month, to £102. On the 12th of September, after the queen's death, a payment of 20*s.* is made to William Ladde, of Shene, on account of the burning of his house by an accident while the queen was staying at Shene.

Under the head of 'Necessaries,' we find a payment of 50*s.* to carpenters, plasterers, and tilers, for works in the queen's chamber. Next are half-yearly payments of 25*s.* 2*d.* to the prioress of St Helen's, in London; and rent for the queen's house in Lombard Street. Next, is a purchase of two small 'catastre,' or cages for birds, in the queen's chamber, and of hemp-seed for the birds; and under the 'Gifts' are two small birds presented to Isabella by the king. Here, likewise, are payments for binding the black carpet in the queen's chamber; for repairs of the castle; lining of the queen's chariot with coloured cloth; repairs of the queen's bath, and gathering of herbs for it; for skins of vellum for writing the queen's books; and for writing a book of divers matters for the queen, 14*s.*, including cost of parchment. Also, to Richard Painter, for azure for illuminating the queen's books. Here payment is entered of the sum of £200, borrowed of Richard, Earl of Arundel. Here are entries of the purchase of an embroidered saddle, with gold fittings, and a black palfrey given to the queen of Scotland; and a payment to Louis de Rocan, merchant, of the Society of Malebaill, in London, for two mules, bought by him at Avignon, for the queen, £28, 13*s.*; the mules arrived after the queen's death, and they were delivered over to the king.

The entries relating to jewels shew that the serious events of Isabella's life, and her increasing years, had not overcome her natural passion for personal display. The total amount expended in jewels is no less than £1399, equivalent to about £16,000 of our present currency; 'and,' says Mr Bond, 'after ample allowance for the acknowledged general habit of indulgence in personal ornaments belonging to the period, we cannot but consider Isabella's outlay on her trinkets as extravagant, and as betraying a more than common weakness for these vain luxuries. The more costly of them were purchased of Italian merchants. Her principal English jewellers appear to have been John de Louthe and William de Berkinge, goldsmiths, of London.' In a general entry of a payment of £421, are included items of a chaplet of gold, set with 'bulays' (rubies), sapphires, emeralds, diamonds, and pearls, price £105; divers pearls, £87; a crown of gold, set with sapphires, rubies of Alexandria, and pearls, price £80; these ornaments being, there is no doubt, ordered for the occasion of Isabella's visit to Windsor, at the celebration of St George's Day. Among others, is a payment of £32 for several articles—namely, for a girdle of silk, studded with silver, 20*s.*; 300 doublets (rubies), at 20*d.* the hundred; 1800 pearls, at 2*d.* each; and a circlet of gold, at the price of £60, bought for the marriage of Katherine Brouart; and another of a pair of tablets of gold, enamelled with divers histories, of the price of £9.

The division of 'Dona,' besides entries of simple presents and gratuities, contains records of gifts to messengers, from acquaintances and others, giving us further insight into the connections maintained by the queen. Notices of messengers bringing letters from the Countesses of Warren and Pembroke are very frequent. Under the head of 'Præstita,' is an entry of £230, given to Sir Thomas de la March, in money paid to him by the hands of Henry Pickard (doubtless, the magnificent lord mayor of that name, who so royally entertained King John of France, the king of Cyprus, and the Prince of Wales at this period), as a loan from Queen Isabella, on the obligatory letter of the said Sir Thomas; for he is known as the victor in a duel, fought at Windsor, in presence of Edward III., with Sir John Viscomte in 1350.

Several payments to couriers refer to the liberation of Charles, king of Navarre; and are important, as proving that the queen was connected with one who was playing a conspicuous part in the internal history of her native country—Charles of Navarre, perhaps the most unprincipled sovereign of his age, and known as 'the Wicked.' Among the remaining notices of messengers and letters, we have mention of the king's butler coming to the queen at Hertford, with letters of the king, and a present of three pipes of wine; a messenger from the king with three pipes of Gascon wine; another with a present of small birds; John of Paris, coming from the king of France to the queen at Hertford, and returning with two volumes of *Lancelot and the Sang Réal*, sent to the same king by Isabella; a messenger bringing a boar's head and breast from the Duke of Lancaster, Henry Plantagenet; Wilson Orloger, monk of St Albans, bringing to the queen several quadrants of copper; a messenger bringing a present of a falcon from the king; a present of a wild-boar from the king, and a cask of Gascon wine; a messenger bringing a present of twenty-four bream from the Countess of Clare; and payments to messengers bringing New-year's gifts from the king, Queen Philippa, the Countess of Pembroke, and Lady Wake.

Payments to minstrels playing in the queen's presence occur often enough, to shew that Isabella greatly delighted in this entertainment; and these are generally minstrels of the king, prince, or of noblemen. We find a curious entry of a payment of 13*s.* 4*d.* to Walter Hert, one of the queen's 'vigiles' (viol-players), going to London, and staying there, in order to learn minstrelsy at Lent time; and, again, of a further sum to the same, on his return from London, 'de scola minstralsie.'

Among the special presents by the queen are New-year's gifts to the ladies of her chamber, eight in number, of 100*s.* to each; and 20*s.* each to thirty-three clerks and squires; a girdle to Edward de Keilbergh, the queen's ward; a donation of 40*s.* to Master Lawrence, the surgeon, for attendance on the queen; a present of fur to the Countess of Warren; a small gift to Isabella Spicer, 'filiolæ reginæ,' her goddaughter; and a present of £66 to Isabella de St Rol, lady of the queen's chamber, on occasion of her marriage with Edward Brouart. Among the 'Messengers' payments we find a letter to the prior of Westminster, 'for a certain falcon of the Count of Tancarville lost, and found by the said prior.'

Respecting Isabella's death, she is stated by chroniclers to have sunk, in the course of a single day, under the effect of a too powerful medicine, administered at her own desire. From several entries, however, in this account, she appears to have received medical treatment for some time previous to her decease. She expired on the 23d of August; but, as early as February 15, a payment had been made to a messenger going on three several occasions to London, for divers medicines for the queen, and for the hire of a horse for Master Lawrence, the physician, and again, for another journey by night to London. On the same day, a second payment was made to the same messenger for two other journeys by night to London, and two to St Albans, to procure medicines for the queen. On the 1st of August, payment was made to Nicholas Thomasyer, apothecary, of London, for divers spices and ointments supplied for the queen's use. Among other entries, is a payment to Master Lawrence of 40*s.* for attendance on the queen and the queen of Scotland, at Hertford, for an entire month.

It is evident that the body of the queen remained in the chapel of the castle until the 23d of November, as a payment is made to fourteen poor persons for watching the queen's corpse there, day and night, from Saturday the 25th of August to the above date; each person receiving twopence daily, besides his food. The queen died at Hertford on August 22, 1358, and was buried in the church of the Grey Friars, within Newgate, the site of the present Christ Church. Large rewards, amounting together to £540, were given after Isabella's death, by the king's order, to her several servants, for their good service to the queen in her lifetime.

## THE AUTUMNAL EQUINOX.

On or about the 21st of September and 21st of March, the ecliptic or great circle which the sun appears to describe in the heavens, in the course of the year crosses the terrestrial equator. The point of intersection is termed the *equinoctial point* or the *equinox*, because at that period, from its position in relation to the sun, the earth, as it revolves on its axis, has exactly one-half of its surface illuminated by the sun's rays, whilst the other half remains in darkness, producing the phenomenon of equal day and night all over the world. At these two periods, termed respectively, from the seasons in which they occur, the *autumnal* and the *vernal* equinox, the sun rises about six o'clock in the morning, and sets nearly at the same time in the evening. From the difference between the conventional and the actual or solar year, the former consisting only of 365 days, while the latter contains 365 days and nearly six hours (making the additional day in leap-year), the date at which the sun is actually on the equinox, varies in different years, from the 20th to the 23d of the month. In the autumnal equinox, the sun is passing from north to south, and consequently from this period the days in the northern hemisphere gradually shorten till, on 21st December, the winter solstice is reached, from which period they gradually lengthen to the spring or vernal equinox on 21st March, when day and night are again equal. The sun then crosses the equator from south to north, and the days continue to lengthen up to the 21st of June, or summer solstice, from which they diminish, and are again equal with the nights at the autumnal equinox or 21st of September.

Owing to the spheroidal form of the earth causing a protuberance of matter at the equator, on which the sun exercises a disturbing influence, the points at which the ecliptic cuts the equator, experience a constant change. They, that is the equinoxes, are always receding westwards in the heavens, to the amount annually of 50″·3, causing the sun to arrive at each intersection about 20′ earlier than he did on the preceding year. The effect of this movement is, that from the time the ecliptic was originally divided by the ancients into twelve arcs or signs, the constellations which at that date coincided with these divisions now no longer coincide. Every constellation having since then advanced 30° or a whole sign forwards, the constellation of Aries or the Ram, for example, occupies now the division of the ecliptic called Taurus, whilst the division known as Aries, is distinguished by the constellation Pisces. In about 24,000 years, or 26,000 from the first division of the ecliptic, the equinoctial point will have made a complete revolution round this great circle, and the signs and constellations as originally marked out will again exactly coincide. The movement which we have thus endeavoured to explain, forms the astronomical revolution called the *precession of the equinoxes*, for the proper ascertainment and demonstration of which, science is indebted to the great French mathematician, D'Alembert.

In connection with the ecliptic and equator, the mutual intersection of which marks the equinoctial point, an interesting question is suggested in reference to the seasons. It is well known that the obliquity of the ecliptic to the equator, at present about 23½°, is diminishing at the rate of about 50 seconds in a century. Were this to continue, the two circles would at last coincide, and the earth would enjoy in consequence a perpetual spring. There is, however, a limit to this decrease of obliquity, which it has been calculated has been going on from the year 2000 B.C., and will reach its maximum about 6600 A.D. From that period the process will be reversed, and the obliquity gradually increase till a point is reached at which it will again diminish. From this variation in the position of the ecliptic, with regard to the equator, some have endeavoured to explain a change of climate and temperature, which it is imagined the world has gradually experienced, occasioning a slighter contrast between the seasons than formerly, when the winters were much colder, and the summers much hotter than they are at present. It is believed, however, that, whatever truth there may be in the allegations regarding a more equable temperature, throughout the year in modern times, it is not to the variation of the obliquity of the ecliptic that we are to look for a solution of the question. The entire amount of this variation is very small, ranging only from 23° 53′ when the obliquity is greatest, to 22° 54′ when it is least, and it is therefore hardly capable of making any sensible alteration on the seasons.

As is well known, both the autumnal and vernal equinoxes are distinguished over the world by the storms which prevail at these seasons. The origin of such atmospheric commotions has never yet been very satisfactorily explained, but is supposed, as stated by Admiral Fitzroy, to arise from the united tidal action of the sun and moon upon the atmosphere; an action which at the time of the equinoxes is exerted with greater force than at any other period of the year.

## THE CATCHPOLE.

Many appellations perfectly clear in the days of their origin, lose significance in course of time, and occasionally become grossly perverted, or absolutely caricatured. Thus a *villain* was originally a distinctive term, applied, with no evil significance, to a serf upon a feudal domain. A *cheater* has, like that, now become equally offensive, though it is simply derived from the officer of the king's exchequer, appointed to receive dues and taxes, and who was called the escheator. One of the best examples of grotesque change is the appellation *beef-eater*, applied to a yeoman of the guard, and which is a caricature of *buffetier*, the guardian of the buffet on occasions of state banqueting. The law-officer whose business was to apprehend criminals, was long popularly known as *the catchpole;* but few remembered that he obtained that designation, because he originally carried with him a pole fitted by a peculiar apparatus to catch a flying offender by the neck. Our cut, copied from a Dutch engraving dated 1626, represents an

CATCHPOLE NO. 1.

officer about to make such a capture. The pole was about six feet in length, and the steel implement at its summit was sufficiently flexible to allow the neck to slip past the V-shaped arms, and so into the collar; when the criminal was at the mercy of the officer to be pushed forward to prison, or dragged behind him. This was the simplest form of the catchpole, sometimes it was a much more formidable thing, as will be more readily understood from our second cut (see next page), copied from the antique instrument itself, obtained at Wurzburg, in Bavaria. The fork at the upper part is strengthened by double springs, allowing the neck to pass freely, but acting as a check against its return; rows of sharp spikes are set round the collar, and would severely punish any violent struggler for liberty, whose neck it had once embraced. The criminal

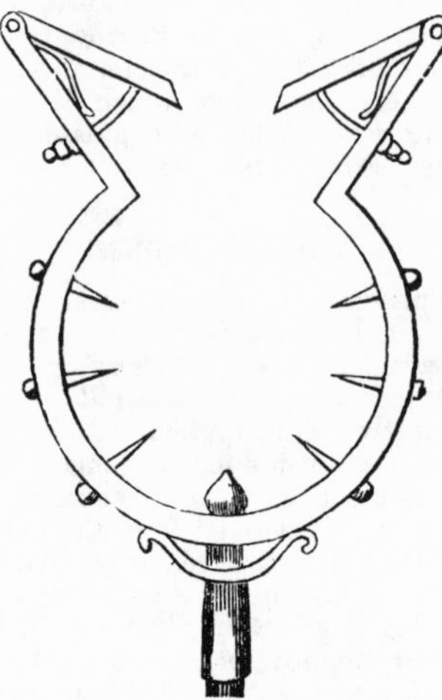

CATCHPOLE NO. 2.

was, in fact, *garrotted* by the officer of the law, according to the most approved fashion of 'the good old times,' when justice was armed with terrors, and indulged in many cruelties now happily unknown.

---

## SEPTEMBER 22.

St Maurice and his companions, martyrs, 286; St Emmeran, bishop of Poitiers, and patron of Ratisbon, martyr, 653.

---

*Born.*—Dr Richard Busby, celebrated head-master of Westminster School, 1606, *Lutton, Lincolnshire;* Philip Dormer Stanhope, Earl of Chesterfield, statesman, and author of *Letters to his Son*, 1694, *London;* John Home, author of *Douglas*, 1722, *Leith;* Peter Simon Pallas, traveller, 1741, *Berlin;* Theodore Edward Hook, novelist, 1788, *London.*

*Died.*—Mardonius, Persian commander, slain at Platæa, 479 B.C.; Virgil, epic poet, 19 B.C., *Brundusium;* John Biddle, 'father of English Unitarianism,' 1662, *Moorfields, London;* François Bernier, eastern traveller, 1688, *Paris;* Pope Clement XIV., 1774; Princess Augusta of England, 1840; Mrs Sherwood, author of numerous works for children, 1851, *Twickenham.*

### VIRGIL THE NECROMANCER.

It is difficult to explain how the fame of the poet Virgil, in its passage through the opening period of the middle ages, became so extraordinarily enveloped in fable. Virgil, as we know, was born at Mantua, but he is said, among other places, to have studied at Naples; and it was with that city that, in the middle ages, the name of the poet was most intimately connected, and there, as early certainly as the twelfth century, numerous stories were told of his wonderful exploits. These, too, were believed by men of the highest rank in theology and science. Our great scholar, Alexander Neckam, has collected some of them in his work, *De Naturis Rerum*, which was published in the latter part of that century; and when, at the beginning of the century following, another of our scholars, Gervase of Tilbury, visited Naples, he listened to similar stories which were told to him by his host, the Archdeacon Pinatellus. Virgil was said to have founded the city of Naples upon eggs, as a magical charm for its protection, and this was the legendary derivation of the name of one of its principal castles, the Castel del' Uovo. On one of the gateways of Naples he set up two brazen statues, one with a merry, the other with a sad and deformed countenance, so enchanted, that if any one entered the town by the side of the gateway on which the merry statue stood, he was certain to prosper in all his affairs; while entering by the other side, produced a contrary effect. On another gate he set up a brazen fly, which remained there eight years, during which period no flies could enter the city; he relieved Naples in a somewhat similar manner from a plague of infectious leeches; he built baths, which cured all disorders; he surrounded his house and gardens with a stream of air, which served for a wall; he constructed a bridge of brass, which took him wherever he pleased. At length, in the fifteenth century, many of these marvellous stories were collected together, and formed into what was called a life of Virgil, which appears to have been first printed in France, but of which an English version was printed in England early in the sixteenth century. It is a curious production, full of very wild adventures, and curiously illustrates the state of intelligence in the middle ages.

After some very fabulous general history, the story tells us that Virgil was the son of a Campanian knight, who had married the daughter of a senator of Rome, and who was powerful and a great enemy to the emperor. Virgil's birth was painful, and was announced by an earthquake in Rome, and they gave him his name from the verb *vigilo*, to watch, 'for by cause that he was a great space of tyme watched so with men.' He was sent to school when a child, to Tolenten (probably meant for Toledo, where people were supposed to go to learn magic in the middle ages), and soon afterwards his father died, and his powerful kinsman dispossessed the widow and her child of their estates, while the emperor refused to give them redress. It was at this time that the event occurred by which Virgil became possessed of his supernatural powers, for, unlike other magicians, he obtained them without subjecting himself to any disagreeable terms.

'An Virgilius was at scole at Tolenten, where he stodyed dyligently, for he was of great understandynge. Upon a tyme the scholers hadde lycence to goo to play and sporte them in the fyldes after the usaunce of the olde tyme; and there was also Virgilius therby also walkynge amonge the hilles all about. It fortuned he spyed a great hole in the syde of a great hyll, wherin he went so depe, that he culde not see no more lyght, and than he went a lytell ferther therin, and than he sawe som lyght agayne, and than wente he fourth streyghte: and within a lytyll wyle after he harde a voice that called, "Virgilius, Virgilius!" and he loked aboute, and he colde nat see no bodye. Than Virgilius spake and asked, "Who calleth me?" Than harde he the voyce agayne, but he sawe no body; then sayd he, "Virgilius, see ye not that lytyll borde lyinge bysyde you there marked with that word?" Than answered Virgilius, "I see that borde well enough." The voyce sayde, "Doo awaye that borde, and lette me oute theratte." Than answered Virgilius to the voyce that was under the lytell borde, and sayd, "Who art thou that talkest me so?" Than answered the devyll, "I am a devyll conjured out of the body of a certeyne man, and banysshed here tyll the day of jugement, without that I be delyvered by the handes of man. Thus, Virgilius, I pray the delyver me out of this payn, and I shall shewe unto the many bokes of nygromancy, and howe thou shalt cum by it lyghtly and knowe the practyse therein, that no man in the scyence of negromancye shall pass the. And moreover I shall showe and enforme you, so that thou shalt have all thy desyre, wherby methynke it is a great gyfte for so lytyll a doynge; for ye may also thus all your power frendys helpen, and make rythe your ennemyes unmyghty." Thorowh that great promyse was Virgilius tempted; he badde the fyend showe the bokes to hym, that he myght have and occupy them at his wyll. And so the fyend shewed hym, and than Virgilius pulled open a borde, and there was a lytell hole, and therat wrange the devyll out lyke a yeel, and cam and stode byfore Virgilius lyke a bygge man; therof Virgilius was astonied and merveyled greatly therof, that so great a man myght come out at so lytell a hole. Than sayd Virgilius, "Shulde ye well passe into the hole that ye cam out of?" "Yes I shall well," sayd the devyll. "I holde the best plegge (*gaze, wager*) that I have ye shall not do it." "Well," sayde the devyll, "thereto I consente." And than the devyll wrange hymselfe into the lytell hole agen, and as he was therein, Virgilius kyvered the hole ageyn with the borde close, and so was the devyll begyled, and myght not there come out agen, but there abydeth shytte styll therin. Than called the devyll dredefully to Virgilius, and sayd, "What have ye done?" Virgilius answered, "Abyde there styll to your day apoynted." And fro thensforth abydeth he there. And so Virgilius becam very connynge in the practyse of the blacke scyence.'

Of the 'cunning' of Virgilius there can be no doubt after this example—at all events, he had evidently more wit than his antagonist. Some time after this, his mother became old and deaf, and she sent for her son home from the school, that he might take steps to recover his inheritance, and to take his rightful place as a senator of Rome; and her messenger proceeded to Tolenten, and 'whan he cam there, he founde Virgilius teching and lernynge the greattest lordes of the lande, and other landes also; for I ensure ye, he was a fayr and a wyse yonge man, and conynge in the scyence of negromancy above all men than lyvynge.' Though Virgilius had now, we are told, made himself immensely rich, and had little need to care for his rights at Rome, yet he obeyed his mother's call, went to Rome, and met with a rebuff from the emperor, which led to a war between them, in which the imperial power was defeated and set at nought by the 'negromancye' of the scholar. The result was a reconciliation, and the restoration of Virgilius, who now became one of the principal men in the emperor's council, and he began to turn his eyes upon the fair ladies of Rome. The first of these to whom he made advances played him false, for, seeking only to mock him, she invited him to visit her one night in her chamber in a high tower, promising to let down a basket attached to a rope, and thus to draw him up. Virgilius came, was drawn half-way up the tower, and then the lady fastened the rope, and left him hanging there to be a spectacle to the populace all the next day. How Virgilius revenged himself is well known to all readers of the old popular literature, and can hardly be related here. Soon after this he took a wife and built himself a magnificent palace, which also possessed many wonders. The emperor now began to be troubled with rebellions in different parts of his empire, and he asked the counsel of Virgilius, who thereupon made in the Capitol a marvellous group of statues, one representing Rome, the others each allotted to a country or province, and each of these turned its back on the statue of Rome and rung a bell, when the province it represented was on the point of rebellion. Thus the emperor was informed of the revolt before it had time to get head, and the group in the Capitol received the name of *Salvatio Romæ*—the safeguard of Rome. It was at length destroyed by an ingenious contrivance of the men of Carthage. The manner in which this was effected will perhaps be best told in the quaint language of the original:

'Than thought they in there mynde to sende iij. men out, and gave them great multytude of golde and sylver; and these iij. men toke theyr leve of the lordes, and went towarde the cytie of Rome, and, when they were come to Rome, they reported themselfe sothesayers and trewe dremers. Upon a tyme wente these iij. men to a hyll that was within the cytie, and there they buryed a great potte of money very depe in the erthe, and when that was done and kyvered ageyne, they went to the brygge of Tyber, and let fall in a certayne place a great barell with golden pense; and when this was done, these thre men went to the seniatours of Rome, and sayd, "Worshypfull lordes, we have this nyghte dremed, that within the fote of a hyll here within Rome, is a great pot with money; wyll ye, lordes, graunte to us, and we shall do the coste to seke thereafter?" And the lordes consented, and than they toke laberours, and delved the money out of the erthe. And when it was done, they went another tyme to the lordes, and sayde, "Worshypful lordes, we have also dremed, that in a certayne place of Tyber lyeth a barell full of golden pense; if that you will graunte to us that we shall go seke it." And the lordes of Rome, thynkynge no dyscepte (deceit), graunted to those sothesayers, and badde them do that they shulde do there best. And than they hyred shyppes and men, and went toward the place where it was; and when they were come, they sowght it in everye place thereabout, and at the laste founde the barelfull of golden pense, whereof they were glade; and than they gave to the lordes costely gyftes. And than to come to theyr purpose, they cam to the lordes ageyne, and sayde to them: "Worshypfull lordes, we have dremed ageyne that under the foundacyon of Capitolium, there where Salvatio Rome standeth, be xij. barelles full of gold; and pleasyeth you, lordes, that you wold graunte us lycense, it shall be to your great avauntage." And the lordes styrred with covytayse, graunted them, bycause ij. tymes afore they told trewe. Whereof they were glad, and gatte laberours, and began to dygge under the foundacyon of Salvatio Rome; and when they thought that they had dygged anoughe, they departed fro Rome, and the next daye folowynge fell that house downe, and all the worke that Virgilius had made, and so the lordes knewe that they were deseyved, and were sorowfull, and after that hade nat no fortune as they had afore tymes.'

Virgilius also gratified the emperor by a contrivance to clear the streets of Rome of night-runners and evil-doers, and by making a wonderful lamp, which stood on a great pillar, and gave light at night to every street in Rome. He also built himself a wonderful orchard attached to his palace, and this brings us to another phase in his adventures.

In a new amour, Virgilius was more successful than on a former occasion. Having heard of the extraordinary beauty of the Soldan's daughter, he resolved to possess himself of her. For this purpose, he 'by his connynge,' built a bridge through the air, and over this passed to the Soldan's court, and gained the lady's love. After some perilous adventures, which we will pass over, he brought the princess home with him, and kept her in his wonderful orchard, for he 'was sore enamoured of that lady.' After a time, he became desirous of finding a husband for the princess, and 'thoughte in his mynde to founde in the myddes of the see, a fayer towne with great landes belongyng to it; and so he dyd by his cunnynge, and called it Napells, and the fundacyon of it was of egges; and in that towne of Napells, he made a tower with iiij. corners, and in the toppe, he set an apell upon a yron yarde, and no man culd pull away that apell without he brake it; thorowghe that yron set he a botel, and on that botel set he a egge; and he henge the apell by the stauke upon a cheyne, and so hangyth it styll. And whenne the egges styrreth, so shulde the towne of Napels quake, and whan the egge brake, then shulde the towne synke.' Such is the legendary origin of the town of Naples! It was no sooner completed, than Virgilius gave it as a dower to the Soldan's daughter, and married her to a certain lord of Spain. But the new town was so fair, that the emperor 'had a great fantasy' to it, and he secretly assembled a great army to take it by force. Virgilius, however, protected Naples against all his designs, and he fortified it, and, leaving all his other houses, he made it his sole residence. Above all, he loved scholars, and endowed there a large school, so richly, that every scholar, while he remained at school, had land allotted to him sufficient for his keep. Thus, under his care, it became the greatest school of necromancy and magic in the world.

Virgilius was again reconciled to the emperor, and performed other marvellous things for his service. At length old age approached, but he was provided even against this. He had built for himself, outside Rome, a strong castle or palace, with only one entrance, which, was protected by images of men with iron flails, which, by his necromancy, he kept in continual motion, so that none but himself could approach the entrance without certain death. Here he came sometimes alone, to secure himself from the emperor's importunities. One day Virgilius took his most trusty servant with him into this palace, and when they were alone, he said to him:

'"My dere beloved frende, and he that I above all men truste, and knowe most of my secret;" and than led he the man into the seller, where he had made a fayer lampe at all seasons burnynge. And than sayd Virgilius to the man, "Se you the barell that standeth here?" and he sayde, "Ye there muste put me; fyrste, ye muste slee me, and hewe smalle to peces, and cut my head in iiij. peces, and salte the heade under in the bottum, and then the peces thereafter, and my hearte in the myddel, and then set the barell under the lampe that nyght and daye therein may droppe and leke; and ye shall ix. dayes longe, ones in the daye fyll the lampe, and fayle nat. And when this is all done, than shall I be renewed and made yonge ageyn, and lyve longe tyme and maney wynters mo, if that it fortune me nat to be taken of above and dye." And when the man harde his master Virgilius speke thus, he was sore abasshed, and sayd, "That wyll I never whyle I lyve, for in no manner wyl I slee you." And then sayd Virgilius, "Ye at this tyme must do it, for it shall be no grefe unto you." And at the last Virgilius entreated his man so muche, that he consented to hym. And then toke the servant Virgilius, and slewe hym, and when he was thus slayn, he hewe hym in peces and salted hym in the barell, and cut his head in iiij. peces as his master bad hym, and than put the herte in the myddell, and salted them wele; and when all this was done, he hynge the lampe ryght over the barell, that it myght at all tymes droppe in thereto. And when he had done all this, he went out of the castell, and turned the vyces [screws—Virgilius had taught him the secret how to stop the movement of the flails, and set them agoing again], and then wente the coper men smyghtynge with theyr flayles so strongly upon the yron anveldes as they dyd afore, and there durste no man enter; and he came every daye to the castell, and fylled the lampe, as Virgilius had bad hym.'

When Virgilius had disappeared from court seven days, the emperor became impatient, and sent for his confidential servant, whose answers were evasive, and made the emperor more resolute to solve the mystery. He therefore compelled the servant, by fear of death, to take him to the castle, and stop the flails, so that he might enter. And he and his courtiers wandered over Virgilius's palace, until he came to the cellar in which he found the remains of the great necromancer salted in a barrel. In his first anger, he slew the faithful servant, by which Virgilius's instructions were lost and could no longer be carried out. 'And when all this was done, than sawe the emperoure and all his folke a naked chylde iij. tymes rennynge aboute the barell, sayinge the wordes, "Cursed be the tyme that ye cam ever here!" and with those wordes vanyshed the chylde away, and was never sene ageyne. And thus abyd Virgilius in the barell dead.'

Such is the legend of the necromancer Virgil, which, there can be no doubt, was the character given by the middle ages to the Roman poet. It is one of the most curious examples of the strange growth of medieval legend, and at the same time shews us the peculiar estimate which people in the darker ages formed of science and learning. At the same time, when we refer this to the darker ages, we must not forget that, in ages considered to be much more enlightened, the Romish Church took advantage of these superstitions and prejudices to persecute science and its followers.

## THE PRINCESS AUGUSTA.

This royal lady, second daughter of George III., combined great sweetness of nature with a propriety of behaviour which is not always accompanied by amiable qualities. There is an anecdote of her Royal Highness well worthy of permanent preservation. 'During the latter part of the reign of George IV., when a certain lady held immense influence over him, the king one day asked the Princess Augusta to come and dine with him. Her Royal Highness asked if Lady —— was to be there, and, on receiving a reply in the affirmative, begged to decline. The king pressed the matter very much, when the princess said: "If you command my attendance as *king*, I will obey you; but if you ask me as a *brother* to come, nothing will induce me." His majesty said no more.' It may further be noted of this good woman, that she was benevolent upon a moderate income, and died so poor as to require no will.

## MRS SHERWOOD.

The children of the present day enjoy immense advantages over their fathers and grandfathers as regards the supply of instructive and entertaining works suited to their tastes and capacities. Foremost among the pioneers of the improved order of things stand the names of Miss Edgeworth and Mrs Sherwood. Aiming both at the same object, these two distinguished writers pursue, nevertheless, a very dissimilar path. Whilst the former occupies herself with the moral, and more especially the reasoning, faculty of human nature, to the almost entire exclusion of the religious element, the latter adopts invariably the peculiar doctrines of Christianity, or what are commonly termed evangelical views, as the only sound basis on which any system of lasting improvement can be founded.

The maiden name of Mrs Sherwood was Butt, and she traced her descent from an ancestor who was said to have come over with William the Conqueror. Her family was certainly one of very old standing in the midland counties. Her grandfather, Dr Butt, resided in Lichfield, at a time when it was the centre of a brilliant literary coterie, including Miss Seward, Richard Lovell Edgeworth, Dr Darwin, and Mr Day, besides being visited occasionally by Dr Johnson and David Garrick from London. His son, George Butt, entered holy orders, and was presented to the rectory of Stanford, in Worcestershire, where his daughter, Mary Martha, the future authoress, was born in 1775. In her autobiography she has given a charming description of this place, where her girlhood's days were spent, and the remembrance of which we see vividly reproduced in her delightful pictures of English country-life in the *Fairchild Family*. Though a sincere affection seems to have subsisted between her and her parents, yet the discipline at Stanford Rectory was, according to her own account, of rather the strictest sort. She was never allowed to sit in the presence of her parents, to come near the fire, or take part in any conversation, and, according to the preposterous discipline of those days, had an iron collar round her neck, to which a back-board was strapped, and thus accoutred, would have to stand the greater part of the day in the stocks, in which position, moreover, she was obliged to learn and repeat her lessons. Yet she says she was a happy child, and such a picture of fresh rosy health that her father used to call her Hygeia. She informs us that at a very early age she began to write stories and plays, but she had the misfortune, shared in by other geniuses, of being originally regarded as a dull child. Little of incident marks her life till after her father's death, which took place when she was about twenty years of age. She then married her cousin, Captain Sherwood, of the 53d Regiment, and accompanied him to India. Here, with the co-operation of Henry Martyn and Mr Corrie, she exerted herself in the founding of schools for the Indian children, besides taking under her more especial care the children of the European soldiers, a labour of love in which she seems to have been eminently successful. Her husband entered cordially with her into all her pious and benevolent exertions. Many of her juvenile works, including the well-known *Henry and his Bearer*, which enjoyed such a diffusion as to be translated even into the Chinese and Cingalese languages, were composed in India. Captain and Mrs Sherwood, returning to England after a residence of many years, took up their abode in the neighbourhood of Worcester, and continued there till a short time before Captain Sherwood's death, when they removed to Twickenham, near London. In this place Mrs Sherwood closed her long and useful life, amid the affectionate ministrations of her daughters, on 22d September 1851. To the last she retained her cheerfulness, and up to within a year or two of her death, her vigour both of body and mind were almost unimpaired.

One distinguishing characteristic of Mrs Sherwood's works is the freshness with which English rural manners and scenes are portrayed. Her descriptions are redolent throughout of violets and wild-roses, green shady lanes, and pleasant walks through woods and fields. Her children, too, are really children—not philosophers in jackets and pinafores, as the young people of Miss Edgeworth are apt to appear to us. Mrs Sherwood must be admitted to possess the descriptive and dramatic, if not the imaginative faculty in a very high degree. Her style is the purest and simplest of English, and the true Christian lady, as well as genial-hearted woman, display themselves unmistakably from beginning to end.

---

## AN EPISODE FROM ZUTPHEN.

The small army which Elizabeth sent in 1585 to aid the Protestant Netherlanders against their Spanish masters, contained other heroes besides Sir Philip Sidney. Of one of these—the Lord Willoughby—we find an interesting anecdote in the modern work, entitled *Five Generations of a Loyal House;* an anecdote, moreover, connected with that skirmish or battle of Zutphen in which Sidney received his mortal wound.

'On the 22d of September 1586, an affray took place, in which Lord Willoughby pre-eminently distinguished himself by valour and conduct, and many others with him upheld the glory of the English name. Sir John Norreis and Sir William Stanley were that day reconciled; the former coming forward to say, "Let us die together in her majesty's cause." The enemy were desirous of throwing supplies into Zutphen, a place of which they entertained some doubt; and a convoy, accordingly, by the orders of the Prince of Parma, brought in a store, though an insufficient one, of provisions. A second, commanded by George Cressiac, an Albanois, was despatched for the same purpose, the morning being foggy. Lord

Willoughby, Lord Audley, Sir John Norreis, and Sir Philip Sidney, encountering the convoy in a fog, an engagement began. The Spaniards had the advantage of position, and had it in their power to discharge two or three volleys of shot upon the English, who, nevertheless, stood their ground. Lord Willoughby himself, with his lance in rest, met with the leader, George Cressiac, engaged with, and, after a short combat, unhorsed him. He fell into a ditch, crying aloud to his victor: "I yield myself to you, for that you be a seemly knight," who, satisfied with the submission, and having other matters in hand, threw himself into the thickest of the combat, while the captive was conducted to the tent of the general, Lord Leicester. The engagement was hot, and cost the enemy many lives, but few of the English were missing. Willoughby was extremely forward in the combat; at one moment his basses, or mantle, was torn from him, but recaptured. When all was over, Captain Cressiac being still in his excellency's tent, refused to acknowledge himself prisoner to any but the knight to whom he had submitted on the field. There is something in this, and the like incidents of the period, which recall us very agreeably to recollections of earlier days of chivalry and romance. Cressiac added, that if he were to see again the knight to whom he had surrendered himself, in the armour he then wore, he should immediately recognise him, and that to him and him only would he yield. Accordingly, Lord Willoughby presenting himself before him, in complete armour, he immediately exclaimed: "I yield to you!" and was adjudged to him as his prisoner.

'It was in this skirmish that the gallant and lamented Sir Philip Sidney, the boast of his age, and the hope of many admiring friends, received the fatal wound which cut short the thread of a brief but brilliant existence. During the whole day he had been one of the foremost in action, and once rushed to the assistance of his friend, Lord Willoughby, on observing him "nearly surrounded by the enemy," and in imminent peril: after seeing him in safety, he continued the combat with great spirit, until he received a shot in the thigh, as he was remounting a second horse, the first having been killed under him.'

---

## MAJOR BERNARDI.

On the 22d of September 1736, there died in the prison of Newgate, at the advanced age of eighty-two, and after a lengthened confinement of forty years, John Bernardi, whose name, as Mr Macaulay observes, has derived a melancholy celebrity from a punishment, so strangely prolonged, that it at length shocked a generation which could not remember his crime. Bernardi was an Englishman, though, as his name implies, of Italian extraction; his father and grandfather having been agents for the republic of Genoa at the court of England. In early life, he had served in the Dutch army under the Prince of Orange, and subsequently in that of James II., during the war of the revolution; in the latter he attained the rank of major, and fought at the battle of the Boyne, and siege of Limerick. In 1696, on the discovery of the plot to assassinate William III., Bernardi was arrested on suspicion of being one of the conspirators, and committed to Newgate. Eight persons were tried, condemned, and executed for their participation in the assassination-plot, as it was termed; but there not being sufficient evidence to ensure a conviction of Bernardi and five other suspected conspirators, the government, to avoid bringing them to a premature trial, and to afford time to procure condemnatory evidence, suspended the Habeas Corpus Act for nine months. At the expiration of that period, Bernardi and his fellow-prisoners applied to be either tried or admitted to bail, according to law; the judges adjourned the consideration of the case for a fortnight, thus affording time for the government to obtain an act of parliament, authorising the imprisonment of the unfortunate men for one year. At the expiration of the year, another act was passed authorising their confinement for another year; and at the end of the second year, a third act was passed authorising their confinement during his majesty's pleasure, parliament, evidently aware of the injustice of its proceedings, evasively throwing the responsibility upon the shoulders of King William.

There were no hopes now for the prisoners till the death of the king in 1702. When that event took place, they again demanded to be tried or admitted to bail; the answer was another act of parliament to confine them during the pleasure of Queen Anne. It happened to be the pleasure of this royal lady to release one of the prisoners, named Counter; so, at her death, there were but five to claim their right of trial or bail; but another act of parliament confined them during the pleasure of George I. When George II. succeeded to the throne, death having mercifully released two of the captives, named Meldrum and Chambers, there were only Bernardi and two fellow-sufferers to claim their legal rights. The counsel who moved their case in the court of King's Bench, stated that his clients had then been imprisoned without trial for thirty-one years; that they had been committed to Newgate, by a secretary of state's warrant, on suspicion of having been concerned in a conspiracy to assassinate King William; that they had never been brought before a magistrate; that there had not been the oath of even one witness sworn against them. It will scarcely be believed that the attorney-general, Sir Philip Yorke, afterwards Lord Hardwicke, opposed the miserable men's claim by a paltry technical quibble. He objected to the motion as irregular, the original commitment not having been produced, or proof given that the claimants were committed to Newgate in 1696. The judges overruled the objection, and there were hopes of justice being done at last; but another act of parliament condemned the unhappy men to imprisonment during the pleasure of George II. The prisoners petitioned parliament, the king and the queen, recounting their sufferings, age, and infirmities, further observing that several, who had been taken in arms against the government in 1714, had been pardoned and liberated, while they, who had never been charged with any crime, were still rotting in a noisome dungeon. The petitions were in vain; death, more compassionate than crowned heads, released two more of the prisoners, Cassels and Blackburne, leaving Bernardi the solitary survivor; and it was not till 1736 that he died in Newgate, after a cruel and unjust, if not exactly illegal, confinement of forty years. He had one solace, however, in his long imprisonment. It appears that he married in 1712, and a writer of the day tells us that his wife, 'by her good management and industry, contributed much to his support and comfort, and to the keeping of his heart from breaking under the worst of his hardships, difficulties, and distresses.' Ten children were the result of this marriage in Newgate, and of them we are told that 'in respect of charge and expense under his strait and narrow circumstances, and under his immurement or being buried alive, they were no small burden to him, yet he esteemed them great blessings.'

A somewhat similar instance of suffering and injustice was perpetrated by the revolution government in Scotland. In 1690, an English gentleman, named Neville Payne, was arrested on suspicion of being implicated in the conspiracy to restore James II., commonly known as Montgomery's Plot. The Scotch privy-council, not, however, without instructions from London, put Payne to the torture, but though considered to be 'a cowardly fellow,' he did not make any disclosures. Severer means were employed to extract confession and the names of accomplices, the torture being applied to both thumbs and one leg, as severely as compatible with the preservation of life, but without success. Although there was nothing against the man, save mere suspicion, he was confined, with more or less severity, in various prisons in Scotland, for more than ten years, till at last the privy-council, apparently puzzled as to what they would do with the 'vain, talking fellow,' liberated him without bail or other security. From the *Domestic Annals of Scotland*, we learn that Payne was an inventor and projector of improvements in ship-building and river navigation; and in all probability he was the same Nevill Payne who figures in the dramatic history of England as the author of three clever plays.

## GEORGE III., AN AUTHOR.

The 22d of September 1761 was the day of that often-described ceremony, the coronation of George III. It is scarcely at all known that this monarch was the author of at least one article, printed in a periodical publication. In the seventh volume of Young's *Annals of Agriculture*, there is a paper giving an account of a farm held by a Mr Ducket, at Petersham, in Surrey, and bearing the signature of Ralph Robinson. This paper, it is asserted on indubitable evidence, was written by George III. Mr Ducket was one of the first to apply machinery to agriculture, and as he was an able mechanician, as well as farmer, the paper was one of no small interest. Mr Ducket's farm, which had thus the honour of a royal description, was for some years held by Dr Ellis, the hydropathist.

During a part of his life, George III. made careful notes on the various persons and circumstances that came more immediately under his observation; illustrating his notes with very apposite quotations from Shakspeare, and other authors. One of these note-books for 1778 happened to fall under the inspection of Mr Willis, the well-known bookseller, who has recorded two instances of apt quotation by the king; both rather different from what might be expected. In allusion to Franklin, he quotes the following words from *Julius Cæsar:*

'O let us have him; for his silver hairs
Will purchase us a good opinion,
And buy men's voices to commend our deeds:
It shall be said his judgment rul'd our hands;
Our youths and wildness shall no whit appear,
But all be buried in his gravity.'

Dr Johnson does not fare so well in the king's estimation. In allusion to his name, the monarch thus quotes from *Love's Labour's Lost:*

'He draweth out the thread of his verbosity finer than the staple of his argument. I abhor such fanatical phantasms; such insociable and point-device companions; such rackers of orthography.'

George III. was accustomed to pay the minutest attention to details, and regulated everything in his own household and family. This habit is illustrated in a remarkable manner by the following arrangements, made by him for a journey to Portsmouth, and a note directing a change in his first plan, carefully copied from the original in his own handwriting. The king made few journeys, but this was on a memorable occasion, being to review the fleet, and present Lord Howe with a sword of honour, on his arrival at Portsmouth, after the glorious battle of the 1st of June. During the time the king stayed at Portsmouth, he resided in the house of Sir Charles Saxton, commissioner of the dock-yard.

'At the Commissioner's.

1. A bedchamber for the King and Queen. If with convenience, a small room for the Queen to dress; if not, can dress in the bedchamber.
2. A chamber for the Princess Royal and Princess Amelia.
3. A bedchamber for Princesses Augusta and Elizabeth.
4. A bedchamber for Princesses Mary and Sophia.

Mrs Clevely, Mrs Sands, Miss Mackenthun, Mrs Turner, Mrs Willis, and Miss Albert.

Brown, Clark, Gisewell, Albert, Dureau, Robinson, Colesham, and Cox.

2 Footmen of the King.
1 Ditto of the Queen.
2 Hobby Grooms,
& 12 Coach-horse servants.
20 Coach-horses.

Horses for three post-coaches, five post-chaises, and two saddle-horses, on the Monday; on the Tuesday, for two post-coaches and six saddle-horses.

Lady Courtown.
Lady Caroline Waldegrave.
Lady Frances Howard.
Lord Harrington.
Mr G. Goldsworthy.
Mr G. Gwynn.
Mr Price.
Prince Ernest—one gentleman and three servants.

'WINDSOR, *June* 16, 1794.

Since I have seen —— this evening, it is settled that Princess Royal will not go to Portsmouth, consequently not Miss Mackenthun, and the two next princesses will take but one servant between them, consequently Mrs Clevely, Mrs Sands, Mrs Willis, and Miss Albert will go in the post-coach, and one post-chaise will be wanting at every stage on Monday.'

# SEPTEMBER 23.

**St Linus, pope and martyr, 1st century. St Thecla, virgin and martyr, 1st century. St Adamnan, abbot, 705.**

*Born*—Octavius Cæsar Augustus, first Roman emperor, 63 B.C., *Aricia;* Dr Jeremy Collier, celebrated author of *A View of the Stage*, &c., 1650, *Stow Qui, Cambridgeshire;* Karl Theodor Körner, German poet, 1791, *Dresden*.

*Died*.—Bishop Jewel, eminent prelate, 1571; Hermann Boerhaavé, distinguished physician, 1738, *Leyden;* Dr Matthew Baillie, eminent physician, 1823; William Upcott, collector of historical manuscripts, 1845, *London;* Edward Wedlake Brayley, topographical and antiquarian writer, 1854.

## KARL THEODOR KÖRNER.

The life-blood of Germany was never roused nor quickened with greater impetus, than when the old fatherland sprung to arms to assert its rights against the tyrannical sway of France, towards the close of the first Napoleon's career. For years she had groaned under the sway; but repeated defeats had taught her to succumb to the oppression which it seemed impossible to resist. Hope at last gleamed upon her from the lights of burning Moscow, and in 1813 she rose, determined to throw off the yoke. In thus vindicating her outraged rights, she was nobly supported by the intellect and genius, as well as military prowess of her sons. The stirring lectures of Fichte, and the martial lyrics of Körner, were no less effective towards the liberation of their country than the valour and strategical skill of Lützow and Blücher.

The father of Karl Theodor Körner held a distinguished position as member of the privy-council of Saxony, and numbered Goethe and Schiller among his personal friends. In his infantine days, Karl was a sickly delicate child, but as he advanced in years, he rapidly outgrew all these signs of weakness, and by the time he approached manhood, was noted for his adroitness in all manly exercises, more especially horsemanship and fencing, besides being renowned for his musical skill, and grace and agility as a dancer. To crown all these, nature had bestowed on him a fine military figure and handsome countenance, with large, full, and expressive eyes. The law was the profession to which his father's wishes would have destined him; but young Körner's tastes inclining more to natural science and engineering, he was sent, when a stripling, to Freiberg, to study mining in the school there presided over by the celebrated geologist, Werner. He pursued his studies in this place in theoretical and practical mining with much enthusiasm, but quitted it in 1810, to attend the university of Leipsic, from which, after remaining for a short time, he proceeded to that of Berlin. In the same year, he made his first appearance before the public, by the issue of a small volume of poems, entitled *Die Knospen*, or 'The Buds.' From Berlin he was sent by his father to Vienna, where he seems to have turned his attention chiefly to dramatic composition, and produced several pieces, one of which, more especially, a tragedy on the subject of Zriny, the Hungarian hero, was performed with immense success. Among his friends in Vienna were included Wilhelm von Humboldt, then ambassador from the Prussian court, and Frederick Schlegel, the celebrated historical commentator and poet. During his stay in Vienna, also, he formed an ardent attachment to a young lady, which met the entire approbation of his family, and arrangements were entered into for their speedy union.

But another bride now claimed the attentions of Körner. The cry to arms which in the spring of 1813 echoed from one end of Germany to the other, found an enthusiastic response in his bosom, and he felt himself impelled to take his place forthwith in the ranks of those patriots who were striving for the liberation of their country in Prussia and the northern states of the confederation. Writing to his father, he says: 'Germany is roused; the Prussian eagle flaps its wings and awakes in all true hearts the great hope of German freedom. My genius sighs for its fatherland; let me be its worthy son. Now that I know what happiness may be realised in this life, and when all the stars of my destiny look down on me with such genial rays, now does a righteous inspiration tell me that no sacrifice can be too great for that highest of all human blessings, the vindication of a nation's freedom.'

In pursuance of this resolve, Körner, in the month of March, quitted Vienna, and proceeded to Breslau, where he joined Lützow's celebrated company of volunteers, or the Black Huntsmen, as they were termed. A few days after his joining the corps, it was solemnly dedicated to the service of its country in the church of Rochau, the services concluding with Luther's noble hymn, *Ein' feste Burg ist unser Gott*. The powers of physical endurance which Körner had acquired in the course of his mining studies at Freiberg, proved of eminent service to him in the fatigues of a military life. His enthusiasm and aptitude for his new duties soon procured his elevation to the post of lieutenant, whilst the geniality and kindliness of his nature made him the idol of his comrades. Here, too, his martial muse was fairly called into action, and some of the noblest of those lyrics which have rendered him the Tyrtæus and Pindar of Germany, were composed beside the bivouac and watch-fires during the intervals of military duty. In the battle of Gorde, near the Elbe, where the French received a signal check, and in the subsequent victorious march of Lützow's volunteers by Halberstadt and Eisleben to Plauen, Körner took a prominent part, acting in the latter movement as adjutant to the commander. Whilst lying at Plauen, an intimation was treacherously conveyed to Lützow of an armistice having been concluded, and he accordingly proceeded to Kitzen, a village in the neighbourhood of Leipsic. Here he found himself surrounded and threatened by a large body of French, and Körner was despatched to demand an explanation from the officer in command, who, instead of replying, cut him down with his sword, and a general engagement ensued. The Black Huntsmen were forced to save themselves by flight; and Körner, who had only escaped death by his horse swerving aside, took shelter in a neighbouring wood, where he was nearly being discovered by a detachment of French, but contrived to scare them away by shouting in as stentorian tones as he could utter: 'The fourth squadron will advance!'

Faint with the loss of blood, and the stunning effects of a severe wound in the head, he at length fell in with some of his old comrades, who procured him surgical assistance, and he managed afterwards to get himself smuggled into Leipsic, then under the rigorous military rule of the French. From this he escaped to Karlsbad, and at last, after visiting various places, reached Berlin, where he succeeded in completely re-establishing his health. Anxious to join again his companions in arms, he now hurried back to the banks of the Elbe, where Marshal Davoust, with a strong reinforcement of Danish troops from Hamburg, was threatening Northern Germany. On 17th August, hostilities were renewed, and Lützow's troops, who guarded the outposts, were brought almost daily into contact with the enemy. On the 25th, the commander resolved to make an attack with a detachment of his cavalry on the rear of the French, but in the meantime received intelligence of an approaching convoy of provisions and military stores escorted by two companies of infantry. This transport had to pass a wood at a little distance from Rosenberg, and here Lützow posted his men, disposing them in two divisions, one of which, with himself at their head, should attack the enemy on the flank, whilst the other remained closed up to cover the rear. During their halt in the thicket, Körner, who acted as Lützow's adjutant, employed the interval of leisure in composing his celebrated *Sword-Song*, which was found in his pocket-book after his death, and has not inaptly been likened to the lay of the dying swan. On the enemy's detachment coming up, it proved stronger than had been anticipated, but it nevertheless broke and fled before the Prussian cavalry, who pursued them across the plain to a thicket of underwood. Here a number of their sharp-shooters ensconced themselves, and for a time galled Lützow's troops by a shower of bullets. One of these passed through the neck of Körner's horse, and afterwards the abdomen and backbone of his rider, who fell mortally wounded. He was conveyed at once by his comrades to a quiet spot in the wood, and assistance was procured, but he never regained consciousness after receiving the wound, and in a few minutes expired. He had met the death which of all others he had vaunted in his lyrics as the most to be desired—that of a soldier in the arms of victory, and in defence of the liberties of his country. This event took place in the gray dawn of an autumn morning, on the 26th August 1813. His body was interred, with all the honours of war, beneath an oak on the roadside near the village of Wobbelin. The tomb has since been surrounded by a wall and a monument erected to his memory, the Duke of Mecklenburg-Schwerin making a present of the ground to Körner's family. Here, a few years later, were deposited the remains of Theodor's beloved sister, Emma, and, at a subsequent period, those of his father.

Thus prematurely terminated, at the age of twenty-two, the career of this young hero whose patriotic lyrics, like those of Moritz Arndt, seem to have entwined themselves round the very heart-strings of the German people. Though somewhat inferior in sonorous majesty to Thomas Campbell's warlike odes, they possess a superiority over them in point of the earnestness with which every line of the German poet is animated. Young, brave, and generous, his effusions are literally the out-breathings of an unselfish and gallant spirit, which disregards every danger, and counts all other considerations as dross in the attainment of some grand and noble end. A collection of his martial poems, under the title of *Leier und Schwert* (Lyre and Sword), was published at Berlin the year following his death. Many of these, including 'My Fatherland,' 'Song of the Black Huntsmen,' 'Lützow's Wild Chase,' 'The Battle-prayer,' and 'The Sword Song' are well known to the English public through translations.

One of Körner's most popular songs is 'The Song of the Sword,' which he wrote only two hours before the engagement in which he was shot. He compares his sword to a bride, and represents it as pleading with him to consummate the wedding. This explains the allusion in the following poem by Mrs Hemans, which we quote as a graceful tribute from one of ourselves to the memory of a noble stranger.

FOR THE DEATH-DAY OF THEODOR KÖRNER.

A song for the death-day of the brave,
A song of pride!
The youth went down to a hero's grave,
With the sword, his bride!

He went with his noble heart unworn,
And pure, and high;
An eagle stooping from clouds of morn,
Only to die.

He went with the lyre, whose lofty tone,
Beneath his hand,
Had thrill'd to the name of his God alone,
And his fatherland.

And with all his glorious feelings yet
In their day-spring's glow,
Like a southern stream that no frost hath met
To chain its flow!

A song for the death-day of the brave,
A song of pride!
For him that went to a hero's grave
With the sword, his bride!

He has left a voice in his trumpet lays
To turn the fight;
And a spirit to shine through the after-days
As a watch-fire's light;

And a grief in his father's soul to rest
'Midst all high thought;
And a memory unto his mother's breast
With healing fraught.

And a name and fame above the blight
Of earthly breath;
Beautiful—beautiful and bright
In life and death!

A song for the death-day of the brave.
A song of pride!
For him that went to a hero's grave
With the sword, his bride!

## UPCOTT, THE MANUSCRIPT-COLLECTOR.

In a work of this nature, it would be improper to omit reference to one so devoted to the collection and preservation of English historical curiosities as William Upcott, sometimes styled the *King of Autograph-collectors*. Ostensibly, he pursued a modest career in life, as under-librarian of the London Institution: the life below the surface exhibited him as acting under the influence of a singular instinct for the acquisition of documents connected with English history—one of those aids to literature whose names are generally seen only in foot-notes or in sentences of prefaces, while the truth is that, but for them, the efforts and the powers of the most accomplished historians would be vain. Upcott was born in Oxfordshire in 1779, and was set up originally as a collector by his godfather, Ozias Humphrey, the eminent portrait-painter, who left him his correspondence. With this as a nucleus, he went on collecting for a long series of years, till, in 1836, his collection consisted of thirty-two thousand letters illustrated by three thousand portraits, the value of the whole being estimated by himself at £10,000. That this was not an extravagant appraisement may now be averred, when we know that, after large portions of the collection had been disposed of, a mere remnant, sold by auction after the collector's death, brought £412, 17*s*. 6*d*. It was to Upcott that the public was indebted for the preservation of the manuscript of the Diary of John Evelyn, a valuable store of matter regarding English familiar life in the seventeenth century. The Correspondence of Henry, Earl of Clarendon, and that of Ralph Thoresby, were also published from the originals in Mr Upcott's collection.

This singular enthusiast spent the last years of his useful and unpretending life in an old mansion in the Upper Street at Islington, which he quaintly denominated *Autograph Cottage*.

## NAVAL ENGAGEMENT OFF FLAMBOROUGH HEAD, SEPTEMBER 23, 1779.

On 23d September 1779, a serious naval engagement took place on the coast of Yorkshire, H.M.S. *Serapis* and *Countess of Scarborough* being the ships on the one side, and a squadron under the command of the celebrated adventurer Paul Jones on the other. It was a time of embarrassment in England. Unexpected difficulties and disasters had been experienced in the attempt to enforce the loyalty of the American colonies. Several of England's continental neighbours were about to take advantage of her weakness to declare against her. In that crisis it was that Jones came and insulted the coasts of Britain. Driven out of the Firth of Forth by a strong westerly wind, he came southwards till he reached the neighbourhood of Flamborough Head, where he resolved to await the Baltic and merchant fleet, expected shortly to arrive there on its homeward voyage under the convoy of the two men-of-war above mentioned. About two o'clock in the afternoon of the 23d September, Jones, on board of his vessel the *Bon Homme Richard* (so called after his friend Benjamin Franklin), descried the fleet in question, with its escort, advancing north-north-east, and numbering forty-one sail. He at once hoisted the signal for a general chase, on perceiving which the two frigates bore out from the land in battle-array, whilst the merchant vessels crowded all sail towards shore, and succeeded in gaining shelter beneath the guns of Scarborough Castle. There was little wind, and, according to Jones's own account, it was nightfall before the *Bon Homme Richard* could come up with the *Serapis*, when an engagement within pistol-shot commenced, and continued at that distance for nearly an hour, the advantage both in point of manageableness and number of guns being on the side of the British ship; whilst the remaining vessels of Jones's squadron, from some inexplicable cause, kept at a distance, and he was obliged for a long time to maintain single-handed a contest with the *two* English frigates. The harvest-moon, in the meantime, rose calm and beautiful, casting its silver light over the waters of the German Ocean, the surface of which, smooth as a mirror, bore the squadrons engaged in deadly conflict. Suddenly, some old eighteen-pounders on board the *Bon Homme Richard* exploded at their first discharge, killing and wounding many of Jones's sailors; and as he had now only two pieces of cannon on the quarter-deck remaining unsilenced, and his vessel had been struck by several shots below the water-level, his position was becoming very critical. Just then, while he ran great danger of going to the bottom, the bowsprit of the *Serapis* came athwart the poop of the *Bon Homme Richard*, and Jones, with his own hands, made the two vessels fast in that position. A dreadful scene at close-quarters then ensued, in which Captain Pearson, the British commander, inflicted signal damage by his artillery on the under part of his opponent's vessel, whilst his own decks were rendered almost untenable by the hand-grenades and volleys of musketry which, on their cannon becoming unserviceable, the combatants on board the *Bon Homme Richard* discharged with murderous effect. For a long time the latter seemed decidedly to have the worst of the contest, and on one occasion the master-gunner, believing that Jones and the lieutenant were killed, and himself left as the officer in command, rushed up to the poop to haul down the colours in the hopelessness of maintaining any longer the conflict. But the flagstaff had been shot away at the commencement of the engagement, and he could only make his intentions known by calling out over the ship's side for quarter. Captain Pearson then hailed to know if the *Bon Homme Richard* surrendered, an interrogation which Jones immediately answered in the negative, and the fight continued to rage. Meantime the *Countess of Scarborough* had been engaged by the *Pallas*, a vessel belonging to Jones's squadron, and after a short conflict had surrendered. The *Bon Homme Richard* was thus freed from the attacks of a double foe, but was at the same time nearly brought to destruction by the *Alliance*, one of its companion-vessels, which, after keeping for a long time at a distance, advanced to the scene of action, and poured in several broadsides, most of which took effect on her own ally instead of the British frigate. At last the galling fire from the shrouds of Jones's ship told markedly in the thinning of the crew of the *Serapis*, and silencing her fire; and a terrible explosion on board of her, occasioned by a young sailor, a Scotchman, it is alleged, who, taking his stand upon the extreme end of the yard of the *Bon Homme Richard*, dropped a grenade on a row of cartridges on the main-deck of the *Serapis*, spread such disaster and confusion that Captain Pearson shortly afterwards struck his colours and surrendered. This was at eleven o'clock at night, after the engagement had lasted for upwards of four hours. The accounts of the losses on both sides are very contradictory, but seem to have been nearly equal, and may be estimated in all at about three hundred killed and wounded. The morning following the battle was extremely foggy, and on examining the *Bon Homme Richard*, she was found to have sustained such damage that it was impossible she

ENGAGEMENT OFF FLAMBOROUGH HEAD.
(From a contemporary print.)

could keep longer afloat. With all expedition her crew abandoned her, and went on board the *Serapis*, of which Paul Jones took the command. The *Bon Homme Richard* sank almost immediately, with a large sum of money belonging to Jones, and many valuable papers. The prize-ships were now conveyed by him to the Texel, a proceeding which led to a demand being made by the English ambassador at the Hague for the delivery of the captured vessels, and the surrender of Jones himself as a pirate. This application to the Dutch authorities was ineffectual, but it served as one of the predisposing causes of the war which not long afterwards ensued with England After remaining for a while at the Texel, the *Serapis* was taken to the port of L'Orient, in France, where she appears subsequently to have been disarmed and broken up, whilst the *Countess of Scarborough* was conveyed to Dunkirk. Meantime, Jones proceeded to France, with the view of arranging his future movements ; but before quitting the Texel, he returned to Captain Pearson his sword, in recognition, as he says, of the bravery which he had displayed on board the *Serapis*. Pearson's countrymen seem to have entertained the same estimate of his merits, as, on his subsequent return to England, he was received with great distinction, was knighted by George III., and presented with a service of plate and the freedom of their corporations, by those boroughs on the east coast which lay near the scene of the naval engagement. In France, honours no less flattering were bestowed on Paul Jones. At the opera and all public places, he received enthusiastic ovations, and Louis XVI. presented him with a gold-hilted sword, on which was engraved, '*Vindicati maris Ludovicus XVI. remunerator strenuo vindici*' (From Louis XVI., in recognition of the services of the brave maintainer of the privileges of the sea).

It may be noted that the true name of Paul Jones was *John Paul*, and that he made the change probably at the time when he entered the American service. His career was altogether a most singular one, presenting phases to the full as romantic as any of those undergone by a hero of fiction. The son of a small farmer near Dumfries, we find him manifesting from his boyhood a strong predilection for the sea, and at the age of twelve commencing life as a cabin-boy, on board the *Friendship* of Whitehaven, trading to Virginia. After completing his apprenticeship, he made several voyages in connection with the slave-trade to the West Indies, and rose to the position of master. He speedily, however, it is said, conceived a disgust to the traffic, and abandoned it. We find him, about 1775, accepting a commission in the American navy, then newly formed in opposition to that of Britain. What inspired Paul with such feelings of rancour against his native country, cannot now be ascertained ; but to the end of his life he seemed to retain undiminished the most implacable resentment towards the British nation. The cause of the colonies against the mother-country, now generally admitted to have been a just one, was adopted by him with the utmost enthusiasm, and certainly he contrived to inflict a considerable amount of damage on British shipping in the course of his cruises.

To the British nation, and to Scotchmen more especially, the name of Paul Jones has heretofore only been suggestive of a daring pirate or lawless adventurer. He appears, in reality, to have been a sincere and enthusiastic partisan of the cause of the colonists, many of whom were as much natives of Britain as himself, and yet have never been specially blamed for their partisanship. In personal respects, he was a gallant and resolute man, of romantically chivalrous feelings, and superior to everything like a mean or shabby action. It is particularly pleasant to remark his disinterestedness in restoring, in after-years, to the Countess of Selkirk, the family-plate which the necessity of satisfying his men had compelled him to deprive her of, on the occasion of his descent on the Scottish coast, and for which he paid them the value out of his own resources. The letters addressed by him on this subject to the countess and her husband, do great credit both to his generosity and abilities in point of literary composition. By the Americans, Admiral Paul Jones is regarded as one of their most distinguished naval celebrities.

## MONEY THAT CAME IN THE DARK.

The following simply-told narrative, though not so very wonderful as to shock our credulity, contains a pleasing spice of mystery, from its want of a direct explanation. It was found, under the date of September 23, 1673, in an old memorandum-book, that had belonged to a certain Paul Bowes, Esq., of the Middle Temple. A little more than a hundred years later, in 1783, the book, and one of the mysteriously-found pieces of money, was in the possession of an Essex gentleman, a lineal descendant of the fortunate Mr Bowes.

'About the year 1658, after I had been some years settled in the Middle Temple, in a chamber in Elm Court, up three pair of stairs, one night as I came into the chamber, in the dark, I went into my study, in the dark, to lay down my gloves, upon the table in my study, for I then, being my own man, placed my things in their certain places, that I could go to them in the dark ; and as I laid my gloves down, I felt under my hand a piece of money, which I then supposed, by feeling, to be a shilling; but when I had light, I found it a twenty-shilling piece of gold. I did a little reflect how it might come there, yet could not satisfy my own thoughts, for I had no client then, it being several years before I was called to the bar, and I had few visitors that could drop it there, and no friends in town that might designedly lay it there as a bait, to encourage me at my studies; and although I was the master of some gold, yet I had so few pieces, I well knew it was none of my number; but, however, this being the first time I found gold, I supposed it left there by some means I could not guess at. About three weeks after, coming again into my chamber in the dark, and laying down my gloves at the same place in my study, I felt under my hand a piece of money, which also proved a twenty-shilling piece of gold; this moved me to further consideration; but, after all my thoughtfulness, I could not imagine any probable way how the gold could come there, but I do not remember that I ever found any, when I went with those expectations and desires. About a month after the second time, coming into my chamber, in the dark, and laying down my gloves upon the same place, on the table in my study, I found two pieces of money under my hand, which, after I had lighted my candle, I found to be two twenty-shilling pieces; and, about the distance of six weeks after, in the same place, and in the dark, I found another piece of gold, and this about the distance of a month, or five or six weeks. I several times after, at the same place, and always in the dark, found twenty-shilling pieces of gold; at length, being with my cousin Langton, grandmother to my cousin Susan Skipwith, lately married to Sir John Williams, I told her this story, and I do not remember that I ever found any gold there after, although I kept that chamber above two years longer, before I sold it to Mr Anthony Weldon, who now hath it (this being 23d September 1673). Thus I have, to the best of my remembrance, truly stated this fact, but could never know, or have any probable conjecture, how that gold was laid there.'

The relationship that existed between cousin Langton and cousin Skipwith does not seem very clear, according to our modern method of reckoning kindred; but it must be recollected that, in former times, the title of cousin was given to any collateral relative more remote than a brother or sister. Probably, cousin Langton was Mr Bowes's grandmother as well as Miss Skipwith's, and, if she liked, could have solved the mystery. For the writer has known more than one instance of benevolent old ladies making presents of money to young relatives, in a similarly stealthy and eccentric manner.

## SEPTEMBER 24.

St Rusticus or Rotiri, bishop of Auvergne, 5th century. St Chuniald or Conald, priest and missionary. St Germer or Geremar, abbot, 658. St Gerard, bishop of Chonad, martyr, 1046.

*Born.*—Sharon Turner, historian, 1768, *London.*

*Died.*—Pepin, king of France, 768; Michael III., Greek emperor, assassinated, 867; Pope Innocent II., 1143; William of Wykeham, founder of Winchester School, 1404, *South Waltham;* Samuel Butler, author of *Hudibras*, 1680, *London;* Henry, Viscount Hardinge, governor-general and commander in India, 1856, *South Park, near Tunbridge.*

### The Feast of Ingathering.

Wherever, throughout the earth, there is such a thing as a formal harvest, there also appears an inclination to mark it with a festive celebration. The wonder, the gratitude, the piety felt towards the great Author of nature, when it is brought before us that, once more, as it has ever been, the ripening of a few varieties of grass has furnished food for earth's teeming millions, insure that there should everywhere be some sort of feast of ingathering. In England, this festival passes generally under the endeared name of *Harvest-Home.* In Scotland, where that term is unknown, the festival is hailed under the name of the *Kirn.* In the north of England, its ordinary designation is the *Mell-Supper.* And there are perhaps other local names. But everywhere there is a thankful joy, a feeling which pervades all ranks and conditions of the rural people, and for once in the year brings all upon a level. The servant sympathises with the success of his master in the great labours of the year. The employer looks kindly down upon his toiling servants, and feels it but due to them that they should have a banquet furnished out of the abundance which God has given him—one in which he and his family should join them, all conventional distinctions sinking under the overpowering gush of natural, and, it may be added, religious feeling, which so well befits the time.

Most of our old harvest-customs were connected with the ingathering of the crops, but some of them began with the commencement of harvest-work. Thus, in the southern counties, it was customary for the labourers to elect, from among themselves, a leader, whom they denominated their 'lord.' To him all the rest were required to give precedence, and to leave all transactions respecting their work. He made the terms with the farmers for mowing, for reaping, and for all the rest of the harvest-work; he took the lead with the scythe, with the sickle, and on the 'carrying days;' he was to be the first to eat, and the first to drink, at all their refreshments; his mandate was to be law to all the rest, who were bound to address him as 'My Lord,' and to shew him all due honour and respect. Disobedience in any of these particulars was punished by imposing fines according to a scale previously agreed on by 'the lord' and all his vassals. In some instances, if any of his men swore or told a lie in his presence, a fine was inflicted. In Buckinghamshire and other counties, 'a lady' was elected as well as 'a lord,' which often added much merriment to the harvest-season. For, while the lady was to receive all honours due to the lord from the rest of the labourers, he (for the lady was one of the workmen) was required to pass it on to the lord. For instance, at drinking-time, the vassals were to give the horn first to the lady, who passed it to the lord, and when he had drunk, *she* drank next, and then the others indiscriminately. Every departure from this rule incurred a fine. The blunders which led to fines, of course, were frequent, and produced great merriment.

In the old simple days of England, before the natural feelings of the people had been checked and chilled off by Puritanism in the first place, and what may be called gross Commercialism in the second, the harvest-home was such a scene as Horace's friends might have expected to see at his Sabine farm, or Theocritus described in his *Idylls.* Perhaps it really was the very same scene which was presented in ancient times. The grain last cut was brought home in its wagon—called the *Hock Cart*—surmounted by a figure formed of a sheaf with gay dressings—a presumable representation of the goddess Ceres—while a pipe and tabor went merrily sounding in front, and the reapers tripped around in a hand-in-hand ring, singing appropriate songs, or simply by shouts and cries giving vent to the excitement of the day.

'Harvest-home, harvest-home,
We have ploughed, we have sowed,
We have reaped, we have mowed,
We have brought home every load,
Hip, hip, hip, harvest-home!'

So they sang or shouted. In Lincolnshire and other districts, hand-bells were carried by those riding on the last load, and the following rhymes were sung:

'The boughs do shake, and the bells do ring,
So merrily comes our harvest in,
Our harvest in, our harvest in,
So merrily comes our harvest in!
Hurrah!'

Troops of village children, who had contributed in various ways to the great labour, joined the throng, solaced with plum-cake in requital of their little services. Sometimes, the image on the cart, instead of being a mere dressed-up bundle of grain, was a pretty girl of the reaping-band, crowned with flowers, and hailed as *the Maiden.* Of this we have a description in a ballad of Bloomfield's:

'Home came the jovial Hockey load,
Last of the whole year's crop,
And Grace among the green boughs rode,
Right plump upon the top.

This way and that the wagon reeled,
And never queen rode higher;
Her cheeks were coloured in the field,
And ours before the fire.'

In some provinces—we may instance Buckinghamshire—it was a favourite practical joke to lay an ambuscade at some place where a high bank or a tree gave opportunity, and drench the hock-cart party with water. Great was the merriment, when this was cleverly and effectively done, the riders laughing, while they shook themselves, as merrily as the rest. Under all the rustic jocosities of the occasion, there seemed a basis of pagan custom; but it was such as not to exclude a Christian sympathy. Indeed, the harvest-home of Old England was obviously and beyond question a piece of natural religion, an ebullition of jocund gratitude to the divine source of all earthly blessings.

Herrick describes the harvest-home of his epoch (the earlier half of the seventeenth century) with his usual felicity of expression.

'Come, sons of summer, by whose toile
We are the Lords of wine and oile;
By whose tough labours, and rough hands,
We rip up first, then reap our lands,
Crown'd with the eares of corne, now come,
And, to the pipe, sing harvest-home.
Come forth, my Lord, and see the cart,
Drest up with all the country art.
See here a maukin, there a sheet
As spotlesse pure as it is sweet:
The horses, mares, and frisking fillies,
Clad, all, in linnen, white as lillies,
The harvest swaines and wenches bound
For joy, to see the hock-cart crown'd.
About the cart heare how the rout
Of rural younglings raise the shout;
Pressing before, some coming after,
Those with a shout, and these with laughter.
Some blesse the cart; some kisse the sheaves;
Some prank them up with oaken leaves:
Some crosse the fill-horse; some with great
Devotion stroak the home-borne wheat:
While other rusticks, lesse attent
To prayers than to merryment,
Run after with their breeches rent.
Well, on, brave boyes, to your Lord's hearth
Glitt'ring with fire, where, for your mirth,
You shall see first the large and cheefe
Foundation of your feast, fat beefe:
With upper stories, mutton, veale,
And bacon, which makes full the meale;
With sev'rall dishes standing by,
As here a custard, there a pie,
And here all-tempting frumentie.
And for to make the merrie cheere
If smirking wine be wanting here,
There's that which drowns all care, stout beere,
Which freely drink to your Lord's health,
Then to the plough, the commonwealth;
Next to your flailes, your fanes, your fatts,
Then to the maids with wheaten hats;
To the rough sickle, and the crookt sythe
Drink, frollick, boyes, till all be blythe,
Feed and grow fat, and as ye eat,
Be mindfull that the lab'ring neat,
As you, may have their full of meat;
And know, besides, ye must revoke
The patient oxe unto the yoke,
And all goe back unto the plough
And harrow, though they 're hang'd up now.
And, you must know, your Lord's word's true,
Feed him ye must, whose food fils you.
And that this pleasure is like raine,
Not sent ye for to drowne your paine,
But for to make it spring againe.'

In the north, there seem to have been some differences in the observance. It was common there for the reapers, on the last day of their business, to have a contention for superiority in quickness of dispatch, groups of three or four taking each a ridge, and striving which should soonest get to its termination. In Scotland, this was called a *kemping*, which simply means a striving. In the north of England, it was a *mell*, which, I suspect, means the same thing (from Fr. *mêlée*). As the reapers went on during the last day, they took care to leave a good handful of the grain uncut, but laid down flat, and covered over; and, when the field was done, the 'bonniest lass' was allowed to cut this final handful, which was presently dressed up with various sewings, tyings, and trimmings, like a doll, and hailed as a *Corn Baby*. It was brought home in triumph, with music of fiddles and bagpipes, was set up conspicuously that night at supper, and was usually preserved in the farmer's parlour for the remainder of the year. The bonny lass who cut this handful of grain, was deemed the *Har'st Queen.* In Hertfordshire, and probably other districts of England, there was the same custom of reserving a final handful; but it was tied up and erected, under the name of a *Mare*, and the reapers then, one after another, threw their sickles at it, to cut it down. The successful individual called out: 'I have her!' 'What have you?' cried the rest. 'A mare, a mare, a mare!' he replied. 'What will you do with her?' was then asked. 'We'll send her to John Snooks,' or whatever other name, referring to some neighbouring farmer who had not yet got all his grain cut down.

This piece of rustic pleasantry was called *Crying the Mare.* It is very curious to learn, that there used to be a similar practice in so remote a district

HARVEST-HOME.

as the Isle of Skye. A farmer having there got his harvest completed, the last cut handful was sent, under the name of *Goabbir Bhacagh* (the Cripple Goat), to the next farmer who was still at work upon his crops, it being of course necessary for the bearer to take some care that, on delivery, he should be able instantly to take to his heels, and escape the punishment otherwise sure to befall him.

The custom of *Crying the Mare* is more particularly described by the Rev. C. H. Hartshorne, in his *Salopia Antiqua* (p. 498). 'When a farmer has ended his reaping, and the wooden bottle is passing merrily round, the reapers form themselves into two bands, and commence the following dialogue in loud shouts, or rather in a kind of chant at the utmost pitch of their voice. First band: *I have her, I have her, I have her!* (Every sentence is repeated three times.) Second: *What hast thee? What hast thee? What hast thee?* First: *A mare, a mare, a mare!* Second: *Whose is her? Whose is her? Whose is her?* First: A. B.'s (naming their master, whose corn is all cut. Second: *Where shall we send her?* &c. First: To C. D. (naming some neighbour whose corn is still standing). And the whole concludes with a joyous shout of both bands united.

'In the south-eastern part of Shropshire, the ceremony is performed with a slight variation. The last few stalks of the wheat are left standing; all the reapers throw their sickles, and he who cuts it off, cries: "*I have her, I have her, I have her!*" on which the rustic mirth begins; and it is practised in a manner very similar in Devonshire. The latest farmer in the neighbourhood, whose reapers therefore cannot send her to any other person, is said to *keep her all the winter*. This rural ceremony, which is fast wearing away, evidently refers to the time when, our county lying all open in common fields, and the corn consequently exposed to the depredations of the wild mares, the season at which it was secured from their ravages was a time of rejoicing, and of exulting over a tardier neighbour.'

Mr Bray describes the same custom as practised in Devonshire, and the chief peculiarity in that instance is, that the last handful of the standing grain is called the Nack. On this being cut, the reapers assemble round it, calling at the top of their voices, 'Arnack, arnack, arnack! we have'n, we have'n, we have'n,' and the firkin is then handed round; after which the party goes home dancing and shouting. Mr Bray considers it a relic of Druidism, but, as it appears to us, without any good reason. He also indulges in some needlessly profound speculations regarding the meaning of the words used. 'Arnack' appears to us as simply 'Our nag,' an idea very nearly corresponding to 'the Mare;' and 'we have'n' seems to be merely 'we have him.'

In the evening of harvest-home, the supper takes place in the barn, or some other suitable place, the master and mistress generally presiding. This feast is always composed of substantial viands, with an abundance of good ale, and human nature insures that it should be a scene of intense enjoyment. Some one, with better voice than his neighbours, leads off a song of thanks to the host and hostess, in something like the following strain:

Here 's a health to our master,
  The lord of the feast;
God bless his endeavours,
  And send him increase!

May prosper his crops, boys,
  And we reap next year;
Here 's our master's good health, boys,
  Come, drink off your beer!

Now harvest is ended,
  And supper is past;
Here 's our mistress's health, boys,
  Come, drink a full glass.

For she 's a good woman,
  Provides us good cheer;
Here 's your mistress's good health, boys,
  Come, drink off your beer!

One of the rustic assemblage, being chosen to act as 'lord,' goes out, puts on a sort of disguise, and comes in again, crying in a prolonged note, *Lar-gess!* He and some companions then go about with a plate among the company, and collect a little money with a view to further regalements at the village ale-house. With these, protracted usually to a late hour, the harvest-feast ends.

In Scotland, under the name of the *Kirn* or *Kirn Supper* (supposed to be from the churn of cream usually presented on the occasion), harvest-home ends in like manner. The description of the feast given by Grahame, in his *British Georgics*, includes all the characteristic features:

'The fields are swept, a tranquil silence reigns,
And pause of rural labour, far and near.
Deep is the morning's hush; from grange to grange
Responsive cock-crows, in the distance heard,
Distinct as if at hand, soothe the pleased ear;
And oft, at intervals, the flail, remote,
Sends faintly through the air its deafened sound.

Bright now the shortening day, and blithe its close,
When to the *Kirn* the neighbours, old and young,
Come dropping in to share the well-earned feast.
The smith aside his ponderous sledge has thrown,
Raked up his fire, and cooled the hissing brand.
His sluice the miller shuts; and from the barn
The threshers hie, to don their Sunday coats.
Simply adorned, with ribands, blue and pink,
Bound round their braided hair, the lasses trip
To grace the feast, which now is smoking ranged
On tables of all shape, and size, and height,
Joined awkwardly, yet to the crowded guests
A seemly joyous show, all loaded well:
But chief, at the board-head, the haggis round
Attracts all eyes, and even the goodman's grace
Prunes of its wonted length. With eager knife,
The quivering globe he then prepares to broach;
While for her gown some ancient matron quakes,
Her gown of silken woof, all figured thick
With roses white, far larger than the life,
On azure ground—her grannam's wedding-garb,
Old as that year when Sheriffmuir was fought.
Old tales are told, and well-known jests abound,
Which laughter meets half-way as ancient friends,
Nor, like the worldling, spurns because threadbare.

When ended the repast, and board and bench
Vanish like thought, by many hands removed,
Up strikes the fiddle; quick upon the floor
The youths lead out the half-reluctant maids,
Bashful at first, and darning through the reels
With timid steps, till, by the music cheered,
With free and airy step, they bound along,
Then deftly wheel, and to their partner's face,
Turning this side, now that, with varying step.
Sometimes two ancient couples o'er the floor,
Skim through a reel, and think of youthful years.

Meanwhile the frothing bickers,* soon as filled,
Are drained, and to the gauntrees † oft return,
Where gossips sit, unmindful of the dance.
Salubrious beverage! Were thy sterling worth
But duly prized, no more the alembic vast
Would, like some dire volcano, vomit forth
Its floods of liquid fire, and far and wide
Lay waste the land; no more the fruitful boon
Of twice ten shrievedoms, into poison turned,
Would taint the very life-blood of the poor,
Shrivelling their heart-strings like a burning scroll.

* Beakers.
† Wooden frames on which beer casks are set.

Such was formerly the method of conducting the harvest-feast; and in some instances it is still conducted much in the same manner, but there is a growing tendency in the present day to abolish this method and substitute in its place a general harvest-festival for the whole parish, to which all the farmers are expected to contribute, and which their labourers may freely attend. This festival is usually commenced with a special service in the church, followed by a dinner in a tent, or in some building sufficiently large, and continued with rural sports; and sometimes including a tea-drinking for the women. But this parochial gathering is destitute of one important element in the harvest-supper. It is of too general a character. It provides no particular means for attaching the labourers to their respective masters. If a labourer have any unpleasant feeling towards his master, or is conscious of neglecting his duty, or that his conduct has been offensive towards his master, he will feel ashamed of going to his house to partake of his hospitality, but he will attend without scruple a general feast provided by many contributors, because he will feel under no special obligation to his own master. But if the feast be solely provided by his master, if he receive an invitation from him, if he finds himself welcomed to his house, sits with him at his table, is encouraged to enjoy himself, is allowed to converse freely with him, and treated by him with kindness and cordiality, his prejudices and asperities will be dispelled, and mutual good-will and attachment established. The hospitality of the old-fashioned harvest-supper, and other similar agricultural feasts, was a bond of union between the farmer and his work-people of inestimable value. The only objection alleged against such a feast, is that it often leads to intemperance. So would the harvest-festival, were not regulations adopted to prevent it. If similar regulations were applied to the farmer's harvest-feast, the objection would be removed. Let the farmer invite the clergyman of his parish, and other sober-minded friends, and with their assistance to carry out good regulations, temperance will easily be preserved.

The modern harvest-festival, as a parochial thanksgiving for the bounties of Providence, is an excellent institution, in addition to the old harvest-feast, but it should not be considered as a substitute for it.

---

# SEPTEMBER 25.

St Firmin, bishop of Amiens, martyr. St Barr or Finbarr, first bishop of Cork, confessor, 6th century. St Aunaire, bishop of Auxerre, about 605. St Colfrid, abbot, 716.

---

*Born.*—Christian Gottlob Heyne, classical editor, 1729, *Chemnitz, Saxony;* William Romaine, eminent divine, 1714, *Hartlepool;* Abraham Gottlieb Werner, geologist, 1750, *Wehrau, Upper Lusatia;* Felicia Dorothea Hemans, poetess, 1794, *Liverpool.*

*Died.*—Philip I. of Spain, 1506, *Burgos;* Lancelot Andrews, eminent prelate and writer, 1626; Ambrosio, Marquis of Spinola, great Spanish captain, 1630; Robert Dodsley, bookseller, and dramatist, 1764, *Durham;* Richard Pococke, bishop of Ossory, oriental traveller, 1765; John Henry Lambert, German philosopher, 1777, *Berlin;* Richard Porson, eminent Greek scholar and professor at Cambridge, 1808, *Old Jewry, London.*



## RICHARD PORSON.

The character of Porson exhibits an extraordinary combination of the highest classical learning and critical acumen, with a strong propensity to coarse drollery and convivial excess. His aberrations were indeed in many respects more ludicrous than repulsive, and notwithstanding the additional disadvantage of a rough and unceremonious temper, we can scarcely find it in our hearts to regard him otherwise than as a very honest fellow, who was nobody's enemy but his own.

A brief sketch will suffice for his history. He was the son of the parish clerk of East Ruston, in Norfolk, and having displayed from childhood the most marked inclination for study, with a wonderfully tenacious memory, he came under the notice of Mr Hewitt, the clergyman of the place, who undertook his instruction along with that of his own sons. The weaver's boy, for such was the occupation of Porson's father on week-days, continued to manifest such indications of classical genius, that a subscription was entered into in the neighbourhood to defray the further expenses of his education. Through these means he was sent first to Eton, and afterwards to Trinity College, Cambridge, where he gained a fellowship, but was afterwards obliged to relinquish it, from a conscientious objection to enter holy orders and subscribe the Thirty-Nine Articles. He then wended his way, a penniless adventurer, to London. Here he is said to have subsisted for nearly six weeks on a guinea, but a number of gentlemen, literary men, and others, clubbed together at last to purchase him an annuity of £100, which placed him beyond the reach of want for the remainder of his days. Shortly afterwards, the Greek chair at Cambridge became vacant, and Porson was at once elected to the professorship, which required no declaration of adherence to any rule of faith. The salary was only £40 per annum. Though no lectures or other services were required of him, it would seem that Porson had fully determined on giving these, but never accomplished his intention, partly owing to his own indolence, partly to the failure of the college authorities in supplying him with proper rooms and accommodation. Most of his subsequent life seems to have been spent in London, where he occupied himself with editing the tragedies of Euripides, and contributing political squibs to the *Morning Chronicle*, relaxing himself by convivialities with his friends, and evenings at the 'Cider Cellars.' In 1806, he was chosen librarian of the London Institution, with a salary of £200 a year, and residence; but his health had now greatly declined, and in about two years after his appointment, he died from the effects of an apoplectic fit, at the age of forty-eight.

The circumstances connected with Porson's marriage are rather curious. He was very intimate with Mr Perry, the editor of the *Morning Chronicle*, for whom his sister, Mrs Lunan, a widow, kept house. One night the professor was seated in his favourite haunt, the Cider Cellars in Maiden Lane, smoking a pipe with a friend, when he suddenly turned to the latter and said: 'Friend George, do you not think the widow Lunan an agreeable sort of personage, as times go?' The party addressed replied that she might be so.

'In that case,' replied Porson, 'you must meet me at St Martin's-in-the-Fields at eight o'clock to-morrow morning,' and thereupon withdrew after having called for and paid his reckoning. His friend was somewhat puzzled, but knowing that Porson generally meant what he said, resolved to obey the summons, and accordingly next morning presented himself at the appointed hour at the church, where he found Porson, with Mrs Lunan and a female friend, and a parson in full canonicals for the solemnisation of matrimony. The service was quickly got through, and thereupon the party quitted the sacred building, the bride and bridegroom going each different ways with their respective friends. The oddity of the affair did not end here. Porson had proposed to Mrs Lunan some time before, but had insisted on her keeping it a secret from her brother; and now that the ceremony was completed, seemed as determined as ever that nothing should be said of the marriage, having apparently also made no preparations for taking his bride home. His friend, who had acted as groomsman, then insisted that Mr Perry should be informed of the occurrence; and Porson, after some opposition, consenting, the two walked together to the residence of the worthy editor, in Lancaster Court, where, after some explanation, an arrangement was effected, including the preparation of a wedding-dinner, and the securing of apartments for the newly-married couple. After dinner, Porson, instead of remaining to enjoy the society of his bride, sallied forth to the house of a friend, and after remaining there till a late hour, proceeded to the Cider Cellars, where he sat till eight o'clock next morning! Notwithstanding what may well be called this most unprecedented treatment of a wife on her wedding-day, it is said that during the year and a half that the marriage subsisted, Porson acted the part of a kind and attentive husband, and had his wife lived, there is great reason to believe that she might have weaned him in time from his objectionable habits.

The worst of these was his propensity to drinking, which seems to have been in a great measure a monomania with him, as he would quaff liquors of all kinds, and apparently with equal gusto. Horn Tooke used to say that Porson would drink ink rather than nothing at all. One day he was sitting with an acquaintance in the chambers of a mutual friend in the Temple, who was confined to bed in another room. His servant came into the room to get a bottle of embrocation for him, which had been left on the chimney-piece. The phial was empty—Porson having drunk up the contents! When dining out, he would not unfrequently return to the dining-room after the company had departed, collect all the driblets of wine which had been left at the bottoms of the glasses, and drink off the aggregate. On one occasion he unexpectedly arrived at the house of his friend Hoppner, the painter, in the vicinity of London. The latter regretted his inability to offer the professor dinner, as Mrs Hoppner had gone to town, and carried with her the key of the cupboard which contained the wine. Porson, however, declared that he could dine very well on a mutton-chop, and beer from the next public-house, and this repast was accordingly procured. Sometime afterwards, he remarked to his host that Mrs Hoppner must assuredly keep some bottle in her bedroom for her own private drinking, and that a search might be made for it. Hoppner protested as to his wife's strict temperance, and the impossibility of any such private mode of refreshing herself being resorted to. To quiet his guest, however, who was becoming obstreperous, an inquisition was made and a bottle discovered, which Porson drained with the utmost glee, declaring it was the best gin he had tasted for a long time. Hoppner, rather discomposed, informed his wife, on her return, that their friend had drank every drop of her hidden flask of cordial. 'Drunk every drop of it!' exclaimed the horrified woman. 'My God, it was spirits of wine for the lamp!'

The dirtiness of his personal attire was very conspicuous, more especially in the latter years of his life. So disreputable an appearance did he at times present, that he would be refused admittance by the servants at the houses of his friends. His favourite beverage at breakfast was porter, and the Cambridge professor of Greek was often seen making his morning-meal on a pot of porter and bread and cheese, with black patches on his nose, and as dirty as if he had been rolling in the kennel. He seemed highly flattered by the compliment paid him by one of his Cider-Cellar associates: 'Dick can beat us all, he can drink all night, and spout all day.'

The memory of this singular man was prodigious, extending not only to classical literature, but to the most opposite productions, such as novels and songs, many of which he would almost have repeated verbatim after having perused them once. In connection with his attainments in Greek, the well-known story has often been related of his encounter in a stage-coach with a Cambridge undergraduate, whom he confounded in a pretended quotation, by producing from his pocket one after the other nearly all the Greek classics, and requesting him to point out in any of them the passage to which he referred. Another anecdote, not so well known, is that of his having called on a friend who was reading *Thucydides*, and consulted him as to the meaning of a word. Porson at once quoted the passage in which it occurred. 'How did you know what passage I referred to?' inquired his friend. 'Oh,' was the reply, 'I know that the word in question occurs only twice in *Thucydides*—once on the right, and once on the left hand page in the edition which you are now reading. I saw you look at the left page, and therefore knew the passage at once.' He used indeed to say sometimes, that the tenacity of his memory was a great misery to him, as it made him remember, whether he would or not, and forced him to retain in his recollection many things which he would gladly have forgotten.

---

## CIDER-MAKING.

Debarred by the adverse influences of climate from the profitable cultivation of the vine, the northern nations of Europe have endeavoured to supply this deficiency by the manufacture of exhilarating liquors from fruits and grains of various kinds, more congenial to their soil and skies. Of these rivals to the grape, with the exception of John Barleycorn and his sons, there is none which may more fairly claim to contest the palm of agreeableness and popularity than the apple and her golden-haired daughter, the bright and sparkling cider, whom some ardent admirers have even exalted to a level with the regal vintage of Champagne. Hear how John Philips, in his poem of *Cider*, eulogises the red-streak apple and its genial produce :

'Let every tree in every garden own
The Red-streak as supreme, whose pulpous fruit
With gold irradiate, and vermilion shines
Tempting, not fatal, as the birth of that
Primeval interdicted plant that won
Fond Eve in hapless hour to taste, and die.
This, of more bounteous influence, inspires
Poetic raptures, and the lowly Muse
Kindles to loftier strains ; even I perceive
Her sacred virtue. See ! the numbers flow
Easy, whilst, cheer'd with her nectareous juice,
Hers and my country's praises I exalt.
Hail Herefordian plant, that dost disdain
All other fields ! Heaven's sweetest blessing, hail !
Be thou the copious matter of my song,
And thy choice nectar ; on which always wait
Laughter, and sport, and care-beguiling wit,
And friendship, chief delight of human life.
What should we wish for more ? or why, in quest
Of foreign vintage, insincere, and mixt,
Traverse th' extremest world ? why tempt the rage
Of the rough ocean ? when our native glebe
Imparts, from bounteous womb, annual recruits
Of wine delectable, that far surmounts
Gallic, or Latin grapes, or those that see
The setting sun near Calpes' towering height.
Nor let the Rhodian, nor the Lesbian vines
Vaunt their rich Must, nor let Tokay contend
For sovereignty ; Phanæus self must bow
To th' Ariconian vales.'

Like hop-picking in the east, the gathering of apples, for cider, forms one of the liveliest and most interesting of rural operations throughout the year in the western counties of England. These comprise mainly Hereford, Monmouth, and Gloucester shires, Somerset and Devon, the first and last counties more especially representing the two great cider districts of England, and also two separate qualities of the liquor, Herefordshire being noted *par excellence* for *sweet*, as Devonshire is for *rough* cider. Both descriptions, however, are made in the two counties. In the sweet cider, the object of the maker is to check the vinous fermentation as far as possible, so as to prevent the decomposition of the saccharine matter, which in the rough cider is more or less destroyed. The cider lauded by Philips in such encomiastic terms, is the sweet Herefordshire cider ; but as a native of the west midland counties, a due allowance must be made for local predilection. It, nevertheless, enjoys a deservedly high reputation, and it is stated as a positive fact that an English peer, when ambassador in France, used frequently to palm it on the *noblesse* as a delicious wine.

In the manufacture of cider, those apples are preferred which are of a small size and have an acid or astringent taste. Red and yellow are the favourite colours, green being avoided as producing a very poor quality of liquor. Where cider is made in small quantities, or where it is desired to have it of a specially fine description, the apples are gathered by the hand when thoroughly ripe, carefully picked, and any rotten portions that may appear, cut away. For general purposes, the fruit is beaten from the trees by the aid of long poles, and collected in baskets beneath, by women and children. It is then spread out in heaps in the open air, and remains exposed to the weather till it becomes mellow. It is then conveyed to the cider-mill, a primitive apparatus, consisting of a stone wheel revolving in a circular trough of the same material, and driven by a horse. The apples are ground as nearly as possible to a uniform consistence, it being especially desirable that the rinds and kernels should be thoroughly pressed, as on the former the colour, and on the latter the flavour of the liquor essentially depend. The resulting pulp, or, as it is termed, *pomage*, is taken to the cider-press, a machine constructed on the principle of the packing-press, on the floor of which the crushed fruit is piled up, between layers of straw or hair-cloth, and subjected to a severe and protracted pressure. The heap thus formed is styled the *cheese*. Wooden tubs or troughs receive the expressed liquor, which is then placed in casks, and left to ferment. This operation being successfully completed, the cider, bright and clear, is racked off into other casks, which are allowed to stand in the open air till the ensuing spring with their bungs lightly fixed, but which are then tightly closed. The best time for bottling it is said to be when it is from eighteen months to two years old, or rather when it has acquired its highest brightness and flavour in the cask. If the proper time for doing this be seized, the liquor thus bottled may be kept for a very long period, but, as a general rule, cider is extremely difficult to preserve, from the readiness with which it turns sour, owing to the development of lactic acid.

As a summer drink, cider is a most palatable and refreshing one, though its extended use seems to be confined to the western counties of England, where it occupies the place in popular favour held, in other parts of the country, by beer. The percentage of alcohol which it contains, varies from 5½ to 9. We retain a most affectionate remembrance of the liquor in connection with the fairy nooks of Devon, and the rich pastures of Somerset, through which, some years ago, it was our fortune to ramble. Enchanted land of the west ! how our fancies are entwined with thy sunny valleys, deep shady lanes, and the beauty and vigour of thy rustic inhabitants. Long may Pomona shed her choicest blessings on thy head, and her refreshing juices cheer the heart of the thirsty and way-worn traveller !

## SEPTEMBER 26.

**Saints Cyprian and Justina, martyrs, 304. St Eusebius, pope and confessor, 310. St Colman Elo, abbot and confessor, 610. St Nilus the Younger, abbot, 1005.**

### ST CYPRIAN THE MAGICIAN.

This saint, so surnamed from his having, previous to his conversion, practised the arts of a magician or diviner, has been coupled in the calendar with Justina, a young Syrian lady, regarding whom a young pagan nobleman applied to Cyprian to assist him with his arts in rendering her more favourable to his suit. Justina was a Christian, and opposed, we are told through the aid of the Virgin, such an effectual resistance to the devices of Cyprian, that the latter was convinced of the weakness of the infernal spirits, and resolved to quit their service. He consulted a priest named Eusebius, who encouraged him in the work of conversion, which he ultimately consummated by burning all his magical books, giving his substance to the poor, and enrolling himself among the Christian catechumens. On the breaking out of the persecution under Dioclesian, Cyprian was apprehended and carried before the Roman governor at Tyre. Justina, who had been the original mover in his change of life, was, at the same time, brought before this judge and cruelly scourged, whilst Cyprian was torn with iron hooks. After this the two martyrs were sent to Nicomedia, to the Emperor Dioclesian, who forthwith commanded their heads to be struck off. The history of St Cyprian and St Justina was recorded in a Greek poem by the Empress Eudocia, wife of Theodosius the Younger, a work which is now lost.

---

*Born.*—Cuthbert, Admiral Lord Collingwood, 1750, *Newcastle-on-Tyne.*

*Died.*—Pope Clement VII. (Giulio de' Medici), 1534; Richard Colley, Marquis Wellesley, statesman, and eldest brother of the Duke of Wellington, 1842, *Kingston House, Brompton.*

## JAM AND JELLY MAKING.

In Galt's *Annals of the Parish*, in which the Rev. Micah Balwhidder quaintly chronicles the occurrences of his district from 1760 downwards, the following entry occurs relative to an important epoch in the parochial history:

'I should not, in my notations, forget to mark a new luxury that got in among the commonalty at this time. By the opening of new roads, and the traffic thereon with carts and carriers, and by our young men that were sailors going to the Clyde, and sailing to Jamaica and the West Indies, heaps of sugar and coffee-beans were brought home, while many, among the kail-stocks and cabbages in their yards, had planted groset and berry bushes; which two things happening together, the fashion to make jam and jelly, which hitherto had been only known in the kitchens and confectionaries of the gentry, came to be introduced into the clachan [village]. All this, however, was not without a plausible pretext; for it was found that jelly was an excellent medicine for a sore throat, and jam a remedy as good as London candy for a cough or a cold, or a shortness of breath. I could not, however, say that this gave me so much concern as the smuggling trade; only it occasioned a great fasherie to Mrs Balwhidder; for in the berry-time, there was no end to the borrowing of her brass-pan to make jelly and jam, till Mrs Toddy of the Cross-Keys bought one, which in its turn came into request, and saved ours.'

This manufacture of jam and jelly may now be said to form an undertaking of some importance in every Scottish household occupying a position in the social scale above the humblest. In South Britain, the process is also extensively carried on, but not with the universality or earnestness of purpose observable in the north. To purchase their preserves at the confectioner's, or to present to their guests sweetmeats, stored in those mendacious pots, which belie so egregiously the expectations entertained of them at first sight, in regard to cubic contents, would in the eyes of the generality of Scottish ladies (those of the old school at least), be held to indicate a sad lack of good housewifeship. Even when the household store was exhausted, as very frequently happens about the months of May or June, we have seen the proposal to remedy the deficiency by purchasing a supply from a shop rejected with scorn.

The jelly-making season may be said to extend over three months—from the beginning of July to the end of September, beginning with strawberries and going out with apples and plums. Great care is exercised in the selection of a dry day for the operation, to insure the proper thickening of the boiled juice. As is well known, this last circumstance constitutes the most critical part of the process; and the obstinate syrup, resolutely refusing to coalesce, not unfrequently tries sadly the patience and temper. In such cases, there is no remedy but to boil the mixture over again with an additional supply of sugar, the grudging of which, by the way, is a fertile cause of the difficulties in getting the juice thoroughly inspissated. We have a vivid recollection of being once in a farmhouse, when the wife of a collier in the neighbourhood, whom the goodwife had endeavoured to initiate in the mysteries of jelly-making, made her appearance with a most woebegone countenance, and dolorous narrative of non-success. 'I can mak naething o' yon thing,' she said with an expression of perfect helplessness; 'it's just stannin' like dub-water!' Whether she was enabled to get this unsatisfactory state of matters remedied, we are unable to say.

Like washing-day, the manufacture of jam and jelly, whilst it lasts, entails a total disregard of the lords of the creation and their requirements, unless, indeed, as not frequently happens, the 'men-folk' of the family are pressed into the service as assistants. A huge pan of fruit and sugar is sometimes a difficult matter to convey to, and place properly on, the fire, and we have seen a great stalwart fellow, now an officer in her Majesty's army, summoned from the parlour to the kitchen, to give his aid in accomplishing this domestic operation. Should a student be spending the recess in the country, during the summer, he is very likely to be pounced on by the ladies of the family to assist them in gathering and sorting the fruit, or snipping off its noses and stalks with a pair of scissors. Of course, in general, the young man is only too happy to avail himself of so favourable an opportunity for flirtation, where the companions of his toils are young, good-looking, and blessed with a fair share of juvenile spirits.

The *Book of Days* is not a cookery-book, and, therefore, any directions or recipes in connection with jelly-making, would here be wholly out of place. Yet in connection with so familiar a custom of Scottish domestic life, we may allude to the difference of opinion prevalent among those versed in jam-lore, as to the proper time which should be allowed for the syrup remaining on the fire, after having reached the point of ebullition. Some recommend the space of twenty minutes, others half-an-hour, whilst a few, determined that the preserves shall be thoroughly subjected to the action of Vulcan, keep the pan bubbling away for three-quarters or even an entire hour. An esteemed relative of our own always insisted on this last period being allowed, with the result, it must be stated, sometimes of the jam becoming a veritable decoction, in which the original shape of the fruit could scarcely be recognised, whilst the substance itself became, after having cooled, so indurated as to be almost impracticable for any other use than as a lollipop. As her old servant was wont to declare, 'she boiled the very judgment out o't!'

In country places, besides the ordinary fruits of the garden, many of the wild products of the woods and fields are made use of in the manufacture of preserves. The bilberry or blaeberry, the barberry, and above all the bramble, are largely employed for this purpose; while in the Highlands and moorland districts, the cranberry, the whortleberry, and even the harsh and unsavoury berries of the *rowan* or mountain-ash are made into jam. On the shores of the Argyleshire lochs, where, from their sheltered position, the fuchsia grows with remarkable luxuriance, its berries are sometimes made into a very palatable *compote*. Bramble-gathering forms a favourite *ploy* amid the juvenile members of a Scottish family, and we have a very distinct recollection in connection therewith, of wild brakes where the purple fruit grew luxuriantly, amid ferns, hazel-nuts, and wild-raspberry bushes, with the invigorating brightness of a September sun overhead, and the brilliant varieties of a September foliage. Faces stained with livid hues, hands scratched with thorns and briers, and shoes and stockings drenched with ditch-water, are among the reminiscences of the joyous days of bramble-gathering.

The inconvenient number of applications recorded by Mr Balwhidder, as having been made to his wife for the use of her brass jelly-pan, is quite consonant with the actual state of matters in a country town in Scotland in former times. These culinary conveniences being rare, the fortunate possessor of one was beset on all sides by her neighbours with requests for it, and if she were good-natured and unselfish, she ran a considerable risk of being entirely excluded herself from participation in its use. Now, however, that these utensils have become an appendage to every kitchen of the least pretension to gentility, such a state of matters has come to be ranked fairly among the legendary reminiscences of the past.

The institution of jelly and jam, as already observed, has experienced a much more extended development in North than in South Britain. In the former division of the island, the condiments in question are regarded as an indispensable appendage to every social tea-drinking, and are also invariably brought out on the occasion of any friend dropping in during the afternoon and remaining to partake of tea. To refrain from producing them, and allow the guest to make his evening repast on bread and butter, would be regarded as in the highest degree niggardly and inhospitable. When no stranger is present, these luxuries are rarely indulged in by the family—that is to say, during the week—but an exception always holds in the case of Sunday evening. On that occasion the children of a Scottish household expect to be regaled *ad libitum* with sweets, and the quantities of jelly then consumed in comparison with the rest of the week might form a curious question for statists. The Sunday-tea, too, is enjoyed with all the more relish that the previous dinner has been generally rather meagre, to avoid as much as possible the necessity of cooking on the Sabbath, and also somewhat hurried, being partaken of 'between sermons,' as the very short interval between the morning and afternoon services is termed in Scotland. Whatever may be said of the rigour of Sunday observance in the north, our recollections of the evening of that day are of the most pleasant description, and will doubtless be corroborated by the memories of many of our Scottish readers. In England, where the great meal of the day is dinner, tea is, for the most part, but a secondary consideration, and neither jams and jellies, nor condiments of any kind, beyond simple bread and butter, are in general to be seen. A young Englishman, studying at the university of Edinburgh, on one occasion rather astonished the lady of the house where he was drinking tea. He had been pressed to help himself to jelly, and having been only accustomed to its use as an accompaniment of the dessert, he very quietly emptied out on his plate the whole dish, causing considerable wonderment to the other guests at this unaccountable proceeding.

## SEPTEMBER 27.

Saints Cosmas and Damian, martyrs, about 303. St Elzear, Count of Arian, and his wife, St Delphina, 14th century.

*Born.*—Louis XIII. of France, 1601, *Fontainebleau;* Jacques Benigne Bossuet, eminent preacher and controversialist, 1627, *Dijon.*

*Died.*—Marco Girolamo Vida, author of Latin poems, &c., 1566, *Alba;* St Vincent de Paul, eminent philanthropist, 1660; Pope Innocent XII., 1700; Dr Thomas Burnet, author of the *Sacred Theory of the Earth*, 1715, *Charterhouse, London;* Admiral René Duguay-Trouin, French naval commander, 1736, *Paris;* James Brindley, celebrated engineer, 1772, *Turnhurst, Staffordshire.*

### ROBERT, DUKE OF NORMANDY.

By the battle of Tinchebrai, fought this day in 1106, was decided the destiny of the dukedom of Normandy, and of its unfortunate ruler Robert, the eldest son of William the Conqueror.

Carried away by the impetuosity of his character, and deceived by evil counsellors, Robert brought trouble into his dominions, and discord into the house of his father, who forgave him only on his dying bed. Leaving to his brother William the care of his Norman subjects, he yielded to the religious and chivalric spirit of the times, and with the choicest of the nobility set out to shew his valour on the plains of Syria, where he was one of the chiefs of the first Crusade.

We can only praise the courage and military exploits of Duke Robert in the east; they were so extraordinary as to obtain him the offer of the crown of Jerusalem, which, on his refusal, was given to Godfrey of Bouillon. A few flags which he had taken from the enemy, were all he brought back from his victories, and these he presented to the Abbey of the Holy Trinity at Caen. During his absence, his brother Henry had seized on the vacant throne of England, and, though deep in debt, Robert was led into further expenses in the vain hope of recovering his lost inheritance. After this, reconciliation between the brothers became impossible, and want of order and economy were the ruin of Robert. He had recourse to arbitrary taxes, not only imposed upon the provinces, but upon the citizens, merchants, and rich people, thus causing general discontent. Numerous and powerful factions were formed; Henry I. was only too ready to obey their call, and arrived in Normandy at the head of his army. His gold bought many partizans; the towns of Bayeux and Caen alone remained faithful to Duke Robert; and after a long siege the first was carried by assault and burned, whilst a conspiracy broke out in Caen, scarcely leaving the unfortunate duke time to escape. A few gallant chevaliers, faithful to their oaths and the principles of legitimacy, rallied round him; but the battle of Tinchebrai was gained by the king, and the duke was taken prisoner.

Become master of his brother, Henry imprisoned him in the castle of Cardiff. For greater security, the eyes of the unhappy duke were put out. His detention lasted from 1106 to 1135, when he died, and it was during this long period that he endeavoured to soothe his weariness by becoming a poet. The songs of the Welsh bards were tried to alleviate his sorrows, and the deep distress he felt at being separated from his only child, whose prospects he had blighted. Forced to learn the language of his jailers, he made use of it to compose several pieces in Welsh, one of which remains, a sort of plaintive elegy. The prince looked on an old oak-tree rising above the forest, which covered the promontory of Penarth, on the Bristol Channel, and from the depths of his prison he thus mournfully addresses it, following the custom of the Welsh bards, who repeat the name of the person or thing they address in each stanza:

Oak, born on these heights, theatre of carnage, where blood has rolled in streams:
Misery to those who quarrel about words over wine.

Oak, nourished in the midst of meadows covered with blood and corpses:
Misery to the man who has become an object of hatred.

Oak, grown up on this green carpet, watered with the blood of those whose heart was pierced by the sword:
Misery to him who delights in discord.

Oak, in the midst of the trefoil and plants which whilst surrounding thee have stopped thy growth and hindered the thickening of thy trunk:
Misery to the man who is in the power of his enemies.

Oak, placed in the midst of woods which cover the promontory from whence thou see'st the waves of the Severn struggle against the sea:
Misery to him who sees that which is not death.

Oak, which has lived through storms and tempests in the midst of the tumult of war and the ravages of death:
Misery to the man who is not old enough to die.

He died at Cardiff, in 1135, in his eightieth year.

### EXPENSE OF A DECENT LODGING IN LONDON IN 1710.

Swift thus writes from London to his friend Stella, 27th September 1710: 'I lodge in Bury Street [St James's], where I removed a week ago. I have the first floor, a dining-room, and bed-chamber, at eight shillings per week; plaguy deep, but I spend nothing for eating, never go to a tavern, and very seldom in a coach; yet, after all, it will be expensive.'—*Works, Scott's edition*, ii. 28.

What seemed to Swift in Anne's days so 'plaguy deep,' would now be found considerably deeper; certainly it would not be less than forty-eight shillings a week.

## SEPTEMBER 28.

St Eustochium, virgin, about 419. St Exuperius, bishop of Toulouse, beginning of 5th century. St Lioba, abbess, about 779. St Wenceslas, Duke of Bohemia, martyr, 938.

*Born.*—Sir William Jones, oriental scholar, 1746, *London.*

*Died.*—Emperor Lothaire I., 855; Henry VI., emperor of Germany, 1197; Jean Baptiste Massillon, celebrated French preacher, 1742; Thomas Day, author of *Sandford and Merton*, 1789, *Wargrave-upon-Thames;* Granville Penn, miscellaneous writer, 1844, *Stoke Park, Bucks;* Thomas Amyot, literary antiquary, 1850, *London;* Dr Karl Ritter, distinguished geographer, 1859, *Berlin.*

### THOMAS DAY.

Rousseau's ideal of education was a cross between the Red Indian and the Spartan. The influence of his fervid advocacy was greatest in France, but he did not lack thorough-going disciples in England, who reduced some of his most questionable dogmas to practice. Mrs Gaskell, in her *Life of Charlotte Brontë*, relates that she had an aunt who, in her childhood, was adopted by a wealthy couple, with the purpose of training her on French and philosophic principles. Her food and clothing were of the simplest and rudest description; but for this she did not mind, being healthy and merry, and indifferent to dress and eating; her hardship lay in the fact, that she and a favourite dog were taken for an airing in the carriage on alternate days; the creature whose turn it was to be left at home being tossed in a blanket—an operation which the girl especially dreaded. Her aversion to the tossing was the reason why it was persevered in. She had grown indifferent to dressed-up ghosts, and so the blanket-exercise was selected as the next mode of hardening her nerves.

One of the most notable of Rousseau's English followers was Thomas Day, the author of *Sandford and Merton*, a book which several generations of children have heartily enjoyed for its stories, without a thought of its philosophy. Day was born in Wellclose Square, London, in 1748. His father held a place in the custom-house, and left him a fortune of £1200 a year. He was educated at the Charterhouse and Oxford, and spent some summers in France, where, with all the enthusiasm of youth, he received the new philosophy of education, condemning old systems as wholly vicious, and believing that no perfection of character was unattainable under Rousseau's. Having resolved on marriage, he determined that his wife should be modelled in accordance with the new light. He therefore went to an orphan asylum at Shrewsbury, and picked out a flaxen-haired girl of twelve, whom he named Sabrina Sidney, after the Severn and Algernon Sidney; and then to the Foundling Hospital in London, where he selected a second, whom he called Lucretia. In taking these girls, he gave a written pledge, that within a year he would place one of them with a respectable tradesman, giving £100 to bind her apprentice, and that he should maintain her, if she should turn out well, until she married or commenced business, in either of which cases he would advance £500. With Sabrina and Lucretia he set off for France, in order that, in quiet, he might discover and discipline their characters. He, however, and the girls quarrelled; next they took small-pox, and he had to nurse them night and day; and by and by he was glad to return to London, and get Lucretia off his hands by apprenticing her to a milliner on Ludgate Hill. It is pleasant to know that she behaved well; and that on her marriage to a substantial linen-draper, Day cheerfully produced his promised dowry of £500. Poor Sabrina was reserved for further trial, but by no means could she qualify for Mrs Day; against the sense of pain and danger no discipline could fortify her. When Day dropped melting sealing-wax on her arms, she flinched; and when he fired pistols at her garments, she started and screamed. When he tried her fidelity by telling her pretended secrets, she divulged them in gossip with the servants. Finally, she exhausted his patience by wearing thin sleeves for ornament, instead of warmth, when out on a visit. He packed her off to an ordinary boarding-school, kept her there for three years, allowed her £50 a year, gave her £500 on her marriage to a barrister; and when she became a widow with two boys, he pensioned her with £30 a year. Failing to educate a wife, he was content to marry, in 1788, Miss Milnes of Wakefield, a lady whose opinions nearly coincided with his own, and who was willing to abjure all vanities in dress. Day was killed in 1789 by a kick from a young horse, which he was trying to train on a new method.

## GHOST WITNESS-SHIP.

In the year 1749, the remote Highland district of Braemar, in Aberdeenshire, was the scene of a murder, which was subsequently alleged to have been discovered through the instrumentality of the ghost of the murdered person; to which effect evidence was given on the trial of two men before the High Court of Justiciary in Edinburgh. From the details of the trial, which have been printed in a separate volume by the Bannatyne Club, Sir Walter Scott framed a brief narrative, which may serve on the present occasion, with the help of a few additional particulars:

'Upon the 10th of June 1754, Duncan Terig *alias* Clark, and Alexander Bain Macdonald, two Highlanders, were tried before the Court of Justiciary, Edinburgh, for the murder of Arthur Davis, sergeant in Guise's Regiment, on the 28th of September 1749. The accident happened not long after the civil war [of 1745], the embers of which were still reeking, so there existed too many reasons on account of which an English soldier, straggling far from assistance, might be privately cut off by the inhabitants of these wilds [Davis had a fowling-piece, and money and rings upon his person, and some of his valuables were afterwards seen in possession of the accused. Robbery seems to have been the sole object of his murderers.] It appears that Sergeant Davis was amissing many years without any certainty as to his fate. At length an account of the murder appeared from the evidence of one Alexander Macpherson [or Macgillies], (a Highlander [a farm-servant at Inverey, and about twenty-six years of age], speaking no language but Gaelic, and sworn by an interpreter), who gave the following extraordinary account of his cause of knowledge: He was, he said, in bed in his cottage, when an apparition came to his bedside, and commanded him to rise and follow him out of doors. Believing his visitor to be one Farquharson, a neighbour and friend, the witness did as he was bid; and when they were without the cottage, the appearance told the witness he was the ghost of Sergeant Davis, and requested him to go and bury his mortal remains, which lay concealed in a place which he pointed out, in a moorland tract, called the hill of Christie. He desired him to take [Donald] Farquharson as an assistant. Next day the witness went to the place specified, and there found the bones of a human body, much decayed. The witness did not at the time bury the bones so found; in consequence of which the sergeant's ghost again appeared to him, upbraiding him with his breach of promise. On this occasion, the witness asked the ghost who were the murderers, and received for answer that he had been slain by the prisoners at the bar. The witness, after this second visitation, called the assistance of Farquharson, and buried the body.

'Farquharson was brought in evidence, to prove that the preceding witness, Macpherson, had called him to the burial of the bones, and told him the same story which he repeated in court. Isabel Machardie, a person who slept in one of the beds which run along the wall in an ordinary Highland hut, declared that upon the night when Macpherson said he saw the ghost, she saw a naked man enter the house, and go towards Macpherson's bed. [More in detail her evidence was this: 'She saw something naked come in at the door; which frighted her so much that she drew the clothes over her head: that when it appeared, it came in a bowing posture; that she cannot tell what it was; that next morning she asked Macpherson what it was that had troubled them the night before? and that he answered, she might be easy, for it would not trouble her any more.']

'Yet, though the supernatural incident was thus fortified, and although there were other strong presumptions against the prisoners, the story of the apparition threw an air of ridicule on the whole evidence for the prosecution. It was followed up by the counsel for the prisoners asking, in the cross-examination of Macpherson: "What language did the ghost speak in?" The witness, who was himself ignorant of the English language, replied: "As good Gaelic as I ever heard in Lochaber." "Pretty well for the ghost of an English sergeant," answered the counsel. The inference was rather smart and plausible than sound, for the apparition of the ghost being admitted, we know too little of the other world to judge whether all languages may not be alike familiar to those who belong to it. It imposed, however, on the jury, who found the accused parties *Not guilty*, although their counsel and solicitor,* and most of the court, were satisfied of their having committed the murder.'

Scott's hypothesis for the explanation of the alleged apparition, is that giving information is unpopular in the Highlands, and Macpherson got up the ghost-story, 'knowing well that his superstitious countrymen would pardon his communicating the commission intrusted to him by a being of the other world.' This hypothesis (whatever other may be adopted) is not only without support in positive fact, but it assumes a degree of anxiety for the execution of justice wholly gratuitous, and certainly far from characteristic of the Braemar Highlander of that day. It also ignores the corroborative evidence of Isabel Machardie. What is even more important, it is out of harmony with the chronology of the story, for Macpherson related his ghostly visitation and buried the sergeant's bones three years before any measures for the vindication of justice were taken, and, for anything that appears, no such measures would ever have been taken, but for the active interference of a retired officer of the army, named Small. This gentleman seems to have been inspired with a strong feeling as a friend of the government and of the army, in contradistinction to the Jacobite sentiments which then largely prevailed. So vigorous were his efforts to make out evidence against the murderers of Davis, that it was taken notice of in the formal defences of the accused, and orally by their counsel, the eminent Mr Lockhart, who was notoriously a Jacobite. Small felt so much exasperated by the insinuations of the counsel, that he next day appeared in the Parliament Close, with his sword by his side, and made an assault upon Mr Lockhart, as the latter was walking to the court; for which offence he was put in prison by the Lords, and only liberated on his making an apology.† It seems to have been to this circumstance that Wedderburn alluded in his famous retort upon Lockhart, in the Court of Session in Edinburgh, when, stung by the overbearing manner of his senior, he reminded him of his having been *disgraced in his person* and dishonoured in his bed—a burst of sarcasm followed by his laying down his gown, and deserting the Scotch for the English bar. (See *Book of Days*, vol. i. p. 39.)

The case of Sergeant Davis, remarkable as it is, does not stand quite singular. A similar one, which occurred in the county of Durham in the year 1631, has been related in many books, and is the subject of a critical historical inquiry in Surtees's *History of Durham*. The circumstances can be made out with tolerable clearness as follows:

One Walker, a yeoman of good estate, and a widower, living at Chester-le-Street, had in his service a young female relative named Anne Walker. The results of an amour which took place between them, caused Walker to send away the poor girl under the care of one Mark Sharp, a collier, professedly that she might be taken care of as befitted her condition, but in reality that she might no more be troublesome to her lover in this world.

Nothing was heard of her till, one night in the ensuing winter, an honest fuller, named James Graham, who lived about six miles from Walker's house, coming down from the upper to the lower floor of his mill, found a woman standing there, with her hair hanging about her head, in which were five bloody wounds. According to the man's evidence, afterwards given,* he asked her who she was, and what she wanted; when she gave an account of her sad fate, having been killed by Sharp on the moor in their journey, and thrown into a coal-pit hard by, while the instrument of her death, a pick, had been hid under a bank, along with his clothes, which were stained with her blood. She demanded of Graham that he should undertake the business of exposing her murder, and having her murderers punished; a task he did not enter upon till she had twice reappeared to him, the last time with a threatening aspect.

The body, the pick, and the bloody clothes being found as Graham described, little doubt remained that Walker and Sharp were the guilty men. They were tried at Durham before Judge Davenport in August 1631. The mode of discovery could not fail in that age to make a great impression, and produce much excitement at the trial. Hence it is not very surprising to hear that one of the jury, named Fairbair, alleged that he saw a child sitting on Walker's shoulder. The men were found guilty, condemned, and executed.

* A brief account of the case is given in the *European Magazine* for May 1793, apparently from the recital of the agent for the prisoners, then surviving. The circumstance of the agent's being fully persuaded of the guilt of his clients is there stated.

† *Scots Magazine*, 1754.

* In Richardson's *Borderer's Table Book* (vi. 351), it is stated that Graham's original deposition is in the Bodleian Library, Oxford.

---

# SEPTEMBER 29.

St Michael and all the Holy Angels. St Theodota, martyr, 642.

## Michaelmas Day.

Michaelmas Day, the 29th of September, properly named the day of St Michael and All Angels, is a great festival of the Church of Rome, and also observed as a feast by the Church of England. In England, it is one of the four quarterly terms, or quarter-days, on which rents are paid, and in that and other divisions of the United Kingdom, as well as perhaps in other countries, it is the day on which burghal magistracies and councils are re-elected. The only other remarkable thing connected with the day is a widely prevalent custom of marking it with a goose at dinner.

Michael is regarded in the Christian world as the chief of angels, or archangel. His history is obscure. In Scripture, he is mentioned five times, and always in a warlike character; namely, thrice by Daniel as fighting for the Jewish church against Persia; once by St Jude as fighting with the devil about the body of Moses; and once by St John as fighting at the head of his angelic troops against the dragon and his host. Probably, on the hint thus given by St John, the Romish church taught at an early period that Michael was employed, in command of the loyal angels of God, to overthrow and consign to the pit of perdition Lucifer and his rebellious associates—a legend which was at length embalmed in the sublimest poetry by Milton. Sometimes Michael is represented as the sole archangel, sometimes as only the head of a fraternity of archangels, which includes likewise Gabriel, Raphael, and some others. He is usually represented in coat-armour, with a glory round his head, and a dart in his hand, trampling on the fallen Lucifer. He has even been furnished, like the human warriors of the middle ages, with a heraldic ensign—namely, a banner hanging from a cross. We obtain a curious idea of the religious notions of those ages, when we learn that the red velvet-covered buckler worn by Michael in his war with Lucifer used to be shewn in a church in Normandy down to 1607, when the bishop of Avranches at length forbade its being any longer exhibited.

Angels are held by the Church of Rome as capable of interceding for men; wherefore it is that prayers are addressed to them and a festival appointed in their honour. Wheatley, an expositor of the Book of Common Prayer, probably expresses the limited view of the subject which is entertained in the Church of England, when he says, that 'the feast of St Michael and All Angels is observed that the people may know what blessings are derived from the ministry of angels.' Amongst Catholics, Michael, or, as he has been named, St Michael, is invoked as 'a most glorious and warlike prince,' 'chief officer of paradise,' 'captain of God's hosts,' 'receiver of souls,' 'the vanquisher of evil spirits,' and 'the admirable general.' It may also be remarked, that in the Sarum missal, there is a mass to St Raphael, as the protector of pilgrims and travellers, and a skilful worker with medicine; likewise an office for the continual intercession of St Gabriel and all the heavenly militia. Protestant writers trace a connection between the ancient notion of tutelar genii and the Catholic doctrine respecting angels, the one being, they say, ingrafted on the other. As to the soundness of this view we do not give any opinion, but it seems certain that in early ages there was a prevalent notion that the affairs of men were much under the direction of angels, good and bad, and men prayed to angels both to obtain good and to avoid evil. Every human being was supposed to have one of these spiritual existences watching over him, aiming at his good, and ready to hear his call when he was in affliction. And, however we may judge this to be a delusion, we must certainly own that, as establishing a connection between the children of earth and something above and beyond the earth, as leading men's minds away from the grossness of worldly pursuits and feelings into the regions of the beautiful and the infinite, it is one of by no means the worst tendency. We must be prepared, however, to find simplicity amidst all the more aspiring ideas of our forefathers.

In time, the sainted spirits of pious persons came to stand in the place of the generally nameless angels, and each place and person had one of these as a special guardian and protector. Not only had each country its particular patron or tutelar saint, but there was one for almost every town and church. Even trades and corporations had their special saints. And there was one more specially to be invoked for each particular ail that could afflict humanity. It will be curious here to descend a little into particulars. First, as to countries, England had St George; Scotland, St Andrew; Ireland, St Patrick; Wales, St David; France, St Dennis and (in a less degree) St Michael; Spain, St James (Jago); Portugal, St Sebastian; Italy, St Anthony; Sardinia, St Mary; Switzerland, St Gall and the Virgin Mary; Germany, St Martin, St Boniface, and St George Cataphractus; Hungary, St Mary of Aquisgrana and St Lewis; Bohemia, St Winceslaus; Austria, St Colman and St Leopold; Flanders, St Peter; Holland, St Mary; Denmark, St Anscharius and St Canute; Sweden, St Anscharius, St Eric, and St John; Norway, St Olaus and St Anscharius; Poland, St Stanislaus and St Hederiga; Prussia, St Andrew and St Albert; Russia, St Nicholas, St Mary, and St Andrew. Then as to cities, Edinburgh had St Giles, Aberdeen St Nicholas, and Glasgow St Mungo; Oxford had St Frideswide; Paris, St Genevieve; Rome, St Peter and St Paul; Venice, St Mark; Naples, St Januarius and St Thomas Aquinas; Lisbon, St Vincent; Brussels, St Mary and St Gudula; Vienna, St Stephen; Cologne, the three kings, with St Ursula and the eleven thousand virgins.

St Agatha presides over nurses. St Catherine and St Gregory are the patrons of literati and studious persons; St Catherine also presides over the arts. St Christopher and St Nicholas preside over mariners. St Cecilia is the patroness of musicians. St Cosmas and St Damian are the patrons of physicians and surgeons, also of philosophers. St Dismas and St Nicholas preside over thieves; St Eustace and St Hubert over hunters; St Felicitas over young children. St Julian is the patron of pilgrims. St Leonard and St Barbara protect captives. St Luke is the patron of painters. St Martin and St Urban preside over tipsy people, to save them from falling into the kennel. Fools have a tutelar saint in St Mathurin, archers in St Sebastian, divines in St Thomas, and lovers in St Valentine. St Thomas Becket presided over blind men, eunuchs, and sinners, St Winifred over virgins, and St Yves over lawyers and civilians. St Æthelbert and St Ælian were invoked *against* thieves.

Generally, the connection of these saints with the classes of persons enumerated took its rise in some incident of their lives, and in the manner of their deaths; for instance, St Nicholas was once in danger at sea, and St Sebastian was killed by arrows. Probably, for like reasons, St Agatha presided over valleys, St Anne over riches, St Barbara over hills, and St Florian over fire; while St Silvester protected wood, St Urban wine and vineyards, and St Osyth was invoked by women to guard their keys, and St Anne as the restorer of lost things. Generally, the patron-saints of trades were, on similar grounds, persons who had themselves exercised them, or were supposed to have done so. Thus, St Joseph naturally presided over carpenters, St Peter over fishmongers, and St Crispin over shoemakers. St Arnold was the patron of millers, St Clement of tanners, St Eloy of smiths, St Goodman of tailors, St Florian of mercers, St John Port-Latin of booksellers, St Louis of periwig-makers, St Severus of fullers, St Wilfred of bakers, St William of hatters, and St Windeline of shepherds. The name of St Cloud obviously made him the patron-saint of nailsmiths; St Sebastian became that of pinmakers, from his having been stuck over with arrows; and St Anthony necessarily was adopted by swine-herds, in consequence of the legend about his pigs. It is not easy, however, to see how St Nicholas came to be the presiding genius of parish-clerks, or how the innocent and useful fraternity of potters obtained so alarming a saint as 'St Gore with a pot in his hand, and the devil on his shoulder.'

The medicating saints are enumerated in the following passage from a whimsical satire of the sixteenth century:—

To every saint they also do his office here assign,
And fourteen do they count, of whom thou may'st have aid divine;
Among the which *Our Lady* still doth hold the chiefest place,
And of her gentle nature helps in every kind of case.
St *Barbara* looks that none without the body of Christ doth die;
St *Cath'rine* favours learned men and gives them wisdom high,
And teacheth to resolve the doubts, and always giveth aid
Unto the scolding sophister, to make his reason staid.
St *Apolin* the rotten teeth doth help when sore they ache;
*Otilia* from the bleared eyes the cause and grief doth take;
*Rooke* healeth scabs and mangins, with pocks, and scurf, and scall,
And cooleth raging carbuncles, and boils, and botches all.
There is a saint, whose name in verse cannot declared be,*
He serves against the plague and each infective malady.
St *Valentine*, beside, to such as do his power despise
The falling-sickness sends, and helps the man that to him cries.
The raging mind of furious folk doth *Vitus* pacify,
And doth restore them to their wit, being called on speedily.
*Erasmus* heals the colic and the griping of the guts,
And *Laurence* from the back and from the shoulder sickness puts.
*Blaise* drives away the quinsy quite with water sanctified,
From every Christian creature here, and every beast beside.
But *Leonard* of the prisoners doth the bands asunder pull,
And breaks the prison-doors and chains, wherewith his church is full.
The quartan ague, and the rest doth *Pernel* take away,
And *John* preserves the worshippers from prison every day;
Which force to *Bennet* eke they give, that help enough may be,
By saints in every place. What dost thou omitted see?
From dreadful unprovided death doth *Mark* deliver his,
Who of more force than death himself, and more of value is.

* Probably St Roque.

St *Anne* gives wealth and living great to such as love her most,
And is a perfect finder out of things that have been lost;
Which virtue likewise they ascribe unto another man,
St *Vincent;* what he is I cannot tell, nor whence he came.
Against reproach and infamy on *Susan* do they call;
*Romanus* driveth sprites away and wicked devils all.
The bishop *Wolfgang* heals the gout, St *Wendlin* keeps the sheep,
With shepherds and the oxen fat, as he was wont to keep.
The bristled hogs doth *Anthony* preserve and cherish well,
Who in his lifetime always did in woods and forests dwell.
St *Gertrude* rids the house of mice, and killeth all the rats;
And like doth Bishop *Huldrick* with his two earth-passing cats.
St *Gregory* looks to little boys, to teach their *a, b, c,*
And makes them for to love their books, and scholars good to be.
St *Nicholas* keeps the mariners from dangers and disease,
That beaten are with boisterous waves, and toss'd in dreadful seas.
Great *Christopher* that painted is with body big and tall,
Doth even the same, who doth preserve and keep his servants all
From fearful terrors of the night, and makes them well to rest,
By whom they also all their life with diverse joys are blest.
St *Agatha* defends the house from fire and fearful flame,
But when it burns, in armour all doth *Florian* quench the same.'

It will be learned, with some surprise, that these notions of presiding angels and saints are what have led to the custom of choosing magistracies on the 29th of September. The history of the middle ages is full of curious illogical relations, and this is one of them. Local rulers were esteemed as in some respects analogous to tutelar angels, in as far as they presided over and protected the people. It was therefore thought proper to choose them on the day of St Michael and All Angels. The idea must have been extensively prevalent, for the custom of electing magistrates on this day is very extensive.

'September, when by custom (right divine)
Geese are ordained to bleed at Michael's shrine'—

says Churchill. This is also an ancient practice, and still generally kept up, as the appearance of the stage-coaches on their way to large towns at this season of the year amply testifies. In Blount's Tenures, it is noted in the tenth year of Edward IV., that John de la Hay was bound to pay to William Barnaby, Lord of Lastres, in the county of Hereford, for a parcel of the demesne lands, *one goose fit for the lord's dinner*, on the feast of St Michael the archangel. Queen Elizabeth is said to have been eating her Michaelmas goose when she received the joyful tidings of the defeat of the Spanish Armada. The custom appears to have originated in a practice among the rural tenantry of bringing a good stubble goose at Michaelmas to the landlord, when paying their rent, with a view to making him lenient. In the poems of George Gascoigne, 1575, is the following passage:

'And when the tenants come to pay their quarter's rent,
They bring some fowl at Midsummer, a dish of fish in Lent,
At Christmas a capon, *at Michaelmas a goose*,
And somewhat else at New-year's tide, for fear their lease fly loose.'

We may suppose that the selection of a goose for a present to the landlord at Michaelmas would be ruled by the bird being then at its perfection, in consequence of the benefit derived from stubble-feeding. It is easy to see how a general custom of having a goose for dinner on Michaelmas Day might arise from the multitude of these presents, as landlords would of course, in most cases, have a few to spare for their friends. It seems at length to have become a superstition, that eating of goose at Michaelmas insured easy circumstances for the ensuing year. In the *British Apollo*, 1709, the following piece of dialogue occurs:

'*Q.*—Yet my wife would persuade me (as I am a sinner)
To have a fat goose on St Michael for dinner:
And then all the year round, I pray you would mind it,
I shall not want money—oh, grant I may find it!
Now several there are that believe this is true,
Yet the reason of this is desired from you.

*A.*—We think you're so far from the having of more,
That the price of the goose you have less than before:
The custom came up from the tenants presenting
Their landlords with geese, to incline their relenting
On following payments, &c.'

---

*Born.*—John Tillotson, archbishop of Canterbury, 1630, *Sowerby, Yorkshire;* Thomas Chubb, freethinking author, 1679, *East Harnham, Wilts;* Robert, Lord Clive, founder of the British empire in India, 1725, *Styche, Shropshire;* William Julius Mickle, translator of Camoens's *Lusiad*, 1734, *Langholm, Scotland;* Admiral Horatio Nelson, naval hero, 1758, *Burnham-Thorpe, Norfolk.*

*Died.*—Pompey the Great, killed in Egypt 48 B.C.; Gustavus Vasa, king of Sweden, 1560, *Stockholm;* Conrad Vorstius, German divine, 1622, *Toningen, Holstein;* Lady Rachel Russell, heroic wife of William, Lord Russell, 1723, *Southampton House;* Charles François Dupuis, astronomer and author, 1809, *Is-sur-Til.*

## SIR HUGH MYDDELTON, AND THE WATER SUPPLY OF OLD LONDON.

Michaelmas Day, 1613, is remarkable in the annals of London, as the day when the citizens assembled to witness, and celebrate by a public pageant, the entrance of the New River waters to the metropolis.

There were present Sir John Swinnerton the lord mayor, Sir Henry Montague the recorder, and many of the aldermen and citizens; and a speech was written by Thomas Middleton the dramatist, who had before been employed by the citizens to design pageants and write speeches for their Lord Mayors' Shows, and other public celebrations. On this occasion, as we are told in the pamphlet descriptive of the day's proceedings, 'warlike music of drums and trumpets liberally beat the air' at the approach of the civic magnates; then 'a troop of labourers, to the number of threescore or upwards, all in green caps alike, bearing in their hands the symbols of their several employments in so great a business, with drums before them, marching twice or thrice about the cistern, orderly present themselves before the mount, and after their obeisance, the speech is pronounced.' It thus commences:

'Long have we labour'd, long desir'd, and pray'd
For this great work's perfection; and by the aid
Of heaven and good men's wishes, 'tis at length
Happily conquer'd, by cost, art, and strength:
After five years' dear expense in days,
Travail, and pains, beside the infinite ways
Of malice, envy, false suggestions,
Able to daunt the spirit of mighty ones
In wealth and courage, this, a work so rare,
Only by one man's industry, cost, and care,
Is brought to blest effect, so much withstood,
His only aim the city's general good.'

A similar series of mere rhymes details the construction of the works, and enumerates the labourers, concluding thus:

'Now for the fruits then: flow forth, precious spring,
So long and dearly sought for, and now bring
Comfort to all that love thee: loudly sing,
And with thy crystal murmur struck together,
Bid all thy true well-wishers welcome hither!'

'At which words,' we are told, 'the flood-gate opens, the stream let into the cistern, drums and trumpets giving it triumphant welcomes,' a peal of small cannon concluding all.

This important work, of the utmost sanitary value to London, was commenced and completed by the indomitable energy of one individual, after it had been declined by the corporate body, and opposed by many upholders of 'good old usages,' the bane of all improvements. The bold man, who came prominently forward when all others had timidly retired, was a simple London tradesman, a goldsmith, dwelling in Basinghall Street, named Hugh Myddelton. He was of Welsh parentage, the sixth son of Richard Myddelton, who had been governor of Denbigh Castle during the reigns of Edward VI., Mary, and Elizabeth. He was born on his father's estate at Galch Hill, close to Denbigh, 'probably about 1555,' says his latest biographer, Mr Smiles,* for 'the precise date of his birth is unknown.' At the proper age, he was sent to London, where his elder brother, Thomas, was established as a grocer and merchant-adventurer, and under that brother's care he commenced his career as a citizen by being entered an apprentice of the Goldsmiths' Company. In due time he took to business on his own account, and, like his brother, joined the thriving merchant-adventurers. In 1597, he represented his native town of Denbigh in parliament, for which he obtained a charter of incorporation, desiring further to serve it by a scheme of mining for coal, which proved both unsuccessful and a great loss to himself. His losses were, however, well covered by his London business profits, to which he had now added cloth manufacturing. On the accession of James I., he was appointed one of the royal

* *Lives of the Engineers.* Until the publication of this work in 1862, there was no good memoir extant of Myddelton, all being overlaid by a mass of inaccuracy and downright fable.

jewellers, being thus one of the most prosperous and active of citizens.

The due supply of pure spring water to the metropolis, had often been canvassed by the corporation. At times it was inconveniently scanty; at all times it was scarcely adequate to the demand, which increased with London's increase. Many projects had been brought before the citizens to convey a stream toward London, but the expense and difficulty had deterred them from using the powers with which they had been invested by the legislature; when Myddelton declared himself ready to carry out the great work, and in May 1609 'the dauntless Welshman' began his work at Chadwell, near Ware. The engineering difficulties of the work and its great expense were by no means the chief cares of Myddelton; he had scarcely began his most patriotic and useful labours, ere he was assailed by an outcry on all sides from land-owners, who declared that his river would cut up the country, bring water through arable land, that would consequently be overflowed in rainy weather, and converted into quagmires; that nothing short of ruin awaited land, cattle, and men, who might be in its course; and that the king's highway between London and Ware would be made impassable! All this mischief was to befall the country-folks of Hertfordshire and Middlesex for Mr Myddelton's 'own private benefit,' as was boldly asserted, with a due disregard of its great public utility; and ultimately parliamentary opposition was strongly invoked. Worried by this senseless but powerful party, with a vast and expensive labour only half completed, and the probability of want of funds, most men would have broken down in despair and bankruptcy; Myddelton merely sought new strength, and found it effectually in the king. James I. joined the spirited contractor, agreed to pay one-half of the expenses in consideration of one-half share in its ultimate profits, and to repay Myddelton one-half of what he had already disbursed. This spirited act of the king silenced all opposition, the work went steadily forward, and in about fifteen months after this new contract, the assembly took place at the New River Head, in the fields between Islington and London, to witness the completion of the great work, as we have already described it.

THE NEW RIVER HEAD, 1665—AFTER HOLLAR.

The pencil of the honest and indefatigable Hollar has preserved to us the features of this interesting locality, and we copy his view above. Mr Smiles observes that 'the site of the New River Head had always been a pond, "an open idell poole," says Hawes, "commonly called the Ducking-pond; being now by the master of this work reduced into a comley pleasant shape, and many ways adorned with buildings." The house adjoining it, belonging to the company, was erected in 1613.' Hollar's view indicates the formal, solid, aspect of the place, and is further valuable for the curious view of Old London in the back-ground; the eye passing over Spa-fields, and resting on the city beyond; the long roof of St Paul's Cathedral appearing just above the boundary-wall of the New River Head; and the steeple of Bow Church to the extreme left. This view was fortunately sketched the year before the great fire, and is consequently unique in topographical value.

Myddelton's autograph, written during the last year of his great labour, is here engraved (see the next page). To it was prefixed the title 'Sir,' by the king's award, at the completion of the undertaking. James I. seems to have been fully aware, at all times, of Myddelton's merit, and anxious to help and honour it. Some years afterwards, when he had temporarily reclaimed Brading Harbour, Isle of Wight, from the sea, the king raised him to the dignity of baronet without the payment of the customary fees, amounting to £1095, a very large sum of money in those days.

A few words must suffice to narrate Myddelton's later career. He sold twenty-eight of his thirty-six shares in the New River soon after its completion. With the large amount of capital this gave him to command, he carried out the work at Brading, just alluded to. He then directed his attention to mining in North Wales, and continued to work the mines with profit for a period of about sixteen years. The lead of these mines contained

AUTOGRAPH OF MYDDELTON.

much silver, and a contemporary declares that he obtained of 'puer silver 100 poundes weekly,' and that his total profits amounted to at least £2000 a month. 'The popular and oft-repeated story of Sir Hugh having died in poverty and obscurity, is only one of the numerous fables which have accumulated about his memory,'* observes Mr Smiles. 'There is no doubt that Myddelton realised considerable profits by the working of his Welsh mines, and that toward the close of his life he was an eminently prosperous man.' He died at the advanced age of seventy-six, leaving large sums to his children, an ample provision for his widow, many bequests to friends and relatives, annuities to servants, and gifts to the poor. All of which it has been Mr Smiles's pleasant task to prove from documentary evidence of the most unimpeachable kind.

In order to fully comprehend the value of Myddelton's New River to the men of London, we must take a retrospective glance at the older water supply. Two or three conduits in the principal streets, some others in the northern suburbs, and the springs in the neighbourhood of the Fleet River, were all they had at their service. The Cheapside conduits were the most used, as they were the largest and most decorative of these structures. The Great Conduit in the centre of this important thoroughfare, was an erection like a tower, surrounded by statuary; the Little Conduit stood in Westcheap, at the back of the church of St Michael, in the Querne, at the north-east end of Paternoster Row. Our cut exhibits its chief features, as delineated in 1585 by the surveyor R. Treswell. Leaden pipes ran all along Cheapside, to convey the water to various points; and the City Records tell of the punishment awarded one dishonest resident, who tapped the pipe where it passed his door, and secretly conveyed the water to his own well. Except where conveyed to some public building, water had to be fetched for domestic use from these ever-flowing reservoirs. Large tankards, holding from two to three gallons, were constructed for this use; and may be seen ranged round the conduit in the cut above given. Many poor men

THE LITTLE CONDUIT IN CHEAPSIDE.

TANKARD-BEARER.

* The favourite fable is, that he was ruined by his connection with the New River, applied for relief to the citizens, and got little, lived in great indigence, and died disregarded. It was even asserted that he hid his decadence beneath the name of Raymond, in a Shropshire village, where he was occasionally employed as a pavior.

lived by supplying water to the householders; 'a tankard-bearer' was hence a well-known London character, and appears in a curious pictorial series of the cries of London, executed in the reign of James I., and preserved in the British Museum. It will be seen from our copy (see engraving on the previous page), that he presents some peculiar professional features. His dress is protected by coarse aprons hung from his neck, and the weight of his large tankard when empty, partially relieved from the left shoulder, by the aid of the staff in his right hand. He wears the 'city flat-cap,' his dress altogether of the old fashion, such as belonged to the time of 'bluff King Hal.' When water was required in smaller quantities, apprentices and servant-girls were sent to the conduits. Hence they were not only gossiping-places, but spots where quarrels constantly arose. A curious print in the British Museum—published about the time of Elizabeth—entitled *Tittle Tattle*, is a satire on these customs, and tells us in homely rhyme:

'At the conduit striving for their turn,
The quarrel it grows great,
That up in arms they are at last,
And one another beat.'

Oliver Cob, the water-bearer, is one of the characters in Ben Jonson's play, ***Every Man in his Humour***, and the sort of coarse repartee he indulges in, may be taken as a fair sample of that used at the London conduits. It was not till a considerable time after the opening of the New River that their utility ceased. Much difficulty and expense awaited the conduct of water to London houses. The owners of the ground near the New River Head exacted heavy sums for permission to carry pipes through their land, and it was not till February 1626, that Bethlehem Hospital was thus supplied. The profits of the New River Company were seriously affected by these expenses, until they secured themselves from exaction by the purchase of the land. The pipes they used for the conveyance of their water were of the simplest construction, formed of the stems of small elm-trees, merely denuded of the bark, drilled through the centre, cut to lengths of about six feet; one end being tapered, so that it fitted into the orifice of the pipe laid down before it; and in this way wooden pipes passed through the streets to the extent of about 400 miles! The fields known as 'Spa-fields,' near the New River Head, were used as a depôt for these pipes; and were popularly termed 'the pipe-fields' by the inhabitants of Clerkenwell. As the conveyance of water by means of these pipes was expensive to the company, and charged highly in consequence, water-carriers still plied their trade. Lauron, an artist who has depicted the street-criers of the time of William III., has left us the figure of the water-carrier he saw about London, crying, 'Any New River water here!' A penny a pail-full was his charge for porterage, and he occasionally enforced the superiority of his mode of serving it by crying, 'Fresh and fair New River water! none of your pipe-sludge!' The wooden pipes leaked considerably, were liable to rapid decay, burst during frosts, and were always troublesome; cast-iron pipes have now entirely superseded them, but this is only within the last thirty-five years; and it may be worth noting here the curious fact, that the rude old elm-tree water-pipes were taken up and removed from before the houses in Piccadilly, extending from the Duke of Devonshire's to Clarges Street, several years ago; and that a similar series were recently exhumed from Pall Mall.

THE WATER-CARRIER.

## CEREMONIES FORMERLY CONNECTED WITH THE ELECTION OF THE MAYOR OF NOTTINGHAM.

On the day the new mayor assumed office (September 29), he, the old mayor, the aldermen, and councillors, all marched in procession to St Mary's Church, where divine service was said. After service the whole body went into the vestry, where the old mayor seated himself in an elbow-chair at a table covered with *black* cloth, in the middle of which lay the mace covered with rosemary and sprigs of bay. This was termed *the burying of the mace*, doubtless a symbolical act, denoting the official decease of its late holder. A form of electing the new mayor was then gone through, after which the one retiring from office took up the mace, kissed it, and delivered it into the hand of his successor with a suitable compliment. The new mayor then proposed two persons for sheriffs, and two for the office of chamberlains; and after these had also gone through the votes, the whole assemblage marched into the chancel, where the senior coroner administered the oath to the new mayor in the presence of the old one, and the town-clerk gave to the sheriffs and chamberlains their oath of office. These ceremonies being over, they marched in order to the New Hall, attended by such gentlemen and tradesmen as had been invited by the mayor and sheriffs, where the feasting took place. On their way, at the Week-day-Cross, overagainst the ancient Guild Hall, the town-clerk proclaimed the mayor and sheriffs; and at the next ensuing market-day they were again proclaimed in the face of the whole market at the Malt Cross.

The entertainment given as a banquet on these occasions will perhaps astonish some of their successors in office. 'The mayor and sheriffs welcomed their guests with *bread and cheese*, fruit in season, and *pipes and tobacco*.' Imagine the present corporation and their friends sitting down to such a feast!

## SEPTEMBER 30.

St Jerome, of Aquileia, doctor of the church, 420. St Gregory, apostle of Armenia, and bishop, beginning of 4th century. St Honorius, archbishop of Canterbury, confessor, 653.

*Born*.—Euripides, tragic dramatist, 480 B.C., *Salamis;* Cneius Pompeius, *Magnus* (Pompey the Great), 106 B.C.; Jacques Necker, financier to Louis XVI., 1734, *Geneva;* William Hutton, miscellaneous writer, 1723, *Derby*.

*Died*.—St Jerome of Aquileia, father of the church, 420; Emperor Rodolph I., 1291; Isabella of Bavaria, queen of Charles VI. of France, 1435, *Paris;* Sir Fulke Greville, Lord Brooke, poet, murdered, 1628; John Reinhold Patkul, Livonian statesman, broken on the wheel, 1707; John Dollond, optician, 1761; George Whitefield, celebrated preacher, 1770, *Newbury Port, New England;* Thomas Percy, bishop of Dromore, author of *Reliques of Ancient English Poetry*, 1811; Auguste Comte, philosophical writer, 1857, *Paris*.

### WILLIAM HUTTON.

Biography records scarcely a finer instance of industry and economy leading their possessor out of the most unpropitious circumstances to affluence and honour, than the story of William Hutton, the Birmingham stationer. His father was a woolcomber, and a dissipated character. William was born in Derby in 1723, and, at the age of seven, was set to earn his living in the Derby silk-mill, and, being too small for his business, he had to move about on a pair of high pattens. In his fifteenth year, he went to Nottingham, and served a second apprenticeship at the stocking-frame, by which, on reaching manhood, he found he could not maintain himself. For amusement, he commenced to practise bookbinding, and, growing expert, resolved to make it his trade. He took a shop at Southwell, fourteen miles from Nottingham, at a rent of 20*s*. a year, and there resorted every Saturday, the market-day. He used to leave Nottingham at five in the morning, carrying a burden of three pounds' weight to thirty, opened shop at ten, dined on bread and cheese and half a pint of ale, took from 1*s*. to 6*s*., shut up at four, and trudged home in the dark, arriving at Nottingham by nine. Southwell was a poor place, and in 1750 he determined to try Birmingham, and engaged half a shop in Bull Street at 1*s*. a week. In Birmingham, he found three booksellers, Aris, Warren, and Wollaston; but he 'judged from the number and intelligence of the inhabitants, that there might be room for a fourth, and hoped that, as an ant, he might escape the envy or notice of the three great men.' Five shillings a week covered all his expenses—food, lodging, washing, and dress, and at the end of the first year he had saved £20. He then ventured to move into a house at £8 a year, and business began to grow rapidly upon him. By and by he relinquished bookselling for stationery, and opened a paper-warehouse, the first ever seen in Birmingham. He made a good marriage; he speculated in lands and houses, sometimes gaining and sometimes losing; he built a country-house and set up a carriage, and was duly recognised as a substantial citizen. He was elected an overseer of the poor and to other civic offices, and as a Commissioner of the Court of Requests he was pre-eminently useful. The Court of Requests was a tribunal for the recovery of small debts, where equity was administered by the common-sense of an unpaid magistrate, and at the trifling cost of a summons. Hutton did his duty as judge with extraordinary assiduity. 'The Court of Requests,' he writes, 'soon became my favourite amusement. I paid a constant attendance, which engrossed nearly two days a week of my time. That my government was not arbitrary will appear from two facts: I never had a quarrel with a suitor, nor the least difference with a brother-commissioner. I attended the Court nineteen years During that time more than a hundred thousand causes passed through my hands! a number possibly beyond what ever passed the decision of any other man. I have had 250 in one day.' Hutton published a collection of cases, with his decisions, in the Court of Requests, and they afford vivid evidence of high judicial faculty, and of a wide and shrewd knowledge of human nature.

In 1781, Hutton made his appearance as an author, in the publication of a *History of Birmingham*. 'I took up the pen,' he says, 'and that with fear and trembling, at the advanced age of fifty-six, a period at which most authors lay it down.' He spared no pains to make his book a good one: 'Pleased as a fond parent with this *History*, as my first literary offspring, I may be said, while in manuscript, to have had the whole by heart. Had a line been quoted, I could have followed it up through the chapter. Frequently, while awake in the night, I have repeated it in silence for two or three hours together without adding or missing a word.' His success with Birmingham tempted him on to other works, such as a *History of Derby*, *The Roman Wall*, *The Battle of Bosworth Field*, and some poetry. 'Having commenced,' he writes, 'I drove the quill thirty years, in which time I published fourteen books.'

Hutton suffered a severe affliction in 1791. The Church-and-King mob, who sacked and burned Priestley's house and chapel, served Hutton in the same style. His warehouse, his stock-in-trade, and country-house at Bennett's Hill, were all destroyed. Hutton was not, like Priestley, a keen politician; his words were always well considered and pacific; but he was a dissenter, he frequented the Unitarian meeting-house, and among the rabble there were probably not a few who bore him no good-will for his judgments in the Court of Requests. The sufferers from the riot had great difficulty in recovering their losses from the Hundred. Hutton laid his claim for £6736, and was awarded only £5390; and others fared even worse. This harsh usage somewhat soured his temper. He confesses, 'The cruel treatment I had met with totally altered my sentiments of man. I had considered him as designed to assist and comfort his species; to reduce the rough propensities of his nature, and to endeavour after perfection, though he could not reach it; but the experience convinced me that the nature of the human species, like that of the brute creation, is to destroy each other. I therefore determined to withdraw from all public business, to spend the small remainder of existence with my little family, and amuse myself with the book and the pen.'

Hutton's nature was too vigorous to remain long under such morbid impressions, and though he continued to be suspected and distrusted as a Jacobin, neither his activity nor his enjoyment of life was seriously affected. He resigned his business as stationer to his son, but he could find little satisfaction away from the warehouse, and every morning, for many years, he walked from Bennett's Hill to town, and spent the day with the same assiduity as when making his fortune. He was a great pedestrian, and his feats, when an old man, were the surprise and alarm of his friends. In his seventy-seventh year, on the 4th July 1800, he set out on foot from Birmingham to make a survey of the Roman Wall. His daughter accompanied him as far as Penrith, riding on a pillion behind a servant, meeting her father in the evening at some appointed inn. He marched from the Solway along the line of the wall to Wallsend, and then back again from Newcastle to Carlisle, 'having,' he says, 'crossed the kingdom twice in one week and six hours, melted with a July sun, and without a drop of rain. By easy marches I arrived at Birmingham, 7th August, after a loss on my part of perhaps one stone weight by perspiration, a lapse of thirty-five days, and a walk of 601 miles.' His daughter describes his manner of walking as 'a steady saunter, by which he got over the ground at the rate of full two miles and a half in an hour. The pace he went did not even fatigue his shoes. He walked the whole 600 miles in one pair, and scarcely made a hole in his stockings.'

William Hutton closed his useful and, on the whole, happy life on the 20th September 1815, at the advanced age of ninety-two. He left an autobiography, giving minute particulars of his habits and career, and in many respects it is not unworthy of a place alongside Franklin's.

## REV. GEORGE WHITEFIELD.

Whitefield was the most effective pulpit orator of last century, and perhaps of any century. He was thoroughly in earnest, and shrank from none of the toils and privations incident to what he thought his path of duty. His voice excelled both in melody and compass. He had a good figure and a fine countenance, and his gestures were always appropriate and full of grace. Franklin, who heard him frequently, learned to distinguish easily between his sermons newly composed, and those which he had often preached in the course of his travels. 'His delivery of the latter,' he says, 'was so improved by frequent repetition, that every accent, every emphasis, every modulation of the voice was so perfectly well turned and well placed, that, without being interested in the subject, one could not help being well pleased with the discourse; a pleasure of much the same kind which one receives from an excellent piece of music.'

Whitefield was born in 1714, at the Bell Inn, in the city of Gloucester. He gave his boyhood a very bad character after the common practice of eminent pietists. His mother was early left a widow, and as soon as George was able, he assisted her in the public-house, and in the end 'put on his blue apron and his snuffers [scoggers or sleeves], washed mops, cleaned rooms, and became a professed and common drawer.' This drudgery was a condition of necessity, not of choice. He had been at a grammar-school, his fine voice had been so praised that he had been tempted to try the stage, and his religious feelings impelled him to the service of the church. Hearing how cheaply a young man might live at Oxford as a servitor, he entered the university at the age of eighteen in that capacity. The students called Methodists, because they lived by rule and method, were then exciting great attention, and Whitefield's heart yearned towards them, and after a while he passed into their fellowship, and rivalled the most ardent in devotion and austerity. 'God only knows,' he writes, 'how many nights I have lain upon my bed groaning under what I felt. Whole days and weeks have I spent in lying prostrate on the ground in silent or vocal prayer.' He chose the worst food, and affected mean apparel; he made himself remarkable by leaving off powder in his hair, when every one else was powdered, because he thought it unbecoming a penitent; and he wore woollen gloves, a patched gown, and dirty shoes, as visible signs of humility. He would kneel under the trees in Christ's Church, walk in silent prayer, shivering the while with cold, till the great bell summoned him to his college for the night. He kept Lent so strictly that, except on Saturdays and Sundays, his only food was coarse bread and sage-tea, without sugar. The end was, that before the termination of the forty days, he had scarcely strength enough left to creep up stairs, and was under a physician for many weeks.

He was ordained deacon in 1736, and after several engagements as curate, sailed for Georgia at the invitation of Wesley. At the end of a year he returned to England, to solicit subscriptions for an orphan-house he had established in Savannah, and which continued to be one of the chief cares of his life. His eloquence was in nothing more apparent than in the ease with which he drew money from the unwilling and indifferent. From a London audience he once took a thousand pounds, then considered a prodigious subscription. Prudence in the person of Franklin could not resist his persuasive appeals. Franklin disapproved of the orphan-house at Savannah, thinking Philadelphia the proper place for its erection, and he says: 'I silently resolved he should get nothing from me. I had in my pocket a handful of copper money, three or four silver dollars, and five pistoles in gold. As he proceeded I began to soften, and concluded to give the copper; another stroke of his oratory made me ashamed of that, and determined me to give the silver; and he finished so admirably, that I emptied my pocket wholly into the collector's dish, gold and all.'

Whitefield's life was spent as a travelling-preacher. He generally made a yearly round through England and Scotland, and went several times to Ireland. He repeatedly visited America, and traversed the whole extent of the British possessions there. Wherever he appeared, crowds flocked to listen to him. In London, he sometimes preached early in the morning, and in the dark and cold of winter the streets near the chapel used to be thronged with eager listeners bearing lanterns in their hands. When he took his departure from a place, he was usually followed by a troop of weeping disciples. In Bristol, especially, the fervour he awakened was extraordinary. There, the churches being closed against him, he commenced preaching in the fields to the savage colliers of Kingswood. His first open-air sermon was preached on the afternoon of Saturday, 17th February 1739, upon a mount, in a place called Rose Green, to an audience of about two hundred. He repeated the experiment, and enormous congregations grew around him. The deep silence of his rude auditors was the first proof that he had impressed them, and soon he saw white gutters made by the tears which plentifully fell down their black cheeks—black as they came out of their coal-pits. 'The open firmament above me,' says he, 'the prospect of the adjacent fields, with the sight of thousands and thousands, some in coaches, some on horseback, and some in the trees, and at times all affected and drenched in tears together; to which sometimes was added the solemnity of the approaching evening, was almost too much for, and quite overcame me.'

The triumphs of many popular preachers have been confined to the vulgar, but the cultivated, and even the sceptical, confessed Whitefield's power. Hume, Chesterfield, and Bolingbroke heard him with surprise and admiration; and the Countess of Huntingdon, who made him her chaplain, introduced him to the highest circles of rank and fashion. He cast his lot among the Methodists, but his aim was to preach the gospel, and not to build up a sect. With Wesley he differed on the question of freewill—Wesley being an Arminian, and Whitefield a Calvinist; but Whitefield, though steadfast in his opinions, was not disposed to waste his energy in wrangling with his able coadjutor. Whitefield by eminence was a preacher; Wesley was more than a preacher—he was a first-rate administrator, and the great religious organisation which bears his name is the attestation of his peculiar genius.

Like Wesley, Whitefield entertained some odd notions about marriage, which, as little in the one case as the other, contributed to happiness. While he was in America in the spring of 1740, he applied to two of his friends, a Mr D. and Mrs D., to ask if they would give him their daughter to wife, at the same time telling them, that they need not be afraid of sending him a refusal, 'for I bless God,' said he, 'if I know anything of my own heart, I am free from that foolish passion which the world calls love. I write, only because I believe it is the will of God, that I should alter my state; but your denial will fully convince me that your daughter is not the person appointed by God for me. But I have sometimes thought Miss E. would be my helpmate, for she has often been impressed upon my heart.' The proposal came to nothing, and the following year he was married in England to Mrs James of Abergavenny, a widow, who was between thirty and forty, and, by his own account, neither rich nor beautiful, but having once been gay, was now 'a despised follower of the Lamb.' They had one child, who died in infancy, and their union was not full of pleasantness. They did not live happily together, and 'her death in 1768 set his mind much at rest.'

Whitefield died in America, at Newbury Port, near Boston, on Sunday morning, 30th September 1770, at the age of fifty-six.

## A CONTEST FOR PRECEDENCE.

Sir John Finett, master of ceremonies to the first two monarchs of the Stuart dynasty that sat on the throne of England, wrote a curious work, entitled *Choice Observations touching the Reception and Precedence of Foreign Ambassadors.* This book, though to us, at the present day, merely an amusing account of court squabbles and pretensions to precedence, was a very important treatise in the ideas of its author; who, if he had lived a little earlier, might have passed as the prototype of Polonius. One great difficulty, never settled in Finett's lifetime, was the placing of the French and Spanish ambassadors, each claiming precedence of the other. James I., on some public festivals, solved the problem by inviting neither of them; but this could not always be done, and so, for many years, the principal courts of Europe were disturbed by unseemly broils between the representatives of France and Spain. At last, the long struggle came to a crisis, formal complaints and courtly protocols being supplemented by swords and pistols; and the battle, which settled the much-disputed point, was fought in the streets of London.

In September 1661, an ambassador from Sweden was expected to arrive at the court of Whitehall. The etiquette and custom then used on the arrival of an ambassador, was for the king's barge to meet him at Gravesend, and convey him up the river to Tower-wharf. He was then received in the king's carriage, his own carriage following next in order, and after that the carriages of the other ambassadors, according to their national precedence. On this occasion, the Marquis d'Estrade, the French ambassador, determined that his carriage should follow next to the Swede's, and the Baron de Batteville, the Spanish ambassador, having made an exactly similar determination, preparations were made for a contest. And, as the populace of London might readily be expected to take part in the fray, the ambassadors applied to King Charles, who, very complaisantly, issued a proclamation, forbidding any Englishman, under penalty of death, from interfering with the quarrel; the ambassadors promising, on their parts, that firearms should not be used.

The 30th of September, the day appointed for the Swedish envoy's reception, having arrived, Tower-hill was crowded with an immense number of the lower classes, anxious to witness the fight; while a strong body of horse and foot guards were posted in the same locality, to prevent any action on the part of the spectators. The hour appointed for the ambassador to land was three o'clock in the afternoon; but the Spanish carriage, guarded by fifty men, armed with swords, was on the wharf five hours earlier, thus obtaining an advantageous position. The French carriage, arriving a little later than its Spanish rival, did not acquire so good a position; it was better guarded, however, being accompanied by one hundred men on foot, and fifty on horseback, most of the latter, in defiance of the arrangement made with the king, being armed with pistols and carabines. All was quiet, till the Swedish ambassador, having landed and been received in the king's carriage, was driven off, his own carriage following. A desperate struggle then commenced. The Spaniards forming across the road to bar the passage of the French, the latter fired a volley, and charged their opponents, sword in hand, yet, in spite of their superior numbers, were bravely repulsed by the cool courage of the Spaniards. Three horses, the postilion, and coachman of the French carriage having been killed, the ambassador's son, who alone occupied it, alighted, and though then severely wounded, drew his sword, stimulating his followers to fresh exertions, but in vain; the Spanish carriage had by this time driven off, next in order to that of the Swede, and the point of precedency, so stoutly contended for, was won and lost. The fight, however, did not cease. For so far, it had been confined to Tower-wharf; now it was extended to Tower-hill. There an outlying detachment of the French were posted, who, rushing on the Spanish carriage, attempted to cut the traces; but were foiled through iron chains, covered with leather, having been prudently provided, instead of the usual traces, for this particular occasion. The Spaniards soon beat this party off, and proceeded on their way without further molestation. Half an hour afterwards, the crest-fallen French, having repaired damages, followed, with only two horses in their carriage.

As each party carried off its own killed and wounded, the amount of casualties could not be accurately ascertained. Rugge, in his curious manuscript, estimates the number of killed at twelve, the wounded at forty. Among the spectators, one Englishman, a poor plasterer, was killed by a shot through the head, and several others were wounded. The bystanders would willingly have taken an active part against the French, if they had not been prevented, by the proclamation and presence of the troops. Pepys did not see the fight, but, after it was over, being, as he says, 'in all things curious,' he 'ran through all the dirt, and the streets full of people, and saw the Spanish coach go by, with fifty drawn swords to guard it, and our soldiers a shouting for joy, strange to see how all the city did rejoice, and indeed we do all naturally love the Spaniards, and hate the French.' He then went to the French embassy to see how they bore their defeat, and tells us they all 'looked like dead men, and not a word among them but shake their heads.'

When tidings of the affray reached Paris, Louis XIV. became extremely indignant, publicly declaring that he would make war upon Spain, if his right of precedence were not conceded in every court of Europe. He at once dismissed the Spanish ambassador from France, and recalled his own ambassador from Madrid. After considerable diplomacy, Louis gained all that he demanded. In the March of the following year, the Marquis of Fuentes was sent from Spain to Paris, in the character of ambassador extraordinary, to formally renounce the long-contested point of precedency. At a grand reception, held at Versailles, Fuentes, in the presence of the Pope's Nuncio, and twenty-six envoys from the various courts of Europe, declared that his master, the king of Spain, had given orders to all his ambassadors to abstain from any kind of rivalry with those of France. Louis, then addressing the foreign ministers, desired them to communicate this declaration to their respective courts. On which the Dutch envoy drily remarked, that he had heard of embassies tendering obedience to the pope, but he had never before known of such from one crowned head to another.

Louis caused a medal to be struck in commemoration of the important event. One side bears the monarch's head, on the other, Louis is represented standing on the dais of his throne, before him is Fuentes, in the humble attitude of one who apologises, the Nuncio and other ambassadors standing round. The motto is 'JUS PRÆCEDENDI ASSERTUM, CONFITENTE HISPANORUM ORATORE,' which may be translated—The right of precedence confirmed by the avowal of Spain.

## THE REVOLUTION OF 1399.

The 30th of September 1399, marks an epoch of some moment in English history—the transference of the crown from the House of Plantagenet to that of Lancaster. On the previous day, a deputation from the Lords and Commons had waited on King Richard II., then a prisoner in the Tower, and had obtained from him a formal renunciation of the throne, in favour of his cousin, Henry of Bolingbroke, who a few weeks before had landed from exile at Ravenspur, in Yorkshire, and in an astonishingly short time made himself master of the kingdom. At the time of Henry's landing, Richard was absent on an expedition to Ireland, and for some time remained in ignorance of what was transpiring at home. On receiving intelligence of Henry's alarming progress, he despatched at once the Earl of Salisbury with an army, but this nobleman after disembarking at Conway, soon found himself deserted by all his forces; and Richard, on landing a few days afterwards at Milford Haven, was soon placed in a similar predicament. Deserted on all hands, the unfortunate monarch was at last compelled to surrender himself to the Earl of Northumberland, and meet at the castle of Flint his cousin Henry. He was then conducted as a prisoner to Chester, from which he was afterwards transferred to the Tower; and then, on 29th September, he received the deputation from parliament already mentioned. The following day, his renunciation of the crown was formally ratified, and himself formally deposed. Whilst this procedure was going on, Henry of Bolingbroke, Duke of Hereford, remained seated in his usual place near the throne, which was empty, and covered with cloth of gold. As soon as eight commissioners had proclaimed the sentence of deposition, he rose, approached the throne, and having solemnly crossed himself, said: 'In the name of God the Father, Son, and Holy Ghost, I, Henry of Lancaster, challenge this realm of England, because I am descended by right line of blood from the good lord King Henry III., and through that right, that God of his grace hath sent me, with help of my kin and of my friends, to recover it; the which realm was in point to be undone for default of government and undoing of the good laws.' He then knelt for a few minutes in apparent devotion on the steps of the throne on which he subsequently took his seat, being conducted thither by the archbishops of Canterbury and York.

Though a manifest usurpation, the seizure of the crown by Henry IV. seems to have been fully in accordance with the will of the English nation, which was disgusted with the corrupt and imbecile administration of Richard II. The vigorous government of Henry and his son, the chivalrous Henry V., may almost appear a vindication of their wisdom in this change of dynasty. But the terrible wars of the Roses, and the miserable end of Bolingbroke's unhappy grandson, Henry VI., amply avenged the wrongs of the Plantagenet family. However we may reverence the ability of Henry IV., and excuse his usurpation of the crown, a dark cloud must ever rest on his memory in connection with the unfortunate Richard II., who was mysteriously murdered by Henry's orders in Pontefract Castle, a short time after his deposition.

Then came October full of merry glee;
For yet his noule was totty of the must,
Which he was treading in the wine-fat's see,
And of the joyous oyle, whose gentle gust
Made him so frolic and so full of lust:
Upon a dreadful Scorpion he did ride,
The same which by Dianæ's doom unjust
Slew great Orion; and eeke by his side
He had his ploughing-share and coulter ready tyde.

SPENSER.

(DESCRIPTIVE.)

OCTOBER IT is now yellow autumn, no longer divided from summer by the plenty sheaf and lingering flowers, but with features of its own, marked with slow decay. There is a rich hectic red on its cheek, too beautiful to last long, and every wind that blows pales the crimson hue, or scatters its beauty on the empty air, for everywhere around us the leaves are falling. But through the openings autumn makes in the foliage, many new beauties are revealed—bits of landscape, which the long close-woven leaves had shut out, of far-away spots, that look like a new country, so strange do they appear when seen for the first time through the faded and torn curtains which have shaded summer. Hill and valley, spire and thatched grange, winding highways and brown bends, over the meadows—with stiles and hedges—shew fresh footpaths, which we have never walked along, and make us long to look at the unvisited places to which they lead. We see low clumps of evergreens, which the tall trees had hidden; nests in hedges, where we were before unable to find one;

and in the orchards a few hardy apples still hang, which only the frost can ripen. The fields seem to look larger, where we saw the grass mown and the corn reaped, for we can now see the bottoms of the hedges. The cherry-trees look as beautiful to the eye as they did when in blossom, such a rich scarlet dyes the leaves, mingled every here and there with golden touches. The elders are still covered with dark purple berries, especially the branches which overhang the water-courses, and are beyond the reach of the villagers. We see flags and rushes and water-plants rocking in the breeze, and reflected in the ripples which were hidden by the entangling grass that now lies matted together, and is beginning to decay. As evening approaches, the landscape seems to assume a sober hue, the colours of the foliage become subdued, and the low sighing of the wind, the call of the partridge, and the few notes uttered by the remaining birds, fall upon the ear with a sad sound at times, and produce a low feeling, which we are seldom sensible of at the change of any other season of the year.

There is still one out-of-door scene beautiful to look at and pleasant to walk through, and that is hop-picking—the last ingathering of autumn that finds employment for the poor; nor are there many prettier English pictures to be seen than a well-managed hop-plantation. The smell of the hop is very delightful, so different from that of new hay and hawthorn-buds, yet quite as refreshing. What a beautiful motion there is in the light and shadow when the breeze stirs the vine-shaped leaves, and the golden coloured hops swaying the bine to and fro, and sharp quiverings in the open net-work where they cross each other, and all pervaded with a soothing aroma, that makes the blood stir like the smell of the rising sap in a forest at spring-time! Merry people, too, are the hop-pickers, whether at their work, or when going or returning from the hop-plantations. The little huts they run up to sleep in, their places of cooking, washing, and other domestic contrivances, tell that they belong to the race who have heralded the way into many a wilderness, lived there, and founded colonies, that are now springing up into great nations. We see them travelling to the hop-grounds with baby on back, and leading children by the hand, carrying cradle and bed, saucepan and kettle, and no doubt nearly everything their humble home contained. We look on and wonder how those tiny bare feet will ever tramp so far, yet while turning the head and watching them, we see them go pit-pat over the ground, three or four steps to the one or two longer strides of their parents, caring no more for the gravel than if they were shod with iron, and we are astonished to see what a way they have gone while we have been watching. Sometimes, in the hop-grounds, we have seen a cradle with the baby asleep in it, swinging between the tall hop-bines, and thought what a pretty picture it would make, if well painted! Often, in the neighbourhood of Farnham, the hop attains the height of from fourteen to sixteen feet, and excepting between a clear hazel-copse, when the leaves are yellowed by autumn, we know nothing more beautiful to walk among than these tall swaying bines. It flowers in June, and in favourable seasons is ripe in September, though many hops remain to be picked in the early part of the present month. There are several varieties of hops grown, known as the red-bind, green-bind, and white-bind; the first of which, though producing small cones, is a hardy plant, and resists the attacks of insects; while the second is very productive in a good season, and will flourish better in a poor soil than the white bind, which is the most difficult of all to grow, and realises the highest price of all the hops. Good practised growers fix upon the time for hop-picking when the cones throw out a strong peculiar scent, which they know the moment the air is filled with it, and they pay more regard to this powerful aroma than they do to the looks of the hops. Nor is it at hop-picking-time only that this beautiful plant gives employment to the poor, though that is the chief season, for in spring the ground has to be well stirred and drawn up about the young shoots; then the poles must be placed in the ground about the end of April, when the shoots are generally five or six inches high. And after all this is done, the shoots must be tied to the poles as they grow higher, and this must be done very lightly and carefully, for if fastened too tight, the shoot would decay, come off, and send out fresh ones from below, which would attain no height, be dwindled, and not bear a bunch of cones worth the gathering. The wild-hop, which may be seen romping about our hedges, is indigenous, and pretty it looks amid the other climbing-plants, many of which bear beautiful berries, nor is there any record of its having been cultivated before the reign of Henry VIII. It was, however, imported from the Low Countries, and used for brewing in England, as early as 1428.

To an observant eye, many little changes are presented, which shew how rapidly autumn is advancing. The flocks are now driven to the fold of an evening, for the nights are becoming too cold and damp for them to remain in the fields, and they will soon be enclosed in ground set apart for their winter-feeding. It is a pleasant sight to see them rush out of the fold of a morning after their confinement, then hurry on and break their closed ranks to feed here and there on the unpalatable and scanty pasturage. Turn wherever we may, we see the face of Nature changing; nowhere does it now wear its old summer-look, the very sound of the falling leaves causes us to feel thoughtful, and many a solemn passage of the Holy Bible passes through the mind, telling us that the time will come when we also 'shall fade as a leaf the wind has taken away. And all thou hast shall fall down as the leaf falleth from the vine.' That we shall soon be 'as oaks when they cast their leaves,' and at no other season of the year do these solemn truths strike us so forcibly as in autumn. As the fallen leaves career before us—crumbling ruins of summer's beautiful halls—we cannot help thinking of those who have perished—who have gone before us, blown forward to the grave by the icy blasts of Death. The scenery of spring awakens no such emotions, there is no sign of decay there, for all seems as if fresh springing into life, after the long sleep of winter. But now, even the sun seems to be growing older, he rises later and sets earlier, as if requiring more rest, instead of increasing in heat and brightness, as he did when the butter-cups looked up at him and 'flashed back gold for gold.' Yet we know this natural decay is necessary to produce the life and beauty of a coming spring, and it is some solace to know, that for every flower autumn rains and blows upon and buries, a hundred will rise up and occupy their places by the time summer returns again, for it is her work to beautify decay.

Nearly all our singing-birds have departed for sunnier lands far over the sea, and the swallows are now preparing to follow them, while, strange interchange, other birds visit us which have been away all spring and summer. Some days before the swallows leave us, they assemble together, at certain places—generally beside a river—where they wait fresh arrivals, until a flock of thousands is mustered; and were not the same gathering going on at other places beside, we might fancy that all the swallows that visit us were assembled in one spot. One place they frequented, which abounded in osier holts, in our younger days, and when up early angling, we have seen them rise in myriads from the willows about six in the morning, and dividing themselves into five or six companies, disperse in contrary directions, when they remained away all day, beginning to return about five, and continuing to come in until it was nearly dark. No doubt this separation took place on account of the scarcity of food, as sufficient could not be found, without flying many miles from the river-side, where they assembled. Every day the flock appeared to augment, and we have no doubt that every division, on its return to this great mustering-ground, brought in many stragglers. We have also often fancied that it was here the young swallows exercised themselves, strengthening their wings for the long journey that lay before them, by circling flights and graceful evolutions, as if trying at times which could come nearest the water at the greatest speed without touching a drop with either breast or pinions. We also came to the conclusion, that all the young ones did not accompany the divisions that went away every day in search of food, but only a portion—as thousands remained—and that those which went out one day rested the next, and had their turn on the second morning, or each alternate day. They seldom remained later than the middle of October, and when they left for good, went away all together, in the direction of the south. A few generally remained for a day or two, then went off in the same direction. Dead swallows were generally picked up among the willows after the flock had migrated. Earliest amongst the fresh arrivals is the wood-cock, who generally reaches the end of his journey in the night, and very weary and jaded he appears. Seldom is he ever seen to land, though he has been found hiding himself near the coast, in so exhausted a state as to be run down, and taken by hand. But he does not remain by the sea-side a day longer than he is compelled, where, having recruited himself a little, he sets off to visit his former haunts. The snipe also arrives about the same time, and is found in the haunts of the wood-cock, on high moors and hills, while the season is mild, and in low, warm, sheltered localities when the weather is severe. In October the redwing reaches us, and if the autumn is fine and warm, its song may often be heard. Its favourite haunts are parks, and secure places, abounding in clumps of trees, where it feeds on worms, and such like soft food, so long as it can be found; never feeding on berries unless they are forced by the frost, then they soon perish. The early arrival of the fieldfare is considered by country-people a sure sign of a hard winter, especially if there is a large crop of heps and haws, which they say, reverentially, Providence has stored up for them beforehand. We think it is a surer sign, that, in the country they have quitted, severe weather has set in earlier than usual. Some naturalists say, that although this bird obtains its food in the hedges, it roosts on the ground; the reason assigned for arriving at this conclusion is, that those who go out at night with nets to capture larks in the field, often find fieldfares amongst the birds thus taken. May not this have been in some neighbourhood where hedges were rare, and caused them to roost, like the rooks on Salisbury Plain, where there is plenty of food, but very few trees, compelling them either to fly miles away at night, or take up their lodgings 'on the cold ground?' Gilbert White is the great authority for this account of the fieldfares.

The woods never look more beautiful than from the close of last month to the middle of October, for by that time it seems as if nature had exhausted all her choicest colours on the foliage. We see the rich, burnished bronze of the oak; red of many hues, up to the gaudiest scarlet; every shade of yellow, from the wan gold of the primrose to the deep orange of the tiger-lily; purple, rising from the light lilac to the darkest velvet of the pansy streaked with jet; and all so blended and softened together in parts, that like the colours on a dove's neck, we cannot tell where one begins and the other ends. And amid this change, the graceful fir-trees seem now to step boldly out, and we are amazed at the quiet beauty we have so long overlooked as we gaze upon these stately and swarthy daughters of autumn, who have been hidden by their fairer sisters of summer. We often wish that a few more of our great landscape-painters had devoted their canvas to the endless tints of 'the fading and many-coloured woods,' as they are seen at no other time excepting this season of the year. Nothing can be grander than the autumnal foliage of the oak, with its variety of tints, which are more numerous than can be found on any other tree, where there are greens of every hue, and browns running into shades, that are almost numberless. The beech again—excepting only one or two of our shrubs—is covered with the richest of all autumn colours—an orange that seems almost to blaze again as you look at it in the sunset, recalling the burning bush before which Moses bowed. Nearly one of the first trees to shed its foliage is the walnut; next the ash, if covered with those keys that make such a rattling in the November wind—if these are wanting, the tree remains much longer in leaf. The ash is one of the most graceful of our forest-trees, with its leaves set in pairs as if made to match one another, while its smooth, tough branches have a gray hue, that seems to make a light through every portion of the tree. The horse-chestnut now wears its changing livery of shining gold, but can hardly be classed amongst our English forest-trees, as it was a stranger to our parks, ornamental-grounds, and copses less than two centuries ago. The lime or linden, though it soon loses its leaves, shews well in an autumn landscape; so does the tall poplar, seeming as if trying to touch the sky with its high up-coned head. How beautiful the elm now looks, especially if its changing foliage is seen from some summit that overlooks a wood, for it is the tallest of our forest-trees, and its topmost boughs may then be seen high above all others! Even so near London as Dulwich, these stately trees may be seen in all their beauty, and some of them look old enough to have thrown their checkered shadows over Shakspeare, when he walked under them with Alleyn the player, in consultation, as they laid out plans for the old hospital which the latter built, and called by the solemn name of 'God's Gift.' And who can walk through our woods and forests without feeling as if in the presence of Shakspeare, moving side by side with him, and Orlando, and Rosalind, and that contented duke who found the woods

'More free from peril than the envious court;'

while the Forest of Arden seems to rise before us with its herd of dappled deer, and in the mind's eye we picture the melancholy Jacques reclining beneath some broad-branched oak, 'whose antique roots peep out upon the brook,' on which the falling leaves go gliding until lost by the overhanging boughs that shut out the receding stream. What a pattering there is now when the wind blows, as the pale golden acorns come rattling out of their beautifully-carved cups—the drinking-vessels of our old fairy-tales, and often forming the tea-service of our country children in the present day, when they play at giving a tea-party on the floor of some thatched cottage! And how grand is the piping of the great autumn winds, sounding like an organ through the forest, and causing us to feel that we are walking through a temple built by an Almighty hand, for there is no sign of the builder man around us! That trellised roof, where, through the openings made by the fallen leaves, we see only the sky, points to a greater Builder than imitative man.

Beautiful as many of our poetical images are, drawn from the fallen leaves, and sad as the sight is to see them lying around our walks, still the fall of the leaf is not its death, no more than that of one flower fading in a cluster is the death of the flower, as it only falls to make room for another blossom. A swelling bud will always be found in autumn above the leaf that is about to fall; and as this bud increases, it pushes down its predecessor, and causes it to break off, or to hang by so light a hold that the wind soon carries away the loosened leaf. This bud, which forces off the old leaf, forms the future stem or branches, which, during the following summer, will bear many leaves in place of the one it has displaced; and though it will cease to increase during the dead winter-months, will be among the foremost to shew itself in the spring. Evergreens retain their leaves throughout the winter, through the new buds not forcing off the old foliage until spring, instead of putting out above the old foliage in autumn as other trees do. This can be proved by transplanting almost any tree; if it lives, the new buds will come out and push off the old leaves, which soon begin to wither after its removal. But if the tree does not retain life, the leaves will still wither, and instead of falling off, remain on the branches, from whence they are not easily removed though dead. The dead leaf remains on the tree; the live leaf falls before it is dead, pressed down by the swelling bud above it, but still retaining a great portion of its leafy moisture. As for the colouring of autumn leaves, it is supposed that the trees absorb oxygen during the night, which, owing to the coldness of the weather, they have not strength enough to throw out again in the daytime, and that this gives an acidity to the juices of the tree, which changes the colour of the leaf, or, that otherwise, they would be pushed down by the new buds, in all their green summer array. Some admit that this may be the case with leaves that are red, but not with others that are brown and yellow. So the question remains open to many doubts, and as we look at the changing foliage in reverence, we feel satisfied in our own minds, that those beautiful touches have been put in by the wonder-working hand of the Creator.

---

## (HISTORICAL.)

This month, so called from being the eighth in the year according to the old Alban or Latin calendar, was, by our Saxon ancestors, styled *Wyn moneth* (modern, *Weinmonat*), or the wine-month. In allusion to this epithet, an old writer remarks, 'and albeit they had not anciently wines made in Germany, yet in this season had they them from divers countries adjoining.' October was also called, by the ancient Germans, *Winter-fyllith*, from the approach of winter with the full moon of the month.

In some of the ancient Saxon calendars, this month is allegorised by the figure of a husbandman carrying a sack on his shoulders and sowing corn, in allusion to the practice of sowing the winter grain, which takes place in October. In other old almanacs, the sport of hawking has been adopted as emblematical of this, the last month of autumn.

## CHARACTERISTICS OF OCTOBER.

On the 23d of the month, the sun enters the sign of *Scorpio*, an astronomical emblem said to typify, in the form of a destructive insect, the increasing power of cold over nature, in the same manner as the equal influence of cold and heat are represented by *Libra*, or the balance, the sign of the preceding month of September. The average temperature for the middle of the month, throughout the British Islands, is about 50°. On the 1st, the sun rises in the latitude of London at 6.11, and sets at 5.49.

Though a melancholy feeling is associated with October, from the general decay of nature by which it is characterised, there occurs, nevertheless, not infrequently in it, some of the finest and most exhilarating weather of the year. Frosts in the mornings and evenings are common, whilst the middle of the day is often enlivened by all the sunshine of July without its oppressiveness, and the clearness of a frosty day in December or January without its piercing cold.

# First of October.

The Festival of the Rosary. St Piat, apostle of Tournay, martyr, about 286. St Remigius, confessor, archbishop of Rheims, 533. St Wasnulf or Wasnon, confessor, patron of Condé, about 651. St Bavo, anchoret, patron of Ghent, 7th century. St Fidharleus of Ireland, abbot, 762.

## FESTIVAL OF THE ROSARY.

The rosary, as is well known, is, in the Roman Catholic Church, a series of prayers, consisting of fifteen *Pater Nosters* and a hundred and fifty *Ave Marias*, which, for the convenience of worshippers, are counted on a string of beads. Each rosary, or string of beads, consists of fifteen decades, each of which decades contains one *Pater Noster*, marked by a large bead, and ten *Ave Marias*, marked by ten smaller beads. The festival of the rosary was instituted to implore the divine mercy in favour of the church and all the faithful, and return thanks for the benefits conferred on them, more especially for the victory of Lepanto, in 1571, over the Turks. This success, believed to be obtained through the intercession of the Virgin, who is so specially invoked in the devotion of the rosary, was ordered by Pius V. to be annually commemorated under the title of St Mary de Victoria. This epithet was, however, changed by his successor, Gregory XIII., into the title of the Festival of the Rosary. The victory of Prince Eugene over the Turks at Belgrade, in 1716, was ordered by Clement XII. to be included in the benefits which this office specially commemorates.

---

*Born.*—Henry III. of England, 1206, *Winchester;* Henry St John, Viscount Bolingbroke, politician and philosophical writer, 1678, *Battersea;* Paul I., emperor of Russia, 1754.

*Died.*—Michael II., the Stammerer, Greek emperor, 829; Pierre Corneille, great tragic dramatist, 1684, *Paris.*

## THE MUSICAL SMALL-COALMAN.

On 1st October 1714, was buried in Clerkenwell churchyard, Thomas Britton, a dealer in coal, whose life presents one of the most curious social anomalies that have ever been recorded. Whilst gaining his livelihood by the active exercise of a humble craft, occupying a habitation and wearing a garb corresponding in plainness to his trade, this singular man contrived by his various talents, and more especially his musical tastes, to assemble around him the most aristocratic company in London, and to be admitted into their society on equal terms, at a time when the principle of exclusion was far more rigidly maintained than it is now, between the upper and lower ranks of the community.

The house occupied by our small-coalman was situated in Aylesbury Street, Clerkenwell, and formed the corner-house of a passage leading by the Old Jerusalem Tavern into St John's Square. On the ground-floor were the coal-stores, and above them a long narrow room, very low in the ceiling, and approached by a break-neck stair from the outside. In this modest saloon, Britton held his musical reunions, which were attended by the great and fashionable, and at which, among other eminent performers, the celebrated Handel did not disdain to exhibit his unequalled skill for the entertainment of the company. The origin of these gatherings is ascribed to Sir Roger l'Estrange, a famous musical dilettante, who, along with other gentlemen, had been taken with the conversation and manners of Britton, so greatly beyond what might have been expected from his station in life. Nor were his guests confined to the male sex. Elegant ladies, from the most fashionable quarters of London, thronged to his humble mansion, and, in the pleasure which they experienced in listening to his concert, forgot the toils which they had undergone in ascending to the hall of performance. It has been said that Britton charged his guests with an annual subscription of ten shillings for the music, and a penny for each cup of coffee drunk. But this was certainly not the case at first, when the entertainment was entirely gratuitous, and no refreshments of any kind were given, though possibly some change may have been introduced at a later period.

In the Augustan age of Queen Anne, the passion for collecting old books and manuscripts began to develop itself among the nobility. Among the most noted bibliophilists of the aristocracy were the Duke of Devonshire, and the Earls of Oxford, Pembroke, Sunderland, and Winchelsea. A favourite Saturday pastime of these noblemen was to make their rounds through the various nooks of the city in which booksellers congregated, and then reassemble at noon at the shop of Christopher Bateman, a bookseller in Paternoster Row. About this time, Thomas Britton would make his appearance, having finished *his* round, and, depositing his sack of small-coal on the ledge of Mr Bateman's window, would go in and join the distinguished company. Here his skill in old books and manuscripts was no less conspicuous than the correctness of his musical taste, and rendered him a most useful acquisition.

As has happened with many greater men, Britton did not escape the shafts of slander and malice, and it was variously asserted that his musical assemblies were merely pretexts for seditious meetings or magical incantations, and that he himself was an atheist or a Jesuit in disguise. There seems, however, to have been really nothing objectionable either in his principles or mode of life, his character being that of a simple and inoffensive, though learned and intelligent man. His death was brought about in a singular manner.

A blacksmith, named Honeyman, who possessed the faculty of ventriloquism, and had almost frightened, by the exercise of it, the notorious Dr Sacheverell into fits, was induced, as a practical joke, to play off his art upon Thomas Britton. Being introduced to the latter, he announced, as if by a supernatural messenger, speaking from a distance, the death of Britton, intimating, moreover, that his only chance of escape was to fall down immediately upon his knees, and repeat the Lord's Prayer. The poor man, terrified out of his senses, did as he was told, and verified the prediction but too soon, as he took to his bed, and died in a few days.

Two pictures of Britton were painted by his friend Woolaston. One of these, which was deposited in the British Museum, represents him in his blue frock, with the small coal-measure in his hand, as he appeared when he went through the town crying his wares. He has also been fortunate enough to secure transmission to posterity in the following lines by Prior:

'Though doomed to small-coal, yet to arts allied,
Rich without wealth, and famous without pride,
Music's best patron, judge of books and men,
Beloved and honoured by Apollo's train.
In Greece or Rome sure never did appear
So bright a genius in so dark a sphere!
More of the man had probably been saved
Had Kneller painted, and had Vertue graved.'

---

## RUMINATING MEN.

'I remember,' says Mrs Piozzi, in her *Tour in Italy*, 'Dr Johnson once said that nobody had ever seen a very strange thing, and challenged the company to produce a strange thing; but I had not then seen Avvocato B——, à la Wyerhere, at Milan, and a man respected in his profession, who actually chews the cud like an ox. He is apparently much like another tall stout man, but has many extraordinary properties, being eminent for strength, and possessing a set of ribs and sternum very surprising, and worthy the attention of anatomists. His body, upon the slightest touch, even through all his clothes, throws out electric sparks; he can reject his meals from his stomach at pleasure; and did absolutely, in the course of two hours, go through, to oblige me, the whole operation of eating, masticating, swallowing, and returning by the mouth a large piece of bread and a peach. With all this conviction, nothing more was wanting; but I obtained, besides, the confirmation of common friends, who were willing likewise to bear testimony of this strange accidental variety. What I hear of his character is, that he is a low-spirited nervous man; and I suppose his ruminating moments are spent in lamenting the peculiarities of his frame.'

This human chewer of the cud was not such a singular being as Mrs Piozzi imagined. Fabricius ab Aquapendente records two similar cases coming under his own observation. One was a monk, who rejoiced in another bovine characteristic, his forehead being adorned with a pair of horns. The other ruminant was not so ornamented himself, but was the son of a one-horned parent; he was a Paduan nobleman, and Fabricius had the satisfaction of dissecting him, and proving the falseness of Bartholin's theory, that human ruminants possessed double stomachs. Lynceus tells us of Anthony Recchi, who was obliged to retire from the dinner-table to ruminate undisturbed, and who declared that the second process of mastication 'was sweeter than honey, and accompanied with a delightful relish.' His son inherited the same faculty, but with him it was under better control, he being able to defer its exercise till a convenient opportunity. Sennert knew a man similarly qualified, and accounted for it by attributing it to the fact of his having been fed on milk warm from the cow, in consequence of the death of his mother at his birth. Pyer believed that two of his countrymen acquired the habit from learning to imitate the calves and sheep with which their vocation associated them. Blumenbach says he knew two men who ruminated their vegetable food, and found great enjoyment in the feat, while one of them had the power of doing so or not as he felt inclined.

In the *Philosophical Transactions* for 1691, there is an account by 'the experienced and learned Frederick Slare, M.D.' of a ruminating man living at Bristol, described as a person of mean parents but of tolerable sense and reason, who had followed the practice from his earliest years, and always found a temporary deprivation of the faculty the sure precursor of illness. He used to commence ruminating about a quarter of an hour after a meal, and the process usually occupied him for an hour and a half, and was attended with greater gratification than the first mastication, after which food always lay heavy in the lower part of the throat. Under the date of October 1, 1767, we find the following in the *Annual Register*: 'We have the following extraordinary account from Winbourne, in Dorsetshire. A few days ago died here Roger Gill, shoemaker, and one of our singing-men, aged about sixty-seven, remarkable for chewing his meat or cud twice over, as an ox, sheep, or cow. He seldom made any breakfast in his latter days; he generally dined about twelve or one o'clock, eat pretty heartily and quickly, without much chewing or mastication. He never drank with his dinner, but afterwards about a pint of such malt liquor as he could get; but no sort of spirituous liquor in any shape, except a little punch, but never cared for that. He usually began his second chewing about a quarter or half an hour, sometimes later, after dinner; when every morsel came up successively, sweeter and sweeter to the taste. Sometimes a morsel would prove offensive and crude, in which case he spat it out. The chewing continued usually about an hour or more, and sometimes would leave him a little while, in which case he would be sick at stomach, troubled with the heartburn, and foul breath. Smoking tobacco would sometimes stop his chewing, but was never attended with any ill consequences. But on the 10th of June last, the faculty entirely left him, and the poor man remained in great tortures till the time of his death.'

Similar cases have been recorded by Messrs Tarbes, Percy, Lawrent, Cullerier, Riche, and Copland. The latter published a full account of a case of rumination in *The London Medical and Physical Journal* (1819-20), and observes in his *Medical Dictionary*, published in 1858, 'since the publication of that case, two others, one of them in a medical man, have been treated by me, and

I have reason to believe that instances of partial or occasional rumination are not so rare in the human subject as is generally supposed.'

---

# OCTOBER 2.

The Feast of the Holy Angel-Guardians. St Leodegarius or Leger, bishop and martyr, 678. St Thomas, bishop of Hereford, confessor, 1282.

*Born.*—Richard III. of England, 1452, *Fotheringay Castle;* Cardinal Charles Borromeo, editor of the *Noctes Vaticanæ,* 1538, *Arona;* The Chevalier d'Eon, celebrated adventurer and pretended female, 1728, *Tonnerre, Burgundy;* Joseph Ritson, antiquary, 1752, *Stockton.*

*Died.*—Aristotle, great Greek philosopher, 322 B. C., *Chalcis;* Major John André, hanged by Washington as a spy, 1780; Admiral Augustus Keppel, 1786; Dr W. E. Channing, Unitarian divine, 1842, *Bennington, Vermont, United States;* Miss Biffin, painter, without hands or arms, 1850, *Liverpool;* Thomas Thomson, legal and literary antiquary, 1852, *Edinburgh.*

## SPAIN BEQUEATHED TO THE BOURBONS.

On 2d October 1700, Charles II. of Spain executed his last will and testament, by which he conveyed his dominions to Philip, Duke of Anjou, second son of the French dauphin, and grandson of Louis XIV. Perhaps no mortuary bequest has excited greater commotions than this celebrated document, occasioning, as it did, the celebrated War of Succession in Spain, and the no less famous campaigns of Marlborough and Prince Eugene in Germany and Italy, in connection with the same cause. The circumstances attending its execution possess both a curious and painful interest, and exemplify strikingly the extremes of priestly machination and political unscrupulousness on the one hand, and of regal misery and helplessness on the other.

Feeble alike in body and mind, wasted by disease, and a prey to the most depressing melancholy and superstition, the unfortunate Charles II. was evidently hastening to the end of his career. Throughout life he had been kept in a state of perpetual tutelage, and had scarcely ever been permitted to have a will of his own. He was the only child of the old age of Philip IV., by that monarch's marriage with his niece, and of two unions which Charles himself had successively contracted, there had never been any issue. The legal right to the Spanish crown now devolved on the descendants of his grandfather Philip III., one of whose daughters was the mother of Louis XIV., and another of the Emperor Leopold. The sympathies of Charles were all in favour of the House of Austria, but he was surrounded by a powerful and unscrupulous faction in the French interest, who left no means untried for the accomplishment of their ends. Working on the superstitious fears of the dying monarch, his ghostly advisers held up before him the terrors of eternal perdition if he failed to make a will in favour of France as the legitimate heir. 'I am partial to my own family,' said poor Charles, when thus badgered, 'but my salvation is dearer to me than the ties of blood.' To relieve in some degree his perplexity, he despatched one of the noblemen of his household to Pope Innocent XII., to request his advice relative to the disposal of the Spanish dominions. The aged pontiff, himself on the brink of the grave, was surrounded by cardinals devoted to the French interest, and he returned a reply that he had no doubt that the rightful heir to the Spanish monarchy was the dauphin; but that to prevent the union of the two crowns of France and Spain, the succession should be vested in his second son, Philip, Duke of Anjou. Yet Charles still clung to his Austrian relatives, and was supported in his predilections by his queen, a sister-in-law of Leopold, who is said sometime previously to have been ineffectually tempted by France to abandon the interests of her family, by the bait held out to her, of marrying the dauphin on Charles's death, and thus continuing to share the Spanish throne. The palace was converted into a bear-garden by the squabbles and uproars which resounded through every quarter, and the noise of which even reached the chamber of the dying king. Intrigues for the post of confessor to the miserable sovereign were eagerly carried on between the partizans of the respective claimants of the succession; and both, as they from time to time gained the ascendency, sought to influence, in opposite directions, the weak and vacillating mind of Charles. Can any condition be imagined more wretched than that of the latter, emaciated with disease and suffering, conscious of his approaching and inevitable end being made the subject of the most calculating and acrimonious discussion, and yet denied the boon, which every Spanish peasant enjoyed, of dying in peace, and even threatened with the vengeance of Heaven in another world if he refused to do violence to his own feelings by gratifying the aspirations of an ambitious court? The victory between the contending factions at last remained with the French, and under the superintendence of Cardinal Portocarrero, the whole armoury of priestly influence and supernatural terror was brought to bear successfully on the mind of the king. He had already been frightened by statements of his being bewitched, and requiring to be exorcised to have the cause of his illness removed. Then it was suggested that his health would be benefited, and the prayers of departed spirits stimulated on his behalf, were he to gaze on and touch the remains of his ancestors, mouldering in the funeral vaults of the Escurial. Urged by his spiritual directors, Charles descended with them to these abodes of the dead, and there witnessed the opening of the marble and jasper coffins which enclosed the relics of royalty. The first opened was that of his mother, for whom he had never entertained any great affection, and at the sight of whose remains he displayed no special emotion. It was different, however, when the tomb of his first queen, Louise of Orleans, was unclosed. The body presented scarcely any traces of dissolution, and the countenance seemed nearly as fresh and blooming as when in life. Charles gazed long and earnestly on the lifeless face, and at last exclaiming, 'I shall soon be with her in heaven!' rushed, in an agony of grief and horror, from the place. Another trial to which he was subjected arose from an insurrection of the Madrid mob, who had been persuaded by the French faction that a famine from which they were suffering had been brought about by the Austrian ministers and their partizans. The rabble destroyed all the bakers' shops, and presenting themselves before the palace, demanded a sight of the king. 'His majesty is asleep,' said one of the courtiers. 'He has slept too long already, and must now awake,' was the angry response. It was judged prudent to gratify the populace in their demand, and the poor king, pale and trembling, and unable to stand on his feet from sickness and fear, was brought out to the balcony in the arms of his attendants. As a capstone to all his sufferings, the last will and testament, appointing Philip of Anjou as his successor, was presented to him for his signature by Cardinal Portocarrero. Coerced and importuned on every side, Charles, with great reluctance, appended his name to the document, and then, bursting into tears, exclaimed: 'I now am nothing!' Immediately on signing it he fainted, and remained for a long time in that condition, inducing the belief that he was dead. He recovered, however, from this fit, and survived for a month longer, expiring on 1st November. The contents of the will were carefully concealed from the queen, the Austrian party, and Europe in general. When the testament came to be read after the king's death, it is said that Blécourt, the French ambassador, aware of its being in favour of his court, advanced confidently towards the Duke of Abrantes, whose office it was to declare the successor to the crown. Rather to the astonishment of the former, the duke, after looking composedly at him, turned aside his head. Then all at once, as if he had not observed Count Harrach, the imperial ambassador, he joyously embraced the latter, saying: 'It is with great pleasure, my lord' (then pausing to give him a closer hug), 'yes, my lord, it is with an extreme joy, and the utmost degree of satisfaction, that I withdraw myself from you, and take leave of the most august House of Austria!'

The success thus attending French diplomacy may, after all, be regarded as of a very dubious kind. Though the grandson of Louis XIV. succeeded ultimately in establishing himself on the Spanish throne, which had been obtained for him by so questionable means, it was only after the expenditure of a vast amount of blood and treasure on the part of his native country, such as rendered the latter years of the reign of the *Grand Monarque* a period of the utmost weakness and misery. The whole circumstances connected with the celebrated will of Charles II. exhibit strikingly the notions then prevalent regarding the relations of sovereigns to their kingdoms, which were considered to be those of hereditary proprietors rather than of responsible first magistrates. Two Spanish nobles, during the discussion in council on the subject of a successor, did indeed suggest a reference of the question at issue to the decision of the national cortes, but such a proposition was at once superciliously negatived as dangerous and disloyal.

## JOSEPH RITSON.

The peculiar tastes and pursuits of the antiquary frequently give him a strong individuality, which, with a little exaggeration, may produce caricature. He seldom appears in the pages of the novelist or dramatist in other than a ridiculous light, being depicted generally either as a foolish collector of despicable trifles, or a half-witted good-natured twaddler. That all this is unjust, will be readily conceded in the present day, when archæological studies have become 'fashionable,' and soirees are given in rooms filled with antiquities as an extra attraction. Among the numerous antiquaries, who, by their labours, have rendered important services to the literature of their country, none has surpassed Joseph Ritson, who was himself an excellent sample of the painstaking and enthusiastic scholar, but unfortunately disfigured by eccentricity and irritability, which 'point a moral' in his otherwise useful career.

Ritson was born October 2, 1752, at Stockton-upon-Tees, Durham, and was bred to the legal profession; he ultimately came to London, entered Gray's Inn, and was called to the bar by the society there in 1789. He appears to have restricted himself to chamber-practice, and to have neglected in a great degree that calling also, that he might indulge in the more congenial study of our older poets. In his readings at the Bodleian

JOSEPH RITSON.

Library and elsewhere, he quietly garnered a multitude of facts—a scrupulous accuracy regarding which was one of his distinguishing characteristics, and an absence of it in any work was deemed by him as little inferior to a moral delinquency. His first appearance in the literary arena, was an attack on Warton's *History of English Poetry*, in which he proved himself a most formidable antagonist. His 'observations' were printed in a quarto pamphlet in 1782, uniform with Warton's volumes, because, as he remarks with a grim jocularity, 'they are extremely proper to be bound up with that celebrated work.' The boldness of his invective, and the accuracy of his objections, at once stamped him as no contemptible critic. But he was unfortunately wanting in temper and charity—errors were crimes with him, and treated accordingly. No better illustration of his mode ot criticism could be given than the passage on the death of Marlow, who died in a fray, from a wound given by his own dagger turned against him by his adversary. Warton, in describing the wound, says it was in his bosom. Ritson at once fires up because he finds no authority for the exact spot, and thus addresses Warton: 'Your propensity to corruption and falsehood seems so natural, that I have been sometimes tempted to believe you often substitute a lie in the place of a fact without knowing it. How else you came to tell us that Marlow was stabbed in the bosom I cannot conceive.' In other instances, Ritson had more justice on his side, and really combated serious error, for Warton by no means understood old English so well as he did; thus, where the sultan of Damascus is described as riding to attack Richard Cœur de Lion, the romance tells us:

'A faucon brode in hand he bare;'

which means, that he came equipped with a broad falchion or sabre. Warton, unfortunately, interprets the import of the passage to be that the sultan carried a falcon on his fist, to shew his contempt for Richard. Ritson, upon this, bursts forth into unmeasured invective: 'such unparalleled ignorance, such matchless effrontery, is not, Mr Warton, in my humble opinion, worthy of anything but castigation or contempt.' To Dr Percy and his *Reliques of Ancient English Poetry*, he is no whit more civil; and, in subsequent publications, he continued his attacks, until the good bishop heartily regretted ever having concocted a work that has given, and will continue to give, pleasure to thousands, and has aided in spreading a knowledge of the beauties of our old ballad-poetry, before comparatively unknown. Percy, unfortunately, worked from an ill-written and imperfect manuscript, and he did not scruple to draw upon his own invention to supply what was wanting. This was a crime not to be forgiven in the eyes of Ritson, who would have walked from London to Oxford to collate a manuscript, or correct an error. Percy desired to make his work popular, an object in which he certainly succeeded, but Ritson's attacks embittered his triumph; and were carried by the antiquary so far, as to needlessly annoy the worthy prelate, for he ultimately denied the existence of the manuscript from which Percy professed to obtain his originals. Ritson had no patience for looseness of diction or assertion; and an amusing anecdote of this is given by Sir Walter Scott, who was intimate with him. He had visited Sir Walter at his cottage near Lasswade, and, in the course of conversation, spoke of the remains of the Roman Wall in the border counties as not above a foot or two in height, on the authority of some friend at Hexham. Sir Walter assured him, that near Gilsland 'it was high enough for the fall to break a man's neck.' Ritson took a formal note, visited the spot afterwards, and then wrote to say he had tested the assertion, and thought it accurate. 'I immediately saw,' says Sir Walter, 'what a risk I had been in, for you may believe I had no idea of being taken quite so literally.'

Ritson's *Select Collection of English Songs* appeared in 1783, and in after-years he published a series of volumes on our Robin-Hood ballads, and ancient popular literature. These were far superior in character to anything of the kind that had before appeared in the literary world, being remarkable alike for their erudition and accuracy. His volumes are elegantly printed, and the few illustrations in them are among the most graceful productions of the pencil of Stothard. It is sad to remember that Ritson lost money by these admirable works. He was too painstaking and accurate for general appreciation, and the public could read easier the books of looser compilation. His last days were clouded by further pecuniary losses, arising from unfortunate speculations, and being obliged to sell his books, he naturally became more irritable than ever. His opinions underwent important changes, and from being a decided Jacobite, he became a liberal in the widest sense of the French Revolution, whose heroes he worshipped, and whose unfortunate religious ideas he also adopted.

Sir Walter Scott said of Ritson, 'he had an honesty of principle about him, which, if it went to ridiculous extremities, was still respectable from the soundness of the foundation. I don't believe the world could have made Ritson say the thing he did not think.' Surtees adds, 'that excessive aspiration after absolute and exact verity, I verily believe, was one cause of that unfortunate asperity with which he treated some most respectable contemporaries.' In Ritson, then, we may study the evil effects of a narrowed view of truth itself, when combined with an irritable temper. Hated as a critic, while respected as a scholar, he rendered himself unnecessarily an object of dislike and aversion, whilst with a little more suavity he might have fulfilled his mission equally well. To him we are undoubtedly indebted for a more exact rendering of our ancient authors, which has guarded them from that loose editorship which was Ritson's abomination. His name and works, therefore, take an important place in literary history. His personal errors, and their consequences, should also be a warning to such critics as needlessly turn their pens to poniards, and their ink to gall.

## THE DUKE OF CUMBERLAND'S MARRIAGE.

On October 2, 1771, Henry Frederic, Duke of Cumberland, younger brother of George III., married the Honourable Mrs Horton, a daughter of Lord Irnham, and widow of Christopher Horton of Catton, a Derbyshire gentleman. She was also the sister of the famous Colonel Luttrel, whom the court-party put forward as the legal possessor of the seat for Middlesex in the House of Commons, in opposition to the claims of Wilkes. The match occasioned the utmost displeasure to George III., who was only informed of it about a month after the event by a letter which he received from his brother, saying that he was married to Mrs Horton, and had gone off with her to Calais. In conjunction with the *mésalliance* avowed shortly after by the Duke of Gloucester, another of the king's brothers, with the Dowager Countess of Waldegrave, this marriage of the Duke of Cumberland occasioned the passing in parliament, by the king's direction, of the well-known Royal Marriage Act, which subsequently rendered null the unions of George IV. and the Duke of Sussex. The bridegroom had, the previous year, made himself unpleasantly conspicuous by figuring as co-respondent in a *crim. con.* trial, in which the wife of Earl Grosvenor was the principal party implicated. It is hinted, also, that he had only married Mrs Horton after having failed in endeavouring to win her on easier terms. The lady is described by Horace Walpole as a young widow of twenty-four, extremely pretty and well made, and remarkable for the great length of her eyelashes, which veiled a pair of most artful and coquettish eyes. In the opinion of that prince of letter-writers, she had no great reason to plume herself on having conquered a man so intellectually weak as the duke. The latter for many years was rigidly excluded from court, as was also his brother, the Duke of Gloucester. He died in 1790, without leaving issue of the marriage. It ought to be remarked that his wife is not to be confounded with a Mrs Anne, or Annabella Horton, better known by the name of Nancy Parsons, who at one period lived with the Duke of Grafton as his mistress, and ultimately became the wife of Lord Maynard.

## STRANGE HISTORY OF THE CHEVALIER D'EON.

Of all the ambassadors or diplomatists who ever served a sovereign, the most extraordinary, perhaps, was the Chevalier d'Eon, who occupied a large space in the public mind at certain periods during the last century: extraordinary, not for his political abilities or services, but for his personal history.

D'Eon first became known in England in 1761, the year after George III. ascended the throne. England and France, after many years of war, had made and received overtures of conciliation; and the Duke de Nivernois was sent by Louis XV. as ambassador extraordinary to negotiate the terms of peace. The chevalier, who accompanied him as secretary, won general favour at court; he was of prepossessing appearance, managed the duties of his position with much ability, and displayed a wide range of accomplishments. When the duke had completed the terms of peace, D'Eon had the honour of communicating the fact from the one sovereign to the other. The court-journal of those days announced as follows, early in 1763: 'M. d'Eon de Beaumont, secretary to the embassy from France, returned this day to London, and was received by the Duke de Nivernois as Knight of the Royal Military Order of St Louis: his Most Christian Majesty having invested him with that order, when he presented to him the ratification of the definitive treaty of peace with England.' Madame de Pompadour, who held an equivocal but influential position at the court of Versailles, wrote about the same time to the Duke de Nivernois, noticing the chevalier in the following terms: 'This M. d'Eon is, I am told, a very good sort of man, who has served the king in more countries than one: and the English have been very polite in giving him the treaty to bring. This, I doubt not, will be of some advantage to him.' When the duke returned to France in 1763, on the completion of his mission, he strongly recommended D'Eon as the temporary representative of France in England, until a permanent ambassador could be appointed. So well had the chevalier conducted himself, that both monarchs assented to this; and soon afterwards we read of the three distinguished French *savans*, Lalande, La Condamine, and Camus, beihg introduced to George III. by the Chevalier d'Eon, as French envoy or representative.

These were the only three brilliant years of D'Eon's life passed in England; they were followed by a period of disgrace. Louis XV. appointed the Count de Guercy his permanent ambassador in England, and directed D'Eon to resume his former position as secretary of embassy, with additional honours as a reward for his services. D'Eon, disappointed in his ambition, or angered in some other way, refused to submit, and published letters exposing a number cf diplomatic secrets relating to the court of France, including an accusation very damaging to the Count de Guercy. The French courtiers were very uneasy at this; and the count brought an action against him in the Court of King's Bench for libel. D'Eon made neither an appearance nor a defence, and a verdict was given against him. The French authorities were very anxious to get hold of him, and even sanctioned a forcible entry into a house in Scotland Yard, where he was supposed to be residing; but he remained for a time hidden. Towards the close of 1764, he applied for a bill of indictment against the Count de Guercy, for a conspiracy to murder or injure him; the count, instead of rebutting the charge, claimed his privileges as a foreign ambassador; and the public remained of opinion that the charge was not wholly without foundation.

Now ensued a strange portion of D'Eon's career. He remained in England several years, little known except by his frequent attendance at fencing-matches, in which art he was an adept. At length, in July 1777, an action was brought in the Court of King's Bench, the decision of which would depend on the *sex* of D'Eon. One man, on evidence which seemed to him conclusive, betted a wager that the chevalier was a woman, and brought an action to recover the amount of the bet. Without touching upon the evidence adduced, or the judge's comments, it will suffice to say that D'Eon from that time became regarded as *Madame* D'Eon, and assumed female attire. A memoir of her was published, from which it appeared that she was born at Tonnerre, in Burgundy, of parents who occupied a good station in society. For the purpose, as is stated, of advancing her prospects in life, she was, with her own consent, treated as a boy, and received the multifarious names of Charles-Genevieve-Louis-Auguste-André-Timothé d'Eon de Beaumont. She was sent to Paris, and educated at the College Mazarin, where she went through the same physical and mental exercises as the other pupils. She became a well-educated person. When past the age of schooling, she became successively doctor in civil law, doctor in canon law, and avocat before the tribunals of Paris; and wrote several books which attracted attention. She was introduced to the Prince de Conti, who introduced her to Louis XV. Louis at that time wished Russia to form a league with France instead of with Prussia; but as this could not be accomplished without a little preliminary intrigue, some secret agent was needed; and D'Eon was selected for this delicate position. The memoir implies, if not directly asserts, that Louis was made acquainted with the real sex of D'Eon. Be this as it may, D'Eon made two distinct visits to Russia, in or about the year 1755; the first time dressed as a woman, the second time as a man, and not known by any one as the same person in the two capacities. So well did D'Eon succeed, that presents and rewards followed—rich gifts from the Empress Elizabeth; and a pension, together with a lieutenancy of dragoons, from Louis. D'Eon served in the campaigns of the Seven Years' War; and then occurred the events in England between 1761 and 1777, already noticed.

The end of D'Eon's life was as strange as the beginning. In woman's dress, D'Eon was in France for a time in 1779, but he resided mostly in England. It was supposed by many that he was largely interested in bets, amounting in various quarters to the enormous sum of £70,000, depending on the question of sex; but a positive denial was given to this insinuation. At length, in 1810, the newspapers announced that the 'celebrated Chevalier d'Eon' died, on the 22d of May, in Millman Street, Foundling Hospital; and then, and not until then, was it decisively known that he was really and properly Chevalier d'Eon, who had so often, and for reasons so little to be comprehended, passed himself off as a woman.

### THE STORY OF MAJOR ANDRE.

There are few monuments in Westminster Abbey which have attracted more attention than that which commemorates the sad fate of Major André. Perhaps no event of the American revolution made more aching hearts on both sides of the Atlantic. Great Britain lost two armies, and thousands of her brave soldiers were slain upon the field of battle, but it may be doubted if so many tears were shed for them all, as for this young soldier, who died upon the gallows.

John André was born in London, the son of a Genevese merchant, in 1751. He was sent to Geneva to be educated, but returned to London at the age of eighteen, and, his talents having introduced him to a literary coterie, he became enamoured of Miss Honora Sneyd, a young lady of singular beauty and accomplishments. As both were very young, the marriage was postponed, and André was induced to engage in trade; but he was ambitious, and, at the age of twenty, entered the army. At the outbreak of the American war he was sent to Canada, and taken prisoner at St John's; but being exchanged, he became the favourite of that gay and gallant officer, General Sir Henry Clinton, who appointed him his aid-de-camp, and soon after adjutant-general.

Young, handsome, clever, full of taste and gaiety, an artist and a poet, he was the life of the army, and the little vice-regal court that was assembled around its chief. The British occupied the American cities, and while the troops of Washington were naked and starving at Valley Forge, Sir Henry was holding a series of magnificent revels in Philadelphia, which were planned and presided over by the gallant Major André.

Philadelphia was evacuated; Sir Henry returned to New York; and Major André, who had known the wife of the American general, Arnold, in Philadelphia, entered into a correspondence with him, and was the agent through whom the British general bargained, under promise of a large reward, for the surrender of Westpoint, the key of the highlands of the river Hudson. André visited Arnold within the American lines, to carry out this treachery; he was captured on his return by three American farmers, who refused his bribes; the papers proclaiming Arnold's treason were found upon him, and, by his own frank confession, he was convicted as a spy, and sentenced to be hanged.

Arnold, by the blunder of an American officer, got warning, and escaped on board the *Vulture*. Sir Henry Clinton, by the most urgent representations to General Washington, tried to save his favourite adjutant, but in vain. There was but one way—the surrender of Arnold, to meet the fate decreed to André. That was impossible; and the young adjutant, then in his twenty-ninth year, after a vain appeal to Washington, that he might die a soldier's death, was hanged on the west bank of the Hudson, almost in sight of the city held by the British army, October 2, 1780. If his life had been undistinguished, he died with heroic firmness. The whole British army went into mourning, and, after the close of the war, his body was deposited near his monument in Westminster Abbey. Even in America, where the name of Arnold is a synonym of treason, the sad fate of Major André excited, and still excites, universal commiseration.

---

## OCTOBER 3.

St Dionysius the Areopagite, bishop of Athens, martyr, 1st century. The Two Ewalds, martyrs, about 695. St Gerard, abbot, 959.

---

*Born.*—Richard Boyle, the great Earl of Cork, 1566, *Canterbury;* Giovanni Baptista Beccaria, natural philosopher, 1716, *Mondovi.*

*Died.*—Robert Barclay, celebrated Scottish Quaker, author of the *Apology* for Quaker tenets, 1690, *Ury, Kincardineshire;* Victor, French dramatic writer, 1846; A. E. Chalon, artist, 1860, *London.*

### WATCHING AND LIGHTING OLD LONDON.

Civilisation, in its slowest progress, may be well illustrated by a glance at the past modes of guarding and lighting the tortuous and dangerous streets of old cities. From the year 1253, when Henry III. established night-watchmen, until 1830, when Sir Robert Peel's police act established a new kind of guardian, the watchman was little better than a person who

'Disturbed your rest to tell you what's o'clock.'

He had been gradually getting less useful from the days of Elizabeth; thus Dogberry and his troop were unmistakable pictures of the tribe, as much relished for the satirical truth of their delineation in the reign of Anne, as in that of her virgin predecessor. Little improvement took place until the Westminster act was passed in 1762, a measure forced on the attention of the legislature by the impunity with which robbery and murder were committed after dark. Before that year, a few wretched oil lamps only served to make darkness visible in the streets, and confuse the wayfarer by partial glimmerings across his ill-paved path. Before the great civil wars, the streets may be said to have been only lighted by chance; by the lights from windows, from lanterns grudgingly hung out by householders, or by the watchmen during their rounds; for by a wonderful stretch of parochial wisdom, and penny-wise economy, the watching and lighting were performed at the same time. The watchman of the olden time carried a fire-pot, called a cresset, on the top of a long pole, and thus marched on, giving light as he bawled the hour, and at the same time, notification of his approach to all thieves, who had thus timeous warning to escape.

THE CRESSET-BEARER.

The appearance of this functionary in the sixteenth century will be best understood from the engraving here copied from one in Sharp's curious dissertation on the Coventry Mysteries. A similar cresset is still preserved in the armoury of the Tower of London. It is an open-barred pot, hanging by swivels fastened to the forked staff; in the centre of the pot is a spike, around which was coiled a rope soaked in pitch and rosin, which sputtered and burned with a lurid light, and stinking smoke, as the watchman went his rounds. The watch was established as a stern necessity; and that necessity had become stern, indeed, before his advent. Roger Hoveden has left a vivid picture of London at night in the year 1175, when it was a common practice for gangs of a 'hundred or more in a company' to besiege wealthy houses for plunder, and unscrupulously murder any one who happened to come in their way. Their 'vocation' was so flourishing, that when one of their number was convicted, he had the surpassing assurance to offer the king five hundred pounds of silver for his life. The gallows, however, claimed its due, and made short work with the fraternity; who continued, however, to be troublesome from time to time until Henry III., as already stated, established regular watchmen in all cities and borough-towns, and gave the person plundered by a thief the right of recovering an equivalent for his loss from the legal guardians of the district in which it occurred; a wholesome mode of inflicting a fine for the non-performance of a parish duty.

The London watchman of the time of James I., as here depicted, differed in no essential point from

WATCHMAN—TEMP. JAMES I.

his predecessors in that of Elizabeth. He carried a halbert and a horn-lantern, was well secured in a frieze gabardine, leathern-girdled; and wore a serviceable hat, like a pent-house, to guard against weather. The worthy here depicted has a most venerable face and beard, shewing how ancient was the habit for parish officers to select the poor and feeble for the office of watchman, in order to keep them out of the poorhouse. Such 'ancient and most quiet watchmen' would naturally prefer being out of harm's way, and warn thieves to depart in peace by ringing the bell, that the wether of their flock carried; 'then presently call the rest of the watch together, and thank God you are rid of a knave,' as honest Dogberry advises. Above the head of the man, in the original engraving from which our cut is copied, is inscribed the cry he uttered as he walked the round of his parish. It is this: 'Lanthorne and a whole candell light, hange out your lights heare!' This was in accordance with the old local rule of London, as established by the mayor in 1416, that all householders of the better class, rated above a low rate in the books of their respective parishes, should hang a lantern, lighted with a fresh and whole candle, nightly outside their houses for the accommodation of foot-passengers, from Allhallows evening to Candlemas day. There is another picture of a Jacobean bellman in the collection of prints in the British Museum, giving a more poetic form to the cry. It runs thus:

'A light here, maids, hang out your light,
And see your horns be clear and bright,
That so your candle clear may shine,
Continuing from six till nine;
That honest men that walk along
May see to pass safe without wrong.'

The honest men had, however, need to be abed betimes, for total darkness fell early on the streets when the rush-candle burned in its socket; and was dispelled only by the occasional appearance of the watchman with his horn lantern; or that more important and noisier official, the bellman. One of these was appointed to each ward, and acted as a sort of inspector to the watchmen and the parish, going round, says Stow, 'all night with a bell, and at every lane's end, and at the ward's end, gave warning of fire and candle, and to help the poor, and pray for the dead.' Our readers have already* been presented with a picture of the Holborn bellman, and a specimen of his verse. He was a regular parish official, visible by day also, advertising sales, crying losses, or summoning to weddings or funerals by ringing his bell. It was the duty of the bellman of St Sepulchre's parish, near Newgate, to rouse the unfortunates condemned to death in that prison, the night before their execution, and solemnly exhort them to repentance with good words in bad rhyme, ending with:

'When Sepulchre's bell to-morrow tolls,
The Lord above have mercy on your souls!'

The watchman was a more prosaic individual, never attempting a rhyme; he restricted himself to news of the weather, such as: 'Past eleven, and a starlight night;' or 'Past one o'clock, and a windy morning.' Horace Walpole amusingly narrates the parody uttered by some jesters who returned late from the tavern on the night when frightened Londoners expected the fulfilment of a prophecy, that their city should be engulfed by an earthquake, and had, in consequence, as many of them as could accomplish it, betaken themselves to country lodgings. These revellers, as they passed through the streets, imitated the voice of the watchmen, calling, 'Past twelve o'clock, and a dreadful earthquake!'

The miserable inefficiency of the watchmen, and the darkness and danger of the streets, continued until the reign of Anne. The apathy engendered by long usage, at last was roused by the boldness of rascaldom. Robberies occurred on all sides, and night-prowlers scarcely waited for darkness to come, ere they began to plunder. It was not safe to be out after dark, the suburbs were then cut off from the town, and a return from London to Kensington or Highgate was a risk to the purse, and probably to the life of the rash adventurer. There was even a plot concocted to rob Queen Anne as she returned to Kensington in her coach. Still the police continued ineffectual, and as long after as 1744, the mayor and aldermen addressed the king, declaring the streets more unsafe than ever, 'even at such times as were heretofore deemed hours of security;' in consequence of 'confederacies of great numbers of evil-disposed persons armed with bludgeons, pistols, cutlasses, and other dangerous weapons,' who were guilty of the most daring outrages. The prison and the gallows now did their work in clearing the streets, the watch was put on a better footing, and a parish tax for lighting led to the establishment of oil-lamps in the streets. The rude character of these illuminations may be seen in Hogarth's view of St James's Street, where the best would naturally be placed. Fig. A of the following group is copied from this view, forming the background of the fourth plate of the 'Rake's Progress' (1735). A rough wooden post, about eight feet high, is stuck in the ground; from this stretches an iron rod and ring, forming a socket for the angular lamp, dimly lighted by a cotton-wick floating in a small pan of oil. Globular lamps were the invention of one Michael Cole, who obtained a patent for them in 1708, and first exhibited one of them the year following at the door of the St James's Coffee-house. He described it as 'a new kind of light, composed of one entire glass of a globular

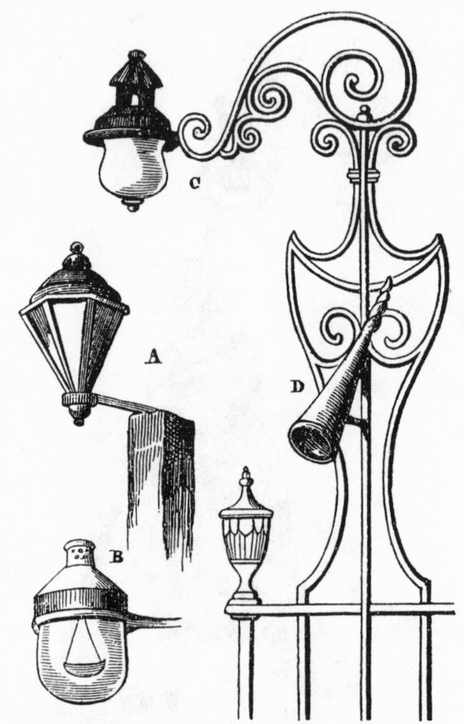

OLD STREET LAMPS.

shape, with a lamp, which will give a clearer and more certain light from all parts thereof, without any dark shadows, or what else may be confounding or troublesome to the sight, than any other lamps that have hitherto been in use.' Cole was an Irish gentleman, and his lamp seems to have won favour; it slowly, but surely, came into general use, and is shewn in our Figure B.

It was customary, in the Hogarthian era, and until the close of the last century, to bestow much cost on the iron-work about aristocratic houses. The lamp-irons at the doors were often of highly-enriched design in wrought metal; many old and curious specimens still remain in the older streets and squares at the west-end of our metropolis. Fig. C depicts one of these in Manchester Square, and the reader will observe the trumpet-shaped implement D attached midway. This is an extinguisher, and its use was to put out the flambeau carried lighted by the footman at the back of the carriage, during a night-progress in the streets. Johnson notices the cowardly bullies of London, who

'Their prudent insults to the poor confine;
Afar they mark the flambeau's bright approach,
And shun the shining train, and golden coach.'

* Vol. i. p. 496.

We give a second, and more ornate example, of a doorway lamp and extinguisher from Grosvenor Square, and it may be remarked as a curious instance of aristocratic self-sufficiency, that this spot, and a few others inhabited by the nobility,

ARISTOCRATIC EXTINGUISHERS.

were the last to adopt the use of the gas-lamp.* This last great improvement was due to a German named Winser, who first publicly exhibited lamps thus lighted on the colonnade in front of Carlton House. Pall Mall followed the example in 1807. The citizens, some time afterwards, lighted Bishopsgate Street in the same manner. Awful consequences were predicted by antiquated alarmists from the extensive use of gas in London: it was to poison the air and blow up the inhabitants! In 1736, one thousand dim oil-lamps supplied with light the whole of the city of London, and there was probably a less number outside; now, there are several thousands of miles of gas-piping laid under the streets for the supply of our lamps; and their light makes an atmospheric change over London, visible at twenty miles' distance, as if from the reflection of one vast furnace.

## A KING ARRESTED BY HIS VASSAL.

The crafty and unscrupulous character of Louis XI. is well known. The great object of his policy, as subsequently with Henry VII. of England, was the reduction of the power of the nobles and great vassals of the crown, so as to strengthen and render paramount the royal prerogative. But the means which he adopted for the accomplishment of this end were of a much darker and more subtle description than those employed by the English monarch. One feudal prince, against whom his machinations were especially directed, was the celebrated Charles the Bold, Duke of Burgundy, than whom, with his ardent impetuous nature, there can scarcely be imagined a greater contrast than the still and wily Louis, whose line of conduct has earned for him the cognomen of the Tiberius of France. Yet on one occasion, the duplicity of the latter found itself at fault, and nearly entailed upon its possessor the most serious consequences.

The burghers of Liège had revolted from their liege lord, the Duke of Burgundy, and been secretly encouraged in their rebellion by the king of France. Louis believed it possible to conceal this circumstance from Charles, but one of his own ministers, the Cardinal Balue, maintained a correspondence with the duke, and kept him informed of everything that transpired at the French court. Through the instigation of this treacherous courtier, Louis was induced to pay his vassal a visit at the town of Peronne, in the territories of the latter. By this mark of confidence, the French king hoped to hoodwink and cajole Charles. The duke received his sovereign with all marks of respect, and lodged him with great splendour in the castle of Peronne. Conferences on state matters were entered into between the two potentates, but in the midst of them Charles received intelligence of Louis's underhand-dealings with the people of Liège, and his rage on learning this was ungovernable. On the 3d October 1468, he laid the French king under arrest, subjected him to close confinement, and was even on the point of proceeding to further extremities. But he ultimately satisfied himself by dictating to Louis a very humiliating treaty, and causing him to accompany him on an expedition against those very citizens of Liège with whom he had been intriguing, and assist in the burning of their town. It is said that so bitter was the mortification which Louis endured in consequence of having thus imprudently placed himself in the power of Charles, that on his return home, he ordered to be killed a number of tame jays and magpies, who had been taught to cry 'Peronne!' The treachery of Cardinal Balue was also punished by the confinement, for many years, of that churchman in an iron cage of his own invention.

---

## ROBERT BARCLAY.

Though not the founder of the Society of Friends, Robert Barclay was one of its earliest and most energetic champions, and did more than any other in vindicating and explaining its principles to the world. The great apologist of the Quakers was the eldest son of Colonel David Barclay of Ury, in Kincardineshire, a Scottish gentleman of ancient family, who had served with distinction in the wars of the great Gustavus Adolphus. Robert received his first religious training in the strict school of Scottish Calvinism, but having been sent to Paris to study in the Scots College there, under the

* It was not till 1842 that gas was permitted to shed its rays over the genteel gloom of this locality; it seems difficult to believe that this prejudice was recently existing in such full force.

rectorship of his uncle, he was led to become a convert to the Roman Catholic faith. Returning, in his fifteenth year, to his native country, he found that his father had joined himself to the new sect of the Quakers, which had only a few years previously sprung into existence under the leadership of George Fox. Robert's faith in the Romish church does not appear to have been very lasting, as, in the course of a few years, we find him following the example of his parent, and adopting enthusiastically the same tenets. Father and son had alike to experience the effects of the aversion with which, in its early days, the Society of Friends was regarded both by Cavalier and Puritan, by Presbyterian and Prelatist. The imprisonment which they underwent is said to have been owing to the agency of the celebrated Archbishop Sharp of St Andrews. It was not, however, of long duration, and through the interposition of the Princess Elizabeth, Princess Palatine, and cousin of Charles II., Robert Barclay was not only liberated from confinement, but seems afterwards to have so far established himself in the favour of the king, that in 1679 he obtained a royal charter erecting his lands of Ury into a free barony, with all the privileges of jurisdiction and otherwise belonging to such an investiture. The remainder of his life was spent in furthering the diffusion of Quakerism, travelling up and down the country in the promulgation of its tenets, and employing his interest with the state authorities in shielding his brethren from persecution. He enjoyed, like Penn, the friendship of James II., and had frequent interviews with him during his visits to London, the last being in 1688, a short time previous to the Revolution. Barclay's own career came to a termination not long afterwards, and he expired prematurely at Ury, after a short illness, on 3d October 1690, at the age of forty-one. He left, however, a family of seven children, all of whom were living fifty years after his death. One of them, Mr David Barclay, who became an eminent mercer in Cheapside, is said, as lord mayor, to have entertained three successive English monarchs—George I., II., and III. The celebrated pedestrian and athlete, Captain Barclay, was a descendant of the great Quaker-champion and the last of the name who possessed the estate of Ury. The old mansion-house having passed, in 1854, into the hands of strangers, was pulled down, and with it 'the Apologist's Study,' which had remained nearly in the same condition as when used by Barclay, and had formed for generations a favourite object of pilgrimage to the Society of Friends.

Barclay's great work, *An Apology for the true Christian Divinity, as the same is held forth and practised by the People called, in scorn, Quakers*, was first published in Latin and afterwards translated by the author into English. It comprises an exposition and defence of fifteen religious propositions maintained by the Quakers, and forms the ablest and most scholarly defence of their principles that has ever been written. The leading doctrine pervading the book is that of the internal light revealing to man divine truth, which it is contended cannot be attained by any logical process of investigation or reasoning. Among other works of the great Quaker were: *A Catechism and Confession of Faith*, and *A Treatise on Universal Love*, the latter being a remonstrance on the criminality of war, and published whilst its author was enduring with his father imprisonment at Aberdeen for conscience' sake. Though so far led away by enthusiasm, on one occasion, as to walk through the streets of Aberdeen, clothed in sackcloth and ashes, as a call on the inhabitants to repentance, Barclay was far from displaying in his ordinary deportment any of that rigour or sourness by which members of his sect have been often supposed to be characterised. He was exemplary in all the relations of life, and was no less distinguished by the gentleness and amiability of his character, than by range and vigour of intellect.

## TREATY OF LIMERICK.

On 3d October 1691, was signed the famous treaty of Limerick, by which the resistance of the Irish to the government of William III. was terminated, and the latter established as undisputed sovereign of the three kingdoms. On the part of the besieged the defence had been conducted by General Sarsfield, one of the bravest and ablest of King James's commanders, who had conducted thither the remains of the army which had continued undispersed after the disastrous engagement of Aghrim, in the preceding month of July. Within the walls of Limerick were contained the whole strength and hope of the Jacobite cause. On the 26th of August, the town was invested by William's Dutch commander, Ginckel, but the garrison made a brave resistance, and it was not till after some terrible encounters that the attacking force was enabled to open its trenches on both sides of the Shannon. On this advantage being gained, Sarsfield, despairing of successfully holding the place, proposed a surrender upon conditions, an offer which was favourably entertained, and by the treaty signed two days subsequently, the war in Ireland was concluded, and tranquillity restored to the country, after a long series of devastating hostilities.

The articles of the treaty of Limerick were highly creditable both to the wisdom and moderation of King William, and also to the valour of the Irish garrison, who had succeeded in obtaining such favourable terms. The troops were allowed to march out of the town with all the honours of war, and had permission, at their option, to embark for France, or enter the service of the English king. The majority, numbering about 10,000, preferred the former alternative, and passing over to the continent, enrolled themselves under the standard of Louis XIV., and became that renowned corps so celebrated in the French service, as 'The Irish Brigade.' The most important stipulation of the treaty, however, in a national point of view, was the clause by which the Roman Catholics were secured in the free exercise of their religion. This stipulation was shamefully violated afterwards by the superimposition of oppressive penal laws, by which was fostered a spirit of hatred and hostility to the English government, who ought rather to have sought to conciliate the inhabitants, and the evil results of whose policy towards Ireland, throughout the eighteenth century, are observable even to the present day.

# OCTOBER 4.

Saints Marcus and Marcian, and their companions, martyrs, beginning of 4th century. The Martyrs of Triers, 4th century. St Ammon, hermit, founder of the Hermitages of Nitria, 4th century. St Petronius, bishop of Bologna, confessor, 5th century. St Edwin, king of Northumberland, martyr, 633. St Aurea, virgin and abbess, 666. St Francis of Assisi, confessor, founder of the Friar Minors, 1226.

## ST FRANCIS.

The memory of no saint is held in affection so mingled with reverence by the Roman Catholic Church as St Francis, 'the gentle and the holy.' He was born in 1182, in the romantic town of Assisi, in Umbria. His father was a merchant, and a hard money-making man. Francis he took into partnership, but he wasted his money in gay living, splendid dress, and banqueting, and made the streets of Assisi ring at night with song and frolic. When about twenty-five, he was seized with a violent illness, and when he rose from his bed, nature looked dreary, and his soul was filled with loathing for his past life and habits. He resolved to be religious, and of course religious after the fashion of his generation. He determined never to refuse alms to a poor person. He met a troop of beggars, and exchanged his dress for the rags of the filthiest. He mortified himself with such severity, that Assisi thought he had gone distracted. His father had been distressed by his luxury, but now he thought he should be ruined by his alms-giving. To bring him, as he thought, to his senses, he beat him unmercifully, put him in fetters, and locked him up. Finding him, however, incorrigible, he carried him before the bishop; and there and then he renounced all his rights of ownership and inheritance, and stripped off his clothes in token of his rejection of the world, and his perpetual choice of poverty.

Francis, thus relieved from all entanglement, pursued his way with a simple energy which nothing could withstand. The fervour of his devotion diffused itself like an epidemic, and crowds parted with their possessions, and followed him into poverty and beggary. He went to Rome, and offered himself and his comrades to the service of the pope. Innocent III., in 1210, incorporated the order, which grew into the mighty and wide-spread fraternity of Franciscans, Grey Friars, or Minor Friars. The first name they had from their founder, the second from their gray clothing, and the third from their humility. Their habit was a loose garment, of a gray colour reaching to the ankles, with a cowl of the same, and a cloak over it when they went abroad. They girded themselves with cords, and went barefooted.

The austerities related of Francis are very much of a piece with those told of other saints. He scarcely allowed his body what was necessary to sustain life. If any part of his rough habit seemed too soft, he darned it with packthread, and was wont to say to his brethren, that the devils easily tempted those who wore soft garments. His bed was usually the ground, or he slept sitting, and for his bolster he had a piece of wood or stone. Unless when sick, he rarely ate any food that was cooked with fire, and when he did, he sprinkled it with ashes. Yet it is said, that with indiscreet or excessive austerity he was always displeased. When a brother, by long fasting, was unable to sleep, Francis brought him some bread, and persuaded him to eat by eating with him. In treating with women, he kept so strict a watch over his eyes, that he hardly knew any woman by sight. He used to say: 'To converse with women, and not be hurt by it, is as difficult as to take fire into one's bosom and not be burned. He that thinks himself secure, is undone; the devil finding somewhat to take hold on, though it be but a hair, raises a dreadful war.'

He was endowed, say his biographers, with an extraordinary gift of tears; his eyes were as fountains which flowed continuously, and by much weeping he almost lost his sight. In his ecstatic raptures, he often poured forth his soul in verse, and Francis is among the oldest vernacular poets of Italy. His sympathy with nature was very keen. He spoke of birds and beasts with all the tenderness due to children, and Dean Milman says the only malediction he can find which proceeded from his lips, was against a fierce swine which had killed a lamb. He had an especial fondness for lambs and larks, as emblems of the Redeemer and the Cherubim. When his surgeon was about to cauterise him for an issue, he said: 'Fire, my brother, be thou discreet and gentle to me.' In one of his hymns, he speaks of his brother the Sun, his sister the Moon, his brother the Wind, his sister the Water. When dying, he said: 'Welcome, Sister Death.' While in prayer it is said that he often floated in the air. Leo, his secretary and confessor, testified that he had seen him, when absorbed in devotion, raised above the ground so high that he could only touch his feet, which he held, and watered with his tears; and that sometimes he saw him raised much higher!

In his ardour for the conversion of souls, he set out to preach to the Mohammedans. A Christian army was encamped before Damietta, in Egypt. He passed beyond its lines, and was seized and carried before the sultan, and at once broke forth in exposition of the mysteries of faith. The sultan is reported to have listened with attention, probably with the Mohammedan reverence for the insane. Francis offered to enter a great fire with the priests of Islam, and to test the truth of their creeds by the result. The offer was declined. 'I will then enter alone,' said Francis. 'If I should be burned, you will impute it to my sins; should I come forth alive, you will embrace the gospel.' This also the sultan refused, but with every mark of honour convoyed the bold apostle to the camp at Damietta.

The crowning glory of the life of Francis is reputed to have occurred in the solitude of Mount Alverno, whither he had retired to hold a solemn fast in honour of the archangel Michael. One morning, when he was praying, he saw in vision a seraph with six wings, and in the midst of the wings the crucified Saviour. As the vision disappeared, and left on his mind an unutterable sense of delight and awe, he found on his hands and feet black excrescences like nails, and in his side a wound, from which blood frequently oozed, and stained his garment. These marks, in his humility, he hid with jealous care, but they became known, and by their means were wrought many miracles. Pope Alexander IV. publicly declared that, with his own eyes, he had seen the stigmata.

These are a few instances out of the mass of legends which made the name of Francis a great power in Europe in the middle ages. He died at Assisi, in 1226, on the 4th of October, which day was appointed as his festival.

*Born.*—Cardinal Robert Bellarmin, eminent controversialist, *Monte Pulciano, Tuscany;* Richard Cromwell, eldest surviving son of the Protector, 1626, *Huntingdon;* Edmond Malone, editor of Shakspeare, 1741, *Dublin.*

*Died.*—Edwin the Great, king of Northumberland, slain at Hatfield, 633; St Francis, founder of the Franciscans or Gray Friars, 1226, *Assisi;* John, Duke of Argyll, statesman and general, 1743; Henry Carey, musician, 1743, *London;* Samuel Horsley, bishop of St Asaph's, divine and controversialist, 1806, *Brighton;* John Vandenhoff, tragedian, 1861, *London.*

## HENRY CAREY.

Carey was a musician and a music-composer of great merit, but not fortunate in his life or affairs. After a long struggle with poverty, he died suddenly, and it has been alleged by his own hand (but this is doubtful), leaving a widow and four small children totally unprovided for. One feels it to have been a sad fate for the man who gave us the charming simple ballad of *Sally in our Alley*, a strain which has been the delight of an infinity of people, and will probably continue so while the English language lasts.

Carey, however, would appear to have conferred a greater musical obligation upon his country than even *Sally in our Alley.* There is now pretty good reason to conclude that he was the author of the Royal Anthem. This noble composition has indeed been attributed to Dr Richard Bull, who lived in the reign of James I., and another history would represent it as originating in honour of James II., at the time when he was threatened with the invasion of the Prince of Orange; but there is in reality no evidence for the words or air having existed before the year 1740. In 1794, a gentleman, named Townsend, was able to report that his father had dined with a party which met in a tavern in Cornhill, in 1740, to celebrate the capture of Portobello, when he heard Henry Carey sing the song as his own composition, with great applause from the company. About the same time, Dr Harington, the celebrated physician and amateur-musician of Bath, took down from the lips of John Christopher Smith, who had composed an opera for which Carey gave the *libretto*, a statement, which Dr Harington had often heard from the old gentleman before—that Henry Carey came to him with the words and music of *God Save the King*, 'desiring him to correct the base, which was not proper'—a request which Mr Smith complied with by writing another base in correct harmony.

The anthem does not seem to have come into notoriety till the first successes of Prince Charles Edward Stuart in the autumn of 1745, called forth a burst of loyal—that is, anti-popish feeling, in the population of London. To gratify this sentiment, the song was brought upon the stage in both Covent Garden and Drury Lane theatres. The *Daily Advertiser* of Monday, September 30, 1745, contains this statement: 'On Saturday night last, the audience at the Theatre-Royal, Drury Lane, were agreeably surprised by the gentlemen belonging to that house performing the anthem of *God Save our Noble King* The universal applause it met with—being encored with repeated huzzas—sufficiently denoted in how just abhorrence they hold the arbitrary schemes of our insidious enemies, and detest the despotic attempts of papal power.' The song and air (the latter with some slight inaccuracies) were printed in the *Gentleman's Magazine* for October of that year; but Mr William Chappell believes that it had seen the light previously, in a collection, entitled *Harmonia Anglicana.**

# OCTOBER 5.

St Placidus, abbot, and companions, martyrs, 546. St Galla, widow, about 550.

*Born.*—Jonathan Edwards, eminent Calvinistic divine, 1703, *Windsor, Connecticut;* Horace Walpole, Earl of Orford, celebrated virtuoso and man of letters, 1717, *Wareham, Dorsetshire;* Dr William Wilkie, author of the *Epigoniad*, 1721, *Dalmeny, Linlithgowshire;* Lloyd, Lord Kenyon, distinguished lawyer, 1732, *Greddington, Flintshire.*

*Died.*—Justin, Roman emperor, 578; Henry III., emperor of Germany, 1056; Philip III., the Bold, king of France, 1285; Edward Bruce, brother of King Robert, killed at Fagher, Ireland, 1318; Augustus III., king of Poland, 1763, *Dresden;* Charles, Marquis Cornwallis, governor-general of India, 1805, *Ghazepore, Benares;* Bernard, Comte de Lacépède, eminent naturalist, 1825.

## HEART-BEQUESTS.

Some curious notions and practices respecting the human heart came into vogue about the time of the first Crusade, and were by many believed to have originated among those who died in that expedition. As the supposed seat of the affections, the heart was magnified into undue importance, and, after the death of a beloved or distinguished person, became the object of more solicitude than all the rest of his body. Thus the heart was considered the most valuable of all legacies, and it became the habit for a person to bequeath it to his dearest friend, or to his most favourite church, abbey, or locality, as a token of his supreme regard. And when no such bequest was made, the friends or admirers of deceased persons would cause their hearts to be carefully embalmed, and then, enclosing them in some costly casket, would preserve them as precious treasure, or entomb them with special honour. This remarkable practice, which has been continued more or less down to the present century, was most prevalent during the medieval ages—numerous instances of which are still on record, and many of them are curious and interesting. Our space will only permit us to give a few specimens:

Robert, the famous Earl of Mellent and Leicester, died in 1118, in the abbey of Preaux, where his body was buried, but his heart, by his own order, was conveyed to the hospital at Brackley, to be

* See Mr Chappell's learned work, *Popular Music in the Olden Time*, ii. 691–707.

there preserved in salt.* He had been among the early Crusaders in the Holy Land, and was, says Henry of Huntingdon, 'the most sagacious in political affairs of all who lived between this and Jerusalem. His mind was enlightened, his eloquence persuasive, his shrewdness acute.' But he was rapacious, wily, and unscrupulous, and acquired much of his vast possessions, which were very extensive, both in England and Normandy, by unjust manœuvres, and acts of cruelty and violence. When he perceived death approaching, he assumed the monastic habit, the usual act of atonement in such characters at that period, and died *a penitent* in the abbey of Praeux, but, while he founded the hospital at Brackley, where his heart was preserved, he stoutly refused to restore any of the possessions which he had unjustly acquired.†

Isabella, daughter of William the Marshal, Earl of Pembroke, and wife of Richard, brother of Henry III., died at Berkhamstead in 1239, and ordered her heart to be sent in a silver cup to her brother, then abbot of Tewkesbury, to be there buried before the high-altar. Her body was buried at Beaulieu, in Hampshire.‡ 'The noble Isabella, Countess of Gloucester and Cornwall,' says Matthew Paris, 'was taken dangerously ill of the yellow jaundice, and brought to the point of death. She became senseless, and after having had the ample tresses of her flaxen hair cut off, and made a full confession of her sins, she departed to the Lord, together with a boy to whom she had given birth. When Earl Richard, who had gone into Cornwall, heard of this event, he broke out into the most sorrowful lamentations, and mourned inconsolably.' Henry, their son, while attending mass in the church of St Lawrence, at Viterbo, in Tuscany, was cruelly murdered by Simon and Guy de Montfort, in revenge for the death of their father at the battle of Evesham, in which, however, he appears to have had no part. His heart was sent in a golden vase to Westminster Abbey, where it was deposited in the tomb of Edward the Confessor. On his monument was a gilt statue holding his heart, labelled with these words: 'I bequeath to my father my heart pierced with the dagger.'§ His father, Richard, king of the Romans, having been thrice married, died in 1272, from grief at his son's murder. His body was buried at the abbey of Hayles, his own foundation, and his heart was deposited in the church of the Minorite Brethren, at Oxford, under a costly pyramid erected by his widow.‖

The heart of John Baliol, Lord of Barnard Castle, who died in 1269, was, by his widow's desire, embalmed and enclosed in an ivory casket richly enamelled with silver. His affectionate widow, Devorgilla, used to have this casket placed on the table every day when she ate her meals, and ordered it to be laid on her own heart, when she was herself placed in her tomb. She was buried, according to her own direction, near the altar in New Abbey, which she herself had founded in Galloway, and the casket containing her husband's heart placed on her bosom. From this touching incident, the abbey received the name of Dolce Cor, or Sweetheart Abbey, and for its arms bore in chief a heart over two pastoral staffs, and in base three mullets of five points.

Hearts were not only bequeathed by Crusaders, who died in the Holy Land, to their friends at home, in testimony of unaltered affection, but were sometimes sent there in fulfilment of an unaccomplished vow. Thus Edward I., after he ascended the throne, again took the cross, promising to return to Jerusalem, and give his best support to the crusade, which was then in a depressed condition. But, being detained by his wars with Scotland, unexpected death, in 1307, prevented the fulfilment of his engagement. He therefore, on his death-bed, charged his son to send his heart to Palestine, accompanied with a hundred and forty knights and their retinues, in discharge of his vow. Having provided two thousand pounds of silver for the support of this expedition, and 'his heart being so conveyed thither, he trusted that God would accept this fulfilment of his vow, and grant his blessing on the undertaking.' He also imprecated 'eternal damnation on any who should expend the money for any other purpose. But the disobedient son little regarded the commandment of his father.'*

It is remarkable that the two sworn foes, Edward I. of England, and Robert Bruce, king of Scotland, should have alike decided to send their hearts to be buried in the Holy Land. Each gave the order on his death-bed; each had the same motive for giving it; and the injunction of each was destined to be unperformed; but had their wishes been realised, the hearts of these two inveterate enemies would have met to rest quietly together for ever, in the same sepulchre.

The account of Bruce's heart is very interesting. As he lay on his death-bed, in 1329, he entreated Sir James Douglas, his dear and trusty friend, to carry his heart to Jerusalem, because he had not, on account of his war with England, been able to fulfil a vow which he had made to assist in the crusade. Sir James, weeping exceedingly, vowed, on the honour of a knight, faithfully to discharge the trust reposed in him. After the king's death, his heart was taken from his body, embalmed, and enclosed in a silver case which, by a chain, Douglas suspended to his neck; and then, having provided a suitable retinue to attend him, he departed for the Holy Land. On reaching Spain, he found the king of Castile hotly engaged in war with the Moors, and thinking any contest with Saracens consistent with his vow, he joined the Spaniards in a battle against the Moors, but, ignorant of their mode of fighting, was soon surrounded by horsemen, so that escape was impossible. In desperation, he took the precious heart from his neck, and threw it before him, shouting aloud: 'Pass on as thou wert wont; I will follow or die!' He followed, and was immediately struck to the earth. His dead body was found after the battle, lying over the heart of Bruce. His body was carried away by his friends, and honourably buried in his own church of St Bride, at Douglas. Bruce's heart was intrusted to the charge of Sir Simon Locard of Lee, who bore it back to Scotland, and deposited it beneath the altar in Melrose Abbey, where, perhaps, it still remains. From this incident, Sir Simon changed

* *Magna Britannia*; published in 1724.

† *Henry of Huntingdon*, p. 309, by Dr Giles.

‡ Dyde's *History of Tewkesbury*, p. 37.

§ Blaauw's *Barons' War*, p. 312.

‖ Chauncy's *History of Herts*, vol. ii. 524; and Matt. Paris, vol. iii. 378.

* Weever's *Funeral Monuments*, p. 462.

his name from Locard to Lockheart (as it used to be spelled), and bore in his arms a heart within a fetterlock, with the motto, 'Corda serrata pando.' From the same incident, the Douglases bear a human heart, imperially crowned, and have in their possession an ancient sword, emblazoned with two hands holding a heart, and dated 1329, the year in which Bruce died. An old ballad, quoted in the notes to Scott's *Marmion*, has this stanza—

> 'I will ye charge, after yat I depart,
> To holy grave, and thair bury my hart;
> Let it remaine ever bothe tyme and howr,
> To ye last day I see my Saviour.'

Mrs Hemans has some beautiful lines on Bruce's heart, in Melrose Abbey, of which the following is the first stanza:

> 'Heart! that didst press forward still,
> Where the trumpet's note rang shrill,
> Where the knightly swords were crossing,
> And the plumes like sea-foam tossing;
> Leader of the charging spear,
> Fiery heart!—and liest thou here?
> May this narrow spot inurn
> Aught that so could beat and burn?'

Sir Robert Peckham, who died abroad, caused his heart to be sent into England, and buried in his family vault at Denham, in Buckinghamshire. He died in 1569, but his heart appears to have remained for many years unburied, as we gather from the following entry in the parish-register of burials: 'Edmundus Peckham, Esqr., sonne of Sir George Peckham, July 18, 1586. On the same day was the harte of Sr Robert Peckham, knight, buried in the vault under the chappell.' The heart is enclosed in a leaden case thus inscribed: 'I. H. S. Robertus Peckham Eques Auratus Anglus Cor suum Dulciss. patrie major. Monumentis commendari. Obiit 1 Septembris MD. XIX.'

Edward Lord Windsor, of Bradenham, Bucks, who died at Spa, January 24, 1574,* bequeathed his body to be buried in the 'cathedral church of the noble city of Liege, with a convenient tomb to his memory, but his heart to be enclosed in lead, and sent into England, there to be buried in the chapel at Bradenham, under his father's tomb, in token of a true Englishman.'† The case containing this heart, which has on it a long inscription, is still in the vault at Bradenham, and was seen in 1848, when Isaac d'Israeli was buried in the same vault.

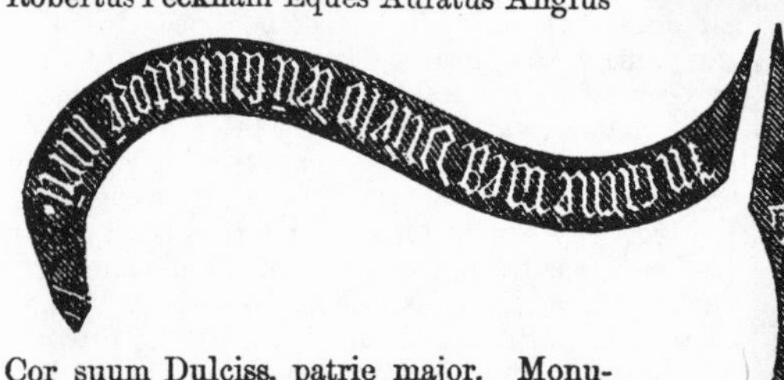

FIGURE OF A HEART DELINEATED ON TOMB IN ST JOHN'S CHURCH, MARGATE.

* Langley's *History of Desborough Hundred, Bucks.*
† Dagdale's *Bar*, vol. ii. p. 308.

The circumstances respecting the heart of Lord Edward Bruce, who was killed in a duel in 1613, are interesting. His body was interred at Bergen, in Holland, where he died, and a monument was there erected to his memory. But a tradition remained in his family, that his heart had been conveyed to Scotland, and deposited in the burial-ground adjoining the old Abbey-Church of Culross, in Perthshire. The tradition had become to many a discredited tale, when, to put it to the test, a search was made in 1806 for the precious relic. Two flat stones, strongly clasped together with iron, were discovered about two feet below the level of the pavement, and partly under an old projection in the wall. These stones had on them no inscription, but the singularity of their being thus braced together, induced the searchers to separate them, when a silver case, shaped like a heart, was found in a cavity between the stones. The case, which was engraved with the arms and name of Lord Edward Bruce, had hinges and clasps, and on being opened, was found to contain a heart carefully embalmed in a brownish-coloured liquid. After drawings of it were taken, it was carefully replaced in its former situation. In another cavity in the stones was a small leaden box, which had probably contained the bowels, but if so, they had then become dust.*

SILVER HEART IN CULROSS ABBEY-CHURCH.

It may be just noticed in passing, as another proof of the undue importance attributed to the

* *Archæologia*, vol. xx., as cited by Bloxam's *Monumental Architecture*, p. 64. See also Chambers's *Domestic Annals of Scotland*, vol. i. p. 450.

heart, that formerly the executioner of a traitor was required to remove the body from the gallows before life was extinct, and plucking out the heart, to hold it up in his hands, and exclaim aloud, 'Here is the heart of a traitor!' 'It was currently reported,' says Anthony Wood, 'that when the executioner held up the heart of Sir Everard Digby, and said, "Here is the heart of a traitor!" Sir Everard made answer and said, "Thou liest!"' This story, which rests solely on A. Wood's authority, is gencrally discredited, though Lord Bacon affirms there are instances of persons saying two or three words in similar cases.

From attaching such importance to the human heart, doubtless arose the practice, which is exemplified in many of our churches, of representing it so freely in sepulchral commemoration. And this occurs, not only where a heart alone is buried, but often the figure of a heart with an inscription is adopted as the sole memorial over the remains of the whole body. An example may be seen in St John's Church, Margate, Kent (see engraving on the previous page). A plate of brass, cut into the shape and size of a human heart, is sunk into the slab which covers the remains of a former vicar of the church. The heart is inscribed with the words 'Credo q^d,' which begin each inscription on three scrolls that issue from the heart, thus:

Credo q^d { Redemptor meus vivit
De terra surrecturus sum
In carne mea videbo deum Salvatorem meum.

Beneath the heart is a Latin inscription, which shews that the whole body of the deceased was interred below. In English it is as follows: 'Here lies Master John Smyth, formerly vicar of this church. He died the thirtieth day of October, A.D. 1433. Amen.'

Sometimes hearts are represented as bleeding, or sprinkled with drops of blood, which was probably

REPRESENTATION OF A HEART IN CHURCH OF LILLINGSTONE DAYRELL.

to symbolise extreme penitence, or special devotedness to a religious life. An example occurs on a brass in the church of Lillingstone Dayrell, Bucks, and is represented in the accompanying wood-cut. The heart is inscribed with the letters J. H. C., and is held in two hands cut off at the wrists, which are clothed in richly-worked ruffles. This heart commemorates the interment of John Merston, rector, who died in 1446. A heart is sometimes placed on the breast, or held in the hands of an effigy representing the person commemorated. The latter case is probably in allusion to Lamentations iii. 41. In such instances, sepulchral hearts are to be regarded as merely emblematic, or, being the chief organ of life, as representatives of the whole body. But in many instances they mark the burial of hearts alone. Thus, in Chichester Cathedral is a slab of Purbeck marble, on which is chiseled a trefoil enclosing hands holding a heart, and surrounded by this inscription:

ICI GIST LE COUER MAUDE DE

The rest of the inscription has been obliterated. Another interesting memorial of the burial of a heart formerly existed in Gaxley Church, Huntingdonshire. This consisted of a small trefoil-headed recess, sculptured in stone, and containing a pair of hands holding a heart. Behind this recess was found a round box, about four inches in diameter, which probably had contained a heart that had perished, as it was empty when discovered.

The burial of hearts appears to have been often attended with some funereal ceremony. The most remarkable instance on record occurred so recently as the 16th of August 1775.

This was the burial, as it was called, of Whitehead's heart. Paul Whitehead was the son of a London tradesman, and was himself apprenticed to a woollen-draper, but having received a superior education, and imbibed a literary bias, he relinquished business as soon as the terms of his apprenticeship were completed. He entered into various literary projects, and published several pieces, both in prose and verse, chiefly of a satirical character. In his poetical satires, he adopted Pope as his model, but, to use his own expression, 'he found that their powers were differently appreciated.' His effusions, however, were not unsuccessful, especially those of a political character, which he supported by the active and zealous part he took at a contested election for Westminster. His talent and services were so far appreciated by his party, that Sir Francis Dashwood, afterwards Lord le Despencer, procured for him an appointment worth about £800 per annum. This, together with his wife's fortune of £10,000, placed him in affluent circumstances, and he passed the remainder of his life in comparative retirement at Twickenham. His compositions were of temporary interest, and he appears to have rightly estimated them himself, for he positively refused to collect them for a standard edition. His moral character, in early life, may be conceived from his being not only a member, but the secretary of the notorious Medmenham Club, or the mock Monks of St Francis. In later life, his habits were respectable, and he possessed a benevolent and hospitable disposition. He died on the 30th of December 1774, aged sixty-four, and among many other legacies, he bequeathed 'his HEART to his noble friend and patron, Lord le Despencer, to be deposited in his mausoleum at West Wycombe, a village two miles from the town of High Wycombe and adjoining Wycombe Park, his lordship's place of residence.'

This mausoleum, which was built with funds bequeathed by George Bubb Dodington, Lord Melcombe Regis, is a large hexagonal roofless building, with recesses in the walls for the reception of busts, urns, or other sepulchral monuments. It stands within the churchyard near the east end of the church, which is also a very singular edifice, built by Lord le Despencer on a remarkably lofty hill, and about half a mile from the village. Whitehead's heart, by order of Lord le Despencer, was wrapped in lead, and enshrined in a marble urn, which cost £50, and on the 16th of August 1775, eight months after Whitehead's death, was conveyed from London to be solemnly deposited within the mausoleum. At twelve o'clock, the precious relic, having arrived within a short distance of Wycombe, was carried forward, accompanied by the following procession :

A grenadier officer in his uniform ;
Nine grenadiers, rank and file, two deep,
the odd one last ;
Two German-flute players ;
Two choristers in surplices, with notes pinned to
their backs ;
Two German-flute players;
Eleven singing-men in surplices, two and two,
the odd one last;
Two French-horn players ;
Two bassoon players ;
Six fifers, two and two ;
Four muffled drums, two and two ;
The urn containing the Heart,
resting on a bier ornamented with
black crape, and borne by six soldiers,
with three others on each side to relieve them ;
Lord le Despencer,
as chief mourner, in his regimentals
as colonel of the Bucks Militia, with crape
round his arm ;
Major Skottowe, Captain Lloyd ;
Seven other militia officers in uniform ;
Two fifers;
Two drummers ;
Twenty soldiers, two and two,
with firelocks reversed.

Dr Arnold, Mr Atterbury, and another walked on the side of the procession all the way, with scrolls of paper in their hands, beating time. The 'Dead March' in *Saul* was played the whole way by the flutes, horns, and bassoons, successively with the fifes and drums. The church-bell continued tolling, and great guns were discharged every three minutes and a half. The hill on which the church stands was crowded with spectators, while the procession, moving very slowly up, was an hour in reaching the mausoleum, and another hour was spent in marching round it, and performing funereal glees. The urn was then borne with much ceremony into the mausoleum, and placed on a pedestal in one of the niches, with this inscription underneath :

PAUL WHITEHEAD OF TWICKENHAM, ESQR.
Ob. 1775.

Unhallowed hands, this urn forbear,
No gems, nor orient spoil
Lie here concealed ; but what 's more rare,
A heart that knew no guile.

The ceremony was concluded by the soldiers firing three volleys, and then marching off with the drums and fifes playing a merry tune. On the next day, a new oratorio, called *Goliah*, composed by Mr Atterbury, was performed in the church.

The heart used to be often taken out of the urn, to be shewn to visitors, and in 1829, notwithstanding the warning epitaph, was stolen, and has never been recovered.*

## OCTOBER 6.

St Faith or Fides, virgin, and her companions, martyrs, 4th century. St Bruno, confessor, founder of the Carthusian monks, 1101.

*Born.*—Dr John Key (Caius), founder of Caius College, Cambridge, 1510, *Norwich ;* Dr Nevil Maskelyne, astronomer, 1732, *London ;* Madame Campan, biographer of Marie Antoinette, 1752, *Paris ;* Louis Philippe, king of France, 1377, *Paris ;* Madame Jenny Lind Goldschmidt, vocalist, 1821, *Stockholm.*

*Died.*—Charles the Bald, king of France, 877 ; Sir John Young, Baron Lisgar, in 1868 Governor-general of Canada, 1876.

### ANCIENT WATCHES.

Many inventions of the greatest value, and ultimately of the commonest use, are sometimes the most difficult to trace to their origin. It is so with clocks and watches. Neither the precise year of their invention, nor the names of their inventors, can be confidently stated. Till the close of the tenth century, no other mode of measuring time than by the sun-dial, or the hour-glass, appears to have existed ; and then we first hear of a graduated mechanism adapted to the purpose, this invention being usually ascribed to the monk Gerbert, who was raised to the tiara in 999, under the name of Sylvester II. These clocks were cumbrous machines ; and it is not till the fourteenth century that we hear of portable clocks. In the succeeding century, they were much more common, and were part of the necessary furniture of a better-class house. They were hung to the walls, and their movements regulated by weights and lines, like the cheap kitchen-clocks of the present day. The invention of the spiral spring as the motive power, in place of the weight and line, gave, about the middle of the fifteenth century, the first great impetus to improvement, which now went on rapidly, and resulted in the invention of the watch —a time-measurer that might be carried about the person.

Southern Germany appears to have been the place from whence these welcome novelties chiefly issued ; and the earliest watches were known as 'Nuremberg Eggs,' a sobriquet obtained as well from the city from whence they emanated, as from their appearance. The works were enclosed in circular metal cases, and as they hung from the girdle, suggested the idea of an egg. Before the invention, or general adoption of the fusee—that is, from about 1500 to 1540—the movements were entirely of steel ; then brass was adopted for the

* In further reference to the subject of this article, we beg to direct the reader to a very elegant and interesting work, recently published, from the pen of Miss Hartshorne, and entitled *Enshrined Hearts of Warriors and Illustrious People.*

plates and pillars, the wheels and pinions only being fabricated of steel; and ultimately the pinions only were of steel. The fusee being universally adopted about 1540, no great change occurred for fifty years, during which time the silversmith seems to have assisted the watchmaker in the production of quaint cases for his works, so that they might become ornamental adjuncts to a lady's waist. Our first example (formerly in the

WATCH NO. 1.

Bernal Collection, and now in that of Lady O. Fitzgerald) tells, after an odd fashion, the classic tale of Jupiter and Ganymede. The works are contained in the body of the eagle, which opens across the centre, and displays the dial-plate, richly engraved with scrolls and flowers on a ground of niello. It will be perceived that this watch is so constructed, that when not suspended to the girdle by the ring in the centre of the bird's back, it can stand on the claws wherever its owner may choose to place it.

Watches were now made of all imaginable shapes and sizes, and the cases of all forms and materials; crystal was very commonly used, through which the mechanism of the watch might be observed. Sometimes stones of a more precious character were cut and adapted to the purpose. The Earl of Stamford possesses one small egg-shaped watch, the cases cut out of jacinths, the cover set round with diamonds on an enamelled border. Mr O. Morgan has in his curious collection of watches one in form of a golden acorn, which discharged a diminutive wheel-lock pistol at a certain hour; another was enclosed in silver cases, taking the form of cockle-shells. We engrave a specimen of

WATCH NO. 2.

a watch in form of a duck (also in Lady O. Fitzgerald's collection); the feathers are chased on the silver. The lower part opens, and the dial-plate, which is likewise of silver, is encircled with a gilt ornamented design of floriated scrolls and angels' heads. The wheels work on small rubies. It is believed to be of the time of Queen Elizabeth.

When the famous Diana of Poitiers became the mistress of Henry II., she was a widow, and the complaisant court not only made her mourning-colours the favourite fashion, but adopted the most lugubrious fancies for personal decoration. Rings in the form of skeletons clasped the finger; other mementos of an equally ghastly description were used as jewels; small coffins of gold contained chased and enamelled figures of death; and watches were made in the form of skulls, of which we

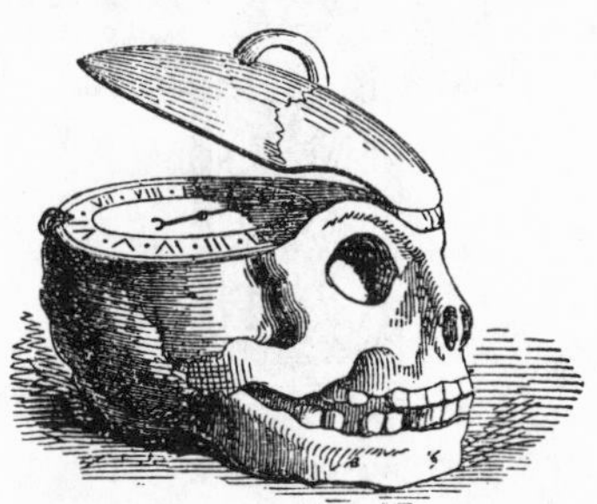

WATCH NO. 3.

engrave an example. All these quaint and *bizarre* forms passed out of fashion at the early part of the seventeenth century, when watchmakers seem to have devoted their attention chiefly to the compact character of their work. About 1620, they assumed a flattened oval form, such as we have seen used to a comparatively recent period; they were sometimes furnished with astronomical dials, and perpetual moving calendars, and often struck the hour; the inner case acting as a silver bell. In Ben Jonson's *Staple of News*, the opening scene exhibits a dissolute junior anxiously awaiting his majority, who 'draws forth his watch, and sets it on the table;' immediately afterwards exclaiming:

'It strikes!—one, two,
Three, four, five, six. Enough, enough, dear watch,
Thy pulse hath beat enough. Now sleep and rest;
Would thou couldst make the time to do so too:
I'll wind thee up no more!'

It appears, then, that until 1670, when the pendulum-spring was invented, the mechanism of the watch had made no advance since the days of Elizabeth. The French makers were among the first to introduce judicious improvements, particularly such as effected weight and size. Lady Fitzgerald possesses a gold enamelled watch manufactured by order of Louis XIII., as a present to our Charles I., which may rival a modern work in its smallness. It is oval; measuring about 2 inches by 1½ across the face, and is an inch in thickness. The back is chased in high-relief with the figure of St George conquering the dragon; the motto of the Garter surrounds the case, which is enriched with enamel colours. Grotesque forms for watch-cases seem to have quite gone out of fashion in the seventeenth century, with one exception; they were occasionally made in the form of a cross to hang at the girdle; and are consequently, but erroneously, sometimes called 'Abbess's watches.' The example here engraved is also from the collection just alluded to. It is covered with elaborate engraving of a very delicate character; the centre of the dial-plate represents Christ's agony in the Garden of Olives,

WATCH NO. 4.

the outer compartments being occupied by the emblems of his passion; a figure of Faith occupying the lowermost. The style of engraving is very like that of the famous Theodore de Bry, who worked largely for the French silversmiths at the commencement of the seventeenth century.

---

# OCTOBER 7.

St Justina of Padua, virgin and martyr. Saints Marcellus and Apuleius, martyrs at Rome. Saints Sergius and Bacchus, martyrs, 4th century. St Mark, pope and confessor, 336. St Osith, virgin, about 870.

*Born.*—William Laud, archbishop of Canterbury, 1573, *Reading;* Charles Abbott, Lord Tenterden, eminent naval and mercantile jurist, 1762, *Canterbury.*

*Died.*—Charles III., the Simple, king of France, 929, *Castle of Peronne;* Margaret, Maid of Norway, 1290, *Orkney;* Sir Thomas Chaloner, statesman and writer, 1565; George Gascoigne, poet and dramatist, 1577, *Stamford, Lincolnshire;* Giovanni Battista Guarini, author of the *Pastor Fido*, 1612, *Venice;* Nicholas Heinsius, scholar and critic, 1681, *Holland;* Antonio Sacchini, composer, 1786, *Paris;* Dr John Brown, founder of the Brunonian system of medicine, 1788, *London;* Dr John George Zimmermann, celebrated author of the treatise on *Solitude*, 1795, *Hanover;* Dr Thomas Reid, eminent Scottish metaphysician, 1796, *Glasgow;* Edgar Allan Poe, American poet, 1849, *Baltimore.*

## THE MAID OF NORWAY.

The fate of this child-sovereign, who only reached her hereditary dominions to die, and through whose decease so protracted a series of disasters was entailed on Scotland, forms one of the interesting events in the history of a nation so noted for the misfortunes of its queens. What we really know of the 'fair maid of Norroway' is very little, however liberally we may draw on imagination to supply the deficiencies, and fill in the lights and shadows to a picture of which the chroniclers of the times have furnished us with nothing but the most meagre outlines. It is not to the brief and sententious records of the thirteenth century, that we are to look for narratives of domestic events, or the personal history of a little girl of seven years old, even though that little girl were a queen in her own right.

Margaret, Princess of Norway, was the only child of Eric, king of that country, by his marriage with the daughter of Alexander III., of Scotland. Her mother died in giving her birth, and on the death of her maternal grandfather in 1285, by a fall from an unruly horse over the cliff at Kinghorn, she became sole inheritrix of the Scottish crown, being already, moreover, heiress-presumptive to that of Norway. Alexander III. had indeed been most unfortunate in his domestic relations, having seen one member of his family after another, including two promising sons, descend into the grave before him, whilst his second marriage, a short time before his death, with the beautiful French princess Joleta, had been unproductive of issue. Feeling sensibly his loneliness, and solicitous also for the careful upbringing of his little granddaughter, in whom all his prospects of a successor rested, he sent over to Norway, shortly after her mother's death, an embassy of Scottish nobles, requesting from his son-in-law the delivery of Margaret to these gallant knights, for the purpose of being brought over to, and educated in, Scotland. Eric refused his consent, and the deputation had to quit the Norwegian court with their master's behest unaccomplished. None of them, however, were destined to set foot again in their native country, the ship in which they were conveyed foundering in sight of the Scottish coast. Margaret may thus be deemed fortunate in having had so narrow an escape of her life, though it was only to lengthen its duration by a very few years.

On the melancholy death of Alexander III., the kingdom was thrown into a most distracted condition; but a great assembly of nobles and dignitaries was held, in which fealty was sworn to Margaret of Norway, as the sovereign of Scotland, and great anxiety expressed to have the young queen brought over to dwell among her subjects. The present conjuncture of affairs presented a strong temptation to the able and ambitious Edward I. of England, to form an advantageous connection with Scotland. A matrimonial alliance was proposed by him, between the young Scottish queen and his own son Edward, Prince of Wales. The offer was favourably entertained both by the Scottish nobles and Margaret's father, King Eric, and negotiations were forthwith instituted for arranging the terms of the match. These were at length settled to the satisfaction of all parties, the principal conditions being that, notwithstanding this union with England, Scotland should retain all the rights and privileges of an independent kingdom, and that its sovereignty in the event of Edward and Margaret having no children, should revert to the young queen's nearest lawful heir. With the view of hastening an adjustment of matters, it is said that money was freely distributed by Edward, in the shape of bribes and pensions among the leading-men of Eric's court.

It may not be a very profitable, but it is certainly a curious speculation, to ponder over the consequences of this marriage to Scotland, had the course of events permitted it to be carried into effect. The union of England and Scotland might thus have been accomplished on most honourable terms to the latter country, which would further have been spared the almost continuous series of wars and devastations, by which she was afflicted during upwards of three hundred years that intervened between Margaret's death and the accession of James VI. to the English throne. The peaceful arts of commerce and agriculture might have been allowed full scope to develop themselves, and the national industry might have raised the country at a much earlier date to that state of prosperity and wealth, which she has only attained in later and more tranquil times. But in that case the purifying influences of adversity would have been unfelt, less occasion would have arisen for the display of manly heroism and independence, the national spirit would have languished, and a Scotchman at the present day would have been unable to quote the deeds of Wallace and Bruce.

In addition to the stipulations regarding the succession to the crown, it had been agreed in the matrimonial treaty, that the young queen should be forthwith sent to Scotland, and be brought up either there or at Edward's court, as might be found most suitable. When the time for her departure arrived, however, her father displayed a great reluctance to part with her; a reluctance which many will regard as a presentiment of the untoward occurrence, by which he was destined so soon to be deprived of her altogether. Both Edward and the Scottish council urged on Eric the fulfilment of his engagement, by sending over his daughter to her future husband and dominions. Two distinguished Scottish knights—Sir David Wemyss, and the famous Sir Michael Scott, of Balwearie, so renowned for his reputed necromantic lore—were despatched to Norway to fetch the young queen, and Eric now gave his consent that she should depart. We can imagine the little girl of seven, wholly unconscious of the important interests which centered in her, sorry to part with a loving and indulgent father, and carried down to the beach, to be intrusted to the care of some weather-beaten Norse admiral, who might possibly, in his youth, have taken part in King Haco's expedition to Scotland, and the battle of Largs. A tender and delicate child, ill fitted, it would seem, for enduring the fatigues of a sea-voyage, she quitted, in September 1290, her father and her native land, never to see either of them again.

Meantime the Scottish nation was expecting the arrival of its young sovereign with all the loyal enthusiasm for which it has ever been distinguished, and a great council was being convened at Perth for deliberating on the affairs of the realm. Suddenly, this august assembly was electrified by a rumour, which reached it from the north, that the young Queen Margaret was no more. The dismal news was soon confirmed, and the country learned with dismay that her father's forebodings regarding her had proved but too true, and that her delicate frame had been unable to support the effects of sickness and exhaustion. Prostrated by illness shortly after commencing her voyage, she gradually sunk, and when at length the vessel reached Orkney, poor Margaret was carried ashore only to breathe her last. At the intelligence of her death, to use the words of an old chronicler, 'the kingdom was troubled, and its inhabitants sunk into despair.' The disastrous interregnum that followed, and the disputes between the descendants of the Earl of Huntingdon, brother of William the Lion, as claimants of the throne, resulting in the attempt of Edward I. to annex Scotland to his dominions, are well known to all readers of history. It may be remarked that a claim to the Scottish crown was also put in by King Eric, as representing his daughter; but no active steps were taken to assert this alleged right. He died a few years afterwards, while only a young man of thirty, having been married to Margaret's mother at an age little above fourteen.

No particulars are known as to the precise spot where the Maid of Norway died, and even her place of burial has never been satisfactorily ascertained. Doubtless, however, she was interred in the venerable cathedral of St Magnus, at Kirkwall, in Orkney; but nothing definite as to this circumstance can be stated, and no known monument or sepulchral stone marks the site of her grave. Amid a number of tombs, however, within that ancient church, bearing no name or inscription, one was discovered, which, on being opened and examined, gave indications of its being the grave of a young person, whilst one or two other circumstances combined to favour the idea of its having been the resting-place of the remains of Margaret of Norway.

## EDGAR ALLAN POE.

Edgar Allan Poe, an eccentric American poet, was born at Boston, January 19, 1809. It may seem absurd to say that he belonged by birth to the aristocracy, in a country where no aristocracy is recognised. Still, it is a fact that Poe was an aristocrat, and it is also true, that no people are more proud of the advantages of birth and breeding, than citizens of the United States, especially those who belong to the southern division of those states. Poe was a Southerner in manners and feelings, as well as by birth; and there is little doubt, that the greater part of the infamy which was heaped upon him after his death, was owing to the fact that as a man of taste he despised, and as an aristocrat, treated with contempt, a tradesman in literature, who lived by making books of biographies, generally laudatory of living literary persons. This man took his revenge when the opportunity came, as any one may kick a dead lion with impunity. Many have echoed, no doubt honestly, the evil fame which was made for the poor poet by this man, whom he had despised and insulted during his life.

Poe's grandfather was a soldier in the war of the American revolution, and a friend of Lafayette. His father was a student at law. He fell in love with an English actress, named Arnold, and married her. They both died young, and at nearly the same time, leaving three orphan children. Edgar was adopted and educated by John Allan, a wealthy merchant of Virginia. At the early age of five years he was brought to England, and was sent to school near London, till he was ten years old.

Poe's life was a series of eccentric adventures. The reason of this is to be found in his temperament, or physical constitution. He lived, from the cradle to the grave, on the verge of madness, when he was not absolutely mad. A half-glass of wine intoxicated him to insanity. His brain was large, almost to deformity, in the region where phrenologists place the imaginative faculties. Under the influence of slight stimulus, such as would have been inappreciable by a person otherwise constituted, Poe was led on to commit acts, the consequences of which were often distressing, and might at any moment have been fatal, as was finally the case.

At an early age he entered college at Charlottesville, Virginia, but he was expelled for dissipation. He also entered the military school at West Point, New York, but he left in a year. During the excitement in favour of the independence of Greece, he started for that country; but he was next found at St Petersburg, where he fell into distress, as was his fortune almost everywhere, and some friends sent him home.

Soon after his return, he published a volume of poems, entitled *Al Aaraaf, Tamerlane, and Minor Poems.* These were written from the age of sixteen to eighteen years.

At one time he enlisted as a soldier, but he soon deserted. He had much partiality for active exercise, and very little for discipline, though he was exceedingly methodical and orderly in all the details of life. He was remarkable for aquatic and gymnastic performances. He was able to leap further than most men, and he once swam seven miles and a half against the tide.

In 1835, Poe was employed to write for the *Southern Literary Messenger*, and about this time he married his cousin, Virginia Clemm, who, at the time of their union, was about fourteen years old. After this, we find him engaged on Benton's *Gentleman's Magazine*, at two pounds a week. This engagement was of brief continuance, and he next was connected with Graham's *Magazine*, and wrote *Some Strange Stories*, nearly all of which seem tinged with a sort of semi-insanity. We next find him engaged with Mr Briggs, in establishing the *Broadway Journal.* This was soon discontinued. In 1845, he published *The Raven*, which has enjoyed a more extended reputation than any other production of his pen.

After the appearance of the *Raven* in transatlantic periodicals, Elizabeth Barrett Browning wrote to Poe, that '*The Raven* had excited a *fit horror* in England.' He was delighted with the compliment. Indeed this sort of impression appeared to be an object of ambition with him. Poe always seemed to consider *The Raven* as his master-piece, and he was fond of reciting it in company, in a sort of sing-song tone, which was very unpleasant to some.

It would be difficult to calculate the amount of fame that Poe might have earned, if he could have lived, and written one year in undisturbed sanity. After the fame of *The Raven* had brought his name upon every lip, he was invited to lecture before the Boston Atheneum—the highest honour the Athens of America could bestow on the poet. He went before an elegant and most intellectual Boston audience, and instead of giving a lecture, he repeated a juvenile poem that had been published! His friends had no doubt of the cause, or occasion of this strange proceeding, but the audience were indignant. Poe declared that 'it was an intentional insult to the genius of the frog-pond, a small pond on Boston Common'—a further evidence of the madness that he often induced, by taking stimulants, though he knew his fearful liability. After this, his irregularities became so much the rule of his life, that Mrs Clemm, who acted the part of a good genius to the poet and his young wife, her daughter, took a cottage at Fordham, near New York. Here she devoted herself to the care of both with tender and unceasing assiduity. Mrs Poe was dying of consumption. Poe was plunged in a deep melancholy, which did not admit of his writing anything. They were in a state of almost utter destitution, and the malady of the poet was constantly aggravated by witnessing the suffering of his fading, lily-like wife, to whom he was tenderly attached. Friends came to their help the moment their condition was known, and it was subsequently brought against Poe, that he took a bribe at this time for a favourable review, which he afterwards wrote of a miserable book of poems. In speaking of this violation of his literary conscience, after he had somewhat recovered the tone of his mind, he said, 'The author gave me a hundred dollars, when my poor Virginia was dying, and we were starving, and *required* me to write a review of that book. What could I do?'

Let those who have judged him harshly for this, and other sins of his life, place themselves in his condition. When sober and sane, Poe was a gentleman of pure taste and elegant manners, whose conversation was always interesting, and often instructive. He had great personal beauty, and the aristocratic manner and bearing of a southern gentleman, and a descendant of the Cavaliers. In 1848, Poe published *Eureka*, which he first gave as a lecture. It is impossible to give a characteristic description of this and other literary performances by Poe. The same sort of extravagance pervades all, and those who knew him most intimately, and were best qualified to judge, believed that he lived and wrote with a shade of madness in all that he did—and yet few men were more methodical and orderly in their habits than Poe. His handwriting was delicately beautiful, and at the same time clear and plain. His study was the perfection of order and neatness. But his fearful proclivities might change all this in a moment. The world cannot believe that half a glass of wine could make a man lose all self-control, and hurry him on to madness, and its fearful consequences. But there is abundant proof that this was true of Poe.

After the death of his wife, Poe gradually recovered from the deep melancholy which had palsied all his mental power during the last portion of her life, and engaged again in literary occupation. Subsequently, he entered into correspondence with a lady of fine genius and high position, with a view to marriage. But here, again, his destiny was against him. The marriage was broken off, and soon after Poe died of delirium tremens, at the age of forty; that critical period at which it seems natural for an irregular life, combined with excessive brain-work, to bring its victims to an end.

# OCTOBER 8.

St Thais, the penitent, about 348. St Pelagia, the penitent, 5th century. St Keyna, virgin, 5th or 6th century. St Bridget, widow, 1373.

*Born.*—Dr John Hoadly, dramatist, 1711, *London.*

*Died.*—Nicolo di Rienzi, tribune of Rome, assassinated, 1354; Sir Richard Blackmore, poet, 1729; Dr Andrew Kippis, miscellaneous writer, 1795, *London;* Vittorio Alfieri, great tragic dramatist of Italy, 1803, *Florence;* Henry Christophe, king of Hayti, 1821; Charles Fourier, Socialist, 1837, *Paris;* Johann H. Dannecker, German sculptor, 1841, *Stuttgardt.*

## RIENZI.

Lord Lytton's noble romance of *Rienzi* has painted in the most attractive and glowing manner the life and actions of the renowned tribune of Rome. It must be admitted, also, that unlike many so-called historical novelists, the author has little, if at all, overstepped the limits of fact and reality in the portraiture of his hero, and presents, both in the delineation of Rienzi's character and the general picture of the political and social condition of Rome at the period, an account which, making due allowance for poetical embellishment, may, on the whole, be relied on as strikingly just and accurate.

It is well known that Rome, in the fourteenth century, was in the most anarchical and deplorable condition. A set of factious and tyrannical nobles had established, in their lawlessness, a perfect reign of terror over the unhappy citizens, and had driven the representatives of St Peter from their seat in the Eternal City, to establish a new pontifical residence at Avignon, in the south of France. Here, during seventy years of the fourteenth century, the papal court maintained itself, and, freed from the restraints by which it was hemmed in and overawed at home by its own subjects, asserted the privileges of the sacred college and the authority of ecclesiastical sway. In the meantime, the general body of Roman citizens groaned under the oppressions of the nobles, which were every day becoming more frequent and intolerable. This scene of violence was unexpectedly changed by one of the most remarkable revolutions that have ever taken place in any state, and which, if carried out with the same success that inaugurated its commencement, might have exercised a lasting and beneficial influence not only on Rome, but the whole of Italy.

Nicolo Gabrini, commonly called Nicolo, or Cola di Rienzi, from an abbreviation of his father's name of *Lorenzo*, was the son of an innkeeper and washerwoman of Rome, who, however, conscious of the natural abilities of their son, bestowed on him a good education, which the young man improved to the best advantage. His enthusiasm was especially excited by the history of the ancient glories of his native city, and he revolved with generous ardour many schemes for raising her from her present degradation to the summit of her primitive greatness. Chosen as one of the thirteen deputies from the Roman commons to the papal government at Avignon, he acquitted himself with great credit in an oration addressed to Pope Clement VI., and received the appointment of apostolic notary, with the daily salary of five gold florins. Stimulated by the success thus achieved, he commenced in earnest, on his return to Rome, his self-imposed task of rousing the citizens to the assertion of their rights and liberties. The death of a much-loved brother, whose assassins, from their aristocratic influence and position, escaped unpunished, added the impulse of revenge to that of patriotism. In animated declamations to the people in the streets and public places of Rome, Rienzi descanted on the greatness of their ancestors, the right and enjoyment of liberty, and the derivation of all law and authority from the will of the governed. The nobles were either too ignorant to comprehend, or too confident in their might, to dread the effect of such addresses, and the designs of the orator were still further veiled by his adopting, like Brutus, the guise of a buffoon or jester, and condescending, in this capacity, to raise a laugh in the palaces of the Roman princes. But, in the month of May 1347, a nocturnal assembly of a hundred citizens was congregated by him on Mount Aventine, and a formal compact was entered into for the re-establishment of *the good estate,* as Rienzi styled his scheme of popular freedom. A proclamation was then made by sound of trumpet, that on the evening of the following day, all persons should assemble unarmed before the church of St Angelo. After a night spent in devotional exercises, Rienzi, accompanied by his band of a hundred followers, issued from the church, and marched in a solemn procession to the Capitol, from the balcony of which he harangued the people, and received, in their acclamations, a ratification of his assumption of supreme power. Stephen Colonna, the most formidable of the nobles, was at this time absent from Rome, and on his return to crush out at once and for ever, as he imagined, the spark of rebellion, he only narrowly saved himself by flight, from falling a victim to the fury of the populace, who supported with the most determined zeal the cause and authority of their champion. A general order was then issued to the great nobles, that they should peaceably retire from the city to their estates; a command which was obeyed with the most surprising unanimity. The title of tribune of Rome, in remembrance of ancient days, was assumed by Rienzi, who forthwith set himself with active earnestness to the task of administrative reformation. In this, for a time, his endeavours were crowned with the most gratifying and signal success. The defences which the nobles had erected around their palaces, and within which, as in robbers' dens, they ensconced themselves to the defiance of all law and order, were levelled to the ground, and the garrisons of troops by which the citizens were overawed, expelled and suppressed. Law and order were everywhere re-established, an impartial execution of justice insured with respect to all ranks of society, and a rigorous and economical management introduced into the departments of revenue and finance. In these days, according to the glowing account of a historian of the times, quoted by Gibbon, the woods began to rejoice that they were no longer infested with robbers; the oxen began to plough; the pilgrims visited the sanctuaries; the roads and inns were replenished with travellers; trade, plenty, and good faith were restored in the markets; and a purse of gold might be exposed without danger in the midst of the highway.

The city and territory of Rome were not the only places comprehended in the patriotic aspirations of Rienzi, who aimed at uniting the whole of Italy into a grand federal republic. In such a scheme, he was five hundred years in advance of his age, and the same difficulties which retarded its accomplishment in modern times, were instrumental in causing its failure in the fourteenth century. The republics and free cities were indeed disposed to look favourably on the projects of the Roman tribune, but the rulers of Lombardy and Naples both despised and hated the plebeian chief. Yet the advice and arbitration of Rienzi were sought by more than one European sovereign, and, as in the case of Cromwell, the aptitude with which he conformed himself to the dignity and general requirements of his high station, formed the theme of universal wonder and applause.

But the judgment and solidity which constituted such essential elements in the character of the English Protector, proved deficient with Nicolo di Rienzi. An injudicious and puerile assumption of regal state, some acts of over-severity in the execution of justice, and a tendency to convivial excess, had all their influence, in conjunction with the proverbial fickleness of popular esteem, in bringing about the overthrow of the tribune. On one occasion, when he caused himself to be created a knight with all the ceremonies of chivalry, he excited prodigious scandal by bathing in the sacred porphyry-vase of Constantine, whilst at the same time the breaking down of the state-bed on which he reposed within the baptistery, the night previous to the performance of the ceremony of investiture, was interpreted as an omen of his approaching downfall. After one or two unsuccessful attempts of the two great factions of the exiled nobles, the Colonna and the Ursini or Orsini, who laid aside their mutual animosities to unite against a common foe, the dethronement of Rienzi was suddenly accomplished by the Count of Minorbino, who introduced himself into Rome at the head of one hundred and fifty soldiers. The tribune, thus surprised, shewed little of the resolution by which his conduct had been hitherto distinguished, and with a lachrymose denunciation of popular ingratitude, he pusillanimously abdicated the government, and was confined for a time in the castle of St Angelo, from which, in the disguise of a pilgrim, he afterwards contrived to escape.

For seven years, Rienzi remained an exile from his native city, wandering about from the court of one sovereign to another, and was at last made a prisoner by the Emperor Charles IV., who sent him as a captive to the papal court at Avignon. The champion of popular rights was for a time treated as a malefactor, and four cardinals were appointed to investigate the charges laid against him of heresy and rebellion. But the magnanimity displayed by him before the pope, seems to have made an impression on the mind of Clement VI., who relaxed the rigours of his confinement by allowing him the use of books, the study of which, more especially of the Holy Scriptures and Titus Livius, served to console the ex-tribune under his misfortunes.

On the accession of Innocent VI. to the pontificate, a new line of policy was adopted by the court of Avignon, who believed that by sending Rienzi to Rome as its accredited representative, with the title of senator, the anarchy and violence which since his deposition had become more rampant than ever, might be suppressed or diminished. The citizens had, indeed, experienced ample cause for regretting the order and impartiality of Rienzi's sway in the tyranny of his successors. His return was celebrated with every appearance of triumph and rejoicing, and for a short period, the benefits which had attended his former government marked his resumption of power. But his relations with the court of Avignon rendered him an object of suspicion to the people, whilst a spirit of jealousy and apprehension led him to the perpetration of several acts of cruelty. To crown his unpopularity, the exigencies of government compelled him to impose a tax, and a fatal commotion was the result. In the closing scene of his career, he displayed a strange combination of intrepidity and cowardice, appearing on the balcony of the Capitol, when it was surrounded by a furious multitude, and endeavouring by his eloquence to calm the passions of the mob. A storm of abuse and more effectual missiles interrupted his address, and after being wounded in the hand with an arrow, he seemed to lose all manly resolution, and fled lamenting to an inner apartment. The populace continued to surround the Capitol till the evening, then burst in the doors, and dragged Rienzi, as he was attempting to escape in disguise, to the platform in front of the palace. Here for an hour he stood motionless before the immense multitude, who for a time stood hushed as if by some spell before the man who had undoubtedly in many respects been well deserving of their gratitude. This feeling of affection and remorse might have shielded the tribune, when a man from the crowd suddenly plunged a dagger in his breast. He fell senseless to the ground, and a revulsion taking place in the feelings of the mob, they rushed upon and despatched him with numerous wounds. His body was ignominiously exposed to the dogs, and the mutilated remains committed to the flames.

Thus perished the celebrated Rienzi, who in after-times has been regarded as the last of the Roman patriots, and celebrated in such glowing language by Lord Byron, with whose lines from *Childe Harold's Pilgrimage* the present notice may not inappropriately close—

'Then turn we to her latest tribune's name,
From her ten thousand tyrants turn to thee,
Redeemer of dark centuries of shame—
The friend of Petrarch—hope of Italy—
Rienzi! last of Romans! While the tree
Of freedom's wither'd trunk puts forth a leaf,
Even for thy tomb a garland let it be—
The Forum's champion, and the people's chief—
Her new-born Numa thou—with reign, alas! too brief.'

## JUDICIAL COMBAT BETWEEN A MAN AND A DOG.

On 8th October 1361, there took place on the Ile Notre Dame, Paris, a combat, which both illustrates strikingly the maxims and ideas prevalent in that age, and is perhaps the most singular instance on record of the appeals to 'the judgment of God' in criminal cases.

M. Aubry de Montdidier, a French gentleman, when travelling through the forest of Bondy, was murdered and buried at the foot of a tree. His dog remained for several days beside his grave, and only left the spot when urged by hunger. The faithful animal proceeded to Paris, and presented himself at the house of an intimate friend of his master's, making the most piteous howlings to announce the loss which he had sustained. After being supplied with food, he renewed his lamentations, moved towards the door, looking round to see whether he was followed, and returning to his master's friend, laid hold of him by the coat, as if to signify that he should come along with him. The singularity of all these movements on the part of the dog, coupled with the non-appearance of his master, from whom he was generally inseparable, induced the person in question to follow the animal. Leading the way, the dog arrived in time at the foot of a tree in the forest of Bondy, where he commenced scratching and tearing up the ground, at the same time recommencing the most piteous lamentations. On digging at the spot thus indicated, the body of the murdered Aubry was exposed to view.

No trace of the assassin could for a time be discovered, but after a while, the dog happening to be confronted with an individual, named the Chevalier Macaire, he flew at the man's throat, and could only with the utmost difficulty be forced to let go his hold. A similar fury was manifested by the dog on every subsequent occasion that he met this person. Such an extraordinary hostility on the part of the animal, who was otherwise remarkably gentle and good-tempered, attracted universal attention. It was remembered that he had been always devotedly attached to his master, against whom Macaire had cherished the bitterest enmity. Other circumstances combined to strengthen the suspicions now aroused.

The king of France, informed of all the rumours in circulation on this subject, ordered the dog to be brought before him. The animal remained perfectly quiet till it recognised Macaire amid a crowd of courtiers, and then rushed forward to seize him with a tremendous bay. In these days the practice of the judicial combat was in full vigour, that mode of settling doubtful cases being frequently resorted to, as an appeal to the 'judgment of God,' who it was believed would interpose specially to shield and vindicate injured innocence. It was decided by his majesty, that this arbitrament should determine the point at issue, and he accordingly ordered that a duel should take place between Macaire and the dog of the murdered Aubry.

We have already explained* that the lower animals were frequently, during the middle ages, subjected to trial, and the process conducted against them with all the parade of legal ceremonial employed in the case of their betters. Such an encounter, therefore, between the human and the canine creation, would not, in the fourteenth century, appear either specially extraordinary or unprecedented.

The ground for the combat was marked off in the Ile Notre Dame, then an open space. Macaire made his appearance armed with a large stick, whilst the dog had an empty cask, into which he could retreat and make his springs from. On being let loose, he immediately ran up to his adversary, attacked him first on one side and then on the other, avoiding as he did so the blows from Macaire's cudgel, and at last with a bound seized the latter by the throat. The murderer was thrown down, and then and there obliged to make confession of his crime, in the presence of the king and the whole court. This memorable combat was depicted over a chimney in the great hall of the château of Montargis. The story has been made the subject of a popular melodrama.

* Vol. i. p. 126–129.

## ELIZABETH CROMWELL:
### THE LADY-PROTECTRESS.

Elizabeth Cromwell, widow of the Protector, after surviving her illustrious husband fourteen years, died in the house of her son-in-law, Mr Claypole, at Norborough, in Northamptonshire, on 8th of October 1672. She was the daughter of Sir James Bourchier, a wealthy London merchant, who possessed a country-house and considerable landed estates at Felsted, in Essex. Granger, who would by no means be inclined to flatter Elizabeth, admits that she was a woman of enlarged understanding and elevated spirit. 'She was an excellent housewife,' he continues, 'as capable of descending to the kitchen with propriety, as she was of acting in her exalted station with dignity; certain it is, she acted a much more prudent part as Protectress than Henrietta did as queen. She educated her children with ability, and governed her family with address.' A glimpse of the Protectorate household is afforded by the Dutch ambassadors, who were entertained at Whitehall in 1654. After dinner, Cromwell led his guests to another room, then the Lady-Protectress, with other ladies, came to them, and they had 'music, and voices and a psalm.' Heath, in his *Flagellum*, 'the little, brown, lying book' stigmatised by Carlyle, acknowledges that Cromwell was a great lover of music, and entertained those that were most skilled in it, as well as the proficients in every other science. But this admission is modified by the royalist writer taking care to remind his readers that 'Saul also loved music.'

At a period when the vilest scurrility passed for loyalty and wit, we hear no evil report of Elizabeth Cromwell. No doubt her conduct was most carefully watched by her husband's enemies, and the slightest impropriety on her part would have speedily been blazoned abroad; yet no writer of the least authority throws reproach on her fair fame. It may be concluded, then, that though probably plain in person, and penurious in disposition, she was a virtuous, good wife and mother. In Cowley's play, *The Cutter of Coleman Street*, there is an allusion to her frugal character and want of beauty, where the Cutter, sneeringly describing his friend Worm, says: 'He would have been my Lady-Protectress' poet; he writ once a copy in praise of her beauty; but her highness gave nothing for it, but an old half-crown piece in gold, which she had hoarded up before these troubles, and that discouraged him from any further applications to court.'

It is a curious though unexplained fact, that we find none of her relatives taking part in the great civil war, nor even any of them employed under the Protectorate administration of public affairs. Nor has any indisputably genuine portrait of Elizabeth been handed down to us, so that the only representation of her features that we have, though universally considered to be a likeness, is found as the frontispiece of one of the most rare and curious of cookery-books, published in 1664, and entitled *The Court and the Kitchen of Elizabeth, commonly called Joan Cromwell, the Wife of the late Usurper, truly Described and Represented.* The accompanying illustration is a copy of this singular

THE LADY-PROTECTRESS.

frontispiece. The reader will notice a monkey depicted at one side of the engraving, and probably may wonder why it was placed there. In explanation, it must be said that the old engravers sometimes indulged in a dry kind of humour, of which this is an example. There is an old vulgar proverb that cannot well be literally repeated at the present day, but its signification is, that on the ground a monkey is passable enough, but the higher it climbs, the more its extreme ugliness becomes apparent. The animal, then, emblematises an ignorant upstart; and as the work is a satire as well as a cookery-book, the monkey is an apposite emblem of one who, according to the author's opinion, 'was a hundred times fitter for a barn than a palace.'

From the peculiar style and matter of this book, one is inclined to think that its author had been a master-cook under the royal *régime*, and lost both his office and perquisites by the altered state of affairs. Or he may have been a discarded servant of Elizabeth herself, for his various observations and anecdotes evince a thorough knowledge of the Protectorate household. Indeed this is the only value the book now possesses, and it must not be forgotten that the only fault or blame implied against Elizabeth by this angry satirist, is her 'sordid frugality and thrifty baseness.'

When the Protectress took possession of the palace of Whitehall, our culinary author tells us that: 'She employed a surveyor to make her some little labyrinths and trap-stairs, by which she might, at all times, unseen, pass to and fro, and come unawares upon her servants, and keep them vigilant in their places and honest in the discharge thereof. Several repairs were likewise made in her own apartments, and many small partitions up and down, as well above stairs as in the cellars and kitchens, her highness-ship not being yet accustomed to that roomy and august dwelling, and perhaps afraid of the vastness and silentness thereof. She could never endure any whispering, or be alone by herself in any of the chambers. Much ado she had, at first, to raise her mind and deportment to this sovereign grandeur, and very difficult it was for her to lay aside those impertinent meannesses of her private fortune; like the Bride Cat, metamorphosed into a comely virgin, that could not forbear catching at mice, she could not comport with her present condition, nor forget the common converse and affairs of life. She very providently kept cows in St James's Park, erected a dairy in Whitehall, with dairy-maids, and fell to the old trade of churning butter and making butter-milk. Next to this covey of milk-maids, she had another of spinsters and sewers, to the number of six, who sat most part of the day in "her privy-chamber sewing and stitching: they were all of them ministers' daughters."'

The dishes used at Cromwell's table, of which our author gives the receipts, sufficiently prove that the magnates of the Commonwealth were not insensible to the charms of good living. *Scotch collops of veal* was a very favourite dish, and *marrow puddings* were usually in demand at breakfast. The remains, after the household had dined, were alternately given to the poor of St Margaret's, Westminster, and St Martin's in the Fields, 'in a very orderly manner without babble or noise.' On great feast-days, Cromwell would call in the soldiers on guard, to eat the relics of his victuals. We are also told, but surely it must be a scullery scandal, that the time-honoured perquisite of kitchen-stuff was endangered, under the rule of the Protectress, she wishing to have it exchanged for candles. Nor was she less penurious with her husband's comforts; we are informed that: 'Upon Oliver's rupture with the Spaniards, the commodities of that country grew very scarce, and oranges and lemons were very rare and dear. One day, as the Protector was private at dinner, he called for an orange to a loin of veal, to which he used no other sauce, and urging the same command, was answered by his wife that oranges were oranges now, that crab [Seville] oranges would cost a groat, and, for her part, she never intended to give it.'

The reason assigned by the Protectress for 'her frugal inspection and parsimony, was the small allowance and mean pittance she had to defray the household expenses. Yet, she was continually receiving presents from the sectaries; such as Westphalia hams, neats' tongues, puncheons of French wines, runlets of sack, and all manner of preserves and comfits.'

It could not be expected that any cook of eminence would serve in such an establishment, and so this chronicler of the backstairs lets us know, that Cromwell's cook was a person of no note, named Starkey, who deservedly came to grief in a very simple manner. One day, when the lord mayor was closeted with the Protector on business of importance, this Starkey, forgetting his high office and professional dignity, took the lord mayor's sword-bearer into the cellar, treacherously intending to make that important official drunk and incapable. But Starkey overrated his own prowess, while underrating that of his guest; for the well-trained bacchanal of the city was little affected by the peculiar atmosphere of the cellar, while Starkey, becoming drunk and disorderly, was overheard by the Protector, and ignominiously discharged upon the spot.

The only state or expense indulged by the Protectress was: 'the keeping of a coach, the driver of which served her for caterer, for butler, for serving-man, and for gentleman-usher, when she was to appear in any public place.' And our author adds, that she had 'horses out of the army, and their stabling and livery in her husband's allotment out of the Mews, at the charge of the state; so that it was the most thrifty and unexpensive pleasure and divertisement, besides the finery and honour of it, that could be imagined. For it saved many a meal at home, when, upon pretence of business, her ladyship went abroad; and carrying some dainty provant for her own and her daughters' own repast, she spent whole days in short visits, and long walks in the air; so that she seemed to affect the Scythian fashion, who dwell in carts and wagons, and have no other habitations.'

The more we read of this scurrilous attack on a prudent mistress, a good wife, and mother, the more we are inclined to admire her true and simple character. It is pleasant to contemplate the Lady-Protectress leaving her palace and banquets of state, to take a long country drive, and a sort of picnic dinner with her daughters. Nor does our author fail, in some instances, to give her credit for good management; he says that: 'Her order of eating and meal-times was designed well to the decency and convenience of her service. For, first of all, at the ringing of a bell, dined the halberdiers, or men of the guard, with the inferior officers. Then the bell rung again, and the steward's table was set for the better sort of those that waited on their highnesses. Ten of whom were appointed to a table or a mess, one of which was chosen by themselves every week for a steward, and he gave the clerk of the kitchen a bill of fare, as was agreed generally every morning. To these ten men, and what friends should casually come to visit them, the value of ten shillings, in what flesh or fish soever they would have, with a bottle of sack, and two of claret was appointed. But, to prevent after-comers from expecting anything in the kitchen, there was a general rule that if any man thought his business would detain him beyond dinner-time, he was to give notice to the steward of his mess, who would set aside for him as much as his share came to, and leave it in the buttery.'

The utmost malignity of the royalists, then, could say no more against the Lady-Protectress, than that she was a thrifty housewife, giving her the appellation of Joan, the vulgar phrase for a female servant. And there is every reason to conclude that Elizabeth Cromwell was a wife well worthy of her illustrious partner.

# OCTOBER 9.

**St Dionysius, or Denis, bishop of Paris, and his Companions, martyrs, 272. St Domninus, martyr, 304. St Guislain, abbot, 681. St Lewis Bertrand, confessor, 1581.**

## ST DENIS.

This saint, properly named St Dionysius, has been sometimes stated as the first who introduced Christianity into France, but this is certainly erroneous, as the martyrdoms at Lyon and Vienne in the second century prove. St Denis was, however, of all the Roman missionaries in Gaul, the individual who, in preaching the doctrines of the Cross, penetrated furthest into the country, and fixed his seat at Paris, of which he became the first bishop. He is said to have been put to death during the persecution of Valerian, and a well-known legend is related regarding him, that, after suffering decapitation, he miraculously took up his head, carried it in his hand for the space of two miles, and then lay down and expired. The *bon mot* uttered regarding this ecclesiastical fable by a witty French lady of the last century, has become proverbial: 'La distance ne vaut rien; c'est le premier pas qui coûte.'

The bodies of St Denis and his companions are recorded to have been interred by a Christian lady named Catalla, not far from the place where they had been beheaded. A chapel was thereafter erected over their tomb, and in the fifth century a church, which was greatly resorted to by pilgrims. In the seventh century, King Dagobert founded on the same spot the famous abbey of St Denis, in which he himself and his successors on the French throne were interred. At the Revolution, this receptacle of the remains of royalty was sacrilegiously violated, and the contents of its tombs ignominiously scattered abroad, whilst the building itself was unroofed, and used for a time as a cattle-market. It was, however, restored with great splendour after the accession of the first Napoleon, and now attracts visitors as one of the most interesting monuments of ancient times, near the French capital.

The French have adopted St Denis as their patron saint, in the same manner as the English have chosen St George. The guardianship of the two countries is thus expressed in the chorus to the old ballad:

> 'St George he was for England,
> St Denis was for France.
> Singing, *Honi soit qui mal y pense.*'

---

*Born.*—Michael Cervantes de Saavedra, author of *Don Quixote*, 1547, *Alcala de Henares;* Jacob Augustus Thuanus (De Thou), historical writer, 1553, *Paris;* Bishop George Tomline, author of *Refutation of Calvinism*, 1753; Charles Comte d'Artois, afterwards Charles X., 1757, *Versailles.*

*Died.*—Pope Clement II., 1047; Gabriel Fallopius, eminent botanist, 1562, *Padua;* Claude Perrault, architect, 1688; Barbara Villiers, Duchess of Cleveland, mistress of Charles II., 1709, *Chiswick;* Dr James Johnson, medical and miscellaneous writer, 1845, *Brighton.*

## MARRIAGE OF LOUIS XII. AND THE PRINCESS MARY.

During the reign of Henry VII. of England, that able and crafty monarch had forced the Archduke Philip of Austria, on the occasion of the latter being driven by a storm on the English coast, to consent to a treaty of marriage between his son Charles, afterwards the celebrated Emperor Charles V., but then a child of six years old, and Henry's daughter, the Princess Mary. Such contracts were extremely common in ancient times, though they seem very frequently to have been entered upon merely for the purpose of securing some present advantage, or evading some present difficulty, and were eventually more generally broken than fulfilled. Henry VIII., several years afterwards, was nevertheless very indignant on ascertaining that Charles, so far from contemplating the completion of the engagement into which his father had entered for him, was on terms with Louis XII. of France for the hand of his second daughter, Renée. The wrath of the English king, however, was quite inoperative, and just at this conjuncture a match was suggested for his sister that soothed his offended dignity whilst it gratified his vanity. Louis XII. of France had, a few months before, lost his wife, Anne of Brittany, who had died without leaving any sons; and in the hope of obtaining male issue, the aged widower of fifty-three sought the hand of the beautiful young English princess of sixteen. Mary had formed an ardent attachment to Charles Brandon, Viscount Lisle, afterwards created Duke of Suffolk, one of the handsomest and most accomplished noblemen of his day; but the indulgence of such private feelings was quite out of the question, and it is not probable that even a murmur was ever uttered by her on the subject to her imperious brother. On 7th August 1514, a marriage-ceremony, by proxy, was celebrated at Greenwich between the princess and Louis XII., the Duke of Longueville representing his master. The French king became very impatient for the arrival of his bride, and wrote pressing letters to hurry her departure. At last the young queen with her attendants, among whom were the Duke of Suffolk and Anne Boleyn, afterwards so famous as the consort of her brother Henry, embarked at Dover, and landed safely in France in the beginning of October. On the 8th of that month, Mary made her public entrance into the town of Abbeville, where she was received with the greatest joy by her impatient husband, King Louis. The following day the marriage was duly solemnised between the parties themselves, and Mary was subsequently crowned with great pomp at the abbey of St Denis, and made her entry into Paris with great splendour. Her married life was by no means a period of unruffled felicity, as the king very ungallantly dismissed all his young wife's English friends and attendants almost immediately after the celebration of the ceremony. Fortunately for Mary, however, her season of probation was but short. Louis was sinking under a complication of infirmities, and at the rejoicings which accompanied his queen's triumphal entry into the capital, was so weak as to be obliged to be carried in a litter. Doubtless the prospect of his speedy demise, which took place on the ensuing New-Year's Day, had its influence in rendering Mary and the Duke of Suffolk, who remained in France as English ambassador, very discreet and circumspect in their conduct. But the former displayed little delicacy in availing herself of the recovery of her liberty, and in less than two months from Louis's death, Mary and the duke were privately wedded at Paris. In thus contracting a union without obtaining the permission of Henry VIII., both parties exposed themselves to the risk of his serious displeasure, which to Suffolk, as his own subject, might have proved fatal. But the dowager French queen and her English husband having crossed the Channel, and taken up their abode in their manor in Suffolk without venturing near the court, a reconciliation was in a short time effected; a consummation the accomplishment of which was greatly owing to the good offices of Cardinal Wolsey, who appears to have been a stanch friend of the young couple.

## CERVANTES.

The age which gave Shakspeare to England gave Cervantes to Spain. Cervantes was Shakspeare's senior by seventeen years, but their lives were otherwise contemporaneous; and nominally, though not actually,* on one day, the 23d of April 1616, both died.

The life of Miguel de Cervantes Saavedra was one of almost continuous hardship and privation. He was born in 1547 at Alcala de Henares, about twenty miles from Madrid. His parents had noble relations, but were poor, and concerning his youth little is positively known beyond what he incidentally tells us in his writings, as that he took great pleasure in attending the theatrical representations of Lope de Rueda, that he wrote verses when very young, and that he read everything within his reach, even as it would seem the torn scraps of paper he picked up in the streets. At Salamanca, he completed his education, and at the age of twenty-three he accompanied Monsignor Aquaviva to Rome, in the capacity of chamberlain. At Rome, in 1571, he entered the papal army as a common soldier, to serve against the Turks. Perhaps with oblique reference to himself, he observes, 'I have always noticed that none make better soldiers than those who are transplanted from the region of letters to the fields of war, and that never scholar became soldier, that was not a good and a brave one.' He was present at the great sea-fight of Lepanto, on the 7th October 1571, when the combined fleets of Spain, Venice, Genoa, Malta, and the pope, in 206 galleys, met the Turks in 250 galleys, and utterly defeated them, checking decisively Turkish intrusion into the west of Europe. Cervantes was in the thickest of the fight, and besides two wounds, received one which deprived him of the use of his left hand and arm during the rest of his life. In 1576, he received a command in a regiment for the Low Countries, but on his voyage thither, he was captured by an Algerine squadron, and he and his comrades were carried to Algiers, and sold as slaves. He served successively three cruel masters—a Greek and a Venetian, both renegadoes, and the dey himself. Many were his plots to escape, and severely did he suffer when detected. He had a grand project for

* See *Book of Days*, vol. i. p. 544.

the insurrection of all the Christian slaves in Algiers, who numbered full 25,000; and the dey declared that 'if he could but keep that lame Spaniard well guarded, he should consider his capital, his galleys, and his slaves safe.' Four times he expected death by impalement or at the stake, and once the hangman's rope was round his neck. After five years of cruel bondage, he was ransomed for the enormous sum of 500 gold ducats, which had been scraped together by friends and relatives in Spain.

Without means, Cervantes resumed the profession of soldier, and served in three expeditions against the Azores. In 1584, at the age of thirty-seven, he married a lady of good family, but with trifling or no fortune. To earn a livelihood, he commenced writing for the stage, and produced, he informs us, thirty dramas, which were all acted with considerable applause. It would appear, however, that the theatre did not pay, for, in 1588, we find him at Seville, then the great market for the vast wealth coming in from America, and as he calls it, 'the shelter for the poor and a refuge for the unfortunate.' At Seville, he acted as agent and money-collector, but did not thrive. In 1590, he made an ineffectual application to the king for an appointment in America, setting forth his adventures, services, and sufferings while a soldier in the Levant, and all the miseries of his life while a slave in Algiers. From Seville he moved to Valladolid, and tradition runs, that he was imprisoned there as a debtor or defaulter, and that, whilst in prison, he commenced writing *Don Quixote*. The tradition may be true, but it is based on no certain evidence. At anyrate, in poverty, at Valladolid, the first part of the immortal romance was written, and at Madrid it was printed and published in 1605.

The book at once attracted attention, and before a year was out a second edition was called for in Madrid, and two editions elsewhere. Successful authorship, however, did little to mend Cervantes's fortune. The Duke of Lerma, minister of Philip III., engaged him to write an account of the festivities and bull-fights with which Lord Howard, ambassador of James I., was received at Valladolid in 1605! Meanwhile, Cervantes went on writing, and produced a number of tales, *Novelas Exemplares*, and *A Journey to Parnassus*, a satire on the bad poets of his time, which made him many enemies, but which, next to *Don Quixote*, is thought his finest production. The second part of *Don Quixote* did not make its appearance till 1615. The author's end was then near. Some years before, he had joined the brotherhood of the Holy Sacrament, one of those religious associations which were then fashionable, and which included among its members Quevedo, Lope de Vega, and other men of letters. Subsequently, he assumed the habit of a Franciscan, and three weeks before his death, he formally entered the sacred order—

'Who, to be sure of Paradise,
Dying put on the weeds of Dominic,
Or in Franciscan think to pass disguised.'

He was buried in the convent of the nuns of the Trinity, Madrid, but, a few years afterwards, this convent was removed to another part of the city, and what became of his ashes is quite unknown. No monument was raised to his memory till 1835, when a bronze statue of him, larger than life, was cast at Rome and set up in Madrid. It may seem incredible, but it is nevertheless the fact, that this statue of Cervantes was the first ever erected in Spain to the honour of a man of letters.

Though Cervantes led a poor life, we shall err if we think of him as miserable. If any inference may be drawn from the tenor of his writings, his was that happy temper, which out of adversity derives not bitterness, but matter for reflection and humorous enjoyment. What to the majority of men would be simple affliction, would, we conceive, to the author of *Don Quixote* be softened in a halo of humorous suggestions. Humour is a rare sweetener of life, and, as Carlyle remarks: 'Cervantes is indeed the purest of all humorists; so gentle and genial, so full, yet so ethereal is his humour, and in such accordance with itself and his whole noble nature.' The world dealt hardly by him, but we shall search in vain for a sour or malignant passage from his pen.

---

# OCTOBER 10.

St Paulinus, archbishop of York, confessor, 644. St John of Bridlington, confessor, 1379. St Francis Borgia, confessor, 1572.

---

*Born.*—Pierre Nicole, logician, of Port Royal, 1625, *Chartres;* John, Duke of Argyll, statesman and commander, 1680; Henry Cavendish, eminent chemist, 1731, *Nice;* Benjamin West, painter, 1738, *Springfield, Pennsylvania;* Rev. Theobald Mathew, Irish apostle of temperance, 1790, *Thomastown, Tipperary.*

*Died.*—Dr John Blow, composer, 1708; Archbishop John Potter, author of *Grecian Antiquities*, 1747, *Croydon;* Dr William Wilkie, author of the *Epigoniad*, 1772, *St Andrews;* Henry Brooke, novelist, 1783, *Dublin;* Jeremiah James Oberlin, philologer, and archæological writer, 1806, *Strasburg;* Varnhagen Von Ense, eminent German writer, 1858, *Berlin.*

## TESTAMENT OF MASTER WILLIAM TRACIE.

'The x daye of October, in the xxii yere of the rayne of King Henry the VIII.' is the date of an interesting document connected with the Reformation in England, 'The Testament of Master Wylliam Tracie, Esquier.'

In the time that immediately preceded the Reformation, many intelligent persons imbibed the opinions of Wycliffe, without making any prominent exhibition of them. This latent degeneracy usually crept out in their last wills, or on their death-beds. The omission of a wish to have masses performed for their souls after death was considered a strong proof of heresy, and dealt with severely. As an instance of this, it is recorded, that the body of William Tracie was taken up in Henry's VIII.'s reign, and publicly burned, by order of the chancellor of Worcester, because the following passage was found in his will: 'And towchyn the wealth of my soule the fayth that I have taken and rehersed, is suffycient (as I suppose) without any other man's worke or workis. My grounde and my beliefe is, that ther is but one god and one mediatour betwene god and man, whych is Jesus Chryste. So that I do not except none in heaven or erthe to be my mediatour between me and god, but only Jesus Chryst, al other be but petitioners in recevinge of grace, but one able to give influence of grace. And therfore wyll I bestowe no part of my goodes for that intent that any man shoulde saye, or do, to healpe my soule, for therein I trust onely to the promyse of God, he that beleveth and is baptized shal be saved, and he that beleveth not shal be damned.'

## HENRY CAVENDISH.

Cavendish has been called the Newton of chemistry, but we must allow that the title is somewhat hyperbolical. Cavendish did not write much; a few papers in the *Philosophical Transactions*, between 1766 and 1809, comprise his publications, but these were composed with such exquisite care, that it has been said each sentence might endure microscopic examination. Sir Humphry Davy, in a lecture delivered shortly after the death of Cavendish, observes, 'his processes were all of a finished nature, perfected by the hand of a master; they required no correction; and though many of them were performed in the very infancy of chemical science, yet their accuracy and beauty have remained unimpaired amidst the progress of discovery.' When Cavendish began his researches, pneumatic chemistry hardly existed. Different gases were recognised, but they were considered to be mere modifications or admixtures of the common air. One by one, cautiously and firmly, he fixed truth after truth beyond dispute. His most notable achievement was his demonstration, in 1781, of the composition of water. Over this discovery there has been considerable controversy, some claiming priority for James Watt; but the fact seems to be, that both Cavendish and Watt reached the same conclusion about the same time by different routes.

The Honourable Henry Cavendish was born in 1731, at Nice, whither his mother, Lady Anne Cavendish, had repaired for the sake of her health, and she died ere her son was two years old. Cavendish was educated at a private school at Hackney, whence he proceeded to Cambridge. In early life his tastes were directed to scientific pursuits, to the ultimate exclusion of politics, and all else in which ordinary men take interest. He became an excellent mathematician, electrician, astronomer, meteorologist, geologist, and as a chemist shot far ahead of his contemporaries. Up to his fortieth year, his income was moderate, perhaps not more than £500 a year, but in 1773 an uncle died and left him an enormous fortune.

This accession of wealth did little to change his habits, which had become irrevocably established as those of a methodic recluse. His shyness, his love of solitude, and aversion to society, bordered on disease. To be looked at or addressed by a stranger seemed to give him positive pain, and when approached abruptly, he would dart away with a cry or ejaculation as if scared or hurt. At Sir Joseph Banks's soirees he would stand for a long time on the landing, afraid to open the door and face the company, nor would he open it till he heard some one ascending the stairs, and then to escape the terror behind faced that in front. At one of these parties Dr Ingenhousz recited the titles and qualifications of Cavendish in a pompous and formal manner, and introduced to him an Austrian gentleman. The Austrian thereon launched out into compliments, saying his chief reason for coming to London was to see and converse with one of the greatest ornaments of the age, and one of the most illustrious philosophers that ever existed. To this high-flown verbiage Cavendish answered not a word, but stood with his eyes cast down, abashed and in misery. At last spying an opening in the crowd, he flew to the door, nor did he stop till he reached his carriage, and drove directly home. Any attempt to draw him into conversation was almost certain to fail, and Dr Wollaston's recipe for treating with him usually answered best: 'The way to talk to Cavendish is never to look at him, but to talk as if it were into vacancy, and then it is not unlikely you may set him going.' Professor Playfair, who visited London in 1782, and was frequently at the meetings of the Royal Society Club, remarks: 'Mr Cavendish is a member of this meeting. He is of an awkward appearance, and has not much of the look of a man of rank. He speaks likewise with great difficulty and hesitation, and very seldom. But the gleams of genius break often through this unpromising exterior. He never speaks at all, but it is exceedingly to the purpose, and either brings some excellent information, or draws some important conclusion.'

Cavendish's town-house was near the British Museum, at the corner of Gower Street and Montague Place. Few visitors were admitted, and some who were permitted to cross its threshold reported that books and apparatus were its chief furniture. He collected a large library of scientific literature, and willing to have it made useful, but not to be troubled with readers and borrowers, he hired a house for its reception in Dean Street, Soho, and kept a librarian. When he wanted one of his own books, he went there as to a circulating library, and left a formal receipt for whatever he took away. His favourite residence was a beautiful villa at Clapham, nearly the whole of which was occupied as workshops. The upper rooms were an observatory; the drawing-room was a laboratory; and in an ante-room was a forge. On the lawn was a wooden stage, from which access could be had to a large tree, to the top of which Cavendish, in the course of his astronomical, meteorological, and electrical experiments, occasionally ascended. For beauty he seemed quite indifferent. His apparatus, always exact and accurate so far as essential, was constructed of the cheapest material, and without any regard for symmetry.

His few guests were treated on all occasions to the same fare—a leg of mutton, and nothing else. Four scientific men were to dine with him one day, and when his housekeeper came to ask him what was to be got for dinner, he said a leg of mutton. 'Sir,' said she, 'that will not be enough for five.' 'Well, then, get two,' was his reply. His heir, Lord George Cavendish, visited him once a year, and was allowed an audience of but half-an-hour. His great income was allowed to accumulate without attention. The bankers where he kept his account found they had a balance of £80,000 on hand, and sent a messenger to confer with him regarding it. The messenger was announced, and

Cavendish, in great agitation, desired him to be sent up, and as he entered the room, cried: 'What do you come here for? What do you want with me?'

'Sir, I thought it proper to wait upon you, as we have a very large balance in hand of yours, and we wish your orders respecting it.'

'If it is any trouble to you, I will take it out of your hands. Do not come here to plague me!'

'Not the least trouble to us, sir, not the least; but we thought you might like some of it to be invested.'

'Well, well. What do you want to do?'

'Perhaps you would like £40,000 invested.'

'Do so, do so! and don't come here to trouble me, or I'll remove it.'

If men were a trouble to him, women were his abhorrence. With his housekeeper he generally communicated by notes deposited on the hall-table. He would never see a female servant, and if an unlucky maid shewed herself, she was instantly dismissed. To prevent inevitable encounters, it is said he had a second staircase erected in his Clapham villa. In all his habits he was punctiliously regular, even to hanging his hat on one peg. From an unvarying walk he was, however, driven by being gazed at. Two ladies led a gentleman on his track, in order that he might obtain a sight of the philosopher. As he was getting over a stile, he saw to his horror that he was watched, and he never appeared in that path again. That he was not quite merciless to the sex, was proved by his saving a lady from the pursuit of a mad cow. The fashion of his dress he never changed, and his appearance was consequently odd and antique, and provoked the attention he so much disliked. The villagers beheld him with awe, and thought him a wizard. His complexion was fair, his temperament nervous, and his voice squeaking. Of course, he would never allow his portrait to be taken, and the only memorial we have of his appearance is a hasty and surreptitious sketch. He died on the 24th of February 1810, aged upwards of seventy-eight. At the time of his death, he was the largest holder of bank-stock in England. He owned £1,157,000 in different public funds, the value of which was estimated at £700,000, and had besides freehold property of £8000 a year, and canal and other personal property. £50,000 lay to his credit at the bankers.

Dr George Wilson, the biographer of Cavendish, sums up his character in saying: 'There was nothing earnest, enthusiastic, heroic, or chivalrous in the nature of Cavendish, and as little was there anything mean, grovelling, or ignoble. He was almost passionless. All that needed for its apprehension more than pure intellect, or required the exercise of fancy, imagination, affection, or faith, was distasteful to Cavendish. An intellectual head thinking, a pair of wonderful acute eyes observing, and a pair of very skilful hands experimenting or recording, are all that I realise in reading his memorials.'

## FATHER MATHEW.

Like Scotland, the island of Ireland has been frequently twitted with the propensity of her children to an over-indulgence in strong liquors, and it cannot be denied that the vice of intoxication has, in past times at least, formed a repulsive characteristic of both countries. With such material to work upon, it will be readily admitted that any one endeavouring to act the part of a reformer of morals, would find an endeavour to convert the masses to sobriety a truly Herculean task. Yet in Ireland such an attempt was made, and the energy and devotedness of one man accomplished what was, temporarily at least, a great moral revolution.

The Rev. Theobald Mathew, who thus proved so successful an apostle of the temperance cause, was related to the family of the Earls of Llandaff, of which his father was an illegitimate scion. Having been ordained a priest in 1814, he was appointed to a missionary charge in Cork, where his zeal and earnestness quickly secured him an immense influence both among rich and poor. Through his means, a benevolent association for visiting the sick and destitute was established in that city, on the model of the societies of St Vincent de Paul. While thus engaged in an active career of usefulness, a temperance society was formed in Cork about 1838, and Father Mathew became its president. The heroic missionary threw himself with all the ardour of his nature into the new movement, and so successful were his efforts, that in a few months he obtained 150,000 converts in Cork alone to temperance principles. Determined to diffuse the benefits of the good cause still further, he commenced a progress through the west of Ireland, in which he was everywhere followed by crowds, who pressed forward to take the vow of total abstinence. The greater part of the island was thus traversed by Father Mathew, and he also visited London and other towns in England. Much of the success that attended his peregrinations is doubtless to be ascribed to that mysterious sympathetic influence by which whole communities have often been swayed. Such was the preaching of Peter the Hermit in the middle ages, and similar effects have recently been witnessed in the 'revival' movement in Britain and America. It is, however, greatly to Father Mathew's credit, that the habitually impulsive temperament of the Irish was thus acted upon for the purest and most beneficial of purposes—their reclamation from a vice which had hitherto constituted with them a national opprobrium. It must also not be forgotten that the good priest was himself a serious sufferer by the results of his philanthropic exertions. A distillery in the south of Ireland, belonging to his family, and from which he himself derived a large income, was shut up in consequence of the disuse of whisky among the lower orders, occasioned by his preaching. His services to the cause of religion and morality were at last recognised by the state, and a pension of £300 a year granted him from the civil list. Notwithstanding this, the expenses attending his benevolent exertions kept him always poor, and even burdened him with a debt, to relieve him from which a subscription was raised. For some years previous to his death, which took place on December 8, 1856, he was incapacitated by ill health from continuing his labours. As a true benefactor of humanity, Father Mathew must ever be regarded as one of the most shining ornaments of the Roman Catholic Church.

# OCTOBER 11.

Saints Tarachus, Probus, and Andronicus, martyrs, 304. St Canicus or Kenny, abbot in Ireland, 599. St Ethelburge or Edilburge, virgin and abbess, about 664. St Gummar or Gomer, confessor, 774.

*Born.*—Erasmus Reinhold, astronomer, 1511, *Salfeldt, Thuringia;* Dr Samuel Clarke, theological writer (*The Being and Attributes of God*), 1675, *Norwich;* James Barry, historical painter, 1741, *Cork;* Philip Astley, founder of Astley's amphitheatre, 1742, *Newcastle-under-Lyne.*

*Died.*—Louis V. emperor of Germany, 1347; Ulrich Zwingli, Swiss reformer, killed at Cappel, 1531; Sir Thomas Wyatt, the Elder, poet and statesman, 1542, *Sherborne;* Thomas Stackhouse, biblical writer, 1752, *Benham, Berkshire;* Anne, Countess of Macclesfield, mother of the poet Savage, 1753, *London;* Samuel Wesley, musician, 1837.

## DEATH OF ZWINGLI.

Inferior to Luther and Calvin in point of genius and mental vigour, Ulrich Zwingli, or as his name is Latinised, Zuinglius, the great Swiss reformer, is better fitted as a man to command our love and esteem. The purity and amiableness of his character are universally admitted, whilst the honour unquestionably belongs to him of being the earliest of the ecclesiastical reformers of the sixteenth century. In his death, too, he may be regarded as a martyr to his principles, having accompanied, at the desire of the council of Zurich, a body of troops, sent during a civil war between the Catholic and Protestant cantons, to the relief of their countrymen at Cappel, where an action ensued, and the devoted pastor was struck down in the act of encouraging the soldiers. The victory turned against the Protestants, and Zwingli, left dying on the battle-field, was run through by the sword of a Catholic soldier, who was ignorant of his quality, but discovered him to be a heretic from his declining, by signs, to avail himself of the offer of a confessor, and recommend his soul to the Virgin. On his body being found and recognised next day, a group of spectators assembled to gaze on the remains of the renowned pastor of Zurich. One of these who had been his colleague in his days of Catholicism, looked long and earnestly on the lifeless face, and then exclaimed: 'Whatever may have been thy faith, I am sure thou wast always sincere, and that thou lovedst thy country. May God take thy soul to his mercy!' The fanatical fury of a bigoted mob was, however, incapable of any such generous appreciation, and a proposal to burn the heretical corpse was received with acclamations, and forthwith carried into execution.

When Zwingli thus met an untimely death, he had only attained the age of forty-seven. As an ecclesiastic of the Roman Catholic Church, he had manifested from the first a decided tendency to the Reformed religion, by inculcating the doctrines of primitive Christianity rather than medieval dogmas, and by referring to the Scriptures as the only authoritative tribunal in religious matters. While a preacher also in the celebrated abbey of Einsiedeln, he discountenanced greatly the superstitious notions which attracted so large a concourse of pilgrims to that celebrated shrine, and procured an erasure of the inscription over the abbey-gate, 'Here plenary remission of all sins is obtained.' His convictions as to the errors of the established faith gained daily ground, and made rapid progress after his transference from Einsiedeln to the post of preacher in the cathedral of Zurich. Here he felt himself called upon, like Luther in a similar position, to denounce the shameless traffic in indulgences, which Samson, a Franciscan friar, was endeavouring to carry on in Zurich, under the authority of Pope Leo X. The papal emissary was obliged to quit the city, and a rebellion against the authority of the holy see having thus been inaugurated, Zwingli was not long in proceeding to shake off its authority altogether. In a work which he published, *On the Observation of Lent*, he disputed with great freedom the obligation of observing particular days, and found himself arraigned in consequence, at the instance of the Bishop of Constance, before the great council of Zurich, to answer the charges of heresy and innovation. Converted, however, already by the preaching of Zwingli to a participation in his sentiments, the decision of the council was a triumphant vindication of the accused, and what may be regarded as the first sanction by state authority of the principles of the Reformation in Switzerland. Shortly afterwards the images were removed from the churches, the celebration of mass abolished, and the practice of marriage introduced among the clergy, Zwingli himself setting an example by wedding, at the age of forty, the widow of an eminent magistrate, by whom he had one son.

As a reformer, Zwingli is certainly entitled to the credit of originality as well as precedence. His views seem to have been matured without any assistance from and co-operation with others, though on after-comparison his formula of faith agreed in all essentials with that of Luther, and was nearly identical with that of Calvin. With the first of these reformers, he maintained a strenuous contest on the subject of consubstantiation, or the presence of the body and blood of Christ in the sacramental elements; but on the occasion of a discussion between them at Marburg, in 1529, the proceedings terminated by the two champions signing their mutual assent to fourteen articles of faith, and expressing a hope that their difference regarding the real presence would not interrupt their harmony, as coadjutors in the same cause. With regard to Calvin, it ought to be observed that his influence has, in reality, been very slight in Switzerland, where the reformed Helvetic church was founded by Zwingli several years before the doctrines of Calvin had been heard of. There is, nevertheless, as already remarked, a close similarity between their tenets, though the characteristic doctrine of predestination is less decidedly expressed by Zwingli.

The amiability of Zwingli's character was no less conspicuous than its intrepidity and uprightness. In many points, he seems to have been in advance of his age, as we find him remonstrating in the assembly of the canton of Schweitz, against that practice which, down to the present day, has formed so unfavourable a trait of the Swiss people—their readiness to hire themselves as mercenary troops to the service of any foreign despot. In this object he so far succeeded, that a law was passed by the assembly of the canton forbidding all foreign alliances and subsidies for the space of twenty-five years. The liberality and large-heartedness of his religious views were remarkable for the sixteenth century. He maintained that no person ought to be molested for his opinions, and ventured even to express a belief in relation to the salvation of heathens, that 'all good men who have fulfilled the laws engraven on their consciences, whatever age or country they may have lived in, will partake of eternal felicity.' One special position that the ecclesiastical must in all respects be subordinated to the secular power, has been made an object of reproach to him, both by Catholics and Protestants. This sentiment contributed perhaps indirectly to his fate, as it was in obedience to the orders of the Zurich magistrates, that he met death on the field of battle, a circumstance with which several of his enemies have thought fit to stigmatise his memory.

---

## SPECTRE-DOGS.

Neither Brand in his *Popular Antiquities*, nor Sir Walter Scott in his *Witchcraft and Demonology*, mentions spectre-dogs as a peculiar class of apparitions, yet they seem to occupy a distinct branch of English mythology. They are supposed to exist in one form or another in almost every county, and few kinds of superstition have more strongly influenced the credulous mind. To have the 'black dog on the back' has become a general phrase, though perhaps few who use it have an idea of its origin. The following anecdotes about spectre-dogs will illustrate this phrase, and shew how generally this branch of superstition is received.

According to popular psychology, the subject may be divided into three parts: 1. Black dogs, which are really fiends that have assumed the form of dogs; 2. The spirits of evil persons, who, as part of their punishment, have been transformed into the appearance of dogs; 3. Evil spirits, that to mimic the sports of men, or to hunt their souls, have assumed the form and habits of hounds. We will begin with the black-dog apparition.

In almost every county there is a popular belief in a spectral dog, which, although slightly varying in appearance in different parts, always bears the same general characteristics. It is described as large, shaggy, and black, with long ears and tail. It does not belong to any species of living dogs, but is severally said to resemble a hound, a setter, a terrier, or a shepherd-dog, though often larger than a Newfoundland. It bears different names, but is always alike supposed to be an evil spirit, haunting places where evil deeds have been done, or where some calamity may be expected. In the Isle of Man, it is called the *Mauthe Doog*, and, according to tradition, was accustomed to haunt Peel Castle, where it was seen in every room, but especially in the guard-chamber. Here, as soon as candles were lighted, it used to go and lie down before the fire, in presence of the soldiers, who became so accustomed to its appearance, that they lost much of the awe which they first felt at its presence. But knowing its malicious character, they never ventured to molest it, till one of them, in a drunken fit, swore that 'he would try whether it were dog or devil!' He made his trial, and was instantly sobered, but rendered speechless. He lived only three days afterwards, and then 'died in agonies more than is common in a natural death.' 'I heard this attested,' says Mr Waldron, 'by several, but especially by an old soldier, who assured me he had seen it oftener than he had then hairs on his head.' Sir Walter Scott, in his *Lay of the Last Minstrel*, thus alludes to this tradition:

> 'For he was speechless, ghastly, wan,
> Like him, of whom the story ran,
> Who spoke the spectre-hound in Man.'

A similar story is related of a man who lived at a village near Aylesbury, in Buckinghamshire. This man was accustomed to go every morning and night to milk his cows in a field, which was some distance from the village. To shorten his walk, he often crossed over a neighbour's field, and passed through a gap in the hedge; but one night, on approaching the gap, he found it occupied by a large, black, fierce-looking dog. He paused to examine the animal, and as he looked at him, his fiery eyes grew larger and fiercer, and he had altogether such a fiend-like and 'unkid' appearance, that he doubted whether he were 'a dog or the bad spirit.' Whichever he was, he thought he would be no pleasant antagonist to encounter. So he turned aside, and passed through a gate at the end of the field. Night after night, he found the same dog in the gap, and turned aside in the same manner. One night, having fallen in with a companion, he returned homeward with him across his neighbour's field, being determined, if he found the dog in the gap, to make an attack upon him, and drive him away. On reaching the gap, there stood the dog looking even fiercer and bigger than ever. But the milkman, wishing to appear valiant before his companion, put down his milk-pails, which were suspended from a yoke across his shoulders, and attempting to speak very bravely, though trembling all over, he exclaimed: 'Now, you black fiend, I'll try what ye're made of!' He raised his yoke in both his hands, and struck at the dog with all his might. The dog vanished, and the milkman fell senseless to the ground. He was carried home alive, but remained speechless and paralytic to the end of his days.

A certain spot near the writer's residence is said to be haunted at midnight by 'the black dog.' Once, at the awful hour of midnight, he happened to pass the dreaded spot, and, sure enough, he met the black-dog apparition. It was a light summer's night, and as he approached the awful apparition, he soon saw it was far too substantial 'to try what it was made of.' He knew it to be a fine black dog, half Newfoundland and retriever, belonging to a gamekeeper, who, doubtless, was near at hand watching his master's preserves. It is no uncommon manœuvre for poachers and such characters to give certain spots the reputation of being haunted.

In the adjoining county of Hertford, the same superstition prevails, and the black-dog apparition is still a dreaded bogie. Within the parish of Tring, but about three miles from the town, a poor old woman was, in 1751, drowned for suspected witchcraft. A chimney-sweep, who was the principal perpetrator of this atrocious deed, was hanged and gibbeted near the place where the murder was effected. While the gibbet stood, and long after it had disappeared, the spot was haunted by a black dog. The writer was told by the village schoolmaster, who had been 'abroad,' that he himself had seen this diabolical dog. 'I was returning home,' said he, 'late at night in a gig with the person who was driving. When we came near the spot, where a portion of the gibbet had lately stood, we saw on the bank of the roadside, along which a ditch or narrow brook runs, a flame of fire as large as a man's hat. 'What's that?' I exclaimed. 'Hush!' said my companion all in a tremble; and suddenly pulling in his horse, made a dead stop. I then saw an immense black dog lying on the road just in front of our horse, which also appeared trembling with fright. The dog was the strangest looking creature I ever beheld. He was as big as a Newfoundland, but very gaunt, shaggy, with long ears and tail, eyes like balls of fire, and large long teeth, for he opened his mouth and seemed to grin at us. He looked more like a fiend than a dog, and I trembled as much as my companion. In a few minutes the dog disappeared, seeming to vanish like a shadow, or to sink into the earth, and we drove on over the spot where he had lain.' The same canine apparition is occasionally still witnessed at the same place or near it.

In Norfolk, and in some parts of Cambridgeshire, the same kind of apparition is well-known to the peasantry by the name of 'Shuck,' the provincial word for shag. Here he is said chiefly to haunt churchyards, but other lonesome places are not secure from his visitations. Thus a dreary lane, in the parish of Overstrand, is called, from his frequent visits there, Shuck's Lane. The spot on which he has been seen, if examined soon after his disappearance, is found to be scorched, and strongly impregnated with the smell of brimstone!

In some districts of the county of Lancaster, this spectre-dog bears the names of 'Trash' and 'Skriker.' Its general appearance is the same as in other parts, but its habits, and the object of its visits, seem somewhat different. It does not haunt particular spots, but appears to certain persons to warn them of the speedy death of some relation or intimate friend. Occasionally, however, it gives its warning, not by its appearance, but only by uttering a peculiar screech, from whence it is called, in the local dialect, Skriker. Its name, Trash, is applied to it, because the noise made by its feet is supposed to resemble that of a person walking with heavy shoes along a miry, sloppy road. If followed, it retreats, but always with its eyes fronting the pursuer, and either sinks into the earth with a frightful shriek, or, if the pursuer averts his eyes from it for a moment, it disappears he knows not how. If struck at with a stick or weapon, it keeps its ground, but, to the horror of the striker, his weapon passes as harmlessly through it as if it were a mere shadow.*

Lyme-Regis, in Dorsetshire, has a famous story about one of these canine apparitions. About a mile from the town stands a farmhouse, which once formed part of an old mansion that was demolished in the parliamentary wars, except the small portion still existing. The sitting-room now used by the farmer, and also by his predecessors for a century or two, retains the large old-fashioned fireplace, with a fixed seat on each side under the capacious chimney. Many years ago, when the then master of the house, as his custom was after the daily toils were over, used to settle himself on one of these snug seats in the chimney-corner, a large black dog as regularly took possession of the opposite one. This dog in all essentials resembled the spectre-dog already described. For many nights, weeks, and months, this mysterious visitor, sitting *vis à vis* to the farmer, cast a gloom over his evening enjoyment. At length, as he received no harm from his companion, and became accustomed to his appearance, he began to look on him as one of the family circle. His neighbours, however, often advised him to drive away the fiend-like intruder; but the farmer, not relishing a contest with him, jestingly replied: 'Why should I? He costs me nothing—he eats nothing, he drinks nothing, he interferes with no one. He is the quietest and frugalest creature in the house.'

One night, however, the farmer, having been drinking too freely with a neighbour, and excited by his taunts about the black dog to an unusual degree of irritation, was determined his courage should no more be called in question. Returning home in a rage, he no sooner saw the dog on his usual seat, than, seizing the poker, he rushed with it towards his mysterious companion. The dog, perceiving his intention, sprang from its seat, and ran up stairs, followed by the infuriated farmer. The dog fled into an attic at the top of the house, and just as the farmer entered the same room, he saw it spring from the floor, and disappear through the ceiling. Enraged at being thus foiled, he struck with the poker the ceiling where the dog had passed through, and down fell a small old-fashioned box, which, on being opened, was found to contain a large sum in gold and silver coins of Charles I.'s reign. The dog was never more seen within doors, but to the present day continues at midnight to haunt a lane which leads to this house, and which has long borne the name of 'Dog Lane,' while a small inn by the roadside still invites the passing stranger by the ominous sign of 'the Black Dog,' portrayed in all his spectral frightfulness. So late as the year 1856, a respectable intelligent woman told the writer that she herself had seen the dog-ghost. 'As I was returning to Lyme,' said she, 'one night with my husband down Dog Lane, as we reached about the middle of it, I saw an animal about the size of a dog meeting us. "What's that?" I said to my husband. "What?" said he, "I see nothing." I was so frightened I could say no more then, for the animal was within two or three yards of us, and had become as large as a young calf, but had the appearance of a black shaggy dog with fiery eyes, just like the description I had heard of the "black dog." He passed close by me, and made the air cold and dank as he passed along. Though I was afraid to speak, I could not help turning round to look after him, and I saw him growing bigger and bigger as he went along, till he was as high as the trees by the roadside, and then seeming to swell into a large cloud, he vanished in the air. As soon as I could speak, I asked my husband to look at his watch, and it was then five minutes past twelve. My husband said he saw nothing but a vapour or fog coming up from the sea.' A case of this kind shews how even a sensible person may become the victim of self-delusion; for in all practical matters this woman was remarkably sober-minded, intelligent, and judicious; and well educated for a person of her calling—that of sick-nurse, the duties of which she discharged in the

* *Notes and Queries.*

writer's house for several weeks to his fullest satisfaction, shewing no symptoms of nervousness or timidity.

The foregoing examples belong to the class of fiends who have assumed the appearance of dogs. We will now give a few instances of human spirits that, as a punishment, have been transformed into similar apparitions.

Lady Howard, a Devonshire notable of the time of James I., was remarkable for her beauty, her wealth, her talents, and accomplishments. But she had many bad qualities. Amongst others, she was unnaturally cruel to her only daughter, and had a sad knack of getting rid of her husbands, having been married no less than four times. At last she died herself, and, for her misdemeanours while living, her spirit was transformed into a hound, and compelled to run every night, between midnight and cock-crowing, from the gateway of Fitz-ford, her former residence, to Oakhampton Park, and bring back to the place from whence she started, a single blade of grass in her mouth; and this penance she is doomed to continue till every blade of grass is removed from the park, which she will not be able to effect till the end of the world. How these particulars were communicated to our living fellow-mortals we are not informed, and we dare not venture a conjecture. Our rustic psychologists have been rather more explicit in the following story:

There once lived in the hamlet of Dean Combe, Devon, a weaver of great fame and skill. After long prosperity he died and was buried. But the next day he appeared sitting at the loom in his chamber, working as diligently as when he was alive. His sons applied to the vicar, who accordingly went to the foot of the stairs, and heard the noise of the weaver's shuttle in the room above. 'Knowles,' he cried, 'come down; this is no place for thee.' 'I will,' replied the weaver, 'as soon as I have worked out my quill' (the quill is the shuttle full of wool). 'Nay,' said the vicar, 'thou hast been long enough at thy work; come down at once.' So when the spirit came down, the vicar took a handful of earth from the churchyard, and threw it in its face. And in a moment it became a black hound. 'Follow me,' said the vicar, and it followed him to the gate of the wood. And when they came there, 'it seemed as if all the trees in the wood were coming together, so great was the wind.' Then the vicar took a nutshell with a hole in it, and led the hound to the pool below the water-fall. 'Take this shell,' said he, 'and when thou shalt have dipped out the pool with it, thou mayest rest—not before!' And at mid-day and at midnight, the hound may still be seen at its work.* It is difficult to understand why the industrious weaver was consigned to such a hopeless doom. Many spectral dogs, believed to be the souls of wicked persons, are said to haunt the sides of rivers and pools, and sometimes their yelping is so dreadful, that all who hear them lose their senses.†

Besides such apparitions of solitary dogs, whole packs of spectral hounds are said to be occasionally heard and seen in full cry in various parts of England and Wales, but chiefly in mountainous districts. They are everywhere described much in the same way, but with different names. In the north, they are called 'Gabriel's Hounds;' in Devon, the 'Wisk,' 'Yesk,' or 'Heath Hounds;' in Wales, 'Cron Annwn,' or 'Cwn Wybir;' and in Cornwall, the 'Devil and his Dandy-dogs.' But few have ever imagined that they have seen these hounds, though popular superstition has described them as black, with fiery eyes and teeth, and sprinkled all over with blood. Generally, they are only heard, and seem to be passing swiftly along in the air, as if in hot pursuit of their prey; and, though not very high up, yet they cannot be seen, because they generally choose cloudy nights. Their yelping is said to be sometimes as loud as the note of a blood-hound, but sharper and more terrific. Why they have anywhere received the name of Gabriel's hounds, appears unaccountable, for they are always supposed to be evil spirits hunting the souls of the dead, or, by their diabolical yelping, to betoken the speedy death of some person. Thus, Mr Holland, of Sheffield, describes in the following sonnet the superstition as held in Yorkshire—

'Oft have I heard my honoured mother say
How she hath listened to the Gabriel Hounds;
Those strange unearthly and mysterious sounds
Which on the ear through murkiest darkness fell;
And how, entranced by superstitious spell,
The trembling villager not seldom heard,
In the quaint notes of the nocturnal bird
Of death premonished, some sick neighbour's knell.
I, too, remember once, at midnight dark,
How these sky-yelpers startled me, and stirred
My fancy so, I could have then averred
A mimic pack of beagles low did bark!
Nor wondered I that rustic fear should trace
A spectral huntsman doomed to that long moonless chase.'

Wordsworth, alluding to another form of this superstition, similar to the German story of the Wild Huntsman, thus writes:

'He oftentimes will start,
For, overhead, are sweeping Gabriel's Hounds,
Doomed, with their impious lord, the flying hart
To chase for ever through aërial grounds.'

Many wild and amusing stories are told respecting these aërial hounds; especially in the secluded districts of Devon and Cornwall. The following is a specimen. A herdsman was journeying homeward across the moors of Cornwall one windy night, when he heard at a distance the baying of hounds, which he was not long in recognising to be the dismal yelp of the Devil's Dandy-dogs. He was three or four miles distant from his home; and, much terrified, he hurried onward as fast as the treacherous nature of the soil and uncertainty of the path would allow; but the melancholy yelping of the hounds and the fiendish shout of the hunter came nearer and nearer. After a long run, they appeared so close upon him, that he could not help turning round to look at them. He was horror-struck, for he could distinctly see the hunter and his dogs. The huntsman was terrible to behold. He was black, had large fiery eyes, horns, a tail, and carried in his clawy-hand a long hunting-pole. The dogs, a numerous pack, blackened the ground as far as it could be seen; each snorting fire, and yelping in the most frightful tone. What was the poor rustic to do? No

* *Notes and Queries*, vol. ii. 515.
† Ibid. vol. i. 295.

cottage was near; no rock, no tree to shelter him —nothing remained but to abandon himself to the fury of these hell-hounds. Suddenly, a happy thought flashed into his mind. He had been told that no evil spirit can resist the power of prayer. He fell on his knees, and at the first holy words he uttered, the hounds stood still, but yelped more dismally than ever; and the huntsman shouted, 'Bo Shrove!' which 'means,' says the narrator, 'in the old language, *The boy prays!*' The black huntsman then drew off his dandy-dogs, and the poor herdsman hastened home as fast as his trembling frame permitted.*

This, and similar stories, strikingly illustrate the creative power of the imagination when excited by fear. The herdsman's vision existed only in his own mind, induced by the terrifying sound, which, although adapted by his imagination to his previous conceptions of the dandy-dogs, was a reality. For it has been fully and satisfactorily ascertained that the goblin-hounds, which have originated such fanciful legends in almost every county, are merely flocks of wild-geese, or other large migratory birds.†

## HARRY ROWE.

In the earlier half of October 1800, there died in the poor-house of York one Harry Rowe, a well-known character in his locality, who made a good deal of noise in the world while he lived, and caused considerable speculation among Shakspearian commentators after his death. For Harry had many years held the distinguished post of trumpet-major to the high-sheriffs of Yorkshire, and was also the reputed author of an ably-commentated edition of *Macbeth*, and a musical farce, entitled *No Cure, no Pay*, a trenchant satire on quack-doctors, and the shameful facility with which medical diplomas and degrees were then obtained by illiterate adventurers. Rowe was born at York in 1726. He served as trumpeter, in the Duke of Kingston's regiment of light horse, at the battle of Culloden; and, after he retired from the army, attended, in the same capacity, the sheriffs and judges at York assizes for nearly half a century. Rowe was also the master of a puppet-show, and, for many successive years, he opened his little theatre at York during the winter months, making a regular circuit to various parts of the country in the summer season. By these means he long supported his poor and aged parents, never allowing them to receive any other aid than that amply provided for them by his own exertions. In his own case he was less fortunate. When overtaken by age and poverty, Rowe was forced to seek an asylum in the poor-house, where he died.

HARRY ROWE.

The puppet-showman had a rough, ready, caustic wit, with which he interlarded the speeches of his wooden comedians, to the great delight of the audience. And so, many actually thought that the edition of *Macbeth*, bearing Rowe's name on the title-page, was really written by him, to the great mystification of later commentators. In the preface, Harry is made to say: 'I am the master of a puppet-show, and as, from the nature of my employment, I am obliged to have a few stock-plays ready for representation whenever I am accidentally visited by a select party of ladies and gentlemen, I have added the tragedy of *Macbeth* to my green-room collection. The alterations that I have made in this play are warranted, from a careful perusal of a very old manuscript in the possession of my prompter, one of whose ancestors, by the mother's side, was rush-spreader and candle-snuffer at the Globe playhouse, as appears from the following memorandum on a blank-page of the manuscript: "This day, March the fourth, received the sum of seven shillings and fourpence, for six bundles of rushes, and two pair of candle-snuffers."'

The work cleverly satirises Johnson's, Steevens's, and Malone's editions of Shakspeare, and was written, as well as *No Cure, no Pay*, by Dr Andrew Hunter of York, a skilful physician and able man of letters. The profits were given to Rowe, to support him in a long and painful illness; and, when unable to manage his wooden company, the old trumpet-major sold the works of the charitable but satirical physician, in all parts of the city of York, as his own composition.

# OCTOBER 12.

**St Wilfrid, bishop of York, confessor, 709.**

*Born.*—Edward VI. of England, 1537, *Hampton Court* Pedro I., emperor of Brazil, 1798; Hugh Miller, geologist, 1802, *Cromarty*.

*Died.*—Pope Honorius I., 638; Pope Boniface VIII., 1303; Maximilian II., emperor of Germany, 1576, *Ratisbon;* Duke of Palmella, Portuguese statesman, 1850, *Lisbon;* Robert Stephenson, engineer, 1859, *London.*

* *Notes and Queries.* † Ibid. vol. v 596.

## DISCOVERY OF AMERICA.

On 12th October 1492, Columbus with his followers landed at last on Watling's Island, one of the Bahama Isles, and planted there the cross in token of gratitude to the Divine mercy, which, after guiding him safely through a perilous voyage, had at last, in the discovery of a western world, crowned with success the darling aspiration of his life. Land had already been descried on the previous evening, but it was not till the ensuing morning that the intrepid admiral beheld the flat and densely-wooded shores gleaming beneath the rays of an autumn sun, and by actually setting his foot on them, realised the fulfilment of his hopes.

It is now well known that although Columbus was unquestionably the first to proclaim to the world at large the existence of a new and vast region in the direction of the setting sun, he cannot literally be said to have been the first European discoverer of America. The ancient Scandinavians or Norsemen, so renowned for their maritime enterprise, had, at the commencement of the 11th century, not only settled colonies in Greenland, but explored the whole east coast of America as far south as lat. 41° 30′ N., and there, near New Bedford, in the state of Massachusetts, they planted a colony. An intercourse by way of Greenland and Iceland subsisted between this settlement and Norway down to the fourteenth century. There is also satisfactory evidence for believing, that in the twelfth century the celebrated Welsh prince, Madoc, having sailed from his native country with a small fleet, landed and founded a colony on the coast of Virginia. But to Columbus still belongs the merit of having philosophically reasoned out the existence of a New World, and by practically ascertaining the truth of his propositions, of inaugurating that connection between the Eastern and Western Hemispheres which has effected so remarkable a revolution in the world's history. It is a little curious, indeed, that the belief which Columbus entertained, at first, as to the land discovered by him being part of India or China, was adhered to by him to the last, and he died in the idea that Cuba formed a portion of the mainland of India. This notion so pertinaciously clung to, both by the great Genoese and Europe in general, was dispelled by Balboa's expedition, in 1513, across the Isthmus of Darien, and discovery of the Pacific Ocean; whilst a few years later, the real position of these countries with respect to America was demonstrated by the expedition of Fernando Magalhaens, whose untimely death, in the Philippine Islands, deprived him of the honour of being the first circumnavigator of the globe.

Much obloquy has been thrown on Amerigo Vespucci, the Florentine navigator, for depriving Columbus of the honour of giving his name to the New World. How the denomination of America arose from Vespucci's Christian name, has never been satisfactorily explained, but it appears to be sufficiently ascertained that he himself is in nowise responsible for the circumstance. Vespucci, who was a man of considerable attainments, wrote an account of his American voyages, which was translated into German, and obtained an immense popularity with that nation. It has been conjectured that the name of America was first applied in Germany to the New World, and from thence was adopted by the other countries of Europe.

## THE 'CURIOSITIES' OF MANCHESTER COLLEGE.

On 12th October 1653, died at Clayton Hall, near Manchester, Humphrey Chetham, who bequeathed the large fortune which, though a gentleman by birth, he had made in trade, for the purpose of establishing a school for the education of forty poor children of Manchester, and also of founding a public library, which till recently was almost the only institution of the kind in Britain. The 'college' as the scholastic establishment and library are termed, was originally a religious foundation, but the buildings were in the sixteenth century sold to the Derby family, from whom they were purchased shortly after the death of Mr Chetham, by the trustees of the latter. The boys are boarded, clothed, and educated from about the age of six to fourteen, after which they are bound apprentices to some trade. Both in a philanthropic and antiquarian point of view, the college forms one of the most interesting public buildings in Manchester, contrasting so markedly, as it does, in its traditions of ancient times, with the bustle of factory-life and the din of mills and machinery. No part of the structure strikes the visitor more forcibly in this respect than the library, which is open daily to the public, with an unlimited right to every one, whether a resident in the town or a stranger, of reading, within a room set apart for the purpose, any book in the collection. The only condition demanded is, that the reader shall enter in a book his name and address. The reading-room is an antique apartment, wainscoted with oak, and adorned with portraits of Humphrey Chetham, the founder, Luther, and other celebrities, and presenting altogether such a quaint and secluded appearance, that it is difficult for the visitor to realise the fact of his being near the centre of such a busy nineteenth-century city as Manchester.

It is a well-known fact that in recent years an odd collection of what were termed 'curiosities' used to be exhibited in the library gallery attached to the college. The visitors were, for the most part, people from the country, who flocked thither to see the wonders of the place. A small fee for admission was charged, the duties of exhibitor being assumed by the college-boys in rotation, and certainly to a stranger the show-boy was the greatest curiosity there. With a loud, shrill voice, in the broad Lancashire dialect, and a tone of wearisome monotony, the boy, with or without a long wand, thus directed attention to the objects exhibited: 'That 's th' skeleton of a mon; that 's a globe; that's a talliscope; that 's a snake; over th' snake's back's two watch-bills; them 's four ancient swooards; that wi' a whoite haft onst belonged to General Wolfe; that 's th' whip that th' snake was kilt wi'; that topmost 's a crocodoile; that bottomost 's a halligator; that boot wonst belonged to Queen Elizabeth; that 's a Hindian pouch; that 's a ancient stiletto; that 's part o' Humphrey Cheetham's armour; that wi' th' white feeace is a munkey; under th' munkey 's a green lizard; side o' th' munkey 's a porpus's skull; under the porpus's skull 's a halligator; under th' halligator 's a turtle; them bows an' arrows belonged to th' Injyans; that 's a porpus's head; them there 's various kinds o' adders, worums, snakes, fishes, and vemenous creeturs; that albine piece was takken from th' deead body of a Frenchmon, that was killed at th' battle o' Waterloo, that was fowt i' th' year eyteen hundert an' fifteen; them's a pair o' eagle's claws; that arrow belonged to one o' th' legions that fowt under th' Duke o' Richmunt at th' battle o' Bosworth Field, i' th' year 1485, when King Richurt th' Third, king of Englund, was slain; them arrows wonst belonged to Robin Hood; that's a sea-hen; that's a sea-weed; that's a unicorn fish; that's part of a Hindian's skull; that's th' top on it; that's Oliver Crummell's stone and tankard; that's part on a loadstone; them two pieces o' wood was almanecks afoare printin' was fun' out; that's a hairy mon; under th' hairy mon's a spaking-trumpet; side o' th' spaking-trumpet's a shark's jaw-bone; that that's leaning against th' spaking-trumpet's Oliver Crummell's swooard; that's a leather-bag; side o' th' leather-bag's two cokey-nut shells; side o' th' cokey-nut shell's a porpus's skull; side o' th' porpus's head's a pumpkin; over th' pumpkin's a turtle; side o' th' turtle's a sea-weed; that top 'un's a crocodile; under th' crocodile's a halligator; under th' halligator's a woman's clog that was split by a thunner-bolt, an' hoo wasn't hurt; side o' th' crocodile's tail's a sea-hen; side o' sea-hen's a Laplander's snow-shoe; that in a box is th' skeleton of a nightingale.'

This brought the show-boy and his gaping auditors to the door of the reading-room, the door of which being thrown open, the company entered to the great annoyance of the readers, and the lad would point out in the same loud, piercing voice, the various curiosities which the apartment contained, including the portrait of Chetham the founder, and finally pointing to the brilliantly painted and gilded cock on a bracket, would exclaim, by way of peroration, 'That's th' cock as crows when he smells roast-beef!' The country-folk at this would stare more and gape wider, as if in momentary expectation of hearing Chanticleer, and then turn away, half disappointed, but consoling themselves with the supposition that just then there was no roast-beef within smelling distance. This ludicrous exhibition is, however, no longer one of the sights of Manchester College. The feoffees, feeling that it was scarcely in accordance with the cloistral quiet, solemn aspect, and studious silence of the place, at length closed the show, and the curiosities have been removed to the Salford Royal Museum, Peel Park.

## ROBERT STEPHENSON.

The lives of George and Robert Stephenson are interwoven, and it is not unlikely that some do not sufficiently recognise the genius of the son in the original glory of the father. 'It was my father's thorough training,' said Robert, 'his example, and his character, which made me the man I am.' And on another occasion, he observed: 'It is my great pride to remember, that whatever may have been done, and however extensive may have been my own connection with railway development, all I know and all I have done is primarily due to the parent whose memory I cherish and revere.' It is pleasant to read these modest and grateful words, yet we must remember that character is as much as education, and in Robert Stephenson it was easy to discern a repetition of those qualities of will and intellect which raised his father from a labourer's cottage to wealth and honours which might satiate any ambition. If Robert rejoiced in his father, George might rejoice in his son. The world will always read their lives together, and behold in the son the crown and perfection of the foundation laid in the father.

Robert Stephenson was born towards the end of 1803, while his father was working as brakesman at Willington Quay, on the north bank of the Tyne, about six miles below Newcastle. George having felt the pinch of ignorance, resolved that his son—his only son—should not suffer in the same way. To cite his own words: 'When Robert was a little boy, I saw how deficient I was in education, and I made up my mind that he should not labour under the same defect, but that I should put him to a good school, and give him a liberal training. I was, however, a poor man; and how do you think I managed? I betook myself to mending my neighbours' clocks and watches at nights, after my daily labour was done, and thus I procured the means of educating my son.' Thus when Robert was twelve, he sent him to a good school in Newcastle, to which he rode daily on a donkey. There are some still living who remember the little boy, dressed in his suit of homely gray stuff, cut out by his father, cantering along to school upon the 'cuddy,' with his wallet of provisions for the day and his bag of books slung over his shoulder.

At the age of fifteen, he was apprenticed to a coal-viewer, and during three years in which he served in that capacity, he spent his evenings with his father in reading, and study, and eager discussions concerning the locomotive-engine, and its growing powers and possible uses. In order that Robert should be well qualified to deal with the world, George took him from business and sent him for six months to Edinburgh University. To what excellent purpose he turned this brief sojourn is proved by an anecdote related by Mr Smiles. One evening, long years afterwards, Mr Robert Stephenson was conversing with a friend in his house in London, and rising from his seat he took down a volume from the shelves. 'What have we here?' was asked, as a book of neatly written manuscript was spread before him. Mr Stephenson's answer was: 'When I went to college, I knew the difficulty my father had in collecting the funds to send me there. Before going I studied short-hand; while at Edinburgh, I took down, verbatim, every lecture; and in the evenings, before I went to bed, I transcribed those lectures word for word. You see the result in that range of books.' One reason for undertaking this great labour was, that his father should share in the instruction he received.

On his return from Edinburgh, Robert assisted his father in the survey of the Stockton and Darlington Railway, entering the figures while his father took the sights. Then he was engaged on the more difficult task of scheming out the line between Liverpool and Manchester over Chat Moss. In 1824, he went to South America, to superintend some mining operations in Columbia; but finding life there dull and unsatisfactory, and his father writing that his help was urgently required at home, he returned to England after an absence of three years, and assumed the management of a locomotive-factory which had been set up in

Newcastle. There he constructed the *Rocket*, that celebrated engine which won the prize of £500 at the competition at Rainhill in 1829, and established the efficiency of the locomotive for working the Liverpool and Manchester Railway, and indeed all future railways. His next great undertaking was the formation of the railway between London and Birmingham, a work of prodigious difficulty and anxiety. In examining the country to ascertain the best line, he walked the whole distance between London and Birmingham upwards of twenty times. Long tunnels and miles of deep excavation had to be driven through unknown strata. The business of railway-making was new, and those who contracted for its execution seldom came to any good. Speaking of the difficulties encountered during the construction of this line, Robert Stephenson observed: 'After the works were let, wages rose, the prices of materials of all kinds rose, and the contractors, many of whom were men of comparatively small capital, were thrown on their beam-ends. Their calculations as to expenses and profits were completely upset. Let me just go over the list. There was Jackson, who took the Primrose-Hill contract—he failed. Then there was the next length—Nowells; then Copeland and Harding; north of them Townsend, who had the Tring cutting; next Stoke Hammond; then Lyers; then Hughes: I think all of these broke down, or at least were helped through by the directors. Then there was that terrible contract of the Kilsby tunnel, which broke the Nowells, and killed one of them. The contractors to the north of Kilsby were more fortunate, though some of them pulled through only with the greatest difficulty. Of the eighteen contracts in which the line was originally let, only seven were completed by the original contractors. Eleven firms were ruined by their contracts, which were re-let to others at advanced prices, or were carried on and finished by the company.'

The skill with which he overcame obstacles between London and Birmingham established Robert Stephenson's reputation beyond cavil, and projectors thought themselves fortunate who could secure his name, and he had only to propose his own terms to obtain them. In one session of parliament he appeared as engineer for no fewer than thirty-three new schemes. His work was enormous, and his income larger than ever fell to any of his profession. His business did not, however, fall into easy routine, but he was continually called to exercise his genius in surmounting difficulties hitherto unattempted by engineers. He designed the Royal Border Bridge, which crosses the Tweed at Berwick, and the High Level Bridge over the Tyne at Newcastle, both of which are marvellous and beautiful works; but as engineer to the Chester and Holyhead Railway he won his chief triumph in carrying the line through tubular bridges over the Straits of Menai and the estuary of the Conway. These Welsh works cost him intense thought and anxiety. When he had got the first tube floated at Conway, and saw all safe, he said: 'Now I shall go to bed!' The Britannia Bridge over the Straits gave him still more trouble. 'It was,' he said, 'a most anxious and harassing time with me. Often at night I would lie tossing about, seeking sleep in vain. The tubes filled my head. I went to bed with them and got up with them. In the gray of the morning, when I looked across the square,* it seemed an immense distance across to the houses on the opposite side. It was nearly the same length as the span of my tubular bridge!' When the first tube had been floated, a friend remarked to him: 'This great work has made you ten years older.' 'I have not slept sound,' he replied, 'for three weeks.'

The tubular bridge he repeated on a grander scale in the Victoria Bridge across the St Lawrence, at Montreal; and in two bridges over the Nile, he varied his plan by running the line *upon* the tubes instead of *within* them. It was from his experience in Egypt that he addressed the House of Commons with so much effect on the Suez Canal scheme. 'I have surveyed the line,' said he, 'I have travelled the whole distance on foot, and I declare there is no fall between the two seas. Honourable members talk about a canal. A canal is impossible—the thing would only be a ditch!'

George Stephenson was once invited to offer himself as member of parliament for South Shields, but he declined the honour, having slight interest in politics. 'Politics,' he used to say, 'are all matters of theory—there is no stability in them; they shift about like the sands of the sea; and I should feel quite out of my element amongst them.' On the question of free-trade, nevertheless, he held a decided opinion. 'England,' said he to Sir Joseph Paxton, 'is, and must be a shopkeeper; and our docks and harbours are only so many wholesale-shops, the doors of which should always be kept open.' Robert, on the other hand, was, strange to say, a thorough-going Protectionist, and represented Whitby in parliament as a Conservative from 1847. He resisted free-trade, and supported the Navigation Laws; and on the 26th of November 1852, he went into the lobby with the famous minority of 53, who voted in disapproval of liberal commercial legislation, and thereby earned the name of 'cannon balls,' their heads being presumed too hard for the entrance of a new idea.

Robert Stephenson died on the 12th of October 1859, in the fifty-sixth year of his age, and was buried by the side of Telford in Westminster Abbey.

## OCTOBER 13.

Saints Faustus, Januarius, and Martialis, martyrs, 304. St Gerald, Count of Aurillac or Orillac, confessor, 909. St Colman, martyr, 1012. Translation of the relics of St Edward the Confessor.† Seven Friar Minors, martyrs in Marocco, 1220.

*Born.*—Edward, Prince of Wales, son of Henry VI., 1453, *Windsor;* Sophia, Electress of Hanover, mother of George I., 1630, *Mayence;* Maurice, Marshal Saxe, eminent general, 1696, *Dresden;* Ferdinand VII., king of Spain, 1784.

*Died.*—Claudius, Roman emperor, poisoned, 54 A.D.; Pope Gregory XII., 1417; Pope Pius III., 1503; Theodore Beza, eminent reformer, 1605, *Geneva;* Thomas Harrison, parliamentary general, executed, 1660; Dr John Gill, eminent Baptist divine, 1771, *Southwark;* Joachim Murat, Bonapartist king of Naples, shot, 1815; Antonio Canova, celebrated sculptor, 1822, *Venice;* Mrs Elizabeth Fry, philanthropist, 1845, *Ramsgate.*

* No. 34 Gloucester Square, Hyde Park, London, where he lived.

† See *Book of Days*, vol. i. p. 54.

## NOTES FROM AUBREY: ON ENGLISH MANNERS IN OLD TIMES.

John Aubrey was an English gentleman-scholar who flourished in the latter half of the seventeenth century, and made many curious collections in history and antiquities. From some papers drawn up by him about the year 1678, and which are preserved in the Ashmole Museum, the following notes are condensed by an eminent historical student—H. T. Riley—who has obligingly communicated them to the editor of the *Book of Days*.

'There were very few free-schools in England before the Reformation. Youths were generally taught Latin in the monasteries, and young women had their education, not at Hackney, as now (1678 A. D.), but at nunneries, where they learned needle-work, confectionary, surgery, physic, writing, drawing, &c. Anciently, before the Reformation, ordinary men's houses had no chimneys, but flues like louvre-holes. In the halls and parlours of great houses were written texts of Scripture, on painted cloths.

'Before the late civil wars, at Christmas, the first dish that was brought to table was a boar's head, with a lemon in his mouth. At Queen's College, in Oxford, they still retain this custom; the bearer of it brings it into the hall, singing to an old tune an old Latin rhyme—*Caput apri defero, &c.* [The boar's head in bring I.] The first dish that was brought to table on Easter-day was a red herring riding away on horseback—*i. e.*, a herring arranged by the cook, something after the manner of a man on horseback, set in a corn-salad. The custom of eating a gammon of bacon at Easter was this—namely, to shew their abhorrence of Judaism at that solemn commemoration of our Lord's resurrection.

'The use of "Your humble servant," came first into England on the marriage of Queen Mary, daughter of Henry IV. of France [to King Charles I.]. The usual salutation before that time was, "God keep you!" "God be with you!" and, among the vulgar, "How dost do?" with a thump on the shoulder. Until this time, the court itself was unpolished and unmannered. King James's court was so far from being civil to women, that the ladies, nay, the queen herself, could hardly pass by the king's apartment without receiving some affront.

'In days of yore, lords and gentlemen lived in the country like petty kings: had their castles and their boroughs, and gallows within their liberties, where they could try, condemn, and execute. They never went to London but in parliament time, or once a year, to do their homage to their king. They always ate in Gothic halls, at the high table or oriel (a little room at the upper end of the hall, where stands a table), with the folks at the side-tables. The meat was served up by watchwords. Jacks are but of late invention; the poor boys did turn the spits, and licked the dripping for their pains. The beds of the men-servants and retainers were in the hall, as now in the grand or privy chamber. The hearth was commonly in the middle, whence the saying,* "Round about our coal-fire."

And burden of a well-known song of former times.

'The halls of the justices of the peace were dreadful to behold; the screen was garnished with corslets and helmets gaping with open mouths, with coats of mail, lances, pikes, halberts, brown-bills, and bucklers. Public inns were rare. Travellers were entertained at religious houses for three days together, if occasion served. The meetings of the gentry were not at taverns, but in the fields or forests, with hawks and hounds, and their bugle-horns in silken baldrics.

'In the last age, every gentleman-like man kept a sparrow-hawk, and a priest kept a bobby,* as Dame Julian Berners teaches us (who wrote a treatise on field-sports, *temp.* Henry VI.); it was also a diversion for young gentlewomen to man † sparrow-hawks and merlins.

'Before the Reformation, there were no poor-rates; the charitable doles given at religious houses, and the church-ale in every parish, did the business. In every parish there was a church-house, to which belonged spits, pots, crocks, &c., for dressing provisions. Here the housekeepers met and were merry, and gave their charity. The young people came there too, and had dancing, bowling, and shooting at butts. Mr Antony Wood assures me, there were few or no alms-houses before the time of King Henry VIII.; that at Oxford, opposite Christ Church, is one of the most ancient in England. In every church was a poor-man's box, and the like at great inns.

'Before the wake, or feast of the dedication of the church, they sat up all night fasting and praying—that is to say, on the eve of the wake. In the Easter-holidays was the clerk's "ale," for his private benefit and the solace of the neighbourhood.

'Glass windows, except in churches and gentlemen's houses, were rare before the time of Henry VIII. In my own remembrance, before the civil wars, copyholders and poor people had none in Herefordshire, Monmouthshire, and Salop: it is so still (1678 A. D.).

'About ninety years ago, noblemen's and gentlemen's coats were [like those] of the bedels and yeomen of the guards—*i. e.*, gathered at the middle.

'Captain Silas Taylor says, that in days of yore, when a church was to be built, they watched and prayed on the vigil of the dedication, and took that point of the horizon where the sun arose, for the east, which makes the variation that so few stand true, except those built between the two equinoxes. I have experimented [with] some churches, and have found the line to point to that part of the horizon where the sun rises on the day of that saint to whom the church is dedicated.

'In Scotland, especially among the Highlanders, the women make a courtesy to the new moon; and our English women, in this country, have a touch of this, some of them sitting astride on a gate or stile the first evening the new moon appears, and saying, "A fine moon, God bless her!" The like I observed in Herefordshire.

'From the time of Erasmus [*temp.* Henry VIII.] till about twenty years last past, the learning was downright pedantry. The conversation and habits of those times were as starched as their bands and square beards, and gravity was then taken for wisdom. The gentry and citizens had little learning of any

* A very small kind of hawk.

† 'To man a hawk' was a current phrase, meaning, to make a hawk tractable.

kind, and their way of breeding up their children was suitable to the rest. They were as severe to their children as their schoolmasters, and their schoolmasters as masters of the house of correction. Gentlemen of thirty and forty years old were to stand, like mutes and fools, bareheaded before their parents; and the daughters—grown women —were to stand at the cupboard-side during the whole time of the proud mother's visit, unless leave was desired, forsooth, that a cushion should be given them to kneel upon, brought them by the serving-man, after they had done sufficient penance in standing. The boys had their foreheads turned up and stiffened with spittle. The gentlewomen had prodigious fans, as is to be seen in old pictures; and it had a handle at least half-a-yard long: with these the daughters were oftentimes corrected. Sir Edward Coke, Lord-Chief Justice, rode the circuit with such a fan; Sir William Dugdale told me he was an eye-witness of it; the Earl of Manchester also used such a fan.

'At Oxford (and, I believe, at Cambridge) the rod was frequently used by the tutors and deans; and Dr Potter, of Trinity College, I know right well, whipped his pupil with his sword by his side, when he came to take his leave of him to go to the Inns of Court.'

---

## TRAGEDY OF THE CALAS FAMILY.

Of all the *Causes Célèbres* of France, there is none which possesses a more painful interest, or points a more instructive moral, than the trial and condemnation of Jean Calas, by the parliament of Toulouse, in the last century. Presenting, on the one hand, a striking instance of the extremities to which even judicial assemblies may be carried by the influence of bigotry and fanaticism, it also gave occasion to the exercise of a powerful effort on the part of Voltaire, whose successful exertions to procure the reversal of an iniquitous sentence, form one of the most meritorious actions in the life of the sceptic philosopher.

In the year 1761, there resided at Toulouse, in the south of France, an old man, sixty-four years of age, named Jean Calas, who for forty years had exercised the vocation of a respectable shopkeeper in that town, and had gained general esteem amid all classes for the amiability and probity of his character. His family, like himself, were all Protestant, with the exception of his third son Louis, who had been converted to the Roman Catholic faith through the instrumentality of an old female servant, who still formed one of the household. The eldest son, Marc-Antoine, was a moody young man of twenty-nine, possessed of great abilities, but depressed and disheartened by finding himself excluded as a Protestant by the tyrannical laws of the time from exercising the profession of an *avocat* or barrister for which he had qualified himself by study. Thus debarred from following out his inclinations, he had no other resource than to fill the post of assistant to his father, whilst his leisure hours were devoted to cards and billiards. At length, on the 13th of October, in the year above mentioned, a young man, named La Vaysse, who had been absent for some time from his native town, called on the Calas family, and was pressed by Marc-Antoine and his father to remain to supper. The family-party, consisting of M. and Madame Calas, Marc-Antoine, and Pierre Calas, and the young La Vaysse, sat down to table. Marc-Antoine appeared rather depressed, ate little, and abruptly quitted the company, entering the kitchen for a few moments before he passed out. The old servant inquired if he were cold. 'On the contrary,' replied he, 'I am burning.' The supper-party imagined that he had gone out to his usual haunt, the billiard-room, and therefore gave themselves no concern for his absence. La Vaysse at last rose to depart, and Pierre Calas followed with a light to shew him the way to the street. On arriving there, they found the shop-door open, and entering to ascertain the cause, were horrified at finding Marc-Antoine Calas suspended from one of the folding-doors which communicated between the shop and a warehouse behind. A cry of consternation, uttered by the two young men, summoned down-stairs the elder Calas and his wife; but La Vaysse, placing himself before her, prevented her from advancing further, whilst her husband and second son cut down the body of her first-born. La Vaysse then ran for a surgeon, who, on arriving, found that life had been extinct for two hours.

The lamentations of the household had meantime reached the surrounding neighbourhood, and a crowd soon gathered, attracted by the intelligence that Marc-Antoine had perished, and in a mysterious manner, for the Calas family, very imprudently for themselves, had agreed to conceal the cause of death, owing to the feeling of infamy which attaches to an act of suicide. Two magistrates speedily arrived to investigate the case, the multitude still increasing around the house, and expressing their opinions on the event, when a voice suddenly called out from the crowd: 'Marc-Antoine has been murdered by his father, because he intended to become a Catholic!'

By one of those electrical impulses, of which numerous instances occur in the history of popular commotions, this monstrous idea at once took possession of the public, including the magistracy, and an order was forthwith given for the arrest of all the members of the Calas family who were in the house on that fatal night, including La Vaysse and the old female-servant, the converter of Louis Calas, who some time before had ceased to reside with his father. The body of Marc-Antoine received, under this belief, the honours due to a martyr, and was interred with the utmost pomp and circumstance in the cathedral of St Stephen, a crowd of twenty thousand persons accompanying the procession, in which an imposing array of priests and monks strove to celebrate, with all the impressiveness of the Roman Catholic Church, the obsequies of a man who had ever regarded their faith with the utmost aversion.

In the meantime the unhappy Calas family were treated with great cruelty. The aged Jean Calas was repeatedly tortured to extort confession, but in vain, and a similar result attended all attempts to terrify the other accused parties into an admission of guilt. The trial of the old man came on shortly before the parliament of Toulouse. Notwithstanding the absolute impossibility of a person, at his time of life, being able to strangle a vigorous young man, in the immediate neighbourhood of a public thoroughfare, and the total absence of any evidence to support the charge, the blind stolidity and fanaticism of his judges pronounced sentence of death, though only by a majority of seven to six in a court of thirteen. It is said that, latterly, the constancy and nerve of Jean Calas forsook him, and that in his last appearance before the parliament, he betrayed such signs of agitation as told strongly against his innocence. In crossing the court of the building, from his place of confinement to the judgment-hall, his attention had been attracted by a flaming pile, to which the public executioner, surrounded by a large crowd, was committing some Protestant treatise. The poor victim of fanatical prejudice imagined that in this spectacle he beheld the preparations for his own death, and was seized by an uncontrollable terror, which influenced him throughout the subsequent judicial procedure. But he persistently as ever maintained his innocence, and by the day of execution, he had regained such firmness as excited the admiration of many, and induced a strong revulsion of feeling in his favour. The cruel sentence was accomplished on 9th March 1762, when the old man endured a lingering death of two hours' duration, by having first his bones broken with an iron bar, and then being stretched on the wheel. He died, maintaining his innocence with his last breath, and rejecting firmly all the adjurations addressed him by the confessor who attended him on the scaffold. The other members of the family were afterwards brought to trial and acquitted, though Pierre Calas was banished on the charge of an offence against religion.

In the last century, news travelled slowly, and consequently it was not till the end of March that the intelligence of this terrible execution was brought to Voltaire, at Ferney, by a traveller from Toulouse to Geneva. The philosopher was horror-struck, and formed at once the resolve to leave no stone unturned for the purpose of establishing the innocence of the Calas family. Through D'Alembert and other friends in Paris, he caused representations of the case to be made to the king and his ministers, and himself sent for Pierre Calas, and a younger brother, who was apprenticed at Geneva, and examined them with the most searching minuteness. The information which he obtained from this and other quarters was carefully sifted and forwarded by him to Paris. He also supplied the widow of Calas with money to convey her to the capital, as a necessary witness for re-establishing her husband's innocence. At last his arduous exertions were successful, the decision of the Toulouse parliament was reversed, and on 9th March 1765, exactly three years from Calas's death, the tribunal which had condemned him pronounced a solemn judgment, annulling their former sentence, and rendering thus a tardy and ineffectual justice to the unfortunate man and his family.

## MRS FRY.

The labours of Howard in effecting an amelioration on the condition of prisons throughout Europe, though signal and important, cannot be said to have accomplished any radical change in the management of these establishments, and derive their highest estimate, in a reformatory point of view, from their directing the attention of the general public to this momentous topic. It was reserved for a woman to carry out what John Howard had so gloriously begun, and, by assuming the mantle which he had dropped, to inaugurate, through her philanthropic exertions, these enlarged views on the subject of prison-discipline by which it is now so conspicuously characterised both in legislative enactment and practice. In recording the name of Elizabeth Fry, we inscribe that of a true heroine, who made the moral and physical wellbeing of her fallen brothers and sisters the aim and study of her life, with the same spirit of devotedness and self-sacrifice which, more recently, has been so nobly exhibited by Miss Florence Nightingale on behalf of our gallant soldiers.

As is well known, Mrs Fry's maiden name was Gurney, and both by the father and mother's side, she inherited eminently the Quaker element; her father, John Gurney of Earlham, in Norfolk, being a distinguished member of the Society of Friends, and her mother, a great-granddaughter of the celebrated Quaker apologist, Robert Barclay. Mr Gurney, however, was not a very strict adherent of his society, and, from the liberal and extended intercourse which he maintained with men of all denominations, there was little of the sectarian or fanatical principle followed in the bringing up of his family. They seem, on the contrary, to have entered freely into all the amusements and pleasures of the world, Elizabeth among the rest. At the age of eighteen, however, she was much impressed by a sermon delivered by William Savery, an American Quaker, and from that period, her religious views became gradually more and more decided. They were more steadfastly established by her marriage, shortly afterwards, to Mr Joseph Fry, a Quaker of the strictest sort, and the junior partner of an extensive mercantile firm in London. It was not, however, till a good many years subsequently that her attention was first directed to the question of prisoners and prison-discipline; a subject which appears first to have been suggested to her mind by a visit paid, along with some members of the Society of Friends, to the condemned cell in Newgate in 1813. The impressions produced upon her by the spectacles which she witnessed in that prison of profligacy, poverty, and filth, was such, that she set her energies seriously forthwith to the task of devising some method for the alleviation of these scenes of horror. With the approbation of the magistrates of Middlesex, she commenced the establishment, in the female wards, of a school for the purpose of affording to the inmates instruction as well as employment. She also succeeded in organising an association of ladies for visiting the female prisoners in Newgate, an occupation in which she herself took a most active share, conversing and praying with them, and by her earnest kindness exercising a softening influence on the hearts of even the most depraved. Through her exertions and representations, a most marked change was effected in the condition of Newgate, more especially the female department, and the improved state of the prison attracted the attention of individuals of the highest authority and position in the land. But Mrs Fry's labours did not cease with Newgate. She gradually extended their sphere, and soon made the general subject of prison-discipline the object of consideration and amendment, and before committees both of the Lords and Commons, she was examined as an important and valuable auxiliary in the cause of criminal reform. The severity of the then law regarding capital punishments, stirred up all the promptings of her benevolent heart, and, among those who contributed by their exertions to the introduction of a more lenient system, her name deserves honourable mention. In the progress of her mission for the improvement of prisons and reclaiming of criminals, Mrs Fry made repeated journeys through Great Britain and Ireland, besides making several excursions to the continent. It is satisfactory, also, to state, that notwithstanding the multifarious and engrossing nature of her philanthropic labours, she never laid herself open to the charge of neglecting her own family, but was throughout most sedulous in the performance of her duties, both as a wife and mother. Her offspring was numerous, and she records herself, that on the occasion of the king of Prussia paying her a visit at her residence of Upton Lane, she presented to him seven of her sons and sons-in-law, eight of her daughters and daughters-in-law, and twenty-five of her grandchildren.

Towards the close of her life, Mrs Fry suffered severely from a neuralgic affection, but, to the last, she retained an undiminished interest in the great philanthropic cause to which she had devoted her life. Though a strict Quaker in every respect, she practised in her dealings with the world at large the most liberal-hearted toleration, and was quite as ready to appreciate the self-denying labours of the Romish Sisters of Charity, as of persons professing sentiments more in accordance with her own. Courageous and energetic as she shewed herself in the prosecution of her mission, she was naturally, in some respects, of a very sensitive and nervous temperament, causing her, when a child, to be unable to go to sleep in the dark, and an insupportable horror at being obliged to enter the sea for the purpose of bathing. As she grew up, much of that timidity of disposition disappeared, and she became noted as a keen and enthusiastic horsewoman; but she still, throughout life, continued to be distinguished in physical constitution by the extremes of timidity and courage. The portrait of Mrs Fry exhibits a most pleasing combination of benevolence and intellect, with a decided expression of humour about the mouth, a quality which, as in most persons of genius, formed a marked characteristic of her organisation.

---

## OCTOBER 14.

St Calixtus or Callistus, pope and martyr, 222. St Donatian, confessor, bishop of Rheims and patron of Bruges, 389. St Burckard, confessor, first bishop of Wurtzburg, 752. St Dominic, surnamed Loricatus, confessor, 1060.

*Born.*—James II. of England, 1633; William Penn, coloniser of Pennsylvania, 1644, *London;* Charles Abbot, Lord Colchester, lawyer and statesman, 1757, *Abingdon.*

*Died.*—Harold, last Saxon king of England, slain at battle of Hastings, 1066; Pierre Gassendi, mathematician and philosopher, 1655, *Paris;* Paul Scarron, humorous writer, 1660, *Paris;* John Henley ('Orator Henley'), 1756, *London;* James, Marshal Keith, killed at Hochkirchen, 1758; Prince Gregory Alexander Potemkin, favourite of Empress Catherine, 1791, *Cherson;* Samuel Phillips, novelist and miscellaneous writer, 1854, *Brighton.*

### BATTLE OF HASTINGS.

The battle of Hastings, fought on Saturday, the 14th of October 1066, was one of those decisive engagements which at various periods have marked the commencement of a new epoch or chapter in the world's history. Gained by the Duke of Normandy, mainly through superiority of numbers, and several well-directed feints, the conduct of the Saxons and their monarch Harold was such as to command the highest admiration on the part of their enemies, and the result might have been very different had Harold, instead of marching impetuously from London with an inadequate army to repel the invaders, waited a little while to gather strength from the reinforcements which were every day pouring in to his standard. But the signal success which, only a few days previous, he had gained over the Norwegians in the north of England, made him over-confident in his own powers, and the very promptitude and rapidity which formed one of his leading characteristics proved the principal cause of his overthrow.

On the 28th of September, sixteen days before the battle, the Normans, with their leader William, had disembarked, totally unopposed, from their ships at a place called Bulverhithe, between Pevensey and Hastings. The future Conqueror of England was the last to land, and as he placed his foot on shore, he made a false step, and fell on his face. A murmur of consternation ran through the troops at this incident as a bad omen, but with great presence of mind William sprang immediately up, and shewing his troops his hand filled with English sand, exclaimed: 'What now? What astonishes you? I have taken seisin of this land with my hands, and by the splendour of God, as far as it extends it is mine—it is yours!'

The invading army then marched to Hastings, pitching their camp near the town, and sallying out from this intrenchment to burn and plunder the surrounding country. Landed on a hostile shore, with a brave and vigorous foe to contend with, all William's prospects of success lay in striking a decisive blow before Harold could properly muster his forces or organise his means of resistance. The impetuosity of the Saxon king, as already mentioned, soon furnished him with such an opportunity. Arriving at *Senlac*, which the bloody engagement a few days subsequently was destined to rechristen by the appellation of *Battle*, Harold pitched his camp, and then received a message from William, demanding that he should either resign his crown in favour of the Norman, submit the question at issue to the decision of the pope, or finally maintain his right to the English crown by single combat with his challenger. All these proposals were declined by Harold, as was also a last offer made by William to resign to his opponent all the country to the north of the Humber, on condition of the provinces south of that river being ceded to him in sovereignty.

On Friday the 13th, the Normans quitted Hastings, and took up their position on an eminence opposite to the English, for the purpose of giving battle on the following day. A singular contrast was noticeable in the manner that the respective armies passed the intervening night. Whilst the Saxons, according to their old convivial custom, spent the time in feasting and rejoicing, singing songs, and quaffing bumpers of ale and wine, the Normans, after finishing their warlike preparations, betook themselves to the offices of devotion, confessed, and received the holy sacrament by thousands at a time.

HASTINGS FROM THE FAIRLIGHT DOWNS.

At early dawn next day, the Normans were marshalled by William and his brother Odo, the warlike bishop of Bayeux, who wore a coat of mail beneath his episcopal robes. They advanced towards the English, who remained firmly intrenched in their position, and for many hours repulsed steadily with their battle-axes the charge of the enemy's cavalry, and with their closed shields rendered his arrows almost inoperative. Great ability was shewn by William and his brother in rallying their soldiers after these reverses, and the attacks on the English line were again and again renewed. Up to three o'clock in the afternoon, the superiority in the conflict remained with the latter. Then, however, William ordered a thousand horse to advance, and then take to flight, as if routed. This stratagem proved fatal to the Saxons, who, leaving their position to pursue the retreating

BATTLE OF HASTINGS—BAYEUX TAPESTRY.

foe, were astounded by the latter suddenly facing about, and falling into disorder, were struck down on every side. The same manœuvre was twice again repeated with the same calamitous results to the English, and on the last occasion Harold, struck by a random arrow which entered his left eye and penetrated to the brain, was instantaneously killed. This still further increased the disorder of his followers, who, however, bravely maintained the fight round their standard for a time. This at last was grasped by the Normans, who then raised in its stead the consecrated banner, which the pope had sent William from Rome, as a sanction to his expedition. At sunset the combat terminated, and the Normans remained masters of the field.

Though by this victory William of Normandy won a kingdom for himself, it was not till years afterwards that he was enabled to sheathe his sword as undisputed sovereign of England. For generations, indeed, the pertinacity so characteristic of the Saxon race displayed itself in a steady though ineffective resistance to their Norman rulers, and for a long time they were animated in their efforts by a legend generally circulated among them, that Harold, their gallant king, instead of being killed, had escaped from the field of battle, and would one day return to lead them to victory. History records many such reports, which, under similar circumstances, have been eagerly adopted by the vanquished party, and are exemplified, among other instances, by the rumours prevalent after the deaths of Don Roderick, the last of the Gothic kings of Spain, and of the Scottish sovereign James IV., who perished at Flodden.

## FIELD-MARSHAL KEITH.

Among the eight generals of Frederick the Great, who, on foot, surround Rauch's magnificent equestrian statue of the monarch in Berlin, one is a Briton. He was descended of a Scotch family, once as great in wealth and station as any of the Hamiltons or the Douglases, but which went out in the last century like a quenched light, in consequence of taking a wrong line in politics. James Edward Keith, and his brother the Earl Marischal, when very young men, were engaged in the rebellion of 1715–16, and lost all but their lives. Abroad, they rose by their talents into positions historically more distinguished than those which their youthful imprudence had forfeited.

The younger brother, James, first served the czar in his wars against Poland and Turkey; but, becoming discontented with the favouritism that prevailed in the Russian army, and conceiving himself treated with injustice, he gave in his resignation in 1747, and was admitted into the Prussian service as field-marshal. Frederick the Great made him his favourite companion, and, together, they travelled *incognito* through Germany, Poland, and Hungary. Keith also invented a game, in imitation of chess, which delighted the king so much, that he had some thousands of armed men cast in metal, by which he could arrange battles and sieges. On the 29th of August 1756, he entered with the king into Dresden, where he had the archives opened to carry away the documents that particularly interested the Prussian court: he also managed the admirable retreat of the army from Olmutz in the presence of a superior force, without the loss of a single gun; and took part in all the great battles of the period. He was killed in that of Hochkirchen, 14th of October 1758. His correspondence with Frederick, written in French, possesses much historical interest. He was of middle height, dark complexion, strongly-marked features, and an expression of determination, softened by a degree of sweetness, marked his face. His presence of mind was very remarkable; and his knowledge, deep and varied in character; whilst his military talents and lively sense of honour made him take rank among the first commanders of the day. His brother, the lord-marshal of Scotland, thus wrote of him to Madame de Geoffrin: 'My brother has left me a noble heritage; after having overrun Bohemia at the head of a large army, I have only found seventy dollars in his purse.' Frederick honoured his memory by erecting a monument to him in the Wilhelmsplatz, at Berlin, by the side of his other generals.

## ORATOR HENLEY.

Possessing considerable power of eloquence, with great perseverance, a fair education, and a good position in life, Henley might have pursued a quiet career of prosperity, had not overweening vanity induced him to seek popularity at any risk, and eventually make himself 'preacher and zany of the age,' according to the satirical verdict of Pope, which he had well earned by his ill-placed buffoonery.

Henley was the son of a clergyman residing at Melton Mowbray, in Leicestershire, where he was born in 1692; he was sent to St John's College, Cambridge, and while an undergraduate there, sent a communication on punning to the *Spectator* (printed in No. 396), which is now the most readily accessible of all his voluminous writings, scattered as they were in the ephemeral literature of his own day. This paper is a strange mixture of sense and nonsense, combined with a pert self-sufficiency, very characteristic of its writer.

On his return to Melton, he was employed as assistant in a school. He preached occasionally, and from the attention which his fluency and earnestness attracted, was induced to betake himself to London, as the proper sphere for the display of his rhetorical talents. He was appointed reader at St George's Chapel, in Queen Square, and afterwards at St John's, Bedford Row; delivered from time to time charity-sermons with great success; and worked at translations for the booksellers. After some years, he was offered a small country living, but would not consent to the obscurity which it entailed. The same exaggeration of style and action in the pulpit, however, which rendered him a favourite with the public, exposed him to animadversion on the part of the clergy and church-patrons. He now attempted political writing, offering his services to the ministry; and when they were declined, made the same offer to their opponents, with no better success. Determined for the future to trust to his own power of eloquence to draw an income from the public, he announced himself as 'the restorer of Ancient Eloquence,' and opened his 'Oratory' in a large room in Butcher Row, Newport Market. Here he preached on Sundays upon theology, and on Wednesdays, on any subject that happened to be most popular. Politics and current events were treated with a vulgar levity that suited the locality. The greatest persons in the land were attacked by him. 'After having undergone some prosecutions, he turned his rhetoric to buffoonery upon all public and private occurrences. All this passed in the same room where at one time he jested, and at another celebrated what he called the "primitive eucharist."'* In a money point of view, he was very successful, his Oratory was crowded, and cash flowed in freely. For the use of his regular subscribers, he issued medals (like the free tickets of theatres and public gardens) with the vain device of a star rising to the meridian, the motto, *Ad summa*; and, beneath it, *Inveniam viam aut faciam*. Pope has immortalised 'Henley's gilt tub,' as he terms the gaudy pulpit from which he poured forth his rhapsodies. There is a caricature of him as a

* Note to Pope's *Dunciad*.

clerical fox seated on his tub; a monkey within it acting as clerk, and peeping from the bung-hole with a broad grin, as he exhibits a handful of coin, the great end for which he laboured. Henley charged one shilling each for admission to his lectures. Another of these caricatures we here copy. It

ORATOR HENLEY.

represents Henley in his pulpit, half-clergyman, half-fox; his pulpit is supported by a pig, emblematic of the 'swinish multitude;' the 'brazen-head' of the popular romance of Friar Bacon;* and a well-filled purse. The lines of *Hudibras* are made to apply to him, beginning—

'Bel and the Dragon's chaplains were
More moderate than you by far.'

In an unlucky hour he attacked Pope, who afterwards held him up to obloquy in the *Dunciad:*

'Imbrown'd with native bronze, lo! Henley stands,
Tuning his voice, and balancing his hands.
How fluent nonsense trickles from his tongue!
How sweet the periods, neither said nor sung!
Still break the benches, Henley, with thy strain,
While Sherlock, Hare, and Gibson preach in vain.
O great restorer of the good old stage,
Preacher at once and zany of thy age!
O, worthy thou of Egypt's wise abodes,
A decent priest, where monkeys were the gods!
But fate with butchers placed thy priestly stall,
Meek modern faith to murder, hack, and maul;
And bade thee live, to crown Britannia's praise,
In Toland's, Tindal's, and in Woolston's * days.'

After some years, Henley left Newport Market, but, faithful to his old friends the butchers, he opened his new Oratory in Clare Market, in the year 1746, and indulged in the most scurrilous censoriousness, and a levity bordering on buffoonery. His neighbours, the butchers, were useful allies, and, it is said, he kept many in pay to protect him from the consequences of his satire. In some instances, he must have run risks of riot and mischief to his meeting-room, which could only be repressed by fear of his brawny protectors. In one instance he tricked a mob of shoemakers, by inducing them to come and hear him describe a new mode by which shoes could be made most expeditiously; the plan really being, simply to cut off the tops of ready-made boots! His reflections on the royal family led to his arrest, but he was liberated, after a few days, on proper bail being tendered, and a promise to curb his tongue in future. His ordinary free-and-easy vulgarity is well hit off in an article on the 'Robin Hood Society,'† published in No. 18 of the *Gray's Inn Journal*, February 17, 1753; he is called Orator Bronze, and exclaims: 'I am pleased to see this assembly; you're a twig from me, a chip of the old block at Clare Market; I am the old block, invincible; *coup de grace*, as yet unanswered. We are brother-rationalists; logicians upon fundamentals! I love ye all—I love mankind in general—give me some of that porter!'

Despite his boldness and impudence, and the daring character of his disquisitions on politics and religion, Henley found a difficulty in keeping up an interest in his Oratory. A contemporary writer says: 'for some years before its author's death, it dwindled away so much that the few friends of it feared its decease was very near. The doctor, indeed, kept it up to the last, determined it should live as long as he did, and actually exhibited many evenings to empty benches. Finding no one at length would attend, he admitted the acquaintances of his door-keeper, runners, &c., gratis. On the 13th of October 1753,‡ the doctor died, and the Oratory ceased, no one having iniquity or impudence sufficient to continue it.'

Irrespective of the improper character of the subjects he chose to descant upon, his inordinate conceit induced him to treat every one as his inferior in judgment; and he enforced his opinions with the most violent gesticulation. Henley's feverish career is a glaring instance of vanity overcoming and degrading abilities, that, properly cultivated, might have insured him a respectable

* In this old tale, the brazen-head was to do wonders when it spoke; but the friar, tired with watching, left his servant to listen while he slept. The head spoke the sentences which appear on the three labels issuing from the mouth, and having spoken the last, fell with a crash that destroyed it. This was typical of the unstable foundation of Henley's popular power.

* Three deistical writers, whose works were published in the early years of the last century.

† A public debating-society, held at the sign of the *Robin Hood*, in Butcher Row, near Temple Bar. Each person paid sixpence for admission, and had a ticket for four pennyworth of drink, the twopence paying the expenses of the society.

‡ This is an error, Henley's death being recorded in the obituary of the *Gentleman's Magazine*, on 14th October 1756.

position, instead of an anxious and fretful life, and an immortality in the pages of a great satirist, of a most undesirable nature.

---

# OCTOBER 15.

St Hospicius or Hospis, anchoret, about 580. St Tecla, virgin and abbess. St Teresa, virgin, foundress of the Reformation of the Barefooted Carmelites, 1582.

---

*Born.*—Virgil, Latin poet, 70 B.C., *Andes, near Mantua;* Evangelista Torricelli, inventor of the barometer, 1608, *Piancaldoli, in Romagna;* Allan Ramsay, Scottish poet, 1686, *Leadhills, Lanarkshire;* Alexander Fraser Tytler, Lord Woodhouselee, author of *Elements of General History*, 1747, *Edinburgh;* Christian, Count Stolberg, poet and dramatist, 1748, *Hamburg;* Frederick William IV., king of Prussia, 1795.

*Died.*—Lucretius, Latin philosophical poet, 55 B.C.; Andreas Vesalius, eminent anatomist, 1564, *Zante;* Pope Gregory XIV., 1591; Dr James Anderson, author of works on political economy, &c., 1808, *London;* Michael Kelly, composer, 1826, *Ramsgate;* Letitia Elizabeth Maclean (*née* Landon), poetess, 1838, *Cape Coast Castle;* Rev. John Foster, celebrated essayist, 1843, *Stapleton, near Bristol.*

## MRS MACLEAN ('L. E. L.').

On New-year's Day morning, 1839, the readers of newspapers were startled by the announcement of the death, at Cape Coast Castle, of Mrs Maclean, wife of Mr George Maclean, the governor of that settlement. But a few months before she had quitted the shores of England with all the gay paraphernalia of a bride, proceeding after the nuptial knot had been tied to her future home by the palm-clad shores, and amid the tropical vegetation of West Africa. Recollections of the young and enthusiastic 'L. E. L.,' whose contributions to the *Literary Gazette* had in their youthful days of romance called forth so many juvenile tributes of admiration both in prose and verse, filled with tears the eyes of many staid men of middle age, whilst to those who had enjoyed the privilege of her society, and the vivacity and charm of her conversation, the shock produced by this sad and unexpected intelligence was overwhelming. Other feelings, however, were speedily to be excited—those of an intense curiosity and interest, not unmingled with horror, by the report that Mrs Maclean had died from the effects of a dose of prussic acid, incautiously taken, and, as some did not hesitate to insinuate, with the intention of self-destruction. The whole affair was involved in the deepest mystery, the sole explanation afforded being that between eight and nine o'clock on the morning of Monday, 15th October, a female servant had gone to Mrs Maclean's room, for the purpose of delivering a note which had just been received. She experienced some difficulty in opening the door, and found that it was occasioned by Mrs Maclean having fallen with her back against it. The unfortunate lady was lying perfectly senseless, with an empty bottle in her hand, labelled as containing hydrocyanic or prussic acid. Assistance was immediately procured, but all in vain—the vital spark had fled. Mr Maclean, her husband, had been suffering from indisposition for a few days previous, and had been most assiduously tended by his wife, who, on the morning of her death, had risen to administer some refreshment to him, and had then retired to her room to resume repose. The servant also who found her in the condition we have mentioned, had seen her about half an hour previously. No one had observed anything peculiar in her demeanour, or any indication of depression of spirits, though from her attendance night and day on her husband, she had become very much exhausted, and was besides liable to spasmodic attacks, for the relief of which, it was stated at the inquest, that she was in the habit of taking in a glass of water a few drops of medicine from the bottle which was found in her hand. The conjecture then come to was, that she had inadvertently taken an overdose, and feeling its effects, had endeavoured to open her door and call for assistance, when she was stricken down helpless. No satisfactory conclusion was ever arrived at, and there the matter rests. It should be stated, however, that all the evidence brought forward went entirely to negative the idea of suicide having been committed. Between Mr Maclean and herself a strong and sincere affection subsisted; there had never been an unkind word between them; and from the tone of all her communications to her friends at home, it was evident that she looked forward with great complacency and cheerfulness to her future career at Cape Coast.

Previous to her marriage, the life of Letitia Elizabeth Landon had not been diversified by much incident. The greater part of it was spent in London, in the neighbourhood of Chelsea and Brompton, in the former of which localities she was born in 1802. Her father, John Landon, the son of a Herefordshire rector, had in his early days gone to sea, but afterwards settled in London as an army-agent. From her earliest years Letitia displayed a most engrossing propensity for reading, and the bent of her genius towards poetry was displayed nearly at as early a date as with Pope and Cowley. When the family resided at Brompton, they happened to have as their near neighbour William Jerdan, the celebrated editor of *The Literary Gazette*, and an acquaintance having been formed, some of Miss Landon's juvenile pieces were shewn to him, approved of, and inserted in his journal. Public attention was soon attracted by the beauty of these pieces; and the mysterious initials 'L. E. L.,' by which the authoress subscribed herself, came soon to be recognised as belonging to the finest lyrics of the day. Thus stimulated, she proceeded to more ambitious undertakings, and the poems of *The Improvisatrice*, *The Troubadour*, *The Golden Violet*, and *The Venetian Bracelet*, procured for her all the fame which their glow and luxuriance of description, with the most melodious harmony of verse, so richly merited. Whether, however, from its essentially artificial character, however natural an appearance it may wear, the poetry of Miss Landon is destined to an abiding immortality, may not unreasonably be questioned. Never was there a poet whose works were *less* a reflex of his own mind than those of L. E. L. With all the enchanting descriptions of woodland glades, sunny gardens, and flowery meadows, beneath the magic of a Provençal or Italian sky, Miss Landon, like Charles Lamb, had little affection for the country, and found herself nowhere in a more congenial atmosphere than amid the smoke and bustle of London. Neither did her disposition partake of the pensive, melancholy cast, so conspicuous in her poems, being, on the contrary, remarkable for its vivacity and cheerfulness. Those who expected to find in her an embodiment of the feelings portrayed in her works, found themselves generally egregiously mistaken in their anticipations. It was said of her, 'that she should write with a crystal pen dipped in dew upon silver paper, and use for pounce the dust of a butterfly's wing;' the real fact being, that her locality for invoking the Muses was her bedroom—a bare homely-looking room facing the street, where she wrote at an old worn-out desk, placed on a little old dressing-table. In person, the impression conveyed was a very pleasing one. Her figure was slight and graceful, and without being artistically beautiful in feature, her face, when she spoke, became handsome in its expressiveness. It is recorded of Hogg the Ettrick Shepherd, that, on being first presented to her at the house of Mrs Hall, he took her hand, and looking earnestly in her face, exclaimed: 'Oh dear! I hae written and thocht mony a bitter thing about ye, but I'll do sae nae mair; I didna think ye'd been sae bonny!'

---

## THE WYNYARD GHOST-STORY.

No modern ghost-story has been more talked of in England, than one in which the seers were two military officers named Sherbroke and Wynyard. The men occupied conspicuous places in society, and were universally known as persons of honour, as well as cool good sense;* the reality of their vision was attested by a remarkable circumstance which afterwards took place; and every effort of their own or on the part of others to give an 'explanation' has been vain.

John Cope Sherbroke and George Wynyard appear in the army list of 1785, the one as a captain and the other a lieutenant in the 33d Regiment —a corps which, some years after, had the honour to be commanded by the Hon. Arthur Wellesley, subsequently Duke of Wellington. The regiment was then on service in Canada, and Sherbroke and Wynyard, being of congenial tastes, had become friends. It was their custom to spend in study much of the time which their brother-officers devoted to idle pleasures. According to a narration resting on the best authority now attainable,† 'They were one afternoon sitting in Wynyard's apartment. It was perfectly light, the hour was about four o'clock; they had dined, but neither of them had drunk wine, and they had retired from the mess to continue together the occupations of the morning. It ought to have been said, that the apartment in which they were had two doors in it, the one opening into a passage, and the other leading into Wynyard's bedroom. There was no other means of entering the sitting-room but from the passage, and no other egress from the bedroom but through the sitting-room; so that any person passing into the bedroom must have remained there, unless he returned by the way he entered. This point is of consequence to the story.

'As these two young officers were pursuing their studies, Sherbroke, whose eye happened accidentally to glance from the volume before him towards the door that opened to the passage, observed a tall youth, of about twenty years of age, whose appearance was that of extreme emaciation, standing beside it. Struck with the presence of a perfect stranger, he immediately turned to his friend, who was sitting near him, and directed his attention to the guest who had thus strangely broken in upon their studies. As soon as Wynyard's eyes were turned towards the mysterious visitor, his countenance became suddenly agitated. "I have heard," says Sir John Sherbroke, "of a man's being as pale as death, but I never saw a living face assume the appearance of a corpse, except Wynyard's at that moment."

'As they looked silently at the form before them, —for Wynyard, who seemed to apprehend the import of the appearance, was deprived of the faculty of speech, and Sherbroke perceiving the agitation of his friend, felt no inclination to address it—as they looked silently upon the figure, it proceeded slowly into the adjoining apartment, and, in the act of passing them, cast its eyes with an expression of somewhat melancholy affection on young Wynyard. The oppression of this extraordinary presence was no sooner removed, than Wynyard, seizing his friend by the arm, and drawing a deep breath, as if recovering from the suffocation of intense astonishment and emotion, muttered in a low and almost inaudible tone of voice, "Great God! my brother!"—"Your brother!" repeated Sherbroke, "what can you mean, Wynyard? there must be some deception—follow me;" and immediately taking his friend by the arm, he preceded him into the bedroom, which, as before stated, was connected with the sitting-room, and into which the strange visitor had evidently entered. It has already been said, that from this chamber there was no possibility of withdrawing but by the way of the apartment, through which the figure had certainly passed, and as certainly never had returned. Imagine, then, the astonishment of the young officers, when, on finding themselves in the centre of the chamber, they perceived that the room was perfectly untenanted. Wynyard's mind had received an impression at the first moment of his observing him, that the figure whom he had seen was the spirit of his brother. Sherbroke still persevered in strenuously believing that some delusion had been practised.*

* Archdeacon Wrangham alludes to them in a note in his edition of Plutarch. 'A very singular story, however,' says he, 'could be told on this head by Generals S—— and W——, both men of indisputable honour and spirit, and honourably distinguished by their exertions in their country's service.' The death of the first is thus noted in *Blackwood's Magazine* for June 1830: 'At Calverton, General Sir John Cope Sherbroke, G.C.B.' The other seer seems to have passed into another branch of the army, and died as lieutenant-colonel of the 24th Light Dragoons, June 13, 1809.

† The narration here given is from *Accredited Ghost Stories*, collected by T. M. Jarvis, Esq. London, 1823. Mr Jarvis adds the following note: 'This story has been read by a relation of General Wynyard, *who states that, in all important circumstances, it is strictly true.*'

* The two gentlemen remarked at the time, that the figure appeared as dressed in a light indoor costume, while they wore furs and wraps owing to the severity of the weather.—*M. E. M., in Notes and Queries, April 3, 1858.*

'They took note of the day and hour in which the event had happened; but they resolved not to mention the occurrence in the regiment, and gradually they persuaded each other that they had been imposed upon by some artifice of their fellow-officers, though they could neither account for the reason, nor suspect the author, nor conceive the means of its execution. They were content to imagine anything possible, rather than admit the possibility of a supernatural appearance. But, though they had attempted these stratagems of self-delusion, Wynyard could not help expressing his solicitude with respect to the safety of the brother whose apparition he had either seen, or imagined himself to have seen; and the anxiety which he exhibited for letters from England, and his frequent mention of his fears for his brother's health, at length awakened the curiosity of his comrades, and eventually betrayed him into a declaration of the circumstances which he had in vain determined to conceal. The story of the silent and unbidden visitor was no sooner bruited abroad, than the destiny of Wynyard's brother became an object of universal and painful interest to the officers of the regiment; there were few who did not inquire for Wynyard's letters before they made any demand after their own; and the packets that arrived from England were welcomed with more than usual eagerness, for they brought not only remembrances from their friends at home, but promised to afford the clue to the mystery which had happened among themselves.

'By the first ships no intelligence relating to the story could have been received, for they had all departed from England previously to the appearance of the spirit. At length the long-wished-for vessel arrived; all the officers had letters except Wynyard. They examined the several newspapers, but they contained no mention of any death, or of any other circumstance connected with his family that could account for the preternatural event. There was a solitary letter for Sherbroke still unopened. The officers had received their letters in the mess-room at the hour of supper. After Sherbroke had broken the seal of his last packet, and cast a glance on its contents, he beckoned his friend away from the company, and departed from the room. All were silent. The suspense of the interest was now at its climax; the impatience for the return of Sherbroke was inexpressible. They doubted not but that letter had contained the long-expected intelligence. After the interval of an hour, Sherbroke joined them. No one dared be guilty of so great a rudeness as to inquire the nature of his correspondence; but they waited in mute attention, expecting that he would himself touch upon the subject. His mind was manifestly full of thoughts that pained, bewildered, and oppressed him. He drew near to the fireplace, and leaning his head on the mantel-piece, after a pause of some moments, said in a low voice, to the person who was nearest him: "Wynyard's brother is no more!" The first line of Sherbroke's letter was—"Dear John, break to your friend Wynyard the death of his favourite brother." He had died on the day, and at the very hour, on which the friends had seen his spirit pass so mysteriously through the apartment.

'It might have been imagined, that these events would have been sufficient to have impressed the mind of Sherbroke with the conviction of their truth; but so strong was his prepossession against the existence, or even the possibility of any preternatural intercourse with the souls of the dead, that he still entertained a doubt of the report of his senses, supported as their testimony was by the coincidence of vision and event. Some years after, on his return to England, he was walking with two gentlemen in Piccadilly, when, on the opposite side of the way, he saw a person bearing the most striking resemblance to the figure which had been disclosed to Wynyard and himself. His companions were acquainted with the story, and he instantly directed their attention to the gentleman opposite, as the individual who had contrived to enter and depart from Wynyard's apartment without their being conscious of the means. Full of this impression, he immediately went over, and at once addressed the gentleman. He now fully expected to elucidate the mystery. He apologised for the interruption, but excused it by relating the occurrence, which had induced him to the commission of this solecism in manners. The gentleman received him as a friend. He had never been out of the country, but he was the twin-brother* of the youth whose spirit had been seen.'

From the interesting character of this narration—the facts of the vision occurring in daylight and to two persons, and of the subsequent verification of likeness by the party not previously acquainted with the subject of the vision—it is much to be regretted that no direct report of particulars has come to us. There is all other desirable authentication for the story, and sufficient evidence to prove that the two gentlemen believed and often told nearly what is here reported. Dr Mayo makes the following statement on the subject: 'I have had opportunities of inquiring of two near relations of this General Wynyard, upon what evidence the above story rests. They told me that they had each heard it from his own mouth. More recently a gentleman, whose accuracy of recollection exceeds that of most people, has told me that he had heard the late Sir John Sherbroke, the other party in the ghost-story, tell it much in the same way at a dinner-table.' †

A writer, signing himself COGNATUS, states in *Notes and Queries* (July 3, 1858), that the brother (not twin-brother) whose spirit appeared to Wynyard and his friend was John Otway Wynyard, a lieutenant in the 3d regiment of Foot-guards, who died on the 15th of October 1785. As this gentleman writes with a minute knowledge of the family-history, we may consider this date as that of the alleged spiritual incident.

In *Notes and Queries*, July 2, 1859, appeared a correspondence, giving nearly the strongest testimony then attainable to the truth of the Wynyard ghost-story. A series of queries on the subject, being drawn up at Quebec by Sir John Harvey, adjutant-general of the forces in Canada, was sent to Colonel Gore, of the same garrison, who was understood to be a survivor of the officers who were with Sherbroke and Wynyard at the time of

* The particular as to this person being a *twin*-brother has been denied. See *Notes and Queries*, June 12, 1858.

† *Letters on the Truths contained in Popular Superstitions.* By Herbert Mayo, M.D. Ed. Frankfort, 1849, p. 62.

the occurrence; and Colonel Gore explicitly replied to the following effect. He was present at Sydney, in the island of Cape Breton, in the latter end of 1785 or 1786, when the incident happened. It was in the then new barrack, and the place was blocked up by ice so as to have no communication with any other part of the world. He was one of the first persons who entered the room after the supposed apparition was seen. 'The ghost passed them as they were sitting at coffee [between eight and nine in the evening], and went into G. Wynyard's bed-closet, the window of which was putt[i]ed down.' He next day suggested to Sherbroke the propriety of making a memorandum of the incident; which was done. 'I remember the date, and on the 6th of June our first letters from England brought the news of John Wynyard's death [which had happened] on the very night they saw his apparition.' Colonel Gore was under the impression that the person afterwards seen in one of the streets of London by Sherbroke and William Wynyard, was not a brother of the latter family, but a gentleman named (he thought) Hayman, noted for being like the deceased John Wynyard, and who affected to dress like him.

---

## SHOW PRODIGIES.

The English newspapers and broadsides of old days preserve to us some curious notices of what have been, from time to time, brought before the public as personal prodigies. We find the grave King William in a novel kind of association in the following account, for example, of a Strong Man. The article is dated, 'London, printed by J. W., near Fleet Street, 1699.'

'THE ENGLISH SAMPSON: HIS STRENGTH PROVED BEFORE THE KING; being an account of the wonderful exploits that Mr William Joyce performed before his majesty at *Kinsington*, the 15th of this instant November, 1699.'

[After a little prefatory flourish, the advertisement thus continues.] 'Being asked how much he was capable of lifting, he reply'd above a tun weight; whereupon a solid piece of lead was prepar'd according to his desire, being shap'd as convenient as possible for his laying hold of, in order to lift it; and being weigh'd, it contained a tun and fourteen pound and an half, which was more than he at first proposed: notwithstanding which he lifted it up at a considerable heighth from the ground, to the admiration of his majesty and his nobles, who were eye-witnes thereof, supposing such an exploit far beyond the ability of any mortal man to perform—after which, at his majesty's command, a rope of incredible thicknes was brought and fastned about his middle, and the other end to an extraordinary strong horse; at which time he told his majesty that the horse could not move him; upon which, to try the experiment, the said horse was order'd to be whip't in order to pull him out of the place; but, notwithstanding all his strength, Mr Joyce stood as immovable as an oak-tree: whereupon, seeing his majesty and others of the nobility to be seemingly astonish'd at this strange action, he thereupon declared that he could, by meer strength, break the same rope in two; whereupon, tying the same to two postes, he twitch'd it in pieces seemingly as easie as another man does a piece of pack-thred; and not only so, but afterwards putting his armes about one of the said postes (which was of extraordinary magnitude), he at one violent pull broke it down, and in the same manner he served the other also, to the extraordinary wonder of all then present. At which strange performances his majesty was mightily well pleas'd (and, 'tis said), has ordred him a considerable gratuity, besides an honorable entertainment for both him and his acquaintance.—We are credibly inform'd that the said Mr Joyce pull'd up a tree of near a yard and half circumferance, by the roots, at Hamstead, on Tuesday last, in the open view of some hundreds of people, it being modestly computed to weigh near 2000 weight;* these, and several other strange and amazing exploytes, he performs almost every day, even to the wonder of all mankind!'

In some degree in contrast with King William's Strong Man, is the account of a wonderfully small Scotsman, who was subjected to public attention in the same reign.

'A SCOTCH DWARF.

'These are to give notice to all persons of quallity, and others, that there is newly come to this place, a little Scotch man, which hath been admired by all that hath yet seen him, he being but two foot and six inches high; and is near upon 60 years of age. He was marry'd several years, and had issue two sons (one of which is with him now). He sings and dances with his son; and has had the honour to be shewn before several persons of note at their houses, as far as they have yet travelled. He formerly kept a writing-school; and discourses of the Scriptures, and of many eminent histories, very wisely; and gives great satisfaction to all spectators; and if need requires, there are several persons in this town that will justifie, that they were his schollars, and see him marry'd. He is to be seen at the lower end of Brookfield Market, near the market-house.' (Further than this, there is no clue to the name of the town).

Other wonders of the same kind follow:

'A "CHANGLING"† CHILD.

'To be seen next door to the *Black Raven*, in *West-Smithfield*, being a living skeleton, taken by a Venetian galley from a Turkish vessel in the Archipelago: This is a fairy child, suppos'd to be born of Hungarian parents, but chang'd in the nursing, aged nine years and more, not exceeding a foot and a half high. The legs, thighs, and arms are so very small that they scarce exceed the bigness of a man's thumb, and the face no bigger than the palm of one's hand; and seems so grave and solid, as if it were threescore years old. You may see the whole anatomy of its body by setting it against the sun. It never speaks. And when passion moves it, it cries like a cat. It has no teeth, but is the most voracious and hungry creature in the world, devouring more victuals

* We take this to mean 2000 lbs., or within about 2 cwt. of a ton; although one would have computed the weight of a tree of this stated circumference, allowing proportionally for its height, branches, &c., at much more.

† *Changeling*, a child left or changed by the fairies for the parents' own child. It was either deformed, mischievous, or idiotic, and hence the term came to be generally applied to a child having those qualities.

than the stoutest man in England.'—The above is headed by the royal arms, and at the foot are the words—*Vivant Rex et Regina*—thus shewing it to be towards the latter end of the seventeenth century.

AN IRISH GIANT.

To the annexed there is no date: '*Miracula Naturæ;* or, a miracle of nature. Being that so much-admired gyant-like young man, aged twenty-three years last June; born in Ireland, of such a prodigious height and bigness, and every way proportionable; that the like hath not been seen in England in the memory of man. He was shewn to his late and present majesty, and several of the nobility at court, five years ago; and his late majesty was pleased to walk under his arm, and he is grown very much since. And it is generally thought, that if he lives three years more, and grows as he has done, he will be much bigger than any of those gyants we read of in story: for he now reaches with his hand three yards and a half, spans fifteen inches, and is the admiration of all that sees him.—He is to be seen at Cow-Lane-End, in Bartholomew Fair, where his picture hangs out.'

THE PAINTED PRINCE.

There is no date to the following, further than that which may be gathered from the style of its typography, which would seem to be of about the period to which most, if not all, of these curious advertisements belong. The one immediately before us runs thus:

'*Prince* Giolo, *Son to the King of* Moangis, *or* Gilolo; *lying under the* Æquator *in the* Long. *of* 152 Deg. 30 Min.; *a Fruitful Island abounding with rich spices and other valuable commodities.*

'This unfortunate prince sailing towards a neighbouring island, with his mother and young sister, to complement the intended marriage betwixt her and the king of that island, a violent tempest surpriz'd them, and drove them on shoar upon the coast of Mindanao, where they were all made prisoners, except the young lady, with whom the king was so inamoured, that he took her to wife; yet suffered the prince and his mother Nacatara to be purchased for money. The mother died, but the prince, her son, is arriv'd in England.

'This famous *Painted Prince* is the first wonder of the age, his whole body (except face, hands, and feet) is curiously and most exquisitely *painted* or *stained*, full of variety of invention, with prodigious art and skill performed. Insomuch, that the antient and noble mystery of painting or staining upon humane bodies seems to be comprised in this one stately piece.

'The pictures, and those other engraven figures copied from him, serve only to describe as much as they can of the foreparts of this inimitable piece of workmanship. The more admirable back-parts afford us a lively representation of one quarter-part of the world upon and betwixt his shoulders, where the arctick and tropick circles center in the north pole on his neck. And all the other lines, circles, and characters are done in such exact symmetry and proportion that it is astonishing, and surmounts all that has hitherto been seen of this kind.

'The paint itself is so durable that nothing can wash it off, or deface the beauty of it. It is prepared from the juice of a certain herb or plant peculiar to that country, which they esteem infallible to preserve humane bodies from the deadly poison or hurt of any venomous creatures whatsoever. This custom they observe—that in some short time after the body is painted, it is carried naked, with much ceremony, to a spacious room appointed, which is filled with all sorts of the most venomous, pernicious creatures that can be found; such as snakes, scorpions, vipers, centapees (centipeds), &c. The king himself [is] present. The grandees and multitudes of spectators seeing the naked body surrounded with so many venomous creatures, and unable to wound or do any mischief to it, seem transported and ready to adore him; for none but those of the royal family are permitted to be thus painted.

'This excellent piece has been lately seen by many persons of high quality, and accurately surveyed by several learned *virtuosi*, and ingenious travellers, who have express'd very great satisfaction in seeing of it.

'This admirable person is about the age of thirty, graceful, and well-proportioned in all his limbs; extreamly modest and civil, neat and cleanly, but his language is not understood, neither can he speak English.

'He will be exposed to publick view every day from the 16th of this instant June, at his lodgings at the Blew Boar's Head, in Fleet Street, near Water Lane; where he will continue for some time, if his health will permit. But if any persons of quality, gentlemen or ladies, do desire to see this noble person, at their own houses or any other convenient place, in or about this city of London, they are to send timely notice, and he will be ready to wait upon them in a coach or chair any time they may please to appoint, if in the day-time.'

---

# OCTOBER 16.

St Gall, abbot, 646. St Mummolin or Mommolin, bishop of Noyon, confessor, 7th century. St Lullus or Lullon, archbishop of Mentz, confessor, 787.

*Born.*—Dr Albert Von Haller, distinguished physiologist, 1708, *Berne;* John George Sulzer, writer on the fine arts, 1720, *Winterthur, in Zurich.*

*Died.*—Bishops Nicholas Ridley and Hugh Latimer, martyred at Oxford, 1555; Roger Boyle, Earl of Orrery, politician and versifier, 1679; Robert Fergusson, Scottish poet, 1774, *Edinburgh;* Marie Antoinette, queen of Louis XVI., guillotined at Paris, 1793; John Hunter, celebrated anatomist, 1793, *London;* Victor Amadeus III. of Sardinia, 1796; Joseph Strutt, antiquary, 1802, *London;* Sharman Crawford, Irish political character, 1861; Henry Martyn, oriental missionary, 1812, *Tokat, Asia Minor;* Thaddeus Kosciusko, Polish patriot, 1817, *Soleure, in Switzerland.*

STORY OF THE DIAMOND NECKLACE.

In connection with the unfortunate Marie Antoinette, whose judicial murder by sentence of the Convention took place on 16th October 1793, we may in this place not inappositely introduce the famous story of the Diamond Necklace, in which the French queen played a conspicuous though involuntary part. This extraordinary affair originated in the profligate state of French society preceding the Revolution, when the upper classes, as if in mockery of the sufferings of the starving poor, displayed a magnificence as insulting as it was reckless and insane. We are told that the officers of the king's *maison militaire* not only wore uniforms, but had the harness and caparisons of their horses covered with gold, and the very manes and tails of these animals plaited with gold braid. Louis XVI. and his queen fell into this strange infatuation; and one of their most serious errors of judgment, was their conduct in the case of the Diamond Necklace, which cast a slur upon the fair fame of the queen, and finally proved one of the most deadly weapons in the hands of her enemies. The details long occupied the attention of the court of France, the College of Cardinals, and the higher ranks of the clergy. Many versions of the facts were given, but the following narrative, compiled from the documents of the case, from the memoirs, pamphlets, and petitions of the accusers and the accused, may be relied on as essentially correct.

THE DIAMOND NECKLACE.

In 1774, Louis XV., wishing to make a present to his mistress, Madame du Barry, commissioned the court-jewellers to collect the finest diamonds to form a necklace that should be unique of its kind. Some time and a considerable outlay were required to make arrangements to procure the largest, purest, and most brilliant diamonds. Unfortunately, before the necklace was completed, Louis XV. was laid in his grave, and the fallen favourite was fain to be content with the riches she possessed, without requiring the execution of the deceased monarch's intentions. The work, however, was too far advanced to permit of its being abandoned without great loss; and in the hope that Louis XVI. might be induced to purchase it for the queen, the jewellers finished the necklace, which was valued at 1,800,000 francs (£72,000 sterling). The new king's finances were in too low a state for him to purchase the necklace; and when it was offered to him, he replied that a ship was more needed than a necklace, which, therefore, remained in the hands of the jewellers for some years, until the occurrence of the event which, by breaking it up and dispersing it, gave it historical celebrity.

To understand by what a complication of circumstances, a woman without position, fortune, favour at court, or even very great charms of person, could have conceived the idea of obtaining an ornament that was beyond the means of sovereigns, can only be explained by reference to events much anterior to her meeting with her victim, and which gave rise to the life-long antipathy of Marie Antoinette to Louis, prince-cardinal of Rohan. In 1772, the prince was appointed ambassador to Vienna. At one of the merry suppers of Louis XV., Madame du Barry drew from her pocket, and read aloud a letter, purporting to be addressed *to her* by the ambassador at Vienna, and giving particulars of the private life of the empress of Austria, whose daughter, Marie Antoinette, had been, three years previously, married to the dauphin. The prince was, however, guiltless of any thought of offending the dauphiness; he had had no correspondence with Madame du Barry, but had merely replied to the king's inquiries as to what was taking place at the imperial court. Louis had left one of the ambassador's private letters in the hands of the Duke d'Aguillon, who was a creature of Du Barry, and had given the letter to her, which she, with her accustomed levity, read to amuse her guests.

The anger of Marie Antoinette, thus unwittingly incurred by M. de Rohan, continued to rankle in her breast after she had succeeded to the throne. Although, being allied to the most powerful families of France, and possessed of a princely income, he had obtained the post of grand-almoner of France, a cardinal's hat, the rich abbey of St Waast, and had been elected *proviseur* of the Sorbonne, the displeasure of the queen effectually disgraced him at court, and embittered his very existence. Such was his disagreeable position when he was introduced to an *intrigante*, who, taking advantage of his desire to regain the royal favour, involved him in the disgraceful transaction that placed him before the world in the attitude of a thief and a forger.

This woman was the descendant of royal blood, and had married a gendarme named Lamotte. Being reduced to beggary, she presented herself before the Cardinal de Rohan, to petition that in his capacity as grand-almoner, he would procure her aid from the royal bounty. Madame Lamotte, without being beautiful, had an intelligent and pleasing countenance and winning manners, and moved the cardinal-prince to advance her sums of money. He then advised her to apply in person to the queen, and, lamenting it was not in his power to procure her an interview, was weak enough to betray the deep chagrin which the sovereign's displeasure had caused him. Some days after, Madame Lamotte returned, stating that she had obtained admittance to the queen's presence, had been questioned kindly, had introduced the name of the cardinal as being one of her benefactors, and, perceiving she was listened to with interest, had ventured to mention the grief he endured, and had obtained permission to lay before her majesty his vindication. This service Madame Lamotte tendered in gratitude to the prince, who intrusted to her the apology, written by himself, which she stated had been placed in the sovereign's hands, and to which a note was vouchsafed in reply, Madame Lamotte having previously ascertained that the cardinal had not seen, or did not remember, the queen's handwriting. The contents were as follows: 'I have seen your note; I am delighted to find you innocent. I cannot yet grant you the audience you solicit; as soon as circumstances will permit, I will let you know. Be discreet.'

The prince was now completely duped. He was convinced that Madame Lamotte was admitted daily into her majesty's private apartments, and he thought it natural that the lively queen should be amused by her quick-witted sallies, and that she should make use of her as a ready tool. Following his guide's advice, he expressed his joy and gratitude in writing, and the correspondence thus commenced was continued, and so worded on the queen's part, that the cardinal had reason to believe that he had inspired unlimited confidence. When he was supposed to be sufficiently prepared, a note was risked from the queen, commissioning the grand-almoner to borrow for a charitable purpose 60,000 francs, and transmit them to her through the medium of Madame Lamotte. Absurd as was this clandestine negotiation, the cardinal believed it; he borrowed the money himself, and remitted it to Madame Lamotte, who brought, in return, a note of thanks. A second loan of a like amount was obtained. With these funds Madame Lamotte and her husband furnished a house handsomely, and started gay equipages, though not until the artful woman had, through her usual medium—a letter from the queen—insinuated to the cardinal that, to prevent suspicion, he should absent himself for a time, when he instantly set out for Alsace.

Meanwhile, Madame Lamotte accounted for her sudden opulence by saying that the queen's kindness supplied her with the means. Her majesty would not allow a descendant of royal blood to remain in poverty. This success emboldened Madame Lamotte to aim at much higher game. The court-jewellers were by this time tired of having the costly necklace lying idle; an emissary of Madame Lamotte had insinuated to them, that an influential lady at court might be able to recommend the purchase of the necklace. A handsome present was promised for such a service. But Madame Lamotte was cautious; she did not meddle with such matters; she would consider the subject. In a few days, she called on the jewellers, and announced that a great lord would that morning look at the necklace, which he was commissioned to purchase. The cardinal, in the meantime, received from his quasi-royal correspondent a note to hasten his return for a negotiation. On reaching Paris, he was informed that the queen earnestly desired to purchase the necklace without the king's knowledge, for which she would pay with money saved from her income. She had chosen the grand-almoner to negotiate the purchase in her name, as a special token of her favour and confidence. He was to receive an authorisation, written and signed by the queen, though the contract was to be made in the cardinal-prince's name. He unsuspectingly hastened to fulfil his mission; and on February 1, 1785, the necklace was placed in the cardinal's hands. Twenty thousand livres of the original price were taken off, quarterly payments agreed to, and the prince's note accepted for the whole amount. The jewellers, however, were made aware that the necklace was being purchased on her majesty's account, the prince having shewn them his authority, and charged them to keep the affair secret from all except the queen.

The necklace was to be delivered on the eve of a great fête, at which Madame Lamotte asserted the queen desired to wear it. The casket containing it was taken to Versailles, to the house of Madame

Lamotte, by whom it was to be handed to the person whom the queen was to send. At dusk, the cardinal arrived, followed by his valet bearing the casket; he took it from the servant at the door, and, sending him away, entered alone. He was placed by Madame Lamotte in a closet opening into a dimly-lighted apartment. In a few minutes a door was opened, a 'messenger from the queen' was announced, and a man entered. Madame Lamotte advanced, and respectfully placed the casket in the hands of the last-comer, who retired instantly. And so adroitly was the deception managed, that the cardinal protested that through the glazed sash of the closet-door, he had perfectly recognised the confidential valet of the queen! To strengthen the cardinal's belief, Madame Lamotte told him that she had taken lodgings at Versailles, as the queen was desirous of having her at hand; and to corroborate this statement, she persuaded the cardinal, disguised, to accompany her, when the queen, as she pretended, desired her attendance at Trianon. On one of these occasions, Madame Lamotte and the cardinal were escorted by the pretended valet, who was the former's accomplice; but it was the *concierge* of the Château of Trianon, and not the queen, whom Madame Lamotte went to visit.

The acknowledgment of the necklace was next artfully planned. Madame Lamotte had noticed that when the queen passed from her own apartment, crossing the gallery, to go to the chapel, she made a motion with her head, which she repeated when she passed the Œil de Bœuf. On the same evening that the necklace was delivered Madame met the cardinal on the terrace of the château, and told him that the queen was delighted. Her majesty could not then acknowledge the receipt of the necklace; but next day, if he would be, as if by chance, in the Œil de Bœuf, her majesty would, by the motion of her head, signify her approbation. The cardinal went, saw, and was satisfied. Meanwhile, as Madame Lamotte informed her dupe, the queen thought it advisable not to wear the necklace until she had mentioned its purchase to the king.

The presence of the cardinal now becoming troublesome, a little note sent him again to Alsace. Madame Lamotte then despatched her husband with the necklace to London, where it was broken up; the small diamonds were reset in bracelets and rings, for the three accomplices; the remainder was sold to jewellers, and the money placed in the Bank of England in a fictitious name.

The cardinal, in the meantime, induced the jewellers to write to the queen (if they could not see her), to thank her for the honour she had done them. They did so, and were soon summoned to explain their letter, which was an enigma to the queen; and the whole affair of the purchase, as far as the cardinal was concerned, was then explained to her majesty. This was in the beginning of July. From that moment Marie Antoinette acted in an unjust and undignified manner. Instead of exposing the manœuvre, and having the authors of the fraud punished, the queen allowed herself to be guided by two of the most inveterate enemies of the cardinal, whom she left to their surveillance; and the jewellers were merely told to bring a copy of the agreement, and leave it with her majesty.

Meanwhile, the first instalment in payment of the necklace was nearly due, and the cardinal being wanted to provide funds for it, he was recalled to Paris in the month of June, by a note assuring him that the realisation of the queen's promises was near at hand, that she was making great efforts to meet the first payment, but that unforeseen expenditure rendered the matter difficult. The prince, however, began to think it strange that no change was apparent in the queen's behaviour towards him in public, nor was the necklace worn; but, to satisfy him, Madame Lamotte arranged a private interview with the queen, between eleven and twelve o'clock, in a grove near Versailles. To personate her majesty at this rendezvous, the conspirators had chosen a certain Mademoiselle Leguet, whose figure, gait, and profile gave her a great resemblance to the queen. This new accomplice was not initiated into the secrets of the plot, but was told that she was to play her little part to mystify a certain nobleman of the court, for the amusement of the queen, who would be an unseen witness of the scene. It was rehearsed in the appointed grove: a tall man, in a blue great-coat and slouched hat, would approach and kiss her hand, with great respect. She was to say in a whisper: 'I have but a moment to spare; I am greatly pleased with all you have done, and am about to raise you to the height of power.' She was to give him a rose, and a small box containing a miniature. Footsteps would then be heard approaching, on which she was to exclaim, in the same low tone: 'Here are Madame, and Madame d'Artois! we must separate.' The scene took place as planned; the queen's relatives being represented by M. Lamotte and a confederate named Villette, who, approaching, cut short the cardinal's interview, of which he complained bitterly to his friends. Nevertheless, understanding that the queen was unable to pay the 300,000 livres, he endeavoured to borrow them; when a note came to say, that if the payment could be delayed one month, the jewellers should receive 700,000 livres at the end of August, in lieu of the 300,000 livres due in July; 30,000 livres being tendered as interest, which Madame Lamotte contrived to pay out of the proceeds of the sale of the diamonds. This the jewellers took and gave the cardinal a receipt on account; but they refused all further delay, and daily pressed the prince for payment, and threatened to make use of the power his note gave them. 'Why,' exclaimed he, 'since you have had frequent access to her majesty, have you not mentioned the disagreeable situation in which her delay places you?' 'Alas! Monseigneur,' they replied, 'we have had the honour of speaking to her majesty on the subject, and she denies having ever given you such a commission, or received the necklace. To whom, my prince, can you have given it?' The cardinal was thunderstruck: he replied, however, that he had placed the casket in Madame Lamotte's hands, and saw her deliver it into those of the queen's valet. 'At any rate,' he added, 'I have in my hands the queen's authorisation, and that will be my guarantee.' The jewellers replied: 'If that is all you count upon, my lord, we fear you have been cruelly deceived.' Madame Lamotte was absent from Paris, but repaired thither, and arriving at the grand-almoner's in the middle of the night, assured him she had just left the queen, who threatened to deny having received the necklace, or authorised its purchase, 'and to make good her own position, would have me arrested, and ruin you;' at the same time entreating his eminence to give her shelter until she could concert with her husband her means of escape. This was, in reality, a *ruse* to clear herself and criminate the cardinal, who, she declared on her arrest, had kept her a close prisoner for four-and-twenty hours, to prevent her disclosing that she had been employed to sell the diamonds for him.

This took place early in August. An enemy of the cardinal now drew up a memorial of the whole affair, which, however, was not presented to the king until the 14th of August; and next morning being a great fête, while the grand-almoner, in his pontifical robes, was waiting to accompany her majesty to the chapel, he was summoned to the royal closet before Louis and Marie Antoinette, the memorialist, and two other court-dignitaries. The king, handing him the depositions of the jewellers, and the financier of whom the cardinal had endeavoured to borrow for the queen 300,000 livres, bade him read them. This being done, the king asked what he had to say to these accusations. 'They are correct in the more material points, sire,' replied the cardinal. 'I purchased the necklace for the queen.' 'Who commanded you?' exclaimed she. 'Your majesty did so by a writing to that effect, signed, and which I have in my pocket-book in Paris.' 'That writing,' exclaimed the queen, 'is a forgery!' The cardinal threw a significant glance at the queen, when the king ordered him to retire, and in a few minutes he was arrested and sent to the Bastile.

A few days after, Madame Lamotte was arrested in the provinces, where she was entertaining a large party of friends; her husband had escaped, and she had sent her other accomplices out of the kingdom. She was taken to the Bastile on the 20th of August: when examined, she at first denied all knowledge of the necklace, though she admitted that she and her husband had been employed by the cardinal to dispose of a quantity of loose diamonds. She afterwards said that the necklace had been purchased by the cardinal to sell in fragments, in order to retrieve his affairs; and that he had acted with the connivance of Cagliostro, into whose hands the funds had passed. She denied all mention of the queen's name, and her tone was ironical and daring. Cagliostro and his wife were sent to the Bastile, where they were kept for many months; but nothing proved that they had been concerned in the affair, though the cardinal used to consult Cagliostro, in whose cabalistic art he had great faith.

At this stage light unexpectedly broke in. Father Loth, a neighbour of Madame Lamotte, whom she had intrusted with her secret, revealed to the friends of the cardinal the parts played by Villette and Mademoiselle Leguet, who were accordingly arrested, one in Geneva, and the other in Belgium. Their evidence was conclusive as to the deception Madame Lamotte had practised upon the cardinal with regard to the queen, and the other facts were easily proved. The testimony of Cagliostro also weighed heavily against her; and when confronted with the witnesses, in a violent rage she exclaimed: 'I see there is a plot on foot to ruin me; but I will not perish without disclosing the names of the great personages yet concealed behind the curtain!'

This strange drama was at length brought to a close on the 31st of May 1786; when, in the trial before the Criminal Court, the prince-cardinal was proved innocent of all fraud, but was ridiculed for his extreme credulity; was ordered by the king to resign his posts at court; and was exiled to his abbey of La Chaise Dieu, in the mountains of Auvergne. The wretched woman, Lamotte, was sentenced to be flogged, branded on both shoulders, and imprisoned for life. When the former part of the sentence was executed, she most foully abused the queen; and though she was gagged, enough was heard to form the ground of the vilest calumnies. Her husband, who had escaped to England, was condemned by default; when he threatened to publish a pamphlet compromising the queen and her minister, Baron de Breteuil, if his wife were not set free. This was treated with contempt; but, ten months after, Madame Lamotte was permitted to escape to England, whither the Duchess of Polignac was sent to purchase the silence of the infamous Lamottes with a large sum of money. The bribe was thrown away, for though one edition of the slanderous pamphlet, or memoir, was burned, a second was published some time after; and the copies which are now extant in the Imperial Library of Paris, were found in the palace of Versailles, when it was taken possession of by the Republican government.

---

## THE WHISTLE DRINKING-CUP.

The drinking-customs of various nations would form a curious chapter in ethnology. The Teutonic races have, however, the most claim to be considered 'potent in potting.' The Saxons were great drinkers; and took with them to their graves their ornamental ale-buckets and drinking-glasses, the latter made without foot or stand, so that they must be filled and emptied by the drinker before they could be set down again on the festive-board. Mighty topers they were, and history records some of their drinking-bouts. Notwithstanding the assertion of Iago, that 'your Dane, your German, and your swag-bellied Hollander, are nothing to your English' in powers of drinking, it may be doubted if the Germans have ever been outdone. Certainly no persons have bestowed more thought on quaint inventions for holding their liquors, or enforcing large consumption, than they have. The silversmiths of Augsburg and Nuremberg, in the sixteenth and seventeenth centuries, devoted a large amount of invention to the production of drinking-cups, taking the form of men, animals, birds, &c., of most grotesque design. Our engraving (see the following page) represents one surmounted by a wind-mill. It will be perceived that the cup must be held in the hand to be filled, and retained there till it be emptied, as then only it can be set upon the table. The drinker having swallowed the contents, blew up the pipe at the side, which gave a shrill whistle, and set the sails of the wind-mill in motion also. The power of the blow, and the length of the gyration, were indicated in a small dial upon the front of the mill, and also in some degree testified to the state of the consumer. Among the songs of Burns is one upon a whistle, used by a Dane of the retinue of Anne of Denmark, which was laid upon the table at the commencement of the orgie, and won by whoever

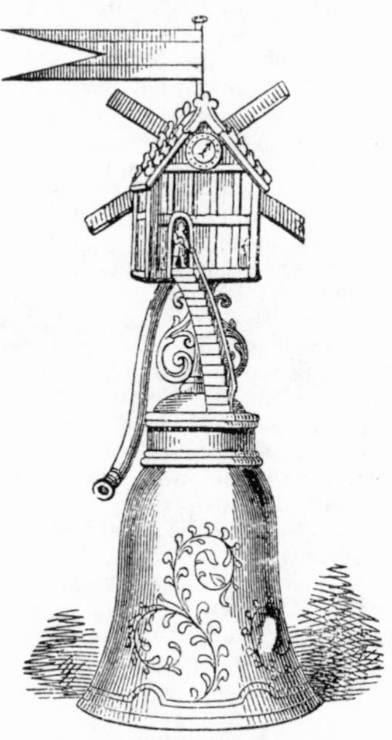

WHISTLE DRINKING-CUP.

was last able to blow it. The Dane conquered all-comers, until Sir Robert Lawrie of Maxwelton, 'after three days and three nights' hard contest, left the Scandinavian under the table.' On 16th October 1789, a similar contest took place, which has been immortalised in Burns's verses.

---

## NATHANIEL LLOYD'S WILL—ODD BEQUESTS.

On the 16th of October 1769, Nathaniel Lloyd, of Twickenham, Middlesex, Esquire, completed his testament in the following terms:

'What I am going to bequeath,
When this frail spark submits to death;
But still I hope the spark divine
With its congenial stars shall shine;
My good Executors, fulfil,
I pray ye, fairly, my last will,
With first and second codicil.
First, I give to dear Lord Hinton,
At Tryford school—not at Winton,
One hundred guineas for a ring,
Or some such memorandum thing;
And truly, much I should have blundered,
Had I not giv'n another hundred
To Vere, Earl Poulett's second son,
Who dearly loves a little fun.
Unto my nephew, Robert Longden,
Of whom none says he ever has wrong done,
Tho' civil law he loves to lash,
I give two hundred pounds in cash.
One hundred pounds to my niece Tuder
(With loving eyes one Matthew view'd her)
And to her children—just among 'em
A hundred more, and not to wrong 'em,
In equal shares I freely give it.
Not doubting but they will receive it.
To Sally Crouch and Mary Lee,
If they with Lady Poulett be,
Because they would the year did dwell
In Twickenham House, and served full well,
When Lord and Lady both did stray
Over the hills and far away:
The first, ten pounds: the other twenty;
And, girls, I hope that will content ye.
In seventeen hundred, sixty-nine,
This with my hand I write and sign,
The sixteenth day of fair October,
In merry mood, but sound and sober;
Past my threescore-and-fifteenth year,
With spirits gay and conscience clear,
Joyous and frolicsome, though old,
And like this day—serene, but cold;
To foes well-wishing, and to friends most kind,
In perfect charity with all mankind.
For what remains, I must desire,
To use the words of Matthew Prior:—
"Supreme! All-wise! Eternal Potentate!
Sole Author! sole Disposer of my Fate!
Enthron'd in Light and Immortality!
Whom no man fully sees, and none can see!
Original of Beings! Power Divine!
Since that I think, and that I live, is thine!
Benign Creator! let thy plastic hand
Dispose of its own effect! Let thy command
Restore, Great Father, thy instructed son,
And in my act, may Thy great will be done."'

To be thus quaint and eccentric in one of the most solemn affairs of life, is of by no means unfrequent occurrence among the denizens of this cloudy island. Some men choose to burden their executors with a great number of injunctions, partly to express certain tastes and prejudices, but mainly, as we may presume, for the vanity of causing some little sensation about themselves when they are no more. The following is a notable example:

'*A True Copy of the Last Will and Testament of* Mr Benjamin Dod, *Citizen and Linen Draper, who lately fell from his Horse, and Dy'd soon after.*

'*In the Name of God*, Amen. I, Benjamin Dod, citizen and mercer of *London*, being in health of body, and good and perfect memory, do make this my last will and Testament in manner and form following (*that is to say*): First, my soul I commend to Almighty God that gave it me, and my body to the earth from whence it came. I desire to be interr'd in the parish church of St John, *Hackney*, in the county of *Middlesex*, about eleven o'clock at night, in a decent and frugal manner, as to Mr Robert Atkins shall seem meet, the management whereof I leave to him. I desire Mr Brown to preach my funeral sermon; but if he should happen to be absent or dead, then such other persons as Mr Robert Atkins shall appoint: and to such minister that preaches my funeral sermon I give five guineas.

'*Item:* I desire four-and-twenty persons to be at my burial, out of which Messrs J. Low, &c. [naming six persons] to be pall-bearers: but if any of them be absent or dead, I desire Mr Robert Atkins to appoint others in their room, to every of which four-and-twenty persons so to be invited to my funeral, I give a pair of white gloves, a ring of ten shillings' value, a bottle of wine at my funeral, and half-a-crown to spent at their return that night, to drink my soul's health, then on her journey to purification in order to eternal rest. I appoint the room where my corps shall lye, to be hung with black, and four-and-twenty wax-candles to be burning. On my coffin to be affixed a cross, and this inscription—

*Jesus Hominum Salvator.*

I also appoint my corps to be carried in a hearse, drawn with six white horses, with white feathers, and follow'd by six coaches, with six horses to each coach, to carry the four-and-twenty persons. I desire Mr John Spicer may make the escutcheons, and appoint an undertaker, who shall be a noted churchman. What relations have a mind to come to my funeral may do it without invitation.

'*Item:* I give to forty of my particular acquaintance, not at my funeral, to every of them a gold ring of ten shillings' value; the said forty persons to be nam'd by Mr Robert Atkins. As for mourning, I leave that to my executors hereafter nam'd; and I do not desire them to give any to whom I shall leave a legacy.'

After enumerating a number of legacies, &c., the testator concludes thus:

'I will have no Presbyterians, moderate Low-churchmen, or occasional Conformists, to be at, or have anything to do with, my funeral. I die in the faith of the true Catholick Church. I desire to have a Tombstone over me, with a Latin inscription; and a lamp, or six wax-candles, to burn seven days and nights together thereon.'

The will of Peter Campbell, of Darley, dated October 20, 1616, contained the following passage: 'Now for all such household goods at Darley, whereof John Howson hath an inventory, my will is, that my son Roger shall have them all towards housekeeping upon this condition, that if, at any time hereafter, any of his brothers or sisters shall find him taking of tobacco, that then he or she, so finding him, and making just proof to my executors, shall have the said goods, or the full value thereof, according as they shall be praised.' *

Some men, again, have an amiable dying satisfaction in charging their wills with a sting or a stab at some relative or other person who has not behaved well, or has (or is supposed to have) been guilty of some special delict towards the testator. Some have a similar pleasure in shewing their contempt for their own kind by careful provision for favourite cats, dogs, and parrots. Others, good easy-natured souls, love to charge their wills with a joke, which they know will provoke a smile from their old friends when they are lying cold in the grave. A few examples of these various testamentary eccentricities follow:

1788.—'I, David Davis, of Clapham, Surrey, do give and bequeath to Mary Davis, daughter of Peter Delaport, the sum of 5*s*., which is sufficient to enable her to get drunk for the last time at my expense.'

1782.—'I, William Blackett, governor of Plymouth, desire that my body may be kept as long as it may not be offensive; and that one or more of my toes or fingers may be cut off, to secure a certainty of my being dead. I also make this request to my dear wife, that as she has been troubled with one old fool, she will not think of marrying a second.'

1781.—'I, John Aylett Stow, do direct my executors to lay out five guineas in the purchase of a picture of the viper biting the benevolent hand of the person who saved him from perishing in the snow, if the same can be bought for that money; and that they do, in memory of me, present it to —— Esq., a King's Counsel, whereby he may have frequent opportunities of contemplating on it, and, by a comparison between that and his own virtue, be able to form a certain judgment which is best and most profitable, a grateful remembrance of past friendship and almost parental regard, or ingratitude and insolence. This I direct to be presented to him in lieu of a legacy of £3000, which I had, by a former will, now revoked and burnt, left him.'

* *Gentleman's Magazine*, April 1769.

*Extract from the Will of S. Church, in* 1793.—'I give and devise to my son, Daniel Church, only *one shilling*, and that is for him to hire a porter to carry away the next badge and frame he steals.'

1813.—'I, Elizabeth Orby Hunter, of Upper Seymour Street, widow, do give and bequeath to my beloved parrot, the faithful companion of 25 years, an annuity for its life of 200 guineas a year, to be paid half-yearly, as long as this beloved parrot lives, to whoever may have the care of it, and proves its identity; but the above annuity to cease on the death of my parrot; and if the person who shall or may have care of it, should substitute any other parrot in its place, either during its life or after its death, it is my positive will and desire, that the person or persons so doing shall refund to my heirs or executors the sum or sums they may have received from the time they did so; and I empower my heirs and executors to recover it from whoever could be base enough to do so. And I do give and bequeath to Mrs Mary Dyer, widow, now dwelling in Park Street, Westminster, my foresaid parrot, with its annuity of 200 guineas a year, to be paid her half-yearly, as long as it lives; and if Mrs Mary Dyer should die before my beloved parrot, I will and desire, that the aforesaid annuity of 200 guineas a year may be paid to whoever may have the care of my parrot as long as it lives, to be always the first paid annuity; and I give to Mrs Mary Dyer the power to will and bequeath my parrot and its annuity to whomsoever she pleases, provided that person is neither a servant nor a man—it must be bequeathed to some respectable female. And I also will and desire that no person shall have the care of it that can derive any benefit from its death; and if Mrs Dyer should neglect to will my parrot and its annuity to any one, in that case, whoever proves that they may have possession of it, shall be entitled to the annuity on its life, as long as it lives, and that they have possession of it, provided that the person is not a servant or a man, but a respectable female; and I hope my executors will see it is in proper and respectable hands; and I also give the power to whoever possesses it, and its annuity, to any respectable female on the same conditions. And I also will and desire, that 20 guineas may be paid to Mrs Dyer directly on my death, to be expended on a very high, long, and large cage for the foresaid parrot. It is also my will and desire, that my parrot shall not be removed out of England. I will and desire that whoever attempts to dispute this my last will and testament, or by any means neglect, or tries to avoid paying my parrot's annuity, shall forfeit whatever I may have left them; and if any one that I have left legacies to attempt bringing in any bills or charges against me, I will and desire that they forfeit whatever I may have left them, for so doing, as I owe nothing to any one. Many owe to me both gratitude and money, but none have paid me either.'

1806.—'I, John Moody, of Westminster, boot-maker, give to Sir F. Burdett, Bart., this piece of friendly advice, to take a special care of his conduct and person, and never more to be the dupe of artful and designing men at a contested election, or ever amongst persons moving in a higher sphere of life; for placemen of all descriptions have conspired against him, and if prudence does not lead him into private life, certain destruction will await him.'

1810.—Richard Crawshay, of Cyfartha, in the

county of Glamorgan, Esq. 'To my only son, who never would follow my advice, and has treated me rudely in very many instances; instead of making him my executor and residuary legatee (as till this day he was), I give him £100,000.'

1793.—'I, Philip Thicknesse, formerly of London, but now of Bologna, in France, leave my right hand, to be cut off after my death, to my son, Lord Audley; and I desire it may be sent to him, in hopes that such a sight may remind him of his duty to God, after having so long abandoned the duty he owed to a father who once affectionately loved him.

1770.—'I, Stephen Swain, of the parish of St Olave, Southwark, give to John Abbot, and Mary, his wife, 6*d.* each, to buy for each of them a halter, for fear the sheriffs should not be provided.'

1794.—'I, Wm. Darley, late of Ash, in the county of Herts, give unto my wife, Mary Darley, for picking my pocket of 60 guineas, and taking up money in my name, of John Pugh, Esq., the sum of one shilling.'

1796.—'I, Catharine Williams, of Lambeth, give and bequeath to Mrs Elizabeth Paxton £10, and £5 a year, to be paid weekly by my husband, to take care of my cats and dogs, as long as any of them shall live; and my desire is that she will take great care of them, neither let them be killed or lost. To my servant-boy, George Smith, £10 and my jackass, to get his living with, as he is fond of traffic.'

1785.—'I, Charles Parker, of New Bond Street, Middlesex, bookseller, give to Elizabeth Parker, the sum of £50, whom, through my foolish fondness, I made my wife, without regard to family, fame, or fortune; and who, in return, has not spared, most unjustly, to accuse me of every crime regarding human nature, save highway-robbery.'

Amongst jocular bequests, that of David Hume to his friend John Home, author of *Douglas*, may be considered as one of the most curious. John Home liked claret, but detested port wine, thinking it a kind of poison; and the two friends had doubtless had many discussions on this subject. They also used to have disputes as to which of them took the proper way of spelling their common family-name. The philosopher, about a fortnight before his death, wrote with his own hand the following codicil to his will: 'I leave to my friend, Mr John Home, of Kilduff, ten dozen of my old claret at his choice, and one single bottle of that other liquor called port. I also leave him six dozen of port, provided that he attests under his hand, signed John *Hume*, that he has himself alone finished that bottle at two sittings. By this concession, he will at once terminate the only two differences that ever arose between us concerning temporal matters.'

Somewhat akin to this humour was that shewn in a verbal bequest of a Scotch judge named Lord Forglen, who died in 1727. 'Dr Clerk, who attended Lord Forglen at the last, told James Boswell's father, Lord Auchinleck, that, calling on his patient the day his lordship died, he was let in by his clerk, David Reid. "How does my lord do?" inquired Dr Clerk. "I houp he's *weel!*" answered David, with a solemnity that told what he meant. He then conducted the doctor into a room, and shewed him two dozen of wine under a table. Other doctors presently came in, and David, making them all sit down, proceeded to tell them his deceased master's last words, at the same time pushing the bottle about briskly. After the company had taken a glass or two, they rose to depart; but David detained them. "No, no, gentlemen; not so. It was the express will of the deceased that I should fill ye a' fou, and I maun fulfil the will o' the dead." All the time the tears were streaming down his cheeks. "And, indeed," said the doctor afterwards in telling the story, "he did fulfil the will o' the dead, for before the end o't there was na ane of us able to bite his ain thoomb!"' *

## JOHN HUNTER'S MUSEUM.

It is doubtful whether any private individual ever formed a museum more complete and valuable than that of John Hunter, now under the care of the Royal College of Surgeons, in Lincoln's Inn Fields. Whatever else the great surgeon was doing, he never forgot or neglected his museum. In 1755, when his brother Dr William Hunter was a surgeon and lecturer of eminence, John was his assistant, and helped him in making anatomical preparations. He soon, however, went far beyond his mere duties as an assistant, and examined all the living and dead animals he could get hold of, to compare their structure with that of the human body. He made friends with the keepers of all the travelling-menageries, and lost no opportunity of profiting by the facilities thus afforded. A mangy dog, a dead donkey, a sick lion, all alike were made contributary to the advancement of science in the hands of John Hunter. He took a house in Golden Square in 1764, and then built a second residence at Earl's Court, where he might carry on experiments in science. After having been made a member of the College of Surgeons, he removed from Golden Square to Jermyn Street, where he packed all the best rooms in the house full of anatomical specimens and preparations. He married in 1771, and his wife thereafter lived at Earl's Court, for there was no room for her among the physiological and pathological wonders of Jermyn Street. Indeed, for more than twenty years, he was accustomed to carry on his favourite researches at Earl's Court, only being in London a sufficient time each day to attend to his practice as a surgeon. His collection increased so rapidly, that the house in Jermyn Street became filled to repletion; insomuch that, in 1782, he took a larger house on the east side of Leicester Square. Here he built a new structure expressly as a museum, comprising a fine room fifty-two feet by twenty-eight, lighted at the top, and provided with a gallery all round. Sir Joseph Banks aided John Hunter out of his own ample store of natural-history specimens, and the museum soon became a wealthy one. Mr Home, a brother-in-law, who had been an assistant army-surgeon, came to reside with him as a sort of curator of the museum. Hunter also employed a Mr Bell for fourteen years, in making anatomical drawings and preparations; while he himself was accumulating a vast mass of MS. papers—building up almost a complete system of physiology and surgery, on the evidence furnished by the specimens in his museum. Hunter was always poor, and very frequently embarrassed, by the expenses which his scientific enterprise entailed upon him, and this notwithstanding the fact that his professional income reached £5000 a year for some years before his death. In 1794, he began to open his museum

* This anecdote is taken from *Boswelliana*, a volume privately printed by R. M. Milnes, Esq.

occasionally to the public, and justly prided himself on the scientific way in which it was arranged. Being a hasty and irritable man, he soon took offence, and was not readily appeased; and he himself predicted that any sudden or violent anger would probably kill him. The result mournfully verified his prediction; for, on the 16th October 1795, having had a very exciting quarrel with some of the members at the College of Surgeons, he dropped down dead in the attempt to suppress his feelings.

In his will, he directed that his museum, the pride of his life, should be offered to the nation if anything like a fair sum were tendered for it; in order that it might be retained in the country. Failing in this, it was to be offered to certain foreign governments, in succession; and if all these attempts failed, it was to be disposed of by private contract. After much negotiation, the government bought the splendid collection, in 1799, for £15,000. The question, what to do with it? had then to be decided, and the following arrangement was come to. The College of Surgeons received a new charter in 1800, constituting it a 'Royal' College, and giving it increased powers. The Hunterian Collection was intrusted to the keeping of the college, on condition of the public being allowed access to it; and twenty-four 'Hunterian Lectures' on surgery being given annually by the college. The government granted £27,500 to construct a building for the reception of the collection; but it was many years before the museum was really opened.

One painful circumstance connected with this museum roused the indignation of the whole medical profession of Europe. John Hunter left a vast mass of manuscripts of priceless value, recording the results of forty years' researches in comparative and pathological anatomy and physiology. This treasure was placed in the museum. Mr (afterwards Sir Everard) Home was one of the executors, and also one of the trustees. He took these manuscripts to his own house, about 1810, under pretence of drawing up a catalogue of them; and no entreaties or remonstrances would ever induce him to return them. He kept them ten or twelve years, and *then burned them!* The only reason he assigned was, that John Hunter had requested him to do so. The world viewed the matter otherwise. Year after year, while the manuscripts were in his possession, Sir Everard poured forth scientific papers in such profusion as astonished all the physicians and anatomists of Europe, who had hitherto been ignorant of his possessing such attainments. Then, after years of surprise and disappointment at the non-return of the Hunter manuscripts, the act of their destruction was openly admitted by Home, and the source of his scientific inspiration now became tolerably manifest. Unhappily, this disgraceful transaction remains beyond a doubt. The trustees and the board of curators indignantly remonstrated with Home in 1824 and 1825, and compelled him to make an attempt to vindicate himself, but none of his excuses or explanations could do away with the one cruel fact, that the invaluable manuscripts were irrevocably gone.

The Hunterian Museum, comprising 22,000 specimens, occupies a fine suite of rooms and galleries at the Royal College of Surgeons, on the south side of Lincoln's Inn Fields. Most of them are valuable only to medical men; but some, such as the skeletons of the Bosjesman, the Irish giant, and the Sicilian dwarf, and the embalmed body of the wife of Martin Van Butchell, a celebrated quack-doctor in the last century, will be viewed by all with the greatest interest.

---

# OCTOBER 17.

St Etheldreda or Audry, abbess of Ely. St Anstrudis or Austru, abbess at Laon, 688. St Andrew of Crete, 761. St Hedwiges or Avoice, Duchess of Poland, widow, 1243.

---

## ST ETHELDREDA OR AUDRY.

This saint, commemorated in the Romish calendar on 23d June, but in the English calendar on 17th October, in celebration of the translation of her relics from the common cemetery of the nuns to a splendid marble coffin within the church of Ely, was the daughter of a king of East Anglia, and earned an exalted reputation both by her piety and good works, and the maintenance of an early vow of virginity which she observed through life, though married successively to two Saxon princes. She founded the convent and church of Ely on the spot where the cathedral was erected at a subsequent period, and died in 679 as its abbess. Various churches throughout England are named after her, among others Ely Cathedral, the patronage of which, however, she shares with St Peter.

From St Etheldreda's more homely appellation of St Audry, is derived an adjective of the English language in familiar use. At the fair of St Audry, at Ely, in former times, toys of all sorts were sold, and a description of cheap necklaces, which, under the denomination of *tawdry laces*, long enjoyed great celebrity. Various allusions to tawdry laces occur in Shakspeare, Spenser, and other writers of their age.

'One time I gave thee a paper of pins,
Another time a tawdry lace,
And if thou wilt not grant me love,
In truth I'll die before thy face.'

*Old Ballad.*

'It was a happy age when a man might have wooed his wench with a pair of kid-leather gloves, a silver thimble, or with a tawdry lace; but now a velvet gown, a chain of pearl, or a coach with four horses, will scarcely serve the turn.'—*Rich's 'My Lady's Looking-glass,'* 1616.

In process of time, the epithet *tawdry* came to be applied to any piece of glittering tinsel or tarnished finery.

*Born.*—Augustus III., king of Poland, 1696; John Wilkes, noted demagogue, 1727, *Clerkenwell, London;* William Scott, Baron Stowell, great consistorial lawyer, 1745, *Heworth, near Newcastle-on-Tyne.*

*Died.*—Pope John VII., 707; Philip de Comines, historian, 1509, *Argenton, in Poitou;* Andrew Osiander, eminent Lutheran divine, 1552, *Königsberg;* Sir Philip Sidney, poet and hero, 1586, *Arnheim, Holland;* Sir Edmundbury Godfrey, mysteriously murdered, 1678; Ninon de Lenclos, celebrated beauty and wit, 1705; Dr John Ward, rhetorician, 1758; Frederic Chopin, musical composer, 1849, *Paris.*

## SIR PHILIP SIDNEY.

Sir Philip Sidney, the idol of his own, and the boast of succeeding ages, was not quite thirty-two when he died. He lived long enough to afford, to all who knew him, unmistakable promise of greatness, but not so long as to leave to posterity any singular proof of it. And yet we can read his character with sufficient clearness, to feel assured that the universal love of him was founded on a solid basis. Though at times we catch glimpses of a certain haughtiness, a hastiness, an ill-tempered boldness of valour, such as in an older man we should not have looked for, we find, on the other hand, unmistakable marks of a true-hearted patriot, a wise statesman, a skilful general, an elegant scholar, a graceful writer, a kind patron, and a Christian gentleman. Ophelia's description of Hamlet has often been applied to him, and it seems to fail in no particular—

'The courtier's, scholar's, soldier's, eye, tongue, sword,
The expectancy and rose of the fair state,
The glass of fashion and the mould of form,
The observed of all observers.'

He was beautiful within and without; elegant as well in fashion of person as in grace of mind. 'Imitate his virtues, studies, and actions,' said his father to Sidney's younger brother, speaking of Sidney; 'he is a rare ornament of this age, the very formular that all well-disposed young gentlemen of our court do form their manners and life by. . . . In truth, I speak it without flattery of him or of myself, he hath the most rare virtues that ever I found in any man.'

Sir Philip Sidney was named *Philip* after Philip of Spain, as well from gratitude to that king, to whom the family was beholden, as in honour of Mary. His mother was a Dudley. Her father, her grandfather, her brother, and her sister-in-law, Lady Jane Grey, had all died on the scaffold; and this was the Dudley blood of which Sidney was proud.

The events of Sidney's short career are not very prominent in history. After leaving the university, he travelled for some years. Being a Protestant, he encountered some personal danger at Paris, where he happened to be during the treacherous massacre of St Bartholomew. Afterwards he was present at Venice, at a time when that already waning power was making peace with the Turk. Besides these particulars, there is nothing worthy of remark in Sidney's travels. After his return, his progress at court was slow. Elizabeth employed him on several important embassies, in which he gave entire satisfaction; but the queen had a way of holding back ambitious youths of merit, and though she was very fond of Sidney, and even took a journey to stand godmother to his daughter Elizabeth, she received his honest, unasked counsels, with considerable coldness, while she appears, at the same time, prudently to have acted on them. At last, she stopped him in the very act of secretly embarking with Sir Francis Drake on a voyage of discovery; and, as she was always whimsical, instead of punishing him, she made him governor of Flushing, a post which some time previously he had applied for in vain. Sidney threw himself heart and soul into the cause of the Low Countries; took an important town by a skilful night-attack; shewed himself apt for war; and received his death-wound in the battle of Zutphen. This battle of Zutphen, so named, was not a battle. A few hundred men were sent to intercept supplies, which the Prince of Parma was conveying into the town, and fell into an ambush of several thousands. Sidney, from a restless thirst for adventure, had joined the troop, unbidden, with other English leaders; and these valiant men, to whom retreat was open, foolishly performed prodigies of valour. Sidney, in a fit of generous boldness, had thrown away his thigh-armour, because a friend had unintentionally come without his own, and a ball shattered his thigh. He had the best of attendance, his wife's nursing, and many tears of true friends; but nothing remained for him but to die a noble and Christian death, and to be borne in a black ship over the still sea and up the Thames, to lie in state many months, to have a national funeral, and be laid in peace in old St Paul's.

A curious contemporary ballad accurately describes the melancholy close:

'The king of Scots bewrayed his grief in learned verse,
And many more their passions penned, with praise to deck his hearse.
The Flushingers made suit his breathless corpse to have,
And offered a sumptuous tomb the same for to engrave;
But O, his loving friends, at their request did grieve,
It was too much he lost his life, his corpse they should not have.
And so from Flushing port, in ship attired with black,
They did embark this perfect knight, that only breath did lack;
The wind and seas did mourn to see this heavy sight,
And into Thames did carry this much lamented knight;
Unto the Minories his body was conveyed,
And there, under a martial hearse, three months or more was laid;
But when the day was come he to his grave must go,
An host of heavy men repaired to see the solemn show.'

Thus the pride of the English people passed out of the view of men, and 'for many months it was counted indecent for any gentleman of quality to appear, at court or in the city, in light or gaudy apparel.'

King James of Scotland, as we have seen, wrote certain sonnets; the two universities between them produced three volumes of mournful elegies; and Spenser honoured his lost friend and patron with the poem of *Astrophel*, which was published in company with several others; the most beautiful of them, to our taste, is *The Dolefull Lay of Clorinda*, because of its true feeling; such true feeling as becomes well Mary, Countess of Pembroke, Sidney's sister, who is said to have been the writer of it.

'O Death! that hast us of such riches reft,
Tell us at least, what hast thou with it done?
What is become of him whose flowre here left
Is but the shadow of his likenesse gone?
Scarse like the shadow of that which he was,
Nought like, but that he like a shade did pas.

But that immortall spirit, which was deckt
With all the dowries of celestiall grace,
By soveraine choyce from th' hevenly quires select,
And lineally derived from Angels' race.
O! what is now of it become aread?
Ay me, can so divine a thing be dead?

Ah no! it is not dead, ne can it die,
But lives for aie, in blisfull paradise:
Where, like a new-borne babe, it soft doth lie,
In bed of lillies wrapt in tender wise;
And compast all about with roses sweet,
And daintie violets from head to feet.

Three thousand birds, all of celestiall brood,
To him do sweetly carol day and night;
And with straunge notes, of him well understood,
Lull him a sleep in angelick delight;
Whilest in sweet dreame to him presented bee
Immortall beauties, which no eye may see.'

Sidney was an author. His *Defence of Poesy* was the earliest offspring of English criticism. His popular romance of *The Arcadia* contains the prayer which Charles I. copied for his own use, and which Milton styled 'heathenish,' when he wished to reproach Charles with the employment of it. The prayer is put in the mouth of a heathen woman, and contains no distinct reference to the cardinal doctrines of Christianity; but as it is both a beautiful composition in itself, and has obtained a singular celebrity through its appearance in *Ikon Basilike*, we take this occasion to quote it:

PAMELA'S PRAYER.—(*Arcadia*, Book iii.)

'O all-seeing Light, and eternal Life of all things, to whom nothing is either so great that it may resist, or so small that it is contemned; look upon my misery with thine eye of mercy, and let thine infinite power vouchsafe to limit out some proportion of deliverance unto me, as to thee shall seem most convenient. Let not injury, O Lord, triumph over me, and let my faults by thy hand be corrected, and make not mine enemy the minister of thy justice. But yet, O Lord, if, in thy wisdom, this be the aptest chastisement for my inexcusable folly; if this low bondage be fittest for my over-high desires; and the pride of my not enough humble heart be thus to be broken, O Lord, I yield unto thy will, and joyfully embrace what sorrow thou wilt have me suffer. Only thus much let me crave of thee—let my craving, O Lord, be accepted of thee, since even that proceeds from thee—let me crave (even by the noblest title which in my great affliction I may give myself, that I am thy creature; and by thy goodness, which is thyself) that thou wilt suffer some beams of thy majesty to shine into my mind, that it may still depend confidently on thee. Let calamity be the exercise, but not the overthrow of my virtue: let their power prevail, but prevail not to destruction. Let my greatness be their prey; let my pain be the sweetness of their revenge; let them (if so seem good unto thee) vex me with more and more punishment. But, O Lord, let never their wickedness have such a hand, but that I may carry a pure mind in a pure body.'

Sidney was a poet also. His sonnets, under the title of *Astrophel and Stella*, were first published some years after his death. Stella had been betrothed to Sidney, but was afterwards compelled to marry Lord Rich; and being ill-treated by him, she eloped with Lord Mountjoy. Her true name was Penelope Devereux: she was sister to Robert, Earl of Essex, beheaded for treason, and who married Sidney's widow.

Lastly, Sidney was a true friend and excellent patron. Spenser owed to him the notice which Elizabeth took of him: and Fulke Greville, Lord Brooke, who wrote his life, felt himself honoured to be able to have such a motto as the following engraved on his tomb:

'Servant to Q. Elizabeth,
Counsellor to K. James,
And Friend to Sir Philip Sidney,
Trophæum Peccati.'

## 'SIDNEY'S SISTER.'

Mary, Countess of Pembroke, the sister of Sir Philip Sidney, made a name for herself by her poetical writings, which, added to her beauty and amiability, have placed her in the Pantheon of notable Englishwomen. All the poets united in singing her praises, Spenser described her as—

'The gentlest shepherdess that lived that day,
And most resembling, both in shape and spirit,
Her brother dear.'

And that brother dedicated to her the celebrated romance, which he wrote at her request, and therefore entitled *The Countess of Pembroke's Arcadia.*

Mary Sidney married Henry, Earl of Pembroke, in 1576; her wedded life was short but happy. After her husband's early death, she retired from the gaieties of the court, devoting herself to the education of her children, the enjoyments of literary leisure, and the exercises of religion. Her longest poem, on the sublime subject of our Saviour's Passion, was written at this time; and though perhaps tinged with poetical exaggeration, thus reflects the pious regrets of her widowed life:

'My infant years misspent in childish toys,
My riper age in rules of little reason,
My better years in all mistaken joys
My present time (O most unhappy season!)
In fruitless labour and in endless love,
O what a horror hath my heart to prove!

I sigh to see my infancy misspent,
I mourn to find my youthful life misled,
I weep to feel my further discontent,
I die to try how love is living dead;
I sigh, I mourn, I weep, I living die,
And yet must live to know more misery.

Sir Philip Sidney concludes his *Apology for Poetry*, with a malediction on all those whose creeping souls cannot look up to the sky of poesy; praying that they may be unsuccessful in love, for lack of skill to compose a sonnet, and that their memories may fade from the earth, for want of an epitaph. His sister neither merited nor obtained such a fate; her memory having been honoured in lines more lasting than brass or marble. Her epitaph, written by Ben Jonson, has never been exceeded in the records of posthumous praise:

'Underneath this sable hearse,
Lies the subject of all verse,
Sidney's sister, Pembroke's mother.
Death! ere thou hast killed another,
Fair, and learned, and good as she,
Time shall throw a dart at thee.'

To these simple and elegant lines, six more, of a rather inferior character, were subsequently added, by an unknown author, supposed to be her son William, Earl of Pembroke:

'Marble piles let no man raise
To her name, for after-days,
Some kind woman, good as she,
Reading this, like Niobe,
Shall turn marble, and become
Both her mourner and her tomb.'

## NINON DE LENCLOS.

This celebrated beauty, who almost enjoyed, like Helen of Troy, the gift of perennial youth, exhibits in her life a striking illustration of French society and morals during the seventeenth century, over nearly the whole of which period her history extends, having been born in 1616 and died in 1706, at the age of ninety. Time seemed hardly to make any impression upon her; and so enduring were her charms of person, that even when she had passed her seventieth year, they still retained the power of attracting admirers and enkindling love. Nor were her attractions restricted solely to those of face and figure. For conversational wit or *esprit*—that special prerogative of the French nation—she occupied a distinguished place, even in the brilliant circles of Parisian society, in the reign of Louis XIV. Of the general laxity which then prevailed in social ethics, we need no more convincing proof than the fact of a person, who led so disreputable a life as Ninon de Lenclos, being openly received into the company of, and courted by individuals, male and female, of the highest respectability and position. Even Madame de Sevigné, whose son was one of Ninon's many lovers, could jestingly address her in her letters as her *belle-fille;* and the prudish and bigoted Madame de Maintenon, after her own elevation to the matrimonial couch of Louis XIV., did not hesitate to invite this Aspasia of France to take up her abode in the palace of Versailles. The latter, however, preferred a life of licence and freedom to the lugubrious restraint and austerity which had just then been inaugurated at court. The great Condé sought repose after his military toils in the society of Ninon, and the subtle La Rochefoucauld could here only satisfy his longing for personal beauty in conjunction with the charms of vivacity and wit. Molière and La Bruyère were constantly to be met in her *salons*, and what she spoke they wrote; in the words of Jules Janin, hers was spoken and theirs was written eloquence. She was well informed on general subjects, spoke several languages, was a thorough and enthusiastic student of Montaigne, and performed with much skill on various musical instruments. Christina, ex-queen of Sweden, paid her a visit, and declared, on leaving Paris, that she had seen nothing more attractive there than the illustrious Ninon. Yet with all her natural advantages, and amid all the splendours by which she was surrounded, Mademoiselle de Lenclos was not happy, and used to declare, in her old age, that were she compelled to live over again her past years, she should certainly commence by hanging herself. So impossible is it to enjoy that serenity of mind, so essential to true happiness, that 'peace of God which passeth all understanding,' where the life is a habitual violation of the precepts of religion and morality, let us bask ourselves as we may in the sunshine of worldly pleasures, honours, and wealth.

The name of *Ninon* was a pet-epithet bestowed on Mademoiselle de Lenclos by her father, her baptismal appellation being *Anne*. To the pernicious lessons inculcated by this relative, who professed unblushingly the grovelling and materialistic doctrines popularly ascribed to Epicurus, most of the subsequent errors of his daughter are to be traced. He was a gentleman of good family in Touraine, and served with distinction in the wars of Louis XIII. against the Huguenots. His wife was also of aristocratic birth from the Orléanais, and, with totally contrary tendencies to her husband, was of a pious and even ascetic turn of mind. Anne's natural disposition to gaiety revolted against such undeviating regularity in religious observances, whilst in her father she found a friend but too ready to encourage her in her determination to free herself from the salutary restraint to which she was subjected by her mother. When a girl of ten years old, it is said he had her dressed in boy's clothes, took her with him to the camp, and instructed her in various military exercises. He died prematurely, and was followed, not long afterwards, by his wife, who had vainly endeavoured to make a nun of her daughter, and expired recommending her to the protection of God, to shield her from the dangers to which she was exposed by her youth and inexperience. These forebodings of affection and maternal piety were but too fully realised. Deprived, at the age of fifteen, of both her parents, left entire mistress of her fortune and actions, with unrivalled mental and personal attractions just beginning to develop themselves, the heedless girl was not long in putting the maxims of her father into practice, and adopting the profession of the regular courtesan. This character, refined no doubt though it might be, but still the Traviata from first to last, she maintained far beyond the usual period enjoyed by women of her class. It must be recorded to her credit, that she betrayed no tendencies to avarice, but was liberal and generous with her money, and was perfectly free from malice in her disposition. There can be no doubt of her possessing naturally many good and amiable qualities, and that, had her early education been more judiciously conducted, her career in life might have been very different. There seemed to be nothing that she dreaded more than forming a permanent connection by marriage. One of the most unfavourable points in her character, was the absence of maternal feeling, which, apparently, had no place in her breast. Of her two sons, one, called La Boissière, became an officer in the French navy, and died at Toulon in 1732. The fate of the other, a son of the Marquis of Gersay, and named Villiers by his father, possesses a singularly tragic interest, rivalling the celebrated story of Oedipus. His parentage, at least on the mother's side, had been carefully concealed from him, and in this state of ignorance he reached the age of nineteen. Having heard of the wondrous charms of Ninon de Lenclos, which were celebrated over France, he sought and obtained an introduction to her, and became desperately enamoured at first sight. It was not long before he declared his passion, and the horror of his mother when he did so may be imagined. Not wishing, if possible, to disclose the secret, she implored the young man to moderate his ardour; but her remonstrances rather adding fuel to the flame, she found herself obliged to state the fact. The confusion and horror experienced by Villiers on hearing this unexpected announcement were so great, that he snatched up a pistol and blew out his brains. Yet the volatile mind of his mother was comparatively little affected by so terrible an incident. This sad story has been introduced by Le Sage as an episode into *Gil Blas.*

## THE POPISH PLOT:

### MYSTERIOUS DEATH OF SIR EDMUNDBURY GODFREY.

One of the most remarkable outbreaks of popular prejudice recorded in British history, is the celebrated so-called Popish Plot in 1678, which for a time may be said to have infected the English people with an absolute frenzy, and was certainly the most wide-spread national delusion under which it ever laboured. The fierceness of religious and political zeal was only exceeded by the astonishing, and all but universal, credulity that prevailed. And yet the ferment excited throughout the country was by no means wholly groundless, however extravagant may have been its development. Let us glance for a moment at the then social and political condition of England.

The eloquent pen of Macaulay has familiarised his countrymen with the remarkable changes inaugurated by the Restoration, from republican theories to the doctrine of passive obedience on the one hand, and from the rigid austerity of puritanical morals to the wildest libertinism and excess on the other. For a time the court had it nearly all its own way, but it was not long before a strong reaction set in, and a jealous watch came to be maintained on the proceedings of the king and government. Foremost among the grounds of suspicion and complaint were the popish leanings of the court, and the influence universally believed to be exercised by Catholics in controlling the affairs of the nation. The avowed adherence by the Duke of York to the Romish faith, the prospect of his ascending the throne in default of heirs of the king's body, and a general disposition on the part of the authorities to relax the penal laws against the papists, excited the most lively apprehensions throughout the kingdom, apprehensions which were intensified from day to day. The dread of Puritans and sectaries began even in the church to be extinguished by the fear of the machinations of Jesuits, and the overthrow of Protestantism. A secret but thoroughly organised conspiracy was believed to be carried on for the destruction of church and state, and no mode of action, it was asserted, would be rejected, however atrocious, provided it were calculated to insure success. The great fire of London, in 1666, and subsequent calamities of a similar nature, were stoutly maintained to have been the work of the papists. The opposition, or country-party, with Shaftesbury at its head, gained rapidly ground in parliament, and a formal impeachment was sent up by the Commons of the Lord-Treasurer Danby, for corrupt and unconstitutional measures. In the midst of the agitation which preceded this last measure, the revelation of the Popish Plot took place.

That a plot was really being carried on by the king and his ministers is indisputable. The secret and disgraceful compact between Charles II. and Louis XIV., by which the former, in return for an annual pension, sold himself and his country to France, would, if successfully carried out, have resulted in the total overthrow of Protestantism by giving free scope to the ambitious schemes of Louis, who would in return have assisted his English brother in trampling into the dust all popular rights, and rendering himself an irresponsible sovereign. But the pretended conspiracy revealed by Titus Oates was only calculated to divert men's minds from the real matter in hand.

This worthy seems to have chosen the most fortunate possible conjuncture for his revelations, as, notwithstanding the gross and palpable contradictions in his statements, the infamy of his previous character, and his entire want of any trustworthy evidence to support his allegations, his monstrous tissue of falsehoods, accusing the Catholics of an atrocious conspiracy to assassinate the king, massacre all Protestants, and establish a popish dynasty in the Duke of York, was received with the utmost gravity and attention. From poverty and obscurity Oates suddenly emerged into wealth and fame, and became the hero and popular favourite of the day. He supplemented his first declaration by additional matter, and from the success which had attended his speculation on the credulity of the public, other informers soon followed in his steps. The ferment spread like wild-fire, and no statement, however absurd, which tended to criminate the Catholics was rejected. Yet the common-sense of the nation might, in a short time, have opened its eyes, had it not been for a mysterious occurrence which goaded to madness its nerves, already so highly strung.

The first deposition of Titus Oates was made on 27th September 1678, before Sir Edmundbury Godfrey, one of the magistrates for Westminster, who, however, does not appear to have been a fanatical partisan of the No-Popery party, as Coleman, an agent of the Duke of York, and seriously criminated by Oates's statements, was a personal friend of his, and warned by him in consequence of the danger to which he was exposed. Godfrey, it has been said, was a man of a melancholy temperament, and suffering at the time from depression of spirits, but this assertion was afterwards denied. He occupied a house in Green's Lane, in the Strand, and about a fortnight after the above deposition was made before him, left home at nine o'clock on the morning of Saturday the 12th of October. Shortly after this, he was seen in the neighbourhood of Marylebone, and at noon of the same day had an interview on business with one of the churchwardens of St Martin's in the Fields. From this time he was never again seen alive. Surprise was felt by his servants at home, at his neither returning in the evening nor sending any message to inform them of his intending to be absent for the night. Sunday came, and no tidings of him; Monday, Tuesday, Wednesday, and Thursday followed with the like result. At six o'clock on the evening of the last-mentioned day (the 17th), as two men were crossing a field on the south side of Primrose Hill, they observed a sword-belt, stick, and pair of gloves lying by the side of the hedge, but paid no attention to them at the time, and continued their journey to the White House in the neighbourhood. Arriving there, they happened to mention what they had seen to the master of the house, who thereupon recommended them to go back to the place, and offered himself to accompany them. The three accordingly started for the spot where they had seen the articles in question; and having arrived there, one of them stooped down to lift them, but happening at the same time to look into the adjoining ditch, saw there the body of a man lying on his face. It was Sir Edmundbury Godfrey, with a sword run through his body, his face bruised, and a livid mark round the neck, as if he had been strangled. He was conveyed at once to the White House, and information sent to the authorities. A jury was impannelled, to inquire into the cause of his death; but no definite conclusion could be come to beyond the evidence furnished by two surgeons, that his death must have been occasioned by strangulation, and his body then pierced with the sword, which had been left sticking in the wound. The ditch was dry, and there were no marks of blood in it, and his shoes were perfectly clean, as if, after being assassinated, he had been carried and deposited in the place where he was found. A large sum of money and a diamond-ring were found in his pockets, but his pocket-book, in which, as a magistrate, he used to take notes of examinations, was missing. Spots of white wax, an article which he never used himself, and which was only employed by persons of distinction, and by priests, were scattered over his clothes; and from this circumstance people were led to conclude that the Roman Catholics were the authors of his death. The whole affair was an inscrutable mystery, but popular impulse seizing hold of the circumstance that Oates had made his deposition before him, and also that no robbery had been committed, attributed at once his murder to the vengeance of the papists.

London was now in a blaze. Here, it was maintained, was a thorough confirmation of what Oates and his companions had asserted of the bloody designs of the Catholics. Stories soon came pouring in to increase and spread the clamour, and among others, informations were sworn to by persons, who pretended to have seen Sir Edmundbury trepanned into an apartment near Somerset House, then strangled, and his body conveyed away in a sedan-chair, and thence conveyed by a man on horseback to the ditch at Primrose Hill. Though the most glaring contradictions appeared in these narratives, they were eagerly caught up and accepted as gospel by an excited and furious people. To doubt the reality of the Popish Plot was regarded as tantamount to a participation in it. Oates, and informers of a similar type, were caressed and encouraged more than ever, and it will be readily believed, that they did not suffer public enthusiasm to languish from a lack of a proper supply of nutriment. It was a time when, as Hume remarks, 'reason could no more be heard than a whisper in the midst of the most violent hurricane.'

From White House, the corpse of Godfrey was carried home to his own residence, where for two days it lay in state, and was visited by vast multitudes. The funeral was attended by an immense procession, at the head of which walked seventy-two clergymen of the Church of England, in full canonicals, whilst the minister who preached a sermon on the occasion, was supported on each side by a stalwart brother-divine, lest he should be killed by the papists! If the murder was really the work of a fanatic Roman Catholic, it was a most ill-judged procedure for the tranquillity of his fellow-religionists, as numbers of them, priests as well as laymen, were ruthlessly immolated to the popular fury. The mere fact of their being Catholics, and being charged as participators in the Popish Plot, was sufficient to insure their condemnation with any jury. The real cause of Godfrey's death has never been discovered, and to this day it remains one of those mysterious occurrences of which no satisfactory explanation can be given. An undoubted fact, it stands out in melancholy prominence amid the tissue of absurdities and falsehoods which compose the substance of the Popish Plot.

## OCTOBER 18.

St Luke the Evangelist. St Justin, martyr, in France, 4th century. St Julian Sabas, hermit. St Monan, martyr, 7th century.

### ST LUKE.

Of the companion and biographer of St Paul, little is recorded in Scripture; but from a passage in the Epistle to the Colossians, we infer that he had been bred to the profession of a physician. In addition to this vocation, he is stated by ecclesiastical writers to have practised that of a painter, and some ancient pictures of the Virgin, still extant, are ascribed to his pencil. In consequence of this belief, which, however, rests on very uncertain foundations, St Luke has been regarded as the patron of painters and the fine arts. He is commonly represented in a seated position, writing or painting, whilst behind him appears the head of an ox, frequently winged. This symbol has been associated with him, to quote the words of an ancient writer, 'because he devised about the presthode of Jesus Christ,' the ox or calf being the sign of a sacrifice, and St Luke entering more largely, than the other Evangelists, into the history of the life and sufferings of our Saviour.

*Born.*—Pope Pius II. (Æneas Silvius), 1405, *Corsignano;* Justus Lipsius, miscellaneous writer, 1547, *Isch, Brabant;* Matthew Henry, eminent divine and commentator, 1662, *Broad Oak, Flintshire;* François de Savoie, Prince Eugene, celebrated imperial general, 1663, *Paris;* Richard Nash (Beau Nash), celebrated master of the ceremonies at Bath, 1674, *Swansea;* Peter Frederik Suhm, Danish archæologist, 1728, *Copenhagen;* Jean Jacques Regis Cambacères, eminent lawyer and statesman, 1753, *Montpellier;* Thomas Phillips, portrait-painter, 1770, *Dudley, Warwickshire.*

*Died.*—John Ziska, Hussite commander, 1424; Sarah Jennings, Duchess of Marlborough, 1744; Réné Antoine de Réaumur, practical philosopher and naturalist, 1757.

### REAUMUR AND HIS THERMOMETER.

Réné Antoine Ferchault de Réaumur is an instance, among many, of those persons who, having devoted the greater part of their lives to scientific investigations, become known to posterity for only one, and that often a very subordinate achievement. Réaumur is now remembered almost exclusively by his thermometer: that is to say, his mode of graduating thermometers—a very small thing in itself. Yet in his day he occupied no mean place among French *savans.* From 1708, when he read his first paper before the Academy of Sciences, till his death on October 18, 1757, he was incessantly engaged in investigations of one kind or other. Geometrical speculations; the strength of cordage; the development of the shells of testaceous animals; the colouring-matter of turquoise-gems; the manufacture of iron, steel, and porcelain; artificial incubation; the imitating of the famous purple dye of the ancients; the graduation of thermometers; the reproduction of the claws of lobsters and crabs; the instincts and habits of insects—all, in turn, engaged the attention of this acute and industrious man, and all furnished him with means for increasing the sum-total of human knowledge.

Scientific men, each in his own department, fully appreciate the value of Réaumur's labours; but to the world at large, as we have said, the thermometric scale is the only thing by which he is remembered. Almost precisely the same may be said of Fahrenheit. Had not the English persisted in using the graduation proposed by the last-named individual, his name would never have become a 'household word' among us; and had not Réaumur's scale been extensively adopted on the continent, his more elaborate investigations, buried in learned volumes, would have failed to immortalise his name.

Till the early part of the last century, the scales for measuring degrees of temperature were so arbitrary, that scientific men found it difficult to understand and record each other's experiments; but Fahrenheit, in 1724, had the merit of devising a definite standard of comparison. He divided the interval between freezing water and boiling water into 180 equal parts or degrees, and placed the former at 32 degrees above the *zero* or point of intense cold, so that the point of boiling-water was denoted by 212°. It is supposed that the extreme cold observed in Iceland in 1709 furnished Fahrenheit with the minimum, or zero which he adopted in his thermometers; but such a limit to the degree of cold would be quite inadmissible now, when much lower temperatures are known to exist. Réaumur, experimenting in the same field a few years after Fahrenheit, adopted also the temperature of freezing water as his *zero,* and marked off 80 equal parts or degrees between that point and the temperature of boiling-water. Celsius, a Swede, invented, about the year 1780, a third mode of graduation, called the *Centigrade;* in which he took the freezing of water as the zero point, and divided the interval between that and the point of ebullition into 100 parts or degrees. All three scales are now employed —a circumstance which has proved productive of an infinite amount of confusion and error. Thus, 212° F. is equal to 80° R., or 100° C.; 60° F. is equal to $12\frac{4}{9}$° R., or $15\frac{1}{2}$° C.; and so on. Like the names of the constellations, it is difficult to make changes in any received system when it has become once established; and thus we shall continue to hear of Réaumur on the continent, and of Fahrenheit in England.



## THE LAST LOTTERY IN ENGLAND.

On the 18th of October 1826, the last 'State Lottery' was drawn in England. The ceremony took place in Cooper's Hall, Basinghall Street; and although the public attraction to this last of a long series of legalised swindles was excessive, and sufficient to inconveniently crowd the hall, the lottery-office keepers could not dispose of the whole of the tickets, although all means, ordinary and extraordinary, had been resorted to, as an inducement to the public to 'try their luck' for the last time.

This abolition of lotteries deprived the government of a revenue equal to £250,000 or £300,000 per annum; but it was wisely felt that the inducement to gambling held out by them was a great moral evil, helping to impoverish many, and diverting attention from the more legitimate industrial modes of money-making. No one, therefore, mourned over the decease of the lottery but the lottery-office keepers, then a large body of men, who rented expensive offices in all parts of England.

The lottery originated among ourselves during the reign of Queen Elizabeth, when 'a very rich lottery-general of money, plate, and certain sorts of merchandise' was set forth by her majesty's order, 1567 A.D. The greatest prize was estimated at £5000, of which £3000 was to be paid in cash, £700 in plate, and the remainder in 'good tapestry meet for hangings, and other covertures, and certain sorts of good linen cloth.' All the prizes were to be seen at the house of Mr Dericke, the queen's goldsmith, in Cheapside; and a wood-cut was appended to the original proclamation, in which a tempting display of gold and silver plate is profusely delineated. The lots, amounting in number to 400,000, appear to have been somewhat tardily disposed of, and the drawing did not take place until January 1568–69. On the 11th of that month, it began in a building erected for the purpose, at the west door of St Paul's Cathedral, and continued, day and night, until the 6th of the following May. The price of the lots was 10*s.* each, and they were occasionally subdivided into halves and quarters; and these were again subdivided for 'convenience of poorer classes.' The objects ostensibly propounded as an excuse to the government for founding this lottery, were the repair of the harbours and fortifications of the kingdom, and other public works. Great pains were taken to 'provoke the people' to adventure their money; and her majesty sent forth a second most persuasive and argumentative proclamation, in which all the advantages of the scheme were more clearly set forth; so that 'any scruple, suspition, doubt, fault, or misliking' that might occur, 'specially of those that be inclined to suspitions,' should be removed, so that all persons have 'their reasonable contentation and satisfaction.' That adventurers had 'certain doubts' still, is apparent from a proclamation issued as a supplement to this from the lord mayor; in which he says, 'though the wiser sort may find cause to satisfy themselves therein, yet to the satisfaction of the scrupler sort' he deigns to more fully explain the scheme. In spite of all this, 'the wiser sort' did not rapidly buy shares, and the 'scrupler sort' held tight their purses, so that her majesty sent a somewhat

The fan-mount, here pictured, was exhibited at the Worcester Congress of the Archæological Institute. The subject, printed in body colours on vellum, represents either the great lottery in 1718, when popular excitement was stimulated in so extravagant a degree, that £1,500,000 was subscribed, or that of 1714, which also presented unusual attractions. The scene, of which so spirited a representation is given on the fan, is probably in Mercer's Hall, Ironmonger Lane, Cheapside, where transactions connected with lotteries usually took place. A dignified person, in black robes, is presiding; over his head is an escutcheon of St George's cross; above are the royal arms, with the initials of Queen Anne. Many officials are in attendance, including three clerks curiously accommodated in a pit in front of the president. There is a platform, with side-boxes conveniently arranged for gay gallants and fashionable ladies in the full costume of the period. The tickets are in the course of being drawn by Blue-coat boys. On one side is the wheel for blanks; on the other, that for prizes—the valve coverings being marked respectively B. P. These wheels, when not in use, appear to have been locked up in cases that separated into two portions when removed from the drawing apparatus, and bore the queen's initials. A precisely similar scene to that here represented, is given in the contemporary engraving, by N. Parr, in six compartments, entitled *Les Divertissements de la Loterie*. It was designed by J. Marchant, drawn by H. Gravelot, and published by Ryland. Ave Maria Lane. Gambling, in private lotteries, was so prevalent about the time, that they were suppressed by act of parliament.

In reference to the subject of fan-decoration, it may here be observed, that the practice of adorning these fashionable appendages with attractive designs, was in great vogue about the middle of the last century. A gentleman, writing in the *Gentleman's Magazine* for May 1753, states the twelve designs upon as many fans held up before as many pretty faces, at a late celebration of the communion 'in a certain church of this metropolis,' as follows: 1. Darby and Joan; 2. Harlequin and Columbine; 3. The prodigal son, with his harlots, copied from the Rake's Progress; 4. A rural dance, with a band of music, consisting of a fiddle, a bagpipe, and a Welsh harp; 5. The taking of Portobello; 6. The solemnities of a filiation; 7. Joseph and his mistress; 8. The humours of Change Alley; 9. Silenus; 10. The first interview of Isaac and Rebecca; 11. The judgment of Paris; 12. Vauxhall Gardens, with the decorations and company.

FAN-MOUNT REPRESENTING A LOTTERY.

fretful mandate to the mayor of London, and the justices of Kent, Sussex, Surrey, and Hampshire, because, 'contrary to her highness' expectation,' there were many lots untaken, 'either of their negligence, or by some sinister disswasions of some not well-disposed persons.' She appoints one John Johnson, gentleman, to look after her interests in the matter, and to 'procure the people as much as maybe to lay in their monies into the lots,' and orders that he 'bring report of the former doings of the principal men of every parish, and in whom any default is, that this matter hath not been so well advanced as it was looked for;' so that 'there shall not one parish escape, but they shall bring in some money into the lots.' This characteristic specimen of royal dragooning for national gambling in opposition to general desire, is a very striking commencement for a history of lottery-fraud.

In the year following, a lottery 'for marvellous rich and beautiful armour,' was conducted for three days at the same place. In 1612, King James I., 'in special favor for the plantation of the English colonies in Virginia, granted a lottery to be held at the west end of St Paul's; wherof one Thomas Sharplys, a tailor of London, had the chief prize, which was 4000 crowns in fair plate.' In 1619, another lottery was held ostensibly for the same purpose. Charles I. projected one in 1630, to defray the expenses of conveying water to London, after the fashion of the New River. During the Commonwealth, one was held in Grocer's Hall by the committee for lands in Ireland. It was not, however, until some years after the Restoration that lotteries became popular. They were then started under pretence of aiding the poor adherents of the crown, who had suffered in the civil wars. Gifts of plate were supposed to be made by the crown, and thus disposed of 'on the behalf of the truly loyal indigent officers.' Like other things, this speedily became a patent monopoly, was farmed by various speculators, and the lotteries were drawn in the theatres. Booksellers adopted this mode to get rid of unsaleable stock at a fancy value, and all kinds of sharping were resorted to. 'The Royal Oak Lottery' was that which came forth with greatest éclat, and was continued to the end of the century; it met, however, with animadversion from the sensible part of the community, and formed frequently, as well as the patentees who managed it, a subject for the satirists of the day. In 1699, a lottery was proposed with a capital prize of a thousand pounds, which sum was to be won at the risk of one penny; for that was to be the price of each share, and only one share to win.

The rage for speculation which characterised the people of England, in the early part of the last century, and which culminated in the South-sea bubble, was favourable to all kinds of lottery speculations; hence there were 'great goes' in whole tickets, and 'little goes' in their subdivisions; speculators were protected by insurance offices; even fortune-tellers were consulted about 'lucky numbers.' Thus a writer in the *Spectator* informs us, 'I know a well-meaning man that is very well pleased to risk his good-fortune upon the number 1711, because it is the year of our Lord.—I have been told of a certain zealous dissenter, who, being a great enemy to popery, and believing that bad men are the most fortunate in this world, will lay two to one on the number 666 against any other number; because, he says, it is the number of the beast.' Guildhall was a scene of great excitement during the time of the drawing of the prizes there, and, it is a fact, that poor medical practitioners used constantly to attend, to be ready to let blood in cases when the sudden proclaiming of the fate of tickets had an overpowering effect.

On the foregoing page, we have copied a very curious representation of a lottery, originally designed for a fan-mount.

Lotteries were not confined to money-prizes, but embraced all kinds of articles. Plate and jewels were favourites; books were far from uncommon; but the strangest was a lottery for deer in Sion Park. Henry Fielding, the novelist, ridiculed the public madness in a farce produced at Drury Lane Theatre in 1731, the scene being laid in a lottery-office, and the action of the drama descriptive of the wiles of office-keepers, and the credulity of their victims. A whimsical pamphlet was also published about the same time, purporting to be a prospectus of 'a lottery for ladies;' by which they were to obtain, as chief prize, a husband and coach-and-six, for five pounds; such being the price of each share. Husbands of inferior grade, in purse and person, were put forth as second, third, or fourth rate prizes, and a lottery for wives was soon advertised on a similar plan. This was legitimate satire, as so large a variety of lotteries were started, and in spite of reason or ridicule, continued to be patronised by a gullible public. Sometimes they were turned to purposes of public utility. Thus in 1736, an act was passed for building a bridge at Westminster by lottery, consisting of 125,000 tickets at £5 each. London Bridge at that time was the only means of communication, by permanent roadway between the City and Southwark. This lottery was so far successful, that parliament sanctioned others in succession until Westminster Bridge was completed. In 1774, the brothers Adam, builders of the Adelphi Terrace and surrounding streets in the Strand, disposed of these and other premises in a lottery containing 110 prizes; the first-drawn ticket entitling the holder to a prize of the value of £5000; the last-drawn, to one of £25,000.

Lotteries, at the close of the last century, had become established by successive acts of parliament; and, being considered as means for increasing the revenue by chancellors of our exchequer, they were conducted upon a regular business-footing by contractors in town and country. All persons dabbled in chances, and shares were subdivided, that no pocket might be spared. Poor persons were kept poor by the rage for speculation, in hopes of being richer. Idle hope was not the only demoralisation produced by lotteries; robbery and suicide came therewith. The most absurd chances were paraded as traps to catch the thoughtless, and all that ingenuity could suggest in the way of advertisement and puffing, was resorted to by lottery-office keepers. About 1815, they began to disseminate hand-bills, with poetic, or rather rhyming, appeals to the public; and about 1820, enlisted the services of wood-engravers, to make their advertisements more attractive. The subjects chosen were generally of a humorous kind, and were frequently very cleverly treated by Cruikshank and the best men of the day. They appealed, for the most part, to minds of small calibre, by depicting people of all grades expressing confidence in the lottery, a determination to try their chances, and a full reliance on 'the lucky office' which issued the hand-bill. Hone, in his *Every-Day Book*, vol. ii., has engraved several specimens of these 'fly-leaves,' now very rare, and only to be seen among the collections of the curious. We add three more examples, selected from a large assemblage, and forming curious specimens of the variety of design occasionally adopted. It is seldom any sentimental or serious subject was attempted, but our first specimen comes in that category. This lottery was drawn on Valentine's Day; Cupid is,

therefore, shewn angling for hearts, each inscribed with their value, £21,000; they float toward him in a stream descending from the temple of Fortune, on a hill in the background; and beneath is inscribed: 'Great chance! small risk! A whole ticket for only eighteen shillings!—a sixteenth for only two shillings! in the lottery to be drawn on Valentine's Day; on which day, three of £2000 will be drawn in the first five minutes, which the public are sure to get for nothing!!'

A whimsical notion of depicting figures of all kinds by simple dots and lines, having originated abroad, was adopted by the keepers of British lottery-offices. The following is a specimen sent out by a large contractor named Sivewright.

When possess'd of sufficient
We sit at our ease;
Can go where we like,
And enjoy what we please.

But when pockets are empty,
If forced to apply
To some friend for assistance,
They 're apt to deny.

Not so with friends Sivewright,
They never say nay,
But lead us to Fortune
The readiest way.

They gallop on gaily;
The fault is your own
If you don't get a good share
Before they 're all gone.

Our third specimen is selected from a series representing the itinerant traders in the streets of London, engaged in conversation on the chances of the lottery. This is the fishwoman, who declares:

'Though a *dab*, I'm not *scaly*—I like a good *plaice*,
And I hope that good-luck will soon smile in my face;
On the 14th of June, when Prizes in *shoals*,
Will cheer up the *cockles* of all sorts of *soals*.'

The English government at last felt the degradation of obtaining revenues by means of the lottery, and the last act which gave it a legal existence received the royal assent on the 9th of July 1823, and soon after 'the last' was drawn in England, as described already.

Lotteries linger still upon the continent; from Hamburg we occasionally get a prospectus of some chateau and park thus to be disposed of, or some lucky scheme to be drawn; but Rome may be fairly considered as the city where they flourish best and most publicly. At certain times, the Corso is gay with lottery-offices, and busy with adventurers. All persons speculate, and a large number are found among the lower grades of the clergy. The writer was present at the drawing of the lottery which took place in November 1856, in the great square termed Piazza Navona. The whole of that immense area was crammed with people, every window crowded, the houses hung with tapestries and coloured cloths, and a showy canopied stage erected at one end of the Piazza, upon which the business of drawing was conducted. As the space was so large, and the mob all eager to know fortune's behests, smaller stages were erected midway on both sides of the square, and the numbers drawn were exhibited in frames erected upon them. Bands of military music were stationed near; the pope's guard, doing duty as mounted police. The last was by no means an unnecessary precaution, for a sham quarrel was got up in the densest part of the crowd for the purpose of plunder, and some mischief done in the turmoil. Of the thousands assembled, many were priests; and all held their numbers in their hands, anxiously hoping for good-fortune. It was a singular sight, and certainly not the most moral, to see people and clergy all eagerly engaged on the Sunday in gambling.

# OCTOBER 19.

Saints Ptolemy, Lucius, and a companion, 166. St Ethbin or Egbin, abbot, end of 6th century. St Frideswide, virgin, and patroness of Oxford, 8th century. St Peter of Alcantara, confessor, 1562.

*Born.*—Sir Thomas Browne, antiquary and philosopher, 1605, *Cheapside, London;* James Butler, Duke of Ormond, commander and statesman, 1610, *Clerkenwell, London;* James Gronovius, scholar and author (*Thesaurus Antiquitatum Græcarum*), 1645, *Deventer;* John Adams, distinguished American statesman, 1735, *Braintree, Massachusetts;* James Henry Leigh Hunt, poet and miscellaneous writer, 1784, *Southgate, Middlesex.*

*Died.*—King John of England, 1216, *Newark Castle;* Jacobus Arminius (Jacob Harmensen), celebrated Dutch theologian, 1609; Sir Thomas Browne, antiquary and philosopher, 1682, *Norwich;* Dean Jonathan Swift, humorous and political writer, 1745, *Dublin;* Henry Kirke White, youthful poet, 1806, *Cambridge;* Francis Joseph Talma, great French tragedian, 1826, *Paris.*

## SIR THOMAS BROWNE.

To many generations of gentle and meditative readers, Sir Thomas Browne has been a choice classic. Southey said, that were his library confined to a dozen English authors, Browne should be one of them. De Quincey describes Donne, Chillingworth, Jeremy Taylor, Milton, South, Barrow, and Sir Thomas Browne, as 'a pleiad or constellation of seven golden stars, such as in their class no literature can match,' and from whose works he would undertake to build up an entire body of philosophy.

Browne was the son of a London merchant, and was born within the sound of Bow Bells in 1605. His father died and left him, in childhood, with a fortune of £6000, out of a great part of which, says Dr Johnson, 'he was defrauded by one of his guardians, according to the common fate of orphans.' He was educated at Winchester and Oxford, and after practising physic for a while in Oxfordshire, he set out on a long tour through Italy, France, and Holland. About 1634, he returned to London, and in the following year he is supposed to have written his *Religio Medici.* In 1636, he settled in Norwich, and commenced business as a physician; and in the enjoyment of an extensive and lucrative practice, he passed in that city the remainder of his long life. Of women he wrote very slightingly, saying, that 'the whole world was made for man, but only the twelfth part of man for woman;' and 'that man is the whole world, but woman only the rib or crooked part of man.' Nevertheless, in 1641, he married a Mrs Mileham, of a good Norfolk family, 'a lady of such symmetrical proportion to her husband, both in the graces of her mind and her body, that they seemed to come together by a kind of natural magnetism,' writes Whitefoot, one of Browne's biographers. Together they lived happily for forty years; she bore him ten children, and lived to be his widow. Charles II., in a visit to Norwich in 1671, knighted Browne. Such, in a few words, is the story of Sir Thomas Browne's life. He died on his seventy-seventh birthday, the 19th of October 1682.

The chief incident in his life was the publication of the *Religio Medici*—the *Religion of a Physician.* It was written, he declares, 'with no intention for the press, but for his own exercise and entertainment.' For some six years it appears to have been handed about in manuscript, and on the plea of its being surreptitiously and imperfectly printed, he gave 'a true and full copy,' under his own hand, to the world in 1643. It at once excited the attention of the public, even in that stormy age, as Johnson says, 'by the novelty of paradoxes, the dignity of sentiment, the quick succession of images, the multitude of abstruse allusions, the subtilty of disquisition, and the strength of language.' In the book he speaks much of himself, but in such terms as to pique rather than satisfy curiosity. He asserts, he understands six languages; that he is no stranger to astronomy; that he has seen many countries; and leaves us to puzzle our heads over the mysterious and solemn announcement, 'that his life has been a miracle of thirty years, which to relate were not history, but a piece of poetry, and would sound like a fable.' So far as concerns the autobiographical portions, the reader of the *Religio Medici* will do well to bear in mind that he is dealing with a humorist; and Browne's humour is so irresistible, that it oozes through some of his gravest passages. Coleridge describes the *Religio Medici* as 'a fine portrait of a handsome man in his best clothes; it is much of what he was at all times; a good deal of what he was only in his best moments. I have never read a book in which I have felt greater similarity to my own make of mind—active in inquiry, and yet with an appetite to believe—in short, an affectionate visionary! It is a most delicious book.'

The success of the *Religio Medici,* which was translated into Latin, and thence into French, German, Dutch, and Italian, probably tempted Browne into the publication of his second work, in 1646, entitled *Pseudodoxia Epidemica,* 'or inquiries into very many received tenets and commonly presumed truths, which examined, prove but vulgar and common errors.' This curious book treats in a pedantic way of a large number of odd notions, such as, that Jews stink; that the forbidden-fruit was an apple; that storks will only live in republics and free states; that the flesh of peacocks corrupteth not; that elephants have no joints; that a pot full of ashes will contain as much water as it would without them; that men weigh heavier dead than alive, and before meat than after; that crystal is nothing but ice strongly congealed, &c. Notwithstanding his zeal to discover old errors, he was a prey to not a few himself. 'Natural diseases,' he writes, 'are heightened to a great excess by the subtlety of the devil co-operating with the malice of those we term witches, at whose instance he doth those villanies.' Sir Matthew Hale fortified himself by this opinion in condemning two poor women as witches. Further he advises, 'that to those who would attempt to teach animals the art of speech, the dogs and cats, that usually speak unto witches, may afford some encouragement.' The motion of the earth he never mentions but with contempt and ridicule, though the opinion was in his time growing popular.

The discovery of some urns in Norfolk, in 1658, induced him to write *Hydriotaphia;* a discourse on urn-burial, in which, with a strange mixture of ideality and pedantry, he describes the funeral rites of ancient nations. 'There is perhaps none of his works,' says Dr Johnson, 'which better exemplifies his reading or memory. It is scarcely to be imagined how many particulars he has amassed, in a treatise which seems to have been occasionally written.' To *Hydriotaphia* he added a disquisition on *The Garden of Cyrus, or the Quincunxial Lozenge or Net-work Plantations of the Ancients artificially, naturally.* Quincunx order is a plantation of trees disposed originally in a square, consisting of five trees, one at each corner, and a fifth in the middle, which disposition, repeated again and again, forms a regular grove, wood, or wilderness. The quincunx, Browne pursues through art and nature with a pertinacity that almost leads his reader to conclude that on that figure the universe was planned.

These were all the writings Sir Thomas Browne published, but after his death a mass of papers was discovered in his study, carefully transcribed, and ready for the press. These miscellanies have been printed, and supply fresh evidence of the versatility and originality of his reading and meditation. Considering the drudgery of his practice as physician, it is surprising that he should have read and written so much; but it is recorded that he was a skilful economist of time, that he could never bear to be a minute idle, and that the hours he could steal from his patients were spent in his study. He was always cheerful, though rarely merry; and, though in his writing garrulous, in speech he was slow and weighty. In his dress he affected plainness, and was averse to all finery; and was a strong advocate for thick and warm garments, as essential to health in the English climate.

The stability the English language had acquired in the age of Elizabeth was lost under her successors, and Browne, along with Milton and others, poured a multitude of exotic words into his compositions, to the great injury of their effect. He uses *commensality*, for the state of many living at the same table; *paralogical*, for an unreasonable doubt; and *arthritical analogies*, for parts that serve some animals in the place of joints; besides a host of other pedantries to even less purpose; so that his style in some parts is rather a tissue of many tongues than honest English.

## DEAN SWIFT.

The life of the celebrated dean of St Patrick's presents a history at once singular and painful. Born and educated in adversity, we find him emerging, after a hard struggle, into prosperity and fame; then disappointed in his canvass for clerical honours, we see him retire from the contest, and devote himself to literature and study; but cursed by a splenetic and morbid disposition, little real enjoyment is seemingly ever derived by him from any source, whilst the cold calculating selfishness which prompted him to trifle with the affections of a loving and self-sacrificing woman, entailed on him the pangs of a secret and agonising remorse. Disease, bodily and mental, comes to complete his miseries, and the last days of the great satirist and politician are characterised by the most melancholy and unqualified idiocy.

'From Marlborough's eyes the streams of dotage flow,
And Swift expires a driveller and a show.'

Though born and resident in Ireland during the greater part of his life, Swift was thoroughly English both by extraction and disposition. His grandfather, the Rev. Thomas Swift, was vicar of Goodrich, in Herefordshire, four of whose sons, of whom he had ten, besides four daughters, settled in Ireland. One of these, Jonathan, who had been bred to the law, was appointed steward of the King's Inns, Dublin, but died about two years afterwards, leaving his widow in great poverty, with an infant daughter, and also pregnant of a son, who was born on 30th November 1667, and received his father's name.

Young Jonathan received his first education at a school in Kilkenny, and was afterwards sent to Trinity College, Dublin, being indebted for these advantages to his uncle, Godwin Swift, who formed the main support of his mother and her family, but seems to have bestowed his bounty in a niggardly and ungracious manner. While at college, Swift made himself specially distinguished in no way, except idling, and the perpetration of many reckless pranks. In 1688, he passed over to England, and joined there his mother, who had been residing for some time in Leicestershire. She was a relation of the wife of Sir William Temple. Introduced to this celebrated statesman, the young man was appointed private secretary, and took up his abode with Sir William, at the latter's seat of Moor Park, in Surrey. Here a reformation took place in his habits; and having both gained the approbation of his patron and his patron's master, King William, who used frequently to visit at Moor Park, he was enabled in 1692 to proceed to Oxford, where he obtained the degree of M.A. in the same year. Returning to his former employment under Sir William, a disagreement arose, and Swift set off to Ireland, with the hope of pushing his way in the church. He had the mortification of being obliged to solicit his patron for a certificate before he could obtain preferment, but in 1695 was made prebend of Kilroot, in the diocese of Connor, with a revenue of a hundred a year. Life, however, in this remote locality was far too dull for him, and he was, consequently, very happy to adjust his difference with Sir William Temple, and return to his secretaryship at Moor Park. On the death of Sir William, he proceeded to London, and superintended there the publication of his patron's posthumous works.

Having accompanied Lord Berkeley to Ireland in 1699, as his chaplain, Swift was presented by him to the rectory of Agher and the vicarages of Rathbeggan and Laracor, in the diocese of Meath. At the last-named of these livings he took up his residence, and continued there, during nearly the whole of the reign of Queen Anne, to pass the life of a country clergyman, varied by occasional visits to England, with which he kept up a constant correspondence; and employing himself, from time to time, in various literary lucubrations, including the celebrated *Tale of a Tub*, and the *Battle of the Books*, published anonymously in 1704, and the *Predictions of Isaac Bickerstaff, Esq.*, in 1708. He also gave to the world several tracts, in one of which, the *Letter on the Sacramental Test*, he opposed strenuously the relaxation of the penal laws regarding dissenters. Swift was thoroughly a High Churchman; and though in politics attached, both by disposition and the connections of early life, to the principles of the Revolution, he became, latterly, the sworn friend and associate of Bolingbroke, Lord Oxford, and the rest of that class of statesmen who maintained a correspondence with the exiled family in France. The utmost, however, which the Tory party bestowed on him, was the deanery of St Patrick's Cathedral, in Dublin; and shortly afterwards, the death of Queen Anne, and the accession of the Hanoverian dynasty, shut him out effectually from all hopes of further preferment. He refrained for many years from visiting England, but earned an immense popularity in Ireland by his denunciation of the unworthy system of restriction imposed on that country by the English parliament. His famous *Drapier's Letters*, on the patent right granted to William Wood to coin farthings and halfpence for Ireland, exposed him to considerable danger from the authorities, but with the Irish raised him to the dignity of a patriot, a position which he ever afterwards maintained in their estimation. A reward of £300 having been offered for the discovery of the author of the Drapier's fourth letter, and a bill against the printer being about to be presented to the grand jury, the following quotation from Scripture was largely circulated in Dublin: 'And the people said unto Saul, shall Jonathan die, who hath wrought this great salvation in Israel? God forbid: as the Lord liveth, there shall not one hair of his head fall to the ground; for he hath wrought with God this day. So the people rescued Jonathan, that he died not.' The grand jury's verdict was *ignoramus*, and the patent was ultimately withdrawn from Wood, who received in compensation a yearly grant of £3000 for twelve years.

In 1726, Swift once more visited England, and in the same year appeared the celebrated *Gulliver's Travels*, which, published anonymously like most of Swift's writings, achieved ere long a European popularity, and more than any other work has conferred on him an immortal reputation. But the moody, misanthropical author cared little for the applause of mankind, whose judgments he regarded with the most withering scorn and contempt. No better proof could be afforded of the general bent of his disposition than the work just alluded to, and more especially the description of the country of the Houynhnhnms. For ironical and sarcastic humour, nothing can be more piquant than his *Directions to Servants*, which, with the utmost gravity, inculcates on domestics the performance of every act which they should *not* do, and the omission of every duty which they *should*. It was about the last literary work in which Swift engaged, and was not published till after his death.

In thus sketching the life of Swift, we have as yet said nothing of a circumstance which has found a prominent place in every biography. Need we say that we allude to his attachments to Stella and Vanessa? The former of these, whose proper name was Esther Johnson, and who is said to have been a natural daughter of Sir William Temple, was a pretty girl of fourteen when she first made Swift's acquaintance at Moor Park, where she was an inmate. The young secretary acted the part of tutor towards her, and a life-long attachment, on the part of Esther at least, was the result. After Swift was settled as vicar of Laracor, Stella and a female friend, named Mrs Dingley, followed him to Ireland. They generally resided in the town of Trim, but took up their abode in the vicarage at Laracor whenever its master was absent. Up to 1716, the intercourse between them seems to have been entirely of a Platonic character, but in that year—Swift having by this time become dean of St Patrick's—they were married in the deanery garden by the bishop of Clogher. This circumstance, however, was carefully concealed, and the cold-blooded indifference with which Swift could thus expose the character of a generous and loving woman to the world's aspersion exhibits him in a very repulsive light. Neither did he remain constant in his attachment to her. During his visits to London about 1712, he made the acquaintance of a young lady of good position, Miss Esther Vanhomrigh, who, like Stella, has been handed down to posterity by a poetic appellation—*Vanessa.* Unlike her rival, however, she appears to have been of a forward, enterprising disposition, and actually made known to Swift the state of her affections; a declaration which he treated at first jestingly, and afterwards replied to by a proffer of everlasting friendship. There can be no doubt that the conduct of the dean in his friendship with Vanessa was wholly unjustifiable, and he reaped the just punishment of his double-dealing in the misery to which he was subjected by the opposing claims of the two rivals on his affections. This embarrassment was considerably increased by the circumstance of Vanessa coming over to Ireland, and fixing her residence in Dublin, from which she afterwards removed to Marley Abbey, near Celbridge. Here Swift used frequently to visit her; and our opinion of his character is by no means heightened, when we know that at the very time when he was indulging in the language of love and affection towards Miss Vanhomrigh, he was himself bound to another by the irrevocable tie of marriage. After the death (about 1720) of a younger sister who lived with her, the attachment of Vanessa to Swift became more violent than ever; and, determined to elicit the nature of his mysterious connection with Stella, she despatched a letter of inquiry to that effect to Mrs Johnson. The tragical consequence is well known. Stella's jealousy being roused by the receipt of this communication, she at once sent the letter to Swift, whom it stirred to a paroxysm of fury. He mounted his horse, rode to Marley Abbey, and entering the apartment where Miss Vanhomrigh was sitting, glared at her with such a terrible expression of countenance, that the unfortunate woman could scarcely muster courage to speak. He threw on the table a packet containing the letter to Stella, quitted the house without a word, and returned to Dublin. Disappointment, indignation, and terror combined, brought Vanessa to her grave in the space of a few weeks after this interview, but not till she had revoked a will by which she had bequeathed the whole of her large fortune to Swift.

Mrs Johnson survived Vanessa by a few years, and died of a decline on the 8th of January 1728. It may be stated, that in addition to these world-renowned names of Stella and Vanessa, there was another lady with whom Swift had contracted an attachment previous to his acquaintance with Stella. She was a Miss Jane Waryng, the sister of a fellow-student at Trinity College, Dublin, and was courted by him under the designation of *Varina*. This,

his first love, Swift regarded for a time with all the ardour of boyish affection, but in a few years his passion cooled, and an estrangement took place. Alluding to these passages in his history, it is beautifully remarked by Mr Thackeray in *The English Humorists*, that the book of Swift's life may be said to open at places kept by these blighted flowers!

One of the best traits in Swift's character, was his large-hearted and unostentatious benevolence. About a third of his income was devoted to charitable objects, and by his will the bulk of his fortune was devised for the foundation of an hospital for idiots, a bequest very suggestive of the melancholy fate of the testator. The anecdotes related of him as a humorist have been so often repeated as to have become, for the most part, utterly threadbare. It may be remarked on this subject, that however fond Swift might be of a joke where the weight of sarcasm rested on the shoulders of another, he had little relish for it when any of the shafts of ridicule rebounded against himself. On such occasions, he would fairly lose temper, and betray a contemptible littleness of mind. Thus he was so incensed at a Catholic priest whom he met in a friend's house, and who smartly replied to his sarcastic interrogation, Why the Catholic Church used pictures and images when the Church of England did not? with the retort: 'Because we are old housekeepers, and you are new beginners,' that he quitted the room, and refused to remain to dinner. Another time, he complained to the mistress of an inn of the sauciness of her cookmaid, who, when the dean asked her how many maggots she had got out of a piece of mutton she was scraping, answered: 'Not so many as are in your head!'

---

## OCTOBER 20.

St Barsabias, abbot, and his companions, martyrs, in Persia, 342. St Artemius, martyr, 362. St Zenobius, bishop of Florence, confessor, 5th century. St Sindulphus or Sendou, of Rheims, 7th century. St Aidan, bishop of Mayo, 768.

---

*Born.*—Sir Christopher Wren, architect of St Paul's, 1632, *East Knoyle, Wilts;* Stanislaus Leczinski, king of Poland, 1677; Henry John Temple, Viscount Palmerston, statesman, 1784, *Broadlands, Hants.*

*Died.*—Charles VI., king of France, 1422; Lord William Howard, 1640, *Naworth Castle, Cumberland;* Henri Basnage du Fraquenet, eminent lawyer, 1695, *Rouen;* Archibald Pitcairn, physician and author, 1713, *Edinburgh;* Charles VI., emperor of Germany, 1740; Michael Dahl, Swedish portrait-painter, 1743, *London;* Philip Astley, author of works on horsemanship, 1814, *Paris.*

### LORD WILLIAM ('BELTED WILL') HOWARD.

One of the most memorable worthies famed in English history is Lord William Howard, commonly known as 'Belted Will,' and one of the most picturesque monuments of Old England is his border stronghold of Naworth Castle, near Brampton, in Cumberland.

He was the third son of Thomas, Duke of Norfolk, the most potent and popular nobleman of his day; and his mother, the duke's second wife, was Margaret, who was daughter and sole heiress of Lord-Chancellor Audley. It was not, however, by this alliance, but by the third marriage of the duke, that the Howard family acquired the magnificent inheritances they enjoy in Cumberland, Northumberland, and Yorkshire. Lord William was born on the 19th December 1563; and in 1566 the duke married, as his third wife, the widow of Thomas, Lord Dacre of Gilsland and Greystoke, whose three daughters and co-heiresses came in ward to the duke, and were prudently destined by him for his three sons. One of the daughters was Elizabeth, who was born in the same year as Lord William Howard, was brought up with him, and became his bride when only fourteen years of age. The duke, however, did not live to see this object of his ambition realised, for Lord William was only in his ninth year when 'good' Queen Bess beheaded his father for his chivalrous devotion to Mary Queen of Scots, and Lord William and his brother were afterwards confined in the Tower for their adherence to the Catholic faith. Naworth Castle and the barony of Gilsland were part of the inheritance of Lord William Howard's youthful bride, but after the attainder of the duke, the crown withheld her estates for many years, and it was not until long after her marriage that they were restored to her, and only then upon her paying Queen Elizabeth a fine of £10,000.

The vindictive persecution thus suffered by Lord William, sadly overclouded his early manhood, and the long and costly litigation for recovery of his young wife's inheritance, impoverished his estate for many years; but adversity served to develop those high qualities of energy, prudence, courage, and perseverance which distinguished him throughout his eventful life. It was not until the accession of James I., when Lord William was in his fortieth year, that the fortunes of the Howard family were restored. He was soon afterwards appointed by the king his lieutenant, and warden of the marches; and it was probably the acquisition of this onerous and martial office, that determined him to repair Naworth Castle and make it his chief abode for the future.

This old stronghold and the adjacent territory had belonged from the days of the Norman kings to the lords of Gilsland—a martial race of barons of the old historic family of Vallibus or De Vaux. By an heiress, the estates came, in the reign of Henry III., to the family of De Malton, and in the following century the marriage of the heiress of the De Maltons to Ralph de Dacre brought Naworth and Gilsland to that nobleman and his posterity.

In those days, a building could not put on castellated dignity without the royal licence; and accordingly, in 1335, Ralph de Dacre obtained license to castellate Naworth. He built his fortress in quadrangular form, enclosing a large courtyard, and at each angle of the south front he built a massive tower; on the other sides the building was naturally fortified by the steep declivities on the edge of which its walls were built. And so in days—

'When English lords and Scottish chiefs were foes,
Stern on the angry confines Naworth rose.
In dark woods islanded its towers looked forth,
And frowned defiance on the growling north.'

For more than two centuries and a half, and until the marriage of Lord William Howard to the co-heiress of Thomas, Lord Dacre, as already mentioned, the property was held by the Dacre family. It does not, however, appear to have been the scene of any very memorable events in our national annals, and the castle had fallen into decay before the reign of Elizabeth. Lord William Howard's repairs seem to have occupied from 1605 to 1620; and the architecture of the chief part of the quadrangle, as it stood down to the time of the fire in 1845, remained as he left it. Much of the massive architecture of the time of Edward III.—that is to say, Lord Dacre's work—was not only preserved at the time of Lord William's repairs, but is standing at the present day; but, conservative as has been the work of restoration, undertaken by the good-hearted Earl of Carlisle after the fire, the aspect of the old stronghold was, in 1845, more medieval than it is now. The characteristic old hall and chapel, and some other antique features of the castle, were destroyed in the fire; but the tower at the south-east angle, known as 'Lord William's Tower,' escaped destruction, and the formidable warden's own chambers, which consisted of his library, his oratory, and his bed-chamber, all reached by a narrow winding-stair, defended by doors strengthened with iron, retained, down to the time of the fire, the very furniture and books he had used, insomuch that these chambers seemed to recall the hour—

'When helmèd warders paced the keep,
And bugler blew for Belted Will.'

And when, as Sir Walter Scott remarked, the lord warden in person might be heard ascending his turret stair, and the visitor was almost led to expect his arrival. And pleasantly does the poet bring the picturesque old chieftain before us:

'Costly his garb, his Flemish ruff
Fell o'er his doublet shaped of buff,
With satin slash'd and lined;
Tawny his boot and gold his spur,
His cloak was all of Poland fur,
His hose with silver twined;
His Bilboa blade, by marchmen felt,
Hung in a broad and studded belt.'

Apropos to his costume, it may be mentioned that the very suit of black in which he is represented in the portrait (attributed to Cornelius Jansen) at

LORD WILLIAM ('BELTED WILL') HOWARD.

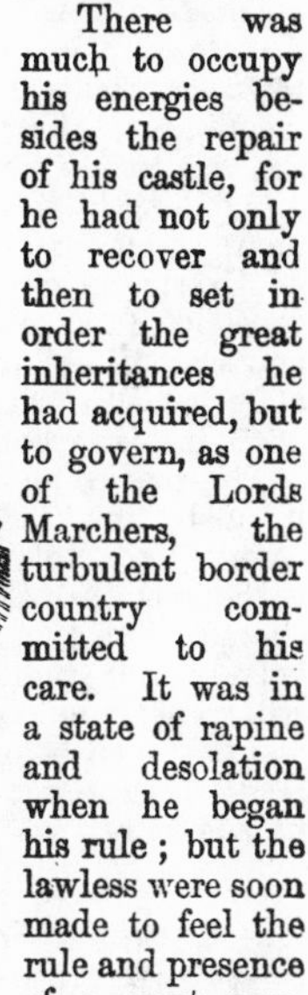

Castle Howard, is mentioned in his steward's account, and appears to have cost £17, 7*s.* 6*d.* The dress is a close jacket of black figured thick silk, with rounded skirts to mid-thigh, and many small buttons; black silk is the material of the hose, and black silk stockings come above the knee; he wears a plain falling shirt-collar, the sleeves turned up at the wrist. His dress-rapier has a gilt basket-hilt, and hangs by a narrow (not broad) belt of black velvet, with gilt hooks. So much for his costume.

There was much to occupy his energies besides the repair of his castle, for he had not only to recover and then to set in order the great inheritances he had acquired, but to govern, as one of the Lords Marchers, the turbulent border country committed to his care. It was in a state of rapine and desolation when he began his rule; but the lawless were soon made to feel the rule and presence of a great man. He maintained at Naworth a garrison of a hundred and forty men at arms, for protection of the country and apprehension of evil-doers, and made his name a word of terror on the border lands. Yet Camden, the great antiquary, found the formidable warden occupied amongst his books, and speaks of him as 'an attentive and learned searcher into venerable antiquity.' His literary tastes and public duties may be said, indeed, to have blended in him the character of scholar and soldier; and it is evident that he was as well practised with the pen as with the sword.

His border stronghold of Naworth stands near the line of the old Roman Wall, and he copied for Camden the inscriptions on Roman altars and tablets, which he had collected from the vicinity. In his days, manuscripts—the spoils of the monasteries—were often to be found scattered in private hands; and Lord William himself collected some manuscripts which are now treasured in the British Museum and the Herald's College, in the collections which bear the name of the great Earl of Arundel, his illustrious nephew. Nor was he a collector only, for the same hand which drew up a list of sixty-eight felons, whom he had captured and hung, edited the chronicle of Florence of Worcester, one of the old monastic historians. A large number of his books are still in his tower at Naworth (unfortunately they have remained stowed in chests ever since the fire); many of them are rare and early printed books, many are great and ponderous tomes, and most of them bear his annotations in his firm and distinct handwriting.

When we view him in

'The tranquil hour
Of social pleasures ill-exchanged for power,'

we see Lord William surrounded by a family circle numbering, on some festive occasions, fifty persons, for sons with their wives, and daughters with their husbands then assembled round their noble parents.

He was accustomed to travel with a large retinue, sometimes numbering eighteen persons, and the expenses of his journeys to London varied from £15 to £30 in the money of the time. When in town, he resided sometimes at Arundel House (then standing on the south side of the Strand), and sometimes in St Martin's Lane.

At length this politic and martial chieftain, having won for himself the honourable distinction of CIVILISER OF THE ENGLISH BORDERS, having consolidated a noble inheritance for his posterity, and seen his children grow to be the comfort of his old age, died at Naworth Castle on the 20th October 1640, in his seventy-seventh year.

The repairs and restorations of Naworth Castle, made by the Earl of Carlisle, have been already adverted to: this notice should not be concluded without stating that, in these works, the original character of the picturesque old stronghold has been so well studied, that an air of antiquity seems still to pervade it, and one might expect to find the warders spell-bound in its gallery or court-yards, ready to issue with their chieftain to repel some hostile foray.

## PHILIP ASTLEY.

The founder of the celebrated amphitheatre, bearing his name, and which, till its metamorphosis by Mr Boucicault into a temple of the regular drama, formed one of the most attractive places of amusement in London to children, great and small, deserves a notice here, both from his own individual merits and the interest attaching to him as the father of the modern circus. He was a native of Newcastle-under-Lyne, and in his early years assisted his father in the occupation of a cabinet-maker; but enlisted when a stripling of seventeen, in the 15th regiment of light-horse, commanded by General Elliot. From his boyhood, he had shewn a marked predilection and aptness for equestrian exercises, for which his new mode of life supplied him with a congenial sphere, and he soon became famous as a regimental rough-rider and instructor in horsemanship. During the last years of the Seven Years' War, he served abroad on the continent, and by his steadiness and intelligence, as well as courage, displayed on numerous occasions, attained the rank of sergeant-major, but, not long afterwards he solicited and obtained his discharge from the army. The object of his doing so, appears to have been the design of turning his equestrian abilities to account in the way of public exhibition; but at first his gains in this line were very scanty, and he was obliged to eke out a living by resuming occasionally his old trade as a cabinet-maker. With a horse, which had been presented to him as a parting-gift and token of esteem by General Elliot, and another which he purchased himself, he conducted his equestrian performances in a field near the Halfpenny Hatch, Lambeth, receiving such trifling gratuities as the liberality of the spectators and passers-by might bestow. From this humble exhibition, he advanced first to the dignity of an unroofed wooden circus, erected by him in the midst of a timber-yard. Here he achieved such success as to attract the patronage of royalty, and a few years later was enabled to erect, on the same site, a spacious wooden building, which he opened in 1780 under the title of the Amphitheatre Riding-House, diversifying his feats by the introduction of musical pieces, and dancing on a regular stage with scenery. Such an interference, however, with dramatic monopoly, was not to be tolerated, and as he had obtained no licence, Astley was prosecuted and imprisoned. Through the influence of Lord Thurlow, whose daughters he had instructed in riding, he was released from confinement, and at the same time granted a licence. A rapid and uninterrupted career of success now attended him, and, from time to time, he enlarged and embellished his amphitheatre, the name of which he changed first to The Royal Grove, and afterwards to the Amphitheatre of Arts; but the title of Astley's Amphitheatre, given it by the public, has proved a more enduring epithet than either. On the breaking out of the war with the French republic, the revival of the old spirit of military enthusiasm in the breast of Astley, induced him to proceed to the Low Countries as a volunteer in the campaign there, under the Duke of York. From him he received the present of two horses, as a mark of esteem for his gallantry at the siege of Valenciennes; but the benevolence and generosity which were as conspicuous characteristics of Astley as courage, induced him to sell the steeds and employ their price in providing winter-comforts for the soldiers of his troop. The news of the burning of his amphitheatre made him hastily quit the seat of war and return to London, but the edifice was soon rebuilt and reopened. A similar disaster befell it a few years afterwards, with the same display of reconstructive energy on the part of the proprietor.

The death of Astley took place at Paris, in October 1814, from gout in the stomach. With the no less celebrated Franconi, he was associated in the establishment of the Cirque Olympique, in the French capital. In physical organisation, Astley presented a fine type of English vigour, being upwards of six feet high, with extraordinary muscular power, and possessing all that love for, and dexterity in managing, the horse, so eminently characteristic of his countrymen. But the warmth and generosity of his heart, so unequivocally evinced during the Low-Country campaign, as well as the unflinching bravery shewn by him on many occasions, inspire us with a much higher respect than any amount of personal ability or worldly success. And as an author, his manuals of horsemanship, and his descriptive account of the theatre of war in the Netherlands, in which he himself had taken a part, if not displaying high merit in a literary point of view, are at least conspicuous for industry and good sense, and the thorough knowledge which the author possesses of his subject.

## GRACE DARLING.

One of the most pleasing incidents in humble life, within the present century, was the heroic achievement of Grace Darling. Her very pretty name, too, had something to do with the popularity which she acquired; for, without attaching over-importance to the matter, there can be little doubt that lovable actions become more fixed in the public mind when connected with such gentle and pleasant names as Grace Darling and Florence Nightingale.

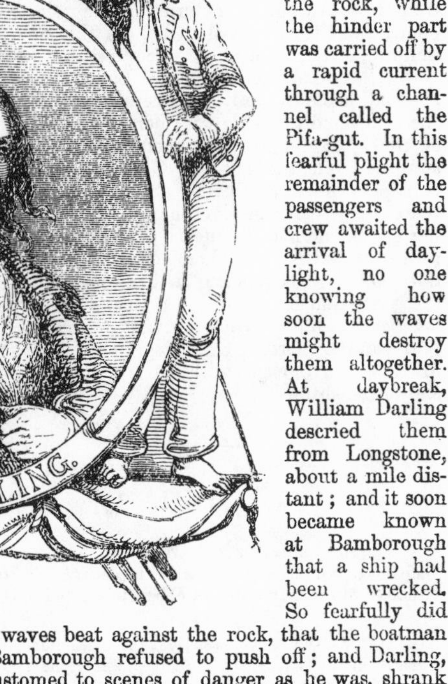

Grace Darling, born in November 1815, was the daughter of William Darling, keeper of the light-house on the Longstone, one of the Farne Islands, off the coast of Northumberland. They are scarcely islands, indeed, being little more than barren and desolate rocks, in most parts very precipitous, and inhabited by little besides sea-fowl. The sea rushes between the islands with great violence; and the spot is so dangerous to ships passing near, that a light-house has long been maintained there. Almost shut out from the world in such a spot, Grace Darling saw very little society; yet her parents managed to give her a fair education for a girl in her station. She was described as being 'remarkable for a retiring and somewhat reserved disposition, gentle in aspect, and mild and benevolent in character; of a fair complexion and comely countenance, with nothing masculine in her appearance.'

It was on the 6th of September 1838, when Grace was about twenty-two years of age, that the event took place which has given her celebrity. The *Forfarshire*, a steamer of about 300 tons, John Humble, master, was on her way from Hull to Dundee. She had a valuable cargo, and sixty-three persons on board—the master and his wife, a crew of twenty men, and forty-one passengers. A slight leak, patched up before her departure, broke out afresh when off Flamborough Head, and rendered it difficult to maintain the fires for the engine. She passed between the Farne Islands and the mainland about six in the evening of the 5th, and then began to encounter a high sea and a strong north wind. The leak increasing, the engine-fires gradually went out; and although the sails were then used, they could not prevent the vessel from being driven southward. Wind, rain, fog, and a heavy sea, all beset the hapless vessel at once. About four o'clock on the morning of the 6th, she struck bows foremost on a precipitous part of one of the rocky islands. Some of the crew and one of the passengers left the ship in one of the boats; two other passengers perished in the attempt to throw themselves into the boat. The females on board clustered round the master, shrieking, and imploring aid which he could not afford them. A heavy wave, striking the vessel on the quarter, raised her from the rock, and then caused her to fall violently on it again; she encountered a sharp ledge, which cut her in twain about midships; the fore-part remained on the rock, while the hinder part was carried off by a rapid current through a channel called the Pifa-gut. In this fearful plight the remainder of the passengers and crew awaited the arrival of daylight, no one knowing how soon the waves might destroy them altogether. At daybreak, William Darling descried them from Longstone, about a mile distant; and it soon became known at Bamborough that a ship had been wrecked. So fearfully did the waves beat against the rock, that the boatman at Bamborough refused to push off; and Darling, accustomed to scenes of danger as he was, shrank from the peril of putting off to the wreck in a boat. Not so his gentle but heroic daughter. She could see, by the aid of a glass, the sufferers clinging to the wreck; and, agonized at the sight, she entreated him to let her go with him in a boat to endeavour to rescue them. At last he yielded; the mother helped to launch the boat into the water, and the father and daughter each took an oar. And so they rowed this fearful mile, at each instant in danger of being swamped by the waves. They reached the wreck, and found nine survivors. One of them, a weaver's wife, was found in the fore-cabin, exposed to the intrusion of the sea, and two children lay stiffened corpses in her arms. The whole nine went with Darling and his daughter into the boat, and safely reached the light-house, where, owing to the severity of the weather, they were forced to remain two days, kindly attended to by the three inmates.

When the news of this exploit reached the coast, all Northumberland was filled with admiration; and speedily the whole kingdom was similarly affected. Grace Darling's name became everywhere known, and she herself received attentions from all quarters. Tourists came from all parts to see the Longstone light-house, and, still more, to see Grace herself. The Duke and Duchess of Northumberland invited her and her father to Alnwick Castle, and gave her a gold watch; the silver medal of the Shipwreck Institution was awarded to her; and testimonials came from various public bodies. A purse of £700 was presented to her by public subscription. Portraits of her were eagerly sought for and purchased; and a speculating manager of a London theatre even offered a large sum to her, if she would merely sit in a boat on the stage for a few minutes, during the performance of a piece written for the occasion. But her modest and retiring disposition revolted from this last-named notoriety; she rejected the offer; and throughout the whole of this novel and tempting career, she never once departed from her gentle, womanly demeanour. Lovers, of course, she had in plenty, but she accepted none of them; she continued to reside with her father and mother at the light-house. And there she died of consumption, on the 20th of October 1842, at the early age of twenty-seven, about four years after the event which had given her fame. Long before her death, she had the means of seeing how literature was invoked in her honour; for memoirs, tales, and poems relating to her were issued from the press—such as *Grace Darling, the Heroine of the Farne Islands; Grace Darling, the Maid of the Isles;* and so forth. One biographer managed to fill 480 octavo pages with an account of her life and of the shipwreck!

# OCTOBER 21.

St Hilarion, abbot, about 371. St Ursula and her companions, virgins and martyrs, 5th century. St Fintan, surnamed Munnu, or Mundus, abbot, in Ireland, 634.

*Born.*—Marshal Augereau, Duke of Castiglione, Bonapartist general, 1757, *Paris;* George Colman, the Younger, dramatist and humorous writer, 1762; Samuel Taylor Coleridge, poet, 1772, *Ottery St Mary, Devonshire;* George Combe, phrenologist, 1788, *Edinburgh.*

*Died.*—Julius Cæsar Scaliger, scholar and critic, 1558, *Agen on the Garonne;* Edmund Waller, poet, 1687, *Beaconsfield, near Windsor;* James Gronovius, scholar and author, 1716, *Leyden;* Tobias Smollett, novelist, 1771, *Leghorn;* Samuel Foote, humorous writer, 1777, *Dover;* Alexander Runciman, Scottish painter, 1785; Horatio, Lord Nelson, killed in Trafalgar Bay, 1805; John Philpot Curran, celebrated Irish orator, 1817, *London;* Charles E. Horn, musical composer, 1849, *Boston, U. S.*

## SAMUEL FOOTE.

This celebrated humorist, whose comic genius procured for him the appellation of the English Aristophanes, and who, by his witty conversation, enjoyed the same pre-eminence in the society of the last, that Sydney Smith did in that of the present century, has nevertheless come now to be nearly forgotten, mainly in consequence of the ephemeral character of much of his writings, which derived a considerable portion of their zest from their stinging personalities, and allusions to events of passing interest.

He was a native of Truro, in Cornwall, where his father held a good position as one of the county magistrates. Having received his primary education at the grammar school of Worcester, he was sent from thence to Oxford, and afterwards entered himself at the Temple, in London, as a law-student, but made little or no progress towards qualifying himself for that profession. The whole bent of his mind was in the direction of fun and frolic, and for several years he led the gay and dissipated life of a man about town, till his pecuniary means were wholly exhausted, and it became necessary to look about seriously for some settled mode of support. From a boy, his talent for mimicry had been conspicuous, its first display, it is said, being a recitation at his father's table, during the Christmas holidays, of a supposed decision by the magisterial bench in an affiliation case, in which the justices, including his own parent, were hit off in the most truthful and ludicrous manner. At college, while under the care of the provost, Dr Gower, his reckless conduct drew down upon him severe lectures from the former, who does not, however, appear to have administered them with much judgment, interlarding his objurgations with many sesquipedalian words and phrases. On such occasions, Foote would appear before his preceptor with a huge folio dictionary under his arm, and on any peculiarly hard word being used, would beg pardon with much formality for interrupting him; turn up his book, as if to find out the meaning of the learned term which had just been uttered; and then closing it, would say with the utmost politeness: 'Very well, sir, now please to go on.' Another of his tricks was setting the bell of the college church ringing at night, by tying a wisp of hay to the bell-rope, which hung down low enough to be within reach of some cows that were turned out to graze in a neighbouring lane. The mishap of Dr Gower and the sexton, who caught hold of the peccant animal, whilst in search of the author of the mischief, and imagined they had made a prisoner of him, provided a rich store of amusement for many days to the denizens of Oxford.

But a life of mirth and pleasantry cannot last for ever, and Foote, having dissipated his fortune, as already mentioned, in London, resolved to turn his talents to account, and with that view tried his fortune on the stage. His first attempt, like Liston, was in tragedy, and he made his appearance in the character of Othello. This, however, was unsuccessful, and a few more impersonations having convinced him of his unfitness for tragedy, he exchanged the buskin for the sock, and gained considerable celebrity by his performance of Lord Foppington in the *Relapse*, Dick in the *Confederacy*, and Bayes in the *Rehearsal.* It then occurred to him to start a performance on his own account, and he accordingly engaged the theatre in the Haymarket, or, as it was then generally termed, the *Little Theatre.* The following advertisement, in consequence, appeared in the *General Advertiser* of 22d April 1747:

'At the Theatre, in the Haymarket, this day, will be performed, a Concert of Music, with which will be given *gratis*, a new entertainment, called the Diversions of the Morning, to which will be added a farce, taken from the Old Bachelor, called the Credulous Husband. Fondlewife by Mr Foote, with an Epilogue, to be spoken by the B—d—d Coffee-house. To begin at 7.'

This entertainment went off with great success, but was stopped in consequence of the opposition of Lacy, the patentee of Drury-Lane Theatre, who procured an interdict against its repetition on the following day, on the ground of Foote having obtained no licence for the Haymarket theatre. The latter, nowise daunted, issued the following advertisement on 24th April:

'On Saturday noon, exactly at 12 o'clock, at the New Theatre, in the Haymarket, Mr Foote begs the favour of his friends to come and drink a dish of chocolate with him; and 'tis hoped there will be a great deal of comedy and some joyous spirits; he will endeavour to make the Morning as diverting as possible. Tickets for the entertainment to be had at George's Coffee-House, Temple Bar, without which no person will be admitted.—*N.B.* Sir Dilbury Diddle will be there, and Lady Betty Frisk has absolutely promised.'

This announcement attracted a considerable audience, many of whom, however, were rather bemuddled in regard to the promise of chocolate, and seem to have expected that they would be served with that refreshment. Whilst waiting in this dubiety, Mr Foote came forward and stated that he had some young performers whom he had been drilling for some time back, and that perhaps the company would have no objections to see them go through their lessons till the chocolate could be got ready. The performance then commenced in earnest, was received with immense applause, and regularly continued with the greatest success, the manager's opponents finding it useless to attempt any further objection. He then altered the time of exhibition to the evening, with the following notice:

'At the request of several persons who are desirous of spending an hour with Mr Foote, but find the time inconvenient, instead of chocolate in the morning, Mr Foote's friends are desired to drink a dish of tea with him at half an hour past 6 in the evening.'

The *tea* proved as popular an entertainment as the *chocolate*, and money flowed liberally into the coffers of the host. But the death, in 1748, of a relative, who bequeathed him a large sum of money, induced Foote to resume the gay life of a gentleman at large, which he indulged for several years, residing principally, during that period, on the continent. In 1752, he again made his appearance in London, and from time to time was engaged as a comedian at the leading theatres, besides contributing to them various dramatic pieces. He resumed the management of the little theatre in the Haymarket in 1760, and retained it, first as lessee and afterwards as proprietor, till a few months previous to his death. A royal patent was granted to him in 1766, through the interest of the Duke of York, for the representation of dramatic pieces during the summer months, from 14th May to 14th September. For this boon he was indirectly indebted to an unlucky horse-accident which had befallen him in the duke's company, and cost him the loss of one of his limbs, necessitating him to use a cork-leg for the remainder of his life. In the eyes of some persons this might appear a judgment for the manner in which he had introduced and ridiculed on the Haymarket stage, under the character of Peter Paragraph, Mr George Faulkner, printer of the *Dublin Journal*, a worthy man, whose chief peculiarity consisted in having lost a leg. But Foote was perfectly reckless how the laugh was raised, and made no exception in favour of either friends or foes.

Subsequent to this misfortune, the pecuniary circumstances of Foote were greatly improved, and for many years he continued to delight the public with his drolleries, and gather thereby a golden harvest. An unfortunate *fracas*, however, in which he got involved with the notorious Duchess of Kingston, whom he had introduced into a farce, *A Trip to Calais*, under the title of Lady Kitty Crocodile, caused him so much annoyance and disquietude, as ultimately to shorten his days. His procedure in this matter is not much to his credit. Though a good deal of obscurity exists in regard to it, it was positively sworn to by the duchess's chaplain in a regular affidavit, that Mr Foote had offered to withdraw the obnoxious piece on receiving the sum of £2000. The lady had interest enough with the lord-chamberlain to get its representation prohibited, though it was afterwards brought out in an altered form as the *Capuchin*. The vindictive feeling, however, of the duchess, led her, through her emissaries, to get a charge of the most odious nature preferred against Foote, which does not appear to have had the slightest foundation in truth. He was honourably acquitted, but the shame and distress which he felt at the imputation of such a crime, completely prostrated him. He sank into a most depressed state of health, both of body and mind; and feeling himself unable longer to attend to his professional duties, he disposed of his theatre to Colman, in the spring of 1777. In the autumn of the same year he resolved to try the restorative effects of a visit to France, and on 20th October arrived at the Ship Inn, Dover, on his way to Calais. Here he is said to have given vent to his last flash of merriment. Going into the kitchen to order a particular dish for dinner, he encountered the cook, who, hearing that he was going to France, boasted that for her part she had never been out of her own country. 'Why, Cooky,' said Foote, 'that is very strange, for they tell me upstairs that you have been several times all over *Greece*.' 'They may say what they like,' she replied, 'but I never was ten miles from Dover in my life.' 'Nay,' rejoined Foote, 'that must be a fib, for I myself have seen you at *Spithead*.' The other servants now perceived the joke, and a universal roar pervaded the kitchen, Foote presenting them with a crown to drink his health and a prosperous voyage. On this, he was destined never to embark, being seized the next morning with a succession of shivering fits, of which he expired in the course of a few hours, at the age of fifty-seven. His body was removed to his house in Suffolk Street, London, and interred in Westminster Abbey.

Respecting Foote's personal character, there is not much to be said. He was one of those beings who seem to be born to be drolls, and whose irresistibly comic powers render it almost impossible to contemplate them in a moral or serious light. The following is Dr Johnson's declaration regarding him, as related to Boswell: 'The first time I was in company with Foote was at Fitzherbert's. Having no good opinion of the fellow, I was resolved not to be pleased; and it is very difficult to please a man against his will. I went on eating my dinner pretty sullenly, affecting not to mind him; but the dog was so very comical, that I was obliged to lay down my knife and fork, throw myself back in my chair, and fairly laugh it out. Sir, he was irresistible.' On another occasion he thus contrasts him with Garrick: 'Garrick, sir, has some delicacy of feeling; it is possible to put him out; you may get the better of him; but Foote is the most *incompressible* fellow that I ever knew: when you have driven him into a corner, and think you are sure of him, he runs through between your legs or jumps over your head, and makes his escape.' It must be recorded to Foote's credit that he was very generous to his poor friends, authors, actors, and others, by whom he was always surrounded, and was really a man of considerable attainments, being both a good classical scholar and well informed on all subjects of general learning.

The literary merit of his dramatic pieces is far from contemptible, and they teem throughout with passages of the raciest humour. Partly owing, however, to their personalities and allusions to events of the day, the interest in which has passed away, and also, it may be, to a certain freedom and levity of language incompatible with modern tastes, his works are now scarcely ever read or represented on the stage. They are all in the comic or satirical vein; and among them may be mentioned the names of *The Author*, *The Liar*, *The Minor*, *The Orators*, *The Nabob*, *The Devil on Two Sticks*, and *The Mayor of Garratt*, in the last of which, the character of Jerry Sneak has become proverbial as an embodiment of a henpecked husband.

We shall be readily excused for introducing here a few of the sayings recorded of Foote.

While present one evening at the *Lectures on the Ancients*, adventured on by Charles Macklin, the lecturer hearing a buzz of laughter in a corner of the room, looked angrily in that direction, and perceiving Foote, said pompously: 'You seem very merry, pray, do you know what I am going to say?' 'No,' replied Foote, 'do you?' On another occasion, while dining at Paris with Lord Stormont, the host descanted volubly on the age of his wine, which was served out in rather diminutive decanters and glasses. 'It is very little of its age,' said Foote, holding up his glass. 'Why do you hum that air?' he said one day to a friend. 'It for ever haunts me,' was the reply. 'No wonder,' he rejoined, 'you are for ever murdering it.' A mercantile friend, who imagined he had a genius for poetry, insisted one day on reading to him a specimen of his verses, commencing with, 'Hear me, O Phœbus and ye Muses Nine;' then perceiving his auditor inattentive, exclaimed, 'Pray, pray, listen.' 'I do,' replied Foote, 'nine and one are ten, go on.' Having made a trip to Ireland, he was asked, on his return, what impression was made on him by the Irish peasantry, and replied that they gave him great satisfaction, as they settled a question which had long agitated his own mind, and that was, what became of the cast-clothes of the English beggars. When bringing out his comedy of *The Minor*, considerable objections were started to its being licensed, and among other parties by the archbishop of Canterbury, Thomas Secker. Foote offered to submit the play to his revisal, with permission to strike out whatever he deemed objectionable; but this proposal the prelate wisely declined, as he observed that he should not like the author to announce the performance of the piece 'as altered and amended by his Grace the Archbishop of Canterbury.' One evening he was asked at a coffee-house if he had attended that day the funeral of a friend, for whom he cherished a great regard, and who happened to be the son of a baker. 'O yes,' he replied, 'poor fellow, I have just seen him shoved into the family oven.'

The celebrated gambler, Baron Newman, having been detected at Bath in cheating at cards, was pitched out at the window. Meeting Foote shortly afterwards, he complained bitterly of the usage to which he had been subject, and asked what he should do to repair his honour. 'Do!' replied Foote, 'never play so *high* again in your life.'

Having once paid a professional visit to Scotland, where he was well received, he was one day dining at a gentleman's house, when an old lady present was called on for a toast, and gave 'Charles the Third.' 'Of Spain, madam?' said Foote. 'No, sir,' she replied somewhat tartly, 'of England.' 'Never mind her,' said one of the company, 'she is one of our old folks who have not got rid of their political prejudices.' 'Oh, dear sir, make no apology,' cried Foote, 'I was prepared for all this; as, from your living so far north, I suppose none of you have yet heard of the Revolution.'

A country gentleman, whom Foote was visiting, was complaining to him of the great expenses to which he had been put by the funeral of a relation, an attorney. 'Why,' said Foote gravely, 'do you bury your attorneys here?' 'Yes, to be sure,' replied the other, 'what should we do?' 'Oh, we never do that in London.' 'How do you manage then?' 'Why, when the patient happens to die, we lay him in a room overnight by himself, lock the door, throw open the sash, and in the morning he is entirely off.' 'Indeed,' said his friend, 'what becomes of him?' 'Why, that we cannot exactly tell, not being acquainted with supernatural causes. All that we know of the matter is, that there's a strong smell of brimstone in the room next morning!'

Foote's mother bore a strong resemblance to her son, both in person and disposition. From her he inherited his mirthful, as well as his extravagant propensities. Though she was heiress to a large fortune, her carelessness in pecuniary matters involved her in such embarrassments, that she at last became dependent on the bounty of Samuel, who allowed her a hundred a year. On one occasion she wrote him as follows:

'DEAR SAM,

I am in prison for debt; come and assist your loving mother, E. FOOTE.'

To this brief note he replied.

'DEAR MOTHER,

So am I; which prevents his duty being paid to his loving mother by her affectionate son, SAM. FOOTE.

'*P.S.*—I have sent my attorney to assist you; in the meantime let us hope for better days.'

One little circumstance remains to be stated in connection with Foote's domestic relations. He is generally said to have been married in early life to a Worcester lady, but the union turned out ill assorted, and his wife was never brought forward among his London friends. They had no children, and so little can now be learned of her history, that it has come to be doubted whether he ever entered the married state at all. He used to say, laughingly, in excuse for bachelorhood, that a lady's age was like a hand at picquet, *twenty-five*, *twenty-six*, *twenty-seven*, *twenty-eight*, *twenty-nine—sixty*, and that he had no idea of finding himself so unequally matched.

## LORD NELSON'S RELICS.

One of the most observable characteristics of English society at the present day, and perhaps of society in general, is the desire of obtaining some memorials of those who have achieved greatness, or have obtained notoriety whether good or bad. From the autograph of Shakspeare or Napoleon, down to the rope with which a notorious criminal was hanged, all such relics have their admirers, according to the varieties of taste in those who collect them. Lord Nelson's relics have been especially sought, and have been made the subject, not only of pamphlets and lengthened correspondence, but of actions at law. We may regard as a *mental* relic that famous saying of Nelson: 'ENGLAND EXPECTS EVERY MAN TO DO HIS DUTY!' Sir Harris Nicolas, in his *Correspondence and Letters of Nelson*, deemed it worth while to ascertain as precisely as he could the circumstances under which those words were uttered. There are three accounts of the matter—one by Mr James, in his *Naval History;* one by Captain Blackwood, who commanded the *Euryalus* at the battle of Trafalgar; and one by Captain Pasco, who had been Nelson's flag-lieutenant in the *Victory*. Sir Harris Nicolas accepts Pasco's version, because that officer had himself to signal the words by means of flags. His account runs thus: 'His lordship came to me on the poop, and after ordering certain signals to be made, about a quarter to noon he said: "Mr Pasco, I wish to say to the fleet, '*England confides that every man will do his duty;*' and he added, "you must be quick, for I have one more to make, which is for close action." I replied: "If your lordship will permit me to substitute '*expects*,' for '*confides*,' the signal will soon be completed, because the word '*expects*' is in the vocabulary, whereas the word '*confides*' must be spelled?" His lordship replied in haste, and with seeming satisfaction: "That will do, Pasco; make it directly!" When it had been answered by a few ships in the van, he ordered me to make the signal for close action.' Captain Blackwood says that the correction suggested by the signal-officer was from '*Nelson* expects' to '*England* expects;' but Captain Pasco's is accepted as being more probable.

Anything which belonged to Nelson at the critical moments of the battles of the Nile and Trafalgar is highly prized. The coat which he wore on the first of these two occasions has been preserved ever since at Greenwich Hospital. The coat which he wore at the battle of Trafalgar has been the theme of some exciting controversies. It was said by many writers, early in this century, that he put on a full-dress uniform-coat, the stars and orders of which were so brilliant as to attract the notice of the enemy's musketeers; and that to this he probably owed his death-wound. A writer in *Notes and Queries*, in 1851, described a copy of Harrison's *Life of Nelson*, which had belonged to Dr Scott, who was the chaplain and friend in whose arms Nelson died on board the *Victory*. Scott had written numerous manuscript notes on the margin of the copy; one of these, relating to the story of the dress-coat, was to the following effect: 'This is wrong. Nelson wore the same coat he did the day before; nor was there the smallest alteration in his dress whatsoever from other days.' He *did* wear his brilliant stars, however (four arranged diamond-wise, thus ⁂, on his breast); but they were embroidered on his undress-coat, and not fixed on temporarily with clasps, as at the present day. This veritable coat fell into the hands of Lady Hamilton, who pledged it with a London alderman for a sum of money. In 1845, after a quarrel between Sir Harris Nicolas and a curiosity-dealer concerning the mode in which the coat was obtained from the widow of the alderman, the late Prince Consort bought the Trafalgar coat and waistcoat for £150, and presented them to Greenwich Hospital, where they are now reverently preserved.

A bit of bullion fringe from Nelson's epaulet is treasured up as a relic. Mr Westphal, who was midshipman on board the *Victory* at the battle of Trafalgar, wrote to the *United Service Magazine*, thirty-seven years afterwards (in 1842), under his higher designation of Sir George Westphal, and gave the following account of one incident on that memorable 21st of October: 'When I was carried down wounded, I was placed by the side of his lordship; and his coat was rolled up and put as the substitute for a pillow under my head, which was then bleeding very much from the wound I had received. When the battle was over, and an attempt was made to remove the coat, several of the bullions of the epaulet were found to be so firmly glued into my hair, by the coagulated blood from my wound, that the bullions, four or five of them, were cut off and left in my hair; one of which I have still in my possession.' The coat to which this epaulet belonged was apparently *the* coat now displayed to visitors at Greenwich Hospital.

The musket-ball that killed the hero is in like manner treasured up as a memento. The late Sir William Beattie was, as Mr Beattie, surgeon on board the *Victory*. In his *Authentic Narrative of the Death of Lord Nelson*, he said: 'The ball struck the forepart of his lordship's epaulet, and entered the left shoulder. . . . . On removing the ball, a portion of the gold lace, and part of the epaulet, together with a small piece of his lordship's coat, were found firmly attached to it.' Indeed this adhesion was almost as close as if the fragments had been inserted into the metal of the bullet while in a molten state. Captain Hardy caused the bullet to be mounted in crystal and silver as a locket, and presented it to Mr Beattie. In 1840, this bullet-locket was in the possession of the Rev. F. W. Baker, of Bathwick. In 1851, it was stated to be in the possession of the Prince Consort.

It is known that when Nelson died, a miniature of Lady Hamilton was found suspended at his breast, with a lock of her hair at the back, and her initials formed in small pearls. This miniature was sold, many years afterwards, among the effects of Sir Alexander Davidson, who had been private secretary to Nelson at the time of his death. There was also a kind of miniature cenotaph made of the guineas which Nelson had in his pocket when he fell. The 'whereabouts' of these two relics was earnestly inquired for a few years ago in *Notes and Queries.* One among a small number of finger-rings has been described, containing, instead of a stone, a small *bas-relief* of Nelson, executed in some dark metal, *said* to be the bullet that killed him; but this is just the sort of story that 'needs confirmation'—especially if the account of the bullet-locket is (as appears to be the case) reliable. The Nelson *car*, in which the body of the hero had been conveyed to its last resting-place in St Paul's Cathedral, was long retained as a relic. It was at first kept in the Painted Hall at Greenwich Hospital, and afterwards at the foot of the dome over the chapel; but it became dilapidated, and then it was picked away piecemeal to form relics.

The Nelson relic which became the subject of a lawsuit was the so-called *Trafalgar Sword;* that which the hero wore at his last great battle. In 1846, Lord Saye and Sele gave a hundred guineas for this sword, and presented it to Greenwich Hospital. Sir Harris Nicolas inspected it, and at once wrote to the *Times*, announcing that the transaction was a fraud, and that the dealer (the same person with whom he had had a dispute in the preceding year) had knowingly deceived the nobleman who had purchased it. It was an undisputed fact that the dealer had bought for £1 that which he sold for a hundred guineas; but he continued to assert that the sword was genuine. Sir Harris asserted, on the contrary, that it was not such a sword as an English admiral was in the habit of wearing in the year 1805; that the scabbard did not belong to the sword; and that *Nelson did not wear any sword at all on the day of Trafalgar.* Dr Scott, in the manuscript notes above adverted to, said: 'In this action he had not his sword with him on deck, which in his other actions he had always carried; the sword was left hanging in the admiral's cabin.' Other testimony corroborates this. The curiosity-dealer then asserted that this was the sword which Nelson *would* have carried at Trafalgar, if he had carried any. A trial for libel arose out of Sir Harris Nicolas's letter to the *Times;* but the curiosity-dealer was twice defeated in it. There was some sort of proof, though indistinct, that the sword had belonged to Nelson; but it was not what it professed to be—the Trafalgar Sword.

---

## S. T. COLERIDGE.

Coleridge and Southey were brothers-in-law, and it would be scarcely possible to bring together two men of letters whose habits were more dissimilar. Southey wrought at literature with all the regularity of a banker's clerk; his day was duly apportioned among separate tasks, and these it was his delight to fulfil with energy and punctuality. Coleridge, on the other hand, did nothing save under strong external compulsion or extraordinary internal impulse. Day after day he dawdled away his time in dreaming and in desultory reading, and his genius was spent in grand designs and small performances.

Samuel Taylor Coleridge was born in 1772 at Ottery St Mary, Devonshire, of which parish his father was vicar. Samuel was the youngest of a numerous family, and at the age of nine he was left an orphan. To Christ's Hospital, London, he was sent for his education, and there he had Charles Lamb for a school-fellow. The man was manifest in the boy: dreamy, solitary, disinclined to the usual amusements of children he was an omnivorous devourer of books. He read straight through a circulating library, folios and all. 'At a very premature age,' he writes, 'even before my fifteenth year, I had bewildered myself in metaphysics and theological controversy. Nothing else pleased me. History and particular facts lost all interest in my mind. Poetry itself, yea novels and romances, became insipid to me.' The perusal of Bowles's *Sonnets*, however, so charmed him, that his lost tastes were thereby restored. Destitute of ambition, he desired to be apprenticed to a shoemaker; but by the advice and efforts of some friends, who appreciated his talents, he went to Cambridge. In a fit of despondency, produced, some say, by slighted love, and others by pecuniary difficulties, he left the university, and after wandering about the streets of London until his last penny was gone, he enlisted as a dragoon under the name of Silas Thompson Comberbatch. An officer discovering his classical attainments, elicited his secret, and his friends being communicated with, they purchased his discharge. Shortly after, in the summer of 1794, he met Southey at Oxford, at that time a fervid republican and Unitarian, and an ardent friendship ensued. Together, they planned a communistic colony, to be called a Pantisocracy, and to be settled on the banks of the Susquehanna. Happily, neither of them had any money, and in the delay requisite for earning some, their vision of social bliss was dissipated, and they were preserved from a bootless adventure. On one day in October 1795, Coleridge and Southey married in Bristol sisters of the name of Fricker, penniless as themselves. Cottle, a Bristol bookseller, had promised Coleridge a guinea and a half for every hundred lines of poetry he should write, and on the strength of this promise he entered on matrimony. He retired with his bride to a small cottage at Clevedon, rented at £5 a year, and was soon lost in a variety of schemes. He projected the *Watchman*, a weekly newspaper, and travelled through the manufacturing districts canvassing for subscribers, and preaching wherever he stayed on Sundays in Unitarian chapels. The *Watchman* was commenced, but it only reached a tenth number. Rising early one morning, he found the servant lighting the fire with an extraordinary quantity of paper. Remonstrating with her on her wastefulness, 'La, sir,' replied Nanny, 'why, it's only *Watchmen!*' From Clevedon he removed to Nether Stowey, at the foot of the Quantock Hills, where he had Wordsworth for a companion, and in that rural retreat he composed most of those pieces which have won for his name an assured place in the register of poets. In 1798, Josiah and Thomas Wedgewood, the potters, provided him with funds to go to Germany to prosecute his studies. After a sojourn there of fourteen months, he returned to England with a renewed passion for metaphysics and theology, and went to live with Southey, who had settled at Keswick. His political and religious opinions about this time underwent a great change; from a Revolutionist he passed into a Conservative, and from a Unitarian into an English Churchman: his politics and theology, however, were both held in a peculiar and philosophic sense, which were very far from being satisfactory to the orthodox. He now sought his livelihood by writing for the newspapers, and by lecturing. He contributed articles to the *Morning Post* and *Courier*. He went to Malta, and served for some months as secretary to the governor of the island. He delivered a course of lectures on poetry and the fine arts at the Royal Institution. He started the *Friend*, a periodical which ran to twenty-seven numbers, and then ceased. The management of a periodical, demanding method and punctuality, was the last thing for a man like Coleridge to succeed with, and to his constitutional indolence he had added the vice of opium-eating. The misery and degradation into which this practice led him were unspeakable. His earnings were spent in the purchase of the pernicious drug. His wife and family dwelt with Southey, and subsisted on his bounty. All dependence on his word was lost, and he became little better than a vagabond upon earth. Of his horrible condition he had the keenest sense, but he had no strength to break his bonds. To Cottle, the Bristol bookseller, he wrote in 1814: 'Conceive a poor miserable wretch, who for many years has been attempting to beat off pain by a constant return to the vice that reproduces it. Conceive a spirit in hell, employed in tracing out for others a road to that heaven from which his crimes exclude him! In short, conceive whatever is most wretched, helpless, hopeless, and you will form as tolerable a notion of my state, as it is possible for a good man to have!' Finally, in 1816, he was induced to place himself under the care of Mr Gilman, a surgeon at Highgate; and on the top of that umbrageous hill, which from the north overlooks London, he found a peaceful and congenial home until his death on the 25th of July 1834.

SAMUEL TAYLOR COLERIDGE.

Mr and Mrs Gilman fully appreciated their patient, and to their house resorted pilgrims from far and near, to listen to the wisdom, metaphysical, theological, and literary, for which his repute was high. If writing was irksome, talking was the pastime and delight of Coleridge's life. Give him but a listener—appreciative or non-appreciative it

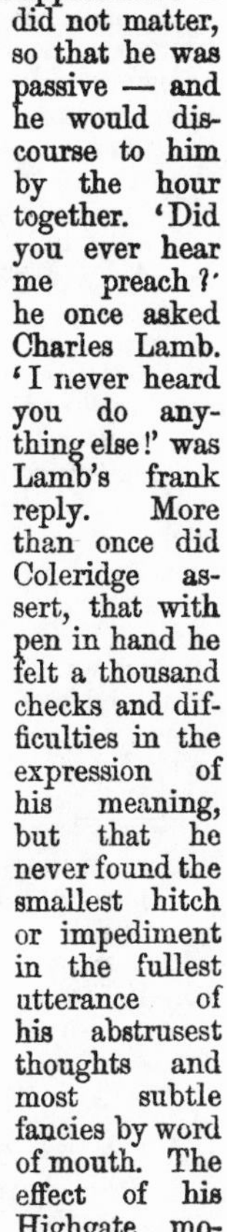

did not matter, so that he was passive — and he would discourse to him by the hour together. 'Did you ever hear me preach?' he once asked Charles Lamb. 'I never heard you do anything else!' was Lamb's frank reply. More than once did Coleridge assert, that with pen in hand he felt a thousand checks and difficulties in the expression of his meaning, but that he never found the smallest hitch or impediment in the fullest utterance of his abstrusest thoughts and most subtle fancies by word of mouth. The effect of his Highgate monologues is variously described by different auditors; by some, they are spoken of as inexpressibly tedious and unintelligible, and by others, as eloquent, profound, and instructive in the highest degree. Carlyle, in his graphic style, relates: 'I have heard Coleridge talk, with eager musical energy, two stricken hours, his face radiant and moist, and communicate no meaning whatsoever to any individual of his hearers. He began anywhere, and nothing could be more copious than his talk. He suffered no interruption, however reverent; hastily putting aside all foreign additions, annotations, or most ingenuous desires for elucidation, as well-meant superfluities which would never do. He had knowledge about many things and topics, much curious reading; but, generally, all topics led him, after a pass or two, into the high-seas of theosophic philosophy, the hazy infinitude of Kantean transcendentalism. Besides, it was talk not flowing anywhither like a river, but spreading everywhither in inextricable currents and regurgitations like a lake or sea; terribly deficient in definite goal or aim, nay, often in logical intelligibility; *what* you were to believe or do, on any earthly or heavenly thing, obstinately refusing to appear from it. So that, most times, you felt logically lost; swamped near to drowning in this tide of ingenious vocables, spreading out boundless as if to submerge the world.'

Coleridge's irresolution shewed itself in his gait: in walking, he rather shuffled than decisively stepped; and a lady once remarked, he never could fix which side of the garden-walk would suit him best, but continually shifted, in cork-screw fashion, and kept trying both. His indolence may, in great part, be accounted for by his lymphatic temperament—a temperament which, according to the degree of its predominance, indisposes its subject to active exertion. De Quincey, describing Coleridge in 1807, draws an accurate picture of a lymphatic man: 'In height, he might seem to be about five feet eight inches; he was in reality about an inch and a half taller, but his figure was of the order which drowns height. His person was broad and full, and tended even to corpulence; his complexion was fair, though not what painters technically style fair, because it was associated with black hair; his eyes were large and soft in their expression, with a peculiar appearance of haze or dreaminess.' Carlyle, speaking of him when about sixty, confirms the observation: 'Brow and head were round, and of massive weight, but the face was flabby and irresolute. The deep eyes, of a light hazel, were as full of sorrow as of inspiration; confused pain looked mildly from them, as in a kind of mild astonishment. The whole figure and air, good and amiable otherwise, might be called flabby and irresolute; expressive of weakness under possibility of strength. He hung loosely on his limbs, with knees bent, and stooping attitude.'

Though Coleridge's prose works are irregular and fragmentary, they have not been without considerable influence at home and in the United States; and the party in the Church of England, of which the late F. D. Maurice was the most notable representative, derives its being from his teaching. How far Coleridge's philosophy was original, is a matter of dispute among metaphysicians. It would seem to be beyond question, that to Schelling he was indebted so far as in some cases to be little more than his translator. Sir William Hamilton—a competent authority, certainly—writing of Coleridge's obligations to the Germans, styles him 'a literary reaver of the Hercynian brakes.'

---

# OCTOBER 22.

St Mark, bishop of Jerusalem, confessor, 2d century. St Philip, bishop of Heraclea, and companions, martyrs, 304. St Mello, or Melanius, bishop of Rouen, confessor, beginning of 4th century. Saints Nunilo and Alodia, virgins and martyrs, in Spain, 9th century. St Donatus, bishop of Fiesoli, in Tuscany, confessor, 9th century.

*Born.*—John Reinhold Forster, traveller and naturalist, 1729, *Dirschau, West Prussia;* Sir Philip Francis, reputed author of the *Letters of Junius*, 1740, *Dublin;* Dr Alexander Murray, distinguished orientalist, 1775, *Dunkitterick, Kirkcudbright.*



*Died.*—Charles Martel, vanquisher of the Saracens, 741, *France;* Athelstan, king of England, 940; Sir Cloudesley Shovel, British admiral, 1707; William Wollaston, author of *The Religion of Nature Delineated*, 1724, *Great Finborough, Suffolk;* John David Michaelis, biblical critic, 1791, *Gottingen;* Dr Samuel Arnold, composer, 1802; Henry Richard, Lord Holland, Whig statesman and man of letters, 1840, *Kensington;* Sir William Molesworth, philosopher and statesman, 1855; Louis Spohr, celebrated composer, 1859, *Cassel.*

## SIR PHILIP FRANCIS.

Though a man of distinguished ability, and playing a prominent part in connection with the history of British India, and the governor-generalship of Warren Hastings, towards the close of the last century, it is very probable that the name of Sir Philip Francis might have ceased to be remembered at the present day, were it not for the interest attaching to him as the supposed author of the celebrated *Letters of Junius.* The question of the individuality of this famous writer has been investigated with the most indefatigable and searching minuteness, and all the powers of literary and critical analysis brought to bear on its decision. To no less than thirty-five persons, including the great Earl of Chatham, the elegant and courtly Lord Chesterfield, the orator and statesman Edmund Burke, the historian Edward Gibbon, the witty politician John Horne Tooke, the demagogue John Wilkes, Horace Walpole, Henry Grattan, and Lord-Chancellor Loughborough, have these vigorous and stinging philippics been ascribed. Never was a literary secret more carefully and successfully kept, or more sedulous efforts employed to trace and ferret it out. But about forty years after the appearance of these Letters, the publication by the son of Mr Woodfall, the printer, of the private letters addressed by Junius to his father, afforded a clue to the identity of the writer, which was most ingeniously followed out by Mr Taylor, and the results given to the world in his *Junius Identified.* The result arrived at was the fixing of the authorship on Sir Philip Francis, then an old man upwards of seventy, whose participation in the matter had scarcely as yet been even suspected. With the position thus laid down by Mr Taylor, though speciously enough controverted by several parties, public opinion has been led generally to coincide, and it may now be almost regarded as established. To the grounds by which this belief is supported we shall shortly advert, but may, in the first place, give a brief sketch of the life of Francis.

He was a native of Dublin, and born there in 1740. His father, Dr Francis, is well known among classical scholars as the translator of Horace, and his grandfather was dean of Lismore. The family removed to England when Philip was a mere boy, and he received his education at St Paul's School, London, where he had as one of his companions Henry Woodfall, who was afterwards to become so famous as the printer and publisher of the *Letters of Junius.* Young Francis was early noted as a remarkably clever lad, and at the age of sixteen obtained a place in the office of the secretary of state, then held by his father's friend, Mr Fox, afterwards Lord Holland. He continued in this place under Fox's successor, Lord Chatham, but quitted it in 1758, to act as secretary to General Bligh, and was present in that capacity at the capture of Cherbourg. Subsequently to this, he became secretary to the Earl of Kinnoul, and in 1763 received an important appointment in the War-Office, which he retained for nine years. The character which he had acquired for diplomatic abilities occasioned his being appointed, along with General Clavering and Colonel Monson, a member of the Supreme Council of Bengal, which was designed to co-operate with, but in reality to act as a check on, the governor-general in the management of affairs. As might have been expected, it proved anything but a harmonious relationship; and Francis, after a six years' residence in India, and a duel with the governor-general, the celebrated Warren Hastings, which nearly proved fatal to the councillor, resigned his office, and returned to England. Not long afterwards he succeeded in getting himself returned to parliament as member for Yarmouth in the Isle of Wight, and from that period till 1807, when he retired from public life, he acted as one of the most active members of the Opposition. Under the Grenville ministry, he was made a knight of the Bath, and it was even said, at one time, that he was going to be sent out to India again as governor-general. He died in St James's Square, London, in 1818.

We have now to consider the evidence as to the identity of Sir Philip with the author of the *Letters of Junius*. There is, first, a remarkable coincidence between the known handwriting of the former and the disguised characters made use of by the latter. Both are the productions of persons having a great command of the pen; but however successfully a person may disguise his writing, it is impossible for him to guard wholly against betraying himself through those minutiæ of penmanship which every one has his own peculiar mode of executing. Thus we find that both Sir Philip Francis and Junius, instead of a round dot over the *i*, make use of an oblique stroke; they mark their quotations not by inverted commas, but by short perpendicular lines; and instead of marking the division of a word at the end of a line by a hyphen, do it by a colon. In the spelling of numerous words, the formation of certain capitals, and the general *style* of the manuscript, there is a great similarity. It has also been found on comparing an envelope addressed by Sir Philip Francis in a feigned hand with the writing of Junius, that they were absolutely identical.

The time at which the *Letters of Junius* appeared coincides very closely with the theory of Francis being the writer. The publication of the first letter in the *Public Advertiser* took place on 21st January 1769, and of the last on 21st January 1772. Letters by the same author, under different names, and also private communications to Woodfall the printer, occur both prior and subsequent to these dates, but none before 1767 or after January 1773. Now we know that from 1763 to 1772, Sir Philip Francis was in the War-Office, and in June 1773, sailed for India as a member of the Supreme Council. The intimate acquaintance of Junius with public matters, inferring often a knowledge of what was transacting behind the scenes of the administrative stage, is thus accounted for, in addition to the coincidence of date. In regard to the style and sentiments of Junius, a great similarity is traceable between them and those of Sir Philip Francis, the same vigour and terseness being conspicuous in each, with the same recklessness of assertion and pungency of sarcasm. Many other circumstances might be mentioned in support of the view we have indicated, but we shall only adduce, in addition, the facts that the authorship of Junius was never formally denied by Sir Philip Francis; that it was firmly believed by his widow, Lady Francis, to whom, on their marriage, he presented an edition of the Letters, with a request never to speak of the book nor let it be seen, but to take it with her to her room. In his drawer, after his death, a parcel containing a book was found sealed up, and directed to his wife. It was *Junius Identified*.

The question may perhaps be asked—why did Sir Philip Francis, supposing him to have been the author of Junius, seek to conceal the fact after all danger of prosecution or party violence had passed away? A sufficient answer may be found in the words of Shylock—'It is my humour;' a reason which Sir Walter Scott very candidly assigns for his long and sedulous endeavours to conceal the authorship of the Waverley Novels. But from a communication of Lady Francis to Lord Campbell, published in the *Lives of the Lord Chancellors*, it would appear that he considered himself in honour bound to secrecy, from his having given a promise to that effect to an eminent person deceased. What share the individual in question had in the matter is not ascertained, but probably some of the letters had been submitted to him before publication by Sir Philip Francis, who had possibly also received in this way some important information. It has since been learned that this mysterious coadjutor of Junius was the Earl of Chatham.

## REVOCATION OF THE EDICT OF NANTES.

The Edict of Nantes is very seldom spoken or written about in modern times; whereas its *Revocation* has become stamped as one of the notable historical events of the seventeenth century. The reason for this distinction will soon be apparent. Towards the close of the sixteenth century, France was troubled both by a war with Spain and by the struggles between the Catholics and Huguenots. Henry IV. had the whole force of the Catholic League against him so long as he was a Protestant or Huguenot; but when, in 1593, he became a convert to Romanism, he had to bear the animosity of Protestants instead of Catholics. This was so perplexing to him, that, after having signed a treaty of peace with Spain in 1598, he promulgated the *Edict of Nantes*. This was a tolerant measure, not tending to disturb the national religion of France, but giving to the Protestants a guarantee that they would not be disturbed in the free exercise of their religion. It gave them, indeed, more than this; for it assured to them a share in the administration of justice, and the privilege of being admitted to various employments of trust, profit, and honour.

After remaining in operation eighty-seven years, this edict was suddenly revoked by Louis XIV. in 1685. It was a gloomy time for the Protestants, seeing that James II. had become king of England; while in France Louis had allowed bigoted advisers to drive him into a cruel course of proceeding towards his Protestant subjects. All the pledges given to them and by the edict were at once revoked, and desolation followed. 'All the iniquities inseparable from persecution,' says Hume, 'were exercised against those unhappy religionists; who became obstinate in proportion to the oppressions which they suffered, and either covered under a feigned conversion a more violent abhorrence of the Catholic communion, or sought among foreign nations for that liberty of which they were bereaved in their native country. Above half a million of the most useful and industrious subjects deserted France; and exported, together with immense sums of money, those arts and manufactures which had chiefly tended to enrich that kingdom. They propagated everywhere the most tragical accounts of the tyranny exercised against them, and revived among the Protestants all that resentment against the bloody and persecuting spirit of popery, to which so many incidents in all ages had given too much foundation. Near fifty thousand refugees passed over into England.'

It is sickening to go through the story of the *Dragonnades*, the forcible conversion of Protestants to Catholicism by means of Louis's dragoons, at Nismes and other French towns. Without dwelling upon those recitals, it may be more to the purpose to say that France injured herself in an incalculable degree by these proceedings: seeing that she drove away from her borders much of that wealth, skill, and industry which was essential to her wellbeing. A numerous body of refugees, as we have said, came to England. Many of them settled in Spitalfields as silk-weavers; and their superior taste, skill, and ingenuity were displayed in the richness and variety of the silks, brocades, satins, and lutestrings which the looms of England afterwards produced. To this day, Spitalfields contains a larger proportion of families, whose names denote a French origin, than is customary in other parts of the metropolis. The art of paper-making, too, was greatly improved in England by this occurrence; for whereas most of our fine papers had until then been imported, now the skilled papermakers themselves were settled in England.

It is singular, indeed, that the king's advisers should not have foreseen the result of these violent measures. First, the Protestants were excluded from all civil employments. Next, they were forbidden to hold any share in the principal silk manufactures. But when an ordinance banished all the pastors, the government were perplexed at finding that the people voluntarily shared in the banishment. It was ordered that all who attempted to leave the kingdom should be sentenced to the galleys; but this did not prevent half a million persons from fleeing to England, Holland, and Germany. The loss of so much capital, skill, and industry to France, was certainly not intended or expected by the ill-advised court.

## SOME STUART STATUES.

On the 22d of October 1635, Viscount Wimbledon, military governor of Portsmouth, wrote the following epistle to the mayor of that town:

'MR MAYOR—Whereas, at my last being at Portsmouth, I did commend it to you most earnestly in regard of his majesty's figure, or statue, that it hath pleased his majesty to honour your town with more than any other; so that these signs of your inns do not only obscure his majesty's figure but outface, as you yourselves may well perceive. Therefore, I desire you that you will see that such an inconveniency be not suffered; but that you will cause, against the next spring, that it be redressed, for that any disgrace offered his majesty's figure is as much as to himself. To which end I will and command all the officers and soldiers not to pass by it without putting off their hats. I hope I shall need to use no other authority to make you do it; for that it concerneth your obedience to have it done, especially now you are told of it by myself.'

The more celebrated statue of the First Charles, now standing at Charing Cross, was treated with much less respect immediately afterwards. Cast by Le Sœur about 1638, it had not been erected when the civil war commenced, and so the parliament sold it for old metal to one John Rivet, a brazier, residing in Holborn, with strict injunctions that it should be broken into pieces. But the brazier, in defiance of those injunctions, preserved the statue intact, exhibiting some fractured bits of brass to the parliamentarians as its mutilated remains, and immediately commenced to drive a brisk trade in brass-handled knives and forks, which he sold as being partly made of the broken statue. These were eagerly purchased by both parties—by the Royalists, as sacred relics of their murdered monarch; by the Roundheads, as triumphal emblems of a vanquished tyranny. After the Restoration, the disgraced statue was exhumed from its concealment in Rivet's back-yard, and in 1674, was erected on a pedestal designed by Grinling Gibbons, on its present site. Waller, 'by four kings beloved,' wrote the following lines on the occasion:

'That the First Charles does here in triumph ride;
See his son reign, where he a martyr died;
And people pay that reverence, as they pass
(Which then he wanted!), to the sacred brass;
Is not the effect of gratitude alone,
To which we owe the statue and the stone.
But heaven this lasting monument has wrought,
That mortals may eternally be taught,
Rebellion, though successful, is but vain;
And kings, so killed, rise conquerors again.
This truth the royal image does proclaim,
Loud as the trumpet of surviving fame.'

Though universally considered to be the finest of our London statues, this specimen of Le Sœur's artistic powers has not escaped adverse criticism. Connoisseurs sometimes differ in opinion, as well as persons of less æsthetic tastes. Walpole proclaims that 'the commanding grace of the figure, and the exquisite form of the horse, are striking to the most unpractised eye.' While, on the other hand, Ralph asserts that 'the man is ill designed and as tamely executed; there is nothing of expression in the face, nor character in the figure; and though it may be vulgarly admired'—(shade of Strawberry Hill! the courtly Horace vulgar!)—'it ought to be generally condemned.'

The next royal statue in chronological order erected in London, possessed less artistic pretensions. The great civil war, though it ruined thousands, was nevertheless the cause of many large fortunes being acquired. Robert Viner, merchant and goldsmith of London, was one of the lucky individuals thus enriched. In a single transaction, recorded by Pepys, he cleared ten thousand pounds by a timely loan to Charles II. Exuberant of loyalty, and rejoicing in the full-blown honour of knighthood, Sir Robert determined to erect a statue to the careless monarch, whose lavish propensities and consequent necessities proved so profitable to the money-lending goldsmith. But, knowing little of art or artists, his principal object was to procure a statue as soon and cheaply as he could, and this he accomplished through one of his mercantile correspondents at Leghorn. The statue was of white marble, and having been executed in honour of John Sobieski, king of Poland, in commemoration of his great victory over the Turks, represented that hero on horseback, the animal trampling upon a prostrate Mussulman. A little alteration—not by any means an improvement—was made on the faces of the figures. Sobieski was converted into an exceedingly bad likeness of Charles, and the prostrate Mussulman transformed into Oliver Cromwell; but the artist leaving the Turkish turban on the head of the latter figure, most ludicrously revealed the original import of the work. The statue was erected on a conduit in Stocks Market in 1674; and Sir Robert Viner, keeping his mayoral-feast on the same day, the king dined with him at Guildhall. On this occasion, the lord mayor, in the pride of his heart and warmth of feeling, did such justice to the various loyal toasts, that he actually began to treat the king more as a familiar friend than a most honoured guest. Charles, with his usual tact, perceiving this conduct, and not altogether unaccustomed to difficulties of the kind, after giving a hint to the nearest courtiers, attempted to steal away to his carriage, then in readiness at the gate. But Viner, seeing the intended retreat, rushed after the monarch, and seizing his hand, exclaimed with an oath: 'Sir! sir! you shall stay and take t'other bottle!' Charles, looking over his shoulder, with a smile and graceful air, repeated the line of an old song—

'He that is drunk is as great as a king,'

and at once returned to the company and 't'other bottle.'

About 1735, the citizens of London, determining to erect a residence for their chief magistrate, two sites, Stocks Market and Leadenhall Market, were proposed for the purpose. Both sites had their advocates, and considerable contention prevailed on the subject, as recorded in the following epigram of the period:

'At Guildhall great debates arose
'Twixt common-council, friends and foes,
About a lord mayor's mansion-house.
Some were for having it erected
At Stocks Market, as first projected;
But others, nor their number small,
Voted for market Leadenhall:
One of the places, all agreed,
Should for their purpose be decreed.
Whence springs this strife we're in the dark yet,
Whether to keep or make a market;
And on the affair all can be said,
They differ but as *stocks* or *lead*.'

One or two circumstances concerning the erection of the Mansion-house may be noticed here. While the discussion was in progress, some one proposed the commanding site formed by the block at the Newgate-street end of Cheapside, but without avail, Stocks Market being ultimately selected. The Earl of Burlington sent a design of Palladio to the lord mayor; but the common-council, discovering, after some inquiry, that Palladio was not a freeman of the city, but a foreigner and papist, rejected his magnificent model with contempt. A citizen was selected for architect of the Mansion-house, and as he had begun life as a ship-builder, he seems not to have forgotten his original profession, the front of the building resembling very much one of the old East India Company's ships, what sailors used irreverently to term 'tea-wagons,' with her clumsy stern and quarter-galleries. The stairs and passages in the interior of the dark edifice were little more than ladders and gangways; and a superstructure on the roof, long since taken down, was an exact resemblance of Noah's ark, as represented by a child's toy. This last appendage to the building was popularly termed 'the Mare's Nest.'

Stocks Market being selected for the mansion-house, the statue that had served to represent four different persons was taken down in 1736. The following rhymes on the occasion allege that the figure on the horse had represented Cromwell also; but this is an anachronism, the Protector being dead before Sobieski won his great battle.

'THE LAST DYING SPEECH AND CONFESSION OF THE HORSE AT STOCKS MARKET.

Ye whimsical people of London's fair town,
Who one day put up what the next you pull down;
Full sixty-one years have I stood in this place,
And never till now met with any disgrace.
What affront to crowned heads could you offer more bare,
Than to pull down a king to make room for a mayor.
The great Sobieski, on horse with long tail,
I first represented when set up for sale;
A Turk, as you see, was placed under my feet,
To prove o'er the sultan my triumph complete.
Next, when against monarchy all were combined,
I for your Protector, Old Noll, was designed.
When the king was restored, you, then, in a trice,
Called me Charles the Second, and by way of device,
Said the old whiskered Turk had Oliver's face,
Though, you know, to be conquered he ne'er felt the disgrace.
Three such persons as these on one horse to ride—
A hero, usurper, and king all astride:
Such honours were mine; though now forced to retire,
Perhaps my next change may be something still higher,
From a fruit-woman's market, I may leap to a spire.
As the market is moved, I'm obliged to retreat,
I could stay there no longer when I'd nothing to eat:
Now the herbs and the greens are all carried away,
I must trot unto those who will find me in hay.'

For many years after the demolition of Stocks Market, the wretched statue was destitute of a fitting resting-place. Long it lay neglected in a builder's shed, till an enterprising innkeeper set it up in his yard. At last, in 1779, the corporation presented it to Robert Viner, a descendant of the loyal lord mayor, who at once took it away to decorate his country seat.

## SHAKSPEARE RELICS AT STRATFORD-ON-AVON.

As one among several steps towards perpetuating the national interest in the great dramatist, the ground of his house at Stratford was purchased by public subscription on the 22d of October 1861, or rather, some of the ground which had belonged to him was purchased. The truth is, there is a difficulty in identifying some of the property; and there have been two separate purchases made in the name of the public. It is believed that the house in which Shakspeare was born still exists. His father, John Shakspeare, bought two freehold houses in Henley Street, Stratford, in 1574; and it is now the cherished theory that William was born in one of these houses ten years earlier, while his father merely rented it. The property remained with John till his death, and then it descended to William; who, in his turn, bequeathed it to his sister, Mrs Hart. It is supposed that she lived in one of the houses till her death in 1646, and that the other was converted into the 'Maidenhead Inn;' this latter became the 'Swan,' and afterwards the 'Swan and Maidenhead.' After many years, that which had been Mrs Hart's portion of the house was divided into two tenements, one of which was a butcher's shop. The butcher who occupied this shop about the year 1807, put up the inscription:

'WILLIAM SHAKSPEARE WAS BORN IN THIS HOUSE.
N.B.—A HORSE AND TAXED CART TO LET.'

In more recent times the inscription was—

'THE IMMORTAL SHAKSPEARE WAS BORN IN THIS HOUSE.'

It ceased to be a butcher's shop, and was rented by an old woman, who made money by shewing the house to visitors. The bedroom, said to be that in which the great dramatist was born, was scribbled all over the walls and ceiling with the names of visitors, some illustrious, but the great portion obscure. The last descendant of the Harts, quitting the house under process of ejectment, took her revenge by whitewashing over all these names; and her successor had much trouble in removing the whitewash. In the condition of a show-place, that which was called Shakspeare's house, comprised about one-fourth of the original building, and consisted of a little shop, a kitchen behind, and two small rooms upstairs. Subsequently, the Royal Shaksperian Club of Stratford-on-Avon purchased some of this property; and another portion of the house was purchased afterwards, to be preserved in the name of the nation. There is no actual proof that William Shakspeare was born in this house; but Stratford has believed it ever since Shakspeare became famous. Washington Irving, delighted with the house and the few so-called relics exhibited in his day, said: 'What is it to us whether these stories be true or false, so long as we can persuade ourselves into the belief of them, and enjoy all the charm of the reality?' And Mr Charles Knight has said: 'Disturb not the belief that William Shakspeare first saw the light in this venerated room!' Here are also preserved, amongst other curiosities, a portrait of Shakspeare, Richard Quiney's letter to the poet asking a loan of £30, and a gold seal ring with the initials 'W. S.' upon it.

The property purchased in 1861, was land rather than houses. At the corner of Chapel Street, Stratford, was an old substantial house called New Place, which belonged to William Underhill in 1597, and was by him sold to William Shakspeare. The property was described as 'one messuage, two barns, two gardens, two orchards, and appurtenances.' In 1643, while occupied by Mrs Nash, Shakspeare's granddaughter, Queen Henrietta Maria stayed three weeks in the house. It was then owned in succession by Edward Nash, Sir Reginald Foote, Sir John Clopton, and the Rev. Francis Gastrell. This last-named owner was a most unsuitable possessor of such a place: for, in 1756, to save himself the trouble of shewing it to visitors, he cut down the celebrated mulberry-tree in the garden which Shakspeare had planted with his own hands; and, in 1759, he pulled down the house itself—which he did not inhabit—in order that he might not have to pay poor-rates for it! A house which stood on the site of New Place, together with about an acre of what had been Shakspeare's garden and orchard, were purchased after some difficulty; and the property was vested in the mayor and corporation of the town, on the conditions—that no building is to be erected on the ground, and that it shall be gratuitously open to the public. At the time of the Shakspeare tercentenary in 1864, his birthplace in Henley Street was renovated, and a fund was started for the erection of a Memorial Hall, which has since been opened and used for the representation of his plays; there is a picture gallery and library attached. The corporation decided in 1883 to acquire some of the adjacent buildings for the purpose of converting the ground into a garden.

---

# OCTOBER 23.

St Theodoret, priest and martyr, 362. St Severin, archbishop of Cologne, confessor, 400. Another St Severin or Surin, bishop. St Romanus, archbishop of Rouen, confessor, 639. St Ignatius, patriarch of Constantinople, confessor, 878. St John Capistran, confessor, 1456.

---

*Born.*—Dr John Jortin, eminent critic, 1698, *London;* Marshal Andoche Junot, French commander, 1771, *Bussy-les-Forges;* Francis, Lord Jeffrey, eminent critic, 1773, *Edinburgh.*

*Died.*—Anicius Manlius Torquatus Severinus Boethius, Latin philosopher, beheaded by King Theodoric, 524; William Prynne, author of *Histrio-Mastix*, or *The Scourge of Players*, 1669, *London;* Jean Foy Vaillant, eminent medallist, 1706; Anne Oldfield, celebrated actress, 1730, *London.*

## WALLER'S SACHARISSA.

Dorothy Sidney, Waller's Sacharissa, lives in the memory of men as a literary curiosity; as one of the brightest ornaments of virtue in the court of Charles I., she is consigned to oblivion.

Dorothy Sidney was born in 1620. She was the eldest of eight daughters, and the favourite of both parents. Her father was Robert Sidney, Earl of Leicester, and her mother, daughter of Henry Percy, ninth Earl of Northumberland.

To compile the lives of poets out of their works, is to build biography with treacherous materials, and little is known of Waller's relations to the lady of his verses, besides the meagre information which is to be found in them. It appears clear, however, that the poet proposed to her, and was somewhat disdainfully rejected. He was then a widower, popular at court, with a large estate and handsome person. The lady was gentle and virtuous, Waller wild and dissolute, and it might be supposed that his loose habits stood in his way. But other suitors of 'dearest Doll,' whose addresses were entertained, were by no means faultless. The truth is, the parents could countenance no one of less rank than a lord.

Waller was not inconsolable; he presently found a comforter, though we would conceive the transfer of his affections to have been a process of some difficulty:

'All that of myself is mine,
Lovely Amoret, is thine:
Sacharissa's captive fain
Would untie his iron chain,
And, those scorching beams to shun,
To thy gentle shadow run.
If the soul had free election
To dispose of her affection,
I would not thus long have borne
Haughty Sacharissa's scorn:
But 'tis sure some power above
Which controls our wills in love.'

Waller was soon afterwards married, as also was Sacharissa herself, on July 11, 1639, to Henry, third Lord Spencer, afterwards Earl of Sunderland. Waller's anathemas on this occasion, conveyed in a letter to Lady Lucy Sidney, another of the sisters, are worthy of quotation:

'May my Lady Dorothy (if we may yet call her so) suffer as much, and have the like passion for this young lord, whom she has preferred to the rest of mankind, as others have had for her; and may this love, before the year go about, make her taste of the first curse imposed on womankind—the pains of becoming a mother. May her first-born be none of her own sex, nor so like her but that he may resemble her lord as much as herself. May she, that always affected silence and retiredness, have the house filled with the noise and number of her children, and hereafter of her grandchildren; and then may she arrive at that great curse, so much declined by fair ladies—old age. May she live to be very old, and yet seem young; be told so by her glass, and have no aches to inform her of the truth; and when she shall appear to be mortal, may her lord not mourn for her, but go hand-in-hand with her to that place where we are told there is neither marrying nor giving in marriage; that, being there divorced, we may all have an equal interest in her again. My revenge being immortal, I wish all this may also befall their posterity to the world's end, and afterwards.' . . .

Lady Sunderland was not so fortunate as to have the poet's curses fulfilled. Her husband was killed at the battle of Newbury, in 1643, and his wife survived a second husband, whom she married in 1652. She died on the 25th February 1684, leaving one son and one daughter by her first, and one son by her second husband.

## THE IRISH MASSACRE.

This fearful event, though its atrocities have been denied or extenuated by party zeal, is nevertheless but too well authenticated, and constitutes a most painful phase in the history of Ireland during the seventeenth century. There can be no doubt that the natives of that country had been harshly and unjustly treated by the English government; they had been insulted and ground down by all kinds of oppressive restrictions; their religion had been proscribed; and large portions of their territory, more especially in the province of Ulster, had been confiscated and transferred to English and Scottish colonists. Yet, even all these provocations, combined with a due allowance for the barbarous condition of the time and country, will be wholly insufficient to excuse or palliate the horrible excesses which took place—excesses reminding us of the worst features of the Bartholomew massacre in France.

The hopes of the Irish had been excited by the successful resistance made by the Scotch to the arbitrary measures of Charles I., and the prospect of re-establishing the supremacy of their religion, as well as of regaining the lands which had been bestowed on the English settlers, stirred them up to the designment of a wide-spread conspiracy and revolt. The principal leaders were Roger Moore, a gentleman of Kildare, with Cornelius Maguire, Baron of Inniskillen, and Sir Phelim O'Neil, two chieftains of Ulster. The plot was successfully matured without the English authorities having any idea of its existence beyond receiving some obscure hints of a conspiracy being in progress; and the 23d of October 1641, was fixed on as a day of general insurrection, to be inaugurated by the surprise of the castle of Dublin. The previous night, one of the confederates getting drunk in a tavern, revealed the whole plot to an Irish Protestant, named Owen O'Connelly, who communicated the information to Sir William Parsons, one of the lords-justices, and the capital was saved. The rising, however, as preconcerted, burst forth in other parts of the country, and most frightful scenes of cruelty and bloodshed ensued. The Ulster colonists, dwelling in profound peace and the prosecution of a prosperous industry, were taken completely by surprise, and butchered promiscuously, without distinction of age or sex, by the savage and infuriated natives. In the words of Lord Clarendon, 'they who escaped best were robbed of all they had, to their very shirts, and so turned naked to endure the sharpness of the season; and by that means, and for want of relief, many thousands of them perished by hunger and cold.' The rebellion spread with frightful rapidity, and in less than a fortnight many of the fairest tracts in Ireland, which the enterprise of the British colonists had reclaimed and adorned, were converted into waste and desolation, as if it had been the object of the devastators to obliterate every trace of English occupancy.

Energetic measures were at once taken by the Long Parliament, on hearing of this outbreak, to effect its suppression, but it nevertheless continued to rage for nearly two years. Great exaggeration was made as to the number of persons who actually perished, but after rejecting all extravagant estimates, it seems to be clearly ascertained, that from the beginning of the insurrection to its end, nearly fifty thousand individuals were murdered in cold blood; and this is exclusive of those who fell with arms in their hands on the field of battle, or endured every indignity and suffering short of death.

### BATTLE OF EDGEHILL: REMARKABLE CASES OF SUSPENDED ANIMATION.

The battle of Edgehill, in which both the Royalist and Parliamentary party claimed the victory, took place on the morning of Sunday, October 23, 1642. Amongst those who fell on the king's side, and were left on the field as dead, was Sir Gervase Scroop, who had fallen covered with wounds about three o'clock on Sunday afternoon. It was not till Tuesday evening that his son, who was also in the king's forces, was able to return to the battle-field to search for the body of his father. When he found it, it was perfectly naked, having been stripped, like the rest of the slain, on Sunday evening, by camp-plunderers. In this state it had lain all Sunday night, all Monday, and Monday night, and was apparently dead, having received no less than sixteen severe wounds. Monday night, it ought to be stated, had been remarkably cold and frosty. Sir Gervase's son carried him to a lodging near at hand, and fancied he felt in the body some degree of heat. 'That heat,' says Fuller, 'was, with rubbing, within few minutes, improved into motion; that motion, within some hours, into sense; that sense, within a day, into speech; that speech, within certain weeks, into a perfect recovery; living more than ten years after, a monument of God's mercy and his son's affection. The effect of his story I received from his own mouth.' * The next day (Wednesday, 26th October), another gentleman, named Bellingham, was found in a like condition among the dead, having received twenty wounds. Being carried off by his friends, he also was restored, and lived for ten days, but died subsequently from one of his wounds terminating in a gangrene. 'The surgeons were of opinion,' says Clarendon, 'that both these gentlemen owed their lives to the inhumanity of those who stripped them, and to the coldness of the nights, which stopped their blood, better than all their skill and medicaments could have done, and that if they had been brought off within any reasonable distance of time after their wounds, they had undoubtedly perished.'

In connection with the subject of unexpected reanimation, the case of Sir Hugh Ackland, of Kellerton, Devonshire, may be mentioned as even more extraordinary. This gentleman was seized with a violent fever, and having apparently expired, had been laid out as dead. The nurse and two footmen were appointed to sit up through the night to watch the corpse. Lady Ackland, to cheer them, had sent them a bottle of brandy, whereupon one of the footmen, 'being an arch rogue,' said to the other: 'Master dearly loved brandy when he was alive, and now, though he is dead, I am determined he shall have a glass with us!' Accordingly, he poured out a bumper, and forced it down Sir Hugh's throat. A gurgling noise immediately ensued, accompanied with a violent motion of the neck and upper part of the chest. A terrible consternation seized the watchers, who rushed violently down stairs; 'the brandy genius' with such speed, that he fell, and rolled head-over-heels, bumping down from step to step till he reached tho bottom; while the nurse screamed with terror. The noise having roused a young gentleman who was sleeping in the house, he immediately got up, and went to the room where the noise had first begun. There, to his astonishment, he saw Sir Hugh sitting upright on the bed. He summoned the servants, and ordering them to place their master in a warm bed, sent off for his medical attendants. In a few weeks, Sir Hugh was restored to perfect health, and lived many years afterwards. He often used to relate this strange story of his own resuscitation by his footman's facetious conceit, for which he is said to have bequeathed him a handsome annuity.

* *Worthies of Lincolnshire.*

---

## OCTOBER 24.

St Felix, bishop and martyr, 303. St Proclus, confessor, archbishop of Constantinople, 447. St Magloire, bishop and confessor, about 575.

*Born.*—Sir James Mackintosh, politician and miscellaneous writer, 1765, *Aldourie, Inverness-shire.*

*Died.*—Hugh Capet, king of France, 996; Jane Seymour, consort of Henry VIII., 1537, *Hampton Court;* Tycho Brahe, celebrated astronomer, 1601, *Prague;* Professor John M'Cullagh, scientific writer, 1847, *Dublin;* Daniel Webster, American statesman, 1852, *Marshfield, Massachusetts.*

### DANIEL WEBSTER.

This distinguished American statesman and orator was born at Salisbury, New Hampshire, January 18, 1782. His father, a descendant of the Puritan settlers of New England, said by Mr Webster to have been the handsomest man he ever saw, except his brother Ezekiel, was a farmer and innkeeper. He owned and cultivated a tract of land, and welcomed travellers to the hospitalities of his log-cabin. He was also a soldier in the French war, and in the revolution he was present at the battles of Saratoga, and the surrender of General Burgoyne. He afterwards became a judge of the court of Common Pleas. The son, Daniel, was educated at Dartmouth College, studied law, taught an academy, and copied deeds, to support himself and aid his brother. He was elected member to congress, became senator for Massachusetts, secretary of state under two presidents, and the first lawyer and orator of his country. He has been considered by many as the greatest man, intellectually, which America has produced. As a lawyer, he had no superior; as senator, only two or three were ever regarded as his equals in ability; while, as an orator, he stands almost alone in a nation of orators. His most remarkable efforts were his speeches in the senate—on the Greek revolution, and in his debate with Mr Hayne, of South Carolina. He has also acquired great fame by two orations—one at the laying of the corner-stone of the Bunker-Hill Monument, on the anniversary of the battle, June 17, 1825, and the other at the completion of that structure, eighteen years after. But, in spite of his great talents, and unbounded local popularity, Mr Webster, like Mr Clay, was disappointed of his highest ambition; and his death was undoubtedly hastened by his failure to receive the nomination of his party to the presidency. Mr Webster's appearance and manner were very impressive. He was a large, massive man, with the head of a giant, deep cavernous eyes, a sallow complexion, and a deep bass voice. His manner of speaking was slow, dignified, and impressive, rising at times to great energy. His character, unfortunately, was marred by some defects. Generous to prodigality, he was a spendthrift, and unreliable in business-matters. Requiring stimulants, he did not always use them in moderation. As a statesman, he was more admired than trusted. Still, his patriotism was undoubted, and his faults were most easily overlooked by those who knew him best. He embodied much of the character, the patriotism, and the ambition of the northern people, and was devoted to the preservation of the Union, as the condition of the future power and greatness of the republic. The following passage from one of his speeches, as a specimen of his oratory, and a proof of his devotion to the Union, may be almost looked upon as a prophecy, too literally and terribly fulfilled. 'When my eyes shall be turned to behold for the last time the sun in heaven, may I not see him shining on the broken and dishonoured fragments of a once glorious union; on states dissevered, discordant, belligerent; on a land rent with civil feuds, or drenched, it may be, in fraternal blood!'

## FOX-HUNTING.

Now that the cornfields have been thoroughly cleared of their produce, that the woods are strewed with fallen leaves, and the shortened days bespeak the near approach of winter, when the fields in the mornings are crisp with the glittering rime which soon dissolves beneath the autumn sunbeams, when angling for the season has fairly closed, and even the sportsman's ardour has begun to languish, then commences the most renowned and exhilarating of all rural pastimes—the thoroughly British sport of fox-hunting. The period over which it extends comprises nearly six months, from the latter part of October to the beginning of April. Much of that space is of course, however, wholly unavailable for hunting-purposes, whilst the ground is either bound by hard frost or covered with snow.

Though this sport requires, for its exercise, the possession both of a considerable amount of physical courage and activity, and of pecuniary means to sustain the expenses which it entails, there is, nevertheless, no amusement which engages so large and universal a sympathy with all classes of the community. No Briton, however unable he may be from the circumstances of his position to take an active part in the chase, can refrain from experiencing a mingled feeling alike of envy and admiration as he witnesses the gallant array of horsemen assemble at the 'meet;' see the grand 'burst' when the fox has been started, and the cry of 'Tallyho! Gone away!' breaks forth; and then follow with his eye the cavalcade in its exciting pursuit, as it sweeps o'er hill and dale, with the hounds in full cry, till the outlines of the figures, becoming rapidly less and less distinct, are fairly lost in the distance. A scene like this stirs the blood in the veins of the most sluggish, whilst with the devotees of the exciting sport, the

FOX-HUNTING—'GONE AWAY!'

enthusiasm felt is such as frequently remains unimpaired by the progress of years or the chills of age, and the grayheaded fox-hunter of threescore may often be seen following the hounds with the same ardour as the stripling of eighteen.

As is well known, much of the success of a 'run' in hunting depends on the condition of the atmosphere. When this is very dry, or when a sharp northerly breeze prevails, the scent or exhalation from the hunted animal is rarefied and dissipated, and becomes consequently impossible to be traced and followed up by the dogs. When, on the other hand, the air is moist, but without the presence of actual rain, and a gentle gale blows from the south or west, then the scent clings to the adjoining soil and vegetation; and a more favourable condition still is, when it is suspended in the air at a certain height from the earth, and the dogs are enabled to follow it *breast high*, at full speed, without putting their heads to the ground. In reference to this subject we may here introduce the celebrated old hunting-song, which depicts very graphically the incidents of a fox-chase:

'A southerly wind and a cloudy sky
Proclaim a hunting-morning;
Before the sun rises we nimbly fly,
Dull sleep and a downy bed scorning.
To horse, my boys, to horse, away;
The chase admits of no delay;
On horseback we've got, together we'll trot:
On horseback, on horseback, together we'll trot:
Leave off your chat, see the cover appear;
The hound that strikes first, cheer him without fear;
Drag on him! ah, wind him, my steady good hounds,
Drag on him! ah, wind him, the cover resounds.

How complete the cover and furze they draw!
Who talks of Jolliffe, or Meynell?
Young Rockwood he flourishes now through the shaw,
And Ringwood roars out in his kennel.
Away we fly, as quick as thought;
The new-sown ground soon makes them fault;

Cast round the sheep's train, cast round, cast round!
Try back the deep lane, try back, try back!
Hark! I hear some hound challenge in yonder spring sedge;
Comfort bitch hits it there, in that old thick hedge.
Hark forward! hark forward! have at him, my boys.
Hark forward! hark forward! zounds, don't make a noise!

A stormy sky, o'ercharged with rain,
Both hounds and huntsmen opposes;
In vain on your mettle you try, boys, in vain,
But down, you must to your noses.
Each moment, now, the sky grows worse,
Enough to make a parson curse:
Pick through the ploughed grounds, pick through, pick through;
Well hunted, good hounds, well hunted, well hunted!
If we can but get on, we shall soon make him quake;
Hark! I hear some hounds challenge in midst of the brake;
Tally-ho! tally-ho, there! across the green plain;
Tally-ho! tally-ho, boys! have at him again!

Thus we ride, whip and spur, for a two hours' chase,
Our horses go panting and sobbing;
See Ranter and Riot begin now to race;
Ride on, sir, and give him some mobbing.
But hold—alas! you'll spoil our sport,
For through the pack you'll head him short.
Clap round him, dear Jack, clap round, clap round!
Hark Lasher, hark Jowler, hark back, hark back!
He's jumping and dangling in every bush;
Little Riot has fastened his teeth in his brush!
Whohoop, whohoop, he's fairly run down!
Whohoop, whohoop, give Tom his half-crown!'

The leaps taken by fox-hunters during the chase form alike the most exciting and perilous part of the pastime. In Leicestershire, which is generally regarded *par excellence* as the hunting-county of England, two specially formidable descriptions of fences require frequently to be surmounted. These are the *ox-fence* and the *bullfinch-fence*. In the former, which is rendered necessary in the locality as an effectual barrier to the roaming of cattle from their pastures during the season of the *œstrus*, or gadfly, the adventurous votary of Diana finds himself confronted by a wide ditch, bordered by a strong blackthorn-hedge, and beyond that by a railing four feet in height, all of which obstacles must be cleared by him and his steed. The bullfinch-fence, on the other hand, of still more frequent occurrence, is a thick and lofty quickset-hedge, of perhaps half a century's growth, with a ditch on one side, and requiring to be charged at full speed by the horseman, who manages to push through, whilst the bushes close after him, leaving no more trace, in the words of 'Nimrod,' 'than if a bird had hopped through.' Brooks also require frequently to be crossed; and from the aversion with which many horses regard them, requiring to be urged to them at full speed, this leap is often considered as the most difficult of any. In many parts of the country, and more especially in Ireland, stone walls are of common occurrence, and to clear these with success, calls forth all the courage and enterprise of the fox-hunter. In connection with this subject, we may here allude to the celebrated feat, achieved in 1792 by Mr Bingham, of

BLOODHUNTER CLEARING A STONE WALL IN GOOD STYLE—FROM BLAINE'S 'ENCYCLOPÆDIA OF RURAL SPORTS.'

leaping a horse over the wall of Hyde Park, the height of which was six feet and a half on the inside, and eight on the outside, where a bed of manure was laid to receive the animal. The high-spirited steed performed the feat twice, merely displacing a few bricks at the last jump. On the subject of accidents, it may likewise here be remarked, that though far from uncommon in the hunting-field, they are generally less disastrous than might be expected, partly from the soft nature of the ground on which they take place, and partly from the skill shewn by riders in evading as much as possible the consequences of a fall. To know 'how to fall' judiciously becomes, therefore, an important accomplishment of the chase.

Of all hunting-enthusiasts, none is more distinguished in sporting annals than the celebrated Thomas Assheton Smith, of Tedworth, in Hampshire, who may be said to have presented the *beau-ideal* of the British fox-hunter and country gentleman in the most splendid type of the character. Possessed of immense wealth in landed property and otherwise, and endowed by nature with the most herculean strength and courage, he continued till the age of eighty to follow the hounds with unabated vigour, having been a votary of the chase for seventy years, and a master of hounds for fifty. Even during the last two years of his life, when he became unable to ride to cover, or even face the inclemency of the weather out of doors, he would still mount his horse, and make the circuit of an extensive conservatory which adjoined to and communicated with his mansion. The extent of his experience in the sport may be estimated from the fact that, as a master of hounds, he had cut off no less than fifteen hundred brushes from as many foxes. In reference to the value set by him on a fox, an amusing anecdote is related that one morning, while at breakfast at Tedworth, he was observed to drop the newspaper with an expression of horror. A lady present inquired what was the matter: 'Good God!' was the reply, 'a fine dog-fox has been burned alive in a barn!' On another occasion, he had been hearing one of the first sermons of Mr Dyson, the clergyman's son at Tedworth, who was no less an adept in fox-hunting than in theological studies. Mr Smith was greatly pleased with the discourse, and on coming out of church after service was over, he slapped the young man on the back, and exclaimed: 'Well done, Frank, you shall have a mount on Rory O'More on Thursday!'

The enthusiasm of the master seems to have imparted itself to his servants, and we find the following instance recorded of his huntsman, George Carter. On Mr Smith's death, it was generally expected that he would be interred in the mausoleum, on the grounds, and under this impression, George made, with great earnestness, the following proposition to the friend in charge of the funeral arrangements: 'I hope, sir, when I, and Jack Fricker, and Will Bryce [the whippers-in] die, we may be laid alongside master in the mausoleum, with Ham Ashley and Paul Potter [two hunters], and a fine couple of his honour's hounds, in order that we may all be ready to start again together in the next world!'

Though the expense of maintaining a hunting-stud is considerable, amounting, in the case of the aristocratic frequenters of Melton-Mowbray, to £1000 per annum and upwards, whilst the yearly sum incurred in keeping up a pack of fox-hounds, with accessory expenses, will fall little short of £5000, there are, nevertheless, some remarkable instances on record of economy in the management of these matters. Thus, the celebrated miser, John Elwes, whose indulgence in hunting formed a solitary exception to his habitually penurious disposition, contrived to maintain a kennel of foxhounds and a stable of hunters, reputed at the time to be the best in the kingdom, at an annual outlay of less than £300. The way in which he managed is said to have been as follows: His huntsman, who acted as servant of all-work, and held no sinecure in his office, rose at four every morning, and after milking the cows, prepared breakfast for his master and any friends that might happen to be staying at the house. He then donned a green coat, saddled the horses, and got out the hounds, and the whole party started for the chase. After the day's 'run' was over, he would return to the stables, rub down the horses as quickly as possible, and then hurry into the house to lay the cloth and wait at dinner. After this, he would betake himself again to his outdoor duties, feed the horses and dogs, litter them down for the night, and milk the cows. Such multifarious avocations would seem almost to have required the hands of a Briareus, and yet Elwes used to call his huntsman an idle dog, that wanted to be paid for doing nothing. Probably the man received occasional assistance in the performance of his duties from his master's tenants, with whom the dogs were boarded during the summer months, as it is almost incredible otherwise that he could have accomplished the herculean task laid on his shoulders.

The other instance of adroit management which we shall quote, is that of Mr Osbaldeston—not the celebrated master of the Quorn hounds of that name, but the younger son of a gentleman of good family in the north of England, who, in consequence of having contracted an imprudent marriage, was turned by his father out of doors, and obliged to support himself by acting as clerk to an attorney in London. His salary amounted only to £60 per annum; and yet on this slender income he contrived not only to maintain himself and large family without running into debt, but also to keep two hunters and a dozen of hounds. This he managed to accomplish by the following method. After business-hours, he acted as accountant to the butchers of Clare Market, who paid him in pieces of meat and offal. With the first he fed himself and family, with the last his hounds, which he kept in the garret of his house. His horses were stabled in the cellar, and fed with grain from an adjoining brewery, and damaged corn from a corn-chandler, to the keeping of whose books Mr Osbaldeston devoted one or two evenings in the week. Serving either an indulgent master, or enabled by circumstances to make arrangements to that effect, he contrived, during the hunting-season, to obtain such leave of absence as permitted him to enjoy his favourite sport.

The enthusiasm for fox-hunting has not always been confined to those whose means enabled them to mount on horseback. A tailor of Cheltenham used to be well known for his pedestrian activity in following Lord Segrave's hounds. Such was his fleetness of foot and knowledge of the country, that, after following the hounds from kennel to cover, he would continue his progress on foot after the fox had been started, and contrived almost always to make his appearance at the death. He would hunt thus five days a week on foot with Lord Segrave, and meet the Duke of Beaufort's hounds on the sixth. On one occasion he walked from Cheltenham to Berkeley, a distance of twenty-six miles, found that the hounds had gone to Haywood, ten miles further off, proceeded thither, and, though rather late, witnessed a splendid run. Lord Segrave, it is said, once offered him a good situation as earth-stopper; but his characteristic answer was, that he could not 'stop earths a-nights and hunt a-days too.' Another pedestrian fox-hunter has been known to travel on foot sixty miles a day.

The reader of the *Spectator* may recollect Sir

Roger de Coverley declining, with thanks, a hound which had been sent him as a present, informing the sender with all courtesy that the dog in question was an excellent *bass*, but that at present he wanted only a *counter-tenor*. Fox-hunters dilate with rapture on the cry of a pack of hounds, more grateful, doubtless, to their ears than the most ethereal warblings of a Lind or a Grisi. A whimsical anecdote is often related of the Cockney, who, when the ardent fox-hunter exclaimed, in reference to the baying of the pack: 'What glorious music! don't you hear it?' replied: 'Music! I can hear nothing of it for the yelping of these confounded dogs!'

Till the end of the seventeenth century, fox-hunting can scarcely be said to have existed as a sport, the stag, the buck, and the hare taking the precedence with our ancestors as objects of the chase, which, at an earlier period, included the wolf and the boar. The county of Leicester, at the present day, constitutes the head-quarters of the sport; a pre-eminence which it owes partly to the nature of the ground, more pastoral than arable, partly to the circumstance of the covers being separated by considerable intervals, preventing the fox from readily getting to earth, and thus securing a good 'run.' The town of Melton-Mowbray, which may be regarded as the fox-hunting metropolis, is thronged during the season by sporting-visitors, who benefit the place to the extent, it is said, of £50,000 a year, and indeed form its main support. The vicinity is the country of the celebrated Quorn or Quorndon pack of hounds, so called from Quorndon Hall, the residence of the great hunter, Mr Meynell, and subsequently of the successive masters of 'the Quorn,' which takes the first place amid the fox-hunting associations of the United Kingdom.

### JOHN DOE AND RICHARD ROE.

The 24th of October 1852, witnessed the deaths of two individuals who, though *personally* unknown to any one, enjoyed, nevertheless, like Mrs Gamp's Mrs Harris, a most extensive reputation by report. Through the whole length and breadth of England, no persons were more frequently referred to (in legal documents) than John Doe and Richard Roe. Their connections with the landed property of the kingdom appeared to be both universal and multiform. In every process of ejectment, instead of the real parties to the suit being named, *John Doe*, plaintiff, sued *Richard Roe*, defendant. Their names were also inserted in criminal proceedings as pledges to prosecute.

This well-known fiction appears to have been introduced into English legal practice about the time of Edward III., in consequence, it is said, of a provision of *Magna Charta* which requires the production of witnesses before every criminal trial. John Doe and Richard Roe were thenceforth inserted as the names of the alleged witnesses. By act 15 and 16 Vic. cap. 76, passed in 1852, sentence of death, to take effect on 24th October of that year, is passed on the two illustrious personages just mentioned, and it is ordered that 'instead of the present proceeding by ejectment, a writ shall be issued, directed to the persons in possession of the property claimed, which property shall be described in the writ with reasonable certainty.'



## OCTOBER 25.

Saints Chrysanthus and Daria, martyrs, 3d century. Saints Crispin and Crispinian, martyrs, 287. St Gaudentius of Brescia, bishop and confessor, about 420. St Boniface I., pope and confessor, 422.

### St Crispin's Day.

St Crispin and his brother Crispinian were natives of Rome, and having become converts to Christianity, travelled northwards into France, to propagate the faith. They fixed their residence at Soissons, where they preached to the people during the day, and at night earned their subsistence by the making of shoes. In this they followed the example of the apostle Paul, who worked at his craft of tent-making, and suffered himself to be a burden to no man. They furnished the poor with shoes, it is said, at a very low price, and the legend adds that an angel supplied them with leather. In the persecution under the Emperor Maximian, they suffered martyrdom, and according to a Kentish tradition, their relics, after being cast into the sea, were washed ashore at Romney Marsh. In medieval art, the two brothers are represented as two men at work in a shoemaker's shop, and the emblem for their day in the Clog Almanacs is a pair of shoes.

From time immemorial, Crispin and Crispinian have been regarded as the patron-saints of shoemakers, who used to observe, and still in many places celebrate, their day with great festivity and rejoicings. One special ceremony was a grand procession of the brethren of the craft with banners and music, whilst various characters representing King Crispin and his court were sustained by different members.

At Tenby, it was customary, on the eve of St Crispin's Day, to make an effigy of the saint, and suspend it from the steeple or some other elevated place. In the morning it was formally cut down, and carried in procession throughout the town. In front of the doors of each member of the craft the procession halted, when a document, purporting to be the last will and testament of the saint, was read, and in pursuance thereof some article of dress was left as a memento of the noisy visit. At length, when nothing remained to be distributed, the padding which formed the body of the effigy was made into a football, and kicked about by the crowd till they were tired. As a sort of revenge for the treatment of St Crispin, his followers hung up on St Clement's Day the effigy of a carpenter, which was treated in a similar way.

*Born.*—Dr James Beattie, poet, 1735, *Laurencekirk, Kincardineshire;* George Stanley Faber, theological writer, and Master of Sherburn Hospital, 1773.

*Died.*—Demosthenes, great Athenian orator, 322 B.C., *Isle of Calauria;* King Stephen of England, 1154, *Canterbury;* Geoffrey Chaucer, poet, 1400, *London;* William Elphinstone, founder of King's College, Aberdeen, 1514, *Edinburgh;* Evangelista Torricelli, inventor of the barometer, 1647, *Florence;* Charles Mordaunt, Earl of Peterborough, celebrated commander in Spain, 1735; Augustine Calmet, biblical commentator, 1757, *Abbey of Senones;* George II. of England, 1760, *Kensington;* William Hogarth, painter and engraver, 1764, *Chiswick;* Sir James Graham, Bart., British statesman, 1861, *Netherby, Cumberland.*

## CHAUCER.

Many biographies of Chaucer have been written at different times, but unfortunately very little which is trustworthy is to be gleaned from them.

If the reader can succeed in deciphering the almost obliterated legend on Chaucer's monument in Westminster Abbey, he will find it recorded that he died in the year 1400, at the age of seventy-two. Some doubt is thrown on this statement, however, by recent research, which fixes the date of his birth about 1340. This monument was not set up until about a century and a half after his death; and the poet's own testimony points to the last-mentioned date as the most correct one.

To decide where Chaucer was born, is a still more puzzling question. Fuller inclines to think that his native place was Woodstock, in Oxfordshire. When Queen Elizabeth 'passed a fair stone house next to her palace in that town' to some tenant or other, this same building was described as *Chaucer's House*, and retained the name long afterwards. But as we find the poet living at Woodstock in Edward III.'s time, and dying there in his old age, the name of the house is accounted for. Another authority (Leland) leans to Berkshire, where Dunnington Castle, near Newbury, is said to have been Chaucer's family property. An oak in the park there, went by the name of *Chaucer's Oak*. But we afterwards find this same property in the possession of a certain Thomas Chaucer—whether he were Chaucer's son or not makes no matter—and thus the place need not by any means have been the poet's birthplace, so far as the name of the oak is concerned. Others maintain that London can justly claim the honours; and it appears from Chaucer's own words, in his *Testament of Love*, that, whether he were born there or not, he was certainly brought up there. His words are these: 'Also in the citie of London, that is to mee soe deare and sweete, in which I was foorth growne; and more kindely love have I to that place than to any other in yerth (as every kindely creature hath full appetite to that place of his kindly engendure).'

Apropos of the poet's origin, Stowe records that 'Richard Chawcer, vintner, gave,' to the church of St Mary Aldermary, 'his tenement and tavern, with the appurtenance, in the Royal Streete the corner of Kerion Lane, and was there buried, 1348.' Mr Furnivall has brought to light a deed of 1380, in which Chaucer describes himself as the son of John Chaucer, vintner; by other documents this John Chaucer is shewn to be the son of Richard Chaucer, also a vintner, and both of London.

Chaucer was educated at Oxford or Cambridge—it cannot be ascertained which—and afterwards travelled—it is not known where, or for how long a period. He returned home to become a courtier, and continued in great favour during the long reign of the third Edward; to all appearance winning honours, gaining friends, and meriting respect, as the first poet of his time.

But Chaucer gained, in Edward's court, something more substantial than honours. He held a succession of offices, which—though under such ambiguous appellations as have come down to us they seem to our ignorance suspicious—were probably of the nature of creditable sinecures, intended to afford the poet competence without toil. He himself informs us, that at this time the profits of his numerous grants enabled him to live with dignity and hospitality. He speaks of himself, looking back, in a sadder time, as 'once glorious in worldly wellfulnesse, and having such godes in welthe as maken men riche.' What would one not give to have been the guest of 'the morning-star of song'—

> 'Which first made to distil and reine
> The gold dewe-dropes of spech and eloquence.'

Wood, in his Annals, describes Chaucer as having been a pupil of Wickliffe, when that enterprising priest was warden of Canterbury Hall. The story is too good to be true. Yet, if we see reason to reject the tradition, it is certain that Chaucer, if not a Wickliffite, sympathised with what we may call the advanced religionists. He considered the pope to be Antichrist, and abhorred the mendicant priests. Nor did these tendencies of his shew themselves only in words. As Chaucer was a good old English yeoman, so we conceive him to be slightly belied by the meek demureness of the likeness which survives of him. Who would expect to find Master Geoffrey Chaucer fined 'two shillings for beating a Franciscane frier in Fleet Street?' Yet such was the fact.

Chaucer had a stanch friend in John of Gaunt, the Duke of Lancaster, and champion of Wickliffe. Not merely an honourable relation of patron and client, but a bond of intimate friendship, existed between them. Duchess Blanche and the duke gave Chaucer to wife a favourite of their own. This was Philippa, sister to Catharine Rouet. Catharine was a knight's daughter, at the time John of Gaunt's mistress, and governess to his children, and afterwards his wife.

In Richard II.'s reign, when the duke's influence declined, Chaucer got into trouble, in consequence of which he found his means considerably straitened. He involved himself in some Wickliffite disturbances, and had to seek safety in flight. Venturing soon after to return to London, he was seized and imprisoned in the Tower. Here, it is said, either faltering in courage through the rigour of his confinement, or provoked by the ingratitude of certain accomplices, he informed against the rest, and regained his liberty. For some time after, though he retained apparently many of his grants, Chaucer seems to have been in rather low water. He describes himself as 'being berafte out of dignitie of office, in which he made a gatheringe of worldly godes.' Soon after his release he disposed of sundry pensions, took his leave of the court, and retired to Woodstock.

It is probable that Chaucer remained for the most part in retirement during the rest of his life. He seems to have written much, if not the whole, of his *Canterbury Tales* during this period. He died an old man, and persisted to the last, says Wood, in his dislike of 'friers.' He is said to have died in the Romish faith. The statement has been disputed, but we scarcely see on what grounds. He does not appear to have been a Wickliffite, although he supported, in certain cases, members of that party. It must be borne in mind that hatred of monks, with their ignorance and licentiousness, and disrespect of reigning popes, worse than the monks, were not by any means in that day, nor indeed long afterwards, inconsistent with strict adherence to the Romish tenets.

Though we have seen that his hatred of the friars was unabated to the last moment, there were some things for which Chaucer, on his dying bed, is said to have been sorry. 'Of that he wrote of love and baudery,' records Wood, 'it grieved him much on his death-bed: for one that lived shortly after his time maketh report, that when he saw death approaching, he did often cry out: 'Woe is me, woe is me, that I cannot recall and annull those things which I have written of the base and filthy love of men towards women: but, alas! they are now continued from man to man, and I cannot do what I desire.'

It is some comfort to find the old man repenting of those blemishes in his works which so often offend the reader of a more refined age. Chaucer's last words, at least, were consistent with his profession. From an old folio edition of his works, dated 1602, presented to the British Museum by Tyrwhitt in 1786, we have gleaned a little tribute to the poet, not unworthy to be recovered from the grasp of oblivion:

'A BALLADE IN THE PRAISE AND COMMENDACION OF MASTER GEFFRAY CHAUCER FOR HIS GOLDEN ELOQUENCE.

Maister Geffray Chaucer, that now lithe in grave,
The noble rhetoricion, and poet of Great Britaine,
That worthy was, the laurer (*sic*) of poetry to have
For this his labour, and the palme to attaine,
Which first made to distil, and reine,
The gold dewe dropes, of spech and eloquence,
Into English tonge, through his excellence.'

It appears that Chaucer had children. He dedicates one of his treatises to a son, Lewis. Fuller mentions a son Thomas—Thomas Chaucer, 'sole son of Geffery Chaucer, that famous poet, from whom he inherited fair lands at Dunnington Castle in this county (*Berkshire*), and at Ewelme, in Oxfordshire. He married Maud, daughter and co-heir of Sir John Burwash, by whom he had one only daughter, named Alice, married unto William de la Pole, Duke of Norfolk. He lyeth buried under a fair tomb in Ewelme Church.' Whether this was really a son of Geoffrey Chaucer, has been doubted, with or without sufficient reason we are unable to say; but if he was, he was not, as we have seen, the 'sole son.'

## THE EARL OF PETERBOROUGH.

Like Charles XII. of Sweden, the character of the great Earl of Peterborough presents a singular combination of the hero and the madman. His career in Spain, as commander of the British forces in the War of Succession, resembles more the history of Amadis or Orlando, than an episode in real warfare; and in the achievements recorded of him, we find ourselves transported once more to the legendary times of chivalry. The conquest of Valencia, more especially, which he commenced with a detachment of 150 dragoons, and accomplished as much to the astonishment of his own army as to the bewilderment of the prostrated enemy, overpowers us with wonderment; and had the narrative only descended to us from antiquity, instead of being the chronicle of an undisputed fact, it would have been infallibly discredited as fabulous and extravagant. Had it not been for the mulishness of the Archduke Charles, as well as the political jealousies and dissensions at home, which prevented his plans from being carried out, and ultimately occasioned his premature recall to England, there seems little reason to doubt that Peterborough might have seated a German monarch on the throne of Madrid, and altered very materially the future arrangements of European diplomacy. But the advantages so surprisingly gained were destined ere long to be as rapidly lost; and in the battle of Almanza, after Peterborough's departure, the prestige, which the British arms had won in the siege of Barcelona and the Valencian campaign, was sadly forfeited.

Peterborough's private life was far from regular; and in all the phases of this extraordinary man's history, we perceive the same enthusiastic bravery and intellectual acumen, the same warmth and generosity of disposition, and the same eccentricities and absurdities, the last two qualities shewing themselves in his love of practical jokes and whimsical adventures. The following anecdote is related in connection with one of his youthful escapades. He was courting a young lady who was remarkably fond of birds, and had taken a fancy to an uncommonly fine canary which belonged to a widow, the keeper of a coffee-house at Charing Cross. She besought Peterborough, then Lord Charles Mordaunt, to procure for her, as a pledge of his affection, this unrivalled songster. He offered, accordingly, an enormous sum to its owner, who, however, was so much attached to it, that she refused to part with it at any price. Determined to gain the prize, he contrived to obtain another bird, of the same size and colour, but a hen, and wholly tuneless. The coveted bird was almost never allowed to be out of sight of its mistress, who sat behind the bar of the coffee-house; but one day Peterborough succeeded in getting her out of the way on some pretext, and made use of the opportunity to effect an exchange of the canaries. This was about the time of James II.'s expulsion. After the Revolution, Peterborough happened to be visiting the coffee-house where he had committed the fraud, and ventured to remark to the landlady: 'I would have bought that bird of yours, and you refused my money for it; I daresay you are by this time sorry for it.' 'Indeed, sir,' she replied, 'I am not, nor would I now take any money for him; for—would you believe it?—from the time that our good king was forced to go abroad and leave us, the dear creature has not sung a note!'

As illustrative of his puerile propensity to petty mischief, it is recorded that, one day while riding in his coach, and seeing a dancing-master, with pearl-coloured silk stockings, and otherwise sprucely attired, picking his steps daintily along the street, he jumped down and pursued him with a drawn sword, forcing the poor man to run ankle-deep into the gutter, into which, however, the earl himself was also forcibly drawn. When stationed at the town of Huete, he learned that a very beautiful young lady had just taken refuge there, in a convent. Peterborough was determined to get a sight of this celebrated fair one, but he was well known as a gay Lothario, and the strictness of the lady-abbess would have opposed an effectual bar to the gratification of his wishes. Procuring the attendance, then, of an engineer-officer, he proceeded with him to the convent, and demanded admission, for the purpose of tracing out a line of defences in the garden, preparatory to converting the place into a fort for protecting his position at Huete. The lady-abbess and her nuns, including the object of Peterborough's curiosity, rushed out in an agony of terror, and besought him to spare their convent. It would seem that the great general was not inexorable, and the construction of the fort was indefinitely postponed. Whether the real purpose of his *ruse* was ever discovered by the fair nun whose beauty prompted the act, or how far she appreciated it, history does not record.

A strong antipathy existed between Peterborough and the Duke of Marlborough. On one occasion, the former was surrounded by an angry mob who took him for the duke, at that time rather unpopular. He ran a chance of receiving some violent usage, when he exclaimed: 'Gentlemen, I shall convince you by two good and sufficient reasons that I am not the Duke of Marlborough. First, I have only five guineas in my pocket; and, second, here they are at your service,' suiting his action at the same time to the word, by scattering the money amongst the crowd. He was then allowed to depart amid loud huzzas, after having thus hurled an ingenious satire both at the wealth and avarice of the great commander.

When very young, Lord Peterborough was married to the daughter of a Kincardineshire baronet, by whom he had two sons, who predeceased their father, being cut off by small-pox within six weeks of each other, and a daughter, who became Duchess of Gordon. Left a widower, and solitary in his old age, he contracted a private marriage with Miss Anastasia Robinson, a celebrated opera-singer, whose beauty and talents were only surpassed by her rare modesty and worth, and who proved to him a most devoted wife. The union was subsequently acknowledged by him, and publicly solemnised. He died at Lisbon, whither he had gone in the hope of re-establishing his failing health, at the age of seventy-seven.

## DEATH OF GEORGE II.: CURIOUS SUPERSTITION.

On the morning of 25th October 1760, George II. expired suddenly at Kensington, at the age of seventy-six. The cause of death was the rupture of the right ventricle of the heart. Though never a popular sovereign, the glories attending the British arms during the latter years of George II.'s reign were such as to conciliate largely the affections of his subjects. Frugal to penuriousness, choleric, and by no means correct in moral deportment, he was, nevertheless, honest and open in character, and possessed of considerable personal courage, as evinced by his bravery at the battle of Dettingen. To both George and his father must be accorded the credit of eminently prudent and judicious management, enabling them alike to preserve the allegiance of their subjects throughout a peculiarly difficult and critical period, and secure for the country a degree of material prosperity such as it had never before enjoyed.

Two years previous to his death, George II. had been attacked by a serious illness, which was expected to prove fatal; but he rallied, and regained for a short period the enjoyment of good health. A curious circumstance, illustrative of popular superstition, is mentioned in connection with this indisposition by Lord Chesterfield, and quoted by Earl Stanhope in his *History of England:* 'It was generally thought his majesty would have died, and for a very good reason—for the oldest lion in the Tower, much about the king's age, died a fortnight ago!'

In old times, it was customary to name the lions in the Tower menagerie after the reigning kings, and the fate of the royal beast was thought to be bound up with that of human majesty. The notion is humorously alluded to by Addison, in the *Freeholder,* where he represents the Jacobite country squire inquiring anxiously at the keeper, at the Tower, whether none of the lions had fallen sick on the taking of Perth and the flight of the Pretender!

---

## THE BATTLE OF AZINCOURT.

In connection with St Crispin's Day occurs one of the most brilliant events of English history—the celebrated battle of Azincourt, gained, like those of Crécy and Poitiers, under an immense disparity in point of numbers on the side of the victors, and also under the most disadvantageous circumstances from the effect of fatigue and privations. The chivalrous Henry V., after proclaiming what can only be designated a most unjustifiable war with France, had embarked on an expedition for its conquest at Southampton, in August 1415, and landed near Harfleur, which he invested and captured after a siege of thirty-six days. So great, however, was the loss sustained by the English army, owing to a terrible dysentery which had broken out in the camp, that the project of re-embarking for England was seriously deliberated in a council of war. The idea was indignantly rejected by Henry, who declared that he must first see a little more of 'this good land of France.' With a greatly reduced army, he accordingly commenced a march through Normandy and Picardy to Calais; and after surmounting numerous difficulties, was engaged on 25th October, near the village of Azincourt or Agincourt, by D'Albret, the Constable of France, at the head of an army which outnumbered that of the English monarch in the proportion of at least six to one. In immediate prospect of the conflict, and in reference to the day on which it was to be fought, Shakspeare represents Henry delivering himself as follows:

'This day is call'd the feast of Crispian:
He that outlives this day, and comes safe home,
Will stand a tip-toe when this day is nam'd,
And rouse him at the name of Crispian.
He that shall live this day, and see old age,
Will yearly on the vigil feast his neighbours,
And say, To-morrow is Saint Crispian:
Then will he strip his sleeve and shew his scars,
And say, These wounds I had on Crispian's day.
Old men forget; yet all shall be forgot,
But he'll remember, with advantages,
What feats he did that day: then shall our names
Familiar in their mouths as household words—
Harry the king, Bedford and Exeter,
Warwick and Talbot, Salisbury and Gloster—
Be in their flowing cups freshly remember'd:
This story shall the good man teach his son;
And Crispin Crispian shall ne'er go by,
From this day to the ending of the world,
But we in it shall be remembered—
We few, we happy few, we band of brothers;
For he to-day that sheds his blood with me
Shall be my brother; be he ne'er so vile,
This day shall gentle his condition:

And gentlemen in England, now a-bed,
Shall think themselves accurs'd they were not here;
And hold their manhoods cheap whiles any speaks
That fought with us upon St Crispin's day.'

As in the two previous great battles between the English and French, the success of the former was mainly owing to their bowmen, whose arrows threw the French cavalry into confusion, and who themselves afterwards broke into the enemy's ranks, and did terrible execution with their hatchets and bill-hooks. The chivalry of France was fearfully thinned, upwards of 7000 knights and gentlemen, and 120 great lords perishing on the field, whilst the loss of the English did not exceed 1600 men. An immense amount of plunder was obtained by the victors, the weakness of whose army, however, prevented them from improving their advantages, and they accordingly continued their march to Calais. From this Henry embarked for England, landed at Dover, and marching in triumph from thence to London, entered that city with a long array of captives, and a pageant of imposing splendour such as had been wholly unprecedented in the case of any previous English monarch.

## PUNCH AND PUNCH-BOWLS.

On the 25th October 1694, Admiral Edward Russell, then commanding the Mediterranean fleet, gave a grand entertainment at Alicant. The tables were laid under the shade of orange-trees, in four garden-walks meeting in a common centre, at a marble fountain, which last, for the occasion, was converted into a Titanic punch-bowl. Four hogsheads of brandy, one pipe of Malaga wine, twenty gallons of lime-juice, twenty-five hundred lemons, thirteen hundredweight of fine white sugar, five pounds' weight of grated nutmegs, three hundred toasted biscuits, and eight hogsheads of water, formed the ingredients of this monster-brewage. An elegant canopy placed over the potent liquor, prevented waste by evaporation, or dilution by rain; while, in a boat, built expressly for the purpose, a ship-boy rowed round the fountain, to assist in filling cups for the six thousand persons who partook of it.

Punch is comparatively a modern beverage, and came to us from India, in the latter part of the seventeenth century. One of the earliest printed notices of it, is in Fryer's Travels, published in 1672, where we are told that punch is an enervating liquor, drunk on the Coromandel Coast, and deriving its name from the Industani word *paunch*, signifying five; the number of ingredients required to form the mixture. Sailors brought the novel compound from the east, and for some time it seems to have been drunk by them alone. On the first day that Henry Teonge joined the ship *Assistance*, as naval chaplain, in 1675, he drank part of three bowls of punch, a liquor very strange to him; and we are not surprised, when he further naïvely informs us, that he had considerable difficulty in finding his pillow when he attempted to go to bed. However great a stranger punch was then to him, they soon became intimately acquainted, for it appears from his amusing *Diary*, that naval officers, in those days, were ready to mix and quaff capacious bowls of punch on the slightest provocation.

The Indian potation, making its way from sea to land, met everywhere with a most welcome reception. In 1680, appeared from the pen of Captain Ratcliff a doggrel poem, entitled *Bacchanalia Cœlestia*, which had an immense popularity, though now almost utterly forgotten. In this effusion, Jupiter is represented with the minor deities on Mount Olympus, hearing for the first time of the novel beverage just invented on earth, and determined to try it. Accordingly, all unite to compound a jovial bowl of punch.

'Apollo despatched away one of his lasses,
Who filled up a pitcher from th' well of Parnassus.
To poets new born, this water is brought;
And this they suck in for their morning's draught.

Juno for lemons sent into her closet,
Which, when she was sick, she infused into posset:
For goddesses may be as qualmish as gipsies;
The sun and the moon we find have eclipses;
These lemons were called the Hesperian fruit,
When vigilant dragon was sent to look to 't.
Three dozen of these were squeezed into water;
The rest of th' ingredients in order came after.

Venus, the admirer of things that are sweet,
Without her infusion there had been no treat,
Commanded her sugar-loaves, white as her doves,
Supported to the table by a brace of young loves,
So wonderful curious these deities were,
The sugar they strained through a sieve of thin air.

Bacchus gave notice by dangling a bunch,
That without his assistance there could be no punch,
What was meant by his sign was very well known,
For they threw in a gallon of trusty Langoon.

Mars, a blunt god, though chief of the briskers,
Was seated at table still twirling his whiskers;
Quoth he, "Fellow-gods and celestial gallants,
I'd not give a fig for your punch without Nantz;
Therefore, boy Ganymede, I do command ye
To put in at least two gallons of brandy."

Saturn, of all the gods, was the oldest,
And we may imagine his stomach was coldest,
Did out of his pouch three nutmegs produce,
Which, when they were grated, were put to the juice.

Neptune this ocean of liquor did crown,
With a hard sea-biscuit well baked in the sun.
This bowl being finished, a health was began,
Quoth Jove, "Let it be to our creature called Man;
'Tis to him alone these pleasures we owe,
For heaven was never true heaven till now."
Since the gods and poor mortals thus do agree,
Here's a health unto Charles his Majesty.'

The toasted biscuit, though long since disused as an ingredient of punch, formed, from a very early period, a favourite addition to many old English drinks. Rochester, when instructing Vulcan how to contrive him a drinking-cup, says:

'Make it so large, that filled with sack
Up to the swelling brim,
Vast toasts, on the delicious lake,
Like ships at sea may swim.'

It was from this use of toasted bread or biscuit, that we acquired the word toast as applied, in the first instance, to a beautiful woman, whose health is often drunk; and, latterly, to the act of drinking the health of any person, or to any idea or sentiment, as it is termed.

The following anecdote, from the *Tatler*, tells us how a piece of toasted bread, in a prepared drink, became ideally connected with a lovely woman. It must be premised that, at one time, it was the fashion for ladies, attired in elegant dresses made for the purpose, to bathe publicly in the baths of the city of Bath. 'It happened, on a public day, a celebrated beauty was in the Cross-bath, and one of the crowd of her admirers took a glass of the water in which the fair one stood, and drank her health to the company. There was in the place a gay fellow, half-fuddled, who offered to jump in, and swore though he liked not the liquor, he would have the toast. He was opposed in this resolution; yet this whim gave foundation to the present honour which is done to the lady we mention in our liquor, who has ever since been called a toast.'

The five ingredients—spirit, water, sugar, lemon, and spice—from which punch derived its name, were in time reduced to four:

'Whene'er a bowl of punch we make
Four striking opposites we take—
The strong, the weak, the sour, the sweet,
Together mixed most kindly meet.
And when they happily unite,
The bowl is pregnant with delight.'

Or, as another minor poet thus describes the 'materials:'

'Whilst I sat pensive in my elbow-chair,
Four nymphs appeared, O how divinely fair!
Unda came first, in water-colours gay;
Brandysia next, as bright as Phœbus' ray.
In a straw gown, then came Limonia keen,
And Saccharissa sweet, was near her seen;
They, to divert my melancholy strain,
Me, all at once agreed to entertain;
And, to relieve my grief-oppressed soul,
To mix their different quotas in a bowl.
First Unda added to the bowl her share,
Water, as crystal clear, her hand as fair:
Brandysia, next her spirit did impart,
To give a warmth and fillip to the heart;
Nor did Limonia make the drink too keen,
For Saccharissa sweetly stepp'd between.
Whilst fairest Unda pours the limpid stream,
And brisk Brandysia warms the vital frame;
Whilst Saccharissa and Limonia meet
To form that grateful contrast, famed sour-sweet,
And all together make the bowl complete;
I'll drink; no longer anxious of my fate,
Nor envy the *poor* rich, nor *little* great.'

During the whole of the last century, punch ruled with sovereign sway. Besides its peculiar attractions, it had a kind of political prestige, as being the favourite beverage of the dominant Whig party; the Tories, at first, regarding it with prejudicial eyes as a foreign interloper coming in about the same time as an alien usurper. The statesmen, generals, and admirals of King William, whether Dutch or English, revelled in 'punch.' The wits and essayists of Anne's Augustan age praised it as the choicest of liquors—need we speak of Johnson, Reynolds, Garrick, Fox, Sheridan, as punch-drinkers! The punch-bowl was an indispensable vessel in every house above the humblest class. And there were many kindly recollections connected with it, it being very frequently given as a present. No young married couple ever thought of buying a punch-bowl; it was always presented to them by a near relative. And the complete change in the feelings of society, as respects drinking-usages, is prominently shewn by the fact, that a punch-bowl was in the last century considered to be a very suitable present from a merchant or banker to a trusty clerk or book-keeper, or from a ship-owner to a sea-captain. Bowls were made and painted with inscriptions and devices for testimonial purposes; the first successful whaling-voyage from Liverpool is commemorated by a punch-bowl, given by the merchants to the fortunate captain. This bowl, on which the ship is depicted in full sail, is now in the collection of Mr Joseph Mayer, the eminent archæologist.

There is no error in saying, that the punch-bowl was frequently one of the most cherished of household effects. In dissenters' families, from its being used as a baptismal-font, it acquired a kind of semi-sacred character; and the head of a household naturally felt a solemn, benignant pride in dispensing hospitality from the vessel in which his father, himself, and his children had been christened. Nor did the high-churchman less esteem the bowl. Punch, as the clergy admitted, was a thoroughly orthodox liquor; for though excess in wine was reprobated by the Scriptures, there was not, from the first chapter of Genesis to the last in Revelation, one word said against punch!

Songs, innumerable, proclaimed the virtues of punch, and extolled it as a panacea for all diseases. Dr Short, a physician of great ability and repute, writing in 1750, says that 'punch is an admirable liquor—the best liquor in the world—the universe cannot afford a better liquor for students.' But doctors differ, and Dr Cheyne, with much better judgment, asserted that there was not one salutary ingredient in it, except the water. Alluding to its Indian origin, he termed it a 'heathenish liquor,' and stigmatised it as being 'nearest arsenic, in its deleterious and poisonous qualities.' It was, no doubt, the unhealthy qualities of punch, the horrible headaches it inflicted, that drove it completely out of use. Besides, it was a terror to tidy housewives; 'the nastiest, sloppiest sluster,' as an old lady once told the writer, ever placed on a dining-room table. For a continual filling of glasses from flowing bowls, with continually increasing unsteadiness of hands, soon made a swimming table and a drenched carpet. Punch-stains, too, were in some materials ineradicable—in black cloth particularly so, leaving small holes, as if the cloth had been burned by a strong acid.

In Scotland, the jolly topers of its western metropolis, the city of Glasgow, long enjoyed an undisputed pre-eminence in the manufacture of punch. The leading ingredients, rum and lemons, were compounded with sugar and cold water, after a peculiarly artistic fashion, which was supposed to be only known to the initiated. This far-famed liquor came into disrepute, on the occasion of the visitation of the cholera to Scotland, about 1833. Being proscribed by the medical faculty, it lost its hold on public favour, a position which it has never since regained. Advanced ideas on the question of temperance have, doubtless, also had their influence in rendering obsolete, in a great measure, this beverage, regarding which some jovial spirits of the old school, reverting sorrowfully to their youthful days, will inform you that gout has considerably increased in the west since the abandonment of punch for claret and champagne.

As may readily be supposed, many of the old tavern-signs displayed a punch-bowl. Addison, in the *Spectator,* notices a sign near Charing Cross, representing a punch-bowl curiously garnished, with a couple of angels hovering over, and squeezing lemons into it. The most popular tavern of the last century that exhibited a punch-bowl on its sign, was the 'Spiller's Head,' in Clare Market. Spiller was a fellow of infinite jest; he started in life as a landscape painter, but taking to the stage, became a very popular actor, and was the original 'Mat of the Mint' in the *Beggars' Opera.* Akerby, his biographer, an artist also, says that Spiller, in the character of Mat, 'outdid his usual outdoings to such a degree, that whenever he sung, he executed his part with so truly sweet and harmonious a tone, and in so judicious and ravishing a manner, that the audience could not avoid putting his modesty to the blush by repeated clamours of encore.' The history of the sign is curious. Spiller, as may be learned from one of his benefit-tickets, engraved by Hogarth, was not unacquainted with the inside of a debtor's prison. During his last confinement, he so charmed one of the turnkeys with his wit, that the man, on Spiller's liberation, resigned office, and took a tavern, so that he might oftener enjoy the laughter-provoking comedian's company. As many notabilities flocked to the house for the same purpose, the original sign was considered scarcely suitable; and so, as Akerby informs us, 'by the concurrent desire of an elegant company, who were assembled there over a bowl of arrack-punch one evening, and by the generous offer of Mr Laguerre, who was one of the company, and as excellent a master in the science of painting as music, the sign was changed from the 'Bull and Butcher' to 'Spiller's Head,' and painted by the said Mr Laguerre gratis, in a manner and with a pencil that equals the proudest performances of those who have acquired the greatest wealth and reputation in the art of painting.'

A PUNCH-BOWL SIGN: THE 'SPILLER'S HEAD.

The accompanying illustration, representing Spiller with a punch-bowl before him, is taken from an engraved copy of the sign in question. But ere this could be painted and set up, Spiller, struck down by apoplexy on the stage, had fallen a victim to the pernicious bowl. And so the following lines were painted beneath the figure:

'View here the wag, who did his mirth impart,
With pleasing humour, and diverting art.
A cheerful bowl in which he took delight,
To raise his mirth, and pass a winter's night.
Jovial and merry did he end his days,
In comic scenes and entertaining plays.

The 'Spiller's Head' was a favourite haunt of the wits and artists of the Hogarthian era. At a later period, when Clare Market was voted low, and 'Old Slaughters' became the artists' house of resort, they were waited on there by a witty waiter, whom they named Suck, from his habit of slily drinking out of the bowls of punch, as he carried them upstairs to the company. This practice, however disgusting it would be considered now, was then looked upon as a mere trifling indiscretion, and forgiven in consideration of the waiter's wit and birth, he being, according to his own account, an illegitimate son of the renowned Spiller.

## THE CHURCH BUILT BY THE PRESIDENT OF THE MEDMENHAM CLUB.

On the 25th of October 1761, the six musical bells of West Wycombe chimed their first merry peal, to announce the completion of the tower which forms part of one of the most extraordinary churches in the kingdom. The old church was entirely demolished, with the exception of a portion of the tower and chancel, which were again united by the new nave, and made to suit its peculiar and original design. The only door into it is through the tower at the west end; and such is the effect of its general appearance, that if a stranger were brought into it blindfolded through the grave-yard, he could scarcely believe himself in a place of Christian worship. It is a large oblong room, sixty feet in length, and forty in width; the ceiling is flat, and painted in mosaic pattern, with a festooned border on the side-walls, where they join the ceiling. The windows, which are large and numerous, are the common sashes of the period, each with a window-seat, that opens, so as to form a cupboard; the floor is paved with black and white marble in lozenges; the seats are mere movable benches; the pulpit and reading-desk, which stand respectively on each side of the entrance to the chancel, are mahogany arm-chairs, with a book-stand in front. Each stands on a low chest of drawers, and when required for divine service, the drawers are pulled out to form steps for the minister to enter. The clerk's desk is somewhat similar, but stands at a distance down the nave. The font, placed in the centre, is of marble; it is about the size, and has the appearance of a small wash-hand basin; four doves are placed round the verge of the font; and it rests on a slender pillar, round which a serpent is entwined, as if pursuing the

INTERIOR OF WEST WYCOMBE CHURCH.

doves. It is said that the nave was thus constructed, that it might be used for convivial and other secular meetings, the window-seats being wine-bins, and cupboards for domestic utensils.

'Ah! well-a-day!—but this seems wondrous strange!
Is this a mart where gossips sell and buy?
A room for lectures, or a stock exchange?
Is that, which seems a pulpit to the eye,
A desk, where auctioneers their labours ply?'

MOULTRIE.

The chancel, which is very small, can scarcely be seen from the nave, for the entrance is so blocked up on both sides by the manorial-pews, or rather galleries, that the passage between is exceedingly narrow. When entered, it has a rich and gorgeous appearance. The ceiling is brilliantly painted with a representation of the Last Supper; the windows are filled with stained glass; the altar-rails are of massive oak, elaborately carved; the communion-table inlaid with mosaic-work; and the floor paved with fine polished marble. Yet the whole has a secular appearance.

The tower, which has large unsightly windows, is surmounted by a low spire, on which is placed a large hollow ball forming a room, with a seat round it that will hold twelve persons. But as it is entered by a ladder outside the spire, few persons have the nerve to make themselves acquainted with its interior. On the north wall, outside the church, which is dedicated to St Lawrence, there is a representation of him suffering martyrdom on a gridiron, with this inscription: 'Though I give my body to be burned, and have not charity, it profiteth me nothing.' And on the south side, there is a sun-dial, with this text: 'Keep thy tongue from evil-speaking, lying, and slandering.' Near the east end of the church is erected a large hexagonal mausoleum, without a roof. This singular building contains niches and recesses for sepulchral urns and monuments, and stands, together with the church, on a very high hill apart from the village. When seen at a distance, it is impossible to describe the odd appearance which the whole pile presents—the ball above the tower looking as if flying in the air.

These remarkable structures were built by the gay and eccentric Sir Francis Dashwood, about the time he became Lord le Despencer. He was the originator and president of the notorious Medmenham Club, or Monks of St Francis, as they named themselves, assuming the garb, but not the austerities, of that order. About half-way down the hill is an excavation, a quarter of a mile long, and running under the church, which is also said to have been his lordship's work, but more probably he only adapted it to his fancy. It is entered by a massive door, formed in an artificial ruin, and consists of a series of lofty caves, connected by a passage, which is in some places divided into two or three parts by huge pillars of chalk, left to support the roof. Near the middle of the excavation, there is a small pool, which is now crossed by stepping-stones, but formerly, it is said, it could only be passed in a boat. The excavation terminates in a large, lofty, circular cavern, with a vaulted roof, in which is a hook for suspending a lamp or chandelier. Here, according to local tradition, the Medmenham Club occasionally held its meetings. And certainly, if its president wished to be near his home, this spot would be convenient, being only half a mile distant. So also, if the club desired special secrecy, no place could be more suitable, seeing that when the door at the entrance was barred from within, and the pool, which the monks called the Styx, was crossed in their boat, their doings in this cavern would be as secure from interruption from the rest of the world, as if they were actually being enacted in the infernal regions themselves. But it is probable, notwithstanding all that has been said on the subject, that nothing was really practised either here, or at Medmenham, their usual place of meeting, more profane or immoral than what was openly practised in most of the convivial societies of that period. This was strenuously maintained in his old age by the last surviving member of the society. And doubtless it was only the mystery and eccentricities with which they chose to invest their proceedings, that gave rise to so many foolish tales and conjectures respecting their doings. As to the assertions and insinuations against them by the author of *Chrysal*, they are unworthy of credit, since his description of their place of meeting shews that he had no personal knowledge of the subject. Medmenham Abbey is not, as he states, in an island, but beautifully situated on the north bank of the Thames; and the room in which the club met remains just as described by Langley in 1797, and is now frequently used by picnic-parties. The rest of the building, though occupied by cottagers, has been so slightly altered externally, that the whole has realised the appearance predicted by Langley seventy years ago. The additional ruined tower, cloister, and other corresponding parts, as he says, were made with so much taste and propriety, that, now they have become clothed with ivy and mosses, they can scarcely be distinguished from the ancient remains; and the whole building has now assumed such a natural and picturesque appearance, that more than one eminent artist has chosen it for the subject of his pencil, probably regarding the whole as the interesting remains of an ancient monastery.

---

# OCTOBER 26.

St Evaristus, pope and martyr, 112. Saints Lucian and Marcian, martyrs, 250.

---

*Born.*—Charles François Dupuis, astronomer, 1742, *Trie-Chateau, near Chaumont;* George James Danton, revolutionary leader, 1759, *Arcis-sur-Aube.*

*Died.*—Abulfeda, Mohammedan historian, 1331, *Syria;* Samuel Puffendorf, distinguished jurist, 1694, *Berlin;* Sir Godfrey Kneller, portrait-painter, 1723; Dr Philip Doddridge, eminent divine and author, 1751, *Lisbon.*

## DANTON.

Danton, more than any man whom the French Revolution threw to the surface, realises the popular idea of a revolutionist. In person he was almost gigantic—tall and muscular. His head was large, and covered with stiff black hair, and his eyebrows bushy. His features were bold and irregular, and were by some called ugly; but when lit up by the fire of his intellect, their coarseness disappeared in harmony. His voice was powerful—in the outbursts of his oratory, terrible—and was likened to thunder and a lion's roar. Courage, audacity, and power were manifest in his bearing, and his careër did not belie his appearance.

He was born in 1759 at Arcis-sur-Aube, of well-to-do farming-people, and was educated for a lawyer. He went to Paris to finish his studies, and there commenced practice as a barrister. He sought the acquaintance of Mirabeau, Camille Desmoulins, Robespierre, Marat, and others, notable for their devotion to revolutionary ideas. He lived economically, and spent his days in the assembly and his nights at the clubs. He ventured to speak, and the discerning were not slow to perceive that in the orator a great power had arisen. Danton attached himself to the Girondists, and, says Lamartine, 'Madame Roland flattered him, but with fear and repugnance, as a woman would pat a lion.'

Daily he grew in popularity, and with Marat led the formidable club of Cordeliers. The court sought his influence by bribes, and in the pride of his strength he exclaimed: 'I shall save the king or kill him!' The revolution, however, was greater than Danton. He who would live in it was forced to run with it or be trampled in its path. After the flight of Louis to Varennes, he advocated his dethronement, and declared in the assembly that hesitation in pronouncing the throne vacant, would be the signal for general insurrection. When Prussia, in 1792, invaded France in vindication of royalty, and spread terror on every side, Danton, by his brave words, gave courage to the nation. 'Legislators!' said he, 'it is not the alarm-cannon that you hear: it is the *pas-de-charge* against our enemies. To conquer them, to hurl them back, what do we require? *Il nous faut de l'audace, et encore de l'audace, et toujours de l'audace*: To dare, and again to dare, and without end to dare!' In a few weeks, fourteen republican armies were in the field, repelling the allied forces with a vigour and success which set Europe aghast. For the king's death Danton voted, but, like the Abbé Sièyes, assigned no reason. In his defiant style, he said: 'The coalesced kings threaten us; we hurl at their feet, as gage of battle, the head of a king.'

Under the Revolution, Danton was first a minister of justice, and then president of the Committee of Public Safety—a body of six men, who were intrusted with absolute executive power, and who therefore bear the infamy of the Reign of Terror. In the course of events, Robespierre and Danton came face to face as rivals for the leadership of Paris, and in Paris, of France. Danton was luxurious, reckless, generous, and frank; on the other hand, Robespierre was ascetic, cold, severe, cautious, and uncompromising. In Robespierre's presence, Danton's power seemed to desert him, as if he were a bird and Robespierre a snake. Feeling that the contest was unequal, he resigned office, and, with his young wife, retired to rural privacy near his native town of Arcis. In domestic confidence, he asserted that the reason of his retreat was horror at the approaching fate of Marie Antoinette.

Robespierre was of far too suspicious and envious a temper to allow an adversary to escape so quietly. Danton likewise had associates who keenly felt his absence from the field of action. He was recalled from Arcis to Paris. He met Robespierre, and was accused by him of embezzling the public money. He retorted by calling Robespierre a sanguinary tyrant. This dispute fixed his doom. His wife and friends urged him to fly. 'Whither fly?' answered he. 'If freed France cast me out, there are only dungeons for me elsewhere. One carries not his country with him at the sole of his shoe.' He heard of the arrest of his friends, and that his own warrant was made out, yet he would not move, saying: 'They dare not, they dare not!' But he forgot that he had Robespierre the merciless, the inflexible, to deal with. He was denounced by St Just as a traitor, and on the night of the 31st March 1794, was arrested. Brought up for trial on the 2d of April, he was asked by Fouquier Tinville his name and place of abode. 'My name,' said he, 'is Danton; a name tolerably well known in the Revolution. I am thirty-five years old. My abode will soon be in nothingness, but my name shall live in the pantheon of history.' He defended himself with wild and scornful words, but was silenced on the ground that he was inciting the people to revolt. No witnesses were called against him, and his own witnesses were refused to be heard. As a matter of course, he was declared guilty.

In prison he affected indifference. 'They think to do without me,' said he; 'they deceive themselves. I was the statesman of Europe. They do not suspect the void which this head leaves' (pressing his cheeks between the palms of his large hands). 'As to me, I laugh at it. I have enjoyed my moments of existence well; I have made plenty of noise upon earth; I have tasted well of life—let us go to sleep!' In the cart in which he was taken to execution, he had thirteen companions, and among them Camille Desmoulins, the sprightliest spirit of the Revolution, who could not believe that he would be allowed to die. He wriggled to get free from the cords which bound him until his clothes came off, crying at the same time: 'Generous people! unhappy people! you are deceived, you are undone, your best friends are sacrificed! Recognise me! save me! I am Camille Desmoulins!' 'Be calm, my friend,' prayed Danton; 'heed not that vile rabble!' At the foot of the scaffold, Danton was heard to ejaculate: 'O my wife, my well-beloved, I shall never see thee more!'—then, interrupting himself—'Danton, no weakness!' He was the last to suffer. His last words were to Samson, the executioner: 'You will shew my head to the people—it is well worth shewing!' As it fell, Samson caught the head from the basket, and carried it round the scaffold amidst the howls of the people.

Danton died on the 5th April 1794. Robespierre's triumph was brief; his own head fell on the 28th of July.

## SIR GODFREY KNELLER.

Sir Godfrey Kneller was the favourite painter of portraits in England, from Charles II.'s time to the reign of George I.

He was born at Lubeck in 1648. After having been some time a painter, he came to England in the ordinary course of his travels. When here, by a series of accidents, he was employed to paint Charles II. and the Duke of Monmouth, and gave such satisfaction, by his portraits of these personages, that he found it profitable to remain in the country.

Horace Walpole maintains that Kneller, had he chosen to turn his attention to high art, would have made an artist of the first class: as it was, he only painted portraits, and some of those in a very inferior manner. The reason which he assigned for his choice of portrait-painting above other branches of art, was that of a man who cared more for his rank on this earth than his rank in the universe. 'Painters of history,' he observed, 'make the dead live, and do not begin to live themselves till they are dead. I paint the living, and they make me live.'

Certainly, so they did. Kneller lived in magnificent style, lost £20,000 by the South-sea affair, and died in possession of £2000 a year. His accumulation of wealth bears witness to his popularity. He had the honour of painting ten crowned heads. These were Charles II., James II. and his queen, William and Mary, Anne, George I., Louis XIV., Peter the Great, and the Emperor Charles VI. Besides these, he painted many other illustrious personages; among whom were Addison, Bishop Burnet, John Locke, Lady Mary Wortley Montagu, Pope, Newton, &c. He painted the beauties of Hampton Court for King William, and likewise perpetuated on canvas the members of the Kit-Cat Club. These celebrated portraits of the most distinguished Whigs of that day were painted for Jacob Tonson, the secretary of the club. Mr Christopher Cat, pastry-cook, of King Street, Westminster, and keeper of the tavern where the club met, was thus immortalised.

James was sitting to Kneller at the very minute that the news reached him of the arrival of the Prince of Orange. The picture was for Pepys, who had been a favourite and faithful servant. James told the painter to proceed with his work, that his good friend Pepys might not be disappointed.

Kneller was knighted in 1692 by William, and made a baronet in 1715 by George I. He was always a vain man, a weakness for which his friend, Pope, incessantly ridicules him in his letters. The poet furnished an inscription (by no means a brilliant specimen of his genius) to Sir Godfrey's monument in Westminster Abbey, for the erection of which the latter himself bequeathed the sum of £300.

## THE FOUNDER OF MERTON COLLEGE.

A codicil to the will of Walter de Merton, leaving the residue of his property to his college, bears date October 26, 1277. This ecclesiastic was one of the four lord-chancellors to whom Oxford is so largely indebted. These were Walter de Merton, who founded Merton College; William de

Wykeham, the founder of New College; William of Waynflete, who founded Magdalen College; and Thomas Wolsey of Ipswich, the founder of Christchurch College. Walter de Merton may be said to have exercised the most influence of the four upon Oxford, because it was he who introduced the collegiate system; the others only elaborated and extended it. In the same way Merton College must be considered the most interesting, if not the most beautiful, because it was the germ whence the rest were developed. The foundation of this establishment appears to have been a scheme to which Chancellor Merton gave his whole heart. There were, doubtless, halls of greater antiquity, but they consisted only of lodgings for the scholars. The scheme of Walter provided a chapel, with residence for chaplains, and accommodation for a warden having charge of the scholars, within the same premises. The endowments speak of a strong influence exerted on behalf of his favourite project, for the lands forming great part of the revenue are widely scattered, marking, it would seem, the gifts of numerous nobles. There are lands and houses and chancels of churches beyond the Tyne, pertaining to Merton College.

Following the rule, that the affix to a Christian name denoted a birthplace, Walter's biographers have mentioned Merton, in Surrey, as the place of his nativity. This is, however, conjectural; and there is equal probability that he was born at Basingstoke, where it is certain his parents lived, died, and were buried. In his after-days, he founded a hospital in Basingstoke to the memory of his father and mother. The day of his death, and the place at which it occurred, are as uncertain as those of his birth; but his will directed that he should be buried in his cathedral of Rochester. The intermediate events of his life are scarcely better known. He was lord-chancellor of England more than once; but whether he received the seals of office twice or thrice, is not quite apparent. Bishop Hobhouse considered he was chancellor twice during the reign of Henry III.; and it is certain that he fulfilled the duties of the chancellorship for the two years preceding the coronation of Edward I. When that event took place, Walter retired from office, and accepted the see of Rochester. A view of his life is a commentary upon his times. Scholar and ecclesiastic, he was chosen by the most powerful nobles in the land, who would not so trust each other, to hold the highest post.

## THE TWO BIG BENS.

No other bell ever underwent such a career of misfortune as that which was intended for use in the new Houses of Parliament. From the time when that immense structure was commenced, it was resolved that both the clock and the hour-bell should be the largest ever seen in this country; but it was not till 1844 that the late Sir Charles Barry solicited tenders for their construction. Through a course of wrangling, which it would be of little use here to elucidate, fifteen years elapsed before the clock was finished and actually at work in its place; this was in 1859. The clock is not only the largest but one of the most accurate we possess. The ponderous weights hang down a shaft 160 feet deep, and require winding-up only once a week. The pendulum, 15 feet long, weighs 680 pounds; and so delicate is its action, that a small weight of only one ounce, placed on a particular part of the apparatus, will alter the rate of the clock one second per week. On the four sides of the clock-tower are dial-rooms, each a large apartment, traversed by mechanism which communicates motion from the clock to the hands. Each of the four clock-dials is 22½ feet diameter; and the mere cast-iron framework of each dial weighs no less than 4 tons. The hour-figures are 2 feet high and 6 feet apart, and the minute-marks are 14 inches apart. The outer point of the minute-hand makes a sudden leap of 7 inches every half minute. The hands weigh more than two hundredweight the pair; the minute-hand being 16 feet long, and the hour-hand 9 feet. In order to render the dials visible at night, each dial-face is glazed with enamelled or opalised glass, with 60 gas-jets behind it.

Such is the magnificent clock, for which suitable bells were sought to be made. The original scheme was for 'a clock that would strike the hours on a bell of eight to ten tons, and chime the quarters upon eight smaller bells.' It was afterwards decided that there should be only four bells for the chimes, in addition to the great hour-bell. In the four corners of the bell-room these bells are placed; the first with a weight of 4½ tons, and yielding the musical note B; the second, weight 2 tons, and note E♯; the third, weight 1½ ton, and note F♯; and the fourth, weight 1¼ ton, and note G♯. By varying the order in which these are struck, they produce four chimes or partial melodies, at the four divisions of each hour; and at the full or completed hour, the whole sixteen sounds form a simple but beautiful melody in the key of E major. These four bells were made and hung nearly in the manner first designed; but the fifth—the king of the belfry, that was to hang in the vacant space between them—has not been so fortunate. It was to have been about 9 feet in diameter, 9 inches thick at the sound-bow, and to weigh 14 tons—nearly three times the weight of the great bell of St Paul's Cathedral; it was to be struck by a hammer of a ton weight, and was then to yield the note E, one octave lower than the E of the chimes, and forming a musical chord with the whole of them. The bell was designed by Mr E. B. Denison, who, as an amateur, has displayed considerable skill in the theory of clock and bell work. After much disputing between commissioners, architects, and others, it was cast in August 1856, at Stockton on Tees, in Yorkshire. The mould was six weeks in preparation. The metal was melted in two furnaces, each containing ten tons. Eighteen out of the twenty tons of molten metal were poured into the mould, producing a bell about 8 feet high and 9½ in diameter at the mouth. When turned and trimmed and finished, it weighed about 15 tons—a little more than had at first been intended. The ponderous mass was then carefully conveyed to London, and placed for a time at the foot of the clock-tower, where it was visited by multitudes of persons. Every Saturday it was struck a certain number of blows, that the quality and loudness of the sound might be tested. On one occasion, the E was found to be a dull and uncertain sound; and this leading to a close scrutiny, it was found that, owing to a flaw in the metal, the bell was practically useless, and would ultimately be broken by the blows of the hammer. It was deemed a fortunate circumstance that the discovery was made before the bell had been raised into the tower. Officially, the bell was to have been named 'St Stephen;' but a random sobriquet used in the *Times*, 'Big Ben,' caught the taste of the public; and in October 1857, it was known all over the country that 'Big Ben was cracked.' There then ensued another series of disputations, accusations, and counter-accusations. Another bell was cast by another bell-founder; it was somewhat less in weight than the former, but was made to yield the same tone. In October 1858, it was raised into its place, a task requiring very perfect appliances; for the weight, raised to a height of nearly 200 feet, was not less than 25 tons, or 56,000 pounds—including bell, cradle, chains, and tackle.

Thus was Big Ben the second cast on the 10th of April, taken out of the mould on the 24th, sent to Westminster on the 31st of May, tried as to tone by Dr Turle on the 18th of June, and finally raised to his destined place in October. During November, Big Ben underwent a long series of blows with hammers weighing from 4 to 7 hundredweight each. The clock was put up in its place, and for some time the inhabitants of the metropolis heard the chime-bells every quarter of an hour, and Big Ben every hour. But another misfortune arose: Ben the second cracked like Ben the first. Then ensued an accusation, a bitter controversy, and a lawsuit; and then fragments of Big Ben were analysed by Professor Tyndall and Dr Percy; while Professor Airey tried to ascertain whether the bell might still be used, though cracked. The subject of Big Ben became almost ludicrous. Not only was the deep E of the bell not to be heard, but the other four were silenced also, and the clock was stopped; insomuch that Earl Derby, in June 1860, said in the House of Lords: 'We all know the circumstances under which we have been deprived of the doubtful advantage of hearing the tones of the great bell; but when a clock ceases to address itself to the sense of hearing, that is no reason it should decline to present itself to the sense of sight. One of the hands has disappeared altogether, and the other stands at twelve; so that it has the merit of being right at least once in the twelve hours.' The earl spoke of the 'doubtful' advantage of hearing the bell. It appears that the tone, when very slowly repeated, had a melancholy and depressing effect on many persons, and was not much liked by those who were attending parliament, or the courts in Westminster Hall. Earl Grey, speaking after the Earl of Derby, 'rejoiced that the great bell had been cracked, and trusted no attempt would be made to make the clock speak to their ears again in the old tones.'

The two Big Bens cost the country nearly £4000, all expenses included. One was broken up and remelted; the other had the flaw or crack for which it was condemned, widened by filing, in order to prevent vibration; in calm weather it can now be heard over the greater part of London.

# OCTOBER 27.

**St Frumentius, apostle of Ethiopia, bishop and confessor, 4th century. St Abban, abbot in Ireland, about 500. St Elesbaan, king of Ethiopia, confessor, 6th century.**

---

*Born.*—Mrs Hester Chapone, moral writer, 1727, *Twywell, Northamptonshire;* Captain James Cook, celebrated voyager, 1728, *Marton, Yorkshire;* Dr Andrew Combe, eminent physiologist, 1797, *Edinburgh.*

*Died.*—Marcus Junius Brutus, assassin of Julius Cæsar, 42 B.C., *Philippi;* Pope Eugenius II., 827; Michael Servetus, burned for heresy at Geneva, 1553; Rev. John Thomson, landscape-painter, 1840, *Duddingston, near Edinburgh;* Madame Ida Pfeiffer, celebrated traveller, 1858, *Vienna.*

## MICHAEL SERVETUS.

The fate of this unfortunate man has evoked an amount of discussion and interest which were doubtless little anticipated by the civil and spiritual rulers of Geneva, when they consigned him to the flames as a heretic and blasphemer. The reputation of Calvin and his followers is deeply concerned in this transaction, which no one, even of his warmest admirers, will at the present day attempt to defend, however much they may try to palliate and excuse. As regards the Reformers, and the right claimed by them of making the Scriptures the sole rule of faith, and interpreting them according to the dictates of private judgment, the burning of Servetus must be pronounced one of the most impolitic acts which they could have perpetrated, seeing that by this proceeding they committed themselves to the same cruel and intolerant system which they denounced so strongly in the Church of Rome.

Servetus was a native of Villanueva, in the kingdom of Aragon, in Spain, and having been destined by his father for the legal profession, was sent to study at Toulouse. Here he devoted himself to theological rather than juristic studies, and the result was a book entitled *De Trinitatis Erroribus*, which he published when only twenty-two. The heterodox views propounded in this work gave deep offence both to Protestants and Catholics, and so threatening to his safety was the hostile feeling excited, that the author deemed it prudent to change his name to Michel de Villeneuve, after his native town. He commenced, too, about this time the study of medicine, in which he made great proficiency, and appears, from a passage in his writings, to have first propounded the theory of the circulation of the blood, which, in the following century, was experimentally demonstrated by Harvey. Such eminence did he attain in his profession, that he came to be regarded as one of the ablest physicians in France, and both practised and lectured with great success at Paris, Lyon, and other places. Having subsequently obtained the post of municipal physician to the town of Vienne, in Dauphiné, he settled down there, and might have lived in tranquillity to the end of his days, were it not for an ardent missionary spirit which led him to fancy himself destined by Heaven for carrying out a sweeping reformation in religious doctrine and belief. With this view he composed, and had stealthily printed, his work entitled

*Restitutio Christianismi*, in which the same views which he had already promulgated regarding the Trinity were advanced afresh. Large consignments of copies were forwarded to Lyon, Frankfort, and Geneva, and in consequence of a representation made by a citizen of Lyon, Guillaume Trie, residing at Geneva, Servetus was arrested at the instance of the ecclesiastical authorities of Vienne, and subjected to a close examination. That Calvin, who had been engaged in a correspondence with Servetus during the composition of the book in question, and been made the subject by the latter of a rather acrimonious attack, was the original mover in this transaction, is a doubtful point; but it would seem that he handed over to Trie various documents which he had received from Servetus, and which were now produced in evidence before the inquisitors. They were, however, balked of their victim, who managed to escape by night from his confinement. For upwards of three months he remained concealed in France, and then took his way for Italy, with the intention of establishing himself at Naples as a physician. Through some unaccountable infatuation, the path which he chose was through Switzerland and Geneva, and in the latter town he arrived about the middle of July 1553. He dwelt in an inn there for about a month, and was on the eve of continuing his journey, when he was arrested in name of the Genevan Council, and committed to prison. A long list of charges, on the ground of heresy, drawn up by Calvin, who then exercised a paramount influence in Geneva, and had taken the initiative steps in procuring the arrest of Servetus by the state authorities, was produced in court against the unfortunate stranger. After a long and protracted trial, in which the magistrates and churches of Zurich, Berne, Basel, and Schaffhausen were consulted, and an unsuccessful demand also made by the authorities of Vienne for the delivery of the prisoner to them, sentence of capital punishment by burning was pronounced on 26th October, and executed the following day. The scene of this memorable event was the eminence of Champel, situated a little distance to the south of Geneva, and commanding a most enchanting view of the lake and surrounding mountains. To the end Servetus maintained, with unflinching constancy, his Unitarian opinions, rejecting firmly the pertinacious exhortations of the reformed pastor, Farel, who attended him to the stake. His last words were: 'Jesus, thou Son of the eternal God, have mercy upon me!'

In passing judgment on the chief actors in this tragedy, we must bear in mind that the principles of religious toleration, as now recognised, were in the sixteenth century not only almost unknown, but reprobated as dangerous and atheistic. Next to professing and disseminating religious error, was the guilt of those who permitted it to exist, and having the power of punishing heretics, refrained from its exercise. Toleration and indifference were, with our earnest-minded and devout ancestors, convertible terms. And it was argued that if treason and disrespect to earthly powers incurred the severest penalties, much more ought these to be inflicted on the guilty parties who, by their maintenance of false doctrine, had both imperilled souls, and done despite to the majesty of Heaven. Such sentiments were not peculiar to the Roman Catholics, but were equally shared by the adherents of the Reformed doctrines, who denounced the cruel persecutions of the papists, not on the ground of religious liberty, but on that of impiety in destroying the holders of the true faith. All sects, and even that to which Servetus belonged, agreed in the duty of exterminating heretics and unbelievers by the sword. Viewed in this light, we can therefore by no means regard Calvin as the unwarranted murderer of Servetus, seeing that he had the approval of the most eminent divines and writers of his day for the deed which was perpetrated under his sanction. But, abstractedly considered, it was a most foul and unjust action, and has left an indelible stain on the memory of the great reformer. An offence was committed, in the first instance, against the law of nations, by assuming jurisdiction over an absolute stranger, a citizen of another country, and who was merely passing through the city of Geneva. No moral or political offences were imputed to the prisoner, who seems, through his whole life, to have been of the most unblemished behaviour, and however offensively he might express himself, had never committed a greater transgression than claiming the right of interpreting the Scriptures according to the dictates of his own judgment. That he was sincere in his belief, is evident from the constancy with which he maintained his principles to the last. And the injustice of refusing to allow him the aid of an advocate—though such an interdiction was in accordance with the laws of the state—and the strong personal animus by which Calvin seemed to be inspired in his procedure towards Servetus, must ever excite the utmost indignation and regret.

The personal character of this victim of intolerance has been variously represented by the partisans and enemies of Calvin—the former depicting him as a man of weak intellect, arrogant and overbearing, but withal cowardly and subservient, and displaying in his conduct a total absence of truth and candour; whilst by the latter he is held up to admiration, as possessing every quality which contributes to form a hero and martyr. Neither of these portraits is correct. It must be admitted that in his defence before the inquisitors at Vienne, he made many statements which, whatever palliation might be made for him on the plea of self-defence, were indubitably false; and that when defending himself before the council of Geneva, he was most intemperate in his abuse of Calvin. But, on the other hand, there can be no doubt of his sincerity in the pursuit of truth, however much opinions may differ as to his having attained that object. His moral purity was unimpeachable, and in point of learning, industry, and scientific skill, he must be admitted to have fallen little, if at all, behind the most distinguished men of his century.

## IDA PFEIFFER.

Among the many travellers who at different times have journeyed over and explored the various countries of our globe, the name of Madame Ida Pfeiffer deserves to be recorded as one of the most extraordinary and peculiar of the class. The mere fact of a woman accomplishing such an amount of travel, would in itself be an unprecedented circumstance; but when we reflect, in addition, that by herself, unattended, and but scantily provided with funds, she forced her way through savage and inhospitable lands, where in some cases the foot of the European had never before trod, and where she experienced every imaginable species of danger and privation, our wonder and interest are heightened tenfold, and we experience a lively curiosity to know something of the personal history of so undaunted and adventurous a wanderer. This feeling is in nowise diminished by the perusal of the various narratives of her journeys, written in the most simple, unpretending style possible, without making the least pretence to scientific or politico-economical knowledge, but displaying, nevertheless, a fund of shrewd observation and sound common sense, combined with great dramatic and descriptive interest.

The maiden-name of this celebrated traveller was Reyer, and she was the third child of a wealthy merchant in Vienna, where she was born in October 1797. Being the only girl in a family of six, she freely shared in childhood in the sports of her brothers, and was encouraged in such tendencies by her parents, who allowed her to dress in boy's clothes, and take part in all sorts of rough games and pranks. This state of matters continued till her father's death, when Ida was about nine years old. A few months after this event, her mother, thinking she had worn the male attire long enough, obliged her to change her trousers for petticoats, an order which occasioned her such grief and indignation, that she actually made herself ill, and by the doctor's advice she was allowed to resume her former costume, and continued to wear it till the age of thirteen. For a time she maintained the character of an incorrigible hoyden. Considering the pianoforte as too much of a feminine instrument, she resisted long being taught its use, and would actually often cut her fingers, or burn them with sealing-wax, to unfit them for practising. Had she been allowed, she would have gladly made herself a proficient on the violin. While she was still a very young girl, a young man was received into Madame Reyer's house as tutor to the family, and it was not long before a warm attachment sprang up between him and Ida. Influenced by this new feeling, she abandoned her old masculine tendencies, and devoted herself assiduously to the acquisition of female accomplishments, useful and ornamental. The object of her attachment was in every way worthy of her, of unblemished character and manners, and greatly beloved by the whole family, her mother included. Having obtained subsequently a good situation in the Austrian civil service, he made a formal offer of his hand; but through some unaccountable caprice, her mother positively refused her consent, and even regarded the young man from that time forward with feelings of the deepest aversion. Ida inherited a considerable fortune from her father, and it was probably with the idea of her contracting a splendid alliance that she was thwarted in her present wishes. But though many other eligible suitors proffered themselves, she would listen to none of them, and the result was a sad series of domestic contentions. Worn out at last by importunity, she consented to receive the proposals of Dr Pfeiffer, an advocate of considerable celebrity in Lemberg, but twenty-four years older than herself, and a widower with a grown-up son. He was a man of the highest honour and integrity, almost too much so, as would seem from his subsequent history; and though there was never any profound feeling of sympathy between him and his wife, he treated her throughout with the most uniform kindness and attention. But his resolute denunciation of abuses stirred him up many enemies, and he was obliged to resign his appointment of counsellor at Lemberg, and remove to Vienna, where from being looked on by the authorities with suspicion, as an enemy of existing institutions, the same star of ill-fortune pursued him, and he was soon reduced to great straits. His generosity also was excessive, rendering him the dupe of numerous individuals, who borrowed large sums of money from him, including his wife's fortune, which was lent to a friend in pecuniary embarrassment, and entirely lost. The distress to which his family was subjected in consequence of these acts of improvidence is thus stated by Madame Pfeiffer.

'Heaven only knows what I suffered during eighteen years of my married life—not, indeed, from any ill treatment on my husband's part, but from poverty and want! I came of a wealthy family, and had been accustomed, from my earliest youth, to order and comfort; and now I frequently knew not where I should lay my head, or find a little money to buy the commonest necessaries. I performed household drudgery, and endured cold and hunger; I worked secretly for money, and gave lessons in drawing and music; and yet, in spite of all my exertions, there were many days when I could hardly put anything but dry bread before my poor children for their dinner. I might certainly have applied to my mother or my brothers for relief, but my pride revolted against such a course. For years I fought with poverty, and concealed my real position: often was I brought so near to despair, that the thought of my children alone prevented me from giving way. At last the urgency of my necessities quite broke my spirit and I had recourse several times to my brothers for assistance.'

Perseverance and self-denial enabled Madame Pfeiffer to struggle through her difficulties, give her two sons a good education, and see them prosperously established in the world. She was now at liberty to indulge that darling wish of her heart, the desire of seeing strange countries, which had haunted her from girlhood, but which circumstances had hitherto prevented her from gratifying. The feeling may indeed be regarded as eccentric, which could prompt the mother of a family, at the age of forty-five, and almost wholly inexperienced in travelling, to set forth on such an expedition. But she quitted no duties at home to embark on it, and as she had so bravely fulfilled these in the day of privation and trial, she may well be excused for following her own inclinations afterwards, when the doing so involved no dereliction of maternal or conjugal obligations. The funds which she possessed were by no means ample, but adversity had taught her economy, and her own nature was one that shrank not from hardship and privation. Her first journey was a visit to the Holy Land, which she accomplished in 1842, proceeding down the Danube to the Black Sea and Constantinople, thence to Syria and Palestine, and returning by way of Egypt, Sicily, and Italy. An account of her tour was published the following year under the title of a *Journey of a Viennese Lady to the Holy Land*, and, meeting with considerable success, provided her with funds for a second journey, which she accomplished in 1845, to Iceland and Scandinavia. Her journal of this expedition was also published, and by the proceeds which she derived from this, as well as from the sale of the geological and botanical specimens which she had collected, she was enabled to effect a third and more ambitious undertaking—that of a voyage round the world. In June 1846, she sailed from Hamburg for Rio Janeiro, from thence rounded Cape Horn to Valparaiso, crossed the Pacific to Otaheite, and afterwards visited China, Ceylon, and India, traversing the latter country from Calcutta to Bombay. She then sailed for Bushire, in Persia, the interior of which country she intended to have visited, but was prevented by the disturbances which had broken out there, and directed her steps instead to Asiatic Turkey, where she visited Bagdad, the ruins of Babylon and Nineveh, and afterwards passed through Armenia and the Caucasus to the Black Sea. In this portion of her journey she underwent the greatest hardships in the shape of heat, discomfort, and scanty fare, besides being exposed to constant danger from the attacks of robbers. After voyaging across the Black Sea to Constantinople, and touching in her way at Sebastopol and Odessa, she returned by Greece and the Ionian Islands to Trieste, and arrived in Vienna in November 1848, in the midst of the confusion after the recapture of the city by Prince Windischgrätz from the revolutionary party.

The interest already excited in Madame Pfeiffer was greatly intensified by the publication of the narrative of her third journey, which, under the title of *A Lady's Voyage Round the World*, was translated both into English and French with much success. Her craving for travel was far from being extinguished, and rather stimulated by what she had gone through. A grant of £150 was made her by the Austrian government, and with her resources thus supplemented, she set out upon a second voyage round the world, proceeding first to London, and thence taking ship for the Cape of Good Hope. Arriving here, she hesitated awhile between an exploring expedition into the interior of the African continent and a voyage to Australia, and at last sailed to Singapore and Sarawak. She was hospitably received by Sir James Brooke, and traversed a great portion of Borneo, including the country of the savage Dyaks. She then visited Java and Sumatra, including in the latter island the cannibal tribes of the Battas, where she made a narrow escape from being killed and eaten, and afterwards voyaged to the Moluccas and Celebes. From this she crossed the Pacific to California, and subsequently sailed to Panama and Lima. Her intention was to cross the Cordilleras to the Amazon, and make her way down that river to the east coast; but after several attempts, in which she visited Quito and witnessed an eruption of the volcano of Cotopaxi, she found herself so thwarted by the treachery of the natives and other causes, besides narrowly escaping death on two occasions by drowning and a fall from her mule, that she abandoned all idea of proceeding further in this direction, and crossing the Isthmus of Panama to Aspinwall, sailed to New Orleans. She then made the tour of the United States and Canada, and having embarked for England, landed at Liverpool in the end of 1854. Before returning home, she made a voyage to the island of St Michael, in the Azores, where one of her sons was settled, and reached Vienna by way of Lisbon, Southampton, and London. An account of her adventures appeared shortly afterwards, under the title of *My Second Journey Round the World*.

After having scarcely rested for a year at home, Madame Pfeiffer set out again on her travels, her main object of curiosity being the island of Madagascar, so thoroughly still an almost *terra incognita* to Europeans. Proceeding through Germany to Berlin and Hamburg, she sailed for Holland, and there, after previously making excursions to London and Paris in quest of information regarding her route, embarked for Cape Town, and from thence made her way to Madagascar by the Mauritius. After landing in the island, and visiting Tananarivo, the capital, she was glad to retreat from it with life, having undergone an attack of the malignant Madagascar fever and a captivity of a fortnight, during which she and her European companions were almost hourly expecting death by the orders of the blood-thirsty queen Ranavola. And from the hardships and malady which had befallen her, Madame Pfeiffer was destined never to recover. Having returned to the Mauritius, she was attacked with such a violent access of fever, that her life was despaired of; she rallied, nevertheless, so far as to be able to embark for London, and arrived there in the month of June 1858. From this she crossed over to Hamburg, and then paid a visit to Berlin and Cracow, in the hope of re-establishing her health. For some time she steadily resisted all the solicitations of her friends to return to her native Vienna; but finding her illness rapidly gaining upon her, she at last consented, and was removed there to the house of her brother, Charles Reyer. Here, after undergoing great suffering for about a month, she expired in October 1858. Her diary of the last and fatal journey to Madagascar was given to the world after her death by her son Oscar.

---

# OCTOBER 28.

**St Simon the Canaanite, apostle. St Jude, apostle. St Faro, bishop of Meaux, confessor, 672. St Neot, anchoret and confessor, 9th century.**

---

*Born.*—Desiderius Erasmus, distinguished scholar and writer, 1467, *Rotterdam;* Dr Nicholas Brady, versifier of the Psalms, 1659, *Bandon, Cork;* Sir David Dalrymple, Lord Hailes, historical writer, 1726, *Edinburgh;* Emanuel, Marshal Grouchy, Bonapartist commander, 1766, *Paris.*

*Died.*—Maxentius, Roman emperor, drowned in Tiber, 312; Alfred the Great, king of England, about 900, *Winchester;* Michael le Tellier, chancellor of France, 1685, *Paris;* John Wallis, eminent mathematician, 1703, *Oxford;* John Locke, philosopher, 1704, *Oates, Essex;* Prince George of Denmark, husband of Queen Anne of England, 1708; John Smeaton, engineer, 1792, *Austhorpe, near Leeds;* Charlotte Smith, novelist, 1806, *Tilford, Surrey.*

## ERASMUS.

Though professedly an adherent of the ancient faith, Erasmus must be regarded as one of the most influential pioneers of the Reformation. His *Colloquies* and *Encomium Moriæ*, or Praise of Folly, in which the superstitions of the day, and the malpractices of priests and friars, are exposed in the wittiest and most ludicrous manner, found thousands of admirers who were unable to appreciate the subtleties of dogmatic theology. It was pithily said of him, that he laid the egg which Luther hatched.

Erasmus was the natural son of a Dutchman, called Gheraerd or Garrit, a name having the same signification as the *Amiable* or the *Beloved;* and from this circumstance he assumed the designation of *Desiderius Erasmus*, which, by reduplication, expresses the same meaning in the Latin and Greek languages. He was educated for the Roman Catholic Church, and entered for a time the monastery of Emaus, near Gouda, but found such a profession very uncongenial, and as he had already given great promise of mental vigour and acumen, he obtained a dispensation from his monastic vows, and travelled through different parts of Europe. While thus journeying from place to place, he supported himself by lecturing and taking charge of pupils, one of whom was Alexander Stuart, a natural son of James IV. of Scotland, who was afterwards slain with his father at Flodden. Among other countries visited by Erasmus was England, where he resided in the house of Sir Thomas More, and also acted for a time as professor of divinity at Cambridge. He afterwards passed over to the Low Countries on an invitation from the Archduke Charles, afterwards Charles V., by whom he was invested with the office of councillor, and a salary of two hundred florins. In 1516, he published his celebrated edition of the Greek Testament, with notes, being the first version which appeared in print. By many this is regarded as the greatest work of Erasmus, who was both an excellent Greek scholar and one of the principal revivers of the study of that ancient language in Western Europe. In 1521, he took up his residence at Basel, where, in the following year, his celebrated *Colloquies* were published. From this he removed in 1529 to Freiburg, but returned again in 1535. He died at Basel on 12th July 1536.

Though a kind-hearted generous-minded man, Erasmus had little of the hero or martyr in his composition, and however clearly his excellent judgment might enable him to form certain conclusions, he wanted still the courage and self-denial to carry them into practice. His indecision in this respect furnished Luther with materials for the most cutting and contemptuous sarcasm. Indeed, in one of his own letters, Erasmus states very candidly his timorous character as follows: 'Even if Luther had spoken everything in the most unobjectionable manner, I had no inclination to die for the sake of truth. Every man has not the courage to make a martyr; and I am afraid, if I were put to the trial, I should imitate St Peter.' He may be regarded in the light of an accomplished, ease-loving scholar, latitudinarian on the subject of religion, and neither disposed to sympathise with the despotism and burdensome ordinances of the old faith, or the austerities and fiery zeal of the new. It is stated, however, that the friends in whose arms he expired were Protestants, and that, in his dying moments, he commended himself to God and Christ alone, rejecting all the ceremonies of the Romish Church.

## THE ALFRED JEWEL.

It may well be said, that of the many monarchs who have been endowed with the appellation *Great*, Alfred of England was one of the very few who really merited the distinguished title. The materials for his history are indeed scanty, yet they teem with romance of the highest and most instructive character—namely, that which represents a good man heroically contending with the greatest difficulties, until, by energy and perseverance, he ultimately overcomes them. His desperate conflicts with the invading Danes, and the various fortunes of the respective parties; Alfred's magnanimity and prudence, whether as conqueror or fugitive; his attachment to literature and the arts; his unwearied zeal to promote the moral, social, and political progress of his subjects—all make even the minutest details of his history of surpassing interest to all educated Britons.

The remarkable jewel, represented in the engraving, was found, in 1693, at Newton Park, a short

THE ALFRED JEWEL.

distance north of the site of Ethelney Abbey, in Somersetshire, near the junction of the rivers Parret and Thone. It is now preserved in the Ashmolean Museum, at Oxford; and, independent of its bearing the name of Alfred, is a most interesting specimen of Anglo-Saxon art. The inevitable melting-pot has left few similar specimens of that age, but we know there must have been many, for the business of a goldsmith was held in high repute by the Anglo-Saxons, and a poem in that language, on the various conditions of men, contains lines that may be translated thus :

'For one a wondrous skill
in goldsmith's art
is provided,
full oft he decorates
and well adorns
a powerful king's noble,
and he to him gives broad
land in recompence.'

Asser, the friend and biographer of Alfred, informs us that, when the great monarch had secured peace and protection to his subjects, he resolved to extend among them a knowledge of the arts. For this purpose he collected, from many nations, an almost innumerable multitude of artificers, the most expert in their respective trades. Among these were not a few workers in gold and silver, who, acting under the immediate instructions of Alfred, executed, with incomparable skill, many articles of these metals. From the circumstance of the jewel having inscribed on it, in Saxon characters, *Ælfred me haet gewercan* (Alfred had me wrought), we may reasonably conclude that it was made under his own superintendence ; and further, from its richness of workmanship and material, that it was a personal ornament worn by the good king himself. The lower end of the jewel, as represented in the engraving, is formed into the head of a griffin, a national emblem of the Saxons. From the mouth of this figure issues a small tube, crossed in the interior by a minute pin of gold. The latter is evidently intended to connect the ornament with the collar or band by which it was suspended round the neck ; the general flatness of form indicating that it was worn in that manner. Antiquaries have not agreed as to the person represented on one side of the jewel. Some have supposed it to be the Saviour, others St Cuthbert, or Pope Martin. But the opinion, that it represented Alfred himself, symbolising his kingly office, is as general and tenable as any yet advanced upon the subject.

## CHARLOTTE SMITH: FLORA'S HOROLOGE.

In the days of our grandfathers, this lady enjoyed a considerable reputation, both as a novelist and poet, though her lucubrations in both capacities are now almost forgotten. Two works of fiction composed by her, *Emmeline, or the Orphan of the Castle*, and the *Old Manor-House*, are mentioned by Sir Walter Scott in terms of high commendation. An ill-assorted marriage proved the source of an infinite series of troubles, and various domestic bereavements, combined latterly with bodily infirmities, saddened an existence which, during the greater part of its course, was more characterised by clouds than sunshine.

The annexed poem exhibits a pleasing specimen of Mrs Smith's talents, and is here introduced as apposite to the character of the *Book of Days*, presenting, as it does, the idea of a clock or dial of Flora. The phenomenon of the *sleep* of plants, or the closing and reopening of the petals of flowers at certain hours, was, as is well known, the discovery of the great botanist Linnæus.

### FLORA'S HOROLOGE.

'In every copse and sheltered dell,
Unveiled to the observant eye,
Are faithful monitors, who tell
How pass the hours and seasons by.

The green-robed children of the spring
Will mark the periods as they pass,
Mingle with leaves Time's feathered wing,
And bind with flowers his silent glass.

Mark where transparent waters glide,
Soft flowing o'er their tranquil bed;
There, cradled on the dimpling tide,
Nymphæa rests her lovely head.

But conscious of the earliest beam,
She rises from her humid nest,
And sees reflected in the stream
The virgin whiteness of her breast.

Till the bright Daystar to the west
Declines, in ocean's surge to lave;
Then, folded in her modest vest,
She slumbers on the rocking wave.

See Hieraciums' various tribe,
Of plumy seed and radiate flowers,
The course of Time their blooms describe,
And wake or sleep appointed hours.

Broad o'er its imbricated cup
The Goatsbeard spreads its golden rays,
But shuts its cautious petals up,
Retreating from the noontide blaze.

Pale as a pensive cloistered nun,
The Bethlehem Star her face unveils,
When o'er the mountain peers the sun,
But shades it from the vesper gales.

Among the loose and arid sands
The humble Arenaria creeps;
Slowly the Purple Star expands,
But soon within its calyx sleeps.

And those small bells so lightly rayed
With young Aurora's rosy hue,
Are to the noontide sun displayed,
But shut their plaits against the dew.

On upland slopes the shepherds mark
The hour, when, as the dial true,
Cichorium to the towering lark
Lifts her soft eyes serenely blue.

And thou, "wee crimson tipped flower,"
Gatherest thy fringed mantle round
Thy bosom, at the closing hour,
When night-drops bathe the turfy ground.

Unlike Silene, who declines
The garish noontide's blazing light;
But when the evening crescent shines,
Gives all her sweetness to the night.

Thus in each flower and simple bell,
That in our path betrodden lie,
Are sweet remembrancers who tell
How fast the winged moments fly.'

## SCHINDERHANNES ('JOHN, THE SCORCHER').

At the close of the last century, and the beginning of the present, the borderland between France and Germany was infested by bands of desperadoes, who were a terror to all the peaceful inhabitants. War, raging with great fury year after year, had brought the Rhenish provinces into a very disorganised state, which offered a premium to every species of lawless violence. Bands of brigands roamed about, committing every kind of atrocity. They were often called *Chauffeurs* or *Scorchers;* because they were accustomed to hold the soles of their victims' feet in front of a fierce fire, to extort a revelation of the place where their property was concealed. Sometimes they were called *Garotters* or *Stranglers* (from *garrot*, a stick which enabled the strangler to twist a cord tightly round the neck of his victim). Each band had a camp or rendezvous, with lines of communication throughout a particular district. The posts on these lines were generally poor country-taverns, the landlords of which were in league with the band. And not only was this the case, but from Holland to the Danube, the chauffeurs could always obtain friendly shelter at these houses, with means for exchanging intelligence with others of the fraternity. The brigands concocted for their own use a jargon composed of French, German, Flemish, and Hebrew, scarcely intelligible to other persons. Not unfrequently, magistrates and functionaries of police were implicated with this confederacy. Names, dress, character, complexion, and feature were changed with wonderful ingenuity by the more accomplished leaders; and women were employed in various ways requiring tact and finesse. The more numerous members of the band, rude and brutal, did the violent work which these leaders planned for them. Many, called *apprentices*, inhabited their own houses, worked at their own trades, but yet held themselves in readiness, at a given signal understood only by themselves, to leave their homes, and execute the behests of the leaders. They were bound by oaths, which were rarely disregarded, an assassin's poniard being always ready to avenge any violation. Most of these apprentices were sent to districts far removed from their homes when lawless work was to be done. A Jewish spy was generally concerned in every operation of magnitude: his vocation was to pick up information that would be useful to the robber-chief, concerning the amount and locality of obtainable booty. For his information, he received a stipulated fee, and then made a profit out of his purchase from the robbers of the stolen property.

Schinderhannes, or 'John the Scorcher,' was the most famous of all the leaders of these robbers. His real name was Johann Buckler; but his practice of *chauffage*, or scorching the feet of his victims, earned for him the appellation of Schinderhannes. Born in 1779, near the Rhine, he from early years loved the society of those who habitually braved all law and control. As a boy, he joined others in stealing meat and bread from the commissariat-wagons of the French army at Kreuznach. He joined a party of bandits, and was continually engaged in robberies: he was often captured, but as frequently escaped with wonderful ingenuity, and his audacity soon led to his being chosen captain of a band. There was something in his manner which almost paralysed those whom he attacked, and rendered them powerless against him. On one occasion, when alone, he met a large party of Jews travelling together. He ordered them imperiously to stop, and to bring him their purses one by one, which they did. He then searched all their pockets; and, finding his carbine in the way, told one of the Jews to hold it for him while he rifled their pockets! This also was done, and the carbine handed to him again. Sometimes he would summon a farmer or other person to his presence, and tell him to bring a certain sum of money, as a ransom, or purchase-price of safety in advance; and such was the terror at the name of Schinderhannes, that these messages were rarely disregarded. As the French power became consolidated on the left bank of the Rhine, Schinderhannes found it expedient to limit his operations to the right bank; and the prisons of Coblentz and Cologne were filled with his adherents. Like Robin Hood, he often befriended the poor at the expense of the rich; but, unlike the hero of Sherwood Forest, he was often cruel. The career of Schinderhannes virtually terminated on the 31st of May 1802, when he was finally captured near Limburg; but his actual trial did not take place till the closing days of October 1803, when evidence sufficient was brought forward to convict him of murder, and he was condemned to death.

Mr Leitch Ritchie has made this redoubtable bandit the hero of a romance—*Schinderhannes, the Robber of the Rhine.* In his *Travelling Sketches on the Rhine, and in Belgium and Holland,* he has also given some interesting details concerning Schinderhannes himself, and the *chauffeurs* generally. Among many so-called wives, one named Julia was especially beloved by him, and she and a brother-robber named Fetzer, were with him when captured. 'At his trial,' says Mr Ritchie in the second of the above-named works, 'he was seen frequently to play with his young infant, and to whisper to his wife, and press her hands. The evidence against him was overpowering, and the interest of his audience rose to a painful pitch. When the moment of judgment drew near, his fears for Julia shook him like an ague. He frequently cried out, clasping his hands: "She is innocent! The poor young girl is innocent! It was I who seduced her!" Every eye was wet, and nothing was heard in the profound silence of the moment, but the sobs of women. Julia, by the humanity of the court, was sentenced first; and Schinderhannes embraced her with tears of joy when he heard that her punishment was limited to two years' confinement. His father received twenty-two years' of fetters; and he himself, with nineteen of his band, was doomed to the guillotine. The execution took place on the 21st of November 1803, when twenty heads were cut off in twenty-six minutes. The bandit-chief preserved his intrepidity to the last.'

Concerning the chauffeurs or bandits generally, it may suffice to say that when Bonaparte became First Consul, he determined to extirpate them. One by one the miscreants fell into the hands of justice. For many years the alarmists in France had been in the habit of insinuating that the bandits were prompted by the exiled royalists, or by the English; but it was perfectly clear that they needed no external stimulus of this kind. After the death of Schinderhannes, the bands quickly disappeared.

## 'RIDING THE STANG;' OR 'ROUGH MUSIC.'

Punishments for minor offences were formerly designed to produce shame in the delinquents by exposing them to public ridicule or indignation. With this view, the execution of the punishment was left very much in the hands of the populace. Such was the practice in the case of the branks, the cucking-stool, the whirligig, the drunkard's cloak, the stocks, the pillory, &c., all of which have been either legally abolished or banished by the progress of civilisation. There is, however, one species of punishment belonging to the above category, which the people seem determined to retain in their own hands, and enforce whenever they judge it expedient so to do. It was exercised, to the knowledge of the writer, on the 28th of October, and ten following days, Sunday excepted, in the year 1862. The punishment in question, called in the north of England 'Riding the Stang,' and in the south 'Rough Music,' is not noticed in the *Popular Antiquities* by Bourne and Brand, but is of frequent occurrence in most of our English counties. If a husband be known to beat his wife, or allow himself to be hen-pecked—if he be unfaithful to her, or she to him—the offending party, if living in a country village, will probably soon be serenaded with a concert of rough music. This harmonious concert is produced by the men, women, and children of the village assembling together, each provided with a suitable instrument. These consist of cows' horns, frying-pans, warming-pans, and tea-kettles, drummed on with a large key; iron pot-lids, used as cymbals; fire-shovels and tongs rattled together; tin and wooden pails drummed on with iron pokers or marrow-bones—in fact, any implement with which a loud, harsh, and discordant sound can be produced. Thus provided, the rustics proceed to the culprit's house, and salute him or her with a sudden burst of their melodious music, accompanied with shouts, yells, hisses, and cries of 'Shame! shame! Who beat his wife? I say, Tom Brown, come out and shew yourself!' and all such kind of taunts and ridicule as rustic wit or indignation can invent. The village humorist, often with his face blacked, or coloured with chalk and reddle, and his body grotesquely clothed and decorated, acts the part of herald, and, in all the strong savour of rustic wit and drollery, proclaims the delinquencies of the unhappy victim or victims. The proclamation, of course, is followed by loud bursts of laughter, shouts, yells, and another tremendous serenade of 'rough music,' to the melody of which the whole party march off, and proceed through the village, proclaiming in all the most public parts the 'burden of their song.' This hubbub is generally repeated every evening, for a week or a fortnight, and seldom fails to make a due impression on the principal auditor; for

'Music hath charms to soothe the savage breast;'

and the writer can testify that, at least in one instance, where police and magistrates had tried in vain to reform a brutal husband who had beaten and ill-treated his wife, his savage breast was tamed by the magic strains of 'rough music.' He was never known to beat his wife again, and acknowledged that the sound of that music never ceased to 'charm' his waking thoughts, and too often formed 'the melody of his dreams.'

A SERENADE OF 'ROUGH MUSIC.'

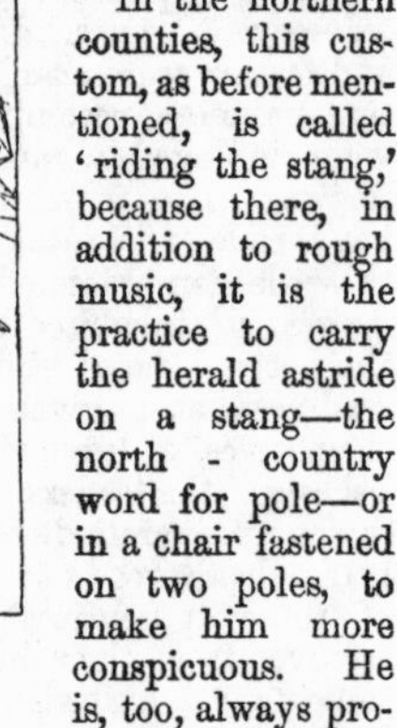

In the northern counties, this custom, as before mentioned, is called 'riding the stang,' because there, in addition to rough music, it is the practice to carry the herald astride on a stang—the north-country word for pole—or in a chair fastened on two poles, to make him more conspicuous. He is, too, always provided with a large frying-pan and key or hammer, and, after beating them together very vigorously, makes his proclamation in rhyme, using the following words, varied only to suit the nature of the offence:

'Ran, tan, tan; ran, tan, tan,  
To the sound of this pan;  
This is to give notice that Tom Trotter  
Has beaten his good wo-man!  
For what, and for why?  
'Cause she ate when she was hungry,  
And drank when she was dry.  
Ran, tan, ran, tan, tan;  
Hurrah—hurrah! for this good wo-man!  
He beat her, he beat her, he beat her indeed,  
For spending a penny when she had need.  
He beat her black, he beat her blue;  
When Old Nick gets him, he'll give him his due;  
Ran, tan, tan; ran, tan, tan;  
We'll send him there in this old frying-pan;  
Hurrah—hurrah! for his good wo-man.'

The 'ran-tan' chorus is shouted by the whole crowd, and repeated after every line. The practice is varied in different places by the addition of an effigy of the culprit riding on an ass, with his face towards the tail, and by other freaks of local humour, suggested perhaps by some peculiarity of the occasion.

This mode of manifesting the popular feeling was in vogue when *Hudibras* was written; and though then often including additions better omitted, was observed in other respects much as at the present day:

'And now the cause of all their fear
By slow degrees approached so near,
They might distinguish different noise
Of horns and pans, and dogs and boys,
And kettle-drums, whose sullen dub
Sounds like the hooping of a tub;
* * * *
And followed with a world of tall-lads,
That merry ditties troll'd, and ballads.
* * * *
Next pans and kettles of all keys,
From trebles down to double base;
* * * *
And at fit periods the whole rout
Set up their throats with clamorous shout.'

Such ceremonies as we have above described are known on the continent by the name of the *Charivari*, and also of *Katzenmusik* (Anglicè, *caterwauling*). Latterly, in France, the *charivari* took a political turn, and gave name to a satirical publication established in Paris in 1832. The same title, as all our readers know, was adopted as an accessory designation by the facetious journalist, Mr Punch.

---

## OCTOBER 29.

St Narcissus, bishop of Jerusalem, 2d century. St Chef or Theuderius, abbot, about 575.

---

*Born.*—George Abbot, archbishop of Canterbury, 1562, *Guildford;* Edmund Halley, astronomer, 1656, *Haggerston, near London;* James Boswell, biographer of Johnson, 1740, *Edinburgh;* William Hayley, poet and biographer of Cowper, 1745, *Chichester;* John Keats, poet, 1796, *Moorfields, London.*

*Died.*—Sir Walter Raleigh, beheaded in Old Palace Yard, 1618; Henry Welby, eccentric character, 1636, *London;* James Shirley, dramatist, 1666, *London;* Edmund Calamy, eminent Puritan divine, 1666, *London;* Admiral Edward Vernon, naval commander, 1757; Jean le Rond d'Alembert, mathematician and encyclopædist, 1783, *Paris;* George Morland, animal-painter, 1806, *London;* Allan Cunningham, poet and miscellaneous writer, 1842, *London.*

### JOHN KEATS.

It is a satisfaction to know that the well-worn story about John Keats being killed by the *Quarterly Review*—a story endorsed by Shelley, and by Byron in *Don Juan:*

'Poor fellow! His was an untoward fate;
'Tis strange the mind, that very fiery particle,
Should let itself be snuffed out by an article'—

is untrue. Croker's criticism did gall the vanity of which Keats, in common with all poets, possessed an ample share; but he was far too self-assured and pugnacious to suffer dangerously from what anybody might say of him.

Keats was the son of a livery-stable keeper, who had risen to comfort by marrying his master's daughter, and was born in Moorfields, London, in 1795. His father, who is described as an active, energetic little man, of much natural talent, was killed by a fall from a horse when John was in his ninth year. His mother, a tall woman with a large oval face and a grave demeanour, after lingering for several years in consumption, died in 1810. A fortune of two thousand pounds was inherited by John.

Keats, as a boy in Finsbury, was noted for his pugnacity. It was the time of the great French war, and children caught the martial spirit abroad. In the house, in the stables, in the streets with his brothers, or with any likely combatant, he was ready for a tussle. He was sent to a boarding-school at Enfield, kept by the father of Mr Charles Cowden Clarke, by whom he is remembered for his terrier-like character, as well as for his good-humour and love of frolic. From school he was taken, at the age of fifteen, and apprenticed for five years to a surgeon and apothecary at Edmonton; an easy distance from Enfield, so that he used to walk over whenever he liked to see the Clarkes and borrow books. He was an insatiable and indiscriminate reader, and shewed no peculiar bias in his tastes, until, in 1812, he obtained in loan Spenser's *Fairy Queen.* That poem lit the fire of his genius. He could now speak of nothing but Spenser. A world of delight seemed revealed to him. 'He ramped through the scenes of the romance,' writes Mr Clarke, 'like a young horse turned into a spring-meadow;' he got whole passages by heart, which he would repeat to any listener; and would dwell with ecstasy on fine phrases, such as that of 'the sea-shouldering whale.' This intense enjoyment soon led to his trying his own hand at verse, and the chief end of his existence became henceforward the reading and writing of poetry. With his friend Cowden Clarke, then a youth like himself, he spent long evenings in enthusiastic discussion of the English poets, shewing a characteristic preference for passages of sweet sensuous description, such as are found in the minor poems of Chaucer, Shakspeare, and Milton, and throughout Spenser, rather than for those dealing with the passions of the human heart. By Clarke he was introduced to Greek poetry, through the medium of translations. They commenced Chapman's *Homer* one evening, and read till daylight, Keats sometimes shouting aloud with delight as some passage of special energy struck his imagination. Therewith began that remarkable affiliation of his mind to the Greek mythology, which gave to his works so marked a form and colour. From Edmonton he removed to the city for the purpose of 'walking the hospitals,' and became acquainted with Leigh Hunt, Shelley, Hazlitt, Godwin, Haydon, and other literary and artistic people, in whose society his mind expanded and strengthened. At Haydon's one evening, when Wordsworth was present, Keats was induced to recite to him his *Hymn to Pan*, which Shelley had praised as 'his surest pledge of ultimate excellence.' Wordsworth listened to the end, and then grimly remarked: 'It is a pretty piece of paganism!'

In 1817, Keats published his first book of poems, which attracted no attention. Next year he tried again, and brought out *Endymion, a Poetic Romance*, for which he was ridiculed as a Cockney-poet in the *Quarterly* and *Blackwood's Magazine*, and recommended 'to go back to his gallipots,' and reminded that 'a starved apothecary was better than a starved poet.' In 1820 appeared *Lamia, the Eve of St Agnes, and other Poems;* these three small volumes, issued within three years, comprised the finished business of his literary life.

Keats was of low stature, considerably under middle size. His shoulders were very broad, and his legs so short, that they quite marred the proportion of his figure. 'His head,' says Leigh Hunt, 'was a puzzle for the phrenologists, being remarkably small in the skull—a singularity he had in common with Byron and Shelley, whose hats I could not get on.' His face was clearly cut, almost feminine in its general form, and delicately mobile; its worst feature was the mouth, which had a projecting upper lip, giving a somewhat savage and pugilistic impression. His eyes were large and blue, and his hair auburn, and worn parted down the middle. Coleridge, who once shook hands with him, when he met him with Leigh Hunt in a Highgate lane, describes him as 'a loose, slack, not well-dressed youth.' At the same time, he turned to Hunt, and whispered: 'There is death in that hand,' although Keats was then apparently in perfect health.

JOHN KEATS.

The senses of Keats were exquisitely developed. In this fact, in conjunction with a fine imagination and copious language, is discovered the mystery of his poetry, which consists mainly in a relation of luxurious sensations of sight, hearing, taste, smell, and touch. Of music he was passionately fond, and in colour he had more than a painter's joy. As to taste, Haydon tells of once seeing him cover his tongue with cayenne pepper, in order, as he said, that he might enjoy the delicious sensation of a cold draught of claret after it. 'Talking of pleasure,' he says in one of his letters, 'this moment I was writing with one hand, and with the other was holding to my mouth a nectarine;' and thereon he proceeds to describe the nectarine in a way which might cause a sympathetic mouth to water with desire. In his *Ode to the Nightingale*, these lines will be remembered:

'O for a draught of vintage, that hath been
Cool'd a long age in the deep-delvèd earth;
Tasting of Flora and the country-green,
Dance, and Provençal song, and sun-burnt mirth!
O for a beaker full of the warm South,
Full of the true, the blushful Hippocrene,
With beaded bubbles winking at the brim,
And purple-stainèd mouth;
That I might drink, and leave the world unseen,
And with thee fade away into the forest dim.'

Observe how every line turns on sensuous delight. With this key, it is truly interesting to examine the poems of Keats, and find how it opens their meaning and reveals their author. In this respect, Keats was the antipodes of Shelley, whose verse is related to mental far more than sensuous emotions.

In 1820, pulmonary consumption appeared in the hitherto healthy constitution of Keats. Getting into bed one night, he coughed, and said: 'That is blood—bring me the candle;' and after gazing on the pillow, turning round with an expression of sudden and solemn calm, said: 'I know the colour of that blood, it is arterial blood—I cannot be deceived in that colour; that drop is my death-warrant. I must die!' He passed through the alternations common to consumptive patients—sometimes better and sometimes worse. His mind, at the same time, was torn with passion and anxiety. His inheritance of £2000 was gone, and he had abandoned the idea of being a surgeon. He was deeply in love, but he had no means of maintaining a wife. A brief and futile attempt was made to earn a living by writing for the magazines. Meanwhile his disease made rapid progress. Accompanied by Mr Severn, a young friend and artist, by whom he was tended with most affectionate care, he set out to spend the winter in Italy. His sufferings, physical and mental, were intense. A keen sorrow lay in the thought that he had done nothing worthy of abiding fame. 'Let my epitaph be,' said he: 'Here lies one whose name was writ in water.' He died at Rome in the arms of Severn on the 23d of February 1821, aged twenty-five years and four months. His last words were: 'Thank God, it has come!' His body was interred in the Protestant cemetery at Rome; a beautiful spot, where violets and daisies blow the winter through, and, in the words of Shelley, 'making one in love with death, to think one should be buried in so sweet a place.' Hither, a few months later, were Shelley's own ashes brought to rest under a stone bearing the inscription: 'Cor Cordium.'

## SIR WALTER RALEIGH.

To trace the career of Sir Walter Raleigh, and extricate his character from the perplexing confusion of contemporary opinion, is an undertaking of considerable difficulty. One principal cause of this is to be found in the heterogeneous qualities of the man. Soldier and poet, sailor and historian, court favourite and roving adventurer, his biographers have been at a loss under what category to place him. He was, says the writer of a little book, printed in London in 1677, and entitled *The Life of the Valiant and Learned Sir Walter Raleigh, Knight, with his Tryal at Winchester*, statesman, seaman, soldier, chemist, chronologer. 'He seemed to be born to that only which he went about, so dexterous was he in all his undertakings, in court, in camp, by sea, by land, with sword, with pen.'

Although Raleigh exerted himself so much in the service of his country, what he did was, for the most part, so out of the way of ordinary men's doings, that even history seems perplexed to discover what to record of him. We are told how he won Elizabeth's favour at the first by laying his rich cloak in the mire to save her majesty's slippers. We are told how he wrote one line of a couplet, when growing restless with the dilatory manner which the queen had in promoting her favourites, and that the queen herself deigned to complete it. We are told how he introduced the poet Spenser to the court, and quarrelled with Essex. Such trivial glimpses as these are almost all we get of him.

The little book above mentioned, by the way, gives a different edition of the far-famed couplet to the one we have been used to. We quote the account given: 'To put the queen in remembrance, he wrote in a window obvious to her eye:

> Fain would I climb, yet fear I to fall.

Which her majesty, either espying or being shewn, under-wrote this answer:

> If thy heart fail thee, climb not at all.'

Raleigh feared no man and no quarrel, and stood his ground against all. He was no sycophant. He must have had a clever wit, joined with his manliness and impetuosity, for he managed to retain Elizabeth's good graces to the last; while the less fortunate Essex died on the scaffold.

Raleigh had a restless spirit, which made him at once innovator and adventurer. He was always making new discoveries. In his dress he was singular, his armour was a wonder, his creed his own concocting. He it was who introduced tobacco; which Elizabeth, strangely enough, judging merely in a commercial spirit, regarded as a useful article, but which seemed to James an execrable nuisance. The El Dorados which he went in search of were innumerable; and as he joined with these mine-finding expeditions a large amount of carrack-stopping, he won himself at last the characteristic appellation of *The Scourge of Spain*, and for this Spain, relentless, had his head in the end.

The day of Elizabeth's death was the birthday of Raleigh's misfortunes. He never was a favourite with James from the first. It is not long before we find him brought up for trial for high treason, in what has always been called *Raleigh's Conspiracy*—so called, it may be, because Raleigh had the least to do with it of any of those involved; or perhaps, which is more likely, because it was a puzzle to every one how such a man as Raleigh could have been connected with it.

Having been previously examined in July, Raleigh was brought to trial at Winchester, on November 17, 1603. Throughout the whole, he is described as conducting himself with spirit, as 'rather shewing love of life than fear of death,' and replying to the insulting language of Sir Edward Coke, the king's attorney, with a dignity which remains Coke's lasting reproach.

Coke's unprovoked insults were abominable. He called Raleigh, for instance, 'the absolutest traitor that ever was.' To which Raleigh only rejoined: 'Your phrases will not prove it, Mr Attourney.' What a speech was this for the king's advocate: 'Thou hast a Spanish heart, and thyself art a spider of hell!' The following is a specimen of the style of bickering which went on on the occasion:

'*Raleigh*. I do not hear yet that you have spoken one word against me; here is no treason of mine done. If my Lord Cobham be a traitor, what is that to me?

*Coke*. All that he did was by thy instigation, thou viper; for I *thou* thee, thou traitor.

*Raleigh*. It becometh not a man of quality and virtue to call me so: but I take comfort in it, it is all you can do.

*Coke*. Have I angered you?

*Raleigh*. I am in no case to be angry.'

Here Lord-Chief Justice Popham seems ashamed, and puts in an apology for his friend on the king's side: 'Sir Walter Raleigh, Mr Attourney speaketh out of the zeal of his duty for the service of the king, and you, for your life: *be valiant on both sides*.' [A curious observation!]

In one instance, Coke was so rude that Lord Cecil rose and remarked: 'Be not so impatient, Mr Attourney, give him leave to speak.' And so we are informed: 'Here Mr Attourney sat down in a chafe, and would speak no more, until the commissioners urged and entreated him. After much ado he went on,' &c.

Raleigh had but one real witness against him, and that was Lord Cobham, the head of the plot, and Raleigh's personal friend. It seems that Cobham, in a temporary fit of anger—Raleigh seems to have inculpated him in the first instance—described Raleigh as the instigator of the whole business. Coke produced a letter, written by Cobham, which seemed to enclose the matter in a nut-shell, for it was very explicit against Raleigh. Raleigh pleaded to have Cobham produced in court, but this was refused. Raleigh had his reasons for this, for at the last minute he pulled out a letter, which Cobham had written to him since the one to Coke, in which that lord begged pardon for his treachery, and declared his friend innocent. And so it appeared that he was, although he evidently had more knowledge of matters than was good for his safety. But a minor point, which was brought forward at last, was like the springing of a mine, and spoiled Raleigh's case. It affirmed that Sir Walter Raleigh had been dealt with to become a spy of Spain, at a pension of £1500 per annum. This might have been a trap set by Spain, but, at anyrate, Raleigh did not deny the fact, and so the evidence turned against him. He was sentenced, with disgraceful severity, to be hanged, drawn, and quartered.

Raleigh wrote a letter to his wife, while in expectation of death. A private communication like this letter gives us a better insight into his conscience, and also into his so-called 'atheism,' than could be got from any other source—

'I sued for my life, but (God knows) it was for you

and yours that I desired it: for know it, my dear wife, your child is the child of a true man, who, in his own respect, despiseth death and his misshapen and ugly forms. I cannot write much. God knows how hardly I steal this time when all sleep, and it is also time for me to separate my thoughts from the world. Beg my dead body, which living was denied you, and either lay it in Sherburn or in Exeter Church, *by my father and mother*.' [Is not this the last wish of all rovers?] 'I can say no more, time and death calleth me away. The everlasting God, powerful, infinite, and inscrutable God Almighty' [Has this an *atheistic* sound?], 'who is goodness itself, the true Light and Life, keep you and yours, and have mercy upon me, and forgive my persecutors and false-accusers' [Why, this is very Christianity!], 'and send us to meet in his glorious kingdom! My dear wife, farewell, bless my boy, pray for me, and let my true God hold you both in his arms.—Yours that was, but now not my own, WALTER RALEIGH.'

After all, Raleigh was not executed. He lived yet a dozen years a prisoner in the Tower, his wife with him, and wrote his famous *History of the World*. When he could no longer rove over the whole earth, he set himself to write its history. He won the friendship of Prince Henry, who could never understand how his father could keep so fine a bird in a cage; and had the young prince lived, he would have set the bird at liberty, but he died. At length James released Raleigh, and sent him on one more mining expedition to South America, with twelve ships and abundance of men. But secretly, out of timidity, James informed Spain of the whole scheme, and the expedition failed. A town was burned, and the Spanish ambassador, Gondomar, became furious. Raleigh knew what to expect; but, having bound himself to return, he did return. He was immediately seized; and, without any new trial, was beheaded on his old condemnation, all to appease the anger of Spain, upon Thursday, the 29th of October 1618, in Old Palace Yard, Westminster.

Raleigh died nobly. The bishop who attended him, and the lords about him, were astonished to witness his serenity of demeanour. He spoke to the Lord Arundel to desire the king to allow no scandalous writings, defaming him, to be written after his death—the only one which was written, strange to say, was James's *Apology*—and he observed calmly: 'I have a long journey to go, therefore must take leave!' He fingered the axe with a smile, and called it 'a sharp medicine,' 'a sound cure for all diseases;' and laid his head on the block with these words in conclusion: 'So the heart be right, it is no matter which way the head lies.'

'Thus,' says our little book, 'died that knight who was Spain's scourge and terror, and Gondomar's triumph; whom the whole nation pitied, and several princes interceded for; Queen Elizabeth's favourite, and her successor's sacrifice. A person of so much worth and so great interest, that King James would not execute him without an apology; one of such incomparable policy, that he was too hard for Essex, was the envy of Leicester, and Cecil's rival, who grew jealous of his excellent parts, and was afraid of being supplanted by him.'

The following is Raleigh's last poem, written the night before his death, and found in his Bible, in the Gate-house, at Westminster:

SIR W. RALEIGH THE NIGHT BEFORE HIS DEATH.

'Even such is time, which takes in trust
Our youth, our joys, and all we have,
And pays us nought but age and dust;
Which in the dark and silent grave,
When we have wandered all our ways,
Shuts up the story of our days!
And from which grave, and earth, and dust,
The Lord shall raise me up, I trust.'

## THE HERMIT OF GRUB STREET.

Amongst the many histories of extraordinary characters, who from various motives have secluded themselves from the world, probably few have created more interest than Mr Henry Welby, the individual about to be recorded. He was a native of Lincolnshire, where, in the neighbourhood of Grantham, his descendants still live. The family is ancient, and of high position, as may be inferred from several of its members having sat in parliament for the county of Lincoln, in the times of the Henrys and the Edwards, and from others having filled the post of sheriff—an office in those days held only by men of the highest status.

About the time of the accession of Queen Elizabeth, we find Mr Henry Welby residing at Goxhill, an ancient village near the Lincolnshire bank of the river Humber, nearly opposite to Kingston-upon-Hull. He was the inheritor of a considerable fortune, and all accounts that have been published concerning him, represent him as a highly-accomplished, benevolent, and popular gentleman. In this neighbourhood, he seems to have lived for a number of years, and then to have quitted it to reside in London, under the singular circumstances now to be detailed, as related in a curious work, published in 1637, under the following title: *The Phœnix of these late Times; or the Life of Henry Welby, Esq., who lived at his House, in Grub Street, Forty-four years, and in that Space was never seen by any: And there died, Oct. 29, 1636, aged Eighty-four. Shewing the first Occasion and Reason thereof. With Epitaphs and Elegies on the late Deceased Gentleman; who lyeth buried in St Giles' Church, near Cripplegate, London.*

In the preface to this singular pamphlet, the following passage occurs: 'This Gentleman, Master Henry Welby, was Forty Years of Age before he took this solitary Life. Those who knew him, and were conversant with him in his former Time, do report, that he was of a middle Stature, a Brown Complexion, and of a Pleasant Chearful Countenance. His Hair (by reason no Barber came near him for the Space of so many Years) was much overgrown; so that he, at his Death, appeared rather like a Hermit of the Wilderness, than Inhabitant of a City. His Habit was plain, and without Ornament; of a sad-coloured Cloth, only to defend him from the Cold, in which there could be nothing found either to express the least Imagination of Pride or Vain-Glory.'

The various accounts which have been published of this remarkable man, agree in the main, but differ in one or two particulars. For instance, in one it is stated that it was his *brother*, whose conduct led to the strange results recorded; and, in another, that it was merely *a kinsman*. In the present notice, we have adhered to the narrative given to the world in 1637. It thus records the history of Mr Welby's eccentricities.

'The Occasion was the Unkindness, or the Unnaturalness and Inhumanity of a younger Brother, who, upon some Discontent or Displeasure conceived against him, rashly and resolutely threatened his Death. The two Brothers meeting Face to Face, the younger drew a Pistol, charged with a double Bullet, from his Side, and presented upon the Elder, which only gave Fire, but by the

HENRY WELBY, THE GRUB-STREET HERMIT.

miraculous Providence of God, no farther Report. At which the Elder, seizing him, disarmed him of his tormenting Engine, and so left him; which, bearing to his Chamber, and desiring to find whether it was merely a false Fire to frighten him, or a Charge speedily to dispatch him, he found Bullets, and thinking of the danger he had escaped, fell into many deep Considerations. He then grounded his irrevocable Resolution to live alone. He kept it to his dying day.

'That he might the better observe it, he took a very fair House in the lower end of *Grub-street*, near unto *Cripplegate*, and having contracted a numerous Retinue into a small and private Family, having the House before prepared for his purpose, he entered the Door, chusing to himself, out of all the Rooms, three private Chambers best suiting with his intended Solitude; the First for his Diet, the Second for his Lodging, and the Third for his Study—one within another. While his Diet was set on the table by one of his servants—an old Maid—he retired into his Lodging-chamber; and while his Bed was making, into his Study; and so on, till all was clear. And there he set up his Rest, and in *forty-four years* never, upon any Occasion how great soever, issued out of those Chambers, till he was borne thence upon Men's shoulders; neither in all that time did Son-in-law, Daughter, Grandchild, Brother, Sister, or Kinsman, Stranger, Tenant, or Servant, Young or Old, Rich or Poor, of what Degree or Condition soever, look upon his Face, saving the ancient Maid, whose Name was Elizabeth, who made his Fire, prepared his Bed, provided his Diet, and dressed his Chamber; which was very seldom, or upon an extraordinary Necessity that he saw her; which Maid-servant died not above Six Days before him.

'In all the Time of his Retirement he never tasted Fish nor Flesh. He never drank either Wine or Strong Water. His chief Food was Oatmeal boiled with Water, which some People call Gruel; and in Summer, now and then, a Sallad of some cool, choice Herbs. For Dainties, or when he would feast himself, upon a High Day, he would eat the Yoke of a Hen's Egg, but no part of the white; and what Bread he did eat, he cut out of the middle part of the Loaf, but of the Crust he never tasted; and his continual Drink was Four-shilling Beer, and no other; and now and then, when his Stomack served him, he did eat some kind of Suckets;* and now and then drank Red Cow's Milk, which Elizabeth fetched for him out of the Fields, hot from the Cow; and yet he kept a bountiful Table for his Servants, with Entertainment sufficient for any Stranger, or Tenant, who had occasion of Business at his House.

'In Christmas holidays, at Easter, and upon other Festival days, he had great Cheer provided, with all Dishes seasonable with the Times, served into his own Chamber, with Store of Wine, which his Maid brought in; when he himself would pin a clean Napkin before him, and putting on a pair of white Holland Sleeves, which reached to his Elbows, called for his Knife, and cutting Dish after Dish up in Order, send one to one poor Neighbour, the next to another, &c., whether it were Brawn, Beef, Capon, Goose, &c., till he had left the Table quite empty. Then would he give thanks, lay by his Linnen, put up his Knife again, and cause the Cloth to be taken away; and this would he do, Dinner and Supper, without tasting one Morsel himself; and this Custom he kept to his dying Day! Indeed, he kept a kind of continual Fast, so he devoted himself unto continual Prayer, saving those Seasons which he dedicated to his Study; For you must know that he was both a Scholar and a Linguist; neither was there any Author worth the Reading, either brought over from beyond the Seas, or published here in the Kingdom, which he refused to buy, at what dear Rate soever; and these were his Companions in the Day, and his Counsellors in the Night; insomuch that the Saying may be verified of him—*Nunquam minus solus, quam cum solus*—He was never better accompanied, or less alone, than when alone. Out of his private Chamber, which had a prospect into the Street, if he spied any Sick, Weak, or Lame, would presently send after them, to Comfort, Cherish, and Strengthen them; and not a Trifle to serve them for the present, but such as would relieve them many Days after. He would, moreover enquire what Neighbours were industrious in their Callings, and who had great Charge of Children; and if their Labour or Industry could not sufficiently supply their Families, to such he would liberally send, and relieve them according to their Necessities.'

Taylor, the 'Water Poet,' thus commemorates the recluse of Grub Street:

'Old *Henry Welby—well be* † thou for ever,
Thy Purgatory 's past, thy Heaven ends never.
Of eighty-four years' life, full forty-four
Man saw thee not, nor e'er shall see thee more.
'Twas Piety and Penitance caus'd thee
So long a Pris'ner (to thyself) to be:
Thy bounteous House within express'd thy Mind;
Thy Charity without, the Poor did find.
From Wine thou wast a duteous *Rechabite*,
And Flesh so long Time shunn'd thy Appetite:
Small-Beer, a Caudle, Milk, or Water-gruel,
Strengthen'd by Grace, maintain'd thy daily Duell
'Gainst the bewitching World, the Flesh, the Fiend,
Which made thee live and die well: there's an End.'

A more recent work gives us the information, that Mr Welby had an only child, a daughter, who was married to Sir Christopher Hildyard, Knight of Winstead, in Yorkshire, and left three sons: 1. Henry, who married Lady Anne Leke, daughter of Francis, first Earl of Scarsdale; and of this marriage the late Right Hon. Charles Tennyson D'Eyncourt is a descendant. 2. Christopher. 3. Sir Robert Hildyard, an eminent royalist commander, who, for his gallant services, was made a knight-banneret, and afterwards a baronet.

* *Suckets*, dried sweet-meats or sugar-plums—in the Scottish dialect, *sunkets*.

† Old Taylor would appear, by these words, to have been a punster.

# OCTOBER 30.

St Marcellus the Centurion, martyr, 298. St Germanus, bishop of Capua, confessor, about 540. St Asterius bishop of Amasea in Pontus, beginning of 5th century.

*Born.*—Jacques Amyot, translator of Plutarch, 1513, *Melun*; Cardinal Cæsar Baronius, historical writer, 1538, *Sora*; George II. of England, 1683, *Hanover*; Richard Brinsley Sheridan, dramatist and politician, 1751, *Dublin*; James Perry, editor of the *Morning Chronicle*, 1756, *Aberdeenshire*.

*Died.*—Antinous, favourite of the Emperor Hadrian, drowned in the Nile, 130 A. D.; James Sturmius, Protestant champion, 1553, *Strasburg*; Charles Alexandre de Calonne, financier to Louis XVI., 1802, *Paris*; Rev. John Whitaker, historical writer, 1808, *Ruan-Lanyhorne, Cornwall*; Edmund Cartwright, inventor of the power-loom, 1823, *Hastings*; Rev. Charles Maturin, dramatist and tale-writer, 1824; Thomas, Earl of Dundonald, distinguished naval commander, 1860, *Kensington*.

## BURNING OF THE TOWER OF LONDON.

On the night of Saturday the 30th of October 1841, the great armory or storehouse, a large and imposing range of buildings, forming part of the Tower of London, and situated on the north side of its precincts, to the east of St Peter's Chapel, was entirely consumed by fire, which had broken out in the Round or Bowyer Tower immediately adjoining. The cause of this calamitous event appears to have been the overheating of the flue of a stove, the prolific origin of so many conflagrations. The edifice destroyed had been founded by James II., and completed in the reign of William and Mary, their majesties celebrating the conclusion of the work by visiting the Tower and partaking of a splendid banquet in the great hall of the new building. This magnificent apartment, occupying the whole of the first-floor, was afterwards employed as a storehouse for small-arms, 150,000 stand of which were destroyed by the fire. On the ground-floor a number of cannon and other trophies, taken in the field, were deposited. Though a loss, estimated at upwards of £200,000, was sustained, it was matter for congratulation that the older portions of the Tower, so interesting by their historical associations, escaped almost uninjured. The Great, or White Tower, was for a time in imminent danger, and the Jewel Tower was so exposed to the flames, that it was believed impossible to avert its destruction. But fortunately both buildings were preserved.

In connection with the Jewel Tower, an interesting incident, as well as a remarkable instance of personal bravery, ought not to be forgotten. We refer to the removal of the Regalia, which, for a second time in their history, though in different circumstances, made as narrow an escape from destruction as when, upwards of a century and a half previously, they were rescued from the fangs of Blood and his associates. On the intelligence of a fire having broken out, Mr W. F. Pierse, superintendent of one of the divisions of the metropolitan police, proceeded with a detachment of constables to the Tower. Shortly after his arrival, the flames made such rapid advances in the direction of the Jewel House, that it was deemed expedient at once to remove the Regalia and crown-jewels to a place of safety. Accompanied by Mr Swifte, the keeper of the Jewel House, and other officials, including several of the Tower warders, Mr Pierse entered the building in question. To get hold of the jewels was now the difficulty, as these treasures were secured by a strong iron grating, the keys of which were in the possession of the lord chamberlain, or elsewhere deposited at a distance, and not a moment was to be lost. Crow-bars were procured, and a narrow aperture made in the grating so as barely to admit one person. Through this opening Mr Pierse contrived, with much difficulty, to thrust himself, and hand through from the inside the various articles of the Regalia. One of these, a silver font, was too large thus to be passed, and it consequently became necessary to break away an additional bar of the grating. While the warders were employed in effecting this, repeated cries were heard from outside, calling to the party within the Jewel House to leave the building as the fire was close upon them. Determined, however, to accomplish the behest which he had undertaken, Mr Pierse unflinchingly retained his post within the grating, and at last succeeded in rescuing the font. The precious articles were all conveyed safely to the governor's house, and a most extraordinary spectacle presented itself in the warders carrying the crowns and other appurtenances of royalty between groups of soldiers, policemen, and firemen.

The heat endured by the party in the Jewel House was such as almost to reduce their garments to a charred state. Some public reward to Mr Pierse, who had thus so gallantly imperilled himself to save the Regalia of the United Kingdom, would, we should imagine, have been a fitting tribute to his bravery. But no such recompense was ever bestowed.

## THE RHYNE TOLL, OR THE CUSTOM OF CHETWODE MANOR.

Many ancient rights and customs, which have long since lost much of their significance, and perhaps now appear to modern notions ridiculous, are nevertheless valuable when viewed in connection with history. For they often confirm and illustrate historic facts, which, from the altered state of the country, would otherwise be unintelligible, and perhaps discredited at the present day. Such a custom or privilege is still possessed and exercised in connection with the manor of Chetwode, in Bucks, which, although very curious both in its origin and observance, has escaped the notice of Blount and other writers on the 'jocular customs of some mannors.'

The manor of Chetwode—a small village about five miles from Buckingham—has been the property of the Chetwode family from Saxon times. Though of small extent, it is the paramount manor of a liberty or district embracing several other manors and villages which are required to do suit and service at the Court-Leet held at Chetwode every three years. The Lord of Chetwode Manor has also the right to levy a yearly tax, called the 'Rhyne Toll,' on all cattle found within this liberty, between the 30th of October and the 7th of November, both days inclusive. The commencement of the toll, which is proclaimed with much ceremony, is thus described in an old document of Queen Elizabeth's reign:

'In the beginning of the said Drift of the Common, or Rhyne, first at their going forth, they shall blow a welke-shell, or horne, immediately after the sunrising at the mansion-house of the manor of Chetwode, and then in their going about they shall blow their horne the second time in the field between Newton Purcell and Barton Hartshorne, in the said county of Bucks; and also shall blow their horne a third time at a place near the town of Finmere, in the county of Oxford; and they shall blow their horne the fourth time at a certain stone in the market of the town of Buckingham, and there to give the poor sixpence; and so, going forward in this manner about the said Drift, shall blow the horne at several bridges called Thornborough Bridge, King's Bridge, and Bridge Mill. And also they shall blow their horne at the Pound Gate, called the Lord's Pound, in the parish of Chetwode. . . . . And also (the Lord of Chetwode) has always been used by his officers and servants to drive away all foreign cattle that shall be found within the said parishes, fields, &c., to impound the same in any pound of the said towns, and to take for every one of the said foreign beasts twopence for the mouth, and one penny for a foot, for every one of the said beasts.' All cattle thus impounded at other places were to be removed to the pound at Chetwode; and if not claimed, and the toll paid, within three days, 'then the next day following, after the rising of the sun, the bailiff or officers of the lord for the time being, shall blow their horne three times at the gate of the said pound, and make proclamation that if any persons lack any cattle that shall be in the same pound, let them come and shew the marks of the same cattle so claimed by them, and they shall have them, paying unto the lord his money in the manner and form before-mentioned, otherwise the said cattle that shall so remain, shall be the lord's as strays.' This toll was formerly so rigidly enforced, that if the owner of cattle so impounded made his claim immediately after the proclamation was over, he was refused them, except by paying their full market price.

Though the custom is still regularly observed, it has undergone some changes since the date of the above document. The toll now begins at nine in the morning instead of at sunrise, and the horn is first sounded on the church-hill at Buckingham, and gingerbread and beer distributed among the assembled boys, the girls being excluded. The officer then proceeds to another part of the liberty on the border of Oxfordshire, and there, after blowing his horn as before, again distributes gingerbread and beer among the assembled boys. The toll is then proclaimed as begun, and collectors are stationed at different parts to enforce it, at the rate of two shillings a score upon all cattle and swine passing on any road within the liberty, until twelve o'clock at night on the 7th of November, when the 'Rhyne' closes.

The occupiers of land within the liberty have long been accustomed to compound for the toll by an annual payment of one shilling. The toll has sometimes been refused, but has always been recovered with the attendant expenses. It realised about £20 a year before the opening of the Buckinghamshire Railway; but now, owing to Welsh and Irish cattle being sent by trains, it does not amount to above £4, and is let by the present lord of the manor for only £1, 5*s*. a year.

The existence of this toll may be traced to remote antiquity, but nothing is known of its origin except from local tradition, which, however, in this case, has been so remarkably confirmed, that it may safely be credited. The parish of Chetwode, as its name implies, was formerly thickly wooded; indeed, it formed a part of an ancient forest called Rookwoode, which is supposed to have been conterminous with the present liberty of Chetwode. At a very early period, says our tradition, this forest was infested with an enormous wild-boar, which became the terror of the surrounding country. The inhabitants were never safe from his attacks; and strangers, who heard of his ferocity, were afraid to visit, or pass through, the district; so that traffic and friendly intercourse were seriously impeded, as well as much injury done to property, by this savage monster. The Lord of Chetwode, like a true and valiant knight, determined to rid his neighbourhood from this pest, or to die in the attempt. Bent on this generous purpose, he sallied forth into the forest, and, as the old song has it—

'Then he blowed a blast full north, south, east, and west—
Wind well thy horn, good hunter;
And the wild-boar then heard him full in his den,
As he was a jovial hunter.

Then he made the best of his speed unto him—
Wind well thy horn, good hunter;
Swift flew the boar, with his tusks smeared with gore,
To Sir Ryalas, the jovial hunter.

Then the wild-boar, being so stout and so strong—
Wind well thy horn, good hunter;
Thrashed down the trees as he ramped him along,
To Sir Ryalas, the jovial hunter.

Then they fought four hours in a long summer day—
Wind well thy horn, good hunter;
Till the wild-boar fain would have got him away
From Sir Ryalas, the jovial hunter.

Then Sir Ryalas he drawed his broad-sword with might—
Wind well thy horn, good hunter;
And he fairly cut the boar's head off quite,
For he was a jovial hunter.'

Matters being thus settled, the neighbourhood rung with the praises of the gallant deed of the Lord of Chetwode, and the news thereof soon reached the ears of the king, who 'liked him so well of the achievement,' that he forthwith made the knight tenant *in capite*, and constituted his manor paramount of all the manors within the limits and extent of the royal forest of Rookwoode. Moreover he granted to him, and to his heirs for ever, among other immunities and privileges, the full right and power to levy every year the Rhyne Toll, which has already been described.

Such is the purport of the Chetwode tradition, which has descended unquestioned from time immemorial, and received, about forty years ago, a remarkable confirmation. Within a mile of Chetwode manor-house there existed a large mound, surrounded by a ditch, and bearing the name of the 'Boar's Pond.' It had long been overgrown with gorse and brushwood, when, about the year 1810, the tenant, to whose farm it belonged, wishing to bring it into cultivation, began to fill up the ditch by levelling the mound. Having lowered the latter about four feet, he came on the skeleton of an enormous boar, lying flat on its side, and at full length. Probably this was the very spot where it had been killed, the earth around having been heaped over it, so as to form the ditch and mound. The space formerly thus occupied can still be traced. It extends about thirty feet in length, and eighteen in width, and the field containing it is yet called the 'Boar's Head Field.' The jaw and other portions of the skeleton are now in the possession of Sir John Chetwode, Bart., the present lord of the manor. There is a somewhat similar tradition at Boarstall, which stands within the limits of Bernewood Forest, as Chetwode does within those of Rookwoode. These forests formerly adjoined, and formed a favourite hunting-district of Edward the Confessor and his successors, who had a palace or hunting-lodge at Burghill (Brill), where the two forests met.*

That the mere killing of a boar should be so richly rewarded, may appear incredible. But many a wild-boar of old was so powerful and ferocious, that he would even attack a lion; while such was his stubborn courage that he would never yield till actually killed or disabled. The classic reader may here recall to mind the celebrated tale, in Greek mythology, of the Calydonian boar that ravaged the fields of Ætolia, and was ultimately slain by Meleager, with the help of Theseus, Jason, and other renowned heroes. Such, indeed, was the nature of the wild-boar, that most of the early poets have chosen it as the fittest animal to illustrate the indomitable courage of their heroes: thus Homer:

'Forth from the portals rushed the intrepid pair,
Opposed their breasts, and stood themselves the war.
So two wild-boars spring furious from their den,
Roused with the cries of dogs and voice of men;
On every side the crackling trees they tear,
And root the shrubs, and lay the forest bare;
They gnash their tusks, with fire their eyeballs roll,
Till some wide wound lets out their mighty soul.'

And Spenser, perhaps not without the charge of plagiarism, has the same illustration:

'So long they fight, and fell revenge pursue,
That fainting, each themselves to breathen let,
And oft refreshed, battle oft renew;
As when two boars with rankling malice met,
Their gory sides fresh bleeding fiercely fret,
Till breathless both, themselves aside retire,
Where foaming wrath their cruel tusks they whet,
And trample the earth the while they may respire;
Then back to fight again, new breathed and entire.'

Such animals were most dangerous, not only to

* See vol. i., 768.

travellers and unarmed rustics, but to the hunting-expeditions of the king and his nobles. It need not, therefore, surprise us to find that the destruction of a wild-boar ranked, in the middle ages, among the deeds of chivalry, and won for a warrior almost as much renown as the slaying an enemy in the open field. So dangerous, indeed, was the hunting of wild-boars, even when the hunter was armed for the purpose, that Shakspeare represents Venus as dissuading Adonis from the practice:

O be advis'd! thou know'st not what it is
With javelin's point a churlish swine to gore,
 Whose tushes never-sheath'd he whetteth still,
 Like to a mortal butcher, bent to kill.
His brawny sides, with hairy bristles arm'd,
Are better proof than thy spear's point can enter;
His short thick neck cannot be easily harm'd;
Being ireful on the lion he will venture.'

Such hunting-expeditions were generally fatal to some of the dogs, and occasionally to one or more of the hunters. Such was the case with Robert de Vere, ninth Earl of Oxford, who was killed in 1395 by the boar he was pursuing.

The knight of Chetwode, then, who from benevolent motives encountered and slew the boar that ravaged his neighbourhood, deserved to be richly rewarded; and what reward could be more appropriate than the privilege of claiming a yearly toll over those roads which he had thus rendered secure? Perhaps, too, the exacting of toll for nine days was to commemorate the period during which the gallant knight persisted before he achieved his object.

Such a custom, as the Rhyne Toll, is not without its use. It is a perpetual memorial, perhaps more convincing than written history, of the dangers which surrounded our ancestors, and from which our country has happily been so long delivered, that we can now scarcely believe they ever existed.

---

## OCTOBER 31.

St Quintin, martyr, 287. St Foillan, martyr, 655. St Wolfgang, bishop of Ratisbon, 994.

### Halloween.

There is perhaps no night in the year which the popular imagination has stamped with a more peculiar character than the evening of the 31st of October, known as All Hallow's Eve, or Halloween. It is clearly a relic of pagan times, for there is nothing in the church-observance of the ensuing day of All Saints to have originated such extraordinary notions as are connected with this celebrated festival, or such remarkable practices as those by which it is distinguished.

The leading idea respecting Halloween is that it is the time, of all others, when supernatural influences prevail. It is the night set apart for a universal walking abroad of spirits, both of the visible and invisible world; for, as will be afterwards seen, one of the special characteristics attributed to this mystic evening, is the faculty conferred on the immaterial principle in humanity to detach itself from its corporeal tenement and wander abroad through the realms of space. Divination is then believed to attain its highest power, and the gift asserted by Glendower of calling spirits 'from the vasty deep,' becomes available to all who choose to avail themselves of the privileges of the occasion.

There is a remarkable uniformity in the fireside-customs of this night all over the United Kingdom. Nuts and apples are everywhere in requisition, and consumed in immense numbers. Indeed the name of *Nutcrack Night*, by which Halloween is known in the north of England, indicates the predominance of the former of these articles in making up the entertainments of the evening. They are not only cracked and eaten, but made the means of vaticination in love-affairs. And here we quote from Burns's poem of *Halloween:*

'The auld guidwife's well-hoordit nits
 Are round and round divided,
And mony lads' and lasses' fates
 Are there that night decided:
Some kindle, couthie, side by side,
 And burn thegither trimly;
Some start awa wi' saucy pride,
 And jump out-owre the chimly
 Fu' high that night.
Jean slips in twa wi' tentie e'e;
 Wha 'twas, she wadna tell;
But this is Jock, and this is me,
 She says in to hersel':
He bleezed owre her, and she owre him,
 As they wad never mair part;
Till, fuff! he started up the lum,
 And Jean had e'en a sair heart
 To see 't that night.'

Brand, in his *Popular Antiquities*, is more explicit: 'It is a custom in Ireland, when the young women would know if their lovers are faithful, to put three nuts upon the bars of the grate, naming the nuts after the lovers. If a nut cracks or jumps, the lover will prove unfaithful; if it begins to blaze or burn, he has a regard for the person making the trial. If the nuts named after the girl and her lover burn together, they will be married.'

As to apples, there is an old custom, perhaps still observed in some localities on this merry night, of hanging up a stick horizontally by a string from the ceiling, and putting a candle on the one end, and an apple on the other. The stick being made to twirl rapidly, the merry-makers in succession leap up and snatch at the apple with their teeth (no use of the hands being allowed), but it very frequently happens that the candle comes round before they are aware, and scorches them in the face, or anoints them with grease. The disappointments and misadventures occasion, of course, abundance of laughter. But the grand sport with apples on Halloween, is to set them afloat in a tub of water, into which the juveniles, by turns, duck their heads with the view of catching an apple. Great fun goes on in watching the attempts of the youngster in the pursuit of the swimming fruit, which wriggles from side to side of the tub, and evades all attempts to capture it; whilst the disappointed aspirant is obliged to abandon the chase in favour of another whose turn has now arrived. The apples provided with stalks are generally caught first, and then comes the tug of war to win those which possess no such appendages. Some competitors will deftly *suck up* the apple, if a small one, into their mouths. Others plunge manfully overhead in pursuit of a particular apple, and having forced it to the bottom of the tub, seize it firmly with their teeth, and emerge, dripping and triumphant, with their prize. This venturous procedure is generally rewarded with a hurrah! by the lookers-on, and is recommended, by those versed in Halloween-aquatics, as the only sure method of attaining success. In recent years, a practice has been introduced, probably by some tender mammas, timorous on the subject of their offspring catching cold, of dropping a fork from a height into the tub among the apples, and thus turning the sport into a display of marksmanship. It forms, however, but a very indifferent substitute for the joyous merriment of ducking and diving.

It is somewhat remarkable, that the sport of ducking for apples is not mentioned by Burns, whose celebrated poem of *Halloween* presents so graphic a picture of the ceremonies practised or

DUCKING FOR APPLES ON HALLOWEEN.

that evening in the west of Scotland, in the poet's day. Many of the rites there described are now obsolete or nearly so, but two or three still retain place in various parts of the country. Among these is the custom still prevalent in Scotland, as the initiatory Halloween ceremony, of pulling *kail-stocks* or stalks of colewort. The young people go out hand-in-hand, blindfolded, into the *kailyard* or garden, and each pulls the first stalk which he meets with. They then return to the fireside to inspect their prizes. According as the stalk is big or little, straight or crooked, so shall the future wife or husband be of the party by whom it is pulled. The quantity of earth sticking to the root denotes the amount of fortune or dowry; and the taste of the pith or *custoc* indicates the temper. Finally, the stalks are placed, one after another, over the door, and the Christian names of the persons who chance thereafter to enter the house are held in the same succession to indicate those of the individuals whom the parties are to marry.

Another ceremony much practised on Halloween, is that of the Three Dishes or *Luggies*. Two of these are respectively filled with clean and foul water, and one is empty. They are ranged on the hearth, when the parties, blindfolded, advance in succession, and dip their fingers into one. If they dip into the clean water, they are to marry a maiden; if into the foul water, a widow; if into the empty dish, the party so dipping is destined to be either a bachelor or an old maid. As each person takes his turn, the position of the dishes is changed. Burns thus describes the custom:

'In order, on the clean hearth-stane,
The luggies three are ranged,
And every time great care is ta'en
To see them duly changed:
Auld uncle John, wha wedlock's joys
Sin' Mar's year did desire,
Because he gat the toom dish thrice,
He heaved them on the fire
In wrath that night.

The ceremonies above described are all of a light sportive description, but there are others of a more weird-like and fearful character, which in this enlightened incredulous age have fallen very much into desuetude. One of these is the celebrated spell of eating an apple before a looking-glass. with the view of discovering the inquirer's future husband, who it is believed will be seen peeping over her shoulder. A curious, and withal, cautious, little maiden, who desires to try this spell, is thus represented by Burns:

'Wee Jenny to her granny says:
"Will ye go wi' me, granny?
I 'll eat the apple at the glass,
I gat frae uncle Johnny."'

A request which rouses the indignation of the old lady:

'She fuff't her pipe wi' sic a lunt,
In wrath she was sae vap'rin',
She notic't na, an aizle brunt
Her braw new worset apron
Out through that night.

"Ye little skelpie-limmer's face!
I daur you try sic sportin',
As seek the foul thief ony place,
For him to spae your fortune:
Nae doubt but ye may get a sight!
Great cause ye hae to fear it;
For mony a ane has gotten a fright,
And lived and died deleeret,
On sic a night."'

Granny's warning was by no means a needless one, as several well-authenticated instances are related of persons who, either from the effects of their own imagination, or some thoughtless practical joke, sustained such severe nervous shocks, while essaying these Halloween-spells, as seriously to imperil their health.

Another of these, what may perhaps be termed *unhallowed*, rites of All Hallows' Eve, is to wet a shirt-sleeve, hang it up to the fire to dry, and lie in bed watching it till midnight, when the apparition of the individual's future partner for life will come in and turn the sleeve. Burns thus alludes to the practice in one of his songs:

'The last Halloween I was waukin',
My droukit sark-sleeve, as ye ken;
His likeness cam' up the house staukin',
And the very gray breeks o' Tam Glen!'

Other rites for the invocation of spirits might be referred to, such as the sowing of hemp-seed, and the winnowing of three *wechts* of nothing, i.e., repeating three times the action of exposing corn to the wind. In all of these the effect sought to be produced is the same—the appearance of the future husband or wife of the experimenter. A full description of them will be found in the poem of Burns, from which we have already so largely quoted. It may here be remarked, that popular belief ascribes to children born on Halloween, the possession of certain mysterious faculties, such as that of perceiving and holding converse with supernatural beings. Sir Walter Scott, it will be recollected, makes use of this circumstance in his romance of *The Monastery*.

In conclusion, we shall introduce an interesting story, with which we have been favoured by a lady. The leading incidents of the narrative may be relied on as correct, and the whole affair forms matter of curious thought on the subject of Halloween divination.

Mr and Mrs M—— were a happy young couple, who, in the middle of the last century, resided on their own estate in a pleasant part of the province of Leinster, in Ireland. Enjoying a handsome competence, they spent their time in various rural occupations; and the birth of a little girl promised to crown their felicity, and provide them with an object of perpetual interest. On the Halloween following this last event, the parents retired to rest at their usual hour, Mrs M—— having her infant on her arm, so that she might be roused by the slightest uneasiness it might exhibit. From teething or some other ailment, the child, about midnight, became very restless, and not receiving the accustomed attention from its mother, cried so violently as to waken Mr M——. He at once called his wife, and told her the baby was uneasy, but received no answer. He called again more loudly, but still to no purpose; she seemed to be in a heavy uneasy slumber, and when all her husband's attempts to rouse her by calling and shaking proved ineffectual, he was obliged to take the child himself, and try to appease its wailings. After many vain attempts of this sort on his part, the little creature at last sobbed itself to rest, and the mother slept on till a much later hour than her usual time of rising in the morning. When Mr M—— saw that she was awake, he told her of the restlessness of the baby during the night, and how, after having tried in vain every means to rouse her, he had at last been obliged to make an awkward attempt to take her place, and lost thereby some hours of his night's rest. 'I, too,' she replied, 'have passed the most miserable night that I ever experienced; I now see that sleep and rest are two different things, for I never felt so unrefreshed in my life. How I wish you had been able to awake me—it would have spared me some of my fatigue and anxiety! I thought I was dragged against my will into a strange part of the country, where I had never been before, and, after what appeared to me a long and weary journey on foot, I arrived at a comfortable-looking house. I went in longing to rest, but had no power to sit down, although there was a nice supper laid out before a good fire, and every appearance of preparations for an expected visitor. Exhausted as I felt, I was only allowed to stand for a minute or two, and then hurried away by the same road back again; but now it is over, and after all it was only a dream.' Her husband listened with interest to her story, and then sighing deeply, said: 'My dear Sarah, you will not long have me beside you; whoever is to be your second husband played last night some evil trick of which you have been the victim.' Shocked as she felt at this announcement, she endeavoured to suppress her own feelings and rally her husband's spirits, hoping that it would pass from his mind as soon as he had become engrossed by the active business of the day.

Some months passed tranquilly away after this occurrence, and the dream on Halloween night had well-nigh been forgotten by both husband and wife, when Mr M——'s health began to fail. He had never been a robust man, and he now declined so rapidly, that in a short time, notwithstanding all the remedies and attentions that skill could suggest, or affection bestow, his wife was left a mourning widow. Her energetic mind and active habits, however, prevented her from abandoning herself to the desolation of grief. She continued, as her husband had done during his life, to farm the estate, and in this employment, and the education of her little girl, she found ample and salutary occupation. Alike admired and beloved for the judicious management of her worldly affairs, and her true Christian benevolence and kindliness of heart, she might easily, had she been so inclined, have established herself respectably for a second time in life, but such a thought seemed never to cross her mind. She had an uncle, a wise, kind old man, who, living at a distance, often paid a visit to the widow, looked over her farm, and gave her useful advice and assistance. This old gentleman had a neighbour named C——, a prudent young man, who stood very high in his favour. Whenever they met, Mrs M——'s uncle was in the habit of rallying him on the subject of matrimony. On one occasion of this kind, C—— excused himself by saying that it really was not his fault that he was still a bachelor, as he was anxious to settle in life, but had never met with any woman whom he should like to call his wife. 'Well, C——,' replied his old friend, 'you are, I am afraid, a saucy fellow, but if you put yourself into my hands, I do not despair of suiting you.' Some bantering then ensued, and the colloquy terminated by Mrs M——'s uncle inviting the young man to ride over with him next day and visit his niece, whom C—— had never yet seen. The proffer was readily accepted; the two friends started early on the following morning, and after a pleasant ride, were approaching their destination. Here they descried, at a little distance, Mrs M—— retreating towards her house, after making her usual matutinal inspection of her farm. The first glance which Mr C—— obtained of her made him start violently, and the more he looked his agitation increased. Then laying his hand on the arm of his friend, and pointing his finger in the direction of Mrs M——, he said: 'Mr ——, we need not go any further, for if ever I am to be married, there is my wife!' 'Well, C——,' was the reply, 'that is my niece, to whom I am about to introduce you; but tell me,' he added, 'is this what you call love at first sight, or what do you mean by your sudden decision in favour of a person with whom you have never exchanged a word?' 'Why, sir,' replied the young man, 'I find I have betrayed myself, and must now make my confession. A year or two ago, I tried a Halloween-spell, and sat up all night to watch the result. I declare to you most solemnly, that the figure of that lady, as I now see her, entered my room and looked at me. She stood a minute or two by the fire and then disappeared as suddenly as she came. I was wide awake, and felt considerable remorse at having thus ventured to tamper with the powers of the unseen world; but I assure you, that every particular of her features, dress, and figure, have been so present to my mind ever since, that I could not possibly make a mistake, and the moment I saw your niece, I was convinced that she was indeed the woman whose image I beheld on that never-to-be-forgotten Halloween.' The old gentleman, as may be anticipated, was not a little astonished at his friend's statement, but all comments on it were for the time put a stop to by their arrival at Mrs M——'s house. She was glad to see her uncle, and made his friend welcome, performing the duties of hospitality with a simplicity and heartiness that were very attractive to her stranger-guest. After her visitors had refreshed themselves, her uncle walked out with her to look over the farm, and took opportunity, in the absence of Mr C——, to recommend him to the favourable consideration of his niece. To make a long story short, the impression was mutually agreeable. Mr C——, before leaving the house, obtained permission from Mrs M—— to visit her, and after a brief courtship, they were married. They lived long and happily together, and it was from their daughter that our informant derived that remarkable episode in the history of her parents which we have above narrated.

*Born.*—John Evelyn, author of *Sylva*, *Memoirs*, &c., 1620, *Wotton, Surrey*; Pope Clement XIV., 1705; Christopher Anstey, author of *The New Bath Guide*, 1724.

*Died.*—John Palæologus, Greek emperor, 1448; John Bradshaw, presiding judge at trial of Charles I., 1659; Victor Amadeus, first king of Sardinia, 1732; William Augustus, Duke of Cumberland, 1765; Jean Pierre Brissot, distinguished Girondist, guillotined, 1793.

## The Luck of Edenhall.

At Edenhall, the seat of the ancient family of Musgrave, near Penrith, in Cumberland, the curious drinking-cup, figured below, is preserved as one of the most cherished heir-looms. It is composed of very thin glass, ornamented on the outside with a variety of coloured devices, and will hold about an

THE LUCK OF EDENHALL.

English pint. The legend regarding it is, that the butler of the family having gone one night to draw water at the well of St Cuthbert, a copious spring in the garden of the mansion of Edenhall, surprised a group of fairies disporting themselves beside the well, at the margin of which stood the drinking-glass under notice. He seized hold of it, and a struggle for its recovery ensued between him and the fairies. The elves were worsted, and, thereupon took to flight, exclaiming:

> 'If this glass do break or fall,
> Farewell the luck of Edenhall!'

The extreme thinness of the glass rendering it very liable to breakage, was probably the origin of the legend, which has been related of this goblet from time immemorial. Its real history cannot now be ascertained, but from the letters I.H.S. inscribed on the top of the case containing it, it has been surmised to have been originally used as a chalice. In the preceding drawing, fig. 1 represents the glass, fig. 2 its leathern case, and fig. 3 the inscription on the top of the latter.

The wild and hair-brained Duke of Wharton is said, on one occasion, to have nearly destroyed the Luck of Edenhall, by letting it drop from his hands; but the precious vessel was saved by the presence of mind of the butler, who caught it in a napkin. The same nobleman enjoys the credit of having composed a burlesque poem in reference to it, written as a parody on *Chevy Chase*, and which commences thus:

'God prosper long from being broke
The Luck of Edenhall!'

The real author, however, was Lloyd, a boon-companion of the duke. Uhland, the German poet, has also a ballad, *Das Glück von Edenhall*, based on this celebrated legend.

## VISIT OF MARIE DE MEDICI TO ENGLAND.

On the 31st of October 1638, Marie de Medici arrived in the city of London, on a visit to the English court. Though she was received with all the honours due to the queen-dowager of France, and the mother of Henrietta, queen of England, yet both court and people considered the visit ill-timed, and the guest unwelcome. Bishop Laud, in his private diary, noticing her arrival, says that he has 'great apprehensions on this business. For indeed,' he continues, 'the English people hate or suspect her, for the sake of her church, her country, and her daughter; and having shifted her residence in other countries, upon calamities and troubles which still pursue her, they think it her fate to carry misfortunes with her, and so dread her as an ill-boding meteor.'

Daughter of the Grand Duke of Tuscany, Marie de Medici, for mere reasons of state, was married to Henry IV., king of France. Henry gained by her the heir he desired, but her unsociable, haughty, and intractable disposition, rendered his life miserable, and it is still considered a doubtful question, whether she were not privy to the plot which caused his death by assassination in 1610. On this event taking place, she attained the height of her power, in acquiring the regency of France; but fully as feeble-minded as she was ambitious, she suffered herself to be ruled by the most unworthy favourites, and the inevitable results quickly followed. She secured, however, for her service, one person of conduct and abilities, who cannot be passed over without notice. Attracted by the eloquent sermons of a young Parisian ecclesiastic, named Armand de Plessis, Marie appointed him to be her almoner, and afterwards made him principal secretary of state; but this man, better known by his later title of Cardinal Richelieu, was fated to become her evil genius and bitterest enemy. During the seven years in which the regency of Marie de Medici lasted, France was convulsed with broils, cabals, and intrigues. At length her son, Louis XIII., assuming the government, caused his mother's unworthy favourite, the Marshal d'Ancre, to be murdered, and his wife to be tried and executed for the alleged crime of sorcery; the wretched woman to the last asserting, that the influence of a strong mind over a weak one was the only witchcraft she had used.

Marie would have contended against her son in open war, but Richelieu joining the king, and threatening to imprison her for life, she was forced, in 1631, to take refuge at Brussels, where she lived for seven years, supported by a pension from the Spanish court, her daughter Elizabeth being wife of Philip IV. of Spain. Restlessly intriguing, but ever foiled by the superior diplomacy of Richelieu, she fled from Brussels to Holland, greatly to the indignation of Philip, who at once stopped her allowance, refusing even to pay the arrears then due to her. It seems as if the fates had combined to punish this miserable old woman, for, besides the popular commotions excited by her intrigues, disasters not attributable to her presence—namely, pestilence, famine, and war—ever dogged her footsteps. Richelieu would have allowed her a liberal annuity, if she would only return to Italy; but this her pride would not permit her to do; moreover, it would be giving up the field to an enemy and rival, whom she still hoped to overcome. So she begged her son-in-law, Charles I., to receive her in England, a request he, with his usual imprudence, generously granted; for he had been forced, by repeated remonstrances of parliament, a few years previous, to dismiss his own queen's foreign chaplains and servants; and it was not likely that her mother, who brought over a new train, should escape unnoticed. There were, indeed, strong reasons for Laud's forebodings and the people's fears. She had a grand reception, however. Waller, the court-poet, dedicated a poem to her, commencing thus:

'Great Queen of Europe! where thy offspring wears
All the chief crowns; where princes are thy heirs:
As welcome thou to sea-girt Britain's shore,
As erst Latona, who fair Cynthia bore,
To Delos was.'

St James's Palace was given to her as a residence, where she kept a petty court of her own, Charles, it is said, allowing her the large sum of £40,000 per annum. But evil days were at hand. The populace ever regarded her as an enemy, and in the excitement caused by Strafford's trial, she was mobbed and insulted, even in the palace of St James's. She applied to the king for protection, but he, being then nearly powerless, could do no more than refer her to parliament. The Commons allowed her a temporary guard of one hundred men, petitioning the king to send her out of the country; and not ungenerously offering, if she went at once, to vote her £10,000, with an intimation that they might send more to her, if she were well out of England. The question was, where could she go? seeing that no country would receive her. At last having secured a refuge in the free city of Cologne, she left England in August 1641, the Earl of Arundel, at the king's request, accompanying her. Lilly, with a feeling one would scarcely have expected, thus notices her departure. 'I beheld the old queen-mother of France departing from London. A sad spectacle it was, and produced tears from my eyes, and many other beholders, to see an aged, lean, decrepit, poor queen, ready for her grave, necessitated to depart hence, having no place of residence left her, but where the courtesy of her hard fate assigned. She had been the only stately magnificent woman of Europe, wife to the greatest king that ever lived in France, mother unto one king and two queens.'

The misfortunes of this woman attended her to

CHEAPSIDE, WITH THE PROCESSION OF MARIE DE MEDICI ON HER VISIT TO CHARLES I. AND HIS QUEEN. FROM LA SERRES'S 'ENTRÉE ROYALE DE REGNE MERE DU ROI,' 1638.

the last. Her friends, under the circumstances, thought it most advisable to invest the £10,000 given her by parliament in an English estate, and as the civil war broke out immediately after, she never received the slightest benefit from it. She died the year following at Cologne, in a garret, destitute of the common necessaries of life. Chigi, the pope's legate, attended her when dying, and induced her to express forgiveness of Richelieu's ingratitude. But when further pressed to send the cardinal, as a token of complete forgiveness, a valued bracelet, that never was allowed to leave her arm, she muttered: 'It is too much!' turned her face to the wall, and expired.

The illustration representing Marie's public entrance into London is considered peculiarly interesting; the engraving from which it is taken being one of the only two street-views extant of the city previous to the great fire. The scene depicted is about the middle of Cheapside; the cross, which stood near the end of Wood Street, forming a conspicuous feature. This was one of the crosses erected by Edward I., in memory of his beloved queen, Eleanor of Castile. It had been frequently repaired and furbished up for various public occasions. Towards the end of Elizabeth's reign, it received some injuries from the ultra-Protestant party; but these were repaired, the iron railing put round the base (as seen in the engraving) and the upper part gilded, in honour of James I.'s first visit to the city. Those were the last repairs it ever received. After sustaining several petty injuries from the Puritans, the House of Commons decreed that it should be destroyed; and in May 1643, the order was carried into effect amid the shouts of the populace.

The building to the right, eastward of the Cross, represents the Standard, which, with a conduit attached, stood nearly opposite the end of Milk Street. Stow describes it exactly as represented in the engraving—a square pillar, faced with statues, the upper part surrounded by a balcony, and the top crowned with an angel or a figure of Fame, blowing a trumpet. The numerous signs seen in the illustration, exhibit a curious feature of old London. The sign on the right is still a not uncommon one, 'the Nag's Head,' and the bush or garland suspended by it, shews that it was the sign of a tavern. When every house had a sign, and the shop-windows were too small to afford any index of the trade carried on within, publicans found it convenient to exhibit the bush. But when a tavern was well established, and had acquired a name for the quality of its liquors, the garland might be laid aside; for, as the old proverb said, 'Good wine needs no bush.'

Next was November; he full grosse and fat
  As fed with lard, and that right well might seeme;
For he had been a fatting hogs of late,
  That yet his browes with sweat did reek and steem,
  And yet the season was full sharp and breem;
In planting eeke he took no small delight:
  Whereon he rode, not easie was to deeme;
For it a dreadful Centaure was in sight,
The seed of Saturne and fair Nais, Chiron hight.

SPENSER.

(DESCRIPTIVE.)

NOVEMBER WHAT an uproar there is in the old forests and woods when the November winds lift up their mighty voices, and the huge trees clashing together, like the fabled giants battling with knotted clubs against the invisible assailant, whose blows they feel but cannot see struck, so wage war on one another! On every hand we hear the crash and fall of mighty branches, and sometime a large tree torn up by the roots comes down, quick as an avalanche, levelling all it falls upon, where it lies with its blackening leaves above the crushed underwood like some huge mammoth that has perished. The sky is low and gloomy and leaden-coloured, and a disheartening shadow seems to fall on everything around. We see swine rooting in the desolate cornfields, among the black and rotten stubble, while the geese come draggled and dirty from the muddy pond, which is half-choked up with fallen leaves. On the cold naked hedge a few ears, which the birds have long since emptied, hang like funeral-wreaths over the departed harvest. The rain raineth every day on the heps and haws and autumn-berries, and beats the brown seed-vessels of the dead-flowers into the earth, while the decayed leaves come rolling up to make a covering for their graves. In some low-lying dank corner a few blackened bean-sheaves, that never ripened, are left to rot; and if you walk near them, you see the white mould creeping along the gaping pods. There is a deathly smell from slimy water-flags and rotting sedge beside the stagnant meres, and at every step your footprint is filled up with the black oozing of the saturated soil the moment it is made. You see deserted sheds in the fields where the cattle sheltered, rent and blown in; and if you enter one to avoid the down-pouring torrent, the dull gray November sky is seen through the gaping thatch, even in the puddle on the floor where the water has lodged. The morsel of hay in the corner you would fain sit down upon is mouldy, and as you look at the beam which spans across, you fancy some one must have hanged himself on it, and hurry out again into the pouring rain.

November is the pioneer of Winter, who comes, with his sharp winds and keen frosts, to cut down every bladed and leafy bit of green that is standing up, so as to make more room for the coming snow-flakes to fall on the level waste, and form a great bed for Winter to sleep upon. He blows all the decaying leaves into dreary hollows, to fill them up, so that when Winter is out on the long dark nights, or half-blinded with the great feathery flakes, he may not fall into them. If a living flower still stands above its dead companions, it bends its head like a mourner over a grave, and seems calling on our mother-earth to be let in. The swollen streams roar and hurry along, as if they were eager to bury themselves in the great rivers, for they have no flowers to mirror, no singing of birds to tempt them to linger among the pebbles and listen, no green bending sprays to toss to and fro, and play with on their way, and they seem to make a deep complaining as they rush along between the high brimming banks. The few cattle that are out, stand head to head, as if each tried to warm the other with its breath, or turned round to shut out the gloomy prospect that surrounds them, laying down their ears at every whistle of the wind through the naked hedges. Even the clouds, when they break up, have a ragged and vagrant look, and appear to wander homeless about the sky, for there is no golden fire in the far west now for them to gather about, and sun themselves in its warmth: they seem to move along in doubt and fear, as if trying to find the blue sky they have lost. The woodman returns home at night with his head bent down, feeling there is nothing cheerful to look round upon, while his dog keeps close behind, seeming to avail himself of the little shelter his master affords from the wind, while they move on together. The pleasantest thing we see is the bundle or fagots he carries on his shoulders, as it reminds us of home—the crackling fire, the clean-swept hearth, and the cozy-looking kettle, that sits 'singing a quiet tune,' on the hob. We pity the poor fellow with the bundle under his arm, who stands looking up at the guide-post where three roads meet, and hope he has not far to go on such a stormy and moonless night.

But amid all these images of desolation, which strike the eye more vividly through missing the richly-coloured foliage that threw such beauty over the two preceding months, November has still its berries which the early frosts have ripened to perfection. Turn the eye wheresoever we may, during our walks, heps and haws abound on the hawthorn-hedges, and where the wild-roses of summer hang swaying in the wind. The bramble-berries, which cottage-children love to gather, besmearing their pretty faces with the fruit, have now their choicest flavour, and melt in the mouth when eaten, looking like beautiful ornaments carved in jet as they rock in the autumn winds. Many a poor village-housewife brings a smile to the children's faces as she places her blackberry pie or pudding on the table, for it is a fruit that requires but little sugar, and is a cheap luxury added to the usual scanty meal. Then there are the sloes and bullaces, almost always to be found in old hedges, which at this season have a misty blue bloom on them, equal to any that we see on the grape. These the country-people gather and keep sound through all the long winter, and they are equal in flavour to the finest damsons our orchards can produce. Though many varieties of plum-trees have been brought to England at different times, yet it is to the sloe and bullace we are indebted for our serviceable plums, as these shrubs are indigenous, and have been brought to perfection by cultivation through many centuries. The dewberry bears so close a resemblance to the blackberry when ripe, that it is not easy to distinguish the difference. When in flower, it is as beautiful as the blossoms of the wild-rose, the fruit has also a blue bloom on it like the plum, which is never found on the blackberry; the divisions of the berry are also larger, and not so numerous. Often, is seen growing among the ling, the pretty cloudberry, only just overtopping the heather, for it is seldom more than a foot high, and its fruit is of a splendid orange colour when ripe, though rather too acid to please every taste. But of all the little berry-bearing beauties, none beat the bilberry when in bloom, for it is then covered with rosy-coloured wax-like flowers, which few of our choice green-house plants excel, and for which we marvel it has not been more cultivated. Birds are partial to this berry, which bears a grape-like bloom, and game fed upon it is said to be as superior in flavour as mutton, fed on pastures abounding in wild-thyme, is to that fattened only on grass. But the fairy of our shrubs—which may rank with the harvest-mouse among animals, and the humming-birds among the feathered race—is the tiny cranberry, which you must bend the back to find, as it only grows three or four inches high. Whether our grandmother had some secret art of preserving these delicious berries, which is now lost—or the fruit has deteriorated in flavour—we cannot tell, but somehow we fancy that cranberries have not the delicious taste now which they had in our boyish days.

The most wonderful plant that bears berries, is the butcher's broom, which may be seen covered with fruit as large as cherries, in the very depth of winter. Both flower and berry grow out of the very middle of the leaf, and it would make a pleasant change in our Christmas decoration, as it is an evergreen, and quite as beautiful as the holly. The black berries of the privet remain on the branches all winter long, and are found there when the sprays are covered with the fresh green leaves of spring. These berries are much harder than our heps and haws, and retain their fulness when all the other hedge-fruits are withered and tasteless, though the birds generally seem to leave them till the last, as if they only ate them when nothing else could be got. They make a grand show with their large clusters amid the nakedness of winter, though almost failing to attract the eye now if seen beside the wild-cornel or dogwood-berries. Autumn has nothing more beautiful than the wild-cornel, with its deep-purple berries hanging on rich red-coloured branches, and surrounded with golden, green, and crimson foliage, as if all the richest hues of autumn were massed together to beautify it, and wreath the black purple of the berries. Another tree, which scarcely arrests the eye in summer, now makes a splendid show, for the seed-vessels appear like roses, the capsules separating like the petals of the Queen of Flowers, for such is the appearance of the spindle-tree. The woody nightshade, whose purple petals and deep golden anthers enriched the hedgerow a few weeks ago, is now covered with clusters of scarlet berries, not unlike our red garden currants; while both the foliage and berries of the guelder-rose seem kindled into a red blaze. But the bird-cherry is the chameleon of shrubs in autumn, its bunches of rich-looking fruit changing from a beautiful green to a rich red, and then to the colour of the darkest of black-heart cherries, and looking equally as luscious to the eye, though it would be dangerous to eat so many as we might of the real cherries without harm. Beside all these, and many other beautiful berries, we have now the ferns all ablaze with beauty—vegetable relics of an old world—and many of them as pleasing to the eye as our choicest flowers. Where is there a grander sight than a long moorland covered with bracken at the close of autumn?—the foliage of the trees is not to be compared with that outspread land of crimson and gold. And there is such a forest smell about it too—that real country aroma, which we get a sniff of in villages where they have only wood-fires—for there is nothing else to compare with the smell of fern where it covers long leagues of wild moorland.

Many little animals are busy, during the autumn, in laying up stores for winter; for though some of them sleep away the greater portion of the cold season, a change in the weather often causes them to awaken, when they have recourse to the provision they have saved; and as soon as the mild warm weather is again succeeded by cold, they coil themselves up, and sleep again. The hibernation of the squirrel is shorter than that of any of our winter-sleeping animals, for he is up and away as soon as he is awakened by a mild atmosphere, and as he has generally more than one larder, enjoys himself until slumber again overtakes him; for we can imagine, from his active habits, that he is not likely to remain in his nest while there is a glimpse of warm sunshine to play in. The hedgehog is a sound sleeper, and stores up no provision, though its hibernation is sometimes broken during a very mild winter, when it may at times be found in the night, searching for food under the sheltered hedges. The pretty dormouse coils itself up like a ball of twine in its winter-nest, curling the tail round the head to the other side of its back, as if tying itself together before going to sleep. Should it awake, there is store of food at hand, which it holds in its forepaws like the squirrel, while sitting up to munch an acorn, hep, or haw, or whatever is stored up, and it is a great hoarder of various kinds of seeds. But few of these torpid animals store their granaries better than the long-tailed field-mouse; considering its smallness, the quantity of corn that has been found in a single nest is amazing. Even if we reckon it to have carried from the harvest-field a full ripe ear at a time, it must have made many journeys to accumulate so much food. Nothing seems to come amiss to it, for if there has been no cornfield at hand, its hoard has been found to consist of nuts, and acorns, gathered from the neighbouring wood, which has sometimes been five or six hundred yards from its nest. Above five hundred nuts and acorns have been taken out of its storehouse; and as it can hardly be supposed that so small an animal could carry more than one at a time, we have proof of its industry in the hoard it must have laboured so hard to get together. One might suppose that, early in autumn, when the weather is fine, these little animals would give themselves up to enjoyment, instead of carrying the many loads they do to their nests, did we not find proof to the contrary. The ant lays up no store at all, though it has so often supplied an image of industry in poetry. It is not only one of the sleepiest of insects in winter, but when applied as chloroform, soon steeps the senses in forgetfulness. The ancient Greeks were acquainted with its drowsy properties, and availed themselves of it. Some naturalists say that the hibernating animals we have glanced at, spread out their provisions in the sun to dry and ripen before carrying them into their nests. That this may be the case, we can hardly doubt, having seen ears of corn, nuts, acorns, and seeds, about the roots of trees, at a considerable distance from the spots where they were grown, and in such positions as they could not have fallen into, even had they been shaken down by the wind. The foresight of these hibernating mammals is proved through their laying up provision against the time they may awaken, long weeks before they retire to their winter-sleep. Nor is it less wonderful to note the going out and coming in of the migrating-birds in autumn; for though all our songsters that are migratory have long since gone, we now hear the screaming of coming flocks in the still night—the clamour of voices high overhead, which is sometimes startling in the star-lighted silence. Most of our aquatic birds land in the night, though long strings of wild-geese are often seen forming a V-like figure in the air, as they wing their way to our fenny and marshy lands in the daytime. If flying low enough, the leader of the van, forming the point of V or Λ, who seems to cleave the air, to make a passage for his followers, will be seen after a time to fall into the rear, when another bird takes his place, until he in time also falls back, as if through fatigue; nor can there be any doubt that the leader, who first pierces the air, through which the whole flock passes, has to exert himself more than his followers. Though the heron may now and then be seen, standing as motionless as if sculptured in marble, at some bend of a river or stream, it is now rather a scarce bird, for there are not more than four or five heronries in England, in which they build and breed close together like rooks. The heron shifts from place to place in search of food, but, like several other of our birds, is not migratory, though it may be seen in some parts of our island at this season, where it rarely appears during any other portion of the year. It flies very high, and in dull weather may often be heard, while on the wing, far beyond the reach of the eye. At first there appears something strange and mysterious in birds coming over to winter with us, and migrating again at the first appearance of spring, and never, or very rarely, staying to breed with us. One of our celebrated naturalists argues that the sun is the great moving-power; that they are again forced northward in spring by the same impulse which brings back again our summer singing-birds; 'all seeking again those spots where they first saw the light, there to rear their young;' and that a failure of temperature and food causes them to follow the sun in autumn. Some think that from the time a bird remains with us, a calculation might be made as to the distance it goes after leaving our shores; that, because some remain a month or so longer with us than others, they do not fly so far away as those which migrate earlier. But the rapidity of the flight of a bird, and its power of remaining on the wing, are objects of consideration; and though the swallow is among the last to leave us, it would fly treble the distance in a few hours than many other birds that leave us earlier, and have neither its strength nor stretch of wing to carry them a great distance. As to the time of departure or arrival of our passenger-birds, that must always depend upon the state of the season at the point of departure; for, as we have before remarked, they can know nothing of the backwardness or forwardness of the autumn or spring in the countries they visit, no more than they can tell before they arrive here whether our April is green, or has had all its buds bitten off by a killing frost, such as we well remember to have seen. Take the dates of the departures and arrivals of our birds from the calendars of some of the most celebrated English naturalists, and they will be found to vary at times a month or more in different years, especially the arrivals. A summer abounding in insect-food will cause birds to leave us earlier, after a forward spring, because their young were sooner hatched, and are stronger and better able to accompany their parents than they would have been had they left the shell later, and been pinched while fed by the parent-birds, through a scarcity of food. The sky-lark, which has long been silent, may now be heard in open sunny places; and we find, from a note made four years ago, that we heard it singing on the downs in Surrey in December.

The poetry of home, which we carry with us unconsciously whithersoever we go, was never more beautifully illustrated than in the poor emigrant's sky-lark, which he carried with him when he left this country for America. Crowds of English settlers used to collect round his hut to hear it sing, and one of them offered all he had in the world—his horse and cart—for the bird, but the owner refused to part with it. We are indebted to the Rev. J. G. Wood for this anecdote, which shews how the hearts of the rudest class of men are touched at times by some trifle which brings back again home with all its old boughs rustling before the 'inward eye.' No matter in what form it appears, but anything which causes us to turn to nature with an affectionate feeling, elevates both mind and heart, inspires love, and makes us better, for we can hardly do so without catching some glimpse of the Great Creator, which carries the mind far beyond the objects that surround us, to the thoughts of those higher destinies which the soul is heir to, and may be ours if we do not sell our godlike birthright.

By the end of this month our gardens look desolate. The few chrysanthemums that have survived have a draggled and dirty look after the frost and rain, and nothing out of doors, excepting the evergreens, remind us of the green flush of departed summer. There is the tapping of rain on our windows, and the roaring of the wind through the long dark nights. The country-roads are soft, and we stick in the mire at every step if we traverse those rutted lanes, which were so delightful to walk along only a few short weeks ago. Even the heart of a brave man beats quicker, who, after passing a treeless and houseless moor, hears the rattling of the bones and irons of the murderer on the gibbet-post, as he turns to enter the high dark wood, which, when he has groped through, still leaves him a long league from the solitary toll-gate—the only habitable spot he will pass before reaching home. For now, in the solemn language of the Holy Bible, we have many a day 'of darkness and of gloominess, of clouds and of thick darkness, even very dark, and no brightness in it, for the land is darkened.'

(HISTORICAL.)

November was styled by the ancient Saxons *Wint-monat*, or the *wind-month*, from the gales of wind which are so prevalent at this season of the year, obliging our Scandinavian ancestors to lay up their keels on shore, and refrain from exposing themselves on the ocean till the advent of more genial weather in the ensuing year. It bore also the name of *Blot-monath*, or the *bloody-month*, from the circumstance of its being customary then to slaughter great numbers of cattle, to be salted for winter use. The epithet had possibly also reference to the sacrificial rites practised at this time.

### CHARACTERISTICS OF NOVEMBER.

On the 22d of this month, the sun enters the sign of *Sagittarius* or *The Archer*, an emblem said to express the growing predominance of cold which now *shoots* into the substance of the earth, and suspends the vegetative powers of nature. The average temperature of the British Islands for the middle of November is about 43°. On the 1st of the month, the sun rises in the latitude of London at 7.11, and sets at 4.49.

November is generally regarded as the gloomiest month of the year, and it is perhaps true that less enjoyment is derivable in it from external objects than in any other of the twelve divisions of the calendar. It is popularly regarded as the month of blue devils and suicides. Leaden skies, choking fogs—more especially in London—and torrents of rain, combined frequently with heavy gusts of wind, which shake down the last remaining leaves from the trees, are phenomena of normal occurrence in November, and certainly by no means conducive to buoyancy and cheerfulness of spirits. Summer and autumn, with their exhilarating influences, have fairly departed, and winter, in its gloomiest phases, is approaching, whilst the hilarity and joyousness of the Christmas-season are still far off. The *negative* character of November, as exemplified in a foggy day of that month in London, is very happily depicted in the following lines, by the prince of modern humorists, Thomas Hood—

'No sun—no moon!
No morn—no noon—
No dawn—no dusk—no proper time of day—
No sky—no earthly view—
No distance looking blue—
No road—no street—no "t'other side the way"—
No end to any row—
No indications where the crescents go—
No top to any steeple—
No recognitions of familiar people—
No courtesies for shewing 'em—
No knowing 'em!
No travelling at all—no locomotion,
No inkling of the way—no notion—
"No go"—by land or ocean—
No mail—no post—
No news from any foreign coast—
No park—no ring—no afternoon gentility—
No company—no nobility—
No warmth, no cheerfulness, no healthful ease—
No comfortable feel in any member—
No shade, no shine, no butterflies, no bees,
No fruits, no flowers, no leaves, no birds,
November!'

# First of November.

The Festival of All-Saints. St Benignus, apostle of Burgundy, martyr, 3d century. St Austremonius, 3d century. St Cæsarius, martyr, 300. St Mary, martyr, 4th century. St Marcellus, bishop of Paris, confessor, beginning of 5th century. St Harold, king of Denmark, martyr, 980.

## All-Saints-Day.

This festival takes its origin from the conversion, in the seventh century, of the Pantheon at Rome into a Christian place of worship, and its dedication by Pope Boniface IV. to the Virgin and all the martyrs. The anniversary of this event was at first celebrated on the 1st of May, but the day was subsequently altered to the 1st of November, which was thenceforth, under the designation of the Feast of All Saints, set apart as a general commemoration in their honour. The festival has been retained by the Anglican Church.

*Born.*—Benvenuto Cellini, celebrated silversmith and sculptor in metal, 1500, *Florence;* Denzil Hollis, reforming patriot, 1597, *Haughton, Northamptonshire;* Sir Matthew Hale, eminent judge, 1609, *Alderley, Gloucestershire;* Nicolas Boileau, poetical satirist, 1636, *France;* Bishop George Horne, biblical expositor, 1730, *Otham, near Maidstone;* Lydia Huntley Sigourney, American poet, 1791, *Norwich, United States.*

*Died.*—Charles II. of Spain, 1700; Dr John Radcliffe, founder of the Radcliffe Library, Oxford, 1714; Dean Humphrey Prideaux, author of *Connection of the History of the Old and New Testament*, 1724, *Norwich;* Louisa de Kerouaille, Duchess of Portsmouth, mistress of Charles II., 1734; Alexander Cruden, author of the *Concordance*, 1770, *Islington;* Edward Shuter, comedian, 1776; Lord George Gordon, originator of the No-Popery Riots of 1780, 1793, *Newgate, London.*

## SIR MATTHEW HALE: DRINKING OF HEALTHS.

The illustrious chief-justice left an injunction or advice for his grandchildren in the following terms: 'I will not have you begin or pledge any health, for it is become one of the greatest artifices of drinking, and occasions of quarrelling in the kingdom. If you pledge one health, you oblige yourself to pledge another, and a third, and so onwards; and if you pledge as many as will be drank, you must be debauched and drunk. If they will needs know the reason of your refusal, it is a fair answer: "That your grandfather that brought you up, from whom, under God, you have the estate you enjoy or expect, left this in command with you, that you should never begin or pledge a health."'

Sir Matthew might well condemn health-drinking, for in his days it was used, or rather abused, for the encouragement of excesses at which all virtuous people must have been appalled. The custom has, however, a foundation and a sanction in the social feelings, and consequently, though it has had many ups and downs, it has always hitherto, in one form or another, maintained its ground. As far back as we can go amongst our ancestors, we find it established. And, notwithstanding the frowns of refinement on the one hand, and tee-totalism on the other, we undoubtedly see it occasionally practised.

Among the earliest instances of the custom may be cited the somewhat familiar one of the health, said to have been drunk by Rowena to Vortigern, and which is described by Verstegan after this fashion: 'She came into the room where the king and his guests were sitting, and making a low obedience to him, she said: "*Waes heal, hlaford Cyning.*" (Be of health, Lord King). Then, having drunk, she presented it [the cup] on her knees to the king, who, being told the meaning of what she said, together with the custom, took the cup, saying: "*Drink heal*" [Drink health], and drank also.'

William of Malmesbury adverts to the custom thus: 'It is said it first took its rise from the death of young King Edward (called the Martyr), son to Edgar, who was, by the contrivance of Elfrida, his step-mother, traitorously stabbed in the back as he was drinking.' The following curious old delineation, from the Cotton Manuscript, seems to agree with the reported custom. The centre figure appears to be addressing himself to his companion, who tells him that he pledges him, holding up his knife in token of his readiness to assist and protect him:

PLEDGING HEALTHS—NO. 1.

In another illustration of the same period, the custom of individuals pledging each other on convivial occasions is more prominently represented:

PLEDGING HEALTHS—NO. 2.

The following account of a curious custom in connection with the drinking of healths, is from a contribution to *Notes and Queries*, by a Lichfield correspondent, who says, that in that ancient city, it has been observed from time immemorial, at dinners given by the mayor, or at any public feast of the corporation. The first two toasts given are 'The Queen,' and 'Weale and worship,' both which are drunk out of a massive embossed silver cup, holding three or four quarts, presented to the corporation in 1666, by the celebrated Elias Ashmole, a native of the city. The ceremony itself is by the same writer thus more particularly described: 'The mayor drinks first, and on his rising, the persons on his right and left also rise. He then hands the cup to the person on his right side, when the one next to him rises, the one on the left of the mayor still standing. Then the cup is passed across the table to him, when *his* left-hand neighbour rises; so that there are always three standing at the same time—one next to the person who drinks, and one opposite to him.' From the curious old letter of thanks for this cup we quote the following lines: 'Now, sir, give us leave to conclude by informing you that, according to your desire (upon the first receipt of your *Poculum Charitatis*, at the sign of the *George for England*), we filled it with Catholic wine, and devoted it a sober health to our most gracious king, which (being of so large a continent) pass the hands of thirty to pledge; nor did we forget yourself in the next place, being our great *Mecœnas*.' This letter of thanks is dated, 'Litchfield, 26th January 1666.' The whole of the original letter appears in *Harwood's Lichfield*.

The custom as practised in the passing of the

renowned 'loving-cup,' at the lord mayor's feasts in London, is too well known to require further notice. Another writer in *Notes and Queries* says, that the same observance always had place at the parish meetings, and churchwardens' dinners, at St Margaret's, Westminster: the cover of the loving-cup being held over the head of the person drinking by his neighbours on his right and left hand.'

It appears from *Barrington's Observations on the Ancient Statutes* (1766), that the custom prevailed at Queen's College, Oxford, where the scholars who wait upon their fellows place their *two thumbs* on the table. The writer adds: 'I have heard that the same ceremony is used in some parts of Germany, whilst the superior drinks the health of the inferior. The inferior, during this, places his two thumbs on the table, and therefore is incapacitated from making any attempt upon the life of the person who is drinking.' The writer on the Lichfield custom also adverts to this, by the by, when he says that, 'he presumes that though the ceremony is different, the object is the same as that at Queen's College—viz., to prevent injury to the person who drinks.'

The practice would appear to have had its origin at the time when the Danes bore sway in this country. Indeed, some authors deduce the expression, 'I'll pledge you,' in drinking, from this period. It seems that the Northmen, in those days, would occasionally stab a person while in the act of drinking. In consequence, people would not drink in company, unless some one present would be their pledge, or surety, that they should come to no harm whilst thus engaged. Nay, at one time, the people became so intimidated that they would not dare to drink until the Danes had actually pledged their honour for their safety!

In Beaumont and Fletcher's days, it was the custom for the young gallants to stab themselves in their arms, or elsewhere, in order to 'drink the healths' of their mistresses, or to write their names in their own blood! The following passage occurs in Pepys's *Diary* relative to 'health-drinking:' 'To the Rhenish wine-house, where Mr Moore shewed us the French manner, when a health is drunk, to bow to him that drunk to you, and then apply yourself to him, whose lady's health is drunk, and then to the person that you drink to, which I never knew before: but it seems it is now the fashion.'

The following remarkable and solemn passage is found in *Ward's Living Speeches of Dying Christians* (in his Sermons): 'My Saviour began to mee in a bitter cup; and *shall I not pledge him?* i. e., drink the same.'

Records of the custom in many countries, and in many ages, might be multiplied *ad infinitum*. It is beyond our present purpose, however, to give any further illustrations, beyond the following curious extract from *Rich's Irish Hvbbvb, or the English Hve and Crie* (1617). After a long and wholesome, though severe, tirade against drunkenness, the quaint old writer says: 'In former ages, they had no conceits whereby to draw on drunkennes; their best was, I drinke to you, and I pledge yee; till at length some shallow-witted drunkard found out the carouse, which shortly after was turned into a hearty draught: but now it is ingined [enjoined] to the drinking of a health, an invention of that worth and worthinesse, as it is pitty the first founder was not hanged, that wee might haue found out his name in the ancient record of the Hangman's Register! The institution in drinking of a health is full of ceremonie, and obserued by tradition, as the papists doe their praying to saints.' The singular writer then adds this description of the performance of the custom: 'He that begins the health, hath his prescribed orders; first vncouering his head, he takes a full cup in his hand, and setling his countenance with a graue aspect, he craues for audience. Silence being once obtained, hee begins to breath out the name, peraduenture of some honorable personage that is worthy of a better regard than to have his name pollvted at so vnfitting a time, amongst a company of drunkards; but his health is drunke to, and hee that pledgeth must likewise of [off] with his cap, kisse his fingers, and bowing himselfe in signe of a reuerent acceptance. When the leader sees his follower thus prepared, he soupes [sups] up his broath, turnes the bottom of the cuppe vpward, and in ostentation of his dexteritie, giues the cup a phylip [fillip], to make it cry *tynge* [a sort of ringing sound, denoting that the vessel was emptied of its contents]. And thus the first scene is acted.—The cup being newly replenished to the breadth of a haire, he that is the pledger must now begin his part, and thus it goes round throughout the whole company, prouided alwaies by a canon set downe by the first founder, there must be three at the least still vncouered, till the health hath had the full passage; which is no sooner ended, but another begins againe, and he drinkes a health to his *Lady of little worth*, or, peraduenture, to his *Light-heel'd mistris*.'

The caustic old writer just referred to, adds the following remarks in a marginal note: 'He that first inuented that vse of drinking healths, had his braines beat out with a pottle-pot: a most iust end for inventers of such notorious abuses. And many in pledging of healths haue ended their liues presently [early], as example lately in London.'

A few notices may be appended of the anathemas which have been hurled at the custom of drinking healths. The first of these is a singular tract published in 1628, 'by *William Prynne, Gent.*, proving the drinking and pledging of Healths to be sinful, and utterly unlawful unto Christians.' At the Restoration, this work had become scarce, and 'it was judged meet that Mr William Prynne's notable book should be reprinted, few of them being to be had for money.' The loyalty of the English to Charles II., was shewn by such a frequency of drinking his health, as to threaten to disturb the public peace, and occasion a royal proclamation, an extract from which is subjoined.

'C. R.

Our dislike of those, who under pretence of affection to us, and our service, assums to themselves a Liberty of Reviling, Threatning, and Reproaching of others. There are likewise another sort of men, of whom we have heard much, and are sufficiently ashamed, who spend their time in Taverns, Tipling-houses, and Debauches, giving no other evidence of their affection to us, but in *Drinking* our HEALTH.'

The following is from a work published about this period:

'*Of Healths drinking, and Heaven's doom thereon: Part of a Letter from* Mr Ab. Ramsbotham.

'Within four or five miles of my house, the first of *July* (as I take it), at a town called *Geslingham*,* there were three or four persons in a shopkeeper's house, drinking of *Strong waters*, and of HEALTHS, as 'tis spoken. And all of a sudden there came a flame of fire down the chimney with a great crack, as of thunder, or of a canon, or granado; which for the present struck the men as dead.

'But afterwards they recovered; and one of them was, as it were, shot in the knee, and so up his Breeches and Doublet to his shoulder; and there it brake out, and split and brake in pieces the window, and set the house on fire; the greater part of which burned down to the ground.

'This hath filled the Country with wonder, and many speak their judgements both on it, and of the persons. ABR. RAMSBOTHAM.'

* Probably Gislingham, in Suffolk.

## DR RADCLIFFE.

John Radcliffe, whose name is perpetuated in so many memorials of his munificence, was born at Wakefield, in Yorkshire, February 7, 1650, and educated in the university of Oxford, where he studied medicine. His books were so few in number, that on being asked where was his library, he pointed to a few vials, a skeleton, and a herbal, in one corner of his room, and exclaimed, with emphasis: 'There, sir, is Radcliffe's library!' In 1675, he took his degree of M.B., and began to practise in Oxford, where, by some happy cures (especially by his cooling treatment of the small-pox), he soon acquired a great reputation. In 1682, he took the degree of M.D., and went out a Grand Compounder; an imposing ceremony in those days, and for a century afterwards, all the members of the college walking in procession, with the candidate himself, bareheaded, to the Convocation House. Radcliffe now removed to London, and settled in Bow Street, Covent Garden, where he soon received daily, in fees, the sum of twenty guineas, through his vigorous and decisive method of practice, as well as his pleasantry and ready wit—many, it is said, even feigning themselves ill, for the pleasure of having a few minutes' conversation with the facetious doctor. The garden in the rear of his house, in Bow Street, extended to the garden of Sir Godfrey Kneller, who resided in the Piazza, Covent Garden. Kneller was fond of flowers, and had a fine collection. As he was intimate with the physician, he permitted the latter to have a door into his garden; but Radcliffe's servants gathering and destroying the flowers, Kneller sent him notice that he must shut up the door. Radcliffe replied peevishly: 'Tell him he may do anything with it but paint it.' 'And I,' answered Sir Godfrey, 'can take anything from him but physic.'

Radcliffe shewed great sagacity in resisting the entreaties of the court-chaplains to change his religion and turn papist; and when the Prince of Orange was invited over, Radcliffe took care that no imputation of guilt could, by any possibility, attach to him afterwards, had the Revolution not succeeded. He had, two years previously, been appointed physician to the Princess Anne; and when King William came, Radcliffe got the start of his majesty's physicians, by curing two of his favourite foreign attendants; for which the king gave him five hundred guineas out of the privy-purse. But Radcliffe declined the appointment of one of his majesty's physicians, considering that the settlement of the crown was then but insecure. He nevertheless attended the king, and for the first eleven years of his reign, received more than 600 guineas annually. In 1689, he succeeded in restoring William sufficiently to enable him to join his army in Ireland, and gain the victory of the Boyne. In 1691, when the young Prince William, Duke of Gloucester, was taken ill of fainting fits, and his life was despaired of, Radcliffe was sent for, and restored the little patient, for which Queen Mary ordered her chamberlain to present him with a thousand guineas. He was now the great physician of the day; and his neighbour, Dr Gibbons, received £1000 per annum from the overflow of patients who were not able to get admission to Radcliffe.

In 1692, he sustained a severe pecuniary loss. He was persuaded by his friend Betterton, the famous tragedian, to risk £5000 in a venture to the East Indies; the ship was captured by the enemy, with her cargo, worth £120,000. This ruined the poor player; but Radcliffe received the disastrous intelligence at the Bull's Head Tavern, in Clare Market (where he was enjoying himself with several persons of rank), with philosophic composure; desiring his companions not to interrupt the circulation of the glass, for that 'he had no more to do but go up so many pair of stairs, to make himself whole again.'

Towards the end of 1694, Queen Mary was seized with small-pox, and the symptoms were most alarming; her majesty's physicians were at their wits' end, and the privy-council sent for Radcliffe. At the first sight of the prescriptions, he rudely exclaimed, that 'her majesty was a dead woman, for it was impossible to do any good in her case, where remedies were given that were so contrary to the nature of the distemper; yet he would endeavour to do all that lay in him to give her ease.' There were some faint hopes for a time, but the queen died. Some few months after, Radcliffe's attendance was requested by the Princess Anne. He had been drinking freely, and promised speedily to come to St James's; the princess grew worse, and a messenger was again despatched to Radcliffe, who, on hearing the symptoms detailed, swore by his Maker, 'that her highness' distemper was nothing but the vapours, and that she was in as good a state of health as any woman breathing, could she but believe it.' No skill or reputation could excuse this rudeness and levity; and he was, in consequence, dismissed. But his credit remained with the king, who sent him abroad to attend the Earl of Albemarle, who had a considerable command in the army; Radcliffe remained in the camp only a week, succeeded in the treatment of his patient, and received from King William £1200, and from Lord Albemarle 400 guineas and a diamond ring. In 1697, after the king's return from Loo, being much indisposed at Kensington Palace, he sent for Radcliffe; the symptoms were dropsical, when the physician, in his odd way, promised to try to lengthen the king's days, if he would forbear making long visits to the Earl of Bradford, with whom the king was wont to drink very hard. Radcliffe left behind him a recipe, by following which the king was enabled to go abroad, to his palace at Loo, in Holland.

In 1699, the Duke of Gloucester, heir-presumptive to the crown, was taken ill, when his mother, the Princess Anne, notwithstanding her antipathy, sent for Radcliffe, who pronounced the case hopeless, and abused the two other physicians, telling them that 'it would have been happy for this nation had the first been bred up a basket-maker (which was his father's occupation), and the last continued making a havock of nouns and pronouns, in the quality of a country schoolmaster, rather than have ventured out of his reach, in the practice of an art which he was an utter stranger to, and for which he ought to have been whipped with one of his own rods.'

At the close of this year, the king, on his return from Holland, where he had not been abstemious, being much out of health, again sent for Radcliffe to Kensington Palace; when his majesty, shewing his swollen ankles, exclaimed: 'Doctor, what think you of these?' 'Why, truly,' said Radcliffe, 'I would not have your majesty's two legs for your three kingdoms.' With this ill-timed jest, though it passed unnoticed at the moment, his professional attendance at court terminated.

Anne sent again for Radcliffe in the dangerous illness of her husband, Prince George. His disease was dropsy, and the doctor, unused to flatter, declared that 'the prince had been so tampered with, that nothing in the art of physic could keep him alive more than six days'—and his prediction was verified.

When, in July 1714, Queen Anne was seized with the sickness which terminated her life, Radcliffe was sent for; but he was confined by a fit of gout to his house at Carshalton. He was accused of refusing to give his professional advice to his sovereign, and in consequence of this report, durst scarcely venture out of doors, as he was threatened with being pulled to pieces if ever he came to London.

Radcliffe died November 1, 1714, 'a victim to the ingratitude of a thankless world, and the fury of the gout.' By his will he left his Yorkshire estate to University College, Oxford, and £5000 for enlargement of the building; to St Bartholomew's Hospital, the yearly sum of £500 towards mending their diet, and £100 yearly for the buying of linen; and £40,000 for the building of a library at Oxford, besides £150 a year for the librarian's salary, £100 a year for the purchase of books, and another £100 for repairs. The smallness of the annual sum provided for the purchase of books is remarkable, and gave occasion to the animadversion, that the main object of the testator was to erect a splendid monument to himself. The bulk of the remainder of his property he left in trust for charitable purposes. The Radcliffe Library is one of the noblest architectural adornments of Oxford. It was designed by Gibbs, and is built on a circular plan, with a spacious dome. It was originally called the Physic Library, and the books which it contains are principally confined to works on medicine and natural science.

## ALEXANDER CRUDEN.

This persevering and painstaking compiler, who was appointed by Sir Robert Walpole bookseller to the queen of George II., died at his lodgings in Camden Street, Islington, November 1, 1770. The Concordance, which has conferred celebrity on his name, was published and dedicated to Queen Caroline in 1737. He was permitted to present a copy of it in person to her majesty, who, he said, smiled upon him, and assured him she was highly obliged to him. The expectations he formed of receiving a solid proof of the queen's appreciation of the work, were disappointed by her sudden death within sixteen days of his reception. Twenty-four years afterwards, he revised a second edition, and dedicated it to her grandson, George III. For this, and a third edition issued in 1769, his booksellers gave him £800.

He was often prominently before the public as a very eccentric enthusiast. Three times, during his life, he was placed in confinement by his friends. On the second of these occasions, he managed to escape from a private lunatic asylum in which he was chained to his bedstead; when he immediately brought actions against the proprietor and physician. Unfortunately for his case, he stated it himself, and lost it. On his third release, he brought an action against his sister, from whom he claimed damages to the amount of £10,000, for authorising his detention. In this suit also he was unsuccessful. In the course of his life, he met with many rebuffs in the prosecution of projects in which he restlessly embarked, as he considered, for the public good; for all of which he solaced himself with printing accounts of his motives, treatment, and disappointments.

One of his eccentricities consisted in the assumption of the title of *Alexander the Corrector*. In the capacity implied by this term, he stopped persons whom he met in public places on Sundays, and admonished them to go home and keep the Sabbath-day holy; and in many other ways addressed himself to the improvement of the public morals. He spent much of his earnings in the purchase of tracts and catechisms, which he distributed right and left; and gave away some thousands of hand-bills, on which were printed the fourth commandment. To enlarge, as he thought, his sphere of usefulness, he sighed for a recognition of his mission in high-places; and, to attain this end, succeeded, after considerable solicitation, in obtaining the signatures of several persons of rank to a testimonial of his zeal for the public good. Armed with this credential, he urged that the king in council, or an act of legislature, should formally constitute him *Corrector of Morals*. However, his chimerical application was not entertained.

Another eccentricity arose out of the decided part he took against Mr Wilkes, when that demagogue agitated the kingdom. He partly expressed his intense feeling in his usual mode—by pamphlet; but more especially evinced his aversion by effacing the offensive numeral No. 45, wherever he found it chalked up. For this purpose, he carried in his pockets a large piece of sponge. He subsequently included in this obliteration all the obscene inscriptions with which idle persons were permitted at that time to disgrace blank walls in the metropolis. This occupation, says his biographer Blackburn, from its retrospective character, made his walks very tedious.

His erratic benevolence prompted him to visit the prisoners in Newgate daily, instruct them in the teachings of the gospel, and encourage them to pay attention, by gifts of money to the most diligent. This good work he was, however, induced to relinquish, by finding that his hardened pupils, directly he had turned his back, spent these sums in intoxicating liquors. While so engaged, he was able to prevail upon Lord Halifax to commute a sentence of death against Richard Potter, found guilty of uttering a forged will, to one of transportation.

Still animated with a desire to regenerate the national morals, he besought the honour of knighthood—not, he declared, for the value of the title, but from a conviction that that dignity would give his voice more weight. In pursuit of the desired distinction, he seems to have given a great deal of trouble to the lords in waiting and secretaries of state, and probably exceeded the bounds of their patience, for, in a commendation of Earl Paulett, he admits that less-afflicted noblemen got quit of his importunities by flight. This earl, he says, in an account of his attendance at court, 'being goutish in his feet, could not run away from the Corrector as others were apt to do.' In 1754, he offered himself as a candidate to represent the city of London in parliament. In this contest, he issued the most singular addresses, referring the sheriffs, candidates, and liverymen to consider his letters and advertisements published for some time past, and especially the appendix to *Alexander the Corrector's Adventures*. 'If there is just ground to think that God will be pleased to make the Corrector an instrument to reform the nation, and particularly to promote the reformation, the peace, and prosperity of this great city, and to bring them into a more religious temper and conduct, no good man, in such an extraordinary case, will deny him his vote. And the Corrector's election is believed to be the means of paving the way to his being a Joseph, and an useful and prosperous man.' He also presented his possible election in the light of the fulfilment of a prophecy. But the be-wigged, and buttoned, and knee-breeched, and low-shoed electors only laughed at him. He consoled himself for the disappointment with which this new effort was attended, as in former ones, by issuing a pamphlet.

The most singular of Cruden's pamphlets detailed his love adventures. He became enamoured of Miss Elizabeth Abney. The father of this lady, Sir Thomas Abney, was a successful merchant, who was successively sheriff, alderman, lord mayor of London, and one of the representatives of the city in parliament. He was a person of considerable consequence, having been one of the founders of the Bank of England, of which he was for many years a director; but his memory is especially honoured from the fact of its being interwoven with that of Dr Watts, who resided with him at Stoke-Newington. His daughter inherited a large fortune; and to become possessed of both, became the Corrector's sanguine expectation. Miss Abney was deaf to his entreaties. For months he pestered her with calls, and persecuted her with letters, memorials, and remonstrances. When she left home, he caused 'praying-bills' to be distributed in various places of worship, requesting the prayers of the minister and congregation for her preservation and safe return; and when this took place, he issued further bills to the same congregations to return thanks. Finding these peculiar attentions did not produce the desired effect, he drew up a long paper, which he called a Declaration of War, in which he declared he should compass her surrender, by 'shooting off great numbers of bullets from his camp; namely, by earnest prayer to Heaven day and night, that her mind might be enlightened and her heart softened.' His grotesque courtship ended in defeat: the lady never relented.

The precision and concentration of thought required in his literary labours, the compilation and several revisings of his *Concordance*, his verbal index of Milton's works, his *Dictionary of the Holy Scriptures*, his *Account of the History and Excellency of the Holy Scriptures*, and his daily employment on the journal in which the letters of Junius appeared, as corrector of the press, render Cruden's aberrations the more remarkable. And a still more curious circumstance, consists in the fact that his vagaries failed to efface the esteem in which he was regarded by all who knew him, more especially by his biographers, Blackburn and Chalmers; the latter of whom said of him, that he was a man to whom the religious world lies under great obligation, 'whose character, notwithstanding his mental infirmities, we cannot but venerate; whom neither infirmity nor neglect could debase; who sought consolation where only it could be found; whose sorrows served to instruct him in the distresses of others; and who employed his prosperity to relieve those who, in every sense, were ready to perish.' Are there many men more worthy of a column in the *Book of Days?*

---

## EXPULSION OF THE JEWS FROM ENGLAND.

In the course of the year of grace, 1290, three daughters of Edward I. were married. The old chroniclers relate wondrous stories of the prodigal magnificence of those nuptials; nor are their recitals without corroboration. Mr Herbert, a late librarian of the city of London, discovered in the records of the Goldsmiths' Company the actual list of valuables belonging to Queen Eleanor, and it reads more like an extract from the *Arabian Nights*, than an early English record. Gold chalices, worth £292 each, an immense sum in those days, figure in it; small silver cups are valued at £118 each—what were the large ones worth, we wonder!—while diamonds, sapphires, emeralds, and rubies, sparkle among all kinds of gold and silver utensils. Modern historians refer to the old chroniclers, and this astounding catalogue of manufactured wealth, as a proof of the attainments in refinement and art which England had made at that early period. But there is a reverse to every medal, and it is much more probable that these records of valuables are silent witnesses to a great crime—the robbery and expulsion of the Jews, proving the general barbarity and want of civilisation that then prevailed.

Not long before this year of royal marriages, Edward, moaning on a sick-bed, made a solemn vow, that if the Almighty should restore him to health, he would undertake another crusade against the infidels. The king recovered; but as the immediate pressure of sickness was removed, and Palestine far distant, he compromised his vow by driving the Jews out of his French province of Guienne, and seizing the wealth and possessions of the unfortunate Israelites.

It may be supposed, from the wandering nature

of the Jewish race, that many members of it had been in England from a very early period; but their first regular establishment in any number dates from the Norman Conquest, William having promised them his protection. The great master of romance has, in *Ivanhoe*, given a general idea how the Jews were treated; but there were particular horrors perpetrated on a large scale, quite unfit for relation in a popular work. In short, it may be said that when the Jews were most favoured, their condition was to our ideas intolerable; and yet it should be recorded in favour of our ancestors, that even then the Jews were rather more mildly treated in England than in the other countries of Europe.

When Edward returned from despoiling and banishing the Jews of Guienne, his subjects received him with rapturous congratulations. The constant drain of the precious metals created by the Crusades, the almost utter deficiency of a currency for conducting the ordinary transactions of life, had caused the whole nation—clergy, nobility, gentry, and commoners—to become debtors to the Jews. If the king, then, would graciously banish them from England as he had from Guienne, his subjects' debts would be sponged out, and he, of course, would be the most glorious, popular, and best of monarchs. Edward, however, did not see the affair exactly in that light. Though, in case of an enforced exodus, he would become entitled to the Jewish possessions, yet his subjects would be greater gainers by the complete abolition of their debts. In fact, the king, besides his own part of the spoil, claimed a share in that of his subjects, but after considerable deliberation the matter was thus arranged. The clergy agreed to give the king a tenth of their chattels, and the laity a fifteenth of their lands; and so the bargain was concluded to the satisfaction and gain of all parties, save the miserable beings whom it most concerned.

On the 31st of August 1290, Edward issued a proclamation commanding all persons of the Jewish race, under penalty of death, to leave England before the 1st of November. As an act of gracious condescension on the part of the king, the Jews were permitted to take with them a small portion

JEW'S HOUSE AT LINCOLN.

of their movables, and as much money as would pay their travelling expenses. Certain ports were appointed as places of embarkation, and safe-conduct passes to those ports were granted to all who chose to pay for them. The passes added more to the royal treasury than to the protection of the fugitives. The people—that is to say, the Christians—rose and robbed the Jews on all sides, without paying the slightest respect to the dearly-purchased protections. All the old historians relate a shocking instance of the treatment the Jews received when leaving England. Holinshed thus quaintly tells the story:

'A sort of the richest of them being shipped with their treasure, in a mighty tall ship which they had hired, when the same was under sail, and got down the Thames, towards the mouth of the river, the master-mariner bethought him of a wile, and caused his men to cast anchor, and so rode at the same, till the ship, by ebbing of the stream, remained on the dry sand. The master herewith enticed the Jews to walk out with him on land, for recreation; and at length, when he understood the tide to be coming in, he got him back to the ship, whither he was drawn up by a cord. The Jews made not so much haste as he did, because they were not aware of the danger; but when they perceived how the matter stood, they cried to him for help, howbeit he told them that they ought to cry rather unto Moses, by whose conduct their fathers passed through the Red Sea; and, therefore, if they would call to him for help, he was able to help them out of these raging floods, which now came in upon them. They cried, indeed, but no succour appeared, and so they were swallowed up in the water. The master returned with his ship, and told the king how he had used the matter, and had both thanks and rewards, as some have written.'

Nearly all over the world this cruel history is traditionally known among the Jews, who add a myth to it; namely, that the Almighty, in execration of the deed, has ever since caused a continual turmoil among the waters over the fatal spot. The disturbance in the water caused by the fall, on ebb-tide, at old London Bridge, was said to be the place; and when foreign Jews visited London, it was always the first wonderful sight they were taken to see. The water at the present bridge is now as unruffled as at any other part of the river, yet Dr Margoliouth, writing in 1851, says that most of the old Jews still believe in the legend regarding the troubled waters.

There are few relics of the Jews thus driven out of England. The rolls of their estates, still among the public records, shew that the king profited largely by their expulsion. Jewry, Jew's Mount, Jew's Corner, and other similarly named localities in some of our towns, denote their once Hebrew occupants. The Jew's House at Lincoln can be undoubtedly traced to the possession of one Belaset, a Jewess, who was hanged for clipping coin, a short time previous to the expulsion. The house being forfeited to the crown by the felony, the king gave it to William de Foleteby, whose brother bequeathed it to the Dean and Chapter of Lincoln, the present possessors. Passing through so few hands, in the lapse of so many years, its history can be easier traced, perhaps, than any other of the few houses of the same age in England. The head of the doorway of this remarkable edifice, as will be seen by the illustration on the preceding page, forms an arch to carry the fireplace and chimney of the upper room. There seems to have been no fireplace in the lower room, there being originally but two rooms—one above, the other below.

The number of banished Jews comprised about 15,000 persons of all ages. English commerce, then in its infancy, received a severe shock by the impolitic measure; nor did learning escape without loss. One of the expelled was Nicolaus de Lyra, who, strange to say in those bigoted days, had been admitted a student at Oxford. He subsequently wrote a commentary on the Old and New Testaments, a work that prepared the way for the Reformation. Both Wickliffe and Luther acknowledged the assistance they had received from it. And though Pope, when describing the Temple of Dulness, says:

'De Lyra there a dreadful front extends,'

both parties, at the period of the Reformation, agreed in saying:

'Si Lyra non lyrasset,
Lutherus non saltasset'—

'If Lyra had not piped, Luther would not have danced.'

From the expulsion down to the period of the Commonwealth, the presence of a few Jews was always tolerated in England, principally about the court, in the capacity of physicians, or foreign agents. Early in 1656, the wise and tolerant Protector summoned a council to deliberate on the policy of allowing Jews to settle once more in England. That all parties might be represented, Cromwell admitted several lawyers, clergymen, and merchants, to aid the council in its deliberation. The lawyers declared that there was no law to prevent Jews settling in England; the clergy asserted that Christianity would be endangered thereby; and the merchants alleged that they would be the ruin of trade. Many of the arguments employed on this discussion were again used in the late debates on the admission of Jews into parliament. The council sat four days without coming to any conclusion: at last Cromwell closed it by saying, that he had sent for them to consider a simple question, and they had made it an intricate one. That he would, therefore, be guided by Providence, and act on his own responsibility. A few days afterwards, he announced to his parliament that he had determined to allow Jews to settle in England, and the affair was accomplished. In May and June 1656, a number of Jews arrived in London, and their first care was to build a synagogue, and lay out a burial-ground. The first interment on their burial-register is that of one Isaac Britto, in 1657.

## THE GREAT EARTHQUAKE AT LISBON IN 1755.

One of the most awful earthquakes ever recorded in history, for the loss of life and property thereby occasioned, was that at Lisbon on the 1st of November 1755. Although equalled, perhaps, in the New World, it has had no parallel in the Old. About nine o'clock in the morning, a hollow thunder-like sound was heard in the city, although the weather was clear and serene. Almost immediately afterwards, without any other warning, such an upheaval and overturning of the ground occurred as destroyed the greater part of the houses, and buried or crushed no less than 30,000 human beings. Some of the survivors declared that the shock scarcely exceeded three minutes in duration. Hundreds of persons lay half-killed under stones and ruined walls, shrieking in agony, and imploring aid which no one could render. Many of the churches were at the time filled with their congregations; and each church became one huge catacomb, entombing the hapless beings in its ruins. The first two or three shocks, in as many minutes, destroyed the number of lives above mentioned; but there were counted twenty-two shocks altogether, in Lisbon and its neighbourhood, destroying in the whole very nearly 60,000 lives. In one house, 4 persons only survived out of 38. In the city-prison, 800 were killed, and 1200 in the general hospital.

The effects on the sea and the sea-shore were scarcely less terrible than those inland. The sea retired from the harbour, left the bar dry, and then rolled in again as a wave fifty or sixty feet high. Many of the inhabitants, at the first alarm. rushed to a new marble quay which had lately been constructed; but this proceeding only occasioned additional calamities. The quay sank down into an abyss which opened underneath it, drawing in along with it numerous boats and small vessels. There must have been some actual closing up of the abyss at this spot; for the poor creatures thus engulfed, as well as the timbers and other wreck,

LISBON.

disappeared completely, as if a cavern had closed in upon them. The seaport of Setubal, twenty miles south of Lisbon, was engulfed and wholly disappeared. At Cadiz, the sea rose in a wave to a height of sixty feet, and swept away great part of the mole and fortifications. At Oporto, the river continued to rise and fall violently for several hours; and violent gusts of wind were actually forced up through the water from chasms which opened and shut in the bed beneath it. At Tetuan, Fez, Marocco, and other places on the African side of the Mediterranean, the earthquake was felt nearly at the same time as at Lisbon. Near Marocco, the earth opened and swallowed up a village or town with 8000 inhabitants, and then closed again. The comparisons which scientific men were afterwards able to institute, shewed that the main centre of the disturbance was far out in the Atlantic, where the bed of the ocean was convulsed by up-and-down heavings, thereby creating enormous waves on all sides. Many of the vessels out at sea were affected as if they had struck suddenly on a sand-bank or a rock; and, in some instances, the shock was so violent as to overturn every person and everything on board. And yet there was deep water all round the ships.

Although the mid-ocean may have been the focus of one disturbance which made itself felt as far as Africa in one direction, England in another, and America in a third, Lisbon must unquestionably have been the seat of a special and most terrible movement, creating yawning gaps in various parts of the city, and swallowing up buildings and people in the way above described. Many mountains in the neighbourhood, of considerable elevation, were shaken to their foundations; some were rent from top to bottom, enormous masses of rock were hurled from their sides, and electric flashes issued from the fissures. To add to the horrors of such of the inhabitants as survived the shocks, the city was found to be on fire in several places. These fires were attributed to various causes—the domestic fires of the inhabitants igniting the furniture and timbers that were hurled promiscuously upon them; the large wax-tapers which on that day (being a religious festival) were lighted in the churches; and the incendiary mischief of a band of miscreants, who took advantage of the terror around them by setting fire to houses in order to sack and pillage. The wretched inhabitants were either paralysed with dismay, or were too much engaged in seeking for the mangled corpses of their friends, to attend to the fire; the flames continued for six days, and the half-roasted bodies of hundreds of persons added to the horrors.

Mr Mallet, in his theory of earthquakes (which traces them to a kind of earth-wave propagated with great velocity), states that the earthquake which nearly destroyed Lisbon was felt at Loch Lomond in Scotland. 'The water, without any apparent cause, rose against the banks of the loch, and then subsided below its usual level: the greatest height of the swell being two feet four inches. In this instance, it seems most probable that the amplitude of the earth-wave was so great, that the entire cavity or basin of the lake was nearly at the same instant tilted or canted up, first at one side and then at the other, by the passage of the wave beneath it, so as to disturb the level of the contained waters by a few inches—just as one would cant up a bowl of water at one side by the hand.'

### ALL-HALLOW-TIDE CUSTOMS AT THE MIDDLE TEMPLE.

In the reign of Charles I., the young gentlemen of the Middle Temple were accustomed at All-Hallow-Tide, which they considered the beginning of Christmas, to associate themselves for the festive objects connected with the season. In 1629, they chose Bulstrode Whitelocke as Master of the Revels, and used to meet every evening at St Dunstan's Tavern, in a large new room, called 'The Oracle of Apollo,' each man bringing friends with him at his own pleasure. It was a kind of mock parliament, where various questions were discussed, as in our modern debating societies; but these temperate proceedings were seasoned with mirthful doings, to which the name of Revels was given, and of which dancing appears to have been the chief. On All-Hallows-Day, 'the master [Whitelocke, then four-and-twenty], as soon as the evening was come, entered the hall, followed by sixteen revellers. They were proper handsome young gentlemen, habited in rich suits, shoes and stockings, hats and great feathers. The master led them in his bar gown, with a white staff in his hand, the music playing before them. They began with the old masques; after which they danced the *Brawls*,* and then the master took his seat, while the revellers flaunted through galliards, corantos, French and country dances, till it grew very late. As might be expected, the reputation of this dancing soon brought a store of other gentlemen and ladies, some of whom were of great quality; and when the ball was over, the festive-party adjourned to Sir Sydney Montague's chamber, lent for the purpose to our young president. At length the court-ladies and grandees were allured—to the contentment of his vanity it may have been, but entailing on him serious expense—and then there was great striving for places to see them on the part of the London citizens. . . . To crown the ambition and vanity of all, a great German lord had a desire to witness the revels, then making such a sensation at court, and the Templars entertained him at great cost to themselves, receiving in exchange that which cost the great noble very little—his avowal that "dere was no such nople gollege in Ghristendom as deirs."'—*Memoirs of Bulstrode Whitelocke, by R. H. Whitelocke*, 1860, p. 56.

* Erroneously written *Brantes* in the authority quoted.



## NOVEMBER 2.

All Souls, or the Commemoration of the Faithful Departed. St Victorinus, bishop and martyr, about 304. St Marcian, anchoret and confessor, about 387. St Vulgan, confessor, 7th century.

### All-Souls-Day.

This is a festival celebrated by the Roman Catholic Church, on behalf of the souls in purgatory, for whose release the prayers of the faithful are this day offered up and masses performed. It is said to have been first introduced in the ninth century by Odilon, abbot of Cluny; but was not generally established till towards the end of the tenth century. Its observance was esteemed of such importance, that in the event of its falling on a Sunday, it was ordered not to be postponed till the Monday, as in the case of other celebrations, but to take place on the previous Saturday, that the souls of the departed might suffer no detriment from the want of the prayers of the church. It was customary in former times, on this day, for persons dressed in black to traverse the streets, ringing a dismal-toned bell at every corner, and calling on the inhabitants to remember the souls suffering penance in purgatory, and to join in prayer for their liberation and repose. At Naples, it used to be a custom on this day to throw open the charnel-houses, which were lighted up with torches and decked with flowers, while crowds thronged through the vaults to visit the bodies of their friends and relatives, the fleshless skeletons of which were dressed up in robes and arranged in niches along the walls. At Salerno, also, we are told, that a custom prevailed previous to the fifteenth century, of providing in every house on the eve of All-Souls-Day, a sumptuous entertainment for the souls in purgatory who were supposed then to revisit temporarily, and make merry in, the scene of their earthly pilgrimage. Every one quitted the habitation, and after spending the night at church, returned in the morning to find the whole feast consumed, it being deemed eminently inauspicious if a morsel of victuals remained uneaten. The thieves who made a harvest of this pious custom, assembling, then, from all parts of the country, generally took good care to avert any such evil omen from the inmates of the house by carefully carrying off whatever they were unable themselves to consume. A resemblance may be traced in this observance, to an incident in the story of *Bel and the Dragon*, in the *Apocrypha*.

*Born.*—Dr William Vincent, scholar and miscellaneous writer, 1739; Marie Antoinette, queen of Louis XVI., 1755, *Vienna;* Field-Marshal Radetzky, celebrated Austrian commander, 1766, *Castle of Trebnitz, Bohemia;* Edward, Duke of Kent, father of Queen Victoria, 1767.

*Died.*—Dr Richard Hooker, author of the *Ecclesiastical Polity*, 1600, *Bishop's Bourne;* Richard Bancroft, archbishop of Canterbury, 1610, *Lambeth;* Sophia Dorothea, consort of George I. of England, 1726, *Castle of Ahlen, Hanover;* Alexander Menzikoff, Russian statesman and general, 1729, *Siberia;* Princess Amelia, daughter of George III., 1810, *Windsor;* Sir Samuel Romilly, eminent lawyer and philanthropist, 1818; Sir Alexander Burnes, diplomatist, murdered at Cabul, 1841; Esaias Tegner, Swedish poet, 1846, *Wexiö, Sweden;* Dr Richard Mant, theological and miscellaneous writer, 1848, *Ballymoney, Antrim.*

## SIR SAMUEL ROMILLY.

The revocation in 1685, by Louis XIV., of Henry IV.'s Edict of Nantes, by which for nearly a hundred years Protestants had enjoyed at least toleration, cost France dearly, but greatly enriched England by the immigration of a multitude of skilful artisans, who introduced to the land of their adoption many forms of useful and elegant industry. Nor did these noble exiles profit England only by their manual skill. The names of their descendants appear with distinction in almost every department of our national life, but few with a more radiant glory than encircles the head of Sir Samuel Romilly.

His grandfather came from Montpellier, and settled in the neighbourhood of London as a wax-bleacher. His father was a jeweller, and in Frith Street, Soho, he was born on the 1st of March 1757. As a boy, he received an indifferent education at the French Protestant school, but as soon as he had left it, he diligently applied himself to self-culture. What business he should follow, he could not decide. A solicitor's was thought of, a merchant's office was tried, and then his father's shop, but none pleased him. Meanwhile, he studied hard and became a good Latin scholar. Eventually, he was articled for five years to one of the sworn clerks in Chancery. In his leisure, he read extensively, but with method, governing himself with a strict rein. At the expiration of the five years, it had been his intention to purchase a seat in the Six Clerks' Office, and there quietly settle for life; but his father needed the requisite funds in his business, and Romilly, deprived of this resource, determined to qualify himself for the bar. Severe mental application brought on ill health, and to recruit his strength he made a journey to Switzerland. In Paris, he formed the acquaintance of D'Alembert, Diderot, and other thinkers of their school, and their influence had considerable effect in moulding his opinions towards liberalism and reform.

In 1783, Romilly was called to the bar, but he had to wait long ere he was rewarded with any practice. When briefs did at last fall to his lot, it very soon became manifest that they were held by a master; he gave his conscience to all he undertook, and wrought out his business with efficiency. Solicitors who trusted him once were in haste to trust him again, and a start in prosperity being made, success came upon him like a flood. His income rose to between £8000 and £9000 a year, and in his diary, he congratulates himself that he did not press his father to buy him a seat in the Six Clerks' Office. Lord Brougham says: 'Romilly, by the force of his learning and talents, and the most spotless integrity, rose to the very heights of professional ambition. He was beyond question or pretence of rivalry the first man in the courts of equity in this country.'

Mirabeau visited London in 1784, and introduced Romilly to the Marquis of Lansdowne, who was so impressed with the young man's genius, that he twice offered him a seat in parliament; but Romilly was too proud to sit under even such liberal patronage. Not until 1806 did he enter the House of Commons, and then as Solicitor General in the Whig government, styled 'All the Talents,' formed after the death of Pitt. That administration lasted little more than a year, but Romilly remained a member of the House for one borough or another to the end of his life. In parliament, he was felt as a great power, and his speeches and votes were invariably on the Whig and progressive side. His oratory, which some competent judges pronounced the finest of his age, was usually listened to with rapt attention; a passage in his speech in favour of the abolition of the slave-trade received the singular honour of three distinct rounds of applause from the House.

Romilly's grand claim to remembrance, however, rests on his humane efforts to mitigate the Draconic code of English law. Nearly three hundred crimes, varying from the most frightful atrocity to keeping company with gipsies, were indiscriminately punishable with death. As a consequence, vice flourished, for, as Lord Coke long ago observed, 'too severe laws are never executed.' He had long meditated over the matter, and after discussing various schemes of procedure, he cautiously ventured, in 1808, to bring in a bill to repeal the statute of Elizabeth, which made it a capital offence to steal privately from the person of another. This he succeeded in getting passed. He next, in 1810, tried a bolder stroke, and introduced three bills to repeal several statutes, which punished with death the crimes of stealing privately in a shop goods to the value of 5*s*., and of stealing to the amount of 40*s*. in dwelling-houses, or in vessels in navigable rivers. All three were lost! He did not despair, however, but kept agitating, and renewed his motions session after session. He did not live to reap success, but he cleared the way for success after him.

Romilly had married, in his forty-first year, Miss Garbett, a lady of rare intelligence, whom he first met at the Marquis of Lansdowne's, and their union proved eminently happy. After twenty years of conjugal felicity, she fell into delicate health. In 1818 there was a dissolution of parliament, and as an evidence of the respect in which Romilly was held, the electors of Westminster placed his name at the head of the poll, although he declined to spend a shilling or solicit a vote. Never, alas! was he destined to sit for Westminster. Public honours were vapid whilst his beloved partner lay nigh unto death. On the 29th of October she died. The shock was dreadful to Romilly. In his agony he fell into a delirium, and in a moment, when unwatched, he sprang from his bed, cut his throat, and expired in a few minutes. The sad event took place in his house, Russell Square, London, 2d November 1818. When Lord Eldon, next morning, took his seat on the bench, and saw the vacant place within the bar where for years Romilly had pleaded before him, iron man though he was, his eyes filled with tears. 'I cannot stay here!' he exclaimed, and rising in great agitation, broke up his court.

In one grave the bodies of husband and wife were laid at Knill, in Herefordshire. It is a singular circumstance, that in the parish church of St Bride, Fleet Street, there is a tablet on the wall with an inscription to the memory of Isaac Romilly, F.R.S., who died in 1759 *of a broken heart*, seven days after the decease of a beloved wife.

Romilly's style of speech was fluent, yet simple, correct and nervous, and without ornament of any kind. His reasoning was clear and accurate, and seemed to the hearer intelligible without an effort. His voice was deep and sonorous, and his presence full of severe and solemn dignity. To these oratorical powers he brought great earnestness; whatever he undertook, he fulfilled with all his might. The cause of his client he made his own, and he was reckoned to run the fairest chance of victory who had Romilly for his advocate.

---

### FUNERAL OF A JEWISH RABBI.

There are not often opportunities, in England, of witnessing the funeral obsequies of the great priests or rabbis among the Jews; because that peculiar people do not form so large a ratio to the whole population here as in many continental countries, and consequently do not comprise so many sacerdotal officers. One of the few instances that have occurred, took place on the 2d of November 1842. Dr Herschel, who had been chief rabbi of England for forty-two years, was buried on this day. At ten o'clock in the morning, the body, in a plain deal-coffin covered with a black cloth, was removed from his residence in Bury Court, St Mary Axe, to the chief synagogue in Duke's Place, Houndsditch. It was supported and followed by twenty-four leading members of the Hebrew persuasion, including Sir Moses Montefiore. During the progress from the door of the synagogue to the ark, a special service was chanted by the Rev. Mr Asher, the principal reader; and after the bier had been placed before the ark, an impressive ceremonial took place. The ark was covered with black cloth; the whole of the windows were darkened; the synagogue was illuminated by wax-tapers; and the whole place assumed a sombre and imposing aspect. This portion of the religious ceremony having been completed, a procession was formed to convey the remains of the venerable rabbi to their last resting-place, the Jews' burial-ground, at Mile End. In the procession were the boys and girls of the German, Spanish, and Portuguese Jewish schools; the youths training up for the priesthood; the readers of the various metropolitan synagogues; and the carriages of the principal Jewish laity. There were nearly a hundred carriages in all. In accordance with a wish expressed by the deceased, there were no mourning-coaches. On arriving at the burial-ground, at Heath Street, Mile End, the body was carried into a sort of hall, in the centre of which it was placed. The reader, then, taking his position at the head of the coffin, repeated a burial-service. At the conclusion of the prayers, the coffin was borne to the grave. Several brown-paper parcels, sealed with wax, containing papers and documents, were thrown into the grave, in obedience to instructions left by the deceased; and a large box, containing one of the laws of Moses, written by Rabbi Herschel himself on parchment, was also, at his special request, consigned to the grave with him. The shops of the Jewish tradesmen along the line of route were closed as the procession passed, the ceremony altogether occupying five hours.

# NOVEMBER 3.

**St Papoul or Papulus, priest and martyr, 3d century. St Flour, bishop and confessor, about 389. St Rumald or Rumbald, confessor, patron of Brackley and Buckingham. St Wenefride or Winifred,* virgin and martyr, in Wales. St Hubert, bishop of Liege, confessor, 727. St Malachy, archbishop of Armagh, confessor, 1148.**

### ST RUMALD.

They who have read Foxe's Martyrology, will perhaps remember that several Lollards who, to save their bodies from the stake, renounced the 'new doctrine,' were nevertheless required to walk to Buckingham, and present an offering at the shrine of St Rumald. Now this St Rumald, whose name is also written Rumbald, and Grumbald, was a very remarkable saint. According to Leland, who copies from a monkish life of him, he was the son of the king of Northumbria by a Christian daughter of Penda, king of Mercia. He was born at Sutton, in Northamptonshire, but not far from the town of Buckingham. Immediately he came into the world, he exclaimed: 'I am a Christian! I am a Christian! I am a Christian!' He then made a full and explicit confession of his faith; desired to be forthwith baptized; appointed his own godfathers; and chose his own name. He next directed a certain large hollow stone to be fetched for his font; and when some of his father's servants attempted to obey his orders, but found the stone far too heavy to be removed, the two priests, whom he had appointed his godfathers, went for it, and bore it to him with the greatest ease. He was baptized by Bishop Widerin, assisted by a priest named Eadwold, and immediately after the ceremony he walked to a certain well near Brackley, which now bears his name, and there preached for three successive days; after which he made his will, bequeathing his body after death to remain at Sutton for one year, at Brackley for two years, and at Buckingham ever after. This done, he instantly expired. After this three-days' existence, the miraculous infant was buried at Sutton by Eadwold the priest; the next year he was translated by Bishop Widerin to Brackley; and the third year after his death, his remains were carried to Buckingham, and deposited in a shrine, in an aisle of the church which afterwards bore his name. Shortly before the year 1477, Richard Fowler, Esq., chancellor to Edward IV., began to rebuild this aisle, but died before its completion. In his will, therefore, he made this bequest: 'Item, I wolle that the aforesaid Isle of St Rumwold, in the aforesaid church prebendal of Bucks, where my body and other of my friends lyen buried, the which isle is begonne of new to be made, be fully made and performed up perfitely in all things att my costs and charge; and in the same isle that there be made of new a toumbe or shrine for the said saint where the old is now standing, and that it be made curiously with marble in length and breadth as shall be thought by myn executors most convenient, consideration had to the rome, and upon the same tombe or shrine I will that there be sett a coffyn or a chest

* See notice of St Winifred at p. 6 of this volume.

curiously wrought and gilte, as it appertaynith for to lay in the bones of the same saint, and this also to be doan in all things at my cost and charge.'* This extreme care for the relics of the infant saint clearly shews that they were held in high veneration at this period, and they continued to be the object of pilgrimages till the middle of the sixteenth century.

There was also a famous image of St Rumald at Boxley, in Kent. This statue or image was very small and hollow, and light, so that a child of seven years old might easily lift it, but, for some reason or other, it occasionally appeared so heavy that persons of great strength were unable to move it. 'The moving hereof,' says Fuller, 'was made the conditions of women's chastity. Such who paid the priest well, might easily remove it, whilst others might tug at it to no purpose. For this was the contrivance of the cheat—that it was fastened with a pin of wood by an invisible stander behind. Now, when such offered to take it who had been bountiful to the priest before, they bare it away with ease, which was impossible for their hands to remove who had been close-fisted in their confessions. Thus it moved more laughter than devotion, and many chaste virgins and wives went away with blushing faces, leaving (without cause) the suspicion of their wantonness in the eyes of the beholders; whilst others came off with more credit (because with more coin) though with less chastity.' Fuller concludes the Legend of St Rumald with this remark: 'Reader, I partly guess by my own temper how thine is affected with the reading hereof, whose soul is much divided betwixt several actions at once:—1. To *frown* at the impudency of the first inventors of such improbable untruths.—2. To *smile* at the simplicity of the believers of them.—3. To *sigh* at that well-intended devotion abused with them.—4. To thank God that we live in times of better and brighter knowledge.'

A memorial of the saint is still preserved at Buckingham in the names of *Well Street* and *St Rumbald's Lane;* and a well at Brackley bears his name.

It is not unworthy of observation, that Butler, in his *Lives of the Saints*, gives but a brief account of Rumald; and though acquainted with Leland's account of him, passes lightly over the miraculous story, only saying: 'He died *very young* on the 3d of November, &c.'

---

*Born.*—Lucan, Latin poet, 39 A.D., *Cordova.*

*Died.*—Constantius, Roman emperor, 361, *Mopsucrene, Cilicia;* Pope Leo the Great, 461; James II., king of Aragon, 1327, *Barcelona;* Thomas de Montacute, Earl of Salisbury, killed in France, 1428; Bishop Robert Lowth, biblical writer, 1787, *Fulham;* Theophilus Lindsey, Unitarian divine, 1808; Dr Felix Mendelssohn Bartholdy, musical composer, 1847, *Leipsic.*

## SPURS AND SPUR-MONEY.

Among the privy-purse expenses of Henry VII., in the year 1495, appears the following item: 'To the children for the king's spurs, 4*s.*' And between June 1530 and September 1532, no less than three payments of 6*s.* 8*d.* are recorded as made by his successor's paymaster 'to the Coristars of Wyndesor in rewarde for the king's spurres.' Apropos of these entries, Mr Markland quotes a note from Gifford's edition of Ben Jonson, stating that from the disturbance of divine service in the cathedrals (more especially in St Paul's) by the jingling of the spurs of persons walking in their precincts, a trifling fine was imposed upon offenders in this way, called 'spur-money,' the collection of which was left to the beadles and singing-boys. It seems to us that the connection between the text and note is rather doubtful—indeed, Mr Markland himself says, 'it must first be shewn that it prevailed at so early a period.' Nicholas supposed that in the above cases the money was paid to redeem the royal spurs from the choristers, who claimed them as their perquisites at installations, or at the annual feast in honour of St George.

Spur-money, as a penalty to be paid for wearing spurs in a cathedral, seems to have been thoroughly established in the seventeenth century. In the *Gull's Horn-Book*, Decker, advising his readers how they should behave in St Paul's, says: 'Be sure your silver spurs clog your heels, and then the boys will swarm about you like so many white butterflies; when you in the open quire, shall draw forth a perfumed embroidered purse—the glorious sight of which will entice many countrymen from their devotion to wondering—and quoit silver into the boy's hands, that it may be heard above the first lesson, although it be read in a voice as big as one of the great organs.' That the custom was not confined to St Paul's, is proved by a passage in *Ray's Second Itinerary*—'July 26, 1661. We began our journey northwards from Cambridge, and that day, passing through Huntingdon and Stilton, we rode as far as Peterborough, twenty-five miles. There I first heard the cathedral service. The choristers made us pay money for coming into the quire with our spurs on.' Another old writer complains that the boys neglect their duties to run about after spur-money. Modern choristers are not so bad as that, but they look sharply after their rights. Some few years ago, a visitor to Hereford Cathedral declined to satisfy the demands of the boys, who thereupon seized his hat, and decamped with it. The indignant despiser of old customs, instead of redeeming his property, laid a complaint before the bench; but the magistrates astonished him by dismissing the case on the grounds that the choristers were justified in keeping the hat as a lien for the payment of the customary fine. There was one way of escaping the tax, the spur-wearer being held exempt if the youngest chorister present failed to repeat his gamut correctly upon being challenged to do so. This curious saving-clause is set forth officially in a notice issued by the dean of the chapel-royal in 1622:

'If any knight or other person entitled to wear spurs, enter the chapel in that guise, he shall pay to the quiristers the accustomed fine; but if he command the youngest quirister to repeat his gamut, and he fail in the so doing, the said knight or other shall not pay the fine.'

By enforcing this rule, the Iron Duke once baffled the young assailants of his purse. When a similar claim was made against the Duke of Cumberland (afterwards king of Hanover) in Westminster Abbey, he ingeniously evaded it by insisting that he was privileged to wear his spurs in the place in which he had been invested with them.

On the belfry-wall of All Saints Church,

* Lipscomb's *Buckinghamshire*, ii. 578.

Hastings, hangs a rhymed notice, declaring the belfry free to 'all those that civil be,' with a proviso—

> 'If you ring in spur or hat,
> Sixpence you pay be sure of that.'

The debtors of Lancaster jail demand largess of any visitor wearing spurs within the castle-walls, and the doorkeeper of the Edinburgh Court of Session is privileged to demand five shillings from any one appearing in that court so accoutred.

Lord Colchester records in his diary (1776), that having inadvertently gone into the House of Commons booted and spurred, he was called to order by an old member for assuming a privilege only accorded to county members. This parliamentary rule is noticed by Sir James Lawrence in his *Nobility of the British Gentry*. 'Though the knights condescended to sit under the same roof with the citizens and burgesses, they were summoned to appear *gladio cincti*, and they always maintained the dignity of the equestrian order. The most trifling distinction suffices to destroy the idea of equality, and the distinction of the spur is still observed. The military members appear no longer in armour, but they alone may wear spurs as a mark of knighthood. The citizen or burgess, who, after a morning-ride, should inadvertently approach the chamber with his spurs on, is stopped by the usher, and must return to divest himself of this mark of knighthood. And to this humiliation any gentleman of the first quality, any Irish peer, nay, the Chancellor of the Exchequer himself, who, whatever might be his authority or dignity elsewhere, should sit in the House in the humble character of citizen or burgess, must submit.'

The first spur worn was merely a sharp goad, afterwards improved by bending the shank to suit the ankle. In the reign of Henry III., the rowelled spur made its first appearance; the rowel was gradually lengthened till it reached its maximum of seven inches and a half, in the time of Henry VI. Then came a change of fashion, and only spurs with close star-shaped rowels were in favour. At this time Ripon, in Yorkshire, was especially famous for the manufacture of spurs: 'As true steel as Ripon rowels,' became a proverbial expression. It was said that Ripon rowels would strike through a shilling, and rather break than bend. When James I. passed through the town in 1617, he was presented with a pair of spurs valued at five pounds. The knights of old, proud of their spurs, were not content with simple steel. Brass and silver were pressed into service, and spurs were chased, gilt, decorated with jewels, and adorned with such mottoes as—

> 'A true knight am I,
> Anger me and try.'

Lady-equestrians adopted spurs at a very early period; Chaucer's wife of Bath is described by him as having 'on her feet a pair of spurs sharp.'

The fops of Shakspeare's day, delighted to hear their spurs jingle as they strutted through the streets:

> 'If they have a tatling spur and bear,
> Heads light as the gay feathers which they wear,
> Think themselves are the only gentlemen.'

So, fastidious Brisk in *Every Man out of his Humour*, praises his horse as 'a fiery little slave, he runs like a—— Oh, excellent, excellent!—with the very sound of the spur!' And when an explanation of the latter phrase is demanded, replies: 'Oh, it's your only humour now extant, sir—a good jingle, a good jingle.'



---

# NOVEMBER 4.

Saints Vitalis and Agricola, martyrs, about **304**. St Joannicius, abbot, 845. St Clarus, martyr, 894. St Brinstan, bishop of Winchester, 934. St Emeric, Hungarian prince, 11th century. St Charles Borromeo, cardinal, archbishop of Milan, and confessor, 1584.

## ST EMERIC.

On this day was honoured St Emeric, the pious son of the pious St Stephen, king of Hungary in the eleventh century. Emeric was a very promising man, both as a prince and an apostle of Christianity; and he might have attained greater eminence if he had not been carried off by death in the lifetime of his father. As it is, this somewhat obscure Hungarian saint has been a person of some consequence in the world, for from his name has come that of one of the great divisions of the earth. Through his celebrity, his name became a popular one: it was conferred, in the fifteenth century, in the Italian form of Amerigo, upon an Italian surnamed Vespucci. Vespucci did the world some service in extending the knowledge of the continent which Columbus had discovered; and by a strange current of circumstances, this continent came to be recognised by the name America, in honour of Signor Vespucci. When St Stephen was choosing a name for his first-born son, how little could he have imagined that the one he chose was to be the parent of the noted word *America!*

In an article on surnames derived from Christian names, which appeared in the *Gentleman's Magazine* for July 1772, *Amory* and *Emery* are set down as derived from Emeric.

---

*Born.*—William III., king of England, 1650, *Hague;* James Montgomery, poet, 1771, *Irvine, Ayrshire.*

*Died.*—John Benbow, British admiral, 1702, *Jamaica;* Charles Churchill, satirical poet, 1764, *Boulogne-sur-Mer;* Josiah Tucker, D.D., dean of Gloucester, political economist, 1799; Paul Delaroche, celebrated painter, 1856, *Paris.*

## 'OLD BENBOW.'

Benbow occupies a place in the naval literature of England which is likely to be permanent. Not because he was a better admiral than many who have lived in later days, but because he had much of that personal daring which is so dear to popular notions. A coarse rough man he was, anything but a gentleman in external demeanour; and, as we shall see, this roughness had something to do with the disaster which cost him his life. Sea story-tellers and sea song-writers, however, are never frightened by such characteristics. Benbow's last fight figures in the *Deeds of*

*Naval Daring.* Dibdin, in his song of *Jervis for Ever*, begins—

'You 've heard, I s'pose, the people talk
Of Benbow and Boscawen,
Of Anson, Pococke, Vernon, Hawke,
And many more then going.'

The immediate object of the song is to praise Jervis, whose great victory in Dibdin's day earned for him the earldom of St Vincent; but the name of Benbow occurs in this and many other sea-songs as that of an unquestioned hero of old times. Born in 1650, he entered the naval service so early that almost his whole life was spent on ship-board; and he was known generally as a rough and ready officer to whom nothing came amiss. On one occasion, when a naval service of some peril was suggested for an aristocratic officer, whose friends expressed apprehension of the result, the king (William III.) laughingly replied: 'Send for honest Benbow!'

The enterprise which is especially associated with Benbow's name was the following. During the war with France in 1702, Admiral Ducasse, with a French squadron of five large ships, threatened one of our West India Islands. Benbow sailed after him with seven ships, and overtook him on the 19th of August. On giving the signal for his ships to engage, there was soon evidence that something was wrong; the ships held back, and Benbow was unable to commence his fight with the enemy. It afterwards appeared that Benbow's offensive manners had led to a rupture between him and most of his captains; and that those officers took the indefensible course of shewing their hostility just when the honour of the country demanded their prompt obedience to orders. Next morning the admiral again put forth the signal to advance; but five out of the seven ships were three or four miles astern of him, as if the captains had agreed that they *could* not assist him. Vexed and irritated, but undaunted as usual, Benbow went into action, two ships against five, and maintained the contest during the whole day. His one coadjutor, the *Ruby*, becoming disabled, he sent that ship to Jamaica to refit. Again he signalled to the five captains, and received some equivocal excuse that the enemy were too strong, and that he had better not attack them. Left still more to his own resources, he renewed the fight on the 21st with one ship, the *Breda*, against five. Three different times did Benbow in person board the French admiral's ship, and three times was he driven back. He received a severe wound in the face, another in the arm, and his right leg was shattered by a chain-shot. Still the heroic man would not give in. He caused his cot to be brought up upon deck; and there he lay, giving orders while his shattered limbs were bleeding. When one of his lieutenants expressed regret at the leg being broken, Benbow replied: 'I am sorry for it too; but I had rather have lost them both than have seen the dishonour brought upon the English nation. But—do you hear?—if another shot should take me off, behave like brave men, and fight it out.' At this time, all the other English ships being inactive and at a distance, most of the French ships concentrated their fire on the *Breda;* and Benbow was only just able to extricate her, and sail to Jamaica. Admiral Ducasse knew very well that his squadron had been saved through the disgraceful conduct of Benbow's captains, and he was too true a sailor to regard it in any but the proper light. He sent the following letter to Benbow:

'SIR—I had little hope on Monday last but to have supped in your cabin;* but it pleased God to order it otherwise, and I am thankful for it. As for those cowardly captains who deserted you, hang them up; for, by God, they deserve it! Yours, &c.,

DUCASSE.'

When Benbow reached Jamaica, he ordered the captains into arrest, and caused a court-martial to be held on them, under the presidency of Rear-Admiral Whetstone. Captain Hudson, of the *Pendennis*, died before the trial; Captains Kirby and Wade were convicted and shot; Captain Constable was cashiered and imprisoned. Two others had signed a paper engaging not to fight under the admiral; but there were extenuating circumstances which led to their acquittal. One of these two was Captain Walton of the *Ruby;* he had signed the paper when drunk (naval captains were often drunk in those days); but he repented when sober, and rendered good service to the admiral. He was the officer who, sixteen years afterwards, wrote a despatch that is regarded as the shortest and most fitting in which a naval victory was ever announced:

'CANTERBURY, OFF SYRACUSE,
16*th August* 1718.

SIR—We have taken and destroyed all the Spanish ships and vessels that were upon the coast; the number as per margin. Yours, &c.,

G. WALTON.

TO SIR GEORGE BYNG,
Commander-in-chief.'

Poor Benbow sank under his mortification. The evidence elicited at the court-martial was sufficient to shew that *he* was not to blame for the escape of the French squadron; but the rough sailor could not bear it; the disgrace to the nation fretted him, and increased the malignancy of his wounds; he dragged on a few weeks, and died on November 4. No monument, we believe, records the fame of 'Old Benbow;' his deeds are left to the writers of naval song and story.

## CHURCHILL.

A short life, a busy, and a notorious, was Churchill's. In a day he found himself famous; for less than four years, from 1761 to 1764, he was one of the most prominent figures in London, and then he died.

The son of a clergyman, he was born in Westminster in 1731, and was destined by his father for his own profession. Educated at Westminster school, he had for companions Warren Hastings; two poets, William Cowper and Robert Lloyd; and two dramatists, George Colman and Richard Cumberland. Ere Churchill was out of his boyhood he marred his life: at the age of seventeen, he married a girl within the rules of the Fleet. For the church he had no inclination, but in addition to pleasing his father, it was now necessary for him to earn a living for himself and family. As soon, therefore,

* That is, to have been taken prisoner.

as he was of canonical age, he was ordained and entered on a country curacy; and, as he says, 'prayed and starved on forty pounds a year.' In 1758, his father died, and out of respect for his memory, his parishioners elected his son to succeed him. At the age of twenty-seven, Churchill returned to London, and was installed as curate and lecturer of St John the Evangelist, Westminster. There he had a better income, but in his duties he had no joy or even satisfaction. He wrote, and wrote truly:

'I kept those sheep,
Which, for my curse, I was ordain'd to keep,
Ordain'd, alas! to keep through need, not choice....
Whilst sacred dulness ever in my view,
Sleep at my bidding crept from pew to pew.'

In London, Churchill met his school-fellow Robert Lloyd, who was serving as usher in Westminster school. Lloyd was a wild fellow, and was as sick of the drudgery of his calling as was Churchill of his. To literary tastes, they both united a passion for conviviality, and together committed many excesses. Mrs Churchill, it is said, was as imprudent as her husband. Their free style of life soon involved them in pecuniary difficulties, and Churchill had to settle with his creditors for 5*s*. in the pound. About the same time, Lloyd threw up his situation as usher, and resolved to seek his living in authorship, and Churchill determined to follow his example.

He first tried his fortune with two poems, with which no bookseller would have anything to do, but he was not to be beaten. For two months he closely attended the theatres, and made the leading actors the theme of a critical and satirical poem, entitled *The Rosciad*. No bookseller would buy it, even for five guineas; but not to be baffled this time, Churchill printed it at his own expense. In March 1761, the *Rosciad* appeared anonymously as a shilling pamphlet, and a few days sufficed to prove that 'a hit' had been made. Who was the author, became the problem of the town. The poor players ran about like so many stricken deer. The reviewers were busy with guesses as to the authorship, and, in self-defence, Colman disowned it, and Lloyd disowned it. Churchill soon put an end to the mystery. In an advertisement, he announced himself as the satirist, and promised a second poem, *An Apology Addressed to the Critical Reviewers*. The *Apology* struck as great terror among the authors as the *Rosciad* among the actors. On every side he was assailed in *Churchilliads*, *Anti-Rosciads*, and such like. In a few months, it is asserted, he cleared a thousand pounds. The money he used well. To his wife, from whom he was now separated, he made a handsome allowance; every man from whom he had borrowed money he repaid with interest; and his creditors, to their glad surprise, received the remaining fifteen shillings in the pound.

His habits now became openly licentious. He doffed the clerical costume, and walked abroad in a blue coat with metal buttons, a gold-laced waistcoat, a gold-laced hat and ruffles. He seduced a young woman, and lived with her as his wife. His parishioners remonstrated, and he resigned his curacy. He published *Night*, a poem, as an apology for his nocturnal orgies, maintaining, as if any excuse could be entertained for his own misdemeanours, that open licentiousness was better than hypocrisy. *Night* was followed by *The Ghost*, a satire on the Cock-Lane spirit-rappings, in which Dr Johnson, who had called Churchill a shallow fellow, was ridiculed as Pomposo.

Satire is a dangerous business. Little Pope had a tall Irishman to attend him when he published the *Dunciad*, but Churchill was well able to take care of himself. Of himself he wrote:

'Broad were his shoulders,
Vast were his bones, his muscles twisted strong,
His face was short, but broader than 'twas long....
His arms were two twin oaks, his legs so stout,
That they might bear a mansion-house about,
Nor were they, look but at his body there,
Design'd by fate a much less weight to bear.'

He stalked about the streets with a bludgeon, and parties who had met to devise retaliation, and who were observed talking loud against the 'Satirical Parson' in the Bedford Coffee-house, quietly dispersed when a brawny figure appeared, and Churchill, drawing off his gloves with a particularly slow composure, called for a dish of coffee and the *Rosciad*.

John Wilkes was in those days at the outset of his career, when it was hard to tell whether he was a patriot or a knave. He sought Churchill's acquaintance, and they became fast friends. Lord Bute was ruler of England under the young king, George III., and a popular cry arose that the revenue had become the prey of Scotchmen. Under the inspiration of Wilkes, Churchill commenced a satire on Scotland, and as he advanced with the work, Wilkes praised it exultingly. 'It is personal, it is poetical, it is political,' cried the delighted demagogue. 'It must succeed!' In January 1763, the *Prophecy of Famine* appeared. It conveyed a thoroughly Cockney idea of Scotland, but in spite, or perhaps because, of its extravagance, it was intensely popular, and spread dismay among the ranks of Scottish place-hunters. It was a new seal of Churchill's power, and his exuberant delight took an odd form. 'I remember well,' says Dr Kippis, 'that Churchill dressed his younger son in a Scottish plaid, like a little Highlander, and carried him everywhere in that garb. The boy being asked by a gentleman with whom I was in company, why he was clothed in such a manner? answered with great vivacity: "Sir, my father hates the Scotch, and does it to plague them!"'

Churchill was associated with Wilkes in the publication of the *North Briton*, and when, in consequence of No. 45 charging the king with falsehood, a general warrant was issued for the apprehension of its authors, printers, and publishers, Churchill was included. He chanced to call on Wilkes whilst he was debating with the officers who had come to arrest him. With much presence of mind, Wilkes addressed him as Mr Thomson, saying: 'Good-morrow, Mr Thomson. How does Mrs Thomson do to-day? Does she dine *in the country?*' Churchill was sharp enough to take the hint. He thanked Wilkes, said Mrs Thomson then waited for him, that he had only come to ask how Mr Wilkes was, and took his leave. He hurried home, secured his papers, and retired to the country, whither no attempt was made to follow him.

To Hogarth's pencil, Churchill owes somewhat of his fame. Hogarth had published a caricature of

Wilkes with his squint, by which the demagogue is better known to posterity than by all the busts and pictures by which his admirers sought to glorify his name. Churchill thereon addressed *An Epistle to William Hogarth,* which appeared in July 1763, and which Garrick described as 'the most bloody performance of my time.' Ere the month was out, Hogarth took his revenge in a shilling print, entitled 'The Bruiser, C. Churchill (once the Rev.), in the character of a Russian Hercules, regaling himself after having killed the monster Caricatura, that so sorely galled his virtuous friend, the heaven-born Wilkes.' All who have turned over Hogarth, will remember the bear in torn clerical bands, and with paws in ruffles, holding a pot of porter and a knotted club with *Lyes* and *North Briton* graven over it, and a pug-dog treating his poems with gross indignity.

Whatever Churchill wrote, sold, and sold for good prices, and he kept publishing pamphlet after pamphlet as occasion moved him. He wrote hastily, and not a little of his work was commonplace and mean, but ever and anon occurred a line or a passage of extraordinary vigour and felicity; and for these he will probably be read as long as English literature endures.

A sudden desire to see Wilkes induced Churchill to set off for Boulogne in October 1764. On the 29th of that month he was seized there with fever. Feeling the hand of death was on him, he sat up in bed and dictated a brief will, leaving to his wife an annuity of £60, and another of £50 to the girl he had seduced, and providing for his two boys. On the 4th of November he died. His body was brought over to Dover, where in the Church of St Martin it lies buried. The news of his death reached Robert Lloyd as he was sitting down to dinner. He sickened, and thrust away his plate untouched. 'I shall follow poor Charles,' was all he said, as he went to the bed from which he never rose again. Churchill's favourite sister, Patty, to whom Lloyd was betrothed, sank next under the double blow, and in a few weeks joined her brother and lover. Thus tragically ended Churchill's brief and boisterous career.

## MARRIAGE OF WILLIAM AND MARY.

Not the least important of the collateral causes, which led to the downfall of the Stuart dynasty in these kingdoms, was the marriage of William Prince of Orange to his fair cousin, the Princess Mary of York, on the 4th of November 1677. William arrived in England on the 19th of October previous, to seek the hand of the princess, and conclude a treaty with England, by which the war between France and Holland could be terminated, and peace restored to Europe. Charles II. was in favour of the marriage; his brother James, the bride's father, was not: both, however, were equally anxious to commit the prince to a treaty before the nuptials were solemnised. But the wise hero of Nassau would not speak of politics till he saw the princess, nor enter into any engagement until the marriage was finally settled. Such being his determination, little time was wasted in diplomacy. Whatever dark forebodings the Duke of York might have entertained, were overruled by the king; and the royal pair were married in St James's Palace, then the residence of the duke, at nine o'clock on a quiet Sunday evening; a passage leading from the bedroom of the princess being fitted up as a temporary chapel for the occasion. The royal etiquette of the day permitted few spectators; those present were the king and queen, the Duke of York and his young wife Mary of Modena, with their pages and personal attendants. Compton, bishop of London, performed the ceremony, the king giving away the bride. On the question being asked, 'Who giveth this woman?' Charles exclaimed, 'I do;' a reply not to be found in the matrimonial service of the church. At the words, 'With all my worldly goods I thee endow,' William, in accordance with the Dutch custom, placed a handful of gold coin on the prayer-book, at which the king cried out to the bride: 'Pick it up—pick it up! it is all clear gain!' Immediately after the ceremony, the royal party received the congratulations of the chief officers of state and foreign ambassadors; and at eleven o'clock the bride and bridegroom retired to rest. All the absurd and indelicate wedding-customs of the olden time were observed on this occasion: the cake was eaten, the bride-posset drunk, the stocking thrown, and the curtain drawn, the last by the king himself, who, as he did it, shouted, 'St George for England!' Indeed, the marriage of the Third George with Queen Charlotte, was the first royal wedding in this country at which those customs, 'more honoured in the breach than in the observance,' were finally dispensed with.

This 'Protestant Alliance,' as it was termed, diffusing a general satisfaction over the land, was celebrated with great rejoicing. At Edinburgh, the Duke of Lauderdale announced the welcome intelligence from the Cross, which was hung with tapestry, and decorated with arbours formed of many hundreds of oranges. Then the duke, several of the nobility, the lord provost and civic magistrates, drank the healths of the royal family; the conduits ran with wine, and sweetmeats were thrown among the crowd; while the guns of the castle thundered in unison with the huzzas of the populace.

William was anxious to return to Holland immediately after his marriage, the more so because small-pox had broken out in St James's Palace, and his wife's beloved sister, the Princess Anne, was lying dangerously ill of it. But the queen's birthday falling on the 15th of November, he was induced to wait for the festivities of that occasion, intended to be celebrated with extra pomp on account of the wedding. On the evening of that day, the following Epithalamium, composed by Waller, was sung by the royal musicians before the assembled company at Whitehall.

'As once the lion honey gave,
  Out of the strong such sweetness came,
A royal hero, no less brave,
  Produced this sweet, this lovely dame.

To her, the prince that did oppose
  Such mighty armies in the field,
And Holland from prevailing foes
  Could so well free himself, does yield.

Not Belgia's fleet (his high command),
  Which triumphs where the sun does rise;
Not all the force he leads by land,
  Could guard him from her conqu'ring eyes.

Orange with youth experience has;
  In action young, in council old:
Orange is what Augustus was—
  Brave, wary, provident, and bold.

On that fair tree, which bears his name,
Blossoms and fruit at once are found;
In him we all admire the same,
His flowery youth with wisdom crowned.'

An easterly wind, much against his inclination, detained William in London four days longer. On the morning of the 19th November, the wind veering to the westward, immediate advantage was taken of the change. At the last moment, previous to her departure, the Princess of Orange took leave of Queen Catherine. Seeing her niece in tears, the queen, by way of consolation, said: 'When I came hither from Portugal, I had not even seen King Charles.' To which the princess replied: 'Remember, however, you came to England, but I am going out of it.' The king, Duke of York, and a large party, taking boats at Whitehall, accompanied the newly-married couple to Erith, where they all dined; then travelling by land to Gravesend, the prince and princess went on board the yacht provided to convey them to Holland. Nat Lee, the more than half-crazy dramatist, saw the embarkation, which he thus describes:

'I saw them launch; the prince the princess bore,
While the sad court stood crowding on the shore.
The prince still bowing on the deck did stand,
And held his weeping consort by the hand,
Which waving oft, she bade them all farewell,
And wept, as if she would the briny ocean swell.'

The wind again becoming unfavourable, William landed at Sheerness, and, accompanied by his bride and four attendants, made an excursion to Canterbury. Here he put up at an inn, and his cash falling short, he despatched his favourite Bentinck to the mayor and corporation, requesting a supply of money. The municipal authorities were taken by surprise. Strongly suspecting that the self-styled royal party were impostors, some of the council advised their immediate arrest and committal to prison; others, with more prudence, recommended less stringent measures; but all agreed not to part with one farthing of money; and so the evasive reply was given to Bentinck, that the corporation had no funds at disposal. In the meantime, Dean Tillotson of the Cathedral, the sharp-witted son of a shrewd Yorkshire clothier, heard of the strange affair, and making his way to the inn, saw and recognised the princess. Rushing back to the deanery, he collected all his ready money and plate, and returning to the inn, presented it to the prince. Twelve years afterwards, when William and Mary were king and queen of England, this service of the far-seeing dean was not forgotten. He was made Clerk of the Closet to their majesties, and soon after consecrated Archbishop of Canterbury.

The dean's interposition made a magical change in the state of affairs. The suspicious landlord, who had been inconveniently pressing his foreign guests for the amount of his bill, became in a moment the most obsequious of mortals. The gentlemen of Kent, now knowing who it was they had among them, crowded with their congratulations, and more substantial presents, to the prince and princess. William remained at the inn four days longer, and then left for Margate, where he embarked on the 28th of November; and after a short but stormy passage, the only lady on board unaffected by sea-sickness being the princess, he arrived safely in Holland.



# NOVEMBER 5.

St Bertille, abbess of Chelles, 692.

*Born.*—Hans Sachs, German poet, 1494, *Nuremberg;* Dr John Brown, miscellaneous writer, 1715, *Rothbury, Northumberland.*

*Died.*—Maria Angelica Kaufmann, portrait-painter, 1807, *Rome.*

## THE GUNPOWDER PLOT.

The 5th of November marks the anniversary of two prominent events in English history—the discovery and prevention of the gunpowder treason, and the inauguration of the Revolution of 1688 by the landing of William III. in Torbay. In recent years, an additional interest has been attached to the date, from the victory at Inkerman over the Russians, in the Crimea, being gained on this day in 1854.

Like the Bartholomew massacre at Paris in 1572, and the Irish massacre of 1641, the Gunpowder Plot of 1605, standing as it were midway, at a distance of about thirty years from each of these events, has been the means of casting much obloquy on the adherents of the Roman Catholic religion. It would, however, be a signal injustice to connect the Catholics as a body with the perpetration of this atrocious attempt, which seems to have been solely the work of some fanatical members of the extreme section of the Jesuit party.

The accession of James I. to the throne had raised considerably the hopes of the English Catholics, who, relying upon some expressions which he had made use of while king of Scotland, were led to flatter themselves with the prospect of an unrestricted toleration of the practice of their faith, when he should succeed to the crown of England. Nor were their expectations altogether disappointed. The first year of James's reign shews a remarkable diminution in the amount of fines paid by popish recusants into the royal exchequer, and for a time they seem to have been comparatively unmolested. But such halcyon-days were not to be of long continuance. The English parliament was determined to discountenance in every way the Roman Catholic religion, and James, whose pecuniary necessities obliged him to court the good-will of the Commons, was forced to comply with their importunities in putting afresh into execution the penal laws against papists. Many cruel and oppressive severities were exercised, and it was not long till that persecution which is said to make 'a wise man mad,' prompted a few fanatics to a scheme for taking summary vengeance on the legislature by whom these repressive measures were authorised.

The originator of the Gunpowder Plot was Robert Catesby, a gentleman of ancient family, who at one period of his life had become a Protestant, but having been reconverted to the Catholic religion, had endeavoured to atone for his apostasy by the fervour of a new zeal. Having revolved in his own mind a project for destroying, at one blow, the King, Lords, and Commons, he communicated it to Thomas Winter, a Catholic gentleman of Worcestershire, who at first expressed great horror, but was afterwards induced to co-operate in the design. He it was who procured the co-adjutorship of the celebrated Guido or Guy Fawkes, who was not, as has sometimes been represented, a low mercenary ruffian, but a gentleman of good family, actuated by a spirit of ferocious fanaticism. Other confederates were gradually assumed, and in a secluded house in Lambeth, oaths of secrecy were taken, and the communion administered to the conspirators by Father Gerard, a Jesuit, who, however, it is said, was kept in ignorance of the plot. One of the party, named Thomas Percy, a distant relation of the Earl of Northumberland, and one of the gentleman-pensioners at the court of King James, agreed to hire a house adjoining the building where the parliament met, and it was resolved to effect the purpose of blowing the legislature into the air by carrying a mine through the wall. This was in the spring of 1604, but various circumstances prevented the commencement of operations till the month of December of that year.

THE GUNPOWDER CONSPIRATORS—FROM A PRINT PUBLISHED IMMEDIATELY AFTER THE DISCOVERY.

In attempting to pierce the wall of the Parliament House, the conspirators found that they had engaged in a task beyond their strength, owing to the immense thickness of the barrier. With an energy, however, befitting a better cause, they continued their toilsome labours; labours the more toilsome to them, that the whole of the confederates were, without exception, gentlemen by birth and education, and totally unused to severe manual exertion. To avert suspicion while they occupied the house hired by Percy, they had laid in a store of provisions, so that all necessity for going out to buy these was obviated. Whilst in silence and anxiety they plied their task, they were startled one day by hearing, or fancying they heard, the tolling of a bell deep in the ground below the Parliament House. This cause of perturbation, originating perhaps in a guilty conscience, was removed by an appliance of superstition. Holy-water was sprinkled on the spot, and the tolling ceased. Then a rumbling noise was heard directly over their heads, and the fear seized them that they had been discovered. They were speedily, however, reassured by Fawkes, who, on going out to learn the cause of the uproar, ascertained that it had been occasioned by a dealer in coal, who rented a cellar below the House of Lords, and who was engaged in removing his stock from that place of deposit to another. Here was a golden opportunity for the conspirators. The cellar was forthwith hired from the coal merchant, and the working of the mine abandoned. Thirty-six barrels of gunpowder, which had previously been deposited in a house on the opposite side of the river, were then secretly conveyed into this vault. Large stones and bars of iron were thrown in, to increase the destructive effects of the explosion, and the whole was carefully covered up with fagots of wood.

These preparations were completed about the month of May 1605, and the confederates then separated till the final blow could be struck. The time fixed for this was at first the 3d of October, the day on which the legislature should meet; but the opening of parliament having been prorogued by the king to the 5th of November, the latter date was finally resolved on. Extensive preparations had been made during the summer months, both towards carrying the design into execution, and arranging the course to be followed after the destruction of the king and legislative bodies had been accomplished. New confederates were assumed as participators in the plot, and one of these, Sir Everard Digby, agreed to assemble his Catholic friends on Dunsmore Heath, in Warwickshire, as if for a hunting-party, on the 5th of November. On receiving intelligence of the execution of the scheme, they would be in full readiness to complete the revolution thus inaugurated, and settle a new sovereign on the throne. The proposed successor to James was Prince Charles, afterwards Charles I., seeing that his elder brother Henry, Prince of Wales, would, it was expected, accompany his father to the House of Lords, and perish along with him. In the event of its being found impossible to gain possession of the person of Prince Charles, then it was arranged that his sister, the Princess Elizabeth, should be seized, and carried off to a place of security. Guy Fawkes was to ignite the gunpowder by means of a slow-burning match, which would allow him time to escape before the explosion, and he was then to embark on board a ship waiting in the river for him, and proceed to Flanders.

The fatal day was now close at hand, but by this time several dissensions had arisen among the conspirators on the question of giving warning to some special friends to absent themselves from the next meeting of parliament. Catesby, the prime mover in the plot, protested against any such communications being made, asserting that few Catholic members would be present, and that, at all events, 'rather than the project should not take effect, if they were as dear unto me as mine own son, they also must be blown up.' A similar stoicism was not, however, shared by the majority of the confederates, and one of them at least made a communication, by which the plot was discovered to the government, and its execution prevented.

Great mystery attaches to the celebrated anonymous letter received on the evening of 26th October by Lord Mounteagle, a Roman Catholic nobleman, and brother-in-law of Francis Tresham, one of the conspirators. Its authorship is ascribed, with great probability, to the latter, but strong presumptions exist that it was not the only channel by which the king's ministers received intelligence of the schemes under preparation. It has even been surmised that the letter was merely a blind, concerted by a previous understanding with Lord Mounteagle, to conceal the real mode in which the conspiracy was unveiled. Be this as it may, the communication in question was the only avowed or ascertained method by which the king's ministers were guided in detecting the plot. It seems also now to be agreed, that the common story related of King James's sagacity in deciphering the meaning of the writer of the letter, was merely a courtly fable, invented to flatter the monarch and procure for him with the public the credit of a subtle and far-seeing perspicacity. The enigma, if enigma it really was, had been read by the ministers Cecil and Suffolk, and communicated by them to various lords of the council, several days before the subject

VAULT BENEATH THE OLD HOUSE OF LORDS—FROM AN ORIGINAL DRAWING.

was mentioned to the king, who at the time of the letter to Lord Mounteagle being received was absent on a hunting-expedition at Royston.

Though the conspirators were made aware, through a servant of Lord Mounteagle, of the discovery which had been made, they nevertheless, by a singular infatuation, continued their preparations, in the hope that the true nature of their scheme had not been unfolded. In this delusion it seems to have been the policy of the government to maintain them to the last. Even after Suffolk, the lord chamberlain, and Lord Mounteagle had actually, on the afternoon of Monday the 4th November, visited the cellar beneath the House of Lords, and there discovered in a corner Guy Fawkes, who pretended to be a servant of Mr Percy, the tenant of the vault, it was still determined to persist in the undertaking. At two o'clock the following morning, a party of soldiers under the command of Sir Thomas Knevett, a Westminster magistrate, visited the cellar, seized Fawkes at the door, and carried him off to Whitehall, where, in the royal bedchamber, he was interrogated by the king and council, and from thence was conveyed to the Tower.

It is needless to pursue further in detail the history of the Gunpowder Plot. On hearing of Fawkes's arrest, the remaining conspirators, with the exception of Tresham, fled from London to the place of rendezvous in Warwickshire, in the desperate hope of organising an insurrection. But such an expectation was vain. Pursued by the civil and military authorities, they were overtaken at the mansion of Holbeach, on the borders of Staffordshire, where Catesby and three others, refusing to surrender, were slain. The remainder, taken prisoners in different places, were carried up to London, tried, and condemned with their associate Guy Fawkes, who from having undertaken the office of firing the train of gunpowder, came to be popularly regarded as the leading actor in the conspiracy. Leniency could not be expected in the circumstances, and all the horrid ceremonies attending the deaths of traitors were observed to the fullest extent. The executions took place on the 30th and 31st of January, at the west end of St Paul's Churchyard.

Some Catholic writers have maintained the whole Gunpowder Plot to be fictitious, and to have been concocted for state purposes by Cecil. But such a supposition is entirely contrary to all historical evidence. There cannot be a shadow of a doubt, that a real and dangerous conspiracy was formed; that it was very nearly successful; and that the parties who suffered death as participators in it, received the due punishment of their crimes. At the same time, it cannot be denied that a certain amount of mystery envelops the revelation of the plot, which in all probability will never be dispelled.

## Guy Fawkes's Day.

Till 1859, a special service for the 5th of November formed part of the ritual of the English Book of Common Prayer; but by a special ordinance of the Queen in Council, this service, along with those for the Martyrdom of Charles I., and the Restoration of Charles II., has been abolished. The appointment of this day, as a holiday, dates from

PROCESSION OF A GUY.

an enactment of the British parliament passed in January 1606, shortly after the narrow escape made by the legislature from the machinations of Guy Fawkes and his confederates.

That the gunpowder treason, however, should pass into oblivion is not likely, as long as the well-known festival of Guy Fawkes's Day is observed by English juveniles, who still regard the 5th of November as one of the most joyous days of the year. The universal mode of observance through all parts of England, is the dressing up of a scare-crow figure, in such cast-habiliments as can be procured (the head-piece, generally a paper-cap, painted and knotted with paper strips in imitation of ribbons), parading it in a chair through the streets, and at nightfall burning it with great solemnity in a huge bonfire. The image is supposed to represent Guy Fawkes, in accordance with which idea, it always carries a dark lantern in one hand, and a bunch of matches in the other. The procession visits the different houses in the neighbourhood in succession, repeating the time-honoured rhyme—

'Remember, remember!
The fifth of November,
The Gunpowder treason and plot;
There is no reason
Why the Gunpowder treason
Should ever be forgot!'

Numerous variations and additions are made in different parts of the country. Thus in Islip, Oxfordshire, the following lines, as quoted by Sir Henry Ellis in his edition of *Brand's Popular Antiquities*, are chanted.

'The fifth of November,
Since I can remember,
Gunpowder treason and plot:
This is the day that God did prevent,
To blow up his king and parliament.
A stick and a stake,
For Victoria's sake;
If you won't give me one,
I 'll take two:
The better for me,
And the worse for you.'

One invariable custom is always maintained on these occasions—that of soliciting money from the passers-by, in the formula, 'Pray remember Guy!' 'Please to remember Guy!' or 'Please to remember the bonfire!'

In former times, in London, the burning of the effigy of Guy Fawkes on the 5th of November was a most important and portentous ceremony. The bonfire in Lincoln's Inn Fields was conducted on an especially magnificent scale. Two hundred cart-loads of fuel would sometimes be consumed in feeding this single fire, while upwards of thirty 'Guys' would be suspended on gibbets and committed to the flames. Another tremendous pile was heaped up by the butchers in Clare Market, who on the same evening paraded through the streets in great force, serenading the citizens with the famed 'marrow-bone-and-cleaver' music. The uproar throughout the town from the shouts of the mob, the ringing of the bells in the churches, and the general confusion which prevailed, can but faintly be imagined by an individual of the present day.

The ferment occasioned throughout the country by the 'Papal Aggression' in 1850, gave a new direction to the genius of 5th of November revellers. Instead of Guy Fawkes, a figure of Cardinal Wiseman, then recently created 'Archbishop of Westminster' by the pope, was solemnly burned in effigy in London, amid demonstrations which certainly gave little evidence of any revolution in the feelings of the English people towards the Romish see. In 1857, a similar honour was accorded to Nana Sahib, whose atrocities at Cawnpore in the previous month of July, had excited such a cry of horror throughout the civilised world. The opportunity also is frequently seized by many of that numerous class in London, who get their living no one exactly knows how, to earn a few pence by parading through the streets, on the 5th of November, gigantic figures of the leading celebrities of the day. These are sometimes rather ingeniously got up, and the curiosity of the passer-by, who stops to look at them, is generally taxed with the contribution of a copper.

## THE REVOLUTION OF 1688: POLITICAL SERVILITY.

On 5th November 1688, William, Prince of Orange, landed in Torbay, an event which, if we consider the important results by which it was followed, may perhaps be regarded as the most critical of any recorded in English history. It forms the boundary, as it were, between two great epochs—those of arbitrary and constitutional government—for the great Civil War, in the middle of the seventeenth century, can scarcely be regarded as more than a spasmodic effort which, carried to excess, overshot the mark, and ended by the re-establishment, for a time, of a sway more odious and intolerable, in many respects, than that whose overthrow had cost so much destruction and bloodshed.

We hear much of the folly of King James, and of all the other causes of his dethronement, but nothing of the culpable conduct of large official bodies, and of many individual subjects, who made it their business to encourage him in his sadly erroneous course, and to flatter him into the conviction that he might go any lengths with impunity. About a month before the landing of the Prince of Orange, the lord mayor, aldermen, sheriffs, &c., of the city of London sent the infatuated monarch an address, containing these words: 'We beg leave to assure your majesty that we shall, with all duty and faithfulness, cheerfully and readily, to the utmost hazard of our lives and fortunes, discharge the trust reposed in us by your majesty, according to the avowed principles of the Church of England, in defence of your majesty and the established government.'

The lieutenancy of London followed in the same strain: 'We must confess our lives and fortunes are but a mean sacrifice to such transcendent goodness; but we do assure your majesty of our cheerful offering of both against all your majesty's enemies, who shall disturb your peace upon any pretence whatever.'

The justices of peace for the county of Cumberland said: 'The unexpected news of the intended invasion of the Dutch fills us with horror and amazement, that any nation should be so transcendently wicked as groundlessly to interrupt the peace and happiness we have enjoyed; therefore, we highly think it our duty, chiefly at this juncture, to offer our lives and fortunes to your majesty's service, not doubting but a happy success will attend your majesty's arms. And if your majesty shall think fit to display your royal standard, which we heartily wish and hope you'll never have occasion to do, we faithfully do promise to repair to it with our persons and interest.'

The privy-council of Scotland express themselves thus: 'We shall on this, as on all other occasions, shew all possible alacrity and diligence in obeying your majesty's commands, and be ready to expose our lives and fortunes in the defence of your sacred majesty, your royal consort, his Royal Highness the Prince of Scotland, &c.' Nor were the Scottish peers, spiritual and temporal, behindhand on this occasion, concluding their declaration as follows: 'Not doubting that God will still preserve and deliver you, by giving you the hearts of your subjects, and the necks of your enemies.'

To the like effect, there were addresses from Portsmouth, Carlisle, Exeter, &c. Nay, so fond was James of this sort of support to his government, that he was content to receive an address from the company of cooks, in which they applaud his 'Declaration of Indulgence' to the skies: declaring that it 'resembled the Almighty's manna, which suited every man's palate, and that men's different gustos might as well be forced as their different apprehensions about religion.'

A very short period elapsed before James was made to comprehend, by fatal experience, the value of such addresses, and to discriminate between the voice of the majority of a nation and the debasing servility of a few trimmers and time-servers.

### ABANDONMENT OF ONE OF THE ROYAL TITLES.

On the 5th of November 1800, it was settled by the privy-council, that in consequence of the Irish Union, the royal style and title should be changed on the 1st of January following—namely, from 'George III., by the grace of God, of Great Britain, France, and Ireland, King, Defender of the Faith;' to 'George III., by the grace of God, of the United Kingdom of Great Britain and Ireland, King, Defender of the Faith.' And thus the title of king of France, which had been borne by the monarchs of this country for four hundred and thirty-two years—since the forty-third year of the reign of the Third Edward—was ultimately abandoned. It was the Salic law which excluded Edward from the inheritance of France; but Queen Elizabeth claimed the title, nevertheless, asserting, as it is said, that if she could not be queen, she would be king of France. And it is the more singular that Elizabeth should have retained the title, for, in the second year of her reign, it was agreed, in a treaty made between France and England, that the king and queen of France [Francis II. and his consort Mary of Scotland] should not, for the future, assume the title of king or queen of England or Ireland.

The abandonment of the title of 'King of France' led to our foreign official correspondence being carried on in the English language instead of in French, as previously had been the custom. A droll story, in connection with this official regulation, is told by an old writer. During the war between England and Spain, in the time of Queen Elizabeth, commissioners were appointed on both sides to treat of peace. The Spanish commissioners proposed that the negotiations should be carried on in the French tongue, observing sarcastically, that 'the gentlemen of England could not be ignorant of the language of their fellow-subjects, their queen being queen of France as well as of England.' 'Nay, in faith, gentlemen,' drily replied Dr Dale, one of the English commissioners, 'the French is too vulgar for a business of this importance; we will therefore, if you please, rather treat in Hebrew, the language of Jerusalem, of which your master calls himself king, and in which you must, of course, be as well skilled as we are in French.'

One of the minor titles held by the kings of England, who were also Electors of Hanover, was very enigmatical to Englishmen, particularly when expressed by the following initials, S.R.I.A.T. Nor even when it was extended thus, *Sacri Romani Imperii Archi-Thesaurus*, and translated into English as, 'Arch-Treasurer of the Holy Roman Empire,' was it less puzzling to the uninitiated. The arch-treasurership of the German empire, was an office settled upon the electors of Hanover, in virtue of their descent from Frederick, Elector Palatine; but its duties were always performed by deputy. Nor had the deputy any concern in the ordinary administration of the imperial treasury, his duties being confined to processions, coronations, and other great public ceremonies, when he carried a golden crown before the emperor, and distributed money and gold and silver medals among the populace.

---

## NOVEMBER 6.

**St Iltutus, abbot. St Leonard, hermit and confessor, 6th century. St Winoc, abbot, 8th century.**

*Born.*—Julian, Roman emperor, 331, *Constantinople;* James Gregory, inventor of the reflecting-telescope, 1638, *Aberdeen;* Colley Cibber, dramatist, 1671, *London.*

*Died.*—Caliph Omar, assassinated at Jerusalem, 644; Pope Innocent VII., 1406; Sir John Falstaff, English knight, 1460, *Norwich;* Prince Henry, son of James I. of England, 1612; Gustavus Adolphus, king of Sweden, killed at battle of Lutzen, 1632; John IV., the Fortunate, king of Portugal, 1656; Bernard de Jussieu, distinguished botanist, 1777, *Paris;* Louis Joseph Philip, Duke of Orleans, guillotined at Paris, 1793; Princess Charlotte of England, daughter of George IV., 1817, *Claremont.*

### GUSTAVUS ADOLPHUS.

Napoleon, than whom there could be no more capable judge, placed Gustavus Adolphus among the eight great captains of the world, a list of warriors which commenced with Alexander and ended with himself. With small means Gustavus was called to do much, and genius eked out the deficiency. By the sternest discipline, by original organisation, tactics, and strategy, he made a little host perform the service of a mighty one, and in the process reconstructed the art of war. Medieval routine vanished under his blows, and modern military science may be said to date from his practice.

He was born in 1594, and, ere he was seventeen, he inherited the Swedish throne by the death of his father, Charles IX. There was a law which pronounced the sovereign a minor until he had attained his twenty-fourth year, but Gustavus had shewn so many signs of manliness, that it was set aside in his favour. It is told of Charles IX., that when abandoning in council designs to which he felt himself unequal, he would, as if in a spirit of prescience, lay his hand on the fair head of his boy Gustavus, and say: 'He will do it; he will!'

Into an inheritance of trouble the young man entered. Denmark, Russia, and Poland were at active enmity with Sweden. First, he beat off the Danes; then he attacked the Russians, and took from them all the territory by which they had access to the Baltic. He next invaded Poland, with which he carried on an eight years' war, and closed the contest with the acquisition of a great part of

Livonia, and the town of Riga. In these conflicts he acquired a rare stock of experience, and trained an army of veterans to his hand. Meanwhile, his home-government was well conducted by his chancellor or prime minister, the sage Oxenstiern—he who wrote to his son when perplexed in some diplomatic entanglement: 'You do not know yet, my son, with how little wisdom mankind is governed.' Gustavus once said to his minister: 'You are too phlegmatic, and if somewhat of my heat did not mingle with your phlegm, my affairs would not succeed so well as they do;' to which Oxenstiern answered: 'Sire, if my phlegm did not mingle some coolness with your heat, your affairs would not be so prosperous as they are;' whereon both laughed heartily. A temper, which on provocation rose to fury, was one of the characteristics of Gustavus. In his wrath against pillage by his followers, it is related that he dragged forth a delinquent soldier by the hair of his head, exclaiming: 'It is better that I should punish thee, than that God should punish thee, and me, and all of us on thy account;' and ordered him off to instant execution. His proneness to anger he confessed. All commanders, he said, had their weaknesses; such a one his drunkenness; such a one his avarice; his own was choler, and he prayed men to forgive him.

That most dreadful war, which lasted for thirty years, from 1618 to 1648, and devastated and depopulated Germany, was raging. Tilly, and the imperial troops, were committing frightful atrocities on the Protestants of Bohemia. Austria, moreover, had menaced and insulted Sweden. Gustavus was not only a Protestant, but a zealous one, and, naturally, the eyes of suffering Protestantism turned to him for help, whose fame as a warrior filled Europe. After fair consideration he determined to intervene, and on the 29th of May 1630, when all his measures were arranged, he appeared in the Diet at Stockholm, to bid its members farewell. Taking his daughter, Christina, in his arms, he presented her as their future queen, amidst the sobs and tears of the assembly. 'Not lightly, or wantonly,' he said, 'am I about to involve myself and you in this new and dangerous war; God is my witness that *I* do not fight to gratify my ambition. The emperor has wronged me most shamefully in the person of my ambassador; he has supported my enemies, persecuted my friends and brethren, trampled my religion in the dust, and even stretched his revengeful arm against my crown. The oppressed states of Germany call loudly for aid, which, by God's help, we will give them. I am fully sensible of the dangers to which my life will be exposed. I have never shrunk from dangers, nor is it likely that I shall escape them all. Hitherto, Providence has wonderfully protected me, but I shall at last fall in defence of my country.' Then adjuring all to do their duties in his absence, he bade them 'a sincere—it may be—an eternal farewell.'

Gustavus led over to Germany an army of 15,000 men, in which were many volunteers from Scotland, and among them David Leslie, one of his ablest officers—he whom Cromwell, in after-years, miraculously defeated at Dunbar. As soon as Gustavus got to work, the fortune of the cause he had espoused began to mend. The courtiers of Vienna consoled themselves in saying, he was a snow-man, and would surely melt as he advanced southwards! Tilly, his antagonist—the ugly, little, Jesuit turned soldier, and esteemed the first general of his age—took his measures more wisely: not to be beaten by Gustavus, he said, was as creditable as to be victorious over other commanders. Tilly soon furnished evidence of the truth of his estimate. Gustavus carried all before him in north Germany, and on the 7th of September 1631, he met Tilly himself before Leipsic, and in a hard-fought field utterly defeated him. A second time, in April 1632, he encountered Tilly on the borders of Bavaria, and again defeated him. In this battle Tilly lost his life by a cannon-ball, which broke his thigh.

The Germans were astonished at the strict discipline which distinguished the Swedish army. All disorders were punished with the utmost severity, particularly impiety, theft, gambling, and duelling. Every regiment assembled round its chaplain for morning and evening prayer. The hardships of the war he shared with his soldiers. The peasants of Bavaria would long tell the tale, how, as he forced them to drag his artillery, he would come among them with kind words, and instructions how to place the lever, accompanied by occasional florins. His attention to trifles, his free intercourse with his men, he used to defend in saying: 'Cities are not taken by keeping in tents; as boys, in the absence of the schoolmaster, shut their books; so my troops, without my presence, would slacken their blows.' In all his actions, he moved under profound religious feeling. 'Pray constantly: praying hard is fighting hard,' was his favourite appeal to his soldiers. 'You may win salvation under my command, but hardly riches,' was his encouragement to his officers. He was often wounded, for he exposed himself freely in battle, and by no entreaty could he be persuaded to be more careful. 'My hour,' he would say, 'is written in heaven, and cannot be reversed on earth.'

Tilly being gone, Wallenstein was appointed to command the Imperialists. The opposing armies met on the field of Lützen, and on the 6th of November 1632, Gustavus opened the battle. In the morning, he knelt in front of his lines and offered up a prayer. Then he gave out Luther's Hymn, and a well-known hymn, said to be his own, beginning—

'Fear not, thou little chosen band.'

'God with us!' was the battle-word. All being ready, he cried aloud: 'Now, in God's name, let us at them! Jesus, Jesus, Jesus, let us fight for the honour of thy holy name!' and dashed at the enemy. A pistol-shot broke his arm. 'It is nothing: follow me!' he exclaimed; but his strength failing, he turned his horse's head, and muttered to the Duke of Lauenburg by his side: 'Cousin, take me hence, for I am wounded.' As he turned, an Austrian trooper shouted: 'Art thou here? I have long sought for thee!' and discharged his carbine into the king's shoulder. Gustavus fell from his horse, with the last words, 'My God!' The tidings flew through the army that the king was slain; that he was taken prisoner; and in revenge and in despair his men fought, as Schiller says, 'with the grim fury of lions,' until victory crowned the day. Defaced with wounds, trodden under feet of horses, the body of Gustavus was drawn from beneath a heap of slain, and laid, amid weeping, with his fathers in Sweden. The neighbourhood of the place where he fell is marked to this day by a porphyritic boulder, with the simple inscription, 'G. A.—1632.'

Thus died Gustavus Adolphus, in his thirty-eighth year, and in the third of his championship of Protestantism. His success had begun to awaken alarms among his allies, who feared in him a possible Protestant emperor; yet of this ambition he gave no signs. 'The devil,' he told his chaplain, who found him reading his Bible—'the devil is very near at hand to those who are accountable to none but God for their actions.' What might be his dreams we can never know, but he has left one of the noblest and purest memories in history. Had he lived, it is likely he would have ended quickly that awful war which afflicted Germany for sixteen years after him. Oxenstiern lived to look after the interests of Sweden, and at the peace succeeded in annexing the Baltic province of Pomerania, held by Sweden until 1815, when it was ceded to Prussia.

## DEATH OF THE PRINCESS CHARLOTTE.

The sensation excited throughout the country by this melancholy event was of no ordinary description, and even at the present day it is still vividly remembered. It was indeed a most unexpected blow, the shining virtues, as well as the youth and beauty of the deceased, exciting an amount of affectionate commiseration, such as probably had never before attended the death of any royal personage in England. A parallel to the feeling thus excited has only appeared in recent years on the occasion of the demise of the consort of our beloved sovereign—the good Prince Albert.

In the Princess Charlotte, the whole hopes of the nation were centered. The only child of the Prince Regent and Caroline of Brunswick, she was

PRINCESS CHARLOTTE.

regarded as the sole security for the lineal transmission to posterity of the British sceptre, her uncles, the Dukes of Clarence, Kent, Cumberland, and Cambridge being then all unmarried. Well-grounded fears were entertained that through her death the inheritance of the crown might pass from the reigning family, and devolve on a foreign and despotic dynasty. These apprehensions were dispelled by the subsequent marriage of the Duke of Kent, and the birth of the Princess Victoria, who, in her actual occupancy of the throne, has realised all the expectations which the nation had been led to entertain from the anticipated accession of her cousin.

In May 1816, the Princess Charlotte was married to Prince Leopold of Saxe-Coburg. Their union had been the result of mutual attachment, not of political expediency, and in the calm tranquillity of domestic life, they enjoyed a degree of happiness such as has not often been the lot of royal personages. The princess's approaching confinement was looked forward to by the nation with affectionate interest, but without the least apprehensions as to the result. Early in the morning of Tuesday the 4th of November, she was taken ill, and expresses were sent off to the great officers of state, including the Archbishop of Canterbury and the Lord Chancellor, who immediately attended. Everything seemed to go on favourably till the evening of the following day (Wednesday), when at nine o'clock the princess was delivered of a still-born child. This melancholy circumstance, however, did not appear to affect the princess so seriously as to give any cause for alarm, and about midnight it was deemed expedient to leave her to repose, and the attentions of the nurse, Mrs Griffiths. Ere half an hour elapsed, the latter observed such an alarming change in her patient, that she at once summoned Prince Leopold and the medical attendants, who hurried to the chamber. The princess became rapidly worse, and in about two hours expired.

After the grief of the nation had somewhat subsided, the feeling of sorrow was succeeded by one of anger. It was said that the medical attendants of the princess had mismanaged the case, and a carelessness and neglect, it was affirmed, had been shewn which would have been scandalous had the fate of the humblest peasant-woman been concerned. Extreme caution must be observed in dealing with these popular reports, considering the general propensity in human nature to slander, and the tendency to find in the deaths of eminent personages food for excitement and marvel. There really appears to have been some blundering in the case, but that this was the occasion of the princess's death, we have no warrant for believing. It is a curious circumstance, that Sir Richard Croft, the physician against whom the public odium was chiefly directed, committed suicide ere many months had elapsed.

## A SAILOR'S LETTER.

When Louis XVIII., under the title of the Count de Lille, was obliged to quit the continent after the peace of Tilsit, and take refuge in England, he landed at Yarmouth from the Swedish frigate, *Freya*, and was rowed ashore by a boat's crew from H.M.S. *Majestic*. Pleased with the attention shewn him, the royal exile left fifteen guineas as a guerdon to the men to drink his health. The honest tars, in obedience to an order which had formerly been issued on the subject of taking money from strangers, refused to avail themselves of this munificence. The present case, however, being rather an exceptional one, the men held 'a talk' on the matter, when they resolved to transmit to Admiral Russell the letter, of which the following is a literal copy:

'MAJESTIC, *6th day of November* 1807.

PLEASE YOUR HONOUR,

We holded a talk about that there £15 that was sent us, and hope no offence, your honour. We don't like to take it, because, as how, we knows fast enuff, that it was the true king of France that went with your honour in the boat, and that he and our own noble king, God bless 'em both, and give every one his right, is good friends now; and besides that, your honour gived an order, long ago, not to take any money from no body, and we never did take none; and Mr Leneve, that steered your honour and that there king, says he won't have no hand in it, and so does Andrew Young, the proper coxen; and we hopes no offence—so we all, one and all, begs not to take it at all. So no more at present

From your honour's dutiful servants.'

(SIGNED) 'Andrew Young, *Coxen;* James Mann; Lewis Bryan; James Lord; James Hood; W. Edwards; Jan. Holshaw; Thomas Laurie; Thomas Siminers; Thomas Kesane; Simon Duft; W. Fairclough; John Cherchil; Thomas Laurence; Jacob Gabriel; William Muzzy.'

How the admiral responded to this communication, we are not informed, but it is to be hoped that the worthy tars were eventually permitted to share among them the gift from Louis. As a specimen of blunt and unadorned honesty, the above composition is perhaps unrivalled.

## THE LITTLECOTE LEGEND.

Aubrey appears to have been the first to put into circulation a romantic story of Elizabeth's time regarding Littlecote Hall, in Wiltshire, which at that period was acquired by the Lord Chief-Justice Popham, in the possession of whose family it has since remained. The account given by Aubrey states that Dayrell, the former proprietor, called a midwife, blindfolded, to his house one night, by whom one of his serving-women was delivered of a child, which she saw him immediately after throw upon the fire; that the poor woman was afterwards able to discover and identify the house where this horrid act had been committed; and that Dayrell, being tried for murder before Chief-Justice Popham, only saved his life by giving Littlecote, and money besides, to the judge as a bribe.*

When Lord Webb Seymour was living in Edinburgh, in the early years of the present century, he communicated a traditionary version of this story to Sir Walter Scott, who wrought up a sketch of it as a ballad in his romance of *Rokeby*, and printed it in full in the notes to that poem. Though Lord Webb's story has thus been brought well into notice, we are induced to have it repeated here.

'It was on a dark rainy night in November, that an old midwife sat musing by her cottage-fireside, when on a sudden she was startled by a loud knocking at the door. On opening it, she found a horseman, who told her that her assistance

* William, Prince of Orange, tarried for a day or two in his advance upon London, November 1688, at Littlecote Hall, which Lord Macaulay speaks of as 'renowned down to our own times, not more on account of its venerable architecture and furniture, than on account of a horrible and mysterious crime which was perpetrated there in the days of the Tudors.' William entertained King James's commissioners in the old hall of the mansion, 'hung,' says Lord Macaulay, 'with coats of mail which had seen the wars of the Roses, and with portraits of gallants who had adorned the court of Philip and Mary.'

was required immediately by a person of rank, and that she should be handsomely rewarded; but that there were reasons for keeping the affair a strict secret, and, therefore, she must submit to be blindfolded, and to be conducted in that condition to the bedchamber of the lady. With some hesitation the midwife consented; the horseman bound her eyes, and placed her on a pillion behind him. After proceeding in silence many miles through rough and dirty lanes, they stopped, and the midwife was led into a house, which, from the length of her walk through the apartments, as well as the sounds about her, she discovered to be the seat of wealth and power. When the bandage was removed from her eyes, she found herself in a bedchamber, in which were the lady on whose account she had been sent for, and a man of a haughty and ferocious aspect. The lady was delivered of a fine boy. Immediately the man commanded the midwife to give him the child, and, catching it from her, he hurried across the room, and threw it on the back of the fire that was blazing in the chimney. The child, however, was strong, and by its struggles rolled itself upon the hearth, when the ruffian again seized it with fury, and, in spite of the intercession of the midwife, and the more piteous entreaties of the mother, thrust it under the grate, and, raking the live coals upon it, soon put an end to its life. The midwife, after spending some time in affording all the relief in her power to the wretched mother, was told that she must be gone. Her former conductor appeared, who again bound her eyes, and conveyed her behind him to her own home: he then paid her handsomely, and departed. The midwife was strongly agitated by the horrors of the preceding night, and she immediately made a deposition of the facts before a magistrate. Two circumstances afforded hopes of detecting the house in which the crime had been committed: one was, that the midwife, as she sat by the bedside, had, with a view to discover the place, cut out a piece of the bedcurtain, and sewn it in again; the other was, that as she had descended the staircase, she had counted the steps. Some suspicions fell upon one Darrell, at that time the proprietor of Littlecote House and the domain around it. The house was examined, and identified by the midwife, and Darrell was tried at Salisbury for the murder. By corrupting his judge, he escaped the sentence of the law; but broke his neck by a fall from his horse while hunting, in a few months after. The place where this happened is still known by the name of Darrell's Stile—a spot to be dreaded by the peasant whom the shades of evening have overtaken on his way.'

Scott further added a legend to much the same purport, which was current in Edinburgh in his childhood. In this case, however, it was a clergyman who was brought blindfolded to the house, the object being to have spiritual consolation administered to a lady newly delivered of an infant. Having performed his part, he was rewarded, enjoined to secrecy on pain of death, and hurried off, but in descending the stair, heard the report of a pistol, and the tragedy is presumed to have been completed when he learned next morning that the house of a family of condition, at the head of the Canongate, had been totally consumed by fire during the night, involving the death of the daughter of the proprietor, 'a young lady eminent for beauty and accomplishments.' After many years, feeling uneasy about the secret, he imparted it to some of his brethren, and it thus acquired a certain degree of publicity. 'The divine, however,' says Scott, 'had been long dead, and the story in some degree forgotten, when a fire broke out again on the very same spot where the house of **** had formerly stood, and which was now occupied by buildings of an inferior description. When the flames were at their height, the tumult, which usually attends such a scene, was suddenly suspended by an unexpected apparition. A beautiful female, in a night-dress extremely rich, but at least half a century old, appeared in the very midst of the fire, and uttered these tremendous words in her vernacular idiom: "*Anes* burned, *twice* burned, the third time I'll scare ye all!"' The narrator adds: 'The belief in this story was formerly so strong, that, on a fire breaking out, and seeming to approach the fatal spot, there was a good deal of anxiety testified lest the apparition should make good her denunciation.'

A correspondent of *Notes and Queries* (April 10, 1858), affirms that this story was current in Edinburgh before the childhood of Sir Walter Scott, and was generally credited, at least as regards the murder part of it. He mentions a person acquainted with Edinburgh from 1743, who used to tell the tale, and point out the site of the house. The present writer knew a lady older than Scott, who had heard the story as a nursery one in her young days, and she offered to point out to him the site of the burned house—which, however, death unexpectedly prevented her from doing. Keeping in view Scott's narration, which assigns the head of the Canongate as the place, it is remarkable that a great fire did happen there at the end of the seventeenth century, and the lofty buildings now on the spot date from that time.

It is not calculated to support the credit of the Littlecote legend, that there is another of the same kind localised in Edinburgh. Nor is this all. A similar tale is told by Sir Nathaniel Wraxall, in which an Irish physician, named Ogilvie, resident at Rome about 1743, is represented as taken with eyes bandaged to a house in the country, where he was called upon to bleed to death a young lady who had dishonoured her family—the family proving afterwards to be that of the Duke de Bracciano. This story was communicated to Wraxall by the celebrated Lady Hamilton, and to support its credibility he relates another incident, of the verity of which he had been assured at Vienna and other German cities. About the year 1774, some persons came to the house of the Strasburg executioner, and engaged him to accompany them on a private professional excursion across the frontier, the object being to put to death a person of high rank. 'They particularly enjoined him to bring the sword with which he was accustomed, in the discharge of his ordinary functions, to behead malefactors. Being placed in a carriage with his conductors, he passed the bridge over the river, to Kehl, the first town on the eastern bank of the Rhine; where they acquainted him that he had a considerable journey to perform, the object of which must be carefully concealed, as the person intended to be put to death was an individual of great distinction. They added that he must not oppose their taking the proper precautions to prevent his knowing the place to which he was conveyed. He acquiesced, and allowed them to hoodwink him. On the second day, they arrived at a moated castle, the draw-bridge of which being lowered, they drove into the court. After waiting a considerable time, he was then conducted into a spacious hall, where stood a scaffold hung with black cloth, and in the centre was placed a stool or chair. A female shortly made her appearance, habited in deep mourning, her face wholly concealed by a veil. She was led by two persons, who, when she was seated, having first tied her hands, next fastened her legs with cords. As far as he could form any judgment from her general figure, he considered her to have passed the period of youth. Not a word was uttered; neither did she utter any complaints, or attempt any resistance. When all the preparations for her execution were completed, on a signal given he unsheathed the instrument of punishment; and her head being forcibly held up by the hair, he severed it at a single stroke from her body. Without allowing him to remain more than a few minutes, he was then handsomely rewarded, conducted back to Kehl by the same persons who had brought him to the place, and set down at the end of the bridge leading to Strasburg.

'I have heard the question frequently agitated, during my residence in Germany, and many different opinions stated, relative to the lady thus asserted to have been put to death. The most generally adopted belief rested on the Princess of Tour and Taxis, Augusta Elizabeth, daughter of Charles Alexander, Prince of Wirtemberg. She had been married, at a very early period of life, to Charles Anselm, Prince of Tour and Taxis. Whether it proceeded from mutual incompatibility of character, or, as was commonly pretended, from the princess's intractable and ferocious disposition, the marriage proved eminently unfortunate in its results. She was accused of having repeatedly attempted to take away her husband's life, particularly while they were walking together near the castle of Donau-Stauff, on the high bank overhanging the Danube, when she endeavoured to precipitate him into the river. It is certain, that about the year 1773 or 1774, a final separation took place between them, at the prince's solicitation. The reigning Duke of Wirtemberg, her brother, to whose custody she was consigned, caused her to be closely immured in a castle within his own dominions, where she was strictly guarded, no access being allowed to her. Of the last-mentioned fact, there is little doubt; but it may be considered as much more problematical, whether she was the person put to death by the executioner of Strasburg. I dined in the autumn of the year 1778 with the Prince of Tour and Taxis, at his castle or seat of Donau-Stauff, near the northern bank of the Danube, a few miles from the city of Ratisbon. He was then about forty-five years of age, and his wife was understood to be in confinement. I believe that her decease was not formally announced as having taken place, till many years subsequent to 1778; but this circumstance by no means militates against the possibility of her having suffered by a more summary process, if her conduct had exposed her to merit it; and if it was thought proper to inflict upon her capital punishment. The private annals of the great houses and sovereigns of the Germanic empire, if they were divulged, would furnish numerous instances of similar severity exercised in their own families during the seventeenth and eighteenth centuries.'*

## NOVEMBER 7.

St Prosdecimus, first bishop of Padua, confessor, 2d century. St Werenfrid, priest and confessor. St Willibrord, confessor, first bishop of Utrecht, 738.

*Born.*—William Stukeley, antiquarian, 1687, *Holbeach, Lincolnshire;* Leopold Frederick, Count Stolberg, miscellaneous writer, 1750, *Bramstedt, Holstein.*

*Died.*—Caius Cilnius Mæcenas, patron of literature and art, 8 B.C.; Sir Martin Frobisher, naval explorer, 1594 A.D., *Plymouth;* Gaspar Tagliacozzi, celebrated surgeon, 1599, *Bologna;* John Kyrle, 'The Man of Ross,' 1724; Jean André Deluc, geologist and natural philosopher, 1817, *Windsor;* Karl Gottlieb Reissiger, composer (Weber's Last Waltz), 1859, *Dresden.*

### JOHN KYRLE, 'THE MAN OF ROSS.'

John Kyrle, an active and benevolent man, whose good deeds ought to win the admiration of all, irrespective of fame derived from other sources, has become notable because Pope called him *The Man of Ross*, and wrote a poem in his praise. Few who visit the pleasant town of Ross, in Herefordshire, fail to inquire about John Kyrle; and their interest in his kind doings mingles with the delight which that beautiful neighbourhood always imparts to strangers. The picturesque church, with the pew in which the good man sat for so many years; the bust and the monumental inscription within the church; the beautiful avenue of trees, called the *Prospect*, or the *Man of Ross's Walk*, in the rear of the church; the house which he built for himself; his arm-chair in the club-room of the little inn—all remain objects of interest to the present day.

John Kyrle was a gentleman of limited means, possessing a small estate in and near Ross, in the latter half of the seventeenth century. A friend from another county once called him 'The Man of Ross;' and Kyrle liked the name, because it 'conveyed a notion of plain, honest dealing and unaffected hospitality.' He formed a terrace, or pleasant walk between a field of his and the river Wye, and planted it with trees. He was always ready to plan walks and improvements for his friends, who were glad to avail themselves of his skill in such matters. Expensive undertakings he could not indulge in, for his income was limited to £500 a year. The town being insufficiently supplied with water, Kyrle dug an oval basin of considerable extent in his field, lined it with brick, paved it with stone, and caused the water from the river to be forced into it by an engine, and conveyed by underground pipes to fountains in

* Wraxall's *Historical Memoirs*, i. 262.

the streets. This was the work noticed by Pope in the lines:

'From the dry rock, who bade the waters flow?
Not to the skies, in useless columns tost,
Or in proud falls magnificently lost;
But clear and artless, pouring through the plain,
Health to the sick, and solace to the swain.'

Kyrle next headed a subscription for making a causeway along the low ground between the town and the bridge. It was so well planned that the county authorities afterwards adopted and extended it as part of the high-road to Hereford and Monmouth. The beautiful spire of the church being in an insecure state, Kyrle devised a mode of strengthening it, procured an assessment to pay for the repairs, contributed himself beyond his share of the assessment, and superintended the execution of the work. Pope was wrong in attributing to him the actual building of the spire:

'Who taught that heaven-directed spire to rise;'

and even of the church itself:

'Who builds a church to God, and not to fame.'

To the renovated church Kyrle presented a great bell, which was cast in his presence at Gloucester; he threw into the crucible his own large silver tankard, having first drunk his favourite toast of 'Church and King!' There was at Ross a grant, renewed by successive lords of the manor, of certain tolls on all corn brought to market; the grant was bestowed as a weekly donation of bread to the poor. Kyrle acted as the almoner to the lords of the manor, and won golden opinions by his manner of fulfilling the duties of that office:

'Behold the market-house, with poor o'erspread;
The Man of Ross divides the weekly bread.'

A multitude of other kindly actions endeared him to his townsmen; and when he died (November 7, 1724), the inhabitants felt that they had indeed lost a friend. It is wonderful what he did with his £500 a year, aided by the liberality which he was the means of developing in other persons.

Many pleasant anecdotes are told of the Man of Ross. When he was planting the elm-walk, it was his wont to sally forth with a spade on one shoulder, and a wooden bottle of liquor for a labourer and himself. On one occasion, this labourer, drinking out of the bottle, did not cease till he had emptied it. Kyrle said to him: 'John, why did not you stop when I called to you?' 'Why, sir,' said the man, 'don't you know that people can never hear when they are drinking?' The next time Mr Kyrle applied himself to the bottle, the man placed himself opposite to him, and opened his mouth as if bawling aloud, till Kyrle had finished. The draught ended, Kyrle asked: 'Well, John, what did you say?' 'Ah, you see, sir,' said the man, 'I was right; nobody can hear when he is drinking!' The Man of Ross lived and died a bachelor, under the housekeeping care of a maiden cousin—Miss Bubb. He disliked crowds and assemblies; but was very fond of snug social parties, and of entertaining his friends on market-days and fair-days. His dishes were plain and according to the season. He liked a goose on his table, liked to carve it, and liked to repeat the well-worn old joke about 'cooking one's goose,' and so forth. Roast-beef he always reserved for Christmas-day. Malt liquor and Herefordshire cider were his only beverages. His 'invitation dinners' comprised nine, eleven, or thirteen persons, including Miss Bubb and himself; and he did not seem satisfied unless the guests mustered one of these aggregates. At his kitchen-fire there was a large block of wood, in lieu of a bench, for poor people to sit upon; and a piece of boiled beef, with three pecks of flour made into loaves, was given to the poor every Sunday. He loved a long evening, enjoyed a merry tale, and always appeared discomposed when it was time to separate. At his death, at the age of eighty-four, he had neither debts nor money, so closely did his income and his expenditure always agree. He left £40 to the Blue Coat School of Ross, and small legacies to the old workmen who had assisted him in his numerous useful works. About a year after John Kyrle's death, a tradesman of the town came to his executor, and said privately to him: 'Sir, I am come to pay you some money that I owed to the late Mr Kyrle.' The executor declared that he could find no entry of it in the accounts. 'Well, sir,' said the tradesman, 'that I am aware of. Mr Kyrle said to me, when he lent me the money, that he did not think I should be able to repay it in his lifetime, and that it was likely you might want it before I could make it up; and so, said he, I won't have any memorandum of it besides what I write and give you with it; and do you pay my kinsman when you can; and when you shew him this paper, he will see that the money is right, and that he is not to take interest.'

---

## TYBURN.

This celebrated place of execution, which figures so prominently in the records of crime, is said to have been first established in the reign of Henry IV., previous to which 'The Elms' at Smithfield seems to have been the favourite locality for the punishment of malefactors. The name is derived from a brook called Tyburn, which flowed down from Hampstead into the Thames, supplying in its way a large pond in the Green Park, and also the celebrated Rosamond's Pond in St James's Park. Oxford Street was, at an earlier period, known as *Tyburn Road*, and the now aristocratic locality of Park Lane, bore formerly the name of *Tyburn Lane*, whilst an iron tablet attached to the railings of Hyde Park, opposite the entrance of the Edgeware Road, informs the passer-by that here stood Tyburn turnpike-gate, so well known in old times as a landmark by travellers to and from London.

The gallows at Tyburn was of a triangular form, resting on three supports, and hence is often spoken of as 'Tyburn's triple tree.' It appears to have been a permanent erection, and there also stood near it wooden galleries for the accommodation of parties who came to witness the infliction of the last penalty of the law, such exhibitions, it is needless to state, being generally regarded by our ancestors as interesting and instructive spectacles. Considerable disputation has prevailed as to the real site of the gallows, but it now appears to be pretty satisfactorily ascertained that it stood at the east end of Connaught Place, where the latter joins the Edgware Road, and nearly opposite the entrance to Upper Seymour Street. A lane led from the Uxbridge Road to the place of execution, in the vicinity of which, whilst excavating the ground for buildings, numerous remains were discovered of the criminals who had been buried there after undergoing their sentence.

Among remarkable individuals who suffered death at Tyburn, were the Holy Maid of Kent, in Henry VIII.'s reign; Mrs Turner, notorious as a poisoner, and celebrated as the inventress of yellow starch; John Felton, the assassin of the Duke of Buckingham; the renowned burglar Jack Sheppard, and the thief-taker Jonathan Wild; Mrs Brownrigg, rendered proverbial by her cruel usage of apprentices; and the elegant and courtly Dr Dodd, whom pecuniary embarrassments—the result of a life of extravagance and immorality—hurried into crime. The last malefactor executed here was John Austin, on 7th November 1783, for robbery with violence. At that period the place of execution for criminals convicted in the county of Middlesex, was transferred from Tyburn to Newgate, where, on the 9th of December following the date just mentioned, the first capital sentence, under the new arrangements, was carried into effect. We are informed that some opposition was made by persons residing around the Old Bailey to this abandonment of the old locality at Tyburn, but the answer returned by the authorities to their petition was, that 'the plan had been well considered; and would be persevered in.' Our readers do not require to be informed that the place thus appointed is still the scene of public executions, now happily of much less frequent occurrence than formerly.

Those curious documents, called *Tyburn Tickets*, were certificates conferred under an act passed in the reign of William III., on the prosecutors who had succeeded in obtaining the capital conviction of a criminal. The object of the enactment was to stimulate individuals in the bringing of offenders to justice; and in virtue of the privilege thus bestowed, the holder of such a document was exempted 'from all manner of parish and ward offices within the parish wherein such felony was committed; which certificate shall be enrolled with the clerk of the peace of the county on payment of 1*s.* and no more.' These tickets were transferable, and sold like other descriptions of property. The act by which they were established was repealed in 1818, but an instance is related by a contributor to *Notes and Queries* of a claim for exemption from serving on a jury being made as late as 1856 by the holder of a Tyburn ticket.

The conveyance of the criminals from Newgate to Tyburn by Holborn Hill and the Oxford Road, afforded, by the distance of space traversed, an ample opportunity to all lovers of such sights for obtaining a view of the ghastly procession. A court on the south side of the High Street, St Giles's, is said to derive its name of *Bowl Yard*, from the circumstance of criminals in ancient times on their way to execution at Tyburn, being presented at the hospital of St Giles's with a large bowl of ale, as the last refreshment which they were to partake of on this side of the grave. Different maxims came ultimately to prevail in reference to this matter, and we are told that Lord Ferrers, when on his way to execution in 1760, for the murder of his land-steward, was denied his request for some wine and water, the sheriff stating that he was sorry to be obliged to refuse his lordship, but that by recent regulations they were enjoined not to let prisoners drink when going to execution, as great indecencies had been frequently committed in these cases, through the criminals becoming intoxicated.

One of the most vigorous drawings by Hogarth represents the execution of the Idle Apprentice at Tyburn—a fitting termination to his disreputable career. Referring to this print, and the remarkable change which has taken place in a locality formerly associated only with the most repulsive ideas, Mr Thackeray makes the following observation in his *English Humorists*: 'How the times have changed! . . . . On the spot where Tom Idle (for whom I have an unaffected pity) made his exit from this wicked world, and where you see the hangman smoking his pipe as he reclines on the gibbet, and views the hills of Harrow or Hampstead beyond—a splendid marble arch, a vast and modern city—clean, airy, painted drab, populous with nursery-maids and children, the abodes of wealth and comfort, the elegant, the prosperous, the polite Tyburnia rises, the most respectable district in the habitable globe!'

# NOVEMBER 8.

The Four Crowned Brothers, martyrs, 304. St Willehad, confessor, bishop of Bremen, and apostle of Saxony, end of 8th century. St Godfrey, bishop of Amiens, confessor, 1118.

*Born.*—Edward Pocock, oriental scholar, 1604, *Oxford;* Captain John Byron, celebrated navigator, 1723, *Newstead Abbey.*

*Died.*—Pope Boniface II., 532; Louis VIII., king of France, 1226, *Montpensier;* Duns Scotus, theologian and scholar, 1308, *Cologne;* Cardinal Ximenes, governor of Spain during minority of Charles V., 1517; John Milton, great English poet and prose writer, 1674, *London;* Madame Roland, revolutionist, guillotined at Paris, 1793; Thomas Bewick, wood-engraver, 1828, *Gateshead;* George Peacock, dean of Ely, mathematician, 1858, *Ely.*

## MADAME ROLAND.

The terrible French Revolution brought many women as well as men into prominence—some for their genius, some for their crimes, and some for their misfortunes. Among the number was Madame Roland. She was born at Paris in 1756; her maiden name being Manon Philipon. Her father was an artist of moderate talent; her mother a woman of superior understanding and great sweetness of disposition. Manon made rapid progress in painting, music, and general literature, and became an accomplished girl. She was very religious at first, but afterwards adopted the views then so prevalent in France, and allowed her imagination to get the better of her religion. Plutarch's *Lives* gave her an almost passionate longing for the fame of the great men of past ages; and at the age of fourteen she is said to have wept because she was not a Roman or Spartan woman. In 1781, she married M. Roland, a man twenty years her senior, and much respected for his ability and integrity. During several years, she divided her time between the education of her young daughter, and assisting her husband in his duties as inspector of manufactures. Together they visited England, Switzerland, and other countries, and imbibed a taste for many liberal institutions and usages which were denied to France under the old Bourbon *régime*.

At length the outburst came—the French struggle for liberty in 1789—so soon to degenerate into ruthless anarchy. The Rolands accepted the new order of things with great avidity. M. Roland was elected representative of Lyon to the National Assembly; and he and his wife soon formed at Paris an intimacy with Mirabeau and other leading spirits, at a time when the Revolution was still in its best days. There was a party among the Revolutionists, called the *Girondists*, less violent and sanguinary than the *Jacobins;* and to this moderate party the Rolands attached themselves. When a Girondist ministry was formed, Roland became Minister of the Interior, or what we should call Home Secretary. He appeared at the court of the unfortunate Louis XVI. in a round hat, and with strings instead of buckles in his shoes—a departure from court-costume which was interpreted by many as symbolic of the fall of the monarchy; while his plain uncompromising language gave further offence to the court. Madame Roland assisted her husband in drawing up his official papers; and to her pen is attributed the famous warning-letter to the king, published in May 1792. It occasioned the dismissal of M. Roland from the ministry, but the dreadful doings on the 10th of August terrified the court, and Roland was again recalled to office. By this time, however, the Revolution had passed into its hideous phase; the populace had tasted blood, and, urged on by the Jacobins, had entered upon a course distasteful to the Rolands and the Girondists generally. When the massacres of the 2d of September took place, Roland boldly denounced them in the National Convention; but Robespierre, Marat, Danton, and the other Jacobins, were now becoming too powerful for him. Especially bitter was the wrath of these men towards Madame Roland, whose boldness, sagacity, and sarcasm had often thwarted them. The lives of herself and her husband were not considered safe; and arrangements were made for them to sleep away from their regular home, the Hotel of the Interior, without making the change publicly known. But this deception was little suited to the high spirit of Madame Roland. She said on one occasion: 'I am ashamed of the part I am made to play. I will neither disguise myself nor leave the house. If they wish to assassinate me, it shall be in my own house.'

The crisis came. On the 31st of May 1793, nearly forty thousand of the rabble were marched against the National Convention by the Jacobins, as the most effectual means of putting down the Girondists. In the evening of the same day, Madame Roland was cast into prison—her husband being at the time away from Paris, for his own safety. She never again obtained her liberty, or saw her husband. Her demeanour was firm and admirable; while ardently advocating what she deemed reasonable individual and national freedom, she never hesitated to denounce the men who, by their sanguinary deeds, were sending a thrill of horror through Europe; but in her more silent hours she grieved for her husband and daughter, and for the many friends who were falling under the guillotine. All her jailers she converted into friends by her fascinating manner and general amiability; but they could do nothing to avert her fate. She devoted all her leisure hours in prison to the composition of her *Mémoires;* in which she delineated, with much sprightliness and grace, the events of her happy youth, and with great judgment and mournful pathos, the fearful turmoil of her later years. At one time, during her three months' imprisonment, she almost determined to take poison, like many miserable creatures around her; but her better nature came to her aid, and she resolved to meet her fate bravely. It was a horrible time. On the 16th of October, the unfortunate Marie Antoinette was guillotined. Later in the same month, twenty of the leading Girondists—all personal friends of the Rolands—shared the same fate. And then came the turn of Madame Roland. After being successively imprisoned in the Abbaye, Sainte Pélagie, and the Conciergerie, she was brought to trial as an accomplice of the Girondists. A few days previous to this, Chauvieu, Madame Roland's advocate, visited her in prison, to confer respecting her defence. Interrupting him in his observations, she took a ring off her finger, and said: 'Do not come to-morrow to the Tribunal; you would endanger yourself without saving me. Accept this ring as a simple token of my gratitude. To-morrow, I shall cease to exist.' At the trial, she appeared dressed carefully in white, with her beautiful black hair descending to her waist. Unmoved by the insults to

MADAME ROLAND.

which she was subjected by her brutal judges, she maintained unruffled a dignity of demeanour which might have suited a Roman matron of old; but her death was a predetermined matter, and she was remorselessly condemned. On the fatal day, and at the same hour and place with herself, a man was to be guillotined. To die first on such an occasion had become a sort of privilege among the wretched victims, as a means of avoiding the agony of seeing others die. Madame Roland waived this privilege in favour of her less courageous companion. The executioner had orders to guillotine her before the man; but she entreated him not to shew the impoliteness of refusing a woman's last request. As she passed to the scaffold, she gazed on a gigantic statue of Liberty erected near it, and exclaimed: 'O Liberty! how many crimes are committed in thy name!' The guillotine then took the life of one who was, perhaps, the most remarkable woman of the French Revolution.

The fate of M. Roland was scarcely less romantically tragical. He had lain concealed for some time in Rouen, but on hearing of his wife's death, he set out on the road to Paris, and walked as far as Baudouin. Here he quitted the highway, entered an avenue leading to a private mansion, and sitting down at the foot of a tree, passed a cane-sword through his body. A paper was found beside him with the following inscription: 'Whoever you are who find me lying here, respect my remains; they are those of a man who devoted his whole life to being useful, and who died as he had lived, virtuous and honest.'

## BEWICK, THE ENGRAVER.

Thomas Bewick owes his celebrity to his knowledge of animals, and the admirable manner in which he applied this knowledge to the production of illustrated works on natural history. Born at Cherryburn, in Northumberland, in 1753, he has left us in his autobiography an interesting account of his introduction to the world of art. Exhibiting some indications of taste in this direction, he was, in 1767, apprenticed to Mr Ralph Beilby, of Newcastle-on-Tyne, an engraver of door-plates and clock-faces, and occasionally of copper-plates for illustrating books. 'For some time after I entered the business,' he says, 'I was employed in copying Copeland's Ornaments; and this was the only kind of drawing upon which I ever had a lesson given me from any one. I was never a pupil to any drawing-master, and had not even a lesson from William Beilby, or his brother Thomas, who, along with their other profession, were also drawing-masters. In the later years of my apprenticeship, my master kept me so fully employed that I never had any opportunity for such a purpose, at which I felt much grieved and disappointed. The first jobs I was put to do were blocking out the wood about the lines on the diagrams (which my master finished) for the *Lady's Diary*, on which he was employed by Charles (afterwards the celebrated Dr) Hutton; and etching sword-blades for William and Nicholas Oley, sword manufacturers, &c., at Shotley Bridge. It was not long till the diagrams were wholly put into my hands to finish. After these, I was kept closely employed upon a variety of other jobs; for such was the industry of my master that he refused nothing, coarse or fine. He undertook everything, which he did in the best way he could. He fitted up and tempered his own tools, and adapted them to every purpose; and taught me to do the same. This readiness brought him in an overflow of work; and the workplace was filled with the coarsest kinds of steel stamps, pipe moulds, bottle moulds, brass-clock faces, door-plates, coffin-plates, bookbinders' letters and stamps, steel, silver, and gold seals, mourning-rings, &c. He also undertook the engraving of arms, crests, and cyphers on silver, and every kind of job from the silversmiths; also engraving bills of exchange, bank-notes, invoices, account-heads, and cards. These last he executed as well as did most of the engravers of the time; but what he excelled in was ornamental silver engraving.' This, of course, was a strange way of introduction to the higher departments of art; but it was not a bad one for such a person as Bewick, who had the germs of a true artist within him. 'While we were going on in this way,' his narrative proceeds, 'we were occasionally applied to by printers to execute wood-cuts for them. In this branch my master was very defective. What he did was wretched. He did not like such jobs. On this account they were given to me; and the opportunity this afforded of drawing the designs on the wood was highly gratifying to me. It happened that one of these, a cut of the "George and Dragon" for a bar-bill, attracted so much notice, and had so many praises bestowed upon it, that this kind of work greatly increased. Orders were received for cuts for children's books; chiefly for Thomas Saint, printer, Newcastle, and successor of John White, who had rendered himself famous for his numerous publications of histories and old ballads. . . . My time now became greatly taken up with designing and cutting a set of wood-blocks for the *Story Teller*, *Gay's Fables*, and *Select Fables;* together with cuts of a similar kind for printers. Some of the Fable cuts were thought so well of by my master, that he, in my name, sent impressions of a few of them to be laid before the Society for the Encouragement of Arts; and I obtained a premium. This I received shortly after I was out of my apprenticeship, and it was left to my choice, whether I would have it in a gold medal or money (seven guineas). I preferred the latter; and I never in my life felt greater pleasure than in presenting it to my mother.'*

Once favoured with the good opportunity thus afforded to him, Bewick did not fail to make use of it. Authors and publishers found him to be useful in wood engraving generally, and he earned a living at this while preparing for higher labours in art. In 1773, he engraved cuts for Dr Hutton's *Mathematics*, and for Dr Horsley's edition of Sir Isaac Newton's works. Coming to London in 1776, he executed work for various persons; but he did not like the place nor the people. 'Wherever I went,' he says in the work already quoted, 'the ignorant part of the Cockneys called me "Scotchman." At this I was not offended; but when they added other impudent remarks, I could not endure them; and this often led me into quarrels of a kind I wished to avoid, and had not been used to engage in. It is not worth while noticing these quarrels, but only as they served to help out my dislike to London.'

Having returned to the north, Bewick applied himself to his favourite pursuit of designing and engraving wood-cuts in natural history, and eking out his income meanwhile by what may be termed commercial engraving. *Æsop's Fables*, *History of Quadrupeds*, *History of Birds*, Hutchinson's *History of Durham*, Parnell's *Hermit*, Goldsmith's *Deserted Village*, Liddell's *Tour in Lapland*—all engaged his attention by turn, whilst at the same time he employed himself in a totally different department of the engraver's art—that of executing copper-plates for bank-notes.

It may be worth mentioning here, that cottages, in Bewick's early days, seem to have been adorned with large wood-cuts, as they are now with cheap coloured lithographs. 'I cannot help lamenting,' he observes, 'that, in all the vicissitudes

* *A Memoir of Thomas Bewick, written by Himself.*

which the art of wood engraving has undergone, some species of it is lost and done away. I mean the large blocks with the prints from them, so common to be seen when I was a boy, in every cottage and farmhouse throughout the country. These blocks, I suppose, from their appearance, must have been cut on the plank way on beech, or some other kind of close-grained wood; and from the immense number of impressions from them, so cheaply and extensively spread over the whole country, must have given employment to a great number of artists in this inferior department of wood-cutting; and must also have formed to them an important article of traffic. These prints, which were sold at a very low price, were commonly illustrative of some memorable exploits; or were, perhaps, the portraits of eminent men who had distinguished themselves in the service of their country, or in their patriotic exertions to serve mankind.'

Bewick has acquired a deserved reputation as well for the lifelike correctness of his drawing, as the allegorical and imaginative charm with which he has invested all his productions. His sense of humour was also remarkably strong, and manifests itself very prominently in the vignettes and tail-pieces with which his *History of Quadrupeds* is embellished, though it is to be regretted that he has not unfrequently allowed this propensity to conduct him beyond the limits of decorum. The amiability and domesticity of his temper is very pleasingly shewn in a letter, addressed to a friend in 1825, of which the following is an extract: 'I might fill you a sheet in dwelling on the merits of my young folks, without being a bit afraid of any remarks that might be made upon me, such as, "Look at the old fool, he thinks there is nobody has *sic bairns as he has!*" In short, my son and three daughters do everything in their power to make their parents happy.'

A visitor to the South Kensington Museum will find a series of Bewick's designs, illustrative of the progress of wood engraving. This reviver of the art in modern times, died in 1828, at the age of seventy-six.

## NOVEMBER 9.

The Dedication of the Church of Our Saviour, or St John Lateran. St Mathurin, priest and confessor, 3d century. St Theodorus, surnamed Tyro, martyr, 306. St Benignus or Binen, bishop, 468. St Vanne or Vitonius, bishop of Verdun, confessor, about 525.

*Born.*—Mark Akenside, poet (*Pleasures of Imagination*), 1721, *Newcastle-on-Tyne;* William Sotheby, poetical translator, 1757, *London.*

*Died.*—William Camden, celebrated scholar, and author of *Britannia*, 1623, *Chiselhurst;* Archbishop Gilbert Sheldon, founder of the Sheldon Theatre, Oxford, 1677, *Croydon;* Paul Sandby, founder of English school of water-colour painting, 1809; Marshal Count de Bourmont, distinguished French commander, 1846.

### The Lord Mayor's Show.

Shorn of its antique pageantry, and bereft of its ancient significance, the procession that passes through London to Westminster every 9th of November, when the mayor of London is 'sworn into' office, becomes in the eyes of many simply ludicrous. It is so, if we do not cast a retrospective glance at the olden glories of the mayoralty, the original importance of the mayor, and the utility of the civic companies, when the law of trading was little understood and ill defined. These companies guarded and enforced the best interests of the traders who composed their fraternities. The Guildhall was their grand rendezvous. The mayor was king of the city, and poets of no mean fame celebrated his election, and invented pageantry for exhibition in the streets and halls, rivalling the court masques in costly splendour. Of all this nothing remains but a few men in armour, and a few banners of the civic companies, to appeal for respect in an age of utilitarianism, already too much inclined to sneer at 'old institutions' and 'the wisdom of our ancestors.' Yet such displays are not without their use in a national as well as historical point of view. The history of trade is the true history of civilisation.

In the great struggle that overthrew feudalism, the most important combatants were the men whose lives and fortunes were endangered in the course of the difficult conduct of trade between the great continental cities. The poor nobility, and their proud and impoverished descendants, frequently lived only by rapacious tolls, exacted from merchantmen passing through their territory, or by their castles. Sometimes these traders and their merchandise were seized and detained till a large ransom was extorted; sometimes they were robbed and murdered outright. In navigating the Rhine and the Danube, the boats were continually obliged to pay toll in passing the castles, then literally dens of thieves; and 'the robber knights' of Germany were the terror of all travellers by land. The law was then powerless to punish these nobles, for they held sovereign power in their petty territories, and kings and emperors cared little to quarrel with them in favour of mere traders. The pages of Froissart narrate the contempt and hatred felt by the nobles for the commonalty, and the jealousy which they entertained of the wealth brought by trade. It became, therefore, necessary for merchantmen to band together, and pay for armed escorts, as they still do in the east; this ultimately led to trading leagues between large towns, ending in the famed Hanseatic League of the North German cities, which first established trade on a secure basis, and gave to the people wealth and municipal institutions, leading to the establishment of Hotels de Ville and Mayoralties, rivalling the chateaux and stately pomp of the old nobility.

The magistrates, chosen by popular voice to protect the municipality, were inaugurated with popular ceremonies; and these public celebrations occupied the same place in the estimation of the people, that the court ceremonies and tournaments did in that of the aristocracy. Ultimately, the wealthy townsmen became as proud as the nobles, and rivalled or outdid them upon all occasions where public display was considered needful. When sovereigns entered the cities, they were received by persons habited in classic or mythological costumes, who welcomed them in set-speeches, the invention of the best poets procurable. Elaborately decorated triumphal arches spanned the streets through which they passed; pageants, arranged on prepared stages, awaited their approach at street-corners; and on the arrival of the august guests, the characters embodied in these poured forth complimentary speeches, or sang choruses with music in their honour.

The trading companies of London imitated their continental brethren in observances of the same kind. In the thirteenth and fourteenth centuries, they rode forth in great state to meet and welcome kings or their consorts, when they came to the 'camera regis,' as they termed the city of London. Foreign potentates and ambassadors received similar honours, in order that the dignity of the city might be properly upheld. When the day came to honour their own chief magistrate, of course they were still more pleased to make public displays. Hence the mayor was inaugurated with much pomp. He went to Westminster in his gilded barge, after a noble fashion; and as he returned, he was greeted by mythological and emblematic personages stationed in pageants by the way, their speeches being prepared by civic poets-laureate, who numbered among them such men as the dramatists Peele, Dekker, Webster, Munday, and Middleton.

Giants seem to have been the most general, as they were always the most popular adjuncts, to these civic displays, at home and abroad. They were intimately connected with the old mythic

THE GIANTS IN GUILDHALL.

histories of the foundation of cities, and still appear in continental pageantry; the London giants being two ponderous figures of wood, stationary in the Guildhall. The giants of Antwerp, Douai, Ath, Lille, and other cities of the Low Countries, are from twenty to thirty feet in height, and still march in great public processions. They occasionally unite to swell the cortège in some town, on very great occasions, except the giant of Antwerp, and he is too large to pass through any gate of the city. In English records, we read of giants stationed on London Bridge, or marching in mayoralty processions; the same thing occurring in our large provincial towns, such as Chester, York, and Norwich. In 1415, when Henry V. made his triumphant entry to London, after the victory of Azincourt, a male and a female giant stood at the Southwark gate of entry to London Bridge; the male bearing the city keys, as if porter of London. In 1432, when Henry VI. entered London the same way, 'a mighty giant' awaited him, at the same place, as his champion. He carried a drawn sword, and by his side was an inscription, beginning:

> 'All those that be enemies to the king,
> I shall them clothe with confusion.'

In 1554, when Philip and Mary made their public entry into London, 'two images, representing two giants, the one named Corineus and the other Gogmagog, holding between them certain Latin verses,' were exhibited on London Bridge. When Elizabeth passed through the city, January 12, 1558—the day before her coronation—'the final exhibition was at Temple Bar, which was "finely dressed" with the two giants, who held between them a poetic recapitulation of the pageantry exhibited.' *

The earliest printed description of the shows on Lord Mayor's Day, is that by George Peele, 1585; when Sir Wolstan Dixie was installed.† The pageants were then occupied by children, appropriately dressed, to personate London, the Thames, Magnanimity, Loyalty, &c.; who complimented the mayor as he passed. One 'apparelled like a Moor,' at the conclusion of his speech, very sensibly reminded him of his duties in these words:

'This now remains, right honourable lord,
That carefully you do attend and keep
This lovely lady, rich and beautiful,
The jewel wherewithal your sovereign queen
Hath put your honour lovingly in trust,
That you may add to London's dignity,
And London's dignity may add to yours.'

A very good general idea of these annual pageants may be obtained from that concocted by Anthony Munday in 1616, for the mayoralty of Sir John Leman, of the Fishmongers' Company. The first pageant was a fishing-boat, with fishermen 'seriously at labour, drawing up their nets, laden with living fish, and bestowing them bountifully upon the people.' These moving pageants were placed on stages, provided with wheels, which were concealed by drapery, the latter being painted to resemble the waves of the sea. This ship was followed by a crowned dolphin, in allusion to the mayor's arms, and those of the company, in which dolphins appear; and 'because it is a fish inclined much by nature to musique, Arion, a famous musician and poet, rideth on his backe.' Then followed the king of the Moors, attended by six tributary kings on horseback. They were succeeded by 'a lemon-tree richly laden with fruit and flowers,' in punning allusion to the name of the mayor; a fashion observed whenever the name allowed it to become practicable. Then came a bower adorned with the names and arms of all members of the Fishmongers' Company who had served the office of mayor; with their great hero, Sir William Walworth, inside; an armed officer, with the head of Wat Tyler, on one side, and the Genius of London, 'a crowned angel with golden wings,' on the other. Lastly, came the grand pageant drawn by mermen and mermaids, 'memorizing London's great day of deliverance,' when Tyler was slain; on the top sat a victorious Angel, and King Richard was represented beneath, surrounded by impersonations of royal and kingly virtues.*

There is still preserved, in Fishmongers' Hall, a very curious contemporary drawing of this show; a portion of it is here copied, depicting the lemon-tree; it will be perceived that the pelican (emblematic of self-sacrificing piety) is in front. 'At the foote of the tree sit five children, resembling the five senses,' according to the words written upon the original; to which is added the information, that this pageant 'remaineth in the Fishmongers' Hall for an ornament' during the mayoralty.

PAGEANT EXHIBITED ON LORD MAYOR'S DAY IN 1616.

Throughout the reign of James I., the inventive faculty of the city poet continued to be thus taxed for the yearly production of pageantry. When the great civil war broke out, men's minds became too seriously occupied to favour such displays; and the gloomy puritanism of the Cromwellian era put a stop to them entirely. For sixteen years no record is given of them; in 1655, the mayor, Sir John Dethick, attempted a restoration of the old shows, by introducing the crowned Virgin on horseback; in allusion to the arms of the Mercers' Company, of which he was a member. In 1657, Sir R. Chiverton restored the galley, two leopards led by Moors, a giant who walked on stilts; and a pageant, with Orpheus, Pan, and the satyrs.

With the Restoration came back the old city-shows in all their splendour. In 1660, the Royal Oak was the principal feature in compliment to Charles II., and no expense was spared to make a good display of other inventions, 'there being twice

* We quote from a small volume devoted to the history of *The Giants in Guildhall, with an Account of other Civic Giants, at Home and Abroad*, by F. W. Fairholt, F.S.A.; to which we must refer the reader who may take an interest in a subject that demands larger space than we have at command. We may here merely add, that the names Gog and Magog, applied to the Guildhall Giants, are comparatively modern, formed by breaking one name into two. The old legendary history of London relates that Gogmagog was an ancient British giant, overcome by Corineus, a gigantic follower of Brutus of Troy, who invaded England, and first founded London, under the name of Troynovant, or New Troy. The oldest figure in the Guildhall is supposed to represent Gogmagog, the younger Corineus. They were carved by the civic carpenter, Richard Saunders, in 1707.

† It may be curious to many readers if we here note the rarity and consequent value of these old pamphlets. The copy bought for the Guildhall Library of Peele's pageant cost £20; it consists of four leaves only, thus valued at £5 each!

* Abridged from Fairholt's *History of Lord Mayors' Pageants*, privately printed by the Percy Society, 1843. In these volumes a succinct account (with extracts) is given of each year's display, as far as it can be ascertained from the examination of the rare descriptive pamphlets, in the Bodleian, Guildhall, and British Museum libraries; or those of private collectors, as well as from notices gleaned from our historians.

as many pageants and speeches as have formerly shewn,' says the author, John Tatham, who was for many years afterwards employed in this capacity. He was succeeded by Thomas Jordan, who enlivened his pageantry with humorous songs and merry interludes, suited to Cavalier tastes. The king often came to the mayor's feast, and when Sir Robert Viner, the great banker (as related in *Spectator*, 462), entertained the king in 1674, both got so merry at the feast, that the mayor lost all notion of rank; followed the king, who was about to depart, and insisted on his returning 'to take t'other bottle.' Charles good-humouredly allowed himself to be half-dragged back to the banqueting hall, humming the words of the old song:

'The man that is drunk is as great as a king!'

A loose familiarity was indulged in by the citizens, rather startling to modern ideas. Thus, when the mayor went in his barge, accompanied by all the civic companies in their barges, as far as Chelsea, in 1662, to welcome and accompany the king in his progress down the river from Hampton Court to Whitehall, their majesties were thus addressed by the speaker in the waterman's barge:—'God blesse thee, King Charles, and thy good woman there; and blest creature she is, I warrant thee, and a true. Go thy ways for a wag! thou hast had a merry time on't in the west; I need say no more! But do'st hear me, don't take it in dudgeon that I am so familiar with thee; thou may'st rather take it kindly, for I am not alwayes in this good humour; though I *thee* thee and *thou* thee, I am no Quaker, take notice of that.'

The Plague, and the Great Fire, were the only causes of interruption to the glories of the lord mayor's show during the reign of Charles, until the quarrel broke out between court and city, which ended in the abrogation of the city charter, and the nomination of mayor and aldermen by the king. When Charles was morally and magisterially at his worst, a song was composed for the inauguration of one of his creatures (Sir W. Pritchard, 1682), declaring him to be a sovereign—

'In whom all the graces are jointly combined,
Whom God as a pattern has set to mankind.'

The citizens were insulted in their own hall when the king was 'pleased to appoint' Sir H. Tulse the following year, and a 'new Irish song' was composed for the occasion, one verse running thus:

'Visions, seditions, and railing petitions,
The rabble believe and are wondrous merry;
All can remember the fifth of November,
But no man the thirtieth of January.
Talking of treason, without any reason,
Hath lost the poor city its bountiful charter;
The Commons haranguing will bring them to hanging,
And each puppy hopes to be Knight of the Garter.'

In 1687, James II. dined with the lord mayor, and introduced the pope's nuncio at the foreign ministers' table. The pageants for the day were got up, as the city poet declares, to express 'the many advantages with which his majesty has been pleased so graciously to indulge all his subjects, though of different persuasions.' The value of this author's flattery may be judged from the fact, that the song he composed in praise of James, was used in praise of William III. two years afterwards, when he and his queen honoured the civic feast.

In 1691, Elkanah Settle succeeded to the post of city-laureate, and contributed the yearly pageants until 1708, when the printed descriptions cease. Settle once occupied an important position in the court of Charles II., and his wretched plays and poems were preferred to those of Dryden; more from political than poetic motives. He occupies a prominent position in Pope's *Dunciad*, where the glories of the mayoralty shows are said to

'Live in Settle's numbers one day more.'

This last of the city bards ultimately wrote drolls for Bartholomew Fair, and in his old age was obliged, for a livelihood, to roar in the body of a painted dragon, which he had invented for one of these shows. His works display 'a plentiful lack of wit;' but he had a sense of gorgeous display, that much pleased the populace. The pamphlet descriptive of his inventions for 1698 contains a spirited engraving (see the next page) of the Chariot of Justice, in which the goddess sits, accompanied by Charity, Concord, and other Virtues; the chariot being drawn by two unicorns, guided by Moors, 'sounding forth the fame of the honourable Company of Goldsmiths.' Settle generally contrived to compliment, however absurdly, the company to which the mayor belonged; and on one occasion, when a grocer was elected, introduced Diogenes in *a currant-butt!*

The last great show was in 1702. The mayor was then a member of the Vintners' Company, and their patron, St Martin, appeared, and divided his cloak among the beggars, according to the ancient legend; an Indian galleon followed, which was rowed by bacchanals, and carried Bacchus on board; then came the Chariot of Ariadne; a Scene at a Tavern; and an 'Arbour of Delight,' with Satyrs carousing. It was a costly and stupid display. An entertainment was prepared for the following year, but the death of Prince George of Denmark, the husband of Queen Anne, frustrated it. The altered taste of the age, and the inutility of such displays, led to their abandonment; the land-procession being restricted to a few occasional impersonations, a few men in armour, and some banner-bearers.

In 1706, the lord mayor's feast was held a few days before Christmas, and is thus described by a contemporary. 'The Duke of Marlborough sat on the right hand of the Lord Mayor, in the middle of an oval table, and the Lord High Treasurer on his left, and the rest of the great men according to their deserts and places. The Queen, Prince, Emperor, Duke of Savoy, and other princes allies' healths were drunk; and when the Lord Mayor offered to begin that of the Duke of Marlborough, his Grace rose up twice at table, and would not permit it till that of Prince Eugene was drunk. His Grace and the rest of the great men, so soon as dinner was over (which was about eight o'clock), took coach and returned to court. The claret that was drunk cost 1*s*. 6*d*. a bottle, and the music 50 libs.'*

The mayor rode on horseback in the civic

* Hearne's *Reliquiæ*, i. 115.

procession until 1712, when a coach was provided for his use. In 1757, the gorgeous fabric which is still used on these occasions was constructed at a cost of £1065, 3*s.*; the panels were painted by Cipriani. Royalty generally viewed the show from a balcony at the corner of Paternoster Row, as depicted in the concluding plate of Hogarth's 'Industry and Idleness,' which gives a vivid picture of this 'gaudy day' in the city. Afterwards Mr Barclay's house, opposite Bow Church, was chosen for the same purpose.

Some few modern attempts have been made to resuscitate the old pageants. In 1837, two colossal figures of the Guildhall Giants walked in the procession. In 1841, a ship fully rigged and manned was drawn through the streets on wheels; the sailors were personated by boys from the naval school at Greenwich. But the most ambitious, and the last of these attempts, was made in 1853, when Mr Fenton, the scenic artist of Sadler's Wells Theatre, and Mr Cooke of Astley's, under the superintendence of Mr Bunning, the city architect, reproduced the old allegorical cars, with modern improvements. First came a 'Chariot of Justice,' drawn by six horses; followed by standard-bearers of all nations on horseback; an Australian cart drawn by oxen, and containing a gold-digger employed in washing quartz; then came attendants carrying implements of industry; succeeded by an enormous car drawn by nine horses, upon which was placed a terrestrial globe, with a throne upon its summit, on which sat Peace and Prosperity, represented by two young ladies from Astley's. Good as was the intention and execution of this pageant, it was felt to be out of place in this modern age of utilitarianism; and this 'turning of Astley's into the streets,' will probably never be again attempted. Soon after this the city barges were sold, and the water-pageant abolished. The yearly procession to Westminster is now shorn of all dignity or significance.

CHARIOT OF JUSTICE IN THE LORD MAYOR'S PAGEANT, 1698.

The banquet in Guildhall is now the great feature of the day. The whole of the cabinet ministers are invited, and their speeches after dinner are expected to explain the policy of their government. The cost of this feast is estimated at £2500. Half of this sum is paid by the mayor, the other half is divided between the two sheriffs. The annual expense connected with the office of mayor is over £25,000. To meet this there is an income of about £8000; other sums accrue from fines and taxes; but it is expected, and is indeed necessary, that the mayor and sheriffs expend considerable sums from their own purses during their year of office; the mayor seldom parting with less than £10,000.

---

## NOVEMBER 10.

Saints Trypho and Respicius, martyrs, and Nympha, virgin, 3d and 5th centuries. Saints Milles, bishop of Susa, Arbrosimus, priest, and Sina, deacon, martyrs in Persia, 341. St Justus, archbishop of Canterbury, confessor, 627. St Andrew Avellino, confessor, 1608.

---

*Born.*—Mahomet, or Mohammed, Arabian prophet, founder of Islamism, 570, *Mecca;* Martin Luther, German reformer, 1483, *Eisleben, Saxony;* Robert Devereux, Earl of Essex, favourite of Queen Elizabeth, 1567, *Netherwood, Herefordshire;* Oliver Goldsmith, poet and dramatist, 1728, *Pallasmore, Ireland;* Granville Sharp, slavery abolitionist and miscellaneous writer, 1734, *Durham;* Friedrich Schiller, poet and dramatist, 1759, *Marbach, Würtemberg.*

*Died.*—Ladislaus VI. of Hungary, killed at Varna, 1444; Pope Paul III. (Alexander Farnese), 1549; Marshal Anne de Montmorency, killed at St Denis, 1567; Gideon Algernon Mantell, geologist, 1852, *London;* Isidore Geoffroy St Hilaire, zoologist, 1861; Prince Leopold George Frederick, King of the Belgians, 1865.

## RALPH ALLEN: FIELDING'S 'ALLWORTHY.'

For his public usefulness in improving the national means of epistolary correspondence, the name of Ralph Allen is entitled to rank with those of John Palmer and Sir Rowland Hill; yet we may in vain search for his name in the biographical dictionaries. But for the notice which Pope has taken of him in his verses, it almost appears as if we should have known nothing whatever of one of the noblest characters of any age or country.

To give the reader an idea of the services which Allen rendered to the postal institutions of the country, it will only be necessary to state that in the reign of Queen Anne (1710), all previous acts relating to the post-office were abrogated, and the entire establishment was remodelled under what is officially spoken of as 'the act of settlement.' Under this new statute, increased powers were given to the post-office authorities, and the entire service rapidly improved; while each year saw considerable sums added to the available revenue of the country. This progress, however, arose from improvements which had been effected on post-roads alone; and although the new act gave facilities for the establishment of 'cross-posts,' they were not attempted till the year 1720, when a private individual undertook to supply those parts of the country, not on the line of the great post-roads, with equal postal facilities. That individual was Mr Ralph Allen, who, at the time, filled the office of deputy-postmaster of Bath. Mr Allen, who, from his position, must have been well aware of the defects of the existing system, proposed to the government to establish cross-posts between Exeter and Chester, going by way of Bristol, Gloucester, and Worcester; connecting, in this way, the west of England with the Lancashire districts and the mail route to Ireland, and giving independent postal inter-communication to all the important towns lying in the direction to be taken. Previous to this proposal, letters passing between neighbouring towns were conveyed by strangely circuitous routes; for instance, letters from Cheltenham or Bath for Worcester or Birmingham, required to go first to the metropolis, and then to be sent back again by another post-road. This manner of procedure, in those days of slow locomotion, caused serious delays, and frequently great inconvenience. Mr Allen's proposition necessitated a complete reconstruction of the mail-routes; but he proved to the Lords of the Treasury that this was a desideratum—that it would be productive to the revenue and beneficial to the country. By his representations, he succeeded in inducing the executive to grant him a lease for life of all the cross-posts that should be established. His engagements bound him to pay a fixed rental of £6000 a year, and to bear all the costs of the new service. In return, the surplus revenue was to belong to him. The enterprise was remunerative from the first. From time to time the contract was renewed, always at the same rental; each time, however, the government required Allen to include other branches of road in his engagement (the new districts were never burdens to him for more than a few weeks), till at his death the cross-posts had extended to all parts of the country. Towards the last, this private project had become so gigantic as to be nearly unmanageable, and the time was anxiously awaited when it should become merged in the general establishment. Mr Allen died in 1764, when the post-office authorities absorbed his department, and managed it so as to quadruple the amount of proceeds in two years.

Mr Allen had reaped golden harvests. In an account which he left at his death, he estimated the net profits of his contract at £10,000 annually—a sum which, during his term of office, amounted, on his own shewing, to nearly half a million sterling! Whilst in official quarters his success was greatly envied, he commanded, in his private capacity, universal respect. In the only short account of this estimable man which we have seen, a contemporary writer states, that he 'was not more remarkable for the ingenuity and industry with which he made a very great fortune, than for the charity, generosity, and kindness with which he spent it.' It is certain that he bestowed a considerable part of his income in works of charity, and in supporting needy men of letters. He was a great friend and benefactor of Fielding; and in *Tom Jones*, the novelist has gratefully drawn Mr Allen's character in the person of Allworthy. He enjoyed the friendship of Chatham; and Pope, Warburton, and other men of literary distinction, were his familiar companions. Pope has celebrated one of his principal virtues, unassuming benevolence, in the well-known lines:

'Let humble *Allen*, with an awkward shame,
Do good by stealth, and blush to find it fame.'

Mr Allen divided his time between the literary society of London and his native city of Bath, near which city stood his elegant villa of Prior Park. A codicil to his will, dated November 10, a short time before his death, contains the following bequest: 'For the last instance of my friendly and grateful regard for the best of friends, as well as for the most upright and ablest of ministers that has adorned our country, I give to the Right Honourable William Pitt the sum of one thousand pounds, to be disposed of by him to any of his children that he may be pleased to appoint.'

---

## THE *TIMES* TESTIMONIAL.

A remarkable instance was afforded, a few years ago, of the power of an English newspaper, and its appreciation by the commercial men of Europe. It is known to most readers at the present day, that the proprietors and editors of the daily papers make strenuous exertions to obtain the earliest possible information of events likely to interest the public, and take pride in insuring for this information all available accuracy and fulness; but it is not equally well known how large is the cost incurred by so doing. None but wealthy proprietors could venture so much, for an object, whose importance and interest may be limited to a single day's issue of the paper.

In 1841, Mr O'Reilly, the *Times* correspondent at Paris, received secret information of an enormous fraud that was said to be in course of perpetration on the continent. There were fourteen persons—English, French, and Italian—concerned, headed by a French baron, who possessed great talent, great knowledge of the continental world, and a most polished exterior. His plan was one by which European bankers would have been robbed of at least a million sterling; the conspirators having reaped about £10,000, when they were discovered. The grand *coup* was to have been this—to prepare a number of forged letters of credit, to present them simultaneously at the houses of all the chief bankers in Europe, and to divide the plunder at once. How Mr O'Reilly obtained his information, is one of the secrets of newspaper management; but as he knew that the chief conspirator was a man who would not scruple to send a pistol-shot into any one who frustrated him, he wisely determined to date his letter to the *Times* from Brussels instead of Paris, to give a false scent. This precaution, it is believed, saved his life. The letter appeared in the *Times* on 26th May. It produced a profound sensation, for it revealed to the commercial world a conspiracy of startling magnitude. One of the parties implicated, a partner in an English house at Florence, applied to the *Times* for the name of its informant; but the proprietors resolved to bear all the consequences. Hence the famous action, *Bogle* v. *Lawson*, brought against the printer of the *Times* for libel, the proprietors, of course, being the parties who bore the brunt of the matter. As the article appeared on 26th May, and as the trial did not come on till 16th August, there was ample time to collect evidence. The *Times* made immense exertions, and spent a large sum of money, in unravelling the conspiracy throughout. The verdict was virtually an acquittal, but under such circumstances that each party had to pay his own costs.

The signal service thus rendered to the commercial world, the undaunted manner in which the *Times* had carried through the whole matter from beginning to end, and the liberal way in which many thousands of pounds had been spent in so doing, attracted much public attention. A meeting was called, and a subscription commenced, to defray the cost of the trial, as a testimonial to the proprietors. This money was nobly declined in a few dignified and grateful words; and then the committee determined to perpetuate the memory of the transaction in another way. They had in their hands £2700, which had been subscribed by 38 public companies, 64 members of the city corporation, 58 London bankers, 120 London merchants and manufacturers, 116 county bankers and merchants, and 21 foreign bankers and merchants. In November, the committee made public their mode of appropriating this sum: namely, £1000 for a '*Times* Scholarship' at Oxford, for boys in Christ's Hospital; £1000 for a similar scholarship at Cambridge, for boys of the city of London School; and the remainder of the money for four tablets, to bear suitable inscriptions—one to be put up at the Royal Exchange, one at Christ's Hospital, one at the City of London School, and one at the *Times* printing-office.

# NOVEMBER 11.

**St Mennas, martyr, about 304. St Martin, bishop of Tours, confessor, 397.**

## Martinmas.

St Martin, the son of a Roman military tribune, was born at Sabaria, in Hungary, about 316. From his earliest infancy, he was remarkable for mildness of disposition; yet he was obliged to become a soldier, a profession most uncongenial to his natural character. After several years' service, he retired into solitude, from whence he was withdrawn, by being elected bishop of Tours, in the year 374. The zeal and piety he displayed in this office were most exemplary. He converted the whole of his diocese to Christianity, overthrowing the ancient pagan temples, and erecting churches in their stead. From the great success of his pious endeavours, Martin has been styled the Apostle of the Gauls; and, being the first confessor to whom the Latin Church offered public prayers, he is distinguished as the father of that church. In remembrance of his original profession, he is also frequently denominated the Soldier Saint.

The principal legend, connected with St Martin, forms the subject of our illustration, which

ST MARTIN DIVIDING HIS CLOAK WITH A BEGGAR.

represents the saint, when a soldier, dividing his cloak with a poor naked beggar, whom he found perishing with cold at the gate of Amiens. This cloak, being most miraculously preserved, long formed one of the holiest and most valued relics of France; when war was declared, it was carried before the French monarchs, as a sacred banner, and never failed to assure a certain victory. The oratory in which this cloak or cape—in French, *chape*—was preserved, acquired, in consequence, the name of *chapelle*, the person intrusted with its care being termed *chapelain:* and thus, according to Collin de Plancy, our English words chapel and chaplain are derived. The canons of St Martin of Tours and St Gratian had a lawsuit, for sixty years, about a sleeve of this cloak, each claiming it as their property. The Count Larochefoucauld at last put an end to the proceedings, by sacrilegiously committing the contested relic to the flames.

Another legend of St Martin is connected with one of those literary curiosities termed a palindrome. Martin, having occasion to visit Rome, set out to perform the journey thither on foot. Satan, meeting him on the way, taunted the holy man for not using a conveyance more suitable to a bishop. In an instant the saint changed the Old Serpent into a mule, and jumping on its back, trotted comfortably along. Whenever the transformed demon slackened pace, Martin, by making the sign of the cross, urged it to full speed. At last, Satan utterly defeated, exclaimed:

'Signa te Signa: temere me tangis et angis:
Roma tibi subito motibus ibit amor.'

In English—'Cross, cross thyself: thou plaguest and vexest me without necessity; for, owing to my exertions, thou wilt soon reach Rome, the object of thy wishes.' The singularity of this distich, consists in its being palindromical—that is, the same, whether read backwards or forwards. *Angis*, the last word of the first line, when read backwards, forming *signa*, and the other words admitting of being reversed, in a similar manner.

The festival of St Martin, happening at that season when the new wines of the year are drawn from the lees and tasted, when cattle are killed for winter food, and fat geese are in their prime, is held as a feast-day over most parts of Christendom. On the ancient clog almanacs, the day is marked by the figure of a goose; our bird of Michaelmas being, on the continent, sacrificed at Martinmas. In Scotland and the north of England, a fat ox is called a mart, clearly from Martinmas, the usual time when beeves are killed for winter use. In Tusser's *Husbandry*, we read:

'When Easter comes, who knows not then,
That veal and bacon is the man?
And Martilmass beef doth bear good tack,
When country folk do dainties lack.'

Barnaby Googe's translation of *Neogeorgus*, shews us how Martinmas was kept in Germany, towards the latter part of the fifteenth century—

'To belly chear, yet once again,
Doth Martin more incline,
Whom all the people worshippeth
With roasted geese and wine.
Both all the day long, and the night,
Now each man open makes
His vessels all, and of the must,*
Oft times, the last he takes,
Which holy Martin afterwards
Alloweth to be wine,
Therefore they him, unto the skies,
Extol with praise divine.'

*New wine not fully fermented.

A genial saint, like Martin, might naturally be expected to become popular in England; and there are no less than seven churches in London and Westminster, alone, dedicated to him. There is certainly more than a resemblance between the Vinalia of the Romans, and the Martinalia of the medieval period. Indeed, an old ecclesiastical calendar, quoted by Brand, expressly states under 11th November: 'The Vinalia, a feast of the ancients, removed to this day. Bacchus in the figure of Martin.' And thus, probably, it happened, that the beggars were taken from St Martin, and placed under the protection of St Giles; while the former became the patron saint of publicans, tavern-keepers, and other dispensers of good eating and drinking. In the hall of the Vintners' Company of London, paintings and statues of St Martin and Bacchus reign amicably together side by side. On the inauguration, as lord mayor, of Sir Samuel Dashwood, an honoured vintner, in 1702, the company had a grand processional pageant, the most conspicuous figure in which was their patron saint, Martin, arrayed, *cap-à-pie*, in a magnificent suit of polished armour; wearing a costly scarlet cloak, and mounted on a richly plumed and caparisoned white charger: two esquires, in rich liveries, walking at each side. Twenty satyrs danced before him, beating tambours, and preceded by ten halberdiers, with rural music. Ten Roman lictors, wearing silver helmets, and carrying axes and fasces, gave an air of classical dignity to the procession, and, with the satyrs, sustained the bacchanalian idea of the affair. A multitude of beggars, 'howling most lamentably,' followed the warlike saint, till the procession stopped in St Paul's Churchyard. Then Martin, or his representative at least, drawing his sword, cut his rich scarlet cloak in many pieces, which he distributed among the beggars. This ceremony being duly and gravely performed, the lamentable howlings ceased, and the procession resumed its course to Guildhall, where Queen Anne graciously condescended to dine with the new lord mayor.

---

*Born.*—John Albert Fabricius, scholar and editor, 1668, *Leipsic;* Firmin Abauzit, celebrated man of learning, 1679, *Uzès, in Languedoc;* Earl of Bridgewater, founder of the Bridgewater Treatise Bequest, 1758; Marie François Xavier Bichat, eminent French anatomist, 1771, *Thoirette;* Dr John Abercrombie, physician and author, 1781, *Aberdeen.*

*Died.*—Canute the Dane, king of England, 1035, *Shaftesbury;* Thomas, Lord Fairfax, Parliamentary general, 1671; Jean Sylvain Bailly, eminent astronomer, guillotined at Paris, 1793; Joshua Brookes, eccentric clergyman, 1821, *Manchester.*

## A FATHER AND SON: SINGULAR SPECIMEN OF A MANCHESTER CLERGYMAN.

On 11th November 1821, died the Rev. Joshua Brookes, M.A., chaplain of the Collegiate Church, Manchester. He was of humble parentage, being the son of a shoemaker or cobbler, of Cheadle Hulme, near Stockport, and he was baptized, May 19, 1754, at Stockport. His father, Thomas

Brookes, was a cripple, of uncouth mien, eccentric manners, and great violence of temper, peculiarities which gained him the sobriquet of 'Pontius Pilate.' Many stories are told of his rude manners and impetuous disposition. He removed to Manchester while Joshua was yet a child, and, in his later years, occupied a house in a passage in Long Millgate, opposite the house of Mr Lawson, then high-master of the Manchester Grammar School. At that school Joshua received his education, and, being a boy of quick parts, was much noticed by the Rev. Thomas Aynscough, one of the Fellows of the Collegiate Church, by whose assistance, and that of some of the wealthier residents of Manchester, his father was enabled to send him to Oxford, where he was entered at Brasenose College. The father went round personally to the houses of various rich inhabitants, to solicit pecuniary aid to send his son to college. Joshua took his degree of M.A. in 1771. In 1789, he was nominated by the warden and fellows of Manchester to the perpetual curacy of the chapelry of Chorlton-cum-Hardy, which he resigned in December 1790, on being appointed to a chaplaincy in the Manchester Collegiate Church, which he held till his death. During his chaplaincy of thirty-one years, he is supposed to have baptized, married, and buried more persons than any other clergyman in the kingdom. He inherited much of his father's mental constitution, especially his rough manners and extreme irascibility; but the influence of education, and a sense of what his position demanded, tended somewhat to temper his eccentricities. It is curious to mark the reflection of the illiterate father's temperament and disposition in the educated son. The father was fond of angling, and having once obtained permission to fish in the pond of Strangeway's Hall, he had an empty hogshead placed in the field, near the brink of the pond, and in this cask—a sort of vulgar Diogenes in his tub—he frequently spent whole nights in his favourite pursuit. In his later years, while sitting at his door, as was his custom, his strange appearance and figure, with a red night-cap on his head, attracted the notice of a market-woman, who, in passing, made some rude remark. Eager for revenge, and yet unable to follow her by reason of his lameness, old Brookes despatched his servant for a sedan-chair, wherein he was conveyed to the market-place; and, having singled out the object of his indignation, he belaboured her with his crutch with such fury, that she had to be rescued by a constable. He was of intemperate habits and extreme coarseness in speech, and was always getting involved in disputes and scrapes. Joshua, to his honour, always treated the old man with respect and forbearance; and, after getting the chaplaincy, he maintained his father for many years till the latter's death. Such was the father. A few traits of the son will complete this strange picture of a pair of Manchester originals in the last century. Young Brookes was at one time an assistant-master at the Grammar School, where he made himself very unpopular with the boys, especially the senior classes, being constantly involved in warfare with them, physical and literary. Sometimes he would singly defy the whole school, and be forcibly ejected from the school-room, fighting with hand and foot against his numerous assailants, and hurling reproaches at them as 'blockheads.' On one occasion, the arrival on the spot of the head-master alone saved him from being pitched over the school-yard parapet-wall, into the river Irk, many feet below. The upper-scholars not only ridiculed him in lampoons, but fathered verses upon him, as that celebrated wit, Bishop Mansel, did upon old Viner. He was sadly vexed by a mischievous rascal writing on his door: 'Odi profanum *Bruks*' [the Lancashire pronunciation of his name] 'et arceo.' Nor was he less annoyed by a satirical effusion occasioned by his inviting a friend to dine with him, and entertaining him only with a black-pudding. The lampoon in question commenced with—

'O Jotty, you dog!
Your house, we well know,
Is head-quarters of prog.'

'Jotty Bruks,' as he was usually called, may be regarded as a perpetual cracker, always ready to go off when touched or jostled in the slightest degree. He was no respecter of persons, but warred equally and indifferently with the passing chimney-sweep, the huxtress, the mother who came too late to be churched, and with his superiors, the warden and fellows. The last-mentioned parties, on one occasion, for some trivial misbehaviour, expelled him from the chapter-house, until he should make an apology. This he sturdily refused to do; but would put on his surplice in an adjoining chapel, and then, standing close outside the chapter-house door, in the south aisle of the choir, would exclaim to those who were passing on to attend divine service: 'They won't let me in. They say I can't behave myself.' At another time, he was seen, in the middle of the service, to box the ears of a chorister-boy, for coming late. Sometimes, while officiating, he would leave the choir during the musical portion of the service, go down to the side-aisles, and chat with any lounger till the time came for his clerical functions being required in person. Once, when surprise was expressed at this unseemly procedure, he only replied: 'Oh! I frequently come out while they're singing *Ta Daum*.' Talking in this strain to a very aged gentleman, and often making use of the expression, 'We old men,' Mr Johnson (in the dialect then almost universal in Manchester) turned upon him with the question: 'Why, how owd art ta?' 'I'm sixty-foive,' says Jotty. 'Sixty-foive!' rejoined his aged interlocutor; 'why t'as a lad; here's a penny for thee. Goo, buy thysel' a penny-poye [pie].' So Jotty returned to the reading-desk, to read the morning-lesson, a penny richer. A child was once brought to him to be christened, whose parents desired to give it the name of Bonaparte. This designation he not only refused to bestow, but entered his refusal to do so in the register of baptisms. In the matter of marriages his conduct was peremptory and arbitrary. He so frightened a young wife, a parishioner of his, who had been married at Eccles, by telling her of consequent danger to the rights of her children, that, to make all right and sure, she was re-married by Joshua himself at the Collegiate Church. Once, when marrying a number of couples, it was found, on joining hands, that there was one woman without any bridegroom. In this dilemma, instead of declining to marry this luckless bride, Joshua required one of the men present to act as bridegroom both to her and his own partner. The lady interested, objecting to so summary a mode of getting over the difficulty, Joshua replied: 'I can't stand talking to thee; prayers' [that is, the daily morning-service] 'will be in directly, thou must go and find him after.' After the ceremony, the defaulter was found drunk in the 'Ring of Bells' public-house, adjoining the church. The churchyard was surrounded by a low parapet-wall, with a sharp-ridged coping, to walk along which required nice balancing of the body, and was one of the favourite 'craddies' [feats] of the neighbouring boys. The practice greatly annoyed Joshua; and one day, whilst reading the burial-service at the grave-side, his eye caught a chimney-sweep walking on the wall. This caused the eccentric chaplain, by abruptly giving an order to the beadle, to make the following interpolation in the solemn words of the funeral-service: 'And I heard a voice from heaven, saying'—— 'Knock that black rascal off the wall!' This *contretemps* was made the subject of a caricature by a well-known character of the day, 'Jack Batty;' who, on a prosecution for libel being instituted, left Manchester. After a long absence he returned, and on his entreating Joshua to pardon him, he was readily forgiven. Another freak of this queer parson was to leave a funeral in which he was officiating, cross the churchyard to the adjacent Half Street, and enter a confectioner's shop, kept by a widow, named Clowes, where he demanded a supply of horehound-lozenges for his throat. Having obtained these, which were never refused, though he never paid for them, he would composedly return to the grave, and resume the interrupted service. In his verbal encounters, he sometimes met with his match. One day, 'Jemmy Watson,' better known by his sobriquet of 'Doctor,' having provoked Joshua by a pun at his expense, the chaplain exclaimed: 'Thou 'rt a blackguard, Jemmy!' The Doctor retorted: 'If I be not a blackguard, Josse, I'm next to one.' On another occasion, he said to Watson: 'This churchyard, the cemetery of the Collegiate Church, must be enclosed; and we shall want a lot of railing.' The Doctor archly replied: 'That can't be, Josse; there's *railing enough* in the church daily.' In his last illness, the parish-clerk came to see him. Joshua had lost the sight of one eye, and the clerk venturing to say that he thought the other eye was also gone, the dying man (who had remained silent and motionless for hours), with a flash of the old fire, shouted twice: 'Thou 'rt a liar, Bob!' A few days afterwards, both eyes were closed in death. He died unmarried, in the sixty-eighth year of his age, and was buried at the south-west end and corner of the Collegiate Church. Poor Joshua! a very 'Ishmael' all his life, he found rest and peace at last. A man of many foibles and failings, he was free from the grosser vices, and in all the private relations of life he was exemplary.

---

## THE DAY OF DUPES:

### TRIUMPH OF CARDINAL RICHELIEU.

This whimsical title has been given to the 11th of November 1630, on the occasion of the triumph of Cardinal Richelieu over his enemies, who imagined that they had succeeded in casting him to the ground, never again to rise. The intriguing and ambitious Marie de' Medici had prevailed on her son, the fickle and weak-minded Louis XIII., to dismiss Richelieu from the office of prime-minister, and raise to that dignity the latter's mortal enemy, the Marshal de Marillac. The wily priest appears to have been fairly rendered prostrate, and unable to avert the ruin which seemed ready to fall on him, when he was persuaded by his friends to make one last effort to recover the favour of the king. With this view he proceeded to Versailles, then only a small hunting-lodge, which Louis XIII. had recently purchased, and had an interview with his sovereign. The result of this memorable visit was that Louis surrendered himself again into the cardinal's hands, with a feebleness similar to what he had previously shewn in dismissing him from his presence. But Richelieu, by this *coup de main*, succeeded in riveting the chains on Louis more firmly than they had been before, and established for himself an absolute sway, which he retained till his death. As may be expected, he did not fail to confirm his power by taking signal vengeance on his enemies, and among others, on the Marshal de Marillac, whom he caused ere long to be brought to the scaffold.

## BURNING OF THE 'SARAH SANDS.'

One of the finest examples on record, of the saving of human life by the maintenance of high discipline, during trying difficulties, was afforded during the burning of the *Sarah Sands*, a transport steamer employed by the government in 1857. She was on her passage from England to India, with a great part of the 54th Regiment of Foot on board, intended to assist in the suppression of the Indian mutiny; the number of persons was about 400, besides the ship's crew. The vessel, an iron steamer of 2000 tons burthen, arrived at a spot about 400 miles from Mauritius; when, at three in the afternoon on the 11th of November, the cargo in the hold was found to be on fire. Captain Castle, commanding the ship, and Lieutenant-Colonel Moffatt, commanding the troops, at once concerted plans for maintaining discipline under this terrible trial. Some of the men hauled up bale after bale of government stores from the hold; some took in sail, and brought the ship before the wind; some ran out lengths of hose from the fire-engine, and poured down torrents of water below. It soon became evident, however, that this water would not quench the flames, and that the smoke in the hold would prevent the men from longer continuing below. The colonel then ordered his men to throw overboard all the ammunition in the starboard magazine. But the larboard or port magazine was so surrounded with heat and smoke, that he hesitated to command the men to risk their lives there; and he therefore called for volunteers. A number of brave fellows at once stepped forward, rushed to the magazine, and cleared out all its contents, except a barrel or two of powder; several of them, overpowered with heat and smoke, fell by the way, and were hauled up senseless. The fire burst up through the decks and cabins, and was intensified by a fierce gale which happened to be blowing at the time. Captain Castle then resolved to lower the boats, and to provide for as many as he could. This was admirably done. The boats were launched without accident, the troops were mustered on deck, there was no rush to the boats, and the men obeyed the word of command with as much order as if on parade—the greater number of them embarking in the boats. A small number of women and children who were on board, were lowered into the life-boat. All these filled boats were ordered to remain within reach of the ship till further orders. The sailors then set about constructing rafts of spare spars, to be ready in case of emergency. Meanwhile the flames had made terrible progress; the whole of the cabins and saloons were one body of fire; and at nine in the evening the flames burst through the upper deck and ignited the mizzen rigging. During this fearful suspense, the barrel or two of powder left in one of the magazines exploded, and blew out the port-quarter of the ship—shewing what would have been the awful result had not the heroic men previously removed the greater part of the ammunition. As the iron bulk-head of the after-part of the vessel continued to resist the flames, Captain Castle resolved to avail himself of this serviceable aid as long as possible; to which end the men were employed for hours in dashing water against the bulk-head, to keep it cool. When fire seized the upper-rigging, soldiers as well as sailors rushed up with wet blankets, and allayed its fearful progress. This struggle between human perseverance and devastating flames continued until two o'clock in the morning, when, to the inexpressible delight of all, the fire was found to be lessening; and by daylight it was extinguished. The horrors of the situation were, however, not yet over. The after-part of the ship was a mere hollow burned shell; and as the gale still continued, the waves poured in tremendously. Some of the men were set to the pumps, some baled out water from the flooded hold with buckets; while others sought to prevent the stern of the ship from falling out by passing hawsers around and under it, and others tried to stop the leak in the port-quarter with spare sails and wet blankets. The water-tanks in the hold, having got loose, were dashed from side to side by the violence of the gale, and battered the poor ship still further. At two in the afternoon (twenty-three hours after the fire had been discovered), the life-boat was hauled alongside, and the women and children taken on board again. All the other boats, except the gig, were in like manner brought alongside, and the soldiers re-embarked; the gig had been swamped, but all the men in her were saved. During thirty-six hours more, nearly all the soldiers were assisting the sailors in working the pumps, and clearing the ship of water; while the captain succeeded at length in getting the ill-fated ship into such trim as to be manageable. He then steered towards the Mauritius, which he reached in eight days. The achievement was almost unparalleled, for the vessel was little else than a burned and battered wreck. Not a single person was lost; the iron bulk-head was the main *material* source of safety; but this would have been of little avail had not discipline and intrepidity been shewn by those on board.

The sense of the 'honour of the flag' came out strikingly during the peril. When the ship was all in a blaze, it was suddenly recollected that the colours of the 54th were in the aft-part of the saloon. Quartermaster Richmond rushed down, snatched the Queen's colours, brought them on deck, and fainted with the heat and smoke; when recovered, he made another descent, accompanied by Private Wills, brought up the regimental colours, and again fainted, with a result which proved nearly fatal.

## CUSTOM OF KNIGHTLOW CROSS.

To the philosophical student of history, and all who feel an interest in the progressive prosperity of our country, and the often slow and painful steps by which that prosperity has been reached, any custom, however insignificant in itself, which tends to throw light upon the doings of our ancestors, is of great interest.

But in our search after such landmarks, as it were, of our country's history, we are too apt to overlook what is most patent to us all, and so it is that a custom which, in all probability, obtained in the days of our Saxon forefathers, long before William of Normandy set foot upon our land, is at the present day carried on close to us, unheeded and unknown to the majority of our readers. The custom to which we refer is the payment to the Lord of the Hundred of Knightlow of Wroth or Ward money for protection, and probably also in lieu of military service.

The scene of these payments is Knightlow Cross, Stretton-on-Dunsmore, near Rugby, Warwickshire. Here, at the northern extremity of the village, in a field by what used to be the Great Holyhead Road, stands a stone, the remains of Knightlow Cross. The stone now to be seen is the mortice-stone of the ancient cross, and is similar to the stone still in existence at St Thomas's Cross, between Clifton-upon-Dunsmore and Newton. The stone stands on a knoll or tumulus, having a fir-tree at either corner, and from it a fine view of the surrounding country is obtained; the spires of the ancient city of Coventry being plainly visible in the distance.

It is a singular circumstance, that the field in which it stands is a freehold belonging to a Mr Robinson of Stretton, but the mound upon which the stone stands belongs to the Lord of the Hundred, his Grace the Duke of Buccleuch and Queensberry. The mound is an ancient British tumulus, one of a chain (still or very lately) to be traced from High Cross—the ancient Roman station Benonis—southward down the Foss Road. The intermediate links are at Wolston Brinklow, near Wittingbrook and Cloudesley Bush, but the latter, we regret to say, has been removed.

Monday morning, the 11th of November 1862, was the day for the payment of this Wroth Silver, as it is called, and a drive in the gray light of a November morning, took us to the spot half an hour before sunrise, but not before groups of villagers and others had begun to collect to witness or take part in this curious old custom. The land-agent of the lord of the hundred arrived soon after, and proceeded at once to read the notice requiring the payment to be made, proclaiming that in default of payment, the forfeit would be 'twenty shillings for every penny, and a white bull with red ears and a red nose.' The names of the parishes and persons liable were then read out, and the amounts were duly thrown into the large basin-like cavity in the stone, and taken from thence by the attendant bailiff. After the ceremony, the actors in the scene—that is, those persons, numbering about forty, who paid the money into the stone—proceeded to the Frog Hall, where a substantial breakfast was provided for them at the expense of the Duke of Buccleuch. There is a tradition in the neighbourhood of the forfeiture of a white bull having been demanded and actually made. Of this, however, there is no record, and it is certain that, of late years, the pecuniary part of the forfeit only has been insisted upon.

Respecting this custom, Dugdale, in his history of Warwickshire, gives the following account:

'There is also a certain rent due unto the Lord of this Hundred, called *Wroth*-money, or *Warth*-money, or *Swarff*-penny, probably the same with *Ward*-penny. Denarii vicecomiti vel aliis castellanis persoluti ob castrorum præsidium vel excubias agendas,* says Sir H. Spelman in his *Glossary*, (fol. 565—566). This rent must be paid every Martinmas-day, in the morning, at Knightlow Cross, before the sun riseth: the party paying it must go thrice about the cross, and say, "The Wrath Money," and then lay it in the hole of the said cross before good witness, for if it be not duly performed, the forfeiture is 30s. and a white bull.'

Altogether, this custom forms a singular and interesting instance of a usage or rite surviving for centuries amidst revolutions, and civil wars, and changes of rulers and circumstances. Though its real origin has been lost, it still remains as a relic of feudal government, and may possibly be handed down to generations yet to come, as a memorial of a state of chronic warfare and depredation.

* Pence paid to a viscount (or smaller lord) or to other lords of castles, for—that is, instead of—keeping garrison-duty, or keeping watch.

## NOVEMBER 12.

St Nilus, anchoret, father of the church, and confessor, 5th century. St Martin, pope and martyr, 655. St Livin, bishop and martyr, 7th century. St Lebwin, patron of Daventer, confessor, end of 8th century.

*Born.*—Richard Baxter, eminent nonconformist divine, 1615, *Rowdon, Shropshire;* Admiral Edward Vernon, naval commander, 1684, *Westminster;* Amelia Opie, novelist, 1769, *Norwich.*

*Died.*—Pope Boniface III., 606; Stephen Gardiner, bishop of Winchester, 1555; Peter Martyr, distinguished reformer, 1562, *Zurich;* Sir John Hawkins, eminent navigator, 1595; William Hayley, biographer of Cowper, 1820, *Felpham;* John M'Diarmid, miscellaneous writer, 1852; Charles Kemble, eminent actor, 1854.

### The Order of Fools.

On 12th November 1381, the above association is said to have been founded by Adolphus, Count of Cleves, under the title of '*D'Order van't Gecken Gesellschaft.*' Though bearing a designation savouring so strongly of absurdity and contempt, the members of which this order was composed were noblemen and gentlemen of the highest rank and renown, who thus formed themselves into a body for humane and charitable purposes. We should be doing these gallant knights a grievous injustice were we to connect them with the *Feast of Fools*, and similar absurdities of medieval times. They were, in fact, not greatly dissimilar to the 'Odd Fellows,' 'Foresters,' and similar associations of the present day, which include within their sphere of operations benevolent and useful as much as convivial and social objects.

The insignia borne by the knights of this order consisted of the figure of a fool or jester, embroidered on the left side of their mantles, and depicted dressed in a red and silver vest, with a cap and bells on his head, yellow stockings, a cup filled with fruits in his right hand, and in his left a gold key, as symbolical of the affection which ought to subsist between the members of the society.

A yearly meeting of the brotherhood of Fools took place at Cleves on the first Sunday after Michaelmas-day, when a grand court was held, extending over seven days, and all matters relating to the welfare and future conduct of the order were revolved and discussed. Each member had some special character assigned to him, which he was obliged to support, and the most cordial equality everywhere prevailed, all distinctions of rank being laid aside.

The Order of Fools appears to have existed down to the beginning of the sixteenth century, but the objects for which it was originally founded seem, as in the case of the Knights Templars, to have gradually been lost sight of, and ultimately became almost wholly forgotten. The latest allusion to it occurs in some verses prefixed to a German translation of Sebastian Brand's celebrated *Navis Stultifera*, or Ship of Fools, published at Strasburg in 1520.

Akin to the Order of Fools was the 'Respublica Binepsis,' which was founded by some Polish noblemen about the middle of the fourteenth century, and derived its name from the estate of its principal originator. Its constitution was modelled after that of Poland, and, like that kingdom, it too had its sovereign, its council, its chamberlain, its master of the chase, and various other offices. Any member who made himself conspicuous by some absurd or singular propensity, received a recognition of this quality from his fellows by having assigned to him a corresponding appointment in the society. Thus the dignity of master of the hunt was conferred on some individual who carried to an absurd extreme his passion for the chase, whilst another person given to gasconading and boasting of his valorous exploits, was elevated to the post of field-marshal. No member could decline acceptance of any of these functions, unless he wished to make himself an object of still greater ridicule and animadversion. At the same time, all persons given to lampooning or personal satire, were excluded from admission to the association. The order rapidly increased in numbers from the period of its formation, and at one time comprised nearly all the individuals attached to the Polish court. Like the German association, its objects were the promotion of charity and good-feeling, and the repression of immoral and absurd habits and practices.

### PLAYGOING-HOURS IN THE OLDEN TIME.

By a police regulation of the city of Paris, dated 12th November 1609, it is ordered that the players at the theatres of the Hôtel de Bourgogne and the Marais shall open their doors at one o'clock in the afternoon, and at two o'clock precisely shall commence the performance, whether there are sufficient spectators or not, so that the play may be over before half-past four. This ordinance, it was enacted, should be in force from the Feast of St Martin to the 15th of the ensuing month of February. Such hours for visiting the playhouse seem peculiarly strange at the present day, when the doors of theatres are seldom opened before half-past six in the evening, or shut before midnight. But our ancestors both closed and opened the day much earlier than we do now, and observed much more punctually the old recipe for health and strength, 'to rise with the lark and lie down with the lamb.' The same early hours for theatrical representations that seem thus to have prevailed in Paris were, during the seventeenth century, no less common in England, where, as we learn from the first playbill issued from the Drury Lane Theatre in 1663, the hour for the commencement of the representation was three o'clock in the afternoon. The badness of the streets, and the danger of traversing them in dark nights from the defective mode of lighting, combined with the absence of an efficient police and the dangers from robbery and violence, all had their influence in rendering it very undesirable to protract public amusements beyond nightfall in those times.

## ANCIENT FORKS.

From a passage in that curious work, Coryate's *Crudities*, it has been imagined that its author, the strange traveller of that name, was the first to introduce the use of the fork into England, in the beginning of the seventeenth century. He says that he observed its use in Italy only 'because the Italian cannot by any means endure to have his dish touched with fingers, seeing all men's fingers are not alike clean.' These 'little forks' were usually made of iron or steel, but occasionally also of silver. Coryate says he 'thought good to imitate the Italian fashion by this forked cutting of meat,' and that hence a humorous English friend, 'in his merry humour, doubted not to call me *furcifer*, only for using a fork at feeding.' This passage is often quoted as fixing the earliest date of the use of forks; but they were, in reality, used by our Anglo-Saxon forefathers, and throughout the middle ages. In 1834, some labourers found, when cutting a deep drain at Sevington, North Wilts, a deposit of seventy Saxon pennies, of sovereigns ranging from Cœnwulf, king of Mercia (796 A.D.), to Ethelstan (878–890 A.D.); they had been packed in a box of which there were some decayed remains, and which also held some articles of personal ornament, a spoon, and *the fork*, which is first in the group here engraved. The fabric and ornamentation of this fork and spoon would, to the practised eye, be quite sufficient evidence of the approximate era of their manufacture, but their juxtaposition with the coins confirms it. In Akerman's *Pagan Saxondom*, another example of a fork, from a Saxon tumulus, is given: it has a bone-handle, like those still manufactured for common use. It must not, however, be imagined that they were frequently used; indeed, throughout the middle ages, they seemed to have been kept as articles of luxury, to be used only by the great and noble in eating fruits and preserves on state occasions. A German fork, believed to be a work of the close of the sixteenth century, is the second of our examples. It is surmounted by the figure of a fool or jester, who holds a saw. This figure is jointed like a child's doll, and tumbles about as the fork is used, while the saw slips up

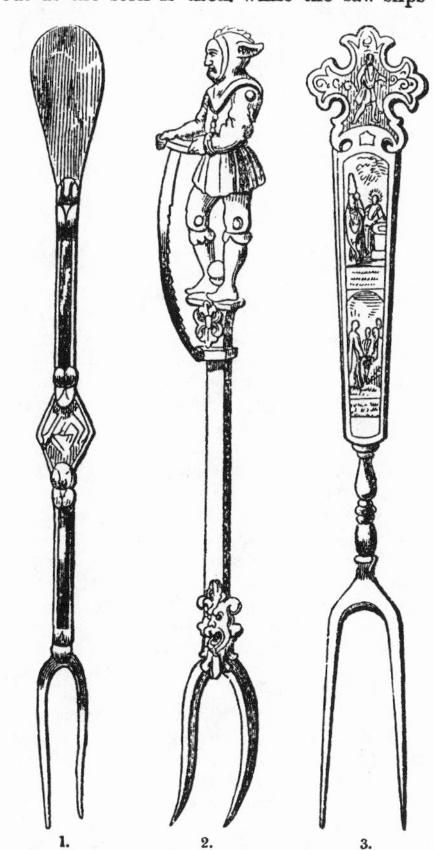

ANCIENT FORKS.

and down the handle. It proves that the fork was treated merely as a luxurious toy. Indeed, as late as 1652, Heylin, in his *Cosmography*, treats them as a rarity: 'the use of silver forks, which is by some of our spruce gallants taken up of late,' are the words he uses. A fork of this period is the third of our selected examples; it is entirely of silver, the handle elaborately engraved with subjects from the New Testament. It is one of a series so decorated, the whole of our engraved examples being at present in the collection of Lord Londesborough. In conclusion, we may observe that the use of the fork became general by the close of the seventeenth century.

---

# NOVEMBER 13.

St Mitrius, martyr, beginning of 4th century. St Brice, bishop and confessor, 444. St Chillen or Killian, priest, 7th century. St Constant, 777. St Homobonus, merchant, confessor, 1197. St Didacus, confessor, 1463. St Stanislas Kostka, confessor, 1568.

*Born*—St Augustine, bishop of Hippo, and father of the Church, 354, *Tagaste, Numidia;* Pelagius, celebrated antagonist of St Augustine, 354; Edward III., king of England, 1312, *Windsor;* Philip Beroaldus, the Elder, scholar and critic, 1450, *Bologna.*

*Died.*—Justinian, Roman emperor, 565; Malcolm Canmore, king of Scotland, 1093, *Alnwick, Northumberland;* Thomas Erpenius, celebrated orientalist, 1624, *Leyden;* William Etty, painter, 1849, *York;* Sir John Forbes, eminent physician and medical writer, 1861, *Whitchurch, near Reading.*

## THE STAMFORD BULL-RUNNING.

From time immemorial down to a late period, the 13th of November was annually celebrated, at the town of Stamford, in Lincolnshire, by a public amusement termed a Bull-running. The sport was latterly conducted in the following manner: About a quarter to eleven o'clock, on the festal-day, the bell of St Mary's commenced to toll as a warning for the thoroughfares to be cleared of infirm persons and children; and precisely at eleven, the bull was turned into a street, blocked up at each end by a barricade of carts and wagons. At this moment, every post, pump, and 'coigne of vantage' was occupied, and those happy enough to have such protections, could grin at their less fortunate friends, who were compelled to have recourse to flight; the barricades, windows, and house-tops being crowded with spectators. The bull, irritated by hats being thrown at him, and other means of annoyance, soon became ready to run; and then, the barricades being removed, the whole crowd, bull, men, boys, and dogs, rushed helter-skelter through the streets. One great object being to 'bridge the bull,' the animal was, if possible, compelled to run upon the bridge that spans the Welland. The crowd then closing in, with audacious courage surrounded and seized the animal; and, in spite of its size and strength, by main force tumbled it over the parapet into the river. The bull then swimming ashore, would land in the meadows, where the run was continued; the miry, marshy state of the fields at that season of the year, and the falls and other disasters consequent thereon, adding greatly to the amusement of the mob. The sport was carried on till all were tired; the animal was then killed, and its flesh sold at a low rate to the people, who finished the day's amusement with a supper of bull-beef.

A local historian thus informs us how the sport was conducted in the seventeenth century. 'The butchers provide the bull, and place him overnight in a stable belonging to the alderman; the next morning, proclamation is made by the bellman that each one shut up his shop-door and gate, and none, under pain of imprisonment, do any violence to strangers; for the preventing whereof (the town being a great thoroughfare), a guard is appointed for the passing of travellers through the same without hurt. None to have any iron upon their bull-clubs, or other staves, which they pursue the bull with; which proclamation being made, and the gates all shut up, the bull is turned out of the alderman's house, and then hivie-skivy, tag-rag, men, women, and children of all sorts and sizes, with all the dogs in the town, running after him, spattering dirt in each other's faces, that one would think them to be so many furies started out of the infernal regions for the punishment of Cerberus, as when Theseus and Perillus conquered the place, as Ovid describes it:

'A ragged troop of boys and girls
Do follow him with stones,
With clubs, with whips, and many nips,
They part his skin from bones.'

According to tradition, the origin of the custom dates from the time of King John; when, one day, William, Earl of Warren, standing on the battlements of the castle, saw two bulls fighting in the meadow beneath. Some butchers coming to part the combatants, one of the bulls ran into the town, causing a great uproar. The earl, mounting his horse, rode after the animal, and enjoyed the sport so much, that he gave the meadow, in which the fight began, to the butchers of Stamford, on condition that they should provide a bull, to be run in that town annually, on the 13th of November, for ever after. There is no documentary evidence on the subject, but the town of Stamford undoubtedly holds certain common rights in the meadow specified, which is still termed the Bull-meadow.

Bull-running was, for a long period, a recognised institution at Stamford. A mayor of the town, who died in 1756, left a sum of money to encourage the practice; and, as appears by the vestry accounts, the church-wardens annually gave money to aid the bull-running. In 1788, the first attempt was made by the local authorities to stop the custom, the mayor issuing a curious proclamation, stating that bull-running was contrary to religion, law, and nature, and punishable with the penalty of death. The Earl of Exeter, who lived

'At Burleigh House, by Stamford town,'

lent his personal influence to the mayor on this occasion; but the bull was run, and both the earl and mayor were insulted by the mob. In 1789, the mayor having obtained the aid of a troop of dragoons, met the bull at St George's Gate, as it was being driven into the town by the bull-woman—a virago dressed in blue ribbons, who officiated on these occasions, and followed by the *bullards*, a name given to the admirers and supporters of bull-running. On the mayor appealing to the officer of dragoons to stop the procession, the latter refused to interfere, alleging that the people were peaceably walking on the highway. 'In that case,' replied the mayor, 'your men are of no use here.' 'Very well,' said the officer, 'I shall dismiss them.' The dismissed dragoons, to their great glee, joined the bullards, and the bull was run as usual. For a long time afterwards, the bullards received no opposition. The towns-people, delighted with the sport, subscribed for a second annual bull-running, which took place on the Monday after Christmas Day; and there were several occasional bull-runnings every year, the candidates for representing Stamford in parliament being always found willing to give a bull for the purpose.

In 1831, the Conservative party canvassed the borough under a flag bearing the representation of a bull. Several clergymen and others remonstrated against this mode of obtaining popular support, distinctly declaring they would not vote, if the obnoxious banner were not laid aside. But many persons of station, and well-known humanity, defended the practice of bull-running, alleging that it was an old-fashioned, manly, English sport; inspiring courage, agility, and presence of mind under danger; and, as regards inhumanity, it was not by any means so cruel to the brute creation, nor so perilous to the life and limb of man, as fox-hunting.

In 1833, the Society for Prevention of Cruelty to Animals made its first public appearance as an opponent of the practice. One of its officers was sent to Stamford on bull-running day, and, being more bold than prudent, was roughly hustled by the crowd. This interference of the society, however well-meant, had a very different effect to that desired; instead of discountenancing the practice, the people of Stamford were thereby stimulated to support it. 'Who or what is this London Society,' they asked, 'that, usurping the place of constituted authorities, presumes to interfere with our ancient amusement?'

In 1836, the society sent several of its officers and agents to Stamford. The 13th falling that year on Sunday, the bull was run on the following day; in the evening, the populace resented the interference of the society's officers, by assaulting them, and breaking some windows. At the following Lent Assizes for Lincolnshire, the society preferred bills of indictment before the Grand Jury, against eight persons, for 'conspiring to disturb the peace by riotously assembling to run and torment a bull' at Stamford, on the 14th of November previous. True bills being found against the men, bench-warrants were obtained, and they were arrested to take their trials at the ensuing midsummer assizes. As is well known, this mode of proceeding behind a man's back, as it were, which deprives the accused of the fair advantage allowed by law, in giving him a copy of the depositions of the witnesses against him, is looked upon with deserved disfavour by both the judges and people of England. Moreover, the conduct of the society in putting the expensive machinery of the higher courts of law in operation against poor labouring-men, for a trumpery street squabble, created a strong feeling in Stamford and its neighbourhood. A subscription was immediately opened, to raise a defence-fund for the prisoners, many subscribing who utterly detested bull-running, but considered the society's proceedings to be over-officious, unjust, and arbitrary. The manager of Stamford theatre, to his immense popularity, gave a benefit in aid of the defence-fund, the piece selected being Colman's comedy of *John Bull;* and altogether, a considerable sum was collected. At the trial, Sergeant Goulbourn, and the leading barristers on the circuit, were retained for the prosecution. The council for the defence could not deny the riot, but pleaded use and custom, and the ignorance of the prisoners, who believed that valuable common rights were preserved to the town by the act of bull-running. Judge Park, when summing up, told the jury that no use or custom could justify a riot. Five of the prisoners were acquitted, three only being found guilty; these last were discharged on giving bail to appear to receive judgment, at the Court of Queen's Bench, when called upon.

The bullards, accepting the result of the trial as a victory, determined to have a grand run in 1837. Influence, however, had been brought to bear on the Home Secretary, who wrote to the mayor of Stamford, impressing upon him the necessity of taking active measures to prevent a proceeding so illegal and disgraceful as bull-running. The mayor, accordingly, swore in more than two hundred special constables to his assistance; but their opposition being lukewarm, the bull was run with greater *éclat* than ever. In 1838, the Home Secretary determined to put down the custom. Several days before the 13th, a troop of the 14th Dragoons, and a strong force of metropolitan police, were sent to Stamford, and a considerable body of special constables were sworn in. The commanders of the military and police, having viewed the field of action, consulted with the mayor. As prevention was better than cure, and there could be no bull-run without a bull, measures were taken accordingly. The town was strictly searched, and two bulls being found, the animals were taken and confined in an inn-yard, under a picket of dragoons. Sentries were then placed on all the outlets of the town, and parties patrolled the roads night and day, to prevent a bull from being brought in. The eventful 13th arrived, and though the streets were crowded with bullards, the authorities were perfectly at their ease. They even heard with complacency the bell of St Mary's toll the time-honoured bull-warning. But at the last stroke of the bell, their fancied security was rudely dissipated by the well-known shouts of 'Hoy! bull! hoy!' from a thousand voices; a noble bull having appeared, as if by magic, in the principal street. There never was such a run! The wild excitement of the scene was enhanced by the bewildered dragoons galloping thither and hither, in vain attempts to secure the animal. The metropolitan police, with greater valour than discretion, formed in a compact phalanx on the bridge; but the bull, followed by the bullards, dashed through them as an eagle might through a cobweb. After a run of some hours, the bull came to bay in the river, and was then captured by the authorities. An attempt was then made to rescue one of the bulls confined in the inn-yard. This led to a collision between the military and the people, stones and brickbats were thrown, and sabre cuts returned in exchange; but, on the dragoons being ordered to load with ball-cartridge, the mob dispersed. Where did the strange bull, a very valuable animal, so miraculously spring from? This enigma was soon solved by its being claimed by a certain noble lord. He had been sending it, in a covered wagon, from one of his estates to another, and, by a 'curious coincidence,' it happened to pass through Stamford on the very day and hour its presence was required by the bullards, who, seizing the wagon, released the animal. Whether the coincidence were accidental or designed, the preceding explanation, if not quite satisfactory, produced a great deal of good-humoured laughter.

In 1839, a stronger force of military and police was sent to Stamford; every precaution was taken, yet some treacherous special constables smuggled a bull into the town, and the bullards had their last run. The animal, however, being young and docile, did not afford much sport, being soon captured by the authorities. In the following year, as bull-running day drew near, the people of Stamford began to count the cost of their amusement. The military, metropolitan police, and special constables of the two previous years, had cost them more than £600—a sum which might, with greater fitness, have been laid out on certain town improvements, then much wanted. So the townsmen forwarded a memorial to the mayor, to be laid before the Home Secretary, pledging themselves that, if no extraneous force of military or police were brought into the town, nor expense incurred by appointing special constables, they, the subscribers, would prevent bull-running from taking place in Stamford during that year. The townsmen were wisely taken at their word, and there never has been a bull-run in Stamford since that time.

The highly-exciting nature of the amusement gave bull-running a charm to vulgar minds, that can scarcely now be understood or appreciated. For weeks before and after the 13th of November, the bullard's song might be heard re-echoing through all parts of Stamford. As a curious and almost forgotten relic of an ancient sport, it cannot be entirely unworthy of a place in these columns.

THE BULLARD'S SONG.

'Come all you bonny boys,
Who love to bait the bonny bull,
Who take delight in noise,
And you shall have your bellyful.
On Stamford's town Bull-running Day,
We 'll shew you such right gallant play,
You never saw the like, you'll say,
As you shall see at Stamford.

Earl Warren was the man,
That first began this gallant sport;
In the castle he did stand,
And saw the bonny bulls that fought.
The butchers with their bull-dogs came,
These sturdy stubborn bulls to tame,
But more with madness did inflame,
Enraged, they ran through Stamford.

Delighted with the sport,
The meadows there he freely gave,
Where these bonny bulls had fought,
The butchers now do hold and have;
By charter they are strictly bound,
That every year a bull be found;
Come, dight your face, you dirty clown,
And stump away to Stamford!

Come, take him by the tail, boys—
Bridge, bridge him if you can;
Prog him with a stick, boys;
Never let him quiet stand;
Through every street and lane in town,
We'll Chevy-chase him up and down,
You sturdy bung-straws* ten miles round,
Come, stump away to Stamford.'

The old bullards are now nearly all dead; but the song, with various additions and variations, may still be occasionally heard. Mr Burton, writing in 1846, says: 'Every incident that calls to the mind of the lower classes their ancient holiday, is seized with enthusiasm, and the old bull-tune is invariably demanded, when anything in the shape of music attracts the attention. At the theatre, whenever there is a full house, "Bull! bull!" is invariably pealed from some corner of the gallery. The magic word immediately fills the mouth of every occupant of that part of the building; it is echoed from the pit, and order and quiet is out of the question till the favourite tune has been played.'

* Threshers.

## SHOOTING-STARS.

During three successive years, from 1831 to 1833, the 13th of November was marked by a magnificent display of shooting or falling stars, those mysterious visitants to our globe respecting whose real nature and origin science is still so perplexed. The first of these brilliant exhibitions was witnessed off the coasts of Spain, and in the country bordering on the Ohio. The second is thus described by Captain Hammond of H.M.S. *Restitution*, who beheld it in the Red Sea, off Mocha. 'From one o'clock A. M. till after daylight, there was a very unusual phenomenon in the heavens. It appeared like meteors bursting in every direction. The sky at the time was clear, the stars and moon bright, with streaks of light, and thin white clouds interspersed in the sky. On landing in the morning, I inquired of the Arabs if they had noticed the above. They said they had been observing it most of the night. I asked them if ever the like had appeared before. The oldest of them replied that it had not.' The area over which this phenomenon was seen extended from the Red Sea westwards to the Atlantic, and from Switzerland to the Mauritius.

But the most imposing display of shooting-stars on record occurred on the third of these occasions—that is, on 13th November 1833. It extended chiefly over the limits comprised between longitude 61° in the Atlantic, and 100° in Central Mexico, and from the latitude of the great lakes of North America, to the West Indies. From the appearance presented, it might be regarded as a grand and portentous display of nature's fireworks. Seldom has a scene of greater or more awful sublimity been exhibited than at the Falls of Niagara on this memorable occasion, the two leading powers in nature, water and fire, engaging, as it were, in an emulative display of their grandeur. The awful roar of the cataract filled the mind of the spectator with an infinitely heightened sense of sublimity, when its waters were lightened up by the glare of the meteoric torrent in the sky. In many parts of the country, the people were terror-struck, imagining that the end of the world was come; whilst those whose education and vigour of mind prevented them from yielding to such terrors, were, nevertheless, vividly reminded of the grand description in the Apocalypse, 'The stars of heaven fell unto the earth, even as a fig-tree casteth her untimely figs, when she is shaken of a mighty wind.'

The most probable theory as to the nature of shooting-stars is, that they form part of the solar system, revolving round the sun in the same manner as the planetoids, but both infinitely smaller in size, and subject to great and irregular perturbations. The latter cause brings them not unfrequently within the limits of the earth's atmosphere, on entering which they become luminous from the great heat produced by the sudden and violent compression which their transit occasions. Having thus approached the earth with great velocity, they are as rapidly again withdrawn from it into the realms of space. It is very possible, moreover, that the fiery showers which we have just described, may be the result of a multitude of these meteors encountering each other, whilst the aërolites, or actual meteoric substances, which

SHOWER OF FALLING STARS AT NIAGARA IN NOVEMBER 1833.

occasionally fall to the surface of the earth, may be such of those bodies as have been brought so far within the influence of terrestrial gravity as to be rendered subject to its effects.

## NOVEMBER 14.

St Dubricius, bishop and confessor, 6th century. St Laurence, confessor, archbishop of Dublin, 1180.

*Born.*—Benjamin Hoadly, bishop of Bangor, eminent Whig prelate, 1676, *Westerham, Kent;* Adam Gottlob Oehlenschläger, Danish poet, 1779, *Copenhagen;* Sir Charles Lyell, geologist, 1797, *Kinnordy, Forfarshire.*

*Died.*—Gottfried Wilhelm Leibnitz, mathematician and moral philosopher, 1716, *Hanover;* George William Frederick Hegel, German philosopher, 1831, *Berlin;* Dr John Abercrombie, physician and moral writer, 1844, *Edinburgh.*

### LEIBNITZ.

Leibnitz is one of the great names of literature:

'A man so various that he seemed to be
Not one, but all mankind's epitome.'

Nevertheless, though his title to fame is everywhere confessed, few at this day, with the exception of some arduous students, are practically conversant with its grounds. Leibnitz was one of the chief intellectual forces of his age, but as a force he was more remarkable for quantity than intensity. He busied himself in a multitude of pursuits and he excelled in all, but he produced no master-piece —nothing of which it could be said, It is the best of its kind. He was a universal genius; his intellect was as capacious as harmonious, and a storehouse for all knowledge; but his mind was lost by reason of its universal sympathies. To be remembered for ever by some work requires that the whole energy, at least for a time, be given to one work. 'Even great parts,' says Locke, writing of Leibnitz in 1697, 'will not master any subject without great thinking.'

Leibnitz was the son of a professor of jurisprudence in the university of Leipsic, in which city he was born in 1646. He was a precocious child, and from his boyhood displayed that love of learning and speculation which distinguished him through life. He gives an amusing account of his efforts when a youth of fifteen, during long solitary walks in the wood of Rosenthal, near Leipsic, to adjust the claims of the Ancients and Moderns—of Aristotle and Descartes, and the reluctance with which, when conciliation was impossible, he was compelled to make an election. His talents, as manifested at the university, and his publications, early brought him into notice, and found him patrons among the princes of Germany. He travelled over the continent, visited England, and everywhere made the acquaintance of men of science and letters. An amusing anecdote is told of him when at sea in a tempest off the Italian coast. The sage captain attributed the storm to the presence of the heretical German, and presuming him ignorant of the Italian language, began to deliberate with the crew on the propriety of throwing the Lutheran Jonah overboard. Leibnitz, with much presence of mind, got hold of a rosary and began to tell his beads with vehement devotion. The ruse saved him. At Nürnberg, he heard of a society of alchemists who were prosecuting a search for the philosopher's stone. He wished to join them, and compiled a letter from the writings of the most celebrated alchemists and sent it to them. The letter consisted of the most obscure terms he could find, and of which, he says, he did not understand a syllable. The illuminati, afraid to be thought ignorant, invited him to their meetings and made him their secretary. Though Leibnitz could thus quiz the alchemists, he believed, to the end of his life, in the reality of the object of their labours.

In the leisure which various pensions secured him, he followed his versatile inclinations with incessant assiduity. Metaphysics, physics, mathematics, jurisprudence, theology, philology, history, antiquities, the classics, all shared his attention, and in all of these branches of knowledge the world heard his voice with respect. The ancient languages he knew well, and was tolerably acquainted with more than half-a-dozen of the modern. He had notions about calculating machines, about improved watches, about a universal alphabet, about hydraulic engines, about swift carriages, by which the journey of one hundred and fifty miles, between Amsterdam and Hanover, might be done in twenty-four hours; and about a hundred other things. He dabbled in medicine, in everything; there was nothing, in fact, in which he could not be interested. In his *Protogena*, he throws out thoughts, which, Dean Buckland observes, contain the germ of some of the most enlightened speculations in geology. His memory was quick and tenacious; he made notes as he read, but he had seldom to refer to them, for he seemed to forget nothing. George I. used to call him his living dictionary. At the age of seventy, he could recite hundreds of lines of Virgil without an error.

In mathematics, if anywhere, his genius shewed itself supreme, and between him and Sir Isaac Newton a bitter controversy broke out as to the credit of the invention of the differential calculus. The question has been thoroughly and tediously debated, but the following points are now considered as tolerably clear: 1st, That the system of fluxions invented by Newton is essentially the same as the differential calculus invented by Leibnitz, differing only in notation; 2d, That Newton possessed the secret of fluxions as early as 1665, nineteen years before Leibnitz published his method, and eleven years before he communicated it to Newton; 3d, That both Leibnitz and Newton discovered their methods independently of each other, but that Newton had priority; and 4th, That although the honour belongs to both, yet, as in every other great invention, they were but the individuals who combined the scattered rays of their predecessors, and gave a method, a notation, and a name to the doctrine of infinitesimal quantities.

As a theologian and metaphysician, Leibnitz was eclectic rather than original. His temper was truly catholic; he differed from others with reluctance; and it seemed to be one of his keenest delights to reconcile apparent contraries. Hence one of his schemes was the incorporation of the various sects of Protestantism, preparatory, if possible, to the inclusion of Rome, with concessions, in one grand Christian community. In philosophy, he had a doctrine called Pre-established Harmony, by which he professed to explain the relations between Deity, the Human Mind, and Nature. It met with wide discussion and some acceptance in the lifetime of Leibnitz, but Pre-established Harmony has long passed out of memory except in histories of philosophy.

One of the warmest admirers of Leibnitz was Sophia Charlotte, wife of Frederick, the first king of Prussia, a great lover of show and ceremony, for which his consort had a quiet contempt. Leibnitz called her 'one of the most accomplished princesses of earth,' and by the world she was known as the republican and philosophic queen. To Leibnitz, '*le grand Leibnitz*,' as she styled him, she resorted for counsel in all her theological and philosophical difficulties, and not seldom to his perplexity, wanting to know, he said: 'le pourquoi du pourquoi' (the why of the why). Wearied with the emptiness of courtiers, she wrote on one occasion: 'Leibnitz talked to me about the infinitely little; *mon Dieu*, as if I did not know enough of that!' This bright soul died at thirty-six, to the great grief of Leibnitz. On her death-bed she said she was very happy; that the king would have a fine opportunity for display at her funeral; and, above all, that now she was going to satisfy her curiosity about a great many things of which Leibnitz could tell her nothing. With many other crowned heads Leibnitz held intercourse more or less intimate. Peter the Great consulted him as to the best means for the civilisation of Russia, and rewarded his suggestions with the title of Councillor of State, and a pension of a thousand roubles.

Leibnitz was only able to get through his multiform business by persistent assiduity. He carried on a most extensive correspondence, and wrote his letters with great care, sometimes three or four times over, and made them the repositories of his most valued ideas and conjectures. His life was sedentary almost beyond example. Sometimes for weeks together he would not go to bed, but sat at his desk till a late hour, then took two or three hours of sleep in his chair, and resumed work at early dawn. He was a bachelor, and had no fixed hours for his meals; but sent to a tavern for food, when hungry and at leisure. His head was large and bald, his hair fine and brown, his face pale, his sight short, his shoulders broad, and his legs crooked and ungainly. He was spare and of middle height, but in walking, he threw his head so far forward as to look from behind like a hunchback. His neglect of exercise told severely on him as he advanced in life. He became plagued with rheumatic gout, his legs ulcerated, and he aggravated his ailment by compressing afflicted parts with wooden vices to stop the circulation of the blood, and dull the sense of pain. He died in Hanover in 1716, in his seventieth year, from the effects, it is said, of an untried medicine of his own concoction. He was buried on the esplanade of his native city of Leipsic, where a monument, in the form of a temple, with the simple inscription, 'Ossa Leibnitii,' marks the spot.

## DISCOVERY OF THE SOURCES OF THE NILE.

It is curious to look back to the days when Bruce the traveller published his celebrated work on Africa, and claimed to have discovered the true sources of the mysterious river which flows so many hundreds of miles through that continent. Comparing that narrative with one which has appeared in 1863, we see that Bruce was in the wrong; that he may have discovered *a* source but not *the* source; and that a long series of intermediate investigations was needed to arrive at a true solution of the interesting problem. No blame to James Bruce for all this. He was really a sagacious and enterprising man; and although some doubt was thrown upon his truthfulness during his life, he is now believed to have been veracious to the extent of his knowledge. His error concerning the sources of the Nile may well be excused, considering the harassing difficulties of the problem.

Glancing at a map of Africa, we see that the Nile is formed by several branches, which meet in Nubia, and flow northward through Egypt into the Mediterranean. The puzzle has been to determine which of the branches ought to be considered as the true Nile, and which mere affluents or tributaries. The easternmost of the chief or important branches, the *Atbara*, rises in about 12° N. lat., 40° E. long; and joins the main river near 18° N. lat., 34° E. long. It was visited by Salt and by Pearce, and has been often noticed by travellers in Abyssinia. The middle, or second of the three branches, known as the *Bahr-el-Azrek*, or *Blue Nile*, is, *par excellence*, the river of Abyssinia, winding through and about that country in a very remarkable way. Bruce traced it upwards until it became a mere streamlet in 11° N. lat., 37° E. long., near the village of Geesh, whence it flows by Sennaar to its junction with the greater Nile at Khartoum. The westernmost, and largest branch, the *Bahr-el-Abiad*, or *White Nile*, is extremely circuitous in its route, winding through the countries of Darfur and Kordofan in a very intricate way.

Now it is the Bahr-el-Azrek, or Blue Nile, which Bruce considered to be the true or original river, and which, on the 14th of November 1770, he believed himself to have traced up to its source. In the preface to his Travels (written in 1790, and, as is supposed, not so accurately as if he had allowed less than twenty years to elapse) he said: 'I hope that what I have said will be thought sufficient to convince all impartial readers that these celebrated sources have, by a fatality, remained to our days as unknown as they were to antiquity; no good or genuine voucher having yet been produced capable of proving that they were before discovered, or seen by the curious eye of any traveller, from the earliest ages to this day. And it is with confidence I propose to my reader, that he will consider me as still standing at the fountain, and patiently hear from me the recital of the origin, course, nature, and circumstances of this the most famous river in the world, which he will in vain seek from books, or from any other human authority whatever, and which by the care and attention I have paid to the subject, will, I hope, be found satisfactory here.'

Bruce was all the more proud of his achievement, because the ancients had believed that the Bahr-el-Abiad was the true Nile, an opinion which he claimed to have shewn fallacious. The ancients were right, however, and Bruce wrong. Step by step the White Nile has been traced to points nearer and nearer to the equator, and therefore nearer to its source. Linant, in 1827, ascended as far as Aleis, in 15° N. lat. In 1842, Werne, heading an expedition sent out by the pacha of Egypt, reached to 5° N. lat., and was told by the natives that the source was still far distant. In 1845, M. D'Abbadie thought he had reached the source of the Nile; but Beke afterwards shewed that the stream traced by D'Abbadie was only an affluent of the Bahr-el-Abiad, and expressed an opinion that the real source is even beyond the equator. M. Knoblecher, who had a missionary establishment at Khartoum, went up the White Nile as far as 4° N. lat., and saw that river still far away to the south-west.

The grand discovery of all, that the Nile really rises in south latitude, and crosses the equator, was made by Captains Grant and Speke, whose names have become thereby renowned throughout Europe. In 1858, Captain Speke reached a very beautiful lake, the *Victoria Nyanza*, while journeying westward from Zanzibar. The head of this lake is three degrees south of the equator. He found the lake to be a large sheet of fresh water, lying on a plateau or table-land, from 3000 to 4000 feet above the level of the sea. The lake, to use the language of Captain Speke, 'looked for all the world like the source of some great river; so much so, indeed, that I at once felt certain in my own mind it was the source of the Nile, and noted it accordingly.' It was the bold guess of a sagacious and experienced man. The Victoria Nyanza is really the head-water of the Nile, being fed immediately by a range of lofty mountains in the interior. Its most southern affluent is the Leewumbu or Shimeeyu. Stanley, who sailed round the lake in 1875, and who explored the head-waters of the Congo, confirmed Speke's discovery. It is thus settled that the Nile flows uninterruptedly from the lake to the Mediterranean, through no less than thirty-four degrees of latitude, and along a course exceeding 2000 miles in length, in a straight line, and perhaps 3000, allowing for windings. Captain Speke was prevented from putting his speculation to the test in 1859 or 1860; but in 1861 and 1862, accompanied by Captain Grant, he traced the course of the grand river down from the lake to the ocean—not actually keeping the stream in view the whole of the way, but touching it repeatedly here and there, in such a way as to leave no doubt that it *is* the Nile.

Thus the somewhat magniloquent terms in which Bruce announced his discoveries have not proved to be justified. The post of honour is to be given, not to the Blue Nile, but to the White Nile, and at a point nearly a thousand miles further south than was reached by Bruce.

---

## NOVEMBER 15.

St Eugenius, martyr, 275. St Malo or Maclou, first bishop of Aleth in Brittany, 565. St Leopold, Marquis of Austria, confessor, 1136. St Gertrude, virgin and abbess, 1292.

---

*Born.*—Andrew Marvell, poet and politician, 1620, *Kingston-upon-Hull;* William Pitt, great Earl of Chatham, 1708, *Boconnoc, Cornwall;* William Cowper, poet, 1731, *Great Berkhamstead, Hertfordshire;* Sir William Herschel, astronomer, 1738, *Hanover;* John Caspar Lavater, physiognomist, 1741, *Zurich;* Rev. James Scholefield, scholar and classic editor, 1789, *Henley on Thames.*

*Died.*—Albertus Magnus, celebrated schoolman, 1280, *Cologne;* Mrs Anne Turner, executed as an accomplice in murder of Sir Thomas Overbury, 1615, *London;* John Kepler, great astronomer, 1630, *Ratisbon;* Henry Ireton, son-in-law of Cromwell, 1651, *Limerick;* James, Duke of Hamilton, killed in a duel in Hyde Park, 1712; Christopher Gluck, composer, 1787, *Vienna;* Bishop Tomline, author of *Refutation of Calvinism,* 1827; Count Rossi, minister of interior, Papal States, assassinated, 1848, *Rome;* Johanna Kinkel, German novelist and musician, 1858.

## ANDREW MARVELL.

It is pleasant to observe how the respect for 'honest Andrew Marvell' outlives all the political changes which succeed each other at fitful intervals in England; it is a homage to manliness and probity. During his life, from 1620 to 1678, he was mixed up with many of the exciting controversies of the times; but it was in the last eighteen years of his life, when Charles II. was king, that Marvell attained his highest reputation. He acted as member of parliament for Kingston-upon-Hull; he trusted the electors, and they trusted him; and there has never been known in the history of our parliament a connection more honourable than that between him and his constituents. He used to write constantly to them about the state of public affairs; and his letters have considerable historical value, insomuch as they supply contemporary evidence of the proceedings in high places. The court-party could not be very much pleased at the publication of such a letter, as the following, from Andrew Marvell to his constitutents at Hull: 'The king having, upon pretence of the great preparations of his neighbours, demanded £300,000 for his navy (though, in conclusion, he hath not sent out any), that the parliament should pay his debts, which the ministers would never particularise to the House of Commons, our house gave several bills. You see how far things were stretched beyond reason, there being no satisfaction how those debts were contracted; and all men foreseeing that what was given would not be applied to discharge the debts, which I hear are, at this day, risen to four millions, but diverted as formerly. Nevertheless, such was the number of the constant courtiers, increased by the apostate patriots, who were bought off for that term, some at six, others at ten, one at fifteen thousand pounds in money; besides what offices, lands, and reversions to others, that it is a mercy they gave not away the whole land and liberty of England. The Duke of Buckingham is again £140,000 in debt; and by this prorogation, his creditors have time to tear all his lands to pieces. The House of Commons have run almost to the end of their line, and are grown extremely chargeable to the king and odious to the people. They have signed and sealed ten thousand a year more to the Duchess of Cleveland, who has likewise near ten thousand a year out of the new farm of the country excise of beer and ale; five thousand a year out of the post-office; and, they say, the reversion of all the king's leases, the reversion of all places in the custom-house, the green wax, and indeed, what not. All promotions, spiritual and temporal, pass under her cognizance.'

The particular incident which has stamped the name of Andrew Marvell with the impress of honesty, has been narrated under different forms; but the following is its substance, as given by one writer: 'The borough of Hull chose Andrew Marvell, a gentleman of little or no fortune, and maintained him in London for the service of the public. His understanding, integrity, and spirit were dreadful to the then infamous administration. Persuaded that he would be theirs for properly asking, the ministers sent his old school-fellow, the Lord Treasurer Danby, to renew acquaintance with him in his garret. At parting, the lord treasurer, out of pure affection, slipped into his hand an order upon the treasury for one thousand pounds, and then went into his chariot. Marvell, looking at the paper, calls after the treasurer: "My lord, I request another moment." They went up again to the garret, and Jack, the servant-boy, was called. "Jack, child, what had I for dinner yesterday?" "Don't you remember, sir? You had the little shoulder of mutton that you ordered me to bring from a woman in the market." "Very right, child. What have I for dinner to-day?" "Don't you know, sir, that you bade me lay by the blade-bone to broil?" "'Tis so; very right, child; go away. My lord, do you hear that? Andrew Marvell's dinner is provided. There's your piece of paper; I want it not. I know the sort of kindness you intended. I live here to serve my constituents; the ministry may seek men for their purpose; I am not one."' The setting of this story is somewhat too dramatic, but there is reason to believe that the substance of it is quite true. It is further said, that, though he thus rejected the money, he was in straitened circumstances at the time, insomuch that he was obliged, as soon as Danby had departed, to send to a friend to borrow a guinea.

## MRS TURNER.

The beauty of this woman, and her connection with the mysterious death of Sir Thomas Overbury, who was poisoned in the Tower through her agency, have invested her name with a species of romance in the annals of crime. Though she undoubtedly merited her fate, both she and her accomplices were merely the minor parties in this nefarious transaction, the principal criminals being the Earl and Countess of Somerset, who, though tried and condemned, received the king's pardon, and after undergoing an imprisonment of some years, were allowed to retire into the country and obscurity. The whole affair forms a singular episode in the reign of James I., and by no means reflects credit on that weak monarch.

When Robert Carr or Ker, a young Scottish adventurer of the border-family of Ferniherst, established himself so rapidly in the good graces of his sovereign, rising suddenly to the most influential posts in the kingdom, Sir Thomas Overbury acted as his bosom-friend and counsellor, and furnished him with most useful and judicious advice as to the mode of comporting himself in the new and unwonted sphere in which he was thus placed. Carr unfortunately, however, cast his eyes on the Countess of Essex, the beautiful and fascinating daughter of the Earl of Suffolk, who had been married when a girl of thirteen to the Earl of Essex, son of the unfortunate favourite of Queen Elizabeth, and who himself afterwards became so noted in the reign of Charles I. as the commander of the parliamentary army. This object of illicit love was but too ready to respond to the addresses of Carr, now created Viscount Rochester, having, it is believed, owed much of the depravity of her disposition to the pernicious lessons of Mrs Turner, who lived as a dependent and companion to his daughter in the house of the Earl of Suffolk. This abandoned Mentor afterwards became the wife of a physician, at whose death, owing to the extravagant manner in which both she and her husband had lived, she was left in very straitened circumstances, and was only too glad to become again the confidante and adviser of the Countess of Essex in her amour with Rochester. Not content with the gratification of their unlawful passion, the guilty pair sought to legalise their connection by a marriage, to effect which it was of course necessary that the countess should, in the first place, obtain a divorce from her husband. Sir Thomas Overbury, who had hitherto concurred with and aided Rochester in his amour, now opposed the marriage-scheme, knowing the odium his pupil would excite by contracting such a union, and dreading also the influence which the countess's relations, the Howards, would thereby obtain. He counselled Rochester strongly against thus committing himself, and enlarged, in rather emphatic terms, on the depraved character of his proposed wife. These speeches were reported by the infatuated favourite to the countess, who thereupon vowed the destruction of Overbury. First, she offered £1000 to Sir John Wood to murder the object of her resentment in a duel. Then Rochester and she concocted a scheme by which, on the favourite's representation to King James, Overbury, on the ground of having shewn contempt for the royal authority, was committed to the Tower, where he was detained a close prisoner under the guardianship of a new lieutenant, wholly in the interest of his enemies, who had procured the removal of the former governor of the fortress.

Meantime a divorce had been instituted by the Countess of Essex against her husband, and a majority of the commission of divines and lawyers, appointed by the king to try the cause, was found servile enough to pronounce sentence of dissolution. The day before this deliverance was given, Sir Thomas Overbury died in the Tower, from an infectious disease, as was alleged, and was hastily and clandestinely buried. No doubt was entertained by the public that he had been poisoned; but the matter was passed over without investigation, and for some months Rochester, now Earl of Somerset, basked with the partner of his guilt in all the sunshine of fashion and royal favour. But the king's fickle temper ere long caused his downfall. The presentation at court of a new minion, George Villiers, afterwards the celebrated Duke of Buckingham, effected such a change in the affections of the king as completely to supplant the old favourite, who was accordingly exposed unshielded to the machinations of his enemies, and the just indignation of the people. On a warrant from the Lord Chief-justice Coke, he and his wife were arrested for having occasioned the death of Sir Thomas Overbury, and along with them the parties of inferior rank who had acted as their accomplices. These were Mrs Turner; Elwes, the lieutenant of the Tower; Weston, the warder who had been intrusted with the immediate custody of the prisoner; and Franklin, an apothecary. The proofs adduced against them were sufficiently strong to insure their condemnation, and their own confessions left subsequently no doubt of their guilt. It appeared that Mrs Turner and the Countess of Somerset had had frequent consultations with a certain Dr Forman, a celebrated conjurer in Lambeth, who enjoyed a high reputation as a compounder of love-philtres, and was consulted in that capacity by many of the most fashionable ladies of the day. He died before the proceedings under notice were instituted, and it does not appear that he had any active concern in the murder of Overbury; but the fact of two of the accused parties having had dealings with a *soi-disant* wizard increased immensely the popular horror. As regards the perpetration of the murder, it was shewn that Mrs Turner procured the poison from Franklin the apothecary, and handing it to the warder, Weston, the latter, under her instructions, and with the complicity of Elwes, the lieutenant of the Tower, administered it to the prisoner in small doses, in various kinds of food, and at different times, extending over a period of some months.

The criminals were all executed at Tyburn. The enduring of the last penalty of the law by Mrs Turner, which took place on 15th November 1615, excited an immense interest. She had made herself famous in the fashionable world as the inventress of a yellow starch, and, in allusion to this circumstance, Lord Chief-justice Coke, who had already addressed her in sufficiently contumelious terms, telling her, categorically, that she had been guilty of the seven deadly sins, declared that as she was the inventor of yellow-starched ruffs and cuffs, so he hoped that she would be the last by whom they would be worn. He, accordingly, gave strict orders that she should be hanged in that attire, which she had rendered so fashionable. This addition to the sentence was fully carried out; and the fair demon, Mrs Turner, on the day of her execution, came to the scaffold arrayed as if for some festive occasion, with her face rouged, and a ruff stiffened with yellow starch round her neck. Numerous persons of quality, ladies as well as gentlemen, went in their coaches to Tyburn to see the last of Mrs Turner. She made a very penitent end, and the object contemplated by the Lord Chief-justice was fully attained, as the yellow ruff was never more worn from that day.

As already mentioned, the principal criminals, the Earl and Countess of Somerset, experienced no further penalty than an imprisonment of some years in the Tower. The partial pardon thus accorded to Carr, seems to have been extorted by fear from the king, who dreaded the revelation, by his former favourite, of some discreditable secret.

## 'OLD PARR.'

Though several sceptical individuals, denying the possibility of the life of man being protracted beyond the period of a hundred years, have maintained that no such instance of longevity can be produced, there is abundant and satisfactory evidence to confute this statement, and establish indisputably the fact of the existence of numerous centenarians both in ancient and modern times. One of these instances, that of 'Old Parr,' whose extreme and almost antediluvian age has become proverbial, rests on such well-authenticated grounds, that no reasonable doubt can be entertained as to its truth.

The Christian name of this venerable patriarch was Thomas, and he was born at Winnington, in the parish of Alberbury, Shropshire, in 1483. His father, John Parr, was an agricultural labourer, and Thomas throughout his long life followed the same occupation. Till the age of eighty, he continued a bachelor, and then married his first wife, with whom he lived for thirty-two years. About eight years after her death, when he himself was a hundred and twenty years old, he married for the second time. Having, in 1635, attained the wonderful age of a hundred and fifty-two years and upwards, he was visited in that year by the Earl of Arundel, who, having gone down to see some estates of his in Shropshire, was attracted by the reports which reached him of so remarkable an old man. His lordship was greatly struck by the intelligence and venerable demeanour of Thomas Parr, who was thereupon induced to pay a visit to London; the earl, as we are informed, 'commanding a litter and two horses (for the more easy carriage of a man so enfeebled and worn with age) to be provided for him; also that a daughter-in-law of his (named Lucye), should likewise attend him, and have a horse for her owne riding with him; and to cheere up the olde man, and make him merry, there was an antique-faced fellow, called Jacke, or John the Foole, with a high and mighty no beard, that had also a horse for his carriage. These all were to be brought out of the country to London, by easie journeys, the charges being allowed by his lordship: and likewise one of his honour's own servants, named Brian Kelly, to ride on horseback with them, and to attend and defray all manner of reckonings and expenses; all which was done accordingly.'

It would have been better, however, had Lord Arundel left the old man undisturbed in his native parish. Partly owing to the fatigues of the journey, partly to the crowds of visitors who thronged to see him, and above all to the unwonted mode of life which he led, Parr, ere many months were over, fell ill and died. He was buried on 15th November 1635, in Westminster Abbey, where a monument was erected to his memory. After death his body was examined by the celebrated Dr Harvey, who found it remarkably stout and healthy, without any trace of decay or organic disease, so that had it not been for the abnormal influences to which he had been subjected for a few months previous to his death, there seems little doubt that Parr might have attained even a much greater age.

OLD PARR'S COTTAGE, NEAR ALBERBURY, SHROPSHIRE.

The principal authority for the history of Old Parr is John Taylor, the 'Water Poet,' who, while the patriarch was residing in London, about a month before he died, published a pamphlet, entitled *The Olde, Olde, very Olde Man; or The Age and Long Life of Thomas Parr.* From the period at which this work was issued, we are warranted in placing considerable reliance on its statements, which appear never to have been controverted. In addition to those above quoted, we are informed by Taylor that, at the age of a hundred and five, Parr was obliged, in consequence of an intrigue with Catharine Milton, whom he afterwards married as his second wife, to do penance in a white sheet at the door of the parish church of Alberbury. When presented to Charles I. at court, that monarch observed to him: 'You have lived longer than other men, what have you done more than other men?' Parr's reply was: 'I did penance when I was a hundred years old.' In the meeting of the venerable patriarch with the British sovereign, a parallel is almost suggested with the grand simplicity in which the presentation of Jacob to Pharaoh is recorded in the Book of Genesis.

Thomas Parr seems, through life, to have been of temperate and industrious habits, of which the following metrical account is given by Taylor:

'Good wholesome labour was his exercise,
Down with the lamb, and with the lark would rise:
In mire and toiling sweat he spent the day,
And to his team he whistled time away:
The cock his night-clock, and till day was done,
His watch and chief sun-dial was the sun.
He was of old Pythagoras' opinion,
That green cheese was most wholesome with an onion;
Coarse meslin bread,* and for his daily swig,
Milk, butter-milk, and water, whey and whig:
Sometimes metheglin, and by fortune happy,
He sometimes sipped a cup of ale most nappy,
Cyder or perry, when he did repair
T' Whitson ale, wake, wedding, or a fair;
Or when in Christmas-time he was a guest
At his good landlord's house amongst the rest:
Else he had little leisure-time to waste,
Or at the ale-house huff-cap ale to taste;
His physic was good butter, which the soil
Of Salop yields, more sweet than candy oil;
And garlick he esteemed above the rate
Of Venice treacle, or best mithridate.
He entertained no gout, no ache he felt,
The air was good and temperate where he dwelt;
While mavisses and sweet-tongued nightingales
Did chant him roundelays and madrigals.
Thus living within bounds of nature's laws,
Of his long-lasting life may be some cause.'

There was doubtless something peculiar in Parr's constitution which enabled him to resist so long the effects of age and natural decay. As a corroboration of the theory of the hereditary transmission of qualities, it is a curious circumstance that Robert Parr, a grandson of this wonderful old man, who was born at Kinver in 1633, died in 1757, at the age of a hundred and twenty-four. Perhaps one of the most ingenious devices in the art of quackery is that by which a well-known medicine, bearing Parr's name, is vaunted to the public as the mysterious preparation by which he was enabled to attain the extraordinary age of a hundred and fifty-two. The portrait which is frequently attached to the puffing placard advertising these drugs, is derived from a likeness of Old Parr, drawn by the celebrated painter Rubens.

In the *Gentleman's Magazine* for March 1814, a view, which we have copied (see the preceding page), is given of Old Parr's cottage, in the parish of Alberbury; Rodney's Pillar, on the Breidden Hill, appears in the distance. It is also stated in the work referred to, that the cottage has undergone very little alteration since the period when Parr himself occupied it, and that a corner beside the huge misshapen chimney is shewn as the place where the Nestor of Shropshire used to sit.

* *Meslin bread*, bread made of a mixture of several kinds of flour. The word is derived from the French *mêler* to mix, and possibly also from the German *mischen*. Other forms of the term are *mastlin*, *maslin*, and *mashlum*, the last of which is well known in Scotland as an epithet for a certain description of bannocks or cakes, made of a mixture of bear or barley and pease meal, and styled from this circumstance *mashlum bannocks*.

## DUEL BETWEEN THE DUKE OF HAMILTON AND LORD MOHUN.

On 15th November 1712, a singularly ferocious and sanguinary duel was fought in Kensington Gardens. The keepers of Hyde Park, on the morning of that day, were alarmed by the clashing of swords, and rushing to the spot whence the sound proceeded, found two noblemen weltering in their blood. These were Lord Mohun, who was already dead, and the Duke of Hamilton, who expired in the course of a few minutes. Nor had the combat been limited to the principals alone. The seconds, Colonel Hamilton on the part of the duke, and General Macartney on that of Lord Mohun, had also crossed swords, and fought with desperate rancour. The former of these remained on the field, and was taken prisoner; but Macartney fled to the continent, from which, however, he afterwards returned, and submitted to a trial.

A prodigious ferment was occasioned by this duel, owing to the circumstance of the Duke of Hamilton being regarded as the head of the Jacobite party both in North and South Britain, whilst Lord Mohun was a zealous champion in the Whig interest. Neither of the men could lay claim to great admiration on the score of integrity or principle, and it is difficult, at the present day, to pronounce any decisive verdict in their case. What, however, seems to have originated merely in personal animosity was represented by the Tory party as a dastardly attempt on the part of their political opponents to inflict a vital wound on the Jacobite cause, then in the ascendant, by removing its great prop, who had just been appointed ambassador to the court of France, and was expected to leave London for Paris in the course of a few days. It was maintained that the duke had met foul-play at the hands of Macartney, by whose sword, and not that of Lord Mohun, he had been slain. But this allegation was never established by sufficient evidence, and the truth of the matter seems to be that both sets of antagonists, principals as well as seconds, were so transported by the virulence of personal enmity as to neglect all the laws both of the gladiatorial art and the duelling code, and engage each other with the fury of savages or wild beasts.

## HALLEY'S COMET OF 1682.

Halley's Comet, so called, has been the means of dispelling many popular illusions concerning the influence of those mysterious bodies on worldly affairs. Before it had been ascertained that comets are *periodical* in their appearance, there was unbounded scope for speculation on the nature of this influence. The excellence of the celebrated vintage of 1811 was attributed to the great comet which appeared in that year; as was also the abundance of the crops. Nay, the number of twins born in the same year, and the fact that a shoemaker's wife in Whitechapel had four children at a birth, were in like manner laid to the charge of the comet; as likewise were the facts that wasps were few, and that flies became blind that year. The Great Plague of London was attributed by some to a comet which appeared in the spring of that year. As there was a comet in 1668, and in the same year a remarkable epidemic among *cats* in Westphalia, some of the wiseacres of that day connected the two phenomena together as probable cause and effect. When Lima and Callao were destroyed by an earthquake in 1746, the disaster was imputed to a small comet in the absence of any more probable delinquent. A church clock, destroyed by a meteoric stone; an unusually large flock of wild pigeons in America; the disasters which were experienced by the Christians at the hands of the Turks in 1456; a fit of *sneezing* that became very prevalent in some parts of Germany; the deaths of eminent persons in various countries—all were believed to have been either produced or presaged by comets which appeared in certain years. That of two things which occurred nearly at the same time, one is the *cause* of the other, is a very popular and easy mode of philosophising. M. Arago adduces, in illustration of this point, the anecdote told by Bayle, of a lady who never looked out of the window of her apartment, situated in the greatest thoroughfare of Paris, and saw the street filled with carriages, without imagining that her appearance at the window was the cause of the crowd!

The reason why Halley's comet, or rather Halley's remarkable prediction concerning the comet, has had some influence in lessening these vague speculations, is because a regular and periodical occurrence of any event takes away from it much of a capricious or uncertain character. After Flamsteed had written down his careful observations on the comet of 1680, Sir Isaac Newton was able to determine what kind of curve it marked out in the heavens; and then Dr Halley proceeded to investigate, in a very elaborate way, whether any two recorded comets were really two successive appearances of the same celestial body. He found reason to believe that the comets of 1531, 1607, and 1682 were in fact one and the same comet, which takes about seventy-six years to perform its remarkable journey round the sun. After making corrections for a few disturbing causes, he boldly declared his belief that that comet would appear again late in 1758 or early in 1759; and, with a pardonable self-respect, he appealed to posterity not to lose sight of the fact, that if the comet should really return about that period, the prediction of such a result was due to an Englishman. As the period approached, the great French mathematicians Clairaut, D'Alembert, and Lalande calculated the probable disturbance which the planets would produce on such a comet; and they agreed that the month of April 1759 would be the probable time of re-appearance, or rather, of the perihelion of the comet—that is, its nearest approach to the sun. The comet was espied on the 25th December 1758, and passed its perihelion on March 13, 1759. This would have been a great triumph to Halley, if he could have lived to see it. All Europe agreed that this particular comet should be called *Halley's Comet*, in honour to the man who had so boldly and successfully predicted its periodicity. Then, as time passed on, arose the question—'Will this comet re-appear after another interval of about seventy-six years, say in 1835?' In 1812, Damoiseau calculated that the comet *ought* to re-appear at perihelion on 4th November in that year. In 1829, Pontécoulant, another great mathematician, explained his reasons for selecting the 14th of November as a more probable date. Two learned Germans, Rosenberger and Lehmann, also investigated the same intricate problem; the one named the 11th of November, the other the 26th, as the day of perihelion. At last, when the year 1835 arrived, all the astronomers in Europe were pointing their telescopes towards the heavens, under the belief that the comet would begin to be visible some time in August. They were right. On the 5th of August MM. Dumouchel and De Vico, at the observatory of Rome, detected the comet; it became visible to the naked eye towards the end of September, attained its greatest brilliancy about the middle of October, and passed its perihelion on 15th November—within one single day of the time calculated by Pontécoulant! All this is very wonderful to persons unskilled in astronomical mathematics; but so certain do savans now feel about it, that they decide that the recorded comets of 1378, 1456, 1531, 1607, 1682, 1759, and 1835 were only so many successive appearances of Halley's comet, at intervals of about seventy-six years apart. There is not the slightest doubt among them that Halley's comet will appear again in or about the year 1911, although possibly not one of our present astronomers will be alive in that year.

By thus substituting regularity for uncertainty, Halley's labours on the subject of comets have effectually reformed popular notions concerning those wondrous visitants.

## NOVEMBER 16.

St Eucherius, bishop of Lyon, confessor, 450. St Edmund, confessor, archbishop of Canterbury, 1242.

*Born.*—Tiberius, Roman Emperor, 42 B. C.; John Freinshemius, scholar and critic, 1608, *Ulm;* Jean le Rond d'Alembert, encyclopædist, 1717, *Paris;* Francis Danby, artist, 1793, *Wexford.*

*Died.*—Aelfric, eminent Saxon prelate, 1005, *Canterbury;* Margaret, queen of Malcolm Canmore of Scotland, 1093; Henry III. of England, 1272, *Westminster;* Perkin Warbeck, pretender to English crown, executed, 1499; Pierre Nicole, logician, of Port Royal, 1695, *Chartres;* James Ferguson, astronomer, 1776, *London;* Jean Lambert Tallien, Terrorist leader, 1820; George Wombwell, celebrated menagerie proprietor, 1850, *Northallerton, Yorkshire;* James Ward, animal painter, 1859, *Cheshunt, Herts.*

### ST MARGARET, QUEEN OF SCOTLAND.

Many of the saints in the Romish calendar rest their claims to the title on grounds either wholly or partially fabulous, or which at best display a merit of a very dubious order. It is, however, satisfactory to recognise in the queen of Malcolm Canmore many of those traits which contribute to form a character of sterling virtue, to whose memory persons of all creeds and predilections must pay a respectful homage. It is true that much of our information regarding her is derived from the report of her confessor Turgot, whom clerical prejudices, as well as the inducements of personal friendship and courtly policy, may have led to delineate her with too flattering a pencil. Enough, however, remains after making all due deductions on this score, to confirm the idea popularly entertained in Scotland of the excellence of Queen Margaret. The niece of King Edward the Confessor, and the granddaughter of Edmund Ironside, the colleague of Canute, her youth was spent in exile, and under the proverbially salutary discipline of adversity. Her father and uncle narrowly escaped destruction at the hands of Canute, who, on the murder of their father, Edmund, sent the two young princes to the court of the king of Sweden, with instructions to put them to death privately. The chivalrous monarch refused to imbrue his hands in innocent blood, and sent the royal youths to Solomon, king of Hungary, by whom they were hospitably received and educated. Edmund the elder brother died, but Edward the younger married Agatha, a German princess, by whom he became the father of Edgar Atheling, Christina, and Margaret. On the death of Harold, at the battle of Hastings, Edgar Atheling made an attempt to vindicate his right to the English crown against William the Conqueror; but his unenergetic character was quite unable to cope with the vigour and resources of the latter, and Edgar and his sister Margaret were consequently obliged to fly the kingdom. They were shipwrecked on the coast of Scotland, and courteously received by King Malcolm Canmore, who was speedily captivated by the beauty and amiable character of Margaret. Her marriage to him took place in the year 1070, at the castle of Dunfermline, a place described by Fordun as surrounded with woods, rocks, and rivers, almost inaccessible to men or beasts by its situation, and strongly fortified by art. Margaret was at this time about twenty-four years of age. On her journey northwards to Dunfermline, she crossed the Firth of Forth at the well-known point where it narrows above Inverkeithing, and which since that event has been known by the designation of the *Queensferry*. A stone is also still shewn on the road, a little below Dunfermline, called *Queen Margaret's Stone*, on which she is traditionally said to have rested. Of the palace or castle where she resided at Dunfermline, a small fragment still remains enclosed within the romantic grounds of Pittencrieff, and known as *Malcolm Canmore's Tower*.

The union thus consummated was followed by a numerous offspring—six sons and two daughters. Three of the sons, Edgar, Alexander, and David ascended successively the throne of Scotland, and the elder daughter Maud or Mathildes married Henry I., king of England. To the education of her children Margaret seems to have devoted herself with the most sedulous attention. She procured for them the best preceptors and teachers that the times afforded, and is said to have been particular in inculcating on them the necessity of restraining and correcting the frowardness of youth, by a proper exercise of discipline. Her own temper, however, appears to have been of the sweetest and most placid kind, and she was beloved among her servants and dependents for her innumerable acts of generosity and complaisance. To the poor also her charity was unbounded. Whenever she walked out, she was besieged by crowds of distressed persons, widows, orphans, and others, to whom she administered relief with a liberality which often exceeded the bounds of prudence. During the various incursions made by Malcolm into England, large numbers of the inhabitants of the country were taken prisoners, and to them the beneficence of Margaret was readily extended. She inquired into, and endeavoured as far as possible to mitigate their unhappy condition, and in many instances secretly paid their ransom out of her own funds, to enable them to return to their homes. She also erected hospitals in various places. With her husband, she seems to have lived on the most affectionate terms. Some of her acts, indeed, bear the marks of that spirit of asceticism and ostentatious humiliation so highly esteemed in that age. Every morning, she prepared a breakfast for nine little orphans, whom she fed on her bended knees; and in the evening, she washed the feet of six poor persons, besides entertaining a crowd of mendicants each day at dinner. The season of Lent was observed by her with more than the wonted austerities of the Roman Catholic Church, allowing herself no food but a scanty meal of the simplest description, before retiring to rest, after a day spent in the closest exercises of devotion. One special act of hers in relation to religious ordinances deserves to be recorded. The observance of the Sabbath, which, previous to her marriage with Malcolm, had fallen greatly into desuetude, was revived and maintained by her influence and example. It is not probable, however, that the staid and decorous observance of Sunday, so characteristic of Scotland, was derived from this incident, as a relapse appears to have taken place in succeeding reigns, and the strictly devotional character of the Sabbath to have been only again established at the Reformation.

Notwithstanding the religious tendencies of Margaret, her court was distinguished by a splendour and elegance hitherto unknown in Scotland. Her own apparel was magnificent, and the feasts at the royal table were served up on gold and silver plate. Her acquaintance with the Scriptures and the writings of the fathers was extensive, and she is reported to have held numerous disputations with doctors of divinity on theological matters. An epitome of her moral excellence is presented in what is related of her, that 'in her presence nothing unseemly was ever done or uttered.'

The last days of this amiable queen were clouded by adversity and distress. The austerity of her religious practices prematurely undermined her health, and she was attacked by a tedious and painful illness, which she bore with exemplary resignation. She listened assiduously to the spiritual consolations of her faithful confessor Turgot, who thus relates her concluding words to him as quoted by Lord Hailes, 'Farewell; my life draws to a close, but you may survive me long. To you I commit the charge of my children, teach them above all things to love and fear God; and whenever you see any of them attain to the height of earthly grandeur, oh! then, in an especial manner, be to them as a father and a guide. Admonish and, if need be, reprove them, lest they be swelled with the pride of momentary glory, through avarice offend God, or by reason of the prosperity of this world, become careless of eternal life. This in the presence of Him, who is now our only witness, I beseech you to promise and to perform.' Her death at the last was accelerated by the news which she received of the death of her husband and eldest son before the castle of Alnwick, in Northumberland, an expedition in which she had vainly endeavoured to dissuade Malcolm from taking part in person. While lying on her couch one day, after having offered up some fervent supplications to the Almighty, she was surprised by the sudden entrance of her third son Edgar, from the army in England. Divining at once that some disaster had happened, she exclaimed: 'How fares it with the king and my Edward?' and then, on no answer being returned: 'I know all, I know all: by this holy cross, by your filial affection, I adjure you, tell me the truth.' Her son then replied: 'Your husband and your son are both slain.' The dying queen raised her eyes to heaven and murmured: 'Praise and blessing be to thee, Almighty God, that thou hast been pleased to make me endure so bitter anguish in the hour of my departure, thereby, as I trust, to purify me in some measure from the corruption of my sins; and thou, Lord Jesus Christ, who through the will of the Father, hast enlivened the world by thy death, oh! deliver me.' In pronouncing the last words, she expired on the 16th of November 1093, at the comparatively early age of forty-seven. She was canonized by Pope Innocent IV. in 1251, but in the end of the seventeenth century, her festival was removed by the orders of Innocent XII., from the day of her death to the 10th of June. She was interred in the church of the Holy Trinity, at Dunfermline, which she had founded, and which, upwards of two hundred years afterwards, received the corpse of the great King Robert. At the Reformation, the remains of Queen Margaret and her husband were conveyed privately by some adherents of the old religion to Spain, and deposited in a chapel which King Philip II. built for their reception, in the palace of the Escurial. Here their tomb is said still to be seen, with the inscription: 'St Malcolm, King, and St Margaret, Queen.' The head of Queen Margaret, however, is stated to be now deposited in the church of the Scots Jesuits, at Douay.

## MR WOMBWELL.

As a celebrity of his kind, George Wombwell deserves notice both for his own untiring industry and skill, and the prominence with which, for a long series of years, his name was familiar to the public, and more especially to the juvenile branches of the community. When a boy, he shewed great fondness for keeping birds, rabbits, dogs, and other animals, but the circumstance which led to his becoming the proprietor of a menagerie was for the most part accidental. A shoemaker by trade, and keeping a shop in Soho, he happened one day to pay a visit to the London Docks, where he saw some of the first boa constrictors which had been imported into England. These reptiles had then no great favour with showmen, as much from fear as ignorance of the art of managing them, and their marketable value was consequently less than it afterwards became. Wombwell purchased a pair for £75, and in the course of three weeks realised considerably more than that sum by their exhibition. He used afterwards to declare, that he entertained rather a partiality for the serpent tribe, as they had been the means of first opening his path to fame and fortune. Stimulated by the success thus achieved, he commenced his celebrated caravan peregrinations through the United Kingdom, visiting all the great fairs, such as those of Nottingham, Birmingham, Glasgow, and Donnybrook. In time, he amassed a handsome independence, but could never be prevailed on to retire to the enjoyment of ease and affluence, and he died, as he had lived, in harness. Neither did he ever abandon the closest attention to all matters

MR WOMBWELL.

connected with the menagerie, and might often be seen scrubbing and working away, as indefatigably as the humblest servant attached to the establishment.

At the time of his death, Wombwell was possessed of three huge menageries, which travelled through different parts of the country, and comprised a magnificent collection of animals, many of them bred and reared by the proprietor himself. The cost of maintaining these establishments averaged at least £35 a day. The losses accruing from mortality and disease form a serious risk in the conduct of a menagerie, and Wombwell used to estimate that from this cause he had lost, from first to last, from £12,000 to £15,000. A fine ostrich, valued at £200, one day pushed his bill through the bars of his cage, and in attempting to withdraw it, broke his neck. Monkeys, likewise, frequently entailed great loss from their susceptibility to cold, which frequently, as in the case of human beings, cut them off by terminating in consumption. As regards the commercial value of wild beasts, we are informed that tigers have sometimes been sold as high as £300, and at other times might be had for £100. A good panther is worth £100, whilst hyenas range from £30 to £40 each, and zebras from £150 to £200. We suspect that the profits of menagerie proprietors are at the present day considerably curtailed, when the establishment of zoological gardens, and the general declension of fairs and shows in the popular estimation, must have sensibly diminished the numbers of persons who used to flock to these exhibitions.

# NOVEMBER 17.

St Dionysius, archbishop of Alexandria, confessor, 265. St Gregory Thaumaturgus, bishop and confessor, 270. St Anian or Agnan, bishop of Orleans, confessor, 453. St Gregory, bishop of Tours, confessor, 596. St Hugh, bishop of Lincoln, confessor, 1200.

---

*Born.*—Vespasian, Roman emperor, 9 A. D.; Jean Antoine Nollet, natural philosopher, 1700, *Pimpré, in Noyon;* Louis XVIII. of France, 1755, *Versailles;* Marshal Macdonald, Duke of Tarentum, Bonapartist general, 1765, *Sancerre.*

*Died.*—Valentinian I., Roman emperor, 375; Sir John de Mandeville, Eastern traveller, 1372, *Liège;* Queen Mary of England, 1558, *St James's Palace;* John Picus, Prince of Mirandola, linguist and miscellaneous writer, 1494, *Florence;* Nicolas Perrot d'Ablancourt, translator of the classics, 1664, *Ablancourt;* John Earle, bishop of Salisbury, author of *Microcosmography*, 1665, *Oxford;* Alain Réné le Sage, author of *Gil Blas*, 1747, *Boulogne-sur-Mer;* Thomas, Duke of Newcastle, statesman, 1768; Empress Catharine the Great of Russia, 1796, *St Petersburg;* Charlotte, queen of George III., 1818, *Kew;* Thomas, Lord Erskine, eminent pleader, 1823, *Almondell, near Edinburgh.*

## SIR JOHN MANDEVILLE.

On 17th November 1372, died at Liège the celebrated Sir John Mandeville or De Mandeville, who may be allowed to take rank as the father of English travellers, and the first in point of time, of that extended array of writers, who have made known to their countrymen, by personal inspection, the regions and peoples of the distant East. The ground traversed by him was nearly similar to that journeyed over in the previous century by the celebrated Venetian, Marco Polo, whose descriptions, however, of the countries which he visited must be admitted to be both much fuller and consonant to truth than those of his English successor. Whilst the Italian traveller restricts himself, in the main at least, to such statements as he was warranted in making, either as eye-witness of the circumstances described, or as communicated to him by trustworthy authorities, it is to be regretted that a great portion of Sir John Mandeville's work is made up of absurd and incredible stories regarding oriental productions and manners, which he has adopted without question, and incorporated into his book, from all sources of legendary information, classic, popular, and otherwise. Yet after carefully winnowing the chaff from the wheat, there remains much curious and interesting matter, which may be accepted as presenting a correct picture of Eastern Asia in the fourteenth century, as it appeared to a European and Englishman of the day. Even the purely romantic and legendary statements in the narrative have their value as illustrating the general ideas prevalent in medieval times on the subject of oriental countries. Many of these travellers' wonders, so familiar to all who have read (and who has not in his childhood?) *Sindbad the Sailor*, will be found referred to in the work of Sir John Mandeville.

Of the history of this enterprising traveller we know little beyond what he himself informs us in the introduction to his narrative. From this, and one or two other sources, we learn that he was born at St Albans, in Hertfordshire, about 1300; devoted himself to mathematics, theology, and medicine (rather a heterogeneous assemblage of studies), and for some time followed the profession of a physician. This last occupation he abandoned after pursuing it for a very short time, and in 1322, he started on an eastern tour, the motives for which seem to have been principally the love of adventure, and desire of seeing strange countries, and above all others, the Holy Land, regarding which the recent fervour of the Crusades had excited an ardent interest in Western Europe. On Michaelmas-day, 1322, he quitted England on his travels, proceeding in the first instance to Egypt, into the service of whose sultan he entered, and fought for him in various campaigns against the Bedouin Arabs. He succeeded in ingratiating himself considerably with his employer, who, according to Mandeville's account, thus testified his sense of the Englishman's merits.

'And he wolde have maryed me fulle highely to a gret princes doughter, gif that I wolde have forsaken my law and my beleve. But, I thank God, I had no wille to don it, for nothing that he behighten me.'

From Egypt Sir John proceeded to the Holy Land, and from thence continued his peregrinations till he reached the dominions of the great Khan of Tartary, a descendant of the celebrated Genghis, whose sovereignty extended over the greater part of Central and Eastern Asia, including the northern provinces of China or Cathay, as it was then termed by Europeans. Under his banners Mandeville took service, and fought in his wars with the king of Manci, whose territories seem to have corresponded to the southern division of the Celestial Empire. He appears subsequently to have travelled over the greater part of the continent of Asia, and also to have visited some of the East Indian Islands. The kingdom of Persia is described by him, and also the dominions of that celebrated medieval, and semi-mythical potentate, Prester John, whom from Mandeville's account we would infer to have been one of the princes of India, whilst other chroniclers seem to point to the sovereign of Abyssinia. After an absence of nearly thirty-four years, Sir John returned to his native country, and published an account of the regions visited by him in the East, which he dedicated to Edward III. It is to be regretted that in this there is so little personal narrative given, all reference to his own adventures being nearly comprised in the meagre and unsatisfactory statements which we have above furnished. Subsequently to its publication, Sir John seems to have gone again abroad on his travels, but the history of his latter days is very obscure. All that can be definitely ascertained is, that he died at Liège, in Belgium, and was buried in a convent in that town.

A manuscript of Sir John Mandeville's travels, belonging to the fourteenth century, is preserved in the Cottonian collection in the British Museum. The first printed English edition was that issued from the Westminster press in 1499, by Winkyn de Worde. During the fourteenth and fifteenth centuries, the work enjoyed a great reputation, second only to Marco Polo's, as an authority on all questions of oriental geography, and was translated into several languages.

## Queen Elizabeth's Day.

Violent political and religious excitement characterised the close of the reign of King Charles II. The unconstitutional acts of that sovereign, and the avowed tendency of his brother toward the Church of Rome, made thoughtful men uneasy for the future peace of the country, and excited the populace to the utmost degree. It had been usual to observe the anniversary of the accession of Queen Elizabeth with rejoicings; and hence the 17th of November was popularly known as 'Queen Elizabeth's Day;' but after the great fire, these rejoicings were converted into a satirical saturnalia of the most turbulent kind. The Popish Plot, the Meal-tub Plot, and the murder of Sir Edmundbury Godfrey, had excited the populace to anti-papistical demonstrations, which were fostered by many men of the higher class, who were members of political and Protestant clubs. Roger North, who lived in these turbulent times, says that the Earl of Shaftesbury was the prime mover in all that opposed the court-party, and the head of the Green Ribbon Club, who held their meetings at the 'King's Head Tavern,' at the corner of Chancery Lane. They obtained their name from the green ribbon worn in their hats, to distinguish them in any street-engagement from clubbists of an opposite party. North says, that 'this copious society were a sort of executive power in and about London; and by correspondence, all over England.' They organised and paid for the great ceremonial processions and pope-burnings that characterised the years 1679-1681, and which were well calculated to keep up popular excitement, and inflame the minds of the most peaceable citizens.

From the rare pamphlet, *London's Defiance to Rome*, which describes 'the magnificent procession and solemn burning of the pope at Temple Bar, November 17, 1679,' we learn that 'the bells generally about the town began to ring about three o'clock in the morning;' but the great procession was deferred till night, when 'the whole was attended with one hundred and fifty flambeaus and lights, by order; but so many more came in volunteers, as made up some thousands. . . . . At the approach of evening (all things being in readiness), the solemn procession began, setting forth from Moorgate, and so passing first to Aldgate, and thence through Leadenhall Street, by the Royal Exchange through Cheapside, and so to Temple Bar. Never were the balconies, windows, and houses more numerously lined, or the streets closer thronged, with multitudes of people, all expressing their abhorrence of popery with continued shouts and exclamations, so that 'tis modestly computed that, in the whole progress, there could not be fewer than two hundred thousand spectators.' The way was cleared by six pioneers in caps and red waistcoats, followed by a bellman bearing his lantern and staff, and ringing his bell, crying out all the way in a loud but dolesome voice: 'Remember Justice Godfrey!' He was followed by a man on horseback, dressed like a Jesuit, carrying a dead body before him, 'representing Justice Godfrey, in like manner as he was carried by the assassins to Primrose Hill.' We copy from a very rare print of the period, this, the most exciting part of the evening's display. Godfrey was a London magistrate, before whom the notorious Titus Oates had made his first deposition; he was found murdered in the fields at the back of Primrose Hill, with a

PROCESSION ON 17TH NOV. 1679 COMMEMORATIVE OF THE MURDER OF SIR EDMUNDBURY GODFREY.

sword run through his body, to make it appear that by falling upon it intentionally, he had committed suicide; but wounds in other parts of his person, and undeniable marks of strangulation, testified the truth. There was little need for a bellman to recall this dark deed to the remembrance of the Londoners. The excitement was increased by another performer in the procession, habited as a priest, 'giving pardons very plentifully to all those that should murder Protestants, and proclaiming it meritorious.' He was followed by a train of other priests, and 'six Jesuits with bloody daggers;' then, by way of relief, came 'a consort of wind-musick.' This was succeeded by a long array of Catholic church dignitaries, ending with 'the pope, in a lofty glorious pageant, representing a chair of state, covered with scarlet, richly embroidered and fringed, and bedecked with golden balls and crosses.' At his feet were two boys with censers, 'at his back his holiness's privy-councillor (the degraded seraphim, *Anglicé*, the devil), frequently caressing, hugging, and whispering him, and ofttimes instructing him aloud to destroy his majesty, to forge a Protestant plot, and to fire the city again, to which purpose he held an infernal torch in his hand.' When the procession reached the foot of Chancery Lane, in Fleet Street, it came to a stop; 'then having entertained the thronging spectators for some time with the ingenious fireworks, a vast bonfire being prepared just overagainst the Inner Temple gate, his holiness, after some compliments and reluctances, was decently toppled from all his grandeur into the flames.' This concluding feat was greeted by 'a prodigious shout, that might be heard far beyond Somerset House,' where the Queen Catharine was lodged at that time, but the ultra-Protestant author of this pamphlet, anxious to make the most of the public lungs, declares ''twas believed the echo, by continued reverberations before it ceased, reached Scotland, France, and even Rome itself, damping them all with a dreadful astonishment.'

This show proved so immensely popular, that it was reproduced next year, with additional political pageantry. Justice Godfrey, of course, was there, but Mrs Celliers and the Meal-tub figured also, accompanied by four Protestants, 'in bipartite garments of black and white,' to indicate their trimming vacillation; followed by a man bearing a banner, on which was inscribed, 'We Protestants in Masquerade usher in Popery.' Then came a large display of priests and clerical dignitaries, winding up with the pope, represented with his foot on the neck of the Emperor Frederick of Germany. After him came Doña Olimpia, and nuns of questionable character; the procession concluding with a scene of the trial, and execution by burning, of a heretic. This procession was also 'lively represented to the eye on a copper-plate,' and we copy as much of it as depicts the doings in Fleet Street, from Temple Bar to Chancery Lane. At the corner of the lane is the King's Head Tavern, the rendezvous of the Green Ribbon Club, agreeing exactly with North's description: 'This house was doubly balconied in the front for the clubsters to issue forth in fresco, with hats and no perukes; pipes in their mouths, merry faces, and diluted throats for vocal encouragement of the *canaglia* below, at the bonfires.' From this house to the Temple Gate, lines cross the street for fireworks to pass. The scene is depicted at the moment when the effigy of the pope is pushed

DEMONSTRATIONS ON QUEEN ELIZABETH'S DAY IN 1679.

from his chair of state into the huge bonfire below, as if in judgment for the fate of the Protestant who is condemned to the stake in the pageant behind him. North speaks of 'the numerous platoons and volleys of squibs discharged' amid shouts that 'might have been a cure of deafness itself.' Dryden alludes to the popularity of the show in the epilogue to his *Œdipus;* when, after declaring he has done his best to entertain the public, he adds:

'We know not what you can desire or hope,
To please you more, but *burning of a pope!*'

In the *Letters to and from the Earl of Derby*, he recounts his visit to this pope-burning, in company with a French gentleman who had a curiosity to see it. The earl says: 'I carried him within Temple Bar to a friend's house of mine, where he saw the show and the great concourse of people, which was very great at that time, to his great amazement. At my return, he seemed frighted that somebody that had been in the room had known him, for then he might have been in some danger, for had the mob had the least intimation of him, they had torn him to pieces. He wondered when I told him no manner of mischief was done, not so much as a head broke; but in three or four hours were all quiet as at other times.' In 1682, the court professed great alarm lest some serious riots should result from these celebrations, and required the mayor to suppress them; but the civic magnates declined to interfere, and the show took place as usual. The following year it was announced that the pageantry should be grander than ever, but the mayor was now the nominee of the king,* and effectually suppressed the display, patrolling all the streets with officers till midnight, and having the City trained-bands in reserve in the Exchange, and a company of Horse Guards on the other side of Temple Bar. 'Thus ended these *Diavolarias*,' says Roger North.

Under somewhat similar excitement, an attempt was made in the reign of Queen Anne to reproduce these inflammatory processions and pageants. The strong feeling engendered by the claims of the High-church party under Dr Sacheverell, and the fears entertained of the Pretender, led their opponents to this course. The pageants were constructed, and the procession arranged; but the secretary of state interfered, seized the stuffed figures, and prevented the display. It was intended to open the procession with twenty watchmen, and as many more link-boys; to be followed by bagpipers playing *Lilliburlero*, drummers with the pope's arms in mourning, 'a figure representing Cardinal Gualteri, lately made by the Pretender Protector of the English nation, looking down on the ground in a sorrowful posture.' Then came burlesque representatives of the Romish officials; standard-bearers 'with the pictures of the seven bishops who were sent to the Tower; twelve monks representing the Fellows who were put into Magdalen College, Oxford, on the expulsion of the Protestants by James II.' These were succeeded by a number of friars, Jesuits, and cardinals; lastly came 'the pope under a magnificent canopy, with

* Charles had suspended the City charter, and the mayor—Sir John Moore—was a mere tool of the court, not elected by the citizens, but placed in office by the king.

a silver fringe, accompanied by the Chevalier St George on the left, and his counsellor the Devil on the right. The whole procession clos'd by twenty men bearing streamers, on each of which was wrought these words:

"God bless Queen Anne, the nation's great defender!
Keep out the French, the Pope, and the Pretender."

'After the proper ditties were sung, the Pretender was to have been committed to the flames, being first absolved by the Cardinal Gualteri. After that, the said cardinal was to have been absolved by the Pope, and burned. And then the devil was to jump into the flames with his holiness in his arms.' The very proper suppression of all this absurd profanity was construed into a ministerial plot against the Hanoverian succession. The accession of George I., a few years afterwards, quieted the fears of the nation, and 'Queen Elizabeth's Day' ceased to be made a riotous political anniversary.

## SIR HENRY LEE.

At a tournament held on the 17th November 1559, the first anniversary of the accession of Queen Elizabeth to the throne, Sir Henry Lee, of Quarendon, made a vow of chivalry, that he would, annually, on the return of that auspicious day, present himself in the tilt-yard, in honour of the queen; to maintain her beauty, worth, and dignity, against all-comers, unless prevented by age, infirmity, or other accident. Elizabeth having graciously accepted Sir Henry as her knight and champion, the nobility and gentry of the court, incited by so worthy an example, formed themselves into an honourable society of Knights Tilters, which, yearly assembling in arms, held a grand tourney on each successive 17th of November. In 1590, Sir Henry, feeling himself overtaken by age, resigned his assumed office of Queen's Knight, having previously received her majesty's permission to appoint the famous Earl of Cumberland as his successor. The resignation was conducted with all due ceremony. The queen being seated in the gallery, with Viscount Turenne, the French ambassador, the Knights Tilters rode slowly into the tilt-yard, to the sound of sweet music. Then, as if sprung out of the earth, appeared a pavilion of white silk, representing the sacred temple of Vesta. In this temple was an altar, covered with a cloth of gold, on which burned wax candles, in rich

SIR HENRY LEE AND HIS DOG.

candlesticks. Certain princely presents were also on the altar, which were handed to the queen by three young ladies, in the character of vestals. Then the royal choir, under the leadership of Mr Hales, sang the following verses, as Sir Henry Lee's farewell to the court:

'My golden locks, time hath to silver turned
(Oh time too swift, and swiftness never ceasing),
My youth 'gainst age, and age at youth have spurned;
But spurned in vain, youth waneth by increasing.
Beauty, strength, and youth, flowers fading bene,
Duty, faith, and love, are roots and ever green.

My helmet, now, shall make a hive for bees,
And lover's songs shall turn to holy psalms :
A man-at-arms must now sit on his knees,
And feed on prayers, that are old age's alms.
And so, from court to cottage, I depart,
My saint is sure of mine unspotted heart.

And when I sadly sit in homely cell,
I 'll teach my swains this carol for a song,
Blest be the hearts, that think my sovereign well,
Cursed be the souls, that think to do her wrong.
Goddess, vouchsafe this aged man his right,
To be your beadsman, now, that was your knight.'

After this had been sung, Sir Henry took off his armour, placing it at the foot of a crowned pillar, bearing the initials E. R. Then kneeling, he presented the Earl of Cumberland to the queen, beseeching that she would accept that nobleman for her knight. Her majesty consenting, Sir Henry armed the earl and mounted him on horseback; he then arrayed himself in a peaceful garb of black velvet, covering his head with a common buttoned cap of country fashion.

At Ditchley, a former seat of the Lees, Earls of Litchfield, collateral descendants of Queen Elizabeth's knight, there was a curious painting of Sir Henry and his dog, with the motto, 'More Faithful than Favoured.' The traditional account of this picture, a copy of which is here engraved, is that Sir Henry, on retiring to rest one night, was followed to his bedroom by the dog. The animal, being deemed an intruder, was at once turned out of the room; but howled and scratched at the door so piteously that Sir Henry, for the sake of peace, gave it readmission, when it crept underneath the bed. After midnight, a treacherous servant, making his way into the room, was seized and pinned to the ground by the watchful dog. An alarm being given, and lights brought, the terrified wretch confessed that his object was to kill Sir Henry and rob the house. In commemoration of the event, Sir Henry had the portrait painted, as a monument of the gratitude of the master, the ingratitude of the servant, and the fidelity of the dog. It is very possible that this anecdote and picture may have given rise to the well-known story of a gentleman rescued from murder, at a lonely inn, by the fidelity and intelligence of his dog, who, by preventing him from getting into bed, induced him to suspect some treacherous design on the part of his landlord, who at midnight, with his accomplices, ascended through a trap-door in the floor of the apartment, but were discomfited and slain by the gentleman, with the aid of the faithful animal.

Sir Henry died at the age of eighty, in the year 1611. About fifty years ago, his epitaph could still be deciphered in the then ruined chapel of Quarendon, in Buckinghamshire.

---

## NOVEMBER 18.

**The Dedication of the Churches of Saints Peter and Paul, at Rome. Saints Alphæus, Zachæus, Romanus, and Barulas, martyrs, about 304. St Hilda or Hild, abbess, 680. St Odo, abbot of Cluni, confessor, 942.**

*Born.*—Pierre Bayle, celebrated critic and controversial writer, author of *Dictionnaire Historique et Critique*, 1647, *Carla-en-Comté*, *Foix;* Sir David Wilkie, painter, 1785, *Manse of Cults*, *Fifeshire.*

*Died.*—Cardinal Reginald Pole, eminent ecclesiastic, 1558; Cuthbert Tunstall, bishop of Durham, 1559; Jacob Böhme, or Böhm, celebrated mystical writer, 1624, *Alt-Seidenberg*, *Upper Lusatia;* Dr T. F. Dibdin, author of numerous bibliographical works, 1847; Charles Heath, line-engraver, 1848; Captain George William Manby, inventor of apparatus for saving life in shipwrecks, 1854, *near Yarmouth;* Professor Edward Forbes, eminent naturalist, 1854, *Edinburgh;* Frank Stone, artist, 1859.

### CARDINAL POLE.

Cardinal Pole was, among many such, the most remarkable man of his time. The unyielding uprightness with which he preserved his conduct true to his convictions, made him many enemies among those he opposed. By his faithful and energetic adherence, during the reigns of Henry and Edward, to the papal see, even, as it must have seemed to many, at the expense of the liberty of his country, as well as by the active share which he took in the retrogressive measures of Mary, he rendered himself unpopular with the English people. But ever adorning the nobility of his birth, with the additional lustre of nobility of mind, he merited respect by his singular learning, his purity of conscience, his uniform consistency, his genuine piety, and the most refined and amiable manners.

Reginald Pole was the son of Richard Pole, Lord Montague, cousin-german to Henry VII.; his mother was Margaret, daughter of George, Duke of Clarence, brother to Edward IV. Born in 1500, he was educated for the church from his earliest years, first by the Carthusians, at Sheen, in Surrey, and afterwards by the Carmelites of Whitefriars. He entered Magdalen College, Oxford, as a nobleman, at the age of twelve. He early obtained various preferments, among others the Deanery of Exeter. He resided abroad several years, under Henry VIII.'s patronage; after which, returning to England, he retired into seclusion to prosecute, uninterrupted, his devotional studies.

Pole's first great trial was his rupture with Henry. After fruitless endeavours, often renewed on the king's part, to induce the churchman to acquiesce in Catharine's divorce, and the rejection of the papal supremacy, and equally vain attempts, and as often reiterated on the side of Pole, to avoid coming to any decision, he was finally induced to declare his opinion, and as he expressed it fully, with the utmost honesty, and with considerable eloquence, he was duly placed under ban, and a price set on his head. Pole kept clear of the danger, and Henry had to content himself with depriving him of all his preferments, and his two brothers and aged mother of their lives.

In the same proportion as the affections of Henry were alienated from the uncompromising counsellor, the Roman see took him into favour. He was created a cardinal, and employed on several important trusts. He actively exerted himself in the formation of a league which should have for its object the restoration of England to the Catholic faith; and, in 1546, along with two other cardinals, he represented the pope at the Council of Trent. In 1549, Pole was elected to the popedom; but as the election was tumultuous, he refused to accept its decision. Upon this the conclave proceeded to elect him again, and this decision also, somewhat arrogantly, he set aside, saying: 'God was a God of light and not of darkness,' and bidding them wait for the morning. The Italians, disconcerted, proceeded once more to an election, and this time the friends of the cardinal were outvoted.

Soon after this, Pole obtained leave to retire from all public offices; but Mary succeeding to the English throne, he accepted the appointment of legate to her court; and being at once freed by parliament from the charge of treason, on which he had been banished, took his seat in the House of Peers. He applied himself with zeal to the furtherance of that cause to which he had always firmly clung, and saw his efforts successful. How far he was instrumental in promoting the cruel persecutions which have invested the reign of Mary with such horror, cannot now be very clearly ascertained, but the general mildness and rectitude of his character warrant us in forming the belief that these atrocities met, at least on his part, with no zealous encouragement.

Gardiner, ambitious to succeed Cranmer as archbishop of Canterbury, endeavoured to hinder Pole from obtaining the vacant office; but dying in the midst of his schemes, the cardinal was consecrated soon afterwards, in February 1556. The reigning pope opposed Pole's promotion, but the queen's support rendered the opposition futile. Brighter times seemed to await him. But falling sick, he only survived to receive the, to him, fatal news of the death of Mary, and followed his mistress in the short space of sixteen hours.

Pole was buried at Canterbury. His funeral was magnificent, but his epitaph was humble, being only: *Depositum Cardinalis Poli.*

## JACOB BÖHME.

Jacob Böhme, or, as commonly written in English, Behmen, is one of the many notable men bred under the tutelage of St Crispin, and in various particulars he resembles his brother-craftsman, George Fox, the first of the Quakers. Böhme was born near Görlitz, in Upper Lusatia, in 1575. His parents being poor, and unable to give him much education, he was employed when a child to herd cattle, and in his twelfth year was apprenticed to a shoemaker. It chanced one day, he relates, when his master and mistress were from home, that a stranger in mean apparel, but with a grave and reverent countenance, came into the shop, and taking up a pair of shoes, desired to buy them. Jacob had never been trusted as a salesman, and knew not what money to ask; but as the stranger was importunate, he named a price which he felt sure would bear him harmless on the return of his master. The stranger took the shoes, and going out of the shop a little way, stood still, and with a loud and earnest voice called: 'Jacob, Jacob, come forth!' Surprised and fascinated, the boy obeyed, and the old man, taking him by his right hand, and fixing his bright and piercing eyes upon him, said: 'Jacob, thou art little, but shalt be great, and become another man, such a one as the world will wonder at; therefore be pious, fear God, and reverence His Word. Read diligently the Holy Scriptures, wherein thou hast comfort and instruction; for thou must endure much poverty, and suffer persecution; but be courageous and persevere, for God loves and is gracious unto thee!'—whereon he departed, and was by Jacob seen no more. The strange messenger and his prediction made a deep impression on the boy's mind. He grew serious beyond his years, and at one time was 'for seven days surrounded with a divine light, and stood in the highest contemplation, and in the kingdom of joys.' He was raised above all frivolity, and in his sacred zeal rebuked his master for light and profane speech. At nineteen he married, and set up as shoemaker in Görlitz on his own account.

Years passed away, four sons were born to Böhme, and he was known only in Görlitz as a pious cobbler, with a taste for reading. Meanwhile he was the subject of remarkable experiences. On one occasion, in his twenty-fifth year, when gazing on a dazzling light produced by the sun's rays breaking on a tin vessel, he fell into a trance, in which he again felt himself encompassed with celestial light, and filled with more than mortal joy. Thereafter when he walked abroad in the fields, there was opened in him a new sense whereby he discerned the essences and uses of plants. He commenced writing, but merely for his own satisfaction, living in peace and silence and speaking to few persons of the mysteries which were opened to him. A volume, called *The Aurora*, which he had in this manner privately composed, he lent to a friend, who made a copy of the work. The treatise found its way to Richter, primate of Görlitz, who denounced it from his pulpit, and had Böhme summoned before the senate, which advised him to leave off scribbling and stick to his last. Strange to say, he took the advice, and for seven years let his pen lie idle. At the mature age of forty-two, however, the prophetic impulse came irresistibly upon him; not from any desire to speak, he says, but because the spirit was strong upon him he resumed his writing, printed *The Aurora*, and followed it up with thirty other publications, great and small. Richter again exerted his influence to silence the unlicensed shoemaker, and the magistrates begged him, for the sake of peace, to leave Görlitz, which, with much good-nature, he did. He had now many friends who recognised his genius, who encouraged him to write, and who read all he produced with avidity. Amongst these admirers was Balthasar Walter, a physician of Dresden, who had travelled through Syria, Egypt, and Arabia in search of magical lore, and after six years of fruitless wandering, had returned home to find more than he sought in the humble shoemaker's booth. He and others would bring Böhme plants, and Böhme would handle them, and instantly reveal their properties. Then they would try him with a Greek or an oriental word, and from the sound he would pronounce its signification. Once when Walter uttered the word *idea*, Jacob sprang up in transport, and declared that the sound presented to him the image of a heavenly virgin of surpassing beauty. He was cited before the Elector of Saxony, who had six doctors of divinity and two professors of mathematics to examine the poor shoemaker. They plied him with many and hard questions, but Böhme had an answer for them all. The elector was so pleased with his demeanour, that he led Böhme aside, and sought from him some information for himself. One of the examiners, Dr Meisner, is reported to have said: 'Who knows but God may have designed him for some extraordinary work? And how can we, with justice, pass judgment against what we understand not? Certainly he seems to be a man of wonderful gifts in the Spirit, though we cannot at present, from any sure ground, approve or disapprove of many things he holds.' After this trial and charitable acquittal, Böhme returned to Görlitz, where he died on Sunday, 18th November 1624. Early in the morning of that day, he called his son Tobias, and asked him whether he did not hear sweet music. Tobias said, 'No.' Then said Böhme: 'Open the door, that you may hear it.' In the afternoon he asked the time, and was told three o'clock. 'My time,' he said, 'is not yet; three hours hence is my time.' When it was near six, he took leave of his wife and son, blessed them, and said: 'Now I go hence into paradise!' and bidding his son turn him, he heaved a sigh, and departed.

Böhme was a little man, withered, and with almost a mean aspect. His forehead was low, and his temples prominent; his nose was large and hooked, his eyes blue and quick, his beard short and scanty, his voice thin and gentle, and his speech and manners modest and pleasing. His writings are voluminous, but they were nearly all composed in the last seven years of his life. They form a wonderful *mélange* of alchemy, astrology, soothsaying, theology, and mystical conceptions concerning things supernal and infernal. He wrote slowly, but steadily, and without revision, and his style is diffuse, immethodical, and obscure. The verdict of a cursory reader of Böhme is commonly one of perplexity or disgust, yet he has never lacked patient students, who have professed to find in his pages a wisdom as profound as unique. Amongst these have been many Germans, and in latter days, Schelling, Hegel, Frederick Schlegel, Novalis, and Tieck. In England, William Law, the author of *A Serious Call to a Devout and Holy Life*, was an ardent disciple of Böhme's; and Henry More, the Platonist, and Sir Isaac Newton, were his reverent admirers. Böhme's works have been translated from the German into Dutch, French, and English, but have long ago ceased to be printed; nevertheless, there exists a demand for them, and second-hand booksellers have seldom one of his volumes long in stock.

Sir David Brewster, in his *Life of Sir Isaac Newton*, observes that Newton, at one period of his life, was a believer in alchemy, and devoted much time to the study and practice of its processes. The Rev. William Law has stated that there were found among Sir Isaac's papers large extracts from Jacob Böhme's works, written with his own hand; and that he had learned, from undoubted authority, that Newton, in the early part of his life, had been led into a search for the Philosopher's Tincture, treated of by Böhme. It would appear that Sir Isaac actually set up furnaces, and spent several months in quest of the tincture.*

* Brewster's *Newton*, vol. ii. p. 371.



# NOVEMBER 19.

**St Pontian, pope and martyr, about 235. St Barlaam, martyr, beginning of 4th century. St Elizabeth of Hungary, widow, 1231.**

*Born.*—Charles I. of England, 1600, *Dunfermline;* Albert Thorwaldsen, great Danish sculptor, 1770.

*Died.*—Caspar Scioppius, scholar and polemical writer, 1649, *Padua;* Nicolas Poussin, painter, 1665, *Rome;* John Wilkins, bishop of Chester, philosopher and writer, 1672, *Chancery Lane, London;* 'The Man in the Iron Mask,'* 1703, *Bastille;* Abraham John Valpy, editor of classics, 1854, *London.*

## PATCHING AND PAINTING.

The beauties of the court of Louis-Quinze thought they had made a notable discovery, when they gummed pieces of black taffeta on their cheeks to heighten the brilliancy of their complexions; but the fops of Elizabethan England had long before anticipated them, by decorating their faces with black stars, crescents, and lozenges:

'To draw an arrant fop from top to toe,
Whose very looks at first dash shew him so;
Give him a mean, proud garb, a dapper grace,
A pert dull grin, a black patch cross his face.'

And the fashion prevailed through succeeding reigns, for Glapthorne writes in 1640: 'If it be a lover's part you are to act, take a black spot or two; 'twill make your face more amorous, and appear more gracious in your mistress's eyes.'†

The earliest mention of the adoption of patching by the ladies of England, occurs in Bulwer's *Artificial Changeling* (1653). 'Our ladies,' he complains, 'have lately entertained a vain custom of spotting their faces, out of an affectation of a mole, to set off their beauty, such as Venus had; and it

A LADY'S FACE ADORNED WITH PATCHES (TEMP. CHARLES I.) —FROM FAIRHOLT'S 'COSTUME IN ENGLAND.'

is well if one black patch will serve to make their faces remarkable, for some fill their visages full of them, varied into all manner of shapes.' He gives a cut (which we copy) of a lady's face patched

* See notice of 'The Man in the Iron Mask' at page 60 of this volume.

† The fashion was common with the Roman dames in the latter days of the Empire.

in the then fashionable style, of which it might well be sung—

'Her patches are of every cut,
For pimples and for scars;
Here's all the wandering planets' signs,
And some of the fixed stars.'

The coach-and-horses patch was an especial favourite. The author of *England's Vanity* (1653) is goaded thereby into a kind of grim humour: 'Methinks the mourning-coach and horses all in black, and plying on their foreheads, stands ready harnessed to whirl them to Acheron, though I pity poor Charon for the darkness of the night, since the moon on the cheek is all in eclipse, and the poor stars on the temples are clouded in sables, and no comfort left him but the lozenges on the chin, which, if he please, he may pick off for his cold.'

Mr Pepys has duly recorded his wife's first appearance in patches, which seems to have taken place without his concurrence, as three months afterwards he makes an entry in his Diary: 'My wife seemed very pretty to-day, it being the first time I had given her leave to wear a black patch.' And a week or two later, he declares that his wife, with two or three patches, looked far handsomer than the Princess Henrietta. Lady Castlemaine, whose word was law, decreed that patches could not be worn with mourning; but they seem to have been held proper on all other occasions, being worn in the afternoon at the theatre, in the parks in the evening, and in the drawing-room at night. Puritanical satirists, of course, did not leave the fair patchers unmolested. One Smith printed *An Invective against Black Spotted Faces*, in which he warned them—

'Hellgate is open day and night
To such as in black spots delight.
If pride their faces spotted make,
For pride then hell their souls will take.
If folly be the cause of it,
Let simple fools then learn more wit.
Black spots and patches on the face
To sober women bring disgrace.
Lewd harlots by such spots are known,
Let harlots then enjoy their own.'

Fashion, however, as usual, was proof against the assaults of rhyme or reason, and spite of both, the ladies continued to cover their faces with black spots. When party-feeling ran high in the days of Anne, we have it on the *Spectator's* authority, that politically-minded dames used their patches as party symbols: the Whigs patching on the right, and the Tories on the left side of their faces, while those who were neutral, decorated both cheeks. 'The censorious say that the men whose hearts are aimed at, are very often the occasion that one part of the face is thus dishonoured and lies under a kind of disgrace, while the other is so much set-off and adorned by the owner; and that the patches turn to the right or to the left according to the principles of the man who is most in favour. But whatever may be the motives of a few fantastic coquettes, who do not patch for the public good so much as for their own private advantage, it is certain that there are several women of honour who patch out of principle, and with an eye to the interests of their country. Nay, I am informed that some of them adhere so steadfastly to their party, and are so far from sacrificing their zeal for the public to their passion for any particular person, that in a late draught of marriage-articles, a lady has stipulated with her husband that whatever his opinions are, she shall be at liberty to patch on which side she pleases.'

This was written in 1711, and in 1754 the patch was not only still in existence, but threatening to overwhelm the female face altogether. A writer in the *World* for that year says: 'Though I have seen with patience the cap diminishing to the size of a patch, I have not with the same unconcern observed the patch enlarging itself to the size of a cap. It is with great sorrow that I already see it in possession of that beautiful mass of blue which borders upon the eye. Should it increase on the side of that exquisite feature, what an eclipse have we to dread! but surely it is to be hoped the ladies will not give up that place to a plaster, which the brightest jewel in the universe would want lustre to supply. . . . All young ladies, who find it difficult to wean themselves from patches all at once, shall be allowed to wear them in whatever number, size, or figure they please, on such parts of the body as are, or should be, most covered from sight. And any lady who prefers the simplicity of such ornaments to the glare of her jewels, shall, upon disposing of the said jewels for the benefit of the foundling or any other hospital, be permitted to wear as many patches on her face as she has contributed hundreds of pounds to so laudable a benefaction, and so the public be benefited, and patches, though not ornamental, be honourable to see.'

This valuable suggestion was lost upon the sex, for Anstey enumerates

'Velvet patches à la grecque,'

among a fine lady's necessities in 1766; they seem, however, to have fallen from their high estate towards the beginning of the present century, for the books of fashion of that period make no allusion to them whatever, but they did not become utterly extinct even then. A writer in 1826, describing the toilet-table of a Roman lady, says: 'It looks nearly like that of our modern belles, all loaded with jewels, bodkins, false hair, fillets, ribbands, washes, and patchboxes;' and the present generation may possibly witness a revival of the fashion, as it has witnessed the reappearance of the ridiculous, ungraceful, intrusive hoop-petticoat.

Long as patching lasted, it was but a thing of a day compared with the more reprehensible custom of painting—a custom common to all ages, and pretty nearly all countries, since Jezebel 'painted her face and tired her head and looked out at a window,' as the avenging Jehu entered in at the gate. There is evidence of Englishwomen using paint as early as the fourteenth century, and the practice seems to have been common when Shakspeare tried his 'prentice hand on the drama. In his *Love's Labour's Lost*, he makes the witty Biron ingeniously defend his dark lady-love—

'If in black my lady's brow be decked,
It mourns that painting and usurping hair,
Should ravish doters with a false aspect
And therefore is she born to make black fair.
Her favour turns the fashion of the days;
For native blood is counted painting now;
And therefore red that would avoid dispraise,
Paints itself black to imitate her brow.'

And when bitter Philip Stubbs complains that his countrywomen are not contented with a face of heaven's making, but must 'adulterate the Lord's workmanship' with far-fetched, dear-bought liquors, unguents, and cosmetics, the worthy Puritan only echoes Hamlet's reproach: 'I have heard of your paintings too, well enough. God hath given you one face, and you make yourselves another.' When Sir John Harrington declared he would rather salute a lady's glove than her lip or her cheek, he justified his seeming bad taste with the rhymes—

'If with my reason you would be acquainted,
Your gloves perfumed, your lip and cheek are painted.'

Overbury describes a lady of the period as reading her face in the glass every morning, while her maid stood by ready to write 'red' here, and blot out 'pale' there, till art had done its best or worst. No wonder the *Stedfast Shepherd* exclaims:

'Shew me not a painted beauty,
Such impostures I defy!'

Court-ladies, nevertheless, continued to wear artificial red and white, till the court itself was banished from England.

As long as the Commonwealth existed, no respectable woman dared to paint her cheeks; but Charles II. had not been a year at Whitehall, before the practice was revived, to the disgust of Evelyn and the discontent of Pepys. The latter vows he loathes Nelly Gwyn and Mrs Knipp (two of his especial favourites), and hates his relative, pretty Mrs Pierce, for putting red on their faces. Bulwer says: 'Sometimes they think they have too much colour, then they use art to make them pale and fair; now they have too little colour, then Spanish paper, red-leather, or other cosmetical rubrics must be had.' A little further on he accuses the gallants of beginning 'to vie patches and beauty spots, nay, painting, with the tender and fantastical ladies.' Among these fantastical dames, we are sorry to say, Waller's Saccharissa must be numbered. The poet complains—

'Pygmalion's fate reversed is mine;
His marble took both flesh and blood;
All that I worshipped as divine,
That beauty—*now 'tis understood,*
Appears to have no more of life
Than that whereof he framed his wife.'

Saccharissa deserved the reproaches of her lover more than Mary of Modena did the rebukes of her confessor, for she rouged, contrary to her own inclination, merely to please her husband.

Painting flourished under Anne. An unfortunate husband writes to the *Spectator* in 1711, asking, if it be the law that a man marrying a woman, and finding her not to be the woman he intended to marry, can have a separation, and whether his case does not come within the meaning of the statute. 'Not to keep you in suspense,' he says; 'as for my dear, never man was so enamoured as I was of her fair forehead, neck, and arms, as well as the bright jet of her hair; but to my great astonishment, I find they were all the effect of art. Her skin is so tarnished with this practice, that when she first wakes in a morning, she scarce seems young enough to be the mother of her whom I carried to bed the night before. I shall take the liberty to part with her by the first opportunity, unless her father will make her portion suitable to her real, not her assumed countenance.' The *Spectator* enters thereupon into a description of the Picts, as he calls the painted ladies. 'The Picts, though never so beautiful, have dead, uninformed countenances. The muscles of a real face sometimes work with soft passions, sudden surprises, and are flushed with agreeable confusions, according as the object before them, or the ideas presented to them, affect their imaginations. But the Picts behold all things with the same air, whether they are joyful or sad; the same fixed insensibility appears on all occasions. A Pict, though she takes all that pains to invite the approach of lovers, is obliged to keep them at a certain distance; a sigh in a languishing lover, if fetched too near, would dissolve a feature; and a kiss snatched by a forward one, might transform the complexion of the mistress to the admirer. It is hard to speak of these false fair ones without saying something uncomplaisant, but it would only recommend them to consider how they like coming into a room newly painted; they may assure themselves the near approach of a lady who uses this practice is much more offensive.'

If Walpole is to be believed, Lady Mary Wortley Montagu not only used the cheapest white paint she could get, but left it on her skin so long, that it was obliged to be scraped off her. More than one belle of his time killed herself with painting, like beautiful Lady Coventry, whose husband used to chase her round the dinner-table, that he might remove the obnoxious colour with a napkin! Would that we could say that rouge, pearl-powder, and the whole tribe of cosmetics were strangers to the toilet-tables of our own day—a glance at the shop-window of a fashionable perfumer forbids us laying the flattering unction to our soul, that ladies no longer strive to

'With curious arts dim charms revive,
And triumph in the bloom of fifty-five;'

and tempts us, in the words of an old author, to exclaim: 'From beef without mustard, from a servant who overvalues himself, and from a woman who painteth herself, good Lord, deliver us!'

---

## NOVEMBER 20.

St Maxentia, virgin and martyr. St Edmund, king and martyr, 870. St Humbert, bishop of the East Angles, martyr, 9th century. St Bernard, bishop of Hildesheim, confessor, 1021. St Felix of Valois, confessor, 1212.

*Born.*—Jean Francois de la Harpe, miscellaneous writer (*Lycée ou Cours de la Littérature*); Thomas Chatterton, poet, 1752, *Bristol;* Louis Alexandre Berthier, Prince of Wagram, general of Napoleon, 1753, *Versailles.*

*Died.*—Sir Christopher Hatton, statesman and courtier of Queen Elizabeth, 1591; Caroline, queen of George II. of England, 1737; Cardinal de Polignac, statesman and man of letters, 1741, *France;* Abraham Tucker, author of *The Light of Nature Pursued*, 1774, *Betchworth Castle, near Dorking;* Roger Payne, celebrated bookbinder, 1797; Mountstuart Elphinstone, Indian diplomatist, &c., 1859, *Hookward Park, Surrey.*

## THE CAPE OF GOOD HOPE DOUBLED BY VASCO DA GAMA.

The doubling of the Cape of Good Hope by Vasco da Gama, on the 20th of November 1497, was a notable event in the world's history—not on account of the actual discovery of that cape, which had been made some years earlier, but from the solution of an important question, whether or not India could be reached from Europe by sea. Columbus, we know, sought to reach that far-famed land of gold and diamonds, perfumes and spices, by a western route across the Atlantic. He discovered America instead, and those islands, which we now call the *West Indies*, owe their name to the geographical error which formerly prevailed regarding their position. The Spanish monarchs, who first fostered and then neglected Columbus, countenanced those projects which led to the discovery, conquest, and settlement of various parts of America; but the kings of Portugal were the great promoters of the enterprises by which South Africa and India were laid open to Europeans.

With the assistance of a map of Africa, the reader can easily trace the steps by which these discoveries were effected. In the year 1412, Prince Henry of Portugal, a man gifted far beyond the average intelligence of his age, determined to send out a ship to explore the west coast of Africa, by sailing southward from the Straits of Gibraltar. The first voyage was not attended with much success; but the prince pursued the scheme at intervals for many years. In 1415, one of the exploring vessels thus sent out reached as far as Cape Non. In 1418, John Gonzales Zano and Tristam Vaz Texeira, two gentlemen of Prince Henry's court, made a voyage which enabled them to discover the island of Madeira. After a period of several years, marked by discoveries of a minor character, Gillianez doubled Cape Bojador in 1433—an event which led Pope Martin V., in the plenitude of liberality and inadvertence, to bestow on the king of Portugal *all* that might be afterwards discovered in Africa and India; a papal concession that gave rise to serious international disputes in after-days. In 1441, Antonio Gonzales and Nuno Tristan advanced as far south as Cape Blanco; a progress which was followed up by Vicente de Lagos and Aloisio de Cada Mosto, who, in 1444, advanced to the river Gambia, and by Cada Mosto, who, in 1446, reached Senegal and Cape de Verde. A long interval now ensued, unmarked by any discoveries of importance on the west African coast. In 1470, the Portuguese discoveries recommenced with a voyage by Fernando Gonaz nearly as far south as the equator. Some years after this, the northern limit of the kingdom of Congo was reached; and in 1484 the river of the same name was attained by Diego Cano. Then came discoveries of a far more important description. King John of Portugal, in 1486, sent out two expeditions to discover an eastern route to India, and likewise the whereabouts of the mysterious potentate known as Prester John. The latter eluded all search, but India did not. One of the expeditions proceeded through Egypt and down the Red Sea, and, amid many difficulties, crossed the Arabian Sea or Indian Ocean to Calicut, in India. The other, under Bartholomew Diaz, comprising two caravals and a small store-ship, proceeded southward beyond the latitude of the Cape of Good Hope; and Diaz doubled it, or went round it from west to east without knowing it. He coasted a thousand miles of the African shores never before seen by Europeans; and though difficulties prevented him from crossing over to India, he had the joy of finding, on his return, that he had really reached and passed the cape which forms the southern extremity of Africa. He called it *Cabo Tormentoso*, the Cape of Torments, or Tempests, on account of the rough weather which he experienced there; but the king said: 'No, it shall be the *Cape of Good Hope*, for the discovery is one of great promise.' At last came the expedition of Vasco da Gama, to which all the above were preliminary. King Emanuel of Portugal (King John's son) sent him out in 1497, in command of three vessels, with 160 men. He doubled the cape on 20th November, sailed northward, and discovered Sofala, Mozambique, and Melinda; and then, guided by an Indian pilot, he crossed the ocean from Melinda to Calicut in twenty-three days. All that followed was a mere finishing of the great problem: Vasco da Gama was the first who made the entire voyage from Western Europe to India, so far as records enable us to judge.

## ROGER PAYNE.

In the last century, when the pursuit of book-collecting was almost approaching to the nature of a mania, a great want was felt of an artist capable of providing suitable habiliments for the treasures of literature—of constructing caskets worthy of the jewels which they enshrined. When the demand comes to be made, the means of supply are seldom far distant; so, at this eventful crisis, as Dr Dibdin informs us, 'Roger Payne rose like a star, diffusing lustre on all sides, and rejoicing the hearts of all true sons of bibliomania.' The individual who could excite such lively enthusiasm was simply a bookbinder, but of such eminence in his art, as to render all his works exceedingly valuable. For taste, judicious choice of ornament, and soundness of workmanship, Payne was unrivalled in his day, and some maintain that he has never been equalled in subsequent times. But whatever lustre Roger may have diffused, it was by his handiwork alone; in person he was a filthy, ragged, ale-sodden creature, with a foolish, and even fierce indifference to the common decencies of life. His workshop was a deplorable filthy den, unapproachable by his patrons; yet, when he waited on his distinguished employers, he made no alteration in his dress. The Countess of Spencer's French maid fainted when she saw such a specimen of humanity in conversation with her mistress. Payne, like others of this kind of temper, thought he thus shewed his manliness, for a Quixotic spirit of independence was one of his failings, though in speech and writing he ever displayed the greatest possible humility.

In spite of his eccentric habits, Payne might have made a fortune by his business, and ridden in a carriage, as finely decorated as the books he bound. The rock on which he split was the excessively ardent devotion which he cherished for strong ale. In one of his account-books, still preserved, we find one day's expenditure thus recorded: 'For bacon, one halfpenny; for liquor, one shilling;' reminding us of a snatch of a song, in the old comedy of *Gammer Gurton's Needle:*

'When I saw it booted not,
Out of doors, I hied me,
And caught a slip of bacon,
When I thought that no one spied me.
Which I intended not far hence,
Unless my purpose fail,
Shall serve for a shoeing-horn,
To draw on two pots of ale.'

Ale may be said to have been meat, drink, washing, and lodging for the wretched Roger. When remonstrated with by his friends and patrons, and told that sobriety, like honesty, was the best policy, and the only road that led to health and wealth, he would reply by chanting a verse of an old song in praise of his favourite beverage, thus:

'All history gathers
From ancient forefathers,
That ale's the true liquor of life;
Men lived long in health,
And preserved their wealth,
Whilst barley-broth only was rife.'

Payne could rhyme on his darling theme; his trade-bills are preserved as great curiosities, for they mostly contain unbusiness-like remarks by this eccentric original. On one, delivered for binding a copy of Barry's work on the Wines of the Ancients, he wrote:

'Homer the bard, who sung in highest strains,
Had, festive gift, a goblet for his pains;
Falernian gave Horace, Virgil fire,
And barley-wine my British muse inspire,
Barley-wine first from Egypt's learned shore,
Be this the gift to me from Calvert's store.'

Payne's chef-d'œuvre is a large paper copy of the famous folio *Æschylus*, known to collectors as the Glasgow *Æschylus*, being printed, with the same types as the equally famous Glasgow *Homer*, by Foulis, in that city in 1795. This book, bound for Lord Spencer, contains the original drawings executed by Flaxman, and subsequently engraved and dedicated to the mother of the earl. Dibdin, in the *Ædes Althorpianæ*, describes it as the most splendid and interesting work in Europe. Payne's bill for binding it is *verbatim*, *literatim*, and *punctuatim*, as follows:

'*Æschylus* Glasguæ. MDCCXCV. Flaxman Illustravit. Bound in very best manner, sewd with strong Silk, every Sheet round every Band, not false Bands; The Back lined with Russia Leather, Cutt Exceeding Large; Finished in the most Magnificent Manner, Em-borderd with ERNAINE expressive of The High Rank of The Noble Patroness of the Designs, The other Parts Finished in the most elegant Taste with small Tool Gold Borders Studded with Gold; and small Tool Plates of the most exact Work, Measured with the Compasses. It takes a great deal of Time, marking out the different Measure-ments; preparing the Tools, and making out New Patterns. The Book finished in compartments with parts of Gold Studded Work. All the Tools except Studded points are obliged to be worked off plain first—and afterwards the Gold laid on and Worked off again. And this Gold Work requires Double Gold, being on Rough Grained Morocco, The Impressions of the Tools must be fitted and covered at the bottom with Gold to prevent flaws and cracks . . . £12 12 0

Fine drawing paper for Inlaying the designs 5*s*. 6*d*. Finest Pickt Lawn paper for Interleaving the Designs 1*s*. 8*d*. One yard and a half of Silk 10*s*. 6*d*. Inlaying the Designs at 8*d*. each 32 Designs £1, 1*s*. 4*d*., . . . . . . . 1 19 0

Mr Morton adding borders to the Drawings . . . . . . . 1 16 0

£16 7 0'

Another bill, delivered to Dr Mosely, Payne's medical attendant, runs thus:

'*Harmony of the World, by Haydon: London* 1642. Bound in the very best manner; the book sewed in the very best manner with white silk, very strong, and will open easy; very neat and strong boards; fine drawing-paper inside stained to suit the colour of the book. The outsides finished in the *Rosie-Crucian taste*—very correct measured work. The inside finished in the *Druid taste*, with *Acorns* and *S S*. studded with *Stars*, &c., in the most magnificent manner. So neat, strong, and elegant as this book is bound, the binding is well worth 13*s*., and the inlaying the frontispiece, cleaning and mending, is worth 2*s*. To Dr Mosely's great goodness, I am so much indebted, that my gratitude sets the price for binding, inlaying, cleaning, and mending at only . . £0 10 6'

Payne, for a long time, lived and worked alone in his filthy den; but towards the close of his career, he took in, as a fellow-labourer, an excellent workman named Weir. This man was a regularly 'dubbed ale-knight,' loved barley-wine to the full as much as his partner, and used to sing:

'Ale is not so costly,
Although that the most lie,
Too long by the oil of the barley,
Yet may they part late,
At a reasonable rate,
Though they come in the morning early.
Sack is but single broth,
Ale is meat, drink, and cloth.'

Sobriety may not be always a bond of union, but inebriation is a certain source of discord, and not only words, but frequently blows were exchanged between the two artists. Weir's wife was a famous cleaner of old books, and she went with her husband to Toulouse, where they exercised their skill and art, for several years, in binding and repairing the valuable library of Count Macarthy. Payne ended his wretched existence on the 20th of November 1797, and was soon followed by Weir to the bourne whence no man returneth. After their deaths, Mrs Weir was employed to clean and repair the books, parchments, vellums, &c., in the Register Office at Edinburgh. Lord Frederick Campbell was so much pleased with her good-conduct, and marvellously successful labours in this capacity, that he had her portrait drawn and engraved. Her *chef-d'œuvre* was a copy of the *Faite of Arms and Chivalrye*, printed by Caxton, and bound by Payne. At the Roxburgh sale, this book was brought to the hammer. As a work printed by Caxton, bound by Payne, and cleaned by Weir does not occur every day, the excitement and sensation when Mr Evans put it up was immense; nor was it finally knocked down till the biddings reached the high figure of three hundred and thirty-six pounds.

## THE BRITISH NIMROD.

In a letter, dated 20th November 1611, from John Chamberlain, a gentleman and scholar, in the reign of James I., to his friend Sir Dudley Carleton, we find, amid other items of news, the following passage regarding the king and queen: 'The king is hunting at Newmarket, and the queen at Greenwich, practising for a new masque.' This brief sentence exhibits very comprehensively the ruling passions of those two royal personages. Queen Anne was no less fond of court masques and balls, than her consort was of the chase. His flatterers bestowed on him the title of the British Solomon, and extolled him as the most profoundly wise sovereign that had ever sat on a throne, but with much greater appropriateness, as far at least as regarded enthusiasm for, and devotedness to sport, they might have dubbed him the British Nimrod. From his early youth in Scotland, the love of the chase was with him an overpowering and absorbing passion, and he gave so much time to it, that the extent of his studies and his knowledge becomes the more a wonder. It took him much away from state business, and proved a serious annoyance to his counsellors — who would be required to accompany him after the stag for six hours in order to get five minutes' conversation with him; but he was never at a loss for something to say in excuse of this misspending of time. 'My health,' he would say, 'is necessary for the state; the chase is necessary for my health: *ergo*, it is doing the public a service if I hunt.' This logic, from royal lips, was irresistible. The king's sports were chiefly pursued in his own parks; but he was not less willing to let his bugle waken the echoes in those of his chief nobles, who were but too happy to contribute to his gratification that they might establish themselves in his favour.

Now and then, some one of the favoured few permitted to ride with him, has, luckily for us, sought to enliven his letters to absent friends with little sketches of the adventures that fell out on these merry hunting-mornings; and in the State Papers we meet with a series of detached photographs, which, brought together, form a not uninteresting picture. Bravely responding to the sharp sting of 'Ripon rowels,' we seem to witness the pure-blooded iron gray that carried England's fortunes, dash onwards, to be again at the head of the field, which he had momentarily lost. Down the steep, along the valley, through the centre of its shallow river's bed, sweep onwards the gallant cavalcade, scattering the shingle with their horses' hoofs, and throwing up the water in broad glistening sheets. A bugle-note from some distant forester falls on the ear. The game's 'at soil.' Another five minutes' sweep round that elbow of the stream, and there stands our 'hart of grease,' knee-deep in the amber pool, his broad dun haunches firm against the lichen-covered rock; his beamy antlers lowering from side to side, as the clustering hounds struggle and swim around him, straining their blood-shot eyes. The king, pleased, yet flushed and pale with excitement, his hunting-garb soiled with mire and bog-water from spur to bonnet plume, reins up just in time to witness the finish, for Bran and Buscar, Ringwood and 'Jewell' (prime leader of the royal pack), have fastened upon the quarry's throat. And when the deer has been broken up, and whilst the foresters, all unbonneted, wind the customary *mort* upon their bugles, our royal woodsman is plunging his unbooted limbs in the beast's warm, reeking entrails:* an extraordinary panacea, recommended by the court-physician, Sir Theodore Mayerne, as the 'sovereign'st thing on earth,' for those gouty and rheumatic twinges, which too emphatically reminded the Stuart in the autumn of his days, how 'every inordinate cup is unblest and the ingredient thereof a devil,' though the warning produced no practical result.

It is amusing enough to note how cheaply and contemptuously James held the judgment of such as presumed to differ from him in their estimation of his favourite sports and his style of indulging in them. Great was his disgust when he heard that his brother-in-law, Christian, king of Denmark, who visited England in 1606, had spoken slightingly of English hunting in general, saying it was an amusement in which more horses were killed in jest, than in the Low-Country wars were consumed in earnest.† James, after indulging in a few expletives, which it is as well to omit, sarcastically growled forth the reply: 'That he knew not what sport the old Danish gods, Thor and Woden, might partake of in their Scandinavian heaven, but flesh and blood could shew no better than he had done.'

A prince thus enamoured of the pleasures of a sportsman's life, could hardly be expected to endure otherwise than impatiently the sedentary duties of his council-chamber. They were, indeed, utterly distasteful to him; and so, likewise, by association, were those assembled there—Egerton, Buckhurst, Dorset, Naunton, Winwood, Nottingham, &c.; lord-keepers, lord-treasurers, lord-admirals, and lord-chamberlains. Debates about the most signal means of curbing Gondomar's haughty insolence, which but reflected the arrogance of his master, or upon the policy of the 'Spanish match,' were often abruptly terminated by the monarch rising from his chair with a yawning remark, that he had worked long enough; so he was off towards Royston, to have a flight with the new Spanish falcon. 'His majesty,' writes Sir Dudley Carleton, already referred to, having broken up the council, rides straight to Royston, 'with all his hunting-crew, a small train of forty persons;' and again: 'the king is at the inn at Ware, with his hawkes.' Unfortunately, he neglects to satisfy inquisitive posterity who read his pleasant letters more than two centuries afterwards, whether James, and his small hunting-crew of forty persons, passed their nights, one and all, in the great bed which is so inseparably associated in our ideas with that town.

Cecil, styled by his master—who had a characteristic nickname for every one about him—'my little beagle,'‡ because, like that diminutive hound, he was small of stature, and indefatigable in hunting

* James's practice invariably, whenever the deer was run down and killed.

† State Papers, 1606.

‡ There is extant a paper in James's handwriting, indorsed, 'A memorial for Sondaye—being the king's notes of various points of business to be dispatched with his Counsall—the little Beagle—and the Bishoppe of Canterburie.'

down—not hares and conies, but conspiracies—(men say he invented far more than he discovered) was almost the only one of his ministers for whom James felt any personal regard, although he often growled at the king's expensive hobbies, which, he said, 'cost more than would build a fleet.' Once when he lay ill of a fever, and the king was about to quit London on a sporting-tour, he received a visit of condolence from his sovereign, who comforted him with these words: 'that he was very sensible of his sickness, and must have a care of his well-doing; "For," quoth James, as he pressed his hand at parting, "should aught untoward occur to thee, my little beagle, there were no more safe hunting for the king of England."'* The probability of being assassinated in his solitary gallops through the lonely forest, was ever present to the royal mind; and his preservation he attributed wholly to the untiring vigilance of his astute state-secretary. Nor were his fears at all unfounded. Among the State Papers is a declaration of one Captain Newell, that a soldier named FitzJames had said, 'There would soone be a puffe, that may send some high enough and low enough to hell ere longe; and that he would shoote the king in the woods of Royston,' with many similar affidavits.

Our modern English sovereigns are satisfied with the modest parade of a single master-huntsman and one pack of buck-hounds. But the first English king of the Stuart race maintained at least seven establishments at the same number of hunting-lodges—at Royston, Hinchinbrooke, Theobalds, Windsor, Newmarket, Nonsuch, Hampton Court—with hounds for the chase in St John's Wood, and the great woods stretching around Newington. Possibly the reader may be rather astonished to hear of great stags and fallow-deer roaming wild in the two last-named suburbs of London, and that James maintained a large staff of foresters and keepers to preserve the pheasants, hares, conies, &c., swarming in their leafy coverts. The one, he now sees covered with pleasant villas, rising from the midst of grounds adorned with all the cunning of horticulture—elegant retirements for the refined and wealthy; the other, chiefly a squalid, densely-populated quarter—possessed by the sons of poverty and toil, and little suggestive of the accessaries to sylvan sport. Our old friend, Sir Dudley Carleton, viewed them under a different aspect. 'The king,' he says, 'went this evening to lie at Lord Arundel's, in Highgate, that he may be nearer and readier to hunt the stag on the morrow, in St John's Wood.' His son, Charles I., one Monday morning unharboured a buck from a great secluded dingle at Newington, where, twenty-four hours previously, a knot of poor trembling Puritans had sheltered themselves and their worship from the persecution of Archbishop Laud. 'We took,' says that zealous churchman in a letter to Windebank, dated Fulham, June 1632—'another conventicle of separatists in Newington Woods, in the very brake where the king's stag was to be lodged, for his hunting next morning.'

But, *revenons à nos chiens.* James had distinct packs of hounds for the several kinds of chase in which he indulged—stag, red deer, roebuck, fox, wolf, hare, and otter—beside ban, bear, and bull-dogs, with a nobleman for their keeper; and teams of spaniels, indispensable to his superb hawking establishments. These necessarily demanded a large suite of attendants, whose names sound strange in the ears of modern sportsmen. There were masters of the game, sergeants of the stag-hounds, 'lumbermen' of the buckhounds, yeomen and children of the leash, tents and toils (the latter being small pages who held relays of fresh dogs at openings of the forest), keepers of the royal fishing-cormorants, of the elephants, camels, and other 'tame beasts,' located in St James's Park. His majesty, we are told, once experienced some inconvenience at his hunting-seats, from the crowding about him of certain over-zealous country gentlemen, eager to gaze upon their sovereign 'taking saye,' or to assist at the ceremony of cutting up a fat stag.

One day when the court was at Rufford, says one of Lord Stafford's letters, 'the loss of a stag, and the hounds hunting foxes instead of deer—put the king into a marvellous chafe, accompanied by those ordinary symptoms (oaths), better known to you courtiers than to us rural swains. In the height whereof comes a clown galloping in, and staring full in his face. "Mass!" quoth the intruder, "am I come forty miles to see a fellow!" and presently turns about his horse, and away he goes faster than he came; the oddness whereof caused his majesty and all the company to burst out into a vehement laugh, and so the fume was for that time happily dispersed.' Yet was his majesty 'merry against the hair,' however genuine might be the glee of his courtiers. 'He that very day,' says John Chamberlain, 'erected a new office, and made Sir Richard Wigmore "marshal of the field." He is to take order that the king be not attended by any but his own followers; nor interrupted nor hindered in his sports by idle spectators.' During one season, the king hunted in the Fen country, where the deer not unfrequently sought safety in the meres, surrounded by dreary marshes, impassable to sportsmen and dogs. The fenmen, like the Bretons dwelling in the *Landes* of France, traversed their boggy soil on stilts; and a party of them being hired on one occasion to drive out the game, and doing their work off-hand and cleverly, James was so gratified thereat, and so amused by their singular appearance when stalking through the water, like a flight of fishing-cranes, that he signified his gracious pleasure to 'erect a new office.' Accordingly, one day after a jovial hunting-dinner, he chose Sir George Carew as leader of the stiltsmen—who was to be ready with his squad in uniform, whenever the royal hounds hunted that district.

Although passing a considerable portion of his life in the saddle, James was not a very skilful horseman, as is testified by the many and dangerous falls recorded of him, through which he was sometimes at the point of death. Every precaution was therefore resorted to, to lessen or avert the perils incident to the headlong pace which the king fearlessly maintained in order to be well-up at the finish. The high-sheriff of Herts, Thomas Wilson, writing to the constables of Sandon, Ketshall, and other towns of the county, informs them of the 'king's express command that they give notice to occupants of arable land, not to plough their fields in narrow ridges, nor to suffer swine to go abroad unringed, and root holes, &c., to the endangering

* State Papers, James I.

of his majesty and the prince in hawking and hunting; they are also to take down the high bounds between lands which hinder his majesty's ready passage.'*

Although his various kennels contained, at a moderate calculation, little short of two hundred couple of hounds, and the cost of their maintenance and equipages was a serious draught upon his privy purse,† James never deemed himself properly furnished, while a single hound of reputation remained in possession of his subjects. The writer has seen a score or two of docquets, empowering his officers everywhere to seize hounds, beagles, spaniels, and 'mongrels' for his majesty's disport; and his chief huntsman had a similar warrant to take by force every canine celebrity known to exist in three counties. On the occurrence of any of those hunting casualties, where his dogs got maimed by horse-kicks, or being ridden over, &c., he vented his indignation in the most outrageous language; yet there, as indeed in almost every transaction of his life, he shewed himself as placable as he was momentarily irate. There is a pleasant instance of this feeling mentioned in one of the letters already quoted. 'The king,' says the writer, 'is at Tibbalds, and the queen gone or going after him. At their last meeting being at Tibbalds, which was about a fortnight since, the queen, shooting at a deer with her crossbow, mistook her mark, and killed Jewell, the king's most special and principal hound, at which he stormed exceedingly awhile, swearing many and great oaths. None would undertake to break unto him the news, so they were fain to send Archie the fool on that errand. But after he knew who did it, he was soon pacified, and with much kindness wished her not to be troubled with it, for he should love her never the worse, and the next day sent her a *jewell* worth £2000, "as a legacy from his dead dog." Love and kindness increase daily between them, and it is thought they were never on better terms.' Doubtless this opportunity of perpetrating a practical joke upon the name of his 'most principal hound,' went a great way in reconciling the royal punster to his loss and to the queen.

---

## NOVEMBER 21.

The Presentation of the Blessed Virgin Mary. St Gelasius, pope and confessor, 496. St Columban, abbot and confessor, 615.

*Born.*—Edmund, Lord Lyons, British admiral, 1790, *Christchurch.*

*Died.*—Marcus Licinius Crassus, Roman triumvir, slain in Mesopotamia, 53 B.C.; Eleanor, queen of Edward I., 1291 A.D.; Sir Thomas Gresham, founder of the London Exchange, 1579, *London;* Thomas Shadwell, poet, 1692, *Chelsea;* Henry Purcell, musician and composer, 1695, *Westminster;* John Hill, noted sarcastic writer and empiric, 1775, *London;* Abraham Newland, celebrated chief cashier of Bank of England, 1807, *Islington;* James Hogg, the Ettrick Shepherd, poet and miscellaneous writer, 1835, *Altrive, Selkirkshire;* Miss Berry, friend of Horace Walpole, 1852, *London;* James Meadows Rendel, engineer, 1856.

* State Papers.

† Wages due to the servants of the royal establishment in this and the following reign, were constantly in arrear. Peter Pett, one of the king's master-shipwrights, memorialised the Lords of the Admiralty, 'that unspeakable abuses are committed in Shotover and Stow woods (Surrey), by cutting off tops for browse for the deer as is pretended; and lopping wood fit for knees for great ships, for firewood. The head-keeper, Sir Thomas Tyrrell's answer was: "How should the keepers live, having but £26, 8s. a year, and that unpaid these *ten* years?"'—*State Papers.*

### SIR THOMAS GRESHAM.

This eminent man was born in London in 1519, and was the second son of Sir Richard Gresham, a member of the Mercers' Company, a prosperous merchant, and lord mayor of London. Although destined for trade, young Gresham received a liberal education, and studied at Cambridge, where he was entered of Gonville College. Subsequently to this, he served an apprenticeship to his brother Sir John Gresham, also a member of the Mercers' Company. A few years after this, we find him employed by the crown in the reign of Edward VI., and afterwards in those of Mary and Elizabeth, in negotiating foreign loans.

Thomas Gresham received the honour of knighthood in 1559. His enjoyment of the queen's confidence, the magnitude of his transactions, and his princely liberality, procured for him the title of the Royal Merchant; and so splendid was his style of living, that he occasionally entertained, at the queen's request, foreign visitors of high rank. Some years previous to his attainment of these honours, he had married Anne, daughter of William Ferneley of West Creting, Suffolk, then the widow of William Read, mercer, of London, by whom he had issue one child, Richard, who died at the age of sixteen in 1564.

On the west side of Bishopsgate Street, in an airy and fashionable quarter, then almost in the fields, Sir Thomas Gresham built for himself a large mansion, which, with its gardens, seems to have extended into Broad Street, and to have occupied what is now the site of the Excise Office. The house was built of brick and timber, and appears to have consisted of a quadrangle enclosing a grass-plot planted with trees; there were two galleries a hundred and forty feet long, and beneath them was an open colonnade. Sir Thomas destined his mansion to become a college, and to form the residence of the seven professors for whose salaries he provided by an endowment. In the Royal Exchange of London, however, he raised a more lasting memorial of his wealth and generosity. In 1566, the site on the north side of Cornhill was bought for £3500, and upon it Sir Thomas Gresham built the Exchange. Its materials, as well as its architect, are stated to have been brought from Flanders, and the *Burse* at Antwerp would seem to have suggested the model. The plan was a quadrangular arcade, with an interior cloister. On the Cornhill front, there was a tower for a bell, which was rung at noon and at six in the evening; and on the north side there was a Corinthian column, which, as well as the tower, was surmounted by a grasshopper—the family crest. On the 23d January 1570, Queen Elizabeth dined at Gresham's house, and visited this new building, which she was pleased to name 'The Royal Exchange.' The shops or stalls in the galleries above the cloister, and surrounding the open court, were, in Gresham's time, occupied by milliners and haberdashers (who sold mouse-traps, bird-cages, shoe-horns, lanterns, and other heterogeneous commodities), armourers, apothecaries, booksellers, goldsmiths, and dealers in glass. The open court below must have presented a curious scene when it was filled by the merchants of different nations, in the picturesque dresses of their respective countries.*

On the 4th July 1575, Sir Thomas Gresham made a will whereby he bequeathed legacies to his nieces and other relations, and to several of his 'preantysses.' He also directed black gowns, of 6*s.* 8*d.* the yard, to be given to a hundred poor men and a hundred poor women, to bring him to his grave in his parish church of St Helen's. By another will, made on the following day, he shewed most memorably that he had never forgotten what he learned at the university, and that it was the wish of his heart to extend to others through all time the aids to learning which he had himself enjoyed. Accordingly, he bequeathed one moiety of his interest in the Royal Exchange to the Corporation of London, and the other moiety to the Mercers' Company, and charged the corporation with the nomination and appointment of four persons to lecture in divinity, astronomy, music, and geometry. To each of these lecturers he directed an annual payment to be made of £50, and another yearly payment of £6, 13*s.* each, to eight 'almefolkes,' to be appointed by the corporation, and who should inhabit his almshouses at the back of his mansion. For the prisoners in each of five London prisons, he provided the annual sum of ten pounds. The wardens and commonalty of the Mercers' Company were charged to nominate three persons to read in law, physic, and rhetoric, within Gresham's dwelling-house; and out of the moiety vested in the company, to pay each lecturer £50 a year; to pay to 'Christ Church Hospital lately the Greyfriars,' to St Bartholomew's Hospital, to 'the Spital at Bedlam nere Bishopsgate Street,' to the hospital for the poor in Southwark, and for the prisoners in 'the Countter in the Powlttrye,' £10 each, annually, and to apply £100 a year, for four quarterly 'feasts or dynnars,' for the whole company of the corporation in the Mercers' Hall. The mansion-house itself, with the garden, stables, and appurtenances, were vested in the mayor, commonalty, and citizens, and in the wardens and commonalty of mercers, in trust to allow the lecturers to occupy the same, and there to inhabit and study, and daily to read the several lectures. He appointed his wife executrix, 'in wyche behalffe' (adds the testator) 'I doe holly put my trust in herr, and have no dowght but she will accomplishe the same accordingly, and all other things as shal be requisite or exspedieant for bothe our honnesties, fames, and good repportes in this transsitory world, and to the proffitt of the comen well, and relyffe of the carfull and trewe poore, according to the pleasseur and will of Allmyghttye God, to whom be all honnor and glorye, for ever and ever!' This will was in the handwriting of Sir Thomas Gresham himself, and was proved on the 26th November 1579, five days after the testator's death. He was honourably interred in the church of St Helen's, and there his sculptured altar-tomb remains.

* See notice and engraving of the old Royal Exchange, in vol. i. pp. 152, 153.

In June 1597, the year after the death of Lady Anne, Sir Thomas's widow, the daily lectures commenced according to his will; and thenceforth, for a long course of years, his mansion-house was known as 'Gresham College,' and the chief part of the buildings were appropriated as the lodgings of the various professors. The house escaped the Great Fire of London; and when the Mansion House of London, and Gresham's Exchange, and the houses of great city companies lay in ruins after that event, Gresham College was for a time employed as the Exchange of the merchants, and afforded an asylum to the lord mayor, and the authorities of the Mercers' Company. But Gresham College acquired a more illustrious association, for it may be regarded as the cradle of the Royal Society, which, in the early part of its history, viz. from 1660 to 1710, held its meetings here, when it numbered among its associates the names of Newton, Locke, Petty, Boyle, Hooke, and Evelyn. In 1768, however, a legislative act of Vandalism put an end to the collegiate character of Gresham's foundation, and the mansion and buildings were sold to government, to form a site for the Excise Office. As compensation to the lecturers for the loss of their lodgings, their salaries were raised to £100 a year. The lectures were afterwards read for some time at the Royal Exchange, but a new college was erected and opened on the 2d November 1843.

Gresham's Royal Exchange was destroyed, as we all know, in the Great Fire. It was rebuilt on a larger scale, but similar plan. This building was accidentally destroyed by fire on the 10th January 1838, and replaced by the present stately structure which visibly perpetuates the memory of the renowned Sir Thomas Gresham.

## JOHN HILL.

Biography, combining instruction with amusement, not unfrequently exhibits, in one and the same character, examples of excellence to be fearlessly followed, and of weaknesses to be as sedulously shunned. As an instance of the advantages to be achieved by unwearied industry and rigid economy of time, the career of John Hill may be adduced as one well worthy of praise and emulation; while it also warningly shews the baleful and inevitable results of an unbridled vanity acting on a weak, malevolent, and contentious disposition. If Ishmael has his hand against every man, he must expect, as a natural consequence, that every man's hand will be against him. One of the various nicknames given to Hill by his contemporaries, was Dr Atall, sufficiently illustrative of his character. For players, poets, philosophers, physicians, antiquaries, critics, commentators, free-thinkers, and divines, were alternately selected by him as objects of satire or invective. And thus it happens, that while Hill's voluminous, and in many instances, useful works, are almost forgotten, and his valuable services to the then infant science of botany scarcely recognised at the present day, his name is principally preserved in the countless satirical squibs and epigrams launched at him by those whom he had wantonly provoked and insulted.

Hill was the son of a worthy Lincolnshire clergyman, and having been educated as an apothecary, he opened a shop in St Martin's Lane, London. Marrying before he had established a business, the *res angusta domi* obliged him to look for other means of support. The fame of Linnæus, and the novelty of his sexual system of botany, then producing a great sensation throughout Europe, Hill determined to turn his attention to that science, for which he undoubtedly had a strong natural taste. Patronised by the Duke of Richmond and Lord Petre, he was employed by them to arrange their gardens and collections of dried plants. He then conceived a scheme of travelling over England to collect rare plants, a select number of which, prepared in a peculiar manner, and accompanied by descriptive letterpress, he proposed to publish by subscription. This plan failing, he tried the stage as an actor, but without success, failing even in the appropriate character of the half-starved apothecary in *Romeo and Juliet.* Relinquishing the sock and buskin, he returned to the mortar and pestle, and while struggling for a living in his original profession, he turned his attention to literature. His first work was a translation of Theophrastus *On Gems*, which, being well and carefully executed, established his reputation as a scholar, and procured him fame, friends, and money. Having at last found the tide that leads to fortune, Hill was not slow to take advantage of it. He wrote travels, novels, plays; he compiled and translated with marvellous activity and industry: works on botany, natural history, and gardening—in short, on every popular subject—flowed, as it were, from his ready pen. From these sources he derived for several years an annual income of £1500.

Obtaining a diploma in medicine from the College of St Andrews, Hill, with this passport to society, set up his carriage, and entered on the gay career of a man of fashion. He commenced the *British Magazine*, and, in addition to his other labours, published a daily essay in the *Advertiser*, under the title of the 'Inspector.' Notwithstanding all this employment, he combined business with pleasure, by being a constant attendant at all places of public amusement, and thus procured the scandalous anecdotes which he so freely dispensed in his periodical writings. About this time he came into collision with Garrick, Hill having composed a farce called the *Route*, and presented it to a charitable institution as 'a piece written by a person of quality.' The play was acted under Garrick's management, for the benefit of the charity, but received little favour; and, on the second night of its representation, it was hissed and hooted through every scene. Wild with rage and disappointment, the doctor disgorged his spite in venomous paragraphs against the manager. To which Garrick simply replied:

'For physic and farces,
His equal there scarce is;
His farces are physic,
His physic a farce is!'

Hill returned to the attack with a paper, entitled *A Petition from the Letters I and U to David Garrick.* In this, these letters are made to complain bitterly of the grievances inflicted on them by the actor, through his inveterate habit of banishing them from their proper places, as in the words virtue, and ungrateful, which he pronounced *vurtie* and *ingratefil.* Garrick again replied with an epigram, in which he had decidedly the best of it:

'If 'tis true, as you say, that I 've injured a letter,
I 'll change my note soon, and I hope for the better.
May the right use of letters, as well as of men,
Hereafter be fixed by the tongue and the pen;
Most devoutly I wish, that they both have their due,
And that *I* may be never mistaken for *U*.'

When all London was gulled by the story of Elizabeth Canning, Hill's natural shrewdness saw through the imposture. In a pamphlet he successfully opposed the current of popular opinion, and was applauded by the discerning few, who had escaped that strange infatuation. One of his opponents in that and other controversies, was Henry Fielding, the goodness of whose heart made him, in this instance, the dupe of female artifice and cunning.

When writing under the character of the 'Inspector,' Hill adopted a whimsically dishonest stratagem, to lash, without manifest inconsistency, some persons whom a little before he had eulogised. He published anonymously the first number of a periodical, entitled the *Impertinent*, in which he violently attacked the poet Smart; but took care, in the next 'Inspector' to defend him with faint praise, and rebuke the cruel treatment of him by the *Impertinent.* When Smart discovered this treacherous trick, he published a keen satire, entitled *The Hilliad*, in which he represents as follows a gipsy fortune-teller inducing Hill to abandon the pestle for the pen:

'In these three lines athwart thy palm I see
Either a tripod or a triple-tree,
For oh! I ken by mysteries profound,
Too light to sink, thou never canst be drowned—
Whate'er thy end, the Fates are now at strife,
Yet strange variety shall check thy life—
Thou grand dictator of each public show,
Wit, moralist, quack, harlequin, and beau,
Survey man's vice, self-praised and self-preferred,
And be th' INSPECTOR of the infected herd;
By any means aspire at any ends,
Baseness exalts, and cowardice defends,
The chequered world's before thee—go—farewell,
Beware of Irishmen—and learn to spell.'

The allusion in the last line refers to an Irish gentleman, named Brown, who, having been libelled in the 'Inspector,' retorted by publicly beating the doctor in the rotunda at Ranelagh Gardens (see cut on the following page). Hill received the buffeting with humility, but to shew that such meekness of conduct was attributable rather to stoicism than to a want of personal courage, he immediately afterwards published an account of himself having once given a beating to a person, whom he named Mario. A wag, doubting this story, wrote—

'To beat one man, great Hill was fated.'
'What man?' 'A man whom he created!'

Indeed, Hill did not claim for himself a high standard of truthfulness; he sometimes acknowledged in the 'Inspector' that he had told falsehoods, thus giving occasion for another epigram:

'What Hill one day says, he, the next, does deny,
And candidly tells us it is all a lie:
Dear doctor, this candour from you is not wanted;
For why should you own it? 'tis taken for granted.'

Hill, however, considered himself a moralist, a friend and supporter of piety and religion. He published a ponderous guinea quarto on *God and Nature*, written professedly against the philosophy of Lord Bolingbroke; and every Saturday's 'Inspector' was devoted to what he termed 'a lay-sermon,' written somewhat in the Orator-Henley style, and affording subject-matter for the following epigrammatic parody:

'Three great wise men, in the same era born,
Britannia's happy island did adorn:
Henley in care of souls, displayed his skill,
Rock shone in physic, and in both John Hill;
The force of nature could no further go,
To make a third, she joined the former two.'

Rock was a notorious quack of the period. Being one day in a coffee-house on Ludgate Hill, a gentleman expressed his surprise that a certain physician of great abilities had but little practice, while such a fellow as Rock was making a fortune. 'Oh!' said the quack, 'I am Rock, and I shall soon explain the matter to you. How many wise men, think you, are in the multitude that pass along this street?' 'About one in twenty,' replied the other. 'Well, then,' said Rock, 'the nineteen come to me when they are sick, and the physician is welcome to the twentieth.'

And to the complexion of quackery did Hill come at last. His mind, from over-production, became sterile; his slovenliness of compilation, and disregard for truth, sank his literary reputation as fast as it had risen. When his works found no purchasers, the publishers ceased to be his bankers. He had lived in good style on the malice and fear of the community, he now found

ASSAULT ON DR HILL AT RANELAGH—FROM A CONTEMPORARY PRINT.

resources in its credulity. He brought out certain tinctures and essences of simple plants, sage, valerian, *bardana*, or water-dock, asserting that they were infallible panaceas for all the ills that flesh is heir to. Their sale was rapid and extensive, and whatever virtues they may have possessed, no one can deny that they were peculiarly beneficial to their author, enabling him to have a town-house in St James' Street, a country-house and garden at Bayswater, and a carriage to ride in from one to the other. The quivers of the epigram-writers were once more filled by these medicines, and thus some of their arrows flew—

'Thou essence of dock, of valerian, and sage,
At once the disgrace and the pest of this age;
The worst that we wish thee, for all of thy crimes,
Is to take thy own physic, and read thy own rhymes.'

To this another wit added:

'The wish must be in form reversed,
To suit the doctor's crimes,
For, if he takes his physic first,
He'll never read his rhymes.'

Hill, or some one in his name, replied:

'Ye desperate junto, ye great, or ye small,
Who combat dukes, doctors, the devil, and all!
Whether gentlemen-scribblers or poets in jail,
Your impertinent wishes shall never prevail;
I'll take neither sage, dock, nor balsam of honey:
Do you take the physic, and I'll take the money.'

The latter end of Hill's life was better than the beginning. Though his first wife was the daughter of a domestic servant, he succeeded in obtaining, as a second helpmate, a sister of Lord Ranelagh. At the parties of the Duchess of Northumberland, he was a frequent guest, and he acquired the patronage of the Earl of Bute. His last and most valuable work, a monument of industry and enterprise, was a complete *Vegetable System*, in twenty-four folio volumes, illustrated by 1600 copper-plates, representing 26,000 plants, all drawn from nature. This work was in every respect far in advance of its period, and entailed a heavy pecuniary loss on its author. A copy of it, however, which he presented to the king of Sweden, was rewarded with the order of the Polar Star, and from thenceforth the quondam apothecary styled himself Sir John Hill. Lord Bute appointed him to the directorship of the royal gardens, with a handsome salary, but it does not seem that the grant was ever confirmed. In spite of the efficacy of his Tincture of Bardana, which Hill warranted as a specific for gout, he died of that disease on the 21st of November 1775. The following is the last fling which the epigrammatists had at him:

'Poor Doctor Hill is dead! Good lack!'
'Of what disorder?' 'An attack
Of gout.' 'Indeed! I thought that he
Had found a wondrous remedy.'
'Why, so he had, and when he tried,
He found it true—the doctor died!'

### MARY BERRY.

This lady, who died in Curzon Street, Mayfair, on 21st November 1852, at the age of ninety, formed one of the last remaining links which connected the life and characters of the latter half of the last century with the present. Both she and her younger sister Agnes enjoyed the acquaintance and friendship of the celebrated Horace Walpole, Earl of Orford, who, after succeeding to that title, made a proffer, though an unaccepted one, of his hand and coronet to Mary Berry. These two ladies were the daughters of Mr Robert Berry, a gentleman of Yorkshire origin, but resident in South Audley Street, London. Walpole first met them, it is said, at Lord Strafford's, at Wentworth Castle, in Yorkshire, and the friendship thus formed was a lasting one. The Misses Berry afterwards took up their abode at Twickenham, in the immediate neighbourhood of Strawberry Hill, with whose master a constant interchange of visits and other friendly offices was maintained. Horace used to call them his two wives, corresponded frequently with them, told them many stories of his early life, and what he had seen and heard, and was induced by these friends, who used to take notes of his communications, to give to the world his *Reminiscences of the Courts of George I. and II.*

On Walpole's death, the Misses Berry and their father were left his literary executors, with the charge of collecting and publishing his writings. This task was accomplished by Mr Berry, under whose superintendence an edition of the works of Lord Orford was published in five volumes quarto. He died a very old man at Genoa, in 1817, and his daughters, for nearly forty years afterwards, continued to assemble around them all the literary and fashionable celebrities of London. Agnes, the younger Miss Berry, predeceased her sister by about a year and a half.

Miss Berry was an authoress, and published a collection of Miscellanies, in two volumes, in 1844. She also edited sixty Letters, addressed to herself and sister by Horace Walpole; and came chivalrously forward to vindicate his character against the sarcasm and aspersions of Lord Macaulay in the *Edinburgh Review.*



## NOVEMBER 22.

Saints Philemon and Appia. St Cecilia, or Cecily, virgin and martyr, 230. St Theodorus the Studite, abbot, 9th century.

### ST CECILIA.

This saint was a Roman lady of good family, and having been educated as a Christian, was desirous of devoting herself to heaven by a life of celibacy. Compelled, however, by her parents to wed a young nobleman named Valerian, she succeeded in converting both her husband and his brother to Christianity, and afterwards shared with them the honours of martyrdom. Accounts differ as to the death which she suffered, some asserting that she was boiled in a caldron, and others that she was left for days to expire gradually after being half decapitated. The legend states that the executioner, after striking one blow, found himself unable to complete his task.

St Cecilia is generally regarded as the patroness of church-music, and, indeed, of music generally; but the reason for her holding this office is not very satisfactorily explained. Butler says that it was from her assiduity in singing the divine praises, the effect of which she often heightened by the aid of an instrument. She is generally represented singing, and playing on some musical instrument, or listening to the performance of an angelic visitant. This last circumstance is derived from an ancient legend, which relates that an angel was so enraptured with her harmonious strains as to quit the abodes of bliss to visit the saint. Dryden thus alludes to the incident in his *Ode for St Cecilia's Day*:

'At last divine Cecilia came,
Inventress of the vocal frame;
The sweet enthusiast from her sacred store,
Enlarg'd the former narrow bounds,
And added length to solemn sounds,
With nature's mother-wit, and arts unknown before.
Let old Timotheus yield the prize,
Or both divide the crown;
He rais'd a mortal to the skies;
She drew an angel down.'

About the end of the seventeenth century, the practice was introduced of having concerts on St Cecilia's Day, the 22d of November. These were highly fashionable for a time; the words of the pieces performed being frequently from the pen of writers like Dryden, Addison, and Pope, and the music composed by artists like Purcell and Blow.

---

*Born.*—Professor Dugald Stewart, celebrated metaphysician, 1753, *Edinburgh.*

*Died.*—Pope John XXIII., 1419, *Florence;* Robert, Lord Clive, founder of the British empire in India, 1774, *Moreton Say, near Drayton;* John Stackhouse, botanist, 1819, *Bath;* François Le Vaillant, African traveller, 1824, *La Neve, near Lauzun;* Sir Henry Havelock, Indian general, 1857, *Lucknow;* Professor George Wilson, author of various scientific works, 1859, *Edinburgh;* Father Lacordaire, eminent French preacher, 1861, *Loreze.*

## FATHER LACORDAIRE.

The Frenchman has an inborn aptitude for oratory, and seldom, for any period, are the pulpit and tribune of his nation deprived of the illumination of genius. Among the greatest of modern French orators was the Abbé Lacordaire. Paris is not a city in which priests are popular, but for years, the delivery of a discourse by him had only to be announced to assemble a crowded audience, waiting with breathless interest for the words from his mouth.

He was the son of a country physician, and was born in 1802. Educated for the law, he went to Paris in 1822, for the purpose of being called to the bar. He evinced remarkable abilities, and his success as an advocate was regarded as certain. Professing deistical opinions, he suddenly, to the amazement of his acquaintance, proclaimed his intention of becoming a priest, and straightway, on his twenty-third birthday, he entered the ecclesiastical seminary of St Sulpice. In after-life, he frequently repeated that neither man nor book was the instrument of his conversion, but that a sudden and secret stroke of grace opened his eyes to the nothingness of irreligion. In a single day he became a believer; and once a believer, he wished to become a priest.

For some years, life passed smoothly with Lacordaire in the fulfilment of a variety of ecclesiastical duties. The only singularity about him was his political liberalism, which he retained as firmly as in the days when a student and barrister. This liberalism drew him into association with Lamennais and Montalembert, and together they started a newspaper, *L'Avenir*, in 1830. Its device was, 'God and Liberty;' that is to say, the pope and the people, ultramontanism in religion and radicalism in politics. *L'Avenir* quickly brought its conductors into a blaze of notoriety, into lawsuits with the government, and into controversy with bishops; but what they gained in fame they lost in money, and they were compelled to stop their newspaper. Prompted by Lamennais, they carried their ecclesiastical controversy to Rome, and insisted on Gregory XVI. pronouncing a decision. To their intense chagrin, the pope issued an encyclical letter condemning the politics of *L'Avenir*. Lacordaire and Montalembert bowed to the papal authority, but Lamennais, after a fierce struggle with himself, passed into open rebellion, in which he continued to the end of his life.

At this time, Lacordaire made the acquaintance of Madame Swetchine, a Russian lady of rank, who, having become a Roman Catholic, resided in Paris, where her house, for more than forty years, was the resort of the most brilliant society of 'the faithful.' To Lacordaire she became more than a mother. 'Her soul,' he wrote, 'was to mine what the shore is to the plank shattered by the waves; and I still remember, after twenty-five years, all the light and strength she afforded to a young man unknown to her. Her counsel preserved me alike from despondency and the opposite extreme.' As long as her health permitted, she was always among Lacordaire's hearers. 'Should you like to see the preacher's mother?' was asked of two persons who were listening to him in Notre-Dame. 'Why, she died ten years ago!' was the answer. 'No, there she is, look at her;' and the speaker pointed to Madame Swetchine, hidden behind a pillar, whose constant attention to, and manifest happiness in, the discourse of the preacher, gave rise to this very natural mistake.

Lacordaire made his first essay as a preacher in 1833, and failed completely. Montalembert and others who heard him unanimously agreed, 'He is a talented man, but will never make a preacher,' and Lacordaire was of the same opinion. Nevertheless, he tried again in the following year, and was instantly successful. By some means his tongue had got loosed, and passion, tenderness, irony, and wit burst freely from his lips. One day, for the benefit of certain scoffers, he exclaimed: 'Gentlemen, God has made you witty, very witty indeed, to shew you how little he cares for the wit of man.' His fame grew daily. The archbishop of Paris called him to mount the pulpit of Notre-Dame; and on one occasion, rising from his throne, in the presence of an immense audience, he greeted the orator with the title of 'our new prophet.'

From this excess of glory he retired for seclusion, for two or three years, to Rome, and, whilst wandering and praying in the basilicas of the Eternal City, he became convinced that it was his mission to revive the order of Dominican friars in France. Having secured the requisite authority, he reappeared in Notre-Dame, clothed in the white woollen habit of the order, with shaven head and black scapular. The novelty lent fresh piquancy to his oratory, and Lacordaire, in Notre-Dame, became one of the lions of Paris, whom everybody, who could possibly do so, felt bound to see and hear. In his zeal, he assumed the name of Dominic, wrote a life of the saint, and defended the Inquisition. At the same time he contended, with all the vigour of a reformer, for freedom of opinion. 'Public conscience,' he said in one of his sermons, 'will always repel the man who asks for exclusive liberty, or forgets the rights of others; for exclusive liberty is but a privilege, and a liberty forgetful of others' rights is nothing better than treason. Yes, Catholics, know this well: if you want liberty for yourselves, you must will it for all men under heaven. If you ask it for yourselves simply, it will never be granted; give it where you are masters, in order that it may be given you wherever you are slaves.' Strange words these, the world thought, from a Dominican monk! Among his last public sayings uttered in Paris was: 'I hope to live and die a penitent Catholic, and an *impenitent liberal.*'

Such being Lacordaire's sentiments, it was nowise surprising that, in the Revolution of 1848, he was selected as member of the Constituent Assembly for the department of Bouches du Rhône. He entered that tumultuous parliament in the garb of St Dominic, and took his seat near the summit of the Mountain, not far from the side of his long-lost friend, Lamennais. His appearance attracted the greatest curiosity, but he was out of his proper sphere. He made several speeches, but they fell flat on his audience, and he had the good sense to perceive his error, and retire after a few weeks' trial. Louis Napoleon's *coup-d'état* was felt by him and his friends as a severe discomfiture, and though his liberty as a preacher was not directly interfered with, he found that it was limited, and that henceforward he must measure and consider every phrase. It was not, therefore, without a sense of relief, that in 1854 he was appointed to the direction of the free college of Soreze, and preached his last sermon in Paris. Once only was he recalled from his provincial solitude. In 1860, he was elected to fill the chair in the French Academy, left vacant by M. de Tocqueville. He was introduced by M. Guizot, and his installation had all the significance of a political demonstration. Montalembert prayed him to remain in Paris for a day or two, but after some little hesitation he answered: 'No, I cannot; it would perhaps prevent some of my children, who are preparing for the coming festival, from going to confession. No one can say what the loss of one communion may be in the life of a Christian.' With such zeal did he give himself to his new duties, that Sorèze, under his care, took rank as the first school in the south of France.

His observance of monastic rule was rigorous in the extreme, and his health suffered by his austerities. 'The great men of antiquity were poor,' he used to say. 'Luxury is the rock on which every one splits to-day. People no longer know how to live on little. A great heart in a little house is of all things here below that which has ever touched me most.' Despite the simplicity and poverty of his habits, there was in him a passion for precision, neatness, and good order, which altogether redeemed them from meanness. During the last two years of his life, he was the subject of a cruel disease, against the influence of which he battled resolutely. Finally, he had to give up, saying: 'This is the first time that my body has withstood my will.' He died on the 22d of November 1861; his last words were: 'My God! open to me—open to me!'

To Protestants and Catholics, Lacordaire was a paradox, and in this lay one reason for the interest he excited. The faithful child of Rome and the democrat were hard to reconcile, yet in him they seemed to be united in all sincerity. In theology, he was no innovator; whatever might be his vehemence, he never lapsed from orthodoxy. He was a sentimentalist, not a philosopher; a patriot, not a statesman. It was his fervour, his fluency, his brilliancy, not depth nor originality of idea, which drew crowds to hear him. He was, what is a very rare thing, a real extempore speaker. He had a wonderful power of improvisation. He prepared his discourses by short but intense labour, and made no notes. Reporters took down what he said, and, with slight revision, he sent their copy to the press. Readers usually feel them tame and abounding in platitudes, but no orator can be judged truly in print. Like an actor, he must be seen to be appreciated. One day, in the pulpit, Lacordaire said: 'By the grace of God, I have a horror for what is commonplace;' whereon, observes his friend and admirer Montalembert, 'He was never more mistaken in his life;' but it demands no ordinary genius to bewitch the world with commonplace.

## ROBIN HOOD.

Much controversy has prevailed with respect to this celebrated outlaw, and the difficulty, or rather impossibility, of now obtaining any information regarding his history that can be relied on as authentic, will, in all likelihood, render him ever a subject for debate and discussion among antiquaries. The utmost attainment that can reasonably be expected in such a matter, is the being enabled, through a judicious consideration and sifting of collateral evidence, to draw some credible inference, or establish some well-grounded probability.

The commonly-received belief regarding Robin Hood is, that he was the captain of a band of robbers or outlaws, who inhabited the forest of Sherwood, in Nottinghamshire, and also the woodlands of Barnsdale, in the adjoining West Riding of Yorkshire. They supported themselves by levying toll on wealthy travellers, more especially ecclesiastics, and also by hunting the deer and wild animals of the forest. Great generosity is ascribed to Robin, who is represented as preying only on the wealthy and avaricious, whilst he carefully eschewed all attacks on poor people or women, and was ever ready to succour depressed innocence and worth by his purse as well as his sword and bow. He is recorded to have cherished a special enmity towards the sheriff of Nottinghamshire, whom, on one occasion, under the guise of a butcher, and pretending that he had some horned cattle to dispose of, he entrapped into the forest of Sherwood, and only released on the payment of a swinging ransom. Bishops and rich ecclesiastics were the objects of his especial dislike and exactions, but he was, nevertheless, a religiously-disposed man, and never failed regularly to hear mass or perform his orisons. He even retained in his band a domestic chaplain, who has descended to posterity by the appellation of Friar Tuck, and been immortalised in *Ivanhoe*. The lieutenant of this renowned captain was a tall stalwart fellow called John Little, but whose name, for the sake of the ludicrous contrast it presented, was transposed into Little John. Other noted members of the band were William Scadlock, George-a-Green, and Much the miller's son. A mistress has also been assigned to Robin Hood, under the epithet of 'Maid Marian,' who followed him to the greenwood, and shared his dangers and toils.

The same popular accounts represent this gay outlaw as living in the period extending from the reign of Henry II., through those of Richard I. and John, to that of Henry III. We are informed that he was born at Locksley, in the county of Nottingham, about 1160 A.D.; that from having dissipated his inheritance through carelessness and extravagance, he was induced to adopt the life of an outlaw in the forests; and that after having, with the band which he had collected around him, successfully conducted his predatory operations for a long course of years, and set all law and magistrates at defiance, he at last, in his eighty-seventh year, felt the infirmities of age coming upon him, and was induced to enter the convent of Kirklees, in Yorkshire, to procure medical assistance. The prioress, who is described as a relation—by some, an aunt—of his own, was led, either through personal enmity or the instigation of another, to cause the death of Robin Hood, an object which she accomplished by opening a vein or artery, and allowing him to bleed to death. The date assigned to this event is November 1247. It is stated that when Robin perceived the treachery which had been practised on him, he summoned all his remaining strength, and blew a loud blast on his bugle-horn. The well-known call reached the ears of his trusty lieutenant, Little John, who forthwith hastened from the adjoining forest, and arriving at the priory, forced his way into the chamber where his dying chieftain lay. The latter, according to the story in the ballad, makes the following request:

'Give me my bent bow in my hand,
And an arrow I'll let free,
And where that arrow is taken up,
There let my grave digged be.'

The bow being then put into his hands by Little John, Robin discharged it through the open casement, and the arrow alighted on a spot where, according to popular tradition, he was shortly afterwards buried. A stone, carved with a florid cross and an obliterated inscription, marks the place of sepulture, and the whole has been in recent times surrounded by an enclosure, as shewn in the accompanying engraving. This probably genuine memorial of Robin Hood, is situated on the extreme edge of Kirklees Park, not far from Huddersfield. The site which it occupies is bold and picturesque, commanding an extensive view of what was formerly forest-land, and which still displays clumps of gnarled oaks, scattered up and down, mingled with furze and scrub.

ROBIN HOOD'S GRAVE.

Finally, we are informed by several old ballads, and also by some writers of a later age, that this prince of robbers was no other than the Earl of Huntingdon, who, from misfortunes or his own mismanagement, had been compelled to adopt a predatory life.

The above statements, with many additions and variations by way of embellishment, are all set forth in the numerous ballads which profess to record the exploits of Robin Hood and his 'merry men.' A collection of these, under the title of *A Lytell Geste* [history] *of Robyn Hood*, from a manuscript apparently of the latter end of the fourteenth century, was printed by Winkyn de Worde, one of the earliest English printers, about 1495. It forms the most satisfactory and reliable evidence that we possess of the life and deeds of the sylvan hero, and comprises one or two circumstances which, as we shall shortly see, go far to substantiate the fact of the actual existence of Robin Hood.

The *Lytell Geste* is divided into eight parts or *fyttes*, as they are called; the seventh of which, and part of the eighth, narrate an adventure of Robin with 'King Edward,' who, at the end of the sixth fytte, is styled 'Edwarde our comly kynge.' The only monarch of that name whom we can consistently believe to be here referred to, is the light-hearted and unfortunate Edward II., who is described as having immediately before made a progress through Lancashire. His father, Edward I., never was in Lancashire after he became king; and Edward III., if he was ever in that county at all, was certainly never there during the earlier years of his reign, whilst, as regards the subsequent years of his government, we have indisputable evidence that Robin Hood had by that time become a historical personage, or at all events an existence of the past. But with respect to Edward II., contemporary proof is furnished that in the autumn of the year 1323, and not long after the defeat and death of his great enemy and kinsman, the Earl of Lancaster, he made a progress through the counties of Lancashire, Yorkshire, and Nottingham. Here a coincidence occurs between a historical fact and the incidents related in the ballad.

According to these last, King Edward having arrived at Nottingham, resolves forthwith on the extermination of Robin Hood and his band, to whose depredations he imputes the great diminution that had lately taken place in the numbers of the deer in the royal forests. A forester undertakes to guide him to the haunts of the outlaw, and Edward and his train, disguised like monks—certainly rather an unkingly masquerade; but Edward II. had little kingliness about him—set out for the place, and on the way thither are suddenly encountered by Robin and his men, to whom the pseudo-abbot represents that he has only with him £40. The half of this he is obliged to give up, but is courteously permitted to retain the remaining moiety. After transacting this little matter of business, Robin invites the abbot and his party to dine with him—an invitation doubtless not to be resisted in the circumstances. After dinner, a shooting-match commences, and in course of this the real rank of the pretended abbot is discovered, and Robin, falling down on his knees, craves forgiveness for himself and retainers. The king grants it, but on condition that the outlaw chief shall quit his present mode of life, and accompany his sovereign to court, where he is promised a place in the royal household. To this he readily consents, and accompanies the king first to Nottingham, and afterwards to London, where, for nearly a year, he 'dwelled in the kynge's courte.'

Now it is at least a singular coincidence, that in the records of the household expenses of Edward II., preserved in Exchequer, the name of 'Robyn Hode' occurs several times as a 'vadlet' or porter of the chamber in the period from the 25th of April to the 22d of November 1324, but no mention of him occurs either previous to the former or subsequent to the latter of these dates. This was the very time during which, according to the ballad, Robin Hood lived at court. The following is the entry on the 22d of November above referred to, which, on the assumption of the ballad-hero and the person there named being the same individual, may be regarded as the latest historical record which we have of that personage. 'Robyn Hod jadys un des porteurs poar cas qil ne poait pluis travailler, de donn par comandement—v s. [To Robin Hood, by command, owing to his being unable any longer to work, the sum of 5*s*.] It is unnecessary to remind the reader, that such a sum represented in those days a much greater value than at the present time.

In the ballad under notice, we are informed that Robert, after having remained in the king's service for about a twelvemonth, became wearied of the court, and longed for the free and joyous life of Sherwood Forest. The king consents to let him go, but only for a short period—a condition which Robin thoroughly disregards after regaining his liberty. Rapturously welcomed by his old associates, and reinstated as their leader, he continues for twenty-two years to lead the life of a robber-chief, and dies at last through treachery in Kirklees Priory, as already mentioned.

For the coincidences above related, between historical facts and the poetical narrative detailed by the compiler of the *Lytell Geste*, we are indebted to the researches of the late Rev. Joseph Hunter, who, in an ingenious tract, entitled *The Ballad-Hero, Robin Hood*, has endeavoured, and we think not unsuccessfully, to vindicate the real existence of this renowned outlaw against the arguments of those who would represent him as a mere poetical abstraction or myth. To the latter view of his character, we shall now advert.

There is no tendency which has been more characteristic of the present century, than that of investigating the foundations by which historical records are supported, sifting the evidence adduced, and endeavouring by an analysis of the materials in the crucible of research, to eliminate whatever has been intermingled of fable or romance. Ruthless and unsparing has been the process, sweeping and stupendous, in many instances, the demolition thereby occasioned, but the results have in the main been beneficial, and the cause of truth, as well as the progress of human knowledge, been signally benefited. In some instances, however, it cannot be denied that this sceptical and overturning tendency has been carried to an extreme. With a rashness, equivalent to the unhesitating faith which made our fathers accept as undoubted fact whatever they found recorded in ancient annals, our critical archæologists of the present day seem not unfrequently to ignore, superciliously, all popular traditions or belief, and transfer, indiscriminately, to the region of myth or fable, the individuals whose actions form the subject of these popular histories. Such a fate has, with other heroes of folk-lore, been shared by the chieftain of Sherwood Forest. It has been maintained by many distinguished antiquaries, including Mr T. Wright, in our own country, and Grimm in Germany, that Robin Hood is a mere fanciful abstraction, a poetical myth, or 'one amongst the personages of the early mythology of the Teutonic people.' It has been gravely conjectured that his name, 'Robin Hood,' is a corruption for 'Robin of the Wood,' and that he is to be only regarded as a mythical embodiment of the spirit of unrestrained freedom and sylvan sport. The principal grounds on which this argument is maintained, are the absence of any direct historical evidence regarding him; the numbers of places in widely-separated parts of the country, which are associated with him and bear his name; and a supposed resemblance between many of the circumstances related of him, and those recorded of various legendary personages throughout Europe.

Where parties have been led to form such views as those above indicated, it requires irrefragable evidence to convert them to an opposite way of thinking. And, doubtless, as far as regards Robin Hood, it is almost hopeless to expect that any more light than what we have hitherto obtained, will be procured to elucidate his history. But the whole weight of inferential evidence seems to be on the side of those who would retain the notion of his having been a real personage. There is nothing, as Mr Hunter remarks, supernatural in the attributes or incidents recorded of him. These are nothing more than what can be supposed to have belonged, or happened to an English yeoman, skilled in all manly sports, more especially in the use of the bow, and naturally endowed with a generous and genial disposition. Much embellishment and romantic fiction has, doubtless, been superadded to his history; but that the leading features of it, as popularly detailed, rest at all events on a basis of fact, is, in our opinion, satisfactorily established.

It will be observed that Mr Hunter, in fixing the reign of Edward II. as the period in which Robin Hood flourished, departs from the commonly-received notion, which represents him as living in the time of Richard I. and John. In this view he is supported by all the evidence that can be gathered from actual documents, and also by the statements in the poem of the *Lytell Geste*; whilst the other notion has no ground to rest on beyond the vague and uncertain authority of tradition, or of chroniclers who wrote long after the events which they profess to record. And it may here also be mentioned, that in the period immediately following Robin Hood's supposed withdrawal from court, Mr Hunter discovered, in the court-rolls of the Manor of Wakefield, the name of a certain 'Robertus Hood,' resident in that town, and a suitor in the manorial court. The adjoining district of Barnsdale, in the West Riding, was no less a haunt of Robin Hood and his followers, than Sherwood Forest, in Nottinghamshire. And another singular circumstance is, that the wife of this Robertus Hood is mentioned under the name of *Matilda*, the title given by some old ballads to Robin Hood's wife, who, however, exchanges it for *Marian* when she follows him to the forest.

The statement that Robin Hood was the Earl of Huntingdon, seems to rest mainly on an epitaph manufactured in after-times, and on one or two obscure expressions found in ancient writers. Upon a flimsy foundation of this kind, Dr Stukeley has built a regular genealogy of Robin Hood, representing his real name as Robert Fitzooth, Earl of Huntingdon. No reliance whatever can be placed on this view of the question, and it is certainly wholly opposed to the few items of historical evidence which have already been adduced.

The earliest demonstrable allusion to Robin Hood in English literature, occurs in Longland's *Vision of Pierce Ploughman*, a poem belonging to the middle of the fourteenth century. A character, allegorising Sloth, is represented as saying:

'I kan not perfitly my paternoster as the prest it sayeth,
But I kan rymes of Robyn Hode and Randolf, Earl of Chester.'

By thus coupling his name with that of the Earl of Chester, a real personage, this passage affords a presumption that Robin Hood was likewise no creation of the imagination. That the fact of his being mentioned at this date, discredits the argument of his having lived only a few years previously, cannot warrantably be maintained, seeing it was a perfectly common practice in the days of minstrelsy to celebrate the deeds of personages, actually living at the time, as well as of those who belonged to a former age.

Assuming Robin Hood and his band to have had a real existence, it becomes a matter of interesting speculation, to conjecture whether any peculiar circumstance in the history of the time can have given rise to this singular society in the forests of Nottinghamshire and the West Riding. M. Thierry, in his *History of the Norman Conquest*, has represented Robin Hood as the chief of a small body of Saxons, who, in these remote fastnesses, defied successfully the authority of the Norman sovereigns. Another writer has imagined them to be a remnant of the followers of the celebrated Simon de Montfort, Earl of Leicester, who was slain at the battle of Evesham. But Mr Hunter's conjecture is at least as plausible as any—that they were persons who had taken part in the rebellion against Edward II., of his cousin, Thomas, Earl of Lancaster, which had been suppressed by the battle of Boroughbridge, in March 1322. A summary vengeance was taken on the earl, who, with a number of his most distinguished followers, was beheaded at his own castle of Pontefract. Many other chiefs were executed in different places. It is reasonable, however, to conjecture that numerous individuals who had taken part in the insurrection, would contrive to evade pursuit by retreating to remote fastnesses. In this way, a band like Robin Hood's might be formed under the leadership of a bold and energetic captain. The immense popularity which the Earl of Lancaster enjoyed in the West Riding, will tend still further to explain the favour and good-will with which Robin Hood and his followers seem to have been generally regarded by the peasantry. And a coincidence is thus established between the date of the battle and the progress of Edward II., already mentioned, in the autumn of the following year, through the northern counties of England.

The circumstance of so many places throughout the country bearing the name of Robin Hood—such as Robin Hood's Hill, Robin Hood's Chair, Robin Hood's Bay, &c.—is derived, with great probability, from the practice which prevailed both in England and Scotland, of celebrating on May-day certain sports under the designation of *Robin Hood Games*. These consisted of a personation of the various characters, which, according to the popular ballads, made up the court or retinue of the king of Sherwood Forest. The reader will find a notice of them at p. 580 of the first volume of this work. From certain places being selected for the observance of these festivities, and also, it may be, from some renowned performer in the games having been connected with a particular locality, the name of Robin Hood has frequently, in all likelihood, been associated with places which he never once visited. Doubtless, however, one or two of these spots are of a more genuine character; such as the grave at Kirklees Priory, and, as Mr Hunter is inclined to believe, the well, known as 'Robin Hood's Well,' a little to the north of Doncaster, on the Great North Road, leading from that town to Ferrybridge.

---

## NOVEMBER 23.

**St Clement, pope and martyr, 100. St Amphilochius, bishop of Iconium, confessor, 100. St Daniel, bishop and confessor, 545. St Tron, confessor, 693.**

*Born*.—**John Wallis, mathematician, 1616,** ***Ashford, Kent*; Dr Thomas Birch, historical and biographical writer, 1705,** ***London*.**

*Died*.—**Louis, Duke of Orleans, brother of Charles VI., assassinated at Paris, 1407; Thomas Tallis, composer of church-music, 1585,** ***Greenwich*; Richard Hakluyt, chronicler of voyages and travels, 1616; William Bentinck, first Earl of Portland, favourite minister of William III., 1709; Antoine François Prevot, novelist, 1763,** ***Forest of Chantilly*; Thomas Henderson, professor of astronomy, &c., 1844; Sir John Barrow, author of biographies and books of travel, 1848,** ***London*.**

### ARDEN OF FAVERSHAM.

One of the most terrible tragedies in private life—afterwards dramatised as a tragedy for the stage by George Lillo—was that known in connection with the name of Arden of Faversham. In 1539, Henry VIII. having ordered the principal part of the monastic buildings at Faversham, in Kent, to be pulled down, granted the site of the abbey, with some adjoining lands, to Sir Thomas Cheyney, who alienated them five years afterwards to Mr Thomas Arden, or Ardern, a gentleman of Faversham. It was this Arden whose atrocious murder, while mayor of the town in 1550, became lastingly impressed on the history of Kent. From Holinshed's *Chronicle* are derived all the later narratives of the event which we now proceed to relate. Arden's wife, 'Mistress Alice, young, tall, and well-favoured of shape and countenance,' formed a criminal connection with a paramour, named Mosbye, 'a black, swart man.' Mosbye had been servant to Sir Edward North, Alice's father-in-law; and then settled as a tailor in London. The infatuated wife, lost to all sense of duty and morality, conspired with Mosbye to put an end to her husband's existence, in order that she might marry the profligate 'black, swart man.' They employed as their confederates one John Green, a Faversham tailor; George Bradshaw, a goldsmith of the same town; and 'one Black Will, of Calyce (Calais), a murderer, which murderer was privily sent for to Calyce by the earnest sute, appoyntment, and confederacye of Alice Arden and Thomas Mosbye.' The conspirators watched Master Arden 'walking in Poule's' (St Paul's Cathedral, the nave of which was a public promenade in those days), but could not find an opportunity to murder him; they then lay in wait for him on Rainham Down, and a second time in the Broomy Close (two places near Faversham), but on all these occasions failed in obtaining an opportunity. The wicked wife then laid a plot for murdering her husband in his own house. She procured the services of Mosbye's sister, Cicely Pounder, and of two of Arden's domestic servants, Michael Saunderson and Elizabeth Stafford. On a particular day selected—Sunday, too—Black Will was hidden in a closet at the end of Arden's parlour. After supper, Arden sat down to play some kind of game with Mosbye; Green stood at Arden's back, holding a candle in his hand, 'to shaddowe Black Will when he should come out;' and the other conspirators had their cue. At a given signal in the game, 'Black Will came with a napkyn in his hand, and sodenlye came behind Arden's back, threw the said napkyn over his hedd and face, and strangled him; and forthwith Mosbye stept to him, and strake him with a taylor's great pressing-iron upon the scull to the braine, and immediately drew out his dagger, which was great and broad, and therewith cut the said Arden's throat.' It is added that 'Mistress Alice herself, with a knife, gave him seven or eight pricks into the breast.' When Black Will had helped to drag the dead body into the closet, he went to Cicely Pounder's house, received eight pounds for his nefarious services, and left Faversham. Cicely then went to Arden's habitation, and assisted in bearing the corpse out into a meadow, called the Almery Croft, behind the house; 'where they laid him on his back in his night-gown, with his slippers on.' We are told by the chronicler, that the doubly-wicked Alice and her companions 'danced, and played on the virginals, and were merrie.' It would appear to have been their intention to make the towns-people aware of an entertainment, with dancing and music, having been given by Arden to his friends on that evening; and to induce them to believe, from the dead body being arrayed in night-clothes, that the unfortunate man had been murdered by some one during the night. On the following morning, Alice seems to have alarmed the town with an announcement of her husband's absence from the house, and her fears for his safety. A search was made by the towns-people, and the dead body was found in the Croft. But here occurred one of those trifling incidents which generally tend to the discovery of a murder. Some of the people 'saw a long rushe or two from the parlour-floor [there were no carpets in those days], stuck between one of his slippers and his foot.' Suspicions being aroused, the house was searched, and it was soon found that Arden had been murdered in his own parlour. Very likely Alice's conduct as a wife had already attracted public attention; for she was at once accused of the murder. Her courage gave way, and she cried out: 'Oh the bloud of God help! for this bloud have I shed!' One by one, as evidence came home to them, the guilty confederates suffered the punishment due to their crimes. Mistress Alice was burned at Canterbury; Mosbye was taken in bed, and was afterwards hung at Smithfield; Green was hung at Faversham; Black Will escaped for many years, but was at length taken, 'and brent on a scaffolde at Flushing;' Bradshaw was hanged in chains at Canterbury; Cicely Pounder was hanged at Smithfield; Saunderson was drawn and hanged at Faversham; and Elizabeth Stafford was burned at the same place. It was, in truth, a time when hanging and burning, drawing and quartering, were fearfully rife as punishments for criminals. It was long said that no grass would grow on the spot where Arden's dead body was found; some, in accordance with the superstitions of the times, attributed this to the murder; while others declared that 'the field he hadde cruelly taken from a widow woman, who had curst him most bitterly, even to his face, wishing that all the world might wonder on him.'

A tragedy, entitled *Arden of Faversham*, was printed in 1592, and was at first attributed to Shakspeare. In after-times, the subject was made the groundwork of a play by Lillo, author of *George Barnwell* and *Fatal Curiosity*. It is believed that an old house, still standing at Faversham, near the Abbey Gateway, is that in which the terrible crime was committed; and a low-arched door, near the corner of the Abbey wall, is pointed out as that through which the murdered Arden was carried out to the Croft.

## PLUGGING LOBSTERS' CLAWS.

There is a curious practice followed by dealers in lobsters, arising out of the action of the wonderful claws with which these crustacea are provided. We do not refer here to the retail-fishmongers of London and other towns, but to the boilers and wholesale-dealers. Concerning the mode of obtaining the supplies of this favourite delicacy, a writer in the *Quarterly Review* (No. 189) says: 'Where do all the lobsters come from? The lovers of this most delicious of all the crustaceous tribe will probably be astonished to learn that they are mainly brought from Norway. France and the Channel Islands, the Orkneys and the Shetlands, do, it is true, contribute a few to the metropolitan market; but fully two-thirds are relentlessly, and with much pinching and twisting, dragged out of the thousand rock-bound inlets which indent the Norway coast. They are conveyed alive in a screw steamer, and by smacks, in baskets, sometimes to the extent of twenty thousand in a night, to Great Grimsby, and are then forwarded to town by the Great Northern Railway: another ten thousand arriving perhaps from points on our own and the

French coasts. The fighting, twisting, blue-black masses are taken, as soon as purchased, to what are termed the "boiling-houses," of which there are four, situated in Dark and Love Lanes, near Billingsgate.'

In 1830, particulars were made public respecting the manner in which these 'fighting, twisting, blue-black masses' are, or were at that time, occasionally treated. Mr Saunders, the leading salesman in the lobster-trade, and Mr Gompertz, secretary to the Society for the Prevention of Cruelty to Animals, waited on the lord mayor on 23d November, to solicit the interference of his lordship with a practice by which needless pain was inflicted on the animals. 'It has been the practice, when lobsters are caught, to tie up the claws with cords, in order to prevent them from doing each other injury; as it is known that shell-fish of this kind will, if some precaution be not taken, tear each other to pieces. The fish are fretted by being thus prevented from grasping whatever they approach; but they sustain no damage in quality as food. To save trouble, however, the persons who deal in shell-fish substitute another mode of preventing the lobsters from fighting, and stick a plug in the spot where the claw is divided. This practice is the cause of great agony to the poor animal; for the moment the shell is removed, the substance appears to have lost its firmness, and the place where the plug has been stuck is completely mortified. Lobsters are very often to be found in fishmongers' shops with the bodies injured materially; and the claws, which are considered the most delicate parts of the fish, absolutely rotten. It was ascertained beyond doubt, that the mortified condition of the fish was attributable to the cruel method of plugging.' The lord mayor might not, perhaps, have been able to check the practice merely because it was unnecessarily cruel; but as it was proved to injure the lobster as an article of food, he had magisterial power to interfere on this ground.

Crabs seem to be more sensitive than lobsters. When the lobsters are taken to the boiling-houses (the *Quarterly Review* informs us), they are plunged into a boiling caldron, basket and all, for twenty minutes. Crabs are boiled in the same way; but their nervous systems are so acute, that they would dash off their claws, in convulsive agony, if plunged in hot water. To prevent this mutilation, they are first killed by the dexterous insertion of a needle through the head.

---

# NOVEMBER 24.

St Chrysogonus, martyr, beginning of 4th century. St Cianan or Kenan, bishop of Duleek, in Ireland, 489. Saints Flora and Mary, virgins and martyrs, 851. St John of the Cross, confessor, 1591.

---

*Born.*—Laurence Sterne, sentimental writer and novelist, 1713, *Clonmel;* John Bacon, sculptor, 1740, *Southwark;* Grace Darling, Northumbrian heroine, 1815, *Bamborough.*

*Died.*—John Knox, Scottish Reformer, 1572, *Edinburgh;* William Sancroft, archbishop of Canterbury, leader of the seven prelates in their celebrated petition to James II., 1693, *Fresingfield, Suffolk;* Dr Robert Henry, historian, 1790, *Edinburgh;* William Lamb, Viscount Melbourne, statesman, 1848, *Melbourne House, Derbyshire;* Rev. Dr George Croly, poet, and romance writer, 1860, *London.*

## THE CIRCE OF CARLISLE HOUSE, SOHO SQUARE.

In the bankrupt list of *The London Gazette* for November 1772, the attention of the public was called, somewhat significantly, to 'Teresa Cornelys, Carlisle House, St Ann, Soho, dealer.' It will not be uninteresting to the reader to have some account of the nature of Teresa Cornelys's dealings.

This lady, by birth a German, and during many years a public singer in Italy and Germany, settled in London somewhere about the year 1756 or 1757: and for twenty years after that time she entertained the public, 'the votaries of fashion of both sexes,' with a series of entertainments, masked balls, and the like, at once 'fascinating and elegant.' These entertainments were held in the suitable mansion of Carlisle House, Soho Square, and figure largely in contemporary papers.

The first printed document referring to Mrs Cornelys, convinces us at once that she must have been a woman of tact. The date of it is, February 18, 1763: 'On Saturday last, Mrs Cornelys gave a ball at Carlisle House, to the upper-servants of persons of fashion, as a token of the sense she has [did not Circe herself insert this little notice?] of her obligations to the nobility and gentry, for their generous subscription to her assembly. The company consisted of 220 persons, who made up fourscore couple in country-dances; and as scarce anybody was idle on this occasion, the rest sat down to cards.'

The nobility and gentry who patronised Carlisle House, did so by paying an annual subscription, in consideration of which they received a ticket, which gave them the run of all that was there, whether it were a ball, or a masked ball, or 'a grand concert of vocal and instrumental music.' Also, it appears, they had the privilege of lending these tickets to friends—a great convenience—provided they wrote 'the name of the person upon the back of the said ticket, to whom they have lent it;' [here the English is again a little Germanized], 'to prevent any mistake.' No doubt single tickets for particular evenings, and the special benefit of non-subscribers, were to be had.

Notwithstanding her great success, for it seems to have been by no means inconsiderable, Mrs Cornelys had her troubles. It was natural that competition should originate opposition establishments. But on her part the best of feeling is always to be premised. 'Whereas it has been industriously reported, to the disadvantage of Mrs Cornelys, that she has expressed herself dissatisfied with a subscription now on foot, to build a large room in opposition to hers; she esteems it her duty, in this public manner, to declare that she never once entertained a thought so unjust and unreasonable.' Nay, so satisfied is she with matters in general, that her longing for 'fatherland' is perceptibly on the decline. 'She humbly hopes she has not been wanting in duty and gratitude to her protectors, and cannot sufficiently be thankful for the comfort she enjoys in this happy country, which she hopes never to leave.'

Mrs Cornelys seems to have spared no money or pains to have everything in keeping with the tastes of her illustrious friends. The expense of the 'alterations and additions to Carlisle House in Soho Square,' and of the 'new embellishments and furniture,' amounted for the year 1765, alone to 'little less than £2000,' and made that house, in the news-writer's opinion, 'the most magnificent place of public entertainment in Europe.' To one of the rooms we find added, 'the most curious, singular, and superb ceiling that ever was executed or even thought of:' and to obviate certain 'complaints of excessive heat,' she arranged to have 'tea below stairs and ventilators above,' and succeeded so admirably, that subscribers were no longer subjected to 'the least danger of catching cold.' To relieve the press of the distinguished crowd, in its entrance and exit, she provided an additional door, and also 'a new gallery for the dancing of cotillons and allemandes, and a suite of new rooms adjoining;' in consequence of which she was most reluctantly compelled to charge subscribers an additional guinea.

On February 27, 1770, Mrs Cornelys's continued efforts were rewarded with a most magnificent masquerade.

First, as to the numbers who attended, 'Monday night the principal nobility and gentry of this kingdom, *to the number of near eight hundred*, were present at the masked ball, at Mrs Cornelys's, in Soho Square.'

Next, as to the stir it made in the neighbourhood. 'Soho Square and the adjacent streets were lined with thousands of people, whose curiosity led them to get a sight of the persons going to the masquerade; nor was any coach or chair suffered to pass unreviewed, the windows being obliged to be let down, and lights held up to display the figures to more advantage.'

One does not wonder at the anxiety of the rabble to see all that was to be seen, for 'the richness and brilliancy of the dresses,' we are told, 'were almost beyond imagination; nor did *any* assembly *ever* exhibit a collection of more elegant and beautiful female figures.'

And now for the company. The reader may form a faint idea: 'Among them were Lady Waldegrave, Lady Pembroke, the Duchess of Hamilton, Mrs Crewe, Mrs Hodges, Lady Almeria Carpenter, &c.'

The characters assumed by the company were extremely various. Sir R. Phillips appeared as 'a double man, half-miller, half-chimney sweeper.' There was also 'a figure of Adam in flesh-coloured silk, with an apron of fig-leaves,' who, in spite of the fig-leaves, must have seemed rather out of keeping. The Earl of Carlisle figured as a running footman; Mr James, the painter, as Midas. The Duke of Devonshire was 'very fine, but in no particular character.' And 'Lord Edg——b, in the character of an old woman, *was full as lovely as his lady*.'

But the ladies were not to be outdone on this festive occasion. 'The Countess-Dowager of Waldegrave wore a dress richly trimmed with beads and pearls, in the character of'—we are sorry to observe it—'Jane Shore.' Many indulged a classical fancy. 'The Duchess of Bolton, in the character of Diana, was captivating.' 'Lady Stanhope, as Melpomene, was a striking fine figure.' 'Lady Augustus Stuart, as a Vestal, and Lady Caroline, as a Fille de Patmos, shewed that true elegance may be expressed without gold and diamonds.' Others took a more modern turn. 'The Countess of Pomfret, in the character of a Greek sultana, and the two Miss Fredericks, who accompanied her, as Greek slaves, made a complete group;' and to eclipse all, 'Miss Monckton, daughter to Lord Galway, appeared in the character of an Indian sultana, in a robe of cloth of gold, and a rich veil. The seams of her habit were embroidered with precious stones, and she had a magnificent cluster of diamonds on her head: the jewels she wore were valued at £30,000.'

But all these brilliant achievements, it seems, were to have an end. The opening of the *Pantheon* shattered Mrs Cornelys to some extent. Then, unfortunately, there were certain 'Bills of Indictment preferred to the Grand Jury.' These indictments insinuated of Mrs Cornelys, 'that she does keep and maintain a common disorderly house, and did permit and suffer divers loose, idle, and disorderly persons, as well men as women, to be and remain during the whole night, rioting and otherwise misbehaving themselves.'

Upon this the nobility and gentry, we presume, to be on the safe side of rumour, transferred their patronage mostly to the *Pantheon*. For in July 1772, 'the creditors of Mrs Cornelys, of Carlisle House, Soho Square,' were 'most earnestly requested to deliver forthwith a particular account of their several and respective demands on the said Mrs Cornelys, to Mr Hickey, in St Alban's Street.' And at last our little register, from *the London Gazette*, of 'Teresa Cornelys, Carlisle House, St Ann, Soho, dealer,' closes the scene.

We hear a great deal more of Carlisle House, and the desperate struggle which it made, apparently with not much success, to regain its position; but it is enough. Mrs Cornelys ultimately retired into private life, and died at a very advanced age, August 19, 1797, in the Fleet Prison.

## MERMAIDS.

Mermaids have had a legendary existence from very early ages; for the Syrens of the ancients evidently belonged to the same remarkable family. Mermen and mermaids—men of the sea, and women of the sea—have been as stoutly believed in as the great sea-serpent, and on very much the same kind of evidence. Sometimes, as expressed in Haydn's *Mermaid's Song*, there is a delightful bit of romance connected with the matter: as where the mermaid offers the tempting invitation:

'Come with me, and we will go
Where the rocks of coral grow.'

But the romance is somewhat damped when the decidedly fishy tail is described. The orthodox mermaid is half-woman, half-fish; and the fishy half is sometimes depicted as being *doubly*-tailed. The heraldry of France and Germany often exhibits mermaids with two tails among the devices; and in the Basle edition of Ptolemy's Geography, dated 1540, a double-tailed mermaid figures on one of the plates. Shakspeare makes many of his characters talk about mermaids. Thus, in the *Comedy of Errors*, Antipholus of Syracuse says:

'Oh, train me not, sweet mermaid, with the note!'

And in another place:

'I'll stop mine ears against the mermaid's song.'

In the *Midsummer-Night's Dream*, Oberon says:

'I heard a mermaid on a dolphin's back.'

In *Hamlet*, the queen, speaking of Ophelia's death, says:

> 'Her clothes spread wide; and mermaid-like,
> Awhile they bare her up.'

In two other passages, he makes his characters say:

> 'I 'll drown more sailors than the mermaids shall.'

And:

> 'At the helm a seeming-mermaid steers.'

But in all these cases Shakspeare, as was his wont, made his characters say what *they* were likely to think, in their several positions and periods of life.

Notices of mermaids are scattered abundantly in books of bygone times; sometimes in much detail, sometimes in a few vague words. In Merollo's *Voyage to Congo*, in 1682, mermaids are said to be very plentiful all along the river Zaire. A writer in *Notes and Queries*, in November 1858, lighted upon an old Scotch almanac, called the *Aberdeen Almanac, or New Prognostications for the Year* 1688; in which the following curious passage occurs: 'To conclude for this year 1688. Near the place where the famous Dee payeth his tribute to the German Ocean, if *curious observers of wonderful things in nature* will be pleased thither to resort the 1, 13, and 29 of May, and in divers other times in the ensuing summer, as also in the harvest-time, to the 7 and 14 October, *they will undoubtedly see a pretty company of* MAR MAIDS, creatures of admirable beauty, and likewise hear their charming sweet melodious voices:

> "In well-tun'd measures and harmonious lays,
> Extol their Maker and his bounty praise;
> That godly honest men, in everything,
> In quiet peace may live, GOD SAVE THE KING!"'

The piety and loyalty of these predicted mermaids are certainly remarkable characteristics. In another part of Scotland, about the same period, a *real* mermaid was seen, if we are to believe *Brand's Description of Orkney and Shetland*, published in 1701. Two fishermen drew up with a hook a mermaid, 'having face, arms, breast, shoulders, &c., of a woman, and long hair hanging down the neck; but the nether-part from below the waist hidden in the water.' One of the fishermen, in his surprise, drew a knife and thrust it into her heart; 'whereupon she cried, as they judged, "Alas!" and the hook giving way, she fell backwards, and was seen no more.' In this case the evidence went thus—Brand was told by a lady and gentleman, who were told by a bailie to whom the fishing-boat belonged, who was told by the fishers; and thus we may infer as we please concerning the growth of the story as it travelled.

In 1775, there was a very circumstantial account given of a mermaid, which was captured in the Grecian Archipelago, in the preceding year, and exhibited in London. 'It has,' as the *Annual Reviewer* of that day said, 'the features and complexion of a European. Its face is like that of a young female; its eyes of a fine light blue; its nose small and handsome; its mouth small; its lips thin, and the edges of them round like those of a codfish; its teeth small, regular, and white; its chin well shaped; its neck full; its ears like those of the eel, but placed like those of the human species; and behind them are the gills for respiration, which appear like curls. Some (mermaids) are said to have hair upon the head; but this has none, only rolls instead of hair, that at a distance may be mistaken for curls. But its chief ornament is a beautiful membrane or fin, rising from the temples, and gradually diminishing till it ends pyramidically, forming a foretop like that of a lady's head-dress. It has no fin on the back, but a bone like that of the human species. Its breasts are fair and full, but without nipples; its arms and hands are well proportioned, but without nails on its fingers; its belly is round and swelling, but no navel. From the waist downwards, the body is in all respects like a codfish. It has three sets of fins, one above another, below the waist, which enables it to swim out upon the sea; and it is said to have an enchanting voice, which it never exerts except before a storm.' Here there is no great intricacy of evidence, for a writer in the *Gentleman's Magazine* also said he saw this particular mermaid—which, however, he described as being only three feet long, tail and all. But a sad blow was afterwards given to its reputation, by a statement that it was craftily made up out of the skin of the angel-shark.

In Mrs Morgan's *Tour to Milford Haven in the Year* 1795, there is an equally circumstantial account of a mermaid observed by one Henry Reynolds, in 1782. Reynolds was a farmer of Pen-y-hold, in the parish of Castlemartin. One morning, just outside the cliff, he saw what seemed to him a person bathing, with the upper part of the body out of the water. Going a little nearer, to see who was bathing in so unusual a place, it seemed to him like a person sitting in a tub. Going nearer still, he found it to resemble a youth of sixteen or eighteen years of age, with a very white skin. The continuation of the body below the water, seemed to be a brownish substance, ending with a tail, which seemed capable of waving to and fro. 'The form of its body and arms was entirely human; but its arms and hands seemed rather thick and short in proportion to its body. The form of the head and all the features of the face were human also; but the nose rose high between the eyes, was pretty long, and seemed to terminate very sharp.' Some peculiarities about the neck and back are then noticed, as also its way of washing its body. 'It looked attentively at him and at the cliffs, and seemed to take great notice of the birds flying over its head. Its looks were wild and fierce; but it made no noise, nor did it grin, or in any way distort its face. When he left it, it was about a hundred yards from him; and when he returned with some others to look at it, it was gone.' We hear nothing further of this merman or merboy; but on looking at the roundabout evidence of the story, we find it to be thus—A paper containing the account was lent to Mrs Morgan; the paper had been written by a young lady, pupil of Mrs Moore, from an oral account given to her by that lady; Mrs Moore had heard it from Dr George Phillips; and he had heard it from Henry Reynolds himself—from all of which statements we may infer that there were abundant means for converting some peculiar kind of fish into a merman without imputing intentional dishonesty to any one. Something akin to this kind of evidence is observable in the account of a mermaid seen in Caithness in 1809, the account of which attracted much attention in

England as well as in Scotland, and induced the Philosophical Society of Glasgow to investigate the matter. The editor of a newspaper who inserted the statement had been told by a gentleman, who had been shewn a letter by Sir John Sinclair, who had obtained it from Mrs Innes, to whom it had been written by Miss Mackay, who had heard the story from the persons (two servant girls and a boy) who had seen the strange animal in the water.

So it is with all these stories of mermaids when investigated. There is always a fish at the bottom of it—either a living fish of peculiar kind, which an ignorant person thinks bears some resemblance to a human being; or a fish which becomes marvellous in the progress of its description from mouth to mouth; or a dead fish's skin manufactured into something that may accord with the popular notions regarding these beings. Mr George Cruikshank, in 1822, made a drawing of a mermaid,* which was exhibited in St James's Street, and afterwards at Bartholomew Fair; it drew crowds by its ugliness, and shewed what wretched things will suffice to gull the public—although, of course, *outside* the booth at the fair there was a picture of the orthodox mermaid, with beautiful features and hair, comb in one hand, mirror in the other, and so forth. This was probably the identical mermaid, respecting which the lord chancellor was called upon to adjudicate, towards the close of November 1822. There was a disputed ownership, and his lordship expressed his satisfaction that he was not called upon to decide whether the animal was 'man, woman, or mermaid,' but only to say to whom it rightfully belonged.

## Thanksgiving-Day in America.

The great social and religious festival of New England, from which it has spread to most of the states of the American republic, is a legacy of the Puritans. They abolished Christmas as a relic of popery, or of prelacy, which they held in nearly equal detestation, and passed laws to punish its observance; but, wanting some day to replace it, the colonial assemblies, and, later, the governors of the states, appointed every year some day in autumn, generally toward the end of November, as a day of solemn prayer and thanksgiving for the blessings of the year, and especially the bounties of the harvest.

Thanksgiving-day is always celebrated on Thursday, and the same day is chosen in most of the states. The governor's proclamation appointing the day, is read in all the churches, and there are appropriate sermons and religious exercises. Families, widely scattered, meet at the bountiful thanksgiving-dinners of roast turkeys, plum-pudding, and mince and pumpkin pies. The evenings are devoted by the young people to rustic games and amusements.

The subjects of the thanksgiving-sermons are not unfrequently of a political character, and in the chief towns of the union, those of the most popular preachers are generally published in the newspapers. The thanksgiving-festival, though widely celebrated, is not so universally respected as formerly, as the influx of Roman Catholics and Episcopalians has brought Christmas again into vogue, which is also kept by the Unitarians with considerable solemnity. As a peculiar American festival it will, however, long be cherished by the descendants of the Puritans.

* See p. 266 of this volume.

# NOVEMBER 25.

St Catharine, virgin and martyr, 4th century. St Erasmus or Elme, bishop and martyr, 4th century.

### ST CATHARINE.

Among the earlier saints of the Romish calendar, St Catharine holds an exalted position, both from rank and intellectual abilities. She is said to have been of royal birth, and was one of the most distinguished ladies of Alexandria, in the beginning of the fourth century. From a child she was noted for her acquirements in learning and philosophy, and while still very young, she became a convert to the Christian faith. During the persecution instituted by the Emperor Maximinus II., St Catharine, assuming the office of an advocate of Christianity, displayed such cogency of argument and powers of eloquence, as thoroughly silenced her pagan adversaries. Maximinus, troubled with this success, assembled together the most learned philosophers in Alexandria to confute the saint; but they were both vanquished in debate, and converted to a belief in the Christian doctrines. The enraged tyrant thereupon commanded them to be put to death by burning, but for St Catharine he reserved a more cruel punishment. She was placed in a machine, composed of four wheels, connected together and armed with sharp spikes, so that as they revolved the victim might be torn to pieces. A miracle prevented the completion of this project. When the executioners were binding Catharine to the wheels, a flash of lightning descended from the skies, severed the cords with which she was tied, and shattered the engine to pieces, causing the death both of the executioners and numbers of the bystanders. Maximinus, however, still bent on her destruction, ordered her to be carried beyond the walls of the city, where she was first scourged and then beheaded. The legend proceeds to say, that after her death her body was carried by angels over the Red Sea to the summit of Mount Sinai. The celebrated convent of St Catharine, situated in a valley on the slope of that mountain, and founded by the Emperor Justinian, in the sixth century, contains in its church a marble sarcophagus, in which the relics of St Catharine are deposited. Of these the skeleton of the hand, covered with rings and jewels, is exhibited to pilgrims and visitors.

A well-known concomitant of St Catharine, is the wheel on which she was attempted to be tortured, and which figures in all pictured representations of the saint. From this circumstance are derived the well-known circular window in ecclesiastical architecture, termed a *Catharine-wheel window*, and also a firework of a similar form. This St Catharine must not be confounded with the equally celebrated St Catharine of Siena, who lived in the fourteenth century.

*Born.*—Lopez de la Vega, great Spanish dramatist, 1562, *Madrid;* Charles Kemble, actor, 1775, *Brecon;* Henry Mayhew, popular writer, 1812, *London.*

*Died.*—Pope Lucius III., 1185; Andrea Doria, Genoese admiral and patriot, 1560, *Genoa;* Edward Alleyn, actor, founder of Dulwich College, 1626, *Dulwich;* John Tillotson, archbishop of Canterbury, eminent Whig divine, 1694, *Lambeth;* Dr Isaac Watts, poet and hymn-writer, 1748, *Stoke-Newington;* Henry Baker, author of *The Microscope made Easy*, 1774, *London;* Richard Glover, poet, 1785; Thomas Amory, eccentric author, 1788; Sir Augustus Wall Calcott, landscape painter, 1844, *Kensington;* John Gibson Lockhart, son-in-law and biographer of Sir Walter Scott, 1854, *Abbotsford;* Rev. John Kitto, illustrator of the Bible and sacred history, 1854, *Cannstadt, near Stuttgardt;* Angus B. Reach, miscellaneous writer, 1856, *London.*

## THE FOUNDER OF DULWICH COLLEGE.

Edward Alleyn, the son of an innkeeper, was born at the sign of the 'Pye,' in Bishopsgate, London. In the days before theatres were specially erected for the purpose, the yards of old inns, surrounded by tiers of wooden galleries, were particularly eligible for the representation of plays. Young Alleyn must, therefore, have been early accustomed to witness stage-performances. His father dying, and his mother marrying again one Browne, an actor and haberdasher, Alleyn was bred a stage-player, and soon became the Roscius of his day. Ben Jonson thus bears testimony to his merit:

'If Rome so great, and in her wisest age,
Feared not to boast the glories of her stage,
As skilful Roscius and grave Æsop, men,
Yet crowned with honours as with riches then;
Who had no less a trumpet of their name
Than Cicero, whose every breath was fame;
How can such great example die in me,
That Alleyn, I should pause to publish thee?
Who both their graces in thy self hast more
Outstript, than they did all that went before:
And present worth in all dost so contract,
As others speak, but only thou dost act.
Wear this renown: 'tis just, that who did give
So many poets life, by one should live.'

Exactly so, the poor player struts and frets his hour upon the stage, then dies, and is heard no more, but the poet lives for all time; and it was a brave thing for rare old Ben to acknowledge this, in the last two of the preceding lines:

'''Tis just that who did give
So many poets life, by one should live.'

Alleyn has been termed the Garrick of Shakspeare's era, and was no doubt intimate with the bard of Avon, as well as with Ben Jonson. A story is told of this grand trio spending their evening, as was their wont, at the Globe, in Blackfriars. On this occasion, Alleyn jocularly accused Shakspeare of having been indebted to him for Hamlet's speech, on the qualities of an actor's excellency. And Shakspeare, seemingly not relishing the innuendo, Jonson said: 'This affair needeth no contention, you stole it from Ned, no doubt; do not marvel: have you not seen him act, times out of number?'

Alleyn's first wife was Joan Woodward, the step-daughter of one Henslowe, a theatrical speculator and pawnbroker; a thrifty man, withal, well calculated to foster and develop the acquisitive spirit, so characteristic of the future life of his step-son-in-law. Soon after his marriage, Alleyn commenced to speculate in messuages and lands—buying and selling—and his exertions seem always to have been attended with profit. Amongst his other purchases, are inns of various signs—as the 'Barge,' the 'Bell and Cock,' at the Bankside; the 'Boar's Head,' probably the very house immortalised by his friend and fellow-actor Shakspeare, in Eastcheap; the parsonage of Firle, in Sussex, and the manor of Kennington in Surrey, may be adduced as instances of the curious variety of Alleyn's property. Being appointed to the office of royal bearward, he became keeper and proprietor of the bear-garden, which, besides bringing him an income of £500 per annum, led him to speculate in bulls, bears, lions, and animals of various kinds. One of the papers in Dulwich College, is a letter from one Fawnte, a trainer of fighting-bulls, who writes as follows:

'Mr Alleyn, my love remembered, I understood by a man, who came with two bears from the garden, that you have a desire to buy one of my bulls. I have three western bulls at this time, but I have had very ill-luck with them, for one has lost his horn to the quick, that I think he will never be able to fight again; that is my old Star of the West, he was a very easy bull; and my bull Bevis, he has lost one of his eyes, but I think if you had him, he would do you more hurt than good, for I protest he would either throw up your dogs into the lofts, or else ding out their brains against the grates, so that I think he is not for your turn. Besides, I esteem him very high, for my Lord of Rutland's man bad me for him twenty marks. I have a bull, which came out of the west, which stands me in twenty nobles. If you should like him, you shall have him of me. Faith he is a marvellous good bull, and such a one as I think you have had but few such, for I assure you that I hold him as good a double bull as that you had of me last is a single, and one that I have played thirty or forty courses, before he hath been taken from the stake, with the best dogs.'

Though Alleyn had, without doubt, a keen eye for a bargain, a ready hand to turn a penny, and an active foot for the main chance, he was, unlike many men of that description, of a true, affectionate, and kindly nature; ever anxious for the welfare and happiness of his home and its inmates. In his letters, when from home, he playfully styles his wife 'mecho, mousin, and mouse;' speaks of her father as 'Daddy Henslowe;' and her sister, as 'Sister Bess,' or 'Bess Dodipoll,' the latter appellation probably derived from some theatrical character. When the plague was raging, in his absence from London, he thoughtfully and playfully writes to his wife:

'My good, sweet mouse, keep your house fair and clean, which I know you will, and every evening throw water before your door; and have in your windows good store of rue and herb of grace, and with all the grace of God, which must be obtained by prayers; and, so doing, no doubt but the Lord will mercifully defend you.'

His interest in home matters, among all his more money-making transactions, never seems to flag. On another occasion he writes:

'Mouse, you send me no news of any things;

you should send me of your domestical matters, such things as happen at home, as how your distilled water proves, or this or that.'

It is little wonder to us, that such a man, when finding himself advanced in years, without an heir, should devote his property to the benefit of the poor. But the bad repute that anciently attached to an actor's profession, made the circumstance appear in his own day a miracle, which, of course, was explained by its consequent myth. According to the latter, Alleyn, when acting the part of a demon on the stage, was so terrified by the apparition of a real devil, that he forthwith made a vow to bestow his substance on the poor, and subsequently fulfilled this engagement by building Dulwich College.

The bad odour in which an actor was formerly held, is clearly exhibited by Fuller, who, speaking of Alleyn, quaintly says: 'In his old age, he made friends of his unrighteous mammon, building therewith a fair college at Dulwich, for the relief of poor people. Some, I confess, count it built on a foundered foundation, seeing, in a spiritual sense, none is good and lawful money, save what is honestly and industriously gotten; but, perchance, such who condemn Master Alleyn herein, have as bad shillings in the bottom of their own bags, if search were made therein. Thus he, who outacted others, outdid himself before his death.'

In further evidence of the disrepute attaching to actors in these days, it may be mentioned here, probably for the first time in print, that Izaak Walton, in his life of Dr Donne, has unworthily suppressed the fact, that Donne's daughter, Constance, was Alleyn's second wife. There were other reasons, however, for maintaining a prudent silence on this point; by a letter preserved at Dulwich, it would appear that Donne attempted to cheat Alleyn out of his wife's dowry.

Exercising his practical genius, Alleyn had his college built during his lifetime. In 1619, it was opened with a sermon and an anthem; then the founder read the Act of creation; and the party, consisting of the Lord Chancellor, the Earl of Arundel, Inigo Jones, and others of similar position and consequence, went to dinner. Each item of the feast, and its price, is carefully recorded in Alleyn's diary. Suffice it to say here, that they had beef, mutton, venison, pigeons, godwits, oysters, anchovies, grapes, oranges, &c., the whole washed down by eight gallons of claret, three quarts of sherry, three quarts of white wine, and two hogsheads of beer.

Alleyn then took upon himself the management of his college of God's Gift; living in it among the twelve poor men and twelve poor children, whom his bounty maintained, clothed, and educated. Here he was visited by the wealthy and noble of the land; and here he lost his faithful partner, Joan Woodward, and soon after married Constance, daughter of Dr Donne. Alleyn administered the affairs of his college till his death, which took place in the sixty-first year of his age, on the 25th of November 1626. With a pardonable wish to preserve his name in connection with the charity he founded, Alleyn appointed that the master and governor thereof should always be of the blood and surname of Alleyn. So strictly was this rule kept, that one Anthony Allen, a candidate for the mastership, was rejected in 1670, for want of a letter *y* in his name; but that objection has since been overruled.

Alleyn did not forget the people among whom he was born, nor those among whom he made his money. By his last will and testament Edward Alleyn, Esquire, Lord of the Manor of Dulwich, founded ten alms-houses, for ten poor people of the parish of St Botolph's, Bishopsgate; and ten alms-houses for ten poor people of the parish of St Saviour's, Southwark, where his bear-garden had so splendidly flourished. And, forgetting the ill-treatment he received from his father-in-law, he amply provided for his widow with a legacy of £1600; no mean fortune according to the value of money in those days.

## DR KITTO.

*Per ardua* was the motto graven on John Kitto's seal, and a more apt one he could scarcely have chosen. He was born in Plymouth in 1804, and as an infant was so puny, that he was hardly expected to live. He was carried in arms long after the age when other children have the free use of their limbs, and one of his earliest recollections was a headache, which afflicted him with various intermissions to the end of his days. His father was a master-builder, but was daily sinking in the world through intemperate habits. Happily the poor child had a grandmother, who took a fancy for him, and had him to live with her. She was a simple and kindly old woman, and entertained her 'little Johnny' for hours with stories about ghosts, wizards, witches, and hobgoblins, of which she seemed to have an exhaustless store. She taught him to sew, to make kettle-holders, and do patch-work, and in fine weather she led him delightful strolls through meadows and country lanes. As he grew older, a taste for reading shewed itself, which grew into a consuming passion, and the business of his existence became, how to borrow books, and how to find pence to buy them. He had little schooling, and that between his eighth and eleventh years, frequently interrupted by seasons of illness. When he was ten, his affectionate grandmother became paralysed, and he had to return to his parents, who found him a situation in a barber's shop. One morning a woman called, and told Kitto she wished to see his master. The guileless boy went to call him from the public-house, and in his absence she made off with the razors. In his rage at the loss, the barber accused Kitto of being a confederate in the theft, and instantly discharged him.

His next employment was as assistant to his father, and in this service occurred the great misfortune of his life. They were repairing a house in Batter Street, Plymouth, in 1817, and John had just reached the highest round of a ladder, with a load of slates, and was in the act of stepping on the roof, when his foot slipped, and he fell from a height of five-and-thirty feet on a stone pavement. He bled profusely at the mouth and nostrils, but not at the ears, and neither legs nor arms were broken. For a fortnight he lay unconscious. When he recovered, he wondered at the silence around him, and asking for a book, was answered by signs, and then by writing on a slate. 'Why do you *write* to me?' exclaimed the poor sufferer. 'Why do you not speak? Speak! speak!'

There was an interchange of looks and seeming whispers; the fatal truth could not be concealed; again the scribe took his pencil, and wrote: 'You are deaf!' Deaf he was, and deaf he remained until the end of his life.

If the prospect of poor Kitto's life was dark before, it was now tenfold darker. His parents were unable to assist him, and left him in idleness to pursue his reading. He waded and groped in the mud of Plymouth harbour for bits of old rope and iron, which he sold for a few pence wherewith to buy books. He drew and coloured pictures, and sold them to children for their half-pence. He wrote labels, to replace those in windows, announcing 'Logins for singel men,' and hawked them about town with slight success. By none of these means could he keep himself in food and raiment, and in 1819, much against his will, he was lodged in the workhouse, and set to learn shoemaking. There his gentle nature and studious habits attracted the attention and sympathy of the master, and procured him a number of indulgences. He commenced to practise literary composition, and quickly attained remarkable facility and elegance of style. He began to keep a diary, and was prompted by the master to write lectures, which were read to the other workhouse-boys. At the end of 1821, he was apprenticed to a shoemaker, who abused and struck him, and made him so miserable, that the idea of suicide not unfrequently arose to tempt him. Here, however, Kitto's pen came to his effectual help, and his well-written complaints were the means of the dissolution of his apprenticeship and re-admission to the workhouse after six months of intolerable wretchedness. Meanwhile the literary ability of the deaf pauper-boy began to be known; he was allowed to read in the Public Library; and some of his essays were printed in the *Plymouth Journal*. In the end there was written in the admission-book of the workhouse—'John Kitto discharged, 1823, July 17th. Taken out under the patronage of the literati of the town.'

Kitto's first book appeared in 1825, consisting of *Essays and Letters, with a short Memoir of the Author*. It brought him little profit, but served to widen his circle of friends. One of these, Mr Grove, an Exeter dentist, invited him to his house, and liberally undertook to teach him his own art; but after a while, hoping to turn his talents to better account, he had him introduced to the Missionary College at Islington, to learn printing. From thence he was sent to Malta, to work at a press there; but Kitto was much more inclined to private study than to mechanical occupation, and his habits not giving satisfaction to the missionaries, he returned to England in 1829, and set out with Mr Grove on a religious mission to the east. For four years he travelled in Russia, the Caucasus, Armenia, and Persia. Whilst living at Bagdad in 1831, the plague broke out, in which about fifty thousand perished, or nearly three-fourths of the inhabitants of the city. In this dreadful visitation, Mr Grove lost his wife. Kitto was restored to his native land in safety in 1833, with a mind enriched and enlarged with a rare harvest of experience.

Anxious, because with no certain means of livelihood, he fortunately procured an introduction to the secretary of the Society for the Diffusion of Useful Knowledge, and was employed by Mr Charles Knight as a contributor to the *Penny Magazine*. Proving a capable and steady workman, he obtained the promise of constant occupation, on the strength of which he married, and in his wife found a helpmate literary and domestic. Mr Knight, in 1835, projected a *Pictorial Bible*, with notes, and intrusted the editorship to Kitto. It was published in numbers, it was praised everywhere, it sold well, and its execution clearly indicated the line in which Kitto was destined to excel. He was next engaged on a *Pictorial History of Palestine*, then on a *Cyclopædia of Biblical Literature*, and finally on eight volumes of *Daily Bible Illustrations*. Besides these, he produced a number of minor works in illustration of the Scriptures, and started and edited a quarterly *Journal of Sacred Literature*. These writings made the name of Kitto a familiar word in every religious household in the land, and in 1850 he was placed for a pension of £100 a year on her Majesty's civil list, in consideration of his services.

Kitto was a ready writer, but at the same time painstaking and correct; and the production of such a mass of literature as lies under his signature, within a period of less than twenty years, entailed the necessity of perpetual labour. 'The working-day of the British Museum,' he wrote to Mr Knight, 'is six hours—mine is sixteen hours.' His deafness,

as well as habits of incessant industry, cut him off from society, and he seldom saw any visitors except such as had actual business to transact. He confessed to a friend, in the summer of 1851, that he had not crossed his threshold for six weeks. His work was his joy, he loved nothing better; but the strain he put upon his fragile constitution was too great. Congestion of the brain set in; he was told his only chance for life lay in perfect rest and abstinence from work for a year or two; but he insisted on completing his literary engagements, and alleged, truly, that he had a wife and ten children to provide for. A number of his admirers subscribed ample funds to justify some years of repose, and in the August of 1854 he retired to Cannstadt, in Würtemberg, but it was too late. On the 25th of November he died at Cannstadt, and was there buried.

In his seventeenth year, Kitto wrote this description of himself, which, making allowance for age, might serve for his picture at fifty, with the addition perhaps of an inch or two to his stature. 'I am four feet eight inches high; my hair is stiff and coarse, of a dark-brown colour, almost black; my head is *very* large, and, I believe, has a tolerable good lining of brain within. My eyes are brown and large, and are the least unexceptionable part of my person; my forehead is high, eyebrows bushy; my nose is large; my mouth very big; teeth well enough; my limbs are not ill-shaped; my legs are *well*-shaped.'

## DOUBLE-CONSCIOUSNESS: ALTERNATE SANITY AND INSANITY.

An inquest, held in London on the 25th of November 1835, afforded illustrative testimony to that remarkable duality, double-action, or alternate action of the mind, which physiologists and medical men have so frequently noticed, and which has formed the basis for so many theories. Mr Mackerell, a gentleman connected with the East India Company, and resident in London, committed suicide by taking prussic acid, while labouring under an extraordinary paroxysm of delusions. During a period of four years, he had had these delusions *every alternate day*. Dr James Johnson, his physician, had bound himself by a solemn promise to the unhappy man, never to divulge to any human being the exact nature of the delusions in question. Fulfilling this promise, he avoided giving to the jury any detailed account. The doctor stated that the delusions under which his patient laboured, while accompanied by most dreadful horrors and depression of mind, 'had not the remotest reference to any act of moral guilt, or to any circumstance in which the community could have an interest, but turned on an idle circumstance equally unimportant to himself and to others, but still were capable of producing a most extraordinary horror of mind.' Mr Mackerell called his two sets of days his 'good days' and 'bad days.' On his bad days he would, if possible, see no one, not even his physician. On his good days he talked earnestly with Dr Johnson concerning his malady; and said that although what he suffered on his bad days in body and mind might induce many men to rush madly upon suicide for relief, yet he himself had too high a moral and religious sense ever to be guilty of such an act. The delusion, Dr Johnson declared, was not of a kind that would have justified any restraint, or any imputation of what is usually called insanity. It was on one subject only, a true *monomania*, that a hallucination prevailed. Whether in London or the country, travelling by road or by sea, this monomania regularly returned every alternate day, beginning when he woke in the morning, and lasting all the day through. The miserable victim felt the first attack of it at a period of unusual excitement and disappointment; and from that time it gradually strengthened until his death—leaving him on the *intermediate* days, however, a clear-headed and perfectly sane man: nay, 'a highly-educated gentleman, of very superior intellectual powers.' On two different occasions, his alternations of good and bad days influenced his proceedings in a curious way, leading him to undo each day what had been done the day before. It was just before the era of railways, when long journeys occupied two or more days and nights in succession. At one time, he secured a passage in the mail to Paisley; but on reaching Manchester he quitted the coach, and returned by the first conveyance to London. Again he quitted London by mail for Paisley, but turned back at Birmingham. A *third* time he engaged a place in the mail to Paisley, but did not start at all, and sent his landlord to make the best bargain he could with the clerk at the coach-office for a return of a portion of the fare. It would appear that his good days gave him an inducement to travel northward, but the bad days then supervened, and changed his plans. He committed suicide, in spite of his oft-expressed religious views, on one of his good days (for the persons in whose house he lived kept a regular account of these singular alternations), having been apparently worn out with the unutterable miseries of one half of his waking existence.

Dr Wigan,* in his curious view of insanity, does not mention this particular case; but he adduces two others of alternate sanity and insanity, or at least double manifestations of mental power. 'We have examples of persons who, from some hitherto unexplained cause, fall suddenly into, and remain for a time, in a state of existence resembling somnambulism; from which, after many hours, they gradually awake—having no recollection of anything that has occurred in the preceding state; although, during its continuance, they had read, written, and conversed, and done many other acts implying an exercise, however limited, of the understanding. They sing or play on an instrument, and yet, on the cessation of the paroxysm, are quite unconscious of everything that has taken place. They now pursue their ordinary business and avocations in the usual manner, perhaps for weeks; when suddenly the somnambulic state recurs, during which all that had happened in the previous attack comes vividly before them, and they remember it as perfectly as if that disordered state were the regular habitual mode of existence of the individual—the healthy state and its events being now as entirely forgotten as were the disordered ones during the healthy state. Thus it passes on for many months, or even years.' Again, in one peculiar form of mental disease, an adult 'becomes a perfect child, is obliged to undertake the labour of learning again to read and write, and passes gradually through all the usual elementary branches of education—makes considerable progress, and finds the task becoming daily more and more easy; but is entirely unconscious of all that had taken place in the state of health. Suddenly she is seized with a kind of fit, or with a sleep of preternatural length and intensity, and wakes in full possession of all the acquired knowledge

* *The Duality of the Mind.* By A. L. Wigan, M.D. 1844.

which she had previously possessed, but has no remembrance of what I will call her *child state,* and does not even recognise the persons or things with which she then became acquainted. She is exactly as she was before the first attack, and as if the disordered state had never formed a portion of her existence. After the lapse of some weeks, she is again seized as before with intense somnolency, and after a long and deep sleep wakes up in the *child state.* She has now a perfect recollection of all that previously occurred in that state, resumes her tasks at the point where she had left off, and continues to make progress as a person would do who was of that age and under those circumstances; but has once more entirely lost all remembrance of the persons and things connected with her healthy [or adult] state. This alternation recurs many times, and at last becomes the established habit of the individual—like an incurable ague.' There are numerous recorded cases in which a person *knows* that he or she is subject to alternate mental states, and can reason concerning the one state while under the influence of the other. Humboldt's servant, a German girl, who had charge of a child, entreated to be sent away; for whenever she undressed it, and noticed the whiteness of its skin, she felt an almost irresistible desire to tear it in pieces. A young lady in a Paris asylum had, at regular intervals, a propensity to murder some one; and when the paroxysm was coming on, she would request to be put in a strait-waistcoat, as a measure of precaution. A country-woman was seized with a desire to murder her child whenever she put it into her cradle, and she used to pray earnestly when she felt this desire coming on. A butcher's wife often requested her husband to keep his knives out of her sight when her children were nigh; she was afraid of herself. A gentleman of good family, and estimable disposition, had a craving desire, when at church, to run up into the organ-loft and play some popular tune, especially one with jocular words attached to it. All these cases, and many others of a kind more or less analogous, Dr Wigan attributes to a *duality of the mind,* connected with a *duality of the brain.* He maintains that the right and left halves of the brain are virtually two distinct brains, dividing between them the organism of the mental power. Both may be sound, both may be unsound in *equal* degree, both may be unsound in *unequal* degree, or one may be sound and the other unsound. The mental phenomena may exhibit, consequently, varying degrees of sanity and insanity. This view has not met with much acceptance among physiologists and psychologists; but, nevertheless, it is worthy of attention.

## NOVEMBER 26.

St Peter, martyr, bishop of Alexandria, 311. St Conrad, bishop of Constance, confessor, 976. St Nicon, surnamed Metanoite, confessor, 998. St Sylvester Gozzolini, abbot of Osimo, institutor of the Sylvestrin monks, 1267.

*Born.*—Sir James Ware, antiquary, 1594, *Dublin;* Dr William Derham, natural philosopher, 1657, *Stowton, near Worcester.*

*Died.*—Prince William, son of Henry I. of England, drowned in the *White Ship,* 1120; John Spotswood or Spotiswood, archbishop of St Andrews, Scottish ecclesiastical historian, 1639; Philippe Quinault, tragic dramatist, 1688, *Paris;* John Elwes, noted miser, 1789, *Marcham, Berkshire;* Dr Joseph Black, eminent chemist, 1799, *Edinburgh;* John Loudoun Macadam, improver of roads, 1836; George, Lord Nugent (poetry, biography, &c.), *Lillies, Bucks;* Marshal Soult, Duke of Dalmatia, 1850, *Soult-Berg;* Vincenz Priessnitz, founder of hydropathy, 1851, *Graefenberg.*

### JOHN ELWES.

On the 26th November 1789, died John Elwes, Esquire, a striking example of the impotent poverty of wealth when it does not enlarge the understanding, or awaken the social affections, and, consequently, cannot purchase common comforts for its wretched possessor. Elwes was the son of a successful brewer in Southwark, named Meggot. Evil tendencies of mind are as hereditary as diseases of the body. Elwes's mother starved herself to death, and his paternal uncle, Sir Harvey Elwes, was a notorious miser, from whom, by one of those fortuitous turns of events that sometimes throws great wealth into the power of those who have least occasion for it, John Elwes derived his name and a vast fortune.

If Elwes had been a mere miser, his name might well have been omitted from this collection; but the extraordinary man possessed qualities which, if they had not been suppressed by the all-absorbing passion of avarice, entitled him to the love and esteem of his friends, and might have advanced him to the respect and admiration of his countrymen. In spite of his penurious disposition, he had an unshaken gentleness of manner, and a pliancy of temper not generally found in a miserable money accumulator. One day he was out shooting with a gentleman who exhibited constant proofs of unskilfulness; so much so, that at last, in firing through a hedge, he lodged several shot in the miser's cheek. The awkward sportsman, with great embarrassment and concern, approached to apologise, but Elwes anticipated apology by holding out his hand, and saying: 'My dear sir, I congratulate you on improving; I thought you would hit something in time!'

Those afflicted by a habitual love of money are seldom scrupulous respecting the means of increasing their stores; yet Elwes abstained from usury on principle, considering it an unjustifiable method of augmenting his fortune. And contrary to an ostentatious meanness, too generally prevalent at the present day, by which many indulge in luxuries at the expense of others, Elwes's whole system of life and saving was founded on pure self-denial. He would walk miles in the rain, rather than hire a conveyance; and sit hours in wet clothes, rather than incur the expense of a fire. He would advance a large sum to oblige a friend, and on the same day risk his life to save paying a penny at a turnpike. He would eat meat in the last stage of putrefaction, 'the charnel-house of sustenance,' rather than allow a small profit to a butcher.

Like most of his class, Elwes was penny-wise and pound-foolish; not unfrequently losing the sheep for the half-penny worth of tar. He suffered his spacious country mansion to become uninhabitable, rather than be at the cost of a few necessary repairs. A near relative once slept at his seat in the country, but the bedchamber was open to wind and weather, and the gentleman was awakened in the night by rain pouring in upon him. After searching in vain for a bell, he was necessitated to move his bed several times, till a place was at last found, where rain did not reach. On remarking the circumstance to Elwes in the morning, the latter said: 'Ay! I don't mind it myself; but to those who do, that is a nice corner in the rain!'

Elwes had an extensive property in houses in London, and as some of his houses were frequently without a tenant, he saved the price of lodgings by occupying any premises that might happen to be vacant. Two beds, two chairs, a table, and an old woman, were all his furniture, and with these, whenever a tenant offered, he was ready to remove at a moment's warning. It was then not easy to find him, or to know what part of the town might be his residence. Colonel Timms, his nephew, and heir to his entailed estates, was on one occasion anxious to see Elwes. After some inquiries, he learned accidentally that his uncle had been seen going into an uninhabited house in Great Marlborough Street. No *gentleman*, however, had been seen about there, but a pot-boy recollected observing an old beggar go into a stable and lock the door after him. Colonel Timms knocked at the door, but no one answering, sent for a blacksmith, and had the lock forced. The lower part of the building was all closed and silent; but, on ascending the staircase, moans were heard, apparently proceeding from a person in great distress. Entering a room, the intruders found, stretched out on an old pallet-bed, seemingly in death, the wretched figure of Elwes. For some time he remained insensible, till some cordials were administered by a neighbouring apothecary; then he sufficiently recovered to be able to say that he had, he believed, been ill for two or three days, and that there was an old woman in the house, but for some reason or other, she had not been near him; that she had been ill herself, but that she had recovered, he supposed, and gone away. On Colonel Timms and the apothecary repairing to the garret, they found the old woman stretched lifeless on the floor, having apparently been dead for two days.

When his inordinate passion for saving did not interfere, Elwes would willingly exert himself to the utmost to serve a friend. He once extricated two old ladies from a long and troublesome ecclesiastical suit, by riding sixty miles at night, and at a moment's warning. Such wonderful efforts would he make with alacrity, and at an advanced age, to serve a person for whom no motives or entreaties could have prevailed on him to part with a shilling. In this, and all his long journeys, a few hard-boiled eggs, a dry crust carried in his pocket, the next stream of water, and a spot of fresh grass for his horse, while he reposed beneath a hedge, were the whole of the travelling expenses of both man and beast. The ladies asked a neighbouring gentleman how they could best testify their thanks for such a service. 'Send him sixpence,' was the reply, 'for then he will be delighted by gaining twopence by his journey.'

So lived John Elwes, encouraging no art, advancing no science, working no material improvement on his estates or country, diffusing no blessings around him, bestowing no benevolence upon the poor and needy, and shewing few signs of parental care or affection. He never was married, but was the father of two natural children, to whom he bequeathed the greater part of his disposable property. Education he despised, and would lay out no money upon it. 'The surest way,' he constantly affirmed, 'of taking money out of people's pockets, is by putting things into their heads.' And no doubt he felt it so, for this strange man was a prey to every sharper who could put a scheme into his head by which he imagined that money might be got. Elwes has been compared to a great pike in a fishpool, which, ever voracious and unsatisfied, clutches at everything, until it is at last caught itself. With a mind incapable of taking comprehensive ideas of money-matters, and a constant anxiety to grasp the tangible results of his speculations, Elwes either disdained or was too indolent to keep regular accounts, and the consequence was that £150,000 of bad debts were owing to him at his death.

As we approach the last scene of all, the cruel tyranny of avarice, over its wretched slave, becomes more and more appalling. Comfortably domiciled in his son's house, Elwes fears that he shall die in poverty. In the night he is heard struggling with imaginary robbers, and crying: 'I will keep my money! I will! Don't rob me! Oh don't!' A visitor hears a footstep entering his room at night, and naturally asks, 'Who is there?' On which a tremulous voice replies: 'Sir, I beg your pardon, my name is Elwes, I have been unfortunate enough to be robbed in this house, which I believe is mine, of all the money I have in the world—of five guineas and a half, and half-a-crown.' A few days after, the money is found, where he had hidden it, behind a window-shutter. And a few days more, Elwes is found in bed, his clothes and hat on, his staff in his hand. His son comes to the bedside, and the father whispers John: 'I hope I have left you as much as you wished.' The family doctor is sent for, and, looking at the dying miser, says: 'That man, with his original strength of constitution, and life-long habits of temperance, might have lived twenty years longer, but for his continual anxiety about money.'

This notice of Elwes cannot be better concluded than in the following summary of his character, by his friend and acquaintance of many years, Mr Topham. 'In one word, his [Elwes] public character lives after him pure and without stain. In private life, he was chiefly an enemy to himself. To others, he lent much; to himself, he denied everything. But in the pursuit of his property, or in the recovery of it, I have it not in my remembrance one unkind thing that ever was done by him.'

## JOHN LOUDOUN MACADAM.

Though neither a soldier nor a statesman, and laying no claim to distinction on the score either of literary or scientific achievement, the practical abilities of Macadam have, nevertheless, added a word to the English language, and earned for him the tribute of a grateful remembrance as one of the most important of our public benefactors. The traveller as he bowls smoothly along the even and well-kept turnpike-road, whether in gig, stage-coach, or chaise, may bless fervently the memory of the great road-reformer of the nineteenth century, whose *macadamised* highways have tended so much to increase the comfort as well as diminish the dangers of vehicular locomotion. The means employed were of the simplest and most efficacious kind, and with an improvement on the original idea, have rendered the public roads throughout the British islands, if not superior, at least second to none in the world.

John Loudoun Macadam was born at Ayr on the 21st September 1756. His father was a landed proprietor, who died when John was about fourteen, and the young man was thereupon sent to the office of an uncle, a merchant in New York. Here he remained for a number of years, and on the war of independence breaking out, established for himself a lucrative business as an agent for the sale of prizes. The termination of hostilities, however, in favour of the colonists, found him nearly penniless, and he returned to his native country. For some time after this he resided in the neighbourhood of Moffat, and subsequently removed to Sauchrie, in Ayrshire, where for thirteen years he acted as deputy-lieutenant of the county, and a member of the commission of the peace. Being here engaged in the capacity of trustee on certain roads, his mind was first led to revolve some scheme for a general amelioration of the system of highways throughout the kingdom, and he continued for many years to study and experiment on the subject. Having been appointed, in 1798, agent for victualling the navy in the western ports of Great Britain, he took up his abode at Falmouth, but afterwards removed to Bristol. In 1815, he was appointed surveyor of the Bristol roads, and here he first seriously set himself to work to carry into actual operation the improvements which he had been pondering over for so many years. The main feature of his plan was to form a bed of fragments of stone—granite, whinstone, or basalt—none of which should be too large to pass through an iron ring two and a half inches in diameter. The stratum or bed of such materials was to be from six to twelve inches in thickness, and it was left to be brought into compactness and smoothness by the action of the vehicles passing over it. Though now approaching sixty years of age, Mr Macadam set himself with all energy to carry out this scheme, and before he died, he had the satisfaction of seeing his system of roadmaking generally adopted, though the only reward he reaped for his labours was a grant of £2000 from parliament, and the repayment of a large sum, amounting to several thousands more, which he proved before a committee of the House of Commons to have been expended by him from his own resources in perfecting his plan. He died at Moffat on 26th November 1836, in the eighty-first year of his age, leaving behind him the reputation of one of the most honourable and disinterested of men.

The great drawback from the virtues of Mr Macadam's plan, lies in the difficulty of obtaining a smooth surface. Without a firm substructure, the subjacent materials are apt to work up amongst those of the macadam bed. It is also found that carriages encounter a prodigious friction from these materials, until they have been somewhat beaten down; and that, even then, the wheels will be found to have left great longitudinal indentations or hollows, with rough ridges between, altogether at issue with true smoothness. The first objection was overcome by the great engineer Telford, who suggested a causewayed substructure as a basis for the bed of small stones. The second difficulty can be to a large extent overcome, by causing a heavy roller to pass in the first place over the bed of macadamised fragments, so as to jam them down into a compact cake, on which the carriages may then pass with comparative facility. But though this plan commends itself to the simplest common sense, and is very generally practised in France, the idea of its advantages seems never yet to have dawned upon the British intellect. Accordingly, the macadamised road is still, with us, a martyrdom to horses; and it is not too much to say, that the thoroughfares of London present, during a third part of all time, frictional difficulties ten times more than there is any just occasion for, and require four times the amount of renewal and expense which is strictly necessary.

## THE HOTTENTOT VENUS.

Early in the present century, a poor wretched woman was exhibited in England under the appellation of the *Hottentot Venus*. With an intensely ugly figure, distorted beyond all European notions of beauty, she was said by those to whom she belonged to possess precisely that kind of shape which is most admired among her countrymen, the Hottentots. Mr Bullock, proprietor of a 'Museum' in which many exhibitions were held in those days, was applied to in 1810 by a Mr Dunlop, surgeon of an African ship, to purchase a beautiful camelopard skin. On account of the high price asked, the negotiation broke off; but at a second interview, Dunlop informed Mr Bullock that he had brought a Hottentot woman home with him from the Cape, whom he had engaged to take back again in two years; that she was an object of great curiosity; and that a person might make a fortune in two years by exhibiting her. Mr Bullock, however, did not close with the offers made to him, and the black woman was sold—for it appears to have been virtually a sale—by the surgeon to another person. Then came forth the advertisements and placards concerning the Hottentot Venus. She was exhibited on a stage two feet high, along which she was led by her keeper, and exhibited like a wild beast; being obliged to walk, stand, or sit, as he ordered her. The exhibition was so offensive and disgraceful, that the attorney-general called for the interference of the lord chancellor on the subject. He grounded his application on the fact, that the poor creature did not appear to be a free agent, and that she was little other than a slave or chattel. She and her keeper both spoke a kind of low Dutch, such as is known on the Hottentot borders of Cape Colony. It was observed, on one occasion, while being exhibited, that on her not coming forward immediately when called, the keeper went to her, and holding up his hand menacingly, said something in Dutch which induced her to come forward. She was often heard, also, to heave deep sighs in the course of the exhibition, and displayed great sullenness of temper. A Dutch gentleman, on one occasion, interrogated her how far she was a willing participator in the exhibition; but her keeper would not allow her to answer the questions. The publicity given to the matter in the Court of Chancery, soon caused the disappearance of the Hottentot Venus from the public gaze, but of the subsequent history of the poor woman herself we have no information.

## WILLIAM OF WYKEHAM.

Manners makyth the Man,
Quoth William of Wykeham.

William of Wykeham, probably one of the most popular characters in English history, was born of humble parents in the obscure Hampshire village from which he derives his surname. Nicholas Uvedale, the lord of the manor, attracted by the child's intelligence, sent him to school at Winchester. When still a youth, William became his patron's secretary, and being lodged in a lofty tower of Winchester Castle, there acquired the enthusiastic admiration of Gothic architecture, which laid the foundation of his future fortune. The young secretary visited the neighbouring churches, cathedrals, and castles; he measured, studied, and compared their various beauties and defects; then considered how such stately edifices had been erected; and figured in his own imagination others of still finer and grander proportions. So, when introduced by his patron to King Edward III., he was qualified to assist that monarch in planning and directing the building of his palatial castle at Windsor. Wykeham thus became the king's favourite and secretary; and subsequently applying himself to politics, he was made keeper of the Privy Seal; then entering the church, he became bishop of Winchester, and soon afterwards lord chancellor of England.

William, however, had nearly lost the favour of the king. When Windsor Castle was completed, the architect caused to be placed over the great gate, the words, THIS MADE WYKEHAM. The inscription was considered to be an arrogant assumption to himself, of all the honour and glory resulting from the great undertaking. The king, at first, was displeased, but William soon satisfied the monarch by the following explanation. In the inscription, the word Wykeham was, according to the idiom of the English language, in the accusative case, and, accordingly, the inscription did not mean that Wykeham made this building, but that the construction of the building made Wykeham, raising him from a poor lad to be the king's favourite architect. And when the heralds were busying themselves to find suitable arms for Wykeham, he gave them as his motto, MANNERS MAKYTH MAN; thereby meaning that a man's real worth is to be estimated, not from the outward and accidental circumstances of birth and fortune, but from the acquirements of his mind and his moral qualifications.

The biography of William of Wykeham, being part of the history of England, is rather beyond our scope. Ever sensible that the education and manners which he acquired at Winchester had made a man of him, he founded Winchester school, for the benefit of future generations. As a necessary adjunct and accessory to the school, he founded New College at Oxford. The publication of the charter of foundation of the latter establishment, bears date the 26th of November 1379.

During his long term of fourscore years, William devoted himself to acts of benevolence and charity. The immense fortune he acquired was expended with equal munificence. He contributed greatly to the promotion of sound education in England, while his skill as an architect was matched by an extraordinary aptitude for civil and ecclesiastical business. His talents and benevolence were not confined to scholastic and ecclesiastical edifices alone; he constructed roads and bridges, and regulated traffic on highways. He was buried in his own oratory in Winchester Cathedral, and whether the result of care or accident, it is pleasing to have to relate that Wykeham's tomb, of white marble, has never been desecrated. Many other tombs have suffered dilapidation in that cathedral, and other places, during the many political and religious changes that have occurred since Wykeham was interred; but his revered effigy, in pontifical robes, seems as if scarcely a few days had elapsed since it left the hand of the sculptor.

# NOVEMBER 27.

St James, surnamed Intercisus, martyr, 421. St Maharsapor, martyr, 421. St Secundin or Seachnal, bishop of Dunseachlin or Dunsaghlin, in Meath, 447. St Maximus, bishop of Riez, confessor, about 460. St Virgil, bishop of Salzburg, confessor, 784.

## Advent Sunday.

The four weeks immediately preceding Christmas are collectively styled *Advent*, a term denoting *approach* or *arrival*, and are so called in reference to the coming celebration of the birth of our Saviour. With this period, the ecclesiastical or Christian year is held to commence, and the first Sunday of these four weeks is termed Advent Sunday, or the first Sunday in Advent. It is always the *nearest* Sunday to the feast of St Andrew,* whether before or after that day; so that in all cases the season of Advent shall contain the uniform number of four Sundays. In 1864, Advent Sunday fell on the 27th of November, the earliest possible date on which it can occur.

*Born.*—Françoise d'Aubigné, Marquise de Maintenon, second consort of Louis XIV., 1635, *Niort;* Henri François d'Aguesseau, chancellor of France, 1668, *Limoges;* Robert Lowth, bishop of London, biblical critic, 1710; John Murray, publisher, 1778.

*Died.*—Horace, lyric and satirical poet, 8 B.C.; Clovis, first king of France, 511, *Paris;* Maurice, Roman emperor, beheaded at Chalcedon, 602; Louis, Chevalier de Rohan, executed at Paris for conspiracy, 1674; Basil Montagu, Q.C. (writings on philosophical and social questions, &c.), 1851, *Boulogne.*

## THE GREAT STORM.

Early on the morning of Saturday, the 27th November 1703, occurred one of the most terrific storms recorded in our national history. It was not merely, as usually happens, a short and sudden burst of tempest, lasting a few hours, but a fierce and tremendous hurricane of a week's duration, which attained its utmost violence on

* See under November 30.

the day above mentioned. The preceding Wednesday was a peculiarly calm, fine day for the season of the year, but at four o'clock in the afternoon a brisk gale commenced, and increased so strongly during the night, that it would have been termed a great storm, if a greater had not immediately followed. On Thursday, the wind slightly abated; but on Friday it blew with redoubled force till midnight, from which time till daybreak on Saturday morning, the tempest was at its extreme height. Consequently, though in some collections of dates the Great Storm is placed under the 26th of November, it actually took place on the following day. Immediately after midnight, on the morning of Saturday, numbers of the affrighted inhabitants of London left their beds, and took refuge in the cellars and lower apartments of their houses. Many thought the end of the world had arrived. Defoe, who experienced the terrors of that dreadful night, says: 'Horror and confusion seized upon all; no pen can describe it, no tongue can express it, no thought conceive it, unless some of those who were in the extremity of it.' It was not till eight o'clock on the Saturday morning, when the storm had slightly lulled, that the boldest could venture forth from the shelter of their dwellings, to seek assistance, or inquire for the safety of friends. The streets were then thickly strewed with bricks, tiles, stones, lead, timber, and all kinds of building materials. The storm continued to rage through the day, with very little diminution in violence, but at four in the afternoon heavy torrents of rain fell, and had the effect of considerably reducing the force of the gale. Ere long, however, the hurricane recommenced with great fury, and in the course of the Sunday and Monday attained such a height, that on Tuesday night few persons dared go to bed. Continuing till noon on Wednesday, the storm then gradually decreased till four in the afternoon, when it terminated in a dead calm, at the very hour of its commencement on the same day of the preceding week.

The old and dangerously absurd practice of building chimneys in stacks, containing as many bricks as a modern ordinary-sized house, was attended by all its fatal consequences on this occasion. The bills of mortality for the week recorded twenty-one deaths in London alone, from the fall of chimneys. After the tempest, houses bore a resemblance to skeletons. Fortunately, three weeks of dry weather followed, permitting the inhabitants to patch up their dwellings with boards, tarpaulins, old sails, and straw; regular repairs being in many instances, at the time, wholly impossible. Plain tiles rose in price from one guinea to six pounds per thousand; and pan-tiles from fifty shillings to ten pounds, for the same number. Bricklayers' wages rose in proportion, so that even in the case of large public edifices, the trustees or managers bestowed on them merely a temporary repair, till prices should fall. During 1704, the Temple, Christ's Hospital, and other buildings in the city of London, presented a remarkable appearance, patched with straw, reeds, and other thatching materials.

At Wells, the bishop of that diocese and his wife were killed, when in bed, by a stack of chimneys falling upon them. Defoe, from personal observation, relates that, in the county of Kent alone, 1107 dwelling-houses and barns were levelled by the tremendous force of the hurricane. Five hundred grand old trees were prostrated in Penshurst, the ancient park of the Sidneys, and numerous orchards of fruit-trees were totally destroyed.

The same storm did great damage in Holland and France, but did not extend far to the northward; the border counties and Scotland receiving little injury from it. The loss sustained by the city of London was estimated at one million, and that of Bristol at two hundred thousand pounds. Great destruction of property and loss of life occurred on the river Thames. The worst period of the storm there, was from midnight to daybreak, the night being unusually dark, and the tide extraordinarily high. Five hundred watermen's wherries, 300 ship-boats, and 120 barges were destroyed; the number of persons drowned could never be exactly ascertained, but 22 dead bodies were found and interred.

The greatest destruction of shipping, however, took place off the coast, where the fleet, under the command of Sir Cloudesley Shovel, had just returned from the Mediterranean. The admiral, and part of his ships anchored near the Gunfleet, rode out the gale with little damage; but of the vessels lying in the Downs few escaped. Three ships of 70 guns, one of 64, two of 56, one of 46, and several other smaller vessels, were totally destroyed, with a loss of 1500 officers and men, among whom was Rear-admiral Beaumont.

It may surprise many to learn that the elaborate contrivances for saving life from shipwreck date from no distant period. Even late in the last century, the dwellers on the English coasts considered themselves the lawful heirs of all drowned persons, and held that their first duty in the case of a wreck was to secure, for their own behoof, the property which Providence had thus cast on their shores. That they should exert themselves to save the lives of their fellow-creatures, thus imperiled, was an idea that never presented itself. Nay, superstition, which ever has had a close connection with self-interest, declared it was unlucky to rescue a drowning man from his fate. In the humane endeavour to put an end to this horrible state of matters, Burke, in 1776, brought a bill into parliament, enacting that the value of plundered wrecks should be levied from the inhabitants of the district where the wreck occurred. The country gentlemen, resenting the bill as an attack on their vested interests, vehemently opposed it. The government of the day also, requiring the votes of the county members to grant supplies for carrying on the war against the revolted American colonies, joined in the opposition, and threw out the bill, as Will Whitehead expresses it:

> 'To make Squire Boobies willing,
> To grant supplies at every check,
> Give them the plunder of a wreck,
> They 'll vote another shilling.'

This allusion to the change which has taken place in public feeling on the subject of wrecks, was rendered necessary to explain the following incident in connection with the Great Storm. At low water, on the morning after the terrible hurricane, more than two hundred men were discovered on the treacherous footing of the Goodwin Sands, crying and gesticulating for aid, well knowing that in a very short time, when the tide rose, they would inevitably perish. The boatmen were too busy, labouring in their vocation of picking up portable property, to think of saving life. The mayor of Deal, an humble slopseller, but a man of extraordinary humanity for the period, went to the custom-house, and begged that the boats belonging to that establishment might be sent out to save some, at least, of the poor men. The custom-house officers refused, on the ground that this was not the service for which their boats were provided. The mayor then collected a few fellow-tradesmen, and in a short speech so inspired them with his generous emotions, that they seized the custom-house boats by force, and, going off to the sands, rescued as many persons as they could from certain death. The shipwrecked men being brought to land, naked, cold, and hungry, what was to be done with them? The navy agent at Deal refused to assist them, his duties being, he said, to aid seamen wounded in battle, not shipwrecked men. The worthy mayor, whose name was Powell, had therefore to clothe and feed these poor fellows, provide them with lodgings, and bury at his own expense some that died. Subsequently, after a long course of petitioning, he was reimbursed for his outlay by government; and this concession was followed by parliament requesting the queen to place shipwrecked seamen in the same category as men killed or wounded in action. The widows and children of men who had perished in the Great Storm, were thus placed on the pension list.

The most remarkable of the many edifices destroyed during that dreadful night was the first Eddystone light-house, erected four years previously by an enterprising but incompetent individual, named Winstanley. He had been a mercer in London, and, having acquired wealth, retired to Littlebury, in Essex, where he amused himself with the curious but useless mechanical toys that preceded our modern machinery and engineering, as

THE GREAT STORM: DESTRUCTION OF THE FIRST EDDYSTONE LIGHT-HOUSE.

alchemy and astrology preceded chemistry and astronomy. As a specimen of these, it is related that, in one room of his house, there lay an old slipper, which, if a kick were given it, immediately raised a ghost from the floor; in another room, if a visitor sat down in a seemingly comfortable arm-chair, the arms would fly round his body, and detain him a close prisoner, till released by the ingenious inventor. The light-house was just such a specimen of misapplied ingenuity as might have been expected from such an intellect. It was built of wood, and deficient in every element of stability. Its polygonal form rendered it peculiarly liable to be swept away by the waves. It was no less exposed to the action of the wind, from the upper part being ornamented with large wooden candlesticks, and supplied with useless vanes, cranes, and other 'top-hamper,' as a sailor would say. It is probable that the design of this singular edifice had been suggested to Winstanley by a drawing of a Chinese pagoda. And this light-house, placed on a desolate rock in the sea, was painted with representations of suns and compasses, and mottoes of various kinds; such as POST TENEBRAS LUX, GLORY BE TO GOD, PAX IN BELLO. The last was probably in allusion to the building's fancied security, amidst the wild war of waters. And that such peace might be properly enjoyed, the light-house contained, besides a kitchen and accommodation for the keepers, a state-room, finely carved and painted, with a chimney, two closets, and two windows. There was also a splendid bedchamber, richly gilded and painted. This is Winstanley's own description, accompanying an engraving of the light-house, in which he complacently represents himself fishing from the state-room window. One would suppose he had designed the building for an eccentric ornament to a garden or a park, were it not that, in his whimsical ingenuity, he had contrived a kind of movable shoot on the top, by which stones could be showered down on any side, on an approaching enemy. Men, who knew by experience the aggressive powers of sea-waves, remonstrated with Winstanley, but he declared that he was so well assured of the strength of the building, that he would like to be in it during the greatest storm that ever blew under the face of heaven. The confident architect had, a short time previous to the Great Storm, gone to the light-house to superintend some repairs. When the fatal tempest came, it swept the flimsy structure into the ocean, and with it the unfortunate Winstanley, and five other persons who were along with him in the building.

There is a curious bit of literary history indirectly connected with the Great Storm. Addison, 'distressed by indigence,' wrote a poem on the victory of Blenheim, in which he thus compares the Duke of Marlborough, directing the current of the great fight, to the Spirit of the Storm—

'So when an angel, by divine command,
With rising tempests shakes a guilty land,
Such as of late o'er pale Britannia past,
Calm and serene, he drives the furious blast.
And pleased th' Almighty's orders to perform,
Rides in the whirlwind, and directs the storm.'

Lord Godolphin was so pleased with this simile, that he immediately appointed Addison to the Commissionership of Appeals, the first public employment conferred on the essayist.

## CIRCUMSTANCES AT THE DEATH OF THOMAS, LORD LYTTELTON.

Thomas, second Lord Lyttelton, who died November 27, 1779, at the age of thirty-five, was as remarkable for his reckless and dissipated life—not to speak of impious habits of thought—as his father had been for the reverse. One of the wicked actions attributed to him, was the seduction of three Misses Amphlett, who resided near his country residence in Shropshire. He had just returned from Ireland—where he left one of these ladies—when, residing at his house in Hill Street, Berkeley Square, he was attacked with suffocating fits of a threatening character. According to one account, he dreamed one night that a fluttering bird came to his window, and that presently after a woman appeared to him in white apparel, who told him to prepare for death, as he would not outlive three days. He was much alarmed, and called for his servant, who found him in a profuse perspiration, and to whom he related the circumstance which had occurred.* According to another account, from a relative of his lordship, he was still awake when the noise of a bird fluttering at the window called his attention; his room seemed filled with light, and he saw in the recess of the window a female figure, being that of a lady whom he had injured, who, pointing to the clock on the mantel-piece, then indicating twelve o'clock, said in a severe tone that, at that hour on the third day after, his life would be concluded, after which she vanished and left the room in darkness.

That some such circumstance, in one or other of these forms, was believed by Lord Lyttelton to have occurred, there can be no reasonable doubt, for it left him in a depression of spirits which caused him to speak of the matter to his friends. On the third day, he had a party with him at breakfast, including Lord Fortescue, Lady Flood, and two Misses Amphlett, to whom he remarked: 'If I live over to-night, I shall have jockeyed the ghost, for this is the third day.' The whole party set out in the forenoon for his lordship's country-house, Pit Place, near Epsom, where he had not long arrived when he had one of his suffocating fits. Nevertheless, he was able to dine with his friends at five o'clock. By a friendly trick, the clocks throughout the house, and the watches of the whole party, including his lordship's, were put forward half an hour. The evening passed agreeably; the ghostly warning was never alluded to; and Lord Lyttelton seemed to have recovered his usual gaiety. At half-past eleven, he retired to his bedroom, and soon after got into bed, where he was to take a dose of rhubarb and mint-water. According to the report afterwards given by his valet,* 'he kept every now and then looking at his watch. He ordered his curtains to be closed at the foot. It was now within a minute or two of twelve by his watch: he asked to look at mine, and seemed pleased to find it nearly keep time with his own. His lordship then put both to his ear, to satisfy himself that they went. When it was more than a quarter after twelve by our watches, he said: "This mysterious lady is not a true prophetess, I find." When it was near the real hour of twelve, he said: "Come, I'll wait no longer; get me my medicine; I'll take it, and try to sleep."' Perceiving the man stirring the medicine with a toothpick, Lord Lyttelton scolded him, and sent him away for a tea-spoon, with which he soon after returned. He found his master in a fit, with his chin, owing to the elevation of the pillow, resting hard upon his neck. Instead of trying to relieve him, he ran for assistance, and when he came back with the alarmed party of guests, Lord Lyttelton was dead.

Amongst the company at Pit Place that day, was Mr Miles Peter Andrews, a companion of Lord Lyttelton. Having business at the Dartford powder-mills, in which he was a partner, he left the house early, but not before he had been pleasingly assured that his noble friend was restored to his usual good spirits. So little did the ghost-adventure rest in Mr Andrews's mind, that he did not even recollect the time when it was predicted the event would take place. He had been half an hour in bed at his partner, Mr Pigou's house at the mill,† when 'suddenly his curtains were pulled open, and Lord Lyttelton

* T. J., the subsequent proprietor of Lord Lyttelton's house, Pit Place, gives this (*Gent. Mag.* 1816, ii. 421), as from a narrative in writing, left in the house as an heirloom, and 'which may be depended on.'

* *Gentleman's Magazine*, 1815, i. 597.

† J. W. Croker (*Notes to Boswell's Life of Johnson*).

appeared before him at his bedside, in his robe-de-chambre and night-cap. Mr Andrews looked at him some time, and thought it so odd a freak of his friend, that he began to reproach him for his folly in coming down to Dartford Mills without notice, as he could find no accommodation. "However," said he, "I'll get up, and see what can be done." He turned to the other side of the bed, and rang the bell, when Lord Lyttelton disappeared. His servant soon after coming in, he inquired: "Where is Lord Lyttelton?" The servant, all astonishment, declared he had not seen anything of his lordship since they left Pit Place. "Pshaw! you fool, he was here this moment at my bedside." The servant persisted that it was not possible. Mr Andrews dressed himself, and with the assistance of the servants, searched every part of the house and garden; but no Lord Lyttelton was to be found. Still Mr Andrews could not help believing that Lord Lyttelton had played him this trick, till, about four o'clock the same day, an express arrived to inform him of his lordship's death, and the manner of it.'

An attempt has been made to invalidate the truth of this recital, but on grounds more than usually weak. It has been surmised that Lord Lyttelton meant to take poison, and imposed the story of the warning on his friends; as if he would have chosen for a concealment of his design, a kind of imposture which, as the opinions of mankind go, is just the most hard of belief. This supposition, moreover, overlooks, and is inconsistent with, the fact that Lord Lyttelton was deceived as to the hour by the tampering with the watches; if he meant to destroy himself, he ought to have done it half an hour sooner. It is further affirmed—and the explanation is said to come from Lord Fortescue, who was of the party at Pit Place—that the story of the vision took its rise in a recent chase for a lady's pet-bird, which Lord Lyttelton declared had been harassingly reproduced to him in his dreams.* Lord Fortescue may have been induced, by the usual desire of escaping from a supra-natural theory, to surmise that the story had some such foundation; but it coheres with no other facts in the case, and fails to account for the impression on Lord Lyttelton's mind, that he had been warned of his coming death—a fact of which all his friends bore witness. On the other hand, we have the Lyttelton family fully of belief that the circumstances were as here related. Dr Johnson tells us, that he heard it from Lord Lyttelton's uncle, Lord Westcote, and he was therefore willing to believe it.† There was, in the Dowager Lady Lyttelton's house, in Portugal Street, Grosvenor Square, a picture which she herself executed in 1780, expressly to commemorate the event; it hung in a conspicuous part of her drawing-room. 'The dove ‡ appears at the window, while a female figure, habited in white, stands at the foot of the bed, announcing to Lord Lyttelton his dissolution. Every part of the picture was faithfully designed, after the description given to her by the valet-de-chambre who attended him, to whom his master related all the circumstances.'* The evidence of Mr Andrews is also highly important. Mr J. W. Croker, in his notes on Boswell, attests that he had more than once heard Mr Andrews relate the story, with details *substantially agreeing* with the recital which we have quoted from the *Gentleman's Magazine*. He was unquestionably good evidence for what occurred to himself, and he may be considered as not a bad reporter of the story of the ghost of the lady which he had heard from Lord Lyttelton's own mouth. Mr Croker adds, that Mr Andrews always told the tale 'reluctantly, and with an evidently solemn conviction of its truth.' On the whole, then, the Lyttelton ghost-story may be considered as not only one of the most remarkable from its compound character—one spiritual occurrence supporting another—but also one of the best authenticated, and which it is most difficult to explain away, if we are to allow human testimony to be of the least value.

## PITT AND HIS TAXES.

The great increase in taxation subsequent to the conclusion of the first American war, is a well-known circumstance in modern British history. The national debt, which, previous to the commencement of the Seven Years' War in 1755, fell short of £75,000,000, was, through the expenses entailed by that conflict, increased to nearly £129,000,000 at the peace of Paris in 1763, while, twenty years subsequently, at the peace of Versailles, in 1783, the latter amount had risen to upwards of £244,000,000, in consequence of the ill-judged and futile hostilities with the North American colonies. When William Pitt, the youngest premier and chancellor of exchequer that England had ever seen, and at the time only twenty-four years of age, came into office in December 1783, on the dismissal of the Coalition cabinet, he found the finances in such a condition as to necessitate the imposition of various new taxes, including, among others, the levying of an additional rate on windows, and also of duties on game-certificates, hackney-coaches, and saddle and race horses. This may be regarded as the commencement of a train of additional burdens on the British nation, which afterwards, during the French war, mounted to such a height, that at the present day it seems impossible to comprehend how our fathers could have supported so crushing a load on their resources. Opposite views prevail as to the expediency of the measures followed by England in 1793, when the country, under the leadership of such champions as Pitt and Burke, drifted into a war with the French republic; a war, however, which, in the conjuncture of circumstances attending the relations between the two countries, must have almost inevitably taken place, sooner or later. At the present day, indeed, when more

* Scott's *Letters on Demonology*, 2d edition, p. 350, note.

† Boswell.

‡ The circumstance of the bird is remarkable. James Howel, in one of his *Familiar Letters*, dated July 3, 1632, gives an account of a tombstone he had seen preparing in a stone-cutter's shop in Fleet Street, on which were stated the deaths of four persons of a family named Oxenham, who had been visited just before their demise by a white-breasted bird, which fluttered over their heads or about the bed on which they lay. At the bottom of the inscriptions were given the names of sundry persons, who attested the fact. 'This stone,' says Howel, 'is to be sent to a town hard-by Exeter, where this happened.' —*Familiar Letters*, 5th ed., p. 232.

* Wraxall's *Memoirs*, i. 315.

liberal and enlightened ideas prevail on international questions, and we have also had the benefit of our fathers' experience, such a consummation might possibly have been avoided. Of the straightforwardness and vigorous ability of Pitt throughout his career, there can be no doubt, however one-sided he may have been in his political sympathies; and a tribute of respect, though opinions will differ as to its grounds, is undoubtedly due to 'the pilot that weathered the storm.'

The taxes imposed by Pitt, as might have been anticipated, caused no inconsiderable amount of grumbling among the nation at large. This grumbling, in many instances, resolved itself into waggish jests and caricatures. The story of the Edinburgh wit, who wrote 'PITT'S WORKS, vol. i., vol. ii.,' &c., on the walls of the houses where windows had been blocked up by the proprietors in consequence of the imposition of an additional duty, is a well-known and threadbare joke. Another jest, which

A DEFIANCE TO PITT'S HORSE-TAX—A FARMER RIDING HIS COW TO STOCKPORT MARKET.

took a practical form, was that concocted by a certain Jonathan Thatcher, who, on 27th November 1784, in defiance of the horse-tax, imposed a few months previously by Pitt, rode his *cow* to and from the market of Stockport. A contemporary caricature, representing that scene, is herewith presented to our readers as a historical curiosity.

---

## NOVEMBER 28.

St Stephen, the Younger, martyr, 764. St James of La Marca of Ancona, confessor, 1476.

---

*Born.*—Captain George William Manby, inventor of life-saving apparatus for shipwrecks, 1765, *Hilgay, Norfolk;* Victor Cousin, moral philosopher, 1792.

*Died.*—Pope Gregory III., 741; Dunois, the Bastard of Orleans, 1468; Edward Plantagenet, Earl of Warwick, beheaded, 1499; Cartouche, celebrated robber, executed at Paris, 1721; Charles Buller, statesman and writer, 1848, *London;* Washington Irving, eminent popular writer, 1859, *Irvington, New York;* Baron C. C. J. Bunsen, Prussian statesman, philosophical writer, 1860, *Bonn.*

### THE REV. LANGTON FREEMAN AND HIS SINGULAR MAUSOLEUM.

Among the numerous individuals who have rendered themselves conspicuous by eccentricities of character, few, perhaps, are more noteworthy than an English clergyman who died about eighty years ago.

The Rev. Langton Freeman, whose baptism is registered on 28th November 1710, was rector of Bilton, in Warwickshire. He resided at the retired and somewhat secluded village of Whilton, in Northamptonshire, some ten or twelve miles distant, from which he rode on Sundays to Bilton, to perform his ministerial duties. He was a bachelor, which may, in some measure, account for the oddities which have rendered his name famous in the neighbourhood where he dwelt. Living, as he did, in an old manor-house, and occupying so honoured a position in society, few persons would suppose that a clergyman and gentleman could be guilty of such meanness as to beg his Sunday-dinner from a labouring-man, and occasionally also help himself from the larder of a richer friend. But, to do him justice, the reverend *sorner* remembered all these petty thefts, and in his will bequeathed a recompense to those whom, in his lifetime, he had robbed.

His will is dated 16th September 1783, and his death took place the 9th of October in 1784. That portion of the testament relating to his burial is very curious, and runs thus :—

'In the name of God, amen. I, the Reverend Langton Freeman, of Whilton, in the county of Northampton, clerk, being in a tolerable good state of bodily health, and of a perfect sound and disposing mind, memory, and understanding (praised be God for the same), and being mindful of my death, do therefore make and ordain this my last Will and Testament, as follows : And principally I commend my soul to the mercy of God through the merits of my Redeemer. And first, for four or five days after my decease, and until my body grows offensive, I would not be removed out of the place or bed I shall die on. And then I would be carried or laid in the same bed, decently and privately, in the summer-house now erected in the garden belonging to the dwelling-house, where I now inhabit in Whilton aforesaid, and to be laid in the same bed there, with all the appurtenances thereto belonging ; and to be wrapped in a strong, double winding-sheet, and in all other respects to be interred as near as may be to the description we receive in Holy Scripture of our Saviour's burial. The doors and windows to be locked up and bolted, and to be kept as near in the same manner and state they shall be in at the time of my decease. And I desire that the building, or summer-house, shall be planted around with evergreen-plants, and fenced off with iron or oak pales, and painted of a dark-blue colour ; and for the due performance of this, in manner aforesaid, and for keeping the building ever the same, with the evergreen-plants and rails in proper and decent repair, I give to my nephew, Thomas Freeman, the manor of Whilton, &c.'

All these instructions appear to have been faithfully carried out, and Mr Freeman was duly deposited in the singular mausoleum which he had chosen. Till within the last few years, the summer-house was surrounded with evergreens ; but now the palings are gone, the trees have been cut down, and the structure itself looks like a ruined hovel.

There is a large hole in the roof, through which, about two years ago, some men effected an entrance. With the aid of a candle they made a survey of the burial-place and its tenant ; the latter, a dried up, skinny figure, having apparently the consistence of leather, with one arm laid across the chest, and the other hanging down the body, which, though never embalmed, seems to have remained perfectly incorrupted.

It is rather singular that there is nothing whatever in the parish register respecting the burial of the Rev. Langton Freeman. This may be accounted for, however, by the circumstance of his having been buried in unconsecrated ground.

## WASHINGTON IRVING.

Were the fact not familiar to every one, most English readers of the *Sketch-Book*, *Bracebridge Hall*, and the lives of Goldsmith and Columbus, would be surprised to learn that they were written by an American ; though, indeed, an American to whom England gave success and fame.

Washington Irving's father was a Scotchman, and his mother an Englishwoman. William Irving went to New York about 1763, and was a merchant of that city during the revolution. His son, Washington, was born April 3, 1783, just as the War of Independence had been brought to a successful termination ; and he received the name of its hero, of whom he was destined to be the, so far, most voluminous biographer. His best means of education was his father's excellent library, and his elder brothers were men of literary tastes and pursuits. At sixteen, he began to study law, but he never followed out the profession. He was too modest ever to address a jury, and in the height of his fame, he could never summon the resolution to make a speech, even when toasted at a public dinner. Irving was early a traveller. At the age of twenty-one, he visited the south of Europe on a tour of health and pleasure. On his return to New York, he wrote for his brother's newspaper ; joined with Paulding, Halleck, and Bryant in the *Salmagundi*—papers in the fashion of the *Spectator;* and wrote a comic history of the early settlement of New York, purporting to be the production of a venerable Dutchman, Diedrich Knickerbocker. This work had a great success, and so delighted Sir Walter Scott, that when the author visited him in 1820, he wrote to thank Campbell, who had given him a letter of introduction, for 'one of the best and pleasantest acquaintances he had met in many a day.' Sir Walter did not stop with compliments. Irving could not find a publisher for his *Sketch-Book*, being perhaps too modest to push his fortunes with the craft. He got it printed on his own account by a person named Miller, who failed shortly after. Sir Walter introduced the author to John Murray, who gave him £200 for the copyright, but afterwards increased the sum to £400. Irving then went to Paris, where he wrote *Bracebridge Hall*, and made the acquaintance of Thomas Moore and other literary celebrities. From thence

RESIDENCE OF WASHINGTON IRVING.

he proceeded to Dresden, and wrote the *Tales of a Traveller;* but he found his richest mine in Spain, where, for three months, he resided in the palace of the Alhambra, and employed himself in ransacking its ancient records. Here he wrote his *Life and Voyages of Columbus* (for which Murray paid him 3000 guineas), the *Conquest of Granada, Voyages of the Companions of Columbus*, &c.

By this time America, finding that Irving had become famous abroad—as American authors and artists mostly do, if at all, according to an old proverb—begged him to accept the post of secretary of legation at London ; a highly honourable office indeed, but, in point of emolument, worth only £500 a year. The Oxford University having conferred on him the honorary degree of D.C.L., and one of George IV.'s gold medals, the Americans, a modest people, always proud of European recognition, made him minister at the court of Spain. On his return to America, he retired to a beautiful country-seat, 'Sunnyside,' built in his own 'Sleepy Hollow,' on the banks of the Hudson, where he lived with his brother and nieces, and wrote *Astoria, Captain Bonneville, Goldsmith, Mahomet,* and his last work, the life of his great namesake, Washington. He was never married. In his youth he loved one who died of consumption, and he was faithful to her memory. He died, November 28, 1859, sincerely mourned by the whole world of literature, and by his own countrymen, who have placed his name at the head of the list of authors whom they delight to honour.

---

## NOVEMBER 29.

St Saturninus, bishop of Toulouse, martyr, 257. St Radbod, bishop of Utrecht, confessor, 918.

*Born.*—Margaret, daughter of Henry VII., and queen of James IV. of Scotland, 1489 ; Sir Philip Sidney, poet, 1554, *Penshurst, Kent;* Dr Peter Heylin, theological and historical writer, 1600, *Burford, Oxfordshire;* John Ray, eminent naturalist, 1628, *Black Notley, Essex.*

*Died.*—Pope Clement IV., 1268, *Viterbo;* Philippe le Bel, king of France, 1314, *Fontainebleau;* Roger Mortimer, paramour of Isabella, Edward II.'s queen, executed at Smithfield, 1330 ; Charles IV., Emperor of Germany, 1378, *Prague;* Cardinal Thomas Wolsey, minister of Henry VIII., 1530, *St Mary's Abbey, Leicester;* Frederick, Elector Palatine, son-in-law of James I. of England, 1632, *Metz;* Brian Walton, bishop of Chester, editor of the Polyglot Bible, 1661, *London;* Prince Rupert, of Bavaria, cavalier-general, 1682, *London;* Marcello Malpighi, eminent anatomist, 1694, *Rome;* Anthony Wood or à Wood, antiquarian writer, 1695, *Oxford;* Maria Theresa, queen of Hungary, 1780, *Vienna.*

### THE EARL OF MARCH: 'MORTIMER'S HOLE.'

To the traveller approaching Nottingham by rail from the Derby side, the commanding position of its ruined castle cannot but be an object of interest. Though commerce has completely surrounded the rock it stands upon with workshops, wharves, and modern dwelling-houses, the castle seems literally 'to dwell alone.' Associations of a character peculiar to itself cluster round it. It has a distinctive existence—claims a distinct parentage from the puny, grovelling erections beneath it—and soars as much beyond them by the events it calls to mind, as by its proud and lofty position. Its history, in fact, is interwoven in the history of the nation ; and part of the glory and shame of its country's deeds rests upon it.

The old castle must have frowned with unusual gloominess when Isabella, queen of Edward II., and her unprincipled paramour, Mortimer, took up their abode in it. The queen had rebelled against and deposed her husband. Mortimer had accomplished his death. And with the young king, Edward III., in their tutelage, they tyrannised over the country, and squandered its treasures as they pleased.

As a fresh instance of her favour, the frail princess had recently elevated Mortimer to the earldom of March. But the encroaching arrogance of the haughty minion was awakening in the minds of the barons a determination to curb his insolence and overgrown power. This spirit of revenge was still further excited by the execution of the king's uncle, the Earl of Kent, who appears to have been slain merely to shew that there was none too high to be smitten down if he dared to make himself obnoxious to the profligate rulers. The bow, however, was this time strained beyond its strength. The blow that was intended to quell the rising storm of indignation, rebounded, with increased force, on the guilty Mortimer, and proved his own destruction. For all parties, weary of his insolence and oppression, were forgetting their former feuds in the common anxiety to work his overthrow, and this last savage act of his government aroused them to a full sense of their danger, and gave increased intensity to their hatred and desire of vengeance. Besides which, they saw in the young king, now in his eighteenth year, signs of growing impatience of the yoke which Mortimer, as regent, had imposed on his authority. Daily they poured complaints into the royal ear of the profligacy, the exactions, and the illegal practices of the paramour, and found in Edward a willing listener. At length he was brought to see his own danger—to look upon Mortimer as the murderer of his father and uncle, the usurper of power which ought to be in his own hands, the spoiler of his people, and the man who was bringing daily dishonour to himself and the nation by an illicit connection with his royal mother. He determined, accordingly, to humble the pride of the arrogant chief, and redress the public grievances.

A parliament was summoned to meet at Nottingham, about Michaelmas 1330. The castle was occupied by the dowager-queen and the Earl of March, attended by a guard of a hundred and eighty knights, with their followers ; while the king, with his queen, Philippa, and a small retinue, took up his abode in the town. The number of their attendants, and the jealous care with which the castle was guarded, implied suspicion in the minds of the guilty pair. Every night the gates of the fortress were locked, and the keys delivered to the queen, who slept with them under her pillow. But with all their precautions, justice was more than a match for their villany. Sir William Mountacute, under the sanction of his sovereign, summoned to his aid several nobles, on whose loyalty and good faith he could depend, and obtained the king's warrant for the apprehension of the Earl of March and others. The plot was now ripe for execution. For a time, however, the inaccessible nature of the castle-rock, and the vigilance with which the passes were guarded, appeared to present an insuperable obstacle to the accomplishment of their designs. Could Sir William Eland, the constable of the castle, be won over, and induced to betray the fortress into their hands? The experiment was worth a trial, and Mountacute undertook the delicate task. Sir William joyfully fell in with a proposition which enabled him at once to testify his loyalty to his sovereign and his detestation of the haughty tyrant. The result of the interview is thus quaintly described by one of the old chroniclers, whose manuscript is quoted by Deering:

'Tho saide Sir William Montagu to the constabill in herynge of all them that were helpyng to the quarrel. "Now certis dere ffrendes us behoveth for to worche and done by your Queyntyse to take the Mortimer, sith ye be the keeper of the castell and have the kayes in your warde." "Sir," quod the constabill, "woll ye understoude that the yats of the castell beth loken with lokys, and Queen Isabell sent hidder by night for the kayes thereof, and they be layde under the chemsell of her beddis hede unto the morrow, and so I may not come into the castell by the yats no manner of wyse; but yet I know another weye by an aley that stretchith oute of the ward under the earthe into the castell that goeth into the west, which aley Queen Isabell, ne none of her meayne, ne the Mortimer, ne none of his companye knowith it not, and so I shall lede you through the aley, and so ye shall come into the castell without spyes of any man that beth your enemies."'

Everything being now arranged, on the night of Friday, October 19, 1330, Edward and his loyal associates were conducted by Sir William Eland through a secret passage in the rock to the interior of the castle. Proceeding at once to a chamber adjoining the queen's apartment, they found the object of their search in close consultation with the bishop of Lincoln and others of his party. The Earl of March was seized; Sir Hugh Turplinton and Sir John Monmouth, two of the state-guards, were slain in attempting to rescue him from the king's associates; and the queen, hearing the tumult, and suspecting the cause, rushed into the room in an agony of terror, exclaiming: 'Fair son, fair son, have pity on the gentle Mortimer!' Notwithstanding the cries and entreaties of the weeping Isabella, her beloved earl was torn from her presence, and hurried down the secret passage by which his captors entered, and which has ever since been designated *Mortimer's Hole.* With so much secrecy and despatch was this stratagem executed, that the guards on the ramparts of the castle were not disturbed, and the good people of Nottingham knew nothing of the enterprise till the following day, when the arrest of Mortimer's sons and several of his adherents by the royalists, gave a significant and acceptable indication that the luxurious and profligate usurpation of the Earl of March had at length been terminated by kingly authority.

MORTIMER'S HOLE, NOTTINGHAM CASTLE—THE PASSAGE THROUGH WHICH MONTACUTE AND HIS PARTY ENTERED.

Mortimer was conveyed by a strong guard to the Tower of London. Edward repaired to Leicester, whence he issued writs for the assembling of a new parliament at Westminster, for the purpose of hearing charges against the late administration, and redressing the grievances under which the kingdom had laboured. At this parliament Mortimer was impeached and convicted in a most summary manner of high treason, and other crimes. No proof in evidence of his guilt was heard, and he was condemned to die as a traitor, by being drawn and hanged on the common gallows; a sentence which was executed at 'The Elms,' in Smithfield, on the 29th of November 1330. His body was allowed to hang two days on the gallows, and was then interred in the church of the Greyfriars.

## THE FALL OF WOLSEY.

Any new information regarding the history of Cardinal Wolsey must ever be welcome. A few items of this description were some years ago obtained from a state manuscript of the reign of Henry VIII., then in the possession of Sir Walter C. Trevelyan, Bart., F.S.A., a junior member of whose family was one of the chaplains to King Henry. Through him it may have found its way to the venerable seat of Nettlecombe, in the county of Somerset, where this manuscript, relating to domestic expenses and payments, has, for some centuries, been deposited.

Mr Payne Collier, in describing this document to the Society of Antiquaries, says: 'We pass over the manner in which Wolsey appears, without check or control, to have issued his written warrants or verbal commandments for payments of money for nearly all purposes, and upon all occasions, even for the despatch of his own letters to Rome; an entry of this kind is made in the first month to which the manuscript applies. Neither is it necessary to dwell upon the items which relate to the known part he took upon the trial of Queen Katherine, since upon this portion of the subject nearly all the authorities, from Hall to Lord Herbert of Cherbury, concur. It is to be observed, with reference to the transactions in which Wolsey was concerned, that no warrant was issued by him for the payment of any sum of money after the 19th of June 1529, when Sir Thomas Fitzgerald, the Irish knight, had a present made to him of £66, 13*s.* 4*d.*, the order for which was given by Wolsey. After this date, the warrants were those of the king, or of particular officers, and it does not seem that the cardinal was allowed to interfere; for his disgrace had then commenced, in consequence of the vexatious postponements in the trial of the divorce. Neither does his name occur again in this document, until we come upon it, as it were, by surprise, where he is spoken of by his double title of Cardinal of York and Bishop of Winchester, in connection with a payment to him of one thousand marks out of the revenues of Winchester. The terms are remarkable. "Item, paide to the Lorde Cardynall of Yorke and Bishope of Wincestre, xviij die Martii, by the Kynge's warraunte, datede at Windesour, xvj. die Martii, in the advancement of his hole yeres pension of M. mrs. by the yeere, out of the bishopricke of Winchester, which yere shall fully ende and ronne at Michilmas next cumming—DClxvj$^{li.}$ xiij$^{s.}$ iiij$^{d.}$"'

This quotation is valuable, both biographically and historically, since it settles the question, whether the sum granted to Wolsey were 1000 marks, as Stow, in his Annals, asserts; or 4000 marks, as it stands in some manuscripts of Cavendish's life of the cardinal. By the above entry, confirmed by a subsequent passage in Cavendish, it is clear that, in consideration of the necessities of the cardinal, it was to be allowed him beforehand. After all his pomp and prosperity—after all his vast accumulations of wealth—after all his piles of plate, and heaps of cloth of gold, and costly apparel—Wolsey, in March 1530 (judging from this entry), was reduced to the necessity of obtaining a loan of a thousand marks; this, too, to carry him to his exile at York, whither his enemies had, by this date, induced the fickle, selfish, and luxurious king to banish his former favourite.

Of Wolsey's subsequent residence at Cawood, we find in this manuscript, an 'Item to David Vincent, by the king's warrant, for his charge, being sent to Cawood, in the north contrie, at suche time as the cardenall was sicke.' As the sum charged was considerable—namely, £35, 6*s.* 8*d.* (more than £200 present money)—we may infer, perhaps, that the messenger, whom Cavendish styles his 'fellow Vincent,' made some stay there, watching the progress of Wolsey's illness, and sending intelligence to the king, who was more anxious for the death than for the life of his victim, in order that he might seize upon the remains of his movables. It is quite evident that the cardinal was not, at this period, so destitute as many have supposed, and that he had carried with him a very large quantity of plate, of which the king possessed himself the moment the breath was out of the body of its owner. Among the payments for January, 22 Henry VIII., we read, in the Trevelyan manuscript, that *two persons were employed three entire days in London, 'weighing the plate from Cawood, late the Cardinalle's.'* Such are the unceremonious terms used in the original memorandum, communicating a striking fact, of which we now hear for the first time.

From Cawood, as is well known, Wolsey was brought to the Earl of Shrewsbury's seat, at Sheffield Park; and thither messengers were unexpectedly sent to convey the cardinal to the Tower. This state manuscript shews that Sir William Kingston, captain of the guard, was sent to arrest the cardinal; and that forty pounds were paid to Kingston in November 1530, for the expenses of his journey, as follows: 'Item, to Sir William Kingston, knight-capitain of the kinges garde, sent to Therle of Shrewsebury with divers of the kinges garde, for the conveyance of the Cardinall of Yorke to the Tower of London, in prest for their charges—xl$^{li.}$'

The cardinal was taken ill on the road: the Earl of Shrewsbury encouraged him to hope for recovery, but the cardinal replied that he could not live, and discoursed learnedly about his ailment, dysentery, which he said, within eight days, if there were no change, would necessarily produce 'excoriation of the entrails, or delirium, or death.' This was on the eighth day, when he confidently expected his death; and he expired after the clock had struck eight, according to his own prediction; 'the very hour,' says Shakspeare, 'himself had foretold would be his last.' He had reached Leicester three days previously: as he entered the gate of the monastery, he said: 'Father abbot, I am come to lay my bones among you;' and so the event proved: the monks carried him to his bed, on which he expired on the 29th of November 1530. Shakspeare has little altered the words he used on his death-bed, though they were spoken to Kingston, and not, as in the play, to Cromwell:

> 'But had I served my God with half the zeal
> I served my king, he would not in mine age
> Have left me naked to mine enemies.'
>
> *Henry VIII.*, Act iii. sc. 2.

It is a curious and novel circumstance, brought to light in the document before us, that, exactly two months before the day of Wolsey's death, the dean and canons of Cardinal's (now Christ-church) College, Oxford, had so completely separated themselves from Wolsey, and from all the interest which he had taken in their establishment, that, instead of resorting to him for the comparatively small sum of £184, for the purpose of carrying on the architectural works, they applied to the king for the loan of the money. The entry of this loan is made in the state document under consideration, 'upon an obligation to be repaid agayne, on this side of Cristinmas next cumming;' so that even this trifling advance could not be made out of the royal purse, filled to repletion by the sacrifice of Wolsey, without an express stipulation that the money was to be returned before Christmas.

Everything in Wolsey (says Mr Collier), his vices and his virtues—were great. He seemed incapable of mediocrity in anything: voluptuous and profuse, rapacious and of insatiable ambition, but too magnanimous to be either cruel or revengeful, he was an excellent master and patron, and a fair and open enemy. If we despise the abjectness which he exhibited in his first fall, let it be remembered from and to what he fell—from a degree of wealth and grandeur which no subject on earth now enjoys, to a condition of ignominy and want, with all the terrible and unknown consequences to which he might be exposed from the merciless and unscrupulous temper of the king.

A picturesque tower or gate-house, the only remains of Wolsey's palace, exists, to this day, at Esher. Its erection has been commonly attributed to the cardinal; he is, however, thought to have had little time for building at Esher; and the architecture of the towers is of an earlier period than Wolsey's. With better authority, the erection of this building is attributed to Bishop Wainfleet, who preceded the cardinal in the possession of the see of Winchester by about eighty years, and is known to have erected 'a stately brick mansion and gate-house' in Esher Park. It is now luxuriantly mantled with ivy: the interior has a very skilfully-wrought newel staircase, of brick; and in the roof is introduced the principle of the oblique arch, a supposed invention of much later date.

In estimating the abjectness of Wolsey, we should also take into account the abject submission which he had long been taught to exhibit before the tyrant—

'Whose smile was transport, and whose frown was fate.'

Of this arbitrary sovereign, one circumstance is disclosed by Cavendish, utterly surpassing all the measures of common iniquity. When Wolsey was sued in a premunire by Henry's order, and all his movables were seized, the chest which contained a dispensation under the king's sign-manual for the very facts on which he was proceeded against, was withheld, and he was prevented from adducing a document, which, if law and reason had any scope, would have preserved him. His misfortunes, and the conversation of some devout and mortified Carthusians, appear to have awakened the first sense of genuine religion in his mind. During his retreat at Cawood, while the king was persecuting him with one refinement of ingenious cruelty after another, he was calm and composed; and here, for the first time, he seems to have exercised, or even comprehended, the character of a Christian bishop. He reconciled enemies, he preached, he visited—nay, he was humble. But this character he was not long permitted to sustain. He had talents for popularity, which, in his delicate and difficult circumstances, he was, perhaps, not sufficiently reserved in displaying. He was preparing to be enthroned at York, with a degree of magnificence which, though far inferior to that which had been practised by his predecessors, was yet sufficient to awaken the jealousy of Henry. The final arrest at Cawood ensued. It is unnecessary, as well as uncharitable, to suppose what there is no proof of—that he died of poison, either administered by himself or others. The obvious and proximate cause of his death was affliction. A great heart, oppressed with indignities, and beset with dangers, at length gave way; and Wolsey, under circumstances affectingly detailed by Cavendish, received, in Leicester Abbey, the two last charities of a death-bed and a grave.

## THE FIRST NEWSPAPER PRINTED BY STEAM.

The 29th of November 1814 forms an important date in the history of printing, and consequently in that of civilisation. It was the day on which a newspaper was for the first time printed by steam, instead of manual power. It seems appropriate that the *Times*, the newspaper which of all others throughout the world is now regarded as the most influential, should have been the one that inaugurated this vast improvement. The common printing-press, though much improved during the second half of the last century, could seldom strike off more than two or three hundred impressions per hour, with one man to ink the types, and another to work the press. To set forth the importance of machine-printing, it is only necessary to remark that, without such an invention, the production of a large impression of a newspaper was mechanically impossible, as the news would have been stale before the end of the impression was accomplished. In 1790, Mr W. Nicholson obtained letters-patent for a machine similar in many respects to those which have been adopted in later years; but it does not appear that he brought his invention into practice. Steam-power, it was known, would effect movements in machinery of almost every imaginable kind; but it was the enterprise of the proprietors of the *Times* that enabled inventors to surmount the difficulties of applying such power to printing-presses.

It was the *second* Mr John Walter (the son of the first and the father of the present proprietor), whose management of the *Times* began in 1803, that gave so immense an impetus to rapid printing. It took many hours to strike off the 3000 or 4000 copies of which the daily issue of the *Times* then consisted; and Mr Walter was dissatisfied with that slow process. In 1804, Thomas Martyn, a compositor in his employment, produced a model of a self-acting machine for working the press; and Walter supplied him with money to continue his ingenious labours. The pressmen, however, were so bitterly hostile to any such innovation, that Martyn was placed almost in fear of his life; and as Walter did not at that time possess a very large capital, the scheme fell to the ground. John Walter, however, was not a man to be beaten by difficulties; he bore in mind Martyn's invention, and bided his time. He encouraged inventors from all quarters; and as his pecuniary means increased, he became able to pay them well for their services. In 1814, he consented that König's patent for a printing-machine should be tried—not in the actual printing-office of the *Times*, but in adjoining premises, for fear of the hostility of the pressmen. König and his assistant, Bauer, worked quietly in these premises for many months, gradually perfecting the machine. The proceedings on the momentous 29th of November were highly characteristic of Mr Walter. 'The night on which this curious machine was first brought into use in its new abode,' says his biographer,* 'was one of great anxiety, and even alarm. The suspicious pressmen had threatened destruction to any one whose inventions might suspend their employment —"destruction to him and his traps." They were directed to wait for expected news from the continent. It was about six o'clock in the morning, when Mr Walter went into the press-room, and astonished its occupants by telling them that the *Times* was already printed by steam; that if they attempted violence, there was a force ready to suppress it; but that if they were peaceable, their wages should be continued to every one of them till similar employment could be procured. The promise was no doubt faithfully performed; and, having so said, he distributed several copies among them. Thus was this most hazardous enterprise undertaken and successfully carried through; and printing by steam, on an almost gigantic scale, given to the world.'

The leading article of the *Times*, on the 29th of November 1814, adverted to the great event in the following terms: 'Our journal of this day presents to the public the practical result of the greatest improvement connected with printing, since the discovery of the art itself. The reader of this paragraph now holds in his hands one of the many thousand impressions of the *Times* newspaper which were taken off last night by a mechanical apparatus. A system of machinery, almost organic, has been devised and arranged, which, while it relieves the human frame of its most laborious efforts in printing, far exceeds all human powers in rapidity and despatch. That the magnitude of the invention may be justly appreciated by its effects, we may inform the public that, after the letters are placed by the compositors, and enclosed in what is called the "form," little more remains for man to do than to attend upon and watch this unconscious agent in its operations. The machine is then merely supplied with paper. Itself places the form, inks it, adjusts the paper to the newly-inked type, stamps the sheet, and gives it forth to the hands of the attendant, at the same time withdrawing the form for a fresh coat of ink, which itself again distributes, to meet the ensuing sheet, now advancing for impression; and the whole of these complicated acts is performed with such a velocity and simultaneousness of movement, that no less than 1100 sheets are impressed in one hour. That the completion of an invention of this kind, not the effect of chance, but the result of mechanical combinations, methodically arranged in the mind of the artist, should be attended with many obstructions and much delay, may be readily admitted. Our share in the event has, indeed, only been the application of the discovery, under an agreement with the patentees, to our own particular business; yet few can conceive, even with this limited interest, the various disappointments and deep anxiety to which we have, for a long course of time, been subjected. Of the person who made this discovery, we have but little to add. Sir Christopher Wren's noblest monument is to be found in the building which he erected; so is the best tribute of praise, which we are capable of offering to the inventor of the printing machine, comprised in the description, which we have feebly sketched, of the powers and utility of the invention. It must suffice to say further, that he is a Saxon by birth; that his name is König; and that the invention has been executed under the direction of his friend and countryman, Bauer.' We have now before us two consecutive numbers of the *Times*—the last that was printed at the hand-press (November 28, 1814), and the first that was printed by machinery (November 29); the latter is far cleaner and more legible than the former—possibly because a new fount of type was used. König's machine was, however, very complicated, and was soon afterwards superseded by one invented by Messrs Applegath and Cowper. As improved, this machine ultimately printed 8000 impressions per hour, but was superseded by the Hoe machine. This in its turn gave way to the famous Walter press, patented in 1866, which prints at an average rate of 12,000 copies per hour, and can do good work at the rate of 17,000 copies.

* In the *Times*, 29th July 1847.

## REMARKABLE WAGERS.

On Monday, 29th November 1773, Mr Foster Powell, an attorney's clerk, commenced a journey from London to York and back again, on foot; a feat which he accomplished in the space of six days, reaching York on the Wednesday evening, and starting again the following morning for London, where he arrived on the evening of Saturday, the 4th December. By this extraordinary effort of pedestrianism, he netted the sum of a hundred guineas, which had been staked on his success.

It has been remarked that a collection of curious or foolish wagers would make an interesting volume. After much ransacking, we have succeeded in unearthing a few of the most remarkable instances, which we now present to our readers.

A wager is said to have been won by Sir Walter Raleigh from the Virgin Queen, on the question of how much smoke is contained in a pound of tobacco. A pound of the article in question was weighed, burned, and then weighed again in ashes. The question was held to be satisfactorily settled by determining the weight of the smoke as exactly that of the tobacco, before being burned, minus the residuum of ashes. The fact of the ashes having received an additional weight by combination with the oxygen of the atmosphere, and also the circumstance of numerous imperceptible gases being evolved by the process of combustion, were alike unthought of by Elizabeth and her knight.

Sir John Pakington, called 'Lusty Pakington,' and by Queen Elizabeth, 'My Temperance,' laid a wager of £3000 to swim against three noble courtiers from Westminster Bridge to Greenwich, but her majesty interposed to prevent any further procedure on the bet. A gentleman of the name of Corbet, a distinguished family near Shrewsbury, betted that his leg was the handsomest in the county or kingdom; and staked immense estates on the point. He won the wager, and a picture is still preserved in the family mansion, representing the process of measuring the legs of the various disputants. A dispute of a similar kind, between two celebrated beauties in the Scottish metropolis, occasioned a considerable amount both of amusement and scandal in the Modern Athens, about half a century ago. It is recorded of Lord Spencer, that he cut off his coat-tails, and laid a successful wager that such a mutilated style of garment would become fashionable. And an amusing bet, though for the very trifling amount of five shillings, is related to have been decided in 1806, in the Castleyard, York, between Thomas Hodgson and Samuel Whitehead, as to which should succeed in assuming the most *singular* and *original* character. Hodgson appeared decorated with ten-guinea, five-guinea, and guinea notes on his coat and waistcoat, a row of five-guinea notes and a purse of gold round his hat, whilst to his back a paper was attached, with the words, 'John Bull.' Whitehead appeared dressed like a woman on one side, with a silk stocking and slipper, and one half of his face painted. The other half of his body resembled a negro in a man's dress, with a boot and spur. One would have thought, that so far as presenting a ridiculous spectacle and making a fool of himself, he ought to have won the wager, but it was decided in favour of his companion. How far the latter owed his success to the prevailing weakness of humanity towards wealth or the display of it, is a question which we think might be fairly mooted.

A gentleman laid a wager to a considerable amount, that he would stand for a whole day on London Bridge with a trayful of sovereigns, fresh from the Mint, and be unable to find a purchaser for them at a penny apiece. Not one was disposed of.

In the roaring, hard-drinking days of the last century, wagers of all kinds were plentiful. Something similar to the case of Hodgson and Whitehead above related was the bet made in relation to Heidegger, Master of the Revels to George II., whose ugliness it was alleged impossible to surpass. The slums of London were ransacked from one end to the other, and at last, in St Giles's an old woman was found, who it was thought would bear away the palm. On being confronted with Heidegger, the judges maintained that the latter, who made himself a party to the dispute with the greatest good-humour, had now fairly met with his match, when it was suggested that he should put on the old woman's bonnet. The additional hideousness thus imparted was such, that Heidegger was unanimously declared as the undoubted holder of the championship of ugliness. A wager of a more intellectual description was laid for a thousand guineas in 1765 between two noblemen, one of whom had constructed a machine which he maintained would propel a boat at the rate of twenty-five miles an hour. A canal was prepared for the experiment near the banks of the Thames; but the tackle broke, and the wager was lost, before the apparatus had an opportunity of being tested. In the *Annual Register* for 1788, we find it stated in the chronicle of occurrences, that a young Irish gentleman, on 21st September of that year, started for Constantinople, having engaged to walk from London to Constantinople and back again within a year. Twenty thousand pounds are stated as being dependent on the issue of the wager, but we have no further accounts of the affair.

The subject-matter of wagers has sometimes taken rather a grim form. A well-known story is related of a member of a party of revellers who engaged, in a fit of bravado, to enter the vault of a church at midnight, and in proof of his having done so, to stick a fork into a coffin which had been recently deposited there. He accomplished his object, and was returning triumphantly, when he felt himself suddenly caught, and was so overpowered by terror that he fell into a swoon, and was found in this condition shortly afterwards on the floor of the vault by his companions, who, alarmed at his long absence, had come out to look for him. The fork which he had stuck into the coffin had caught hold of his long cloak, and thus occasioned a fit of terror which had nearly proved fatal. An incident of this nature is credibly recorded to have taken place in London in the last century, the scene being one of the vaults beneath Westminster Abbey.

It is only consistent with the British propensity for sport and athletic effort, that so many wagers should be recorded in connection with feats of pedestrianism. Thus we are told that on the 24th July 1750, a man upwards of forty years of age, for a wager of fifty guineas, ran from Shoreditch to the eight mile-stone beyond Edmonton in fifty minutes, having been allowed an hour for performing the exploit. In 1763, one of the Gloucestershire militia undertook, for a wager of £300, to walk from London to Bristol in twenty hours. This he accomplished in nineteen hours and thirty-five minutes, having quitted London at midnight, and arrived at Bristol the following evening. In the same year, a shepherd ran on Moulsey Hurst, fifteen miles in one hour and twenty-eight minutes, having engaged to do so in an hour and a half. And in July 1809, was completed the famous pedestrian feat of Captain Barclay, who won £3000 on a wager that he would walk a thousand miles in a thousand successive hours. The captain's entry into Newmarket after the accomplishment of his undertaking, was heralded by a peal of bells. Numerous other pedestrian bets of a similar character to Barclay's have subsequently been made, and are familiar to all readers of sporting literature.

Till recently, the fulfilment of an obligation constituted by wager, contrary to what has all along prevailed in Scotland, could be enforced in English courts of law. Latterly, indeed, they were looked upon with great disfavour; but the judges, nevertheless, still found themselves bound to take cognizance of them, however contrary such matters might seem to legal seriousness and dignity. A few of the cases recorded are curious enough. Perhaps one of the most noted is the action tried before Lord Mansfield in July 1777, on a wager which had been laid regarding the sex of the celebrated Chevalier D'Eon. A great deal of evidence, much more curious than edifying, was brought forward; and it was maintained by the defendant, that the action ought to be dismissed as a gambling, indecent, and unnecessary proceeding. The lord chief-justice, however, took a different view; and while expressing a strong disapprobation of such cases, laid down that pactions proceeding on wagers were not contrary to the law of England, and that therefore the jury should find a verdict for the plaintiff. A verdict for £700 was accordingly returned. In another case before Lord Mansfield, in the Court of King's Bench, the sum of 500 guineas was sought to be recovered by Lord March from Mr Pigott, on a wager which the plaintiff had laid with the defendant as to whether Sir William Codrington or old Mr Pigot should first die. The latter died suddenly of gout in the head the morning previous to the laying of the wager. Owing to this circumstance, the defendant maintained that there was no bet; but the court and jury ruled otherwise, and a verdict was returned for the full amount claimed, and costs. An amusing case is related to have been tried at the Kingston assizes, where a Mr Courtney was sued for the payment of 100 guineas on a wager which had been laid that the plaintiff should furnish three horses which should go ninety miles in three hours. This he performed to the letter, but it was by starting all the three horses together, so that they had only thirty miles each to run within the three hours, an undertaking which they accomplished with the utmost ease. The court supported the defendant's view of the transaction, that it was an unfair bet, and a verdict in his favour was consequently given. In another action, tried before the Court of Common Pleas, the plaintiff sought to enforce a claim on a wager for 'a rump and dozen,' which Sir James Mansfield was inclined to dismiss, because he did not *judicially* know the meaning of 'a rump and dozen,' but he was overruled by Mr Justice Heath, who remarked that they knew quite well *privately* that 'a rump and dozen' meant a dinner and wine, an agreement, as his lordship observed, in which he could discover no illegality.

Many similar cases might be related, but we shall restrict ourselves to two more. One of these was an action brought at the York assizes in 1812, by the *Reverend* B. Gilbert against Sir Mark M. Sykes, Bart. At a dinner-party in his own house, the latter, in the course of a conversation on the hazard to which the life of Bonaparte was exposed, had offered, on receiving a hundred guineas, to pay a guinea a day as long as Napoleon should remain alive. Mr Gilbert suddenly closed with the proposal, sent the hundred guineas to the baronet, and the latter continued to pay the clergyman a guinea a day for nearly three years. At last he declined to pay any longer, and an action was brought to enforce the fulfilment of the obligation. It was contended by the defendant's counsel, that he had been surprised into the bet by the clergyman's hasty acceptance of it, and also that the transaction was an illegal one, seeing that Mr Gilbert, having a beneficial interest in the life of Bonaparte, might, in the event of invasion, be tempted to use all means for the preservation of the life of an enemy of his country. The jury returned a verdict for the defendant; but on the case being brought before the Court of King's Bench, a rule was granted by Lord Ellenborough, to shew cause why the verdict should not be set aside and a new trial granted, as in his lordship's opinion the fact of a contract was clearly established, and unless anything of an immoral or impolitic tendency could be proved, the agreement must be supported. On the ground last mentioned, the rule was ultimately discharged and a new trial refused; the judges finding that such a wager was illegal, from its tendency to produce public mischief, as, on the one hand, an undue interest was created in the preservation of the life of a public enemy, and on the other, a temptation might be induced to plot the assassination of Bonaparte, any suspicion of which ought to be carefully guarded against by the nation at large.—The other case to which we have referred, was an action brought on a wager, that the celebrated Johanna Southcott would be delivered of a son, on or before the 1st of November 1814. As the party in question was a single woman, it was held that no claim of action could be sustained, as the wager involved the perpetration of an immorality. On similar grounds, it has been ruled that no action was maintainable on a bet respecting the issue of a boxing-match, such a proceeding being a breach of the peace.

By the gambling act passed in 1845, all agreements whatever founded on any gaming or betting transaction, are declared absolutely null and void, and no action for their enforcement can be sustained. The courts of law have thus been saved the expenditure of much valuable time, to the postponement often of important business, on the discussion of frivolous and unedifying questions.

---

# NOVEMBER 30.

St Andrew, apostle. Saints Sapor and Isaac, bishops; Mahanes, Abraham, and Simeon, martyrs, 339. St Narses, bishop, and companions, martyrs, 343.

## ST ANDREW.

St Andrew was the son of Jonas, a fisherman of Bethsaida, in Galilee, and was the brother of Simon Peter, but whether elder or younger we are not informed in Scripture. He was one of the two disciples of John the Baptist, to whom the latter exclaimed, as he saw Jesus pass by: 'Behold the Lamb of God!' On hearing these words, we are informed that the two individuals in question followed Jesus, and having accosted him, were invited by the Saviour to remain with him for that day. Thereafter, Andrew went in quest of his brother Simon Peter, and brought him to Christ, a circumstance which has invested the former apostle with a special pre-eminence.

After the Ascension, the name of St Andrew is not mentioned in the New Testament, but he is believed to have travelled as a missionary through Asiatic and European Scythia; to have afterwards passed through Thrace, Macedonia, and Epirus into Achaia; and at the city of Patra, in the last-named region, to have suffered martyrdom about 70 A.D. The Roman proconsul, it is said, caused him to be first scourged and then crucified. The latter punishment he underwent in a peculiar manner, being fastened by cords instead of nails to the cross, to produce a lingering death by hunger and thirst; whilst the instrument of punishment itself, instead of being T-shaped, was in the form of an X, or what is termed a cross decussate. We are further informed that a Christian lady of rank, named Maximela, caused the body of St Andrew to be embalmed and honourably interred; and that in the earlier part of the fourth century, it was removed by the Emperor Constantine to Byzantium, or Constantinople, where it was deposited in a church erected in honour of the Twelve Apostles. The history of the relics does not end here, for we are informed that, about thirty years after the death of Constantine, in 368 A. D., a pious Greek monk, named Regulus or Rule, conveyed the remains of St Andrew to Scotland, and there deposited them on the eastern coast of Fife, where he built a church, and where afterwards arose the renowned city and cathedral of St Andrews. Whatever credit may be given to this legend, it is certain that St Andrew has been regarded, from time immemorial, as the patron saint of Scotland; and his day, the 30th of November, is a favourite occasion of social and national reunion, amid Scotchmen residing in England and other places abroad.

The commencement of the ecclesiastical year is regulated by the feast of St Andrew, the nearest Sunday to which, whether before or after, constitutes the first Sunday in Advent,* or the period of four weeks which heralds the approach of Christmas. St Andrew's Day is thus sometimes the first, and sometimes the last festival in the Christian year.

---

*Born.*—Sir Henry Savile, eminent scholar and mathematician, 1549, *Over Bradley, Yorkshire;* Jonathan Swift, humorous and political writer, 1667, *Dublin;* John Toland, sceptical writer, 1669, *Ireland;* Mark Lemon, dramatist and miscellaneous writer, 1809, *London.*

*Died.*—Euripides, tragic dramatist, 406 B.C.; Edmund Ironside, colleague of King Canute, assassinated 1016; William Gilbert, celebrated writer on magnetism, 1603, *Colchester;* John Selden, politician, and legal writer, author of *Table-talk*, 1654, *London;* Maurice, Marshal Saxe, 1750, *Castle of Chambord;* James Sheridan Knowles, dramatist, 1862, *Torquay.*

## SELDEN.

The seventeenth century was rich in great lawyers, but few could take precedence of John Selden. In the contests between the Stuarts and their parliaments he was constantly referred to for advice, and his advice he gave without fear or favour. James I., in 1621, cast him into prison for counselling the Commons to resist his will, and in 1629 Charles I. committed him to the Tower for a similar offence; yet neither the tyranny of the crown nor the applause of the people could make him swerve from his persistent integrity. He was not a cold-blooded reasoner, but a patriot, whose motto was 'Liberty above all;' nevertheless his proud distinction was, that in the tumults and excitement of a stormy age he preserved his reason and independence unimpaired. A mediator is usually an unpopular character, but Selden commanded the respect alike of Royalist and Roundhead. Clarendon writes of him: 'Mr Selden was a person whom no character can flatter, or transmit in any expressions equal to his virtue. He was of so stupendous learning in all kinds, and in all languages, that a man would have thought he had been entirely conversant among books, and had never spent an hour but in reading and writing; yet his humanity, courtesy, and affability was such, that he would have been thought to have been bred in the best courts, but that his good-nature, charity, and delight in doing good, and in communicating all he knew, exceeded that breeding.'

Selden's learning was indeed prodigious. From his youth he was a hard student, and having a rare memory, he seldom forgot what he had read. While quite a young man, he had earned a high reputation as a jurist. He was no orator, but men resorted to him for his opinion rather than his rhetoric, and his practice lay rather in his chamber than in the law-courts. He wrote many books; and a *History of Tithes*, published in 1618, provoked much excitement in consequence of his denying the divine, while admitting the legal right of the clergy to tithes. He was summoned in consequence before the High Commission Court, but without further result than the exaction from him of an expression of sorrow for creating disturbance, no retractation being made of the opinion which he had expressed. Few except antiquaries at this day disturb Selden's works, but his memory is kept green in literature by means of a collection of his *Table-talk* made by Milward, his secretary for twenty years. Of this choice volume Coleridge in a somewhat extravagant vein says: 'There is more weighty bullion sense in Selden's *Table-talk* than I ever found in the same number of pages in any uninspired writer.' The *Table-talk* affords a fine idea of Selden, and confirms Clarendon's eulogy when he says: 'In his conversation Selden was the most clear discourser, and had the best faculty of making hard things easy, and of presenting them to the understanding of any man that hath been known.' Not unfrequently also, over some bright saying, will the reader be ready to exclaim with Coleridge: 'Excellent! Oh! to have been with Selden over his glass of wine, making every accident an outlet and a vehicle for wisdom.' Throughout the *Table-talk* there are evidences of his independent and impartial temper; High Churchmen and Puritans suffer equally from his blows. Of women his opinion is generally contemptuous. For instance, he says:

'*Of Marriage.*—Marriage is a desperate thing. The frogs in Esop were extreme wise; they had a great mind to some water, but they would not leap into the well, because they could not get out again.'

The experience of his times would suggest this bit of wisdom about

'*Religion.*—Alteration of religion is dangerous, because we know not where it will stay; it is like a millstone that lies upon the top of a pair of stairs; it is hard to remove it, but if once 'tis thrust off the first stair, it never stays till it comes to the bottom.'

Thus would Selden have justified the execution of a witch:

'*Witches.*—The law against witches does not prove there be any; but it punishes the malice of those people that use such means to take away men's lives. If one should profess that by turning his hat thrice, and crying "Buz," he could take away a man's life, though in truth he could do no such thing, yet this were a just law made by the state, that whosoever should turn his hat thrice, and cry "Buz," with the intention to take away a man's life, shall be put to death.'

* See p. 622 of this volume.

Here is an anecdote about King James:

'*Judgments.*—We cannot tell what is a judgment of God; 'tis presumption to take upon us to know. Commonly we say a judgment falls upon a man for something we cannot abide. An example we have in King James, concerning the death of Henry IV. of France. One said he was killed for his wenching, another said he was killed for turning his religion. "No," says King James (who could not abide fighting), "he was killed for permitting duels in his kingdom."'

The following have their application to the scruples and asceticism of the Puritans:

'*Conscience.*—A knowing man [a wise man] will do that which a tender conscience man dares not do, by reason of his ignorance; the other knows there is no hurt: as a child is afraid of going into the dark, when a man is not, because he knows there is no danger.

*Pleasure.*—'Tis a wrong way to proportion other men's pleasure to ourselves; 'tis like the child's using a little bird, "O poor bird! thou shalt sleep with me!" so lays it in his bosom, and stifles it with his hot breath: the bird had rather be in the cold air. And yet, too, it is the most pleasing flattery, to like what other men like.'

After a banishment of nearly four centuries, Cromwell allowed the Jews to settle in England. Selden no doubt approved his liberality, for, said he:

'*Jews.*—Talk what you will of the Jews, that they are cursed, they thrive where ere they come, they are able to oblige the prince of their country by lending him money; none of them beg, they keep together, and for their being hated, my life for yours, Christians hate one another as much.'

In the following, he gives his judgment against those who hold that genius is an acquirement of education or industry:

'*Learning and Wisdom.*—No man is wiser for his learning: it may administer matter to work in, or objects to work upon; but wit and wisdom are born with a man.'

These morsels may give some notion of the flavour of the *Table-talk;* there is no better book to have at hand and dip into at an odd half-hour.

Selden was born at Salvington, on the Sussex coast, near Worthing, in 1584. In the house where he spent his boyhood, on the lintel of the door withinside, is a Latin distich, rudely cut in capitals intermixed with small letters, reputed to have been the work of Selden when ten years old. The inscription runs:

'Gratus, honeste, mihi; non claudar, initio, sedeque:
Fur abeas, non sum facta soluta tibi.'

Which may be rendered:

'Thou 'rt welcome, honest friend, walk in, make free:
Thief, get thee hence, my doors are closed to thee!'

His father was a musician, or as he is called in the parish register, 'a minstrell.' Young Selden was educated at Oxford, and from thence removed to London, and entered the Inner Temple in 1604. His early rise in life he owed simply to his own diligence and ability. When asked, in his old age, to whom he should leave his fortune, he said he had no relation but a milk-maid, and she would not know what to do with it. He died on the last day of November 1654, within sixteen days of the completion of his seventieth year. He was buried in the Temple Church, and Archbishop Usher preached his funeral sermon, in the course of which he observed, that he 'looked upon the deceased as so great a scholar, that he was scarce worthy to carry his books after him.' In person Selden was tall, being in height about six feet; his face was thin and oval, his nose long and inclining to one side; and his eyes gray, and full, and prominent.

## MARSHAL SAXE.

Though not a general of the highest order, Marshal Saxe is still the most distinguished commander that appeared in France during the greater part of the last century. The victory of Fontenoy, in which he repulsed the combined forces of England and Holland under the Duke of Cumberland and Prince Waldeck, was followed by a series of successes which compelled the allies to enter into negotiations with France for peace, resulting in the treaty of Aix-la-Chapelle in 1748. Honours of all sorts were showered on him by Louis XV.; and among other rewards, the magnificent castle of Chambord, twelve miles from Blois, with an annual revenue of 100,000 francs, was bestowed on the hero of so many achievements.

Marshal Saxe was the natural son of Augustus II., king of Poland, and was born at Dresden on 19th October 1696. From boyhood he was inured to arms, having, when only twelve years of age, served under Count Schulembourg before Lisle. He first entered the French army about 1720, when the Duke of Orleans appointed him to the command of a regiment. Subsequently to this he succeeded in getting himself elected Duke of Courland; but through the influence of the Czarina Catharine I. in the Polish Diet, he was deprived of his sovereignty, and compelled to retreat to France. After some vicissitudes of fortune, he took service, in 1733, again with France, under whose banners, with the exception of an interval spent in vainly prosecuting his claim to the duchy of Courland, he continued for the remainder of his days.

A foreigner by birth, Marshal Saxe was, in religious belief, a Lutheran; and as he died in the Protestant faith, it was impossible to bury him with all the rites and ceremonies due to his distinguished position and services. A lady of rank remarked on hearing of his death: 'How vexatious that we cannot say a *De profundis* for him who made us so often sing *Te Deum!*' Louis XV., however, caused his corpse to be conveyed with great pomp from Chambord to Strasburg, where it was interred in the Lutheran church in that town.

## THE GREAT RAILWAY MANIA-DAY.

Never had there occurred, in the history of joint-stock enterprises, such another day as the 30th of November 1845. It was the day on which a madness for speculation arrived at its height, to be followed by a collapse terrible to many thousands of families. Railways had been gradually becoming successful; and the old companies had, in many cases, bought off, on very high terms, rival lines which threatened to interfere with their profits. Both of these circumstances tended to encourage the concoction of new schemes. There is always floating capital in England waiting for profitable employment; there are always professional men looking out for employment in great engineering works; and there are always scheming moneyless men ready to trade on the folly of others. Thus the bankers and capitalists were willing to supply the capital; the engineers, surveyors, architects, contractors, builders, solicitors, barristers, and parliamentary agents, were willing to supply the brains and fingers; while, too often, cunning schemers pulled the strings. This was especially the case in 1845, when plans for new railways were brought forward literally by hundreds, and with a recklessness perfectly marvellous.

By an enactment in force at that time, it was necessary for the prosecution of any railway scheme in parliament, that a mass of documents should be deposited with the Board of Trade on or before the 30th of November in the preceding year. The multitude of these schemes, in 1845, was so great, that there could not be found surveyors enough to prepare the plans and sections in time. Advertisements were inserted in the newspapers, offering enormous pay for even a smattering of this kind of skill. Surveyors and architects from abroad were attracted to England; young men at home were tempted to break the articles into which they had entered with their masters; and others were seduced from various professions into that of railway engineers. Sixty persons in the employment of the Ordnance Department left their situations to gain enormous earnings in this way. There were desperate fights in various parts of England between property-owners who were determined that their land should not be entered upon for the purpose of railway-surveying, and surveyors who knew that the schemes of their companies would be frustrated unless the surveys were made and the plans deposited by the 30th of November. To attain this end, force, fraud, and bribery were freely made use of. The 30th November 1845 fell on a Sunday; but it was no Sunday near the office of the Board of Trade. Vehicles were driving up during the whole of the day, with agents and clerks bringing plans and sections. In country districts, as that day approached, and on the morning of the day, coaches-and-four were in greater request than even at race-time, galloping at full speed to the nearest railway-station. On the Great Western Railway an express train was hired by the agents of one new scheme; the engine broke down; the train came to a stand-still at Maidenhead, and in this state, was run into by another express train hired by the agents of a rival project; the opposite parties barely escaped with their lives, but contrived to reach London at the last moment. On this eventful Sunday, there were no fewer than *ten* of these express trains on the Great Western Railway, and *eighteen* on the Eastern Counties! One railway company was unable to deposit its papers, because another company surreptitiously bought, for a high sum, twenty of the necessary sheets from the lithographic printer; and horses were killed in madly running about in search of the missing documents before the fraud was discovered. In some cases the lithographic stones were stolen; and in one instance the printer was bribed by a large sum not to finish, in proper time, the plans for a rival line. One eminent house brought over four hundred lithographic printers from Belgium, and even then, and with these, all the work ordered could not be executed. Some of the plans were only two-thirds lithographed, the rest being filled up by hand. However executed, the problem was to get these documents to Whitehall before midnight on the 30th of November. Two guineas a mile were in one instance paid for post-horses. One express train steamed up to London 118 miles in an hour and a half, nearly 80 miles an hour. An established company having refused an express train to the promoters of a rival scheme, the latter employed persons to get up a mock funeral cortège, and engage an express train to convey it to London; they did so, and the plans and sections came *in the hearse*, with solicitors and surveyors as mourners!

Copies of many of the documents had to be deposited with the clerks of the peace of the counties to which the schemes severally related, as well as with the Board of Trade; and at some of the offices of these clerks, strange scenes occurred on the Sunday. At Preston, the doors of the office were not opened, as the officials considered the orders which had been issued to keep open on that particular Sunday, to apply only to the Board of Trade; but a crowd of law-agents and surveyors assembled, broke the windows, and threw their plans and sections into the office. At the Board of Trade, extra clerks were employed on that day, and all went pretty smoothly until nine o'clock in the evening. A rule was laid down for receiving the plans and sections, hearing a few words of explanation from the agents, and making certain entries in books. But at length the work accumulated more rapidly than the clerks could attend to it, and the agents arrived in greater number than the entrance-hall could hold. The anxiety was somewhat allayed by an announcement, that whoever was inside the building before the clock struck twelve should be deemed in good time. Many of the agents bore the familiar name of Smith; and when 'Mr Smith' was summoned by the messenger to enter and speak concerning some scheme, the name of which was *not* announced, in rushed several persons, of whom, of course, only one could be the right Mr Smith at that particular moment. One agent arrived while the clock was striking twelve, and was admitted. Soon afterwards, a carriage with reeking horses drove up; three agents rushed out, and finding the door closed, rang furiously at the bell; no sooner did a policeman open the door to say that the time was past, than the agents threw their bundles of plans and sections through the half-opened door into the hall; but this was not permitted, and the policeman threw the documents out into the street. The baffled agents were nearly maddened with vexation; for they had arrived in London from Harwich in good time, but had been driven about Pimlico, hither and thither, by a post-boy who did not, or would not, know the way to the office of the Board of Trade.

The *Times* newspaper, in the same month, devoted three whole pages to an elaborate analysis, by Mr Spackman, of the various railway schemes brought forward in 1845. They were no less than 620 in number, involving an (hypothetical) expenditure of 560 millions sterling; besides 643 other schemes which had not gone further than issuing prospectuses. More than 500 of the schemes went through all the stages necessary for being brought before parliament; and 272 of these became acts of parliament in 1846—to the ruin of thousands who had afterwards to find the money to fulfil the engagements into which they had so rashly entered.

And after him came next the chill December;
Yet he through merry feasting which he made,
And great bonfires, did not the cold remember;
His Saviour's birth his mind so much did glad.
Upon a shaggy-bearded goat he rode,
The same wherewith Dan Jove on tender yeares,
They say, was nourisht by th' Idæan mayd;
And in his hand a broad deepe bowle he beares,
Of which he freely drinks an health to all his peeres.

SPENSER.

(DESCRIPTIVE.)

# DECEMBER

DARK December has now come, and brought with him the shortest day and longest night: he turns the mist-like rain into ice with the breath of his nostrils: and with cold that pierces to the very bones, drives the shivering and houseless beggar to seek shelter in the deserted shed. He gives a chilly blue steel-like colour to the shrivelled heps and haws, and causes the half-starved fieldfares to huddle together in the naked hedge for warmth; while the owl, rolling himself up like a ball in his feathers, creeps as far as he can into the old hollow tree, to get out of the way of the cold. Even the houses, with their frosted windows, have now a wintery look; and the iron knocker of the door, covered with hoary rime, seems to cut the fingers like a knife when it is touched. The only cheering sight we see as we pass through a village, is the fire in the blacksmith's forge, and boys sliding—as they break the frosty air with merry shouts—on the large pond with its screen of pollard-willows, broken now and then by the report of the sportsman's gun, and the puff of smoke which we see for a few moments floating on the air like a white cloud in the distant valley. We see the footprints of the little robin in the snow, and where it lies deep, the long-eared hare betrays her hiding-place by the deep indentments she makes in the feathery flakes. The unfrozen mere looks black through the snow that lies around it, while the flag-like sedges that stand upright appear like sharp sword-blades frosted with silver. The trees mirrored deep down seem as if reflected on polished ebony, until we draw nearer and look at the cold gray sky, that appears to lie countless fathoms below. When the wind shakes the frosted rushes and the bending water-flags, they seem to talk to one another in hoarse husky whispers, as if they had lost their voices through standing so long in the cold by the water-courses, and forgotten the low murmurings they gave utterance to in summer. We pity the few sheep that are still left in the fields, burrowing for the cold turnips under the snow, and almost wish their owners had to procure their own food in the same way, for having neglected to fold them. The falling snow from some overladen branch, under which we are passing, makes us shake our heads as we feel it thawing about the neck. Now the mole is compelled to work his way deeper underground in search of food, as the worms he feeds upon are only to be found beyond the reach of the frost, below which he must penetrate or starve, for his summer hunting-grounds are now tenantless. During a severe frost, myriads of fish perish for want of air in our ponds and rivers, and those who value their stock will not neglect to make holes through the ice, and throw food into the water, for unless this is done, they will devour one another. Cattle also gather about their usual drinking-place, and wait patiently until the ice is broken for them. That lively little fellow, the water-wagtail—the smallest of our birds that walk—may now be seen pecking about the spots of ground that are unfrozen in moist places, though what he finds to feed upon there, unless it be loosened bits of grit and gravel, is difficult to ascertain. Many a shy bird, but seldom seen at any other season, now draws near to our habitations in search of food; and sometimes, when entering an outhouse, we are startled by the rush of wings, as the pretty intruder escapes by the open doorway we are entering. The black-bird dashes out of the shed as the farmer's boy enters to fodder the cattle, frightening him for the moment, so unexpected and sudden is the rush; for cattle must now be attended to early and late, and the farmer finds plenty to do, although there is but little labour going on in the fields. Sometimes he has to hurry out half-dressed in the night, for there is a cry of 'murder' in the hen-roost, and he well knows that the fox has broken in someway, and will not retire supperless in spite of the loud outcry. The housewife, when she counts her chickens next morning, and reckons up her loss, wishes the old earth-stopper had been laid up with rheumatism instead of being out all night as he is, blocking up the fox-holes, while Reynard is out feeding, to prevent him from running in when he is hunted. Poor old fellow! we have often felt sorry for him, as we have passed him on a cold winter's night, with his lantern and spade, making the best of his way to some fox's burrow, to block up the entrance, and have often wondered what the fox thinks when he returns home, and finds the doorway filled in with thorns and furze, over which the earth is shovelled. Though a thief, he is a beautifully formed animal, and I like to see him trailing his long bush through the snow, and to hear his feet stirring the fallen leaves as he steals through the wood.

How few and apt are the words Shakspeare has used to paint a perfect picture of winter in *Love's Labour's Lost!* He begins by describing the icicles hanging down the wall, and Dick the shepherd blowing his nails to warm them, with the same breath that he blows into his porridge to cool it. Next he tells us how Tom drags huge logs to the great hall-fire, which he would rear on the andirons, for grates and coal were not in use in Shakspeare's time; then follows Marian with her red, raw nose, the milk frozen in the pail she carries, pitying the poor birds she saw outside shivering in the snow. Neither do matters mend at church, where there is such a noise of coughing as to drown the parson's 'sixteenthly,' one aisle answering to another, as if the congregation were playing at catching colds instead of balls, for as soon as one has ceased to cough, it is taken up by another, until it goes the whole round of the church. Outside, at night, the owl keeps crying, 'To-whit, too-whoo,' hidden, perhaps, among the ivy of centuries, which has overgrown the picturesque and ornamented gable. Every line here of the great poet is a picture of winter, though only painted in words; and so distinct is each outline, that any artist, with a poetical eye, might transfer every figure, with such action as Shakspeare has given to each, to canvas. Now is the time to sit by the hearth and peruse his immortal works; and few, we think, will read a page attentively without discovering something new—some thought that assumes a fresh form, or presents itself to the mind in a new light. For out-of-door pleasure, at times, is not to be found, as the days are short, cold, comfortless, and almost dark; lanes, fields, and woods naked, silent, and desolate; while the dull gray sky seems, at times, as if sheeted with lead. What a brave heart the pretty robin must have to sing at such a season! and if anything can tempt us out of doors, it is a hope that we may hear his cheerful song.

Beside the song of the robin, the green ivy gives a life to the nakedness, especially when we see it clambering up a gigantic tree, whose branches are bald. In summer we could not see it for the intervening foliage, though it was then green with young leaves. We love to see it romping about our gray old churches, and old English manor-houses; sometimes climbing up the old square tower of the one, and burying under its close-clinging stems the twisted chimneys of the other, forming a warm shelter for the little wrens and titmice from the biting frosts and cutting winds of winter. Then there are the bright holly-bushes, with their rich clusters of crimson berries, which throw quite a cheerful warmth around the places in which they grow, and recall pleasant visions of the coming Christmas, and the happy faces they will flash upon when reflecting the sunny blaze from the snug warm hearth. Here and there, though never very common, we see the mirth-making mistletoe, generally growing on old apple and hawthorn trees, and very rarely on the oak; and it is on records which have been written from ancient traditions, that wherever the Druids selected a grove of oaks for their heathen worship, they always planted apple-trees about the place, so that the mistletoe might be trained around the trunks of the oaks. The black hellebore, better known as the Christmas-rose, is one of the prettiest flowers now seen out of doors, though but seldom met with in the present day, excepting in old gardens, which we much wonder at, as it is a large, handsome, cup-shaped flower, sometimes white, but more frequently of a rich warm pink colour, and quite as beautiful as any single rose that is cultivated. But few gardens are without evergreens, and the winter-blooming laurustinus, mixed with other shrubs, now make a pretty show, though a noble, old, high holly-hedge is, after all, one of the grandest of green objects we now meet with. Another curious shrub that now occasionally flowers, is the Glastonbury-thorn, which our forefathers believed never bloomed until Christmas-day. It may sometimes be found now covered with blossom, although, like the rest of the thorns, it had bloomed before in May, as will be seen by the berries hanging on it at its second time of flowering, though this after-crop of bloom is not general. All we can see in the kitchen-garden is a little green above the ridge, where the celery is earthed up; a few savoys and kale, with a refreshing rim of parsley here and there, if it has been protected from the frost; and these, excepting the autumn-sown cabbage plants, are about all that now look green. Still there are occasionally days when the sun comes out, and a mild south wind blows, shaking the icicles that hang from the gray beard of grim old Winter, as if to tell him that he must not sleep too sound, for the shortest day has come, and the snow-drops will soon be in flower, and then a flush of golden crocuses will be seen, that will make his dim eyes dance again as he rubs the hoary rime from his frosted eyelashes. And on these fine December days, great enjoyment may be found in a good bracing country-walk, which will send a summer glow through the system, and cause us to forget the cold. The sky appears of a more brilliant blue, and looks as if higher up than at any other season, while the winter moon, often seen at noonday, appears to have gone far away beyond her usual altitude. We see a new beauty in the trees which we beheld not before—the wonderful ramification of the branches as they cross and interlace each other, patterns fit for lace, nature's rich net-work—scallop and leaf, that seem as if worked on the sky to which we look up; and we marvel that some of our pattern-drawers have not made copies of these graceful intersections of spray and bough as seen amid the nakedness of winter. Sometimes the branches are hung with frost, which, were it not of so pure a white, we might fancy was some new kind of beautiful shaggy moss, in form like what is often seen on trees. The bushes, sedge, and withered grasses are covered with it, and look at times as if they were ornaments cut out of gypsum or the purest marble; while some portions of the hedges, where only parts of the branches are seen, look like the blackthorn, which is sheeted with milk-white blossoms long before a green leaf appears.

We often wonder how, during a long and severe frost, the birds contrive to live. That many perish through cold and want of food, is well known through the number that are picked up dead and frozen, though a greater number are eaten by the animals that prey upon everything they can find. Many pick up insects in a dormant state from out the stems of decayed trees, old walls, and the thatched roofs of cottages and outhouses, and they also forage among furze-bushes, the underneath portions of which being dead, form a warm shelter for such insects as the gnats, which may be seen out in every gleam of sunshine; for there are numbers of birds that never approach the habitation of man, no matter how severe the winter may be. But most mysterious of all is the manner the waterfowl manage to subsist, when every stream, lake, and river is frozen, which has happened at times, and lasted for several weeks. It is very possible that they then leave our inland waters, and have recourse to the sea, though many naturalists have come to the conclusion that they then return to the countries from whence they came. There is but little doubt that birds feed on many things we are ignorant of. We have startled them, many a time, from some spot where they were pecking at something as fast as their little heads could go up and down; but even with the aid of a powerful magnifying-glass, we were unable to discover anything but small grit, sand, and portions of fine gravel on the spot. Wood-pigeons, we know well, eat the eyeshoots out of the tops of turnips, and devour the tenderest portion of winter-greens. Larks and other birds find a living in the autumn-sown corn-fields, and make sad havoc among the seed. Other birds tear the thatch off corn-stacks, and eat until they are hardly able to fly. Country lads know that there is good shooting to be found in places like these. Nor does the farmer care so much about what they devour, as the injury they cause to what is left; for where the thatch is off, the rain penetrates, and runs down to the very lowest sheaves in the rick, which, after getting wet, soon become black and rotten. One thing we must consider, birds require less food during these short, dark days than they do at any other season of the year, as they are asleep more than double the time they pass in slumber in summer, nor when awake do they exert themselves so much on the wing as during the long days.

How dreary must have been the winters through which our forefathers passed, no further back even than a century ago! But few of our towns were then lighted at night; here and there an oil-lamp flickered, which the wind soon blew out; and these cast such a dull light, and were so far apart, that few old people ventured through the streets on dark nights without carrying lanterns in their hands. Those who could afford it, followed their servants, who were the lantern-bearers. Then the roads were almost impassable in winter, and a few may still be found in the remote corners of England, bad enough, to tell what the generality of highways were in those old days. Coaches were almost unknown, and unless people rode on horseback, there was only the slow-paced stage-wagon, which even a cripple might pass on the road; for the great lumbering tilted vehicle, when it did not stick fast, seldom crept along at the rate of more than two miles an hour. All the miles of villages and roads that went stretching away from the little town, were in darkness; for when the last dim lamp was left behind at the town-end, no more light was to be seen, unless from the window of some solitary farmhouse, where they had not retired to rest, until you reached your own home in the far-away hamlet; and fortunate you were if you did not lose your shoes in the knee-deep muddy roads. Men have been known, in those old winters, to stick fast in the roads that run through clay lands, where they were sometimes found dead, or if they survived, were unable to move when pulled out in the following morning, until warmth was restored to the system. On lonesome moors, wide unenclosed commons, and hedgeless heaths, wayfarers, unable to travel along the deep-rutted and muddy roads, lost their way, trying to find a firmer footing elsewhere, and wandered about until the cold gray dawn of winter broke, fortunate if in the night they stumbled upon some dilapidated field-shed or sheepfold. Goods were carried from one town to another on the backs of packhorses; and the mounted traveller who had to journey far, carried all his necessaries in his saddle-bags, considering himself very fortunate if he had not to give them up, with all his money, to some daring highwayman, who generally rode up, pistol in hand, demanding without ceremony 'Your money, or your life!' Any one glancing over the files of country newspapers that appeared about a century ago, would be startled to read of the number of highway robberies that then took place, and the many wayfarers that perished through cold on the roads during those old hard winters. We, who travel by rail, and live in towns lighted by gas, are not subject to these calamities. We have, in our day, seen men compelled to cross the wide fens and marshes when snow has fallen after a hard frost, and it was impossible to tell where the water-courses lay in places that drained these wide low-lying lands, as all appeared alike a level waste buried under a white snowy pall. For safety they bestrode long leaping-poles, which they used for clearing the dikes in summer, and now employed in throwing themselves across the trenches, so that if the ice broke with them, they were seldom immersed above the legs. And across those long, wide, white windy marshes, where there was neither hoof, wheel, nor footmark to guide them, would these hardy men travel on their errands, with nothing to guide them but some bush or embankment or taller tuft of sedge, whose forms were so altered by the fallen snow, that they went along in doubt as to whether they were the same landmarks they were accustomed to trust to. And sometimes they fell into deep hollows, where the snow drifted over them in the night, and were not found again for weeks after they were lost, when their bodies were borne back for burial. From some of these old newspapers now before us, describing the winters a hundred years ago in the country, we find such passages as the following: 'The frost was so severe, the street-lamps could not be lighted on account of the oil being frozen; many people were found frozen to death in the fields and roads, and thousands of birds were picked up dead.' —'So severe was the weather, that only eight or nine people came from the country on market-day; none of the carriers arrived, nor any sheep or cattle; the town has been without water three weeks, except what is got through melting down the ice and snow. Many people have been found dead in the stackyards and sheds without the town.' —And during this severe weather, the quartern-loaf was selling for 1*s.* 4*d.*, and wheat fetching £6 and £7 a quarter, and that was no longer ago than the first year of the present century. Another of these old papers says: 'The weather was so severe, and the snow so deep, that the judges were detained on the road, and could not come in time to open the assizes.'

Flocks of sheep perished in the snow-drifts during these hard winters, and shepherds who went out to look after them, were sometimes lost, nor were their bodies found until spring came and all the snow had melted away. We were shewn a deep dell in the wild wolds, where one of the shepherds was found, after the snow had gone, and all around where he had so long lain dead, there were thousands of primroses in bloom. Even in the present day, when winters are generally milder, we have often with difficulty climbed some hill, that we might look over the snow-clad country at our feet. The cottages in the distance seem half-buried, as if the snow stood as high as the window-sills and reached half up the doorways, and you wonder how the inhabitants can get out, and make their way over those white untrodden fields, so deep as they are covered with snow. The rick-yard looks like mounds of up-coned snow, yet so smooth and equally distributed that no human hand could pile flake above flake in such level and beautiful slopes, so unindented and unbroken, out of any material mechanical art can contrive; and yet so lightly do the flakes lie on one another, that the first gust of wind shakes them loose, and disperses them on the air like full-blown May-blossoms. One might fancy that the long rows of level hedges were thick marble walls, and that the black line far beyond which marks the river, was the deep chasm from which all those miles of upheaving marble has been quarried. We look behind, where hills ascend above hills, with level table-lands between, telling where, for unknown epochs, the ocean spread and sank in desolate silence; and we seem as if looking upon a dead country, from which everything living has long since passed away, and nothing could find sustenance on those cold terraces and bald high uplands of snow, to whose sides the few bare trees that lean over seem to cling in agony, as the wind goes moaning through their naked branches. But, like the blue of heaven seen through the rift of clouds beyond, there is hope before us, for the shortest day is passed, and soon some little hardy flower will be seen here and there, and far across the snow we shall hear the faint bleating of new-born lambs, and the round green daisies will begin to knock under the earth to be let out, and so frighten grim old Winter in his sleep, that he will jump up and hurry away, looking with averted head over his shoulder, for fear he should be overtaken by Spring.

---

(HISTORICAL.)

December, like the three preceding months, derives its name from the place which it held in the old Roman calendar, where the year was divided, nominally, only into ten months, with the insertion of supplementary days, to complete the period required for a revolution of the earth round the sun. In allusion to the practice of lighting fires in this month for the purpose of warmth, and the consequent inconveniences which resulted, Martial applies to it the epithet of *fumosus* or *smoky*. He also characterises it as *canus* or *hoary*, from the snows which then overspread the high grounds. By the ancient Saxons, December was styled *Winter-monat* or *winter month;* a term which, after their conversion to Christianity, was changed to *Heligh-monat* or *holy month* from the anniversary, which occurs in it, of the birth of Christ. Among the modern Germans, December is still, from this circumstance, distinguished by the epithet of *Christmonat*.

### CHARACTERISTICS OF DECEMBER.

On the 22d of December, the sun enters the sign of *Capricornus* or the *Goat*. The idea thus allegorised by a *climbing* animal is said to be the ascent of the sun, which, after reaching its lowest declination at the winter-solstice, on the 21st of this month, recommences its upward path, and continues to do so from that date till it attains its highest altitude at the summer-solstice, on the 21st of June.

The average temperature for the middle of December, throughout the British Islands, is about 39°. On the 1st of the month, in the latitude of London, the sun rises at 7.57 and sets at 4.3. As regards meteorological characteristics, December bears in its earlier portion a considerable resemblance to the preceding month of November. Heavy falls of snow and hard frosts used to be of normal occurrence at the season of Christmas, but in recent years Britain has witnessed such a cycle of mild winters, that, as a general rule, snow rarely descends in any quantity before the commencement of the New Year.

# First of December.

St Eligius or Eloy, bishop of Noyon, confessor, 659.

*Born.*—Princess Anna Comnena, historian, 1083, *Constantinople ;* John Keill, mathematician and natural philosopher, 1671, *Edinburgh*.

*Died.*—Henry I. of England, 1135, *Rouen ;* Pope Leo X., 1521 ; Sir James Ware, antiquary, 1666, *Dublin ;* Susanna Centlivre, dramatist, 1723, *London ;* Alexander I., Emperor of Russia, 1825, *Taganrog ;* Dr George Birkbeck, promoter of scientific education, 1841, *London ;* Ebenezer Elliott, poet ('the anti-cornlaw rhymer'), 1849, *Barnsley*.

### MRS CENTLIVRE.

Literary success presupposes talent and industry, but dramatic success not only talent and industry, but patience and tact in dealing with the world. An author, when he has acquired the confidence of the publishers, may live quietly at home and transact his business from his desk ; but a dramatist, when he has finished his work as a man of letters, often finds himself at the beginning of his troubles. He has to adapt his piece to the style and caprice of the actors, to submit to the excision of what he considers the finest efforts of his wit and fancy, and to the insertion of what he thinks clap-trap or commonplace. Hence, whatever may be thought of the theatre, the writer of a dozen or two of successful plays cannot but be regarded with a certain reverence, as one who has passed through an ordeal of which only a character of equal sweetness and energy is capable.

Of the private life and character of Mrs Centlivre, not much is known ; but, in an age when female authorship was far from being so common as in our own, she wrote some score of plays, two or three of which hold their place on the stage to the present day. With few advantages of education, she managed to acquire a respectable stock of learning, to write with sprightliness and ease, and to find herself a welcome guest wherever literature was had in honour.

The date and place of her birth are both uncertain. Her father, Mr Freeman, had an estate at Holbeach, Lincolnshire, was a zealous dissenter and republican, and, after the Restoration, sought refuge from persecution in Ireland. There, about 1680, it is supposed his daughter Susannah was born. Whilst she was yet a girl, he died, leaving her quite destitute. There is a romantic story, that Susannah set out for London alone, either to find some friends, or earn a livelihood ; and that, when near Cambridge, she was seen by a young gentleman, who was so charmed by her loveliness, that he persuaded her to dress as a boy, and live with him as a fellow-student at the university. There seems no doubt that, at sixteen, she was married to a nephew of Sir Stephen Fox, and that, within a year, she was a widow. Soon after, Colonel Carrol made her his wife ; but ere two years were out, he was killed in a duel, and thus, before she was twenty, the beauty was twice widowed. Very fond of the theatre, she thought she would try her hand at a tragedy, and was fortunate enough to have it performed at Drury Lane in 1700, under the title of *The Perjured Husband*. Thus encouraged, she persevered, but abandoned tragedy for comedy, finding it the line in which she could excel. At the same time she procured an engagement as an actress, but, like Mrs Inchbald at a later date, she discovered that her pen was a more effective instrument than her voice and face. Nevertheless, it was on the stage that she gained her third husband. She was at Windsor in 1706, performing as Alexander the Great in Lee's *Rival Queens*, when she won the heart of Joseph Centlivre, Yeoman of the Mouth, or, in other words, chief cook to Queen Anne. They were married, and lived happily together until her death, in 1723, at his house in

Spring Gardens, Charing Cross. She was buried in St Martin's in the Fields.

Mrs Centlivre was lively if not witty, and, for her good-humour, was loved wherever she was known. The language of her plays has little in it to attract the reader, but her plots are well constructed, the scenes full of action, and her characters natural and well marked. By these qualities they sometimes succeeded in spite of the prognostics of the players. In rehearsal, *The Busy Body* was decried; but it ran for thirteen nights, then thought an extraordinary success, whilst Congreve's *Way of the World*, sparkling with wit and smartness, was a failure. Mrs Centlivre shares in the sin of her time, in the occasional licentiousness of her dialogue. During the rehearsal of her *Bold Stroke for a Wife*, a comedy which, as well as the *Busy Body*, still appears occasionally on modern play-bills, Wilks, the actor, declared that not only would it be dee'd, but that she would be dee'd for writing it. Her *Wonder, or a Woman keeps a Secret*, if not her best, is the most popular of her productions. In it, as Don Felix, Garrick took his farewell in 1776. As became the daughter of a suffering dissenter, Mrs Centlivre was an ardent Whig and advocate of the Hanoverian succession, and not unfrequently introduced her politics into her plays. Pope gave her a line in the *Dunciad*—

'At last Centlivre found her voice to fail'—

for writing a ballad against his Homer before she had read it.

## THE YOUNG ROSCIUS.

Precocity of genius, or of ability, has always a certain attraction for the world; partly on account of a kindly feeling towards the young, but principally owing to a love of the marvellous, which leads most of us to run after that which is new and wonderful. If the encouragement thus afforded to precocious boys and girls had the effect of strengthening the powers thus early developed, this would be a great point in its favour; but such is certainly not the case. The youthful prodigy generally becomes, if he or she lives, a very prosaic adult. This was illustrated in the instance of *The Young Roscius*, a boy-actor who made the public almost crazy in the early part of the present century. William Henry West Betty, the boy in question, was born near Shrewsbury in 1791. Almost from a child he evinced a taste for dramatic recitations, which was encouraged by a strong and retentive memory. Having been taken to see Mrs Siddons act, he was so powerfully affected, that he told his father 'he should certainly die if he was not made a player.' He gradually got himself introduced to managers and actors; and at eleven years of age, he learned by heart the parts of Rollo, Young Norval, Osman, and others high in popular favour in those days. On the 16th of August 1803, when under twelve years of age, he made his first public appearance at Belfast in the character of Osman; and went through the ordeal without mistake or embarrassment. Soon afterwards he undertook the characters of Young Norval and Romeo. His fame having rapidly spread through Ireland, he soon received an offer from the manager of the Dublin theatre. His success there was prodigious, and the manager endeavoured, but in vain, to secure his services for three years. Addresses were presented to the *Young Roscius*, as he was now called; and pamphlets were written in advocacy of plans for insuring the happiness and completing the education of one who was to be the bright star of the age. He next played nine nights at the small theatre at Cork, whose receipts, averaging only ten pounds on ordinary nights, amounted to a hundred on each evening of Master Betty's performance. In May 1804, the manager of the Glasgow theatre invited the youthful genius to Scotland. When, a little after, Betty went to the sister-city of Edinburgh, one newspaper announced that he 'set the town of Edinburgh in a flame;' and, at a loss apparently how to account for so brilliant a phenomenon, put forth a theory that the boy's 'pleasing movements of perfect and refined nature, had been incorporated with his frame previous to his birth!' Mr Home went to see the character of Young Norval in his own play of *Douglas* enacted by the prodigy, and is said to have declared: 'This is the first time I ever saw the part played according to my ideas of the character. He is a wonderful being!' The manager of the Birmingham playhouse then sent an invitation, and was rewarded with a succession of thirteen closely-packed audiences. Here the *Roscio-mania*, as Lord Byron afterwards called it, appears to have broken out very violently; it affected not only the inhabitants of that town, but all the iron and coal workers of the district between Birmingham and Wolverhampton. In an article in one of the early volumes of the *Penny Magazine*, descriptive of the South Staffordshire district and its people, it is said: 'One man, more curious or more idle than his fellows, determined to leave his work, and see the prodigy with his own eyes. Having so resolved, he proceeded, although in the middle of the week, to put on a clean shirt and a clean face, and would even have anticipated the Saturday's shaving, but he was preserved from such extravagance by the motive which prevented Mrs Gilpin from allowing the chaise to draw up to her door on the eventful morning of the journey:

——"lest all
Should say that she was proud."

But, notwithstanding this moderation, he did not pass unobserved. The unwonted hue of the shirt and face were portents not to be disregarded, and he had no sooner taken the road to Birmingham, than he was met by an astonished brother, whose amazement, when at last it found vent in words, produced the following dialogue: "Oi say, sirree, where be'est thee gwain?" "Oi 'm agwain to Brummajum." "What be'est thee agwain there for?" "Oi 'm agwain to see the Young Rocus." "What?" "Oi tell thee oi 'm agwain to see the Young Rocus." "Is it aloive?"' The 'Young Rocus,' who was certainly 'aloive' to a very practical end, then went to Sheffield, and next to Liverpool.

Such was the boy who, on December 1, 1804, made his first bow to a London audience. After a desperate competition between the managers of Drury Lane and Covent Garden theatres, the former succeeded in securing the treasure. The flaming accounts from the country newspapers had driven the Londoners to a high pitch of excitement. The pressure at the theatre was unparalleled. As early as one o'clock in the day, persons began to take their stations near the doors; and the inhabitants in the neighbouring streets looked out from their upper windows upon the tremendous array of people that assembled by six o'clock. Bow-Street officers were posted in great force within the theatre, and Foot-guards without, to endeavour to maintain order. At the opening of the door, after many faintings in the crowd, hundreds were in danger of suffocation from the mad endeavours of those behind them to force themselves forward. Although no places were unlet in the boxes, gentlemen paid box-prices to have a chance of jumping over the fronts of the boxes into the pit; and then others who could not find room for a leap of this sort, fought for standing-places with those who had hired the boxes days or weeks before. In short, it was a frightful scene, which long impressed itself on the memories of those who were present. The play, Browne's *Barbarossa*, in which the Young Roscius played the part of Selim, was to have been preceded by an address from Mr Charles Kemble; but as not a word of it could be heard in the tumultuous house, he wisely gave up the attempt. Half the first scene of the play was then gone through; nothing could be heard. Kemble came forward again, but again could not be heard; and the first act of the play proceeded in dumb-show. At length, in the second act, Selim appeared, and the perspiring audience gave up their frantic noise for equally frantic admiration. Audiences as full as the theatre could hold, though without such wild paroxysms, afterwards witnessed his performance of Tancred, Romeo, Frederick, Octavian, Hamlet, Osman, Achmet, Young Norval, and other favourite characters. An arrangement was made by the patrons and managers of the two Theatres Royal, that this golden talisman should be made available for both; and he played at the two theatres on alternate nights—earning about £1000 a week altogether. Young Betty was 'presented to the king, and noticed by the rest of the royal family and the nobility, as a prodigy. Prose and poetry were put in requisition to celebrate his praise; prints of his person were circulated throughout the kingdom; and even the university of Cambridge was sufficiently hurried away by the tide of the moment, to make the subject of Sir William Browne's prize-medal, *Quid noster Roscius eget?* It was even in public contemplation to erect statues to him; and Opie painted a full-length portrait of him, in which the Young Roscius was represented as having drawn inspiration from the tomb of Shakspeare. But the best proof of the sensation he created is the fact, that the amount which twenty-eight nights of his performances at Drury Lane brought into the house was £17,210, an average of nearly £615 per night.'* It is supposed that the receipts at Covent Garden were nearly as much, and that thus £30,000 was earned by this boy for the managers in fifty-six performances.

Fortunately for young Betty, his friends took care of his large earnings for him, and made a provision for his future support. He soon retired from the stage, and then became a person of no particular note in the world, displaying no more genius or talent than the average of those about him. When he became a man, he appeared on the stage again, but *utterly failed;* he would not and could not 'draw.' The Young Roscius and Mr Betty were two entirely different persons in the public estimation.

* *The Georgian Era*, vol. iv.

---

## MR HEBER'S LIBRARY: BIBLIOMANIACS.

The sale by auction of Mr Richard Heber's library, the disposal of one department of which commenced on the 1st of December 1834, illustrated in a significant way that exclusive fondness for books which is frequently styled *Bibliomania*, or *book-madness*. If the collectors were in the habit of reading the works which they buy, all would be well; or if, when collected, the books were sold or given in a mass to those who would know how to value them, this again would be well; but the real bibliomaniac collects books merely for the pleasure of collecting, and the collection is generally dispersed after a time. Mr Heber was a man of great learning, whose knowledge really extended over a vast range of literature; and it is a pity that there is no 'Heber's Library' in existence, as a testimony to his taste and knowledge; the library which he formed having shared the usual fate of such ponderous collections. Born in 1773, Mr Heber (who was half-brother to the celebrated bishop of Calcutta, of the same name) inherited property which permitted him to spend immense sums in the purchase of books, and he received an education which enabled him to appreciate the books when purchased. He formed the habit of making excursions from the family-seats in Yorkshire and Shropshire to London, to attend book-sales; and the first collection which he made, consisted of curious old works relating to early English poets and dramatists. When the termination of the war, in 1815, opened the continent to English travellers, Heber visited France, Belgium, and the Netherlands, making large purchases of books in each country. Again, in 1825, he went abroad, purchasing books everywhere; and at the same time he kept an agent employed in buying largely for him at all the book-sales in England. All the hopes once entertained of him as a public man, or a country gentleman, were disappointed; he cared for nothing but books. Libraries which he possessed in different localities, sale-rooms, and booksellers' shops, were almost the only places which had attractions for him. He kept up a correspondence with all the great dealers in old books throughout the kingdom, and had all their catalogues regularly sent to him. On hearing of a curious book, he was known to have put himself into a mail-coach, and travelled three or four hundred miles to obtain it, fearful to intrust his commission to any one else. One of his biographers says: 'He has been known to seriously say to his friends, on their remarking on his many duplicates, "Why, you see, sir, no man can do comfortably without *three* copies of a work. One he must have for a *show*-copy, and he will probably keep it at his country-house. Another, he will require for his own use and reference; and unless he is inclined to part with this, which is very inconvenient, or risk the injury of his best copy, he must needs have a third at the service of his friends! This was a handsome speech to address to a borrower; but it cannot be denied that Mr Heber's duplicates were often purchased, through that passion of collectors which demands not only that an article should be possessed, but that it should also be kept from the possession of others. The fact was, that collecting had grown into an uncontrollable habit; and that it was only satisfied in him, as in others, by an almost unlimited indulgence. The desire of possessing duplicates, or (which is the same thing under another name) preventing other collectors obtaining them, was not peculiar to Mr Heber, but was more remarkable in him, because exhibited on a large scale and with ample means.'

The taste strengthened as he grew older. Not only was his collection of old English literature unprecedented, but he brought together a larger number of fine copies of Latin, Greek, French, Spanish, Italian, and Portuguese books than had ever been possessed by a private individual. His house at Hodnet, in Shropshire, was nearly all library. His house in Pimlico (where he died in 1833) was filled with books from top to bottom: every chair, table, and passage containing 'piles of erudition.' A house in York Street, Westminster, was similarly filled. He had immense collections of books, in houses rented merely to contain them, at Oxford, Paris, Antwerp, Brussels, and Ghent. When he died, curiosity was naturally excited to know what provision he had made in reference to his immense store of books; but when his will was discovered, after a long and almost hopeless search among bills, notes, memoranda, and letters, it was found, to the astonishment of every one on reading it, that the library *was not even mentioned!* It seemed as if Heber cared nothing what should become of the books, or who should possess them, after his decease; and as he was never married, or influenced greatly by domestic ties, his library was considered by the executors of his will as merely so much 'property,' to be converted into cash by the aid of the auctioneer. What was the number of books possessed by him, or the amount of money paid for them, appears to have been left in much doubt. Some estimated the library at 150,000 volumes, formed at a cost of £100,000; others reckoned it at 500,000 volumes, at an aggregate value of £250,000. The truth was, his executors did not know in how many foreign towns his collections of books were placed. Thus it could not accurately be ascertained what portion of the whole was sold by auction in London in 1834—6; but the mere catalogue of that portion fills considerably more than two thousand printed octavo pages. The sales were conducted by Mr Evans, Messrs Sotheby, and other book-auctioneers, and occupied two hundred and two days, extending through a period of upwards of two years from April 10, 1834, to July 9, 1836. One copy of the catalogue has been preserved, with marginal manuscript notes relating to almost every lot; and from this a summary of very curious information is deducible. It appears that, whatever may have been the number of volumes sold by auction, or otherwise got rid of abroad, those sold at this series of auctions in London were 117,613 in number, grouped into 52,672 lots. As regards the ratio borne by the prices obtained, to those which Mr Heber had paid for the books in question, the account as rendered shewed that the auctioneer's hammer brought £56,775 for that which had cost £77,150. It would appear, therefore, that the losses accruing to Mr Heber's estate through his passion for book-collecting, amounted to upwards of £20,000, and this irrespective of the fate, whatever it may have been, of the continental libraries. We can hardly come to any other conclusion, than that Mr Heber's life was nearly a useless one—performing unnecessary work, which was undone soon after his death.

---

# DECEMBER 2.

St Bibiana, virgin and martyr, 363.

*Born.*—Francis Xavier Quadrio, learned Jesuit, and historical writer, 1695, *Valtellina;* Henry Gally Knight, illustrator of architectural antiquities, 1786.

*Died.*—Hernan Cortes, conqueror of Mexico, 1547, *near Seville;* Margaret of Navarre, grandmother of Henri IV., 1549; St Francis Xavier, Catholic missionary, 1552, *China;* Gerard Mercator (Kaufmann), geographer, 1594, *Doesburg;* Philip, Duke of Orleans, Regent of France, 1723; Amelia Opie, novelist, 1853, *Norwich.*

## ST FRANCIS XAVIER.

St Francis Xavier was born on the 7th of April 1506, in a castle at the base of the Spanish side of the Pyrenees, not far from which his future comrade and director, Ignatius Loyola, was then living, a gay youth of fifteen. Xavier was sent to the university of Paris, and there shared a room with Peter Faber, a Savoyard, to whom he became tenderly attached. In 1528, Loyola arrived at their college, a middle-aged man, meanly clad, worn with austerities, and burning with zeal. Loyola made friends with Faber, but Xavier could not endure him, and repulsed his approaches. Loyola, discerning a desirable spirit in Xavier, nevertheless persevered. One day Xavier had been lecturing on philosophy, and having met with much applause, was walking about in a high state of elation, when Loyola whispered in his ear: 'What shall it profit a man if he gain the whole world and lose his own soul?' The question startled Xavier, and changed the current of his feelings towards Loyola. He associated with him and Faber in study and devotion. Three other students joined them—Lainez, Bobadilla, and Rodriguez—and on the 15th of August 1534, the six met in a subterranean chapel of the church of Montmartre, and took vows of perpetual celibacy, poverty, and labour for the conversion of infidels. Such was the humble beginning of the Society of Jesuits. They resolved to place their lives at the service of the pope, and when preaching at Rome, in 1540, Xavier was chosen to go as a missionary to India. With joy he started, and on his way to Lisbon came within a few miles of his birthplace, and was pressed to turn aside and bid his mother farewell. He refused, lest his ardour should suffer loss in the regrets of filial affection. A voyage to India was a tedious enterprise in the sixteenth century. He sailed from Lisbon on the 7th of April 1541, wintered in Africa on the coast of Mozambique, and his ship did not reach Goa until the 6th of May 1542. The Portuguese of Goa, he found, were leading worse lives than the heathen, except that they did not worship idols, and their conversion was his first business. He learned the language of Malabar, and went preaching among the pearl-fishers; and entering the kingdom of Travancore, he met with such success, that he reported baptising 10,000 Indians in a month. At Malacca, then a great centre of trade, he met three Jesuits, whom Loyola had sent to his aid, and with them made a tour through the Moluccas. At Malacca, he had met a Japanese, whose account of his strange and populous country had decided Xavier to visit it. He picked up as much of the language as he could, and in August 1549 landed in Japan, and for about two years travelled through the islands, making a host of converts. His mission was continued with great vigour by the Jesuits for nearly a century, when, for some cause or other, the government took fright, massacred the Christians, foreign and native, and sealed Japan against Europeans until our own day. He next determined to plant his faith in China, but the Portuguese merchants pleaded with him not to make the attempt, as he would assuredly be the cause of their utter destruction. Xavier was not to be moved by such alarms, and persuaded a Chinaman to run him ashore by night near Canton. This plan the Portuguese frustrated, and in the midst of his disappointment, on the barren island of Sancian, within sight of the desired Chinese mainland, he took fever, and died on the 2d of December 1553, aged only forty-seven, and in the twelfth year of his Asiatic ministry. His body was carried to Goa, and his shrine is to Catholics the holiest place in the Far East. In 1662, he was canonized, and by a papal brief in 1747, was pronounced the patron-saint of the East Indies. His festival is observed on the 3d of December.

The story of Xavier in Asia, as told by Catholics, is a long record of miracle on miracle; and by his miracles they account for the otherwise incredible statements regarding his success as a propagandist.

## MECHANICS' INSTITUTIONS.

On the 2d December 1824, an institution was opened in London concerning which very warm anticipations were entertained, but which has not fully borne the fruit hoped for. After one or two minor attempts in various towns, it was resolved to establish a place in the metropolis, where workmen could acquire a knowledge of science, and of the principles of those arts on which they were daily employed. Scarcely any books on such matters were then accessible to persons of limited means, and popular lectures were nearly unknown. Many men in high places dreaded such innovations; insomuch that one declared, that 'science and learning, if universally diffused, would speedily overturn the best-constituted government on earth.' It is to the credit of Scotland that she took the lead of England in this matter. The Andersonian Institution at Glasgow had a mechanics' class, at which the late benevolent Dr Birkbeck lectured to large audiences on scientific subjects connected with the occupations of working-men; and the School of Arts at Edinburgh, under the auspices of Mr Leonard Horner and other enlightened men, furnished similar instruction, though to smaller audiences. In October 1823, proposals were put forth for establishing a Mechanics' Institution in London; and in the following month a public meeting on the subject was held at the Crown and Anchor Tavern. The object was declared to be 'the instruction of mechanics at a cheap rate in the principles of the art they practise, as well as in all other branches of useful knowledge;' and the means for obtaining this object were 'lectureships on the different arts and sciences, a library of reference and circulation, a reading-room, a museum of models, a school of design, an experimental workshop and laboratory, and a supply of instruments and apparatus.' Mr (afterwards Lord) Brougham, in a letter addressed to Dr Birkbeck as chairman, said: 'The plan will prosper in exact proportion to the interest which the mechanics themselves take in its detail. It is for their benefit, and ought to be left in their hands as soon as possible after it is begun.' And Mr Cobbett supported this view by saying: 'If they'—the working-men—'allowed other management to interfere, men would soon be found who would put the mechanics on one side and make use of them only as tools.' The scheme having been favourably received, the *London Mechanics' Institution* was formed, and was opened on the day above named. Men of great attainments offered their services as lecturers, and the lecture-hall frequently contained a thousand persons, listening with the greatest attention to discourses on astronomy, experimental philosophy and chemistry, physiology, the steam-engine, &c. Many persons, who afterwards attained to a more or less distinguished position in society, owed their first knowledge of the principles of science to the London Mechanics' Institution. The novelty and the success of the enterprise were so great, that similar institutions sprang up rapidly in various parts of the kingdom. At a public meeting in London, in July 1824, Mr Brougham said: 'Scarcely three days ever elapse without my receiving a communication of the establishment of some new Mechanics' Institution. At the beginning of May last, I made a calculation that since the preceding July I had received accounts of no less than thirty-three being established.' They extended far and wide, until at length there were at the very least four hundred such institutions in Great Britain.

It will not be suitable, in a work like this, to investigate fully the question why Mechanics' Institutions have comparatively failed; why, when the first enthusiasm had worked off, they failed to realise the expectations of their founders; a few words, nevertheless, may be said on the subject. Of the fact itself, there can be little doubt. 'In large towns,' a careful observer remarks, 'they [Mechanics' Institutions] have usually sprung from the exertions and wishes, not so much of the working-classes, as of the more wealthy. The energy and enthusiasm that originated them carried them on for a time; but as the novelty wore off, the members and revenue decreased, modifications of plan had to be adopted, new features introduced, and radical changes made. If these proved acceptable to the public, the institution flourished; if not, it decayed. If the original idea of giving scientific education only were strictly carried out, the number of members was small; while if amusement took the place of study, the institution lived in jeopardy, from the fickle and changing taste for amusement on the part of the public.' But *why* have mechanics shewn themselves, except in a few special instances, unwilling to give to these institutions such a measure of support as is necessary to their profitable working? The reasons assigned are many. In some places where bickerings have existed between employers and employed on the subject of wages, and where the employers have lent aid towards establishing Mechanics' Institutions, the men have persuaded themselves that there is some secret design lurking underneath, and have suspiciously held aloof. Then, as to natural bias, most working-men shew a stronger taste for social and political subjects than for scientific and educational questions; they would rather attend a political meeting than a scientific lecture; rather read a party-newspaper than a dispassionate book; rather invest a little money in a benefit society or a building club, than in an institution for mental improvement; and although it may be a wise rule to exclude politics and theology, many men find such topics more 'exciting' and attractive than science or education. Next, a very large class of workmen consists of persons who really do not care at all for such subjects as those last named; when their work is done, theatres, public-houses, music-halls, smoking-rooms, &c., are their regular places of resort; and they would deem it almost as strange to go to a scientific lecture as to church on a week-day evening. The quarterly payments for Mechanics' Institutes are chargeable with another portion of the comparative failure; for a workman who receives weekly wages would more readily pay a subscription weekly, than save up for thirteen weeks in order to pay in one sum. Uncertainty of employment is another unfavourable circumstance; if a workman is out of employ when his subscription becomes due, the Mechanics' Institute is one of the first things he would give up. When the subscription is made small enough to attract numerous members, it is often too small to carry on the institute efficiently, and the instruction degenerates both in quantity and quality. One more circumstance must be noticed—unless working-men subscribe in sufficient number to form a majority, they cannot retain the management in their own hands; and unless they do, it ceases to be suitable to the wants and wishes of their class; and thus they have a further excuse for staying away.

Some among the above causes have rendered the London Mechanics' Institution, and most others of its kind, less successful than the early promoters had anticipated.

# DECEMBER 3.

St Lucius, king and confessor, end of second century. St Birinus, bishop and confessor, 650. St Sola, hermit, 790. St Francis Xavier, Apostle of the Indies, confessor, 1552.

*Born.*—Luigi Pulci, Italian poet, 1431, *Florence;* John Gruter, eminent scholar and critic, 1560, *Antwerp;* Matthew Wren, bishop of Ely, 1585, *London;* Samuel Crompton, inventor of the *mule* for spinning cotton, 1753, *Firwood, near Bolton;* Robert Bloomfield, poet, 1766, *Honington, Suffolk.*

*Died.*—Alexander Farnese, Duke of Parma, distinguished commander, 1592; Giovanni Belzoni, explorer of Egyptian antiquities, 1823, *Gato, in Guinea;* John Flaxman, sculptor, 1826, *London;* Frederick VI., king of Denmark, 1839; Robert Montgomery, poet, 1855, *Brighton;* Christian Rauch, sculptor, 1857, *Dresden.*



## SAMUEL CROMPTON.

Muslins, until near the close of last century, were all imported from India. English spinners were unable to produce yarn fine enough for the manufacture of such delicate fabrics. Arkwright had invented spinning by rollers, and Hargreaves the spinning-jenny, when, in 1779, Crompton succeeded in combining both inventions in his *mule.* He thereby enabled spinners to draw out long threads, in large numbers, to more than Hindu tenuity, and helped Lancashire effectually to her high and lucrative office of cotton-spinner-in-chief to the world.

Samuel Crompton was born on the 3d of December 1753, at Firwood, near Bolton. His father was a farmer, and the household, after the custom of Lancashire in those days, employed their leisure in carding, spinning, and weaving. While Samuel was a child, his father died. Shortly before his death, he had removed to a portion of an ancient mansion called Hall-in-the-Wood, about a mile from Bolton. It was a large rambling building, built in different styles and at different periods, and full of rooms, large and small, connected by intricate stairs and corridors. The picturesque site and appearance of Hall-in-the-Wood has made it a favourite subject with artists, and it has been painted and engraved again and again. Seldom has a mechanical invention had a more romantic birthplace.

Widow Crompton was a strong-minded woman, and carried on her husband's business with energy and thrift. She was noted for her excellent butter, honey, and elder-berry wine. So high was her repute for management, that she was elected an overseer of the poor. Her boy Samuel she ruled straitly. He used to tell that she beat him occasionally, not for any fault, but because she *so* loved him. He received an ordinary education at a Bolton day-school, and when about sixteen, his mother set him to earn his living by spinning at home, and she exacted from him a certain amount of work daily. His youth at Hall-in-the-Wood was passed in comparative seclusion. All day he was alone at work, his mother doing the bargaining and fighting with the outer world. He was very fond of music, and managed to construct a violin, on which he learned to play with proficiency. His evenings he spent at a night-school in the study of mathematics. A virtuous, reserved, and industrious youth was Crompton's.

At Hall-in-the-Wood lived his uncle, Alexander Crompton, a remarkable character. He was so lame that he could not leave the room in which he slept and worked. On his loom he wove fustians, by which he earned a comfortable living. Like the rest of the family, his piety was somewhat austere; and as he was unable to go to church, he was accustomed on Sundays, as soon as he heard the bells ringing, to put off his working-coat and put on his best. This done, he slowly read from the prayer-book the whole of the morning-service and a sermon, concluding about the same time as the church was coming out, when his good coat was laid aside, and the old one put on. In the evening, the same solitary solemnity was gone through.

With one of Hargreaves's jennies, Crompton

span. The yarn was soft, and was constantly breaking; and if the full quantity of allotted work was not done, Mrs Crompton scolded, and the time lost in joining broken threads kept the gentle spinner from his books and his darling fiddle. Much annoyance of this kind drove his ingenuity into the contrivance of some improvements.

Five years—from his twenty-first year, in 1774, to his twenty-sixth in 1779—were spent in the construction of the mule. 'My mind,' he relates, 'was in a continual endeavour to realise a more perfect principle of spinning; and though often baffled, I as often renewed the attempt, and at length succeeded to my utmost desire, at the expense of every shilling I had in the world.' He was, of course, only able to work at the mule in the leisure left after each day's task of spinning, and often in hours stolen from sleep. The purchase of tools and materials absorbed all his spare cash; and when the Bolton theatre was open, he was glad to earn eighteenpence a night by playing the violin in the orchestra. The first mule was made, for the most part, of wood, and to a small roadside smithy he used to resort, 'to file his bits o' things.'

Crompton proceeded very silently with his invention. Even the family at Hall-in-the-Wood knew little of what he was about, until his lights and noise, while at work in the night-time, excited their curiosity. Besides, inventors of machinery stood in great danger from popular indignation. The Blackburn spinners and weavers had driven Hargreaves from his home, and destroyed every jenny of more than twenty spindles for miles round. When this storm was raging, Crompton took his mule to pieces, and hid the various parts in a loft or garret near the clock in the old Hall. Meanwhile, he created much surprise in the market by the production of yarn, which, alike in fineness and firmness, surpassed any that had ever been seen. It immediately became the universal question in the trade, How does Crompton make that yarn? It was at once perceived that the greatly-desired muslins, brought all the way from the East Indies, might be woven at home, if only such yarn could be had in abundance.

At this time Crompton married, and commenced housekeeping in a cottage near the Hall, but still retained his work-room in the old place. His wife was a first-rate spinner, and her expertness, it is said, first drew his attention to her. Orders for his fine yarn, at his own prices, poured in upon him; and though he and his young wife span their hardest, they were quite unable to meet a hundredth part of the demand. Hall-in-the-Wood became besieged with manufacturers praying for supplies of the precious yarn, and burning with desire to penetrate the secret of its production. All kinds of stratagems were practised to obtain admission to the house. Some climbed up to the windows of the work-room, and peeped in. Crompton set up a screen to hide himself, but even that was not sufficient. One inquisitive adventurer is said to have hid himself for some days in the loft, and to have watched Crompton at work through a gimlet hole in the ceiling.

If Crompton had only possessed a mere trifle of worldly experience, there is no reason why, at this juncture, he might not have made his fortune. Unhappily his seclusion and soft disposition placed him as a babe at the mercy of sharp and crafty traders. He discovered he could not keep his secret. 'A man,' he wrote, 'has a very insecure tenure of a property which another can carry away with his eyes. A few months reduced me to the cruel necessity either of destroying my machine altogether, or giving it to the public. To destroy it, I could not think of; to give up that for which I had laboured so long, was cruel. I had no patent, nor the means of purchasing one. In preference to destroying, I gave it to the public.'

Many, perhaps the majority of inventors, have lacked the means to purchase a patent, but have, after due inquiry, usually found some capitalist willing to provide the requisite funds. There seems no reason to doubt, that had Crompton had the sense to bestir himself, he could easily have found a friend to assist him in securing a patent for the mule, or the Hall-i'-th'-Wood-Wheel, as the people at first called it.

He says he 'gave the mule to the public;' and virtually he did, but in such a way that he gained no credit for his generosity, and was put to inexpressible pain by the greed and meanness of those with whom he dealt. Persuaded to give up his secret, the following document was drawn up.

'We, whose names are hereunto subscribed, have agreed to give, and do hereby promise to pay unto, Samuel Crompton, at the Hall-in-the-Wood, near Bolton, the several sums opposite our names, as a reward for his improvement in spinning. Several of the principal tradesmen in Manchester, Bolton, &c., having seen his new machine, approve of it, and are of opinion that it would be of the greatest public utility to make it generally known, to which end a contribution is desired from every well-wisher of trade.'

To this were appended fifty-five subscribers of one guinea each, twenty-seven of half a guinea, one of seven shillings and sixpence, and one of five shillings and sixpence—making, together, the munificent sum of £67, 6*s.* 6*d.*, or less than the cost of the model-mule which Crompton gave up to the subscribers! Never, certainly, was so much got for so little. The merciless transaction receives its last touch of infamy, from the fact recorded by Crompton in these words:—'Many subscribers would not pay the sums they had set opposite their names. When I applied for them, I got nothing but abusive language to drive me from them, which was easily done; for I never till then could think it possible that any man could pretend one thing and act the direct opposite. I then found it was possible, having had proof positive.'

Deprived of his reward, Crompton devoted himself steadily to business. He removed to Oldhams, a retired place, two miles to the north of Bolton, where he farmed several acres, kept three or four cows, and span in the upper story of his house. His yarn was the best and finest in the market, and brought the highest prices; and, as a consequence, he was plagued with visitors, who came prying about under the idea that he had effected some improvement in his invention. His servants were continually bribed away from him, in the hope that they might be able to reveal something that was worth knowing. Sir Robert Peel (the first baronet) visited him at Oldhams, and offered him a situation, with a large salary, and the prospect of a partnership; but Crompton had a morbid dislike to Peel, and he declined the overtures, which might have led to his lasting comfort and prosperity.

In order to provide for his increasing family, he moved into Bolton in 1791, and enlarged his spinning operations. In 1800, some gentlemen in Manchester commenced a subscription on his behalf, but, what with the French war, the failure of crops, and suffering commerce, their kindly effort stuck fast between four and five hundred pounds. The amount collected was handed over to Crompton, who sunk it in the extension of his business.

Aided by the mule, the cotton manufacture prodigiously developed itself; but thirty years elapsed ere any serious attempt was made to recompense the ingenuity and perseverance to which the increase was owing. At last, in 1812, it was resolved to bring Crompton's claims before parliament. It was proved that 4,600,000 spindles were at work on his mules, using up 40,000,000 lbs. of cotton annually; that 70,000 persons were engaged in spinning, and 150,000 more in weaving the yarn so spun; and that a population of full half a million derived their daily bread from the machinery his skill had devised. The case was clear, and Mr Perceval, the chancellor of the exchequer, was ready to propose a handsome vote of money, when Crompton's usual ill-luck intervened in a most shocking manner. It was the afternoon of the 11th of May 1812, and Crompton was standing in the lobby of the House of Commons conversing with Sir Robert Peel and Mr Blackburne, when one of them observed: 'Here comes Mr Perceval.' The group was instantly joined by the chancellor of the exchequer, who addressed them with the remark: 'You will be glad to know that I mean to propose £20,000 for Crompton; do you think it will be satisfactory?' Hearing this, Crompton moved off from motives of delicacy, and did not hear the reply. He was scarcely out of sight when the madman Bellingham came up, and shot Perceval dead. This frightful catastrophe lost Crompton £15,000. Six weeks intervened before his case could be brought before parliament, and then, on the 24th June, Lord Stanley moved that he should be awarded £5000, which the House voted without opposition. Twenty thousand pounds might have been had as easily, and no reason appears to have been given for the reduction of Mr Perceval's proposal. All conversant with Crompton's merits felt the grant inadequate, whether measured by the intrinsic value of his service, or by the rate of rewards accorded by parliament to other inventors.

With the £5000 Crompton entered into various manufacturing speculations with his sons; but none turned out well, and as he advanced in years some of his friends found it necessary to subscribe, and purchase him an annuity of £63. A second application to parliament on his behalf was instituted, but it came to nothing. Worn out with cares and disappointments, Crompton died at his house in King Street, Bolton, on the 26th of June 1827, at the age of seventy-four.

The unhappiness of Crompton's life sprung from the absence of those faculties which enable a man to hold equal intercourse with his fellows. 'I found to my sorrow,' he writes, 'that I was not calculated to contend with men of the world; neither did I know there was such a thing as protection for me on earth!' When he attended the Manchester Exchange to sell his yarns or muslins, and any rough-and-ready manufacturer ventured to offer him a less price than he had asked, he would invariably wrap up his samples, put them into his pocket, and quietly walk off. During a visit to Glasgow, the manufacturers invited him to a public dinner; but he was unable to muster courage to go through the ordeal, and, to use his own words, 'rather than *face up*, I first hid myself, and then fairly bolted from the city.' One day a foreign count called on him in Bolton. Crompton sent a message that he was in bed, and could not be seen. A friend, who accompanied the count, thereon ran up stairs, and proposed to Crompton that they should pay their visit in the bedroom; but he would not be persuaded, and vowed that if the count was brought up, he would hide under the bed! His excessive pride made him extremely sensitive to the very appearance of favour or patronage. To ask what was due to him always cost him acute pain. When in London, in 1812, prosecuting his claims, he wrote to Mr Giddy, one of his most steadfast supporters in parliament, 'Be assured, sir, there will be no difficulty in getting rid of me. The only anxiety I now feel is, that parliament may not dishonour themselves. *Me* they cannot dishonour. All the risk is with them. I conceived it to be the greatest honour I can confer on them, to afford them an opportunity of doing me and themselves justice. I am certain my friends and family would be ashamed of me, were I to consider myself come here *a-begging*, or on the contrary *demanding*. I only request that the case may have a fair and candid hearing, and be dealt with according to its merits.'

Crompton's habits were simple and frugal in the extreme, and by his industry he readily procured every comfort he cared to possess. Well would it have been for him when he lost the ownership of his invention, if he had been able to sweep every expectation connected with it into oblivion. The operation of these hopes were even less mischievous on him than on his sons and daughters, who unhappily were deprived of the guidance of their mother's good sense in their childhood. Before their eyes was continually dangling the possibility of their father being raised to affluence; and when poor Crompton came back to Bolton with £5000 instead of a great fortune, he heard the bitterest reproaches in his own household. His family he loved very tenderly, and we can fairly imagine that it was goaded by desire to satisfy them, that he spent five weary months in London in 1812, dancing attendance on members of parliament.

Crompton has been described by those who knew him in the strength and beauty of manhood, as a singularly handsome and prepossessing man; all his limbs, and particularly his hands, were elegantly formed, and possessed great muscular power. He could easily lift a sack of flour by the head and tail, and pitch it over the side of a cart. His manners and motions were at all times guided by a natural politeness and grace, as far from servility as rudeness. His portrait displays a beautiful face and head, in which none can fail to discern a philosopher and gentleman.

Crompton's memory, until lately, has been strangely neglected. In 1859, Mr Gilbert J. French, of Bolton, published an excellent biography of his townsman, from which work our facts have been drawn. A statue of Crompton, in bronze, by

Mr W. Calder Marshall, was erected in the market-place of Bolton in 1862.

## GIOVANNI BATTISTA BELZONI.

In 1778, a son was born to a poor barber in the ancient city of Padua. There was little room for this novel addition to an impoverished family of fourteen, and the youth's earliest aspirations were to push his fortune far distant from his father's house. A translation of *Robinson Crusoe* falling into the lad's hands, excited an adventurous spirit, that clung to him through life; for, strange to say, Defoe's wonderful romance, though seemingly written with a view to deter and discourage wandering spirits, has ever had the contrary effect. When quite a boy, the barber's son ran away from home, but, after a few days' poverty, hardship, and weary travelling, he was fain to return to the shelter of the parental roof. He now settled for a season, learned his father's business, and, becoming an able practitioner with razor and scissors, he once more set off with the determination of improving his fortunes in the city of Rome. There a love disappointment induced him to enter a Capuchin convent, where he remained till the arrival of the French army threw the monks homeless and houseless on the world. Of an almost gigantic figure, and endowed with commensurate physical power, the barber-monk now endeavoured to support himself by exhibiting feats of strength and dexterity. The old inclination for wandering returning with increased force, he travelled through Germany to Holland and England, reaching this country in 1802. In the same year he performed at Sadler's Wells Theatre, in the

BELZONI AT SADLER'S WELLS AS THE PATAGONIAN SAMSON.

character of the Patagonian Samson, as represented in the accompanying engraving, copied from a very rare character portrait of the day. His performance is thus described in a contemporary periodical: 'Signor Belzoni's performance consists in carrying from seven to ten men in a manner never attempted by any but himself. He clasps round him a belt, to which are affixed ledges to support the men, who cling round him; and first takes up one under each arm, receives one on either side, one on each of his shoulders, and one on his back; the whole forming a kind of a pyramid. When thus encumbered, he moves as easy and graceful as if about to walk a minuet, and displays a flag in as flippant a manner, as a dancer on the rope.'

In some unpublished notes of Ellar, the Harlequin and contemporary of Grimaldi, the pantomimist observes that he saw Belzoni in 1808, performing in Sander's Booth, at Bartholomew Fair, in the character of the French Hercules. In 1809, he continues, 'Belzoni and I were jointly engaged at the Crow Street Theatre, Dublin, in the production of a pantomime—I as Harlequin, he as artist to superintend the last scene, a sort of hydraulic temple, that, owing to what is frequently the case, the being overanxious, failed, and nearly inundated the orchestra. Fiddlers generally follow their leader, and Tom Cook, now leader at Drury Lane, was the man; out they ran, leaving Columbine and myself, with the rest, to finish the scene in the midst of a splendid shower of fire and water. The young lady who played the part of Columbine was of great beauty, and is now the wife of the celebrated Thomas Moore, the poet. Signor Belzoni was a man of gentlemanly but very unassuming manners, yet of great mind.'

There are few towns in England, Scotland, or Ireland in which Belzoni did not exhibit about this period. The following is an exact copy of one of his hand-bills, issued in Cork early in 1812. The GRAND CASCADE, mentioned in the bill, was in all probability the splendid shower of fire and water recorded in the preceding passage from Ellar's note-book.

*Theatre, Patrick Street.*

CUT

*A Man's Head*

OFF!!!

AND PUT IT ON AGAIN!

This present Evening MONDAY, Feb. 24, 1812.

*And positively and definitively the* LAST NIGHT.

SIG. BELZONI

RESPECTFULLY acquaints the Public, that by the request of his Friends, he will Re-open the above *Theatre* for one night more—*i. e.*, on MONDAY Feb. 24, and although it has been announced in former *Advertisements*, that he would perform for Two Nights —he pledges his word that this present Evening, will be positively and definitively the last night of his Re-presentations, and when he will introduce a FEAT OF LEGERDEMAIN, which he flatters himself will astonish the Spectators, as such a feat never was attempted in Great Britain or Ireland. After a number of Entertainments, he will

CUT

*A Man's Head Off!!*

And put it on Again!!!

ALSO THE

GRAND CASCADE.

Belzoni married in Ireland, and continuing his wandering life, exhibited in France, Spain, and Italy. Realising a small capital by his unceasing industry, he determined to visit Egypt, a country that for ages has been the *El Dorado* of the Italian race. Belzoni's object in visiting Egypt was to make a fortune by instructing the natives to raise water, by a very dangerous method, now abandoned—a kind of tread-wheel, formerly known to English mechanics by the technical appellation of 'the monkey.' Being unsuccessful in this endeavour, he turned his attention to removing some of the ancient Egyptian works of art, under the advice and patronage of Mr Salt, the British consul. The various adventures he went through, and how he ultimately succeeded, are all detailed by Belzoni in the published account of his travels, entitled *Narrative of the Operations and recent Discoveries in the Pyramids, Temples, Tombs, and Cities of Egypt and Nubia.*

Scarcely four years' exertions in Egypt had made Belzoni comparatively wealthy and famous. On his way to England, to publish his book, he visited Padua, and was received with princely honours. The authorities met him at the city gates, presented him with an address, and ordered a medal to be struck in his honour. Arriving in London, he became the fashionable lion of the day; and with a pardonable reticence, Belzoni took care not to allude to the character he had formerly sustained when in England. On this point the late Mr Crofton Croker tells an interesting story, published in Willis's *Current Notes.* He says, 'I remember meeting Belzoni, the last day of 1821, at the late Mr Murray's, in Albemarle Street, where we saw the New Year in, and "glorious John" brewed a special bowl of punch, for the occasion. Beside the juvenile family of our host, the whole D'Israeli family were present. We all played a merry game of Pope Joan, and when that was over, Murray presented to each a pocket-book, as a New-year's gift. Murray was engaged, at a side-table, making the punch, upon tasting the excellence of which he uttered something like the sounds made by a puppet-showman, when about to collect an audience. The elder D'Israeli thereupon took up my pocket-book, and wrote with his pencil the following impromptu:

"Gigantic Belzoni at Pope Joan and tea,
What a group of mere puppets we seem beside thee;
Which our kind host perceiving, with infinite jest,
Gives us Punch at our supper, to keep up the jest."

'Indifferent as the epigram itself was, I smiled at it, and observed: "Very true—excellent!" Which Belzoni perceiving, said: "Will you permit me to partake of your enjoyment?" "Certainly," I replied, handing him the book. Never shall I forget his countenance after he had read the four lines. He read the last line twice over, and then his eyes actually flashed fire. He struck his forehead, and muttering: "I am betrayed!" abruptly left the room.'

At a subsequent interview between Mr Croker and Belzoni, the latter accounted for his strange conduct by stating that he had considered the lines to be an insulting allusion to his early life as a showman. On Mr Croker explaining that they could not possibly have any reference to him, Belzoni requested the former to accompany him to Mr Murray, with the view of making an explanation. They went, and then the great publisher knew, for the first time, that the celebrated Egyptian explorer had been an itinerant exhibitor.

The active mind of Belzoni soon tired of a mere London existence. In 1822, he determined to embark in the too fatal field of African adventure. In the following year, when passing from Benin to Houssa, on his way to Timbuctoo, he was stricken with dysentery, carried back to Gato, and put on board an English vessel lying off the coast, in hopes of receiving benefit from the sea-air. He there died, carefully attended by English friends, to whom he gave his amethyst ring, to be delivered to his wife, with his tender affection and regrets that he was too weak to write his last adieux.

The kindly sailors, among whom he died, carried his body ashore, and buried it under an arsama-tree, erecting a monument with the following inscription:

'Here
Lie the Remains
of
G. Belzoni, Esq.

Who was attacked with dysentery on the 20th Nov. at Benin, on his way to Houssa and Timbuctoo, and died at this place on the 3d December 1823.

'The gentlemen who placed this inscription over the remains of this celebrated and intrepid traveller, hope that every European visiting this spot, will cause the ground to be cleared and the fence around repaired if necessary.'

The people of Padua have since erected a statue to the memory of their townsman, the energetic son of a poor barber; but it was not till long after his death that the government of England bestowed a small pension on the widow of Belzoni.

---

## 'CROSSING THE LINE.'

Among the festivals of the old Roman calendar, in pagan times, we find one celebrated on the 3d of December, in honour of Neptune and Minerva. In connection with the former of these deities, we may here appropriately introduce the account of a well-known custom, which, till recently, prevailed on board ship, and was regarded as specially under the supervision of Neptune, who, *in propriâ personâ*, was supposed to act the principal part in the ceremony in question. We refer to the grand marine saturnalia which used to be performed when 'crossing the line:' that is, when passing from north to south latitude, or *vice versâ*. The custom, in some form or other, is believed to be very ancient, and to have been originally instituted on the occasion of ships passing out of the Mediterranean into the Atlantic, beyond the 'Pillars of Hercules.' It had much more absurdity than vice about it; but sometimes it became both insulting and cruel. When the victims made no resistance, and yielded as cheerfully as they could to the whim of the sailors, the ceremony was performed somewhat in the following way, as related by Captain Edward Hall, and quoted by Hone: 'The best executed of these ceremonies I ever saw, was on board a ship of the line, of which I was lieutenant, bound to the West Indies. On crossing the line, a voice, as if at a distance, and at the surface of the water, cried: "Ho, ship ahoy! I shall come on board!" This was from a person slung over the bows, near the water, speaking through his hands. Presently two men of large stature came over the bows. They had hideous masks on. One represented Neptune. He was naked to the waist, crowned with the head of a large wet swab, the end of which reached to his loins, to represent flowing locks; a piece of tarpaulin, vandyked, encircled the head of the swab and his brows as a diadem; his right hand wielded a boarding-pike, manufactured into a trident; and his body was smeared with red ochre, to represent fish-scales. The other sailor represented Amphitrite, having locks formed of swabs, a petticoat of the same material, with a girdle of red bunting; and in her hand a comb and looking-glass. They were followed by about twenty fellows, naked to the waist, with red ochre scales, as Tritons. They were received on the forecastle with much respect by the old sailors, who had provided the carriage of an eighteen-pounder gun as a car, which their majesties ascended: and were drawn aft along the gangway to the quarter-deck by the sailors. Neptune, addressing the captain, said he was happy to see him again that way; adding that he believed there were some "Johnny Raws" on board who had not paid their dues, and whom he intended to initiate into the salt-water mysteries. The captain answered, that he was happy to see him, but requested he would make no more confusion than was necessary. They then descended to the main-deck, and were joined by all the old hands, and about twenty "barbers," who submitted the shaving-tackle to inspection.' This shaving-tackle consisted of pieces of rusty hoop for razors, and very unsavoury compounds as shaving-soap and shaving-water, with which the luckless victim was bedaubed and soused. If he bore it well, he was sometimes permitted to join in performing the ceremony upon other 'Johnny Raws.' See engraving on the following page.

It was not always, however, that neophytes conformed without resistance to such rough christening ceremonies. A legal action, instituted in 1802, took its rise from the following circumstances. When the ship *Soleby Castle* was, in the year mentioned, crossing the equator on the way to Bombay, the sailors proceeded to the exercise of their wonted privilege. On this occasion, one of the passengers on board, Lieutenant Shaw, firmly resisted the performance of the ceremony. He offered to buy off the indignity by a present of money or spirits; but this was refused by the men, and it then became a contest of one against many. Shaw shut himself up in his cabin, the door of which he barricaded with trunks and boxes; and he also barred the port or small window. After he had remained some time in this voluntary imprisonment, without light or air, during the hottest part of the day, and 'under the line,' the crew, dressed as Neptune and his satellites, came thundering at his cabin-door, and with oaths and imprecations demanded admission. This he refused, but at the same time renewed his offer of a compromise. Mr Patterson, the fourth mate, entreated the crew, but in vain, to accept the offer made to them. The men, becoming chafed with the opposition, resolved now to obtain their way by force, regardless of consequences. They tried to force the door, but failed. Mr Raymond, third mate, sanctioned and approved the conduct of the men; and suggested that while some were engaged in wrenching the door off its hinges, others should effect an entry through the port. A sailor, armed with a sword and bludgeon, was lowered by a rope down the outside of the ship; and he succeeded in getting into the cabin, just at the moment when the other sailors forced open the door. Lieutenant Shaw defended himself for a time with his sword, and fired off his pistols—more for the sake of summoning assistance than to do injury, for they were not loaded. The whole gang now pressed round him, and after wresting the sword from his hand, dragged him upon deck. There he clung for some time to the post of the cuddy-door; and, finding the first and third mates to be abetting the seamen, he called out loudly for the captain. The captain's cabin-door, however, was shut, and he either did not or would not hear the appeal. So impressed was the sensitive mind of the lieutenant with the indignity in store for him, that he actually endeavoured to throw himself overboard, but this was prevented by Mr Patterson. Unmoved by all

MARINE CEREMONIES AT 'CROSSING THE LINE.'

his entreaties, the crew proceeded with the frolic on which they had set their hearts, and which, after the resistance they had encountered, they resolved not to forego on any terms. They seized the lieutenant, dragged him along the quarter-deck to the middle of the ship, and placed him sitting in a boat half-filled with filthy liquid. His eyes being bandaged with a dirty napkin, a nauseous composition of tar and pitch was rubbed over his face, as 'Neptune's shaving soap,' and scraped off again by means of a rusty hoop, which constituted 'Neptune's razor.' He was then pushed back with violence into the boat, and there held struggling for some seconds, with his head immersed in the noisome liquid. Injured in body by this rough treatment, he was much more wounded in his mental feelings; and when the ship arrived at Bombay, he brought an action against the first and third mates. The fourth mate bore witness in his favour; and the captain, as a witness, declared that he did not hear the cry for assistance; but it is known that captains, at that time, were mostly unwilling to interfere with the sailors on such occasions. The damages of 400 rupees (£40), though more than the mates relished being called upon to pay, could scarcely be deemed a very satisfactory recompense for the inflictions which the lieutenant had undergone.

The improvement wrought among seafaring-men during the last few years, has tended to lessen very much the frequency of this custom. Not only naval officers, but officers in the mercantile marine, are better educated than those who filled such posts in former times; and the general progress of refinement has led them to encourage more rational sports among the crew. The sailors themselves are not much more educated than formerly; but improvement is visible even here; and the spirit which delighted in the coarse fun of this equatorial 'shaving,' is now decidedly on the wane.

# DECEMBER 4.

St Clement of Alexandria, father of the church, beginning of 3d century. St Barbara, virgin and martyr, about 306. St Maruthas, bishop and confessor, 5th century. St Peter Chrysologus, archbishop of Ravenna, confessor, 450. St Siran or Sigirannus, abbot in Berry, confessor, 655. St Anno, archbishop of Cologne, confessor, 1075. St Osmund, bishop and confessor, 1099.

---

*Born.*—Thomas Carlyle, historical and miscellaneous writer, 1795, *near Ecclefechan, Dumfriesshire;* Dr John Kitto, Biblical illustrator, 1804, *Plymouth.*

*Died.*—Pope John XXII., 1334, *Avignon;* Cardinal Richelieu, celebrated minister of Louis XIII., 1642, *Paris;* William Drummond, poet, 1649, *Hawthornden;* Thomas Hobbes, philosopher, author of *Leviathan,* 1679; John Gay, poet and dramatist, 1732, *London;* John Shute, Lord Barrington, 1734; James Perry, editor of the *Morning Chronicle,* 1821, *Brighton;* Robert Jenkinson, Earl of Liverpool, statesman, 1828; Samuel Butler, bishop of Lichfield, great scholar, 1839.

## HOBBES.

Hobbes was the plague of the theologians and philosophers of the seventeenth century. Charles II. likened him to a bear against whom the church played its young dogs in order to exercise them. Warburton, writing a century later, said: 'The philosopher of Malmesbury was the terror of the last age, as Tindall and Collins are of this. The press sweat with controversy, and every young churchman-militant would try his arms in thundering on Hobbes's steel cap.' A library might, indeed, be formed of the literature Hobbes provoked; and supposing it were admitted that he was altogether in the wrong, yet we should see a beneficent end in the means which stimulated so much mental activity. Faith is strengthened and assured in free contest with error; belief would lapse into mere hearsay if not sharply tested by question and denial; and we all must own, that 'truth like a torch the more it 's shook it shines.'

Thomas Hobbes was born at Malmesbury, in Wilts, on Good Friday, 1588, the year of the Spanish Armada. It is said his birth was hastened by his mother's terror of the enemy's fleet; and it may be, that a timidity with which through life he was afflicted, was thus induced. He and Fear, he was wont to say, were born together. He was a precocious child; he learned much and easily, and while yet a boy, translated the *Medea* of Euripides from the Greek into Latin verse. At the age of fifteen he was sent to Oxford, and at twenty he entered the Cavendish family as tutor to Lord Hardwicke, and with scarcely an intermission remained in the service of that noble house as tutor and secretary to the end of his long life. Born under Elizabeth, he lived through the reigns of James and Charles; he saw the rise and fall of the Commonwealth; and died in 1679, at the great age of ninety-two, within six years of the accession of James II. The latter part of his life was spent in Derbyshire, in the charming retreat of Chatsworth, and from Bishop Kennet we have a minute account of his habits there. 'His professed rule of health was to dedicate the morning to his exercise, and the afternoon to his studies. At his first rising, therefore, he walked out and climbed any hill within his reach; or, if the weather was not dry, he fatigued himself within doors by some exercise or other, to be a sweat. . . . . After this he took a comfortable breakfast; and then went round the lodgings to wait upon the earl, the countess and the children, and any considerable strangers, paying some short addresses to all of them. He kept these rounds till about twelve o'clock; when he had a little dinner provided for him, which he ate always by himself without ceremony. Soon after dinner, he retired to his study, and had his candle with ten or twelve pipes of tobacco laid by him; then shutting his door, he fell to smoking, thinking, and writing for several hours.' Hobbes was tall and spare; his forehead was massive, and in old age deeply wrinkled; his hair was a bright black, till time grizzled it; his eyes were quick and sparkling, and his nose long. His countenance, he tells us, was 'not beautiful, but when I am speaking, far from disagreeable.'

Hobbes's temper was naturally and intensely conservative, and his lot was cast in times when the whole current of events seemed destined to disturb it. His first work, a translation of Thucydides, in which he had the assistance of Ben Jonson, was published in 1628, in order that the absurdities of the Athenian democrats might serve as a warning to turbulent Englishmen. As civil troubles thickened, he was glad to seek refuge in Paris, where he enjoyed the acquaintance of Descartes, Gassendi, and other eminent Frenchmen. But though he had no inclination for a personal share in the strife which was rending his country into warring factions, he was far from indifferent to it. His mind was absorbed in the questions it suggested; he was asking himself, what was the origin of society? and what were the true relations between rulers and their subjects? The first result of his meditations appeared in a Latin treatise, *De Cive,* printed in Paris in 1642, and afterwards translated into English as *Philosophical Rudiments concerning Government and Society.* Descartes wrote of *De Cive,* 'I can by no means approve of its principles or maxims, which are very bad and extremely dangerous, because they suppose all men to be wicked, or give them occasion to be so. His whole design is to write in favour of monarchy, which might be done to more advantage than he has done, upon maxims more virtuous and solid.' The principles set forth in the *De Cive,* Hobbes more fully developed in the celebrated *Leviathan; or the Matter, Form, and Power of a Commonwealth, Ecclesiastical and Civil,* published in London, in folio, in 1651. In this work he describes man in a state of nature, or of isolation, as in a state of war, which in society he exchanges for a state of amity or peace. God made man, and man, in his turn, makes society, which is a sort of artificial man; a man on a large scale, in which the ruler is the brain, and his subjects, according to their various offices, the members. To the monarch he accords absolute power, and to his subjects unconditional obedience, not only in matters civil but religious. It might be supposed that such a doctrine would have proved highly acceptable to a generation in which the divine right of kings was in common vogue, but it was quickly discerned that though Hobbes rendered a useful defence of absolutism, it was a defence, spite of Hobbes's protests, which might serve a

Cromwell as well as a Stuart. Hence, in 1666, parliament passed a censure on the *Leviathan* and *De Cive*.

Hobbes's pen, to the end of his life, was never idle. He wrote in advocacy of necessity against free-will. He translated the *Iliad* and *Odyssey* into very ordinary verse. He composed a history of the civil wars from 1640 to 1660. He had a controversy with Dr Wallis, professor of geometry at Oxford, which lasted twenty years, and in which he was thoroughly worsted. Hobbes had commenced the study of mathematics in middle life, and imagined he had discovered the quadrature of the circle. Wallis told him he was mistaken, and the dispute which ensued was acrimonious to a laughable degree. Hobbes published *Six Lessons to the Professors of Mathematics in Oxford*, to which Wallis replied in *Due Correction for Mr Hobbes for not Saying his Lessons Right*.

Though the parliament condemned Hobbes, he was a favourite with Charles II. and his court. The aversion in which he was held by the pious, was a fair title to their esteem; and his sharp sayings and low estimate of human motives, were perfectly suited to their tastes. Moreover, he had been mathematical tutor to Charles when in exile; and though, after the publication of the *Leviathan*, he had been forbidden the royal presence, the king had a real fondness for his old master, and, seeing him one day in London, as he passed along in his coach, he sent for Hobbes, gave him his hand to kiss, ordered his portrait to be taken, and settled on him a pension of £100 a year.

Hobbes was freely denounced as an atheist, but solely by inference, and in direct opposition to his own confession. He expressly acknowledged God as 'the Power of all powers, and First Cause of all causes;' but, at the same time, denied that any could know '*what* He is, but only that He *is*.' What gave great handle to some to treat him as an atheist, was the contempt he expressed for many of those scholastic terms invented by theologians, in their endeavour to define the Infinite, and his determination to pursue his reasoning on politics and philosophy in thorough independence of their dogmas. Consistently with his principles, he conformed to the Church of England, and partook of its sacraments; but he seldom remained to listen to the sermon after the prayers.

Perhaps no writer has treated questions of polity and metaphysics with greater terseness and clearness than Hobbes, and lovers of a manly English style receive deep gratification from his pages. The late Sir William Molesworth collected and edited the works of Hobbes in sixteen volumes. When he stood as candidate for parliament for Southwark in 1845, one of the election cries was, 'Will you vote for Molesworth, the editor of Atheist Hobbes?'

## JOHN GAY: ORIGIN OF A POPULAR NURSERY RHYME.

Gay is chiefly remembered as the author of the *Fables* and the *Beggar's Opera*, both of which, though not productions evincing the highest order of genius, have, by their sparkling vivacity and humour, secured for themselves transmission to posterity. He appears to have been wild and improvident in conduct, but nevertheless of a most amiable and genial disposition, which endeared him to a wide circle of literary friends, one of whom, Pope, thus touchingly commemorates him in the well known elegy on Gay:

> 'Of manners gentle, of affections mild;
> In wit a man, simplicity, a child.'

A mock-heroic poem, by Gay, entitled *Trivia, or the Art of Walking the Streets of London*, gives a very lively description of the city of London as it existed in the reign of Queen Anne, and of the dangers and inconveniences to which a pedestrian was exposed in those days while traversing its thoroughfares. This poem is indirectly connected with a well-known nursery rhyme. Few of our readers are unacquainted with the effusion commencing:

> 'Three children sliding on the ice,
> Upon a summer's day;'

with its tragi-comical catastrophe, and its moral of like character, addressed to—

> 'Parents that have children dear,
> And eke they that have none.'

Like many other tales of that class, both in prose and verse, its origin, we believe, has long remained unknown. A little old book, however, which we had occasion to quote in our first volume (p. 173), *The Loves of Hero and Leander* (London, 1653 and 1677), enlightens us on this point, and gives these lines in their primitive form.

In the latter part of the work, we find a rambling story, in doggerel rhymes, attempting the comical, and no less than eighty-four lines in length: it begins thus:

> '*Some* Christian people, *all* give ear
> Unto the grief of us:
> Caus'd by the death of three children dear,
> The which it hapned thus.'

And, elsewhere in the narrative, we meet with three other quatrains, the origin evidently of the rhyme in question:

> 'Three children sliding thereabout,
> Upon a place too thin,
> That so at last it did fall out,
> That they did all fall in.
>
> * * * *
>
> For had these at a sermon been,
> Or else upon dry ground,
> Why then I would ne'er have been seen,
> If that they had been drown'd.
>
> Ye parents all that children have,
> And ye that have none yet,
> Preserve your children from the grave,
> And teach them at home to sit.'

From the concluding verse of the story, as told in the original, it would seem that these lines were composed in the early part of the Civil Wars of Charles I.

In connection with this homely production, we have now to advert to an instance in which a more recent writer has evidently been indebted to it. Among the other incidents of the narrative, we are told that these unlucky children were sliding upon the Thames, when frozen over, and that one of them had the misfortune to lose his head by the inopportune closing of the ice :

'Of which one's head was from his should-
Ers stricken, whose name was John,
Who then cry'd out as loud as he could,
"O Lon—a, Lon—a, London,
Oh ! tut—tut, turn from thy sinful race,"
Thus did his speech decay.'

If we turn to a passage in Gay's *Trivia* (book ii. ll. 388–392), descriptive of a frost on the Thames, near a century later, we find the following account of the tragic death of Doll the apple-woman :

'The cracking crystal yields, she sinks, she dies,
Her head, chopt off, from her lost shoulders flies;
"Pippins," she cry'd, but death her voice confounds,
And "Pip, pip, pip," along the ice resounds!'

The severing of the head from the shoulders, the half-articulated words, and the 'speech decaying,' or 'voice confounded,' in death, are, all of them, points so extremely similar, that there can hardly be room for supposing this to be a case of accidental coincidence.

## MR PERRY OF THE *MORNING CHRONICLE.*

James Perry was one of those silent workers whose works do not perish ; and who, even when the worker and the work both have disappeared, exert a lasting influence on those who follow them. He was an Aberdeen man, born in 1756. After receiving a good education, and commencing the study of the law, he was suddenly thrown upon his own resources through commercial disasters in his family. Coming to England, he obtained an engagement as clerk to a manufacturer in Manchester ; and while thus employed, he greatly improved himself, during his leisure hours, by joining a literary association. The essays and papers which he contributed as a member of this society attracted much attention at the time. He went to London in 1777, to seek a wider sphere of usefulness ; and feeling a kindred sympathy towards a newspaper called the *General Advertiser*, he wrote essays and fugitive-pieces, dropped them into the letter-box at the office of that journal, and had the pleasure of seeing them in print a day or two afterwards. An accidental circumstance brought him into communication with the proprietors. Calling one day at the shop of Messrs Richardson and Urquhart, booksellers, to whom he had letters of recommendation, he found the latter busily engaged reading, and apparently enjoying an article in the *General Advertiser.* After Mr Urquhart had finished the perusal, Perry delivered his message ; and Urquhart said : 'If you could write articles such as this, I could give you immediate employment.' When Urquhart (who was one of the proprietors of the paper) heard that Perry was the author of the article, and had another of a similar kind with him in his pocket, they soon came to terms. Urquhart offered and Perry accepted a situation of a guinea a week, with an extra half-guinea for aiding in the *London Evening Post*, issued from the same establishment. Installed now in a regular literary capacity, Mr Perry threw the whole of his energies into his work. During the memorable trials of Admirals Keppel and Palliser, he, for six successive weeks, by his own individual efforts, managed to transmit daily, from Portsmouth, eight columns of a report of the proceedings, taken by him in court. These contributions, so very acceptable to the general public, raised the circulation of the *General Advertiser* largely. Even this arduous labour did not exhaust his appetite for study ; and he wrote, in addition, papers on a large variety of subjects. In 1782, he conceived the plan, and commenced the publication, of the *European Magazine*, a monthly journal, intended to combine a review of new books with a miscellany on popular subjects. After conducting this for twelve months, he was appointed editor to a newspaper called the *Gazetteer*, with a salary of four guineas a week, and a proviso that he should be allowed to advocate those political opinions which he himself held, and which were those of Charles James Fox. To understand an innovation which he at once introduced, it will be necessary to bear in mind what constituted parliamentary reporting in those days. Both Houses of parliament, for a long series of years, had absolutely forbidden the printing of the speeches in newspapers ; and it was only in an indirect way that the public could learn what was going on with the legislature. No facilities were offered to reporters ; there was no 'Reporters' Gallery ;' the 'Strangers' Gallery' was the only place open to them, and no one was allowed to use a note-book. William Woodfall, of the *Morning Chronicle*, became quite famous for his success in overcoming these difficulties. He used to commit a debate to memory, by attentively listening to it, and making here and there a secret memorandum ; when the House rose, he went home, and wrote out the whole of the speeches, trusting a little to his memoranda, but chiefly to his memory. Though generally accurate, mistakes, of course, occurred ; and now and then the report contained evidence of 'poking fun' at an honourable member. Mr Wilberforce once explained to the House, that in a report of a speech of his concerning the cultivation of the potato, he was made to say : 'Potatoes make men healthy, vigorous, and active ; but what is still more in their favour, they make men tall ; more especially was he led to say so, as being rather under the common size ; and he must lament that his guardians had not fostered him under that genial vegetable !' Woodfall's reputation became considerable ; and when strangers visited the House, their first inquiry often was : 'Which is the Speaker, and which is Mr Woodfall ?' As the visitors were locked into the gallery, and not allowed to leave it, or partake of any refreshment, till the debate was ended, Woodfall often had a very exhausting night of it. He would draw a hard-boiled egg from his pocket, take off the shell in his hat, and stoop his head to make a hasty meal, before the serjeant-at-arms could witness this infraction of the rules of the House. He was not a favourite with the other reporters ; and on one occasion the well-known hard egg was filched from his pocket, and an unboiled one substituted by a practical joker who owed him a grudge. One of the reporters who had thus to retain in his memory the substance of the speeches, was Mark Supple, an Irishman full of wit and humour, and often full of wine likewise.

One evening, being in his usual place in the gallery, a dead silence happened to occur for a few seconds, when he suddenly called out: 'A song from Mr Speaker!' William Pitt was nearly convulsed with laughter; Mr Addington, the speaker, could with difficulty retain his gravity; but the serjeant-at-arms had to punish the offender.

Mr Perry, we have said, in the *Gazetteer* introduced a great improvement—that of employing several reporters in each House of parliament, instead of one only, as had been the usual custom. Many of the speeches had been wont to appear in print some days after they had been delivered; but Perry rightly thought that the public ought to be served more promptly. By employing, accordingly, a larger staff, he was enabled to surprise and gratify the readers of his paper each morning with very fair reports of the speeches of the previous evening. He conducted the *Gazetteer* for eight years, and also edited Debrett's *Parliamentary Debates*. Mr Woodfall, who had gained celebrity in connection with the *Morning Chronicle*, sold it (apparently in 1790) to Mr Perry and Mr Gray, who had the money lent to them by Mr Bellamy, a wine-merchant, and housekeeper to the House of Commons. Perry at once took a high tone; he advocated steady liberal principles, avoiding alike bigoted Toryism on the one hand, and rabid Republicanism on the other; and at the same time, kept equally aloof from scandal and from venality. Although nearly always opposed to the minister of the day, he was only twice, in his newspaper career of forty years, exposed to *ex officio* prosecution, and was in both cases honourably acquitted. During a critical period of the French Revolution, Perry lived for twelve months at Paris, and acted there as reporter and correspondent for the *Chronicle*. He had many eminent men to assist him in the editorship; at one time, Mr (afterwards Serjeant) Spankie; at another, Mr (afterwards Lord) Campbell; at another, Thomas Campbell, the poet; and at another, William Hazlitt. Perry was a general favourite, and he was thus characterised by a contemporary: 'He was a highly honourable and brave man: confidence reposed in him was never abused. He was the depositary of many most important secrets of high personages. Generous in the extreme, he was ever ready with his purse and his services. His manner was manly, frank, and cordial; and he was the best of proprietors. Walter, of the *Times*, was a better man of business; and Daniel Stuart, of the *Post* and *Courier*, knew better how to make money; but Perry was a thorough gentleman, who attracted every man to him with whom he was connected.'

Soon after Mr Perry's death, the *Morning Chronicle* was sold for £42,000 to Mr Clements, proprietor of the *Observer*. In 1834, Sir John Easthope bought it for a much smaller sum. In later years, it sunk greatly in reputation; and the sale became so small, that it could no longer be carried on without loss. The proprietorship changed frequently; and an attempt was made to revive the sale by establishing the journal as a penny-paper. This also failing, the *Morning Chronicle* disappeared from the public eye altogether. Mr Perry's reputation is not affected by these failures; he made the paper the best of all the London journals; the decadence was due to others.



# DECEMBER 5.

St Crispina, martyr, 304. St Sabas, abbot, 532. St Nicetius, bishop of Triers, confessor, about 566.

---

*Born.*—Robert Harley, Earl of Oxford, minister of Queen Anne, 1661.

*Died.*—Francis II. of France, husband of Queen of Scots, 1560; Sir Henry Wotton, poet and miscellaneous writer, 1639, *Eton;* Johann Wolfgang Theophilus Mozart, celebrated composer, 1792, *Vienna;* John Bewick, wood-engraver, 1795, *Ovingham;* Carlo Giovanni Maria Denina, historical writer, 1813, *Paris;* Leopold Frederick, Count Stolberg, poet and miscellaneous writer, 1819, *Sondermühlen, near Osnabrück;* Captain S. A. Warner, inventor of projectiles, 1853, *Pimlico.*

## MOZART.

Mozart appears as a being eccentrically formed to be a medium for the expression of music and no grosser purpose. In this he was strong: in everything else of body and mind, he remained a child during the thirty-six years to which his life was limited.

'When three years old, his great amusement was finding concords on the piano; and nothing could equal his delight when he had discovered a harmonious interval. At the age of four, his father began to teach him little pieces of music, which he always learned to play in a very short time; and, before he was six, he had invented several small pieces himself, and even attempted compositions of some extent and intricacy.

'The sensibility of his organs appears to have been excessive. The slightest false note or harsh tone was quite a torture to him; and, in the early part of his childhood, he could not hear the sound of a trumpet without growing pale, and almost falling into convulsions. His father, for many years, carried him and his sister about to different cities for the purpose of exhibiting their talents. In 1764, they came to London, and played before the late king. Mozart also played the organ at the Chapel Royal; and with this the king was more pleased than with his performance on the harpsicord. During this visit he composed six sonatas, which he dedicated to the queen. He was then only eight years old. A few years after this he went to Milan; and at that place was performed, in 1770, the opera of *Mithridates*, composed by Mozart at the age of fourteen, and performed twenty nights in succession. From that time till he was nineteen, he continued to be the musical wonder of Europe, as much from the astonishing extent of his abilities, as from the extreme youth of their possessor.

'Entirely absorbed in music, this great man was a child in every other respect. His hands were so wedded to the piano, that he could use them for nothing else: at table, his wife carved for him; and, in everything relating to money, or the management of his domestic affairs, or even the choice and arrangement of his amusements, he was entirely under her guidance. His health was very delicate; and, during the latter part of his too short life, it declined rapidly. Like all weak-minded people, he was extremely apprehensive of death; and it was only by incessant application to his favourite study, that he prevented his spirits sinking totally under the fears of approaching dissolution. At all other times, he laboured under a profound melancholy, which unquestionably tended to accelerate the period of his existence. In this melancholy state of spirits, he composed the *Zauberflöte*, the *Clemenza di Tito*, and the celebrated mass in D minor, commonly known by the name of his *Requiem*. The circumstances which attended the composition of the last of these works are so remarkable, from the effect they produced upon his mind, that we shall detail them; and, with the account, close the life of Mozart.

'One day, when his spirits were unusually oppressed, a stranger, of a tall, dignified appearance, was introduced. His manners were grave and impressive. He told Mozart that he came from a person who did not wish to be known, to request he would compose a solemn mass, as a requiem for the soul of a friend whom he had recently lost, and whose memory he was desirous of commemorating by this solemn service. Mozart undertook the task, and engaged to have it completed in a month. The stranger begged to know what price he set upon his work, and immediately paid him one hundred ducats, and departed. The mystery of this visit seemed to have a very strong effect upon the mind of the musician. He brooded over it for some time; and then suddenly calling for writing materials, began to compose with extraordinary ardour. This application, however, was more than his strength could support; it brought on fainting-fits; and his increasing illness obliged him to suspend his work. "I am writing this Requiem for myself!" said he abruptly to his wife one day; "it will serve for my own funeral-service;" and this impression never afterwards left him. At the expiration of the month, the mysterious stranger appeared, and demanded the Requiem. "I have found it impossible," said Mozart, "to keep my word; the work has interested me more than I expected, and I have extended it beyond my first design. I shall require another month to finish it." The stranger made no objection; but observing, that for this additional trouble it was but just to increase the premium, laid down fifty ducats more, and promised to return at the time appointed. Astonished at his whole proceedings, Mozart ordered a servant to follow this singular personage, and, if possible, to find out who he was: the man, however lost sight of him, and was obliged to return as he went. Mozart, now more than ever persuaded that he was a messenger from the other world, sent to warn him that his end was approaching, applied with fresh zeal to the Requiem; and, in spite of the exhausted state both of his mind and body, completed it before the end of the month. At the appointed day the stranger returned; but Mozart was no more.' *

## NOTES ON AN ANCIENT GOTHIC CROWN.

Towards the close of 1858, or early in 1859, in the course of excavations at La Fuente de Guarraz, near Toledo, on the property of some private individual, a hoard of treasure of great value and interest was brought to light. No particulars of the discovery are recorded It seems, however, that there were not found any remains of a case or casket in which the relics had been enclosed; in several parts the ornamentation had been filled with the soil in which they were found; it has, therefore, been supposed that those relics of royalty had been buried in some time of confusion without any enclosure. The spot where the crowns were found was uncultivated land, which the peasants were breaking up when the discovery was made. The treasure consisted of eight crowns: four are of gold richly jewelled; from the front of the crowns jewelled crosses are suspended by gold chains; there are also chains of the same metal for the purpose of hanging the crowns in some convenient situation. These ancient and precious objects were brought to Paris in the month of January 1859, by the proprietor of the land where they were found, and the crowns were immediately purchased by the Minister of Public Instruction, for the national collection at the Hotel de Cluny, a museum which is already possessed of many valuable examples of medieval art, besides specimens of more ancient date. The largest of the crowns bears the following inscription, in letters jewelled and appended by little chains to its lower margin, 'RECCESVINTHVS REX OFFERET;' the letters are about two inches in length each—they are separately hung, and to each is attached a pendant pearl and sapphire. The gold letters are beautifully incrusted with precious stones, and engraved in the same manner as some of the gold work of the Anglo-Saxon period. By means of the inscription, we are able to arrive at a knowledge of the date of this crown, for King Reccesvinthus governed Spain from 653 to 675; the inscription also shews that it has been an offering (probably to some religious shrine) by this ruler; and the seven other crowns, of smaller dimensions and value, may have been those of the queen and the princes and princesses of the family; some of them, judging by their size, are intended for children of early age—the whole being a solemn offering on some important occasion.

In ancient times it was customary to enrich the saintly shrines with choice and valuable gifts; amongst these, however, there were often imitation crowns and other objects given as votive-offerings, to be placed over the altars, or in some other conspicuous position. There are, however, instances of the crowns which were actually worn by kings and queens having been devoted to this purpose—amongst these may be mentioned the Iron Crown of Lombardy. It is to be observed that the gold chains by which those relics were suspended, have been added to the simple circlets which were no doubt actually worn by royal personages about twelve hundred years ago, since they are formed with hinges and fastenings to facilitate the fastening of them to the heads of the wearers.

The crown of the king measures about nine inches in diameter, and twenty-seven in circumference; it is a hoop about four inches in breadth, and upwards of half an inch in thickness; it is, however, not solid, but formed of massive gold plates soldered together. The margins of this hoop consist of two bands of *cloisonné* work, with incrustations of carnelian; and it is still further enriched with thirty oriental sapphires of large size, set in collets, giving to the gems a very prominent relief. Thirty very large pearls are arranged alternately with the

* *Edinburgh Review*, xxxiii. 380.

sapphires. The intervening spaces are pierced in open work and engraved, so as to represent foliage and flowers, and to the lower margin is appended the fringe of letters already mentioned. The golden chains are united above with foliated ornaments, which are enriched with numerous pendant pearls and sapphires, and surmounted by a capital, in the form of a knot of crystal, elaborately carved and polished, and terminating in a globe of the same material. The Latin shaped cross, suspended from the crown by a slender chain, is set with six fine sapphires and eight pearls of remarkable dimensions, mounted in very high relief; jewelled pendants are also attached to the limbs and foot of the cross. This has been worn as a fibula or brooch, the acus by which it has been fastened to the royal robes

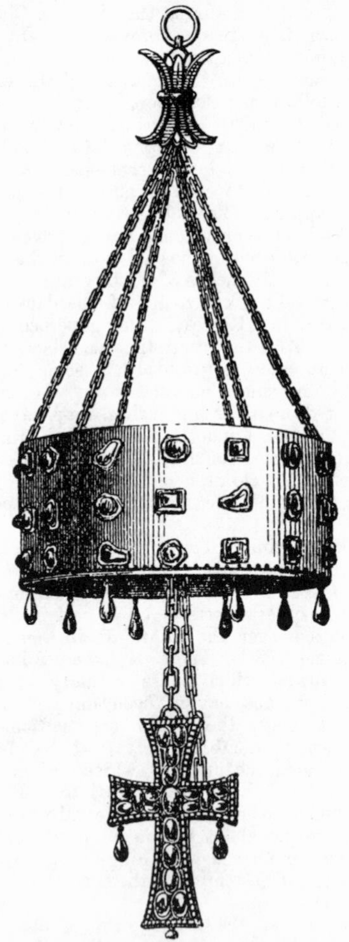

ANCIENT GOTHIC CROWN.

being still visible. The entire length of this combination of ornament, from the gold hook to which it is fastened to the lowest pendant sapphire attached to the cross, is about three feet. The crown is composed of the purest gold, the colour of which, with the violet sapphires alternating with the pearls, &c., presents a most gorgeous appearance.

The crown of which we give an engraving was probably worn by the queen of Reccesvinthus. The broad circlet is set with fifty-four rubies, sapphires, emeralds, and opals, whilst pendant sapphires fringe its lower margin. Above and below, near both edges of this circlet, there are little loops which seem to have been used for fastening a lining or cap of some costly tissue within the golden hoop, to protect the forehead of the wearer. The pendant cross is not so much decorated as that above mentioned, being, however, richly set on both sides with sapphires. The same jewels are also suspended from the cross. The other six crowns are of several fashions. Three are essentially different from the others, for instead of a broad band, the circlet consists of open framework of gold, formed of three horizontal hoops and numerous traverses, with gems set at the points of intersection; all the crowns are enriched with not less than fifty-four precious stones and pearls, and have also hanging fringes of sapphires.

On the pendant crosses of one of the crowns is engraved the following dedication: 'IN DEI NOMINE OFFERET SONNICA SANCTÆ MARIÆ IN SORBACES.' After the word NOMINE, a leaf is introduced as a stop; M. Du Sommerards considers that *Sonnica* is a male appellation. The three smallest crowns had no pendant crosses. As an example of ancient art-workmanship, this may be regarded as one of the most remarkable discoveries which have been made in recent times. The articles are in excellent preservation, and the French have reason to congratulate themselves that they have gained possession of such a prize.

## DR SHEBBEARE.

A person happening to pass by Charing Cross, on the 5th of December 1758, would have witnessed an extraordinary spectacle—a vast crowd surrounding a scaffold, on which stood two men and a pillory. A man in the pillory was no unusual sight in those days, but, in this particular case, the culprit's head and hands were not enclosed in the holes provided for the purpose; unconfined, he stood at his ease, and, to prevent even the rains of heaven from visiting him too roughly, a servant, dressed in a rich livery, carefully held an umbrella over his revered head. The man whose legally inflicted punishment was thus turned into a triumph, was Dr John Shebbeare. The son of a country attorney in Devonshire, Shebbeare was educated as a surgeon, but, being unsuccessful in his profession, turned his attention to literature. Having resolved, as he admitted, to write himself into a pension or the pillory, his political tracts were of an exceedingly virulent character, most galling to the king and ministry of the day. His best-known work is a series of *Letters to the People of England*, which had a wide circulation, and was eagerly read by all classes. The leading idea in the *Letters*, was the then not unpopular one, that the grandeur of France and the misfortunes of England, were wholly attributable to the undue influence of Hanover in the British council-chamber. In allusion to the White Horse being the armorial ensign of Hanover, Shebbeare's motto prefixed to his *Letters*, was the well-known verse from the *Apocalypse*—'And I looked and beheld a pale horse; and his name that sat upon him was Death, and Hell followed.'

In consequence of these *Letters*, the Attorney-general Pratt, afterwards Lord Camden, filed an information against Shebbeare in the Court of King's Bench, at the Easter term, 1758. At the trial, the officers of the crown admitted a point, then and afterwards much disputed, but now incontrovertibly established, that the jury have the right to determine both the *law* and the *fact* in cases of libel. Shebbeare was found guilty, and sentenced to be fined five pounds, to stand in the pillory one hour, to be imprisoned in the Marshalsea for three years, and to give security for his good-behaviour for seven years, himself in £500, and two others in £250 each. The under-sheriff at that time was a Mr Beardmore, a person of exactly the same political principles as Shebbeare; so he brought the culprit to the pillory in one of the city state-coaches, handing him out and in with the greatest demonstrations of respect. This gave Churchill occasion to write in the *Author:*

'Where is Shebbeare? O let not foul reproach,
Travelling thither in a city-coach,
The pillory dare to name; the whole intent
Of that parade was fame, not punishment,
And that old stanch Whig, Beardmore, standing by
Can in full court give that reproach the lie.'

The last line refers to a trial that arose out of this affair. Beardmore was arraigned in the Court of King's Bench for not doing his duty on the occasion. He contended that he had fulfilled the letter of the law by pillorying Shebbeare, and brought forward a number of witnesses to prove it. The judge, however, ruled that Shebbeare had not been put *in* the pillory, and the too-indulgent sub-sheriff was sentenced to pay a fine of £50, and suffer two months' imprisonment. Beardmore afterwards had his revenge, when solicitor to Wilkes; by an overstretch of legal power, he and his clerk were taken into custody, and recovered heavy damages from the secretary of state, for false imprisonment.

The footman who held the umbrella over Shebbeare, was an Irish chairman, hired and dressed in livery for the occasion. The following day, he called on the doctor, representing that the guinea he received for his trouble was scarcely sufficient; for, as he put it, 'only think of the disgrace, your honour.' Shebbeare gave him five shillings more, and the man went away satisfied.

Shebbeare remained three years, the full term of his sentence, in prison. On the expiration of that time, a new reign had commenced: George III., young and inexperienced, had ascended the throne; and his minister, Lord Bute, was the most unpopular of men. So it was thought best to make a friend of such a virulent and unscrupulous writer as the doctor, and a pension was granted to him accordingly. Thus his words were made good—he wrote himself into the pillory, and into a pension. Dr Johnson was pensioned shortly after, causing the wits to say that the king had first pensioned a *she* bear, and afterwards a *he* bear. In a satirical poem, entitled the *Masquerade*, Johnson and Shebbeare are thus alluded to:

'Much beared and much flattered by people of note
With cash in his pockets for turning his coat,
Surly Johnson as Crispin the Second comes pat in,
Talking Latin in English, and English in Latin,
Successor of Shebbeare, but missing the wood,
Where, pampered by Bute, his prototype stood.'

Shebbeare's plays, novels, political, satirical, and medical works, are thirty-four in number, but now all utterly forgotten. He died at a good old age in 1788, greatly lamented by his friends; for this Ishmael of politics and public life is represented as a very amiable and worthy man in all his private relations, as husband, son, father, brother, and friend. So little do we know of each other, so little do we probably know of our ownselves and characters.

---

# DECEMBER 6.

St Theophilus, bishop of Antioch, confessor, 190. St Nicholas, confessor, archbishop of Myra, 342. Saints Dionysia, Dativa, Aemilianus, Boniface, Leontia, Tertius, and Majoricus, martyrs, 484. St Peter Paschal. bishop and martyr, 1300.

## ST NICHOLAS.

St Nicholas belongs to the fourth century of the Christian era, and was a native of the city of Patara, in Lycia, in Asia Minor. So strong were his devotional tendencies, even from infancy, that we are gravely informed that he refused to suck on Wednesdays and Fridays, the fast-days appointed by the church! Having embraced a religious life by entering the monastery of Sion, near Myra, he was in course of time raised to the dignity of abbot, and for many years made himself conspicuous by acts of piety and benevolence. Subsequently he was elected archbishop of the metropolitan church of Myra, and exercised that office with great renown till his death. Though escaping actual martyrdom, he is said to have suffered imprisonment, and otherwise testified to the faith under the persecution of Diocletian.

As with St Cuthbert, the history of St Nicholas does not end with his death and burial. His relics were preserved with great honour at Myra till the end of the eleventh century, when certain merchants of Bari, on the Adriatic, moved by a pious indignation similar to what actuated the Crusaders, made an expedition to the coast of Lycia, and landing there, broke open the coffin containing the bones of the saint, and carried them off to Italy. They landed at Bari on the 9th of May 1087, and the sacred treasure which they had brought with them was deposited in the church of St Stephen. On the day when the latter proceeding took place, we are told that thirty persons were cured of various distempers through imploring the intercession of St Nicholas, and since that time his tomb at Bari has been famous for pilgrimages. In the ensuing article a description is given of the annual celebration of his festival in that seaport.

Perhaps no saint has enjoyed a more extended popularity than St Nicholas. By the Russian nation, he has been adopted as their patron, and in England no fewer than three hundred and seventy-two churches are named in his honour. He is regarded as the special guardian of virgins, of children, and of sailors. Scholars were under his protection, and from the circumstance of these being anciently denominated *clerks*, the fraternity of *parish clerks* placed themselves likewise under the guardianship of St Nicholas. He even came to be regarded as the patron of robbers, from an alleged adventure with thieves, whom he compelled to restore some stolen goods to their proper owners. But there are two specially celebrated legends regarding this saint, one of which bears reference to his protectorship of virgins, and the other to that of children. The former of these stories is as follows: A nobleman in the town of Patara had three daughters, but was sunk in such poverty, that he was not only unable to provide them with suitable marriage-portions, but was on the point of abandoning them to a sinful course of life from inability to preserve them otherwise from starvation. St Nicholas, who had inherited a large fortune, and employed it in innumerable acts of charity, no sooner heard of this unfortunate family, than he resolved to save it from the degradation with which it was threatened. As he proceeded secretly to the nobleman's house at night, debating with himself how he might best accomplish his object, the moon shone out from behind a cloud, and shewed him an open window into which he threw a purse of gold. This fell at the feet of the father of the maidens, and enabled him to portion his eldest daughter. A second nocturnal visit was paid to the house by the saint, and a similar present bestowed, which procured a dowry for the second daughter of the nobleman. But the latter was now determined to discover his mysterious benefactor, and with that view set himself to watch. On St Nicholas approaching, and preparing to throw in a purse of money for the third daughter, the nobleman caught hold of the skirt of his robe, and threw himself at his feet, exclaiming: 'O Nicholas! servant of God! why seek to hide thyself?' But the saint made him promise that he would inform no one of this seasonable act of munificence. From this incident in his life is derived apparently the practice formerly, if not still, customary in various parts of the continent, of the elder members and friends of a family placing, on the eve of St Nicholas's Day, little presents, such as sweetmeats and similar gifts, in the shoes or hose of their younger relatives, who, on discovering them in the morning, are supposed to attribute them to the munificence of St Nicholas. In convents, the young lady-boarders used, on the same occasion, to place silk-stockings at the door of the apartment of the abbess, with a paper recommending themselves to 'Great St Nicholas of her chamber.' The next morning they were summoned together, to witness the results of the liberality of the saint who had bountifully filled the stockings with sweetmeats. From the same instance of munificence recorded of St Nicholas, he is often represented bearing three purses, or three gold balls; the latter emblem forming the well-known pawnbrokers' sign, which, with considerable probability, has been traced to this origin. It is true, indeed, that this emblem is proximately derived from the Lombard merchants who settled in England at an early period, and were the first to open establishments for the lending of money. The three golden balls were also the sign of the Medici family of Florence, who, by a successful career of merchandise and money-lending, raised themselves to the supreme power in their native state. But the same origin is traceable in both cases—the emblematic device of the charitable St Nicholas.

The second legend to which we have adverted is even of a more piquant nature. A gentleman of Asia sent his two sons to be educated at Athens, but desired them, in passing through the town of Myra, to call on its archbishop, the holy Nicholas, and receive his benediction. The young men, arriving at the town late in the evening, resolved to defer their visit till the morning, and in the meantime took up their abode at an inn. The landlord, in order to obtain possession of their baggage, murdered the unfortunate youths in their sleep; and after cutting their bodies to pieces, and salting them, placed the mutilated remains in a pickling-tub along with some pork, under the guise of which he resolved to dispose of the contents of the vessel. But the archbishop was warned by a vision of this horrid transaction, and proceeded immediately to the inn, where he charged the landlord with the crime. The man, finding himself discovered, confessed his guilt, with great contrition, to St Nicholas, who not only implored on his behalf the forgiveness of Heaven, but also proceeded to the tub where the remains of the innocent youths lay in brine, and then made the sign of the cross, and offered up a supplication for their restoration to life. Scarcely was the saint's prayer finished, when the detached and mangled limbs were miraculously reunited, and the two youths regaining animation, rose up alive in the tub, and threw themselves at the feet of their benefactor. We are further informed, that the archbishop refused their homage, desiring the young men to return thanks to the proper quarter from which this blessing had

LEGENDARY REPRESENTATION OF ST NICHOLAS—FROM A MANUSCRIPT IN THE BODLEIAN LIBRARY.

descended; and then, after giving them his benediction, he dismissed them with great joy to continue their journey to Athens. In accordance with this legend, St Nicholas is frequently represented, as delineated in the accompanying engraving, standing in full episcopal costume beside a tub with naked children.

An important function assigned to St Nicholas, is that of the guardianship of mariners, who in Roman Catholic countries regard him with special reverence. In several seaport towns there are churches dedicated to St Nicholas, whither sailors resort to return thanks for preservation at sea, by hanging up votive pictures, and making other offerings. This practice is evidently a relic of an old pagan custom alluded to by Horace :

> Me tabulâ sacer
> Votivâ paries indicat uvida
> Suspendisse potenti
> Vestimenta maris Deo.

The office of protector of sailors, thus attributed in ancient times to Neptune, was afterwards transferred to St Nicholas, who is said, on the occasion of making a voyage to the Holy Land, to have caused by his prayers a tempest to assuage, and at another time to have personally appeared to, and saved some mariners who had invoked his assistance.

## The Feast of St Nicholas.

The Feast of St Nicholas, at Bari, is one of the chief ecclesiastical festivals of Southern Italy. It is attended by pilgrims in thousands, who come from considerable distances. From the Tronto to Otranto, the whole eastern slope of the Apennines sends eager suppliants to this famous shrine, and nowhere is there more distinctly to be seen how firm and deep a hold the faith in which they have been educated has on the enthusiastic nature of the Italian peasantry, than at this sanctuary, and on this occasion.

Bari is a city of considerable importance, in the compartment of Apulia. It is situated on the Adriatic coast, half-way between the spur, formed by Monte Gargano, and the heel of the boot. It contains some 58,000 inhabitants, and is capital of the province of Terra di Bari, which contains more than half a million of population. The city occupies a small peninsula, which escapes, as it were, into the blue waters of the Adriatic, from the bosom of the richest and most fertile country in Italy. The whole seaboard, from the mouths of the Ofanto to within a few miles of the renewed 'overland-route' harbour of Brindisi, recalls the descriptions given of Palestine in its ancient and highly-cultivated state. The constant industry of the people—in irrigation, in turning over the soil, in pruning the exuberant vegetation—is rewarded by a harvest in every month of the year, and the wealth of the soil is expressed by the contented aspect, the decent clothing, and the personal adornment with rings, chains, and ear-rings, of both men and women. Stockings and even gloves are commonly worn, and that not as being needed for defence against the climate, but as marks of decent competence. At Barletta, the great grain-port, which is situated between this garden of Italy and the great pastoral plain of Apulia, there is a labour-market held daily, during the summer months, at four A.M. There the labourers meet, before going to their daily toil, to settle the price of labour, and to arrange for the due distribution of workmen through the country. Each man is attended by his dog, and most of them mount their asses, at the conclusion of this ancient and admirable congress, to ride to the scene of their occupation.

The harvests of this fertile country commence, in the latter part of April and earlier portion of May, by the gathering of the pulse crops, those of beans especially, on which the people subsist for some weeks, and of vetches. Oranges and lemons succeed during the month of May, and the country affords many species of these fruit, one at least of which, as large as a child's head, and with a thick and edible rind, is unknown in other parts of Europe. In June, succeeds the harvest of oats, barley, and wheat, and the gathering of flax. In July, the maize is harvested; a plant which has been regarded as of American origin, but which is represented in the frescoes of Pompei as boiled and eaten precisely as we see it used at the present day. July is also the chief month for the making of cheese, as well as for the silk crop, or the tending of the silk-worm till it forms its cocoons. August produces cotton, tobacco, and figs. September yields grapes and a second shearing of wool, the first having taken place in May. The next five months, in fertile years, supply a constant yield of olives; and the plucking and preserving of the fruit, as well as the manufacture of oil, afford continual occupation. The olive, which, in the south of France, appears as a small shrub, covers the hills to the south of the Ofanto with trees about the size of the apple-trees of the Gloucestershire and Herefordshire orchards; and yet further south, in the Terra di Otranto, it rises into the magnitude of a forest-tree, and covers large districts of country with a rich and shady woodland. The culture and the varieties of the olive are the same with those that are so minutely described by Virgil, and the flavour of the edible species, and the delicacy and filbert-like aroma of the new-made oil, can only be appreciated by a visit to a country like Apulia. In March, the latest addition to the production of the country, the little Mandarin orange, becomes ripe; a delicious fruit, too delicate to export. Introduced into Italy during the present generation, it has already much increased in size, at the expense, it is said, of flavour. In April is the season for the slaughtering of fatted animals, which brings us round again to the wool-crop.

Bari is an archiepiscopal city, but its ancient cathedral, with its almost picturesque architecture, is outshone by the splendour of the Church of St Nicholas, the 'protector of the city.' The grand prior of St Nicholas is one of the chief ecclesiastical dignitaries in Italy, claiming to rank with the bishop of Loretto, the archbishop of Milan, and the cardinal of Capua. The king of Italy for the time is, when he enters the precincts of St Nicholas, a less person than the grand prior, ranking always, however, as the first canon of the chapter, and having a throne in the choir erected for his occupation in that capacity. It so chanced that the writer was in Bari, and was the guest of the grand prior, who was a man every way fitted to sustain such a dignity—courteous and affable, erect and vigorous in form and gait, and clear and bright in complexion, although hard on fourscore years of age. He was the very counterpart of the pictures of Fénélon, but of Fénélon unworn by the charge of the education of a dauphin.

The two great festivals that are distinctive of the

city are those of St Mark and St Nicholas. On St Mark's Day, the chief peculiarity is the procession of the clergy and municipality to the walls of the ancient castle that overlook the sea, and the solemn firing of a cannon thrice in the direction of Venice, in acknowledgment of the relief afforded by the Venetian fleet when Bari was besieged by the Saracens in 1002 A.D. The ricochet of the cannon-ball over the surface of the Adriatic is watched with the greatest interest by the people, and the distance from the shore at which the water is struck appears to be regarded as ominous.

But on the festa of St Nicholas, in addition to the rejoicings of the citizens and to the influx of the *contadini*, the city is absolutely invaded by an army of pilgrims. With staves bound with olive, with pine, or with palm, each bearing a suspended water-bottle formed out of a gourd, frequently barefoot, clothed in every variety of picturesque and ancient costume, devotees from many different provinces of the kingdom seek health or other blessings at the shrine of the great St Nicholas. The priory gives to each a meal, and affords shelter to many. Others fill every arch or sheltered nook in the walls, bivouac in the city, or spend the night in devotion. The grand vicar of the priory said that on that morning they had given food to nine thousand pilgrims, and there are many who never seek the dole, but travelling on horseback or in carriages to within a few miles of Bari, assume the pilgrim habit only to enter the very precincts of the shrine.

The clergy composing the chapter of St Nicholas are not slow to maintain the thaumaturgic character of their patron, and seem to believe in it. The bones of the saint are deposited in a sepulchre beneath the magnificent crypt, which is in itself a sort of subterranean church, of rich Saracenic architecture. Through the native rock which forms the tomb, water constantly exudes, which is collected by the canons on a sponge attached to a reed, squeezed into bottles, and sold to the pilgrims, as a miraculous specific, under the name of the 'Manna of St Nicholas.' As a proof of its supernatural character, a large bottle was shewn to me, in which, suspended from the cork, grew and floated the delicate green bladder of one of the Adriatic *ulvæ*. I suppose that its growth in fresh water had been extremely slow, for a person, whose word I did not doubt, assured me that he remembered the bottle from his childhood, and that the vegetation was then much less visible. 'This,' said the grand vicar, a tall aquiline-featured priest, who looked as if he watched the effect of every word upon a probable heretic—'this we consider to be conclusive as to the character of the water. If vegetation takes place in water that you keep in a jar, the water becomes offensive. This bottle has been in its present state for many years. You see the vegetation. But it is not putrid. Taste it, you will find it perfectly sweet. *Questa è prodigiosa*.' I trust that all the water that was sold to the pilgrims was really thus afforded by St Nicholas, if its efficacy be such as is asserted to be the case; but on this subject the purchasers must rely implicitly on the good faith of the canons, as mere human senses cannot distinguish it from that of the castle well.

The pilgrims, on entering the Church of St Nicholas, often shew their devotion by making the circuit once, or oftener, on their knees. Some are not content with this mark of humility, but actually move around the aisles with the forehead pressed to the marble pavement, being generally led by a child, by means of a string or handkerchief, of which they hold the corner in the mouth. It is impossible to conceive anything more calculated to stir the heart with mingled feelings of pity, of admiration, of sympathy, and of horror than to see these thousands of human beings recalling, in their physiognomy, their dialects, their gesticulations, even their dresses, the *Magna Græcia* of more than two thousand years ago, urged from their distant homes by a strong and intense piety, and thinking to render acceptable service by thus debasing themselves below the level of the brute. The flushed face, starting eyes, and scarred forehead, fully distinguish such of the pilgrims as have thus sought the benediction of the saint.

The mariners of Bari take their own part, and that a very important one, in the functions of the day, and go to a considerable expense to perform their duty with *éclat*. Early in the morning, they enter the church in procession, and receive from the canons the wooden image of the saint, attired in the robes and mitre of an archbishop, which they bear in triumph through the city, attended by the canons only so far as the outer archway of the precincts of the priory. They take their charge to visit the cathedral and other places, and then fairly embark him, and carry him out to sea, where they keep him until nightfall. They then return, disembark under the blaze of illumination, bonfires, and fireworks, and the intonation, by the whole heaving mass of the population, of a Gregorian Litany of St Nicholas; parade the town, visit by torchlight, and again leave, his own church; and finally, and late in the night, return the image to the reverend custody of the canons, who, in their purple robes and fur capes turned up with satin, play only a subordinate part in the solemnity. 'It is the only time,' said a thickly-moustached bystander—'it is the only occasion, in Italy, on which you see the religion of Jesus Christ in the hands of the people.' The conduct of the festa was, indeed, in the hands of the mariners and of the pilgrims; the character of the religion is a different question.

Those who have witnessed the festa of St Januarius at Naples, will err if they endeavour thence to realise the character of the festa of St Nicholas at Bari. The effect on the mind is widely different. Without the frantic excitement that marks the Neapolitan festival, there is a deep, serious, anxious conviction that pervades the thousands who assemble at Bari, which renders the commemoration of St Nicholas an event unique in its nature. The nocturnal procession, the flashing torches, the rockets, the deep-toned litany, the hum and surge of the people through the ancient archways, the thousands of pilgrims that seem to have awakened from a slumber of seven centuries, all tend powerfully to affect the imagination. But the chief element of this power over the mind is to be found in the deep earnestness of so great a mass of human beings, while the stars look down calm and solemn on their time-honoured rite, and a deep bass to their litany rolls in from the waves of the Adriatic.

## The Boy-Bishop: Eton Montem.

On St Nicholas's Day, in ancient times, a singular ceremony used to take place. This was the election of the *Boy-bishop*, or *Episcopus Puerorum*, who, from this date to Innocents' or Childermas Day, on 28th December, exercised a burlesque episcopal jurisdiction, and, with his juvenile dean and prebendaries, parodied the various ecclesiastical functions and ceremonies. It is well known that, previous to the Reformation, these profane and ridiculous mummeries were encouraged and participated in by the clergy themselves, who, confident of their hold on the reverence or superstition of the populace, seem to have entertained no apprehension of the dangerous results which might ultimately ensue from such sports, both as regarded their own influence and the cause of religion itself.

The election of the Boy-bishop seems to have prevailed generally throughout the English cathedrals, and also in many of the grammar-schools, but the place where, of all others, it appears to have specially obtained, was the episcopal diocese of Salisbury or Sarum. A full description of the mock-ceremonies enacted on the occasion is preserved in the *Processional of Salisbury Cathedral*, where also the service of the Boy-bishop is printed and set to music. It seems to have constituted literally a mimic transcript of the regular episcopal functions; and we do not discover any trace of parody or burlesque, beyond the inevitable one of the ludicrous contrast presented by the diminutive bishop and his chapter to the grave and canonical figures of the ordinary clergy of the cathedral. The actors in this solemn farce were composed of the choristers of the church, and must have been well drilled in the parts which they were to perform. The boy who filled the character of bishop, derived some substantial benefits from his tenure of office, and is said to have had the power of disposing of such prebends as fell vacant during the period of his episcopacy. If he died in the course of it, he received the funeral honours of a bishop, and had a monument erected to his memory, of which latter distinction an example may be seen on the north side of the nave of Salisbury Cathedral, where is sculptured the figure of a youth clad in episcopal robes, with his foot on a lion-headed and dragon-tailed monster, in allusion to the expression of the Psalmist: '*Conculcabis leonem et draconem*—[Thou shalt tread on the lion and the dragon].'

Besides the regular buffooneries throughout England of the Boy-bishop and his companions in church, these pseudo-clergy seem to have perambulated the neighbourhood, and enlivened it with their jocularities, in return for which a contribution, under the designation of the 'Bishop's subsidy,' would be demanded from passers-by and householders. Occasionally, royalty itself deigned to be amused with the burlesque ritual of the mimic prelate, and in 1299, we find Edward I., on his way to Scotland, permitting a Boy-bishop to say vespers before him in his chapel at Heton, near Newcastle-on-Tyne, on the 7th of December, the day after St Nicholas's Day. On this occasion, we are informed that his majesty made a handsome present to this mock-representative of Episcopacy, and the companions who assisted him in the discharge of his functions. During the reign of Queen Mary of persecuting memory, we find a performance by one of these child-bishops before her majesty, at her manor of St-James-in-the-Fields, on St Nicholas's Day and Innocents' Day, 1555. This queen restored, on her accession, the ceremonial, referred to, which had been abrogated by her father, Henry VIII., in 1542. We accordingly read in Strype's *Ecclesiastical Memorials*, quoted by Brand, that on 13th November 1554, an edict was issued by the bishop of London to all the clergy of his diocese to have the procession of a boy-bishop. But again we find that on 5th December, or St Nicholas's Eve, of the same year, 'at even-song time, came a commandment that St Nicholas should *not go abroad or about*. But notwithstanding, it seems so much were the citizens taken with the mock of St Nicholas—that is, a boy-bishop—that there went about these St Nicholases in divers parishes, as in St Andrew's, Holborn, and St Nicholas Olaves, in Bread Street. The reason the procession of St Nicholas was forbid, was because the cardinal had, this St Nicholas Day, sent for all the convocation, bishops, and inferior clergy, to come to him to Lambeth, there to be absolved from all their perjuries, schisms, and heresies.' Again Strype informs us that, in 1556, on the eve of his day, 'St Nicholas, that is, a boy habited like a bishop *in pontificalibus*, went abroad in most parts of London, singing after the old fashion, and was received with many ignorant but well-disposed people into their houses, and had as much good cheer as ever was wont to be had before, at least, in many places.'

With the final establishment of Protestantism in England, the pastime of the Boy-bishop disappeared; but the well-known festivity of the *Eton Montem* appears to have originated in, and been a continuance under another form, of the medieval custom above detailed. The Eton celebration, now abolished, consisted, as is well known, in a march of the scholars attending that seminary to Salt Hill, in the neighbourhood [AD MONTEM—'To the Mount'—whence the name of the festivity], where they dined, and afterwards returned in procession to Eton in the evening. It was thoroughly of a military character, the mitre and ecclesiastical vestments of the Boy-bishop and his clergy of former times being exchanged for the uniforms of a company of soldiers and their captain. Certain boys, denominated *salt-bearers*, and their *scouts* or deputies, attired in fancy-dresses, thronged the roads in the neighbourhood, and levied from the passers-by a tribute of money for the benefit of their captain. This was supposed to afford the latter the means of maintaining himself at the university, and amounted sometimes to a considerable sum, occasionally reaching as high as £1000. According to the ancient practice, the salt-bearers were accustomed to carry with them a handkerchief filled with salt, of which they bestowed a small quantity on every individual who contributed his quota to the subsidy. The origin of this custom of distributing salt is obscure, but it would appear to have reference to those ceremonies so frequently practised at schools and colleges in former times, when a new-comer or *freshman* arrived, and, by being *salted*, was, by a variety of ceremonies more amusing to his companions than himself, admitted to a participation with the other scholars in their pastimes and privileges. A favourite joke at Eton in former times was, it is said, for the salt-bearers to fill with the commodity which they carried, the mouth of any stolid-looking countryman, who, after giving them a trifle, asked for an equivalent in return.

About the middle of the last century, the Eton Montem was a *biennial*, but latterly it became a *triennial* ceremony. One of the customs, certainly a relic of the Boy-bishop revels, was, after the procession reached Salt Hill, for a boy habited like a parson to read prayers, whilst another officiated as clerk, who at the conclusion of the service was kicked by the parson downhill. This part of the ceremonies, however, was latterly abrogated in deference, as is said, to the wishes of Queen Charlotte, who, on first witnessing the practice, had expressed great dissatisfaction at its irreverence. The Eton-Montem festival found a stanch patron in George III., who generally attended it with his family, and made, along with them, liberal donations to the salt-bearers, besides paying various attentions to the boys who filled the principal parts in the show. Under his patronage the festival flourished with great splendour; but it afterwards fell off, and at last, on the representation of the master of Eton College to her Majesty and the government, that its continuance had become undesirable, the Eton Montem was abolished in January 1847. This step, however, was not taken without a considerable amount of opposition.

In recent times, the Eton-Montem festival used to be celebrated on Whit-Tuesday, but previous to 1759, it took place on the first Tuesday in Hilary Term, which commences on 23d January. It then not unfrequently became necessary to cut a passage through the snow to Salt Hill, to allow the procession to pass. At a still remoter period, the celebration appears to have been held before the Christmas holidays, on one of the days between the feasts of St Nicholas and the Holy Innocents, the period during which the Boy-bishop of old, the precursor of the 'captain' of the Eton scholars, exercised his prelatical functions.

---

*Born.*—Henry VI. of England, 1421, *Windsor;* Baldassarre Castiglione, diplomatist and man of letters, 1478, *Casatico, near Mantua;* General George Monk, Duke of Albemarle, 1608, *Potheridge, Devonshire;* Sir David Baird, hero of Seringapatam, 1757, *Newbyth, Scotland;* Rev. Richard Harris Barham, author of the *Ingoldsby Legends*, 1788, *Canterbury*.

*Died.*—Otho II., Emperor of Germany, 983, *Rome;* Alphonso I. of Portugal, 1185, *Coimbra;* Pope Clement VI., 1352, *Avignon;* Dr John Lightfoot, divine and commentator, 1675, *Great Munden, Herts;* Nicholas Rowe, dramatist, 1718, *London;* Florent Carton Dancourt, comic dramatist, 1726; Catharine Clive, celebrated comic actress, 1785, *Strawberry Hill, Twickenham.*

## THE INTRODUCTION OF TEA.

Dr Johnson gives Earls Arlington and Ossory the credit of being the first to import tea into England. He says that they brought it from Holland in 1666, and that their ladies taught women of quality how to use it. Pepys, however, records having sent for a cup of tea, a China drink of which he had never drunk before, on the 25th of September 1660; and by an act of parliament of the same year, a duty of eightpence a gallon was levied on all sherbert, chocolate, and tea made for sale. Waller, writing on some tea commended by Catherine of Braganza, says:

'The best of herbs and best of queens we owe
To that bold nation, which the way did shew
To the fair region where the sun does rise.

The Muses' friend, Tea, does our fancy aid,
Repress the vapours which the head invade,
And keeps the palace of the soul serene.'

Her majesty may have helped to render tea-drinking fashionable, but the beverage was well known in London before the Restoration. The *Mercurius Politicus* of September 30, 1658, contains the following advertisement:—'That excellent, and by all physicians approved, China drink, called by the Chineans *Tcha*, by other nations *Tay*, alias Tee, is sold at the Sultaness Head Coffee-House, in Sweeting's Rents, by the Royal Exchange, London.' Possibly this announcement prompted the founder of Garraway's to issue the broadsheet, preserved in the British Museum Library, in which he thus runs riot in exaltation of tea: 'The quality is moderately hot, proper for winter or summer. The drink is declared to be most wholesome, preserving in perfect health until extreme old age. The particular virtues are these. It maketh the body active and lusty. It helpeth the headache, giddiness and heaviness thereof. It removeth the obstructions of the spleen. It is very good against the stone and gravel. . . . . It taketh away the difficulty of breathing, opening obstructions. It is good against lippitude distillations, and cleareth the sight. It removeth lassitude, and cleanseth and purifieth adust humours and a hot liver. It is good against crudities, strengthening the weakness of the stomach, causing good appetite and digestion, and particularly for men of a corpulent body, and such as are great eaters of flesh. It vanquisheth heavy dreams, easeth the brain, and strengtheneth the memory. It overcometh superfluous sleep, and prevents sleepiness in general, a draught of the infusion being taken; so that, without trouble, whole nights may be spent in study without hurt to the body. It prevents and cures agues, surfeits, and fevers by infusing a fit quantity of the leaf, thereby provoking a most gentle vomit and breathing of the pores, and hath been given with wonderful success. It (being prepared and drunk with milk and water) strengtheneth the inward parts and prevents consumptions. . . . . It is good for colds, dropsies, and scurvies, and expelleth infection. . . . . And that the virtue and excellence of the leaf and drink are many and great, is evident and manifest by the high esteem and use of it (especially of late years), by the physicians and knowing men in France, Italy, Holland, and other parts of Christendom, and in England it hath been sold in the leaf for six pounds, and sometimes for ten pounds the pound-weight; and in respect of its former scarceness and dearness, it hath been only used as a regalia in high treatments and entertainments, and presents made thereof to princes and grandees till the year 1657.'

Having furnished these excellent reasons why people should buy tea, Mr Garway proceeds to tell them why they should buy it of him: 'The said Thomas Garway did purchase a quantity thereof, and first publicly sold the said tea in leaf and drink, made according to the directions of the most knowing merchants and travellers into those Eastern countries; and upon knowledge and experience of the said Garway's continued care and industry in obtaining the best tea, and making drink thereof, very many noblemen, physicians, merchants, and gentlemen of quality, have ever since sent to him for the said leaf, and daily resort to his house in Exchange Alley, to drink the drink thereof. And to the end that all persons of eminency and quality, gentlemen and others, who have occasion for tea in leaf, may be supplied, these are to give notice that the said Thomas Garway hath tea to sell from sixteen shillings to fifty shillings the pound.'

*Rugge's Diurnal* tells us that tea was sold in almost every street in London, in 1659, and it stood so high in estimation, that, two years later, the East India Company thought a couple of pounds a gift worthy the acceptance of the king. Its use spread rapidly among the wealthier classes, although the dramatists railed against it as only fit for women, and men who lived like women. In 1678, we find Mr Henry Saville writing to his uncle, Secretary Coventry, in disparagement of some of his friends who have fallen into 'the base unworthy Indian practice' of calling for tea after dinner in place of the pipe and bottle, seeming to hold with *Poor Robin* that

'Arabian tea
Is dishwater to a dish of whey.'

The enemies of the new fashion attacked it as an innocent pretext for bringing together the wicked of both sexes, and ladies were accused of slipping out of a morning:

'To Mrs Thoddy's
To cheapen tea, without a bodice.'

Dean Swift thus sketches a tea-table scene:

'Let me now survey
Our madam o'er her evening tea,
Surrounded with the noisy clans
Of prudes, coquettes, and harridans.
Now voices over voices rise,
While each to be the loudest vies.
They contradict, affirm, dispute;
No single tongue one moment mute;
All mad to speak and none to hearken,
They set the very lapdog barking,
Their chattering makes a louder din,
Than fishwives o'er a cup of gin;
Far less the rabble roar and rail,
When drunk with sour election ale!'
*Journal of a Modern Lady.*

Scandal, if the poets are to be believed, was always an indispensable accompaniment of the cheering cup:

'Still, as their ebbing malice it supplies,
Some victim falls, some reputation dies.'

And Young exclaims:

'Tea! how I tremble at thy fatal stream!
As Lethe dreadful to the love of fame.
What devastations on thy banks are seen,
What shades of mighty names that once have been!
A hecatomb of characters supplies
Thy painted altars' daily sacrifice!'

Other writers denounced tea on economical grounds. *The Female Spectator* (1745) declares the tea-table 'costs more to support than would maintain two children at nurse; it is the utter destruction of all economy, the bane of good-housewifery, and the source of idleness.' That it was still a luxury rather than a necessity, is plain from the description of the household management of a model country rector, as given in *The World* (1753). 'His only article of luxury is tea, but the doctor says he would forbid that, if his wife could forget her London education. However, they seldom offer it but to the best company, and less than a pound will last them a twelvemonth.' What would the frugal man have thought of the country lady mentioned by Southey, who, on receiving a pound of tea as a present from a town-friend, boiled the whole of it in a kettle, and served up the leaves with salt and butter, to her expectant neighbours, who had been invited specially to give their opinions on the novelty! They unanimously voted it detestable, and were astonished that even fashion could make such a dish palatable.

Count Belchigen, physician to Maria Theresa, ascribed the increase of new diseases to the weakness and debility induced by daily drinking tea; but as a set-off, allowed it to be a sovereign remedy for excessive fatigue, pleurisy, vapours, jaundice, weak lungs, leprosy, scurvy, consumption, and yellow fever. Jonas Hanway was a violent foe to tea. In an essay on its use, he ascribes the majority of feminine disorders to an indulgence in the herb, and more than hints that the same vice has lessened the vigour of Englishmen, and deprived Englishwomen of beauty. He is horrified at the fact of no less than *six* ships and some five hundred seamen being employed in the trade between England and China! Johnson reviewed the essay in the *Literary Magazine*, prefacing his criticism with the candid avowal that the author 'is to expect little justice from a hardened and shameless tea-drinker, who has for twenty years diluted his meals with only the infusion of this fascinating plant; whose kettle has scarcely time to cool; who with tea amuses the evening, with tea solaces the midnight, and with tea welcomes the morning.' Spite of this threatening exordium, the doctor's defence of his beloved drink is but weak and lukewarm. He admits that tea is not fitted for the lower classes, as it only gratifies the taste without nourishing the body, and styles it 'a barren superfluity,' proper only to amuse the idle, relax the studious, and dilute the meals of those who cannot use exercise, and will not practise abstinence. For such an inveterate tea-drinker, the following is but faint praise: 'Tea, among the greater part of those who use it most, is drunk in no great quantity. As it neither exhilarates the heart, nor stimulates the palate, it is commonly an entertainment merely nominal, a pretence for assembling to prattle, for interrupting business or diversifying idleness.' He gives the annual importation then (1757) as about four million pounds, 'a quantity,' he allows, 'sufficient to alarm us.' What would the doctor say now, when, as evening closes in, almost every English household gathers round the table, where

'The cups
That cheer but not inebriate wait on each,'

and the quantity of the article imported is nearly fortyfold what he regards in so serious a light?

# DECEMBER 7.

St Ambrose, bishop and confessor, doctor of the church, 397. St Fara, virgin and abbess, 655.

*Born.*—Giovanni Lorenzo Bernini, architect and sculptor, 1598, *Naples;* Rev. Richard Valpy, D.D., compiler of classic grammars, &c., 1754, *Jersey.*

*Died.*—Cicero, Roman orator, assassinated 43 B.C.; Algernon Sidney, republican and patriot, beheaded on *Tower Hill,* 1683; Marshal Ney, general of Napoleon, shot at *Paris,* 1815; Dr John Aikin, popular author, 1822, *Stoke-Newington;* Abbé Macpherson, rector of the Scotch College, Rome, 1846.

## SINGULAR DISPENSATION GRANTED BY LUTHER AND OTHER PROTESTANT DIVINES.

Philip, landgrave of Hesse, one of the stanchest protectors of Luther, had married Catherine of Saxony; but this princess, though beautiful and accomplished, had never succeeded in finding favour in his eyes. After having, for several years, paid his addresses to various beauties, the inconstant husband at last formed a more abiding intimacy with Marguerite de Staal. A severe illness, from which he only recovered with great difficulty, had the effect of inspiring him with some scruples relative to his course of life—he resolved to have his conscience set at rest.

To attain this object, the landgrave addressed a memorial to Luther, in which, fortified by the authority of the Old Testament, he demanded from the Reformer permission to have *two wives* at the same time—one who, in public, should receive the honours due to a princess and his consort, and another who, without scandal, might be regarded as his legal mistress. Although, in this remarkable document, Philip supplicates the doctors to grant him this favour, he at the same time threatens to appeal to the emperor, or even the pope, should he fail in having his request complied with by the Protestant divines. Moreover, he makes most liberal promises. 'Let them grant me,' he says, 'in the name of God, what I ask, so that I may be able to live and die more cheerfully for the cause of the gospel, and be more ready to undertake its defence. I engage to perform, on my part, all that may be required of me in reason, whether as regards *the property of convents,* or matters of a similar description.'

The conduct of this singular negotiation was intrusted to the celebrated reformer, Bucer. The Protestant clergy were embarrassed. On the one part, they feared to bring their profession of belief into discredit by so extended a compliance; while, on the other hand, they were desirous to retain a patron of such power and influence as Philip. At last Melanchthon, as principal scribe, drew up a resolution, which was approved by the other divines. An extract from this curious document is subjoined.

It is drawn up with considerable care and address. The theologians begin by laying down, according to the gospel, the position that no man ought to have more than one wife; the landgrave is requested to take notice what confusion would result, if this fundamental law of society were overthrown; and it also represents to him that the princess, his consort, is a pattern of virtue; that she has presented him with several children, &c.

'But, in conclusion,' continues the reverend conclave through their spokesman, 'if your highness is thoroughly determined to marry a second wife, we are of opinion that it ought to be done secretly; that is to say, there should be none present beyond the contracting parties, and a few trustworthy persons, who should be bound to secrecy. There is no opposition or real scandal to be dreaded here, for it is no unusual thing for princes to maintain mistresses, *nihil enim est inusitati principes concubinas alere;* and even though the people in general were scandalised, the most enlightened of the community would doubt the truth of the story, whilst prudent persons would always prefer this moderate course of procedure to adultery and other brutal actions. We ought not to care greatly for what the world will say, provided our own conscience is clear: *nec curandi aliorum sermones, si rectè cum conscientiâ agatur.* It is thus that we approve of the proceeding in question, though only in the circumstances which we have just indicated, for the gospel has neither recalled nor forbidden what the law of Moses permitted with regard to marriage.'

This warrant of approval is subscribed by eight doctors of divinity, including Luther, Melanchthon, and Bucer, and is dated the 7th of December 1539.

On the 4th of March of the ensuing year, Philip espoused Marguerite de Staal in the castle of Rothemburg. The marriage-contract is a no less curious document than the resolution of the Protestant divines above quoted.

'Considering that the eye of God' (so says this precious manifesto) 'penetrates everything, and that little of the workings of Omniscience comes to the knowledge of men, his highness declares his intention of marrying Marguerite de Staal, notwithstanding that the princess, his consort, is still alive; and in order to prevent this proceeding being imputed to inconstancy or whim, to avoid scandal, and preserve the honour of the said Margaret and the reputation of her family, he here swears before God, and on his soul and conscience, that he neither takes her to wife through levity or caprice, nor from any contempt of law or superiors, but because he is compelled to this step by certain necessities so important and inevitable of health and conscience, that it is impossible for him to preserve his existence and live according to the law of God, unless he espouse a second wife in addition to the consort whom he already possesses. That his highness has explained the matter to many learned divines, men of Christian piety and prudence, and has taken the advice of these reverend persons, who, after investigating the circumstances laid before them, have recommended his highness to place his soul and conscience at rest by a double marriage. That the same cause and the same necessity have induced the most serene Princess Christina, Duchess of Saxony, first wife of his highness, through the exalted prudence and sincere devotion which render her so estimable, to consent with readiness *that a companion should be given to her,* so that the soul and health of her beloved spouse may run no further risk, and that the glory of God may be promoted, as the writing under the hand of the said princess sufficiently testifies.'

It will be recollected that the very same year

(1540) in which the above marriage of Philip of Hesse took place, Henry VIII. of England obtained, or rather commanded, the sanction of his clergy and parliament to his divorce from Anne of Cleves, merely because she did not happen to be to his liking. A still more liberal dispensation from the ordinary rules of morality was, in the last century, accorded by the Calvinistic clergy of Prussia to the reigning king, Frederick William II., nephew and successor of Frederick the Great, to have *three* wives at the same time—Elizabeth of Brunswick, the Princess of Hesse, and the Countess of Euhof. The authorisation granted by the divines was, like that of Luther and his brethren, founded on the principle, that it was better to contract an illegal marriage than to pursue habitually a course of immorality and error.*

## CUT-PURSES AND PICKPOCKETS.

In the olden time, ere pockets were invented, the *gipciere*, or purse, containing money and other valuables, being worn at the girdle, became a much-coveted prize for the dishonest, who managed to obtain possession of it by deftly cutting the strings by which it was suspended. Autolycus said, and we can well believe him, that 'an open ear, a quick eye, and a nimble hand, is necessary for a cut-purse.' Subsequently, however, when pockets came into fashion, the cut-purses—moving with the times, as the saying is—became pickpockets; still, down to the period of the Restoration, both branches of the light-fingered art flourished contemporaneously. And, though the days of the girdle-purse are long since past, its remembrance is not even yet lost. In the language of vulgar contumely, the opprobrious epithet of 'cut-purse rogue' is still applied to a person whose ill-favoured countenance is not belied by the honesty of his character. The thieves of London have long enjoyed the reputation of being exceedingly dexterous in the art of stealing from the person. Paul Hentzner, who visited England in 1598, in the capacity of tutor to a young German nobleman, tells us that, at Bartholomew Fair, one of his company, a Dr Tobias Solander, 'had his pocket picked of his purse, containing nine crowns *du soleil*, which, without doubt, was so cleverly taken from him by an Englishman, who always kept very close to him, that the doctor did not in the least perceive it.'

Such dexterity is not, altogether, to be wondered at in the street-thieves of the period, seeing that they were regularly trained to the exercise of their profession. Stow informs us that, in 1585, a person named Wotton, 'kept an academy for the education and perfection of pickpockets and cut-purses.' This man was of gentle birth, and had been a merchant of good credit, but becoming reduced in circumstances, he set up an ale-house at Smart's Quay, near Billingsgate. Here 'he commenced a new trade in life,' by opening a school to teach young boys to cut purses. 'Two devices,' continues Stow, 'were hung up—one was a pocket, and the other was a purse. The pocket had in it certain counters, and was hung about with hawk's bells, and over the top did hang a little sacring bell. The purse had silver in it, and he that could take out a counter, without noise of any of the bells, was adjudged a judicial *nypper*, according to their terms of art; a *foyster* was a pickpocket, a *nypper* was a pick-purse or cut-purse.

Mr John Selman, a celebrated 'nypper and foyster,' whose portrait is here presented to the

SELMAN, THE CUT-PURSE.

reader, with the purse, the fatal fruit of his dishonesty, still in his hand, was in all probability trained at Wotton's academy, on Smart's Quay. His history, so far as it is known, is short and simple, and in some places reads very like a police report of the present day. On Christmas-day, 1611, when King James, Queen Anne, the Duke of York, and several of the nobility, were receiving the sacrament in the Chapel Royal of Whitehall, a Mr Dubbleday observed a stranger in the sacred edifice, whose honesty he had some reason to suspect. Seeing this person swiftly but quietly leaving the chapel, after hovering for a short time round a Mr Barrie, Dubbleday went up to Barrie, and in the stereotyped phrase of a modern policeman, asked him if he had lost anything. Barrie at first said, 'No;' but on feeling his pockets, found that his purse, containing forty shillings, was gone. The two immediately followed the stranger, and arresting him, found in one of his pockets the stolen purse, in the other, a small knife used for cutting. After service was over, Sir Richard

* The above article is, for the most part, translated from *Ephémérides Politiques Littéraires et Religieuses*, a French work already quoted. Strange as the facts appear, they are perfectly authentic.

Banister, clerk of the Green Cloth, as the crime had been committed within the precincts of the court, examined the prisoner. The man, having been taken *flagrante delicto*, could not deny his crime He gave his name John Selman, resident in Shoe Lane, of no trade or profession, and acknowledged that he had gone to the royal chapel with an evil intention. He wore 'a fair black cloak, lined and faced with velvet, the rest of his apparel being suitable thereto.' In short, Selman was a prototype of the modern swell-mob's-man; and the short cloak he is represented wearing in the engraving, greatly resembles the cape which detectives tell us is used as a 'cover' by pickpockets at the present time. Six days afterwards, Selman was tried by royal commission, and found guilty. Being asked why sentence of death should not be passed upon him, he fell on his knees, submitted himself to the king's mercy, and begged that his body might have Christian burial. Then Sir Francis Bacon delivered sentence, not without taking the opportunity of pandering to the king's love of gross flattery, by saying: 'The first and greatest sin that ever was committed was done in heaven; the second was done in paradise, being heaven upon earth; and truly I cannot choose but place this in the third rank, in regard it was done in the house of God, and also God's lieutenant here on earth, being in God's house there present ready to receive the holy sacrament, all which being considered, the time, the place, and person there present, I do advise thee, that as thou hast submitted thyself to the king's mercy, so thou wilt crave pardon at God's hands.' Seven days more, and the sentence was carried into execution between Charing Cross and the Court Gate. Selman's last speech we may pass over; but it appears that the crowd at the execution behaved much as such crowds now do. 'See,' exclaims the chronicler to whom we are indebted for Selman's history, 'see the graceless and unrepenting minds of such livers; for one of his quality, a pickpocket, even at his execution, grew master of a true man's purse, who being presently taken, was imprisoned, and is like, the next sessions, to wander the long voyage after his grand captain, Monsieur John Selman.'

Ben Jonson humorously introduces a pickpocket in his play of *Bartholomew Fair*. A simple country squire, who fancies himself a match for all kinds of roguery, asks a ballad-singer for a song. The vocalist proposing to sing, '*A caveat against Cut-purses*,' the squire exhibits, boastingly, his well-lined purse, defying any thief to take it from him, and the singer commences thus:

'My masters, and friends, and good people, draw near,
And look to your purses, for that I do say;
And though little money, in them you do bear,
It costs more to get, than to lose in a day,
    You oft have been told,
    Both the young and the old,
And bidden beware of the cut-purse so bold.
Then if you take heed not, free me from the curse,
Who both give you warning, you, and the cut-purse.
Youth, youth, you had better been starved by thy nurse,
Than live to be hanged for cutting a purse!'

In another verse allusion is evidently made to Selman.

'At plays, and at sermons, and at the sessions,
'Tis daily their practice such booty to make;
Yea, under the gallows, at executions,
They stick not the stare-abouts' purses to take.
    Nay, one without grace,
    At a better place,
At court, and in Christmas, before the king's face,
Alack! then, for pity, must I bear the curse,
That only belongs to the cunning cut-purse.
Youth, youth, thou hadst better been starved by thy nurse,
Than live to be hanged for stealing a purse!'

While the squire stands listening to the song, his purse in his pocket, and one hand holding it firmly, a thief tickles his ear with a straw. As the hand is lifted to brush away the supposed insect, the purse is stolen and passed to the ballad-singer, who is an accomplice. The surprise and discomfiture of the silly squire may be imagined, but only rare Ben himself can describe it.

The most noted pickpocket in what Dr Johnson termed the *Biographia Flagitiosa*, was a woman named Mary Frith, but better known as Mall Cut-purse. This 'Sybilla Tyburnia' was born in 1585, and soon became an accomplished cut-purse. There is little new under the sun. She used to *work* in company with two other thieves, just as pickpockets do now. One called the '*bulk*,' created an obstruction; Mary, the '*file*,' cut the purse, and handed it to a third named the '*rub*,' who carried it off. When Mary was quite young, she, for a bet of £20, rode Banks's famous horse Morocco,* from Charing Cross to Shoreditch, dressed in doublet, breeches, boots, and spurs, carrying a trumpet in her hand and a banner hanging over her back. For wearing men's clothes on this occasion, Mall was tried by the ecclesiastical court, and forced to do penance at the door of St Paul's Cathedral. Having thus atoned for her offence, and finding a great convenience in male attire, she wore it ever after. She soon became an adroit fencer and bold rider, and in the character of a highwayman, robbed the Parliamentary general, Fairfax, of 200 gold jacobuses on Hounslow Heath. This, however, she considered merely robbing a Philistine who had stolen the crown from her king; for Mall was the stanchest of Cavaliers, and this trait in her character throws an air of romance over her strange history. She had established herself opposite the Conduit, in Fleet Street, as a broker or negotiator between thieves and the public, when Charles I. passed her door, on his return from the Border in 1639. Rushing out, she caught the king's hand, and kissed it; the same day she caused the Conduit to run with wine at her own expense. When Wentworth's trial was in progress, she sent a bull to the Bear Garden to be baited. As the sport was about to commence, she said: 'Gentlemen, that noble animal, the bull, is named Strafford; the wretched curs going to bait him are named Pym and St John; and if any one feels offended at what I say, here am I ready to maintain it by sword or cudgel.'

Mall's deeds were not all done in defiance of the law. She was instrumental in bringing to justice the notorious 'five women barbers,' who used a young girl in a very cruel and indescribable manner. With less good taste and feeling, Killigrew composed a song on this affair, which he sang to

* See *Book of Days*, vol. i. p. 225.

Charles II., till tears of laughter ran down the too merry monarch's cheeks. Antiquaries would give almost anything for a perfect copy of this song, which thus commences:

'Did you ever hear the like?
Did you ever hear the fame?
Of the five women barbers,
Who lived in Drury Lane.'

One of these five women barbers was the mother of Nan Clarges, who, marrying Monk, when his fortunes were at a low ebb, lived to hear herself styled Duchess of Albemarle.

Mall is said to have been the first Englishwoman who smoked tobacco. A portrait, representing her in the act of indulging in the luxury, adorns the frontispiece of Middleton's play of the *Roaring Girl*, in which she figures as the principal character. Another portrait represents her with a

MALL CUT-PURSE.

dog, an ape, and a parrot; for, like her friend Banks, she delighted in training animals, and made money by exhibiting their tricks. It is said that she was at one time worth £3000, but her generosity to distressed Cavaliers left her little more than £100 at her death. This sum she left to her relative, John Frith, a shipmaster at Rotherhithe; advising him to spend it in good wine, like a man, rather than venture it at sea, at the risk of being drowned in vile salt-water, like a dog. She died of a dropsy when upwards of seventy years of age, after having composed the following epitaph on herself, in the form of an acrostic:

'M erry I lived, and many pranks I played,
A nd, without sorrow, now in grave am laid;
R est, and the sleep of death, doth now surcease
Y outh's active sins, and their old-aged increase.

F amous I was for all the thieving art,
R enowned for what old women ride in cart,
I n pocket and in placket, I had part,
T his life I lived in a man's disguise,
H e best laments me that with laughter cries.'

An instance of a female acquiring a considerable sum of money by picking pockets, occurred in the last century. In 1783, a Miss West, a noted pickpocket, died; leaving, according to a magazine obituary, £3000 to her two children—'one of whom was born in Clerkenwell Bridewell, while the mother was imprisoned for picking pockets in Exeter Change, when Lord Baltimore' (another infamous character) 'was lying in state.'

---

# DECEMBER 8.

The Conception of the Blessed Virgin Mary. St Romaric, abbot, 653.

## Conception of the Virgin Mary.

This is one of the festivals of the Roman Catholic Church, in connection with which a long controversy prevailed. It is well known that the doctrine of the *immaculate* conception of the Virgin, or her conception without the taint of original sin, was, till recently, a theological dogma on which the Church of Rome had pronounced no positive decision. Though accepted by the majority of doctors, and strenuously maintained by many theological writers, it was, nevertheless, denied by some, more especially by the Dominicans, and was pronounced by several popes to be an article of faith which was neither to be absolutely enforced nor condemned—a point, in short, on which the members of the church were free to use their private judgment. But the question, which for centuries had been allowed to remain an open subject for discussion, was determined in the affirmative by a deliverance of Pope Pius IX. on 8th December 1854. The doctrine of the Immaculate Conception of the Virgin forms accordingly, now, an essential article in the Roman Catholic system of belief.

---

*Born.*—Mary, Queen of Scots, 1542, *Linlithgow;* Queen Christina of Sweden, 1626; Charles Wentworth Dilke, editor of the *Athenæum*, &c., 1789; Johann Georg von Zimmermann, celebrated author of treatise on *Solitude*, 1728, *Brug, Switzerland.*

*Died.*—Emperor Sigismund of Germany, 1437; Henry Jenkins, aged 169, 1670, *Ellerton-upon-Swale, Yorkshire;* Richard Baxter, Nonconformist divine, 1691, *London;* Scaramouche, celebrated zany, 1694, *Paris;* Barthélemi d'Herbelot, distinguished orientalist, 1695, *Paris;* Thomas Corneille, dramatist, brother of Pierre, 1709, *Andelys;* Vitus Behring, navigator, 1741, *Behring Island, off Kamtchatka;* Thomas de Quincey, miscellaneous writer, 1859, *Edinburgh.*

### THOMAS DE QUINCEY.

In Mrs Gordon's *Memoir of Christopher North*, published towards the close of 1862, we meet with several curious illustrations of De Quincey's singular character.

De Quincey's confirmed habit of taking opium, which, at one time, held complete mastery over his powerful intellect, caused him to be distinguished by the undesirable title of 'the Opium Eater.' He may be said to have given himself the appellation in the first instance, by his book, entitled *The Confessions of an Opium Eater*, in which he professes to describe his experience as such, vividly portraying the wretchedness and the ecstasies of those extraordinary conditions of mind and body, with which, from his constant use of the drug, he became familiar. In 1829, De Quincey made a protracted stay at Professor Wilson's house. In the later years of his life, he almost entirely shook off an indulgence which pain, in the first instance, had led him to acquire, and which use had made habitual, and, to some extent, necessary; but at the time of this visit, he was still a slave. Mrs Gordon thus describes his daily routine, on the occasion of his visit to her father, above referred to:

'An ounce of laudanum per diem prostrated animal life in the early part of the day. It was no unfrequent sight to find him in his room lying upon the rug in front of the fire, his head resting upon a book, with his arms crossed over his breast, plunged in profound slumber. For several hours he would lie in this state, until the effects of the torpor had passed away. The time when he was most brilliant, was generally towards the early morning-hours; and then, more than once, in order to shew him off, my father arranged his supper-parties, so that, sitting till three or four in the morning, he brought Mr De Quincey to that point at which, in charm and power of conversation, he was so truly wonderful.'

A less painful and more amusing anecdote is told of that wordy, wandering manner, which renders his impassioned and beautiful prose sometimes tedious in the extreme. Being obliged, from delicacy of constitution, to be careful about his food, as Mrs Gordon tells us, he used to dine in his own room, and at his own hour. His invariable diet was 'coffee, boiled rice and milk, and a piece of mutton from the loin.' 'The cook, who had an audience with him daily, received her instructions in silent awe, quite overpowered by his manner; for, had he been addressing a duchess, he could scarcely have spoken with more deference. He would couch his request in such terms as these: "Owing to dyspepsia afflicting my system, and the possibilities of any additional disarrangement of the stomach taking place, consequences incalculably distressing would arise; so much so, indeed, as to increase nervous irritation, and prevent me from attending to matters of overwhelming importance, if you do not remember to cut the mutton in a diagonal rather than in a longitudinal form." The cook—a Scotchwoman—had great reverence for Mr De Quincey as a man of genius; but after one of these interviews, her patience was pretty well exhausted, and she would say: "Weel, I never heard the like o' that in a' my days; the body has an awfu' sicht o' words. If it had been my ain maister that was wanting his dinner, he would ha' ordered a hale tablefu' wi' little mair than a waff o' his haun, and here 's a' this claver aboot a bit mutton nae bigger than a prin. Mr De Quinshey would mak' a gran' preacher, though I 'm thinking a hantle o' the folk wouldna ken what he was driving at."'

The cook's view of the opium-eater's style was anything but superficial. During the last seventeen years of his life, De Quincey resided at the village of Lasswade, near Edinburgh. He died in the Scottish metropolis on 8th December 1859.

---

## SPOTS IN THE SUN.

December 8, 1590, at sunset, James Welsh of the ship *Richard of Arundel*, sailing off the coast of Guinea, observed a great black spot on the sun, and found the same appearance visible next morning.—*Hakluyt's Voyages*, ii. 618. Similar phenomena had been observed on several previous occasions. They did not, however, become a subject for scientific remark till about 1611.

'When viewed with a telescope and coloured glasses, the sun is observed to have large black spots upon it, surrounded with a band or border less completely dark, called a *penumbra.* This penumbra is partially luminous, and terminated by distinct edges, presenting no apparent gradations of luminosity: it is mostly of a shape nearly corresponding to that of the spot it surrounds, but occasionally occupying a considerable space, and including several spots. Though the sun's radiant disc is sometimes clear, it very frequently, indeed generally, exhibits these *maculæ;* they are of various magnitudes—some of them I have myself found, by careful measurement, to be several times larger than the earth. These solar spots are usually confined within 35° of his equator, and in a zone parallel; but I have often seen them much nearer to the polar regions. . . . . The extreme difficulty of watching such changes with the telescope, in the sun's brilliant glare, is a very serious obstacle to minute scrutiny. Nor is it wholly without danger; the illustrious Sir William Herschel lost an eye in this service; and I myself had a narrow escape from a similar disaster, by neglecting to reduce the aperture of the instrument.'

As to the spots—'From their generally preserving the same position *inter se*, and continuing visible during equal times, it is held that they are component parts of the sun's solid body, seen through vast accidental openings in the luminous substance which encompasses that immense orb. Hence the variability of the maculæ, which in some cases are seen to contract, dilate, and disappear, at short intervals, in a manner only compatible with the atmospheric or gaseous state of matter.' The sun is thus to be 'regarded as a black solid nucleus, surrounded by two atmospheres, the one obscure, the other luminous. In the instance of a spot, the penumbra is the extremity of the inner and dark atmosphere, a fissure exposing the bare nucleus, but not so wide as that in the outer luminous medium above.'—*Smythe's Cycle of Celestial Objects*, i. 89.

The ingenious Mr James Nasmyth, in 1860, made an interesting addition to our knowledge of the surface of the sun. He discovered that the luminous envelope is composed of masses of bright matter, of the shape of willow-leaves. They become particularly distinct in this form, in the narrow straits of luminous matter which are often seen crossing through the dark maculæ.

# DECEMBER 9.

**The Seven Martyrs at Samosata, 297. St Leocadia, virgin and martyr, 304. St Wulfhilde, virgin and abbess, 990.**

---

*Born.*—Gustavus Adolphus the Great, of Sweden, 1594; John Milton, poet, 1608, *London;* William Whiston, divine, translator of Josephus, 1667, *Norton, Leicestershire;* Philip V. of Spain, 1683, *Versailles.*

*Died.*—Pope Pius IV., 1565; Sir Anthony Vandyck, painter, 1641, *London;* Pope Clement IX., 1669; Edward Hyde, Earl of Clarendon, 1674, *Rouen;* John Reinhold Forster, naturalist, and voyager, 1798, *Halle;* Joseph Bramah, inventor of the Bramah press, &c., 1814, *Pimlico;* Charles Macfarlane, historian, 1858, *London;* John O'Donovan, LL.D., Irish historical antiquary, 1861, *Dublin.*

## MILTON'S BIRTHPLACE, AND ITS VICINITY.

The house in which John Milton was born, on the 9th December 1608, no longer exists; but its site can be determined within a few yards. His father was a scrivener, who carried on business in Bread Street, Cheapside; and here was born the child who was destined to become one of the world's greatest poets. 'In those days,' says Professor Masson in his *Life of Milton*, 'houses in cities were not numbered, as now; and persons in business, to whom it was of consequence to have a distinct address, effected the purpose by exhibiting over the door some sign or emblem. This fashion, now left chiefly to publicans, was once common to all trades and professions. Booksellers and printers, as well as grocers and mercers, carried on their business at the "Cross Keys," the "Dial," the "Three Pigeons," the "Ship and Black Swan," and the like, in such and such streets; and every street in the populous part of such a city as London presented a succession of these signs, fixed or swung over the doors. The scrivener Milton had a sign as well as his neighbours. It was an eagle with outstretched wings; and hence his house was known as the "Spread Eagle," in Bread Street.' Now, it appears that there is a little inlet or court on the east side of Bread Street, three or four doors from Cheapside, which was once called 'Spread Eagle Court,' but which has now no name distinct from that of the street itself; and Professor Masson thinks, not without good grounds, that this spot denotes pretty nearly the site of John Milton's birthplace. Bread Street is almost exactly in the centre of that large area of buildings which was consumed by the great fire of 1666; and the house in question was one of those destroyed. Before that year (although *Paradise Lost* was not yet published), Milton's name had become famous; and Anthony à Wood states that strangers liked to have pointed out to them the house where he first saw the light. The church of Allhallows, close by, still contains the register of Milton's baptism.

It is interesting to trace the changes which that part of the city has undergone since the old days. Courtiers, poets, wits, and gallants were once quite at home in a place where almost every house is now a wholesale warehouse for textile goods. Milton himself, as we know from the details of his life, after his boyish-days in Bread Street, lived in Barbican, in Jewin Street, in Bartholomew Close, and in Little Britain, besides various places at the west end of the town. Bread Street was occupied as a bread-market in the time of Edward I.; and other streets turning out of Cheapside or situated near it, such as Milk Street, Wood Street, and Hosier Lane, were in like manner markets for particular kinds of commodities. William Stafford, Earl of Wiltshire, had a mansion in Bread Street, towards the close of the fifteenth century. Stow says: 'On the west side of Bread Street, amongst divers fair and large houses for merchants, and fair inns for passengers, had ye one prison-house pertaining to the sheriffs of London, called the Compter, in Bread Street; but in the year 1555, the prisoners were removed from thence to one other new Compter in Wood Street, provided by the city's purchase, and built for that purpose.' The 'fair inns for travellers' were the 'Star,' the 'Three Cups,' and the 'George.' But more famous than these was the 'Mermaid,' thought by some writers to have been in Friday Street, but more generally considered to have been in Bread Street. It was a tavern where Shakspeare, Ben Jonson, Beaumont, Fletcher, Donne, and other choice spirits assembled, in the time of Queen Elizabeth.

> 'What things have we seen
> Done at the Mermaid!'

said one of them; and there can be little doubt that wit flashed and sparkled there merrily; for witty courtiers, as well as witty authors, swelled the number. All are gone now—the bread-market, the Compter, the earl's mansion, the inns for travellers, the renowned 'Mermaid,' and the poet's birthplace; no wealthy merchants, even, 'live' in Bread Street, for their private residences are far away from city bustle. Bread Street is now almost exclusively occupied by the warehouses of wholesale dealers in linens, cottons, woollens, silks, and all the multifarious articles, composed of these, belonging to dress. Not only are nearly all the sixty or seventy houses so occupied, but in some cases as many as seven wholesale firms will rent the rooms of one house.

And so it is in nearly all the streets that surround Bread Street. Where almost every house is now a warehouse, there were once places or people that one likes to read and hear about. Take Cheapside ('Chepe,' or 'West Cheaping') itself. This has always been the greatest thoroughfare in the city of London; and nearly all the city pageants of old days passed through it. It contained the shops of the wealthy mercers and drapers from very early times. Lydgate, in his *London Lykpenny*, written in the fifteenth century, makes his hero say:

> 'Then to the Chepe I began me drawne,
> Where moch people I saw for to stand.
> One ofred me velvet, sylke, and lawne;
> An other he taketh me by the hande,
> "Here is Parys thread, the finest in the land!"'

This is curious, as tending to shew that the mercers or their apprentices were wont to solicit custom at their shop-doors, as butchers still do. There was once the 'Conduit' in Cheapside, near which Wat Tyler beheaded some of his prisoners in 1381, and Jack Cade beheaded Lord Saye in 1450. The cross in Cheapside, one of those erected by Edward in memory of his queen, Eleanor, was near the

Poultry. Where Bow Church now stands, Edward I. and his queen sat in a wooden gallery to see one of the city pageants pass through Cheapside. An accident on that occasion led to the construction of a stone gallery; and when all this part of the city was laid in ashes in 1666, Sir Christopher Wren included a pageant-gallery in the front of his beautiful steeple of Bow Church, just over the arched entrance. That gallery, in which Charles II. and Queen Anne were royal visitors, is still existing, though no longer used in a similar way. Concerning the street itself, Howes, writing about 1631, said: 'At this time and for divers years past, the Goldsmith's Row' (a jutting row of wooden tenements), 'in Cheapside, was very much abated of her wonted store of goldsmiths, which was the beauty of that famous street; for the young goldsmiths, for cheapnesse of dwelling, take their houses in Fleet Street, Holborne, and the Strand, and in other streets and suburbs; and goldsmiths' shops were turned to milliners, linen-drapers, and the like.' Two centuries or more ago, therefore, Cheapside, which had already been a mart for mercery and drapery, became still more extensively associated with those trades. It was about that time that Charles I. dined on one occasion with Mr Bradborne, one of the wealthy Cheapside mercers. If we turn into any one of the streets branching from this great artery, we should find strange contrasts to the old times now exhibited. In Friday Street, now occupied much in the same way as Bread Street, there was at one time a fish-market on Fridays; the 'Nag's Head,' at the corner of Cheapside, was concerned in some of the notable events of Elizabeth's reign; and a club held the meeting which led eventually to the establishment of the Bank of England. In Old Change—once the 'Old Exchange,' for the receipt of bullion to be coined; and where dealers in 'ventilating corsets' and 'elastic crinolines' now share most of the houses with mercers and drapers—Lord Herbert, of Cherbury, had a fine house and garden in the time of James I.; and early in the last century, there was a colony of Armenian merchants there. In Bow Lane, Tom Coryat, the eccentric traveller, died in 1617. In Soper's Lane, changed, after the great fire, to Queen Street, the 'pepperers' used to reside in some force; they were the wholesale-dealers in drugs and spices. In the Old Jewry, Sir Robert Clayton had a fine house in the time of Charles II.; and in this street Professor Porson died. Bucklersbury, where Sir Thomas More lived, and where his daughter Margaret was born, was a famous place for druggists, apothecaries, herbalists, and dealers in 'simples.'

---

## BRAMAH LOCK-PICKING.

Joseph Bramah, the mechanical engineer, is better remembered, perhaps, in connection with lock-making than with any other department of his labours, although others were of a more important character. Born in 1749, he was intended, like his brothers, to follow the avocation of their father, who was a farmer in Yorkshire; but a preference for the use of mechanical tools led him to the trade of a carpenter and cabinet-maker. He became an inventor, and then a manufacturer, of valves and other small articles in metal-work; and in 1784, he devised the 'impregnable' lock, which has ever since obtained so much celebrity. Then ensued a long series of inventions in taps, tubes, pumps, fire-engines, beer-engines for taverns, steam-engines, boilers, fire-plugs, and the like. His hydraulic-press is one of the most valuable contributions ever made by inventive skill to manufacturing and engineering purposes. His planing-machine for wood and metal surfaces has proved little less valuable. He made a machine for cutting several pen-nibs out of one quill, and a machine for numbering bank-notes, and devised a new mode of rendering timber proof against dry-rot. In the versatile nature of his mechanical genius, he bears a strong resemblance to the elder Brunel. His useful life, passed in an almost incessant series of inventions, was brought to a close, characteristically enough, on December 9, 1814, by a cold caught while using his own hydraulic-press for uprooting trees in Holt Forest.

The reason why Bramah's locks have been more publicly known than any other of his inventions is, because there was a mystery or puzzle connected with them. How to lock a door which can be opened only by means of a proper key, is a problem nearly four thousand years old; for Denon, in his great work on Egypt, has given figures of a lock found depicted among the bas-reliefs which decorate the great temple at Karnak: it is precisely similar in principle to the wooden locks now commonly used in Egypt and Turkey. The principle is simple, but exceedingly ingenious. Shortly before Mr Bramah's time, English inventors sought to improve upon the old Egyptian locks; but he struck into a new path, and devised a lock of singularly ingenious and complex character. To open it without its proper key, would be (to use his own language) 'as difficult as it would be to determine what kind of impression had been made in any fluid, when the cause of such impression was wholly unknown; or to determine the separate magnitudes of any given number of unequal substances, without being permitted to see them; or to counterfeit the tally of a banker's cheque, without having either part in possession.' One particular lock made by him, having thirteen small pieces of mechanism called 'sliders,' was intended to defy lock-pickers to this extent: that there were the odds of 6,227,019,500 to 1, against any person, unprovided with the proper key, finding the means of opening the lock without injuring it! Mr Chubb, and many other persons both in England and America, invented locks which attained, by different means, the same kind of security sought by Mr Bramah; and it became a custom with the makers to challenge each other—each daring the others to pick *his* lock. The Great Exhibition of 1851 brought this subject into public notice in a singular way. An American lockmaker, Mr Hobbs, declared openly at that time that *all* the English locks, including Bramah's, might be picked; and, in the presence of eleven witnesses, he picked one of Chubb's safety-locks in twenty-five minutes, without having seen or used the key, and without injuring the lock. After much controversy concerning the fairness or unfairness of the process, a bolder attempt was made. There had, for many years, been exhibited in the shop-window of Messrs Bramah (representatives of the original Joseph Bramah), a padlock of great size, beauty, and complexity; to which an announcement was affixed, offering a reward of two hundred guineas to any person who should succeed in picking that lock. Mr Hobbs accepted the challenge; the lock was removed to an apartment specially selected; and a committee was appointed, chosen in equal number by Messrs Bramah and Mr Hobbs, to act as arbitrators. The lock was screwed to, and between two boards, and so fixed and sealed that no access could be obtained to any part of it except through the keyhole. Mr Hobbs, without once seeing the key, was to open the lock within thirty days, by means of groping with small instruments through the keyhole, and in such way as to avoid injury to the lock. By one curious clause in the written agreement, Messrs Bramah were to be allowed to use the key in the lock at any time or times when Mr Hobbs was not engaged upon it; to insure that he had not, even temporarily, either added to or taken from the mechanism in the interior, or disarranged it in any way. This right, however, was afterwards relinquished; the key was kept by the committee during the whole of the period, under seal; and the keyhole was also sealed up whenever Mr Hobbs was not engaged upon it. This agreement, elaborate enough for a great commercial enterprise, instead of merely the picking of a lock, was signed in July 1851; and Mr Hobbs began operations on the 24th. For sixteen days, spreading over a period of a month, he shut himself in the room, trying and testing the numerous bits of iron and steel that were to enable him to open the lock; the hours thus employed were fifty-one in number, averaging rather more than three on each of the days engaged. On the 23d of August Mr Hobbs exhibited the padlock *open*, in presence of Dr Black, Professor Cowper, Mr Edward Bramah, and Mr Bazalgette. In presence of two of these gentlemen, he then both locked and unlocked it, by means of the implements which he had constructed, without ever having once seen the key. On the 29th he again locked and unlocked it, under the scrutiny of all the members of the committee. On the 30th the proper key was unsealed, and the lock opened and shut with it in the usual way: thus shewing that the delicate mechanism of the lock had not been injured. Mr Hobbs then produced the instruments which he used. The makers of the lock took exception to some of the proceedings, as not being in accordance with the terms of the challenge; but the arbitrators were unanimous in their decision that Mr Hobbs had fairly achieved his task. The two hundred guineas were paid. Of the stormy controversy that arose among the lock-makers, we have not here to speak: suffice it to say, that the lock which was thus picked was one which Joseph Bramah had made forty years earlier. All the intricate details on which the lock-picker was engaged, were contained within a small brass barrel about two inches long.

## THE FORTUNE THEATRE.

'1621, Dec. 9, Md.—This night att 12 of the clock the Fortune was burnt.' Such is the brief account given by Alleyn, in his diary, of the destruction of his theatre after an existence of twenty-one years. In two hours the building was burned to the ground, and all its contents destroyed.

The Fortune stood on the east of Golding (now Golden) Lane, Barbican, and was built in the year 1599 for Alleyn and his partner Henslowe, by Peter Streete, citizen and carpenter. The contract for its erection has been preserved, and we find it therein stipulated that the frame of the house was to be set square, and contain fourscore feet 'every way square' without, and fifty feet square within. The foundation, reaching a foot above the ground, was of brick, the building itself being constructed of timber, lath, and plaster. It consisted of three stories; the lowest, twelve, the second, eleven, and the upper one, nine feet in height; with four convenient divisions for 'gentlemen's rooms' and 'twopenny rooms.'* The stage was forty-three feet wide, and projected into the middle of the yard—the open space where the groundlings congregated. The theatre was covered with tiles, instead of being thatched like the Globe, and the supports of the rooms or galleries were wrought like pilasters, and surmounted by carved satyrs. Streete contracted to do all the work, except the painting, for £440, but the entire cost was considerably more. Alleyn's pocket-book contains the following memorandum, made in 1610:

'What the Fortune cost me in November 1599:

| | |
|---|---|
| First for the lease to Brews, . . | £240 |
| Then for building the playhowse, . | 520 |
| For other private buildings of myne own, | 120 |
| So it hath cost me in all for the leas, . | £880 |

Bought the inheritance of the land of the Gills of the Isle of Man within the Fortune, and all the howses in Wight Cross Street, June 1610, for the sum of £340.

Bought John Garret's leas in reversion from the Gills for twenty-one years, for £100, so in all it cost me £1320.

Blessed be the Lord God Everlasting.'

While the Fortune was in course of erection, a complaint was laid by sundry persons against 'building of the new theatre,' which led to an order in council limiting the theatres to be allowed to the Globe on the Surrey side, and the Fortune on the Middlesex side of the river—the latter being licensed, contingent on the Curtain Theatre, in Shoreditch, being pulled down or applied to other uses. The performances were only to take place twice a week; and the house was on no account to be opened on Sundays, during Lent, or 'at such time as any extraordinary sickness shall appear in or about the city.'

In May 1601, the 'Admiral's servants' were transferred from the Curtain to Alleyn's new house, where they appear to have prospered. After it was burned down, it was rebuilt with brick, and the shape altered from square to round; and, in 1633, Prynne speaks of it as lately re-edified and enlarged. When Alleyn founded Dulwich College (the charity from which his own profession have been so strangely excluded), the Fortune formed part of its endowment, and the funds of the college suffered greatly when the theatre was closed during the Civil War. In 1649,

* The gentlemen's rooms are represented by our modern boxes, and the twopenny rooms by our gallery—taking their name from the charge for admission—

'I'll go to the Bull or Fortune, and there see
A play for twopence, and a jig to boot.'

Goffe's *Careless Shepherdess*, 1656.

some Puritan soldiers destroyed the interior of the house; and the trustees of the college finding it hopeless to expect any rent from the lessees, took the theatre into their own hands. A few years later, they determined to get rid of it altogether, and inserted an advertisement in the *Mercurius Politicus* of February 14, 1661, to the following effect: 'The Fortune Playhouse, situate between White Cross Street and Golding Lane, in the parish of St Giles, Cripplegate, with the ground belonging, is to be let to be built upon; where twenty-three tenements may be erected, with

HOUSE OCCUPYING THE SITE OF THE FORTUNE THEATRE, GOLDEN LANE, IN 1790.

gardens, and a street may be cut through for the better accommodation of the buildings.' From this, it may be judged that the theatre occupied considerable space. There are no signs of any gardens now, the site of the theatre is marked by a plaster-fronted building bearing the royal arms, represented in the accompanying engraving; and the memory of the once popular playhouse is preserved in the adjacent thoroughfare called Playhouse Yard.

## DECEMBER 10.

St Eulalia, virgin and martyr, about 304. St Melchiades, pope, 314.

*Born.*—Thomas Holcroft, dramatist and translator, 1745, *London;* General Sir William Fenwick Williams, hero of Kars, 1800, *Nova Scotia.*

*Died.*—Llewellyn, Prince of Wales, killed, 1282; Edmund Gunter, mathematician, 1626; Jean Joseph Sue, eminent physician, 1792, *Paris;* Casimir Delavigne, French dramatist, 1843, *Lyon;* William Empson, editor of *Edinburgh Review*, 1852, *Haileybury;* Tommaso Grossi, Italian poet, 1853, *Florence;* Dr Southwood Smith, author of works on sanitary reform, 1861, *Florence.*

### LLEWELLYN, THE LAST NATIVE PRINCE OF WALES.

The title of 'Prince of Wales' has entirely changed its character. Originally, it was applied to a native sovereign. In the ninth century, when the Danes and Saxons had completely broken the power of the Britons in England, Wales was still in the hands of the *Cymri*, a branch of the same stock as the Britons; and it was governed by three brothers, with the dignity of princes—the prince of North Wales having precedence of the others in rank. It was, however, a very stormy and unsettled rule; for we find that, during the next three centuries, the princes of Wales were often obliged to pay tribute to the Saxon, Danish, and Norman rulers of England; and, moreover, the princes were frequently quarrelling among themselves, overstepping each other's landmarks, and breaking agreements without much scruple. At length one prince, Llewellyn, rose superior to the rest, and was chosen by the general voice of the people sovereign of Wales in 1246. The border district between the two countries, known as the *Marches*, was the scene of almost incessant conflicts between the English and Welsh, let who might be king in the one country, or prince in the other. There is a passage in Fuller, illustrative of the hardships endured by the English soldiers during a raid across the Marches nearly to the western part of the principality: 'I am much affected with the ingenuity [ingenuousness] of an English nobleman, who, following the camp of King Henry III. in these parts (Caernarvonshire), wrote home to his friends, about the end of September 1245, the naked truth, indeed, as followeth: "We lie in our tents, watching, fasting, praying, and freezing. We watch, for fear of the Welshmen, who are wont to invade us in the night; we fast, for want of meat, for the half-penny loaf is worth five pence; we pray to God to send us home speedily; and we freeze for want of winter garments, having nothing but thin linen between us and the wind."' On the other hand, the Welsh were always ready to take advantage of any commotions across the border. In 1268, Llewellyn was compelled to accept terms which Henry III. imposed upon him, and which rendered him little else than a feudal vassal to the king of England. When Henry died, and Edward I. became king, Llewellyn was summoned to London, to render homage to the new monarch. The angry blood of the Welshman chafed at this humiliation; but he yielded—more especially as Edward held in his power the daughter of Simon de Montfort, Earl of Leicester, to whom Llewellyn was betrothed, and he could only obtain her by coming to London. In 1278, Llewellyn and the lady were married, the king himself giving away the bride. The Prince and Princess of Wales went to their future home in the principality. Their happiness, however, was short-lived: the princess died in giving birth to a daughter, who afterwards ended her days as a nun in a Lincolnshire convent. Peace did not long endure between Llewellyn and Edward. A desolating war broke out, marked by much barbarity on both sides. Llewellyn's friends fell away one by one, and made terms with the powerful king of England. The year 1282 saw the close of the scene. While some of his adherents were combating the Earl of Gloucester and Sir Edmund Mortimer in South Wales, Llewellyn himself was fighting in the north. Leaving the bulk of his soldiers, and coming almost unattended to Builth, he fell into an ambush, which cost him his life. Dr Powel, in 1584, translated into English an account of the scene, written by Caradoc of Llanfargan: 'The prince departed from his men, and went to the valley with his squire alone, to talk with certain lords of the country, who had promised to meet him there. Then some of his men, seeing his enemies come down from the hill, kept the bridge called the Pont Orewyn, and defended the passage manfully, till one declared to the Englishmen where a ford was, a little beneath, through the which they sent a number of their men with Elias Walwyn, who suddenly fell upon them that defended the bridge, in their backs, and put them to flight. The prince's esquire told the prince, as he stood secretly abiding the coming of such as promised to meet him in a little grove, that he heard a great noise and cry at the bridge; and the prince asked whether his men had taken the bridge, and he said, "Yes." "Then," said the prince, "I pass not if all the power of England were on the other side." But suddenly, behold the horsemen about the grove; and as he would have escaped to his men, they pursued him so hard that one Adam Francton ran him through with a staff, being unarmed, and knew him not. And his men being but a few, stood and fought boldly, looking for their prince, till the Englishmen, by force of archers, mixed with the horsemen, won the hill, and put them to flight. And as they returned, Francton went to despoil him whom he had slain; and when he saw his face, he knew him very well, and stroke off his head, and sent it to the king at the abbey of Conway, who received it with great joy, and caused it to be set upon one of the highest turrets of the Tower of London.'

Thus closed the career of Llewellyn, the last native sovereign of Wales. Edward I. speedily brought the whole principality under his sway, and Wales has ever since been closely allied to England. Edward's queen gave birth to a son in Caernarvon Castle; and this son, while yet a child, was formally instituted Prince of Wales. It thenceforward became a custom, departed from in only a few instances, to give this dignity to the eldest son, or heir-apparent of the English king or queen. The title is not actually inherited; it is conferred by special creation and investiture, generally soon after the birth of the prince to whom it relates. It is said, by an old tradition, that Edward I., to gratify the national feelings of the Welsh people, promised to give them a prince without blemish on his honour, Welsh by birth, and one who could not speak a word of English. He then, in order to fulfil his promise literally, sent Queen Eleanor to be confined at Caernarvon Castle, and the infant born there had, of course, all the three characteristics. Be this tradition true or false, the later sovereign cared very little whether the Princes of Wales were acceptable or not to the people of the principality. In the mutations of various dynasties, the Prince of Wales was not, in every case, the eldest son and heir-apparent; and in two instances, there was a princess without a prince. Henry VIII. gave this title to his two daughters, Mary and Elizabeth, in succession; but the general rule has been as above stated. It may be useful here to state, in chronological order, the eighteen Princes of Wales, from the time of Edward I. to that of Victoria. We shall construct the list from details given in Dr Doran's *Book of the Princes of Wales*. Each prince has a kind of surname, according to the place where he was born. (1.) *Edward of Caernarvon*, son of Edward I., born 1284; died, 1327, as Edward II. (2.) *Edward of Windsor*, son of Edward II., born 1312; died, 1377, as Edward III. (3.) *Edward of Woodstock*, son of Edward III., born 1330; known as Edward the Black Prince, and died 1376. (4.) *Richard of Bordeaux*, son of Edward the Black Prince, born 1367; died, 1399, as Richard II. (5.) *Henry of Monmouth*, son of Henry IV., born 1387; died, 1422, as Henry V.; (6.) *Edward of Westminster*, son of Henry VI., born 1453; died 1471. (7.) *Edward of the Sanctuary*, son of Edward IV., born 1470; died, 1483, as Edward V. (8.) *Edward of Middleham*, son of Richard III., born 1474; died 1484. (9.) *Arthur of Winchester*, eldest son of Henry VII., born 1486; died 1502. (10.) *Henry of Greenwich*, second son of Henry VII., born 1491; died, 1547, as Henry VIII. (11.) *Henry of Stirling*, eldest son of James I., born 1594; died 1612. (12.) *Charles of Dunfermline*, second son of James I., born 1600; died, 1649, as Charles I. (13.) *Charles of St James's*, son of Charles I., born 1630; died, 1685, as Charles II. (14.) *George Augustus of Hanover*, son of George I., born 1683; died, 1760, as George II. (15.) *Frederick Louis of Hanover*, son of George II., born 1707; died 1751. (16.) *George William Frederick of Norfolk House*, son of the last named, born 1738; died, 1820, as George III. (17.) *George Augustus Frederick of St James's*, son of George III., born 1762; died, 1830, as George IV. (18.) *Albert Edward*, son of Queen Victoria, born 1841; and came of age, 1862. Besides the above, there were two wanderers, who were regarded in many parts of Europe as Princes of Wales, and certainly were so in right of birth. These were the son and grandson of the fugitive James II.—*James Francis Edward*, born 1688, and known afterwards as the 'Old Pretender,' died 1765; and his son, *Charles Edward*, born 1720, and for a long period known as the 'Young Pretender,' died 1788.

### FACSIMILES OF INEDITED AUTOGRAPHS: CHRISTIANA OR 'CHRESTIENN,' DUCHESS OF LORRAINE.

This princess was the daughter of Christiern II., of Denmark, surnamed, from his atrocities, the Nero of the North, and Isabel of Austria. She was a woman of keen intellect and great ability.

Henry VIII. of England sought her hand, but Christiana repulsed him, with the sarcastic observation, that 'had she possessed two heads, *one* should have been at his grace's service.' She died December 10, 1590.

### THE MISSISSIPPI SCHEME.

On the 10th of December 1720, John Law, late comptroller-general of the finances of France, retreated from Paris to his country-seat of Guermande, about fifteen miles distant from the metropolis, and in a few days afterwards quitted the kingdom, never again to return. A few months before, he had enjoyed a position and consideration only comparable with that of a crowned monarch—if, indeed, any sovereign ever received such eager and importunate homage, as for a time was paid to the able and adventurous Scotchman.

The huge undertaking projected by Law, and known by the designation of the Mississippi Scheme, was perhaps one of the grandest and most comprehensive ever conceived. It not only included within its sphere of operations the whole colonial traffic of France, but likewise the superintendence of the Mint, and the management of the entire revenues of the kingdom. The province of Louisiana, in North America, then a French possession, was made over by the crown to the 'Company of the West,' as the association was termed, and the most sanguine anticipations were entertained of the wealth to be realised from this territory, which was reported, amid other resources, to possess gold-mines of mysterious value. In connection with the same project, a bank, established by law, under the sanction of the Duke of Orleans, then regent of France, promised to recruit permanently the impoverished resources of the kingdom, and diffuse over the land, by an unlimited issue of paper-money, a perennial stream of wealth.

For a time these sanguine anticipations seemed to be fully realised. Prosperity and wealth to a hitherto unheard of extent prevailed throughout France, and Law was, for a short period, the idol of the nation, which regarded him as its good genius and deliverer. Immense fortunes were realised by speculations in Mississippi stock, the price of which rose from 500 livres, the original cost, to upwards of 10,000 livres by the time that the mania attained its zenith. A perfect frenzy seemed to take possession of the public mind, and to meet the ever-increasing demand, new allotments of stock were made, and still the supply was inadequate. Law's house in the Rue Quinquempoix, in Paris, was beset from morning to night by eager applicants, who soon by their numbers blocked up the street itself and rendered it impassable. All ranks and conditions of men—peers, prelates, citizens, and mechanics, the learned and the unlearned, the plebeian and the aristocrat—flocked to this temple of Plutus. Even ladies of the highest rank turned stockjobbers, and vied with the rougher sex in eagerness of competition. So utterly inadequate did the establishment in the Rue Quinquempoix prove for the transaction of business, that Law transferred his residence to the Place Vendôme, where the tumult and noise occasioned by the crowd of speculators proved such a nuisance, and impeded so seriously the procedure in the chancellor's court in that quarter, that the monarch of stockjobbers found himself obliged again to shift his camp. He, accordingly, purchased from the Prince of Carignan, at an enormous price, the Hôtel de Soissons, in which mansion, and the beautiful and extensive gardens attached, he held his levees, and allotted the precious stock to an ever-increasing and enthusiastic crowd of clients.

With such demands on his time and resources, it became absolutely impossible for him to gratify one tithe of the applicants for shares, and the most ludicrous stories are told of the stratagems employed to gain an audience of the great financier. One lady made her coachman overturn her carriage when she saw Mr Law approaching, and the *ruse* succeeded, as the gallantry of the latter led him instantly to proffer his assistance, and invite the distressed fair one into his mansion, where, after a little explanation, her name was entered in his books as a purchaser of stock. Another female device to procure an interview with Law, by raising an alarm of fire near a house where he was at dinner, was not so fortunate, as the subject of the trick suspecting the motive, hastened off in another direction, when he saw the lady rushing into the house, which he and his friends had emerged from on the cry of fire being raised.

The terrible crash at last came. The amount of notes issued from Law's bank more than doubled all the specie circulating in the country, and great difficulties were experienced from the scarcity of the latter, which began both to be hoarded up and sent out of the country in large quantities. Severe and tyrannical edicts were promulgated, threatening heavy penalties for having in possession more than 500 livres or £20 in specie; but this ukase only increased the embarrassment and dissatisfaction of the nation. Then came an ordinance reducing gradually the value of the paper currency to one half, followed by the stoppage of cash-payments at the bank; and at last the whole privileges of the Mississippi Company were withdrawn, and the notes of the bank declared to be of no value after the

1st of November 1720. Law had by this time lost all influence in the councils of government, his life was in danger from an infuriated and disappointed people, and he was therefore fain to avail himself of the permission of the regent (who appears still to have cherished a regard for him) to retire from the scene of his splendour and disgrace. After wandering for a time through various countries, he proceeded to England, where he resided for several years. In 1725, he returned again to the continent, fixed his residence at Venice, and died there almost in poverty, on 21st March 1729.

Such was the end of the career of the famous John Law, who, of all men, has an undoubted title to be ranked as a prince of adventurers. In him the dubious reputation formerly enjoyed by Scotland, of sending forth such characters, was fully maintained. He was descended from an ancient family in Fife; but his father, William Law, in the exercise of the business of a goldsmith and banker in Edinburgh, gained a considerable fortune, enabling him to purchase the estate of Lauriston, in the parish of Cramond, which was inherited by his eldest son John. The ancient mansion of Lauriston Castle on this property, beautifully situated near the Firth of Forth, is believed to have been erected in the end of the sixteenth century, by Sir Archibald Napier of Merchiston, father of the celebrated inventor of logarithms, and then proprietor of Lauriston. It is represented in the accompanying engraving. In recent years, the building was greatly enlarged and embellished by

LAURISTON CASTLE, AS IT APPEARED AT THE CLOSE OF THE LAST CENTURY.

Andrew Rutherfurd, Lord Advocate for Scotland, and subsequently one of the judges of the Court of Session. Law is said to have retained throughout a strong affection for his patrimonial property, and a story in reference to this is told of a visit paid to him by the Duke of Argyle in Paris, at the time when his splendour and influence were at the highest. As an old friend, the duke was admitted directly to Mr Law, whom he found busily engaged in writing. The duke entertained no doubt that the great financier was busied with a subject of the highest importance, as crowds of the most distinguished individuals were waiting in the anterooms for an audience. Great was his grace's astonishment when he learned that Mr Law was merely writing to his gardener at Lauriston regarding the planting of cabbages at a particular spot!

Of Law's general character, it is not possible to speak with great commendation. He appears to have been through life a libertine and gambler, and in the latter capacity he supported himself for many years, both before and after his brief and dazzling career as a financier and political economist. In his youth, he had served an apprenticeship to monetary science under his father, and a course of travel and study, aided by a vigorous and inventive, but apparently ill-regulated intellect, enabled him subsequently to mature the stupendous scheme which we have above detailed, and succeed in indoctrinating with his views the regent of France. His first absence from Great Britain was involuntary, and occasioned by his killing, in a duel, the celebrated Beau Wilson (see following article), and thus being obliged to shelter himself by flight from the vengeance of the law. He then commenced a peregrination over the continent, and after a long course of rambling and adventure, settled down at Paris about the period of death of Louis XIV. A pardon for the death of Wilson was sent over to him from England in 1719.

## BEAU WILSON.

Towards the end of the reign of William III., London society was puzzled by the appearance of a young aspirant to fashionable fame, who soon became the talk of the town from the style in which he lived. His house was furnished in the most expensive manner; his dress was as costly as the most extravagant dandy could desire, or the richest noble imitate; his hunters, hacks, and racers were the best procurable for money; and he kept the first of tables, dispensing hospitality with a liberal spirit. And all this was done without any ostensible means. All that was known of him was, that his name was Edward Wilson, and that he was the fifth son of Thomas Wilson, Esq., of Keythorpe, Leicestershire, an impoverished gentleman. Beau Wilson, as he was called, is described by Evelyn as a very young gentleman, 'civil and good-natured, but of no great force of understanding,' and 'very sober and of good fame.' He redeemed his father's estate, and portioned off his sisters. When advised by a friend to invest some of his money while he could, he replied, that however long his life might last, he should always be able to maintain himself in the same manner, and therefore had no need to take care for the future.

All attempts to discover his secret were vain; in his most careless hours of amusement he kept a strict guard over his tongue, and left the scandalous world to conjecture what it pleased. Some good-natured people said he had robbed the Holland mail of a quantity of jewelry, an exploit for which another man had suffered death. Others said he was supplied by the Jews, for what purpose they did not care to say. It was plain he did not depend upon the gaming-table, for he never played but for small sums—and he was to be found at all times, so it was not to be wondered at that it came to be believed that he had discovered the philosopher's stone.

How long he might have pursued his mysterious career, it is impossible to say: it was cut short by another remarkable man on the 9th of April 1694. On that day, Wilson and a friend, one Captain Wightman, were at the 'Fountain Inn,' in the Strand, in company with the celebrated John Law (see preceding article), who was then a man about town. Law left them, and the captain and Wilson took coach to Bloomsbury Square. Here Wilson alighted, and Law reappeared on the scene; as soon as they met, both drew their swords, and after one pass the Beau fell wounded in the stomach, and died without speaking a single word. Law was arrested, and tried at the Old Bailey for murder. The cause of the quarrel did not come out, but there is little doubt that a woman was in the case. Evelyn says: 'The quarrel arose from his (Wilson's) taking away his own sister from lodging in a house where this Law had a mistress, which the mistress of the house thinking a disparagement to it, and losing by it, instigated Law to this duel.' Law declared the meeting was accidental, but some threatening letters from him to Wilson were produced on the trial, and the jury believing that the duel was unfairly conducted, found him guilty of murder, and he was condemned to death. The sentence was commuted to a fine, on the ground of the offence amounting only to manslaughter; but Wilson's brother appealed against this, and while the case was pending a hearing, Law contrived to escape from the King's Bench, and reached the continent in safety, notwithstanding a reward offered for his apprehension. He ultimately received a pardon in 1719.

Those who expected Wilson's death would clear up the mystery attached to his life, were disappointed. He left only a few pounds behind him, and not a scrap of evidence to enlighten public curiosity as to the origin of his mysterious resources.

While Law was in exile, an anonymous work appeared which professed to solve the riddle. This was *The Unknown Lady's Pacquet of Letters*, published with the Countess of Dunois' *Memoirs of the Court of England* (1708), the author, or authoress of which, pretends to have derived her information from an elderly gentlewoman, 'who had been a favourite in a late reign of the then she-favourite, but since abandoned by her.' According to her account, the Duchess of Orkney (William III.'s mistress) accidentally met Wilson in St James's Park, incontinently fell in love with him, and took him under her protection. The royal favourite was no niggard to her lover, but supplied him with funds to enable him to shine in the best society, he undertaking to keep faithful to her, and promising not to attempt to discover her identity. After a time, she grew weary of her expensive toy, and alarmed lest his curiosity should overpower his discretion, and bring her to ruin. This fear was not lessened by his accidental discovery of her secret. She broke off the connection, but assured him that he should never want for money, and with this arrangement he was forced to be content. The 'elderly gentlewoman,' however, does not leave matters here, but brings a terrible charge against her quondam patroness. She says, that having one evening, by her mistress' orders, conducted a stranger to her apartment, she took the liberty of playing eaves-dropper, and heard the duchess open her strong-box and say to the visitor: 'Take this, and your work done, depend upon another thousand and my favour for ever!' Soon afterwards poor Wilson met his death. The confidante went to Law's trial, and was horrified to recognise in the prisoner at the bar the very man to whom her mistress addressed those mysterious words. Law's pardon she attributes to the lady's influence with the king, and his escape to the free use of her gold with his jailers. Whether this story was a pure invention, or whether it was founded upon fact, it is impossible to determine. Beau Wilson's life and death must remain among unsolved mysteries.

---

## DECEMBER 11.

Saints Fuscian, Victoricus, and Gentian, martyrs, about 287. St Damasus, pope and confessor, 384. St Daniel the Stylite, confessor, about 494.

---

*Born.*—Dr William Cullen, illustrious professor of medicine, 1712, *Hamilton;* Paul Joseph Barthez, physiologist, 1734, *Montpellier;* Charles Wesley, musician, 1757, *Bristol.*

*Died.*—Michael VIII. Palæologus, Greek emperor, 1282; Louis, Prince of Condé (the Great Condé), 1686, *Fontainebleau;* Sir Roger l'Estrange, translator of classic authors, 1704; Charles XII. of Sweden, killed at Frederickshall, 1718; Theodore Neuhoff, ex-king of Corsica, 1756, *London.*

### PRECOCIOUS MUSICIANS.

There are several unquestionable examples of an almost instinctive musical genius manifesting itself in early infancy. Probably the most remarkable of these, is the instance of the two brothers Wesley, occurring as it did in one family. Charles Wesley, son of a well-known clergyman of the same name, and nephew of the better known founder of Methodism, was born at Bristol on the 11th of December 1757. Nearly from his birth, his mother used to quiet and amuse the infant with her harpsichord. Even before he could speak, his musical ear was so nice, that he would not permit his mother to play with one hand only, but would take the other and place it on the keys. Soon attempting to play himself, his mother used to tie him in a chair at the harpsichord, where he would amuse himself for hours together. When only two years and nine months old, he astonished his parents by playing a tune in correct time. Soon afterwards, he could play any air he chanced to hear, with a true bass added, as if spontaneously, without study or hesitation. He then seemed to have little respect or reverence for any one not a musician. When asked to play to a stranger, he would inquire, in his childish prattle, 'Is he a musicker?' and, if the answer were in the affirmative, would run to the instrument with ready eagerness.

Samuel Wesley was born in 1766, and evinced a talent for music almost as early as his elder brother Charles. He could play a tune when but two years and eleven months old, and could put a correct bass to airs long before he had acquired a knowledge of musical notation. He constantly attended his brother, playing, or rather making believe to play, on a chair or table, while Charles played the harpsichord. With the advantage of such an example, he soon outstripped his brother. He learned to read from the words of songs in music-books, and could compose music long before he could write. At the age of eight years, he surprised the musical world by an oratorio, entirely his own composition, which he entitled *Ruth*.

As not unfrequently happens in cases of premature development, the flattering promises of youth were not fulfilled, as far as regards Charles Wesley, at least, in riper years. He soon became an excellent player on the organ and harpsichord, at a time, it must be remembered, when the art of playing on keyed instruments, far behind what it is at the present day, was only advancing towards the perfection which, comparatively speaking, it may be said to have now attained. In early life, Charles was brought under the notice of George III., and often had the honour of entertaining the royal leisure by performances of Handel's music. Of great moral worth, amiable qualities, and simplicity of manners, Charles Wesley made many friends in his day, though as a musician, were it not for his precocious exhibition of talent, he would be now quite forgotten. After attaining a certain degree of excellence as a performer, he remained stationary; none of his compositions ever soared above mediocrity, and the height of his eminence was the appointment of organist to the fashionable church of St George's, Hanover Square.

Samuel Wesley attained much greater eminence, both in point of musical and general acquirement. He was possessed by an absorbing passion for music, but this did not prevent him from becoming, in addition, a good Greek, Latin, and Italian scholar. Sheridan said of him: 'I am no judge of Mr Wesley's musical abilities, but I will venture to assert that his intellectual powers and education would enable him to distinguish himself in any walk of life.' These brilliant prospects were clouded by an unhappy misfortune. Mr Wesley, one night, accidentally fell into an excavation for building purposes, that had shamefully been left unguarded, in one of the London streets. The effects of this fall depressed his mental energies; for seven years he remained in a low despondent state of mind, refusing the solace even of his beloved art. He subsequently experienced several recoveries and relapses, before being finally relieved by death. His musical compositions were generally of too elevated a character to please the public at large. He composed a grand mass for Pope Pius VI., for which the pontiff returned thanks in a flattering Latin letter; and, as if to make the *amende honorable* to Protestantism, Wesley composed thereafter a complete cathedral service for the Church of England, on which his fame as a musician now principally rests.

Mozart, already noticed in a previous article, was another striking instance of precocious musical genius. An exception also must be admitted in his case to the general comparison between juvenile prodigies, and those trees, that, blossoming out of season, seldom produce good fruit. Mozart's father was an eminent musician, and his sister an accomplished player on the harpsichord, so it may almost be said, that he and Samuel Wesley were nursed on music; their early attentions stimulated, and their ears soothed with harmony. There is an instance, however, of another precocious musician, who never possessed any such advantages.

William Crotch was born at Norwich, in July 1775. His father, by trade a carpenter, though he had no knowledge of music, was fond of the art, and with great ingenuity succeeded in building an organ, on which he learned to play *God save the King*, and a few other common tunes. About Christmas 1776, when the infant Crotch was not more than a year and a half old, he discovered a great inclination for music, by leaving even his food to attend to it, when the organ was playing; and six months afterwards, he would touch the key-note of his favourite tunes, to induce his father to play them. Soon after this, as he was still unable to name the tunes, he would play the two or three first notes of them, when he thought the key-note did not sufficiently express the one he wished to be played. It seems to have been owing to his having heard the superior performance of a Mrs Lulman, a lady of musical attainments, who tried his father's organ, and who played and sang to her own accompaniment, that young Crotch first attempted to play a tune himself. The same evening, when being carried through the room where the organ was, on his way to bed, the infant screamed and struggled violently to go to the instrument; and, on his wish being complied with, he eagerly beat down the keys with his little fist. The next day, being left with his brother, a youth of fourteen, in the same room, he persuaded the latter to blow the bellows, whilst he himself struck the keys of the organ. At first, he played at random, but presently he produced, with one hand, so much of *God save the King* as to awaken the curiosity of his father, then in his workshop, who came into the room to know who it was that played the instrument. When he found that it was his infant son, he could scarcely credit his ears and eyes. At this time young Crotch, as proved by his baptismal register, was no more than two years and three weeks old. Next day, he made himself master of the treble of the second part, and the day after he attempted the bass, which he performed correctly in every particular, excepting the note immediately before the close; this being an octave below the preceding sound, was beyond the reach of his little hand. After the lapse of a few more months, he mastered both the treble and bass of 'Hope, thou nurse of young desire,' the well-known song from *Love in a Village*, and ere long, from this period, he could extemporise the bass to any melody, whether performed by himself or others.

The infantine attainments of Crotch could scarcely be described without entering into technical details; but, unlike many infant prodigies, he did much to fulfil the promise of his earlier years, and became thoroughly versed in musical art, and a skilful composer. In 1797, when in his twenty-second year, he was appointed Professor of Music in the university of Oxford, and in 1822 principal of the Academy of Music. He was the author of many pieces for the organ and pianoforte, including the opera *Palestine;* he also issued *Elements of Musical Composition and Thorough-bass;* and *Specimens of various styles of Music of all Ages.* In addition to his great musical talent, Dr Crotch also excelled as a painter, many of his pictures being above mediocrity. That he was not better known may be set down to his very retiring habits.

## SIR ROGER L'ESTRANGE.

Roger L'Estrange, born in 1611, was the youngest son of a Norfolk baronet and stanch Royalist. He was educated at Cambridge, and went with Charles I. to the North in 1639. Faithful to his family principles, he obtained from the king a commission for taking the town of Lynn; and falling into the hands of the Parliamentary army, he was arrested, tried, and condemned to be hanged as a spy. Petitioning the Lords, he was reprieved for fourteen days, and the respite being afterwards prolonged, he spent a dreary four years in the prison of Newgate, in the daily expectation of being executed. He then contrived to escape to the continent, where he remained to the dissolution of the Long Parliament, when he adopted the bold expedient of returning to England, and appealing to Cromwell in person. The appeal was successful; he received an indemnity, and was discharged on giving security. His enemies afterwards alleged that he had served Cromwell as a musician, giving him the nickname of 'Oliver's fiddler.' L'Estrange's explanation of this affair affords us a curious peep at the manners of the times. He says, that while the question of indemnity was pending, he one day walked in St James's Park. Hearing an organ touched in a low tone, in the house of a Mr Hickson, he went in, and found a company of five or six persons, about to practise music. They immediately requested him to take a viol and bear a part, which he did; and, soon after, Cromwell walked in, stayed, and listened a while to the music, and then departed, without saying a word to any one.

At the Restoration, L'Estrange finding himself, with many other royalists, forgotten, published his *Memento,* which was the means of obtaining for him the appointment of licenser of the press. He subsequently started and conducted more than one newspaper, and published a great number of political tracts. From James II. he received the honour of knighthood, 'in consideration of his eminent services and unshaken loyalty to the crown;' and, about the same time, he obtained a seat in parliament. At the Revolution, he was deprived of the commission of the peace, and after seeing so many changes of government, wisely retired into private life. Queen Mary condescended to perpetrate a stupid anagram on his name; but a distich, really shewing smartness, was written by one Lee, who by years was so altered as scarcely to be recognised by his old friend Sir Roger:

'Faces may alter, but names cannot change,
I am *strange Lee* altered, you are still *Lee strange.*'

Besides his numerous political tracts, Sir Roger published many translations from the Greek, Latin, and Spanish. His translations, written in a semi-slang style, are full of curious old-English colloquialisms. It has been alleged that he thus aided in corrupting the English language, but a contemporary writer says, 'those who consider the number and greatness of his books will admire he should ever write so many; and those who have read them, considering the style and method they are writ in, will more admire he should write so many.' Dr Johnson was greatly indebted to L'Estrange, as is evidenced from the numerous quotations given in his dictionary. Sir Roger lived to the good old age of eighty-seven, dying on the 11th of December 1704, and his epitaph is still to be seen on one of the pillars in his parish church of St Giles in the Fields.

## THEODORE, KING OF CORSICA.

Monarchs have occasionally been deposed, put to death, and subjected to various indignities, but we question much whether any individual, who had once exercised sovereign sway, ever presented so pitiable a spectacle as Theodore von Neuhoff, ex-king of Corsica. His memory is chiefly preserved by the sympathy which his misfortunes excited in England in the last century, and the exertions of Horace Walpole and other eminent personages on his behalf.

This temporary holder of regal power was the son of a Westphalian gentleman of good family, who had held a commission in the French army. His son, who was born in Metz about 1696, entered the same service, but appears afterwards to have quitted it, and rambled, as an adventurer, over the greater part of Europe. At last he was thrown into prison for debt at Leghorn, and on emerging from this confinement, he made the acquaintance of several leaders among the Corsican insurgents, then endeavouring to effect the independence of their country by shaking off the yoke of Genoa. Neuhoff accepted their proffer of the sovereignty of the country in return for assistance to be furnished by himself, and he accordingly, in March 1736, made his appearance on the Corsican coast with a supply of ammunition and money which he had succeeded in obtaining from the Bey of Tunis, by holding out to the latter the promise of an exclusive trade with Corsica, and permission to have a station there for his pirate ships. Eagerly welcomed at first by the Corsicans, Neuhoff was, in the following month of April, elected king by their general assembly, and, at the same time, swore to observe the tenor of a constitution which was then proclaimed. For some months he exercised all the acts of an independent sovereign, coining money, distributing patents of nobility, and instituting an order of knighthood. He is stated also, with the view of shewing an example of firmness, to have put to death three persons belonging to distinguished families. Among other military enterprises, he undertook successfully the capture of Porto Vecchio from the Genoese, but was foiled in an attempt on Bastia. His popularity ere long diminished, and finding his position both an arduous and insecure one, he made arrangements for conducting the government in his absence, and quitted the island with the intention, as he asserted, of obtaining fresh succour. But his sovereignty of Corsica was never to be resumed. After visiting successively Italy, France, and Holland, he was at last arrested for debt at Amsterdam. Some Jews and foreign merchants, settled in that city, procured his release, and also furnished him with means to equip an armament for the recovery of his dominions. With this he appeared off Corsica in 1738, but was unable to land in consequence of the depression of the insurgents' cause through the assistance furnished to the Genoese by the French. A similar unsuccessful attempt was made by him in 1742.

Neuhoff now proceeded to London, where he met with great kindness and sympathy as an exiled monarch. Additional mishaps, however, befell him here, and he was obliged, in consequence of money which he had borrowed, to endure an imprisonment of some years' duration in the King's Bench Prison. Here, it is said, he used to affect a miserable display of regal state, sitting under a tattered canopy, and receiving visitors with great ceremony. Smollett has introduced a description of him in prison in his novel of *Ferdinand Count Fathom.* At last the exertions of Walpole and others succeeded in raising a sum of money, which enabled Neuhoff to obtain his release from confinement, after making over to his creditors, as an asset, his kingdom of Corsica. The advertisement in the papers of the day announcing the opening of the subscription for the ex-sovereign, was prefixed by the words in which, as is alleged, the great general of Justinian used, in his old age, to solicit alms—'*Date obolum Belisario.*'

Neuhoff did not long survive his liberation, and died in London on 11th December 1756. He was buried in the churchyard of St Ann's, Westminster, where the following epitaph, composed by Horace Walpole, was inscribed on a tablet, with a diadem carved at the summit:

'NEAR THIS PLACE IS INTERRED
THEODORE, KING OF CORSICA,
WHO DIED IN THIS PARISH, DECEMBER 11, 1756,
IMMEDIATELY AFTER LEAVING
THE KING'S BENCH PRISON,
BY THE BENEFIT OF THE ACT OF INSOLVENCY;
IN CONSEQUENCE OF WHICH
HE REGISTERED THE KINGDOM OF CORSICA
FOR THE USE OF HIS CREDITORS.

The grave, great teacher, to a level brings
Heroes and beggars, galley-slaves and kings.
But Theodore this moral learned ere dead:
Fate poured its lessons on his living head,
Bestowed a kingdom, and denied him bread.'

# DECEMBER 12.

Saints Epimachus, Alexander, and others, martyrs, 250. St Corentin, bishop and confessor, 5th century. St Columba, abbot in Ireland, 548. St Finian, or Finan, confessor, bishop of Clonard, in Ireland, 6th century. St Cormac, abbot in Ireland. St Valery, abbot, 622. St Colman, abbot in Ireland, 659. St Eadburge, abbess of Menstrey, in Thanet, 751.

*Born.*—Nicholas Sanson, geographer, 1599, *Abbeville;* Samuel, Viscount Hood, British admiral, 1724, *Butley, Somersetshire;* Dr Erasmus Darwin, poet and physiologist, 1731, *Elston, near Newark;* Sir William Beechey, artist, 1753; Archduchess Maria Louisa, second wife of Napoleon, 1791.

*Died.*—Darius Nothus, of Persia, 405 B.C.; Henry St John, Viscount Bolingbroke, political and philosophical writer, 1751, *Battersea;* Colley Cibber, dramatist, 1757, *Islington;* Sir Mark Isambard Brunel, engineer of Thames Tunnel, 1849, *London.*

## THE TWO EMPRESSES, JOSEPHINE AND MARIA LOUISA.

An historical parallel has sometimes been drawn between Queen Catharine and the Empress Josephine: the one having been divorced by Henry VIII., in order that he might marry Anne Boleyn; and the other divorced by the Emperor Napoleon, in order that he might marry the Archduchess Maria Louisa. But, beyond these points of similarity, the parallel fails. Henry sought to throw a stigma on her of whom he was tired as a wife; Napoleon had political reasons only for what he did. Josephine bowed meekly to her fate; but Catharine felt keenly that she was an injured woman. A little has been said, in a former article (vol. i. p. 731), concerning a prophecy or fortune-teller's story to which Josephine gave credence; but something may be added here relating more nearly to Maria Louisa.

In 1809, Napoleon was approaching the zenith of his power. His conquests had made nearly all the sovereigns of Europe suppliants for his favour. Austria had long held out, but the terrible defeat at Wagram had brought her, too, into subjection. Napoleon's ambition, never satisfied, sought for still more and more of the adjuncts of imperial power. He had married a lady with no royal blood in her veins, and by this lady he had no child to inherit his imperial throne; thus a double reason was afforded to a man of his character for getting rid of his poor wife. And, in addition, the French themselves were uneasy at the future prospects of their country, in the event of the emperor dying without issue. M. Thiers, though a glorifier of Napoleon, does not hide the real character of the line of conduct adopted by him on this occasion. On the 26th of October 1809, Napoleon stated his views to the Chancellor Cambacérès: 'He loved that old companion of his life, Josephine,' says the historian, 'though he was not scrupulously faithful to her, and it wrung his heart to part from her; but, as his popularity declined, he liked to suppose that it was not his fault, but the want of a future, which menaced his glorious throne with premature decay. To consolidate what he felt trembling under his feet, was his engrossing thought; if a new wife were chosen, obtained, placed in the

Tuileries, and became the mother of a male heir, the faults which had set all the world against him might, perchance, be disarmed of their consequences. It was well, no doubt, to have an indisputable heir; but better, a hundredfold better, would it have been to be prudent and wise! However this may be, Napoleon, who, notwithstanding his want of a son, at the zenith of his glory and power after Tilsit, had been unable to bring himself to sacrifice Josephine, now at last resolved to do so; because he felt the empire shaken, and was about to seek, in a new marriage, the security which he ought to have derived from an able and moderate course of conduct.'* Cambacérès ventured to urge that the proceeding was in various ways objectionable; but Napoleon haughtily silenced him. The emperor had long before secretly sounded Alexander concerning an alliance with the House of Russia. On the 9th of December, at a painful interview between Napoleon, Josephine, and her son and daughter by her first marriage, the separation was agreed upon—the inflexible will of the emperor overbearing all opposition. On the 15th, the civil contract of marriage was formally dissolved, in presence of most of the emperor's relations; and a conclave of obsequious bishops soon afterwards found arguments for annulling the spiritual or religious marriage. Meanwhile negotiations were going on between Napoleon and Alexander for the marriage of the former to the Princess Anna of Russia, the Emperor Alexander's sister. Austria and Saxony had each thrown out hints that an alliance with the great military conqueror would be acceptable; and as there was some hesitation on the part of Russia, Napoleon suddenly changed his plan, and, on the 5th of February 1810, demanded in marriage the youthful Archduchess Maria Louisa of Austria. The demand was eagerly responded to by the court of Vienna, and the lady herself seems to have urged no objection. M. Thiers states that the emperor, Francis II., delighted at the prospect, nevertheless desired that the wishes of his daughter should be consulted, and sent M. Metternich to tell her the news. 'The young princess was eighteen, of a good figure, excellent health, and a fair German complexion. She had been carefully educated, had some talent, and a placid temper; in short, the qualities desirable in a mother. She was surprised and pleased, far from being dismayed, at going into that France where, but lately, the revolutionary monster devoured kings; and where a conqueror, now mastering the revolutionary monster, made kings tremble in his turn. She accepted with becoming reserve, but with much delight, the brilliant lot offered to her. She consented to become the consort of Napoleon, and mother to the heir of the greatest empire in the world.' A marriage by proxy took place in Vienna on the 11th of March; a civil marriage at St Cloud on the 1st of April; and a final spiritual marriage at the Tuileries on the 2d.

Maria Louisa became a mother in due course, and Napoleon seems to have had no particular affection for her in any other light. She was a princess of neutral or negative qualities, kind in private life, but a little embarrassed when her husband wished her to take the lead in splendid court-ceremonies. Poor Josephine, of course, was not likely to be brought into her society. There was nearly thirty years' difference in their ages (Josephine was born June 24, 1763, and Maria Louisa December 12, 1791); and still more difference in their antecedents. Both empresses were alike in this, they ceased to be empresses while Napoleon was still alive; though Maria Louisa succeeded still in retaining a certain rank, being made Duchess of Parma by the allies, after the fall of Bonaparte.

* *History of the Consulate and the Empire*, vol. ii., book xxxvii.

## BRUNEL.

Mark Isambard Brunel was born at Hacqueville, a few miles from Rouen, in 1769—that notable year which gave to the world Napoleon and Wellington, Humboldt and Cuvier. Like so many other inventors, Brunel displayed from childhood a passion for construction. His father, who was a prosperous farmer, determined to make him a priest; but Mark shewed no inclination whatever for literary studies, devoting his attention to drawing, mathematics, and mechanics, and amusing himself in making boats, clocks, and musical instruments, while a carpenter's shop was to him a paradise. There was little gained by contending with such impulses, and Brunel, having been allowed in 1786 to enter the navy, made several voyages to the West Indies. In 1793, his ship was paid off, and happening shortly afterwards to visit Paris, he imprudently, in a moment of excitement, made a royalist speech at a political club, and was counselled to seek safety in flight. He escaped to Rouen, and sailed for New York, where he was naturalised as an American citizen. He found easy and abundant employment as an engineer; and was appointed to make a survey for a canal between Lake Champlain and the Hudson, to design and build a theatre in New York, and to plan the defence and fortification of that city. There was every reason for him to remain in the United States, but whilst at Rouen he had made the acquaintance of Sophia Kingdom, an English lady, for whose sake he abandoned his professional prospects. In 1799, he accordingly recrossed the Atlantic, settled in England, and married.

The story of Brunel's life, for years hereafter, is comprised in a list of inventions over which he bestowed a world of pains and anxiety, but from which he reaped little beyond a bare subsistence. One of the most useful was a plan for making block-pulleys for ships by machinery. It was adopted by the government in 1803, and he was employed to carry it into execution in the dockyard at Portsmouth. The ingenuity of the contrivance was not less remarkable than the accuracy and economy with which its operations were performed. It comprises, so to speak, sixteen different machines, all driven by the same steam-power; seven of which cut and shape logs of elm or ash into the shells of blocks of any required size, while nine fashion stems of lignum-vitæ into pulleys or sheaves, and form the iron pin, on the insertion of which the block is complete. Four men with this machine turn out as many blocks as fourscore did formerly; and although 1500 blocks are required in the rigging of a single ship of the line, the supply has never failed even in time of war; and sixty years' experience has suggested scarcely an improvement on Brunel's original design. The service he thus rendered to the navy he endeavoured to repeat for the army, in devising machinery for the manufacture of shoes, in which pins took the place of thread, so that the rubbish supplied by rascally contractors might be superseded. The peace of 1815 removed the pressing necessity for great numbers of soldiers' shoes, and it was reserved for American enterprise to develop into commercial practice shoe-making by machinery. The circular-saw, worked by the steam-engine, was brought to its present high degree of force and efficiency by Brunel, and the saw-mill in Chatham dock-yard was erected under his care. He devised a machine for twisting cotton and forming it into balls; another for hemming and stitching; another for knitting; another for copying letters; another for ruling paper; another for nail-making; another for making wooden boxes; a hydraulic packing-press; besides new methods and combinations for suspension-bridges, and a process for building wide and flat arches without centerings. He was employed in the construction of the first Ramsgate steamer, and was the first to suggest the use of steam-tugs to the Admiralty. At the playful request of Lady Spencer, he produced a machine for shuffling cards. The cards were placed in a box, a handle was turned, and in a few seconds the sides flew open, and presented the pack divided into four parts, thoroughly mixed. This enumeration may give some idea of the versatility of Brunel's inventive powers, but he lacked mercantile faculty whereby to turn them to pecuniary advantage. In 1821, he was actually imprisoned for debt, and was only released by a vote of £5000 from government.

In the construction of an engine with carbonic acid gas for the motive-power, Brunel, assisted by his son, spent nearly fifteen years and £15,000 in experiments. They overcame most of the mechanical difficulties—they obtained an intense power at a low temperature—and the hopes of the scientific and commercial worlds were alike strongly excited; but in the end they had to confess a failure, and admit, 'that the effect of any given amount of caloric on gaseous bodies was not greater than that produced by the expansion of water into steam;' and that, therefore, 'the practical application of condensed gases, including common air, was not so advantageous as that derived from the expansive force of steam.'

The great enterprise by which Brunel became popularly distinguished, was the Thames Tunnel. Two or three attempts had been made to connect the shores of Essex and Kent by a subaqueous passage, but all had failed. One day, when Brunel was passing through the dock-yard at Chatham, his eye was caught by a piece of ship-timber perforated by the destructive worm—the *Teredo Navalis;* and the study of its mode of operation suggested the construction of a cast-iron shield, which should bore like an auger by means of strong hydraulic screws, while as fast as the earth was cut away, bricklayers should be at hand to replace it with an arch. He patented the plan, and revived the project of a road under the Thames. In 1824, a Thames Tunnel Company was formed, and in 1825, the work commenced, and was pursued through many difficulties from explosions of gas and irruptions of water, until 1828. At the beginning of that year about 600 feet were completed, when, on the 12th of January, the river broke through, six men were drowned, and Brunel's son, also so distinguished in after-days as an engineer, only escaped by being washed up the shaft. The tunnel was emptied, but the funds of the company were exhausted. In an 'Ode to M. Brunel,' Hood wrote:

'Other great speculations have been nursed,
Till want of proceeds laid them on the shelf:
But thy concern was at the worst
When it began to *liquidate* itself.'

For seven years, until 1835, work was suspended, when, at the solicitation of the Duke of Wellington, government advanced the company, on loan, £246,000. At last the entire 1200 feet, from Wapping to Rotherhithe, were completed, and on the 25th of March 1843 the tunnel was opened to the public. Brunel was knighted by the Queen, and his fame was borne to the ends of the earth. As an engineer, the work reflected great credit on him, but commercially it was a failure. It cost well-nigh £500,000, and the tolls produced annually something less than £5000, a sum which proved barely sufficient to keep the tunnel in repair. [The tunnel consists of two parallel arched passages, 14 feet broad, 16 feet high, and 1200 feet long. In 1865, the East London Railway Company purchased the Thames Tunnel for £200,000, and about 40 trains pass through it daily.]

Brunel died in 1849, in his eighty-first year, leaving behind him a son, Isambard Kingdom Brunel, who fully inherited his father's genius. Brunel was a little man, with a head so large, that an Irishman once said, 'Why that man's face is all head!' Many amusing anecdotes are told of his blunders during his moods of inventive abstraction; as, for instance, caressing a lady's hand, who sat next him at table, thinking it his wife's; forgetting his own name, and handing in other people's cards at houses he visited; and getting into wrong coaches, and travelling long distances ere he discovered his mistake. At other times he shewed rare presence of mind. Once when inspecting the Birmingham railway, trains, to the horror of the bystanders, were observed to approach from opposite directions. Brunel, seeing retreat to be impossible, buttoned his coat, brought the skirts close round him, and placing himself firmly between the two lines of rail, the trains swept past, and left him unscathed.

## PRAISE-GOD BAREBONES' PARLIAMENT.

When Charles I. had been put to death by the Revolutionists, on the 30th January 1649, the nation was governed, for four or five years, by the parliament, more or less under the control of the successful military leaders. Circumstances gave these military leaders more and more influence; for, owing to the contentions of Royalists, Presbyterians, Levellers, Covenanters, Fifth-Monarchy Men, Antinomians, and other parties, the civil power was very much distracted. Cromwell soon gained an ascendency over all the other active men of the day, on account both of his military successes, and of the force of his character generally. After the battle of Worcester (September 3, 1651), and the flight of Charles II., Cromwell made gradual strides towards supreme power. The parliament grew jealous of him and the army, and he jealous of their preference for the navy. At length, on April 20, 1653, he forcibly dissolved that celebrated parliament, known in history as the *Long Parliament:* a most violent proceeding, which made him practically dictator over the whole kingdom.

Cromwell, in his self-assumed capacity as 'captain-general and commander-in-chief of all the armies and forces raised and to be raised within this commonwealth,' summoned a sort of parliament, by an order dated June 6: the parliament or council to consist of persons nominated by him, and not elected by the people. A hundred and forty of these summonses were issued, and all but two of the persons summoned attended. Bulstrode expressed wonder, when recording these events, that so many persons of good-fortune and education accepted the summons from such a man as Oliver. Mr Carlyle comments on Bulstrode's perplexity, and on the constitution of the assembly generally, in one of his most characteristic passages: 'My disconsolate friend, it is a sign that Puritan England, in general, accepts this action of Cromwell and his officers, and thanks them for it, in such a case of extremity; saying, as audibly as the means permitted: Yea, we did wish it so! Rather mournful to the disconsolate official mind! Lord Clarendon, again, writing with much latitude, has characterised this convention as containing in it "divers gentlemen who had estates, and such a proportion of credit in the world as might give some colour to the business;" but consisting, on the whole, of a very miserable beggarly sort of persons, acquainted with nothing but the art of praying; "artificers of the meanest trades," if they even had any trade: all which the reader shall, if he please, add to the general *guano*-mountains, and pass on, not regarding. The undeniable fact is, these men were, as Whitelock intimates, a quite respectable assembly; got together by anxious "consultation of the godly clergy," and chief Puritan lights in their respective counties; not without much earnest revision, and solemn consideration in all kinds, on the part of men adequate enough for such a work, and desirous enough to do it well. The list of the assembly exists; not yet entirely gone dark for mankind. A fair proportion of them still recognisable to mankind. Actual peers one or two: founders of peerage families, two or three, which still exist among us—Colonel Edward Montague, Colonel Charles Howard, Anthony Ashley Cooper. And better than kings' peers, certain peers of nature; whom, if not the king and his pasteboard Norroys have had the luck to make peers of, the living heart of England has since raised to the peerage, and means to keep there—Colonel Robert Blake, the Sea-King, for one. "Known persons," I do think, "of approved integrity, men fearing God;" and perhaps not entirely destitute of sense any one of them! Truly it seems rather a distinguished parliament—even though Mr Praise-God Barebone, "the leather merchant in Fleet Street," be, as all mortals must admit, a member of it. The fault, I hope, is forgivable? Praise-God, though he deals in leather, and has a name which can be misspelt, one discerns to be the son of pious parents; to be himself a man of piety, of understanding, and weight—and even of considerable private capital, my witty flunky friends! We will leave Praise-God to do the best he can, I think.—And old Francis Rouse is there from Devonshire; once member for Truro; provost of Eton College; whom by-and-by they make speaker; whose psalms the northern kirks will sing. Richard, mayor of Hursley, is there, and even idle Dick Norton; Alexander Jaffray of Aberdeen, Laird Swinton of the College of Justice in Edinburgh; Alderman Ireton, brother of the late Lord Deputy, colleague of Praise-God in London. In fact, a real assembly of the notables in Puritan England; a parliament, *parliamentum*, a real *speaking apparatus* for the now dominant interest in England, as exact as could well be got—much more exact, I suppose, than any ballot-box, free hustings, or ale-barrel election usually yields. Such is the assembly called the *Little Parliament*, and wittily *Barebones' Parliament*. Their witty name survives; but their history is gone all dark.' *

This was, indeed, a little parliament of only five months' duration. Hume casts unsparing ridicule on its proceedings; Carlyle praises it, saying that its mission was 'to introduce Christianity into private life.' It failed. 'No wonder,' says Carlyle. 'Fearful impediments lay against that effort of theirs: the sluggishness, the half-and-half-ness, the greediness, the cowardice, the general opacity of ten million men against it—alas, the whole world, and what we call the devil and all his angels, against it! Considerable angels, human and others.' Cromwell found his Little Parliament often going beyond his wishes in reform; and at length a bill to abolish tithes, because the clergy were lazy, and another to abolish the Court of Chancery, raised such a storm against them that Cromwell was glad to get rid of them. By a sort of party-manœuvre, on December 12, the parliament voted its own death, in a resolution: 'That the sitting of this parliament any longer, as now constituted, will not be for the good of the commonwealth; and that therefore it is requisite to deliver up unto the Lord-general Cromwell the powers which we received from him.' The minority insisted on maintaining 'a house,' and continued the sittings with a new speaker. But General Harrison entered with a few soldiers, and asked what they were doing. 'We are seeking the Lord,' said they. 'Then you may go elsewhere,' said he: 'for to my certain knowledge, He has not been here these many years.' Thus the 'Barebones' Parliament' died: four days afterwards, Oliver Cromwell became Protector.

## THE TRADESCANTS.

The following lines are inscribed upon a tomb in Lambeth churchyard:

'Know, stranger, ere thou pass; beneath this stone,
Lye John Tradescant, grandsire, father, son;
The last dy'd in his spring; the other two
Lived till they had travelled Art and Nature through,
As by their choice collections may appear,
Of what is rare, in land, in sea, in air;
Whilst they (as Homer's Iliad in a nut)
A world of wonders in one closet shut.
These famous antiquarians that had been
Both Gardeners to the Rose and Lily Queen,
Transplanted now themselves, sleep here; and when
Angels shall with their trumpets waken men,
And fire shall purge the world, these hence shall rise
And change this garden for a paradise.'

The grandsire of the above epitaph came of Flemish origin. After travelling through Europe

* *Oliver Cromwell's Letters and Speeches, with Elucidations by Thomas Carlyle*, vol. ii. p. 388.

and in the East, he settled in England; and was at one time gardener to the Duke of Buckingham, and afterwards to Charles I. He formed a large 'physic garden' at South Lambeth, and was the means of introducing many plants into this country. So ardent was he in the acquisition of rarities, that he is said to have joined an expedition against the Algerine corsairs, in order to obtain a new sort of apricot from North Africa, which was known thence as the Algier apricot. He was also an enthusiastic collector of curiosities, with which he filled his house, and earned for it the popular name of 'Tradeskin's Ark.' He died at an advanced age, in 1652 or 1653. His son, another John Tradescant, followed in his father's footsteps. In 1656, he published a catalogue of his collection under the title of *Museum Tradescantianum.* From this we learn that it was indeed a multifarious assemblage of strange things—stuffed animals and birds, chemicals, dyeing materials, idols, weapons, clothes, coins, medals, musical instruments, and relics of all sorts. We here enumerate a few of the strangest articles—'Easter eggs of the patriarchs of Jerusalem; two feathers of the phœnix tayle; claw of the bird Roc, who, as authors report, is able to truss an elephant; a natural dragon above two inches long; the Dodad, from the isle of Mauritius, so big as not to be able to fly; the bustard, as big as a turkey, usually taken by greyhounds on Newmarket Heath; a cow's tail from Arabia; half a hazel-nut, with seventy pieces of household stuff in it; a set of chessmen in a peppercorn; landskips, stories, trees, and figures, cut in paper by some of the emperors; a trunnion of Drake's ship; knife wherewith Hudson was killed in Hudson's Bay; Anna Bullen's night-vail; Edward the Confessor's gloves.'

In Ashmole's diary, under date 12th December 1659, occurs this entry: 'Mr Tradescant and his wife told me they had long been considering upon whom to bestow their closet of curiosities when they died, and at last resolved to give it unto me.' Tradescant died in 1672, and bequeathed his house to Ashmole, who, after some litigation with his friend's widow, took possession of the ark in 1674. The collection was left by Ashmole to the university of Oxford, and was the nucleus of the museum bearing his name.

In May 1747, Sir W. Watson visited the long-neglected garden of Tradescant, and found it entirely grown over with weeds, with which, however, a few of the old gardener's favourites yet struggled for life. Among them were 'two trees of the arbutus, the largest which I have seen, which from their being so long used to our winters, did not suffer by the severe colds of 1729 and 1740, when most of their kind were killed throughout England.'

## DECEMBER 13.

St Lucy, virgin and martyr, 304. St Jodoc or Josse, confessor, 666. St Aubert, bishop of Cambray and Arras, 669. St Othilia, virgin and abbess, 772. St Kenelm, king and martyr, 820. Blessed John Marinoni, confessor, 1562.

### ST LUCY.

St Lucy was a native of Syracuse, and sought in marriage by a young nobleman of that city; but she had determined to devote herself to a religious life, and persistently refused the addresses of her suitor, whom she still further exasperated by distributing the whole of her large fortune among the poor. He thereupon accused her to the governor, Paschasius, of professing Christian doctrines, and the result was her martyrdom, under the persecution of the Emperor Dioclesian. A curious legend regarding St Lucy is, that on her lover complaining to her that her beautiful eyes haunted him day and night, she cut them out of her head, and sent them to him, begging him now to leave her to pursue, unmolested, her devotional aspirations. It is added that Heaven, to recompense this act of abnegation, restored her eyes, rendering them more beautiful than ever. In allusion to this circumstance, St Lucy is generally represented bearing a platter, on which two eyes are laid; and her intercession is frequently implored by persons labouring under ophthalmic affections.

### The Ember-days.

The Ember-days are periodical fasts originally instituted, it is said, by Pope Calixtus, in the third century, for the purpose of imploring the blessing of Heaven on the produce of the earth; and also preparing the clergy for ordination, in imitation of the apostolic practice recorded in the 13th chapter of the Acts. It was not, however, till the Council of Placentia, 1095 A.D., that a uniformity as regards the season of observance was introduced. By a decree of this assembly, it was enacted that the Ember-days should be the first Wednesday, Friday, and Saturday following, respectively, the first Sunday in Lent, or Quadragesima Sunday, Whitsunday, Holyrood Day (14th September), and St Lucy's Day (13th December). The term is said to be derived from the Saxon *emb-ren* or *imbryne*, denoting a course or circuit, these days recurring regularly, at stated periods, in the four quarters or seasons of the year. Others, with some plausibility, derive the epithet from the practice of sprinkling dust or embers on the head, in token of humiliation; and also from the circumstance that at such seasons it was only customary to break the fast by partaking of cakes baked on the embers, or *ember-bread.* In accordance with a canon of the English Church, the ordination of clergymen by the bishop generally takes place on the respective Sundays immediately following the ember-days. The weeks in which these days fall, are termed the *Ember-weeks,* and in Latin the ember-days are denominated *Jejunia quatuor temporum,* or 'the fasts of the four seasons.'

*Born.*—Pope Sixtus V., 1521, *Montalto;* Henri IV. of France, 1553, *Pau;* Maximilien de Bethune, Duke of Sully, minister of Henri IV., 1560, *Rosny;* William Drummond, poet, 1585, *Hawthornden;* Rev. Arthur Penrhyn Stanley, biographer of Dr Arnold, 1815.

*Died.*—Emperor Frederick II. of Germany, 1250; Emanuel the Great, king of Portugal, 1521; James V. of Scotland, 1542, *Falkland;* Conrad Gesner, eminent naturalist, 1565, *Zurich;* Anthony Collins, freethinking writer, 1729; Rev. John Strype, historical writer, 1737, *Hackney;* Christian Furchtegott Gellert, writer of fables, 1769, *Leipsic;* Peter Wargentin, Swedish astronomer, 1783, *Stockholm;* Dr Samuel Johnson, lexicographer, 1784, *London;* Charles III. of Spain, 1788.

## THE COUNCIL OF TRENT.

This celebrated council, one of the most important ever summoned by the Roman Catholic Church, was formally opened on 13th December 1545, and closed on 4th December 1563. Its sittings extended thus, with various prorogations, over a period of eighteen years, and through no less than five pontificates, commencing with Paul III., and ending with Pius IV.

The summoning of a general council had been ardently desired by the adherents both of the Roman Catholic and Reformed systems, partly from a desire to have many great and scandalous abuses removed, partly from the hope of effecting a reconciliation between the opposite faiths, through mutual concession and an adjustment of the points in dispute by the decision of some authoritative assembly. The requisition to convoke such a meeting was first made to Clement VII., and was seconded, with all his influence, by the Emperor Charles V.; but, as is well known, popes have ever had the greatest dislike of general councils, regarding them as dangerous impugners of their pretensions, and at the present conjuncture no proposal could have been more distasteful. Well knowing the ecclesiastical abuses that prevailed, and fearful of the consequences of inquiry and exposure, Clement, by various devices, contrived, for the short remainder of his life, to elude compliance with the unpalatable proposition. But his successor, Paul III., found himself unable, with any appearance of propriety, to postpone longer a measure so earnestly desired, and he accordingly issued letters of convocation for a general ecclesiastical council. After much disputation, the town of Trent, in the Tyrol, was fixed on as the place of meeting of the assembly.

But with all the preliminary arrangements entered into, the German Protestant subjects of Charles V. were thoroughly dissatisfied. The place chosen for the meeting was unsuitable from its remote situation, and an infinitely weightier objection was made to the right assumed by the pope of presiding in the council and directing its deliberations, together with the refusal to guarantee, throughout the proceedings, the recognition of the Scriptures, and the usage of the primitive church, as the sole standards of faith. After some abortive attempts to accommodate these differences, the Protestants finally declined to attend or recognise in any way the approaching council, which was accordingly left wholly to the direction of the Catholics. One of the first points determined was: 'That the books to which the designation of *Apocryphal* hath been given, are of equal authority with those which were received by the Jews and primitive Christians into the sacred canon; that the traditions handed down from the apostolic age, and preserved in the church, are entitled to as much regard as the doctrines and precepts which the inspired authors have committed to writing; that the Latin translation of the Scriptures, made or revised by St Jerome, and known by the name of the *Vulgate* translation, should be read in churches, and appealed to in the schools as authentic and canonical.' In virtue of its infallible authority, claimed to be derived from the immediate inspiration of the Holy Spirit, the council denounced anathemas against all those who should impugn or deny the validity of its decisions. The ancient formula, however, prefixed by ecclesiastical councils to their deliverances—*It has seemed good to the Holy Spirit and to us*—was, on the occasion of the assembly at Trent, exchanged for the milder phrase—*In the presence of the Holy Spirit it has seemed good to us.*

This specimen, given by the council at the commencement of its proceedings, was sufficiently indicative of the results to be eventually expected. So far from any modification being effected in the tenets or claims of the Roman Catholic Church and its ministers, these, on the contrary, were more rigorously enforced and defined. In the words of Dr Robertson: 'Doctrines which had hitherto been admitted upon the credit of tradition alone, and received with some latitude of interpretation, were defined with a scrupulous nicety, and confirmed by the sanction of authority. Rites, which had formerly been observed only in deference to custom, supposed to be ancient, were established by the decrees of the church, and declared to be essential parts of its worship. The breach, instead of being closed, was widened and made irreparable.' While thus so antagonistic to Protestant views, the decrees of the Council of Trent are generally regarded as one of the principal standards and completed digests of the Roman Catholic faith.

## ANTIQUARIAN HOAXES.

One of the most amusing traits in the character of Sir Walter Scott's kind-hearted antiquary, the estimable Monkbarns, is his perfect reliance on his own rendering of the letters A. D. L. L., on a stone he believes to be antique, and which letters he amplifies into *Agricola dicavit libens lubens;* a theory rudely demolished by Edie Ochiltree, who pronounces 'the sacrificial vessel,' also on the stone, to be the key to its true significance, *Aikin Drum's lang ladle.* Scott had 'ta'en the antiquarian trade' (as Burns phrases it) early in life, and commenced his literary career in that particular walk; his early rambles on the line of the great Roman Wall, in the Border counties, would familiarise him with inscriptions; and his acquaintance with antiquarian literature lead him to the knowledge of a few mistakes made in works of good repute. In depicting the incident above referred to, he might have had in his mind the absurd error of Vallancey, who has engraved in his great work on Irish Antiquities, a group of sepulchral stones on the hill of Tara, having upon one an inscription which he reads thus: BELI DIVOSE, 'To Belus, God of Fire.' He indulges, then, in a long and learned disquisition on this remarkable and unique inscription;

ALTAR TO BAAL.

which he has also so carefully engraved, that its *real* significance may easily be tested. It turned out to be the work of an idler, who lay upon the stone, and cut his name upside down with the date of the year: E. CONID. 1731; and if the reader will turn the engraving on the preceding page, the whole thing becomes clear, and Baal is deprived of his altar.

Dean Swift had successfully shewn how a choice of words, and their arrangement, might make plain English look exceedingly like Latin. The idea was carried out further by some wicked wit, who, aided by a clever engraver, produced, in 1756, a print called 'The Puzzle,' which has never been surpassed in its peculiar style. 'This curious inscription is humbly dedicated,' says its author, 'to the penetrating geniuses of Oxford, Cambridge, Eton, and the learned Society of Antiquaries.' The first, fourth, sixth, and three concluding lines are particularly happy imitations of a Latin inscription. It is, however, a simple English epitaph; the key, published soon afterwards, tells us: 'The inscription on the stone, without having regard to the stops, capital letters, or division of the words, easily reads as follows: "Beneath this stone

THE MYSTERIOUS INSCRIPTION: ANTIQUARIES PUZZLED.

reposeth Claud Coster, tripe-seller of Impington, as doth his consort Jane."'

Such freaks of fancy may fairly be classed with Callot's *Impostures Innocentes*; not so when false inscriptions and forged antiques have been fabricated to mislead the scholar, or make him look ridiculous. One of the most malicious of these tricks was concocted by George Steevens, the Shakspearian commentator, to revenge himself on Gough, the director of the Society of Antiquaries of London, and author of the great work on our Sepulchral Monuments. The entire literary life of Steevens has been characterised as displaying an unparalleled series of arch deceptions, tinctured with much malicious ingenuity. He scrupled not, when it served his purpose, to invent quotations from old books that existed only in his imagination, and would deduce therefrom corroboration of his own views. Among other things, he invented the famous description of the poisonous upas-tree of Java, and the effluvia killing all things near it. This account, credited by Darwin, and introduced in his *Botanic Garden*, spread through general literature as a fact; until artists at last were induced to present pictures of the tree and the deadly scene around it. Steevens chose the magazines, or popular newspapers, for the promulgation of his inventions, and signed them with names calculated to disarm suspicion. It is impossible to calculate the full amount of mischief that may be produced by such means—literature may be disfigured, and falsehood take the place of fact.

The trick on Gough was the fabrication of an inscription, purporting to record the death of the Saxon king, Hardicanute, and was done in revenge for some adverse criticism Gough had pronounced on a drawing of Steevens. Steevens vowed that, wretched as Gough deemed his work, it should have the power to deceive him. He obtained the fragment of a chimney-slab, and scratched upon it an inscription in Anglo-Saxon letters, to the effect that 'Here Hardcnut drank a wine-horn dry, stared about him, and died.' It was alleged to have been discovered in Kennington Lane, where the palace of the monarch was also said to have been, and the fatal drinking-bout to have taken place. The stone was placed carelessly among other articles in a shop where Gough frequently called. He fell fairly into the trap; and brought forward his imagined prize, as a great historic curiosity, to the notice of the Society of Antiquaries. One of the ablest members of the association—the Rev. S. Pegge—was induced to write a paper on the subject. Schnebbelie, the draughtsman of the society, was employed to draw the inscription carefully, and it was engraved, and published in vol. lx. of the *Gentleman's Magazine*, from which our cut is copied.

THE HARDICANUTE MARBLE.

The falsely-formed letters, and absurd tenor of the whole inscription, would deceive no one now. Luckily, before its publication in the *Magazine*, its history was discovered; but as the plate contained other subjects, it was nevertheless issued, with a note of warning appended. Steevens, however, followed up his success with a bitter description of the triumph of his fraud, and the impossibility of Gough's 'wriggling off the hook on which he is so archæologically suspended.'

Instances might be readily multiplied of similar deceptive inventions; indeed, the history of falsehood and forgery in connection with antiquities is as vast as it is still unceasing. Rome and Naples are to-day what Padua was in the sixteenth century—the birthplace of spurious curiosities, manufactured with the utmost art, and brought forth with the greatest apparent innocence. Nothing is forgotten to be done that may effectually deceive; and the unguarded stranger may see objects dug out of ruins apparently ancient, that have been recently made, and placed there for his delectation. A brisk trade in painted vases has always been carried on; and many of them, evidently false, have been published in works of high character.

FAME ELUDING HER FOLLOWER.

Birch, in his *History of Ancient Pottery*, speaks of this, and adds: 'One of the most remarkable fabricated engravings of these vases was that issued by Brondsted and Stackelberg, in a fit of archæological jealousy. A modern archæologist is seen running after a draped female figure called ΦΗΜΗ, or *Fame*; who flies from him, exclaiming ΕΚΑΣ ΠΑΙ ΚΑΛΕ, "Be off, my fine fellow!" This vase, which never existed except upon paper, deceived the credulous Inghirami, who, too late, endeavoured to expunge it from his work.' Consequently his valuable book on *Vasi Fittili* is disfigured by this absurd invention, and our cut is traced from his plate. These mischievous tricks compel the student to double labour—he has not only to use research, but to be assured that what he finds may be depended on. Supposed facts may turn out to be absurd fictions, and the stream of knowledge be poisoned at its very source.

## THE NINE WORTHIES OF LONDON.

Everybody has read, or at least heard, of the famous *History of the Seven Champions of Christendom*, but few, we suspect, have either read or heard of another work by the same author, which, if less interesting than the chivalric chronicle dear to boyhood, has the merit of being to some extent founded on fact. In the year 1592, Mr Richard Johnson gave to the world *The Nine Worthies of London; explaining the honourable Exercise of Arms, the Virtues of the Valiant, and the Memorable Attempts of Magnanimous Minds; pleasant for Gentlemen, not unseemly for Magistrates, and most profitable for 'Prentices.*

This chronicle of the deeds of city-heroes is a curious compound of prose and verse. The Worthies are made to tell their own stories in rhyme, to a prose accompaniment unique in its way. What that way is, may be judged by the following quotation from the fanciful prelude: 'What time Fame began to feather herself to fly, and was winged with the lasting memory of martial men; orators ceased to practise persuasive orations, poets neglected their lyres, and Pallas herself would have nothing painted on her shield save mottoes of Mars, and emblems in honour of noble achievements. Then the ashes of ancient victors, without scruple or disdain, found sepulture in rich monuments; the baseness of their origin shaded by the virtue of their noble deeds.' Fame, however, was still fearful of her honour growing faint, and, in her fear, betook herself to Parnassus, and invoked the aid of the Muses in order to revive 'what ignorance in darkness seems to shade, and hateful oblivion hath almost rubbed out of the book of honour—the deeds not of kings, but of those whose merit made them great.' Choosing Clio as her companion, Fame re-entered her chariot, and speedily reached the Elysian Fields, where, upon a rose-covered bank, nine handsome knights lay asleep; waking them up, she desired them to tell their several adventures, that Clio might take them down for the benefit of mankind in general, and London 'prentices in particular.

Then forth stepped Sir William Walworth, fishmonger, twice lord mayor of London (in 1374 and 1380). His narrative begins and ends with the great event of his second mayoralty—the rebellion of Wat Tyler. He relates how the malcontents advanced to London, mightily assailed the Tower walls, and how—

'Earle's manner houses were by them destroyed;
The Savoy and S. Jones by Smithfield spoiled.'

While—

'All men of law that fell into their hands
They left them breathless, weltering in their blood;
Ancient records were turned to firebrands,
Any had favour sooner than the good:
So stout these cut-throats were in their degree,
That noblemen must serve them on their knee.'

To protect the person of the young king when he went to meet the rebels at Smithfield, Walworth attended with

'A loyal guard of bills and bows
Collected of our tallest men of trade.'

During the parley with Wat Tyler, the sturdy magistrate sat chafing with anger at the audacity of the blacksmith's followers, but refrained from interfering, because his betters were in place, till he could control himself no longer—

'When I saw the rebels' pride increasing,
And none control or counter-check their rage;
'Twere service good (thought I) to purchase peace,
And malice of contentious brags assuage,
With this conceit all fear had taken flight,
And I, alone, pressed to the traitors' sight.

Their multitude could not amaze my mind,
Their bloody weapons did not make me shrink,
True valour hath his constancy assigned,
The eagle at the sun will never wink.
Among their troops incensed with mortal hate,
I did arrest Wat Tyler on the pate.

The stroke was given with so good a will,
I made the rebel couch unto the earth;
His fellows that behind (though strange) were still.
It marred the manner of their former mirth.
I left him not, but ere I did depart,
I stabbed my dagger to his damned heart.'

For which daring deed Richard immediately dubbed him a knight.

'A costly hat his Highness likewise gave;
That London's maintainance might ever be,
A sword also he did ordain to have,
That should be carried still before the mayor,
Whose worth deserved succession to the chair.'

The second speaker is Sir Henry Pitchard, who commences his story with an atrocious pun:

'The potter tempers not the massive gold,
A meaner substance serves his simple trade,
His workmanship consists of slimy mould,
Where any placed impression soon is made.
His *Pitchards* have no outward glittering pomp,
As other metals of a firmer stamp.'

After serving in the wars of Edward III., Pitchard set up as a vintner, and throve so well that he was elected lord mayor (1356); he hints that he could speak of liberal deeds, but prefers to rest his claim to honourable consideration upon his anxiety for the advance of London's fame, and the part he played on Edward's return from France with 'three crowns within his conquering hand.'

'As from Dover with the prince his son,
The kings of Cyprus, France, and Scots did pass,
All captive prisoners to this mighty, one,
Five thousand men, and I their leader was,
All well prepared, as to defend a fort,
Went forth to welcome him in martial sort.
When the city 'peared within our sights,
I craved a boon, submisse upon my knee,
To have his grace, these kings, with earls and knights
A day or two, to banquet it with me,
The king admired, yet thankfully replied:
"Unto thy house, both I and these will ride."

The royal guests and their followers were right hospitably entertained:

'For cheer and sumptuous cost no coin did fail,
And he that thought of sparing did me wrong.'

This truly civic achievement is at once admitted by Clio to justify Pitchard's enrolment among the Worthies Nine.

Sir William Sevenoke tells how he was found under seven oaks, near a small town in Kent, and after receiving some education, was apprenticed to a grocer in London. His apprenticeship having expired, he went with Henry V. to France, where—

'The Dolphyne [Dauphin] then of France, a comely knight,
Disguised, came by chance into a place
Where I, well wearied with the heat of fight,
Had laid me down, for war had ceased his chace;
And, with reproachful words, as lazy swain
He did salute me ere I long had lain.

I, knowing that he was mine enemy,
A bragging Frenchman (for we termed them so),
Ill brooked the proud disgrace he gave to me,
And therefore lent the Dolphyne such a blow,
As warmed his courage well to lay about,
Till he was breathless, though he were so stout.

At last the noble prince did ask my name,
My birth, my calling, and my fortunes past;
With admiration he did hear the same,
And so a bag of crowns he to me cast;
And, when he went away, he said to me:
"Sevenoke, be proud, the Dolphyne fought with thee!"'

The war over, Sevenoke determined to turn grocer again, and in time became famous for his wealth. [In 1413, Sevenoke was made sheriff; in 1418, he was elected lord mayor; and, two years later, he represented London in parliament. By his will, he set apart a portion of his wealth to build and maintain twenty almshouses, and a free-school at Seven-oaks. In Elizabeth's reign, the school was named 'Queen Elizabeth's Grammar School,' and received a common seal for its use. It still exists, and possesses six exhibitions wherewith to reward its scholars.]

Sir Thomas White, merchant-tailor, lived in the days of Queen Mary. He says he cannot speak of arms and blood-red wars—

'My deeds have tongues to speak, though I surcease,
My orators the learned strive to be,
Because I twined palms in time of peace,
And gave such gifts that made fair learning free;
My care did build these bowers of sweet content,
Where many wise their golden times have spent.

The English cities and incorporate towns
Do bear me witness of my country's care;
Where yearly I do feed the poor with crowns,
For I was never niggard yet to spare;
And all chief boroughs of this blessed land,
Have somewhat tasted of my liberal hand.'

Sir John Bonham's life seems not to have lacked excitement. Born of gentle parents, he was apprenticed to a mercer, and shewed such qualities that he was intrusted with a valuable cargo of merchandise for the Danish market. He was received at the court of Denmark, and there made such progress in the favour of the king's daughter, with whom every knight was in love, that she gave him a favour to wear in his helmet at a grand tournament—

'They that have guiders cannot choose but run,
Their mistress's eyes do learn them chivalry,
With those commands these tournays are begun,
And shivered lances in the air do fly.
No more but this, there Bonham had the best,
Yet list I not to vaunt how I was blest.'

Despite his success in arms, Bonham did not neglect business, and as soon as he had sold his cargo and refilled his ship, he made preparations for returning home. Just as he was about to leave Denmark, the Great Solyman declared war, and began to ravage the country. Bonham was offered the command of an army destined to arrest the progress of the invader; he accepted it, and soon joined issue with the foe, half of whose army—

'Smouldered in the dust,
Lay slaughtered on the earth in gory blood;
And he himself compelled to quell his lust
By composition, for his people's good.
Then at a parley he admired me so,
He made me knight, and let his army go.'

The generosity of the Turk did not stop here; he loaded the new-made knight with chains of gold and costly raiment, to which the monarch he had served so well added—

'Gifts in guerdon of his fight,
And sent him into England like a knight.'

Our sixth Worthy rejoiced in the alliterative appellation of Christopher Croker. He was bound 'prentice to a vintner of Gracechurch Street, and, according to his own account, must have been a fascinating young fellow—

'My fellow-servants loved me with their hearts;
My friends rejoiced to see me prosper so,
And kind Doll Stodie (though for small deserts),
On me vouchsafed affection to bestow.'

Still, Croker was not satisfied. He burned with a desire to raise his sweetheart to high estate, and when he was pressed for the army—believing his opportunity had arrived—he was proof against the arguments of his master, and the tears of his master's daughter. To France he went, and there, he says—

'To prove my faith unto my country's stay,
And that a 'prentice, though but small esteemed,
Unto the stoutest never giveth way
If credit may by trial be redeemed.
At Bordeaux siege, when others came too late,
I was the first made entrance through the gate.'

When that famous campaign was ended, our brave 'prentice was one of ten thousand men chosen by the Black Prince to aid him in restoring Don Pedro to the Castilian throne; and when he returned to England, he returned a knight.

'Thus labour never loseth its reward,
And he that seeks for honour sure shall speed.
What craven mind was ever in regard?
Or where consisteth manhood but in deed?
I speak it that confirmed it by my life,
And in the end, Doll Stodie was my wife.'

Sir John Hawkwood was born to prove it does not always take nine tailors to make a man.

His conduct in action won the notice of the Black Prince, who gave him a noble steed; and he made such good use of the gift, that he was knighted by that great captain, and enrolled among 'the Black Prince's knights.' When there were no more battles to be fought in France, Sir John collected together a force of 15,000 Englishmen, with which he entered the service of the Duke of Milan, and immortalised himself in Italian history as 'Giovanni Acuti Cavaliero.' He afterwards fought on the side of Spain against the pope, and having acquired riches and reputation, returned to Padua to die.

Like most of his co-worthies, Sir Hugh Caverley, silk-weaver, won his knighthood in France. He then went to Poland, and became renowned as a hunter, and earned the gratitude of the people by terminating the career of a monstrous boar that troubled the land. For many years he lived in honour in Poland, but ultimately left that country for France, where he died. The last of the Nine Worthies was Sir Henry Maleverer, grocer, commonly called Henry of Cornhill, who lived in the days of Henry IV. He became a crusader, and did not leave the field till he saw the Holy City regained from the infidels. He stood high in favour with the king of Jerusalem, till that monarch's ears were poisoned against him, when, to avoid death, the gallant knight was compelled to seek a hiding-place. This he found in the neighbourhood of Jacob's Well, of which he assumed the guardianship.

'For my pleasure's sake
I gave both knights and princes heavy strokes;
The proudest did presume a draught to take
Was sure to have his passport sealed with knocks.
Thus lived I till my innocence was known,
And then returned; the king was pensive grown,

And for the wrong which he had offered me,
He vowed me greater friendship than before;
My false accusers lost their liberty,
And next their lives, I could not challenge more.
And thus with love, with honour, and with fame,
I did return to London, whence I came.

When the last of the Worthies thus concluded his story, Fame gently laid his head upon a soft pillow, and left him and his companions to the happiness of their sweet sleep, and enjoined Clio to give the record of their lives to the world, 'that every one might read their honourable actions, and take example by them to follow virtue and aspire.'

# DECEMBER 14.

**St Spiridion, bishop and confessor, 348. Saints Nicasius, archbishop of Rheims, and his companions, martyrs, 5th century.**

*Born.*—Michael Nostradamus, famous prophet, 1503, *St Remy, in Provence;* Tycho Brahe, astronomer, 1546, *Knudsthorp, near the Baltic;* Barthélemi d'Herbelot, orientalist, 1625, *Paris;* Daniel Neal, divine and author (*History of the Puritans*), 1678, *London;* James Bruce, Abyssinian traveller, 1730, *Kinnaird, Stirlingshire;* Rev. Charles Wolfe, author of *The Burial of Sir John Moore,* 1791, *Dublin.*

*Died.*—Pope Anastasius I., 402; Sir John Oldcastle, Lord Cobham, burned as a Lollard, 1417, *St Giles' Fields, London;* Dean Henry Aldrich, of Christ-Church, Oxford, eminent scholar and divine, 1710; Thomas Rymer, historical writer, 1713; Thomas Tenison, archbishop of Canterbury, 1715, *Lambeth;* Sir William Trumbull, statesman and man of letters, 1716; General George Washington, American patriotic commander and statesman, 1799, *Mount Vernon, Virginia;* Conrad Malte-Brun, geographer, 1826, *Paris;* J. C. Loudon, botanical writer, 1843, *Bayswater, London;* Earl of Aberdeen, statesman, 1860, *London;* Prince Albert, consort of Queen Victoria, 1861, *Windsor Castle.*

## J. C. LOUDON.

There is quite as much difference between a gardener of the old school, and one of the modern era, as exists between the old sea-captain, and the scientific naval officer of the present day; Andrew Fairservice has paired off with Commodore Trunnion, and we are very well rid of both of them. There can be no doubt that the eminent position to which the art of gardening and its professors have of late years attained, is mainly due to the teachings of John Claudius Loudon. The writer well remembers the terrible outcry among the old-school gardeners when Loudon's Encyclopædia first appeared. 'This bookmaking-fellow,' they cried, 'will teach the gentry everything, and the masters and mistresses will know more than we do!' Their words were verified; but the consequence was, that the young gardeners had to study, in order to keep pace with their employers, and doing so speedily raised their craft to a higher platform. Having commenced this movement, Loudon devoted his whole life to urge it forward. He incessantly laboured to shew, that horticulture and botany were merely the foundations of the gardener's calling; that something more than a smattering of a dozen other arts and sciences was necessary to complete the superstructure. And now, when the grave has closed over him for twenty years, it is amply testified by the most convincing proofs that his ideas were correct.

It was in 1822 that Loudon gave to the world the most important and comprehensive publication ever written on horticulture—*The Encyclopædia of Gardening;* a work fully meriting its pretentious title; and though, of necessity, a compilation, enriched with much useful original matter, the result of his continental travels. The success of this work induced him to undertake a series of encyclopædias on agriculture, botany, and cognate subjects, the last of which appeared in 1832. The herculean toils of these ten years are beyond description. 'The labour,' says Mrs Loudon, 'was immense; and for several months he and I used to sit up the greater part of every night, never having more than four hours sleep, and drinking strong coffee to keep ourselves awake.' Undeterred, however, he next commenced a more extended and labour-exacting work than any of his previous productions, an *Arboretum et Fruticetum Britannicum,* embracing every particular relative to the trees and shrubs—whether native or introduced—of the British islands. It is scarcely credible, but no less true, that during the time these vast works were in course of production, Loudon edited several periodicals. In 1826, he established the *Gardener's Magazine,* which he continued till his death. In

1826, he commenced his *Magazine of Natural History*, and edited it until 1836, when it passed into other hands. In 1834, he commenced the *Architectural Magazine*, discontinuing it in 1838; but in 1836 he began publishing his *Suburban Gardener*. It may be safely said, that such multifarious and incessant labours are without a parallel in literature.

A quaint old farmer of our acquaintance, when speaking of a person who worked very hard without deriving much profit from his labours, said that he had turned over a great deal of grass, but made very little hay. It is painful to relate, that the very same words might be applied to Loudon's heroic undertakings. When the Arboretum was completed in 1838, Loudon, who published at his own expense and risk, found himself indebted to printer, paper-maker, and engraver no less a sum than £10,000.

Loudon's literary labours would appear excessive, even for a man in perfect health, and with the vigorous use of his limbs; but they seem little less than miraculous, when the circumstances under which they were carried on are taken into consideration. A severe attack of rheumatic fever when in his twenty-third year, produced a permanent stiffness of the left knee. Subsequently his right arm became affected, and Loudon was advised to try the curative effects of shampooing. During this process, the arm was broken so close to the shoulder as to render setting it in the usual mode impossible. Shortly after, the arm was again broken; and then, in 1826, amputation became unavoidable. In this year, it will be observed, he established the *Gardener's Magazine*, and entered on that career of herculean mental effort already detailed; nor was it carried on without a still further shattering of his frame, for now his left hand became so disabled, that the use of only the third and little finger remained. Maimed and infirm of body, his mind retained its unabated vigour, and he had recourse to the employment of an amanuensis and draughtsman. Thus did he yield ground only inch by inch, as death advanced; and when his last hour arrived, death still found him hard at work, for 'he died standing on his feet.' Chronic inflammation of the lungs terminated his life on the 14th of December 1843. The work on which he was employed at the time of his death, is entitled *Self-instruction for Young Gardeners*, the class of persons whose interests his lifelong labours were devoted to promote. Let his faithful wife, who best knew him, and who has since followed him to the last resting-place, utter his requiem—'Never did any man possess more energy and determination; whatever he began he pursued with enthusiasm, and carried out notwithstanding obstacles that would have discouraged any ordinary person. He was a warm friend; most affectionate in all his relations of son, husband, father, and brother; and never hesitated to sacrifice pecuniary considerations to what he considered his duty.'

---

## VEGETABLES, HERBS, AND FRUITS IN ENGLAND IN THE THIRTEENTH CENTURY.

In connection with the improvements in the art of gardening, effected by Mr Loudon, the subject of the foregoing article, it may not be uninteresting to contemplate the condition of horticulture in England in the thirteenth century; and the nature and extent of the supplies of fruit, vegetables, and similar produce procurable by our ancestors. From the roll of the household expenses of Eleanor, Countess of Leicester, third daughter of King John, and wife of the celebrated Simon de Montfort, who fell at Evesham, we gather the following curious details; this roll being the earliest known memorial of the expenditure of an English subject.

It cannot fail to be remarked, in perusing the roll, that very few esculent plants are mentioned. Dried pease and beans, parsley, fennel, onions, green-pease, and new beans, are the only species named. Pot-herbs, of which the names are not specified, cost 6*d.*; and here, on the authority of Mr Hardy, we may mention that one shilling then would purchase as much as fifteen now. If any other vegetables were in general use at the time, they were, perhaps, comprised under the term *potagium*. There is, however, much uncertainty upon the subject of the cultivation of vegetables, in this country, during the thirteenth and fourteenth centuries. Cresses, endive, lettuce, beets, parsneps, carrots, cabbages, leeks, radishes, and cardoons, were grown in France during the reign of Charlemagne; but it is doubtful whether many of these varieties had penetrated into England at an early period. The most skilful horticulturists of the Middle Ages were ecclesiastics, and it is possible that in the gardens of monasteries many vegetables were raised which were not in common use among the laity. Even in the fifteenth century, the general produce of the English kitchen-garden was contemptible, when compared with that of the Low Countries, France, and Italy. Gilbert Kymer can enumerate only, besides a few wild and forgotten sorts, cabbage, lettuce, spinach, beet-root, trefoil, bugloss, borage, celery, purslaine, fennel, smallage, thyme, hyssop, parsley, mint, a species of turnip, and small white onions. According to him, all these vegetables were boiled with meat. He observes that some were eaten raw, in spring and summer, with olive-oil and spices, but questions the propriety of the custom. This is, perhaps, the earliest notice extant of the use of salads in England.

The roll furnishes but little information respecting fruit. The only kinds named are apples and pears; three hundred of the latter were purchased at Canterbury, probably from the gardens of the monks. It is believed, however, that few other sorts were generally grown in England before the latter end of the fifteenth century; although Matthew Paris, describing the bad season of 1257, observes that 'apples were scarce, and pears scarcer, while quinces, vegetables, cherries, plums, and all shell-fruits were entirely destroyed.' These shell-fruits were, probably, the common hazel-nut, walnuts, and perhaps chestnuts: in 1256, the sheriffs of London were ordered to buy two thousand chestnuts for the king's own use. In the Wardrobe Book of the 14th of Edward I., we find the bill of Nicholas, the royal fruiterer, in which the only fruits mentioned are pears, apples, quinces, medlars, and nuts. The supply of these from Whitsuntide to November, cost £21, 14*s.* 1½*d.*

This apparent scarcity of indigenous fruits naturally leads to the inquiry, what foreign kinds, besides those included in the term spicery, such as almonds, dates, figs, and raisins, were imported into England in this and the following century. In the time of John, and of Henry III., Rochelle was celebrated for its pears, and conger-eels; the sheriffs of London purchased a hundred of the former for Henry in 1223. In the 18th of Edward I., a large Spanish ship came to Portsmouth; out of the cargo of which the queen bought one frail of Seville figs, one frail of raisins or grapes, one bale of dates, and two hundred and thirty pomegranates, fifteen citrons, and seven *oranges.* The last item is important, as Le Grand d'Aussy could not trace the orange in France to an earlier date than 1333; here we find it known in England in 1290; and it is probable that this was not its first appearance. The marriage of Edward with Eleanor of Castile naturally led to a greater intercourse with Spain, and, consequently, to the introduction of other articles of Spanish produce than the leather of Cordova, olive-oil, and rice, which had previously been the principal imports from that fertile country, through the medium of the merchants of Bayonne and Bordeaux.

It is to be regretted that the series of wardrobe books is incomplete, as much additional information on this point might have been derived from them. At all events, it appears certain that Europe is indebted to the Arab conquerors of Spain for the introduction of the orange, and not to the Portuguese, who are said to have brought it from China. An English dessert in the thirteenth century must, it is clear, have been composed chiefly of dried and preserved fruits, dates, figs, apples, pears, nuts, and the still common dish of almonds and raisins.

With respect to spices, the arrival of a ship laden with them was an event of such importance, and perhaps rarity, that the king usually hastened to satisfy his wants before the cargo was landed. Thus, in the reign of Henry III., the bailiffs of Sandwich were commanded to detain, upon their coming into port, two great ships laden with spices and precious merchandises, which were exported from Bayonne; and not to allow anything to be sold until the king had had his choice of their contents.

Returning to the roll, cider is mentioned only once, and in such a manner as to convey the impression that it was not in much estimation, the Countess having distributed one ton among eight hundred paupers.

## ALBERT, PRINCE CONSORT.

On no occasion subsequent to the death of the Princess Charlotte of Wales, in 1817, was any royal demise so deeply lamented in England as that of Albert, Prince Consort to Queen Victoria. Born on the 26th of August 1819—only two months after the royal lady whom he was destined to espouse—he passed his early days in receiving an education unusually complete in all that could grace a prince and a gentleman, both as regards solid learning and high-bred accomplishments. He and his elder brother, Ernest Augustus, had lasting reason to be grateful for the care bestowed upon them by their father, the reigning Duke of Saxe Coburg Gotha. The two young princes visited England in 1836, while William IV. was king; and then, it is understood, took place the interview between Albert and Victoria, which led ultimately to their union. On the return of the two brothers to Germany, both princes continued their studies with great assiduity, at various universities. Albert is believed, too, to have profited greatly during a temporary residence with his uncle, Leopold, the sagacious king of the Belgians; who, being uncle to Victoria as well as to Albert, was well fitted to instruct the young man concerning the delicate and responsible position of one who might become husband to the Queen of England. In 1839, when he was declared of age, Prince Albert came into possession of estates worth about £2500 a year: and this was all the patrimonial property which he inherited. On the 10th of October in that year, Ernest and Albert again visited England. Victoria was then Queen. Her ministers had already agreed on the suitableness of Albert as her husband, in all that concerned political, national, and religious considerations; and the graces and accomplishments of the Prince now fairly won the heart of the young Queen. It was not for an almost portionless young Prince to pay addresses to the greatest queen in Europe; nor was it an easy matter for an English maiden, at twenty, to shew her preference towards him; but one of the many memoirs of the Prince gives the *denouement* in the following form. On a certain occasion, at one of the palace balls, the Queen presented her bouquet to the Prince at the conclusion of a dance; his close uniform, buttoned up to the throat, did not permit him to place the bouquet where the Persian-like compliment would dictate; but he drew forth a penknife, ripped a hole in the breast of his coat, and placed the treasure there. On another occasion, when he was thanking the Queen for the very kind and gracious reception which he had met with in England, she replied: 'If, indeed, your Highness is so much pleased with this country, perhaps you would not object to remaining in it and making it your home.' These narrations may not either of them, perhaps, be strictly correct, but there is not a doubt that the alliance proceeded from mutual affection. On the 14th of November, Prince Albert left England; and on the 23d, at a privy council summoned for the purpose, the Queen said: 'I have caused you to be summoned, in order that I may acquaint you with my resolution in a matter which deeply concerns the welfare of my people, and the happiness of my future life. It is my intention to ally myself in marriage with Prince Albert of Saxe Coburg Gotha. Deeply impressed with the solemnity of the engagement which I am about to contract, I have not come to this decision without mature consideration, nor without feeling a strong assurance that, with the blessing of Almighty God, it will at once secure my domestic felicity, and serve the interests of my country.' By an unusual combination of circumstances, the Tory, or Church-and-King party of the day, appeared in the character of economical reformers; for they, in the House of Commons, cut down to £30,000 a year, an allowance to Prince Albert, which Viscount Melbourne's government had proposed should be £50,000. On the 24th of January 1840, the Prince was made Knight of the Garter; on the 9th of February, he arrived in England; and on the next day he became husband to Queen Victoria.

During the twenty-two years of his married

life, this exemplary man laboured incessantly to be worthy of his high position, and to foster all good and ennobling schemes. His merits were partially known to the nation during his lifetime, but never so fully as after his decease. He went through a regular course of study of the system of English law and jurisprudence, and of the rise and progress of the English constitution, under Mr Selwyn. He studied agriculture, both scientifically and practically, and became a regular exhibitor at agricultural shows. He revived the drooping Society of Arts, and made it more flourishing than it had ever been before. He was, more than any other person, the originator of International Exhibitions; and to him the world owed especially the Great Exhibition of 1851. He took a decided part in the establishment of the South Kensington Museum, and of schools of art in various parts of the country. He advocated popular education in various ways, calculated to shew the liberal tendency of his mind. He made speeches and addresses at the York and Aberdeen meetings of the British Association for the Advancement of Science, which shewed a very extensive acquaintance with science in its principles, its history, and its practical applications. He had something to say worth hearing and attending to at the Educational, Statistical, and Social Science Congresses. He was the promoter of a new branch or department of the Order of the Bath, designed to recognise civil in addition to military and naval merit. He might, at one time, have become commander-in-chief of the Queen's armies; but his own appreciation of the delicate position which he occupied towards her Majesty—at once a husband and a subject—led him to decline the honour, although urged to accept it by the Duke of Wellington. There were two or three occasions in his life when he was a little misunderstood; especially in 1851 and 1854, during political discussions, which led many persons to accuse him of using 'German' influence injurious to English interests; but the leaders of both parties, in and out of office, uniformly acknowledged the purity of his intentions, and the care with which he sought always to keep strictly within the constitutional limits of his position.

Such was the Prince whose death, on the 14th of December 1861, was a source of great national grief.

Mr Tennyson published a new edition of his *Idylls of the King* a few weeks after the death of the Prince; to whose memory he dedicated it in lines which are likely to take a permanent place in the poetry of this country. In the following extract, the leading characteristics of the Prince's mind are well set forth:

'He seems to me
Scarce other than my own ideal knight,
"Who reverenced his conscience as his king;
Whose glory was, redressing human wrongs;
Who spake no slander, no, nor listen'd to it;
Who lov'd one only and who clave to her"—
Her, over all whose realms to their last isle,
Commingled with the gloom of imminent war,
The shadow of His loss moved like eclipse,
Darkening the world. We have lost him: he is gone:
We know him now: all narrow jealousies
Are silent; and we see him as he moved,
How modest, kindly, all-accomplish'd, wise,
With what sublime repression of himself,
And in what limits, and how tenderly;
Not swaying to this faction or to that;
Not making his high place the lawless perch
Of wing'd ambitions, nor a vantage-ground
For pleasure; but through all this tract of years
Wearing the white flower of a blameless life,
Before a thousand peering littlenesses,
In that fierce light which beats upon a throne,
And blackens every blot: for where is he,
Who dares foreshadow for an only son
A lovelier life, a more unstain'd, than his?
Or how should England, dreaming of *his* sons,
Hope more for these than some inheritance
Of such a life, a heart, a mind, as thine,
Thou noble father of her kings to be,
Laborious for her people and her poor—
Voice in the rich dawn of an ampler day—
Far-sighted summoner of War and Waste
To fruitful strifes and rivalries of peace—
Sweet nature gilded by the gracious gleam
Of letters, dear to science, dear to art,
Dear to thy land and ours, a Prince indeed,
Beyond all titles, and a household name,
Hereafter, through all times, Albert the Good.'

And the closing lines, addressed to the royal widow, are equally beautiful:

'Break not, O woman's heart, but still endure;
Break not, for thou art royal, but endure,
Rememb'ring all the beauty of that star
Which shone so close beside thee, that ye made
One light together, but has past and left
The crown a lonely splendour.
May all love,
His love, unseen but felt, o'ershadow thee,
The love of all thy sons encompass thee,
The love of all thy daughters cherish thee,
The love of all thy people comfort thee,
Till God's love set thee at his side again.'

---

## THE 'SACHEVERELL' FERMENT IN QUEEN ANNE'S TIME.

The effect of particular sermons has often been remarked upon in rousing the feelings of large multitudes of persons, but it seldom extended far beyond the immediate hearers; this of Dr Sacheverell's, however, rung through the whole nation; little else was spoken of for months, and in its consequences it influenced a general election, and turned out the Whig ministry. The preacher, Henry Sacheverell, was descended from a good Derbyshire family, who had taken part with the Puritans, and struggled for the very principles which the subject of the present memoir so warmly opposed; but his father had become a clergyman of the Church of England, and held the living of Marlborough, where his son Henry was born in the year 1672. The father dying in poverty, and leaving a large family, Henry was adopted by a Mr Hearst, who sent him to Magdalen College, Oxford, where he became the intimate friend of Addison, gained a fellowship, and was celebrated as a college tutor. Thus when, in after-days, we find him spoken of as an ignorant, bombastical fellow, 'who had not learning enough to write or speak true English;' and we are informed that the learned doctors of the university of Oxford, in holding a high-feast to welcome their champion after his trial, were soon disgusted at his unspeakable ignorance, we cannot help suspecting that these accounts must have arisen from the violence of party-spirit. It is said that he began life as a Whig, but not getting the promotion he wanted, he became a Tory, and, like all renegades, poured out boundless abuse on his late friends. In 1705, he was presented to the living of St Saviour's, Southwark, where his loud voice, great impudence, and graceful, well-dressed person, gained him many admirers. The popular cry at the time was, that the church was in danger from the wickedness of the ministry, and Sacheverell, taking up the cry, seized the opportunity, when preaching the assize sermon at Derby, on 15th August 1709, of making a violent attack on the government; and again, on the 5th of November, when addressing the corporation of London in St Paul's Cathedral, he chose for his text: 'Perils from false brethren,' and used the expression, 'the crafty insidiousness of such wily Volpones,' which was then a popular nickname for Godolphin, the lord treasurer. Foaming at the mouth, and striking the pulpit with his clenched hand, he denounced the bishops who approved of toleration to dissenters, and the supporters of the Revolution as men who had committed the unpardonable offence. The corporation gave their thanks, as usual, for the sermon, and do not generally seem to have been aware of the treason they had been listening to; but when the sermon was printed, and the Tories praised it up to the skies, setting no less than forty thousand copies in circulation, the ministry took alarm, and Marlborough and Godolphin urged an impeachment. In the following month of December, the House of Commons passed a resolution denouncing both this and the previous discourse, delivered by Sacheverell at Derby, as 'malicious, scandalous, and seditious libels, highly reflecting upon her majesty and government, the late happy revolution, and the Protestant succession as by law established, and both Houses of parliament, tending to alienate the affections of her majesty's good subjects, and to create jealousies and divisions among them.' The author and printer of the discourses in question were at the same time ordered to attend at the bar of the House, a command which was complied with by them on the following day (14th December); and thereupon a motion was made and carried that Sacheverell should be impeached of high crimes and misdemeanours. In the meantime, the people were roused to the greatest excitement by the High-Church party, who asserted that the Puritans were regaining the ascendency, the Whigs would pull down the church, and Sacheverell was to be prosecuted in order to try their strength; money and strong-ale gained them numerous partisans among the lower orders.

After some delays, the trial began on the 27th of February 1710. When the doctor had previously made his appearance in the House of Commons, he was accompanied by no less than one hundred of the most eminent clergymen in London; but the House of Lords determined that Westminster Hall would be a more suitable place for the trial than their own house; and that had been prepared with greater show than perhaps was necessary. The queen had her box near the throne, and attended as a private individual; numbers of ladies, of every station, crowded to support their favourite preacher; and the populace rushed in such numbers, that it was much feared the galleries would give way. Out of doors, the scene was no less striking; London had been in a sort of riot ever since the arrest of Sacheverell; the lowest of the people were his greatest supporters; butchers' boys, chimney-sweeps, costermongers, formed his body-guard, and the respectable citizens wished the trial well over, so much did they dread that the drunken and riotous crowd would find vent for their passions in setting fire to their houses and murdering the Whigs. The subject of all this uproar entered the hall, attended by Dr Atterbury and Dr Smalridge, and inflated with his own importance in no small degree; the old Duchess of Marlborough declaring 'that his clean gloves, good assurance, and white handkerchief well-managed, moved the hearts of many at his appearance.' Four articles of impeachment were brought against him, and Robert Walpole distinguished himself much by the speech he made in support of them. Sacheverell made a speech in his own defence: 'exquisitely contrived to move pity, full of impious piety, denying the greatest part of the charge, with solemn appeals to God and such applications of Scripture as would make any serious person tremble;' whilst the beautiful daughter of the Duchess of Marlborough, who thus writes, was so much affected at his calling God to witness what was a falsehood, that she burst into tears; but other noble ladies sympathised with the accused, and saw a halo of truth and innocence around the head of the injured priest.

The doctor's return home, after the first day's trial, was one continued ovation; but on the evening of the second day, the riot broke out by the pillaging and burning of some dissenting chapels; a bonfire was made in Lincoln's Inn Fields, of the books and cushions, the mob shouting around: 'High Church and Sacheverell!' Bishop Burnet, who was well known for his tolerant views, and had been denounced by Sacheverell, had a narrow escape; the mob rushed upon his house, but some of the guards arrived in time to save it. There was a movement upon the bank; happily the mob was cowardly, and dispersed as soon as the troops appeared; no blood was shed, but it was generally believed that many gentlemen, in disguise, directed and encouraged the people; the queen was suspected of being on their side, and on one of the days of the trial, as she was on her way to Westminster, they gathered round her chair, shouting: 'God bless your majesty and the church; we hope your majesty is for Dr Sacheverell.' On the 20th of March, the trial came to an end; the doctor was found guilty by a majority of sixty-eight to fifty-two; three days after, he was placed on his knees at the bar, and the lord chancellor pronounced this judgment: 'You, Henry Sacheverell, are enjoined not to preach during the term of three years next ensuing, and your two printed sermons shall be burned before the Royal Exchange, at one of the clock in the afternoon, by the common hangman, in the presence of the lord mayor and sheriffs of London.' As this very mild sentence was considered equivalent to an acquittal, the illuminations and rejoicings were on a splendid scale, and every passer-by was compelled to drink to the health of the popular champion. He, on his side, was more inflated with vanity than ever; his vulgar attendants huzzaed him through the streets like a successful parliamentary candidate. For some days, he employed himself in calling upon those noblemen who had voted in his favour; but the Duke of

Argyle refused him admittance, desiring his servant to tell him that what he did in parliament was not done for his sake. On the other hand, Lord Weymouth presented him with fifty pounds, and many gifts were sent to him. After exhausting the enthusiasm of the metropolis, he set off on a sort of progress through the kingdom; Oxford, as the focus of high-churchism, or as the Whigs called it, 'the nursing-place of slavery,' was loud in its approbation and warm in its reception; in every town feasts were provided, and, strange to say, when a clergyman was in the case, drunkenness prevailed; three bottles and a magnum were pure orthodoxy, and since the restoration of Charles II., such scenes had not been witnessed. Sacheverell was received by the mayors, and escorted by a mounted train; garlands and flags adorned the streets, and medals, with his picture engraved, were struck.

Happily, after a few weeks, people recovered their senses, and acknowledged the justice of the Duchess of Marlborough's remark: 'Oh, what dreadful things do we undergo for the sake of the church!' At Ely, the doctor was pelted with stones and curses; and on wishing to make a speech to the Company of the Bank of England, the directors ordered him to be turned out: nevertheless, the affair had a most powerful influence on the elections, and the Tory ministry were brought back to their places. The living of Salatin, in Shropshire, was presented to him; and a month after the three years' suspension had expired, the queen, who at heart was always on his side, gave him the valuable living of St Andrews, Holborn. Like many who owe their popularity to circumstances rather than any merit of their own, Sacheverell dropped into private life, and nothing worthy of note is told of him, but that his quarrels with his parishioners were by no means unfrequent; just what might be expected from so pugnacious a disposition. He inherited a considerable fortune, and died on the 5th of June 1724, having lived in comfort and affluence during his later years.

---

## DECEMBER 15.

St Eusebius, bishop of Vercelli, 371.

*Born.*—George Romney, portrait painter, 1734, *Dalton, Lancashire;* Jerome Bonaparte, youngest brother of Napoleon, 1784, *Ajaccio.*

*Died.*—Timoleon, liberator of Syracuse, 337 B.C.; Pope John VIII., 82 A.D.; Izaak Walton, author of *The Complete Angler,* 1683, *Winchester;* George Adam Struvius, jurist, 1692, *Jena;* Benjamin Stillingfleet, naturalist, 1771, *Westminster;* Jean Baptiste Carrier, revolutionary terrorist, guillotined, 1794; Mrs Sarah Trimmer, authoress of juvenile and educational works, 1810, *Brentford;* David Don, botanist, 1841, *London;* Leon Faucher, eminent French statesman and publicist, 1854, *Marseille.*

### WILLIAM HOGARTH.

Were it desired to select from the distinguished men of Great Britain, one who should approach most nearly to the type of the true-born Englishman, with all his uprightness and honesty, his frank-hearted vivacity and genial joviality of temperament, and, at the same time, his roughness, obstinacy, and inveteracy of prejudice, no fitter representative of such aggregate qualities could be obtained than William Hogarth, our great pictorial moralist. Repulsive and painful as many of his subjects are, seldom exhibiting the pleasing or sunny side of human nature, their general fidelity and truthfulness commend themselves alike to the hearts of the most illiterate and the most refined, whilst the impressive, if at times coarsely-expressed, lessons which they inculcate, place the delineator in the foremost rank of those who have not inaptly been termed 'week-day preachers.'

With the exception of two memorable excursions—one with a company of friends to Rochester and Sheerness, and another to Calais—Hogarth's life appears to have been almost exclusively confined to London and its immediate vicinity. His father, Richard Hogarth, was the youngest son of a Westmoreland yeoman, who originally kept a school at St Bees, in Cumberland, but came up when a young man to London, and settled as a schoolmaster in Ship Court, in the Old Bailey. He married and had three children—William, afterwards the celebrated artist, and two girls, Mary and Anne.

Young Hogarth, having early shewed a turn for drawing, was bound apprentice to a silversmith, and initiated in the art of engraving arms and cyphers on plate. The employment did not satisfy the aspirations of his genius, and he accordingly, on the expiration of his indentures, entered Sir James Thornhill's academy, in St Martin's Lane, where he occupied himself in studying drawing from the life. In the mere delineation, however, of the external figure, irrespective of the exhibition of character and passion, Hogarth never acquired any great proficiency. During the first years of his artistic career, he supported himself by engraving arms and shop-bills; and then gradually ascending in the professional scale, he turned his attention successfully to portrait-painting, and in the course of a few years derived both a considerable income and reputation from this source. An amusing and characteristic anecdote of him is related in connection with this period of his life. A certain nobleman, remarkable for ugliness and deformity, employed Hogarth to paint his picture—a behest which the artist executed with only too scrupulous fidelity. The peer was disgusted at so correct a representation of himself, and refused to take or pay for the picture. After numerous ineffectual negotiations with his lordship on the subject, Hogarth addressed him the following note: 'Mr Hogarth's dutiful respects to Lord —— ; finding that he does not mean to have the picture which was drawn for him, is informed again of Mr Hogarth's pressing necessities for the money. If, therefore, his lordship does not send for it in three days, it will be disposed of, with the addition of a tail and some other appendages, to *Mr Hare, the famous wild-beast man;* Mr H. having given that gentleman a conditional promise on his lordship's refusal.' The *ruse* was successful; the price agreed on was paid for the picture, which was forthwith destroyed.

Having attained the age of thirty-three, Hogarth contracted, in 1730, a secret marriage with the only daughter of the celebrated painter, Sir James Thornhill, who was at first extremely indignant at the match. He afterwards, however, relented, and lived till his death in great harmony with his son-in-law.

With the publication of the 'Harlot's Progress,' in 1733, Hogarth commenced those serial prints which have rendered his name immortal. From the first, his success in this department of art was assured. The 'Harlot's Progress' was followed, after the interval of two years, by the still more famous 'Rake's Progress,' and this again by the series of 'Marriage à la Mode,' 'Industry and Idleness,' the 'Stages of Cruelty,' and the 'Election Prints.' Numerous other individual pieces might be mentioned, such as the 'March to Finchley,' which excited the wrath of George II., by the ludicrous light in which his soldiers were presented; 'Modern Midnight Conversation,' 'Strolling Players in a Barn,' and 'Beer Street,' and 'Gin Lane;' the former a plea for the liquor which Hogarth, like a true Englishman, deemed the most wholesome and generous beverage; the latter, a fearfully repulsive, but at the same time salutary delineation of the dreadful miseries resulting from the abuse of ardent spirits. To another picture by Hogarth, 'The Gate of Calais,' a curious anecdote is attached. He had made an excursion thither with some friends, but with the determination apparently to find nothing in France either pleasing or commendable. Like Smollett, Hogarth seems to have entertained a thorough contempt for the French nation, and he was unable to refrain from giving vent to his sentiments even in the open street. The lank and grotesque figures which presented themselves everywhere, and by their appearance gave unmistakable evidence of the poverty and misery of the country, under the old *régime*, called forth all his powers of ridicule; whilst the light-heartedness and vivacity with which, like the Irish, the French people could forget or charm away their wretchedness, raised only to a higher pitch his feeling of contempt. Very speedily and summarily, however, he himself was obliged to quit the country which he so heartily despised. Ignorant of foreign jealousies on the subject of bulwarks and fortifications, he began to make a sketch of the gate of Calais, as a curious piece of architecture. This action being observed, he was arrested as a spy, and conveyed by a file of musketeers before the governor of the town. There his sketch-book was examined, but nothing whatever was discovered to warrant the suspicion entertained against him. The governor, however, assured him with the utmost politeness, that were it not for the circumstance of the preliminaries of a treaty of peace having actually been signed between England and France, he should have been under the disagreeable necessity of hanging Mr Hogarth on the ramparts of Calais. As it was, he must insist on providing him with a military escort whilst he continued in the dominions of Louis XV. The discomfited artist was then conducted by two sentinels to his hotel, and from thence to the English packet in the harbour. Hogarth's guard of honour accompanied him to the distance of about a league from the shore, and then seizing him by the shoulders, and spinning him round upon the deck, they informed him that he was now at liberty to pursue his voyage without further molestation. Hogarth reproduced this adventure in the print above referred to, where, in addition to the grotesque figures who fill up the centre and foreground of the picture, he himself is delineated standing in a corner, and making a sketch of the gateway of the town, whilst the hand of a sentinel is in the act of being laid on the artist's shoulder. Though he thus perpetuates the recollection of the circumstance, it is said that he never liked to hear any reference to the mortifying incident that ensued. In a letter from Horace Walpole to Sir Horace Mann, dated 15th December 1748, this misadventure of Hogarth is communicated as a piece of news which had just transpired.

Hogarth's prints are thus admirably epitomised by Mr Thackeray in his *English Humorists:* 'They give us the most complete and truthful picture of the manners, and even the thoughts, of the past century. We look, and see pass before us the England of a hundred years ago—the peer in his drawing-room, the lady of fashion in her apartment, foreign singers surrounding her, and the chamber filled with gewgaws in the mode of that day; the church, with its quaint florid architecture and singing congregation; the parson with his great wig, and the beadle with his cane: all these are represented before us, and we are sure of the truth of the portrait. We see how the lord mayor dines in state; how the prodigal drinks and sports at the bagnio; how the poor girl beats hemp in Bridewell; how the thief divides his booty, and drinks his punch at the night-cellar, and how he finishes his career at the gibbet. We may depend upon the perfect accuracy of these strange and varied portraits of the bygone generation; we see one of Walpole's members of parliament chaired after his election, and the lieges celebrating the event, and drinking confusion to the Pretender; we see the grenadiers and trainbands of the city marching out to meet the enemy; and have before us, with sword and firelock, and white Hanoverian horse embroidered on the cap, the very figures of the men who ran away with Johnny Cope, and who conquered at Culloden. The Yorkshire wagon rolls into the inn-yard; the country parson, in his jack-boots, and his bands and short cassock, comes trotting into town, and we fancy it is Parson Adams, with his sermons in his pocket. The Salisbury fly sets forth from the old "Angel"—you see the passengers entering the great heavy vehicle, up the wooden steps, their hats tied down with handkerchiefs over their faces, and under their arms, sword, hanger, and case-bottle; the landlady—apoplectic with the liquors in her own bar—is tugging at the bell; the hunchbacked postilion—he may have ridden the leaders to Humphry Clinker—is begging a gratuity; the miser is grumbling at the bill; Jack of the Centurion lies on the top of the clumsy vehicle, with a soldier by his side—it may be Smollett's Jack Hatchway—it has a likeness to Lesmahago. You see the suburban fair, and the strolling-company of actors; the pretty milkmaid singing under the windows of the enraged French musician—it is such a girl as Steele charmingly described in the *Guardian*, a few years before this date, singing, under Mr Ironside's window in Shire Lane, her pleasant carol of a May morning. You see noblemen and blacklegs bawling and betting in the cock-pit; you see Garrick as he was arrayed in *King Richard;* Macheath and Polly in the dresses which they wore when they charmed our ancestors, and when noblemen in blue ribbons sat on the stage, and listened to their delightful music. You see the ragged French soldiery, in their white coats and cockades, at Calais Gate—they are of the regiment, very likely, which friend Roderick Random joined before he was rescued by his preserver, Monsieur de Strap, with whom he fought on the famous day of Dettingen. You see the judges on the bench : the audience laughing in the pit ; the student in the Oxford theatre ; the citizen on his country-walk ; you see Broughton the boxer, Sarah Malcolm the murderess, Simon Lovat the traitor, John Wilkes the demagogue, leering at you with that squint which has become historical, and that face which, ugly as it was, he said he could make as captivating to woman as the countenance of the handsomest beau in town. All these sights and people are with you. After looking in the *Rake's Progress* at Hogarth's picture of St James's Palace-gate, you may people the street, but little altered within these hundred years, with the gilded carriages and thronging chairmen that bore the courtiers, your ancestors, to Queen Caroline's drawing-room, more than a hundred years ago.'

Hogarth was not only a painter and an engraver, but likewise an author, having published, in 1753, a quarto volume, entitled the *Analysis of Beauty*, in which he maintains the fundamental principle of beauty to consist in the curve or undulating line, and that round swelling figures are the most attractive to the eye. This idea appears to have been cherished by him with special complacency, as in that characteristic picture which he painted of himself and his dog Trump, and of which a

WILLIAM HOGARTH.

copy is here engraved, he has inscribed, in association with the curve, 'The Line of Beauty and Grace,' as his special motto.

A very curious and interesting memorial of Hogarth and his associates, exists in the narration of a holiday excursion down the river as far as Sheerness. Though Hogarth himself is not the chronicler, we are favoured, by one of the party, with a most graphic description of this merry company, who seem to have enjoyed their trip with all the zest of school-boys or young men 'out on a lark.' Hogarth acted as draughtsman, making rough sketches of many of the incidents of the journey, which seems to have been as jovial an expedition as good-humour, high spirits, and beer, could have contributed to effect.

One of the members of this party was Hogarth's brother-in-law, John Thornhill, who afterwards became sergeant-painter to the king, but resigned his office in favour of Hogarth in 1757. It has been imagined that this connection with the court, in his latter years, led the artist into that pictorial warfare with Wilkes and Churchill, in which certainly no laurels were gathered by any of the parties engaged. Hogarth's health began now visibly to decline, and after languishing in this state about two years, he expired suddenly, of aneurism in the chest, on 25th October 1764. He was interred in the churchyard at Chiswick, where a monument, recently restored, was erected to his memory. He never had any family, and was survived for twenty-five years by his wife, who died in 1789.

## The Society of the Piu.

At the beginning of the fourteenth century, London contained many foreigners, whose business it was to frequent the various fairs and markets held in England, and with whom their idle time hung heavily for want of some congenial amusement. To meet this want, they formed a semi-musical, semi-friendly association, called the Company or Brotherhood of the Piu—'in honour of God, our Lady Saint Mary, and all saints both male and female ; and in honour of our lord the king, and all the barons of the country.' Both the name and nature of the association were derived from similar societies then existing in France and Flanders, which are supposed to have taken their titles from the city of Le Puy, in Auvergne, a city rejoicing in the possession of a famous statue of the Virgin, popular with the pilgrims of the age.

The rules and regulations of the London society are preserved in the *Liber Custumarum*, one of the treasures of the Guildhall library. From these we learn that the avowed object of the loving companions of the Piu, was to make London renowned for all good things ; to maintain mirth, peace, honesty, joyousness, and love ; and to annihilate wrath and rancour, vice and crime. The brotherhood, which was not confined to foreigners, consisted of an unlimited number of members, each of whom paid an entrance-fee of sixpence, and an annual subscription of one shilling, towards the expenses of the yearly festival. The management of the society's affairs was intrusted to twelve companions, who held office till removed by death or their secession from the brotherhood, but the president or prince, as he was called, was changed every year. Any member was eligible to serve, and none could decline the office if chosen by the outgoing prince—his choice being ratified by eleven of the twelve companions declaring him, upon oath, to be 'good, loyal, and sufficient.' The expense entailed by accepting the honour was not very burdensome, consisting merely in paying for the official costume, 'a coat and surcoat without sleeves, and mantle of one suit, with whatsoever arms he may please.' The crown was provided by the society at the cost of one mark, and was passed from one prince to another. The only other officers were a clerk to keep the accounts, register the names of the members, and summon them to the meetings of the company; and a chaplain, 'at all times singing mass for living and dead companions.'

To suit the convenience of the mercantile community, the great festival of the Piu was held on the first Sunday after Trinity, in a room strewed with fresh rushes, and fairly decked with leaves. As soon as the company were assembled, the investiture of the new prince took place, with the following simple ceremony: 'The old prince and his companions shall go through the room, from one end to the other, singing; and the old prince shall carry the crown of the Piu upon his head, and a gilt cup full of wine in his hands. And when they shall have gone round, the old prince shall give to drink unto him whom they shall have chosen, and shall give him the crown, and such person shall be prince.' The blazon of the new chief's arms were then hung in a conspicuous place, and the most important business of the day commenced.

This was the choosing of the best song. The competitors—who were exempted from paying the festival-fee—were ranged on a seat covered with cloth of gold, the only place allowed to be so decorated. The judges were the two princes and a jury of fifteen members, who took an oath not to be biassed in their judgment, 'for love, for hate, for gift, for promise, for neighbourhood, for kindred, or for any acquaintanceship old or new, nor yet anything that is.' Further to insure the prize being properly awarded, it was decreed that, 'there be chosen two or three who well understand singing and music, for the purpose of trying and examining the notes, and the points of the songs, as well as the nature of the words composed thereto. For without singing, no one ought to call a composition of words, a song; nor ought any royal song to be crowned without the sweet sounds of melody sung.' When the song had been chosen, it was hung beneath the arms of the prince, and its author crowned. Then dinner was served, each guest receiving good bread, ale and wine, pottage, one course of solid meat, double roast in a dish, cheese, 'and no more.' At the conclusion of this moderate banquet, the whole company rose, mounted their horses, and went in procession through the city, headed by the princes past and present, between whom rode the musical champion of the meeting. On arriving at the house of the new prince, the brethren dismounted, had a dance 'by way of a hearty good-bye,' and departed homeward on foot.

None but members of the company were invited to the festival, and ladies were especially excluded from taking part in it, by a clause which is a curiosity in its way, as a gallant excuse for an ungallant act. It runs thus: 'Although the becoming pleasances of virtuous ladies is a rightful theme and principal occasion for royal singing, and for composing and furnishing royal songs, nevertheless it is hereby provided that no lady or other woman ought to be at the great feast of the Piu, for the reason that the companions ought hereby to take example and rightful warning to honour, cherish, and commend all ladies, at all times, in all places, as much in their absence as in their presence.'

The day after the feast a solemn mass was sung at the priory of St Helen's for the souls of all Christian people in general, and those of the brotherhood in particular. The accounts were audited, and any surplus left, added to the treasury of the company; if the expenses of the feast exceeded the receipts, the difference was made good by contributions from the members. The names of absentees in arrears were published, and those who had neglected paying their subscription for seven years were expelled the society, the same sentence being passed against evil-minded companions, respecting whom there was this emphatic statute: 'If there be any one who is unwilling to be obedient to the peace of God, and unto the peace of our lord the king—whom God preserve—the community of the companions do not wish to have him or his fees, through whom the company may be accused or defamed.'

Members were also expected to attend at the wedding or funeral of a brother, and were furthermore enjoined always to aid, comfort, and counsel one another in faith, loyalty, peace, love, and concord as brethren in God and good love.

## NEGRO AUTHORS.

There are so very few instances on record of any of the pure African negro race exhibiting a taste or ability for literary composition, that their names seem not unworthy of notice in this collection. First in the list stands Ignatius Sancho, who was born in 1729, on board of a slave-ship, a few days after leaving the coast of Guinea, for the Spanish-American colonies. At Carthagena, he was christened Ignatius; his mother died soon after, and his father, unable to survive her, avoided the miseries of slavery by suicide. When two years of age, Ignatius was brought to England, and given by his owner as a present to three elderly maiden-sisters, residing near Greenwich. These ladies, having just previously read *Don Quixote*, gave their little slave the name of Sancho; but, however fond of reading themselves, they denied that advantage to Ignatius, believing that ignorance was the only security for obedience; that to cultivate the mind of their slave, was equivalent to emancipating his person. Happily, the Duke of Montague, then residing at Blackheath, near Greenwich, saw the little negro, and admired in him a native frankness of manner, as yet unimpaired by servitude, if unrefined by education. Learning that the child was trying to educate himself, the duke lent him books, and strongly recommended to his three mistresses the duty of cultivating a mind of such promising ability. The ladies, however, remained inflexible; it was of no use to educate the lad, they said, as they had determined to send him back to West Indian slavery. At this crisis, the duke died; and, the duchess declining to interfere between the negro-lad and his mistresses, Sancho, in the immediate prospect of being sent away, fell into a state of despair. With four shillings, all the wealth he possessed, he bought a pistol, and threatened to follow the example of his father. The ladies, now terrified in their turn, gave up all claim to their slave, and he was taken into the service of the Duchess of Montague. In this family Sancho served, principally in the capacity of butler, for many years, till corpulence and gout rendered him unfit for duty. He then set up a small grocer's shop, and by care and industry gained a decent competence to support his family till his death, which took place on the 15th of December 1780.

Sancho corresponded with many notabilities of his day, such as Sterne, Garrick, and the few persons who then took an interest in the abolition of the slave-trade. His letters were published after his death, edited by a Miss Crewe, who, as she says, did not give them to the public till she had obviated an objection which had been advanced, that they were originally written with the view of publication. She declares that no such idea was ever entertained by Sancho; that not one letter was printed from a copy or duplicate preserved by himself, but all collected from the various friends to whom he had written them. She also adds, that her reasons for publishing them, were her desire of shewing that an African may possess abilities equal to a European; and the still superior motive of serving a worthy family. In this undertaking Miss Crewe had the happiness of finding that the world was not inattentive to the voice of obscure merit. The first and second editions of Sancho's letters produced £500 to his widow and family, and the writer has seen a fifth edition, published more than twenty years after his death, by his son, William Sancho, then a respectable bookseller in Westminster.

Attobah Cugoana, a Fantin negro, was carried as a slave to Grenada, when quite a child. Meeting with a benevolent master, he was subsequently liberated and sent to England, where he entered the service of Mr Cosway, the celebrated portrait-painter. Little is known of this negro's history, though it would seem that he was a much abler man than Sancho, with less advantages of education and the assistance of influential friends. He was the author of a work of considerable celebrity in its day, entitled *Thoughts and Sentiments on the evil and wicked Traffic of the Slavery and Commerce of the Human Species: Humbly submitted to the Inhabitants of Great Britain.* This is certainly an ably composed book, containing the essence of all that has been written against slavery from a religious point of view; and though the matter is ill arranged, and some of the arguments scarcely logical, it was translated into French, and obtained great consideration among the continental philanthropists.

Another interesting example of literary distinction achieved by what Thomas Fuller, with a quaintness and benevolence of phrase peculiarly his own, styles 'God's image cut in ebony,' is afforded by Phillis Wheatley, an African negress, who, when about seven years of age, was brought to Boston as a slave in 1761. She was purchased by a respectable merchant, named Wheatley, who had her christened Phillis, and, according to custom, her master's surname was bestowed on her. She never received any instruction at school, having been taught to read by her master's family; the art of writing she acquired herself. Phillis composed a small volume of poems, which was published in her nineteenth year. Like many others of her race, she vainly hoped that the quarrel between the mother-country and the American colonies would be beneficial to African freedom; that when independence was gained by the white man, the black would be allowed some share in the precious boon. In a poem on *Freedom*, addressed to the Earl of Dartmouth, the secretary of state for the colonies, she thus writes—

'Should you, my lord, while you pursue my song,
Wonder from whence my love of freedom sprung,
Whence flow those wishes for the common good,
By feeling hearts alone best understood—
I, young in life, by seeming cruel fate,
Was snatched from Afric's fancied happy seat.
What pangs excruciating must molest,
What sorrows labour in my parent's breast?
Steeled was that soul, and by no misery moved,
That from a father seized the babe beloved.
Such, such my case—and can I then but pray,
Others may never feel tyrannic sway?'

Phillis married a person of her own complexion, a tradesman in comfortable circumstances in Boston. Her married life was unhappy. From the notice bestowed on Phillis by persons of station and influence, her husband, with the petty jealousy common to his race, felt hurt that his wife was respected more than himself. In consequence, he behaved to her harshly and cruelly, and she, sinking under such treatment, died in her twenty-sixth year, much regretted by those capable of appreciating her modest talents and virtues.

---

# DECEMBER 16.

St Ado, archbishop of Vienne, confessor, 875. St Alice or Adelaide, empress of Germany, 999.

*Born.*—John Selden, lawyer and politician, 1584, *Salvington, Sussex;* George Whitefield, celebrated preacher, 1714, *Bell Inn, Gloucester;* Elizabeth Carter, distinguished literary lady, 1717, *Deal;* Chrétien Guillaume Lamoignon de Malesherbes, minister and defender of Louis XVI., 1721, *Paris;* Bernard, Comte de Lacépède, eminent naturalist, 1756, *Agen;* Jane Austen, novelist, 1775, *Steventon, Hampshire;* Carl Maria Von Weber, composer of *Der Freischütz*, 1786, *Eutin, in Holstein.*

*Died.*—Sir William Petty, eminent political economist, 1687, *Westminster;* Abbé Desfontaines, translator of Virgil and Horace, 1745; Thomas Pennant, naturalist, 1798, *Downing, Flintshire;* Antoine François de Fourcroy, distinguished French chemist, 1809; Rev. Samuel Lee, orientalist, 1852, *Barley, Herts;* Wilhelm Grimm, writer of fairy tales, &c., 1859, *Berlin.*

## SIR WILLIAM PETTY.

In the small town of Romsey or Rumsey, in Hampshire, William Petty, the son of a humble tradesman, was born in 1623. Like Franklin, the boy took great delight in watching artificers working at their various occupations, and when little more than twelve years of age, he acquired a facility and dexterity in handling tools, which proved of great advantage to him in after-life. At the age of fifteen, having mastered all the education afforded by the grammar-school of Rumsey, Petty proceeded to the college of Caen, in Normandy. An orphan, without patrimony or patron, the young student took a small venture of English goods with him to France, and during the four years he remained at college there, he supported himself by engaging in trade. Josiah Wedgewood used to say, that there was no pleasanter occupation than making money by honourable industry; and Petty always alleged that making money was the very best kind of employment to keep a man out of mischief. Having acquired French, mathematics, astronomy, and navigation, Petty returned to England and entered the sea-service; but being reproved for not reporting a certain landmark he was ordered to look out for, he discovered, for the first time, that he was near-sighted, and, in consequence, determined to abandon the sea. In the very curious autobiographical preamble Petty attached to his will, we learn that when he gave up the sea-service, his whole fortune consisted of sixty pounds. Having chosen medicine as his future profession, he went and studied at Leyden, Utrecht, Amsterdam, and Paris. At the last place he devoted his attention particularly to anatomy, the subsequently celebrated Hobbes being his class-fellow. Petty, during this sojourn on the continent, supported and educated a younger brother named Anthony, and was sometimes so reduced, that in Paris he is said to have lived for two weeks on three penny-worth of walnuts. His ingenuity and industry extricated him from such difficulties, and he very probably exercised his favourite method of keeping out of mischief; for when he and his brother returned to England, after a three years' absence, and all charges of travel, subsistence, and education, for two persons had been paid, Petty's sixty pounds, instead of being diminished, had increased to seventy.

He then invented an instrument for double writing, which seems to have been merely a copying-machine. Four years afterwards, he obtained the degree of Doctor of Medicine. His seventy pounds were then reduced to twenty-eight; but being appointed to the professorship of anatomy at Oxford, and the Readership of Gresham College, in two more years he was worth four hundred pounds. And then, being appointed physician to the army in Ireland, with an outfit of one hundred pounds, he went to that country with five hundred pounds at his command, and a salary of one pound per day, in addition to which he soon acquired a private practice of four hundred pounds per annum.

The tide which bore him to fortune, was the appointment of physician to the army in Ireland. This, however, was no mere lucky accident. Petty, by hard industry, rigid economy, and great ingenuity, had prepared himself to take advantage of such a flood, to swim and direct his course upon it at pleasure, not to be swept away by it. His reputation as a man of great ability obtained the appointment. A contemporary writer tells us, that 'the war being nearly ended in Ireland, many endeavours were used to regulate, replant, and reduce that country to its former flourishing condition, as a place most wanting such contrivances as tended to the above-mentioned ends, and for which Dr Petty had gained some reputation in the world.'

The state of Petty's money-affairs, previous to and on his arrival in Ireland in 1652, as above detailed, are taken from his will, and we find, from the same document, that by undertaking contracts, speculating in mines, ships, and timber, 'making advantageous bargains,' and 'living within his income,' in the course of thirty-five years, he had increased his store to a fortune of £15,000 per annum.

Petty is best known by his admirable survey of Ireland. Soon after his arrival in that country, observing that the admeasurement and division of the forfeited estates, granted to the Cromwellian soldiery, was very much mismanaged, he applied and obtained a contract for the execution of this important work, which he performed not more for his own advantage than that of the public. The maps of this survey, comprising a large proportion of the kingdom, were all drawn by Petty, and entitled by him the 'Down Survey,' from the trivial, though in one sense important, reason, that all was laid *down* on paper. And, considering the time and circumstances in which these maps were executed, their accuracy is surprising, and they continue to be referred to as trustworthy evidence in courts of law even at the present day.

The changes of governments and parties, appeared rather to have contributed to the success in life, than to the discomfiture of this remarkable man. He was secretary to Henry Cromwell, when lord-lieutenant of Ireland, and sat in Richard Cromwell's parliament, as member for West Looe, in Cornwall; yet, at the Restoration, he received the honour of knighthood from Charles II. That model of an English gentleman, Evelyn, who knew Petty well, thus speaks of him:

'The map of Ireland, made by Sir William Petty, is believed to be the most exact that ever yet was made of any country. There is not a better Latin poet living, when he gives himself that diversion; nor is his excellence less in council and prudent matters of state; but he is so exceeding nice in sifting and examining all possible contingencies, that he adventures at nothing that is not demonstration. There were not in the whole world his equal, for a superintendent of manufacture and improvement of trade, or to govern a plantation. If I were a prince, I should make him my second councillor at least. He was, with all this, facetious and of easy conversation, friendly and courteous, and had such a faculty of imitating others, that he would take a text and preach, now like a grave orthodox divine, then falling into the Presbyterian way, then to the fanatical, the Quaker, the monk, the friar, the popish priest, with such admirable action, and alteration of voice and tone, as if it were not possible to abstain from wonder, and one would swear to hear several persons, or forbear to think he was not in good earnest an enthusiast, and almost beside himself; then he would fall out of it into a serious discourse; but it was very rarely he would be prevailed on to oblige the company with this faculty, and that only amongst intimate friends.'

Petty invented a double-bottomed ship, and patented inventions for the improvement of carriages, cannon, and pumps. During all those occupations, he found time to write treatises on statistics and political economy, being one of the first to elevate the latter study to the rank of a science. His *Political Anatomy of Ireland* gives the first authentic account of the population of that country, and affords valuable information of its state towards the close of the seventeenth century. He clearly foresaw the great advantages of a union between England and Ireland, and of a free commercial intercourse between the two kingdoms. His treatise on *Taxes and Contributions* is far in advance of his time, and in this work is first demonstrated the now universally recognised doctrine, that the labour required for the production of commodities alone determines their value. In his *Quantulumcunque* (a treatise on money), he condemns laws regulating the rate of interest, observing that there might just as well be laws to regulate the rate of exchange; and he exposes the then prevailing fallacy, that a country might be drained of cash by an unfavourable balance of trade.

Petty, in that remarkable document, his will, shews that he well understood the true principles of political economy as respects mortuary charities; clearly foreseeing the many evils that have since arisen from injudicious bequests. He says:

'As for legacies to the poor, I am at a stand; as for beggars by trade and election, I give them nothing; as for impotents by the hand of God, the public ought to maintain them; as for those who have no calling nor estate, they should be put upon their kindred; as for those who can get no work, the magistrates should cause them to be employed, which may be well done in Ireland, where is fifteen acres of improvable land for every head; prisoners for crimes, by the king; for debts, by their prosecutors; as for those who compassionate the sufferings of any object, let them relieve themselves by relieving such sufferers—that is, give them alms *pro re nata*, and for God's sake, relieve the several species above mentioned, if the above-mentioned obligees fail in their duties. Wherefore, I am contented that I have assisted all my poor relations, and put many in a way of getting their own bread, and have laboured in public works, and by inventions have sought out real objects of charity; and I do hereby conjure all who partake of my estate, from time to time, to do the same at their peril. Nevertheless, to answer custom, and to take the surer side, I give £20 to the most wanting of the parish, in which I may die.'

He further concludes his will with the following profession of his religious opinions:

'I die in the profession of that faith, and in the practice of such worship, as I find established by the laws of my country; not being able to believe what I myself please, nor to worship God better than by doing as I would be done unto, and observing the laws of my country, and expressing my love and honour of Almighty God by such signs and tokens as are understood to be such by the people with whom I live, God knowing my heart, even without any at all; and thus begging the Divine Majesty to make me what he would have me to be, both as to faith and good works, I willingly resign my soul into his hands, relying only on His infinite mercy, and the merits of my Saviour, for my happiness after this life, where I expect to know and see God more clearly than by the study of the Scriptures, and of his works, I have hitherto been able to do. Grant me, O Lord, an easy passage to thyself, that as I have lived in thy fear, I may be known to die in thy favour, Amen.'

Petty died on the 16th of December 1687, and was interred beside his humble parents at Rumsey; a flat stone in the church pavement, cut by an illiterate workman, records—

'HERE LAYES
SIR WILLIAM
PETTY.'

He left three children; his eldest son, Charles, was created Baron Shelburne by William III., and, dying without issue, was succeeded by his younger brother, Henry, created Viscount Dunkeron, and Earl of Shelburne. Henry was succeeded by a sister's son, who adopted his name and arms, and the noble family of Lansdowne, seemingly inheriting the talents with the estates, have ever proved themselves worthy namesakes and representatives of Sir William Petty.

## WILHELM GRIMM'S MARRIAGE.

The renowned literary copartnership, known as the 'Brothers Grimm,' was, on the 16th of December 1859, dissolved by the death of the younger member of the firm. The year 1863 witnessed the death of the surviving elder brother, Jacob Grimm; and in the decease of these two eminent men, Germany has been deprived of the two greatest philologers and critical archæologists which even she can boast of. The learning and industry of the brothers was only surpassed by the beautiful simplicity and affection which characterised their progress and mutual intercourse through life. An interesting epitome of their history, as well as some curious circumstances connected with the marriage of Wilhelm Grimm, are given in a letter which lately appeared in the columns of a widely-circulated newspaper, from its Prussian correspondent. The story, from its piquancy, merits being preserved, and we accordingly quote it as follows:

'From morn till night they [Jacob and Wilhelm Grimm] worked together in contiguous rooms for nearly sixty years. United in literary labour, they never separated socially. A librarian's office, or a professorship, conferred upon one of them, was never accepted until an analogous post had been created for the other. William installed Jacob in the library of Marburg, Jacob drawing William after him to the university of Göttingen. They lived in the same house, and it is more than a fable they intended to marry the same lady; or rather they intended not. The story is, that an old aunt, taking commiseration on the two elderly bachelors, and apprehensive of the pecuniary consequences of their students' life, resolved to provide them with partners fit to take care of them after her death. After great reluctance, the two philological professors were brought to see the sense of the plan. They agreed to marry, but on this condition, that one of them should be spared, and the wife of the other obliged to look after the finances and linen of both. A young lady being produced, the question of who should be the victim was argued for many an hour between the unlucky candidates. Nay, it is even alleged that the publication of one of their volumes was delayed full eight days by the matrimonial difference. At length Jacob, being the elder, was convinced of his higher duty to take the leap. But he had no idea how to set to work, and ingratiate himself with the lady. Half from a desire to encourage his brother, and half from a wish to take some share of the burden, William offered to come to the rescue in this emergency, and try to gain favour with the future Mrs Grimm. Then Cupid interfered, and took the matter into his own hands. The lady being a lovely girl of twenty-two, distinguished by qualities of heart and head, proved too many for the amateur. She had been entirely ignorant of the honours intended for her, and the fraternal compact to which she had given occasion; and it is, perhaps, for this very reason that, falling in love with her resolute antagonist, she so changed the feelings of the latter as to convert him into a slave and admirer before the end of the week. Then arose a difficulty of another but equally delicate nature. Over head and ears in love, William dared not make a clean breast of it to the fair lady. In his conscience he accused himself of felony against his brother. He had broken their agreement; he had robbed him of his bride. He felt more like a villain than ever he did in his life. But heaven knew what it did in furnishing him with an old aunt. Stepping in at the right moment, and acquainting Jacob with what had been going on before his eyes, this useful creature cut the Gordian-knot in a trice. So far from getting into a fury, and hating his brother for what he could not help, Jacob was barbarous enough to declare this the most joyous tidings he had ever received. So William was married, Jacob making off for the Harz, and roving about among the hills and vales with the feelings of an escaped convict. The marriage was happy. Of the two sons resulting from it, the younger, a poet of great promise, many years after married the second daughter of Bettina von Arnim. After, as before it, the two brothers continued to keep house together.'

In further reference to the Brothers Grimm, who, as is well known, have acquired great popularity with juvenile readers by their collection of fairy tales and legends, the following amusing anecdote may here also be introduced. It is related in the *Athenæum* for 1859, and is given on the authority of Jacob Grimm himself. A little girl of about eight years old, evidently belonging to an upper-class family, called one day at Dr Grimm's house, and desired to see the 'Herr Professor.' The servant shewed her into the study, where Dr Grimm received her, and inquired, with great kindness, what she had to say to him. The little maiden, looking very earnestly at the professor, said: 'Is it thou who hast written those fine Märchen' [fairy tales]?

'Yes, my dear, my brother and I have written the Haus Märchen.'

'Then thou hast also written the tale of the clever little tailor, where it is said, at the end, who will not believe it must pay a thaler' [dollar]?

'Yes, I have written that too.'

'Well, then, I do not believe it, and so, I suppose, I have to pay a thaler; but as I have not so much money now, I'll give thee a groschen [about three-halfpence] on account, and pay the rest by and by.'

The professor, as may be expected, was highly amused with this combination of childish simplicity and conscientiousness. He inquired the name of his little visitor, and took care that she reached home in safety. Doubtless also the kind old man must have felt ever afterwards something like a paternal affection for the tiny critic, who had thus taken so warm an interest in one of his own bantlings.

---

## A CONVIVIAL ENTHUSIAST OF THE OLD SCHOOL.

December 16, 1813, died at his house, in Welbeck Street, William Bosville, of Gunthwaite, Esq., at the age of sixty-nine; in some respects a notable man. According to the report of his grand-nephew, the Rev. John Sinclair, in the memoirs of his father, Sir John Sinclair, he shone as an eccentric *habitué* of London during a large part of the reign of George III. 'My grand-uncle's exterior,' says Mr Sinclair, 'consisted of the single-breasted coat, powdered hair and queue, and other paraphernalia, of a courtier in the reign of George II.; but within this courtly garb was enclosed one of the most ultra-liberal spirits of the time. He assembled every day at his house, in Welbeck Street, a party of congenial souls, never exceeding twelve in number, nor receiving the important summons to dinner a single moment after five o'clock. . . . . A slate was kept in the hall, on which any intimate friend (and he had many) might inscribe his name as a guest for the day. . . . He scarcely ever quitted the metropolis; he used to say that London was the best residence in winter, and that he knew no place like it in summer. But though he seldom really travelled, he sometimes made imaginary journeys. He used to mention, as a grave fact, that he once visited the Scilly Isles, and attended a ball at St Mary's, where he found a young lady giving herself great airs, because her education had received a "finish" at the Land's End. Another of his stories was that, having been at Rome during the last illness of Clement XIV., he went daily to the Vatican, to ascertain what chance he had of enjoying the spectacle of an installation. The bulletins, according to my uncle's playful imagination, were variously expressed, but each more alarming than its predecessor. First, "his Holiness is very ill;" next, "his Excellency is worse;" then, "his Eminence is in a very low state;" and at last, the day before the pope expired, came forth the startling announcement, "his Infallibility is delirious." This pleasant original occasionally coined anecdotes at the expense of his own guests, and related them to their face, for the amusement of the company. Parson Este was once editor of a paper called the *World;* and Bosville alleged of him, before a large party, that one day a gentleman in deep mourning came to him at the office, requesting the insertion of a ready-made panegyric upon his brother, who had died a few days before. "No!" answered the reverend editor; "your brother did not choose to die in our newspaper, and that being the case, I can find no room for eulogies upon him." It was a favourite saying of Bosville, which my father borrowed from him, when he wanted to give encouragement to a diffident friend, "Il faut risquer quelque chose." The origin of this catch-word was a story told by Bosville of a party of

French officers, each of whom outvied the rest in relating of himself some wonderful exploit. A young Englishman, who was present, sat with characteristic modesty in silence. His next neighbour asked him why he did not contribute a story in his turn, and, being answered, "I have done nothing like the feats that have been told us," patted him on the back, and said with a significant look: "Eh, bien, monsieur, il faut risquer quelque chose."

'[Bosville] wished his dinner-parties to be continued to the very last. His health declined, and his convivial powers deserted him; but the slate hung as usual in the hall, and he felt more anxiety than ever that the list of guests upon it should not fail of its appointed number. . . . . Even during his last hours, when he was confined to his chamber, the hospitable board was regularly spread below. He insisted upon reports from time to time of the jocularities calling forth the laughter which still assailed his ear; and on the very morning of his decease, gave orders for an entertainment punctually at the usual hour, which he did not live to see.'—*Rev. John Sinclair's Memoirs of Sir John Sinclair*, 2 vols. 1837.

Though, as Mr Sinclair informs us above, his grand-uncle clung most pertinaciously to the metropolis and rarely quitted it to any distance, there was, nevertheless, a series of country excursions which he long continued to make with great regularity. We allude to the famous Sunday-parties given by John Horne Tooke to his friends at his mansion at Wimbledon. Among the numerous guests who, on the first day of the week, might be seen ascending the hill from Putney, or crossing Wimbledon Common, to their host's residence, Mr Bosville was one of the most constant; and we are informed by Mr Stephens, in his life of Horne Tooke, that for 'many years a coach-and-four, with Mr Bosville and two or three friends, punctually arrived within a few minutes of two o'clock; and, after paying their respects in the parlour, walked about an hour in the fine gardens, with which the house was, all but on one side, surrounded. At four, the dinner was usually served in the parlour looking on the common.' To such festive reunions, presided over by the great wit and *bon vivant* of the day, Mr Bosville's own parties seem to have borne a close resemblance, though doubtless his social and conversational powers paled before those of the author of *The Diversions of Purley*.

## ABOLITION OF THE PASSPORT-SYSTEM IN FRANCE.

A wise and liberal measure adopted by the emperor of the French, in 1861, had the effect of drawing public attention to an international system which travellers had ample reason to remember with bitterness. This was the system of *passports*—'that ingenious invention,' as a writer in the *Quarterly Review*, in 1855, characterised it, 'for impeding the tourist and expediting the fugitive.' From early times, sovereigns claimed the right of prohibiting, if they chose, the entrance into their dominions of the subjects of another sovereign; and of equally prohibiting the exit of their own subjects. Hence, when states were at peace, the sovereigns adopted a plan of permitting the relaxation of this rule, through the medium of their respective ambassadors or representatives. Hall, in his *Chronicle*, adverts to these sovereign rights in the reign of Edward IV.; and the rules are known to have been very strict in the times of Elizabeth and James I. Passports are a very ancient institution. It is mentioned by some of the old monkish chroniclers as an achievement on the part of King Canute, that he obtained *free passes* for his subjects through various continental countries, on their pilgrimages to the shrines of the Apostles Peter and Paul at Rome. Each pilgrim was furnished with a document in the nature of a passport, called *Tracturia de Itinere Peragenda.* The general form of these documents was as follows: 'I [here comes the name of the person granting the passport], to our holy and apostolic and venerable fathers in Christ, and to all kings, bishops, abbots, priests, and clerks in every nation of Christendom, who devote themselves to the service of the Creator, in monasteries, in cities, in villages, or in hamlets. Be it known to you that this our brother [here comes the name of the person holding the passport] and your servant, has obtained permission from us to proceed on a pilgrimage to the Church of St Peter, your father, and to other churches, to pray for his soul's sake, for yours, and for ours. Therefore do we address this to you, begging that you will, for the love of God and of St Peter, give him hospitable treatment, aiding, consoling, and comforting him—affording to him free ingress, egress, and regress, so that he may in safety return to us. And for so doing, may a fitting reward be bestowed on you, at the last day, by Him who lives and reigns for ever!' This was something more than a passport, however, seeing that it entreated hospitality for the pilgrims.

Those perplexing people, the Chinese, who have anticipated us in so many things, had a passport-system nearly a thousand years ago. The Abbé Renaudot, in his translation of the Travels of Ebn Wahab, in the tenth century, gives the following passage: 'If a man travel from one place to another, he must take two passes with him—the one from the governor, the other from his deputy or lieutenant. The governor's pass permits him to set out on his journey, and takes notice of the name of the traveller and of those of his company; the age and family of the one and the other. And this is done for the information of the frontier places, where these two passes are examined; for whenever a traveller arrives at any of them, it is registered: "That such a one, the son of such a one, of such a family, passed through this place on such a day," &c.' The reason assigned by the Arabian traveller for this custom is the following: 'By this means they prevent any one from carrying off the money or effects of other persons, or their being lost.' It is not difficult to see that a system of registry, by which the movements and location of the subjects of a sovereign could be known, may be made applicable to some useful purposes; but when nations have advanced in civilisation, when their trading transactions bring them more and more into correspondence, the system becomes an impediment, productive of far more harm than good.

The *Moniteur*, the official French newspaper, contained the following announcement on the 16th of December 1860: 'The Emperor has decided that after the 1st of January next, and by reciprocity, the subjects of her Majesty the Queen of Great Britain and Ireland coming into France, shall be admitted and allowed to travel about without passports. The Minister of the Interior will give instructions to his agents to see this matter carried out.' It had been long known that the Emperor's personal opinions were opposed to the passport-system, and that he had only waited for the current of French thought to flow in the same direction as his own. A leading article in the *Times*, two days afterwards, forcibly depicted the evils of the system which has thus been happily abolished: 'The passport-system was a standing annoyance to British subjects in France. It involved the two things which Englishmen detest most—vexatious stoppages for the sake of small exactions, and constant liability to official interference. You might seldom experience the actual evil, but you never got rid of the risk. At any hour of the day, or night, on any pretence, or on no pretence, you might be required to produce your "papers," like a suspicious-looking vessel on the high-seas; and, if this manifest of your person and purposes did not satisfy the inquirer, you were liable to detention and imprisonment at his discretion. It was a right of search in the most offensive form, hanging over the traveller at every stage of his journey. At the best, you could never escape molestation or fine. You might compound with a *commissionaire*, and be quit of the job for a two-franc piece and a couple of hours' delay; but that much was inevitable, and, as it might recur at every town you came to, you were never safe. Above all—and this was the most exasperating feature in the case—the system placed you, as a matter of course, under the notice and control of the police, from the first moment of your arrival in the country, to the moment of your departure. The very fact of your travelling was regarded as a proceeding requiring justification. You had to clear yourself of a *primâ facie* case against you, and the passport was your ticket-of-leave. Unluckily, it was impossible to insure the completeness of this precious document. No man could ever take it for granted that his passport was in perfect order; and, consequently, he was always at the mercy of the police, who, from whim, suspicion, zeal, or spite, might deal with him as they chose, on no other warrant than some alleged defect in the cabalistic form of the passport. Passports were to police agents what the confessional is to the Romish priesthood—the instrument of power and action.' If this mode of keeping out the unoffending had the effect of keeping out offenders also, something might be said in its favour; but this is precisely what it did *not* do. 'None knew this better than the police themselves. They understood perfectly that all the fish they pretended to catch, slipped always, and, as a matter of course, through their meshes. We think we may defy any one to produce an instance of a conspirator, malefactor, or other evil-minded person who was arrested upon the evidence of his passport. On the contrary, as the police were bound, by the conditions of their own system, to take the shewing of the passport as conclusive, and as the papers of these gentry were invariably in order, the disguise proved exceedingly convenient to them. Except for their passports, they might have had to give some account of themselves, but these documents saved them all trouble and risk together. There they were, stamped and ticketed as lawful travellers by the police themselves, bearing the police-mark, and covered by the police certificate. As they had taken excellent care to observe every formality, there was nothing to be done with them; and the weight of the system consequently fell on the unsuspecting victims, whose very innocence had prevented them from providing against its snares.' The truth is, that a swarm of officials lived and prospered upon the profits of the system; and as the destruction of those gains would be equivalent to the destruction of a profession, all those who practised the profession had a strong reason for maintaining the system, and staving off reform as long as possible. Hence the oft-repeated assertions that the passport-system was the palladium, the ægis, the shield of good government.

The probabilities are, that other governments will, one by one, abandon the absurd restrictions which have thus been abolished by France.

## DECEMBER 17.

St Olympias, widow, about 410. St Begga, widow and abbess, 698.

*Born.*—Anthony Wood or à Wood, antiquarian writer, 1632, *Oxford;* Gabrielle Emilie, Marquise du Chastelet, translator of Newton's *Principia*, 1706; Ludwig Beethoven, eminent composer, 1770, *Bonn;* Sir Humphry Davy, chemist, 1779, *Penzance.*

*Died.*—Sir William Gascoigne, lord chief-justice, 1413; Simon Bolivar, liberator of South America, 1831, *Carthagena;* Kaspar Hauser, mysterious foundling, from the stroke of an assassin on the 14th, 1833, *Anspach, Bavaria;* Maria Louisa, archduchess of Parma (ex-empress of the French), 1847, *Parma.*

### KASPAR HAUSER.

Like the 'Man in the Iron Mask,' the identity of the unfortunate Kaspar Hauser, the foundling of Nuremberg, has formed the subject of much curious speculation. To the present day, the mystery hanging over his origin remains undispelled, and the whole affair is beset with such anomalies and contradictions, that it is almost impossible to form even a well-grounded conjecture on the subject. The following are the ascertained facts of the case.

Between four and five o'clock in the afternoon of 26th May 1828, a young lad, apparently of about sixteen or seventeen years of age, was found in a helpless and forlorn condition in the market-place of Nuremberg, by a citizen of that town. He was dressed like a peasant-boy, and had with him a letter addressed to the captain of the sixth regiment of horse at Nuremberg. Being conducted to this officer and interrogated, it soon became evident that he could speak very little, and was almost totally ignorant. To all questions he replied, 'Von Regensburg' (from Regensburg), or 'Ich woais nit' (I don't know). On the other hand, he wrote his name in firm legible characters on a sheet of paper, but without adding the place of his birth, or anything else, though requested to do so. Though short and broad shouldered, his figure was perfectly well-proportioned. His skin was very white; his limbs delicately formed, the hands and feet small and beautiful, the latter, however, shewing no marks of his having ever worn shoes. With the exception of dry bread and water, he shewed a violent dislike to all kinds of meat and drink. His language was confined to a few words or sentences in the old Bavarian dialect. He shewed entire ignorance of the most ordinary objects, and great indifference to the conveniences and necessaries of life. Among his scanty articles of clothing was a handkerchief marked K. H.; he had likewise about him some written Catholic prayers. In the letter which he carried, dated 'From the confines of Bavaria, place unknown, 1828,' the writer stated himself to be a poor day-labourer, the father of ten children, and said that the boy had been deposited before his door by his mother, a person unknown to the writer. He stated further, that he had brought up the boy secretly, without allowing him to leave the house, but had instructed him in reading, writing, and the doctrines of Christianity; adding that it was the boy's wish to become a horse-soldier. The letter enclosed a line, apparently from the mother, stating that she, a poor girl, had given birth to the boy on the 30th April 1812, that his name was Kaspar, and that his father, who had formerly served in the sixth regiment, was dead.

The poor boy having been taken before and attended to by the magistrates, his story was soon made known to the public, and he himself became the object of general sympathy. Binder, a burgomaster, exerted himself, in particular, to throw some light on the obscurity in which the origin of the young man was involved. In the course of many conversations with him, it came out that Hauser, from his childhood, had worn only a shirt and trousers; that he had lived in a dark place underground, where he was unable to stretch himself out at full length; that he had been fed upon bread and water by a man who did not shew himself, but who cleaned and dressed him, and provided him with food and drink while he was in a state of natural or artificial sleep. His sole occupation was playing with two wooden horses. For some time before he was conveyed to Nuremberg, the man had come oftener to his dungeon, and had taught him to write by guiding his hand, and to lift his feet and walk. This narrative gave rise to various suppositions and rumours. According to some, this mysterious foundling was the natural son of a priest, or of a young lady of high rank, while others believed him to be of princely origin, or the victim of some dark plot respecting an inheritance. Some incredulous persons believed the whole affair to be an imposition. On the 18th July 1828, Hauser was handed over to the care of Professor Daumer, who afterwards acted the part of his biographer. The history of his education is remarkable in a pedagogic point of view, as his original desire for knowledge, his extraordinary memory, and acute understanding decreased in proportion as the sphere of his knowledge extended. His progress was, on the whole, small. On the 17th October 1829, he was found bleeding from a slight wound on the brow, which he said had been inflicted by a man with a black head. All efforts made to discover the perpetrator were ineffectual. The incident excited a great sensation; Hauser was conveyed to the house of one of the magistrates, and constantly guarded by two soldiers. Among the many strangers who came to see him was Lord Stanhope, who became interested in him, and sent him to be educated at Anspach. Here he was employed in an office of the court of appeal, but he by no means distinguished himself either by industry or talent, and was gradually forgotten, till his death again made him the subject of attention. This event took place under the following singular circumstances. A stranger, under the pretext of bringing him a message from Lord Stanhope, and informing him of the circumstances of his birth, engaged to meet Hauser in the palace garden at three o'clock in the afternoon of the 14th December 1833. The hapless young man was faithful to the rendezvous, but he had scarcely commenced to converse with the unknown emissary, when the latter stabbed him in the left side, and he fell mortally wounded. He had, however, sufficient strength left to return home and relate the circumstances of his assassination, and three days afterwards, on the 17th December 1833, he died. Among the many surmises current regarding the unfortunate Hauser, the latest is that he was the scion of a noble family in England, and that his dark and mysterious history, with its atrocious termination, had its origin in this country. But nothing beyond mere conjecture has ever been adduced.

## THE DAY OF THE ANCIENT BRITON.

Ancient Britain is not so entirely a thing of the past as is generally supposed. When the ancient Britons were driven out of their territory, they could not carry their old homes with them; these were abandoned, and it is probable that the sites of many of them were occupied by the Roman conquerors. But in inaccessible places, beyond the Roman Wall, this was not the case; and to this day, among the Cheviot Hills, may be seen one of their deserted towns, several strong forts, numerous isolated huts, a monolithic ring temple, terraces on the steep hill-sides on which they grew their corn, barrows and cairns innumerable. These remains of ancient Britain yield a vivid realisation of the day of our Celtic predecessors.

The deserted town just mentioned, is situated on the southern slope of one of the Cheviot Hills, called Greenshaw. It consists of a group of stone huts, between sixty and seventy in number, divided into three clusters. The largest cluster, containing upwards of thirty huts, is surrounded by two strong stone rampiers, a fact which suggests the supposition that on report of coming foe, all the inhabitants would take shelter within the enclosure. Time has clothed the summits of the walls with vegetation, and heaped up earth on the ruins; but this has not destroyed the identity of the place. The huts are of a circular form, built of large pieces of unhewn porphyry. This is the stone of the district; and is still to be seen in enormous quantities, lying, in blocks, among the heather and ferns on the sides of the hills. There was no quarrying required. All the ancient Briton had to do, was to collect pieces of suitable and portable sizes. To every hut there is a doorway; and to one of them an indication of a sill, or similar arrangement, to receive a door. They are all roofless; and the question of what material the roofs were formed, is the only one about which there is any doubt; whether they were simply thatched with the abundant gorse, heather, or ferns, as the shepherds' huts are to this day in the same district, or whether they possessed conical roofs of stone or timber, we shall probably never know. In the extreme north of Scotland, there are circular stone-houses of a similar antiquity with conical stone roofs; yet, when several of these huts were cleared of the accumulations within them, for the purpose of an antiquarian survey,* at which the writer was present, no traces of roof stones were discovered. In nearly every instance, charred wood was found upon the flat stones with which the floors were rudely paved. There is a burn, called Linhope, near this town, from which, as well as from a couple of springs close by, water could be procured; and it is noticeable, that the distance to this stream is protected by a length of rampier. Several pieces of rough clay-pottery, found in the soil of the town, prove that pitchers were broken in going to the water in that day as in this. There is an ancient roadway, sunken two or three feet deep, and fortified by a rampier, down to the neighbouring river Breamish; and two others of a similar construction, lead from the west and from the east into the town.

On another of the Cheviot Hills, Yeavering Bell, are further traces of ancient Britain. On the summit of this hill, about two thousand feet above the level of the sea, is an area of twelve acres, enclosed by a stone wall, upwards of ten feet thick, having four entrances into it, one of which is defended by a guard-house; and within this area is an inner fort, excavated out of the rock, of an oval form, measuring thirteen feet across the widest part. On the sides of the hill, and in a high valley between the Bell and the next hill, called Whitelaw, there are many remains of stone huts rudely flagged, some in groups surrounded by rampiers, and others isolated. Barrows, too, are numerous here. On Ingram Hill, several of these old-world tumuli have been opened; but nothing but charred wood has been found in them.

In the valley of the Breamish, where there are many more camps, there are traces of ancient British agriculture. These are terraces cut out of the hillsides, rising one above another. On some hills there are a dozen or more of these primitive cornfields, or hanging gardens. It is supposed that as the valleys were boggy and liable to floods, this was the mode of culture which presented less difficulty than any other to the Celtic mind.

The Celtic temple, or monolithic ring, in the same district, consists of thirteen huge stones, which once marked an oval enclosure on the bank of the Three Stone Burn. There were, probably, fourteen originally; as between the first and thirteenth there is a space double the extent that exists between any of the others. Several are overthrown, and lie bedded in heather. They are of different heights; the tallest being upwards of five feet; the shortest, scarcely two feet above the ground. As this could not have been a place of residence, nor of defence, we may reasonably conclude that it was a place of worship. What rites were celebrated within its mystic oval we can but imagine; but the temple itself we may see with our eyes.

In fine, among the gorse, ferns, scarlet-leaved bilberries, mountain pinks, mosses, tall foxgloves, and heather of the Cheviot district, with its myriads of blocks of porphyry strewn upon the hills, and valleys covered with sea-green lichens, we have a considerable tract of ancient Britain still. We may enter the ancient Briton's fort, or his hut; we may climb the rampiers raised by his hands, scan his vast hunting-grounds and his terraced cornfields; and we may saunter, as we have seen, in his temple—so rudely grand with its background of hills and canopy of sky. We may search the *debris* of his deserted home, and find the flint arrow-head with which he shot; the horns of the deers so slain; the flint javelin-head he reserved for hostile tribes; the handmills with which his women ground corn; pieces of the pottery they used for domestic purposes; and, maybe, a portion of a discarded armlet worn by a Celtic princess.

* The Berwickshire Naturalists' Club, assisted by a contribution from the Duke of Northumberland, surveyed the Celtic antiquities of the Cheviot district, in the summers of 1861 and 1862. An elaborate report of the survey was written by Mr Geo. Tate, F.G.S., Alnwick, one of the secretaries for the transactions of that body.

## THE 'O. P. RIOTS.'

The disturbance known in theatrical annals as the *O. P. Riots*, or the *O. P. Row*, was perhaps the most remarkable manifestation of the popular will ever displayed at any of our places of amusement, ending with a concession to public opinion rather than to rightful claim.

On the 20th of September 1808, Covent Garden Theatre was burned to the ground, involving the loss of many lives, and the destruction of property valued at little less than a quarter of a million sterling. As it had belonged to a sort of joint-stock company, money was soon found to rebuild the theatre; and great admiration was bestowed on the magnitude and beauty of the new structure, when it was opened to the public on the 17th of September 1809. But a storm was impending. The proprietors had issued an address or prospectus, announcing that, in consequence of the great expense incurred in rebuilding the theatre, the increased ground-rent charged by the Duke of Bedford, and the enhanced prices of almost everything needed for stage purposes, they would be compelled to raise the prices of admission to the boxes and pit. They appealed to the kindness and consideration of the public under these circumstances; and Mr John Kemble, in an opening address, adverted to the matter in the following very unpoetical terms:

'Solid our building, heavy our expense;
We rest our claim on your munificence;
What ardour plans a nation's taste to raise,
A nation's liberality repays.'*

If there had been anything like 'free-trade' in theatres, the audience would have had no right to

* The following parody on these clumsy lines—testifying how the public were disposed to view the matter—appeared in the *Times*:

'Heavy our building, but not so th' expense;
We rest our hopes upon your want of sense;
What av'rice spends, new mines of wealth to raise,
A gen'rous people's folly soon repays.'

complain, but simply to stay away if they did not choose to pay the enhanced prices. As matters stood, however, in those days, the two 'Patent' or 'Royal' theatres, Covent Garden and Drury Lane, claimed great privileges over all the minor establishments; the public were forbidden to see Shakspeare represented except at the two great houses; and therefore they claimed, rightly or wrongly, to have some voice in determining the prices of admission. To assert this right, was evidently the purpose of a large number of the visitors on the opening night. They received Kemble with volleys of hooting, groaning, whistling, 'cat-calls,' and cries of 'Old Prices!'—the last soon abbreviated to 'O. P.!' The opening address passed over in dumb show; and so did the tragedy of *Macbeth* and the farce of the *Quaker*. The mob outside sympathised with the audience within, and Bow Street was a scene of tremendous commotion. Excited by the accounts given in the newspapers, the public prepared to go to the theatre on the second night in a spirit more warlike than ever; and on the third night, Kemble gave still greater offence to the audience by saying to them: 'I wait to know what you want.' So matters continued for a week: the actors and actresses bravely bearing the storm, instead of receiving the applause to which they were accustomed; and the audience determining that not a single word of the performances should be heard. At length, on the 23d, Mr Kemble made an announcement from the stage, which was certainly a fair one under the circumstances, to this effect—that a committee of gentlemen should be appointed to examine the accounts of the theatre, with a view of determining whether the new prices were or were not equitable; that the theatre should be closed until that committee had reported on their proceedings; and that the report should be accepted as conclusive by the two belligerents, the public and the proprietors. The audience took this proposal in good part; and on the following day a committee was formed, consisting of Alderman Sir Charles Price, Sir Thomas Plumer (solicitor-general), Mr Sylvester (recorder of the City of London), Mr Whitmore (governor of the Bank of England), and Mr Angerstein. The report of the committee was decidedly in favour of the proprietors; shewing that, if the new house were fully insured, and all expenses honourably paid, the probable gross receipts at the new prices would not yield more net profit than three and a half per cent. on the capital sunk; and that at the old prices, there would be no profit whatever. This report was printed on the play-bill for the re-opening night, October 4. The public had evidently expected a different decision, and manifested signs of turbulence before the curtain rose. The malcontents were of two kinds—those who insisted on the old prices, whether right or wrong; and those who doubted whether the committee had satisfactorily explained their meaning, and their mode of reasoning. The report said that the 'future profits' would probably be three and a half per cent. or *nil*, according as the new or the old prices were adopted. But there arose a doubt whether five per cent. had been implied as regular *interest* on the capital sunk, in addition to the *profit* named. This produced an explanation, to the effect that no such interest had been implied; and that the proprietors, in the opinion of the committee, would obtain no return whatever for their money, unless the new prices were adopted.

According to all principles of fairness, the opposition should have ended here, unless some other fallacy or error had been detected. But it did not. On the contrary, the O. P. advocates formed themselves into a party, resolved to disturb the performances night after night, until their demands were acceded to. Then ensued a series of struggles which lasted during the extraordinary period of ten weeks, and which were not ended till the 'Treaty of Peace' was framed on the 17th of December. It became a regular part of the duty of the daily newspapers to notice the state of affairs at the theatre on the previous evening. Sometimes there were merely speeches *pro* and *con* by the pit-orators and Mr Kemble; sometimes cries and shouts, such as 'Old Prices!' 'No humbug for John Bull!' 'No garbled extracts!' &c.; while on other occasions the malcontents went to the expense of placards to the following effect: 'Mr Kemble, let your monopoly cease, and then raise your prices as high as you please!' 'No private boxes for intriguing!' 'A long pull, a strong pull, and a pull altogether, for old prices!' 'John Bull, be very bold and resolute! never depart from your resolution, but firmly keep your station.' The word 'monopoly' gives a clue to one motive for the opposition—the patent rights which Mr Kemble haughtily claimed in reference to the legitimate drama. As to the private boxes, they had increased in number, as a source of additional profit; and the dissatisfied public chose to stigmatise them on other than financial grounds. In addition to cries and placards, there was a continuous tumult of groaning, singing, laughing, and whistling; with an occasional accompaniment of coachmen's horns, showmen's trumpets, dustmen's bells, and watchmen's rattles. Many came with the symbolic initials, 'O. P.,' on their hats or coats. The malcontents got up a gymnastic exercise, which was known as the 'O. P. dance,' and which consisted in an alternate stamping of the feet, accompanied with the regular cry of 'O. P.!' in noisy and monotonous unison. As it was rather expensive to keep on this system night after night, the rioters began to adopt the plan of coming in at half-price; the curious effect of which was, that three acts of a play were listened to in the usual orderly manner by peaceful visitors; while of the remaining two acts not a word could be heard.

If the proprietors had remained quiescent, the disturbances would probably have died out after a few nights; and the new prices would have been adhered to or not, according as the house was well or ill filled. But they adopted a most reprehensible step—that of hiring prize-fighters, to convince the public by the force of fists. This gave a wholly new aspect to the struggle; many persons who had hitherto held aloof, now took part in the contest, for they felt exasperated at procedure so insulting. Dutch Sam, a noted pugilist of those days, organised his corps; and the pit became a scene of fighting. On one particular evening, Mr Clifford, a barrister, who had taken an active part in the opposition, entered the pit with the letters O. P. on his hat; he was received with cheers, and the old 'O. P. dance' again commenced. The proprietors now thought themselves strong enough to adopt decisive measures; at least this was the view of Mr Brandon, the box-keeper, for he caused Mr Clifford to be arrested. Then ensued new scenes of excitement. Mr Brandon failed to get Mr Clifford convicted as a rioter; whereupon Mr Clifford succeeded in obtaining a verdict against Mr Brandon for false imprisonment. A meeting took place at the Crown and Anchor Tavern, with the view of obtaining subscriptions to defend any persons against whom, like Mr Clifford, proceedings might be instituted as rioters. Mr Kemble, feeling that the public were taking up the matter rather seriously, requested and obtained admission to this assembly. He offered, on the part of the proprietors, to concede most of the objects demanded, and to drop all prosecutions. The meeting demanded also the dismissal of Mr Brandon, who seems to have made himself unnecessarily offensive; but a supplicatory letter from him pacified the public. A few weeks afterwards, a public dinner was held, in which Mr Kemble took part, as a sort of ratification of the Treaty of Peace.

One of the most remarkable circumstances connected with the O. P. Riots is, that these enabled Stockdale, the publisher, to fill two entire octavo volumes, forming a compilation called the *Covent Garden Journal*. This work comprises, first, a statement of the cause of the quarrel; then a Journal of the sixty-seven nights' disturbances, numbered with all the regularity of Scheherazade's narrations in the *Arabian Nights' Entertainments;* and then an appendix of documents. These documents are valuable, in so far as they shew the tone of public feeling on the subject, as reflected in the newspaper-press. The *Times, Chronicle, Post, Examiner, Herald, Public Ledger*, and *Evening Post*, all are represented in these documents, and generally as opponents of the Kemble party. Some of the newspaper *jeux d'esprit*, and some of the placards distributed in the theatre, shewed how heartily many of the public entered into the comicality which formed one aspect of the affair. One commenced:

'Cease, cease the public here to knock, sirs;
The pit was never made for box-ers.'

Another:

'Surely the manager devoid of grace is;
He pigeons both our pockets and our places.'

A third: 'In consequence of the general hoarseness in town, occasioned by a clamour for Old Prices, the confectioners, it is said, have determined, in the sale of their pectoral lozenges, to follow Mr Kemble's plan, by charging an advance.' The *Morning Chronicle* appeared with:

'Since naught can appease Johnny Bull but O. P.,
And the promised suppression of every P. B.,
The playhouse, no doubt, will continue M. T.,
For King John has declar'd he 'd be sooner D. D.'

The following was a parody on Gray's *Bard*, beginning:

'Ruin seize thee, ruthless John,
Confusion on thy banners wait.'

And another on *Chevy Chase:*

'God prosper long our noble king,
Our cash and comforts all;
In Covent Garden while I sing
The row that did befall.'

One effusion was to be sung to the tune of 'Said a Smile to a Tear:'

'Said a P to an O,
Where d' ye intend to go?
Said the O, I've not fixed upon whither.
O then, said the P,
You and I will agree,
To kick up a row both together.'

A second to the air of 'Derry Down:'

'They send in their ruffians, who saucily sit,
With their doxies in front-seats of boxes and pit,
With orders to stifle the voice of the town,
And convince us of error by knocking us down.
Derry down.'

A third to that of *The Frog in an Opera Hat:*

'John Kemble would an acting go;
Heigho, says Rowley.
He raised the price which he thought too low,
Whether the public would let him or no,
With his roly-poly,
Gammon, and spinage,
Heigho, says Kemble.'

The *House that Jack Built* was brought into requisition, with stanzas which commenced with—

'This is the House that Jack built.
These are the Boxes, let to the great, that
Visit the House that Jack built.'

And so on to the last cumulative clause, which ran thus:

'This is the Manager full of scorn, who raised the price to the People forlorn, and directed the Thief-taker, shaven and shorn, to take up John Bull with his Bugle-horn, who hissed the Cat engaged to squall, to the poor in the Pigeon-holes, over the Boxes, let to the Great, who visit the House that Jack built.'

The 'Cat' was Madame Catalani, a little out of favour at that time with some of the public. Nor did the *National Anthem* fail in the hands of these parodists:

'God save great Johnny Bull,
Long live our Johnny Bull,
God save John Bull!
Send him victorious,
Loud and uproarious,
With lungs like Boreas,
God save John Bull!'

---

# DECEMBER 18.

Saints Rufus and Zozimus, martyrs, 116. St Gatian, first bishop of Tours, confessor, about 300. St Winebald, abbot, and confessor, 760.

*Born.*—Prince Rupert, military commander, 1619, *Prague.*
*Died.*—Robert Nanteuil, celebrated engraver, 1678, *Paris;* Heneage Finch, Earl of Nottingham, 1682; Veit Ludwig von Seckendorf, political and theological writer, 1692, *Halle;* Soame Jenyns, religious and general writer, 1787; Pierre Louis de Préville, celebrated French comedian, 1799; Johann Gottfried Von Herder, German theologian and philosopher, 1803; Dr Alexander Adam, eminent classic scholar and teacher, 1809, *Edinburgh;* Thomas Dunham Whitaker, antiquarian writer, 1821, *Blackburn;* General Lord Lynedoch, 1843, *London;* Samuel Rogers, poet, 1855, *London.*

## SUN-DIALS AND HOUR-GLASSES.

When the philanthropist Howard was on his death-bed, he said: 'There is a spot near the village of Dauphiney, where I should like to be buried; suffer no pomp to be used at my funeral, no monument to mark the spot where I am laid; but put me quietly in the earth, place a sun-dial over my grave, and let me be forgotten.' A similar affection was evinced by Sir William Temple, who desired that his heart might be placed in a silver box and deposited under the sun-dial in his garden, where he had experienced so much pleasure in contemplating the works of nature.

Sun-dials are of very ancient date, and the honour of inventing them is claimed for the Phœnicians. The earliest mention of them occurs in the well-known incident recorded in Scripture of King Hezekiah, who, when sick and penitent, is granted, in miraculous evidence of the Lord's intention to restore him to health, that the shadow shall go backward ten degrees on the sun-dial of Ahaz. Homer, too, often supposed to be a contemporary of Hezekiah, states, in his *Odyssey*, that there was a dial in the Island of Syra, upon which was represented the sun's annual race.

Two centuries ago, sun-dials attracted more attention than they do at the present time. The great sculptor, Nicholas Stone, mentions, under date 1619, the making of a dial at St James's, the king finding stone and workmanship only, for the which he had £6, 13*s*. 4*d*. 'And in 1622,' he says, 'I made the great diall in the privy-garden, at Whitehall, for the which I had £46.' 'And in that year, 1622,' he continues, 'I made a diall for my Lord Brook, in Holbourn, for the which I had £8, 10*s*.' And for Sir John Daves, at Chelsey, he made a dial and two statues of an old man and a woman, for which he received £7 a piece.*

In Joseph Moxon's *Tutor to Astronomie and Geographie, or An easie way to know the use of both the Globes* (1659), there are ample directions for the making of sun-dials of many various kinds, and among others 'a solid ball or globe that will shew the hour of the day without a gnomon.' The principle followed in this case, was to have a globe marked round the equator with two series of numbers from 1 to 12, and to erect it, rectified for the latitude, with one of the 12's set to the north, the other to the south. When the sun shone on this globe, the number found under the place where the shadowed and illuminated parts met, was the hour of the day.

Mr Moxon has fortunately given us a representation, here copied, of a dial of this kind perched on the top of a columnar fountain, which was erected by Mr John Leak, at Leadenhall Corner, in London, in the mayoralty of Sir John Dethick, knight, and thus has preserved to us, incidentally, an object much more important than the dial—namely, a beautiful fountain which once adorned one of the principal thoroughfares of the metropolis, furnishing those supplies of healthful beverage which the charity of our age has again offered through the medium of our so-called 'drinking fountains.'

However invaluable sun-dials might be as chronometers, they could only be of use in daylight, and when the sun was actually shining. Some mode had to be devised for supplying their place in cloudy weather, at night, or within doors. One contrivance employed by the ancients for this end

SUN-DIAL AND FOUNTAIN, FORMERLY AT LEADENHALL CORNER, LONDON.

was the *clepsydra*, or water-clock, which noted the passing of time by the escape of water through a vessel, with a hole at the bottom, into a cistern beneath. Another method, designed on a similar principle, was that of the hour-glass, by which the lapse of time was ascertained through the passing of a small quantity of sand from the upper to the

* *Anecdotes of Painting in England.*

lower part of the glass. Hour-glasses are said to have been invented at Alexandria about the middle of the third century, and we are informed that persons used to carry them about as we do watches. They are familiar to us as an accompaniment, in pictorial representations, of the solitary monk or anchorite, where the hour-glass is generally exhibited along with the skull and crucifix. They were also attached to pulpits, in order to regulate the length of sermons.

But this last mode of employing hour-glasses seems to have been chiefly introduced after the Reformation, when long sermons came much into fashion. Previous to that period, pulpit-discourses appear to have been generally characterised by brevity. Many of St Austin's might be easily delivered in ten minutes; nor was it usual in the church to devote more than half an hour to the most persuasive eloquence. These old sermons were of the nature of homilies, and it was only when the church felt called upon to explain tenets attacked, or eliminate doctrinal disputes, that they altered in character; and the pulpit became a veritable 'drum-ecclesiastic.' From the days of Luther, the length of sermons increased, until the middle of the seventeenth century; when the Puritan preachers inflicted discourses of two hours or more in duration on their hearers. In some degree to regulate these enthusiastic talkers, hour-glasses were placed upon the desks of their pulpits, and in 1623, we read of a preacher 'being attended by a man that brought after him his book and hour-glass.' Some churches were provided with half-hour glasses also, and we may imagine the anxiety with which the clerk would regard the choice made by the parson, as upon this would depend the length of his attendance. L'Estrange tells an amusing story of a parish clerk, who had sat patiently under a preacher, 'till he was three-quarters through his second glass,' and the auditory had slowly withdrawn, tired out by his prosing; the clerk then arose at a convenient pause in the sermon, and calmly requested 'when he had done,' if he would be pleased to close the church-door, 'and push the key under it,' as himself and the few that remained were about to retire.

In the sixteenth century, pulpits began to be regularly furnished, with iron-work stands, for the

PULPIT HOUR-GLASS—NO. 1.

reception of the hour-glass. One of these in Compton Bassett Church, Wilts, is here represented; the large fleur-de-lys, in the centre of the iron bar, acts as a handle by which the hour-glass may be turned in its stand. Sometimes these stands and glasses were very elaborate in design, and of costly materials. At Hurst, in Berkshire, is a wrought-iron work of the kind most intricately designed. It has the date 1636, and the words, 'as this glass runneth, so man's life passeth,' amid foliations of oak and ivy. The frame of the hour-glass of St Dunstan's, Fleet Street, was of solid silver, and contained enough of the precious metal to be melted down, and converted into staff-heads for the parish beadles.

The lonely church of Cliffe, on the Kentish coast, between Gravesend and the Nore, furnishes us with a second example of the stand alone. The pulpit is of carved wood, dated 1634. This stand is affixed thereto by a bracket, which bears upon the shield the date 1636. It is on the preacher's left side.

PULPIT HOUR-GLASS—NO. 2.

In the book of St Katherine's Church, Aldgate, date 1564, we find, 'Paid for an Hour-glass that hangeth by the pulpit where the preacher doth make a sermon, that he may know how the hour passeth away, one shilling;' and in the same book, among the bequests of date 1616, is 'an hower-glass with a frame of irone to stand in.' In the time of Cromwell, the preacher, having named the text, turned up the glass; and if the sermon did not last till the sand had run down, it was said by the congregation that the preacher was lazy; but if, on the other hand, he exceeded this limit, they would yawn and stretch themselves till he had finished.

Many humorous stories originated from this clerical usage. There is a print of Hugh Peter's preaching, holding up the hour-glass, as he utters the words, 'I know you are good-fellows, so let's have another glass!' A similar tale is told of Daniel Burgess, the celebrated Nonconformist divine, at the beginning of the last century. Famous for the length of his pulpit harangues, and the quaintness of his illustrations, he was at one time declaiming with great vehemence against the sin of drunkenness, and in his ardour had fairly allowed the hour-glass to run out before bringing his discourse to a conclusion. Unable to arrest himself in the midst of his eloquence, he reversed the monitory horologe, and exclaimed, 'Brethren,

I have somewhat more to say on the nature and consequences of drunkenness, *so let's have the other glass—and then!*'—the usual phrase adopted by topers at protracted sittings.

Mr James Maidment, in his *Third Book of Scottish Pasquils*, has given a somewhat similar anecdote. 'A humorous story,' he observes, 'has been preserved of one of the Earls of Airly, who entertained at his table a clergyman, who was to preach before the Commissioner next day. The glass circulated, perhaps, too freely; and whenever the divine attempted to rise, his lordship prevented him, saying: "Another glass—and then!" After conquering his lordship, his guest went home. The next day the latter selected as his text, "The wicked shall be punished and right *airly!*" Inspired by the subject, he was by no means sparing of his oratory, and the hour-glass was disregarded, although he was repeatedly warned by the precentor, who, in common with Lord Airly, thought the discourse rather lengthy. The latter soon knew why he was thus punished, by the reverend gentleman (when reminded) always exclaiming, not *sotto voce*, "Another glass—and then!"'

Fosbroke, in his *British Monachism*, tells a quaint tale of a mode by which long sermons were avoided: 'A rector of Bibury used to preach two hours, regularly turning the glass. After the text, the esquire of the parish withdrew, smoked his pipe, and returned to the blessing.'

Hogarth, in his 'Sleeping Congregation,' has introduced an hour-glass on the left-hand side of the preacher. They lingered in country churches; but they ceased to be in anything like general use after the Restoration.

---

# DECEMBER 19.

St Nemesion, and others, martyrs, 250. St Samthana, virgin and abbess, 738.

*Born.*—Charles William Scheele, distinguished chemist, 1742, *Stralsund;* Captain William Edward Parry, Arctic navigator, 1790, *Bath.*

*Died.*—Frederick Melchior, Baron Grimm, statesman and wit, 1807, *Gotha;* Benjamin Smith Barton, American naturalist, 1815; Augustin Pugin, architectural draughtsman, 1852; Joseph Mallard William Turner, painter, 1851, *Chelsea.*

## J. M. W. TURNER.

Joseph Mallard William Turner, R.A., was the son of a barber, and was born at his father's shop, in Maiden Lane, in London, in 1775. The friendly chat of the celebrities of the time in that room of frizzling and curling, persuaded Turner, the father, that his son would become a great man; so he gave him a very fair education, and in his rude way encouraged the lad's taste for art. The son formed a close friendship with a clever young artist like himself, Girtin, who would have been, had he lived, some critics say, his great rival. Turner himself used good-naturedly to assert: 'If poor Tom had lived, I should have starved.'

In 1789, Turner entered the Royal Academy as a student. After remaining there in that capacity for five years, and working actively at his profession for other five, during which periods he sent to the exhibition no less than fifty-nine pictures, he was elected in 1799 an associate of the Royal Academy. In the two following years he exhibited fourteen pictures, and in 1802 was elected an academician. Till this date he had chiefly been known as a landscape painter in water-colours, but thenceforth he turned his attention to oil-painting, and in the ensuing half-century produced at the Academy exhibitions upwards of two hundred pictures. In 1807, he was elected professor of perspective in the Royal Academy, and the following year appeared his *Liber Studiorum*, or Book of Studies, which Charles Turner, Mr Lupton, and others, engraved. Other engraved works by him are his illustrations of Lord Byron's and Sir Walter Scott's poems; Rogers' Italy and Poems; The Rivers of England; The Rivers of France, and Scenery of the Southern Coast. To enumerate the different paintings of Turner would be impossible. They have established him as the greatest of English landscape painters, and earned for him the appellation of the 'English Claude,' to whom, indeed, many of his admirers pronounce him superior. Among his more famous pictures, reference may specially be made to his 'Kilchurn Castle, Loch Awe;' 'The Tenth Plague of Egypt;' 'The Wreck of the *Minotaur;*' 'Calais Pier;' 'The Fighting *Temeraire* Tugged to her Last Berth;' 'The Grand Canal, Venice;' 'Dido and Eneas;' 'The Golden Bough;' 'Modern Italy;' 'The Fall of Carthage,' and 'The Building of Carthage.' The sea in all its varied aspects, but chiefly under that of gloom or tempests; bright sunny landscapes and noble buildings, lighted up by the glowing rays of the setting sun; and generally nature in her weird-like and unwonted moods, form the favourite themes of this great artist. Through all his productions the genius of a poet declares itself, impressing us with the same mysterious feeling of ineffable grandeur that we experience in reading the works of Dante or Milton. The eccentricity of his colouring and indefiniteness of his figures, rendering many of his later pictures, to ordinary observers, nothing more than a splash or unmeaning medley, have been frequently animadverted on; and with respect to the pictures executed during the last twenty years of his life, it cannot be denied, notwithstanding their unfailing suggestiveness, that much of this censure is well founded.

The Royal Academy treated Turner well, and he, in return, adhered to it devotedly to his death. But the prime of his life was spent in struggles with poverty, in unmerited obscurity, and battles with his employers. He had a rigid sense of justice, and a proud consciousness of his own merits and the dignity of his art. The pertinacity with which he exacted the last shilling in all cases made him seem mean. The natural way in which he continued to retain the simple, we might say uncouth, habits which poverty taught him, after he became wealthy, caused him to be branded as a miser. His gruff and peculiar ways, his honesty, as well as his proficiency, made him many enemies. But he lived to reach a high pinnacle of popularity, and to know himself fairly appreciated.

Turner's life is a strange story, a narrative at once painfully and pleasingly interesting. Many seeds of human frailty, many taints of a vulgar origin were never uprooted, though ever kept in check by a truly noble soul. Turner was emphatically a child of nature. His faults were natural frailties not restrained, his virtues rather good impulses than acquired principles. When he rudely dismissed a beggar-woman, and then ran after her with a five-pound note, he furnished a key which unlocks his whole life.

We must set one thing against another. Turner was rough and blunt; yet of how many could it be said, that 'he was never known to say an ill word of any human being, never heard to utter one word of depreciation of a brother-artist's work?' Let the reader learn to wonder at Turner's greatness, by applying to himself such a test. A curious tale is told of his obstinacy. He was visiting at Lord Egremont's. He and his host quarrelled so desperately as to whether the number of windows in a certain building was six or seven, that the carriage was ordered, and Turner driven to the spot, to count them for himself, and be convinced of his mistake. But on another occasion, when Lord Egremont ordered up a bucket of water and some carrots, to settle a question about their swimming, Turner proved to be in the right.

He was fond of privacy, and on this subject Chantrey's stratagem, by which he got into the artist's studio, long remained a standing joke against Turner. There were some things, unhappily, connected with his private life, which were wisely kept concealed; and when, to an unknown residence, which he had at Chelsea, the old man retired at last to die, he was only discovered by his friends the day before his final journey.

Undoubtedly, Turner was fond of hoarding, but he was too great to become a miser. He hoarded his sketches even more eagerly than his sixpences. If he amassed £140,000, it was to leave it to found a charity for needy artists. This was his life's wish. If his grasping was great, his pride was greater. For when his grand picture of 'Carthage' was refused by some one, for whom it was painted to order, at the price of £100, Turner, in his pride, resolved to leave it to the nation. 'At a great meeting at Somerset House, where Sir Robert Peel, Lord Hardinge, and others were present, it was unanimously agreed to buy two pictures of Turner, and to present them to the National Gallery, as monuments of art for eternal incitement and instruction to artists and all art-lovers. A memorial was drawn up, and presented to Turner by his sincere old friend, Mr Griffiths, who exulted in the pleasant task. The offer was £5000 for the two pictures, the 'Rise,' and 'Fall of Carthage.' Turner read the memorial, and his eyes brightened. He was deeply moved: he shed tears; for he was capable, as all who knew him well knew, of intense feeling. He expressed the pride and delight he felt at such a noble offer from such men, but he added sternly, directly he read the word 'Carthage'—'No, no; they shall not have it,' at the same time informing Mr Griffiths of his prior intention.

All his friends loved him, and he was really, as we have stated, no miser. There was silver found under his pillow, when he left any place he had been staying at; but this was because he was too sensitive to offer it to the servants in person. We read of him paying, of his own accord, for expensive artist-dinners, of his giving a merry picnic, of his sending upwards of £20,000 secretly to the aid of a former patron.

Turner was generous-hearted, too, in other than pecuniary matters. He pulled his own picture down, to find a place for the picture of some insignificant young artist, whom he wished to encourage. He blackened a bright sky in one of his academy pictures, which hung between two of Lawrence's, so as to cast its merits into the shade. In this befouled condition, he allowed his own production to remain throughout the exhibition; and whispered to a friend, to allay his indignation: 'Poor Lawrence was so distressed; never mind, it'll wash off; it's only lampblack!'

His genuine affections were never drawn out. The history of his first love is a sad story of disappointment, enough to darken a life. He always stuck close to his old 'dad,' as he called him; but quitted, much to the old man's disappointment, a pleasant country-house and garden, for a dull house in town. The reason for this proceeding oozed out one day in conversation with a friend: 'Dad would work in the garden, and was always catching cold.'

This great artist's will, after all, was so loosely expressed, that its intentions were to a great extent frustrated, and the bulk of his property, which he had bequeathed for national and artistic purposes, was successfully claimed by his relatives. By a compromise, however, effected with the latter, the magnificent series of oil-paintings and drawings, known as the Turner Collection, have been secured for our national galleries as the most exalted trophies of British art.

## 'ALMANACS FOR THE ENSUING YEAR.'

The year is now drawing to its close, the Christmas festivities are in active preparation, and almost every one is looking forward with cheerful anticipation to the welcome variety from the regular pursuits and monotonous routine of ordinary life, which characterises the death of the Old year, and the birth of the New one. Youngsters at school are looking eagerly forward to the delights of home and the holidays—the intermission from study and scholastic restraint; the sliding, skating, and other sports of the season; the mince-pies, the parties, and the pantomimes. A universal bustle and anticipation everywhere prevails. Hampers with turkeys, geese, bacon, and other substantial provisions are coming up in shoals to town as presents from country friends; whilst barrels of pickled oysters, and boxes of cakes, dried fruits, and *bonbons* find their way in no less force to the provinces. Nor in thus providing for material and gastronomic enjoyment, are the more refined and intellectual cravings of humanity neglected. Christmas-books of all shapes, sizes, and subject-matter blaze forth magnificently in booksellers' windows, decked in all the colours of the rainbow, resplendent in all the gorgeousness of modern bookbinding, and displaying the grandest trophies of typographic and illustrative skill. The publishers of the various popular periodicals now put forth the 'extra Christmas number,' and the interest and curiosity excited by this last are shared with the graver and more business-like 'almanacs for the ensuing year.'

The time-honoured street-cry just quoted, may still be heard echoing through many of our public thoroughfares, though it is probably much less common now than it used to be, when itinerant venders of all kinds found a greater toleration from the authorities, and a far readier market with the public for their wares. In the present day, people generally resort to the regular booksellers or stationers for their almanacs. Here purchasers of all means and tastes may be suited, whether they desire a large and comprehensive almanac, which, in addition to the mere calendar, may furnish them with information on all matters of business and general utility throughout the year, or whether they belong to that class whose humble wants in this direction are satisfied by the expenditure of a penny.

It is well known that the Stationers' Company of London enjoyed, in former times, a monopoly of the printing of all books; and long after this privilege had gradually been withdrawn from them, they continued to assert the exclusive right of publishing almanacs; but this claim was successfully contested in 1775 by Thomas Carnan, a bookseller in St Paul's Churchyard, who obtained a decision against the company in the Court of Common Pleas, and this judgment was subsequently concurred in by parliament, after an animated discussion. The Stationers' Company continued the publication of almanacs with considerable profit to themselves, notwithstanding this infringement of what they deemed a vested right; and to the present day this branch of trade, the sole relic of a business which formerly comprehended the whole world of literature, forms, in spite of competition, a most profitable source of revenue to the association. The day on which the Stationers' Company issue their almanacs to the public (on or near the 22d November) presents a very animated and exciting scene, and is delineated

'ALMANAC DAY' AT STATIONERS' HALL.

in the accompanying engraving. We quote the following description from Knight's *London:* 'Let us step into Ludgate Street, and from thence through the narrow court on the northern side to the Hall. The exterior seems to tell us nothing, to suggest nothing, unless it be that of a very commonplace looking erection of the seventeenth century, and therefore built after the fire which destroyed everything in this neighbourhood; so we enter. Ha! here are signs of business. The Stationers cannot, like so many of its municipal brethren, be called a dozing company; indeed it has a reputation for a quality of a somewhat opposite kind. All over the long tables that extend through the hall, which is of considerable size, and piled up in tall heaps on the floor, are canvas bales or bags innumerable. This is the 22d of November. The doors are locked as yet, but will be opened presently for a novel scene. The clock strikes, wide asunder start the gates, and in they come, a whole army of porters, darting hither and thither, and seizing the said bags, in many instances as big as themselves. Before we can well understand what is the matter, men and bags have alike vanished—the hall is clear; another hour or two, and the contents of the latter will be flying along railways, east, west, north, and south; yet another day, and they will be dispersed throughout every city and town, and parish and hamlet of England; the curate will be glancing over the pages of his little book to see what promotions have taken place in the church, and sigh as he thinks of rectories, and deaneries, and bishoprics; the sailor will be deep in the mysteries of tides and new moons that are learnedly expatiated upon in the pages of his; the believer in the stars will be finding new draughts made upon that Bank of Faith, impossible to be broken or made bankrupt—his superstition as he turns over the pages of his Moore—but we have let out our secret. Yes, they are all *almanacs*—those bags contained nothing but almanacs: Moore's and Partridge's, and Ladies' and Gentlemen's, and Goldsmiths', and Clerical, and White's celestial, or astronomical, and gardening almanacs—the last, by the way, a new one of considerable promise and we hardly know how many others. It is even so. The—at one time—printers and publishers of everything, Bibles, prayer-books, school-books, religion, divinity, politics, poetry, philosophy, history, have become at last publishers only of these almanacs and 'prognostications,' which once served but to eke out the small means of their poorer members. And even in almanacs they have no longer a monopoly. Hundreds of competitors are in the field. And, notwithstanding, the Stationers are a thriving company. In the general progress of literature, the smallest and humblest of its departments has become so important as to support in vigorous prosperity, in spite of a most vigorous opposition, the company, in which all literature—in a trading sense—was at one time centered and monopolised!'

It is not necessary here to enter into the history of almanacs, a subject which has already been thoroughly discussed in the introduction to this work. We may remark, nevertheless, that till a comparatively recent period, the general subject-matter of which the majority of almanacs was composed, reflected little credit, either on the general progress of the nation in intelligence, or the renowned company by whom these books were supplied. The gross superstitions and even indecencies which disfigured *Poor Robin's Almanac*, and the predictions and other absurdities of the publications bearing the names of Partridge and Moore, continued to flourish with unimpaired vigour up to 1828. In that year, the Society for the Diffusion of Useful Knowledge issued in the *British Almanac* a quiet protest against the worthless pabulum hitherto supplied to the public. This new work both found extended favour with the public, and produced a signal reform in most of the popular almanacs. In the following year, *Poor Robin* disappeared altogether from the stage; a great portion of the astrology which pervaded the other almanacs was retrenched; and since that period the publications of the Stationers' Company have kept pace with the growing requirements and improved tastes of the age.

## LONDON STREET NOMENCLATURE.

The sponsors of Old London performed their duties more conscientiously than most of their successors; as a consequence, the names of the older streets of the capital serve not only as keys to their several histories, but as landmarks by which we can measure the changes wrought by time in the topographical features of the city. The streams which once murmured pleasantly near the abodes of the Londoners have long since been degraded into sewers, but their memory is preserved in the streets of Fleet, Walbrook, and Holborn (from the Saxon *Hulbourne*, the stream at the foot of the hill), and the parish of St Marylebone—a corruption of St Mary-le-bourne. The favourite trysting-places of the youthful citizens, the wells to which they flocked in the sweet summer-time, have left their names to Clerkenwell, Holywell Street, Bridewell, and Monkwell Street; as the mineral springs have to Spa-fields and Bagnigge Wells Road. The wall that encompassed the city has disappeared, with all its gates, but London Wall, Aldgate, Aldersgate, Moorgate, Bishopsgate, Newgate, Cripplegate, and Ludgate, are still familiar words. Barbican marks the site of the ancient burgh-kenning or watch-tower. Covent Garden and Hatton Garden remind us that trees bore fruit and flowers once bloomed in these now stony precincts, while Vine Street (the site of the vineyard of the royal palace at Westminster), and Vinegar Yard, Drury Lane (originally Vine-garden Yard), speak of the still more distant day when the grape was cultivated successfully in town.

Cheapside was the principal market or chepe in London; the fish-market was held in Fish Street, the herb-market in Grass (Grace) Church Street, corn-dealers congregated in Cornhill, bakers in Bread Street, and dairymen in Milk Street. Friday Street takes its name from a fish-market opened there on Fridays. Goldsmith's Row, Silver Street, Hosier Street, Cordwainer Street (now Bow Lane), and the Poultry, were inhabited respectively by goldsmiths, silversmiths, stocking-sellers, bootmakers, and poulterers. Garlick Hill was famous for its garlic. In Sermon, or Shermonier's Lane, dwelt the cutters of the metal to be coined into pence. Ave-Maria Lane, Creed Lane, and Paternoster Row, were occupied principally by the writers and publishers of books containing the alphabet, aves, creeds, and paternosters. Cloth-fair was the resort of drapers and clothiers, and the Haymarket justified its name until 1830, when the market was removed to another quarter.

Till a few years ago, the Northumberland lion still looked over Charing Cross, and a peer of the realm resided in Islington; yet no one would look for a duke in Clerkenwell, or expect to find aristocratic mansions just out of the lord mayor's jurisdiction. Such associations were not always incongruous, the town-houses of the Earls of Aylesbury and the Dukes of Newcastle stood on the ground now occupied by Aylesbury and Newcastle Streets, Clerkenwell; Devonshire House did not give way to the square of that name (Bishopsgate Without) till the year 1690, and in earlier times the kingmaker feasted his dependents where Warwick Lane abuts on Newgate Street. Succumbing to fashion's constant cry of 'Westward ho!' the old mansions of the nobility have been pulled down one by one, bequeathing their names to the houses erected on their sites. To this aristocratic migration London owes its squares of Bedford, Berkeley, Leicester, and Salisbury, and the streets rejoicing in the high-sounding names of Exeter, Grafton, Newport, Albemarle, Montague, Arundel, Argyll, Brooke, Burleigh, Chesterfield, and Coventry. Clare-market tells where the town-house of the Earls of Clare stood. Essex Street (Strand) takes its name from the mansion of Elizabeth's ill-fated favourite; Dorset Court (Fleet Street), from that of the poetical earl; and Scotland Yard marks the site of the lodging used by the kings of Scotland and their ambassadors. Bangor Court (Shoe Lane), Durham Street (Strand), Bonner's Fields, Ely Place (Holborn), and York Buildings (Strand) are called after long-vanished episcopal palaces. The religious houses of the Dominican, Augustine, White and Crouched Friars, have their memory preserved in Blackfriars, Austin-friars, Whitefriars, and Crutched-friars. Mincing-lane derived its name from certain tenements belonging to the nuns or *minchuns* of St Helen, and Spitalfields took its appellation from the neighbouring priory of St Mary Spital.

Euston Square, Fitzroy Square, Russell Square, Tavistock Street, Portland Place, and Portman Square, are named after the titles of the ground-landlords; one celebrated nobleman has thus commemorated both name and dignity in George Street, Villiers Street, Duke Street, Of Alley, and Buckingham Street. Woburn Square, Eaton Square, and Ecclestown Street, Pimlico, were named after the country-seats of the landowners who built them. Sometimes street names have been conferred in compliment to individuals more or less famous. Charles, King, and Henrietta Streets, Covent Garden, and Queen's Street, Lincoln's Inn Fields, were so styled in honour of Charles I. and his consort; Charles Street, James Square, was named after the Merry Monarch; York and James Streets (Covent Garden), after his brother. Rupert Street (Haymarket) was so designated after fiery Rupert of the Rhine; Princes Street, Wardour Street, after James I.'s eldest son, whose military garden occupied a portion of the site; Nassau Street, Soho, was so called in compliment to William III.; Queen's Square (Bloomsbury), after Caroline, consort of George II.; and Hanover Square in honour of George I. Later still, we have Regent Street, King William Street, Adelaide Street, with Victoria and Albert Streets without number. Theobald's Road was James I.'s route to his Hertfordshire hunting-seat; King's Road, Chelsea, George III.'s favourite road to Kew. The famous 'Mr Harley,' afterwards Earl of Oxford, gave Oxford Street its name; Denzil Street (Clare Market) was called after one of the five members whose attempted arrest by Charles I. was the commencement of the momentous struggle between King and Commons. The list of 'In Memoriam' streets is a long one; among them are Greville Street, Holborn—from Fulke Greville, the friend of Sir Philip Sidney; Hans Place and Sloane Street—after Sir Hans Sloane, Lord of Chelsea Manor, whose library formed the nucleus of the British Museum; Southampton Street, Strand—in honour of Lady Rachel Russell, the model wife, who was a daughter of the Earl of Southampton; Suffolk Street, Southwark—after Brandon, the earl of that name, who married Henry VIII.'s sister, Mary; Stafford Row, Pimlico—from Lord Stafford, one of Oates's victims; Throgmorton Street—from Sir Nicholas Throgmorton, said to have been poisoned by the Earl of Leicester; Hare Court Temple—after Sir N. Hare, Master of the Rolls in the reign of Elizabeth; Cumberland Street and Gate—after the victor of Culloden Field. Literary celebrities come in for but a small share of brick-and-mortar compliments. Mrs Montagu, the authoress, lives in Montagu Place (Portman Square); Killigrew, the wit, has given his name to a court in Scotland Yard; and Milton has received the doubtful compliment of having the notorious Grub Street of the Dunciad days re-dedicated to him. The founder of the Foundling Hospital is justly commemorated in Great Coram Street; and Lamb, the charitable cloth-worker, who built a conduit at Holborn in 1577, has his munificence recorded in Lamb's Conduit Street. Downing Street takes its name from Sir George Downing, secretary to the treasury in 1667; and the once fashionable Bond Street was called after Henrietta Maria's comptroller of the household. Barton Booth, the Cato of Addison's tragedy, has left his name in Barton Street, Westminster; the adjacent Cowley Street, being called after his birthplace. These are not the only thoroughfares connected with the drama; the site of the old Fortune Theatre is marked by Playhouse Yard (Central Street); and that of the Red Bull Theatre, by Red Bull Yard (St John's Street Row). Globe Alley and Rose Alley are mementoes of those famous playhouses; while the Curtain Theatre is represented by the road of that name. Apollo Court, Fleet Street, reminds us of Jonson's glorious sons of Apollo. Spring Gardens (Charing Cross) was a favourite resort of pleasure-seekers in Pepy's time, but nought but its name is left now to recall its fame, a fate that has befallen its rival Vauxhall.

Old Street was the old highway to the north-eastern parts of the country. Knight Rider Street was the route of knights riding to take part in the Smithfield tournaments. Execution Dock, Wapping, was the scene of the last appearance of many a bold pirate and salt-water thief. Bowl Yard (St Giles's) was the spot where criminals were presented with a bowl of ale on their way to Tyburn. Finsbury and Moorfields were originally fens and moors; Houndsditch was an open ditch noted for the number of dead dogs cast into it; Shoreditch was known as Soersditch long before the goldsmith's frail wife existed. Paul's Chain owes its name to a chain or barrier that used to be drawn across St Paul's Churchyard, to insure quietness during the hours of divine worship. The Great and Little Turnstiles were originally closed by revolving barriers, in order to keep the cattle pastured in Lincoln's Inn Fields from straying into Holborn. The Sanctuary (Westminster) was once what its name implies. The Birdcage-Walk (St James's Park) derived its name from an aviary formed by James I. The aristocratic neighbourhood of May Fair is so called from the annual fair of St James, which was held there till the year 1809.

Corruption has done its work with street-names. The popular love of abbreviation has transformed the Via de Alwych (the old name for Drury Lane) into Wych Street, and Guthrum into Gutter Lane, while vulgar mispronunciation has altered Desmond into Deadman's Place, Sidon into Sything and Seething Lane, Candlewick into Cannon Street, Strypes Court (named after the historian's father) into Tripe Court, St Olave's into Tooley Street, Golding into Golden Square, Birchover into Birchin Lane, Blanche-Appleton into Blind-chapel Court, and Knightenguild Lane (so called from tenements pertaining to the knighten-guild created by Edgar the Saxon) into Nightingale Lane. Battersea figures in Domesday Book as Patricesy, passing to its present form through the intermediate ones of Baltrichsey and Battersey; Chelsea, known to the Saxons as Cealchythe, and to Sir Thomas More as Chelcith, is, according to Norden, 'so called from the nature of the place, whose strand is like the chesel, cœsel or cesol, which the sea casteth up, of sand and pebble stones, thereof called Cheselsey, briefly Chelsey.' In the fourteenth century, Kentish-town was known as Kaunteloe; Lambeth assumes the various shapes of Lamedh, Lamhee, Lamheth, and Lambyth; Stepney was once Stebenhede, and afterwards Stebonhethe; Islington took the form of Isendune, Iseldon or Eyseldon; Kensington was Chenesitune, and Knightsbridge appears in the reign of Edward III. as 'the town of Knighbrigg.' Other changes have been wrought by mere caprice. There may have been reasons for converting Petty France into New Broad Street, Dirty Street into Abingdon Street, Stinking Lane, otherwise Chick Lane, otherwise Blow-bladder Lane, otherwise Butcher-hall Lane, into King Edward Street, Knave's Acre into Poultney Street, Duck Lane into Duke Street, and Pedlar's Acre into Belvedere Road; but Cato Street (the scene of Thistlewood's conspiracy), Monmouth Street (celebrated for its frippery and second-hand garments), Dyot Street, and Shire Lane (which marked the line of boundary between the city and the county), might well have been left in possession of these old names; nothing has been gained by re-christening them Homer Street, Dudley Street, George Street, and Lower Scarle's Place.

---

# DECEMBER 20.

St Philogonius, bishop of Antioch, confessor, 322. St Paul of Latrus, or Latra, hermit, 956.

---

*Born.*—John Wilson Croker, reviewer and miscellaneous writer, 1780, *Galway*.

*Died.*—Ignatius, bishop of Antioch, martyred at Rome, 107 A.D.; Bernard de Montfaucon, French antiquary, 1741; Louis the Dauphin, father of Louis XVI., 1765; Thomas Hill, patron of literary men, and prototype of *Paul Pry*, 1840, *Adelphi, London*.

## THE SUPPRESSION OF STAGE-PLAYS.

On December 20, 1649, 'some stage-players in St John Street were apprehended by troopers, their clothes taken away, and themselves carried to prison.'—*Whitelocke's Memorials*.

When England was torn by civil strife, the drama had a hard struggle for existence. Its best supporters had more serious matters to attend to, and while its friends were scattered far and wide, its foes were in authority, and wielded their newly-won power without mercy. When the civil war broke out, one of the first acts of parliament was the issuing, in September 1642, of the following:

'*Ordinance of the Lords and Commons concerning Stage-plays.*

Whereas the distressed estate of Ireland, steeped in her own blood, and the distracted estate of England, threatened with a cloud of blood by a civil war, call for all possible means to appease and avert the wrath of God appearing in these judgments; amongst which fasting and prayer, having been often tried to be very effectual, have been lately, and are still, enjoined; and whereas public sports do not well agree with public calamities, nor public stage-plays with the seasons of humiliation, this being an exercise of sad and pious solemnity, and the other being spectacles of pleasure too commonly expressing lascivious mirth and levity; it is therefore thought fit, and ordered by the Lords and Commons in this Parliament assembled, that while these sad causes and set times of humiliation do continue, public stage-plays shall cease and be forborne. Instead of which are recommended to the people of this land the profitable and seasonable consideration of repentance, reconciliation, and peace with God, which probably will produce outward peace and prosperity, and bring again times of joy and gladness to these nations.'

It was not to be expected that this unwelcome ordinance would be submitted to in silence. *The Actors' Remonstrance* soon appeared, complaining of the inconsistency of parliament in closing well-governed theatres, used only by the best of the nobility and gentry, while it permitted the bear-gardens to remain unmolested, patronised, as they were, by boisterous butchers, cutting cobblers, hard-handed masons, and the like riotous disturbers of the public peace; and gave uncontrolled allowance to puppet-shows. After defending the play-houses against sundry charges of their assailants, the pamphleteer promises, on behalf of the poor disrespected players, that if they are re-invested in their houses, they will not admit any female whatsoever unless accompanied by her husband or some near relative; that they will reform the abuses in tobacco, and allow none to be sold, even in the threepenny galleries, except the pure Spanish leaf; that all ribaldry shall be expelled the stage; and for the actors, 'we will so demean ourselves as none shall esteem us of the ungodly, or have cause to repine at our actions or interludes; we will not entertain any comedian that shall speak his part in a tone as if he did it in derision of some of the pious, but reform all our disorders and amend all our amisses.'

The author of *Certain Propositions offered to the Consideration of the Honourable Houses of Parliament*, advises that (as there must necessarily be amusements at Christmas, whether parliament likes it or not) the authorities should declare they merely intended to reform, and not abolish the actor's calling, and to that end confine the plots of plays to scriptural subjects. He is evidently a royalist, and satirically suggests: 'Joseph and his brethren would make the ladies weep; that of David and his troubles would do pretty well for the present; and, doubtless, Susannah and the elders would be a scene that would take above any that were ever yet presented. It would not be amiss, too, if, instead of the music that plays between the acts, there were only a psalm sung for distinction sake. This might be easily brought to pass, if either the court playwriters be commanded to read the Scriptures, or the city Scripture-readers be commanded to write plays.'

One half-serious argument used in favour of re-opening the theatres was that, by so doing, the ranks of the royal army would be materially weakened. Most of the leading actors of the day had, in fact, exchanged their stage-foils for weapons of a deadlier sort. Prince Rupert's regiment had in its ranks three of the most popular representatives of feminine parts—Burt being a cornet, Hart a lieutenant, and Shatterel quartermaster. Mohun became captain in another regiment; and Allen of the Cockpit was quartermaster-general at Oxford. Other players contrived, spite of the law, to eke out a precarious living by practising their profession by stealth. In 1644, the sheriffs dispersed an audience assembled at the Salisbury Court Theatre to witness Beaumont and Fletcher's *King and No King;* but the poor players still found such encouragement in defying the law, that a second ordinance was issued, instructing the civic authorities to seize all actors found plying their trade, and commit them to the common jail, to be sent to the sessions, and punished as rogues. This proving inefficacious, in 1647 a more stringent act was passed, by which it was enacted 'that all stage-players, and players of interludes, and common plays are, and shall be, taken for rogues, whether they be wanderers or no, and notwithstanding any licence whatsoever from the king, or any other person or persons, to that purpose.' The lord mayor, the sheriffs, and the justices of the peace were ordered to have all galleries, boxes, and seats, in any building used for theatrical representations, at once pulled down and demolished. A fine of five shillings was inflicted upon any person attending such illegal performances, all money taken at the doors was to be confiscated for the benefit of the poor of the parish; and last, but not least, any player caught in the act was to be publicly whipped, and compelled to find sureties for future good-behaviour. If he dared to offend a second time, he was to be considered an incorrigible rogue, 'and dealt with as an incorrigible rogue ought to be.'

For a time parliament seems to have attained its object in completely suppressing the drama, but as soon as the war was over, the actors who had passed through it unscathed returned to their old haunts; and these waifs and strays of the various old companies, uniting their forces in the winter of 1648, obtained possession of the *Cockpit* in Drury Lane, and attempted, in a quiet way, to supply the town with its favourite recreation. For a few days they were allowed to act without interference, but one afternoon, during the performance of *The Bloody Brother*, a troop of soldiers entered the house, turned the disappointed playgoers out, and carried the actors to prison in their stage-clothes. To prevent further infraction of the law, a provost-marshal was appointed, who was expressly instructed to seize all ballad-singers, and suppress all stage-plays.

Under the Protectorate, this stringency seems to have been relaxed. Plays were acted privately a little way out of town, and at Christmas and Bartholomew-tide, the players managed, by a little bribery, to have performances at the Red Bull, in St John Street. Friendly noblemen, too, often allowed them to make use of their houses; Goffe, the woman-actor of the Blackfriars theatre, being employed to notify the time and place to all persons whom it might concern. As soon as Cromwell was dead, and the signs of the time gave augury of a restoration of the monarchy, the players grew bolder. Several plays were acted at the above-mentioned theatre in 1659, and by June 1660, the Cockpit was again opened by Rhodes, and the Salisbury Court Theatre by Beeston. When Charles was fairly seated on the throne, the drama was soon legalised by the granting of two patents, one to Sir W. Davenant, and the king's servants at Drury Lane, and the other to Killigrew and the duke's servants at Dorset Gardens—and so ended the puritanical suppression of stage-plays.

In the reign of Elizabeth, somewhere about the year 1580, there had been a partial suppression of theatres. Certain 'godly citizens and well-disposed gentlemen of London,' brought such a pressure to bear upon the city magistrates, that the latter petitioned her majesty to expel all players from London, and permit them to destroy every theatre within their jurisdiction. Their prayer was granted, and the several playhouses in Gracechurch Street, Bishopsgate Street, Whitefriars, Ludgate Hill, and near St Paul's, 'were quite put down and suppressed by these religious senators.' The houses outside the city-boundaries were, fortunately, in no way molested, or English literature would have been the poorer by some of Shakspeare's greatest works.

Whenever the plague made its appearance in London, the drama went to the wall; and as long as it stayed in town, the players were forced to be idle. Sir Henry Herbert's office-book contains the following memorandum:

'On Thursday morning the 23d of February, the bill of the plague made the number of forty-four, upon which decrease the king gave the players their liberty, and they began the 24th February 1636.

'The plague increasing, the players lay still until the 2d of October, when they had leave to play.'

Of course the closing of the theatres was rigidly enjoined during the Great Plague, but the court was only too glad to seize the earliest opportunity of opening them again. Pepys says, in his *Diary*, under date 20th November 1666.—'To church, it being Thanksgiving-day for the cessation of the plague; but the town do say, that it is hastened before the plague is quite over, there being some people still ill of it; but only to get ground of plays to be publicly acted, which the bishops would not suffer till the plague was over.'

---

## A FLYING SHIP IN 1709.

In No. 56 of the *Evening Post*, a newspaper published in the reign of Queen Anne, and bearing date 20–22d December 1709, we find the following curious description of a *Flying Ship*, stated to have been lately invented by a Brazilian priest, and brought under the notice of the king of Portugal in the following address, translated from the Portuguese:

'Father Bartholomew Laurent says that he has found out an Invention, by the Help of which one may more speedily travel through the Air than any other Way either by Sea or Land, so that one may go 200 Miles in 24 Hours; send Orders and Conclusions of Councils to Generals, in a manner, as soon as they are determined in private Cabinets; which will be so much the more Advantageous to your Majesty, as your Dominions lie far remote from one another, and which for want of Councils cannot be maintained nor augmented in Revenues and Extent.

Merchants may have their Merchandize, and send Letters and Packets more conveniently. Places besieged may be Supply'd with Necessaries and Succours. Moreover, we may transport out of such Places what we please, and the Enemy cannot hinder it:

The Portuguese have Discovered unknown Countries bordering upon the Extremity of the Globe: And it will contribute to their greater Glory to be Authors of so Admirable a Machine, which so many nations have in vain attempted.

Many Misfortunes and Shipwrecks have happened for want of Maps, but by this Invention the Earth will be more exactly Measur'd than ever, besides many other Advantages worthy of your Majesty's Encouragement.

But to prevent the many Disorders that may be occasioned by the Usefulness of this Machine, Care is to be taken that the Use and full Power over the same be committed to one Person only, to whom your Majesty will please to give a strict Command, that whoever shall presume to transgress the Orders herein mentioned shall be Severely punished.

May it please your Majesty to grant your humble Petitioner the Priviledge that no Person shall presume to Use, or make this Ship, without the Express Licence of the Petitioner, and his Heirs, under the Penalty of the loss and Forfeiture of all his Lands and Goods, so that one half of the same may belong to the Petitioner, and the other to the Informer. And this to be executed throughout all your Dominions upon the Transgressors, without Exception or Distinction of Persons, who likewise may be declared liable to an Arbitrary punishment, &c.'

Of this much-vaunted invention an engraving is

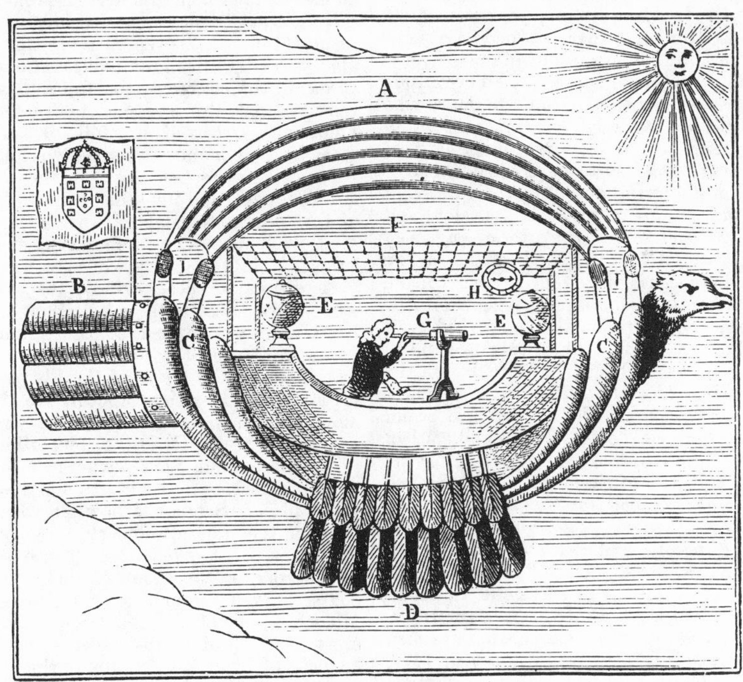


THE FLYING SHIP.

given in the same newspaper, and is here presented to the reader, who may probably be equally amused by the figure delineated, and the explanation of its uses, as subjoined.

*An Explanation of the Figure.*

A. *Represents the Sails wherewith the Air is to be divided, which turn as they are directed.*

B. *The Stern to govern the Ship, that She may not run at random.*

C. *The Body of the Ship which is formed at both ends Scollopwise; in the concavity of Each is a pair of Bellows, which must be blown when there is no Wind.*

D. *Two Wings which keep the Ship upright.*

E. *The Globes of Heaven and Earth containing in them Attractive Virtues. They are of Metal, and serve for a Cover to two Loadstones, placed in them upon the Pedestals, to draw the Ship after them, the Body of which is of Thin Iron Plates, covered with Straw Mats, for conveniency of* 10 *or* 11 *men besides the Artist.*

F. *A cover made of Iron Wire in form of a Net, on which are Fastened a good number of Large Amber Beads, which by a Secret Operation will help to keep the Ship Aloft. And by the Sun's heat the aforesaid Mats that line the Ship will be drawn towards the Amber Beads.*

G. *The Artist who by the help of the Celestial Globe, a Sea Map, and Compass, takes the Height of the Sun, thereby to find out the spot of Land over which they are on the Globe of the Earth.*

H. *The Compass to direct them in their Way.*

I. *The Pulleys and Ropes that serve to hoist or Furl the Sails.*

This extraordinary aërial locomotive is perhaps one of the most curious of these apparatuses for the purpose of flying, of which we find numerous instances from the middle ages downwards. A more extended knowledge of the laws of gravity, and the relations subsisting between us and the atmosphere surrounding our globe, has induced us to discard all such attempts at emulating the powers of the feathered tribes of creation as chimerical. By means of balloons, indeed, first made available by Montgolfier in the latter half of the eighteenth century, we have been enabled to overcome, in a limited degree, the obstacles which prevent us from soaring above the surface of the earth. But it is very significant, that whilst in all other means of locomotion we have made such rapid strides within the last hundred years, the science of aëronautics has advanced little beyond the point which it attained in the days of our grandfathers.

In connection with this subject, we may allude to a well-known story of an Italian charlatan who visited Scotland in the reign of James IV., and insinuated himself so successfully into the good graces of that monarch, as to be created abbot of Tungland. The following account of his proceedings is thus quaintly given by Bishop Lesley, and quoted by Mr Wilson in his *Prehistoric Annals of Scotland*. 'He causet the king believe that he, be multiplyinge and utheris his inventions, wold make fine golde of uther metall, quhilk science he callit the quintassence; quhairupon the king maid greit cost, bot all in vaine. This Abbott tuik in hand to flie with wingis, and to be in Fraunce befoir the saidis ambassadouris; and to that effect he causet mak ane pair of wingis of fedderis, quhilkis beand fessenit apoun him, he flew of the Castell wall of Striveling [Stirling], bot shortlie he fell to the ground and brak his thee-bane. *Bot the wyt* [blame] *thairof he ascryvit to that thair was sum hen fedderis in the wingis, quhilk yarnit and covet the mydding* [dunghill] *and not the skyis.*' How far this very philosophical mode of accounting for the failure of his project was successful in maintaining his credit with James we are not informed, but we opine it were but a sorry solace for a broken limb. It is a little curious that, in the year 1777, a similar experiment is recorded to have been made at Paris, on a convict from the galleys. The man was surrounded with whirls of feathers, curiously interlaced, and extending gradually at suitable distances, in a horizontal direction from his feet to his neck. Thus accoutred, he was let down from a height of seventy Paris feet, descended slowly, and fell on his feet uninjured, in the presence of an immense body of spectators. He complained of a feeling like sea-sickness, but experienced no pain otherwise.

## THE COMMONWEALTH OF HADES.

The aberrations of the human intellect have, perhaps, never assumed more extraordinary forms than in the history of magic and witchcraft. The belief in demons has existed in all ages of known history, and among the pagan peoples, it was almost a more important part of the vocation of the priesthood to control the evil spirits than to conduct the worship of the beneficent deities; at all events, it was that ascribed faculty which gave them the greatest influence over their ignorant votaries. The introduction of Christianity did not discourage the belief in demons, but, on the contrary, it was the means of greatly increasing their numbers. Not only were the multiform spirits of the then popular creeds, such as satyrs, wood-nymphs, elves, &c., accepted as demons, but all the false gods of the pagans were placed in the same category, and thus was introduced into medieval magic a host of names of individual demons, taken from all countries, to the effect, necessarily, of creating very confused ideas on a subject which, in the olden time, had been tolerably clear even to the vulgar. When the learned men of the middle ages began to take demonology into their hands, they sought to reduce this confusion into order by arranging and classifying, and they soon produced an elaborate system of orders and ranks, and turned the infernal regions into a regular monarchy, modelled upon the empires of this world, with offices and dignities imitated from the same pattern. It was in the course of the fifteenth and sixteenth century that this system of a demoniacal commonwealth received its full development; and men like Johannes Wierus, who published his *Pseudomonarchia Dæmonum* in the latter of these two centuries, and the other writers of his class and of that period, were able to give a minute account of all its details. They are amusing enough, and the subject is, in many points of view, very interesting.

According to these writers, the emperor of the demons was Belzebuth or Belzebub. He is said to have been worshipped by the people of Canaan under the form of a fly, and hence he is said to have founded the Order of the Fly; the only order of knighthood which appears to have existed among the demons. When these writers became acquainted with Hades, a revolution had taken place there, and Satan, who had formerly been monarch, had been dethroned and Belzebub raised to his place. Satan had now placed himself at the head of the opposition party. Among the great princes were: 1. Eurynome, prince of death, and grand-cross of the order of the Fly. He was of course taken from the Greek mythology.—2. Moloch, prince of the country of tears, also grand-cross of the order, and member of the imperial council of state.—3. Pluto, prince of fire, and superintendent of the infernal punishments.—4. Leonard, grand-master of the Sabbaths, and inspector-general of magic and sorcery. He was a knight of the order of the Fly, and appeared often as a black man or negro.—5. Baalberith, 'master of the alliances,' and, according to some, secretary-general, and keeper of the archives of hell. The four previous named princes were demons of the first order; Baalberith was only of the second. —6. Proserpine, archduchess of Hades, and sovereign princess of the evil spirits.

The ministers of state of Belzebuth's court were: 1. Adramelec, grand-chancellor, and grand-cross of the order of the Fly.—2. Astaroth, grand-treasurer. 3. Nergal, chief of the secret police.—4. Baal, general-in-chief of the armies, and grand-cross of the order of the Fly.—5. Leviathan, grand-admiral, and knight of the Fly.

Belzebuth had his ambassadors also, and their different appointments were, perhaps, intended to convey a little satire on the different countries to which they were sent. They were: 1. To France, Belphegor, an unclean demon, who often appeared in the form of a young woman; he was the demon of discoveries and ingenious inventions, and gave riches.—2. To England, Mammon, the demon of avarice, and the inventor of mining for metals.—3. To Turkey, Belial, one of the most vicious of all the demons.—4. To Russia, Rimmon, who was the chief physician at the court of Belzebuth.—5. To Spain, Thammuz, who was the inventor of artillery. —6. To Italy, Hutgin, a familiar demon, who took pleasure in obliging people.—7. To Switzerland, Martinet, who was especially familiar with magicians, and assisted travellers who had lost their way.

Among other high officers were, Lucifer, who was grand-justiciary and minister of justice; and Alastor, who held the distinguished office of executioner. The officers of the household of the princes were: Verdelet, master of the ceremonies, whose duty it was to convey the witches to the Sabbath; Succor Benoth, chief of the eunuchs, and the demon of jealousy; Chamos, grand-chamberlain, and the demon of flattery—he was knight of the Fly; Melchom, treasurer and payer of the public servants; Nisroch, chief of the kitchen; Behemoth, grand-cupbearer; Dagon, master of the pantry; and Mullin, principal valet-de-chambre. There were also certain ministers or officers of the privy-purse of Belzebuth, such as Kobal, director of the theatres, who was in this world the patron of comedians; Asmodeus, the superintendent of the gambling-houses; Nybbas, the grand-parodist, and who had also the management of dreams and visions; and Antichrist, who was the great juggler and necromancer of the shades.

With a court so complicated in its arrangements, and numerous in its officers, we might, perhaps, like to know what was the population of Belzebuth's empire. Wierus has not left us without full information, for he tells us that there are in hell, 6666 legions of demons, each legion composed of 6666 demons, which, therefore, makes the whole number amount to 44,435,556.

Whoever wishes for further information, need only have recourse to Johannes Wierus, and he may obtain as much as he can possibly desire. It must not be forgotten that these statements were at one time fully believed in by men of education and intellect.

## DECEMBER 21.

St Thomas, apostle. St Edburge, virgin, 9th century.

### St Thomas's Day

The festival of St Thomas was instituted in the twelfth century, and, as an old author alleges, was assigned an early place in the ecclesiastical calendar from this apostle having been vouchsafed the most indisputable evidence of the resurrection. In pictorial art, St Thomas is represented holding a builder's square, and in accordance with the following legend, he is regarded as the patron saint of architects and builders.—When St Thomas was at Cæsarea, our Lord appeared unto him, and said: 'The king of the Indies, Gondoforus, hath sent his provost, Abanes, to seek for workmen well versed in the science of architecture, who shall build for him a palace finer than that of the emperor at Rome. Behold now, I will send thee to him.' And St Thomas went, and Gondoforus commanded him to build a magnificent palace, and gave him much gold and silver for the purpose. The king went to a distant country, and was absent for two years; and St Thomas, meanwhile, instead of building a palace, distributed all the treasures intrusted to him among the poor and sick; and when the king returned he was full of wrath, and commanded that St Thomas should be seized and cast into prison, while he meditated for him a horrible death. Meantime, the brother of the king died, and the king resolved to erect for him a magnificent tomb; but the dead man, after that he had been dead four days, suddenly rose, sat upright, and said to the king: 'The man whom thou wouldst torture is a servant of God; behold, I have been in Paradise, and the angels shewed unto me a wondrous palace of gold, silver, and precious stones; and they said: This is the palace that Thomas the architect has built for thy brother King Gondoforus.' And when the king heard those words, he ran to the prison, and delivered the apostle, and then St Thomas said to him: 'Knowest thou not that they who would possess heavenly things have little care for the goods of this world? There are in heaven rich palaces without number, which were prepared from the beginning of the world for those who purchase the possession thereof through faith and charity. Thy riches, O king, may prepare thy way to such a place, but they cannot follow thee thither.' Like many other of the old saintly legends, this was never meant or assumed to be a matter-of-fact relation, but simply a parable or religious fiction, invented for the instruction of the people, and rendered the more impressive and striking by an exalted apostle being made the hero of the tale.

It is said that after the dispersion of the apostles, St Thomas preached the gospel to the Medes, Persians, Bactrians, Ethiopians, and Indians, among the latter of whom he suffered martyrdom at Melapoor, and was buried in a church, which he had caused to be erected in that city. Marco Polo, who travelled in the thirteenth century, says: 'In that province of Malabar, is the body of the glorious martyr St Thomas, the apostle, who there suffered martyrdom. It rests in a small city, not frequented by many merchants, because unsuited for the purposes of commerce; but, from devotional motives, a vast number both of Christians and Saracens resort thither. The Christians who perform this pilgrimage collect earth, which is of a red colour, from the spot where he was slain, and reverentially carry it away with them, often employing it afterwards in miracles, and giving it with water to the sick, by which many disorders are cured. A variety of miracles are daily performed at the tomb of St Thomas, through the interposition of the blessed apostle.'

Sir John Mandeville, in his travels, describes the

same country as 'a great kingdom containing many fair cities and towns. In that kingdom lies the body of St Thomas the apostle in flesh and bone, in a fair tomb, in the city of Calamy; for there he was martyred and buried. But men of Assyria carried his body into Mesopotamia, into the city of Edessa; and afterwards he was brought thither again. And the arm and the hand that he put to our Lord's side, when he appeared to him after his resurrection, is yet lying in a vessel without the tomb. By that hand they there make all their judgments. For, when there is any dissension between two parties, and each of them maintains his own cause, both parties write their causes on two bills, and put them in the hand of St Thomas; and, anon, the hand casts away the bill of the wrong cause, and holds still the bill with the right cause, and therefore men come from far countries to have judgments of doubtful causes.' The accompanying engraving, from an illumination in an ancient manuscript of Mandeville's travels, preserved in the Bibliothèque Imperiale of Paris, represents the judgment of St Thomas. And if the story be considered incredible, the writer can only quote Mandeville's own lines addressed to unbelievers thus:

'If scanty be my laud and praise,
And witless folk should call me liar,
For that my book contains strange lays,
I will not storm nor burst with ire.
Let him who credits not my tales,
Travel as far as I have been,
Then, may he tell if truth prevails,
In what I say that I have seen.'

St Thomas's Day falls on the winter solstice, the shortest day in the year, as expressed in the following couplet:

'St Thomas gray, St Thomas gray,
The longest night and the shortest day.'

In some parts of the country the day is marked by a custom, among poor persons, of *going a gooding*, as it is termed—that is to say, making the round of the parish in calling at the houses of their richer neighbours, and begging a supply either of money or provisions to procure *good things*, or the means of enjoying themselves at the approaching festival of Christmas. From this circumstance St Thomas's Day is in some places designated 'Doleing Day,' and in others 'Mumping [begging] Day.' In Warwickshire, the custom under notice used to be called *going a corning*, from the poor people carrying with them a bag in which they received a contribution of corn from the farmers. By a correspondent of *Notes and Queries*, in 1857, we are informed that the custom of 'Gooding' exists in full force in Staffordshire, where not only the old women and widows, but representatives from every poor family in the parish, make their rounds in quest of alms. The clergyman is expected to give a shilling to each person, and at all houses a subsidy is looked for either in money or kind. In some parts of the same county a sum of money is collected from the wealthier inhabitants of the parish, and placed in the hands of the clergyman and churchwardens, who on the Sunday nearest to St Thomas's Day, distribute it in the vestry under the name of 'St Thomas's Dole.' We learn also from another communication of the writer just quoted, that at Harrington, in Worcestershire, it is customary for children on St Thomas's Day to go round the village begging for apples, and singing—

THE JUDGMENT OF ST THOMAS—FROM AN ILLUMINATION IN AN ANCIENT FRENCH MANUSCRIPT.

'Wassail, wassail, through the town,
If you 've got any apples, throw them down;
Up with the stocking, and down with the shoe,
If you 've got no apples, money will do;
The jug is white and the ale is brown,
This is the best house in the town.'

In return for the alms bestowed during these 'gooding' peregrinations, it was customary for the recipients, in former times, to present to their benefactors a sprig of holly or mistletoe. A liberal dole was distributed at the 'great house,' or the mansion of the principal proprietor in the parish; and at the kitchens of all the squires and farmers' houses, tankards of spiced-ale were kept for the special refection of the red-cloaked old wives who made in procession these foraging excursions on St Thomas's Day. It is said that the hospitality shewn on such occasions proved sometimes rather overpowering, and the recipients of this and other charitable benefactions found themselves occasionally wholly unable to find their way back to their own habitations, having been rendered, through the agency of John Barleycorn, as helpless as the 'Wee bit Wifikie' immortalised in Scottish song.

---

## THE 'ADVENT IMAGES' AND THE 'VESSEL-CUP.

In connection with the practice of 'going a gooding' on St Thomas's Day, described in the foregoing article, an account may here be given of a kindred custom which appears not yet to be extinct—that of the 'Advent Images.' These are two dolls, dressed the one to represent the Saviour, and the other the Virgin Mary, and during the week before Christmas they are carried about the country by poor women, who, in return for their exhibition, expect a halfpenny, which it is considered as insuring the height of ill-luck to deny. The following carol is sung on the occasion by the bearers of the images:

'The first good joy that Mary had, it was the joy of one,
To see her own son Jesus to suck at her breast-bone;
It brings tidings of comfort and joy!

The next good joy that Mary had, it was the joy of two,
To see her own son Jesus to make the lame to go.
It brings, &c.

The next good joy that Mary had, it was the joy of three,
To see her own son Jesus to make the blind to see.
It brings, &c.

The next good joy that Mary had, it was the joy of four,
To see her own son Jesus to read the Bible o'er.
It brings, &c.

The next good joy that Mary had, it was the joy of five,
To see her own son Jesus to make the dead alive.
It brings, &c.

The next good joy that Mary had, it was the joy of six,
To see her own son Jesus to bear the crucifix!
It brings, &c.

The next good joy that Mary had, it was the joy of seven,
To see her own son Jesus to wear the crown of Heaven.
It brings, &c.'

This custom is also termed going about with a 'vessel-cup,' and the performers are styled 'vessel-cup singers.' The word 'vessel-cup' is evidently a corruption for 'wassail-cup,' and denotes the wish expressed on the occasion for the health and happiness of the party who bestows his charity on the exhibitor of the images. It may here be stated that in Yorkshire only one image used to be carried about—that of the Saviour, which was placed in a box surrounded by evergreens, and such flowers as could be procured at the season. The party to whose house the figure was carried was at liberty to take from the decorations of the image a leaf or a flower, which was carefully preserved, and regarded as a sovereign remedy for the toothache! The following was one of the stanzas of the quaint old carol sung by the old women who carried the image:

'God bless the master of this house,
The mistress also,
And all the little children
That round the table go.'

Not only was it considered peculiarly unlucky to refuse the tribute claimed by the image-bearer, but it was even deemed an augury of bad fortune if any household was not visited by the 'Advent Images' before Christmas Eve at the latest. The expression, 'As unhappy as the man who has seen no Advent Images,' was at one time proverbial in Yorkshire.

---

*Born.*—Thomas Becket, archbishop of Canterbury, 1117, *London;* John Kepler, distinguished astronomer, 1571, *Weil, Würtemberg.*

*Died.*—Giovanni Boccaccio, celebrated tale-writer, 1375, *Certaldo;* Maximilien, Duke of Sully, minister of Henri IV., 1641, *Villebon;* Catherine of Braganza, queen of Charles II. of England, 1705, *Lisbon;* James Harris, author of *Hermes*, 1780; Arnauld de Berquin, author of *L'Ami des Enfants*, 1791, *Paris;* Rev. Dr Harris, author of *Mammon, The Great Teacher*, &c., 1856, *London.*

## CATHERINE OF BRAGANZA.

Many other women besides queens live miserable lives, but the insignificant possess one advantage over those nobler born—their sufferings are unobserved and uncommented on. The woman of rank is a subject for perpetual remark among those of her own class, the journals of the day keep the public well informed as to the minutest particulars of her history, and the rabble at the corners of every street shrug their shoulders as she passes.

Catherine of Braganza, the wife of Charles II., began life under favourable auspices. Reared in a palace, beautiful, possessed of ample dowry, the daughter of one king and the wife of another, loving her husband devotedly, and not herself unpleasing in his eyes, she must have cast no unhopeful glance into the future; yet at that very minute, fortune's wheel was turning. Twenty-three miserable years awaited her, each one worse and more hopeless than the one which preceded it The neglect of the king, the scorn of his mistresses, the plots of courtiers, and the laughter of the world, combined to make the childless Catherine the most wretched of all women in her own gay and dissolute court.

Queen Catherine was born on the Festival of St Catherine, the 25th of November, in the year 1638. She arrived at Portsmouth in May 1662, where Charles was waiting to receive her. The marriage-ceremony was performed privately by the archbishop of Canterbury, and also a second time, with greater secrecy, according to the Romish ritual; for the queen, who was a stanch Catholic, did not hold the first bond to be valid. After staying some weeks at Hampton Court, she made her public entry into London on the 23d of August. 'The queen,' says Evelyn, 'arrived, with a train of Portuguese ladies, in their monstrous fardingales, or guard-infantas; their complexions olivader, and sufficiently disagreeable: her majesty in the same habit; her foretop long, and turned aside very strangely. She was yet of the handsomest countenance of all the rest, and, though low of stature, prettily shaped; languishing and excellent eyes; her teeth wronging her mouth by sticking a little too far out; for the rest, lovely enough.'

Many queens have arrived in England to be hated from the first moment of their appearance, but it was not so with Catherine. Charles had not made the first advances. The king of Portugal, having with difficulty recovered his crown out of the hands of Spain, found the same difficulty in retaining possession of it. Cromwell had driven him to great straits, in revenge for assistance which he extended to Charles I. France, an old ally, had recently abandoned him. Thus, by proposing a marriage between Charles II. and the Infanta, he hoped to establish his power. On the other hand, Charles found the marriage profitable. He procured for England the possession of two important islands, and for himself the acceptable present of £500,000. All this was in the usual course of things. But the Infanta was pretty and agreeable, and a good Catholic, and Charles good-naturedly took a liking to her; and in this it was that her reception differed from that of Queen Caroline, or Anne of Cleves.

But twenty-three years of annoyance embittered the remembrance of their pleasant days. Charles, by wit and neglect, by urbanity and threats, broke her into her position; so that, from having treated his mistresses with disdain and resentment, she learned to endure them with coldness, and saw the Duchess of Cleveland a lady of the bed-chamber with patience. Despair prompted at length a sacrifice of self-respect, and she made them friends and confidantes; and finally, says Burnet, 'she went about masked, and came into houses unknown, and danced there, with a great deal of wild frolic.'

Strange to say, Charles never seems to have entertained any serious ill-feeling towards her, though we generally hate those whom we injure. He rejected, with disgust, the offer of Buckingham to carry her off to the West Indies, and procure a divorce on the plea of desertion, and despised the insinuations and charges of several who accused her of plotting with the Jesuits to take the king's life. And when he was on his death-bed, and the queen, whose grief drove her to distraction, asked pardon of her husband, if by any chance she had ever offended him, she gained at last this one poor consolation: 'Alas, poor woman,' he exclaimed, 'she beg my pardon! I beg hers with all my heart.'

Catherine survived the Revolution, remaining in England till the arrival of the Prince of Orange, and ultimately died at Lisbon on 21st December 1705.

## THE MAIMING OF SIR JOHN COVENTRY.

A strange scene was enacted in London on the night of the 21st December 1669. Near Suffolk Street were assembled fifteen or twenty of his majesty's guards, mounted and unmounted, under the command of Sir Thomas Sands and the son of the Earl of Inchiquin. From ten o'clock to two, they waited impatiently for the coming of Sir John Coventry, whom they expected to pass on his way home from the tavern at which he supped. At length he came, and divining their hostile purpose at a glance, Sir John snatched a flambeau from his servant, and drawing his sword, placed his back against the wall, and bravely defended himself with both weapons. He succeeded in disabling O'Brian and some others of his assailants, but was forced to succumb to superior numbers. After they had disarmed him, the cowardly crew threw him down, and cutting his nose to the bone, left him.

This atrocious outrage was perpetrated in accordance with the orders of the Duke of Monmouth, Coventry's professed friend; but the actual instigator was Charles II. himself. In a parliamentary committee of Ways and Means, a motion had been made: 'That towards the Supply, every one that resorts to any of the Playhouses who sits in the boxes, shall pay 1*s.*; every one who sits in the pit, shall pay 6*d.*; and every other person, 3*d.*' This was opposed by the court-party, on the ground that the players were the king's servants, and a part of his pleasure. Whereupon Sir John Coventry pertinently, but indiscreetly, asked: 'Whether the king's pleasure lay among the men or the women that acted?' This was touching Old Rowley too nearly to be pleasant, and it did not need much argument to persuade Charles, that if the offence was allowed to pass unpunished, reflections on royal weaknesses would become dangerously common. And so the king, forgetful of obligations incurred by the fugitive Charles Stuart, determined to make an example of Coventry, and carried out his resolve despite the remonstrances of his brother.

Bold Andrew Marvell could not let his pen lie idle upon such an event. In his *Instructions to a Painter*, he says:

'While the king of France with powerful arms,
Gives all his fearful neighbours strange alarms,
We, in our glorious bacchanals, dispose
The humbled fate of a plebeian nose.
Which to effect, when thus it was decreed,
Draw me a champion mounted on a steed;
And after him a brave brigade of horse
Armed at all points, ready to reinforce
His; this assault upon a single man.
* * * * *
'Tis this must make O'Brian great in story,
And add more beams to Sands's former glory.'

Parliament was furious at the indignity offered to one of its members on the very night after its adjournment, and made it the first subject for consideration upon re-assembling. The result of their deliberations was the passing of an act banishing the principal actors in the affair, with a special clause rendering them incapable of receiving the royal pardon; while to prevent a recurrence of the offence, the cutting, maiming, and disfiguring of any man was made felony without benefit of clergy, and punishable with death. The Coventry Act, as it was called, remained on the statute-book till the year 1828, when it was repealed.

It is a curious circumstance that Pepys records the fact of Sir William Coventry, uncle to Sir John, meditating, about nine months previous to the outrage on his nephew, a similar revenge to that taken by Charles. Sir William fancied that Killigrew intended to bring him upon the stage; and he accordingly gave the dramatist to understand that if any of his actors 'did offer anything like representing him, that he would not complain to my Lord Chamberlain, which was too weak, nor get him beaten as Sir Charles Sedley is said to have done, but that he would cause his nose to be slit.'

## The Halcyon Days.

The seven days preceding, and the seven days following the shortest day, or the winter-solstice, were called by the ancients the *Halcyon Days*. This phrase, so familiar as expressive of a period of tranquillity and happiness, is derived from a fable, that during the period just indicated, while the halcyon bird or king-fisher was breeding, the sea was always calm, and might be navigated in perfect security by the mariner. The name *halcyon* is derived from two Greek words—ἅλς, the sea; and κυω, to conceive; and, according to the poetic fiction, the bird was represented as hatching her eggs on a floating nest, in the midst of the waters. Dryden thus alludes to the notion:

'Amidst our arms as quiet you shall be,
As halcyons brooding on a winter's sea.'

---

# DECEMBER 22.

St Ischyrion, martyr, 253. Saints Cyril and Methodius, confessors, end of 9th century.

---

*Died.*—Emperor Vitellius, beheaded at Rome, 69 A.D.; Richard Plantagenet, alleged son of Richard III., 1550, *Eastwell, Kent;* Richard Allein, Nonconformist divine, 1681; Michael Baron, celebrated actor, 1729, *Paris;* Sir Philip Francis, reputed author of *Junius*, 1818, *London;* Dr James Cowles Prichard, distinguished ethnologist, 1848, *London;* Rev. M. J. Routh, D.D., president of Magdalen College, Oxford, in his 100th year, 1854, *Oxford.*

## THE ORIGINAL BLUEBEARD.

For more than a century and a half, Bluebeard has been a favourite melodramatic hero: favourite, that is, with those who wish to find a tyrant as a foil to some ill-used damsel or heroine; and the more savage he is, the more intense is the interest felt in the story—by boys and girls, if not by 'children of larger growth.' In this, as in some other histories, the more thoughtful readers occasionally ask—Is it true? There certainly was no real lady to say: 'Sister Anne, sister Anne, do you see anybody coming?' but nevertheless Mezeray, and other French writers, tell us of a man who really suggested to Perrault the idea for the story of *Bluebeard.*

Giles de Laval, Seigneur de Retz, better known in French history as Marshal de Retz, was born in or about the year 1396. Losing his father in 1416, Giles entered the service of his sovereign-prince, the Duc de Bretagne; and his name is found mentioned in connection with events in 1420 and 1425. He next entered the service of the French king, Charles VII., and was actively engaged in the defensive war maintained by that monarch against the English; distinguishing himself in many engagements. In 1429, he was one of the captains under the celebrated Joan of Arc; and aided her in bringing provisions into Orleans. We then hear of Giles, and his brother René, accompanying the king to Rheims; and it is supposed that Giles was on this occasion created Marshal of France, in recognition of his military merits. It was he who carried the holy *ampoule*, at the consecration of the king, from the abbey of St Remi to the cathedral. He appears also at this time to have been counsellor and chamberlain to the king. Again we hear of him commanding troops against the English in 1430 and 1433, in which last-named year his martial services appear to have terminated.

Now, there is nothing whatever in this career to denote a cruel or depraved taste: on the contrary, Giles de Laval presents himself to us as the Marshal de Retz, a man of high birth, successful as a military commander, and in high favour at the court of the king of France. Yet the French annals tell us that this man, at the age of thirty-seven, commenced the abominable course of life which has brought infamy upon his name. When twenty years of age, he had inherited large estates from his father; at twenty-four, he had married Catherine de Thouars, who brought him still larger property; and when his maternal grandfather, Jean de Craon, died in 1432, another set of estates fell to him: insomuch that Giles became the richest subject in France. This immense fortune was the grand cause of his ruin. He plunged into a course of profligacy and debauchery which diminished his wealth rapidly; and he sold one estate after another to defray his lavish expenses. He maintained a guard of honour of two hundred horsemen; and his suite, of fifty persons, comprised chaplains, choristers, musicians, pages, and *serviteurs;* most of whom were made ministers or accomplices in his acts of libertinism. Yet, withal, he affected great pomp and magnificence in religious ceremonies. His chapel was hung with cloth of gold and silk; the sacred vessels were of gold, and enriched with precious stones. His chaplains, habited in scarlet robes adorned with fur, bore the titles of dean, chanter, archdeacon, and bishop; and he even sent a deputy to the pope, to ask permission for a cross to be carried before him! These, and other extravagances, made such inroads on his wealth that he began to dispose of his estates one after another. His family, alarmed at this prodigal waste of means, in which they all had an interest, obtained a decree from the parliament of Paris, forbidding him to make any further alienations of his property.

Even at this stage we do not recognise in Giles de Retz what the world would call a monster; we see in him only a profligate spendthrift, who joined licentiousness with religious observances in a way not at all unusual in the middle ages. But the worst was approaching. Craving for wealth to supply his extravagance, he had recourse to alchemy. Failing, then, to discover the grand art of transmuting base metals into gold, he next turned his attention to magic or sorcery, under the guidance of an Englishman, named Messire Jean, and an Italian, named Francisco Prelati. He is reported to have now made a compact with Satan, offering to give, in return for boundless wealth, everything except his own life and soul: as regarded the lives and souls of others, he felt no scruple. It was at this time, according to the accounts which have descended to us, that he began to immolate children—even while fulfilling his religious duties in his chapel with careful precision. The poor little creatures, made the victims of his iniquity in various ways, were finally put to death, and their blood and hearts used as charms in diabolical rites. His myrmidons inveigled boys and girls from the neighbouring villages into his castle, and they were never afterwards seen. Other agents of his, during his tours from one to another of his castles in Bretagne, were wont to persuade poor peasants, who had beautiful children, to intrust them to the care of the marshal, who promised to attend to their advancement in life. The children were never again seen; and when outcries were made in consequence, the accomplices in De Retz's iniquities sought to stifle them by threats or bribery. This continued so long, and the number of children who disappeared became so large, that the matter came under the notice and interference of the authorities. In 1440, the marshal was arrested, together with two of his men, Henri and Etienne Corillant. Confronted with his two accomplices, Giles at first denied all knowledge of them; but a threat of the torture having alarmed him, he made what is called a 'clean breast of it' by revealing everything. The judges were frozen with horror at the obscene and atrocious recital which he made. There is no doubt as to the authenticity of the horrible transactions; and a biographer of the marshal, in the *Biographie Universelle*, states that manuscript reports of the trial (which lasted a month) exist in the Bibliothèque Imperiale at Paris, and also among the archives of the Chateau at Nantes. What the wretched young victims (who varied from eight to eighteen years of age) were made to endure before being put to death, cannot be described here. During a period of at least eight years, and at his several castles of Machecoul, Chantocé, and Tiffanges, as well as in his mansions at Nantes and Suze, were these atrocities carried on. In most cases he burned the bodies; but sufficient remains were found to indicate forty-six victims at Chantocé, and eighty at Machecoul. Giles did not boast of his atrocities; he confessed them, and publicly asked pardon of the parents of the murdered innocents. Condemned to be strangled, he exhibited once more a characteristic of his strange nature, by begging that the bishop of Nantes would head the procession which was formed on this occasion. His execution took place in 1440, about or a little before Christmas-day—some say December 22.

Probably on account of some personal peculiarity, Giles de Laval became remembered as *Barbe-bleue*, whence our *Bluebeard*. It seems to have speedily become a name of terror; for Holinshed, speaking of the committal of the Duke of Suffolk to the Tower, in the reign of Henry VI., says: 'This doing so much displeased the people, that if politic provision had not been made, great mischief had immediately ensued. For the commons, in sundry places of the realm, assembled together in great companies, and chose to them a captain, whom they called *Bluebeard;* but ere they had attempted any enterprise, their leaders were apprehended, so that the matter was pacified without any hurt committed.'

As to the children's *Bluebeard*, it was written by Perrault in the time of Louis XIV., and has been translated from the French into nearly all the languages of Europe. This Bluebeard's propensity is not to kill children, but to marry wife after wife in succession, kill them, and deposit them in the fatal closet which curiosity would not leave untouched. We all know how another victim was saved, and how Bluebeard met his death.

## RICHARD PLANTAGENET.

December 22, 1550, died a poor working-man, named Richard Plantagenet, who was believed to be a son of Richard III., king of England. The story has been preserved by Dr Thomas Brett, who saw the entry of the man's death in the parish register of Eastwell, and who, about 1720, obtained other particulars from the Earl of Winchelsea at Eastwell House.

Sir Thomas Moyle having, about 1545, purchased the estate of Eastwell, began to build the mansion alluded to. He was surprised to observe that one of the bricklayers, a man well advanced in years, was accustomed, on leaving off work, to take out a book and begin to read. Sir Thomas's curiosity was excited to know what book occupied the man's attention; but the extreme shyness of the student for some time baffled his desires. At length, taking him by surprise, he found, to his increased astonishment, that the man perused a Latin book. He then inquired how he came to be able to read a book in that language, and after some conversation, obtained from him a series of particulars which he said had hitherto been told to none.

He was, in his earliest years, boarded with a schoolmaster, and there was occasionally visited by a gentleman, who paid regularly for his maintenance and education, but who did not let him know his parentage. At length, when he was about sixteen, this gentleman took him on a journey, and introduced him to a stately house, where another personage of distinguished appearance, and wearing a star and the order of the Garter, came to see him, conversed kindly with him, and then dismissed him. Some time after, he was conducted into Leicestershire, and brought before the king in his tent, in the midst of an army, and was surprised to find that the king was the same distinguished person whom he had lately seen. Richard embraced him, acknowledged him as his son, and said that if he should, as he hoped, survive the battle about to be fought, the son should be duly provided for; after which he was desired to take a position at some distance till the end of the conflict. The king also warned him, in the event of his defeat and death, to conceal the relationship now acknowledged, as it would be sure to be fatal to him.

Finding the battle go against King Richard, he made his way from the field, and as he entered Leicester, he saw a dead man brought in naked, laid across a horse, and learned that it was the monarch he had yesterday seen at the head of a gallant army.

Chance directed him into the occupation of a bricklayer, in which he had spent his life in contented obscurity.

Sir Thomas Moyle, feeling for the misfortunes of this scion of royalty, built a small house for him on his grounds, and requested him to take what food he should henceforth require from his kitchen. But it would appear that the old man did not live above three or four years in the enjoyment of the ease at last accorded to him.*

This story is of so romantic a nature, that it might well be doubted. Mr Jesse, however, in his *Memoirs of King Richard III.* (8vo, 1861), expresses a general faith in it, and shews several reasons for thinking it true. 'Anciently, when any person of noble family was interred at Eastwell, it was the custom to affix a special mark against the name of the deceased in the register of burials. The fact is a significant one, that this aristocratic symbol is prefixed to the name of Richard Plantagenet. At Eastwell, his story still excites curiosity and

* From Dr Brett's letter, in Peck's *Desiderata Curiosa*, 4to, p. 250.

interest. . . . . A well in Eastwell Park still bears his name; tradition points to an uninscribed tomb in Eastwell churchyard as his last resting-place; and, lastly, the very handwriting which, more than three centuries ago, recorded his interment, is still in existence.'

In further connection with the subject of the Plantagenet family, Sir Bernard Burke, in his work, entitled *Vicissitudes of Families*, remarks: 'What race in Europe surpassed in royal position, personal achievement, or romantic adventure, our Plantagenets, equally wise as valiant, no less renowned in the cabinet than the field? Yet, as late as 1637, the great-grandson of Margaret Plantagenet, herself daughter and heir of George, Duke of Clarence, was following the cobbler craft at Newport, in Shropshire. Among the lineal descendants of Edmund Woodstock, Earl of Kent, son of Edward the First, entitled to quarter the royal arms, occur a butcher and a toll-gatherer, the first a Mr Joseph Smart, of Hales Owen (Salop), the latter Mr G. Wymot, keeper of the turnpike-gate, Cooper's Bank, Dudley. Among descendants of Thomas Plantagenet, Duke of Gloucester, son of Edward III., we discover Mr Penny, late sexton at St George's, Hanover Square—a strange descent from sword and sceptre to spade and pick.'

## MRS MAPP, THE BONE-SETTER.

'Died last week, at her lodgings, near the Seven Dials, the much-talked of Mrs Mapps, the bone-setter, so miserably poor, that the parish was obliged to bury her.'—*London Daily Post*, 22d December 1737.

The subject of this melancholy obituary notice was for a time the object of popular wonder and enthusiasm. The daughter of a country bone-setter, she had, after wandering about from place to place, settled herself at Epsom, where she soon became famed for wonder-working cures—cures apparently effected more by boldness and personal strength than skill. She married a mercer's servant, but the match seems to have been an unfortunate one, for the *Grub-Street Journal* of April 19, 1736, says: 'We hear that the husband of Mrs Mapp, the famous bone-setter at Epsom, ran away from her last week, taking with him upwards of a hundred guineas, and such other portable things as lay next to his hand. Several letters from Epsom mention that the footman, whom the fair bone-setter married the week before, had taken a sudden journey from thence with what money his wife had earned; and that her concern at first was very great, but as soon as the surprise was over, she grew gay; and seems to think the money well disposed of, as it was like to rid her of a husband.' He must have been a bold man to marry her, and still bolder to have ventured to incur her wrath, if her portrait does her justice—a more ill-favoured, or a stronger-framed woman, it would have been difficult to find.

Her professional success, however, must have gone far to solace her for matrimonial failure. Besides driving a profitable trade at home, she used to drive to town once a week, in a coach-and-four, and return again bearing away the crutches of her patients as trophies of honour. She held her levees at the Grecian Coffee-house, where she operated successfully upon a niece of Sir Hans Sloane. The same day, she straightened the body of a man whose back had stuck out two inches for nine years; and a gentleman who went into the house with one shoe-heel six inches high, came out again cured of a lameness of twenty years' standing, and with both his legs of equal length. She was not always so successful. One Thomas Barber, tallow-chandler, of Saffron Hill, thought proper to issue the following warning to her would-be patients:

'Whereas it has been industriously (I wish I could say truly) reported that I had found great benefit from a certain female bone-setter's performance, and that it was from a want of resolution to undergo the operation that I did not meet with a perfect cure;—This is to give notice, that any persons afflicted with lameness (who are willing to know what good and harm others may receive, before they venture on desperate measures themselves), will be welcome any morning to see the dressing of my leg, which was sound before the operation, and they will then be able to judge of the performance, and to whom I owe my present unhappy confinement to my bed and chair.'

The cure of Sir Hans Sloane's niece made Mrs Mapp the town-talk, and if it was only known that she intended to make one of the audience, the theatre favoured with her presence was sure to be crowded to excess. A comedy was announced at the Lincoln's Inn Fields Theatre, called *The Husband's Relief, or The Female Bone-setter and the Worm-doctor*. Mrs Mapp attended the first night, and was gratified at hearing a song in her praise, of which we give two verses as a specimen:

'You surgeons of London who puzzle your pates,
To ride in your coaches and purchase estates;
Give over for shame, for your pride has a fall,
And the doctress of Epsom has outdone you all.

Dame Nature has given her a doctor's degree,
She gets all the patients and pockets the fee;
So if you don't instantly prove it a cheat,
She'll loll in a chariot whilst you walk the street.'

She seems to have been accompanied on this occasion by two noted quacks—Ward the worm-doctor, and Taylor the oculist. A rhymster in the *Grub-street Journal*, alluding to this strange conjunction, says:

'While Mapp to th' actors shewed a kind regard,
On one side sat Taylor, on th' other side Ward.
When their mock persons of the drama came,
Both Ward and Taylor thought it hurt their game.
Wondering how Mapp could in good-humour be—
Zounds! cries the manly dame, it hurts not me,
Quacks, without art, may either blind or kill,
But demonstration shews that mine is skill.'

Mrs Mapp soon afterwards removed from Epsom to Pall Mall, but she did not forget her country friends. She gave a plate of ten guineas to be run for at Epsom, and went to see the race. Singularly enough, the first heat was won by a mare called 'Mrs Mapp,' which so delighted the doctress, that she gave the jockey a guinea, and promised to make it a hundred if he won the plate, but to his chagrin he failed to do so. The fair bone-setter's career was but a brief one. In 1736, she was at the height of her prosperity, and at the end of 1737, she died in the miserable circumstances set forth in our opening paragraph.

## DECEMBER 23.

St Servulus, confessor, 590. The Ten Martyrs of Crete, 3d century. St Victoria, virgin and martyr, 250.

*Born.*—Heneage Finch, Earl of Nottingham, 1621; Robert Barclay, celebrated Quaker, author of the *Apology*, 1648, *Gordonstown, Morayshire;* Frederick Augustus of Saxony, 1750; Sir Martin Archer Shee, portrait-painter, 1770, *Dublin;* Alexander I., Emperor of Russia, 1777.

*Died.*—Childebert I., of France, 558, *Paris;* Henri de Lorraine, Duke of Guise, assassinated at Blois, 1588; William Davison, secretary of state to Queen Elizabeth, 1608; Michael Drayton, poet, 1631; James Sargent Storer, engraver, 1854, *London.*

### THE EIKON BASILIKÉ.

'On the 23d of December 1648, Richard Royston, the royal bookseller at the "Angel" in Ivy Lane, received the MS. copy of the *Eikon Basiliké* for the press.' Such is the earliest date we find in connection with a book which became very famous during the turbulent times of the Commonwealth. Whether any copies were printed by the 30th of the ensuing month, the day when Charles I. was executed, is doubtful; but there is no doubt that it was largely in circulation soon afterwards, and that it produced a powerful effect on the Royalists. Most of them believed that the king wrote it; the peculiar character of the book, and the publishing of it by the king's bookseller, encouraged this belief; nor were the active members of the court-party (for reasons presently to be noticed) at all anxious to disturb this favourite and favourable impression.

The work itself, which was the chief means of obtaining for Charles I. the designation of the 'Royal Martyr,' is a remarkable composition, by whomsoever written. M. Guizot, in his history of the events of those times, thus characterises it: 'The manuscript had probably been perused, perhaps even corrected, by Charles himself, during his residence in the Isle of Wight. In any case, it was the real expression, and true portraiture of his position, character, and mind, as they had been formed by misfortune. It is remarkable for an elevation of thought which is at once natural and strained; a constant mingling of blind royal pride and sincere Christian humility; heart-impulses struggling against habits of obstinate self-consciousness; true piety in the midst of misguided conduct; invincible though somewhat inert devotion to his faith, his honour, and his rank; and as all these sentiments are expressed in monotonous language, which, though often emphatic, is always grave, tranquil, and even unctuous with serenity and sadness—it is not surprising that such a work should have profoundly affected all royalist hearts, and easily persuaded them that it was the king himself who addressed them.'

There can be no doubt that Royalists and Parliamentarians were alike attracted by the *Eikon Basiliké*, though for different reasons. Appearing directly after the king's death, and purporting to be a 'Portraiture of his Sacred Majesty in his Solitudes and Sufferings,' it could not fail to excite a deep interest in the faithful adherents of the House of Stuart. Even among many of Charles's opponents his fate had excited strong sympathy; he was regarded as having been less in error than some of his advisers; and there was a general tendency to forget his faults, and remember his virtues. 'Hence,' says Lord Macaulay ('Milton,' *Encyclopædia Britannica*), 'the appearance of a work, professedly by his own hand—in which he is represented in the constant exercise of prayer, asserting the integrity of his motives before the Great Searcher of Hearts, and urging a fervent appeal from the injustice and cruelty of man to the justice and clemency of God—was eminently calculated to agitate the public mind in his favour, and to make every tongue vibrate in execration of his enemies.' The Royalists unquestionably relied greatly on the effect which they expected to be produced by the book; and nearly fifty thousand copies of it were sold in England. On the other hand, the Puritans or Parliamentarians, alarmed at the effect on the public mind, desired Milton to write an answer to the *Eikon Basiliké*, with the view of shewing that, whether written by the king or not, its political reasonings were invalid. Milton accepted the duty; and hence his *Eikonoclastes*, or *Image Breaker*, one of the most celebrated of his works. The two books should be read together: the *Eikon Basiliké*, not as the production of the unfortunate king, but of the bishop of Exeter, Dr Gauden; and the *Eikonoclastes* (more frequently spelled *Iconoclastes* or *Iconoclast*) of Milton. There is reason to believe that Milton suspected the author of the *Eikon* to be some bishop or clergyman; but still he answered it as if it had been a royal production. Macaulay, less favourable than Guizot to the Royalists, thus characterises the *Iconoclast:* 'Pressing closely on his antagonist, and tracing [tracking ?] him step by step, he either exposes the fallacy of his reasonings, or the falsehood of his assertions, or the hollowness of his professions, or the convenient speciousness of his devotions. He discovers a quickness which never misses an advantage, and a keenness of remark which carries an irresistible edge. In argument and in style, the *Iconoclast* is equally masterly, being at once compressed and energetic, perspicuous and elegant. It is a work, indeed, which cannot be read by any man whose reason is not wholly under the dominion of prejudice, without producing a conviction unfavourable to the royal party; and it justly merited the honourable distinction conferred upon it by royalist vengeance, of burning in the same flames with the *Defence of the People of England.*'

We have mentioned Dr Gauden, bishop of Exeter, as the author of the *Eikon Basiliké*. This is now known to have been the case, but the Royalists and High-Church party continued, to an advanced period, to foster the popular belief that the First Charles wrote it. The question was long a matter of literary discussion, and in the last century, we find Hume, in his *History of England*, advocating the claims of the king to the authorship, in preference to those of Dr Gauden. Moreover, it was a species of pious fraud, which the statesmen and churchmen deemed politic to encourage 'for the public advantage.' The late Sir James Mackintosh was of opinion that, irrespective of other testimony, the Eikon reads more like the production of a priest than of a king. 'It has more of dissertation than effusion. It has more regular division and systematic order than agree with the habits of Charles. The choice and arrangement of words shew a degree of care and neatness which are seldom attained but by a practised writer. The views of men and affairs, too, are rather those of a bystander than an actor; they are chiefly reflections, sometimes in themselves obvious, but often ingeniously turned, such as the surface of events would suggest to a spectator not too deeply interested. It betrays none of those strong feelings which the most vigilant regard to gravity and dignity could not have uniformly banished from the composition of an actor and a sufferer. It has no allusions to facts not accessible to any moderately-informed man: though the king must have (sometimes rightly) thought that his superior knowledge of affairs would enable him to correct vulgar mistakes.'*

Numerous copies of the *Eikon Basilikê* are preserved in the public and private libraries of this country—not only on account of the curious circumstances connected with the work itself, but because it was customary to write on the fly-leaves, during the troubled period of the Commonwealth, melodies and other verses on the hapless monarch who had been decapitated. These inscriptions shewed that the grief was deep and sincere among those who thought the cry of 'Church and King' was the only one which could save the nation. Some went to the very extreme of adulation. One ran thus:

'Nec Carolus Magnus
Nec Carolus Quintus,
Sed Carolus Agnus
Hic jacet intus.'

Mr E. S. Taylor has described, in *Notes and Queries*, a copy of the work, containing two very curious *Chronosticons* in manuscript: that is, enigmas in which certain dates are denoted. Roman numerals, as most persons are aware, are letters of the alphabet, and may thus be used in two different ways. In one of the chronosticons here adverted to, the praises of Charles I. are celebrated, and at the same time the year 1648, in which, according to the old method of reckoning the commencement of the year he was executed, is denoted:

ReX pIVs et greX VerVs
ConDemnantVr InIqVe

The other embodies the year of the world (according to one system of chronology), namely, 5684, as that in which the king was executed:

TrIstIa perCharI Deploro fVnera RegIs
Inferna Ingratæ Detestor MVnera pLebIs
ReX DeCoLLatVr serVIs; qVIs taLIa VerbIs
EXpLICet aVt possIt LaChryMIs æqVare Labores
HIC pIetatIs honos, sIC RegeM In sCeptra reponVnt

These are to be thus understood. The letters in thick capitals denote the numerals; M, D, C, L, X, I, are to be interpreted in the way usual in Roman numerals; V serves both for *v* and *u* as a letter, and for 5 as a numeral. Each symbol is used separately: thus I X are 1 and 10, not 9; and I V are 1 and 5, not 4. We rather suspect that, in *Notes and Queries*, the (*m*) in the first chronosticon should have been printed in large type as a numeral; and that an additional (*l*) in the second should also be in large type, to make up the quantities.

* *Edinburgh Review*, 1826.

## FAMILY OMENS OF DEATH.

The popular omens of death are almost innumerable, yet the appearance of any one of them is, according to rustic credulity, sufficient to foreshew the decease of any ordinary person in the middle or lower classes of society. For common people must be satisfied with common things. Even superstition knows how to pay due deference to rank and genealogy, and cunningly insinuates herself among the aristocracy, by contributing her mysterious influence to enhance the honours of rank and birth. Thus, among the *élite*, death-omens assume a special and distinctive shape, and, becoming a sort of household dependents, are never heard of but when they appear to do 'suit and service' to the respective families with which they are severally connected. So that the family, thus supernaturally honoured, while disdaining all vulgar omens of mortality, beholds the appearance of its own with dismay, feeling assured that death will soon visit some one of its members. Some of these family omens are curious and interesting. There still exists in Devon a family named Oxenham, with which such an omen is said to be connected. Prince, in his *Worthies of Devon*, speaking of this, says: 'There is a family of considerable standing of this name at South Tawton, near Oakhampton, of which is this strange and wonderful thing recorded, that at the death of any of them, a bird with a white breast is seen for awhile fluttering about their beds, and then suddenly to vanish away. Mr James Howell tells us that, in a lapidary's shop in London, he saw a large marble slab to be sent into Devonshire, with an inscription: "That John Oxenham, Mary his sister, James his son, and Elizabeth his mother, had each the appearance of such a bird fluttering about their beds as they were dying."'*

There is a local ballad on this subject which is too long for insertion, but, as it is little known, a few extracts from it may be interesting. It begins thus:

'Where lofty hills in grandeur meet,
And Taw meandering flows,
There is a sylvan, calm retreat,
Where erst a mansion rose.

There dwelt Sir James of Oxenham,
A brave and generous lord;
Benighted traveller never came
Unwelcome to his board.

In early life his wife had died,
A son he ne'er had known,
And Margaret, his age's pride,
Was heir to him alone.'

Margaret became affianced to a young knight, and their marriage-day was fixed. On the evening preceding it, her father gave a banquet to his friends, who, of course, congratulated him on the approaching happy union. He stood up to thank them, and in alluding to the young knight, so soon

* See Howell's *Familiar Letters*.

to be his daughter's husband, he jestingly called him his son:

'But while the dear, unpractised word
Still lingered on his tongue,
He saw a silvery-breasted bird
Fly o'er the festive throng.

Swift as the lightning's flashes fleet,
And lose their brilliant light,
Sir James sank back upon his seat,
Pale and entranced with fright.'

He, however, managed to conceal the cause of his embarrassment, and the next day the wedding-party assembled in the church, and the priest had begun the marriage-service:

'When Margaret with terrific screams
Made all with horror start—
Good heavens! her blood in torrents streams,
A dagger's in her heart!'

The deed had been done by a discarded lover, who, by the aid of disguise, had stationed himself just behind her. He drew the dagger from her breast, and, with a frantic laugh, exclaimed:

'Now marry me, proud maid, he cried;
Thy blood with mine shall wed;
He dashed the dagger in his side,
And at her feet fell dead.

Poor Margaret, too, grows cold with death,
And round her hovering flies
The phantom-bird for her last breath,
To bear it to the skies.'

The owl is one of the most usual omens of death among the commonalty; so, of course, it could not be received as a family omen among the aristocracy. As an honourable distinction, therefore, the dispenser of omens has assigned two owls, of enormous size, to premonish the noble family of Arundel of Wardour of approaching mortality. Whenever these two solemn spectres are seen perched on a battlement of the family mansion, it is too well known that one of its members will soon be summoned out of this world.

The ancient baronet's family of Clifton, of Clifton Hall, in Nottinghamshire, is forewarned that death is about to visit one of its members, by a sturgeon forcing itself up the river Trent, on whose bank their mansion is situated near to Clifton Grove, the scene of Henry Kirke White's poem of that title.

There is an ancient Roman Catholic family in Yorkshire, of the name of Middleton, which is said to be apprised of the death of any one of its members by the apparition of a Benedictine nun. Camden, in his *Magna Britannia*, after speaking of the illustrious antiquity of the Brereton family, says 'this wonderful thing respecting them is commonly believed, and I have heard it myself affirmed by many, that for some days before the death of the heir of the family, the trunk of a tree has always been seen floating in the lake adjoining their mansion.' On this omen, Mrs Hemans has some spirited stanzas, among which occur the following:

'Yes! I have seen the ancient oak
On the dark deep water cast,
And it was not felled by the woodman's stroke,
Or the rush of the sweeping blast;
For the axe might never touch that tree,
And the air was still as a summer sea.

'Tis fallen! but think thou not I weep
For the forest's pride o'erthrown;
An old man's tears lie far too deep,
To be poured for that alone!
But by that sign too well I know
That a youthful head must soon be low!

He must, he must! in that deep dell,
By that dark water's side,
'Tis known that ne'er a proud tree fell
But an heir of his father's died.
And he—there's laughter in his eye,
Joy in his voice—yet he must die!

Say not 'tis vain! I tell thee, some
Are warned by a meteor's light,
Or a pale bird flitting calls them home,
Or a voice on the winds by night;
And they must go! and he too, he—
Woe for the fall of the glorious Tree!'

In a note to the *Lady of the Lake*, Sir Walter Scott gives the following curious account from the manuscript memoirs of Lady Fanshaw. Her husband, Sir Richard, and herself, chanced, during their abode in Ireland, to visit a friend, the head of a sept, who resided in his ancient baronial castle, surrounded with a moat. At midnight, Lady Fanshaw was awakened by a ghastly and supernatural scream; and, looking out of bed, beheld, by the moonlight, a female face and part of the form hovering at the window. The distance from the ground, as well as the circumstance of the moat, excluded the possibility that what she beheld was of this world. The face was that of a young and rather handsome woman, but pale; and the hair, which was reddish, was loose and dishevelled. The dress, which Lady Fanshaw's terror did not prevent her remarking accurately, was that of the ancient Irish. This apparition continued to exhibit itself for some time, and then vanished with two shrieks similar to that which had first excited Lady Fanshaw's attention. In the morning, with infinite terror, she communicated to her host what she had witnessed, and found him prepared not only to credit, but to account for the apparition. 'A near relation of my family,' said he, 'expired last night in this castle. We disguised our certain expectation of the event from you, lest it should throw a cloud over the cheerful reception which was your due. Now, before such an event happens in this family and castle, the female spectre, whom you have seen, always is visible. She is believed to be the spirit of a woman of inferior rank, whom one of my ancestors degraded himself by marrying, and whom afterwards, to expiate the dishonour done to his family, he caused to be drowned in the castle-moat.' In his *Peveril of the Peak*, Sir Walter mentions a similar female spirit or ban-shee, said to attend on the Stanley family, warning them, by uttering a shriek, of some approaching calamity; and especially, 'weeping and bemoaning herself before the death of any person of distinction belonging to the family.'

It is unfortunate that so many of these ancient family omens have come down unaccompanied with the particulars that gave rise to them, which would have rendered them far more interesting. Now, we can scarcely see any connection between the omen and the family, or conceive why the things specified should have been considered omens of death at all.

# DECEMBER 24.

St Gregory of Spoleto, martyr, 304. Saints Thrasilla and Emiliana, virgins.

## Christmas Eve.

The eves or vigils of the different ecclesiastical festivals throughout the year are, according to the strict letter of canonical rule, times of fasting and penance; but in several instances, custom has appropriated them to very different purposes, and made them seasons of mirth and jollity. Such is the case with All-Saints' Eve, and perhaps even more so with Christmas Eve, or the evening before Christmas Day. Under the latter head, or 25th of December, will be found a special history of the great Christian festival; though the observances of both days are so intertwined together, that it becomes almost impossible to state, with precision, the ceremonies which are peculiar to each. We shall, however, do the best we can in the circumstances, and endeavour, under the 24th of December, to restrict ourselves to an account of the popular celebrations and customs which characterise more especially the eve of the Nativity.

With Christmas Eve, the Christmas holidays may practically be said to commence, though, according to ecclesiastical computation, the festival really begins on the 16th of December, or the day which is distinguished in the calendar as *O Sapientia*, from the name of an anthem, sung during Advent. It is proper, however, to state that there seems to be a discrepancy of opinion on this point, and that, in the judgment of some, the true Christmas festival does not commence till the evening before Christmas Day. The season is held to terminate on 1st of February, or the evening before the Purification of the Virgin (Candlemas Day), by which date, according to the ecclesiastical canons, all the Christmas decorations must be removed from the churches. In common *parlance*, certainly, the Christmas holidays comprehend a period of nearly a fortnight, commencing on Christmas Eve, and ending on Twelfth Day. The whole of this season is still a jovial one, abounding in entertainments and merry-makings of all sorts, but is very much changed from what it used to be with our ancestors in feudal times, when it was an almost unintermitted round of feasting and jollity.

For a picture of Christmas Eve, in the olden time, we can desire none more graphic than that furnished by Sir Walter Scott in *Marmion*.

'On Christmas Eve the bells were rung;
On Christmas Eve the mass was sung;
That only night, in all the year,
Saw the stoled priest the chalice rear.
The damsel donned her kirtle sheen;
The hall was dressed with holly green;
Forth to the wood did merry-men go,
To gather in the mistletoe.
Then opened wide the baron's hall
To vassal, tenant, serf, and all;
Power laid his rod of rule aside,
And Ceremony doffed his pride.
The heir, with roses in his shoes,
That night might village partner choose;
The lord, underogating, share
The vulgar game of 'post and pair.'
All hailed, with uncontrolled delight,
And general voice, the happy night,
That to the cottage, as the crown,
Brought tidings of salvation down!

The fire, with well-dried logs supplied,
Went roaring up the chimney wide;
The huge hall-table's oaken face,
Scrubbed till it shone, the day to grace,
Bore then upon its massive board
No mark to part the squire and lord.
Then was brought in the lusty brawn,
By old blue-coated serving-man;
Then the grim boar's-head frowned on high,
Crested with bays and rosemary.
Well can the green-garbed ranger tell,
How, when, and where the monster fell;
What dogs before his death he tore,
And all the baiting of the boar.
The wassail round in good brown bowls,
Garnished with ribbons, blithely trowls.
There the huge sirloin reeked: hard by
Plum-porridge stood, and Christmas-pie;
Nor failed old Scotland to produce,
At such high-tide, her savoury goose.
Then came the merry masquers in,
And carols roared with blithesome din;
If unmelodious was the song,
It was a hearty note, and strong.
Who lists may in their mumming see
Traces of ancient mystery;
White shirts supplied the masquerade,
And smutted cheeks the visors made;
But, oh! what masquers, richly dight,
Can boast of bosoms half so light!
England was merry England, when
Old Christmas brought his sports again.
'Twas Christmas broached the mightiest ale;
'Twas Christmas told the merriest tale;
A Christmas gambol oft could cheer
The poor man's heart through half the year.'

To investigate the origin of many of our Christmas customs, it becomes necessary to wander far back into the regions of past time, long ere Julius Cæsar had set his foot on our shores, or St Augustine preached the doctrines of Christianity to the men of Kent. We have frequently, in the course of this work, had occasion to remark on the numerous traces still visible in popular customs of the old pagan rites and ceremonies. These, it is needless here to repeat, were extensively retained after the conversion of Britain to Christianity, partly because the Christian teachers found it impossible to wean their converts from their cherished superstitions and observances, and partly because they themselves, as a matter of expediency, ingrafted the rites of the Christian religion on the old heathen ceremonies, believing that thereby the cause of the Cross would be rendered more acceptable to the generality of the populace, and thus be more effectually promoted. By such an amalgamation, no festival of the Christian year was more thoroughly characterised than Christmas; the festivities of which, originally derived from the Roman Saturnalia, had afterwards been intermingled with the ceremonies observed by the British Druids at the period of the winter-solstice, and at a subsequent period became incorporated with the grim mythology of the ancient Saxons. Two popular observances belonging to Christmas are more especially derived from the worship of our pagan ancestors—the hanging up of the mistletoe, and the burning of the Yule log.

As regards the former of these practices, it is well known that, in the religion of the Druids, the mistletoe was regarded with the utmost veneration, though the reverence which they paid to it seems to have been restricted to the plant when found growing on the oak—the favourite tree of their divinity Tutanes—who appears to have been the same as the Phenician god Baal, or the sun, worshipped under so many different names by the various pagan nations of antiquity. At the period of the winter-solstice, a great festival was celebrated in his honour, as will be found more largely commented on under our notice of Christmas Day. When the sacred anniversary arrived, the ancient Britons, accompanied by their priests, the Druids, sallied forth with great pomp and rejoicings to gather the mystic parasite, which, in addition to the religious reverence with which it was regarded, was believed to possess wondrous curative powers. When the oak was reached on which the mistletoe grew, two white bulls were bound to the tree, and the chief Druid, clothed in white (the emblem of purity), ascended, and, with a golden knife, cut the sacred plant, which was caught by another priest in the folds of his robe. The bulls, and often also human victims, were then sacrificed, and various festivities followed. The mistletoe thus gathered, was divided into small portions, and distributed among the people, who hung up the sprays over the entrances to their dwellings, as a propitiation and shelter to

THE YULE LOG.

the sylvan deities during the season of frost and cold. These rites in connection with the mistletoe, were retained throughout the Roman dominion in Britain, and also for a long period under the sovereignty of the Jutes, Saxons, and Angles.

The following legend regarding the mistletoe, from the Scandinavian mythology, may here be introduced: Balder, the god of poetry and eloquence, and second son of Odin and Friga, communicated one day to his mother a dream which he had had, intimating that he should die. She (Friga), to protect her son from such a contingency, invoked all the powers of nature—fire, air, earth, and water, as well as animals and plants—and obtained an oath from them that they should do Balder no hurt. The latter then went and took his place amid the combats of the gods, and fought without fear in the midst of showers of arrows. Loake, his enemy, resolved to discover the secret of Balder's invulnerability, and, accordingly, disguising himself as an old woman, he addressed himself to Friga with complimentary remarks on the valour and good-fortune of her son. The goddess replied that no substance could injure him, as all the productions of nature had bound themselves by an oath to refrain from doing him any harm. She added, however, with that awkward simplicity which appears so often to characterise mythical personages, that there was one plant which, from its insignificance, she did not think of conjuring, as it was impossible that it could inflict any hurt on her son. Loake inquired the name of the plant in question, and was informed that it was a feeble little shoot, growing on the bark of the oak, with scarcely any soil. Then the treacherous Loake ran and procured the mistletoe, and, having entered the assembly of the gods, said to the blind Heda: 'Why do you not contend with the arrows of Balder?' Heda replied: 'I am blind, and have no arms.' Loake then presented him with an arrow formed from the mistletoe, and said: 'Balder is before thee.' Heda shot, and Balder fell pierced and slain.

The mistletoe, which has thus so many mystic associations connected with it, is believed to be propagated in its natural state by the *missel-thrush*, which feeds upon its berries. It was long thought impossible to propagate it artificially, but this object has been attained by bruising the berries, and by means of their viscidity, causing them to adhere to the bark of fruit-trees, where they readily germinate and take root. The growth of the mistletoe on the oak is now of extremely rare occurrence, but in the orchards of the west-midland counties of England, such as the shires of Gloucester and Worcester, the plant flourishes in great frequency and luxuriance on the apple-trees. Large quantities are annually cut at the Christmas season, and despatched to London and other places, where they are extensively used for the decoration of houses and shops. The special custom connected with the mistletoe on Christmas Eve, and an indubitable relic of the days of Druidism, handed down through a long course of centuries, must be familiar to all our readers. A branch of the mystic plant is suspended from the wall or ceiling, and any one of the fair sex, who, either from inadvertence, or, as possibly may be insinuated, *on purpose*, passes beneath the sacred spray, incurs the penalty of being then and there kissed by any lord of the creation who chooses to avail himself of the privilege.

The burning of the Yule log is an ancient Christmas ceremony, transmitted to us from our Scandinavian ancestors, who, at their feast of *Juul*, at the winter-solstice, used to kindle huge bonfires in honour of their god Thor. The custom, though sadly shorn of the 'pomp and circumstance' which formerly attended it, is still maintained in various parts of the country. The bringing in and placing of the ponderous block on the hearth of the wide chimney in the baronial hall was the most joyous of the ceremonies observed on Christmas Eve in feudal times. The venerable log, destined to crackle a welcome to all-comers, was drawn in triumph from its resting-place at the feet of its living brethren of the woods. Each wayfarer raised his hat as it passed, for he well knew that it was full of good promises, and that its flame would burn out old wrongs and heartburnings, and cause the liquor to bubble in the wassail-bowl, that was quaffed to the drowning of ancient feuds and animosities. So the Yule-log was worthily honoured, and the ancient bards welcomed its entrance with their minstrelsy. The following ditty, appropriate to such an occasion, appears in the Sloane Manuscripts. It is supposed to be of the time of Henry VI.:

'WELCOME YULE.

Welcome be thou, heavenly King,
Welcome born on this morning,
Welcome for whom we shall sing,
Welcome Yule,

Welcome be ye Stephen and John,
Welcome Innocents every one,
Welcome Thomas Martyr one,
Welcome Yule.

Welcome be ye, good New Year,
Welcome Twelfth Day, both *in fere*,*
Welcome saints, lovèd and dear,
Welcome Yule.

Welcome be ye, Candlemas,
Welcome be ye, Queen of Bliss,
Welcome both to more and less,
Welcome Yule.

Welcome be ye that are here,
Welcome all, and make good cheer,
Welcome all, another year,
Welcome Yule.'

And here, in connection with the festivities on Christmas Eve, we may quote Herrick's inspiriting stanzas:

'Come bring with a noise,
My merry, merry boys,
The Christmas log to the firing,
While my good dame she
Bids ye all be free,
And drink to your heart's desiring.

With the last year's brand
Light the new block, and,
For good success in his spending,
On your psalteries play
That sweet luck may
Come while the log is a teending.†

Drink now the strong beer,
Cut the white loaf here,
The while the meat is a shredding;
For the rare mince-pie,
And the plums stand by,
To fill the paste that's a kneading.'

The allusion at the commencement of the second stanza, is to the practice of laying aside the half-consumed block after having served its purpose on Christmas Eve, preserving it carefully in a cellar or other secure place till the next anniversary of Christmas, and then lighting the new log with the charred remains of its predecessor. The due observance of this custom was considered of the highest importance, and it was believed that the preservation of last year's Christmas log was a most effectual security to the house against fire. We are further informed, that it was regarded as a sign of very bad-luck if a squinting person entered the hall when the log was burning, and a similarly evil omen was exhibited in the arrival of a bare-footed person, and, above all, of a flat-footed woman! As an accompaniment to the Yule log, a candle of monstrous size, called the *Yule Candle*, or *Christmas Candle*, shed its light on the festive-board during the evening. Brand, in his *Popular Antiquities*, states that, in the buttery of St John's College, Oxford, an ancient candle socket of stone still remains, ornamented with the figure of the Holy Lamb. It was formerly used for holding the Christmas Candle, which, during the twelve nights of the Christmas festival, was burned on the high-table at supper.

* In company. † Burning.

In Devonshire, the Yule log takes the form of the *ashton fagot*, and is brought in and burned with great glee and merriment. The fagot is composed of a bundle of ash-sticks bound or hooped round with bands of the same tree, and the number of these last ought, it is said, to be nine. The rods having been cut a few days previous, the farm-labourers, on Christmas Eve, sally forth joyously, bind them together, and then, by the aid of one or two horses, drag the fagot, with great rejoicings, to their master's house, where it is deposited on the spacious hearth which serves as the fireplace in old-fashioned kitchens. Fun and jollity of all sorts now commence, the members of the household—master, family, and servants—seat themselves on the settles beside the fire, and all meet on terms of equality, the ordinary restraint characterising the intercourse of master and servant being, for the occasion, wholly laid aside. Sports of various kinds take place, such as jumping in sacks, diving in a tub of water for apples, and jumping for cakes and treacle; that is to say, endeavouring, by springs (the hands being tied behind the back), to catch with the mouth a cake, thickly spread with treacle, and suspended from the ceiling. Liberal libations of cider, or *egg-hot*, that is, cider heated and mixed with eggs and spices, somewhat after the manner of the Scottish *het-pint*, are supplied to the assembled revellers, it being an acknowledged and time-honoured custom that for every *crack* which the bands of the *ashton fagot* make in bursting when charred through, the master of the house is bound to furnish a fresh bowl of liquor. To the credit of such gatherings it must be stated that they are characterised, for the most part, by thorough decorum, and scenes of inebriation and disorder are seldom witnessed. One significant circumstance connected with the vigorous blaze which roars up the chimney on Christmas Eve ought not to be forgotten. We refer to the practice of most of the careful Devonshire housewives, at this season, to have the kitchen-chimney swept a few days previously, so as to guard against accidents from its taking fire. In Cornwall, as we are informed by a contributor to *Notes and Queries*, the Yule log is called 'the mock,' and great festivities attend the burning of it, including the old ceremony of lighting the block with a brand preserved from the fire of last year. We are informed also that, in the same locality, Christmas Eve is a special holiday with children, who, on this occasion, are allowed to sit up till midnight and 'drink to the mock.'

Another custom in Devonshire, still practised, we believe, in one or two localities on Christmas Eve, is for the farmer with his family and friends, after partaking together of hot cakes and cider (the cake being dipped in the liquor previous to being eaten), to proceed to the orchard, one of the party bearing hot cake and cider as an offering to the principal apple-tree. The cake is formally deposited on the fork of the tree, and the cider thrown over the latter, the men firing off guns and pistols, and the women and girls shouting—

'Bear blue, apples and pears enow,
Barn fulls, bag fulls, sack fulls.
Hurrah! hurrah! hurrah!'

A similar libation of spiced ale used to be sprinkled on the orchards and meadows in Norfolk; and the author of a very ingenious little work, published some years ago,* states that he has witnessed a ceremony of the same sort, in the neighbourhood of the New Forest in Hampshire, where the chorus sung was—

'Apples and pears with right good corn,
Come in plenty to every one,
Eat and drink good cake and hot ale,
Give Earth to drink and she 'll not fail.'

From a contributor to *Notes and Queries*, we learn that on Christmas Eve, in the town of Chester and surrounding villages, numerous parties of singers parade the streets, and are hospitably entertained with meat and drink at the different houses where they call. The farmers of Cheshire pass rather an uncomfortable season at Christmas, seeing that they are obliged, for the most part, during this period, to dispense with the assistance of servants. According to an old custom in the county, the servants engage themselves to their employers from New-Year's Eve to Christmas Day, and then for six or seven days, they leave their masters to shift for themselves, while they (the servants) resort to the towns to spend their holidays. On the morning after Christmas Day hundreds of farm-servants (male and female) dressed in holiday attire, in which all the hues of the rainbow strive for the mastery, throng the streets of Chester, considerably to the benefit of the tavern-keepers and shopkeepers. Having just received their year's wages, extensive investments are made by them in smock-frocks, cotton dresses, plush-waistcoats, and woollen shawls. Dancing is merrily carried on at various public-houses in the evening. In the whole of this custom, a more vivid realisation is probably presented than in any other popular celebration at Christmas, of the precursor of these modern jovialities—the ancient Roman Saturnalia, in which the relations of master and servant were for a time reversed, and universal licence prevailed.

Among Roman Catholics, a mass is always celebrated at midnight on Christmas Eve, another at daybreak on Christmas Day, and a third at a subsequent hour in the morning. A beautiful phase in popular superstition, is that which represents a thorough prostration of the Powers of Darkness as taking place at this season, and that no evil influence can then be exerted by them on mankind. The cock is then supposed to crow all night long, and by his vigilance to scare away all malignant spirits. The idea is beautifully expressed by Shakspeare, who puts it in the mouth of Marcellus, in *Hamlet*—

'It faded on the crowing of the cock.
Some say, that ever 'gainst that season comes
Wherein our Saviour's birth is celebrated,
The bird of dawning singeth all night long:
And then, they say, no spirit can walk abroad;
The nights are wholesome; then no planets strike,
No fairy takes, nor witch hath power to charm;
So hallow'd and so gracious is the time.'

A belief was long current in Devon and Cornwall, and perhaps still lingers both there and in other remote parts of the country, that at midnight, on Christmas Eve, the cattle in their stalls fall down on their knees in adoration of the

* *The Christmas Book: Christmas in the Olden Time: Its Customs and their Origin* (London, 1859).

infant Saviour, in the same manner as the legend reports them to have done in the stable at Bethlehem. Bees were also said to sing in their hives at the same time, and bread baked on Christmas Eve, it was averred, never became mouldy. All nature was thus supposed to unite in celebrating the birth of Christ, and partake in the general joy which the anniversary of the Nativity inspired.

### THE CHRISTMAS-TREE : CHRISTMAS EVE IN GERMANY AND AMERICA.

In Germany, Christmas Eve is for children the most joyous night in the year, as they then feast their eyes on the magnificence of the Christmas-tree, and rejoice in the presents which have been provided for them on its branches by their parents and friends. The tree is arranged by the senior members of the family, in the principal room of the house, and with the arrival of evening the children are assembled in an adjoining apartment. At a given signal, the door of the great room is thrown open, and in rush the juveniles eager and happy. There, on a long table in the centre of the room, stands the Christmas-tree, every branch glittering with little lighted tapers, while all sorts of gifts and ornaments are suspended from the branches, and possibly also numerous other presents are deposited separately on the table, all properly labelled with the names of the respective recipients. The Christmas-tree seems to be a very ancient custom in Germany, and is probably a remnant of the splendid and fanciful pageants of the middle ages. Apparently since the marriage of Queen Victoria with Prince Albert, previous to which time it was almost unknown in this country, the custom has been introduced into England with the greatest success, and must be familiar to most of our readers. Though thoroughly an innovation on our old Christmas customs, and partaking, indeed, somewhat of a prosaic character, rather at variance with the beautiful poetry of many of our Christmas usages, he would be a cynic indeed who could derive no pleasure from contemplating the group of young and happy faces who cluster round the Christmas-tree to share its pleasant fruit.

S. T. Coleridge, in a letter from Ratzeburg, in North Germany, published in the *Friend*, and quoted by Hone, mentions the following Christmas customs as observed in that locality. Part of them seems to be derived from those ceremonies proper to St Nicholas's Day, already described under 6th December. 'There is a Christmas custom here which pleased and interested me. The children make little presents to their parents, and to each other, and the parents to their children. For three or four months before Christmas, the girls are all busy, and the boys save up their pocket-money to buy these presents. What the present is to be, is cautiously kept secret; and the girls have a world of contrivances to conceal it—such as working when they are out on visits, and the others are not with them; getting up in the morning before daylight, &c. Then, on the evening before Christmas-day, one of the parlours is lighted up by the children, into which the parents must not go; a great yew-bough is fastened on the table at a little distance from the wall, a multitude of little tapers are fixed in the bough, but not so as to burn it till they are nearly consumed, and coloured paper, &c., hangs and flutters from the twigs. Under this bough the children lay out, in great order, the presents they mean for their parents, still concealing in their pockets what they intend for each other. Then the parents are introduced, and each presents his little gift; they then bring out the remainder, one by one, from their pockets, and present them with kisses and embraces. Where I witnessed this scene, there were eight or nine children, and the eldest daughter and the mother wept aloud for joy and tenderness; and the tears ran down the face of the father, and he clasped all his children so tight to his breast, it seemed as if he did it to stifle the sob that was rising within it. I was very much affected. The shadow of the bough and its appendages on the wall, and arching over on the ceiling, made a pretty picture; and then the raptures of the *very* little ones, when at last the twigs and their needles began to take fire and *snap*—O! it was a delight to them! On the next day (Christmas-day), in the great parlour, the parents lay out on the table the presents for the children; a scene of more sober joy succeeds; as on this day, after an old custom, the mother says privately to each of her daughters, and the father to his sons, that which he has observed most praiseworthy, and that which was most faulty, in their conduct. Formerly, and still in all the smaller towns and villages throughout North Germany, these presents were sent by all the parents to some one fellow, who, in high-buskins, a white robe, a mask, and an enormous flax-wig, personates *Knecht Rupert*—i. e., the servant Rupert. On Christmas-night, he goes round to every house, and says that Jesus Christ, his Master, sent him thither. The parents and elder children receive him with great pomp and reverence, while the little ones are most terribly frightened. He then inquires for the children, and, according to the character which he hears from the parents, he gives them the intended presents, as if they came out of heaven from Jesus Christ. Or, if they should have been bad children, he gives the parents a rod, and in the name of his Master recommends them to use it frequently. About seven or eight years old, the children are let into the secret, and it is curious how faithfully they keep it.'

In the state of Pennsylvania, in North America, where many of the settlers are of German descent, Christmas Eve is observed with many of the ceremonies practised in the Fatherland of the Old World. The Christmas-tree branches forth in all its splendour, and before going to sleep, the children hang up their stockings at the foot of the bed, to be filled by a personage bearing the name of *Krishkinkle* (a corruption of *Christ-kindlein*, or the Infant Christ), who is supposed to descend the chimney with gifts for all good children. If, however, any one has been naughty, he finds a birch-rod instead of sweetmeats in the stocking. This implement of correction is believed to have been placed there by another personage, called *Pelsnichol*, or Nicholas with the fur, in allusion to the dress of skins which he is supposed to wear. In this notion, a connection is evidently to be traced with the well-known legendary attributes of St Nicholas, previously described, though the benignant character of the saint is in this instance wofully belied. It is further to be remarked, that though the general understanding is that *Krishkinkle* and *Pelsnichol* are distinct personages—the one the rewarder of good children, the other the punisher of the bad—they are also occasionally represented as the same individual under different characters, the prototype of which was doubtless the charitable St Nicholas.

---

## CHRISTMAS GAMES: SNAPDRAGON.

SOME interesting particulars relative to the indoor diversions of our ancestors at Christmas, occur in the following passage quoted by Brand from a tract, entitled *Round about our Coal-fire, or Christmas Entertainments*, which was published in the early part of the last century. 'The time of the year being cold and frosty, the diversions are within doors, either in exercise or by the fireside. Dancing is one of the chief exercises; or else there is a match at Blindman's Buff, or Puss in the Corner. The next game is Questions and Commands, when the commander may oblige his subjects to answer any lawful question, and make the same obey him instantly, under the penalty of being smutted [having the face blackened], or paying such forfeit as may be laid on the aggressor. Most of the other diversions are cards and dice.'

From the above we gather that the sports on Christmas evenings, a hundred and fifty years ago, were not greatly dissimilar to those in vogue at the present day. The names of almost all the pastimes then mentioned must be familiar to every reader, who has probably also participated in them himself at some period of his life. Let us only add *charades*, that favourite amusement of modern drawing-rooms (and of these only the name, not the sport itself, was unknown to our ancestors), together with a higher spirit of refinement and delicacy, and we shall discover little difference between the juvenile pastimes of a Christmas-party in the reign of Queen Victoria, and a similar assemblage in the reign of Queen Anne or the first Georges.

One favourite Christmas sport, very generally played on Christmas Eve, has been handed down to us from time immemorial under the name of 'Snapdragon.' To our English readers this amusement is perfectly familiar, but it is almost unknown in Scotland, and it seems therefore desirable here to give a description of the pastime. A quantity of raisins are deposited in a large dish or bowl (the broader and shallower this is, the better), and brandy or some other spirit is poured over the fruit and ignited. The bystanders now endeavour, by turns, to grasp a raisin, by plunging their hands through the flames; and as this is somewhat of an arduous feat, requiring both courage and rapidity of action, a considerable amount of laughter and merriment is evoked at the expense of the unsuccessful competitors. As an appropriate accompaniment we introduce here

### The Song of Snapdragon.

'Here he comes with flaming bowl,
Don't he mean to take his toll,
Snip! Snap! Dragon!
Take care you don't take too much,
Be not greedy in your clutch,
Snip! Snap! Dragon!

With his blue and lapping tongue
Many of you will be stung,
Snip! Snap! Dragon!
For he snaps at all that comes
Snatching at his feast of plums,
Snip! Snap! Dragon!

But Old Christmas makes him come,
Though he looks so fee! fa! fum!
Snip! Snap! Dragon!
Don't 'ee fear him, be but bold—
Out he goes, his flames are cold,
Snip! Snap! Dragon!'

Whilst the sport of Snapdragon is going on, it is usual to extinguish all the lights in the room, so that the lurid glare from the flaming spirits may exercise to the full its weird-like effect. There seems little doubt that in this amusement we retain a trace of the fiery ordeal of the middle ages, and also of the Druidical fire-worship of a still remoter epoch. A curious reference to it occurs in the quaint old play of *Lingua*, quoted by Mr Sandys in his work on Christmas.

'*Memory*. Oh, I remember this dish well; it was first invented by Pluto to entertain Proserpine withal.

*Phantastes*. I think not so, Memory; for when Hercules had killed the flaming dragon of Hesperia, with the apples of that orchard he made this fiery meat; in memory whereof he named it Snapdragon.'

Snapdragon, to personify him, has a 'poor relation' or 'country cousin,' who bears the name of *Flapdragon*. This is a favourite amusement among the common people in the western counties of

England, and consists in placing a lighted candle in a can of ale or cider, and drinking up the contents of the vessel. This act entails, of course, considerable risk of having the face singed, and herein lies the essence of the sport, which may be averred to be a somewhat more arduous proceeding in these days of moustaches and long whiskers than it was in the time of our close-shaved grandfathers.

## The Mummers.

The mummers, or, as they are styled in Scotland, the *guisers* or *guizards*, occupied a prominent place in the Christmas revels of the olden time, and their performances, though falling, like the other old customs of the season, into desuetude, are still kept up in several parts of the country. The passion for masquerade, like that for dramatic representation, seems an inherent one in human nature; and though social progress and fashion may modify and vary the peculiar mode of development, the tendency itself remains unaltered, and only adopts from age to age a new, and, it may be, more intellectual phase. Thus the rude and irreverent mysteries and miracle plays which delighted our ancestors, have been succeeded in the gradual course of improvement by the elaborate stage mechanism and display of our own times; and the coarse drolleries which characterised the old Christmas festivities, have made way for the games and charades, and other refined amusements of modern drawing-rooms. But in all these changes we only find an expression under altered and diversified forms of certain essential feelings and tendencies in the constitution of humanity.

Looking back to the Roman *Saturnalia*, from which so many of our Christmas usages are derived, we find that the practice of masquerading was greatly in vogue at that season among the people of Rome. Men and women assumed respectively the attire of the opposite sex, and masks of all kinds were worn in abundance. The early Christians, we are informed, used, on the Feast of the Circumcision or New-year's Day, to run about in masks in ridicule of the pagan superstitions; but there can be no doubt that they also frequently shared in the frolics of their heathen neighbours, and the fathers of the church had considerable difficulty in prevailing on their members to refrain from such unedifying pastimes. Afterwards, the clergy endeavoured to metamorphose the heathen revels into amusements, which, if not really more spiritual in character than those which they supplanted, had at least the merit of bearing reference to the observances, and recognising the authority of the church and its ministers. The mysteries or miracle plays in which even the clergy occasionally took part as performers, were the results, amid numerous others, of this policy. These singular dramas continued for many centuries to form a favourite amusement of the populace, both at Christmas and other seasons of the year; and in the first volume of this work (p. 633) will be found an account of the celebration of the Whitsuntide mysteries at Chester. The Christmas *mumming* was in many respects a kindred diversion, though it appears to have partaken less of the religious element, and resembled more nearly those medieval pageants in which certain subjects and characters, taken from pagan mythology or popular legends, were represented. Frequently, also, it assumed very much the nature of a masquerade, when the sole object of the actors is to disguise themselves, and excite alternately laughter and admiration by the splendid or ridiculous costumes in which they are arrayed.

The term *mummer* is synonymous with *masker*, and is derived from the Danish, *mumme*, or Dutch, *momme*. The custom of mumming at the present day, such as it is, prevails only at the Christmas season, the favourite and commencing night for the pastime being generally Christmas Eve. Formerly, however, it seems to have been practised also at other times throughout the year, and Stow, in his *Survey of London*, has preserved to us an account of a splendid 'mummerie,' which, in 1377, was performed shortly before Candlemas by the citizens of London, for the amusement of Prince Richard, son of the Black Prince, and afterward the unfortunate monarch Richard II. In the year 1400, we are informed that Henry IV., holding his Christmas at Eltham, was visited by twelve aldermen and their sons as mummers, and that these august personages 'had great thanks' from his majesty for their performance. But shortly afterwards, as Fabyan tells us, a conspiracy to murder the king was organised under the guise of a Twelfth-night mumming. The plot was discovered only a few hours before the time of putting it in execution. Henry VIII., who ruthlessly demolished so many ancient institutions, issued an ordinance against mumming or guising declaring all persons who went about to great houses arrayed in this fashion, liable to be arrested as vagabonds, committed to jail for three months, and fined at the king's pleasure. The reason assigned for this edict, is the number of murders and other felonies which have arisen from this cause. But we hear of no permanent or serious check sustained by the mummers in consequence.

In the tract, *Round about our Coal-fire, or Christmas Entertainments*, already quoted, the following passage occurs in reference to the practice of mumming at a comparatively recent period: 'Then comes mumming or masquerading, when the squire's wardrobe is ransacked for dresses of all kinds. Corks are burnt to black the faces of the fair, or make deputy-moustaches, and every one in the family, except the squire himself, must be transformed.' And in further illustration of an old English pastime, the subjoined verses on mumming, in the characteristic form of the madrigal, from *La Musa Madrigalesca*, may here be introduced:

'To shorten winter's sadness,
See where the folks with gladness
Disguised all are coming,
Right wantonly a-mumming.
Fa la.

Whilst youthful sports are lasting,
To feasting turn our fasting;
With revels and with wassails,
Make grief and care our vassals.
Fa la.

For youth it well beseemeth,
That pleasure he esteemeth;
And sullen age is hated,
That mirth would have abated.
Fa la.'

The grand and special performance of the mummers from time immemorial, has been the representation of a species of drama, which embodies the time-honoured legend of St George and the dragon, with sundry whimsical adjuncts, which contribute to give the whole affair an aspect of 'very tragical mirth.' The actors, chiefly young lads, having arrayed themselves in the costumes proper to the allegorical characters which they are to support, sally forth in company on Christmas Eve, to commence their round of visits to the houses of the principal inhabitants of the parish. Arriving at the first residence in their way, they knock at the door, and claim the privilege of Christmas in the admission of St George and his 'merrymen.' The accompanying engraving delineates a motley group on such an occasion as we are describing. First is seen Old Father Christmas, bearing, as emblematic devices, the holly bough, wassail-bowl, &c. Beside him stands a pretty little girl, carrying a branch of mistletoe. Then come the Grand Turk, the gallant knight, St George, and the latter's antagonist, the

A PARTY OF MUMMERS.

devouring dragon. A doctor is also present with a large box of pills to cure the wounded. Drums and other music accompany the procession, which, moreover, in the above engraving is represented as accompanied by the parish-beadle, whose command of the stocks, in days gone by, rendered him a terror to evil-doers, and insured the maintenance of order and decorum.

The institution of the mummers, as already intimated, is one that has considerably declined, but it still flourishes in some of the remoter districts of England. As regards the *guisers* in Scotland, where the festivities of the winter-season cluster chiefly around the New Year, we shall have occasion to make special reference to them under the 31st of December.

In conclusion, we present our readers with a specimen of the mumming-drama, as exhibited at the present day at Tenby, in South Wales. At this town, for three weeks at the Christmas season, the mummers are accustomed to go their rounds, mostly three in company, in a quaint guise, when every house is visited by them, and leave to enter requested. Upon being admitted, they commence the performance of the following drama, which has already been printed in *Tales and Traditions of Tenby.* As each of the three represents various characters, they shall be designated Nos. 1, 2, and 3.

No. 1.—'Here come I, Old Father Christmas,
Christmas or not,
I hope Old Father Christmas
Will never be forgot.
A room—make room here, gallant boys,
And give us room to rhyme,
We 're come to shew activity
Upon a Christmas time.
Acting youth or acting age,
The like was never acted on this stage;
If you don't believe what I now say,
Enter St George, and clear the way.'

No. 2.—'Here come I, St George, the valiant man,
With naked sword and spear in hand,
Who fought the dragon, and brought him to the slaughter,
And for this won the king of Egypt's daughter.
What man or mortal will dare to stand
Before me with my sword in hand;
I 'll slay him, and cut him as small as flies,
And send him to Jamaica to make mince-pies.'

St George's challenge is soon taken up, for says No. 3:

'Here come I, a Turkish knight,
In Turkish land I learned to fight,
I 'll fight St George with courage bold,
And if his blood 's hot, will make it cold.'

To this rejoins No. 2, who says:

'If thou art a Turkish knight,
Draw out thy sword, and let us fight.'

A battle is the result; the Turk falls, and St George, struck with remorse, exclaims:

'Ladies and gentlemen,
You 've seen what I 've done,
I 've cut this Turk down
Like the evening sun;
Is there any doctor that can be found,
To cure this knight of his deadly wound?'

No. 1 re-enters, metamorphosed.

'Here come I, a doctor,
A ten-pound doctor;
I've a little bottle in my pocket,
Called hokum, shokum, alicampane;
I 'll touch his eyes, nose, mouth, and chin,
And say: "Rise, dead man," and he 'll fight again.'

After touching the prostrate Turk, the latter leaps up, ready again for the battle. St George, however, thinks this to be a favourable opportunity for sounding his own praises, and rejoins:

'Here am I, St George, with shining armour bright,
I am a famous champion, also a worthy knight;
Seven long years in a close cave was kept,
And out of that into a prison leaped,
From out of that into a rock of stones,
There I laid down my grievous bones.
Many a giant did I subdue,
And ran a fiery dragon through.
I fought the man of Tillotree,
And still will gain the victory.
First, then, I fought in France,
Second, I fought in Spain,
Thirdly, I came to Tenby,
To fight the Turk again.'

A fight ensues, and St George, being again victor, repeats his request for a doctor, who succeeds, as before, in performing a miraculous cure, and at once comes forward as the Protector:

'Here come I, Oliver Cromwell,
As you may suppose,
Many nations I have conquered,
With my copper nose.
I made the French to tremble,
And the Spanish for to quake,
I fought the jolly Dutchmen,
And made their hearts to ache.'

No. 2 then changes his character into that of the gentleman in black.'

'Here come I, Beelzebub,
Under my arm I carry a club,
Under my chin I carry a pan,
Don't I look a nice young man?'

Having finished his speech, the main object of the visit is thus delicately hinted by No. 3:

'Ladies and gentlemen,
Our story is ended,
Our money-box is recommended;
Five or six shillings will not do us harm,
Silver, or copper, or gold if you can.'

After this appeal has been responded to, St George, the Turk, Doctor, Oliver Cromwell, and Beelzebub, take their departure, and the 'guising' is at an end.

## The Lord of Misrule.

The functionary with the above whimsical title played an important part in the festivities of Christmas in the olden time. His duties were to lead and direct the multifarious revels of the season, or, as we should say at the present day, to act as Master of the Ceremonies. The following account of him is given by Stow: 'In the feast of Christmas, there was in the king's house, wheresoever he lodged, a *Lord of Misrule*, or Master of Merry Disports, and the like had ye in the house of every nobleman of honour or good worship, were he spiritual or temporal. The Mayor of London, and either of the Sheriffs, had their several *Lords of Misrule*, ever contending, without quarrel or offence, who should make the rarest pastime to delight the beholders. These lords beginning their rule at Allhallond Eve, continued the same till the morrow after the Feast of the Purification, commonly called Candlemas Day, in which space there were fine and subtle disguisings, masks and mummeries, with playing at cards for counters, nayles and points, in every house, more for pastimes than for gain.'

In the university of Cambridge, the functions of the Lord of Misrule were performed by one of the Masters of Arts, who was regularly elected to superintend the annual representation of Latin plays by the students, besides taking a general charge of their games and diversions during the Christmas season, and was styled the *Imperator* or *Præfectus Ludorum*. A similar Master of Revels was chosen at Oxford. But it seems to have been in the Inns of Court in London that the Lord of Misrule reigned with the greatest splendour, being surrounded with all the parade and ceremony of royalty, having his lord-keeper and treasurer, his guard of honour, and even his two chaplains, who preached before him on Sunday in the Temple Church. On Twelfth Day, he abdicated his sovereignty, and we are informed that in the year 1635, this mock-representative of royalty expended in the exercise of his office about two thousand pounds from his own purse, and at the conclusion of his reign was knighted by Charles I. at Whitehall. The office, indeed, seems to have been regarded among the Templars as a highly-honourable one, and to have been generally conferred on young gentlemen of good family.

The following is an extract from the 'articles' drawn up by the Right Worshipful Richard Evelyn, Esq., father of the author of the *Diary*, and deputy-lieutenant of the counties of Surrey and Sussex, for appointing and defining the functions of a Christmas Lord of Misrule over his estate at Wotton:—'*Imprimis*, I give free leave to Owen Flood, my trumpeter, gentleman, to be Lord of Misrule of all good orders during the twelve days. And also, I give free leave to the said Owen Flood to command all and every person or persons whatsoever, as well servants as others, to be at his command whensoever he shall sound his trumpet or music, and to do him good service, as though I were present myself, at their perils. . . . . I give full power and authority to his lordship to break up all locks, bolts, bars, doors, and latches, and to fling up all doors out of hinges, to come at those who presume to disobey his lordship's commands. God save the king!'

In the accompanying engraving, one of these Lords of Misrule is shewn with a fool's bauble as his badge of office, and a page, who acts as his assistant or confederate in conducting the jocularities. We are informed that a favourite mode for

THE LORD OF MISRULE.

his lordship to enter on the duties of his office was by explaining to the company that he absolved them of all their wisdom, and that they were to be just wise enough to make fools of themselves. No one was to sit apart in pride or self-sufficiency, to laugh at others. Moreover, he (the Lord of Misrule) came endowed with a magic power to turn all his auditory into children, and that, while his sovereignty lasted, he should take care that they conducted themselves as such. So fealty was sworn to the 'merry monarch,' and the reign of fun and folly forthwith commenced. In the pantomime of the present day, we see in the mischievous pranks of the Clown, who parodies all the ordinary occupations of grave and serious life, a reproduction under a modern form of the extravagances of the Lord of Misrule.

There can be no doubt that scandalous abuses often resulted from the exuberant licence assumed by the Lord of Misrule and his satellites. It need, therefore, occasion no surprise to find their proceedings denounced in no measured terms by Prynne and other zealous Puritans. 'If,' says the author of the *Histrio-Mastix*, 'we compare our Bacchanalian Christmasses and New-year's Tides with these Saturnalia and Feasts of Janus, we shall find such near affinitye betweene them both in regard of time (they being both in the end of December and on the first of January) and in their manner of solemnising (both of them being spent in revelling, epicurisme, wantonesse, idlenesse, dancing, drinking, stage-plaies, masques, and carnall pompe and jollity), that we must needes conclude the one to be but the very ape or issue of the other. Hence Polydore Virgil affirmes in express tearmes that our Christmas Lords of Misrule (which custom, saith he, is chiefly observed in England), together with dancing, masques, mummeries, stage-playes, and such other Christmass disorders now in use with Christians, were derived from these Roman Saturnalia and Bacchanalian festivals; which (concludes he) should cause all pious Christians eternally to abominate them.'

In Scotland, previous to the Reformation, the monasteries used to elect a functionary of a similar character, for the superintendence of the Christmas revels, under the designation of the Abbot of Unreason. The readers of the Waverley Novels will recollect the graphic delineation of one of these mock-ecclesiastics in *The Abbot*. An ordinance for suppressing this annual burlesque, with other festivities of a like kind, was passed by the Scottish legislature in 1555. In France, we find the congener of the Lord of Misrule and the Abbot of Unreason in the *Abbas Stultorum*—the Abbot or Pope of Fools.

---

*Born.*—Galba, Roman empero. 3 B.C.; John, king of England, 1166, *Oxford;* William Warburton, bishop of Gloucester, 1698, *Newark;* George Crabbe, poet, 1754, *Aldborough;* Eugene Scribe, French dramatist, 1791, *Paris.*

*Died.*—George of Cappadocia, noted Arian bishop, slain at Alexandria, 361 A.D.; Thomas Beaufort, Duke of Exeter, 1426, *Bury St Edmunds;* Vasco da Gama, celebrated Portuguese navigator, 1525, *Cochin, in Malabar;* Madame de Genlis, popular authoress, 1830, *Paris;* Davies Gilbert, antiquarian and man of science, 1839, *Eastbourne, Sussex;* Archdeacon Henry John Todd, editor of Johnson's *Dictionary*, &c., 1845, *Settrington, Yorkshire;* Dr John Ayrton Paris, chemist, 1856, *London;* Hugh Miller, geologist, 1856, *Portobello.*

## The Waits.

It is a curious circumstance, that no one appears clearly to know whether the term *Waits* denoted originally musical instruments, a particular kind of music, or the persons who played under certain special circumstances. There is evidence in support of all these views. At one time, the name of Waits was given to minstrels attached to the king's court, whose duty it was to guard the streets at night, and proclaim the hour—something in the same manner as the watchmen were wont to do in London before the establishment of the metropolitan police. A regular company of waits was established at Exeter as early as the year 1400, and in relation to the duties and emoluments of such personages in the reign of Edward IV., the following curious account is furnished by Rymer: 'A wayte, that nightelye from Mychelmas to Shreve Thorsdaye pipethe the watche withen this courte fower tymes;

in the somere nyghtes iij tymes, and makethe bon gayte at every chambere-dore and offyce, as well for feare of pyckeres and pillers. He eateth in the halle with mynstrielles, and takethe lyverye [allowance] at nyghte a loffe, a galone of alle, and for somere nyghtes ij candles pich, a bushel of coles; and for wintere nyghtes half a loafe of bread, a galone of alle, iiij candles piche, a bushel of coles; daylye whilste he is presente in courte for his wages in cheque roale allowed iiijd. ob. or else iijd. by the discreshon of the steuarde and tressorere, and that, aftere his cominge and diservinge; also cloathinge with the household yeomen or mynstrielles lyke to the wages that he takethe; and if he be syke he takethe twoe loves, ij messe of great meate, one gallon of alle. Also he parteth with the housholde of general gyfts, and hathe his beddinge carried by the comptrollers assygment; and under this yeoman to be a groome watere. Yf he can excuse the yeoman in his absence, then he takethe rewarde, clotheinge, meat, and all other things lyke to other grooms of houshold. Also this yeoman waight, at the makinge of Knyghtes of the Bath, for his attendance upon them by nyghte-time, in watchinge in the chappelle, hath he to his fee all the watchinge clothing that the knyght shall wear upon him.' This statement is interesting, as it shews that the *Wait*, or *Yeoman-wait*, at court was a kind of page, paid partly in money and partly in board-wages; and it may be a fair question whether the *yeoman-waiter* of later days is not to be traced to some such origin.

In Mr Thoms's edition of *The famous History of Dr Faustus*, the term under notice is clearly applied to a musical instrument: 'Lastly was heard by Faustus all manner of instruments of music—as organs, clarigolds, lutes, viols, citterns, *waits*, hornpipes, anomes, harps, and all manner of other instruments of music.' Butler, also, in his *Principles of Musick*, published in 1636, mentions 'the *waits* or *hoboys*'—implying that that which was called the *waits* or *wayghtes*, was the same instrument as the one long known as the hoboy, hautboy, hautbois, or oboe. Some trace the name *wait* to the German *wacht*, which signifies a watchman or night-guard; a meaning not necessarily connected with music in any way. Dr Rimbault states that, in a roll of officers in the service of Henry VII., one of the entries is 'Musicians for the Wayghtes.'

Dr Busby, in his *Musical Dictionary*, speaking of the waits, says: 'This noun formerly signified *hautboys*, and (which is remarkable) has no singular number. From the instruments, its signification was, after a time, transferred to the performers themselves; who, being in the habit of parading the streets at night with their music, occasioned the name to be applied generally to all musicians who followed a similar practice.'

In the following extract from a communication to the *Gentleman's Magazine* in 1756, describing the mode of constituting freemen at Alnwick, the waits are distinctly spoken of as persons. After describing certain ridiculous ceremonies, the writer proceeds to say: 'They [the freemen in prospect] are generally met by women dressed up with ribbons, bells, and garlands of gum-flowers, who welcome them with dancing and singing, and are called *timber-waits*—perhaps a corruption of *timbrel-waits*, players on timbrels.' Mr H. Coleridge also has expressed a belief that the original waits were wind-instrument players, as shewn by the use of the word in the romances of *Kyng Alysaunder* and *Sir Eglamour*.

A writer in *Notes and Queries* draws attention to the analogy between the words *waits* and *waith*, the latter of which, in Scotland, means wandering or roaming about from place to place. Such wanderers were the minstrels of Scotland, who, three centuries ago, were under the patronage of the civic corporation of Glasgow, and at the city's expense were clothed in blue coats or outer garments. 'A remnant of this custom, still popularly called *waits*, yet exists in the magistrates annually granting a kind of certificate or diploma to a few musicians, generally blind men of respectable character, who perambulate the streets of the city during the night and morning, for about three weeks or a month previous to New-year's Day, in most cases performing on violins the slow, soothing airs peculiar to a portion of the old Scottish melodies; and in the solemn silence of repose the effect is very fine. At the commencement of the New-year, these men call at the houses of the inhabitants, and, presenting their credentials, receive a small subscription.'

It is evident that considerable confusion prevails on the subject of the waits, but if we abide by the modern meaning of the term, we shall find that it refers exclusively to a company of musicians whose performances bear a special relation to the season of Christmas. In Scotland, perhaps, they are more associated with the New Year, but in England their functions belong certainly to a period which ends with Christmas-day.

When the waits became town-musicians, instead of court-pages, they were sometimes civic servants, employed as watchmen to call the hour at night, sometimes serenaders or nocturnal minstrels, who looked for a living from private liberality. There is a paper in the *Tatler* (No. 222), which speaks of waits as they were a century and a half ago, and introduces the subject in the following manner: 'Whereas, by letters from Nottingham, we have advice that the young ladies of that place complain for want of sleep, by reason of certain riotous lovers, who for this last summer have very much infested the streets of that eminent city with violins and bass-viols, between the hours of twelve and four in the morning;' with more to the same purport. It then proceeds to state that the same practice existed in other towns, and accounts for it thus: 'For as the custom prevails at present, there is scarce a young man of any fashion in a corporation who does not make love with the town music; the waits often help him through his courtship.'

At present, and in London, the waits are musicians who play during the night-hours for two or three weeks before Christmas, terminating their performances usually on Christmas Eve. They use generally wind-instruments, and play any tunes which happen to be popular at the time. They call at the houses of the inhabitants soon afterwards for Christmas donations.

Down to the year 1820, perhaps later, the waits had a certain degree of official recognition in the cities of London and Westminster. In London, the post was purchased; in Westminster, it was an appointment under the control of the High Constable and the Court of Burgesses. A police inquiry about Christmas-time, in that year, brought the matter in a singular way under public notice. Mr Clay had been the official leader of the waits for Westminster; and on his death, Mr Monro obtained the post. Having employed a number of persons in different parts of the city and liberties of Westminster to serenade the inhabitants, trusting to their liberality at Christmas as a remuneration, he was surprised to find that other persons were, unauthorised, assuming the right of playing at night, and making applications to the inhabitants for Christmas-boxes. Sir R. Baker, the police magistrate, promised to aid Mr Monro in the assertion of his claims; and the result, in several police cases, shewed that there really was this 'vested right' to charm the ears of the citizens of Westminster with nocturnal music. At present (as stated in the last paragraph), there is nothing to prevent any number of such itinerant minstrels from plying their midnight calling.

---

# DECEMBER 25.

The Nativity of Jesus Christ. St Eugenia, virgin and martyr, about 257. St Anastasia, martyr, 304. Another St Anastasia.

## Christmas-Day.

The festival of Christmas is regarded as the greatest celebration throughout the ecclesiastical year, and so important and joyous a solemnity is it deemed, that a special exception is made in its favour, whereby, in the event of the anniversary falling on a Friday, that day of the week, under all other circumstances a fast, is transformed to a festival.

That the birth of Jesus Christ, the deliverer of the human race, and the mysterious link connecting the transcendent and incomprehensible attributes of Deity with human sympathies and affections, should be considered as the most glorious event that ever happened, and the most worthy of being reverently and joyously commemorated, is a proposition which must commend itself to the heart and reason of every one of His followers, who aspires to walk in His footsteps, and share in the ineffable benefits which His death has secured to mankind. And so though at one period denounced by the Puritans as superstitious, and to the present day disregarded by Calvinistic Protestants, as unwarranted by Scripture, there are few who will seriously dispute the propriety of observing the anniversary of Christ's birth by a religious service.

A question, however, which has been long and eagerly agitated, is here brought forward. Is the 25th of December really the day on which our Saviour first shewed himself in human form in the manger at Bethlehem? The evidence which we possess regarding the date is not only traditional, but likewise conflicting and confused. In the earliest periods at which we have any record of the observance of Christmas, we find that some communities of Christians celebrated the festival on the 1st or 6th of January; others on the 29th of March, the time of the Jewish Passover; while others, it is said, observed it on the 29th of September, or Feast of Tabernacles. There can be no doubt, however, that long before the reign of Constantine, in the fourth century, the season of the New Year had been adopted as the period for celebrating the Nativity, though a difference in this respect existed in the practice of the Eastern and Western Churches, the former observing the 6th of January, and the latter the 25th of December. The custom of the Western Church at last prevailed, and both of the ecclesiastical bodies agreed to hold the anniversary on the same day. The fixing of the date appears to have been the act of Julius I., who presided as pope or bishop of Rome, from 337 to 352 A.D. The circumstance is doubted by Mosheim, but is confirmed by St Chrysostom, who died in the beginning of the fifth century. This celebrated father of the church informs us, in one of his epistles, that Julius, on the solicitation of St Cyril of Jerusalem, caused strict inquiries to be made on the subject, and thereafter, following what seemed to be the best authenticated tradition, settled authoritatively the 25th of December as the anniversary of Christ's birth, the 'Festorum omnium metropolis,' as it is styled by Chrysostom. It is true, indeed, that some have represented this fixing of the day to have been accomplished by St Telesphorus, who was bishop of Rome 128–139 A.D., but the authority for the assertion is very doubtful. Towards the close of the second century, we find a notice of the observance of Christmas in the reign of the Emperor Commodus; and about a hundred years afterwards, in the time of Diocletian, an atrocious act of cruelty is recorded of the last-named emperor, who caused a church in Nicomedia, where the Christians were celebrating the Nativity, to be set on fire, and by barring every means of egress from the building, made all the worshippers perish in the flames. Since the end of the fourth century at least, the 25th of December has been uniformly observed as the anniversary of the Nativity by all the nations of Christendom.

Thus far for ancient usage, but it will be readily comprehended that insurmountable difficulties yet exist with respect to the real date of the momentous event under notice. Sir Isaac Newton, indeed, remarks in his *Commentary on the Prophecies of Daniel*, that the feast of the Nativity, and most of the other ecclesiastical anniversaries, were originally fixed at cardinal points of the year, without any reference to the dates of the incidents which they commemorated, dates which, by the lapse of time, had become impossible to be ascertained. Thus the Annunciation of the Virgin Mary was placed on the 25th of March, or about the time of the vernal equinox; the feast of St Michael on the 29th of September, or near the autumnal equinox; and the birth of Christ and other festivals at the time of the winter-solstice. Many of the apostles' days—such as St Paul, St Matthias, and others—were determined by the days when the sun entered the respective signs of the ecliptic, and the pagan festivals had also a considerable share in the adjustment of the Christian year. To this last we shall shortly have occasion to advert more particularly, but at present we shall content ourselves by remarking that the views of the great astronomer just indicated, present at least a specious explanation of the original construction of the ecclesiastical calendar. As regards the observance of Easter indeed, and its accessory celebrations, there is good ground for maintaining that they mark tolerably accurately the anniversaries of the Passion and Resurrection of our Lord, seeing that we know that the events themselves took place at the period of the Jewish Passover. But no such precision of date can be adduced as regards Christmas, respecting which the generally received view now is, that it does *not* correspond with the actual date of the nativity of our Saviour. One objection, in particular, has been made, that the incident recorded in Scripture, of shepherds keeping watch by night on the plains of Bethlehem, could not have taken place in the month of December, a period generally of great inclemency in the region of Judæa.

Though Christian nations have thus, from an early period in the history of the church, celebrated Christmas about the period of the winter-solstice or the shortest day, it is well known that many, and, indeed, the greater number of the popular festive observances by which it is characterised, are referrible to a much more ancient origin. Amid all the pagan nations of antiquity, there seems to have been a universal tendency to worship the sun as the giver of life and light, and the visible manifestation of the Deity. Various as were the names bestowed by different peoples on this object of their worship, he was still the same divinity. Thus, at Rome, he appears to have been worshipped under one of the characters attributed to *Saturn*, the father of the gods; among the Scandinavian nations he was known under the epithet of Odin or Woden, the father of Thor, who seems afterwards to have shared with his parent the adoration bestowed on the latter, as the divinity of which the sun was the visible manifestation; whilst with the ancient Persians, the appellation for the god of light was Mithras, apparently the same as the Irish *Mithr*, and with the Phœnicians or Carthaginians it was Baal or Bel, an epithet familiar to all students of the Bible.

Concurring thus as regards the object of worship, there was a no less remarkable uniformity in the period of the year at which these different nations celebrated a grand festival in his honour. The time chosen appears to have been universally the season of the New Year, or, rather, the winter-solstice, from which the new year was frequently reckoned. This unanimity in the celebration of the festival in question, is to be ascribed to the general feeling of joy which all of us experience when the gradual shortening of the day reaches its utmost limit on the 21st of December, and the sun, recommencing his upward course, announces that mid-winter is past, and spring and summer are approaching. On similar grounds, and with similar demonstrations, the ancient pagan nations observed a festival at mid-summer, or the summer-solstice, when the sun arrives at the culminating-point of his ascent on the 21st of June, or longest day.

By the Romans, this anniversary was celebrated under the title of *Saturnalia*, or the festival of Saturn, and was marked by the prevalence of a universal licence and merry-making. The slaves were permitted to enjoy for a time a thorough freedom in speech and behaviour, and it is even said that their masters waited on them as servants. Every one feasted and rejoiced, work and business were for a season entirely suspended, the houses were decked with laurels and evergreens, presents were made by parents and friends, and all sorts of games and amusements were indulged in by the citizens. In the bleak north, the same rejoicings had place, but in a ruder and more barbarous form. Fires were extensively kindled, both in and out of doors, blocks of wood blazed in honour of Odin and Thor, the sacred mistletoe was gathered by the Druids, and sacrifices, both of men and cattle, were made to the savage divinities. Fires are said, also, to have been kindled at this period of the year by the ancient Persians, between whom and the Druids of Western Europe a relationship is supposed to have existed.

In the early ages of Christianity, its ministers frequently experienced the utmost difficulty in inducing the converts to refrain from indulging in the popular amusements which were so largely participated in by their pagan countrymen. Among others, the revelry and licence which characterised the Saturnalia called for special animadversion. But at last, convinced partly of the inefficacy of such denunciations, and partly influenced by the idea that the spread of Christianity might thereby be advanced, the church endeavoured to amalgamate, as it were, the old and new religions, and sought, by transferring the heathen ceremonies to the solemnities of the Christian festivals, to make them subservient to the cause of religion and piety. A compromise was thus effected between clergy and laity, though it must be admitted that it proved anything but a harmonious one, as we find a constant, though ineffectual, proscription by the ecclesiastical authorities of the favourite amusements of the people, including among others the sports and revelries at Christmas.

Ingrafted thus on the Roman Saturnalia, the Christmas festivities received in Britain further changes and modifications, by having superadded to them, first, the Druidical rites and superstitions, and then, after the arrival of the Saxons, the various ceremonies practised by the ancient Germans and Scandinavians. The result has been the strange medley of Christian and pagan rites which contribute to make up the festivities of the modern Christmas. Of these, the burning of the Yule log, and the superstitions connected with the mistletoe have already been described under Christmas Eve, and further accounts are given under separate heads, both under the 24th and 25th of December.

The name given by the ancient Goths and Saxons to the festival of the winter-solstice was *Jul* or *Yule*, the latter term forming, to the present day, the designation in the Scottish dialect of Christmas, and preserved also in the phrase of the 'Yule log.' Perhaps the etymology of no term has excited greater discussion among antiquaries. Some maintain it to be derived from the Greek, ουλοι or ιουλος, the name of a hymn in honour of Ceres; others say it comes from the Latin *jubilum*, signifying a time of rejoicing, or from its being a festival in honour of Julius Cæsar; whilst some also explain its meaning as synonymous with *ol* or *oel*, which in the ancient Gothic language denotes a feast, and also the favourite liquor used on such occasion, whence our word *ale*. But a much more probable derivation of the term in question is from the Gothic *giul* or *hiul*, the origin of the modern word *wheel*, and bearing the same signification. According to this very probable explanation, the Yule festival received its name from its being the turning-point of the year, or the period at which the fiery orb of day made a revolution in his annual circuit, and entered on his northern journey. A confirmation of this view is afforded by the circumstance that in the old clog almanacs, a *wheel* is the device employed for marking the season of Yule-tide.

Throughout the middle ages, and down to the period of the Reformation, the festival of Christmas, ingrafted on the pagan rites of Yule, continued throughout Christendom to be universally celebrated with every mark of rejoicing. On the adoption of a new system of faith by most of the northern nations of Europe in the sixteenth century, the Lutheran and Anglican churches retained the celebration of Christmas and other festivals, which Calvinists rejected absolutely, denouncing the observance of all such days, except Sunday, as superstitious and unscriptural. In reference to the superstition anciently prevalent in Scotland against spinning on Christmas or Yule day, and the determination of the Calvinistic clergy to put down all such notions, the following amusing passage is quoted by Dr Jamieson from *Jhone Hamilton's Facile Traictise:* 'The ministers of Scotland—in contempt of the vther halie dayes obseruit be England—cause their wyfis and seruants *spin* in oppin sicht of the people upon Yeul day; and their affectionnate auditeurs constraines their tennants to yok thair pleuchs on Yeul day in contempt of Christ's Natiuitie, whilk our Lord has not left vnpunisit; for thair oxin ran wod [mad], and brak their nekis, and leamit [lamed] sum pleugh men, as is notoriously knawin in sindrie partes of Scotland.' In consequence of the Presbyterian form of church-government, as constituted by John Knox and his coadjutors on the model of the ecclesiastical polity of Calvin, having taken such firm root in Scotland, the festival of Christmas, with other commemorative celebrations retained from the Romish calendar by the Anglicans and Lutherans, is comparatively unknown in that country, at least in the Lowlands. The tendency to mirth and jollity at the close of the year, which seems almost inherent in human nature, has, in North Britain, been, for the most part, transferred from Christmas and Christmas Eve to New-year's Day and the preceding evening, known by the appellation of *Hogmenay*. In many parts of the Highlands of Scotland, however, and also in the county of Forfar, and one or two other districts, the day for the great annual merry-making is Christmas.

From a curious old song preserved in the Harleian Manuscripts in the British Museum, we learn that it was considered peculiarly lucky when Christmas-day fell on a Sunday, and the reverse when it occurred on a Saturday. The intermediate days are, for the most part, characterised by a happy uniformity of propitious augury. The versification is of the rudest and most rugged description, but as an interesting specimen of medieval folk-lore, we subjoin the stanzas relating to Sunday and Saturday:

'Lordinges, I warne you al beforne,
Yef that day that Cryste was borne,
Falle uppon a Sunday;
That wynter shall be good par fay,
But grete wyndes alofte shalbe,
The somer shall be fayre and drye;
By kynde skylle, wythowtyn lesse,
Throw all londes shalbe peas,
And good tyme all thyngs to don.
But he that stelyth he shalbe fownde sone;
Whate chylde that day borne be,
A great lord he shalbe.

* * * * *

If Crystmas on the Saterday falle,
That wynter ys to be dredden alle,
Hyt shalbe so fulle of grete tempeste
That hyt shall sle bothe man and beste,
Frute and corne shal fayle grete won,
And olde folke dyen many on;
Whate woman that day of chylde travayle
They shalbe borne in grete perelle;
And chyldren that be borne that day,
Within half a yere they shall dye par fay,
The summer then shall wete ryghte ylle:
If thou awght stele, hyt shel the spylle;
Thou dyest, yf sekenes take the.'

Somewhat akin to the notions above inculcated, is the belief in Devonshire that if the sun shines bright at noon on Christmas-day, a plentiful crop of apples may be expected in the following year.

From the Diary of that rare old gossip, Mr Pepys, we extract the following entries relative to three Christmas-days of two hundred years ago:

'Christmas-day (1662).—Had a pleasant walk to Whitehall, where I intended to have received the communion with the family, but I came a little too late. So I walked up into the house, and spent my time looking over pictures, particularly the ships in King Henry the Eighth's Voyage to Bullaen; marking the great difference between those built then and now. By and by, down to the chapel again, where Bishop Morley preached on the song of the angels, "Glory to God on high, on earth peace and good-will towards men." Methought he made but a poor sermon, but long, and reprehending the common jollity of the court for the true joy that shall and ought to be on those days. Particularised concerning their excess in plays and gaming, saying that he whose office it is to keep the gamesters in order and within bounds, serves but for a second rather in a duel, meaning the groome porter. Upon which it was worth observing how far they are come from taking the reprehensions of a bishop seriously, that they all laugh in the chapel when he reflected on their ill actions and courses. He did much press us to joy in these public days of joy, and to hospitality. *But one that stood by whispered in my eare, that the bishop do not spend one groate to the poor himself.* The sermon done, a good anthem followed with vialls, and the king came down to receive the sacrament.

'Christmas-day (1665).—To church in the morning, and there saw a wedding in the church, which I have not seen many a day; and the young people so merry one with another, *and strange to see what delight we married people have to see these poor fools decoyed* into our condition, every man and woman gazing and smiling at them.

'Christmas-day (1668).—To dinner alone with my wife, who, poor wretch! sat undressed all day till ten at night, altering and lacing of a noble petticoat; while I by her making the boy read to me the Life of Julius Cæsar, and Des Cartes's book of Music.'

The geniality and joyousness of the Christmas season in England, has long been a national characteristic. The following poem or carol, by George

Wither, who belongs to the first-half of the seventeenth century, describes with hilarious animation the mode of keeping Christmas in the poet's day:

'So now is come our joyfulst feast;
 Let every man be jolly;
Each room with ivy leaves is drest,
 And every post with holly.
Though some churls at our mirth repine,
Round your foreheads garlands twine;
Drown sorrow in a cup of wine,
 And let us all be merry.

Now all our neighbours' chimneys smoke,
 And Christmas blocks are burning;
Their ovens they with baked meat choke,
 And all their spits are turning.
Without the door let sorrow lye;
And if for cold it hap to die,
We'll bury't in a Christmas-pie,
 And evermore be merry.

Now every lad is wond'rous trim,
 And no man minds his labour;
Our lasses have provided them
 A bagpipe and a tabor;
Young men and maids, and girls and boys,
Give life to one another's joys;
And you anon shall by their noise
 Perceive that they are merry.

Rank misers now do sparing shun;
 Their hall of music soundeth;
And dogs thence with whole shoulders run,
 So all things then aboundeth.
The country-folks, themselves advance,
With crowdy-muttons out of France;
And Jack shall pipe and Jyll shall dance,
 And all the town be merry.

Ned Squash hath fetcht his bands from pawn,
 And all his best apparel;
Brisk Nell hath bought a ruff of lawn
 With dropping of the barrel.
And those that hardly all the year
Had bread to eat, or rags to wear,
Will have both clothes and dainty fare,
 And all the day be merry.

Now poor men to the justices
 With capons make their errants;
And if they hap to fail of these,
 They plague them with their warrants:
But now they feed them with good cheer,
And what they want, they take in beer,
For Christmas comes but once a year,
 And then they shall be merry.

Good farmers in the country nurse
 The poor, that else were undone;
Some landlords spend their money worse,
 On lust and pride at London.
There the roysters they do play,
Drab and dice their lands away,
Which may be ours another day,
 And therefore let's be merry.

The client now his suit forbears,
 The prisoner's heart is eased;
The debtor drinks away his cares,
 And for the time is pleased.
Though others' purses be more fat,
Why should we pine or grieve at that?
Hang sorrow! care will kill a cat,
 And therefore let's be merry.

Hark! now the wags abroad do call,
 Each other forth to rambling;
Anon you'll see them in the hall,
 For nuts and apples scrambling.
Hark! how the roofs with laughter sound,
Anon they'll think the house goes round,
For they the cellar's depth have found,
 And there they will be merry.

The wenches with their wassel-bowls
 About the streets are singing;
The boys are come to catch the owls,
 The wild mare in it bringing,
Our kitchen-boy hath broke his box,
And to the dealing of the ox,
Our honest neighbours come by flocks,
 And here they will be merry.

Now kings and queens poor sheepcotes have,
 And mate with every body;
The honest now may play the knave,
 And wise men play the noddy.
Some youths will now a mumming go,
Some others play at Rowland-bo,
And twenty other game boys mo,
 Because they will be merry.

Then, wherefore in these merry daies,
 Should we, I pray, be duller?
No, let us sing some roundelayes,
 To make our mirth the fuller.
And, while thus inspired we sing,
Let all the streets with echoes ring;
Woods and hills and every thing,
 Bear witness we are merry.'

At present, Christmas-day, if somewhat shorn of its ancient glories, and unmarked by that boisterous jollity and exuberance of animal spirits which distinguished it in the time of our ancestors, is, nevertheless, still the holiday in which of all others throughout the year, all classes of English society most generally participate. Partaking of a religious character, the forenoon of the day is usually passed in church, and in the evening the re-united members of the family assemble round the joyous Christmas-board. Separated as many of these are during the rest of the year, they all make an effort to meet together round the Christmas-hearth. The hallowed feelings of domestic love and attachment, the pleasing remembrance of the past, and the joyous anticipation of the future, all cluster round these family-gatherings, and in the sacred associations with which they are intertwined, and the active deeds of kindness and benevolence which they tend to call forth, a realisation may almost be found of the angelic message to the shepherds of Bethlehem—'Glory to God in the highest, and on earth peace, good-will toward men.'

## Christmas Carols.

Amid so many popular customs at Christmas, full of so much sweet and simple poetry, there is perhaps none more charming than that of the Christmas carols, which celebrate in joyous and yet devout strains the Nativity of the Saviour. The term is believed to be derived from the Latin *cantare* (to sing), and *rola!* an interjection expressive of joy. The practice appears to be as ancient as the celebration of Christmas itself, and we are informed that in the early ages of the church, the bishops were accustomed to sing carols on Christmas-day among their clergy. The quaint and inestimable Jeremy Taylor, referring in his *Great Exemplar* to the *Gloria in Excelsis*, or hymn sung by the angels on the plains of Bethlehem, says: 'As soon as these blessed choristers had sung their *Christmas Carol*, and taught the Church a hymn to put into her offices for ever in the anniversary of this festivity, the angels returned into heaven.' Milton also, in the twelfth book of *Paradise Lost*, thus alludes to what may be regarded as the first Christmas carol:

'His place of birth a solemn angel tells
To simple shepherds, keeping watch by night;
They gladly thither haste, and by a quire
Of squadron'd angels hear his *carol* sung.'

In process of time, these Christmas hymns became very much secularised, and latterly, were frequently nothing more than festal chants, sung during the revelries of the Christmas season. The earliest specimen which we possess of the medieval carol, belongs to this class, and is preserved in a manuscript in the British Museum. It is composed in Norman-French, and belongs to the thirteenth century. The same convivial quality characterises a 'sett of carols,' the earliest printed edition of these Christmas chants, published by Wynkyn de Worde in 1521. The 'Boar's Head' song, quoted in a subsequent article, occurs with others of a similar class in the collection referred to.

As with the generality of our popular ballads, we find the earlier specimens of Christmas carols often extremely rugged and unadorned in point of

CHILDREN'S CAROL ON CHRISTMAS MORNING.

composition, and perceive them gradually assume a more polished and harmonious form with the progress of education and refinement. This improvement is chiefly to be remarked after the commencement of the sixteenth century. The following carol, belonging to that period, is frequently sung on Christmas-morning by children, as represented in the accompanying engraving—

'When Christ was born of Mary free,
In Bethelem, in that fair citie,
Angels sang there with mirth and glee,
*In Excelsis Gloria.*

Herdsmen beheld these angels bright,
To them appearing with great light,
Who said: "God's Son is born this night,"
*In Excelsis Gloria.*

This King is come to save mankind,
As in scripture truths we find,
Therefore this song have we in mind,
*In Excelsis Gloria.*

Then, Lord, for Thy great grace,
Grant us the bliss to see thy face,
Where we may sing to Thy solace,
*In Excelsis Gloria.*'

In his *History of English Poetry*, Warton notices a licence, granted in 1562, to John Tysdale for printing 'Certayne goodly Carowles to be songe to the glory of God;' and again 'Crestenmas Carowles auctorisshed by my lord of London.' This may be regarded as a specimen of the endeavours made at the time of the Reformation, to supplant the old popular carols, by compositions of a more devout and less popish character, and in Scotland we find instances of the same policy in the famous *Gude and Godly Ballates*, and *Ane compendious Book of godly and spirituall Sangs;* the latter printed at Edinburgh in 1621. The Puritans, indeed, denounced not only the singing of Christmas carols, but the observance of the festival of Christmas itself, as pernicious and unscriptural, and to their influence has been ascribed much of the seriousness characterising this department of popular poetry in later times.

It will be recollected that Goldsmith's *Vicar of Wakefield*, describing the unsophisticated character of his parishioners, says: 'They kept up the Christmas carol.' Such a composition as the following might have been sung by these simple swains. It is one of the most popular of the class of chants under notice.

'God rest you merry, gentlemen,
Let nothing you dismay,
For Jesus Christ our Saviour
Was born upon this day,
To save us all from Satan's power,
When we were gone astray.
O tidings of comfort and joy!
For Jesus Christ our Saviour
Was born on Christmas-day.

In Bethlehem, in Jewry,
This blessed babe was born,
And laid within a manger
Upon this blessed morn;
The which his mother Mary
Nothing did take in scorn.
O tidings, &c.

From God our Heavenly Father,
A blessed angel came,
And unto certain shepherds,
Brought tidings of the same,
How that in Bethlehem was born,
The Son of God by name.
O tidings, &c.

Fear not, then said the angel,
Let nothing you affright,
This day is born a Saviour
Of virtue, power, and might;
So frequently to vanquish all,
The friends of Satan quite.
O tidings, &c.

The shepherds at those tidings,
Rejoiced much in mind,
And left their flocks a-feeding
In tempest, storm, and wind,
And went to Bethlehem straightway,
This blessed babe to find.
O tidings, &c.

But when to Bethlehem they came,
Whereas this infant lay,
They found Him in a manger,
Where oxen feed on hay,
His mother Mary kneeling,
Unto the Lord did pray.
O tidings, &c.

Now to the Lord sing praises,
All you within this place,
And with true love and brotherhood,
Each other now embrace;
This holy tide of Christmas
All others doth deface.
O tidings, &c.'

Another of these carols is presented to the reader. Without laying claim to literary merit of an exalted order, it has all that simplicity and melodiousness which render ballad-poetry so charming:

'I saw three ships come sailing in
On Christmas-day, on Christmas-day;
I saw three ships come sailing in
On Christmas-day in the morning.

And what was in those ships all three,
On Christmas-day, on Christmas-day?
And what was in those ships all three,
On Christmas-day in the morning?

Our Saviour Christ and his Lady,
On Christmas-day, on Christmas-day:
Our Saviour Christ and his Lady,
On Christmas-day in the morning.

Pray whither sailed those ships all three,
On Christmas-day, on Christmas-day?
Pray whither sailed those ships all three,
On Christmas-day in the morning?

O they sailed into Bethlehem,
On Christmas-day, on Christmas-day;
O they sailed into Bethlehem,
On Christmas-day in the morning.

And all the bells on earth shall ring,
On Christmas-day, on Christmas-day;
And all the bells on earth shall ring,
On Christmas-day in the morning.

And all the angels in heaven shall sing,
On Christmas-day, on Christmas-day;
And all the angels in heaven shall sing,
On Christmas-day in the morning.

And all the souls on earth shall sing,
On Christmas-day, on Christmas-day,
And all the souls on earth shall sing,
On Christmas-day in the morning.

Then let us all rejoice amain,
On Christmas-day, on Christmas-day;
Then let us all rejoice amain,
On Christmas-day in the morning.'

The next carol, which we proceed to quote, is of a very different character, being one of those doggerel rhymes sung by children, when they go on a *gooding* excursion on Christmas-morning. An explanation of the term in italics has been already given in our notice of St Thomas's Day, to which such expeditions are more strictly appropriate. The carol, as subjoined, is sung on Christmas-morning by children in Yorkshire, who bear along with them, on the occasion, a Christmas-tree as a badge of their mission. The scene is also pictorially delineated on the following page.

'Well-a-day! well-a-day!
Christmas too soon goes away,
Then your *gooding* we do pray,
For the good time will not stay—
We are not beggars from door to door,
But neighbours' children known before,
So gooding pray,
We cannot stay,
But must away,
For the Christmas will not stay,
Well-a-day! well-a-day.'

Christmas carols are sung on Christmas Eve as well as on the morning of Christmas-day, and indeed the former is regarded by many as the more appropriate occasion. Then the choristers, attached to the village-church, make their rounds to the principal houses throughout the parish, and sing some of those simple and touching hymns. The airs to which they are sung are frequently no less plaintive and melodious than the words, and are often accompanied by instruments. The writer retains a vivid recollection of a carol which he heard sung, some years ago, on Christmas Eve by a detachment of the village choir, in front of a country-house in Devonshire, where he was at the time a visitor. The sweet and pathetic melody, which was both remarkably well sung and played, the picturesqueness of the group of singers, whose persons were only rendered visible, in the darkness of the night, by the light of one or two lanterns which they carried, and the novelty and general interest of the scene, all produced an impression which was never to be forgotten. These Christmas-eve carols are very general in Devonshire, and the usual custom for the singers is to club the money which they receive on such occasions, and expend it in a social merry-making on Twelfth Day, a fortnight afterwards.

CHRISTMAS-MORNING CAROL BY CHILDREN IN YORKSHIRE.

One or two poets of note have essayed carol-writing, among whom may be mentioned Bishop Hall and Robert Herrick, both belonging to the earlier half of the seventeenth century. And here, though we have already quoted so largely, we cannot refrain from introducing the following singularly beautiful effusion of Herrick, forming the first part of a poem, entitled the *Star Song*, written as a hymn for the Epiphany, but of which the first three stanzas, as here presented, are fully as applicable to Christmas. It glows with an imagery truly oriental:

'*A flourish of music: then follows the Song.*

Tell us, thou clear and heavenly tongue,
Where is the Babe that lately sprung?
Lies he the lily-banks among?

Or say, if this new Birth of ours
Sleeps, laid within some ark of flowers,
Spangled with dew-light; thou canst clear
All doubts, and manifest the where.

Declare to us, bright star, if we shall seek
Him in the morning's blushing cheek,
Or search the beds of spices through,
To find him out?'

These charming verses are introduced in a very beautiful *Book of Christmas Carols*, published in 1846, adorned with splendid illuminations from manuscripts preserved in the British Museum. The typography of the lyric in question is literally *bedded* among a most lovely and characteristic group of fruits and flowers.

We find scarcely any traces of the singing of Christmas carols in Scotland, though from time immemorial it has been so universally prevalent, not only in England, but in France, Italy, and other countries of the continent. In England, at one time, it was customary on Christmas-day, more especially at the afternoon-service, to sing carols in churches, instead of the regular psalms and hymns. We are, moreover, informed that at the end of the service it was the usage on such occasions for the clerk in a loud voice to wish all the congregation A Merry Christmas and a Happy New-Year.

## The Three Magi.

In connection with the birth of the Saviour, and as a pendant to the notice under Twelfth Day, or the Epiphany, of the observances commemorative of the visit of the Wise Men of the East to Bethlehem (see vol. i. p. 61), we shall here introduce some further particulars of the ideas current in medieval times on the subject of these celebrated personages.

The legend of the Wise Men of the East, or, as they are styled in the original Greek of St Matthew's gospel, Μαγοι (the Magi), who visited the infant Saviour with precious offerings, became, under monkish influence, one of the most popular during the middle ages, and was told with increased and elaborated perspicuity as time advanced. The Scripture nowhere informs us that these individuals were kings, or their number restricted to three. The legend converts the Magi into kings, gives their names, and a minute account of their stature and the nature of their gifts. Melchior (we are thus told) was king of Nubia, the smallest man of the triad, and he gave the Saviour a gift of gold. Balthazar was king of Chaldea, and he offered incense; he was a man of ordinary stature. But the third, Jasper, king of Tarshish, was of high stature, 'a black Ethiope,' and he gave myrrh. All came with 'many rich ornaments belonging to king's array, and also with mules, camels, and horses loaded with great treasure, and with multitude of people,' to do homage to the Saviour, 'then a little childe of xiii dayes olde.'

THE OFFERING OF THE MAGI.

The barbaric pomp involved in this legend made it a favourite with artists during the middle ages. Our engraving is a copy from a circular plate of silver, chased in high-relief, and partly gilt, which is supposed to have formed the centre of a morse, or large brooch, used to fasten the decorated cope of an ecclesiastic in the latter part of the fourteenth century. The subject has been frequently depicted by the artists subsequent to this period. Van Eyck, Durer, and the German schools were particularly fond of the theme—the latest and most striking work being that by Rubens, who revelled in such pompous displays. The artists of the Low Countries were, probably, also biassed by the fact, that the cathedral of Cologne held the shrine in which the bodies of the Magi were said to be deposited, and to which the faithful made many pilgrimages, greatly to the emolument of the city, a result which induced the worthy burghers to distinguish their shield of arms by three crowns only, and to designate the Magi as 'the three kings of Cologne.'

It was to the Empress Helena, mother of Constantine the Great, that the religious world was indebted for the discovery of the place of burial of these kings in the far east. She removed their bodies to Constantinople, where they remained in the church of St Sophia, until the reign of the Emperor Emanuel, who allowed Eustorgius, bishop of Milan, to transfer them to his cathedral. In 1164, when the Emperor Frederick conquered Milan, he gave these treasured relics to Raynuldus, archbishop of Cologne, who removed them to the latter city. His successor, Philip von Heinsberg, placed them in a magnificent reliquary, enriched with gems and enamels, still remaining in its marble shrine in the cathedral, one of the chief wonders of the noble pile, and the principal 'sight' in Cologne. A heavy fee is exacted for opening the doors of the chapel, which is then lighted with lamps, producing a dazzling effect on the mass of gilded and jewelled sculpture, in the centre of which may be seen the three skulls, reputed to be those of the Magi. These relics are enveloped in velvet, and decorated with embroidery and jewels, so that the upper part of each skull only is seen, and the hollow eyes which, as the faithful believe, once rested on the Saviour.

The popular belief in the great power of intercession and protection possessed by the Magi, as departed saints, was widely spread in the middle ages. Any article that had touched these skulls was believed to have the power of preventing accidents to the bearer while travelling, as well as to counteract sorcery, and guard against sudden death. Their names were also used as a charm, and were inscribed upon girdles, garters, and finger-rings. We engrave two specimens of such rings, both works of the fourteenth century. The upper one is of silver, with the names of the Magi engraved upon it; the lower one is of lead simply cast in a mould, and sold cheap for the use of the commonalty. They were regarded as particularly efficacious in the case of cramp. Traces of this superstition still linger in the curative properties popularly ascribed to certain rings.

Bishop Patrick, in his *Reflections on the Devotions of the Roman Church*, 1674, asks with assumed *naïveté* how these names of the three Wise Men—Melchior, Balthazar, and Jasper—are to be of service, 'when another tradition says they were Apellius, Amerus, and Damascus; a third, that they were Megalath, Galgalath, and Sarasin; and a fourth calls them Ator, Sator, and Peratoras; which last I should choose (in this uncertainty) as having the more kingly sound.'

---

*Born.*—Jesus Christ, Saviour of the world;* Sir Isaac Newton, natural philosopher, 1642, *Woolsthorpe, near Grantham*; Johann Jacob Reiske, oriental scholar, 1716, *Zorbig, Saxony*; William Collins, poet, 1720, *Chichester*; Richard Porson, Greek scholar, 1759, *East Ruston, Norfolk.*

*Died.*—Persius, satiric poet, 62 A.D.; Pope Adrian I., 795; Emperor Leo V., the Armenian, slain at Constantinople, 820; Sir Matthew Hale, eminent judge, 1676; Rev. James Hervey, author of the *Meditations*, 1758, *Weston Favell, Northamptonshire*; Mrs Chapone, moral writer, 1801, *Hadley, Middlesex*; Colonel John Gurwood, editor of Wellington's *Dispatches*, 1854, *Brighton.*

## CHRISTMAS CHARITIES.

We have already, in commenting on Christmas-day and its observances, remarked on the hallowed feelings of affection and good-will which are generally called forth at the celebration of this anniversary. Quarrels are composed and forgotten, old friendships are renewed and confirmed, and a universal spirit of charity and forgiveness evoked. Nor is this charity merely confined to acts of kindness and generosity among equals; the poor and destitute experience the bounty of their richer neighbours, and are enabled like them to enjoy themselves at the Christmas season. From the Queen downwards, all classes of society contribute their mites to relieve the necessities and increase the comforts of the poor, both as regards food and raiment. Even in the work-houses—those abodes of short-commons and little ease—the authorities, for once in the year, become liberal in their housekeeping, and treat the inmates on Christmas-day to a substantial dinner of roast-beef and plum-pudding. It is quite enlivening to read the account in the daily papers, a morning or two afterwards, of the fare with which the inhabitants of the various work-houses in London and elsewhere were regaled on Christmas-day, a detailed chronicle being furnished both of the quality of the treat and the quantity supplied to each individual. Beggars, too, have a claim on our charity at this season, maugre all maxims of political economy, and must not be turned from our doors unrelieved. They may, at least, have their dole of bread and meat; and to whatever bad uses they may possibly turn our bounty, it is not probable that the deed will ever be entered to our discredit in the books of the Recording Angel. Apropos of these sentiments, we introduce the following monitory lines by a well-known author and artist:

* We place here this record of the Saviour's birth in accordance with the popular belief, which assigns the 25th of December as the date of that event. The reader will find the question discussed under the article on Christmas-day.

### SCATTER YOUR CRUMBS.

BY ALFRED CROWQUILL.

Amidst the freezing sleet and snow,
  The timid robin comes;
In pity drive him not away,
  But scatter out your crumbs.

And leave your door upon the latch
  For whosoever comes;
The poorer they, more welcome give,
  And scatter out your crumbs.

All have to spare, none are too poor,
  When want with winter comes;
The loaf is never all your own,
  Then scatter out the crumbs.

Soon winter falls upon your life,
  The day of reckoning comes:
Against your sins, by high decree,
  Are weighed those scattered crumbs.

In olden times, it was customary to extend the charities of Christmas and the New Year to the lower animals. Burns refers to this practice in 'The Auld Farmer's Address to his Mare,' when presenting her on New-Year's morning with an extra feed of corn:

'A guid New-year, I wish thee, Maggie!
Hae, there's a ripp to thy auld baggie!'

The great-grandfather of the writer—a small proprietor in the Carse of Falkirk, in Scotland, and an Episcopalian—used regularly himself, every Christmas-morning, to carry a special supply of fodder to each individual animal in his stable and cow-house. The old gentleman was wont to say, that this was a morning, of all others in the year, when man and beast ought alike to have occasion to rejoice.

## CHRISTMAS DECORATIONS.

The decking of churches, houses, and shops with evergreens at Christmas, springs from a period far anterior to the revelation of Christianity, and seems proximately to be derived from the custom prevalent during the Saturnalia of the inhabitants of Rome ornamenting their temples and dwellings with green boughs. From this latter circumstance, we find several early ecclesiastical councils prohibiting the members of the church to imitate the pagans in thus ornamenting their houses. But in process of time, the pagan custom was like others of a similar origin, introduced into and incorporated with the ceremonies of the church itself. The sanction of our Saviour likewise came to be pleaded for the practice, he having entered Jerusalem in triumph amid the shouts of the people, who strewed palm-branches in his way.

It is evident that the use of flowers and green boughs as a means of decoration, is almost instinctive in human nature; and we accordingly find scarcely any nation, civilised or savage, with which it has not become more or less familiar. The Jews employed it in their Feast of Tabernacles, in the month of September; the ancient Druids and other Celtic nations hung up the mistletoe and green branches of different kinds over their doors, to propitiate the woodland sprites; and a similar usage prevailed, as we have seen, in Rome. In short, the feeling thus so universally exhibited, is one of natural religion, and therefore not to be traced exclusively to any particular creed or form of worship.

Stow, that invaluable chronicler, informs us in his *Survey of London*, that 'against the feast of Christmas every man's house, as also their parish churches, were decked with holme [the evergreen oak], ivy, bayes, and whatsoever the season of the year afforded to be green. The conduits and standards in the streets were likewise garnished: among the which I read, that in the year 1444, by tempest of thunder and lightning, towards the morning of Candlemas-day, at the Leadenhall, in Cornhill, a standard of tree, being set up in the midst of the pavement, fast in the ground, nailed full of holme and ivie, for disport of Christmass to the people, was torne up and cast downe by the malignant spirit (as was thought), and the stones of the pavement all about were cast in the streets, and into divers houses, so that the people were sore aghast at the great tempest.'

The favourite plants for church decoration at Christmas are holly, bay, rosemary, and laurel. Ivy is rather objectionable, from its associations, having anciently been sacred to Bacchus, and employed largely in the orgies celebrated in honour of the god of wine. Cypress, we are informed, has been sometimes used, but its funereal relations render it rather out of place at a festive season like Christmas. One plant, in special, is excluded—the mystic mistletoe, which, from its antecedents, would be regarded as about as inappropriate to the interior of a church, as the celebration of the old Druidical rites within the sacred building. A solitary exception to this universal exclusion, is mentioned by Dr Stukeley, who says that it was one time customary to carry a branch of mistletoe, in procession to the high-altar of York Cathedral, and thereafter proclaim a general indulgence and pardon of sins at the gates of the city. We cannot help suspecting that this instance recorded by Stukeley, is to be referred to one of the burlesques on the services of the Church, which, under the leadership of the Boy-bishop, or the Lord of Misrule, formed so favourite a Christmas-pastime of the populace in bygone times.

A quaint old writer thus spiritualises the practice of Christmas decorations. 'So our churches and houses decked with bayes and rosemary, holly and ivy, and other plants which are always green, winter and summer, signify and put us in mind of His Deity, that the child that now was born was God and man, who should spring up like a tender plant, should always be green and flourishing, and live for evermore.' Festive carols, we are informed, used to be chanted at Christmas in praise of the evergreens, so extensively used at that season. The following is a specimen:

'HOLLY.

Here comes holly that is so gent,
To please all men is his intent.
Allelujah!

Whosoever against holly do cry,
In a rope shall be hung full high.
Allelujah!

Whosoever against holly do sing,
He may weep and his hands wring,
Allelujah!

IVY.

Ivy is soft and meek of speech,
Against all bale she is bliss,
Well is he that may her reach.

Ivy is green, with colours bright,
Of all trees best she is,
And that I prove will now be right.

Ivy beareth berries black,
God grant us all his bliss,
For there shall be nothing lack.'

The decorations remain in the churches from Christmas till the end of January, but in accordance with the ecclesiastical canons, they must all be cleared away before the 2d of February or Candlemas-day. The same holds good as a custom with regard to private dwellings, superstition in both cases rendering it a fatal presage, if any of these sylvan ornaments are retained beyond the period just indicated.* Herrick thus alludes to the popular prejudice.

'Down with the rosemary, and so
Down with the baies and mistletoe;
Down with the holly, ivie, all
Wherewith ye drest the Christmas hall;

That so the superstitious find
No one least branch there left behind;
For look, how many leaves there be
Neglected there, maids trust to me,
So many goblins you shall see.'

Aubrey informs us that in several parts of Oxfordshire, it was the custom for the maid-servant to ask the man for ivy to decorate the house; and if he refused or neglected to fetch in a supply, the maids stole a pair of his breeches, and nailed them up to the gate in the yard or highway. A similar usage prevailed in other places, when the refusal to comply with such a request incurred the penalty of being debarred from the well-known privileges of the mistletoe.

* See p. 53 of this volume.

## OLD ENGLISH CHRISTMAS FARE.

THE 'brave days of old' were, if rude and unrefined, at least distinguished by a hearty and profuse hospitality. During the Christmas holidays, open-house was kept by the barons and knights, and for a fortnight and upwards, nothing was heard of but revelry and feasting. The grand feast, however, given by the feudal chieftain to his friends and retainers, took place with great pomp and circumstance on Christmas-day. Among the dishes served up on this important occasion, the boar's head was first at the feast and foremost on the board. Heralded by a jubilant flourish of trumpets, and accompanied by strains of merry minstrelsy, it was carried—on a dish of gold or silver, no meaner metal would suffice—into the banqueting-hall by the sewer; who, as he advanced at the head of the stately procession of nobles, knights, and ladies, sang:

'*Caput apri defero,*
*Reddens laudes Domino.*
The boar's head in hand bring I
With garlands gay and rosemary;
I pray you all sing merrily,
*Qui estis in convivio.*

The boar's head, I understand,
Is the chief service in this land;
Look wherever it be found,
*Servite cum cantico.*

Be glad, both more and less,
For this hath ordained our steward,
To cheer you all this Christmas—
The boar's head and mustard!
*Caput apri defero,*
*Reddens laudes Domino.*'

---

The brawner's head was then placed upon the table with a solemn gravity befitting the dignity of such a noble dish:

'Sweet rosemary and bays around it spread;
His foaming tusks with some large pippin graced,
Or midst those thundering spears an orange placed,
Sauce, like himself, offensive to its foes,
The roguish mustard, dangerous to the nose.'

The latter condiment was indispensable. An old book of instruction for the proper service of the royal table says emphatically: 'First set forth mustard with brawn; take your knife in your hand, and cut brawn in the dish as it lieth, and lay on your sovereign's trencher, and *see there be mustard!*'

When Christmas, in the time of the Commonwealth, was threatened with extinction by act of parliament, the tallow-chandlers loudly complained that they could find no sale for their mustard, because of the diminished consumption of brawn in the land. Parliament failed to put down Christmas, but the boar's-head never recovered its old supremacy at the table. Still, its memory was cherished in some nooks and corners of Old England long after it had ceased to rule the roast. The lessee of the tithes of Horn Church, Essex, had, every Christmas, to provide a boar's-head, which, after being dressed and garnished with bay, was wrestled for in a field adjoining the church. The custom of serving up the ancient dish at Queen's College, Oxford, to a variation of the old carol, sprung, according to the university legend, from a valorous act on the part of a student of the college in question. While walking in Shotover forest, studying his Aristotle, he was suddenly made aware of the presence of a wild-boar, by the animal rushing at him open-mouthed. With great presence of mind, and the exclamation, 'Græcum est,' the collegian thrust the philosopher's ethics down his assailant's throat, and having choked the savage with the sage, went on his way rejoicing.

The Lord Jersey of the Walpolian era was a great lover of the quondam Christmas favourite, and also—according to her own account—of Miss Ford, the lady whom Whitehead and Lord Holdernesse thought so admirably adapted for Gray's friend, Mason, 'being excellent in singing, loving solitude, and full of immeasurable affectations.' Lord Jersey sent Miss Ford a boar's head, a strange first present, at which the lady laughed, saying she 'had often had the honour of meeting it at his lordship's table, and would have ate it had it been eatable!' Her noble admirer resented the scornful insinuation, and indignantly replied, that the head in question was not the one the lady had seen so often, but one perfectly fresh and sweet, having been taken out of the pickle that very morning; and not content with defending his head, Lord Jersey revenged himself by denying that his heart had ever been susceptible of the charms of the fair epicure.

Next in importance to the boar's-head as a Christmas-dish came the peacock. To prepare Argus for the table was a task entailing no little trouble. The skin was first carefully stripped off, with the plumage adhering; the bird was then roasted; when done and partially cooled, it was sewed up again in its feathers, its beak gilt, and so sent to table. Sometimes the whole body was covered with leaf-gold, and a piece of cotton, saturated with spirits, placed in its beak, and lighted before the carver commenced operations. This 'food for lovers and meat for lords' was stuffed with spices and sweet herbs, basted with yolk of egg, and served with plenty of gravy; on great occasions, as many as three fat wethers being bruised to make enough for a single peacock.

The noble bird was not served by common hands; that privilege was reserved for the lady-guests most distinguished by birth or beauty. One of them carried it into the dining-hall to the sound of music, the rest of the ladies following in due order. The bearer of the dish set it down before the master of the house or his most honoured guest. After a tournament, the victor in the lists was expected to shew his skill in cutting up inferior animals. On such occasions, however, the bird was usually served in a pie, at one end of which his plumed crest appeared above the crust, while at the other his tail was unfolded in all its glory. Over this splendid dish did the knights-errant swear to undertake any perilous enterprise that came in their way, and succour lovely woman in distress after the most approved chevalier fashion. Hence Justice Shallow derived his oath of 'By cock and pie!' The latest instance of peacock-eating we can call to mind, is that of a dinner given to William IV. when Duke of Clarence, by the governor of Grenada; when his royal highness was astonished by the appearance of the many-hued bird, dressed in a manner that would have delighted a medieval Ude or Soyer.

Geese, capons, pheasants drenched with ambergrease, and pies of carps-tongues, helped to furnish the table in bygone Christmases, but there was one national dish—neither flesh, fowl, nor good red herring—which was held indispensable. This was furmante, frumenty or furmety, concocted—according to the most ancient formula extant—in this wise: 'Take clean wheat, and bray it in a mortar, that the hulls be all gone off, and seethe it till it burst, and take it up and let it cool; and take clean fresh broth, and sweet milk of almonds, or sweet milk of kine, and temper it all; and take the yolks of eggs. Boil it a little, and set it down and mess it forth with fat venison or fresh mutton.' Venison was seldom served without this accompaniment, but furmety, sweetened with sugar, was a favourite dish of itself, the 'clean broth' being omitted when a lord was to be the partaker.

Mince-pies were popular under the name of 'mutton-pies,' so early as 1596, later authorities all agreeing in substituting neats-tongue in the place of mutton, the remaining ingredients being much the same as those recommended in modern recipes. They were also known as shred and Christmas pies:

'Without the door let sorrow lie,
And if for cold it hap to die,
We'll bury it in a Christmas-pie,
And evermore be merry!'

In Herrick's time it was customary to set a watch upon the pies, on the night before Christmas, lest sweet-toothed thieves should lay felonious fingers on them; the jovial vicar sings:

'Come guard the Christmas-pie,
That the thief, though ne'er so sly,
With his flesh-hooks don't come nigh,
To catch it,
From him, who all alone sits there,
Having his eyes still in his ear,
And a deal of nightly fear,
To watch it.'

Selden tells us mince-pies were baked in a coffin-shaped crust, intended to represent the cratch or manger in which the Holy Child was laid; but we are inclined to doubt his statement, as we find our old English cookery-books always style the crust of a pie 'the coffin.'

When a lady asked Dr Parr on what day it was proper to commence eating mince-pies, he answered, 'Begin on O. Sapientia (December 16th), but please to say Christmas-pie, not mince-pie; mince-pie is puritanical.' The doctor was wrong at least on the last of these points, if not on both. The Christmas festival, it is maintained by many, does not commence before Christmas Eve, and the mince-pie was known before the days of Praise-God Barebones and his strait-laced brethren, for Ben Jonson personifies it under that name in his *Masque of Christmas.* Likely enough, the name of 'Christmas-pie' was obnoxious to puritanical ears, as the enjoying of the dainty itself at that particular season was offensive to puritan taste:

'All plums the prophet's sons deny,
And spice-broths are too hot;
Treason's in a December-pie,
And death within the pot.'

Or, as another rhymster has it:

'The high-shoe lords of Cromwell's making
Were not for dainties—roasting, baking;
The chiefest food they found most good in,
Was rusty bacon and bag-pudding;
Plum-broth was popish, and mince-pie—
O that was flat idolatry!'

In after-times, the Quakers took up the prejudice, and some church-going folks even thought it was not meet for clergymen to enjoy the delicacy, a notion which called forth the following remonstrance from Bickerstaffe.—'The Christmas-pie is, in its own nature, a kind of consecrated cake, and a badge of distinction; and yet it is often forbidden, the Druid of the family. Strange that a sirloin of beef, whether boiled or roasted, when entire is exposed to the utmost depredations and invasions; but if minced into small pieces, and tossed up with plumbs and sugar, it changes its property, and forsooth is meat for his master.'

Mortifying as Lord Macartney's great plum-pudding failure may have been to the diplomatist, he might have consoled himself by remembering that plum-porridge was the progenitor of the pride and glory of an English Christmas. In old times, plum-pottage was always served with the first course of a Christmas-dinner. It was made by boiling beef or mutton with broth, thickened with brown bread; when half-boiled, raisins, currants, prunes, cloves, mace and ginger were added, and when the mess had been thoroughly boiled, it was sent to table with the best meats. Sir Roger de Coverley thought there was some hope of a dissenter, when he saw him enjoy his porridge at the hall on Christmas-day. Plum-broth figures in *Poor Robin's Almanac* for 1750, among the items of Christmas fare, and Mrs Frazer, 'sole teacher of the art of cookery in Edinburgh, and several years' colleague, and afterwards successor to Mrs

M'Iver,' who published a cookery-book in 1791, thought it necessary to include plum-pottage among her soups. Brand partook of a tureenful of 'luscious plum-porridge' at the table of the royal chaplain in 1801, but that is the latest appearance of this once indispensable dish of which we have any record.

As to plum-pudding, we are thoroughly at fault. Rabisha gives a recipe in his *Whole Body of Cookery Dissected* (1675), for a pudding to be boiled in a basin, which bears a great resemblance to our modern Christmas favourite, but does not include it in his bills of fare for winter, although 'a dish of stewed broth, if at Christmas,' figures therein. It shared honours with the porridge in Addison's time, however, for the *Tatler* tells us: 'No man of the most rigid virtue gives offence by an excess in plum-pudding or plum-porridge, because they are the first parts of the dinner;' but the Mrs Frazer above mentioned is the earliest culinary authority we find describing its concoction, at least under the name of 'plumb-pudding.'

While Christmas, as far as eating was concerned, always had its specialities, its liquor *carte* was unlimited. A carolist of the thirteenth century sings (we follow Douce's literal translation):

'Lordlings, Christmas loves good drinking,
  Wines of Gascoigne, France, Anjou,
English ale that drives out thinking,
  Prince of liquors, old or new.
Every neighbour shares the bowl,
  Drinks of the spicy liquor deep;
Drinks his fill without control,
  Till he drowns his care in sleep.'

And to attain that end every exhilarating liquor was pressed into service by our ancestors.

## THE CHRISTIAN AND OTHER ERAS IN CHRONOLOGY.

The *Christian Era* adopts a particular year as a commencement or starting-point, from which any subsequent year may be reckoned. It has no particular connection with *Christmas-day*, but it may suitably be noticed in this place as associated with that great festival.

All nations who have made any great advance in civilisation, have found it useful to adopt some particular year as a chronological basis. The Romans adopted for this purpose the year, and even the day, which some of their historians assigned as the date for the foundation of Rome. That particular date, designated according to our present chronology, was the 21st of April, in the year 754 B.C. They were wont to express it by the letters A. U. C., or *Ab urbe condita*, signifying 'from the foundation of the city.' The change effected in the calendar by the first two Cæsars, and which, with the alteration afterwards rendered necessary by the lapse of centuries, forms, to the present day, the standard for computing the length and divisions of the year, took place 47 B.C. or 707 A.U.C.

The *Olympiads* were a Greek mode of computing time, depending on chronological groups, each of which measured respectively four years in length. They began in 776 B.C., in commemoration of an event connected with the Olympic Games. Each period of four years was called an *Olympiad;* and any particular date was denoted by the number of the Olympiad, and the number of the year in it; such as the third year of the first Olympiad, the first year of the fourth Olympiad, and so on. The Greeks, like the Romans, made in ancient times their civil years a little longer or a little shorter than the true year, and were, like them, forced to reform their calendar occasionally. One of these reforms was made by Meton in 432 B.C., a year which corresponded to the fourth year of the eighty-sixth Olympiad; and another in 330 B.C. When the power of Greece sank to a shadow under the mighty influence of that of Rome, the mode of reckoning by Olympiads gradually went out of use.

The *Christian Era*, which is now adopted by all Christian countries, dates from the year in which Christ was born. According to Greek chronology, that year was the fourth of the 194th Olympiad; according to Roman, it was the year 753 A.U.C.—or 754, if the different dates for beginning the year be rectified. It is remarkable, however, that the Christian era was not introduced as a basis of reckoning till the sixth century; and even then its adoption made very slow progress. There is an ambiguity connected with the Christian era, which must be borne in mind in comparing ancient dates. Some chronologists reckon the year immediately *before* the birth of Christ, as 1 B.C.; while others call it 0 B.C., reserving 1 B.C. for the actual year of the birth. There is much to be adduced in favour of each of these plans; but it suffices to say that the former is the one most usually adopted.

The *Julian Period* is a measure of time proposed by Joseph Scaliger, consisting of the very long period of 7980 years. It is not, properly speaking, a chronological era; but it is much used by chronologists on account of its affording considerable facilities for comparing different eras with each other, and in marking, without ambiguity, the years before Christ. The number of years (7980) forming the Julian period, marks the interval after which the sun, moon, and earth will come round to exactly the same positions as at the commencement of the cycle. The exact explanation is too technical to be given here; but we may mention the following two rules:—To convert any date B.C. into the Julian system, subtract the year B.C. from 4714, and the remainder is the corresponding year in the Julian period; to convert any date A.D. into the Julian system, add 4713 to the year of the Christian era.

The *Mohammedan Era*, used by most or all Mohammedan nations, dates from the flight of Mohammed to Medina—the 15th of July, 622 A.D. This date is known as the *Hegira*, or flight. As the Christian era is supposed to begin on the 1st of January, year 0, a process of addition will easily transfer a particular date from the Mohammedan to the Christian era.

For some purposes, it is useful to be able to transfer a particular year from the Roman to the Christian era. The rule for doing so is this: If the given Roman year be less than 754, deduct it from 754; if the given Roman year be *not* less than 754, deduct 753 from it; the remainder gives the year B.C. in the one case, and A.D. in the other.

In like manner it may be useful to know how to convert years of the Greek Olympiads to years of the Christian era. It is done thus: Multiply the next preceding Olympiad by 4, and add the odd years; subtract the sum from 777 if before Christ, or subtract 776 from the sum if after Christ; and the remainder will be the commencement of the given year—generally about the middle of July in the Christian year.

In regard to all these five eras (and many others of less importance), there is difficulty and confusion in having to count sometimes backwards and sometimes forward, according as a particular date is before or after the commencement of the era. To get over this complexity, the *Creation of the World* has been adopted, by Christians and Jews alike, as the commencement of a universal era. This would be unexceptionable, if authorities agreed as to the number of years which elapsed between that event and the birth of Christ; but so far are they from agreeing, that, according to competent authorities, there are *one hundred and forty* different computations of this interval! The one most usually adopted by English writers is 4004 years; but they vary from 3616 up to 6484 years. The symbol A.M., or *Anno Mundi*, signifying 'year of the world,' is arrived at by adding 4004 to the Christian designation for the year—that is, if the popular English chronology be adopted. There are, however, three other calculations for the year of the world that have acquired some historical note; and the best almanacs now give the following among other adjustments of eras—taking the year 1863 as an example.

| | |
|---|---|
| Christian Era (A. D.), . . . . . | 1863 |
| Roman Year (A. U. C.), . . . . . | 2616 |
| Anno Mundi (Jewish account), . . | 5623 |
| " " (Alexandrian account), . | 7355 |
| " " (Constantinopolitan), . | 7371 |
| " " (Popular Chronology), . . | 5867 |
| Mohammedan Era (A. H.), . . . . | 1279 |
| Julian Period, . . . . . . . | 6576 |

## SIR ISAAC NEWTON AND THE APPLE.

The Christmas-day of 1642 was marked by the birth of one of the world's greatest men—one who effected more than any other person in rendering the world familiar to us, in an astronomical point of view. During his long and invaluable life, which extended to the 20th of March 1727 (he presided at the meeting of the Royal Society so late as the 28th of February in that year, when more than eighty-four years of age), his researches extended over an illimitable domain of science, and are imperishably written on the page of philosophy. One or two incidents connected with his life will be found narrated in a previous article (vol. i. p. 399); but we may suitably notice, in this place, the remarkable way in which the grandest and most sublime of all his discoveries has become popularly associated with a very trivial circumstance—the fall of an apple.

It is curious to trace the manner in which this apple-story has been told by different writers, and the different opinions formed concerning it. Pemberton, who received from Newton himself the history of his first ideas of gravitation, does not mention the apple, but speaks simply of the idea having occurred to the philosopher 'as he sat alone in a garden.' Voltaire says: 'One day, in the year 1666, Newton went into the country, and seeing fruit fall from a tree (as his niece, Madame Conduit, has informed me), entered into a profound train of thought as to the causes which could lead to such a drawing-together or attraction.' Martin Folkes speaks of the fruit being an apple. Hegel, referring to this subject, alludes contemptuously to the story of the apple, as a modern version of the history of the tree of knowledge, with whose fruit the serpent beguiled Eve. Gauss, a great mathematician, who believes that a philosopher worthy of the name would not need to have his attention drawn to the subject by so trivial an incident, says: 'The history of the apple is too absurd. Whether the apple fell or not, how can any one believe that such a discovery could in that way be accelerated or retarded? Undoubtedly, the occurrence was something of this sort. There comes to Newton a stupid importunate man, who asks him how he hit upon his great discovery. When Newton had convinced himself what a noodle he had to do with, and wanted to get rid of the man, he told him that an apple fell on his nose; and this made the matter quite clear to the man, and he went away satisfied.'

Sir David Brewster, in his *Life of Newton*, does not expressly declare either his acceptance or rejection of the apple-legend; but his tone denotes the former rather than the latter. He considers the date to have been more probably 1665 than 1666, when 'the apple is said to have fallen from the tree at Woolsthorpe, and suggested to Newton the idea of gravity. When sitting alone in the garden, and speculating on the power of gravity, it occurred to him that as the same power by which the apple fell to the ground was not sensibly diminished at the greatest distance from the centre of the earth to which we can reach, neither at the summits of the loftiest spires, nor on the tops of the highest mountains, it might extend to the moon and retain her in her orbit, in the same manner as it bends into a curve a stone or a cannon ball, when projected in a straight line from the surface of the earth. If the moon was thus kept in her orbit by gravitation to the earth, or, in other words, its attraction, it was equally probable, he thought, that the planets were kept in their orbits by gravitating towards the sun. Kepler had discovered the great law of the planetary motions, that the squares of their periodic times were as the cubes of their distances from the sun; and hence Newton drew the important conclusion, that the force of gravity or attraction, by which the planets were retained in their orbits, varies as the square of their distances from the sun. Knowing the force of gravity at the earth's surface, he was, therefore, led to compare it with the force exhibited in the actual motion of the moon, in a circular orbit; but having assumed that the distance of the moon from the earth was equal to sixty of the earth's semidiameters, he found that the force by which the moon was drawn from its rectilineal path in a second of time was only 13·9 feet, whereas, at the surface of the earth it was 16·1 feet. This great discrepancy between his theory and what he then considered to be the fact, induced him to abandon the subject, and pursue other subjects with which he had been previously occupied.' In a note, Sir David adverts to the fact that both Newton's niece and Martin Folkes (who was at that time president of the Royal Society) had mentioned the story of the apple; but that neither Whiston nor Pemberton had done so. He speaks of a proceeding of his own, which denotes an affection towards Newton's tree at Woolsthorpe, such as might be felt by one who believed the story: 'We saw the apple-tree in 1814, and brought away a portion of one of its roots. The tree was so much decayed that it was taken down in 1820, and the wood of it carefully preserved by Mr Turner of Stoke Rocheford.'

Professor De Morgan, in a discussion which arose on this subject a few years ago in the pages of *Notes and Queries*, points out somewhat satirically, that the fact of such a tree having stood in Newton's garden, goes very little way towards proving that the fall of an apple from that tree suggested the mighty theory to the philosopher; and he illustrates it by the story of a man who once said: 'Sir, he made a chimney in my father's house, and the bricks are alive to this day to testify it; therefore deny it not.' Mr De Morgan believes that the current story grew out of a conversation, magnified in the way of which we have such a multitude of instances. Sir Isaac, in casual talk with his niece, may have mentioned the fall of some fruit as having once struck his mind, when he was pondering on the moon's motion; and she, without any intention of deceiving, may have retailed this conversation in a way calculated to give too much importance to it. 'The story of the apple is pleasant enough, and would need no serious discussion, if it were not connected with a remarkable misapprehension. As told, the myth is made to convey the idea that the fall of an apple put into Newton's mind what had never entered into the mind of any one before him—namely, the same kind of attraction between several bodies as exists between an apple and the earth. In this way, the real glory of such men as Newton is lowered. It should be known that the idea had been for many years floating before the minds of physical inquirers, in order that a proper estimate may be formed of the way in which Newton's power cleared away the confusion, and vanquished the difficulties which had prevented very able men from proceeding beyond conjecture.' Mr De Morgan proceeds to shew that Kepler, Bouillard, and Huyghens, had all made discoveries, or put forth speculations, relating to the probable law by which the heavenly bodies attract each other; and that Newton, comparing those partial results, and bringing his own idea of universal gravitation to bear upon them, arrived at his important conclusions, without needing any such aid as the fall of an apple.

It may be mentioned as a curious circumstance, that a controversy arose, a few years ago, on the question whether or not Cicero anticipated Newton in the discovery or announcement of the great theory of gravitation. The matter is worthy of note, because it illustrates the imperfect way in which that theory is often understood. In the Tusculan Disputations of Cicero, this passage occurs: '*Quâ omnia delata gravitate medium mundi locum semper expetant.*' The meaning of the passage has been regarded as somewhat obscure; and in some editions *In quâ* occurs instead of *Qua;* nevertheless the idea is that of a *central point*, towards which all things gravitate. In all probability, others preceded Cicero in enunciating this theory. But Newton's great achievement was to dismiss this idea of a *fixed* point altogether, and to substitute the theory of *universal* for that of *central* gravitation; that is, that *every* particle gravitates towards every other. If this principle be admitted, together with the law that the force of the attraction varies inversely as the square of the distance, then the whole of the sublime system of astronomy, so far as concerns the movements of the heavenly bodies, becomes harmonious and intelligible. Assuredly Cicero never conceived the Newtonian idea, that when a ball falls to meet the earth, the earth rises a little way to meet the ball—which is one consequence of the law, that the ball attracts the earth, as well as being attracted by it.

We may expect, in spite of all the arguments of the sages, that the story of the apple will continue in favour. In the beautiful new museum at Oxford, the statue of Newton is sculptured with the renowned pippin at the philosopher's feet.

## LEGEND OF THE GLASTONBURY THORN.

The miraculous thorn-tree of Glastonbury Abbey, in Somersetshire, was stoutly believed in until very recent times. One of the first accounts of it in print was given in Hearne's *History and Antiquities of Glastonbury*, published in 1722; the narration consists of a short paper by Mr Eyston, called 'A little Monument to the once famous Abbey and Borough of Glastonbury, . . . . with an Account of the Miraculous Thorn, that blows still on Christmas-day, and the wonderful Walnut-tree, that annually used to blow upon St Barnaby's Day.' 'My curiosity,' he says, 'having led me twice to Glastonbury within these two years, and inquiring there into the antiquity, history, and rarities of the place, I was told by the innkeeper where I set up my horses, who rents a considerable part of the enclosure of the late dissolved abbey, that St Joseph of Arimathea landed not far from the town, at a place where there was an oak planted in memory of his landing, called the *Oak of Avalon;* that he (Joseph) and his companions marched thence to a hill near a mile on the south side of the town, and there being weary, rested themselves; which gave the hill the name of *Weary-all-Hill;* that St Joseph stuck on the hill his staff, being a dry hawthorn-stick, which grew, and constantly budded and blowed upon Christmas-day; but, in the time of the Civil Wars, that thorn was grubbed up. However, there were, in the town and neighbourhood, several trees raised from that thorn, which yearly budded and blowed upon Christmas-day, as the old root did.'

Eyston states that he was induced, by this narration, to search for printed notices of this famous thorn; and he came to a conclusion, that 'whether it sprang from St Joseph of Arimathea's dry staff, stuck by him in the ground when he rested there, I cannot find, but *beyond all dispute it sprang up miraculously!*' This tree, growing on the south ridge of Weary-all-Hill (locally abbreviated into *Werrall*), had a double trunk in the time of Queen Elizabeth; 'in whose days a saint-like Puritan, taking offence at it, hewed down the biggest of the two trunks, and had cut down the other body in all likelihood, had he not been miraculously punished by cutting his leg, and one of the chips flying up to his head, which put out one of his eyes. Though the trunk cut off was separated quite from the root, excepting a little of the bark which stuck to the rest of the body, and lay above the ground above thirty years together, yet it still continued to flourish as the other part of it did which was left standing; and after this again, when it was quite taken away, and cast into a ditch, it flourished and budded as it used to do before. A year after this, it was stolen away, not known by whom or whither.' We are then, on the authority of a Mr Broughton, told how the remaining trunk appeared, after its companion had been lopped off and secretly carried away. 'The remaining trunk was as big as the ordinary body of a man. It was a tree of that kind and species, in all natural respects, which we term a white thorn; but it was so cut and mangled round about in the bark, by engraving people's names resorting hither to see it, that it was a wonder how the sap and nutriment should be diffused from the root to the branches thereof, which were also so maimed and broken by comers thither, that I wonder how it could continue any vegetation, or grow at all; yet the arms and boughs were spread and dilated in a circular manner as far or further than any other trees freed from such impediments of like proportion, bearing haws as fully and plentifully as others do. The blossoms of this tree were such curiosities beyond seas, that the Bristol merchants carried them into foreign parts.' But this second trunk—which bore the usual infliction of the names of silly visitors—was in its turn doomed to destruction. 'This trunk was likewise cut down by a military saint, as Mr Andrew Paschal calls him, in the rebellion which happened in King Charles I.'s time. However, there are at present divers trees from it, by grafting and inoculation, preserved in the town and country adjacent; amongst other places, there is one in the garden of a currier, living in the principal street; a second at the White Hart Inn; and a third in the garden of William Strode, Esquire.' Then ensues a specimen of trading, by no means rare in connection with religious relics: 'There is a person about Glastonbury who has a nursery of them, who, Mr Paschal tells us he is informed, sells them for a crown a piece, or as he can get.' Nothing is more probable. That there *was* a thorn-tree growing on the hill, is undoubted; and if there was any religious legend concerning its mode of getting there, a strong motive would be afforded for preparing for sale young plants, after the old one had disappeared. Down to very recent times, thorn-trees have been shewn in various parts of Somersetshire, each claiming to be *the* Glastonbury thorn. In Withering's *Arrangement of British Plants*, the tree is described botanically, and then (in the edition of 1818) the author says: 'It does not grow within the abbey at Glastonbury, but in a lane beyond the churchyard, on the other side of the street, by the side of a pit. It appears to be a very old tree: an old woman of ninety (about thirty years ago) never remembers it otherwise than it now appears. There is another tree of the same kind, two or three miles from Glastonbury. It has been reported to have no thorns; but that I found to be a mistake. It has thorns, like other hawthorns, but which also in large trees are but few. It blossoms twice a year. The winter blossoms, which are about the size of a sixpence, appear about Christmas, and sooner if the winter be severe.' Concerning the alleged flowering of the tree on Christmas-day especially, there is a curious entry in the *Gentleman's Magazine* for January 1753, when the public were under some embarrassment as to dates, owing to the change from the old style to the new. 'Glastonbury.—A vast concourse of people attended the noted thorn on Christmas-day, new style; but, to their great disappointment, there was no appearance of its blowing, which made them watch it narrowly the 5th of January, the Christmas-day, old style, when it blowed as usual.' Whether or not we credit the fact, that the tree *did* blossom precisely on the day in question, it is worthy of note that although the second trunk of the famous legendary tree had been cut down and removed a century before, some one particular tree was still regarded as the wonderful shrub in question, the perennial miracle.

A thorn-tree was not the only one regarded with reverence at Glastonbury. Mr Eyston thus informs us of another:—'Besides the Holy Thorn, Mr Camden says there was a miraculous Walnut-Tree, which, by the marginal notes that Mr Gibson hath set upon Camden, I found grew in the Holy Churchyard, near St Joseph's Chappel. This tree, they say, never budded forth before the Feast of St Barnabas, which is on the eleventh of June, and on that very day shot out leaves and flourish't then as much as others of that kind. Mr Broughton says the stock was remaining still alive in his time, with a few small branches, which continued yearly to bring forth leaves upon St Barnabas's Day as usual. The branches, when he saw it, being too small, young, and tender to bring forth fruit, or sustain their weight; but now this tree is likewise gone, yet there is a young tree planted in its place, but whether it blows, as the old one did, or, indeed, whether it was raised from the old one, I cannot tell. Doctor James Montague, Bishop of Bath and Wells in King James I.'s days, was so wonderfully taken with the extraordinariness of the Holy Thorn, and this Walnut-Tree, that he thought a branch of these trees was worthy the acceptance of the then Queen Anne, King James I.'s consort. Fuller, indeed, ridicules the Holy Thorn; but he is severely reproved for it by Doctor Heylin (another Protestant writer), who says "he hath heard from persons of great worth and credit, dwelling near the place, that it had budded and blowed upon Christmas Day," as we have above asserted.'

A flat stone, with certain initials cut in it, at the present day marks the spot where the famous tree once stood, and where, according to the legend, Joseph of Arimathea stuck his pilgrim's staff into the ground.

## CHRISTMAS CUSTOM AT CUMNOR.

There is a pleasant Christmas custom connected with the parish of Cumnor, in Berkshire, the church of which is a vicarage, and a beautiful specimen of the venerable parochial edifices of that kind in England. On Christmas-day, after evening-service, the parishioners, who are liable to pay any tithes, repair to the vicarage, and are there entertained with bread, cheese, and ale. It is no benefaction on the part of the vicar, but claimed as a right on the part of the parishioners, and even the quantity of the good things which the vicar brings forward is specified. He must have four bushels of malt brewed in ale and small-beer, two bushels of wheat made into bread, and half a hundredweight of cheese; and whatever remains unconsumed by the vicarage-payers is distributed next day, after morning-prayers, among the poor.

In connection with this parish, there is another curious custom, arising from the fact that Cassenton, a little district on the opposite side of the Thames, was once a part of it. The Cassenton people had a space on the north side of the church set apart for their burials, and on this account paid sixpence a year to Cumnor. They had to bring their dead across the Thames at Somerford Mead, where the plank stones they used in crossing remained long after visible; thence they came along a 'riding' in Cumnor Wood, which they claimed as their church-way, beginning the psalm-singing at a particular spot, which marked the latter part of the ceremonial.

CUMNOR CHURCH, BERKSHIRE.

Not less curious is the perambulation performed in this parish during Rogation week. On arriving at Swinford Ferry, the procession goes across and lays hold of the twigs on the opposite shore, to mark that they claim the breadth of the river as within the bounds of the parish. The ferryman then delivers to the vicar a noble (6*s.* 8*d.*), in a bowl of the river-water, along with a clean napkin. The vicar fishes out the money, wipes his fingers, and distributes the water among the people in commemoration of the custom. It seems a practice such as the Total Abstinence Society would approve of; but we are bound to narrate that the vicarage-dues collected on the occasion, are for the most part diffused, in the form of ale, among the thirsty parishioners.*

* *Bibliotheca Topographica*, iv. 23, 24.

## THE SEVERE CHRISTMAS OF 1860: INTENSE COLD AND ITS EFFECTS.

The Christmas of 1860 is believed to have been the severest till then experienced in Britain. At nine o'clock in the morning of Christmas-day in that year, the thermometer, at the Royal Humane Society's Receiving House, in Hyde Park, London, marked 15° Fahrenheit, or 17° below the freezing-point, but this was a mild temperature compared with what was prevalent in many parts of the country during the preceding night. Mr E. J. Lowe, a celebrated meteorologist, writing on 25th December to the *Times*, from his observatory at Beeston, near Nottingham, says: 'This morning the temperature at four feet above the ground was 8° below zero, and on the grass 13·8° below zero, or 45·8° of frost. . . . The maximum heat yesterday was only 20°, and from 7 P.M. till 11 A.M. the temperature never rose as high as zero of Fahrenheit's thermometer. At the present time (12.30 P.M.), the temperature is 7° above zero at four feet, and 2·5° above zero on the grass.' Other observations recorded throughout England correspond with this account of the intensity of the cold, by which, at a nearly uniform rate, the three days from the 24th to the 26th December were characterised. The severity of that time must still be fresh in the memory of our readers. In the letter of Mr Lowe, above quoted, he speaks of having 'just seen a horse pass with icicles at his nose three inches in length, and as thick as three fingers.' Those who then wore mustaches must remember how that appendage to the upper-lip became, through the congelation of the vapour of the breath, almost instantaneously stiff and matted together, as soon as the wearer put his head out of doors.

What made this severity of cold the more remarkable, was the circumstance that for many years previously the inhabitants of the British Islands had experienced a succession of generally mild winters, and the present generation had almost come to regard as legendary the accounts which their fathers related to them of the hard frosts and terrible winters of former times. Here, therefore, was an instance of a reduction of temperature unparalleled, not only in the recollection of the oldest person living, but likewise in any trustworthy record of the past.

During the three days referred to, the damage inflicted on vegetation of all kinds was enormous. The following account of the effects of the frost in a single garden, in a well-wooded part of the county of Suffolk, may serve as a specimen of the general damage occasioned throughout England. The garden referred to is bounded on the west by a box-hedge, and on the south by a low wall, within which was a strip of shrubbery consisting of laurels, Portugal laurels, laurustinus, red cedar, arbor vitæ, phillyrea, &c. Besides these, there stood in the garden some evergreen oaks, five healthy trees of some forty years' growth, two yews (which were of unknown age, but had been large trees beyond the memory of man), and a few younger ones between thirty and forty years old. All these, with the exception of the young yew-trees, the red cedars, the box, some of the arbor vitæ, and some little evergreen oaks, were either killed outright, or else so injured that it became necessary to cut them down. Nor was this done hastily without waiting to see whether they would recover themselves; ample time was given for discovering whether it was only a temporary check from which the trees and shrubs were suffering, or whether it was an utter destruction of that part of them which was above ground. In some cases, it was found that the root was still alive, and this afterwards sent forth fresh shoots, but in other cases it turned out to be a destruction literally 'root and branch.' Some of the trees, indeed, after having been cut down level with the ground, made a desperate attempt to revive, and sent up apparently healthy shoots; but the attempt was unsuccessful, and the shoots withered.

Nor was the damage confined to the evergreens: fruit-trees suffered also; for instance, apple-trees put forth leaves and flowers, which looked well enough for a time, but, before the summer was over, these withered, as if they had been burned; while one large walnut-tree, half a century old, not only had its young last year's shoots killed, but lost some of its largest branches.

Beyond the limits of the garden referred to, the effects of this frost were no less remarkable. Elm-trees were great sufferers; they, along with the very oaks, had many of their outer twigs killed; and a magnificent, perhaps unique, avenue of cedars of Lebanon, which must have been among the oldest of their kind in the kingdom (they were only introduced in Charles II.'s reign) was almost entirely ruined.

Notwithstanding this unexampled descent of temperature, the nadir,* as it may be termed, of cold till then experienced in Britain, the period during which it continued to prevail was of such short duration that there was no time for it to effect those wonderful results which we read of in former times as occasioned by a severe and unusually protracted frost. In a former part of this work (vol. i. p. 108), we have given an account of several remarkably hard frosts, which are recorded to have taken place in England. From a periodical work we extract the following notice of similar instances which occurred chiefly on the continent of Europe in past ages. 'In the year 401, the Black Sea was entirely frozen over. In 462, the Danube was frozen, so that Theodomer marched on the ice to Swabia, to avenge his brother's death. In 763, the cold was so intense that the Strait of Dardanelles and the Black Sea were entirely frozen over. The snow, in some places, drifted to the depth of fifty feet, and the ice was heaped in such quantities on the cities as to cause the walls to fall down. In 860, the Adriatic was entirely frozen over. In 891 and 893, the vines were killed by frost, and cattle died in their stalls. In 991, the winter lasted very long and was extremely severe. Everything was frozen over, and famine and pestilence closed the year. In 1067, the cold was so intense that most of the travellers in Germany were frozen to death on the roads. In 1133, it was excessively cold in Italy; the Po was frozen from Cremona to the sea, while the heaps of snow rendered the roads impassable; wine-casks burst and trees split by frost with an immense noise. In 1234, a pine-forest was killed by frost at Ravenna. In 1269, the frost was intense in Scotland, and the Cattegat was frozen between Norway and Jutland. In 1281, the houses in Austria were covered with snow. In 1292, the Rhine was frozen; and in Germany 600 peasants were employed to clear the way for the Austrian army. In 1344, all the rivers in Italy were frozen. In 1468, the winter was so severe in Flanders that the wine was cut with hatchets to be distributed to the soldiery. In 1594, the winter was so severe that the Rhine and Scheldt were frozen, and even the sea at Venice. In 1670, the frost was very intense in England and Denmark; both the Little and Great Belt were frozen over. In 1684, many forest-trees and oaks in England were split with the frost. In 1691, the cold was so intense, that the starved wolves entered Vienna. The cold of 1740 was scarcely inferior to that of 1709. In 1776 there was very keen cold.'

In the winter of 1848—1849, the public journals

* Since 1860, the winters of 1870–71, 1878–79, 1879–80, and 1880–81 have been very severe.

recorded that the mercury, on one occasion, froze in the thermometers at Aggershuus, in Sweden. Now, as mercury freezes at 39° below zero, marked scientifically as —39°, that is, 71° *below the freezing-point*, we know that the temperature must have been at least as low as this—perhaps several degrees lower. And yet, as we shall afterwards shew, lower degrees of temperature even than this have been experienced by the Arctic voyagers.

As might be expected, it is from the latter voyagers that we obtain some of the most interesting information concerning low temperatures. In the long and gloomy winter of the polar regions, the cold assumes an intensity of which we can form little conception. Mercurial thermometers often become useless; for when the mercury solidifies, it can sink no further in the tube, and ceases to be a correct indicator. As a more available instrument, a spirit-thermometer is then used, in which the place of mercury is supplied by rectified spirit of wine. With such thermometers, our Arctic explorers have recorded degrees of cold far below the freezing-point of mercury. Dr Kane, the American Arctic explorer, in his narrative of the Grinnell Expedition in search of Franklin, records having experienced —42° on the 7th February 1851; that is, 74° of frost, or 3° below the freezing-point of mercury.

Let us conceive what it must have been to *act a play*, in a temperature only a few degrees above this! A week after the date last mentioned, the crew of the ship engaged in the expedition referred to, performed a farce called *The Mysteries and Miseries of New York!* The outside temperature on that evening was —36°; in the 'theatre' it was —25° behind the scenes, and —20° in the audience department. One of the sailors had to enact the part of a damsel with bare arms; and when a cold flat-iron, part of the 'properties' of the theatre, touched his skin, the sensation was like that of burning with a hot-iron. But this was not the most arduous of their dramatic exploits. On Washington's birthday, February 22, the crew had another performance. 'The ship's thermometer outside was at —46°; inside, the audience and actors, by aid of lungs, lamps, and hangings, got as high as —30°, *only* 62° below the freezing-point—perhaps the lowest atmospheric record of a theatrical representation. It was a strange thing altogether. The condensation was so excessive, that we could barely see the performers; they walked in a cloud of vapour. Any extra vehemency of delivery was accompanied by volumes of smoke. Their hands steamed. When an excited Thespian took off his coat, it smoked like a dish of potatoes.'

Dr Kane records having experienced as low a temperature as —53°, or 85° below the freezing-point; but even this is surpassed in a register furnished by Sir Edward Belcher, who, in January 1854, with instruments of unquestioned accuracy, endured for *eighty-four consecutive hours*, a temperature never once higher than —50°. One night it sank to —59¼°; and on another occasion the degree of cold reached was —62½°, or 94½° below the freezing-point!

* Lieutenant Schwatka, during his memorable sleighing expedition in 1879–80, experienced an average cold of 100° F. below freezing-point on sixteen days.

Dr E. D. Clarke, the celebrated traveller, told Dr Whiting that he was once nearly frozen to death—not in any remote polar region, but in the very matter-of-fact county of Cambridge. After performing divine service at a church near Cambridge, one cold Sunday afternoon in 1818, he mounted his horse to return home. Sleepiness came upon him, and he dismounted, walking by the head of his horse; the torpor increased, the reins dropped from his hand, and he was just about sinking—probably never again to rise—when a passing traveller rescued him. This torpor is one of the most perilous accompaniments of extreme cold, and is well illustrated in the anecdote related of Dr Solander in a previous article.*

Sir Edward Parry remarks, in reference to extremely low temperatures: 'Our bodies appeared to adapt themselves so readily to the climate, that the scale of our feelings, if I may so express it, was soon reduced to a lower standard than ordinary; so that after being for some days in a temperature of —15° or —20°, it felt quite mild and comfortable when the thermometer rose to zero'—that is, when it was 32° below the freezing-point. On one occasion, speaking of the cold having reached the degree of —55°, he says: 'Not the slightest inconvenience was suffered from exposure to the open air by a person well clothed, so long as the weather was perfectly calm; but in walking against a very light air of wind, a smarting sensation was experienced all over the face, accompanied by a pain in the middle of the forehead, which soon became rather severe.' As a general remark, Parry on another occasion said: 'We find it necessary to use great caution in handling our sextants and other instruments, particularly the eye-pieces, of telescopes, which, if suffered to touch the face, occasioned an intense burning pain.' Sir Leopold M'Clintock, while sledging over the ice in March 1859, trudged with his men eight hours at a stretch, over rough hummocks of ice, without food or rest, at a temperature of —48°, or *eighty degrees below the freezing-point*, with a wind blowing too at the time. In one of the expeditions a sailor incautiously did some of his outdoor work without mittens; his hands froze; one of them was plunged into a basin of water in the cabin, and the intense cold of the hand instantly *froze the water*, instead of the water thawing the hand! Poor fellow: his hand required to be chopped off.

Dr Kane, who experienced more even than the usual share of sufferings attending these expeditions, narrates many anecdotes relating to the cold. One of his crew put an icicle at —28° into his mouth, to crack it; one fragment stuck to his tongue, and two to his lips, each taking off a bit of skin—*burning* it off, if this term might be used in an inverse sense. At —25°, 'the beard, eyebrows, eyelashes, and the downy pubescence of the ears, acquire a delicate, white, and perfectly enveloping cover of venerable hoar-frost. The moustache and under-lip form pendulous beads of dangling ice. Put out your tongue, and it instantly freezes to this icy crusting, and a rapid effort, and some hand-aid will be required to liberate it. Your chin has a trick of freezing to your upper-jaw by the luting aid of your beard; my eyes have often been so glued, as to shew that even a wink may be unsafe.' In

* See vol. i. p. 642.

reference to the torpor produced by extreme cold, Dr Kane further remarks: 'Sleepiness is *not* the sensation. Have you ever received the shocks of a magneto-electric machine, and had the peculiar benumbing sensation of "Can't let go," extending up to your elbow-joints? Deprive this of its paroxysmal character; subdue, but diffuse it over every part of the system—and you have the so-called pleasurable feelings of incipient freezing.' One day he walked himself into 'a comfortable perspiration,' with the thermometer seventy degrees below the freezing-point. A breeze sprang up, and instantly the sensation of cold was intense. His beard, coated before with icicles, seemed to bristle with increased stiffness; and an unfortunate hole in the back of his mitten 'stung like a burning coal.' On the next day, while walking, his beard and moustache became one solid mass of ice. 'I inadvertently put out my tongue, and it instantly froze fast to my lip. This being nothing new, costing only a smart pull and a bleeding afterwards, I put up my mittened hands to "blow hot," and thaw the unruly member from its imprisonment. Instead of succeeding, my mitten was itself a mass of ice in a moment; it fastened on the upper side of my tongue, and flattened it out like a batter-cake between the two disks of a hot gridle. It required all my care with the bare hands to release it, and then not without laceration.'

The following remarkable instances of the disastrous results of extreme cold in Canada are related by Sir Francis Head:—'I one day inquired of a fine, ruddy, honest-looking man, who called upon me, and whose toes and insteps of each foot had been truncated, how the accident happened? He told me that the first winter he came from England, he lost his way in the forest, and that after walking for some hours, feeling pain in his feet, he took off his boots, and from the flesh immediately swelling, he was unable to put them on again. His stockings, which were very old ones, soon wore into holes, and as rising on his insteps he was hurriedly proceeding he knew not where, he saw with alarm, but without feeling the slightest pain, first one toe and then another break off, as if they had been pieces of brittle stick; and in this mutilated state he continued to advance till he reached a path which led him to an inhabited log-house, where he remained suffering great pain till his cure was effected. On another occasion, while an Englishman was driving, one bright beautiful day, in a sleigh on the ice, his horse suddenly ran away, and fancying he could stop him better without his cumbersome fur-gloves than with them, he unfortunately took them off. As the infuriated animal at his utmost speed proceeded, the man, who was facing a keen north-west wind, felt himself gradually, as it were, turning into marble; and by the time he stopped, both his hands were so completely and so irrecoverably frozen, that he was obliged to have them amputated.'

Englishmen, take them one with another, bear up against intense cold better than against intense heat, one principal reason being, that the air is in such circumstances less tainted with the seeds of disease. They are then more lively and cheerful, feel themselves necessitated to active and athletic exertion, and become, consequently, better able to combat the adverse influences of a low degree of temperature.

# DECEMBER 26.

**St Stephen, the first martyr. St Dionysius, pope and confessor, 269. St Iarlath, confessor, first bishop of Tuam, in Ireland, 6th century.**

## St Stephen's Day.

To St Stephen, the Proto-martyr, as he is generally styled, the honour has been accorded by the church of being placed in her calendar immediately after Christmas-day, in recognition of his having been the first to seal with his blood the testimony of fidelity to his Lord and Master. The year in which he was stoned to death, as recorded in the Acts of the Apostles, is supposed to have been 33 A.D. The festival commemorative of him has been retained in the Anglican calendar.

A curious superstition was formerly prevalent regarding St Stephen's Day—that horses should then, after being first well galloped, be copiously let blood, to insure them against disease in the course of the following year. In Barnaby Googe's translation of *Naogeorgus*, the following lines occur relative to this popular notion:

'Then followeth Saint Stephen's Day, whereon doth every man
His horses jaunt and course abrode, as swiftly as he can,
Until they doe extreemely sweate, and then they let them blood,
For this being done upon this day, they say doth do them good,
And keepes them from all maladies and sicknesse through the yeare,
As if that Steven any time tooke charge of horses heare.'

The origin of this practice is difficult to be accounted for, but it appears to be very ancient, and Douce supposes that it was introduced into this country by the Danes. In one of the manuscripts of that interesting chronicler, John Aubrey, who lived in the latter half of the seventeenth century, occurs the following record: 'On St Stephen's Day, the farrier came constantly and blouded all our cart-horses.' Very possibly convenience and expediency combined on the occasion with superstition, for in *Tusser Redivivus*, a work published in the middle of the last century, we find this statement: 'About Christmas is a very proper time to bleed horses in, for then they are commonly at house, then spring comes on, the sun being now coming back from the winter-solstice, and there are three or four days of rest, and if it be upon St Stephen's Day it is not the worse, seeing there are with it three days of rest, or at least two.'

In the parish of Drayton Beauchamp, Bucks, there existed long an ancient custom, called *Stephening*, from the day on which it took place. On St Stephen's Day, all the inhabitants used to pay a visit to the rectory, and practically assert their right to partake of as much bread and cheese and ale as they chose at the rector's expense. On one of these occasions, according to local tradition, the then rector, being a penurious old bachelor, determined to put a stop, if possible, to this rather expensive and unceremonious visit from his parishioners. Accordingly, when St Stephen's Day arrived, he ordered his housekeeper not to open the window-shutters, or unlock the doors of the house, and to remain perfectly silent and motionless whenever any person was heard approaching. At the usual time the parishioners began to cluster about the house. They knocked first at one door, then at the other, then tried to open them, and on finding them fastened, they called aloud for admittance. No voice replied. No movement was heard within. 'Surely the rector and his housekeeper must both be dead!' exclaimed several voices at once, and a general awe pervaded the whole group. Eyes were then applied to the keyholes, and to every crevice in the window-shutters, when the rector was seen beckoning his old terrified housekeeper to sit still and silent. A simultaneous shout convinced him that his design was understood. Still he consoled himself with the hope that his larder and his cellar were secure, as the house could not be entered. But his hope was speedily dissipated. Ladders were reared against the roof, tiles were hastily thrown off, half-a-dozen sturdy young men entered, rushed down the stairs, and threw open both the outer-doors. In a trice, a hundred or more unwelcome visitors rushed into the house, and began unceremoniously to help themselves to such fare as the larder and cellar afforded; for no special stores having been provided for the occasion, there was not half enough bread and cheese for such a multitude. To the rector and his housekeeper, that festival was converted into the most rigid fast-day they had ever observed.

After this signal triumph, the parishioners of Drayton regularly exercised their 'privilege of Stephening' till the incumbency of the Rev. Basil Woodd, who was presented to the living in 1808. Finding that the custom gave rise to much rioting and drunkenness, he discontinued it, and distributed instead an annual sum of money in proportion to the number of claimants. But as the population of the parish greatly increased, and as he did not consider himself bound to continue the practice, he was induced, about the year 1827, to withhold his annual payments; and so the custom became finally abolished. For some years, however, after its discontinuance, the people used to go to the rectory for the accustomed bounty, but were always refused.

In the year 1834, 'the commissioners appointed to inquire concerning charities,' made an investigation into this custom, and several of the inhabitants of Drayton gave evidence on the occasion, but nothing was elicited to shew its origin or duration, nor was any legal proof advanced shewing that the rector was bound to comply with such a demand.* Many of the present inhabitants of the parish remember the custom, and some of them have heard their parents say, that it had been observed—

'As long as the sun had shone,
And the waters had run.'

In London and other places, St Stephen's Day, or the 26th of December, is familiarly known as *Boxing-day*, from its being the occasion on which those annual guerdons known as *Christmas-boxes* are solicited and collected. For a notice of them, the reader is referred to the ensuing article.

* See the Report of the Charity Commissioners, vol. xxvii., p. 83, in the British Museum.

## CHRISTMAS-BOXES.

The institution of Christmas-boxes is evidently akin to that of New-year's gifts, and, like it, has descended to us from the times of the ancient Romans, who, at the season of the Saturnalia, practised universally the custom of giving and receiving presents. The fathers of the church denounced, on the ground of its pagan origin, the observance of such a usage by the Christians; but their anathemas had little practical effect, and in process of time, the custom of Christmas-boxes and New-year's gifts, like others adopted from the heathen, attained the position of a universally recognised institution. The church herself has even got the credit of originating the practice of Christmas-boxes, as will appear from the following curious extract from *The Athenian Oracle* of John Dunton; a sort of primitive *Notes and Queries*, as it is styled by a contributor to the periodical of that name.

'*Q.* From whence comes the custom of gathering of Christmas-box money? And how long since?

*A.* It is as ancient as the word *mass*, which the Romish priests invented from the Latin word *mitto*, to send, by putting the people in mind to send gifts, offerings, oblations; to have masses said for everything almost, that no ship goes out to the Indies, but the priests have a box in that ship, under the protection of some saint. And for masses, as they cant, to be said for them to that saint, &c., the poor people must put in something into the priest's box, which is not to be opened till the ship return. Thus the mass at that time was *Christ's-mass*, and the box *Christ's-mass-box*, or money gathered against that time, that masses might be made by the priests to the saints, to forgive the people the debaucheries of that time; and from this, servants had liberty to get *box-money*, because they might be enabled to pay the priest for masses—because, *No penny, no paternoster*—for though the rich pay ten times more than they can expect, yet a priest will not say a mass or anything to the poor for nothing; so charitable they generally are.'

The charity thus ironically ascribed by Dunton to the Roman Catholic clergy, can scarcely, so far as the above extract is concerned, be warrantably claimed by the whimsical author himself. His statement regarding the origin of the custom under notice may be regarded as an ingenious conjecture, but cannot be deemed a satisfactory explanation of the question. As we have already seen, a much greater antiquity and diversity of origin must be asserted.

This custom of Christmas-boxes, or the bestowing of certain expected gratuities at the Christmas season, was formerly, and even yet to a certain extent continues to be, a great nuisance. The journeymen and apprentices of trades-people were wont to levy regular contributions from their masters' customers, who, in addition, were mulcted by the trades-people in the form of augmented charges in the bills, to recompense the latter for gratuities expected from them by the customers' servants. This most objectionable usage is now greatly diminished, but certainly cannot yet be said to be extinct. Christmas-boxes are still regularly expected by the postman, the lamplighter, the dustman, and generally by all those functionaries who render services to the public at large, without receiving payment therefor from any particular individual. There is also a very general custom at the Christmas season, of masters presenting their clerks, apprentices, and other *employés*, with little gifts, either in money or kind.

St Stephen's Day, or the 26th of December, being the customary day for the claimants of Christmas-boxes going their rounds, it has received popularly the designation of *Boxing-day*. In the evening, the new Christmas pantomime for the season is generally produced for the first time; and as the pockets of the working-classes, from the causes which we have above stated, have commonly received an extra supply of funds, the theatres are almost universally crowded to the ceiling on Boxing-night; whilst the 'gods,' or upper gallery, exercise even more than their usual authority. Those interested in theatrical matters await with considerable eagerness the arrival, on the following morning, of the daily papers, which have on this occasion a large space devoted to a chronicle of the pantomimes and spectacles produced at the various London theatres on the previous evening.

In conclusion, we must not be too hard on the system of Christmas-boxes or *handsels*, as they are termed in Scotland, where, however, they are scarcely ever claimed till after the commencement of the New Year. That many abuses did and still do cling to them, we readily admit; but there is also intermingled with them a spirit of kindliness and benevolence, which it would be very undesirable to extirpate. It seems almost instinctive for the generous side of human nature to bestow some reward for civility and attention, and an additional incentive to such liberality is not unfrequently furnished by the belief that its recipient is but inadequately remunerated otherwise for the duties which he performs. Thousands, too, of the commonalty look eagerly forward to the forthcoming guerdon on Boxing-day, as a means of procuring some little unwonted treat or relaxation, either in the way of sight-seeing, or some other mode of enjoyment. Who would desire to abridge the happiness of so many?

## CHRISTMAS PANTOMIMES.

Pantomimic acting had its place in the ancient drama, but the grotesque performances associated with our English Christmas, are peculiar to this country. Cibber says that they originated in an attempt to make stage-dancing something more than motion without meaning. In the early part of the last century, a ballet was produced at Drury Lane, called the *Loves of Mars and Venus*, 'wherein the passions were so happily expressed, and the whole story so intelligibly told by a mute narration of gesture only, that even thinking-spectators allowed it both a pleasing and rational entertainment. From this sprung forth that succession of monstrous medleys that have so long infested the stage, and which arise upon one another alternately at both houses, outvying in expense, like contending bribes at both sides at an election, to secure a majority of the multitude.' Cibber's managerial rival, Rich, found himself unable, with the Lincoln's-Inn-Fields' company, to compete with Drury Lane in the legitimate drama, and struck out a path of his own, by the invention of the comic pantomime. That he was indebted to Italy for the idea, is evident from an advertisement in the *Daily Courant*, for the 26th December 1717, in which his *Harlequin Executed* is described as 'A new Italian Mimic Scene (never performed before), between a Scaramouch, a Harlequin, a Country Farmer, his Wife, and others.' This piece is generally called 'the first English pantomime' by theatrical historians; but we find comic masques 'in the high style of Italy,' among the attractions of the patent-houses, as early as 1700. Rich seems to have grafted the scenic and mechanical features of the old masque upon the pantomimic ballet. Davies, in his *Dramatic Miscellanies*, describes Rich's pantomimes as 'consisting of two parts—one serious, the other comic. By the help of gay scenes, fine habits, grand dances, appropriate music, and other decorations, he exhibited a story from *Ovid's Metamorphoses*, or some other mythological work. Between the pauses or acts of this serious representation, he interwove a comic fable, consisting chiefly of the courtship of Harlequin and Columbine, with a variety of surprising adventures and tricks, which were produced by the magic wand of Harlequin; such as the sudden transformation of palaces and temples to huts and cottages; of men and women into wheel-barrows and joint-stools; of trees turned to houses; colonnades to beds of tulips; and mechanics' shops into serpents and ostriches.'

Pope complains in *The Dunciad*, that people of the first quality go twenty and thirty times to see such extragavances as—

'A sable sorcerer rise,  
Swift to whose hand a winged volume flies:  
All sudden, gorgons hiss and dragons glare,  
And ten-horned fiends and giants rush to war.  
Hell rises, Heaven descends, and dance on earth,  
Gods, imps and monsters, music, rage, and mirth,  
A fire, a jig, a battle and a ball,  
Till one wide conflagration swallows all.  
Thence a new world to Nature's laws unknown,  
Breaks out refulgent, with a heaven its own;  
Another Cynthia her new journey runs,  
And other planets circle other suns.  
The forests dance, the rivers upward rise,  
Whales sport in woods, and dolphins in the skies;  
And last, to give the whole creation grace,  
Lo! one vast egg produces human race.'

The success of the new entertainment was wonderfully lasting. Garrick and Shakspeare could not hold their own against Pantomime. The great actor reproaches his aristocratic patrons because—

'They in the drama find no joys,  
But doat on mimicry and toys.  
Thus, when a dance is in my bill,  
Nobility my boxes fill;  
Or send three days before the time,  
To crowd a new-made pantomime.'

And *The World* (1st March 1753) proposes that pantomime shall have the boards entirely to itself. 'People of taste and fashion have already given sufficient proof that they think it the highest entertainment the stage is capable of affording; the most innocent we are sure it is, for where nothing is said and nothing is meant, very little harm can be done. Mr Garrick, perhaps, may start a few objections to this proposal; but with those universal talents which he so happily possesses, it is not to be doubted but he will, in time, be able to handle the wooden sword with as much dignity and dexterity as his brother Lun.'

The essayist does Rich injustice; the latter's Harlequin was something more than a dexterous performance. Rich was a first-rate pantomimic actor, to whom words were needless. Garrick bears impartial witness to the genius of the exhibitor of the eloquence of motion. In the prologue to a pantomime with a talking-hero, produced after Rich's death, he says:

'''Tis wrong,
The wits will say, to give the fool a tongue.
When Lun appeared, with matchless art and whim,
He gave the power of speech to every limb;
Though masked and mute, conveyed his quick intent,
And told in frolic gestures all he meant.'

At this time the *role* of Harlequin was not considered derogatory to an actor as it is now—Woodward, who established his reputation by playing such characters as Lord Foppington, Marplot, and Sir Andrew Aguecheek, was equally popular as the party-coloured hero.

In the hands of Lun's successors, Harlequin sadly degenerated; and when Grimaldi appeared upon the scene, his genius elevated the Clown into the principal personage of the pantomime. The harlequinade still remained the staple of the piece, the opening forming a very insignificant portion. John Kemble himself did not disdain to suggest the plot of a pantomime. Writing to Tom Dibdin, he says: 'The pantomime might open with three Saxon witches lamenting Merlin's power over them, and forming an incantation, by which they create a Harlequin, who is supposed to be able to counteract Merlin in all his designs against King Arthur. If the Saxons come on in a dreadful storm, as they proceeded in their magical rites, the sky might brighten, and a rainbow sweep across the horizon, which, when the ceremonies are completed, should contract itself from either end, and form the figure of Harlequin in the heavens. The wizards may fetch him down as they will, and the sooner he is set to work the better.'—Dibdin's *Reminiscences*.

Dibdin himself was a prolific pantomime author; and we cannot give a better idea of what the old-fashioned pantomime was, than by quoting the first scene of his *Harlequin in his Element; or Fire, Water, Earth, and Air*, performed at Covent Garden Theatre in 1807. The *dramatis personæ* consist of Ignoso, the spirit of Fire; Aquina, the fairy of the Fountain; Aurino, genius of Air; Terrena, spirit of Earth; Harlequin (Mr Bologna, Junr.); Columbine (Miss Adams); Sir Amoroso Sordid, guardian to Columbine (Mr Ridgway); and Gaby Grin, his servant (Mr Grimaldi).

SCENE I.

*A beautiful garden, with terraces, arcades, fountains, &c. The curtain rises to a soft symphony.* AURINO *is seen descending on a light cloud; he approaches a fountain in the centre of the garden, and begins the following duet:*

*Aurino.* Aquina! Fountain Fairy!
The genius of the Air
Invites thee here
From springs so clear,
With love to banish care.

AQUINA, *rising from fountain.*

*Aquina.* Aurino, airy charmer,
Behold thy nymph appear.
What peril can alarm her,
When thou, my love, art near?

TERRENA *rises from the earth, and addresses the other two.*

*Terr.* Why rudely trample thus on Mother Earth?
Fairies, ye know this ground 's my right by birth.
These pranks I 'll punish: Water shall not rise
Above her level; Air shall keep the skies.

*It thunders:* IGNOSO *descends.*

*Igno.* 'Tis burning shame, such quarrels 'mong you three,
Though I warm you, you 're always cold to me.
The sons of Earth, on every slight disaster,
Call me good servant, but a wicked master.
Of Air and Water, too, the love I doubt,
One blows me up, the other puts me out.
Nay, if you 're angry, I 'll have my turn too,
And you shall see what mischief I can do!

IGNOSO *throws the fire from his wand; the flowers all wither, but are revived by the other fairies.*

*Terr.* Fire, why so hot? Your bolts distress not me,
But injure the fair mistress of these bowers;
Whose sordid guardian would her husband be,
For lucre, not for love. Rather than quarrel,
let us use our powers,
And gift with magic aid some active sprite,
To foil the guardian and the girl to right.

*Quartett.*

*Igno.* About it quick!
*Terr.* This clod to form shall grow,
*Aqui.* With dew refreshed—
*Aur.* With vital air—
*Igno.* And warm with magic glow.

HARLEQUIN *is produced from a bed of party-coloured flowers; the magic sword is given him, while he is thus addressed:*

*Terr.* This powerful weapon your wants will provide;
Then trip,
*Aur.* Free as air,
*Aqui.* And as brisk as the tide.
*Igno.* Away, while thy efforts we jointly inspire.
*Terr.* Tread lightly!
*Aur.* Fly!
*Aqui.* Run!
*Igno.* And you'll never hang fire!

IGNOSO *sinks.* AQUINA *strikes the fountains; they begin playing.* TERRENA *strikes the ground; a bed of roses appears.* Harlequin *surveys everything, and runs round the stage.* Earth *sinks in the bed of roses, and* Water *in the fountain.* Air *ascends in the car.* Columbine *enters dancing; is amazed at the sight of* Harlequin, *who retires from her with equal surprise; they follow each other round the fountain in a sort of pas de deux. They are surprised by the entrance of* Columbine's Guardian, *who comes in, preceded by servants in rich liveries.* Clown, *as his running-footman, enters with a lapdog.* Old Man *takes snuff—views himself in a pocket-glass.* Clown *imitates him, &c.* Old Man *sees* Harlequin *and* Columbine, *and pursues them round the fountains, but the lovers go off, followed by* Sir AMOROSO *and servants.*

And so the lovers are pursued by Sir Amoroso and Clown through sixteen scenes, till the fairies unite them in the *Temple of the Elements*. The harlequinade is full of practical jokes, but contains no hits at the follies of the day throughout it all; the relative positions of Clown and Sir Amoroso, Pantaloon, or the Guardian (as he is styled indifferently), as servant and master, are carefully preserved.

Since Dibdin's time, the pantomime has undergone a complete change. The dramatic author furnishes only the opening, which has gradually become the longest part of the piece; while the harlequinade—left to the so-called pantomimists to arrange—is nothing but noise. Real pantomime-acting is eschewed altogether; Harlequin and Columbine are mere dancers and posturers; and Clown, if he does not usurp the modern Harlequin's attribute, is but a combination of the acrobat and coarse buffoon. The pantomime of the present day would certainly not be recognised by Rich or owned by Grimaldi.

---

*Born.*—Gulielmus Xylander, translator of the classics, 1532, *Augsburg;* Thomas Gray, poet, 1716, *Cornhill, London.*

*Died.*—Antoine Houdart de la Motte, dramatist, 1731, *Paris;* Joel Barlow, American author and diplomatist, 1812, *near Cracow;* Stephen Girard, millionaire, 1831.

## STEPHEN GIRARD.

In a country, destitute of a titled and hereditary aristocracy, wealth is distinction. The accumulation of great wealth is evidence of strong character; and when the gathered riches are well used and well bestowed, they give celebrity and even renown.

Stephen Girard was the son of a common sailor of Bourdeaux, France, and was born May 21, 1750. At the age of ten he went, a cabin-boy, to New York, where he remained in the American coasting trade until he became master and part-owner of a small vessel, while he was still a youth. During the American Revolution, he kept a grocery and liquor-shop in Philadelphia, and made money enough from the American and British armies, as they successively occupied the city, to embark largely in trade with the West Indies. Fortune comes at first by slow degrees. The first thousand pounds is the step that costs. Then, in good hands, capital rolls up like a snow-ball. In 1790, Girard had made £6000. Now the golden stream began to swell. The misfortunes of others were his gain. At the time of the terrible massacre of St Domingo, he had some ships in a harbour of that island. The planters sent their plate, money, and valuables on board his vessels, and were preparing to embark, with their families, when they were massacred by the infuriated negroes. Property to the value of £10,000 was left in the hands of Girard, for which he could find no owners.

He married, but unfortunately, and soon separated from his wife, and he had no children and no friends. Yet this hard, money-making man was a hero in courage and in charity. When professing Christians fled from the yellow fever in Philadelphia, in 1793, 1797, and 1798, Girard, who had no religious belief, stayed in the city, and spent day and night in taking care of the sick and dying. As his capital accumulated, he became a banker; and when the United States government, in the war of 1812 with England, wanted a loan of £1,000,000, and only got an offer of £4000, Girard undertook the entire loan. When he died, December 26, 1831, he left £1,800,000, nearly the whole of which was bequeathed to charitable institutions, £400,000 being devoted to the foundation of a college for orphan boys. The buildings of this college, in the suburbs of Philadelphia, are constructed of white marble, in the Grecian style, and are among the most beautiful in the world.

Girard was a plain, rude man, without education, frugal and friendless; yet kind to the sick, generous to the poor, and a benefactor to the orphan.

## LONDON LIFE A CENTURY AGO.

Hogarth has bequeathed us the most perfect series of pictures possessed by any nation, of the manners and custom of its inhabitants, as seen by himself. They go lower into the depths of everyday life than is usually ventured upon by his brethren of the brush. The higher-class scenes of his 'Marriage à la Mode' teach us little more than we can gather from the literature of his era; but when we study 'Gin Lane' in all its ghastly reality, we see—and shudder in contemplating it—the abyss of vice and reckless profligacy into which so large a number of the lower classes had fallen, and which was too disgusting as well as too familiar, to meet with similar record in the pages of the annalist.

There exists a curious octavo pamphlet—dedicated by its author to Hogarth himself—which minutely describes the occupation of the inhabitants of London during the whole twenty-four hours. It is unique as a picture of manners, and though rude in style, invaluable for the information it contains, and which is not to be met elsewhere. It appears to have been first published in 1759, and ran through several editions. It is entitled *Low Life: or, one half the World knows not how the other half Live;* and purports to be 'a true description of a Sunday as it is usually spent within the Bills of Mortality, calculated for the 21 day of June,' the anniversary (new style) of the accession of King George II. Mr G. A. Sala, in his volume entitled *Twice Round the Clock*, acknowledges that his description therein of the occupation of each hour of a modern London day, was suggested by the perusal of a copy of this old pamphlet, lent to him by Mr Dickens, and which had been presented to that gentleman by another great novelist, Mr Thackeray. Under such circumstances, we may warrantably assume that there is something valuable in this unpretentious *brochure*, and we therefore proceed to glean from it as much as may enable our readers to comprehend London life a century ago; premising that a great part of it is too gross, and a portion likewise too trivial, for modern readers.

Our author commences his description at twelve o'clock on Saturday night, at which hour, he says: 'The Salop-man in Fleet Street shuts up his gossiping coffee-house.'* Almost the next incident reminds us of the old roguery and insecurity

* The liquid known as *salop* or *saloop*, kept hot, was at one time much sold at street-corners in London, but the demand ceased about thirty years since. It was made from an infusion of sassafras, and said to be very nutritive.

of London—'watchmen taking fees from house-breakers, for liberty to commit burglaries within their beats, and at the same time promising to give them notice if there is any danger of their being taken, or even disturbed in their villanies.' The markets begin to swarm with the wives of poor journeymen shoemakers, smiths, tinkers, tailors, &c., who come to buy great bargains with little money. Dark-house Lane, near Billingsgate, in an uproar, with custom-house officers, sailors' wives, smugglers, and city-apprentices, waiting to hear the high-water bell ring, to go in the tilt-boat to Gravesend.* Ballad-singers, who have encumbered the corners of markets several hours together, repairing to the houses of appointed rendezvous, that they may share with pickpockets what had been stolen from the crowd of fools, which had stood about them all the evening. Houses which are left open, and are running to ruin, filled with beggars; some of whom are asleep, while others are pulling down the timber, and packing it up to sell for firing to washerwomen and clear-starchers. Tapsters of public-houses on the confines of London, receiving pence and twopences from those sottish citizens they have light to town from over the fields, and who were too drunk and fearful to come by themselves.'

From two till three o'clock, our author notes—'Most private shops in and about London (as there are too many), where Geneva is publicly sold in defiance of the act of parliament, filled with the worst classes. Young fellows who have been out all night *on the ran-dan*, stealing staves and lanterns from such watchmen as they find sleeping on their stands. The whole company of *Finders* (a sort of people who get their bread by the hurry and negligence of sleepy tradesmen), are marching towards all the markets in London, Westminster, and Southwark; to make a seizure of all the butchers, poulterers, green-grocers, and other market-people have left behind them, at their stalls and shambles, when they went away. Night-cellars about Covent Garden and Charing-Cross, fill'd with mechanics, some sleeping, others playing at cards, with dead-beer before them, and link-boys giving their attendance. Men who intend to pretend to walk thirty or forty miles into the country, preparing to take the cool of the morning to set out on their journeys. Vagabonds who have been sleeping under hay-ricks in the neighbouring villages and fields, awaken, begin to rub their eyes, and get out of their nests.'

From three to four o'clock.—'Fools who have been up all the night, going into the fields with dogs and ducks, that they may have a morning's diversion at the noisy and cruel amusement.† Pigeon-fanciers preparing to take long rambles out of London, to give their pigeons a flight. The bulks of tradesmen's houses crowded with vagabonds, who having been picking pockets, carrying links, fetching spendthrifts from taverns, and beating drunken-men, have now got drunk themselves and gone to sleep.* Watchmen crying "Past four o'clock," at half-an-hour after three, being persuaded that scandalous pay deserves scandalous attendance.† Poor people carrying their dead children, nailed up in small deal-boxes, into the fields to bury them privately, and save the extravagant charge of parish dues. The streets, at this time, are beginning to be quiet—the fishwomen gone to Billingsgate to wait the tide for the arrival of the mackerel-boats.'

From four till five o'clock.—'Early risers, with pipes stuck in their jaws, walking towards Hornsey Wood, Dulwich Common, Marybone, and Stepney, in order to take large morning-draughts, and secure the first fuddle of the day. Beggars going to parish nurses, to borrow poor helpless infants at fourpence a day, and persuade credulous charitable people they are their own, and have been sometime sick and fatherless. The wives and servant-girls of mechanics and day-labourers, who live in courts and alleys, where one cock supplies the whole neighbourhood with water, taking the advantage before other people are up, to fill their tubs and pans with a sufficiency to serve them the ensuing seven days.'

From five till six o'clock.—'The several new-built bun-houses about the metropolis, at Chelsea, Stepney, Stangate, Marybone, &c., are now open. People who keep she-asses about Brompton, Knightsbridge, Hoxton, and Stepney, getting ready to run with their cattle all over the town, to be milked for the benefit of sick and infirm persons. Poor people with fruit, nosegays, buns, &c., making their appearance. Petty equipages preparing to take citizens country journeys. The pump near St Antholin's Church, in Watling Street, crowded with fishwomen who are washing their stinking mackerel, to impose them on the public for fish come up with the morning's tide. Bells tolling, and the streets beginning to fill with old women and charity-children, who attend the services of the church.'

From six to seven o'clock.—'A great number of people of both sexes, especially fanciers and dealers in birds, at the Birds Nest Fair held every Sunday morning, during the season, on Dulwich Common. Beggars who have put on their woful countenances, and also managed their sores and ulcers so as to move compassion, are carrying wads of straw to the corners of the most public streets, that they may take their seats, and beg the charity of all well-disposed Christians the remaining part of the day.'

From seven to eight o'clock.—'Country fellows, newly come to London, running about to see parish churches, and find out good ale and new acquaintances. Chairmen at the court-end of the town, fast asleep in their chairs, for want of business or a better lodging. Common people going to quack-doctors, and petty barbers, in order to be let blood (and perhaps have their arms lamed) for threepence. Abundance of lies told in barbers' shops by those who come to be shaved, many fools taking those places to be the repositories of polite education.

* The journey to Gravesend was a serious adventure in those days, always occupying twelve hours, and frequently more; if the tide turned, the passengers met with great delay, and were sometimes put ashore far from their destination. The only accommodation in these open boats, was a litter of straw, and a sail-cloth over it.

† For a further account of this *sport*, and one favourite London locality where it was chiefly indulged in, see p. 74 of the present volume.

* These bulks were the stalls of the open shops then very common in London—for an account of which see vol. i. p. 350.

† We may refer to p. 410 of the present volume for some further notice of these old night-guardians.

The whole cities of London, Westminster, and the borough of Southwark, covered by a cloud of smoke, most people being employed at lighting fires.'

From eight to nine.—'People in common trade and life, going out of town in stage-coaches to Edmonton, Stratford, Deptford, Acton, &c.; tradesmen who follow the amusement of angling, preparing to set out for Shepperton, Carshalton, Epping Forest, and other places of diversion; to pass away the two or three feast-days of the week. Servants to ladies of quality are washing and combing such lapdogs as are to go to church with their mistresses that morning.'

From nine to ten.—'Pupils belonging to surgeons going about their several wards, letting blood, mending broken bones, and doing whatever else they think necessary for their poor patients. Citizens who take a walk in the morning, with an intent to sleep away the afternoon, creeping to Sadler's Wells, or Newington, in order to get drunk during the time of divine service. French artificers quit their garrets, and exchange their greasy woollen caps and flannel shirts for swords and ruffles; and please themselves with a walk in St James's Park, the Temple, Somerset House gardens, Lincoln's Inn walks, or Gray's Inn; and then look sharp after an eleemosynary dinner at some dirty public-house. The new breakfasting-hut near Sadler's Wells crowded with young fellows and their sweethearts, who are drinking tea and coffee, telling stories, repeating love-songs, and broken scraps of low comedy, till towards dinner-time. The great room at the "Horns," at Hornsey Wood, crowded with men, women, and children, eating rolls and butter, and drinking of tea, at an extravagant price.'

From ten till eleven.—'Crowds of old country fellows, women, and children, about the lord-mayor's coach and horses, at the south side of St Paul's Churchyard.* Much business done on the custom-house quays, Temple piazzas, and the porch of St Mary-le-Bow Church, in Cheapside, since the nave of St Paul's has been kept clear, by order of the bishop of London.† The churchyards about London, as Stepney, Pancras, Islington, &c., filled with people reading the tombstones, and eating currants and gooseberries. Actors and actresses meeting at their apartments to rehearse the parts they are to perform. Fine fans, rich brilliants, white hands, envious eyes, and enamelled snuff-boxes, displayed in most places of divine service, where people of fashion endure the intolerable fatigue with wonderful seeming patience.'

From eleven till twelve.—'Poor French people, about the Seven Dials and Spitalfields, picking dandelion in the adjacent fields, to make a salad for dinner. The organ-hunters running about from one parish church to another, to hear the best masters, as Mr Stanley, &c., play.‡ The wives of genteel mechanics, under pretence of going to prayers in their apartment, take a nap and a dram, after which they chew lemon-peel to prevent being smelt. Ladies about St James's reading plays and romances, and making paint for their faces.'

From twelve till one.—'Idle apprentices, who have played under gateways during the time of divine service, begging the text of old women at the church-doors to carry home to their inquisitive masters and mistresses. Young tradesmen, half-starved gentlemen, merchants' clerks, petty officers in the customs, excise, and news-collectors, very noisy over their half-pints and dumplings in tavern-kitchens about Temple Bar and the Royal Exchange. Nosegay-women, flying-fruiterers, and black-shoe boys come again into business as the morning-service is over. The south side of the Royal Exchange, in Cornhill, very much crowded with gentlemen doing business and hearing news. The Mall, in St James's Park, filled with Frenchmen picking their teeth, and counting the trees for their dinner. All the common people's jaws in and about this great metropolis in full employment.'

From one till two.—'The friends of criminals under sentence of death in Newgate, presenting money to the turnkeys to get to the sight of them, in order to take their last farewell, and present them with white caps with black ribbons, prayer-books, nosegays, and oranges, that they may make a decent appearance up Holborn, on the road to the other world. Church bells and tavern bells keep time with each other. Men and boys who intend to swim in the River Lea near Hackney, the ponds near Hampstead, and the river Thames near Chelsea, this afternoon, are setting out according to their appointments. Pickpockets take their stands at the avenues of public places, in hopes of making a good booty during the hurry of the afternoon.'

From two till three.—'Strollers, posture-masters, puppet-show men, fiddlers, tumblers, and toy-women, packing up their affairs, and preparing to set out for such fairs as Wandsworth, &c., which will, according to the custom of the nation, begin the next day. Pawnbrokers' wives dressing themselves in their customers' wearing-apparel, rings and watches, in order to make a gay appearance in the fields, when evening-service is over. Citizens who have pieces of gardens in the adjacent villages, walking to them with their wives and children, to drink tea, punch, or bottled-ale; after which they load themselves with flowers for bean-pots; and roots, salads, and other vegetables for their suppers. The paths of Kensington, Highgate, Hampstead, Islington, Stepney, and Newington, found to be much pleasanter than those of the gospel.'

From three till four.—'Tallow-chandlers who do business privately in back-cellars and upper-rooms to evade the king's duty, taking advantage of most people being at church, in the fields, or asleep, to make mould-candles, known by the name of "running the buck." A general jumble from one end of London to another of silks, cottons, printed linens, and calicoes. Merchants get into their counting-houses with bottles of wine, pipes and tobacco before them, studying schemes for the advancement of their several stocks, both in trade and the public funds.'

From four till five.—'Some hundreds of people, mostly women and children, walking backward

* The mayor at that time attended every Sunday morning-service at St Paul's.

† This is a very curious notice of a very old custom, that of making the nave the scene of gossip and business, which prevailed in the days of Elizabeth, to the disregard of common decency in a sacred edifice, and which appears to have been customary even to this late date.

‡ Mr Stanley was the famous *blind* organist of the Temple church, and a friend of Handel. There is a portrait and memoir of him in the *European Magazine* for 1784.

and forward on Westminster Bridge for the benefit of the air. Eel-pies most unmercifully devoured at Green's Ferry, Jeremy's Ferry, and Bromley Lock on the River Lea; and at Clay Hall, near Old Ford, at Bow. The office-keepers of the Theatres Royal, tracing the streets from the houses of noblemen, ladies, and the principal actors and actresses, to let them know what is to be performed the ensuing day. The cider-cellar, in Spring Gardens, crowded with people of all nations.'

From five till six.—'People who have the conveniency of flat leaded roofs on the tops of their houses, especially such as have prospects of the river Thames, drinking tea, beer, punch, and smoking tobacco there till the dusk of the evening. Well-dressed gentlewomen, and ladies of quality, drove out of St James's Park, Lincoln's Inn Gardens, and Gray's Inn Walks, by milliners, mantua-makers, sempstresses, stay-makers, clear-starchers, French barbers, dancing-masters, gentlemen's gentlemen, tailors' wives, conceited old maids, and butchers' daughters. Great numbers of footmen near the gate-entrance of Hyde Park, wrestling, cudgel-playing, and jumping; while others who have drank more than their share are swearing, fighting, or sleeping, till their ladies return from the Ring.'

From six till seven.—'Children in back-alleys and narrow passages very busy at their several doors, shelling pease and beans for supper; and making boats, as they call them, with bean-shells and deal-matches. New milk and biscuits plentifully attacked by old women, children, and fools, in St James's Park, Lamb's Conduit Fields, and

ST MONDAY IN THE DAYS OF HOGARTH.

St George's Fields, Southwark. Westminster Abbey crowded with people, who are admiring the monuments, and reading their inscriptions.'

From seven till eight.—'Fishermen out with their boats on the river Thames, and throwing out their nets to catch under-sized fish, contrary to act of parliament. The drawers at Sadler's Wells, and the Prospect House, near Islington; Jenny's Whim at Chelsea; the Spring Gardens at Newington and Stepney; the Castle at Kentish Town; and the Angel at Upper Holloway; in full employment, each of them trying to cheat, not only the customers, but even the person who has the care of the bar; and every room in those houses filled with talk and smoke. The taverns about the Royal Exchange filled with merchants, underwriters, and principal tradesmen, who oftentimes do as much business on the Sunday evenings, as they do when they go upon the Exchange.

From eight to nine.—'Black eyes and broken heads exhibited pretty plentifully in the public streets, about precedency. Great struggling at Paris-Garden stairs, and the Barge-House stairs in Southwark, to get into the boats that ply to and from Blackfriars and the Temple. Young highwaymen venturing out upon the road, to attack such coaches, chaises, and horsemen as they think are worth meddling with on their return to London.'

From nine till ten.—'Masters of private mechanic families reading to them chapters from *The Whole Duty of Man* before they go to bed. The streets hardly wide enough for numbers of people, who about this time are reeling to their habitations. Great hollowing and whooping in the fields, by such persons as have spent the day abroad, and are now returning home half-drunk, and in danger of losing their company.'

From ten till eleven.—'Link-boys who have

been asking charity all day, and have just money sufficient to buy a torch, taking their stands at Temple Bar, London Bridge, Lincoln's-Inn-Fields, Smithfield, the City Gates, and other public places, to light, knock down, and rob people. The gaming-tables at Charing Cross, Covent Garden, Holborn, and the Strand, begin to fill with men of desperate fortunes, bullies, fools, and gamesters.'

From eleven till twelve.—'People of quality leaving off gaming in order to go to supper. Night-houses begin to fill. One-third of the inhabitants of London fast asleep, and almost penniless. The watch-houses begin to fill with young fellows shut out of their apartments, who are proud of sitting in the constable's chair, holding the staff of authority, and sending out for liquor to treat the watchmen. Bell-ringers assembling at churches to usher in the 22d of June, the day of the king's accession.'

Such are a few of the items illustrative of past manners, afforded by a pamphlet characterised by Mr Sala as 'one of the minutest, the most graphic, the most pathetic pictures of London life a century since that has ever been written.' The author tells us that he chose Sunday for his descriptive day, in order that he might not be accused of any invidious choice: 'hardly can it be expected that the other six begin or end in a more exemplary manner.' To the third edition of 1764 is appended a picture of St Monday, that universal day of debauch among the working-classes (see the engraving on the preceding page). Here we see tradesmen of all denominations idling and drinking, while a busy landlady chalks up double scores. Each man is characterised by some emblem of his trade. To the left, a shoemaker and tailor are seated on a bench, the former threatening his ragged wife, who urges him home, with the strap; the tailor quietly learns a new song. The butcher, busy at cards, has his game deranged by a termagant wife, who proceeds to blows. The sturdy porter in front defies the staggering leather-cutter, who upsets the painter's colours; the painter, stupidly drunk on a bench behind, is still endeavouring to lift another glass. On the walls, 'King Charles's Golden Rules' are hung up with all the pretentious morality of low haunts; another paper, inscribed 'Pay to-day, I trust to-morrow,' is the most likely to be appealed to and enforced by the busy hostess.

We gather from this slight review of a curious work, that London hours were earlier, and London habits in some degree more natural, as regards rising and walking, than among ourselves; but we also see greater coarseness of manners, and insecurity of life and property. Altogether, we may congratulate ourselves on the changes that a century has produced, and leave to unreasoning sentimentalists the office of bewailing the 'good old times.'

---

## DECEMBER 27.

**St John, apostle and evangelist. St Theodorus Grapt, confessor, 9th century.**

### St John the Evangelist's Day.

A special reverence and interest is attached to St John—'the disciple whom Jesus loved.' Through a misapprehension of the Saviour's words, a belief, we are informed, came to be entertained among the other apostles that this disciple should never die, and the notion was doubtless fostered by the circumstance, that John outlived all his brethren and coadjutors in the Christian ministry, and was indeed the only apostle who died a natural death. He expired peacefully at Ephesus, it is stated, at the advanced age of ninety-four, in the reign of the Emperor Trajan, and the year of our Lord 100; thus, as Brady observes, 'making the first century of the Christian Era and the Apostolical Age, terminate together.'

Though John thus escaped actual martyrdom, he was, nevertheless, called upon to endure great persecution in the cause of his Friend and Master. Various fathers of the church, among others Tertullian and St Jerome, relate that in the reign of Domitian, the Evangelist, having been accused of attempting to subvert the religion of the Roman Empire, was transported from Asia to Rome, and there, in presence of the emperor and senate, before the gate called *Porta Latina*, or the Latin Gate, he was cast into a caldron of boiling oil, which he not only remained in for a long time uninjured, but ultimately emerged from, with renovated health and vigour. In commemoration of this event, the Roman Catholic Church retains in its calendar, on the 6th of May, a festival entitled 'St John before the Latin Gate.' Domitian, we are further informed, notwithstanding this miraculous interposition, continued obdurate, and banished St John to Patmos, a lonely island in the Grecian Archipelago, where he was employed in working among the criminals in the mines. In this dreary abode, the apostle, as he informs us himself, witnessed those sublime and wondrous visions, which he has recorded in the Apocalypse.

On the assassination of Domitian, and the elevation of Nerva to the imperial throne, John was released from his confinement at Patmos, and returned to Ephesus, where he continued till his death. A tradition obtains, that in his last days, when unable to walk to church, he used to be carried thither, and exhorted the congregation in his own memorable words, 'Little children, love one another.' Partly in reference to the angelic and amiable disposition of St John, partly also, apparently, in allusion to the circumstance of his having been the youngest of the apostles, this evangelist is always represented as a young man, with a heavenly mien and beautiful features. He is very generally represented holding in his left hand an urn, from which a demoniacal figure is escaping. This device appears to bear reference to a legend which states that, a priest of Diana having denied the divine origin of the apostolic miracles, and challenged St John to drink a cup of poison which he had prepared, the Evangelist, to remove his scepticism, after having first made on the vessel the sign of the cross, emptied it to the last drop without receiving the least injury. The purging of the cup from all evil is typified in the flight from it of Satan, the father of mischief, as represented in the medieval emblem. From this legend, a superstitious custom seems to have sprung of obtaining, on St John's Day, supplies of hallowed wine, which was both drunk and used in the manufacture of *manchets* or little loaves; the individuals who partook of which were deemed secure from all danger of poison throughout the ensuing year. The subjoined allusion to the practice occurs in Googe's translation of *Naogeorgus:*

'Nexte John the sonne of Zebedee hath his appoynted day,
Who once by cruell Tyrannts' will, constrayned was they say
Strong poyson up to drinke; therefore the Papistes doe beleeve
That whoso puts their trust in him, no poyson them can greeve:
The wine beside that halowed is in worship of his name,
The Priestes doe give the people that bring money for the same.
And after with the selfe same wine are little manchets made
Agaynst the boystrous Winter stormes, and sundrie such like trade.
The men upon this solemne day, do take this holy wine
To make them strong, so do the maydes to make them faire and fine.'

---

*Born.*—Jacques Bernouilli, mathematician, 1654, *Basle;* Dr Conyers Middleton, philosophical and controversial writer, 1683, *Hinderwell, near Whitby;* Pope Pius VI., 1717; Arthur Murphy, dramatist and miscellaneous writer, 1727, *Ireland.*

*Died.*—Pierre de Ronsard, poet, 1585, *St Cosme Priory, near Tours;* Thomas Cartwright, Puritan divine, 1603; Captain John Davis, navigator, killed near *Malacca,* 1605; Thomas Guy, founder of Guy's Hospital, 1724, *London;* Henry Home, Lord Kames, lawyer and metaphysician, 1782; Prince Lee Boo, of Pelew, 1784, *London;* John Wilkes, celebrated demagogue, 1797; Dr Hugh Blair, eminent divine, 1800, *Edinburgh;* Joanna Southcott, female enthusiast and prophet, 1814, *London;* Charles Lamb, poet and essayist, 1834, *Edmonton;* Rev. William Jay, eminent dissenting preacher, 1853, *Bath;* Josiah Conder, editor and miscellaneous writer, 1855.

## THOMAS GUY, AND GUY'S HOSPITAL: 'BOOKSELLERS AND STATIONERS.'

There is one noble institution in the metropolis, *Guy's Hospital,* which renders a vast amount of good to the poor, without any appeal either to the national purse or to private benevolence. Or, more correctly, this is a type of many such institutions, thanks to the beneficence of certain donors. Once now and then, it is necessary to bring public opinion to bear upon these charities, to insure equitable management; but the charities themselves are noble.

Thomas Guy was the son of a coal-merchant and lighterman, at Horseleydown, and was born in 1645. He did not follow his father's trade, but was apprenticed to a bookseller, and became in time a freeman and liveryman of the Stationers' Company. He began business on his own account as a bookseller, in a shop at the corner of Cornhill and Lombard Street, pulled down some years ago when improvements were made in that neighbourhood. He made large profits, first by selling Bibles printed in Holland, and then as a contractor for printing Bibles for Oxford University. He next made much money in a way that may, at the present time, seem beneath the dignity of a city shopkeeper, but which in those days was deemed a matter of course: viz., by purchasing seamen's tickets. The government, instead of paying seamen their wages in cash, paid them in bills or tickets due at a certain subsequent date; and as the men were too poor or too improvident to keep those documents until the dates named, they sold them at a discount to persons who had ready cash to spare. Mr Guy was one of those who, in this way, made a profit out of the seamen, owing to a bad system for which the government was responsible. About that time, too, sprung up the notorious scheme called the South-sea Company, which ultimately brought ruin and disgrace to many who had founded or fostered it. Guy did not entangle himself in the roguery of the company; but he bought shares when low, and had the prudence to sell out when they were high. By these various means he accumulated a very large fortune. Pennant deals with him rather severely (in his *History of London*) for the mode in which a great part of his fortune was made; but, taking into consideration the times in which he lived, his proceedings do not seem to call for much censure. When his fortune was made, he certainly did good with it. He granted annuities to many persons in impoverished circumstances; he made liberal benefactions to St Thomas's Hospital; he founded an almshouse at Tamworth, his mother's native town; he left a perpetual annuity of £400 to Christ's Hospital, to receive four children yearly nominated by his trustees; and he gave large sums for the discharge of poor debtors. The following anecdote of him may here be introduced: '[Guy] was a man of very humble appearance, and of a melancholy cast of countenance. One day, while pensively leaning over one of the bridges, he attracted the attention and commiseration of a bystander, who, apprehensive that he meditated self-destruction, could not refrain from addressing him with an earnest entreaty "not to let his misfortunes tempt him to commit any rash act;" then, placing in his hand a guinea, with the delicacy of genuine benevolence, he hastily withdrew. Guy, roused from his reverie, followed the stranger, and warmly expressed his gratitude; but assured him he was mistaken in supposing him to be either in distress of mind or of circumstances: making an earnest request to be favoured with the name of the good man, his intended benefactor. The address was given, and they parted. Some years after, Guy, observing the name of his friend in the bankrupt-list, hastened to his house; brought to his recollection their former interview; found, upon investigation, that no blame could be attached to him under his misfortunes; intimated his ability and full intention to serve him; entered into immediate arrangements with his creditors; and finally re-established him in a business which ever after prospered in his hands, and in the hands of his children's children, for many years, in Newgate Street.'

The great work for which Thomas Guy is remembered, is the hospital bearing his name, in the borough. In connection with the foundation of this building, a curious anecdote has been related, which, though now somewhat hackneyed, will still bear repetition. Guy had a maid-servant of strictly frugal habits, and who made his wishes her most careful study. So attentive was she to his orders on all occasions, that he resolved to make her his wife, and he accordingly informed her of his intention. The necessary preparations were made for the wedding; and among others many little repairs were ordered, by Mr Guy, in and about his house. The latter included the laying down a new pavement opposite the street-door. It so happened that Sally, the bride-elect, observed a portion of the pavement, beyond the boundary of her master's house, which appeared to her to require mending, and of her own accord she gave orders to the workmen to have this job accomplished. Her directions were duly attended to in the absence of Mr Guy, who, on his return, perceived that the workmen had carried their labours beyond the limits which he had assigned. On inquiring the reason, he was informed that what had been done was 'by the mistress's orders.' Guy called the foolish Sally, and telling her that she had forgotten her position, added: 'If you take upon yourself to order matters contrary to my instructions before we are married, what will you not do after? I therefore renounce my matrimonial intentions towards you.' Poor Sally, by thus assuming an authority to which she then had no claim, lost a rich husband, and the country gained the noble hospital; named after its founder, who built and endowed it at a cost of £238,292.* Guy was seventy-six years of age when he matured the plan for founding an hospital. He procured a large piece of ground on a lease of 999 years, at a rent of £30 per annum, and pulled down a number of poor dwellings which occupied the site. He laid the first stone of his new hospital in 1722, but did not live to witness the completion of the work; for he died on the 27th of December 1724—just ten days before the admission of the first sixty patients. His trustees procured an act of parliament for carrying out the provisions of his bequest. They leased more ground, and enlarged the area of the hospital to nearly six acres; while the endowment or maintenance fund was laid out in the purchase of estates in Essex, Herefordshire, and Lincolnshire.

The building itself is large and convenient, but not striking as an architectural pile. This has indeed been a lucky hospital; for, nearly a century after Guy's death, an enormous bequest of nearly £200,000 was added to its funds. Mr Hunt, in 1829, left this sum, expressly to enlarge the hospital to the extent of one hundred additional beds. The rental of the hospital estates now exceeds £30,000 per annum. In the open quadrangle of the hospital is a bronze statue of Guy by Scheemakers; and in the chapel, a marble statue of him by Bacon.

In connection with Thomas Guy, who, of all the members of the Stationers' Company of London, may certainly be pronounced to have been one of the most successful in the acquisition of wealth, an interesting circumstance regarding the original import of the term *stationer* calls here for notice. Up to about the commencement of the last century, the term in question served almost exclusively to denote a bookseller, or one who had a *station* or *stall* in some public place for the sale of books. An instance of this application of it occurs in the following passage in Fuller's *Worthies of England:* 'I will not add that I have passed my promise (and that is an honest man's bond) to my former *stationer*, that I will write nothing for the future, which was in my former books so considerable as may make them interfere one with another to his prejudice.'

* *Lawson's History of Banking.*

The annexed engraving exhibits a stationer's stall or bookseller's shop in ancient times, when books were generally exposed for sale in some public place in the manner here represented. A parallel to this mode of conducting business still exists in the book-fairs at Leipsic and Frankfort, in Germany. In medieval days, the *stationarius* or *stationer* was an official connected with a university, who sold at his stall or *station* the books written or copied by the *librarius* or book-writer. From this origin is derived the modern term *stationer*, which now serves exclusively to denote an individual whose occupation consists in supplying the *implements* instead of the *productions* of literary labour.

A STATIONER'S STALL, OR BOOKSHOP IN THE OLDEN TIME.

## JOANNA SOUTHCOTT.

Joanna Southcott was born about the year 1750, of parents in very humble life. When about forty years old, she assumed the pretensions of a prophetess, and declared herself to be the woman mentioned in the twelfth chapter of the Book of Revelation. She asserted that, having received a divine appointment to be the mother of the Messiah, the visions revealed to St John would speedily be fulfilled by her agency and that of the son, who was to be miraculously born of her. Although extremely illiterate, she scribbled much mystic and unintelligible nonsense as visions and prophecy, and for a time carried on a lucrative trade in the sale of seals, which were, under certain conditions, to secure the salvation of the purchasers. The imposture was strengthened by her becoming subject to a rather rare disorder, which gave her the appearance of pregnancy after she had passed her grand climacteric. The faith of her followers now rose to enthusiasm. They purchased, at a fashionable upholsterer's, a cradle of most expensive materials, and highly decorated, and made costly preparations to hail the birth of the miraculous babe with joyous acclamation. The delusion spread rapidly and extensively, especially in the vicinity of London, and the number of converts is said to have amounted to upwards of one hundred thousand. Most of them were of the humbler order, and remarkable for their ignorance and credulity; but a few were of the more educated classes, among whom were two or three clergymen. One of the clergymen, on being reproved by his diocesan, offered to resign his living if 'the holy Johanna,' as he styled her, failed to appear on a certain day with the expected Messiah in her arms. About the close of 1814, however, the prophetess herself began to have misgivings, and in one of her lucid intervals, she declared that 'if she had been deceived, she had herself been the sport of some spirit either good or evil.' On the 27th of December in that year, death put an end to her expectations—but not to those of her disciples. They would not believe that she was really dead. Her body was kept unburied till the most active signs of decomposition appeared; it was also subjected to a *post-mortem* examination, and the cause of her peculiar appearance fully accounted for on medical principles. Still, numbers of her followers refused to believe she was dead; others flattered themselves that she would speedily rise again, and bound themselves by a vow not to shave their beards till her resurrection. It is scarcely necessary to state, that most of them passed to their graves unshorn. Several families of her disciples resided together near Chatham, in Kent, remarkable for the length of their beards, and the general singularity of their manners and appearance. In 1851 there were four congregations, comprising 198 persons. Joanna Southcott was interred, under a fictitious name, in the burial-ground attached to the chapel in St John's Wood, London. 'A stone has since been erected to her memory, which, after reciting her age and other usual particulars, concludes with some lines, evidently the composition of a still unshaken believer, the fervour of whose faith far exceeds his inspiration as a poet.'

## CHARLES AND MARY LAMB.

The lives of literary men are seldom characterised by much stirring adventure or variety of incident. The interest attaching to them consists mainly of the associations with which they are intertwined—the joys, trials, and sorrows of their domestic history, and the tracing of the gradual development of their genius to its culminating-point, from its first unfledged essays. In contemplating their career, much benefit may be derived both by the philosopher and moralist—the former of whom will gain thereby a deeper and more thorough knowledge of the workings of human nature, and the latter reap many an instructive and improving lesson.

Few biographies display so much beauty, or are more marked by a touching and lively interest, than those of Charles Lamb and his sister Mary. Devotedly attached to each other, united together by a strong sympathy both in mental and physical temperament, and a highly-refined and cultivated literary taste, they passed from youth to age; and when first the brother, and afterwards the sister, were laid in the same grave, in the peaceful churchyard of Edmonton, it might truly be said of them, that they 'were lovely and pleasant in their lives, and in their death they were not divided.' We shall now present the reader with a brief sketch of their history.

Their father, John Lamb, was a clerk to Mr Salt, a bencher of the Inner Temple; and in Crown Office Row of this classic locality, Charles was born in February 1775. His sister Mary was ten years older than himself, and there was also an elder brother, John. Young Lamb's early associations were thus all of a quaint and antiquarian nature. The grand old Temple church, so impressive, both from its architectural beauty and the romantic interest attached to its former possessors, the Knights Templars, who repose in its precincts; the dim walks and passages of the inns-of-court, redolent alike of learning and jurisprudence; and the pleasant sunny gardens descending to the noble Thames, where King Edward of yore had mustered a gallant array of knighthood and men-at-arms, ere setting forth on his last expedition to Scotland—all combined to stamp their impress on the mind of a sensitive, affectionate, and poetic child. At the age of seven, he obtained a presentation to Christ's Hospital, where the ensuing seven years of his life were spent, and a lasting friendship formed with the poet Coleridge, then a student at the same institution. Lamb made here considerable progress in classical learning; but an impediment of speech, which clung to him through life, prevented him, as originally intended, from entering the church, a profession indeed to which his inclinations were not adapted; and he accordingly quitted school at fourteen, and was placed for a time in the South-sea House, where his brother John held a situation. From this he was, in a year or two, transferred to a clerkship in the East India House, an establishment in which he gradually rose to the enjoyment of a large salary; and was ultimately pensioned off on a handsome allowance, a few years previous to his death. Shortly after entering on this employment, his parents removed from the Temple to Little Queen Street, Holborn. The pecuniary resources of the family were at this time but scanty, consisting of Charles's then small salary from the East India House, an annuity enjoyed by his father from the liberality of his old master, Mr Salt, and the scanty returns which his sister Mary could procure by her industry with the needle. Old Mr Lamb was now sinking into dotage, and his wife was stricken by an infirmity which deprived her of the use of her limbs. An old maiden-aunt, whom Charles has affectionately commemorated, resided with them, and paid them a small board. Notwithstanding all the difficulties with which they had to struggle, the affection which bound the different members of the family together, and, more especially, Mary and Charles, secured their enjoyment of a large share of happiness; but a fearful misfortune was about to overtake them.

A predisposition to insanity seems to have been inherited by the Lambs. At the age of twenty, Charles was seized by a fit of this malady, which compelled his removal, for a few weeks, to a lunatic asylum. His recovery, however, was complete and final; and till the end of his life his intellect remained sound and unclouded. A sadly different fate was that of poor Mary, his sister. Worn out by her double exertions in sewing and watching over her mother, who required constant attention, her mind which, on previous occasions, had been subject to aberration, gave way, and burst into an ungovernable frenzy. One day after the cloth had been laid for dinner, the malady attacked her with such violence, that, in a transport she snatched up a knife, and plunged it into the breast of her mother, who was seated, an invalid, in a chair. Her father was also present, but unable from frailty to interpose any obstacle to her fury; and she continued to brandish the fatal weapon, with loud shrieks, till her brother Charles entered the room, and took it from her hand. Assistance was procured, and the unfortunate woman was conveyed to a madhouse, where, in the course of a few weeks, she recovered her reason. In the meantime, her mother was dead, slain, though in innocence, by her hand; her father and aunt were helpless; and her brother John disposed to concur with the parish authorities and others in detaining her for life in confinement. In this conjuncture, Charles stepped forward, and by pledging himself to undertake the future care of his sister, succeeded in obtaining her release. Nobly did he fulfil his engagement by the sedulous and unremitting care with which he continued ever afterwards to watch over her, abandoning all hopes of marriage to devote himself to the charge which he had undertaken. It was a charge, indeed, sufficiently onerous, as Miss Lamb's complaint was constantly recurring after intervals, necessitating her removal for a time to an asylum. It was a remarkable circumstance connected with her disease, that she was perfectly conscious of its approach, and would inform her brother, with as much gentleness as possible, of the fact, upon which he would ask leave of absence from the India House, as if for a day's pleasuring, and accompany his sister on her melancholy journey to the place of confinement. On one of these occasions, they were met crossing a meadow near Hoxton by a friend, who stopped to speak to them, and learned from the weeping brother and sister their destination. In setting forth on the excursions which at first they used to make annually, during Lamb's holidays, to some place in the country, Mary would always carefully pack up in her trunk a strait-waistcoat, to be used in the event of one of her attacks coming on. Latterly, these jaunts had to be abandoned, as they were found to exercise on her an injurious influence.

The attendance required from Lamb at the India House was from ten to four every day, leaving him in general the free enjoyment of his evenings. These were devoted to literary labours and studies, diversified not unfrequently by social meetings with his friends, of whom his gentle and amiable nature had endeared to him an extensive circle. On Wednesday evenings, he usually held a reception, at which the principal literary celebrities of the day would assemble, play at whist, and discuss all matters of interest relating to literature, the fine arts, and the drama. Among those present on these occasions, in Lamb's younger days, might be seen Godwin, Hunt, and Hazlitt, and when in town, Wordsworth, Southey, and Coleridge. At a later period, Allan Cunningham, Cary, Edward Irving, and Thomas Hood would be found among the guests. Shortly after Miss Lamb's first release from confinement, her brother and she removed from Holborn to Pentonville, where, however, they did not remain long, and in 1800 took up their abode in the Temple, in which locality, dear to the hearts of both of them from early associations, they resided about seventeen years, probably the happiest period of their existence. From the Temple, they removed to Russell Street, Covent Garden, and thence to Colebrook Cottage, Islington, on the banks of the New River, where, rather curious to say, Lamb, for the first time in his life, found himself raised to the dignity of a householder, having hitherto resided always in lodgings. Not long, too, after his settling in this place, he exchanged the daily drudgery of the desk for the independent life of a gentleman at large, having been allowed to retire from the India House on a comfortable pension. In a few years, however, his sister's increasing infirmities, and the more frequent recurrence of her mental disorder, induced him to quit London for the country, and he took up his abode at Enfield, from which he afterwards migrated to Edmonton. Here, in consequence of the effects of a fall, producing erysipelas in the head, he expired tranquilly and without pain, after a few days' illness, in December 1834. His sister was labouring at the time under one of her attacks, and was therefore unable to feel her loss with all the poignancy which she would otherwise have experienced. She survived her brother for upwards of twelve years, and having been latterly induced by her friends to remove from Enfield to London, died quietly at St John's Wood on 20th May 1847.

It is now proper to refer to Lamb's literary works. Being independent of the pen as a main support, his writings are more in the character of fugitive pieces, contributed to magazines, than of weighty and voluminous lucubrations. As an author, his name will principally be recollected by his celebrated *Essays of Elia*, originally contributed to the *London Magazine*, and a second series, even superior to the first, entitled the *Last Essays of Elia*. These delightful productions, so racy and original, place Lamb incontestably in the first rank of our British essayists, and fairly entitle him to contest the palm with Addison and Steele. Egotistical they may in one sense be termed, as the author's personal feelings and predilections, with many of his peculiar traits of character, are brought prominently forward; but the egotism is of the most charming and unselfish kind—a sentiment which commends itself all the more winningly to us when he comes to speak of his sister under the appellation of his Cousin Bridget. Other essays and pieces were contributed by him to various periodicals, including Leigh Hunt's *Reflector*, *Blackwood's Magazine*, and the *Englishman's Magazine*, and bear all the same character of quaintness, simplicity, and playful wit. In his early days, his tendencies had been principally exerted in the direction of poetry, in the production of which there was a sort of copartnership betwixt him and Coleridge, along with Charles Lloyd, and a volume of pieces by the trio was published at Bristol in 1797. As a votary of the Muses, however, Lamb's claims cannot be highly rated, his poems, though graceful and melodious, being deficient both in vigour and originality of thought. The one dramatic piece, the farce of *Mr H.*, which he succeeded in getting presented on the boards of Drury Lane, was shelved on the first night of its representation. The disappointment was borne manfully by him, and as he sat with his sister in the pit, Lamb joined himself in the hisses by which the fate of his unfortunate bantling was sealed.

Allusion has already been made to Lamb's amiability of disposition. Through the whole course of his life he never made a single enemy, and the relations between him and his friends were scarcely ever disturbed by the slightest *fraças*. To use a favourite expression of Lord Jeffrey, he was eminently 'sweet-blooded.'

Though of a highly poetic and imaginative temperament, Lamb took little pleasure in rural scenery. A true child of London, no landscape, in his estimation, was comparable with the crowded and bustling streets of the great metropolis, Covent-Garden Market and its piazzas, or the gardens of the inns of court. A visit to Drury Lane or Covent-Garden Theatre in the evening, a rubber at whist, or a quiet fireside-chat with a few friends, not unaccompanied by the material consolations of sundry steaming beverages and the fragrant fumes of the Virginian weed, were among his dearest delights. One unfortunate failing must here be recorded—his tendency, on convivial occasions, to exceed the limits of temperance. This, however, can scarcely be regarded as a habitual error on his part, and has probably received a greater prominence than it merited, from his well-known paper, *The Confessions of a Drunkard*, in which he has so graphically described the miserable results of excess. Another predilection, his addiction to the use of tobacco, was ultimately overcome by him after many struggles. His tastes, in the consumption of the fragrant weed, were not very delicate, inducing him to use the strongest and coarsest kinds. On being asked one day by a friend, as he was puffing forth huge volumes of smoke, how he had ever managed to acquire such a practice, he replied: 'By striving after it as other men strive after virtue.' His convivial habits leading him not unfrequently to 'hear the chimes at midnight,' his appearance at business next morning was sometimes considerably beyond the proper hour. On being one day reproved by his superior for his remissness in this respect, the answer was: 'True, sir, very true, I often come *late*, but then, you know, I always go away *early*.' To a man of his disposition, it can be readily supposed that the dull routine of his duties at the India House was a most distasteful drudgery, and we accordingly find him often bewailing humorously his lot in letters to his correspondents. His good sense, however, rendered him perfectly aware of the benefits of regular employment and a fixed income, and his complaints must therefore be regarded in a great measure as ironical, the offspring of the spirit of grumbling, so characteristic of the family of John Bull.

During the intervals of her malady, Miss Lamb appeared in her natural and attractive aspect, the well-bred mistress of her brother's house, doing its honours with all grace, and most tenderly solicitous and careful in everything relating to his comfort. Her conversation and correspondence were both lively and genial, and possessing the same literary tastes as Charles, she was often associated with him in the production of various works. These were chiefly of a juvenile nature, including the charming collection of *Tales from Shakspeare; Mrs Leicester's School;* and *Poetry for Children.*

---

# DECEMBER 28.

**The Holy Innocents. St Theodorus, abbot of Tabenna, confessor, 367.**

## Innocents' Day.

This festival, which is variously styled Innocents' Day, The Holy Innocents' Day, and Childermas Day, or Childermas, has been observed from an early period in the history of the church, as a commemoration of the barbarous massacre of children in Bethlehem, ordered by King Herod, with the view of destroying among them the infant Saviour, as recorded in the Gospel of St Matthew. It is one of those anniversaries which were retained in the ritual of the English Church at the Reformation.

In consequence probably of the feeling of horror attached to such an act of atrocity, Innocents' Day used to be reckoned about the most unlucky throughout the year, and in former times, no one who could possibly avoid it, began any work, or entered on any undertaking, on this anniversary. To marry on Childermas Day was especially inauspicious. It is said of the equally superstitious and unprincipled monarch, Louis XI., that he would never perform any business, or enter into any discussion about his affairs on this day, and to make to him then any proposal of the kind, was certain to exasperate him to the utmost. We are informed, too, that in England, on the occasion of the coronation of King Edward IV., that solemnity, which had been originally intended to take place on a Sunday, was postponed till the Monday, owing to the former day being in that year the festival of Childermas. This idea of the inauspicious nature of the day was long prevalent, and is even yet not wholly extinct. To the present hour we understand the housewives in Cornwall, and probably also in other parts of the country, refrain scrupulously from scouring or scrubbing on Innocents' Day.

In ancient times, the 'Massacre of the Innocents' might be said to be annually re-enacted in the form of a smart whipping, which it was customary on this occasion to administer to the juvenile members of a family. We find it remarked by an old writer, that 'it hath been a custom, and yet is elsewhere, to whip up the children upon Innocents' Day Morning, that the memorie of Herod's murder of the Innocents might stick the closer, and in a moderate proportion to act over the crueltie again in kinde.' Several other ancient authors confirm the accuracy of this statement. The idea is naturally suggested that these unfortunate 'innocents' might have escaped so disagreeable a commemoration by quitting their couches betimes, before their elders had risen, and we accordingly find that in some places the whole affair resolved itself into a frolic, in which the lively and active, who managed to be first astir, made sport to themselves at the expense of the lazy and sleepy-headed, whom it was their privilege on this morning to rouse from grateful slumbers by a sound drubbing administered *in lecto.*

In reference to the three consecutive commemorations, on the 26th, 27th, and 28th of December, theologians inform us that in these are comprehended three descriptions of martyrdom, all of which have their peculiar efficacy, though differing in degree. In the death of St Stephen, an example is furnished of the highest class of martyrdom; that is to say, both in *will and deed.* St John the Evangelist, who gave practical evidence of his readiness to suffer death for the cause of Christ, though, through miraculous interposition, he was saved from actually doing so, is an instance of the second description of martyrdom—in *will* though not in *deed.* And the slaughter of the Innocents affords an instance of martyrdom in *deed* and not in *will,* these unfortunate children having lost their lives, though involuntarily, on account of the Saviour, and it being therefore considered 'that God supplied the defects of their will by his own acceptance of the sacrifice.'

---

*Born.*—Thomas Henderson, astronomer, 1798, *Dundee;* Alexander Keith Johnstone, geographer, 1804.

*Died.*—Mary of Orange, queen of William III., 1694, *Kensington;* Pierre Bayle, critic and controversialist, 1706, *Rotterdam;* Joseph Piton de Tournefort, distinguished botanist, 1708, *Paris;* Dr John Campbell, miscellaneous writer, 1775, *London;* John Logan, poet, 1788, *London;* Thomas Babington Macaulay, Lord Macaulay, historian, essayist, &c., 1859, *Kensington.*

## JOHN LOGAN.

The name of John Logan, though almost entirely forgotten in South Britain, is not likely to pass into oblivion in Scotland, as long as the church of that country continues to use in her services those beautiful Scripture paraphrases and hymns, undoubtedly the finest and most poetical of any *versified* collection of chants for divine worship employed by any denomination of Christians in the United Kingdom. Some of the finest of these, including the singularly solemn and affecting hymn, 'The hour of my departure's come,' are from the pen of Logan.

The history of this gifted man forms one of those melancholy chapters which the lives of men of genius have but too often furnished. The son of a small farmer near Fala, in Mid-Lothian, he was educated for the Scottish Church in the Edinburgh University, and almost immediately after being licensed as a preacher, was presented to a church in Leith, where for several years he enjoyed great renown as an eloquent and popular preacher. He delivered a course of lectures in Edinburgh with much success on the 'Philosophy of History,' published a volume of poems, and had a tragedy called *Runnamede* acted at the Edinburgh theatre in 1783. The times were now somewhat changed since the days when the production of Home's tragedy of *Douglas* had excited a ferment in the Scottish Church, which has become historical. We are informed by Dr Carlyle, who himself had to encounter the violence of the storm which burst forth against Home and the clerical brethren who supported him, that about 1784, so complete a revulsion of feeling had taken place on the subject of theatricals, owing to the predominance gained by the Moderate over the Evangelical party, that when Mrs Siddons made her first appearance in Edinburgh, the General Assembly of the Scottish Church was obliged to adjourn its sittings at an early hour to enable its reverend members to attend the theatre and witness the performance of the great tragic actress. Yet, notwithstanding this altered state of public opinion, Logan did undergo some obloquy and animadversion in consequence of the play above referred to, and the annoyance thereby occasioned, combined with a hereditary tendency to hypochondria, seems to have induced a melancholy and depression of spirits which prompted him to seek relief in the fatal solace of stimulating liquors. The habit rapidly gained strength; and having so far forgotten himself as on one occasion to appear in the pulpit in a state of intoxication, the misguided man was glad to make an arrangement with the ecclesiastical authorities, by which he was allowed to resign his ministerial charge, and retain for his maintenance a portion of its revenues. He then proceeded to London, where he eked out his income by literary labour of various kinds, but did not long survive his transference to the metropolis, dying there on 28th December 1788. Two posthumous volumes of his sermons long enjoyed great popularity.

Whilst yet a student at Edinburgh College, Logan acted for a time as tutor to a boy who afterwards became Sir John Sinclair of Ulbster, famous for his many public-spirited undertakings. The following anecdote of this period of his life exhibits an amusing instance of a tendency to practical joking in the disposition of the future divine and poet. About 1766, the Sinclair family, with whom he resided, made a progress from Edinburgh to its remote Caithness home; and owing to the badness of the roads, it was necessary to employ two carriages, the heaviest of them drawn by six horses. 'When the cavalcade reached Kinross, the natives gathered round in crowds to gaze upon it, and requested the tutor to inform them who was travelling in such state. Logan affected a suspicious reluctance to give an answer; but at last took aside some respectable bystander, and, after enjoining secrecy, whispered to him, pointing to the laird: "You observe a portly stout gentleman, with gold lace upon his clothes. That is (but it must not be mentioned to mortal) the great Duke William of Cumberland; he is going north *incog.* to see the field of Culloden once more." This news was, of course, soon spread, and brought the whole population to catch a glimpse of the hero.' *

---

## The White Horse of Berkshire.

In a previous article,† we took occasion to describe the celebrated Berkshire monument known as 'Wayland Smith's Cave,' the history of which is shrouded in a mysterious antiquity. About a mile from this famous cromlech exists a no less remarkable memorial of bygone times—the renowned White Horse of Berkshire.

The colossal representation which bears this name consists of a trench, about two feet deep,

* *Memoir of Sir John Sinclair, by his Son.* 2 vols. 1837.
† Volume ii. p. 82.

cut in the side of a steep green hill, which is called White Horse Hill, and rises on the south of the vale known as the Vale of the White Horse. It is situated in the parish of Uffington, in the western district of Berkshire, about five miles from Great Farringdon. Though rudely cut, the figure, excavated in the chalk of which the hill is composed, presents, when viewed from the vale

THE WHITE HORSE OF BERKSHIRE.

beneath, a sufficiently recognisable delineation of a white horse in the act of galloping. Its length is about 374 feet, and the space which it occupies is said to be nearly two acres.

No exact evidence can be adduced regarding the origin of this remarkable figure, but there seems to be little doubt that, in accordance with the popular tradition, it was carved to commemorate the victory of King Ethelred and his brother Alfred, afterwards Alfred the Great, over the Danes at Ashdown, in the year 871. The actual site of this great battle is not known, and has been the subject of some discussion; but the balance of probability is in favour of its having been fought in the neighbourhood of White Horse Hill, on the summit of which, at the height of 893 feet above the sea, is an ancient encampment, consisting of a plain of more than eight acres in extent, surrounded by a rampart and ditch. This enclosure is called Uffington Castle, and immediately beneath it is the stupendous engraving of the White Horse.

Were the preservation of this curious monument dependent only on the persistency of the original figure, it would probably have long since been obliterated by the washing down of debris from above into the trench, and the gradual formation of turf. From time immemorial, however, a custom has existed among the inhabitants of the neighbouring district, of assembling periodically, and scouring or cleaning out the trench, so as to renew and preserve the figure of the horse. This ceremony is known as 'The Scouring of the White Horse,' and, according to an ancient custom, the scourers are entertained at the expense of the lord of the manor. The festival which concludes their labours, forms a fête of one or two days' duration. Rustic and athletic games of various kinds, including wrestling, backsword-play, racing, jumping, and all those pastimes included in the general category of 'old English sports,' are engaged in on this occasion with immense enthusiasm, and prizes are distributed to the most successful competitors. A most interesting and graphic description of one of these rural gatherings, which took place in September 1857, is given in *The Scouring of the White Horse*, from the spirited pen of Mr Hughes, the well-known author of *Tom Brown's School-days*.

## CARD-PLAYING AND PLAYING-CARDS.

A universal Christmas custom of the olden time was playing at cards; persons who never touched a card at any other season of the year, felt bound to play a few games at Christmas. The practice had even the sanction of the law. A prohibitory statute of Henry VII.'s reign, forbade card-playing save during the Christmas holidays. Of course, this prohibition extended only to persons of humble rank; Henry's daughter, the Princess Margaret, played cards with her suitor, James IV. of Scotland; and James himself kept up the custom, receiving from his treasurer, at Melrose, on Christmas-night, 1496, thirty-five unicorns, eleven French crowns, a ducat, a *ridare*, and a *leu*, in all about equal to £42 of modern money, to use at the card-table. One of Poor Robin's rhythmical effusions runs thus:

'Christmas to hungry stomachs gives relief,
With mutton, pork, pies, pasties, and roast-beef;
And men, at cards, spend many idle hours,
At loadum, whisk, cross-ruff, put, and all-fours.'

Palamedes, it is said, invented the game of chess to assuage the bitter pangs of hunger, during the siege of Troy; and, similarly, Poor Robin, in another doggerel rhyme, seems to imply that a pair—an old name for a pack—of cards may even cheer a comfortless Christmas—

'The kitchen that a-cold may be,
For little fire you in it may see.
Perhaps a pair of cards is going,
And that's the chiefest matter doing.'

The immortal Sir Roger de Coverley, however, took care to provide both creature-comfort and amusement for his neighbours at Christmas; by sending 'a string of hog's puddings and a pack of cards' to every poor family in the parish.

Primero was the fashionable game at the court of England during the Tudor dynasty. Shakspeare represents Henry VIII. playing at it with the Duke of Suffolk; and Falstaff says: 'I never prospered, since I forswore myself at Primero.' In the Earl of Northumberland's letters about the Gunpowder-plot, it is noticed that Joscelin Percy was playing at this game on Sunday, when his uncle, the conspirator, called on him at Essex House. In the Sidney papers, there is an account of a desperate quarrel between Lord Southampton, the patron of Shakspeare, and one Ambrose Willoughby. Lord Southampton was then 'Squire of the Body' to Queen Elizabeth, and the quarrel was occasioned by Willoughby persisting to play with Sir Walter Raleigh and another at Primero, in the Presence Chamber, after the queen had retired to rest, a course of proceeding which Southampton would not permit. Primero, originally a Spanish game, is said to have been made fashionable in England by Philip of Spain, after his marriage with Queen Mary. Rogers elegantly describes the fellow-voyagers of Columbus engaged at this game:

'At daybreak might the caravels be seen,
Chasing their shadows o'er the deep serene;
Their burnished prows lashed by the sparkling tide,
Their green-cross standards waving far and wide.

And now once more, to better thoughts inclined,
The seaman, mounting, clamoured in the wind.
The soldier told his tales of love and war;
The courtier sung—sung to his gay guitar.
Round at Primero, sate a whiskered band;
So fortune smiled, careless of sea or land.'

Maw succeeded Primero as the fashionable game at the English court. Sir John Harrington notices it as—

'Maw,
A game without civility or law;
An odious play, and yet in court oft seen,
A saucy Knave to trump both King and Queen.'

Maw was the favourite game of James I., who appears to have played at cards, just as he played with affairs of state, in an indolent manner; requiring in both cases some one to hold his cards, if not to prompt him what to play. Weldon, alluding to the poisoning of Sir Thomas Overbury, in his *Court and Character of King James*, says: 'The next that came on the stage was Sir Thomas Monson, but the night before he was to come to his trial, the king being at the game of Maw, said: "To-morrow comes Thomas Monson to his trial." "Yea," said the king's card-holder, "where if he do not play his master's prize, your majesty shall never trust me." This so ran in the king's mind, that at the next game, he said he was sleepy, and would play out that set the next night.' The writer of a contemporary pamphlet, entitled *Tom Tell-truth*, shews that he was well acquainted with James's mode of playing cards, and how, moreover, his majesty was tricked in his dawdling with state matters, where the friendly services of a card-holder were less to be depended on. This pamphleteer, addressing James, observes: 'Even in the very gaming ordinaries, where men have scarce leisure to say grace, yet they take a time to censure your majesty's actions, and that in their old-school terms. They say you have lost the fairest game at Maw that ever king had, for want of making the best advantage of the five-finger, and playing the other helps in time. That your own card-holders play booty, and give the sign out of your own hand.' This gives us a suspicion of what the game of Maw was like, which is fully verified by the following verses under a caricature of the period, representing the kings of England, Denmark, and Sweden, with Bethlem Gabor, playing at cards against the pope and some monks.

'Denmark, not sitting far, and seeing what hand
Great Britain had, and how Rome's loss did stand,
Hopes to win something too: Maw is the game
At which he plays, and challengeth at the same
A Monk, who stakes a chalice; Denmark sets gold
And shuffles; the Monk cuts; Denmark being bold,
Deals freely round; and the first card he shews
Is the five-fingers, which, being turned up, goes
Cold to the Monk's heart; the next Denmark sees
Is the ace of hearts; the Monk cries out I lees!
Denmark replies, Sir Monk shew what you have;
The Monk could shew him nothing but the knave.'

From the preceding allusions to the five-fingers (the five of trumps), the ace of hearts, and the knave, it is evident that Maw differed very slightly from Five Cards, the most popular game in Ireland at the present day. As early as 1674, this game was popular in Ireland, as we learn from Cotton's *Compleat Gamester*, which says: 'Five Cards is an Irish game, and is much played in that kingdom, for considerable sums of money, as All-fours is played in Kent, and Post-and-pair in the west of England.' Games migrate and acquire new names, as well as other things. Post-and-pair, formerly the great game of the west of England, has gone further west, and is now the Poker of the south-western states of America; and the American backwoodsman, when playing his favourite game of *Euker*, little thinks that he is engaged at the fashionable Parisian *Écarté*.

Noddy was one of the old English court games, and is thus noticed by Sir John Harrington:

'Now Noddy followed next, as well it might,
Although it should have gone before of right;
At which I say, I name not any body,
One never had the knave, yet laid for Noddy.'

This has been supposed to have been a children's game, and it was certainly nothing of the kind. Its nature is thus fully described in a curious satirical poem, entitled *Batt upon Batt*, published in 1694.

'Shew me a man can turn up Noddy still,
And deal himself three fives too, when he will;
Conclude with one-and-thirty, and a pair,
Never fail ten in Stock, and yet play fair,
If Batt be not that wight, I lose my aim.'

From these lines, there can be no doubt that the ancient Noddy was the modern Cribbage—the Nob of to-day, rejoicing in the name of Noddy, and the modern Crib, being termed the Stock. Cribbage is, in all probability, the most popular English game at cards at the present day. It seems as if redolent of English comfort, a snug fireside, a Welsh-rabbit, and a little mulled something simmering on the hob. The rival powers of chance and skill are so happily blended, that while the influence of fortune is recognised as a source of pleasing excitement, the game of Cribbage admits, at the same time, of such an exertion of the mental faculties, as is sufficient to interest without fatiguing the player. It is the only game known to the writer that still induces the village surgeon, the parish curate, and two other old-fashioned friends, to meet occasionally, on a winter's evening, at the village inn.

Ombre was most probably introduced into this country by Catherine of Portugal, the queen of Charles II.; Waller, the court-poet, has a poem on a card torn at Ombre by the queen. This royal lady also introduced to the English court the reprehensible practice of playing cards on Sunday. Pepys, in 1667, writes: 'This evening, going to the queen's side to see the ladies, I did find the queen, the Duchess of York, and another at cards, with the room full of ladies and great men; which I was amazed at to see on a Sunday, having not believed, but contrarily flatly denied the same, a little while since, to my cousin.'

In a passage from Evelyn's *Memoirs*, already quoted (vol. i. p. 226), the writer impressively describes another Sunday-evening scene at Whitehall, a few days before the death of Charles II., in which a profligate assemblage of courtiers is represented as deeply engaged in the game of Basset. This was an Italian game, brought by Cardinal Mazarin to France; Louis XIV. is said to have lost large sums at it; and it was most likely brought to England by some of the French ladies of the court. It did not stand its ground, however, in this country; Ombre continuing the fashionable game in England, down till after the expiration of the first quarter of the last century. It is utterly forgotten now, but being Belinda's game in the *Rape of the Lock*, where every incident in the deal is minutely described, it could be at once revived from that delightful poem. Pope's Grotto and Hampton Court excited in Miss Mitford's mind 'vivid images of the fair Belinda and the game of Ombre.' The writer, who resides in that classic neighbourhood, sometimes sees at auctions in old houses, the company puzzling their brains over a curious three-cornered table, wondering what it possibly could have been made for. It is an Ombre-table, expressly used for playing this game, and is represented, with an exalted party so engaged, on the frontispiece of Seymour's *Compleat Gamester*, published in 1739. From the title-page we learn that this work was written 'for the use of the young princesses.' These were the daughters of George, Prince of Wales, afterwards George II. One of them, Amelia, in her old-maidenhood, was a regular visitor at Bath, seeking health in the pump-room, and amusement at the card-table.

Quadrille succeeded Ombre, but for a curious reason did not reign so long as its predecessor. From the peculiar nature of Quadrille, an unfair confederacy might be readily established, by any two persons, by which the other players could be cheated. In an annual publication, the *Annals of Gaming*, for 1775, the author says, 'this game is most commonly played by ladies, who favour one another by making signs. The great stroke the ladies attempt is keeping the pool, when by a very easy legerdemain they can serve themselves as many fish as they please.'

While the preceding games were in vogue, the magnificent temple of Whist, destined to outshine and overshadow them, was in course of erection.

'Let India vaunt her children's vast address,
Who first contrived the warlike sport of Chess;
Let nice Piquette the boast of France remain
And studious Ombre be the pride of Spain;
Invention's praise shall England yield to none,
When she can call delightful Whist her own.'

All great inventions and discoveries are works of time, and Whist is no exception to the rule; it did not come into the world perfect at all points, as Minerva emerged from the head of Jupiter. Nor were its wonderful merits early recognised. Under the vulgar appellations of Whisk and Swobbers, it long lingered in the servants-hall, ere it could ascend to the drawing-room. At length, some gentlemen, who met at the Crown coffee-house, in Bedford Row, studied the game, gave it rules, established its principles, and then Edward Hoyle, in 1743, blazoned forth its fame to all the world.

'Whilst Ombre and Quadrille at court were used,
And Basset's power the city dames amused,
Imperial Whist was yet but light esteemed,
And pastime fit for none but rustics deemed.
How slow, at first, is still the growth of fame!
And what obstructions wait each rising name!
Our stupid fathers thus neglected, long,
The glorious boast of Milton's epic song;
But Milton's muse, at last, a critic found,
Who spread his praise o'er all the world around;
And Hoyle, at length, for Whist performed the same,
And proved its right to universal fame.'

Many attempts have been made, at various times, to turn playing-cards to a very different use from that for which they were originally intended. Thus, in 1518, a learned Franciscan friar, named Murner, published a *Logica Memorativa*, a mode of teaching logic, by a pack of cards; and, subsequently, he attempted to teach a summary of civil law in the same manner. In 1656, an Englishman, named Jackson, published a work, entitled the *Scholar's Sciential Cards*, in which he proposed to teach reading, spelling, grammar, writing, and arithmetic, with various arts and sciences, by playing-cards; premising that the learner was well grounded in all the games played at the period. And later still, about the close of the seventeenth century, there was published the *Genteel Housekeeper's Pastime; or the Mode of Carving at Table represented in a Pack of Playing-Cards, by which any one of Ordinary Capacity may learn how to Carve, in Mode, all the most usual Dishes of Flesh, Fish, Fowl, and Baked Meats, with the several Sauces and Garnishes proper to Every Dish of Meat.* In this system, flesh was represented by hearts, fish by clubs, fowl by diamonds, and baked meat by spades. The king of hearts ruled a noble sirloin of roast-beef; the monarch of clubs presided over a pickled herring; and the king of diamonds reared his battle-axe over a turkey; while his brother of spades smiled benignantly on a well-baked venison-pasty.

A still more practical use of playing-cards can be vouched for by the writer. Some years ago, a shrewd Yankee skipper, bound for New York, found himself contending against the long westerly gales of winter with a short and inefficient crew, but a number of sturdy Irish emigrants as passengers. It was most desirable to make the latter useful in working the ship, by pulling and hauling about the deck; but their utter ignorance of the names and positions of the various ropes rendered the project, at first sight, apparently impossible. The problem, however, was readily solved by placing a playing-card, as a mark or tally, at each of the principal ropes; the red cards in the fore-part of the ship, the black cards in the after; hearts and clubs on the starboard side, spades and diamonds on the larboard. In five minutes, every Irishman knew his station, and the position of the cards; there was no mysterious nautical nomenclature of tacks, sheets, halliards, braces, bowlines, &c., to bother the Hibernian mind. The men who were stationed at the ace of spades, for instance, well knew their post, and when called to tack ship, were always found at it; when orders were given to haul down the king of clubs, the rope was at once seized by ready hands. The writer has seen the after-guard and waisters of a newly-commissioned crack ship-of-war, longer in learning their stations, and becoming efficient in their duties, than those card-taught Irishmen were.

Even the pulpit has not disdained to turn playing-cards to practical use. Bishop Latimer, preaching at Cambridge on the Sunday before Christmas, 1527, suited his sermon to the card-playing practice of the season rather than the text. And Fuller gives another example of a clergyman preaching from Romans xii. 3—'As God hath dealt to every man the measure of faith.' The reverend gentleman in question adopted as an illustration of his discourse the metaphor of *dealing* as applied to cards, reminding his congregation that they should follow suit, ever play above-board, improve the gifts dealt out to them, take care of their trumps, play promptly when it became their turn, and so forth.

The familiar name of the nine of diamonds has already been noticed in these pages (vol. i. p. 75). In Ireland, the six of hearts is still termed 'Grace's card.' The Honourable Colonel Richard Grace, an old Cavalier, when governor of Athlone for James II., was solicited, by promises of royal favour, to betray his trust, and espouse the cause of William III. Taking up a card, which happened to be the six of hearts, Grace wrote upon it the following reply, and handed it to the emissary who had been commissioned to make the proposal. 'Tell your master I despise his offer, and that honour and conscience are dearer to a gentleman, than all the wealth and titles a prince can bestow.'

Short notes were frequently written on the back of playing-cards. In an old collection of poetry is found the following lines:

TO A LADY, WHO SENT HER COMPLIMENTS TO A CLERGYMAN ON THE TEN OF HEARTS.

'Your compliments, dear lady, pray forbear,
Old English services are more sincere;
You send ten hearts—the tithe is only mine,
Give me but one, and burn the other nine.'

The kind of advertisements now called circulars, were often, formerly, printed on the backs of playing-cards. Visiting-cards, too, were improvised, by writing the name on the back of playing-cards. About twenty years ago, when a house in Dean Street, Soho, was under repair, several visiting-cards of this description were found behind a marble chimney-piece, one of them bearing the name of Isaac Newton. Cards of invitation were written in a similar manner. In the fourth picture, in Hogarth's series of 'Marriage-à-la-Mode,' several are seen lying on the floor, upon one of which is inscribed: 'Count Basset begs to no how Lade Squander sleapt last nite.' Hogarth, when he painted this inscription, was most probably thinking of Mrs Centlivre's play, *The Basset Table*, which a critic describes as containing a great deal of plot and business, without much sentiment or delicacy.

An animated description of a round game at cards, among a party of young people in a Scottish farmhouse, is given in Wilson's ever-memorable *Noctes*. It is the Shepherd who is represented speaking in this wise:

'As for young folks—lads and lasses, like—when the gudeman and his wife are gaen to bed, what's the harm in a ggem at cairds? It's a chearfu', noisy, sicht o' comfort and confusion. Sic luckin' into anither's hauns! Sic fause shufflin'! Sic unfair dealin'! Sic winkin' to tell your pairtner that ye hae the king or the ace! And when that wunna do, sic kickin' o' shins and treadin' on taes aneath the table—aften the wrang anes! Then down wi' your haun' o' cairds in a clash on the boord, because you've ane ower few, and the coof maun lose his deal! Then what gigglin' amang the lasses! What amicable, nay, love-quarrels, between pairtners! Jokin', and jeestin', and tauntin', and toozlin'—the cawnel blawn out, and the soun' o' a thousan' kisses!—That's caird-playing in the kintra, Mr North; and where's the man amang ye that wull daur to say that it's no a pleasant pastime o' a winter's nicht, when the snaw is cumin' doon the lum, or the speat's roarin' amang the mirk mountains.'

A curious and undoubtedly authentic historical anecdote is told of a pack of cards. Towards the end of the persecuting reign of Queen Mary, a commission was granted to a Dr Cole to go over to Ireland, and commence a fiery crusade against the Protestants of that country. On coming to Chester, on his way, the doctor was waited on by the mayor, to whom he shewed his commission, exclaiming, with premature triumph: 'Here is what shall lash the heretics of Ireland.' Mrs Edmonds, the landlady of the inn, having a brother in Dublin, was much disturbed by overhearing these words; so, when the doctor accompanied the mayor down stairs, she hastened into his room, opened his box, took out the commission, and put a pack of cards in its place. When the doctor returned to his apartment, he put the box into his portmanteau without suspicion, and the next morning sailed for Dublin. On his arrival, he waited on the lord-lieutenant and privy council, to whom he made a speech on the subject of his mission, and then presented the box to his lordship; but on opening it, there appeared only a pack of cards, with the knave of clubs uppermost. The doctor was petrified, and assured the council that he had had a commission, but what was become of it he could not tell. The lord-lieutenant answered: 'Let us have another commission, and, in the meanwhile, we can shuffle the cards.' Before the doctor could get his commission renewed, Queen Mary died, and thus the persecution was prevented. We are further informed that, when Queen Elizabeth was made acquainted with the circumstances, she settled a pension of £40 per annum on Mrs Edmonds, for having saved her Protestant subjects in Ireland.

There are few who sit down to a quiet rubber that are aware of the possible combinations of the pack of fifty-two cards. As a curious fact, not found in Hoyle, it is worth recording here, that the possible combinations of a pack of cards cannot be numerically represented by less than forty-seven figures, arrayed in the following order: 16, 250, 563, 659, 176, 029, 962, 568, 164, 794, 000, 749, 006, 367, 006, 400.

An old work on card-playing sums up the morality of the practice, very concisely, in the following lines:

'He who hopes at cards to win,
Must never think that cheating 's sin;
To make a trick whene'er he can,
No matter how, should be the plan.
No case of conscience must he make,
Except how he may save his stake;
The only object of his prayers
Not to be caught and kicked down stairs.'

A more summary process of ejectment, even, than kicking down stairs, seems to have been occasionally adopted in the olden time; sharpers having sometimes been thrown out of a window. A person so served at Bath, it is said, went to a solicitor for advice, when the following conversation took place:

'Says the lawyer: "What motive for treatment so hard?"
"Dear sir. all my crime was but—slipping a card."

"Indeed! For how much did you play then, and where!"
"For two hundred, up two pair of stairs at the Bear."
"Why, then, my good friend, as you want my advice,
T'other guinea advanced, it is yours in a trice."
"Here it is, my dear sir."—"Very well, now observe,
Future downfalls to shun, from this rule never swerve,
When challenged upstairs, luck for hundreds to try,
Tell your frolicsome friends, that you don't play so *high!*"'

The card-player has had his epitaph. Let us conclude with it:

'His card is cut—long days he shuffled through
The game of life—he dealt as others do:
Though he by honours tells not its amount.
When the last trump is played, his tricks will count.'

## DECEMBER 29.

St Marcellus, abbot of the Acœmetes, confessor, about 485. St Evroul, abbot and confessor, 596. St Thomas Becket, archbishop of Canterbury, 1170.

*Born.*—Sir Archibald Alison, Bart., historian, 1792, *Kenley, Shropshire.*

*Died.*—Thomas Becket, archbishop of Canterbury, murdered, 1170; Sebastian Castalio, scholar and controversialist, 1563, *Basle;* Viscount William Stafford, victim of 'Popish Plot,' executed, 1680; Dr Thomas Sydenham, distinguished physician, 1689, *London;* Brook Taylor, algebraist, 1731, *London;* Joseph Saurin, mathematician and natural philosopher, 1737, *Paris;* Jacques Louis David, painter, 1825, *Brussels;* Rev. T. R. Malthus, political economist, 1834, *Bath;* William Crotch, musical composer, 1847, *Taunton;* W. H. Maxwell, novelist and historian, 1850, *Musselburgh;* James, Marquis of Dalhousie, statesman, 1860.

### THOMAS BECKET.

The career and fate of this celebrated ecclesiastic, form one of the most remarkable episodes of English history in the twelfth century. The leading incidents of his life are familiar to all, but a brief and comprehensive recapitulation may nevertheless not be unacceptable to our readers.

Thomas Becket or à Becket, as his name is sometimes written, was the son of a London merchant, who bestowed on him a good education. For a time young Becket was employed in the office of the sheriff of London, and there made the acquaintance of Theobald, archbishop of Canterbury, who sent him to study civil law in Italy and France, and afterwards, besides presenting him with two ecclesiastical livings, intrusted him with the management of certain negotiations with the see of Rome, requiring the utmost tact and address. The young clerk succeeded so well in this mission as not only to justify the confidence reposed in him by his patron, but also in attracting the notice of Henry II., who conceived rapidly such an attachment to Becket personally, and so exalted an estimate of his abilities, that in 1158 he promoted his new favourite to the dignity of chancellor of the realm. The king had no occasion to accuse himself of injudiciousness in taking this step, for Becket proved not only a most accomplished courtier and delightful companion, but likewise a clear-headed and sagacious statesman. He even gave evidence of military tastes and prowess by accompanying the king on an expedition to France, where, at the head of a company of knights, he took active part in several sieges, and unhorsed in single combat a French knight of high renown for bravery and feats of arms.

But Henry was not content with the position to which he had raised Becket, and in which, if he had been allowed to remain, his life would, in all probability, have ultimately terminated in tranquillity and honours, instead of the awful tragedy by which it was prematurely brought to a close. Desirous of curbing the growing pretensions of the church, and believing that in his chancellor he would find a ready coadjutor in this project, the king insisted on the latter accepting the archbishopric of Canterbury, which had just then become vacant. Becket, it is said, would have declined this accession of honours, and frankly warned the king of the consequences which he must expect. Henry however insisted, and Becket was forthwith installed in his new dignity.

A most extraordinary change of conduct now took place. From the gay and worldly chancellor, who joined in all his sovereign's amusements, and indulged in every obtainable luxury and splendour, Becket was transformed to the austere and enthusiastic monk, whose sole aim is the exaltation of his order, and the extension of the power of the church. The first sign of this altered procedure was the resigning of the office of chancellor, an act which likewise occasioned the first coldness between him and the king. Then followed an exhibition of self-mortification and asceticism, such as in medieval times was regarded as the most conclusive evidence of goodness and piety. Yet much exaggeration seems to have taken place on this subject, as Becket, notwithstanding his numerous charities, and those ostentatious but highly-esteemed acts of humility which he now practised, maintained to the close of his life a great magnificence in establishment and retinue.

After many causes of dissension and ill-will between Henry and the archbishop, produced by the zeal and energy of the latter in prosecuting the interests of the church and the claims of his own see in particular, an open rupture was at last occasioned by the immunity which the clergy claimed from secular jurisdiction, and which Becket vehemently urged and supported. The king was no less resolute in asserting the subjection of priests to the authority of the ordinary courts, in the event of crimes committed by ecclesiastics, and a vital struggle ensued, in which Henry had for a time the advantage. Becket was forced to quit the country as an exile, and remained abroad for several years. Through the influence of the pope and the king of France, a seeming reconciliation was at last effected in July 1170, and in the beginning of the ensuing month of December, the formidable champion of ecclesiastical rights returned to England, and entered again amid acclamations the archiepiscopal metropolis of Canterbury.

The reconciliation had proved but hollow with both parties, neither of whom were disposed to recede from what they considered their rights.

Three prelates, the archbishop of York, and the bishops of London and Salisbury, had given inexpiable offence to Becket by performing, in the absence of the latter, the coronation of the king's eldest son, Prince Henry, an act which the archbishop of Canterbury resented as an unpardonable encroachment on his exclusive privileges. He published letters of excommunication against the offending bishops, who forthwith made their way to France, where Henry II. was then residing, in the castle of Bur, near Bayeux, and reported this fresh instance of Becket's resistance to the authority of the crown. Henry's rage on receiving this intelligence was tremendous, and vented itself in complaints against those lukewarm and spiritless courtiers, who, he said, allowed this upstart priest to treat their sovereign with such insolence. These fatal words proved Becket's death-warrant. Four courtiers, named respectively Reginald Fitzurse, Hugh de Morville, William de Tracy, and Richard le Breton, understanding these expressions as an authorisation of the murder of Becket, quitted forthwith the castle, and took their way to the coast, where they embarked for England. Arriving there, they assembled on the 28th of December 1170, at the castle of Saltwood, occupied by Randulph de Broc, a mortal enemy of Becket, and here, it is said, they concocted in darkness, without seeing each other's faces, the scheme for the murder of Becket. The next day, the party proceeded to Canterbury, and in the afternoon made their way into the archbishop's palace and the apartment where Becket was sitting with his clergy. Fitzurse acted as the spokesman, and announcing that he and his companions had come to the archbishop with a message from the king, demanded satisfaction in the absolution of the three bishops, and compliance with the royal will in that and other matters. Becket defended his conduct, and a scene of violent and mutual recrimination ensued. The conspirators then, boiling with passion, quitted the palace, which they had entered unarmed, and thereupon girded on their swords, one or two of the party, moreover, arming themselves with hatchets. Having returned to the archbishop's residence, they found the avenues of admission barred against them, but they at last succeeded in forcing an entrance. Becket, meantime, had been urged by a small band of faithful adherents to take refuge within the cathedral, and though, for a time, he rejected this proposal as cowardly and undignified, he was at last induced to do so on being reminded that it was now five o'clock, and the time of vesper-service. Quitting the palace by a private door, he gained the cloisters of the cathedral, and from thence entered the church by a door in the north transept. His enemies, who had now by this time succeeded in making their way into the cloisters, followed him by the same entrance into the sacred building, and here Becket and his foes were again confronted. A scene of altercation similar to what had already taken place in the palace now recommenced, and after much invective on both sides, Fitzurse struck Becket a blow on the head with his sword, which, however, did no further damage than knocking off his cap. Tracy followed with a more deadly stroke, and several additional blows left the archbishop a lifeless corpse on the pavement of the church.

It is needless to pursue the terrible story any further. No punishment beyond excommunication and the enforced pilgrimage of one or two of the conspirators to the Holy Land, seems to have befallen the murderers; for by a singular reciprocity, it would appear that, by the same principle for which Becket contended so stoutly—the immunity of the clergy from sacred jurisdiction—crimes committed by laymen against priests were, like the offences of the clergy themselves, only cognisable before ecclesiastical courts, where, in both cases, the highest sentence that could be pronounced was excommunication. But the benefit accruing to the church from the archbishop's death was incalculable. Becket was now regarded as, and received the honours of, a martyr, and it was with great difficulty that Henry succeeded in obtaining absolution from the pope for the passionate expressions which had indirectly authorised the archbishop's murder. The king's subsequent pilgrimage to Canterbury, and his painful penance of a day and a night at the tomb of the sainted Thomas, exhibited thoroughly the church's triumph over the secular power. The victory which the latter had gained in the celebrated 'Constitutions of Clarendon,' at the commencement of the rupture between Becket and Henry II., was now more than avenged. In the advanced supremacy of ecclesiastical over temporal sway, which reached its climax in the reign of Henry's son, King John, it may well be averred of Becket's murder that 'it was more than a crime; it was a blunder.'

From the period of Becket's death to the Reformation, his shrine in Canterbury Cathedral continued to be visited by crowds of pilgrims, whose offerings proved as valuable a source of clerical revenue as those of the worshippers at the no less celebrated tomb of St Cuthbert, in the cathedral of Durham. The Canterbury pilgrimages have been immortalised by Chaucer, from whose *Canterbury Tales* we learn that piety and devotion were by no means uniformly characteristic of the visitors who flocked, on such occasions, to the shrine of St Thomas. On the overthrow of the Roman Catholic religion in the sixteenth century, Becket's shrine was dismantled and plundered, and the name of the saint himself excluded from the calendar, in the reformed liturgy. An entire revulsion of feeling now took place regarding him, and from the rank of a holy man and a martyr he descended in general estimation to the level of a scheming priest and audacious rebel, whilst his murder, if not actually approved, was regarded in the light of a righteous judgment for his overweening ambition. This view of his character prevailed generally up to the present day, when a second revolution in public opinion took place; and Becket has found several able panegyrists, not only on grounds of Roman Catholic or Anglican high-church predilections and sympathies, but in reference to principles of a different nature—motives of patriotism and resistance to feudal tyranny. These last-mentioned views are advocated by M. Thierry and Mr Froude; the former of whom regards Becket in the same aspect that he does Robin Hood, as the vindicator of Saxon rights and liberties against Norman oppression; the latter sees in him a bulwark to the people against monarchical and baronial outrage, such as the power of the church actually often was in medieval times. M. Thierry's view seems to be entirely fanciful; and neither in this light, nor in the view taken by Mr Froude, is it possible to attribute to Becket the character either of a martyr or a hero. That he was not a hypocrite, may be fairly conceded; and he appears to have been in many respects a really charitable and generous-minded man. But his disposition was both obstinate and headstrong in the highest degree; and in his machinations to render the church paramount, we can only see the promptings of an ambition alike undeserving of commendation on religious or moral grounds, and most dangerous to the progress of the intellectual and personal liberties of mankind. The *Constitutions of Clarendon*, against which he protested so strenuously, contained nothing more objectionable than what has come to be universally recognised as essential to the maintenance of good order and liberty in the various relations of church and state. In the opinions of certain parties, it is impossible to exalt too highly the power of the church, and under no circumstances can any procedure be deemed inexcusable whose object is the furtherance of this holy cause. To persons of this way of thinking, Becket must of course ever appear as a hero.

## LEGEND OF BECKET'S PARENTS.

In connection with the renowned Thomas Becket, noticed in the preceding article, a curious story is related of the marriage of his parents. It is said that Gilbert, his father, had in his youth followed the Crusaders to Palestine, and while in the East had been taken prisoner by a Saracen or Moor of high rank. Confined by the latter within his own castle, the young Englishman's personal attractions and miserable condition alike melted the heart of his captor's daughter, a fair Mohammedan, who enabled him to escape from prison and regain his native country. Not wholly disinterested, however, in the part which she acted in this matter, the Moor's daughter obtained a promise from Gilbert, that as soon as he had settled quietly in his own land, he should send for, and marry his protectress. Years passed on, but no message ever arrived to cheer the heart of the love-lorn maiden, who thereupon resolved to proceed to England and remind the forgetful knight of his engagement. This perilous enterprise she actually accomplished; and though knowing nothing of the English language beyond the Christian name of her lover and his place of residence in London, which was Cheapside, she contrived to search him out; and with greater success than could possibly have been anticipated, found him ready to fulfil his former promise by making her his wife. Previous to the marriage taking place, she professed her conversion to Christianity, and was baptized with great solemnity in St Paul's Cathedral, no less than six bishops assisting at the ceremony. The only child of this union was the celebrated Thomas Becket, whose devotion in after-years to the cause of the church, may be said to have been a befitting recompense for the attention which her ministers had shewn in watching over the spiritual welfare of his mother.

This singular story has found credence in recent times with Dr Giles, M. Thierry, Mr Froude, and M. Michelet; but by one of the most judicious modern biographers of Becket, Canon Robertson, it is rejected as a legendary tale, wholly unsupported by the evidence of those chroniclers who were Becket's contemporaries. It gave rise, both in England and Scotland, to more than one ballad, in which the elder Becket's imprisonment in the East, his liberation by the aid of the Moorish damsel, and the latter's expedition to Britain in quest of him, are all set forth with sundry additions and embellishments. In one of these, which bears the name of *Lord Beichan*, the fair young Saracen, who, by some extraordinary corruption or misapprehension, is recorded under the designation of *Susie Pye*, follows her lover to Scotland, and there surprises him at the very hour when he is about to unite himself in marriage to another lady. The faithless lover on being reminded of his previous compact, professes the utmost contrition, and declares at once his resolve to wed the Saracen's daughter, who had given such evidence of her love and attachment to him, by making so long and dangerous a journey. The hapless bride, who would otherwise have speedily become his wife, is unceremoniously dismissed along with her mother; and the nuptials of Lord Beichan and Susie Pye are then celebrated with great magnificence. Another ballad on the same subject is entitled *Young Bekie*, but the heroine here is represented as the daughter of the king of France, and distinguished by the title of *Burd Isbel*. By such romantic embellishments, and so incongruous and ridiculous a nomenclature, did the ballad-writers of a later age embody in verse the story of the parents of the renowned archbishop of Canterbury.

## MALTHUS.

This celebrated writer, whose theory on population has been the subject of so much unmerited abuse, was the son of a gentleman of independent fortune, who possessed a small estate in the county of Surrey. Young Malthus received his early education mainly from a private tutor, and subsequently entered Jesus' College, Cambridge, where he studied for the church, and obtained a fellowship in 1797. For a time, he held the incumbency of a small parish in Surrey near his native place.

It was not in the church, however, that Mr Malthus was to become famous. Through life, the bent of his genius seems to have led him in the direction of political economy and statistics; and in pursuit of information on this subject, he made extensive journeys and inquiries through various countries of Europe. The first edition of the work, which has conferred on him such notoriety, appeared in 1798, under the title of *An Essay on the Principle of Population, as it affects the Future Improvement of Society, with Remarks on the Speculations of Mr Godwin, M. Condorcet, and other Writers*. In subsequent issues, the title of the work was changed to its present form: *An Essay on the Principle of Population; or a View of its Past and Present Effects on Human Happiness, with an Inquiry into our Prospects respecting the Future Removal or Mitigation of the Evils which it occasions*. The leading principle in this work is, that population, when unchecked, doubles itself at the end of every period of twenty-five years, and thus increases, in a *geometrical* progression, or the ratio of 1, 2, 4, 8, 16,

32; whilst the means of subsistence increases only, in an *arithmetical* progression, or the ratio of 1, 2, 3, 4, 5, 6. The author discusses the question of the various restrictions, physical and moral, which tend to keep population from increasing, and thus prevent it outstripping the means of subsistence in the race of life. A misapprehension of the writer's views, combined with his apparent tendency to *pessimism* in the regarding of misery and suffering as the normal condition of humanity, has contributed, notwithstanding the philosophical soundness of many of his theories, to invest the name of Malthus with much opprobrium.

When the common or vulgar impression regarding Mr Malthus's celebrated essay is considered, it is surprising to find that *the man* was one of the most humane and amiable of mortals. His biographer tells us, it would be difficult to overestimate the beauty of his private life and character. His life 'a perpetual flow of enlightened benevolence, contentment, and peace;' 'his temper mild and placid, his allowances for others large and considerate, his desires moderate, and his command over his own passions complete.' 'No unkind or uncharitable expression respecting any one, either present or absent, ever fell from his lips. . . . . All the members of his family loved and honoured him; his servants lived with him till their marriage or settlement in life; and the humble and poor within his influence always found him disposed, not only to assist and improve them, but to treat them with kindness and respect.' 'To his intimate friends, his loss can rarely, if ever, be supplied; there was in him a union of truth, judgment, and warmth of heart, which at once invited confidence, and set at nought all fear of being ridiculed or betrayed. You were always sure of his sympathy; and wherever the case allowed it, his assistance was as prompt and effective as his advice was sound and good.' *

Shortly after his marriage in 1805 to Miss Eckersall, Mr Malthus was appointed professor of modern history and political economy at the East India College at Haileybury, and held this office till his death. He expired on 29th December 1834, at Bath, at the age of sixty-eight, leaving behind him a son and daughter.

---

# DECEMBER 30.

St Sabinus, bishop of Assisium, and his companions, martyrs, 304. St Anysia, martyr, 304. St Maximus, confessor, about 662.

---

*Born.*—Titus, Roman emperor, 41 A. D.; Sir John Holt, lord chief-justice, 1642, *Thame, Oxfordshire;* John Philips, poet (*The Splendid Shilling*), 1676, *Bampton.*

*Died.*—Richard, Duke of York, killed at Wakefield, 1460; Roger Ascham, eminent scholar and writer, 1568; John Baptist Van Helmont, alchemist, 1644, *Holland;* Jacques Saurin, eminent Protestant divine, 1730, *Hague;* James Francis Edward, the elder Pretender, 1765, *Rome;* Paul Whitehead, poet, 1774, *London;* Olaus Gerhard Tychsen, orientalist, 1815, *Rostock;* Samuel Hibbert Ware, miscellaneous writer, 1848, *Altrincham, Cheshire.*

* Memoir prefixed to Malthus's *Political Economy,* 2d edition, 1836.



## ROGER ASCHAM.

Roger Ascham, instructor of Queen Elizabeth in Latin and Greek, was born in 1515, at the village of Kirby-Wiske, near Northallerton, in Yorkshire, the youngest of the three sons of John Ascham, who was house-steward to the Scroope family. Educated at Cambridge University, he in time rose to be the university orator, and became noted for his zeal in promoting, what was then a novelty in England—the study of the Greek language. In 1545, he published *Toxophilus,* a treatise on archery, for which Henry VIII. rewarded him with a pension of £10 per annum—a sum then of much higher value than it appears to us now. This work was written not only as a specimen of an improved style of composition in English, but with a view to recommend the continuance of the use of the bow as a weapon of war, which the hand-gun, or musket, was then beginning to supersede, and also as an invigorating and healthful exercise. It is composed in the form of a dialogue between Toxophilus and Philologus, and besides praising and teaching the practice of archery, contains a large admixture of philosophical disquisition. In 1548, Ascham, on the death of William Grindall, who had been his pupil, was appointed instructor in the learned languages to the Lady Elizabeth, afterwards queen; but at the end of two years, on some dispute or disgust with her attendants, he resigned his situation, and returned to his college. Soon afterwards, he accepted the post offered to him of secretary to Sir Richard Morrisine, who was about to proceed on an embassy to the court of the Emperor Charles V., in Germany. He remained abroad till the death of Edward VI., in 1553, when the embassy was recalled to England. During his absence, he was appointed Latin secretary to King Edward. It is somewhat extraordinary that though Queen Mary and her ministers were papists, and Ascham a Protestant, he was retained in his office of Latin secretary, his pension was increased to £20, and he was allowed to retain his fellowship and his situation as university orator. Soon after his return, however, he married, and then, of course, resigned his fellowship. On the death of Mary, in 1558, Queen Elizabeth not only required his services as her Latin secretary, but as her instructor in Greek, and he resided at court during the remainder of his life. He died December 30, 1568, in the fifty-third year of his age.

Only two works were published by Ascham during his lifetime, *Toxophilus,* and a *Report of the Affairs of Germany and of the Emperor Charles's Court,* which contains some curious descriptions of the personal appearance and manners of the principal persons whom he saw and conversed with. His most valuable work, *The Schoolmaster,* was published by his widow. Dr Johnson has remarked that the system of instruction recommended in this work is perhaps the best ever given for the study of languages. His Latin letters were collected and published by his friend, Edward Grant, master of Westminster School, who prefixed to them a Life of Ascham written in Latin. The English works were reprinted in a collected form in 4to, in 1761, and to this volume was prefixed a life, written by Dr Johnson, which has served as a basis for all subsequent notices of Ascham.

## THE STORY OF THE *RESOLUTE*.

Perhaps the most remarkable voyage on record, was that of the arctic exploring-ship *Resolute*. Abandoned by her officers and crew to anticipated destruction, she, as if instinct with life, made a voyage of a thousand miles *alone*, back to regions of civilisation—as if in indignant protest against her abandonment.

In April 1852, Sir Edward Belcher, with the ships *Assistance*, *Pioneer*, *Resolute*, *Intrepid*, and *North Star*, left England to search for Sir John Franklin and his companions. Captain M'Clure, in the *Investigator*, was at that time struggling against appalling difficulties in the ice-bound seas north of the American continent. On the 6th of April 1853, Captain M'Clure and Lieutenant Pim had their memorable meeting on the ice; the former having come from the Pacific, the latter from the Atlantic. Lieutenant Pim belonged to Captain Kellett's ship *Resolute*, part of Belcher's squadron. The *Investigator*, the ship with which M'Clure had practically solved the problem of the North-west Passage, was abandoned in the ice, and her commander and the remainder of the crew were received on board the *Resolute*. With the exception of this single fact of rescuing M'Clure, Belcher was singularly unfortunate: achieving little or nothing in other ways. On the 15th of May 1854, at his express command, but sorely against their will, Captain Kellett and Commander M'Clintock finally abandoned the *Resolute* and *Intrepid*, locked in ice off the shores of Melville Island. On the 24th of August, in the same year, again at the express command of Belcher, Commander Sherard Osborn abandoned the *Pioneer*, while Belcher himself abandoned the *Assistance*, both ships being ice-locked in Wellington Channel. The officers and crews of no less than five abandoned ships reached England before the close of the year.

It was one of these five deserted ships which, we may almost say, came to life again many months afterwards; to the astonishment of every one conversant with the arctic region. Late in the year 1855, Captain Buddington, in the American whaler *George Henry*, was sailing about in Davis's Strait, when, on the 17th of September, about forty miles from Cape Mercy, he descried a ship presenting unusual appearances; no signals were put out or answered; and, when he approached, no crew were visible. It was the *Resolute*, as sound and hearty as ever, with the exception of a little water which had got into the hold, and the spoiling of some of the perishable articles inside. Any one with a map of the arctic regions before him, will see what a lengthened voyage the good old ship must have made from Melville Island, through Barrow Straits, Lancaster Sound, and Baffin's Bay, during the period of 474 days which intervened between her abandonment and her recovery. The probable track is marked in a map attached to Mr M'Dougall's *Eventful Voyage of the Resolute*. It is supposed that ice, loosened during the short summers of 1854 and 1855, drifted with the current into Davis's Strait, and carried along with it the ship.

The gift of the adventurous old ship by America to England was gracefully managed. The United States congress, on the 28th of August 1856, passed the following resolution: 'Whereas it has become known to Congress, that the ship *Resolute*, late of the navy of Her Majesty the Queen of the United Kingdom of Great Britain and Ireland, on service in the Arctic Seas in search of Sir John Franklin and the survivors of the expedition under his command, was rescued and recovered in those seas by the officers and crew of the American whale-ship, the *George Henry*, after the *Resolute* had been necessarily abandoned in the ice by her officers and crew, and after drifting still in the ice for more than one thousand miles from the place where so abandoned—and that the said ship *Resolute*, having been brought to the United States by the salvors at great risk and peril, had been generously relinquished by them to Her Majesty's government. Now, in token of the deep interest felt in the United States for the service in which Her Majesty's said ship was engaged when thus necessarily abandoned, and of the sense entertained by Congress of the act of Her Majesty's government in surrendering said ship to the salvors: Be it resolved by the Senate and House of Representatives of the United States of America in Congress assembled, That the President of the United States be, and he is hereby requested to cause the said ship *Resolute*, with all her armament, equipment, and property on board when she arrived in the United States, and which has been preserved in good condition, to be purchased of her present owners, and that he send the said ship with everything pertaining to her as aforesaid, after being fully repaired and equipped at one of the navy-yards of the United States, back to England under control of the secretary of the navy, with a request to Her Majesty's government, that the United States may be allowed to restore the said ship *Resolute* to Her Majesty's service—and for the purchase of said ship and appurtenances, as aforesaid, the sum of forty thousand dollars, or so much thereof as may be required, is hereby appropriated, to be paid out of any money in the treasury not otherwise appropriated.'

The final incident in the story was the formal presentation of the ship to the Queen of England, on the part of the government of the United States. This presentation was delayed no less than 469 days after the discovery or recovery of the ship by Captain Buddington, owing to various causes, some avoidable and others unavoidable. On the 13th of November 1856, the *Resolute*, in excellent trim after her repairs, set sail, and arrived near Cowes on December the 12th, under the care of Captain Hartstein of the United States navy. Sir George Seymour, naval commander-in-chief at Portsmouth, made arrangements for a royal visit to the recovered ship. The Queen, the Prince Consort, the Prince of Wales, the Princess Royal, and Princess Alice, left Osborne House, and steamed out to the old ship, which was decked out in colours, with the English and American flags flying at the peak. Captain Hartstein and the officers, in full uniform, received the royal party, to whom they were severally introduced. Captain Hartstein then said to the Queen: 'Allow me to welcome your Majesty on board the *Resolute*, and, in obedience to the will of my countrymen and of the President of the United States, to restore her to you, not only as an evidence of friendly feeling to your sovereignty, but as a token of love.

admiration, and respect to your Majesty personally.' The Queen made a short but kindly recognition of this address. The royal party then went over the ship, and examined it with great interest. Captain Hartstein, with a map spread out before him, traced the course which the deserted ship had followed, and the relation which that course bore to arctic voyages generally. Captain Hartstein, in reply to a question from the Prince Consort, expressed a belief that Sir John Franklin, or some of his companions, might still be alive, among the Esquimaux—a belief which many persons entertained at that time, but which gradually gave way to hopelessness. After the departure of the royal visitors, a *dejeûner* was given in the ward-room, during which one 'toast' was, 'The future success of the *Resolute*, and may she be again employed in prosecuting the search for Sir John Franklin and his comrades.'

The Americans had done their self-imposed work well and gracefully. With such care had the repairs and re-equipment been performed, that not only had the ship's stores—even to flags—been replaced, but the officers' libraries, pictures, musical-boxes, &c., had been preserved, and with excellent taste had all been restored to their original positions. The royal family were touched at the sight of these little memorials, as they went from cabin to cabin of the ship. Captain Hartstein was invited to visit the Queen at Osborne that evening. On the following day the *Resolute* was brought into Portsmouth harbour, amid great rejoicings, and complimentary salutes to the American flag. Many banquets were given to Captain Hartstein and his officers on subsequent days; the chief of which, for grandeur and importance, was given by the mayor and corporation of Portsmouth. A deputation from the Shipowners' Association of Liverpool came to Portsmouth, with an invitation for the American officers; which, however, their limited time prevented them from accepting. The prime minister entertained Captain Hartstein at his seat in Hampshire; the government gave a dinner to the American sailors on Christmas-day; and Lady Franklin invited all the officers to an entertainment provided by her for them at Brighton.

At length, on the 30th of December, the formal transfer of the interesting old ship took place. Captain George Seymour, of the *Victory*, with two subordinate officers, and small parties of seamen and marines, went on board the *Resolute*. Precisely at one o'clock, the *Victory* hoisted the American flag at her main, and fired a salute of twenty-one guns; while Captain Hartstein hauled down the American colours from the *Resolute*, and substituted the British, and the American crew manned the yards to give three cheers to the *Victory*. Captain Hartstein, with his officers around him, then addressed Captain Seymour: 'Sir, the closing scene of my most pleasant and important mission has now to be performed. And permit me to hope that, long after every timber in her sturdy frame shall have perished, the remembrance of the old *Resolute* will be cherished by the people of the respective nations. I now, with a pride totally at variance with our professional ideas, strike my flag, and to you, sir, give up the ship.' Captain Seymour made a suitable reply; and soon afterwards the whole of the American officers and seamen were conveyed on board the United States' mail steam-ship *Washington*, in which they returned to their own country. The British government offered to convey them in the war-steamer *Retribution*, in friendly compliment to the American government; but arrangements previously made interfered with this plan.

The issue of this affair was, after all, not a pleasant one. The Admiralty, with indecorous haste, ordered the brave old ship to be dismantled and reduced to the state of an unsightly hulk. This was a bit of paltry economy, which assorted ill with extravagance in other matters. It was injudicious in many ways; for the old ship would have formed a memento of arctic expeditions; it would have afforded testimony concerning the currents and drift-ice of those regions; it would have been a pleasant object for Englishmen to visit, side by side with Nelson's famous ship in Portsmouth harbour; and it would have been gratifying to Americans visiting England, to see that the liberality of their government had been appreciated.

### PRIMITIVE STYLE OF SKATING.

Fitz-Stephen, in his account of the sports of the young citizens of London on the ice in the twelfth century (as quoted by us under January 20), notes their expertness in using the bones of animals as a means of increasing their velocity, 'taking in their hands poles shod with iron, which at times they strike against the ice, they are carried along with as great rapidity as a bird flying, or a bolt discharged from a cross-bow.' The cut here given illustrates this practice. A child is using the jaw-bones of a horse or cow as a sledge, and propelling himself with pointed staves. It is copied from a Dutch engraving, representing sports on the ice in the town-ditch at Antwerp, 1594.

---

## DECEMBER 31.

St Sylvester, pope and confessor, 335. St Columba, virgin and martyr, 3d century. St Melania the Younger, 439.

### New-year's Eve, or Hogmanay.

As a general statement, it may be asserted that neither the last evening of the old year nor the first day of the new one is much observed in England as an occasion of festivity. In some parts of the country, indeed, and more especially in the northern counties, various social merry-makings take place; but for the most part, the great annual holiday-time is already past. Christmas Eve, Christmas-day, and St Stephen's or Boxing Day have absorbed almost entirely the tendencies and opportunities of the community at large in the direction of joviality and relaxation. Business and the ordinary routine of daily life have again been resumed; or, to apply to English habits the words of an old Scottish rhyme still current, but evidently belonging to the old times, anterior to the Reformation, when Christmas was the great popular festival:

'Yule 's come and Yule 's gane,
And we hae feasted weel;
Sae Jock maun to his flail again,
And Jenny to her wheel.'

Whilst thus the inhabitants of South Britain are settling down again quietly to work after the festivities of the Christmas season, their fellow-subjects in the northern division of the island are only commencing their annual saturnalia, which, till recently, bore, in the license and boisterous merriment which used to prevail, a most unmistakable resemblance to its ancient pagan namesake. The epithet of the *Daft* [mad] *Days*, applied to the season of the New Year in Scotland, indicates very expressively the uproarious joviality which characterised the period in question. This exuberance of joyousness—which, it must be admitted, sometimes led to great excesses—has now much declined, but New-year's Eve and New-year's Day constitute still the great national holiday in Scotland. Under the 1st of January, we have already detailed the various revelries by which the New Year used to be ushered in, in Scotland. It now becomes our province to notice those ceremonies and customs which are appropriate to the last day of the year, or, as it is styled in Scotland, *Hogmanay*.

This last term has puzzled antiquaries even more than the word Yule,* already adverted to; and what is of still greater consequence, has never yet received a perfectly satisfactory explanation. Some suppose it to be derived from two Greek words, ἁγια μηνη (the holy moon or month), and in reference to this theory it may be observed, that, in the north of England, the term used is *Hagmena*, which does not seem, however, to be confined to the 31st of December, but denotes generally the period immediately preceding the New Year. Another hypothesis combines the word with another sung along with it in chorus, and asserts 'Hogmanay, trollolay!' to be a corruption of '*Homme est né—Trois Rois là*' ('A Man is born—Three Kings are there'), an allusion to the birth of our Saviour, and the visit to Bethlehem of the Wise Men, who were known in medieval times as the 'Three Kings.' But two additional conjectures seem much more plausible, and the reader may select for himself what he considers the most probable. One of these is, that the term under notice is derived from *Hoggu-nott*, *Hogenat*, or *Hogg-night*, the ancient Scandinavian name for the night preceding the feast of Yule, and so called in reference to the animals slaughtered on the occasion for sacrificial and festal purposes—the word *hogg* signifying *to kill*. The other derivation of Hogmanay is from '*Au gui menez*' ('To the mistletoe go'), or '*Au gui l'an neuf*' ('To the mistletoe this New Year'), an allusion to the ancient Druidical ceremony of gathering that plant. In the *patois* of Touraine, in France, the word used is *Aguilanneu*; in Lower Normandy, and in Guernsey, poor persons and children used to solicit a contribution under the title of *Hoguinanno* or *Oguinano*; whilst in Spain the term, *Aguinaldo*, is employed to denote the presents made at the season of Christmas.

* See p. 745 of this volume.

In country places in Scotland, and also in the more retired and primitive towns, it is still customary on the morning of the last day of the year, or Hogmanay, for the children of the poorer class of people to get themselves swaddled in a great sheet, doubled up in front, so as to form a vast pocket, and then to go along the streets in little bands, calling at the doors of the wealthier classes for an expected dole of oaten-bread. Each child gets one quadrant section of oat-cake (sometimes, in the case of particular favourites, improved by an addition of cheese), and this is called their *hogmanay*. In expectation of the large demands thus made upon them, the housewives busy themselves for several days beforehand in preparing a suitable quantity of cakes. The children on coming to the door cry, 'Hogmanay!' which is in itself a sufficient announcement of their demands; but there are other exclamations which either are or might be used for the same purpose. One of these is:

'Hogmanay,
Trollolay,
Give us of your white bread, and none of your gray.'

And another favourite rhyme is:

'Get up, goodwife, and shake your feathers,
And dinna think that we are beggars;
For we are bairns come out to play,
Get up and gie 's our hogmanay!'

The following is of a moralising character, though a good deal of a truism:

'Get up, goodwife, and binna sweir,
And deal your bread to them that 's here;
For the time will come when ye 'll be dead,
And then ye 'll neither need ale nor bread.'

The most favourite of all, however, is more to the point than any of the foregoing:

'My feet's cauld, my shoon 's thin;
Gie 's my cakes, and let me rin!'

It is no unpleasing scene, during the forenoon, to see the children going laden home, each with his large apron bellying out before him, stuffed full of cakes, and perhaps scarcely able to waddle under the load. Such a mass of oaten alms is no inconsiderable addition to the comfort of the poor man's household, and enables him to enjoy the New-year season as much as his richer neighbours.

In the primitive parish of Deerness, in Orkney, it was customary, in the beginning of the present century, for old and young of the common class of people to assemble in a great band upon the evening of the last day of the year, and commence a round of visits throughout the district. At every house they knocked at the door, and on being admitted, commenced singing, to a tune of its own, a song appropriate to the occasion. The following is what may be termed a *restored* version of this chant, the imagination having been called on to make up in several of the lines what was deficient in memory. The 'Queen Mary' alluded to is evidently the Virgin:

'This night it is guid New'r E'en's night,
We're a' here Queen Mary's men;
And we're come here to crave our right,
And that's before our Lady.

The very first thing which we do crave,
We're a' here Queen Mary's men;
A bonny white candle we must have,
And that's before our Lady.

Goodwife, gae to your butter-ark,
And weigh us here ten mark.

Ten mark, ten pund,
Look that ye grip weel to the grund.*
Goodwife, gae to your geelin vat,
And fetch us here a skeel o' that.

Gang to your awmrie, gin ye please,
And bring frae there a yow-milk cheese.

And syne bring here a sharping-stane,
We'll sharp our whittles ilka ane.

Ye'll cut the cheese, and eke the round,
But aye take care ye cutna your thoom.

Gae fill the three-pint cog o' ale,
The maut maun be aboon the meal.

We houp your ale is stark and stout,
For men to drink the auld year out.

Ye ken the weather's snaw and sleet,
Stir up the fire to warm our feet.

Our shoon's made o' mare's skin,
Come open the door, and let's in.'

The inner-door being opened, a tremendous rush was made *ben* the house. The inmates furnished a long table with all sorts of homely fare, and a hearty feast took place, followed by copious libations of ale, charged with all sorts of good-wishes. The party would then proceed to the next house, where a similar scene would be enacted. How they contrived to take so many suppers in one evening, heaven knows! No slight could be more keenly felt by a Deerness farmer than to have his house passed over unvisited by the New-year singers.

The doings of the *guisers* or *guizards* (that is, masquers or *mummers* †) form a conspicuous feature in the New-year proceedings throughout Scotland. The favourite night for this exhibition is Hogmanay, though the evenings of Christmas, New-year's Day, and Handsel Monday, enjoy likewise a privilege in this respect. Such of the boys as can lay any claim to the possession of a voice have, for weeks before, been poring over the collection of 'excellent new songs,' which lies like a bunch of rags in the window-sill; and being now able to screech up 'Barbara Allan,' or the 'Wee cot-house and the wee kail-yardie,' they determine upon enacting the part of guisers. For this purpose they don old shirts belonging to their fathers, and mount mitre-shaped casques of brown paper, possibly borrowed from the Abbot of Unreason; attached to this is a sheet of the same paper, which, falling down in front, covers and conceals the whole face, except where holes are made to let through the point of the nose, and afford sight to the eyes and breath to the mouth. Each vocal guiser is, like a knight of old, attended by a sort of humble squire, who assumes the habiliments of a girl, with an old-woman's cap and a broomstick, and is styled 'Bessie.' Bessie is equal in no respect, except that she shares fairly in the proceeds of the enterprise. She goes before her principal, opens all the doors at which he pleases to exert his singing powers; and busies herself, during the time of the song, in sweeping the floor with her broomstick, or in playing any other antics that she thinks may amuse the indwellers. The common reward of this entertainment is a halfpenny, but many churlish persons fall upon the unfortunate guisers, and beat them out of the house. Let such persons, however, keep a good watch upon their cabbage-gardens next Halloween!

The more important doings of the guisers are of a theatrical character. There is one rude and grotesque drama which they are accustomed to perform on each of the four above-mentioned nights; and which, in various fragments or versions, exists in every part of Lowland Scotland. The performers, who are never less than three, but sometimes as many as six, having dressed themselves, proceed in a band from house to house, generally contenting themselves with the kitchen for an arena; whither, in mansions presided over by the spirit of good-humour, the whole family will resort to witness the spectacle. Sir Walter Scott, who delighted to keep up old customs, and could condescend to simple things without losing genuine dignity, invariably had a set of guisers to perform this play before his family both at Ashestiel and Abbotsford. The drama in question bears a close resemblance, with sundry modifications, to that performed by the mummers in various parts of England, and of which we have already given a specimen.*

Such are the leading features of the Hogmanay festivities in Scotland. A similar custom to that above detailed of children going about from house to house, singing the *Hagmena* chorus, and obtaining a dole of bread or cakes, prevails in Yorkshire and the north of England; but, as we have already mentioned, the last day of the year is not in the latter country, for the most part, invested with much peculiar distinction. One or two closing ceremonies, common to both countries—the requiem, as they may be termed, of the dying year—will be more appropriately noticed in the concluding article of this work.

## BURNING OF 'THE CLAVIE.'

A singular custom, almost unparalleled in any other part of Scotland, takes place on New-year's Eve (old style) at the village of Burghead, on the southern shore of the Moray Firth, about nine miles from the town of Elgin. It has been observed there from time immemorial, and both its origin, and that of the peculiar appellation by which it is distinguished, form still matter of conjecture and dispute for antiquaries. The following extract from the *Banffshire Journal* presents a very interesting

* In stooping into a deep ark, or chest, there is of course a danger of falling in, unless the feet be kept firm to the ground.

† For an account of the English mummers, see p. 739 of this volume.

* See p. 740 of this volume.

and comprehensive view of all that can be stated regarding this remarkable ceremonial:

'Any Hogmanay afternoon, a small group of seamen and coopers, dressed in blue overfrocks, and followed by numbers of noisy youngsters, may be seen rapidly wending their way to the south-western extremity of the village, where it is customary to build the Clavie. One of the men bears on his shoulders a stout Archangel tar-barrel, kindly presented for the occasion by one of the merchants, who has very considerately left a quantity of the resinous fluid in the bottom. Another carries a common herring-cask, while the remainder are laden with other raw materials, and the tools necessary for the construction of the Clavie. Arrived at the spot, three cheers being given for the success of the undertaking, operations are commenced forthwith. In the first place, the tar-barrel is sawn into two unequal parts; the smaller forms the groundwork of the Clavie, the other is broken up for fuel. A common fir prop, some four feet in length, called the "spoke," being then procured, a hole is bored through the tub-like machine, that, as we have already said, is to form the basis of the unique structure, and a long nail, made for the purpose, and furnished gratuitously by the village blacksmith, unites the two. Curiously enough, no hammer is allowed to drive this nail, which is "sent home" by a smooth stone. The herring-cask is next demolished, and the staves are soon undergoing a diminution at both extremities, in order to fit them for their proper position. They are nailed, at intervals of about two inches all round, to the lower edge of the Clavie-barrel, while the other ends are firmly fastened to the spoke, an aperture being left sufficiently large to admit the head of a man. Amid tremendous cheering, the finished Clavie is now set up against the wall, which is mounted by two stout young men, who proceed to the business of filling and lighting. A few pieces of the split-up tar-barrel are placed in a pyramidal form in the inside of the Clavie, enclosing a small space for the reception of a burning peat, when everything is ready. The tar, which had been previously removed to another vessel, is now poured over the wood; and the same inflammable substance is freely used, while the barrel is being closely packed with timber and other combustible materials, that rise twelve or thirteen inches above the rim.

'By this time the shades of evening have begun to descend, and soon the subdued murmur of the crowd breaks forth into one loud, prolonged cheer, as the youth who was despatched for the fiery peat (for custom says no sulphurous lucifer, no patent congreve dare approach within the sacred precincts of the Clavie) arrives with his glowing charge. The master-builder relieving him of his precious trust, places it within the opening already noticed, where, revived by a hot blast from his powerful lungs, it ignites the surrounding wood and tar, which quickly bursts into a flame. During the short time the fire is allowed to gather strength, cheers are given in rapid succession for "The Queen," "The Laird," "The Provost," "The Town," "The Harbour," and "The Railway," and then Clavie-bearer number one, popping his head between the staves, is away with his flaming burden. Formerly, the Clavie was carried in triumph round every vessel in the harbour, and a handful of grain thrown into each, in order to insure success for the coming year; but as this part of the ceremony came to be tedious, it was dropped, and the procession confined to the boundaries of the town. As fast as his heavy load will permit him, the bearer hurries along the well-known route, followed by the shouting Burgheadians, the boiling tar meanwhile trickling down in dark sluggish streams all over his back. Nor is the danger of scalding the only one he who essays to carry the Clavie has to confront, since the least stumble is sufficient to destroy his equilibrium. Indeed, this untoward event, at one time looked on as a dire calamity, foretelling disaster to the place, and certain death to the bearer in the course of next year, not unfrequently occurs. Having reached the junction of two streets, the carrier of the Clavie is relieved; and while the change is being effected, firebrands plucked from the barrel are thrown among the crowd, who eagerly scramble for the tarry treasure, the possession of which was of old deemed a sure safeguard against all unlucky contingencies. Again the multitude bound along; again they halt for a moment as another individual takes his place as bearer—a post for the honour of which there is sometimes no little striving. The circuit of the town being at length completed, the Clavie is borne along the principal street to a small hill near the northern extremity of the promontory called the "Doorie," on the summit of which a freestone pillar, very much resembling an ancient altar, has been built for its reception, the spoke fitting into a socket in the centre. Being now firmly seated on its throne, fresh fuel is heaped on the Clavie, while, to make the fire burn the brighter, a barrel with the ends knocked out is placed on the top. Cheer after cheer rises from the crowd below, as the efforts made to increase the blaze are crowned with success.

'Though formerly allowed to remain on the Doorie the whole night, the Clavie is now removed when it has burned about half an hour. Then comes the most exciting scene of all. The barrel is lifted from the socket, and thrown down on the western slope of the hill, which appears to be all in one mass of flame—a state of matters that does not, however, prevent a rush to the spot in search of embers. Two stout men, instantly seizing the fallen Clavie, attempt to demolish it by dashing it to the ground: which is no sooner accomplished than a final charge is made among the blazing fragments, that are snatched up in total, in spite of all the powers of combustion, in an incredibly short space of time. Up to the present moment, the origin of this peculiar custom is involved in the deepest obscurity. Some would have us to believe that we owe its introduction to the Romans; and that the name Clavie is derived from the Latin word *clavus*, a nail—witches being frequently put to death in a barrel stuck full of iron spikes; or from *clavis*, a key—the rite being instituted when Agricola discovered that *Ptoroton*, *i.e.*, Burghead, afforded the grand military key to the north of Scotland. As well might these wild speculators have remarked that Doorie, which may be spelled *Durie*, sprang from *durus*, cruel, on account of the bloody ceremony celebrated on its summit. Another opinion has been boldly advanced by one party, to the effect that the Clavie is

Scandinavian in origin, being introduced by the Norwegian Vikings, during the short time they held the promontory in the beginning of the eleventh century, though the theorist advances nothing to prove his assumption, save a quotation from Scott's *Marmion;* while, to crown all, we have to listen to a story that bears on its face its own condemnation, invented to confirm the belief that a certain witch, yclept, "Kitty Clavers," bequeathed her name to the singular rite. Unfortunately, all external evidence being lost, we are compelled to rely entirely on the internal, which we have little hesitation, however, in saying points in an unmistakable manner down through the long vistas of our national history to where the mists of obscurity hang around the Druid worship of our forefathers. It is well known that the elements of fire were often present in Druidical orgies and customs (as witness their cran-tara); while it is universally admitted that the bonfires of May-day and Midsummer eve, still kept up in different parts of the country, are vestiges of these rites. And why should not the Clavie be so too, seeing that it bears throughout the stamp of a like parentage? The carrying home of the embers, as a protection from the ills of life, as well as other parts of the ceremony, finds a counterpart in the customs of the Druids; and though the time of observance be somewhat different, yet may not the same causes (now unknown ones) that have so greatly modified the Clavie have likewise operated in altering the date, which, after all, occurs at the most solemn part of the Druidical year?'

---

*Born.*—Hermann Boerhaave, distinguished physician, 1668, *Voorhout, near Leyden;* Charles Edward Stuart, younger Pretender, 1721, *Rome;* Charles, Marquis Cornwallis, Indian commander, 1738; Dr Johann Gaspar Spurzheim, phrenologist, 1776, *Longwich, near Treves.*

*Died.*—Commodus, Roman emperor, murdered, 192 A. D.; John Wycliffe, early reformer, 1384, *Lutterworth, Leicestershire;* Thomas Erastus, physician, and author of treatise on *Excommunication*, 1583, *Basle;* Giovanni Alfonso Borelli, physician and anatomist, 1679; Robert Boyle, natural philosopher, 1691, *London;* John Flamsteed, astronomer, 1719, *Greenwich;* Jean-François Marmontel, tale-writer, 1799; William Gifford, reviewer and satirist, 1826, *London.*

## WYCLIFFE.

Of Wycliffe, 'the morning-star of the Reformation,' very little is with certainty known beyond what is gathered from his writings; hence he has been compared to 'the voice of one crying in the wilderness'—a voice and nothing more—a mighty agency manifest only in its effects. A portrait of the reformer is preserved at Lutterworth, but it can scarcely be of the age assumed; it is probably the copy of a contemporary picture. At any rate, it fulfils our ideal of Wycliffe. We behold, in what was said to be his 'spare, frail, emaciated frame,' the countenance of a Yorkshireman, firm and nervous; of one who could form his own opinion and hold it against the world, and all the more resolutely because against the world.

The year of Wycliffe's birth is usually stated as 1324, three years before the accession of Edward III. His name he took from his native village, situated about six miles from Richmond in Yorkshire, and thus it is sometimes written John *de* Wycliffe. In his time there were in truth but two professions—arms and the church; most lawyers, physicians, and even statesmen, were ecclesiastics. The universities were therefore thronged with crowds of students, perhaps as numerous (if medieval statistics are to be credited) as the entire populations of Oxford and Cambridge at this day. Wycliffe was sent to Oxford, where, in course of time, he rose to high distinction as a lecturer, became a consummate master in dialectics, and the pride of the university. 'He was second to none in philosophy,' writes Knighton, a monk, who abhorred him; 'and in the discipline of the schools he was incomparable.' He was promoted to various dignities—to the wardenship of Baliol and Canterbury Halls, to the living of Fillingham, and finally to that of Lutterworth in Leicestershire, with which his name is most intimately associated, as where he dwelt longest, and where he died.

Wycliffe first rose into national publicity by his bold denunciations of the mendicant friars, who were swarming over the land, and interfering with the duties of the settled priesthood. In this contest he carried with him the sympathy, not only of the laity, but of the clergy, who saw in the friars troublesome interlopers. He treated all the orders with asperity. He branded the higher as hypocrites, who, professing beggary, had stately houses, rode on noble horses, and had all the pride and luxury of wealth, with the ostentation of poverty. The humbler, he rated with indignation as common able-bodied vagabonds, whom it was a sin to permit to saunter about, and fatten on the thrift of the pious.

Edward III., in 1366, called on Wycliffe for his advice as to his relation to the pope. Urban V. had demanded payment of the tribute due under the convention of King John, and which had fallen thirty-three years into arrear. With many subtle and elaborate arguments, Wycliffe counselled resistance of the claim. He was still further honoured by his appointment, in 1374, as a member of a deputation sent by Edward to Gregory XI. to treat as to the adjustment of differences between English and ecclesiastical law. It is supposed that the experience gained in this journey sharpened and intensified Wycliffe's aversion to the papacy, for on his return he began to speak of the pope as 'Antichrist, the proud worldly priest of Rome, and the most cursed of clippers and cut-purses.' This daring language soon brought him into conflict with the authorities, and in 1377 he was cited to appear at St Paul's, to answer the charge of holding and publishing certain heretical doctrines. Wycliffe presented himself on the appointed day, accompanied by his friend John of Gaunt, Duke of Lancaster; but an altercation arising between Gaunt and Courtney, the bishop of London, the crowd broke into a tumult, and the court separated without doing anything. Other attempts were made to bring him to judgment, but with no decisive results. His teaching was condemned by convocation; Richard II., by letter, commanded his silence at Oxford, but at Lutterworth he wrote and preached with undaunted spirit. He owed something of this impunity to the great schism which had broken out in 1378 in consequence of the election of two popes, by which for several years the papal power was paralysed. Wycliffe seized the occasion for writing a tract, in which he called upon the kings of Christendom to use the opportunity for pulling down the whole fabric of the Romish dominion, 'seeing that Christ had cloven the head of Antichrist, and made the two parts fight against each other.' The favour of John of Gaunt was likewise a strong defence, but it is doubtful whether he would have cared to stand between Wycliffe and the terrible penalty of proven heresy. Gaunt was no theologian; he rejoiced in humbling the clergy, but he shewed no desire to tamper with the faith of the people.

Wycliffe's opinions are difficult to define, first, because they were progressive, changing and advancing with experience and meditation; and second, because the authorship of many manuscripts ascribed to him is doubtful. He commenced by questioning the polity of Roman Catholicism, and ended in asserting its theology to be erroneous. In doctrine, Calvin might have claimed Wycliffe as a brother, but far beyond Calvin he was ready to accord perfect freedom of conscience. 'Christ,' he said, 'wished his law to be observed willingly, freely, that in such obedience men might find happiness. Hence he appointed no civil punishment to be inflicted on the transgressors of his commandments, but left the persons neglecting them to the suffering which shall come after the day of doom.' In the matter of church-government, he advocated principles which would almost identify him with the Independents. The whole framework of the hierarchy he pronounced a device of priestly ambition—the first step in the ascending scale, the distinction between bishop and presbyter being an innovation on the practice of the primitive church, in which all were equal. He was opposed to establishments and endowments, insisting that pastors should depend on the free offerings of their flocks. As a missionary, he was the director of a number of zealous men, styled 'poor priests,' who received and busily diffused his doctrines. 'Go and preach,' he said to them; 'it is the sublimest work: but imitate not the priests, whom we see after the sermon sitting in the ale-houses, or at the gaming-table, or wasting their time in hunting. After your sermon is ended, do you visit the sick, the aged, the poor, the blind, and the lame, and succour them according to your ability.'

His industry was astonishing. The number of his books, mostly brief tracts, baffles calculation. Two hundred are said to have been burned in Bohemia. His great work was the translation of the Scriptures from the Vulgate into English. Of this undertaking, Lingard says: 'Wycliffe multiplied copies with the aid of transcribers, and his poor priests recommended it to the perusal of their hearers. In their hands it became an engine of wonderful power. Men were flattered with the appeal to their private judgment; the new doctrines insensibly acquired partisans and protectors in the higher classes.' Wycliffe's translation did much to give form and permanence to the English language, and it will for ever remain a mighty landmark in its history.

Dean Milman thus pithily sums up Wycliffe's merits as an author: 'He was a subtle schoolman, and a popular pamphleteer. He addressed the students of the university in the language and logic of the schools; he addressed the vulgar, which included no doubt the whole laity and the vast number of the parochial clergy, in the simplest and most homely vernacular phrase. Hence he is, as it were, two writers: his Latin is dry, argumentative, syllogistic, abstruse, obscure; his English rude, coarse, but clear, emphatic, brief, vehement, with short stinging sentences and perpetual hard antithesis.'

In 1379, Wycliffe was attacked with an illness which his physicians asserted would prove fatal. A deputation of friars waited on him to extort a recantation, but the lion sat up in bed and sternly dismissed them, saying: 'I shall not die, but recover, and live to expose your evil deeds;' and he did live until 1384. On the 29th of December of that year, he was in his church hearing mass when, just as the host was about to be elevated, he was struck down with palsy. He never spoke more, and died on the last day of the year, aged about sixty.

Wycliffe's influence appeared to die with him; more than a century elapsed between his death and the birth of Latimer; yet his memory, his manuscripts, and above all his version of the Scriptures, gave life to the Lollards, whom no persecution could extirpate, and whose faith at last triumphed in the supremacy of Protestantism. In 1415, the Council of Constance, which consigned John Huss and Jerome of Prague to the flames, condemned forty-five articles, said to be extracted from the works of Wycliffe, as erroneous and heretical. Wycliffe they designated an obstinate heretic, and ordered that his bones, if they could be distinguished from those of the faithful, should be dug up and cast on a dunghill. Thirteen years later, this sentence was executed by the bishop of Lincoln, at the command of the pope. The Reformer's bones were disinterred and burned, and the ashes cast into the Swift, whence, says Fuller, 'they were conveyed to the Avon, by the Avon to the Severn, by the Severn to the narrow seas, and thence to the main ocean. Thus the ashes of Wycliffe are the emblem of his doctrine, which is now dispersed all the world over.'

## STRUGGLE FOR A CASK OF WINE.

There are many curious circumstances connected with the ownership of abandoned, lost, or unclaimed property. In such cases the crown generally comes forward as the great claimant, subject of course to such pretensions as other parties may be able to substantiate in the matter. If a man finds or picks up treasure, it becomes a knotty point to determine whether he may keep it. If the owner has thrown it away, the finder may keep it; but if the owner hides it or loses it, without an intention of parting with it, there is often much legal difficulty in deciding whether the crown or any one else acquires a right to it.

And so it is out at sea, and on the British coasts. The laws concerning *wrecked* property are marked by much minuteness of detail, on account of the great diversity of the articles forming the cargoes of ships, and the relation they bear to the 'sink or swim' test. As a general rule, the king or queen is entitled to wrecks or wrecked property, unless and until a prior claimant appears. The main object of this prerogative was, not to grasp at the property for emolument, but to discourage the barbarous custom of wrecking, by which ships and human life were often purposely sacrificed as a means of giving booty to the wreckers who lived on shore. Then, to determine who shall obtain the property if the crown waives its claim, shipwrecked goods are divided into four classes—*flotsam*, *jetsam*, *ligan*, and simple *wreck*. *Flotsam* is when the ship is split, and the goods float upon the water between high and low water marks. *Jetsam* is when the ship is in danger of foundering, and the goods are cast into the sea for the purpose of saving it. *Ligan*, *ligam*, or *lagan*, is when heavy goods are thrown into the sea with a buoy, so that mariners may know where to retake them. *Wreck*, properly so called, is where goods shipwrecked are cast upon the land. By degrees, as the country became more amenable to law, the sovereign gave up the claim to some of these kinds of wrecked property, not unfrequently vesting them in the lords of adjacent manors. *Ligan* belongs to the crown if no owner appears to claim it; but if any owner appears, he is entitled to recover the possession; for even if the goods were cast overboard without any cask or buoy, in order to lighten the ship, the owner is not, by this act of necessity, construed to have renounced his property. All the goods called *flotsam*, *jetsam*, and *ligan* become *wreck* if thrown upon the land, instead of floating, and subject to the laws of wreck. By a very curious old law, if a man, or a dog, or a cat escape 'quick' or alive out of a ship, that ship shall not be regarded as wreck; it still continues the property of the same owner as before; the words man, dog, or cat, are interpreted to mean any living animals by which the ownership of the vessel might be ascertained. Lord Mansfield put a very liberal interpretation upon this old statute. A case was brought before him for trial, in which the lord of a manor claimed the goods of a wrecked ship cast on shore, on the ground that no living creature had come alive from the ship to the shore. But Lord Mansfield disallowed this claim. He said: 'The coming to shore of a dog or a cat alive can be no better proof than if they should come ashore dead. The escaping alive makes no sort of difference. If the owner of the animal were known, the presumption of the goods belonging to the same person would be equally strong, whether the animal were living or not.'

The records of our law and equity courts give some curious information concerning the struggles between the crown and other persons, concerning the right to property thrown ashore. One famous case is known by the title *Rex* v. *Two Casks of Tallow*. Another, *Rex* v. *Forty Nine Casks of Brandy*, shews the curious manner in which the judgment of the court awarded some casks to the crown and some to the lord of the manor—according as the casks were found floating beyond three miles from the shore, floating *within* that distance, lying on the wet foreshore, lying on the dry foreshore, or alternately wet and dry.

A still more curious case was tried at the end of December 1809, between the crown and Mr Constable, lord of the manor of Holdernesse, in Yorkshire. It was a struggle who should obtain a cask of wine, thrown ashore on the coast of that particular manor. The lord's bailiff, and some custom-house officers, hearing of the circumstance, hastened to the spot, striving which should get there first. The officers laid hold of one end of the cask, saying: 'This belongs to the king.' The bailiff laid hold of the other end, and claimed it for the lord of the manor. An argumentative dispute arose. The officers declared that it was smuggled, 'not having paid the *port* duty.' The bailiff retorted that he believed the wine to be *Madeira*, not port. The officers, smiling, said that they meant port of entry, not port wine—a fact that possibly the bailiff knew already, but chose to ignore. The bailiff replied: 'It has been in no port, it has come by itself on the beach.' The officers resolved to go for further instructions to the custom-house. But here arose a dilemma: what to do with the cask of wine in the interim? As the bailiff could not very well drink the wine while they were gone, they proposed to place it in a small hut hard by. They did so; but during their absence, the bailiff removed it to the cellar of the lord of the manor. The officers, when they returned, said: 'Oh, ho! now we have you; the wine is the king's *now*, under any supposition; for it has been removed *without a permit*.' To which the bailiff responded: 'If I had not removed the wine without a permit, the sea would have done so the next tide.' The attorney-general afterwards filed an information against the lord of the manor; and the case came on at York—on the question whether the bailiff was right in removing the wine without a custom-house 'permit?' The arguments *pro* and *con* were very lengthy and very learned; for although the cask of wine could not possibly be worth so much as the costs of the case, each party attached importance to the decision as a precedent. The decision of the court at York was a special verdict, which transferred the case to the court of Exchequer. The judgment finally announced was in favour of the lord of the manor—on the grounds that no permit is required for the removal of wine unless it has paid duty; that wine to be liable to duty, must be imported; that wine cannot be imported *by itself*, but requires the agency of some one else to do so; and that therefore wine wrecked, having come on shore by itself, or without human volition or intention, was not 'imported,' and was not subject to duty, and did not require a permit for its removal. The trial virtually admitted the right of the lord of the manor to the wine, as having been thrown ashore on his estate; the only question was whether he had forfeited it by the act of his servant in removing it from the spot without a permit from the custom-house officers; and the decision of the court was in his favour on this point. But it proved to be by far the most costly cask of wine he ever possessed; for by a strange arrangement in these Exchequer matters, even though the verdict be with the defendant, he does not get his costs.

## RINGING OUT THE OLD YEAR: CONCLUSION.

The close of the year brings along with it a mingled feeling of gladness and melancholy—of gladness in the anticipation of brighter days to come with the advent of the New Year, and of melancholy in reflections on the fleeting nature of time, and the gradual approach to the inevitable goal in the race of life. That so interesting an occasion should be distinguished by some observance or ceremony appears but natural, and we accordingly find various customs prevail, some sportive, others serious, and others in which both the mirthful and pensive moods are intermingled.

One of the best known and most general of these customs is, that of sitting up till twelve o'clock on the night of the 31st December, and, then, when the eventful hour has struck, proceeding to the house-door, and unbarring it with great formality to 'let out the Old, and let in the New Year.' The evening in question is a favourite occasion for social gatherings in Scotland and the north of England, the assembled friends thus welcoming together the birth of another of Father Time's ever-increasing, though short-lived progeny. In Philadelphia, in North America, we are informed that the Old Year is there 'fired out,' and the New Year 'fired in,' by a discharge of every description of firearm—musket, fowling-piece, and pistol. In the island of Guernsey, it used to be the practice of children to dress up a figure in the shape of a man, and after parading it through the parish, to bury it on the sea-shore, or in some retired spot. This ceremony was styled '**enterrer le vieux bout de l'an.**'

A custom prevails, more especially among English dissenters, of having a midnight service in the various places of worship on the last night of the year, the occasion being deemed peculiarly adapted both for pious meditations and thankfulness, and also for the reception and retention of religious impressions. And to the community at large, the passing away of the Old Year and the arrival of his successor is heralded by the peals of bells, which, after twelve o'clock has struck, burst forth from every steeple, warning us that another year has commenced. At such a moment, painful reflections will obtrude themselves, of time misspent and opportunities neglected, of the fleeting nature of human existence and enjoyment, and that ere many more years have elapsed, our joys and sorrows, our hopes and our forebodings, will all, along with ourselves, have become things of the past. Such is the dark side of the question, but it has also its sunny side and its silver lining:

'For Hope shall brighten days to come
And Memory gild the past.'

And on such an occasion as we are contemplating, it is both more noble and more profitable to take a cheerful and reassuring view of our condition, and that of humanity in general—laying aside futile reflections on past imprudence and mismanagement, and resolving for the future to do our utmost in fulfilling our duty to God and our fellow-men.

With the 'Ringing out of the Old Year' we now conclude our labours in *The Book of Days;* and in reference to the aspirations just alluded to, which every generous mind must feel, we take leave of our readers, in the subjoined utterance of our greatest living poet:

'Ring out, wild bells, to the wild sky,
The flying cloud, the frosty light:
The Year is dying in the night;
Ring out, wild bells, and let him die.

Ring out the old, ring in the new,
Ring, happy bells, across the snow:
The Year is going, let him go;
Ring out the false, ring in the true.

Ring out the grief that saps the mind,
For those that here we see no more;
Ring out the feud of rich and poor,
Ring in redress to all mankind.

Ring out a slowly-dying cause,
And ancient forms of party strife;
Ring in the nobler modes of life,
With sweeter manners, purer laws.

Ring out the want, the care, the sin,
The faithless coldness of the times;
Ring out, ring out my mournful rhymes,
But ring the fuller minstrel in.

Ring out false pride in place and blood,
The civic slander and the spite;
Ring in the love of truth and right,
Ring in the common love of good.

Ring out old shapes of foul disease;
Ring out the narrowing lust of gold;
Ring out the thousand wars of old,
Ring in the thousand years of peace.

Ring in the valiant man and free,
The larger heart, the kindlier hand;
Ring out the darkness of the land,
Ring in the Christ that is to be.'